Overview of Parts & Units · Register der Abschnitte & Module

Part 1 Basic Medical Terms

Unit 1 Health & Fitness, Unit 2 Diet & Dieting, Unit 3 Food & Drink, Unit 4 Illness & Recovery, Unit 5 Injuries, Unit 6 Accidents & Emergencies, Unit 7 States of Consciousness, Unit 8 First Aid, Unit 9 Drugs & Remedies, Unit 10 Alcohol & Smoking, Unit 11 Substance Abuse, Unit 12 Death & Mortality

Part 2 Health Care

Unit 13 Health Care Administration, Unit 14 Hospitals & Medical Facilities, Unit 15 Medical Staff & Specialties, Unit 16 Nurses & Paramedical Staff, Unit 17 Basic Medical Equipment & Supplies, Unit 18 At the Doctor's, Unit 19 On the Ward, Unit 20 Hospital Routines

Part 3 Body Structures & Functions

Unit 21 Head & Neck, 22 The Trunk, 23 Extremities, 24 Body Height & Weight, 25 Build & Appearance, 26 Teeth, 27 Dentition & Mastication, 28 Bones, 29 Joints, 30 Muscles & Tendons, 31 Musculoskeletal Function, 32 The Heart, 33 Cardiac Function, 34 Blood Vessels, 35 The Lymphatic System, 36 Blood & Lymph Circulation, 37 The Blood, 38 Hematopoiesis & Coagulation, 39 The Immune System, 40 The Nervous System, 41 The Brain, 42 Nerve Function, 43 Lungs & Airways, 44 Respiration, 45 Digestive Tract, 46 Digestion, 47 Liver & Biliary System, 48 Kidneys & Urinary Tract, 49 Urine Production & Elimination, 50 Female Sexual Organs, 51 Menstrual Cycle, 52 Male Sexual Organs, 53 Male Sexual Function, 54 Endocrine Glands, 55 Hormones, 56 The Skin, 57 The Senses, 58 Eyes, 59 Vision, 60 Ears, 61 Hearing, 62 Smell, Taste & Touch

Part 4 Complex Body Functions

Unit 63 Posture & Position, Unit 64 Body Movement, Unit 65 Walking & Locomotion, Unit 66 Human Sounds & Speech, Unit 67 Gestures & Body Language, Unit 68 Sexuality, Unit 69 Fertility & Reproductive Medicine, Unit 70 Pregnancy, Unit 71 Childbirth, Unit 72 Sleep, Unit 73 Mental Activity, Unit 74 Memory, Unit 75 Personality & Behavior, Unit 76 Mood & Attitude, Unit 77 Mental Health, Unit 78 Metabolism, Unit 79 Nutrition, Unit 80 Growing Up & Aging

Part 5 Medical Science

Unit 81 Biochemistry & Molecular Biology, Unit 82 Biochemical Elements & Compounds, Unit 83 Cytology & Cell Biology, Unit 84 Clinical Genetics, Unit 85 Medical Embryology, Unit 86 Histology, Unit 87 Anatomy, Unit 88 General Physiology, Unit 89 General Pathology, Unit 90 Pathogens & Parasites, Unit 91 Toxicology, Unit 92 Pharmacologic Agents, Unit 93 Anesthetics, Unit 94 Infectious Diseases, Unit 95 Childhood Diseases, Unit 96 Sexually Transmitted Diseases, Unit 97 General Oncology, Unit 98 Tumor Types, Unit 99 Radiology, Unit 100 Medical Statistics, Unit 101 Medical Studies & Clinical Trials

Part 6 Clinical Terms

Unit 102 History Taking, 103 Clinical Symptoms, 104 Pain, 105 Fever & Sweating, 106 Fractures, 107 Physical Examination, 108 Clinical Signs, 109 Gastrointestinal Symptoms, 110 Cardiovascular Symptoms, 111 Respiratory Symptoms, 112 Urologic Symptoms, 113 Neurologic Findings, 114 Skin Lesions, 115 Clinical Abbreviations, 116 Lab Studies, 117 Diagnosis, 118 Diagnostic Procedures, 119 Etiology, Course & Prognosis, 120 Therapeutic Intervention, 121 Pharmacologic Treatment, 122 Immunization, 123 Resuscitation, 124 Medical & Surgical Emergencies, 125 Critical Care, 126 Surgical Treatment, 127 Basic Operative Techniques, 128 Minimally Invasive Surgery, 129 Plastic & Reconstructive Surgery, 130 Grafts & Flaps, 131 The Surgical Suite, 132 Surgical Instruments, 133 Laparoscopic Equipment, 134 Perioperative Management, 135 Anesthesiology, 136 Blood Transfusion, 137 Sutures & Suture Materials, 138 Endoscopic Suturing, 139 Asepsis, 140 Wound Healing, 141 Fracture Management, 142 Physical Therapy & Rehabilitation

KWiC-Web

Fachwortschatz Medizin

Englisch

Sprachtrainer & Fachwörterbuch in einem
KWiC – Key Words in Context

Ingrid & Michael Friedbichler

2. überarbeitete Auflage
69 Abbildungen

Dipl. Übers. Mag. Ingrid Friedbichler
Mag. Michael Friedbichler, M. A.
Medizinische Universität Innsbruck und
Institut für Translationswissenschaft
Leopold-Franzens-Universität Innsbruck
Herzog-Siegmund-Ufer 15
Österreich, 6020 Innsbruck

Bibliographische Information der Deutschen Nationalbibliothek

Die Deutsche Nationalbibliothek verzeichnet diese Publikation in der Deutschen Nationalbibliographie; detaillierte bibliographische Daten sind im Internet über http://dnb.d-nb.de abrufbar.

1. Auflage 2003

Wichtiger Hinweis: Wie jede Wissenschaft ist die Medizin ständigen Entwicklungen unterworfen. Forschung und klinische Erfahrung erweitern unsere Erkenntnisse, insbesondere was Behandlung und medikamentöse Therapie anbelangt. Soweit in diesem Werk eine Dosierung oder eine Applikation erwähnt wird, darf der Leser zwar darauf vertrauen, dass Autoren, Herausgeber und Verlag große Sorgfalt darauf verwandt haben, dass diese Angabe **dem Wissensstand bei Fertigstellung des Werkes** entspricht.

Für Angaben über Dosierungsanweisungen und Applikationsformen kann vom Verlag jedoch keine Gewähr übernommen werden. **Jeder Benutzer ist angehalten,** durch sorgfältige Prüfung der Beipackzettel der verwendeten Präparate und gegebenenfalls nach Konsultation eines Spezialisten festzustellen, ob die dort gegebene Empfehlung für Dosierung oder die Beachtung von Kontraindikationen gegenüber der Angabe in diesem Buch abweicht. Eine solche Prüfung ist besonders wichtig bei selten verwendeten Präparaten oder solchen, die neu auf den Markt gebracht worden sind. **Jede Dosierung oder Applikation erfolgt auf eigene Gefahr des Benutzers.** Autoren und Verlag appellieren an jeden Benutzer, ihm etwa auffallende Ungenauigkeiten dem Verlag mitzuteilen.

© 2007 Georg Thieme Verlag
Rüdigerstr. 14
D-70469 Stuttgart
Telefon: +49/0711/8931-0
Unsere Homepage: www.thieme.de

Printed in Germany

Cartoons: Dr. Stephan Schreieck, Innsbruck
Umschlaggestaltung: Thieme Verlagsgruppe
XML-Aufbereitung: Hübner EP, 65343 Eltville
Satz: Druckhaus Götz GmbH, 71636 Ludwigsburg
  Satzsystem: 3B2 Version 6.05
Druck: Westermann Druck, 08058 Zwickau

Geschützte Warennamen werden **nicht** besonders kenntlich gemacht. Aus dem Fehlen eines solchen Hinweises kann also nicht geschlossen werden, dass es sich um einen freien Warennamen handle.

Das Werk, einschließlich aller seiner Teile, ist urheberrechtlich geschützt. Jede Verwertung außerhalb der engen Grenzen des Urheberrechtsgesetzes ist ohne Zustimmung des Verlages unzulässig und strafbar. Das gilt insbesondere für Vervielfältigungen, Übersetzungen, Mikroverfilmungen und die Einspeicherung und Verarbeitung in elektronischen Systemen.

ISBN 978-3-13-117462-8   1 2 3 4 5 6

Zum Geleit

Unsere gegenwärtige Kultur bevorzugt seit dem vergangenen Jahrhundert in der internationalen Verständigung die englische Sprache in ungeahntem Ausmaß. War im Mittelalter und auch noch zur Zeit der Aufklärung Latein die alleinige Wissenschaftssprache, konnten sich in der Vergangenheit Französisch, Deutsch, Spanisch und andere so genannte Weltsprachen nur begrenzt durchsetzen.

Erst im 20. Jahrhundert haben sich einige Technologien so durchgesetzt, dass z. B. in der Luftfahrt Englisch wirklich zur Weltsprache geworden ist. Auch in Ländern wie Russland und China, die sich nach dem Zweiten Weltkrieg als autonome Großmächte abschotten wollten, gilt sie heute im Luftverkehr als unentbehrliches Kommunikationsmittel.

Ein weiterer Bereich in der internationalen Kommunikation sind Medizin und Naturwissenschaften, die vom hohen Niveau der Wissenschaft im angloamerikanischen Raum beeinflusst werden. Zeitschriften und Bücher brauchen hohe Auflagen, um überleben zu können. Der englischsprachige Kulturbereich ist ein Vielfaches der europäischen und asiatischen Regionen. Kein Verlag kann sich der Expansion in diesen Raum entziehen. In vielen europäischen Ländern werden wichtige Kongresse und Symposien nur noch in englischer Sprache abgehalten. Wer aus falschem Patriotismus diese Entwicklung ablehnt, bleibt sicher auf der Strecke.

Die Autoren dieses Buches haben die Notwendigkeit von Fachenglischkenntnissen für Mediziner schon vor zwei Jahrzehnten wahrgenommen und seit 1978 am Aufbau des Lehrangebots und der Entwicklung einschlägiger Unterrichts- und Lernmaterialien zur Vermittlung der englischen Fachsprache an der medizinischen Fakultät der Universität Innsbruck mit großem Erfolg gearbeitet.

Zu dieser Pionierarbeit kann man ihnen gratulieren und wünschen, dass das nun vorliegende Werk, welches aus dieser jahrelangen Aufbauarbeit hervorgegangen ist, vielen Medizinstudenten und Ärzten den Zugang zur internationalen Fachkommunikation erleichtern möge.

Univ.-Prof. i. R. Dr. Franz Dienstl
Ehrenpräsident der Österr. Gesellschaft für Internistische und Allgem. Intensivmedizin, ehem. Leiter der Kardiolog. Intensivstation, Universitätsklinik Innsbruck

Foreword

It is a pleasure to write this foreword for *KWiC-Web: Fachwortschatz MEDIZIN Englisch*, a book intended to help German-speaking medical professionals to communicate with colleagues around the globe.

The world of medicine has rapidly become integrated on both clinical and basic scientific levels. A clear understanding of the English terminology and phraseology is essential to accurate interchange of ideas.

The organization and content of this book should prove very helpful to medical students and German physicians who acquire information in English textbooks and journals as well as those who seek some of their clinical training in the United States and other English-speaking countries. This project is the brainchild of Michael and Ingrid Friedbichler, both of whom have more than twenty years of experience in teaching English to medical students and young doctors at Innsbruck University. In addition, they have been involved in medical translation for many years, and as linguistic advisors have helped prepare countless papers for publication in American and British medical journals. Owing to their extensive experience in the field they are familiar with the challenges that German speakers encounter when studying international medical journals and textbooks, interviewing English-speaking patients, and writing or presenting papers in English.

KWiC-Web: MEDIZIN provides a combination of more than 140 integrated topic-related English glossaries covering all fields of medicine on the one hand and a bilingual medical dictionary on the other. The common use basic keywords are presented in a semantic network of easy-to-learn units (e.g. hormones, childhood diseases, urologic signs and symptoms, etc.) together with explanations and synonyms, related terms, sample sentences, illustrated English uses, and German translations.

This book is an extremely useful asset for those who are learning medical English, undergoing English-based clinical training, writing articles or communicating at medical meetings in English. The authors are to be congratulated for an outstanding contribution.

Anthony J. Schaeffer, MD
Herman L. Kretschmer Professor of Urology,
Chair, Department of Urology
Northwestern University, Chicago, USA

Vorwort zur 2. Auflage

Als wir im Herbst 2003 dieses Fachwörterbuch unseren Mitarbeitern, den Studierenden und dem interessierten Fachpublikum an der Universität Innsbruck präsentierten, gab es zunächst manch verdutztes Gesicht, denn ein solches Wörterbuch hatten sie noch nicht gesehen. Es bedurfte einiger Zeit, aber schließlich erkannten alle, die sich mit dem Konzept näher befassten, dass dieses etwas andere Fachwörterbuch vieles kann, was sie bisher vergeblich gesucht hatten. Ähnlich waren auch die ersten Reaktionen, die uns von Benutzern und Rezensenten erreichten.

Es freut uns daher ganz besonders, dass das neuartige Konzept unseres Sprachtrainers inzwischen weithin Anerkennung gefunden hat und mittlerweile an mehreren Universitäten im deutschsprachigen Raum in Fachenglischkursen verwendet bzw. zum Selbststudium empfohlen wird. Dass mit KWiC-Web ein zukunftsweisendes Projekt entstanden ist, zeigt auch die Tatsache, dass sich mittlerweile Verlagshäuser in Japan, Brasilien und den Niederlanden dafür interessieren.

Wir bedanken uns für die wertvollen Rückmeldungen von Benutzern und Rezensenten im In- und Ausland. In der nun vorliegenden 2. Auflage konnten wir die Verbesserungsvorschläge in vielen Details berücksichtigen. So wurden z.B. die für Österreich spezifischen Ausdrücke in den Übersetzungen durchgehend als solche gekennzeichnet und die Unterschiede zwischen einzelnen britischen und amerikanischen Benennungen noch exakter herausgearbeitet. Auch aktuelle Entwicklungen in den Gesundheitssystemen der englisch- und deutschsprachigen Länder seit 2002 wurden berücksichtigt. Als Ergänzung zum Buch können wir auch die inzwischen im Handel erhältliche elektronische Version auf CD-ROM empfehlen, die durch eine integrierte Volltextsuche eine effiziente Nutzung direkt auf dem PC ermöglicht.

Unser Dank gebührt dem gesamten Redaktionsteam im Georg Thieme Verlag, das uns wie schon bei der 1. Auflage bestens unterstützt hat, allen voran Herrn Dr. Urbanowicz für seine Bemühungen um eine reibungslose Kooperation, sowie Herrn Elm, der für die sorgfältige Einarbeitung der Änderungen gesorgt hat.

Wir freuen uns mit diesem Buch unsere Erfahrung beim Erwerb professioneller Englischkenntnisse anbieten zu können und wünschen allen Benutzern viel Erfolg damit. Rückmeldungen, ob Korrektur- oder Erweiterungsvorschläge, sind uns sehr willkommen und können an folgende e-Mail Adresse gerichtet werden: med-english@i-med.ac.at

Innsbruck, Ingrid & Michael Friedbichler
im Frühjahr 2007

Vorwort zur 1. Auflage

Obwohl die englische Fachsprache heute in der Medizin zu einer wichtigen Zusatzqualifikation geworden ist, gab es bislang kaum Hilfsmittel, mit denen sich Mediziner gezielt die für ihr Fachgebiet relevante sprachliche Kompetenz aneignen konnten.
Nach mehr als 5-jähriger Entwicklungsarbeit ist es uns daher eine große Freude, nun nach dem Band zur Zahnmedizin mit *KWiC-Web: Fachwortschatz Medizin Englisch* auch Materialien zur Aktivierung der produktiven Sprachkompetenz für den gesamten medizinischen Bereich präsentieren zu können. Auf der Grundlage von computergestützten lexikographischen Methoden und den neuesten Erkenntnissen der Spracherwerbsforschung, wurde ein zukunftsweisendes Konzept entwickelt, welches Medizinern aller Fachrichtungen die Möglichkeit bietet, sich zwischendurch oder auf der Anreise zu einem Kongress mit den englischen Fachausdrücken und Wendungen bestimmter Fachbereiche rasch und effizient vertraut zu machen.
Neuland zu betreten bedeutet immer eine Potenzierung des Aufwandes. Wenngleich wir durch unsere Lehrtätigkeit an der Universität Innsbruck auf einen wertvollen Erfahrungsschatz in der Fachsprachenvermittlung zurückgreifen konnten, wäre dieses Buch ohne die Unterstützung eines ganzen Teams von Fachleuten und Beratern, denen wir an dieser Stelle unseren besonderen Dank aussprechen möchten, nicht realisierbar gewesen. An erster Stelle gebührt dieser Dank William B. Gallagher, M.D. (FACS), Tucson, AZ., USA, der für uns die englischen Termini und Texte auf deren fachliche und sprachliche Richtigkeit überprüft hat.
Des Weiteren bedanken wir uns bei einem Team von niedergelassenen und wissenschaftlich arbeitenden Fachärzten, die jeweils die deutschen Entsprechungen der übersetzten Termini in ihren Fachgebieten überprüft haben und uns darüber hinaus beratend zur Seite standen. Ganz besonders haben uns unser langjähriger Mentor Univ.-Prof. i.R. Dr. Franz Dienstl (Kardiologie, Innere Medizin), Dr. Hans Hausdorfer (Infektiologie, Pharmakologie) und Ass.-Prof. Dr. Alexander Alge (Gynäkologie, Embryologie, Onkologie, bildgebende Diagnostik) unterstützt. Unser Dank gilt auch folgenden Fachleuten von der Medizinischen Universität Innsbruck: MR Univ.-Prof. Dr. Gernot Helweg† (Radiologie), ao. Univ.-Prof. Dr. Reinhard Höpfl (Dermatologie, Venerologie), Dr. Christian Hoser (Unfallchirurgie), Univ.-Prof. Dr. Helmut Klocker (Biochemie, Genetik, Labormedizin), Univ.-Prof. Dr. Günther Putz (Anästhesie, Notfall- u. Intensivmedizin), und Dr. Hanno Ulmer (Biostatistik).
Im weiteren bedanken wir uns für die hilfreiche Fachberatung bei Dr. Peter Huemer, Wolfurt/Vlbg. (Zahnmedizin), Univ.-Prof. Dr. Günter Janetschek, Linz (minimal-invasive Chirurgie), Dr. Erich Köhler, Wien (Psychiatrie), Dr. Birgit Krecy, Telfs/Tirol (Neurologie), Dr. Wolfgang Oberthaler, Innsbruck (Orthopädie), Univ.-Prof. Dr. Arnulf Stenzl, Tübingen (Urologie, Chirurgie), Dr. Christa Them, Pflegedirektorin am AZW Innsbruck (Krankenpflege), und Mag. rer. nat. Katrin Friedbichler, Wien (Zellbiologie), sowie bei Dr. Stephan Schreieck für die humorvollen Zeichnungen, die zur Auflockerung der fachlichen Materie beitragen sollen.
Last but not least verdankt dieses Buch seine Veröffentlichung dem Pioniergeist von Dr. Thorsten Pilgrim und seinen Mitarbeitern vom Thieme Verlag, die sich nicht gescheut haben, mit *KWIC-Web* zu neuen Ufern aufzubrechen. Wir bedanken uns für das Vertrauen, das sie in uns und unsere Arbeit gesetzt haben und die weiten Wege, die sie bei der Konzeption einer benutzerfreundlichen graphischen Gestaltung und der Entwicklung einer speziellen Datenbank mit uns gegangen sind, um nur zwei der Punkte zu erwähnen, die für alle Pionierarbeit bedeutet haben.
Bleibt zu hoffen, dass dieses Buch all jenen, die sich mit der englischen Fachsprache der Medizin vertraut machen wollen, ein effizientes Hilfsmittel sein möge, das ihnen das Tor zur internationalen Fachwelt öffnet.

Innsbruck, im Juni 2003   Ingrid & Michael Friedbichler

Table of Contents · Inhaltsübersicht

Part 1 Basic Medical Terms

Unit 1	Health & Fitness • Gesundheit & Fitness	1
Unit 2	Diet & Dieting • Nahrung & Diät	6
Unit 3	Food & Drink • Essen & Trinken	10
Unit 4	Illness & Recovery • Krankheit & Genesung	14
Unit 5	Injuries • Verletzungen	18
Unit 6	Accidents & Emergencies • Unfälle & Notfälle	22
Unit 7	States of Consciousness • Bewusstseinslagen	30
Unit 8	First Aid • Erste Hilfe	33
Unit 9	Drugs & Remedies • Medikamente & Heilmittel	38
Unit 10	Alcohol & Smoking • Alkohol & Nikotin	42
Unit 11	Substance Abuse • Substanzmissbrauch	46
Unit 12	Death & Mortality • Tod & Mortalität	51

Part 2 Health Care

Unit 13	Health Care Administration • Gesundheitswesen	56
Unit 14	Hospitals & Medical Facilities • Krankenhäuser & medizinische Einrichtungen	59
Unit 15	Medical Staff & Specialties • Fachärzte & ärztliches Personal	62
Unit 16	Nurses & Paramedical Staff • Pflegepersonal & medizinische Hilfsberufe	67
Unit 17	Basic Medical Equipment & Supplies • Medizinische Grundausstattung	71
Unit 18	At the Doctor's • Beim Arzt	75
Unit 19	On the Ward • Auf der Station	80
Unit 20	Hospital Routines • Von der Aufnahme bis zur Entlassung	84

Part 3 Body Structures & Functions

Unit 21	Parts of the Body: Head & Neck • Körperteile: Kopf & Hals	89
Unit 22	The Trunk • Der Rumpf	92
Unit 23	Extremities • Extremitäten	95
Unit 24	Body Height & Weight • Körpergröße & Gewicht	98
Unit 25	Build & Appearance • Körperbau & Erscheinungsbild	101
Unit 26	Teeth • Zähne	104
Unit 27	Dentition & Mastication • Zahnen & Kauen	108
Unit 28	Bones • Knochen	111
Unit 29	Joints • Gelenke	117
Unit 30	Muscles & Tendons • Muskeln & Sehnen	120
Unit 31	Musculoskeletal Function • Funktion des Bewegungsapparats	125
Unit 32	The Heart • Das Herz	130
Unit 33	Cardiac Function • Herztätigkeit	134
Unit 34	Blood Vessels • Blutgefäße	136
Unit 35	The Lymphatic System • Das lymphatische System	140
Unit 36	Blood & Lymph Circulation • Blut- & Lymphzirkulation	142
Unit 37	Components of the Blood • Blutbestandteile	146
Unit 38	Hematopoiesis & Coagulation • Blutbildung & Blutgerinnung	151
Unit 39	The Immune System • Das Immunsystem	155
Unit 40	The Nervous System • Das Nervensystem	162
Unit 41	Brain & Spinal Cord • Gehirn & Rückenmark	166
Unit 42	Nerve Function • Nervenfunktion	171
Unit 43	Lungs & Airways • Lunge & Atemwege	175
Unit 44	Respiration • Atmung	179
Unit 45	Digestive Tract • Der Verdauungstrakt	182
Unit 46	Digestion • Verdauung	186

Unit 47	Liver & Biliary System • Leber & Gallenwege		191
Unit 48	Kidneys & the Urinary Tract • Nieren & Harnwege		195
Unit 49	Urine Production & Elimination • Harnproduktion & -ausscheidung		198
Unit 50	Female Sexual Organs • Das weibliche Genitale		201
Unit 51	Menstrual Cycle • Menstruationszyklus		206
Unit 52	Male Sexual Organs • Das männliche Genitale		209
Unit 53	Male Sexual Function • Männliche Sexualfunktion		213
Unit 54	Endocrine Glands • Endokrine Drüsen		215
Unit 55	Hormones • Hormone		219
Unit 56	The Skin & its Appendages • Haut & Hautanhangsgebilde		225
Unit 57	The Senses • Sinnesorgane		231
Unit 58	Eyes • Augen		235
Unit 59	Vision • Gesichtssinn		239
Unit 60	Ears • Ohren		244
Unit 61	Hearing • Gehörsinn		248
Unit 62	Smell, Taste & Touch • Geruchs-, Geschmacks- & Tastsinn		250

Part 4 Complex Body Functions

Unit 63	Posture & Position • Körperhaltung & -lage		253
Unit 64	Body Movement • Körperbewegung		255
Unit 65	Walking & Locomotion • Fortbewegung & Gang		260
Unit 66	Human Sounds & Speech • Sprache & menschliche Laute		264
Unit 67	Gestures & Body Language • Gestik & Körpersprache		268
Unit 68	Sexuality • Sexualität		271
Unit 69	Fertility & Reproductive Medicine • Fertilität & Reproduktionsmedizin		275
Unit 70	Pregnancy • Schwangerschaft		279
Unit 71	Childbirth • Geburt		282
Unit 72	Sleep • Schlaf		288
Unit 73	Mental Activity • Mentale Funktionen		292
Unit 74	Memory • Gedächtnis		295
Unit 75	Personality & Behavior • Persönlichkeit & Verhalten		300
Unit 76	Mood & Attitude • Stimmungslagen		306
Unit 77	Mental Health • Mentale Gesundheit		310
Unit 78	Metabolism • Stoffwechsel		319
Unit 79	Nutrition • Ernährung		324
Unit 80	Growing Up & Aging • Aufwachsen & Altern		328

Part 5 Medical Science

Unit 81	Biochemistry & Molecular Biology • Biochemie & Molekularbiologie		332
Unit 82	Biochemical Elements & Compounds • Biochemische Elemente & Verbindungen		340
Unit 83	Cytology & Cell Biology • Zytologie & Zellbiologie		350
Unit 84	Clinical Genetics • Klinische Genetik		356
Unit 85	Medical Embryology • Medizinische Embryologie		367
Unit 86	Histology • Histologie		372
Unit 87	Anatomy • Anatomie		378
Unit 88	General Physiology • Allgemeine Physiologie		384
Unit 89	General Pathology • Allgemeine Pathologie		389
Unit 90	Microbes, Pathogens & Parasites • Krankheitserreger & Parasiten		396
Unit 91	Toxicology • Toxikologie		402
Unit 92	Pharmacologic Agents • Arzneimittel & pharmazeutische Wirkstoffe		408
Unit 93	Anesthetics • Betäubungsmittel		413
Unit 94	Infectious Diseases • Infektionskrankheiten		416
Unit 95	Childhood Diseases • Kinderkrankheiten		422
Unit 96	Sexually Transmitted Diseases • Sexuell übertragbare Krankheiten		425
Unit 97	General Oncology • Allgemeine Onkologie		428

Unit 98	Tumor Types • Tumorarten	433
Unit 99	Radiology • Radiologie	438
Unit 100	Medical Statistics • Biostatistik	442
Unit 101	Medical Studies & Clinical Trials • Medizinische Forschung & klinische Studien	448

Part 6 Clinical Terms

Unit 102	History Taking • Anamnese	453
Unit 103	Nonspecific Clinical Symptoms • Unspezifische klinische Symptome	456
Unit 104	Pain • Schmerz	461
Unit 105	Fever & Sweating • Fieber & Schweißproduktion	465
Unit 106	Fractures • Knochenbrüche	469
Unit 107	Physical Examination • Klinische Untersuchung	473
Unit 108	Common Clinical Signs • Allgemeine klinische Zeichen	478
Unit 109	Gastrointestinal Signs & Symptoms • Magen-Darm-Symptomatik	481
Unit 110	Cardiovascular Signs & Symptoms • Herz-Kreislauf-Symptomatik	485
Unit 111	Respiratory Signs & Symptoms • Atemwegssymptomatik	490
Unit 112	Urologic Signs & Symptoms • Urologische Symptomatik	495
Unit 113	Neurologic Findings • Neurologische Befunde	498
Unit 114	Skin Lesions • Hautläsionen	504
Unit 115	Clinical Abbreviations & Acronyms • Klinische Abkürzungen & Akronyme	508
Unit 116	Routine Lab Studies • Routinelaboruntersuchungen	513
Unit 117	Diagnosis • Diagnose	518
Unit 118	Diagnostic Procedures & Investigations • Diagnostische Verfahren	523
Unit 119	Etiology, Course & Prognosis • Ätiologie, Krankheitsverlauf & Prognose	529
Unit 120	Therapeutic Intervention • Therapeutische Maßnahmen	534
Unit 121	Pharmacologic Treatment • Medikamentöse Behandlung	537
Unit 122	Immunization • Immunisierung	540
Unit 123	Resuscitation • Reanimation	543
Unit 124	Medical & Surgical Emergencies • Medizinische & chirurgische Notfälle	548
Unit 125	Critical Care • Intensivmedizin	555
Unit 126	Surgical Treatment • Der operative Eingriff	562
Unit 127	Basic Operative Techniques • Chirurgische Basistechniken	565
Unit 128	Minimally Invasive Surgery • Minimal-invasive Chirurgie	568
Unit 129	Plastic & Reconstructive Surgery • Plastische & Wiederherstellungschirurgie	572
Unit 130	Grafts & Flaps • Transplantate	575
Unit 131	The Surgical Suite • Der Operationstrakt	578
Unit 132	Surgical Instruments • Chirurgische Instrumente	581
Unit 133	Laparoscopic Equipment • Laparoskopische Geräte & Instrumente	584
Unit 134	Perioperative Management • Perioperative Maßnahmen	587
Unit 135	Anesthesiology • Anästhesiologie	590
Unit 136	Blood Transfusion • Bluttransfusion	594
Unit 137	Sutures & Suture Materials • Chirurgische Nahttechniken & -materialien	599
Unit 138	Endoscopic Suturing • Endoskopische Nahttechniken	603
Unit 139	Medical & Surgical Asepsis • Medizinische & chirurgische Asepsis	606
Unit 140	Wound Healing • Wundheilung	608
Unit 141	Fracture Management • Frakturbehandlung	612
Unit 142	Physical Therapy & Rehabilitation • Physikalische Therapie & Rehabilitation	616

Index – English Terms • Index der englischen Fachtermini ... 625

Index – English Abbreviations • Index der englischen Abkürzungen ... 694

Index – German Terms • Index der deutschen Fachtermini ... 700

Quellenverzeichnis zu den Abbildungen ... 848

Benutzeranleitungen

Wozu wurde KWiC-Web Fachwortschatz Medizin entwickelt?

In den letzten Jahren ist die englische Fachsprache zu einer wichtigen Zusatzqualifikation für Mediziner geworden. In diesem Bereich gibt es inzwischen eine Reihe von Materialen, größtenteils sind es jedoch medizinische Fachwörterbücher. Ob umfassend oder als Taschenbuch, gebunden oder auf CD-ROM, alle diese herkömmlichen Wörterbücher haben für den Sprachlernenden allerdings einen entscheidenden Nachteil. Durch die alphabetische Auflistung der Wörter sind sie zwar als Nachschlagewerke ideal, für den Erwerb eines einschlägigen Fachwortschatzes jedoch ungeeignet.

Was Sie hier in Händen halten ist eine völlig andere Art von Wörterbuch. Es ist nach dem Bausteinprinzip auf der Grundlage fachlicher Zusammenhänge aufgebaut und ermöglicht es sowohl Medizinstudenten, die sich mit den grundlegenden Termini auseinandersetzen, als auch Fachärzten, die sich mit den Begriffen ihres Fachbereichs vertraut machen wollen, und Pflegefachkräften ebenso wie Therapeuten und Übersetzern von medizinischen Texten, gezielt den jeweils relevanten Wortschatz aus den entsprechenden Bausteinen (Modulen) ihren speziellen Bedürfnissen entsprechend zu aktivieren. Da sich jedes Modul auf eine überschaubare Anzahl von Fachtermini beschränkt, lassen sich diese Baustein für Baustein in „schöpferischen Pausen" zwischendurch oder auf Reisen leicht einprägen oder auffrischen.

Wie ist der Wortschatz in KWiC-Web strukturiert?

KWiC steht für *Key Words In Context* und **Web** für die Vernetzung in semantischen Netzwerken. **KWiC-Web** setzt in zweierlei Hinsicht neue Maßstäbe.

1. Keywords. Der medizinische Wortschatz in **KWiC-Web** ist in 142 Kapitel (Module), die in semantische Netzwerke (sinnzusammenhängende Termini, Ausdrücke und Wendungen, die ähnlich wie im sog. mentalen Lexikon des menschlichen Gedächtnisses miteinander verbunden sind) gegliedert sind, aufbereitet. Diese Module umfassen die gängigen Begriffe der verschiedenen medizinischen Fachgebiete in baumdiagrammartigen Verknüpfungen – von medizinisch relevanten Wörtern aus der Allgemeinsprache, wie z.B *tooth decay* (Zahnkaries), bis hin zu spezifischen Fachtermini, wie z.B. *initial stab incision*, einem wichtigen Ausdruck in der minimal-invasiven Chirurgie.

Zusätzlich wurden die elektronisch herausgefilterten Schlüsselwörter auf ihren didaktischen Wert hin geprüft, d.h. typische englische Bezeichnungen und Wendungen werden gegenüber medizinischen Internationalismen und Termini, die dem Nicht-Native-Speaker weder in der Bedeutung noch in der Aussprache oder Verwendung Probleme bereiten, bevorzugt berücksichtigt.

Obwohl Vollständigkeit ein unerreichbares Ziel bleibt, findet man in **KWiC-Web** alle wichtigen Fachtermini und darüber hinaus viele fachspezifische Wortverbindungen, die zwar gängig sind, bisher aber noch nirgends beschrieben wurden.

2. Context. KWiC-Web geht weit über eine Liste von englisch-deutschen Wortgleichungen hinaus. Da die adäquate Einbettung der Fachtermini im Kontext für Fachleute wie auch Übersetzer meist die größte Hürde im aktiven Sprachgebrauch darstellt, ist die Kontextualisierung der Termini ein wesentliches Kriterium. Spracherwerb findet schließlich immer im Kontext statt, und Übersetzungen bieten meist nur in begrenztem Maß Hilfe.

Deshalb werden in **KWiC-Web** die Schlüsselwörter nicht nur mit deutschen Entsprechungen, sondern jeweils samt ihrem typischen semantischen Umfeld in englischen Erklärungen, Beispielsätzen, und den gebräuchlichsten Wortverbindungen (Kollokationen) und Phrasen präsentiert, die alle einer riesigen Fachtextsammlung entnommen sind. Dies gibt dem Benutzer Einblick in die authentische Verwendung der Fachausdrücke in der medizinischen Literatur.

Fachwörterbuch, Kollokationswörterbuch und Wissensdatenbank in einem

KWiC-Web vereint die Vorzüge eines englischen Erklärungswörterbuches mit jenen einer einsprachigen Phraseologiesammlung und eines zweisprachigen Nachschlagewerkes.

Jedes Modul beinhaltet rund 200 morphologisch oder semantisch verwandte Ausdrücke, Phrasen, und Kollokationen, die mit verwandten Modulen durch Verweise verbunden sind, sodass ein einprägsames semantisches Netzwerk (= Web) von miteinander in enger Beziehung stehenden Termini, Erläuterungen, Wortverbindungen, lexikalischen Clustern und Fakten entsteht, das einer Wissensdatenbank gleicht. Dadurch wird nicht nur die Verwendung der Schlüsselwörter veranschaulicht, sondern auch deren Verknüpfung und Beziehung mit anderen Fachtermini aufzeigt. So wird jedes Modul zu einer Zusammenschau der wichtigsten Schlüsselwörter und Wendungen, denen man in einschlägigen Fachtexten und im Klinikalltag immer wieder begegnet. Vertraute Ausdrücke und solche, die man schon einmal gehört aber wieder vergessen hat, stehen dabei neben unbekannten, und **KWiC-Web** zeigt, wie sie untereinander vernetzt sind. Es entstehen im Unterbewusstsein Assoziationen, die das Wiedererkennen und Behalten auf lange Sicht wesentlich verbessern. Dadurch kommt das Arbeiten mit **KWiC-Web** dem Studium bzw. „Querlesen" tausender Seiten von Fachtexten gleich – allerdings in kürzester Zeit, da es sich um einen stark verdichteten Auszug handelt (deshalb auch KWIC-!).

Korpusgestütztes Erfassen

Ohne die Verwendung von repräsentativen elektronischen Korpora von authentischen englischen Fachtexten wäre die Selektion der Schlüsselwörter, Kontextbeispiele, und Kollokationen nur mit Qualitätseinbußen und einem riesigen Zeitaufwand zu bewältigen. **KWiC-Web** basiert auf einem über 20 Mio. Wörter umfassenden medizinischen Textkorpus. Um die Verlässlichkeit hoch und die Fehlerhaftigkeit gering zu halten, wurden ausschließlich authentische Quellen (Standard-Handbücher, Fachartikel, und Fachtexte englischsprachiger Autoren herangezogen.

Die moderne Computerlinguistik ermöglicht es uns, spezifische Fragen des Sprachgebrauchs, v.a. die Verwendung und Verbreitung von Fachausdrücken und Wendungen, anhand von authentischen Fachtexten per Knopfdruck zu prüfen. Da **KWiC-Web** auf der Grundlage solcher Textanalysen erstellt wurde, sind die Sprachdaten nicht nur aktuell sondern geben auch die Sprache wieder, die in der Fachkommunikation tatsächlich verwendet wird.

Welches Englisch?

Die Weltsprache Englisch hat viele Ausprägungen und Varianten. In **KWiC-Web** wird grundsätzlich *Standard American* als Ausgangssprache verwendet, es wird aber auf regionale Varianten – besonders auf Unterschiede zwischen amerikanischem und britischem Englisch – verwiesen und diese fallweise auch erläutert (besonders bei unterschiedlicher Bedeutung oder Verwendung; s. auch Hinweise zur Aussprache und Schreibweise, letzte Seite).

Wie sind die Module aufgebaut?

Die Aufbereitung des medizinischen Fachwortschatzes in übersichtliche Module erfolgte analog zur fachlichen Strukturierung in einzelne Fachbereiche. Auch innerhalb der Module sind die Wortfelder nach fachlich-semantischen Kriterien angeordnet. Ähnlich wie bei einem guten Lehrbuch gelangt man den Begriffssystemen folgend von den grundlegenden Schlüsselwörtern zu immer spezifischeren Termini. Das zweite Ordnungsprinzip folgt didaktischen Kriterien. Grundlegende und häufig verwendete Ausdrücke werden jeweils vor den komplexen und seltenen angeführt. Durch den ansteigenden Schwierigkeitsgrad kann jeder Benutzer die Eindringtiefe individuell bestimmen und einfach zum nächsten Modul weitergehen, wenn er den Eindruck hat, es wird zu spezifisch. Durch diese Anordnung der Schlüsselwörter (den Bedeutungszusammenhängen statt dem Alphabet folgend) ergeben sich zusätzliche Kopplungseffekte, wodurch die Effizienz von **KWiC-Web** weiter gesteigert wird, da die Behaltensquote vor allem für Benutzer, die mit dem betreffenden Fachgebiet in der Muttersprache bereits vertraut sind, noch höher wird. Die Einträge decken jedes Gebiet so ab, dass zwischen den Modulen keine wesentlichen Überschneidungen oder Lücken entstehen.

Die Module sind mit treffenden Überschriften versehen, die den jeweiligen Bereich klar umreißen. So findet man beispielsweise Termini wie *teeth grinding*, *exfoliated* und *gag reflex* im Modul **Dentition & Mastication**, und Einträge wie *ache*, *tender*, und *analgesic* im Modul **Pain**. Wenn sich auch in inhaltlich angrenzenden Modulen manche Ausdrücke wiederfinden, als Keywords sind sie jeweils nur einem Modul zugeordnet.

Querverweise: Am Beginn jedes Moduls wird auf Zusammenhänge mit verwandten Modulen verwiesen, in denen der Benutzer viele Termini samt ausführlichen Erklärungen und Übersetzungen wiederfinden kann. Auf zusätzliche Querverbindungen zwischen einzelnen Termini verschiedener Module wird jeweils beim betreffenden Wort verwiesen

(z. B. → **U23**-14). Damit wird das Modul (Unit 23) und die Eintragsnummer (14) bezeichnet.

Wie sind die einzelnen Einträge strukturiert?

Die Einträge enthalten folgende Komponenten:

Das Hauptstichwort (Schlüsselwort): Jedes Modul wurde so angelegt, dass es 10 bis 35 Einträge (Hauptstichwörter und deren Wortfelder) umfasst. Nominalformen und Nominalverbindungen machen den Großteil der Schlüsselwörter aus; die dazugehörigen Adjektive, Präpositionen und Verben findet man in den Beschreibungen, Beispielsätzen, Wortverbindungen und Phrasen (z. B. *an elective operation, to undergo an operation for a tumor, to be operated on, operative approach, operating room*). Deshalb scheint z. B. das Verb *perform* zwar nirgends als Haupteintrag auf, im Kontext taucht es allerdings immer wieder in Verbphrasen wie *to perform a study/an operation/a biopsy* bei den betreffenden Nomina auf.

Verwandte Ausdrücke: Bei jedem Schlüsselwort sind Synonyme (*syn*), Fast-Synonyme (*sim*), Antonyme (*opposite*) und verwandte Ausdrücke (*rel*) wie z. B. Unter- und Nebenbegriffe des Haupteintrags angeführt. Bei Vorliegen mehrerer synonymer Ausdrücke werden die häufiger verwendeten zuerst genannt, selten gebrauchte Benennungen werden gekennzeichnet (*rare*). Zusammen mit den Angaben zur Sprachebene und den Kontextbeispielen wird dadurch für den Benutzer ersichtlich, welcher Terminus in welchem Zusammenhang verwendet wird.

Deutsche Übersetzungen (Marginalspalte): Für jedes Schlüsselwort und die verwandten Ausdrücke werden in der Marginalspalte die deutschen Entsprechungen angeführt. Zusätzlich werden Wörter oder Passagen im Kontext, die für den Benutzer schwer aus dem Zusammenhang erschließbar bzw. besonders wichtig oder nützlich sind, übersetzt. Die übersetzten Passagen sind im englischen Text blau markiert und über Hochzahlen den Übersetzungen in der Marginalspalte zugeordnet. Dadurch bekommt der Benutzer auch Einblick in spezielle Bedeutungen der Termini im authentischen Kontext.

Worterklärungen: Hier handelt es sich weniger um Definitionen als um beschreibende Erklärungen bzw. Paraphrasen in einfachem Englisch. Diese sind für Fachleute als Formulierungshilfe ebenso nützlich wie für Translatoren, die die Bedeutung des Fachausdrucks weder im Englischen noch in der Muttersprache kennen. Außerdem enthalten diese Umschreibungen weitere Neben-, Über- und Unterbegriffe zu den Haupteinträgen.

Authentische Beispielsätze (>>-Symbol): Diese sind dem medizinischen Korpus entnommen und geben dem Benutzer Einblick in die authentische Verwendung der Fachtermini in der medizinischen Literatur. Bei der Auswahl der Beispiele wurde sowohl auf die sprachliche als auch die fachliche Relevanz geachtet.

Wortfamilie: Bei jedem Schlüsselwort und dessen verwandten Ausdrücken werden auch die dazugehörigen Wortfamilien (Verben, Adjektive, etc.) angeführt. Man findet also beim Eintrag *diagnosis* auch *to (over)diagnose, misdiagnosis, (non)diagnostic*, etc.

Hinweise zur Grammatik und Stilebene: Neben Angaben zu Wortart und grammatikalischen Besonderheiten (Plural, unregelmäßiges Verb, etc.) wird auch auf die Sprachebene, in der die Ausdrücke vorwiegend verwendet werden, verwiesen (z. B. Fachterminus, Fachjargon, klinischer oder umgangssprachlicher Ausdruck). Bei Wörtern, die in mehr als zwei Stilebenen verwendet werden, wurde auf eine Angabe verzichtet. Aus Platzgründen konnte die Stilebene bei den verwandten Termini und den Wortfamilien nur dann angegeben werden, wenn diese von jener der Wörter davor bzw. danach abweicht. Die Kennzeichnung der Sprachebenen und deren Bedeutung ist auf der Umschlagklappe erläutert.

Phrasen und Kollokationen (*Use*): Diese werden ähnlich wie in Kollokationswörterbüchern jeweils in Blöcken von linken bzw. rechten Kollokationen dargestellt. Aus Platzgründen wurde auf die Tilde verzichtet; das zu ergänzende „Tildewort" ist kursiv/fett hervorgehoben. Der Eintrag *saline / IV / bolus **infusion** • **infusion** rate / bottle / tubing* ist also wie folgt zu lesen: *saline infusion, IV infusion, bolus infusion* <neuer Block> *infusion rate, infusion bottle, infusion tubing*. Bei Aneinanderreihungen von Verbphrasen, z. B. *to relieve/blunt/alleviate **pain*** (*to* ist jeweils zu ergänzen) und bei zusammengesetzten Wörtern, wie z. B. *hypo/ hyper**esthesia*** oder ***patho**genesis /physiology* steht der Schrägstrich direkt beim betreffenden Wort(teil).

Klinische Phrasen: In vielen Fachbereichen gibt es wiederkehrende klinische Situationen, in denen bestimmte Wendungen und Aussagen ständig vorkommen. Solche Standardphrasen sind jeweils am Ende des Moduls unter **Clinical Phrases** in ganzen Sätzen mit der deutschen Entsprechung angeführt (in 21 Modulen).

Aussprache: Bei englischen Wörtern, deren Aussprache bzw. Betonung Probleme bereiten kann, ist die internationale Lautschrift bzw. die Betonung angegeben. Eine Erklärung der Lautschriftsymbole anhand von Beispielen findet sich in der Umschlagklappe.

Tipps und Hinweise auf Besonderheiten (*Note*): Bei Stichwörtern, die in Bezug auf Verwendung, Bedeutung oder Grammatik besondere Schwierigkeiten bereiten, werden diese in leicht verständlichem Englisch erläutert (Hinweise auf „falsche Freunde", Verwechslungsgefahren, Nebenbedeutungen, etc.).

Kann ich KWiC Web auch zum Nachschlagen bestimmter Suchwörter verwenden?

Alle englischen Schlüsselwörter und Übersetzungsäquivalente sind auch über einen deutschen und englischen Index auffindbar, wodurch **KWiC-Web** auch wie ein zweisprachiges Fachwörterbuch zum Nachschlagen geeignet ist. Zudem bietet ein Index der englischen Abkürzungen direkten Zugang zu den medizinischen Akronymen im Text.

Wie kann ich mit KWiC-Web arbeiten?

Es gibt grundsätzlich drei Zugangswege zu den in **KWiC-Web** aufbereiteten Materialien.

1. Über das Inhaltsverzeichnis und das Modulregister. Im Inhaltsverzeichnis finden Sie eine Übersicht der einzelnen Module (Units), Abschnitte und Fachbereiche in englischer und deutscher Sprache. Hier können Sie die für Sie relevanten Bereiche auswählen und dann die betreffenden Module in der gewünschten Tiefe durchgehen. Mit Hilfe des Griffregisters finden Sie schnell zu den gesuchten Modulen.

2. Über die Querverweise. Jedes Modul sowie viele Schlüsselwörter stehen mit anderen Modulen bzw. Einträgen in Verbindung. Auf Querverbindungen zu anderen Units wird jeweils am Beginn des Moduls verwiesen (***Related Units***). Wollen Sie also ein spezielles Fachgebiet umfassend erarbeiten, folgen Sie einfach diesen Verweisen, um zu jenen Fachbereichen zu gelangen, die damit in Verbindung stehen. Auch die Querverweise zwischen einzelnen Termini sind nützliche Wegweiser zu weiteren fachlichen Zusammenhängen.

3. Über die Indices. Suchen Sie spezielle Termini oder wollen deren Bedeutung, Übersetzung, Verwendung, oder Wortverbindungen nachschlagen, können Sie dies mit Hilfe des deutschen bzw. englischen Index tun. Über den Index können Sie auch schnell zu allen Schlüsselwörtern und ihrem sprachlichen Umfeld gelangen.

Wer kann mit KWiC-Web arbeiten?

Grundsätzlich jeder, der über grundlegende Englischkenntnisse aus der Schulzeit verfügt (B1-B2 Niveau, gemeinsamer Referenzrahmen des Europarates). Durch die differenzierte Aufbereitung des reichhaltigen Sprachmaterials ist **KWiC-Web** für verschiedene Benutzergruppen optimal verwendbar.

Studenten und Ärzte in Ausbildung, die mit englischen Lehrbüchern und internationalen Fachzeitschriften arbeiten, Ihre Dissertation in englischer Sprache verfassen, oder eine Famulatur in Edinburg, Boston, Kapstadt, Singapur oder Sydney anstreben.

Ärzte in Klinik und Forschung, die sich mit Hilfe von englischen Fachartikeln weiterbilden, internationale Kongresse besuchen, sich auf ein Auslandsjahr vorbereiten, oder einen Artikel in einer internationalen Fachzeitschrift veröffentlichen wollen.

Pflegefachkräfte, Therapeuten, MTA, Rettungshelfer, etc., die sich mit den englischen Begriffen in ihrem Fachbereich vertraut machen wollen. Durch die didaktische Gliederung des Wortschatzes (Grundlegendes zuerst) müssen die relevanten Termini nicht erst mühsam aus einer Fülle von Texten herausgefiltert werden.

Übersetzer und Dolmetscher, die im medizinischen Bereich arbeiten. Ob Sie sich in ein neues Fachgebiet einarbeiten oder spezielle Wortverbindungen oder Phrasen suchen, in **KWiC-Web** finden Sie auf kleinstem Raum eine Fülle von sprachlichen und fachlichen Informationen, die Sie sonst aus verschiedenen Nachschlagewerken erst mühsam zusammensuchen müssen oder überhaupt in keinem anderen Behelf finden können.

Unit 1   Health & Fitness

Related Units: 2 Diet & Dieting, 4 Illness & Recovery, 64 Body Movement, 102 History Taking, 142 Physiotherapy

health [helθ] *n*   opposite **illness**[1], **sickness**[1], **ill health**[2] *n* → U4-1

condition of physical [fɪzɪkᵊl], mental, and social well-being; being free from disease, complaints [eɪ] or abnormalities

healthful[3] [helθfᵊl] *adj* • **healthfulness** *n* • **healthcare**[4] [helθkeɚ] *n*

» This may be important to your health. She was in good health until 4 days before she was admitted to the hospital[5]. Antibiotics [aɪD:] should be given for wounds [u:] in persons with general ill health. Is there a pattern of overconcern[6] [sɜː] about the child's health?

Use **to be in** good/the best of[7]/excellent[7]/perfect[7]/poor **health** • **to have a** strong/sound **health** • **to be** a picture of / to be good/bad for one's[8] **health** • **to** jeopardize[9] [dʒep-] /restore **sb.'s health** • general / mental / emotional [oʊʃ]/ public **health** • child / maternal [ɜː]/ family / adolescent [es] **health** • state / preservation **of health** • **health** problem / education[10] / policy[11] / care (costs) • **health** insurance[12] / risk or hazard [æ]/ threat [e]/ status[13] / food[14] • **health** history / habits / behavior[15] [eɪ]/ assessment • **health** screening [iː] / tests[16] / certificate[17] / professional / check[18] [tʃek] • **healthful** diet[19] [daɪət]/ habits / living / body weight • to provide **health care** • **health care** services / system[20] / provider [aɪ]/ worker • **health**-compromising behavior

Gesundheit
Krankheit[1] Krankheit, Kränklichkeit[2] gesund, bekömmlich[3] medizin. Versorgung[4] ins Krankenhaus eingeliefert[5] übertriebene Sorge[6] sich bester Gesundheit erfreuen[7] ungesund/ gesundheitsschädlich sein[8] die Gesundheit gefährden[9] Gesundheitserziehung[10] Gesundheitspolitik[11] Krankenversicherung[12] Gesundheitszustand[13] Reform-, Biokost[14] Gesundheitsverhalten[15] Reihenuntersuchungen[16] Gesundheitszeugnis, -attest[17] Vorsorgeuntersuchung[18] gesunde Nahrung[19] Gesundheitswesen[20]

1

healthy [helθi] - healthier - healthiest *adj*
opposite **not healthy** or **unhealthy**[1] *adj*

(i) not ill, strong and well and/or showing good health (ii) good for your health

healthy-looking *adj* • **healthy-appearing** [ɪɚ] *adj* • **healthiness**[2] *n*

» A chronic course is more often seen in previously [iː] healthy adults. I'm much healthier now. Adolescence is one of the physically healthiest periods in an individual's life. All unhealthy granulation tissue must be removed.

Use to be/get/remain/appear/be considered **healthy** • **healthy** tissue[3] / body / skin and hair • **healthy** appetite[4] / eating • **healthy** lifestyle[5] / baby / child • **healthy** individuals or subjects [ʌ]/ patients • **healthy** climate [aɪ]/ attitude[6] /-appearing organ • generally / apparently[7] [eɚ]/ relatively **healthy** • physically[8] [ɪ]/ otherwise **healthy** • **unhealthy** person / attitude /-looking[9]

(i) gesund
(ii) heilsam, bekömmlich
ungesund[1] Gesundheit[2] gesundes Gewebe[3] guter Appetit[4] gesunde Lebensweise[5] gesunde Einstellung[6] scheinbar gesund[7] körperlich gesund[8] ungesund aussehend[9]

2

well *adv*   *syn* **sound** [saʊnd], **fine** [faɪn] *adj*, opposite **unwell**[1], **sick**[2] *adj*

to be in good health and without injuries or any other health problems

good - better - best *adj* • **to do sb. good**[3] *phr* • **be bad/ good for**[4] *phr*

» The patient seemed to be doing well. I'm quite fine, thanks. I had a minor injury but it feels fine now and shouldn't cause me any problems. This is a common cause of acute hemolysis in a previously well adult patient. Immobilization must be continued until bone healing [iː] is sound[5]. Some sleep will do you good. Garlic[6] is said to be good for the heart [ɑː].

Use to be or feel/appear/recover [ʌ] /get **well** • systemically / seemingly[7] / otherwise **well** • to be **fine** • **sound** healing[8] [iː]/ sleep[9] • **well** baby care • **get well** card • **well**-nourished[10] [ɜː] (*abbr* W/N) /-developed /-trained • **well**-tolerated[11] /-preserved[12] [ɜː]/-balanced diet[13] • **well**-adjusted [dʒʌ]/-disposed[14]

gesund/ wohlauf sein, sich wohl fühlen
unwohl, unpässlich[1] krank[2] jem. gut tun/ helfen[3] jem. gut tun, gesund sein[4] abgeschlossen[5] Knoblauch[6] scheinbar gesund[7] gute Heilung[8] tiefer Schlaf[9] in gutem Ernährungszustand[10] gut verträglich[11] gut erhalten[12] ausgewogene Kost[13] gewogen, freundlich gesinnt[14]

3

thriving [θraɪvɪŋ] *adj*   *sim* **flourishing**[1][ɜː‖*BE* ʌ], **bouncing**[2] [baʊn'sɪŋ] *adj*

growing stronger, developing well, being healthy and successful

» This is a common cause of loose stools[3] [uː] in thriving children. Some breast-fed [e] infants fail to thrive. How can children who are apparently not getting enough calories in their diets be flourishing? He ran a flourishing private practice until 2003. Due to a relative lack of WBCs[4] in the CSF[5], the infection flourishes. Bouncing babies make healthier grown-ups.

Use **thriving** child / infant • **flourishing** practice[6] / business [ɪ] • **bouncing** baby[7] • with health[8] / gait[9] [ɡeɪt]

gut gedeihend, kräftig, (auf)blühend
gut gedeihend, blühend, florierend[1] stramm, kräftig[2] Durchfall[3] Leukozyten[4] Zerebrospinalflüssigkeit, Liquor[5] gutgehende Praxis[6] strammer Säugling[7] vor Gesundheit strotzend[8] federnder Gang[9]

4

2 BASIC MEDICAL TERMS — Health & Fitness

hygienic [haɪdʒiː‖enɪk] *adj* *syn* **s**a**nitary** *adj, rel* **wh**o**lesome**[1], **benef**i**cial**[2] *adj*

to preserve[3] [ɜː] or promote a person's health, esp. by keeping the body and/or the environment [aɪ] free from agents [eɪdʒ] that are deleterious[4] [ɪɚ] to health

hygie**ne**[5] *n* • **hygienist** *n* • **sanit**a**tion**[5] [eɪ] *n* • **s**a**nitize**[6] *v* • **uns**a**nitary**[7] *adj*
• **wh**o**lesomeness**[8] *n* → U2-13 • **unwh**o**lesome**[9] *adj* • **b**e**nefit**[10] *vt & vi & n*

» The normal microbial flora is influenced by factors such as the diet, hygienic habits[11], sanitary conditions, or air pollution [uː∫]. Wholesome natural food contains plenty of proteins and vitamins. Exercise programs are also beneficial. Some postmenopausal [ɒː] women benefit from chemotherapy [kiːm-]. There may be a benefit in hospitalized patients.

Use **hygienic** practices[11] / conditions / problem • **sanitary** measures [eʒ]/ precautions [ɒː]/ regulations • **sanitary** facilities[12] [sɪ]/ napkin *or* pad[13] *or (BE)* towel[13] [taʊəl] • **personal**[11] / good foot / genital **hygiene** • bronchial [k]/ oral *or* dental / fecal [iːk]/ mental[14] **hygiene** • level of / (in)adequate / poor **sanitation** • environmental / food / fecal[15] **sanitation** • **wholesome** diet / entertainment [eɪ] • **beneficial** effect[16] / results / response • **to benefit** from • to be of (great[17]/ little/ lasting/ limited) **benefit for** • health / clinical / therapeutic / cosmetic **benefit** • considerable / questionable[18] / survival[19] [aɪ] **benefit**

hygienisch, sauber, sanitär, gesund(heitlich)
gesund, bekömmlich, gut[1] zuträglich, förderlich[2] erhalten[3] schädlich[4] Gesundheitspflege, Hygiene[5] keimfrei machen, sterilisieren[6] unhygienisch[7] Gesundheit, Bekömmlichkeit[8] ungesund, ungut[9] guttun, nützen; profitieren, Nutzen ziehen; Vorteil, Nutzen[10] Körperpflege[11] sanitäre Einrichtungen[12] Damenbinde[13] Psychohygiene[14] Abwasserreinigung[15] günstige Wirkung[16] von großem Nutzen/ sehr vorteilhaft sein für[17] zweifelhafter Nutzen[18] Überlebensvorteil[19]   5

---

lively [laɪvli] *adv* *sim* **vital**[1] [vaɪtᵊl], **vivacious**[2] [vɪveɪ∫əs] *adj*
rel **energetic**[3] [dʒe], **vigorous**[4] [ɪ], **ex**u**berant**[5] [uː] *adj*

very active and full of life, spirit, and energy

live**liness** *n* • **vit**a**lity**[6] *n* • **energy** [enɚdʒi] *n* • **vigor**[7] [vɪgɚ] *n*

» Her lively manner lends itself to easily established relationships, but she is rarely deeply involved emotionally. Hyperthymic [aɪ] individuals[8] tend to be cheerful, exuberant, overconfident, energetic, vigorous, and full of plans. Pain-induced immobility began to compromise[9] the patient's energy, spirit, appetite, and vitality. The extent of lactic acidosis[10] depends on the duration and vigor of muscular [ʌ] activity.

Use **lively** character / mind[11] / humor / interest[12] / discussion • **vital** personality / signs[13] / organs • **vital** capacity[14] / statistics • **vivacious** girl / manner / personality • **energetic** patient / walking[15] • **vigorous** infant[16] / exercise • **vigorous** coughing[17] [kɒːf-]/ cry / treatment[18] • **exuberant** youth [juːθ]/ mood[19] [uː] • **exuberant** behavior / energy / life force • youth and / lost **vitality** • full of / to burst [ɜː] with **energy** • sexual[20] **vigor**

lebhaft, lebendig, vital
vital; (lebens)wichtig[1] lebhaft, munter[2] schwungvoll, aktiv, voller Energie[3] dynamisch, kraftvoll, energisch[4] ausgelassen, (über)sprudelnd[5] Vitalität[6] Kraft, Energie, Dynamik[7] Hyperthymiker/ hyperthyme Persönlichkeiten[8] beeinträchtigen[9] Lakt(at)azidose[10] wacher Geist[11] reges Interesse[12] Vitalfunktionen/ -zeichen[13] Vitalkapazität[14] flottes/ rasches Gehen[15] kräftiges Kind[16] starker Husten[17] intensive Behandlung[18] ausgelassene Stimmung[19] sexuelle Spannkraft[20]   6

---

well-being *n* *sim* **wellness**[1] *n, rel* **welfare**[2] [welfeɚ] *n* → U13-6

achievement [t∫] of a state of good health as defined [aɪ] by the individual

» A regular exercise program consistent with life-style, age, and cardiac status certainly enhances general well-being. Also elderly people participate [ɪs] in our wellness program.

Use **overall**[3] / **physical**[4] [ɪ]/ emotional / mental **well-being** • fetal [iː]/ long-term / personal **well-being** • feeling / improved sense[5] **of well-being** • emotional / dental **wellness** • **wellness** clinic / plan / walking / body treatment • to be on[6] / social / employee's / child[7] **welfare** • **welfare** benefits[8] / worker[9] / work • **welfare** officer / agency [eɪdʒ]/ policy / state[10]

Wohl(befinden), Gesundheit
Wellness[1] Wohl(ergehen); Wohlfahrt, Sozialhilfe, Fürsorge[2] allgemeines Wohlbefinden[3] körperl. Gesundheit/ Wohlbefinden[4] größeres Wohlbefinden[5] Sozialhilfe beziehen[6] Kinderfürsorge[7] Sozialhilfe[8] Sozialarbeiter(in)[9] Wohlfahrtsstaat[10]   7

---

constitution [(j)uː∫] *n clin & term* *rel* **phenotype**[1] [fiːnətaɪp], **somatotype**[2] [soʊmətə-‖-mætətaɪp] *n term* → U25-3

inborn physical or psychological makeup of an individual modified by environmental factors

constitu**tional**[3] *adj term* • **phenotypic** [fiːnətɪpɪk] *adj* • **somatotyping**[4] *n*

» Patients who have a stoic [stoʊɪk] constitution will persevere[5] with tremendous pain. In children with constitutional short stature[6] [stæt∫ɚ], birth weight [weɪt] and length are not affected, but typically the rate of growth is decreased during infancy.

Use to have a strong[7]/good **constitution** • male / chromosomal[8] / XXY / psychopathic [saɪkə-]/ **constitution** • **constitutional** cause / weakness [iː]/ symptoms[9] • **constitutional** disease[10] / delay [eɪ] of growth[6] [groʊθ]/ psychology

Konstitution, Verfassung
Phänotyp, (äußeres) Erscheinungsbild[1] Körperbau-, Konstitutionstyp[2] konstitutionell, anlagebedingt, Konstitutions-[3] Einteilung in verschiedene Körperbautypen[4] durchhalten[5] konstitutionelle(r) Wachstumsverzögerung/ Minderwuchs[6] eine robuste Konstitution haben[7] Chromosomenkonfiguration[8] Allgemeinsymptome, konstitutionelle S.[9] konstitutionelle Krankheit[10]   8

Health & Fitness BASIC MEDICAL TERMS 3

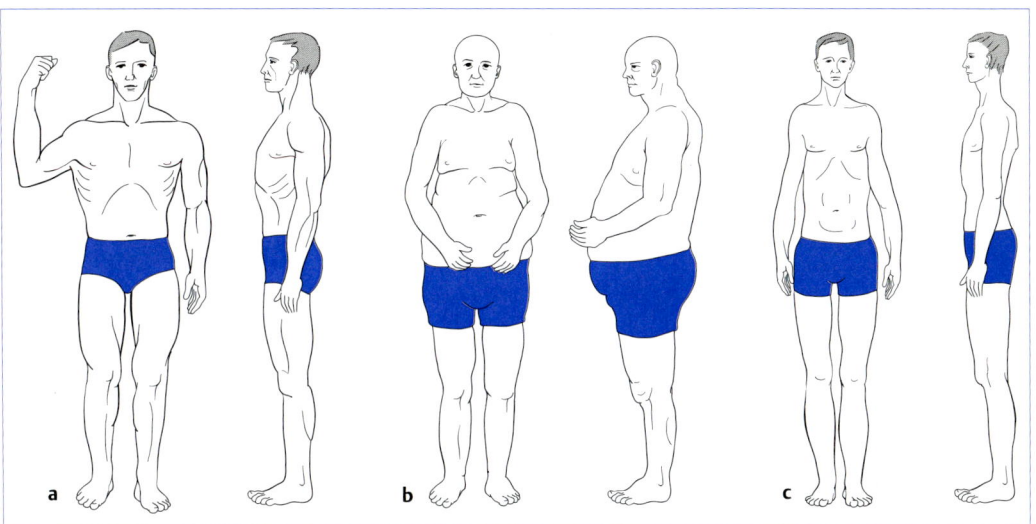

Chief constitutional types according to Kretschmer

(physical) fitness [fɪzɪkəl fɪtnəs] n   sim condition¹ [kəndɪʃən], shape² n

gute körperliche Verfassung/ Gesundheit, Fitness
körperl. Verfassung, Kondition, Form¹ Verfassung, Form² fit, durchtrainiert, in Form³ Konditi-on(straining)⁴ Fitnesstraining⁵ Fitnessfanatiker(in)⁶ Fitnesstest⁷ Fitnessraum⁸ Fitnesstrainer(in)⁹ Arbeitsfähigkeit¹⁰ Reisefähigkeit¹¹ keine Kondition haben¹² schlechter konditioneller Zustand¹³ in Form bleiben¹⁴

physically strong, and in good condition; esp. as a result of exercise
fit³ adj • **well-conditioned**³ adj • **conditioning**⁴ n

» How much does she spend on fitness training and beauty [bjuːti] treatments. Every week of rest usually requires at least two weeks of exercising to reach preinjury [priːɪndʒəri] fitness level. Supervised fitness walking was advised [aɪ] to patients with osteoarthritis [aɪ] of the knee. In fit patients, surgery was associated with a lower frequency of complications.

Use to build/test/prove/judge [ʌ] **sb's fitness** • biologic / aerobic / cardiopulmonary [uːʌ] / psychologic **fitness** • **fitness** program / exercise or routine⁵ [iː] / equipment / freak⁶ [iː] • **fitness** test⁷ / level / gym⁸ [dʒɪm] / problem / room⁸ / center / club / **fitness** instructor⁹ [ʌ] / guru / for work¹⁰ / to travel¹¹ • to keep **fit** • to be in good/stable/out of¹² **condition** • exercise / abdominal / poor¹³ **conditioning** • to be/get/keep/stay¹⁴ **in shape**

9

recreation [rekrieɪʃən] n
sim **relaxation¹** [eɪʃ], **diversion²** [dɪvɜːrʃən] n, **rest³** n & v
rel **regeneration⁴** [rɪdʒənəreɪʃən] n

Erholung, Entspannung
Entspannung, Erschlaffung, Relaxation¹ Unterhaltung, Zerstreuung² Ruhe, Erholung; ruhen, s. ausruhen, schonen³ Erneuerung, Neubildung, Regeneration⁴ Freizeit⁵ (sich) regenerieren, sich erholen⁶ verstauchter Knöchel⁷ Erholung im Freien⁸ Spiel-, Sportplatz⁹ Entspannung fördern¹⁰ Beckenbodenentspannung¹¹ Entspannungstechniken¹² Freizeiteinrichtungen¹³ Freizeitbeschäftigung¹⁴ Freizeitdrogen¹⁵ ruhig sein; s. in Ruhelage befinden¹⁶ s. ausruhen¹⁷ Gelenkschonung¹⁸ Alters-, Pflegeheim¹⁹

engaging in activities that divert, amuse or stimulate during one's leisure [liːʒər‖BE leʒə] time⁵
recreate v • **relax** [rɪlæks] v • **divert** [ɜː] v • **regenerate⁶** v • **recreational** adj

» Are you aware of the health risks associated with the ever-increasing demands made by the duty-rest-recreation schedules [sk‖ʃedjuːlz] in our round-the-clock society? He attributes his return to normality to deep relaxation therapy. I find a tremendous relaxation in fishing. The sprained [eɪ] ankle⁷ should be rested sufficiently [ɪʃ] to allow complete healing [iː].

Use physical / healthy [e] / outdoor⁸ / leisurely [iː] **recreation** • **recreation** center / ground⁹ • pleasant [e] / entertaining [eɪ] / welcome **diversion** • teenage / occasional [eɪʒ] / summer-time **diversion** • to promote¹⁰/achieve **relaxation** • muscle / pelvic floor¹¹ **relaxation** • period / ritual / state / degree **of relaxation** • **relaxation** techniques¹² [tekniːks] • activities • **recreational** facilities¹³ / activity¹⁴ / water sports / skiing • **recreational** sun exposure / interests / drugs¹⁵ • to be at¹⁶/have or take a¹⁷ /be relieved by/seek **rest** • (complete/ strict/ prolonged) bed / joint¹⁸ / adequate **rest** • **rest** period / day / home¹⁹

10

4 BASIC MEDICAL TERMS   Health & Fitness

able-bodied *adj*   *rel* **robust**[1] [ʌ], **firm**[1] [ɜː] *adj, opposite* **disabled**[2] [eɪ] *adj & n*
healthy, strong, physically fit, and without injuries [ɪndʒəːiːz] or **infirmity**[3] [ɜː]
firmness *n* • **robustness**[4] *n* • **disability**[5] [dɪsəbɪləti] *n* → U142-3 • **able-bodied** *n*
» It's often difficult for the able-bodied to understand the problems the disabled experience in their lives. The patient **swiftly**[6] returned to remarkably robust health and remained free of illness. Join our health club to maintain a youthful, radiant [eɪ], and firm body year round.
Use **able-bodied** man • **robust** health[7] / child / **immune response**[8] • **firm** body / muscles / belly[9] / handshake • tissue / abdominal / skin / breast [e] / stool [uː] **firmness**

gesund, körperlich leistungsfähig, kräftig
robust, widerstandsfähig[1] behindert; Behinderte[2] Gebrechlichkeit[3] Robustheit, Widerstandsfähigkeit[4] Behinderung[5] rasch[6] robuste Gesundheit[7] starke Immunantwort/-reaktion[8] Waschbrettbauch, straffer Bauch[9]

11

---

workout *n*   *sim* **training**[1] [eɪ] *n, rel* **physical exercise**[2], **sport(s)**[3] *n* → U64-18
activity of **exerting**[4] [ɜː] one's muscles in various ways to keep fit, trim one's body or lose weight
to work out[4] *v phr* • **exercise**[4] *v* • **train**[4] *v* • **sportsman**[5] *n* • **sporting**[6] *adj*
» If an athlete [iː] trains twice a day, each hard **workout**[7] should be followed by at least 3 easy ones. Dyspnea [ɪ] in this situation is similar to that **brought on**[8] by exercise. You should exercise every morning and get plenty of fresh air. He is allowed several hours a day of relaxation or recreation and can occasionally exercise by playing ball. Cooling [uː] down (gradually slowing down before stopping the exercise) can help prevent **dizziness**[9].
Use intense or vigorous[7] / light / frequent **workout** • weight-lifting / a 30-minute aerobic **workout** • to do[10]/try/prescribe/advise **exercises** • (regular) physical / stretching / respiratory[11] **exercises** • (an)aerobic / leg / back / neck **exercises** • stomach / light / strenuous[12] **exercises** • **exercise** program / bicycle[13] [baɪsɪkl]/ test[14] / (in)tolerance[15] • contact / competitive[16] **sports** • alternate[17] **sport** • **sport** physical[18] • **sports** medicine[19] / activities / shoes /-related fracture • **sporting** event[20] / accident • interval[21] / weight / strength[22] **training** • altitude[23] [æ]/ autogenic[24] [dʒe]/ biofeedback **training** • **training** session / schedule[25]

(Körper)training, Trainingseinheit
Übung, Training[1] körperl. Ertüchtigung, Turnübungen[2] Sport[3] trainieren[4] Sportler[5] sportlich[6] hartes Training[7] verursacht[8] Schwindel[9] Gymnastik machen[10] Atemübungen[11] anstrengende Übungen[12] Standrad, Heimtrainer[13] Belastungstest[14] physische Belastbarkeit[15] Leistungssport[16] Ausgleichssport, Ersatzsportart[17] sportmedizin. Untersuchung[18] Sportmedizin[19] Wettkampf[20] Intervalltraining[21] Krafttraining[22] Höhentraining[23] autogenes Training[24] Trainingsplan[25]

12

---

warm *or* **tune** *or* **tone up** *v phr*   *sim* **limber** *or* **loosen** [uː] **up**[1] *v phr,*
                                                      rel **stretching**[2] *n*
to do preliminary exercises (skipping[3], stretching) to optimize muscle performance and prevent injury
warm-up *n* • **tone**[4] [toʊn] *v & n* • **toning** *n* • **stretch** [stretʃ] *v* • **limber**[5] [ɪ] *adj*
» Stretching should be done after a warm-up and after exercise. Active warm-up by exercise, preferably by performing a sport at a relaxed pace[6] [peɪs], prepares muscles for competition more effectively than passive heating [iː] with a heating pad[7], ultrasound [ʌ], or infrared lamp. Limber up with a good stretching routine led by a qualified instructor [ʌ]. To avoid direct injury, athletes should never stretch further than they can hold for a count of 10. Stretching helps eliminate stress and tension [ʃ] and increase flexibility.
Use **to warm up** the muscles • thorough **warm-up** • to feel[8] **toned up** • **to limber up** one's legs / before the match • **limber** body • to do a lot of / regular **stretching** • **stretching** exercises[2] / out • and straining[9] [eɪ] • **to tone** one's body / oneself / selected muscles[10] • body / muscle / tissue **toning** • **toning** effect • muscle / resting[11] **tone**

aufwärmen
aufwärmen, Lockerungsübungen machen[1] Dehnen, Dehnungsübungen[2] Hüpfen, Hopsen, Traben, Seilspringen[3] stärken, kräftigen; Tonus, Spannungszustand[4] gelenkig, beweglich[5] Tempo[6] Heizkissen[7] sich gut in Form fühlen[8] Dehnen und Belasten[9] einzelne Muskeln kräftigen[10] Ruhetonus[11]

13

---

jogging *n*   *sim* **running**[1] [ʌ] *n, rel* **circuit** [sɜːrkɪt] **training**[2], **spinning**[3] [ɪ] *n*
running at a moderately swift pace as a form of exercise
jog [dʒɒːg] *v & n* • **jogger** *n* • **run**[4] - ran - run *v irr & n* • **runner**[5] [rʌnə] *n*
» Brisk walking[6], jogging, fast cycling [saɪklɪŋ] and doing heavy chores[7] [tʃ] are more effective than playing golf. I had a little jog this morning and the pain has gone. I was told to pedal out[8] a 100-mile day and follow that up with the ritual evening jog or yoga work-out.
Use to go/do a bit of/take up[9] **jogging** • daily / steady [e] **jogging** • **jogging** injury / in place[10] / shoes • **to jog** along • morning / 5-mile / gentle[11] [dʒ] / 12-minute **jog**

Lauftraining, Jogging
Lauf(en)[1] Zirkeltraining[2] Ergometertraining, Spinning[3] laufen, Lauf[4] Läufer(in)[5] rasches Gehen, Walken[6] schwere körperl. Arbeit[7] mit d. Fahrrad zurücklegen[8] zu joggen anfangen[9] Joggen an Ort und Stelle[10] lockerer Lauf[11]

14

Health & Fitness   BASIC MEDICAL TERMS **5**

aerobics [eəˈɔːbɪks] n   rel **gymnastics¹** [dʒɪmˈnæstɪks],
                    calisthenics¹, isometrics² [aɪsə-] n → U142-17

series of rhythmic [ɪ] exercises performed to music that stimulate the aerobic capacity of the body

gymnasium³ [eɪ] n • **gymnast⁴** n • **(an)aerobic⁵** adj term • **isometric** adj

» My doctor recommends 20-30 minutes of vigorous, continuous aerobic exercise 3-5 times a week. Calisthenics is a combination of controlled exercises, gymnastics, and simplified ballet [bæleɪ], which combines fitness, flexibility, poise⁶ [pɔɪz], and graceful [eɪs] movement. Many women use calisthenics as a physique [fɪziːk] builder⁷. Isometrics is an exercise that involves muscle contraction through pressing and pulling [ʊ] against an immovable object. Are there isometric exercises² I can do while using cruise control on long trips?

Use step / low intensity / water or aqua⁸ **aerobics** • **anaerobic** threshold (abbr AT) exercise⁹ • **anaerobic** respiration¹⁰ / training • **aerobic** exercises / appliances¹¹ [aɪ] • group / eye¹² / bodyweight¹³ **calisthenics** • muscular [ʌ] endurance / roadside¹⁴ / computer¹⁵ **calisthenics** • **calisthenic** exercises or drills • general / therapeutic or remedial¹⁶ / water **gymnastics** • competitive¹⁷ / rhythmic [ɪ] (sportive)¹⁸ / vocal / mental **gymnastics**

Aerobic
Gymnastik¹ isometrische Übungen² Sport-, Turnhalle³ Kunstturner(in)⁴ (an)aerob⁵ (Körper)haltung⁶ zur Verbesserung d. Figur⁷ Wassergymnastik, Wasser-Aerobic, Aquarhythmik⁸ anaerobes Schwellentraining⁹ anaerobe (Zell)atmung¹⁰ Aerobicgeräte¹¹ Augengymnastik¹² Trimmübungen (z. Gewichtsreduktion)¹³ Entspannungsübungen f. Autofahrer¹⁴ Haltungsgymnastik f. Bildschirmarbeiter¹⁵ Heilgymnastik¹⁶ Kunstturnen¹⁷ rhythmische Sportgymnastik¹⁸

15

yoga [jougə] n   rel **meditation¹** [eɪʃ], **deep muscle relaxation²** n

system of physical exercises focused on muscle tone, holding of postures, breathing [iː] exercises³, and meditation to achieve physical and mental well-being and tranquility⁴ [kwɪ]

meditate⁵ v • **meditative⁶** adj • **relaxing⁷** adj

» Lessening response to stress by various techniques [k] such as yoga, hypnosis [hɪp-], transcendental meditation, or biofeedback is helpful for many patients. There has been an upsurge [-sɜːrdʒ] in demand⁸ for yoga and Tai Chi which combine meditation with physical activity to help relieve [iː] stress and increase self-awareness⁹ [eəʳ].

Use hatha¹⁰ / Tantric **yoga** • **yoga** position / classes¹¹ / healing center • transcendental¹² (abbr TM)/ Mantra / Zen / Christian¹³ **meditation**

Yoga, Joga
Meditation¹ Tiefenmuskelentspannung² Atemübungen³ Ruhe, Gelassenheit⁴ meditieren⁵ meditativ⁶ entspannend, erholsam⁷ verstärkte Nachfrage⁸ Selbsterkenntnis⁹ Hatha-Yoga¹⁰ Yogakurse¹¹ transzendentale Meditation¹² christl. Meditation¹³

16

sauna (bath) [sau‖ˈsɔːnə bæθ] n   syn **Finnish bath** n,
                       rel **steam** [iː] **room** or **bath¹** n

wooden room in which hot steam is used to open the pores [ɔː] and eliminate toxins through sweat [e] followed by rubbing [ʌ] the body and a cold shower [ʃauəʳ]

bathe² [beɪð] v • **bathing** [beɪðɪŋ] n

» A one-day membership at our health club includes a swim, supervised gym session, sauna, steam bath, massage, manicure, wash, blow dry³, and make-up. Don't plunge⁴ [plʌndʒ] into icy water after a steamy sauna. I enjoyed steam baths and saunas at the leisure center⁵.

Use to go for/have a **sauna** • communal⁶ / private **sauna** • vapor¹ [eɪ]/ whirlpool [ɜː] or jacuzzi [dʒəkuːzi]/ sitz⁷ **bath** • bubble⁸ [ʌ]/ Turkish⁹ / [ɜː]/ hot¹⁰ / ice(-water) **bath** • to take a¹¹ **bath**

Sauna(bad)
Dampfbad¹ baden, waschen² Fönen³ springen⁴ Freizeitzentrum⁵ öffentliche Sauna⁶ Sitzbad⁷ Schaumbad⁸ türkisches Bad⁹ heißes Bad¹⁰ ein Bad nehmen, baden¹¹

17

health spa n   rel **health club¹** n, **health farm²** n BE, **bodywork³** n → U142-20

health resort near a spring⁴ or at the seaside where people go to become more healthy

» Close by is a health spa with an indoor pool, steam room and gymnasium⁵. This is not a medical spa, but it does focus on total well-being. He looks trim after his month in a health farm. Based on the premise that physical illness is often emotionally based, healing centers have increasingly been outdoing⁶ health farms. Biomechanical therapy is a gentle and relaxing type of bodywork used to integrate and realign⁷ [aɪ] the body's structural framework.

Use bathing [eɪ]/ thalassotherapy⁸ / hot springs⁹ **spa** • fitness / hiking¹⁰ / elegant **spa** • **spa** water / bath / hotel¹¹ • **spa** treatment¹² / therapist / effect • **health** ranch² • women-only **health farm** • therapeutic / (w)holistic / deep tissue / aquatic [æ] **bodywork**

Kurort, -anstalt, Heilquelle
Fitness-Zentrum¹ Gesundheitszentrum² Bodywork, Körperarbeit³ Quelle⁴ Sporthalle, Fitnessraum⁵ übertreffen⁶ (wieder) einrichten⁷ Thalassotherapiezentrum⁸ Thermalbad⁹ Wanderkur¹⁰ Kurhotel¹¹ Balneotherapie, Badekur¹²

18

6 BASIC MEDICAL TERMS — Diet & Dieting

Kneipp cure [kjʊɚ] or **Kur** n   rel **flo(a)tation**[1] [eɪʃ], **Swiss shower**[2] n term
system of treatments combining applications of cold water, herbology[3], and diet of natural foods which was developed in Germany in the mid-1800s by Pastor Sebastian Kneipp
kneippism[4] n term • **float**[5] [floʊt] v • **showering** [ʃaʊɚɪŋ] n clin
» Floatation therapy can produce complex reactions in the body due to reduced gravity and the concentration of salts. A Vichy shower uses 5 or more shower nozzles[6] [ɒː] in a horizontal pattern over the client to create a gentle or vigorous rain shower[7].
Use **Kneipp** herbal [ɜː] baths[8] / Kur baths / (hydro)therapy[9] / wellness • **Kneipp** health resort[10] / garden herbs[11] / wellness center • water / rest **cure** • **flotation** therapy / tank[12] • to take/have **a shower** • cold / hot / Vichy[7] **shower** • jet[13] [dʒet]/ laser / evening **shower** • **shower** bath / room[14] / cap[15] / curtain[16] [ɜː]/ head[17]

Kneippkur
Flotation[1] Massagedusche[2] Kräuterkunde[3] Kneipp-Kur, Kneippbewegung[4] floaten, im Wasser schweben[5] Düsen[6] Regendusche[7] Kneippsche Kräuterbäder[8] Kneippsche Hydrotherapie[9] Kneipp-Kurort[10] Kneippsche Gartenkräuter[11] Schwebetank[12] Strahldusche[13] Duschraum[14] Duschhaube[15] Duschvorhang[16] Duschkopf[17]   19

mud [mʌd] **treatment** or **moortherapy** [muː-] n term
   rel **gommage**[1] [-ɑːʒ], **scrub**[2], **parafango**[3], **paraffin wrap**[4] [ræp] n term
treatment with mineral-rich moor mud[5] containing over 800 plants many of which have known medicinal [ɪs] properties
scrub[6] [skrʌb] v • **fango** [fæ‖fɑːŋgoʊ] n
» Seaweed [iː], mud or clay [kleɪ] body masks[7] are the domain [eɪ] of the health spa. The mud is applied to the body as hot packs[8] to detoxify the body, loosen[9] [uː] muscles and stimulate circulation. Mud treatments remineralize, hydrate [aɪ] and exfoliate the skin leaving [iː] it with a vital, healthy glow [oʊ].
Use **mud** bath[10] / bed • **moor** bath[10] /-mud facial [eɪ] mask /-drink therapy[11] • moor mud[12] / seaweed / aromatic **wrap** • body[13] / compression[14] **wrap** • (herbal) body / Loofah[15] / lymphatic[16] **scrub** • abrasive[1] [eɪ]/ lid / 2-minute **scrub** • **parafango** treatment / (body) wrap • **fango** bath / (mud) treatment[17] / total body[18] / foot exfoliating [oʊ] **gommage** • purifying / sea mineral[19] **gommage**

Moorbehandlung
Peeling[1] Abreibung[2] Parafango[3] Paraffinpackung[4] Moorerde[5] abreiben[6] Schlamm- oder Lehm-Ganz(körper)packungen[7] heiße Packungen[8] lockern[9] Moorbad[10] Moortrinkkur[11] Moorpackung[12] Ganzpackung[13] Kompresse, Wickel[14] Abreibung mit einem Luffaschwamm[15] manuelle Lymphdrainage[16] Fangobehandlung[17] Ganzkörperpeeling[18] Meersalzpeeling[19]   20

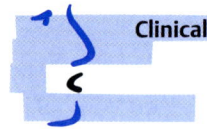

Clinical Phrases

How has your health been? Wie geht es Ihnen gesundheitlich? • I'm as fit as a fiddle. Ich bin kerngesund. • Walking the dog is the only exercise I get. Der Spaziergang mit dem Hund ist meine einzige körperliche Betätigung.• Is she still enjoying good health? Ist sie noch immer bei guter Gesundheit? • My wife nursed me back to health. Meine Frau hat mich gesund gepflegt. • How do you feel today? Wie geht es ihnen heute? • Thanks, I'm fine. Danke, gut. • For a 70-year-old he is quite well-preserved. Für einen Siebzigjährigen ist er gut erhalten.• I'm working hard at getting back into shape. Ich tue alles, um wieder in Form zu kommen. • I haven't been too well lately. Mir geht es in der letzten Zeit nicht gut.

Unit 2   Diet & Dieting
Related Units: 3 Food & Drink, 79 Nutrition, 27 Dentition & Mastication, 46 Digestion, 28 Metabolism

ingest [ɪndʒest] v term   syn **take in** v phr,
   sim **eat**[1] [iːt] - **ate** [eɪt‖et]   eaten v irr
to take in food, drink or medication via the mouth for digestion[2] [dɪ‖daɪdʒestʃən]
ingestion[3] n term • **ingestants**[4] n • **intake**[5] n • **overeat**[6] v clin • **eater** n • **eating** n
» Ingested food is mixed with salivary amylase [eɪ] before it reaches the stomach [k]. Hospitalize patients who have ingested mushrooms[7] [ʌ] known to cause serious [ɪə] poisoning[8]. Adequate intake of fluids should be encouraged [ɜː] in immobilized patients. Many depressed patients eat little and are frequently constipated[9]. Eat up[10] before it gets cold. You should not eat a late meal before bedtime.
Use **to ingest** food / foreign [fɒrɪn] bodies[11] • **ingested** eggs / fluid / drugs / poison • milk / accidental[12] / toxin / caustic[13] [ɒː]/ co**ingestion** • **to eat** less / enough / well / like a horse[14] / without help / cooked foods / a regular diet[15] / out[16] / to have sth./be unable/to refuse **to eat** • ready[17]-**to-eat** • to be a big / small / fussy [ʌ] or picky[18] / compulsive [ʌ] **eater** • **eating** habits[19] / disorder[20] • binge[21] [bɪndʒ] **eating** • obsessive, compulsive[22] **overeating**

einnehmen, zu sich nehmen
essen[1] Verdauung[2] (Nahrungs)aufnahme, Einnahme (Medikament)[3] aufgenommene Nahrung, Ingesta[4] Ein-, Aufnahme, Zufuhr[5] s. überessen[6] Pilze[7] Vergiftung[8] verstopft, obstipiert[9] iss auf[10] Fremdkörper verschlucken[11] akzidentelle / versehentliche Einnahme[12] E. von Ätzmitteln[13] essen für vier[14] normale Kost zu s. nehmen[15] (ins Restaurant) essen gehen[16] fertig zubereitet[17] heikel b. Essen[18] Essgewohnheiten[19] Essstörung[20] E. mit Heißhungerattacken / Essanfällen[21] Fresssucht[22]   1

Diet & Dieting　　　　　　　　　　　　　　　　　　　　　　　　　　　　BASIC MEDICAL TERMS　7

consume [uː] v　　sim **have**[1], **dine**[2] [aɪ] v, **lunch**[3] [lʌntʃ] v & n

　consumption[4] [ʌ] n • **dining** n • **dinner**[5] [ɪ] n • **diner**[6] [aɪ] n

» Nutritional [ɪʃ] needs can be met quite easily by adults who consume dairy [eə] products[7]. Alcohol when consumed in excess for prolonged periods typically causes these symptoms. Why don't you have another toast? They lunched on fast food every day.

Use **to consume** a varied diet [daɪət]/ little dietary fiber[8] / large quantities of beer • **consumption of** contaminated food[9] / heavy [e] meals[10] • coffee / alcohol / seafood[11] / excessive **consumption** • safe for **consumption**[12] • **to dine** out with sb. • **dining** hall[13] / room / table / car[14] / to have/go out for **lunch** • buffet [eɪ]/ business **lunch** • **lunch**time / break or hour[15] • candlelight **dinner**

konsumieren, verzehren, zu sich nehmen
essen, trinken, zu sich nehmen[1] speisen, dinieren[2] (zu) Mittag essen, Mittagessen[3] Konsum, Verzehr[4] Hauptmahlzeit, Abendessen[5] Esslokal[6] Milchprodukte[7] wenig Ballaststoffe zu s. nehmen[8] Konsum verdorbener Lebensmittel[9] K. schwerverdaulicher Gerichte[10] Konsum v. Meeresfrüchten[11] für den Verzehr geeignet / mindestens haltbar bis[12] Speisesaal[13] Speisewagen[14] Mittagspause[15]　　2

---

feed [fiːd] - fed - fed [e] v irr　　sim **nourish**[1] [nɜːrɪʃ] v → U79-1

(i) to give food to a baby, animals or persons who cannot eat without help
(ii) to supply with nutriment[2] [uː]

　feed(ing)[3] n • **underfeeding**[4] n • **underfed** adj

» Generally, infants[5] weighing [eɪ] less than 1200g require 2-hour feedings, whereas larger infants are fed at 3-hour intervals. How often does your baby feed[6]?

Use **to feed** sb. honey [ʌ]/ sb. with a spoon / poorly[7] • **feeding** bottle[8] / cup[9] / method / pattern[10] / problem / tube [uː]/ regimen[11] [dʒ] • breast[12]- [e]/ bottle-/ adequately[13] / well / tube-**fed** • tube[14] / intravenous [iː]/ forced[15] / breast **feeding** • to be a heavy[16] [e]/ poor **feeder**

(i) füttern, Nahrung zuführen
(ii) (er)nähren, mit Nahrung versorgen
(er)nähren[1] Nahrung[2] Stillen, Füttern, Ernährung[3] Unterernährung[4] Säuglinge[5] trinken, nach d. Brust / Flasche verlangen[6] wenig zu sich nehmen / trinken (Baby)[7] Saugflasche[8] Schnabeltasse[9] Stillzeiten[10] Ernährungsplan[11] gestillt[12] ausreichend ernährt[13] Sondenernährg.[14] Zwangsernährg.[15] e. starker Esser sein[16]　　3

---

wolf [ʊ] **down** v phr inf　　sim **gulp** [ʌ] **down**[1], **bolt down**[2], **gobble (up)**[2] v phr inf

to take big bites[3] and swallow[4] hurriedly or greedily[5] [iː] without chewing [tʃuːɪŋ] or drink in one swallow[6] [swɒloʊ]

(Speisen) hinunterschlingen
hinunterstürzen (Getränk), -schlingen (Essen)[1] gierig essen, verschlingen[2] Bissen[3] schlucken[4] gierig[5] Zug[6]　　4

---

nonedible or **inedible** [e] adj　　opposite **edible**[1] adj, rel **palatable**[2] adj

unfit for human consumption, e.g. past its sell-by date[3]

　unpalatable[4] adj • **palatability**[5] n

» Vitamin K1 is present in most edible vegetables, especially in green leaves. A diet with normal fat content is more palatable and just as effective as a low-fat diet.

Use **nonedible** plants

nicht essbar, ungenießbar
ess-, genießbar[1] wohlschmeckend, schmackhaft[2] nach dem Ablaufdatum[3] nicht schmackhaft; ungenießbar[4] Schmackhaftigkeit[5]
　　5

---

food [fuːd] n　　sim **foodstuffs**[1], **groceries**[2] [oʊs], **victuals**[3] n BE,
　　　　　　　　　　　*****grub**[4] [ʌ] n inf

any substance [ʌ] that can be metabolized[5] by an organism to give energy and build up tissue

» Enjoy your food. Asking the patient to keep a diary[6] [daɪəɪ] of foods eaten may prove helpful. Fortification[7] of foodstuffs with vitamins etc. has nearly eliminated once-common deficiency states[8] [ɪʃ].

Use **to** refuse/prepare[9]/(BE) be off one's[10] **food** • **food** intake[11] / additives[12] / preservatives[13] / supplement • bolus[14] of / fatty / ingested / junk[15] [dʒʌŋk]/ fast / health[16] [e] **food** • (un)cooked / solid[17] / spicy [spaɪsi]/ spoiled[18] **food** • **food** craving[19] [eɪ] / intolerance[20] / particles / poisoning[21] • **food** aversion[22] / debris[23] [iː]/ choices / sources / chain[24] [tʃeɪn] • undigested / baby[25] / regurgitated[26] [ɜːrdʒ] **food** • **food**-borne infection[27] • fortified / contaminated[28] / aspiration of **foodstuffs**

Nahrung, Essen
Nahrungsmittel[1] Lebensmittel[2] Lebensmittel, Proviant[3] Fressalien[4] abbauen, umwandeln[5] Tagebuch[6] Anreicherung[7] Mangelzustände[8] E. zubereiten[9] keinen Appetit haben[10] Nahrungsaufnahme[11] Lebensmittelzusatzstoffe[12] Konservierungsmittel[13] Bolus, Bissen[14] N. mit geringem Nährwert[15] Reformkost[16] feste N.[17] verdorbene N.[18] Essensgelüste[19] Nahrungsmittelunverträglichkeit[20] Nahrungsmittelvergiftung[21] Abneigung gegen Speisen[22] Speisereste[23] Nahrungskette[24] Säuglingsnahrung[25] erbrochenes Essen[26] Lebensmittelinfektion[27] kontaminierte Lebensmittel[28]　　6

　Note: Food is normally used in the singular. In the plural it is used synonymously with foodstuffs to refer to different types of food.

8 BASIC MEDICAL TERMS — Diet & Dieting

meal [miːl] *n*

food served and eaten at one time (e.g. breakfast, brunch[1] [ʌ], lunch, barbeque[2], afternoon tea, supper[3], dinner[4])

» *Cafeterias* [ɪɚ] *and buffet* [eɪ] *meals should be avoided by anyone on a weight-reducing* [weɪt] *diet. Certain foods or meal patterns can change drug effectiveness.*

Use to eat/ingest[5]/miss[6] **a meal** • the major[7] **meal** • before / after / in-between **meals** • at **meal**time • **meals** on wheels[8] [iː] • large / light / heavy[9] / fatty / solid[10] / test / evening / bedtime **meal** • **meal** planning / patterns[11]

Mahlzeit; Essen, Kost

Brunch, Frühstück u. Mittagessen in einem[1] Grillen (im Freien)[2] Abendessen[3] Hauptmahlzeit, (Fest)essen[4] Mahlzeit einnehmen[5] M. auslassen[6] Hauptmahlzeit[7] Essen auf Rädern[8] schwerverdauliches Gericht[9] feste Kost[10] Essgewohnheiten[11]   7

---

dish [dɪʃ] *n*

(i) food prepared in a particular way (ii) dishware for serving food (pl) (iii) a shallow[1] container, e.g. a Petri dish

dish out[2] / **up**[3] *v phr* • **dish towel** [aʊ]/ **cloth**[4] [ɒː] *n or* **tea towel**[4] *BE*

» *These infections are mostly due to raw* [rɒː] *fish dishes. This dish is best when served cold. They dished up the finest of meals.*

Use to do or wash[5] **the dishes** • favorite[6] [eɪ] **dish** • **dish** washer[7] / water[8] / rack[9]

(i) Gericht, Speise (ii) Geschirr (iii) Schale, Schüssel

flach[1] austeilen[2] anrichten, auftragen[3] Geschirrtuch[4] Geschirr spülen / abwaschen[5] Lieblingsspeise[6] Spülmaschine, Geschirrspüler[7] Abwasch-, Spülwasser[8] Geschirrkorb, -ständer[9]   8

---

serving [ɜː] *n*   *syn* **helping** *n, sim* **course**[1] [kɔːrs] *n*

a portion of food or drink

serve[2] *v* • **service**[3] *n* • **server**[4] *n*

» *Do you want a second helping? Frying*[5] [aɪ] *the food before serving may not destroy the toxins.*

Use standardized **serving** size [aɪ] • **serving** spoon [uː] • salad **server**[6] • a four-**course** meal[7]

Portion

Gang[1] servieren[2] Bedienung[3] Vorlegebesteck[4] (ab)braten[5] Salatbesteck[6] 4-gängiges Menü[7]

9

---

snack *n & v*

(n) a light informal meal, e.g. tea or coffee break[1] [eɪ] where you have some refreshments[2]

» *Dietary strategies to increase appetite or intake include providing salty foods, nutrient-dense beverages*[3] [rɪdʒɪz] *such as fruit juice, and easy-to-eat snacks. What are you snacking on?*

Use to have a[4] **snack** • **snack** food / bar[5]

Imbiss, Zwischenmahlzeit; Imbiss zu sich nehmen

Kaffeepause[1] Erfrischungen[2] nährstoffreiche Getränke[3] eine Kleinigkeit essen[4] Imbissstube[5]

10

---

appetite [æpətaɪt] *n*   *rel* **hungry**[1] [ʌ], **thirsty**[2] [ɜː] *adj*, **hunger**[3], **thirst**[4] *n & v*

(i) normal desire to eat (ii) to have a craving[5] [eɪ] for special foods

appetizer[6] *n* -iser *espBE* • **appetizing**[7] *adj* -ising *BE*

» *The patient's appetite is poor. Are you hungry for*[8] *some meat? Some medications enhance the sensation of thirst*[9] *by causing a dry mouth.*

Use to work up[10] / it gives me[11] **an appetite** • loss of[12] / healthy[13] / inability to control one's **appetite** • to spoil or ruin[14] / lose **your appetite** • to be/feel **hungry** • wolfish[15] [ʊ] / salt / air **hunger** • **hunger** pain[16] / strike / cry / behavior [eɪ] • **appetite** suppressant[17] • to experience **thirst** • **thirst** mechanism [k]/ center / sensation[9]

Appetit

hungrig[1] durstig[2] Hunger; hungern[3] Durst; dürsten[4] Verlangen, Lust[5] Appetitanreger, -happen, Vorspeise[6] appetitanregend, lecker[7] A./ Lust haben auf[8] Durstgefühl[9] s. einen Appetit holen[10] A. anregen[11] Appetitlosigkeit[12] guter/gesunder A.[13] A. verderben[14] Wolfshunger[15] Nüchtern-, Hungerschmerz[16] Appetitzügler[17]   11

---

diet [daɪət] *v & n*

v to eat sparingly[1] [eə]

n (i) prescribed selection of foods (ii) usual food and drink consumed by a person

dietary[2] *adj & n* • **dietician** *or* **-tian**[3] *n* • **dietetics**[4] *n* • **dietetic**[2] *adj*

» *A healthy person consuming a variety* [aɪə] *of foods is unlikely to have a dietary deficiency*[5] [ɪʃ]. *I have been on this diet for weeks but to no effect. Regaining body weight after dieting is referred to as weight cycling.*

Use to be on[6]/go on/observe[6]/follow[6]/adhere [ɪə] to[6] **a diet** • to put sb. on[7]/prescribe/tolerate[8] **a diet** • strict[9] / well-balanced[10] / a 1000-calorie / high-fiber[11] [aɪ] **diet** • low-fat / diabetic [e]/ bland [æ] or ulcer[12] [ʌlsɚ] **diet** • full- or clear-liquid[13] / modified / (weight [weɪt]) reducing or slimming down[14] / soft[15] **diet** • changes in / staple[16] [eɪ] **diet** • dietary assessment / history / allowance[17] [aʊ]/ risk factors / service / counselor[18] [aʊ] • **dieting** with exercise / patient • **diet** free of / high in proteins / of fruits[19]

Diät halten;
(i) Diät, Schon-, Krankenkost
(ii) Nahrung, Kost

in Maßen, wenig[1] diätetisch; Diätvorschrift[2] Diätetiker(in)[3] Diätetik, Ernährungslehre[4] Mangelernährung[5] D. halten[6] auf D. setzen[7] Kost vertragen[8] strenge D.[9] ausgewogene K.[10] ballaststoffreiche K.[11] reizarme / blande Diät[12] flüssige Nahrung[13] Schlankheitsdiät, Reduktionskost[14] leichte K., Breikost[15] Hauptnahrung[16] Diätempfehlung, empfohlene Nahrungszufuhr[17] Ernährungsberater(in)[18] Obstdiät[19]   12

Diet & Dieting BASIC MEDICAL TERMS 9

wholesome [hoʊlsəm] *adj*   *syn* **healthy** [helθi], **healthful** *adj* → U1-2

food supposed to be good for your health because it is rich in nutrients[1] or low in artificial ingredients [iː]
wholefood(s)[2] *n espBE* • whole wheat[3] [wiːt] *n* • whole bread[4] [e] *n*
» The wholesome ingredients[5] of their breads are well documented.

gesund, bekömmlich
reich an Nährstoffen[1] Vollwertprodukte[2] Voll(korn)weizen[3] Vollkornbrot[4] Zutaten[5]
13

starve [stɑːrv] *v*

(i) to die or–informally–suffer (extremely) from lack of food (ii) not to give someone any food
(semi-)starvation[1] [eɪ] *n* • **starving**[2] *adj & n*
» She has been starving herself. They died of starvation. Total starvation causes a loss of approximately 0.4 kg of body weight per day.
Use to be **starving**[3] • **to starve** to death[4] • **starvation** diet[5] • to die of / total / prolonged / oxygen[6] [ɒksɪdʒən] **starvation**

(ver)hungern (lassen), fasten
(Ver)hungern, Hungertod[1] (ver)hungernd; (Aus)hungern[2] halb verhungert sein, vor Hunger umkommen[3] verhungern[4] Hungerkur[5] Sauerstoffhunger[6]
14

fast [fæst] *v & n*   *sim* **fasting**[1] [fæstɪŋ] *adj & n*

to abstain [eɪ] from[2] (certain) food over a specific period of time for therapeutic [juː] or religious [dʒ] reasons
» Patients are fasted under close supervision [ɪʒ] for up to 72 h. Diarrhea [daɪəriːə] of any cause often improves or resolves with fasting[3]. They also recommend obtaining a fasting lipid profile.
Use prolonged periods of / avoidance of / after **fasting** • **fasting** blood sugar or glucose levels[4] • in the fed and **fasted** states[5] • under **fasting** conditions

fasten, hungern; Fasten(zeit)
nüchtern, hungernd; Fasten[1] sich enthalten[2] sistiert bei Nahrungskarenz[3] Nüchternblutzucker[4] nüchtern und mit vollem Magen[5]
15

vegetarian [vedʒɪteəriən] *n & adj*   *sim* **vegan**[1] [viːɡən] *adj & n*,
   rel **vegetarianism**[2] *n*

(n) person who does not eat meat or fish or (often) any animal products (adj) excluding meat
» A vegan diet can be nutritionally adequate, although more thoughtful [3] [θɔːtfᵊl] food choices and supplementation[4] with fortified foods[5] may be necessary.
Use **vegetarian** food • ovo-/ ovo-lacto/ strictly **vegetarian** diet[6]

Vegetarier(in); vegetarisch
streng vegetarisch; strenge(r) V.[1] Vegetarismus, veget. Lebensweise[2] wohlüberlegt[3] Ergänzung[4] angereicherte Nahrungsmittel[5] streng vegetarische Kost[6]
16

health freak [iː] *n inf*

person very enthusiastic [uː] about a healthy life-style, esp. health food, often to the point of being obsessed[1] with it
» Oat bran[2] [oʊt bræn] has become the favorite [eɪ] of health freaks.

Gesundheitsapostel
besessen sein[1] Haferkleie[2]
17

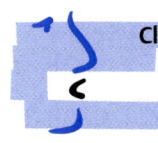

Clinical Phrases

Try to keep off salty food. Salzhaltige Speisen sollten Sie nach Möglichkeit meiden. • She has a sweet tooth. Sie isst gern Süßigkeiten. • I don't have a stomach for milk any more. Mir schmeckt die Milch nicht mehr. • I couldn't stomach it. Ich habe es nicht vertragen. • Thanks, I'm full. Danke, ich bin satt. • I made a real pig of myself stuffing myself with sweets. Ich habe mir den Bauch mit Süßigkeiten vollgeschlagen. • He just couldn't stay off the booze. Er griff immer wieder zur Flasche. • I've hardly touched any food for a week. Ich habe schon eine Woche kaum etwas gegessen. • Most infants will want to feed every two or three hours. Die meisten Säuglinge wollen alle 2–3 Stunden gefüttert werden. • The baby's refused the bottle ever since. Seither hat das Baby die Flasche verweigert. • It seems the boy's practically living on chips and sweets. Der Bub ernährt sich anscheinend nur von Chips und Süßigkeiten. • It makes my mouth water. Mir läuft das Wasser im Mund zusammen. • I've been off my food for the past few weeks. (BE) Ich hatte in den letzten paar Wochen keinen Appetit. • I am starved / starving. Ich komme fast um vor Hunger. • For them lunch is just a snack. Sie essen mittags nicht viel.

Unit 3 Food & Drink

Related Units: 2 Diet & Dieting, 27 Dentition & Mastication, 46 Digestion, 78 Metabolism, 79 Nutrition

meat [iː] n

flesh of animals that is cooked and eaten; types include pork (from pigs), beef[1] (cows), veal[2] [iː] (calf [kæf]), mutton[3] [ʌ] (sheep), lamb, poultry[4] [oʊ] (chicken, turkey[5], etc.), and venison or game[6] (from wild animals, e.g. deer[7] [ɪ]). Meat can be eaten as bacon[8], ham[9], steak, cutlet[10] [ʌ], chop[11], hamburger, sausage[12] [sɔːsɪdʒ], hot dog[13], etc.

meaty adj • meatloaf[14] [oʊ] n • meatballs[15] n

» Do you like your steak medium-rare[16] or well-done? Excessive intake of purine from meat, fish and poultry may favor stone formation. You should not pour any gravy[17] [eɪ] on your meat. Tofu is used as a meat substitute.

Use raw / (under)cooked[18] / fried / roast / lean[19] [iː] meat • fatty / red / white / ground[20] [aʊ] / tough[21] [tʌf]/ tender[22] meat • meat tenderizer / substitute[23] • corned[24] beef • chicken soup

Fleisch
Rindfl.[1] Kalbfl.[2] Schaffl.[3] Geflügel[4] Truthahn[5] Wild[6] Rotwild[7] Speck[8] Schinken[9] Schnitzel[10] Kotelett[11] Wurst[12] Würstchen[13] Fleischkäse[14] Fleischklöße[15] halb durch[16] Soße[17] (nicht) durchgegartes Fl.[18] mageres Fl.[19] Hackfleisch[20] zähes Fl.[21] zartes Fl.[22] Fleischersatz[23] Dosenfleisch[24]

1

fish v & n usu sing

types of fish commonly eaten include trout[1] [aʊ], cod[2], herring, sardine, salmon[3] [sæmən], mackerel, and tuna[4]

» Shall we have fish for lunch? I'd like the cod fillets. Do you like tuna canned in oil?

Use freshwater[5] / marine[6] / fatty / smoked[7] / baked / broiled[8] / canned[9] / breaded[10] [e] fish • fish stick or finger[11] • filleted sole[12] [soʊl]

fischen; Fisch
Forelle[1] Dorsch[2] Lachs[3] Thunfisch[4] Süßwasserfisch[5] Meeres-, Seefisch[6] Räucherfisch[7] gegrillter F.[8] Dosenfisch[9] panierter F.[10] Fischstäbchen[11] Seezungenfilet[12]

2

seafood n

edible marine fish and shellfish[1], e.g. octopus or squid[2], shrimps[3], roe[4] [roʊ], lobster[5] [ɒː], crab, mussel[6] [ʌ], oyster[7]

» Most cases of food poisoning[8] were linked to ingestion[9] [dʒ] of undercooked seafood.

Use seafood restaurant / consumption[9] / ingestion • raw [ɒː] seafood

Meeresfrüchte
Schalentiere[1] Tintenfisch[2] Garnelen[3] Rogen[4] Hummer[5] Miesmuscheln[6] Austern[7] Lebensmittelvergiftung[8] Konsum v. Meeresf.[9]

3

milk n & v

» The patient should not drink any cold milk. This milk has turned / gone sour[1] [saʊɚ]. A glass of milk usually relieves[2] the pain.

Use whole[3] [hoʊl]/ skim(med)[4] / raw / cow / goat's[5] / breast[6] [e] milk • (un)pasteurized [tʃɚ]/ certified[7] / fortified vitamin D[8] / butter milk • scalded[9] [ɒː]/ low-fat[4] / condensed[10] / acidophilus[11] / coconut / dry or instant[12] milk • milkshake / sugar / powder [aʊ]

Milch; melken
sauer werden[1] lindert[2] Vollmilch[3] Magermilch[4] Ziegenmilch[5] Muttermilch[6] Vorzugsmilch[7] mit Vitamin D angereicherte M.[8] abgekochte M.[9] Kondens-, Dosenmilch[10] Sauermilch[11] Trockenmilch[12]

4

dairy [deɚi] products or espBE produce n

foods made from milk such as cheese, cream[1] [iː], butter, curd[2] [ɜː], yog(ho)urt [joʊgɚt], and whey[3] [ʰweɪ]

» The fruit custard[4] [ʌ] may have been mouldy[5] and the mildew[6] [duː] has probably precipitated[7] his symptoms.

Use peanut[8] / melted[9] butter • (un)grated[10] [eɪ] / cream[11] / soft[12] / Swiss / cottage cheese • (un)whipped / whipping[13] cream • dairy farm / cow

Milch-, Molkereiprodukte
Obers, Sahne[1] Quark, Topfen[2] Molke[3] Fruchtcreme[4] schimmelig[5] Schimmel[6] auslösen[7] Erdnussbutter[8] zerlassene B.[9] geriebener Käse[10] (Doppelrahm-)frischkäse[11] Weichkäse[12] Schlagsahne, -rahm (öst.)[13]

5

vegetable [vedʒətəbl] n usu sing   rel legumes[1] [legjuːmz] n

edible seeds[2], roots[3], stems[4] or leaves of many plants such as potatoes, beets[5], asparagus[6], cabbage[7], cauliflower[8] [ɒː], lettuce[9] [letɪs], cucumbers[10], rhubarb, horseradish[11], carrots, beans[12], peppers[13], sweet corn[14], onions[15] [ʌ], green peas[16], turnips[17], egg plants[18], pumpkins[19], spinach [ɪtʃ], broccoli, lentils[20], etc.

» Travelers can reduce their risk of diarrhea [daɪəriːə] by avoiding uncooked vegetables, salads, and unpeeled[21] fruit. Vitamin K1 is present in most edible vegetables, particularly in green leaves.

Use fresh / (green) leafy / root / starchy[22] [tʃ] / raw / grated[23] vegetables • vegetable proteins / oils / soup • salad dressing[24] • dried beans • mashed potatoes[25]

Gemüse
Hülsenfrüchte[1] Samen[2] Wurzeln[3] Stiele[4] Rüben, Bete[5] Spargel[6] Kohl[7] Blumenkohl[8] Kopfsalat[9] Gurken[10] Meerrettich[11] Bohnen[12] Paprika[13] Zuckermais[14] Zwiebel[15] grüne Erbsen[16] weiße Rüben[17] Auberginen[18] Kürbisse[19] Linsen[20] ungeschält[21] stärkehaltiges Gemüse[22] geraspeltes G.[23] Salatsoße[24] Kartoffelpüree[25]

6

Food & Drink   BASIC MEDICAL TERMS 11

fruit [fruːt] n usu sing

ripened[1] [aɪ], mostly edible reproductive parts of a plant containing the seeds, e.g. apples, pears[2] [eə], peaches[3] [iːtʃ], tangerines[4] [dʒ], cherries[5], pineapples[6] [aɪ], apricots, grapes[7] [eɪ], plums[8] [ʌ], prunes[9] [uː], dates[10] [eɪ], figs[11], melons, etc.

» Fructose is a natural or added sweetener in fruit. Many fruits are a good source of vitamin C and dietary [aɪə] fiber[12] [aɪ]. Consume at least 5 – 9 servings of fruits and vegetables per day.

Use fresh / dried[13] / canned[14] / (un)peeled[15] fruit • citrus [saɪ]/ kiwi / tropical / raw / unripened / fallen[16] fruit • fruit sugar / juice / pulp[17] / salad / in heavy/light syrup • fruitcake • apple pie[18] [paɪ]/ sauce[19] • sliced [aɪ] peaches[20]

berries n pl

pulpy[1] [ʌ] and mostly edible small fruit from low bushes [ʊ], e.g. strawberry[2] [ɔː], blueberry[3], blackberry[4], black and red currant[5] [ɜː], cranberry[6], raspberry[7] [ræzberɪ]

Use raspberry tart[8] / pie[9] / jam[10] / jello[11] [dʒeloʊ] • poisonous[12] berry

bread [bred] n   sim breadstuff[1] n

food made from flour[2] [flaʊɚ], water and yeast[3] [jiːst] mixed into a dough[4] [doʊ] and baked in the oven[5] [ʌ]; bread products include rolls[6], buns[7] [ʌ], doughnuts[8], wafers[9] [eɪ], waffles[9] [ɒː], toasts, etc.

breading[10] n • breaded[11] adj

» In patients with heart failure specially processed breads[12] and salt substitutes are advisable.

Use white / dark / rye[13] [raɪ]/ barley / wheat[14] [iː] (un)enriched / whole grain[15] / crispbread[16] • garlic[17] / French / raisin[18] [eɪ]/ sourdough[19] / gluten(-free) / gingerbread[20] [dʒ] • a slice[21] of / loaf[22] [oʊ] of bread • bread products / crumbs[23] [krʌmz]

pastry [peɪstri] n   rel frosting[1] n, BE icing [aɪsɪŋ] n

dough of flour, water, baking powder[2], and shortening[3] to make pies[4], cakes, strudel, pancakes[5], soufflés [sufleɪz], etc.

» Apple pie and custard[6] [ʌ] was his staple food[7] [eɪ]. You should avoid cookies[8] and pastries.

Use French pastry • pastry cook[9] • apple / pumpkin[10] / meat / rhubarb / deep-dish pie • chocolate[11] [tʃɒːklət] frosting

pasta n

types of pasta include spaghetti, noodles [uː], macaroni, tortellini, etc.

» The Food Guide Pyramid recommends 6 – 11 daily servings of bread, pasta, rice, and cereals.

Use spaghetti with meatballs[1] / in tomato sauce[2] • egg[3] / tender-stage[4] noodles

cereals [sɪəɪəlz] n pl   syn cornflakes n espBE

(i) starchy [tʃ] grains[1] used as food, e.g. rice[2], wheat, rye, barley[3], oats[4] [oʊ], corn[5], buckwheat[6] [ʌ], millet[7], etc. (ii) breakfast food prepared from grain

» Oatmeal[8] is among the most nourishing [ɜː] ingredients[9] in cereals. How about Graham crackers[10]?

Use whole-grain[11] cereals • cereal-based formulation / grains

egg n

thin-shelled female reproductive body laid by e.g. hens containing the ovum or embryo together with nutritive[1] (yolk[2] [joʊk]) and protective envelopes (egg white[3] and shell[4])

» Some gastric infections are associated with ingestion of cracked[5] eggs.

Use hard-boiled[6] / soft-boiled / raw / whole [hoʊl] / scrambled[7] / fried[8] [aɪ] egg • hen's / half a dozen [ʌ] / ham and / free-range[9] / commercial henhouse[10] eggs • egg protein / products / nog[11] / cup /-timer[12] / allergy

---

Obst, Früchte; Frucht

gereift[1] Birnen[2] Pfirsiche[3] Mandarinen[4] Kirschen[5] Ananas[6] Weintrauben[7] Zwetschgen, Pflaumen[8] gedörrte Zwetschgen, Dörrpflaumen[9] Datteln[10] Feigen[11] Ballaststoffe[12] Trockenfrüchte[13] Dosenfrüchte[14] (un)geschältes Obst[15] Fallobst[16] Fruchtfleisch[17] Apfelkuchen[18] Apfelmus[19] Pfirsichspalten[20]   7

Beeren

fleischig[1] Erdbeere[2] Heidel-, Blaubeere[3] Bromb.[4] Johannisb.[5] Preiselb.[6] Himb.[7] Himbeertörtchen[8] Himbeertorte[9] Himbeermarmelade[10] Himbeergelee[11] giftige B.[12]   8

Brot

Brot(getreide)[1] Mehl[2] Hefe, Germ[3] Teig[4] Backofen, -rohr[5] Brötchen, Semmeln[6] süße Brötchen[7] Krapfen, Berliner[8] Waffeln[9] Paniermehl[10] paniert[11] speziell hergestellte Brotsorten[12] Roggenbrot[13] Weizenb.[14] Vollkornb.[15] Knäckeb.[16] Knoblauchb.[17] Rosinenb.[18] Sauerteigbrot[19] Lebkuchen[20] eine Scheibe Brot[21] Brotlaib[22] Brotkrümel, Brösel[23]   9

(Fein)gebäck

Zuckerguss, Glasur[1] Backpulver[2] Backfett[3] Törtchen, Obstkuchen, Pasteten[4] Pfannkuchen, Omelette[5] Vanillesoße, -pudding[6] Hauptnahrung[7] Kekse, Plätzchen[8] Konditor(in)[9] Kürbiskuchen[10] Schokoladeglasur[11]   10

Teigwaren

Spaghetti bolognese[1] Pasta asciuta[2] Eiernudeln[3] Nudeln al dente[4]

11

(i) Getreideflocken (ii) Mü(e)sli

stärkehaltige Getreidesorten[1] Reis[2] Gerste[3] Hafer[4] Mais[5] Buchweizen[6] Hirse[7] Haferflocken[8] nahrhafte Bestandteile[9] Graham-, Weizenschrotcrackers[10] Vollkornflocken[11]
12

Ei

nahrhaft[1] Eigelb, Dotter[2] Eiweiß[3] Schale[4] gesprungen[5] hart gekochtes E.[6] Rührei, Eierspeise[7] Spiegelei[8] Freilandeier[9] Batterieeier[10] Eierlikör[11] Eieruhr[12]
13

12 BASIC MEDICAL TERMS — Food & Drink

nuts [nʌts] n usu pl

large, hard-shelled seeds, e.g. peanuts[1], walnuts[2] [ɒː], almonds[3] [ɑːl], pignolia[4], cashew nuts or coconuts
nutcracker[5] n • **nutshell**[6] n

» Seeds and nuts are good sources of vitamin E .

Nüsse
Erdnüsse[1] Walnüsse[2] Mandeln[3] Pinienkerne[4] Nussknacker[5] Nussschale[6]
14

oil n & v   sim (cooking) fats[1] n

(n) greasy[2] [iː], viscous [vɪskəs] liquid used for cooking, in ointments[3], lubricants[4] [uː], etc.
oily[5] adj • **oilcloth**[5] n • **fatty**[6] adj

» Take margerine [dʒ] instead of lard[7] or butter as a cooking fat, but use it sparingly.
Use animal / vegetable[8] / dietary[1] **fats** • soybean / olive / corn[9] / wheat germ[10] [dʒ]/ rapeseed[11] **oil** • fish[12] / cod [ɒː] / liver[13] / greasy **oil**

Öl; (ein)ölen
Speisefette[1] fett(ig), schmierig[2] Salben[3] Schmier-, Gleitmittel[4] Wachstuch[5] fett(haltig)[6] Schweineschmalz[7] pflanzliche Fette[8] Maiskeimöl[9] Weizenkeimöl[10] Rapsöl[11] Tran[12] Lebertran[13]
15

sugar n & v   sim (mono-/di- [aɪ])saccharide[1] [k] n, rel molasses[2] n term

sweet crystalline [ɪ] carbohydrate [aɪ] (fructose [uː], lactose, sucrose [uː], dextrose, and glucose) which works as a sweetener and a source of energy for the body
sugared[3] adj • **sugary**[4] adj • **sugar-coated**[5] adj

» High-fiber, sugar-free cereals should be encouraged. Aspartame (NutraSweet) is an artificial sweetener very popular with diabetics [aɪə].
Use a lump [ʌ] of[6] **sugar** • table / brown[7] / refined[8] / granulated / powdered[9] / cane[10] [eɪ]/ maple[11] [eɪ]/ invert[12] **sugar** • **sugar** beet[13] [iː]/ cube[6] / substitute[14] / uptake /-containing foods • **sugared** almonds[15]

Zucker, Saccharose; süßen, zuckern
Saccharid[1] Melasse[2] gezuckert[3] zuckerhaltig, süß[4] m. Z. überzogen, dragiert[5] e. Stück Zucker[6] brauner Zucker[7] raffinierter Z.[8] Staubzucker[9] Rohrzucker[10] Ahornsirup[11] Invertzucker[12] Zuckerrübe[13] Zuckerersatz[14] kandierte Mandeln[15]
16

candy n sing   syn sweet(ie) n BE

rich sweet made of flavored[1] [eɪ] sugar often with chocolate, caramel, honey, liquorice[2] [lɪkɚɪs], nougat [uː], fruit or nuts; merchandized [tʃ] as candy bars, lollipops[3] or suckers[3], pralines, crisps[4], marshmellows, chewing gum, etc.
sweetener[5] n • **sweet** adj • **sweeten**[6] v

» Younger children may suck on hard candy[7]. A high intake of sucrose (table sugar) in such items [aɪ] as soft drinks, candy, syrup[8], and sweetened cereals is a major risk factor for caries.
Use artificial / nonnutritive[9] **sweetener** • **candy** bar[10] / store / floss[11] (BE) • hard / cotton[11] **candy** • **sweet** smelling[12] / potatoes[13] • to have a **sweet** tooth[14]

 Note: In BE a sweet[15] can also be the last course of a meal (dessert[15] in AE).

Süßigkeiten, Bonbons
aromatisiert[1] Lakritze, Süßholz[2] Lutscher[3] Knabbergebäck[4] Süßstoff[5] (ver)süßen[6] Bonbon[7] Sirup[8] kalorienarmer Süßstoff[9] Riegel[10] Zuckerwatte[11] wohlriechend[12] Süßkartoffeln[13] e. Schwäche für Süßigkeiten haben[14] Nachspeise, Dessert[15]
17

seasoning [iː] n   syn seasoner n, rel salt[1] n

substances added to food to give it more flavor[2], including salt, pepper, herbs [ɜːrbz] and spices
season[3] v • **(un)salted**[4] adj • **salt-rich**[5] adj • **salt-restricted**[6] adj

» Counseling should be offered about seasoning the food with spices (e.g. pepper).
Use well **seasoned**[7] • table / rock[8] / a pinch [tʃ] of[9] **salt** • **salt** intake[10] • **salted** butter / water • **salt**-restricted diet[11] • depletion[12] [iː]

Würze, Würzen
Salz[1] Geschmack[2] würzen[3] (un)gesalzen[4] stark gesalzen[5] salzarm[6] gut gewürzt[7] Steinsalz[8] eine Prise Salz[9] Salzkonsum[10] salzarme Diät[11] Salzmangel, -verlust[12]
18

herbs [ɜːrbz‖hɜːbz] n pl   syn potherbs n

(i) dried aromatic plants used in cookery[1] for its savory[2] [eɪ] qualities (chives[3] [tʃaɪvz], parsley[4], basil[5], dill, fennel[6], thyme[7] [θaɪm], sage[8] [seɪdʒ], rosemary[9], mint[10] etc. (ii) plants used for medicinal purposes, e.g. camomile[11], arnica, etc.
herbal[12] adj & n • **herbaceous**[12] [hɚˈbeɪʃəs] adj • **herbarium**[13] n • **herbalist**[14] n

» Clinical research showed that Chinese herbal medicine is effective in controlling eczema [eks]. Many herbal folk remedies[15] are prepared by immersing[16] dried leaves or flowers in hot water.
Use **herbal** tea[17] / extract / remedies / medicines • garden / officinal[18] [fɪʃ] **herbs**

(Küchen)kräuter
Kochen[1] schmackhaft[2] Schnittlauch[3] Petersilie[4] Basilikum[5] Fenchel[6] Thymian[7] Salbei[8] Rosmarin[9] Minze[10] Kamille[11] krautartig, Kräuter-; Kräuterbuch[12] Herbarium, Kräutersammlung[13] Kräutersammler, -doktor[14] pflanzliche Hausmittel[15] ansetzen[16] Kräutertee[17] pflanzliche Drogen, Heilkräuter[18]
19

Food & Drink   BASIC MEDICAL TERMS **13**

spices [spaɪsiːz] *n usu pl*

intensely aromatic vegetable substances used for seasoning food, e.g. mustard[1] [ʌ], garlic[2], cinnamon[3], ginger[4] [dʒ], cloves[5] [oʊ], nutmeg[6], cayenne pepper, chili powder[7], curry, etc.

spicy[8] *adj* • **spice (up)**[9] *v*

» *The veal was spiced with black pepper. Rely on a mild and bland diet[10] and avoid spicy food.*
Use hot and **spicy**[11] • to cut down on **spicy** dishes[12]

Gewürze
Senf[1] Knoblauch[2] Zimt[3] Ingwer[4] Gewürznelken[5] Muskat[6] Chilipulver[7] würzig[8] (pikant) würzen[9] blande/ reizarme Diät[10] scharf gewürzt[11] Konsum stark gewürzter Speisen reduzieren[12]   20

food substitute *or* **replacer** *n*   *rel* **food exchange list**[1] *n*

foods similar in nutritive value and/or taste that are used to replace foodstuffs a person must strictly avoid[2]

substitute[3] *v* • **substitution**[4] *n* • **replace**[3] *v* • **replacement**[4] *n*

» *Substitution with any food low in saturated fat such as bran[5] or nuts will have positive effects.*
Use fat / meat / coffee / milk[6] **substitute** • **substitution** of margarine for butter

Nahrungsmittelersatz(stoff)
Nährwert-, Lebensmitteltabelle[1] meiden[2] ersetzen[3] Ersatz, Substitution[4] Kleie[5] Milchersatz[6]

21

nutritional supplement *n term*   *rel* **food additives**[1] *n term*

enrichment of foods with nutrients[2] such as vitamins to improve dietary intake according to specific needs

supplement[3] *v* • **supplementary, -al**[4] *adj* • **additional**[5] *adj*

» *The first dietary measure [eɪ] is a low-fat diet supplemented with medium-chain triglycerides [aɪ]. Claims that dyes[6] [daɪz], emulsifiers[7], stabilizers[8], and other food additives may contribute to hyperactivity in children are controversial.*
Use diet(ary) / (multi)vitamin / mineral / calcium / iron[9] / daily high fiber[10] / weight-loss **supplement** • iron-**supplemented** • dietary bulk[10] **additive** • **additive**-free baby food[11]

Nährstoffanreicherung
Lebensmittelzusatzstoffe, Additive[1] Nährstoffe[2] ergänzen[3] ergänzend[4] zusätzlich[5] Lebensmittelfarbstoffe[6] Emulgatoren[7] Stabilisatoren[8] Eisenanreicherung[9] Ballaststoffanreicherung[10] zusatzstofffreie Kindernahrung[11]

22

cooked *adj*   *opposite* **raw**[1] [ɒː], **uncooked**[1] *adj*

food prepared for consumption by heating; it can be baked[2] (dry oven heat), boiled[3] (in hot water) fried[4] (in hot oil), steamed[5] [iː] (in water vapor [eɪ]), stewed[6] [stuːd], roasted[7], broiled[8] or barbequed (abbr BBQ)

(pre/ over/ pressure-)cook[9] *v* • **cooking** *n* • **cookery** *n* • **cookbook** *n*

» *Do you want your chicken roasted, fried or with stuffing[10]?*

gekocht
roh, ungekocht[1] gebacken[2] gekocht, -sotten[3] gebraten[4] gedünstet[5] gedünstet, -schmort[6] geröstet[7] gegrillt[8] (vor-/ ver-/ mit Dampf) kochen[9] Füllung[10]

23

beverage [bevərɪdʒ] *n*   *syn* **drinks** *n usu pl*

any liquid suitable for drinking including mineral water, fruit juice[1], tea, carbonated[2] and alcoholic drinks

drink - drank - drunk *v irr* • **drinkable**[3] *adj* • **drinking**[4] *adj & n* • **drinker**[5] *n*

» *How much do you ordinarily drink? Did you have any artificially sweetened beverages? He is a heavy drinker[6].*
Use carbonated / alcoholic **beverages** • to have a **drink**[7] • hard / long / soft[8] **drinks** • **drinking** water[9] / soda / age / bout[10] [aʊ] / beer / wine / tea / social[11] **drinker**

> **Note:** Both in colloquial and clinical situations *drink*, *drinking* and *drinker* are frequently used to refer to alcohol intake (esp when not further specified).

Getränk
Fruchtsaft[1] kohlensäurehaltig[2] trinkbar[3] Trink-; (Be)trinken[4] Trinker(in)[5] Alkoholiker(in), Säufer(in)[6] etwas trinken[7] alkoholfreie G.[8] Trinkwasser[9] Trinkgelage, Zecherei[10] Gesellschaftstrinker(in)[11]

24

juice [dʒuːs] *n*

(i) liquid that can be extracted from fruit and vegetables (ii) body fluid, e.g gastric juice[1]

juicy[2] *adj*

» *Pour [ɔː] some lemon juice[3] over the cutlet[4] [ʌ]. Is your steak juicy?*
Use orange / grapefruit / apple / tomato [eɪ] **juice** • **juice** bar

(i, ii) Saft
Magensaft[1] saftig[2] Zitronensaft[3] Schnitzel[4]

25

caffein(e) [kæfiːn] *n*

bitter alkaloid contained in coffee, cocoa[1] [koʊkoʊ], and tea that is responsible for their stimulating effects

caffeinism[2] *n* • **caffea**[3] *n* • **café**[4] [kæfeɪ] *n* • **(de)caffeinated**[5] *adj*

» *A few cups of coffee can significantly disturb sleep in some patients.*
Use **caffeine** withdrawal[6] [ɒːl] • ground[7] [aʊ] **coffee** • **coffee** bean[8] • black / green / iced **tea**

Koffein
Kakao[1] Koffeinvergiftung[2] Kaffeestrauch[3] Kaffeehaus[4] koffeinhaltig; -frei[5] Koffeinentzug[6] gemahlener Kaffee[7] Kaffeebohne[8]

26

14 BASIC MEDICAL TERMS — Illness & Recovery

alcoholic drinks n sim **brew(age)**¹ [bruːɪdʒ] n , **booze²** [buːz] n inf
fermented brew or distilled alcohol-containing drinks, e.g. beer, wine, cider³ [saɪdɚ], etc.
alcohol n • **alcoholic⁴** adj & n • **alcoholism⁵** n
» Alcohol consumption also raises [eɪ] the blood pressure. He's been an alcoholic for years.
Use **alcoholic** excess⁶ / patient • **alcohol** ingestion or consumption⁷ / abuse⁸ /-dependent⁹ • **Alcoholics** Anonymous¹⁰

alkoholische Getränke
Gebräu¹ Alkohol, Schnaps² Apfelwein, Most³ alkoholisch, -haltig; Alkoholiker(in)⁴ Alkoholabhängigkeit, Alkoholismus⁵ Alkoholexzess⁶ Alkoholkonsum⁷ Alkoholmissbrauch⁸ alkoholabhängig⁹ Anonyme Alkoholiker¹⁰ 27

liquor [lɪkɚ] n   syn **spirits** n pl BE
hard (alcoholic) drinks¹ which are distilled² rather than fermented³, e.g. whiskey, brandy, gin
» Heavy users of hard liquor and wine account for⁴ 40% of cases of pancreatitis [aɪtɪs].
Use **liquor** store⁵ • to drown in⁶ [aʊ]/ intoxicating⁷ / bottles of **liquor**

Spirituosen
harte Getränke¹ gebrannt² vergoren³ ausmachen⁴ Spirituosengeschäft⁵ (Sorgen) im A. ertränken⁶ berauschendes Getränk⁷ Zerebrospinalflüssigkeit, Liquor (cerebrospinalis)⁸ 28

> Note: In medical English *liquor* is practically never used to refer to body fluids, e.g. the amniotic or the cerebrospinal [aɪ] fluid⁸.

Unit 4 Illness & Recovery
Related Units: 1 Health & Fitness, 89 General Pathology, 102 History Taking, 119 Etiology, Course & Prognosis, 77 Mental Health, 94 Infectious Diseases, 104 Pain, 134 Perioperative Care, 142 Physical Therapy & Rehabilitation

sick adj → U103-11 syn **ill** adj, sim **unwell¹, not well², unhealthy³** [e] adj
(i) not feeling well or in poor physical or mental health
(ii) to feel nauseated [ɔː] and about to vomit (BE)
illness⁴ n • **sickness⁴** n • **-sick** comb • **sickening⁵** adj • **sickly⁶** adj
» She is rather pale—is she sick? She's ill with measles [iː]. He is too sick to care for himself. I'm beginning to feel sick to my stomach⁷ [k]. If you don't feel well, you should stay in bed. There's too little time being spent treating the ill. Have you had any major [eɪdʒ] illnesses⁸?
Use to fall or get⁹/become or be taken⁹/be/feel **ill** • air/ brain¹⁰/ car**sick** • morning / x-ray **sickness** • **sickness** benefit¹¹ / leave¹² • **sick**-pay¹¹ / bed / room / leave¹² /-list • acutely / seriously [ɪɚ]/ mentally / chronically / critically / terminally¹³ [ɜː] **ill** • sudden / mild / severe / life-threatening [e]/ pre-existing¹⁴ • acquired¹⁵ [aɪ]/ physical [ɪ]/ psychiatric [saɪk-] **illness** • systemic / viral¹⁶ [aɪ]/ febrile **illness** • prolonged / associated / (in)curable / fatal¹⁷ [eɪ] **illness** • **sickly** child¹⁸ • **unhealthy** food

**(i) krank
(ii) übel sein, erbrechen**
unwohl¹ nicht gesund² nicht gesund, schädlich, ungesund³ Krankheit, Erkrankung⁴ ekelerregend, abscheulich⁵ kränklich⁶ übel sein⁷ schwere Krankheiten⁸ krank werden⁹ geisteskrank, verrückt¹⁰ Krankengeld¹¹ Krankenurlaub, Krankenstand (öst.)¹² im Endstadium¹³ Vorerkrankung¹⁴ erworbene Krankheit¹⁵ Viruserkrankung¹⁶ tödl. Krankheit¹⁷ kränkliches Kind¹⁸ schlechter Gesundheitszustand, Kränkeln¹⁹ 1

> Note: In BE **to be/feel sick** refers to vomiting while **feel ill** means to be coming down with an illness; **ill** is rarely used before a noun–except **ill** (=**bad**) **effects** or **ill** health¹⁹.

catch - caught - caught v irr inf   syn **get, pick up** v inf, **contract** v → U94-2f
to get a disease, esp. an easily transmitted¹ one such as an infection
» Did you catch a cold²? Where did she pick up that bug³? He contracted an infection when swimming in the polluted⁴ water. You can get all kinds of illnesses if you take a swim here.
Use **to catch** measles / the flu⁵ • **to contract** an illness / gonorrhea⁶ [rɪə] • **to contract** an upper respiratory infection / tuberculosis / HIV infection

bekommen, sich zuziehen
ansteckend¹ sich erkälten² Bazillus³ verseucht⁴ die Grippe bekommen⁵ sich e. Gonorrhö/ Tripper zuziehen⁶ 2

suffer (from) [ʌ] v   sim **sustain¹** [eɪ], **endure²** [ɪndjʊɚ] v clin, **go through³** v
(i) to have a disease (ii) to be affected or afflicted by harmful events, influences, disease, etc.
suffering⁴ n clin • **sufferer⁵** n clin & jar → U104-2
» He is suffering from high blood pressure. I suffered a mild attack of epilepsy. She sustained a neck injury when diving into shallow water⁶. She's been going through a spell⁷ of ill health.
Use **to suffer from** an illness / late complications / malnutrition⁸ [uː] • **to suffer from** dehydration [aɪ]/ heat stroke⁹ [oʊ] • **to sustain a** burn [ɜː]/ fracture / stroke¹⁰ / heart [ɑː] attack • chronic tinnitus / hay [eɪ] fever¹¹ [iː]/ diabetes¹² [iː] **sufferer** • burden [ɜː] of¹³ / unbearable¹⁴ [eɚ] **suffering** • **to endure** pain

erleiden, leiden an/ unter
erleiden, davontragen¹ erleiden, ertragen, aushalten² durchmachen³ Leid(en)⁴ Leidende(r)⁵ seichtes Wasser⁶ Phase⁷ an Unterernährung leiden⁸ einen Hitzschlag erleiden⁹ einen Schlaganfall erleiden¹⁰ Heuschnupfenpatient(in)¹¹ Diabetiker(in)¹² Leidensdruck¹³ unerträgliches Leiden¹⁴ 3

Illness & Recovery BASIC MEDICAL TERMS **15**

disease [dɪziːz] *n*   *syn* **dis**o**rder** *n*, *sim* **condition**¹ *n*, **dysfunction**² [ɪ] *n term*
specific impairment [eəʳ] of health or disturbance [ɜː] of normal function [ʌ]
disea**sed**³ *adj term* • **dis**o**rdered**⁴ *adj* • **dis**ea**se-free**⁵ *adj* • **dysfunctional** *adj*
» He *suffers from a rare heart condition. Does he have a medical condition that could account* [aʊ] *for the fatigue*⁶ [fətiːg]? *Patients with associated conditions*⁷ *may benefit from*⁸ *this mode of therapy.*
Use to eradicate⁹ *a disease* • heart / lung / viral [aɪ] *disease* • crippling¹⁰ / advanced / rare *disease* • progressive / no evidence of (*abbr* NED) *disease* • systemic / underlying¹¹ / predisposing *condition* • in a critical *condition* • *diseased* organ / area • mental / behavior¹² [eɪ] / affective¹³ / attention deficit *disorder* • autonomic / (borderline/ antisocial) personality¹⁴ / emotional *disorder* • organic / functional / psychosomatic [saɪkə-] *disorder* • congenital [dʒe] / anxiety¹⁵ [aɪ] *disorder* • panic / posttraumatic stress *disorder* • eating¹⁶ / substance abuse *disorder* • multiorgan / motor / endocrine / erectile¹⁷ *dysfunction* • *dysfunctional* uterine bleeding (*abbr* DUB)/ labor¹⁸ [eɪ] • *dysfunctional* state / sphincter / voiding¹⁹

> **Note:** While **illness** is a broad term for any health problem, **disease** is used with distinct pathologic entities and **condition** preferably with chronic or multiple disorders.

Krankheit, Erkrankung, Störung
Krankheit, Leiden; Zustand, Befinden¹ Funktionsstörung, Dysfunktion² krank, erkrankt, befallen³ krank, gestört⁴ rezidivfrei⁵ Müdigkeit⁶ Begleiterkrankungen, Komorbidität⁷ profitieren von⁸ eine Krankheit ausrotten⁹ zur Invalidität führende K.¹⁰ Grunderkrankung, -leiden¹¹ Verhaltensstörung¹² Affektstörung¹³ dissoziale Persönlichkeitsstörung¹⁴ Angstneurose¹⁵ Essstörung¹⁶ Erektionsstörung, erektile Impotenz¹⁷ Dystokie¹⁸ Miktionsstörung¹⁹

4

ailment [eɪlmənt] *n clin usu pl*   *syn* **malady** [mælədi] *n inf*
  rel **malaise**¹ [məleɪz] *n term* → U103-7, **a touch of**² [tʌtʃ] *phr inf*
chronic complaints [eɪ] which are not very serious, esp. very common ones such as a cold
ailing³ [aɪlɪŋ] *adj inf* • **ail**⁴ *vt & vi*
» *She has a long history of vague medical ailments. What's been ailing you, Mrs Brown? He'd been ailing for months before he died. It is just a* touch of indigestion⁵—*nothing serious.*
Use job-related⁶ / physical *ailments* • *ailing* father • childhood⁷ / chronic *maladies*

> **Note:** Clinical and informal expressions referring to being slightly ill include: **not being/ feeling yourself**, **to feel run down**, **to be off colour** (*BE*), **to be or feel under the weather**⁸, **be out of sorts**⁸, **to be/feel indisposed**. **Malady** is mostly used figuratively for a social or structural problem, while **malaise** is a symptom.

Krankheit, Leiden
Unpässlichkeit¹ Anflug von, leicht² kränklich, leidend³ plagen, laborieren an; kränkeln⁴ leichte Verdauungsstörung⁵ Berufskrankheiten⁶ Kinderkrankheiten⁷ nicht ganz auf der Höhe/ angeschlagen sein⁸

5

bedridden *adj*   *syn* **bedfast** *adj*, **laid** [eɪ] **up, be down with** *v phr inf*,
  rel **prostration**¹ [prɒstreɪʃᵊn] *n term*
severely affected by an illness that you are confined [aɪ] to bed², unable to get up and do anything
prostrate³ [prɒstreɪt] *v term* • **prostrating** *adj* • **bed rest**⁴ *n*
» *Pressure sores*⁵ *generally occur* [ɜː] *in patients who are bedridden and unable or unwilling to change position. She was acutely ill, appeared* exhausted [ɔː] *and prostrated*⁶. *The skin reaction may be accompanied by fever, malaise and even prostration, but this is very rare. She's laid up with acute rheumatism* [ruː-]. *Bedfast, paralyzed and* moribund⁷ [-bʌnd] *patients who are candidates for* decubiti⁵ [aɪ] *must be turned frequently.*
Use **bedridden** elderly patients • heat⁸ / extreme / severe *prostration* • *prostrating* headaches [k]/ pain • to order strict⁹/require/institute/be at/place at/keep at **bed rest**

bettläg(e)rig (sein)
Prostration, Erschöpfung, extreme Kraftlosigkeit¹ ans Bett gefesselt, bettläg(e)rig² zu Boden werfen³ Bettruhe⁴ Wundliegen, Dekubitus⁵ erschöpft und kraftlos⁶ im Sterben liegend⁷ Hitzeerschöpfung⁸ absolute Bettruhe verordnen⁹

6

infirmity [ɪnfɜːrməti] *n clin*   *syn* **feebleness** [fiːblnəs] *n inf*
being weak, frail¹ [eɪ], or bedridden, esp. used for referring to elderly people
infirm¹ *adj term* • **feeble**¹ *adj* • **infirmary**² *n* • **feeble-minded**³ *adj pej*
» *Elderly people tend to ignore their infirmities. Her aging infirm husband was moved to a* retirement facility⁴. *Heat stroke*⁵ *may occur in the elderly, infirm or* susceptible⁶ [sʌse-] *individuals in the absence of unusual exposure* [oʊʒ] *to heat. Her hand moved feebly across the desk.*
Use chronically **infirm** • *feeble* old man / pulse⁷ [ʌ]/ urinary stream⁸ [iː]

Schwäche, Gebrechlichkeit, Gebrechen
schwach, gebrechlich¹ Krankenzimmer; -haus² schwachsinnig³ Altersheim⁴ Hitzschlag⁵ empfindlich⁶ schwacher Puls⁷ schwacher (Harn)strahl⁸

7

16 BASIC MEDICAL TERMS — Illness & Recovery

disabled [eɪ] adj & n   syn **handicapped** adj & n, sim **invalid**[1] adj & n → U142-3

person in need of long-term care because (s)he is incapacitated[2] [æs] by a chronic illness
disability[3] n • **disabling**[4] adj • **invalidism**[5] n term • **invalidity**[5] n BE

» Thousands of workers are disabled by back pain each year. Reintegration and social adjustment [dʒʌ] for the disabled and disfigured[6] may be slow. He has been an invalid all his life.

Use **disabled** from birth [ɜː] • **disabling** illness / pain • physically [ɪ] / developmentally **disabled** • partially [ʃ] / completely or totally[7] **disabled** • life-long / level of / learning[8] **disability** • mental / permanent [ɜː] / severe[9] **disability** • **disability** benefit or pension[10] • mentally / physically / severely / multiply[11] [ʌ] **handicapped** • **invalid** chair (BE) or wheelchair[12] / car[13]

> **Note:** In modern usage the terms **disabled** and **handicapped** are considered politically correct, while **invalid** is dated and considered offensive by many handicapped people.

behindert; Behinderte
erwerbsunfähig, invalide; Invalide(r)[1] behindert, arbeitsunfähig[2] Behinderung, Invalidität[3] funktionell beeinträchtigend, behindernd[4] Erwerbsunfähigkeit, Invalidität[5] entstellte Menschen[6] vollinvalide[7] Lernschwäche[8] schwere Behinderung[9] Invalidenrente[10] mehrfach behindert[11] Rollstuhl[12] Behindertenfahrzeug[13]

8

malingerer [məlɪŋɡɚ] n clin   rel **hypochondriac**[1] [haɪpoʊkɒːndriæk] n

person who tends to avoid responsibilities or duties, e.g. by pretending to be ill
malinger[2] v term • **malingering** n & adj • **hypochondriac(al)**[3] adj

» Malingerers consciously seek a real or imagined gain [eɪ] from their illness[4]. Her family doctor[5] thought she was malingering. Hypochondriacs are preoccupied with[6] a fear of serious [ɪɚ] illness.

Use **hypochondriacal** patient / beliefs / delusion[7] [uː] / preoccupation

Simulant(in)
Hypochonder, eingebildete(r) Kranke(r)[1] sich krank stellen, simulieren[2] hypochondrisch[3] Krankheitsgewinn[4] Hausarzt[5] besessen von[6] hypochondrischer Wahn[7]

9

affect [əfekt] v   syn **involve** [ɒː], **afflict** v

to influence in a negative way or cause pain, suffering and/or disease
affliction[1] [əflɪkʃən] n • **(un)involved** adj • **involvement**[2] n

» The right kidney was not affected. In most patients the affliction is short-lived. Boys are afflicted twice as commonly as girls. Large areas of the spinal [aɪ] cord[3] were involved.

Use **affected** side / area / parts • **(un)involved** side / nodes[4] [oʊ] / joints [dʒ] / ear / by tumor[5] • local / extensive / systemic / renal [iː] / liver **involvement** • vascular / lymph [lɪmf] node or nodal[7] **involvement** • **afflicted** joint • chronic / debilitating / life-long / hip **affliction** • **afflictions of** old age[8] / aging[8] [eɪdʒɪŋ]

schädigen, betreffen, befallen
Leiden, Beschwerden[1] Befall, Beteiligung[2] Rückenmark[3] befallene Lymphknoten[4] tumorbefallen[5] Mitbeteiligung d. Niere[6] Lymphknotenbeteiligung, -befall[7] Altersbeschwerden[8]

10

impaired [ɪmpeɚd] adj → U142-3   syn **compromised** [-aɪzd] adj term & clin

made worse, weaker or less effective, inefficient [ɪʃ] or reduced in function
impairment[1] n • **impair** v • **unimpaired**[2] n • **compromise**[3] v & n

» Olfaction[4] [æ] and taste are impaired in smokers. About 20% of patients with lung involvement suffer irreversible lung impairment. There was transient impairment of consciousness and confusion. Almost any pathogen can cause pneumonia [n(j)uː-] in a compromised host [oʊ].

Use **impaired** sensation / function / ability to swallow[5] [ɒː] • mentally / mildly / severely **impaired** • visual [ɪʒ] / speech [tʃ] / hearing[6] / cognitive **impairment** • **impairment of** consciousness[7] [ʃ] / memory / liver function • (non)immuno**compromised**[8] • (life-threatening) hemodynamic[9] [aɪ] / cardiovascular **compromise** • respiratory / neurologic [ʊɚ] **compromise**

beeinträchtigt, gestört
Beeinträchtigung, Störung, Schädigung[1] ungestört, intakt[2] gefährden; Gesundheitsgefährdung, akute Komplikation/ Krise[3] Geruchssinn[4] Schluckstörung[5] Schwerhörigkeit[6] Bewusstseinsstörung[7] immungeschwächt[8] hämodynamische Komplikation[9]

11

deteriorate vi   syn **worsen** [ɜː] vi/vt inf, **decline** [dɪklaɪn] vi, rel **aggravate**[1] vt

to get progressively worse (symptoms, the patient's status/ condition)
deterioration[2] n • **aggravation**[2] n • **decline**[3] n • **worse**[4] adj • **worsening**[5] n & adj

» His health is steadily [e] deteriorating. I'm afraid he's worse[6] today. Her condition worsened overnight. There was sudden deterioration of vision [ɪʒ]. Voluntary activity declined due to weakness and fatigue. The pain is aggravated by shoulder motion [oʊʃ]. Dairy [eɚ] products[7] may aggravate diarrhea [daɪəriːə].

Use sudden / progressive[8] / clinical / neurologic / cerebral / mental[9] **deterioration** • **to worsen** symptoms [ɪ]/ the condition[10] / quickly / by day • steady / rapid / gradual / intellectual[9] / functional **decline** • **to aggravate** acne [ækni]/ a disorder • **aggravating** factors • to make/be/become **worse** • to make things / transiently[11] / progressively **worse** • clinical[12] / radiographic / neurologic / marked[13] **worsening** • **worsening** asthma [æzmə]/ clinical status[12] / of joint pain

sich verschlechtern – sich verschlimmern
etw. verschlimmern[1] Verschlechterung, Verschlimmerung[2] Verschlechterung, Verfall; Abnahme[3] schlechter[4] Verschlechterung; fortschreitend, progredient[5] es geht ihm schlechter[6] Milchprodukte[7] zunehmende Verschlechterung[8] geistiger Verfall[9] den Gesundheitszustand verschlechtern[10] vorübergehend schlechter[11] Verschlechterung d. klin. Status[12] deutl. Verschlechterung[13]

12

Illness & Recovery BASIC MEDICAL TERMS **17**

improve [uː] v   syn **ameliorate** [əmiːljəreɪt] v, sim **alleviate**¹ [iː], **mitigate**¹ v
(i) to get better after an illness
(ii) to cause symptoms or a condition to get better (e.g. by therapy)
improvement² n clin • **amelioration**² n • **alleviation**³ n • **mitigation**³ n
» His condition has improved markedly. The drug did not seem to improve symptoms. Treatment is directed toward alleviating renal insufficiency [ɪʃ]. This will improve perfusion and ameliorate some of his rest pain⁴. Overall, improvement in symptoms was quite dramatic.
Use **to improve** skin function / blood flow / outcome • **to improve** with age⁵ / over time / with exercise • **to ameliorate** behavior problems / pruritus [aɪ] signs • **to alleviate** symptoms / pain⁶ / headache [hedeɪk] • **to alleviate** anxiety⁷ [aɪ]/ spasm / heartburn [hɑːrtbɜːrn] • to show no⁸ **improvement** • gradual / little⁹ / partial / marked or definite¹⁰ **improvement** • clinical / subjective / signs of¹¹ **improvement** • symptomatic / dramatic **alleviation** • **alleviation of** symptoms / pain¹²

(sich) bessern, besser werden, s. erholen, Fortschritte machen
lindern, (ver)mindern¹ Besserung² Linderung, Erleichterung³ Ruheschmerz⁴ sich auswachsen, mit zunehmendem Alter besser werden⁵ Schmerz lindern⁶ Ängste abbauen/ Angst mindern⁷ keine Besserung zeigen⁸ leichte Besserung⁹ deutliche B.¹⁰ Anzeichen einer Besserung¹¹ Schmerzlinderung¹²

13

subside [aɪ] vi → U140-4   syn **abate** [eɪ], **fade** [eɪ] vi, rel **revert**¹, **reverse**¹ [ɜː] vt
to lessen, become less pronounced [aʊ] or return to normal² (e.g. signs of shock, fever [iː])
subsidence³ n clin • **abatement**³ n • **reversal**⁴ n • **(ir)reversible** adj
» Her swelling has subsided completely without residual discomfort⁵. Nausea [ɔː] and vomiting usually disappear as the cramps in the lower abdomen subside. Continue treatment until the resulting intense anxiety abates. Spontaneous [eɪ] reversal occurs slowly, over many weeks. Failure of the fever to subside indicates inadequate drainage [-ɪdʒ].
Use **to subside** gradually⁶ [ædʒ]/ promptly / rapidly / without sequelae⁷ [sɪkwɛliː]/ within 2 days • **to revert** to(ward) normal² / spontaneously • **to abate** with remission • **to reverse** a process / a deficit⁸ / drug effects / a chemical injury / the catabolic state • temporary⁹ **subsidence** • **reversible** disease / impairment / ischemia [ɪskiːmɪə]

nachlassen, abklingen, (ab)sinken, sich bessern
bessern, normalisieren¹ s. normalisieren² Rückgang, Abklingen, Remission³ (Auf)lösung, Besserung⁴ Restbeschwerden⁵ allmählich abklingen⁶ komplikationslos abklingen⁷ einen Mangel beheben⁸ vorübergehende Besserung⁹

14

resolve [rɪzɒːlv] vi   syn **settle (down)** v,
sim **disappear**¹ [-ɪɚ], **go away**¹ v phr clin
to lessen and return to normal (e.g. a swelling, eruption [ʌ], etc.)
resolution² [uːʃ] n term • **unresolved** adj • **disappearance**² n
» The abscess resolved with antibiotic therapy alone. Most cases resolve in 4-6 weeks with conservative management. This rash³ has settled down nicely. Extrapyramidal syndromes increase with anxiety, wax and wane⁴ [eɪ], and disappear with sleep. The fever went away for more than 24 hours and then returned. You can rest assured that this numbness⁵ [ʌ] will settle spontaneously [eɪ].
Use **to resolve** spontaneously⁶ / uneventfully / without sequela / within hours • edema [iː] / palsy⁷ [ɔː]/ hematuria / vasospasm⁸ [eɪ] **resolves** • **to settle** with rest⁹ / one's nerves / down at night¹⁰ • **resolution of** signs / symptoms¹¹ / the infection / the edema • to hasten¹² [heɪsⁿn] /promote **resolution** • clinical / histologic / partial / full¹³ / (in)complete¹³ **resolution** • rapid / prompt / spontaneous¹⁴ / eventual¹³ / pain **resolution** • **unresolved** pneumonia¹⁵ [n(j)uː-]/ enigma¹⁶ / uremia [iː]/ conflict¹⁷ / issue¹⁸

abklingen, sich zurückbilden, (sich) beruhigen
verschwinden, abklingen¹ Besserung, Rückbildung, Abklingen² Ausschlag³ zu- u. abnehmen⁴ Taubheitsgefühl⁵ spontan abklingen⁶ Lähmung bildet sich zurück⁷ Gefäßkrampf löst sich⁸ in Ruhe abklingen⁹ über Nacht abklingen¹⁰ Abklingen d. Symptome¹¹ Abheilen/ Abklingen beschleunigen¹² vollkommene Rückbildung, Vollremission¹³ Spontanremission¹⁴ persistierende Pneumonie¹⁵ ungelöstes Rätsel¹⁶ nicht bewältigter Konflikt¹⁷ ungelöstes Problem¹⁸

15

recover [rɪkʌvɚ] v clin   syn **recuperate** [uː], **convalesce** [kɒnvəles] v clin
rel **get over**¹ v phr, **overcome**¹ v inf
to get better or well again after an illness as the condition improves and symptoms resolve and disappear and the patient returns to normal activities
recovery² n • **recuperation**² n • **convalescence**² n • **convalescent**³ adj & n
» Most children recover from hepatitis without sequelae⁴. The infant is still recovering from birth shock. You badly need some weeks of rest and recuperation. I was just getting over the flu when I caught another bug [ʌ]. Otherwise the patient's convalescence was smooth⁵ [uː].
Use **to recover from** shock / frostbite⁶ / arthritis [aɪ]/ anesthesia [iːʒ]/ surgery [ɜː] • to make a full⁷ /achieve [ətʃiːv] **recovery** • to accelerate or hasten or speed up **recovery** • full or complete⁸ / partial⁹ **recovery** • early / prompt / good **recovery** • uneventful or uncomplicated / spontaneous¹⁰ / time to¹¹ **recovery** • **recovery** period¹¹ / room¹² • to be on the way to¹³ **recovery** • prolonged / surgical **convalescence** • **convalescent** serum¹⁴ [ɪɚ]/ period¹¹ / carrier¹⁵ / care / home¹⁶ • prolonged / surgical **recuperation**

genesen, sich erholen
überwinden, überstehen¹ Genesung, Erholung, Rekonvaleszenz² genesend; Rekonvaleszent(in)³ Folgen, Folgeerscheinungen⁴ problemlos⁵ von Erfrierungen genesen⁶ völlig wiederhergestellt sein⁷ vollständige Genesung, Restitutio ad integrum⁸ Defektheilung⁹ Spontanheilung¹⁰ Rekonvaleszenz¹¹ Aufwachraum¹² auf d. Weg d. Besserung sein¹³ Rekonvaleszentenserum¹⁴ rekonvaleszenter Ausscheider¹⁵ Erholungsheim¹⁶

16

18 BASIC MEDICAL TERMS   Injuries

Clinical Phrases

Ever since that accident he's been in a pretty bad way. Seit seinem Unfall geht es ihm gesundheitlich ziemlich schlecht. • I've not been feeling myself for a while. Ich bin schon einige Zeit gesundheitlich nicht ganz auf der Höhe. • I've been feeling under the weather for some days, doctor. Herr Doktor, ich fühle mich schon ein paar Tage etwas angeschlagen. • Are you feeling better today? Geht es Ihnen heute besser? • Do you feel up to going back to work? Glauben Sie, dass Sie wieder zur Arbeit gehen können? • She seems to be on the mend again. Sie scheint auf dem Weg der Besserung zu sein. • I've been up and about for two days now. Seit zwei Tagen bin ich wieder auf den Beinen. • I wish you a speedy recovery. Baldige Besserung! • I suppose the child is sickening for measles. Das Kind brütet vermutlich die Masern aus. • Her health has been declining. Ihr Gesundheitszustand ist zusehends schlechter geworden. • His progress has suffered a setback. Er hatte einen Rückfall. • In the last 48 hours Mrs. Miller has been pursuing a constant downhill course. Mit Frau M. ging es in den letzten 48 Stunden ständig bergab. • I hope she'll get well soon. Ich hoffe, sie ist bald wieder auf den Beinen.

Unit 5   Injuries
Related Units: 106 Fractures, 104 Pain, 89 General Pathology, 140 Wound Healing, 141 Fracture Management

injure [ɪndʒɚ] *v usu pass*   *syn* **hurt, wound** [uː] *v* → U104-3
to hurt oneself or harm somebody else
injury[1] *n* • **(un)injured / (un)hurt** *adj* • **the injured**[2] *n*
» *Do not rub or massage* [-ɑː(d)ʒ] *injured tissues or apply ice or heat. The injured area should be cleansed* [e] *with soap or antiseptic and sterile* dressings[3] *applied.*
Use badly / seriously [ɪɚ]/ critically / fatally[4] **injured** • **injured** extremity / area / head / party[5] / tissue / epithelium [iː] • **to hurt** oneself / one's back

   Note: Do not confuse *to injure* and *injury* with insure[6] [ɪnʃʊɚ] and insurance[7].

(sich) verletzen, verwunden
Verletzung[1] Verletzte[2] Verband[3] tödlich verletzt[4] verletzte Person/Partei[5] versichern (lassen)[6] Versicherung[7]

1

injury [ɪndʒɚi] *n*   *syn* **trauma** [trɒːmə] *n term*
damage or wound inflicted[1] on the body by external forces
injurious[2] [ɪndʒʊɚɪəs] *adj* • **injury-free** *adj*
» *Many patients find even minor injuries (such as venipuncture)* unbearable[3] [eɚ]. *Tell me about the circumstances of your injury. Where is your injury? Excess carotene is not injurious.*
Use to sustain[4]/receive **an injury** • **injury** to the breast[5] [e]/ from exposure to cold[6] / site / type / degree / mechanism [k]/ pattern **of injury** • head / brain / spinal [aɪ] cord[7] / blast[8] / whiplash[9] / facial [feɪʃəl] **injury** • work(-related) / sports / thermal / cold[6] / radiation / renal [iː]/ self-inflicted[10] / bodily[11] **injury** • superficial / blunt[12] [ʌ]/ closed / penetrating / needle stick[13] / crush(ing)[14] [ʌ]/ soft tissue[15] / impalement[16] [eɪ] **injury** • **injured** extremity / area / head • **injurious** effect / agent[17]

Verletzung, Trauma
zugefügt[1] schädlich[2] unerträglich[3] V. erleiden[4] Brustverletzung[5] Erfrierung[6] Rückenmarkverletzung[7] Explosionstrauma[8] Schleudertrauma[9] Selbstverstümmelung[10] Körperverletzung[11] stumpfe V.[12] Nadelstichverletzung[13] Quetschung[14] Weichteilverletzung[15] Pfählungsverletzung[16] schädliche Substanz[17]

2

wound [wuːnd] *v & n*   *syn* **traumatize** *v term*, **injure** *v*, *sim* **harm**[1] *v*
(v) to cause an injury, esp one that breaks the skin (n) injury to the skin or an internal organ caused by violence [aɪ] or a surgical incision
wounded[2] *n & adj* • **harm** *n* • **unharmed**[3] *adj*
» *The wound was dressed with a plain* pad[4] *and bandage. It was a simple* through-and-through bullet [ʊ] wound[5]. *The* wound exudate[6] *was quite* frothy[7]. *Explore and* debride [iː] *the wound carefully.*
Use to inflict/cause/approximate[8]/clean/cover/dress[9]/swab[10] [ɒː]/close **a wound** • **wound** healing / care[11] / cleanser[12] [e]/ closure • deep / burn / bite / flesh / open / penetrating **wound** • gunshot / puncture or stab[13] / clean / contaminated / gaping[14] [eɪ]/ surgical **wound** • **wound** cavity / abscess / discharge[6] / margins[15] [dʒ]/ edges[15] / surface • to do sb.[16] / to come to / bodily[17] **harm**

verletzen, verwunden; Wunde, Verwundung
verletzen, Schaden zufügen[1] Verletzte; verwundet[2] unverletzt, -versehrt[3] Wundauflage[4] Durchschuss[5] Wundsekret[6] trüb[7] Wundränder adaptieren[8] W. verbinden[9] W. abtupfen[10] Wundversorgung[11] Wundreinigungsmittel[12] Stichwunde[13] klaffende W.[14] Wundränder[15] jem. Schaden/ e. Verletzung zufügen[16] Körperverletzung[17]

3

Injuries   BASIC MEDICAL TERMS 19

trauma [trɒːmə] *n term, pl* **-s** *or* **-ata**   *syn* **injury, wound** *n*

physical or psychic [saɪkɪk] injury caused by accidents, violent action, toxic substances, emotional shock, etc.

traumatic *adj term* • **traumatize** *v* • **-trauma, trauma(to)-** *comb*

» There was eyelid swelling from blunt trauma to the orbit. The CNS bleeding occurred without evidence of antecedent [siː] trauma or of a specific lesion.

Use **trauma** center / care / index • high risk for **trauma** • acoustic[1] [kuː]/ birth / facial / arterial trauma • emotional / major[2] [eɪdʒ] / multiple[3] **trauma** • a/ non/ post-**traumatic** • *traumatic* death[4] [e]/ in origin / pain / shock / event[5] / (brain) injury / sexual experience • *traumatized* zone [zoʊn]/ patient[6] • **traumato**logy /genic • baro/ micro**trauma**

Trauma, Wunde, seelische Erschütterung
Schalltrauma[1] schweres T.[2] Polytrauma[3] Unfalltod[4] traumatisches Ereignis[5] Traumapatient(in)[6]

4

---

lesion [liːʒᵊn] *n term* → U89-3   *sim* **sore**[1] [sɔːr] *n clin* → U104-11

(i) wound or injury (ii) broad term for all kinds of tissue damage (skin sores[2], ulcers [ʌls], tumors, etc.)

» If the carious lesion progresses, infection of the dental pulp may occur, causing acute pulpitis [-aɪtɪs].

Use gross[3] [oʊ]/ deep seated / occult / palpable / nodular / localized / focal[4] / irritative / polypoid / premalignant[5] / necrotic **lesion** • skin[2] / scalp[6] / vaginal [dʒ] wall / rib / solitary[7] / recurrent[8] [ɜːǁʌ] **lesions** • bed *or* pressure[9] / running[10] / oriental / cold[11] *sore*

(i) Verletzung
(ii) Läsion, Schädigung, Tumor
wunde Stelle, Geschwür[1] Hautläsionen[2] makroskopische Läsion[3] Herdläsion[4] Präkanzerose[5] Kopfhautverletzungen[6] Solitärläsionen[7] Rezidive[8] Dekubital-, Druckgeschwür[9] eiternde Wunde[10] Herpes simplex, Fieberbläschen[11]

5

---

cut *n & v*   *sim* **slash**[1], **slice**[2] [aɪ] *n & v clin,* **incision**[3] *n term* → U126-9

(n) wound made by cutting (v) incise the skin or tissue by accident[4] or intention with a knife [naɪf], scalpel, scissors [sɪzəz], etc.

cutdown[5] *n term* → U127-18 • **cut** through/ away/ off[6]/ in *v phr jar*

» He had a bad cut on his shin[7]. She cut her soles[8] on the broken glass. Cut the umbilical cord[9].

Use slight / superficial / deep **cut** • venous[5] [iː] **cutdown** • **cut** edge[10] / surface[11] / section / ends / into slices [aɪ] • vein [eɪ] was **cut** and ligated[12] [aɪ] • **to slash** one's wrists[13] [rɪsts]

Schnittwunde, -verletzung; (ein/ab/durch/zer)schneiden
(langer/ tiefer) Schnitt; aufschlitzen[1] Scheibe; (Scheiben) schneiden[2] (Ein)schnitt, Inzision[3] versehentlich[4] Venae sectio, Venenschnitt[5] ab-, wegschneiden[6] Schienbein[7] Fußsohlen[8] Nabelschnur[9] Schnittrand[10] Schnittfläche[11] V. wurde ligiert u. durchtrennt[12] s. die Pulsadern aufschneiden[13]

6

---

laceration [læsəreɪʃᵊn] *n term*   *sim* **tear**[1] [teə] *n clin* → U5-19

(i) a torn external or internal wound with rough [rʌf] margins[2]; not a cut or incision
(ii) the act of lacerating

lacerated[3] *adj term* • **lacerate** *v usu pass* • **lacerable** *adj* • **torn** *adj*

» Bleeding from the external ear is most commonly due to[4] local laceration or abrasion. A tear had developed in the intima of the aorta [eɪ].

Use *lacerated* wound / tendon[5] • scar from / skin / pelvic floor[6] / puncture[7] / flap-type **laceration** • *laceration of the* liver / pleura [ʊ]/ cervix / perineum[8] • **torn** dura / vessel[9] • retinal / esophageal [dʒɪəl] **tear**

Riss-, Platzwunde; Zerreißung
(Ein)riss, Ruptur[1] ausgefranste Ränder[2] ein-, aufgerissen, zerfetzt[3] zurückzuführen auf[4] Sehnenriss, -ruptur[5] Beckenbodenriss[6] Stichwunde[7] Dammriss[8] Gefäßruptur[9]

7

---

abrasion [əbreɪʒᵊn] *n term*   *syn* **graze** [eɪ] *n & v clin,*
  sim **chafe**[1] [tʃeɪf] *v & n,* **excoriation**[2] *n term*

(i) wound caused by scraping [eɪ] the skin against a rough object (ii) pathologic or therapeutic grinding or wearing [eə] away[3] of superficial tissue layers, e.g. of tooth substance, skin layers, uterine mucosa, etc.

abrasive[4] *adj & n term* • abrade[5] *v* • **excoriated** *adj*

» Abrasions such as a skinned knee[6] [niː] or a floor burn[7] should be washed, a mild antiseptic ointment[8] applied, and covered with sterile gauze[9] [ɒː].

Use superficial [ɪʃ]/ facial / scalp / corneal[10] / multiple **abrasion** • **abrasions and/or** contusions [juː]/ lacerations • derm**abrasion**

(i) Schürfwunde, Abschürfung, Schramme (ii) Abrieb, Abrasion, Abschabung
aufscheuern, wundreiben; wundgeriebene Stelle[1] Exkoriation[2] Abtragung[3] abreibend; Schleifmittel[4] abschürfen, -reiben[5] aufgeschürftes Knie[6] Abschürfung durch mechan. Reibung[7] Salbe[8] (Verbands)mull[9] Hornhautabschabung, Abrasio corneae[10]

8

scratch [skrætʃ] *v & n clin*   *syn* **scrape** [eɪ] *v & n clin*

(v) (i) to inflict small shallow cuts[1] with a sharp object (ii) scrape or rub oneself with one's fingernails to relieve itching [ɪtʃɪŋ] (n) a small abraded area where the skin is torn or worn off

» The lesions were found along linear scratch marks[2]. The itch[3] provokes a desire to scratch.

Use **scratch**-type incision / test[4] • vigorously [ɪg] **scraped** area • skin / tissue / corneal / uterine[5] **scrapings** • iris [aɪ] **scraped** free • cat-**scratch** fever[6] [iː]

sting [stɪŋ] - stung - stung *v irr & n*   *sim* **bite**[1] - bit - bitten *v irr & n*, **prick**[2] *v & n*, **puncture**[3] [ʌ] *v & n term*

(n) wound caused by certain insects (e.g. hornets[4], wasps [ɒː], fire ants[5]), plants (e.g. nettles[6], poison ivy[7] [aɪvi]) and animals (esp marine animals like jellyfish[8] [dʒ], stingrays[9], etc.) typically associated with exposure to irritating chemicals or venoms[10]

stinging[11] *adj* • **biting** *adj* • **stinger**[12] *n* → U91-16 • **punctured** *adj term*

» Usually the barbed venomous stinger[13] can be found in place after a bee sting. The girl was stung by several honeybees. Hospitalize all patients who have been bitten by poisonous snakes.

Use insect / scorpion **stings** • animal / dog / cat / mosquito / snake / tick[14] / human / stork[15] **bite** • **bite** wound[16] / injury • flea[17]- [iː] / frost[18]-**bitten** • **biting** sensation / louse [aʊ] • **puncture** wound / site[19] • needle / lumbar[20] [ʌ]/ acu**puncture** • to **prick** one's finger • **prick** (skin) test[21]

burn [bɜːrn] *n & v clin*   *sim* **scald**[1] [skɔːld] *v & n clin*

(n) injury to tissues resulting from fire, hot liquids, steam[2] [iː], acid chemicals, lightning[3], electricity or radiation (v) to cause a lesion by heat exposure or suffer pain from heat

scalding[4] *adj clin* • **sunburn**[5] *n* • **postburn** *adj term*

» Burn scars are often unsightly[6] [saɪt] and total resolution[7] is not possible in many cases. The mainstay of treatment of any chemical burn is copious[8] irrigation with large amounts of tap water[9]. Be careful not to scald the anesthetized tissues.

Use minor / major / deep thermal / 1st degree[10] / contact / friction[11] [kʃ] **burns** • chemical *or* acid[12] / electrical / depth of **burn** • **burn** victim / trauma / coma / care • **burned** body surface • **burning** pain / sensation[13] / feet / tongue [tʌŋ]/ on urination[14] • **scald(ing)** burn[1] • **scalded** skin[15]

frostbite [frɒstbaɪt] *n clin*   *sim* **chilblain** [tʃɪlbleɪn] *or* **(erythema)** [iː] **pernio**[1] *n term*

blanching[2], paresthesias[3] [iː], edema [ɪdiːmə] and local tissue destruction as a result of exposure to extreme cold

frostbitten[4] *adj clin* • **frostnip**[5] *n*

» After rewarming the frostbitten area becomes purple [ɜː], painful and tender. Chilblains are red, itching, blistering[6] skin lesions without actual freezing of the tissues.

Use deep / superficial / severe[7] **frostbite** • **frostbitten** toes / digits [dʒ]

bruise [bruːz] *n & v clin*   *syn* **contusion** [uː] *n*, *sim* **hematoma**[1] [hiːmətoʊmə] *n term* → U89-26

(n) injury to soft tissues produced by blunt trauma (e.g. a blow[2], kick, or fall) producing a subcutaneous hematoma from ruptured blood vessels
(v) to cause a contusion, e.g. by bumping [ʌ] into[3] sth.

bruising[4] *n* • **contuse** *v* • black eye *or* shiner[5] [aɪ] *n clin*

» How did you bruise your forearm? She was treated for cuts and bruises. The left kidney is mildly contused. How do you differentiate subdural hematomas from cerebral contusion without hematoma?

Use skin **bruises** • to be easily[6] **bruised** • ecchymosis [kɪ] and **bruising** • cerebral[7] contusion • **contusion** of the spinal [aɪ] cord • **contused** wound[8]

(sich) kratzen, schaben; Kratzer, Schramme
oberflächliche Schnittverletzungen[1] Kratzspuren[2] Jucken, Juckreiz[3] Skarifikations-, Kratztest[4] Kürettagematerial a. d. Uterus[5] Katzenkratzkrankheit[6]   9

stechen, brennen; (Insekten)stich, Biss, Stachel *(BE)*
beißen; Biss[1] (ein-, auf-, durch) stechen; (Ein)stich[2] punktieren, (durch)stechen; Punktion, Einstich[3] Hornissen[4] Feuerameisen[5] (Brenn)nessel[6] Giftefeu[7] Quallen[8] Stachelrochen[9] tierische Gifte[10] stechend, brennend[11] Stachel[12] Giftstachel m. Widerhaken[13] Zeckenbiss[14] Storchenbiss[15] Bisswunde[16] voller Flohbisse[17] erfroren[18] Punktionsstelle[19] Lumbalpunktion[20] Pricktest[21]   10

Verbrennung, Brandwunde; (sich) verbrennen
(sich) verbrühen; Verbrühung[1] Dampf[2] Blitzschlag[3] siedend (heiß)[4] Sonnenbrand[5] hässlich, unansehnlich[6] Rückbildung[7] gründlich[8] Leitungswasser[9] V. 1. Grades[10] Verbrennungen durch mech. Reibung[11] Verätzung[12] Brennen, brennendes Gefühl[13] Brennen beim Urinieren[14] verbrühte Haut[15]   11

Erfrierung, Congelatio
Frostbeule, Pernio[1] Blässe, Blasswerden[2] Parästhesien, Sensibilitätsstörungen[3] erfroren[4] leichte Erfrierung[5] mit Blasenbildung[6] schwere/ hochgradige Erfrierung[7]
   12

Quetschung, Prellung, Kontusion, Bluterguss; quetschen, s. einen blauen Fleck holen
Hämatom, Bluterguss[1] Schlag, Stoß[2] stoßen gegen[3] Prellungen, blaue Flecke(n)[4] blaues Auge, Veilchen[5] leicht blaue Flecke(n) bekommen[6] Hirnprellung, Contusio cerebri[7] Quetschwunde[8]
   13

Injuries   BASIC MEDICAL TERMS **21**

---

concussion [kənkʌʃ³n] *n clin & term*   *syn* **commotio** [kəmoʊʃioʊ] *n term rare*
(i) generally, a collision [ɪʒ] or violent shaking
(ii) the resulting injury to soft tissues, esp. the brain or retina
be concussed[1] *phr term* • **concussive**[2] *adj* • **postconcussion** *adj*
» Concussion affects only mentation[3], with return of consciousness moments or minutes after impact[4]. Amnesia[5] [iː] after concussion typically follows a few moments of unresponsiveness[6].
Use **concussion of the** brain[7] / spinal cord[8] • to suffer a[9] / cerebral / cochlear [k]/ grade 3 **concussion** • **concussive** effect / blow / (head) injury / state • **postconcussion** headache / syndrome[10]

(Gehirn)erschütterung, Commotio
(Gehirn)erschütterung haben[1] erschütternd[2] mentale Funktionen[3] Aufprall, Stoß[4] Amnesie, Erinnerungslücke[5] Nichtansprechbarkeit[6] Commotio cerebri[7] Commotio spinalis, Rückenmarkerschütterung[8] eine Gehirnerschütterung erleiden[9] postkommotionelles Syndrom[10]   14

---

swelling *n clin*   *sim* **puffiness**[1] [ʌ] *n clin*,
                 tumescence[2], **edema**[3] [iˈdiːmə] *n term*
abnormal localized enlargement due to accumulation of fluid[4] in the tissue
swell[5] - swelled - swollen *v irr* • **puffy**[6] *adj* • **edematous**[7] [e] *adj*
» Is the painful swelling in her breast [e] due to bruising? Venous stasis [eɪ] may sometimes affect lymphatic vessels, producing a permanent swelling called solid edema[8].
Use **swelling** subsides[9] • **swollen** lymph nodes / joints / ankle / nasal mucosa • acute / local(ized) / diffuse / inflammatory[10] / marked[11] / painful or tender **swelling** • facial / soft tissue / ankle / eyelid[12] / cloudy[13] [aʊ] **swelling** • **puffiness** about the eyes

(An)schwellung
Aufgedunsenheit[1] Tumeszenz, (diffuse) Anschwellung[2] Ödem[3] Flüssigkeitsansammlung[4] (an)schwellen[5] verschwollen[6] ödematös[7] Myxödem[8] Schwellung klingt ab[9] entzündliche Schwellung[10] starke Schwellung[11] Lidschwellung[12] trübe Schwellung[13]

15

---

sprain [eɪ] *n & v clin*   *sim* **torsion**[1] [ʃ] *n term*
(n) injury to the tendons[2], ligaments[3] and/or capsule around a joint (v) to twist[4] a joint
torsional[5] *adj term* • **distort**[6] *v* • **distortion**[7] *n*
» It was just a sprain, the ligament was not torn and there was no avulsion fracture[8]. How did you sprain your ankle?
Use ankle / foot / knee / collateral ligament[9] / (un)stable **sprain** • **sprain** fracture[8] • **sprained** ankle[10] / wrist [ɪst] • (internal/external) tibial / testicular[11] **torsion** • **torsional** movement / displacement[12] / stress • outward / medial / radiographic / mandibular[13] **distortion** • **distorted** face[14] / anatomy / body image

▪ **Note:** In English medical usage *distortion* and *sprain* are not synonymous.

Verstauchung, Zerrung, Distorsion; zerren, verstauchen, überdehnen
Torsion, (Ver)drehung[1] Sehnen[2] Bänder[3] verdrehen, -stauchen, umknicken[4] Dreh-, Torsions-[5] verdrehen, -zerren[6] Verzerrung[7] Abrissfraktur[8] Seitenbandzerrung[9] verstauchter Knöchel[10] Hodentorsion[11] Drehfehlstellung[12] Unterkieferasymmetrie[13] verzerrtes Gesicht[14]

16

---

strain [eɪ] *v & n clin*   *sim* **pull**[1] *v*, **sprain**[1] *v & n clin*
(v) to overstretch[2] or overexercise a muscle [mʌsl] or ligament
(n) damage (usually muscular [kjʊ]) resulting from excessive physical effort[3]
straining[4] *n* • **strenuous**[5] [e] *adj*
» You must avoid flexing[6], lifting and straining. Causes of chronic low back pain may also include back strain due to poor posture[7] [pɒːstʃɚ] or poor conditioning[8] that is aggravated[9] by mechanical factors (e.g. overuse[10] or obesity [iː]).
Use to strain or pull[1] **a muscle** • (low) back[11] / muscle[12] / abduction / right heart[13] / emotional[14] **strain** • abdominal[15] **straining**

überdehnen, -lasten, zerren; Überdehnung, -belastung, Zerrung
(Muskel) zerren[1] überdehnen[2] körperliche Überanstrengung[3] Anstrengung, Belastung[4] anstrengend[5] Beugen, Bücken[6] schlechte Haltung[7] schlechter Trainingszustand[8] verschlechtert[9] Überbelastung, -training[10] überanstrengter/s Rücken/ Kreuz[11] Muskelzerrung[12] Rechtsherzbelastung[13] seelische Belastung[14] Bauchpresse[15]

17

---

hemorrhage [heməridʒ] *n term*   *syn* **bleeding** *n clin*, **bleed** *n jar* → U89-26
internal or external bleeding usually from a ruptured vessel, e.g. prolonged minor oozing [uːzɪŋ] of blood[1] from minute[2] [maɪnjuːt] vessels or acute and massive extravasation[3]
hemorrhagic *adj term* • **nosebleed**[4] *n clin* • **bleeder**[5] *n* • **bleed** - bled - bled *v irr*
» In an arterial [ɪɚ] hemorrhage the blood is bright red in color and comes in spurts[6].
Use to arrest or stop a[7] **hemorrhage** • acute / major[8] / brisk[8] / profuse[8] / intracranial / internal[9] **hemorrhage** • petechial [k] / capillary / postextraction / postpartum[10] / essential / concealed[11] [iː]/ secondary[12] **hemorrhage** • **hemorrhagic** disease of the newborn[13] / fever

Blutung, Hämorrhagie
Sickerblutung[1] kleinste[2] Blutaustritt, Blutung[3] Nasenbluten[4] Bluter(in), Hämophile(r)[5] pulssynchron spritzen[6] Blutung stillen[7] starke B.[8] innere B.[9] Nachgeburtsblutung[10] okkulte B.[11] Nachblutung[12] hämorrhagische Diathese d. Neugeborenen[13]

18

22 BASIC MEDICAL TERMS — Accidents & Emergencies

rupture [rʌptʃɚ] n & v term   syn **tear** [teɚ] - tore - torn n & v irr clin, sim **disruption**[1] [ʌ] n term

(n) a break [eɪ] or tear in continuity[2] of soft tissues (tendons, vessels)
(un)ruptured adj • **tearing** n • disrupt[3] v • disruptive[4] adj
» On laparoscopy blunt diaphragmatic rupture was diagnosed. There was a tear of the middle meningeal artery.
Use traumatic / spontaneous[5] [eɪ] **rupture** • tendon[6] / partial[7] / delayed [eɪ]/ free / contained[8] [eɪ] **rupture** • splenic[9] [e]/ bladder[10] / aortic [eɪ] **rupture** • **rupture of** the diaphragm [æm]/ an aneurysm [ænjərɪzᵊm]/ membranes[11] / longitudinal ligaments • **ruptured** eardrum[12] / vessels / scar[13] • ligamentous[14] / partial[15] / neural / family[16] **disruption** • **disrupted** muscle / sleep[17] / speech • **disruptive** behavior[18] / child / patient • **tear** injury • wear-and-[19] [eɚ]/ hamstring[20] / meniscal **tear**

Note: Mark the difference in pronunciation and meaning in tear[21] [ɪɚ] and tearing[22] [ɪɚ].

Ruptur, Riss, (Durch)bruch, Hernie; reißen, platzen, rupturieren
Zerreißung, Spaltung[1] Kontinuität[2] (zer)stören, zerreißen, spalten[3] zerreißend, -störend[4] Spontanruptur[5] Sehnenriss, -ruptur[6] Einriss[7] gedeckte Ruptur[8] Milzruptur[9] Blasenruptur[10] Blasensprung[11] Trommelfellruptur[12] Narbenbruch[13] Bänderriss[14] Zerrung[15] zerrüttete Familienverhältnisse[16] gestörter Schlaf[17] störendes/ destruktives Verhalten[18] Abnutzung, Verschleiß[19] Zerrung/ Riss d. Oberschenkelbeuger[20] Träne[21] Tränen(träufeln); tränend[22]

19

dislocation n term   rel **displacement**[1] n, **fracture**[2] n & v term → U106-1ff

displacement of the articular surface of a bone from its joint; in displaced fractures the main bony fragments are widely separated
dislocate[3] v term • **displace**[4] v • **(un)displaced** adj
» Proper positioning of the x-ray tube[5] will improve identification of the radial head dislocation. Swelling may mask the bone displacement.
Use hip / elbow (joint) / carpal / traumatic / fracture-[6]/ (un)complicated / recurrent[7] [ɜːǁʌ] **dislocation** • **dislocation of the** shoulder / jaw [dʒɔː]/ thumb[8] [θʌm] • downward / anterior / medial / lateral **displacement** • degree[9] / direction **of displacement** • double / (non)displaced[10] / old (healed) / (un)stable[11] **fracture** • **fracture** site[12] [aɪ]/ fragments / reduction[13] / nail / healing • **fractured** rib / limb [lɪm]/ jaw[14]

Verrenkung, Luxation
Verschiebung, Fehlstellung, Dislokation[1] (Knochen)fraktur, -bruch; (Knochen) brechen / frakturieren[2] verrenken, luxieren[3] verschieben, dislozieren[4] Röntgenröhre[5] Luxationsfraktur[6] habituelle L.[7] Daumenluxation[8] Grad der Fehlstellung[9] dislozierte Fraktur[10] (in)stabile F.[11] Bruchstelle[12] Reposition d. Fraktur[13] Kieferbruch[14]

20

Unit 6   Accidents & Emergencies

Related Units: 5 Injuries, 7 States of Consciousness, 106 Fractures, 104 Pain, 8 First Aid, 123 Resuscitation, 124 Medical & Surgical Emergencies

accident [æksɪdᵊnt] n   sim **incident**[1] n

misfortune [-tʃən] or unexpected and unplanned event resulting in property damage[2], injury, or loss of life (e.g. a car or plane crash[3], a shipwreck[4], train derailment[5] [eɪ] or capsize[6] [kæpsaɪz] of a boat)
accidental[7] adj • **by accident**[8] phr • **accident-prone**[9] [proʊn] adj
» Burns [ɜː] are the leading cause of accidental death in children. This will help decrease the risk of future accidents in your home. How many people are involved in the accident? An incident involving a hazardous material requires specialty management because a threat [e] to rescue workers exists that may create additional casualties [kæʒ-].
Use to have/cause/get killed in[10] **an accident** • automobile or road or motor vehicle [iː] or traffic[11] **accident** • railway / bicycle [aɪ]/ motorcycle [saɪ] **accident** • skiing / riding[12] / shooting / diving[13] [aɪ] **accident** • industrial[14] [ʌ]/ radiation [eɪ]/ bathtub[15] / aviation [eɪ] **accident** • bad or nasty[16] / major [meɪdʒɚ]/ fatal[17] **accident** • at the scene of the[18] **accident** • **accident** prevention[19] / and emergency (abbr A & E) department[20] (BE) • **accidental** injury / poisoning / overdose / needle stick[21] • **accidental** fire / death[22] / hypothermia [ɜː]/ contamination • biting[23] / hazardous [ɑː] material / submersion[24] [ɜː] **incident** • suicidal [saɪ]/ mass casualty or multicasualty[25] / life-threatening [e] **incident** • **incident** commander[26] • **accident-prone** patients

Unfall, Unglück
Vorfall, Zwischenfall[1] Sachschaden[2] Flugzeugabsturz[3] Schiffbruch[4] Zugentgleisung[5] Kentern[6] Unfall-, akzidentell; zufällig, versehentlich[7] zufällig, durch Zufall; aus Versehen[8] unfallgefährdet[9] tödl. verunglücken[10] Auto-, Verkehrsunfall[11] Reitunfall[12] Tauchunfall[13] Arbeits-, Betriebsunfall[14] Unfall i. d. Badewanne[15] schwerer U.[16] tödl. Unfall[17] am Unfallort[18] Unfallverhütung[19] Unfallambulanz[20] akzidentelle Nadelstichverletzung[21] Unfalltod[22] Bissverletzung[23] Ertrinkungsunfall[24] Massenunfall[25] Einsatzleiter[26]

1

Accidents & Emergencies   BASIC MEDICAL TERMS 23

collide (with) [kəlaɪd] v   rel **crash**[1], **smash**[2], **hit**[3] v,
                                      knock [nɒːk] **down/ over**[4], **run into**[5]/ **over**[6] v

to crash with a violent impact, esp. in accidents of automobiles, planes, or ships traveling at great speed

collision[7] [kəlɪʒ³n] n • **crash**[8] [kræʃ] n • **smash-up**[8] n inf BE • **aircrash**[9] n

» They collided at the intersection[10]. The momentum of the collision caused the victim's head to hit the dashboard[11]. I crashed into the door. The car smashed into a tree. He was run over by a car. I was hit by pieces of the falling cargo[12] [kɑːrɡoʊ]. He was knocked to the ground [aʊ] by the blow [oʊ]. The surfer was run over by a motorboat. The car behind ran into me when I braked [eɪ].

Use automobile [ɒː]/ head-on[13] / rear [rɪɚ] end (automobile)[14] **collision** • high-speed vehicular / motor vehicle-pedestrian [e] **collision** • to be in a/involved in a/come into[15] **collision** • to have a **crash** • train / (air)plane[16] [eɪ] **crash** • **crash** helmet[17] / barrier[18] /-landing[19] • **hit-and-run** accident[20] / driver • car[8] **smash** • **to be knocked** down by a car / over on the zebra [iː] crossing[21]

zusammenstoßen, kollidieren
verunglücken, e. Unfall haben; knallen/ krachen gegen/ in[1] prallen; zerschlagen[2] (zusammen)stoßen, anfahren[3] nieder-, umstoßen, an-, überfahren[4] rennen/ fahren gegen[5] überfahren[6] Zusammenstoß, Kollision[7] Zusammenstoß, Unfall, Karambolage[8] Flugzeugabsturz[9] Kreuzung[10] Armaturenbrett[11] Fracht, Ladung[12] Frontalzusammenstoß[13] Auffahrunfall[14] zusammenstoßen, kollidieren[15] Flugzeugabsturz[16] Sturzhelm[17] Leitplanke[18] Bruchlandung[19] Unfall m. Fahrerflucht[20] auf d. Zebrastreifen ange-/ überfahren werden[21]   2

---

heavy (goods) vehicle [hevi ɡuːds viːɪkl] n, abbr **HGV**
                      syn **truck** [trʌk] n, rel **automobile**[1] [ɒːtəmoʊbiːl], **car**[1] n

large truck (BE lorry) with a separate part for the driver designed to transport heavy loads[2] [oʊ]

vehicular adj • **trucker**[3] n • **trucking** n • **truckage**[4] n • **automobilist**[5] n

» Shear [ʃɪɚ] forces are common when the victim is run over by a heavy goods vehicle. When the child is the pedestrian[6] in a motor vehicle collision, the case-fatality rate increases threefold. The American Automobile Association in the US and the Royal Automobile Club in Britain are organizations which offer advice [aɪ] and repair [eɚ] services to motorists.

Use to drive a **vehicle** • motor[1] / farm[7] / recreational[8] [ieɪʃ] (abbr RV) **vehicle** • emergency[9] [ɜː]/ military **vehicle** • **vehicle** accident / headlights[10] / mile - exhaust[11] [ɒː] • oncoming[12] / incoming / submerged[13] [ɜː] **vehicle** • pickup[14] / trailer[15] [eɪ] / overturned **truck** • **truck** driver[3] /-trailer[15] • **vehicular** accident or collision / access[16] / emissions[17] / traffic • **automobile** ride / driving / occupants[18] / insurance [ʃʊɚ] • passenger[19] / patrol[20] [oʊ] / tank **car** • refrigerator / stock[21]/ sport(s) **car** • five-door / hatchback[22] / broken-down / damaged **car** • street[23] / railroad / freight[24] [freɪt] / cable[25] / **car** seat / keys / phone • **car** use / sickness[26] / park[27] • safe / (rear-)facing[28] [eɪs] / infant / lumbar[28] [ʌ] **car seat** • front / passenger[29] • back **seat** • **seat** belt or restraint[30] [eɪ]

Lastkraftwagen, LKW
Auto, Wagen, (Kraft)fahrzeug[1] Lasten[2] LKW-Fahrer(in)[3] LKW-Transport[4] Fahrzeuglenker(in), Autofahrer(in)[5] Fußgänger(in)[6] landwirtschaftl. Fahrzeug[7] Wohnmobil[8] Einsatzfahrzeug[9] Autoscheinwerfer[10] Auspuff[11] entgegenkommender Wagen[12] versunkenes Fahrzeug[13] Pritschenwagen, Kleintransporter[14] Sattelschlepper[15] Zufahrt[16] Abgase[17] Autoinsassen[18] Personenkraftwagen, PKW[19] Streifenwagen[20] Viehtransporter[21] Auto m. Heckture[22] Straßenbahn[23] Güterwagen[24] Seilbahn[25] Übelkeit b. Autofahren[26] Parkplatz[27] Autositz m. Lendenstütze[28] Beifahrersitz[29] Sicherheitsgurt[30]   3

---

blow [bloʊ] n   rel **strike**[1] [aɪ], **impact**[2], **shock**[3], **bang**[4], **punch**[5] [ʌ], **kick**[6] n

(i) hard hit with the fist[7] or a weapon [e] (ii) sudden frustrating [ʌ] or disappointing event

strike[8] - struck - struck/ stricken v irr • **bang**[9] v • **punch** [pʌntʃ] v • **kick** v

» There is a history of a blow to the nose. A fatal [eɪ] diagnosis in a child is a severe blow to the family. "Hangman's fractures" are typically produced by striking the chin [tʃ] on the steering [ɪɚ] wheel [iː] in a head-on collision. Most handgun projectiles [dʒe] strike tissue at a speed below 274 m/sec. He banged his head against the windshield.

Use to deliver or strike[10] a **blow** • hammer / direct / sharp / forceful[11] / neck[12] **blow** • back / crushing[13] [ʌʃ]/ concussive [ʌ] **blow** • lightning[14] **strike** • panic[15]-/ drought-[16] [draʊt]/ famine- [æ]/ poverty[17]-**stricken** • **to bang** your knee against/ on sth. • **a bang** on the head[18] • **shock** wave[19] / absorber[20] • **punch** ball[21] (BE) • **punching** bag[21] • **punch-up**[22] (espBE)

(i) **Schlag, Stoß**
(ii) **Unglück, Schicksalsschlag**
Schlag, Treffer[1] Auf-, Zusammenprall[1] Auswirkung[2] Stoß, Schlag[3] Schlag; Knall[4] (Faust)schlag[5] Tritt, Stoß[6] Faust[7] schlagen, stoßen, treffen[8] s. anschlagen[9] e. Schlag versetzen[10] kräftiger S.[11] Genickschlag[12] zermalmender S.[13] Blitzschlag[14] in Panik[15] dürregeplagt[16] notleidend[17] Schlag auf d. Kopf[18] Stoßwelle[19] Stoßdämpfer[20] Sandsack[21] Schlägerei[22]   4

fall n clin usu pl   rel **collapse**[1] [kəlæps], **breakdown**[1] [breɪkdaʊn] n
   accidental drop to the ground or free descent [dɪsent] from a higher position
   falling adj & n • **fall**[2] - fell - fallen v irr • **collapse**[3] v • **break down**[3] v
   » Most calcaneal [eɪ] fractures[4] are the result of a fall, with force borne primarily by the patient's heels [iː]. Falls constitute 40% of home accidents, more than those from burns, scalds[5] [ɔː], cuts and scratches, or strangulation. The wrist[6] [r] is usually injured by falling on an outstretched hand. Your wife might suffer a nervous [ɜː] breakdown. In severe burns, circulatory collapse may result.
   Use to have or take[2] **a fall** • accidental / minor [aɪ] **fall** • to stumble [ʌ] and[7] **fall** • **to fall** over / forward / off the roof / down the stairs[8] • **to fall** down on your knees [niːz]/ from a height[9] [haɪt] • **to fall** out of a window / into the water / flat on the face[10] • **to fall** head first[11] / to one's death • **falling** sickness[12] / debris [iː] • **to collapse** from the heat[13] • circulatory[14] [sɜːrk-]/ lung[15] [ʌ]/ structural[16] [ʌ] **collapse** • nervous[17] / emotional [oʊʃ] **breakdown**

Sturz
Zusammenbruch, Kollaps[1] fallen, stürzen[2] zusammenbrechen, kollabieren[3] Fersenbeinfrakturen[4] Verbrühungen[5] Handgelenk[6] stolpern u. stürzen[7] d. Treppe hinunterstürzen[8] aus großer Höhe stürzen[9] auf d. Nase fallen[10] kopfüber stürzen[11] Fallsucht, Epilepsie[12] einen Hitzekollaps haben[13] kardiovaskulärer Kollaps, Kreislaufkollaps[14] Lungenkollaps[15] Gebäudeeinsturz[16] Nervenzusammenbruch[17]
5

compression n   rel **contusion**[1] [-t(j)uːʒən], **crush** [krʌʃ] **injury**[1], **constriction**[2] n
   squeezing [iː] and pressing or otherwise applying [aɪ] pressure to body structures, organs or tissues
   compress[3] v & n • **crushing**[4] adj & n • **constrict**[5] v • **constrictive**[6] adj
   » Compression injuries (e.g. falling from a height and landing on a foot, crushing the distal tibial physis [ɪ]) may substantially affect bone growth. The vertebral bodies are often sites of compression fractures. The crush injuries are due to structural collapse and falling debris. Cerebral contusion can be demonstrated by CT scan as small areas of hemorrhage [e] in the cerebral parenchyma.
   Use nerve / chest[7] [tʃ]/ (nerve) root[8] [uː]/ (spinal) [aɪ] cord [kɔːrd] **compression** • brain[9] / tracheal [k] **compression** • **compression** injury / fracture[10] • **compression** neuropathy / paralysis[11] / atelectasis[12] • **to crush** tablets[13] / sb. against an object / sth. between two objects • **crushed** bone / tissue [tʃ‖BE sjuː]/ ice[14] • **crush** fracture[10] / injury [ɪndʒɚi]/ wound[15] [uː] • **crushing** blow / force • cerebral [s] or brain[16] / lung or pulmonary [ʊ‖ʌ] **contusion** • myocardial / severe **contusion** • vessel / pupillary [pjuː-]/ bronchial [k] **constriction** • **contused** wound[15]

Kompression, Quetschung, Druck
Quetschung, Prellung, Kontusion[1] Einengung, -schnürung, Konstriktion[2] zusammendrücken, komprimieren; Umschlag, Kompresse[3] zerschmetternd, vernichtend; Quetschung[4] zusammenziehen, ein-, verengen[5] einengend[6] Brustkorb-, Thoraxkompression, Compressio thoracis[7] Wurzelkompression[8] Compressio cerebri[9] Kompressionsfraktur, Stauchungsbruch[10] Druck-, Kompressionslähmung[11] Kompressionsatelektase[12] Tabletten zerdrücken/-stoßen[13] zerstoßenes Eis[14] Quetschwunde[15] Contusio cerebri[16]
6

stab [stæb] v   sim **penetrate**[1], **pierce**[2] [pɪɚs] v, **sting**[3], **puncture**[4] [pʌŋktʃɚ] v & n, rel **cut**[5] v & n
   to injure a person by a thrusting [ʌ] blow with a sharp pointed object, e.g. a knife [naɪf]
   stabbing[6] adj & n • **penetration**[7] n • **penetrating**[8] adj • **stinging**[9] adj
   » Cat bites cause deep puncture wounds with little crush injury. The tympanic membrane may be punctured and the tympanum penetrated by objects placed in the ear canal. Air leaked [iː] from the lung which was punctured by a fractured rib. These insects sometimes bite before stinging. Pneumothorax [n(j)uː-] may result from blunt [ʌ] or penetrating chest trauma [ɔː]. There is usually a palpable feeling of resistance when the needle [iː] pierces the parietal [aɪ] pericardium.
   Use **to stab sb.** in the back / to death[10] • **stab** wound[11] [uː]/ incision[12] [sɪʒ] • **stabbing** pain[13] • **puncture** wound[11] / site[14] [aɪ] • **penetrating** injury[15] / object / foreign [fɒːrən] body[16] • **penetrating** (chest/ back) trauma[15] / head wound • **to penetrate** deeply (into tissue) / the skin / the gut [ʌ] wall[17] • **to pierce** the skin[18] / subcutaneous [eɪ] tissue / liver • **piercing** pain[13] / ear[19] **piercing** • bee [iː]/ wasp[20] [ɒː]/ scorpion **sting** • **to cut oneself** with a knife / on the glass • **cut** surface[21]

(ein-, er)stechen
ein-, durchdringen[1] durchstechen, -bohren[2] stechen; brennen; Stechen, Stich, Brennen[3] durch-, einstechen, punktieren; Einstich, Punktion[4] schneiden; Schnitt[5] stechend; Messerstecherei[6] Eindringen; Penetration[7] durchdringend, penetrierend[8] stechend, brennend[9] jem. erstechen[10] Stichwunde[11] Stichinzision[12] stechender Schmerz[13] Punktionsstelle[14] penetrierende Verletzung[15] penetrierender Fremdkörper[16] d. Darmwand durchdringen[17] d. Haut durchstoßen/ -bohren[18] Stechen v. Ohrlöchern[19] Wespenstich[20] Schnittfläche[21]
7

Accidents & Emergencies   BASIC MEDICAL TERMS **25**

gunshot [ʌ] **wound** [uː] *or* **injury** *n, abbr* **GSW**

rel **firearms**[1] *n pl,* **weapon**[2] [wepən] *n*

lesion [iː] caused by a missile[3] [mɪsᵊl] or bullet[4] [bʊlət] fired from a weapon

handgun[5] *n* • shoot[6] [uː] - shot - shot *v irr* • shot[7] [ʃɒːt] *n* • (un)armed[8] *adj*

» *Patients with gunshot wounds to the torso*[9] *often present in hemorrhagic* [ædʒ] *shock with multiple organ injury. Deaths from firearms will soon surpass deaths from motor vehicle accidents in numbers. Mangling injuries*[10] *include gunshot and blast wounds, severe open crush wounds, and bites by large animals. The type of weapon must be ascertained*[11] [eɪ]*.*

Use small-caliber / penetrating[12] / civilian / cardiac[13] **gunshot wound** • **gunshot wound** complications / to the head[14] / **firearm** deaths / safety / violence [aɪə] / (-related) injuries[15] • to check sb. for[16] / low-velocity **weapons** • chemical / biological / nuclear [uː] **weapons** • to hand in *or* relinquish[17] **the weapon** • to have/fire[6] **a gun** • shot[18] / pump / air[19] / small-caliber / paint[20] **gun** • **gun**fire / control legislation[21] / ownership[22] • **shotgun** blast • **handgun** wound / projectile

explosion [ɪksploʊʒᵊn] *n* *syn* **blast** [æ] *n, rel* **burst**[1] [ɜː] *n & v,* **detonation**[2] *n*

violent release of energy caused by a chemical or nuclear reaction

explode[3] *v* • explosive[4] *adj & n* • blast[5] *v* • detonate[6] [detᵊneɪt] *v*

» *Large explosions cause multiple* [ʌ] *foreign body impregnations*[7] *and lacerations* [s]*. Blast injuries in civilians*[8] *occur* [ɜː] *as a result of fireworks, household explosions, or industrial* [ʌ] *accidents. It only needs a spark*[9] *for the explosives in here to blow up*[3]*. Luckily the TNT*[10] *failed to detonate.*

Use gas / atomic (bomb)[11] / reactor **explosion** • enclosed space / deafening[12] [e] **explosion** • **explosive** device[13] [dɪvaɪs] / expert / charge [tʃ] / plastic / home-made[14] **explosive** • **blast** effect / trauma *or* injury[15] / wound • **to detonate a** bomb / mine [maɪn] • accidental / (underground) nuclear[11] **detonation** • **detonation** size

fire [faɪɚ] *n* *sim* **blaze**[1] [bleɪz] *n & v*

rel **flame**[2] [eɪ]**, smoke**[3]**, arson**[4] [ɑːrsᵊn] *n,* **burn**[5] [ɜː] *n & v* → U5-11

(i) combustion[6] [ʌ] of inflammable[7] [æ] materials producing heat, light, and (often) smoke
(ii) burning object set afire[8] by accident (destructive fire) or on purpose (e.g. for cooking or warmth)

firefighter[9] *n* • flammable[7] *adj* • ablaze[10] *adj* • arsonist[11] *n* • **burning** *adj*

» *Where's the fire? Smoke inhalation* [eɪʃ] *kills more fire victims*[12] *than does thermal* [ɜː] *injury. The fire was due to a utility failure*[13]*. Firefighters took two hours to control the blaze. Most fire deaths are due to burns and asphyxia* [æsfɪksɪə] *from carbon monoxide. Smoke from a wood fire is extremely irritating because it contains aldehyde* [-aɪd] *gases. Flame burns from ignited*[14] [aɪ] *clothing are often the most serious part of the injury.*

Use accidental / major[15] [eɪdʒ]/ minor [aɪ]/ structural[16] [ʌ] **fire** • forest[17] / bush [ʊ]/ camp / open **fire** • to light a/catch[18]/be on[19]/be trapped in a **fire** • to set a/fight a/put out a **fire** • **fire** trauma / drill[20] / escape[21] / exit • **fire** alarm[22] /wall / extinguisher[23] • **fire**man[9] / department *or (BE)* brigade[24] [eɪ]/ station[25] • **fire** crew[26] [kruː]/ engine /-plug[27] [ʌ]/ proof / damage • **fire**ball[28] /works /bomb[29] / storm / disaster[30] [æ] • to be in[19]/extinguish **flames** / a cloud *or* pall of[31] / kerosene **smoke** • **smoke** inhalation / detector[32] / helmet • **blazing** fire • **flammable** liquids [lɪkwɪds]/ materials

Schussverletzung, -wunde
Schusswaffen[1] Waffe[2] Geschoß[3] Kugel[4] Handfeuerwaffe[5] schießen[6] Schuss; Schütze[7] (un)bewaffnet[8] Rumpf[9] Verstümmelungen[10] festgestellt[11] Durchschuss[12] Herzschuss[13] Kopfschuss[14] Schussverletzungen[15] jem. auf Waffen untersuchen[16] d. Waffe aushändigen/abgeben[17] Schrotflinte[18] Luftgewehr[19] Spritzpistole[20] Waffengesetze[21] Waffenbesitz[22]

8

Explosion
Explosion, Ausbruch; platzen, (zer)bersten; sprengen[1] Explosion, Knall, Detonation[2] explodieren, in d. Luft fliegen[3] explosiv, Spreng-; Explosiv-; Sprengstoff[4] sprengen[5] explodieren (lassen), detonieren[6] Einschläge[7] Zivilbevölkerung[8] Funken[9] Trinitrotoluol[10] Atomexplosion[11] ohrenbetäubende E.[12] Sprengkörper, Bombe[13] selbstgebastelter S.[14] Knall-, Explosionstrauma[15]

9

(i) Feuer (ii) Brand(stelle)
Feuer(sbrunst), Brand; brennen, lodern[1] Flamme[2] Rauch, Qualm[3] Brandstiftung[4] Verbrennung; (ver)brennen[5] Verbrennung[6] leicht brennbar, feuergefährlich[7] angezündet, in Brand gesteckt[8] Feuerwehrmann[9] in Flammen[10] Brandstifter(in), Pyromane/-in[11] Brandopfer, -verletzte[12] defekte Anlage[13] brennend[14] Großbrand[15] Gebäudebrand[16] Waldbrand[17] Feuer fangen[18] brennen[19] Brandschutz-, Feuerwehrübung[20] Feuerleiter[21] Feueralarm, -melder[22] Feuerlöscher[23] Feuerwehr[24] Feuerwache[25] Löschmannschaft[26] Hydrant[27] Feuerball, Kugelblitz[28] Brandbombe[29] Brandkatastrophe[30] Rauchwolke[31] Rauchmelder[32]

10

BASIC MEDICAL TERMS — Accidents & Emergencies

damaged [dæmɪdʒd] adj   rel **harmful**[1], **detrimental**[1], **pernicious**[2] [ɪʃ] adj
injured, harmed, broken, or blemished[3] → U91-1
damage[4] n & v • **harm**[4] n & v • **harmless**[5] adj • **detriment** n • **damages**[6] n pl

» Such an accident may damage both the knee joint and the hip. Damage from electrical injury[7] may be extensive even though the outward signs of injury are minimal. Long-term cortico-steroid therapy often does more harm than good. Tachycardia [k] can be particularly detrimental, because it shortens diastolic filling and increases myocardial oxygen demand.

Use sun-/ brain / radiation-[8] [eɪ]/ severely **damaged** • **damaged** equipment[9] / nerve[10] / heart valves [æ] • **harmful** substance [ʌ] or agent[11] [eɪdʒ]/ stimuli [aɪ]/ exposure [oʊ] • **harmful** habits / inhalation / (health) effects[12] • **harmless** snake / scorpion sting • **detrimental** effects / to wound healing [iː]/ to health[13] • **pernicious** anemia [iː]/ vomiting / effect[14] • **to damage** target organs • to cause or inflict[15]/repair [eə] **damage** • tissue[16] / cellular / skin / endothelial [iː] **damage** • skeletal / joint / (neuro)vascular / (irreversible) [ɜː] brain[17] **damage** • eye / liver / spinal [aɪ] cord **damage** • massive / fetal [iː]/ hypoxic-ischemic [kiː]/ radiation[18] **damage** • permanent[19] [ɜː]/ functional / multiple / sublethal [iː] **damage** • **damage** to nerve roots[20] / to the spinal cord / award[21] [ɔː] • to cause or do (no) /suffer[22] [ʌ] /avoid **harm** • **harm** to sth./sb. / to others • physical [ɪ] or bodily[23] / personal / emotional / self-inflicted[24] **harm** • to award / to pay[25] / money / general **damages**

---

casualty [kæʒʊəlti] n   rel **victim**[1], **injured party**[2] n
person injured or killed in an accident or missing or captured in military engagement [eɪdʒ]
multicasualty[3] [ʌ] adj • **victimize**[4] [vɪktɪmaɪz] v

» Most casualties were related to trauma from structural collapse, flying debris, or being knocked to the ground. The victim was pinned[5] under a car for a long time. Victims are collected and treated in field hospitals that can stabilize them pending distant evacuation[6]. The simple act of moving a victim from one position to another, if done improperly, may convert [ɜː] a simple injury into a major one.

Use to report/reduce or mitigate[7] [ɪ] **casualties** • **casualty** collection point / department[8] • **multicasualty** event/ incident • to fall[9] **victim** (to sth.) • trauma[10] / burn[11] / flood [ʌ]/ accident[12] **victim** • hurricane [ʌ]/ lightning [aɪ]/ rape[13] [eɪ]/ child **victim** • (un)conscious [ʃ]/ alleged[14] [edʒ]/ moribund / dazed[15] [eɪ] **victim** • **victim of** (child) abuse / a disaster[16] • **victim of** a rabid [eɪ‖æ] wolf / a crime [aɪ]

---

eyewitness n   syn **percipient** [sɪ] **witness** n leg, rel **bystander**[1], **onlooker**[1] n
a person at the scene [siːn] of an accident or crime [aɪ] who can describe what happened
witness[2] [wɪtnəs] n & v • **(un)witnessed**[3] adj

» The amount of ground movement felt by eyewitnesses of the quake[4] [kweɪk] was determined. Testimonial [oʊ] evidence[5] is presented by percipient witnesses, who relate their first-hand experience of relevant subjects within lay [eɪ] comprehension[6]. Obtain as much information as possible about the details of the injury from any witnesses. The site should be secure from bystanders and clear of loose debris[7].

Use **eyewitness** account[8] [aʊ] • to be a/bear [beə] **witness** to sth.[9] • key / child **witness** • prosecuting[10] / expert (medical)[11] **witness** • **witness** stand or box[12] (BE) / fee[13] [fiː] • to take the **witness** stand[14] • innocent / lay / ill-informed **bystanders** • **bystander** intervention /-initiated[15] CPR • **witnessed** trauma / apneas • **unwitnessed** death / cardiac arrest[16]

---

geschädigt, lädiert, verletzt
nachteilig, schädlich[1] schädlich, bösartig, perniziös[2] entstellt, verunstaltet[3] Schaden, (Be)schädigung, Verletzung; schaden, (be)schädigen[4] unschädlich, harmlos[5] Schadensersatz[6] Elektrotrauma[7] strahlengeschädigt[8] beschädigte/ schadhafte Geräte[9] geschädigter Nerv[10] Schadstoff[11] gesundheitsschädl. Auswirkungen[12] gesundheitsschädlich[13] schädl. Wirkung[14] Schaden zufügen[15] Gewebeschädigung[16] irreversibler Hirnschaden[17] Strahlenschaden[18] Dauerschaden, bleibender Sch.[19] Nervenwurzelschädigung[20] Zuerkennung v. Schadenersatzansprüchen[21] Schaden erleiden[22] Körperverletzung[23] selbstzugefügte Verletzung[24] Schadenersatz leisten[25]   11

Unfallopfer, Verletzte(r), Tote(r)
Opfer[1] Verletzte(r), Geschädigte(r)[2] m. vielen Verletzten/ Opfern[3] ungerecht behandeln, schikanieren[4] eingeklemmt[5] bis z. Abtransport[6] d. Verluste/ Opferzahl verringern[7] Unfallstation[8] zum Opfer fallen[9] Verletzte(r), Traumapatient(in)[10] Verbrennungspatient(in), -opfer[11] Unfallopfer[12] Vergewaltigungsopfer[13] angebliches Opfer[14] benommenes Opfer[15] Katastrophenopfer[16]   12

Augenzeuge/-in
Anwesende(r), Zuschauer/-in[1] Zeuge/-in, Zeugnis; bezeugen, bestätigen; (mit)erleben[2] (un)beobachtet[3] (Erd)beben[4] Zeugenaussage[5] Laienverständnis[6] lose Trümmer[7] Augenzeugenbericht[8] etw. bezeugen, Zeugnis ablegen über[9] Belastungszeuge/-in[10] med. Sachverständige(r)[11] Zeugenstand[12] Zeugengeld[13] i. d. Zeugenstand treten[14] von e. Zuschauer(in) eingeleitete Reanimation[15] unbemerkter Herzstillstand[16]   13

Accidents & Emergencies

BASIC MEDICAL TERMS 27

accidental electric shock n   syn **electrical accident** n,
   rel **electrocution**[1][-kjuːʃən], **lightning (strike)**[2] [laɪtnɪŋ straɪk] n clin
sudden violent impact caused by the passage of an electric current[3] [ɜː|‖BE ʌ] through the body
electricity n • **electrocute** v • **electroshock**[4] n • **countershock**[5] [aʊ] n

» Electric shock may produce loss of consciousness [ʃ]. The death rate from high-voltage electrocution[6] is high, but resuscitation[7] [ʌs] should always be initiated [ɪʃ] as soon as the victim is safely removed from the energy source. Suspect lightning injury in a person found dazed[8], unconscious, or injured in the vicinity [sɪ] of a thunderstorm[9] [ʌ]. In flashover, the lightning travels on the outside of the body.

Use low-voltage[10] / high-voltage[6] **electric shock injury** • **electric(al)** injury[11] / burn / field • **electric(al)** energy / charge[12] [tʃɑːrdʒ]/ power • **electric(al)** force / cord[13] [k]/ blanket[14] • **electrical** current[3] / cardioversion[15] [ɜː]/ stimulation / cautery[16] [ɒː] • to be struck by[17] [ʌ]/ death by / streak[18] [iː] **lightning** • a flash of[19] / thunder and **lightning** • **lightning** injury[20] / victim / current / rod[21] • **electroshock** therapy[22] • to deliver a / administer **countershock** • electrical / synchronized [ɪ] direct current[23] (abbr DC) **countershock**

Elektro-, Stromunfall, elektr. Schlag, Stromstoß
Tod durch elektr. Strom; Hinrichtung durch d. elektr. Stuhl[1] Blitzschlag[2] elektr. Strom[3] Elektroschock, elektr. S.[4] Defibrillation[5] Starkstromverletzung[6] Reanimation[7] benommen[8] Gewitter[9] Niederspannungsverletzung[10] Elektrotrauma[11] elektr. Ladung[12] Stromkabel[13] Heizdecke[14] elektr. Kardioversion[15] Elektrokoagulation, -kauterisation[16] vom Blitz getroffen werden[17] Linienblitz[18] Blitz[19] Verletzung durch Blitzschlag[20] Blitzableiter[21] Elektroschock-, Elektrokonvulsionstherapie[22] synchrone Defibrillation[23]   14

---

hypovolemic [iː] **shock** n term   rel **hemorrhage**[1] [e], **dehydration**[2] n term
shock caused by a reduction in circulating blood volume from massive blood loss or fluid depletion[3] [iːʃ]
hypovolemia[4] [haɪpoʊ-] n term • **hemorrhagic** [ædʒ] adj → U5-18 • **dehydrated** [aɪ] adj → U78-22

» Hypovolemic shock may be the sole presenting sign of blunt [ʌ] trauma to organs such as the spleen [iː], liver, or kidneys. Shock in the traumatized patient is usually due to hypovolemia from hemorrhage. Heat exhaustion[5] [ɒː] consists of fatigue[6] [fətiːg], tachycardia, nausea[7] [ɔː], and an urge to defecate [e] caused by dehydration and hypovolemia from heat stress.

Use (non)hemorrhagic / early / suspected[8] **hypovolemic shock** • apparent[9] [eɚ]/ severe **hypovolemic shock** • rapidly progressive / mild **hypovolemic shock** • cellular / generalized / hypertonic[10] / hypernatremic[11] [iː] **dehydration** • rapid / chronic / profound [aʊ] or severe[12] **dehydration** • acute / intravascular **hypovolemia** • arterial [ɪɚ]/ relative **hypovolemia** • true or effective[13] / prolonged **hypovolemia** • mild / diuretic-induced[14] [daɪjəretɪk] **hypovolemia**

hypovolämischer Schock, Volumenmangelschock
Blutung[1] Dehydratation[2] Flüssigkeitsverlust[3] Hypovolämie[4] Hitzeerschöpfung[5] Müdigkeit[6] Übelkeit[7] Verdacht auf hypovolämischen Schock[8] manifester hypovolämischer Schock[9] hypertone Dehydratation[10] hypernatriämische D.[11] schwere D.[12] effektive Hypovolämie[13] diuretikabedingte Hypovolämie[14]   15

---

near-drowning [draʊnɪŋ] n   rel **drowning**[1], **submersion**[2] [-ɜːrʒən] n
accident in which the victim survives [aɪ] asphyxiation[3] due to prolonged submersion in water
drown[4] vi & vt clin • **(near-)drowned**[5] adj • **submerge**[6] v • **submerged**[7] adj

» Submersion incidents[8] are classified according to outcome: drownings are those with death occurring within 24 hours, while survival for over 24 hours constitutes near-drowning. The pH in near-drowned victims is commonly significantly acidotic. Drowning victims[9] should be moved to land or to some other hard surface before chest compression is attempted.

Use child(hood) or pediatric / adult **drowning** • freshwater[10] / sea water[11] / dry[12] **drowning** • **drowning** accidents[8] / episode / medium [iː]/ deaths[9] • prolonged / duration of **submersion** • ice-water / depth of[13] **submersion** • **submersion** accidents[8] / hypoxemia [iː]/ deaths[9]

Beinahe-Ertrinken
Ertrinken[1] Unter-, Eintauchen[2] Erstickungszustand[3] ertrinken; ertränken[4] ertrunken[5] untertauchen[6] unter Wasser[7] Bade-, Ertrinkungsunfälle[8] Ertrunkene[9] Ertrinken im Süßwasser[10] Ertrinken im Salzwasser[11] trockenes Ertrinken[12] Tauchtiefe[13]   16

28 BASIC MEDICAL TERMS — Accidents & Emergencies

decompression sickness n term, abbr **DCS**
  syn **the bends** n pl clin, **Caisson** [keɪsən] **disease** n term
  rel **barotrauma**[1] [æ] n, **high-altitude** [æ] or **mountain sickness**[2] n term
  life-threatening condition occurring in divers[3] or aviators[4] [eɪ] moving too quickly from higher to lower atmospheric pressures which causes nitrogen [aɪ] to accumulate in the tissue and impair oxygenation
  decompress v term • **(re)compression**[5] n
» Sensory hearing loss, which develops during the ascent [əsent] phase[6] of a saturation [eɪ] dive[7] [daɪv], may be the first symptom of decompression sickness. The severity [e] of acute mountain sickness correlates with altitude and rate of ascent. Underwater diving represents even a greater barometric stress to the ear than flying.
Use pulmonary or respiratory[8] / inner-ear / cerebral [s] **decompression sickness** • musculoskeletal / serious **decompression sickness** • gradual / surgical[9] [ɜː]/ cerebral[10] / cardiac[11] **decompression** • **decompression** symptoms / chamber[12] [tʃeɪ] • air[13] / motion[14] [oʊʃ] **sickness** • otic or inner ear[15] / pulmonary **barotrauma** • ventilator / extreme / sinus[16] [aɪ] **barotrauma** • (sub)acute[17] / chronic / progressive **mountain sickness** • high-altitude pulmonary edema[18] [iː]/ encephalopathy

Dekompressions-, Druckfall-, Caisson-Krankheit
Barotrauma, Druckverletzung[1] Höhen-, Bergkrankheit[2] Taucher(in)[3] Flugzeugpilot(in)[4] (Re)kompression[5] Aufstieg, -tauchen[6] Gerätetauchen[7] Lungenbarotrauma[8] chir. Dekompression/ Entlastung[9] Hirndekompression[10] Herzdekompression[11] Dekompressionskammer[12] Fliegerkrankheit[13] Reise-, Bewegungskrankheit, Kinetose[14] Aero-, Barootitis[15] Aero-, Barosinusitis[16] akute Höhenkrankheit[17] Höhenlungenödem[18]

17

emergency [ɪmɜːrdʒənˈsi] n   rel **urgency**[1] [ɜː] n, **exigency**[2] [eksɪdʒənˈsi] n
  sudden unforeseen crisis [aɪ] that threatens [e] the lives or welfare of those involved and requires immediate action
  urgent[3] [ɜːrdʒənt] adj • **on an emergency basis**[4] phr • **semi-emergency** adj
» Obtain emergency neurosurgical consultation [ʌ]. Percutaneous [eɪ] catheter drainage [eɪ] may convert [ɜː] a potential emergency operation[5] to an elective[6] one. Assign [aɪ] victims for transport in order of relative priority based on the urgency of their condition.
Use to be admitted as an[7] **emergency** • **Emergency** Medical Service[8] (abbr EMS) • medical[9] / cardiac / cardiovascular[10] / acute abdominal **emergency** • eye / diabetic / acid-base / surgical **emergency** • dire [daɪə] or grave[11] [eɪ]/ life-threatening [e] **emergency** • **emergency** room[12] (abbr E.R.) or department or ward[12] [ɔː]/ care[13] / call[14] • **emergency** intubation / endoscopy[15] • **emergency** operation or surgery[5] / measures[16] [eʒ] • **emergency** hospitalization / treatment or management[13] / medicine[17] • in an **emergency** setting[18] • clinical / urinary / fecal[19] [iː] **urgency** • **urgency** of treatment • clinical **exigency**

Notfall
Dringlichkeit[1] Erfordernis, Notlage, Dringlichkeit[2] dringend[3] notfallmäßig[4] Notoperation, -eingriff[5] Elektivoperation[6] als Notfallpatient(in) eingeliefert werden[7] Notfalldienst[8] internistischer Notfall[9] kardiovaskulärer N.[10] ernster/ schwer(wiegend)er N.[11] Notaufnahme[12] Notfallbehandlung[13] Notruf[14] Notfallendoskopie[15] Notmaßnahmen[16] Notfallmedizin[17] im Notfall[18] Stuhldrang[19]

18

Stop messing around, Mr. Wriggly!
The faster you let me fill in all these forms,
the sooner we'll be able to fix you up.

SOS call or **message** [mesɪdʒ] n   rel **Mayday! Mayday!**[1] [meɪdeɪ] n
  internationally recognized distress call[2] (short for Save Our Souls) sent out via radio[3] or Morse code (3 short, 3 long followed by 3 short signals) by ships or aircraft in urgent need of help
» You should send out an SOS call for extra blood supplies[4] [aɪ]. Mayday! Mayday! is the radio signal used by ships in distress. Go get the lifejackets[5] while I make the Mayday call.
Use to send out[6]/make/transmit **an SOS call** • **Mayday** call / message

Hilferuf, SOS-Signal
Mayday (int. Funknotruf abgeleitet von franz. m'aidez)[1] Notruf[2] über Funk[3] Blutkonserven[4] Schwimmwesten[5] einen SOS-Ruf senden[6]

19

Accidents & Emergencies BASIC MEDICAL TERMS

(natural) disaster [æ] n   syn catastrophe [kətæstrəfi] n, rel devastation[1] n

sudden extremely destructive events like (earth)quakes, floods[2] [ʌ], landslides[3], tidal [aɪ] waves[4], etc. which cause a high toll of casualties[5] and damage in the social and physical environment of a region

disastrous[6] adj • **catastrophic**[6] adj • **devastating**[6] [e] adj • **devastate**[7] v

» How many rescue workers were deployed[8] [ɔɪ] to the disaster area? The earthquake has devastated the town. The city, 15 miles from the epicenter, was a scene of devastation.

Use to avert [ɜː] a[9] **disaster** • **disaster** area[10] / site [saɪt]/ victim / assistance[11] • **disaster** drills or exercises[12] / medicine[13] • **disaster** plan / training[12] / severity [e] scale • **disaster** cache [kæʃ] medical supplies[14] [aɪ] • **disastrous** impact / sequelae[15] [sɪkwiːliː] • to be disastrous for sb. • **devastating** news / effect / injury • a trail [eɪ] of[16] / widespread [aɪ] **devastation** • **catastrophic** results / drought[17] [draʊt]/ birth defects • civil [sɪ]/ family / clinical **catastrophe** • ecological or environmental[18] / nuclear **catastrophe**

(Natur)katastrophe

Verwüstung[1] Überschwemmungen, Flutkatastrophe[2] Erdrutsche[3] Flutwellen[4] große Opferzahl[5] verheerend, katastrophal[6] verwüsten, -nichten[7] eingesetzt[8] e. Katastrophe abwenden[9] Katastrophengebiet[10] Katastrophenhilfe[11] Katastrophenübung[12] Katastrophenmedizin[13] bereitgehaltene medizinische Hilfsgüter[14] verheerende Folgen[15] Spuren d. Verwüstung[16] katastrophale Dürre[17] Umweltkatastrophe[18]

20

panic [pænɪk] n & v clin & term   rel **terror**[1], **dread**[2] [dred], **fright**[3] [fraɪt] n

overwhelming feeling of fear[2] and apprehension[4] resulting in paralyzed apathy or hysteric behavior

panicky[5] adj • **dread**[6] v • **dreadful**[7] adj • **frightening**[8] [fraɪtᵊnɪŋ] adj → U77-5

» Don't panic, it's O.K. As the patient comes closer to the phobic [foʊbɪk] stimulus, the anxiety [aɪ] mounts [aʊ] to an intensity reaching panic. Panic spread through the crowd as the shooting continued. Sleep terror is an abrupt [ʌ], terrifying arousal [aʊ] from sleep. The anxiety may be related to a dread of leaving home (i.e. separation anxiety). Primary [aɪ] shock is usually caused by psychic [saɪkɪk] or nervous stimuli such as fright or sudden pain.

Use to get into[9] **panic** • mass[10] **panic** • **panic** reaction[11] /-stricken / situation • **panic** state / attack[12] / disorder • **panicky** feeling / person / decision[13] [sɪ] • **to panic** over a problem • to live in/be filled with **dread** • a dread of leaving home / dark alleys[14] [ɪ] • to live in/flee [iː] in/feel/have a **terror** • **terror** of spiders / drowning[15] • night or sleep[16] **terror** • stage[17] / severe / feeling of **fright** • **frightening** experience[18]

Panik; in Panik geraten

panische Angst, Schrecken[1] Angst, Furcht[2] Schreck(en)[3] Befürchtung, Sorge[4] überängstlich[5] s. fürchten, Angst haben[6] schrecklich, furchtbar[7] erschreckend, furchterregend[8] in Panik geraten[9] Massenpanik[10] Angst-, Kurzschlussreaktion[11] Panikattacke, -anfall[12] panikartiger Entschluss[13] Angst vor dunklen Gängen[14] panische Angst vor d. Ertrinken[15] Pavor nocturnus, Nachtangst[16] Lampenfieber[17] schreckliches Erlebnis[18]

21

trauma [ɒː] or **accident prevention** n
rel **precaution**[1] [ɒːʃ], **prophylaxis**[2] n → U9-18; U120-6

programs designed to reduce the incidence of accidents, e.g. by fencing off[3] unsafe areas, warning signs, health teaching and instruction about danger zones and risk activities, safety rules[4], etc.

preventive[5] adj • **prevent**[6] v • **precautionary** adj • **caution**[7] [kɒːʃᵊn] v & n • **traumatic** adj

» Trauma prevention is still not receiving enough attention, although laws requiring the use of seatbelts and motorcycle helmets have demonstrated a clear-cut survival benefit[8]. Spinal [aɪ] precautions must be maintained [eɪ] where indicated. For contaminated wounds [uː] antibiotic prophylaxis is recommended.

Use injury / workplace exposure[9] [oʊʒ]/ poison **prevention** • sudden death / suicide[10] / disease **prevention** • cancer[11] [s]/ HIV / pressure sore[12] **prevention** • **prevention** measures[13] [e]/ program[14] / and control • **preventive** medicine[15] / (health) care[16] • **preventive** therapy or treatment[16] / measures[13] • **trauma** center / patient • **traumatic** asphyxia [ɪ]/ event[17] • primary[18] / secondary / tertiary [tɜːrʃəri] **prevention** • to take[19] **precautions** • biohazard[20] / sanitary / isolation **precautions** • barrier[21] / blood / universal **precautions**

Unfallverhütung

Sicherheitsvorkehrung, Vorsichtsmaßnahme[1] Vorbeugung, Prophylaxe[2] Absperren[3] Sicherheitsbestimmungen[4] vorbeugend, Präventiv-[5] verhindern; vorbeugen[6] warnen; Vorsicht, Warnung[7] klarer Überlebensvorteil[8] Arbeitsplatzschutzmaßnahmen[9] Suizidprophylaxe[10] Krebsvorsorge[11] Dekubitusprophylaxe[12] Präventivmaßnahmen, vorbeugende M.[13] Präventionsprogramm[14] Vorsorge-, Präventivmedizin[15] Prophylaxe[16] Trauma, traumat. Ereignis[17] primäre Prophylaxe[18] (Sicherheits)vorkehrungen treffen[19] Schadstoffschutzmaßnahmen[20] Verwendung v. Schutzvorrichtungen[21]

22

Unit 7 States of Consciousness

Related Units: 5 Injuries, 8 First Aid, 10 Alcohol, 107 Physical Examination, 113 Neurologic Findings, 123 Resuscitation, 126 Surgical Treatment, 134 Perioperative Management, 135 Anesthesiology

conscious [kɒːnʃəs] *adj*, **-ly** *adv*   opposite **unconscious**[1] *adj*

(i) associated with thought, will, or perception[2] (ii) related to consciousness (iii) awareness undulled[3] [ʌ] by sleep, faintness, or stupor

(un/ sub)consciousness[4] *n* • **semiconsciousness**[5] *n* • **self/ subconscious** *adj*

» Some patients may consciously or unconsciously engage in forceful air swallowing. She became conscious[6] after the anesthesia wore off[7]. The clinical definition of consciousness ranges from alert wakefulness[8], to mild lethargy, stupor, and deep coma.

Use loss of / to lose / to regain or return to[9] / clouding of[11] [aʊ] **consciousness** • alteration of[10] [ɔː] / altered state of[10] / to assess the level of **consciousness** • full / impaired[11] [eə] / compromised[11] / dull[11] / waxing-waning[12] [eɪ] **consciousness** • to lapse or fall into[13]/verify **unconsciousness** • to become[13]/be **unconscious** • **unconscious** patient / guilt[14] [ɡɪlt]/ motivation [eɪ] • **(un)conscious** process / control • weight [weɪt]/ health[15] [helθ] **conscious**

> Note: Do not confuse *self-conscious (inhibited)*[16] and *self-confident (=self-reliant)*[17] [aɪ] as well as *conscious* and *conscience*[18] [kɒːnʃəns] and *conscientious*[19] [-ʃienʃəs].

bewusst
bewusstlos; unbewusst[1] Wahrnehmung[2] ungetrübt[3] (Unter)bewusstsein[4] Dämmerzustand[5] B. erlangen[6] nachlassen[7] Vigilanz, Wachheit[8] B. wiedererlangen[9] Bewusstseinsstörung, -veränderung[10] Bewusstseinstrübung[11] schwankende Bewusstseinslage[12] Bewusstsein verlieren, bewusstlos werden[13] nicht bewusste Schuld[14] gesundheitsbewusst[15] befangen, gehemmt[16] selbstbewusst[17] Gewissen[18] gewissenhaft[19]

1

alert [əlɜːrt] *adj & v & n term & clin*   sim **arousal**[1][aʊ], **vigilance**[2] [dʒ] *n term*

(adj) be wide awake[3] [eɪ], watchful or mentally responsive, fully aware,
(v) to alarm (n) warning signal

alertness[2] *n clin* • **arouse**[4] [aʊ] *v* • **vigilant**[5] *adj*

» An alert, wakeful patient responds immediately and appropriately to all stimuli [aɪ]. A stuporous patient responds only when aroused by vigorous[6] [vɪɡərəs] stimulation.

Use quiet/active **alert** state • patient is awake, **alert** and oriented/cooperative • medic-**alert** tag[7] • be **alert** to • be on the[8] **alert** • mental **alertness** and arousal

wach, rege; warnen, alarmieren; Alarm
Erwachen, Erhöhung d. Wachheitsgrades, Arousal[1] Wachheit, Vigilanz[2] hellwach[3] (auf)wecken, erregen[4] wach, rege[5] stark[6] mediz. Informationsplakette[7] einsatzbereit/ auf der Hut sein[8]

2

lucid [luːsɪd] *adj clin*

mentally clear, not confused, and able to be understood, esp between periods of clouded consciousness

lucidity[1] *n clin* • **lucidness**[1] *n*

» The level of alertness fluctuated considerably[2] with the occurrence of episodic confusion and lucid intervals[3] suggesting delirium.

Use **lucid** periods[3] [ɪɚ] / intervals[3] / lethargy • periods of[3] **lucidity**

bei Bewusstsein, hell, klar (denkend)
Klarheit, bei klarem Verstand[1] stark schwanken[2] helle Augenblicke/ Phasen[3]

3

faint [feɪnt] *v & n & adj term & clin*   sim **blackout**[1], **breakdown**[2] *n clin*, **syncope**[3] [sɪŋkəpi] *n term* → U110-11

(v) to collapse[6] or pass out[4]
(n) temporary loss of consciousness usually due to cerebral hypoxia

faintness[5] *n clin* • **break down**[6] *v phr* • **syncopal** *adj term*

» Shouting and gentle shaking are usually enough to revive[7] [rɪvaɪv] a person who may have fainted or may be just sleeping. The pain may be so severe that the patient faints.

Use to precipitate/produce[8] *a faint* • **syncopal** attack[1] • **fainting** fit or spell[1] • cardiac / vasovagal [eɪ]/ sudden **faint**

> Note: As an adjective *faint* is also used in medicine to mean *weak* or *hard to hear, see etc.* (faint pulse[9]/heart sound/macules)

ohnmächtig werden; Ohnmacht; schwach
(kurze) Ohnmacht, Blackout[1] Kollaps[2] Synkope[3] ohnmächtig werden[4] Schwäche(gefühl)[5] kollabieren[6] ins Bewusstsein zurückholen[7] Ohnmacht verursachen/ auslösen[8] schwacher Puls[9]

4

light-headed *adj clin*   sim **(to feel) faint**[1]*phr*, **drowsy**[2] [draʊzi], **dizzy**[3] [dɪzi] *adj clin*

to feel weak or dizzy and likely to lose consciousness

light-headedness[4] *n clin* • **drowsiness**[5] *n*

» Both drowsiness and stupor are usually attended by[6] some degree of mental confusion. Faintness, dizziness, or light-headedness may indicate an impending[7] loss of consciousness.

benommen
einer Ohnmacht nahe sein[1] schläfrig, benommen[2] schwindlig[3] Benommenheit[4] Schläfrigkeit[5] einhergehen mit[6] bevorstehend, drohend[7]

5

States of Consciousness

BASIC MEDICAL TERMS 31

pass out v phr inf   sim **be out**[1] v jar,
         opposite **come to**[2] v clin, BE **come round**[2] phr

to lose consciousness

» When she heard [hɜːrd] about her father's death she passed out.

in Ohnmacht fallen, ohnmächtig werden
bewusstlos/ weg sein[1] wieder zu sich kommen[2]   6

unresponsive adj term & jar   opposite **responsive**[1] adj term & jar

(i) failing to respond to sensations or verbal stimuli (ii) failing to respond to treatment

(un)responsiveness[2] n term • **respond (to)**[3] v • **response**[4] n

» Certain psychiatric [saɪkɪætrɪk] states can mimic[5] coma by producing an apparent [ɛɚ] unresponsiveness.

Use **unresponsive** pupils[6] [pjuːpᵊlz]/ to stimuli / to light • not **responsive** to therapy

(i) nicht ansprechbar (ii) nicht reagierend/ ansprechend
ansprechbar[1] Ansprechbarkeit, Reaktionsfähigkeit, Reagibilität[2] reagieren, ansprechen (auf)[3] Reaktion[4] vortäuschen[5] lichtstarre Pupillen[6]   7

disorientation n   sim **confusion**[1] [-fjuːʒᵊn] n,
         lose one's bearings[2] [ɛɚ] phr inf

be bewildered[3] [ɪ] or perplexed[4]; reactions to one's surroundings[5] (esp. time, place, person) are inappropriate

(dis)oriented adj • **confused**[3] adj • **orientation** n

» Patients with psychotic disorders may be fully oriented or exhibit a disorientation as to person that is at least as great as their disorientation as to time and place.

Use patient is **disoriented** and confused • well-**oriented** to time, place, and person[6] • **disoriented** behavior • acute **disorientation** • **confusional** state[7]

Desorientiertheit, fehlende Orientierung
Verwirrtheit, Verwirrung[1] Orientierung verlieren[2] verwirrt[3] verblüfft, perplex[4] Umgebung[5] orientiert zu Zeit, Raum, Person[6] Verwirrtheitszustand[7]   8

stunned [stʌnd] adj inf   sim **dazed**[1] [deɪzd] adj inf,
         ****spaced out**[2] [eɪ] adj → U11-10

(i) knocked out by a heavy blow
(ii) mental numbness[3] [nʌmnəs] esp. due to a shock, great surprise or intense light

» Suspect lightning injury[4] in persons found dazed or unconscious after a thunderstorm[5].

(i) betäubt (durch einen Schlag) (ii) benommen, (wie) gelähmt, fassungslos
benommen, verwirrt[1] (wie) unter Drogen, weg, high[2] Benommenheit[3] Verletzung durch Blitzschlag[4] Gewitter[5]   9

obtunded [ʌ] adj term   sim **blunt**[1] [ʌ], **dull**[2] [ʌ] adj & v clin

reduced level of consciousness; insensitive to pain as a result of an analgesic[3] [-dʒiːsɪk] or anesthetic[4]

obtundent[5] adj & n • **obtundation** n

» If lavage [ləvɑːʒ] is done in an obtunded or comatose patient, prophylactic insertion of a cuffed [ʌ] endotracheal [eɪk] tube[6] is recommended to prevent aspiration. Brain function may range from alertness to obtundation.

Use be/become **obtunded** • deeply[7] **obtunded** • state of mental / prolonged **obtundation**

teilnahmslos, abgestumpft, gedämpft
abgestumpft; abstumpfen[1] teilnahmslos; abstumpfen, dämpfen[2] Schmerzmittel[3] Narkotikum[4] dämpfend; dämpfendes Mittel[5] Endotrachealtubus m. Cuff[6] stark gedämpft[7]   10

stupor [st(j)uːpɚ] n term

impaired[1] [ɛɚ] or reduced consciousness with marked decrease in responsiveness to stimulation

(semi-)stuporous[2] adj term • **stupefaction**[3] n • **stupefacient**[4] [-feɪʃᵊnt] adj & n

» In stuporous catatonia the patient is subdued[5], mute[6] [mjuːt], and negativistic, accompanied by varying combinations of staring [ɛɚ], rigidity [dʒɪ], and cataplexy.

Use alcoholic / anergic [ənɜːrdʒɪk] benign [aɪn] catatonic[7] / depressive / delusion[8] / epileptic / postseizure[9] [iːʒ] **stupor** • **stuporous** patient

Stupor, Reaktionsunfähigkeit
eingeschränkt[1] stuporös[2] Betäubung, Benommensein[3] betäubend; Betäubungsmittel[4] gedämpft[5] stumm[6] katatoner Stupor[7] schizophrener S.[8] Stupor nach epileptischem Anfall[9]   11

lethargy [leθɚdʒɪ] n term   sim **apathy**[1] [æ] n, → U113-2f
         opposite **hyperactivity**[2], **agitation**[3] [dʒ] n term

a state of abnormal indifference[4], listlessness[5], sluggishness[6] [ʌ], lassitude[6], languor[6] [gɚ] or stupor

lethargic adj term • **apathetic** adj • **hyperactive** adj • **agitated**[7] adj

» Apathy, drowsiness, and confusion improve more gradually. Hepatic encephalopathy may begin with irritability[8] and mild confusion and slowly progress to agitation, lethargy, change in personality and difficulties in judgment[9] and orientation.

Use fatigue [fətiːg] and[10] **lethargy** • depression, withdrawal[11] [-drɔːᵊl] and **apathy** • **apathetic** state / hyperthyroidism [aɪ]

Lethargie
Apathie[1] Hyperaktivität[2] psychomotor. Unruhe, Agitiertheit[3] Gleichgültigkeit[4] Antriebs-, Teilnahmslosigkeit[5] Trägheit, Mattigkeit[6] agitiert[7] Gereiztheit[8] Urteilsvermögen[9] Müdigkeit u. Lethargie[10] Zurückziehen[11]   12

32 BASIC MEDICAL TERMS — States of Consciousness

somnolence n term & clin → U72-1   sim **sopor**[1] [soʊpɚ] n term
(i) semicomatose state (ii) state of unnatural drowsiness
somnolent adj term • **soporific**[2] adj & n • **soporiferous**[2] adj
» The patient complained of excessive daytime somnolence, morning sluggishness and fatigue. Her lethargy deepened into somnolence.
Use episodes of **somnolence** • **somnolent** and lethargic / metabolic rate

(i) schläfrige Teilnahms-losigkeit
(ii) **Somnolenz**
Sopor, schlafähnl. Zustand[1] einschläfernd; Schlafmittel[2]
13

coma [koʊmə] n term & clin
profound [aʊ] unconsciousness[1] from which a patient cannot be aroused even by powerful stimuli [aɪ]
comatose[2] [-toʊs] adj term • **semi-comatose** adj • **coma-like**[3] adj
» CNS symptoms include lethargy, coma, and convulsions [ʌ]. Pinpoint pupils[4], coma, and hypertension are suggestive [dʒe] of[5] cerebellar hemorrhage [e].
Use to lapse into[6]/be in/lie in / induced[7] **coma** • alcoholic / deep hepatic / diabetic [e] or hypoglycemic [-glaɪsiː]/ thyrotoxic[8] [aɪ]/ uremic [iː] **coma** • Glasgow **coma** scale[9] [eɪ] • to be/become **comatose** • deeply[10] **comatose**

Koma
tiefe Bewusstlosigkeit[1] komatös[2] komaartig[3] stecknadelkopfgroße Pupillen[4] sind ein Anzeichen für[5] ins Koma fallen[6] künstl. Tiefschlaf[7] thyreotoxisches Koma[8] Glasgow-Komaskala[9] tief komatös[10]
14

trance [trænts‖trɑːnts] n term
(i) altered state of consciousness as in hypnosis [ɪ], hysteria [ɪ], or ecstasy (ii) dazed or stuporous state (iii) detachment[1] [ætʃ] from one's surroundings (e.g. in deep concentration or daydreaming[2])
» A history of trancelike states[3] during which simple motor behaviors persist corroborates[4] the presence of daytime somnolence.
Use alcoholic / hypnotic[5] / induced[5] / death[6] **trance** • **trance**-like state / attack

Trance(zustand)
Losgelöstsein[1] Tag-, Wachträumen[2] tranceähnliche Zustände[3] bestätigt, erhärtet[4] hypnotischer Schlaf[5] Scheintod[6]
15

delirium n term
clouded state of consciousness and confusion, marked by difficulty in sustaining attention to stimuli, anxiety[1] [æŋzaɪəti], illusions and hallucinations, disordered sleep-wakefulness cycles[2] [saɪklz], motor disturbances; etc.
delirious[3] adj term
» Delirium is an acute confusional state associated with a change in level of consciousness ranging from lethargy and withdrawal to agitation. Symptoms and signs of delirium tremens include profoundly delirious states associated with tremulousness[4] and agitation.
Use delirious patient • **delirium** tremens[5] (abbr DT) / of persecution[6] • acute / exhaustion[7] [ɪgzɔːstʃən]/ traumatic / febrile[8] [e‖iː] **delirium**

Delir, Delirium
ängstl. Erregung, Angst(zustände)[1] gestörter Schlaf-Wach-Rhythmus[2] delirant[3] Zittern[4] Delirium tremens, Alkohol-, Entzugsdelir[5] Verfolgungswahn[6] Erschöpfungsdelirium[7] Fieberdelir[8]
16

persistent vegetative [vedʒ-] **state** n term, abbr **PVS**   syn **vigil** [dʒ] **coma** n, rel **akinetic** [eɪkaɪnetɪk] **mutism**[1] [juː] n term
state of unresponsiveness due to diffuse cortical or brain stem damage[2]
» PVS patients may show some improvement from an initially comatose state and appear to be awake but lie motionless and without evidence of awareness or higher mental activity.

apallisches Syndrom, Coma vigile, Wachkoma
akinetischer Mutismus[1] Hirnstammschädigung[2]
17

brain death [deθ] n term   syn **irreversible coma** n term
cessation [s] and irreversibility[1] of brain function; legal definitions vary from state to state
brain-dead[2] adj term
» The criteria [aɪ] for brain death must persist[3] for 6 hours with a confirmatory isoelectric [aɪ] (flat) EEG[4].
Use to confirm/declare/establish[5]/mimic **brain death** • diagnosis of / diagnostic criterion [kraɪtɪəɪᵊn] for **brain death** • **brain death** legislation [dʒ]

Hirntod
irreversibler Ausfall[1] hirntot[2] bestehen, andauern[3] isoelektr./ Nulllinien-EEG[4] Hirntoddiagnose sicherstellen[5]
18

First Aid   BASIC MEDICAL TERMS **33**

Unit 8   First Aid
Related Units: 5 Injuries, 6 Accidents & Emergencies, 16 Paramedical Staff, 17 Medical Equipment, 7 Consciousness,
                106 Fractures, 63 Posture & Position, 108 Clinical Signs, 140 Wound Care, 123 Resuscitation, 125 Critical Care

first aid [eɪd] *n*   *rel* **field measures**[1] [eʒ], **help**[2],
                           assistance[2], **attention**[3] *n* → U142-29

emergency [ɜː] care [keɚ] given before regular medical aid can be obtained [eɪ]
aid[4] (in) *v* • **aid**[5] *n* • **aide**[6] *n* • **self-help**[7] *n* • **assist**[4] *v* • **attend** (**to**)[8] *v*
» As a first aid measure [meʒɚ], place the patient in a shady [eɪ], cool place, and remove clothing. First aid at the scene [siːn] of an accident should be administered by trained personnel whenever possible. Field placement of intravenous [iː] lines[9] may increase the chances of infection. Patients commonly seek [iː] emergency medical attention for hemarthroses [iː], hematuria, and epistaxis.
Use to give or provide[10] [aɪ] /seek **first aid** • basic / emergency / life-saving / advanced (*abbr* AFA) **first aid** • **first aid** measures[11] / techniques / instruction [ʌ] program[12] • **first aid** kit[13] • post or station[14] • **aid** and attendance • **to aid** in diagnosis • hearing[15] / mutual [juː] food / Band®-**aid** • home health • nurse's[16] [ɜː] **aide** • **first** responder • **field** conditions / hospital[17] / personnel • **field** paramedics[18] / treatment • sterile / surgical[19] [ɜː] **field** • to call for/summon[20] [ʌ] /request/ seek **help** • emergency **help** • to ask for/seek/lend or provide[21] **assistance** • disaster[22] (medical) / military / aeromedical[23] **assistance** • **assistance** team • to require/ seek/ get/focus[24]/pay[25] **attention** • in need of / urgent [ɜː] to seek medical[26] **attention**

rescue [ˈreskjuː] *v & n*   *rel* **save**[1] [seɪv], **secure**[2] [sɪkjʊɚ], **relieve**[3] [rɪliːv] *v*

(v) to save a person who is in a dangerous situation or remove [uː] a victim from the danger zone [zoʊn]
rescuer[4] *n* • **life-saving** *adj* • (un)**safe**[5] *adj* • **relief**[6] *n* • **safeguard**[7] [eɪ] *v & n*
» They were rescued from the blazing [eɪ] drilling rig[8]. It must not interfere [-ɪɚ] with[9] the rescue efforts[10]. Wearing a safety belt[11] can save your life. Immobilization is not complete until the patient is secured to the spine [aɪ] board[12] with straps. The tiring [aɪ] rescuer must signal for a change. It is erroneous to assume that during storms it is safe to leave the shelter and venture [-tʃɚ] into the open[13] once lightning strikes.
Use to come to the or sb.'s[14] **rescue** • victim / air-sea[15] / fire **rescue** • cave [eɪ] / avalanche [-æntʃ] **rescue** • **rescue** team or squad[16] [skwɒd]/ worker / personnel • **rescue** services / activities[10] / treatment • **rescue** operation[10] / attempt[17] / vessels[18] • **rescue** breathing[19] [iː] / blanket • **search-and-rescue** (*abbr* SAR) mission / dog • **to save** the patient's life / sb. from drowning[20] [aʊ] • **to save** the eye / a finger • **to relieve** suffering [ʌ]/ distress / pain • **to secure** the patient's well-being / the airway[21] • **to secure** sth. with tapes [eɪ]/ it to the arm • life/ limb[22]- [ɪm] / time-**saving** • **safe** distance / location / travel / procedure [siː] • professional **rescuer** • **rescuer's** skills[23] / hand / arm / mouth • **rescuer** exhaustion [ɔː] or fatigue[24] • **2-rescuer** CPR[25] • disaster[26] / famine [æ] **relief** • **relief** work / supplies [aɪ] agency [eɪdʒ] or organization[27]

evacuate [ɪˈvækjʊeɪt] *v*   *sim* **extricate**[1], **retrieve**[1] [iː], **free**[1] *v*,
                                rel **transport**[2] *v*

(i) move out of an unsafe location into safety (ii) to excrete [iː] or discharge from the body
evacuation[3] *n* • **extrication**[4] *n* • **retrieval**[4] *n* • **transport(ation)**[5] *n*
» A helicopter equipped for medical evacuation should be requested. To conserve [ɜː] oxygen, lower flow rates may be used until the victim can be evacuated to a lower altitude [æ]. Casualty mitigation[6] through early warning and evacuation is hard to manage, since tornadoes are difficult to predict and the time frame for evacuation or protective cover is brief. This will help you to reach and extricate persons who are trapped[7]. Ensure that the airway remains patent[8] while the victim is transported to the hospital.
Use **to evacuate** victims / homes[9] / from danger • emergency / victim[10] / surgical[11] **evacuation** • emergency / rescue and / (aero-)medical **retrieval** • **retrieval** team / flight • ground / air / aeromedical[12] **transport** • (non)medical / emergency **transport** • prompt / rapid **transport** • **transport** officer[13] • victim[14] **extrication** • **extrication** time[15] / device[16] [-aɪs]/ from the vehicle

---

erste Hilfe
Maßnahmen vor Ort[1] Hilfe[2] Aufmerksamkeit, Beachtung; med. Behandlung, Versorgung[3] unterstützen, beistehen, helfen[4] Hilfe(stellung); Hilfsmittel[5] Helfer(in), Berater(in)[6] Selbsthilfe[7] s. kümmern um[8] Venenkatheter[9] erste Hilfe leisten[10] Erste-Hilfe-Maßnahmen[11] Erste-Hilfe-Kurs[12] Verbandskasten[13] Erste-Hilfe-Station[14] Hörgerät[15] Krankenpflegehelfer(in)[16] Feldlazarett[17] Sanitäter[18] Operationsfeld[19] Hilfe holen[20] Hilfe leisten[21] Katastrophenhilfe[22] Hilfe durch d. Flugrettungsdienst[23] Aufmerksamkeit richten[24] Beachtung schenken[25] s. in ärztl. Behandlung begeben, einen Arzt aufsuchen[26]   1

retten (aus), bergen, befreien; Rettung, Bergung
retten, bewahren, -schützen[1] sichern, sicherstellen; festmachen[2] helfen, befreien; erleichtern, lindern[3] Retter(in)[4] sicher, in Sicherheit[5] Erleichterung, Hilfe[6] schützen; Schutz[7] brennende Bohrinsel[8] behindern[9] Rettungsmaßnahmen, -aktion[10] Sicherheitsgurt[11] Rettungstrage[12] s. ins Freie wagen[13] jem. z. Hilfe kommen[14] Luftrettung über See[15] Rettungsmannschaft[16] Rettungsversuch[17] Bergungsschiffe[18] Mund-zu-Mund-Beatmung[19] jem. vor d. Ertrinken retten[20] d. Atemwege freihalten[21] zur Rettung d. Arms/ Beins[22] Können d. Retters/-in[23] Ermüdung d. R.[24] Zwei-Helfer-Reanimationsmethode[25] Katastrophenhilfe[26] Hilfsorganisation[27]   2

(i) evakuieren, bergen
(ii) (aus)räumen, entleeren
befreien (aus)[1] (ab)transportieren, befördern[2] Evakuierung, Räumung[3] Befreiung[4] Transport, Beförderung[5] Reduktion d. Opferzahl[6] eingeschlossen sein, festsitzen[7] frei[8] Wohnhäuser evakuieren/ räumen[9] Evakuierung d. Opfer[10] chir. Ausräumung[11] Flugrettungstransport[12] Transportleiter[13] Befreiung d. Opfer(s)[14] Dauer d. Bergung[15] Bergevorrichtung[16]

3

BASIC MEDICAL TERMS — First Aid

safety [seɪfti] n   sim **security**[1] [sɪkjʊərəti] n
opposite **danger**[2], **risk**[3], **hazard**[3] [hæzərd] n → U124-2; U91-5

a place or state in which there is no danger; security refers to protection against potential threats[4] [e]

(in)secure[5] adj • insecurity[6] n • endanger[7] v • dangerous[8] adj • risky[9] adj

» The press cannot be denied [aɪ] access[10] to a disaster site[11] unless they interfere [-ɪər] with ongoing rescue efforts, even if they jeopardize[7] [dʒepərdaɪz] their own safety in the process. My life was in danger. "Splint[12] them where they lie" is a time-honored rule[13] of emergency care of fractures unless it is necessary to remove an injured patient from imminent danger[14] of fire, explosion, etc.

Use to run for/bring into/be in/reach/ensure[15] [ɪnʃʊər] **safety** • a place of[16] / public[17] [ʌ]/ child **safety** • helicopter / firearm / radiation[18] [eɪ] **safety** • **safety** needs / precautions[19] [ɔː]/ regulations • **safety** first program[20] / buoy[21] [buːi‖bɔɪ]/ belt • **safety** goggles[22] / check / pin[23] / valve[24] [æ] • airport / (false) sense of[25] **security** • **security** measures / provisions[19] [ɪʒ] • **security** risk[26] / considerations / guard[27] [ɑː] • **security** personnel / check[28] / system [ɪ] / alert[29] [ɜː] / financial / social[30] **security** • to be in/pose little **danger** • **danger** zone[31] / signal[32] / list / to travelers • to take the/be at **risk** • **risk** factor / assessment[33] / reduction [ʌ] • to pose a potential[34] **hazard** • health[35] / environmental / safety **hazard** • radiation / contamination **hazard** • occupational[36] / without undue[37] **hazard** • **hazard** area[31] • to feel **secure** • **dangerous** activities / chemicals [ke-] / poisons[38] • **dangerous** situations / disease • **risky** maneuver [uː]/ procedure [siː]/ test

Sicherheit, Gefahrlosigkeit
Sicherheit, Geborgenheit, Sicherung, Schutz[1] Gefahr[2] Risiko, Gefahr[3] Bedrohungen[4] (un)sicher[5] Ungewissheit, -sicherheit, Verunsicherung[6] gefährden[7] gefährlich, nicht sicher[8] risikoreich, riskant[9] Zutritt verwehrt[10] Unglücksort[11] schienen[12] altbewährte Regel[13] drohende Gefahr[14] Sicherheit gewährleisten[15] sicherer Ort[16] öffentl. Sicherheit[17] Strahlensicherheit[18] Sicherheitsvorkehrungen[19] Unfallverhütungsprogramm[20] Rettungsboje[21] Schutzbrille[22] Sicherheitsnadel[23] Sicherheitsventil[24] Gefühl d. Sicherheit[25] Sicherheitsrisiko[26] Wache, Sicherheitsbeamte(r)[27] Sicherheitskontrolle[28] Sicherheitsalarm[29] Sozialhilfe[30] Gefahrenzone[31] Warnsignal[32] Risikoeinschätzung[33] e. mögl. Gefahr/ Risiko darstellen[34] Gesundheitsrisiko[35] Berufsrisiko[36] ohne großes Risiko[37] gefährl. Gifte[38]

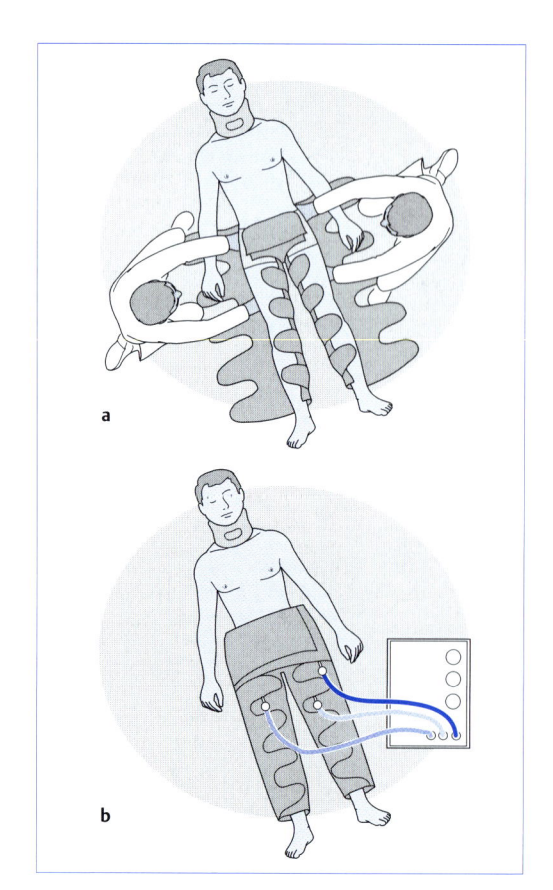

Military antishock trousers:
(a) the garment is placed around the patient's legs
(b) the MAST garment is inflated

First Aid BASIC MEDICAL TERMS **35**

ambulance n   rel **emergency medical service** (abbr **EMS**) **helicopter**[1] n term
  specially equipped automobile to transport casualties and patients to and from hospitals
» The loading (transport) officer maintains [eɪ] a log[2] of each departing ambulance's destination. Obtain [eɪ] and deploy[3] [ɔɪ] additional ambulance resources through reserve [ɜː] units, back-up arrangements[4] [eɪ], mutual [mjuːtʃʊəl] aid[5], etc. Request assistance from the aeromedical helicopter[1] unit.
Use to call an **ambulance** • community / air[6] / first-in[7] / EMS[8] **ambulance** • **ambulance** car / service[9] /men or crew[10] [kruː]/ driver[11] / attendant or technician[12] [ɪʃ] • **ambulance** dispatch center / carry(ing) chair • **ambulance** trolley[13] / loading bay[14] [beɪ] • to approach a **helicopter** • **helicopter** rotor vibrations / landing zone

Rettungs-, Krankenwagen
Notarzt-, Rettungshubschrauber[1] Aufzeichnungen[2] einsetzen[3] Hilfseinrichtungen[4] gegenseitige Hilfe[5] Flugrettung[6] ersteintreffender Rettungswagen[7] Notarztwagen[8] Rettungsdienst[9] Mannschaft d. Rettungswagens[10] Krankenwagenfahrer(in)[11] Rettungssanitäter(in)[12] Fahrgestell f. Patiententrage[13] Laderampe f. Rettungswagen[14]   **5**

paramedic n   sim **emergency medical technician**[1] [teknɪʃən] n term, abbr **EMT**
  person (not a physician [ɪʃ] or nurse [ɜː]) trained to give emergency medical treatment before or during transportation to hospital and to assist medical professionals (e.g. in the military)
  paramedical[2] [pærəmedɪkəl] adj term • **paramedic**[3] adj → U16-9
» One paramedic assumes the role of medical commander. Endotracheal [k] intubation is a skill typically learned at the paramedic level. Check if radio contact[4] with the emergency transport technicians is available. Well-trained EMTs can prepare patients for transport quickly and perform life-support procedures en route.
Use EMT / field / first-in[5] **paramedic** • **paramedical** staff[6] / personnel[6] / specialist • certified / basic[7] / trained **EMT** • intermediate [iː]/ paramedic or advanced[8] **EMT** • **paramedic** team / unit / manual • **paramedic** services[9] / division

Rettungsassistent(in)
Rettungssanitäter, -helfer(in)[1] paramedizinisch[2] Sanitäts-, Assistenz-[3] Funkkontakt[4] erster Sanitäter am Unfallort, Ersthelfer(in)[5] ärztl. Hilfspersonal[6] Rettungshelfer(in)[7] Rettungsassistent(in)[8] Sanitätsdienst[9]

6

alarm [əlɑːrm] n & v   sim **alert**[1] [ɜː] n & v, **warning**[2] n & adj, rel **report**[3] n & v
  (v) to warn others to a danger or fill sb. with apprehension[4] or anxiety [ænzaɪəti]
  alarming[5] adj • **alerting**[5] adj • **hyperalert**[6] [aɪ] adj • **(fore)warn**[7] v
» There was a brief false alarm when a rescue worker reported hearing a voice in the wreckage[8] [r]. Be alert for possible concurrent [ɜː] trauma[9] [ɔː] with occult internal bleeding. The laboratory must be alerted. Provide advance warning to receiving [iː] hospitals so that appropriate measures [eʒ] may be taken. When there is a report of a trapped victim, a fire rescue team is dispatched in addition to the EMS unit to clear fire hazards, wash away spilled gasoline, etc.
Use **to be alarmed** by the cries • to give or raise [eɪ] or sound the[10] **alarm** • to cause/set the[11]/trigger an **alarm** • smoke / fire / security / false **alarm** • **alarm** bell[12] / system[13] / response[14] / clock[15] • **to be alert** to danger • to be on the[16]/put sb. on **alert** • red[17] **alert** • to raise/issue [ɪʃ‖ɪsjuː]/heed[18] [iː] **warnings** • early / advance / without[19] **warning** • **warning** sign[20] / label [eɪ]/ symptoms [ɪ] • initial [ɪʃ]/ preliminary[21] • red[17] **report** • **alarming** figures[22] / rate / level / increase

Alarm, Besorgnis; alarmieren, warnen, beunruhigen
Alarm; alarmieren[1] Warnung; warnend, Warn-[2] Bericht; Meldung, Reportage; berichten, melden[3] Besorgnis[4] alarmierend, beunruhigend[5] aufgeputscht, hypervigil[6] (vor)warnen[7] Trümmer, Wrack(teile)[8] Begleitverletzung[9] Alarm schlagen[10] d. Wecker stellen[11] Alarmglocke[12] Alarmanlage[13] Alarmreaktion[14] Wecker[15] einsatzbereit/ auf der Hut sein[16] Alarmstufe Rot[17] Warnungen beachten[18] ohne Vorwarnung[19] erstes Anzeichen[20] vorläufiger Bericht[21] besorgniserregende Zahlen[22]

7

tourniquet [tɜːr‖tʊərnɪkɪt] n term
  compression bandage applied to arrest a hemorrhage or to facilitate obtaining blood samples
» Control bleeds by pressure or elevation or by tourniquet if these are not successful. Use a tourniquet to obtain a bloodless field. Correct tightness [taɪt-] of the tourniquet is hard to assess.
Use to apply or place[1] **a tourniquet** • to tighten [taɪtən]/inflate [eɪ]/deflate[2]/release [iː]/remove **the tourniquet** • **tourniquet** control / effect / time[3] / constriction • **tourniquet** ischemia[4] [ɪskiːmɪə]/ injury / test[5] / arm / limb [lɪm]/ pneumatic[6] [n(j)uː-]/ rotating / multiple [ʌ] **tourniquets**

Tourniquet, Druckmanschette, Stauschlauch, -binde
einen Stauschlauch anlegen[1] Luft aus d. Manschette ablassen[2] Dauer d. Blutleere[3] tourniquetbedingte Ischämie[4] Rumpel-Leede Stauversuch[5] Druckluftmanschetten[6]

8

ambulance dispatch center [dɪspætʃ sentər] n term
  communications center which receives incoming emergency calls, assesses capacity needs[1] and resources available at local hospitals and coordinates the rescue operation
  dispatch[2] v • **dispatcher**[3] n
» The first paramedic on the scene of a multicasualty event[4] provides an initial report by radio to the dispatch center, relaying[5] such information as type of incident, estimated number of victims and severity of injuries[6], presence of any hazard, additional resources needed, etc.
Use central[7] / (local) EMS **dispatch center** • **dispatch** information[8] / personnel / system[9] • **to dispatch** ambulances / mobile EMS personnel • central **dispatcher**

Rettungsleitstelle
erhebt Bedarf an Ressourcen[1] (ent)senden[2] Einsatzleiter(in)[3] Massenunfall[4] weiterleiten[5] Schweregrad d. Verletzungen[6] zentrale Rettungsleitstelle[7] Einsatzmeldung[8] Verteilersystem[9]

9

foreign body *n term, abbr* **FB**   *sim* **foreign** [fɒːrən] **material** *or* **matter**[1] *n clin*

material that has been introduced into the tissues or cavities of the body and is not readily absorbable

» In choking [tʃoʊkɪŋ] victims[2] cardiac arrest may respond promptly to removal of foreign bodies by the Heimlich maneuver. The abrupt [ʌ] onset of cough [kɒːf] or choking in toddlers[3] should heighten [haɪtᵊn] suspicion of foreign body aspiration. The foreign body lodges[4] [lɒːdʒɪz] in the supraglottic airway.

Use to aspirate/search for/locate[5] **a foreign body** • to dislodge/remove[6] **a foreign body** • tracheobronchial[7] [k]/ esophageal [dʒiː]/ intraocular[8] / conjunctival [dʒʌ] **FB** • intravesical[9] / corneal / nasal [eɪ] **FB** • urethral [iː]/ vaginal [dʒ] **FB** • ingested [dʒe]/ swallowed / aspirated / impacted[10] **FB** • retained [eɪ]/ infected / sharp **FB** • penetrating / migratory[11] [aɪ]/ minute[12] [maɪn(j)uːt] **FB** • **foreign body** aspiration[13] / obstruction [ʌ]/ extraction *or* removal[14] [uː] • **foreign body** sensation[15] / granuloma[16] / reaction[17] • **foreign body** giant [dʒaɪᵊnt] cells[18] / embolus[19] • **foreign object**[1] / protein[20] / particle[1] • **foreign** antigen / serum [ɪə]/ organism / cells

Heimlich maneuver [mənuːvɚ] *n term*

syn **subdiaphragmatic** [sʌbdaɪəfræg-] *or* **abdominal thrusts** [ʌ] *n term*

technique [tekniːk] for dislodging[1] and clearing[2] [ɪə] a foreign body from the airway of a choking victim by forceful upward thrusts[3] to the victim's upper abdomen just below the rib cage[4] [keɪdʒ]

maneuver[5] *v* • **maneuverability** *n* • **thrust**[6] [ʌ] *v* • **thrusting** *adj & n*

» Foreign bodies obstructing the airway may be relieved by performing the Heimlich maneuver repeatedly until successful. Back blows[7] [oʊ] or the Heimlich maneuver may clear the obstruction. In children younger than one year back blows and chest thrusts are recommended instead of the Heimlich maneuver, which should not be attempted.

Use to perform the **Heimlich maneuver** • supine[8] [aɪ]/ prompt **Heimlich maneuver** • life-saving / manual[9] / resuscitative[10] [ʌs] **maneuvers** • respiratory / airway (clearance) **maneuvers** • airway foreign body / jaw-thrust [dʒɒː] and chin-lift[11] [tʃɪn] **maneuver** • to deliver[12] **thrusts** • upper[13] / forcible **abdominal thrusts** • manual / chest / upward **thrusts**

breathing bag [briːðɪŋ bæg] *n clin*

syn **resuscitation** [rɪsʌsɪteɪʃᵊn] *or* **reservoir bag, Ambu bag**® *n term*

self-refilling device [dɪvaɪs] used to assist in manual ventilation

» Provide supplemental oxygen by mask (nonrebreathing, if available), nasal prongs[1] [ɒː], or Ambu bag. Maintain [eɪ] ventilation with oxygen delivered by a bag-mask combination at a high flow rate until tracheal [k] intubation can be performed.

Use manual resuscitation[2] / rebreathing[3] **bag** • self-refilling / nonrebreather reservoir **bag** • **bag**-valve-mask [æ] device *or* combination[4] • **bag**-(valve)-mask unit[4] /-breathing[5] /-(valve)-mask ventilation[5] • hand **bag** respiratory assistance[5]

medical *or* **military antishock trousers** *n term, abbr* **MAST** → U124-4f

inflatable garment placed around a patient's legs and abdomen to reduce perfusion to the lower body and thereby direct cardiac output to the vital organs, e.g. for field treatment of hypovolemia, shock, etc.

» MAST also raise peripheral resistance and therefore increase coronary blood flow. We have an ET tube[1] in place, 2 IVs with lactated Ringer's[2] wide open, and MAST garment inflated. The MAST suit [suːt] is of proved value for in-hospital tamponade of bleeding in patients with severe pelvic fractures and massive pelvic bleeding. If a patient arrives with MAST in place, it should be deflated slowly and only after the patient has been stabilized hemodynamically.

Use to apply/remove/deflate [eɪ] **the MAST garment** • **MAST** garment *or* suit[3] / device[3] • **antishock** measures [eɪ] • pneumatic [n(j)uː-] **antishock** garment[3]

logroll [lɒːgroʊl] *v term*

special rolling technique used to transfer patients with suspected spinal [aɪ] lesions[1] [iːʒ] to preclude[2] [uː] further injury [ɪndʒɚi]

» Logroll the patient to maintain axial orientation if cervical spine injury is suspected. She was logrolled onto the spine board with manual cervical spine traction maintained throughout[3].

Use **logroll(ing)** technique[4] [tekniːk]

Fremdkörper, FK
Fremdsubstanz, -körper, körperfremdes Material[1] Erstickungsopfer[2] Kleinkinder[3] sitzt fest[4] e. Fremdkörper lokalisieren[5] e. Fremdkörper entfernen[6] tracheobronchialer F.[7] intraokulärer F.[8] intravesikaler F.[9] festsitzender F.[10] wandernder F.[11] winziger F.[12] Fremdkörperaspiration[13] Fremdkörperentfernung[14] Fremdkörpergefühl[15] Fremdkörpergranulom[16] Fremdkörperreaktion[17] Fremdkörperriesenzellen[18] Fremdkörperembolus[19] Fremdprotein[20]   **10**

Heimlich-Handgriff
Mobilisieren[1] Beseitigen, Entfernen[2] nach oben gerichtete Druckstöße[3] Brustkorb[4] manövrieren[5] drücken, stoßen[6] Schläge zw. d. Schulterblättern[7] Heimlich-Handgriff beim liegenden Patienten[8] Handgriffe, manuelle Methoden[9] Reanimationsmaßnahmen[10] Anheben d. Kinns u. Vorschieben d. Unterkiefers, Esmarch-Handgriff[11] Stöße versetzen[12] Druckstöße auf den Oberbauch[13]

11

Beatmungs-, Ambu-Beutel
Nasenklemme[1] Handbeatmungs-, Atembeutel[2] Rückatmungsbeutel[3] Beatmungsbeutel mit Maske[4] Maskenbeatmung[5]

12

Antischockhose
Endotrachealtubus[1] Ringer-Laktat-Lösung[2] Antischockhose[3]

13

atraumatisch umlagern (bei Verdacht auf WS-Verletzung)
mit Verdacht auf Wirbelsäulenverletzungen[1] verhindern[2] die ganze Zeit über[3] en-bloc Umlagerungstechnik/ Mobilisation (bei WS-Verletzten)[4]   **14**

First Aid   BASIC MEDICAL TERMS **37**

extrication collar [kɒːlɚ] *n term* → U141-9   *rel* **vacuum mattress¹** *n term*

rigid cervical collar for prehospital use² when a casualty is suspected to have sustained [eɪ] spinal trauma

» *Proper sizing³ of the extrication collar is extremely important. The 2ⁿᵈ care provider⁴ [aɪ] should then place a firm extrication collar around the neck. Split-scoop [uː] stretchers and vacuum mattresses are more appropriate for transfer than rigid spinal boards, which should be reserved for primary extrication from vehicles, rather than as devices for transporting patients.*

Use to apply an⁵ / cervical [sɜː]/ adjustable [ʌ] **extrication collar** • one-piece / Stifneck®⁶ **extrication collar** • semirigid [semɪrɪdʒɪd] cervical⁷ / stiff / c-/ floatation⁸ **collar** • **vacuum** (limb) [lɪm] splint⁹ / pump¹⁰ [ʌ]

HWS-Stützkrawatte, -Schiene, Immobilisationskragen
Vakuummatratze¹ Einsatz im präklin. Bereich² Wahl d. richtigen Größe³ Helfer(in)⁴ HWS-Schiene anlegen⁵ Stifneck⁶ Halskrause⁷ Rettungskragen⁸ Vakuum-Schiene⁹ Absaugpumpe¹⁰

15

stretcher [stretʃɚ] *n*   *syn* **litter** *n BE*,
         rel **spine** [aɪ] **board¹, backboard¹, scoop** [skuːp] **stretcher²** *n term*

equipment for transporting people who are ill, wounded [uː] or dead which usually consists of a sheet of canvas³ stretched between two poles⁴; spine boards are used for prehospital patient transport and extrication from vehicles

» *Gently* [dʒ] *maneuver the stretcher under the patient without rolling or lifting. Transfer the patient from the ambulance stretcher⁵ to the emergency department stretcher, taking care to maintain cervical spine and back immobilization in multiple blunt* [ʌ] *injuries⁶. Immobilize the patient on a rigid spine board using tape and lateral restraints⁷ [eɪ] (sandbags). Prolonged use of spine boards can rapidly lead to pressure injuries.*

Use to place on⁸/strap on/fall from **a stretcher** • road / folding / split scoop⁹ **stretcher** • **stretcher** bearer¹⁰ [eɚ] case¹¹ • long¹² / short / wood / plastic **spine board** • fiber-glass / helicopter / rigid¹³ **spine board** • pediatric **backboard** • rescue¹ **board** • orthopedic [iː] **scoop stretcher** • **scoop and run** time / attitude / versus stay & play¹⁴

(Kranken)trage, Tragbahre
Rettungstrage, Spine-Board¹ Schaufeltrage, -bahre² Leinentuch³ Stangen⁴ Rettungstrage⁵ stumpfe Verletzungen⁶ seitliche Abstützung⁷ auf eine Trage legen⁸ zweiteilige Schaufeltrage⁹ Krankenträger¹⁰ nicht gehfähige(r) Patient(in)¹¹ langes Rettungsbrett¹² Rettungsbrett¹³ möglichst rasch einladen u. abtransportieren oder am Unfallort stabilisieren¹⁴

16

sniffing position *n jar* → U63-7f
         rel **stable side/lateral position¹, jaw thrust²** [ʌ]**, head tilt³** *n term*

the head is extended on the slightly flexed neck and the chin is elevated to align [əlaɪn] the oral, pharyngeal, and tracheal [k] planes which ensures patency [eɪ] of the airway and allows for endotracheal intubation

» *Place the patient in the sniffing position. The sniffing position permits visualization of the glottis and vocal cords and allows passage of the endotracheal tube⁴. After managing life-threatening problems turn the casualty to a stable side position. Place the victims in a stable lateral position and keep them warm until they can be transported to a medical facility. Jaw thrust without head tilt should be done if cervical spine injury is possible.*

Use prone⁵ [oʊ]/ semiprone or lateral recumbent⁶ [ʌ] **position** • (dorsal) recumbent⁷ / recovery⁸ / semi-Fowler⁹ **position** • (left/ right) lateral (decubitus)¹⁰ / supine¹¹ **position**

Schnüffelstellung
stabile Seitenlage, NATO-Lagerung¹ Vorschieben d. Unterkiefers² Überstrecken d. Kopfes³ Endotrachealtubus⁴ Bauchlage⁵ Sims-Position⁶ Rückenlage m. angewinkelten, gespreizten Beinen⁷ Erholungs-, Recoveryposition⁸ halbsitzende Lagerung⁹ Seitenlage(rung)¹⁰ Rückenlage¹¹

17

salvage [sælvɪdʒ] *v*   *sim* **preserve¹** [prɪsɜːrv]**, spare²** [speɚ] *v term*

to save from death, damage or destruction

salvage³ *n term* • salvageable⁴ *adj* • **salvageability** *n* • preservation⁵ *n*

» *Intensive care salvages some critically ill head-injured patients. By the time shock develops the opportunity for salvage has been lost. These patients may be spared emergency endoscopy. The nerve-sparing approach [-oʊtʃ] usually results in preservation of potency.*

Use **to salvage** vision⁶ [ɪʒ]/ a kidney • to merit⁷ / limb / foot / bladder **salvage** • **salvage** therapy / surgery⁸ / rate • salvageable⁹ blood / teeth⁹ / case • to be worth⁷ **salvaging** • organ-/ nerve¹⁰-**sparing** • **to preserve** blood supply¹¹ / the spleen [iː] • **to preserve** potency¹² [oʊ]/ cognitive functions • **preservation of** sight¹³ [saɪt]/ (renal) function¹⁴ • **preservation of** host [oʊ] tissue / cellular integrity

retten, erhalten
erhalten, schonen¹ (ver)schonen, ersparen² Rettung, Erhaltung³ erhaltungsfähig⁴ Erhaltung, Schonung⁵ d. Sehkraft erhalten⁶ erhaltenswert sein⁷ Erhaltungsoperation⁸ (noch) zu rettende Zähne⁹ nervschonend¹⁰ d. Blutversorgung erhalten¹¹ d. Potenz erhalten¹² Erhaltung d. Sehkraft¹³ Erhaltung d. Nierenfunktion¹⁴

18

triage [trɪɑːʒ] *n term*

process of classifying patients by categories and allocating[1] aid on the basis of relative urgency[2] [ɜːrdʒ°nˈsi] of or likely benefit from medical treatment

» *Triage at the accident scene seeks to identify the patients who are most at risk of dying from their injuries and thus would benefit most from[3] a trauma center.*

Use to perform/begin/permit **triage** • disaster / prehospital[4] / telephone **triage** • emergency room / 4-level[5] / psychiatric [saɪkɪætrɪk] **triage** • **triage** examination / system / decision / category • **triage** location / tag[6] / priority [aɪɔː]/ officer[7]

Sichtung, Triage
zuteilen[1] Dringlichkeit[2] am meisten profitieren von[3] präklinische Triage[4] Vierstufen-Triage, Triage m. vier Kategorien[5] Triage-Anhängekarte[6] Triageleiter(in)[7]

19

Unit 9 Drugs & Remedies

Related Units: 121 Pharmacologic Treatment, 92 Pharmacologic Agents, 93 Anesthetics, U 102 History

medication *n term*   *syn* **medicine** *n clin & inf,* **medicament** *n rare*

(i) medicinal preparations[1]
(ii) administration[2] of remedies

medicinal[3] *adj term* • **medical**[4] *adj* • **medicate**[5] *v* • **self-medication** *n*

» *Relapses[6] can be treated with a second course[7] of these medications. Don't forget to take your medicine! Are you on any medication?*

Use to take/start/receive [iː]/continue/discontinue[8]/review[9] [rɪvjuː] **medication** • oral / pre[10]/ transdermal / sodium-containing[11] / pain **medication** • preoperative / daily schedule [skǁʃ] of / life-long[12] **medication** • **medicinal** drug[13] / herbs[14] [ɜːrbz]/ iron supplementation [ʌ] • **medical** therapy[15] • **medicated** bath / shampoo[16] / soap [oʊ]/ area

(i) Medikament(e)
(ii) Arznei(mittel)verordnung, -anwendung, Medikation
Präparate[1] Verabreichung[2] medizinisch, Heil-[3] medizinisch, ärztlich[4] medikamentös behandeln[5] Rückfälle, Rezidive[6] Zyklus, Kur[7] Medikament absetzen[8] Med. überprüfen[9] Prämedikation[10] natriumhaltiges Med.[11] Dauermedikation[12] Arzneidroge[13] Heilkräuter[14] medikamentöse Behandlung[15] medizinisches Shampoo[16]

1

remedy [remədi] *n & v clin*   *rel* **remediation**[1] [iː] *n term*

(n) substance or treatment that can cure[2] [kjʊɚ] a disease or relieve[3] pain or other symptoms
(v) to cure

remediable[4] [iː] *adj clin* • **remedial**[5] *adj*

» *The cause of his hearing loss (impaction of ear wax[6]) was easily remediable. Hot showers are an age-old remedy for itching disorders[7]. Obstructive [ʌ] causes must be excluded or remedied.*

Use pain-relieving / herbal[8] (folk) / home[9] / over-the-counter[10] / cold[11] **remedy** • **remedy for** internal/external use[12] / burns • **remediable** condition

(Heil-/ Arznei)mittel; bessern, heilen
Behandlung, Besserung[1] kurieren, heilen[2] lindern[3] heil-, behebbar[4] heilend, Heil-[5] Zeruminalpfropf[6] bewährtes Mittel gegen Juckreiz[7] pflanzliche Droge[8] Hausmittel[9] rezeptfreies Arzneimittel[10] Mittel gegen Erkältungen[11] M. zur äußeren Anwendung[12]

2

drug [ʌ] *n term & clin & inf*   *sim* **agent**[1] [eɪdʒənt] *n term* → U11-1; U92-2

n (i) any substance other than food used for preventing, diagnosing, treating, and curing disease
(ii) in genE it also refers to stimulating or depressing substances that can be addictive[2], esp. narcotics[3]

drug-induced [uːs] *adj* • **drug-related** *adj* • **drug**[4] *v usu pass*

» *This is the drug of choice[5] for the treatment of uncomplicated urinary tract infections.*

Use to administer[6]/be on *or* take[7] **drugs** • street *or* illicit[8] / recreational[9] / designer / potent[10] / powerful **drug** • crude[11] / scheduled / (non)prescription[12] / over-the-counter[13] **drug** • oral / experimental *or* investigational new[14] (*abbr* IND) **drug** • **drugs** for hay [heɪ] fever[15] [iː] • **drug** administration / dependence[16] / dispensing[17] / incompatibility[18] / interaction /-related deaths[19] • sustained/prolonged release[20] **drug** • **adverse** drug event (*abbr* ADE) *or* drug reaction[21] (*abbr* ADR) • therapeutic / blocking / antiallergic **agent** • **drug-induced** jaundice[22] [dʒɒːndɪs] / parkinsonism

> **Note:** In view of its double meaning the expression *drug* is best avoided when talking to patients about *medication* as it may give rise to misunderstandings. Among physicians and in the literature, however, the term is widely used. While patients are likely to interpret *Is he on drugs?* as a reference to cocaine or LSD, doctors commonly use terms like *drug-related disease* or *drug therapy*[23].

(i) Medikament, (Arznei)mittel
(ii) (Rausch)droge, Suchtgift
Wirkstoff[1] abhängig/ süchtig machend[2] Narkotika, Rausch-, Betäubungsmittel[3] (starke) Medikamente geben, D. nehmen, betäuben[4] M. der Wahl[5] M. verabreichen[6] D. nehmen, drogenabhängig sein[7] illegale Droge[8] Psychopharmakon[9] hochwirksames M.[10] Ausgangsdroge[11] rezeptpflichtiges Medikament[12] rezeptfreies M.[13] Testmed.[14] M. gegen Heuschnupfen[15] Drogenabhängigkeit[16] Arzneimittelhandel[17] Arzneistoffinkompatibilität[18] Drogentote[19] Depot-, Retardpräparat[20] Nebenwirkung, unerwünschte Arzneimittelwirkung[21] Drogenikterus[22] medikamentöse Behandlung[23]

3

Drugs & Remedies BASIC MEDICAL TERMS 39

pharmacy [fɑːrməsi] *n clin & term*   *sim BE* **chemist('s)**[1] [kemɪst] *n*
   (i) retail[2] store where medicinal preparations and supplies[3] are sold
   (ii) a branch of pharmacology
   pharmacist[4] *n term* • **druggist**[5] *n inf* • **pharma(co)-** *comb* → U92-1
» In general, the prescribing physician[6] provides or asks the dispensing pharmacist to provide written drug use information for the patient.
Use hospital[7] **pharmacy** • **pharmacist**-on-call[8] • **pharmaco**chemistry /therapy[9] /logy

> Note: In America *drugstores* are retail shops which sell drinks, snack, cosmetics, household goods, etc.; they may, however, include a *pharmacy* where prescription drugs are dispensed.

(i) Apotheke
(ii) Pharmazie, Pharmazeutik
Apotheke u. Drogerie[1] Einzelhandels-[2] Arzneimittel u. Ärztebedarf[3] Apotheker(in), Pharmazeut(in)[4] Apotheker(in), Drogist(in)[5] verschreibende(r) Arzt/ Ärztin[6] Anstalts-, Klinikapotheke[7] diensthabende(r) Apoth.[8] medikamentöse Behandlung[9]

4

dispense *v term*
   to prepare, compound[1] [aʊ], label[2] [eɪ], sell and give out medications to patients
   dispensatory[3] *n term* • **dispensary**[4] *n clin* • **dispenser**[5] *n*
» Today these drugs are increasingly dispensed without prescription[6]. It may not be sold or dispensed directly to the patient. Dispense in dropper bottle[7] or amber[8] [æ] glass container.
Use **dispensing** chemist[9] *(BE)* • soap **dispenser**

(Arznei) (zu)bereiten u. abgeben
(ab)mischen[1] etikettieren[2] Arzneimittel-Codex, Ergänzung z. amtl. Arzneibuch[3] Anstalts-, Klinikapotheke[4] Spender, Dispenser[5] rezeptfrei[6] Tropfflasche[7] bernsteinfarben[8] Apotheker(in), Drogist(in)[9]

5

dosage [doʊsɪdʒ] **form** *n term*   *sim* **dosage formulation**[1] *n term*
   describes how a drug is supplied[2] (as a tablet or cream [iː], powdered [aʊ], in liquid form, etc.)
   formulate[3] *v term*
» Special coatings[4] [oʊ] are used to retard[5] the disintegration[6] of solid dosage forms in the gut[7] [ʌ]. This solution is specifically formulated for exclusive application to the oral mucosa.
Use oral[8] / topical / solid[9] / liquid / oral suspension[10] **dosage form** • parenteral / pediatric [iæ]/ controlled- or slow-release[11] **dosage form** • commercial [ɜː]/ metered [iː] spray[12] / water-in-oil / delayed-[11] [eɪ]/ extended-[11] / prompt-release[13] / capsule **formulation**

Arznei-, Darreichungsform
Zubereitungsform[1] hergestellt, vertrieben[2] zubereiten[3] Überzug[4] verzögern[5] Zerfall[6] Darm[7] perorale Arzneiform[8] feste A.[9] Mixtur[10] Retardpräparat[11] Dosieraerosol[12] schnell zerfallende Arzneizubereitung[13]

6

... strictly for the birds!

tablet *n & v, abbr* **tabs**   *sim* **capsule**[1] [kæpsəl‖sjuːl] *n term & clin,* **pill**[2] *n clin & inf*
   solid dosage form varying in shape (disk-like) and size, and method of manufacture (molded[3] [oʊ], compressed[4]); a caplet is a mixture between a tablet and a capsule-shaped dosage form
» Dissolve[5] the tablet under the tongue. Swallow [ɒː] the capsule whole[6]. Take the tablet with a glass of water.
Use enteric-coated[7] / chewable[8] [uː]/ scored[9] / sublingual **tablet** • buffered [ʌ]/ half-, regular-, double-strength[10] / rapidly dissolving **tablet** • dispersible[11] [ɜː]/ slow-release[12] [iː]/ coated[13] / dry-coated[14] / film-coated[15] **tablet** • (hard/soft) gelatin [dʒe]/ translucent [uːs] **capsule** • sleeping / contraceptive[16] [se]/ multiphasic[17] [eɪ] **pill**

Tablette; tablettieren
Kapsel[1] Pille[2] geformt[3] gepresst[4] zergehen lassen[5] unzerkaut schlucken[6] magensaftresistente T.[7] Kautablette[8] T. m. Teilungs-/ Bruchkerbe[9] forte Tabl.[10] Brause-, Lösungstablette[11] Retardpräparat[12] überzogene Tabl., Dragee[13] Manteltablette[14] Filmtablette[15] Antibabypille[16] Mehrphasenpille[17]

7

ointment [ɔɪ] *n term or* **salve** [sæv] *n clin, abbr* **oint.** *or* **UNG**   *sim* **gel**[1] [dʒel], **paste**[2] [eɪ], **cream**[3], **balm** [bæˡm‖bɑːm] *or* **balsam**[4] [ɒː] *n clin*

semisolid medicinal preparations for application to the skin which are suspended[5] in fatty or greasy[6] [iː] material

creamy *adj*

» *Oils, powders[7], and ointments should not be routinely used. Lindane 1% cream is also effective but may irritate the skin. Apply[8] the ointment topically and spread[9] [e] it with gauze[10] [ɡɒːz].*

Use to use/rub in **an ointment** • ophthalmic [ɒːfθæl-] *or* eye[11] / rectal / emulsifying[12] [ʌ]/ 5% / water-soluble **ointment** • emollient *or* soothing[13] [uːð]/ steroid [ɪə]/ iodine[14] [aɪ] **ointment** • ointment dosage form / tube / application • coal tar / lidocaine / film-forming / regular-strength **gel** • (emollient) dental / zinc[15] (oxide) / gelatin [dʒe] **paste** • corticosteroid / (sun block) lip **balm** • vaginal [dʒ]/ moisturizing[16] [tʃ]/ cold[17] **cream**

Salbe, Unguentum
Gel[1] Paste[2] Creme[3] Balsam[4] suspendiert[5] fettig, schmierig[6] Puder[7] auftragen[8] verteilen[9] Gaze, Verbandsmull[10] Augensalbe[11] emulgierende S.[12] weiche Salbe, Ung. molle[13] Iodsalbe[14] Zinkpaste[15] Feuchtigkeitscreme[16] Kühlsalbe[17]

8

---

powder [paʊdɚ] *n & v term & clin*   *sim* **pellet**[1] *n term & clin*

solid preparation dispensed in the form of small particles; pellets are small cylindrical or ovoid pills of compressed agents, e.g. steroid hormones for subcutaneous implantation and slow release

powdery[2] *adj* • **powdered**[3] *adj*

» *Dissolve one 2-gram package [pækɪdʒ] of powder in a full glass (8 ounces [aʊ]) and stir [stɜːr] well[4]. The diluent[5] [ɪ] is slowly injected into the vial [vaɪᵊl] which is then gently [dʒ] swirled[6] [ɜː] until the pellet is dissolved.*

Use absorbent / oral / topical / antifungal[7] / activated charcoal[8] [tʃ]/ sprinkle[9] / aerosol [eɚ] **powder** • freeze-dried[10] [aɪ] **pellets**

Puder, Pulver; (ein)pudern, pulverisieren
Granulat, Pellet[1] pulverförmig[2] pulverisiert[3] gut umrühren[4] Verdünnungsmittel[5] vorsichtig schwenken[6] fungizider Puder[7] Aktivkohle, Carbo medicinalis[8] Streupuder[9] gefriergetrocknete Granula[10]

9

---

tincture [tɪŋktʃɚ] *n term*   *sim* **lotion**[1] [oʊʃ] *n term & clin*

medicinal agents suspended in an alcohol-containing solution

» *Preparations containing tincture of benzoin can be removed by swabbing[2] them with rubbing alcohol. The gel is spread onto the ulcer as a thin continuous film. Apply enough gel and rub in[3] gently.*

Use iodine[4] [aɪə]/ hydroalcoholic[5] / benzoin [z] opium[6] **tincture** • shake[7] / drying / (back) rub[8] / antifungal [ʌŋg]/ cleansing[9] [e]/ aftershave **lotion**

Tinktur
Lotion[1] Wegwischen[2] einreiben[3] Iodtinktur[4] Äthanol-Wassergemisch[5] benzoesäurehalt. Opiumtinktur[6] Schüttelmixtur[7] Einreibemittel[8] Reinigungslotion[9]

10

---

drops *n term & inf usu pl, abbr* **gtt.**   *sim* **solution**[1] [uːʃ], → U81-25
syrup[2] [sɪrəp] *n term & clin, abbr* **Liq**

(i) dosage for medications (ii) popular term for tinctures, eyewashes[3], etc.

solvent[4] *n term* • **solute**[5] *n* • **soluble**[6] *adj* • **solubility**[7] *n*

» *Some recommend a dose of 2 drops of ophthalmic solution. 5mL of a 20% solution should be instilled[8] with a syringe[9] [dʒ] connected to the catheter. Ipecac [ɪ] syrup[10] is now used as a centrally acting emetic[11] in acute oral drug overdose.*

Use eye / nose / stomach[12] [k] **drops** • maple[13] [eɪ]/ flavored [eɪ]/ demulcent [ʌls]/ glucose / cough[14] [kɒːf] **syrup** • clear / cloudy[15] [aʊ]/ discolored / diluted[16] [uː]/ aqueous[17] [eɪkwɪəs] **solution** • concentrated / IV / nasal / oral / saline[18] [eɪ] **solution**

Tropfen, Guttae
Lösung[1] Sirup[2] Augenwässer, Collyria[3] Lösungsmittel[4] gelöster Stoff[5] löslich[6] Löslichkeit[7] eingeträufelt, instilliert[8] Spritze[9] Ipecacuanha-, Brechwurzelsirup[10] Emetikum[11] Magentropfen[12] Ahornsirup[13] Hustensaft, -sirup[14] trübe Lösung[15] verdünnte L.[16] wässrige L.[17] Kochsalzlösung[18]

11

---

suppository [səpɒːzətɔːri] *n term*

solid cone-shaped[1] [oʊ] dosage form for introduction into the rectum or vagina [dʒ] that readily [e] melts[2] at body temperature

» *Moisten[3] the suppository by placing it in a cup of water for 10s before rectal insertion. For best results the suppository should be retained[4] for at least 3 hours.*

Use to place/insert[5] **a suppository** • vaginal[6] / intraurethral / pile[7] [aɪ] / laxative[8] **suppository**

Zäpfchen, Suppositorium
kegelförmig[1] schmilzt[2] befeuchten[3] im Körper verbleiben[4] Z. einführen[5] Vaginalzäpfchen[6] Hämorrhoidenzäpfchen[7] Stuhlzäpfchen[8]

12

---

vial [vaɪəl] *or* **phial** [faɪəl] *n term*
sim **ampul(e)** *or* **ampoule**[1] [æmpʲuːl] *n term*

small receptacle[2] [se] (usually of glass) for holding liquids, and esp. medicines which are typically withdrawn[3] [ɒːn] with syringes for IV or IM injection; ampuls are hermetically sealed[4] [iː] vials which need to be broken for use

» *Discard[5] opened vials after 96 hours. Remove the vial from packaging[6] just before use and shake well. The vial should be rolled not shaken to dissolve the drug. 0.05 mg/mL is packaged as single-use ampuls[7], all other strengths[8] as multiple-dose vials.*

Use plastic / reaction / diluent [ɪ] / multiple dose[9] **vial** • opened / 4-mL size **ampul**

Stechampulle, Vial, Ampullenflasche
Ampulle[1] Behälter[2] entnommen[3] verschlossen[4] entsorgen[5] Verpackung[6] Einzeldosisampullen[7] Konzentrationen[8] Mehrfachentnahmeflasche[9]

13

Drugs & Remedies   BASIC MEDICAL TERMS 41

lozenge [lɒːzəndʒ] *n clin*   *syn* **pastil(le)** [pæstəl‖pæstiːəl] *n clin*
   (i) a dose of medicine in the form of a small pellet (ii) a small aromatic or medicated candy
» *Dissolve slowly in the mouth, do not bite or chew* [tʃuː] *lozenges or* swallow [ɒː]
   them whole[1] [hoʊl]. *He was* sucking[2] [ʌ] *a lozenge.*
Use menthol / iron / cough[3] [kɒːf] / sore throat[4] / benzocaine [keɪ]/ chloraseptic
   lozenge • fruit / throat[4] **pastille**

Pastille, Lutschtablette
ganz schlucken[1] lutschen[2] Hustenpastille, -bonbon[3] Lutschtablette gegen Halsschmerzen[4]
14

antidote [æntɪdoʊt] *n & v*
   drugs that can neutralize [uː] toxic substances[1] or counteract[2] [aʊ] their effects
» *This medication is to be used as an antidote for emergency use in poisoning[3].*
Use universal / physiologic [fɪz]/ chemical[4] [ke] **antidote** • **antidote** to / against

Gegenmittel, -gift, Antidot; G. verabreichen
Gift(stoff)e[1] entgegenwirken[2] bei Vergiftungsnotfällen[3] chemisches Gegenmittel[4]
15

pack(age) [pækɪdʒ] *n & v*   *sim* **packet**[1][pækɪt], **carton**[2] [ɑː] *n*
   (n) container (glass bottle, carton, packets for powders etc.) for dispensing drugs in adequate doses
   packaging[3] *n* • **repackaging** *n*
» *Keep in the protective packaging until used. Each* blister card[4] *contains one day's dosage (14 cards per package). Dispense in the original carton to protect the solution from light.*
Use dose / triple [ɪ] card / hospital[5] **pack** • double-barrier / child-resistant[6] / unitdose[7] **packaging**

Packung; verpacken
Schachtel, Packung[1] (Papp)karton[2] Verpackung[3] Blisterpackung[4] Klinik-, Anstaltspackung[5] kindersichere Verpackung[6] Einzeldosispackung[7]
16

package insert *n term*   *syn* **patient instruction** [ʌ] **leaflet** [iː] *n clin & inf*
   important product information for the patient (composition[1], mode of action[2], dosage[3], administration[4], indications, contra-indications[5], side effects[6], precautions [ɒː] etc.)
» *Carefully read the package insert for specific dosing guidelines[7] [aɪ].*

Packungsbeilage, Beipackzettel
Zusammensetzung[1] Wirkungsweise[2] Dosierung[3] Anwendungsweise[4] Gegenanzeigen, Kontraindikationen[5] Nebenwirkungen[6] Dosierungsrichtlinien[7]
17

precautions [prɪkɒːʃənz] *n*
   these are warnings to take preventive[1] or security measures[2] [eɜ], e.g. not to exceed [iː] the recommended dosage[3], do not take with alcohol, avoid excessive heat, keep drugs out of the reach of children, etc.
   precautionary[1] *adj* • **caution**[4] [kɒːʃən] *n & v*
» *Caution in increasing dosage is recommended. These precautions do not apply to short-term IV use unless otherwise specified. Use caution when driving or operating machinery because of possible* drowsiness[5] [aʊz], impairment [eɚ] *of motor skills*[6] *and/or* judgement [dʒʌdʒ-] *of* distance[7], *etc.*
Use **precautions** to consider[8] / while using this medication • to **caution** against[9]

Vorsichtsmaßnahmen
vorbeugende Maßnahmen[1] Sicherheitsmaßn.[2] empfohlene Dosis nicht überschreiten[3] Vorsicht; warnen[4] Schläfrigkeit, Benommenheit[5] Beeinträchtigung d. Fahrtüchtigkeit[6] Distanzeinschätzung[7] zu berücksichtigende V.[8] warnen vor[9]
18

storage [stɔːrɪdʒ] *n*
   the conditions under which drugs are kept[1] are decisive [aɪ] for their shelf life[2] and stability[3]
» *Store below 40°C (104°F) in a tight* [taɪt], light-resistant[4] *container and protect from freezing. Fomepizole is stable* [eɪ] *for at least 48 hs when refrigerated* [dʒ] *or if* stored[1] *at room temperature. The tablet will* maintain potency[5] *through the expiration date*[6] *provided the bottle cap is replaced tightly after each use.*

Lagerung
gelagert/ aufbewahrt werden[1] Haltbarkeit[2] Stabilität[3] lichtundurchlässig[4] Wirkung behalten[5] über das Verfalldatum hinaus[6]
19

Clinical Phrases

These tablets should be taken on an empty stomach. Diese Tabletten sollten auf nüchternen Magen eingenommen werden. • Take these capsules with meals. Nehmen Sie diese Kapseln zu den Mahlzeiten ein. • The drug is well tolerated. Das Medikament ist gut verträglich. • Protect from light! Lichtschutz erforderlich. • This drug has a particularly swift onset of action. Dieses Medikament wirkt besonders rasch. • Consult your family doctor if symptoms persist. Bei anhaltenden Beschwerden sollten Sie Ihren Hausarzt aufsuchen. • Store in a cool, dry place. Protect from heat and moisture. Kühl und trocken aufbewahren! • For expiration date see bottom of container. Verfalldatum auf der Unterseite des Behälters beachten!

Unit 10 Alcohol & Smoking

Related Units: 11 Substance Abuse, 3 Food & Drink, 9 Drugs & Remedies, 91 Toxicology, 7 Consciousness, 44 Respiration, 65 Walking, 66 Speech, 75 Behavior, 111 Respiratory Signs & Symptoms, 113 Neurologic Findings

drunk(en) [ʌ] *adj*   *syn* **boozed(-up)** [uː] *adj inf, rel* **tipsy**[1] [tɪpsi] *adj*

suffering from the effects of excessive alcohol intake (also termed acute alcohol intoxication[2])
drunk[3] *n* • **drink**[4] - drank - drunk *v irr* • **drinking**[5] *adj & n* • **drunkenness**[6] *n*

» He had an argument with a friend while drunk. How much do you ordinarily drink? Perform a systematic intraoral examination in patients over 45 who smoke tobacco or drink immoderately. He keeps drinking to the point of drunkenness. He's half asleep and a bit boozed up. Drinking sherry always makes me tipsy.

Use **drunken** behavior • bum[7] [ʌ]/ husband / gait [eɪ]/ brawl[8] [ɔː] • to get/be/appear **drunk** • blind *or* dead[9] • roaring[9] [ɔː] **drunk** • **drunk** driver • as a lord[9] *(BE)* • **drunk** driving[10] (arrest) / and disorderly • **to drink** greedily[11] [iː]/ excessively / up[12] / sb. under the table • **drink** oneself into oblivion[13] / and drive[10] • chronic / problem **drinking** • inability to control / surreptitious[14] [ɪʃ] **drinking** • **drinking** binge[15] [bɪndʒ]/ habits[16] / problem • **drinking** pattern • friends[17] / water • **to drink** daily / to sb.'s health[18] • **to drink** alcoholic beverages / without control

> Note: **Drinking**, **drinks** and **to drink** (unless specified otherwise) normally refer to alcohol. **Drunken** is only used in front of nouns. Informal and slang expressions for **drunk** include: **smashed, tight, pickled, loaded,** **pissed,** *plastered (BE)*.

betrunken, alkoholisiert
beschwipst[1] akute Alkoholvergiftung /-intoxikation[2] Betrunkene(r), Säufer(in)[3] trinken[4] Trink-, Sauf-; Trinken[5] (Be)trunkenheit, Trunksucht[6] Saufbold, Penner[7] Schlägerei v. Betrunkenen[8] sternhagelvoll, total blau[9] Trunkenheit/ Alkohol am Steuer[10] gierig trinken[11] austrinken[12] bis zur Bewusstlosigkeit trinken[13] heimliches Trinken[14] Saufgelage[15] Trinkgewohnheiten[16] Saufkumpanen[17] auf jem. trinken, jem. zuprosten[18]

1

---

alcohol [ælkəhɒːl] *n*   *syn* **booze** [buːz] *n inf*, **drink** *n*
rel **liquor**[1] [lɪkɚ] *n, BE* **spirits**[1] *n pl* → U3-27f

(i) alcohol-containing drinks (beer, wine, gin, etc.) (ii) volatile hydroxyl [aɪ] compounds, e.g. ethanol [e]

(non)-alcoholic[2] *adj* • **booze**[3] *v* • **boozer**[4] *n* • **boozy** *adj* • **spirit**[5] *n*

» No alcohol is allowed on the ward[6] [ɔː]. Moderate alcohol intake is not harmful. Quite honestly, he's been too fond of[7] the booze lately. On a day when you drink alcohol, how many drinks do you have?

Use to drink/ingest[8] [dʒe] /abuse/avoid **alcohol** • grain[9] [eɪ]/ ethyl [eθɪl‖BE iːθaɪl]/ methyl / 70% / rubbing[10] [ʌ] **alcohol** • **alcohol** use / consumption [ʌ] *or* intake *or* ingestion[11] / excess • **alcohol** abuse[12] / sponging [ʌ] *or* rub[13] / withdrawal[14] [ɔː] • **alcohol**-induced /-related • **alcohol-related** blackouts[15] / traffic accident / gastritis [aɪ] • to stay off the[16] **booze** • big[17] **boozer** • intoxicating / hard[18] / distilled **liquor** • **liquor** store[19] • surgical[20] **spirit** • to give up / be given to[3] **drink** • soft[21] **drinks** • to have/take a **drink** • methylated[22] **spirits** *(BE)*

Alkohol
Spirituosen[1] alkoholfrei[2] saufen[3] Säufer(in); Kneipe *(BE)*[4] Spiritus, Weingeist[5] (Krankenhaus)station[6] gerne mögen[7] Alkohol konsumieren[8] Äthylalkohol[9] Alkohol für Ein-/ Abreibungen[10] Alkoholkonsum[11] Alkoholmissbrauch, -abusus[12] Alkoholabreibung[13] Alkoholentzug[14] alkoholbedingte Erinnerungslücken[15] Alkohol meiden[16] starke(r) Trinker(in)[17] harte Getränke, Schnaps[18] Spirituosengeschäft[19] Wundbenzin[20] alkoholfreie Getränke[21] denaturierter Alkohol, Brennspiritus[22]

2

---

blood alcohol level *n*, *abbr* **BAL**   *syn* **blood alcohol content** *n*, *abbr* **BAC**

» In habitual [ɪtʃ] drinkers[1] the rate of ethanol[2] metabolism can be sufficiently [ɪʃ] high to permit the consumption of large quantities of spirits without raising [eɪ] the blood alcohol level over 80 mg/dL, at which the conventional breath analyzer[3] begins to detect ethanol. Estimate the blood alcohol level by taking a breath [e], blood or urine [jʊɚɪn] sample.

Use **blood alcohol** sample[4] [æ]/ concentration • to raise [eɪ] /determine[5] [ɜː] /reduce **the blood alcohol level** • high / low / rising[6] [aɪ]/ falling **blood alcohol content**

Blutalkoholspiegel, -konzentration
Gewohnheitstrinker, notorische T.[1] (Äthyl)alkohol, Äthanol[2] (Atem)alkoholmessgerät, Alkomat[3] Alkoholblutprobe[4] d. Blutalkoholgehalt bestimmen[5] steigender Blutalkoholspiegel[6]

3

---

sober [soʊbɚ] *adj*   *rel* **dry**[1] [draɪ], **clean**[2] [kliːn] *adj inf*

(i) not under the influence of alcohol or any other intoxicant (ii) serious and realistic

sober up[3] *v* • **dry out**[3] *v* • **sobriety**[4] [səbraɪəti] *n* • **soberness**[4] *n*

» Breathalyzers [e] are a very rough [rʌf] means of determining whether a person is sober or not. Alcoholics Anonymous[5] (*abbr* AA) helps alcoholics maintain sobriety through group support. He thought the coffee would sober him up. The road to sobriety is often long and bumpy [ʌ]. Is New York a dry state?

Use stone-cold[6] **sober** • **sober** as a judge[6] [dʒʌdʒ]/ mood [uː]/-minded[7] [aɪ] • to be/ stay **dry** • **dry** hotel / bar[8] / party / campus policy • **drying-out** cell[9] / period of[10] / long-term / maintenance [eɪ] of **sobriety** • **sobriety** test / checkpoint / from alcohol • standard field **sobriety** test[11] (*abbr* SFST)

(i, ii) nüchtern
trocken, keinen Alkohol mehr trinken[1] clean, nicht mehr drogenabhängig[2] ausnüchtern, nüchtern machen/ werden[3] Nüchternheit, Alkoholabstinenz[4] Anonyme Alkoholiker[5] vollkommen nüchtern[6] besonnen, nüchtern[7] Bar ohne Alkoholausschank[8] Ausnüchterungszelle[9] trockene Phase[10] Blutalkoholtest[11]

4

Alcohol & Smoking   BASIC MEDICAL TERMS **43**

intoxicated [ɪntɒːksɪkeɪtɪd] *adj*   *syn* **inebriated** [iː] *adj* → U91-14

showing signs of temporary deterioration in mental function, emotional lability, flushed [ʌ] face¹, unsteady [e] gait² [eɪ], loud incoherent [ɪɚ] speech, esp. as a result of rapid or excessive ingestion of alcoholic beverages

intoxicate *v* • **inebriate** *v* • **intoxication**³ *n term* • **inebriation**⁴ *n*
• **intoxicant**⁵ *n & adj* • **inebriant**⁵ *n & adj*

» *Typical intoxication states* [eɪ] *include euphoria* [juː-], *slurred* [ɜː] *speech⁶, hallucinations, and confusion* [(j)uːʒ]. *Inhaling of gases produces a form of inebriation similar to that of the volatile* [-aɪl] *anesthetics⁷.*

Use driving while (abbr DWI)/ to appear **intoxicated** • **intoxicated** individuals / driver⁸ / with alcohol / by drugs⁹ • **intoxicating** effect¹⁰ / (acute) alcohol / ethanol [e] **intoxication** • methanol / carbon monoxide [-aɪd]/ drug¹¹ **intoxication** • lead¹² [e]/ narcotic¹³ / systemic **intoxication** • mild / moderate **intoxication** • acute / chronic / overt¹⁴ [ɜː] **intoxication** • severe¹⁵ [ɪɚ] pathologic / water¹⁶ **intoxication** • signs / severity [e]/ period / reversal [ɜː] *of intoxication* • **intoxication** state¹⁷ • drug¹¹ / alcohol **inebriation** • **inebriated** patient

berauscht, im Rausch, unter Alkoholeinfluss

gerötetes Gesicht¹ unsicherer Gang² Intoxikation, Trunkenheit, Rausch(zustand)³ Trunkenheit, betrunkener Zustand⁴ Rauschmittel; berauschend⁵ verwaschene Sprache⁶ (volatile) Inhalationsanästhetika⁷ alkoholisierte(r) (Auto)lenker(in)⁸ im Drogenrausch⁹ berauschende Wirkung¹⁰ Arzneimittelintoxikation, -vergiftung¹¹ Bleivergiftung¹² Rauschmittel-, Betäubungsmittelintoxikation¹³ klin. manifeste I.¹⁴ schwere Vergiftung¹⁵ Wasserintoxikation¹⁶ Rauschzustand¹⁷   5

temperance *n*   *syn* **moderation** *n*

(i) to control one's behavior, esp. with regard to avoiding extremes such as alcohol excess
(ii) being in the habit of not drinking alcohol because of one's principles

intemperance¹ *n* • **temper**² *v* • **immoderate**³ *adj* • **(in)temperate**⁴ *adj*

» *Temperance and self-control are the virtues⁵* [ɜː] *he preaches to reformed alcoholics⁶. Temperance supporters regarded alcohol the way people today view heroin—as an inherently addicting substance. Alcohol use in moderation need not be discouraged* [ɜː]‖*BE* ʌ. *Moderate alcohol intake does not retard the healing* [iː] *process. She used to drink immoderately.*

Use to advocate or promote⁷ **temperance** • **temperance** movement⁸ / activists / society / hotel • to drink in⁹/allow salt in/show **moderation** • **moderation** in alcohol use / of alcohol intake • to drink⁹ (**im**)**moderately** • **moderate** alcohol intake¹⁰ / amounts [aʊ] of fat • **moderate** calorie restriction / cholesterol elevation¹¹

**(i) Mäßigkeit, Zurückhaltung
(ii) Abstinenz**

Unmäßigkeit, Zügellosigkeit¹ mäßigen² unmäßig, maßlos³ gemäßigt, maßvoll⁴ Tugenden⁵ ehemalige Akoholiker(innen)⁶ sich für Mäßigung aussprechen⁷ Abstinenzbewegung⁸ in Maßen trinken⁹ mäßiger/ maßvoller Alkoholkonsum¹⁰ mäßiggradige Erhöhung d. Cholesterinspiegels¹¹   6

abstinence [æbstɪnənᵗs] *n*   *syn* **abstention** [æbstenʃᵊn] *n*

practice of refraining [eɪ] from pleasurable [eʒ] activities that might have a negative effect, esp. alcohol

abstain [eɪ] (**from**)¹ *v* • **abstinent**² *adj* • **abstainer**³ [eɪ] *n*

» *Delirium tremens syndrome typically appears after 3-4 days of abstinence. Abstention from alcohol is essential while you are on this medication. He's managed to remain abstinent for more than a month now. His prognosis is poor if he is unable to abstain from drinking.*

Use to maintain/warrant⁴ [ɔː] **abstinence** • relative / absolute or complete or total⁵ **abstinence** • continued / periodic **abstinence** • **abstinence** rate / from alcohol / from food⁶ • **abstinence** symptoms [ɪ]/ syndrome⁷ [ɪ] • **abstention from** alcohol / tobacco / coitus • **to abstain from** alcohol⁸ / drinking / sexual contact • **to abstain from** strenuous physical [ɪ] exercise⁹

Abstinenz, Enthaltsamkeit

s. enthalten, verzichten auf¹ abstinent² Abstinenzler(in)³ Abstinenz erfordern⁴ vollkommene Abstinenz⁵ Nahrungskarenz⁶ Abstinenz-, Entzugssyndrom⁷ keinen Alkohol trinken, Alkohol meiden⁸ keinen anstrengenden Sport betreiben⁹   7

teetotaler [tiːtoʊtᵊlɚ] *n*   *syn* **teetotalist** *n & adj*, *rel* **prohibitionist**¹ [ɪʃ] *n & adj*

person who totally abstains from all intoxicating beverages

teetotal² *adj* • **teetotaling** *n* • **teetotalism** *n* • **prohibition**³ *n*

» *He was a teetotaler in an era* [iː] *when alcoholism was widespread* [e]. *More than 10% of physicians said they were teetotal. The prohibition era was the period from 1920 to 1933 when the production of alcoholic beverages in the U.S. was illegal* [iː].

Use habitual / confirmed⁴ [ɜː]/ strict⁵ **teetotaler** • anti-**teetotalist** • **teetotalist** state⁶ • anti-**prohibitionist** • **prohibitionist** movement / policies⁷ • to advocate / promote **teetotalism** • fanatical / state-enforced **teetotalism** • alcohol **prohibition**

Antialkoholiker(in), Abstinenzler(in)

Alkoholgegner(in)¹ abstinent² Verbot; Prohibition³ überzeugte(r) Antialkoholiker(in)⁴ strenge(r) A.⁵ Land/ Bundesstaat mit Alkoholverbot⁶ Prohibitionspolitik⁷   8

hangover [hæŋoʊvɚ] *n clin*   *rel* **hung-over**¹ [hʌŋ oʊvɚ] *adj clin*

disagreeable² aftereffects (headache, heartburn³, etc.) from the use of alcohol or recreational drugs⁴

» *Simple intoxication lasts less than 12 hours and is usually followed by a hangover. This is not a stomach* [k] *upset⁵, you simply got a hangover. I'm feeling really hungover today.*

Kater, Katzenjammer

verkatert¹ unangenehm² Sodbrennen³ Freizeitdrogen⁴ Magenverstimmung⁵   9

alcoholic n syn **drinker**, *****dr*u*nk(ard)** n, *****l*u*sh** [ʌ], *****dipso(m*a*niac)** [eɪ] n inf
a person who is given to excessive drinking
alcoh*o*lic[1] adj • **low-*a*lcohol**[2] adj • **non-dr*i*nker**[3] n • **non-drinking** adj
» G*ou*t[4] [aʊ] att*a*cks in chr*o*nic alcoh*o*lics occur [ɜː] at lower s*e*rum [ɪɚ] urate [jʊɚeɪt] levels than in non*a*lcoholics[3]. Even in moderate drinkers *a*lcohol is likely to result in repeated awakenings [eɪ] and a sense of r*e*stless sleep. Her father was a dr*u*nkard.
Use **alcoh*o*lic** b*e*verages or drinks[5] / extract / tincture • **alcoh*o*lic** f*a*mily / stupor [-(j)uː] / halluci*osis*[6] / p*oi*soning[7] • **alcoh*o*lic** c*o*ma [oʊ]/ cirrh*o*sis [sərousɪs]/ fatty l*i*ver[8] • **alcoh*o*lic** hepat*i*tis [aɪ]/ pancreat*i*tis / psych*o*sis[9] [saɪk-] • active / chronic / t*ee*nage[10] **alcoh*o*lic** • add*i*cted[11] • homeless **alcoh*o*lic** • *a*bstinent / well-n*ou*rished [ɜː]/ ref*o*rmed[12] **alcoh*o*lic** • **Alcoh*o*lics** An*o*nymous • h*ea*vy or hard[13] / m*o*derate / wine **dr*i*nker** • whiskey / pr*o*blem / soci*a*l[14] **dr*i*nker** • inc*u*rable [kjʊɚ] **dr*u*nkard**

alcohol habituation [həbɪtʃʊeɪʃən] n term → U11-5
habit-forming pr*o*cess referring generally to t*o*lerance[1] and psycholog*i*cal [saɪkə-] dependence on cont*i*nued *a*lcohol intake to maintain a sense of well-being which may result in add*i*ction
habit*u*al[2] [həbɪtʃuəl] adj • **h*a*bit**[3] [hæbɪt] n • **hab*i*tuated to**[4] adj
» Unlike dep*e*ndency, *a*lcohol habitu*a*tion is not ass*o*ciated with a t*e*ndency to incr*ea*se *a*lcohol consumption [ʌ]. We use the term 'dep*e*ndency' in a broad sense to include both *a*lcohol add*i*ction and habitu*a*tion.
Use **a*l*cohol** add*i*ction[5] / tolerance / *o*verdose / *o*dor [oʊ] on breath[6] [e] • drug[7] **habitu*a*tion** • drinking / smoking[8] / drug **h*a*bits** • poor d*ie*tary [aɪ] or eating[9] / n*o*xious[10] [nɒːkʃəs]/ living **h*a*bits** • to kick or give up a[11] **h*a*bit** • **h*a*bit**-forming[12]

alcoholism n term syn **alcohol dependence** or **addiction** [əd*ɪ*kʃən] n term
chronic *a*lcohol ab*u*se, depend*e*nce, or add*i*ction resulting in imp*ai*rment [eɚ] of health and social or occupa*t*ional [eɪʃ] functioning [ʌ], and incr*ea*sing adaptation to the effects of *a*lcohol
» L*i*ver f*ai*lure[1] [eɪ] may be prec*i*pitated[2] [sɪ] by *a*lcoholism. Is there any *e*vidence for a genetic predisposi*t*ion [ɪʃ] to *a*lcoholism? *A*lcohol dep*e*ndency frequently coex*i*sts with depr*e*ssion.
Use chronic / acute / long-st*a*nding[3] / gen*e*tic **alcoholism** • alpha[4] / type I / type II / tr*ea*tment-resistant **alcoholism** • primary [aɪ]/ secondary / par*e*ntal[5] **alcoholism** • alcohol dependence[6] / excess[7] / addict[8] / counseling [aʊ] • to produce/develop **dependency** • mild / sev*e*re [ɪɚ]/ phys*i*cal[9] / psychol*o*gic [saɪkə-] **dependency**

fetal alcohol syndrome [fiːtəl ælkəhɒːl sɪndroʊm] n term
specific pattern of fetal malform*a*tion with growth defi*c*iency[1] [ɪʃ], craniof*a*cial [eɪ] an*o*malies, and limb d*e*fects [iː] found among *o*ffspring[2] of alcoh*o*lic women
» In f*e*tal *a*lcohol syndrome the f*e*tuses [iː] are very quiet in *u*tero [juː], and there is a higher *i*ncidence of delayed [eɪ] postn*a*tal [eɪ] growth and beh*a*vior devel*o*pment.

delirium tremens [dəlɪɚɪəm triː‖tremənz] n term, abbr **DT**
  rel **withdr*a*wal syndrome**[1] [wɪðdrɒːəl sɪndroʊm] n term → U11-12
acute org*a*nic psych*o*sis following *a*lcohol withdr*a*wal marked by mental conf*u*sion, r*e*stlessness, tremor, sw*ea*ting [e], elec*t*rolyte [-laɪt] dist*u*rbances [ɜː], anx*i*ety [ænzaɪəti], and prec*o*rdial distress
delirious[3] adj term • **withdraw**[4] - withdr*e*w [uː] - withdr*a*wn v irr → U75-14
» The spectrum of manifest*a*tions in alcoh*o*lic withdr*a*wal, ranges from anx*i*ety, decr*ea*sed cogni*t*ion[5], and tr*e*mulousness[6], incr*ea*sing irritab*i*lity[7] to full-blown delirium tr*e*mens. *A*lcohol withdr*a*wal should be suspected in every unexpl*ai*ned del*i*rium.
Use *a*lcohol withdr*a*wal / toxic[8] / s*e*nile [iː‖e] **del*i*rium** • traum*a*tic / exh*au*stion[9] [ɒː]/ postoperative **del*i*rium** • acute[10] / transient / unexpl*ai*ned / *a*gitated[11] [ædʒ] **del*i*rium** • **delirious** patient / state[12] / dep*e*ndence • *a*lcohol[13] / c*a*ffeine / drug **withdr*a*wal** • heroin / gr*a*dual[14] / abr*u*pt [ʌ] **withdr*a*wal** • **withdr*a*wal** sympt*o*ms[15] / re*a*ctions / h*ea*dache • **withdr*a*wal** state / ins*o*mnia / program[16] • **withdr*a*wal from/of** st*i*mulants / hall*u*cinogens [uːs] • **withdr*a*wal from/of** depr*e*ssants[17] / *a*lcohol[13]

Alkoholiker(in), Alkoholkranke(r), Trinker(in), Trunkenbold
alkoholisch, -haltig, -süchtig[1] alkoholarm[2] Nichttrinker(in)[3] Gicht[4] alkohol. Getränke, Alkoholika[5] Alkoholhalluzinose[6] Alkoholvergiftung, -intoxikation[7] Alkoholfettleber[8] Alkoholpsychose[9] jugendl. Alkoholiker(in)[10] Alkoholkranke(r), -süchtige(r)[11] ehemalige(r) Alkoholiker(in)[12] starke(r) Trinker(in), Säufer(in)[13] Gesellschaftstrinker(in)[14]

Alkoholgewöhnung, -toleranz
Toleranz[1] gewohnheitsmäßig, habituell[2] (An)gewohnheit[3] gewöhnt an[4] Alkoholkrankheit, Alkoholismus[5] Alkoholfahne[6] Arzneimittelgewöhnung[7] Rauchgewohnheiten[8] schlechte Essgewohnheiten[9] gesundheitsschädl. Gewohnheiten[10] eine Gewohnheit ablegen[11] suchterzeugend[12]

Alkoholismus, -krankheit, -abhängigkeit, -sucht
Leberinsuffizienz[1] herbeigeführt[2] langjähriger Alkoholismus[3] Alpha-Alkoholismus[4] Alkoholabhängigkeit eines Elternteils[5] Alkoholabhängigkeit, -krankheit[6] Alkoholmissbrauch, -abusus[7] Alkoholiker(in)[8] physische Abhängigkeit[9]

embryofetales Alkoholsyndrom, Alkoholembryopathie
Minderwuchs[1] Kinder[2]

Alkoholdelir, Delirium tremens
Entzugs-, Abstinenzsyndrom[1] Angst[2] delirant, deliriös[3] entziehen[4] vermindertes Wahrnehmungs- u. Denkvermögen[5] Zittern[6] Reizbarkeit[7] toxisches Delir(ium)[8] Erschöpfungsdelir[9] akutes Delir, Delirium acutum[10] rasendes Delir(ium)[11] deliranter Zustand[12] Alkoholentzug[13] allmählicher Entzug[14] Entzugserscheinungen[15] Entziehungskur[16] Barbituratentzug[17]

Alcohol & Smoking   BASIC MEDICAL TERMS **45**

alcohol detoxi(fi)cation *n term*   *syn* **treated** [iː] **withdrawal** [ɔː] *n clin*

(i) gradual recovery from the toxic effects of alcohol
(ii) treatment assisting in the elimination of alcohol

detoxify[1] [dɪtɔːksɪfaɪ] *v term* • **detoxicate**[1] *v* → U91-23

» *The immediate objectives of alcohol detoxification are to help the patient relieve the immediate symptoms of withdrawal and achieve* [tʃ] *a substance-free state. The* drugs of choice[2] *for alcohol detoxification are benzodiazepines* [aɪæ]. *Ingested alcohol is detoxified by the liver. While alcohol withdrawal is often treated in a hospital,* outpatient detoxification[3] *has been proposed for alcoholics with mild abstinence syndromes in an attempt to save costs.*

Use long-term / short-term / metabolic[4] **detoxification** • inpatient[5] / chemical **detoxification** • **detoxification** from stimulants / center[6] • **detoxification** treatment[7] / program[8] / of addicts

Alkoholentgiftung, Entziehungskur, Alkoholentzug(stherapie)
entgiften[1] Medikamente der Wahl[2] ambulante Entgiftung/ Entziehungskur[3] physiolog. Entgiftung[4] stationäre Entgiftung/ Entziehungskur[5] Entgiftungszentrum, Entzugsanstalt[6] Entgiftungstherapie[7] Entziehungskur[8]

15

smoke [smoʊk] *v & n*   *sim* **puff (on)**[1] [pʌf], **draw on**[2] [drɔː] *v phr*

(v) to inhale [eɪ] and exhale smoke from cigarettes, cigars, pipes, etc.

(non-)smoker[3] *n* • **smoking**[4] *n & adj* • **smoke-free**[5] *adj* • **smokeless**[5] *adj*

» *It is estimated that women smokers who quit smoking by age 35 add about 3 years to their life expectancy. The drug may help reduce anxiety* [aɪ] *generated by smoking cessation.*

Use **to smoke** like a chimney[6] [tʃ]/ tobacco / marihuana • parental cigarette / exposure [oʊʒ] to passive[7] **smoke** • **smoke** inhalation /-filled room • chain[8] [tʃeɪn]/ pipe / heavy[9] **smoker** • long-term / ex- or former[10] **smoker** • **smoker's** heart[11] [ɑː]/ palate / cough[12] [kɒf] • to start/stop or quit[13] [kwɪt] /discontinue[13]/refrain [eɪ] from/continue **smoking** • passive[7] / involuntary / maternal [ɜː] **smoking** • heavy / no[14] / cigarette **smoking** • **smoking** history / area / restrictions / habit • **smoking** cessation [s] (treatment)[15] • **smoke-free** environment [aɪ]/ work site[16] [aɪ] • **smokeless** tobacco

rauchen; Rauch
rauchen (ohne zu inhalieren)[1] ziehen an[2] (Nicht)raucher(in)[3] Rauchen, Raucher-[4] rauchfrei[5] wie ein Schlot rauchen[6] passives Rauchen[7] Kettenraucher(in)[8] starke(r) Raucher(in)[9] ehemalige(r) R.[10] Raucherherz[11] Raucherhusten[12] mit dem Rauchen aufhören[13] Rauchen verboten[14] Raucherentwöhnung[15] rauchfreier Arbeitsplatz[16]

16

tobacco [təbækoʊ] *n*   *rel* **nicotine**[1] [nɪkəti:n] *n*

leaves[2] of the tobacco plant[3] dried and prepared for smoking or ingestion [ɪndʒestʃən]

tobacco-stained[4] [eɪ] **/-related /-free** *adj* • **tobacconist**[5] *n* • **nicotinic**[6] *adj*

» *Inhalation is the most addictive form of nicotine use. Nicotine is a poisonous volatile alkaloid which is responsible for many of the effects of tobacco.*

Use **tobacco** exposure [oʊʒ]/ use / addiction[7] / smoke[8] / products[9] • **tobacco** and marihuana mix / control program[10] • **tobacco-stained** fingers[11] • **tobacco-related** cancer • chewing[12] [tʃuːɪŋ]/ smokeless **tobacco** • **nicotine** craving[13] [eɪ]/ (blood) level / dependence[7] • **nicotine** withdrawal / replacement therapy[14] / (-containing chewing) gum[15] [ʌ] • **nicotine** (skin) patches[16] / patch [pætʃ] therapy • **nicotinic** acid[17] [æsɪd]/ receptor

Tabak
Nikotin[1] Blätter[2] Tabakpflanze[3] nikotingelb[4] Tabak(waren)händler[5] nikotinhaltig; Nikotin-[6] Nikotinabhängigkeit, -abusus[7] Tabakrauch[8] Tabakwaren[9] Raucherentwöhnung(sprogramm)[10] Raucherfinger[11] Kautabak[12] starkes Verlangen nach e. Zigarette[13] Nikotinentwöhnung, -ersatztherapie[14] nikotinhalt. Kaugummi[15] Nikotinpflaster[16] Nikotinsäure[17]

17

light - lit - lit [laɪt - lɪt] *v irr*   *syn* **light up** *v phr*

light[1] [laɪt] *n* • **give sb. a light**[2] *phr* • **lighter**[3] [laɪtɚ] *n*

» *Sorry, have you got a light? You can't light up in here! He lit the cigar with a* match[4].

Use cigarette[5] **lighter** • lit cigarette[6]

anzünden
Feuer[1] jem. Feuer geben[2] Feuerzeug[3] Streichholz[4] Zigarettenanzünder[5] brennende Zigarette[6] 18

cigarette [sɪgɚet] *n*   *syn* **fag** [æ] *n inf BE*,
                              rel **cigar**[1] [sɪgɑːr], **pipe**[2] [paɪp], **cigarillo**[3] [ɪ] *n*

finely ground [aʊ] tobacco wrapped [r] in paper, usually with a filter tip[4] for smoking

» *Cigarette smoking should be avoided. Patients should* anticipate[5] [ɪs] *situations that stimulate cigarette craving* [eɪ] *and use the gum* [ʌ] *prophylactically.*

Use a packet **of cigarettes** • **cigarette** smoke / smoking / burns [ɜː]/ butt [ʌ] or end[6] • **cigarette** holder[7] / lighter / ash[8] [æʃ] • filter-tipped[9] / low-tar [ɑː] and -nicotine[10] / marihuana **cigarette** • **pipe** stem[11] / cleaner[12] / tobacco • a pack-a-day **cigarette** smoker • **cigar** smoker / box / cutter[13] [ʌ]

Zigarette
Zigarre[1] Pfeife[2] Zigarillo[3] Filter[4] vorhersehen[5] Zigarettenstummel, Kippe[6] Zigarettenspitze[7] Zigarettenasche[8] Filterzigarette[9] leichte Zigarette[10] Pfeifenhals, -rohr[11] Pfeifenreiniger[12] Zigarrenabschneider[13]

19

snuff [snʌf] *n*   *rel* **sniffing**[1] [ɪ], **snorting**[2] [ɔː] *n* → U11-23; U44-2

finely powdered [aʊ] tobacco taken by sniffing it up the nose
sniff[3] *v & n* • **sniffer**[4] *n* • **sniffle**[5] [ɪ] *v* • **snuffle**[5] [ʌ] *v*

» *It's about time you stopped taking snuff, don't you think. With the eyes closed, the patient sniffs and tries to identify the stimulus. Ask about the use of illicit drugs, reviewing major techniques of use (e.g. pills, smoking, sniffing or huffing [ʌ], snorting, injecting [dʒe]).*

Use to take[6] / a pinch [tʃ] of[7] **snuff** • **snuff** box[8] / glue[9] [uː]/ gasoline [gæsᵊliːn]/ solvent[10] **sniffing** • cocaine[11] [eɪ]/ chronic **snorting**

Schnupftabak
Schnüffeln, Schnupfen, Inhalation[1] Schnupfen[2] schnüffeln, schnupfen; Schnüffeln[3] Schnüffler(in)[4] schniefen[5] schnupfen[6] eine Prise Schnupftabak[7] Schnupftabakdose[8] Klebstoffschnüffeln[9] Inhalation v. Lösungsmitteln[10] Cocainschnupfen[11]   20

Unit 11   Substance Abuse
Related Units: 9 Drugs & Remedies, 10 Alcohol & Smoking, 7 States of Consciousness, 77 Mental Health, 91 Toxicology, 135 Anesthesiology, 124 Medical Emergencies

dope [doʊp] *n inf*   *syn* **stuff** [ʌ] *n inf,* **(street) drug** [ʌ], **narcotic** *n* → U9-3

slang expression for illicitly[1] bought, self-administered substances [ʌ] taken for mood-altering purposes
dope[2] *v inf* • **drugged**[3] [drʌgd] *adj* • **drug-related** *adj* • **narcotic**[4] *adj*

» *Do you think he is pushing dope? Somebody must have doped her drink. He was drugged to the eyeballs[5]. Where did you get the stuff from? "Street drugs" are almost always adulterated[6] [ʌ] with one or more other compounds. They were all arrested on drug charges[7]. Though controversial, decriminalization of drug use, particularly of narcotics, and registration of addicts would probably decrease drug-related handgun violence [aɪ].*

Use to smoke[8]/push[9] **dope** • **dope** dealer or pusher[10] / test • to be **doped up** • to do/be on or take[11]/push[9] **drugs** • narcotic[12] / depressant[13] / illegal [iː] or illicit [ɪs] **drug** • soft[14] / hard[15] / recreational[16] [eɪ] **drug** • hallucinogenic [dʒe] / mood [uː] elevating / designer [aɪ] **drugs** • **drug** (ab)use[17] (pattern) / habit / needle / intoxication[18] • **drug** addiction / addict[19] • **drug** trafficking[20] / counselor[21] [aʊ]/-related death • **Drug** Abuse Warning Network (*abbr* DAWN) • heavily[5] [e] **drugged** • **narcotic** effect / addict[19] / agent[12] [eɪdʒᵊnt] • **narcotic** analgesics [dʒiː]/ premedication[22] • opioid[23] [oʊpɪɔɪd]/ parenteral / IV[24] / long-acting **narcotics**

Rauschmittel, -gift, (illegale) Droge, Stoff
illegal[1] betäuben, dopen, Rauschmittel beimischen[2] unter Drogeneinfluss stehend[3] betäubend, -rauschend, narkotisch[4] mit Drogen vollgepumpt[5] verunreinigt[6] Drogendelikte[7] Haschisch rauchen[8] mit Drogen handeln, dealen[9] Drogenhändler(in), Dealer(in)[10] drogensüchtig sein, Drogen nehmen[11] Rauschgift, Betäubungsmittel, Narkotikum[12] Beruhigungsmittel, Sedativum[13] leichte Droge[14] harte D.[15] Freizeitdroge[16] Drogenmissbrauch[17] Arzneimittelvergiftung[18] Drogenabhängige(r), Rauschgiftsüchtige(r)[19] Drogenhandel[20] Drogenberater(in)[21] medikamentöse Narkosevorbereitung[22] Opioide[23] Injektionsnarkotika[24]   1

craving [kreɪvɪŋ] *n clin*   *sim* **urge**[1] [ɜːrdʒ], **compulsion**[2] [ʌ] *n* → U73-11, U77-19

strong, often uncontrollable desire [aɪ] for sth., e.g. drugs, cigarettes, or certain foods
crave[3] [eɪ] *v clin* • **urge**[4] *v* • **compel**[5] *v* • **compulsive**[6] *adj* • **compelling**[7] *adj*

» *These infants are often found to crave salt [ɔː]. Factors contributing to relapse include craving for nicotine[8] [ɪ] and social pressures. They crave nicotine and have a strong urge to smoke. Elimination of drug craving and withdrawal [ɔː] symptoms may not be possible initially.*

Use **craving** for sugar [ʃ]/ for attention[9] / to be loved / for fresh air • carbohydrate [aɪ]/ alcohol[10] / drug / cigarette[8] **craving** • to have/produce **a craving** • to reduce/ satisfy[11] / [-faɪ] lose **one's craving** • food[12] / urges and **cravings** • to feel an / strong / compelling[13] **urge** • sucking [ʌ] / sexual[14] **urge** • **urge to** smoke / void[15] [vɔɪd]/ defecate [defəkeɪt] • **compulsive** eating disorder[16] / use of drugs / urge[13] / neurosis[17] [n(j)ʊəroʊsɪs]

Appetenz, starkes/ unbezwingbares Verlangen
Verlangen, Drang[1] (innerer) Zwang, Druck[2] s. sehnen/ verlangen nach[3] eindringlich bitten, drängen[4] zwingen[5] zwanghaft, Zwangs-[6] zwingend[7] Nikotinsucht[8] starkes Bedürfnis nach Aufmerksamkeit[9] Alkoholsucht, Alkoholismus[10] seine Gelüste befriedigen[11] Essensgelüste[12] unwiderstehlicher Drang[13] Sexualtrieb[14] Harndrang[15] Essstörung[16] Zwangsneurose[17]   2

Substance Abuse   BASIC MEDICAL TERMS

addiction [əˈdɪkʃən] n   syn **dependence, dependency** n, → U10-12
rel **abuse**¹ [əˈbjuːs] n & v

chronic, relapsing disease characterized by compulsive drug seeking [iː] and dependency on a substance that is psychologically [saɪkə-] or physically [fɪz-] habit-forming² (esp. alcohol or narcotic drugs)

dependent³ **(up)on** adj • **drug-dependent**⁴ adj • **abuser** n • **abused** adj

» The most troublesome [ʌ] complication is addiction to narcotics. Drugs with little or no potential for addiction⁵ or significant dependence should be used to treat chronic benign [aɪ] pain. Two members of the family have known and untreated substance abuse disorders.

Use to develop/overcome **an addiction** • drug / methadone / nicotine **addiction** • iatrogenic [aɪə-]/ some level of⁶ **addiction** • **addiction** to narcotics / potential⁵ / to cause/produce/develop/diminish/be predisposed to⁷ **dependence** • physical or physiologic⁸ [fɪzɪ-]/ psychologic(al) **dependence** • narcotic / prescription drug⁹ **dependence** • **dependence** liability¹⁰ [aɪ] • to detect¹¹ **abuse** • adolescent / multiple / IV¹² **drug abuse** • recreational / physician¹³ **drug abuse** • substance¹⁴ / alcohol / cocaine [eɪ] **abuse** • stimulant / polydrug / child **abuse** • drug / narcotics / child **abuser**

addicted (to) adj clin & term   syn **hooked** [ʊ] **(on), turned on** [ɜː] adj inf

addictive¹ adj clin & term • **addicting**¹ adj

» The infant of a woman addicted to opioids (e.g. heroin, morphine, methadone) should be observed [ɜː] for the development of withdrawal [ɔː] symptoms² within 72 h after delivery. Many patients become addicted to the narcotics prescribed [aɪ] for pain. She's hooked on cocaine³.

Use to be/become **addicted** • heroin- / cocaine³-/ physically [ɪ] **addicted** • psychologically⁴ [saɪkə-]/ moderately **addicted** • to be/get **hooked** on a drug⁵ • **addictive** properties⁶ / potential⁷ / medications⁸ • **addictive** disorder⁹ / behavior¹⁰ [eɪ]/ illness • **addictive** personality / daily dose • highly **addictive/ing** • **addicting** agent¹¹ [eɪdʒənt]

tolerance n clin   rel **habituation¹, physical dependence²** n term

condition in which higher doses of a drug are required to produce the same effect as during initial use

tolerate³ [tɒləreɪt] v • **tolerant**⁴ adj • **tolerable**⁵ [tɒlərəbl] adj
habit⁶ [hæbɪt] n • **habitual**⁷ [həbɪtʃʊəl] adj • **habituating**⁸ adj → U10-11

» Physical [fɪzɪkəl] dependence and tolerance do not accompany all forms of drug dependence. All available hypnotics [hɪp-] involve some risk of overdose, habituation, tolerance, and addiction. Before developing the drug dependence, he did not demonstrate the pleasure-oriented [eɪ] behavior usually attributed to⁹ addicts.

Use drug / alcohol / opiate [oʊpieɪt] **tolerance** • potential for / cross¹⁰-/ development of¹¹ / risk of **tolerance** • **tolerance to** opioids / alcohol • to do sth. out of or from¹²/pick up a¹³/get into the **habit** • smoking / methadone **habit** • **habit**-forming⁸ / change • **habitual** drug user • to cause / risk of / drug¹⁴ **habituation** • **habituating** potential¹⁵ / medications / dependence¹⁶

addict n   syn **substance** [ʌ] **abuser** n term, **junkie** or **junky** [dʒʌŋki] n inf

person who is physiologically dependent on a substance that so abrupt [ʌ] deprivation¹ [eɪ] of the substance produces withdrawal [ɔː] symptoms [ɪ]

nonaddict² n clin • **abused**³ adj • **drug-abusing**⁴ adj

» Addicts have been described as escapists who cannot face realities or as withdrawn⁵ [-ɔːn] or depressed individuals with a history of suicide [suːɪsaɪd] attempts and self-inflicted injuries⁶.

Use narcotic / drug / heroin / teenage⁷ **addict** • **substance abuse** problem / prevention⁸ • **substance abuse** disorder / treatment⁹ (program) • **abused** drugs¹⁰ • drug / opioid **abuser**

Abhängigkeit, Sucht
Missbrauch, Abusus; missbrauchen¹ suchterzeugend, süchtigmachend² abhängig³ drogenabhängig⁴ Abhängigkeits-, Suchtpotential⁵ eine gewisse Abhängigkeit⁶ suchtgefährdet sein⁷ physische Abhängigkeit⁸ Medikamentenabhängigkeit⁹ Suchtneigung, -gefahr¹⁰ Missbrauch aufdecken¹¹ intravenöser Drogengebrauch/ -missbrauch¹² ärztl. Arzneimittelmissbrauch¹³ Drogenmissbrauch, -gebrauch¹⁴

süchtig, abhängig
süchtigmachend, suchterzeugend¹ Entzugserscheinungen² kokainabhängig³ psychisch abhängig⁴ drogenabhängig werden⁵ suchtbildende Eigenschaften⁶ Abhängigkeits-, Suchtpotential⁷ suchterzeugende Medikamente⁸ Sucht(krankheit)⁹ Suchtverhalten¹⁰ suchterzeugende Substanz, Suchtmittel¹¹

Toleranz
Gewöhnung¹ physische Abhängigkeit² (er)dulden, tolerieren, vertragen³ widerstandsfähig; nachsichtig, tolerant⁴ erträglich, tolerierbar⁵, (An)gewohnheit, Sucht⁶ gewohnheitsmäßig, habituell⁷ suchterzeugend, -bildend⁸ nachgesagt, zugeschrieben⁹ Kreuztoleranz¹⁰ Toleranzentwicklung¹¹ etw. aus Gewohnheit tun¹² s. etw. angewöhnen¹³ Arzneimittel-, Drogengewöhnung¹⁴ Suchtpotential¹⁵ psychische Abhängigkeit¹⁶

Drogengebraucher(in), (Drogen)süchtige(r), -abhängige(r)
Entzug¹ nicht-abhängige(r) Drogengebraucher(in)² missbraucht³ süchtig⁴ verschlossen⁵ Selbstverstümmelungen⁶ drogenabhängige(r) Jugendliche(r)⁷ Suchtmittelprophylaxe⁸ Suchtentwöhnungsbehandlung, Drogenentzugsbehandlung⁹ missbräuchl. verwendete Medikamente¹⁰

BASIC MEDICAL TERMS — Substance Abuse

drug dealer [iː] n clin
    syn **pusher** [ʊ], **trafficker** [æ] n, sim **smuggler**[1] [ʌ] n inf
person who sells illegal [iː] drugs in the streets
» It was only a minor [aɪ] incident[2] in the unending battle between drug dealers and undercover [ʌ] agents[3] [eɪdʒ]. The thugs[4] [ʌ] posing [oʊ] as security guards [gɑːrdz] were the pushers at parties where drugs were portrayed [eɪ] as harmless.
Use major / to arrest a **drug dealer** • a ring of[5] / drug / hashish **smugglers** • **drug** baron or lord / cartel[6] / control • **drug** enforcement agency [eɪ] or administration[7] (abbr DEA) • **drug** clinic / smuggling[8] • **drug** charge[9] [tʃɑːrdʒ]/ counselor[10] [aʊ]

Drogenhändler(in), -dealer(in)
Schmuggler(in)[1] Zwischenfall[2] verdeckte Ermittler[3] Schlägertypen[4] Schmuggelring[5] Drogenkartell[6] U.S. Drogenaufsichtsbehörde[7] Drogenschmuggel[8] Anklage wegen Drogenmissbrauchs[9] Drogenberater(in)[10]

7

shoot (up) [ʃuːt ʌp] v inf   syn **fix** v, sim **mainline**[1] [meɪnlaɪn], **pop**[2] [ɒː] v inf
to inject narcotics with a needle and syringe either subcutaneously or intravenously
shot[3] [ʃɒt] n inf • **fixer**[4] n • **fix**[3] n • **mainline**[5] n
» We saw him shooting up in the bathroom. She is shooting heroin five times a week. From this time on he needed his regular fix of heroin. I could have done anything for a shot of heroin. With mainlining the initial thrill[6] is more immediate. The classic routes of administration are sniffing[7], skin popping[8] and mainlining, each being associated with a more intense experience as well as addiction liability [laɪəbɪləti].

fixen, schießen, Schuss setzen, Drogen injizieren
i.v. spritzen, fixen[1] subkutan spritzen, (Pillen) schlucken[2] Schuss (Drogeninjektion); Spritze (Injektion), Impfung[3] Fixer(in)[4] (i.v.) Schuss[5] Kick[6] Schnüffeln[7] subkutanes Spritzen[8]

8

rush [rʌʃ] n clin & inf   syn **flash** [flæʃ], **bang** [æ], **buzz** [bʌz] n inf,
    rel **flashback**[1] n → U74-11
surge [sɜːrdʒ] of euphoric [juːf-] pleasure[2] [pleʒɚ] that rapidly follows administration of a drug
» The warm, glowing sensation [eɪ] rapidly spreading [e] over the body which is comparable to sexual release[3] [iː] is called rush. Mental imagery from a "bad trip" later triggered by mild stimuli [aɪ] such as marijuana, alcohol, or psychic [saɪkɪk] trauma [ɒː] are termed flashbacks.

Flash
Flashback, Echorausch, Rauschzustand ohne Drogeneinnahme[1] Euphoriewelle[2] Orgasmus[3]

9

trip (out) v inf   rel **spaced** [speɪst] **out**[1], **high**[1], **stoned**[2] [oʊ] adj inf → U7-9
to have an imaginary [ædʒ] experience while under the influence of a hallucinogenic [dʒe] substance
trip[3] n inf • **high**[4] [haɪ] n
» Has she been tripping out on LSD again? She was as high as a kite[1] [kaɪt]. He looks totally spaced out. With "free-base" cocaine [eɪ] (one version is now widely labeled [eɪ] as "crack") the speed [iː] of onset is shortened and the intensity of the high is magnified.
Use bad[5] / horror[5] **trip** • to block the / moderate / opiate / cocaine **high** • **to get/be high** on drugs[1]

(auf) einen Trip gehen/ einwerfen
im Drogenrausch/ auf dem Trip/ high sein[1] stoned, im Drogenrausch, unter Drogeneinfluss stehend, angetörnt[2] Drogenrausch, Trip[3] High-Gefühl, Hochgefühl[4] Horrortrip[5]

10

overdose [oʊvɚdoʊs] n term & clin, abbr **OD**   rel **golden shot**[1] n inf → U122-4
an excessive dosage of a drug the effects of which may range from mania [eɪ] to coma and death
overdose[2] v term & clin • **overdosage**[3] n • **overdosing** n & adj → U121-7
» The patient was overdosed with cannabinoids. If opioid overdose is strongly suspected, give additional doses of naloxone. The overdosed patient should be screened for ethanol [e].
Use to die of[4]/take an **OD** • narcotic / drug / barbiturate[5] **overdose** • digitalis [dʒ]/ opiate / heroin **overdose** • accidental[6] / intentional / (sub)acute [ʌ] **overdose** • **overdose** of medication • **overdosed** patient / with stimulants • symptoms [ɪ] of / treatment for **overdosing** • differential diagnosis with[7] **overdosing**

Überdosis
goldener Schuss, tödl. Überdosis (v. Heroin)[1] überdosieren, eine Überdosis verabreichen[2] Überdosierung[3] an einer Überdosis sterben[4] Barbituratüberdosis[5] akzidentelle Überdosis[6] Differentialdiagnose bei Überdosierung[7]

11

withdrawal or **abstinence symptoms** n clin → U10-12
    rel **cold turkey**[1] [ɜː] n inf
unpleasant [e] or life-threatening [e] reactions (e.g. anxiety, insomnia, tremor, etc.) occurring [ɜː] in an addict who is deprived [aɪ] of his accustomed [ʌ] dose of alcohol, narcotics etc.
» Patients receiving [iː] regular doses of opioids for two weeks or more frequently develop a physiologic dependence with the development of withdrawal symptoms (agitation [dʒ], tachypnea [iː], tachycardia [k], diarrhea) upon acute termination of the drug. I've gone through three days of cold turkey.
Use to lead to/show/precipitate[2] [sɪ] /avert[3] [ɜː] /relieve[4] [iː] **withdrawal symptoms** • acute / severe / mild / alcohol **withdrawal symptoms** • substance or drug[5] / neuroleptic / barbiturate / gradual[6] **withdrawal** • **withdrawal** syndrome[7] / sickness / seizures[8] [siːʒɚz]/ from methadone • permanent [ɜː] / drug / sexual[9] **abstinence** • **abstinence** period / from drug products[10]

Entzugserscheinungen
kalter Entzug, körperl. Entzug ohne flankierende Medikation[1] Entzugserscheinungen auslösen[2] Entzugserscheinungen vermeiden[3] Entzugserscheinungen abschwächen/ mildern[4] Drogenentzug[5] schrittweise Entziehung[6] Entzugs-, Abstinenzsyndrom[7] Krampfanfälle bei Entzug[8] sexuelle Abstinenz/ Enthaltsamkeit[9] Drogen-, Suchtmittelabstinenz[10]

12

Substance Abuse — BASIC MEDICAL TERMS 49

halfway house n clin   rel **sheltered** [ʃeltəd] **workshop**[1] n clin → U142-28

specialized treatment facility for alcoholics, drug addicts, or psychiatric patients who no longer require full hospital care but are not yet prepared to adjust [ʌ] to living independently

» Social and therapeutic environments [aɪ] such as day hospitals, halfway houses, and self-help communities[2] utilize peer pressure[3] to modify the self-destructive [ʌ] behavior. Appropriate care includes providing information about legal [iː] services, shelters[4] and safe houses, hotlines, support groups[2], and counseling [aʊ] services.

Use **halfway house for** drug addicts / alcoholics / mentally retarded[5] / runaways [ʌ] • **halfway house for** physically handicapped[5] / penal [iː] rehabilitation[6] • **sheltered** environment[7] / living arrangement[8] / job

Rehabilitationseinrichtung
geschützte Werkstatt[1] Selbsthilfegruppen[2] Gruppendynamik[3] Zufluchtsstätten, Wohnheime[4] Behindertenintegrationszentrum[5] Rehabilitationszentrum f. Straffällige[6] geschützte Umgebung[7] betreutes Wohnen[8]

13

joint [dʒɔɪnt] n inf   syn **reefer** [riːfə], **spliff** n, sim **roach**[1] [roʊtʃ] n inf

marihuana leaves rolled into a cigarette for smoking

» He claimed [eɪ] that smoking joints is less harmful than chronic alcohol abuse.

Use to smoke[2]/pass[3]/roll[4]/blast **a joint** • to blast a **roach**

selbstgedrehte Marihuana-, Haschischzigarette, Joint
Joint-Stummel[1] einen Joint rauchen[2] e. Joint herumgehen lassen[3] e. Joint drehen[4]

14

marijuana or **marihuana** n   syn **cannabis** n term, rel **hashish**[1] n

dried leaves or pressed resin[2] (hashish) of the hemp plant[3]; smoked or chewed[4] for its euphoric effects

cannabinoid[5] n term • **cannabinol**[6] n

» Marihuana derivatives such as tetrahydrocannabinol (abbr THC) are about as effective as oral prochlorperazine. It is wise for nursing mothers[7] to avoid marijuana. Phencyclidine[8] (abbr PCP) — a common adulterant[9] of marihuana, amphetamines, and street hallucinogens) — is also called "angel dust" or "crystal." Hashish is the most potent of the cannabis preparations.

Use smoked / sniffed[10] / ingested[11] [dʒɛ]/ occasional [eɪʒ] use of[12] **marijuana** • **marijuana** cigarette[13] / smoking / derivatives[14] • **marijuana** intoxication /-induced tachycardia • high-potency **cannabis** • **cannabis** compound [aʊ]/ users /-induced brain atrophy • **cannabinoid** abuse • flashback reactions with **cannaboids**

Note: Street names for cannabis include **grass**, **pot**, **weed**, **tea**, **dope**, and **Mary Jane**, while hashish may be referred to as **hash**, **ganga**, or **Goma de Mota**.

Marihuana, Cannabis
Haschisch, Kiff[1] Harz[2] Hanf[3] gekaut[4] Cannabinoid[5] Cannabinol[6] stillende Mütter[7] Phencyclidin, PCP[8] unreine Mischung[9] geschnupftes Marihuana[10] oral aufgenommenes M.[11] gelegentl. Marihuanagebrauch[12] Marihuanazigarette[13] Marihuanaprodukte[14]

15

barbiturates [ɪtʃ] n pl term   syn **barbs, downers** [aʊ], **(Mexican) reds** n inf

addictive derivatives of barbituric acid[1] (e.g. phenobarbital) which have sedative[2] and hypnotic effects → U92-24; U93-14

barbed up[3] adj inf • **barbiturism**[4] n term • **barbituric** adj • **-barbital** comb

» Because alcohol, barbiturates, and benzodiazepines [aɪæ] are cross-tolerant, benzodiazepines are substituted [ʌ] for alcohol in the treatment of alcohol withdrawal.

Use ingested / injected [dʒɛ]/ high-dose **barbiturates** • (ultra-)short-acting[5] / long-acting[6] **barbiturates** • **barbiturate** poisoning[7] / therapy • **barbiturate** withdrawal[8] / overdose / coma • pheno[9] [fiːnə-] /seco/ pento/ hexo**barbital** • thio**barbituric** [θaɪə-] acid

Barbiturate, Beruhigungs-, Schlaf-, Narkosemittel
Barbitursäure[1] sedierend[2] unter Barbiturateinfluss stehend[3] Barbiturateabhängigkeit, -vergiftung[4] kurzwirkende Barbiturate[5] langwirkende B.[6] Barbituratvergiftung[7] Barbituratentzug[8] Phenobarbital[9]

16

amphetamine n term   rel **stimulant**[1], **Ecstasy**[2] n, abbr **XTC**

one of a group of addictive stimulants including dextroamphetamine[3] and methamphetamine[4]

» MDMA (methylenedioxymethamphetamine), an amphetamine derivative[5] better known as "ecstasy," is a designer drug[6] with high abuse potential and neurotoxicity. Illicitly obtained stimulants may contain caffeine, ephedrine, methylenedioxyamphetamine (abbr MDA), and phencyclidine. XTC, the "peace and love" drug of the rave party culture, is similar to MDA in its chemistry and may have effects similar to other amphetamines. The amount [aʊ] of MDMA in XTC needed to get high is close to the toxic dose.

Use dextro/ meth**amphetamine** • **amphetamine** intake[7] / toxicity / poisoning • **amphetamine** abuse / epidemic[8] • **amphetamine**-barbiturate combination tablet • **amphetamine** withdrawal / psychosis[9] [saɪk-]/ overdose • over-the-counter[10] [aʊ] (abbr OTC)/ CNS[11] **stimulant** • respiratory[12] / appetite[13] **stimulant** • to try/experiment with/deal with/be high on **XTC** • **XTC** pills[14] / trade[15] / user • **XTC**-related violence / smuggling route

Note: Street names for various types of amphetamines include **black beauties**, **lid poppers**, **pep pills**, **speed** (injectable), and **ice** (crystalline [ɪ]).

Amphetamin, Weckamin
Stimulans, Aufputschmittel[1] Ecstasy, Extasy, XTC[2] Dextroamphetamin[3] Methamphetamin[4] Amphetaminderivat[5] Designerdroge[6] Amphetamineinnahme[7] Amphetaminepidemie[8] Amphetaminpsychose[9] rezeptfreies Stimulans/ Aufputschmittel[10] ZNS-stimulierende Substanz[11] Atemstimulans[12] appetitanregendes Mittel[13] Ecstasy-Tabletten[14] Ecstasy-Handel[15]

17

morphine [mɔːrfɪn] *n term*   *rel* **opiate**[1], **codeine**[2], **papaverine**[3] *n term*

main and most powerful narcotic alkaloid of opium which is highly addictive and is used as an analgesic[4] [dʒiː] and respiratory depressant in medicine

morphinism[5] *n* • **morphinist**[6] *n* • **opium** [oʊpɪəm] *n* • **opioid** *adj & n* → U135-5

» Morphine is not only more potent than codeine [iː] but also has a higher maximal ceiling [siː] effect[7]. At least 25% of persistent opiate abusers are likely to die within 10-20 years of abuse. Opiate antagonists (e.g. naloxone) compete [iː] with heroin and other opiates for opioid receptors[8].

Use intravenous [iː]/ oral / topical / epidural / controlled-release[9] [iː] **morphine** • **morphine** sulfate [ʌ]/ dependence[10] / hydrochloride • **morphine** cocktail / tablet / addiction[10] • **opium** alkaloid[11] / derivative / tincture[12] • smoked[13] / synthetic / exogenous [ɒːdʒ]/ endogenous **opiates** • **opiate** drugs[14] /-dependent / tolerance • **opiate** overdose / antagonists[15] / withdrawal • potent / weak **opioid** • **opioid** addict / medication /-like effects • **opioid** analgesic / maintenance [eɪ] therapy[16]

Morphium, Morphin
Opiat[1] Kodein[2] Papaverin[3] Analgetikum, Schmerzmittel[4] Morphinabhängigkeit; Morphinismus, (chron.) Morphinvergiftung[5] Morphiumsüchtige(r), Morphinist(in)[6] Ceiling-, Sättigungseffekt[7] Opioidrezeptoren[8] kontrollierte Gabe v. Morphium[9] Morphinabhängigkeit, Morphinismus[10] Opiumalkaloid[11] Tinctura Opii, Laudanum[12] Rauchopiate, Chandu, Tschandu[13] Opiate[14] Opiatantagonisten[15] Opioiderhaltungstherapie[16]   18

heroin [heroʊɪn] *n*   *syn* **diacetylmorphine** [daɪəsiːtˀl-] *n term*, *rel* **methadone**[1] *n term*

highly addictive opioid (morphine derivative[2]) prohibited in most countries due to its potential for abuse

» Most opioids, including heroin, methadone, meperidine, morphine, and codeine, are excreted in the urine within 24 hours and can be readily [e] detected. Currently, methadone substitution is the preferred method of opioid withdrawal.

Use **heroin** user / injection [dʒe]/ addiction[3] • **heroin** withdrawal / substitute[4] [ʌ]/ overdose /-addicted[5] • intravenous [iː]/ dependent on[5] / street / black tar[6] **heroin** • **methadone** maintenance program[7] / (use in) detoxification • **heroin**-associated nephropathy /-addicted mother[8] • **heroin**-dependent person /-induced euphoria

   Note: Street names for heroin include *junk* [dʒʌŋk], *smack*, *big H*, and *mud*.

Heroin, Dia(cetyl)morphin
Methadon[1] Morphinderivat[2] Heroinabhängigkeit[3] Heroinersatz[4] heroinabhängig[5] schwarzes Teerheroin, schwarzer Teer[6] Methadonsubstitutionstherapie, -ersatztherapie[7] heroinsüchtige Mutter[8]   19

cocaine [koʊkeɪn] *n*   *rel* **crack**[1] [æ] **(cocaine), speedballs**[2] [iː] *n inf*

alkaloid obtained from coca leaves[3] or by synthesis from ecgonine or its derivatives; it has moderate vasoconstrictor activity and pronounced [aʊ] psychotropic effects; its salts are used as a local anesthetic

cocainization[4] *n term* • **cocaine-induced** *adj*

» Cocaine is a stimulant and local anesthetic [e] not a narcotic. There is an increased incidence of developmental delay [eɪ] in cocaine-exposed, very low birth weight infants. Cocaine smugglers [ʌ] may swallow small packets of cocaine in balloons [uː] or condoms. Cocaine cannot be safely used while breastfeeding[5], as it persists in the milk for up to 24 h. Persistent hemorrhage required topical cocainization[4].

Use to snort[6]/inject/abuse **cocaine** • free-base or volatilized[7] **cocaine** • street[8] / smokable **cocaine** • topical / adulterated[9] [ʌ] **cocaine** • urine level of **cocaine** • **cocaine** ingestion / inhalation / base[10] • **cocaine** snorting / exposure / user / spray • **cocaine** solution[11] / toxicity / intoxication[12] • **cocaine** anesthesia[4] /-saturated cotton pledget[13] [dʒ] • **cocaine**-addicted mother / freebase smoking /-to-crime connection

   Note: Street names for cocaine include *coca*, *coke*, *snow*, *lady*, *flake*, and *paradise*.

Kokain, Koks, Schnee
Crack, Kokainbase[1] Speedballs, Mixtur aus Heroin und Kokain[2] Cocablätter[3] Kokainisierung, Kokain-Lokalanästhesie[4] Stillen[5] Kokain schnupfen[6] rauchbares/ gelöstes Kokain, Free-Base[7] illegales K.[8] unreines K.[9] Kokainbase[10] Kokainlösung[11] Kokainvergiftung[12] mit Kokain getränkter Wattebausch[13]   20

hallucinogen [həluːsɪnədʒˀn] *n term*   *syn* **hallucinogenic drug** *n*
   sim **psychedelic**[1] [saɪkədelɪk] *n term*

mind-altering substance whose most potent pharmacologic action is on the CNS (e.g. mescal) **hallucinogenic**[2] [dʒe] *adj term* • **psychedelic**[3] *adj* • **hallucinosis**[4] *n*

» In normal subjects hallucinogens typically elicit[5] [s] optical or auditory hallucinations[6], depersonalization, perceptual [sep] disturbances[7] [ɜː], and disturbances of thought processes.

Use **hallucinogen** abuse / user / poisoning • **hallucinogenic** mushrooms[8] [ʌ] • **psychedelic** drug[1] / effect /-induced / experience / usage[9] [juːsɪdʒ] • substance-induced / alcoholic[10] **hallucinosis**

Halluzinogen
Psychedelikum, Psychodelikum, -dysleptikum, Psychotomimetikum[1] Halluzinationen auslösend, halluzinogen[2] psychodelisch, psychedelisch, bewusstseinserweiternd[3] Halluzinose[4] lösen aus[5] akust. Halluzinationen[6] Wahrnehmungsstörungen[7] halluzinogene Pilze[8] Konsum v. Psychodysleptika[9] Alkoholhalluzinose[10]   21

Death & Mortality   BASIC MEDICAL TERMS **51**

LSD n   syn **acid** [æsɪd] n inf, rel **mescaline**[1] n or **mesc(al)**[1] n inf

psychedelic drug (lysergic [ɜː] acid diethylamide[2]) which induces hallucinatory states of a visual nature

» Because it is simple to produce and mimics[3] to some degree the traditional psychedelic drugs, PCP has become a common deceptive substitute for LSD, THC[4], and mescaline. Tolerance develops rapidly for LSD-induced changes in psychological function when the drug is used over a course of 4 days or more.

Use **LSD** intake / addict[5] / habit[6] / dependency[6] • **LSD**-induced changes / withdrawal • paper[7] **acid** • **acid**head[5] • ingested / smoked / snorted **mescaline**

> Note: Street names for LSD include **blotter**, **Orange Sunshine**, **Purple Haze**, and **Blue Dragon**, while mescaline is also called **Big Chief** or **Cactus**.

LSD, Acid
Mescalin[1] Lysergsäurediäthylamid[2] wirkt wie[3] Tetrahydrocannabinol, THC[4] LSD-Abhängige(r)[5] LSD-Sucht, -abhängigkeit[6] LSD-Blotter/ Pappen, auf Löschblatt geträufeltes LSD[7]

22

solvent [ɒː] **sniffing** n   syn **glue** [gluː] **huffing** [ʌ] n inf, → U10-20
       inhalant [eɪ] **abuse** n term, **volatile substance abuse** n term, abbr **VSA**

inhaling [eɪ] volatile substances contained in many household products[1] in order to get high

» Sniffing of solvents and inhaling of gases (e.g. toluene, paint thinners[2], nail polish[3], aerosols) produce a form of inebriation[4] similar to that of volatile anesthetics[5]. Solvent abuse via paint, lacquer[6], or glue sniffing is a relatively common form of substance abuse. Abuse of inhalants includes sniffing glue[7], gasoline[8], petroleum ether[9] [iː], spray paints[10], and other hydrocarbons.

Use gasoline [gæsəliːn]/ glue / hydrocarbon[11] **sniffing** • household / organic[12] / lipid / volatile **solvents** • chlorinated[13] / aromatic hydrocarbon **solvent** • **solvent** user / exposure / intoxication[14] /-dependent • toxic **inhalant** • **inhalant** irritant / neurotoxicity

Schnüffeln v. Lösungsmitteln
Haushaltschemikalien[1] Farbverdünnungsmittel[2] Nagellack[3] Rauschzustand[4] Inhalationsanästhetika, -narkotika[5] Lack[6] Klebstoff[7] Benzin[8] Petroläther[9] Spritzlacke[10] Schnüffeln v. Kohlenwasserstoffen[11] organische Lösungsmittel[12] chlorhalt. Lösungsmittel[13] Lösungsmittelintoxikation, -vergiftung[14]

23

doping [doʊpɪŋ][1] n   rel **anabolic steroids**[1] [stɪə‖stərɔɪdz] n term

use of banned[2] substances by athletes to improve their performance[3] in sporting competitions
anti-doping adj & n

» He claimed that he had nothing to do with doping. Had the athletes actually undergone blood doping procedures? Doping undermines[4] the integrity of sport and is a real danger to the health of athletes. We need to develop new anti-doping policies[5].

Use inadvertent[6] [ɜː]/ (holistic) blood[7] / erythropoietin [oʊ] (abbr EPO) **doping** • **doping** substance[8] / agent[8] / charges[9] • **doping** infractions[10] [ækʃ]/ scandal / test[11] / expert • **anti-doping** regulations or statutes[5] / policy / commission[12]

Doping
Anabolika[1] verboten[2] Leistung[3] untergräbt[4] Dopingbestimmungen[5] unbeabsichtigtes/ ungewolltes Doping[6] Blutdoping[7] Dopingmittel[8] Dopingvorwürfe[9] Dopingvergehen[10] Dopingkontrolle, -test[11] Dopingkommission[12]

24

Unit 12   Death & Mortality
Related Units: 6 Accidents, 8 First Aid, 7 Consciousness, 89 Pathology, 123 Resuscitation, 125 Critical Care, 97 Oncology

moribund [mɔːrɪbʌnd] adj
       syn **on one's deathbed** [deθbed], **close to death, at death's door** phr

>to be in a very critical condition, close to death or in the terminal stages of a fatal illness[1]

» Bedfast[2], paralyzed, and moribund patients must be turned frequently. Ms Kim is close to death now. When he was on his deathbed, he asked to see me a last time.

Use **moribund** patient [eɪʃ]/ victim[3] / state

im Sterben liegend; todkrank
tödliche Krankheit[1] bettlägerig[2] sterbendes Opfer[3]

1

fatal [feɪtəl] adj   syn **lethal** [liːθəl] adj, rel **terminal**[1] [tɜːrmɪnəl] adj term

leading to death or having extremely unfortunate, dire[2] [daɪə] or ruinous consequences
fatality[3] n • fate[4] [feɪt] n • **sublethal** adj term • nonlethal adj • lethality n

» Hepatitis [aɪ] A is more severe and more likely to be fatal in adults. Small amounts of this synthetic [sɪn-] narcotic are potentially lethal in children. In the terminal stages patients should be kept as comfortable as possible.

Use **fatal** accident / illness / heart [hɑːrt] attack / virus [aɪ] / infection • **fatal** dose[5] / complications / outcome[6] / injury[7] • **fatally** wounded[8] [uː] • to cause[9] **fatality** • motor vehicle[10] [iː]/ traffic[10] **fatalities** • **fatality** rate[11] • **lethal** injury[7] / damage / injection [dʒe] • **lethal** dose[5] / factors[12] / concentration • **lethal** complications / mutation[13] • **terminal** cancer[14] ['s]/ illness • **terminal** stage[15] / care / sedation [eɪʃ] • **terminally** ill patient[16]

tödlich, letal, mit tödl. Ausgang
im Endstadium, End-, terminal[1] schrecklich[2] Todesfall, -opfer;[3] Schicksal[4] tödl./ letale Dosis[5] tödl. Ausgang[6] tödl. Verletzung[7] tödl. verwundet[8] zum Tode führen[9] Verkehrstote[10] Sterbe-, Sterblichkeitsziffer, Mortalität[11] Letalfaktoren, -gene[12] Letalmutation[13] Krebs im Endstadium[14] Endstadium[15] Patient(in) im Endstadium[16]

2

BASIC MEDICAL TERMS — Death & Mortality

mortal [mɔːrtᵊl] *adj & n*   *opposite* **immortal**[1] *adj & n*

(adj) unrelenting[2] and deadly, unable to live on forever (n) a human being
mortality[3] [mɔːrtælət̬i] *n* • **immortality** *n* • **immortalize** *v*

» The commander was mortally wounded[4] [uː]. He is struggling [ʌ] to come to grips[5] with his own mortality. Regular screening for breast [e] cancer helps decrease the mortality rate[6]. Telomerase [-eɪz] might be at least in part responsible for tumor cell immortality.

Use **mortal** danger / injury / enemy[7] • **mortally** offended[8] • perinatal[9] [eɪ]/ operative / overall[10] **mortality** • infant[11] / child(hood)[12] / treatment-related **mortality** • age-specific[13] / cause-specific / disease-specific[14] **mortality** • maternal[15] [ɜː]/ reduction [ʌ] in / to reduce [-uː] **mortality** • high / low / cancer[16] [kænˈsɚ] **mortality** • **mortality** statistics[17] / study • **immortal** cells [s]

---

sterblich, tödlich, Tod-, Sterbe-; Sterbliche

unsterblich; Unsterbliche[1] unerbittlich[2] Sterblichkeit(sziffer), Mortalität[3] tödl. verwundet[4] klarkommen mit[5] Mortalitätsrate[6] Todfeind[7] tödl. beleidigt[8] perinatale Mortalität[9] Gesamtmortalität[10] Säuglingssterblichkeit[11] Kindersterblichkeit[12] altersspezifische Mortalität[13] krankheitsspez. M.[14] Müttersterblichkeit[15] Krebssterblichkeit[16] Mortalitätsstatistik[17]   3

---

die [daɪ] *v no pass*   *syn* **pass away** *v phr*
   sim **expire**[1] [ɪkspaɪɚ], **depart**[2] [dɪpɑːrt], **succumb** [səkʌm] **(to)**[3] *v*

process of gradual or sudden deterioration of vital [vaɪtᵊl] functions that ends in death
dying[4] [daɪɪŋ] *adj & n* • **to breathe one's last**[5] [briːð] *phr*

» He's afraid of dying a violent [aɪ] death[6]. What did his father die of? You should realize that your father is a dying man. Mrs Johns has been nursing[7] [ɜː] her dying husband for months. The patient quietly expired in his sleep. When did your mother pass away?

Use **to die** unexpectedly / young / in one's sleep • **to die** by one's own hand[8] / for your beliefs • **to die from** hunger[9] / injuries • **to die of** cancer / heart disease[10] / natural causes[11] [ɒː] • **dying** day / words[12] / process • **dying** patient • process [s]/ fear[13] / risk **of dying** • **to succumb to** cancer[14]

> **Note:** In clinical situations (e.g. when speaking to the patient's next of kin[15]) **to pass away** (rarely **to succumb to** and **expire**) is most commonly used.

---

sterben, entschlafen

seinen Geist aufgeben[1] aus d. Leben scheiden[2] erliegen[3] sterbend, im Sterben liegend; Sterbende[4] seinen letzten Atemzug tun[5] gewaltsamer Tod[6] pflegen[7] Hand an sich legen, Selbstmord begehen[8] verhungern[9] an einer Herzkrankheit sterben[10] eines natürl. Todes sterben[11] die letzten Worte[12] Angst vor d. Sterben[13] einem Krebsleiden erliegen[14] Angehörige[15]

4

---

dead [ded] *adj & n*   *syn* **deceased** [dɪsiːst] *adj & n*,
   opposite **(a)live**[1] [aɪ] *adj, rel* **late**[2] *adj*

(adj) not showing any signs of life (n) people who have died (**the dead**, pl and always with the article)
deaden[3] [dedᵊn] *v* • **deadly**[4] [dedli] *adj* • **lifeless**[5] [laɪfləs] *adj* • **living**[1] [lɪvɪŋ] *adj*

» Survival time from onset of symptoms [ɪ] ranges from 5 to 16 months, and about 75% of patients are dead within one year after diagnosis. The doctors are keeping him alive on a life support machine[6] [iː]. He's still alive! I am the proudest person alive. This is a matter of life and death. This is a deadly form of skin cancer. The morphine will deaden her pain[7].

Use to drop[8]/be shot/pronounce [aʊ] /be left for **dead** • to bury [e] /honor [ɒː] /rise [aɪ] from the **dead** • brain[9] / declared / considered **dead** • **dead** on arrival[10] [aɪ] (*abbr* DOA)/ body[11] / space[12] [speɪs]/ tissue • **deadly** poison / trap[13] • **live** birth / virus / vaccine[14] [ks] • to reach hospital/be discharged [tʃ] **alive** • **alive and** well[15] (*abbr* A & W)/ kicking[15] • **lifeless** body[16] • your **late** husband[17]

---

tot, verstorben; Tote, Verstorbene

lebend(ig)[1] verstorben[2] lindern, mildern, dämpfen, abtöten[3] tödlich[4] leblos, tot[5] Herz-Lungen-Maschine[6] Schmerz(en) lindern[7] tot umfallen[8] hirntot[9] tot bei d. Einlieferung[10] Leiche, Leichnam[11] Totraum[12] tödl. Falle[13] Lebendimpfstoff, -vakzine[14] gesund u. munter[15] lebloser Körper[16] Ihr verstorbener Gatte[17]

5

---

survive [sɚvaɪv] *v*   *sim* **outlive**[1] [aʊtlɪv] *v,* **live on**[2] [lɪv ɒn] *v phr*

(i) to stay alive, esp. after being close to death (ii) to live longer than sb. else
survival[3] [sɚvaɪvᵊl] *n* • **survivor**[4] *n* •
surviving *adj* • **survivable**[5] *adj* → U100-25

» If he survives one week, recovery [ʌ] is likely. Starvation[6] [eɪ] can be survived for 2-3 months. The patient is not likely to outlive the beneficial [ɪʃ] effects of such surgery [ɜː]. I can't live on like this. Some survivors of the acute illness recover surprisingly well. Airway injuries are survivable with immediate [iː] treatment only.

Use **to survive** an accident / a heart attack • patient / disease-free[7] **survival** • **survival rate**[8] / time or period[9] / curve[10] [ɜː] • **survival** probability[11] / benefit[12] / of the fittest • long-term[13] / cancer / polio / neonatal [niːoʊneɪtᵊl] **survivor** • **survivor** of heart transplant • **surviving** children / patients • **survivable** trauma [ɒː] or injury

---

(jem.) überleben, am Leben bleiben

jem. überleben, etwas überdauern[1] weiterleben[2] Überleben(szeit)[3] Überlebende(r), Hinterbliebene(r)[4] überlebbar[5] Hungern[6] rezidivfreie Überlebenszeit[7] Überlebensrate[8] Überlebenszeit[9] Überlebenskurve[10] Überlebenswahrscheinlichkeit[11] Überlebensvorteil[12] Langzeitüberlebende(r)[13]

6

Death & Mortality   BASIC MEDICAL TERMS 53

death [deθ] n   sim **end**[1] n inf, **eternal** [ɜː] **rest**[2] n phr,
                decease[3] [dɪsiːs], **demise**[3] [-aɪz] n form
   permanent [ɜː] end of all life functions [ʌ] in an organism or part of it
   deceased[4] [dɪsiːst] adj & n • **departed**[4] [ɑː] adj & n • **deathbed**[5] n
» Her family wanted to be present at the time of her death. Most deaths[6] are due to
   strokes[7]. Emotional stages that may occur when a patient learns of approaching
   death are denial[8] [aɪ], anger, bargaining[9], depression, and acceptance. He died a
   natural death aged 79.
Use to be close to/face/meet one's **death** • to escape/resist[10]/deny [dɪnaɪ] /long for
   death • (un)natural / untimely[11] / tragic [dʒ] / sudden [ʌ] **death** • instant / accidental[12] / violent [aɪ]/ imminent[13] **death** • brain[14] / alcohol-related **death** • risk /
   (leading) cause[15] (abbr COD)/ time / circumstances [ɜː] **of death** • denial / pro-
   nouncement [aʊ] / notification[16] **of death** • to put sb. to[17] **death** • starved /
   choked[18] [tʃ]/ frightened [aɪ] **to death** • frozen / burned [ɜː]/ beaten / trampled[19]
   to death • **death** toll[20] / penalty[21] / wish / instinct • **death** rattle[22] / notice[16] /
   with dignity • **death due to** drug abuse / strangulation / suffocation[23] • **death by**
   poisoning / fire / electrocution[24] [kjuː]

suicide [suːɪsaɪd] n   syn **self-inflicted death** n term
   the act of taking one's own life[1] voluntarily and intentionally
   suicidal [suːɪsaɪdᵊl] adj • **-cide** [-saɪd] comb
» Suicide attempts[2] with overdoses of other drugs are less often successful. He could
   see no way out but to take his own life. He tried to kill himself by slashing his wrists[3]
   [r]. The immediate [iː] goal [goʊl] of psychiatric [saɪk-] evaluation is to assess the
   current suicidal risk.
Use to consider/contemplate[4]/attempt/commit[5] **suicide** • apparent [eə] prevention
   of[6] / teen / (physician-)assisted[7] **suicide** • **suicide** risk / hotline / victim / survivor
   • **suicidal** depression / individual[8] / thoughts or ideation[9] [aɪdɪeɪʃᵊn] • **suicidal**
   intent[10] / overtures[11] [-tʃɚz] / tendencies / threat[12] [θret] • **suicidal** overdose / act /
   death / rate[13] • geno[14] / [dʒenəsaɪd] infanti[15]/ pesti**cide**

mercy killing [mɜːrsi kɪlɪŋ] n clin   syn **euthanasia** [juːθəneɪʒ(ɪ)ə] n term,
                                          rel **right-to-die**[1] n
   to bring about[2] the death of a person suffering from an incurable disease by administering a
   lethal drug (active)or allowing the person to die by withholding treatment[3] or withdrawing life
   support (passive)
   kill[4] v • **killer**[5] n & adj • **killing** adj & n
» Do you think euthanasia should be legalized [iː]? If we support a mentally competent[6] patient's right to request that life support be withdrawn, this may open the
   door to a more general acceptance of euthanasia. What are the public attitudes
   toward the right to die? Malaria kills a million children each year. She was killed
   in an aircrash[7].
Use active / passive[8] **euthanasia** • **killer** disease / instinct / virus [aɪ] / cells[9] • **kill** off[10]
   / yourself • serial[11] [sɪəɪəl]/ pain[12] **killer** • **right-to-die** debate [eɪ]/ case

manslaughter n leg   sim **murder**[1] [ɜː] n & v, **homicide**[2] [hoʊmɪsaɪd] n leg
   to kill sb. by accident (e.g. by reckless driving[3]) or while trying to defend one's own life (in
   self-defense[4])
   slaughter[5] [slɔːtɚ] v & n • **murderer**[6] n • **murderous**[7] adj • **homicidal**[8] adj
» The driver will be charged [tʃɑːrdʒd] with manslaughter. The incidence of violent
   crime—murder, rape[9] [reɪp], and assault[10] [əsɔːlt] —has doubled [ʌ] within the past
   five years. For every teenager who dies of heart [hɑːrt] disease, 8 die as a result of
   homicide.
Use to commit/be charged with[11] **manslaughter** • **manslaughter** charges • involuntary[12] **manslaughter** • attempted[13] / brutal / first-degree **murder** • mass / convicted[14] **murderer** • **homicide** investigation / by misadventure[15] • **homicidal**
   tendencies • **murderous** intentions[16]

Tod
Tod, Ende[1] ewige Ruhe[2] Ableben, Tod[3] verstorben; Verstorbene(r)[4] Sterbe-, Totenbett[5] Todesfälle[6] Schlaganfälle[7] Verleugnung[8] Verhandeln[9] nicht sterben wollen[10] vorzeitiger/ allzu zu früher Tod[11] Unfalltod[12] nahe/ kurz bevorstehender T.[13] Hirntod[14] Haupttodesursache[15] Todesanzeige[16] jem. hinrichten[17] erstickt[18] zu Tode getrampelt[19] Zahl d. Todesopfer[20] Todesstrafe[21] Todesröcheln[22] Tod durch Ersticken[23] Tod auf dem elektrischen Stuhl[24]

7

Selbsttötung, Freitod, Suizid
sich d. Leben nehmen[1] Suizidversuche[2] sich d. Pulsadern aufschneiden[3] s. mit Selbstmordgedanken tragen[4] Selbstmord begehen[5] Suizidprophylaxe, -prävention[6] ärztl. Beihilfe zum Suizid[7] Suizidgefährdete(r)[8] Suizidgedanken[9] Suizid-, Selbsttötungsabsicht[10] Suizidphantasien[11] Suizid-, Selbstmorddrohung[12] Suizidrate[13] Völkermord[14] Kindestötung[15]

8

Sterbehilfe, Euthanasie
Recht auf selbstbestimmtes Sterben[1] herbeiführen[2] Behandlungsverzicht, -abbruch[3] töten[4] Mörder(in); tödlich, Killer-[5] geistig voll zurechnungsfähig, i. Vollbesitz s. geistigen Kräfte[6] kam bei einem Flugzeugabsturz ums Leben[7] passive Sterbehilfe[8] Killer-, K-Zellen[9] vernichten, (ab)töten[10] Serienmörder(in)[11] Schmerzmittel, Analgetikum[12]

9

Totschlag
Mord; ermorden[1] Tötung, Totschlag, Mord[2] rücksichtsloses Fahren[3] Selbstverteidigung[4] abschlachten, Blutbad[5] Mörder(in)[6] blutrünstig, Mord-[7] mörderisch, Mord-[8] Vergewaltigung[9] Körperverletzung[10] wegen Totschlags angeklagt sein[11] fahrlässige Tötung[12] versuchter Mord[13] verurteilte(r) Mörder(in)[14] Unfall m. Todesfolge[15] Mordabsichten[16]

10

54 BASIC MEDICAL TERMS — Death & Mortality

capital punishment [ʌ] n term   syn **death penalty** [penəlti] n inf,
                                      rel **execution**¹ [eksɪkjuːʃən] n

to put to death (officially [ɪʃ] execute) a person who has been convicted of a capital crime² [aɪ]
execute³ v • **punish**⁴ [pʌnɪʃ] v • **punishable**⁵ adj

» Is capital punishment indeed an effective deterrent⁶ [ɜː]? This crime carries the death penalty.
Use to sentence⁷/put sb. **to death** • **death** row⁸ [roʊ]/ sentence⁹ • **punishable** by death

Todesstrafe
Exekution, Vollstreckung¹ Kapitalverbrechen, schweres V.² hinrichten, vollstrecken³ (be)strafen⁴ strafbar⁵ Abschreckungsmittel⁶ zum Tode verurteilen⁷ Todestrakt (Gefängnis)⁸ Todesurteil⁹

11

grieve [griːv] v   syn **mourn** [mɔːrn] v, rel **condole** [oʊ] **with**¹ v phr

feel or show sorrow in reaction to an actual, perceived [siː] or anticipated loss
grief² [griːf] n • **grieving** adj & n • **mourning**³ n • **mourner**⁴ n • **condolence**⁵ n

» I can understand your grief. It grieved me to learn about my husband's infidelity⁶. May I offer my sincere [-sɪɚ] condolences to you and your family. Relatives who are grieving should be given an opportunity to talk about it. You have to give yourself time to mourn now.
Use **to grieve** deeply⁷ / for sb. / over sth. • to cause/feel/suffer/express/ease [iːz] sb.'s **grief** • normal / deep⁸ / profound⁸ [aʊ]/ overwhelming⁹ / inconsolable [oʊ] **grief** • **grief** therapist¹⁰ / assessment / and loss counseling [aʊ] • dysfunctional¹¹ / acute / anticipatory¹² **grieving** • **grieving** process¹³ • **mourn** for / over • to be in / period of **mourning** • letter of¹⁴ **condolence** • to extend¹⁵/offer one's heartfelt **condolences**

trauern (um), sich grämen
jem. kondolieren/ sein Mitgefühl aussprechen¹ Leid, Kummer² Trauer(zeit, -kleidung)³ Trauernde(r), Trauergast⁴ Beileid, Anteilnahme⁵ Untreue⁶ zutiefst bekümmert sein⁷ tiefe Trauer⁸ unsagbare Trauer⁹ Trauertherapeut(in)¹⁰ pathologische Trauer¹¹ antizipatorische Trauer¹² Trauerprozess¹³ Kondolenz-, Beileidsbrief¹⁴ seine Kondolenz erweisen, kondolieren, sein Beileid aussprechen¹⁵

12

bereavement [bɪriːvmənt] n   sim **loss**¹ n, rel **sorrow**² [sɔːroʊ] n

state of sadness and regret over the death or departure of a loved one
bereaved³ [bɪriːvd] adj & n • **sorrow**⁴ v • **sorrowful**⁵ adj

» Elderly patients who are bereaved are at greater risk of rapid deterioration. She has suffered a bereavement recently. It's a question of showing sympathy⁶ [ɪ] for the bereaved. His death is a great loss to all of us. How did she get over⁷ the loss of her son?
Use to suffer a/get over one's **bereavement** • **bereavement** assessment / counseling / support group⁸ • period of⁹ / natural process **of bereavement** • **bereaved** family¹⁰ • to express one's **sorrow**

schmerzl. Verlust, Trauer(fall)
Verlust¹ Traurigkeit, Trauer, Kummer² leidtragend, trauernd; die Hinterbliebenen³ sich grämen⁴ traurig⁵ Mitgefühl⁶ hinwegkommen über⁷ Selbsthilfegruppe für Trauernde⁸ Trauerzeit⁹ Trauerfamilie¹⁰

13

corpse [kɔːrps] n clin   syn **body** n, **cadaver** n term, *****stiff** n inf,
                                      rel **ashes**¹ [æʃɪz] n pl

(i) the bodily remains [eɪ] of a dead person (ii) physical [ɪ] object or structure [ʌ]
cadaveric² [kədævɚɪk] adj • **stiff** adj

» Did you find any traces of violence on the body of Mr Morgan? Dissecting cadavers³ is an essential component of teaching surgical skills. Her ashes were scattered over the lake.
Use to embalm⁴ [-ɑːm] /bury [e] /exhume [uː] **a body** • dead / decomposing⁵ [oʊ] **body** • foreign⁶ (abbr FB) **body** • **a corpse** decays [dɪkeɪz] or rots⁷ • **cadaver** organ / transplant or graft⁸ • kidney / donor⁹ [oʊ] • **cadaver** scent¹⁰ [s]/ preserved [ɜː] for anatomic study • **cadaveric** rigidity¹¹ [rɪdʒɪdəti]

(toter) Körper, Leichnam, Leiche
Asche, sterbl. Hülle¹ Leichen-² Sezieren von Leichen³ einen Leichnam einbalsamieren⁴ verwesende Leiche⁵ Fremdkörper⁶ eine Leiche verwest⁷ Leichentransplantat⁸ Leichenspender(in)⁹ Leichengeruch¹⁰ Totenstarre¹¹

14

rigor mortis [rɪgɚ mɔːrtɪs] n term   rel **livor** [laɪvɚ] **mortis**¹, **lividity**² [ɪ] n term

rigid stiffening of cardiac and skeletal muscles shortly after death (due to depletion³ of ATP)
rigor⁴ n term → U105-9 • **rigid**⁵ [rɪdʒɪd] adj • **rigidity**⁶ n • **livid**⁷ [lɪvɪd] adj

» Rigor mortis is well-developed in the cold body and livor mortis is dorsally distributed, cherry-pink in coloration and unfixed. Hypothermic [ɜː] patients who have been exposed to prolonged or extreme cold may appear to be in a state of rigor mortis. Livor mortis can be confused with bruises⁸ [uː]. Fixed lividity darkened the victim's mangled⁹ legs.
Use **rigor mortis** sets in • in a state of / degree of / resolved¹⁰ **rigor mortis** • algor¹¹ **mortis** • cherry-pink / postmortem¹ / fully developed **lividity** • pattern of / fixed / dependent **lividity** • to become **rigid** • postmortem or cadaveric¹² / muscle [mʌsl] **rigidity** • **livid** skin / areas¹³ / scar¹⁴

Totenstarre, Rigor mortis
Toten-, Leichenflecke, Livores¹ bläuliche Hautverfärbung, Lividität² Mangel³ Rigor, Muskelsteifigkeit; Schüttelfrost⁴ steif, starr, unbeweglich, rigid⁵ Rigidität, Steifheit, Starre⁶ livid, (blass)bläulich (verfärbt)⁷ blaue Flecke, Hämatome⁸ verstümmelt⁹ gelöste Totenstarre¹⁰ Algor mortis, Totenkälte¹¹ Rigor mortis¹² livide Bereiche¹³ bläulich verfärbte Narbe¹⁴

15

Death & Mortality   BASIC MEDICAL TERMS 55

morgue [mɔːrg] n
    sim **mortuary**[1] [mɔːrtʃʊɚi], **funeral home** or **parlor**[1] [fjuːnəl pɑːrlɚ] n
facility [sɪ] where the dead are kept before being identified or examined by the medical examiner[2] or before they are released[3] [iː] for burial [e] or cremation[4] [krimeɪʃⁿn]
» A mix-up in the hospital morgue resulted [ʌ] in a woman burying a man she thought was her husband–but was not. Mr Kelly's son, who died from natural causes an hour after delivery, went missing from the hospital mortuary four days before his funeral.
Use body transferred to [ɜː]/ a city / hospital **morgue** • **mortuary** gown[5] [gaʊn]

Leichenschauhaus
Leichenhalle[1] Leichen(be)schauer(in)[2] freigegeben[3] Feuerbestattung, Einäscherung, Kremation[4] Totenkleid[5]

16

burial [beriəl] n syn **interment** [ɜː] n,
    sim **funeral**[1] n, rel **obituary**[2] [-bɪtʃʊɚi] n
the ritual placing of a corpse or cremated ashes in a grave
bury[3] [beri] v • **buried** adj • **burying** n • **inter**[3] v • **funerary**[4] [fjuː-] adj
» The burial takes place on Monday. He is afraid of being buried alive. She'd buried her husband a year earlier. He lies buried over there.
Use **burial** ground[5] [aʊ] • decent [iː] **burial** • to attend[6]/conduct **a funeral** • state **funeral** • **funeral** service[7] / home or parlor / procession[8] [se]/ director[9]

Bestattung, Beerdigung, Beisetzung
Begräbnis[1] Nachruf[2] begraben, beerdigen[3] Begräbnis-[4] Begräbnisstätte, Friedhof[5] einem Begräbnis beiwohnen, an einem Begräbnis teilnehmen[6] Trauergottesdienst[7] Leichenzug[8] Beerdigungsunternehmer[9]

17

casket [kæskɪt] n syn **coffin** [kɒfɪn] n,
    rel **grave**[1] [eɪ], **tomb**[1] [tuːm], **cemetery**[2] [se-] n
box in which a corpse is buried or cremated [kriːmeɪtɪd]
» They lowered the casket into the grave. If you go on smoking you're digging your own grave[3]. It's not the cough that carries you off[4], it's the coffin they carry you off[5] in.
Use to dig[6]/pray at/desecrate[7] [desɪkreɪt] **a grave** • unmarked[8] / mass[9] **grave** • **grave**yard[2] /stone[10] /side /digger[11] • from the cradle [eɪ] to the[12] / to turn in one's **grave** • **tomb**stone[10] • military **cemetery**

Sarg
Grab(stätte)[1] Friedhof[2] sich sein eigenes Grab schaufeln[3] hinwegraffen[4] wegtragen[5] e. Grab ausheben/ schaufeln[6] Grab schänden[7] Grab eines/r Unbekannten[8] Massengrab[9] Grabstein[10] Totengräber[11] von der Wiege bis zur Bahre[12]

18

posthumous [pɒstʃəməs] adj
    sim **postmortem** or **post mortem**[1] adj term & n jar
occurring [ɜː] after a person's death
» His suicide was seen as a means of getting posthumously the affection[2] that was not forthcoming during his lifetime.
Use **posthumous** honors [ɒnɚz]/ publication[3] • **postmortem** changes[4] / delivery / graft • **postmortem** examination[5] / lividity / rigidity • to do a[6] **postmortem**

post(h)um
post mortem, postmortal; Obduktion, Autopsie[1] Zuneigung[2] postume Veröffentlichung[3] postmortale Veränderungen[4] Autopsie, Obduktion[5] eine Obduktion durchführen[6]

19

autopsy [ɒtəpsi] n term syn **postmortem examination, necropsy** n term
examination of the organs of a dead body to determine [ɜː] the cause of death (esp. when death took place under suspicious [ɪʃ] circumstances [sɜː]) or for pathologic study
autopsy[1] v term • autopsic(al) adj • autopsist[2] n • antemortem adj
» The anomaly was only discovered at autopsy. Vasculitis of the coronary arteries is seen in almost all fatal cases of Kawasaki disease that have been autopsied. Atrophy of the cerebellum was evident on gross[3] postmortem inspection of the brain. Renal artery stenosis was found at postmortem. Necropsy revealed cardiac enlargement with mural thrombi [aɪ].
Use to request an/do or perform an[1]/discover at[4] **autopsy** • hospital / epidemiologic / perinatal [eɪ]/ forensic[5] **autopsy** • complete / nondiagnostic **autopsy** • **autopsy** examination[6] / room odor [oʊdɚ]/ material • **autopsy** findings[7] / report[8] / confirmation • **autopsy** pathology / series / tissue / specimen [es] • **autopsy** consent form[9] / permit[10] [ɜː]/ limited to the brain • **autopsied** patient[11] • **post-mortem** dissection[6] / inspection / study[6] / diagnosis • **postmortem** (anatomic) specimen[12] / tissue cultures [ʌ]

Leichenöffnung, Obduktion, Autopsie, Sektion, Nekropsie
eine Obduktion/ Sektion vornehmen, obduzieren[1] Obduzent(in)[2] makroskopisch[3] bei d. Autopsie feststellen[4] gerichtl. Sektion[5] Autopsie, Obduktion, Sektion[6] Obduktionsbefund[7] Obduktionsbericht[8] schriftl. Einverständniserklärung f. d. Obduktion[9] Obduktionsgenehmigung[10] obduzierte(r) Patient(in)[11] Autopsiepräparat[12]

20

coroner [kɔːrⁿnɚ] n rel **medical examiner**[1] n term → U15-21
local official who investigates the causes and circumstances of sudden, violent or unexplained deaths
» Unless demanded by the coroner or medical examiner, an autopsy cannot be performed without the permission of the patient's next of kin[2]. The medical examiner agreed that using rigor mortis to determine the time of death is an inexact formula.
Use to report a case to the **coroner** • **coroner's** investigation or inquest[3] (BE)/ case / office / court / staff / documents • **coroner**-on-call[4]

Leichen(be)schauer(in)
Gerichtsmediziner(in)[1] nächste Angehörige[2] Leichenschau, Totenschau[3] diensthabende(r) Leichenbeschauer(in)[4]

21

Unit 13   Health Care Administration
Related Units: 14 Hospitals, 18 At the Doctor's, 15 Medical Staff & Specialties, 16 Paramedical Staff, 20 Hospital Routines

health care [helθ keɚ] n   sim **health service**[1] [sɜːrvɪs] n
care encompassing social, economic, and environmental influences, in addition to medical care
health-related adj • **self-care**[2] n • **aftercare**[3] [æftɚkeɚ] n
» Newly diagnosed [aɪ] patients were started on a medical regimen [edʒ] and referred [ɜː] to a clinic or private medical care. On-scene [siːn] management of casualties [æʒ] was performed by disaster medical assistance teams[4] consisting of volunteer [ɪɚ] health care and rescue [reskjuː] workers[5].
Use national / quality / professional **health care** • home / primary[6] [aɪ] **health care** • **health care** system[7] [ɪ]/ facility [sɪ]/ administration • **health care** provider [aɪ]/ institution • **health care** organization[8] (abbr HCO)/ policy[9] / plan • **health care** professional / team / costs • primary (acute)[10] / secondary / tertiary [tɜːrʃɚi] **care** • specialized / long-term (abbr LTC)/ uncompensated **care** • **care** program / plan[11] • standard / duty[12] / quality **of care** • National[13] (abbr NHS)/ School / preventive[14] **health service** • **health-related** services • **Health Service** Commissioner or Ombudsman[15] [ɒː]

health authorities [əθɔːrɪtiz] n   rel **health administration**[1] [eɪʃ] n
administrative bodies responsible for organizing health care in a given area
» Most cases of viral [aɪ] meningitis [dʒaɪ] in the U.S. go unreported[2] to public health authorities. If botulism is suspected, the local health authority should be notified[3]. An anxious [kʃ] parent or institutional authority may request a drug screen on an asymptomatic adolescent.
Use public / federal / state / regional[4] [iːdʒ]/ local **health authorities** • emergency [ɜː] medical services / state / child welfare[5] **authorities** • Mental / Occupational Safety and **Health Administration** • **health** agency[6] [eɪdʒ]/ department[7] / official

Public Health Service [pʌblɪk helθ sɜːrvɪs] n, abbr **PHS**
rel **National Institutes of Health**[1] n, abbr **NIH**
nationwide administration of health programs headed by the Department of Health and Human Services[2] (abbr DHHS) which is responsible for government hospitals, publication of sanitary reports, quarantine [ɒː], statistics, medical research, etc.; the NIH, the National Library of Medicine and the Centers for Disease Control[3] (abbr CDC) are associated institutions
» What are the recommendations of the Public Health Service Advisory [aɪ] Committee on diptheria [ɪɚ] and tetanus immunization. This quick reference guide on acute pain management was published by the Agency for Health Care Policy and Research (abbr AHCPR), Public Health Service, U.S. Department of Health and Human Services.
Use United States (abbr USPHS) **Public Health Service** • health care / (routine) clinical **service** • blood transfusion[4] [juːʒ]/ nursing[5] [ɜː]/ food / dietary [aɪə] **service** • community / ambulance[6] / emergency (medicine)[7] **service** • pain / crisis [aɪ] intervention[8] / mental health **service** • supportive / counseling[9] [aʊ] geriatric [dʒerɪ-] **service** • medical social[10] / rehabilitation **service** • Chief [tʃ] of[11] **Service** • **service**-connected disability[12] (abbr SCD) / request • fee [iː]-for-**service** reimbursement[13] [ɜː]

Surgeon General [sɜːrdʒən dʒenɚəl] n term
(i) chief medical officer of the DHHS[1] in the U.S.
(ii) chief of medical services in the armed forces[2]
» The U.S. Surgeon General summarized [ʌ] the immediate [iː] health benefits of smoking cessation[3] [s] that are valid for[4] men and women of all ages. Surgeon General Heaton reported a 2.5% incidence of infection[5] in patients with contaminated[6] battle wounds [uː].
Use U.S. **Surgeon General** • **Surgeon General** of the United States

> **Note:** Mark the difference between a general surgeon[7] and the **Surgeon General**.

Gesundheitsfürsorge
Gesundheitsdienst[1] selbstständige Versorgung u. Gesunderhaltung/ Gesundheitsbewusstsein, -pflege[2] Nachbehandlung, -sorge[3] katastrophenmedizin. Hilfsteams[4] Rettungshelfer[5] med. Grundbetreuung[6] Gesundheitswesen[7] Gesundheitsorganisation[8] Gesundheitspolitik[9] Erstversorgung[10] Pflegeplan[11] Behandlungspflicht[12] staatl. Gesundheitsdienst in GB[13] präventiver Gesundheitsdienst[14] Beschwerdebeauftragter/ Ombudsmann für das Gesundheitswesen[15]   **1**

Gesundheitsbehörden
Gesundheitsverwaltung[1] werden nicht gemeldet[2] verständigt[3] Regionalbehörden d. staatl. brit. Gesundheitsdienstes[4] Jugendwohlfahrtsbehörden[5] Gesundheitseinrichtung[6] Gesundheitsamt, -ministerium[7]   **2**

öffentl. Gesundheitsdienst
®Nationale biologisch-medizinische Forschungseinrichtungen d. U.S. Gesundheitsministeriums[1] U.S. Gesundheits- u. Sozialministerium[2] ®U.S. Seuchenschutzzentren[3] Blutspendedienst[4] Pflegedienst[5] Rettungsdienst[6] Notfalldienst, ärztl. Notdienst[7] Kriseninterventionsdienst[8] Beratungsdienst[9] sozialmed. Dienst[10] Obmann/ Obfrau d. Personalvertretung[11] Invalidität durch einen Arbeitsunfall[12] Vergütung nach Fallpauschalen[13]   **3**

(i) **Leiter(in) d. U.S. Gesundheitswesens,**
(ii) **Generalstabsarzt/-ärztin**
oberster Beamter i. Gesundheitsministerium[1] Streitkräfte[2] Abgewöhnung d. Rauchens[3] gelten für[4] Infektionsrate[5] verunreinigt, kontaminiert[6] Allgemeinchirurg(in)[7]   **4**

HEALTH CARE

Health Care Administration

health insurance [ɪnˈʃʊɚənˈs] n *rel* **Medicare**[1], **Medicaid**[2] [ˈmɛdɪkeɪd] *n term*

insurance covering [ʌ] losses due to ill health

insure[3] *v* • **insurer**[4] *n* • **insured** [ɪnˈʃʊɚd] *adj & n* • **reinsurance**[5] *n*

» Traditional fee-for-service insurance reimburses [ɜː] the hospital and the physician [ɪʃ] for services rendered but frequently does not cover preventive care. Medicare covers approximately 80% of home oxygen expenses. A federal law requires Medicare or Medicaid providers to give their adult patients information on advance directives[6] at the time of initial care.

Use to take out an[7] **insurance** • private / adequate **health insurance** • universal [ɜː] health care **insurance** • hospitalization / professional liability[8] [laɪə-]/ medical malpractice[8] **insurance** • life[9] / trip cancellation[10] [kænsə-]/ evacuation[11] / social[12] **insurance** • **insurance** policy[13] / company[14] / carrier[15] / plan • **insurance** contract[16] / claim • premiums[17] [iː] • **insurance** coverage[18] [kʌvɚɪdʒ] / rate / funds [ʌ]/ physical [ɪ] examination • un/ under**insured**[19] • the **insured**[20] • **Medicare** funds / coverage / reimbursement [ɜː]

> Note: Mark the difference in pronunciation and stress between **to insure** [ɪnˈʃʊɚ] and **to injure** [ˈɪndʒɚ].

(public *or* **social) welfare** [soʊʃəl ˈwɛlfɚ] *n* *rel* **social security**[1] [sɪkjʊɚəti] *n*

economic assistance to persons in need provided by the state or an organization

» The legal [iː] counsel [aʊ] of the welfare department filed [aɪ] a court [ɔː] petition[2] [ɪʃ] for temporary removal of the father of the abuse victim from the home. Huge [hjuːdʒ] surpluses[3] [ɜː] in the US Social Security system are supposed to finance [aɪ] the deficit.

Use to be on[4] **welfare** • **welfare** state / benefits[5] / authorities • **welfare** officer / policy / work • Department of Health, Education and[6] **Welfare** • **child welfare** consultation / authorities / personnel[7] • **Social Security** administration / days / payments[8] / statistics • **social** services • insurance[9] / support (system) • **social** agency [eɪdʒ]/ medicine[10] • **social** network[11] / life / functioning • **social** contacts / independence • **social** conflicts / maladjustment[12] [dʒʌ] • **social** isolation / diseases[13] / stigma

health maintenance [ˈmeɪntənənˈs] **organization** *n term, abbr* **HMO**

prepaid system of health care to individuals and families enrolled on a voluntary basis which offers continuity of care by member physicians[1] and limited referral[2] [ɜː] to outside specialists

» The federal Patient Self-Determination Act[3] requires hospitals and HMOs to inform patients of their right to make health care decisions [sɪ] and to provide advance directives.

Use routine [iː]/ appropriate **health maintenance** • preferred [ɜː] provider[4] (*abbr* PPO) **organization** • **health maintenance** needs / care / visit[5] / measures [eʒ]

managed care [ˈmænɪdʒd keɚ] *n term*

health care system in which redundant[1] [ʌ] services are eliminated and costs are minimized by administrative control[2] over medical services[3] provided in a health care facility[4]

» By 1995, about 20% of the U.S. population was in managed care plans, and in some parts of the U.S. the enrollment[5] [oʊ] was above 50 percent.

Use **managed care** organization (*abbr* MCO)/ plan (*abbr* MCP)

Food and Drug Administration *n term, abbr* **FDA**

U.S. agency of the DHHS responsible for the purity[1] and wholesomeness[2] of foods, effectiveness and safety of drugs, therapeutic devices [aɪ], and cosmetics as well as their correct packaging[3] and labeling[4]

» In the USA, regulations for collecting, storing, and transporting blood and its components are established by the FDA. The tool [uː] was FDA-approved [uː] in 1988 and is currently [ɜː] undergoing FDA trials[5] [traɪəlz] of gallstone [ɔː] lithotripsy[6] [ɪ].

Use U.S. **Food and Drug Administration** • **FDA**-approved[7] / regulations / study group • **FDA** patient data collection / adverse [ɜː] drug reaction monitoring program[8] / warning

---

Krankenversicherung
U.S. Krankenversicherung bes. f. Senioren[1] U.S. Gesundheitsfürsorgeprogramm f. Bedürftige[2] versichern (lassen)[3] Versicherer, Versicherungsgesellschaft, -geber[4] Rückversicherung[5] Patiententestament[6] eine Versicherung abschließen[7] Arzthaftpflichtversicherung[8] Lebensversicherung[9] Reiserücktrittsversicherung[10] Rückholversicherung[11] Sozialversicherung[12] Versicherungspolice, -schein[13] Versicherungsgesellschaft[14] Versicherungsträger[15] Versicherungsvertrag[16] Versicherungsbeiträge, -prämien[17] Versicherungsschutz[18] unterversichert[19] d. Versicherte, Versicherungsnehmer(in)[20] 5

Fürsorge, Wohlfahrt
Sozialhilfe[1] e. Antrag bei Gericht einreichen[2] Überschüsse[3] Sozialhilfe beziehen[4] Sozialleistungen, -hilfe[5] US Ministerium f. Gesundheitswesen, Ausbildung u. Wohlfahrt[6] Kinderfürsorger(innen)[7] Sozialhilfeleistungen, Sozialbeiträge[8] Sozialversicherung[9] Sozialmedizin[10] soziales Netz[11] Verhaltensstörung[12] (sozial) stigmatisierte Erkrankungen[13] 6

®private Krankenversicherungsorganisation
HMO-Vertragsärzte[1] Überweisung[2] ®Verordnung z. Selbstbestimmungsrecht v. Patienten[3] ®bevorzugte med. Versorgungsorganisation[4] Vorsorgeuntersuchung[5] 7

®Managed Care
nicht zwingend erforderlich[1] verwaltungstechnisches Management[2] med. Versorgung[3] Gesundheitseinrichtung[4] Beteiligung[5] 8

®U.S. Arznei- u. Lebensmittelbehörde
Reinheit[1] Bekömmlichkeit[2] Verpackung[3] Kennzeichnung[4] FDA-Studien[5] Cholelithotripsie, Gallensteinzertrümmerung[6] von d. FDA zugelassen[7] FDA-Überwachungsprogramm v. unerwünschten Nebenwirkungen[8] 9

58 HEALTH CARE

Cancer Registry [kænˈsɚ redʒɪstri] *n term* *syn* **tumor registry** *n term*

central agency collecting data on the prevalence[1] and/or incidence[2] of specific malignancies[3]

» *The problem is that there is no nationwide cancer registry[4]. The National Nosocomial Infections Surveillance Registry has been monitoring nosocomial infection[5] rates since 1970.*

Use trauma [ɒː]/ multicenter / national / state-wide[6] **registry** • Testicular Tumor Panel and / International Bone Marrow Transplant[7] / Organ Replacement[8] **Registry** • **Registry of** Myocardial [maɪə-] Infarction

World Health Organization *n term, abbr* **WHO** *or* **OMS** *(French)*

United Nations agency based in Geneva (SUI) that is concerned with promoting worldwide health standards and regulations, coordinating international cooperation and research, epidemiologic studies[1], etc.

» *Since the start of the WHO eradication[2] [eɪʃ] program, the number of infected persons has declined [aɪ] by 97%. The WHO list of reportable diseases[3] is widely regarded as a satisfactory minimum.*

Use Pan American (*abbr* PAHO) **Health Organization** • **WHO** guidelines[4] [aɪ]/ certificate / formulation / classification • **WHO** recommendations[5] / criteria [kraɪtɪɚɪə] • **WHO** grading [eɪ] system / expert committee • **WHO** case-control study[6] / scientific group[7] / workshop report

International [æʃ] **Red Cross** *n term, abbr* **IRC**

worldwide humanitarian organization founded to relieve human suffering of victims of war and calamity[1]; volunteers make a major contribution to many of its activities, e.g. collection of blood donations[2], public health and community programs such as maternity courses[3]

» *Various disaster relief [iː] organizations[4], e.g. the IRC, the Salvation [eɪʃ] Army[5], and various private or nonprofit organizations[6] provide assistance in the form of shelter[7], food, clothing, and services to victims. The American National Red Cross and the American Heart Association teach CPR techniques[8] both to lay [leɪ] persons[9] and to paramedical professionals.*

Use (national) American / regional **Red Cross** • **IRC** Society[10] [saɪ] • **Red Cross** organization / Blood Center[11] / Children's Hospital

American Medical Association [æsoʊsieɪʃ(ə)n] *n term, abbr* **AMA**
rel **Infectious Diseases Society** [səsaɪəti] **of America**[1] *n term, abbr* **IDSA**

professional association of licensed physicians[2] in the U.S.

» *The AMA guidelines define domestic violence[3] as "an ongoing, debilitating experience of physical, psychologic, and/or sexual abuse[4] in the home, associated with increasing isolation from the outside world and limited personal freedom and accessibility to resources."*

Use **AMA** Council on Scientific Affairs / Guidelines for Adolescent Preventive Services (*abbr* GAPS) • **AMA** Handbook of Poisonous and Injurious Plants[5] • British Medical[6] (*abbr* BMA)/ California Medical **Association** • American Urologic (*abbr* AUA) **Association** • British Pediatric / British Dental (*abbr* BDA) **Association** • American Dental[7] (*abbr* ADA)/ New York Heart (*abbr* NYHA) **Association** • American Nurses'[8] (*abbr* ANA)/ Visiting Nurse (*abbr* VNA) **Association** • **Association of** Poison Control Centers • Undersea Medical / International Continence (*abbr* ICS)/ American Cancer[9] (*abbr* ACS) **Society** • Canadian Pediatric / Child Neurology **Society** • **Society of** Critical Care Medicine / Pediatric Oncology

Medical Board [medɪkəl bɔːrd] *n term*
rel **General Medical Council**[1] [kaʊnˈsəl] *n term BE, abbr* **GMC**

the state agency that licenses[2] [aɪs] MDs, investigates complaints [eɪ], disciplines[3] those who violate [aɪə] the law[4], conducts physician evaluations, and facilitates rehabilitation

» *The Medical Board of California performs similar functions [ʌ] for affiliated healing [iː] arts professions[5] such as registered dispensing opticians[6] [ɪʃ], licensed midwives[7] [ɪ], and research psychoanalysts [saɪkoʊ-]. The GMC licenses doctors to practice medicine in the UK, protects patient's rights, fosters[8] good medical practice, promotes a high standard of medical education, and deals with doctors whose fitness to practice is in doubt [daʊt].*

Use North Carolina / State of Ohio / Arkansas State / New South Wales / Veterinary **Medical Board** • **Medical Board** of California • Australian / South African / Singapore **Medical Council** • **Medical Council of** Canada / New Zealand / India

---

Krebsregister
Prävalenz[1] Inzidenz[2] bösartige Tumoren[3] nationales Krebsregister[4] Krankenhaus-, Nosokomialinfektion[5] US-bundesstaatl. Register[6] Internat. Register für Knochenmarktransplantationen[7] Register f. Organtransplantationen[8]   10

Weltgesundheitsorganisation
epidemiolog. Studien[1] Ausrottung[2] meldepflichtige Krankheiten[3] WHO-Richtlinien[4] Empfehlungen der WHO[5] von der WHO durchgeführte Fallkontrollstudie[6] WHO-Forschungsgruppe[7]

11

Internationales Komitee des Roten Kreuzes
Katastrophe[1] Blutspenden[2] Geburtsvorbereitungskurse[3] Katastrophenhilfsorganisationen[4] Heilsarmee[5] gemeinnützige Organisationen[6] Unterkunft[7] Reanimationstechniken[8] Laien[9] Rot-Kreuz-Gesellschaft[10] Blutspendedienst d. Roten Kreuzes[11]   12

®Amerik. Ärzteverband
®Amerikanische Gesellschaft für Infektionskrankeiten[1] approbierte Ärzte[2] Gewalt i. d. Familie[3] sexueller Missbrauch[4] AMA-Handbuch d. Giftpflanzen u. pflanzl. Schadstoffe[5] Brit. Ärzteverband[6] ®Amerikanischer Zahnärzteverband[7] ®Amerikanischer Krankenschwesternverband[8] ®Amerikanische/ US-Krebsgesellschaft[9]

13

U.S. Ärztekammer
Brit. Ärztekammer[1] approbieren[2] zur Rechenschaft ziehen[3] das Gesetz verletzen, widerrechtlich handeln[4] nichtärztliche Heilberufe[5] Augenoptiker[6] staatl. geprüfte Hebammen/ Geburtshelfer(innen)[7] fördert[8]

14

Unit 14 Hospitals & Medical Facilities

Related Units: 13 Health Care Administration, 15 Medical Staff, 16 Nurses, 20 Hospital Routines

hospital [hɒːspɪtᵊl] n   syn **medical center** [mɛdɪkᵊl sɛntɚ] n

health facility [sɪ] or medical institution where the sick or injured receive medical or surgical treatment

hospitalize[1] v • **hospitalization**[2] n term • **hospitalism**[3] n term • **prehospital**[4] adj

» Patients with first-degree [iː] burns [3ː] may be discharged [tʃ] from the hospital[5] after a short period of observation. No benefit of hypertonic saline [eɪ] was demonstrated for in-hospital resuscitations[6] [ʌs]. The patient must be moved to a medical center that has an artificial [ɪʃ] kidney program[7].

Use to send to/admit sb. to[1] *(the)* **hospital** • general[8] / specialty / teaching[9] **hospital** • university / state / private **hospital** • army[10] / urban [3ː]/ city / country [ʌ] **hospital** • field[11] / accredited / acute (care)[12] **hospital** • affiliated / AHA-registered / certified [3ː] **hospital** • chronic disease / closed-staff **hospital** • children's[13] / sole community *(abbr SCH)* **hospital** • day (care)[14] / night / hotel[15]-/ rehabilitation **hospital** • maternity[16] [3ː]/ psychiatric [saɪk-] **hospital** • long-term[17] / in-/ out-of **hospital** • community health[8] *(abbr CHC)*/ drug treatment **center** • burn / cancer [ˈs] / retirement [aɪ] **center** • trauma [ɒː]/ childbirth or birthing[16] [3ː] **center** • stone / free-standing emergency [3ː] *(abbr FEC)* **center** • **hospital** stay[18] / day / facilities [fəsɪlətiːz]/ bed • **hospital** setting / environment [aɪ]/ diet / nursing [3ː] care / air • **hospital**-acquired [aɪ] infection[19] / course / attendant[20] • **hospital** administration / birth certificate / mortality rate • **prehospital** care[21] / treatment / phase [feɪz]/ transport

> Note: In *AmE* a patient is **in the hospital** while in *BE* a patient is **in hospital**.

clinic n   sim **outpatient department**[1] n term, abbr **OPD**
        ambulatory care center[1] n term, rel **infirmary**[2] [3ː] n

(i) health facility providing [aɪ] outpatient care or group practice run by several specialists [ef]
(ii) medical instruction held at the bedside or cases presented to physicians with discussion

(pre)clinical [priːklɪnɪkᵊl] adj term • **clinician**[3] [klɪnɪʃᵊn] n • **clinico-** comb

» Neck pain is a common complaint in most outpatient clinics. Most of these patients can be treated in the clinic, but a few severe refractory[4] cases may require treatment in the hospital under anesthesia [iː3]. Dr. Pit will hold a clinic on the subject next week. The infirmary is the place to go to have ticks[5] removed or headaches and other minor problems handled.

Use free / pain[6] / walk-in[7] / venereal [ɪɚ] disease *(abbr VDC)*/ group[8] **clinic** • quit-smoking[9] / maternal [3ː] and infant care[10] **clinic** • volunteers in medicine *(abbr VIM)* **clinic** • outpatient clinic[1] / facility / service / care / treatment[11] • outpatient follow-up[12] / visit / contact • ambulatory clinic[1] (visit) / care[13] system • ambulatory patient[14] / ECG (monitoring) / surgery [3ː] (center) • clinical test / cases / course[15] / findings[16] • clinical picture[17] / suspicion [ɪʃ]/ features[18] [fiːtʃɚz] / trial[19] [aɪ] • experienced **clinician** • **clinico**pathologic • school / campus / prison **infirmary** • Eye and Ear / Leeds General **Infirmary** • **infirmary** room[20] / report

sanatorium or **sanitarium** n   rel **skilled nursing facility**[1] n term, abbr **SNF**

hospital for recuperation[2] [k(j)uː] or posthospital treatment of chronic diseases, esp. in combination with dietary [daɪətɚi] or exercise regimens[3] [rɛdʒɪmənz]

» The sanatorium is not equipped to handle major [meɪdʒɚ] medical problems. She took a medical cure [kjʊɚ] at a sanatorium. The insurance will pay for care in a hospital and a SNF, and for home health and hospice care. After each injection [dʒɛ] visit you have to remain at the treatment facility [sɪ] for at least 30 minutes.

Use private [aɪ]/ TB[4] **sanatorium** • **sanatorium** doctor / treatment • Medicaid / (non-)hospice **SNF** • **SNF** care / services[5] / resident • **SNF** administrator / rates[6] / reimbursement[7] [3ː] / day[8] / acute *(abbr ACF)*/ intermediate [iː] *(abbr ICF)* **care facility** • chronic[9] / long-term **care facility** • hospital / dialysis [daɪælɪsɪs]/ health care[10] **facilities** • outpatient / psychiatric [saɪk-]/ x-ray[11] [ɛksreɪ] **facilities** • toilet / sanitary[12] • free-standing **facilities** • supportive / independent living *(abbr ILF)* **facilities**

Krankenhaus, Klinik, Hospital, Spital

ins Krankenhaus einweisen/ -liefern, stationär aufnehmen, hospitalisieren[1] Krankenhauseinweisung, stationäre Aufnahme, Hospitalisierung[2] Hospitalismus[3] präklinisch[4] aus d. Krankenhaus entlassen[5] Reanimation[6] Dialyseeinheit, -programm[7] allgem. Krankenhaus[8] Lehrkrankenhaus[9] Militärkrankenhaus, -spital, Lazarett[10] Feldlazarett, -spital[11] Akutkrankenhaus[12] Kinderkrankenhaus[13] Tagesklinik[14] Hostel[15] Entbindungsanstalt, -heim, Geburtsklinik[16] Langzeitkrankenhaus[17] Krankenhausaufenthalt[18] Nosokomialinfektion, nosokomiale Infektion[19] Krankenpfleger(in)[20] präklin. Versorgung/ Betreuung[21]

1

(i) Poliklinik, Ambulanz, Ambulatorium
(ii) klin. Unterricht, Klinikum

Ambulanz[1] Krankenzimmer, -station; Krankenhaus *(BE)*[2] Kliniker(in)[3] hartnäckig, therapieresistent[4] Zecken[5] Ambulanz m. Behandlung ohne Voranmeldung[6] Schmerzklinik[7] Gemeinschaftspraxis, Ärztehaus[8] Raucherentwöhnungsseminar[9] Mütterberatung[10] ambulante Behandlung[11] ambulante Nachsorge[12] ambulante Betreuung[13] gehfähige(r) Patient(in)[14] klin. Verlauf[15] klin. Befund[16] klin. Bild, Krankheitsbild[17] klin. Symptome[18] klin. Studie[19] Krankenzimmer[20]

2

Sanatorium, Genesungsheim, (Lungen)heilstätte

Pflegeheim[1] Genesung, Erholung[2] therapeut. Übungen, Krankengymnastik[3] Lungenheilstätte[4] Pflegedienste[5] Pflegesätze[6] Pflegekostenrückerstattung[7] Tagesklinik, -heim[8] Pflegeheim/ Krankenheim f. chronisch Kranke[9] medizin. Einrichtungen, Gesundheitseinrichtungen[10] Röntgeneinrichtungen[11] sanitäre Einrichtungen/ Anlagen[12]

3

HEALTH CARE

hospice [hɒːspɪs] n → U12-1f   rel nursing home¹ [nɜːrsɪŋ hoʊm] n

health facility or program providing palliative and supportive care for the terminally [ɜː] ill²

» Many patients prefer to be cared for in their homes or in a hospice setting rather than a hospital. Only 20% of people over age 85 reside [aɪ] in a nursing home.

Use free-standing **hospice** • **hospice** care³ / medicine / facility • **hospice** support / team / nurse [ɜː]/ volunteer [ɪɚ] • **nursing home** stay / care / resident⁴ • **nursing home** placement⁵ / admission • rest or old people's⁶ / foster or adoptive⁷ / funeral⁸ [fjuː] **home**

Sterbeklinik, Hospiz

Pflegeheim¹ Patienten i. Endstadium, Terminalkranke² Sterbebegleitung, -betreuung³ Pflegeheimbewohner(in)⁴ Einweisung ins Pflegeheim⁵ Alters-, Seniorenheim⁶ Kinderheim⁷ Leichenhalle⁸

4

mental institution [mentᵊl ɪnstɪt(j)uːʃᵊn] n   syn psychiatric [saɪkɪætrɪk] hospital, (mental) asylum [əsaɪləm] n → U77-24

medical facility for providing care and treatment for mentally incompetent or unbalanced clients [aɪ]

(de)institutionalize¹ v term • institutionalism² n • hospitalism² n

» Decide whether to start procedures for involuntary commitment³ to a mental institution. The disadvantages of psychiatric hospitalization⁴ include decreased self-confidence⁵, the stigma of being a "psychiatric patient", possible increased dependency⁶ and regression⁷. If inpatient care⁸ is needed, units that are divisions of general hospitals and those in psychiatric hospitals are equally effective.

Use **mental** hospital⁹ / home⁹ • closed¹⁰ **hospital** • pediatric • educational¹¹ **institution** • **institution** for mental diseases⁹ (abbr IMD)/ of therapy¹² • **psychiatric** patient / disorder¹³ / emergency service • **psychiatric** hold³ / hospitalization / practice • **psychiatric** nursing / inpatient unit¹⁴ / outpatient treatment¹⁵ • **psychiatric** home care / social worker (abbr PSW) • **mental** patient / disorder¹⁶ / confusion¹⁷ [juː] • **mental** clarity [eɚ]/ disability or handicap¹⁸ • **institutional** care⁸ (facility) • to become **institutionalized** • **institutionalized** elderly / children • *insane⁹ [eɪ] or *lunatic⁹ [uː] **asylum** • **asylum** for the mentally ill⁹

Note: Among the numerous colloquial expressions, which mostly have a negative connotation, the most widely used ones are: **sanatorium**, *funny farm*, *mad-house*, *nuthouse*, *(loony) bin*, *booby hatch*, and *cuckoo's nest*.

Nervenheilanstalt, psychiatrische Klinik

in e. Heim/ Anstalt einweisen; institutionalisieren¹ Hospitalismus² Zwangseinweisung³ stationäre Aufnahme⁴ Selbstvertrauen, -bewusstsein⁵ Abhängigkeit⁶ Regression⁷ stationäre Betreuung/ Pflege⁸ Nervenheilanstalt, psychiatr. Klinik⁹ geschlossene Anstalt¹⁰ Erziehungsanstalt¹¹ Therapieeinleitung, -beginn¹² psychiatrische Störung¹³ psychiatr. Station¹⁴ ambulante psychiatr. Behandlung¹⁵ psychische Störung, Geisteskrankheit¹⁶ geistige Verwirrtheit¹⁷ geistige Behinderung¹⁸

5

emergency [ɪmɜːrdʒənˈsi] room or department n, abbr ER or ED   syn casualty [kæʒʊəlti] (department) n BE → U6-12,18

hospital area equipped and staffed to treat patients or trauma victims requiring urgent care

emergency¹ n • casualty² n • multicasualty³ adj

» On arrival in the ER, a reliable IV route was established⁴, and blood drawn⁵ for enzyme [aɪ] analysis. The patient was evaluated by an obstetrician⁶ [ɪʃ] before being discharged⁷ from the emergency department. If a doctor treats a patient while performing normal duties in the ER or as part of the responding "crash cart" team⁸ in a hospital, the Good Samaritan statute does not apply.

Use hospital / pediatric [iː] **ED** • **emergency** center / measures⁹ [eʒ]/ care / call¹⁰ • **emergency** management¹¹ / medical service¹² (abbr EMS)/ physician¹³ [ɪʃ] • accident and emergency¹⁴ (A&E)/ hospital / clinical / surgical¹⁵ **department** • records / central supply [aɪ]/ radiology or x ray¹⁶ **department** • **Department of** Pediatrics / Urology • mass **casualty** incident¹⁷ • arriving / bomb / military¹⁸ **casualties** • **multicasualty** event

Unfallstation, Notaufnahme

Notfall¹ (Unfall)opfer, Verletzte(r); Unfallstation (BE)² Katastrophen-³ venöser Zugang wurde gelegt⁴ Blut abgenommen⁵ Geburtshelfer(in)⁶ entlassen⁷ Notarztteam⁸ Notmaßnahmen⁹ Notruf¹⁰ Not(fall)behandlung¹¹ Notfalldienst, Notdienst¹² Notarzt/-ärztin¹³ allgemeine Notaufnahme/ Unfallambulanz¹⁴ chirurg. Abteilung¹⁵ radiolog. Abteilung¹⁶ Massenunfall¹⁷ Kriegsverletzte, Gefallene¹⁸

6

intensive care unit n term, abbr ICU   syn critical care unit n term → U125-1f

hospital facility equipped with sophisticated monitoring and resuscitative [sʌs] equipment¹ and staffed for high-quality continuous nursing and medical supervision of critically ill patients

» Patients who show no favorable response to aggressive therapy should be hospitalized in an intensive care unit. Transport the patient to an ICU with one-on-one nursing².

Use medical / surgical / prenatal [eɪ]/ neonatal³ [iː] (abbr NICU) **intensive care unit** • patient (abbr PCU)/ transitional [ɪʃ] (abbr TCU) **care unit** • extended (abbr ECU) / special **care unit** • (mobile) coronary⁴ (abbr MCCU) **care unit** • **ICU** admission⁵ / patient / setting / management • ambulatory / tropical disease / EMS⁶ **unit** • paramedic⁷ / psychiatric / neurological **unit** • trauma⁸ / burn [ɜː]/ hematology **unit** • preoperative holding⁹ / ambulatory surgery **unit** • advanced life support **unit** • cardiac surveillance [eɪ]/ dialysis¹⁰ [æ]/ tuberculosis **unit** • intermediate [iː] (medical) care / intensive observation¹¹ **unit**

Intensivstation

Reanimationsausrüstung, -geräte¹ Einzelpflege, individuelle Pflege² Neugeborenenintensivstation³ kardiolog. Intensivstation⁴ Aufnahme in d. Intensivstation⁵ notärztliches Team⁶ Arzthelfer-, Sanitäterteam⁷ Frischverletztenstation⁸ Wartebereich (vor OP-Schleuse)⁹ Dialysestation¹⁰ Intensivbeobachtungsstation, IBS¹¹

7

Hospitals & Medical Facilities   HEALTH CARE **61**

newborn nursery [n(j)uːbɔːrn nɜːrsəri] n

hospital section where newborn infants are taken care of

nurse[1] [nɜːrs] n & v • **nursling**[2] n • **nursing**[3] adj • **nursing**[4] n → U16-2

» The single most important principle in nursery infection control is good hand washing. Otitis [oʊtaɪtɪs] media[5] [iː] may be present in a significant number of long-term nursery residents. Rooming-in promotes [oʊ] breast [e] feeding while bottle supplements[6] [ʌ] in the nursery at night undermine[7] [aɪ] it.

Use well-baby[8] / transitional [ɪʃ]/ intensive care / level 2 / level 3 **nursery** • **nursery** staff or personnel[9] / care / epidemic • **nursery**-acquired [aɪ] pneumonia [n(j)uː-]/ infection rate / outbreak • day[10] **nursery** • **nursery** school[11] / rhyme [aɪ] • **nursing** mother[12] / infant • bra(ssiere)[13] • **nursing** diarrhea [iː]/ bottle (caries)[14] [keəriːz]/ home[15] (BE) / wet[16] **nurse**

Säuglingsstation, -zimmer, Neugeborenenstation
Krankenschwester, -pfleger; pflegen[1] Säugling; Pflegekind[2] stillend[3] Krankenpflege[4] Mittelohrentzündung[5] zusätzl. Flaschennahrung, Zufüttern[6] untergräbt[7] allgem. Säuglingsstation[8] Kinderschwestern[9] Kindertagesstätte, Kinderhort, -krippe[10] Kindergarten[11] stillende Mutter[12] Still-BH[13] Flaschenkaries[14] priv. Entbindungsklinik, Privatklinik; Pflegeheim[15] Amme[16]   8

radiology suite [reɪdɪŋːlədʒi swiːt] n term → U99-1f
                                                    rel **section**[1], **division**[2] [ɪʒ] n

series of connected rooms in a medical facility equipped for radiographic diagnosis and/or treatment

» The patient is then moved from the radiology suite to an operating room that has fluoroscopic capabilities. The room temperature in the delivery suite[3] should be raised (esp. for infants weighing < 1500 g). He's professor and chairman of the Division of Neurosurgery [ɜː].

Use surgical or operating[4] / obstetrical[3] **suite** • labor-delivery-recovery-postpartum[3] (abbr LDRPS) **suite** • ultrasonography[5] / endoscopy **suite** • bronchoscopy [kɒ]/ trauma[6] [ɒː]/ urologic **suite** • **Section of** Genetics / Pulmonary [ʊ‖ʌ] Medicine • **Division of** Vascular Surgery[7] / Orthopedic [iː] Trauma • **Division of** Plastic and Reconstructive [ʌ] Surgery[8] • **Division of** Gynecologic [gaɪn‖dʒɪnɪkə-] Oncology / Infectious Diseases

radiologische Abteilung
Abteilung, Trakt[1] Abteilung, Institut[2] Entbindungsstation, -abteilung[3] Operationstrakt[4] Ultraschallraum[5] Schockraum, Frischverletztenambulanz[6] Abteilung für Gefäßchirurgie[7] Abteilung für Plastische u. Wiederherstellungschirurgie[8]

9

quarantine ward or **station** [kwɔːrəntiːn wɔːrd] n term
                                            rel **isolation**[1] [aɪsəleɪʃən] n term → U94-1ff; U139-9ff

facility for isolating [aɪ] persons with highly contagious[2] [eɪdʒ] diseases (e.g. Lassa fever[3]) [iː] quarantine (off)[4] v term • quarantinable[5] adj • isolate[6] v & n • isolette[7] n

» As a well-trained pathologist she knew the quarantine would not be lifted[8]. All patients must be managed under conditions of strict barrier isolation. Reassure [ʃ] the patient that it's the pathogen, not the person, that is being isolated.

Use to be in/establish[9]/put sb. in[4] **quarantine** • detention in / involuntary / full-scale[10] **quarantine** • **quarantine** facility / hospital / ship / period[11] • **quarantine** measures[12] [eʒ]/ officer / procedure [siː] • **quarantined** patient • **quarantinable** disease[13] • contact[14] / respiratory / protective[15] **isolation** • patient / disease-specific **isolation** • **isolation** precautions [ɒː]/ room / from peers[16] [ɪə] • infant placed in an **isolette**

Quarantäne-, Isolierstation
Isolierung[1] hochinfektiös[2] Lassa-Fieber[3] unter Quarantäne stellen, isolieren[4] quarantänepflichtig[5] isolieren; Isolat[6] Brutkasten[7] aufgehoben[8] Quarantäne verhängen[9] strenge/ vollkommene Isolierung[10] Quarantänezeit[11] Quarantänemaßnahmen[12] quarantänepflichtige Krankheit[13] Isolierung[14] protektive Isolierung[15] Isolierung v. Gleichaltrigen/ Kollegen[16]

10

tissue typing laboratory [tɪʃjuː‖tɪsjuː taɪpɪŋ læbrətɔːri] n term → U136-10
                                                    sim **path lab**[1] [pæθ læb] n jar → U116-1

room or unit equipped for the performance of tests, and investigative procedures and for the preparation of reagents [eɪdʒ], etc. used in the identification of tissue types, esp. for evaluating compatibility[2] of tissues from a donor[3] [oʊ] and a recipient[4] [sɪ] before transplantation

» A battery of screening laboratory tests cannot substitute [ʌ] for[5] a thorough[6] initial [ɪʃ] evaluation. Take the specimen[7] to the lab and ask for a complete tumor tissue type as soon as possible. Which role does the toxicology lab have in the treatment of acute poisoning?

Use clinical / bacteriology[8] / microbiology / toxicology **laboratory** • pathology[1] / venereal [ɪə] disease research (VDRL) **laboratory** • catheterization / maximum containment [eɪ] **laboratory** • forensic[9] / central / sleep[10] **laboratory** • **laboratory** tests or examinations[11] / data / workup[11] / diagnosis • **laboratory** findings[12] / values[13] / technician[14] [ɪʃ]/ techniques [iː] • tissue specimen / culture [ʌ] **sent to the lab** • **lab** work[15] / study / tests[11] / report[16]

HLA-Labor
Pathologielabor[1] Verträglichkeit[2] Spender(in)[3] Empfänger(in)[4] ersetzen[5] gründlich[6] Gewebeprobe[7] bakteriolog. Labor[8] gerichtsmedizin. Labor[9] Schlafforschungslabor[10] Labordiagnostik[11] Laborbefund(e)[12] Laborwerte[13] (med. techn.) Laborassistent(in)[14] Laboruntersuchungen[15] Laborbericht[16]

11

HEALTH CARE

blood bank [blʌd bæŋk] *n term* → U136-15f

hospital unit or free-standing[1] facility [sɪ] in which blood is collected from donors, typed[2], stored and/or prepared for transfusion [juː3] to recipients [sɪ]

bank[3] *v term* • **blood banking** *n* • **banked**[4] *adj*

» Most hospitals have a blood bank program whereby the patient can donate [oʊ] blood[5] prior [praɪɚ] to admission to replace the units[6] used. A clotted sample of the patient's blood should be sent to the blood bank for retyping and cross-matching[7].

Use hospital-based / regional / commercial [ɜː]/ community **blood bank** • tissue[8] [tɪʃ‖sjuː]/ skin[9] / bone[10] **bank** • sperm[11] [ɜː]/ eye[12] / stroke [oʊ] data **bank** • **blood bank** procedure / technology specialist[13] • **blood bank** services[14] / physician [fɪzɪʃᵊn]/ support • **blood bank** immunohematology / and donor center • **banked** blood[6] / serum [ɪɚ]/ plasma[15] • **bank** blood • autologous blood[16] / tissue[17] / skin **banking**

Blutbank, Blutdepot

eigenständig[1] Blutgruppe bestimmt[2] konservieren u. lagern[3] konserviert[4] Blut spenden[5] Blutkonserve(n)[6] Durchführung einer Kreuzprobe[7] Gewebebank[8] Hautbank[9] Knochenbank[10] Samenbank[11] Augenbank[12] Blutbanktechniker(in)[13] Blutspendedienst[14] Plasmakonserve[15] Herstellung v. Eigenblutkonserven[16] Zell-, Gewebekonservierung[17]

12

Unit 15 Medical Staff & Specialties
Related Units: 14 Hospitals, 18 At the Doctor's, 16 Nurses & Paramedical Staff

physician [fɪzɪʃᵊn] *n clin & term*   *syn* **(medical) doctor, MD, Dr.** *n*, **doc** *n inf*

(i) person trained at a college of medicine who is licensed [aɪs] to practice medicine[1]
(ii) practitioner [ɪʃ] of medicine[2], as contrasted with a surgeon[3] [sɜːrdʒᵊn] → U131-5

physic[4] [fɪzɪk] *n* • **physics**[5] [ɪ] *n* • **doctorate**[6] [dɒːktɚət] *n* • **doctoral** *adj*

» These patients should be referred[7] [ɜː] to their primary physician for outpatient follow-up[8]. The doctor said it would never get better by itself and could lead to arthritis [aɪ]. Doc, I hardly eat anything. This section was contributed by Mary T. Holmes, MD.

Use to seek [iː] help from/present to/visit[9]/consult [ʌ] **a physician** • primary [aɪ] (care)[10] (*abbr* PCP)/ house[11] (*BE*)/ family[10] (practice) **physician** • board-certified[12] [ɜː]/ office-based / woman / salaried **physician** • full-time / contract[13] / treating [iː] or attending[14] / referring[15] [ɜː] **physician** • specialty care (*abbr* SPC) / emergency[16] [ɜː] (*abbr* EP)/ chest [tʃ]/ osteopathic / general[17] **physician** • **physician's** private office / assistant (*abbr* P.A.) • **physician**-directed / on call[18] / to see[9]/call **a doctor** • family[10] / country [ʌ] **doctor** • **doctor**-patient relationship[19] • **doctor's** office[20] / bill / duty / signature • **Doctor of** Medicine or Medical Doctor (*abbr* MD)/ Philosophy (*abbr* PhD) • **doctoral** thesis[21] [iː]/ candidate

Note: Mark the difference between **physician** and **physicist**[22]. **Physical** can refer to both the body (e.g. physical [ɪ] fitness) or to physics (e.g. physical laws[23]).

Arzt, Ärztin

(in diesem Kapitel wird zur besseren Übersichtlichkeit Arzt für beide Formen verwendet)
d. Arztberuf ausüben[1] innere Medizin[2] Chirurg(in)[3] Arzneimittel, Medikament, Abführmittel[4] Physik[5] Doktorat, Doktortitel[6] überwiesen[7] ambulante Nachsorge[8] einen Arzt aufsuchen[9] Hausarzt, prakt. Arzt[10] ®PJ-Student(in), Turnusarzt (öst.) im 1. Turnusjahr (interne Abt.)[11] approbierter Arzt[12] Vertragsarzt[13] behandelnder Arzt[14] überweisender Arzt[15] Notarzt[16] Allgemeinmediziner(in)[17] diensthabender Arzt[18] Arzt-Patient-Beziehung[19] (Arzt)praxis[20] Doktorarbeit[21] Physiker(in)[22] physikalische Gesetze[23]

1

medical staff [stæf‖*BE* stɑːf] *n*   *rel* **hospital staff**[1] *n*

physicians, residents, physician's assistants, and interns employed by a medical facility [sɪ]

staff[2] *v* • **(well-/under)staffed**[3] *adj* • **staffing**[4] *n*

» Staff members hurrying [ɜː] by who are calling to each other can be extremely disturbing [ɜː] to an acutely ill patient. At least one physician on duty[5] in the emergency [ɜː] care area is available [eɪ] within 30 minutes through a medical staff call roster[6] [ɒː].

Use to be on the[7] **staff** • open / closed / active / associate [oʊʃ]/ honorary [ɒː] **medical staff** • provisional [ɪʒ]/ president of the **medical staff** • health care / professional / in-service[8] **staff** • OR / emergency department / intensive care[9] / obstetric **staff** • laboratory / nursing[10] [ɜː]/ office / senior[11] [iː]/ chief of **staff** • **staff** member[12] / nurse[13] / orientation • **staff**-to-patient transmission / privilege • **staffing** problems • **medical** profession[14] / assistant (*abbr* MA)/ director[15] • **medical** oncologist / assistance (team)

ärztl. Personal (i. Krankenhaus)

Krankenhaus-, Klinikpersonal[1] Mitarbeiter finden für, besetzen[2] unterbesetzt[3] Stellenbesetzung[4] diensthabender Arzt[5] Dienstplan[6] zum Mitarbeiterstab gehören[7] Belegschaft[8] Intensivpflegepersonal[9] Pflegepersonal[10] dienstältere Mitarbeiter(innen)[11] Mitarbeiter(in), Kollege/-in[12] ausgebildete Kranken-/ Stationsschwester[13] Arztberuf, Ärzteschaft[14] ®Klinikdirektor[15]

2

Medical Staff & Specialties   HEALTH CARE 63

attending (physician or **surgeon)** *n term*   *syn* **consultant** [ʌ] *n term BE*

(i) physician or surgeon on the staff of a hospital who regularly attends patients at the hospital, supervises and teaches house staff, fellows[1], medical students, etc.
(ii) doctor who is responsible for a particular (usually private) patient

attend[2] [ətɛnd] *v* • **attend to**[3] *v* • **attendance**[4] *n* • **consult**[5] *v* • **consultation**[6] *n*

» The child must be hospitalized and the attending physician informed of the emergency physician's suspicions [ɪʃ]. Physicians can also relieve suffering [ʌ] by spending time with dying patients, listening to them, and attending to their psychological [saɪk-] distress. A skilled anesthesiologist should be in attendance[7] during labor[8] [eɪ].

Use **attending** staff / cardiologist • full-time / assistant[9] **attending** • **to attend** clinics / a day care center[10] / school • **to attend to a** patient's needs / task[11] • **consultant** radiologist / neuro-ophthalmologist • house[12] (*BE*)/ plastic / vascular / transplant / oral **surgeon**

   Note: In the U.S. a **consultant**[13] is a physician or surgeon who acts in an advisory capacity counseling the attending doctors.

(i) ®Chefarzt, Primar(arzt) (öst.)
(ii) Behandelnder Arzt
Fachärzte i. Ausbildung[1] versorgen, behandeln; besuchen, anwesend sein[2] s. kümmern um[3] Anwesenheit, Dienst, Bereitschaft[4] konsultieren, zu Rate ziehen[5] Beratung, Besprechung, Konsultation[6] anwesend[7] bei d. Entbindung[8] stellvertretende(r) Leiter(in)[9] ein Tagesheim besuchen[10] s. einer Aufgabe widmen[11] PJ-Student, Turnusarzt (öst.) im 1. Turnusjahr (chirurg. Abt.)[12] Konsiliararzt[13]   3

resident [rɛzɪdᵊnt] *n term*   *syn* **registrar** [rɛdʒɪstrɑːr] *n term BE*
                                  rel **PGY-2, 3** or **4**[1] *n jar*

(i) medical doctor who has completed medical school and internship and is receiving [siː] training in a specialized area; completion [iːʃ] of a residency program is required for board [ɔːrd] certification in a medical or surgical specialty
(ii) someone living at a particular place for a prolonged period

residency[2] *n term* • **residence**[3] *n* • **resident**[4] *adj* • **residential** [rɛzɪdᵊntʃᵊl] *adj*

» The length of residency varies according to the specialty. Then the monocytes [-saɪts] penetrate the endothelial [iː] layer and take up residence[5] in the intima.

Use medical (specialty) / surgical [ɜː]/ first year / PGY-2 / senior[6] [iː]/ chief [tʃiːf] **resident** • medical[7] / administrative **residency** • **residency** (training) program[2] / Review Committee (*abbr* RRC) • senior[6] [iː] **registrar** • **resident** bacteria[8] [ɪɚ]/ flora[9] / cells • **residential** care[10] / center • nursing home[11] / rural [rʊɚᵊl]/ long-term **residents** • place / area / change / history **of residence**

   Note: In the U.S. a **registrar** is an administrative officer whose chief responsibility is to maintain the medical records. **PGY** stands for '**postgraduate year'**.

(i) Assistenzarzt i. d. Fachausbildung
(ii) Bewohner(in)
Assistenzarzt i. 2., 3., 4. Ausbildungsjahr[1] Facharztausbildung[2] Wohnort[3] wohnhaft, ansässig[4] sich ansiedeln[5] Assistenzarzt in einem fortgeschrittenen Ausbildungsjahr, Oberarzt[6] internistische Ausbildung[7] Bakterienflora[8] Residentflora[9] stationäre Pflege[10] Bewohner eines Pflegeheims[11]   4

(medical) intern [ɪntɜːrn] *n term*
         syn **houseman** [haʊsmən‖mæn], **house officer** *n term BE*, *abbr* **H.O.**
physician in the first postgraduate year (PGY-1) gaining supervised [uː] practical experience before beginning a residency program

internship[1] *n term* • **subintern**[2] *n* • **intern(e)** *v* • **in-house**[3] *adj*

» The medical intern is responsible for primary patient care. I was the intern assigned [aɪ] to the case. The internship year is often quite rigorous [ɪ]. It's hard to describe an intern's typical day since we rotate through different services, each with its own schedule.

Use to work as an[4] / nurse [ɜː] **intern** • senior[5] (*abbr* SHO) **house officer** • student **internship** • preregistration[6] [dʒ]/ junior[7] [dʒuː] (*abbr* JHO) **house officer** • **house** surgeon (*abbr* HS)/ staff

®Assistenzarzt, Turnusarzt (öst.)
®Assistenzarztausbildung, Turnus (öst.)[1] ®PJ-Student(in) i. letzten Studienjahr, der/die das sog. praktische Jahr i. Krankenhaus absolviert[2] (haus)intern, im Haus[3] den Turnus machen (öst.), das prakt. Jahr absolvieren[4] ®Turnusarzt i. 3. Turnusjahr (öst.), Assistenzarzt[5] PJ-Student, Arzt im 1. Turnusjahr (öst.), Assistenzarzt[6] ®Turnusarzt im 2. Turnusjahr (öst.)[7]   5

extern [ɛkstɜːrn] *n term*   *syn* **medical clerk** [ɑː] or **elective** *n term BE*
                                rel **locum (tenens)**[1] [loʊkəm tiːnənz] *n term*
nonresident advanced medical student assisting with patient care as an extracurricular activity

externship[2] [ɛkstɜːrnʃɪp] *n term* • **clerkship**[2] [ɑː] *n BE* • **medical student** *n*

» An extern who was infected with AIDS by a needle sued [uː] the hospital for negligence[3]. Medical clerks perform clerical work[4] to support the care given to patients in a ward[5] [ɔː].

Use medical[6] **extern** • surgical / hospital / clinic / unit / ward[7] **clerk** • supply [aɪ]/ admissions / medical records[8] / office **clerk** • to do[9]/require **a locum** • medical / dental / pharmacy **locum** • **locum** post[10] / doctor / recruitment[11] [uː] • 3rd-year / 4th-year **medical student** • **medical** graduate[12] / assistant • to do an[13] **elective** • to work as an[13] **extern**

Famulant(in)
(Urlaubs)vertreter(in)[1] Famulatur[2] klagte d. KH wegen Fahrlässigkeit[3] Schreibarbeit[4] Station[5] Famulant(in) i. d. medizin. Abteilung[6] Stationshelferin, -gehilfe[7] med. Dokumentationsassistent(in)[8] e. Vertretung übernehmen[9] Vertretungsstelle[10] Einstellung e. Vertreters(in)[11] promovierter Arzt[12] famulieren[13]   6

fellow [fɛloʊ] *n term*　*syn* **PGY-4** *or* **5** *n jar*, **trainee** [treɪniː] *n term BE*
(i) medical school graduate who has completed residency and is undergoing specialized training in a subspecialty (ii) member of a learned [ɪ] society
fellowship¹ *n term* • **traineeship**² *n BE*
» The Division of Transplantation is staffed by 3 transplant fellows, a fourth-year surgical resident, 2-3 interns, and one medical fellow. Most patients, when informed, allow trainees to play an active role in their care.
Use postdoctoral / senior [iː]/ (non)medical / clinical **fellow** • infectious diseases / research³ / visiting **fellow** • anesthesia [iːʒ]/ graduate **trainee** • **trainee** dentist / nurse⁴ [ɜː] • to supervise **trainees** • **fellow** in nephrology / specialist⁵

Note: In the U.S. everybody receiving specialized training can be referred to as a **trainee**.

(i) **Facharzt (FA) i. Ausbildung**
(ii) **Forschungsstipendiat(in)**
Facharztausbildung; Forschungsstipendium¹ Ausbildung(szeit)² Forschungsstipendiat(in)³ Krankenpflege-, Schwesternschüler(in)⁴ Fachkollege/ -in⁵

7

general practitioner [præktɪʃənɚ] *n term abbr* **GP**
　syn **family** *or* **primary-care physician** *n, opposite* **specialist**¹ *n*
doctor who is not a specialist but treats all illnesses
practice² *v & n* • **generalist**³ *n & adj* • (**sub**)**specialty**⁴ *n* • **specialize (in)**⁵ *v*
» While the majority of family physicians and general practitioners do treat HIV-infected patients, many feel uncomfortable doing so. Fifty percent of women presenting to GPs with a variety of symptoms suggestive [dʒe] of acute UTI⁶ were found to have upper tract infection.
Use to see/consult [ʌ] **a practitioner** • primary-care / dental⁷ / medical⁸ / emergency **practitioner** • pediatric / mental health / experienced / nurse⁹ **practitioner** • **family** practice (*abbr* FP)/ medicine / doctor / counseling [aʊ] • **primary-care** patient / provider [aɪ] • mental health¹⁰ / infectious disease / pain / cancer¹¹ **specialist** • medical / hand / pulmonary [ʊ‖ʌ] disease¹² **specialist** • **specialist in** blood bank technology (*abbr* SBBT) • **specialist in** nuclear [uː] medicine / otorhinolaryngology¹³ • medical / surgical **specialty** • **specialty** management¹⁴ / referral¹⁵ [ɜː]/ training

praktischer Arzt, Arzt für Allgemeinmedizin
Facharzt, Spezialist(in)¹ praktizieren, ausüben; Praxis² Allgemeinmediziner(in); allgemeinmedizinisch³ Spezial-, Fachgebiet⁴ s. spezialisieren auf⁵ Harnwegsinfektion⁶ Zahnarzt⁷ prakt. Arzt⁸ ®selbstständige(r) Diplomkrankenschwester/ -pfleger (allgem. Krankenpflege)⁹ Psychiater(in)¹⁰ Krebsspezialist(in)¹¹ Lungenfacharzt¹² HNO-Facharzt¹³ fachärztl. Behandlung¹⁴ Überweisung an e. Facharzt¹⁵

8

(general) internist [ɪntɜːrnɪst] *n term*　*rel* **internal** [ɜː] **medicine**¹ *n term*
physician specialized in the medical diagnosis and treatment of disorders of the internal organs; subspecialties² include cardiology, hematology [hiː-], gastroenterology, endocrinology, and nephrology
» Refer the patient to an internist or gastroenterologist within 4-5 days. Unfortunately, internists frequently do not examine the breasts [e] in women, they are apt to³ refer this to gynecologists. What is the internist's role in the management of cardiovascular trauma [ɒː]?
Use **the internist's** role / approach [-oʊtʃ] to diagnosis / perspective • **internal** anatomy / organs⁴ / structures [ʌ]/ disease / injury⁵

Facharzt für innere Medizin, Internist(in)
innere Medizin¹ Teilbereiche² neigen dazu³ innere Organe⁴ innere Verletzung⁵

9

dermatologist [dɜːrmətɒːlədʒɪst] *n term*　*rel* **venereologist**¹ [vənɪɚ-] *n term*
physician specialized in disorders of the skin; venereologists specialize in sexually transmitted disease
dermatology² *n term* • **venereology** *n* • **venereal**³ *adj* • **derm(a)-** *comb*
» Rather than using systemic steroids in difficult cases, consultation should be sought from a dermatologist or allergist with experience in managing severe urticaria [ɜːrtɪk-]. If the lesions [iːʒ] do not resolve⁴, referral [ɜː] to a dermatologist or venereologist is necessary.
Use to refer to/see⁵/be treated by **a dermatologist** • department of⁶ / pediatric **dermatology** • **dermatologic** consultation / manifestations⁷ / disorders⁸ • **venereal** infection / transmission⁹ / disease • **derma**tologic /titis [aɪ] /tosis¹⁰

Hautfacharzt, Dermatologe, -login
Facharzt f. Geschlechtskrankheiten/ Venerologie¹ Dermatologie² Geschlechts-, sexuell, venerisch³ abklingen⁴ e. Dermatologen/-in konsultieren⁵ dermatolog. Abteilung⁶ Hautmanifestationen⁷ Hautkrankheiten⁸ Übertragung durch Sexualkontakt⁹ Dermatose, Hautkrankheit¹⁰

10

anesthesiologist [ænəsθiːzɪɒːlədʒɪst] *n term*
　syn **anesthetist** [e‖iː] *n term BE*　→ U131-6
physician trained in administering anesthetics [e] and caring for people who are anesthetized
anesthesiology¹ *n term* • **anesthetic**² [e] *adj & n* • **anesthesia**³ [-θiːʒə] *n* → U135-1
» It is essential that the anesthesiologist continuously assess the depth of anesthesia⁴. The anesthesiologist should be aware of the severity [e] of ventricular dysfunction.
Use physician⁵ / pediatric / geriatric / experienced / skilled **anesthesiologist** • nurse⁶ **anesthetist** • **anesthetic** drugs² / spray / solution [uːʃ]/ properties • general / local⁷ / volatile **anesthetic**

FA f. Anästhesiologie, Anästhesist(in), Narkosefacharzt
Anästhesiologie¹ anästhetisch, Narkose-; Anästhetikum² Anästhesie, Ausschaltung d. Schmerzempfindlichkeit, Schmerzunempfindlichkeit³ Narkosetiefe⁴ Narkosefacharzt⁵ Narkoseschwester⁶ Lokalanästhetikum⁷

11

Medical Staff & Specialties HEALTH CARE **65**

psychiatrist [saɪkaɪətrɪst] *n term* *syn* **analyst,** ***shrink,** ***alienist** [eɪliən-] *n inf*
rel **psychologist**[1] [saɪkɒːlədʒɪst] *n term* → U77-16

physician trained in the diagnosis and treatment of mental, emotional [oʊʃ] and behavioral disorders[2]

psychiatry[3] *n term* • **psychology** *n* • **psychiatric**[4] *adj* • **psych(o)-** *comb*

» Optimally, evaluation of the child who is failing [eɪ] to thrive[5] [aɪ] is performed by a team including a physician, nutritionist, child developmentalist[6], social worker, and psychiatrist or psychologist. Formerly the province[7] of psychiatrists and psychoanalysts[8], psychotherapy[9] is now also practiced by social workers, clinical psychologists, nurses [ɜː], clergymen[10] [klɜːrdʒɪmen], and many paraprofessionals.

Use consulting [ʌ] **psychiatrist** • **psycho**therapist[11] /analysis • social / child / biologic / adolescent[12] [es]/ geriatric[13] [dʒeri-] **psychiatry** • descriptive / dynamic [daɪ-]/ forensic[14] **psychiatry** • **psychiatric** care[15] / disorder / evaluation / consultant • **psych**otic [saɪkɒːtɪk] /ogenic [saɪkoʊdʒenɪk] /ic[16] /ologic /omotor /osocial • **psych**osomatic /otropic /ostimulant[17] /edelic drug[18]

Facharzt f. Psychiatrie, Psychiater(in)
Psychologe, -login[1] Verhaltensstörungen[2] Psychiatrie[3] psychiatrisch[4] m. Gedeihstörungen[5] Entwicklungspsychologe/-in[6] Kompetenzbereich[7] Psychoanalytiker[8] Psychotherapie[9] Geistliche[10] Psychotherapeut(in)[11] Jugendpsychiatrie[12] Gerontopsychiatrie[13] forensische Psychiatrie[14] psychiatr. Betreuung[15] psychisch, seelisch[16] Psychostimulans, -tonikum[17] Psychedelikum, Psychotomimetikum, halluzinogene Substanz[18] 12

radiologist [reɪdɪŋːlədʒɪst] *n term* → U99-1f
rel **x-ray technician**[1] [teknɪʃən] *n term*

physician trained in the use of radioactive substances, x-rays, and other imaging techniques[2]

radiology[3] *n term* • **radiologic(al)** *adj* • **radiation**[4] [eɪ] *n* • **radio-** *comb*

» Thorough cleansing[5] [e] of the colon and examination by a skilled radiologist are essential if small polyps are to be demonstrated. The diagnosis of bone tumors is most precise [saɪ] when made by the clinician [ɪʃ], the radiologist, and the pathologist in close consultation.

Use diagnostic / pediatric / experienced **radiologist** • **radiation** therapist[6] / oncologist • diagnostic / interventional *or* invasive[7] [eɪ]/ therapeutic [juː] **radiology** • **radiologic** technologist[1] / examination • **radio**biology /activity /graph[8] /isotope [aɪ] /nuclide /dense[9] /paque[9] [-peɪk] /therapist[6] • **radiologically** detectable / guided[10] [aɪ]/ normal

Facharzt f. Radiologie, Radiologe, -login
Röntgenassistent(in)[1] bildgebende Verfahren[2] Radiologie[3] Strahlung, Bestrahlung[4] gründl. Reinigung[5] Strahlentherapeut(in)[6] Interventionsradiologie[7] Röntgenbild, -aufnahme[8] strahlendicht, -undurchlässig[9] unter Röntgendurchleuchtungskontrolle[10]

13

neurologist [n(j)ʊəˈrɒːlədʒɪst] *n term* *rel* **neurosurgeon**[1] *n term*

physician specializing in the diagnosis and treatment of nervous [ɜː] system disease

neurology *n term* • **neurologic(al)**[2] *adj* • **neuro-** *comb*

» If the headache persists refer the patient to a neurologist. Consult [ʌ] a neurologist or vascular surgeon[3] about evaluation and definitive treatment of transient ischemic [kiː] attacks[4]. If the fracture is more than a week old and there are no abnormal symptoms or signs, referral to a neurologist or neurosurgeon is satisfactory.

Use pediatric *or* child[5] / clinical **neurologist** • **neurologic** assessment *or* examination[6] / status [æ|eɪ] • **neurologic** function [ʌ]/ abnormalities / impairment[7] [eɚ]/ deficit[8] • **neuro**pathologist /psychologist[9] /radiologist /-oncologist

Facharzt für Neurologie, Neurologe, -login
Facharzt f. Neurochirurgie, Neurochirurg(in)[1] neurologisch[2] Facharzt f. Gefäßchirurgie, Gefäßchirurg(in)[3] transitorische ischämische Attacken[4] Facharzt f. Kinderneurologie[5] neurolog. Untersuchung[6] neurolog. Schädigung[7] neurolog. Ausfall[8] Neuropsychologe/-in[9] 14

orthopedist [ɔːrθəpiːdɪst] *n term* *syn* **orthopod** [ɔːrθəpɒːd] *n jar*
rel **orthotist**[1], **podiatrist**[2] [poʊdaɪətrɪst] *n term*

physician and surgeon specializing in the prevention, diagnosis and correction of disorders in the skeleton, muscles, joints and associated tissues

orthopedics[3] [iː] *n term* • **orthopedic**[4] [iː] *adj* • **orthotics**[5] [ɒː] *n* • **ortho-** *comb* • **podiatry**[6] [aɪə] *n* • **podiatric** [æ] *adj*

» Open injuries [ɪndʒəriːz] and complex dislocations require prompt examination by an orthopedist in the ER[7]. Most patients with tendinitis [aɪ] can be treated on an outpatient basis[8], with referral [ɜː] to a rheumatologist [ruːmə-] or orthopedist as necessary.

Use pediatric **orthopedist** • **orthopedic** surgeon[9] / nurse / consultation / referral • **orthopedic** appliances[10] [aɪ]/ prosthesis [iː]/ shoes[11] / surgery[12] / custom-made[13] [ʌ] **orthotics** • **orthotic** devices[10] [aɪs]/ protection • practising / sports **podiatrist** • **podiatry** clinic • **podiatric** patient / ultrasound [ʌ]/ medicine

FA f. Orthopädie, Orthopäde, Orthopädin
Bandagist(in), Orthopädiemechaniker(in)[1] Fußpfleger(in), Podologe, -login[2] Orthopädie[3] orthopädisch[4] Orthopädietechnik, orthopäd. Geräte/ Hilfsmittel[5] Fußpflege, Pediküre[6] Notaufnahme[7] ambulant[8] Orthopäde/-in, Unfallchirurg(in), Orthopäde u. Chirurg[9] orthopädische Geräte[10] orthopädische Schuhe[11] orthopäd. Chirurgie[12] individuell angefertigte orthopäd. Hilfsmittel[13] 15

gynecologist [gaɪnə‖dʒɪnɪkɒːlədʒɪst] n term
rel **obstetrician**[1] [ɒːbstətrɪʃən] n, rel **neonatologist**[2] [niːəneɪtɒːlədʒɪst] n term
physician and surgeon specializing in disorders of sexual or reproductive function in women; in most countries it is practised in conjunction with obstetrics, the care of the mother and fetus [iː] during pregnancy, labor[3] [eɪ], childbirth and the puerperium[4] [ɪə]
gynecology[5] n term • **gynecologic(al)** adj • **obstetrics**[6] n • **neonatal** [eɪ] adj
» Questionable abnormalities were noted on routine ultrasound examination done in the obstetrician's office. Multiple pregnancy should always be identified prenatally to allow the obstetrician and pediatrician or neonatologist to plan their management jointly [dʒ].
Use American College of Obstetricians and **Gynecologists** (abbr ACOG) • **gynecologist-in-chief**[7] • **gynecologic** emergency[8] / consultation / examination[9] / oncologist

pediatrician [piːdɪətrɪʃən] n term   opposite **geriatrician**[1] [dʒerɪətrɪʃən] n term
physician concerned with the development and care of children, childhood diseases and their treatment
pediatrics[2] [æ] n term • **geriatrics**[3] n • **pediatric** adj • **geriatric** [æ] adj
» If the pediatrician is in attendance[4] in the delivery room[5] for a normal delivery, the physical examination is largely based on observation coupled [ʌ] with auscultation of the chest. In case the nightmares[6] recur, the pediatrician has to make a more extensive investigation.
Use general **pediatrician** • **pediatric** cardiologist / nurse practitioner[7] (abbr PNP) • **pediatric** dentistry[8] / neurosurgery • **pediatric** urology[9] / otolaryngology / dietitian[10] [daɪətɪʃən]/ intensive care unit[11] • **pediatric** advanced life support (abbr PALS)/ anesthesia / surgery[12] • **pediatric** hospitalization / nursing / nutrition [ɪʃ]/ dosage[13] [doʊsɪdʒ]/ ward[14] [ɔː]

ophthalmologist [ɒːfθælmɒːlədʒɪst] n term, abbr **ophth**
syn **oculist** [ɒːkjəlɪst] n dated, **eye specialist** n clin
physician trained in the anatomy, physiology and treatment of diseases of the eyes
ophthalmology[1] n term • **ophthalmic**[2] adj • **ophthalmologic** adj • **ophthalm(o)-** comb
» Many facial [eɪʃ] injuries, if not promptly attended to[3] by an ophthalmologist, may lead to loss of vision[4] [ɪʒ]. Acute care by an eye specialist, including examination of the optic nerve head, is essential if blood is noted in the anterior chamber[5] [tʃeɪ] (hyphema[6] [haɪfiːmə]).
Use neuro-**ophthalmologist** • general / clinical / pediatric / preventive **ophthalmologist** • **ophthalmic** surgeon / ointment[7] [ɔɪ]/ examination / infection / solutions[8] • **ophthalmologic** assessment / referral / consultation / care • **ophthalmo**scopy[9] /dynamometry[10] [aɪ] /pathy /plegia[11] [ɒːfθælmoʊpliːdʒ(ɪ)ə]

oto(rhino)laryngologist [oʊtoʊraɪnoʊlærɪŋgɒːlədʒɪst] n term
syn **ENT specialist** n clin
physician trained in the diagnosis and treatment of diseases of the ear, the nose, and throat [oʊ]
otorhinolaryngology[1] n term • **ot(o)-, rhin(o)-, laryng(o)-** comb
» Some otolaryngologists recommend prophylactic tympanoplasty [ɪ] tubes for children with cleft palate[2] and recurrent or persistent otitis [aɪ] media[3] [iː]. If cerebrospinal [aɪ] fluid rhinorrhea[4] [raɪnɔriːə] is suspected, a CT scan followed by ENT and neurosurgical consultation is indicated.
Use pediatric **otolaryngologist** • **ENT** chair[5] / examination / trauma [ɒː]/ emergency [ɜː] • **rhin**itis[6] [raɪnaɪtɪs] /orrhea /oplasty[7] /ovirus [aɪ] • **oto**toxic /scope[8] /rrhea

pharmacist [fɑːrməsɪst] n → U9-4   rel **pharmacologist**[1] n → U92-1
professional trained in formulating and dispensing drugs and medications
pharmaceutical[2] [-suːtɪkəl] adj & n • **pharmacy**[3] n • **pharma(co)-** comb
» Issues of grief and loss are addressed by all members of the hospice team (physician, nurse coordinator, psychosocial worker, chaplain[4] [tʃæplɪn], and pharmacist). Prior to discharge[5] from the hospital nurses and pharmacists will instruct patients on their medications.
Use clinical **pharmacist** • clinical[6] **pharmacy** • **pharmaco**poeia[7] [iː] /logy /therapy[8]

Frauenarzt, FA f. Frauenheilkunde, Gynäkologe, -login
Facharzt f. Geburtshilfe, Geburtshelfer(in)[1] Neonatologe, -login[2] Wehen[3] Wochenbett, Puerperium[4] Gynäkologie[5] Geburtshilfe[6] Vorstand d. gyn. Abteilung[7] gynäkolog. Notfall[8] gynäkolog. Untersuchung[9]

16

FA f. Kinderheilkunde, Kinderarzt, Pädiater(in)
Geriater(in)[1] Kinderheilkunde, Pädiatrie[2] Altersheilkunde, Geriatrie[3] anwesend[4] Kreißsaal[5] Alpträume[6] selbstständige(r) Kinderkrankenschwester/ -pfleger[7] Kinderzahnheilkunde[8] Kinderurologie[9] Kinderdiätassistent(in)[10] Kinderintensivstation[11] Kinderchirurgie[12] Kinderdosierung[13] Kinderstation[14]

17

Facharzt f. Augenheilkunde, Augenarzt
Augenheilkunde, Ophthalmologie[1] ophthalmisch, Augen-[2] behandelt, versorgt[3] Verlust d. Sehkraft, Visusverlust[4] vordere Augenkammer[5] Hyphaema[6] Augensalbe[7] Augenwässer[8] Augenspiegelung, Ophthalmoskopie[9] Ophthalmodynamometrie[10] Augenmuskellähmung, Ophthalmoplegie[11]

18

FA f. Hals-Nasen-Ohren-Heilkunde, HNO-Arzt
Otorhinolaryngologie, Hals-Nasen-Ohren-Heilkunde, HNO[1] Gaumenspalte[2] Mittelohrentzündung, Otitis media[3] Liquorrhoe a. d. Nase[4] HNO-(Patienten)stuhl[5] Nasenschleimhautentzündung, Rhinitis[6] Nasen-, Rhinoplastik[7] Otoskop, Ohrenspiegel[8]

19

Apotheker(in)
Pharmakologe, -login[1] pharmazeutisch; Arzneimittel[2] Apotheke, Pharmazie[3] Krankenseelsorger(in)[4] Entlassung[5] Klinik-, Anstaltsapotheke[6] Arzneibuch, Pharmakopoe[7] Pharmakotherapie, medikamentöse Therapie[8]

20

Nurses & Paramedical Staff   HEALTH CARE **67**

pathologist [pəθɒːlədʒɪst] *n term*

rel **medical examiner**[1] *n term* → U12-21

physician trained in the nature, cause, process and effects of disease; examines samples of tissue removed during surgery [ɜː] to make an exact diagnosis and/or performs postmortem examinations[2]

pathology[3] *n term* • **pathologic(al)**[4] *adj* • **patho-** *comb* → U89-1

» Microscopically, the lesion can be confused with malignant melanoma by the inexperienced pathologist. Cervical polyps should be examined by a pathologist to exclude malignancy.

Use clinical or laboratory / surgical / neuro/ forensic[1] / speech[5] [spiːtʃ] **pathologist** • forensic / armed forces / aviation / independent **medical examiner** • **medical examiner's** investigation[6] • to notify the[7] **medical examiner** • cellular[8] / clinical / brain / benign [bɪnaɪn]/ negative for[9] **pathology** • **patho**physiology[10] /gen[11]

Pathologe, Pathologin
Gerichtsmediziner(in)[1] Autopsien[2] Pathologie, Lehre v. d. Krankheiten; patholog. Abteilung[3] pathologisch, krankhaft[4] Logopäde/ -pädin[5] gerichtliche Sektion[6] d. Gerichtsmediziner(in) verständigen[7] Zellularpathologie[8] kein patholog. Befund[9] Pathophysiologie[10] Krankheitserreger[11]

21

chiropractor [kaɪrəpræktɚ] *n term*   rel **osteopath(ist)**[1] [ɒːstɪɒːpəθɪst] *n term*

specialist who treats disorders by manipulating the bones of the spine[2] [aɪ]

chiropractic[3] *adj & n term* • **osteopathy**[4] *n* • **osteopathic** *adj*

» Try to find a chiropractor whose practice is limited to conservative treatment of back pain and other musculoskeletal problems. Chiropractic treatment has been in existence for more than a hundred years. She is a practising osteopathist as well as a physiotherapist[5] [fɪzɪoʊ-]. A registered osteopath is an expert in the use of soft tissue techniques [tekniːks], and gentle [dʒe] mobilization and manipulation techniques[6].

Use qualified[7] / straight [streɪt] **chiropractor** • trained[8] **osteopathist** • **chiropractic** manipulation / treatment[9] / care • **chiropractic** healing [iː]/ medicine[10] / college / professional[11] • holistic[12] [oʊ]/ cranial [eɪ]/ naturopathic **osteopathy** • **osteopathic** practitioner or physician[1] / surgeon

Chiropraktiker(in)
Osteopath(in)[1] Wirbelsäule[2] chiropraktisch; Chiropraktik, -praxis[3] Osteopathie[4] Physiotherapeutin[5] vorsichtige Mobilisations- und Manipulationstechniken[6] ausgebildete(r) Chiropraktiker(in)[7] ausgebildete(r) Osteopath(in)[8] Chirotherapie[9] Chiropraktik, manuelle Medizin, Chirotherapie[10] Chiropraktiker(in)[11] ganzheitl. Osteopathie[12]

22

quack (doctor) [kwæk dɒːktɚ] *n*   rel **healer**[1] [hiːlɚ] *n*

untrained person pretending to be a physician and claiming [eɪ] to cure diseases by useless procedures [siː], secret [iː] remedies, and worthless [ɜː] therapeutic [juː] machines [məʃiːnz]

quackery[2] [kwækəri] *n* • **healing**[3] *n & adj*

» He was one of the most notorious [ɔː] cancer-cure quacks[4] of the day. Weight loss schemes [skiːmz] and devices [aɪs] probably are the most popular form of quackery.

Use **quack** treatment / cures [kjʊɚz]/ remedies[5] • faith[6] [feɪθ] **healer** • **healing** power[7] / period / process / rate[8] • medical **quackery**

Kurpfuscher, Quacksalber
Heiler(in)[1] Kurpfuscherei, Quacksalberei[2] Heilung; heilend, Heil-[3] berühmt-berüchtigter Krebsheiler[4] quacksalberische Mittel[5] Gesundbeter(in)[6] Heilkraft[7] Heilungsrate[8]

23

Unit 16   Nurses & Paramedical Staff
Related Units: 14 Hospitals, 15 Medical Staff, 20 Hospital Routines, 134 Perioperative Management, 140 Wound Healing, 142 Physical Therapy

health care worker *n, abbr* **HCW**   *syn* **health professional** *n*
             sim **allied** [ælaɪd] **health** *or* **paramedical personnel**[1] *n*

general term for professionals in medical, social, and paramedical services and supportive health care, e.g. physicians, dentists, podiatrists[2], nurses, audiologists[3] [ɒː], and therapists

» Almost all hospitals have implemented body substance [ʌ] isolation, which requires use of gloves [ʌ] whenever a health care worker anticipates contact with body secretions [iː]. Hospitals may be categorized by their ability to provide acute care as determined by the availability of physicians [ɪʃ], nurses, allied health personnel, and other hospital resources.

Use hospital / ancillary[4] [sɪ]/ occupationally [eɪʃ] exposed **health care worker** • pregnant / infected / (non)immunized **HCW** • emergency[5] [ɜː]/ social[6] / rescue[7] **worker** • laboratory[8] / mental health / grief[9] **worker** • **health care** team / professional / services[10] • **health care** provider / center / facilities[11] [sɪ] • **health care** consumer / proxy[12] / costs / system[13] • **paramedical** professions[14] / specialists • emergency medical services[15] (*abbr* EMS)/ (hospital) auxiliary [ɒːgz-] *or* ancillary[16] **personnel**

Mitarbeiter(in) im Gesundheitswesen
paramediz. Personal, ärztl. Hilfspersonal[1] Fusspfleger[2] Audiologen[3] medizinische Hilfskraft[4] Rettungsarbeiter(in)[5] Sozialarbeiter(in)[6] Rettungshelfer(in)[7] Laborant(in)[8] Trauerbegleiter(in)[9] Gesundheitsfürsorge, med. Versorgung[10] Gesundheitseinrichtungen[11] Betreuungsvollmacht, Patientenverfügung, Vorsorgevollmacht[12] Gesundheitswesen[13] Heilhilfsberufe[14] Notfalldienst[15] Hilfspersonal[16]

1

HEALTH CARE — Nurses & Paramedical Staff

nurse [nɜːrs] n & v   sim **sister**¹ [sɪstɚ] n BE

(n) person trained in health care of sick, injured or handicapped people (usually under the direction of a physician)

n**u**rsing² [ɜː] n & adj • n**u**rsery³ n • nurs**o**logy⁴ n term • nursem**ai**d⁵ [eɪ] n inf

» Examine the nurses' notes from the preceding [siː] evening. Authorize [ɔː] the nurse to dispense a mild analgesic [dʒiː] as necessary. As patients become progressively incapacitated⁶ [æs], visiting nurse assistance or part-time nurses⁷ are almost invariably required.

Use **to nurse** sb. back to health⁸ • public [ʌ] health (abbr PHN) or community (BE)/ general duty⁹ [(j)uː] **nurse** • charge¹⁰ [tʃɑːrdʒ]/ school / trained office¹¹ **nurse** • specially trained / surgical [ɜː] or scrub¹² [ʌ] **nurse** • staff¹³ / assisting¹⁴ **nurse** • **nurse**-patient relationship /-client [aɪ] interaction • **nurse**-patient ratio [reɪʃioʊ]/ educator • **nursing** auxiliary¹⁴ / assistant¹⁴ • special care (abbr SCN)/ newborn nursery • well-baby / observation **nursery** • director of¹⁵ / team **nursing** • ward¹⁰ [ɔː] **sister** (BE) • nurses' station¹⁶ • **nursing** home¹⁷ / staff¹⁸ / mother¹⁹ • **nursing** assessment²⁰ / diagnosis / intervention • **nursing** goal²¹ [goʊl]/ care plan / audit²² [ɔː] • skilled²³ / home²⁴ / supportive / intensive **nursing care** • respiratory / orthopedic [iː]/ constant **nursing care** • inadequate / psychiatric [saɪkɪ-] **nursing care**

(Kranken)schwester, -pfleger; pflegen; stillen

Oberschwester, (Ordens)schwester¹ Krankenpflege; Pflege² Kindergarten; Kinder-, Säuglingszimmer³ Pflegeforschung⁴ Kindermädchen⁵ behindert⁶ Teilzeitkrankenschwestern, -pfleger⁷ gesund pflegen⁸ Hilfsschwester⁹ Stationsschwester¹⁰ ausgebild. Arzthelfer(in)¹¹ OP-Schwester, -Pfleger¹² stellvertr. Stationsschwester, ausgebild. Krankenschwester¹³ Schwesternhelfer(in)¹⁴ Pflegedienstleiter(in), leitende Krankenpflegekraft¹⁵ Schwesternzimmer¹⁶ Pflegeheim; (BE) Privatklinik¹⁷ Pflegepersonal¹⁸ Pflegemutter; stillende M.¹⁹ Pflegeanamnese²⁰ Pflegeziel²¹ Pflegeevaluation²² professionelle Krankenpflege²³ häusl. Krankenpflege²⁴

2

---

student [st(j)uːdᵊnt] **nurse** n   syn **trainee** [treɪniː] or **pupil** [pjuːpᵊl] **nurse** n, syn **probationer** [eɪʃ] (**nurse**) n BE

nursing student who is enrolled at a school of nursing¹ and is undergoing training at a hospital

» The student nurse was asked to hold the patient's ankles. She planned to become a registered nurse but she only worked as a nurse probationer [eɪʃ]. The purpose of assignments² [aɪ] is to provide nursing care to patients in a learning environment for the trainee nurse.

Use 2ⁿᵈ year **trainee nurse** • practical / graduate³ [ædʒ] **nurse** • nurse's aide⁴ [eɪd]

Schwesternschülerin, Lernschwester

Krankenpflegeschule¹ prakt. Übungen² diplomierte(r) Krankenschwester/ -pfleger³ Schwesternhelfer(in)⁴

3

---

registered nurse [redʒɪstɚd nɜːrs] n term, abbr **RN**
                        sim **certified** [sɜːrtɪfaɪd] **nurse**¹ n term, abbr **CN**

professional nurse trained at an approved school of nursing and licensed [aɪs] by state authorities

» The enterostomal therapist is usually a RN who has taken specialized training and is certified in the field. Student nurses help to ease² [iːz] the work load of certified nurses.

Use certified (abbr CRN)/ state³ (abbr SRN) **registered nurse** • qualified **nurse** • licensed practical⁴ (abbr LPN)/ licensed vocational⁴ (abbr LVN) **nurse**

diplom. Gesundheits- und Krankenschwester/-pfleger

geprüfte(r) Krankenschwester/-pfleger¹ erleichtern² staatl. geprüfte(r) Gesundheits- u. Krankenschwester/ -pfleger³ geprüfte(r) Krankenpflegehelfer(in)⁴

4

---

nurse specialist n term   sim **nurse practitioner**¹ n, rel **nurse clinician**² n term

registered nurse with advanced training in a particular area of patient care; e.g. neurosurgery

» Once the diagnosis of cancer is made, management of the patient is best undertaken in collaboration with medical and surgical oncologists, oncology nurse specialists, and a number of other consulting³ professionals. Functions of the clinical nurse specialist include providing direct patient care, teaching patients and their families, and conducting research⁴.

Use clinical² **nurse specialist** • **nurse** anesthetist⁵ [e]/ epidemiologist [e‖iː] (abbr NE)/ coordinator • pediatric⁶ (abbr PNP)/ family (abbr FNP) **nurse practitioner**

Fach(kranken)schwester, -pfleger

®selbstständige(r) Diplomkrankenschwester/ -pfleger (allgem. Krankenpflege)¹ selbstständige(r) Klinikschwester/ -pfleger² beratende³ Forschung betreiben⁴ Narkoseschwester⁵ Kinderkrankenschwester, -pfleger⁶

5

---

nurse-midwife n term   sim **midwife**¹ [mɪdwaɪf] n, rel **wet nurse**², **dry nurse**³ n clin

registered nurse qualified by advanced training to assist women during pregnancy, labor [eɪ], delivery and the postpartum period

(**nurse**) midwifery⁴ n term • dry-nursing⁵ n clin

» Nurse-midwives conduct delivery independently, care for the newborn, procure⁶ [-kjʊɚ] medical assistance when necessary, and execute emergency measures [eʒ] as required. A dry nurse is a female who is in charge of another woman's child but does not breast-feed⁷ [e] it.

Use certified nurse- (abbr CNM)/ lay⁸ **midwife** • American College of **Nurse-Midwives**

diplomierte(r) Hebamme/ Entbindungspfleger

Hebamme, Entbindungspfleger, Geburtshelfer(in)¹ Amme² Säuglingsschwester³ Geburtshilfe⁴ Säuglingspflege⁵ beziehen⁶ stillen⁷ Laienhebamme⁸

6

Nurses & Paramedical Staff   HEALTH CARE **69**

---

visiting nurse n, abbr **VN**   syn **public** or **community health nurse** n

nurse specialized in public health and primary care nursing who is employed by the local health authorities[1] to treat patients in their homes; in Britain also called **district nurse**

» The visiting nurse can administer medications[2] and monitor[3] the patient's physical condition. If there are further problems a public health nurse will be sent to the home.

Gemeindeschwester, -pfleger
regionale Gesundheitsbehörden[1] Medikamente verabreichen[2] überprüfen[3]

7

---

social worker n   sim **welfare worker**[1] n, **health visitor**[2] n BE → U13-6

individual, usually with a university degree in social work, who provides counsel[3] and aid to individuals with emotional and family problems

social [souʃəl] **work**[4] • socio- comb • society [səsaɪəti] n • **welfare**[5] [welfeə] n

» Have a social worker assess the ability of the family, friends, and community agencies [eɪdʒ] to provide [aɪ] the support that will allow the patient to remain at home. The families refused assistance from a social worker but accepted community nurse intervention. Home visiting by welfare workers or a public health nurse was needed.

Use family[6] / medical[7] / clinical / psychiatric[8] **social worker** • psychological **worker** • community service **work** • social network[9] / isolation / interaction • social medicine[10] / security[11] / child[12] **welfare** • sociology /genic /economic status

Sozialarbeiter(in)
Fürsorger(in)[1] Krankenschwester m. Zusatzqualifikation in häusl. Krankenpflege u. Geburtshilfe[2] berät[3] Sozialarbeit[4] Sozialhilfe, Wohlergehen[5] Familienhelfer(in), -fürsorger(in)[6] Sozialbetreuer(in) i. Krankenhaus[7] psychiatr. Betreuer(in)[8] soziales Netz[9] Sozialmedizin[10] Sozialversicherung, -hilfe[11] Kinderfürsorge[12]

8

---

medic [medɪk] n inf   syn **medical corpsman** n term
                           rel **paramedic**[1], **medical officer**[2] n term → U8-6

(i) member of a medical unit in the military or police forces
(ii) more broadly also used to refer to paramedics in the emergency medical services[3], medical students, or any person involved in medical work

» She's a medic with the 545th Military Police Company, Fort Hood, TX. Central Hospital, this is medic 19, how do you copy[4]? We analyzed the factors contributing to paramedic on-scene time during evaluation and management of blunt [ʌ] trauma[5].

Use army or military / special forces / combat[6] **medic** • **medic** unit or team / bag • emergency medical technician[7] [ɪʃ] (abbr EMT)-/ field / well-trained **paramedic** • medic-alert [ɜː] tag[8] /-alert bracelet[9] [eɪs] • **paramedic** unit / (rescue) team • transport or loading[10] [oʊ]/ triage[11] [trɪɑːʒ] **officer** • public relations[12] / (pediatric) house[13] **officer**

(i) Sanitätssoldat(in)
(ii) med. Helfer(in)
Rettungsassistent(in)[1] Amtsarzt/-ärztin; Stabsarzt[2] Notfalldienst[3] wie ist d. Empfang[4] stumpfes Trauma[5] Feldsanitäter(in)[6] Rettungssanitäter(in)[7] med. Informationsplakette[8] med. Informationsarmband[9] Logistikleiter(in)[10] ärztl. Einsatzleiter(in)[11] Pressesprecher(in)[12] ®Assistenzarzt/-ärztin, Turnusarzt/-ärztin (öst.)[13]

9

---

medical technologist [teknɒːlədʒɪst] n term, abbr **MT**
                          rel **medical laboratory technician** [teknɪʃən] or **assistant**[1] n term

health care worker trained in clinical laboratory procedures; technologists mostly hold the highest rank in the field while technicians carry out routine work under the supervision of technologists or physicians

» All technologists involved in urography should be well trained in the recognition of the early signs of contrast reactions and in resuscitation[2]. Transfer clearly labeled specimens directly to the clinical pathologist in charge[3] or to the responsible laboratory technician.

Use emergency[4] (abbr EMT)/ ophthalmic (abbr OMT) **medical technician** • dental (laboratory)[5] / tissue typing **technician** • x-ray or radiology[6] / respiratory care / parasitology **technician** • urodynamic / emergency transport or ambulance[4] **technician** • CT-scan / histologic (abbr HT) **technician** • medical record[7] / dietetic[8] (abbr DT)/ cardiac rescue **technician** • office or physician's[9] / dental[10] **assistant** • surgical[11] / respiratory therapy **assistant** • medical (abbr MT)/ registered care (abbr RCT)/ chemistry **technologist** • certified surgical[12] (abbr CST) / cardiovascular (abbr CVT) **technologist** • cyto/ electroneurodiagnostic (abbr ENDT) **technologist**

medizinisch-technische(r) Assistent(in), MTA
Labor(atoriums)assistent(in)[1] Reanimation, Wiederbelebung[2] leitend, verantwortlich[3] Rettungssanitäter(in)[4] Zahntechniker(in)[5] radiolog.-techn. Assistent(in)/ Röntgenassistent(in)[6] med. Dokumentationsassistent(in)[7] Diätassistent(in)[8] Arzthelfer(in)[9] Zahnarzthelfer(in), -assistent(in)[10] Operationsassistent(in), zweite(r) Chirurg(in)[11] technische(r) Operationsassistent(in)[12]

10

---

perfusionist [pɚfjuːʒənɪst] n term, abbr **PERF**
                           syn **perfusion technologist** n term, abbr **PFT**

highly skilled health professional who operates a heart-lung machine [ʃiː] under the supervision of a physician or assists extracorporeal [iː] circulation[1]

perfuse[2] [pɚfjuːz] v term • **perfusion**[3] [pɚfjuːʒən] n

» During open heart [hɑːrt] surgery, the perfusionist operates[4] the heart/lung bypass [aɪ] machine[5]. The perfusion technologist is also trained in the administration of blood products, anesthetic [e] agents [eɪdʒənts] and drugs.

Use certified clinical (abbr CCP)/ cardiovascular **perfusionist** • **perfusionist** training program / instructor [ʌ] • tissue / arterial [ɪɚ]/ cardiac / lung[6] [ʌ] **perfusion** • poor) skin[7] / renal[8] [iː] **perfusion** • **perfusion** lung scan[9] / rate / catheter[10]

Kardiotechniker(in)
extrakorporaler Kreislauf[1] durchströmen, perfundieren[2] Durchblutung, -strömung, Perfusion[3] bedient[4] Herz-Lungen-Maschine[5] Lungenperfusion[6] schlechte Hautdurchblutung[7] Nierendurchblutung, -perfusion[8] Lungenperfusionsszintigramm[9] Perfusor, Spritzenpumpe[10]

11

16

HEALTH CARE — Nurses & Paramedical Staff

therapist [θerəpɪst] n   rel **counselor**¹ [kaʊnˈsələr] n

specialist trained in methods of therapy other than operative and drug treatment

(**chemo**)**therapeutic**² [kiːmoʊ-] adj term • **therapy** n & comb • **counseling**³ n

» Close follow-up and a close patient-therapist relationship are necessary for sustained⁴ [eɪ] dietary [daɪətəri] change. Family members may need outside help in dealing with their grief through supportive counseling services.

Use physical⁵ / home / occupational⁶ [eɪʃ] (abbr OT)/ rehabilitation nurse **therapist** • speech (and language)⁷ / behavior⁸ / grief⁹ / activity **therapist** • enterostomal (abbr ET)/ sex / radiation **therapist** • registered respiratory¹⁰ (abbr RRT)/ psycho-**therapist** [saɪk-] • (balance)/ joint mobility/ ambulation/ muscle [mʌsl] control/ exercise¹¹ **therapy** • inhalation / play¹² / art¹³ / group **therapy** • family / behavior / nutrition¹⁴ [ɪʃ] **therapy** • diet¹⁵ / drug¹⁶ / genetic [dʒ] **counselor** • vocational¹⁷ [eɪʃ] (rehabilitation) / grief⁹ [griːf] **counselor** • family / pastoral / weight control / genetic **counseling** • marital¹⁸ / psychologic / smoking cessation¹⁹ **counseling**

Therapeut(in)
Berater(in)¹ therapeutisch² Beratung³ langfristig⁴ Physiotherapeut(in), Krankengymnast(in)⁵ Ergo-, Beschäftigungstherapeut(in)⁶ Logopäde/-in⁷ Verhaltenstherapeut(in)⁸ Trauerbegleiter(in), -therapeut(in)⁹ gepr. Atemtherapeut(in)¹⁰ Übungstherapie¹¹ Spieltherapie¹² Kunsttherapie¹³ Ernährungstherapie¹⁴ Ernährungsberater(in)¹⁵ Drogenberater(in)¹⁶ Berufsberater(in)¹⁷ Eheberatung¹⁸ Raucherentwöhnungsberatung¹⁹   12

dietitian [daɪətɪʃən] n   syn **dietician** n,
    rel **nutritionist**¹ [nuːtrɪʃᵊnɪst] n → U2-12; U79-3

professional specialized in nutritional care and food-service supervision

dietetics² n term • **dietetic**³ adj • **dietary**⁴ adj & n clin • **nutrition**⁵ n • **nutritional** adj

» If initial [ɪʃ] evaluation suggests dietary inadequacy⁶, formal assessment by a registered dietician is indicated. Dietary counseling by a trained dietitian is essential. Most nutritionists say that huge⁷ [hjuːdʒ] doses of vitamin C do not decrease the incidence of the common cold⁸.

Use registered (abbr RD)/ clinical / licensed [aɪs]/ consulting [ʌ]/ pediatric [iː] **dietitian** • public health **nutritionist** • **dietetic** assistant⁹ / technician⁹ [ɪʃ]/ food¹⁰ • **dietary** fiber¹¹ [aɪ]/ allowance [aʊ] • to provide/maintain [eɪ] (adequate/ enteral) **nutrition** • **nutritional** counseling¹²

Diätspezialist(in), Diätetiker(in)
Ernährungswissenschaftler(in)¹ Diätetik, Ernährungstherapie² diätetisch, Ernährungs-, Diät-³ diätetisch; Diätplan, -vorschrift⁴ Ernährung⁵ Mangel-, Fehlernährung, Malnutrition⁶ sehr hohe⁷ Schnupfen⁸ Diätassistent(in)⁹ Diätkost, -nahrung¹⁰ Ballaststoffe¹¹ Ernährungsberatung¹²   13

OPERATING ROOM

Overstaffed!? Don't make me laugh. This is the third operation I've carried out this morning – and I'm only the janitor!

orderly n   rel **medical attendant**¹, **porter**², **diener**² [iː], **janitor**³ [dʒæ-] n

untrained male hospital attendant¹ who works under the directions of a registered nurse and performs general non-medical duties, e.g. patient transports to and from the OR, preoperative shaving, etc.

» Send all available personnel resources such as doctors, nurses, orderlies, and registration clerks [ɜː] to the emergency department where the incoming casualties⁴ [æʒ] will arrive. Instruct an attendant to accompany the patient to the bathroom.

Use **orderly**-on-call⁵ • hospital / domestic **orderly** • morgue⁶ [mɔːrg] **diener** • nursing / ambulance / day care center⁷ **attendant**

Krankenpflegehelfer, Pfleger, Sanitäter (mil.)
Krankenpfleger(in)¹ Pflegehelfer² Hausmeister³ eingelieferte Frischverletzte⁴ diensthabender Krankenpflegehelfer⁵ Angestellte(r) im Leichenschauhaus⁶ Tagesstättenbetreuer(in)⁷   14

hospital volunteer [vɒːləntɪər] n
    sim **hospital auxiliary**¹ [ɒːgzɪləri], **ancillary** [ænˈsələri] **personnel**² n

nonprofessional helping out at a medical facility, e.g. operating the switchboard³ on weekends

volunteer⁴ v • **voluntary**⁵ adj • **auxiliary** adj • **volunteerism**⁶ n term

» Volunteer services, including homemakers⁷, visiting nurses, and adult protective services may be helpful in maintaining the patient at home. Volunteerism by both health care professionals and lay [leɪ] individuals is common during a disaster.

Use hospice / adult / emergency [ɜː] department⁸ **volunteer** • Peace Corps / Good Samaritan **volunteer** • **volunteer** health care / blood donor⁹ [oʊ] • nursing¹⁰ **auxiliary** • **ancillary** health care worker¹¹ / procedure [siː]/ measures¹² [eʒ]

freiwillige(r)/ ehrenamtl. Krankenhaus-Helfer(in)
med. Hilfskraft¹ Hilfspersonal² Telefonvermittlung³ etw. freiwillig tun⁴ freiwillig; willkürlich⁵ freiwilliger Einsatz⁶ Haus- und Familienpflegerinnen⁷ freiwillige(r) Helfer(in) i. d. Notaufnahme⁸ freiwillige(r) Blutspender(in)⁹ Krankenpflege-, Schwesternhelfer(in)¹⁰ Fürsorgehelfer(in)¹¹ Zusatzmaßnahmen¹²   15

Unit 17   Basic Medical Equipment & Supplies
Related Units: 18 At the Doctor's, 107 Physical Examination, 127 Basic Operative Techniques, 132 Surgical Instruments

doctor's bag n   syn doctor's case [dɒːktəs keɪs] n

portable case which holds items [aɪ] a doctor needs to handle a day's emergencies, e.g. a flashlight, tape measure¹ [eʒ], calipers², BM sticks³, tablets, pain drugs, prescription pad⁴, injectables⁵ [dʒe], thermometer, lancets⁶ ['s], neurological pins⁷, surgical masks & gloves⁸ [ʌ], catgut [ʌ], bandages⁹, swabs¹⁰, specimen collecting containers¹¹, and medical alert [ɜː] bracelets [eɪs] & tags¹²

» Keep your doctor's bag locked when not in use and check the expiration [eɪʃ] dates¹³ of all drugs six monthly. His worn-out doctor's bag is packed with measles [iː] vaccines¹⁴ [ks]. Benzylpenicillin [sɪ] and erythromycin [aɪs] are listed as 'Doctor's Bag' items.

Use full-sized / large-capacity [æs]/ state-of-the-art¹⁵ **doctor's bag** • old-style / leather [e] **doctor's bag** • doctor's bag supplies¹⁶ [aɪ]

Arzt-, Bereitschaftstasche
Maßband, Bandmaß¹ Greif-, Tastzirkel² Stuhlteststäbchen³ Rezeptblock⁴ Injektionsmittel⁵ Lanzetten⁶ neurolog. Testnadeln⁷ Mundschutz u. OP-Handschuhe⁸ Verbandmaterial⁹ Tupfer¹⁰ Abstrichröhrchen¹¹ med. Informationsarmbänder u. -plaketten¹² Ablaufdatum¹³ Masernimpfstoff¹⁴ d. neuesten Stand entsprechende Arzttasche¹⁵ Inhalt d. Arzttasche¹⁶   1

stethoscope [steθəskoʊp] n term

instrument to hear and amplify the sounds produced by the heart [ɑː], lungs, and other internal organs, it consists of the bell (piece¹), a flexible rubber [ʌ] tube and binaural [ɔː] earpieces²

stethoscopic adj term • stethoscopy³ [steθɒːskəpi] n rare

» Heart sounds⁴ are audible by stethoscope, most prominently beneath the sternum [ɜː]. A pericardial friction [frɪkʃən] rub⁵ [ʌ] was elicited [ɪs] when firm pressure with the diaphragm [daɪəfræm] of the stethoscope is applied to the chest wall at the left lower sternal border.

Use to be audible [ɒː] with/hear through/listen with **a stethoscope** • chest / binaural⁶ / differential / electronic⁷ / Doppler (ultrasonic)⁸ / esophageal [-dʒiːəl]/ obstetrical⁹ / diaphragm of the¹⁰ **stethoscope** • **stethoscope** placement • **the stethoscope** is placed over or on a part of the body • stethoscopic examination / auscultation [ɒːskəl-]/ headset

Stethoskop
Bruststück, Schalltrichter¹ Ohroliven² Abhören, Auskultation³ Herztöne⁴ perikardiales Reibegeräusch⁵ Schlauchstethoskop⁶ elektron. Stethoskop⁷ Doppler-Stethoskop⁸ Hebammen-Stethoskop⁹ Stethoskopmembran¹⁰   2

tongue depressor or blade [tʌŋ bleɪd] n term   rel spatula¹ [spætʃələ] n term

broad wooden blade with rounded ends used for pressing down the tongue to allow for inspection of the fauces² [fɔːsiːz] or for scraping³ [eɪ] or lifting and mixing or spreading⁴ [e] soft substances [ʌ]

depressed adj term • spatulate⁵ v • spatulation n

» Assess⁶ tongue size and function with a flashlight and tongue blade. Check occlusion⁷ [uːʒ] by retracting each cheek [tʃiːk] with a tongue depressor while the patient bites normally. One layer of the cream is applied with sterile technique [tekniːk], using a sterile tongue blade as an applicator⁸.

Use to insert [ɜː] or place/wipe [aɪ] away with⁹ **a tongue blade** • sterile / splinting with a padded¹⁰ **tongue blade** • laryngoscope¹¹ [ɪ]/ scalpel¹² **blade** • wooden¹³ / plastic / metal **spatula** • depressed scar¹⁴ [skɑːr]/ skull [ʌ] fracture¹⁵ / mood¹⁶ [uː]/ reflexes¹⁷ • to spatulate vessels / the ureter [jʊɚ]/ an anastomosis¹⁸

Mund-, Zungenspatel
Spatel¹ Schlund, Rachen² Abschaben³ Auftragen⁴ spatulieren⁵ feststellen⁶ Verzahnung, Okklusion⁷ Applikator⁸ mit einem Zungenspatel abstreifen⁹ Schienen mit e. gepolsterten Z.¹⁰ Laryngoskop-Spatel¹¹ Skalpellklinge¹² Holzspatel¹³ leicht eingedellte Narbe¹⁴ Impressionsfraktur¹⁵ gedrückte Stimmung¹⁶ abgeschwächte Reflexe¹⁷ e. Anastomose spatulieren¹⁸   3

flashlight n   syn torch [tɔːrtʃ] n BE, rel headlight¹, head mirror¹ n term

small portable battery-powered electric lamp

lighted² [laɪtɪd] adj • lighting³ n • penlight⁴ n • sunlight [ʌ] n

» Using a hand flashlight, shine⁵ the light obliquely⁶ [iː] and parallel to the plane of the iris [aɪ] across the cornea and anterior chamber⁷ [eɪ]. Make sure that suction and adequate lighting are available. Illumination⁸ with a penlight is necessary. Use a headlight, head mirror or other bright light source⁹ and a suction device¹⁰ [-aɪs] to determine [ɜː] the site of bleeding.

Use hand-held **flashlight** • fiberoptic **headlight** • laryngeal¹¹ [dʒ]/ dental¹² / hand-held **mirror** • exposure [oʊʒ] to sunlight

Taschenlampe
Stirnspiegel, -reflektor¹ be-, ausgeleuchtet² Beleuchtung³ Diagnostikleuchte⁴ leuchten⁵ schräg⁶ vordere Augenkammer⁷ Be-, Ausleuchten⁸ starke Lichtquelle⁹ Absaugvorrichtung¹⁰ Kehlkopfspiegel, Laryngoskop¹¹ Mund-, Zahnspiegel¹²   4

eye chart [tʃ] n clin   syn Snellen or visual acuity chart n term → U59-8

symbols of graduated size for measuring visual acuity¹ [əkjuːəti] for far or near vision

» The Amsler chart² (a finely squared [skweəd] grid viewed from a distance of 35 cm) is the easiest method of detecting central field abnormalities³ due to macular disease⁴. Snellen charts are used to test acuity at a distance of 6 m (20 ft).

Use Amsler² / color vision [ɪʒ] test⁵ **chart** • reading / wall⁶ / hand-held / growth⁷ [groʊθ] **chart** • **Snellen** test types⁸ • eye speculum / bandage⁹ [-ɪdʒ] drops / bank

(Snellen-)Sehprobentafel
Sehschärfe¹ Amsler-Netz, Gitternetz² Anomalien d. zentralen Gesichtsfeldes³ Makulaerkrankung⁴ pseudo-isochromat./ Ishihara-Tafeln⁵ Wandkarte⁶ Wachstumstabelle⁷ Snellen-Sehproben⁸ Augenverband⁹   5

nasal speculum *n term*   *syn* **rhinoscope** [ˈraɪnəskoʊp] *n term*
                                rel **retractor**[1] *n term* → U132-16

a retractor designed to be inserted into the nasal [eɪ] cavity to facilitate[2] [sɪ] inspection and/or medication

rhinoscopy[3] [raɪnˈɒːskəpi] *n term* • **rhino-** *comb* • **-scope** *comb*

» Use a narrow speculum lubricated[4] [uː] with water only. The speculum inserted into the patient's ear canal must be large enough to provide an airtight [aɪ] seal[5] [siːl]. Use the nasal speculum to systematically examine the walls of the nasal cavity for bleeding points.

Use ear[6] / eye or lid[7] / vaginal[8] [dʒ] / rectal[9] **speculum** • bivalve [æ] or duckbill[10] [ʌ]/ metal / three-pronged[11] [ɒː] **speculum** • water-lubricated / moistened / largest possible **speculum** • **speculum** examination / tip[12] • laryngo [ləˈrɪŋɡəskoʊp]/ ophthalmo[7]/ gastro[13]/ endo**scope** • broncho[14] [k]/ colono/ arthro**scope** • to perform **rhinoscopy** • evident on / conventional **rhinoscopy** • **rhino**rrhea[15] [raɪnəˈriːə] /phyma [raɪnoʊˈfaɪmə] /sinusitis [aɪ] /virus [aɪ] • **rhino**scleroma /tomy /plasty[16]

Nasenspekulum, Rhinoskop
(Wund)spreizer[1] ermöglichen[2] Rhinoskopie, Nasenspiegelung[3] gleitfähig gemacht[4] luftdichter Verschluss[5] Otoskop, Ohrenspekulum[6] Augenspiegel, Ophthalmoskop[7] Scheidenspekulum[8] Mastdarmspekulum[9] Doppelspekulum[10] 3-Blatt-Spekulum[11] Spekulumspitze[12] Gastroskop[13] Bronchoskop[14] Rhinorrhoe, Nasenausfluss[15] Nasenplastik, Rhinoplastik[16]

6

otoscope [ˈoʊtəskoʊp] *n term*   *syn* **auriscope** [ɔː] *n term*, *rel* **tuning fork**[1] *n clin*

instrument for examining the ear and the drum [ʌ] membrane[2]
otoscopic *adj term* • **otoscopy**[3] [ɒː] *n* • **oto-** *comb*

» A pneumatic [n(j)uːm-] otoscope[4] with a rubber suction [ʌ] bulb and tube is used to assess mobility of the tympanic membrane[2]. The fissure [ɪʃ] can be identified by inspecting the anal [eɪ] canal with an anoscope [eɪ] or an otoscope, using a large speculum. The tines[5] [aɪ] of a vibrating [aɪ] tuning fork are held first near the pinna[6], then the stem of the still-vibrating fork is placed in contact with the mastoid process.

Use pneumatic[4] **otoscope** • vibrating / 128-cycle / 256-Hz **tuning fork** • **tuning fork** test[7] • **otoscopic** examination[3] / findings[8] / signs of inflammation [eɪʃ] • pneumatic **otoscopy** • **oto**laryngologist[9] /logic emergency /toxic[10] /rrhea

Otoskop, Ohrenspekulum
Stimmgabel[1] Trommelfell[2] Ohr(en)spiegelung, Otoskopie[3] Otostroboskop, Otoskop m. Anschluss für pneumat. Trommelfelltest[4] Zinken[5] Ohrmuschel, Auricula[6] Stimmgabelprüfung[7] Otoskopiebefund[8] HNO-Arzt/ Ärztin, Facharzt/-ärztin f. Hals-Nasen-Ohrenheilkunde[9] ototoxisch[10]

7

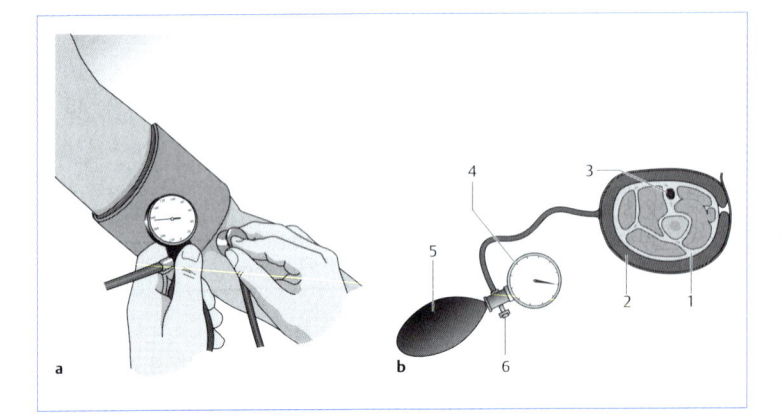

Blood pressure measurement: **(a)** the blood pressure measuring cuff, **(b)** sphygmomanometer in place: upper arm **(1)**, cuff **(2)**, brachial artery **(3)**, manometer **(4)**, bulb **(5)**, air vent valve **(6)**

sphygmomanometer [sfɪɡmoʊməˈnɒːmətɚ] *n term*
                        rel **blood pressure cuff**[1] [ʌ], **tourniquet**[2] [tʊɚˈtɜːrnɪkɪt] *n term*

instrument consisting of an inflatable [eɪ] cuff[3], inflating bulb[4] [ʌ], and a gauge[5] [ɡeɪdʒ] for measuring [eʒ] blood pressure

(**sphygmo**)man**ometry**[6] *n term* • **sphygmo-** *comb*

» Hearing Korotkoff sounds by stethoscope and sphygmomanometer is the most common measure of blood pressure. If an extremity is to be catheterized, apply [aɪ] the tourniquet above the site. Rotating tourniquets are effective with BP cuffs applied to three limbs [lɪmz].

Use well-calibrated[7] **sphygmomanometer** • **sphygmomanometer** bulb • BP[1] / rubber[8] [ʌ]/ arm **cuff** • leg / endotracheal [eɪk] tube[9] **cuff** • **cuff** (inflation) pressure[10] / deflation / size[11] • to apply or place[12]/act as/inflate/release [iː] /remove **a tourniquet** • arterial [ɪɚ]/ orthopedic [iː]/ limb **tourniquets** • arm / rotating **tourniquets** • **tourniquet** time[13] / effect / ischemia[14] [ɪskiː-] • **tourniquet** test[15] / injury[16] • indirect cuff[6] **sphygmomanometry** • **sphygmomanometric** measurement[6] [eʒ] • **sphygmo**manometric /graph[17] /gram

Blutdruckmessgerät, Sphygmomanometer
Blutdruckmanschette[1] Tourniquet, Stauschlauch, -manschette[2] aufblasbare Manschette[3] Ballon[4] Messgerät[5] indirekte/ unblutige Blutdruckmessung, RR-Messung[6] geeichtes Blutdruckmessgerät[7] Gummimanschette[8] Tubusmanschette, Cuff[9] Manschettendruck[10] Manschettenbreite[11] e. Staumanschette anlegen[12] Dauer d. Staudrucks[13] Esmarch-Blutleere[14] Rumpel-Leede-Test/-Stauversuch[15] Tourniquetsyndrom[16] Sphygmograph, Pulsschreiber[17]

8

Basic Medical Equipment & Supplies	HEALTH CARE **73**

reflex hammer [riːfleks hæmɚ] n	syn **neurologic hammer** n term → U113-1
　　rel **percussion** [ʌ] **mallet**[1] [mælᵊt], **percussor**[1], **plessor**[1] n term → U107-8
　small hammer with soft rubber head used to tap[2] tendons, nerves [ɜː], or muscles [mʌslz] directly or indirectly (e.g. with a plessimeter in mediate [iː] percussion[3] of the chest)
　　plexor[1] [pleksɚ] n term • **plessimeter** or **pleximeter**[4] [ples‖pleksɪmətɚ] n
» With the arm gently [dʒ] flexed at the elbow, tap the biceps [baɪseps] tendon with a reflex hammer. The reflex hammer is a percussion hammer which can be used to test reflexes. Using a reflex hammer, deep tendon reflexes are elicited[5] [ɪs] in all four extremities.
Use triangular **reflex hammer** • patella / percussion[1] / Babinski hammer • **hammer** technique • to trigger or elicit[6]/test **a reflex** • deep tendon[7] / knee (jerk) [dʒɜːrk] or patellar[8] / plantar[9] **reflex** • **reflex** arc[10] [ɑːrk]/ response[11] / movement / contraction[12] • **reflex** latency [eɪ]/ inhibition[13] / testing[14] • light or gentle[15] / deep[16] / forceful[17] / vigorous[17] **percussion** • fist / muscle / abdominal / chest / vertebral [ɜː] **percussion** • **percussion** note[18] / tympany[19] [ɪ] / tenderness[20] • dull [ʌ] **percussion** note[21] • hyperresonance[22] / dullness[21] **to percussion**

Reflexhammer
Perkussionshammer[1] beklopfen[2] indirekte/ mittelbare Perkussion[3] Plessimeter[4] ausgelöst[5] e. Reflex auslösen[6] Sehnenreflex[7] Patellarsehnenreflex[8] Plantar-, Fußsohlenreflex[9] Reflexbogen[10] Reflexantwort[11] reflektor. Kontraktion[12] Reflexhemmung[13] Reflexprüfung[14] leise Perkussion[15] Tiefenperkussion[16] kräftige P.[17] Perkussions-, Klopfschall[18] tympanitischer Klopfschall[19] Perkussionsempfindlichkeit[20] gedämpfter Klopfschall[21] hypersonorer Klopfschall[22]
9

syringe [sɪrɪndʒ] n	rel **Vacutainer (tube)**[1] [vækjuteɪnɚ t(j)uːb] n term
　instrument for injecting [dʒe] or withdrawing [ɒː] fluids which consists of a barrel[2] [bærᵊl], plunger[3] [plʌndʒɚ], barrel tip, and hub [ʌ] opening[4] to which the needle shaft [ʃæft] is connected
» A separate syringe and needle should be used for each vaccine[5] [væksiːn]. Grasp the syringe or Vacutainer in the dominant hand while palpating the vein [eɪ] with the index finger[6] of the other hand. Pus[7] [ʌ] was aspirated into a syringe percutaneously.
Use to fill[8]/draw up into or load[8]/empty/(dis)connect/remove **a syringe** • attached [ætʃ]/ sterile • disposable[9] / glass / plastic **syringe** • heparinized[10] / prefilled [iː] or preloaded / 10-mL **syringe** • bulb[11] / tuberculin / suction[12] [sʌkʃᵊn] **syringe** insertion [-sɜːrʃᵊn]/ irrigating[13] / **syringe** • **syringe** opening / plunger / holder • **syringe** irrigation / fluid[14] • **Vacutainer** equipment / system [ɪ]

Spritze
Blutentnahmeröhrchen, Vacutainer-Kanüle[1] Zylinder[2] Kolben[3] Kanülenansatz[4] Impfung[5] Zeigefinger[6] Eiter[7] eine Spritze aufziehen[8] Einweg-, Einmalspritze[9] heparinisierte Spritze[10] Ballonspritze[11] Aspirationsspritze[12] Spülspritze[13] Injektionsflüssigkeit[14]
10

hypodermic (needle) [haɪpədɜːrmɪk niːdᵊl] n clin & jar → U132-5, U136-6
　hollow needle, similar to but smaller than an aspirating needle, used primarily for injection
　　needle[1] v jar & clin • **needling**[2] n • **needlestick**[3] n
» Are you sure he did not engage [-geɪdʒ] in nonsterile practices such as recycling[4] hypodermic needles? Check the skin for evidence of trauma [ɒː] or hypodermic injections. Insert the needle just under the skin and pull the plunger back gently to create a slight vacuum.
Use **hypodermic** equipment[5] / syringe / injection[6] / administration[7] • to grasp/hold /insert or introduce[8]/advance[9]/guide **the needle** • to direct/push/rotate/remove or withdraw[10] **the needle** • syringe and / disposable / large-bore[11] **needle** • fine / 22-gauge[12] [geɪdʒ]/ 6.5-cm or 2 1/2-in steel[13] [iː] **needle** • bevel[14] / lumen [uː]/ shaft / tip • hub[15] **of the needle** • introducing / tapered[16] [eɪ] / probing[17] [oʊ] • butterfly [ʌ] **needle** • catheter-clad or catheter-over **needle** • blunt[18] [ʌ]/ anesthetizing [e]/ spinal [aɪ] **needle** • thoracentesis [iː]/ scalp vein / Vacutainer[19] **needle** • **needle** point / size / hub[15] / holder[20] • **needle** insertion / placement / entry[21] • **needle** site[21] / pressure / aspiration / biopsy [aɪ] • **needle** puncture [ʌ] mark[22] / sharing[23] [eɚ]/ puncture • **needlestick** injury[24]

Subkutan-, Injektionsnadel
durchstechen, punktieren[1] Punktion[2] Nadelstich[3] wiederverwenden[4] Injektionsbesteck[5] subkutane Injektion[6] subk. Applikation/ Verabreichung[7] d. Nadel einführen/ einstechen[8] d. N. vorschieben[9] d. N. herausziehen[10] großlumige Hohlnadel[11] 22er-Nadel (N. m. 0,71mm Außendurchmesser)[12] Metallnadel[13] abgeschrägte Nadelspitze[14] Nadel-, Kanülenansatz[15] spitze N.[16] chirurg. Sonde[17] stumpfe Nadel[18] Spritzennadel[19] Nadelhalter[20] Einstichstelle[21] Punktionsnarbe[22] gemeinsame Verwendung v. Nadeln (bei Drogengebrauch)[23] Nadelstichverletzung[24]
11

kidney dish [kɪdni dɪʃ] n term	syn **kidney tray** [treɪ] n term
　　rel **specimen jar**[1] [spesɪmᵊn dʒɑːr], **tray**[2], **lotion bowl**[3] [loʊʃᵊn boʊl] n term
　kidney-shaped receptacle commonly used as an emesis basin[4] [eɪ] and for many other clinical purposes
» I quickly grabbed a kidney dish from a nearby trolley[5] and held it to her mouth. Place these instruments in a sterile kidney dish. The placenta [se] is delivered into a kidney dish and the midwife[6] will examine it carefully to make sure that it is complete.
Use stainless [eɪ] steel[7] / sterling [ɜː] silver / enamel[8] **kidney dish** • plastic / reusable[9] [juː] **kidney dish** • Petri[10] **dish** • instrument[11] / catheter **tray** • bedside[12] / ash[13] **tray** • grinding [aɪ] / denture[14] [-tʃɚ]/ toilet[15] **bowl** • sterile **specimen jar**

Nierenschale
Probenglas[1] Auflagetablett, Tray, Schale[2] Testschälchen[3] Speischale[4] Rollwagen[5] Hebamme[6] Nierenschale aus Edelstahl[7] N. aus Email[8] wiederverwendbare N.[9] Petri-Schale[10] Instrumentenschale, -tray[11] Essenstablett[12] Aschenbecher[13] Behälter f. Zahnprothese[14] Toilettenbecken[15]
12

17

74 HEALTH CARE   Basic Medical Equipment & Supplies

swab [swɒːb] *n & v clin & term*   *syn* **cotton applicator** [kɒːtʰn æplɪkeɪtɚ] *n term*
                                        rel **pad**[1] [pæd], **glass slide**[2] [slaɪd] *n* → U116-5

(n, i) stick-like instrument with absorbent gauze[3] [gɔːz] or cotton used for cleansing [e] or drying the skin, applying[4] topical medications, or for collecting specimens for analysis in the lab (ii) a specimen taken with a swab

swabbing *n* • **apply** [aɪ] *v* • **application**[5] *n* • **pad**[6] *v* • **padded**[7] *adj* → U140-19

» Swab the mouth around the molars and cheeks. Positive areas should be swabbed with a premoistened[8] swab. Use one applicatorful of this cream vaginally [dʒ] at bedtime for 7 days. Wash the area with sterile gauze pads soaked [oʊ] in a cleansing agent [eɪdʒ].

Use to apply/cleanse[9]/collect **with a swab** • (sterile) cotton / cotton-tipped[10] **swab** • plastic-shafted bulb **swab** • throat [oʊ]/ nasal[11] / pharyngeal [dʒ] **swab** • anal / vaginal / cervical[12] [ɜː]/ urethral [iː]/ **swab** • **swab** sample or specimen[13] / culture [ʌ] • sterile / moist / wet **cotton applicator** • cotton-tipped[10] / wooden **applicator** • fluoride[14] / silver nitrate [aɪ] **applicator** • cotton gauze / alcohol **pad** • plastic-coated absorbent / alcohol prep[15] **pad** • electrode / eye[16] / nasal [eɪ] drip / heel[17] [iː] **pad** • (volar) fat[18] / finger / protective[19] **pad** • knee[20] [niː]/ shoe / note[21] / prescription / heating **pad** • gentle / throat **swabbing** • **to apply** a dressing[22] / a cream[23] / ice bags • **to apply** a tourniquet[24] / a cast[25] [kæst]/ pressure[26] / suction[27]

(i) **(Stiel)tupfer, Watteträger**
(ii) **Abstrich; abtupfen**

Bausch; Kissen, Polster; Kompresse[1] Objektträger[2] Gaze, Mull[3] aufbringen, applizieren[4] Anwendung, Applikation[5] (aus)polstern, füttern, wattieren[6] gepolstert, -füttert[7] befeuchtet[8] mit e. Tupfer reinigen[9] Wattestäbchen[10] Nasenabstrich[11] Zervixabstrich[12] Abstrichmaterial[13] Fluoridapplikator[14] Alkoholtupfer z. Desinfektion[15] Augenklappe[16] Fersenfettgewebe; Fersenpolster[17] Fettpolster[18] Schutzpolster[19] Knieschützer[20] Notizblock[21] e. Verband anlegen[22] e. Creme auftragen[23] e. Stauschlauch anlegen[24] e. Gipsverband anlegen[25] Druck ausüben[26] absaugen[27]

13

lubricant [luːbrɪkənt] *n & adj* → U9-8

(n) substance capable [eɪ] of reducing friction[1] [frɪkʃən] by making surfaces smooth[2] [uː] or slippery[3]

lubricate[4] *v* • **lubricating** *adj* • **lubrication**[5] *n* → U56-9

» Insert the warmed, water-lubricated speculum into the upper vagina [dʒaɪ]. Lubricating jelly[6] [dʒeli] should not be used, since it may interfere [-fɪɚ] with the Pap test[7]. Lubricate the end of the tracheal [k] tube.

Use to apply/inject/act as[8] **a lubricant** • artificial [ɪʃ]/ high-viscosity / bland[9] **lubricant** • water-soluble[10] / hydrophobic **lubricant** • coital / spermatotoxic[11] / sterile **lubricant** • glove [ʌ]/ anesthetic / ocular[12] **lubricant** • **lubricant** fluid • **lubricating** ointment[6] [ɔɪ]/ lotion [oʊʃ]/ eye drops[12] • (decreased) vaginal[13] / insufficient [ɪʃ]/ generous[14] [dʒe] **lubrication**

Gleitmittel; schmierend, Gleit-
Reibung[1] glatt, geschmeidig[2] gleitfähig, schlüpfrig[3] (ein)fetten, -schmieren, gleitfähig machen[4] Schmieren, Ölen, Lubrikation[5] Gleitgel[6] Pap-Test, -Abstrich[7] als Gleitmittel wirken/ fungieren[8] reizarmes Gleitmittel[9] wasserlösl. Lubrikans[10] spermizides Gleitmittel[11] benetzende Augentropfen[12] Scheidenlubrikation[13] reichliches Einfetten/ Einschmieren[14]

14

disinfectant *n & adj term* → U139-5   *syn* **germicide** [dʒɜːrmɪsaɪd] *n term*

(n) antiseptic chemical capable of killing vegetative forms of germs[1] but usually not bacterial spores[2]

disinfect[3] *v* • **disinfection**[4] *n* • **germicidal** *adj* • **-cide, -cidal** *comb* → U90-5

» Contaminated surfaces may be easily disinfected with household bleach[5] [bliːtʃ], commercial disinfectants (e.g. Lysol), or 70% isopropyl [aɪsəproʊpəl] alcohol. Is there a history of skin reactions to iodine[6] [aɪədɪn], thimerosal [θaɪmɛrəsæl] or other germicides?

Use chemical / skin[7] / organic iodine / halogenated [dʒə]/ mild **disinfectant** • **disinfectant** soap [oʊ]/ solution[8] [uːʃ] • **germicidal** soap / action or effect[9] • **to disinfect** the hands / the skin / equipment[10] / heat[11] / chlorine / high-level[12] **disinfection** • amebi [iː]/ fungi[13] [ʌ]/ pesti**cide** • insecti/ herbi [(h)ɜːrbɪsaɪd]/ rodenti**cide** • bacteri[14]/ viru/ microbi**cidal**

Desinfektionsmittel; Desinfiziens, keim(ab)tötendes Mittel; desinfizierend
Keime[1] Bakteriensporen[2] desinfizieren, entseuchen, -keimen[3] Desinfektion[4] haushaltsübliches Bleichmittel[5] Iod[6] Hautdesinfektionsmittel[7] Desinfektionslösung[8] keimtötende Wirkung[9] Gegenstände/ Geräte desinfizieren[10] Heißluftdesinfektion[11] high-level Desinfektion[12] Fungizid, Antimykotikum[13] bakterizid, bakterienabtötend[14]   15

(doctor's) white coat [koʊt] *n*   *sim* **medical tunic**[1] [t(j)uːnɪk] *n*
                                       rel **name tag** or **ID badge**[2] [bædʒ] *n*

garment with long sleeves that covers the body from shoulder down and is worn over normal clothes

» When on duty[3], you must wear your white doctor's coat with your ID badge attached to the left breast pocket. Orientation to person is helped by medical personnel wearing large name tags. When I see a doctor or a nurse in a white coat I become apprehensive[4] and my blood pressure soars[5] [ɔː]. This doctor's coat, with its wrinkle-resistant fabric[6] and three spacious[7] [eɪʃ] pockets, functions nicely as a portable office. This excellent 'how-to' book of challenging medical interviews[8] belongs in every doctor's coat pocket.

Use lab[9] / (unisex) doctor's / clean **coat** • to put on/wear[10]/be (dressed) in **a doctor's coat** • white coat ceremony[11] / response • white coat effect / syndrome[12] / hypertension • to wear a **name tag** • identification[13] / Medic-Alert[14] / triage tag

Arztkittel, weißer Kittel
OP-Schutzkittel[1] Namensschild[2] im Dienst[3] ängstlich[4] schnellt in die Höhe, steigt rapide[5] knitterfreier Stoff[6] groß und tief[7] schwierige Anamnesegespräche[8] Labormantel[9] e. weißen Kittel tragen[10] Promotionsfeier[11] Angst vor Ärzten, Arztphobie[12] Erkennungsmarke[13] medizin. Informationsplakette[14]

16

At the Doctor's   HEALTH CARE **75**

pager n   *syn* **beeper, bleep** n *jar BE, rel* **intercom system**[1], **loudspeaker**[2] n
device [dɪvaɪs] that makes a bleeping [iː] noise when the doctor is wanted on the phone
page[3] vt • **paging** [peɪdʒɪŋ] n • **bleep**[3] [bliːp] v *inf & jar BE* • **beep**[4] [biːp] n
» You are asked to carry this pager with you so that you can quickly respond in case of an emergency. For wireless[5] [aɪ] instant messaging, most hospital doctors carry a pager. Make sure you don't leave the hospital with a beeper that is needed on the next shift[6]. My bleep went off[7] but it was a false alarm.
Use to carry/be available [eɪ] on[8]/turn off **the pager** • in-hospital[9] / on-call[10] / digital [ɪdʒ] **pager** • **pager** number / authorization list[11] / relay [eɪ] • **paging** system • hospital-wide[9] **beeper** • **beeper** service / call • hospital[9] **bleep**

▪ Note: In the U.S. **bleep** refers to the noise used to drown obscenities on TV.

Funkrufempfänger, Piepser
Gegensprechanlage[1] Lautsprecher[2] (jem.) auspiepsen[3] Piepston, -signal[4] drahtlos[5] Dienst[6] ertönte, klingelte[7] über d. Piepser erreichbar sein[8] krankenhausinterner Piepser[9] Piepser für d. Bereitschaftsdienst[10] Piepsergenehmigungsliste[11]

17

Unit 18   At the Doctor's
Related Units: **15** Medical Staff, **17** Medical Equipment, **19** On the Ward, **20** Hospital Routines, **102** History Taking, **9** Drugs & Remedies

doctor's *or* **physician's office** [fɪzɪʃ⁽ə⁾nz ɒːfɪs] n
   syn (**doctor's) surgery** [sɜːrdʒɚi] n *BE, rel* (**doctor's) practice**[1] [præktɪs] n
facility [sɪ] or room where a physician sees and treats [iː] patients
official[2] [ɪʃ] n & adj • **officer** n • **practice**[3] v, BE **–ise**
malpractice n • **practitioner**[4] [ɪʃ] n
» Patients who cannot be depended on should be asked to come to the physician's office for a shot[5]. Beginning at 3 years of age, office screening [iː] of vision [ɪʒ] should be performed. Office BP is often higher than that obtained [eɪ] at home. It is now common practice in obstetrics[6] to obtain antenatal [eɪ] ultrasonography [ʌltrə-]. The amount of depot fat is best estimated in office practice by measuring [eʒ] body weight [weɪt] and relating it to height [haɪt].
Use to attend/be brought to/arrive at/return to **the doctor's office** • primary [aɪ] care[7] / GP's[7] / urologic / obstetrician's [ɪʃ] **office** • **office**-based physician[8] / personnel / assistant[9] / nurse[9] [ɜː] hours[10] [aʊɚz]/ equipment / supplies [aɪ] • **office** schedule[11] [sk‖ʃedjuːl]/ visit / management / evaluation[12] • **office** protocol book / file [aɪ]/ practice[13] / procedure[14] [siː] • **office** population[15] • to see[16]/call in a **doctor** • to run a[17] **practice** • to establish a[18] / to go into[18] **practice** • doctor in private/ general/ family/ group[19] **practice** • obstetric / surgical [ɜː]/ pediatric / urologic / dental **practice** • (in everyday/ current [ɜː]/ good) clinical / routine medical[20] **practice** • medical[21] **malpractice** • **malpractice** case / law(suit) [lɔːsuːt]/ insurance [ʃʊɚ]/ damage awards[22] [ɔː] • **practice** guideline [aɪ]/ advisory[23] [aɪ]/-oriented • **practice** patterns / settings[24] / standards • **to practice** medicine / safer sex • **surgery** hours[10] • medical / general[25] (*abbr* GP)/ infection-control **practitioner** • mental health[26] [helθ]/ dental / folk[27] [foʊk] **practitioner** • nurse[28] / rural[29] [rʊɚl]/ experienced [ɪɚ] **practitioner** • health care[30] / state **official** • **official** policy [pɒːlɪsi] • public [ʌ] health / medical[31] / house[32] / police **officer**

(Arzt)praxis
Ordination, (Arzt)praxis; Praxisalltag[1] Beamter/-in; offiziell, amtlich, Amts-, Dienst-[2] praktizieren, ausüben; üben[3] prakt. Arzt/ Ärztin, Praktiker(in)[4] Injektion[5] Geburtshilfe[6] Praxis d. Hausarztes/ -ärztin[7] niedergelassene(r)/ praktizierende(r) Arzt/ Ärztin[8] Arzthelfer(in)[9] Ordinationszeiten[10] Praxisablauf[11] ambulante Abklärung[12] Praxisalltag[13] ambul. Eingriff[14] Patienten(gut)[15] e. Arzt aufsuchen/ konsultieren[16] e. Praxis führen[17] e. Praxis eröffnen[18] Gemeinschaftspraxis[19] ärztl. Routinetätigkeiten[20] ärztl. Behandlungs-/ Kunstfehler[21] Schadensersatz f. ärztl. Kunstfehler[22] prakt. Ratgeber[23] i. der Praxis[24] prakt. A., Allgemeinmediziner(in)[25] Psychiater(in)[26] Heilpraktiker(in), Naturarzt/-ärztin[27] Arzthelfer(in), Krankenschwester[28] Landarzt/-ärztin[29] Beamter/-in i. Gesundheitsdienst[30] Amtsarzt/ -ärztin[31] ®Assistenzarzt/-ärztin, Turnusarzt/ -ärztin (öst.)[32]

1

(medical) appointment n   *rel* **office visit**[1], **cancellation**[2] [kænˈs-] n
visit to a physician's office, clinic or outpatient department[3] arranged [eɪ] in advance[4]
(**re)appoint**[5] v • **interappointment** adj • **previsit** adj • **visitor** n • **cancel**[6] v
» She was discharged[7] [dɪstʃɑːrdʒd] with an appointment for a neurologist the next day. A complete history should be obtained at the first office visit. In the busy [ɪ] practice a previsit questionnaire helps to streamline[8] [iː] history taking. We'll have to reappoint Mr. Hill. We need a backup list of patients who will come in at short notice[9] for last-minute cancellations.
Use to make[10]/seek [iː] /fix[10]/schedule/arrange[10] [eɪ] /give sb./have/keep **an appointment** • broken[11] / examination / dental[12] / return[13] / follow-up[14] **appointment** • **appointment** date / scheduling[15] / keeping • book[16] / card[17] • by **appointment** only[18] • medical[1] / patient / physician **visit** • clinic / outpatient / dental / home[19] **visit** • monthly / twice-yearly / initial [ɪʃ] or first **visit** • repeat / return[20] **visit** • (un)scheduled / follow-up **visit** • preoperative / postsurgical / pre- or antenatal[21] [eɪ] **visit** • acute care / emergency department **visit** • well-child / preschool [iː]/ health supervision[22] [ɪʒ] **visit** • hospital **visitor** • **to cancel** an appointment / elective surgery

(Arzt-, Behandlungs)termin
Arztbesuch[1] Terminabsage[2] Ambulanz[3] im Voraus[4] einen (neuen) Termin geben[5] absagen, stornieren[6] entlassen[7] effizienter gestalten[8] auf Abruf[9] e. Termin vereinbaren[10] nicht eingehaltener T.[11] Zahnarzttermin[12] Kontrolltermin[13] Nachsorgetermin[14] Terminvereinbarung[15] Terminkalender[16] Bestellkarte (f. Arzttermin)[17] nur nach Vereinbarung[18] Hausbesuch[19] Kontrolluntersuchung, Kontrolle[20] Schwangerschaftsvorsorgeuntersuchung[21] Vorsorgeuntersuchung[22]

2

receptionist [rɪsepʃ⁽ə⁾nɪst] n   rel **reception room** or **waiting room**¹ n
assistant at the reception desk² who manages the appointments, telephone calls, office schedule, etc.
» My receptionist will give you a new appointment. The receptionist is not only the up-front contact for the patient but is also involved in book-keeping or backing up³ in the lab. All right, I'll try to squeeze⁴ [iː] you in today. Please complete this checklist in the waiting room. A list of the scheduled [ʃǁskedjuːld] patients and appointment times should be prepared and ready for the receptionist as each patient arrives.
Use medical / patient / clinic / admitting⁵ / radiology section **receptionist** • **receptionist's** window⁶ • **receptionist** training • **waiting** area⁷ / list⁸ / period⁹ / time⁹

(medical) advice [-aɪs] n   sim **counseling**¹ [aʊ] n, rel **(medical) attention**² n
recommendation or proposal [oʊ] for an appropriate course [kɔːrs] of action
advise³ [ədvaɪz] v • **(in)advisable**⁴ adj • **attend (to)**⁵ v • **counsel** v • **counselor**⁶ n
» A frank discussion of the patient's status should be coupled [ʌ] with sound [aʊ] advice⁷ about smoking, diet [daɪət], and work habits. She was strongly advised to prevent conception [se] during the 90 days following rubella vaccination [ks]. Any deterioration of vital [aɪ] signs demands prompt attention. Sexually active adolescents [es] should be counseled to use condoms. Postoperatively, the surgeon must attend to⁸ the patient's emotional [oʊʃ] needs.
Use to seek⁹/offer/give/provide/obtain [eɪ] /reject [dʒe] *(medical) advice* • to leave the hospital against medical¹⁰ (abbr AMA) **advice** / health / expert / travel **advice** • dietary¹¹ / practical / telephone / late-at-night **advice** • **advice** regarding air travel / on tobbacco use • **advice** from a physician¹² / for patients • to seek¹³ **medical attention** • to pay/draw¹⁴/require/bring to¹⁵/receive **attention** • to come to/attract¹⁶/escape/divert¹⁷ [ɜː] /focus/gain sb.'s **attention** • clinical / surgical **attention** • *to advise* rest / elevation of the leg¹⁸ / the use of crutches [ʌ] • *to advise* against lavage¹⁹ [ɑːʒ]/ sb. of a poor prognosis²⁰ • *to counsel* a patient / sb. about risks²¹ • office-based / diet / risk-reduction • smoking cessation²² **counseling** • premarital / parental / family **counseling** • contraceptive²³ / cancer / genetic²⁴ / psychologic [saɪk-] / marriage²⁵ **counseling** • nutritional²⁶ / weight control / supportive / behavioral [eɪ] **counseling** • bereavement [iː] or grief²⁷ / pastoral / rape²⁸ [reɪp] **counseling** • **counseling** services²⁹ / team / session³⁰ / program / strategies • drug³¹ / grief **counselor**

recommend v   rel **advocate**¹, **propose**², **urge**³ v → U73-11
to suggest a course of action, option, or plan because it is suitable in a particular situation
recommended⁴ adj • **commendable**⁵ adj • **recommendation**⁶ n
» Many physicians recommend aspirin in doses of 300 mg per day. He denied⁷ [aɪ] coughing in order to avoid recommendations to quit smoking⁸. Urologic referral is recommended for women with frequent recurrences of cystitis⁹. Lower dosages are advocated for patients with renal insufficiency¹⁰. Your physician proposed this therapy on the basis of his clinical judgment¹¹. Urge patients to report undesired effects before stopping medication.
Use **to reommend** a change of life-style / hospitalization • **to reommend** a follow-up¹² / dry skin care / against sth.¹³ • *to advocate* immobilization / surgery¹⁴ / steroids • *to propose* an exercise program • **recommended** dosage / regimen¹⁵ [edʒ]/ for children / dietary [aɪ] allowance¹⁶ (abbr RDA) • dosing / vaccination¹⁷ [ks]/ therapeutic [juː]/ WHO **recommendations**

reassurance [riːəʃʊ⁽ə⁾nʔs] n   rel **comfort**¹ [kʌmfɚt] n & v → U19-11, 142-29
things said to help patients overcome their fears and worries and strengthen their confidence
reassure² v • **reassuring** adj • **comforting** adj & n
» Patients with dyspepsia require reassurance that the condition is not serious but may be chronic. Reassure the patient that no organic lesion [iː] is present and explain the emotional basis of the headache. Mild contrast material reactions usually do not require treatment except reassurance and comforting. Patients can be comforted by the knowledge that the course [kɔːrs] of the disease³ is not progressive.
Use to provide or give/call for/need⁴/respond to **reassurance** • medical⁵ / verbal [ɜː]/ therapeutic [juː] **reassurance** • supportive⁶ / repeated [iː]/ continued **reassurance** • explanation / support / encouragement⁷ [ɜː] **and reassurance** • **to reassure** the patient / parents • *to comfort* a baby⁸

---

76 HEALTH CARE   At the Doctor's

Sprechstundenhilfe
Warteraum, -zimmer¹ Anmeldung² aushelfen³ einschieben⁴ Aufnahmesekretärin⁵ Anmeldeschalter⁶ Wartebereich⁷ Warteliste⁸ Wartezeit⁹   3

ärztlicher Rat
Beratung¹ (ärztliche) Behandlung² raten; empfehlen³ ratsam, empfehlenswert⁴ s. kümmern um⁵ Berater(in)⁶ kompetenter Rat⁷ sich kümmern um⁸ e. Arzt zu Rate ziehen, e. ärztl. Rat einholen⁹ d. Krankenhaus gegen Revers verlassen¹⁰ Diätempfehlung¹¹ ärztl. Rat¹² s. in ärztl. Behandlung begeben, e. Arzt aufsuchen¹³ d. Aufmerksamkeit lenken (auf)¹⁴ zur Kenntnis bringen¹⁵ Aufmerksamkeit erregen¹⁶ ablenken¹⁷ Hochlagern d. Beins empfehlen¹⁸ von e. Lavage abraten¹⁹ jem. über e. ungünstige Prognose unterrichten²⁰ jem. über mögl. Risiken aufklären²¹ Raucherentwöhnungsberatung²² Empfängnisverhütungsberatung²³ genetische B.²⁴ Eheberatung²⁵ Ernährungsberatung²⁶ Trauerarbeit²⁷ Beratung v. Vergewaltigungsopfern²⁸ Beratungsdienst²⁹ Beratungsgespräch³⁰ Drogenberater(in)³¹   4

empfehlen, raten
befürworten, empfehlen, eintreten für¹ vorschlagen; beabsichtigen² drängen auf, nahelegen³ empfohlen⁴ empfehlens-, lobenswert⁵ Empfehlung⁶ verschwieg⁷ nicht mehr zu rauchen⁸ häufig wiederkehrende Blasenentzündungen⁹ Niereninsuffizienz¹⁰ klin. Beurteilung¹¹ e. Nachuntersuchung empfehlen¹² von etw. abraten¹³ e. chir. Eingriff befürworten¹⁴ empfohlene(s) Behandlung(sschema)¹⁵ empf. Nahrungszufuhr¹⁶ Impfempfehlungen¹⁷   5

Beruhigung, Zuspruch, Bestätigung
Trost, Beruhigung; Beistand leisten, trösten, beruhigen¹ beruhigen, versichern² Krankheitsverlauf³ Zuspruch brauchen⁴ ärztl. Zuspruch⁵ gutes Zureden, Beschwichtigung⁶ Zuspruch und Ermutigung⁷ ein kl. Kind beruhigen⁸   6

At the Doctor's   HEALTH CARE 77

house call [haus kɔːl] n   syn **home visit** [houm vɪzɪt] n

to provide [aɪ] medical care to a patient at his/her home

visit v • **visiting** adj • **visitation**[1] [eɪʃ] n • **visitor** n • **call**[2] v & n • **caller**[3] n

» She started getting house calls after a few falls prevented her from driving to her monthly check-ups. A home visit is of great value in assessing the frail[4] [eɪ] patient's ability to function in his or her own environment. What initially appeared to be a 10-minute visit for a throat [θroʊt] culture [ʌ] turned into a 1-hour visit spent counseling an anxious [ænkʃəs] pregnant teenager. Plan a return visit in 6 weeks and at 3-4 months after that.

Use to make/require **a visit** • **home visit** schedule • to make[5] **a house call** • **visiting hours**[6] / list / policies[7] / nurse[8] (service) • pastoral / home **visitation** • **visitation** rate • **home** care[9] / assessment • **to call** the doctor / for further investigation[10] / attention to a problem • **to call** in sick[11] (BE)/ (upon sb.) for help[12] • **call** button [ʌ] • emergency[13] / nighttime **call** • to be[14] / doctor[15] **on call** • **on-call** physician[15]

Hausbesuch

Besuch[1] (an)rufen; Besuch, Anruf[2] Besucher(in), Anrufer(in)[3] schwach, gebrechlich[4] einen Hausbesuch machen[5] Besuchszeiten[6] Besuchs-zeit(en)regelung[7] Hauskranken-pfleger(in)[8] häusliche Pflege, Haus-krankenpflege[9] weitere Unter-suchungen erfordern[10] sich krank melden[11] jem. um Hilfe bitten[12] Notruf[13] Bereitschaftsdienst ha-ben[14] diensthabende(r) Arzt/Ärztin[15]

7

doctor-patient relationship n   sim **physician-patient rapport**[1] [rəpɔːr] n

relation based on the unavoidable reliance[2] [aɪ] of the lay person on the physician's skill and help until healing [iː] and/or rehabilitation are complete

relate [rɪleɪt] (**to**)[3] v • **relation**[4] [rɪleɪʃən] n • **relative**[5] n • (**un**)**related**[6] adj

» Efforts should be directed toward firm [ɜː] and empathetic psychosocial support in the context of a sustained[7] [eɪ] physician-patient relationship. Check the patient's capacity to relate to others in a meaningful [iː] way. He was unable to establish rapport with the child. The rapport between patient and physician is a key factor to therapeutic success.

Use to establish[8]/maintain/renew **a relationship** • patient-physician / parent-child[9] / marital **relationship** • confidential[10] / trusting[10] [ʌ]/ personal / therapeutic **rela-tionship** • working[11] / contractual / legal [iː]/ sexual **relationship** • supportive / stable [eɪ] **relationship** • **relationship** of trust[10] • to establish[12]/build[12]/gain **rap-port with the patient** • to have difficulty establishing **rapport** • good[13] / poor **rapport**

Arzt-Patient-Beziehung

Vertrauensverhältnis zw. Arzt u. Patient[1] Vertrauen[2] zusammenhän-gen mit; sich verhalten[3] Bezie-hung[4] Verwandte(r)[5] verwandt; zusammenhängend[6] länger dau-ernd[7] eine Beziehung aufbauen[8] Eltern-Kind-Beziehung[9] Vertrau-ensverhältnis[10] Zusammenarbeit[11] e. Vertrauensbasis schaffen[12] gutes Einvernehmen[13]

8

(medical) checkup [tʃekʌp] n clin   syn **medical** n jar
                                      rel **follow-up (examination)**[1] n term → U134-15

thorough [θɜːroʊ] physical examination[2] of an individual to assess his/ her health status [eɪ‖æ]

check[3] [tʃek] v & n • (**re**/ **un**)**checked** adj • **double-check**[4] [ʌ] v • **checklist** n

» The patient did not come for a regular checkup—this was an out-of-hours emergency [ɜː] visit[5]. Further investigation can be delayed [eɪ] until the 6-wk checkup, when appropriate treatment can be instituted. You should have your hearing [hɪɚɪŋ] checked.

Use to have[6]/go for[6] **a checkup** • annual / routine[7] [iː]/ adolescent [es]/ dental **check-up** • regular **checkups** • health[8] / well-baby / wound [uː] **check** • **check** of pro-gress[9]/ • **to check** the vital [aɪ] signs[10] / for a pulse [ʌ] • to arrange **follow-up** • careful / close / appropriate / frequent **follow-up** • postoperative / prolonged[11] / long-term[11] / outpatient[12] **follow-up** • **follow-up** care[13] / visit / examination[14] / x-ray [eksreɪ]/ period[15] • child behavior / FUO[16] **checklist**

ärztl. Untersuchung, Vorsorgeuntersuchung

Nachsorge, -untersuchung[1] gründ-liche körperl. Untersuchung[2] über-prüfen, kontrollieren; Überprüfung, Kontrolle[3] nachprüfen[4] Notfall-behandlung außerhalb d. Ordinati-onszeit[5] sich durchuntersuchen lassen[6] Routineuntersuchung[7] Vor-sorge-, Gesundenuntersuchung[8] Verlaufskontrolle[9] d. Vitalfunktio-nen (über)prüfen[10] Langzeitkon-trolle[11] ambulante Nachsorge[12] Nachsorge[13] Nachuntersuchung[14] Nachuntersuchungszeitraum[15] Checkliste b. Fieber unbekannter Genese[16]

9

(doctor's) medical certificate n   rel **leave** [liːv] **of absence**[1] n, abbr **LOA**

official document issued [ɪs‖ɪʃuːd] by a physician

certify[2] [sɜːrtɪfaɪ] v • **certification** [sɜːrtɪfɪkeɪʃən] n • **certifiable**[3] [aɪ] adj

» Passengers will be required to present a medical certificate from their doctor. There is an incongruence[4] between the sex recorded on the birth certificate and gender [dʒ] identity[5]. This 56-year-old pilot is applying for renewal of his medical certificate. The Medical Certificate states that an individual has been found to be free of communi-cable[6] syphilis [ɪ].

Use to record sth. on/issue[7]/complete/sign [saɪn] **a medical certificate** • driver's / airman / confidential **medical certificate** • **medical certificate** of fitness[8] / holder • health[8] / sick[9] / (hospital) birth[10] / death[11] **certificate** • to file [aɪ] a death[12] **certificate** • **certificate** of need [iː] (abbr CON) • to be/go **on leave** • medical / sick[13] / family / maternity[14] [ɜː]/ annual / (un)paid **leave** • preadmission[15] (abbr PAC)/ board / CPR[16] **certification** • **certification** examination • **certified** EMT (emergency medical technician)[17]

ärztl. Attest/ Bescheinigung

Beurlaubung[1] bescheinigen, attes-tieren[2] meldepflichtig; unzurech-nungsfähig[3] Diskrepanz[4] Ge-schlechtsidentität[5] ansteckend[6] e. ärztl. Attest ausstellen[7] Gesund-heitszeugnis, -attest[8] Krankschrei-bung[9] Geburtsurkunde[10] Toten-schein[11] einen Totenschein ausstel-len[12] Krankenurlaub, -stand[13] Mut-terschaftsurlaub[14] Überprüfung d. Einweisungsindikation[15] Reanima-tionsbescheinigung[16] ausgebilde-te(r)/ geprüfter Rettungs-sanitäter(in)[17]

10

78 HEALTH CARE

At the Doctor's

confidentiality [kɒːnfɪdenˈʃɪælətɪ] n   *rel* **privacy**[1] [ˈpraɪvəsɪ], **disclosure**[2] [dɪskloʊʒɚ] n

discretion [eʃ] owed by the doctor to his patient to keep the information revealed to a health care provider private [aɪ]; this basic duty of medical ethics was initially set out in the Hippocratic Oath[3] [oʊθ]

confidential[4] *adj* • **confidence**[5] *n* • **confide**[6] [aɪ] *v* • **private** *adj* • **disclose** *v*

» Confidentiality is fundamental to any doctor-patient relationship. Prior to queries[7] [ɪɚ] about sexual behavior, it may be useful to restate the confidential nature of the questioning. Information contained in the patient's medical record is confidential and should not be disclosed to the police or other parties unless the patient has consented in writing[8] to its disclosure.

Use to maintain or observe[9]/sacrifice/preserve[9]/respect/honor [ɒːnɚ] /override[10] **confidentiality** • absolute / breach [briːtʃ] of[11] **confidentiality** • **confidentiality** of records / regulations / violation[11] • **confidential** information[12] / report / relationship / counseling • to provide **privacy** • the patient's right to / invasion [eɪʒ] of[13] **privacy** • overt[14] [ɜː]/ full / wrongful[15] **disclosure** • **disclosure of** risks[16] / sexual abuse • to build[17]/develop/(re)gain/lose/have **confidence** • lack of self-**confidence**[18] • **private** practice[19] / physician / hospital / room / insurance[20]

referral [rɪfɜːrəl] n *term & clin*   *rel* **second opinion**[1] [əˈpɪnjən] n *term*

directing or redirecting patients to a specialist or specialized medical care for further treatment

refer [rɪfɜːr] (**to/ for**)[2] *v term* • **referring** [ɜː] *adj*

» Arrange [eɪ] for orthopedic [iː] referral within 3-5 days. The patient should be referred for further gynecologic [dʒɪnə-] evaluation. Patients with serious conjunctival [aɪ] or corneal injury should be immediately referred to an ophthalmologist. This gives patients time to adjust [ədʒʌst] to the diagnosis of cancer and seek a second opinion if they wish.

Use to make/plan/require [aɪ] **a referral** • to require/need/warrant **referral** • early / prompt[3] / urgent / written **referral** • specialty[4] / emergency / immediate / early / sex-partner[5] **referral** • surgical / ophthalmologic[6] / neurologic **referral** • self-[7]/ burn center / dental **referral** • **to refer patients** to a specialist / for neurologic evaluation[8] • **to refer patients** to a support group / for treatment / for a surgical opinion • **referring** physician[9] / surgeon / laboratory / clinic[10] • **referral** form[11] / center / practice[12] / process / pattern / assistance • **referred** inpatient admission • to desire [aɪ] /request/seek[13] [iː] **a second opinion** • expert medical[14] / psychiatric [saɪk-] opinion • **second opinion** program

consultation [kɒːnsʌlteɪʃ³n] n *clin & term*

(i) seeking [iː] the help of a specialist to evaluate the nature and progress of disease in a particular patient (ii) talk session between clinician and patient which involves history taking, medical advice, etc.

consult[1] [ʌ] *v* • **consultant**[2] [ʌ] *n* • **consulting**[3] *adj* • **consultative**[3] *adj*

» Pressure sores[4] require surgical consultation for debridement, cleansing [e], and dressing[5]. At the end of this consultation, the doctor will discuss his findings with you and make recommendations for treatment. This must be decided in consultation between the blood bank physician and the patient's physician. Splint[6] the injury and consult an orthopedist. Have you had a good consultation with your physician?

Use to have a/require/seek/obtain **consultation** • telephone / online / telemedicine[7] **consultation** • medical[8] / prompt / emergency / expert[9] / surgical **consultation** • hematologic / neurologic / ophthalmologic / preoperative anesthesia[10] [iː] **consultation** • **to consult** a doctor / a urologist / with colleagues[11] [-liːgz] • **consultation** form / report / fee[12] [fiː] / room[13] / hours[14] • **consulting** room[13] / hours[14]

Vertraulichkeit, Schweigepflicht

Privatsphäre[1] Bekanntgabe, Aufklärung[2] hippokratischer Eid[3] vertraulich[4] Vertrauen[5] anvertrauen[6] Fragen[7] schriftlich einwilligen[8] s. an d. Schweigepflicht halten[9] s. nicht a. d. S. halten[10] Verletzung d. Schweigepflicht[11] vertraul. Information(en)[12] Eindringen i. d. Privatsphäre[13] Offenlegung[14] unbefugte Preisgabe (v. Daten)[15] Aufklärung über mögl. Risiken[16] Vertrauen aufbauen[17] mangelndes Selbstvertrauen[18] Privatpraxis[19] Privatversicherung[20]

11

Überweisung

zweite Meinung, Zweitgutachten[1] überweisen zu/ wegen; verweisen auf; s. wenden an/ beziehen auf[2] sofortige Überweisung[3] Ü. zu e. Facharzt/-ärztin[4] Ü. d. Sexualpartners/-in[5] Ü. zu/ an e. Augenarzt/-ärztin[6] erwünschte Ü.[7] Patienten z. neurolog. Abklärung überweisen[8] überweisende(r) Arzt/ Ärztin[9] Überweisungsklinik[10] Überweisungsschein[11] Überweisungspraxis[12] e. zweite Meinung/ Zweitgutachten einholen[13] Fachgutachten, fachärztl. Meinung[14]

12

(i) Konsilium, konsiliarische Beratung
(ii) ärztl. Beratung, Konsultation

zu Rate ziehen, konsultieren, bei-, zuziehen[1] Konsiliarius; Chefarzt (i. brit. Krankenhaus)[2] beratend[3] Dekubitus, Dekubitalgeschwüre[4] Verbinden[5] schienen[6] telemedizin. Konsultation[7] Konsultation e. Internisten/-in[8] fachärztl. Beratung/ Konsultation[9] präoperative Anästhesiesprechstunde[10] Fachkollegen bei-/ zuziehen[11] Beratungshonorar[12] Sprechzimmer[13] Sprechstunde[14]

13

At the Doctor's   HEALTH CARE **79**

medical or **patient's chart** [tʃɑːrt] n   syn **treatment** or **medical card** n BE
                                             rel **medical record**[1] [e] n → U20-5; U102-12

index card[2] or computer file used to record the patient's history, treatment, progress, etc.
• **chart**[3] v term • **charting** n • **record**[4] [rɪkɔːrd] v

» The number of x-rays[5] [eksreɪz] should be recorded in the patient's chart. The growth of an infant should be charted weekly against one of the standard postnatal growth curves [ɜː].

Use wall / hand-held / electronic / growth[6] [groʊθ]/ weight [weɪt]/ temperature[7] **chart** • progress / flow[8] / fluid balance / eye[9] / visual acuity [əkjuːɪti] or Snellen[9] **chart** • **chart** review[10] / number • **to chart** patient observations • frequent travelers' medical / insurance[11] **card** • identity[12] / followup appointment[13] **card** • **card** index[14]

Krankenblatt, Karteikarte
Krankenakte[1] Karteikarte[2] aufzeichnen, erfassen[3] aufzeichnen, festhalten, niederschreiben[4] Röntgenaufnahmen, -bilder[5] Wachstumstabelle, -kurve[6] Fieberkurve[7] Flussdiagramm[8] Sehprobentafel[9] Durchsicht d. Krankenblätter[10] Versicherungskarte[11] (Personal)ausweis[12] Nachsorgeeinbestellung[13] Kartei[14]

14

If the doctor's bill is higher than expected,
patients may experience a sudden short-lived improvement
of symptoms before they see a new health care provider.

doctor's or **medical bill** n   rel **health** or **medical insurance**[1] [ɪnʃʊəʳnts] n

written statement of charges [tʃɑːrdʒiːz] for medical services [ɜː].
• **bill**[2] v • **billing**[3] [bɪlɪŋ] n • **insure**[4] [ɪnʃʊəʳ] v • **insurer**[5] n → U13-5

» How can I get a claim [eɪ] form[6] so I can submit my doctor's bill? Identification of an occupational [eɪʃ] etiology [iːtɪ–] may have important economic ramifications[7], e.g. the awarding [ɔː] of worker's compensation, which covers[8] [ʌ] medical bills as well as lost wages [eɪdʒ]. Even when insurance provides coverage for a service, the patient may be responsible for an initial "deductible"[9] [ʌ] and a copayment. Traditional fee-for-service insurance[10] reimburses[11] [ɜː] the hospital and the physician for services rendered but frequently does not cover preventive care. While preparing to submit the doctor's bill for reimbursement, she discovered [ʌ] a previous [iː] surgery was revealed [iː] to her employer.

Use to record sth. on/issue[2]/sign/send sb./pay **a bill** • in-hospital[12] **bill** • **bill** of health[13] / life[14] / travel / automobile / liability[15] / medical malpractice **insurance** • **insurance** plan / company[5] / carrier[16] • **insurance** policy[17] / premium[18] [iː]/ coverage[19] [kʌvərɪdʒ] • **to bill** sb. for services • private [aɪ]/ state-sponsored[20] / for-profit[21] **insurer** • **insured** (party)[22]

Arztrechnung
Krankenversicherung[1] Rechnung ausstellen[2] Rechnungslegung[3] versichern[4] Versicherungsgesellschaft, -geber[5] Antragsformular[6] weitreichende wirtschaftl. Konsequenzen[7] (ab)decken[8] Selbstbehalt[9] leistungsbezogene Versicherung[10] refundiert[11] Rechnung f. d. stationären Aufenthalt[12] Gesundheitssattest[13] Lebensversicherung[14] Haftpflichtversicherung[15] Versicherungsträger[16] Versicherungspolice, -schein[17] Versicherungsbeitrag, -prämie[18] Versicherungssumme[19] staatl. Versicherungsanstalt[20] privatwirtschaftl. Versicherung[21] Versicherungsnehmer(in), Versicherte(r)[22]

15

Clinical Phrases

Come in, Mrs. Blythe, have a seat. Kommen Sie nur herein, Frau B. und nehmen Sie Platz. • What brings you to my office today? Was kann ich für Sie tun? • How are you this morning? Wie geht es Ihnen heute? • How long has this been troubling you? Seit wann haben Sie diese Beschwerden? • Have you ever been under a physician's care? Waren Sie schon einmal in ärztlicher Behandlung? • I will ask a gynecologist to see you. Ich werde Sie zu einem/r Gynäkologen/-in überweisen. • Have you had any more spells of dizziness since I last saw you? Hatten Sie wieder Schwindelanfälle seit Sie das letzte Mal bei mir waren? • Please step onto the scale. Bitte steigen Sie auf die Waage. • First I'd like to examine your throat, then I'll advise some treatment for you. Lassen Sie mich zuerst in den Hals schauen, dann werde ich eine Behandlung vorschlagen. • Open your mouth wide, please. Den Mund weit aufmachen, bitte. • Tell me if you've ever experienced trouble with your balance. Hatten Sie schon einmal Gleichgewichtsstörungen? • Have you had a tetanus shot recently? Wurden Sie in der letzten Zeit gegen Tetanus geimpft? • Does Dr Sting have a large practice? Hat Dr. S. viele Patienten?

Unit 19 On the Ward

Related Units: **20** Hospital Routines, **16** Nurses **15** Medical Staff, **134** Perioperative Management, **142** Physical Therapy

(hospital) ward [wɔːrd] *n, abbr* **Wd**   *sim* **unit**[1] *n, rel* **cubicle**[2] [kjuːbɪkl] *n*

division [ɪʒ] of a hospital (or suite [swiːt]) shared by patients who need a similar kind of care

» The patient was elated[3] [eɪ] and overcheerful and disturbed [ɜː] the ward by loud shouting and singing. We are going to take an elevator to the ward, where you can get some sleep. Use cubicle drapes[4] [eɪ] or screens[5] [iː] when caring for patients who are not in private rooms.

Use to send/transfer[6] **to the ward** • general / surgical [ɜː] / medical or internal medicine[7] / emergency[8] [ɜː] **ward** • children's or pediatric[9] / nursing[10] [ɜː]/ adult / psychiatric [saɪkɪ-] **ward** • open / secure [sɪkjʊɚ] or locked[11] **ward** • oncology / chronic-care / isolation[12] [aɪsə-] **ward** • accident or casualty[13] [kæʒ-]/ maternity[14] [ɜː] **ward** • **ward** nurse [ɜː] or (BE) sister[15] / staff / doctor / maid[16] [eɪ] • **ward** clerk [ɜː‖BE ɑː]/ round[17] [aʊ] • ambulatory care[18] / intensive or critical care[19]/ burn [ɜː] **ward** • dialysis [daɪələsɪs]/ trauma [ɔː]/ inpatient[20] / living-in **unit**

Station, Abteilung

Abteilung; Krankensaal; Team[1] abgetrennte Zelle i. Krankensaal; Untersuchungskabine[2] in Hochstimmung[3] Vorhänge[4] Trennwände[5] auf d. Station verlegen[6] innere Abteilung[7] Notaufnahme[8] Kinderstation[9] Pflegestation[10] geschlossene Station[11] Isolierstation[12] Unfallstation[13] Wöchnerinnenstation[14] Stationsschwester[15] Stockmädchen[16] Visite[17] Ambulanz[18] Intensivstation[19] Bettenstation[20]   **1**

---

patient's room [peɪʃənts ruːm] *n*   *rel* **rooming-in**[1], **living-in**[1] *n clin*

room in a ward designed [aɪ] and equipped for occupancy[2] by one or more inpatients[3]

» Hospitalize the patient in a private room at bed rest. The baby should room-in with the mother whenever possible. If seclusion [uːʒ] rooms[4] and restraints[5] [eɪ] have to be used patients must be observed [ɜː] at frequent intervals.

Use ward / separate / single[6] / semi-private [aɪ]/ isolation[7] **room** • treatment[8] / prep[9] / darkened / (postoperative) recovery[10] [ʌ] **room** • delivery or labor[11] [eɪ]/ birth(ing)[11] [ɜː]/ waiting / emergency [ɜː] (abbr ER) **room** • examination[12] / x-ray [eksreɪ]/ outpatient[13] / operating **room** • resuscitation[14] [ʌs]/ soundproof(ed)[15] [uː] **room** • **room** temperature / air[16] • **patient** load [oʊ]/ interview / identification bracelet[17] [eɪs]

Kranken-, Patientenzimmer

Rooming-in[1] Belegung[2] stationäre Patienten[3] geschlossene Zimmer[4] Fuß-, Handfesseln[5] Einzelzimmer[6] Isolierzimmer[7] Behandlungsraum[8] OP-Vorbereitungsraum[9] Aufwachraum[10] Kreißsaal[11] Untersuchungszimmer, -raum[12] Ambulanzraum[13] Reanimationszimmer[14] schalldichter Raum[15] Raumluft[16] Patienten-Identifikationsarmband[17]   **2**

---

hospital bed *n*   *sim* **gurney**[1] [gɜːrni], **crib**[2], **cot**[2] [kɒt] *BE n*

bed with adjustable [ʌ] head and foot ends equipped to optimize care for the hospitalized patient

bedcover[3] [ʌ] *n* • bedding[4] *n* • bed rest[5] *n* • bedrails[6] [eɪ] *n pl* • bedtime[7] *n*

» Use a padded armboard[8] [-bɔːrd] which fits under the mattress of the patient's gurney. Clothing should be loose and bed clothing[4] light. Elevation[9] of the legs in bed minimizes postoperative swelling. Complete bed rest with the head of the bed[10] elevated on blocks is necessary. Bed side rails[6] help to prevent patients from falling out of bed.

Use electric / acute[11] **hospital bed** • to roll over in/ be confined [aɪ] to[12]/be kept in/rest on a firm [ɜː] **bed** • to sit up in[13]/get out of/leave **bed** • to put a child to/strip the[14]/make the[15] **bed** • to elevate the head / foot[16] / side / edge[17] **of the bed** • (un)occupied / adjustable [ədʒʌ-] **bed** • water or (full-)flotation[18] [eɪ] / newborn / incubator[19] **bed** • surgical[20] / adult / pediatric / specialty[21] / circular [sɜː] **bed** • swing / night / oscillating / temporary **bed** • at[22] (abbr h.s)/ nothing by mouth at **hedtime** • **bedtime** medication • **bed** wedge[23] [wedʒ] /clothes[4] [oʊ]/ blocks / board [ɔː]/ net / utilization[24] • **hed**bound [aʊ] or bedridden patient[25] / sore[26] [sɔːr]/ mobility / wetting • to order[27] (complete) [iː]/ strict[28] **hed rest** • **cot** death[29] [e] • **crib** death[29]

Krankenhausbett

Rollbett[1] Kinderbett[2] Bettdecke[3] Bettzeug, -wäsche[4] Bettruhe[5] seitl. Bettrahmen[6] Schlafenszeit[7] gepolsterte Armstütze[8] Hochlagern[9] Kopfteil d. Bettes[10] Akutbett[11] ans Bett gefesselt/ bettlägrig sein[12] s. im Bett aufsetzen[13] d. Bett abziehen[14] d. Bett machen[15] Fußende d. Bettes[16] Bettkante[17] Wasserbett[18] Wärmebett[19] Bett m. verstellbarem Kopf- u. Fußteil[20] Spezialbett[21] vor d. Schlafengehen[22] Bettkeil[23] Bettenauslastung[24] bettlägrige(r) Patient(in)[25] Wundliegen, Dekubitalgeschwür[26] Bettruhe verordnen[27] strenge Bettruhe[28] plötzl. Kindstod, Krippentod[29]   **3**

---

overhead or **overbed trapeze** [trəpiːz] *n*   *syn* **T** or **trapeze bar** [bɑːr] *n*
   rel **frame**[1] [eɪ], **cradle**[2] [eɪ], **footboard** [ɔː] or **foot rest**[3] *n*

bar suspended over the patient's bed to help with sitting up and shifting [ʃɪftɪŋ] position

» Due to her respiratory condition the patient needs a trapeze bar to sit up. When you are at home, you will not have the T bar any longer. The hand pendant control[4] also adjusts bed frame height [haɪt] for safe transfers. The use of a cradle to reduce contact with bedclothes may be helpful. During active poliomyelitis [-maɪəlaɪtɪs], rest on a firm bed with footboards is indicated to help prevent footdrop[5].

Use bed[1] / Stryker (wedge)[6] [dʒ] **frame** • bed[2] **cradle** • **foot** block[3] • padded[7] **foot rest**

Aufricht(e)hilfe, Bettgalgen

Bettgestell[1] Bettbogen, Reifenbahre[2] Fußstütze[3] Handsteuerung[4] Spitzfußstellung[5] Spezialbett zum atraumatischen Umlagern von Patienten mit instabilen WS-Frakturen[6] gepolsterte Fußstütze[7]   **4**

On the Ward   HEALTH CARE 81

mattress [mætrəs] n   rel **pillow¹** [pɪloʊ], **cushion²** [kʊʃᵊn], **linen³** [lɪnᵊn] n
comfortable supportive layer of padding on a bed which permits good body alignment [aɪ] • **cushion⁴** [ʊ] v • **well-cushioned⁵** adj
» Water and air mattresses, sheepskin pads⁶, and foam [oʊ] cushions⁷ may help relieve pressure but are not substitutes [ʌ] for frequent turning of bedridden patients. The skin and the bed linens should be kept clean and dry.
Use firm⁸ [ɜː]/ soft / foam⁹ [oʊ]/ silicone gel [dʒel]/ egg-crate¹⁰ [eɪ] **mattress** • rotating aid [eɪd]/ thermal¹¹ [ɜː]/ hypothermia [ɜː] **mattress** • **mattress** cover¹² [ʌ]/ pad¹³ • to rest on/ insert [ɜː] /be propped up on¹⁴/support with **a pillow** • rubber [ʌ]/ pressure-relieving / knee **pillow** • **pillow** case¹⁵ / splint¹⁶ • clean / folded / soiled¹⁷ / contaminated **linen** • **linen** storage / change • egg crate¹⁸ / foam / seat¹⁹ / wheel chair **cushion**

Matratze
Kopfkissen¹ Kissen, Polster² Betttuch, -laken³ polstern, dämpfen⁴ gut gepolstert⁵ Schaffellauflagen⁶ Schaumstoffkissen⁷ harte Matratze⁸ Schaumstoffmatratze⁹ Wabenmatratze¹⁰ Wärmematratze¹¹ Matratzenbezug¹² Matratzenauflage¹³ durch Kissen gestützt¹⁴ Kopfkissenbezug¹⁵ Polsterschiene¹⁶ schmutziges Bettlaken¹⁷ Wabenkissen¹⁸ Sitzkissen¹⁹   5

heating blanket [hiːtɪŋ blæŋkɪt] n   rel **heating pad¹** [æ], **heat lamp²** n clin
wool [ʊ] cover with electric wires [aɪ] inside for warming the patient
» Active external rewarming involves direct application of heat sources [ɔː] (heating blankets, heat lamps, warm water immersion [ɜː]) to external body surfaces [ɜː]. Do not apply [aɪ] heat in the form of hot water bottles³, or heating pads without a physician's [ɪʃ] consent.
Use heating lamp² / system • surface⁴ heating • electric (warming)⁵ / thermal⁵ [ɜː]/ cooling⁶ [uː] **blanket** • warm / rolled-up⁷ **blanket** • infrared² / sun or ultraviolet⁸ [aɪ] **lamp**

Heizdecke
Heizkissen¹ Infrarotlicht, Wärmelampe² Wärmeflaschen³ Oberflächenerwärmung⁴ Heizdecke⁵ Kühldecke⁶ zusammengerollte Decke⁷ Höhensonne, UV-Lampe⁸   6

bedside stand or **table** n   syn **side tray** [saɪd treɪ] n
rel **overbed table¹, food tray²** n
cabinet with a drawer [ɔː] for the patient's personal care items [aɪ], belongings, etc.
» The patient fails to eat food placed on the left side of the tray. Right heart [ɑː] catheterization can be carried out at the bedside³. Your overbed table can be tilted⁴ when you want to read or write something and has a mirror on the back for combing hair, shaving, etc.
Use instrument⁵ / disposable / catheter / ash tray • **bedside** cabinet⁶ / unit / manner⁷ • **bedside** examination / test⁸ / diagnosis⁹ / monitoring / procedure [siː]

Nachttisch, -schränkchen
Betttisch¹ (Essens)tablett² am Krankenbett³ schräg gestellt⁴ Instrumentenschale⁵ Nachtschränkchen⁶ Umgang m. Kranken, Verhalten (d. Arztes) am Krankenbett⁷ Bedside-Test⁸ Bedside-Diagnostik⁹   7

urinal [jʊɚɪnᵊl] n term   syn **urine bottle** n, rel **commode¹** [oʊ], **bed pan²** n clin
receptacle [se] for collecting urine³ in male or catheterized patients who are confined to bed
» If mobility cannot be improved, access [ækses] to a urinal or commode may restore continence. Bed rest with convenient [iː] access to a bathroom, commode, or bedpan is desirable [aɪ]. Have the patient use a bedside commode rather than a bedpan.
Use to assist with the **urinal** • urine drainage [eɪ] bag / collecting container³ [eɪ] • to sit on/position on/transfer to **the commode** • bedside¹ **commode** • **commode** privileges • to offer/remove/empty/clean/lift the patient onto⁴ **the bedpan** • to slip the **bedpan** into place⁵ • regular / fracture⁶ **bedpan** • **bedpan** liner⁷ [aɪ]

Urinflasche, Urinal
Nachtstuhl¹ Bettschüssel, -pfanne, Schieber² Harnsammelbehälter³ d. Patienten/-in auf die Bettpfanne heben⁴ die Bettpfanne unterschieben⁵ Spezialbettpfanne für Frakturierte⁶ Urinschiffchen⁷   8

bathroom [bæθruːm] n   sim **toilet¹**, BE **lavatory¹** n, rel **bathing²** [beɪðɪŋ] n
(i) room with a bathtub³ [ʌ] and/or a shower
(ii) common euphemism for toilet in AE and AusE
bathe⁴ [eɪ] v • bath⁵ [æ] n → U142-20 • afterbath adj • toileting⁶ n
» We have to maintain [eɪ] a regimen [edʒ] of bed-to-chair with bathroom privileges⁷ and meals in bed. I didn't reach the toilet in time. Give the bed bath⁸ in a setting that provides privacy [aɪ] for the patient. Determine [ɜː] the patient's ability to perform basic activities of daily life like bathing, dressing, toileting, feeding, getting in and out of chairs and bed, and walking.
Use to go to⁹/walk to/reach/accompany the patient to **the bathroom** • **bathroom** privileges⁷ (abbr BRP) • **bathroom** aids [eɪdz]/ scales¹⁰ [eɪ]/ safety devices [aɪs] • joint¹¹ [dʒ] **toilet** • **toilet** facilities [sɪ]/ seat¹² / bowl¹³ [boʊl] • **toilet** tissue or paper / transfer / function / training¹⁴ • **toileting** habits¹⁵ • regular / sink-side¹⁶ **bathing** • tub¹⁷ [ʌ]/ complete / partial¹⁸ / vapor [eɪ]/ medicated¹⁹ **bath** • daily / cool / contrast²⁰ / tepid²¹ **bath** • **bath** mat²² /time / towel [taʊəl]/ period • **afterbath** massage [-sɑːʒ]

(i) Badezimmer
(ii) Toilette
Toilette¹ Baden² Badewanne³ baden, waschen⁴ Bad, Badewanne⁵ Toilettenbenutzung⁶ Erlaubnis auf d. Toilette zu gehen⁷ e. Waschung durchführen⁸ auf d. Toilette gehen⁹ Personenwaage¹⁰ gemeinsame Toilette¹¹ Toilettensitz¹² Toilettenbecken, WC-Muschel¹³ Erziehung z. Sauberkeit¹⁴ Stuhlgewohnheiten¹⁵ Waschen i. Waschbecken¹⁶ Wannenbad¹⁷ Teilbad¹⁸ medizinisches Bad¹⁹ Wechselbad²⁰ lauwarmes Bad²¹ Bademattte²²   9

82 HEALTH CARE — On the Ward

grooming [uː] *n term* → U142-27   *rel* **hygiene**[1] [haɪdʒiːn], **washing**[2] *n*
rel **douche**[3] [duːʃ], **soak**[4] [oʊ] *v & n* → U1-17ff

caring for the external appearance [ɪɚ] and cleanliness [e] (showering [aʊ], combing [koʊmɪŋ], shaving [eɪ], trimming nails[5], skin care, etc.)

groom[6] *v* • **well-groomed**[7] *adj* • **hygienic** *adj* • **wash**[8] *v & n* • **washcloth**[9] *n*

» Inpatients often need help from the nurse as they cannot groom themselves independently. The patient's hygiene and grooming are deteriorating [ɪɚ]. Patients with severe neglect[10] may fail to dress or groom the left side of the body. The patient's hygienic habits should be determined [ɜː]. To remove excess calluses[11] or corns[12], soak the feet in lukewarm [uː] water for about 10 minutes and then rub [ʌ] off the excess tissue with a towel or file [aɪ].

Use dressing, bathing, feeding and **grooming** • **grooming** implements[13] / and washing • thorough[14] / hand / mouth[15] / hair / soap [oʊ]/ shampoo [uː] **washing** • good / careful / proper **hygiene** • (over)meticulous[16] / adequate / poor **hygiene** • general / personal[17] / feminine / penile [iː]/ (ano)genital [dʒe] **hygiene** • perineal [iː]/ bronchial [k]/ oral[18] / dental **hygiene** • standard / lack **of hygiene** • **hygienic** conditions / habits / care / measures[19] [eʒ] / problem • vaginal[20] [dʒ]/ anal [eɪ] **douching** • nasal / vinegar / jet[21] [dʒ]/ air **douche** • warm / hot / cool / tap-water **soak** • wet[22] / saline [eɪ]/ soothing[23] [uː] **soak**

cueing [kjuːɪŋ] *n term*   *rel* **assistance**[1] *n*, **support**[2], **aid**[3] [eɪd], **help**[3] *n & v*

helping patients with activities of daily living by suggesting the next steps

cue[4] [kjuː] *n & v* • **assist**[5] *v* • **supportive** *adj* • **self-help**[6] *n* • **aide**[7] *n* → U142-29

» The patient is able to use a quad cane[8] [kwɒːd keɪn] with verbal cueing. You can call for assistance by activating the signal device [aɪs] next to your pillow. The family will need continued assistance and support in adjusting [dʒʌ] to the diagnosis. This organization provides aid to victims of rape[9] [reɪp].

Use **cueing** assistance / for activities of daily living (*abbr* ADL) • to read/take[10]/miss **cues** • visual [ɪʒ]/ auditory [ɒː]/ a baby's **cues** • assisted living center[11] / coughing [kɒfɪŋ] • to require/need/provide/refuse[12] **assistance** • medical[13] / standby / minimal **assistance** • general nursing (*abbr* GNA)/ homemaking[14] / visiting nurse **assistance** • **assistance** for upper body dressing / in transfers / with walking • family / nutritional [ɪʃ]/ spiritual • emotional[15] [oʊʃ] **support** • **support** group[16] • **supportive** care / measures[17] [eʒ] • walking[18] / mutual [juː]/ hearing / low-vision[19] **aid** • with the **aid** or **help** of • home health[20] **aide** • to be of (great/ limited/ little) **help** • **self-help** group[16] / devices[21] / program

ambulation [æmbjəleɪʃən] *n term* → U65-1; 134-13; 142-13

walking about, esp. mobilization programs of patients who have been confined [aɪ] to bed[1]

ambulate[2] *v* • **(semi)ambulatory**[3] *adj* → U14-2

» Graduated [æ] ambulation[4] with elastic support is permitted, but standing is forbidden. The distance a patient can walk varies [eɚ] with the rate of walking.

Use to advise/start/resume/permit/be allowed/occur [ɜː] with[5] **ambulation** • early[6] / gradual indoor / limited **ambulation** • progressive / crutch[7] / full / independent / free **ambulation** • **ambulation** balance / goal [oʊ]/ on crutches[7] • **to ambulate with a walker**[8] / with minimal assistance / on parallel bars[8] • to be/become **ambulatory**

wheelchair [ʰwiːltʃeɚ] *n, abbr* **wc**
rel **motorized invalid carriage**[1] [kerɪdʒ] *n*, **hoist**[2] [hɔɪst] *n & v*

mobile seat with wheels, a steering mechanism, and brakes for non-ambulatory persons

» One-half of amputees [iː] who were ambulatory before injury became wheelchair-bound[3] [aʊ] afterward. Eventually he may be mobilized on crutches or in a wheelchair. The patient must be lifted out of bed and into a chair.

Use to be confined [aɪ] to a[3] **wheelchair** • customized[4] [ʌ] **wheelchair** • **wheelchair** cushion [ʊ]/ pad / ramp[5] / transfer / mobility • to sit in/rest in/get (up) out of/(a)rise from **a chair** • arm[6]/ easy[7] / upholstered[8] / roll-in shower[9] / potty[10] / swivel[11] [ɪ] **chair** • **chair** rest / with arm rests[6] / bottom[12] / back[13]

Körperpflege
Hygiene[1] Waschen[2] spülen; Spülung, Guss[3] einweichen, (durch)tränken; (Eintauch)bad, Einweichen[4] Schneiden d. Nägel[5] sich pflegen[6] gepflegt[7] waschen; Wäsche[8] Waschlappen[9] Neglect, halbseitige Vernachlässigung[10] Hornhaut[11] Hühneraugen[12] Körperpflegeutensilien[13] gründl. Waschen[14] Mundspülung[15] übertriebene Hygiene[16] Körperpflege[17] Mundpflege, -hygiene[18] hygienische Maßnahmen[19] Scheidenspülung[20] Wasserstrahldusche[21] Einweichen[22] wohltuendes Bad, Entspannungsbad[23]

10

Hilfestellung durch schrittweise Anleitungen
Hilfe[1] Stütze, Unterstützung; (unter)stützen[2] Hilfe; helfen[3] Hilfe(stellung) (geben)[4] helfen, behilflich sein, assistieren[5] Selbsthilfe[6] Helfer(in)[7] Vierfuß-Gehhilfe[8] Vergewaltigungsopfer[9] sich richten nach[10] Beihilfe zum Selbstmord[11] Hilfe ablehnen[12] ärztl. Hilfe[13] Hilfestellung b. d. Haushaltsführung[14] seelische Unterstützung[15] Selbsthilfegruppe[16] unterstützende Maßnahmen[17] Gehhilfe[18] Sehhilfe[19] Hauskrankenpfleger(in)[20] Selbsthilfevorrichtungen[21]

11

(Umher)gehen, Mobilisation
bettlägrig[1] umhergehen[2] gehfähig; ambulant[3] dosiertes Gehen[4] beim Gehen auftreten/ feststellbar sein[5] Frühmobilisation[6] Gehen an Krücken[7] mit einem Gehgestell umhergehen[8]

12

Rollstuhl
Behindertenfahrzeug[1] Hebekran, Lifter; hochheben[2] an d. Rollstuhl gefesselt (sein)[3] individuell angepasster Rollstuhl[4] Rollstuhl-Rampe[5] Lehnstuhl[6] Stuhl, Sessel[7] Polstersessel[8] Dusch(roll)stuhl[9] Leibstuhl, Töpfchen[10] Drehsessel[11] Sitzfläche[12] Sessellehne[13]

13

On the Ward   HEALTH CARE **83**

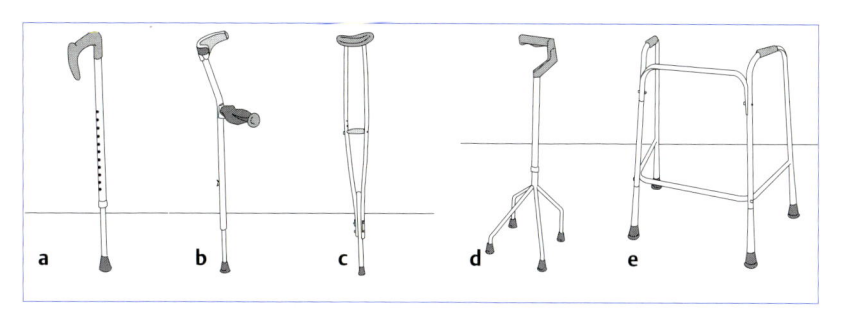

Walking aids: **(a)** adjustable cane, **(b)** below-elbow or forearm crutch, **(c)** underarm crutch, **(d)** quad cane, **(e)** fixed walker

---

crutches [krʌtʃiːz] n, usu pl   rel **cane¹** [keɪn], **walker(ette)²** [wɒːkəret] n

type of support³ typically fitting under the armpit⁴ for use as a walking aid
walk [wɒːk] v & n • **walking** adj & n → U65-1

» *Comfort can be enhanced⁵ by limitation of weight* [weɪt] *bearing⁶* [eə˞] *with the aid of crutches. When degeneration in a weight-bearing joint is mild, symptoms are relieved by use of external supports such as a cane, crutches, or a walker. Advise the use of crutches and avoidance of weight bearing. Younger patients usually prefer to be ambulatory on crutches.*

Use to walk with⁷/support on/be on⁷/provide/mobilize sb. on **crutches** • axillary⁸ / elbow extension or Canadian / platform or forearm⁹ / Lofstrand **crutches** • **crutch** use / support / gait¹⁰ [ɡeɪt]/ palsy¹¹ [pɔːlzi] • **walking** stick¹² / frame² / to use a / quad¹³ [kwɒːd] **cane** • to go for a /be unable to **walk** • platform **walker** • **walker** applied to cast¹⁴ [æ]/ placement • to have difficulty in / brisk / crutch / cessation [se-] of **walking** • **walking** distance / speed [iː]/ capacity¹⁵ [æs]/ exercise / aid¹⁶ • **walking** brace¹⁷ [breɪs]/ cast¹⁸ / barefoot [eə˞]/ without support / uphill¹⁹

Krücken, Stockstützen
Gehstock¹ Gehgestell, -wagen, -bock² Stütze³ Achselhöhle⁴ erhöht⁵ Belastung⁶ an Krücken gehen⁷ Achselkrücken⁸ Unterarmkrücken⁹ Krückengang¹⁰ Krückenlähmung¹¹ Spazierstock¹² Vierfuß-Gehhilfe¹³ am Gips befestigte(r) Sohlenplatte/ Gehstollen¹⁴ Gehfähigkeit¹⁵ Gehhilfe¹⁶ Funktionsschiene¹⁷ Gehgips¹⁸ bergauf Gehen¹⁹

14

---

occupancy (rate) [ɒːkjəpənˈsi reɪt] n   rel **hospital stay¹** [hɒːspɪtˀl steɪ] n

number of average daily inpatients relative to the number of hospital beds available in a care facility
(un)occupied² adj • **occupant³** n • **hospitalization⁴** [eɪ] n • **stay⁵** v & n

» *Of the 1.5 million nursing home beds 90% are occupied by Americans older than 65, yet less than 5% of them live in nursing* [ɜː] *homes or other institutions. Most ureteroscopy cases incur⁶* [ɜː] *a hospital stay of 1 to 2 days. Following laparoscopic appendectomy the postoperative hospital stay averages one day less⁷ than in open appendectomy.*

Use **occupied** hospital beds⁸ • postoperative / shorter⁹ **hospital stay** • length of¹⁰ (abbr LOS)/ average length of (abbr ALOS)/ duration of¹⁰ **stay** • nursery / ICU¹¹ / nursing home **stay** • **stay** charges¹² [tʃɑːrdʒiːz] • **short stay** surgery • **to stay** indoors / in bed / home from work / awake • **to stay** seated / in close proximity¹³ / near the child / with therapy¹⁴

Krankenhausbelegung, Bettenauslastung
Krankenhausaufenthalt¹ (nicht) belegt² Bewohner(in), Insasse/-in³ Krankenhausaufenthalt, Hospitalisierung⁴ bleiben; Aufenthalt⁵ in Kauf nehmen müssen⁶ ist i. Durchschnitt 1 Tag kürzer⁷ belegte Krankenhausbetten⁸ kürzerer Krankenhausaufenthalt⁹ Dauer d. K.¹⁰ Aufenthalt auf d. Intensivstation¹¹ Aufenthaltskosten¹² ganz i. d. Nähe bleiben¹³ s. weiterbehandeln lassen¹⁴

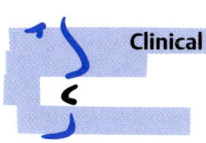

15

Clinical Phrases

Good morning, Mrs. Walters. It's good to see that you're up and about. Guten Morgen, Frau W. Schön dass Sie schon auf sind und herumgehen können. • Has he been making progress? Hat sich sein Zustand gebessert? • Can the patient be allowed to bathe himself or does he require assistance with getting in and out of the shower? Kann sich der Patient alleine waschen oder muß ich ihm beim Duschen helfen? • Sorry to wake you, Dr. Poole but Mr. James in room 5 has been very restless. Entschuldigen Sie, dass ich Sie aufwecke, Dr. P., aber Herr J. auf Zimmer 5 ist sehr unruhig. • First move the crutches and your injured leg forward. Zuerst müssen Sie beide Krücken aufsetzen und das verletzte Bein nach vorne stellen. • Let the nurse know, if you have difficulty lying on one pillow. Sagen Sie es der Schwester, wenn Sie noch ein zweites Kopfkisssen brauchen.

Unit 20   Hospital Routines
Related Units: 13 Health Care Administration, 14 Hospitals, 18 At the Doctor's, 102 History Taking, 107 Physical Examination, 118 Diagnostic Procedures, 127 Operative Techniques

(hospital) admission n term   sim **hospitalization**[1] [hɒːspɪtᵊlɪzeɪʃᵊn] n
process of a person's confinement [aɪ] in a hospital as an inpatient[2] for observation or care
admit (to)[3] v term • **admitting** adj • **pre/ readmission**[4] n • **hospitalize** v [-ləɪz]
» The dysfunction often disappears on the way to the ward[5] [ɔː] or shortly after admission. Most of these patients have repeated hospital admissions for overdose or withdrawal [ɔː] problems[6]. The patient was examined, admitted, and sent to the ward by the surgeon [ɜː]. In hospital-acquired [aɪ] pneumonia [n(j)uː-] initial empiric therapy with antibiotics is determined [ɜː] by the severity [e] of illness, risk factors, and the length of hospitalization.

Use to require or warrant [ɔː] /decline[7] [aɪ] **admission** • (up)on / at the time of / 6 wks prior [aɪ] to / within 24 hs of **admission** • (in)voluntary / elective / urgent [ɜː] **admission** • emergency[8] [ɜː]/ transfer / previous [iː] **admission** • same-day / initial[9] [ɪʃ]/ overnight / short-term **admission** • nursing [ɜː] home / hospice / ICU[10] / surgical[11] **admission** • pediatric / psychiatric / geriatric [dʒe] / asthma [z] **admission** • **admission** to (the) hospital[12] / criteria / process • **admission** physical [ɪ] examination[13] / note[14] / blood work / diagnosis[15] • **to be admitted** as an emergency / directly / promptly / for evaluation and workup[16] • **to be admitted** for observation[17] / for medical reassessment • **to be admitted** to a dialysis program / for terminal [ɜː] care / in dazed [eɪ] condition[18] • **Admissions or Admitting Office** • **admitting** physician [ɪʃ] or doctor[19] / officer / manager / department • to require/warrant/ necessitate/consider/avoid **hospitalization** • brief / overnight / prolonged[20] / length or duration of **hospitalization** • immediate [iː]/ emergency / initial / involuntary[21] **hospitalization** • **preadmission** screening [iː] (abbr PAS) • indications / need / reason[22] / criteria **for hospitalization** • necessity / symptoms calling[23] **for hospitalization**

outpatient [aʊtpeɪʃᵊnt] adj & n term, abbr **OP**   opposite **inpatient**[1] adj & n term
rel **patient**[2] n, **case**[3] [keɪs] n term & jar, **client**[4] [klaɪᵊnt] n term
(n) patient who is treated in a doctor's office, clinic, or other ambulatory care facility
» Patients with these findings may be spared[5] [eə] emergency endoscopy and discharged from the hospital early to undergo outpatient workup[6]. Fiberoptic bronchoscopy can be done for in- or outpatients, even at the bedside or with patients on ventilatory support[7] in the ICU.

Use **outpatient** department[8] / case / care / clinic[9] • **outpatient** management[10] / therapy / procedure • **outpatient** analgesia [dʒiː]/ (cataract) surgery[11] • **outpatient** counseling [aʊ]/ follow-up[12] / visit[13] • medical / pediatric [iː] **outpatients** • **inpatient** service day • male / adult / pregnant / elderly **patient** • geriatric / low-risk / private [aɪ] **patient** • alert [ɜː]/ cooperative / disoriented / immunocompromised[14] **patient** • untreated / cancer / surgical **patient** • **patient** care / comfort / well-being / day[15] / **patient** identification / satisfaction[16] / compliance [aɪ] • **client**-centered therapy • mild / acute / borderline / severe **cases** • caseload[17] [oʊ]/ presentation / report[18] / conference • **case** study[19] [ʌ]/ abstract / summary [ʌ]/ series [sɪəriːz]

medical care [medɪkᵊl keə] n   sim **health care**[1] [helθ keə] n → U13-1
providing professional treatment (i.e. under a physician's [ɪʃ] direction) for the sick or injured
care (for)[2] v • **caregiver**[3] n • **take care**[4] phr • **careful**[5] adj • **careless** adj
» Women 20-40 years of age should have a breast [e] examination as part of routine [uː] medical care every 2-3 years. Weight [weɪt] loss may be marked[6] if the patient has delayed [eɪ] seeking [iː] medical care. Today, the vast majority [dʒɔː] of mental health care already takes place outside hospitals.

Use to seek/give or provide/be under or receive[7] [siː] /refuse/monitor **medical care** • state-of-the-art / emergency / austere[8] [ɔːstɪə] **medical care** • prompt / ambulatory[9] / quality of **medical care** • **medical care** system [ɪ]/ neglect[10] • **to care** for the sick • **to take care** of a patient / not to injure the nerve / of one's health[11] • (out)patient[9] / nursing [ɜː]/ supportive **care** • acute / prehospital[12] [iː]/ initial **care** • stabilizing / emergency / surgical / postoperative[13] or after**care** • intensive / critical or intensive[14] / 24-hour / long-term[15] **care** • foot / mouth / wound[16] [uː]/ trauma [ɔː]/ followup[13] / self[17]-**care** • home[18] / hospice / terminal [ɜː]/ bereavement[19] [iː]/ pastoral **care**

(stationäre) Aufnahme
Einweisung/ -lieferung/ Aufnahme i. Krankenhaus, Hospitalisierung; Krankenhausaufenthalt[1] stationäre(r) Patient(in)[2] (stationär) aufnehmen; Zutritt gewähren[3] erneute Einweisung, Wiederaufnahme[4] Station[5] Entzugserscheinungen[6] eine stationäre Aufnahme ablehnen[7] Notaufnahme[8] Erstaufnahme[9] Aufnahme f. d. Intensivstation[10] Aufnahme f. e. Operation[11] stationäre Aufnahme[12] Aufnahmeuntersuchung[13] Aufnahmebericht[14] Aufnahmediagnose[15] z. Abklärung stationär aufgenommen werden[16] zur Beobachtung aufgenommen werden[17] i. benommenem Zustand aufgenommen w.[18] Aufnahmearzt/-ärztin[19] längerer Krankenhausaufenthalt[20] Zwangseinweisung[21] Einweisungsgrund[22] Symptome, die e. Einweisung erfordern[23]

1

ambulant;
ambulante(r) Patient(in)
stationär; stationäre(r) Patient(in)[1] Kranke(r), Patient(in)[2] (Krankheits)fall[3] Klient(in)[4] erspart[5] ambulante Untersuchungen[6] mechan. Atemhilfe[7] Ambulanz[8] Ambulanz, Poliklinik, Ambulatorium[9] ambulante Behandlung[10] ambulante Staroperation[11] ambulante Nachsorge[12] Ambulanzbesuch[13] immungeschwächte(r) Patient(in)[14] Beleg(ungs)tag[15] Patientenzufriedenheit[16] Patientenzahl[17] Fallbericht, Kasuistik[18] Fallstudie[19]

2

ärztliche Behandlung, medizinische Versorgung
Gesundheitsfürsorge[1] pflegen, betreuen, versorgen[2] Betreuer(in), Sorgeberechtigte(r)[3] s. kümmern, aufpassen, vorsichtig sein[4] sorgfältig, vorsichtig[5] beträchtlich[6] i. ärztl. Behandlung sein[7] notdürftig medizin. Versorgung[8] ambulante Behandlung[9] unterlassene Hilfeleistung[10] auf seine Gesundheit achten[11] präklin. Behandlung[12] Nachsorge[13] Intensivpflege[14] Langzeitbehandlung[15] Wundversorgung, -behandlung[16] Selbstbehandlung[17] häusliche Pflege[18] Trauerarbeit[19]

3

Hospital Routines   HEALTH CARE **85**

on call [ɒːn kɒːl] *phr term*   *syn* **on duty** [d(j)uːti] *phr, opposite* **off duty**¹ *phr*

keeping ready to provide [aɪ] medical services when needed, esp. in case of an emergency [ɜː]
duty² *n* • **duty-bound**³ [aʊ] *adj*

» *The surgeon on call and operating room personnel should be notified. Anesthesiology services must be immediately available on call⁴. Which physician was charged⁵ with the duty to disclose the necessary information to the patient? Dr Martin is out on a call⁶ right now.*

Use to be⁷ **on call** • doctor⁸ / physician⁸ / intern [ɜː]/ resident⁹ / pharmacist **on call** • pathologist / x-ray technician¹⁰ [ɪʃ]/ (surgical) nurse [ɜː] **on call** • **on-call** consultation¹¹ / specialist • to be on⁷/go off **duty** • hospital / reporting / legal [iː] **duty** • breach [briːtʃ] of¹² / night¹³ **duty** • **duty** of (due) [d(j)uː] care¹⁴

diensthabend, im Dienst, in Bereitschaft
dienstfrei, außer Dienst¹ Pflicht² verpflichtet³ auf Abruf⁴ beauftragt⁵ macht e. Krankenbesuch⁶ Dienst haben⁷ diensthabende(r) Arzt/ Ärztin⁸ diensthab. Assistenzarzt/-ärztin⁹ diensthab. Röntgenassistent(in)¹⁰ Konsiliar-, Liaisondienst¹¹ Pflichtverletzung¹² Nachtdienst¹³ Behandlungspflicht¹⁴   4

medical record *n term*   *sim* **patient('s) chart**¹, **flow sheet**² [floʊʃiːt] *n term*

chronologic documentation of the patient's presenting complaint(s) and medical history, the findings on examination, results of diagnostic procedures, and medications and/or therapy
record³ [rɪkɔːrd] *v* • **recording** *adj&n* • **chart**⁴ [tʃɑːrt] *v* • **charting** *n* → U18-9

» *Medical records are the most constantly reviewed [juː] documents in the hospital. Record the character of the patient's voice and examine the vocal cords. Some offices enter a note in the patient's chart whenever a prescription is refilled. All patients should be followed with a flow sheet including amounts and timing of insulin and fluid, together with a record of vital [aɪ] signs, urine volume, and blood chemistries.*

Use to maintain [eɪ] a⁵/enter into the **medical record** • written / the patient's / problem-oriented (*abbr* POMR) **medical record** • electronic (*abbr* EMR)/ online (*abbr* OMR)/ traditionally organized **medical record** • **medical record** entry⁶ / index / database [eɪ] • **medical record** documentation⁷ / technician⁸ [k] (*abbr* MRT) • **record** keeping⁹ • **to record** vital signs¹⁰ / drug use / family history / observations¹¹ • hospital / clinical / patient (care) **record** • treatment¹² / permanent [ɜː]/ anesthesia¹³ [iː] **record** • **recording** technique [tekniːk]/ machine [-ʃiːn] or device¹⁴ • all-night EEG / pH / sleep¹⁵ **recording** • temperature¹⁶ / blood pressure **chart** • dosage / flow¹⁷ / order on **chart** • **patient** or **medical** card¹ (*BE*)/ data set • problem-centered **charting**

Krankenakte, -unterlagen
Krankenblatt, Patientenbogen, Karteikarte¹ Ergebnistabelle, Parameterübersicht² aufzeichnen, registrieren, protokollieren³ ein-, auftragen⁴ e. Krankenakte führen⁵ Eintrag i. d. Krankenakte⁶ Patientendokumentation⁷ med. Dokumentationsassistent(in)⁸ Führen e. Krankenakte⁹ Vitalfunktionen protokollieren¹⁰ Beobachtungen schriftl. festhalten¹¹ Behandlungsunterlagen¹² Anästhesieprotokoll¹³ Registriergerät¹⁴ Schlafaufzeichnungen¹⁵ Fieberkurve¹⁶ Flussdiagramm¹⁷   5

Is that you Dr. Scrabble?
Just want to make sure the medication order for Mrs. Kyme in room 15 is actually yours. The staff nurse says she is not used to your handwriting being so readable.

progress report or **note** *n term*   *syn* **SOAP note** *n* , *rel* **problem list**¹ *n jar*

summary [ʌ] of a patient's hospital course [ɔː] including his/her current [ɜː] status and any recent developments
report² *v&n* • **note**³ *v* • **reportable**⁴ *adj* • **notify**⁵ *v* • **notifiable**⁴ *adj* • **list**⁶ *v*

» *The signed consent form should be backed up by the physician's own brief entry in the progress notes, with date and time. Enter a note in the patient's chart when a prescription is refilled⁷. The patient's smoking status should be noted on the problem list.*

Use written (*abbr* WPR) **progress report** • status [eɪ∥æ]/ case⁸ / consultation **report** • telephone / self⁹-/ autopsy [ɒː]/ laboratory¹⁰ **report** • **to report** an incident¹¹ / uniform **reporting** • **reportable** disease¹² / admit¹³ / preoperative **note** • clinical / nurse's [ɜː] **note** • operating¹⁴ / critical / waiting **list** • to be/put sb.¹⁵ **on the waiting list** • **notifiable** disease¹²

tägliche Zusammenfassung, Tagesbericht, Verlaufsbericht
Übersichtsliste (d. gesundheitl. Probleme)¹ berichten, melden, anzeigen; Bericht² notieren; zur Kenntnis nehmen, beachten³ melde-, anzeigepflichtig⁴ benachrichtigen, mitteilen⁵ aufschreiben, -listen, notieren⁶ ein 2. Mal ausgestellt⁷ Fallbericht, Kasuistik⁸ Selbstanzeige⁹ Laborbericht¹⁰ e. Vorfall melden¹¹ meldepflichtige Krankheit¹² Aufnahmeprotokoll¹³ Operationsliste¹⁴ jem. auf d. Warteliste setzen¹⁵   6

Note: A soap note is a narrative progress note containing the four components, subjective data (S), objective data (O), assessment (A), and plan (P).

86 HEALTH CARE — Hospital Routines

medication order *n term*   *rel* **policy**[1] [pɒːləsi], **rule**[2] [ruːl], **authorization**[3] *n*

prescription[4] written on a hospital form stating the name of the patient and the drug, the dosage, the time, frequency and route of administration, the date, and the signature of the physician

order[5] [ɔːrdɚ] *v* • **authorize**[6] [ɒːθəraɪz] *v* • **(un)authorized**[7] *adj*

» *Foresight*[8] [-saɪt] *in the adjustment* [dʒʌ] *of medication orders will minimize the risk of overdosage of drugs. Do not order these tests routinely with spirometry. The care they deliver is authorized by standing orders. Unauthorized touching* [tʌtʃ-] *of a patient is termed battery*[9].

Use to carry out/write/have/give or issue[10]/review **orders** • doctor's / medical[11] **order** • admission / diagnostic / treatment **order** • preoperative / catheter care / monitoring / nursing[12] [ɜː] **orders** • single / written / (constant) verbal (*abbr* VO) **orders** • standard / (tele)phone **orders** • (predesignated) standing[13] / PRN[14] **orders** • do not resuscitate[15] [ʌ] (*abbr* DNR)/ stat[16] **orders** • **to order** strict bed rest[17] / a test / an ECG / a drug • **order** book • **orders** on admission / on the chart / with(out) termination date • public [ʌ] health / vaccination[18] [ks]/ transfusion [juːʒ] **policies** • insurance [ʃʊɚ]/ discharge[19] [tʃ]/ visiting[20] **policies** • hospital / disclosure[21] [oʊʒ] legal [iː] **rules** • **rule** of thumb[22] [θʌm] • to obtain [eɪ] **authorization** • parental / express[23] / verbal **authorization** • **authorization** form[24]

Verschreibung, Rezept
Richtlinie, Regelung[1] Regel, Vorschrift, Bestimmung[2] Ermächtigung[3] Verschreibung, Rezept[4] veranordnen[5] ermächtigen, autorisieren[6] nicht berechtigt, unbefugt[7] Weitblick[8] Körperverletzung[9] Anweisungen geben, anordnen[10] ärztl. Verordnung/ Anordnung[11] Pflegeanweisungen[12] festgelegte Handlungs-/ Verfahrensanweisungen[13] bei Bedarf anzuwenden[14] DNR-Order[15] sofort durchzuführende Anordnungen[16] strenge Bettruhe verordnen[17] Impfrichtlinien[18] Entlassungsbestimmungen[19] Besuchszeitregelung[20] Bestimmungen z. Aufklärungspflicht[21] Faustregel[22] ausdrückliche Erlaubnis[23] Ermächtigungsformular[24]   7

---

diagnostic procedure [prəsiːdʒɚ] *n term*

       rel **diagnostic** [daɪəgnɒːstɪk] **workup**[1] *n jar*

laboratory test and/or investigation performed for identifying a patient's disease or condition

» *When the physician's treatment entails*[2] *invasive* [eɪ] *diagnostic procedures or drug treatment involving the risk of special harm, the consent*[3] *of the patient must first be obtained* [eɪ].

Use examination or assessment[4] / operative[5] **procedure** • surgical[5] / elective[6] / emergency[7] **procedure** • dental / imaging[8] / corrective / office[9] **procedure** • cosmetic or esthetic / facelift **procedure** • (non-)invasive / experimental[10] / exposure-prone[11] [oʊ] **procedures** • **diagnostic** evaluation / tool [uː] or aid[12] / measure [eʒ] • **diagnostic** modality / imaging[13] / study / test • clinical / initial [ɪʃ]/ preoperative[14] / routine [ruːtiːn] **workup** • thorough [θɜːroʊ]/ complete or comprehensive[15] **workup** • urologic / laboratory[16] **workup**

diagnostisches Verfahren
Diagnostik, diagnost. Untersuchungen[1] erfordert[2] Einwilligung[3] Untersuchungsverfahren[4] chirurg. Eingriff[5] Elektiveingriff[6] Notmaßnahme, -operation[7] bildgebendes Verfahren[8] ambulanter Eingriff[9] experimentelle Verfahren[10] V. m. hohem Expositionsrisiko[11] diagnost. Hilfsmittel[12] bildgebende Diagnostik[13] präoperative diagnost. Abklärung[14] eingehende diagnost. Untersuchungen[15] labordiagnost. Untersuchungen[16]   8

---

ward round [wɔːrd raʊnd] *n clin & jar usu pl*   *sim* **walking rounds**[1] *n clin & jar*

regular visits the attending physician[2] and his team make to all the inpatients they are responsible for

» *In some hospitals nurses participate in walking rounds instead of or in addition to report. During ward rounds, a didactic discussion* [ʌ] *of each patient's problems is conducted, emphasizing the appropriate use of diagnostic procedures. The team visits each child during walking rounds and discusses the plan of care*[3] *and any concerns*[4] [ɜː] *with the patient and family. Your physicians will make walking rounds on the unit*[5] *every morning.*

Use to be on/do or make[6]/attend **ward rounds** • medical ward[7] / surgical / post-OP **rounds** • attending[8] / uroradiology / teaching or professor's[9] **rounds** • (medical/ neurosurgery) grand[10] **rounds** • nursing[11] / chart **rounds** • **post-round** lecture session

(Stations)visite
Visite[1] leitende(r) Oberarzt/-ärztin[2] Behandlungsplan[3] Anliegen[4] Station[5] Visite machen[6] Visite auf d. internen Station[7] Chefvisite[8] Lehrvisite[9] Seminar m. klin. Fallbesprechung[10] Pflegevisite[11]   9

---

morbidity & mortality conference *n term, abbr* **M & M conference**

occasional [eɪɜ] meeting of the medical staff at which treatment errors are discussed

» *Sometimes objects like toothpicks remain within the GI tract for many years, only to turn up in a granuloma or abscess, particularly at a clinicopathologic conference.*

Use patient care / noon[1] [uː]/ consecutive case[2] / clinicopathologic[3] (*abbr* CPC) **conference** • medical staff[4] / face-to-face[5] **conference**

interne Besprechung (v. Behandlungsfehlern)
Mittagsbesprechung[1] Fallbesprechung[2] klin.-patholog. B.[3] Ärztebesprechung[4] Vieraugengespräch[5]   10

Hospital Routines   HEALTH CARE **87**

intervention [ɪntə·venʃən] *n term*   *sim* **medical measures**[1] [medɪkəl meʒɚz] *n*
action addressing a patient's health problem in order to alter [ɒː] the course of the pathologic process
interventional[2] [e] *adj term* • **intervene**[3] [iː] *v* • **measure**[4] [eʒ] *v*
» Early intervention in childhood asthma [z] may help prevent chronicity [ɪs]. The dietary [aɪ] interventions resulted in an 8% decrease in serum cholesterol. Assess the response to the therapeutic interventions. In this situation conservative measures should be employed.
Use to require [aɪ] **intervention** • nursing[5] [ɜː]/ therapeutic[6] [juː] **intervention** • pharmacologic / surgical or operative **intervention** • social / on-site[7] / crisis[8] [aɪ]/ early **intervention** • **intervention** program / strategies • **interventional** angiography / radiology[9] / immunotherapy • to take/institute/withhold[10]/forego[11] **measures** • active / conventional / invasive [eɪ] **measures** • adjunctive[12] [ədʒʌŋk-]/ temporizing[13] **measures** • emergency[14] [ɜː]/ conservative / therapeutic[15] / supportive[12] **measures** • dietary [aɪ]/ palliative / preventive or prophylactic[16] **measures** • isolation [aɪsə-]/ first aid [eɪd] **measures** • life support[17] / CPR[18] **measures**

Eingriff, Intervention, Behandlung
medizin. Maßnahmen[1] Interventions-[2] eingreifen, -schreiten[3] messen, bestimmen[4] Pflegeintervention[5] therapeut. Eingriff[6] Eingriff vor Ort[7] Krisenintervention[8] Interventionsradiologie[9] Maßnahmen vorenthalten[10] auf Maßnahmen verzichten[11] zusätzl./ unterstützende M.[12] M. um Zeit zu gewinnen[13] Notmaßnahmen[14] therapeut. M.[15] Präventivmaßnahmen, vorbeugende M.[16] lebenserhaltende M.[17] Wiederbelebungsmaßnahmen[18]
11

(medical) audit [ɒːdɪt] *n term, abbr* **MA**
   sim **review**[1] [riːvjuː], **quality assessment**[2] *n term*
systematic review and evaluation of health care procedures to determine [ɜː] the quality of care
» An audit of experience [ɪɚ] with pyogenic [paɪədʒenɪk] liver abscess [s] over the past decade revealed [iː] that the mortality rate in a referral center is still as high as 18%.
Use nursing[3] / medical / treatment **audit** • quality management / patient care[3] (*abbr* PCA) **audit** • claims[4] [eɪ]/ (pre)admission[5] / medical services **review** • concurrent[6] [ɜː]/ continued stay [eɪ] **review** • peer[7] [ɪɚ]/ retrospective / private [aɪ] **review** • (drug) utilization[8] [juːtəlaɪzeɪʃən] (*abbr* UR) **review**

Überprüfung d. ärztl. Handlungen u. Pflegemaßnahmen
(Über)prüfung[1] Qualitätsbeurteilung[2] Pflegeevaluation[3] Anspruchsprüfung[4] Überprüfung d. Aufnahmeindikation[5] Begleitkontrolle[6] Kontrolle durch KollegInnen[7] Evaluation d. Verschreibungen/ Medikamenteneinnahme[8]
12

medical negligence [neglɪdʒənˈs] *n term*   *sim* **medical care neglect**[1]
   abandonment [æ] **of care**[1] *n, rel* **malpractice**[2] [mæl-] *n term*
harmful professional action or inaction that deviates [iː] from accepted standards of care
neglect[3] *v* • **negligible**[4] [neglɪdʒəbl] *adj* • **neglected** *adj* • **neglectful**[5] *adj*
» A physician injuring a patient by conduct[6] that fails to meet the legal standard of due care may be liable[7] [laɪəbl] for negligence in an action[8] for malpractice. Allegations[9] of medical malpractice may include other torts[10] [tɔːrts], e.g. assault[11] [ɒː], battery[11], and breach [briːtʃ] of confidentiality[12].
Use to be liable [aɪ] or sued[13] [suːd] **for negligence** • to be guilty [gɪlti] of/prove **negligence** • professional / gross[14] [oʊ]/ imputed[15] [juː] **negligence** • mistreatment [iː] and **neglect** • emotional [oʊʃ]/ physical [ɪ]/ parental / self-**neglect** • **neglected** appendicitis[16] [saɪ] • medical / plastic surgery **malpractice** • **malpractice** claim [eɪ]/ action • **malpractice** suit [suːt]/ litigation[17] [lɪtɪɡeɪʃən]/ insurance [ɪnʃʊəᵊnts]

Fahrlässigkeit, Verletzung der Sorgfaltspflicht
Behandlungsverweigerung, unterlassene Hilfeleistung[1] Behandlungs-, Kunstfehler[2] vernachlässigen, nicht befolgen[3] unwesentlich, unbedeutend[4] nachlässig[5] Verhalten[6] haftbar sein[7] Klage[8] Beschuldigungen[9] Delikte[10] Körperverletzung[11] Verletzung d. Schweigepflicht[12] wegen Fahrlässigkeit angeklagt s.[13] grobe F.[14] Vorwurf d. Fahrlässigk.[15] verschleppte Appendizitis[16] Schadenersatzprozess wegen e. ärztl. Kunstfehlers[17]
13

living will *n term*   *syn* **advance** *or* **medical directive** [dɪrektɪv] *n term*
   rel **incompetence**[1], **power of attorney**[2] [ɜː] *n term*
written document signed by a legally [iː] competent[3] patient giving advance directives that no heroic measures be taken in case he/ she should be suffering [ʌ] from an irreversible [ɜː] terminal [ɜː] illness
incompetent [ɪnkɒːmpətənt] *adj term* • **competent** *adj* • **will**[4] *v* • **direct**[5] *v*
» Incompetence may be caused by mental or physical [ɪ] incapacities[6] such as mental illness, senility, alcoholism, or unconsciousness from trauma. This document, which is commonly known as health care proxy[2] or powers of attorney grants you the authority to consent to care for your incompetent father. These written, signed, and witnessed[7] instructions by the competent patient are termed advance directives and include durable powers of attorney for health care, living wills, and natural death directives.
Use to draw up a/make one's[8]/witness a **will** • mentally[9] / legally[10] **incompetent** • **competent** adult • advance health care / natural death **directive**

Patientenverfügung, -testament, Vorsorgevollmacht
Unfähigkeit[1] (Handlungs)vollmacht, Sachwalterschaft[2] geschäftsfähig[3] verfügen; vermachen, -erben[4] anweisen, befehlen[5] Beeinträchtigungen[6] durch Zeugen bestätigt[7] sein Testament machen/ errichten[8] unzurechnungsfähig[9] geschäftsunfähig[10]
14

(patient) transfer [trænˈsfɜːr] *n term* *sim* **transport**[1] *n & v*
moving a patient from one place, position, hospital unit, or care facility [sɪ] to another
transferral[2] [ɜː] *n term* • **transfer** *v* • **transferring** *n* • **transporter cart** *n*

» Whenever possible, patients should assist with their own positioning, transferring, and self-care. It is preferable to determine the best institution for definitive treatment (inpatient facility, day care, etc) and transfer the patient there before starting antipsychotics [-saɪkɒːtɪks].

Use to arrange for/await/tolerate[3]/survive/delay **transfer** • (inter/intra)**hospital**[4] / sliding [aɪ] board[5] [bɔːrd] **transfer** • supine [aɪ] to sit / sit-to-stand / pivot **transfer** • **transfer** diagnosis / agreement / to hospital / to wheelchair [ʰwiːltʃɚ] • **transfer** with standby assistance / to ICU[6] / to nursing [ɜː] home • **to be transferred** from bed to chair / for definite care • **to be transferred** for custodial [oʊ] care[7] / to the OR / to the morgue[8] [mɔːrg] • **to transfer** in / out / independently • **transported** on gurney[9] [gɜːrni]

verlegen, umlagern, überstellen; Umlagerung, Verlegung, Überstellung
Transport, Beförderung; transportieren, befördern[1] Überstellung, Umlagerung[2] verlegungsfähig sein[3] Überstellung in e. anderes Krankenhaus[4] Umlagerung m. d. Rutschbrett[5] Verlegung auf d. Intensivstation[6] in e. geschlossene psychiatr. Einrichtung verlegt werden[7] ins Leichenschauhaus gebracht werden[8] mit e. Rollbett transportiert (werden)[9] 15

discharge [n dɪs-‖v dɪstʃɑːrdʒ] *vt & n term* → U42-6, U88-11
sim **sign out**[1] *v phr*, **release**[2] [iː] *v & n jar*

(i) to release a hospitalized patient from care, custody [ʌ] or confinement [aɪ]
(ii) to release a substance [ʌ] (e.g. pus [ʌ]) or emotions [oʊʃ] (e.g. repressed anxiety[3] [aɪ])

» After a brief period of observation the patient was discharged in good condition. A high percentage of patients developed bacteriuria [jʊɚ] after discharge from the hospital. Competent patients can sign out of the emergency department without treatment and against medical advice. He discharged[4] his aggressions.

Use criteria [kraɪ-] for / timing of / ready for **discharge** • at the time of hospital[5] / home evaluation prior to[6] **discharge** • **to discharge a patient** from the emergency department / home • **to discharge a patient** to the care of his family physician • **to discharge a patient** to office follow-up[7] / to a convalescent [es] treatment center • inpatient / outpatient (*abbr* OP)/ wrongful[8] **discharge** • **discharge by death** / transfer • **discharge** date[9] / diagnosis / medication / note[10] • **discharge** process / summary[11] [ʌ]/ abstract[11] / planning • blood-stained[12] [eɪ]/ purulent [jʊɚ]/ nasal **discharge** • vaginal / menstrual / aural[13] [ɔː] **discharge** • **discharge** from the wound[14] [uː] • **discharged** against medical advice[15] (*abbr* AMA) • **to sign** oneself out • patient **release** form[16] • **release** slip[17] • **to be released** on an overnight pass

(i) entlassen; Entlassung
(ii) absondern; Sekret
s. abmelden, verlassen[1] freisetzen, abgeben; entlassen; Freisetzung; Entlassung[2] unterdrückte Angst[3] freien Lauf lassen[4] bei d. Entlassung[5] Überprüfung d. Wohnverhältnisse vor d. Entlassung[6] e. Pat. z. ambulanten Nachsorge entlassen[7] verfrühte Entlassung[8] Entlassungstermin, -datum[9] Entlassungsbrief[10] Entlassungsprotokoll[11] blutig tingierter Ausfluss[12] Ohrenfluss, Otorrhoe[13] Wundsekret[14] gegen Revers entlassen[15] Entlassungsformular[16] Entlassungsschein[17]

16

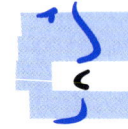

Clinical Phrases

We should admit him for observation overnight. Wir sollten ihn die Nacht über zur Beobachtung aufnehmen. • Don't worry, Mrs Kim. Everything will work out fine. Sie brauchen sich keine Sorgen zu machen, Frau K. Das wird schon wieder. • Nurse, will you attend to Mr Hiller's pressure sores. Schwester, würden Sie sich bitte um den Dekubitus von Herrn H. kümmern. • Be sure that Mrs. Kay is NPO. Sorgen Sie dafür, dass Frau K. nüchtern ist. • The physician's order for you is 'activity as tolerated'. Der Arzt hat angeordnet, dass Sie aufstehen und herumgehen können, solange Sie keine Schmerzen haben. • We may be able to discharge you soon. Wir werden Sie vielleicht bald entlassen können. • I've got another round to do before I turn in. Ich muss noch eine Visite machen, bevor ich mich schlafen legen kann.

Unit 21   Parts of the Body: Head & Neck
Related Units: 26 Teeth, 28 Bones, 43 Airways, 58 Eyes, 60 Ears, 66 Speech

head [hed] n

(i) top part of the body on the neck including the face, skull[1] [ʌ], and brain (ii) major end of long bones, e.g. the femoral [e] head[2] (iii) top position in a team or a department

head[3] v • **bareheaded**[4] [eɚ] adj • **headache** [hedeɪk] n • **headless** adj

» Tilt[5] your head backward and elevate the chin. It's important to keep his head covered.

Use to shake/turn/flex[6]/hold **one's head** • **head** and neck region [riːdʒ°n] • **head** position / rotation / elevation[7] / examination / injury / film[8] • **head** rest or support[9] / mirror[10] / screw[11] [skruː]/ implant **head** • sense of **head** fullness • to be big-[12]/ bald-[13] [ɔː] **headed** • to lose one's **head** • **head** first • to **head** for[14]

face [feɪs] n & v → U25-10ff

(n) the front of the head including the forehead[1] [fɔːrhed], the chin, the temples[2], and cheeks

facial [feɪʃ°l] adj • **-faced** adj • **facies**[3] [feɪʃiːz] n term

» The first eruptions[4] are seen on the face around the eyes and nose. Did you notice the puzzled expression on her face[5]?

Use **facial** expression or gestures[6] /dʒestʃɚz/ muscles [mʌslz]/ nerve / hair / injuries / deformity / palsy[7] [pɔːlzi] • coarse [kɔːrs] **facial** features[8] [fiːtʃɚz] • sad / angry / flushed[9] [ʌʃ]/ mask-like **face** • to lose one's / to make a[10] **face** • **face** mask / lift / pack[11] / cream [iː] • abnormal / moon / bird-like[12] / adenoid **facies** • red-/purple-/ round-**faced** • to **face** a problem / death

eye [aɪ] n & v → U58-1ff

paired organ of sight [saɪt] located in the eye sockets [ɒː] (orbits)[1] including the pupil[2], lense and retina

(eye)lid[3] n • **eyebrow** [aʊ] n • **eyelashes**[4] [æ] n • **eyeball**[5] n • **cross-eyed**[6] adj

» Keep your eyes closed. There was infrequent blinking and fluttering[7] [ʌ] of the closed eyelids. This is not visible to the naked [neɪkɪd] eye[8].

Use to close/open the **eyes** • bags under the[9] **eyes** • watery / red / bloodshot[10] / dry **eyes** • black[11] / glass **eye** • **eye** contact / blinking[12] / charts[13] [tʃ]/ patch[14] [tʃ]/ drops /-sight[15] / piece[16] / witness[17] • to raise [eɪ] the / upper / lower **eyelids**

nose [noʊz] n & v

covering of the nasal cavity[1] with the nostrils or nares[2] [neɚiːz] (term) through which we breathe [briːð] and smell

nasal [neɪz°l] adj • **naso-** comb • **nosebleed**[3] n

» A nose with a markedly depressed bridge is called saddle nose. These patients have coarse facial features, a broad, flat nose, and widely set eyes. There is blood in the nasal sinuses[4] [aɪ].

Use to blow one's[5] **nose** • to speak/breathe through **the nose** • tip / root[6] [uː]/ back or bridge[7] **of the nose** • runny / blocked-up[8] **nose** • **nasal** height [haɪt]/ concha[9] [kɒːŋkə]/ septum / bone / cavity / decongestant [dʒe] spray[10] • **nose** job[11]

jaws [dʒɒːz] n   sim **jawbone**[1] n → U28-10

bones of the skull (maxilla[2] and mandible[3]) and adjacent [ədʒeɪs°nt] soft tissues that frame the mouth and hold the teeth

» In edentulous [-tʃələs] jaws[4] of elderly persons, atrophy of the alveolar process is common. The skin of the lateral cheeks, jawline[5], and neck is dissected free in the subcutaneous plane. The pain is localized to the jaw, base of the tongue, pharynx or larynx, tonsillar area, and ear.

Use upper[2] / lower[3] / opposing / broken / protrusive **jaw** • both / clenched[6] [tʃ]/ retrusive **jaws** • angle[7] [æŋgl]/ spasms / weakness **of the jaw** • **jaw** position / relation[8] / movement / muscle / (jerk [dʒɝːrk]) or reflex[9] / clenching[10] / support / exercises • **jaw** stiffness / clicking[11] / fracture / winking[12] • **jawbone** anatomy / architecture / defect / resorption / segment

---

(i) Kopf; (ii) Caput; (iii) Leiter

Schädel[1] Oberschenkelkopf, Caput femoris[2] an d. Spitze stehen[3] ohne Kopfbedeckung[4] neigen[5] d. Kopf nach vorne neigen[6] Hochlagerung d. Kopfes[7] Schädelröntgen[8] Kopfstütze[9] Stirnspiegel[10] Schraubenkopf[11] eingebildet[12] glatzköpfig[13] zusteuern auf[14]

1

Gesicht; gegenüberstehen, konfrontiert sein

Stirn[1] Schläfen[2] Gesicht(sausdruck), Facies[3] Ausschlag[4] verdutzter Gesichtsausdruck[5] Gesichtsausdruck, Mimik[6] Gesichts-, Fazialislähmung[7] grobe Gesichtszüge[8] gerötetes G.[9] d. Gesicht verziehen[10] Gesichtspackung[11] Vogelgesicht[12]

2

Auge; ansehen, mustern

Augenhöhlen, Orbitae[1] Pupille[2] (Augen)lid[3] Wimpern[4] Augapfel[5] schielend[6] Zucken[7] mit bloßem Auge[8] Tränensäcke, Ringe unter den Augen[9] blutunterlaufene A.[10] blaues Auge[11] Blinzeln, Augenzwinkern[12] Sehprobentafeln[13] Augenklappe[14] Sehkraft[15] Okular[16] Augenzeuge[17]

3

Nase; herumschnüffeln

Nasenhöhle[1] Nasenlöcher, Nares[2] Nasenbluten[3] Sinus paranasales, Nasennebenhöhlen[4] s. d. Nase putzen, s. schnäuzen[5] Nasenwurzel[6] Nasenrücken[7] verstopfte N.[8] Nasenmuschel, Concha nasalis[9] Nasenspray[10] Nasenoperation[11]

4

Kiefer

Kieferknochen[1] Oberkiefer, Maxilla[2] Unterkiefer, Mandibula[3] zahnlose Kiefer[4] Unterkieferrand[5] zusammengepresste K.[6] (Unter)kieferwinkel, Angulus mandibulae[7] Kieferrelation[8] Masseterreflex[9] Zähnepressen[10] Kiefergelenkknacken[11] Kiefer-Lid-Phänomen[12]

5

BODY STRUCTURES & FUNCTIONS — Parts of the Body: Head & Neck

chin [tʃɪn] *n* *syn* **mentum** *n term*

the protruding¹ front portion of the lower jaw² formed by the mental protuberance³
mental *adj term* • **genial** [dʒɪnaɪᵊl] *adj* •
mento-, genio- [dʒiːnioʊ] *comb*

» Test eyebrow elevation, smiling, lip pursing⁴, cheek puff⁵ and chin muscle contraction. The head must be tilted and the chin lifted so that the oropharynx can be explored.

Use **chin** reflex⁶ / protuberance³ / tilt / lift / rest⁷ / musculature / cap⁸ • unshaven / prominent⁹ / firm [ɜː]/ sagging¹⁰ / double¹¹ **chin** • square¹²-**chinned** • **mental** foramen [eɪ] or canal¹³ / nerve / region • **genial** tubercle¹⁴ / **genio**plasty¹⁵ /hyoid [aɪ] muscle • **mento**labial /plasty¹⁵

Kinn, Mentum
vorspringend¹ Unterkiefer² Kinnvorsprung, Protuberantia mentalis³ Mundspitzen, Vorstülpen d. Lippen⁴ Aufblasen d. Wangen⁵ Masseterreflex⁶ Kinnstütze⁷ Kinnkappe⁸ vorspringendes K.⁹ schlaff herabhängendes K.¹⁰ Doppelkinn¹¹ m. kantigem K.¹² Foramen mentale¹³ Tuberculum mentale, Kinnhöcker¹⁴ Kinn-, Genioplastik¹⁵   6

cheek [tʃiːk] *n* *syn* **bucca** [bʌkə] *n term*

the fleshy part at either side of the face below the eyes
-cheeked *adj clin* • **buccal**¹ *adj term* • **bucco-** *comb*

» The lower lid sagged² [sægd] permitting tears [tɪɚz] to spill over the cheeks. Her cheeks had a rosy hue³ [hjuː].

Use fat / upper / lateral / sunken⁴ [ʌ]/ rosy⁵ **cheeks** • **cheek**bone⁶ / contours / biting⁷ [aɪ]/ bite • red-/ chubby⁸-**cheeked** [tʃʌbi] • **buccal** mucosa⁹ / surface / vestibule • **bucco**labial [eɪ]/lingual

Wange, Backe, Bucca
bukkal¹ hing herunter² Farbe³ eingefallene W.⁴ gerötete Wangen⁵ Joch-, Wangenbein, Os zygomaticum⁶ Wangenbeißen⁷ pausbäckig⁸ Wangenschleimhaut⁹

7

mouth [maʊθ] *n* *sim* **oral** [ɔː] **cavity**¹ *n term*

opening to the lungs and stomach [k] including the throat, soft and hard palate², teeth, tongue [tʌŋ], the upper and lower lips
mouthful³ *n* • **mouthwash**⁴ *n* •
oral⁵ *adj term* • **stomat-, oro-**⁶ *comb*

» These patients should not be given barium [eɚ] by mouth⁵. The patient complained of a sore mouth⁷ and difficulty swallowing.

Use to open/close **one's mouth** • wide / dry / nothing by⁸ (*abbr* NPO) **mouth** • to make one's **mouth** water⁹ • roof / floor / corner¹⁰ **of the mouth** • **mouth** opening / rinse⁴ / breathing¹¹ [iː]/-watering¹² / flora / guard¹³ [gɑːrd] • **oral** health / mucosa / hygiene [haɪdʒiːn]/ status [eɪ]/ administration¹⁴ / contraceptive • **oro**pharynx /antral /nasal /facial • **stomat**ology /itis⁷ [aɪ]/ognathic system

Mund
Mundhöhle, Cavitas oris¹ weicher/harter Gaumen² Bissen, Schluck³ Mundwasser⁴ oral⁵ d. M. betreffend, Stomato-⁶ Mundschleimhautentzündung, Stomatitis⁷ nüchtern⁸ d. Mund wässrig machen⁹ Mundwinkel¹⁰ Mundatmung¹¹ lecker¹² Zahnschutz¹³ orale Verabreichung¹⁴

8

lip *n* *syn* **labium** [eɪ] *n term, pl* **labia**, *sim* **prolabium**¹ *n term*

(i) one of the two fleshy muscular folds with an outer mucosa surrounding the mouth (ii) a liplike structure bounding² [aʊ] a cavity or groove³ [uː]:
lipstick⁴ *n* • **labial**⁵ [eɪ] *adj term* • **labio-** or **cheil(o)-** [kaɪl] *comb*

» The oral cavity is bounded anteriorly by the vermilion border of the lips⁶. Vesiculation⁷, scabbing⁸, and crusting around the lips occurred over the next few days. The infranasal groove in the midline of the upper lip is called the philtrum⁹ [f].

Use to pout¹⁰ [aʊ]/chew [tʃuː]/bite/suck [ʌ]/lick or smack¹¹/burn **one's lips** • (short) upper / lower / double / cleft¹² or hare**lip** [eɚ] • inner / red of the / open / closed / pouted / dry **lips** • cracked or fissured¹³ / thick¹⁴ / swollen / scaling¹⁵ [eɪ] **lips** • **lip** of a wound¹⁶ [uː]/ reading / balm¹⁷ [bɑːlm] • **lip** mucosa / musculature / support / contour¹⁸ / closure¹⁹ [oʊʒ]/ line²⁰ / (in)competence²¹ / biting / retractor²² • **labial** tooth surface / vestibule²³ / margin / frenulum²⁴ / consonant²⁵ / ulcer [ʌ] • **labio**palatal /buccal space • **cheil**osis /itis²⁶ [aɪ]/oplasty

Lippe, Labium
Lippenwulst, -rot, Prolabium¹ begrenzen² Furche, Sulcus³ Lippenstift⁴ labial, Lippen-⁵ Lippensaum⁶ Bläschenbildung⁷ Schorfbildung⁸ Oberlippengrübchen, Philtrum⁹ Lippen schürzen/ vorstülpen¹⁰ sich d. L. lecken¹¹ Lippenspalte, Labium fissum, Hasenscharte¹² aufgesprungene L.¹³ breite/ wulstige L.¹⁴ s. schuppende L.¹⁵ Wundrand¹⁶ Lippenbalsam¹⁷ Lippenprofil¹⁸ Lippenschluss¹⁹ Lippenschlusslinie²⁰ Lippen(in)kompetenz²¹ Lippenhalter²² labialer Mundvorhof²³ Lippenbändchen, Frenulum labii²⁴ Labial-, Lippenlaut²⁵ Lippenentzündung, Cheilitis²⁶   9

(oral) vestibule [vestɪbjuːl] *n term* *syn* **buccal** [ʌ] **cavity**, **vestibulum oris** *n term*

part of the mouth ouside the teeth and/or gums bounded¹ [aʊ] laterally by the lips and the cheeks, and by the reflections of the mucosa² from the lips and cheeks to the gums
vestibular³ *adj term* • **vestibulo-** *comb*

» The patient presented with a severely resorbed mandible and a shallow vestibule⁴. The local vestibular swelling responded well to antibiotic therapy.

Use to extend into⁵/reconstruct/deepen **the vestibule** • **vestibule of the** mouth / nose⁶ • labial / (labio)buccal **vestibule** • **vestibular** surface / space / depth⁷ / mucosa / incision / sulcus [ʌ] • **vestibulo**plasty⁸

(Mund)vorhof, Vestibulum oris
begrenzt¹ Umschlagfalten d. Schleimhaut² vestibulär³ flaches V.⁴ i. d. Mundvorhof hineinreichen⁵ V. nasi, Naseneingang⁶ Mundvorhoftiefe⁷ Vestibulum-, Mundvorhofplastik⁸

10

Parts of the Body: Head & Neck — BODY STRUCTURES & FUNCTIONS

tongue [tʌŋ] *n*   *syn* **lingua** [lɪŋgwə], **glossa** [ɒː‖ɔː] *n term*

(i) mobile muscular organ of taste[1] and speech on the floor of the oral cavity covered with mucous membrane[2] which assists in chewing, swallowing[3], and articulation[4] (ii) language

lingual[5] *adj term* • **glossal**[5] *adj* • **gloss-, -glossia** *comb*

» The anterior two-thirds of the tongue (oral tongue) is limited posteriorly by the circumvallate [-væleɪt] papillae[6] [iː] and includes the tip, dorsum, lateral borders, and undersurface of the mobile tongue. To increase mobility of the tongue, the lingual frenum [iː] may need cutting. Untreated tongue-tie[7] may affect speech and interfere with[8] mastication and passive cleansing [e] of the teeth.

Use to put out[9]/hold[10]/bite **one's tongue** • clean / furred [ɜː] or coated[11] / moist / parched [tʃ] or dry / fissured [ɪʃ] or scrotal or grooved[12] [uː]/ burning / bald [ɔː] or glossy or glazed[13] [eɪz] **tongue** • tip / base[14] / margin [dʒ]/ anterior/posterior third / thickening **of the tongue** • mappy or geographic[15] / bitten / inflamed [eɪ]/ strawberry[16] / smoker's / black hairy[17] / cleft or bifid[18] **tongue** • **tongue** space / function / movement / pressing / depressor[19] • **lingual** nerve / tonsil[20] / artery • **linguo**labial • **glossal** surface / ulcer • **glosso**pharyngeal muscle /epiglottic folds /palatine nerve /dynia [ɪ]/ptosis • **gloss**itis[21]

(i) **Zunge, Lingua, Glossa**
(ii) **Sprache**
Geschmacksorgan[1] Schleimhaut[2] Schlucken[3] Aussprache, Artikulation[4] lingual, zungenseitig[5] Zungenpapillen, Papillae linguales[6] Ankyloglossie, Zungenverwachsung[7] behindern[8] Z. herausstrecken/ zeigen[9] d. Mund halten[10] belegte Z.[11] Faltenzunge, L. plicata[12] Lackzunge[13] Zungengrund, Radix linguae[14] Landkartenz., L. geographica[15] Himbeer-, Erdbeerz.[16] schwarze Haarzunge, Melanoglossie[17] Spaltzunge, L. bifida[18] Zungenspatel, -halter[19] Zungenmandel, Tonsilla lingualis[20] Zungenentzündung, Glossitis[21]   **11**

---

throat [θroʊt] *n*   *syn* **pharynx** [færɪŋks] *n*, *sim* **fauces**[1] [fɔːsiːz] *n pl term*

(i) the fauces and pharynx
(ii) in genE, the front part of the neck between the chin and the clavicle[2]

throaty[3] *adj clin* • **pharyngeal** [-dʒɪəl] *adj term* • **faucial** [fɔːʃəl] *adj*

» Wrap[4] [ræp] this scarf[5] around your throat. You need warm throat irrigations[6] or gargles[7].

Use to clear one's[8] **throat** • sore[9] / scratchy[10] [tʃ]/ dry **throat** • **throat** swab[11] [ɒː]/ infection / culture • ear, nose and **throat** (*abbr* ENT)[12] • injected[13] [dʒe] **fauces** • pharyngeal or faucial[14] **tonsil** • **throaty** voice[15]

(i) **Rachen, Schlund, Pharynx**
(ii) **Hals, Kehle**
Schlund(enge), Fauces[1] Schlüsselbein, Clavicula[2] heiser, rau; guttural[3] wickeln[4] Schal[5] Halsspülungen[6] Gurgelmittel[7] s. räuspern[8] Halsschmerzen[9] Halskratzen[10] Rachenabstrich[11] HNO[12] entzündeter/ geschwollener Rachen[13] Rachenmandel, Tonsilla pharyngealis[14] raue Stimme[15]   **12**

---

neck *n*   *syn* **cervix** [sɜːrvɪks] *n*, *sim* **nape** [neɪp] *or* **nucha**[1] [njuːkə] *n term*

(i) narrowed connection between the trunk [ʌ] and the head
(ii) neck-like narrowing in bones, teeth, etc.

cervical[2] *adj term* • **nuchal**[3] *adj* • **neckline**[4] *n clin*

» The neck was supple[5] [ʌ]. Her neck muscles [mʌslz] were tight[6] [taɪt] and she complained of a headache. Pruritic lesions are particularly common around the neckline.

Use to twist[7]/break **one's neck** • back of the[1] **neck** • **neck** pain / stiffness[8] / tie[9] /lace[10] [-ləs]/ veins / extension • bladder[11]/ femoral[12] [e] **neck** • **nuchal** rigidity[8] [rɪdʒɪdəti] • **cervical** rib[13] / spine[14] [aɪ]/ nodes [oʊ]/ collar[15]

(i) **Hals, Nacken**
(ii) **Zervix, Collum**
Nacken[1] zervikal, Hals-[2] Nacken-[3] Ausschnitt, Dekolletee[4] beweglich, weich[5] verspannt[6] H. (ver)drehen[7] Nackensteifigkeit[8] Krawatte[9] Halskette[10] Blasenhals[11] Oberschenkelhals, Collum femoris[12] Halsrippe, Costa cervicalis[13] Halswirbelsäule[14] Halskrause[15]   **13**

Adam's apple *n clin*   *syn* **laryngeal** [-dʒ(ɪ)əl] **prominence** *n term*

cartilage[1] [kɑrtəlɪdʒ] of the voice box (larynx)[2] [lærɪŋks] moving up and down in the front of the neck, esp prominent in men

» The cricothyroid [aɪ] membrane is about 1.5 fingerwidths below the laryngeal prominence and is bounded[3] [aʊ] caudally by the cricoid cartilage[4].

Adamsapfel, Prominentia laryngea
Knorpel[1] Kehlkopf, Larynx[2] begrenzt[3] Ringknorpel, Cartilago cricoidea[4]   **14**

---

ear [ɪɚ] *n*

organ of hearing [ɪɚ] and equilibrium[1] consisting of the outer, middle, and inner or sensory ear[2]

eardrum[3] [ʌ] *n* • **earlobe**[4] [oʊ] *n* •
auditory[5] [ɒː] *adj term* • **aural**[5] [ɔː] *adj* • **oto-, oro-** *comb*

» The rash[6] typically begins at the hairline[7] and behind the ears. One patient had lost a natural ear in an accident.

Use inner[1] / middle[8] / external **ear** • **ear** plugs[9] [ʌ] /ache [eɪk]/ muffs[10] [ʌ]/ drops / wax[11] • cauliflower[12] [ɒː] **ears** • **auditory** canal or meatus[13] [ɪeɪ]/ ossicles[14] / threshold[15] [θreʃhoʊld] • **aural** discharge[16] / pressure

Ohr
Gleichgewicht[1] Innenohr[2] Trommelfell, Membrana tympani[3] Ohrläppchen[4] (Ge)hör-, auditiv[5] Ausschlag[6] Haaransatz[7] Mittelohr[8] Ohrschutz, Wattepfropf[9] Ohrenschützer[10] Ohrenschmalz, Cerumen[11] Boxerohren[12] Gehörgang, Meatus acusticus[13] Gehörknöchelchen, Ossicula auditus[14] Hörschwelle[15] Ohr(en)fluss, Otorrhoe[16]   **15**

hair [heɚ] *n usu sing*

slender thr<u>ea</u>dlike[1] [e] outgrowth [-ouθ] covering the human scalp[2], face (b<u>ea</u>rd [ɪɚ], mustache[3] [mʌstæʃ]) and body hair; hair loss leads to a receding [iː] hairline[4] and finally to b<u>a</u>ldness[5] [ɒː]; artificial hair is called a toupee [tuːpeɪ] or wig[6]

hairy *adj* • **hairless** *adj* • **hairdo** or **hairstyle**[7] *n* • **haircut** *n*

» Drugs can cause diffuse hair loss. This disease favors hairy areas like the scalp. There was a patch[8] of gray-white hair. These patients typically have sp<u>a</u>rse [ɑː] ax<u>i</u>llary and p<u>u</u>bic hair[9].

Use to grow/cut/comb **hair** • blond or fair [feɚ]/ <u>au</u>burn[10] [ɒː]/ graying / dry / gr<u>ea</u>sy[11] [iː]/ curly[12] [ɜː]/ brittle[13] **hair** • **hair** turns gray / falls out • scalp / body / pubic / t<u>a</u>ste[14] **hair** • **hair** brush / spray / root[15] / shaft / f<u>o</u>llicle / thinning / growth

Haar

fadenförmig[1] Kopfhaut[2] Schnurrbart[3] Haaransatz[4] Glatzköpfigkeit[5] Haarteil, Perücke[6] Frisur[7] Fleck[8] spärliche Achsel- u. Schambehaarung[9] kastanienbraunes H.[10] fettiges H.[11] gelocktes H.[12] brüchiges H.[13] Geschmacksstiftchen[14] Haarwurzel[15]

16

Unit 22   The Trunk

Related Units: 21 **Head & Neck,** 23 **Extremities,** 50 **Female Sexual Organs,** 52 **Male Sexual Organs,** 87 **Anatomy**

tr<u>u</u>nk [ʌ] *n clin & term*   *syn* **torso** [tɔːrsou] *n, sim* **truncus**[1] [trʌŋkəs] *n term*

(i) central part of the body excluding the head, neck, and limbs
(ii) the main part of a vessel or nerve

tr<u>u</u>ncal[2] [trʌŋkəl] *adj term* • **truncated**[3] *adj*

» El<u>e</u>vate the legs and keep the trunk horiz<u>o</u>ntal. These nerves [ɜː] are inv<u>o</u>lved in the maint<u>e</u>nance [eɪ] of p<u>o</u>sture[4] and <u>i</u>ntegrated m<u>o</u>vements of the limbs[5] [lɪmz] and trunk. In truncus arteri<u>o</u>sus, a single large v<u>e</u>ssel overr<u>i</u>des [aɪ] the ventricular septum and distributes all of the blood ejected [dʒe] from the heart.

Use forward fl<u>e</u>xion of the **trunk** • brachiocephalic [breɪkɪousəfælɪk]/ p<u>u</u>lmonary[6] [ʊ][ʌ]/ nerve[7] / lower **trunk** • upper / lower **torso** • **trunk** m<u>u</u>scles[8] [ʌ]/ move-ment • **truncal** ob<u>e</u>sity[9] [iː]/ abr<u>a</u>sions [eɪʒ]/ r<u>a</u>sh / at<u>a</u>xia[10] • **truncus** arteri<u>o</u>sus[11]

(i) Rumpf, Stamm
(ii) Truncus

Truncus (gemeinsamer Gefäß- oder Nervenstamm)[1] Rumpf-, Stamm-[2] gekürzt, amputiert, trunkiert[3] (Körper)haltung[4] Extremitäten[5] Truncus pulmonalis[6] Nervenstamm[7] Rumpfmuskulatur[8] Stammfettsucht[9] Rumpfataxie[10] Truncus arteriosus[11]

1

chest [tʃ] *n clin*   *syn* **th<u>o</u>rax, p<u>e</u>ctus** *n term,*
  rel **br<u>ea</u>st**[1] [e], **b<u>u</u>st**[2] [ʌ], **b<u>o</u>som**[3] [ʊ] *n* → U50-17

body region between the neck and the di<u>a</u>phragm encl<u>o</u>sed by the ribs

thor<u>a</u>cic[4] [θəræsɪk] *adj term* • **pect<u>o</u>ral**[5] *adj*
br<u>ea</u>stbone[6] *n clin* • **-chested, thoraco-** *comb*

» P<u>e</u>ctus carin<u>a</u>tum[7] [eɪ] is a b<u>o</u>wing [ou] out of the st<u>e</u>rnum [ɜː]. There are no breath [e] sounds[8] over the left chest. Grafts from the subclavicular regions of the thorax provide a better color match than those from the lower trunk or the b<u>u</u>ttocks[9] [ʌ] and thighs[10] [θaɪz].

Use to bring out your[11]/get sth. off one's[12] **chest** • **chest** wall / c<u>a</u>vity[13] / m<u>u</u>scle[14] [s] • **chest** hair / di<u>a</u>meter [daɪæ-]/ pain • flat / asth<u>e</u>nic [e]/ f<u>u</u>nnel[15] [ʌ]/ pigeon[7] [dʒ] • **chest** • b<u>a</u>rrel(-shaped)[16] / fl<u>ai</u>l[17] [eɪ] **chest** • ant<u>e</u>rior / l<u>a</u>teral / lower **chest** • **chest** medicine / compr<u>e</u>ssion / x-ray[18] / l<u>ea</u>d[19] [iː]/ **pectus** deformity / excav<u>a</u>tum[15] / thor<u>a</u>cic cage[20] [keɪdʒ]/ nerve / aorta [eɪ] • thor<u>a</u>cic c<u>a</u>vity[13] / vertebrae [ɜː]/ spine[21] [aɪ] • pect<u>o</u>ral region / muscle[14] / girdle[22] [ɜː] • pect<u>o</u>ral spine[21] / fascia [fæʃ(i)ə] • intr<u>a</u>thoracic • th<u>o</u>racoabd<u>o</u>minal • flat[23]-/ bare[24]-**chested** • **breast** abnorm<u>a</u>lities / feeding[25] [iː]/ cancer / rec<u>o</u>nstruction [ʌ]

Thorax, Brust(korb)

Mamma, (weibl.) Brust[1] Busen, Oberweite[2] Busen[3] thorakal; Brust-[4] Brust-, Pektoral-[5] Brustbein, Sternum[6] Kiel-, Hühnerbrust, Pectus carinatum[7] Atemgeräusche[8] Gesäß[9] Oberschenkel[10] die Brust herausstrecken[11] sich etw. von d. Seele reden[12] Brustraum[13] Brustmuskel, M. pectoralis[14] Trichterbrust, Pectus excavatum[15] Fassthorax[16] instabiler T., Thoraxinstabilität[17] Thoraxröntgen[18] Brustwandableitung[19] Brustkorb[20] Brustwirbelsäule[21] Schultergürtel, Cingulum membri superioris[22] flachbrüstig[23] mit nacktem Oberkörper[24] Stillen[25]

2

> **Note:** Mark the difference between **chest** and **breast**, which are common words in clinical usage, while **bosom** (poetic) and **bust** (clothing) are rare.

epig<u>a</u>strium *n term*   *syn* **epig<u>a</u>stric r<u>e</u>gion** *n, rel* **prec<u>o</u>rdium**[1] *n term*

central upper abd<u>o</u>minal region [riːdʒən] below the st<u>e</u>rnum [ɜː] and the c<u>o</u>stal [ɒː] margin[2] [mɑːrdʒɪn] between the right and left hypochondriac [haɪpəkɒːndriæk] regions

precordial[3] [priːkɔːrdɪəl] *adj term*

» There was v<u>o</u>miting with t<u>e</u>nderness of the epig<u>a</u>strium and later of the entire abd<u>o</u>men. The liver enlargement may pres<u>e</u>nt subcostally, in the epigastrium, or as a l<u>o</u>calized b<u>u</u>lging[4] [bʌldʒɪŋ] of the rib cage[5]. She compl<u>ai</u>ns of a sense of epig<u>a</u>stric h<u>ea</u>viness[6] [e].

Use to compress the **epigastrium** • **epigastric** fold[7] / reflex / vein [eɪ]/ discomfort • **epigastric** bloating[6] [oʊ]/ fullness[6] / hernia[8] [ɜː] • central / active / hyperdyn<u>a</u>mic [aɪ]/ quiet **precordium** • **precordial** chest wall / l<u>ea</u>ds[9] [iː]/ pain[10] / palp<u>a</u>tion

Epigastrium, Oberbauch(gegend)

Präkordialregion, Herzgegend[1] Rippenbogen[2] präkordial, vor d. Herzen gelegener Brustwandbereich[3] Vorwölbung[4] Brustkorb, (knöcherner) Thorax[5] Druck/ Völlegefühl in d. Oberbauchgegend[6] Plica umbilicalis lateralis, Plica epigastrica[7] Hernia epigastrica[8] Brustwandableitungen (bei EKG)[9] Präkordialschmerz[10]

3

The Trunk   **BODY STRUCTURES & FUNCTIONS 93**

abdomen n term   syn **belly** n, sim **stomach**[1] [k], **tummy**[1] [ʌ] n clin → U45-6

region between the thorax and the pelvis which is divided into 4 quadrants or into 9 abdominal regions (epigastric, umbilical [ʌ], hypogastric, lumbar [ʌ], iliac, and the right and left hypochondriac regions)[2]

abdominal [æbdɒːmɪnəl] adj term • **abdomino-** comb • **pot-bellied**[3] adj inf

» The gallbladder[4] [ɔː] is palpable in the right upper abdomen. The length of the hospital stay for patients undergoing abdominal surgery was reduced. In massive ascites [saɪ] the belly is taut [ɒː]. Lie down flat on your stomach, please. Was that your tummy rumbling [ʌ]?

Use protuberant[5] / pendulous[6] / surgical or acute[7] **abdomen** • **abdominal** cavity[8] / muscles / wall[9] / girth[10] [ɜː] • **abdominal** breathing[11] [iː]/ aorta / distention[12] • **abdominal** cramps[13] / tenderness[14] • **belly** ache[15] [eɪk]/ laugh[16] [læf] • muscle[17] / swollen **belly** • **abdomino**perineal [iː] /plasty /jugular [dʒʌ] reflux [iː] test[18] • pit of the[19] **stomach**

> Note: Although **belly** and **stomach** are clinically used to refer to the abdominal region, both mostly relate to the gastric pouch[20] [paʊtʃ]; **tummy** (has both meanings as well) is used mainly when talking with children.

Abdomen, Bauch, Venter
Bauch; Magen[1] Regio hypochondriaca sinistra[2] dickbäuchig[3] Gallenblase[4] vorstehender Bauch[5] Hängebauch[6] akutes Abdomen[7] Bauchraum, -höhle[8] Bauchdecke[9] Bauchumfang[10] Bauchatmung[11] geblähtes Abdomen[12] Bauchkrämpfe[13] Druckschmerzhaftigkeit d. Abdomens[14] Bauchschmerzen[15] dröhnendes Lachen[16] Muskelbauch, Venter musculi[17] hepatojugulärer Refluxtest[18] Magengrube[19] Magen(sack)[20]

4

navel [eɪ] n clin   syn **umbilicus** [ʌmbɪlɪkəs‖laɪkəs] n term, **belly button** [ʌ] n inf

depression in the center of the abdomen at which the umbilical cord joined the fetal [iː] abdomen; the expression **belly button** is used mainly when talking with children

umbilical[1] [ʌmbɪlɪkəl‖bɪlaɪkəl] adj term • **para/ infraumbilical** adj

» Place the first hand midway between the navel and the xiphisternal [z] notch[2]. The injection sites include a U-shaped area around the umbilicus. Show me your belly button, Billy.

Use everted[3] [ɜː]/ (abnormally) low-placed / wet[4] **umbilicus** • lateral to / above the **umbilicus** • **umbilical** region / fold[5] / fissure[6] / cord[7] [kɔːrd]/ tape[8] / hernia[9] • **umbilical** ring[10] / fistula / sinus [aɪ]/ stump [ʌ] • tummy[11] **button**

(Bauch)nabel, Umbilicus, Omphalos
umbilikal, Nabel-[1] Schwertfortsatzspitze[2] vorstehender/ vorgewölbter Nabel[3] nässender Nabel[4] Plica umbilicalis, Nabelfalte[5] Incisura lig. teretis[6] Nabelschnur[7] Nabelbinde[8] Nabelbruch, Hernia umbilicalis[9] Nabelring, Anulus umbilicalis[10] Bauchnabel[11]

5

22

waist [weɪst] n   syn **waistline** n, sim **beltline**[1] n clin, rel **flank**[2] [æ] n clin & term

the narrowing of the body between the ribs and hips

waisted[3] [weɪstɪd] adj & comb

» Your belt is fastened to tightly around your waist. Upper body obesity (excess fat around the waist and flank) is a greater health risk than lower body obesity (thighs and buttocks).

Use small[4] / narrow[4] / slim[4] / thick / wasp[5]-**waist** [ɔː] • **waistline** area • **waist** circumference[6] [ʌ]/ level /-high[7] • **waist** belt[8] / band[9] / pack /-deep[7] • **flank** pain[10] / area / compression • **flank** wound [uː]/ incision[11] [sɪ]/ mass • to strip to the[12] **waist** • slender-/ high[13]-**waisted**

Taille, Mitte
Gürtellinie[1] Flanke, Seite, Lende[2] tailliert[3] schlanke Taille[4] Wespentaille[5] Taillenumfang[6] hüfthoch, bis zur Taille[7] Hüftgurt, -gürtel[8] Rock-, Hosenbund[9] Flankenschmerz[10] Flankenschnitt[11] Oberkörper freimachen[12] hochtailliert[13]

6

hip n clin usu pl   rel **os coxae**[1] [ɒːs kɒːksi], **innominate bone**[1], **pelvis**[2] n term

(i) region on either side of the body at and lateral to the hip joint [dʒ]
(ii) informally, the hip joint itself

narrow-hipped[3] adj clin • **pelvic**[4] [pelvɪk] adj term → U28-21

» Resisted abduction [ʌ] of the hip elicits[5] pain. While hip arthritis [aɪ] usually produces groin pain[6], some patients have buttock or low back symptoms[7]. Several osteotomies of the innominate bone have been described for improving acetabular [æsɪ-] coverage [ʌ] of the femoral [e] head. The epididymis drains [eɪ] into the vas deferens, which courses [ɔː] through the inguinal canal into the pelvis.

Use to sway[8] [eɪ]/wiggle or shake[8]/abduct/extend **one's hips** • **hip** area / joint / bone[1] • **hip** girdle[9] [ɜː]/ bath[10] / musculature • **hip** motion [ʊʃ]/ adduction / stiffness • **hip** click[11] / spica cast[12] [spaɪkə kæst] • **hip** arthroplasty[13] / replacement[13] / prosthesis[13] [iː]/ pain[14] • flexed / dislocated[15] / snapping[11] **hip** • **coxa** vara / valga / plana • flat[16] / beaked[17] [iː]/ brim of the[18] **pelvis** • **pelvic** ring or girdle[9] / floor[19] • **pelvic** cavity[20] / examination / organs

(i) Hüfte, Coxa
(ii) Hüftgelenk
Hüftbein, -knochen, Os coxae[1] Pelvis, Becken[2] schmalhüftig[3] Becken-, pelvin[4] löst aus, verursacht[5] Schmerzen in d. Leistengegend[6] Kreuzschmerzen[7] m. d. Hüften wackeln[8] Beckengürtel[9] Sitzbad[10] Schnapphüfte, schnellende Hüfte, Coxa saltans[11] Becken-Bein-Gips[12] Hüftgelenksatz, Hüftendoprothese[13] Hüft(gelenk)schmerz, Koxalgie[14] Hüftgelenkluxation[15] plattes Becken, Pelvis plana[16] Schnabelbecken[17] Beckeneingang, Apertura pelvica superior[18] Beckenboden[19] Beckenhöhle, Cavitas/ Cavum pelvis[20]

7

BODY STRUCTURES & FUNCTIONS — The Trunk

hypogastrium n term   syn **(supra)pubic** [pjuː] or **hypogastric region** n term
lowermost abdominal region between the umbilical region and the pubic symphysis [sɪmfɪsɪs]
hypogastric[1] [haɪpoʊgæstrɪk] adj term
» Sympathetic fibers [aɪ] emerging [dʒ] from T11-L2 travel through the paravertebral sympathetic chain [tʃeɪn] ganglia[2], superior hypogastric plexus, and hypogastric nerves to enter the pelvic plexus along with parasympathetic fibers.
Use **hypogastric** pressure / vein[3] [eɪ]/ plexus[4] • retro/ infra/ ilio/ trans**pubic** • **pubic** hair[5] / fat pad / margin • **pubic** bone / tubercle [(j)uː]/ lice[6] [laɪs]/ ramus[7] [eɪ] • **suprapubic** compression / catheter / cystostomy[8]

Unterbauch(gegend), Hypogastrium
hypogastrisch; Unterbauch-[1] Grenzstrangganglien, Ganglia trunci sympathici[2] Vena iliaca interna, V. hypogastrica[3] Plexus hypogastricus[4] Schamhaare, -behaarung[5] Filz-, Schamläuse[6] Schambeinast, Ramus pubicus[7] suprapubische Blasenfistel[8]
8

groin [grɔɪn] n clin   syn **inguinal region** [ɪŋgwɪnəl riːdʒən] n term
region at the crease[1] [kriːs] where the inner part of the thigh [θaɪ] joins the trunk
inguinal[2] adj term • **inguino-** comb
» Colicky[3] flank pain radiating [eɪ] to the groin suggests acute ureteric obstruction. In pseudoxanthoma [suːdoʊzænθoʊmə] elasticum, the flexural [ekʃ] areas such as the axillae [iː] and inguinal area are the primary [aɪ] sites of involvement.
Use to strain [eɪ] one's[4] **groin** • ipsilateral / uninvolved **groin** • **groin** crease / exploration • **groin** incision / swelling / hernia[5] [ɜː] • **inguinal** canal[6] / ring[7] / hernia[5] • **inguinal** ligament[8] [ɪg]/ lymph [lɪmf] nodes / testis[9]

Leiste(nbeuge), Leistengegend, Regio inguinalis
Hautfalte[1] Inguinal-, Leisten-[2] kolikartig[3] sich die Leiste zerren[4] Leistenbruch, -hernie, Hernia inguinalis[5] Leistenkanal, Canalis inguinalis[6] Leistenring, Anulus inguinalis[7] Leistenband, Poupart-Band, Lig. inguinale[8] Leistenhoden[9]
9

crotch [krɒtʃ] n clin   sim **perineum**[1] [iː], **pudendum**[2] n term, rel **lap**[3] n clin
angle [æŋgl] formed by the inner sides of the thighs where they join the trunk (including the external genitals)
perineal[4] [perɪniːəl] adj term • **pudendal**[5] [pjuːdendəl] adj
» Make sure the patient's crotch is over the crotch of the MAST garment[6]. Keep the child on the parent's lap. The vulva [ʌ] and perineum are inflamed [eɪ].
Use a kick in the **crotch** • (deep/ superficial) [ɪʃ] transverse [ɜː] muscle of the **perineum** • **perineal** body[7] / area / care / support[8] / fistula[9] / **perineal** mass / nerves / muscles[10] / prostatectomy[11] • **pudendal** vessels / nerve / block or anesthesia[12] [iːʒ] • to be on mother's **lap** • **lap** belt or restraint[13] [eɪ]

Schritt, Dammgegend
Damm, Perineum[1] (weibl) Scham(gegend), Vulva[2] Schoß[3] perineal; Damm-[4] Scham-, Pudendus-[5] Antischockhose[6] Centrum tendineum perinei[7] Dammschutz[8] Dammfistel[9] Dammmuskulatur[10] perineale Prostatektomie[11] Pudendusanästhesie, -block[12] Beckengurt[13]
10

back n clin   syn **dorsum** [dɔːrsəm] n term, pl **dorsa**
(i) posterior part of the body from the neck to the end of the spine
(ii) backside of body parts
backache[1] [bækeɪk] n clin • **dorsal**[2] adj term • **dorso-** comb
» Lower back pain[3] ranks second among the reasons for doctor office visits. Are there any lesions [iːʒ] on the back? Pain is localized to the back. Lie down on your back. Stand with your back flat against the wall.
Use to turn[4]/flex/arch[5] [ɑːrtʃ]/lie on **one's** back • the small of the[6] / to have a bad **back** • **back** muscles[7] /bone[8] / strain[9] [eɪ] • **back** stiffness / injury [ɪndʒəri]/ exercises • upper / lower[6] / tense[9] / rigid [rɪdʒɪd] **back** • **back of the** head[10] / tongue[11] [tʌŋ]/ neck[12] • **dorsum of the** hand[13] / foot

Rücken; Rückseite, Dorsum
Rückenschmerzen[1] dorsal[2] Kreuzschmerzen[3] jem. den Rücken zuwenden; den Rücken kehren[4] den Rücken krümmen[5] Kreuz[6] Rückenmuskulatur[7] Wirbelsäule[8] verspannter Rücken[9] Hinterkopf[10] Zungenrücken[11] Nacken[12] Handrücken[13]
11

spine [aɪ] n   syn **vertebral** [vɜːrtəbrəl] [tiːbrəl] or **spinal column** [ɒː] n clin,
       backbone n inf → U28-19
(i) series of bones in the midline of the back which form the axis of the skeleton and protect the spinal cord[1] [kɔːrd]
(ii) pointed prominence or process of a bone
spinal[2] [aɪ] adj term • **vertebra**[3] [ɜː] n, pl **-ae** [eɪ‖iː] • **intervertebral**[4] adj
» The spine protects the spinal cord from trauma [ɒː]. Dislocation of the cervical vertebrae involves the risk of spinal cord injury. Stand with your backbone rigid, please.
Use cervical [sɜː]/ thoracic [æs]/ lumbar[6] [ʌ]/ sacral [eɪ] **spine** • flexion / (compensatory) curvature[7] [ɜː] **of the spine** • concavity / convexity **of the spine** • **spine** movement / injury[8] • **spine** board[9] / immobilization • **spinal** cord / fluid[10] / nerves[11] / reflex • **vertebral** body[12] / foramen[13] [eɪ]/ fracture / compression • **intervertebral** disk[14] (space) • para/ costo**vertebral** • to have no[15] **backbone**

(i) Wirbelsäule;
(ii) Dorn; Spina
Rückenmark[1] Wirbel-, Spinal-[2] Wirbel[3] intervertebral, Zwischenwirbel-[4] Brustwirbelsäule[5] Lendenwirbelsäule[6] Wirbelsäulenkrümmung[7] Wirbelsäulenverletzung[8] Rettungstrage[9] Zerebrospinalflüssigkeit, Liquor[10] Spinal-, Rückenmarksnerven, Nervi spinales[11] Wirbelkörper, Corpus vertebrae[12] Wirbelloch, Foramen vertebrale[13] Band-, Zwischenwirbelscheibe[14] kein Rückgrat besitzen[15]
12

Extremities BODY STRUCTURES & FUNCTIONS 95

buttock [bʌtək] *n clin usu pl*   *syn* **natis** *n term, pl* **nates** [neɪtiːz]
  rel **bottom**¹, **behind**¹, **backside**¹, **bum**¹ [ʌ] *(BE)* *****butt**¹, *****ass**¹ *n inf*
  either of the two large fleshy cheeks at the bottom of the torso comprised of the gluteal muscles
  gluteal² [gluːtɪəl‖tiːəl] *adj term* → U30-15
» *Avoid girdles* [ɜː] *or body stockings³ that press the buttocks together. She fell on her behind. Slightly spank the baby's bottom⁴. My backside still aches. The hemorrhoids were visible on spreading⁵ [e] the buttocks. There is abundant [ʌ] hair⁶ in the gluteal fold of the buttocks.*
Use right/ left **buttock** • wasted⁷ [eɪ] **buttocks** • **buttock** muscle⁸ [mʌsl]/ crease⁹ [kriːs] • **gluteal** region¹⁰ / fold *or* cleft⁹

Gesäßbacke, Natis
Gesäß, Hintern, Po¹ gluteal, Gesäß-² Bodystockings³ d. Kind einen Klaps auf d. Po geben⁴ Auseinanderziehen⁵ starke Behaarung⁶ Gesäßmuskelschwund⁷ Gesäßmuskel⁸ Gesäßfurche, -spalte⁹ Gesäßgegend, Regio glutaea¹⁰

13

Unit 23   Extremities
Related Units: **22** Trunk, **28** Bones, **29** Joints, **30** Muscles, **87** Anatomy, **63** Posture, **64** Body Movement, **65** Walking

limb [lɪm] *n*   *syn* **extremity** [ɪkstremətɪ] *n, pl* **-ies**
  (i) one of the projecting [dʒe] paired [eə] appendages, i.e. arms and legs
  (ii) branch or arm of an anatomic part, e.g. the descending [se] limb of Henle's loop¹ [uː]
  -limbed *comb*
» *The patient drags² his right lower extremity. A purpuric [pjuɚ] rash³ appeared over the trunk⁴ and extremities. Amputation of the limb may be required.*
Use right upper *(abbr* RUE)/ lower / unaffected **extremity** • flaccid⁵ [(k)s]/ cachectic [k]/ flail⁶ [eɪ] **extremity** • **extremity** vessels / abrasions [eɪʒ]/ immobilized in cast⁷ • ischemic [kiː]/ paralyzed / severed⁸ [e] **limb** • missing / phantom⁹ / artificial¹⁰ **limb** • involuntary trembling / elevation¹¹ / loss *of* **limb** • **limb** amputation / movement / temperature /-threatening [e] • **limb** deformity / girdle¹² [ɜː]/ loss • **limb** length / pain / venography • **limb** lead¹³ [iː]/ perfusion [juːʒ] • **limb** weakness [iː]/ salvage¹⁴ [-ɪdʒ] • short-**limbed**

(i) Extremität, Glied(maße)
(ii) Ast, Schenkel
absteigender Ast d. Henle-Schleife¹ zieht nach² Ausschlag³ Rumpf⁴ schlaffe Extremität⁵ abnorm bewegl. Extremität⁶ eingegipster/s Arm/ Bein⁷ abgetrenntes Glied⁸ Phantomglied⁹ Arm-, Bein-Prothese¹⁰ Hochlagern d. Arms/ Beins¹¹ Gliedmaßen-, Extremitätengürtel¹² Extremitätenableitung (EKG)¹³ Erhaltung/ Rettung d. Arms/ Beins¹⁴

1

arm *n*   *syn* **upper extremity** *n term*
  (i) clinically and popularly, either of the two upper limbs from the shoulder to the hands
  (ii) anatomically, the upper extremity from the shoulder to the elbow
  forearm¹ *n* • **armful** *or* **armload**² *n* • **brachial** [eɪk] *adj term* • **brachio-** *comb*
» *Stretch out your left arm. What are you carrying under your arm? There was persistent upper extremity hypertension [haɪpɚ-]. The patient complains of pain when the arm is raised [eɪ] above the shoulder, but not with the arm held down by the side. The brachial pulse [ʌ] was palpated.*
Use to walk arm in³/twist sb.'s⁴ **arm** • upper / needle-marked **arm** • **arm** motion [oʊʃ]/ hair / sling⁵ • **arm** span⁶ / bone / swing⁷ • **arm** numbness⁸ [ʌ]/ cuff⁹ [ʌ]/ board¹⁰ • **arm** rest¹¹ / cast / electrode • *with* folded *or* crossed¹² / open **arms** • *to* keep *or* hold¹³ sb. *at* **arm's** length • plump- [ʌ] / short-**armed** • **brachial** artery / vein [eɪ]/ nerve / muscle¹⁴ [mʌsl] • **brachio**cephalic trunk [ʌ] /radial [eɪ] muscle /ulnar [ʌ] articulation¹⁵

(i) Arm, obere Extremität
(ii) Oberarm, Brachium
Unterarm¹ Handvoll, Portion² ein-/ untergehakt spazieren gehen³ jem. d. Arm verdrehen⁴ Armtragetuch, Mitella, Dreieckstuch⁵ Armspannweite⁶ Mitschwingen d. Arme⁷ Taubheit d. Arms⁸ Armmanschette⁹ Armstütze¹⁰ Armlehne¹¹ m. verschränkten Armen¹² jem. auf Distanz halten¹³ Musculus brachialis¹⁴ Articulatio humeroulnaris¹⁵

2

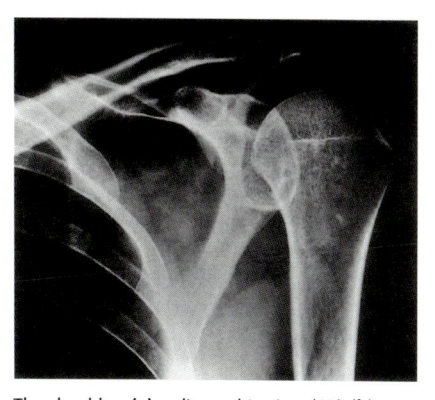

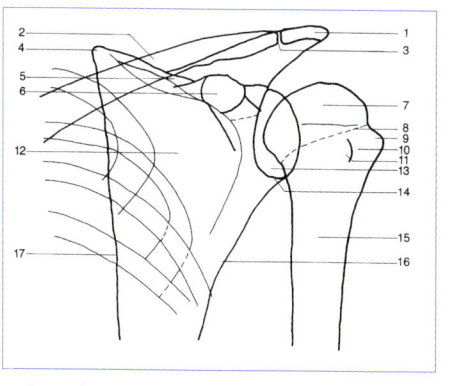

The shoulder: **(a)** radiographic view (AP) **(b)** corresponding schematic drawing: acromion (process) **(1)**, clavicle **(2)**, acromioclavicular joint **(3)**, superior scapular angle **(4)**, spine of the scapula **(5)**, coracoid process **(6)**, humeral head **(7)**, anatomic humeral neck **(8)**, greater humeral tuberosity **(9)**, intertubercular sulcus **(10)**, lesser tuberosity **(11)**, shoulder blade **(12)**, glenoid cavity **(13)**, inferior glenoid lip *or* labrum **(14)**, surgical neck **(15)**, axillary border of the scapula **(16)**, vertebral border **(17)**

shoulder [ʃoʊldɚ] n   rel **armpit**[1] n clin, **axilla**[1] [æks‖ˈægzɪlə] n term

joint [dʒ] formed by the clavicle, scapula and humerus [hjuː-] where the arm is attached [ætʃ] to the trunk; it is covered by the rounded mass of the deltoid muscle

shoulder[2] v inf • **shoulder-high** adj • **axillary**[3] [ˈægzɪləri‖ɪləri] adj term

» The shoulder girdle [ɜː] was affected first. This caused adduction [ʌ] and internal rotation of the shoulder with pronation of the forearm. Adhesive [iː] capsulitis[4] [aɪ], which is often referred to as frozen shoulder, is characterized by pain and restricted movement of the shoulder. The widest cuff [ʌ] that would fit between the axilla and the antecubital [kjuː] fossa was used. The pain radiates[5] [eɪ] toward the left axilla.

Use to shrug[6] [ʌ] /lift or elevate **one's shoulders** • to pull back/roll[7]/carry sth. on **one's shoulders** • **shoulder** girdle[8] / joint • **shoulder** blade[9] [eɪ]/ motion • **shoulder** dislocation[10] / belt[11] • **shoulder** spica [spaɪkə] cast[12] / width[13] / strap[14] • **shoulder** pad[15] /-hand syndrome[16] • flexed / loose[17] [uː]/ slip[18] **shoulder** • dislocated / frozen[4] **shoulder** • broad / narrow[19] **shoulders** • **axillary** region [iːdʒ]/ folds[20] / vein [eɪ]/ line[21] • **axillary** (lymph) nodes[22] [lɪmf noʊdz]/ temperature / hair

Schulter, Achsel
Achselhöhle, Axilla[1] auf d. Schulter nehmen, schultern[2] Achsel-, axillär[3] Periarthropathia/ Periarthrosis humeroscapularis, schmerzhafte Schultersteife[4] strahlt aus[5] m. d. Schultern zucken[6] Schulterkreisen[7] Schultergürtel, Cingulum membri superioris[8] Scapula, Schulterblatt[9] Schulter(gelenk)luxation[10] Träger, Schultergurt[11] Spica humeri, Schulter-Arm-Gipsverband[12] Schulterbreite[13] Träger, Schulterriemen[14] Schulterpolster[15] Zervikobrachialsyndrom, Schulter-Hand-S. [16] lose Schulter[17] instabile Schulter[18] schmale Schultern[19] Achselfalten, Plica axillaris anterior u. posterior[20] Axillarlinie, Linea axillaris[21] Achsellymphknoten[22]

3

elbow [ˈelboʊ] n   syn **cubitus** [ˈkjuːbɪtəs] n term

bend of the arm at the hinged [hɪndʒd] articulation[1] joining the upper arm with the forearm

elbow[2] v • **elbowed**[3] adj • **(ante)cubital**[4] adj term

» A cane[5] [keɪn] should provide 25 degrees of elbow flexion [ekʃ]. Swelling, deformity, and limited elbow motion, either on flexion-extension or on supination-pronation, suggest significant elbow injury. The injury in tennis usually occurs when hitting a backhand with the elbow flexed.

Use to bend or flex/injure/dislocate **the elbow** • semiflexed / lateral / tennis[6] **elbow** • pulled or nursemaid's[7] [ɜː] **elbow** • **elbow** joint / jerk [dʒɜːrk] or reflex[8] [iː]/ room[9] • **elbowed** catheter • **antecubital** fossa[10] / space [speɪs]/ veins • **cubital** tunnel [ʌ]/ lymph nodes[11] • **cubitus** valgus[12] [æ]/ varus [eɚ]

Ell(en)bogen, Cubitus
Scharniergelenk[1] s. durchboxen[2] gebogen[3] kubital, Ellbogen-[4] (Spazier)stock[5] Tennisellbogen[6] Radiusköpfchensubluxation, Chassaignac-Lähmung[7] Trizepssehnenreflex[8] Ellbogen-, Bewegungsfreiheit[9] Ellenbeuge, Armbanduhr[9] Handwurzelkanal, Fossa cubitalis[10] Nodi lymphatici cubitales[11] Cubitus valgus[12]

4

carpus [ˈkɑːrpəs] n term   sim **wrist**[1] [rɪst] n → U28-17

part of the hand between the forearm and the metacarpus[2] which consists of 8 carpals[3] in two rows [oʊ]

carpal adj term • **carp(o)-** comb

» The carpus was displaced volarly and proximally with the articular fragment. Exercises to strengthen the wrist extensors should be started. The radial [eɪ] artery distal to the wrist is patent[4] [eɪ]. Across the wrist, the dense volar carpal ligament closes the bony carpal tunnel [ʌ] through which pass all eight finger flexors as well as the flexor pollicis longus and median [iː] nerve.

Use **wrist** bone / joint[5] / splint / scars [ɑː] • **wrist** restraints[6] [eɪ] /drop[7] /watch[8] / injuries [ɪndʒ-] • flexed / immobilized **wrist** • **carpal** bones[3] / fracture / tunnel or canal[9] • **carpo**metacarpal /pedal spasm[10]

Handwurzel, Carpus
Handwurzel, Carpus; Handgelenk[1] Mittelhand, Metacarpus[2] Handwurzelknochen, Ossa carpi[3] durchgängig[4] Handgelenk[5] Handfesseln[6] Fallhand[7] Armbanduhr[8] Handwurzelkanal, Karpaltunnel, Canalis carpi[9] Karpopedalspasmus[10]

5

hand n & v   syn **manus** [ˈeɪ‖ɑː] n term, rel **palm**[1] [pɑːm], **fist**[2] n → U28-17

(n) terminal [ɜː] part of the arm used to grasp[3] and hold objects; formed by 27 bones, namely 8 carpals in the wrist, 5 metacarpals[4] (main part of the hand) and 14 phalanges [-dʒiː] (fingers)

manual[5] adj • **handedness**[6] n • **handful** n • **handy**[7] adj • **palmar**[8] adj term

» The patches occurred [ɜː] on the patient's dominant hand. Hand me Mr Green's chart[9] [tʃ], please. With the palm flat on the table, have the patient abduct [ʌ] and adduct the fingers. In the adult hand, the dorsal skin stretches about 4 cm in the longitudinal and transverse planes when the fist closes.

Use to flex **the hands** • **hand** steadiness [e]/ grip[10] /shake[11] / strength / writing[12] • **hand** clapping / washing / surgery[13] • **hand** controls /-held device[14] [-aɪs] • cold **hands** • callus on[15] **the hands** • palms / digits / dorsum / edema **of the hands** • blanching[16] [ˈʃ]/ tremor **of the hands** • left-**handed** • **manual** activity / compression / dexterity[17] • **manual** exploration / manipulation / traction • give sb. a[18] **hand** • **palmar** surface / muscle / fascia [ʃ] or aponeurosis[19] • **palmar** flexion / erythema [iː]/ side[20] / crease[21] [kriːs] • to make a[22] (full) **fist**

Hand, Manus; reichen, geben
Handfläche[1] Faust[2] (er)greifen[3] Mittelhandknochen[4] manuell, Hand-[5] Händigkeit[6] praktisch, handlich[7] palmar, volar, Handflächen-[8] Krankenblatt[9] Händedruck, (Hand)griff[10] Händedruck[11] Handschrift[12] Handchirurgie[13] Handgerät[14] Schwielen a. d. Händen[15] Abblassen d. Hände[16] Handgeschicklichkeit[17] jem. behilflich sein[18] Palmaraponeurose, A. palmaris[19] Handfläche, -teller[20] Querfurche d. Handfläche[21] eine Faust machen[22]

6

Extremities   BODY STRUCTURES & FUNCTIONS 97

finger n   syn **digit** [dɪdʒɪt] n term, rel **knuckles¹** [nʌklz] n inf

any of the terminal [ɜː] members of the hand (sometimes excepting the thumb² [θʌm])

fingertip³ n • **fingerwidth⁴** n • **fingernail⁵** n • **digital⁶** adj term

» Tiny hemorrhagic [ædʒ] infarcts were seen in the nail folds⁷ and finger pulps⁸ [ʌ]. Anatomically the digits of the hand are numbered 1 to 5 starting with the thumb. Amputation of the digit is necessary. Hyperpigmentation is especially prominent over the knuckles, elbows, knees, and posterior neck and in palmar creases and nail beds⁹.

Use index or fore¹⁰/ middle / ring / little **finger** • flexed / waxy / trigger¹¹ / mallet¹² [æ]/ well-lubricated¹³ [uː] **finger** • webbed¹⁴ **fingers** • **finger** print¹⁵ / extension / food / exercises • **finger**-sucking / clubbing¹⁶ / fracture / percussion • **finger**-(to-)nose test¹⁷ /-like projection¹⁸ • volar region of the **fingers** • **digital** palpation • frostbite¹⁹ / cyanosis [saɪə-]/ tingling (sensation)²⁰ / amputation **of the fingertips** • knuckle pads²¹

Finger

(Finger)knöchel¹ Daumen² Fingerspitze³ Fingerbreite⁴ Fingernagel⁵ digital, Finger-⁶ Nagelfalz⁷ Fingerbeere, -kuppe⁸ Nagelbett⁹ Zeigefinger¹⁰ federnder/ schnellender/ schnappender/ Trigger-F.¹¹ Hammerfinger¹² gut eingefetteter F.¹³ kutane Syndaktylie, häutige Verwachsung d. F.¹⁴ Fingerabdruck¹⁵ Trommelschlägelfingerbildung¹⁶ Finger-Nase-Versuch¹⁷ fingerförm. Fortsatz¹⁸ Erfrierungen a. d. Fingerspitzen¹⁹ Kribbeln i. d. F.²⁰ Fingerknöchelpolster²¹   7

leg n   syn **lower extremity** n term

commonly used to refer to the whole lower limb but technically only the part between the knee and ankle

long-/ bow¹-/ frog-legged adj clin • **bowlegs²** n • **leggy³** adj inf

» In older patients fracture may be prevented by interventions that strengthen the legs. The patient should be placed in a sitting position with legs dangling⁴ over the side of the bed.

Use to cross⁵/straddle⁶ **one's legs** • lower⁷ / wooden⁸ **leg** • **leg** muscles⁹ / motion / pain / cramp • **leg** edema¹⁰ / exercises / raising [eɪ]/ cast / brace¹¹ [breɪs] • delicate / bowed² [boʊd]/ spider [aɪ] **legs** • (disproportionally) long / edematous / restless¹² **legs** • **lower extremity** amputation¹³ / edema¹⁰ / weakness / pulses [ʌ]

Bein, untere Extremität

O-beinig¹ O-Beine² langbeinig³ baumelnd⁴ d. Beine übereinanderschlagen/ überkreuzen⁵ d. Beine spreizen⁶ Unterschenkel⁷ Holzbein⁸ Beinmuskulatur⁹ Beinödem, -schwellung¹⁰ Beinschiene¹¹ Wittmaack-Ekbom-Syndrom, unruhige/ ruhelose Beine, restless legs-Syndrom¹² Beinamputation¹³   8

thigh [θaɪ] n   syn **upper leg** n

the leg between the hip and the knee formed by the thigh bone or femur [iː] and its surrounding muscles

» Flex¹ your thighs on your abdomen. Erythema [iː] was seen on the posterior surfaces of the upper legs. Fresh thrombi [aɪ] were detected in the lower thigh, calf, and popliteal [iː] veins².

Use inner / outer / lower / anterior **thigh** • **thigh** injury / bone³ • deep vein / biceps [baɪseps] muscle / quadrate [kwɒː-] muscle⁴ **of the thigh**

(Ober)schenkel

anwinkeln¹ Kniekehlenvene, Vena poplitea² Oberschenkelknochen, Femur³ Musculus quadratus femoris⁴   9

lower leg n   syn **shank** [ʃæŋk] n inf,
             rel **shin¹** [ʃɪn], **calf²** [kæf‖BE kɑːf] n, pl **calves**

the leg from the knee to the foot

» There is an exquisitely tender³ red plaque [plæk] on the medial lower leg above the malleolus [iː]. Bring your right heel to your left shin. There was myalgia⁴ [maɪældʒ(i)ə] affecting mainly the calves.

Use right **lower leg** • calf muscles⁵ [mʌslz]/ bone⁶ / pain⁷ / vein [eɪ]/ compression • **shin** bone⁸ / splint /guard⁹ [ɑː] • heel-**shin** test¹⁰

Unterschenkel

Schienbein(bereich)¹ Wade² sehr druckschmerzhaft³ Muskelschmerzen, Myalgie⁴ Wadenmuskulatur⁵ Wadenbein, Fibula⁶ Wadenschmerz⁷ Schienbein, Tibia⁸ Schienbeinschützer⁹ Ferse-Schienbein-Test¹⁰   10

knee [niː] n   syn **genu** [dʒe‖dʒiːn] n term, rel **knee cap¹** n clin, **patella¹** n term

joint connecting the thigh (with the lower leg which consists of 3 condyloid [kɒndəlɔɪd] articulations², 12 ligaments (patellar, collateral, popliteal [iː], and cruciate [uːʃ] ligaments³), 4 menisci [-kaɪ‖-saɪ], 13 bursae⁴ [iː] and the patella

kneel⁵ [niːl] v • **knock-knees⁶** [nɒːkniːz] n clin • **knock-kneed** adj

» Ligamentous tears⁷ [eɚ] in the knee (e.g. torn menisci⁸) are extremely common in athletes. Slight flexion of the knees is desirable [aɪ]. The arthritis [aɪ] involves the large weight-bearing [eɚ] joints (chiefly the knee and ankle). Comminuted fracture⁹ of the patella is caused only by direct violence.

Use to bend¹⁰/flex¹⁰/extend **one's knee** • **knee** joint¹¹ / motion /-hip flexion • **knee**-ankle interaction • **knee**-elbow position¹² /-jerk [dʒɜːrk] (abbr KJ) or reflex¹³ • **knee** stiffness / pain / sling • **knee** pad¹⁴ / replacement¹⁵ /-high (socks)¹⁶ • immobilized / fluid in **knee** • **genu** varum [eɚ]/ valgum⁶

Knie, Genu

Kniescheibe, Patella¹ Ellipsoid-, Eigelenke² Kreuzbänder, Ligamenta cruciata genus³ Schleimbeutel, Bursae⁴ knien⁵ X-Beine⁶ Bänderrisse⁷ Meniskusrisse⁸ Trümmerfraktur⁹ d. Knie beugen¹⁰ Kniegelenk, Articulatio genus¹¹ Knie-Ell(en)bogen-Lage¹² Patellarsehnenreflex¹³ Knieschützer¹⁴ Knieendoprothese¹⁵ Kniestrümpfe¹⁶   11

ankle [æŋkl] *n*   *rel* **malleolus**[1] [məliːəlᵊs] *n term* → U28-24f
(i) part of the lower leg just above the foot in the region of the ankle joint
(ii) the joint of the tibia, the talus [eɪ], and the fibula [fɪbjʊlə]

» *Bedsores*[2] *may also be seen over the heels* [iː] *and ankles. Patients complain of pain, usually of a burning* [ɜː] *and tingling*[3] *quality, in and around the ankle and often extending to the toes. Sterilize the skin around the medial malleolus.*

Use to sprain [eɪ] or twist[4] **one's ankle** • **ankle** joint[5] / bone[6] /-deep / dorsiflexion • **ankle** fracture[7] / injury • **ankle** swelling or edema[8] [iː] / sprain / jerk or reflex[9] • medial[10] / lateral[11] **malleolus**

(i) (Fuß)knöchel, Fessel
(ii) oberes Sprunggelenk, Art. talocruralis

Knöchel, Malleolus[1] Dekubitus, Wundliegen[2] Kribbeln[3] sich d. Knöchel verstauchen[4] oberes Sprunggelenk[5] Sprungbein, Talus[6] Knöchelfraktur[7] Knöchelödem[8] Achillessehnenreflex[9] Innenknöchel, Malleolus medialis[10] Außenknöchel, M. lateralis[11]   12

---

foot [fʊt] *n, pl* **feet** [fiːt]   *rel* **sole**[1] [soʊl], **heel**[2] [hiːl], **instep**[3] *n*
the pedal extremity at the distal end of the leg consisting of the tarsus, metatarsus and phalanges [-dʒiːz]
bare-footed[4] [beəfʊtɪd] *adj clin* • **footprint**[5] *n* • **plantar**[6] [æ] *adj term*

» *All infants are footprinted in the delivery room*[7]. *Careful examination of the feet and assessment of shoe fit are also important in the patient with gait* [eɪ] *disturbance*[8] [ɜː]. *In psoriasis* [səraɪəsɪs] *the entire skin surface, including the nails, scalp, palms, and soles must be evaluated. Dupuytren's contracture is also frequently found in the plantar fascia* [ʃ] *of the instep.*

Use to go on[9]/tread on sb.'s [10] **foot** • ball[11] / dorsal digital veins **of the foot** • fore[12] / club[13] / claw[14] [ɔː] **foot** • flat**footed**[15] • **foot**drop[16] /board[17] /plate • **foot** pain / care / wear[18] [weə] • **heel** bone[19] / cord[20] / pad / spur[21] [ɜː] • **heel** protector /-toe walking[22] /-tap reflex[23] • anterior / painful **heel** • high / wedge[24] [dʒ] **heels** • **plantar** aspect (of foot) / flexor / aponeurosis or fascia[25] • **plantar** nerve / reflex / wart[26] [ɔː] • **footprint** identification • **sole** creases [iː]/ stroking[27] [oʊ]/ wedge

Fuß
Fußsohle[1] Ferse[2] Rist[3] barfuß[4] Fußabdruck[5] plantar, Fußsohlen-[6] Kreißsaal[7] Gangstörung[8] zu Fuß gehen[9] jem. auf d. Fuß treten[10] Fußballen[11] Vorfuß[12] Klumpfuß[13] Klauenfuß[14] plattfüßig[15] Spitzfuß, Pes equinus[16] Fußstütze[17] Schuhwerk[18] Fersenbein, Kalkaneus[19] Achillessehne[20] Fersen-, Kalkaneussporn[21] Abrollen[22] Achillessehnenreflex[23] Keilabsätze[24] Plantaraponeurose, A. plantaris[25] Fußsohlenwarze, Verruca plantaris[26] Bestreichen d. Fußsohle[27]   13

---

toe [toʊ] *n*   *rel* **toenail**[1] [toʊneɪl] *n*
one of the five digits [dɪdʒɪts] of the foot
tiptoe[2] *n & v* • **intoe**[3] *n* • **wide-toed** *adj*

» *Callosities and corns*[4] *of feet and toes are caused by pressure and friction. Sandals or open-toed shoes should be worn if possible. Toenails should be cut straight across, not too close to the skin. Common foot problems include plantar warts* [ɔː], *ulceration, bunions*[5] [ʌ], *corns, and ingrown and overgrown toenails.*

Use **toe** bone / drop • big or first / fourth / little **toe** • hammer[6] / claw[7] / pigeon[3] [ɪdʒ] **toe** • to tread [e] or step on sb.'s **toes** • fanning of[8] / webbed[9] **toes** • to cut one's **toenails** • long / curved [ɜː]/ swollen / infected / ingrown[10] **toenails** • **toenail** changes / fungal [ʌ] infection • **toeing-in**[11] • **intoe** gait[12] [eɪ] • **wide-toed** shoes

Zehe
Zehennagel[1] Zehenspitze; auf Z. gehen[2] Sichelfuß(haltung), Pes adductus[3] Hühneraugen, Clavi[4] chron. entzündete Großzehenballen (b. Hallux valgus)[5] Hammerzehe[6] Krallen-, Klauenzehe[7] Zehenspreizung[8] kutane Syndaktylie d. Zehen[9] eingewachsene Zehennägel[10] Einwärtsgang, -gehen[11] Gang über d. Großzehe, innenrotierter Gang[12]   14

Unit 24   Body Height & Weight
Related Units: 25 Build, 80 Growing up, 102 History Taking, 107 Physical Examination, 79 Nutrition, 1 Fitness, 2 Dieting

(body) weight [bɒːdi weɪt] *n*

weigh[1] [weɪ] *v* • **weighing** *adj & n* • **weight-bearing**[2] [eə] *n & adj* • **weightless**[3] *adj*

» *A recent change in body weight is a better index of undernutrition*[4] *than a low relative weight. How much do you weigh? Weight loss*[5] *was due to physiologic changes in body composition, e.g. loss of height and lean* [iː] *body mass. The patient should be weighed in only a gown* [aʊ] *after voiding*[6]. *A large amount of weight was lost on a rigid* [ɪdʒ] *dieting program*[7].

Use to lose or take off[8]/gain [eɪ] or put on[9] **weight** • ideal[10] / normal / baseline[11] / altered [ɔː] **(body) weight** • total / desired[12] [aɪ]/ excess(ive)[13] **(body) weight** • **weight** history / change / table[14] / control • **weight** check[15] / curve [ɜː]/ gain[16] / fluctuation[17] [ʌ] • **weight** reduction / goal [goʊl]/-lifting[18] / persistent / (un)intentional[19] **weight loss** • **weighing** procedure [siː] • underwater **weighing** • birth[20] [ɜː]/ heavy / normal-**weight** • full / partial [ʃ] / (un)protected[21] **weight-bearing** • progressive[22] / avoidance of **weight-bearing**

Körpergewicht
wiegen[1] Belastung, lasttragend[2] schwerelos[3] Unter-, Mangelernährung[4] Gewichtsverlust[5] Blasenentleerung[6] strenge Diät[7] abnehmen[8] zunehmen[9] Idealgewicht[10] Ausgangs-, Anfangsgewicht[11] Sollgewicht[12] Übergewicht[13] Gewichtstabelle[14] Gewichtskontrolle[15] Gewichtszunahme[16] Gewichtsschwankungen[17] Gewichtheben[18] bewusste Gewichtsreduktion[19] Geburtsgewicht[20] vorsichtige Belastung[21] zunehmende Belastung[22]   1

> **Note:** Weight is often measured in **pounds** (lb), **ounces** (oz.) and **stone(s)** (BE); 1 lb is 0.454 kg, 1 ounce is 28.35 grams, 1 stone equals 14 lb or 6.35 kg.

Body Height & Weight   BODY STRUCTURES & FUNCTIONS 99

(body) height [heɪt] n   sim **body size**¹, **stature**² [stætʃɚ], **(body) length**³ n

natural height of a person in an upright position; body length is measured [eɪ] lying down (esp. in infants)

statural [stætʃɚəl] adj term

» The pubertal [ɜː] height spurt⁴ [ɜː] accounts for about 25% of final adult height. Bloom's syndrome is characterized by small body size, immunodeficiency and light-sensitive facial erythema. Both parents are of short stature⁵. Examination should include measurements of arm span⁶ and height. What height are you? By 25 years of age, the head measures one-eighth of the body length.

Use to reach a /grow in **height** • to rise to one's⁷ **full height** • to be above⁸/below **average height** • full / mean [iː]/ mature / final⁹ / predicted adult¹⁰ **height** • **height** age¹¹ / chart [tʃ]/ status / spurt¹² / percentile • **height** attainment¹³ [eɪ]/ -to-weight ratio [eɪʃ] • **height**-weight table / velocity¹⁴ • standing / sitting¹⁵ / shoulder / anterior facial **height** • crown-rump¹⁶ [ʌ]/ average / birth¹⁷ **length** • foot / recumbent¹⁸ [ʌ] **length** • leg **length** discrepancy¹⁹ • to be of normal **stature** • tall / above-average / imposing²⁰ [oʊ] **stature** • stunted²¹ [ʌ]/ short / (marked) shortness of **stature** • to grow / small or short²¹ in **stature** • **statural** growth suppression • large / small²² / ideal **body size**

> Note: In many English-speaking countries height is still measured in **foot** (ft.), which is about 30.48 cm, and in **inches** (in.) which equals 2.54 cm.

short adj   opposite **tall**¹ - taller - tallest [ɒː] adj, rel **big**² - bigger - biggest adj

tallish³ adj • **tallness**⁴ n • **shortening**⁵ n • *shorty⁶ n inf

» Obesity [iː] and short stature may be signs of Cushing's [ʊ] syndrome. In Western societies there is a preference for tallness in both males and females. Her father is a big, burly⁷ [ɜː] man.

Use to be on the⁸ **short side** • **short** limb dwarfism⁹ [ɒː] • **tall** men / girls • disproportionately¹⁰ **tall** • childhood / adult / constitutional¹¹ / pathologic **short stature** • hereditary / genetic [dʒ-]/ primordial¹² [praɪm-] **short stature** • limb [lɪm]/ truncal¹³ [trʌŋkəl] **shortening**

dwarfism [dwɔːrfɪzəm] n term   opposite **gigantism**¹ [dʒaɪɡæntɪzəm] n term

condition of being extremely short and undersized due to genetic defects, endocrine dysfunction, etc.

dwarf² n & adj term, pl **-ves** • **giant**³ [dʒaɪənt] n & adj • **dwarfed**⁴ adj

» Tall stature may be due to eunuchoidism [juː] or gigantism. A whole-baby x-ray study should be obtained in every newborn short-limbed dwarf. Patients with Laron dwarfism⁵ have severe proportionate growth retardation and elevated growth hormone levels.

Use (a)sexual / deprivation [ɪ] or psychosocial⁶ [saɪk-]/ pituitary⁷ [t(j)uː] **dwarfism** • renal [iː]/ cachectic [kɛ]/ thanatophoric⁸ **dwarfism** • short-limbed / achondroplastic / Seckel's⁹ **dwarfism** • congenital [dʒɛ]/ overall / cerebral¹⁰ [s]/ heart / mammary¹¹ **gigantism** • bird-headed [ɛ]/ short-limbed / cretin¹² [iː] **dwarf** • **giant** cell¹³ / bladder stone¹⁴

body fat [bɒdi fæt] n   rel **fat pad**¹ [fæt pæd] n

fatty or adipose tissue that forms soft pads between various organs, serves to outline body contours, and provides a reserve [ɜː] energy supply [səplaɪ]

fatty² adj • *fatness³ n • **high/ low-fat**⁴ adj

» Regional distributions of body fat play an important role in the risk factors of obesity. At birth, body fat is about 12% of body weight. Examination shows that most of the patient's fat is distributed in the hips, thighs [θaɪz], and legs. A felon⁵ is an abscess of the distal fat pad of the digit [dɪdʒɪt].

Use to accumulate/burn⁶/decrease **body fat** • mean [iː] / total⁷ / excessive / distribution of **body fat** • marrow / (firm [ɜː]/ abundant) [ʌ] subcutaneous⁸ [eɪ]/ abdominal / visceral [ɪs] **fat** • properitoneal [iː] / retroperitoneal / pararenal [iː] **fat** • renal sinus [aɪ]/ periarticular **fat** • perjorbital / depot⁹ / dietary [aɪə]/ neutral¹⁰ [(j)uː]/ fecal [iː] **fat** • **fat** cell¹¹ (number) / breakdown¹² / **fat** deposit¹³ / layer¹⁴ / content¹⁵ • **fat**-storing cells¹⁶ / distribution¹⁷ • **fat** intake / digestion¹⁸ / accumulation¹⁹ • **fat** metabolism²⁰ / depletion²¹ [iː] • **fat** embolism²² / necrosis /-soluble²³ • buccal²⁴ [ʌ]/ labial / axillary / suprapubic / infrapatellar **fat pad** • **fatty** (connective) tissue²⁵ / weight gain • **fatty** streaks²⁶ [iː]/ breasts [e]/ liver²⁷ / meal / meat • **fatty** stools²⁸ / acids²⁹ / degeneration

---

(Körper)größe
Körpergröße, Körpermaße¹ Wuchs, Statur, Größe² (Körper)größe, -länge³ pubertärer Wachstumsschub⁴ klein(gewachsen, -wüchsig)⁵ Armspannweite⁶ sich zu voller Größe aufrichten⁷ überdurchschnittlich groß sein⁸ Endgröße⁹ prognostizierte Endgröße¹⁰ Längenalter¹¹ Wachstumsschub¹² Erreichen einer Körpergröße¹³ Wachstumsgeschwindigkeit, Tempo d. Längenwachstums¹⁴ Sitzhöhe¹⁵ Scheitel-Steiß-Länge¹⁶ Geburtslänge¹⁷ Körperlänge im Liegen¹⁸ Beinlängenunterschied¹⁹ stattliche Größe²⁰ Minder-, Kleinwuchs²¹ kleinwüchsig²²

2

klein(gewachsen)
groß¹ groß und schwer² ziemlich groß³ Größe⁴ Verkürzung⁵ Knirps⁶ stämmig⁷ eher klein sein⁸ Kleinwuchs mit kurzen Gliedmaßen⁹ unverhältnismäßig groß¹⁰ konstitutioneller Klein-/ Minderwuchs¹¹ primordialer Minderwuchs¹² Rumpfverkürzung¹³

3

Klein-, Zwergwuchs
Riesenwuchs, Gigantismus¹ Zwerg; zwergenhaft² Riese; riesig, riesenhaft³ kleinwüchsig, unterentwickelt⁴ Laron-Syndrom⁵ psychosozialer Minderwuchs⁶ hypophysärer Kleinwuchs⁷ thanatophorer Kleinwuchs⁸ Seckel-Syndrom⁹ zerebraler Gigantismus, Sotos-Syndrom¹⁰ Mammahypertrophie, Gigantomastie¹¹ hypothyreote(r) Minderwüchsige(r)¹² Riesenzelle¹³ (sehr) großer Blasenstein¹⁴

4

Körperfett
Fettpolster¹ fett(haltig), fettig² Fettleibigkeit³ fettarm⁴ Panaritium⁵ Körperfett verbrennen⁶ Gesamtkörperfett⁷ Unterhautfettgewebe⁸ Depotfett⁹ Neutralfett¹⁰ Fettzelle, Adipozyt¹¹ Fettabbau¹² Fetteinlagerung¹³ Fettschicht¹⁴ Fettgehalt¹⁵ Fettspeicherzellen¹⁶ Fettverteilung¹⁷ Fettverdauung¹⁸ Fettansammlung¹⁹ Fett-, Lipidstoffwechsel²⁰ Fett(gewebe)schwund²¹ Fettembolie²² fettlöslich²³ Bichat-Wangenfettpropf, Corpus adiposum buccae²⁴ Fettgewebe²⁵ fetthaltige Plaques, Fettplaques²⁶ Fettleber²⁷ Fettstühle²⁸ Fettsäuren²⁹

5

slim adj → U25-5,8   syn **slender** adj, rel **slight**¹ [slaɪt], **delicate**², **narrow**³ adj
delicate, graceful⁴ [eɪ] and thin in an attractive way
slim (down)⁵ v phr • **slenderize**⁵ v • **slenderness**⁶ n • **slightness**⁶ n

» Males with Klinefelter's [aɪ] syndrome are usually tall and slim. She was a slim, supple⁷ [ʌ] creature [kriːtʃɚ], and rather tall for her age. Absorption of fat, carbohydrate [aɪ], and protein is just as complete in the obese [iː] patient as in the slender individual. The patient's fingers are long and slender and have a spider-like [aɪ] appearance [ɪɚ].
Use **slim** body / legs / hands / hips⁸ / girl • to keep **slim** • **slender** people / habitus / figure⁹ / children • **slender** waist¹⁰ [eɪ]/ arms / fingers • **slight** build¹¹ • **narrow** face¹² / head / neck / spinal canal / shoulders¹³

schlank, schmal, dünn
schmächtig, dünn¹ zierlich, grazil, zart(gliedrig)² schmal³ anmutig, graziös⁴ schlank werden/ machen, trimmen, abnehmen, -specken⁵ Zierlichkeit, Schlankheit⁶ geschmeidig⁷ schmale Hüften⁸ schlanke Figur⁹ schlanke Taille¹⁰ schmächtiger/ zarter Körperbau¹¹ schmales Gesicht¹² schmale Schultern¹³   **6**

body mass index n term   abbr **BMI**
a measure [eʒ] of quantifying obesity (weight in kg divided by height in meters squared¹)
» Assessment of BMI is useful for determining both under- and overnutrition. A BMI of 13-15 kg/m² suggests that total body fat content² is lower than 5% of weight.
Use to determine [ɜː] /influence **the BMI** • increased / initial [ɪʃ]/ preoperative **BMI** • lean³ [iː]/ mean [iː] **body mass** • **body** size [aɪ]/ surface [ɜː] (area)⁴ / composition

Körpermasse-, Körperbauindex, Quetelet-Index, BMI
zum Quadrat¹ Körperfettanteil² fettfreie Körpermasse³ Körperoberfläche⁴   **7**

overweight adj & n   sim **heavy**¹ [e], ***fat**², **corpulent**³, **stout**³ [aʊ] adj
more than 10-20% above a person's desirable body weight, as seen in large-framed⁴, fat persons
corpulence⁵ n clin • **stoutness**⁵ [aʊ] n • **heavyset**³ [hɛvɪsɛt] adj
» She has a long-standing history of being overweight. This typically presents in middle-aged men who are overweight and hypertensive. The operative risk rises proportionately to the extent of overweight. Have you always been this heavy?
Use to be/become **overweight** • mild⁶ / moderate / severe⁷ **overweight** • **heavyset** individual • **heavy** weight⁸ / load⁹ / lifting / meal¹⁰ [iː] • **heavy** exercise / drinker¹¹

Note: In clinical settings the expression *to be fat is avoided and replaced by more polite expressions such as **heavy**, **plump**¹², **fleshy**¹² or **well-rounded**¹².

übergewichtig; Übergewicht
schwer; stark¹ dick, fett(leibig)² korpulent, untersetzt, vollschlank³ grobknochig⁴ Korpulenz, Beleibtheit⁵ leichtes Übergewicht⁶ starkes Übergewicht⁷ Schwergewicht⁸ schwere Last⁹ schwerverdauliches Essen¹⁰ starke(r) Trinker(in), Alkoholiker(in)¹¹ rundlich, mollig¹²   **8**

Well, Mrs. Plym, concerning your weight
... let me put it this way. For your body mass index to be normal you'd have to be about seventeen feet tall.

obesity [oʊbiːsəti] n term & clin   syn **adiposity** [ædɪpɒːsəti], **adiposis** n term
overall excess of body fat, esp. in the subcutaneous [eɪ] connective tissues; adiposity mostly refers to an accumulation of fat cells in an organ or specific tissues
(non)obese¹ [oʊbiːs] adj term & clin • **adipose**¹ [ædɪpoʊs] adj term
» Weight reduction in the obese lowers blood pressure modestly. Serial photographs can document a shift in fat distribution even if the patient is not obese. Fatigue² [fətiːɡ] is most often due to overexertion³, poor physical conditioning, inadequate rest, obesity, or stress.
Use to be/become / markedly / frankly **obese** • extremely / grossly [oʊ] massively **obese** • **obese** patient / diabetic⁴ [e]/ abdomen / state • constitutional⁵ [t(j)uːʃ]/ childhood / early-onset **obesity** • mild / moderate / extreme or massive⁶ **obesity** • simple⁷ / gross or marked **obesity** • parental / morbid⁸ / alimentary⁹ **obesity** • exogenous / hypothalamic [haɪp-] **obesity** • generalized¹⁰ / central or truncal¹¹ [ʌ] **adiposity** • abdominal / gluteofemoral¹² [e] **adiposity** • **adiposis** dolorosa¹³ / hepatica / cerebralis • **adipose** tissue¹⁴ / cells / mass / depots¹⁵ / deposit¹⁶

Adipositas, Fettleibigkeit, -sucht, Obesitas
fettleibig, adipös¹ Müdigkeit, Erschöpfung² Überanstrengung³ fettleibige(r) Diabetiker(in)⁴ konstitutionelle Fettsucht⁵ extreme Fettsucht⁶ primäre Fettsucht⁷ krankhafte F.⁸ alimentäre Fettsucht⁹ universelle Adipositas¹⁰ Stammfettsucht¹¹ Reithosenfettsucht¹² Adipositas dolorosa, Dercum-Krankheit¹³ Fettgewebe¹⁴ Fettdepots¹⁵ Fetteinlagerung¹⁶   **9**

Build & Appearance **BODY STRUCTURES & FUNCTIONS** 101

underweight adj & n   rel **thin¹, lean¹** [iː], **skinny¹, gaunt²** [ɒː] adj → U25-7

less than normal body weight (after adjustment [dʒʌ] for height, age, sex, body build³, etc.)

» *Protein requirements for normal and underweight patients are calculated using actual weights. In lean young men body fat is less than 20%. The affected side of the face is gaunt, and the skin is thin, wrinkled⁴ [r], and rather brown. You are a bit on the skinny side.*

Use markedly⁵ / severely **underweight** • **thin** body habitus / neck⁶ / fingers / layer⁷ [eɪ] • **lean** tissue [tɪʃjuː]/ abdominal wall / meat⁸ • **lean** muscle [mʌsl] mass⁹ / body mass or weight¹⁰ • **skinny** legs¹¹

untergewichtig; Untergewicht
dünn, mager¹ hager, ausgemergelt² Körperbau³ runzlig⁴ deutlich untergewichtig⁵ dünner Hals⁶ dünne Schicht⁷ mageres Fleisch⁸ fettfreie Muskelmasse⁹ fettfreie Körpermasse¹⁰ dünne Beine¹¹   10

---

scale [skeɪl] n   syn **(a pair of) scales, weighing machine** [məʃiːn] n espBE

(i) device [aɪs] for determining a person's body weight
(ii) marked off strip for measuring¹ (iii) standardized test

» *Would you mind stepping on the scales? Coma is graded [eɪ] on a scale of 0-4.*

Use to step on the² **scales** • bathroom³ / hospital / chair / in-bed⁴ **scale** • measuring / millimeter / temperature⁵ / body-satisfaction **scale** • **scale** reading⁶ [iː]

**(i) (Personen)waage
(ii) Maßstab (iii) Skala**
Maßstab, -band, Messstreifen¹ sich auf d. Waage stellen² Personenwaage³ Bettwaage⁴ Temperaturskala⁵ Anzeige; Ablesung⁶   11

---

calipers [kælɪpɚz] n pl term   syn **callipers** n BE

gauge¹ [geɪdʒ] with a calibrated screw for the measurement of diameters [aɪæ], e.g. skinfold thickness²

» *Caliper measurements [meʒ-] of skinfold thickness provide a useful index of fat mass. Calipers were used to make six bilateral measurements.*

Use triceps [aɪs] skinfold³ / slide [aɪ]/ electronic⁴ **calipers** • **caliper** distance

Kaliper, Greif-, Tastzirkel
Messgerät¹ Hautfaltendicke² Kaliper zur Messung d. Hautfaltendicke am Trizeps³ elektronischer Kaliper⁴   12

Unit 25   Build & Appearance

Related Units: 24 Body Height & Weight, 63 Posture, 64 Body Movement, 21 Head & Neck, 67 Gestures, 107 Physical Examination, 114 Skin Lesions

---

(body) build [bɪld] or **shape** n   syn **physique** [fɪziːk] n, rel **figure¹** [fɪgɚ] n inf

individual shape given to the human body by the muscles [mʌslz] and bony [oʊ] framework [eɪ]

well-built² adj • **body-building** n • **physical³** [fɪzɪkəl] adj & n

» *The body build is asthenic [e] with evidence of weight [weɪt] loss. First observe the patient's general physique and habitus and then inspect the hands. He needs to add strength [streŋkθ] to his physique. Jane is a natural blonde with a good figure.*

Use heavy⁴ [e]/ powerful⁴ / medium [iː]/ slight [slaɪt] or slender⁵ **build** • slightly [aɪ]/ strongly⁶ **built** • **body building** exercises • powerful⁷ / ideal / remarkable **physique** • to keep one's⁸ **figure** • trim⁹ / handsome¹⁰ / striking¹¹ [aɪ] **figure** • fine or good¹⁰ / imposing [oʊ] / ridiculous¹² **figure** • **physical** fitness / activity / exam(ination)¹³ • **physical** complaints¹⁴ [eɪ]/ punishment [ʌ]/ therapy¹⁵

Körperbau, Statur
Figur¹ gut gebaut² physisch, körperlich; physikalisch; körperl. Untersuchung³ kräftiger Körperbau⁴ zarter/ schmächtiger Körperbau⁵ kräftig gebaut⁶ kräftige Statur⁷ schlank bleiben⁸ schlanke F.⁹ hübsche F.¹⁰ gute/ tolle Figur¹¹ lächerliche Figur¹² körperl. Untersuchung¹³ körperl. Beschwerden¹⁴ Physiotherapie, physikalische Therapie¹⁵   1

(body) habitus [hæbɪtəs] n term   rel **somatotype¹** n, **endomorph²** adj term

(i) physical characteristics of a person (ii) posture [pɒːstʃɚ] or position of the body

type [taɪp] n • **somatotyping³** n term • **ectomorph⁴** adj • **mesomorph⁵** [eǁiː] adj

» *Pubic [pjuːbɪk] hair and habitus are female in character. In pubertal [ɜː] girls body habitus changes, and the percentage of body fat increases.*

Use to evaluate **body habitus** • large / thin / female⁶ **body habitus** • slender⁷ / athletic / asthenic⁷ [e] **habitus** • masculinized / eunuchoid [juː] / marfanoid⁸ **habitus** • pyknic⁹ [pɪknɪk] / asthenic¹⁰ / athletic¹¹ **type**

Habitus, äußeres Erscheinungsbild
Körperbautyp¹ pyknisch² Einteilung in Konstitutionstypen³ asthenisch, leptosom⁴ athletisch⁵ weibl. Habitus⁶ leptosomer/ asthenischer Habitus⁷ marfanoider Habitus⁸ pyknischer Körperbautyp⁹ asthenischer K.¹⁰ athletischer K.¹¹   2

---

frame size [freɪm saɪz] n   rel **constitution¹** [(j)uːʃ] n → U1-8

body outline as determined [ɜː] by skeletal dimensions (measured [eʒ] by wrist circumference² [ʌ] or the breadth of the humeral epicondyle)

constitutional³ adj

» *The triceps [aɪ] skin-fold thickness⁴ differs with frame size and height [haɪt]. The BMI does not take into account differences in frame size.*

Use small⁵ / medium / large⁶ / weight-for⁷-**frame size** • overall⁸ / small head / heart / breast **size** • genetic / female / chromosomal **constitution** • **constitutional** cause / short stature⁹ [stætʃɚ]/ obesity¹⁰ • **constitutional** symptoms¹¹ / disorder¹² / delay [eɪ] of growth • **constitutional** type¹³

Knochenbau
Konstitution¹ Handgelenksumfang² konstitutionell, anlagebedingt³ Hautfaltendicke⁴ zarter Knochenbau⁵ kräftiger K.⁶ Körpermasse(n)-index⁷ Gesamtgröße⁸ konstitutioneller Minderwuchs⁹ konstitutionelle Fettsucht¹⁰ Allgemeinsymptome¹¹ konstitutionelle Störung/ Krankheit¹² Konstitutionstyp¹³   3

BODY STRUCTURES & FUNCTIONS — Build & Appearance

athletic [e] *adj*   *rel* **muscular**¹[mʌskjʊləʳ], **brawny**² [brɔːni], **sturdy**² [ɜː], **trim**³ *adj*

muscular, fit, well proportioned body typically seen in athletes
athlete [æθliːt] *n* • **trim (down)**⁴ *v* • **muscle** [mʌsl] *n*

» This treatment [iː] alternative is also suitable in the younger, more athletic individual. She's sturdy enough for tough [tʌf] physical activities⁵. Only hard training will make you more muscular.

Use **athletic** build⁶ / body / habitus / activity • **athletic** prowess⁷ [aʊ]/ training / injury⁸ / heart⁹ • **sturdy** woman / shoulders • **muscular** arms¹⁰ / activity¹¹ / youngster¹² / work • **brawny** man • **trim** girl • to be in (good)¹³ **trim**

athletisch, sportlich
muskulös¹ kräftig, robust² gepflegt, adrett, durchtrainiert³ etw. für seine Figur tun, s. trimmen⁴ anstrengende sportliche Aktivitäten⁵ athletischer Körperbau⁶ Sportlichkeit⁷ Sportverletzung⁸ Sportherz⁹ muskulöse Arme¹⁰ Muskeltätigkeit¹¹ muskulöser Junge¹² gut in Form sein¹³   **4**

---

lanky [læŋki] *adj*   *syn* **asthenic** *adj term*,
sim **slim**¹, **slender**¹, **wiry**² [waɪri] *adj*

ungracefully³ thin with long slender limbs; slim and slender are approving expressions (attractively thin)
slenderness⁴ *n* • **slimness**⁴ *n* • **slim (down)**⁵ *v* • **slimming** *adj & n* → U24-6

» The feminine ideal of delicacy⁶, slimness, and grace⁷ [ɡreɪs] is outdated. In slender or muscular individuals these veins [eɪ] stand out and are easy to enter.

Use **lanky** frame⁸ / figure⁸ • **asthenic** body build / appearance [ɪəʳ] • **slender** people / children / neck⁹ / habitus / fingers¹⁰ • to be on a **slimming** diet¹¹ [daɪət] • **wiry** frame / marathon runner

asthenisch, leptosom, schlaksig
schlank, schmal¹ drahtig² unattraktiv³ Schlankheit⁴ abnehmen⁵ Zartheit⁶ Anmut⁷ schlaksige Figur⁸ schlanker Hals⁹ schlanke Finger¹⁰ eine Schlankheitskur machen¹¹   **5**

---

stocky [stɒki] *adj*   *sim* **plump**¹ [ʌ], **chubby**¹ [ʌ] *adj clin*, **pyknic**² [ɪ] *adj term*

heavy and strong with broad shoulders³ and chest, short and compact in body frame and/or stature
stockiness⁴ *n clin* • **plumpness**⁵ [ʌ] *n* • **chubbiness**⁵ [tʃʌbɪnəs] *n*

» He is a stockily-built man who looks heavier than he really is. The typical patient may be stocky but not morbidly obese⁶ [iː]. She is rather plump around the hips.

Use **stocky** man • **plump** figure⁷ • **chubby** cheeks⁸ [tʃiːks]/ face / fingers

stämmig, untersetzt
mollig, pummelig, rundlich¹ pyknisch² breite Schultern³ Stämmigkeit⁴ Rundlichkeit, Stämmigkeit⁵ krankhaft fettsüchtig⁶ rundliche/ mollige Figur⁷ Pausbacken⁸   **6**

---

emaciated [ɪmeɪs‖ɪmeɪʃieɪtɪd] *adj term* → U108-14   *syn* **gaunt** [ɡɒnt] *adj*
sim **bony**¹ [bəʊni], **haggard**² [hæɡəʳd], **drawn**³ [drɔːn] *adj*

weak [iː], pinched³ [ʃ], extremely thin or wasting [eɪ] away⁴ physically, esp. from disease, hunger or cold
emaciation⁵ [ɪmeɪs‖ɪmeɪʃieɪʃən] *n term* • **gauntness**⁵ *n clin*

» Alcoholics frequently put on weight, whereas drug addicts are usually emaciated. His face is gaunt, the skin is thin and wrinkled⁶ [r]. She was haggard with shadows under the eyes.

Use to become **emaciated** • **bony** hand • **gaunt** face⁷ • **drawn** face⁸ • **haggard** face⁸ • extreme [iː] **emaciation**

abgemagert, ausgezehrt
knochig¹ ausgezehrt, abgespannt² eingefallen, verhärmt³ abgemagert, ausgezehrt⁴ Abmagerung, Auszehrung⁵ faltig, runzlig⁶ ausgemergeltes Gesicht⁷ verhärmtes Gesicht⁸   **7**

---

petite [pətiːt] *adj*   *sim* **slight**¹, **delicate**², **frail**² [eɪ], **fragile** [ædʒ] *adj*

short and slender (approving [uː] expression for females)
delicacy³ [delɪkəsi] *n clin* • **fragility**⁴ [frədʒɪlɪti] *n* • **frailty**⁴ *n*

» The patient is dark-haired and petite and complains of excessive body hair. She is too delicate physically for this sport. At 79 there are still no signs of frailty and senility in him. She still seems a bit fragile after her recent illness. Tom is a bit slighter [aɪ] than his sister.

Use **delicate** hands / features [iː] / skin⁵ / membrane / health⁶ • to look/become **frail** • physical⁷ / human **frailty** • **fragile** patients / tissue / bones⁸ / health⁶ • condition • tissue [ʃ‖s] / bone / vascular / skin⁹ **fragility**

zierlich, zart, anmutig
schmächtig¹ zart, zer-, gebrechlich² Zartheit³ Zartheit, Zer-, Gebrechlichkeit⁴ zarte Haut⁵ schwache Gesundheit, Kränklichkeit⁶ körperl. Gebrechlichkeit⁷ brüchige Knochen⁸ erhöhte Verletzlichkeit d. Haut⁹   **8**

---

barrel-chested *adj clin*   *rel* **broad-shouldered**¹, **narrow-waisted**² [eɪ] *adj*
rel **slim-hipped**³, **long-legged**⁴ *adj*

increased AP diameter of the chest typical of patients with chronic obstructive pulmonary [ʊ‖ʌ] disease

» A barrel-chested appearance is often noted in elderly patients without major respiratory problems. He was round-shouldered, with stooped [uː] posture⁵, and an asthenic appearance.

Use thin⁶-**chested** • round-/ narrow⁷-**shouldered** • slim²-**waisted** • one-/ bow⁸- [oʊ]/ cross-/ short-/ thin-**legged** • **long-legged** underwear⁹ [eəʳ]

mit einem Fassthorax
breitschultrig¹ m. schlanker Taille² schmalhüftig³ langbeinig⁴ gebeugte Haltung⁵ schmalbrüstig⁶ schmalschultrig⁷ O-beinig⁸ lange Unterhose⁹   **9**

Build & Appearance — BODY STRUCTURES & FUNCTIONS

(facial) features [feɪʃ⁽ə⁾l fiːtʃɚz] n pl → U103-3
  rel **countenance**[1] [kaʊntənənˈs] n, **facies**[1] [feɪʃiːz], **physiognomy**[2] [fɪziˈɒnəmi] n term
characteristic parts of a person's face, esp. the nose, eyes, forehead[3], mouth, and chin[4] [tʃ]
facial[5] adj • **face**[1] n • **midface** [mɪdfeɪs] n & adj • **physiognomic**[6] adj term
» Close relatives tend to resemble each other with respect to height [haɪt], weight, shape of nose and other facial features. This is associated with characteristic facies, esp. a high forehead, upturned nose[7], puffy [ʌ] cheeks[8], and low-set ears[9]. The face has fine wrinkles and an apathetic countenance. He has a typical Irish physiognomy.
Use coarse[10] [ɔː]/ typical / unusual **facial features** • physical / anatomic / phenotypic[11] [fiːnə-] **features** • dysmorphic [dɪs-]/ cushingoid[12] [ʊ] **features** • coarse / anxious [æŋkʃəs]/ flushed[13] [ʌ]/ moon(-shaped)[14] **facies** • stern[15] [ɜː]/ shining / impassive **countenance** • apathetic[16] / flushed[13] **countenance** • adenoid(al)[17] / Parkinson's or mask(ed)[18] / leonine[19] [liːənaɪn] **facies** • **facial** expression[20] / wrinkling[21] [r]/ asymmetry [ɪ]/ acne [ækni] • typical Latino **physiognomy** • red or flushed[13] / round or moon[14] / characteristic **face** • immobile / symmetrical / bird-like[22] **face**

complexion [kəmplekʃ⁽ə⁾n] n → U21-2
skin color, texture[1] [tekstʃɚ] and appearance of a person's face
» Men of light complexion[2] who work outdoors are twice as likely as women to develop skin cancer. Fair-complexioned[2] persons should use a sunscreen[3] with a sun protective factor of at least 15.
Use healthy[4] [e]/ clear / flawless[5] [ɔː]/ smooth [uː] **complexion** • fair or light[6] / dark / ruddy[4] **complexion** • florid[7] [ɔː]/ pale[8] / sallow[8] [æ] **complexion**

ruddy [rʌdi] adj rel **pale**[1] [peɪl], **pallid**[1] [pælɪd], **dusky**[2] [ʌ] adj → U108-5
a rosy, healthy or reddish complexion
ruddiness[3] n clin • **duskiness**[4] n • **red-faced**[5] adj • **paleness**[6] n • **pallor**[6] [æ] n
» In the first few hours after birth the skin is usually ruddy. The skin has a bronze to dusky discoloration[4] that darkens with time. The surrounding tissue changed from pale to dusky.
Use **ruddy** face /-cheeked[7] • **dusky**-red / yellow / purplish [ɜː] hue[8] [hjuː] • **dusky** edema [iː] • **pale** face / skin[9] / nail beds / green[10] • **duskiness** of the nail bed

fair [feɚ] adj sim **blond(e)**[1] adj,
  rel **auburn**[2] [ɔː], **ginger**[3] [dʒ], **brunette**[4] adj
(i) pale or light-colored (of hair or skin) (ii) good looking
» Individuals with fair complexions, freckles[5] and blond or red hair tan[6] [æ] poorly and sunburn easily. She is a tall woman with long auburn hair.
Use **fair**-haired[1] /-skinned children[7] / patients • the **fair** sex[8] • **auburn** hair • ash [æʃ]/ natural **blonde** • **blond** curls[9] [ɜː] • actor • **ginger** hair

beard [bɪɚd] n rel **m(o)ustache**[1] [mʌstæʃ‖BE mʊstɑːʃ] n, **whiskers**[2] n pl
hair growing on the lower part of a man's face
bearded[3] adj • **beardless**[4] adj • **moustached** adj
» The beard, brows[5] [aʊ] and lashes[6] were also involved. It was due to several ingrowing hairs[7] in the beard area. The characteristic hair growth of male puberty involves development of mustache and beard, and upward extension of pubic hair in a diamond-shaped pattern.
Use to grow a[8] **beard** • bushy [ʊ] **beard** • **beard** growth[9] / region [iːdʒ] • white-**bearded** • drooping[10] [uː] **moustaches** • side[11]-**whiskers**

hairline [heɚlaɪn] n & adj rel **hair**[1], **scalp**[2] [skælp] n
edge of the area where the hair grows on the head
hairy[3] adj • **hairiness**[4] [heɚrnes] n • **scalp**[5] v
» In these patients the neck is short, the hairline is low, and the ears are often low-set. He had fashioned his hair into a pony-tail[6] [poʊni teɪl]. This diffuse folliculitis [aɪ] favors [eɪ] hairy areas, including the scalp and the area under the beard.
Use receding[7] [siː]/ low[8] / scalp / posterior **hairline** • nuchal [n(j)uːk⁽ə⁾l]/ occipital [ksɪ] **hairline** • **hairline** fracture[9] / scar [ɑː] • cropped[10] / gray / silver **hair** • straight [streɪt]/ curled[11] [ɜː]/ collar-length[12] [ɒː] **hair** • body / axillary / pubic[13] [pjuːbɪk] **hair** • **hairdo** or style[14] /piece[15] /cut[16] • **scalp** line / abrasions[17] [eɪʒ]/ oil / electrode • dandruff [dændrəf‖ʌf] of the[18] **scalp**

Gesichtszüge
Gesicht(sausdruck), Miene[1] Gesichtsausdruck, Physiognomie[2] Stirn[3] Kinn[4] Gesichts-, fazial[5] physiognomisch[6] Stupsnase[7] Pausbacken[8] tiefsitzende Ohren[9] grobe Gesichtszüge[10] phänotypische Merkmale[11] cushingoides Aussehen[12] gerötetes Gesicht[13] Mondgesicht[14] strenge Miene[15] apathischer Gesichtsausdruck[16] Facies adenoidea[17] Maskengesicht[18] Facies leontina, Löwengesicht[19] Mimik[20] Faltenbildung im Gesicht[21] Vogelgesicht[22]

10

Gesichtsfarbe, Teint
Beschaffenheit, Struktur[1] hellhäutig[2] Sonnenschutz[3] gesunde Gesichtsfarbe[4] makelloser Teint[5] heller Teint[6] blühendes Aussehen[7] fahle Gesichtsfarbe, blasser Teint[8]

11

gesund, rot
blass, bleich, fahl[1] dunkel(häutig)[2] Röte, gesunde Gesichtsfarbe[3] dunkle Verfärbung[4] rotgesichtig, m. rotem Kopf[5] Blässe[6] rotbackig[7] dunkelvioletter Farbton[8] blasse Haut[9] blass-, zartgrün[10]

12

**(i) blond, hell
(ii) schön, liebreizend**
blond[1] rotbraun[2] rotblond[3] brünett[4] Sommersprossen[5] bräunen, braun werden[6] hellhäutige Kinder[7] das schöne Geschlecht[8] blonde Locken[9]

13

Bart
Schnurrbart[1] Backen-Kinnbart[2] bärtig[3] bartlos[4] Augenbrauen[5] Wimpern[6] einwachsende Haare[7] sich einen Bart wachsen lassen[8] Bartwuchs[9] gezwirbelter Schnurrbart[10] Backenbart[11]

14

Haaransatz; sehr fein, Haar-
Haar(e)[1] Kopfhaut[2] haarig, stark behaart[3] Behaartheit[4] skalpieren[5] Pferdeschwanz[6] Stirnglatze, Geheimratsecken[7] niedriger Haaransatz[8] Haarbruch, Knochenfissur[9] kurz geschnittenes Haar[10] lockiges/ krauses H.[11] halblanges H.[12] Schamhaar, -behaarung[13] Frisur[14] Haarteil[15] Haarschnitt[16] Kopfhautabschürfungen[17] Kopfschuppen[18]

15

104 BODY STRUCTURES & FUNCTIONS — Teeth

bald [bɔːld] *adj* *syn* **bald-headed** *adj, rel* **shave¹** - shaved - shaven *v irr*

having lost or lacking hair on all or most of the scalp

baldness² [ɔː] *n* • **balding³** *adj* • **shave⁴** [ʃeɪv] *n* • **shaving⁵** *n & adj*

» I have noticed a bald spot above my right ear. Male-pattern baldness, the most common form of alopecia [-piːʃiə], is of genetic predetermination. You need a shave. Don't you shave under your arm? In this setting shaving of the operative field increases the risk of infection.

Use to grow⁶ **bald** • **bald** patch / tongue⁷ [tʌŋ] • premature / frontal⁸ / temporal **balding** • to develop / total / male-pattern⁹ **baldness** • **shave** biopsy¹⁰ [aɪ] • razor¹¹ [reɪzɚ] **shave** • **shaven** head • **shaving** cream [iː]/ kit¹² / foam [oʊ])

glatzköpfig, kahl

rasieren¹ Kahlheit² schütter werdend³ Rasur⁴ Rasieren; Rasier-⁵ e. Glatze bekommen⁶ Möller-Hunter-Glossitis⁷ Ausbildung einer Stirnglatze⁸ männl. Glatzenbildung, männl. Typ d. Alopecia androgenetica⁹ Bürstenbiopsie¹⁰ Elektrorasur¹¹ Rasierzeug¹²   16

wrinkle [rɪŋkl] *n & v*   *rel* **fold¹** [foʊld], **pucker²** [ʌ] *n & v* → U56-17

(n) small fold in the skin that increases with age

wrinkled³ *adj* • **wrinkly³** *adj* • **puckered³** *adj* • **puckering** *n*

» During the process of aging natural wrinkle lines appear perpendicular [ɪ] to the direction of contraction of the underlying facial muscles [mʌslz]. The patient's skin has a puckered appearance.

Use facial⁴ [eɪ] skin / fine **wrinkles** • anti**wrinkle** cream⁵ • **to wrinkle your** brow [braʊ] *or* forehead⁶ / nose⁷ / skin⁸ / nasolabial [eɪ] alar [eɪ]/ nail⁹ / (inter)gluteal¹⁰ [uː] **fold** • **wrinkled** skin¹¹ / tongue¹² • **puckered** face¹³ / lips / scar / appearance¹⁴ • macular **puckering**

Falte, Runzel; Falten bekommen, knittern

Falte; Falz, Plica; (zusammen)falten¹ Fältchen; runzeln, verziehen² faltig, runzlig³ Gesichtsfalten⁴ Antifalten-Creme⁵ d. Stirn runzeln⁶ d. Nase rümpfen⁷ Hautfalte⁸ Nagelfalz⁹ Gesäßfurche, -spalte¹⁰ runz(e)lige/ faltige Haut¹¹ Faltenzunge, Lingua plicata¹² faltiges/ runz(e)liges Gesicht¹³ runz(e)liges Aussehen¹⁴   17

skin blemish [blemɪʃ] *n*   *rel* **spot¹, pimple¹** *n inf,* **freckles²** *n usu pl*

small mark spoiling the appearance, esp. of the skin → U56-17, 114-5f,9

blemished *adj* • **spotless³** *adj* • **freckled⁴** *adj* • **freckling** *n* • **pimply⁵** *adj*

» You should use a skin tonic for oily, blemished complexions⁶. Use make-up to conceal⁷ [-siːl] spots, freckles, scars, and minor skin blemishes.

Use to camouflage / minor [aɪ] **skin blemishes** • cherry-red / white **spot** • hypopigmented / cafe-au-lait⁸ **spot** • dark / multiple / juvenile [dʒuː]/ senile⁹ **freckles** • **blemished** complexion • **pimply** face¹⁰ / nose • axillary / inguinal **freckling**

Schönheitsfehler, Hautunreinheit

Fleck, Pickel¹ Sommersprossen, Epheliden² makellos³ sommersprossig⁴ pickelig⁵ unreine Haut⁶ abdecken⁷ Cafe-au-lait-, milchkaffeefarbener Fleck⁸ Altersflecke, Lentigines seniles⁹ Pickelgesicht¹⁰   18

birthmark [ɜː] *n clin*   *syn* **mole** [moʊl] *n clin & term,* **nevus** [niːvəs] *n term* *sim* **stain¹** [steɪn] *n* → U114-3

spot or blemish on the skin which is visible at or shortly after birth

» Birthmarks may involve an overgrowth of pigment cells, lymph [lɪmf] or blood vessels. Moles on the palms [pɑːmz], soles and genitalia [eɪ] are usually junctional nevi² [niːvaɪ].

Use vascular³ / connective tissue / pigment⁴ **birthmark** • pigmented⁴ **mole** • hairy⁵ / blue⁶ / spider⁷ [aɪ]/ junctional² [dʒʌ] **nevus** • **nevus** flammeus⁸ [æ] • portwine⁸ **stain**

Muttermal, Nävus

Fleck, Mal¹ Junktionsnävus/-nävi² Blutgefäßnävus, Naevus vasculosus³ Pigmentnävus, N. pigmentosus⁴ Haar-, Tierfellnävus, N. pilosus⁵ blauer Nävus, N. coeruleus⁶ Spinnen-, Sternnävus, N. araneus⁷ Feuermal, Weinfleck, Naerus flammeus⁸   19

Unit 26 Teeth

Related Units: 21 Head & Neck, 27 Dentition & Mastication, 46 Digestion, 66 Human Sounds & Speech

tooth [tuːθ] *n,* **teeth** [tiːθ] *pl*   *syn* **dens** *n term,* **dentes** *pl*

one of the bony structures set in the alveoli [aɪ] of the jaws [dʒɔːz], used in mastication and assisting in articulation¹

dental *adj*

» The tooth may become sensitive to hot or cold, and then severe continuous throbbing pain² follows. Oral features [fiːtʃɚz] of vitamin C deficiency include loosening³ of teeth, swelling, bleeding, ulceration [s] and a burning sensation in the tongue⁴ [tʌŋ].

Use tooth loss / mobility⁵ / surface / socket [ɒː]/ retention / ache [eɪk]/ position • adjacent⁶ [dʒeɪs]/ opposing⁷ **teeth** • artificial / natural / poorly aligned⁸ [aɪn]/ residual **teeth** • mandibular / maxillary / devitalized *or* non-vital⁹ [aɪ]/ tender¹⁰ / spaced **teeth** • pegged¹¹ / broken **tooth**

Zahn, Zähne; Dens, Dentes

Artikulation, Aussprache¹ pochender/ klopfender Schmerz² Lockerung³ Zungenbrennen⁴ Zahnbeweglichkeit⁵ Nachbarzähne⁶ Gegenzähne, Antagonisten⁷ Zahnfehlstellung⁸ devitale Zähne⁹ empfindliche Z.¹⁰ Zapfenzahn¹¹   1

Teeth BODY STRUCTURES & FUNCTIONS **105**

front or **anterior** [ɪɚ] **teeth** n clin   opposite **posterior teeth**[1] n clin

the cutting teeth (centrals, laterals, cuspids [ʌ]); the posterior teeth are the bicuspids [aɪ] and molars

Vorder-, Frontzähne
Backenzähne[1]

2

incisor [sɪ] or **incisal tooth** n term   syn **cutting tooth** n clin

one of the four front teeth–the centrals and laterals–with cutting (incisal) edges in each jaw at the apex [eɪ] of the dental arch [tʃ]
incisal adj term
» *A cavity was prepared in the right central incisor. The maxillary right lateral was missing.*
Use right / left first or central **incisor** or **central**[1] • second or lateral **incisor** or **lateral**[2] • maxillary / mandibular **incisors** • **incisor** crown / area / position / point[3] / contact • **incisal** edge[4] / embrasure[5] [-eɪʒɚ]

Schneidezahn, Dens incisivus
linker mittlerer Schneidezahn[1] lateraler/ seitlicher S.[2] Inzisalpunkt[3] Schneidekante[4] Einziehung am Schneidezahn[5]

3

(tooth) cusp [kʌsp] n clin   syn **cuspis dentis** n term

elevated chewing [tʃuːɪŋ] or tearing [eɚ] points of the cuspids, bicuspids, and molars
cuspal[1] adj • **cuspless** adj
» *The cuspal angle*[2] *[æŋɡl] of the restoration must be increased. The lingual cusp had to be sacrificed.*
Use **cusp** tip[3] • **cusp(al)** inclination[4] • **cusp** -to-fossa relationship • short / distobuccal [ʌ] **cusp**

Zahnhöcker, Cuspis dentis
Höcker-, höckrig[1] Höckerwinkel[2] Höckerspitze[3] Höckerneigung[4]

4

canine [keɪnaɪn] **(tooth)** n & adj clin   syn **eye tooth** n inf, **cuspid (tooth)** n rare

one of the corner teeth in the arch next to the laterals with by a pointed cusp for tearing food
» *A fixed prosthesis* [iː] *extended from the canine to the first molar region.*
Use **canine** eminence[1] / alveolus [ɪə]/ guidance[2] [aɪ]/ mandible • primary [aɪ] **canines**

Eck-, Augenzahn;
Dens caninus
Eckzahnspitze[1] Eckzahnführung[2]

5

premolar [priːmoʊlɚ] n & adj clin   syn **bicuspid** [aɪ] **(tooth)** n & adj term

one of the teeth just behind the cuspids which have two cusps or points
» *On statistical average, premolar teeth are retained for a longer period than molar teeth. All molars and the mandibular premolars were missing.*
Use mandibular / maxillary **premolar** • first / second **bicuspid** • unrestored / fully erupted[1] [ʌ] **premolars** • at the second **premolar** site

Prämolar, vorderer Backen-, Stockzahn, Bikuspidat,
Dens praemolaris
vollständig durchgebrochene Prämolaren[1]

6

molar (tooth) n & adj clin   syn **cheek** [iː] **tooth** n inf, **dens molaris** n term

one of the teeth behind the second bicuspids with flattened surfaces and four or five cusps
» *The shape and occlusal relation of the denture* [dentʃɚ] *was similar to natural molars.*
Use first or 6-year[1] **molars** • second or 12-year **molars** • premolar-**molar** region • single-**molar** restoration • abscessed lower **molar** • **molar** occlusal force[2]

Molar, Mahlzahn, großer Backenzahn, Dens molaris
Sechsjahrmolaren[1] molare Kaukraft[2]

7

third molar (tooth) n term & clin   syn **wisdom tooth** n inf

one of the most posterior teeth that erupt in late adolescence and have four cusps; their roots are often fused[1] [fjuːzd]
» *The incidence of trauma* [ɒː] *to the mental nerve during removal of third molars is 3–5.5%.*
Use impacted[2] / partially erupted **3rd molar** • **third molar** tuberosity

3. Molar, Weisheitszahn,
Dens serotinus
verschmolzen[1] impaktierter/ retinierter Weisheitszahn[2]

8

(dental) arch [ɑːrtʃ] n term & clin

(i) horseshoe-shaped[1] ridge supporting the teeth (ii) collectively all upper or lower teeth
» *The prosthesis frequently loosened when the patient, who had an atrophic* [eɪtrɒ:fɪk] *dental arch, yawned*[2] *[jɔːnd].*
Use upper / lower / shortened[3] **(dental) arch** • in both **arches** • **arch** width[4] [wɪdθ]/ length • full **arch** prosthesis[5] • opposing **arch** impression • U-shaped **arch** form

(i) Zahnbogen
(ii) Zahnreihe
hufeisenförmig[1] gähnte[2] verkürzter Zahnbogen[3] Zahnbogenbreite[4] Vollprothese[5]

9

palate [pælət] n clin   syn **roof of the mouth** n clin, **palatum** [eɪ] n term

the bony (hard) and muscular (soft) partition between the oral and nasal cavities; popularly used to refer to the uvula[1] which is also termed pendulous palate[1]
palatal adj term • **palatine** [aɪn] adj • **palato-** comb
» *The boneless soft palate should rise symmetrically when the patient says "ah."*
Use soft[2] / hard[3] / high-arched[4] / cleft[5] **palate** • **palatine** tonsil[6] [ɒː]/ arch[7] • **palatal** wall / vault[7] [vɔːlt] • **palato**pharyngeal [dʒiːəl] /nasal [eɪ]/glossal

Gaumen, Palatum
Uvula, Zäpfchen[1] weicher G., Gaumensegel, Velum palatinum[2] harter G., Palatum durum[3] Spitz-, Steilgaumen, hoher G.[4] Gaumenspalte[5] Gaumenmandel[6] Gaumenbogen[7]

10

26

fren(ul)um [friːnəm‖frenjələm] *n term,* **fren(ul)a** *or* **frenums** *pl*
   fold of mucous membranes attaching the lips, cheeks and tongue to the gums
   » *The* lingual frenum[1] *may need cutting to increase mobility of the* tongue [ʌ].

Frenulum, Bändchen
Zungenbändchen, Frenulum linguae[1]

11

gums [gʌmz] *n clin usu pl*   *syn* **gingiva** [dʒɪndʒəvə] *n term,* **gingivae** [iː] *pl*
   epithelial and connective tissues attached to the tooth and alveolar bone
   gingival[1] *adj term* • **gingivo-**[1] *comb* • **gummy**[1] *adj jar*
   » *The effect of local anesthesia was checked by pricking the gums. There is a band of red, inflamed gingiva along the necks of the teeth.*
   Use **gingival** tissue / margin[2] [dʒ]/ tenderness • free / attached[3] **gingiva** • marginal **gingivae** • **gingival** gumline[2] / discoloration[4] / massage [ɑː(d)ʒ]/ stippling[5] • receding[6] [iː] **gums** • **gummy** smile[7]

   ▌ **Note:** In the singular *gum* most commonly refers to *chewing gum*.

Zahnfleisch, Gingiva
die G. betreffend[1] Zahnfleischrand[2] befestigte G.[3] Zahnfleischverfärbung[4] Zahnfleischtüpfelung[5] Zahnfleischschwund[6] Zahnfleischlächeln, gummy smile[7]

12

(dental) alveolus [ælvɪələs] *n term,* **alveoli** [aɪ‖iː] *pl*
                          syn **(tooth) socket** [ɒː] *n clin & inf*
   opening in the maxilla or mandible in which the tooth is attached by the periodontal ligament[1] (abbr PDL)
   alveolar *adj term* • **alveolo-** *comb*
   » *The tooth must be sectioned and atraumatically extracted to preserve socket anatomy. The vertical bite force induces a bending moment as the tooth moves in its alveolus.*
   Use **alveolar** process[2] / ridge [dʒ] *or* crest[3] / bone / socket • extraction[4] **socket**

Alveole, Zahnfach
Wurzelhaut, Desmodont[1] Alveolarfortsatz[2] Alveolarkamm[3] Extraktionshöhle[4]

13

(dental) crown [kraʊn] *n clin*   *syn* **corona dentis** *n term*
   (i) part of the tooth above the gums covered with enamel (ii) an artificial substitute for that part
   » *Decalcification of dental crowns occurs with chronic* vomiting[1] *(the lingual surfaces of the lower anterior teeth are primarily* affected[2]).
   Use artificial[3] / natural (tooth-) **crown**

   ▌ **Note:** The term *crown* more commonly refers to restorations. The expression *dental* or *tooth crown* is used when referring to natural teeth.

(Zahn)krone, Corona dentis
Erbrechen[1] betroffen[2] prothetische Krone[3]

14

(dental *or* **tooth) enamel** [ɪnæməl] *n clin*   *syn* **enamelum** *n term*
   hard ceramic layer covering the exposed part of teeth
   » *These enamel changes range from whitish opaque areas to severe brown discoloration.*
   Use **enamel** formation[1] / changes / hypoplasia [eɪʒə]/ powder[2] • saliva-coated [aɪ] **enamel** • **enamel** cuticle[3] [kjuːtɪkl]/ organ

(Zahn)schmelz, Enamelum
Schmelzbildung, Amelogenese[1] Schmelzpulver[2] Schmelzoberhäutchen[3]

15

dentin(e) [dentɪn‖dentiːn] *n clin*   *syn* **dentinum** [aɪ] *n term*
   calcium [s] part of a tooth below the enamel containing the pulp chamber [tʃeɪ] and root canals
   dentinal *adj term* • **dentino-** *comb* • **dentinogenesis** [dʒe] *n*
   » *Caries spreads rapidly in dentin because of its lower mineral content. The pulp is surrounded by hard dentinal walls.*
   Use exposed[1] / root[2] / softened **dentin** • **dentin(al)** tubules[3] / surface • **dentinal** pain • **dentino**enamel junction[4] [dʒʌŋkʃən] /blasts[5]

Zahnbein, Dentin
freigelegtes D.[1] Wurzeldentin[2] Dentinkanälchen[3] Schmelz-Dentin-Grenze[4] Odonto-, Dentinoblasten[5]

16

cementum [sɪmentəm] *n term*   *syn* **(tooth) cement** *n clin*
   layer of mineralized connective tissue covering the dentin of the roots and neck of a tooth
   » *Cementum functions as an anchoring substance for the tooth to the alveolar bone. Noncarious teeth can become painful when enamel and cementum do not quite contact each other.*
   Use **cementum** deposition • **cemento**enamel junction[1] • **cementum**-like tissue

   ▌ **Note:** Unlike *cementum* the term *cement*[2] also refers to a nonmetallic adhesive [iː] material[3] used for various restorations.

Wurzelzement (das), Cementum
Schmelz-Zement-Grenze[1] Zement (der)[2] Befestigungsmaterial[3]

17

Teeth　　　　　　　　　　　　　　　　　　　　　　　　　　　　　BODY STRUCTURES & FUNCTIONS　**107**

(dental) pulp [pʌlp] *n clin*　　*syn* **pulpa (dentis)** *n term*

soft, spongy [spʌndʒɪ] tissue in the center of the tooth containing blood vessels and nerves
pulpal *adj term* • **pulpless** *adj*

» Teeth with decay¹ [dɪkeɪ] involving the pulp are a potential source of alveolar bone infection.
Use **pulp** chamber [tʃ] *or* cavity² / canal • **pulpal** reaction / exposure³ [-ouʒɚ] • **pulp** testing⁴ / capping⁵

(Zahn)pulpa, Pulpa dentis
Karies¹ Zahnhöhle, Pulpakavum² Pulpafreilegung³ Vitalitäts-, Sensibilitätsprüfung⁴ Pulpaüberkappung⁵

18

root (of tooth) [uː] *n clin & term*　　*syn* **radix** [eɪ] **dentis** *n term*

part of a tooth below the neck¹; covered by cementum rather than enamel

» The tooth demonstrated extensive occlusal root caries. The abscess was located at the root apex of a nonvital tooth.
Use **root** apices² [eɪpɪsiːz]/ bifurcation [aɪ] • **root canal** filling³ / treatment⁴ (*abbr* RCT) • crown-to-**root** ratio [eɪ] • single-/ two-/ multi⁵-**rooted tooth**

Zahnwurzel, Radix dentis
Zahnhals¹ Wurzelspitzen² Wurzelfüllung³ Wurzelbehandlung⁴ mehrwurzeliger Zahn⁵

19

quadrant [kwɒːdrᵊnt] *n term*

the oral cavity is divided anatomically into the upper left and right and the lower left and right quadrants

» The patient had six implants placed per quadrant.
Use mandibular left / opposing¹ / right posterior **quadrant**

Quadrant
Gegenquadrant¹

20

mesial [miːzɪᵊl] *adj term*　　*opposite* **distal¹** *adj term*

front or forward toward the median [iː] plane [eɪ] following the curvature [kɜːrvətʃɚ] of the dental arch

» The mesial surface of the bicuspid is the portion which is adjacent to² [dʒeɪs] the cuspid.

mesial
distal¹ neben, benachbart²

21

proximal [ɒː] *adj term*　　*sim* **interproximal¹** *adj term*

denoting the surface between adjacent teeth

» Interproximal caries and periapical [eɪ] lesions [iːʒ] are best visualized [ʒ] by posterior bitewing [aɪ] radiographs² [eɪ].
Use **interproximal** space³ [eɪ]/ surface / brush⁴ [ʌ]

proximal
Interdental-, Approximal-¹ Bissflügelaufnahmen² Interdentalraum, Approximalbereich³ Interdentalbürstchen⁴

22

labial [eɪ] *adj term*　　*sim* **buccal¹** [ʌ] *adj, opposite* **lingual², palatal³** *adj term*

towards, referring or adjacent to the lips (labial), cheek [iː] (buccal), tongue [tʌŋ] (lingual) and palate (palatal)
labio- *comb* • **bucco-** *comb* • **linguo-** *comb*

» To restore the labial profile, lip support is obtained from labial denture flanges⁴ [dʒ] optimally extended into the vestibule. The maxillary anterior teeth tend to erupt⁵ labially.
Use **labial** aspect *or* surface⁶ / gingiva / muscle [mʌsl] • **labio**buccal /palatal /lingual • **buccal** cavity⁷ / cusp [ʌ] tip⁸ / crown margin [dʒ] / mucosa • **bucco**alveolar /labial /gingival [dʒ] /lingual • **lingual** nerve⁹ / cusp¹⁰ / tipping¹¹ / to the alveolar crest • **linguo**palatal

labial
bukkal¹ lingual² palatal³ Prothesenrand⁴ durchbrechen⁵ Labialfläche⁶ Mundvorhof⁷ bukkale Höckerspitze⁸ Lingualnerv, Nervus lingualis⁹ Lingualhöcker¹⁰ Lingualkippung¹¹

23

occlusal [əkluːzᵊl] *adj term*

referring to the chewing [tʃuːɪŋ] or grinding [aɪ] surface of the bicuspid and molar teeth

» Occlusal and chewing forces were mainly directed in the vertical and horizontal dimensions.
Use **occlusal** plane¹ [eɪ]/ surface²

okklusal
Bissebene¹ Kaufläche²

24

intraoral [ɔː] *adj term*　　*opposite* **extraoral¹** *adj term*

inside as opposed to (from) outside the mouth

» The intraoral approach has the disadvantage of temporary paresthesia [-θiːʒə] from stretching the mental nerve.
Use **intraoral** anchorage² [æŋk]/ environment³ [aɪ]/ local anesthesia⁴ [-θiːʒə]/ camera

intraoral
extraoral¹ intraorale Befestigung² Mundmilieu³ intraorale Leitungsanästhesie⁴

25

maxillofacial [mæksɪloʊfeɪʃᵊl] *adj term*

referring to the dental arches, jaws and face

» An oral-maxillofacial surgeon¹ was consulted because of persistent malocclusion.
Use **maxillofacial** surgery / prosthetics² / restoration / defect / augmentation • **maxillo**palatine /mandibular /labial /turbinal

Gesicht u. Kiefer betreffend, maxillofazial
Mund-Kiefer-Gesichtschirurg(in)¹ Kiefer-Gesichtsprothetik²

26

26

Unit 27 Dentition & Mastication
Related Units: 26 Teeth, 46 Digestion, 66 Human Sounds & Speech, 3 Food & Drink

dentition [dentɪʃᵊn] *n term*
(i) collective term for the teeth in the dental arch
(ii) the teething [tiːðɪŋ] process (from calcification to eruption)
» His dentition is in poor repair[1]. The situation when both deciduous and permanent teeth are present is termed mixed dentition[2].
Use deciduous / permanent / natural / artificial[3] **dentition** • retarded[4] / precocious[5] [prɪkoʊʃəs] **dentition**

(i) Gebiss, Dentition
(ii) Zahndurchbruch
in schlechtem Zustand[1] Misch-, Übergangsgebiss[2] Zahnersatz[3] verzögerte D., Dentitio tarda[4] vorzeitige D., Dentitio praecox[5]
[1]

deciduous [dɪsɪdjʊəs] **teeth** *n term*   *syn* **baby** or **milk teeth** *n clin & inf*
also called primary [aɪ] or temporary (set of) teeth which fall out in childhood and are replaced by the permanent teeth
» The deciduous teeth begin to calcify [s] about the 16th week of prenatal life.
Use to cut[1]/shed[2]/lose **deciduous teeth** • spaced[3] **deciduous teeth**

Milchzähne, -gebiss
Milchzähne bekommen[1] M. fallen aus[2] lückiges Milchgebiss[3]
[2]

erupt [ɪrʌpt] *vi term*   *syn* **come in** *v phr clin & inf*
(i) when a tooth elongates and breaks the gums (ii) generally, to break through the skin
eruption [ʌ] *n term* • **unerupted** *adj*
» A significant change in arch width[1] [wɪdθ] occurs with eruption of the permanent teeth.
Use tooth / delayed[2] [eɪ]/ impeded[3] [iː]/ ectopic **eruption** • fully / partially **erupted** • ectopically **erupting** molar

durchbrechen
Zahnbogenbreite[1] verzögerter Zahndurchbruch[2] erschwerter Zahndurchbruch, Dentitio difficilis[3]
[3]

teething [tiːðɪŋ] *n clin & term*   *syn* **cutting of teeth** *n clin & inf*
process of eruption of the primary teeth normally beginning around the 6th month of life
» Your baby may be teething. Look, he's cut his first tooth. Teething is often associated with excessive drooling[1] [uː] irritability, and biting on hard objects. This problem cannot be ascribed to teething.
Use **teething** problems / process / ring or teether[2] / powders [aʊ]

Zahnen, Zahndurchbruch
Sabbern[1] Beißring[2]
[4]

exfoliate *vi term*   *syn* **shed** *vt*, **fall out** *vi phr clin & inf*
physiologic shedding of primary teeth in childhood; first the teeth loosen[1] and eventually[2] fall out
exfoliation[3] *n term* • **(non)exfoliated** *adj*
» The first baby teeth are usually shed when the child is six, but it is not uncommon for them to be retained much longer. By age 9 the permanent incisors reach the dental height [haɪt] of the exfoliated incisors.

(Zähne) verlieren, ausfallen
sich lockern[1] schließlich[2] Zahnwechsel[3]
[5]

permanent or **secondary teeth** or **dentition** *n term*
adult set of teeth which erupt between about the 6th and 13th year of life
» Once erupted, many permanent teeth do not maintain[1] a fixed position.

bleibende(s) Zähne/ Gebiss
beibehalten[1]
[6]

edentulous [ɪdentʃələs] *adj term*   *syn* **toothless** *adj clin & inf*
having lost all natural teeth
edentulous *adj term* • **edentulism** *n* • **edent(ul)ation**[1] *n* • **edentulousness** *n*
» She received a freestanding prosthesis[2] in each edentulous quadrant [ɒː].
Use partially or semi-/ totally or completely **edentulous** • **edentulous** patient / adult / arch / alveolar ridge[3] [dʒ]/ jaw [dʒɔː]/ maxilla / site

zahnlos
Zahnlosigkeit (durch Zahnentfernung)[1] Freiendprothese[2] Alveolarkamm (nach Zahnverlust)[3]
[7]

denture [dentʃɚ] *n term*   *syn* **plates** [eɪ] *n pl*, **artificial** or **false teeth** *n clin & inf*
artificial replacement for some or all natural teeth
» The existing denture was readapted 14 days after fixture installation.
Use full (set of) / partial / upper or maxillary / fixed[1] / removable / temporary or transitional[2] **denture** • **denture** base[3] / satisfaction / wearer [eɚ]/-bearing [eɚ] area[4] / retention / (in)stability / cleanser[5] [e]/ patient

Zahnprothese, künstliches Gebiss
festsitzende Zahnprothese[1] Interimsprothese[2] Prothesenbasis[3] prothesentragende Fläche[4] Prothesenreiniger[5]
[8]

Dentition & Mastication — BODY STRUCTURES & FUNCTIONS 109

salivation [eɪ] *n term*   *sim* **drooling**[1] [uː] *n clin & inf*
   the secretion of saliva as the mouth waters, e.g. at the sight or smell of tasty food
   saliva [səlaɪvə] *n term* • **saliva(to)ry** *adj* • **salivate**[2] *v*
» *Salivary control was slightly hampered[3] and this led to drooling.*
Use **saliva** flow • artificial **saliva** • **salivary** pellicle[4] / gland / secretion / proteins • reduced / increased / profuse[5] **salivation**

Speichelbildung, -fluss, Salivation
Sabbern[1] Speichel produzieren[2] beeinträchtigt[3] exogenes Schmelzoberhäutchen[4] starker/ übermäßiger Speichelfluss[5]   9

spit - spit - spit *v irr & n inf*
   (v) to force out the contents of the mouth, usually saliva (n) saliva
   spitoon[1] [uː] *n term BE*
» *Rinse[2] and then spit out. Some patients deny production of sputum because spitting is socially unacceptable.*
Use **to spit** out • blood **spitting**

(aus)spucken; Spucke
Mundspül-, Speibecken[1] ausspülen[2]   10

bite - bit - bitten *v irr*   *sim* **nibble**[1] *v clin & inf* → U5-10
   to seize [iː] with the teeth or jaws
   bite off/ through/ into[2] *v*
» *The patient was asked to bite as if he was chewing [uː]. Bite into this material.*
Use nail[3] **biting** • **bitten** tongue / lips / cheeks [iː]

(zu)beißen
knabbern[1] ab-, durch-, hineinbeißen[2] Nägelbeißen, -kauen[3]   11

Great job correcting that overbite of yours, isn't it Mr. Wilde!

bite [baɪt] *n clin & term & jar*   *syn* **morsel** *n inf*
   (i) in genE, a mouthful of solid food
   (ii) forced closure of the jaws or the pressure developed thereby
   (iii) jargon for various dental terms like interocclusal record[1] and interarch distance
» *He only took a bite and then the tooth was loose[2].*
Use to take/have a **bite** • **bite** wing[3] / opening[4] / plane / block / force / registration[5] / guard [ɑːrd] splint[6] / fork /-sized[7] [aɪ] • check**bite**[8]

(i) Bissen, Happen (ii) Biss
Okklusionsbefund, -diagnostik, -analyse[1] locker, lose[2] Bissflügel[3] Bisshöhe[4] Bissnahme[5] Aufbissschiene[6] mundgerecht[7] Checkbiss[8]   12

occlude [əkluːd] *v term*
   to bring the teeth of both jaws into contact
   occlusion *n term* • **malocclusion**[1] *n* • **occlusal** *adj*
» *As they occlude, all teeth should contact their opponents[2]. The molars occclude normally. The patient was asked to occlude with as much force as possible. First the vertical dimension of occlusion was registered.*
Use balanced / in habitual / centric[3] / interfered[4] **occlusion** • **occlusal** contact / force / level / load / plane[5] / surface

okkludieren, Zahnreihen schließen
Okklusionsstörung, Malokklusion[1] Gegenzähne, Antagonisten[2] zentrische Okklusion[3] gestörte Okklusion[4] Okklusionsebene[5]   13

freeway space *n term*   *syn* **interarch** or **interocclusal distance** *n term*
   gap between the occluding surfaces of opposing teeth with the jaws in physiologic resting position[1]
» *The vertical dimension of occlusion should allow for adequate freeway space.*
Use anterior / inadequate **freeway space** • excessive **interarch distance**

Interokklusalabstand
Ruhe(schwebe)lage[1]   14

BODY STRUCTURES & FUNCTIONS — Dentition & Mastication

masticate [mæstɪkeɪt] *v term*   *syn* **chew** [tʃuː], **munch** [ʌ] *v clin & inf*
chewing food and mixing it with saliva to prepare it for swallowing¹ [ɔː] and digestion [dʒe]
mastication² *n term* • **masticatory** *adj*
» While the patient chewed standardized pieces of crispbread, seated upright in a dental chair, recordings of masticatory sequences from start to swallowing were performed.
Use **masticatory** muscles / process² / load³ / mandibular movement / oral mucosa⁴ / function / improvement • **masticatory** cycle [saɪk] duration⁵ / ability / apparatus • mean [iː] **masticatory** force⁶ • **masticatory** silent period • **chewing** efficiency⁷ [ɪʃ]/ pattern / stroke⁸ / ability / contacts / force⁶ • **chewing** test food / gum / tobacco

(zer)kauen
Schlucken¹ Kauvorgang² Kaubelastung³ mastikatorische Schleimhaut⁴ Kauzyklusdauer⁵ mittlere Kaukraft⁶ Kauleistung⁷ Kaubewegung⁸

15

gag [gæg] *v & n*   *syn* **retch** [retʃ], **heave** [iː] *v*, *sim* **choke¹** [tʃoʊk] *v clin & inf*
v (i) to retch or cause to retch, e.g. by touching the soft palate²
 (ii) to keep the mouth from closing by placing a mouth prop between the teeth
gag *or* **pharyngeal** [-ɪndʒiːəl] **reflex³** *n term* • **gagging** *adj & n*
» He started gagging every time I inserted an instrument. The patient gags reflexively.
Use to experience a **gagging** sensation • a severe **gagger**

(i) würgen, Brechreiz haben (ii) mit Mundsperrer öffnen; Mundsperrer
(er)würgen; ersticken¹ weicher Gaumen² Würg(e)reflex³

16

clench [klentʃ] *v clin*
to squeeze [iː] together tightly [taɪtli], e.g. the upper and lower teeth or the hand to make a fist¹
teeth clenching² *n term*
» He was encouraged [ɜː] to clench as hard as possible. The patient was a clencher who habitually³ kept his teeth tightly together.
Use **clenching** force / habit / level / in centric [s] occlusion • nighttime⁴ **clenching**

zusammenbeißen, -pressen
Faust ballen¹ Zahnpressen² ständig, gewohnheitsmäßig³ nächtliches Zahnpressen⁴

17

grind [aɪ] - ground - ground [aʊ] *v irr clin*   *rel* **bruxism¹** [ʌ] *n term*
(i) making a grating sound by clenching and rubbing the teeth
(ii) to crush food
(iii) wearing [eə] away by polishing or abrasion, e.g. to reshape the contour of a tooth
teeth grinding¹ *n clin* • **grinding wheel²** [iː] *n* • **grinder³** *n jar*
» If the patient is a **grinder³** there will be continuous movement of opposing tooth surfaces.
Use **grinding** movement / habit⁴ / equipment⁵ • **ground** section⁶

(i) knirschen (ii) (zer)mahlen (iii) (ab-, ein)schleifen
(Zähne)knirschen, Bruxismus¹ Schleifstein² Knirscher, Schleifmaschine³ habituelles Knirschen⁴ Schleifkörper⁵ (ab)geschliffene Fläche⁶

18

attrition *n term*   *sim* **demastication¹**, **abrasion²** [-eɪʒ°n] *n term*
wearing away the biting surfaces in the process of normal mastication; loss of tooth structure from mechanical wear other than chewing is termed abrasion
abrade³ [eɪ] *v term* • **abrasive** [eɪ] *adj & n*
» The teeth were replaced because of attrition. With age the biting surfaces become worn⁴ (attrition) so that chewing becomes less effective.
Use mechanical [k] **abrasion** • **abrasive** polishing paste⁵ / paper⁶ / wear

Attrition, Abrieb
Demastikation, Abkauung¹ Abrasion, Abrieb, -nutzung² abreiben, abradieren, abkauen, abtragen³ abgenutzt⁴ Polierpaste⁵ Schleifpapier⁶

19

resorption [rɪzɔːrpʃ°n] *n term*
removal of bone or tooth structure by pressure; gradual destruction of dentin and cementum of the root, e.g. of the primary teeth prior to shedding
bone resorption¹ *n term* • **bone-resorptive** *adj* • **resorb²** *v*
» Clearly the microdamage induced by the high stresses is one cause of bone resorption.
Use severely **resorbed** edentulous jaws • advanced / extensive / alveolar³ / (jaw)**bone resorption** • **resorption** of tooth roots⁴ • **resorptive** pattern / state [eɪ]/ process / changes

Resorption, Abbau
Knochenabbau¹ resorbieren² Alveolarkammabbau³ Wurzelresorption⁴

20

erosion [ɪroʊʒ°n] *n term*   *sim* **abfraction¹** *n term*
loss of tooth structure due to processes not related to bacterial action
erode² *v term* • **erosive** *adj*
» Tooth grinding erodes and eventually reduces the height [haɪt] of the dental crowns.
Use **eroded** areas³ / cement • chemical [k]/ spark⁴ **erosion** • **erosive** process

Erosion
Ausbrechen (v. Schmelz, Dentin)¹ abtragen, erodieren² usurierte Bereiche³ Funkenerosion⁴

21

Bones
BODY STRUCTURES & FUNCTIONS

decalcification [dɪkæls-] *n term*   *opposite* **calcification**[1] *n term* → U31-14

loss of calcium salts from teeth or bone; may be the result of a pathologic process or part of a bone grafting procedure

(de)calcify[2] *v term* • **(de)calcified** *adj* • **non-decalcified** *adj*

» Chronic *cocaine* [koʊkeɪn] *snorting*[3] may result in widespread decalcification of teeth. Decalcified teeth are more *susceptible* [sə] to *decay*[4] [dɪkeɪ]. The bone products were freeze-dried, decalcified, and *sealed* [iː]. As the permanent teeth calcify, the roots of the baby teeth are gradually resorbed.

Use **calcified** tissue / *deposits*[5] / bone • **decalcified** section / *specimen*[6] [es] • **decalcifying** solution

Dekalzifikation, -zierung, Entkalkung
Verkalkung, Kalzifikation[1] (ent-,) verkalken[2] Kokainschnupfen[3] kariesanfällig[4] verkalkte Ablagerungen[5] dekalzifiziertes Präparat[6]

22

Unit 28   Bones
Related Units: 21 Head & Neck, 26 Teeth, 22 The Trunk, 23 Extremities, 29 Joints, 30 Muscles & Tendons, 31 Musculoskeletal Function, 106 Fractures, 141 Fracture Management

skeleton [skelətᵊn] *n*   *syn* **bony** [boʊni] **framework** [eɪ] *n clin*

(i) supporting framework of the body (ii) all 206 bones of the body taken collectively

skeletal[1] [skelətᵊl ‖ *espBE* -liːtl] *adj* • **skeleto-, -skeletal** *comb* • **skeletonize**[2] *v term*

» The X-rays revealed [iː] demineralization of the skeleton. In children, the *facial* [eɪʃ] skeleton heals so fast that *fractures* must be *reduced*[3] within 4-5 days to avoid *malunion* [juː].

Use bony / *axial*[4] / *appendicular*[5] / *infantile* / *craniofacial* [eɪ] **skeleton** • endo/ exo-**skeleton** • **skeleton** hand[6] • **skeletal** system [ɪ]/ muscle[7] [mʌsl]/ maturation[8] • **skeletal** mineralization / stability • **skeletal** changes / deformity / growth / development[9] • **skeletal** proportions / X-ray [ekreɪ] / age[10] / traction[11] [trækʃᵊn] • **musculoskeletal** system[12] / pain / disorder

Skelett, Knochengerüst
skelettartig, Skelett-, Knochen-[1] skelettieren[2] eingerichtet, reponiert[3] Achsen-, Stammskelett[4] Gliedmaßen-, Extremitätenskelett[5] Skeletthand[6] Skelettmuskel[7] Knochenreifung[8] Skelettentwicklung[9] Skelett-, Knochenalter[10] Knochenextension[11] Stütz- u. Bewegungsapparat[12]

1

os *n term, pl* **ossa** [ɒːsə]   *syn* **bone** [boʊn] *n, rel* **periosteum**[1] [ɒː] *n term*

hard connective tissue consisting mainly of calcium [s] salts covered by a fibrous [aɪ] membrane

osseous[2] [ɒːsɪəs] *adj term* • **ossicle**[3] *n* • **ost(eo)-, -osteum** *comb* • **bony**[2] *adj*

» Bones are composed of an outer hard layer (*compact bone*[4]) and a softer inner part (*spongy* [spʌndʒi] *bone*[5]) which contains the marrow. Fracture of the scaphoid bone is the most common injury to the carpus. Immature bone is less brittle than that of adults. Unless the periosteum is torn, displacement cannot occur [ɜː].

Use cortical[6] / cancellous[5] [kænsələs]/ subchondral [kɒː]/ webbed[7] **bone** • innominate or hip[8] / facial [eɪʃ]/ nasal [eɪ] **bone** • cranial[9] / funny or crazy[10] / sesamoid[11] **bone** • long / short[12] / flat / irregular **bone** • weight-bearing [weɪtbeərɪŋ]/ growing / immature / brittle[13] **bones** • **bone** marrow[14] / formation / density[15] / resorption • **bone** destruction [ʌ]/ fracture / pain • **bone** healing [iː]/ scan[16] / auditory [ɒː] or ear[17] **ossicles** • **osteo**cyte [-saɪt] /genic [-dʒenɪk] /blast /genesis • **osteo**dystrophy [ɪ] /malacia[18] [-məleɪ(ɪ)ə] /myelitis [aɪ] • **bony** anatomy / pelvis[19] / labyrinth / trabecular pattern[20] • **bony** attachment[21] [ætʃ]/ fragments / spur[22] [ɜː]/ erosion [oʊʒ]

> **Note:** Terminologically bones are referred to as ***os lunatum***, *os hyoideum*[23], etc. but more generally as the ***lunate bone*** and ***hyoid bone***[23], and clinically often just as the ***lunate*** and the ***hyoid***[23].

Os, Knochen
Knochenhaut, Periost[1] knöchern, ossär, Knochen-[2] Knöchelchen, Ossiculum[3] Substantia compacta, Kompakta, Os compactum[4] Os spongiosum, (Subst.) spongiosa[5] Kortikalis, Subst. corticalis[6] Geflechtknochen[7] Hüftbein, Os coxae[8] Schädelknochen[9] Musikantenknochen[10] Sesambein, Os sesamoideum[11] kurzer Knochen, Os breve[12] brüchige K., Osteogenesis imperfecta[13] Knochenmark, Medulla ossium[14] Knochendichte[15] Knochenszintigrafie, -gramm[16] Gehörknöchelchen[17] Osteomalazie, Knochenmineralisationsstörung[18] knöchernes Becken[19] Anordnung d. Knochenbälkchen[20] knöcherner Ansatz[21] Knochensporn[22] Zungenbein, Os hyoideum[23]

2

diaphysis [daɪæfɪsɪs] *n term, pl* **-ses**   *rel* **epiphysis**[1] *n term, pl* **-ses** [epɪfɪsiːz]

the tube-like shaft of the long bones enclosing the endosteum and the medullary cavity[2]

epiphyseal/-ial[3] [epɪfɪzɪəl ‖ fɪsiːəl] *adj term* • **diaphyseal** *adj* • **metaphyseal**[4] *n*

» The films show increased density of the femoral [e] head epiphysis. The exudate[5] [eksjuːdeɪt] continued to spread [e] under the periosteum along the diaphysis. The fracture line followed the growth plate[6], separating epiphysis from metaphysis.

Use ulnar [ʌ] **diaphysis** • proximal / distal / radial [eɪ] head[7] / slipped[8] **epiphysis** • **epiphyseal** (growth) plate[6] [eɪ]/ line / fracture • **epiphyseal** center / separation[8] / closure[9] [oʊʒ]/ arrest[10] • **diaphyseal** portion / dysplasia [eɪ] aclasis[11] /-epiphyseal fusion [fjuːʒᵊn]

Diaphyse, Knochenschaft
Epiphyse, Knochenende[1] Markhöhle, Cavitas medullaris[2] epiphysär[3] Metaphyse, Längenwachstumszone[4] Exsudat[5] Epiphysen-, Wachstumsfuge[6] Radiusköpfchenepiphyse[7] Epiphysenlösung, Epiphyseolyse[8] Epiphysenschluss[9] vorzeitiger E.[10] multiple kartilaginäre Exostosen/ Osteochondrome[11]

3

BODY STRUCTURES & FUNCTIONS — Bones

tuberosity [tuːbəˈrɪːsəti] *n term*   *rel* **tubercle**[1], **trochanter**[2] [troʊˈkæntɚ] *n term*   *rel* **condyle**[3] [kɒndaɪl‖dᵊl], **promontory**[4] *n term*

large rounded prominence on long bones to which ligaments [ɪ] and muscles attach[5] [tʃ]

trochanteric *adj term* • **epicondyle**[6] *n* • (**epi**/ **inter**/ **supra**)**condylar**[7] *adj*

» Violent contraction of the quadriceps [ɔː] muscle caused avulsion[8] [ʌ] of the tibial tuberosity. Place your examining finger on the pubic tubercle. He has a displaced lateral condylar fracture. Decubitus ulcers [ʌlsɚz] vary in depth and often extend from skin to a bony pressure point such as the greater trochanter or the sacrum [eɪ]. Using the gluteal cleft to mark the midline, locate the sacral promontory[9], which is palpable even in obese [iː] patients.

Use ischial [ɪskɪᵊl]/ gluteal[10] / calcaneal [keɪ]/ scaphoid / ungual[11] [ʌ]/ tibial[12] **tuberosity** • **tuberosity** of the tibia[12] • femoral / medial [iː]/ lateral **condyle** • **condylar** fossa / prominence / screw[13] [uː]/ fracture[14] • medial / humeral [hjuː] **epicondyle** • intercondylar[15] / pubic[16] [pjuː]/ tibial **tubercle** • greater[17] / lesser[18] **trochanter of the femur**

Tuberositas, Knochenhöcker
Tuberculum, kl. Höcker[1] Trochanter, Rollhügel[2] Kondylus, Gelenkknorren[3] Promontorium[4] ansetzen[5] Epikondylus[6] suprakondylär[7] Abriss[8] Promontorium (ossis sacri)[9] Tuberositas glutaealis[10] Tuberositas phalangis distalis[11] Tuberositas tibiae[12] Kondylenschraube[13] Kondylenfraktur[14] Eminentia intercondylaris (tibiae)[15] Tuberculum pubicum[16] großer Trochanter, T. major[17] kl. Trochanter, T. minor[18]

4

---

crest [krest] *n*   *syn* **crista** *n term*
   rel **process**[1], **spine**[2] [aɪ], **ramus**[3] [reɪməs] *n term, pl* **-i**

a ridge[4] [ɪdʒ] or elevated line projecting [dʒe] from a level or evenly [iː] rounded surface [ɜː]

» If a sufficient [ɪʃ] number of cells cannot be obtained [eɪ] from the posterior iliac crest, marrow can also be harvested from the anterior iliac crest and sternum. Mandibular fractures generally occur [ɜː] in the region of the mid body at the mental foramen, the angle of the ramus, or at the neck of the condyle. The avulsion [ʌ] fracture[5] involved the anterior inferior iliac spines and a portion of the iliac crest epiphysis anteriorly. If the mastoid process is tender[6], obtain mastoid x-rays to determine whether suppurative[7] [ʌ] mastoiditis [aɪ] has developed.

Use iliac[8] / tibial[9] / lacrimal **crest** • spinous[10] [aɪ]/ styloid [aɪ]/ mastoid[11] / intercondylar **process** • (right) pubic[12] [pjuːbɪk]/ superior / descending[13] [se] **ramus** • iliac[14] / ischial [k]/ vertebral[15] [ɜː]/ lumbosacral [ʌ] **spine**

Crista, Kamm, Leiste
Processus, Fortsatz[1] Spina, Dorn[2] Ramus, Ast, Zweig[3] Leiste[4] Abrissfraktur[5] druckschmerzhaft[6] eitrig[7] Darmbeinkamm, Crista iliaca[8] Margo ant. tibiae, Schienbeinkante[9] Dornfortsatz, Proc. spinosus[10] Warzenfortsatz, Proc. mastoideus, Mastoid[11] Schambeinast, Ramus ossis pubis[12] R. descendens, absteigender Ast[13] Darmbeinstachel, Spina iliaca[14] Wirbelsäule[15]

5

---

foramen [fəˈreɪmən] *n term, pl* **-ina** [fəˈræmɪnə]
   rel **sinus**[1] [saɪnəs], **cavity**[2], **fossa**[3] *n, pl* **-ae** [fɒːsiː‖aɪ], **notch**[4] [nɒːtʃ] *n term*

an opening or aperture [æpətʃɚ] through a bone or a membranous structure

» An outpouching[5] [-paʊtʃɪŋ] of abdominal contents through the greater sciatic [saɪætɪk] foramen[6] was detected. The medial [iː] head of the gastrocnemius [kniː] was passed through the posterior capsule and intercondylar notch[7]. CSF leakage[8] [liːkɪdʒ] was due to fracture of the roof of the ethmoid sinus[9]. There was a palpable mass in the right iliac fossa. Minor [aɪ] fragments of the posterior margin [dʒ] of the acetabulum may be disregarded unless they are in the hip joint cavity.

Use obturator / (inter)vertebral[10] [ɜː]/ infraorbital **foramen** • mental / carotid / mandibular[11] **foramen** • optic / epiploic [oʊ]/ apical[12] [eɪ] **foramen** • **foramen** magnum[13] / ovale [eɪ]/ spinosum • air[14] / accessory [kse] nasal or paranasal[14] [eɪ] **sinuses** • frontal[15] / sphenoid [iː]/ maxillary **sinuses** • urogenital [dʒe] **sinus** • antecubital[16] [kjuː]/ glenoid[17] [iː]/ iliac[18] **fossa** • supraclavicular / (anterior/ middle) cranial **fossa** • joint[19] [dʒɔɪnt]/ peritoneal [iː]/ pleural [ʊ]/ oral **cavity** • nasal / abdominal / thoracic [æs] **cavity** • (supra)sternal [ɜː]/ jugular[20] [dʒʌgjəlɚ]/ great sciatic[21] [saɪætɪk] **notch**

Foramen, Loch
Sinus, Höhle[1] Cavitas, Cavum, Höhle[2] Fossa, Grube[3] Kerbe, Fissur, Incisura[4] Ausstülpung[5] Foramen ischiadicum majus[6] Fossa intercondylaris (femoris)[7] Liquoraustritt[8] Sinus/ Labyrinthus ethmoidalis, Siebbeinhöhle[9] Foramen vertebrale, Wirbelloch[10] F. mandibulae[11] F. apicis dentis, Wurzelkanalöffnung[12] F. magnum, großes Hinterhauptloch[13] Nasennebenhöhlen, Sinus paranasales[14] S. frontales, Stirnhöhlen[15] Ellenbeuge, Fossa cubitalis[16] Cavitas glenoidalis[17] Fossa iliaca[18] Gelenkhöhle, Cavitas articularis[19] Incisura jugularis (ossis occipitalis)[20] I. ischiadica major[21]   6

---

cranium [eɪ] *n term, pl* **-ia**   *syn* **skull** [skʌl] *n, rel* **fontanelle**[1] *n term*

(i) bony case surrounding the brain (ii) broad term for all 28 bones of the head, esp. of the cranial floor[2] and vault[3] [ɔː] (the frontal, occipital, two parietal and temporal, the sphenoid and ethmoid bones)

cranial[4] [kreɪnɪəl] *adj term* • **cranio-** *comb* • **-cranial** *comb*

» The origin of the headache is superficial [ɪʃ], external to the skull, rather than originating deep within the cranium. Patients with open cranial wounds[5] [uː] should be given prophylactic antibiotics as soon as possible. Check the size [aɪ] and presence of the fontanelles.

Use anterior **cranium** • base[2] / sutures[6] [uː] **of the skull** • **skull** plate / cap[3] / fracture / film[7] / anterior[8] / posterior / mastoid[9] / open / bulging [bʌldʒɪŋ] **fontanelle** • **cranial** bones / vault[3] [vɔːlt]/ occiput[10] [ɒːksɪpət] • **cranial** base[2] / sutures[6] / fossa[11] / diameter [daɪæ-] • **cranial** nerves[12] [ɜː]/ foramina / growth • **cranio**facial deformity /cerebral trauma • **cranio**spinal [aɪ] axis /tomy[13] • intra/ extra**cranial**

Kranium, Cranium, Schädel
Fontanelle[1] Schädelbasis, Basis cranii[2] Schädeldach, Kalotte, Calvaria[3] kranial; Hirn-, Schädel-[4] offene Schädelverletzungen[5] Schädelnähte, Suturae cranii[6] Schädelröntgen[7] große Fontanelle, Fonticulus anterior[8] hintere Seitenfontanelle, F. mastoideus/ posterolateralis[9] Hinterhaupt[10] Schädelgrube, Fossa cranii[11] Hirnnerven, Nn. craniales[12] Schädeleröffnung, Kraniotomie, Trepanation[13]

7

Bones

BODY STRUCTURES & FUNCTIONS 113

parietal (bone) [pəraɪət̬əl] *n term*   *rel* **occipital (bone)**¹ [ɒksɪpɪt̬əl], **frontal** [ʌ] **(bone)**², **temporal (bone)**³, **sphenoid**⁴ [sfiːnɔɪd], **ethmoid (bone)**⁵ *n term*

one of the two large bones between the frontal and occipital bones that are joined by the sagittal suture

parietal⁶ *adj term* • **parieto-** *comb* • **sphenoid(al)** *adj* • **spheno-** *comb*

» The third fontanelle is a bony defect along the sagittal [ædʒ] suture⁷ in the parietal bones. The frontal bone forms the roof of the eye sockets⁸ (orbits⁸). The occipital bone surrounds the foramen magnum [æ] and bears [beɚz] the condyles that articulate with the atlas. Facial nerve palsies [ɔː] after temporal bone fracture may require decompression and repair [-eɚ] of the injured 7ᵗʰ cranial nerve. Fracture of the ethmoid bone most frequently occurs [ɜː] with blunt [ʌ] trauma to the orbit.

Use anterior **parietal** • **occipital** condyle / protuberance [(j)uː]/ foramen • **occipital** crest⁹ / fontanelle¹⁰ / lobe [oʊ] • **frontal** sinus¹¹ /-parietal region [iːdʒ]/ gyrus¹² [dʒaɪrəs]/ vein • **frontal** nerve / headache / sinusitis [aɪ] • **sphenoid** bone / body¹³ / wings¹⁴ / ridge¹⁵ • **parietal**-occipital region / lobe¹⁶ (lesion) [iːʒ] • **parietal** pleura¹⁷ / cell¹⁸ (mucosa) • **parieto**frontal /occipital /sphenoid /temporal • **sphenoidal** concha [kɒŋkə]/ yoke¹⁹ [joʊk]/ process • **spheno**orbital suture /palatine artery

Scheitelbein, Os parietale
Hinterhauptbein, Os occipitale¹ Stirnbein, Os frontale² Schläfenbein, Os temporale³ Keilbein, Os sphenoidale⁴ Siebbein, Os ethmoidale⁵ wandständig, parietal⁶ Pfeilnaht, Sutura sagittalis⁷ Augenhöhlen, Orbitae⁸ Crista occipitalis⁹ kleine/ hintere Fontanelle, Fonticulus posterior¹⁰ Stirnhöhle, Sinus frontalis¹¹ Stirnwindung, Gyrus frontalis¹² Keilbeinkörper, Corpus ossis sphenoidalis¹³ Alae ossis sphenoidalis, Keilbeinflügel¹⁴ Crista sphenoidalis¹⁵ Parietal-, Scheitellappen, Lobus parietalis¹⁶ parietales Pleurablatt¹⁷ Beleg-, Parietalzelle¹⁸ Jugum sphenoidale¹⁹

8

facial skeleton *n*   *syn* **facial bones** *n clin, rel* **zygoma**¹ [zaɪgoʊmə] *n term*

includes the zygomatic² (malar [eɪ] or cheek [tʃiːk] bone²), lacrimal, nasal and turbinate [ɜː] bones³, the upper and the lower jaw, the vomer⁴ [oʊ], and the palatine bones⁵–6 ear bones, and the hyoid⁶ [haɪɔɪd]

zygomatic [zaɪgəmæt̬ɪk] *adj term* • **midfacial** [mɪdfeɪʃəl] *adj* • **-facial** *comb*

» In Le Fort III fracture, the entire facial skeleton, including the zygoma, infraorbital rim⁷, nasal skeleton, maxillary alveoli, and teeth, is dislocated from the base of the skull. Displacement of the body of the zygoma results in flattening of the cheek and depression of the orbital floor⁸ and rim. The lateral orbital rim is fractured at the frontozygomatic suture [uː].

Use **facial** nerve / palsy⁹ [pɔːlzi]/ deformity / cleft¹⁰ [kleft] • body of the **zygoma** • **zygomatic** bone² / arch¹ [ɑːrtʃ] • **zygomatic** process [ɒːs]/ fracture / pain • **midfacial** fracture¹¹ / hypoplasia [eɪʒ] • cranio/ hemi [e]/ maxillo**facial** • bucco [ʌ]/ oro/ cervico**facial**

Gesichtsschädel, Viscerocranium
Jochbogen, Zygoma, Arcus zygomaticus¹ Joch-, Wangenbein, Os zygomaticum² Nasenmuscheln, Conchae nasales³ Pflugscharbein, Vomer⁴ Gaumenbein, Os palatinum⁵ Zungenbein, Os hyoideum⁶ unterer Augenhöhlenrand, Infraorbitalrand, Margo infraorbitalis⁷ Orbitaboden⁸ Fazialislähmung, -parese, Gesichtslähmung⁹ Gesichtsspalte¹⁰ Mittelgesichtsfraktur¹¹

9

maxilla [mæksɪlə] *n term, pl* **-ae**   *syn* **upper jaw** [dʒɔː] *n* → U26-10, 21-7
  rel **mandible**¹ *n term*

one of the paired bones forming the upper jaw, hard palate², and the floor of the orbits

(sub)maxillary [mæksǁɪlɚi] *adj term* • **premaxilla**³ *n* • **mandibular** *adj*

» Torus palatinus⁴ is a common benign [aɪn] overgrowth of bone in the midline of the hard palate where the maxillae [iːaɪ] fuse [fjuːz]. Malocclusion [uːʒ] often reflects a disproportion between jaw and tooth size. Mandibular fractures generally occur in the region of the mid body⁵ at the mental foramen⁶, the angle of the ramus, or at the neck of the condyle.

Use anterior / alveolar [ɪə] process of the **maxilla** • lower or mandibular¹ / prominent / edentulous⁷ **jaw** • **jaw** muscles / movement / opening • **jaw** fracture / thrust [ʌ] (maneuver)⁸ [uː] • body⁵ / angle [æŋgl]/ (inferior) border or rim **of the mandible** • coronoid process⁹ / condyle **of the mandible** • anterior / protruding [uː]/ receding [iː]/ dislocated¹⁰ **mandible** • **maxillary** sinus¹¹ / artery / midline • **maxillary** antrum¹¹ / alveoli [aɪ]/ teeth • inter**maxillary** • **mandibular** incisors [sɪ]/ arch¹² [ɑːrtʃ] / condyle • **mandibular** angle / fracture • **maxillo**facial surgeon¹³ [ɜː] /mandibular

Oberkiefer(knochen), Maxilla
Unterkiefer(knochen), Mandibula¹ harter Gaumen, Palatum durum² Prämaxilla, Zwischenkieferknochen³ Torus palatinus, Gaumenwulst⁴ Corpus mandibulae, Unterkieferkörper⁵ Foramen mentale⁶ zahnloser Kiefer⁷ Esmarch Handgriff⁸ Proc. coronoideus mandibulae⁹ Kiefer(gelenk)luxation, Unterkieferverrenkung¹⁰ (Ober)kieferhöhle, Sinus maxillaris¹¹ Mandibularbogen; Unterkieferzahnreihe, Arcus dentalis inferior¹² Mund-Kiefer-Gesichts-Chirurg(in)¹³

10

clavicle [klævɪkl] *n*   *syn* **clavicula** *n term*, **collar bone** [kɒlɚ boʊn] *n clin*

doubly [ʌ] curved [ɜː] long bone forming part of the shoulder girdle¹ [ɜː]; it articulates with the manubrium² [uː] and the acromion³ [oʊ] of the scapula

(supra/ mid/ infra)clavicular⁴ [kləvɪkjəlɚ] *adj term* • **collar**⁵ *n & v clin*

» Maintenance [eɪ] of reduction [ʌ] and adequate immobilization of the clavicle can be achieved [tʃ] with the help of braces⁶ [breɪsiːz] and strapping⁷ [æ] for depressing the clavicle and elevating the shoulder.

Use right / distal / dislocated⁸ **clavicle** • **clavicular** head / region / notch⁹ / fracture¹⁰ • **acromioclavicular** joint¹¹ / ligament [ɪ]/ dislocation • **supraclavicular** fossa / (lymph) [lɪmf] nodes [oʊ]

Schlüsselbein, Klavikula, Clavicula
Schultergürtel¹ Manubrium sterni² Akromion³ Klavikula-, Kleido-⁴ Kragen; am K. packen⁵ Stützkorsett⁶ Tapeverband⁷ Klavikulaluxation⁸ Incisura clavicularis⁹ Schlüsselbeinbruch¹⁰ äußeres Schlüsselbeingelenk, Schultereckgelenk, Articulatio acromioclavicularis¹¹ 11

28

BODY STRUCTURES & FUNCTIONS — Bones

scapula n term   syn **scapular bone** n term, **shoulder blade** [ʃoʊldɚ bleɪd] n clin

flat triangular [aɪæ] bone overlying the ribs posteriorly on either side; it articulates laterally with the clavicle via the acromion process and with the humerus at the glenoid [e‖iː] cavity¹ or arm socket¹

scapular [skæpjəlɚ] adj term • **scapulo-** comb

» The prominent dorsal spinous [aɪ] process which is continuous with the acromion of the scapula forms the summit [ʌ] of the shoulder².

Use winged³ / elevated or high⁴ / angle of **scapula** • **scapular** region⁵ • **shoulder** girdle⁶ [ɜː] • **scapulo**humeral reflex [iː] /dynia [-dɪniə] • **scapulo**clavicular joint⁷ /thoracic [æs] motion [oʊʃ]

Schulterblatt, Skapula, Scapula

Cavitas glenoidalis, Schultergelenkpfanne¹ Schulterhöhe² flügelförm. abstehendes Schulterblatt, Scapula alata³ Schulterblatthochstand⁴ Regio scapularis⁵ Schultergürtel⁶ äußeres Schlüsselbeingelenk, Art. acromioclavicularis⁷   12

---

sternum [stɜːrnəm] n term   syn **breastbone** [brɛstboʊn] n clin

long flat bone forming the central part of the anterior chest [tʃest] wall; it consists of the corpus or body¹, the manubrium² [uː], and the xiphoid [zɪfɔɪd] process³

(supra/ para)sternal [suːprəstɜːrnᵊl] adj term • **sterno-** comb

» The sternum articulates with the cartilages⁴ of the first seven ribs and with the clavicle. The ventral wall of the bony thorax extends from the suprasternal notch⁵ to the xiphoid.

Use depressed⁶ / costal notches of **sternum** • **sternal** depression⁶ / border or edge⁷ • **sternal** ribs⁸ / muscle / line • **sternal** cleft⁹ / puncture¹⁰ [ʌ]/ retraction¹¹ • **sterno**costal ligament /clavicular joint

---

Brustbein, Sternum

Corpus sterni¹ Manubrium (sterni), Handgriff² Schwertfortsatz, Proc. xiphoideus³ Knorpel⁴ Incisura jugularis sterni⁵ Trichterbrust, Pectus excavatum⁶ Sternalrand⁷ echte Rippen, Costae verae⁸ Sternumspalte, Fissura sterni⁹ Sternalpunktion¹⁰ (inspirator.) Einziehung über d. Brustbein¹¹   13

---

rib [rɪb] n   syn **costa** [kɒstə] n term, pl **-ae** rare

one of the 12 pairs of curved bones forming the main portion of the bony wall of the chest

(inter)costal¹ [ɪntɚkɒstᵊl] adj term • **-costal** comb • **costo-** comb

» The metaphyses of long bones, the ribs, and the sternum are common sites of tuberculous osteomyelitis. When the abdominal muscles contract, the rib cage is pulled downward.

Use cervical² [sɜː]/ true³ / false⁴ [ɔː] **ribs** • floating⁵ [oʊ]/ supernumerary⁶ [uː] **ribs** • **rib** cage⁷ [keɪdʒ]/ notches / fracture / resection • **rib** hump⁸ [ʌ]/ tenderness / retractor / spreader⁹ [e] • **costal** arch¹⁰ / cartilage / margin¹¹ / angle / pleura¹² [ʊɚ] • **intercostal** space¹³ / muscles / nerves / arteries • **costo**vertebral angle tenderness¹⁴ (abbr CVAT) /chondral separation¹⁵ • **costo**clavicular ligament /axillary vein [eɪ]

Rippe, Costa

interkostal¹ Halsrippen, Costae cervicales² echte Rippen, C. verae³ falsche R., C. spuriae⁴ fliegende R., Costae fluctuantes⁵ überzählige R.⁶ Brustkorb⁷ Rippenbuckel⁸ Rippenspreizer⁹ Rippenbogen, Arcus costalis¹⁰ Rippen(bogen)rand¹¹ Rippenfell, Pleura costalis¹² Interkostalraum¹³ Nierenlagerschmerzen¹⁴ kostochondraler Abriss¹⁵   14

---

humerus [hjuːmɚəs] n term, pl **-i** [aɪ‖iː]   syn **(upper) arm bone** n clin
rel **trochlea**¹ [trɒːkliə] n term

the bone forming the upper arm; its head articulates with the glenoid cavity of the scapula and its condyle at the distal end forms the elbow joint with the radius and ulna

humeral² adj term • **humer(o)-** comb • **trochlear**³ adj → U30-8

» The surgical neck of the humerus⁴ is frequently the site of fractures. Fractures of the humerus often extend into the trochlear surface [ɜː] of the elbow joint.

Use adducted [ʌ]/ fractured **humerus** • (internal/ external) rotation / head⁵ of the **humerus** • capitellum⁶ / longitudinal [uː] axis of the **humerus** • **humeral** epicondyle / neck / shaft [ʃæft] (fracture)⁷ • **humero**ulnar /radial

---

Humerus, Oberarmknochen

Trochlea¹ Oberarm-, Humerus-² rollenförmig, trochlearis³ Collum chirurgicum (humeri), chirurg. Hals d. Oberarmknochens⁴ Caput humeri⁵ Capitulum humeri, Oberarm-, Humerusköpfchen⁶ Humerusschaft(fraktur)⁷

15

---

radius [reɪdiəs] n term, pl **radii** [reɪdiaɪ]   rel **ulna**¹ [ʌlnə], **olecranon**² n term

lateral and shorter of the two bones of the forearm³ lying parallel to the ulna

radial⁴ adj term • **ulnar**⁵ adj • **radio-** comb • **ulno-** comb

» While the head of the radius is much smaller than the olecranon process of the ulna, the styloid [aɪ] process⁶ of the distal radius, which forms the greater part of the wrist [r] joint⁷, is much larger than the styloid process of the ulna.

Use dislocation / longitudinal axis **of the radius** • **radial** tuberosity / pulse⁸ [ʌ]/ head • **radio**ulnar joint /carpal • trochlear notch / coronoid process⁹ **of the ulna** • proximal third / bowing [oʊ] **of the ulna** • **ulnar** aspect / antebrachial [eɪk] region / ligament • **ulnar** nerve¹⁰ / artery / pulse / deviation¹¹ [diːvieɪʃᵊn] • **ulno**carpal ligament¹² • **olecranon** fossa / bursa¹³ [ɜː]/ ligament / process²

Radius, Speiche

Ulna, Elle¹ Olekranon, Olecranon Ell(en)bogen² Unterarm³ Radius-, Radialis-⁴ ulnar, Ulnaris-⁵ Proc. styloideus (radii/ ulnae)⁶ Handgelenk⁷ Radialispuls⁸ Processus coronoideus ulnae⁹ Nervus ulnaris¹⁰ Ulnardeviation¹¹ Lig. ulnocarpale¹² Bursa subcutanea olecrani¹³

16

Bones
BODY STRUCTURES & FUNCTIONS

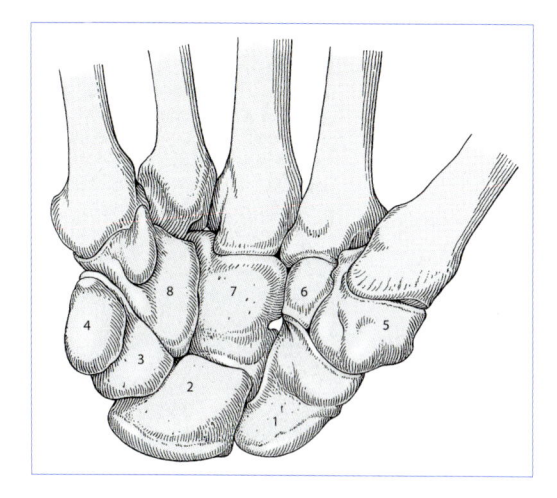

Palmar view of the right wrist:
scaphoid (bone) (1),
lunate (2),
triquetrum (3),
pisiform (4),
trapezium (5),
trapezoid (6),
capitate (7),
hamate (8)

---

carpals [kɑːrpəlz] *n term pl*   *syn* **carpal bones** *n, rel* **metacarpals**[1] *n term pl*

two rows [rouz] of 8 bones (scaphoid[2], [skæfɔɪd] lunate[3] [luːneɪt], triquetrum[4] [traɪkwiːtrəm], pisiform[5], trapezium [iː], trapezoid, capitate[6], and hamate[7]) that articulate proximally with the radius and (indirectly) the ulna and distally with the 5 metacarpals

carpus[8] *n term* • **(meta/ inter)carpal** [metəkɑːrpəl] *adj* • **(meta)carpo-** *comb*

» It looks like an intra-articular fracture of the volar margin[9] of the carpal surface of the radius. A dorsal transverse skin incision over the heads of the metacarpals (sparing[10] [eɚ] the veins) allows the MP joints[11] of the swollen [ou] hand to flex and assume the functional position.

Use distal **carpals** • fourth / thumb [θʌm]/ ulnar **metacarpals** • **carpal** ligament / canal [kənæl]/ articulations[12] • **carpal** spasm / tunnel [ʌ] (syndrome)[13] [ɪ] • **metacarpal** head / neck / shaft / vein [eɪ] • **carpo**metacarpal ligament /pedal spasms[14] • **metacarpo**phalangeal (*abbr* MCP) joints[11]

Handwurzelknochen, Ossa carpi
Mittelhandknochen, O. metacarpalia[1] Kahnbein, Os scaphoideum[2] Mondbein, O. lunatum[3] Dreiecksbein, O. triquetrum[4] Erbsenbein, O. pisiforme[5] Kopfbein, O. capitatum[6] Hakenbein, O. hamatum[7] Handwurzel, Carpus[8] Margo anterior[9] schonen[10] Fingergrundgelenk(e), Artic. metacarpophalangeales[11] Interkarpalgelenke, Artic. intercarpales[12] Karpaltunnel(syndrom)[13] Karpopedalspasmen[14]   17

---

phalanx *n term, pl* **-anges** [fəlændʒiːz], *abbr* **phal**   *rel* **knuckle**[1] [nʌkl] *n*

one of the 14 long bones of the digits[2] [dʒ] of the hand and foot (2 for the thumb [θʌm] or great toe, and 3 each for the other 4 digits; arranged in 3 tapering[3] [eɪ] rows distal to the metacarpus and metatarsus

(inter)phalangeal[4] [fəlændʒɪəl|dʒiːəl] *adj term* • **-phalangia** *comb* → U23-7

» He has several spiral [aɪ] fractures of the phalanges of the lesser toes[5]. We have to remove the entire phalanx or to excise [eksaɪz] the distal portion of the metatarsal.

Use proximal / middle / distal *or* terminal[6] [ɜː] **phalanx** • **phalangeal** head / shaft (fracture) • distal (*abbr* DIP)/ proximal[7] (*abbr* PIP) **interphalangeal joint**

Phalanx, Finger-, Zehenknochen
(Finger)knöchel[1] Finger; Zehen[2] spitz auslaufend[3] (inter)phalangeal[4] kleine Zehen[5] Endphalanx[6] proximales Interphalangealgelenk, PIP-Gelenk[7]   18

---

vertebra [vɜːrtəbrə] *n term, pl* **-ae** [eɪ‖iː]

rel **backbone**[1], **spine**[1] [spaɪn] *n clin* → U22-12

one of the 33 bony segments of the spinal column (7 cervical[2], 12 thoracic[3], 5 lumbar[4], 5 sacral[5] (fused into the sacrum), and 4 coccygeal [kɒksɪdʒɪəl] vertebrae[6] (fused into the coccyx)

(inter)vertebral[7] [vɜːrtəbrəl‖tiːbrəl] *adj term* • **spinal**[8] [aɪ] *adj* • **spinous**[9] *adj* **vertebr(o)-** *comb*

» The atlas or first cervical vertebra articulates with the occipital bone and rotates around the dens of the axis[10]. The nerve root[11] [uː] emerging [ɜː] between the C5 and C6 vertebrae is the C6 root. A patient complaining [eɪ] of back or neck pain and inability to move the legs may have a spine [aɪ] fracture. Please stand with your backbone rigid [rɪdʒɪd]. The anterior spinal column—the vertebral bodies and disks—is the commonest site of skeletal involvement in tuberculosis.

Use cervical [sɜːrvɪkəl]/ thoracic [æs]/ lumbar [ʌ] (*abbr* L1-L5) **vertebrae** • atlas *or* C-1 / axis *or* C-2[12] / fused[13] [juː]/ adjacent[14] [ədʒeɪsənt] **vertebra** • **vertebral** body[15] / column[1] [kɒləm] • **vertebral** foramen / arch[16] [ɑːrtʃ]/ ribs[17] • **vertebro**chondral [kɒ] ribs[17] • **spinous** process[18] • **spinal** canal / column[1] • **spinal** cord[19] [kɔːrd]/ tap[20] • **intervertebral** disk[21]

Wirbel, Vertebra
Wirbelsäule, Columna vertebrae[1] Halswirbel, V. cervicales[2] Brustwirbel, V. thoracicae[3] Lendenwirbel, V. lumbales[4] Kreuz(bein)wirbel, V. sacrales[5] Steiß(bein)wirbel, V. coccygeae[6] Intervertebral-, Zwischenwirbel-[7] spinal, Wirbel-[8] dorn-, stachelförmig[9] Dens axis[10] Nervenwurzel[11] Axis, 2. Halswirbel[12] Blockwirbel[13] benachbarter Wirbel[14] Wirbelkörper, Corpus vertebrae[15] Wirbelbogen, Arcus vert.[16] fliegende Rippen[17] Dornfortsatz, Proc. spinosus[18] Rückenmark, Medulla spinalis[19] Lumbalpunktion[20] Zwischenwirbel-, Bandscheibe, Discus intervertebralis[21]   19

116 BODY STRUCTURES & FUNCTIONS — Bones

(os) sacrum [ˈseɪkrəm] n term
rel **(os) coccyx**[1] [ˈkɒksɪks] n term, **tail** [eɪ] **bone**[1] n clin

curved, spade-shaped[2] segment of the spine forming the posterior part of the pelvic girdle [ɜː]

(lumbo)sacral [lʌmbəʊˈseɪkrəl] adj term • **coccygeal**[3] [-ɪdʒɪəl] adj • **sacro-** comb

» The sacrum is formed by the fusion[4] of five originally separate sacral vertebrae. The levator [eɪ] muscle passes from the tip of the coccyx to the pubic symphysis [ɪ] anteriorly.

Use **sacral** spine / prominence / edema [iː]/ anesthesia[5] [iːʒ] • **coccygeal** muscles / nerve / pain / segment • **sacro**coccygeal joint /genital fold[6] • **sacro**iliac joint /pubic diameter[7] [aɪæ] • **lumbosacral** spine / nerve roots / plexuses / back pain[8] • **lumbosacral** sprain[8] [eɪ]/ flexion exercises / corset / cord[9]

pelvis n clin & term pl -es   rel os coxae[1] [ˈkɒksi] n term, hip bone[1] n clin
(i) massive cup-shaped ring of bone at the hip formed by the pubis, ilium, and ischium laterally and anteriorly and the sacrum and coccyx posteriorly
(ii) the pelvic cavity[2] (iii) any basin-like [eɪ] cavity

pelvic[3] [ˈpelvɪk] adj term • **coxal** [ˈkɒksəl] adj • **pelvi-** comb → U22-7

» The femoral head was driven medially [iː] toward the pelvis and through the acetabulum[4] [æsə-]. The pelvic girdle[5] [ɜː] is shaped differently in men and women. Demineralization caused flattening of the pelvic bones, which contracted the pelvic outlet.

Use true or lesser[6] / greater or false[7] [ɔː] / renal[8] [iː] **pelvis** • bony[9] / android / gynecoid[10] [ɡaɪnǁdʒɪnɪkɔɪd] **pelvis** • acetabulum of the[4] **pelvis** • flexed[11] / right / ipsilateral **hip** • pain-free / dislocated[12] / dysplastic[13] [ɪ] **hip** • **hip** joint[14] / socket[4] / capsule • **hip** motion / abduction [ʌ]/ flexors • **hip** pain[15] / replacement[16] / prosthesis[16] [iː] • **pelvic** cavity / brim[17] / diameter • **pelvic** inlet[18] / outlet[19] / ring[20] • **pelvic** muscles / vein [eɪ]/ floor[21] (relaxation) • **pelvic** organs or viscera[22] [ɪs]/ diaphragm [ˈdaɪəfræm]/ fracture • **coxal** bone[1] / articulation[14] • **coxa** vara / valga / plana • **pelvi**rectal /metry

pubic bone n clin   syn pubis n term, rel ilium[1] [ˈɪliəm] n, ischium[2] [ˈɪskiəm] n term
anterior portion of the hip bone

(supra/ retro)pubic [ˈpjuːbɪk] adj term • **ischial** adj • **iliac** adj • **ilio-**, **ischio-** comb

» The urogenital [dʒe] diaphragm bridges the perineum [iː] anterior to the ischial tuberosities between the descending [se] rami [ˈreɪmaɪ] of the pubis. The inguinal ligament passes between the pubic tubercle and anterior iliac spine[3]. Posterior disruptions [ʌ] of the pelvic ring are often hard to distinguish regardless of whether they are due to dislocations of the sacroiliac joint or to fractures of the ilium.

Use **pubic** symphysis[4] [ɪ]/ ramus [eɪ]/ tubercle[5] / region / hair • **ischial** tuberosity[6] / spine / ramus • **iliac** bone[1] (graft) / crest / fossa[7] / artery • **iliac** bifurcation [aɪ]/ lymph [ɪ] node chain [tʃeɪn]/ graft • ischio/ trans**pubic** • **ilio**pubic tract[8]

femur [ˈfiːmə] n term, pl femora [e]   syn thigh bone [θaɪ boʊn] n clin
long bone of the thigh articulating with the hip bone proximally and the tibia distally

femoral[1] [ˈfemərəl] adj term • **femoro-** comb

» The large round head of the femur articulates with the acetabulum [s] of the hip. The femoral head[2] was adequately relocated beneath [iː] the roof of the acetabulum.

Use distal / opposing / ipsilateral / fractured[3] **femur** • **femoral** shaft / neck[4] / vein [eɪ] • **femoral** condyle / epiphysis / pulse[5] • **femoro**tibial joint /popliteal bypass[6]

tibia (bone) [ˈtɪbiə] n term   syn shin [ʃɪn] or shank bone n clin
rel **fibula**[1] [ˈfɪbjələ], **patella**[2], **malleolus**[3] [məˈliːələs] n term, pl –i [aɪ]

larger bone of the lower leg articulating with the femur, fibula (calf [kæf] bone[1]), and talus

(mid)tibial[4] adj term • **tibio-** comb • **fibular** [ɪ] adj • **(infra)patellar**[5] adj

» The nodules were located over the tibia. The medial meniscus and the fibular collateral ligament are torn. The medial malleolus is fractured in the horizontal plane.

Use saber[6] [ˈseɪbə]/ proximal **tibia** • **tibia** vara[7] / **tibial** shaft / condyle / crest[8] / spine • **tibial** fracture / nerve / vein • **tibio**fibular joint[9] / distal / intact / unstable [eɪ] **fibula** • **fibular** collateral ligament [ɪ] • lateral / medial[10] [iː] **malleolus** • high-riding[11] / floating[12] [oʊ] **patella** • **patellar** dome [doʊm] / tendon[13] / cartilage [-lɪdʒ] • **patellar** instability / reflex[14] [iː]/ dislocation[15] • **patello**femoral

---

Sakrum, Os sacrum, Kreuzbein
Steißbein, Os coccygis[1] schaufelförmig[2] kokzygeal, Steißbein-[3] Verschmelzung[4] Sakral-, Kaudalanästhesie[5] Plica rectouterina[6] Distantia sacropubica[7] Hexenschuss, Lumbago[8] Truncus lumbosacralis[9]

20

Pelvis, Becken(knochen)
Hüftbein, Os coxae[1] Beckenhöhle, Cavitas pelvis[2] pelvin, Becken-[3] Hüftgelenkpfanne, Acetabulum[4] Beckengürtel[5] kl. Becken, Pelvis minor[6] gr. Becken, P. major[7] Nierenbecken, P. renalis, Pyelon[8] knöchernes B.[9] feminine Beckenform[10] gebeugte Hüfte[11] Hüft(gelenk)luxation[12] Hüft(gelenk)dysplasie[13] Hüftgelenk, Art. coxae[14] Hüft(gelenk)schmerz, Koxalgie[15] Hüftgelenkersatz, Hüftendoprothese[16] Beckenrand[17] Beckeneingang, Apertura pelvis superior[18] Beckenausgang, A. pelvis inferior[19] Beckenring[20] Beckenboden[21] Beckenorgane[22]

21

Os pubis, Pubis, Schambein
Darmbein, Os ilium[1] Sitzbein, Os ischii[2] vorderer Darmbeinstachel, Spina iliaca anterior[3] Schambeinfuge, Symphysis pubis/ pubica[4] Tuberculum pubicum, Schambeinhöcker[5] Sitzbeinhöcker, Tuber ischiadicum[6] Fossa iliaca[7] Tractus iliopubicus[8]

22

Femur, Oberschenkelknochen
femoral, Femur-[1] Femurkopf, Caput femoris[2] Oberschenkelfraktur[3] Schenkelhals, Collum femoris[4] Femoralispuls[5] femoropoplitealer Bypass[6]

23

Tibia, Schienbein
Fibula, Wadenbein[1] Kniescheibe, Patella[2] Knöchel, Malleolus[3] tibial, Tibia-[4] patellar, Patella-[5] Säbelscheidentibia[6] Blount-Krankheit[7] Margo ant. tibiae[8] Tibiofibulargelenk, Art. tibiofibularis[9] Innenknöchel, Malleolus medialis[10] Patellahochstand[11] tanzende Patella, Ballottement d. P.[12] Patellarsehne[13] Patellarsehnenreflex[14] Patellaluxation[15]

24

Joints   BODY STRUCTURES & FUNCTIONS **117**

tarsus [tɑːrsəs] *n term, pl* **-i**   *rel* **tarsal (bone)¹, metatarsus²** *n term*
the root of the foot at the instep³ which is made up of 7 tarsal bones, the talus, calcaneus, and navicular bone⁴, 3 wedge-shaped⁵ cuneiform [kjʊniːə-] bones⁶, and the cuboid [kjuːbɔɪd] bone⁷
(mid)tarsal⁸ *adj term* • **(inter)metatarsal** *adj* • **tarso-** *comb*
» Minor [aɪ] avulsion [ʌ] fractures⁹ of the tarsal navicular may occur [ɜː] as a feature [fiːtʃɚ] of severe midtarsal sprain [eɪ]. The fourth metatarsal is least rigidly [ɪdʒ] anchored¹⁰ [k] at its base.
Use **tarsal** navicular (bone)⁴ / tunnel [ʌ] syndrome¹¹ [ɪ] • **metatarsal** phalangeal [dʒ] joint¹² / arch [ɑːrtʃ] • **tarso**metatarsal joint • *intermetatarsal* ligaments¹³ / space

Tarsus, Fußwurzel
Fußwurzelknochen, Os tarsi¹ Mittelfuß, Metatarsus² Rist³ Kahnbein, Os naviculare⁴ keilförmig⁵ Keilbeine, Ossa cuneiformia⁶ Würfelbein, Os cuboideum⁷ tarsal, Fußwurzel-⁸ Ab-, Ausrissfraktur⁹ verankert¹⁰ Tarsaltunnelsyndrom¹¹ Zehengrundgelenk, Art. metatarsophalangealis¹² Lig. metatarsalia¹³
25

talus [teɪləs] *n term*   *syn* **ankle** [æŋkl] **bone** *n clin,* **astragalus** [æ] *n term rare*
the tarsal bone that articulates with the malleoli of the tibia and fibula to form the ankle joint¹
(sub/ tibio)talar *adj term* • **talo-** *comb* • **astragalar** *adj*
» The posterior tibial tendon was interposed between the medial malleolus and the talus.
Use vertical [ɜː] **talus** • **talar** neck² / body³ / head / tilt⁴ / fracture / displacement • **talo**calcaneal joint⁵ /navicular /crural [teɪloʊkruəɹəl] • *subtalar* joint⁵

Talus, Sprungbein
oberes Sprunggelenk, Artic. talocruralis¹ Collum tali, Sprungbeinhals² Corpus tali, Sprungbeinkörper³ Taluskippung⁴ Articulatio talocalcanea/ subtalaris⁵
26

calcaneus [kælkeɪnɪəs] *n term*
   syn **calcaneum, (os) calcis** [ɒːs kælsɪs] *n term,* **heel** [iː] **bone** *n clin*
largest of the tarsal bones; it articulates with the cuboid¹ [kjuː] and the talus above
calcaneal *adj term* • **calcaneo-** *comb*
» The calcaneus must be dissected from the heel pad² with great care in order to avoid injury to the heel flap. Most fractures of the calcaneal body are comminuted ones³.
Use axial fixation / (tali)pes⁴ [tælɪpiːz] of the calcaneus • **calcaneal** region / bursa [ɜː] / tuberosity⁵ • **calcaneal** dorsiflexion / spur⁶ [ɜː] • **calcaneo**cuboid joint⁷ /fibular ligament (*abbr* CFL) • **calcaneo**navicular /valgus position • *retrocalcaneal* space / bursitis⁸ [aɪ]

Fersenbein, Calcaneus, Kalkaneus
Würfelbein, Os cuboideum¹ Fersenfettgewebe; Fersenpolster² Trümmerfrakturen³ Hakenfuß, Pes calcaneus⁴ Fersenhöcker, Tuber calcanei⁵ Fersen-, Kalkaneussporn⁶ Articulatio calcaneocuboidea⁷ Achillobursitis⁸
27

Unit 29 Joints
Related Units: **28** Bones, **30** Muscles, **22** Trunk, **23** Extremities, **31** Musculoskeletal Function, **64** Body Movement, **106** Fractures

articulation [ɑːrtɪkjʊleɪʃⁿn] *n term*   *syn* **joint** [dʒɔɪnt] *n clin* → U66-1
(i) more or less movable [uː] place of junction [dʒʌŋkʃⁿn] between two or more bones of the skeleton
(ii) speech [spiːtʃ]
articulate with¹ *v term* • **(intra/ supra)articular²** *adj* • *disarticulation³ n*
» The needle is introduced more distally, at the talonavicular [teɪloʊ-] articulation. Make sure the lunate⁴ [uː] articulates with the distal radius [eɪ] and the capitate⁵ with the lunate.
Use (distal) radio-ulnar [ʌ]/ patellofemoral [e]/ tibiofibular [ɪ] **articulation** • intervertebral [ɜː]/ costosternal [ɜː] **articulation** • speech **articulation** • **articulation** pain • fibrous [aɪ] *or* immovable⁶ *joint* • cartilaginous [ædʒ] *or* slightly movable⁷ / synovial [aɪ] *or* freely movable⁸ *joint* • wrist [r]/ shoulder / ankle⁹ / small hand *joint* • large (weight-bearing) [eə]/ false¹⁰ *joint* • *joint* space *or* cleft¹¹ / cavity¹¹ / capsule¹² • *joint* line / surface¹³ [ɜː] motion [moʊʃⁿn] • *joint* stiffness / aspiration¹⁴ / alignment¹⁵ [aɪ] • *joint* dislocation¹⁶ / replacement¹⁷ / effusion¹⁸ [juː] • *articular* cartilage¹⁹ / surface¹³ / facet¹³ [fæsət] / fracture • poly/ mon/ osteo/ non/ peri/ trans**articular** • knee / hip²⁰ *disarticulation*

> Note: Most joints are named after the bones they join using compound adjectives (first part ending in **-o**), e.g. acromio**calvic**ular / costosternal joint. Sometimes both forms are used (iliosacral *or* sacroiliac joint).

(i) **Articulatio, Gelenk**
(ii) **Aussprache; Lautbildung**
artikulieren, Gelenk bilden¹ artikulär, Gelenk-² Exartikulation, Absetzen im Gelenk³ Os lunatum, Mondbein⁴ Os capitatum, Kopfbein⁵ Syndesmose, Bandhaft, Art. fibrosa⁶ Art. cartilaginea, straffes Gelenk, Knorpelhaft⁷ Art. synovialis, bewegliche Knochenverbindung, Diarthrose⁸ Art. talocruralis, oberes Sprunggelenk⁹ Pseudarthrose, Falschgelenk¹⁰ Gelenkhöhle, -spalt, Cavitas articularis¹¹ Gelenkkapsel, Capsula art.¹² Gelenkfläche¹³ Gelenkpunktion¹⁴ Gelenkreposition¹⁵ Gelenkluxation¹⁶ Gelenkersatz, Alloarthroplastik¹⁷ Gelenkerguss¹⁸ Gelenkknorpel¹⁹ Hüftgelenksexartikulation²⁰
1

Joints

cartilage [kɑːrtªlɪdʒ] *n*   *rel* **perichondrium**[1] [perɪkɒːndrɪəm] *n term*

avascular connective tissue[2] characterized by its firm consistency; consists of cells (chondrocytes[3]), an interstitial matrix[4] [eɪ] of collagen fibers [aɪ], and a ground substance

cartilaginous[5] [ædʒ] *adj term* • **chondral**[5] [kɒːndrªl] *adj* • **chondr(o)-** *comb*

» There are three kinds of cartilage: hyaline [aɪ] cartilage, elastic cartilage, and fibrocartilage[6]. The cricoid [kraɪkɔɪd] cartilage[7] is the only complete cartilaginous ring in the respiratory tract. Bleeding [iː] between the auricular cartilage and perichondrium frequently follows contusions [(j)uːʒ] or other injuries to the auricle [ɔː].

Use (intra)articular[8] / epiphysial [ɪ]/ rib **cartilage** • sternal / xiphoid [z]/ intervertebral[9] **cartilage** • (accessory) nasal / conchal[10] / annular[7] **cartilage** • arytenoid / thyroid[11] [aɪ]/ auricular[10] **cartilage** • falciform[12] [s]/ interosseous **cartilage** • septal / sesamoid / epiglottic **cartilage** • costal[13] [ɒː]/ tracheal [k] **cartilages** • **cartilage of the** larynx / nasal septum / pharyngotympanic tube / ear[10] • white / yellow **fibrocartilage** • **endochondral** ossification[14] • **perichondrium** graft

Knorpel, Cartilago

Knorpelhaut, Perichondrium[1] Bindegewebe[2] Knorpelzellen, Chondrozyten[3] Interzellularsubstanz[4] knorpelig, verknorpelt, Knorpel-[5] Faser-, Bindegewebeknorpel, Cartilago fibrosa[6] Cartilago cricoidea, Ringknorpel[7] Gelenkknorpel[8] Zwischenwirbel-, Bandscheibe[9] Cart. auricularis, Ohr(muschel)knorpel, Knorpelgerüst d. Ohrmuschel[10] Schildknorpel, Cart. thyroidea[11] Meniscus medialis[12] Rippenknorpel[13] enchondrale Ossifikation[14]   2

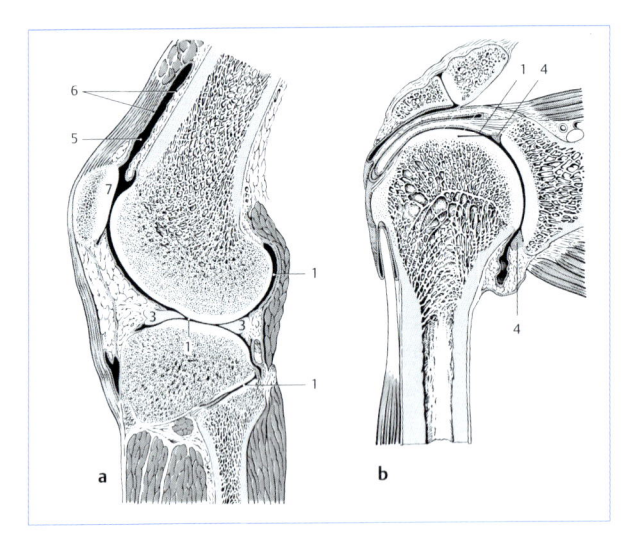

Synovial joints:
(a) cross-section of the knee,
(b) cross-section of the shoulder;
articular space (1), knee menisci (3), glenoid lip (4), suprapatellar synovial bursa (5), synovial membrane (6), articular cartilage (7)

---

synovial joint [sɪnouvɪəl dʒɔɪnt] *n term*
   syn **diarthrodial joint, diarthrosis** [daɪɑːrθrousɪs] *n term*

union of bony elements surrounded by an articular capsule lined by synovial membrane[1]

arthro- *comb* • **-arthrosis** *comb* • **synov-** [sɪnouv-] *comb*

» Inflammation from the synovial joints and bursae [iː] of the upper cervical spine may lead to atlanto-axial subluxation [ʌ]. Osteoarthritis (abbr OA) represents failure of a diarthrodial joint.

Use **synovial** (joint) **fluid**[2] / (tendon) sheath[3] [ʃiːθ]/ bursa[4] [ɜː] • multi-axial / affected **joint** • proximal interphalangeal [dʒ] (*abbr* PIP) **joint** • **joint** mouse[5] / position sense (*abbr* JPS) • **arthro**pathy /scopy /graphy /gram /desis[6] [iː] • hem[7]/ pseud [suːd]/ py [paɪ]/ hydr[8] [haɪdr]/ osteo**arthrosis** • tendon / bulging[9] [bʌldʒɪŋ] **synovium** • inflamed [eɪ]/ rheumatoid [ruːmətɔɪd] **synovium** • **synovium**-lined • **synov**itis [aɪ]/ectomy

Articulatio synovialis, Diarthrose, echtes Gelenk

Gelenkinnenhaut, Synovialhaut, (Membrana) Synovialis[1] Synovia, Gelenkschmiere[2] Sehnenscheide, Vagina synovialis tendinis[3] Schleimbeutel, Bursa synovialis[4] Gelenkmaus, freier Gelenkkörper, Corpus liberum[5] Arthrodese, op. Gelenkversteifung[6] Hämarthros, blutiger Gelenkerguss[7] Hyd(r)arthros, seröser G.[8] Ausstülpung der Gelenkskapsel[9]   3

---

ball-and-socket joint *n*   *rel* **pivot joint**[1] *n*, **trochoid** [troukɔɪd] **joint**[1] *n term*

freely movable joint which is lined with synovial membrane and enclosed within a joint capsule; it allows multiaxial [ʌ] movement in all planes [eɪ] (e.g. hip, shoulder joints)

» The shoulder and the hip are typical ball-and-socket joints. An example for a pivot joint is the articulation between the atlas [æ] and the axis [æ] in which the process of the atlas rotates within a bony ring of the second cervical vertebra [ɜː].

Use hip[2] / tooth[3] [uː]/ molar / dry / eye[4] **socket** • **pivot** shift test[5] / transfer[6] / tooth[7]

Kugelgelenk, Art. sphaeroidea

Radgelenk, A. trochoidea[1] Hüftgelenkpfanne, Acetabulum[2] Zahnfach, Alveole[3] Augenhöhle, Orbita[4] Pivotshift Test, Subluxationstest[5] Patiententransfer durch Drehen[6] Stiftzahn[7]   4

Joints BODY STRUCTURES & FUNCTIONS **119**

hinge [dʒ] **joint** n syn **hinged articulation, ginglymus** [dʒɪ‖gɪ] **joint** n term
synovial joint which allows forward and backward movement in one plane only, e.g. the knee
» *The jaw* [dʒɒː] *is primarily a hinge joint but it can also move somewhat from side to side. The ankle and knee are hinge joints which also allow some rotary movement.*
Use **hinge** knee prosthesis [iː]/ axis¹ / point • **hinged** flap² / prosthesis³ • superiorly [ɪɚ] **hinged**

Scharniergelenk, Ginglymus
Scharnierachse¹ Rotationslappen² Scharnierprothese³

5

saddle [æ] **joint** n sim **condyloid** [kɒːndəlɔɪd] or **condylar joint**¹ n term
biaxial synovial joint in which the double motion is effected by the opposition of two surfaces, each of which is concave in one direction and convex in the other; e.g. the thumb [θʌm] carpometacarpal joint
(**epi**)**condyle**² [kɒːndaɪl] n term • (**epi/ inter/ supra/ trans**)**condylar**³ adj
» *The saddle joint at the base of the thumb allows more complex movement than with the other fingers. A condyloid joint is found at the base of the* index finger⁴.
Use **saddle** (-back) nose⁵ (deformity) / block (anesthesia)⁶ [iː] • **condyloid** process⁷ • tibial [ɪ]/ (lateral) femoral [e] **condyle** • medial [iː]/ mandibular⁷ / prosthetic **condyle** • **condylar** groove⁸ [uː]/ neck / hinge axis / guidance [aɪ] • **condylar** flattening⁹ / spurring [ɜː]/ erosion¹⁰ [oʊʒ] • **condylar** deformity / fracture / replacement • **intercondylar** notch¹¹ [nɒːtʃ]/ region [iːdʒ]/ fracture

Sattelgelenk, Art. sellaris
Articulatio condylaris, Ellipsoidgelenk¹ Kondylus, Gelenkknorren² kondylär, Kondylen-³ Zeigefinger⁴ Sattelnase⁵ Sattelblock⁶ Proc. condylaris mandibulae, Gelenkkopf d. Kiefergelenks⁷ Fossa condylaris⁸ Kondylenabflachung⁹ Abnützung d. Kondylus¹⁰ Fossa intercondylaris¹¹

6

gliding [glaɪdɪŋ] or **plane** [pleɪn] **joint** n syn **arthrodial** [oʊ] **joint** n term
synovial joint in which the opposing surfaces are nearly plane allowing only slight gliding motion
» *Many of the small bones of the wrist and ankle meet in gliding joints.*
Use **gliding** mechanism¹ [ek]/ movement • anterior / posterior **gliding** • occlusal² [uːz]/ mandibular **glide** • **arthrodial** cartilage³

Gleitgelenk, Art. plana
Gleitmechanismus¹ Okklusionsbewegung, dynam. Okklusion² Gelenkknorpel, Cartilago articularis³

7

synovial fluid [sɪnoʊvɪəl fluːɪd] n clin & term syn (**articular**) **synovia** n term
transparent viscous [ɪsk] fluid serving as a lubricant¹ [uː] in a joint, tendon sheath, or bursa
» *Synovial fluid from involved joints was not inflammatory and contained no crystals* [ɪ]. *Pressure on the opposite side of the joint will make the synovium bulge* [ʌ] *more prominently.*
Use hemorrhagic [ædʒ]/ extravasation [eɪʃ] of² **synovial fluid** • **synovial fluid** analysis³ / aspirate / smear⁴ [smɪɚ] • **synovial fluid** volume / glucose [uː] level / leukocyte [luːkəsaɪt] count⁵ [aʊ] • **synovial** cavity / lining cells / villi⁶ [aɪ]/ biopsy [aɪ] • **synovial** thickening / effusion⁷ [juːʒ]/ proliferation

Gelenkschmiere, Synovia, Synovial-, Gelenkflüssigkeit
Gleit-, Schmiermittel¹ Austreten v. Gelenkflüssigkeit² Synovialanalyse³ Synovialabstrich⁴ Leukozytenanzahl i. d. Synovia⁵ Synovialzotten, Villi synoviales⁶ Gelenkerguss, intraartikuläre Effusion⁷

8

joint capsule [kæpsəl‖BE sjuːl] n clin syn **capsula articularis** n term
sac enclosing a joint formed by the outer fibrous [aɪ] capsule and the inner synovial membrane
(**extra/ intra**)**capsular**¹ adj term • **capsulectomy**² n • **encapsulated**³ adj
» *These fibers did not provide the necessary tensile strength for ligaments and joint capsules. Immobilization should not be used for more than a few days, since capsular adhesions* [iːʒ] *and prolonged stiffness may result.*
Use (posterior) hip / (medial) knee / pathologically attenuated⁴ **joint capsule** • **joint capsule** thickening / distention⁵ • palpation / contracture⁶ / fibrosis **of the joint capsule** • prostatic⁷ / renal⁸ **capsule** • **capsular** ligaments / contracture⁶

Gelenkkapsel, Capsula articularis
intrakapsulär¹ operative Kapselentfernung, Kapsulektomie² eingekapselt³ pathol. dünne Gelenkkapsel⁴ Kapseldehnung⁵ Gelenkskapselschrumpfung, arthrogene Kontraktur, Gelenkkontraktur⁶ Prostatakapsel⁷ Nierenkapsel⁸

9

(**synovial**) **bursa** [bɜːrsə] n term, pl **bursas, bursae** [bɜːrsiː‖aɪ]
closed sac or envelope lined with synovial membrane and containing fluid, usually found or formed in areas subject to friction¹ [frɪkʃⁿn], e.g. over a prominent part or where a tendon passes over a bone
bursal adj term • **bursitis**² [bɜːrsaɪtɪs] n
» *Bursae facilitate* [sɪ] *normal movement, minimize friction between moving parts, and may communicate* [juː] *with joints. Padding³* [æ] *placed around the bursa often relieves* [iː] *pressure. Patients with septic bursitis require hospitalization.*
Use extra-articular / prepatellar / omental⁴ **bursa** • ulnar [ʌ]/ paratendinous / anserine⁵ [-aɪn] **bursa** • lubricating [uː]/ trochanteric [(subcutaneous) [eɪ] olecranon⁶ **bursa** • **bursa of the** hyoid⁷ [aɪ] • **bursal** wall / effusion⁸ / injection [dʒe] • retromalleolar [iː]/ subdeltoid⁹ **bursitis** • iliopsoas [ɪlɪoʊsoʊəs]/ anserine **bursitis**

Schleimbeutel, Bursa synovialis
Reibung¹ Schleimbeutelentzündung, Bursitis² Polsterwatte, Polsterung³ Bursa omentalis, Netzbeutel, Bauchfelltasche⁴ Bursa anserina⁵ Bursa subcutanea olecrani⁶ Bursa infrahyoidea⁷ Bursaerguss⁸ Bursitis subdeltoidea⁹

10

BODY STRUCTURES & FUNCTIONS — Muscles & Tendons

synovial membrane n term   syn **synovium** n term, pl **-a**
  membrane of connective tissue lining the cavities of synovial joints
» The synovial membrane does not cover the articular cartilage of the bones. Biopsy of inflamed synovial membrane shows nonspecific edema [iː] and hyperemia [iː]. The Achilles [k] tendon does not have a true synovial sheath[1] [ʃiːθ] but is surrounded by a paratendon[2].
Use delicate / regenerated [dʒe] **synovial membrane** • **synovial membrane** blood vessels / inflammation[3] [eɪʃ]/ histopathology • **synovial** (tendon) sheath [iː]/ fold[4] / hernia[5] [ɜː].

Synovialhaut, Membrana synovialis, Synovialis
Sehnenscheide[1] Sehnengleitgewebe, Paratendineum[2] Synovi(al)tis, Entzündung d. Synovialis[3] Synovialfalte, Plica synovialis[4] Synovialhernie[5]

11

cartilaginous joint [kɑːrtɪlædʒɪnəs dʒɔɪnt] n term
  rel **synchondrosis**[1] [sɪŋkɒːndrousɪs] n, **symphysis**[2] [sɪmfəsɪs] n term, pl **-ses**
  slightly movable joint connected by hyaline [haɪəlɪn‖aɪn] cartilage
» In symphyses [-siːz] the bones are connected by a flat disk of fibrocartilage which remains unossified, e.g., the intervertebral [ɜː] disk[3] and the symphysis pubis[4]. In most synchondroses, the connecting cartilage is converted [ɜː] to bone, as between epiphyses [-fɪsiːz] and diaphyses of long bones, except for the sternal synchondroses and the cartilaginous union [juː] of the first rib and the manubrium [uː] of the sternum [ɜː].
Use **cartilaginous** joint structures [ʌ]/ growth plate[5] / disk • **cartilaginous** acetabulum [æsə-] / matrix[6] [eɪ]/ tissue[7] • **cartilaginous** cap[8] / ring / airways • sternal[9] / cranial [eɪ] **synchondrosis** • pubic[4] [pjuː]/ pleural[10] [ʊə] **symphysis**

Articulatio cartilaginea, Knorpelgelenk
Synchondrose[1] Symphyse[2] Zwischenwirbel-, Bandscheibe, Discus intervertebralis[3] Schambeinfuge, Symphysis pubica[4] knorpelige Wachstumszone, Epiphysenknorpel, -fuge[5] Knorpelgrundsubstanz, -matrix, Matrix cartilaginea[6] Knorpel(gewebe)[7] Knorpelkappe[8] Synchondrosis sternocostalis[9] Pleuraverwachsung[10]

12

syndesmosis n term, pl **-ses**   syn **syndesmotic joint** n, rel **synarthrosis**[1] n term
  immovable fibrous joint[1] united by ligaments, e.g. the distal ends of the tibia and fibula
  syndesmotic [sɪndesmɒːtɪk] adj term • **syndesmo-** comb
» Tenderness of the deltoid ligament and syndesmosis can be difficult to identify. Damage to the syndesmotic ligaments between the distal tibia and fibula is demonstrated by distal tibiofibular diastasis[2] [daɪæstəsɪs].
Use tibiofibular[3] / radioulnar [ʌ] **syndesmosis** • **syndesmo**phyte[4] [-faɪt] • disruption [ʌ] of the[5] **syndesmosis**

Syndesmose, -is, Bandhaft
Synarthrose[1] Auseinanderweichen d. Articulatio tibiofibularis[2] Syndesmosis tibiofibularis[3] Syndesmophyt[4] Syndesmosensprengung[5]

13

suture (joint) [suːtʃɚ dʒɔɪnt] n   syn **sutura**, pl **-ae** n term
  rel **gomphosis**[1] [gɒːmfousɪs], **synostosis**[2] n term
  immovable joint between cranial [eɪ] bones which are united [aɪ] by fibrous [aɪ] tissue
  synostotic [sɪnɒːstɒːtɪk] adj term • **gompholic** adj
» Premature closure of the coronal sutures[3] causes brachycephaly [brækɪsefəli]. Some forms of craniosynostosis may result from constraints [eɪ] to the developing fetal [iː] head (e.g. sagittal [ædʒ] synostosis).
Use cranial[4] [eɪ]/ frontozygomatic [aɪ]/ frontolacrimal **suture** • interparietal [aɪ]/ occipitoparietal [ɒːks-] **suture** • spheno-occipital [sfiːnoʊ-]/ sagittal[5] **suture** • lambdoidal[6] / serrated[7] **suture** • prematurely fused[8] [juː]/ scalp **sutures** • cranial **suture** defect • tarsal / radioulnar[9] **synostosis** • closed / wide[10] **cranial sutures**

(Knochen)naht, Sutura
Gomphosis, Einkeilung, -zapfung[1] Knochenhaft, Synostose[2] Suturae coronales, Kranznähte[3] Sutura cranii, Schädelnaht[4] Pfeilnaht, Sut. sagittalis[5] Lambdanaht, Sut. lambdoidea[6] Zackennaht, Sut. serrata[7] vorzeitige Verknöcherung d. Schädelnähte[8] radioulnare Synostose[9] offene Schädelnähte[10]

14

Unit 30   Muscles & Tendons
Related Units: 28 Bones, 29 Joints, 31 Musculoskeletal Function, 64 Body Movement, 21 Head & Neck, 22 Trunk, 23 Extremities, 106 Fractures

muscle fiber [faɪbɚ] n, BE **fibre**   rel **fascicle**[1] [fæsɪkl] n term
  multinucleated contractile filaments [ɪ] containing actin and myosin [maɪəsɪn] which are arranged [eɪ] in sheathed [ʃiːθt] bundles[2] [ʌ]
  fascicular[3] [fəsɪkjʊlɚ] adj term • **fasciculation**[4] n
» Human skeletal muscles are a mixture of red, white, and intermediate [iː] type fibers. Muscle fibers contain sarcoplasm[5] and striated myofibrils[6] [aɪ‖ɪ] which consist of myofilaments[7]. Hyperextension may lead to nerve compression by the posterior fascicle of the ligament.
Use striated[8] / smooth / red[9] / white[10] **muscle fibers** • longitudinal / circularly [ɜː] oriented[11] **muscle fibers** • diaphragmatic / detrusor / denervated **muscle fiber** • slow-twitch (ST) or type I[12] / fast-twitch (FT) or type II[13] **muscle fibers** • **muscle fiber** length / membrane / action potential • **muscle fiber** damage[14] / atrophy • **fascicular** area / block[15] • surrounding / anterior **fascicle** • muscle[16] **fasciculation**

Muskelfaser
Faszikel, Fasciculus, Muskelfaserbündel[1] v. Faszien umhüllte Bündel[2] faszikulär[3] Faszikulation[4] Sarkoplasma[5] Myofibrillen[6] Myofilamente[7] Skelettmuskelfasern[8] rote Muskelfasern[9] weiße M.[10] zirkulär angeordnete Muskelfasern[11] ST-Fasern, langsam zuckende/ Typ I-Fasern[12] FT-Fasern, schnelle Zuckungsfasern, Typ II-Fasern[13] Muskelfaserverletzung[14] Faszikelblock[15] Muskelzuckungen, faszikuläre Zuckungen[16]

1

Muscles & Tendons — BODY STRUCTURES & FUNCTIONS

muscle [mʌsl] *n*   *syn* **musculus** [mʌskjʊləs] *n term, pl* **-i**

contractile body tissue by which movements [uː] of the various organs and parts are effected
muscular[1] [mʌskjʊlɚ] *adj* • **musculature**[2] [-tʃɚ] *n term* • **musculo-, myo-** *comb*

» Clinically the term muscle spasm refers to a brief, unsustained[3] [eɪ] contraction of a single or multiple [ʌ] muscles. There is bilateral ptosis [t] because the levator [eɪ] muscle is innervated by a single central subnucleus. Motor examination should include appraisal[4] [eɪ] of muscular bulk[5] [ʌ]. He complains of stiffness and pain in his shoulder and hip musculature [ʌ].

Use striated [aɪeɪ] or voluntary or skeletal[6] / smooth [uː] or involuntary or plain[7] [eɪ] muscles • muscle strength / spindle[8] / tone[9] / relaxants • extensor / adductor [ʌ]/ strap[10] muscle • two-bellied[11] / cardiac[12] / sternomastoid muscle • muscle belly[13] / circumference [ʌ]/ mass[5] / cramp • muscle fatigue[14] [iː]/ weakness / rigidity[15] [dʒɪ]/ pump [ʌ] • muscles of facial [eɪʃ] expression[16] / the neck / mastication[17] / muscular system / tension[18] [ʃ]/ tremor / dystrophy [ɪ] • facial[19] / limb [lɪm]/ lumbar [ʌ]/ pelvic floor[20] musculature • musculoskeletal /cutaneous [eɪ] /tendinous /fascial • myocardial [maɪoʊ] /clonus [oʊ] /electric complex • myocutaneous flap /pathy /neural junction [dʒʌ] /tomy

> **Note:** Muscles are named in two ways: the **musculus rectus abdominis** (anatomic term) is clinically called the **rectus muscle** or just the **rectus**.

Muskel, Musculus
muskulös, muskulär, Muskel-[1] Muskulatur[2] kurzfristig, -zeitig[3] Bestimmung[4] Muskelmasse[5] quergestreifte/ willkürl. M., Skelettmuskulatur[6] glatte M., Eingeweidemuskulatur[7] Muskelspindel, Fusus neuromuscularis[8] Muskeltonus[9] Haltemuskel[10] zweibäuchiger Muskel, Musculus biventer[11] Herzmuskel[12] Muskelbauch, Venter musculi[13] Muskelermüdung[14] Muskelstarre, -steifigkeit, -verspannung[15] mimische Muskulatur[16] Kaumuskulatur[17] Muskelspannung[18] Gesichtsmuskulatur[19] Beckenbodenmuskulatur[20]

2

insertion [ɪnsɜːrʃən] *n term*   *syn* **attachment** [ətætʃmənt] *n term*
   opposite **origin**[1] [ɔːrədʒɪn] *n term, rel* **head**[2] [hed] *n term*

the more distal or more movable attachment of a muscle to a bone or other structure by means of a tendon; the more proximal or more fixed attachment is called the origin

insert[3] [ɪnsɜːrt] *v term* • **originate**[4] [ərɪdʒɪneɪt] *v* • **arise**[4] [əraɪz] *v*

» Fluffy[5] [ʌ] periosteal new bone may be marked, especially at the insertion of muscles and ligaments [ɪg]. Spurs[6] [ɜː] at the insertion of the plantar fascia [ʃ] are common. The serratus [eɪ] anterior inserts on the anteromedial [iː] aspect of the scapula.

Use muscle / tendon[7] / (musculo)tendinous[7] insertion • torn off at / detached [tʃ] from[8] its origin • long / lateral / medial head • to originate from the pubis / in / along the iliac crest • to arise from • muscle[9] / ligamentous / bony[10] attachment

Ansatz
Ursprung[1] Muskelkopf, Caput musculi[2] inserieren, ansetzen[3] seinen Ursprung haben/ ausgehen von[4] spongiös[5] Sporne[6] Sehnenansatz[7] am knöchernen Ursprung ausgerissen[8] Muskelansatz[9] knöcherner Ansatz[10]

3

motor end plate [moʊɾɚ end pleɪt] *n term* → U40-13
syn **myoneural** or **neuromuscular junction** [nʊɚoʊmʌskjʊlɚ dʒʌŋkʃən] *n term*

large and complex end-formation by which several terminal [ɜː] branches[1] of a motor axon establish synaptic contact[2] with a striated muscle fiber cell

» Acetylcholine [koʊ] serves as the neurotransmitter at the skeletal muscle end plate. Nicotinic receptors are located on motor end plates of skeletal muscle. Magnesium [iː] acts directly on the myoneural junction. If the virus enters the muscle, it can travel across the neuromuscular junction up the axon to the anterior horn cells[3].

Use cartilaginous [ædʒ]/ skeletal muscle **end plate** • to travel across the / postsynaptic[4] / (para)sympathetic **neuromuscular junction** • **end plate** potential[5] • **neuromuscular junction** transmission / block[6] • **motor** sense[7] / nerve / neuron[8] • **motor** root [uː]/ tract / unit / pathway[9]

motor./ neuromuskuläre Endplatte, myoneurale/ Neuro-Effektor-Synapse
Nervenendigungen[1] eine synaptische Verbindung herstellen[2] Vorderhornzellen[3] postsynaptischer Teil d. neuromuskulären Synapse[4] Enplattenpotential[5] Blockierung d. motor. Endplatte[6] Bewegungsgefühl[7] Motoneuron[8] motorische Bahn[9]

4

tendon [tendən] *n*   *syn* **tendo** *n term, pl* **tendines, sinew** [sɪnjuː] *n inf*
   rel **aponeurosis**[1] [æpən(j)ʊɚoʊsɪs] *n term*

fibrous [faɪbrəs], densely arranged fascicles[2] connecting muscles with their bony attachments
(pre)tendinous[3] *adj term* • **ten(d)o-** *comb* • **aponeurotic**[4] [ɒː] *adj*

» A tap[5] on a tendon stretches muscle spindles and activates the primary spindle afferent fibers. Fibrinous [ɪ‖aɪ] deposits on the surfaces of tendon sheaths and in the overlying fascia may lead to audible creaking [iː] over moving tendons. Ptosis [toʊsɪs] can be due to dysgenesis [dʒe] of the levator [eɪ] palpebrae [-iː] superioris or abnormal insertion of its aponeurosis into the eyelid.

Use hamstring [æ]/ heel [iː] or Achilles[6] [k]/ flexor[7] / extensor finger **tendon** • deep[8] / absent / weak / hyperactive **tendon reflexes** • **tendon** sheath[9] [ʃiːθ]/ nodule[10] / lengthening / grafting[11] • **tendinous** cords[12] [kɔːrdz] • **aponeurotic** tendon / closure [oʊʒ] • plantar[13] / extensor / external [ɜː] oblique[14] [oʊbliːk] **aponeurosis** • **tend**ovaginitis[15] [dʒɪ] /initis • **teno**synovitis[15] [tenəsɪnəvaɪtɪs] /rrhaphy[16] [-rəfi]

Sehne, Tendo
Aponeurose, Sehnenhaut, flächenhafte Sehne[1] Faserbündel, Fasciculi[2] sehnig; Sehnen-[3] aponeurotisch, Aponeurosen-[4] Beklopfen[5] Achillessehne[6] Beugesehne[7] Sehnenreflexe[8] Sehnenscheide, Vagina tendinis[9] Sehnenknötchen[10] Sehnentransplantation, -plastik[11] Sehnenfäden, Chordae tendineae[12] Plantaraponeurose, A. plantaris[13] Aponeurose d. M. obliquus externus abdominis[14] Sehnenscheidenentzündung, Tendovaginitis, Tenosynovitis[15] Sehnennaht[16]

5

ligament [lɪgəmənt] *n*   *syn* **ligamentum** *n term, pl* **-a**

band or sheet [ʃiːt] of fibrous tissue connecting two or more bones, cartilages[1] [-lɪdʒiːz], or other structures [ʌ], or serving as support for fasciae or muscles

ligamentous[2] *adj term*

» If the posterior ligaments of the uterus [juː] are involved, endometriosis pain increases with intercourse[3]. Operative division of the volar [oʊ] carpal ligament achieved lasting pain relief.

Use collateral / suspensory / anterior cruciate[4] [uːʃ] (*abbr* ACL)/ annular[5] **ligament** • periodontal[6] / falciform [s]/ inguinal[7] / ruptured[8] [ʌ] **ligament** • **ligament** of Treitz[9] • **ligamentum** collaterale radii • **ligamentous** attachment / structures[10] / support / capsular bands • **ligamentous** laxity[11] / injury / tear[8] [teɚ]/ disruption[8] [ʌ]/ calcification

fascia [fæʃ(ɪ)ə] *n term, pl* **-ae** [fæʃiː]

sheet of fibrous tissue enclosing muscles and muscle groups and separating their layers [eɪ]

(**myo/ musculo/ extra/ sub**)**fascial** [fæʃ(ɪ)əl] *adj term* • **fasci(o)-** *comb*

» Many deep tissue compartments in the arms and legs are contained [eɪ] by unyielding[1] [jiː] fascia. The fascial edges of the defect should be cleaned. Fasciotomy[2] is effective treatment for compartment syndrome[3] [ɪ] only if performed within a few hours after onset.

Use muscle / plantar[4] / aponeurotic **fascia** • Gerota's[5] / endopelvic / rectus **fascia** • deep[6] / superficial [ɪʃ]/ transversalis [eɪ]/ dense **fascia** • **fascia** lata[7] • **fascial** layer [leɪɚ] *or* plane [eɪ]/ compartment[8] / **fascial** strands[9] / attachment / fibers • **fascial** edge[10] / sling / closure[11] [oʊʒ] • **fascial** defect [iː]/ contracture • **fasciotomy**[2] /octaneous [eɪ] /itis [fæʃɪaɪtɪs]

muscular pulley [puli] *n clin*   *sim* **retinaculum**[1] *n, rel* **trochlea**[2] [trɒːk-] *n term*

a fibrous loop [uː] or tunnel [ʌ] through which a muscle tendon passes, e.g. in the fingers

pulley-enhanced[3] [æ‖*BE* ɑː] *adj term* • **retinacular** *adj* • **trochlear**[4] *adj*

» There is local tenderness of the proximal digital [ɪdʒ] pulleys in the distal palm [pɑːm]. In the form of sheaths [ʃiːθs] and pulleys, fascias hold tendons in the concavity[5] [kæ] of arched [tʃ] joints[6] to convey [eɪ] mechanical [kæ] efficiency [ɪʃ] and power. The extensor tendons are ensheathed [iː] in six compartments at the wrist [r] beneath the extensor retinaculum. Isolated fractures of the trochlea of the humerus [hjuː] are very unusual.

Use (digital) tendon / flexor / A2[7]-**pulley** • **pulley** of the talus[8] [eɪ] / ligaments / rupture • **trochlear** notch [nɒːtʃ] (of the ulna)[9] [ʌ]/ nerve (palsy)[10] [pɔːlzi]• **trochlea** muscularis / of the humerus[11] / femoris / tali[12] [teɪlaɪ] • extensor[13] / flexor / medial [iː] patellar[14] / inferior peroneal[15] **retinaculum** • **retinacular** tissue / blood supply / tear [teɚ]/ avulsion[16] [ʌ]

sphincter (muscle) *n clin & term*   *syn* **musculus sphincter** [sfɪŋktɚ] *n term*

muscle encircling a duct [ʌ], tube [t(j)uːb] or orifice in a way that its contraction constricts the lumen [uː] or orifice

sphincteric[1] *adj term* • **rhabdosphincter**[2] [ræbdoʊ-] *n* • **sphinctero-** *comb*

» It interfered [ɪɚ] with the ability of the sphincters to close the anal [eɪ] canal. In the female urethra [iː] there is no purely circular [sɜː] sphincteric entity but abundant[3] [ʌ] circularly oriented muscle fibers. Refractory diabetic [e] diarrhea [iː] is often associated with impaired [eɚ] sphincter control and fecal [iː] incontinence.

Use internal anal[4] / external urethral[2] **sphincter** • pyloric [paɪlɒːrɪk]/ (lower) esophageal [dʒ] **sphincter** • incompetent[5] / hypertonic[6] [ɒː] **sphincter** • **sphincter** tone[7] [oʊ]/ pressure / length • **sphincter** function / competence / of Oddi[8] • **sphincteric** ring / activity / musculature [ʌ] • **sphincteroplasty**[9] /tomy

pectoral muscle *n clin*   *syn* **musculus pectoralis** [eɪ] *n term,* **pec** [pek] *n inf*

paired thick, fan-shaped muscle of the upper chest wall acting on the shoulder joint (greater pectoral[1]) and the thin triangular muscle underneath which arise from the 3rd, 4th and 5th ribs (smaller pectoral[2])

» The pectoralis major inserts by a flat wide tendon into the crest of the greater tubercle of the humerus. The pectoralis minor acts to raise [eɪ] the 3rd, 4th and 5th ribs in forced inspiration.

Use greater[1] / smaller[2] **pectoral muscle** • **pectoralis** major[1] [meɪdʒɚ] / minor[2] [aɪ] (muscle) / fascia • **pectoral** region [iːdʒ]/ girdle[3] [ɜː]/ lymph node [lɪmf noʊd] • **pectoral** nerve / muscle motion [oʊʃ]/ pedicle flap[4]

Band, Ligamentum

Knorpel[1] ligamentär, Band-[2] Geschlechtsverkehr, Koitus[3] vorderes Kreuzband, Lig. cruciatum anterius[4] Lig. anulare radii[5] Desmodont[6] Leistenband, Lig. inguinale Pouparti[7] Bänderriss, Bandruptur[8] Treitz-Band, Plica duodenalis superior/ duodenojejunalis[9] Bandstrukturen[10] Bandinstabilität, lockere Bänder[11]

6

(Muskel)faszie, Muskelhülle

nicht dehnbar[1] Faszienspaltung, Fasziotomie[2] Logen-, Kompartment-Syndrom[3] Plantarafaneurose, Aponeurosis plantaris[4] Gerota-Faszie[5] tiefe Faszie[6] Oberschenkelfaszie, Fascia lata[7] Faszienloge[8] Faszienstränge[9] Faszienrand[10] Fasziennaht[11]

7

Ringband

Halteband, Retinaculum[1] Trochlea, Rolle[2] durch e. Ringband verstärkt[3] rollenförmig, trochlear(is)[4] Krümmung, Wölbung[5] Beugegelenke[6] A2-Ringband, -Pulley[7] Sustenaculum tali[8] Incisura trochlearis (ulnae)[9] Trochlearislähmung[10] Trochlea humeri[11] Trochlea tali, Talusrolle[12] Retinaculum extensorum[13] R. patellae mediale[14] Retinaculum musculorum peronaeorum inferius[15] Ausriss d. Haltebands[16]

8

Sphinkter, Musculus sphincter, Schließmuskel

Sphinkter-[1] Rhabdosphinkter, äußerer Harnröhrenschließmuskel, M. sphincter urethrae externus[2] zahlreich[3] Musculus sphincter ani internus, innerer Afterschließmuskel[4] Sphinkterinsuffizienz[5] Sphinkterhypertonie[6] Sphinktertonus[7] M. sphincter Oddii/ ampullae (hepatopancreaticae)[8] Sphinkterplastik[9]

9

Brustmuskel

M. pectoralis major, großer Brustmuskel[1] M. pectoralis minor, kleiner Brustmuskel[2] Schultergürtel, Cingulum membri superioris[3] gestielter Pectoralislappen[4]

10

Muscles & Tendons   BODY STRUCTURES & FUNCTIONS

biceps [baɪseps] **(muscle of the arm)** *n clin*   *syn* **biceps brachii** *n term*
            rel **(musculus) triceps** [aɪ] **brachii**[1] [breɪkɪaɪ‖kiː] *n term*
   its long head[2] originates from the supraglenoid tuberosity of the scapula, its short head[3] from
   the coracoid process[4] and inserts at the radial tuberosity; the biceps flexes and supinates [uː]
   the forearm
   bicipital[5] [baɪsɪpɪtᵊl] *adj term*
» Decrease [iː] *in a deep tendon reflex (biceps or triceps jerk[6]* [dʒɜːrk]*) is common.
   Bicipital tendinitis* [aɪ] *results from inflammation of the tendon sheath surrounding
   the long head of the biceps. Does this involve repetitive biceps flexion* [flekʃᵊn]
   against resistance?
Use **biceps** femoris (muscle)[7] / tendon • **biceps** reflex [iː] or jerk[8] / muscle strength •
   bicipital tendinitis / groove[9] [uː] • long head[2] / short head[3] *of the biceps* • **triceps**
   muscle of the arm[1] / skinfold measurement[10] [eɪ]/ weakness [iː]

M. biceps brachii, Bizeps (brachii)
M. triceps brachii, Trizeps (brachii)[1] Caput longum, langer Kopf[2] Caput breve[3] Rabenschnabelfortsatz, Proc. coracoideus[4] zweiköpfig; Bizeps-[5] Trizepssehnenreflex[6] M. biceps femoris[7] Bizepssehnenreflex[8] Sulcus intertubercularis[9] Trizepshautfaltenmessung[10]

11

(musculus) latissimus dorsi [dɔːrsaɪ] *n term, abbr* **LD**
                  rel **musculus levator scapulae**[1] [lɪveɪtɚ skæpjuliː] *n term*
   broadest muscle of the back (paired); originates via large lumbar aponeuroses at the spinous
   processes of the lower 5-6 thoracic and the lumbar vertebrae, the median ridge of the sacrum,
   and the outer lip of the iliac crest and inserts into the posterior lip[2] of the bicipital groove of the
   humerus with the teres major
» *The fibers of the latissimus dorsi twist as they pass the scapula and converge* [-ɜːrdʒ]
   at the intertubercular groove[3] [uː] *of the humerus. With incision of the LD and its
   aponeurosis, the serratus* [eɪ] *posterior inferior muscle and the quadratus* [eɪ] *lumborum* [ʌ] *are exposed.*
Use **latissimus dorsi** musculature / (musculocutaneous [eɪ]/ free) flap[4] • **levator** ani
   [eɪnaɪ] (muscle)[5] / sling[6] / sling gap • **levator muscle of the** ribs[7] • **levator muscle
   of the** scapula / upper lip[8] / prostate[9]

M. latissimus dorsi, Latissimus, breiter Rückenmuskel
M. levator scapulae[1] Rand[2] Sulcus intertubercularis[3] (freier) Latissimus dorsi-Lappen[4] M. levator ani[5] Levatorschlinge[6] Mm. levatores costarum[7] M. levator labii superioris[8] M. levator prostatae, M. pubovaginalis[9]

12

trapezius [trəpiːzɪəs] **(muscle)** *n term*   *rel* **deltoid** [deltɔɪd] **(muscle)**[1] *n term*
   flat, triangular muscle which originates at the nuchal [n(j)uːkᵊl] ligament[2], occipital bone, and
   spinous [aɪ] processes of the 7th cervical and all thoracic [æs] vertebrae and inserts at the
   clavicle, acromion, and the spine of the scapula; it draws the head backward, raises the shoulder, and rotates the scapula
   trapezoid[3] *adj term* • **(sub)deltoid** [sʌbdeltɔɪd] *adj*
» *Bruits[4]* [bruːiːz] *were most prominent over the lower portion of the trapezius muscle
   at the back of the neck. Spasm within the trapezius may be palpable as a firm knot*
   [nɒːt]. *Subdeltoid soreness[5] frequently radiates* [eɪ] *along the lateral humerus to the
   deltoid insertion.*
Use **trapezius** fibers / ridge[6] [rɪdʒ]/ musculocutaneous [eɪ] flap • superior / lower
   trapezius • **deltoid** region / ridge or tuberosity[7] / tendon / ligament[8] / insertion[9]

M. trapezius, Kapuzenmuskel
M. deltoideus, Deltamuskel[1] Lig. nuchae, Nackenband[2] trapezförmig[3] Bruits, Geräusche[4] Muskelschmerzen, -kater[5] Linea trapezoidea[6] Tuberositas deltoidea (humeri)[7] Lig. deltoideum/ mediale, inneres Knöchelband[8] Ansatz d. Musculus deltoideus[9]

13

rectus (muscle of the abdomen) *n*   *syn* **(musc.) rectus abdominis** *n term*
            rel **internal** [ɜː] **oblique**[1]**/ external oblique**[2] [oʊbliːk] **(muscle)** *n*
   pair of straight muscles arising from the pubic [pjuːbɪk] crest[3] [k] and inserting at the xiphoid
   [z] process[4] and the 5th-7th costal [ɒː] cartilages; at the linea alba they are joined by a medial
   [iː] tendon
» *The rectus functions to flex the vertebral* [ɜː] *column[5]* [kɒːləm]*, draw the thorax
   forward, tense[6] the anterior abdominal wall and help compress the abdominal
   contents. A broad, flat aponeurosis extends medially to the midline, forming the
   anterior layer of the rectus sheath.*
Use **(musculus) rectus** femoris / capitis anterior[7] / sheath[8] [ʃiːθ]/ diastasis[9] [æ] •
   rectus / transversus [ɜː] **abdominis (muscle)**

Rectus abdominis, gerader Bauchmuskel
M. obliquus internus abdominis, innerer schräger Bauchmuskel[1] M. obliquus externus abd., äußerer schräger B.[2] Crista pubica[3] Schwertfortsatz, Proc. xiphoideus[4] Wirbelsäule[5] anspannen, straffen[6] M. rectus capitis anterior, vorderer gerader Kopfmuskel[7] Rektusscheide[8] Rektusdiastase[9]

14

gluteal muscles [gluːtɪəl‖tiːəl] *n*   *rel* **iliopsoas** [ɪlɪəsoʊəs] **(muscle)**[1] *n term*
   three paired muscles that form the buttocks[2] [ʌ] and extend, abduct [ʌ] and rotate the thigh[3]
   gluteus maximus (muscle)[4] *n term* • **(musculus) psoas**[5] [soʊəs] *n*
» *Pain was referred down the leg from a trigger point in the gluteus medius [iː]. The
   iliopsoas is the paired group of muscles at the loin[6]* [lɔɪn] *which consists of the
   iliacus* [ɪlaɪəkəs] *and the psoas major muscle. The psoas minor is a long, slender
   muscle that lies ventral to the psoas major which joins the iliopsoas deep in the
   pelvis and inserts in the lesser trochanter.*
Use **gluteus** medius / minimus[7] • **gluteal** tuberosity / area / gait[8] [geɪt]/ fold or cleft[9] •
   iliopsoas fascia / bursitis [ɜː] sign[10] • **psoas** major [eɪdʒ] / minor [aɪ] abscess[11]
   [s] sign[10] • **ilio**femoral /lumbar [ʌ] ligament[12] /pectinal line[13] /tibial band[14]

Gesäßmuskeln
M. iliopsoas[1] Gesäß[2] Oberschenkel[3] M. glutaeus maximus, großer Gesäßmuskel[4] M. psoas, Lendenmuskel[5] Lende[6] M. glutaeus minimus, kleiner Gesäßmuskel[7] Trendelenburg-Zeichen[8] Gesäßfurche, -spalte[9] Psoaszeichen[10] Psoasabszess[11] Lig. iliolumbale[12] Linea arcuata ossis ilii[13] Tractus iliotibialis, Maissiat-Streifen[14]

15

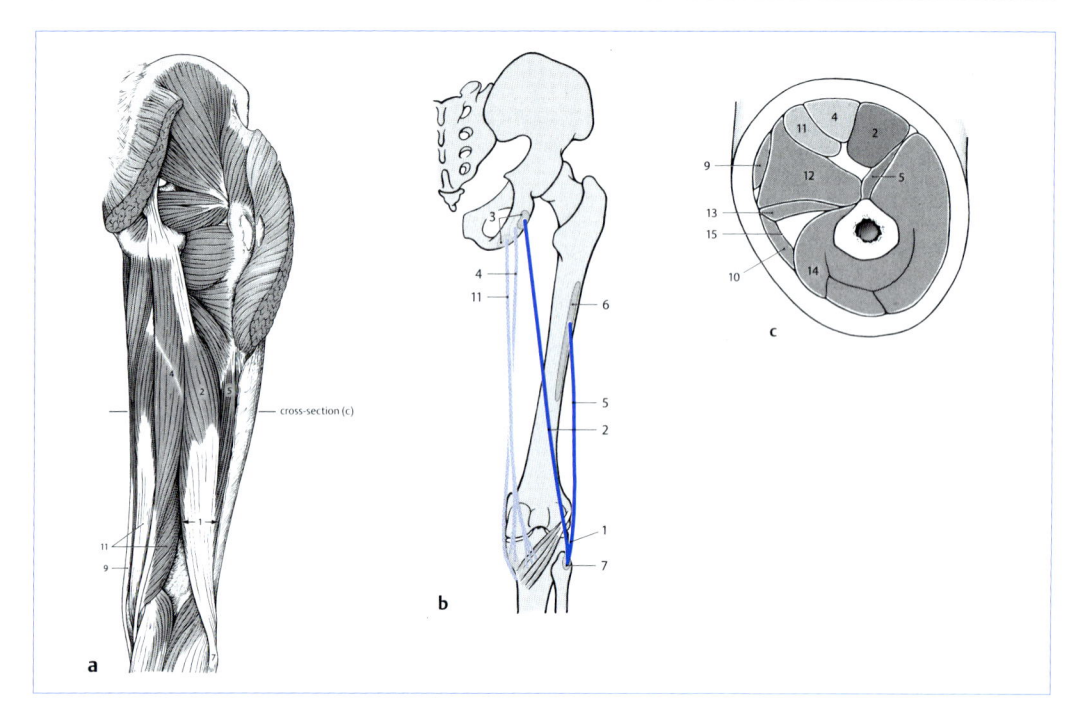

124 BODY STRUCTURES & FUNCTIONS — Muscles & Tendons

Hamstring muscles: (a) muscles of the posterior thigh, (b) schematic drawing of the hamstrings, (c) cross-section of the thigh: biceps femoris (1), long head of the biceps femoris (2), ischial tuberosity (3), semitendinosus (4), short head of the biceps femoris (5), lateral lip of linea aspera (6), head of the fibula (7), pes anserinus (8), gracilis (9), sartorius (10), semimembranosus (11), adductor magnus (12), adductor longus (13), medial vastus (14), vasto-adductor membrane (15)

hamstrings [hæmstrɪŋz] n   syn **hamstring muscles** n clin
rel **quadriceps** [kwɒdrɪseps] **(femoris** [e] **muscle)**[1] n term, **quads**[1] n pl inf

muscles at the back of the thigh [θaɪ] responsible for flexing the knee [niː] and moving the leg backward; includes the biceps (femoris)[2], the semitendinosus[3], and the semimembranosus[4]

» Risk factors for lumbar [ʌ] strain[5] include a forward-tipped pelvis (bottom to top), weak abdominal muscles and tight[6] [taɪt] inflexible hamstrings[7]. Significant weakness may develop in the quadriceps muscle group. The quadriceps femoris is the great extensor muscle of the anterior thigh which comprises [aɪ] the vastus lateralis[8], medialis and intermedius [iː].

Use to contract/build or develop/stretch/injure/pull[9] **the hamstrings** • weak / sore[10] / swollen **hamstrings** • **hamstring** strain[11] / tear [teɚ] • **quadriceps** musculature / jerk [ɜː] or reflex[12] • **quadriceps** expansion / exercises • rectus[13] / biceps **femoris**

ischiokrurale Muskulatur, Bein-, Knie-, Oberschenkelbeuger
Oberschenkelstrecker, M. quadriceps femoris[1] M. biceps femoris[2] M. semitendinosus[3] M. semimembranosus[4] Hexenschuss, Lumbago[5] verspannt[6] verkürzte Beinbeuger[7] M. vastus lateralis[8] sich d. Beinbeuger zerren[9] schmerzhafte B.[10] Zerrung d. Beinbeuger[11] Quadrizepssehnen-, Patellarsehnenreflex[12] M, rectus femoris[13]

16

peroneus [perəniːəs] **(muscles)** n term
syn **peroneal (muscles)** n clin & term, **calf muscles** n clin

lateral muscles of the lower leg, the longer one overlying the short peroneal muscle[1] which inserts into the 5th metatarsal; both act to pronate [oʊ] and plantarflex the foot

peroneal adj term • **calf**[2] [kæf‖BE kɑːf] n inf, pl **calves**

» Activity of the peroneus brevis muscle may increase displacement of the avulsed [ʌ] proximal fragment. Weakness of the peroneals is an occasional [eɪʒ] predisposing [iː] factor.

Use **(musculus) peroneus** longus[3] / brevis[1] / tertius[4] [ɜːrʃɪəs] • **peroneus** brevis muscle[1] • **peroneal** muscles / fibers / tendon / sheath [iː]/ groove [uː] • **peroneal** nerve / vein [eɪ]/ palsy[5] [ɔː]/ muscular atrophy • **calf muscle** group / pump[6] / strain[7] [eɪ]/ cramp[8] / tenderness • posterior • anterior • tight **calf muscles** • triceps muscle of the[9] **calf**

Mm. peroneaei/ fibulares, Waden(bein)muskeln
Musculus peroneus/ fibularis brevis[1] Wade[2] M. peroneaus/ fibularis longus[3] M. peroneaus/ fibularis tertius[4] Peronäus-, Fibularislähmung[5] (Waden)muskelpumpe[6] Wadenmuskelzerrung[7] Wadenkrampf[8] M. triceps surae[9]

17

Musculoskeletal Function　　　　　　　　　　　　　　　BODY STRUCTURES & FUNCTIONS **125**

Unit 31　Musculoskeletal Function
Related Units: **64** Movement, **65** Walking, **28** Bones, **29** Joints, **30** Muscles, **113** Neurologic Findings, **142** Physical Therapy

contraction [kənˈtrækʃən] *n*　　*opposite* **relaxation**[1] [riːlækˈseɪʃən] *n* → U1-11

(i) shortening or increase in tension of muscular [ʌsk] tissue, e.g. of the ventricle (heart beat), the smooth [uː] muscles [mʌslz] in the intestine, the anal [eɪ] sphincter, or the uterus in labor [eɪ]
(ii) shrinkage[2] [ʃrɪŋkɪdʒ] or reduction [ʌ] in size [saɪz]

contract[3] *v* • **relax**[4] *v* • **relaxed** *adj* • **relaxing** *adj* • **relaxant**[5] *n term*
contractile[6] [-aɪl‖-ᵊl] *adj term* • **contractility**[7] *n* • **contracture**[8] [kənˈtræktʃə] *n*

» Segmental contractions of the colon form, relax, and reform in different locations. When the displaced tendons[9] contract, they create [krieɪt] a bowstring [oʊ] effect. Muscle relaxants were needed to facilitate skeletal muscle relaxation.

Use to trigger[10]/inhibit/limit **contraction** • muscle or muscular[11] / anal / bladder / peristaltic **contraction** • phasic [ˈfeɪzɪk]/ sustained[12] [eɪ]/ wound [uː]/ cardiac[13] **contraction** • active / passive / (in)voluntary[14] / ATP-induced [(j)uːs] **contraction** • isometric[15] [aɪsə-]/ isotonic[16] / twitch[17] **contraction** • rapid / spastic [æ]/ rhythmic [ɪ] / forceful[18] **contraction** • process / vigor [ˈvɪɡə]/ speed **of contraction** • wave / rate / coordination **of contraction** • **contracted** abdomen / bladder[19] / gallbladder [ɔː] • non- or a**contractile** • **contractile** tissue[20] / fiber [aɪ]/ element / force • ligamentous / muscle or muscular[21] **relaxation** • active / gradual [ˈɡrædʒʊəl]/ difficulties in motor **relaxation** • mental / biofeedback-assisted[22] / jaw [dʒɔː]/ pelvic floor[23] **relaxation** • **relaxation** training / response[24] / phase[25] [feɪz] • **relaxed** muscle / body posture[26] / patient / attitude • (smooth) [uː] muscle / (non)depolarizing muscle[27] **relaxant**

(i) Kontraktion, Zusammenziehen (ii) Schwindung
Relaxation, Entspannung, Erschlaffung[1] Schrumpfung, Verminderung[2] kontrahieren, zusammenziehen[3] entspannen, erschlaffen[4] Relaxans, entspannungsförderndes Mittel[5] kontraktionsfähig, kontraktil[6] Kontraktilität[7] Kontraktur[8] Sehnen[9] e. Kontraktion auslösen[10] Muskelkontraktion[11] anhaltende K., Dauerkontraktion[12] Herzkontraktion, Systole[13] (un)willkürl. K.[14] isometr. K.[15] isotonische K.[16] Muskelzuckung[17] starke Kontraktion[18] Schrumpfblase[19] kontraktiles Gewebe[20] Muskelerschlaffung, -entspannung[21] biofeedbackunterstützte Entspannung[22] Beckenbodenentspannung[23] Entspannungsreaktion[24] Entspannungsphase[25] entspannte/ lockere Körperhaltung[26] depolarisierendes Muskelrelaxans[27]　　　　　　　　1

---

flex *v clin & term*　　*syn* **bend** - bent - bent *v irr*, *sim* **bow**[1] [*vt* boʊ‖*vi* baʊ] *vt & vi*

to move a joint [dʒɔɪnt] in a way to decrease the angle [æŋɡl] between the two adjoining bones

flexion[2] *n term* • **flexible**[3] *adj* • **flexor**[4] *n* • **-flect** *comb* • **bow**[5] [baʊ] *n*

» Have the patient flex both wrists[6] [r] to 90 degrees. The hand was splinted[7] in 45° flexion. I can't bend down[8] to tie my shoes. In traumatic bowing [oʊ] the shaft of a bone is bent.

Use **to flex** your muscles • slightly [slaɪtli]/ partly / acutely [juː]/ fully / forward **flexed** • **to bend** down / over (forward)[9] / your knee • **bent**-knee sit-up exercise • ante**flect**[10] • **to bow** one's head[11] / down / to the audience [ɔː] • lateral / dorsal / forward / palmar[12] **flexion** • plantar[13] [æ]/ volar[12] [oʊ]/ (ab)normal **flexion** • angle of greatest[14] / forceful / full **flexion** • (gentle) [dʒ] active / passive **flexion** • degrees / loss / limitation[15] **of flexion** • **flexion** position / reflex[16] / crease[17] [kriːs] • **flexion** exercise / deformity / contracture[18] • **flexed** muscles / wrist / shoulders • **flexor** muscle[4] / tendon[19] / pulley[20] [ˈpʊli] • **flexor** spasm / weakness [iː] • toe / digital[21] [ɪdʒ]/ forearm[22] **flexors**

beugen, biegen, flektieren
beugen; neigen, senken, s. verneigen/ (ver)beugen[1] Flexio(n), Beugung[2] biegsam, elastisch[3] Beuger, Beugemuskel, Flexor[4] Verbeugung[5] Handgelenke[6] geschient[7] s. bücken[8] s. nach vorne beugen[9] anteflektieren, vor(wärts)neigen[10] d. Kopf senken/ neigen[11] Palmar-, Volarflexion[12] Plantarflexion[13] max. Beugewinkel[14] Beugungseinschränkung[15] Beuge(-Rückzieh)reflex[16] Beugefurche[17] Beugekontraktur[18] Beugesehne[19] Ringband (d. Beugeseite)[20] Fingerbeuger[21] Unterarmbeuger[22]　　　　　　2

---

extend [ɪkˈstend] *v clin & term*　　*syn* **stretch** [tʃ] *v*, *sim* **straighten**[1] [ˈstreɪtᵊn] *v clin*

(i) to straighten a limb, diminish the angle of flexion, or bring the distal segment of a limb in such a position that its axis is parallel with that of the proximal part
(ii) to reach or broaden

outstretched[2] *adj* • **stretching** *n* • **stretch**[3] *n* • **straight**[4] *adj*
extension[5] *n term* • **hyperextension**[6] *n* • **extensor**[7] *n* → U141-3

» The straight leg-raising [eɪ] test[8] is performed by lifting the extended leg of the supine[9] [aɪ] patient. Arch[10] [ɑːrtʃ] your back and try to stretch a little more. Examine the affected arm at full stretch. Reduction[11] [ʌ] of greenstick fractures is achieved [tʃ] by straightening [eɪ] the arm into normal alignment [aɪ].

Use **to extend** both arms • **extended** anteriorly [ɪə]/ outward / 30 degrees • **to stretch** your body / the arms / (yourself) out / a muscle • muscle **stretch** reflex[12] • **stretch** marks[13] / receptor[14] [se]/ reflex[12] [iː] • **stretch** injury / test • muscle / passive / active **stretching** • excessive or undue[15] **stretching** • **stretching** exercises[16] • **to straighten** up[17] / your back • **to straighten** your arm / out a curvature[18] [ɜː] • **to stand**[19]/remain **straight** • active finger / neck **extension** • knee / joint / full **extension** • **extension** splint[20] • **hyperextension** exercise / injury[21]

(i) (aus)strecken
(ii) sich erstrecken/ ausdehnen (bis)
strecken, (sich) aufrichten, gerade machen[1] ausgestreckt, -gebreitet[2] Dehnen, Strecken[3] gerade[4] Streckung, Extension[5] Hyperextension, Überstreckung[6] Strecker, Extensor[7] Lasègue-Test[8] auf d. Rücken liegend[9] krümmen[10] Reposition[11] (Muskel)dehnungsreflex[12] Schwangerschaftsstreifen[13] Dehnungsrezeptor[14] Überdehnung, übermäßige D.[15] Dehnungsübungen[16] s. aufrichten[17] begradigen[18] gerade stehen[19] Extensionsschiene[20] Überstreckungsverletzung[21]　　　3

BODY STRUCTURES & FUNCTIONS — Musculoskeletal Function

agonist n term　　rel **antagonist**[1] [æntǽgənɪst], **synergist**[2] [sɪnɚdʒɪst] n term

(i) muscle in a state of contraction opposed by its antagonist (ii) a drug with a specific effect **(ant)agonistic**[3] adj term • **antagonism**[4] n • **synerg(ist)ic**[5] adj → U92-6 **synergy**[6] n term • **synergism**[7] n • **asynergy**[8] n • **dyssynergia**[8] [dɪsɪnɜːrdʒ(ɪ)ə] n

» Rigidity [dʒɪ] involved both the agonist and antagonist muscles of the extremity. This is due to the antagonistic action of the pronator teres [tɪəːiːz] on the biceps [aɪs] and supinator. The coordination of activity by agonists, antagonists, synergists, and fixators is regulated by a three-level hierarchy [aɪ] of motor control.

Use **agonist** properties • **agonist(ic)** muscle • physiologic / metabolic / adrenergic [ɜː]/ competitive[9] **antagonist** • **antagonistic** reflexes [iː]/ action • **antagonist(ic)** muscle[1] • **synergistic** muscles • flexor-extensor[10] **synergy**

Agonist
Antagonist, Gegenspieler[1] Synergist[2] (ant)agonistisch[3] Antagonismus, gegensinnige Wirkung[4] synergistisch[5] Synergie, Zusammenwirken[6] Synergismus[7] A-, Dyssynergie, Koordinationsstörung[8] kompetitiver Antagonist[9] Zusammenspiel zwischen Beuger u. Strecker[10]

4

---

twitch [twɪtʃ] v & n clin　　rel **fasciculation**[1], **tic**[2] n term → U64-7, U113-1, 4f

(v) to make an uncontrolled, jerky[3] [dʒɜːrki] motion, esp. due to a muscle contraction caused by a nervous [ɜː] condition

fast-twitch[4] adj term • **twitching** adj & n • **tic-like**[3] adj • **fascicular**[5] [sɪ] adj

» Isolated small twitches were felt clinically and recorded by EMG[6]. A fasciculation is a visible or palpable twitch within a single muscle due to the spontaneous [eɪ] discharge[7] of one motor unit. If tics are mild, anxiolytic [ɪ] agents may be used to reduce tic frequency [iː].

Use **twitch** tension / response • **twitching** muscles / movements • muscle or muscular[8] / fascicular[1] / facial[9] [eɪʃ]/ eyelid[10] **twitching** • motor / convulsive[9] [ʌ]/ facial[9] / spasmodic **tic** • **tic** frequency / intensity / disorder • douloureux[11] • **fast-twitch** fibers[12] [aɪ] • **tic-like** or jerky movements • facial / lingual / muscle / repetitive [e] **fasciculation** • **fasciculation** potentials[13] • **fascicular** block[14] / twitchings[1]

zucken; Zuckung
Faszikulation, faszikuläre Zuckungen[1] Muskelzucken, (nervöses) Zucken, Tic(k)[2] ruckartig[3] schnell zuckend[4] faszikulär[5] Elektromyografie[6] Entladung[7] Muskelzuckung(en)[8] Tic convulsif, Fazialiskrämpfe[9] Lidkrampf, Blepharospasmus[10] Trigeminusneuralgie[11] FT-, schnell zuckende Fasern[12] Faszikulationspotentiale[13] Faszikelblock[14]

5

---

abduct [æbdʌkt] v term　　rel **spread**[1] - spread - spread [e] v irr clin　　opposite **adduct**[2] [ədʌkt] v term

move away from the median [iː] plane of the body (limbs) or of the hand or foot (digits)

abduction[3] [æbdʌkʃən] n term • **adduction**[4] n • **abductor**[5] n • **adductor**[6] n

» In the lithotomy position[7] the thighs [θaɪz] are flexed and abducted. Spread the patient's nostrils apart using the nasal [eɪ] speculum. There is evidence of adduction of the vocal cords[8] on inspiration. The pupil constricted[9] on attempted adduction.

Use **to abduct** slightly / moderately / passively / to 90° • to be held / with the arms[10] **abducted** • radial [eɪ]/ ulnar [ʌ]/ full / forced **abduction** • decreased [iː]/ hip / shoulder **abduction** • **abduction** exercises / plaster cast[11] • **abduction** splint[12] / limitation[13] • **to spread one's** arms / fingers[14] / legs • **to spread** the ribs apart • forefoot / toe / thumb [θʌm] **adduction** • **adduction** position / contracture[15] • **adductor** muscle of the thumb / hallucis tendon • **adductor** magnus[16] / reflex[17] / spasm[18]

abduzieren, abspreizen, seitwärts wegführen
spreizen, ausbreiten[1] heranführen, adduzieren[2] Abduktion, Abspreizung[3] Adduktion, seitl. Heranführen[4] Abzieh-, Abspreizmuskel, Abduktor[5] Adduktor, Anzieher[6] Steinschnittlage[7] Stimmbänder[8] verengte sich[9] m. ausgebreiteten Armen[10] Abduktionsgips[11] Abduktionsschiene[12] Abduktionshemmung, -einschränkung[13] die Finger spreizen[14] Adduktionskontraktur[15] M. adductor magnus[16] Adduktorenreflex[17] Adduktorenspasmus[18]

6

---

rotation [eɪʃ] n　　rel **circumduction**[1] [sɜːrkəmdʌkʃən] n term, **twist**[2] v & n clin

combination of all movements of a ball-and-socket joint[3]

rotate[4] v term • **rota(to)ry, rotational**[5] adj • **circumduct**[6] v • **untwist**[7] v

» There is pain on the inner aspect of the thigh with abduction, extension, and internal rotation of the knee. The twist was 360 degrees. Epiphyseal [ɪ] fractures usually occur as a result of severe twisting, pulling or shaking [eɪ] of a child's limbs [lɪmz].

Use to control/avoid **rotation** • external / inward **rotation** • (counter)clockwise[8] [aʊ]/ reversed[9] [ɜː] **rotation** • rapid or brisk / (in)complete **rotation** • forearm / head / ocular **rotation** • mal/ de/ counter**rotation** • **to twist one's** ankle[10] / neck • **rotational** (mal)alignment[11] [aɪ]/ forces / instability[12] • **rotational** control / deformity / osteotomy[13] • **rota(to)ry** motion[14] • subluxation [ʌ]/ chair[15] • **twisting** forces[16] / injury[17] / motion[14]

Rotation, Drehung
Zirkumduktion, Kreisbewegung[1] torquieren, (ver)drehen; Verdrehung, Torsion[2] Kugelgelenk[3] (sich) drehen, rotieren[4] Rotations-, Dreh-[5] kreisen[6] detorquieren[7] D. gegen d. Uhrzeigersinn[8] Gegendrehung[9] s. d. Knöchel verstauchen[10] Rotationsfehlstellung[11] Rotationsinstabilität[12] Drehosteotomie[13] Drehbewegung[14] Drehsessel[15] Torsionskräfte[16] Torsionsverletzung[17]

7

---

eversion [ɪvɜːrʒən] n term　　opposite **inversion**[1] [ɪnvɜːrʒən] n term

turning laterally or outward, e.g. the sole [soʊl] of the foot or the eyelids

evert[2] v term • **invert**[3] v • **-version** [ɜː] comb

» Occult [ʌ] lesions [iːʒ] can be demonstrated by x-rays under eversion or inversion stress. The foot was slightly inverted to relax the tension on the deltoid ligament [ɪ].

Use forced / gentle / excessive / subtalar [eɪ] **eversion** • **eversion** position / tape strapping[4] / fracture[5] • forced **inversion** • **inversion of the** (hind)foot [aɪ]/ heel [iː]/ subtalar joint • **inversion** stress / ankle sprain[6] [eɪ]/ range • **inversion** instability / deformity • **everted** foot / lid[7] / umbilicus • femoral [e] ante[8]/ uterine[9] [juː] retro**version**

Eversion, Auswärtsdrehung, Ausstülpung
Inversion, Einwärtsdrehung, Einstülpung[1] auswärtsdrehen[2] einwärtsdrehen[3] Eversionstapeverband[4] Eversionsfraktur[5] Inversionsverstauchung d. Knöchels[6] Augenlidektropium[7] Antetorsion[8] Rückwärtsneigung d. Gebärmutter, Retroversio uteri[9]

8

Musculoskeletal Function · BODY STRUCTURES & FUNCTIONS

supination [suːpɪneɪʃən] *n term* *opposite* **pronation**¹ [proʊneɪʃən] *n term*

(i) rotation of the forearm so that the palm [pɑːm] faces upward
(ii) elevation of the medial [iː] edge of the foot

supinate² *v term* • **pronate**³ *v* • **pronator**⁴ *n* • **supine**⁵ [aɪ] *adj* • **prone**⁶ *adj*

» Reduction was accomplished by forced supination of the forearm. The more proximal the amputation, the less pronation and supination is possible. The forearm was pronated and the elbow extended. Immobilize the wrist in pronation. Have the patient pronate the thumb.

Use to be in / full / relative / forearm⁷ **supination** • to permit/limit or restrict⁸/preclude **pronation** • limited / repetitive / rhythmic [ɪ]/ complete **pronation** • to **supinate** against resistance • **supinator** longus reflex⁹ • **pronator** teres¹⁰ / quadratus [eɪ] (muscle) • **supine** position or posture¹¹ / X-rays) • **supine** exercise / patient / hypotension • **prone** sleeping position /-sleeping infants

(i) Supination
(ii) Auswärtsdrehung des Fußes

Pronation; Einwärtsdrehung/ Senkung d. inneren Fußrandes¹ supinieren, auswärtsdrehen² pronieren, einwärtsdrehen³ Pronator, M. pronator⁴ supiniert, in Rückenlage⁵ proniert, in Bauchlage⁶ Unterarmsupination⁷ die Pronation einschränken⁸ Radiusperiostreflex⁹ M. pronator teres¹⁰ Rückenlage¹¹

9

---

muscle *or* **muscular tone** [toʊn] *n* *syn* **tonus** [toʊnəs] *n term*
rel **tension**¹ [tenʃən] *n*, **turgor**² [tɜːrgɚ] *n term*

continuous activity of muscles which helps maintain body posture, venous [iː] return, etc.

tonic³ *adj & n term* • **tonicity**⁴ *n* • **tense**⁵ *adj* • **tensile**⁶ *adj* • **tono-**, **-tonic** *comb*

» The sphincter maintains urethral [iː] closure [oʊʒ] by its passive tone. Neuropathy is also responsible for the loss of tone⁷ of intrinsic foot muscles. The bright red spot which appears first spreads to form a tense, glistening⁸ [ɪs], hot area.

Use skeletal / abdominal / uterine [juː] **muscle tone** • smooth [uː]/ myogenic [maɪədʒenɪk]/ decreased⁹ **muscle tone** • to lose/regain/restore **tone** • increase in¹⁰ / poor / normal / passive **tone** • **tonic** spasm /-clonic seizure¹¹ [siːʒɚ] • hypo [haɪpoʊ]/ hyper/ iso**tonic** [aɪ] • sphincter / flexor / postural / vascular¹² / vesical / rectal / resting¹³ **tone** • anal [eɪ] **tonus** • **tono**meter¹⁴ • **to tense** up¹⁵ • **tense** patient / back¹⁶ / abdomen • (chronic) muscle • nervous¹⁷ [ɜː]/ skin **tension** • **tension** headache¹⁸ • **tensile** strength¹⁹

Muskeltonus

(An)spannung¹ Turgor, Gewebespannung² tonisch, tonisierend; Tonikum, Stärkungsmittel³ Tonizität, Spannungszustand⁴ gespannt, straff; verkrampft, nervös⁵ dehnbar; Zug-⁶ Tonusverlust⁷ glänzend⁸ herabgesetzter Muskeltonus⁹ Tonuserhöhung¹⁰ tonisch-klonischer (Krampf)anfall¹¹ Gefäßtonus¹² Ruhetonus¹³ Tonometer, Druckmesser¹⁴ s. verkrampfen¹⁵ verspannter Rücken¹⁶ Nervenanspannung¹⁷ Spannungskopfschmerz¹⁸ Zugfestigkeit¹⁹

10

---

supple [sʌpl] *adj inf & clin* *sim* **pliable**¹ [plaɪəbl], **limber**² [lɪmbɚ] *adj clin*

(i) bending and stretching easily without tearing [eɚ]
(ii) not unduly³ [(j)uː] stiff or tense (esp. on palpation)

suppleness⁴ *n* • **pliability**⁵ *n* • **limber up**⁶ *v phr clin* → U1-13

» This exercise will keep your shoulders supple. Are you supple enough to reach your toes? The patient's neck is supple. The 1ˢᵗ heart [hɑːrt] sound may be palpable in patients with pliable valves [æ]. Go for frequent short walks to limber up your legs.

Use **supple** neck / foot / tissue [tɪʃ‖sjuː] • **supple** limbs⁷ [lɪmz]/ skin / mind⁸ • **pliable** skin⁹ / valves¹⁰ / vagina [dʒ]/ bladder wall • **limber** body

geschmeidig, elastisch, beweglich

biegsam, formbar¹ beweglich, gelenkig² übermäßig³ Geschmeidigkeit, Beweglichkeit⁴ Biegsamkeit, Geschmeidigkeit⁵ aufwärmen, Lockerungsübungen machen⁶ bewegliche Glieder⁷ reger Geist⁸ geschmeidige Haut⁹ nicht kalizifizierte Herzklappen¹⁰

11

---

flaccid [flæ(k)sɪd] *adj* *syn* **limp** [ɪ] *adj*, *sim* **flabby**¹ [æ], **floppy**² [flɒːpi] *adj inf*
rel **paralyzed**³ [pærəlaɪzd] *adj term* → U135-11

soft, weak [iː], not firm [ɜː] and lacking normal tone

flaccidity⁴ *n term* • **paralysis**⁵ [pəræləsɪs] *n* • **limpness**⁴ *n* • **flabbiness** *n*

» Upper motor neuron [n(j)ʊərɒːn] deficit was associated with lower limb numbness⁶ [ʌ], flaccid tone, and absent tendon reflexes⁷. In a paralyzed extremity, loss of vasomotor control leads to a lowered tone in the vascular bed. Pain may precede [siː] the onset of paralysis.

Use **flaccid** muscles / penis [iː]/ bladder / weakness / paralysis⁸ • to become/go⁹ **limp** • **limp** handshake¹⁰ / spell¹¹ • **paralyzed** muscle / limb / cord¹² • **paralyzed** diaphragm¹³ [daɪəfræm]/ child / by fear¹⁴ / facial [eɪʃ]/ muscular / sleep¹⁵ **paralysis** • **floppy** infant¹⁶ (syndrome) / valve [æ] syndrome¹⁷ / foot

Note: Do not confuse **limpness** with **limping**¹⁸ or a **limp**¹⁸.

schlaff, weich

wabbelig, schlaff¹ schlaff, schlapp² gelähmt, paralysiert³ Schlaffheit⁴ Lähmung, Paralyse⁵ Taubheit⁶ Sehnenreflexe⁷ schlaffe Lähmung⁸ ohnmächtig werden⁹ schlaffer Händedruck¹⁰ Synkope¹¹ Stimmlippenlähmung¹² Zwerchfelllähmung¹³ vor Angst wie gelähmt¹⁴ Schlaflähmung¹⁵ extrem schlaffes/ hypotones Kind, floppy infant¹⁶ Mitralklappenprolaps-, Barlow-Syndrom¹⁷ Hinken, Humpeln¹⁸

12

muscle strength [mʌsl strenkθ] n   syn muscle power [pauɚ] n
opposite muscle weakness[1] [iː] n

ability of muscles to resist or produce physical [fɪzɪkᵊl] force
strengthen[2] v • strengthening[3] adj & n • strong[4] adj • weaken[5] v • weak[6] adj
» Continue treatment until muscle strength and full joint motion are recovered[7] [ʌ]. Abdominal conditioning[8] and spinal muscle strengthening exercises are prescribed [aɪ] when pain subsides[9] [aɪ]. Profound [au] magnesium [iː] depletion [iːʃ] can cause acute muscle weakness.
Use to build or improve[10]/maintain/lose muscle strength • to test/recover/(re)gain muscle strength • abdominal / biceps [aɪs]/ expiratory muscle strength • diminished / improved / momentary loss of[11] muscle strength • (proximal) leg / hand grip or grasp[12] / upper extremity strength • full / half / maximal[13] / normal strength • asymmetric leg / upper arm / focal (motor) weakness • diffuse / (bi)facial / episodic weakness • strengthening exercise[14] • muscle mass / stamina[15] [æ]/ action potential[16]

Muskelkraft
Muskelschwäche[1] stärken, kräftigen[2] stärkend, Kräftigungs-; Kräftigung, Stärkung[3] stark, kräftig[4] (ab)schwachen; schwächer w., erlahmen[5] empfindlich, schwach[6] wiederhergestellt[7] Bauchmuskeltraining[8] nachlässt[9] die Muskelkraft verbessern[10] vorübergehender Verlust d. Muskelkraft[11] Greifkraft[12] Maximalkraft[13] Kräftigungsübung[14] Muskelausdauer[15] Muskelaktionspotential[16]

13

ossification [ɒsɪfɪkeɪʃᵊn] n term   rel calcification[1] [kælsɪfɪkeɪʃᵊn] n term
bone formation which in long bones occurs by the replacement of calcified cartilage [kɑːrtᵊlɪdʒ] at the epiphysial plate where osteoblasts form bone trabeculae[2] [-iː]
ossified[3] adj term • osseo-, osteo- comb → U106-15
(de)calcify[4] v • calcific adj • (de)calcification[5] n
» Femoral [e] head ossification is usually present by 6 months of age. Many of the pertinent [ɜː] structures in the elbow ossify late in childhood. Children with rickets[6] have defective calcification of growing bone and hypertrophy of the epiphyseal [ɪ] cartilages.
Use en(do)chondral[7] [ɒː] paravertebral / delayed [eɪ] ossification • ossification center[8] • central / peripheral / articular cartilage / ectopic calcification • soft tissue / subcutaneous [eɪ] calcification • degenerative [dʒe] / atherosclerotic[9] / metastatic[10] calcification • calcific density / deposits[11] / tendinitis [aɪ] • calcified cartilage[12] / woven[13] [ou] bone • osteoblast[14] /clast[15] /genesis[16] /lytic [ɪ] /periosteal • osteoarthrosis /chondritis /porosis /tomy /sclerosis • osseointegration[17]

Ossifikation, Verknöcherung
Kalzifikation, Verkalkung, Kalkeinlagerung[1] Knochenbälkchen, Trabeculae[2] verknöchert, ossifiziert[3] verkalken, Kalk ablagern, kalzifizieren[4] Entkalkung, Dekalzifizierung[5] Rachitis[6] enchondrale Ossifikation[7] Ossifikationskern[8] Arterienverkalkung, Arteriosklerose[9] Calcinosis metastatica[10] Kalkablagerungen[11] verkalkter/ kalzifizierter Knorpel[12] verkalkter Geflechtknochen[13] Osteoblast, Knochenbildungszelle[14] Osteoklast, Knochenfresszelle[15] Knochenbildung, Osteogenese[16] Osseointegration[17]

14

stability [stəbɪləti] n   opposite instability[1] n
ability to resist change and remain constant despite disturbing [ɜː] influences, esp.
(de)stabilize[2] [eɪ] v term • (de)stabilization[3] n • (un)stable[4] [eɪ] adj
» Dislocations require immediate reduction [ʌ], followed by tests for stability and tendon function. Adjustable [dʒʌ] supports help reduce deformities, soft tissue contracture, or instability of the ligaments. Both arms need to be held in a stable position. Muscles that stabilize the arm position [ɪʃ] are termed fixators.
Use to provide[5]/maintain [eɪ] /restore stability • postural / clinical / psychosocial [saɪkə-] stability • physical [ɪ]/ joint[6] [dʒɔɪnt]/ chest [tʃ] wall[7] / vasomotor [eɪ] instability • cervical spine / surgical[8] [ɜː] / stabilization • stable fracture[9] / weight [weɪt] • unstable joint[10] / ankle injury / tendon / dislocation[11] / gait[12] [geɪt]

Stabilität, Festigkeit
Instabilität[1] stabilisieren[2] Stabilisierung[3] (in)stabil[4] für Stabilität sorgen[5] Gelenkinstabilität[6] Thoraxinstabilität[7] operative Stabilisierung[8] stabile Fraktur[9] instabiles Gelenk[10] instabile Luxation[11] unsicherer Gang[12]

15

elasticity [iːlæstɪsəti] n   sim resilience or resiliency[1] [rɪzɪliənˈsi] n
rel friability[2] [fraɪəbɪləti], brittleness[2] [ɪ], fragility[2] [frədʒɪləti] n
physical and physiologic quality (e.g. of muscles or bones) that enables tissues to yield[3] [jiːld] to passive physical stretch or pressure and subsequently [ʌ] return to their original shape
elastic[4] adj • elastin[5] n • resilient[4] adj • brittle[5] adj • fragile[6] adj • friable[6] adj
» Elasticity is lost with age. The nails are lusterless[7] [ʌ], brittle, and the substance of the nail is friable. The intervertebral disks[8] are elastic in youth and allow the bony vertebrae to move easily upon each other. Due to the resiliency of the proximal femur [iː] a fracture in this region can only occur [ɜː] with severe trauma [ɒː].
Use to lose/reduce/have good elasticity • skin / tissue elasticity • long-lasting[9] resiliency • elastic fibers[10] [aɪ] / tissue[11] / properties / recoil of the lung[12] / elastic bandage[13] [-ɪdʒ]/ stockings[14] • brittle bones / nails[15] / diabetes[16] [iː]

Elastizität, Biegsamkeit
Spannkraft, Elastizität[1] Brüchigkeit, Sprödigkeit[2] nachgeben[3] elastisch[4] Elastin[5] brüchig, zerbrechlich, spröde[6] glanzlos[7] Zwischenwirbel-, Bandscheiben[8] Dauerelastizität[9] elastische Fasern[10] elast. Bindegewebe[11] Lungenwiderstand[12] elastische(r) Binde/ Verband[13] Gummi-, Stützstrümpfe[14] brüchige Nägel[15] Brittle Diabetes, instabiler juveniler Diabetes (mellitus)[16]

16

Musculoskeletal Function BODY STRUCTURES & FUNCTIONS **129**

flexibility n   opposite **inflexibility¹, rigidity¹** [dʒɪ] n term, **stiffness¹** n clin

ability to bend and move one's body without undue restrictions or pain

(**in**)**flexible²** adj • **rigid³** [rɪdʒɪd] adj • **flexure⁴** [flekʃɚ] n term
stiff adj clin • **stiffen⁵** [stɪfᵊn] v

» *Joint flexibility and motor function [ʌ] were regularly assessed. The rigidity of cata-lepsy may be overcome by slight external force but returns at once. This leads to local pain, stiffness, and restricted activity.*

Use to provide/improve/promote/require **flexibility** • normal / joint / waxy⁶ / mental **flexibility** • **flexible** flatfoot⁷ / endoscope • **inflexible** hamstrings⁸ • **flexible** rib cage [keɪdʒ]/ deformity • **rigid** posture [pɒːstʃɚ]/ erection / cervical [sɜːr-] collar⁹ • **rigidly** extended arm • nuchal¹⁰ [n(j)uːkᵊl]/ spastic / abdominal / board-like¹¹ [ɔː]/ penile [iː] **rigidity** • morning¹² / muscle / neck¹⁰ **stiffness** • hand / back / sensation of¹³ **stiffness** • progressive **stiffening**

Flexibilität, Beweglichkeit, Biegsamkeit
Starrheit, Steifigkeit, Steifheit¹ flexibel, beweglich, biegsam² steif, starr, rigid³ Biegung, Krümmung, Flexur⁴ steif werden, versteifen⁵ wachsartige Biegsamkeit, Flexibilitas cerea⁶ kindl. Knick-Senkfuß⁷ unbewegliche/ steife Beinbeuger⁸ HWS-Stützkrawatte⁹ Nackensteifigkeit¹⁰ bretthartes Abdomen¹¹ Morgensteifigkeit¹² Steifigkeitsgefühl¹³

17

range of motion [reɪndʒ əʊv moʊʃᵊn] n term, abbr **ROM**
                         syn **range of movement** [muːvmənt] n term

maximum extent (measured in degrees of a circle) to which a joint can be extended or flexed

» *When all pain has resolved¹, ROM exercises are added to improve flexibility. A mild to moderate increase in ROM of the knee can be expected. If stable [eɪ] fixation is obtained [eɪ], active ROM exercises can be started at 5-7 days postoperatively.*

Use to assess/control/restrict or curtail² [eɪ] /preserve [ɜː] or maintain **ROM** • to re-establish or recover/augment³ **ROM** • functional / joint⁴ / full **ROM** • abnormal / loss of **ROM** • gentle [dʒe] **ROM** exercises • active⁵ / passive⁶ **ROM** • normal / restricted or limited **ROM** • joint⁷ / body / leg / hip / lumbar [ʌ] spine⁸ [aɪ] **motion** • right ventricular wall / rotatory⁹ / slight [aɪ] **motion** • extremes [iː] of / pain-free / pain aggravated by¹⁰ **motion** • loss of / restriction or limitation of¹¹ **motion** • **range** of knee [niː] motion¹²

Bewegungsausmaß
abgeklungen¹ d. Bewegungsausmaß einschränken² das Bewegungsausmaß vergrößern/ steigern³ Bewegungsausmaß im Gelenk⁴ aktives B.⁵ passives B.⁶ Gelenkbewegung⁷ Bewegung d. Lendenwirbelsäule⁸ Drehbewegung, Rotation⁹ Bewegungsschmerz¹⁰ Bewegungseinschränkung¹¹ Bewegungsausmaß im Kniegelenk¹²

18

motor coordination [koʊɔːrdɪneɪʃᵊn] n term
                         rel **motor dexterity¹** [deksterəti] n term

harmonious coworking of the motor apparatus [eɪ], esp. in the execution of purposeful [ɜː] movements²

(**un/ well-**)**coordinated³** adj • **coordinate⁴** v • **incoordination⁵** n term

» *Motor dysfunction may result from weakness, imbalance, and other disturbances [ɜː] in the initiation or coordination of movement. Absorption of nutrients⁶ [uː] in the GI tract⁷ also depends on the deeper muscular layers for the coordinated propulsion [ʌ] of food through the lumen. Upper motor neuron lesions cause incoordination that is manifest as slow, coarse [ɔː] movements⁸. Neurologic abnormalities of fine motor coordination are common.*

Use poor / lack of⁵ / impaired⁵ [eɚ]/ fine⁹ / visual-**motor coordination** • eye-hand¹⁰ / proper¹¹ **coordination** • **coordinated** reflexes¹² • motor **incoordination** • manual¹³ / loss of **dexterity** • **uncoordinated** eye movements / contractions

Bewegungskoordination
motorische Geschicklichkeit¹ zielgerichtete Bewegungen² gut koordiniert³ koordinieren, aufeinander abstimmen⁴ Inkoordination, fehlende K., Koordinationsstörung⁵ Nährstoffe⁶ Verdauungstrakt⁷ unkoordinierte Bewegungen⁸ Feinkoordination, feinmotor. K.⁹ Auge-Hand-K.¹⁰ richtige Koordination¹¹ koordinierte Reflexe¹² manuelle Geschicklichkeit¹³

19

fine motor skills n term   opposite **gross** [groʊs] **motor skills¹** n term

precisely [aɪ] coordinated movements, e.g. writing, cutting, sewing² [oʊ], visual tracing [eɪs]

» *Changes in gross motor skills have a great impact on the child's exploration of the environment [aɪ]. These neurons are involved in the execution [juːʃ] of learned, fine movements. Is there any difficulty with eating and fine facial [eɪʃ] movements?*

Use **fine** coordination / motor control / dexterity³ • **fine** movements / twitching⁴ [ɪ]/ tremor⁵ • **gross** deformity⁶ / facial asymmetry / instability / hematuria⁷ • **motor** abilities⁸ / activity / behavior⁹ [eɪ]/ fiber [aɪ]/ neuron¹⁰ • **motor** pathways¹¹ / control / power / abnormality • **motor** function¹² [ʌ]/ development¹³ / deficit / restlessness¹⁴ / seizure [siːʒɚ] • **motor** dysphagia [dɪsfeɪdʒ(ɪ)ə]/ axon / cortex¹⁵ / end plate¹⁶

Feinmotorik
Grobmotorik¹ Nähen² feinmotor. Geschicklichkeit³ leichtes Zucken⁴ feinschlägiger Tremor⁵ schwere Fehlbildung⁶ Makrohämaturie⁷ motor. Fähigkeiten⁸ motor. Verhalten⁹ Motoneuron¹⁰ motor. (Nerven)bahnen¹¹ Motorik¹² motor. Entwicklung¹³ motor. Unruhe¹⁴ Motorkortex, motor. Rinde(nfeld)¹⁵ motor. Endplatte¹⁶

20

Unit 32 The Heart
Related Units: 33 Cardiac Function, 36 Blood & Lymph Circulation, 43 Lungs, 110 Cardiovascular Signs & Symptoms

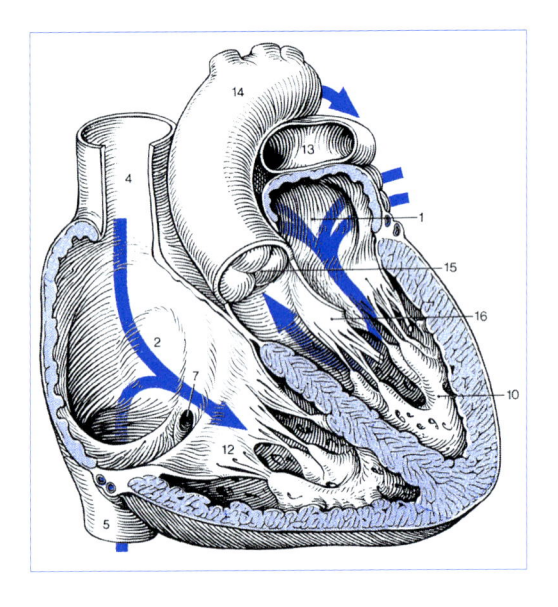

The heart:
left atrium (**1**), right atrium (**2**),
superior vena cava (**4**), inferior vena cava (**5**),
coronary sinus (**7**), trabeculae carneae (**10**),
anterior papillary muscle (**11**), tricuspid valve (**12**),
pulmonary trunk (**13**), aorta (**14**), aortic valve (**15**),
mitral valve (**16**)

heart [hɑːrt] *n*   *syn* **cor** *n term, gen* **cordis,** *rel* **precordium**[1] *n term*

(i) hollow muscular organ that is divided into four chambers which receive the blood from the veins and pump it into the arteries
(ii) in genE, a person's character, emotions and feelings, courage, or the central, most important part

heartache[2] [-eɪk] *n clin* • **cordial**[3] *adj* • **precordial** *adj term* • **heartburn**[4] [ɜː] *n*

» Your heart sounds fine. The heart is more centrally placed in the chest in newborns. I have a weak [iː] heart, doctor. Is the heart beating? The chest wall is often the source of hemorrhage [-ɪdʒ], but the lung, heart, pericardium, and great vessels account for 15-25% of cases.

Use to examine/listen to/supply[5] [aɪ]/innervate/compress **the heart** • right / left / fetal [iː]/ large / artificial[6] [ɪʃ] **heart** • **palpitating** *or* **thumping** [ʌ] *or* **pounding**[7] [aʊ] **heart** • **boot**-shaped[8] [uː] **heart** • **donor**[9] [oʊ]/ normal-sized [saɪzd]/ transplanted **heart** • **brave** [eɪ]/ **passionate** / **faithful** [eɪ] **heart** • **heart** muscle [mʌsl]/ function / action[10] / beat[11] [iː]/ **heart**-sick / rate[12] [eɪ]/ sounds[13] [aʊ]/ size • **heart** disease [iː]/ murmur[14] [ɜː]/ attack[15] • **heart** failure[16] / block / surgery • **heart**-lung machine[17] • **precordial** lead[18] [iː]/ chest pain / thump[19] [ʌ]

heartless *adj*   opposite **kind-hearted**[1], **hearty**[2], **heartfelt**[3] *adj*

to be lacking in feeling, pity[4], warmth, courage [kɜːrdʒ] or enthusiasm [uː]
heart-broken[5] *adj* • **heartening**[6] *adj* • **open-heartedness**[7] *n*

» How could he be so heartless as to leave his family when they needed him most. His wife was heartbroken when she heard the prognosis. A hearty breakfast would be better for your health. Ms. Morgan is a grim-faced but kind-hearted and very cooperative elderly spinster[8].

Use to open one's/lose one's/have no/take[9]/take sth. to/learn by[10] **heart** • at[11] / a change of[12] / with all my **heart** • open-/ light-[13]/ broken-/ faint-[14] [eɪ] **hearted** • half-/ hard-/ cold-**hearted** • kind-/ warm-/ light-**heartedness** • **heart**-sick /-rending[15] /-throb[16] • **heart**-shaped /-searching[17] /-warming • **hearty** appetite / meal[18] [iː]/ soup / health / voice / laugh [læf‖ *BE* lɑːf] • **heartfelt** thanks • **heart** of gold / of stone /-to-heart[19] / and soul • **heart-breaking** report

---

(i) **Herz, Cor, Cardia**
(ii) **Herz, (Mit)gefühl**
Präkordialgegend[1] Kummer[2] herzlich[3] Sodbrennen[4] das Herz versorgen[5] künstliches Herz, Kunstherz[6] (heftig) klopfendes Herz[7] Coeur en sabot, Holzschuhherz[8] Spenderherz[9] Herztätigkeit[10] Herzschlag[11] Herzfrequenz[12] Herztöne[13] Herzgeräusch[14] Herzanfall, -infarkt[15] Herzversagen[16] Herz-Lungen-Maschine[17] Brustwandableitung[18] präkordialer Faustschlag[19]

herz-, gefühllos, grausam
gutherzig[1] herzlich; herzhaft, kräftig[2] tief empfunden, herzlich[3] Mitleid, -gefühl[4] todunglücklich, untröstlich[5] ermutigend[6] Offenherzigkeit[7] unverheiratete ältere Frau[8] Mut fassen[9] auswendig lernen[10] i. Grunde d. Herzens[11] Gesinnungswechsel, Meinungsänderung[12] heiter, unbekümmert[13] zaghaft[14] herzzerreißend[15] Herzensbrecher[16] Gewissenserforschung[17] kräftige Mahlzeit[18] ganz offen[19]

The Heart — BODY STRUCTURES & FUNCTIONS

cardiac [kɑːrdɪæk] *adj term*
related to or acting on the heart
non/ intracardiac *adj term* • **card(io)-** *comb* • **-cardia(c)** *comb*
» Careful preoperative assessment of cardiac patients[1] undergoing noncardiac surgical procedures [siː] is of crucial [kruːʃᵊl] importance. The stroke syndrome[2] [ɪ] that can be clinically recognized as embolic is that of cardiac origin.
Use **cardiac** muscle / chamber[3] [tʃeɪmbɚ]/ valve[4] [æ]/ rate • **cardiac** rhythm [ɪ]/ cycle [saɪkl]/ contraction / output[5] • **cardiac** disease / arrest[6] / enlargement • **cardiac** silhouette[7] / failure[8] / massage [ɑː] • **cardiac** tamponade[9] [eɪ]/ enzymes [zaɪ]/ compression • catheter • **cardiac** pacemaker[10] [eɪ]/ work (load)[11] [oʊ]/ valvular disease or valvulopathy[12] • **noncardiac** chest pain / surgery • **cardio**gram /logist /megaly /vascular • **cardio**pulmonary bypass[13] /version /plegia[14] [pliːdʒ(ɪ)ə] • tachy[15] [tækɪ-]/ brady**cardia**

> Note: The term **cardia**[16] denotes the portion of the stomach at the esophageal opening, therefore **cardiac** and **cardio-** may also refer to the stomach.

kardial, Herz-
Herzpatienten[1] Schlaganfall, apoplekt. Insult[2] Herzkammer[3] Herzklappe[4] Herzminutenvolumen[5] Herz(-Kreislauf-)stillstand[6] Herzsilhouette[7] Herzversagen[8] Herz(beutel)-, Perikardtamponade[9] Herzschrittmacher[10] Herzarbeit[11] Herzklappenerkrankung[12] kardiopulmonaler Bypass[13] (künstl.) induzierter Herzstillstand, Kardioplegie[14] Tachykardie[15] Kardia, Mageneingang, Pars cardiaca ventriculi[16]

3

---

cardiac apex [eɪ] *n term* *syn* **apex cordis** *n, opposite* **base**[1] [beɪs] *n term*
rounded lower border of the heart formed by the left ventricle; usually located at the 5th intercostal space[2] (*abbr* ICS)
» In most patients, the left anterior descending [se] artery wraps [ræps] the apex of the heart. The murmur [ɜː] of aortic stenosis in the elderly is sometimes heard only at the cardiac apex. The opening snap[3] was heard best at the lower left sternal [ɜː] border and radiated [eɪ] to the base of the heart.
Use left/right ventricular / bladder / lung **apex** • **apex** beat[4] / murmur[5] / cardiogram[6]

Apex (cordis), Herzspitze
Herzbasis, Basis cordis[1] Zwischenrippen-, Interkostalraum[2] Öffnungston[3] Herzspitzenstoß[4] Herzspitzengeräusch[5] Apexkardiogramm[6]

4

---

endocardium *n term* *rel* **pericardium**[1], **epicardium**[2] *n term, pl* **-cardia**
innermost layer of endothelium which lines[3] the walls of the heart chambers [tʃeɪmbɚz]
endocardial *adj term* • **pericardial** *adj* • **pericard-**, **endocard-** *comb*
» The depolarization wavefronts[4] then spread [e] through the ventricular wall, from endocardium to epicardium, triggering ventricular contraction. In patients with small effusions [juː] the presence of pericardial fluid is recorded by transthoracic [-æsɪk] echocardiography as a relatively echo-free [k] space between the posterior pericardium and left ventricular epicardium.
Use ventricular / mural [jʊ]/ infarcted **endocardium** • **endocardial** inflammation[5] [-eɪʃᵊn]/ fibrosis / fibroelastosis[6] [aɪ] • **endocardial** cushion [ʊ] defect[7] • sub**endocardial** • **endocardi**tis[5] [aɪ] • parietal [aɪə]/ posterior [ɪɚ]/ engorged[8] [-gɔːrdʒd] **pericardium** • thickened / constricting / inelastic **pericardium** • ventricular **epicardium** • **pericard**itis /iotomy /iectomy[9] /iocentesis[10] [iː] • **pericardial** sac[1] / space / fluid / effusion[11] [juː] • **pericardial** friction rub[12] [ʌ]/ tamponade[13] [eɪ]/ window[14] • **epicardial** vessels / coronary arteries / layer [eɪ]/ electrodes

Endokard, Endocardium, Herzinnenhaut
Perikard, Herzbeutel[1] Epikard, viszerales Blatt d. Perikards[2] ausgekleidet[3] Depolarisationswelle(nfront)[4] Endokarditis[5] Endokardfibroelastose[6] Endokardkissendefekt[7] prall gefülltes Perikard[8] Perikardektomie, operative Entfernung d. Perikards[9] Perikardpunktion[10] Perikarderguss[11] perikardiales Reibegeräusch[12] Herzbeutel-, Perikardtamponade[13] Perikardfenster[14]

5

---

myocardium [maɪoʊ-] *n term* *syn* **heart** or **cardiac muscle** [mʌsl] *n clin*
middle layer of the heart consisting of a network of contractile (striated[1] [aɪeɪ]) muscle fibers
(non/ post/ trans)myocardial *adj term* • **myocard-** *comb*
» The bundles [ʌ] of myocardial fibers which function to contract the heart are spiral-shaped [aɪ]. The increase in the adrenergic [-ɜːrdʒɪk] nerve impulses to the myocardium, the increased concentration of circulating catecholamines [koʊ], and the tachycardia [k] that all occur during exercise combine to augment the contractile state of the myocardium.
Use to oxygenate[2]/involve/infiltrate/extend into **the myocardium** • ventricular / functioning / contracting **myocardium** • viable [aɪ]/ infarcted / ischemic [ɪskiː-] **myocardium** • hypertrophied / damaged[3] **myocardium** • jeopardized[4] [dʒep-]/ inflamed [eɪ]/ failing [eɪ] **myocardium** • **myocardial** muscle damage[5] / failure / infarct(ion)[6] (*abbr* MI) • **myocardial** perfusion [juː]/ rupture[7] [rʌptʃɚ] • **myocardial** revascularization[8] / scintigraphy[9] • **myocard**iopathy[10] /itis /iograph

Myokard, Myocardium, Herzmuskel
gestreift[1] d. Herzmuskel m. Sauerstoff versorgen[2] geschädigter Herzmuskel[3] gefährdetes Herzmuskelgewebe[4] Myokardschädigung[5] Myokard-, Herzinfarkt[6] Herzmuskelriss[7] Myokardrevaskularisation[8] Myokardszintigrafie[9] Kardiomyopathie[10]

6

BODY STRUCTURES & FUNCTIONS

atrium [eɪ] **(cordis)** n term, pl **atria**   syn **atrial chamber** [tʃeɪmbɚ] n, rel **auricle**[1] [ɔːrɪkl] n term

one of the two upper chambers of the right and the left heart which receives blood from the vena [iː] cava [eɪ] (right) and the pulmonary [u‖ʌ] veins [eɪ] (left) and is emptied into the corresponding ventricle during diastole [daɪæstəli]

atrial[2] [eɪ] adj term • **atrio-** comb • **auricular**[2] adj • **auriculo-** comb

» The atrioventricular valves prevent reflux of blood into the atria during ventricular systole. The only estimate of atrial filling pressure we have is the central venous (right atrial) pressure.

Use right (abbr RA)/ left (abbr LA)/ dilated [aɪ]/ thin-walled **atrium** • **atrial** wall / pressure / contraction[3] / systole [sɪstəli]/ rate • **atrial** enlargement / fibrillation[4] [ɪ‖aɪ] (abbr AF)/ flutter[5] [ʌ]/ tachycardia [k] • **atrial** septal defect[6] (abbr ASD)/ gallop / premature beats[7] • **atrioventricular** septum / orifice / valve[8] [æ]/ node[9] [oʊ]/ bundle[10] [ʌ]/ groove[11] [uː] • **auriculo**venous [iː] pulse [ʌ] / ventricular rhythm[12] [rɪðᵊm]

Note: The term **auricle** was formerly also used as a synonym for **atrium**, above all in BE.

ventricle (of the heart) n term   syn **heart chamber** n clin

one of the two lower chambers in the right and the left heart that receives blood from the atrium and pumps it into the pulmonary artery (right) and the aorta [eɪ] (left), respectively

ventricular[1] adj term • **ventriculo-** comb

» In infants, severe valvular stenosis may be associated with a poorly developed right ventricle. Manual chest compression during CPR[2] causes raised [eɪ] pressure in the left ventricle with resultant forward flow of blood across the aortic [eɪ] valve.

Use right / left / cerebral **ventricle** • **ventricular** apex [eɪ]/ wall / beat[3] / volume[4] / rhythm • **ventricular** systole[3] / ejection [iːdʒekʃᵊn] fraction[5] • **ventricular** dysfunction / tachycardia[6] / gallop • **ventricular** hypertrophy [haɪpɜːr-]/ extrasystole • **ventricular** fibrillation[7] [ɪ‖aɪ] (abbr VF)/ septal defect[8] (abbr VSD) • **ventriculo**atrial shunt [ʌ]

(inter)ventricular septum n term, pl **septa**   rel **atrial septum**[1] n term

wall separating the cardiac ventricles of the heart

septal adj term • **septate**[2] [septeɪt] adj • **sept-** comb • **midventricular** adj

» Thrombosis in the anterior descending branch of the left coronary artery results in infarction of the anterior left ventricle and interventricular septum. The leaflets[3] [iː] were not attached [tʃ] directly to the ventricular septa, so that a large defect is located between the top of the ventricular septum and the common leaflets of the mitral [aɪ] and tricuspid [aɪ] valves.

Use right / left / muscular[4] [ʌ]/ upper / intact / ruptured [ʌ] **ventricular septum** • myocardial / membranous[5] **septum** • intraventricular / interatrial[1] / intra-atrial **septum** • **septal** wall / leaflet[6] / rupture / defect / hypertrophy[7]

heart or **cardiac valve** [vælv] n clin   rel **leaflet**[1] [liːflət], **cusp**[1] [kʌsp] n term

one of the four structures in the heart which by opening and closing with each heartbeat prevent reflux

valv(ul)ar adj term • **valv(ulo)-** comb • bi/ tricuspid [aɪ] adj

» In a healthy [e] valve, approximation of the cusps[2] during diastole is complete. The pulmonary valve ring is usually small. The aortic valve which is located between the outflow tract of the left ventricle and the ascending [s] aorta, is usually composed of three cusps, a fibrous skeleton, and the sinuses [aɪ] of Valsalva[3]. The aortic (anterior) leaflet of the mitral valve was cleft.

Use mitral [aɪ] or bicuspid or left atrioventricular[4] / tricuspid or right atrioventricular[5] **valve** • semilunar[6] [uː]/ pulmonary[7] / aortic[8] **valve** • infected / prosthetic or artificial[9] [ɪʃ] **heart valve** • coronary or thebesian[10] [-iːʒᵊn] venous[11] [iː] **valve** • **valve** leaflet or cusp[1] / closure / opening • **valve** disease / insufficiency[12] [ɪʃ]/ incompetence[12] • **valve** regurgitation[12] [rɪgɜːrdʒɪ-]/ replacement[13] / reconstruction[14] / repair[14] / system[15] • stenotic / incompetent / prolapsed **valve** • aortic / tricuspid / semilunar [uː]/ fused / redundant [ʌ]/ ruptured [ʌ] **cusp** • **cusp**-like / **valvular** heart disease / endocarditis [aɪ] • **valvo**tomy /ulitis /uloplasty[14]

Atrium, (Herz)vorhof

Auricula, Herzohr; Ohrmuschel[1] atrial, Vorhof-[2] Vorhofkontraktion[3] Vorhofflimmern[4] Vorhofflattern[5] Vorhofseptumdefekt[6] Vorhofextrasystolen[7] Atrioventrikularklappe[8] Atrioventrikular-, AV-, Aschoff-Tawara-Knoten[9] Atrioventrikular-, His-Bündel[10] Sulcus coronarius, (Herz-)Kranzfurche[11] Atrioventrikularrhythmus[12]

[7]

(Herz)kammer, Ventrikel

ventrikulär,*Kammer-[1] kardiopulmonale Reanimation[2] Kammersystole[3] Ventrikelvolumen[4] Ventrikelejektionsfraktion[5] ventrikuläre Tachykardie[6] Kammerflimmern[7] Ventrikel-, Kammerseptumdefekt[8]

[8]

Septum interventriculare, Kammerscheidewand

Vorhofseptum, -scheidewand, Septum interatriale[1] septiert, durch ein Septum getrennt[2] Segel[3] Pars muscularis/ muskulöser Teil d. Septum interventriculare[4] Pars membranacea/ membranöser Teil d. Septum interventriculare[5] septales Segel[6] Septumhypertrophie[7]

[9]

Herzklappe

Klappensegel, Herzklappenzipfel, Cuspis[1] Klappenschluss[2] Sinus aortae/ Valsalvae[3] Mitralklappe, Valva atrioventricularis sinistra[4] Trikuspidalklappe, V. atrioventricularis dextra[5] Semilunar-, Taschenklappe, V. semilunaris[6] Pulmonalklappe, V. trunci pulmonalis[7] Aortenklappe[8] künstl. Herzklappe, Herzklappenprothese[9] Thebesius-Klappe, Valvula sinus coronarii[10] Venenklappe[11] Herzklappeninsuffizienz[12] Herzklappenersatz[13] Herzklappenrekonstruktion, Valvuloplastik[14] Klappenapparat[15]

[10]

The Heart

foramen [eɪ] **ovale** [ouvɛrli‖-æli] *n term* *rel* **ductus** [ʌ] **arteriosus**[1] *n term*
opening in the atrial septum through which the blood bypasses the lungs in fetal [iː] life
» In the fetal circulation a considerable amount of this blood is shunted across the foramen ovale into the left atrium. After the neonatal period of cardiovascular adaptation with closing of the foramen ovale and ductus arteriosus there is complete separation of the systemic and pulmonary circuits and all right heart pressures are lower than those in the left heart.
Use patent[2] [eɪ]/ small / reopened *foramen ovale* • fossa[3] *ovalis* • fetal / persistent or patent[4] (*abbr* PDA) *ductus arteriosus* • ligated[5] [aɪ]/ closure of a patent *ductus arteriosus* • persistent truncus[6] *arteriosus* • ligamentum[7] *arteriosum*

Foramen ovale cordis
Ductus arteriosus / Botalli[1] offenes Foramen ovale[2] Fossa ovalis[3] offener Ductus Botalli, persistierender Ductus arteriosus, Ductus arteriosus apertus[4] ligierter Ductus arteriosus[5] Truncus arteriosus persistens[6] Ligamentum arteriosum[7]

11

chordae [kɔːrdi] **tendineae** [-ɪi] (**cordis**) *n term*   *syn* **tendinous cords** *n jar*
tendinous strands[1] that anchor [k] the cusps of the atrioventricular valves to the papillary muscles and prevent them from prolapsing into the atria during ventricular contraction
» The chordae tendineae of the tricuspid valve are finer than the coarse[2] [ɔː] strands of the chordae tendineae of the left ventricle. Nonrheumatic [uː] mitral regurgitation[3] [gɜːrdʒ] may develop abruptly [ʌ], such as with ruptured chordae tendineae in mitral valve prolapse[4].
Use elongated / shortened / thickened / fused[5] [fjuːzd]/ weakened [iː]/ ruptured[6] [ʌ] *chordae tendineae*

Chordae tendineae
Sehnenfäden[1] derb[2] Mitralinsuffizienz[3] Mitralklappenprolaps[4] Sehnenfädenverwachsung[5] Sehnenfädenabriss[6]

12

papillary muscle [mʌsl] *n term*   *rel* **trabeculae carneae**[1] [-ɪi] *n term pl*
one of the muscular projections in the ventricles of the heart that maintain tension on the chordae tendineae during ventricular contraction and help to open and close the atrioventricular valves
» A low-pitched[2] third heart sound (S3) is believed to be caused by the sudden tensing[3] of the papillary muscles, chordae tendineae, and valve leaflets.
Use anterior[4] / posterior[5] / right ventricular *papillary muscle*

Papillarmuskel
Trabekeln, Trabeculae carneae[1] niederfrequent[2] Anspannung[3] vorderer Papillarmuskel, Musculus papillaris anterior[4] hinterer P., M. papillaris posterior[5]

13

coronary [kɔːrəneri] *adj term*   *rel* **coronary**[1] [kɔːrənᵊri] *n clin BE*
(i) related to encircling structures, esp. the coronary blood vessels (ii) related to the heart
intra/ noncoronary *adj term*
» The left main coronary artery is usually about 1 cm long and gives rise to the left anterior descending and left circumflex [ɜː] coronary arteries. Her husband died of a coronary last year. Epinephrine provides a high diastolic aortic root pressure that improves coronary perfusion.
Use **coronary** circulation[2] / vessels[3] • **coronary** artery / arterial tree / vein [eɪ] • **coronary** valve / ostium / sinus [aɪ] • plexus • to have/suffer[4] *a coronary* • **coronary artery** occlusion[5] / obstruction [ʌ]/ stenosis[6] • right / posterior descending [se] **coronary artery** • left (main) / left anterior descending (*abbr* LAD) **coronary artery** • **coronary** perfusion or blood flow[7] • **coronary** pressure / risk[8] • **coronary** insufficiency[9] [ɪʃ]/ (vaso)spasm [eɪ] • **coronary** thrombosis[10] / atherosclerosis / artery disease (*abbr* CAD) • **coronary** heart disease[11] (*abbr* CHD) • **coronary** aortic bypass (graft)[12] (*abbr* CABG)/ care unit[13] (*abbr* CCU) • **coronary** arteriography / angioplasty / dilator [aɪ] drugs[14] • *intracoronary* injection [dʒe]/ stent

koronar, (Herz)kranz-, Koronar-
Herzanfall, -infarkt[1] Koronarkreislauf[2] Herzkranz-, Koronargefäße[3] einen Herzinfarkt erleiden[4] Koronararterienverschluss[5] Koronarstenose[6] Koronardurchblutung, -perfusion[7] Herzinfarktrisiko[8] Koronarinsuffizienz[9] Koronarthrombose[10] koronare Herzkrankheit[11] aortokoronarer Bypass[12] kardiolog. Intensivstation[13] Koronarmittel, -dilatanzien[14]

14

sinus [aɪ] *or* **S-A node** *n term*   *syn* **sinoatrial** [eɪ] *or* **Keith-Flack node** *n term*
rel **bundle of His** *or* **AV bundle**[1] [ʌ], **Purkinje's fibers**[2] [aɪ] *n term*
excitable component of the cardiac conduction system[3] containing pacemaker cells that regulate the heartbeat independently of any stimulation by nervous impulses from the brain or the spinal cord[4]
» The S-A node normally fires at a rate of 70-75 beats per minute. If the sinus node fails to generate [dʒe-] an impulse, the pacemaker function shifts to the AV node or Purkinje's fibers.
Use atrioventricular (*abbr* A-V) or Aschoff-Tawara[5] / His-Tawara / Keith's *node* • A-V **nodal** activation / pathways / conduction • *sinoatrial* block[6] • *sinus node* recovery time[7] • *sinus* function / activity / arrest / arrhythmia[8] [eɪ]/ rhythm [ɪ] • *His bundle* electrocardiography[9] /-Purkinje system[10] • **Purkinje** cells / fiber action potential

Sinus-, SA-, Sinoatrialknoten, Keith-Flack-Knoten
His-/ AV-Bündel, Fasciculus atrioventricularis[1] Purkinje-Fasern[2] Erregungsleitungssystem d. Herzens[3] Rückenmark[4] Atrioventrikularknoten, Aschoff-Tawara-, AV-Knoten, Nodus atrioventricularis[5] sinoatrialer/ sinoauriculärer/ SA-Block[6] Sinusknotenerholungszeit[7] Sinusarrhythmie[8] His-Bündel-Elektrokardiographie[9] His-Purkinje-System[10]

15

Unit 33 Cardiac Function

Related Units: 32 Heart, 36 Blood Circulation, 42 Nerve Function, 110 Cardiovascular Signs & Symptoms

heart sound [aʊ] n term abbr **HS**   sim **heart tones**[1] n term,
    rel **heartbeat**[2] n clin

any of the normal noises produced by the heart [hɑːrt] which can be heard on auscultation [ɒː] over the precordium [iː]

beat[3] - beat - beaten v irr • **beat**[4] [iː] n • **beating** adj & n • **interbeat**[5] adj term

» The first heart sound occurs with the closure of the mitral [aɪ] and tricuspid [ʌ] valves [æ] and marks the onset of ventricular systole. Pathologic heart sounds include murmurs[6] [ɜː], clicks[7], rubs[8] [ʌ], and snaps[9]. Ventricular work increases with exercise, both per beat and per minute. Is the heart beating? The atrium is paced[10] [peɪst] at a rate of about 80 beats/min.

Use first (abbr S₁)/ second (abbr S₂)/ third (abbr S₃)/ fourth (abbr S₄)/ split[11] **heart sound** • diminished[12] / absent / distant / muffled[12] [ʌ]/ faint[13] [eɪ] **heart sounds** • fetal [iː] (abbr FHT) **heart tones** • forceful[14] / arrested[15] / irregular **heartbeat** • apex[16] / atrial[17] / (supra)ventricular sinus [aɪ] **beat** • slow / dropped or missed[18] / irregular / premature[19] / escape[20] **beats** • ventricular ectopic (abbr VEBs)/ pacemaker / fusion[21] [juː] **beats** • **interbeat** interval

cardiac cycle [saɪkl] n term, abbr **CC**

complete sequence of events occurring during one heartbeat including electrical impulse conduction[1] [ʌ], contraction of the heart muscle, opening and closure of the heart valves and the subsequent systole

» The combination of retraction of the left ventricle and expansion of the left atrium [eɪ] during systole may produce a characteristic rocking motion [oʊ] of the chest with each cardiac cycle.

Use phase [feɪz] of[2] / late in / throughout[3] [uː] **the cardiac cycle** • **cardiac** activity[4] / index[5] (abbr CI)/ size [saɪz]/ standstill[6] • **cardiac** conduction (abnormality or defect)[7] [iː]/ dullness[8] [ʌ] • **cardiac** performance[9] / enzymes [zaɪ]/ work (load)[10]

systole [sɪstəlɪ] n term   opposite **diastole**[1] [daɪæstəlɪ] n term

contraction of the heart, which pumps the blood into the aorta [eɪ] and the pulmonary [ʊ‖ʌ] arteries

(pre-/ mid-/ end)**systolic**[2] adj term • (pan)**diastolic**[3] adj • extra/ **asystole**[4] n

» Heart murmurs may be systolic, diastolic, or continuous. Continuous murmurs begin in systole, peak [iː] near S₂, and continue into all or part of diastole. Atherosclerotic vessels have reduced systolic expansion and abnormally rapid wave propagation.

Use early / late / mid/ atrial[5] [eɪ]/ ventricular[6] **systole** • at / in / during / premature[7] **systole** • early / late / end-**diastole** • **systolic** (blood) pressure[8] (abbr SBP)/ sound / murmur [ɜː]/ click[9] • **systolic** contraction / hypertension / (dys)function [ʌ]/ thrill[10] • **diastolic** (blood) pressure (abbr DBP)/ depolarization / failure [eɪ] • **diastolic** filling[11] (time/ volume/ pressure) / flow murmur[12] • pan[13]- or holo**systolic** • ventricular / atrial / nodal[14] [oʊ]/ occasional[15] [eɪ] **extrasystoles**

point of maximal impulse n term, abbr **PMI**   rel **apex** [eɪ] **beat**[1] [iː] n term

point on the chest wall at which the maximal cardiac impulse is seen and/or palpated as strongest; usually in the 5th intercostal space[2] just medial to the left midclavicular line[3]

» Breath sounds in the affected hemithorax are absent, with displacement[4] of the PMI. The PMI was palpated in the 5th intercostal space. The apex beat is sustained (begins to fall with the S2) and is not displaced. A right ventricular heaving [iː] impulse[5] is palpable. Palpation revealed [iː] precordial activity, right ventricular lift, and a diffuse point of maximal impulse[6].

Use diffuse[6] / laterally displaced **point of maximal impulse** • location of the **maximal impulse** • cardiac / apex or apical[1] [eɪ]/ triple [ɪ] apical / atrial / (brisk) systolic **impulse** • (left/ right) ventricular / (double-peaked) [iː] carotid[7] **impulse** • (prominent/ sustained [eɪ]) left ventricular **impulse** • well-defined [aɪ]/ poorly defined[8] / displaced[9] / palpable **apex beat** • **apex beat** site

---

Herzton (HT)

(kindl.) Herztöne[1] Herzschlag[2] schlagen, pochen[3] Schlag[4] zwischen den Schlägen[5] (Herz)geräusche[6] Clicks, Klicks[7] Reiben, Reibegeräusche[8] Öffnungs- bzw. Schlusstöne[9] stimuliert[10] gespaltener Herzton[11] gedämpfte Herztöne[12] schwache H.[13] kräftiger Herzschlag[14] Herzstillstand[15] Herzspitzenstoß[16] Vorhofsystole[17] ausgefallene Systolen[18] Extrasystolen[19] Ersatzsystolen[20] Fusionssystolen[21]

1

Herzzyklus, -periode

Erregungsleitung[1] Phase d. Herzschlags[2] über die gesamte Herzperiode[3] Herztätigkeit[4] Herzindex, CI[5] Herzstillstand, Asystolie[6] Erregungsleitung(sstörung)[7] Herzdämpfung[8] Herzleistung[9] Herzarbeit[10]

2

Systole

Diastole[1] (end)systolisch[2] diastolisch[3] Herzstillstand, Asystolie[4] Vorhofsystole[5] Kammer-, Ventrikelsystole[6] Extrasystole[7] systolischer (Blut)druck[8] systol. Klick[9] systol. Schwirren[10] diastolische Füllung[11] diastol. (Herz)geräusch[12] holosystolisch, d. ganze Systole andauernd[13] AV-Extrasystolen[14] vereinzelte Extrasystolen[15]

3

Punctum maximum (d. Herzspitzenstoßes)

Herzspitzenstoß[1] Zwischenrippenraum[2] Medioklavikularlinie[3] Verlagerung[4] hebender Herzspitzenstoß[5] großflächiges Punctum maximum[6] Carotis-, Karotispuls[7] verbreiterter/ breiter Herzspitzenstoß[8] verlagerter Herzspitzenstoß[9]

4

Cardiac Function **BODY STRUCTURES & FUNCTIONS** 135

heart rate *n term*   *syn* **cardiac rate** *n*, *rel* **tachycardia**[1] [tækɪ-] *n term* → U110-2

rate of ventricular contractions recorded as the pulse or number of (heart)beats per minute

bradycardia[2] *n term* • **tachy/ bradycardi(a)c**[3] *adj* • **brady-, tachy-** *comb*

» *The initial response to hypoxia [aɪ] is an increase in frequency of respiration and a rise in heart rate and blood pressure. An increase in heart rate shortens diastole proportionately more than systole and diminishes the time available for flow across the mitral [aɪ] valve.*

Use fetal / resting[4] / exercise[5] / intrinsic **heart rate** • rapid / slow / maximal **heart rate** • elevated *or* increased / irregular **heart rate** • (sleeping) pulse[6] **rate** • decrease / fluctuations[7] [ʌ]/ alterations [ɔː] **in heart rate** • **heart rate** and rhythm [rɪðᵊm]/ variability (*abbr* HRV) • relative / reflex [iː]/ vagally [eɪ] mediated [iː]/ fetal / sinus[8] **bradycardia** • symptomatic / transient **bradycardia** • persistent / marked[9] / life-threatening [e] **bradycardia** • **bradycardia-tachycardia**-syndrome[10] • sinus / (paroxysmal [ɪ]/ multifocal) atrial[11] **tachycardia** • (supra)ventricular[12] / ectopic / paroxysmal **tachycardia** • orthostatic *or* postural[13] / compensatory / mild **tachycardia** • **brady**arrhythmia[14] [ɪ] • **tachy**arrhythmia

Herz(schlag)frequenz
Tachykardie[1] Bradykardie[2] bradykard[3] Ruhe(herz)frequenz, H. i. Ruhe[4] Herzfrequenz bei Belastung[5] Pulsfrequenz[6] Herzfrequenzschwankungen[7] Sinusbradykardie[8] deutliche/ ausgeprägte Bradykardie[9] Bradykardie-Tachykardie-Syndrom, Sick-Sinus-Syndrom[10] Vorhoftachykardie[11] (supra)ventrikuläre Tachykardie[12] orthostatische/ lageabhängige Tachykardie[13] Bradyarrhythmie, arrhythmische Bradykardie[14]

5

sinus [aɪ] **rhythm** [rɪðᵊm] *n term*   *rel* **cardiac** *or* **heart rhythm**[1] *n term*

normal cardiac rhythm generated by the sinoatrial node; it consists of a normal P wave (represents atrial depolarization) followed by a PR interval and a QRS complex (ventricular depolarization)

ar/ dysrhythmia[2] *n term* • **(anti)arrhythmic**[3] *adj & n* • **rhythmic**[4] *adj*

» *Resting sinus rates between 60-100 beats/min have been considered to represent the limits of the normal range [eɪ]. Exercise and emotion are potent [oʊ] accelerators of sinus rhythm.*

Use to be in/remain in/maintain/restore[5]/return to/revert [ɜː] to **sinus rhythm** • normal (*abbr* NSR) / (un)stable [eɪ] **sinus rhythm** • spontaneous [eɪ]/ conversion to normal[6] **sinus rhythm** • irregular *or* abnormal / (S₃/ S₄) gallop[7] / escape[8] **rhythm** • idioventricular[9] / atrioventricular[10] **rhythm** • atrial [eɪ]/ ventricular / His bundle [ʌ] *or* junctional[11] [dʒʌ]/ pacemaker **rhythm** • **rhythm** disturbance[2] [ɜː]/ strip[12] / monitoring[13] / tracings[14] [eɪs] • **sinus** impulse

Sinusrhythmus
Herzrhythmus[1] Rhythmusstörung, Dysrhythmie[2] antiarrhythmisch; Antiarrhythmikum[3] rhythmisch, regelmäßig[4] d. Sinusrhythmus wiederherstellen[5] Wiederherstellung d. Sinusrhythmus[6] protodiastolischer/ Dritter-Ton-Galopp[7] Ersatzrhythmus[8] idioventr. R. (z. B. Kammerautomatie)[9] atrioventrikulärer Rhythmus[10] His-Bündel-R.[11] Herzrhythmusanalysestreifen, Langer Streifen[12] Herzrhythmusüberwachung[13] Herzrhythmusaufzeichnungen[14]

6

cardiac output *n term, abbr* **CO**   *rel* **(cardiac) stroke** [oʊ] **volume**[1] *n term*

volume of blood ejected from the left heart at each beat (the stroke output[1] *or* volume) multiplied by the heart rate per minute (also called minute volume[2], *abbr* MV)

high-output *adj term* • **low-output** *adj*

» *The volume of blood ejected by the heart per minute is the cardiac output; the normal range in the resting state is 4 to 8 L/min. Usually the cardiac output is expressed in relation to the body surface area[3] (BSA) as the cardiac index (CI). Heart size and output are reduced.*

Use (in)adequate / effective / good / high / low / decreased[4] / resting[5] **cardiac output** • (left/ right) ventricular / atrial / stroke (volume)[1] **output** • ventricular end-diastolic[6] **volume** • left ventricular / total / forward[7] / impaired [eə]/ poor / increased[8] **stroke volume** • **low-output** state[9] / septic shock • **high-output** murmur[10] / (heart) failure

Herzminuten- (HMV), Herzzeit- (HZV), Minutenvolumen
Schlagvolumen[1] Minutenvolumen, MV[2] Körperoberfläche[3] vermindertes Herzminutenvolumen[4] HMV i. Ruhe[5] enddiastolisches Volumen[6] Vorwärtsvolumen[7] erhöhtes Schlagvolumen[8] Low-output-Syndrom[9] Herzgeräusch infolge e. erhöhten HMV[10]

7

ventricular ejection [ɪdʒekʃᵊn] *n term*   *rel* **ejection period**[1] [ɪɚ] *n term*

forceful expulsion of blood from the ventricles through the semilunar valves into the aorta

preejection *adj term* • **eject**[2] *v* • **ejection-type** *adj*

» *Even though the stroke volume is diminished, patients with mitral [aɪ] regurgitation [ɜː] may have a bounding [aʊ] pulse[3], since vigorous [ɪ] left ventricular ejection produces a rapid upstroke[4] in the arterial [ɪɚ] pulse. Determination of the ejection fraction at rest and during exercise by echocardiography is helpful in the differential diagnosis of dyspnea [dɪspniːə].*

Use left / right **ventricular ejection** • ejection time[1] / fraction[5] (*abbr* EF)/ sound[6] / click[7] / murmur[6] [ɜː] • abbreviated [iː]/ pre**ejection period** • **ejection-type** systolic murmur[8]

Ventrikel-, Kammerauswurf
Austreibungsphase, -zeit[1] auswerfen, ausstoßen[2] schnellender Puls, Pulsus celer[3] Druckanstieg[4] Auswurf-, Ejektionsfraktion[5] Austreibungsgeräusch[6] Ejektionsklick[7] frühsystolisches Herzgeräusch[8]

8

33

ventricular filling pressure n term   rel **cardiac filling pressure**[1] n term
  pressure in the ventricle as it fills with blood at the end of diastole
  » ACE inhibitors[2] reduce left ventricular filling pressure and right atrial pressure and moderately increase cardiac output. Venodilators, which are similar in cardiac action to diuretics [aɪ], decrease ventricular filling pressure or preload and thus reduce congestive symptoms.
  Use elevated[3] [e]/ left / right / monitoring of **ventricular filling pressure** • inadequate / impaired [eɚ]/ early **ventricular filling** • cardiac / left ventricular (abbr LV)/ chamber[4] **filling** • early diastolic[5] / rapid / slow / presystolic **filling** • atrial / left ventricular / diastolic coronary artery **filling pressure** • **filling** phase[6] / period[6] / rate

Kammerfüllungsdruck
Füllungsdruck d. Herzens[1] ACE-Hemmer[2] erhöhter enddiastolischer Füllungsdruck[3] Ventrikel-, Kammerfüllung[4] frühdiastolische Füllung[5] Füllungsphase, -periode[6]

9

(cardiac) preload [priːloʊd] n term   rel **(cardiac) afterload**[1] n term
  stretched condition of the myocardial [aɪ] fibers [aɪ] at end-diastole just before contraction; it is estimated by the ventricular end-diastolic volume and pressure
  load[2] v & n term • **overload**[3] n • **(over)loading** adj & n
  » The end-systolic left ventricular pressure-volume relationship is a particularly useful index of ventricular performance since it is independent of both preload and afterload. Treatment consists of fluid loading[4] to improve left ventricular filling.
  Use (left) ventricular **preload** • **preload** filling pressure / reduction [ʌ] • (right/ left) ventricular / systemic / systolic **afterload** • fluid / pressure[5] / work[6] / left ventricular[7] volume / mechanical [k] **load** • right atrial / circulatory or fluid[8] **overload** • circulatory [sɜːr-]/ sodium[9] **overloading**

Vorlast, Preload
Afterload, Nachbelastung, Nachlast[1] (be)laden, belasten; Belastung, Last[2] Über(be)lastung[3] Flüssigkeitszufuhr[4] Druckbelastung[5] Arbeit(slast), Arbeitsbelastung[6] Linksherzbelastung[7] Flüssigkeitsbelastung, Hyperhydratation[8] Natriumüberbelastung[9]

10

Unit 34 Blood Vessels
Related Units: 36 Blood Circulation, 35 Lymphatic System, 32 Heart, 33 Cardiac Function, 43 Lungs, 44 Respiration

(blood) vessel n [vesᵊl]   syn **vas** [væz] n term, pl **vasa** [eɪ]
  one of the network of muscular tubes through which blood circulates through the body
  (intra/ extra)vascular[1] [sk] adj term • **vasculature**[2] [æ] n • **vas(o)-** [eɪ] comb
  » In vasculitis [aɪ] any type and size [aɪ] of vessel may be involved—arteries, arterioles, veins, venules, or capillaries. What is the procedure [siː] of choice[3] for revascularization of single-vessel disease? Severe cardiovascular shock was caused by loss of autonomic control of the vasculature [-tʃ(j)ʊɚ].
  Use superficial [fɪʃ]/ major[4] [meɪdʒɚ]/ small (caliber) **blood vessels** • great / peripheral collecting / afferent[5] **vessels** • efferent[6] / collateral[7] / nutrient [uː] or feeding[8] **vessels** • cerebral / retinal / coronary / mammary **vessels** • visceral [ɪs] / iliac / pulmonary [ʊ‖ʌ]/ renal [iː]/ cutaneous [eɪ] **vessels** • dilated [eɪ]/ constricted / engorged[9] [ɡɔːrdʒ] **vessels** • patent[10] [eɪ]/ occluded [uː] **vessels** • thin-walled / ruptured [ʌ]/ bleeding **vessels** • aberrant[11] / tortuous[12] [-tʃʊəs] **vessels** • lymph or lymphatic[13] [ɪ] **vessels** • **vessel** wall / lumen [uː] • cardio**vascular** • **vascular** bud[14] [ʌ]/ bed[15] / endothelium [iː]/ perfusion [juː] • **vascular** supply[16] [aɪ]/ tone [oʊ]/ resistance[17] / volume • **vascular** collapse / spasm / congestion[18] [dʒe] • **vascular** obstruction [ʌ]/ insufficiency [ɪʃ] • **vascular** damage[19] / injury or lesion[19] [iːʒ]/ accident • **vascular** disease / access[20] [ækses]/ pedicle[21] / occlusion[22] • **vasa** vasorum[8] • **vaso**constrictor /motor nerves[23] /sensory • **vaso**spasm /pressor reflex [iː] • **vascul**arity[16] /arization[24] /opathy /ogenic [dʒe] • systemic / cerebral / coronary **vasculature** • dermal / pulmonary **vasculature** • renal[25] / splanchnic [k]/ penile [piːnaɪl]/ local **vasculature**

(Blut)gefäß
vaskulär, Gefäß-[1] Gefäßsystem[2] Methode der Wahl[3] große Blutgefäße[4] zuführende Gefäße, Vasa afferentia[5] abführende Gefäße, Vasa efferentia[6] Kollateralgefäße[7] versorgende Gefäße, Vasa vasorum[8] gestaute Gefäße[9] durchgängige G.[10] aberrierende G.[11] geschlängelte G.[12] Lymphgefäße[13] Gefäßanlage, -knospe[14] Gefäßbett[15] Gefäßversorgung[16] Gefäßwiderstand[17] vaskuläre Stauung[18] Gefäßschädigung, -läsion[19] vaskulärer Zugang[20] Gefäßstiel[21] Gefäßverschluss[22] vasomotorische Nerven, Vasomotoren[23] Vaskularisation, Gefäß(neu)bildung[24] Nierengefäße[25]

1

adventitial layer or **coat** n   syn **(tunica)** [t(j)uː-] **adventitia** [-tɪʃ(ɪ)ə] n term
  outermost layer [eɪ] of vessels which is composed of connective tissue with elastic and collagenous [ædʒ] fibers; it encloses the (tunica) intima[1] and the middle layer of smooth [uː] muscle tissue, the (tunica) media[2] [iː]
  (sub/ peri)adventitial [-tɪʃᵊl] adj term • **subintima** n • **(sub)intimal** adj
  » This is a vasculitis [aɪ] of the medium-sized arteries with fibrinoid [aɪ] degeneration [dʒ] in the media extending to the intima and adventitia. Minor neck trauma [ɒː] may produce stripping of the intima or media of the internal carotid or vertebral arteries.
  Use aortic **adventitia** • **adventitial** scar (tissue) / thickening[3] / cystic disease[4] • arterial [ɪɚ] **intima** • **intimal** flap[5] / tear[6] [teɚ]/ injury or damage[7] / thickening / hyperplasia [eɪʒ] • **intimal** proliferation / fibrosis[8] / dissection • **medial** thinning / necrosis[9] / hypertrophy

Adventitia, Tunica adventitia/ externa
Intima, Tunica interna/ intima[1] Media, Tunica media[2] Verdickung d. Adventitia[3] zystische Adventitiadegeneration[4] Intimalappen[5] Intimaläsion[6] Intimaschädigung[7] Intimafibrose[8] Medianekrose[9]

2

Blood Vessels   BODY STRUCTURES & FUNCTIONS **137**

---

artery [ɑːrtɚɪ] *n clin & term*   *rel* **arteriole¹** [ɑːrtɪɚıoʊl] *n term*

blood vessel carrying oxygenated blood from the heart to the periphery

(intra)ar**ter**ial² *adj term* • **arteri**olar³ *adj* • **arteri**(o)-, **ather**(o)- [æθ-] *comb*

» Auscultation [ɒː] of the epigastrium revealed a murmur⁴ [ɜː] due to obstruction of the celiac [siː] artery. Renal angiography revealed stretching and bowing [oʊ] of arterioles. Fortunately, vascular occlusion does not involve a major artery or vein. Acute arterial occlusion is characterized by pain, pallor⁵ [æ], paralysis, paresthesia [iːʒ], and pulselessness.

Use pulmonary / coronary⁶ / innominate **artery** • (middle) cerebral / subclavian [eɪ] / brachial [eɪk] **artery** • (external/ internal/ common) iliac⁷ / popliteal [iː] **artery** • (inferior/ superior) mesenteric / (deep) femoral⁸ [e] **artery** • nutrient / patent / obliterated **artery** • **arterial** blood (flow) / wall / diameter [aɪæ] • **arterial** branch⁹ / spasm / supply¹⁰ / insufficiency • **arterial** pressure¹¹ / pulse / catheter • pulmonary / retinal / afferent glomerular¹² **arterioles** • **arteriolar** (nephro)sclerosis¹³ / resistance • **arterio**venous [iː] /capillary /pathy¹⁴ /graphy • **athero**sclerosis /sclerotic plaque [æ‖ɑː]

---

vein [veɪn] *n clin & term*   *rel* **venule¹** [venjuːl] *n term*

vessel returning deoxygenated blood to the heart (except for the pulmonary vein)

(intra)venous² [iː] *adj term* • **ven**ular [e] *adj* • **ven-, phleb**(o)- [fliː-] *comb*

» If percutaneous [eɪ] insertion is not possible, the antecubital vein should be exposed by venous cutdown³. Effort thrombosis of the axillary⁴ vein and innominate vein obstruction from elongation and buckling⁵ [ʌ] of the innominate artery should be considered in the differential.

Use to feel for⁶ /insert into **a vein** • deep / superficial⁷ / varicose⁸ **vein** • pulmonary / portal⁹ / femoral / saphenous [fiː] **vein** • **vein** stripping¹⁰ • splenic / retinal / portal / hepatic / intrarenal **venules** • pulmonary / terminal / postcapillary / high endothelial¹¹ (*abbr* HEV) **venules** • **venous** system / blood / pressure¹² / return¹³ [ɜː]/ pulse¹⁴ / drainage • **venous** stasis¹⁵ / thrombosis / bleeding / occlusion¹⁶ / access¹⁷ • central **venous** line¹⁸ / **ven**ipuncture¹⁹ /ectomy • **phleb**itis /ography /othrombosis²⁰ /otomy³

(blood) capillary *n term*   *rel* **plexus¹** *n term, pl* **plexuses** [pleksəsiːz]

one of the microscopic thin-walled vessels which joins the arterioles and venules

(pre/ post/ intra/ extra/ peri/ trans)**capillary**² *adj term* • **capillar**ity³ *n*

» The slow, pulseless movement of blood allows for the exchange of vital [aɪ] and waste products at the capillary level. Use an epinephrine-containing solution to control capillary oozing⁴ [uː].

Use blood / arterial / venous / alveolar [ɪə]/ glomerular / skin **capillary** • retinal / brain / lymphatic⁵ / pulmonary⁶ / bile⁷ [aɪ] **capillaries** • **capillary** blood⁸ / bed / wall / system / loop⁹ [uː]/ refill (time) • **capillary** pressure¹⁰ / pulse¹¹ [ʌ]/ flow / permeability¹² [ɪə] / drainage • cutaneous [eɪ]/ fenestrated¹³ **capillary** • **capillary** bleeding /-sized vessel • **precapillary** arteriole / resistance • **postcapillary** venule / sphincter • **transcapillary** exchange / pressure gradient [eɪ] • **arteriocapillary** junction [dʒʌ] • **alveolocapillary** barrier [æ]/ membrane¹⁴ / block¹⁵ / vascular¹⁶ / nerve **plexus** • arterial / venous / capillary¹⁷ / brachial **plexus** • celiac or solar¹⁸ / pampiniform **plexus**

---

collateral *n & adj term*   *rel* **communicate¹, anastomose²** *v term* → U129-6

(n) small side branch, accessory or subsidiary of a blood vessel or nerve axon

collateralization³ *n term* • **anastom**osis⁴ *n, pl* **–ses** • **communicat**ing *adj*

» This dissection easily may injure the collateral blood supply immediately adjacent⁵ [dʒeɪs] to the testis. Cirrhotic patients with collateral anastomoses may also develop arterial desaturation. These incompetent perforating branches communicate with tributaries of the main trunk⁶ rather than the main trunk itself. The venous tributaries anastomose freely and usually drain into one renal vein. The communicating veins perforate the deep muscular [ʌsk] fascia [ʃ] to connect the superficial and deep venous systems.

Use **collateral** circulation⁷ / (arterial) vessels⁸ / veins / (blood) flow⁷ • **collateral** blood supply⁹ / channels [tʃ] • **collateral** anastomoses / (venous) network / pathways [æ] • arterial / venous / bronchial [k] **collaterals** • abdominal wall / intercostal / ulnar **collaterals** • large / well-developed¹⁰ **collaterals** • **to anastomose** freely • **communicating** vessels / artery / veins¹¹ / branches¹² / cavities • intra-arterial / intravenous / arteriovenous¹³ / fistulous¹⁴ / direct **communication**

Arterie, -ia, Puls-, Schlagader
Arteriole¹ arteriell, Arterien-² arteriolär, Arteriolen-³ Geräusch⁴ Blässe⁵ Koronararterie, Kranzschlagader, Arteria coronaria⁶ A. iliaca communis, gemeinsame Hüftschlagader⁷ A. profunda femoris, tiefe Oberschenkelarterie⁸ Arterienast⁹ arterielle Versorgung¹⁰ Arteriendruck, arterieller Druck¹¹ Arteriola glomerularis afferens, zuführendes Gefäß d. Nierenglomeruli¹² Arteriolosklerose¹³ Arterienerkrankung, Arteriopathie¹⁴

3

Vene, Vena, Blutader
Venula, Venole¹ intravenös² Venae sectio, Phlebotomie, Venenschnitt³ Achselvenenthrombose⁴ Aufwölbungen⁵ eine Vene ertasten⁶ oberflächl. Vene⁷ Krampfader, Varize⁸ Pfortader, Vena portae⁹ Venenstripping¹⁰ HEV¹¹ Venendruck¹² venöser Rückstrom¹³ Venenpuls¹⁴ venöse Stauung, Venostase¹⁵ Venenverschluss¹⁶ venöser Zugang¹⁷ zentraler Venenkatheter¹⁸ Venenpunktion¹⁹ Phlebothrombose, tiefe Venenthrombose²⁰

4

Kapillar-, Haargefäß, Kapillare, Vas capillare
Plexus, Geflecht¹ kapillär, Kapillar-² Kapillarität, Kapillarwirkung³ Sickerblutung⁴ Lymphkapillaren⁵ Lungenkapillaren⁶ Gallenkapillaren, Canaliculi biliferi⁷ Kapillarblut⁸ Kapillarschlinge⁹ Kapillardruck¹⁰ Kapillarpuls¹¹ Kapillarpermeabilität¹² fenestrierte Kapillare¹³ alveolokapilläre Membran¹⁴ alveolopillärer Block¹⁵ Plexus vasculosus, Gefäßgeflecht, -netz¹⁶ Kapillarnetz¹⁷ Sonnengeflecht, Plexus solaris/ coeliacus¹⁸

5

Kollateralgefäß; (Axon)kollaterale; kollateral, Neben-
in Verbindung stehen¹ anastomosieren² Kollateralisierung, Ausbildung eines Kollateralkreislaufs³ Anastomose⁴ angrenzend, -liegend⁵ Hauptgefäß⁶ Kollateralkreislauf⁷ Kollateralgefäße⁸ Kollateralversorgung⁹ gut ausgebildete Kollateralgefäße¹⁰ Venae communicantes¹¹ Verbindungsäste¹² arteriovenöse Verbindung/ Anastomose/ Shunt¹³ Fistel¹⁴

6

34

(vena) [iː] cava [keɪvə] *n term, pl* **venae cavae** [viːni: keɪviː]

one of the two major veins returning blood from the periphery to the right atrium [eɪ]

(sub/ peri/ para/ porta/ interaorto/ retro)caval¹ *adj term* • **cavo-** [eɪ] *comb*

» The superior vena cava, which is formed by the union of the two brachiocephalic veins, returns blood from the head and neck, upper limbs², and thorax. The inferior vena cava, which originates at the level of the 5th lumbar [ʌ] vertebra on the right side, pierces the diaphragm at the level of the 8th thoracic [æs] vertebra. The renal arteries originate laterally from the aorta, the left running directly to the kidney and the right crossing behind the cava.

Use inferior³ [ɪɚ]/ superior⁴ **vena cava** • suprahilar [aɪ]/ intrahepatic **cava** • **vena cava filter⁵** / wall • **(vena) caval** pressure / flow / system / ligation [eɪ] • superior **vena cava** syndrome⁶ [ɪ]/ obstruction [ʌ] • **venocavo**graphy⁷ • **cavo**pulmonary [ʊ‖ʌ]

Vena cava, Hohlvene
retrokaval¹ obere Extremitäten² untere Hohlvene, Vena cava inferior³ obere Hohlvene, Vena cava superior⁴ Kavafilter, -sieb⁵ Vena-cava-superior-Syndrom⁶ Kavografie⁷

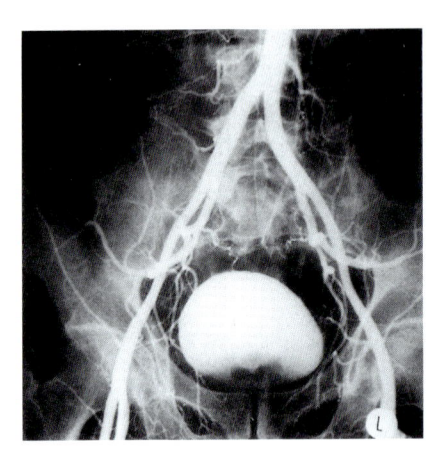

Angiography of the pelvic arteries demonstrating the aortic bifurcation with the iliac and femoral arteries

aorta [eɪɔːrtə] *n term* *rel* **aortic arch**¹ [ɑːrtʃ] *n term*

main trunk [ʌ] of the systemic arterial system which arises from the base of the left ventricle and divides into the right and left common iliac arteries at the level of the 4th lumbar vertebra (aortic bifurcation)

(sub/ para/ peri/ intra)aortic² [eɪɔːrtɪk] *adj* • **aorto-** *comb*

» Oxygen saturation³ in the left ventricle, right ventricle, pulmonary artery, and aorta is identical to that in the left atrium [eɪ]. Most aneurysms of the abdominal aorta⁴ involve the segment of the aorta between the takeoff of the renal arteries and the aortic bifurcation. Intraoperative staging should include biopsies [aɪ] of celiac [siː] and para-aortic lymph nodes.

Use ascending⁵ [se]/ descending⁶ / thoracic⁷ [æs]/ infrarenal **aorta** • abdominal / distal / overriding⁸ **aorta** • **aortic** valve⁹ [æ]/ sinus [aɪ]/ hiatus¹⁰ [aɪeɪ] • **aortic** body¹¹ / root¹² / bifurcation¹³ [aɪ] • **aortic** thrill¹⁴ / rupture *or* tear¹⁵ [teɚ]/ insufficiency *or* regurgitation¹⁶ • **aortic** stenosis *(abbr AS)*/ aneurysm • **aortic** coarctation¹⁷ / dissection¹⁸ • **aortic arch** vessels • **subaortic** obstruction / (valve) stenosis • **aorto**coronary /pulmonary /caval /iliac /graphy

Aorta, große Körperschlagader
Aortenbogen, Arcus aortae¹ aortal, Aorten-² Sauerstoffsättigung³ Bauchaorta, Pars abdominalis aortae⁴ aufsteigende A., P. ascendens aortae⁵ absteigende A., P. descendens aortae⁶ Brustaorta, P. thoracica aortae⁷ reitende A.⁸ Aortenklappe⁹ Aortenschlitz, Hiatus aorticus¹⁰ Glomus aorticum¹¹ Aortenwurzel¹² Aortenbifurkation¹³ Aortenschwirren¹⁴ Aortenruptur¹⁵ Aorten(klappen)insuffizienz¹⁶ Aorten(isthmus)stenose, Coarctatio aortae¹⁷ Aortendissektion, Aneurysma dissecans d. Aorta¹⁸

innominate artery *n term* *syn* **brachiocephalic** [eɪk] **trunk** *or* **artery** *n term*

one of the three arteries arising from the aortic arch which divides into the right subclavian [eɪ] and the right common carotid artery

» Most atherosclerotic plaques [plæks] occur at the origin of the internal carotid, but the innominate artery and ascending aorta are implicated¹ occasionally. The first anterior branch, the common trunk of the umbilical and superior vesical arteries, was ligated [aɪ] and divided.

Use **brachiocephalic** vessels / veins / bruit² [bruiː‖bruːt] • **innominate** veins³ • pulmonary⁴ / celiac⁵ [siː]/ tibioperoneal [iː]/ nerve **trunk**

Truncus brachiocephalicus
betroffen¹ Strömungsgeräusch über dem T. brachiocephalicus² Venae brachiocephalicae³ Truncus pulmonalis⁴ Truncus coeliacus⁵

Blood Vessels   BODY STRUCTURES & FUNCTIONS 139

common carotid (artery) n term & jar   syn **arteria carotis communis** n term

one of the major arteries supplying the head and neck which arises from the brachiocephalic trunk (right) and from the aortic arch (left) and branches into the external and internal carotid arteries

» Erosion of the internal, external, or common carotid arteries causes profuse [juː] hemorrhage[1]. Injured carotid arteries that have produced a neurologic deficit[2] should be ligated.

Use right / left / extracranial [eɪ]/ external[3] / internal[4] **carotid artery** • **carotid** pulse[5] [ʌ]/ sinus[6] [aɪ] / plexus / body[7] • **carotid** bifurcation[8] / sheath[9] [ʃiːθ]/ bruit[10]

Arteria carotis communis, Karotis, gemeinsame Kopfschlagader
starke Blutung[1] neurolog. Ausfälle[2] äußere Kopfschlagader, A. carotis externa[3] innere K., A. carotis interna[4] Karotispuls[5] Karotissinus, S. caroticus[6] Karotisdrüse, Paraganglion/ Glomus caroticum[7] Karotisgabel[8] Vagina carotica[9] Strömungsgeräusch über d. A. carotis[10]   10

external jugular [dʒʌ-] **vein** n term & jar   syn **vena jugularis externa** n term

superficial [ɪʃ] vein passing down the side of the neck which is formed by the junction[1] of the posterior auricular and the retromandibular vein below the parotid gland and empties into the subclavian vein

» The right internal jugular is the best vein to use for accurate estimation of the central venous pressure. The external jugular vein courses from behind the angle [æŋgl] of the mandible across the sternocleidomastoid [aɪ] muscle and superficial to it to join the subclavian [eɪ] vein. Guide the wire around the bends in the course of the external jugular vein-subclavian vein junction into the intrathoracic portion of the subclavian vein-superior vena cava system.

Use (right/ left) internal[2] / external[3] / distended **jugular vein** • **jugular** venous pressure (abbr JVP)/ pulse[4] • **jugular** venous distention[5] / chain nodes[6] / foramen [eɪ]/ puncture[7]

dorsale oberfläch. Drosselvene, Vena jugularis externa
Vereinigung[1] innere Drosselvene, Vena jugularis interna[2] hintere oberflächl./ äußere Drosselvene, Vena jugularis externa[3] Jugularvenenpuls[4] Jugularvenendehnung, Distension d. Jugularvenen[5] Jugularislymphknoten[6] Jugularispunktion[7]

11

venous valve [vælv] n clin   syn **valv(ul)a venosa** n term → U32-10

one of the small folds in the tunica intima of veins [eɪ] which prevent the reflux [iː] of blood

valvar[1] [vælvɚ] adj term • **valved**[2] adj • **valveless**[3] adj • **valvul(o)-** comb

» The venae cavae and the hepatic, portal, splenic [e], renal [iː], pulmonary, mesenteric, cerebral, and superficial head and neck veins have no valves or possess only functionally incompetent intimal folds. Fibrinolytic [ɪ] agents help preserve competency and function of venous valves.

Use popliteal [iː]/ diseased / defective or incompetent[4] **venous valves** • caval[5] / truncal [ʌ]/ saphenofemoral [fiː]/ heart[6] **valve** • **valveless** veins • **valve** damage / cusp[7] / system

Venenklappe, Valvula venosa
klappenförmig, Klappen-[1] mit Klappen versehen, Klappen-[2] klappenlos[3] insuffiziente Venenklappen, Venenklappeninsuffizienz[4] Valvula venae cavae inferioris, Valvula Eustachii[5] Herzklappe[6] Klappentasche[7]

12

branch [bræntʃ‖brɑː-] n & v   syn **ramus** [eɪ] n term, rel **tributary**[1] n & adj

one of the primary divisions of a blood vessel or nerve

branched[2] adj • **rebranch** v • **branching**[3] n & adj

» These arteries may give off secondary branches that form arterial plexuses in the adventitial layer of the ureter. The first main branch off the renal artery serving[4] the renal parenchyma supplies the posterior segment of the kidney. Infection spread along the vein and necessitated its removal [uː] up to the next major tributary.

Use **to branch** off • arterial / main or major[5] / small / ascending[6] **branch** • descending / deep / superficial / terminal[7] **branch** • anastomotic[8] **branches** • major / draining / portal[9] / saphenous [fiː] **tributary** • **tributary** vein / from the pancreas / of the main trunk

(Haupt)ast, Ramus, Verzweigung; s. gabeln/ verzweigen
Nebenast, Aufzweigung; untergeordnet, Neben-[1] verzweigt, verästelt[2] Verzweigung, -ästelung; s. verzweigend[3] versorgend[4] Hauptast[5] aufsteigender Ast, Ramus ascendens[6] Endast, -aufzweigung[7] anastomosierende Äste[8] Seitenast d. Pfortader[9]

13

vascular lumen [uː] n term, pl **lumina**   rel **patency**[1] [peɪtənˈsɪ] n term

space inside a vessel (or any other tubular [(j)uː] structure, e.g. a duct [ʌ] or the intestine)

(trans/ intra)luminal[2] adj term • **patent**[3] adj

» Once the needle [iː] is in the lumen of the vein, the required amount of blood can be withdrawn[4] with a steady [e], even pull on the plunger[5] [ʌndʒ] of the syringe[6] [sɪrɪndʒ]. Systemic infusion of fibrin-specific agents over 6 h restored coronary artery patency in approximately 75% of patients.

Use to have **a lumen** • to grow across/fill/block/occlude[7]/enlarge/reestablish **the lumen** • vessel / arterial / aortic / intravascular / capillary **lumen** • patent / narrowed[8] **lumen** • caliber or size[9] / patency / obstruction / distention **of the lumen** • **luminal** diameter[9] / narrowing / fluid • **intraluminal** pressure[10] / thrombus / growth / mass / lesion [iːʒ] • percutaneous [eɪ] **transluminal** coronary angioplasty[11] (abbr PTCA) • to determine/confirm/maintain[12]/reestablish **patency** • coronary arterial / airway[13] / ductal [ʌ] **patency** • **patent** celiac artery[14] / bronchus / biliary tree[15] / foramen [eɪ] ovale[16] [oʊveɪli]

Gefäßlumen, lichte Weite
Durchgängigkeit[1] intraluminal[2] offen, durchgängig[3] entnommen[4] Kolben[5] Spritze[6] d. Lumen verschließen[7] verengtes Lumen[8] Lumendurchmesser[9] intraluminaler Druck[10] perkutane transluminale koronare Angioplastie[11] d. Durchgängigkeit gewährleisten[12] Freisein d. Atemwege[13] durchgängige(r) A. coeliaca/ Truncus coeliacus[14] durchgängiges Gallengangsystem[15] offenes Foramen ovale[16]

14

34

Unit 35 The Lymphatic System

Related Units: 36 Blood & Lymph Circulation, 34 Blood Vessels, 37 Components of the Blood, 39 The Immune System

lymphatic [lɪmfætɪk] **system** *n term*   *rel* **lymph(atic) vessels**[1] *n clin*

tissue [tɪʃjuː‖tɪsjuː] and organs which produce, store and transport cells that fight infection; these include the bone marrow, spleen, thymus, lymph nodes, and channels [tʃænᵊlz] that carry lymph fluid

lymphatics[1] *n term & jar* • **lymphoid**[2] *adj* • **lymph(o)-** *comb*

» This procedure [siː] allows connections to form between blocked superficial dermal lymphatics and the normal deep lymphatic system. Tumor cells may spread [e] via the lymphatic system to the preauricular and submandibular lymph nodes.

Use **lymphatic** tissue[3] / duct [ʌ] / channels / pathways[4] • **lymphatic** chain[5] [tʃeɪn]/ plexus / sinuses [aɪ] • **lymphatic** flow / drainage[6] [eɪ]/ obstruction [ʌ] • **lymph** capillaries[7] / circulation[8] / spaces [eɪs] / regional [iː]/ peripheral **lymphatics** • superficial dermal [ɜː]/ groin[9] **lymphatics** • mesenteric / diaphragmatic **lymphatics** • cervical [ɜː]/ breast [e] **lymphatics** • **lymphoid** tissue[3] / follicle[10] / hyperplasia [-eɪʒ(ɪ)ə] • **lympho**cyte [-saɪt] /cytosis /blast /cele [-siːl] • **lymphangio**graphy[11] /tis • **lymph**edema[12] [iː]

lymphatisches System
Lymphgefäße, Vasa lymphatica[1] lymphoid, -atisch, Lymph-[2] lymphat. Gewebe[3] Lymphbahnen[4] Lymphknotenstrang[5] Lymphdrainage, -abfluss[6] Lymphkapillaren[7] Lymphkreislauf[8] Lymphgefäße i. d. Leistengegend, Nodi lymphatici inguinales[9] Lymphfollikel, -knötchen, Folliculus lymphaticus[10] Lymph(angi)ografie[11] Lymphödem[12]

1

lymph [lɪmf] *or* **lymphatic fluid** *n clin*   *rel* **chyle**[1] [kaɪl] *n term*

clear fluid in the lymphatic vessels that is collected from the tissues throughout the body and contains varying numbers of white blood cells (chiefly lymphocytes) and a few red blood cells

chylous *or* **chyliform**[2] *adj term* • **(endo/ peri)lymphatic** *adj* • **chylo-** *comb*

» The accumulation of free chyle in the peritoneal cavity is a rare form of ascites. Lymphatic obstruction resulted in a loss of protein-rich chylous fluid from the mucosal lacteals.

Use composition / accumulation / leakage [iː] **of chyle** • **lymph** cell *or* lymphocyte / flow[3] • **lymph** formation[4] / resorption / stasis[5] [eɪ] • **endolymphatic** duct / system[6] / sac • **endolymphatic** pressure / hydrops[7] [aɪ] • **chylous** fluid / effusion[8] [juːʒ]/ ascites[9] [aɪ] • **chylo**thorax /microns[10] [aɪ] /pericardium[11] /peritoneum • **chylomicron** formation / triglycerides [ɪs] / remnants[12]

Lymphe
Chylus, Milchsaft[1] chylös, chylusartig[2] Lymphfluss[3] Lymphbildung[4] Lymphstauung[5] endolymphatisches System[6] Meniere-Krankheit[7] chylöses Exsudat, chylöser Erguss[8] chylöser Aszites[9] Chyloperikard[10] Chylomikronen[11] Chylomikronenfragmente[12]

2

lymph node [noʊd] *n clin & term*   *syn* **lymph gland** *n clin & jar*

one of the round or oval bodies found along the course [ɔː] of lymphatic vessels which vary greatly in size and contain numerous [uː] lymphocytes which filter the lymph fluid passing through the node

» Like the spleen, lymph nodes filter and cleanse [e] the lymph by removing cellular debris[1] [dəbriː], bacteria [ɪə], parasites [-saɪts], and other noxious [nɒkʃəs] agents[2].

Use perivascular / periaortic / regional[3] [iːdʒ] / local **lymph nodes** • axillary[4] / pectoral *or* anterior axillary / cervical [ɜː] **nodes** • supraventricular / parasternal [ɜː]/ submental **nodes** • hilar [aɪ]/ pulmonary / iliac [ɪliæk]/ pelvic **nodes** • (superficial/ deep) inguinal[5] / lateral aortic / popliteal [iː] **nodes** • palpable / swollen / affected *or* involved[6] / tender[7] **lymph nodes** • **lymph node** enlargement[8] / dissection[9] / involvement[10] • **lymph node** sampling[11] / biopsy[11] [aɪ]/ metastasis • **lymphaden**itis /opathy /ectomy[9]

Lymphknoten, Nodi lymphaticus
Zelltrümmer, -fragmente[1] Schadstoffe[2] regionäre Lymphknoten[3] Achsel-, axilläre Lymphknoten, Nodi lymphatici axillares[4] N. lymph. inguinales profundi[5] befallene L.[6] druckdolente/ druckschmerzempfindl. L.[7] Lymphknotenvergrößerung[8] Lymphknotendissektion, Lymphadenektomie[9] Lymphknotenbefall, -beteiligung[10] Lymphknotenbiopsie[11]

3

spleen [spliːn] *n clin & term*   *syn* **lien** [laɪən] *n term rare*

vascular lymphatic organ between the stomach [k] and the diaphragm [-æm]; its white pulp[1] [ʌ] consists of lymphatic nodules and diffuse lymphatic tissue while the red pulp[2] is composed of venous sinusoids [aɪ]

splenic[3] [splɛnɪk] *adj term* • **splen(o)-** [iː] , **lien(o)-** *comb* • **-splenia** [e] *comb*

» Normal blood cells pass rapidly through the spleen, while abnormal and senescent[4] [es] cells are retarded and entrapped. The spleen is particularly well suited to antibody formation, since plasma is skimmed by the trabecular arteries and delivered to the lymphoid follicles, bringing soluble[5] antigens into direct contact with immunologically competent cells.

Use hilum [aɪ] of the[6] / accessory[7] / palpable / ruptured[8] [ʌ] **spleen** • normal-sized [aɪ]/ (massively) enlarged **spleen** • **spleen** tip / scan[9] • **splenic** artery / blood flow / vein [eɪ] • **splenic** red pulp [ʌ]/ portography[10] • **splenic** cell cords / sinuses[11] [aɪ] • capsule[12] / flexure of the colon[13] • **splenic** abscess / injury / infarct(ion)[14] / macrophages [-feɪdʒiːz] • **spleno**megaly[15] /renal • **splen**ectomy[16] /ectomize

Milz, Splen, Lien
weiße Pulpa, Pulpa alba[1] rote Pulpa, Pulpa rubra[2] Milz-[3] überaltert[4] löslich[5] Milzhilus, Hilum splenicum[6] Lien accessorius, Nebenmilz[7] Milzruptur[8] Milzszintigrafie[9] Splenoportografie[10] Milzsinus, Sinus splenici[11] Milzkapsel[12] linke Kolonflexur, Flexura coli sinistra[13] Milzinfarkt[14] Milzvergrößerung, Splenomegalie[15] Milzentfernung, Splenektomie[16]

4

The Lymphatic System

BODY STRUCTURES & FUNCTIONS

thymus (gland) [θaɪməs glænd] *n term*

primary [aɪ] lymphoid organ located in the superior [ɪɚ] mediastinum [aɪ] and lower part of the neck that is essential in early life for the normal development of immunological function

thymic[1] [θaɪmɪk] *adj term* • **thym(o)-** *comb*

» The thymus reaches its greatest absolute weight at puberty [juː], then it begins to involute, and much of the lymphoid tissue is replaced by fat. Childhood non-Hodgkin's lymphomas can arise in any lymphoid tissue including lymph nodes, Waldeyer's ring[2], Peyer's patches, thymus, liver, and spleen.

Use fetal [iː]/ enlarged[3] / small / absent **thymus** • **thymic** tissue / macrophages / involution[4] • **thymus**-derived [aɪ] or -dependent lymphocytes[5] / enlargement[3] • **thymic** tumor[6] / hypoplasia [eɪ]/ aplasia • **thym**ectomy /idine kinase /ocytes[7] /oleptic drugs[8] /oma[6]

Thymus

Thymus-[1] Waldeyer-Rachenring, lymphat. Rachenring[2] Thymusvergrößerung[3] Thymusrückbildung, -involution[4] thymusabhängige Lymphozyten, T-Lymphozyten[5] Thymustumor, Thymom[6] Thymozyten[7] Thymoleptika, Antidepressiva[8]

5

tonsil [tɒnˈsᵊl] *n clin*   *syn* **tonsilla** *n, pl* **–ae**, *rel* **adenoids**[1] *n term*

large oval mass of lymphoid tissue in the lateral wall of the oropharynx [ɔːroʊfærɪŋks] on either side between the pillars [ɪ] of the fauces[2] [fɔːsiːz]

(peri)tonsillar[3] *adj term* • **tonsill-** *comb* • **adenoid(al)** *adj*

» The tonsil bulges [ʌ] medially [iː], and the anterior pillar is prominent. Gentle [dʒ] palpation of the peritonsillar and tonsillar tissues intraorally revealed swelling. Throat [oʊ] inspection revealed increased pharyngeal lymphoid tissue and enlarged tonsillar and adenoid tissue.

Use lingual[4] / palatine[5] / pharyngeal[6] / tubal[7] **tonsil** • **tonsillar** lymphatic tissue / pillars[2] / fossa • **tonsillar** enlargement / exudate / abscess / crypts[8] [ɪ] • large / hypertrophied **adenoids** • **adenoidal** lymphoid hyperplasia[1] • **tonsill**itis[9] /ectomy and adenoidectomy (*abbr* T & A) *or* tonsilloadenoidectomy[10] /opharyngitis [dʒaɪ]

Tonsille, Mandel

adenoide Wucherungen, Nasen-Rachenpolypen[1] Gaumenbögen[2] peritonsillär[3] Zungenmandel, Tonsilla lingualis[4] Gaumenmandel, T. palatina[5] Rachenmandel, T. pharyngealis/ adenoidea[6] Tubenmandel, T. tubaria[7] Tonsillarkrypten[8] Tonsillitis, Mandelentzündung[9] Tonsilloadenoidektomie[10]

6

thoracic duct [θɔːræsɪk dʌkt] *n term*   *rel* **right lymphatic duct**[1] *n term*

largest lymph vessel in the body originating at the cisterna chyli; it passes through the aortic opening of the diaphragm, crosses the posterior mediastinum to open into the left brachiocephalic vein at its origin

» The jugular [dʒʌgjʊlɚ] chain [tʃeɪn] and transverse [ɜː] cervical [sɜː] lymphatics drain [eɪ] into the thoracic duct on the left side of the neck. Oral feedings with medium-chain triglycerides[2] [ɪs] help reduce lymphatic flow through the thoracic duct postoperatively.

Use endolymphatic / perilymphatic[3] / bronchomediastinal[4] [aɪ] **duct** • arch [tʃ] of the **thoracic duct** • **thoracic duct** lymphocytes / drainage[5] / obstruction / injury / fistula

Ductus thoracicus, Milchbrustgang

Ductus lymphaticus dexter[1] mittelkettige Triglyzeride[2] Ductus perilymphaticus[3] Truncus bronchomediastinalis[4] Ductus-thoracicus-Drainage[5]

7

receptaculum chyli [kaɪlaɪ] *n term*   *syn* **cisterna chyli** [sɪstɜːrnə] *n term*

dilated [eɪ] sac at the lower end of the thoracic duct into which the intestinal trunk and two lumbar [ʌ] lymphatic trunks[1] open; when present it is located behind the aorta opposite the 1st and 2nd lumbar vertebrae[2]

» Lymphatic channels [tʃæ-] within the mesentery drain through regional lymph nodes and terminate in the cisterna chyli. The cisterna chyli should be ligated [aɪ] to prevent chylous [aɪ] ascites with its attendant[3] excessive protein loss in the postoperative period.

Cisterna chyli

Trunci lumbales[1] Lendenwirbel[2] damit verbunden[3]

8

bronchomediastinal trunk [brɒːŋkoʊmiːdɪəstaɪnᵊl trʌŋk] *n term*

lymph vessel arising [aɪ] from the junction [dʒʌŋkʃᵊn] of the efferent lymphatics from the bronchial and mediastinal nodes on either side

» From the renal pedicle[1] the lymphatic channels, usually 4 or 5 trunks, drain to lymph nodes along the inferior vena cava [viːnə keɪvə] and to the lateral aortic nodes.

Use lumbar [ʌ] (lymphatic)[2] / intestinal[3] / subclavian[4] [eɪ] **trunk**

Truncus bronchomediastinalis

Nierenstiel[1] Truncus lumbalis[2] Truncus intestinalis[3] Truncus subclavius[4]

9

lacteal (vessel) *n & adj term*

one of the lymph vessels in the intestinal villi[1] [aɪ] transporting milky-white chyle to the thoracic [æs] duct

» The entrance of the nutrients[2] [uː] into the general circulation is achieved via [vaɪə‖viːə] the capillaries into the portal system or via the lacteals into the intestinal lymphatics. The chylomicron [kaɪloʊmaɪkrɒːn], a fat droplet containing 80-95% triglycerides [aɪ], is secreted [iː] into lacteals and transported to the circulation via the thoracic duct.

Use central / mucosal [mjuːkoʊsᵊl]/ dilated [eɪ] **lacteal**

Lymphkapillare d. Dünndarms; milchig, chylös

Darmzotten, Villi intestinales[1] Nährstoffe[2]

10

35

Peyer's patches [paɪɚz pætʃiːz] *n term* syn **Peyer's gland** *n term*
submucosal collections of numerous [uː] lymphoid nodules closely packed together in the intestinal wall (esp. the ileum [ɪliəm]) that partially or completely disappear in advanced life
» *Submucosal lymphoid aggregates (so-called Peyer's patches) are much more numerous in the ileum than in the jejunum* [dʒɪdʒuːnəm]. *With invasion* [eɪʒ] *of the gallbladder*[1] [ɔː] *and Peyer's patches, bacteria regain entry to the bowel* [baʊəl] *lumen.*
Use gut [ʌ] or intestine / mucosal / hypertrophied **Peyer's patches** • **Peyer's patch** lymphoid aggregates[2] / follicle capillaries

Peyer-Plaques, Folliculi lymphatici aggregati
Gallenblase[1] Folliculi lymphatici aggregati, Haufen v. Lymphfollikeln[2]

11

reticuloendothelial [iː] **system** *n term, abbr* **RES** syn **mononuclear phagocyte** [fægəsaɪt] **system, lymphoreticular system** *n term*
functional body system comprising the macrophages [-feɪdʒɪz], reticulum cells in the spleen, lungs, bone marrow and lymph nodes, bone marrow, and the fibroblastic [aɪ] reticular cells of hematopoietic tissues
transendothelial *adj term* • **reticular**[1] *adj* • **reticulo-** *comb* • **reticulocyte**[2] *n*
» *Measles* [miːzlz] *virus*[3] [aɪ] *invades the respiratory epithelium* [iː] *and spreads via the bloodstream to the reticuloendothelial system, from which it infects all types of white blood cells. The predominant cellular sources of these cytokines*[4] [saɪtəkiːnz] *are T-lymphocytes and cells of the reticuloendothelial system (circulating monocytes, tissue macrophages).*
Use **reticuloendothelial** organ / tissues / cell (function) / iron [aɪ] stores[5] / neoplasm [iː] • **reticuloendothel**iosis[6] • **mononuclear** phagocytic [sɪ] system[7] • **transendothelial** migration [aɪ] • **reticulo**nodular /granular • **reticulocyte** count[8]

Monozyten-Makrophagen-/ retikuloendotheliales System, RES
retikulär, netzartig[1] Retikulozyt, Proerythrozyt[2] Masernvirus[3] Zytokine[4] retikuloendotheliale Eisendepots[5] Retikuloendotheliose[6] Monozyten-Makrophagen-System[7] Retikulozytenzählung, -zahl[8]

12

Unit 36 Blood & Lymph Circulation
Related Units: 34 Blood Vessels, 35 Lymphatic System, 37 Components of the Blood, 32 Heart, 33 Cardiac Function, 110 Cardiovascular Signs & Symptoms

(blood) circulation [sɜːrkjʊleɪʃən] *n* sim **bloodstream**[1] [blʌdstriːm] *n*
flow of blood from the heart [ɑː] through the arteries, capillaries, and veins [eɪ] back to the heart
circulatory[2] *adj term* • **(re)circulate** *v* • **circulating**[3] *adj* • **microcirculation**[4] [aɪ] *n*
» *Diabetics* [e] *with diminished sensation of the toes do not necessarily have diminished circulation to the feet. Feedback inhibition results in a restoration of the circulating concentrations of pituitary* [(j)uː] *hormones*[5] *to normal. Acute adrenal* [iː] *insufficiency* [ɪʃ] *may result in inadequate cardiac output despite normal circulatory volume.*
Use blood / lymph [lɪmf]/ cerebrospinal [aɪ] fluid[6] / extracorporeal[7] [iː] **circulation** • systemic[8] / pulmonary[9] / peripheral **circulation** • collateral[10] / maternal [ɜː]/ fetal [iː] **circulation** • arterial [ɪɚ]/ venous [iː]/ capillary **circulation** • bronchial / coronary[11] / enterohepatic[12] / renal[13] [iː] **circulation** • impaired [eɚ] **circulation** • **circulatory** system (function) / fluid / status / overload[14] / collapse • **circulatory** shock / compromise[15] [-aɪz] / arrest[16] / failure[17] / support • **circulating** (blood) volume / platelets[18] [eɪ] / hemoglobin • **circulating** immune complexes / inhibitor / toxin • local / coronary / pulmonary / skin **microcirculation** • portal **bloodstream** • **bloodstream** infection / invasion [eɪʒ]/ dissemination

(Blut)kreislauf, -zirkulation
Blut(bahn), -kreislauf[1] zirkulierend, Kreislauf-[2] zirkulierend[3] Mikrozirkulation[4] Hypophysenhormone[5] Liquorzirkulation[6] extrakorporaler Kreislauf[7] großer oder Körperkreislauf[8] kleiner oder Lungenkreislauf[9] Kollateralkreislauf[10] Koronarkreislauf[11] enterohepatischer Kreislauf[12] Nierenkreislauf, -durchblutung[13] Kreislaufüberbelastung[14] Kreislaufstörung[15] Kreislaufstillstand[16] Kreislaufversagen[17] zirkulierende Thrombozyten[18]

1

pulmonary [ʊ‖ʌ] **circulation** *n term* syn **lesser circulation** *n term*
passage of blood from the right ventricle through the pulmonary arteries to the alveoli [aɪ] of the lungs for oxygenation and removal of CO_2 and back through the pulmonary veins to the left atrium [eɪ]
» *About 95% of pulmonary blood circulation is supplied by the pulmonary artery and its branches, a low-pressure system, while bronchial circulation originates from the aorta and usually provides about 5% of blood to the airways and supporting structures of the lungs.*
Use pulmonary blood **circulation** • injured [ɪndʒɚd] **pulmonary circulation** • **pulmonary** arterial trunk[1] [ʌ]/ perfusion[2] [juːʒ]/ venous [iː] return • **pulmonary** capillary wedge [dʒ] pressure[3] • **pulmonary** microvascular pressure / microcirculation • **pulmonary** vascular congestion[4] [dʒe]/ hypertension[5] • **pulmonary** angiography / (thrombo)embolism[6] / shunt [ʃʌnt]

Lungen-, kleiner Kreislauf
Truncus pulmonalis[1] Lungendurchblutung, -perfusion[2] pulmokapillärer Verschlussdruck, Wedge-Druck[3] Lungenstauung[4] pulmonale Hypertension/ Hypertonie[5] Lungenembolie[6]

2

Blood & Lymph Circulation — BODY STRUCTURES & FUNCTIONS 143

hepatic or portal circulation n term   sim portal system[1] n term → U47-5

circulation of blood to the liver from the intestine and spleen [iː] via the portal vein and its tributaries[2]

periportal adj term • **intra/ hepatoportal** [hepətoʊpɔːrtᵊl] adj • **porto-** comb

» Splenic [e] MRI[3], which may demonstrate or exclude extrahepatic portal obstruction, aids in diagnosis. These esophageal [-dʒiːəl] varices [værɪsiːz] are portosystemic collateral vessels which carry blood from the coronary veins of the portal system into the azygos-hemiazygos [hemɪeɪzaɪɡəs] veins[4].

Use **portal** blood(stream) / vein [eɪ] / venous [iː] anatomy / collateral circulation • **portal** flow velocity / pressure[5] / hypertension[6] • **portal** vein occlusion[7] [uːʒ]/ inflammation[8] [eɪ]/ hypertensive ascites [əsaɪtiːz] • **portal** decompression / phlebitis[8] [aɪ]/ vein thrombosis[9] • **portal** system surgery /-systemic shunt[10] [ʌ] • hypothalamic(-pituitary)[11] [(j)uː] **portal system** • **periportal** fibrosis / necrosis • **porto**caval shunt[10] /systemic pressure gradient [eɪ] • **porto**hepatic /pulmonary /graphy[12]

Portal-, Pfortaderkreislauf

Pfortadersystem[1] Nebenäste[2] Kernspintomografie d. Milz[3] Vv. azygos u. hemiazygos[4] Pfortaderdruck[5] Pfortaderhochdruck, portale Hypertension[6] Pfortaderverschluss[7] Pfortaderentzündung, Pylephlebitis[8] Pfortaderthrombose[9] portokavale(r) Shunt/ Anastomose[10] hypophysäres Pfortadersystem[11] Portografie, Röntgenkontrastdarstellung d. Pfortader[12]

3

hemodynamics [hiːmoʊdaɪnæmɪks] n term

physical properties of circulation such as cardiac output, BP, peripheral resistance, etc. and their study

hemodynamic[1] adj term • **hyperdynamic** adj • **hemo-** [hiːmoʊ] comb

» Bicarbonate[2] does not improve hemodynamics in critically ill patients who have lactic acidosis[3]. Stabilize a hemodynamically unstable patient before performing diagnostic procedures.

Use (ab)normal / altered [ɒː]/ (un)stable [eɪ]/ deranged[4] [eɪ] **hemodynamics** • systemic / venous / (intra)renal **hemodynamics** • glomerular / portal / capillary **hemodynamics** • **hemodynamic** (pressure) monitoring[5] / burden[6] [ɜː] • **hemodynamic** (in)stability / support • **hyperdynamic** state • **hemo**dilution[7] [uːʃ] /dialysis [æ] /lysis[8] [hɪmɒːləsɪs] /lytic [ɪ]

Hämodynamik

hämodynamisch[1] Bikarbonat[2] Laktatazidose, Laktazidose[3] hämodynamische Störungen[4] hämodynam. Überwachung[5] hämodynamische Belastung[6] Blutverdünnung, Hämodilution[7] Hämolyse, Auflösung/ Abbau v. Erythrozyten[8]

4

blood flow [floʊ] n   sim perfusion[1] [pɚfjuːʒᵊn] n term → U88-3

amount of blood passing through an organ, specific tissues or vessels

inflow[2] n term • **outflow**[3] n • **backflow**[4] n • **flowmetry** n • **perfusate**[5] n • **perfuse**[6] v term • (non)**perfused** adj • re/ hyper/ hypoperfusion[7] n

» Surrounding this was a zone of stasis [eɪ], characterized by sluggish[8] [ʌ] capillary blood flow. Wound [uː] healing is profoundly influenced by local blood supply, vasoconstriction, and all factors that govern perfusion and blood oxygenation. The goal is to increase blood pressure to the point that coronary perfusion is sustained[9] [eɪ].

Use to check for/impede[10] [iː] /maintain/restore **blood flow** • coronary / cerebral[11] / arterial **blood flow** • diminished or decreased[7] mechanisms [k]/ direction **blood flow** • interruption[12] / stasis[13] [eɪ]/ cessation[12] [s] **of blood flow** • hepatic arterial / renal plasma[14] (abbr RPF) **flow** • capillary / collateral / retrograde [eɪ]/ lymph(atic) **flow** • sluggish / stagnant **flow** • **flow** rate / pattern / stasis[13] • vascular / portal **inflow** • left ventricular / hepatic venous [iː] **outflow** • **outflow** tract / resistance / obstruction[15] • regional / arterial / cardiac **perfusion** • lung[16] / cutaneous[17] [eɪ]/ brain[11] / cerebral cortex **perfusion** • impaired[18] [eɚ] **perfusion** • **perfusion** rate / pressure / scan or scintigraphy[19] / support

Durchblutung, Blutfluss

Perfusion, Durchströmung, -blutung[1] Zufluss, Einströmen[2] Ab-, Ausfluss[3] Rückfluss[4] Perfusionsflüssigkeit[5] perfundieren, durchströmen[6] Minder-, Mangeldurchblutung, Hypoperfusion[7] langsam[8] aufrechterhalten[9] d. Blutfluss/ Durchblutung behindern[10] Hirndurchblutung[11] Unterbrechung d. Blutzufuhr, Ischämie[12] Blutstase, -stau(ung)[13] renaler Plasmafluss[14] Abflussbehinderung[15] Lungenperfusion[16] Hautdurchblutung[17] Perfusionsstörung[18] Perfusionsszintigrafie[19]

5

blood supply [səplaɪ] n clin

opposite (**venous**) **drainage**[1][dreɪnɪdʒ], **venous return**[2] [ɜː] n term

transport of oxygen-rich arterial blood to the tissues of the body providing them with nutrients

supply[3] v • **supplying** adj • **drain**[4] [dreɪn] v & n • (un)**drained** adj

» The phrenic [e] arteries arising directly from the aorta supply the diaphragm. Interruption of the blood supply to the humeral [juː] head may cause avascular [eɪ] necrosis. Venous drainage [-ɪdʒ] is more apt to be interrupted[5] than arterial inflow when the mesentery is trapped[6]. Promote venous drainage by elevating the foot of the bed[7] 15-20 degrees.

Use adequate[8] / abundant [ʌ] or rich[9] / (in)sufficient[8] [ɪʃ]/ poor / impaired **blood supply** • arterial / collateral / local / dual [d(j)uːəl] **blood supply** • **blood supply** to the brain / of the heart [ɑː]/ from the aorta [eɪ] • arterial[10] **supply** • collateral / cerebral / hepatic / penile [piːnaɪl] **venous drainage** • **venous drainage** system / route [aʊ‖uː] • lymphatic / lacrimal[11] / bile[12] [aɪ]/ surgical **drainage** • central[13] / systemic / coronary / pulmonary **venous return** • interrupted [ʌ]/ unimpaired[14] [eɚ] **venous return** • **venous return** to the heart / from the extremities

Blutversorgung, -zufuhr

venöser Abfluss[1] venöser Rückstrom/ -fluss[2] versorgen, liefern, zuführen[3] ableiten, drainieren; Drain[4] wird eher unterbrochen[5] eingeklemmt[6] Hochstellen d. Fußendes[7] ausreichende Blutversorgung[8] gute Durchblutung[9] arterielle Blutzufuhr[10] Abfluss d. Tränenflüssigkeit[11] Gallenabfluss[12] zentralvenöser Rückstrom/ -fluss[13] ungehinderter venöser Rückstrom[14]

6

144 BODY STRUCTURES & FUNCTIONS — Blood & Lymph Circulation

blood volume n clin & term
　　　　　　rel **euvolemia**[1] [juːvəliːmɪə], **hypovolemia**[2] [haɪpoʊ-] n term
total amount of blood in the body controlled by capillary fluid exchange, hormones, and renal filtration
volumetric[3] [e] adj • **-volemia** comb • **-volemic** [iː] comb

» Normally, mean intrathoracic pressure is negative, which increases thoracic [æs] blood volume and ventricular end-diastolic volume. In acute blood loss, the blood volume must be restored through preoperative fluid administration and/or pharmacologic manipulation.

Use central[4] / (intra)arterial [ɪɚ]/ mean [iː] arterial **blood volume** • cerebral / pulmonary capillary[5] **blood volume** • total / circulating / distribution [juːʃ] of **blood volume** • **blood volume** nomogram / loss / deficit / expansion[6] / replacement • (intra)vascular / plasma[7] / circulating **volume** • mean corpuscular[8] [ʌ]/ red blood cell[9] **volume** • end-diastolic [aɪə]/ stroke[10] / extracellular (fluid) **volume** • **volume** replacement[11] / expander / depletion[12] [iːʃ] • **volume** excess / overload[13] / repletion[11] • iso**volumetric** • hypo**volemic**

Blutvolumen, Gesamtblutmenge
Normovolämie[1] Hypovolämie, Verminderung d. zirkulierenden Blutmenge[2] volumetrisch[3] zentrales Blutvolumen[4] pulmonal-kapilläres Blutvolumen[5] Vergrößerung d. Blutvolumens[6] Plasmavolumen[7] mittleres Erythrozyteneinzelvolumen[8] Erythrozytenvolumen[9] Schlagvolumen[10] Volumenersatz, -substitution[11] Volumenverlust[12] Volumenüberlastung[13]

7

blood pressure [blʌd preʃɚ] n clin & term, abbr **BP** → U107-14
　　　　　　rel **hypertension**[1] [haɪpɚtenʃˢn], **hypotension**[2] [haɪpoʊ-] n term → U124-6
tension of the blood within the arteries that is dependent on left ventricular contraction, arterial elasticity, the resistance of the arterioles and capillaries as well as blood volume and viscosity
normo/ hypo/ **hypertensive**[3] adj & n term • **hypertonicity** n • **hypotonicity**[2] n • **-tonic** comb

» A systolic pressure of 60 mm Hg usually means that flow is sufficient to maintain viability [aɪ] of the extremity. Overall blood pressure is maintained by ventricular contraction, vascular resistance and elasticity, and the viscosity and volume of the blood. Sympatholytic [ɪ] antihypertensive agents [eɪdʒ] may be required to control hypertension.

Use **blood pressure** readings[4] [iː] • arterial / systolic[5] / diastolic[6] / adequate **blood pressure** • high / elevated[7] / unstable **blood pressure** • mean arterial / left ventricular **pressure** • central venous[8] / (coronary) perfusion **pressure** • (systemic/ capillary/ interstitial [ɪʃ]/ net) hydrostatic[9] / (atrial/ ventricular) filling **pressure** • osmotic / hydrostatic [aɪ] venous / plasma oncotic[10] **pressure** • **pressure** wave / gradient[11] [eɪ] / falls / measurements[12] [eʒ] • arterial / venous / portal[13] **hypertension** • pulmonary / intracranial [eɪ]/ renal **hypertension** • essential[14] / malignant[15] / mild / moderate **hypertension** • postural[16] / systemic **hypotension** • **hypertensive** patient[3] / episode / crisis[17] [aɪ] • muscular[18] [ʌ]/ serum [ɪɚ] **hypertonicity** • **hypertonic** saline [eɪ] solution / state / dehydration[19]

Blutdruck
Bluthochdruck, Hypertension, Hypertonie[1] niedriger Blutdruck, Hypotension, Hypotonie; Tonusverminderung[2] hypertensiv; Hypertoniker(in)[3] Blutdruckwerte[4] systolischer Blutdruck[5] diastolischer Blutdruck[6] erhöhter Blutdruck[7] zentralvenöser Druck, zentraler Venendruck[8] hydrostat. Druck[9] kolloidosmotischer Druck d. Plasmas[10] Druckgefälle[11] Druckmessungen[12] Pfortaderhochdruck, portale Hypertension[13] essentielle/ primäre Hypertonie[14] maligne Hypertonie[15] orthostatische Hypotonie[16] hypertensive Krise, Blutdruckkrise[17] muskuläre Hypertonie[18] hypertone Dehydratation[19]

8

pulse pressure [pʌls] n term　　rel **pulse wave**[1] [eɪ] n term,
　　　　　　upstroke[2] [ʌ] n jar
difference between the systolic and the diastolic blood pressure during the cardiac cycle
pulsate[3] [pʌlseɪt] v term • **pulsation** n • **pulseless**[4] adj • **pulsatile**[5] [aɪ] adj

» A narrow pulse pressure (more than half the systolic pressure), distended neck veins, and pulsus paradoxus[6] were present. The presence of arterial pulses distal to penetrating wounds [uː] does not preclude[7] arterial injury as pulse waves may be transmitted through soft clots. Palpation and quantification of lower extremity vascular pulsations should be performed. In aortic regurgitation[8] [ɜː], the pulse has a rapid upstroke and then collapses.

Use arterial / wide [aɪ]/ large / widened / increased / narrow[9] **pulse pressure** • **pulse pressure** fall • **pulse** volume / quality / rate[10] / measurement [eʒ] • **pulse** oximetry[11] / rise / deficit[12] • **pulse wave** velocity[13] / transmission time[14] / jugular [dʒʌgjʊlɚ] venous[15] / paradoxic(al)[6] **pulse** • epigastric[16] / precordial / capillary **pulsations** • presystolic / jugular venous **pulsations** • **pulsatile** arterial blood flow / perfusion / mass / tinnitus[17] [ɪ] • **pulse wave**[18] / carotid / delayed [eɪ]/ brisk or rapid[19] **upstroke** • **pulseless** extremities / disease[20] / electrical activity

Pulsdruck
Pulswelle[1] Druckanstieg[2] pulsieren[3] pulslos[4] pulsierend, pulssynchron schlagend[5] paradoxer Puls[6] ausschließen[7] Aorten(klappen)insuffizienz[8] flacher Puls[9] Pulsfrequenz[10] Pulsoximetrie[11] Pulsdefizit[12] Pulswellengeschwindigkeit[13] Pulswellenlaufzeit[14] Jugularispuls[15] epigastrische Pulsationen[16] pulssynchrone Ohrgeräusche[17] Pulswellenanstieg[18] plötzlicher Druckanstieg[19] Aortenbogensyndrom[20]

9

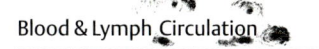

(total) peripheral resistance n term, abbr **TPR**

rel **vascular resistance**[1], **arteriolar tone**[2] [ɑːrtɪɚioʊlɚ toʊn] n term

opposition to blood flow in the systemic circulation calculated as the mean [iː] arterial pressure[3] minus the central venous pressure divided by the cardiac output[4]

» Valvular [æ] insufficiency [ɪʃ] decreased because of the fall in peripheral resistance. Tachy-cardia and a low BP due to elevated systemic resistance are early signs of a drop in cardiac output.

Use total pulmonary / low / increased / high **peripheral resistance** • pulmonary[5] / systemic[6] / coronary / renal **vascular resistance** • venous[7] [iː]/ arteriolar / capillary[8] **resistance** • cerebrovascular / urethral [iː] **resistance** • **resistance** to flow[9] • vascular[10] / venous / (peripheral) [ɪ] vasomotor [veɪzoʊ-] **tone**

peripherer Widerstand
Gefäßwiderstand[1] arteriolärer Tonus[2] mittlerer Aortendruck[3] Herzminutenvolumen[4] Lungengefäßwiderstand[5] systemischer Gefäßwiderstand[6] venöser Widerstand[7] kapillärer Widerstand[8] Strömungswiderstand[9] Gefäßwiderstand[10]

10

vasoconstriction [veɪzoʊkənstrɪkʃən] n term

opposite **vasodilation**[1] [-daɪleɪʃən] n term

narrowing of the vascular lumen by an increase in smooth [uː] muscle[2] tone of the wall of a vessel

dila(ta)tion[3] n term • dilate[4] [eɪ] v • constrict[5] v • vaso- [veɪzoʊ-] comb

» Splanchnic [k] vasoconstriction caused ischemia [ɪskiːmɪə] secondary to a low-flow state. What can cause symptoms of vasodilation such as headache, flushing[6] [ʌ], palpitations, and peripheral edema [iː]?

Use localized / neurogenic [dʒe]/ pulmonary **vasoconstriction** • profound[7] [aʊ] venous [iː] **vasoconstriction** • renal / splanchnic [æ] **vasoconstriction** • uterine [juː]/ nasal **vasoconstriction** • passive[8] / active[9] / arteriolar **vasodilation** • reflex [iː]/ muscular [ʌ] **vasodilation** • systemic / cerebral **vasodilation** • peripheral / exercise-induced[10] **vasodilation** • vasomotor reflex[11] /dilators[12] /constrictive • **vaso**congestion /constrictor[13] • **vaso**active /spasm[14] /stimulation

Gefäßverengung, Vasokonstriktion
Gefäßerweiterung, Vasodilatation[1] glatte Muskulatur[2] Dehnung, Erweiterung, Dilatation[3] erweitern, dehnen, dilatieren[4] ver-, einengen, zusammenziehen[5] Hitzewallungen[6] starke Gefäßverengung[7] passive Gefäßerweiterung[8] aktive G.[9] belastungsbedingte Gefäßerweiterung[10] vasomotor. Reflex[11] Vasodilatanzien, gefäßerweiternde (Arznei)mittel[12] gefäßverengend; vasokonstr. Nerv, Vasokonstriktor; Vasokonstringens, gefäßvereng. Mittel[13] Gefäßkrampf, Vaso-, Angiospasmus[14]

11

blood viscosity [vɪskɒːsɪti] n clin   rel **plasma** [æ] **viscosity**[1] n term

internal resistance of blood to flow resulting from friction (shearing [ɪɚ] forces[2]) of its cellular components

(hyper)**viscous**[3] [vɪskəs] adj • **viscid**[3] [s] adj • **hyperviscosity** n • **visco-** comb

» Resistance to the flow of blood in a vessel is proportional to vessel length and viscosity of blood. Increased viscosity due to a high hematocrit may result in stasis [eɪ] of blood within vessels, and predispose patients to pulmonary congestion[4] and vascular thrombosis.

Use elevated or increased[5] / decreased **blood viscosity** • serum [ɪɚ]/ sputum / seminal [e] fluid[6] / relative[7] **viscosity** • high / low / dynamic[8] [daɪ-] / kinematic[9] **viscosity** • **low-viscosity** fluid • **viscous** secretions[10] [iːʃ]/ effusion [juːʒ] / cervical [sɜːr-] mucus[11] [mjuːkəs]/ sputum • **highly viscous** mucus[12] • **visco**elasticity /elastic properties

Blutviskosität
Plasmaviskosität[1] Scherkräfte[2] viskös, zähflüssig[3] Lungenstauung[4] erhöhte Blutviskosität[5] Viskosität d. Samenflüssigkeit[6] relative Viskosität[7] dynam. Viskosität[8] kinematische Viskosität[9] zähflüssiges Sekret[10] visköser Zervixschleim[11] hochvisköser Schleim[12]

12

hemodilution [hiːmədaɪluːʃən] n term   opposite **hemoconcentration**[1] n term

decrease in the concentration of red blood cells in the circulation in relation to plasma volume

dilute[2] [dɪ‖daɪluːt] v & adj • **(un/pre)diluted** adj • **dilutional**[3] adj • concentrate[4] v & n & adj

» Young patients without heart disease tolerate hemodilution well, as long as the plasma volume is fully expanded. Hemoconcentration is reflected by elevated hemoglobin [hiːmə-] and hematocrit values. The blood is hemoconcentrated because of plasma loss into the peritoneal [iː] cavity.

Use normovolemic [iː]/ isovolumetric[5] [aɪsoʊ-]/ preoperative **hemodilution** • progressive / excessive **hemodilution** • **hemoconcentration** nomogram • **undiluted** plasma / serum / suspension • **dilutional** hyponatremia[6] [iː]/ acidosis • **thermodilution**[7] • to reveal [iː] /minimize **hemoconcentration** • platelet[8] / antihemophilic factor (abbr AHF)/ factor VIII **concentrate**

Blutverdünnung, Hämodilution
Bluteindickung, Hämokonzentration[1] verdünnen, diluieren; verdünnt[2] Verdünnungs-[3] konzentrieren, anreichern; Konzentrat; konzentriert[4] isovolumetrische Hämodilution[5] Verdünnungshyponatriämie[6] Thermodilution[7] Thrombozytenkonzentrat[8]

13

shunt [ʃʌnt] *n term* → U129-6 *rel* **anastomosis¹, bypass²** [baɪpæs] *n term*

diversion [ɜː] of fluids to an absorbing [iː] system by fistulation or a mechanical device [-aɪs]
shunt³ *v term* • **shunting** *n* • **bypass⁴** *v* → U125-11

» In patients with a left-to-right shunt at the atrial [eɪ], ventricular, or pulmonary artery levels, pulmonary blood flow will exceed [iː] systemic blood flow. These collateral vessels result in shunting of portal blood into the systemic circulation.

Use ateriovenous⁵ [iː]/ bidirectional / cavomesenteric [eɪ] / right-to-left⁶ **shunt** • aorta-to-pulmonary artery *or* aortopulmonary [eɪ] **shunt** • portal-systemic *or* portosystemic⁷ / ventriculoperitoneal⁸ [iː] **shunt** • splenorenal [e]/ cerebrospinal [aɪ] fluid⁹ **shunt** • hemodialysis¹⁰ [æ]/ reversed¹¹ [ɜː] **shunt** • **shunt** function / surgery / implantation • **shunt** infection¹² • reversal¹¹ • **to shunt** blood

Shunt, Kurzschluss
Anastomose¹ Bypass, Umgehung² einen Shunt anlegen, shunten³ umgehen, umleiten⁴ arteriovenöser Shunt⁵ Rechts-Links-Shunt⁶ portosystemischer Shunt⁷ ventrikuloperitonealer Shunt⁸ Liquorshunt⁹ Hämodialyseshunt¹⁰ Shuntumkehr¹¹ Shuntinfektion¹²

14

blood-brain barrier [blʌd breɪn bærɪɚ] *n term, abbr* **BBB**

selective mechanism [ek] keeping many compounds [aʊ] in the blood from entering the parenchyma [pərɛŋkɪmə] of the CNS

» Cytokines [saɪtə-] generated by the exudate disrupt¹ [ʌ] the blood-brain barrier to cause brain edema, which is further aggravated by ischemic [kiː] brain damage. Permeability of the blood-brain barrier tends to increase after return of flow to the ischemic area.

Use to cross²/penetrate³/break down **the blood-brain barrier** • disrupted **BBB** • **BBB** permeability⁴ / defect • blood-CSF⁵ / placental⁶ [se]/ gastric mucosal⁷ **barrier**

Blut-Hirn-Schranke
schädigen¹ d. Blut-Hirn-Schranke passieren² d. Blut-Hirn-Schranke durchdringen³ Durchlässigkeit d. Blut-Hirn-Schranke⁴ Blut-Liquor-Schranke⁵ Plazentaschranke, -barriere⁶ Magenschleimhautbarriere⁷

15

(vascular) permeability [ɜː] *n term*   *sim* **capillary permeability¹** *n term*

extent to which the vascular wall permits the passage of substances [ʌ]
(im/ semi)permeable² *adj term* • **permeate³** [-ieɪt] *v* • **(hyper/ im)permeability** *n*

» Burns [ɜː] lead to a loss of intravascular fluid volume due to increased vascular permeability. Venous [iː] obstruction, vasodilatation, muscular exercise, and increased capillary permeability all increase the rate of lymph flow.

Use microvascular / artery wall / venular / endothelial [iː] **permeability** • membrane / ion⁴ [aɪən]/ water **permeability** • intestinal / glomerular / blood-brain barrier⁵ **permeability** • relative / selective⁶ / low or poor **permeability** • **permeability** factor • impermeable to glucose⁷ / membrane • gas-**permeable** membrane⁸

Gefäßpermeabilität, -durchlässigkeit
Kapillarpermeabilität¹ semipermeabel, halbdurchlässig² durchdringen³ Ionenpermeabilität⁴ Durchlässigkeit d. Blut-Hirn-Schranke⁵ selektive Permeabilität⁶ glukoseundurchlässig⁷ gasdurchlässige Membran⁸

16

Unit 37   Components of the Blood
Related Units: **36** Blood Circulation, **38** Hematopoiesis & Coagulation, **78** Metabolism, **55** Hormones, **39** The Immune System, **47** The Liver & Biliary System, **49** Urine Production

blood [blʌd] *n*   *syn* **sanguis** [sæŋgwɪs] *n term rare*

the fluid and its suspended particles that are circulated through the heart [ɑː], blood vessels, and tissues [ʃ|s] by which oxygen and nutritive [uː] materials¹ are transported to the tissues, while carbon dioxide [aɪ] and various metabolic products² are removed for excretion [iːʃ]
bloody *adj* • **bloodless³** *adj* • **half-blood⁴** *n* • **hem(ato)-, sangui(n)-** *comb*

» The peripheral blood smear⁵ [smɪɚ] reveals [iː] target cells, nucleated red cells, and a hypochromic microcytic [sɪ] anemia [iː]. The carotid body⁶ responds to a decrease in oxygen tension, an increase in blood acidity [sɪ] and in blood temperature.

Use to spill⁷/(with)draw [ɒː] *or* obtain⁸/cross-match⁹/donate/transfuse¹⁰ **blood** • arterial¹¹ [ɪɚ]/ bright red / venous [iː] **blood** • intracranial [eɪ]/ peripheral [ɪf]/ portal / cord¹² / maternal [ɜː] **blood** • citrated¹³ / defibrinated [aɪ]/ oxygenated¹¹ / whole¹⁴ **blood** • (fecal) [iː] occult [ʌ]/ autologous¹⁵ [ɒː] **blood** • **blood** vessel / group / supply¹⁶ [aɪ]/ pressure • **blood** clotting *or* coagulation¹⁷ / clot¹⁸ • **blood** sample¹⁹ / test / count²⁰ [aʊ]/ gas analysis • **blood** chemistry [ke-]/ urea nitrogen [aɪ] (*abbr* BUN) • **blood** donor [oʊ]/ bank / loss / typing²¹ • **blood** transfusion / products • **blood**-stained²² [eɪ] /-shot eyes²³ /-borne infection /-brain-barrier²⁴ • **bloody** sputum / diarrhea [iː]/ stools [uː] • **bloody** vaginal [dʒ] discharge²⁵ / rhinorrhea [aɪ] • **bloodless** phlebotomy [flɪ-]/ field • **hemo**globin /chrome /dynamics /lysis /ptysis [ɪ] • **hem**orrhage²⁶ /rrhoid /dialysis [æ] /stasis [eɪ] /philia²⁷ [-fɪlɪə] • **hemato**crit /toxic /penia [iː] /genic • **hemat**oma /uria /temesis²⁸ /ngioma [-dʒɪoʊmə] • **(sero)sanguin**ous material / discharge • **asanguinous** fluid • **exsanguinating** hemorrhage²⁹ [e] • fatal³⁰ [eɪ] **exsanguination** • **consanguinous** marriage / mating³¹ [eɪ]

Blut, Sanguis
Nährstoffe¹ Stoffwechselprodukte² blutleer; unblutig³ Mischling, Halbblut⁴ Blutausstrich⁵ Paraganglion/ Glomus caroticum⁶ Blut vergießen⁷ Blut abnehmen⁸ d. Kreuzprobe machen⁹ Blut transfundieren¹⁰ sauerstoffreiches/ arterielles Blut¹¹ Nabelschnurblut¹² Zitratblut¹³ Vollblut¹⁴ Eigenblut¹⁵ Blutversorgung¹⁶ Blutgerinnung¹⁷ Blutgerinnsel, Thrombus¹⁸ Blutprobe¹⁹ Blutbild²⁰ Blutgruppenbestimmung²¹ blutig, blutbefleckt²² blutunterlaufene Augen²³ Blut-Hirn-Schranke²⁴ blutiger Scheidenausfluss²⁵ Blutung²⁶ Bluterkrankheit, Hämophilie²⁷ Bluterbrechen, Hämatemesis²⁸ Massenblutung²⁹ Verblutung³⁰ Inzest³¹

1

Components of the Blood — BODY STRUCTURES & FUNCTIONS

-(h)emia [iːmɪə] *comb*, BE **-(h)aemia**

word ending describing a blood condition, e.g. hyperglycemia[1] [-glaɪsiːmɪə] refers to an excess of glucose in the blood

-emic [iːmɪk] *comb*

» Hyponatremia[2] may develop in patients with marked hyperlipidemia or hyperproteinemia, as fat and protein contribute to plasma bulk[3] [ʌ] although they are not dissolved in plasma water. Hypochloremia, hypokalemia[4], and alkalosis may result from fluid and electrolyte [-laɪt] losses.

Use an/ hypercalc/ hyperlipoprotein**emia** • hyperkal/ hypercholesterol[5]/ bilirubin**emia** • hypox/ hyponatr/ hypoalbumin**emia** • hypogammaglobulin/ bacter[6]/ ur[7]/ azot**emia** • an/ hyperchlor/ hypokal**emic** • normocalc/ ur[8]/ hyperprolactin**emic**

-ämie

Hyperglykämie[1] Hyponatr(i)ämie, verminderter Natriumgehalt d. Blutes[2] Plasmavolumen[3] Hypokaliämie[4] Hypercholesterinämie, erhöhte Serumcholesterinwerte[5] Bakteriämie[6] Harnvergiftung, Urämie[7] urämisch[8]

[2]

(blood) plasma *n term*   *sim* **(blood) serum**[1] [sɪəːəm] *n term*, *pl* **sera, serums**

noncellular fluid portion in circulating blood; serum refers to plasma after the fibrin [aɪ] clot has been removed in the process of coagulation but is sometimes also used as a synonym for plasma and antiserum

antiserum[2] [æntɪsɪəːəm] *n term* • **plasm(a)-** *comb* • **sero-** [sɪəːoʊ-] *comb*

» Plasma is a clear, straw-colored[3] fluid which contains transport proteins, inorganic salts, nutrients[4], gases, enzymes [aɪ], hormones and waste [eɪ] materials[5] from the cells in the body.

Use circulating [ɜː]/ fresh frozen[6] **plasma** • **plasma** cells / derivatives[7] / fractions[8] • **plasma** products / substitute[9] • **plasma** concentration or level / osmolality / volume[10] • **plasma** protein[11] (binding) / albumin[12] / glucose / bicarbonate / renin activity • **plasma** expander[9] / infusion / exchange[13] • **serum** cholesterol / amylase [æmɪleɪz] /-bound [au] / iron[14] / sodium • **serum** potassium / lipase [lɪpeɪz] / bilirubin / sickness[15] • **serum** complement level / protein-bound iodine[16] [aɪə] (*abbr* SPBI)/ alkaline phosphatase • antilymphocyte [ɪ] (*abbr* ALS)/ antirabies[17] [eɪ] **serum** • **plasma**cyte /blast /cytosis /pheresis[18] [iː] • serology /logic test[19] /positive /negative /group • sero**type** /conversion[20] /vaccination[21] [ks] /therapy

Blutplasma

(Blut)serum[1] Antiserum[2] gelblich[3] Nährstoffe[4] Stoffwechselschlacken, -abfallprodukte[5] tiefgefrorenes Frischplasma[6] Plasmaderivate[7] Plasmafraktionen[8] Plasmaersatz(stoff), -expander[9] Plasmavolumen[10] Plasmaprotein[11] Plasmaalbumin[12] Plasmaaustausch[13] Serumeisen[14] Serumkrankheit[15] proteingebundenes Jod im Serum[16] Tollwut-Antiserum[17] Plasmapherese[18] serolog. Untersuchung[19] Serokonversion[20] Serovakzination[21]

[3]

(blood) corpuscle [kɔːrpʌsl] *n term*   *syn* **blood cell** *n clin*, **hematocyte** *n term*

one of the formed elements suspended in the blood which normally make up 45% of its volume

(intra/ extra)corpuscular *adj term*

» Such high erythrocyte [ɪ] counts are possible only when the red corpuscles are smaller than normal. Red blood cells can be frozen and stored for up to 3 years. The causes of acute hemolysis can be extracorpuscular or intracorpuscular.

Use red[1] / white **corpuscle** • **mean corpuscular** volume[2] (*abbr* MCV)/ hemoglobin (concentration)[3] (*abbr* MCHC)/ diameter [daɪæ-] (*abbr* MCD) • **extracorpuscular** hemolysis • **intracorpuscular** hemolytic [ɪ] anemia[4] [əniːmɪə]

Blutkörperchen, -zelle, Hämozyt

rotes Blutkörperchen, Erythrozyt[1] mittleres Erythrozyteneinzelvolumen, MCV[2] mittlere korpuskuläre Hämoglobinkonzentration, MCHC[3] korpuskuläre hämolyt. Anämie[4]

[4]

---

red blood cell *n clin*, *abbr* **RBC**   *syn* **erythrocyte** [ɪrɪθrəsaɪt] *n term*

biconcave [eɪ] hemoglobin-containing disk formed in the red bone marrow (from megalo-, erythro-, normoblasts[1] and reticulocytes[2]) which performs the task of transporting oxygen from the lungs to the tissues

erythroid[3] *adj term* • **erythrocytic**[4] [ɪ] *adj* • **erythroblast** *n* • **erythro-** *comb*

» With ischemia [kiː], blood viscosity increases and red blood cells sludge[5] [slʌdʒ] within capillaries. The blood smear [ɪə] was diagnostic, with large numbers of nucleated erythroblasts, target cells, and small pale RBCs. This can lead to acute hemolytic anemia with increased erythrocyte fragility[6] [dʒɪ], impaired oxygen delivery to tissues, and increased susceptibility [sʌs-] to infection[7].

Use circulating / (im)mature[8] / young / aged[9] / senescent[9] [sɪnes-]/ type 0 **RBCs** • dysmorphic / teardrop-shaped / nucleated[10] / hypochromic **RBCs** • fragmented / extravasated / packed[11] / frozen **RBCs** • **red blood cell** production[12] / release [iː]/ destruction / agglutination • **red blood cell** indices / size / mass / count[13] / morphology • **red blood cell** distribution curve[14] [ɜː]/ folate [foʊleɪt] level / smear / survival[15] / sickled[16] / infected **erythrocytes** • **erythrocyte** maturation factor (*abbr* EMF)/ membrane[17] • **erythrocyte** (proto)porphyrin / antigen / sedimentation rate[18] (*abbr* ESR) • **erythroid** precursor[19] [ɜː]/ cell / activity / hyperplasia [eɪ] • eosinophilic [ɪəsɪnə-] **erythroblast** • **erythro**cytosis /blastosis /poiesis[12] [poʊiːsɪs]

Erythrozyt, rotes Blutkörperchen

Normoblasten[1] Retikulozyten[2] erythroid, rötlich[3] erythrozytär[4] zusammenlagern[5] Erythrozytenfragilität[6] Infektionsanfälligkeit[7] unreife Erythrozyten[8] überalterte Erythrozyten[9] kernhaltige E.[10] Erythrozytenkonzentrat[11] Erythro(zyto)poese[12] Erythrozytenzählung, -zahl[13] Erythrozytenverteilungskurve[14] Erythrozytenüberlebensdauer, -zeit[15] Sichelzellen[16] Erythrozytenmembran[17] Blutkörperchensenkungsgeschwindigkeit, BKS[18] Erythrozytenvorläufer, -stufe, Erythroblast[19]

[5]

hemoglobin n term, abbr **Hb**　　rel **heme**[1] [hiːm], **transferrin**[2] n term
　iron-containing red protein consisting of approximately 6% heme and 94% globin which attracts and loosely binds to free oxygen which it transports from the lungs to the tissues
　oxyhemoglobin[3] [ɒksɪ-] n term • **carboxyhemoglobin** n [-hiːməɡloʊbɪn]
　» When the iron [aɪ] in Hb is oxidized from the ferrous to ferric state, e.g. in poisoning with nitrates, a nonrespiratory compound, methemoglobin (MetHb), is formed. Oxidized hemoglobin denatures[4] [eɪ] and forms so-called Heinz bodies[5]. Arterial blood gases and arterial O_2 saturation of hemoglobin and carboxyhemoglobin levels should be measured.
　Use free / (non)oxygenated[3] / total circulating / muscle **hemoglobin** • glycosylated[6] [aɪ]/ embryonic[7] / fetal[8] / adult[9] **hemoglobin** • **hemoglobin** A1c / A2 / C / E / F[8] / H / S • **hemoglobin**-binding capacity / molecules • **hemoglobin**-oxygen dissociation curve [ɜː]/ SC disease[10] • hepatic / (non)hemoglobin **heme** • **heme**-bound iron / precursor[11] [ɜː]/ synthesis[12] [ɪ]/ oxygenase / catabolism • iron-laden[13] [eɪ]/ plasma / serum / carbohydrate-deficient[14] [ɪʃ] (abbr CDT) **transferrin** • **transferrin** saturation / receptor / iron-binding capacity[15] • **hemoglobin**emia /uria[16] /opathy

Hämoglobin, Hb, roter Blutfarbstoff
Häm[1] Transferrin, Siderophilin[2] Oxyhämoglobin[3] denaturiert[4] Heinz-(Innen)körper[5] glykolisiertes Hämoglobin[6] embryonales/ frühfetales Hämoglobin, H. Gower, HbP[7] fetales Hämoglobin, HbF[8] adultes Hämoglobin, HbA[9] Hämoglobin S-C-Krankheit[10] Hämpräkursor, Vorstufe d. Häm[11] Hämsynthese[12] m. Eisen beladenes Transferrin[13] kohlenhydratdefizientes T., Desialotransferrin[14] Eisenbindungskapazität v. Transferrin[15] Hämoglobinurie[16]　　6

white (blood) cell n clin, abbr **WBC**　　syn **leukocyte** [luːkəsaɪt] n term
　one of several types of colorless nucleated[1] blood cells which are capable of ameboid [iː] movement and have a key role in fighting infections; unlike RBCs they are able to migrate [aɪ] through capillary walls
　leukocytic [-sɪtɪk] adj term • **leuk(o)-**, BE **leuc(o)-** [luːkoʊ‖BE ljuːkoʊ] comb
　» Platelet and white cell aggregates formed in response to injury were trapped in the lungs, where they engendered[2] [dʒe] an inflammatory response. An elevated synovial [sɪn-] fluid white count and low glucose (relative to plasma glucose) suggest sepsis. The lab tests revealed elevated leukocyte and eosinophil counts.
　Use abundant[3] [ʌ]/ (ab)normal / transfused **WBCs** • **WBC** (dys)function / production / casts[4] [æ‖BE ɑː] • **WBC** differential (count)[5] / breakdown[6] / aplasia [eɪ] • (non)granular / peripheral blood **leukocytes** • fecal [iː]/ CSF / urine / wound [uː]/ phagocytic[7] [ɪ] **leukocytes** • **leukocyte** count / alkaline phosphatase[8] (abbr LAP)/ chemotaxis [iː] • **leukocyte**-poor washed red cells[9] / infiltration • **leukocyte** transfusion / antigens[10] / adhesion [iːʒ] deficiency[11] [ɪʃ] • **leukocytic** cellular infiltration / migration[12] [aɪ] • **leukocyte** proteolytic [ɪ] enzymes[13] / cytokines [aɪ] • **leuko**penia[14] [iː] /penic /cytoclastic vasculitis [aɪ] • **leuko**cytosis[15] /dystrophy [ɪ] • **leuk**emia [iː] /emic /apheresis[16] [iː]

Leukozyt, weißes Blutkörperchen
kernhaltige[1] hervorriefen[2] zahlreiche Leukozyten[3] Leukozytenzylinder[4] Leukozytendifferentialzählung[5] Leukozytenabbau[6] phagozytierende Leukozyten[7] alkalische Leukozytenphosphatase[8] leukozytenarme gewaschene Erythrozyten[9] Leukozytenantigene[10] Leukozytenadhäsionsmangel[11] Leukozytenwanderung, Leukodiapedese[12] Leukoproteasen[13] Leuko(zyto)penie, Verminderung d. Leukozytenzahl i. Blut[14] Leukozytose, Vermehrung d. Leukozytenzahl i. Blut[15] Leukapherese[16]　　7

polymorphonuclear leukocyte n term　　syn **poly** n jar, **granulocyte** n term
　mature granular leukocyte which contains a segmented multilobed nucleus; the 3 types of polymorphonuclear (abbr PMN) cells are the neutrophils[1] [(j)uː], eosinophils[2] [ɪəsɪnəfɪlz], and basophils[3] [eɪ]
　(a)granulocytic[4] adj term • **neutropenia** [iː] n • **eosinophilia** n • **basophilic**[5] adj
　» Polymorphonuclear leukocytes in the bladder wall also appear to play a role in clearing bacteriuria. Eosinophils are granulocytes derived [aɪ] from the same progenitor [dʒe] cells[6] as neutrophils, basophils, and monocytes-macrophages [mækroʊfeɪdʒiːz]. When tissue is damaged, basophils release [iː] histamines [-miːnz] and heparin. Moving between endothelial [iː] cells, neutrophils migrate [aɪ] toward the offending agent [eɪdʒᵊnt].
　Use **polymorphonuclear** WBCs / cells / neutrophils / chemotaxis / leukocytosis • **granulocyte**-macrophage colony-stimulating factor (abbr GM-CSF) • **granulocyte** stem cells / transfusion[7] / (im)mature[8] / circulating **granulocytes** • **granulocytic** cells / series[9] [ɪəriːz] / precursor[10] / neutrophil • **agranulocyt**osis • marrow [æ]/ blood **basophils** • **basophilic** leukocytes[3] / stippling[11] [ɪ] • juvenile[12] [dʒuː]/ mature / band[13] / activated **neutrophils** • (hyper)segmented[14] / aggregated / adherent [ɪə] **neutrophils** • **neutrophil** life cycle / pool[15] • **neutrophilic** leukocytes[1] / predominance / pleocytosis • anti-**neutrophil** cytoplasmic antibody (abbr ANCA)

polymorph-/ segmentkerniger Granulozyt
neutrophile Granulozyten[1] eosinophile G.[2] basophile G.[3] granulozytär, Granulozyten-[4] basophil[5] Stammzellen[6] Granulozytentransfusion[7] reife Granulozyten[8] Granulozytenzellreihe[9] Granulozytenvorläuferzelle[10] basophile Tüpfelung (d. Erythrozyten)[11] junge (neutrophile) Granulozyten, Metamyelozyten[12] stabkernige neutrophile Granulozyten[13] übersegmentierte Granulozyten[14] Granulozytenspeicher[15]　　8

Components of the Blood   BODY STRUCTURES & FUNCTIONS **149**

---

monocyte [mɒːnəsaɪt] *n term*   *syn* **endothelial** [iː] **leukocyte** *n term dated*

relatively large phago**cy**tic [sɪ] mono**nu**clear leukocyte formed in the bone marrow which circulates in the blood for about 24 hours before it migrates to the tissues where it develops into a macrophage[1]

monocytic [mɒːnəsɪtɪk] *adj term* • **promonocyte**[2] *n* • **monocyt-** *comb*

» Monocytes are usually indented[3] or horseshoe-shaped[4] but also rounded or ovoid; their nuclei [aɪ] are usually large and centrally placed and are surrounded by at least a small band of cytoplasm [saɪ]. Tissue macrophages[5] arise by migration of monocytes from the circulation.

Use circulating[6] / (peripheral) blood[7] / infiltrating **monocytes** • antigen-presenting / (non-)activated / virus-infected [aɪ] **monocyte** • **monocyte** activation / phagocytosis [fægəsaɪtousɪs] • **monocyte** cell marker /-macrophage [-feɪdʒ] system[8] • **monocyte** chemotaxis [kiːmoʊ-]/ precursor [ɜː] cell /-(derived) [aɪ] macrophage • **monocytic** leukemia[9] [iː]/ ehrlichiosis • **monocyt**osis[10] /openia [iː]

Monozyt
Makrophage[1] Promonozyt[2] eingebuchtet[3] hufeisenförmig[4] Gewebemakrophagen[5] zirkulierende Monozyten[6] Blutmonozyten[7] Monozyten-Makrophagen-System[8] Monozytenleukämie[9] Monozytenvermehrung, Monozytose[10]

9

---

lymphocyte [lɪmfə-] *n term*   *syn* **agranulocyte** *or* **non-granular leukocyte** *n rel* **plasma cells**[1] *n term* → U39-12

mostly small (7-8 mm) WBC formed in lymphatic tissue with a round or slightly indented, eccentrically situated nucleus normally comprising about 22-28% of all leukocytes in circulating blood of adults

lymphocytic [sɪ] *adj term* • **lymphoblast**[2] *n* • **lymphokines**[3] *n* • **lympho-** *comb*

» His eosinophil and basophil concentrations are strikingly increased[4], but lymphocytes and monocytes are normal. Hodgkin's infiltrates are heterogeneous and consist of abnormal lymphoreticular cells, histiocytes, lymphocytes, monocytes, plasma cells, and eosinophils.

Use B-cells *or* B[5]- / T-cells *or* T[6]- / helper-T *or* T helper[7] / cytotoxic T[8]-/ CD4[7] / CD8[9] **lymphocytes** • peripheral blood / mature[10] [juɚ]/ sensitized[11] **lymphocyte** • atypical [eɪ]/ transformed **lymphocyte** • immunocompetent / tumor-infiltrating (*abbr* TIL) **lymphocyte** • **lymphocyte** count / population[12] / transformation[13] / subsets[14] • **lymphocyte** response / antigen / proliferation / recirculation[15] [ɜː] • **lymphocyte**-mediated [iː] cytotoxicity /-activated killer (*abbr* LAK) cells • bone marrow / IgA-secreting [iː]/ malignant / occasional[16] **plasma cells** • **plasma cell** dyscrasia[17] [dɪskreɪ(ɪ)ə]/ leukemia / myeloma [maɪə-] • **lympho**cytoma /ma /cytopenia /cytosis • **agranulo**cytosis

Lymphozyt
Plasmazellen[1] Lymphoblast[2] Lymphokine[3] deutlich erhöht[4] B-Zellen, B-Lymphozyten[5] T-Lymphozyten, T-Zellen[6] T-Helferzellen, CD4+-Zellen[7] zytotoxische T-Zellen, Killerzellen[8] Suppressorzellen, CD8+-Zellen[9] reifer Lymphozyt[10] sensibilisierter Lymphozyt[11] Lymphozytenpopulation[12] Lymphozytentransformation[13] Lymphozyten-Subpopulationen[14] Lymphozytenrezirkulation[15] vereinzelte Plasmazellen[16] Plasmazelldyskrasie[17]

10

(blood) platelet [pleɪtlɪt] *n clin & term*   *syn* **thrombocyte** [θrɒːmbəsaɪt] *n term*

disk-shaped, non-nucleated fragment of a megakaryocyte which is released from the bone marrow into the blood where it initiates blood clotting[1] and aggregates to occlude small leaks in blood vessels

antiplatelet[2] [eɪ] *adj term* • **megathrombocyte**[3] *n* • **thrombocyt(o)-** *comb*

» These megathrombocytes are young platelets produced in response to enhanced platelet destruction. At any given time about a third of all platelets can be found in the spleen[4] [iː].

Use adherent [ɪɚ]/ antibody-coated [oʊ]/ HLA-matched[5] / single-donor [oʊ] **platelets** • **platelet** response / adhesion [iːʒ]/ aggregation[6] / transfusion • **platelet**-activating factor (*abbr* PAF)/ factors[7] / cofactor I *or* factor VIII / cofactor II *or* factor IX • **platelet**-derived [aɪ] growth factor[8] (*abbr* PDGF) • **platelet** life span *or* survival[9] [aɪ]/ thrombus *or* plug[10] [ʌ] • **antiplatelet** agent / antibodies[11] • **thrombo**(cyto)poiesis[12] [-pɔɪiːsɪs] /lytic [ɪ] • **thrombocyt**openia [iː] /openic /osis /emia[13] [iː]

Blutplättchen, Thrombozyt
Blutgerinnung[1] Antithrombozyten-[2] Makrothrombozyt[3] Milz[4] histokompatible Thrombozyten[5] Thrombozytenaggregation[6] Plättchen-, Thrombozytenfaktoren[7] Plättchenwachstumsfaktor[8] Thrombozytenlebenszeit, -dauer[9] Plättchenthrombus, Abscheidungsthrombus, weißer T.[10] Thrombozyten-, Plättchenantikörper[11] Thrombo(zyto)poese[12] Thrombozythämie[13]

11

---

fibrinogen [faɪbrɪnədʒən] *n term*   *syn* **clotting factor I** *n, rel* **fibrin**[1] [aɪ] *n term*

plasma globulin that is converted[2] into fibrin by the action of thrombin in the presence of ionized calcium

cryofibrinogen[3] [kraɪə-] *n term* • **(anti)fibrinolytic**[4] [ɪ] *adj & n* • **fibrino-** *comb*

» This may lead to bleeding secondary to low fibrinogen and platelet levels. A useful clinical test is to look for the rapid fibrinogen consumption seen in disseminated intravascular coagulation by obtaining serial fibrinogen levels. Venous thrombi are composed principally of erythrocytes trapped in a fine fibrin mesh with few platelets.

Use to cleave[5] [iː]/ bind **fibrinogen** • plasma / functional / lack of[6] **fibrinogen** • **fibrinogen** binding / level / synthesis /-related clot formation • **fibrinogen** degradation *or* split products[7] / fragments • **fibrinogen** deficiency[6] / scanning / uptake test[8] • **fibrin** clot[9] / glue[10] [uː]/ foam[11] / strands[12] / mesh[13] • **fibrin**olysis[14] /lytic

Fibrinogen, Faktor I, F-I
Fibrin[1] umgewandelt[2] Fibrinogen-Kryopräzipitat[3] antifibrinolytisch, Antifibrinolytikum, Fibrinolyseinhibitor, -hemmstoff[4] Fibrinogen spalten[5] Fibrinogenmangel[6] Fibrinogenspaltprodukte[7] Fibrinogenaufnahmetest[8] Fibringerinnsel[9] Fibrinkleber[10] Fibrinschaum[11] Fibrin-Monomere[12] Fibrinnetz[13] Fibrinolyse[14]

12

BODY STRUCTURES & FUNCTIONS — Components of the Blood

prothrombin [-θrɒːmbɪn] *n term*   *syn* **clotting factor II** *n, rel* **thrombin**[1] *n term*

glycoprotein [glaɪkə-] formed and stored in the liver parenchyma and present in plasma which is converted [ɜː] to thrombin by the action of extrinsic thromboplastin[2]

prothrombinogenic [-dʒenɪk] *adj term* • **antithrombin**[3] *n*

» In the presence of thromboplastin and calcium ions [aɪə], prothrombin is converted to thrombin, which in turn converts fibrinogen to fibrin, a process resulting in coagulation of blood.

Use plasma **prothrombin** • **prothrombin** level / activity / activator[2] / time[4] (*abbr* PT)/ consumption test[5] [ʌ]/ complex concentrate[6] • clot-bound [aʊ]/ free / circulating **thrombin** • **thrombin** time[7] / generation[8] / fibrinogen reaction • **thrombin** inhibitor /-antithrombin complex • **antithrombin** III

Prothrombin, Faktor II
Thrombin[1] Prothrombinaktivator, Thrombokinase, Thromboplastin[2] Antithrombin[3] Prothrombin-, Thromboplastinzeit[4] Prothrombinverbrauchstest[5] Prothrombinkomplexkonzentrat[6] (Plasma)thrombinzeit[7] Thrombinbildung[8]

13

thromboplastin *n term*   *syn* **thrombokinase** [θrɒːmbəkaɪneɪz] *n term*
rel **tissue** [tɪʃjuː‖tɪs] **factor**[1], **factor III**[1] *n term*

enzyme present in platelets required for the conversion of prothrombin to thrombin

thrombokinetics [θrɒːmboʊkɪnetɪks] *n term*

» Tissue thromboplastin (factor III) interacts[2] with factor VII[3] and calcium to activate factor X[4]; active factor X combines [aɪ] with factor V[5] in the presence of calcium and phospholipid to produce thromboplastin activity.

Use intrinsic / extrinsic / factor III or tissue[1] **thromboplastin** • partial [-ʃəl] **thromboplastin** time[6] (*abbr* PTT) • plasma **thromboplastin** antecedent[7] [siː]/ component[8]

Thromboplastin, -kinase
Gewebethromboplastin, -faktor, Faktor III[1] zusammenwirken[2] Prokonvertin[3] Stuart-Prower-Faktor[4] Proakzelerin[5] partielle Thromboplastinzeit, Partialthromboplastinzeit, PTT[6] Faktor XI, Rosenthal-Faktor[7] Faktor IX, Christmas-Faktor[8]

14

plasmin [plæzmɪn] *n term*   *syn* **fibrinolysin** [faɪbrɪnəlaɪsɪn] *n term*
rel **plasminogen**[1] [plæzmɪnədʒən], **urokinase**[2] [jʊəroʊkaɪneɪz] *n term*

active proteolytic enzyme which dissolves fibrin in blood clots; plasminogen or profibrinolysin is its inactive precursor in plasma which is converted to plasmin by the action of urokinase

antiplasmin[3] *n term* • **fibrinolysis**[4] *n* • **staphylokinase** *n* • **streptokinase** *n*

» Plasmin directly lyses[5] [aɪ] thrombi [aɪ] both in the pulmonary artery and in the venous [iː] circulation. Free plasminogen cannot be activated by single-chain urokinase plasminogen activator but, like tPA, scuPA can readily [e] activate plasminogen bound [aʊ] to fibrin.

Use to (in)activate[6]/generate/neutralize [(j)uː] **plasmin** • alpha-2 / active **plasmin** • **plasmin** inhibitor[7] /-mediated [iː] destruction of fibrin • thrombus [θrɒːmbəs]/ bound [aʊ]/ serum **plasminogen**[8] • plasma zymogen [zaɪmədʒən] **plasminogen** • **plasminogen** activator inhibitor[8] • anisoylated **plasminogen** streptokinase [-kaɪneɪz] activator complex (*abbr* APSAC) • tissue[9] (*abbr* tPA)/ recombinant tissue-type[10] **plasminogen activator** • single-chain [tʃeɪn] urokinase[11] (*abbr* scuPA) **plasminogen activator**

Plasmin, Fibrinolysin
Plasminogen[1] Urokinase[2] Antiplasmin, Antifibrinolysin[3] Fibrinolyse[4] löst auf[5] Plasmin inaktivieren[6] Plasmininhibitor[7] Plasminogenaktivatorinhibitor[8] Gewebeaktivator[9] rekombinanter Gewebeaktivator, t-PA[10] einkettiger Urokinase-Plasminogen-Aktivator[11]

15

agglutinogen [æɡluːtənədʒən] *n term* → U38-11
syn **blood group** or **RBC antigen** [æntɪdʒən] *n term*

genetically determined antigen on the surface of RBCs that forms agglutinins in response to incompatible cells of a different blood group which bring about[1] a transfusion reaction

agglutinogenic [-dʒenɪk] *adj term* • **(hem)agglutinin** *n* • **blood type**[2] *n*

» Although more than 300 different blood antigens have been identified, only the ABO and Rh types are antigenic enough to cause concern in pregnancy and transfusion. Antibodies against ABO or Rh antigens cause hemolytic transfusion reactions or fetal erythroblastosis.

Use cold[3] / filamentous / specific **agglutinins** • **agglutinin** absorption / titer • ABO[4] **blood groups** • **blood group** system / substances[5] / incompatibility[6] • **blood typ**ing[7]

Agglutinogen
auslösen[1] Blutgruppe[2] Kälteagglutinine[3] ABO-/ ABNull-Blutgruppen[4] Blutgruppenantigene[5] Blutgruppenunverträglichkeit, -inkompatibilität[6] Blutgruppenbestimmung[7]

16

Rhesus factor [riːsəs fæktə] *n term, abbr* **Rh factor**

one of at least 8 highly immunogenic agglutinogens that may be present on the surface of RBCs and plays a major [eɪdʒ] role in pregnancy as well as blood transfusion and cross-matching[1]

Rh-negative /-positive *adj term* • **anti-Rh agglutinin** [uː] *n*

» Red blood cells are tested against anti-A, anti-B, and anti-D serum, so that the patient's blood may be classified as one of the 4 ABO types and as either Rh-positive or Rh-negative. If the mother is Rh-negative, an Rh antibody titer should be repeated at 26 to 27 weeks.

Use **Rhesus** blood groups / factor positive incompatibility / monkey • **Rh**-negative blood / immune [juː] globulin[2] /-negative mother[3] • **Rh** antibody titer[4] [aɪ]/ antigen system / antiserum[5] [ɪə] • **Rh** isoimmunization [aɪ]/ gene [dʒiːn]/ sensitization[6] (in pregnancy) / hemolytic [hiːməlɪtɪk] disease[7]

Rhesus-Faktor, Rh
Durchführung einer Kreuzprobe[1] Anti-D-Immunglobulin[2] Rh-negative Mutter[3] Rhesusantikörpertiter[4] Anti-D-Serum[5] Rhesussensibilisierung[6] Neugeborenenerythroblastose, Morbus haemolyticus neonatorum[7]

17

Unit 38 Hematopoiesis & Coagulation

Related Units: 37 Blood, 36 Blood Circulation, 78 Metabolism, 33 Cardiac Function, 47 Liver, 49 Urine Production, 110 Cardiovascular Signs & Symptoms

---

hem(at)opoiesis [hiːmətoupɔiːsɪs] *n term*   *syn* **blood formation** *n clin*

process of formation of blood cells in the bone marrow, spleen, liver and lymph nodes
hematopoietic[1] [-pɔiɛtɪk] *adj term* • **hematopoietin**[2] *n* • **-poiesis, -poietic** *comb*

» In these transplants hematopoietic stem cells are infused into a peripheral vein of the recipient[3] and the stem cells home to[4] the marrow to reestablish hematopoiesis. The turnover of differentiated hematopoietic cells in an adult weighing 70 kg (154 lbs) is over 0.5 trillion cells per day including 200 billion red blood cells and 70 billion neutrophilic leukocytes [uː].

Use to stimulate/suppress **hematopoiesis** • constitutive[5] / extramedullary[6] / normal[5] **hematopoiesis** • ineffective / megaloblastic[7] / deficient [ɪʃ]/ dys**hematopoiesis** • **hematopoietic** tissue [ʃ]/ system / growth factor • **hematopoietic** colony-stimulating factor / stem cells[8] • **hematopoietic** progenitor [dʒe] cell[8] (*abbr* HPC)/ cytokine [saɪtəkaɪn] • **hematopoietic** suppression / disease / malignancy • erythro[9] [ɪ] / thrombo(cyto)/ lympho(cyto)[10] [ɪ] / myelo**poiesis** [maɪəloupɔiːsɪs]

Häm(at)opoese, Blutbildung
hämatopoetisch, blutbildend[1] Erythropoetin[2] Empfänger(in)[3] wandern zum[4] konstitutive/ normale Hämatopoese[5] extramedulläre Blutbildung[6] megaloblastische Blutbildung[7] Blutstammzellen, hämatopoetische Stammzellen/ Progenitorzellen[8] Erythro(zyto)poese[9] Lympho(zyto)poese[10]

(bone) marrow [mærou] *n clin & term*   *syn* **medulla** [ʌ‖ʊ] **(ossium)** *n term rare*

spongy [spʌndʒi] tissue filling the cavities of bones which produces erythrocytes [ɪ], leukocytes [uː] and platelets[1] [eɪ] (red marrow); yellow marrow consists chiefly of fat and is found mainly in the long bones

(intra/ extra)medullary[2] *adj term* • **myeloid**[3] [maɪəlɔɪd] *adj* • **myelo-** *comb*

» A reticulocyte count is useful in assessing the ability of the patient's bone marrow to respond to anemia [iː]. Leukemic [iː] cells accumulate in the bone marrow and replace normal hematopoietic cells. Tumors involving the bone marrow may be associated with leukocytosis and the presence of immature myeloid cells in the peripheral blood.

Use red[4] / yellow[5] / sternal [ɜː] **marrow** • autologous / tibial [ɪ] **bone marrow** • **(bone) marrow** fat / space[6] / megakaryocytes[7] [æ] • **bone marrow** hemosiderin / fibrosis[8] / sensitivity • **bone marrow** plasmacytosis / aplasia [eɪ]/ purging[9] [pɜːrdʒ-]/ graft[10] • **bone marrow** cavity[6] / neutrophil [(j)uː] storage pool (*abbr* NSP) • **bone marrow**-derived [aɪ] cells / toxicity / depression[11] • **bone marrow** failure[11] / biopsy[12] [aɪ]/ aspiration[13] • **bone marrow** transplant[10] / suppression / culture[14] [ʌ] • medullary cavity or canal[6] / space[6] • **myeloid** precursor [ɜː]/ tissue[4] / series • **myeloid** maturation / metaplasia [eɪ]/ leukemia[15] [iː] • **myelo**cyte /blast /cytic leukemia[15] /genous[16] /culture[14] • **myelo**pathy /suppression /sis[15] /dysplasia /ma /fibrosis • **myelo**cele [-siːl] /meningocele /graphy

▌ Note: Both **myeloid** and the combining form **myelo-** may refer to bone marrow and the spinal [aɪ] cord[17].

Knochenmark, Medulla ossium
Thrombozyten[1] extramedullär[2] knochenmarkähnlich, markartig, Rückenmark-, myeloid, myeloisch[3] rotes Knochenmark, Medulla ossium rubra[4] gelbes Knochenmark, Medulla ossium flava[5] Markhöhle, Cavitas medullaris[6] Knochenmarkriesenzellen, Megakaryozyten[7] Knochenmarkfibrose[8] (Tumorzell)Purging, Aufreinigungstechnik des Knochenmarks[9] Knochenmarktransplantat[10] Knochenmarkdepression[11] Knochenmarkbiopsie[12] Knochenmarkaspiration[13] Knochenmarkkultur[14] myeloische Leukämie[15] myelogen[16] Rückenmark[17]

---

blast cells [blæst selz] *n term*   *rel* **hematocytoblast**[1], **stem cell**[2] *n term*

immature precursor [ɜː] cells for erythroblasts, lymphoblasts [ɪ], neuroblasts
blastic *adj term* • **-blast, -blastic, blast(o)-** *comb* • **stem (from)**[3] *v clin*

» Before peripheral stem cell harvest[4] the stem cell content of the blood is augmented. In leukemia blast cells can be classified as myeloid, lymphoid, erythroid, or undifferentiated. The differential showed neutropenia along with a small percentage of blasts amid[5] normal lymphocytes.

Use circulating / peripheral / leukemic [iː] **blast cells** • **blast** count / phase[6] / morphology / crisis[6] • **stem cell** population / activation / factor[7] (*abbr* SCF)/ defect [iː]/ leukemia[8] • (bone) marrow[9] / pluripotent[10] / peripheral / purified **stem cells** • myelo[11]/ (definitive) erythro/ lympho**blast** • normo[12]/ mono/ sidero/ megalo**blast** • **blastic** reaction / transformation[13] / sites / foci / phase[6] • osteo/ normo/ megalo**blastic** • **blasto**genesis[14] /cyst

Blasten
Hämozytoblast, Hämatoblast[1] Stammzelle[2] stammen (von)[3] Stammzellenentnahme[4] unter[5] Blastenkrise, -schub, -phase[6] Stammzellfaktor[7] Stammzellenleukämie, akute undifferenzierte Leukämie[8] Knochenmarkstammzellen[9] pluripotente Stammzellen[10] Myeloblast[11] Normoblast[12] Blastentransformation[13] Blastogenese, Blastenbildung[14]

hemolysis [hɪmɒːlɪsɪs‖əlaɪsɪs] *n term*
    rel **anemia**[1] [əniːmɪə] *n term, BE* **anaemia**
dissolution or destruction of red blood cells by liberation of hemoglobin, e.g. by specific complement-fixing antibodies, toxins, various chemical agents, or alteration of temperature
hemolytic[2] *adj term* • **hemolysin**[3] *n* • **anemic**[4] *adj* • **-lysis, -emia** *comb*
» The essential feature of hemolysis is a shortened RBC life span[5]. Hemolytic anemia results when bone marrow production can no longer compensate for RBC destruction. A high reticulocyte count confirms the hemolytic nature of the anemia.
Use immune[6] / intravascular / microangiopathic / alpha / beta[7] / auto**hemolysis** • chronic / episodic / severe / mild / increased[8] **hemolysis** • excessive / self-limited / low-grade **hemolysis** • **hemolytic** disorder / anemia[9] / jaundice[10] [dʒɒː] transfusion reaction • **hemolytic**-uremic syndrome[11] / crisis[12] [aɪ] • dia/ fibrino/ thrombo[13] / hydro**lysis** • chronic / iron-deficiency[14] / aplastic / sickle cell **anemia** • pernicious[15] / megaloblastic / nutritional[16] [ɪʃ]/ sideroblastic **anemia** • hypochromic / immunohemolytic[17] / mild / moderate **anemia**

Hämolyse, Erythrozytenabbau, -auflösung
Anämie, Blutarmut[1] hämolytisch, Hämolyse auslösend[2] Hämolysin[3] anämisch, blutarm[4] verkürzte Erythrozytenlebensdauer[5] Immunhämolyse[6] Betahämolyse[7] gesteigerte Hämolyse[8] hämolyt. Anämie[9] hämolyt. Ikterus[10] hämolytisch-urämisches Syndrom[11] hämolyt. Krise[12] Thrombolyse[13] Eisenmangelanämie[14] perniziöse Anämie, Morbus Biermer, Vitamin B$_{12}$-Mangelanämie[15] ernährungsbedingte/ alimentäre Anämie[16] immunhämolyt. Anämie[17]   **4**

---

cytopenia [saɪtəpiːnɪə] *n term*   *syn* **hypocytosis** [haɪpoʊsaɪtoʊsɪs] *n rare,*
    opposite **hypercytosis**[1] *n term*
deficiency [ɪʃ] in the number of any of the cellular elements in the circulating [ɜː] blood
-penia, -penic [piːnɪk] *comb* • **-osis, -otic** *comb*
» Many drugs affect the bone marrow and may cause single or multiple cytopenias. The hallmark[2] [ɔː] of aplastic [eɪ] anemia is pancytopenia. Anemia, leukopenia [uː], and thrombocytopenia may develop during the course of cancer therapy.
Use single / multiple [ʌ]/ peripheral / profound [aʊ] **cytopenia** • granulo[3] / (immune/ drug-induced) thrombo**cytopenia** • (febrile [e‖iː]/ chronic) pan[4] / reticulo**cytopenia** • erythroblasto/ lympho [lɪmfə]/ leuko[5] / neutro**penia** • erythro/ (hyper)leuko/ thrombo[6] / lympho**cytosis** • reticulo/ macro/ micro/ pleo[7] [pliːoʊ]/ agranulo**cytosis** • aniso/ poikilo[8] / sphero/ ellipto**cytosis**

Zytopenie, Verminderung der Zellzahl
Hyperzytose, erhöhte Zellzahl[1] Kennzeichen[2] Granulozytopenie[3] Panzytopenie[4] Leuko(zyto)penie[5] Thrombozytose, temporäre Vermehrung d. Thrombozytenzahl[6] Pleozytose, erhöhte Zellzahl (bes. im Liquor)[7] Poikilozytose, Vielgestaltigkeit d. Erythrozyten[8]

   5

---

extravasate *v term* → U136-7   *rel* **bleed**[1] [iː] - bled - bled *v irr & n* → U140-13
to pass out of a vessel into tissues; the term is used in connection with blood, lymph, or urine
extravasation[2] *n term* • **rebleed** *v* • **bleeder**[3] *n jar* • **nosebleed**[4] *n clin* → U5-18
» Erythrocytes had extravasated from the involved vessels, leading to palpable purpura [ɜː]. Urethrography demonstrates free extravasation of blood in the pelvis. Delayed bleeding[5], persistent extravasation with hematoma, and the potential for infection cause concern. About 60-80% of variceal [s] **bleeders**[6] will stop spontaneously [eɪ]; however, without therapy, over half of these will rebleed within one week.
Use **to extravasate** into the interstitial space / from the arterioles • **extravasated** fluid / bile[7] [aɪ]/ blood • **extravasated** red blood cells / sweat [e]/ urine • vascular / urinary[8] / fluid **extravasation** • bloody [ʌ]/ contrast or dye [daɪ] **extravasation** • intraperitoneal / focal **extravasation** • scrotal / self-limited / gross[10] [oʊ] **extravasation** • **to bleed** briskly[11] / profusely[11] / massively • **to bleed** slightly[12] / excessively / readily[13] [e] • **to bleed** spontaneously / uncontrollably / intermittently • small / initial / torrential[14] / lower GI / variceal[6] **bleed** • **rebleed** rate • ligated [aɪ]/ coagulated **bleeder**

(aus einem Gefäß) austreten
bluten; Blutung[1] Austritt v. Flüssigkeit, Extravasat[2] Bluter(in), Hämophile(r); blutendes Gefäß[3] Nasenbluten[4] Spätblutung[5] Varizenblutung(en)[6] extravaskuläre Galle[7] Harnaustritt[8] Kontrastmittelaustritt[9] massiver Flüssigkeitsaustritt/ Gefäßaustritt[10] stark bluten[11] ein wenig bluten[12] leicht bluten, zu Blutungen neigen[13] Massenblutung[14]

   6

---

ooze [uːz] *v & n*   *sim* **seep**[1] [iː] *v, rel* **squirt**[2], **spurt**[2] - spurt - spurt [ɜː] *v irr*
to pass gradually or leak through, esp. small quantities of blood from a wound or bleeding site
oozing *n term* • **seepage**[3] [siːpɪdʒ] *n* • **spurting** *n* • **spurter**[4] *n jar*
» If the wound [uː] oozes or bleeds excessively, a gentle [dʒ] compression dressing[5] should be applied. The varices may be actively spurting or oozing blood or show evidence of recent bleeding. The intestine became severely congested [dʒe], and blood began to seep into the intestinal lumen.
Use to cause/control/dry up **oozing** • mild / bloody[6] / serous [ɪə]/ capillary / venous [iː] **oozing** • microvascular / persistent[7] / diffuse **oozing** • **oozing** lesion[8] [iːʒ]/ arterial[4] **spurter** • to be forced out in[9] **squirts** • fluid / intermittent **seepage**

sickern; Sickerblutung
sickern, entweichen, auslaufen[1] (heraus)spritzen[2] (Durch)sickern[3] arterielle Blutung[4] Kompressions-, Druckverband[5] Sickerblutung[6] persistierende Sickerblutung[7] nässende/ leicht blutende Wunde[8] stoßweise herausspritzen[9]

   7

Hematopoiesis & Coagulation — BODY STRUCTURES & FUNCTIONS

bleeding n & adj   syn hemorrhage [hemərɪdʒ] n, → U5-18
rel **hematoma**[1] [hiːmətoumə] n term → U5-13

(n) blood loss as a result of a rupture [ʌ] of blood vessels
(non)hemorrhagic[2] [hemɔrædʒɪk] adj term • **cephal(o)hematoma** n

» Some patients bleed rapidly, but the bleeding stops spontaneously after only a small amount of blood is lost. Bleeding was manifested by petechiae [pətiːkiiː] and easy bruisability[3] [uː] with mucous membrane hemorrhage (e.g. epistaxis). The surgical landmarks have been distorted by urinary extravasation and massive hematomas. Expansion of the hematoma may place pressure on the femoral [e] nerve.

Use internal[4] / arterial / variceal / uterine [juː]/ vaginal [dʒ]/ intermenstrual[5] **bleeding** • intra-abdominal / urethral [iː]/ rectal / occult [ʌ] **bleeding** • acute / brisk / massive **bleeding** • **bleeding** site [aɪ] or point / time[6] / abnormality[7] / tendency[8] • **bleeding** episodes / complications / ulcer [ʌlsɚ] • to cause/control/arrest or stop[9] *(a)* **hemorrhage** • external / punctate[10] [ʌ]/ (major) internal / upper gastrointestinal **hemorrhage** • postoperative / secondary[11] / life-threatening[12] [e]/ fatal [eɪ] **hemorrhage** • deep muscle / thigh[13] [θaɪ]/ flank / nasal septum **hematoma** • intracerebral / epidural[14] [(j)ʊ]/ subcapsular splenic[15] [e] **hematoma** • perineal [iː]/ subungual / pulsatile [ʌ] or pulsating[16] **hematoma** • dissecting / expanding / (un)contained[17] [eɪ] **hematoma** • **hematoma** formation • oto**hematoma** • **hemorrhagic** shock[18] / exudate[19] / esophageal [dʒiː] varices • **hemorrhagic** pancreatitis [aɪ]/ diathesis[8] [daɪæθəsɪs]/ fever [iː]

exsanguinate [ɪksæŋgwɪneɪt‖adj -nɪt] v & adj term
(v) to drain [eɪ] blood from the body or bleed massively causing life-threatening [e] blood loss
(non)exsanguinating adj term • **exsanguination**[1] n

» Prevent asphyxiation by exsanguinated blood. Rupture [ʌ] with exsanguination is the major complication of infrarenal [iː] abdominal aortic [eɪ] aneurysms [ænjɚɪzᵊmz]. Only patients with exsanguinating hemorrhage must be rushed to the OR immediately.

Use to die from[2] / to prevent / rapid / fatal [eɪ]/ high risk of[3] **exsanguination** • **exsanguination** due to internal bleeding / transfusion[4] • **exsanguinating** hemorrhage[5] / trauma [ɔː]/ patient

(blood) coagulation [kouægjʊleɪʃᵊn] n term → U127-10
syn **(blood) clotting** [klɒtɪŋ] n clin, rel **hemostasis**[1] [hiːməsteɪsɪs] n term

cascade of events inducing formation of a fibrin [aɪ] clot in response to vascular endothelial damage
coagulate[2] v term • **coagulant**[3] adj & n • **coagulase** [eɪ] n • **coagul(o)-** comb

» Disordered hemostasis in von Willebrand's disease is due to a combination of extrinsic platelet [eɪ] dysfunction and impairment [eɚ] of the intrinsic coagulation pathway. Christmas disease[4] is due to deficient levels of factor IX, a coagulant in the intrinsic pathway.

Use plasma / impaired[5] / disseminated intravascular[6] *(abbr DIC)* **coagulation** • **coagulation** mechanism / cascade or pathway[7] / process • **coagulation** factor[8] / test / time[9] / defect[5] / disorder[5] • **clotting** abnormality[5] / factor[8] / time[9] / defect[5] • **coagulant** dysfunction[5] [ɪ] • (ab)normal / primary[10] / immediate / secondary **hemostasis** • platelet[10] / coagulant-specific **hemostasis** • **coagul**ability[11] /um[12] /opathy[5]

platelet aggregation [pleɪtlɪt ægrɪgeɪʃᵊn] n term
sim **platelet agglutination**[1] n term

clumping [ʌ] together of thrombocytes due to the action of platelet agglutinins, e.g. ADP[2]
aggregate[3] v & n term • **agglutinate**[4] v
hemagglutination[5] [hiːm-] n term • **(hem)agglutinin** n

» Fibrinogen is required for platelet aggregation and fibrin [aɪ] formation. Platelet aggregability is increased after arising in the early morning hours. Platelet antiaggregation agents[6] inhibit the formation of intraarterial platelet aggregates that can form on diseased arteries.

Use to promote/stimulate/inhibit[7]/suppress **platelet aggregation** • decreased [iː]/ impaired [eɚ]/ ADP-induced / intravascular / in vitro [iː‖ɪ] **platelet aggregation** • **platelet aggregation** study or test[8] / inhibitors[6] / abnormality • cold[9] / febrile / specific **agglutinins** • **hemagglutination** titer [aɪ]/ inhibition [ɪʃ] test[10]

Blutung, Hämorrhagie; blutend
Hämatom, Bluterguss[1] hämorrhagisch, Blutungs-[2] Neigung zu Hautblutungen/ blauen Flecken[3] innere Blutung[4] Zwischenblutung[5] Blutungszeit, BZ[6] Blutgerinnungsstörung[7] Blutungsneigung, hämorrh. Diathese[8] Blutung stillen[9] punktförm. Blutung, Petechie[10] Nachblutung[11] lebensbedrohliche Blutung[12] Oberschenkelhämatom[13] Epiduralhämatom, epidurales H.[14] subkapsuläres Milzhämatom[15] pulsierendes Hämatom[16] organisiertes Hämatom[17] hämorrh. Schock[18] hämorrh. Exsudat[19]

aus-, verbluten; blutleer; blutleer machen
Exsanguination, Aus-, Verblutung[1] verbluten[2] hohes Verblutungsrisiko[3] Blutaustausch, Austauschtransfusion[4] Massiv-, Massenblutung[5]

(Blut)gerinnung, Koagulation
Blutstillung, Hämostase[1] gerinnen, koagulieren[2] gerinnungsfördernd; gerinnungsförd. Mittel, Koagulans[3] Christmas-Krankheit, Hämophilie B[4] Gerinnungsstörung, Koagulopathie[5] disseminierte intravasale Gerinnung, Verbrauchskoagulopathie[6] Koagulationskaskade[7] (Blut)gerinnungsfaktor[8] (Blut)gerinnungszeit[9] primäre Hämostase[10] Gerinnbarkeit, Koagulabilität[11] Koagulum, Blutgerinnsel[12]

Thrombozytenaggregation
Thrombozytenagglutination[1] Adenosindiphosphat[2] zusammenballen, sich anhäufen; Aggregat[3] zusammenkleben, verklumpen[4] Hämagglutination, Verklumpung v. Erythrozyten[5] Thrombozytenaggregationshemmer[6] d. Thrombozytenaggregation hemmen[7] Plättchen-, Thrombozytenaggregationstest[8] Kälteagglutinine[9] Hämagglutinationshemmtest[10]

blood clot [klɒːt] n clin   syn **coagulum** n,
rel **thrombus**[1], **embolus**[2] n term, pl **-i** n term → U124-13

jelly-like mass formed by the conversion of fibrinogen to fibrin that entraps red blood cells

clot[3] v clin • **clotted**[4] adj • **embolic** adj term • **embolism**[5] n • **embolization**[6] n

» Emboli [aɪ] may arise from clots within aneurysms anywhere in the aortofemoral system. There is little difference between hemostatic plugs [ʌ], which are a physiologic response to injury, and pathologic thrombi [aɪ]. Cleansing [e] removes the adherent [ɪɚ] coagulum from the suture-skin [suːtʃɚ] juncture [dʒʌŋktʃɚ] and lowers the risk of stitch abscess[7] formation.

Use precipitating [sɪ]/ obstructing[8] / intrarenal **blood clot** • fibrin[9] [aɪ]/ mucin [mjuːsɪn]/ intravascular **clot** • intra-arterial / mural[10] [mjʊəl]/ perivascular **clot** • fresh[11] / soft / free-floating[12] [oʊ]/ laminated[13] **clot** • **clot** formation[14] / size / retraction[15] / lysis [laɪsɪs] • **clotted** (whole) blood • partially / recently **clotted** • fibrinous[9] [aɪ]/ wound [uː] **coagulum** • venous [iː]/ popliteal [ɪ]/ fresh[11] / vena caval **thrombus** • deep-vein / obstructing [ʌ] or occlusive[8] **thrombus** • arterial / atheromatous / cardiac **emboli** • pulmonary / retinal **emboli** • cerebral / bacterial[16] [ɪɚ]/ septic[16] / multiple **emboli** • **embolic** stroke[17] / occlusion [uːʒ]/ infarction • **embol**ectomy[18] • hepatic artery / splenic [e] **embolization** • peripheral / cholesterol / tumor **embolization**

coagulation or **clotting factor** n term   syn **coagulant** [koʊægjələnt] n term

plasma components involved in the clotting process; they were numbered in the order of their discovery and are part of the intrinsic, extrinsic or common pathways of the coagulation cascade

» The patient may have reduced levels of factor VIII coagulant activity. Warfarin blocks synthesis in the liver of at least four vitamin [aɪ‖ɪ] K-dependent clotting factors: prothrombin, factor VII, factor IX, and factor X. In patients who already have decreased levels of clotting factors, hemodilution[1] [hiːmədaɪluːʃⁿn] can result in significant further reduction in coagulation factors.

Use plasma[2] / vitamin K-dependent / depleted[3] [iː] **coagulation factors** • (inherited / acquired) [aɪ] abnormality of / consumption [ʌ] of[4] **coagulation factors** • blood / activated[5] / purified [pjʊɚɪ-]/ defective **clotting factors** • **clotting factor** precursor / synthesis [ɪ]/ concentrate / assay • antihemophilic[6] (abbr AHF)/ von Willebrand **factor** • **factor** VII level / VIII antigen / XII deficiency / IX hemophilia[7] • arterial [ɪɚ]/ venous [iː] **clotting** • **clotting** mechanism [ek]/ time[8] / process / parameters • **clotting** protein / disturbance[9] / abnormality[9] • **coagulant** factors[10]

fibrinolysis [faɪbrɪnəlaɪsɪs‖nɒːlɪsɪs] n term
rel **anticoagulant**[1], **thrombolytic**[2] [θrɒːmbəlɪtɪk] n & adj term

dissolution of thrombi [aɪ] by enzymatic [zə] activity that splits the peptide bonds between fibrin chains

(anti)fibrinolytic[3] [ɪ] adj term • defibrination[4] n
fibrinolysin[5] [aɪ] n • lyse[6] [laɪs] v

» The pulmonary endothelium [iː] contains potent fibrinolysins that can break up any poorly organized embolus. Although fibrinolysis begins immediately after vascular injury, clot lysis[7] and vessel recanalization may not be complete for 7 to 10 days. The fibrinolytic pathway is important in normal hemostasis, as defects can predispose patients to either hemorrhage or recurrent [ɜː‖ʌ] thrombosis.

Use to stimulate/suppress **fibrinolysis** • endogenous / primary / secondary / systemic **fibrinolysis** • impaired / excessive[8] / increased[9] / unchecked[10] **fibrinolysis** • **fibrinolytic** activity / enzyme[11] [enzaɪm]/ defect / therapy • **defibrination** syndrome[12] [ɪ] • **defibrinated** blood[13] / oral / heparin **anticoagulant** • **anticoagulant** protein / activity[14] / effect[14] / therapy • **thrombolytic** agent[15] / therapy[7]

(Blut)gerinnsel, -koagulum
Thrombus[1] Embolus[2] gerinnen, koagulieren[3] geronnen[4] Embolie[5] Embolisation[6] Nahtabszess[7] obturierender Thrombus[8] Fibringerinnsel[9] wandständiger Thrombus[10] frischer Thrombus[11] frei flottierender Thrombus[12] Abscheidungsthrombus[13] Thrombenbildung[14] Blutgerinnselretraktion[15] septische Emboli[16] embolischer Insult[17] Embolektomie, operative Embolusentfernung[18]

12

(Blut)gerinnungsfaktor
Hämodilution, Blutverdünnung[1] plasmatische Blutgerinnungsfaktoren[2] fehlende Gerinnungsfaktoren[3] Verbrauch von Gerinnungsfaktoren[4] aktivierte Gerinnungsfaktoren[5] antihämophiler Faktor, antihämophiles Globulin[6] Hämophilie B, Christmas-Krankheit[7] (Blut)gerinnungszeit[8] Gerinnungsstörung[9] Gerinnungsfaktoren[10]

13

Fibrinolyse
Antikoagulans, gerinnungshemmendes Mittel; gerinnungshemmend[1] Thrombolytikum, Fibrinolytikum; thrombolytisch[2] fibrinolysehemmend, antifibrinolytisch[3] Defibrinierung[4] Fibrinolysin, Plasmin[5] auflösen[6] Thrombolyse[7] überschießende Fibrinolyse[8] vermehrte Fibrinolyse, Hyperfibrinolyse[9] unkontrollierte Fibrinolyse[10] fibrinspaltendes Enzym[11] Defibrinisierungssyndrom[12] defibriniertes Blut[13] gerinnungshemmende Wirkung[14] Thrombolytikum, Fibrinolytikum[15]

14

Unit 39 The Immune System
Related Units: 35 Lymphatic System, 37 Blood, 122 Immunization, 136 Blood Transfusion, 84 Genetics, 89 Pathology, 90 Pathogens, 94 Infectious Diseases, 97 Oncology, 129 Plastic Surgery

immune system [ɪ] n term   syn **body** or **host** or **immune defense system** n

interrelated cellular, molecular, and genetic system which protects an organism from the effects of foreign materials such as bacteria, viruses [aɪ], or aberrant native [eɪ] cells[1]

immune[2] [ɪmjuːn] adj & comb term & clin • **immunization**[3] n • **immun(o)-** comb

» How does the immune system recognize invaders? Impairment [eə] of the immune system, especially T-cell function, has been linked to increased susceptibility to infection[4]. Influenza renders the patient temporarily immune to reinfection [iː] with the same virus serotype [ɪə].

Use to control/compromise[5] **the immune system** • cellular / humoral [hjuː]/ the patient's / immature **immune system** • suppressed[6] / intact / compromised [-aɪzd]/ native[7] **immune system** • **immune system** function / components • **immune** cell[8] (population) / activity / function • **immune** mechanism / process / defect [iː] or deficiency[9] [ɪʃ] • **to be immune** to measles[10] [iː] • non-/ hyper**immune** • **immuno**gen[11] /aggregated /assay • **immuno**reactive /sorbent[12] /histochemistry • **immuno**fluorescence test[13] /logy /logic • **immuno**competent[14] /compromised [-aɪzd] • **immuno**deficiency[9] (syndrome [ɪ]) /therapy /stimulation • **immuno**suppressants[15] /suppression or -depression[16] • radio**immuno**assay

Immunsystem
Körperzellen[1] immun[2] Immunisierung[3] Infektionsanfälligkeit[4] d. Immunsystem schwächen[5] supprimiertes Immunsystem[6] körpereigenes Immunsystem[7] Immunzelle, Immunozyt, immunkompetente Zelle[8] Immundefekt, -defizienz, -mangelkrankheit[9] gegen Masern immun sein[10] Immunogen, Antigen[11] Immunadsorbens[12] Immunfluoreszenztest[13] immunkompetent[14] Immunsuppressiva[15] Immunsuppression, Unterdrückung/ Abschwächung d. Immunantwort[16]

1

immune response n clin & term   syn **immune reaction** n clin & term

(i) response of the immune system to an antigen [æntɪdʒən] (immunogen) that leads to the condition of induced sensitivity, esp. from the viewpoint of antibody (Ig) production
(ii) response of previously [iː] sensitized tissue[1] to an antigen, esp. to resist infection

(hyper/ hypo)responsiveness[2] [haɪpərɪspɔːnsɪvnəs] n term → U120-11
• **reactant** n term • **react (to/ with)**[3] v • **(cross-)reactivity**[4] n → U121-11

» The route of administration in part determines the nature of the immune responses to vaccines[5] [æks]. As a rule, the immune response to the initial antigenic exposure [oʊʒ] is serologically detectable only after a lag period[6] of several days or weeks.

Use to evoke [oʊ] or elicit[7]/stimulate/exhibit **immune reaction** • to suppress/interrupt [ʌ] /modulate[8] **immune reaction** • cellular or cell-mediated[9] [iː]/ humoral [hjuː] **immune reaction** • B-cell / T-cell / pathologic / vaccine-induced **immune reaction** • local / systemic / immediate / delayed[10] **immune response** • cross-reactive / host / adequate **immune response** • altered [ɒː]/ hyperactive[11] / exaggerated[11] **immune response** • dysregulated / poor[12] / abnormal / initial / primary[13] **immune response** • secondary / potent[14] [oʊ]/ antitumor **immune response** • **immune response** genes[15] [iː]/ factor (directed) against HIV / to the virus [aɪ] • immunologic / primary[13] / autoimmune[16] [ɒː] **response** • antibody / host [oʊ]/ inflammatory [æ]/ bone marrow **response** • **response** to shock • **immune** recognition / surveillance[17] [eɪ(1)]/ defense[18] • **immune** responsiveness / adherence[19] [ɪə]/ resistance • **immune** tolerance[20] / regulation / elimination • **immune status**[21] [eɪ‖æ]/ recovery [ʌ] or reconstitution / deficiency / suppression[22] • **immune**-related /-mediated /-stimulating drugs[23] • immune / acute-phase[24] / nucleophilic **reactant** • immunologic / antibody / T helper cell **reactivity** • allergic [ɜː]/ tissue [tɪʃ‖sjuː] / metabolic / skin(test) **reactivity**

Immunantwort, -reaktion
sensibilisiertes Gewebe[1] Reaktionsfähigkeit, Reagibilität; Ansprechbarkeit[2] reagieren auf/ mit[3] Kreuzreaktivität[4] Impfstoffe, Vakzinen[5] Latenzphase[6] eine Immunreaktion auslösen/ hervorrufen[7] die Immunantwort verändern[8] zelluläre Immunreaktion[9] verzögerte Immunreaktion[10] überschießende Immunreaktion[11] schlechte Immunreaktion[12] Primärantwort, -reaktion, primäre Immunantwort[13] starke Immunreaktion[14] Immune-response-Gene, Ir-Gene[15] Autoimmunreaktion[16] immunolog. Überwachung[17] Immunabwehr[18] Immunadhärenz[19] Immuntoleranz[20] Immunstatus[21] Immunsuppression[22] Immunstimulanzien[23] Akute-Phase-Substanz[24]

2

Fab fragment or **portion** [pɔːrʃən] n term   rel **Fc fragment** or **region**[1] n term

antigen-binding fragment of an Ig molecule consisting of both a light chain and the N-terminal[2] of a heavy chain

fragment[3] [frægmənt] vi term • **fragmentation**[4] n

» The idiotype is defined as the specific region of the Fab portion of the Ig molecule to which antigen binds. Digoxin-specific Fab-fragment antibodies should be administered. An IgM antibody directed against the Fc fragment of IgG (rheumatoid [uː] factor[5]) is present in the serum. The patient secretes [iː] a defective heavy chain that has an intact Fc fragment and a deletion [iːʃ] in the Fd region.

Use protein / F(ab)₂ / peptide / amino terminal[2] [ɜː] **fragment** • carboxyl or C-terminal[6] / (double-stranded) DNA[7] **fragment** / HLA / genetic / variable[8] / constant[9] **region** • **Fab** antibody **fragment**[10] • **Fc** portion[1] / receptor (expression) / binding site[11] • RBC / DNA **fragmentation**

Fab-Fragment, Fab-Anteil
FC Fragment, -Anteil[1] N-terminales Ende, Amino-Terminal[2] in Bruchstücke zerfallen[3] Fragmentation[4] Rheumafaktor[5] C-terminales Ende, Carboxy-Terminal[6] doppelsträngiges DNA-Fragment[7] variable Region, VL/ VH-Region[8] konstante Region, CH/ CL-Region[9] Fab-Antikörperfragment[10] Fc-Bindungsstelle[11]

3

156 BODY STRUCTURES & FUNCTIONS — The Immune System

humoral [hjuː-] **immunity** n term   rel **cell-mediated** [iː] **immunity**[1] n term

immune response mediated mainly by antibodies circulating [sɜːrk-] in the body fluids

auto-/ cross-immunity[2] n term • **autoimmune** [ɒːtɔɪmjuːn] adj

» Defects in humoral immunity predispose [iː] mainly to bacterial [ɪɚ] infections, while defects in cellular immunity predispose to infections with fungi [fʌndʒaɪ‖-gaɪ], viruses, mycobacteria [maɪ-], and protozoa. One attack of herpes [ɜː] zoster usually confers [ɜː] immunity. The new epidemic cholera strain [eɪ] exhibits no cross-immunity with the traditional O1 serotype [ɪɚ].

Use to develop/induce/confer or provide[3] **immunity** • to attain[4] [eɪ] /lack/guarantee [iː] /determine **immunity** • protective / serologic / natural[5] **immunity** • tissue / mucosal[6] / T-cell or cellular[1] **immunity** • active / passive / congenital[7] [dʒe]/ acquired[8] [aɪ] **immunity** • permanent[9] / herd[10] [ɜː]/ tumor / host / antitoxic **immunity** • deficient [ɪʃ]/ compromised / vaccine-induced[11] **immunity** • (non)specific[12] / relative **immunity** • partial [pɑːrʃ°l]/ depressed / waning[13] [eɪ] **immunity** • temporary / lasting[9] / life-long[14] **immunity** • **immunity** against reinfection / to rubella • antibody-mediated / cell-mediated **autoimmunity** • thyroid [aɪ]/ sperm [ɜː] **autoimmunity** • **autoimmune** process / reaction[15] / disease[16] • **autoimmune** hemolytic [ɪ] anemia[17] [iː]/ hepatitis [aɪ] • **autoimmune** mechanism [ek]/ component / destruction [ʌ]

immunoglobulin n term, abbr **Ig**   syn **immune globulin** n term
  rel **antiglobulin**[1] [æntɪglɒːbjəlɪn], **isotype**[2] [aɪsətaɪp], **idiotype**[3] [ɪdɪə-] n term

glycoprotein with antibody activity consisting of two pairs of polypeptide chains; they are classified as IgG (80%), IgA (10-15%), IgM, IgD (less than 0.1%), and IgE (< 0.01%)

» Based on differences in the H chains, subclasses of immunoglobulins are referred to as IgG1, etc. Immunoglobulins bind to specific antigenic targets and elicit a biologic response from the host. Antibodies of the IgG or IgM isotype can form complexes with the allergen and thereby activate complement to generate [dʒe] mediators [iː] of inflammation [eɪʃ].

Use membrane-bound[4] [aʊ]/ monoclonal[5] / polyclonal **immunoglobulins** • thyroid-stimulating / native[6] [eɪ]/ Rh / surface **Ig** • **Ig** class[7] / level[8] /-bearing [eɚ] B-cells • **Ig** synthesis [ɪ] /-forming cells / defects [iː]/ deficiency[9] [ɪʃ] • **Ig** preparations / administration[10] / therapy • L-chain / IV / maternally derived[11] [aɪ]/ thyroid [aɪ] growth **immunoglobulins** • high-titer CMV[12] / host [oʊ] **immunoglobulins** • gamma[13] / tetanus immune[14] (abbr TIG)/ alpha-1 **globulin** • hyperimmune anti-hemophilic[15] (abbr AHG) **globulin** • antithymocyte[16] [aɪ] (abbr ATG)/ cortisol-binding (abbr CBG) **globulin** • IgG4 / heavy-chain **isotype** • **isotype** composition

H or **heavy chain** [hevi tʃeɪn] n term   opposite **L** or **light-chain**[1] [laɪt] n term

polypeptide chain of high molecular weight Ig determining[2] [ɜː] its class and subclass [ʌ]

» The large number of possible combinations of L and H chains make up the "libraries" [aɪ] of antibodies of each individual. Approximately 60% of human Igs have k light chains, and 40% have l light chains. L chains are divided into a region of variable sequence [iː] (VL) and one of constant sequence (CL), each comprising[3] about half the length of the L chain.

Use DNA / α-globin[4] **chain** • **chain** terminator [ɜː] • **heavy chain** genes[5] [dʒiːnz]/ locus / class • **heavy chain** disease[6] / components / isotype • **light chain** excretion[7] [iːʃ]/ (deposition) disease[8] (abbr LCDD)

hapten(e) [hæpten] n term   rel **epitope**[1], **paratope**[2], **determinant**[3] [ɜː] n term

compound [aʊ] that is not itself immunogenic but, after conjugation [dʒə] to a carrier molecule, becomes immunogenic and induces antibody, which can bind the hapten alone in the absence of carrier

haptenic adj term • **antihapten** adj

» This supports the theory that contrast material may act as haptens and induce specific antihapten antibodies. Viral [aɪ] protein epitopes expressed on the cell surface in the context of histocompatibility proteins can attract T cells. The bacteria [ɪɚ] fight back by cloaking[4] [oʊ] antigenic determinants on their surface.

Use immune / conjugated[5] **hapten** • **hapten** conjugation[6] • **haptenic** allergen / free radicals • antigenic / surface / T cell / mast cell / conformational[7] / viral [aɪ] epitope • type-specific / cross-reactive / determinant **epitope** • genetic / antigenic[1] / group[8] **determinant** • MHC class II / self MHC / HLA-C locus **determinant** • hidden / immunogenic / cross-reactive **determinant** • isotypic[9] [ɪ]/ cluster[8] [ʌ] (abbr CD) **determinant** • serotype-specific / target / resistance / virulence [ɪ] **determinant**

---

humorale Immunität
zellvermittelte Immunität[1] Kreuzimmunität[2] Immunität verleihen[3] Immunität erlangen[4] natürliche Immunität[5] Schleimhautimmunität[6] angeborene Immunität[7] erworbene Immunität[8] bleibende/ persistierende Immunität[9] kollektive Immunität[10] vakzineinduzierte Immunität[11] unspezifische Immunität[12] abnehmende Immunität[13] lebenslängliche/ lebenslange Immunität[14] Autoimmunreaktion[15] Autoimmunkrankheit, -erkrankung[16] autoimmunhämolyt. Anämie[17]

4

Immunglobulin, Ig
Antiglobulin[1] Isotyp[2] Idiotyp[3] membrangebundene Immunglobuline[4] monoklonale Ig[5] natürliche/ native Ig[6] Immunglobulinklasse[7] Immunglobulinkonzentration[8] Immunglobulinmangel[9] Immunglobulinapplikation, Ig-Gabe[10] mütterl. Immunglobuline[11] hochkonzentrierte Zytomegalievirusimmunglobuline[12] Gammaglobulin[13] Tetanusimmunglobulin[14] antihämophiles Globulin[15] Antithymozytenglobulin[16]

5

H-Kette, schwere Kette
L-Kette, leichte Kette[1] festlegen[2] umfassen[3] α-Globinkette[4] H-Kettengene[5] Schwerkettenkrankheit[6] Ausscheidung leichter Ketten[7] Leichtkettenkrankheit[8]

6

Hapten, Halbantigen, unvollständiges Antigen
antigene Determinante, Epitop[1] Antigenbindungsstelle, Paratop[2] Determinante[3] maskieren[4] Haptenkonjugat[5] Haptenkonjugation[6] Konformationsdeterminante[7] Gruppendeterminante[8] isotypische Determinante[9]

7

The Immune System   BODY STRUCTURES & FUNCTIONS 157

antibody [ˈæntɪbɒːdi] n term, abbr **Ab**   rel **antigen**[1] [ˈæntɪdʒ³n] n term, abbr **Ag**
immunoglobulin that binds [aɪ] to and reacts with a specific antigen
autoantibody n term • **antigenic** adj • **antigenicity**[2] n • **antitoxin** n → U91-15
» A person with type A blood has circulating antibodies to B antigen. Despite the vigorous[3] serologic response to measles [iː] virus [aɪ], the patient did not develop antibodies to the M protein of the measles virion [aɪ‖ɪ]. His initial cerebrospinal [aɪ] fluid antigen titer was greater than 1:32. Antigenic coupling [ʌ] of IgE molecules on the surface of mast cells and basophils [eɪ] causes the release [iː] of eosinophil chemotactic [kiːmoʊ-] factors.
Use antinuclear[4] (abbr ANA)/ IgA / blocking[5] **antibodies** • fluorescent / allo[6]/ anti-receptor **antibodies** • monoclonal / neutralizing [(j)uː] **Ab** • complement-fixing[7] / cross-reactive[8] **Ab** • **antibody**-coated [oʊ] cell • histocompatibility[9] / somatic **antigen** • thymus-(in)dependent[10] / human leukocyte[11] [saɪ] (abbr HLA) **antigen** • self-[12]/ cross-reacting / private[13] **antigen** • ubiquitous[14] / sequestered[15] **antigen** • endogenous [ɒːdʒ]/ exogenous or foreign[16] **antigen** • C-locus / platelet(-specific)[17] [eɪ]/ viral capsid (abbr VCA) **antigen** • carcinoembryonic (abbr CEA)/ prostate-specific[18] (abbr PSA) **antigen** • **antigen**-antibody reaction[19] / processing /-presenting cell[20] (abbr APC) • **antigen** presentation /-forming cell (abbr AFC)/-dependent cell-mediated cytotoxicity (abbr ADCC) • **antigen**-specific response / detection[21] / titer / recognition[22] [ɪʃ] • **antigen** skin testing /-binding site • **antigenic** stimulus / determinant[23] / characteristics or properties[24] • **antigenic** coupling [ʌ]/ drift / shift[25]

immune complex n term   syn **antigen-antibody complex** n term
antigen combined with a specific antibody to which complement may be fixed
» Complement activation resulting from non-IgE immune complex formation may lead to mediator release with resultant urticaria [ɜː] and angioedema [iː], e.g. in serum sickness[1] or transfusion [juː] reactions. Erythema [iː] nodosum leprosum is a consequence of immune injury from antigen-antibody complex deposition in skin and other tissues.
Use circulating[2] [ɜː]/ IgM-IgG **immune complex** • **immune complex** formation[3] / precipitation / deposition[4] • **immune complex**-like reaction /-dependent • **immune complex** level / assay / (-mediated) disease or disorder[5] • **immune complex** glomerulonephritis[6] [aɪ]/ vasculitis / allergic [ɜː] disease • Ag-Ab[7] / IgA-containing / soluble[8] **immune complex** • HLA or MHC[9] / protein / multienzyme [aɪ] **complex** • **antigen-antibody** binding [aɪ]/ interactions / complement complex[10] / system

complement pathway [pæθweɪ] n term   syn **complement system** [ɪ] n term
cascading series of plasma enzymes, regulatory proteins, and proteins capable of cell lysis[1] [aɪ]
» Activation of the classic complement pathway via C1, C4, and C2 and activation of the alternative complement pathway via factor D, C3, and factor B both lead to cleavage[2] [kliːvɪdʒ] and activation of C3. Antitumor activity is not dependent on mechanisms involving complement or host effector cells such as natural killer cells or macrophages. Complement can also be activated on the surface of microorganisms via the alternative pathway[3].
Use classic(al)[4] / alternative[3] **complement pathway** • to activate/bind or fix[5]/coat [oʊ] **complement** • first / 3rd / C4 / Bf / terminal[6] [ɜː] / early[7] / late **complement component** • activated / lysing [aɪ] by / hemolytic [ɪ] / chromosome[8] **complement** • **complement** cascade / factors[9] / component • **complement** fragment / proteins[10] / activation[11] • **complement** activity[12] / fixation (abbr CF) test[13] /-fixing antibody[14] • **complement** level / titer / receptor / product • **complement** consumption[15] / deficiency[16] / opsonins • **complement**-mediated lysis /-independent mechanism

antigen-presenting cell n term, abbr **APC**   rel **dendritic** [ɪ] **cell**[1] n term
cell (e.g. a B-cell or macrophage) capable [eɪ] of transforming an antigen so that when displayed at the cell surface with an MHC molecule it is recognized by a helper T cell and serves to activate it
» Any cell that expresses MHC class II can serve as an antigen-presenting cell to CD4+ lymphocytes. The three cell types that are the primary presenters of antigen peptide fragments to T cells are dendritic/Langerhans cells, monocytes-macrophages [-feɪdʒiːz], and B cells. Follicular dendritic cells are APCs for B cells and are distinct from the dendritic/Langerhans cells[2], which are APCs for T cells.
Use APC-T cell interaction • **antigen-presenting** monocyte / macrophage / pathway • **antigen-**reactive T cell[3] / blood or circulating[4] / bone marrow **dendritic cells** • follicular[5] (abbr FDCs)/ mucosal **dendritic cells**

Antikörper, Ak
Antigen, Ag[1] Antigenität[2] stark[3] antinukleäre Antikörper, ANA[4] blockierende/ inkomplette/ konglutinierende Ak[5] Alloantikörper[6] komplementbindender Ak[7] kreuzreaktiver Ak[8] Histokompatibilitätsantigen[9] thymusabhängiges Antigen[10] humanes Leukozytenantigen, HLA[11] Autoantigen[12] familiäres Ag[13] ubiquitäres Ag[14] sequestriertes Ag[15] exogenes/ körperfremdes Ag[16] Thrombozytenantigen[17] prostataspezifisches Ag[18] Antigen-Antikörper-Reaktion[19] antigenpräsentierende Zelle[20] Antigennachweis[21] Antigenerkennung[22] antigene Determinante[23] Antigeneigenschaften[24] Antigenshift[25]

8

Immun-, Antigen-Antikörper-, AgAk-Komplex, AAK
Serumkrankheit[1] zirkulierender AAK[2] Immunkomplexbildung[3] Ablagerung v. Immunkomplexen[4] Immunkomplexkrankheit[5] Immunkomplexglomerulonephritis[6] AAK[7] löslicher Immunkomplex[8] HLA-Genkomplex, Majorhistokompatibilitätskomplex[9] Antigen-Antikörper-Komplement-Komplex[10]

9

Komplementsystem
Zytolyse[1] Spaltung[2] klassischer Komplementaktivierungsweg[3] alternativer Komplementaktivierungsweg[4] Komplement binden[5] terminale Komplementkomponente[6] frühe Komplementkomponente[7] Chromosomensatz[8] Komplementfaktoren[9] Komplementproteine[10] Komplementaktivierung[11] Komplementaktivität[12] Komplementbindungsreaktion[13] komplementbindender Antikörper[14] Komplementverbrauch[15] Komplementdefekt, -mangel[16]

10

antigenpräsentierende Zelle
dendritische Zelle[1] Langerhans-Zellen[2] antigenreaktive T-Zelle[3] zirkulierende dendritische Zellen[4] follikuläre dendritische Zellen[5]

11

B-lymphocyte [lɪmfəsaɪt] n term → U37-10

syn **B-cell** n, rel **plasma cell**[1] n term

immunocompetent lymphocyte that is not thymus-dependent [aɪ] and is responsible for Ig production

» B-lymphocytes are the precursors[2] [ɜː] of plasma cells and express[3] surface Igs[4] but do not release[5] [iː] them and thus do not play a direct role in cell-mediated [iː] immunity. The adult spleen[6] [iː] produces monocytes, lymphocytes, and plasma cells. BCG vaccine [æks] stimulates both B-cell and T-cell immune responses.

Use normal / circulating / tissue / (im)mature[7] / IgA / transformed **B-lymphocytes** • short-lived[8] / atypical [ɪ]/ antibody-producing **lymphocytes** • tumor-infiltrating (abbr TIL)/ autoreactive **lymphocytes** • **lymphocyte** transforming factor[9] (abbr LTF) • anti-**lymphocyte** serum[10] • lymphomatous / precursor[11] **B-cell** • **B-cell** immune response / differentiation[12] • **B-cell** precursor or progenitor[11] / growth factor[13] • **B-cell** antigen receptor complex / function • **B-cell** leukemia[14] [luːkiːmɪə]/ lymphoma • antibody-secreting[15] [iː]/ bone marrow / malignant **plasma cells** • **plasma cell** dyscrasias[16] [eɪ]/ leukemia[17] / granuloma

T lymphocyte n term   syn **T cell** n, rel **cytokine**[1] [saɪtəkaɪn] n term

long-lived thymocyte-derived lymphocyte responsible for cell-mediated immunity which has a typical T3 surface marker and differentiates and divides in the presence of transforming agents (mitogens[2] [aɪ])

anti-T cell adj term • **-kine** comb

» Precursors of T cells migrate [aɪ] to the thymus [aɪ], where they develop some of the functional and cell surface characteristics of mature T cells. The immune effect attributed[3] to cyclosporine[4] includes inhibition of T-lymphocyte response to alloantigen or exogenous interleukin-2 [uː]. Is there any molecular evidence for a clonal T-cell disorder?

Use suppressor[5] / cytotoxic[6] (abbr CTL) **T lymphocytes** • CD8+ (regulatory)[5] / thymic[7] quiescent[8] [es] **T lymphocytes** • mature[9] / peripheral / lung / donor [oʊ] **T lymphocytes** • tumor-specific / effector **T-cell** • **T-cell** activation[10] (pathway) / response • **T-cell** (-mediated) immunity[11] / subset[12] [ʌ] • **T-cell** surface marker / proliferation • **T-cell** count[13] [aʊ]/ cytokine / dependent • **T-cell** assay / receptor[14] / repertoire • **T-cell** abnormality / memory / deficiency[15] [ɪʃ] • **T-cell** clones[16] / depression /-targeted immunotherapy / lymphoma[17] / anti-**T-cell** antibodies[18] • immunoregulatory / chemoattractant [kiːmoʊ-] or chemotactic[19] **cytokines** • T cell(-derived) [aɪ]/ (pro/ anti-)inflammatory [æ] **cytokines** • pyrogenic / membrane-associated **cytokine** • lympho/ chemo[19]/ mono**kines**

helper T cell n term   syn **CD4+ T cell, T helper cell** or **lymphocyte** n term

class of T cells that triggers other T and B lymphocytes, and macrophages to promote antibody formation

» For thymus-dependent antigens, T helper lymphocytes control the switch from IgM to IgG. Activated T helper-inducer cells release a variety [aɪ] of mediators [iː] (lymphokines) including proteins capable of recruiting blood monocytes to the local milieu of the activated T cells. Functional T cell subsets are generally divided into helper T lymphocytes, which preferentially recognize[1] class II antigens, cytotoxic T lymphocytes, which preferentially recognize class I antigens, and suppressor cells, which act to enhance graft survival[2].

Use TH1(-type) or type 1[3] / precursor / activated[4] **helper T cells** • **helper T cell** function[5] / activity / count[6] / response • **T helper**-inducer cells[7] / to suppressor ratio[8] [eɪʃ] • **T helper** cell phenotype [iː]/ infiltration

memory cell n term   syn **memory lymphocyte** [meməri lɪmfəsaɪt] n term

long-lived[1] T- and B-lymphocyte formed by exposure [oʊ3] to antigens that carries the specific antibody until stimulated by a second exposure

» After primary infection antibody-producing lymphocytes persist in small numbers as memory cells and begin to proliferate[2] rapidly in response to reexposure[3]. Resting memory CD4+ T cells[4] are thought to continuously circulate between various lymphoid tissue compartments.

Use sensitized[5] / latently [eɪ] infected / resting[4] **memory T lymphocytes** • immunologic(al)[6] / T cell / B cell **memory** • **memory** B cell[7] / T cell[8]

B-Lymphozyt, B-Zelle
Plasmazelle[1] Vorläufer[2] exprimieren[3] Oberflächenimmunglobuline[4] freisetzen[5] Milz[6] (un)reife B-Lymphozyten[7] kurzlebige Lymphozyten[8] Lymphozytentransformationsfaktor[9] Antilymphozytenserum[10] B-Zellenvorläufer, B-Zellblasten[11] B-Zellendifferenzierung[12] B-Zell-Wachstumsfaktor[13] B-Zell-Leukämie[14] antikörperbildende Plasmazellen[15] Plasmazelldyskrasie[16] Plasmazellenleukämie[17]

12

T-Lymphozyt, T-Zelle
Zytokin[1] Mitogene[2] zugeschrieben[3] Ciclosporin[4] Suppressorzellen[5] zytotoxische T-Lymphozyten[6] thymusabhängige Lymphozyten, T-Lymphozyten[7] ruhende T-Lymphozyten[8] reife T-Lymphozyten[9] T-Lymphozytenaktivierung[10] zellvermittelte/ zelluläre Immunität[11] T-Zell-Subpopulation[12] T-Zellzahl[13] T-Zell-Rezeptor[14] T-Lymphozytenmangel[15] T-Lymphozytenklone[16] T-Zell-Lymphom[17] T-Zellen-Antikörper[18] Chemokine[19]

13

Helferzelle, T-Helfer-Lymphozyt, CD4+ Zelle
erkennen[1] die Transplantatüberlebenszeit verbessern[2] TH1-Zellen[3] aktivierte T-Helferzellen[4] T-Helferzellenfunktion[5] T-Helfer-Zellzahl[6] T-Helfer/ Induktor-Lymphozyten[7] CD4/CD8-Quotient[8]

14

Gedächtniszelle, Memory cell
langlebig[1] s. vermehren[2] erneute Exposition[3] ruhende T-Gedächtniszellen[4] sensibilisierte T-Gedächtniszellen[5] immunologisches Gedächtnis[6] B-Gedächtniszelle[7] T-Gedächtniszelle[8]

15

The Immune System

BODY STRUCTURES & FUNCTIONS

cytotoxic or **killer cell** n term, abbr **K cell**   rel **null** [ʌ] **cell**[1] n term

T cell involved in antibody-dependent cell-mediated immunity with receptors for the Fc portion of IgG molecules which enable it to lyse IgG-coated target cells without mediation of complement

cytoxicity[2] [saɪtətɒːksɪsəti] n term • **kill** n & v • **killing** n

» Normally redundancy[3] [ʌ] in host resistance allows interferon [ɪɚ], natural killer cell, B or T lymphocyte responses to compensate for a deficiency in one of these factors. CD8+ cytotoxic T cells are induced to become active killer cells by IL-2[4]. NK cells[5] kill target cells with low or negative levels but not those with high levels of MHC class I expression.

Use natural[5] (abbr NK) / active / lymphokine-activated[6] (abbr LAK) **killer cell** • **killer cell** differentiation / cytotoxicity • **killer** T cells[7] / T lymphocytes[7] • **null cell** lineage[8] [lɪnɪɪdʒ]/ deficiency / tumor / adenomas[9] • **cytotoxic** antibodies[10] / reaction / effector cell • **cytotoxic** lineage / agent[11] / therapy • antibody-dependent cellular[12] (abbr ADCC)/ direct / lymphocyte **cytotoxicity** • cytokine-mediated [iː]/ complement-mediated / tumor[13] **cytotoxicity** • bacterial / single-cell / tumor cell[14] **kill** • microbial / parasite / phagocytic [fægəsɪtɪk] **killing** • oxidative / complement-mediated **killing** • macrophage-mediated / intracellular bacterial[15] [ɪɚ] **killing** • **killing** ability or capacity • bacterial **killing** test[16]

Killerzelle, K-Zelle, zytotoxische Zelle

Nullzelle[1] Zytotoxizität[2] Reserven[3] Interleukin-2[4] natürl. Killerzellen[5] lymphokinaktivierte Killerzelle[6] zytotoxische T-Zellen[7] Nullzelllinie[8] Nullzelladenome[9] zytotoxische Antikörper[10] zytotoxische/ zellschädigende Substanz[11] antikörperabhängige zellvermittelte Zytotoxizität[12] Antitumor-(Zyto)toxizität[13] Zerstörung von Tumorzellen[14] intrazelluläre Bakterienabtötung[15] Bestimmung d. Keimabtötungsrate[16]

16

Phagocytosis: (a) the affixed antibody reacts with Fc receptors on macrophages which bind the target to the destroyer and activate phagocytic processes that internalize the target,

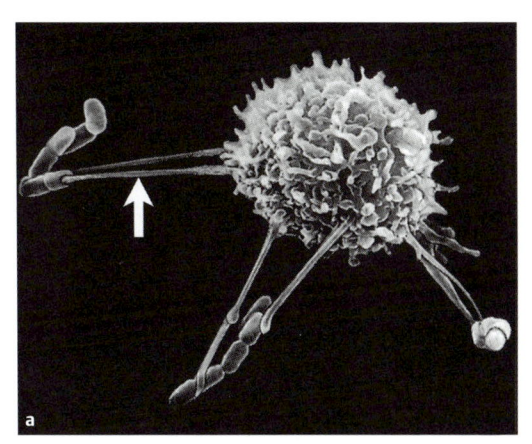

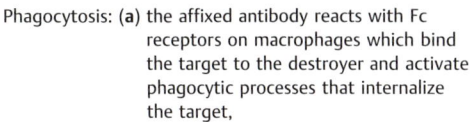

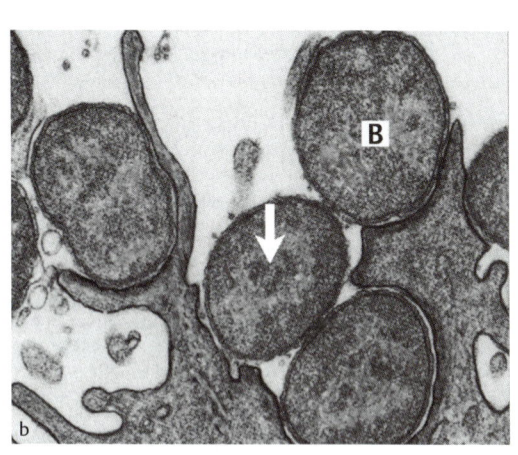

(b) phagocyte engulfing bacteria (B)

---

scavenger cell [skævəndʒɚ sel] n term   syn **phagocyte** [fægəsaɪt] n term

cell possessing the property of ingesting[1] [dʒe] bacteria, foreign particles, and other cells

phagocytic adj term • **phagocytosis**[2] n • **phagocytose/-tize**[1] v • **scavenge**[1] v • **phago-** comb

» Phagocytes are divided into microphages (polymorphonuclear leukocytes[3] which ingest chiefly bacteria) and macrophages which are largely scavengers, ingesting dead tissue and degenerated [dʒe] cells. Plasmin degrades [eɪ] fibrin [aɪ] polymer into small fragments, which are cleared by the monocyte-macrophage scavenger system[4]. Chemotactic factors[5] are substances [ʌ] that attract phagocytes to sites of microbial invasion [eɪʒ].

Use antioxidant / peroxyl / free radical[6] **scavenger** • **scavenger** macrophage / function / activity[7] • **scavenger** system[8] / receptor pathway • mononuclear / activated / circulating **phagocyte** • CNS[9] / peripheral blood **phagocyte** • **phagocyte** system[8] / chemotaxis / aggregation[10] • **phagocyte** function / defect[11] [iː] • **phagocytic** cell (adherence) / process[2] / killing • **phagocytic** clearance [ɪɚ]/ defect[11] / vacuole or vesicle[12] • white cell / neutrophil / monocyte / macrophage / marrow **phagocytosis** • bacterial / impaired[11] [eɚ]/ resistance to **phagocytosis** • **phago**some[12] /lysosome[13]

Fresszelle, Phagozyt

phagozytieren[1] Phagozytose[2] polymorphkernige Granulozyten[3] Monozyten-Makrophagen-System[4] chemotaktische Faktoren, Chemotaxine[5] Radikalfänger[6] Phagozytoseaktivität[7] phagozytäres System[8] Mikrogliazelle[9] Phagozytenaggregation[10] Phagozytosedefekt[11] Phagozytosevakuole, Phagosom[12] Phagolysosom[13]

17

BODY STRUCTURES & FUNCTIONS — The Immune System

macrophage [-feɪdʒ] n term   rel **histiocyte**[1], **lysosome**[2] [aɪ], **monocyte**[3] n term

actively phagocytic mononuclear cell arising from monocytic stem cells in the bone marrow; these cells are widely distributed in the body (e.g. Kupffer cells[4] in the liver), vary in morphology and motility, and have abundant [ʌ] endocytic vacuoles[5], lysosomes, and phagolysosomes

macrophagic [æ] adj term • **microphage**[6] n • **monokine**[7] n • **-phage** comb

» Macrophages are involved in the production of antibodies and in cell-mediated immune responses, participate in presenting antigens to lymphocytes, and secrete [iː] a variety of immunoregulatory molecules. Lysosomes are cellular organelles in which complex macromolecules are degraded [eɪ] by specific acid hydrolases [aɪ].

Use activated / host / tissue[1] / splenic [e]/ alveolar[8] [ɪə]/ dermal [ɜː] **macrophage** • lipid-containing (foamy)[9] [oʊ]/ hemosiderin-laden[10] [eɪ] **macrophage** • dendritic / monocyte-derived [aɪ] **macrophage** • parasite-infected / PAS-positive **macrophage** • **macrophage**-activating factor[11] (abbr MAF)/ activating response • **macrophage** precursor [ɜː]/ activity /-secreted products • **macrophage**-derived foam cell[9] / enzyme / mobility[12] • **macrophage** chemotactic [kiːm-] factor (abbr MCF)/ migration inhibition [ɪʃ] test[13] • **macrophage**-monocyte stimulation / invasion [eɪʒ] mechanism • **macrophage**-inflammatory protein (abbr MIP) • **macrophage**-produced neurotoxin /-tropic virus [aɪ] • foamy[9] / multi-nucleated / Langerhans[14] **histiocyte** • reactive / crystal-laden [ɪ]/ meningeal [dʒiː] **histiocyte** • neutrophil [(j)uː]/ (extra)cellular / hepatic **lysosome** • thyroid [aɪ]/ swollen / iron-laden[15] [aɪ] **lysosome** • **lysosomal** membrane / enzyme[16] / storage disease[17] / degradation[18] • (peripheral) blood / infected / virus-altered [ɒː] **monocytes** • infiltrating / antigen-presenting / circulating[19] **monocytes** • **monocyte**-macrophage scavenger system[20] /-lineage [lɪnɪɪdʒ] cell • count[21] [aʊ])

immune agglutination n term   rel **immune adherence**[1] [ɪə] n term → U38-11

process caused by agglutinating antibodies[2] that is specific for the suspended microorganism which causes erythrocytes [ɪ] and suspended bacteria to adhere and form clumps [ʌ]

agglutinate[3] [uː] v term • **agglutinin** n • **adhere**[4] [ɪə] v • **adherent** adj

» Complement-mediated immune adherence involves the interaction of C3b and C4b with a series of receptors [se] on the macrophage. Rapid enzyme immunoassays and latex [eɪ] agglutination tests[5] for both toxin A and toxin B have been developed.

Use passive or indirect[6] / bacterial / nonimmune / red cell[7] **agglutination** • platelet[8] [eɪ]/ latex / hem[7] [iː]/ auto [ɒː]/ micro [aɪ]/ co**agglutination** • **agglutination** reaction[9] / test[9] / inhibition[10] / titer [aɪ‖iː] • immune / cold[11] / iso(hem)/ phytohem [faɪtəhiːm]/ hem[12]/ leuko**agglutinin** • **agglutinin** titer

major [meɪdʒɚ] **histocompatibility complex** n term, abbr **MHC**
syn **HLA complex** or **system** [ɪ] n term

cluster [ʌ] of genes, termed HLA complex in humans, which codes for cell-surface histocompatibility antigens and is the principal determinant of tissue type and transplant compatibility

» The MHC genes [dʒiːnz] expressed in the thymus [aɪ] play a crucial [uːʃ] role[1] in the selection of the T cell receptor repertoire during maturation. Three clearly defined loci are recognized within the HLA complex for class I HLA antigens. The principal role of the CD4 molecule is to promote interaction of T cells with class II HLA molecules on antigen-presenting cells.

Use human / disease-associated / donor **major histocompatibility complex** • **MHC** class I antigens /-encoded molecules[2] • **major histocompatibility** antigens[3] / gene complex[4] • **histocompatibility** antigens[3] / leukocyte [uː] antigens[3] (abbr HLA)/ genes • **histocompatibility** locus[5] / determinants / haplotype / typing or testing[6] / match • human leukocyte antigen[3] (abbr HLA) **complex** • **HLA** allele [iː]/ molecule / antigens[3] / locus[5] / class II genes /-D region • **HLA** phenotype[7] [iː]/ type / allotype / haplotype /-matched • **HLA** identical siblings[8] /-antibody screen /-linked disease

---

Makrophage

Histiozyt, Macrophagocytus stabilis[1] Lysosom[2] Monozyt[3] Kupffer-Sternzellen, Macrophagocytus stellatus[4] zahlreiche intrazelluläre Vakuolen[5] Mikrophage, neutrophiler Granulozyt[6] Monokin[7] Alveolarmakrophage[8] Xanthom-, Schaumzelle, lipidbeladener/-speichernder Histiozyt[9] Sideromakrophage[10] Makrophagenaktivierungsfaktor[11] Makrophagenmobilität[12] Makrophagenmigrationshemmtest[13] Langerhans-Zelle[14] eisenspeicherndes Lysosom[15] lysosomales Enzym[16] lysosomale Speicherkrankheit[17] lysosomaler Abbau[18] zirkulierende Monozyten[19] Monozyten-Makrophagensystem[20] Monozytenzählung, -zahl[21]

18

Immunhämagglutination

Immunadhärenz[1] agglutinierende Antikörper[2] zusammenballen, verklumpen, agglutinieren[3] (an)haften, verkleben[4] Latex(agglutinations)test[5] indirekte/ passive Agglutination[6] Erythrozyten-, Hämagglutination[7] Thrombozytenagglutination[8] Agglutinationsreaktion, -test[9] Agglutinationshemmung[10] Kälteagglutinin[11] Hämagglutinin[12]

19

Haupt-, Majorhistokompatibilitätskomplex

Schlüsselrolle[1] MHC-Moleküle[2] HLA-Antigene, Histokompatibilitäts-, Transplantationsantigene, MHC-Antigene[3] HLA-Genkomplex[4] HLA-Lokus[5] Histokompatibilitätstestung[6] HLA-Phänotyp[7] HLA-identische Geschwister[8]

20

The Immune System   BODY STRUCTURES & FUNCTIONS **161**

self *n & adj & comb term*   *syn* **auto-** *comb,*
                        opposite **foreign**[1] [fɒːrᵊn] *adj or* **nonself**[1] *adj & n term*

(n) an individual's autologous cell components as contrasted with exogenous (nonself) constituents; recognition of self from non-self serves to protect the host from an immunologic attack on his own antigenic constituents, as opposed to immune system destruction or elimination of foreign antigens

» *Self versus nonself discrimination[2], based upon moderate affinity to self-peptide + MHC, is imprinted on the T cell repertoire. In the thymus, the recognition [ɪʃ] of self-peptides on thymic epithelial [iː] cells, macrophages and dendritic cells is thought to play an important role. Foreign antigens are degraded and their peptide fragments presented in the context of MHC class I or class II molecules on APC[3].*
Use **self** antigen[4] /-recognition[5] /-tolerance[6] /-MHC antigens /-protein /-infection[7] • recognition of[5] **self** • **nonself** substances / antigen[8] • anti**self** response[9] • **foreign** antigen[8] (binding site) • **foreign** antigenic stimuli [aɪ]/ cells / body[10] (*abbr* FB) • **foreign** histocompatibility antigens / DNA / proteins[11] / to the body[12] • **auto-** immunity /antibody[13] /agglutinins[14] /inoculation[15] /logous /immune disease[16]

(körper)eigen, Selbst, Selbst-, Auto-
fremd, Nichtselbst[1] Selbst-Nicht-Selbst-Erkennung[2] antigenpräsentierende Zellen[3] Autoantigen[4] Erkennung körpereigener Strukturen[5] Immuntoleranz[6] Selbst-, Autoinfektion[7] Fremdantigen[8] Autoimmunreaktion[9] Fremdkörper[10] Fremdproteine[11] körperfremd[12] Autoantikörper[13] Autoagglutinine[14] Autoinokulation[15] Autoimmunkrankheit[16]

21

immune resistance *n term* → U120-13   *rel* **rejection**[1] [rɪdʒekʃᵊn] *n term*
                rel **anergy**[2] [ænɚdʒi], **immune tolerance**[3] *n term* → U130-21, U121-12

natural or acquired [əkwaɪəd] ability of an organism to maintain its immunity against the effects of pathogenic microorganisms, toxins, drugs, and non-self substances[4]
resist [rɪzɪst] *v term* • **resistant**[5] *adj* • **reject** [rɪdʒekt] *v* • **antirejection** *adj*
» *Changing the patient to a less antigenic insulin may make possible a dramatic reduction in insulin dosage or at least may shorten the duration of immune resistance.*
Use to develop[6]/confer[7] [ɜː] /show or display/impair/decrease **resistance** • immune insulin / local tissue / antigen **resistance** • inborn or natural[8] / acquired[9] / antibiotic[10] / host **resistance** • enhanced or increased[11] / relative / high-level **resistance** • **resistance to** infection / ampicillin [sɪ] / to prevent[12]/control/diagnose/ confirm [ɜː]/ abort[13]/result in **rejection** • (hyper)acute[14] / signs of / tissue / transplant[15] **rejection** • (immediate/ delayed) [eɪ] graft[15] / organ / accelerated[16] [əksel-] **rejection** • cell-mediated / mild / steroid-resistant[17] / irreversible [ɜː] **rejection** • **rejection** response[18] / activity / process / episode • **antirejection** therapy[19] / medication • immunologic[3] / self[3]-/ drug **tolerance** • cross[20]/ exercise[21] / glucose **tolerance**

immunologische Resistenz
Abstoßung, Rejektion[1] Anergie, fehlende Reaktion auf Antigene[2] Immuntoleranz[3] Fremdsubstanzen, körperfremde S.[4] widerstandsfähig, resistent[5] eine Resistenz entwickeln[6] R. verleihen[7] angeborene R.[8] erworbene R.[9] Antibiotikaresistenz[10] erhöhte Resistenz[11] eine Abstoßung verhindern[12] d. Abstoßung unterdrücken[13] (hyper)akute Abstoßung[14] Transplantatabstoßung[15] akzelerierte/ beschleunigte A.[16] steroidresistente A.[17] Abstoßungsreaktion[18] Rejektionstherapie[19] Kreuztoleranz[20] phys. Belastbarkeit[21]

22

hypersensitivity [haɪpɚ-] *n term*   *syn* **allergy** [ælɚdʒi] *n term* → U124-3

exaggerated[1] immunologically mediated inflammatory response to a normally innocuous[2] antigen
hypersensitive (to)[3] *adj term* • **sensitive** *adj* → U57-8 • **sensitivity (to)** *n*
(hyper)sensitization *n term* • **sensitize**[4] *v* • **allergic**[5] [ɜː] *adj* • **allergen**[6] *n*
» *Test for hypersensitivity before injecting [dʒe] antitoxin or drugs (e.g. penicillin) to which the patient has had a severe reaction in the past. In some asthma [æzmə] patients, offensive allergens cannot be identified by history[7] or by allergy testing. Is there a history of parental allergy?*
Use IgE-mediated or immediate (type)[8] / delayed (type)[9] (*abbr* DTH)/ cutaneous **hypersensitivity** • bronchial [k]/ cellular or cell-mediated[9] **hypersensitivity** • vitamin D / drug[10] / food **hypersensitivity** • **hypersensitivity** reaction / to cold[11] • hypo/ light-**sensitive** • **hypersensitive** child / skin / intestine • to rule out[12]/in- quire [aɪ] about **allergies** • contact / seasonal [iː]/ nasal[13] [eɪ]/ food[14] **allergy** • (intestinal) protein / drug[10] **allergy** • penicillin [sɪ]/ chronic / IgE-mediated **allergy** • de[15]/ self-/ HLA / photo/ cross- pre**sensitization** • **to be allergic to** milk / antibiotics / nickel[16] • **allergic** factor / patient[17] / reaction[18] • **allergic** sensitization[19] / (eye) disease / contact dermatitis [aɪ] • contact[20] / atopic / airborne / inhaled[21] [eɪ] **allergen** • injected[22] / animal / ingested[23] [dʒe] **allergen** • **allergen** exposure[24] [oʊʒ] testing • challenge[25] [dʒæl-]/ ingestion • **allergen** inhalation /-specific antibody /-free environment [aɪ] • **allergen**-induced asthma[26] / immunotherapy[15] / extract

Überempfindlichkeit, Allergie
übermäßig[1] harmlos, unschädlich[2] überempfindlich, allergisch; hypersensibel[3] sensibilisieren[4] allergisch[5] Allergen[6] anamnestisch[7] Soforttypreaktion, IgE-vermittelte Reaktion vom Soforttyp[8] Spätreaktion, zellvermittelte Reaktion vom Spättyp, Typ IV-Immunantwort[9] Arzneimittelallergie[10] Kälteallergie[11] Allergien ausschließen[12] allerg. Rhinitis[13] Nahrungsmittelallergie[14] Desensibilisierung[15] auf Nickel allergisch sein[16] Allergiker(in)[17] allerg. Reaktion[18] Allergisierung[19] Kontaktallergen[20] Inhalationsallergen[21] Injektionsallergen[22] Ingestionsallergen[23] Allergenexposition[24] Allergenprovokation[25] allergisches Asthma[26]

23

Unit 40 The Nervous System
Related Units: 41 Brain, 42 Nerve Function, 31 Musculoskeletal Function, 73 Mental Activity

nerve (cell) [nɜːrv sel] *n*   *syn* **neuron(e)** [n(j)ʊərɒːn] *n term*,
                                   rel **interneuron¹** *n term*

morphological and functional unit of the nervous system consisting of a cell body and several processes

nervous² *adj* • **neural³** [n(j)ʊərəl] *adj term* • **neuronal⁴** *adj* • **neur(o)-** *comb*

» The vena [iː] caval [eɪ] foramen [eɪ] allows passage of the inferior vena cava and small branches of the phrenic [frenɪk] nerve. The C6 root [ruːt] is the nerve root emerging [ɜː] between the C5 and C6 vertebrae [iːǁeɪ]. This causes damage to nervous tissue⁵ which may lead to deterioration of vision⁶ [ɪʒ]. There is a regular turnover of the bipolar receptor cells, which function [ʌ] as the primary [aɪ] sensory neurons.

Use cranial⁷ [eɪ]/ phrenic⁸ / spinal⁹ [aɪ] (accessory) [kse]/ sciatic¹⁰ [saɪætɪk] **nerve** • lumbosacral [eɪ]/ median [iː]/ peripheral / cutaneous [eɪ] **nerve** • facial [eɪʃ]/ trigeminal [dʒe]/ optic **nerve** • auditory [ɒː] or acoustic¹¹ [uː]/ olfactory¹² **nerve** • sensory¹³ / (oculo)motor¹⁴ / somatic / bipolar [aɪ]/ multipolar **nerve** • **nerve** root¹⁵ / fiber [aɪ]/ ending¹⁶ / canal [æ] • **nerve** head / bundle [ʌ]/ trunk¹⁷ [ʌ]/ pathways¹⁸ • **nerve** plexus / distribution [juː]/ branch¹⁹ / sheath²⁰ [ʃiːθ] • **nerve** (dys)function / supply²¹ [aɪ]/ conduction [ʌ]/ stimulation • **nerve** block / injury / palsy²² [ɔː]/ compression / paralysis²² • sensory / (upper/ lower) motor²³ **neuron** • preganglionic²⁴ / second-order / adrenergic²⁵ [ɜː] **neuron** • pain-transmission / internuncial [ʌ] or connector¹ / olfactory receptor **neuron** • **neuron** synapse /-effector interaction • **nervous** system / tension²⁶ [ʃ]/ exhaustion [ɒː] or prostration²⁷ [eɪ] • **nervous** depression / breakdown²⁸ • **neural** crest²⁹ [k]/ foramen [eɪ]/ tube defect³⁰ / tissue⁵ • **neural** damage / reflexes / repair • **neuronal** tissue / innervation / activation / excitability • **neuronal** network³¹ / circuit³² [ɜː]/ signal / loss • **neuro**logy /logic /genic /endocrine • **neuro**fibril³³ /glial /nitis [aɪ] /muscular [ʌ] /effector

Nervenzelle, Neuron
Zwischen-, Interneuron¹ Nerven-, nervös² neural³ Neuronen-, neuronal⁴ Nervengewebe, Textus nervosus⁵ Visusverschlechterung⁶ Hirnnerv, N. cranialis⁷ Phrenikus, N. phrenicus⁸ Spinal-, Rückenmarknerv, N. spinalis⁹ Ischiasnerv, N. ischiadicus¹⁰ Akustikus, VIII. Hirnnerv, N. acusticus/ vestibulocochlearis¹¹ Riechnerv, N. olfactorius¹² sensorischer/ sensibler Nerv¹³ motor. Nerv, N. motorius¹⁴ Nervenwurzel¹⁵ Nervenendigung¹⁶ Nervenstamm¹⁷ Nervenbahnen¹⁸ Nervenast¹⁹ Nervenscheide²⁰ Nervenversorgung²¹ Nervenlähmung²² unteres motorisches Neuron, spinales Motoneuron²³ präganglionäres N.²⁴ adrenerges N.²⁵ Nervenanspannung²⁶ Neurasthenie, psychovegetatives Syndrom²⁷ Nervenzusammenbruch²⁸ Neuralleiste²⁹ Neuralrohrdefekt³⁰ neuronales Netz³¹ Neuronenkreis, -schaltung³² Neurofibrille³³

1

axon [æksɒːn] *n term*   *syn* **axon/ axis cylinder** [sɪ-] *n term*,
                            rel **dendrite¹** [-raɪt] *n term*

single process of a nerve cell that normally conducts [ʌ] impulses away from the cell body

(peri/ neuro)axonal² *adj term* • **dendritic³** [ɪ] *adj* • **ax(io)-** *comb*

» In contrast to dendrites, which rarely exceed 1.5 mm in length, axons can extend great distances from the parent cell body (some axons of the pyramidal tract are 40-50 cm long). Each alpha motor axon arborizes⁴ just before reaching the muscle fibers that it innervates.

Use afferent / efferent / motor / peripheral / somatic **axon** • (un)myelinated [aɪ]/ pyramidal [æ] **axon** • postsynaptic⁵ / proprioceptive [se]/ sudomotor **axon** • **axon** hillock⁶ / reflex⁷ / loss / transport / sheath⁸ [iː] • **axonal** process / degeneration / neuropathy / terminal⁹ • cochlear [k] nerve **dendrite** • **axi**petal¹⁰ • **axo**plasm¹¹ /dendritic /somatic synapse¹² /onopathy

Axon, Neuraxon, Neurit, Achsenzylinder
Dendrit¹ axonal, Axon-² dendritisch³ verzweigt sich⁴ postsynaptisches Axon⁵ Axonhügel, Colliculus axonis⁶ Axonreflex⁷ Axonscheide⁸ Axonterminal⁹ axipetal¹⁰ Axoplasma¹¹ axosomatische Synapse¹²

2

nerve *or* **neural pathway** [nɜːrv pæθweɪ] *n term*

collection of axons establishing a conduction route [aʊǁuː] for the transmission of nervous impulses from one group of nerve cells to another or to an effector organ¹

» Behavior [eɪ] and mood are modulated by noradrenergic [-ɜːrdʒɪk], serotonergic, and dopaminergic pathways. The voiding [ɔɪ] reflex² is dependent on intact neural pathways to the micturition [ɪʃ] center³ in the brain stem⁴. The central auditory pathway is a complex system with many crossovers and relay [iː] stations to the auditory cortex.

Use sensory *or* afferent⁵ / motor⁶ / excitatory [ɪksaɪ-]/ inhibitory / reflex⁷ **pathways** • ascending⁸ [s]/ descending⁹ / sympathetic **pathways** • proprioceptive [se]/ nociceptive [noʊsɪ-] *or* pain(-sensitive)¹⁰ **pathways** • visual [ɪʒ] *or* optic¹¹ / conduction¹² **pathways** • cerebrospinal [aɪ] fluid¹³ / accessory **pathways** • lymphatic¹⁴ / metabolic¹⁵ / catabolic **pathways** • enzymatic/ T-cell activation **pathways**

Nervenbahn
Erfolgsorgan¹ Miktionsreflex² Miktionszentrum³ Hirnstamm⁴ sensorische/ afferente Bahnen⁵ motor. Bahnen⁶ Reflexbahnen⁷ aufsteigende Bahnen⁸ absteigende Bahnen⁹ Schmerzbahnen¹⁰ Sehbahnen¹¹ Leitungsbahnen¹² Liquorwege¹³ Lymphbahnen¹⁴ Stoffwechselwege¹⁵

3

The Nervous System

BODY STRUCTURES & FUNCTIONS 163

afferent [æfɚənt] *or* **sensory fibers** [sensəɹi faɪbɚz] *n term*
opposite **efferent** *or* **motor** [moutɚ] **fibers**[1] *n term*

neurons conveying [eɪ] impulses from a peripheral sense organ toward the CNS

afferents[2] *n pl term* • **efferents**[3] *n pl* • **deefferented** *adj* • **deafferentation**[4] *n*

» Visceral [ɪs] abdominal pain is mediated by visceral afferent nerves that accompany the sympathetic pathways. There are no efferent somatic nerve cell body synapses outside of the CNS. The function of the first dorsal interosseus muscle must be checked to establish the integrity of the deep motor branch of the ulnar [ʌ] nerve.

Use **afferent** impulse / signals / limb[5] [lɪm]/ innervation / stimulus[6] • **afferent** nociceptor / terminal [ɜː]/ feedback • **sensory** action potential / input / acuity[7] [kjuː] • **sensory** branch / perception[8] [se]/ examination • **sensory** deficit / disturbances[9] [ɜː]/ impairment [ɚ] • **sensory** (hearing) loss / neuropathy • hemi/ neuro/ psycho**sensory** [saɪkoʊ-] • **efferent** vagal [eɪ] tone / signals / pathways[10] / impulses / nerves • **motor** area or cortex[11] / activity / skills[12] • **motor** coordination[13] / center[14] / behavior[15] • vaso [veɪzoʊ]/ psycho[16] / sensori/ oro/ visual- oculo**motor** • primary / vagal / (somato)sensory[17] / mechanoreceptor **afferents** • (muscle) [ʌ] spindle / visceral [s] / taste *or* gustatory[18] [ʌ] **afferents** • propriospinal / pain / nociceptive **afferents** • sympathetic **efferents**

afferente/ sensible/ sensorische (Nerven)fasern
efferente/ motorische (Nerven)fasern[1] Afferenzen[2] Efferenzen[3] Deafferenzierung[4] afferenter Ast[5] afferenter Reiz[6] Sinnesschärfe[7] Sinneswahrnehmung[8] Sensibilitätsstörungen[9] efferente Bahnen[10] motor. Rindenfeld, motor. Cortex[11] motor. Fertigkeiten[12] Bewegungskoordination[13] motor. Zentrum[14] motor. Verhalten[15] psychomotorisch[16] sensorische Afferenzen[17] Geschmacksafferenzen[18]

4

central nervous system [sentrəl nɜːrvəs sɪstəm] *n term, abb* **CNS**
rel **peripheral** [pərɪfəɹəl] **nervous system**[1] *n term, abb* **PNS**

the brain and the spinal cord[2] which coordinate and control the entire nervous system

» All local anesthetics [e] have CNS toxicities including confusion [juː], coma, and seizures[3] [iː]. The peripheral nervous system consists of the cranial [eɪ] and spinal [aɪ] nerves from their points of exit from the CNS to their terminations in peripheral structures [ʌ].

Use intracranial part of the **CNS** • **CNS** function / depression / disease[4] / involvement[5] • **CNS** stimulant / syphilis[6] / trauma / bleeding / infection[7] • **CNS** metastases[8] / symptoms / mass lesion • metastases to the[9] **peripheral nervous system** • **peripheral nervous system** changes / diseases / involvement / dysfunction [ɪ]/ complications

Zentralnervensystem, ZNS
peripheres Nervensystem, PNS[1] Rückenmark[2] Krampfanfälle[3] Erkrankung d. Zentralnervensystems[4] Beteiligung/ Befall d. ZNS[5] Syphilis cerebri, Neurolues[6] ZNS-Infektion[7] ZNS-Metastasen[8] Metastasierung in das periphere Nervensystem[9]

5

autonomic [ɔːtənɒːmɪk] **nervous system** *n term*
syn **involuntary** *or* **visceral** [vɪsəɹəl] **nervous system** *n term*

part of the nervous system which innervates smooth [uː] and cardiac muscle, glandular tissue[1], governs intestinal peristalsis, the heartbeat, etc. and is not under voluntary control

dysautonomia[2] [dɪs-] *n term* • **voluntary**[3] [vɒːləntəri] *adj*

» The innervation of the bladder and its involuntary sphincter is via the autonomic nervous system. The activity of autonomic nerves is regulated by central neurons responsive to diverse afferent inputs.

Use **autonomic** centers[4] / plexus[5] / (dys)function / (hyper)activity / response • **autonomic** control / arousal[6] [aʊ]/ discharge[7] • **autonomic** effector cells / tone / reflexes / lability • **autonomic** insufficiency / disturbances[8] / denervation / blockade • **involuntary** body functions / movement / contraction • **involuntary** muscles[9] / guarding[10] [ɑː]/ weight loss[11] • **voluntary** sphincter / muscle activity[12] / (motor) control / eye movements

autonomes/ vegetatives Nervensystem
Drüsengewebe[1] Dysautonomie[2] willkürlich, willentlich; freiwillig[3] vegetative Zentren[4] vegetatives Nervengeflecht[5] vegetativer Erregungszustand[6] autonome Entladung[7] vegetative Störungen[8] unwillkürliche Muskulatur[9] unwillkürliche/ reflektorische Anspannung[10] unbeabsichtigter Gewichtsverlust[11] willkürliche Muskelaktivität/ -tätigkeit[12]

6

somatic (nerve) fibers [aɪ] *n term*
opposite **secretory** [siːkrətəɹi] **fibers**[1] *n term*

nerves of sensation or motion as distinguished from those exciting secretory activity

psychosomatic [saɪkoʊ-] *n term* • **somatization**[2] *n* • **somato-, secreto-** *comb*

» During voiding[3], somatic fibers relax the pelvic floor and external sphincter. The anal canal is generously supplied with somatic sensory nerves which are highly susceptible[4] [se] to painful stimuli [aɪ]. There are no efferent somatic nerve cell body synapses outside of the CNS.

Use **somatic** nervous system[5] / (motor) neuron / sensory nerve[6] • **somatic** nerve supply / innervation • **somatic** pathways / stimuli / pain / sensations • **somatic** response / reflexes / complaints[7] [eɪ] • **psychosomatic** illness / factors / disorder[8] • **somat**algia [-ældʒ(ɪ)ə] /osensory evoked potentials[9] /oform (pain) disorder • **secreto**motor /inhibitory[10]

somatische (Nerven)fasern
sekretorische (Nerven)fasern[1] Somatisierung[2] Blasenentleerung, Miktion[3] empfindlich[4] animales Nervensystem[5] somatosensorische/ -sensible Faserbahnen[6] somatische Beschwerden[7] psychosomatische Störung[8] somatosensibel/ -sensorisch evozierte Potentiale, SEP[9] sekretionshemmend[10]

7

40

BODY STRUCTURES & FUNCTIONS

adrenergic fibers [ædrənɜːrdʒɪk faɪbəz] n term
opposite **cholinergic** [koʊlənɜːrdʒɪk] **fibers**[1] n term
autonomic nerve cells or fibers that employ norepinephrine[2] as their neurotransmitter
(anti)cholinergic[3] adj & n term • **(non/ anti)adrenergic**[4] adj & n • **-ergic** comb
» These agents [eɪdʒ] accumulate [kjuː] in postganglionic adrenergic neurons and inhibit norepinephrine release [iː]. Cholinergic stimuli [aɪ], either vagal [eɪ] or intramural [jʊə], are the most potent pepsigogues[5] [pepsɪgɒːgz], though gastrin and secretin [iː] are also effective.
Use **adrenergic** activity / stimulation / (blocking) agent[4] • agonist[6] • alpha-/ beta-**adrenergic** [iː]‖[eɪ] • **cholinergic** neurons[7] / receptor / innervation / crisis[8] [aɪ] • dopamin**ergic**[9]

sympathetic fibers n term
opposite **parasympathetic** [pærəsɪmpəθetɪk] **fibers**[1] n term
part of the autonomic nervous system that chiefly contains adrenergic fibers and acts to constrict blood vessels, accelerates [əkse-] the heart rate, and raises [eɪ] the blood pressure
sympath(o)- [sɪmpəθoʊ] comb
» Sympathetic fibers emerging [ɜː] from the gray areas of T11-L2 travel through the paravertebral sympathetic chain ganglia, superior hypogastric plexus, and hypogastric nerves to enter the pelvic plexus along with parasympathetic fibers.
Use **sympathetic** nerves / chain [tʃeɪn] or trunk[2] [ʌ]/ ganglion • **sympathetic** component / efferent activity • nerve endings[3] • **sympathetic** innervation / (over)stimulation / block or blockade[4] [eɪ]/ reflex • **sympathetic** (hyper)activity / outflow[5] / vasoconstriction [veɪzoʊ-]/ irritation[6] • **parasympathetic** activity / tone[7] / agent • **parasympathetic** agonist / inhibition / palsy[8] • **sympatho**mimetic[9] /lytic[10] [lɪtɪk] /adrenal [iː]

vagus (nerve) [veɪgəs nɜːrv] n term
syn **pneumogastric** [n(j)uːmoʊ-] or **tenth cranial** [kreɪnɪəl] nerve n term
paired cranial nerve which supplies the pharynx, larynx, lungs, heart, esophagus, stomach and most of the abdominal viscera and controls speech, swallowing[1], and numerous sensory and motor functions
(-)vagal [veɪgəl] adj & comb • **vago-** comb
» Maneuvers [uː] such as gagging[2], the Valsalva maneuver[3], or placing the face in cold water stimulate the vagus nerve. Sensory innervation of the epiglottis is supplied by the internal branch of the superior laryngeal [dʒ] nerve that branches from the vagus bilaterally.
Use right / left / jugular [dʒʌ] ganglion of the[4] **vagus** • **vagus** reflex[5] [iː]/ arrhythmia [ɪ]/ pulse[6] [ʌ] • **vagal** trunk[7] [ʌ]/ nerve terminals[8] / efferent activity • **vagal** tone[9] / hypertonicity [ɪs]/ syncope[10] [sɪŋkəpi] • **vagal** stimulation[11] / bradycardia[12] / symptoms • vaso**vagal** • **vago**tomy /lytic drug[13] /tonic

ganglion [gæŋglɪən] n term, pl **-ia** [gæŋglɪə]
aggregation of nerve tissue in the PNS mainly at the site of junction or division of neurons
(pre/ post/ a)ganglionic[1] adj term • **ganglionated**[2] adj • **gangli(o)-** comb
» Urogenital [dʒe] ganglia include a complex intraganglionic network of cholinergic and adrenergic fibers that either pass uninterruptedly through the ganglion or terminate in it as neuron synapses.
Use sensory / spinal[3] / autonomic / (para)sympathetic **ganglion** • (dorsal) root[3] [uː]/ basal[4] [eɪ] **ganglia** • cervical [sɜː]/ stellate[5] / trigeminal[6] [traɪdʒe-] **ganglion** • otic / pelvic plexus / geniculate[7] **ganglion** • **ganglion** cell[8] / of the vagus [eɪ] nerve • **ganglionic** crest[9] / synapse / transmission • **ganglionic** stimulation / blocking agent[10] • **postganglionic** nerve endings[11] / sudomotor [uː] axon • **postganglionic** parasympathetic cholinergic neurons / neurotransmitter • **ganglio**nectomy /neuroma[12] /nitis [aɪ] /cytoma [saɪ] /sides[13]

The Nervous System

adrenerge (Nerven)fasern
cholinerge Fasern[1] Noradrenalin[2] anticholinerg; Anticholinergikum, Parasympatholytikum[3] antiadrenerg, sympatholytisch; Adrenozeptorblocker, -antagonist, Antiadrenergikum, Sympatholytikum[4] die Pepsinproduktion stimulierende Reize[5] Adrenozeptoragonist, Sympathomimetikum[6] cholinerge Neurone[7] cholinergische Krise[8] dopaminerg[9]
8

sympathische (Nerven)fasern
parasympathische (Nerven)fasern[1] Grenzstrang, Truncus sympathicus[2] sympathische Nervenendigungen[3] Sympathikusblockade, -ausschaltung[4] sympath. Erregungsübertragung[5] Sympathikusirritation[6] Parasympathikotonus[7] Parasympathikuslähmung[8] Sympath(ik)omimetikum, Adrenozeptoragonist[9] Sympath(ik)olytikum, Adrenozeptorantagonist[10]
9

Nervus vagus, Vagus
Schluckakt[1] Würgen[2] Valsalva-Manöver, Bauchpresse[3] oberes Vagusganglion, Ganglion superius nervi vagi[4] Vagusreflex[5] Vaguspuls[6] Vagusstamm, Truncus vagalis[7] vagale Nervenendigungen[8] Vagustonus[9] vasovagale Synkope[10] Vagusstimulation[11] parasympathische Bradykardie[12] Vagolytikum, Parasympatholytikum[13]
10

Ganglion
ganglionär, Ganglien-[1] m. Ganglien versehen[2] Spinalganglien[3] Basalganglien[4] Ganglion stellatum/ cervicothoracicum[5] Ganglion trigeminale/ semilunare/ Gasseri[6] Ganglion geniculatum/ geniculi[7] Ganglienzelle[8] Neuralleiste, Ganglienleiste[9] Ganglienblocker, Ganglioplegikum[10] postganglionäre Nervenendigungen[11] Ganglioneurom[12] Gangliosid[13]
11

The Nervous System

BODY STRUCTURES & FUNCTIONS 165

(nerve) plexus [plɛksəs] *n term, pl* **-es**   *rel* **neurovascular bundle**[1] [ʌ] *n term*
a network of interconnected nerves, veins, and/or or lymph [lɪmf] vessels
plexiform[2] *adj* • **plex(o)-** *comb* → U34-5
» *The testicular plexus is derived* [aɪ] *from the aortic* [eɪɔː] *plexus. The inferior hypogastric plexus consists of freely interconnected nerves in the pelvic fascia* [fæʃ(ɪ)ə] *that is lateral to the rectum, internal genitalia* [eɪ]*, and lower urinary organs.*
Use brachial [eɪk]/ autonomic / cervical sympathetic / celiac [siː] or solar[3] **plexus** • inferior hypogastric [aɪ] *or* pelvic[4] / lumbosacral [lʌm-] **plexus** • myenteric [maɪ-] *or* Auerbach's[5] / choroid[6] **plexus** • vascular[7] / venous [iː] **plexus** • **plexus** anesthesia[8] [iːʒ]/ paralysis[9] • **plexiform** nerve arrangement / neuroma • **plexo**pathy /genic • **bundle** branch block[10]

Plexus, Geflecht
Gefäßnervenbündel, neurovaskuläres Bündel[1] geflecht-, plexusartig, plexiform[2] Plexus coeliacus/ solaris, Sonnengeflecht[3] Plexus hypogastricus inferior, P. pelvinus[4] Auerbach-Plexus, P. myentericus[5] P. choroidei[6] Plexus vasculosus, Gefäßgeflecht[7] Plexusanästhesie[8] Plexuslähmung[9] Schenkelblock[10]

12

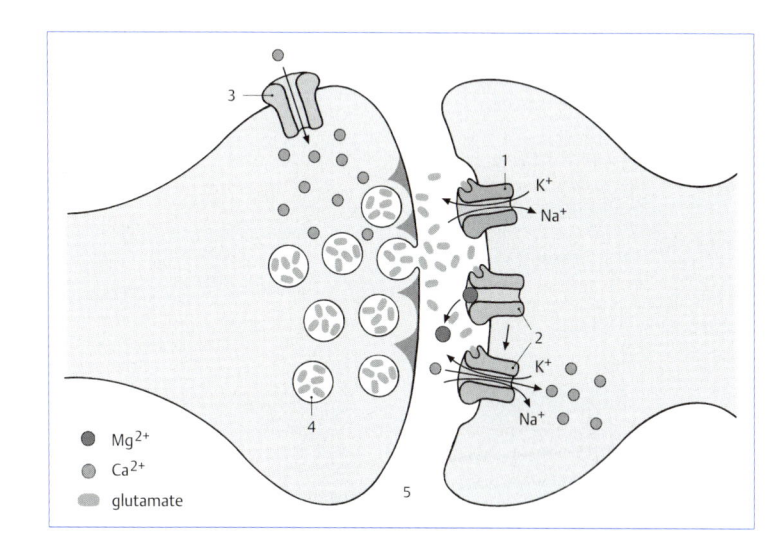

Glutamatergic synaptic transmission: synaptic AMPA receptor (**1**), NMDA receptor channel (**2**), calcium channel (**3**), synaptic vesicle (**4**), synaptic cleft (**5**)

---

synapse [sɪ‖sɪnæps] *n & v term*   *rel* **synaptic gap** *or* **cleft**[1] [sɪnæptɪk] *n term*
region of membrane-to-membrane contact between two neurons (or a nerve cell and an effector organ) across which transmission of nerve impulses takes place
(**pre**/ **post**)**synaptic**[2] *adj term* •(**poly**/ **mono**)**synaptic**[3] *adj*
» *Postganglionic fibers from these synapses innervate the pancreatic acini* [æsɪnaɪ]*, the islets* [aɪ]*, and the ducts* [ʌ]*. Acetylcholine is released into the synaptic cleft, and interacts with postganglionic receptor sites to elicit*[4] [ɪs] *a functional response. Muscle relaxants depress spinal synaptic reflexes, prolong synaptic recovery time, and reduce repetitive discharges.*
Use axodendritic[5] [ɪ]/ axosomatic / dendrodendritic[6] / autonomic / electrical[7] **synapse** • ganglionic / spinal / excitatory[8] [aɪ] / inhibitory[9] **synapse** • **synaptic** junction[10] [dʒʌŋkʃᵊn]/ input / (neuro)transmission[11] • **synaptic** transmitter / relay [riːleɪ]/ recovery [ʌ] time[12] / vesicle[13] • **presynaptic** (nerve) terminal [ɜː]/ membrane / depolarization • **postsynaptic** membrane[14] / (alpha/ dopamine) [oʊ] receptor • **postsynaptic** potential[15] / inhibition[16]

Synapse; Synapse bilden
Synapsenspalt[1] postsynaptisch[2] monosynaptisch[3] auslösen[4] axodendritische Synapse[5] dendrodendritische Synapse[6] elektr. Synapse, Synapsis nonvesicularis[7] erregende/ exzitatorische Synapse[8] hemmende/ inhibitorische Synapse[9] Synapsen-/ synapt. Verbindung[10] synapt. Erregungsübertragung[11] synaptische Latenzzeit[12] synapt. Bläschen/ Vesikel[13] postsynapt. Membran[14] postsynapt. Potential[15] postsynapt. Hemmung[16]

13

---

myelin sheath [maɪəlɪn ʃiːθ] *n term*   *rel* **Schwann cell**[1] [ʃwɑːn sel] *n term*
lipoprotein envelope[2] surrounding most axons larger than 0.5-mm in diameter [æ]; composed of Schwann cells in peripheral nerves and of oligodendroglia cells in the brain and spinal cord
(**un**)**myelinated**[3] [aɪ] *adj term* • (**re**/**de**)**myelination**[4] *n* • **demyelinate** *v*
» *The myelin sheath can regenerate rapidly, esp. after segmental demyelination. Each Schwann cell maintains* [eɪ] *the myelin sheath along one segment of nerve fiber.*
Use multilamellated[5] / thin / patchy degeneration of the[6] / breakdown of [7]**myelin sheath** • transient / optic / perivascular / segmental / selective[8] **demyelination** • CNS / peripheral **myelin** • **myelin** membrane / protein / wrapping[9] [r] • **myelin** destruction[10] [ʌ]/ loss[4] • **demyelinated** axon • **demyelinating** lesion [iːʒ]/ plaques [plæks] • **demyelinating** cord disorder / diseases[11] / polyneuropathy

Mark-, Myelinscheide
Schwann-Zelle[1] Hülle[2] markhaltig, -reich[3] Demyelinisation, -sierung, Entmarkung[4] mehrschichtige Markscheide[5] Demyelinisierungs-, Entmarkungsherde[6] Markscheidenzerfall, Myelinabbau[7] selektive Entmarkung[8] Markscheide, Myelinmantel, -hülle[9] Zerstörung d. Marksubstanz[10] Entmarkungskrankheiten[11]

14

node of Ranvier [noʊd əv rɑːvieɪ] *n term* *rel* **saltatory conduction**[1] *n term*
short unmyelinated interval in the myelin sheath between successive segments of the myelin sheath
» This indicates antibody deposition on the motor axon at the nodes of Ranvier and distal motor nerve terminals. Posterior pharyngeal wall tumors drain bilaterally to jugular [dʒʌ] chain nodes and retropharyngeal nodes of Ranvier. Slowing of evoked [oʊ] response latencies [eɪ] in MS[2] is thought to result from loss of saltatory conduction along demyelinated axons.

Ranvier-Schnürring
saltatorische Erregungsleitung[1]
multiple Sklerose[2]

15

Unit 41   Brain & Spinal Cord
Related Units: 40 Nervous System, 58 Eyes, 60 Ears, 42 Nerve Function, 73 Mental Activity

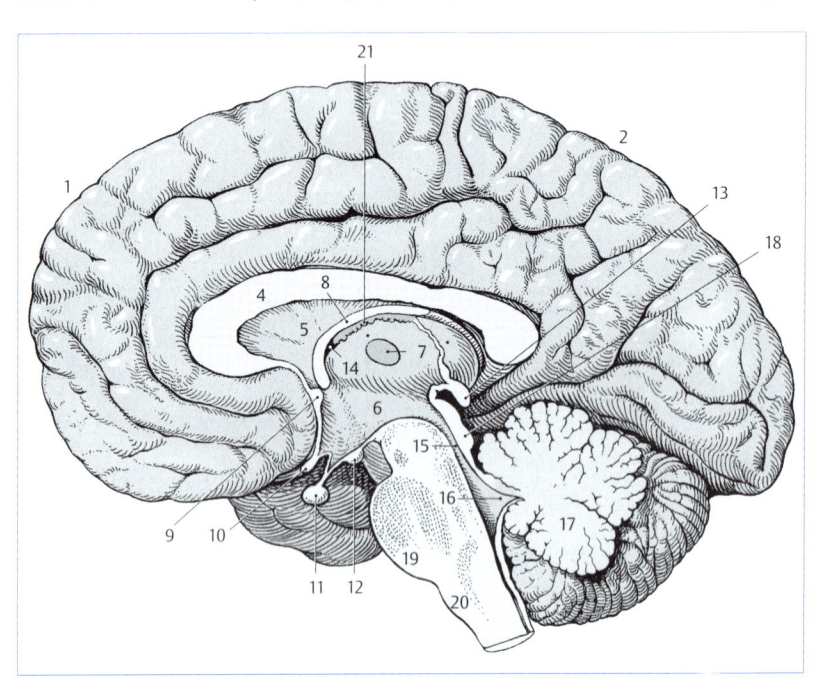

The brain (median cross-section of the right hemisphere): frontal lobe (**1**), parietal lobe (**2**), diencephalon (**3**), corpus callosum (**4**), septum pellucidum (**5**), third ventricle (**6**), interthalamic adhesion (**7**), fornix (**8**), anterior commissure (**9**), optic chiasm (**10**), pituitary (**11**), mamillary bodies (**12**), pineal gland (**13**), interventricular foramen of Monro (**14**), cerebral aqueduct (**15**), fourth ventricle (**16**), cerebellum (**17**), quadrigeminal plate (**18**), pons (**19**), medulla oblongata (**20**), choroid plexus (**21**)

brain [breɪn] *n*   *syn* **encephalon** [ɪnsefəlɒːn] *n term, rel* **brains**[1] *n inf pl only*
portion of the central nervous [ɜː] system in the cranium [eɪ] consisting of the forebrain[2], midbrain[3] [ɪ] and hindbrain[4] [haɪndbreɪn]
brainy[5] *adj clin* • **brainpower**[6] *n* • **brainwash**[7] *v* • **encephal(o)-** *comb*
» Although focal signs may be found in metabolic brain disease, asymmetric findings should be assumed to reflect a structural brain lesion [iː] until proved otherwise. There was no anatomic damage to brain tissue. In status epilepticus the brain suffers from hypoxia [haɪ-] and acidosis.
Use to use/rack[8] **one's brain** • cranial [eɪ]/ spinal[9] [aɪ]/ fetal [iː]/ left side of the **brain** • **brain** region / center[10] / tissue / cells • **brain** capillaries / activity / waves[11] • **brain** function / growth / development[12] • **brain** maturation / metabolism[13] / teaser[14] [iː] • **brain** disease / injury[15] / abscess / damage[16] / **brain** edema [iː]/ tumor / hemorrhage[17] [-ɪdʒ] • **brain** death[18] / imaging / scan[19] / electrical activity mapping[20] (*abbr* BEAM) • **encephal**itis [aɪ] /ocele /opathy • rhomb[4]/ pros[2]/ mes[3]/ tel**encephalon**

Gehirn, Hirn, Cerebrum, Encephalon
Intelligenz, Verstand, Köpfchen[1]
Vorderhirn, Prosencephalon[2] Mittelhirn, Mesencephalon[3] Rautenhirn, Rhombencephalon[4] gescheit[5] Intelligenz[6] e. Gehirnwäsche unterziehen[7] sich d. Kopf zerbrechen[8] Nachhirn, verlängertes Mark, Myelencephalon[9] Hirnzentrum[10] Hirnströme[11] Hirnentwicklung[12] Gehirnstoffwechsel[13] Denk(sport)-aufgabe[14] Hirnverletzung, (Schädel)hirntrauma[15] Hirnschaden, -schädigung[16] (Ge)hirnblutung[17] Hirntod[18] Hirnszintigrafie[19] BEAM[20]

1

Brain & Spinal Cord   BODY STRUCTURES & FUNCTIONS 167

cerebrum [səriːbrəm‖serəbrəm] *n term*

rel **cerebellum**[1] [serəbeləm] *n term*

main portion of the brain including all parts of the brain within the skull except the medulla [ʌ], pons, and cerebellum; strictly speaking it refers only to the parts derived [aɪ] from the telencephalon[2] and includes mainly the cerebral hemispheres (cerebral cortex and basal ganglia)

cerebral[3] [serə‖səriːbrəl] *adj term* • **cerebellar**[4] *adj*
cerebr(o)- *comb* • **cerebell(o)-** *comb*

» The surface of the cerebrum is convoluted[5]. The cerebellum lies above the pons and medulla and beneath the posterior portion of the cerebrum. The hemispheres of the cerebellum are united by a narrow middle portion, the vermis[6] [ɜː].

Use **cerebral** aqueduct[7] [æ]/ peduncle[8] [ʌ]/ vasculature / blood flow or perfusion[9] [juː]/ perfusion pressure (*abbr* CPP) • **cerebral** vasospasm [eɪ]/ anoxia / contusion[10] / edema / palsy[11] [ɔː] • crus[12] [uː‖ʌ]/ falx[13] [æ‖ɔː]/ commotio[14] [oʊʃ] **cerebri** • tonsils[15] / central lobule / quadrangular lobule **of the cerebellum** • anterior / midline / lateral / injured [ɪndʒɚd] **cerebellum** • **cerebellar** vein [eɪ]/ Purkinje cells / tentorium[16] / vermis[6] [ɜː]/ fossa • **cerebellar** (dys)function / sign[17] / ataxia[18] / infarction / degeneration • **cerebro**vascular accident[19] (*abbr* CVA) /spinal fluid[20] /cortical /retinal • **cerebello**pontine [aɪ] angle[21] [æŋgl] /medullary cistern[22] [sɪ]

cerebral hemisphere [hemɪsfɪɚ] *n term*   rel **commissure**[1] [kɒmɪʃʊɚ] *n term*
rel **corpus callosum**[2], **fornix cerebri**[3] *n term*

one of the two parts of the cerebrum on either side of the cerebral fissure in the midline which consists of the cerebral cortex (gray matter[4]), the centrum semiovale, and the subcortical nuclei[5] (i.e. basal ganglia)

(bi/ intra)hemispheric [e] *adj term* • **hemispheral** *adj* • **(trans)callosal** *adj*

» Language function resides predominantly in the left hemispheres of most persons, including the left-handed. The neural [(j)ʊɚ] organization of spatial [eɪʃ] orientation[6] displays a right hemisphere dominance pattern. The corpus callosum is the great commissural plate of nerve fibers interconnecting the cortical hemispheres. The anterior commissure connects the middle and inferior temporal gyri [dʒaɪraɪ] of the hemispheres and runs across the midline just in front of the fornix.

Use right / left / (non)dominant[7] / opposite / cerebellar[8] **hemisphere** • **hemispheral** convexity[9] / lesion [iː] • **hemispheric** disease / stroke[10] / infarct / injury • splenium[11] [iː]/ truncus[12] [ʌ]/ genu[13] [dʒ] **of the corpus callosum** • **callosal** involvement[14] • **transcallosal** pathways • rostral or anterior[15] (*abbr* AC)/ posterior[16] **commissure** • (dorsal) hippocampal or fornical[17] / habenular[18] / middle or soft[19] **commissure** • optic / interhemispheric **commissure** • severed **commissure** • **commissural** pathways[20]

cerebral ventricle *n term*
rel **cerebral aqueduct**[1] [ækwədʌkt] *n term*

one of a system of irregularly shaped communicating cavities located within the cerebral hemispheres, diencephalon [aɪ] and brain stem that are continuous with the central canal of the spinal cord

(inter/ intra)ventricular[2] [ɪ] *adj term* • **aqueductal** [ʌ] *adj*

» The lateral ventricles communicate with the third ventricle through the interventricular foramen[3]. Cranial CT scan can readily [e] identify blood within the ventricles but thin layers of subarachnoid [æk] or subdural blood lying over the hemispheres may be missed. Obstruction of the outlet foramina of the fourth ventricle may produce hydrocephalus [haɪdrɒse-] or may be associated with aqueductal stenosis.

Use (left/ right) lateral[4] / third[5] / fourth[6] **ventricle** • **ventricular** puncture[7] [ʌ]/ drainage[8] [-ɪdʒ] • **intraventricular** hemorrhage[9] [-rɪdʒ] • patent[10] [eɪ] **aqueduct** • **aqueduct** of Sylvius[1] • **aqueductal** stenosis[11]

Großhirn, Cerebrum
Kleinhirn, Cerebellum[1] Endhirn, Telenzephalon[2] zerebral, (Ge)hirn-, Zerebral-, Zerebro-[3] zerebellar[4] gewunden[5] Kleinhirnwurm, Vermis[6] Aquaeductus cerebri/ mesencephali/ Sylvii[7] Hirnstiel, Pedunculus cerebri[8] Hirndurchblutung[9] Hirnprellung, Contusio cerebri[10] Zerebralparese[11] Hirnschenkel, Crus cerebri[12] Großhirnsichel, Falx cerebri[13] Gehirnerschütterung, Commotio cerebri[14] Kleinhirntonsillen, Tonsillae cerebelli[15] Kleinhirnzelt, Tentorium cerebelli[16] Kleinhirnzeichen[17] zerebellare Ataxie[18] Schlaganfall, Gehirnschlag, apoplektischer Insult[19] Liquor (cerebrospinalis)[20] Kleinhirnbrückenwinkel[21] Cisterna cerebromedullaris[22]

2

Großhirnhälfte, -hemisphäre
Kommissur, Commissura, Verbindung(sstelle)[1] Balken, Corpus callosum[2] Hirngewölbe, Fornix cerebri[3] graue Substanz[4] subkortikale Kerne[5] räumliche Orientierung[6] dominante Großhirnhemisphäre[7] Kleinhirnhälfte, -hemisphäre[8] Hemisphärenkonvexität[9] Gehirnschlag in e. Hemisphäre[10] Balkenwulst, Splenium corporis callosi[11] Balkenstamm, Truncus corporis callosi[12] Balkenknie, Genu corporis callosi[13] Mitbeteiligung des Corpus callosum[14] Commissura anterior[15] C. posterior[16] C. fornicis[17] C. habenularum[18] Adhaesio interthalamica[19] Kommissurenbahnen[20]

3

Hirnventrikel, -kammer, Ventriculus cerebri
Aquaeductus cerebri/ Sylvii[1] ventrikulär, Ventrikel-[2] Foramen interventriculare[3] Seitenventrikel, Ventriculus lateralis[4] dritter Ventrikel, V. tertius[5] vierter Ventrikel, V. quartus[6] Ventrikelpunktion[7] Ventrikeldrainage[8] Ventrikelblutung[9] durchgängiger Aquaeductus cerebri[10] Aquäduktstenose[11]

4

gyrus [dʒaɪrəs] *n term, pl* **-i** [dʒaɪraɪ]

    rel **lobe**[1] [loʊb], **(cerebral) sulcus** [sʌlkəs] *or* **fissure**[2] [fɪʃɚ] *n term*

prominent rounded convolution of the cerebral cortex bounded [aʊ] by the wall and floor of the sulcus

gyral *adj term* • **pachygyria**[3] [k] *n* • **agyria**[4] [eɪdʒaɪriə] *n* • **lobar** *adj* • **sulcal** *adj*

» The prerolandic-precentral gyrus[5] on one side of the cerebrum plus the immediately more anterior areas of frontal lobe cortex regulate skilled muscular [ʌ] activities that occur [ɜː] on the opposite side of the body. Most of the temporal lobes are interconnected by the anterior commissure. The CT showed an associated [oʊʃ] mass effect distorting adjacent[6] [ədʒeɪs-] sulci [sʌlsaɪ‖kaɪ] and the lateral ventricles.

Use (sub)callosal / supracallosal [uː]/ cingulate[7] [sɪ]/ left angular / dentate[8] **gyrus** • (left inferior) frontal / parahippocampal[9] **gyrus** • (superior) temporal / supramarginal[10] [dʒ] **gyrus** • (pre)frontal / parietal[11] [aɪ]/ temporal[12] / occipital [ksɪ] **lobe** • **lobe**ctomy[13] • central[14] / oculomotor / chiasmatic[15] [kaɪ-]/ lateral[16] / calcarine[17] **sulcus** • longitudinal cerebral[18] / (primary) cerebellar **fissure** • choroid / calcarine[17] / sylvian[16] **fissure** • **gyral** flattening • **lobar** hemorrhage / gliosis[19] [aɪ] • **sulcal** enlargement

Gyrus, (Ge)hirnwindung
Hirnlappen, Lobus cerebri[1] Sulcus cerebri[2] Pachy-, Makro-, Megagyrie[3] Agyrie[4] Sulcus praecentralis[5] benachbart[6] Gyrus cinguli[7] G. dentatus[8] G. parahippocampalis[9] G. supramarginalis[10] Scheitel-, Parietallappen, Lobus parietalis[11] Schläfen-, Temporallappen, L. temporalis[12] Lobektomie, operative Entfernung e. Hirnlappens[13] Sulcus centralis/ Rolandi[14] Sulcus chiasmatis[15] Sulcus lateralis, Fissura Sylvii, Sylvius-Furche[16] Sulcus calcarinus[17] Fissura longitudinalis cerebri[18] lobäre/ lappenbegrenzte Gliose[19]

5

cerebral cortex [kɔːrteks] *n term*   *syn* **pallium** *n term rare, pl* **-ia**

gray outer coating 1-4 mm in thickness covering the entire surface of the cerebral hemispheres; characterized by a laminar organization such that the nerve cells are stacked[1] in defined layers

(sub)cortical[2] *adj term* • **neocortex**[3] *n* • **cortic(o)-** *comb*

» The cerebral cortex has been mapped into 47 areas which, in functional terms, can be classified into 3 categories: motor cortex[4] (areas 4 and 6) with a poorly developed inner granular layer [eɪ] (agranular cortex[5]) and prominent pyramidal cell layers, sensory cortex comprising the somatic sensory cortex (areas 1 to 3), auditory cortex[6], and visual cortex[7], and finally association cortex, the vast remaining expanses of the cerebral cortex.

Use prefrontal **cerebral cortex** • occipital[8] / occipitotemporal / cerebellar[9] **cortex** • cingulate [sɪ]/ posterior parietal / prepiriform **cortex** • (primary/ supplementary) motor[4] / sensorimotor **cortex** • somatosensory / sensory[10] / primary visual *or* striate[7] [straɪeɪt] **cortex** • **cortical** white matter / arteries / perfusion / function • **cortical** sensory deficit / visual impairment / blindness[11] / atrophy • **corticospinal** tract[12]

Großhirnrinde, Cortex cerebri
angeordnet[1] kortikal, Rinden-[2] Neocortex[3] motor. Cortex/ Rinde(nfeld/ -zentrum)[4] agranuläre Rinde[5] Hörrinde, akustischer Cortex[6] (primäre) Sehrinde, visueller Cortex, primäres Sehzentrum, Area striata[7] okzipitaler Cortex[8] Kleinhirnrinde, Cortex cerebelli[9] sensibles/ sensorisches Rindenfeld[10] Rindenblindheit[11] Pyramidenbahn, Tractus corticospinalis[12]

6

gray matter [greɪ mæt̬ɚ] *n term*

    rel **white matter** *or* **substance**[1] [ʌ] *n term*

regions of the brain and spinal cord which are made up primarily of the cell bodies and dendrites of nerve cells rather than myelinated [aɪ] nerve fibers[2] (also referred to as substantia alba[1])

» MRI is better than CT at distinguishing between gray and white matter. The inflammation involves the posterior and anterior horns of the gray matter. Axons of the upper motor neurons [n(j)ʊɚːnz] descend [se] through the subcortical white matter and the posterior limb [lɪm] of the internal capsule.

Use subcortical / periaqueductal[3] [ʌ] **gray matter** • **gray matter** nuclei [nuːkliaɪ]/ -white matter junction[4] [dʒʌŋkʃən]/ necrosis • **gray matter of the** brain / brainstem / (spinal) cord[5] • cerebral / cerebellar[6] / frontal orbital **white matter** • **white matter** tract / changes / lesion [iːʒ]/ disease • **gray** *or* unmyelinated [aɪə] fibers[7] [aɪ]/ commissure[8] / columns[9] [kɒːləmz]

graue Substanz, Substantia grisea
weiße Substanz, Substantia alba[1] markhaltige Nervenfasern[2] S. grisea centralis, zentrales Höhlengrau[3] Rinden-Mark-Grenze[4] graue Rückenmarksubstanz, S. grisea medullae spinalis[5] Marksubstanz d. Kleinhirns, Corpus medullare[6] marklose Nervenfasern[7] Substantia intermedia centralis[8] Columnae griseae, säulenartige Anteile der grauen Rückenmarksubstanz[9]

7

Brain & Spinal Cord BODY STRUCTURES & FUNCTIONS 169

meninges [mənɪndʒiːz] n pl term   rel **dura (mater)**[1] [d(j)ʊə·ə meɪ‖mɑːtɚ] n,
 rel **arachnoid** [əræknɔɪd] **(mater)**[2], **pia** [paɪə‖piːə] **(mater)**[3] n term
 one of the three membranous coverings [ʌ] of the brain and spinal [aɪ] cord
 meningeal[4] [menɪndʒiːəl] adj term • **mening(o)-** comb • **(sub/ epi)dural** adj
 • **(sub)arachnoid** adj • **pial** [paɪ‖piːəl] adj
» Between the arachnoid and the pia mater lies the subarachnoid space. The pia mater and the arachnoid are collectively called *leptomeninges*[5], as distinguished from the dura mater or *pachymeninx*[1] [k]. The pia mater also *invests*[6] the cerebellum but not so intimately as it does the cerebrum, not dipping down into all the smaller sulci. Check for signs of meningeal irritation[7] (nuchal [n(j)uːkᵊl] rigidity[8] [dʒɪ], Kernig's sign, or Brudzinski's sign).
Use inflamed[9] **meninges** • **meningeal** membranes / vessels / infection • **meningeal** inflammation[9] / signs / biopsy [aɪ]/ syndrome[10] • cranial[11] [eɪ]/ spinal / underlying / torn[12] **dura** • **dura** mater transplantation • **dural** sinus [aɪ] (occlusion) [uːʒ]/ defect [iː]/ sac[13] / tear[12] [teə] • **epidural** space[14] / hematoma / abscess / anesthesia [iːʒ] or block[15] / **subdural** space / effusion[16] [juːʒ]/ empyema [aɪiː]/ tap[17] • **arachnoid** membrane[2] / villi[18] [aɪ]/ cyst [sɪst] / **subarachnoid** space[19] / exudate / hemorrhage[20] • **pial** arteries • **mening**itis[9] [aɪ] /ioma /ism(us) /oencephalitis /ovascular

Meningen, Hirn- und Rückenmarkhäute
Dura (mater), Pachymeninx, harte Hirn-/ Rückenmarkshaut[1] Arachnoidea, Spinnwebenhaut[2] Pia mater, weiche Hirn-/ Rückenmarkshaut[3] meningeal, Hirnhaut-[4] Leptomeningen, weiche Hirnhäute[5] hüllt ein[6] Hirnhautreizung[7] Nackensteifigkeit[8] Hirnhautentzündung, Meningitis[9] meningeales Syndrom[10] Dura mater encephali[11] Durazerreißung[12] Duralsack[13] Epi-, Periduralraum[14] Epi-, Periduralanästhesie[15] Subduralerguss[16] subdurale Punktion[17] Arachnoidalzotten[18] Subarachnoidalraum, Spatium subarachnoideum[19] Subarachnoidalblutung[20]
8

thalamus [θæləməs] n term   rel **epi**[1]/ **meta**[2]/ **sub**[3]/ **hypothalamus**[4] n term
 one of two ovoid masses of gray matter forming the lateral wall of the third ventricle; the hypothalamus is situated at the base of the thalamus and influences neuroendocrine function and body water balance
 (hypo/ sub/ spino/ intra)thalamic adj term • **thalam(o)-** comb → U54-4
» Exteroceptive sensory impulses travel in the spinothalamic tracts[5] and synapse in the thalamus, which projects [dʒe] to the sensorimotor cortex. Secondary diabetes [iː] insipidus is due to[6] damage to the hypothalamus or pituitary [(j)uː] stalk[7] [stɔːk]. The presumed cause of transient total amnesia [iːʒ] is the result of transient ischemia affecting the posteromedial thalamus or hippocampus bilaterally.
Use ventral / dorsal / optic / dominant **thalamus** • medial [iː]/ ipsilateral **subthalamus** • **subthalamic** stimulation / nucleus[8] / posterior / mamillary tubercle of the[9] **hypothalamus** • **hypothalamic** sulcus /-pituitary axis[10] / dysfunction [dɪs-]

Thalamus, Sehhügel
Epithalamus[1] Metathalamus[2] Subthalamus[3] Hypothalamus[4] Tractus spinothalamicus ventralis und lateralis[5] zurückzuführen auf[6] Hypophysenstiel[7] Nucleus subthalamicus, Luys-Körper[8] Corpus mamillare, Mamillarkörper[9] Hypothalamus-Hypophysensystem[10]
9

(corpus) striatum [kɔːrpəs straɪeɪtᵊm] n term   syn **striate** [straɪeɪt] **body** n,
 rel **substantia nigra**[1] [aɪ‖ɪ] n term
 paired subcortial mass consisting of the caudate [ɔː] nucleus[2] and the outer segment of the lentiform nucleus[3] (putamen[4] [eɪ]), and a large-celled globus pallidus[5]
 striatal adj term • **striato-** comb • **nigral** adj • **pallidal** adj • **pallid-** comb
» The direct pathway from the striatum to the substantia nigra pars reticulata and the globus pallidus interna is GABA-ergic [-ɜːrdʒɪk] and inhibitory. In primary parkinsonism there is loss of the pigmented neurons of the substantia nigra, locus ceruleus[6] [səˈuːlɪəs], and other brainstem dopaminergic cell groups.
Use **striatal** neurons / dopamine [oʊ] uptake[7] • **striato**nigral degeneration[8] • fetal [iː]/ pigmented **substantia nigra** • **substantia nigra** pars compacta (abbr SNc)/ pars reticulata (abbr SNr)/ cells / tissue / neurons • **nigral** involvement[9] / transplantation • dominant / lateral[10] / medial[11] globus pallidus • globus pallidus interna[11] (abbr Gpi)/ externa[10] • **pallid**othalamic /otomy

(Corpus) striatum, Streifenkörper
Substantia nigra[1] Schweifkern, N. caudatus[2] Linsenkern, N. lentiformis[3] Putamen[4] Pallidum, Globus pallidus[5] Locus caeruleus/ coeruleus[6] Dopaminaufnahme im Striatum[7] striatonigrale Degeneration[8] Beteiligung/ Befall d. Substantia nigra[9] Globus pallidus lateralis[10] Globus pallidus (pars) medialis[11]
10

hippocampus [hɪpəkæmpəs] n term   rel **amygdala**[1] [əmɪgdələ] n term
 internally convoluted structure bordering the choroid [kɔː] fissure [fɪʃɚ] of the lateral ventricle
 hippocampal adj term • **amygdaloid** adj
» The limbic system[2] comprises [aɪ] the amygdala, the hippocampal formation, and the neurons of the cingulate [sɪ] gyrus [aɪ]. Encephalitis [ɪnsefəlaɪtɪs] was most extensive in the hippocampus and amygdala, producing affective changes in personality.
Use ventral / dorsal / dominant **hippocampus** • **hippocampal** fissure or sulcus[3] / formation[4] • **amygdaloid** nuclei[5] / complex[6]

Hippokampus, Ammonshorn, Cornu ammonis
Amygdala, Corpus amygdaloideum, Mandelkern[1] limbisches System[2] Sulcus hippocampi[3] Hippokampusformation[4] Corpora amygdaloidea[5] Mandelkernkomplex[6]
11

41

brain stem *n term*   *syn* **brainstem** *n, rel* **diencephalon**[1] [daɪ-], **pons**[2] *n term*
unpaired portion of the brain composed of the pons, medulla oblongata, and mesencephalon [sɛ] (some also include the diencephalon)

diencephalic[3] [daɪɛnsəfælɪk] *adj term* • **pontine**[4] [pɒːntaɪn] *adj* • **ponto-** *comb*

» A positive ciliospinal reflex indicates that the spinothalamic tracts and their connections to sympathetic fibers in the brain stem are intact. Vertebrobasilar TIAs[5] are characterized by brain stem and cerebellar symptoms, including dysarthria, diplopia[6], vertigo, and ataxia.

Use lower / upper / descending [sɛ] **brain stem** • **brain stem** nerves [ɜː]/ nuclei / activity / signs • **brain stem** reflexes[7] [iː]/ (dys)function[8] / perfusion / injury / lesion[9] • **brain stem** compression / contusion[10] / ischemia [ɪskiː-]/ herniation • **brain stem** auditory evoked potentials[11] (*abbr* BAEPs)/ stroke[12] • caudal / upper / low **diencephalon** • **diencephalic** region / level / structures • **diencephalic**-midbrain dysfunction / compression / syndrome[13] • anterior / rostral / lateral / dorsal / mid/ base of the **pons** • **pontine** fibers [aɪ]/ tegmentum[14] • reticular formation[15] / arteries • **pontine**-mesencephalic regulatory tracts / myelinosis [maɪəlɪn-] • **pontine**-level dysfunction / apoplexy • **ponto**medullary junction [dʒʌ]

cerebellar peduncle [piː‖pədʌŋkəl] *n term*
rel **(corpora) quadrigemina**[1] [kwɒːdrɪdʒɛmɪnə] *n term*
one of the three paired stalk-like[2] structures composed exclusively of white matter that connect the cerebellum to the midbrain, pons and medulla oblongata, respectively

peduncular [ʌ] *adj term* • **pedunculotomy** *n* • **quadrigeminal** *adj*

» Short circumferential branches of the basilar [æ‖eɪ] artery supply the lateral two-thirds of the pons and middle and superior cerebellar peduncles. The oculomotor nerves, the cerebral peduncles, the cerebral aqueduct, and the midbrain are vulnerable [ʌ] to compression from the displaced temporal lobe.

Use superior[3] / middle[4] / inferior[5] **cerebellar peduncle** • (rostral) cerebral[6] **peduncle** • quadrigeminal plate[1]

medulla [mɪdʌlə] **(oblongata)** [ɑː] *n term*
rel **pyramidal decussation**[1] [pəræmɪdəl dɪkəseɪʃən] *n term*
most caudal [kɒːdəl] portion of the brainstem continuous with the spinal cord which extends from the lower border of the pyramidal decussation to the pons

(ponto/ intra)medullary[2] [mɪdʌ-‖mɛdʒələɪ] *adj term* • **decussate**[3] [dekə‖dɪkʌ] *v*

» Motor nuclei [aɪ] of the medulla oblongata include the hypoglossal nucleus[4], the dorsal motor nucleus, and the nucleus ambiguus of the vagus [eɪ]. Partial lesions in this area may interrupt decussating pyramidal tract fibers[5] destined for the legs. The second-order neuron decussates and ascends in the medial lemniscus[6] located medially in the medulla and in the tegmentum of the pons and midbrain and synapses in the ventral posterolateral nucleus.

Use reticular formation / inferior olives **of the medulla oblongata** • rostral ventrolateral (*abbr* RVLM) **medulla** • **medullary** center of the cerebellum[7] / vomiting center / respiratory center / ischemia [iː] • **intramedullary** spinal cord tumor[8] • Forel's tegmental[9] / optic[10] **decussation** • **decussation** of the superior cerebellar peduncles[11]

(spinal) cord [spaɪnəl kɔːrd] *n term*
rel **anterior horn**[1], **cauda** [kaʊ-‖kɔːdə] **equina**[2] [aɪ‖iː] *n term*
portion of the CNS extending in the vertebral canal[3] from the medulla to the lumbar region

paraspinal *adj term* • **-spinal** *comb* • **spin(o)-** *comb* • **caudate**[4] [kɔːdeɪt] *adj*

» High cervical cord lesions may cause death from respiratory insufficiency [ɪʃ]. Compression of the spinal cord may result in paraplegia [-pliːdʒ(ɪ)ə] or quadriplegia, depending on the segment involved, whereas compression of a spinal root[5] [uː] may cause weakness [iː] and sensory loss in structures innervated by it. The spinal cord terminates [ɜː] in the cauda equina at the spinal column[6] level of approximately L2.

Use cervical **spinal cord** • **spinal cord** sympathetic pathways / center / reflexes[7] [iː] • **spinal cord** injury[8] / trauma[8] [ɔː]/ lesion[8] [iːʒ]/ damage[9] / ischemia [ɪskiː-]/ stimulation • **spinal** canal / nerves[10] [ɜː]/ nerve root / shock • **spinal** block[11] / anesthesia[11] [iːʒ]/ tap[12] / deformity / fusion[13] [juːʒ] • central / anterior / posterior **cord** • cervical [sɜː]/ lumbar [ʌ]/ (lumbo)sacral [eɪ] **cord** • **cord** segment[14] / compression[15] / edema • cranio/ neuro/ cilio/ intra**spinal** • **paraspinal** ganglia • **spino**thalamic tract *or* pathway[16] /bulbar [ʌ] muscular [ʌ] atrophy[17] /cerebellar degeneration

---

Hirnstamm, Truncus cerebri
Zwischenhirn, Diencephalon[1] Brücke, Pons cerebri[2] dienzephal, Zwischenhirn-[3] pontin, Brücken-[4] transitorische ischämische Attacken, TIA[5] Diplopie, Doppeltsehen, Doppelbilder[6] Hirnstammreflexe[7] Hirnstammfunktion[8] Hirnstammläsion[9] Hirnstammkontusion[10] akustisch evozierte Hirnstammpotentiale[11] Hirnstamminfarkt[12] dienzephales Syndrom[13] Brückenhaube, Tegmentum pontis[14] pontine Formatio reticularis[15]

12

Kleinhirnstiel, Pedunculus cerebellaris
Vierhügelplatte, Lamina tecti/ quadrigemina[1] stielförmig[2] oberer Kleinhirnstiel, P. c. superior/ rostralis[3] mittlerer Kleinhirnstiel, P. c. medius[4] unterer Kleinhirnstiel, P. c. inferior/ caudalis[5] Hirnstiel, Pedunculus cerebri[6]

13

Medulla oblongata, verlängertes Mark, Nachhirn, Myelencephalon
Pyramidenkreuzung, Decussatio pyramidum[1] medullär, Medullar-[2] kreuzen[3] Nucleus nervi hypoglossi[4] Pyramidenfasern[5] Lemniscus medialis[6] Corpus medullare, Marksubstanz d. Kleinhirns[7] intramedullärer Rückenmarktumor[8] Forel-, Haubenkreuzung[9] Sehnenkreuzung, Chiasma opticum[10] Kreuzung d. oberen Kleinhirnstiele, Decussatio pedunculorum cerebellarium rostralium/ superiorum[11]

14

Rückenmark, Medulla spinalis
Vorderhorn[1] Cauda equina, Pferdeschweif[2] Wirbelkanal[3] schwanzförmig, geschwänzt, caudatus[4] Rückenmarkwurzel[5] Wirbelsäule[6] Rückenmarkreflexe[7] Rückenmarkverletzung[8] Rückenmarkschädigung[9] Spinalnerven, Nervi spinales[10] Spinal-, Lumbalanästhesie[11] Lumbalpunktion[12] op. Versteifung v. Wirbelsäulensegmenten, Spondylodese[13] Rückenmarksegment[14] Rückenmarkkompression[15] Tractus spinothalamicus[16] bulbospinale Muskelatrophie[17]

15

Nerve Function   BODY STRUCTURES & FUNCTIONS **171**

pyramidal tract [pərǽmɪdᵊl trækt] *n term*   *syn* **corticospinal** [aɪ] **tract** *n term*
bundle [ʌ] of fibers [aɪ] originating from pyramidal cells in the fifth layer of the precentral motor (area 4), the premotor area (area 6), and to a lesser extent from the postcentral gyrus
extrapyramidal[1] *adj term* • **pyramid** [pɪrəmɪd] *n*
» *The corticospinal or pyramidal tracts pass through the medullary pyramids to connect the cerebral cortex to lower motor centers of brainstem and spinal cord. Extrapyramidal disorders are characterized by dyskinesias* [iː3], *ballismus, tremors, rigidity* [dʒɪ], *or dystonias in the waking* [eɪ] *state. The neurologic examination elicited*[2] *signs of bilateral corticospinal tract involvement.*
Use direct or anterior[3] / lateral or crossed[4] **pyramidal tract** • **pyramidal tract** fibers / signs[5] / lesion[6] / involvement • medullary / renal **pyramid** • **pyramidal** cells[7] • **extrapyramidal** motor system[8] / syndrome[9] (*abbr* EPS)/ deficits / symptoms / crisis [aɪ] • ascending[10] / descending / (contra)lateral[4] **corticospinal tract** • **corticospinal** motor neuron / tract involvement • fiber / sensory[11] / spinal **tract** • spinocerebellar / cerebellar vestibular[12] **tract** • spinothalamic / bulbospinal[13] / corticobulbar **tract**

Pyramidenbahn, Tractus corticospinalis
extrapyramidal[1] ergab[2] Pyramidenvorderstrangbahn, Tractus corticospinalis anterior[3] Pyramidenseitenstrangbahn, Tractus corticospinalis lateralis[4] Pyramidenbahnzeichen[5] Pyramidenbahnläsion[6] Pyramidenzellen[7] extrapyramidales System[8] extrapyramidales Syndrom[9] aufsteigende Pyramidenbahn[10] sensible/ sensorische Bahn[11] Tractus cerebellovestibularis[12] Tractus spinobulbaris[13]

16

cerebrospinal [aɪ] **fluid** *n term, abbr* **CSF**
rel **cisterna magna**[1] *n term*
fluid filling the ventricles and the subarachnoid cavities of the brain and the central canal of the spinal cord which is largely secreted [iː] by the choroid plexuses[2] of the ventricles of the brain
cisternal [sɪstɜːrnᵊl] *adj term* • **cistern** [sɪstɜːrn] *n*
» *The ratio* [eɪʃ] *of blood glucose* [uː] *to cerebrospinal fluid glucose*[3] *is helpful in the diagnosis of inflammatory* [æ] *disease. Lumbar* [ʌ] *puncture*[4] [ʌ] *should be performed to document elevated CSF pressure. If standard lumbar puncture is unrewarding*[5]*, a cervical cisternal tap to sample CSF near to the basal meninges may be more promising.*
Use abnormal / bloody[6] / hemorrhagic[6] / xanthochromic[7] [zænθə-]/ centrifuged **cerebrospinal fluid** • **cerebrospinal fluid** flow[8] / pathways / circulation[8] / drainage / absorption[9] • **cerebrospinal fluid** pressure[10] / volume / leak[11] [iː]/ rhinorrhea[12] [iː] • **cerebrospinal fluid** otorrhea / examination or analysis[13] / cell count • **CSF** proteins[14] / antigen titer / pleocytosis [pliːəsaɪ-] • **CSF** cytology[15] / culture [ʌ]/ abnormality / acidosis • **cerebrospinal** nerves / axis[16] / pressure[10] • cerebellomedullary / basal or interpeduncular[17] **cistern** • **cisternal** puncture *or* tap[18] / compression

Liquor (cerebrospinalis), Gehirn-Rückenmark-Flüssigkeit
Cisterna magna/ cerebromedullaris[1] Plexus choroidei[2] Liquorzucker[3] Lumbalpunktion[4] nicht zielführend[5] blutiger Liquor[6] gelblich verfärbter/ xanthochromer L.[7] Liquorpassage[8] Liquorresorption[9] Liquordruck[10] Liquoraustritt[11] Liquorrhoe aus d. Nase[12] Liquoruntersuchung[13] Liquorproteine[14] Liquorzytologie[15] Zentralnervensystem[16] Cisterna interpeduncularis[17] Subokzipital-, Zisternenpunktion[18]

17

Unit 42 Nerve Function
Related Units: 40 The Nervous System, 41 The Brain, 57 The Senses, 7 Consciousness, 73 Mental Activity, 77 Mental Health, 113 Neurologic Findings

innervate [ɪnɜːr‖ɪnɚveɪt] *vt clin & term*
sim **subserve**[1] [sʌbsɜːrv] *v term*
to supply [səplaɪ] an organ or body region with nerves [ɜː] or nervous stimuli [aɪ]
innervation[2] *n term* • **reinnervate**[3] *v* • **denervate** *v* • **denervation**[4] *n*
» *Sympathetic fibers* [aɪ] *to the pancreas pass from the splanchnic* [k] *nerves through the celiac* [siː] *plexus to innervate the pancreatic vessels. All digital extensors are innervated by the radial* [eɪ] *nerve. The blood supply and innervation of the chest wall are via the intercostal vessels and nerves. The chorda* [k] *tympani* [tɪmpənaɪ] *branch of the facial* [feɪʃᵊl] *nerve subserves taste from the anterior two-thirds of the tongue* [tʌŋ]*.*
Use to supply/provide/receive/influence/block/disrupt[5] [ʌ] **innervation** • autonomic / (para)sympathetic / vagal [eɪ] **innervation** • motor[6] / neuronal / sensory *or* afferent[7] **innervation** • somatic / cholinergic [-ɜːrdʒɪk]/ adrenergic / segmental[8] **innervation** • neuromuscular [ʌ]/ inhibitory[9] / reciprocal[10] [sɪ] **innervation** • bladder / antral / double / altered [ɔː]/ aberrant[11] **innervation** • density[12] / degree / loss **of innervation** • richly *or* densely / autonomically / somatically **innervated**

innervieren
zuständig sein für, versorgen[1] Innervation, nervale Versorgung[2] reinnervieren[3] Denervierung[4] die nervale Versorgung unterbrechen/ stören[5] motorische Innervation[6] sensorische/ sensible Innervation[7] segmentale/ segmentäre Innervation[8] inhibitorische Innervation[9] reziproke Innervation[10] aberrierende Innervation[11] Innervationsdichte[12]

1

transmit v → U94-3   sim **conduct**¹ [ʌ], **convey**¹ [kənveɪ] v

to transfer or deliver information (e.g. electrical impulses) or serve as the medium [iː] for transmission

transmission n term • **conduction**² n • **conductance**³ n • **conductive**⁴ adj

» The pain of parietal peritoneal inflammation is transmitted by somatic nerves. Sensory stimuli from this part of the head are conveyed to the CNS via the trigeminal [traɪdʒe-] nerves. The smaller fibers in peripheral nerves convey pain, temperature, and autonomic impulses.

Use **to transmit** sensations of temperature / (motor/ pain) signals / sound⁵ / infections • (pain) impulse⁶ / neuro/ neuromuscular⁷ [n(j)ʊɚoʊ-] **transmission** • synaptic / cholinergic / ganglionic **transmission** • nociceptive [se] spinal / (para)-sympathetic **transmission** • **transmission** neuron / pathways⁸ • **to convey** afferent neurons⁹ / proprioceptive impulses¹⁰ / taste sensations • **to conduct** electrical impulses • to slow/prolong **conduction** • (peripheral) nerve / motor / sensory / myogenic [maɪədʒenɪk] **conduction** • atrial [eɪ] / retrograde¹¹ / K+ **conduction** • aberrant¹² / A-V nodal¹³ / concealed¹⁴ [siː] **conduction** • **conduction** velocity¹⁵ / capacity / delay¹⁶ • **conduction** block / disturbances¹⁷ / defect • sodium¹⁸ / ion [aɪ] channel [tʃ] **conductance** • **conductance** change • **conductive** hearing loss¹⁹

saltatory conduction [ʌ] n term   rel **electrotonic current flow**¹ n term

propagation of action potentials in myelinated² [aɪ] neurons from one node of Ranvier³ to the next

» Saltatory conduction significantly increases the conduction velocity. Propagation⁴ [eɪʃ] occurs [ɜː] by electrotonic current flow and saltatory conduction in all neurons [n(j)ʊɚ-]. What is the function of myelin [aɪ] in saltatory conduction?

Use **saltatory** propagation⁵ / process

relay [riːleɪ] v clin   sim **propagate**¹ v, rel **modulate**², **mediate**³ [iː] v

to hand over or pass a signal along a pathway or fiber [aɪ], e.g. a nerve impulse

relay⁴ n term • **propagation** n • **(neuro)modulation** n • **modulatory** adj

» The reticular activating system receives afferent impulses from sensory pathways and relays the impulses to the thalamic reticular nucleus. The relays between the RAS⁵ and the thalamic and cortical areas are accomplished by neurotransmitters. The visual image impinging [dʒ] upon⁶ the retina is translated into a continuously varying barrage⁷ [-ɑːʒ] of action potentials that propagates along the primary optic pathway to visual [ɪʒ] centers within the brain. Receptive gastric relaxation is an active process mediated by vagal [eɪ] reflexes.

Use **to relay** information • CNS / auditory [ɒː]/ gustatory⁸ [ʌ] **relays** • **relay** station / nucleus⁹ [uː] • **to propagate** an action potential • electrical impulse / wave **propagation** • prejunctional¹⁰ [dʒ]/ supraspinal [aɪ]/ pain¹¹ **modulation** • **modulatory** neuron / substance¹² [ʌ]/ influence

nerve or **neur(on)al impulse** [ɪmpʌls] n

rel **action potential**¹ n term, abbr **AP**

an electrochemical [ke] process which is propagated via the nervous [ɜː] tissue

» The myelin sheath² [maɪəlɪn ʃiːθ] serves to promote transmission of nervous impulses along the axon. The carotid sinus [aɪ] gives rise to sensory impulses carried to the medulla oblongata via a branch of the glossopharyngeal [dʒ] nerve. Autonomic nerve impulses, integrated in the pelvic plexus, project [dʒe] to the penis [iː] through the cavernous nerves.

Use to generate/respond to/receive/inhibit **impulses** • neurovascular / afferent / visual / auditory³ **impulse** • brain / apical [eɪ] or cardiac⁴ / vagal⁵ [eɪ] **impulse** • electric(al) / pacing [eɪs] **impulse** • facili(ta)tory⁶ / inhibitory / sensory / reflex / pain **impulse** • **impulse** activity / conduction⁷ / transmission / generation⁸ [dʒ] **impulses** to the brain • to generate a nerve⁹ **action potential** • intestinal / motor unit / sensory nerve **action potentials** • **action potential** duration • (cell) membrane¹⁰ / pacesetter¹¹ / resting¹² / threshold¹³ **potential** • after**potential**¹⁴ • late / (visual/ average/ brainstem auditory¹⁵/ somatosensory) evoked¹⁶ [oʊ] (abbr EP) **potentials** • (electrical) **potential** difference¹⁷ (abbr PD)

übertragen, (weiter)leiten

leiten¹ Leitung² Leitfähigkeit³ leitend, Leitungs-⁴ Schall leiten⁵ Reizübertragung⁶ neuromuskuläre (Erregungs)übertragung⁷ Leitungsbahnen⁸ afferente Neuronen enthalten⁹ propriozeptive Reize leiten¹⁰ retrograde Leitung¹¹ aberrierende Leitung¹² atrioventrikuläre/ AV-Überleitung¹³ verborgene Leitung¹⁴ Leit(ungs)geschwindigkeit¹⁵ Leitungsverzögerung, verzögerte Reizleitung¹⁶ Leitungsstörungen¹⁷ Leitfähigkeit für Natrium(ionen)¹⁸ Schallleitungsschwerhörigkeit¹⁹

saltator. Erregungsleitung

elektrotonische Ausbreitung des Stroms¹ markhaltig² Ranvier-Schnürring³ Fort-, Weiterleitung⁴ saltatorische Fortleitung⁵

weiterleiten, verschalten, übermitteln

weiterleiten, übertragen, s. ausbreiten/ fortpflanzen¹ abwandeln, modulieren² vermitteln³ Relais, Verschaltung⁴ aufsteigendes retikuläres (aktivierendes) System/ Aktivierungssystem⁵ auftreffen⁶ Salve⁷ Umschaltstellen f. Geschmacksreize⁸ Relaiskern⁹ präsynaptische Modulation¹⁰ Schmerzmodulation¹¹ Modulator¹²

Nervenimpuls, Reiz

Aktionspotential¹ Markscheide² akust. Reiz³ Herzspitzenstoß⁴ Vagusreiz⁵ Erregungsimpuls⁶ Reizleitung⁷ Reizbildung⁸ ein Aktionspotential auslösen⁹ Membranpotential¹⁰ Schrittmacherpotential¹¹ Ruhepotential¹² Schwellenpotential¹³ Nachpotential¹⁴ akustisch evozierte Hirnstammpotentiale¹⁵ somatosensibel evozierte Potentiale¹⁶ Potentialdifferenz¹⁷

Nerve Function   BODY STRUCTURES & FUNCTIONS **173**

depolarization n term   syn **(nervous) discharge** n clin & jar, sim **firing**[1] n jar

destruction and neutralization of membrane potential or change in the direction of its polarity

hyperpolarization n term • **hyper/ depolarize**[2] v • **depolarizing** adj • **fire** v

» Dilated pupils must not be the only criterion [ɪɔ-] for terminating CPR[3], as they may merely reflect transient autonomic sympathetic discharge or parasympathetic inhibition. Binding of sulfonylureas to the receptor causes depolarization, calcium influx[4], and insulin secretion. Acetylcholine is released in response to nerve impulses that depolarize the nerve terminals.

Use cardiac cell / atrial [eɪ]/ dendritic [ɪ]/ (muscle) membrane **depolarization** • **afterdepolarization**[5] • slow / electrical / spontaneous [eɪ]/ biphasic [baɪfeɪzɪk] **depolarization** • repetitive[6] / presynaptic / premature[7] / partial **depolarization** • **depolarization** wave / phase[8] / block[9] • **depolarizing** current / muscle relaxants[10] / postsynaptic receptor [se] • wave / rate / spread[11] [eɪ]/ loss **of depolarization** • electrical / autonomic / adrenergic [-ɜːrdʒɪk] / phasic[12] **discharge** • neuronal[13] / spontaneous **firing** • reflex [iː]/ burst[14]- [ɜː]/ multiunit **firing** • **firing** frequency

Depolarisation
Entladung, Feuern[1] depolarisieren[2] kardiopulmonale Reanimation[3] Kalziumeinstrom[4] Nachdepolarisation[5] wiederholte Depolarisation[6] vorzeitige Depolarisation[7] Depolarisationsphase[8] Depolarisationsblock[9] depolarisierende Muskelrelaxanzien[10] Depolarisationsausbreitung[11] phasische Entladung[12] neuronale Entladung[13] phasische/rhythmische Gruppenentladung, Burst-Zyklus[14]

6

refractory period [pɪɔ-iəd] n term   rel **repolarization**[1] [ɹipoʊləɹzeɪʃ°n] n term

period of depressed excitability following depolarization during which excitable tissue such as nerve or muscle fiber fails to respond to further stimuli [aɪ] of threshold intensity

refractoriness[2] [ɹɪfræktə-ɪnəs] n term • **repolarize** [oʊ] v

» These drugs interfere with the potassium channel[3] [tʃ] to alter the plateau [-toʊ] phase[4] [feɪz] of the AP and increase refractoriness. Early atrial premature complexes may reach the AV conduction system while it is still in its relative refractory period. Why is the repolarization not as steep as the depolarization? Then the cell reverses the depolarization and begins to repolarize.

Use to prolong/shorten[5] **the refractory period** • absolute[6] / effective **refractory period** • functional[7] [ʌ] / relative[8] / long **refractory period** • AV node / accessory [kse] pathway **refractoriness** • myocardial [maɪə-]/ ventricular **repolarization** • **repolarization** changes / phase[9]

Refraktärphase
Repolarisation[1] Refraktärverhalten[2] Kaliumkanal[3] Plateauphase[4] die Refraktärphase verkürzen[5] absolute Refraktärphase[6] funktionelle Refraktärphase[7] relative Refraktärphase[8] Repolarisationsphase[9]

7

excitation [eksaɪteɪʃ°n] n term   syn **nerve stimulation** n term → U57-1

complete response (i.e. according to the all-or-none principle[1]) of a nerve or muscle to an adequate stimulus, ordinarily including propagation of excitation along the membranes

excite[2] [aɪ] v term • **excitatory** adj • **excitability**[3] n • **(hyper)excitable**[4] adj • **stimulatory**[5] [ɪ] adj term • **stimulate** v • **stimulus**[6] n • **excito-** comb

» Excitation may also occur [ɜː] with no depolarization at all through so-called receptor-dependent channels. Slow conduction via an alternative pathway allows time for the initially blocked pathway to recover excitability. With diminished inhibition, the resting firing rate[7] of the alpha motor neuron increases. With progressive muscle contraction, each motor unit fires at a more rapid rate.

Use to lead to/delay [eɪ] **excitation** • neural [ʊɚ-]/ electrical[8] / vagal [eɪ] **excitation** • CNS[9] / smooth [uː] muscle **excitation** • visual / paradoxical / sexual / indirect / pre**excitation** • **excitation** contraction coupling[10] [ʌ] • state **of excitation** • (phrenic) nerve[11] / vagal / adrenergic **stimulation** • galvanic[12] / electro/ over/ under**stimulation** • **excitatory** impulse[13] / nerve / output / receptor • **excitatory** response / neurotransmitter / postsynaptic potential[14] (abbr EPSP) • electrical / nerve / membrane / neuromuscular[15] **excitability** • reflex / increased or hyper[16]/ emotional **excitability** • **excito**motor /glandular /secretory[17] [iː] /vascular /toxic

Erregung, Exzitation
Alles-oder-Nichts-Prinzip[1] reizen, erregen[2] Erregbarkeit[3] übererregbar[4] stimulierend[5] Reiz, Stimulus[6] Ruhepotential[7] elektr. Erregung[8] zentralnervöse Erregung[9] elektromechanische Kopp(e)lung[10] Phrenikusstimulation[11] galvanische Reizung[12] Erregungsimpuls[13] exzitatorisches postsynaptisches Potential[14] neuromuskuläre Erregbarkeit[15] erhöhte Erregbarkeit, Hyperexzitabilität[16] sekretionsanregend, -fördernd[17]

8

ionic current [aɪɒnɪk kɜːkʌrənt] n term

rel **calcium channel**[1] [tʃænəl] n term

electrical current generated by the flow of ions through Na+ and K+ channels in the axonal membrane

» The ionic currents producing spontaneous diastolic depolarization appear to involve the inward current of either sodium or calcium. Phenytoin [ɪ] appears to suppress seizure [siːʒɚ] spread through inhibition of specific voltage-gated Ca2+ channels.

Use to generate a **current** • electric(al) / action[2] / excitatory **current** • stimulating / piezoelectric [pɪeɪzoʊ‖espBE paɪiːz-] **current** • gating[3] [eɪ] / outward **current** • high / low / high-frequency[4] **current** • **ionic** concentration[5] / gradient[6] [eɪ]/ imbalance • **ionic** pump[7] [ʌ]/ strength[8] / complex / diffusion [juː]/ membrane / ion[9] [aɪ] / (ATP-sensitive) potassium[10] / K+ **channel** • voltage-gated calcium[11] / cation [kætaɪən]/ chloride [klɔːraɪd] **channel** • **calcium channel**-blocking agent or blocker or antagonist[12] • **channel** activity or action

Ionenstrom
Kalziumkanal[1] Aktionsstrom[2] Tor-, Gating-Strom[3] Hochfrequenzstrom[4] Ionenkonzentration[5] Ionengradient, -gefälle[6] Ionenpumpe[7] Ionenstärke[8] Ionenkanal[9] ATP-abhängiger Kalium-Kanal[10] spannungsgesteuerter Kalziumkanal[11] Kalziumblocker, -antagonist[12]

9

neurotransmitter [ʊɚ] *n term, abbr* **NT** *syn* **transmitter substance** [ʌ] *n term*

chemical substance (e.g. acetylcholine or GABA) that is released by a presynaptic cell following excitation and crosses the synapse to stimulate or inhibit the postsynaptic cell

» A neurotransmitter is selectively released from a nerve terminal [ɜː] by an action potential. Transmitter secretion by neuroendocrine cells is frequently episodic or pulsatile [ʌ].

Use excitatory *or* stimulatory[1] / inhibitory[2] / adrenergic[3] [ɜː] **neurotransmitter** • nonadrenergic-noncholinergic [dʒ] (*abbr* NANC) **neurotransmitter** • preganglionic / postganglionic[4] **neurotransmitter** • **neurotransmitter** system / pathway[5] / response / secretion • neuroinhibitory / co-**transmitter** • substance P[6] • **transmitter** action[7] / release[8] [iː]/ agonist[9] / antagonist[10] • acetylcholine-/ pain**transmitting**

(Neuro)transmitter, Überträgersubstanz
erregender/ exzitator. (Neuro)transmitter[1] hemmender/ inhibitorischer N.[2] adrenerger Neurotransmitter[3] postganglionärer N.[4] Neurotransmitterbahn[5] Substanz P[6] Transmitterwirkung[7] Transmitterfreisetzung[8] Transmitteragonist[9] Transmitterantagonist[10]

10

acetylcholine [əsetɪl-‖əsiːtl-‖æsətɪlkouliːn] *n term, abbr* **Ach**
rel **norepinephrine**[1] *n, abbr* **NE, serotonin**[2]**, dopamine**[3] [doupəmiːn] *n term*

neurotransmitter at cholinergic synapses causing parasympathetic effects, e.g. vasodilation, cardiac inhibition, and intestinal peristalsis; NE is the postganglionic adrenergic [ɜː] mediator

(non)cholinergic[4] [kɒːlɪnɜːrdʒɪk] *adj term* • **(non)adrenergic** *adj* • **-ergic** *comb*

» Acetylcholine serves as the neurotransmitter at all autonomic ganglia, at the postganglionic parasympathetic nerve endings, at the postganglionic sympathetic nerve endings innervating the eccrine sweat [e] glands[5], and at the neuromuscular junction[6] [ʌ]. Hydrolysis of ACh by acetylcholinesterase inactivates the neurotransmitter at cholinergic synapses.

Use CSF / intracoronary **acetylcholine** • **acetylcholine** receptor[7] (*abbr* AchR)/ activity / content • **acetylcholine**-like drug / injection [dʒ] • **acetylcholin**esterase[8] [e] (*abbr* AchE)/-dependent /-induced [uːs] • serotonin secretion [iːʃ]/-selective reuptake [ʌ] inhibitor[9] (*abbr* SSRI) • **serotonin** agonist / antagonist[10] /-rich food • **serotonin** uptake / concentration / level[11] • **dopamine** metabolism / activity / depletion[12] [iːʃ] • **dopamine** excess / blocker[13] / precursor[14] [ɜː] • catecholamin [koʊ]/ antiadren/ GABA-**ergic**[15] • anticholin/ (hyper)dopamin/ seroton(in)**ergic**[16]

Acetylcholin
Noradrenalin, Norepinephrin[1] Serotonin[2] Dopamin[3] cholinerg[4] merokrine Schweißdrüsen[5] neuromuskuläre Synapse[6] Acetylcholinrezeptor[7] Acetylcholinesterase[8] selektiver Serotoninwiederaufnahme-Hemmer[9] Serotoninantagonist[10] Serotoninspiegel[11] Dopaminentleerung, -depletion[12] Dopaminantagonist[13] Dopaminvorstufe[14] GABAerg[15] serotoninerg[16]

11

reflex arc [ɑːrk] *n term*
rel **reflex**[1] [riːfleks] *n term* → U113-1

afferent and efferent pathways along which nerve impulses travel from the sensory receptor to the CNS and back to the effector organ to produce a reflex action[2]

reflexive[3] [rɪfleksɪv] *adj term* • **a/ dys/ hypo/ hyperreflexia**[4] *n*

» Additional regulation is provided by local reflex arcs within the autonomous enteric nervous system. Coughing may be initiated [ɪʃ] either voluntarily or reflexively.

Use simple / monosynaptic[5] / multisynaptic[6] [ʌ] sympathetic **reflex arc** • sacral [eɪ] micturition [ɪʃ] or voiding [ɔɪ] **reflex arc** • defecation / baroreceptor / glossopharyngeal-vagal **reflex arc** • light[7] / accommodation / gag[8] [æ] **reflex** • bladder / erectile / conditioned[9] **reflex** • **reflex** mechanism / center[10] / hammer[11] • to elicit or trigger[12]/test **reflexes** • **reflex** activity or function [ʌ]/ response[13] / fainting[14] [eɪ] • **reflex** latency[15] [eɪ]/ pattern • **reflex** movement[16] / testing / time[17] / muscle contraction[18] • **reflex** spasm[19] /-induced /-stimulated /-mediated [iː] • brain stem[20] / spinal [aɪ] cord **reflexes** • deep tendon (*abbr* DTR)/ postural[21] **reflexes** • sluggish[22] [ʌ]/ depressed *or* diminished[22] **reflexes** • absent[23] / brisk[24] / hyperactive[25] **reflexes** • **reflexive** movement[16] / tachycardia

Reflexbogen
Reflex[1] Reflexhandlung[2] reflektorisch[3] Hyperreflexie[4] monosynaptischer Reflexbogen[5] polysynapt. Reflexbogen[6] Lichtreflex[7] Würg(e)reflex[8] bedingter/ konditionierter R.[9] Reflexzentrum[10] Reflexhammer[11] Reflexe auslösen[12] Reflexantwort[13] Reflexabschwächung[14] Reflexlatenz[15] Reflexbewegung[16] Reflexzeit[17] reflektor. Muskelkontraktion[18] Reflexkrampf[19] Hirnstammreflexe[20] Haltungsreflexe[21] abgeschwächte Reflexe[22] erloschene/ nicht auslösbare R.[23] lebhafte R.[24] gesteigerte R.[25]

12

reflex inhibition [ɪʃ] *n term* *rel* **motor inhibition**[1]**, Renshaw cell**[2] *n term*

situation in which sensory stimuli [-laɪ] decrease reflex activity

inhibit[3] [ɪnhɪbɪt] *v* • **inhibitory** *adj term* • **inhibitor**[4] *n*

» We have only indirect evidence to support reflex inhibition of smooth [uː] muscle sphincter activity during bladder contraction. Renshaw cells are inhibitory interneurons[5] [ʊɚ] excited by a collateral branch of an alpha motor neuron that causes the neuron to stop firing, thus preventing excessive muscle [mʌsl] contraction.

Use parasympathetic / presynaptic[6] / feedback[7] **inhibition** • reflex muscular [ʌsk]/ Renshaw cell[7] **inhibition** • **motor** activity / center / cortex / neuron • **motor** nuclei[8] [nuːklɪaɪ]/ branch [tʃ]/ unit[9] (action potential) • **motor** axon(al loss) / end-plate[10] / conduction velocity / pattern / weakness [iː] • **inhibitory** neuron / concentration / neuropeptide [-aɪd] • **inhibitory** effect[11] / postsynaptic neurotransmission • peripheral sympathetic / cholinesterase [e]/ serotonin [sɪɚ-] transport / MAO[12] **inhibitor**

Reflexhemmung
motorische Hemmung[1] Renshaw-Zelle[2] hemmen[3] Hemmer, Inhibitor[4] Zwischen-, Interneurone[5] präsynaptische Hemmung[6] Feedback-/ rückgekoppelte Hemmung, Renshaw-Hemmung[7] motorische Kerne[8] motorische Einheit[9] motorische Endplatte[10] hemmende Wirkung[11] Monoamin(o)oxidasehemmer, MAO-Hemmer[12]

13

Lungs & Airways   BODY STRUCTURES & FUNCTIONS 175

reciprocal [resɪ-] **innervation** n term   rel **anterior horn cells**[1] n term

contraction in a group of muscles accompanied by relaxation in its antagonists

» *The coordinated interplay[2] of muscle activity necessary for balance and skilled movements is governed by the principle of reciprocal innervation. A motor unit consists of a single anterior horn cell, its efferent axon, and all the muscle fibers innervated by that axon.*

Use double [ʌ]/ inhibitory **innervation** • **reciprocal** inhibition[3] [ɪʃ]/ activity • **anterior horn** (motor) neuron / cell damage / cell disease[4]

reziproke Innervation
Vorderhornzellen[1] Zusammenspiel[2] reziproke Hemmung[3] Vorderhornzellerkrankung[4]

14

Unit 43   Lungs & Airways
Related Units: 44 Respiration, 21 Head & Neck, 22 Trunk, 32 Heart, 45 Digestive Tract,
66 Human Sounds & Speech, 111 Respiratory Signs & Symptoms

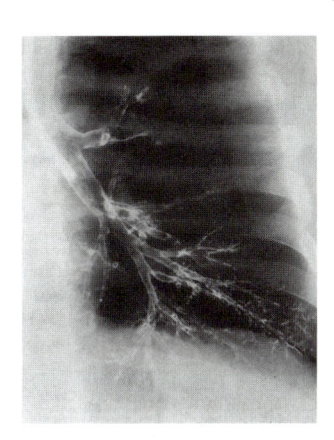

Bronchography of the left lung depicting the bronchial tree with the upper and lower lobe segments

lung(s) [lʌŋz] n clin & term, abbr **L**

paired [eɚ], highly elastic organ of respiration in the lateral thorax in which gas exchange[1] takes place

» *Each lung is irregularly conical in shape, presenting a blunt[2] [ʌ] upper extremity (the apex) [eɪ], and a concave [eɪ] base following the curve [ɜː] of the diaphragm [daɪəfræm]. At birth the color of the lungs is pinkish white.*

Use right / left / well aerated[3] [eɚ]/ contralateral / dependent[4] **lung** • **lung** tissue / apices [eɪpɪsiːz]/ segment / sounds[5] / function • **lung** volume / perfusion [juːʒ]/ capacity / compliance [aɪ]/ maturity[6] [tjʊɚ] • **lung** disease / injury / collapse[7] / abscess[8] / cancer • **lung** scan[9] / biopsy [aɪ]/ transplant[10] • iron[11] [aɪɚn]/ airless or drowned[7] [aʊ]/ wet[12] **lung**

Lunge(nflügel), Pulmo(nes)
Gasaustausch[1] abgerundet[2] gut belüftete Lunge[3] periphere Lungenbezirke[4] Atemgeräusche[5] Lungenreife[6] Lungenkollaps[7] Lungenabszess[8] Lungenszintigrafie[9] Lungentransplantat(ion)[10] eiserne Lunge[11] interstitielles Lungenödem, feuchte Lunge[12]

1

pulmonary [ʊ∥ʌ] adj term   syn **pulmonic** [pʊlmɒːnɪk], **pneumonic** adj term

relating to or associated [oʊʃ] with the lungs or the pulmonary artery

-**pulmonary** [pʊlmənɛɚi∥pʌl-] comb • **pneum(on)- [n(j)uːm]** comb

» *Reduced pulmonary arterial [ɪɚ] blood flow stimulates enlargement of bronchial [k] and mediastinal [aɪ] arteries. All pneumonic plague[1] [pleɪɡ] contacts should be kept under medical surveillance[2] [sɚveɪlənˡs]. Pulmonic flow murmurs [ɜː] are rarely seen in elderly patients.*

Use **pulmonary** artery / vein [eɪ]/ valve[3] [æ]/ function (test)[4] • **pulmonary** circulation[5] / secretions [iːʃ] • **pulmonary** vascular resistance[6] / hypertension • **pulmonary** embolism[7] / edema[8] [iː]/ contusion[9] / **pneumonic** complications / infiltrate[10] / consolidation[11] / plague[1] / **pulmonic** valve[3] / stenosis / regurgitation[12] [ɜː] • broncho [k]/ cardio/ aorto**pulmonary** • **pneumo**nia[13] / nitis[14] /thorax /peritoneum

pulmonal, Lungen-
Lungenpest[1] Überwachung[2] Pulmonalklappe, Valva trunci pulmonalis[3] Lungenfunktionsprüfung[4] Lungenkreislauf, kleiner Kreislauf[5] Lungengefäßwiderstand[6] Lungenembolie[7] Lungenödem[8] Lungenkontusion[9] Lungeninfiltrat[10] Lungenverdichtung[11] Pulmonal(klappen)insuffizienz[12] Lungenentzündung, Pneumonie[13] (interstitielle plasmazelluläre) Pneumonie, Pneumonitis[14]

2

pulmonary lobe [loʊb] *n term*

rel **bronchopulmonary** [brɒːnkoʊ-] **segment** *or* **lobule**¹ [lɒːbjuːl] *n term*

one of the 5 major divisions of the lungs which are supplied with air by the lobar bronchi

lobar² *adj term* • **(inter)lobular** *adj* • **(sub/ non)segmental** *adj* • **segmentation**³ *n*

» The bronchopulmonary segments make up large lung units called the lobes. The right lung is divided into the upper, middle, and lower or basal [eɪ] lobes. Each lobe is subdivided [ʌ] into 2-5 bronchopulmonary segments. A primary lobule consists of a terminal bronchiole, respiratory bronchioles, and alveolar [ɪə] ducts [ʌ] which communicate with many alveoli [aɪ].

Use right upper (*abbr* RUL)/ right middle⁴ (*abbr* RML)/ left lower (*abbr* LLL) **lobe of the lung** • **pulmonary**⁵ / primary / liver **lobule** • **lobule of the** breast [e]/ liver • superior⁶ / (broncho)pulmonary¹ / posterior / anterior **segment** • antero-apical [eɪ]/ (medial) basal / basilar / flail⁷ [eɪ] **segment** • **segmental** divisions / bronchi [aɪ] • **subsegmental** bronchial obstruction • inter/ intra/ extra/ multi**lobar** • **lobar** bronchus⁸ [k]/ pneumonia⁹ [n(j)uːmoʊnjə] • **interlobar** septa / fissure [ɪʃ]/ effusion¹⁰ [juːʒ] • **interlobular** pleurisy [plʊərəsi]/ emphysema [emfɪsiːmə]

pulmonary hilum [aɪ] *n term*

rel **root** [uː] **of the lung**¹, **lung base**² [eɪ] *n*

opening on the mediastinal [aɪ] surface of each lung where the bronchus, nerves, blood and lymph vessels enter and/or leave; the root of the lung refers to the pedicle³ of structures entering the lung at the hilum

(peri/ supra/ extra)hilar⁴ *adj term* • **basal** *adj* • **pulmo(no)-** *comb*

» Friction rubs⁵ are most commonly heard over the lung bases, because the lower lobes are the most frequent location of pulmonary emboli. The base of the lung rests on the diaphragm with which it moves up and down during respiration.

Use **hilum of the** lung⁶ / spleen⁷ [iː]/ renal [iː]/ liver or hepatic / widening [aɪ] of the⁸ **hilum** • **hilar** area / vessels⁹ / arteries / branches • **hilar** lymph [ɪ] nodes¹⁰ / calcification / (lymph)adenopathy • **perihilar** region / infiltrates • **suprahilar** vena cava [viːnə keɪvə] • **base** of the lung² • heard over the **lung bases**

upper airways [eəˈweɪz] *n clin*

rel **respiratory** *or* **air passages**¹ *n clin*

part of the respiratory tract² extending from the nares³ [neəriːz] or the mouth to the larynx

» The lower airways extend from the subglottis to and including the terminal [ɜː] bronchioles [k]. The patient requires assistance with bag and mask ventilation⁴ until the airway is intubated.

Use to open/clear⁵/assess/protect **the airways** • to secure [-kjʊə]/ or establish/maintain (the patency [eɪ] of)⁶ **the airways** • nasal [eɪ]/ lower or intrathoracic [æs]/ large / small / terminal [ɜː] **airways** • artificial [ɪʃ]/ oropharyngeal⁷ [-færɪndʒiːəl]/ laryngeal⁸ [dʒiː]/ surgical **airway** • clear⁹ / patent [eɪ]/ swollen **airways** • **airway** resistance¹⁰ / pressure / secretions / collapse • **airway** compression / obstruction¹¹ / injury • **airway** control • nasal **air passages** • nasal **passages**

paranasal *or* air sinuses [aɪ] *n term*

rel **maxillary antrum** *or* **sinus**¹ *n term*

four pairs of cavities in the frontal, ethmoid, maxillary, and sphenoid [sfiː-] bones which communicate with the nasal air passages; they also have a role in adding resonance to the voice

(post/ oro/ sino)nasal² [neɪzᵊl] *adj term* • **antral** [æ] *adj* • **naso-, antr-** *comb*

» The paranasal sinuses help the nose in warming and moistening³ the air.

Use frontal⁴ [ʌ]/ ethmoid [eθ-]/ sphenoid⁵ **sinus** • maxillary / involved / affected **sinus** • **paranasal sinus** infection / cancer / tumors⁶ • **nasal** vestibule [-bjuːl]/ mucous [juː] membrane⁷ • **nasal** septum / septal deformity⁸ • **nasal** secretions / stuffiness⁹ [ʌ] • **nasal** obstruction / voice¹⁰ / spray • frontal / ethmoid / mastoid *or* tympanic **antrum** • **postnasal** drip¹¹ / discharge / pack(ing)¹² • **sinonasal** tract • **naso**(oro)pharyngeal /tracheal [k] /labial [eɪ] /lacrimal

---

Lungenlappen, Lobus pulmonis

Lungensegment¹ lobär, Lappen-² Segmentbildung, Segmentation³ (rechter) Mittellappen, Lobus medius pulmonis dextri⁴ Lungenläppchen, Lobulus pulmonis⁵ Oberlappensegment⁶ übermäßig bewegliches Segment⁷ Lappenbronchus, Bronchus lobaris⁸ Lobärpneumonie⁹ Interlobärerguss¹⁰

3

Lungenhilus, Hilum pulmonis

Lungenwurzel, Radix pulmonis¹ Basis pulmonis² Stiel³ hilär, Hilus-⁴ Reibegeräusche⁵ Lungenhilus, Hilum pulmonis⁶ Milzhilus, Hilum splenicum⁷ Hilusvergrößerung⁸ Hilusgefäße⁹ Hiluslymphknoten¹⁰

4

obere Atemwege

Atem-, Luftwege¹ Atem-, Respirationstrakt² Nasenlöcher, Nares³ Maskenbeatmung⁴ Atemwege freimachen⁵ Atemwege freihalten⁶ Oropharyngealtubus⁷ Kehlkopfmaske⁸ freie Atemwege⁹ Atemwegswiderstand, Resistance¹⁰ Atemwegsobstruktion¹¹

5

Nasennebenhöhlen, Sinus paranasales

Kieferhöhle, Sinus maxillaris¹ nasal, Nasen-² Anfeuchten³ Stirnhöhle, S. frontalis⁴ Keilbeinhöhle, S. sphenoidalis⁵ Nasennebenhöhlentumoren⁶ Nasenschleimhaut⁷ Nasenseptumdeviation⁸ verstopfte Nase⁹ Rhinolalie, Näseln¹⁰ Schleimstraße im Nasenrachenraum¹¹ hintere Nasentamponade¹²

6

Lungs & Airways   BODY STRUCTURES & FUNCTIONS 177

epiglottis [epɪglɒːtɪs] *n term*   *rel* **laryngeal** [ləɾɪndʒɪəl‖lærɪndʒiːəl] **inlet**[1], **glottis**[2], **larynx**[3] *n term* → U21-14

thin plate of elastic cartilage, covered with mucous membrane at the root of the tongue which together with the arytenoid cartilage serves to cover the glottis during the act of swallowing[4]

(ary)epiglottic *adj term* • **glottic**[5] *adj* • **glottal**[5] *adj* • **laryng(o)-** *comb*

» The epiglottis stands erect when liquids are being swallowed, but is passively bent over the aperture by solid foods being swallowed. In the newborn the trachea from the glottis to the carina is 5-7.5 cm long. The lingual surface of the epiglottis is part of the supraglottic larynx.

Use cherry-red / swollen / normal-sized / enlarged **epiglottis** • **epiglottic** cartilage / inflammation[6] • closed / patent [eɪ] **glottis** • **glottal** reflex[7] / edema [ɪdiːmə] • **glottic** dysfunction [ɪ]/ spasm[8] • atrium [eɪ] or vestibule / aperture[1] / dilatation / cancer **of the larynx** • **laryngeal** reflex[7] / prominence[9] / stridor [aɪ] • **laryngo**logy /ologist /ospasm[8] /ectomy /otomy /oscope[10]

Epiglottis, Kehldeckel
Kehlkopfeingang, Aditus laryngis [1] Glottis, Stimmapparat[2] Kehlkopf, Larynx[3] Schluckakt[4] Glottis-[5] Epiglottitis[6] Kehlkopfreflex[7] Stimmritzenkrampf, Laryngospasmus[8] Adamsapfel, Prominentia laryngea[9] Kehlkopfspiegel, Laryngoskop[10]

7

trachea [treɪkɪə‖trəkiːə] *n term*   *syn* **windpipe** [wɪndpaɪp] *n clin & inf*

air tube extending from the larynx into the thorax where it divides into the right and left main bronchi

(broncho/ naso/ endo)tracheal[1] [k] *adj term* • **tracheo-** *comb*

» The trachea is stiffened by 16 to 20 rings of hyaline [aɪ] cartilage which are incomplete posteriorly. The internal lining[2] of the trachea is composed of ciliated [sɪ] columnar [ʌ] epithelium[3] [iː].

Use membranous / lower **trachea** • bifurcation [baɪ-]/ carina [aɪ‖iː]/ compression **of the trachea** • perforation / shift / intubation **of the trachea** • **tracheal** cartilages or rings[4] / mucosa [mjuː-]/ wall • **tracheal** muscle [s]/ orifice [-fɪs]/ lumen / diameter [aɪæ] • **tracheal** midline / reflex / washings[5] • **tracheal** deviation [eɪʃ]/ narrowing / rales[6] [ɑː‖æ]/ obstruction • **bronchotracheal** tree[7] / secretions[8] • **endotracheal** tube[9] • **nasotracheal** intubation / airway / route [aʊ‖uː] • **tracheot**omy[10] /stomy[11] /scopy /esophageal [iː] /pulmonary

Trachea, Luftröhre
endotracheal[1] Auskleidung[2] hohes zilienbesetztes Zylinderepithel[3] Knorpelspangen d. Luftröhre, Luftröhrenknorpel[4] Lavagematerial aus der Trachea[5] Trachealrasseln[6] Tracheobronchialbaum[7] Tracheobronchialsekret[8] Endotrachealtubus[9] Luftröhrenschnitt, Tracheotomie[10] Tracheostoma[11]

8

bronchus [brɒnkəs] *n term, pl* **-i** [aɪ]   *rel* **bronchiole**[1] [brɒnkɪoʊl] *n term*

subdivision [ʌ] of the trachea conveying [eɪ] air to and from the right and left lung; in the lungs the right and left main bronchi divide into the lobar, segmental, and subsegmental bronchi

bronchial *adj term* • **bronchiolar** *adj* • **bronch(o)-** *comb*

» Edema of the lung parenchyma narrows small bronchi and increases resistance in the pulmonary vasculature. Respiratory insufficiency was due to plugging[2] of bronchi with mucus.

Use right / left / primary or main(stem)[3] / segmental[4] / lobar **bronchus** • proximal / distal / major **bronchi** • **bronchial** tubes[5] / cartilage / branches or branchings[6] / tree[7] / lumen • **bronchial** breath sounds or breathing[8] / secretion / washing or lavage • **bronchial** toilet or suctioning[9] / biopsy [aɪ] • **bronchial** obstruction / foreign body[10] / asthma[11] / carcinoma / lobular / small / alveolar or terminal[12] **bronchiole** • **bronchiolar** edema [iː]/ spasm • **broncho**tracheal /stenosis /spasm /scope /gram • **broncho**pulmonary /spirometry[13] /dilatation /genic • **bronch**itis [aɪ]/iolitis /iectasis[14]

Bronchus
Bronchiole[1] Verlegung, Obstruktion[2] Haupt-, Stammbronchus, B. principalis[3] Segmentbronchus, B. segmentalis[4] Bronchien[5] Bronchialäste[6] Bronchialbaum[7] Bronchialatmen[8] Bronchialtoilette[9] Bronchialfremdkörper[10] Bronchialasthma, Asthma bronchiale[11] Bronchiolus terminalis[12] Bronchospirometrie[13] Bronchiektase[14]

9

alveolar sac *or* **alveolus** [ælvɪələs] *n term, pl* **-i** [aɪ]   *syn* **air sac** [sæk] *n clin*

one of the thin-walled saclike terminal dilations [eɪʃ] of the pulmonary bronchioles and alveolar ducts [ʌ] where gas is exchanged between the alveolus and the pulmonary blood

(inter/ intra/ broncho)alveolar[1] [ælvɪələ˞] *adj term* • **alve(olo)-** *comb*

» Each alveolus is surrounded by a network of capillary blood vessels. The air spaces and alveolar ducts underwent fibrosis, while the peripheral [ɪf] bronchi became dilated [aɪ].

Use pulmonary or lung / dental **alveolus** • perfused / poorly ventilated[2] / collapsed / patent **alveoli** • **alveolar** duct[3] / spaces[4] / wall /-capillary membrane / septum • **alveolar** air or gas[5] / ventilation / pressure[6] / dead space • **intra-alveolar** pressure[6] / exudate / hemorrhage [-ɪdʒ] • **interalveolar** septum / vessels • **air** spaces[7] / exchange / entry / flow /-fluid level • **air** / leak[8] / embolism[9] / trapping[10]/ hunger / swallowing[11]

Lungenbläschen, Alveolus pulmonis
alveolär, Alveolar-[1] schlecht belüftete Alveolen[2] Alveolargang, Ductus alveolaris[3] Alveolarräume[4] Alveolarluft, -gas[5] Alveolardruck[6] Lufträume[7] Luftverlust (bei künstl. Beatmung)[8] Luftembolie[9] Lufteinschluss[10] Luftschlucken, Aerophagie[11]

10

BODY STRUCTURES & FUNCTIONS — Lungs & Airways

pleura [plʊɚə] *n term, pl* **pleurae** [plʊɚiː]

thin serous [ɪɚ] membrane enclosing each lung and lining [aɪ] the walls of the pleural cavity

(-)pleural [plʊɚəl] *adj term & comb* • **pleuritic**¹ [plʊɚɪtɪk] *adj* • **pleur(o)-** *comb*

» The pulmonary pleura² dips into the fissures [ɪʃ] between the different lobes. Thoracoscopy offers the opportunity to view the entire pleura, superior sulcus [ʌ], interlobar fissures, hilar area, diaphragm, and pericardium. About 500 mL of blood had accumulated in the pleural space.

Use parietal [aɪ] *or* outer³ / visceral [s] *or* inner² / diaphragmatic **pleura** • cervical⁴ [sɜː]/ mediastinal⁵ / pericardiac / costal⁶ [ɒː] **pleura** • overlying / weeping⁷ [iː] **pleura** • **pleural** space⁸ / cavity⁹ / fluid • **pleural** leak [iː]/ effusion⁷ [uːʒ]/ (friction) rub¹⁰ [ʌ] • **pleural** peel¹¹ [iː]/ plaques [plæks‖ɑː]/ pressure • **pleural** biopsy [aɪ]/ involvement • **pleur**isy¹² /itis¹² [aɪ] /odynia [ɪ] /opericardial cyst [sɪst] • broncho/ extra/ intra**pleural**

diaphragm [daɪəfræm] *n term & clin*   *syn* **diaphragma** *n term*

musculomembranous partition between the thoracic [æs] and abdominal cavities which contracts and flattens with inspiration and relaxes during expiration

(sub/ supra)diaphragmatic¹ [daɪəfrægmætɪk] *adj term* • hemidiaphragm² [e] *n*

» The acutely distended stomach pushed the diaphragm upward causing collapse of the lower lobe of the left lung. X-rays show an elevated right diaphragm and pleural fluid in the right hemithorax³.

Use elevated⁴ / depressed / flattened / ruptured⁵ [ʌ]/ paralyzed [-laɪzd] **diaphragm** • left / immobile **hemidiaphragm** • pelvic / urogenital [dʒe]/ contraceptive⁶ [se] **diaphragm** • dome⁷ / tenting⁸ / undersurface / descent [dɪsent] *of the diaphragm* • contraction / relaxation / elevation⁴ / rupture⁵ [ʌ] *of the diaphragm* • **diaphragm** excursion⁹ [ɜː] • **diaphragmatic** muscle [ʌ]/ pleura / lymphatics [lɪmfætɪks]/ breathing [iː] *or* respiration¹⁰ • **diaphragmatic** elevation⁴ / adhesions [iːʒ]/ pleurisy • **diaphragmatic** hernia¹¹ [ɜː]/ defect / irritation / weakness • elevated *or* raised [eɪ] **hemidiaphragm**

mediastinum [miːdɪəstaɪ-] *n term, pl* **-a**   *syn* **interpulmonary septum** *n term*

compartment between the pleural cavities extending anteriorly from the suprasternal notch¹ to the xiphoid [zɪf-] process² and posteriorly from the first to the 11th thoracic vertebrae

mediastinal³ *adj term* • **pneumomediastinum**⁴ *n* • **mediastin(o)-** *comb*

» The superior mediastinum is the area above the pericardium that is bordered inferiorly by an imaginary [ædʒ] line from the manubrium to the fourth thoracic [æs] vertebra [ɜː].

Use anterior⁵ / middle / posterior [ɪɚ]/ upper *or* superior⁶ **mediastinum** • adjacent⁷ [ədʒeɪs-]/ contralateral / widened⁸ [aɪ] **mediastinum** • **mediastinal** compartment / structures • **mediastinal** lymph [lɪmf] nodes / widening⁸ • **mediastinal** flutter⁹ [ʌ]/ shift¹⁰ / infection • **mediastinal** masses *or* tumors / fibrosis [aɪ] • **mediastin**itis [aɪ] /oscopy /otomy

---

Pleura, Brustfell

pleuritisch¹ Lungenfell, Pleura pulmonalis/ visceralis² parietales Pleurablatt, P. parietalis³ Pleurakuppel, Cupula pleurae⁴ Mittelfell, P. mediastinalis⁵ Rippenfell, P. costalis⁶ Pleuraerguss⁷ Pleuraspalt⁸ Pleurahöhle, Cavitas pleuralis⁹ Pleurareiben¹⁰ Pleuraschwarte¹¹ Brustfellentzündung, Pleuritis¹²

Diaphragma, Zwerchfell

diaphragmatisch, Zwerchfell-¹ (rechte oder linke) Zwerchfellkuppel/ -hälfte² rechte Thoraxhälfte³ Zwerchfellhochstand⁴ Zwerchfellruptur⁵ Scheidenpessar⁶ Zwerchfellkuppel⁷ Zwerchfellwölbung⁸ Atemexkursion, Zwerchfellbewegung⁹ Zwerchfellatmung¹⁰ Zwerchfellhernie, Hernia diaphragmatica¹¹

Mediastinum, Mittelfell

Incisura jugularis sterni¹ Schwertfortsatz, Processus xiphoideus² mediastinal³ Mediastinalemphysem, Pneumomediastinum⁴ vorderes Mediastinum, M. anterius⁵ oberes Mediastinum, M. superius⁶ anliegendes Mediastinum⁷ Mediastinalverbreiterung⁸ Mediastinalflattern⁹ Mediastinalverziehung, -verschiebung¹⁰

Unit 44 Respiration

Related Units: 43 Airways, 21 Head & Neck, 22 Trunk, 46 Digestion, 36 Blood Circulation, 66 Human Sounds, 72 Sleep, 103 Clinical Symptoms, 111 Respiratory Symptoms, 123 Resuscitation

breathe [briːð] v

rel **yawn**[1] [jɒːn], **snore**[2] [snɔːr], **sigh**[3] [saɪ] v & n → U72-13; U66-4f

to draw air into the lungs (through the nose or mouth) and then expel it again

br**ea**th[4] [e] n • br**ea**thing[5] [iː] n & adj • br**ea**thless[6] [e] adj • br**ea**thy[7] [e] adj • br**ea**ther[8] [iː] n

» Take a slow, deep breath, please. The chest should rise with each breath, and airflow should be unimpeded [iː]. A musty[9] [ʌ] sweet odor [oʊ] was noted on the breath. On the evening before surgery the patient should be encouraged [ɜː] to sit up, cough, breathe deeply, and walk around.

Use **to breathe** in / out / through one's mouth / with one's mouth open[10] • to take a (short/ quick/ deep[11]) **breath** • to catch[12]/hold[13] one's **breath** • to have bad[14] **breath** • exhaled [eɪ]/ short(ness) of[15] (abbr SOB)/ alcohol on **breath** • **breath** sounds[16] / odor[14] / freshener /-holding • **breath**alyzer or analyzer[17] / test • shallow[18] [æ]/ deep / to have difficulty (in) **breathing** • **breathing** rate[19] / exercises / pattern • **breathing** cycle [saɪkl]/ problems • **breathy** voice[20] • mouth **breather** • loud / heavy or severe / habitual[21] [ɪtʃ]/ cyclic / occasional [eɪʒ] **snoring** • **sighing** respirations • **to sigh** frequently

atmen
gähnen; Gähnen[1] schnarchen; Schnarchen[2] seufzen; Seufzer[3] Atem[4] Atmen, Atmung; Atem-[5] atemlos, außer Atem[6] rauchig, belegt[7] Atem-, Verschnaufpause; Atmende(r)[8] faulig[9] m. offenem Mund atmen[10] tief einatmen[11] Atem holen, verschnaufen[12] Atem anhalten, nicht atmen[13] Mundgeruch (haben)[14] Kurzatmigkeit[15] Atemgeräusche[16] Atemalkoholtestgerät, Alkomat[17] flache Atmung[18] Atemfrequenz[19] belegte Stimme[20] gewohnheitsmäßiges/ habituelles Schnarchen[21]

1

inhale [ɪnheɪl] v clin   rel **sniff**[1], **sniffle**[2], **snuffle**[2] [ʌ] v clin → U10-20; U11-23

opposite **exhale**[3] v clin

to draw in air by breathing

inhalation [eɪ] n • exhalation n • inhalant[4] [eɪ] n & adj term • inhalational adj • inhaler[5] [eɪ] n

» The patient is instructed to take several deep breaths and then inhale deeply before coughing [kɒːfɪŋ] vigorously[6]. The dose is 2-4 inhalations by metered-dose inhaler[7] every 6 hours. Have the patient take a deep breath and forcibly exhale against a closed glottis (Valsalva maneuver[8]) [uː]. He reported an inability to take in a sufficiently [ɪʃ] deep breath rather than difficulty in exhaling.

Use **to inhale** deeply / droplets / aerosol [eɚ] • nasal [eɪ] / O₂ / steam[9] [iː]/ involuntary / smoke **inhalation** • noxious [ɒkʃ]/ toxic chemical[10] / dust [ʌ] **inhalation** • **inhalational** route [aʊ‖uː]/ agent [eɪdʒ]/ anesthetic[11] / exposure [oʊʒ]/ provocation • **inhalation** therapy[12] / anesthesia [iːʒ]/ analgesia [dʒiː]/ injury[13] • complete / active / passive / pursed-lip [ɜː]/ forced[14] [s] **exhalation** • **exhaled** air or breath or gas [æ] / carbon monoxide [-aɪd] • glue[15] [uː]/ solvent [ɒ]/ **sniffing** • **to sniff** leaded [e] gasoline[16] [-iːn]

einatmen, inhalieren
schnüffeln, schnuppern, schniefen[1] schnüffeln, schniefen[2] ausatmen, exhalieren[3] Inhalat, Inhalationsmittel; Inhalations-[4] Inhalationsapparat, Inhalator[5] stark, kräftig[6] Dosierinhalator[7] Valsalva-Versuch[8] Dampfinhalation[9] Einatmung giftiger Chemikalien[10] Inhalationsanästhetikum, -narkotikum[11] Inhalationstherapie[12] Inhalationsschaden[13] forcierte Exspiration[14] Klebstoffschnüffeln[15] bleihaltiges Benzin einatmen[16]

2

inspiration [ɪnspɪreɪʃᵊn] n term   opposite **expiration**[1] n term

rel **aspiration**[2] n term → U127-16

the act of drawing in the breath in order to exchange oxygen for carbon dioxide [daɪɒːksaɪd]

inspire[3] [ɪnspaɪɚ] v • inspiratory adj • expire[4] v • (end-)expiration n (end-)expiratory[5] adj • aspirate[6] [v æspɪreɪt‖n -rɪt] v & n • spiro-[a] comb

» Inspiration is accomplished chiefly by diaphragmatic excursion[7] [ɜː], while the intercostal and accessory [əkses-] muscles[8] contribute little to ventilation. In sucking [ʌ] chest wounds [uː] a valve-like[9] [æ] effect may allow entry of air on inspiration but not exit on expiration. The ability to expire to a normal RV[10] was limited because of expiratory muscle [s] weakness [iː]. Guard [ɑː] against[11] aspiration of vomitus by having the patient lie on one side.

Use deep / spasmodic [ɒː]/ maximal / full / during[12] / (up)on[12] **inspiration** • active / passive / forced[13] / prolonged[14] **expiration** • duration / speed **of expiration** • **inspiratory** dyspnea [ɪ] / film or chest x-ray / reserve [ɜː] volume[15] • **to expire** rapidly[16] • **expiratory** phase [feɪz]/ flow (abbr EF)/ pressure • **expiratory** muscle (strength) / stridor[17] [aɪ]/ airway obstruction [ʌ] • spirometry[18] /meter /gram • **to aspirate** vomitus[19] / a small object • to avoid/protect against **aspiration** • bronchial [k] **aspirate** • pulmonary [u‖ʌ] foreign [fɒːrᵊn] body[20] / tracheal [k] **aspiration**

Inspiration, Einatmung
Exspiration, Exspirium, Ausatmung[1] Aspiration[2] einatmen[3] ausatmen, exspirieren[4] exspiratorisch, Exspirations-[5] aspirieren; Aspirat[6] Zwerchfellexkursion[7] Atemhilfsmuskulatur[8] ventilartig[9] Residualvolumen[10] vorbeugen[11] beim Einatmen[12] forcierte Exspiration[13] verlängertes Exspirium[14] inspirator. Reservevolumen[15] kräftig ausatmen[16] exspiratorischer Stridor[17] Spirometrie[18] Erbrochenes aspirieren[19] Fremdkörperaspiration[20]

3

BODY STRUCTURES & FUNCTIONS — Respiration

respiration [respɪreɪʃən] *n term* *rel* **gas exchange**[1] [gæs ɪkstʃeɪndʒ] *n term*
process of the molecular exchange of oxygen and CO_2 in the lungs [ʌ] and in the tissues
respiratory[2] [respɪr‖rɪspaɪrətɔːri] *adj term* • **-pnea** [iː], **-pneic** *comb* • **respirator**[3] *n*
» *Between acute attacks, breath sounds may be normal during quiet respiration. Respirations are labored[4] [eɪ], and rales [ɑː‖æ] are widely dispersed [ɜː] over both lung fields anteriorly and posteriorly.*
Use external[5] [ɜː]/ internal[6] / costal[7] [ɒː] abdominal[8] / tissue[9] [tɪʃ‖sjuː] **respiration** • spontaneous [eɪ]/ deep / shallow / slowed[10] **respiration** • artificial[11] / assisted[12] / mouth-to-mouth[13] **respiration** • controlled / accessory muscles of **respiration** • **respiration** rate • (ir)regular / noisy / gasping [æ] / sighing[14] **respirations** • rapid / wheezing[15] [iː]/ Kussmaul('s) **respirations** • **respirations** have ceased[16] [siːst] (*abbr* RHC)/ per minute • **respiratory** system or passages or tract[17] / failure[18] [eɪ]/ quotient [ouʃ] (*abbr* RQ) • cardio**respiratory** • tachy [tækɪ]/ hyper/ dys[19] [ɪ]/ a/ ortho**pnea** • tachy/ hyper/ dys/ a/ ortho**pneic** • to wean [iː] from[20]/be off **the respirator** • **respirator** dependence / mask • to maintain/optimize/improve/participate in /impair[21] [eə]/ **gas exchange** • adequate / impaired / decreased [iː]/ normal **gas exchange**

Respiration, Atmung
Gasaustausch[1] respiratorisch, Atmungs-, Atem-[2] Respirator, Beatmungsgerät[3] erschwert[4] Lungenatmung, äußere A.[5] Zellatmung, innere A.[6] Brust-, Thorax-, Thorakalatmung[7] Bauch-, Zwerchfellatmung[8] Gewebeatmung[9] verlangsamte Atmung, Bradypnoe[10] künstl. Beatmung[11] assistierte B.[12] Mund-zu-Mund-B.[13] Seufzeratmung[14] Giemen, pfeifendes Atmen[15] Atemstillstand[16] Respirationstrakt, Atemwege[17] Ateminsuffizienz[18] Atemnot, Dyspnoe[19] vom Respirator entwöhnen[20] den Gasaustausch beeinträchtigen[21]   4

---

inflate [ɪnfleɪt] *v term*   *opposite* **deflate**[1] [ɪ] *v term, rel* **ventilate**[2] *v clin*
to distend a hollow structure like the lungs by blowing in air or gas
(hyper)**inflation**[3] *n term* • **deflation** *n* • **ventilation**[4] *n* • **ventilatory** *adj*
hyperventilate [haɪpɚ-] *v* • **ventilator**[5] *n* → U123-9; U125-10f
» *Adequacy of ventilation is best assessed by observing [ɜː] chest wall motion [ouʃ]. Apnea [æpnɪə‖æpniːə] means cessation [s] of ventilation[6] for 20 seconds.*
Use **to inflate the** lungs / balloon [uː]/ blood pressure cuff[7] [ʌ] • **inflated** alveoli [aɪ]/ cuff • completely *or* fully **deflated** • **to deflate** the MAST garment[8] • well[9] **ventilated** • **ventilatory** pattern / effort[10] / support or assistance[11] • lung *or* pulmonary / alveolar **ventilation** • collateral / (expired/ total) minute[12] **ventilation** • (in)adequate / assisted *or* mechanical [k]/ bag-valve-mask[13] [æ] **ventilation** • intermittent mandatory[14] (*abbr* IMV)/ positive-pressure[15] **ventilation** • distribution / adequacy[16] / failure **of ventilation** • adequate airway / oxygenation / intubation **and ventilation**

aufblasen, -blähen, -pumpen
Luft ablassen[1] belüften, ventilieren, beatmen[2] Überblähung[3] Ventilation, Belüftung, Beatmung[4] Respirator, Beatmungsgerät[5] Atemstillstand[6] die Blutdruckmanschette aufpumpen[7] Luft aus d. Antischockhose ablassen[8] gut belüftet[9] Atemarbeit[10] Atemhilfe, assistierte Beatmung[11] Atemminutenvolumen[12] manuelle Beatmung (m. Handbeatmungsbeutel)[13] intermittierende maschinelle B.[14] Überdruckbeatmung[15] ausreichende Belüftung[16]   5

---

aerate [eəeɪt] *v term*   *sim* **oxygenate**[1] [ɒːksɪdʒəneɪt] *v term* → U82-11
to supply [aɪ] a substance (esp. blood) with or expose it to oxygen or carbon dioxide
(hyper)**aeration**[2] *n term* • (an)**aerobic**[3] *adj* • **aerated** *adj* • **oxygenation** *n* **oxygenator** *n term* • (de)**oxygenated**[4] *adj* • **-oxia** *comb* → U125-11
» *Chest x-rays indicated lack of aeration in some areas. There were blood gas abnormalities due to perfusion of poorly aerated lung resulting in hypoxemia and a respiratory alkalosis. Maintain oxygenation by giving 100% oxygen by a cannula inside the endotracheal [eɪ] tube.*
Use alveolar **aeration** • **aeration of** the lungs • well / over/ non**aerated** • **aerobic** conditions / bacteria[5] [ɪɚ]/ exercises • **anaerobic** microorganisms / flora / metabolism • **anaerobic** coverage[6] / lung abscess / infection • (de)**oxygenated** hemoglobin / blood/ • to facilitate/ensure[8]/improve/impair/assess **oxygenation** • poor / adequate / arterial / systemic / tissue[9] **oxygenation** • extracorporeal membrane (*abbr* ECMO)/ fetal **oxygenation** • hyperbaric[10] (*abbr* HBO) **oxygenation** • membrane[11] / pump[12] / bubble[13] **oxygenator** • an/ hyper/ hyp**oxia**

(be)lüften
m. Sauerstoff anreichern, oxygenieren[1] übermäßige Belüftung[2] (an)aerob[3] sauerstoffarm, desoxygeniert[4] Aerobier[5] Abschirmung gegen anaerobe Erreger[6] sauerstoffreiches/ arterielles Blut[7] d. Sauerstoffversorgung sicherstellen[8] Gewebeoxygenation[9] hyperbare Oxygenation[10] Membranoxygenator[11] Herz-Lungen-Maschine[12] Bubble-Oxygenator[13]
6

---

gasp *v & n clin*   *rel* **pant**[1] , **puff**[2] [ʌ] *v & n clin,* **wheeze**[3] [ʰwiːz] *v & n term & clin*
(v) noisy, short and labored[4] breathing with the mouth open, e.g. when one is exhausted, in shock or pain
gasping *adj & n* • **panting** *adj & n* • **puffing** *adj & n* • **wheezing** *adj & n term*
» *In paroxysmal nocturnal dyspnea, the patient awakens gasping and must sit or stand to get his breath, which may be dramatic and terrifying. A pack-a-day cigarette smoker puffs[5] more than 70,000 times a year. It is simpler to use longer-acting formulas that contain high concentrations of medication/puff, so the patient can take fewer puffs throughout the day.*
Use **to gasp** for breath *or* air[6] / forcefully • severe **panting** • **gasping** respirations[7] / puffing of the cheeks[8] • **to be out of**[9] **puff** (BE) • expiratory / stridor or inspiratory **wheezes** • audible [ɒː]/ high-pitched[10] **wheezes** • localized / diffuse / persistent / unilateral **wheezes** • **wheezing and** dyspnea / coughing / stridor [aɪ] • **wheezing and** rales *or* rhonchi[11] [rɒŋkaɪ]/ crackles[12]

keuchen, schwer atmen; Keuchen, Schnappatmung
keuchen, hecheln[1] schnaufen; paffen, ausstoßen; Schnappatmung, Inhalationsstoß[2] keuchen, pfeifend atmen; pfeifendes Atemgeräusch, Giemen[3] erschwert[4] raucht[5] nach Atem ringen/ Luft schnappen[6] Schnappatmung[7] Aufblasen d. Wangen[8] außer Atem sein[9] hochfrequente Atemgeräusche[10] Giemen u. Rasselgeräusche[11] G. u. krepitierendes Knistern[12]
7

Respiration | BODY STRUCTURES & FUNCTIONS 181

suffocate [sʌfəkeɪt] v → U123-6 *syn* **asphyxiate** [əsfɪksɪeɪt] v term → U111-4
rel **choke¹** [tʃoʊk], **gag²** [æ] v & n clin → U27-16
to struggle [ʌ] for breath because of obstructed air passages or lack of oxygen (e.g. in drowning³) [aʊ]
suffocation⁴ n • **suffocating⁵** adj • **asphyxia⁴** n term • **asphyxiation** n
» Large amounts of blood in the airways does not only seriously disturb [ɜː] gas exchange but may cause the patient to suffocate. Rare cases of laryngeal [dʒ] obstruction with suffocation have been described. Vomiting due to gagging on tenacious [eɪʃ] mucus⁶ is seen in whooping [uː] cough.
Use **to suffocate** sb. / in the fire • impending⁷ / sense or feeling of⁸ / death due to⁹ **suffocation** • **suffocating** sensation⁸ • **suffocative** bronchitis [kaɪ]/ goiter¹⁰ [ɔɪ] • to become/be **asphyxiated** • fetal [iː]/ neonatal¹¹ [eɪ]/ traumatic [ɒ] **asphyxia** • **to choke** to death / up¹² • nocturnal [ɜː] **choking** • **choking** sensation⁸ / while eating • **gag** reflex¹³ • **gagging and** coughing [kɒːfɪŋ]/ vomiting

ersticken
ersticken, (er)würgen; Würgen¹ würgen; Mundsperrer² Ertrinken³ Erstickung, Asphyxie⁴ erstickend, Erstickungs-⁵ zäher Schleim⁶ drohende Erstickung, Erstickungsgefahr⁷ Erstickungsgefühl⁸ Tod durch Ersticken⁹ d. Trachea einengende Struma¹⁰ Neugeborenenasphyxie¹¹ verstopfen, ersticken (Stimme)¹² Würg(e)reflex¹³

8

mucociliary clearance [mjuːkoʊsɪliəri klɪəənˡs] n term
rel **pulmonary surfactant¹** [səfæktənt] n term
tracheobronchial [k] mechanism which cleanses² [e] the respiratory passages by entrapping³ inhaled particles in airways secretions and sweeping⁴ them toward the oropharynx by ciliary [sɪl] motion⁵ [oʊ]
mucus⁶ [mjuːkˢs] n term • **mucous⁷** adj • **mucoid** adj • **mucosa⁸** n • **muco-** comb
» Cigarette smoking, lung disease, or alcoholism impair⁹ [-ɚ] mucociliary clearance. His recurrent¹⁰ respiratory tract infections are due to the lack of mucociliary clearance. Freshwater aspiration alters the surface tension¹¹ properties of pulmonary surfactant and causes alveoli [aɪ] to collapse and become atelectatic¹².
Use inadequate or defective **mucociliary clearance** • nasal ciliary / bronchopulmonary / (lower/ ineffective) airway¹³ **clearance** • sputum¹⁴ / mucus¹⁵ / aerosol [eɚ-] **clearance** • **clearance** of secretions / mechanism¹⁶ • **mucociliary** transport / function / (escalator) system¹⁷ • inflammatory [æ] mediators [iː] • production / loss **of surfactant** • artificial¹⁸ / exogenous / aerosolized **surfactant** • **surfactant** production / deficiency¹⁹ [ɪʃ]/ (replacement) therapy²⁰ • nasal / sinus [aɪ]/ bronchial [k]/ green **mucus** • tenacious²¹ [eɪʃ]/ excess / hypersecretion of²² **mucus** • **mucus**-secreting glands²³ • plug²⁴ [ʌ] • **mucoid** secretions²⁵ / discharge²⁵ / rhinorrhea [aɪ]/ material • **mucous** cells / blanket²⁶ / membrane⁸ / layer²⁶ [eɪ]/ glands²³ • **muco**cutaneous [eɪ] /epidermoid [ɜː] /lytic [ɪ] /purulent²⁷ [pjʊɚ]

muköziliäre Clearance/ Reinigung
Surfactant, Antiatelektasefaktor¹ reinigen² einschließen³ spülen, transportieren⁴ Zilienbewegung⁵ Schleim⁶ mukös, schleimig⁷ Schleimhaut, Mukosa⁸ behindern⁹ rezidivierend¹⁰ Oberflächenspannung¹¹ atelektatisch¹² Atemwegsreinigung¹³ Expektoration¹⁴ Abtransport d. Schleims¹⁵ Reinigungsmechanismus¹⁶ muköziliäres Transportsystem¹⁷ künstliches Surfactant¹⁸ Surfactantmangel¹⁹ Surfactantsubstitutionstherapie²⁰ zäher Schleim²¹ übermäßige Schleimsekretion/ -produktion²² Schleimdrüsen, muköse Drüsen, Glandulae mucosae²³ Schleimpfropf²⁴ schleimiges Sekret²⁵ Schleimschicht²⁶ schleimig-eitrig²⁷

9

respiratory excursion [ɪkskɜːrʒᵊn] n term
rel **lung expansion¹** [ɪkspænʃᵊn], **lung compliance²** [kəmplaɪənˡs] n term
complete movement of expansion and contraction of the lungs during respiration
(re)**expand³** v term • **expanded** adj • **hyperexpansion⁴** n • **compliant** adj
» Acute respiratory distress syndrome is best recognized by its effects, namely decreased lung compliance, arterial [ɪɚ] hypoxemia [iː], and reduced lung volume. Pain may cause diminished respiratory excursion (chest splinting⁵) on the affected side. On palpation, the symmetry [ɪ] of lung expansion can be assessed.
Use inspiratory / maximum / chest / diaphragmatic⁶ **excursion** • free / equal **excursion** • poor / low / decreased [iː]/ increased **lung compliance** • airway / pulmonary² / chest wall or thoracic⁷ [æs] **compliance** • ventricular / bladder **compliance** • **poorly compliant** chest wall / lungs • (asymmetric/ diminished/ bilaterally equal/ full) chest⁸ **expansion** • unilateral **hyperexpansion** • **hyperexpanded** lung fields

Atemexkursion
Lungenausdehnung¹ Dehnbarkeit/ Compliance d. Lunge² sich ausdehnen/ entfalten³ Überdehnung⁴ Behinderung d. Thoraxexkursion⁵ Zwerchfellexkursion, -bewegung⁶ thorakale Compliance, Thorax-Compliance⁷ beidseitig gleichmäßige Thoraxausdehnung⁸

10

vital [aɪ] **capacity** [æs] n term, *abbr* **VC** *syn* **respiratory capacity** n term
greatest volume of air that can be forcibly exhaled from the lungs after maximum inspiration
» Direct compression of abdominal contents, elevation of the diaphragm¹ [aɪ], and restriction of rib cage [keɪdʒ] motion² all reduce vital capacity. Obstructive dysfunction is graded according to the reduction in the ratio [ʃ] of forced expiratory volume in 1 second (FEV1) to FVC.
Use forced³ (*abbr* FVC)/ decreased **vital capacity** • total lung (*abbr* TLC)/ residual lung (*abbr* RLC) **capacity** • functional residual⁴ [ɪd] (*abbr* FRC) **capacity** • inspiratory⁵ (*abbr* IC)/ ventilatory **capacity** • carbon monoxide diffusing⁶ (*abbr* DLCO)/ oxygen-carrying⁷ **capacity**

Vitalkapazität
Zwerchfellhochstand¹ Brustkorb-, Thoraxbeweglichkeit² forcierte Vitalkapazität³ funktionelle Residualkapazität⁴ Inspirationskapazität⁵ CO-Diffusionskapazität⁶ Sauerstoffbindungskapazität⁷

11

182 BODY STRUCTURES & FUNCTIONS — Digestive Tract

tidal [taɪdᵊl] **volume** or **air** n term, abbr V_t
　　　　　　　　　　　rel **residual** [rɪzɪdʒʊəl] **volume**¹ n term, abbr **RV**
　volume of air that is inspired or expired in a single breath during regular breathing
» Respiratory rate and tidal volume are unchanged. An acute asthmatic [z] attack is associated with air trapping and increased residual volume, which result in hyperinflation of the lungs.
Use spontaneous [eɪ]/ high / low / maximal / end-**tidal volume** • lung / respiratory minute² / forced expiratory³ (abbr FEV) **volume** • expiratory reserve⁴ [ɜː] (abbr ERV)/ inspiratory reserve⁵ (abbr IRV) **volume** • expired / humidified / insufflated / trapped **air** • pleural [ʊɚ] / free / compressed⁶ / swallowed **air** • **air**borne⁷ /flow /ways⁸ /tight⁹ [taɪt]/ passages⁸ • **air** exchange / sac¹⁰ / embolism¹¹ / leak [iː]/ hunger¹² • **tidal** breathing¹³ • **residual** air¹ / function

Atem(zug)volumen
Residualvolumen¹ Atemminutenvolumen, AMV² Sekundenkapazität³ exspirator. Reservevolumen⁴ inspirator. Reservevolumen⁵ Druckluft⁶ durch d. Luft übertragen, aerogen⁷ Luft-, Atemwege⁸ luftdicht⁹ Alveolarsäckchen, Sacculus alveolaris¹⁰ Luftembolie¹¹ Lufthunger¹² Cheyne-Stokes-Atmung¹³

12

Unit 45　Digestive Tract
Related Units: 46 Digestion, 47 Liver & Biliary System, 26 Teeth, 27 Dentition & Mastication, 21 Head & Neck, 22 Trunk, 109 Gastrointestinal Signs & Symptoms

digestive tract [daɪdʒestɪv trækt] n term
　　　　　　syn **gastrointestinal** or **alimentary tract** or **canal** [kənæl] n term
　passage leading from the mouth to the anus [eɪ]
　alimentation¹ n term • **enteral**² adj • -**enteric**² adj & comb • **enter(o)**- comb
» The foreign body in the intestinal tract was directly visualized [ɪʒ] and removed with a GI endoscope. The mucosa [oʊ] in the alimentary canal was severely damaged.
Use gastrointestinal (abbr GI)/ upper GI **tract** • upper **GI** series³ [sɪɚiːz] • **intestinal** cells / mucosa [koʊ]/ villi⁴ [aɪ]/ wall • **intestinal** segment / flora⁵ / bacteria⁶ [ɪɚ] • **intestinal** juice⁷ [dʒuːs]/ secretions [iːʃ]/ contents⁸ / glands or crypts⁹ [ɪ] • **intestinal** loops¹⁰ [uː]/ gas / motility • **intestinal** transit (time) / tube¹¹ / obstruction • **intestinal** hernia [ɜː]/ bleeding or hemorrhage¹² • **intestinal** perforation / infection / inflammation • **digestive** tract disorder / process¹³ / enzymes [zaɪ]/ juices¹⁴ • **alimentary** bolus¹⁵ [oʊ]/ obesity [iː]/ edema¹⁶ [iː] • intravenous [iː] hyper¹⁷/ parenteral **alimentation** • **enteric** bacteria⁶ / flora⁵ / infection /-coated aspirin¹⁸ • **entero**genic [dʒe] /toxin /colitis [-aɪtɪs]

Verdauungstrakt, -kanal, Magen-Darm-Trakt
Ernährung, Alimentation¹ enteral, intestinal, Darm-² Magen-Darm-Passage³ Darmzotten, Villi intestinales⁴ Darmflora⁵ Darmbakterien⁶ Darmsaft⁷ Darminhalt⁸ Darmdrüsen, Lieberkühn-Krypten, Glandulae intestinales⁹ Darmschlingen¹⁰ Darmrohr¹¹ Darmblutung¹² Verdauungsvorgang¹³ Verdauungssäfte¹⁴ Bolus, Bissen¹⁵ Hungerödem¹⁶ intravenöse Hyperalimentation¹⁷ magensaftresistentes Aspirin¹⁸

1

oral cavity [kævɪti] n term → U46-7
　the cavity of the mouth including the narrow cleft¹ between the lips and cheeks [tʃiːks], the teeth, gums² [gʌmz], and tongue [tʌŋ] which communicates³ with the nasal [eɪ] and pharyngeal cavity (nasopharynx⁴)
　oral [ɔːrəl] adj term • **oro-** comb • (**naso-**)**oropharyngeal** adj
» In children the tongue is quite large relative to their oral cavity. Difficulty emptying material from the oral pharynx into the esophagus [ɪ] is termed pre-esophageal dysphagia⁵ [-feɪdʒ(ɪ)ə].
Use **oral cavity** infection / cancer [ˈs] • proper⁶ **oral cavity** • **oral** flora / mucosa⁷ / secretions • **oral** enzyme / hygiene [aɪdʒ]/ vaccine⁸ [ks]/ temperature⁹ • **oral** intake¹⁰ / feedings / contraceptive [se]/ dose • **oral** route [oʊ‖uː] of infection / thermometer / intubation • **orally** ingested [dʒe] • **oro**tracheal [k] tube¹¹ / nasal reflux [iː]

Mundhöhle, Cavitas/ Cavum oris
Spalte¹ Zahnfleisch² verbunden ist mit³ Nasenrachenraum, Nasopharynx⁴ oropharyngeale Dysphagie⁵ Cavum oris proprium, eigentliche Mundhöhle⁶ Mundschleimhaut⁷ Schluckimpfung⁸ Oral-, Sublingualtemperatur⁹ orale Nahrungsaufnahme¹⁰ Orotrachealtubus¹¹

2

salivary glands [sælɪvɚi glændz] n term & clin
　saliva-secreting exocrine [aɪ] glands of the oral cavity including the parotid¹, submandibular and sublingual glands which secrete [iː] most of the saliva and the labial [eɪ], buccal [ʌ], molar, lingual, and palatine [-aɪn] glands
　saliva² [səlaɪvə] n term • **salivate**³ [sælɪveɪt] v • **salivation**⁴ n
» The minor salivary glands are widely distributed in the mucosa of the lips, cheeks, hard and soft palate⁵, uvula [juː], floor of mouth⁶, tongue and peritonsillar region. Symptoms of mushroom [ʌ] poisoning⁷ include sweating [e], salivation, lacrimation⁸, vomiting, abdominal cramps, diarrhea [iː], confusion⁹ [juː], coma, and occasionally convulsions¹⁰ [ʌ].
Use minor¹¹ [aɪ]/ major¹² [eɪdʒ] **salivary glands** • **salivary** duct¹³ [ʌ]/ flow⁴ / stones / secretion [iː] • **salivary gland** tumor¹⁴ / diminished secretion of / artificial¹⁵ [ɪʃ]/ resting / viscous¹⁶ [sk] • **saliva** / to drool³ [uː]/swallow¹⁷ [ɒː] • **saliva** / **saliva** output / production • substitute¹⁵ [ʌ] • excessive or hyper**salivation**¹⁸ [aɪ]

Speicheldrüsen, Glandulae salivariae
Parotis, Ohrspeicheldrüse¹ Speichel² S. produzieren, sabbern³ Speichelfluss, Salivation⁴ weicher Gaumen⁵ Mundboden⁶ Pilzvergiftung⁷ Tränensekretion⁸ Verwirrtheit⁹ Krämpfe¹⁰ kl. Speicheldrüsen, Gg. salivariae minores¹¹ große S., Gg. salivariae majores¹² Speichelgang¹³ Speicheldrüsentumor¹⁴ Speichelsubstitution¹⁵ zähflüssiger S.¹⁶ s. schlucken¹⁷ patholog. gesteigerte Speichelsekretion, Hypersalivation, Ptyalismus, Sialorrhoe¹⁸

3

Digestive Tract — BODY STRUCTURES & FUNCTIONS 183

pharynx [færɪŋks] *n term, pl* **-ges/-xes** [fərɪndʒiːz]   *syn* **throat** [θroʊt] *n*,
                                              sim **fauces**¹ [fɔːsiːz] *n pl term* → U21-12
portion of the digestive tube between the esophagus and the oro- and nasopharynx [neɪzoʊ-]
pharyngeal² [færɪndʒiːəl‖fərɪndʒ(ɪ)əl] *adj term* • **faucial**² [fɔːʃəl] *adj*
-pharynx, -pharyngeal, pharyngo- *comb*

» The human swallowing apparatus [eɪ] consists of the pharynx, cricopharyngeal [kraɪk-] *(upper esophageal)* sphincter, and the body and lower sphincter of the esophagus. A topical anesthetic [e] is gargled³ or sprayed into the pharynx. Herpangina [dʒaɪ] is characterized by an acute onset of fever [iː] and posterior pharyngeal ulcers [s], often linearly arranged on the anterior fauces. In severe croup [uː], fever persists, with worsening [ɜː] coryza⁴ [kəraɪzə] and sore throat.

Use laryngeal⁵ / oral⁶ / nasal⁷ / inflamed [eɪ] / injected⁸ [dʒe] **pharynx** • **pharyngeal** reflex⁹ / mucosa / tonsil / pack¹⁰ / oro/ hypo⁵/laryngo**pharynx** • **pharyngo**epiglottic fold¹¹ /esophageal [dʒ] **pharyngo**palatine arch¹² [tʃ] /tympanic tube¹³ • naso**pharyngeal** obstruction • **faucial** arch • area / tonsil¹⁴ / isthmus¹⁵ [ɪsməs]/ pillars¹⁶ [ɪ] • muscles of palate and fauces • sore¹⁷ **throat**

Pharynx, Rachen
Fauces, Schlund(enge), Pharynx¹ pharyngeal, Rachen-² gurgeln mit³ Schnupfen⁴ Hypopharynx, Pars laryngea⁵ Mesopharynx, P. oralis⁶ Epipharynx, P. nasalis⁷ geröteter/ hyperämischer Rachen⁸ Würg(e)reflex⁹ Halswickel¹⁰ Plica glossoepiglottica lateralis/ mediana¹¹ hinterer Gaumenbogen, Arcus palatopharyngeus¹² Tuba auditiva, Ohrtrompete¹³ Gaumenmandel, Tonsilla palatina¹⁴ Schlundenge, Isthmus faucium¹⁵ Gaumenbögen, Arcus palatoglossus u. A. palatopharyngeus¹⁶ Halsschmerzen¹⁷   4

esophagus [ɪsɒːfəgˢs] *n term*, BE **oesophagus**   *syn* **gullet** [gʌlɪt] *n clin & inf*
tube about 25 cm in length through which food passes from the pharynx to the stomach [k]
esophageal¹ [-fədʒiːəl] *adj term* • **megaesophagus** *n* • **esophag(o)-** *comb*

» Incompetence of the lower esophageal sphincter² rather than sliding hiatus [aɪeɪ] hernia³ is the primary cause of acid reflux. Dysphagia for both solids and liquids was due to impaired [eɚ] esophageal peristalsis, which interrupted the smooth [uː] esophageal transport of a bolus.

Use cervical⁴ [ɜː]/ distal / lower / upper / thoracic⁵ [æs]/ proximal **esophagus** • border / stretching / rupture⁶ [ʌ] **of esophagus** • **esophageal** hernia [ɜː]/ opening / motility / peristalsis⁷ / tube / tear⁶ [teɚ] • **esophageal** obstruction / dysphagia [dɪsfeɪdʒ(ɪ)ə]/ varices⁸ [værɪsiːz]/ reflux [iː]/ speech⁹ • **esophag**itis /ectomy • **esophago**gastric sphincter² /salivary reflex¹⁰ /scopy /stomy

Ösophagus, Speiseröhre
ösophageal, Speiseröhren-¹ unterer Ösophagussphinkter² Gleitbruch, -hernie³ Pars cervicalis, Halsabschnitt d. Speiseröhre⁴ P. thoracica, Brustabschnitt d. Speiseröhre⁵ Ösophagusruptur⁶ Ösophagusperistaltik⁷ Ösophagusvarizen⁸ Ösophagus(ersatz)stimme, -sprache⁹ Roger-Reflex¹⁰

5

abdomen [æbdəmˢn‖æbdoʊmˢn] *n term* → U22-4
                                 syn **belly, tummy** [ʌ] *n clin*, **abdo** *n jar, abbr* **abd**
anterior part of the trunk [ʌ] between the thorax and the pelvis divided into regions (epigastric, umbilical, pubic, hypochondriac¹ [kɒː], lateral, and inguinal² regions) or four quadrants
abdominal [æbdɒːmɪnˢl] *adj term* • **intra-abdominal** *adj*

» The abdomen is divided into right upper and lower, and left upper and lower quadrants [ɒː] by horizontal and vertical lines intersecting at the umbilicus [ʌ]. The abdomen was supple³ [ʌ] and without masses or organomegaly. Plain [eɪ] abdominal films⁴ showed mucosal edema [iː] and an abnormal haustral [ɔː] pattern⁵. On palpation the abdomen was not tender⁶.

Use lower / protuberant⁷ [(j)uː]/ pendulous⁸ / surgical [ɜː]/ acute⁹ **abdomen** • **abdominal** breathing¹⁰ [iː]/ wall / cavity¹¹ • **abdominal** girth¹² [ɜː]/ aorta [eɪ]/ pain / contents • **abdominal** bloating [oʊ] or distention¹³ / tenderness / cramps / compression • **abdominal** reflex¹⁴ / aneurysm [ænjə-]/ muscle guarding¹⁵ [gɑːrdɪŋ] • **abdominal** rigidity¹⁶ [dʒɪ]/ straining¹⁷ [eɪ] • **belly**ache / tap¹⁸ / button¹⁹ [ʌ] • **intra-abdominal** pressure

Abdomen, Bauch, Unterleib
Hypochondrium¹ Leiste(ngegend)² weich³ Abdomenleeraufnahme, -übersichtsaufnahme⁴ Haustrenmuster, -anordnung⁵ druckschmerzhaft, -dolent⁶ hervortretender Bauch⁷ Hängebauch⁸ akutes Abdomen⁹ Bauch-, Zwerchfellatmung¹⁰ Bauchhöhle, Cavitas abdominalis¹¹ Bauchumfang¹² gebähtes Abdomen, Trommelbauch¹³ Bauchhaut-, Bauchdeckenreflex¹⁴ Bauchdecken-, Abwehrspannung¹⁵ bretthartes Abdomen¹⁶ Bauchpresse¹⁷ Bauchpunktion¹⁸ Bauchnabel¹⁹   6

peritoneum [perɪtˢniːəm] *n term*   *rel* **mesentery**¹, **omentum**² *n term*
serous [ɪɚ] sac lining the abdominal and pelvic cavities
peritoneal *adj term* • **mesent**eric *adj* • **oment**al *adj* • **peritoneo-** *comb*

» One side of the herniated [ɜː] stomach was covered by peritoneum. Long-lasting peritoneal drains tend to become infected and lead to peritonitis. Although the mesentery joins the intestine along one side, the peritoneal layer of the mesentery envelops the bowel and is called the visceral peritoneum, or serosa. The greater omentum is a double-leafed apron [eɪ] that extends from the greater curvature [ɜː] of the stomach to the transverse mesocolon.

Use intestinal or visceral³ / parietal⁴ [aɪ] / pelvic⁵ **peritoneum** • double fold of⁶ **peritoneum** • **peritoneal** fluid / cavity⁷ / irritation • intra/ retro**peritoneal** • **peritoneal** reflection⁸ / lavage⁹ [ɑː]/ tap / dialysis¹⁰ [daɪælɪsɪs] / pneumo¹¹ [n(j)uːmoʊ]/ retro**peritoneum** • **periton**eoscopy /itis¹² [aɪ] • inferior **mesenteric** artery (*abbr* IMA) • **mesenteric** lymph [ɪ] nodes / plexus / vessels / (lymph)adenitis • **mesenteric** cyst [sɪst]/ infarction¹³ / vascular occlusion¹⁴ / vein [eɪ] thrombosis • appendiceal¹⁵ [siː]/ **mesentery** • greater¹⁶ / lesser¹⁷ **omentum** • **omental** flap / bursa¹⁸ [ɜː]/ patch / cyst / hernia¹⁹ [ɜː]/ torsion

Peritoneum, Bauchfell
Mesenterium, Dünndarmgekröse¹ Omentum, Netz, Epiploon² Peritoneum viscerale³ P. parietale⁴ Beckenperitoneum⁵ Peritonealduplikatur⁶ Bauchfellhöhle, Cavitas peritonealis⁷ peritoneale Umschlagfalte⁸ Peritoneallavage, -spülung⁹ Peritonealdialyse¹⁰ Pneumoperitoneum¹¹ Bauchfellentzündung, Peritonitis¹² Mesenterialinfarkt¹³ Mesenterialgefäßverschluss¹⁴ Mesenteriolum, Mesoappendix¹⁵ großes Netz, Omentum majus¹⁶ kl. Netz, O. minus¹⁷ Netzbeutel, Bauchfelltasche, Bursa omentalis¹⁸ Netzbruch¹⁹   7

184 BODY STRUCTURES & FUNCTIONS — Digestive Tract

stomach [stʌmᵊk] *n clin & inf*

rel **curvature**[1] [kɜːrvətʃɚ], **pylorus**[2] [paɪlɔːrᵊs] *n term*

(i) bag-shaped reservoir for food between the esophagus and the duodenum beneath the diaphragm that consists of the cardiac opening[3], fundus [ʌ], antrum, body[4], and pylorus
(ii) the epigastric region[5]

(**epi/ hypo**)**gastric** *adj term* • **gastr**(**o**)- *comb* • **pyloric** *adj* • **stomach**[6] *v inf*

» The stomach which lies just beneath the diaphragm, has a capacity of about 1 liter; its wall has a mucous [juː], submucous, muscular [ʌsk], and a peritoneal coat. Endoscopy revealed erosions on the ridges [dʒ] of thickened folds in the antrum of the stomach. Most gastric ulcers[7] [s] occur along the lesser curvature at the junction [ʌ] of antral and fundic [ʌ] mucosa.

Use to cleanse [e]/upset[8] **the stomach** • acid [æsɪd]/ full / distended / on an empty[9] **stomach** • **stomach** trouble[10] / ache [eɪk]/ tube[11] / pump / aspirate / capacity • **stomach** contents[12] / lining[13] [aɪ]/ cramp / acidity • **gastric** fold / (acid) secretion[14] • **gastric** juice[15] [dʒuːs]/ motility / tube[11] • **gastric** emptying (rate)[16] / suction [sʌkʃᵊn]/ parietal [pəraɪətᵊl] cells[17] • greater[18] / lesser[19] **curvature** • **gastro**intestinal /esophageal /duodenal /enteritis [aɪ] /scopy • **gastr**ectomy /itis[20] • **pyloric** channel [tʃænᵊl]/ antrum / glands[21] • **pyloric** sphincter / obstruction[22] [ʌ]/ stenosis

(i) **Magen, Gaster**
(ii) **Magengrube, Epigastrium**
Curvatura, Magenkrümmung[1] Pylorus, (Magen)pförtner[2] Kardia, Mageneingang[3] Corpus ventriculi[4] Epigastrium, Oberbauchgegend, Magengrube, Regio epigastrica[5] verdauen, -tragen[6] Magengeschwüre, Ulcera ventriculi[7] sich d. Magen verderben[8] auf nüchternen/ leeren M.[9] Magenbeschwerden[10] Magensonde, -schlauch[11] Mageninhalt[12] Magenauskleidung[13] Magensekretion, -sekret[14] Magensaft[15] Magenentleerungszeit[16] Belegzellen[17] Curvatura major, linker Magenrand[18] C. minor, rechter M.[19] Magenschleimhautentzündung, Gastritis[20] Pylorusdrüsen, Glandulae pyloricae[21] Pylorusobstruktion[22]

8

gut [gʌt] *n*   *syn* **bowel(s)** [baʊəlz], **intestine(s)** [ɪntestɪnz] *n clin & term*

digestive tube from the stomach to the anus distinguished into the small and the large intestine

intestinal[1] *adj term*

» Gas is present in the gut as a result of swallowed air, bacterial metabolism of ingested[2] [dʒe] fermentable materials in the intestinal lumen, or diffusion from the blood into the bowel. These agents tend to stabilize the water content of the bowel and provide bulk[3] [ʌ].

Use small[4] / large[5] **intestine** or **bowel** • proximal / distal / entire **gut** • primitive[6] / obstructed / plain[7] **gut** • **gut** wall / flora[8] / bacteria[9] / motility • **gut** absorption / inflammation / perforation • irritable[10] / lazy[11] / (un)prepared **bowel** • **bowel** mucosa[12] / contents / lumen / loop[13] [uː]/ gas[14] • **bowel** sounds[15] / tone / movement[16] / habits[17] / obstruction • **intestinal** absorption / anastomosis / flora[8] / bacteria[9] / gas[14] • **intestinal** mucosa[12] / obstruction / parasites / volvulus[18]

Darm, Eingeweide
intestinal, Darm-[1] aufgenommen[2] wirken darmfüllend[3] Dünndarm[4] Dickdarm[5] Urdarm[6] einfaches Catgut[7] Darmflora[8] Darmbakterien[9] Reizkolon, -darm, Colon irritabile[10] träger Darm[11] Darmschleimhaut[12] Darmschlinge[13] Darmgas[14] Darmgeräusche[15] Darmentleerung, Stuhlgang[16] Stuhlgewohnheiten[17] Darmverschlingung, Volvulus[18]

9

duodenum [d(j)ʊɒːdᵊnᵊm‖d(j)ʊədiːnᵊm] *n term*

first segment of the small intestine about 25 cm or 12 fingerbreadths (hence the name) in length, it extends from the pylorus to the junction [dʒʌ] with the jejunum at the level of the 1ˢᵗ or 2ⁿᵈ lumbar [ʌ] vertebra[1]

duodenal [d(j)ʊədiːnᵊl‖ d(j)ʊɒːdᵊnᵊl] *adj term* • **duodeno-** *comb*

» The first part of the duodenum is known as the duodenal cap[2]. The bile [aɪ] duct[3] and the pancreatic duct[4] open into the descending portion of the duodenum at the ampulla of Vater[5]. Villous adenomas of the duodenum may obstruct the papilla of Vater[6]. There was a reflux [iː] of bile[7] from the duodenum to the stomach.

Use descending[8] [s]/ proximal / distal / widened [aɪ] **duodenum** • **duodenal** loop / bulb[2] [ʌ] / ampulla[5] [ʊ]/ sphincter / glands • **duodenal** secretions [iːʃ]/ villi[9] / smear[10] [ɪɚ] • **duodenal** biopsy [aɪ]/ folds[11] / bands[12] / ulcer[13] [ʌlsɚ] • **duodeno**jejunal junction[14] /graphy /scopy

Duodenum, Zwölffingerdarm
Lendenwirbel[1] Bulbus duodeni, Pars superior[2] Ductus choledochus[3] Ductus pancreaticus[4] Ampulla hepatopancreatica[5] Papilla duodeni major/ Vateri[6] Galle(nflüssigkeit)[7] Pars descendens[8] Zwölffingerdarmzotten[9] Duodenalabstrich[10] Plicae duodenalis superior et inferior[11] Strikturen im Duodenum[12] Zwölffingerdarmgeschwür, Ulcus duodeni[13] Flexura duodenojejunalis[14]

10

jejunum [dʒiːdʒuːnᵊm] *n term*

part of the small intestine (approx. 8 feet in length) between the duodenum and the ileum

-jejunal *adj & comb term* • **jejun**(**o**)- [dʒiːdʒun] *comb*

» Bleeding lesions of the duodenum or proximal jejunum may be biopsied or coagulated enteroscopically. Magnesium [iː] is absorbed primarily in the jejunum and ileum.

Use dilated [eɪ]/ distal / proximal or upper / mid**jejunum** • **jejunal** villi / loop / ulcer / diverticula[1] / feeding (tube)[2] • **jejunoileal** bypass or shunt[3] [ʌ]/ junction • **jejuno**ileal /gastric /plasty /tomy /stomy[4] • **jejun**itis[5] [-aɪtɪs] /ectomy

Jejunum, Leerdarm
Jejunaldivertikel[1] jejunale Ernährungsfistel[2] jejunoilealer Bypass/Shunt[3] Jejunostomie[4] Jejunitis, Entzündung d. Jejunums[5]

11

45

Digestive Tract | **BODY STRUCTURES & FUNCTIONS** 185

ileum [ɪlɪəm] *n term*   *rel* **cecum¹** [siːkəm] *n term, BE* **caecum**

portion of the small intestine extending from the jejunoileal junction to the ileocecal opening²
ileal [ɪlɪəl] *adj term* • **cecal** [siːkəl] *adj* • **ileocecal** *adj* • **ile(o-)** *adj*

» Adhesions [iːʒ], hernias, tumors, FBs³ (esp. gallstones⁴) [ɔː] are common causes of mechanical [k] obstruction of the duodenum, jejunum, ileum, colon, or rectum. There was no increase in mouth-to-cecum transit times in colicky⁵ infants.

Use distal / reflux into terminal [ɜː] **ileum** • **ileal** vein [eɪ]/ reabsorption / atresia [iːʒ]
• **ileal** loop reservoir⁶ / conduit⁶ • **ileo**rectal anastomosis⁷ /gastric reflex /jejunitis
• **ileo**colic fold /cecal valve⁸ [æ] • **cecal** size / diameter [aɪæ]/ perforation⁹ • **cecal** volvulus / gangrene/ diverticulitis • contiguous¹⁰ / high¹¹ / mobile¹² **cecum**

▪ Note: Mark the difference between **ileum** (ileal), **ilium**¹³ (iliac) and **ileus**¹⁴.

Ileum, Krummdarm
Zäkum, Zökum, Blinddarm¹ Ostium ileocaecale² foreign bodies = Fremdkörper³ Gallensteine⁴ an Koliken leidend⁵ Ileum-Conduit, Ileumblase⁶ Ileorektostomie⁷ Ileozäkal-, Bauhin-Klappe⁸ Blinddarmdurchbruch⁹ angrenzendes Zäkum¹⁰ Zäkumhochstand¹¹ sehr bewegl. Zäkum, Caecum mobile¹² Ilium, Darmbein¹³ Ileus, Darmverschluss¹⁴
12

appendix (vermiformis) *n term, pl* **-ces** [əpendɪsiːz]
                                syn **vermiform** [ɜː] **appendix** *n term*

wormlike [ɜː] intestinal diverticulum extending from the blind end of the cecum ending in a blind extremity

appendiceal [-siːəl] *adj term* • **appendicitis**¹ [-saɪtɪs] *n* • **append-** *comb*

» A large inflammatory mass was found involving the appendix, terminal ileum, and cecum, requiring a resection of the entire mass and ileocolostomy. Rebound [aʊ] tenderness² may be suggestive of acute appendicitis.

Use to free³/visualize/remove/bury [e] the stump of⁴ **the appendix** • high-lying⁵ / (acutely) inflamed⁶ [eɪ]/ retrocecal⁷ **appendix** • base / mesentery⁸ / tip **of the appendix** • **appendiceal** lumen / wall / perforation / stump [ʌ] / abscess⁹ / acute¹⁰ / chronic / (non)perforated¹¹ / suspected¹² **appendicitis** • uncomplicated / retrocecal / atypical [eɪ] **appendicitis** • catarrhal¹³ / gangrenous **appendicitis** • **appendectomy**¹⁴

Appendix vermiformis, Wurmfortsatz
Appendizitis, sog. Blinddarmentzündung¹ Loslassschmerz² die Appendix freilegen³ den Appendixstumpf versenken⁴ hochliegende Appendix⁵ entzündete A.⁶ retrozäkale A.⁷ Mesenteriolum, Mesoappendix⁸ appendizitischer Abszess⁹ akute Appendizitis¹⁰ perforierende A.¹¹ Verdacht auf A.¹² katarrhalische Appendizitis¹³ Appendektomie, sog. Blinddarmoperation¹⁴
13

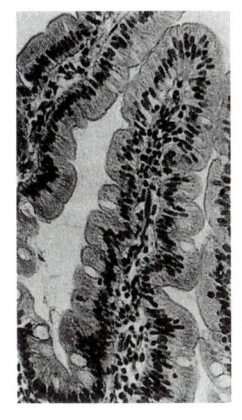

Normal-appearing jejunal villi
in a 3-year-old boy:
(a) histologic section,
(b) scanning electron microscopic view

intestinal villi [vɪlaɪ] *n pl*   *syn* **villi (intestinales)** *n term, sing* **villus**

projections of the mucous membrane of the intestine; they are leaf-shaped [iː] in the duodenum and become shorter, more finger-shaped, and sparser¹ in the ileum

(inter)villous² [vɪləs] *adj term* • **villo-** *comb* • **microvilli**³ [maɪkroʊvɪlaɪ] *n pl*

» Jejunal tissue may be otherwise normal or show clubbing [ʌ] of the villi⁴, dilated lymphatics, or even partial villous atrophy. Jejunal biopsy shows broadening and shortening of the villi and lengthening of the crypts [krɪpts].

Use interstitial [ɪʃ]/ duodenal / ischemic [ɪskiːmɪk]/ shortened⁵ / thickened **villi** • **villous** features [iːtʃ]/ histology / tumor • **villous** adenoma or polyp⁶ [pɒːlɪp]/ surface / atrophy⁷ • **villoglandular** polyp⁶ • **intervillous** space⁸

Darmzotten, Villi intestinales
weniger zahlreich¹ villös, zottenreich² Mikrovilli³ trommelschlägelartige Auftreibung d. Darmzotten⁴ verkürzte Zotten⁵ Zottenpolyp, Zottenadenom, villöser Darmpolyp⁶ Zottenatrophie⁷ intervillöser Raum/ Spalt⁸
14

colon [koʊlən] n term
rel **large intestine** *or* **bowel**¹ [baʊəl] *n clin*, **haustrum**² [ɔː] *n term, pl* **-a**

portion of the gut extending from the cecum to the rectum

col(on)ic [kɒlɪk‖kəlɒnɪk] *adj term* • **colo-** *comb* • **haustral** [hɔːstrəl] *adj*
haustration³ *n term*

» The ascending colon extends between the ileocecal orifice and the hepatic flexure. Barium [eə] enema⁴ [enɪmə] revealed absence of haustrations.

Use ascending⁵ [se]/ transverse⁶ / descending⁷ / sigmoid⁸ [ɪ]/ meso/ irritable⁹ **colon** • **colon** conduit / interposition¹⁰ / cancer / massage¹¹ • **colonic** absorption / gas / motility • **colonic** contraction / dila(ta)tion • **colonic** mucosa / flora / pH / contents / transit¹² • **colonic** dysfunction / inertia¹³ [ɪnɜːrʃə]/ obstruction / bleeding (episodes) • **colonic** irrigation *or* lavage¹⁴ [-ɑːʒ]/ polyp • hepatic *or* right¹⁵ / splenic [e] *or* left¹⁶ **colic flexure** • **haustral** pattern • **col**orectal cancer /ovaginal [dʒ] /ostomy bag¹⁷ /itis /olysis • **colono**scope /scopy¹⁸

rectum [rektəm] n term
rel **proctoscopy**¹ [prɒktɒːskəpi] *n term*

terminal portion of the digestive tube extending from the sigmoid colon to the anal canal

rectal² [rektəl] *adj term* • **recto-** [rektoʊ] *comb* • **proct(o)-** *comb*

» A phosphate enema³ may be given to empty the rectum. Following DRE⁴, the perianal area was examined, and the lubricated⁵ [uː] scope was gently inserted 3-4 cm past the anal sphincter.

Use per⁶ (*abbr* PR)/ prolapsed / stool [uː] in / fold of / flexure [ekʃ] of **rectum** • **rectal** temperature⁷ / folds / canal / examination • **rectal** biopsy⁸ / swab⁹ [ɒː]/ skin tags¹⁰ • **rectal** suppository¹¹ / enema • **rectal** burning / prolapse¹² / bleeding • **rectal** polyp / hemorrhoids [e]/ mass • **proct**itis /ology /ologist /osigmoidoscopy /oscope • **recto**uterine pouch¹³ [paʊtʃ]/ -vesical pouch¹⁴ • **rectovaginal** septum¹⁵ / fold / examination • **rectosigmoid** sphincter / junction¹⁶ • **rectouterine** ligament [ɪ]/ muscle

anus [eɪnəs] n term, pl & gen ani [eɪnaɪ]   syn **back passage** n clin

opening of the digestive tract in the fold between the buttocks¹ [ʌ] through which the feces² [fiːsɪz] are evacuated

anal *adj term* • **perianal** *adj* • **ano-** *comb*

» These preparations sometimes help to prevent anal irritation by increasing stool firmness. Venous [iː] drainage [eɪ] above the anorectal juncture³ is through the portal system. A smear [ɪə] of the anal mucosa⁴ was examined for WBCs⁵.

Use artificial⁶ / imperforate⁷ [ɜː] **anus** • external/internal sphincter of the **anus** • **anal** canal / region / orifice⁸ / verge⁹ [vɜːrdʒ] • **anal** sphincter / tone / reflex¹⁰ • **anal** fissure¹¹ [fɪʃər]/ cancer / intercourse¹² / **anal** atresia⁷ [iːʒ]/ pruritus¹³ [aɪ] • levator [eɪ]/ pruritus¹³ [aɪ] **ani** • **ano**coccygeal [-kɒksɪɡɪəl] /cutaneous [eɪ] • **perianal** area / itching¹³ [tʃ]

Kolon, Grimmdarm
Dickdarm¹ Haustrum² Haustrenbildung, Haustrierung³ Bariumeinlauf⁴ Colon ascendens⁵ C. transversum⁶ C. descendens⁷ C. sigmoideum⁸ Reizkolon, C. irritabile⁹ Koloninterposition, -zwischenschaltung¹⁰ Kolonmassage¹¹ Kolontransit¹² Darmträgheit¹³ Kolonlavage, Dickdarmreinigung¹⁴ rechte Kolonflexur, Flexura coli dextra/ hepatica coli¹⁵ linke K., F. coli sinistra/ lienalis coli¹⁶ Kolostomiebeutel¹⁷ Kolo(no)skopie¹⁸

15

Rektum, Mastdarm
Proktoskopie¹ rektal, Rektum-² Einlauf³ digitale rektale Untersuchung, DRU⁴ m. Gleitmittel versehen⁵ rektal⁶ Rektaltemperatur⁷ Rektumbiopsie⁸ Rektalabstrich⁹ Mariskien, Analfalten¹⁰ Rektalzäpfchen¹¹ Rektumprolaps¹² Excavatio rectouterina, Douglas-Raum¹³ E. rectovesicalis¹⁴ Septum rectovaginale¹⁵ rektosigmoidale Übergangszone¹⁶

16

Anus, After
Gesäß¹ Stuhl, Fäkalien² anorektale Übergangszone³ Analabstrich⁴ weiße Blutkörperchen, Leukozyten⁵ künstlicher After, Anus praeter(naturalis)⁶ Anus imperforatus, Analatresie⁷ Anus, After⁸ Analring⁹ Analreflex¹⁰ Analfissur¹¹ Analverkehr¹² Afterjucken, Analpruritus, Pruritus ani¹³

17

Unit 46   Digestion
Related Units: **2** Diet, **3** Food & Drink, **27** Mastication, **45** Digestive Tract, **47** Liver, **78** Metabolism, **79** Nutrition, **109** Gastrointestinal Signs & Symptoms

ingestion [ɪndʒestʃən] n term → U2-1   syn **(food) intake** n clin,
rel **imbibition**¹ [ɪʃ] *n term*

introduction of food and drink into the stomach [k]

ingest² *v term* • **ingestants**³ *n* • **ingesta**³ *n pl* • **ingestive** *adj* • **imbibe** [aɪ] *v*

» Acute toxicity can result from ingestion of massive doses of vitamin A. Patients are encouraged to ingest fluids during meals. A high intake of saturated fat⁴ increases the risk of prostate cancer. Many drinkers occasionally imbibe to excess.

Use food / rapid / drug⁵ / barbiturate [ɪ]/ aspirin / caustic⁶ [ɒː] **ingestion** • deliberate⁷ / excessive / prolonged **ingestion** • oral / dietary [aɪə]/ salt **intake** • (excessive) fluid¹ / (adequate) water **intake** • increased caloric⁸ / alcohol⁹ **intake** • **ingested** material / food particles¹⁰ / poison

(Nahrungs)aufnahme, -zufuhr, Ingestion
Flüssigkeitsaufnahme¹ Nahrung zu sich nehmen² aufgenommene Nahrung, Ingesta³ gesättigte Fette⁴ Medikamenteneinnahme⁵ Ätzmittelingestion⁶ absichtl. Einnahme⁷ erhöhte Kalorienzufuhr⁸ Alkoholkonsum⁹ ingestierte Nahrungspartikel¹⁰

1

Digestion   BODY STRUCTURES & FUNCTIONS   **187**

swallowing [swɒ:louɪŋ] n   syn **deglutition** [-ʊtɪʃᵊn] n term,
                            rel **suck**[1], **suckle**[2] [ʌ] v

passing anything through the mouth, pharynx, and esophagus into the stomach; to perform deglutition

swallow[3] v & n • **sucker**[4] n • **suction** n • **suckling**[5] n • **deglutitive** adj term

» Do you have any difficulty in speaking and swallowing[6]? Have the patient swallow and advance the tube into the esophagus. The deglutition reflex[7] [iː] is a complex series [ɪɚ] of events that serves both to propel food through the pharynx and the esophagus and to prevent its entry into the airway.

Use **to swallow sth.** down / up[8] / whole[9] • barium[10] [eɚ]/ (impaired) [eɚ] ability to[11] **swallow** • **swallowing** reflex[7] / center[12] / mechanism [ek]/ function • act of / painful[6] / impaired[11] / air[13] **swallowing** • normal / impaired[11] **deglutition** • **deglutitive** inhibition • **to suck on** candy / the bottle / the breast [e]/ fingers / a pacifier[14] [æs] • **sucking** reflex[15] / urge [ɜːrdʒ]/ action[16] / chest wound[17] [uː] • **suck-swallow** dysfunction [ɪ] • thumb[18] [θʌm]/ blanket / fist / blood-**sucking** • thumb[19] **sucker**

(Ver)schlucken, Schluckakt, Deglutition

(ein-, auf)saugen, nuckeln, lutschen[1] saugen, trinken; stillen, säugen[2] (ver)schlucken; Schluck[3] Sauger[4] Säugling[5] Schluckbeschwerden[6] Schluckreflex[7] verschlucken, -schlingen[8] unzerkaut/ ganz schlucken[9] Bariumschluck, Ösophagus-Breischluck[10] Schluckstörung[11] Schluckzentrum[12] Luftschlucken, Aerophagie[13] am Schnuller saugen, nuckeln[14] Saugreflex[15] Saugakt[16] offener Pneumothorax[17] Daumenlutschen[18] Daumenlutscher(in)[19]

2

---

belch [beltʃ] n   syn **burp** [bɜːrp] n inf, **eructation** [ɪrʌkteɪʃᵊn] n term
                          rel **hiccup**[1] or BE **hiccough** [hɪkʌp] n clin

bringing up gas from the stomach, sometimes with acid [æsɪd] fluid and a characteristic sound

belch[2] v clin • **burp**[2] v inf • **hiccup**[3] v clin • **eructate**[2] [ɪrʌkteɪt] v term

» The patient presented with fatty food intolerance, belching, flatulence, a sense of epigastric heaviness [e], heartburn[4] [hɑːrtbɜːrn], and upper abdominal pain of varying intensity. Swallowed air that is not belched passes through the gut [ʌ] and leaves as flatus[5] [eɪ].

Use (in)voluntary / gaseous [eɪ]/ nervous [ɜː]/ repetitive[6] **eructation** • **to burp** a baby[7] • chronic excessive **belching** • **belching** and bloating[8] [oʊ]/ indigestion[9] [ɪndɪdʒestʃᵊn] • intractable[10] **hiccup**

▪ Note: The expression **burp** is used predominantly in connection with babies.

Aufstoßen, Rülpser, Eruktation, Ruktus

Schluckauf, Singultus[1] aufstoßen, rülpsen[2] Schluckauf haben[3] Sodbrennen[4] Flatus, Wind[5] ständiges Aufstoßen[6] Bäuerchen machen lassen[7] Aufstoßen und Blähungen[8] Aufstoßen u. Verdauungsstörung[9] hartnäckiger Schluckauf[10]

3

---

regurgitate [rɪgɜːrdʒɪteɪt] v term   sim **bring up**[1] (food) phr clin, **vomit**[1] v

to flow backward, esp. to bring up swallowed food spontaneously and without effort

regurgitation[2] n term • **vomiting** n clin • **vomitus**[3] n term → U103-12; U109-3f

» Infants commonly regurgitate a portion of feedings. Was there any blood in what you brought up? Vomiting should be distinguished from regurgitation, which is the effortless reflux[2] [riːflʌks] of liquid or food stomach contents. The patient noted regurgitation of undigested food, nocturnal [ɜː] choking[4] [tʃoʊkɪŋ], and gurgling[5] [ɜː] in the throat.

Use **to bring up** blood from the stomach[6] / phlegm [flem] from the lungs[7] • **to vomit** (up) food / gastric contents / bile-stained [eɪ] material[8] • **to vomit** spontaneously / persistently • to cause/avoid **regurgitation** • effortless / acid[9] / spontaneous [eɪ] / postprandial[10] **regurgitation** • mild / severe / excessive **regurgitation** • **regurgitated** material / gastric contents[11] / bile[12] [baɪl]

regurgitieren, zurückströmen; erbrechen (ohne Antiperistaltik)

(er)brechen, s. übergeben[1] Rückströmen, -fluss, Regurgitation[2] Erbrochenes[3] würgendes Gefühl[4] Gurgeln[5] Blut (er)brechen[6] Schleim aushusten[7] galliges Erbrechen, Galle erbrechen[8] saures Regurgitieren[9] postprandialer Reflux[10] regurgitierter Mageninhalt[11] Gallenrückfluss[12]

4

---

retch [retʃ] v clin   sim **heave**[1] [hiːv] v inf → U44-8

strong involuntary effort to vomit without actually bringing up anything

retching[2] n clin • **heaving**[3] n

» Vomiting is often preceded [siː] by nausea[4] [nɔːzɪə] and by retching, spasmodic respiratory and abdominal movements (so-called dry heaves[2]). I thought I'd heard her heaving in the bathroom. My stomach heaved[5] at the sight of food.

Use postoperative / preceding / vomiting and / nonproductive[2] **retching** • early-morning / bouts of[6] **retching** • vigorous[7] [ɪg]/ forceful[7] **retching** • **to heave** a sigh[8]

würgen, Brechreiz haben

Brechreiz haben, s. übergeben; (hoch)heben, ausstoßen[1] Brechreiz[2] Brechreiz, Erbrechen[3] Übelkeit[4] es drehte mir d. Magen um[5] Brechreizanfälle[6] starker Brechreiz[7] einen Seufzer ausstoßen[8]

5

---

peristalsis [perɪstælsɪs] n term   rel **gastrointestinal motility**[1] n term

wave-like smooth [uː] muscle contraction that moves food through the digestive tract

antiperistalsis[2] n term • peristaltic[3] adj
hypo/ dysmotility[4] [ɪ] n term • motile[5] [moʊtaɪl‖-ᵊl] adj

» Determine the presence of adequate esophageal peristalsis. Neuroleptics have anxiolytic [ɪ] and antiemetic effects[6] and do not inhibit gastrointestinal motility.

Use hyperactive[7] [aɪ]/ (ab)normal / swallowing-induced **peristalsis** • propulsive[8] [ʌ]/ retrograde or reversed[2] [ɜː] **peristalsis** • **peristaltic** waves[9] / activity / movements[9] / contractions[9] • **peristaltic** sounds / rushes[10] [ʌ]/ unrest[5] • esophageal[11] [dʒ]/ impaired[4] **motility** • intestinal / gastric / esophageal **dysmotility**

Peristaltik

Magen-Darmmotilität[1] Antiperistaltik[2] peristaltisch[3] Motilitätsstörung[4] beweglich[5] antiemetische Wirkung[6] Hyperperistaltik[7] propulsive/ vorwärtsbewegende Peristaltik[8] peristaltische Wellen[9] Borborygmen[10] Ösophagusmotilität[11]

6

46

BODY STRUCTURES & FUNCTIONS — Digestion

aboral or **aborad** adj term   opposite **orad**[1] adj term → U45-2

away from the mouth, usually referring to the propulsion[2] of food in the intestinal tract

» The circular [sɜː] smooth muscle orad to the bolus contracts. The propulsive movement of phasic [feɪzɪk] and peristaltic contractions[3] slowly pushes chyme[4] in an aboral direction.

Use **aborad** direction / progression • **orad** waves • to move **orad**

---

aboral, v. Mund weg/ entfernt
adoral, mundwärts[1] Vorwärtsbewegung[2] propulsive Peristaltik[3] Speisebrei, Chymus[4]

[7]

---

gastric emptying rate or **time** n term
    rel **orocecal** [-siːkəl] **transit time**[1] n term

time required for solids[2] or liquids[3] to pass on from the stomach into the small intestine

empty[4] v & adj

» Dietary fiber [aɪ] slows transit through the jejunum [dʒ]. Mean orocecal transit time for a solid meal is 35 hours. The colon empties satisfactorily. You must take this on an empty stomach[5]. Empty the stomach by gastric lavage[6] [-ɑːʒ] and administer activated charcoal[7] [tʃ].

Use early / delayed[8] [eɪ]/ rapid / inadequate **gastric emptying** • normal / prompt[9] / partial **emptying** • rapid / (postprandial) intestinal / gut [ʌ]/ colonic[10] **transit** • to increase/ speed **transit time** • small bowel[11] [aʊ]/ gastrointestinal **transit time** • **transit** study

---

Magenentleerungszeit
Mund-Blinddarm-Zeit[1] feste Nahrung[2] Flüssigkeiten[3] entleeren; leer, nüchtern[4] auf leeren/ nüchternen Magen[5] Magenspülung[6] Aktivkohle, Carbo medicinalis[7] verzögerte Magenentleerung[8] sofortige Entleerung[9] Kolontransit[10] Dünndarmpassagezeit[11]

[8]

---

chyme [kaɪm] n   rel **bolus**[1] [bəʊləs] n term, pl **boluses**

semi-liquid mass of partially digested food particles and gastric juices [dʒuːsiːz] passing from the stomach through the pyloric [paɪlɔːrɪk] sphincter into the duodenum

» Gastric chyme is forced into the funnel-shaped[2] [ʌ] antral chamber [tʃeɪ-] by peristalsis. As the bolus enters the esophagus, a peristaltic wave propels it toward the stomach [k].

Use to mix/move **chyme** • prolonged transit time for / gastric **chyme** • **bolus of** food / dye[3] [daɪ] • food / fluid / large / impacted[4] / meat[5] **bolus** • **bolus** feeding / injection[6] [dʒe] / therapy • **bolus** obstruction[7] [ʌ]/ death[8]

Chymus, Speisebrei
Bolus, Bissen; große Pille[1] trichterförmig[2] Farbbolus[3] steckengebliebener/ impaktierter Bissen[4] Fleischbolus[5] Bolusinjektion, intravenöse Schnellinjektion[6] Bolusobstruktion[7] Bolustod[8]

[9]

---

gastric juice [dʒuːs] n clin   rel **intestinal juices**[1] n clin

digestive secretions of the gastric glands producing mainly pepsin, hydrochloric [haɪ-] acid[2], and mucin [mjuːsɪn]

» The output of gastric juice in a fasting subject varies from 500 to 1500 mL/d. Antacids[3] were given to reduce acid-stimulated release [iː] of secretin [iː], which increases the flow of pancreatic juice. Take a sample of jejunal juice for microbiologic testing of the intestinal flora[4].

Use pancreatic[5] [æ]/ duodenal / jejunal[6] [dʒiːdʒuːnəl] **juice** • **intestinal** secretions[1] [iːʃ]/ fluid / tract gas[7] / loop[8] [uː]/ disturbance [ɜː] / **intestinal** tube[9] / hypermotility[10] / obstruction • **intestinal** infection / villi[11] [aɪ] • **gastric** mucosa [oʊ]/ mucus [mjuːkəs] / cardia[12] / distention[13] / acidity [sɪ]

Magensaft
Darmsäfte[1] Salzsäure[2] Säureblocker, Antazida[3] Darmflora[4] Pankreassaft[5] Jejunumsekret[6] Darmgas[7] Darmschlinge[8] Darmrohr[9] gesteigerte/ übermäßige Darmmotilität[10] Darmzotten[11] Mageneingang, -mund, Kardia[12] Magenblähung[13]

[10]

---

digest [daɪdʒest] v   rel **break down**[1], **split up**[1] v phr clin,
    hydrolyze[2] [haɪdrəlaɪz] v term → U78-10

mechanical and chemical [ke] breakdown[3] [eɪ] of food into absorbable substances in the GI tract

digestion[4] n • **digestive**[5] adj & n • **(in)digestible**[6] adj •
digestant[7] n term • **hydrolysis** [-drɒːlɪsɪs] n

» Pancreatic enzymes [zaɪ] digest protein to form free amino acids[8] and oligopeptides. Dietary fiber[9] [aɪ] cannot be digested by the human intestine. Fats, proteins, and carbohydrates[10] [aɪ] are hydrolyzed and solubilized[11] by pancreatic and biliary secretions[12]. By the action of these enzymes, lactose is split into glucose and galactose.

Use to aid/ induce/promote[13]/accelerate [əkse-] /inhibit/be resistant to[14] **digestion** • protein / fat[15] / carbohydrate / lactose / proteolytic [ɪ] **digestion** • colonic bacterial / (intra)luminal[16] **digestion** • **digestive** system or tract[17] / glands / enzymes[18] • **digestive** process / tube[17] / tonic / disturbance[19] • easily / partially **digested** • pre**digest**[20] / mal[19] or in**digestion** • un**digested** • protein[21] / tissue [tɪʃjuː] **breakdown** • products[22] / rate **of hydrolysis** • fat-**splitting** enzyme[23] [enzaɪm]

---

verdauen
aufspalten[1] hydrolysieren[2] Aufspaltung, Abbau[3] Verdauung, Digestion[4] digestiv, Verdauungs-; verdauungsförderndes Mittel, Digestivum[5] (un)verdaulich[6] verdauungsförd. Mittel, Digestivum[7] Aminosäuren[8] Ballaststoffe[9] Kohlenhydrate[10] löslich gemacht[11] Gallensäfte, -sekrete[12] Verdauung fördern[13] unverdaulich sein[14] Fettverdauung[15] luminale Verdauung[16] Verdauungskanal, -trakt[17] Verdauungsenzyme[18] Verdauungsstörung, Maldigestion[19] vorverdauen[20] Eiweißabbau[21] Spalt-, Hydrolyseprodukte[22] fettspaltendes Enzym, Lipase[23]

[11]

Digestion BODY STRUCTURES & FUNCTIONS **189**

fermentation [fɜːrmenteɪʃᵊn] *n term*

anaerobic conversion [ɜː] of foods by the action of enzymes which split them up into simpler compounds

ferment[1] *v term* • **fermenter**[2] *n* • **fermentable**[3] *adj*

» The majority of bacterial [ɪɚ] *fermentation*[4] takes place in the colon. Colonic bacteria ferment mannitol to produce hydrogen [aɪ]. Malabsorbed lactose is fermented by intestinal bacteria, producing gas and organic acids.

Use acetic[5] / alcoholic[6] / amylic[7] / butyric[8] [ɪ] ***fermentation*** • lactic acid[9] / ammoniacal[10] / storing / colonic[11] ***fermentation*** • ***fermentable*** fiber[12] [aɪ] • ***fermentation*** product[13]

Gärung; Fermentation, Fermentierung

(ver)gären, fermentieren[1] Fermenter, Fermentator[2] Gärungs-; fermentierbar[3] bakterielle Zersetzung[4] Essigsäuregärung[5] alkoholische G.[6] Stärkeabbau, Zuckergärung[7] Buttersäuregärung[8] Milchsäuregärung[9] ammoniakalische G.[10] Fermentation i. Dickdarm[11] fermentierbare Faserstoffe[12] Gärungsprodukt[13]

12

---

absorb [æbsɔːrb] *v*   *syn* **incorporate** *v*, **take up** *v phr*

taking substances into the bloodstream [iː] from the bowels[1] [baʊəlz]

absorptive[2] *adj* • **(re/ mal)absorption**[3] *n* • **incorporation** *n* • **uptake**[4] *n*

» The proximal colon absorbs electrolytes [aɪ] and water more efficiently [ɪʃ] than the descending colon. More than 80% of protein absorption occurs [ɜː] in the proximal 100cm of jejunum [dʒuː].

Use well / efficiently / readily [e] / rapidly / poorly ***absorbed*** • fat[5] / iron[6] [aɪ]/ carbohydrate [-haɪdreɪt] ***absorption*** • calcium [s]/ colonic / delayed[7] [eɪ] ***absorption*** • ***absorptive*** cells / surface [ɜː] • ***absorption*** rate[8] • gastrointestinal / glucose / hepatic[9] / ammonia[10] / substrate [ʌ] ***uptake*** • calcium ***incorporation*** • ***incorporation of*** amino acids [æs]/ lipid material / iodine [aɪə] • glucose-galactose / carbohydrate[11] / fat / intestinal / nutrient[12] [uː] ***malabsorption***

ab-, resorbieren, aufnehmen

Darm[1] absorbierend, Ab-, Resorptions-[2] Malabsorption, Ab-, Resorptionsstörung[3] Aufnahme[4] Fettresorption[5] Eisenresorption[6] Resorptionsverzögerung[7] Resorptionsgeschwindigkeit[8] Aufnahme in die Leber[9] Ammoniakaufnahme[10] Kohlenhydratmalabsorption[11] unzureichende Nährstoffresorption[12]

13

---

bowel sounds *n pl*   *syn* **borborygmi** [aɪ] *n term*
                   rel **stomach rumbles**[1] [ʌ] *n pl inf*

high-pitched[2] bubbling[3] [ʌ] and gurgling[4] [ɜː] noises caused by the propulsion [ʌ] of chyme [kaɪm] through the lower gut [ʌ]

rumble[5] [ʌ] *v clin*

» In the presence of distention from flatus the bowel sounds are hyperresonant and can be heard over the entire abdomen. My stomach rumbled as I hadn't eaten any breakfast.

Use normal / (normo)active / hyperactive[6] [aɪ]/ decreased[7] [iː]/ diminished[7] ***bowel sounds*** • sluggish[7] [ʌ] / hypoactive[7] / absent[8] / high-pitched[9] ***bowel sounds*** • ***bowel*** habits[10] / function / movement[11] / contents[12] • absence of[8] ***bowel sounds*** • audible [ɔː] / loud [aʊ] / high-pitched[9] ***borborygmi***

Darmgeräusche, Borborygmen

Magenknurren[1] hochfrequent[2] blubbernd[3] gurgelnd[4] knurren, kollern[5] verstärkte Darmgeräusche[6] verminderte/ träge Darmgeräusche[7] fehlende Darmgeräusche[8] hochfrequente Darmgeräusche[9] Stuhlgewohnheiten[10] Stuhlgang[11] Darminhalt[12]

14

---

wind or **gas** [gæs] *n clin*   *syn* **flatus** [fleɪtəs] *n term, sim* *****fart**[1] [ɑː] *v & n inf*

clinical euphemism for gases in the intestine expelled[2] through the anus [eɪ] → U109-7

flatulence[3] [ætʃ] *n term* • **flatulent**[4] *adj* • **gaseous**[5] [eɪ] *adj* • **gaseousness**[6] *n*

» Flatulence is caused by undigested carbohydrates reaching the lower bowel where gases are produced by bacterial flora. A major [eɪdʒ] source of intestinal gas is the fermentative action of intestinal bacteria [ɪɚ] on carbohydrates and proteins.

Use to break[7] [eɪ] ***wind*** • to expel or pass[7] ***flatus*** • increased / excessive ***flatus*** • passage or expulsion[8] [ʌ] ***of flatus*** • to experience[9] ***flatulence*** • (overlying) [aɪ] intestinal or bowel[10] / stomach ***gases*** • ***gas***-forming food[11] /-distended intestinal loops [uː]/ formation[12] • ***gaseous*** eructations

     Note: The expression ***fart*** should be avoided in clinical settings.

Blähung, (Darm)wind, Flatus

furzen; Furz[1] entweichend, abgehend[2] Flatulenz, Blähung(en)[3] flatulent, blähend[4] gasförmig, Gas-[5] Gasförmigkeit, -zustand[6] einen Wind/ Blähung abgehen lassen[7] Windabgang[8] Blähungen haben[9] Darmwinde, Blähungen[10] blähende Kost[11] Gasbildung[12]

15

---

intestinal flora *n term*   *syn* **bowel** [baʊᵊl] or **gut** [gʌt] **flora** *n clin*

normal population of microorganisms (microbial associates, esp. bacteria) inhabiting[1] the gut

» These organisms compete with the normal bowel flora that colonize[1] the mucosa. This gram-negative bacillus is probably part of the endogenous intestinal flora.

Use ammonia-producing ***intestinal flora*** • ***intestinal*** bacteria / protozoa [-zoʊə] • bacterial overgrowth[2] • bacterial[3] / oral[4] / normal mouth / colonic[5] ***flora*** • typical nasopharyngeal [dʒ]/ skin[6] / vaginal[7] [dʒ] ***flora*** • fecal[8] [fiːkᵊl]/ (an)aerobic / gram-negative ***flora*** • enteric[9] / intestinal bacterial[9] ***flora***

Darmflora

besiedeln[1] bakterielle(s) Overgrowth/ Überwucherung[2] Bakterienflora, Keimbesiedelung[3] Mundflora[4] Dickdarmflora[5] Hautflora[6] Scheidenflora[7] Stuhlflora[8] Darmflora[9]

16

putrefaction [pjuːtrɪˈfækʃᵊn] n term
　　　　　　　　　syn **decomposition** n term, **rotting** [ɒː] n inf

decay[1] [dɪkeɪ] of organic matter (enzymes, proteins) by bacterial action in the gut producing foul-smelling[2] [aʊ], toxic compounds [aʊ], e.g. ammonia[3] and hydrogen [aɪ] sulfide[4] [ʌ], and mercaptans [kæ]

putrefactive[5] adj term • **putrefy**[6] [aɪ] v • **putrid**[7] adj • **decompose**[6] v • **rot**[6] v inf

» Food-borne botulism can occur [ɜː] when preservation does not inactivate the spores but kills other putrefactive bacteria[8] that might inhibit their growth. Infection with B. dermatitidis appears to be acquired by inhalation of the fungus [ʌ] from soil, decomposed vegetation, or rotting wood.

Use bacterial[9] **putrefaction** • anaerobic / thermic[10] / tissue / protein[11] **decomposition** • **putrid** empyema [aɪiː]/ odor[12] / sputum / lung abscess • **rotten** teeth[13]

---

defecate [ˈdefɪkeɪt] v term, BE **defaecate**　　syn **eliminate, evacuate** v

to empty or remove and discharge[1] material from the body, esp. via the bowels

evacuation n • **elimination** n • **defecation**[2] n term • **defecatory**[3] adj

» Is there a change in the pattern of bowel elimination[2]? The urge [ɜːdʒ] to defecate[4] is perceived [siː] when small amounts of feces enter the rectum and stimulate stretch receptors in the rectal wall. To decrease straining [eɪ] with defecation[5], patients should be given instructions for a high-fiber diet[6] [daɪət].

Use **to evacuate** the stomach[7] / fecal material[8] • surgical[9] [ɜː] **evacuation** • normal pattern of[10] / altered [ɔː] **bowel elimination** • to attempt/initiate/perform/aid **defecation** • pain on[11] / (increased) frequency of / obstructed [ʌ] **defecation** • **defecatory** difficulties[12] / reflex[13] [iː] • incomplete / fecal[2] **evacuation**

> **Note:** The expressions **shit** and **crap** are substandard synonyms for **defecate** and **feces** which are to be avoided in clinical contexts.

---

bowel movement n clin, abbr **BM**　　syn **stool** [uː], BE **motion** [moʊʃᵊn] n clin usu pl

the solid waste products evacuated from the bowels or the act of passing fecal matter

to open one's bowels[1] [baʊᵊlz] phr clin BE → U109-10

» Do your bowels open regularly? Are your motions well-formed? Fiber [aɪ] increases the bulk[2] [ʌ] of the stool and facilitates excretion [iː]. Enemas[3] [e] may be required to relieve fecal impaction, and the regular use of stool softeners and a high-fiber diet may help prevent recurrences [ɜː] BE [ʌ].

Use (ir)regular[4] / frequency [iː] of / (in)frequent **BMs** • bloody[5] [ʌ]/ loose[6] [uː] painful **bowel movements** • incontinent of[7] **stool** to pass or evacuate[1]/hold back or retain[8] [eɪ] **stools** • pencil-shaped[9] / (semi-)formed[10] / bulky [ʌ] **or** voluminous[11] [uː] **stools** • clay-colored [eɪ] or light-colored or pale [eɪ] or acholic[12] [k] **stool** • dark / hard / fatty or greasy[13] [iː] **stools** • bilious [ɪ]/ impacted / residual **stools** • inability to control[14] / change in **stools** • number / digital [dʒ] removal **of stools** • **stool** collection / retention[15] • **bowel** training[16] / function / obstruction [ʌ]/ irrigation[17]

---

feces [ˈfiːsiːz] n term, BE **faeces**　　syn **excrement** n clin, **excreta** [iː] n term

body wastes [eɪ] discharged from the bowels

fecal[1] [ˈfiːkᵊl] adj term • **feculent**[2] [e] adj • **excretion**[3] n • **excrementitious**[1] adj

» Feces consist of water, food residue[4], bacteria, and intestinal and hepatic secretions. Fecal specimens should be examined for occult [ʌ] blood[5]. The vomitus was feculent. The usual dietary intake of calcium [s] is 1-3 g/d, most of which is excreted unabsorbed in the feces.

Use normal / semiliquid **feces** • gas and / discharge of[6] **feces** • passed in[7] / incontinence of[8] **feces** • **fecal** material or matter[9] / mass / output / contents • **fecal** fat / flora / loss / frequency / specimens[10] • **fecal** impaction / incontinence[8] / softener[11] • **fecal** vomiting[12] / contamination • **feculent** vomiting[12] / odor [oʊ] • fecal[6] / urinary [jʊ]/ renal [iː] **excretion**

Fäulnis, Zersetzung, Putreszenz

Zersetzung, Zerfall[1] faulig, übelriechend[2] Ammoniak[3] Schwefelwasserstoff[4] fäulniserregend, Fäulnis-[5] (ver)faulen, verrotten, verwesen[6] faulig[7] Fäulnisbakterien[8] bakterielle Zersetzung[9] thermische Zersetzung[10] Eiweißfäulnis[11] übler Mundgeruch, Foetor ex ore[12] kariöse Zähne[13]

17

(den Darm) entleeren, ausscheiden

ausscheiden[1] Darmentleerung, Stuhlgang, Defäkation[2] Stuhl-, Defäkations-[3] Stuhldrang[4] Pressen b. Stuhlgang[5] ballaststoffreiche Kost[6] den Magen aushebern[7] Stuhl/ Kot ausscheiden[8] chirurg. Entfernung, Ausräumung[9] normaler Stuhlgang[10] schmerzhafter Stuhlgang[11] Stuhlentleerungsprobleme[12] Defäkationsreflex[13]

18

Stuhl(gang), Darmentleerung

Stuhlgang haben[1] Volumen[2] Einläufe[3] regelmäßiger Stuhlgang[4] Blutstuhl, blutiger S.[5] dünnflüssiger S., Durchfall[6] stuhlkontinent[7] den Stuhl verhalten[8] Bleistiftstuhl[9] geformter Stuhl[10] voluminöse Stühle[11] kalk-/ lehmfarbener/ acholischer/ heller Stuhl[12] Fettstuhl, Steatorrhoe[13] Stuhlinkontinenz[14] Stuhlverhaltung[15] Darmtraining[16] Darmreinigung, -spülung[17]

19

Stuhl, Kot, Exkremente, Fäzes

fäkal, Kot-, Stuhl-[1] fäkulent, kotartig[2] Ausscheidung, Exkret, Excretum[3] Nahrungsreste, unverdaute Nahrungsbestandteile[4] okkultes Blut[5] Stuhlentleerung[6] im Stuhl ausgeschieden[7] Stuhlinkontinenz[8] Stuhl, Fäkalien[9] Stuhlproben[10] Laxans[11] Koterbrechen, Kopremesis, Miserere[12]

20

Unit 47 Liver & Biliary System

Related Units: 45 Digestive Tract, 46 Digestion, 54 Endocrine Glands, 78 Metabolism, 79 Nutrition, 37 Components of the Blood, 109 Gastrointestinal Signs & Symptoms

liver [lɪvɚ] n clin & term

largest glandular [æ] organ of the body situated in the right hypochondrium [k] and upper part of the epigastrium beneath the diaphragm [daɪəfræm]

hepatic[1] [hɪpætɪk]] adj term • pre/ posthepatic adj • hepat(o)- comb

» The liver is almost entirely covered by peritoneum [iː]. So-called hepatic pain[2] is due to compression of the swelling liver by its capsule. These gallstones[3] [ɔː] result from secretion [iːʃ] by the liver of bile[4] supersaturated with cholesterol. In cirrhosis [s] the liver edge is usually firm, blunt[5] [ʌ], and irregular. The patient presents with jaundice[6] [dʒɒːndɪs] and hepatic tenderness[7].

Use infantile / enlarged / firm [ɜː]/ hard **liver** • nodular / tender / congested[8] [dʒe] **liver** • compromised [aɪ]/ cirrhotic / shrunken[9] [ʌ] **liver** • bed • edge[10] / segment **of the liver** • central veins [eɪ]/ biopsy[11] [aɪ] **of the liver** • infiltration / enlargement[12] / cirrhosis[13] [ou] **of the liver** • **liver** edge[10] / surface [ɜː]/ cells[14] / parenchyma[15] [eŋkɪ]/ capsule / scan[16] • **liver** enzymes [zaɪ]/ function tests[17] / biopsy[11] / damage[18] / failure[19] • **hepatic** cells[14] / vein / arterial flow / flexure[20] • **hepatic** disease / cyst [sɪst]/ congestion[8] • **hepatic** cirrhosis[13] / failure / adenoma / coma[21] • **hepato**cellular /cytes[14] /biliary system /megaly[12] /logist • **hepato**toxic /duodenal [iː] ligament [ɪɡ] /jugular [dʒʌ] reflux[22] [iː] • **hepat**itis[23] [-aɪtɪs] /ectomy /icojejunostomy [dʒɪdʒuː]

Leber, Hepar

hepatisch, Leber-[1] Leberschmerz[2] Gallensteine[3] Galle[4] stumpf[5] Ikterus, Gelbsucht[6] Druckschmerzhaftigkeit d. Leber[7] Stauungsleber[8] Schrumpfleber[9] Leberrand[10] Leberbiopsie[11] Lebervergrößerung, Hepatomegalie[12] Leberzirrhose[13] Leber(parenchym)zellen[14] Leberparenchym[15] Leberszintigrafie[16] Leberfunktionstests[17] Leberschaden[18] Leberversagen[19] rechte Kolonflexur, Flexura coli dextra[20] Leberkoma, hepatisches K., Coma hepaticum[21] hepatojugulärer Reflux[22] Leberentzündung, Hepatitis[23]

hepatic lobe [loub] n term   syn lobe of the liver n clin

one of the four main portions of the liver named the right, left, caudate[1], and quadrate[2] lobes

lobar[3] [loubɚ] adj term • uni/ bilobar [aɪ] adj • lobectomy[4] [loubektəmi] n

» The falciform [s] ligament[5] [ɪ] containing the ligament of teres[6] (the obliterated umbilical [ʌ] vein[7]) divides the liver into lobes. The right lobe of the liver which is subdivided into the anterior and posterior segments is six times larger than the left. The caudate lobe often becomes palpable as an epigastric mass. The left hepatic vein drains the lateral segment of the left lobe.

Use left[8] / caudate[1] [kɔːdeɪt] / quadrate[2] [kwɒːdreɪt] **lobe of the liver** • right[9] **liver lobe** • **lobar** branch [æ]/ duct [ʌ]/ fissure [fɪʃɚ] • hepatic[4] **lobectomy**

Leberlappen, Lobus hepatis

Lobus caudatus[1] Lobus quadratus[2] lobär[3] Lobektomie, Leberlappenresektion[4] Ligamentum falciforme hepatis[5] Ligamentum teres hepatis[6] obliterierte Nabelvene[7] linker Leberlappen, Lobus hepatis sinister[8] rechter Leberlappen, Lobus hepatis dexter[9]

hepatic lobule [lɒːbjuːl] n term   syn liver lobule or acinus n term, pl –i [æsɪnaɪ]

polygonal functional [ʌ] unit of the liver consisting of hepatocytes[1] [-saɪts] arranged around a central vein bounded [au] by the preterminal [ɜː] and terminal branches of portal triad[2]

lobular[3] adj term • interlobular adj • acinar adj

» Bile [aɪ] formed in the hepatic lobules is secreted into a complex network of canaliculi [-aɪ], small bile ductules, and larger bile ducts that run with lymphatics and branches of the portal vein and hepatic artery in portal tracts[2] situated between hepatic lobules. The hepatic veins represent the final common pathway for the central veins of the lobules of the liver. Small branches of the terminal portal venule and hepatic arteriole enter each acinus at the portal triad [aɪ].

Use caudate **lobule** • **lobular** hepatitis • **interlobular** bile ducts[4] / veins of the liver[5]

Leberläppchen, Lobulus hepatis

Leberparenchymzellen, Hepatozyten[1] Periportalfeld(er), Glisson-Dreieck(e)[2] lobulär, läppchenförmig[3] interlobuläre Gallengänge, Ductuli interlobulares[4] Vv. interlobulares hepatis[5]

hepatic sinusoid [saɪnəsoɪd] n term   rel hepatic cord[1], Kupffer cells[2] n term

sinusoidal capillaries radiating [eɪ] from the center of the liver lobule which are lined by Kupffer cells

sinusoidal adj • pre/ postsinusoidal adj term • perisinusoidal adj

» Portal venous [iː] and hepatic arterial blood becomes pooled after entering the periphery of the hepatic sinusoid. Nutrients[3] [uː] are exchanged across the spaces of Disse[4], which separate hepatocytes from the porous sinusoidal lining [aɪ]. Sinusoidal flow from adjacent[5] [dʒeɪs] acini merges [ɜː] at the terminal [ɜː] hepatic venule. Spindle-shaped Kupffer cells which line the sinusoids serve as tissue macrophages[6] [-feɪdʒiːz].

Use blood-filled **sinusoid** • **sinusoidal** pressure[7] / resistance / hypertension [aɪ]/ dilatation[8] • **sinusoidal** lining[9] [aɪ] (cells) / endothelial [θiː] cells / cell damage • liver or hepatic / phagocytosing[10] [fæɡəsaɪ-] **Kupffer cells** • **Kupffer cell** function

Lebersinusoid

Leberzellbalken[1] Kupffer-Sternzellen, Macrophagocytus stellatus[2] Nährstoffe[3] Disse-Räume[4] benachbart[5] Gewebemakrophagen[6] intrahepatischer Druck[7] Sinusoid-Erweiterung, Dilatation der Sinusoide[8] Sinusoidauskleidung[9] phagozytierende Kupffer-Sternzellen[10]

portal triad [traɪæd] *or* **tract** *n term*   *rel* **portal fissure** *or* **porta hepatis**[1] *n term*
branches of the portal vein, hepatic artery, and the biliary [ɪ] ducts[2] bound [aʊ] together in the perivascular fibrous [aɪ] capsule as they enter at the liver hilum[1] [aɪ] (portal fissure)
portal[3] *adj term* • **triaditis** [aɪ] *n* • **port(a)-** *comb*

» The bile ducts[2] run with branches of the portal vein and hepatic artery in portal tracts situated between hepatic lobules. Hepatocytes are arranged in sheets or plates that radiate [eɪ] from each portal triad toward adjacent central veins. The portal vein terminates in the porta hepatis between the caudate and quadrate lobes by dividing into right and left lobar branches.

Use **portal** vein [eɪ] (*abbr* PV)/ vein thrombosis[4] (*abbr* PVT)/ lobule[5] • **portal** pressure[6] / (venous) tract / bile duct [ʌ]/ ductules [-juːlz] • **portal** venous flow (*abbr* PVF)/ inflow / system • **portal** circulation[7] /-systemic shunt[8] [ʌ]/ triaditis [aɪ]/ hypertension[9] • **portal** hypertensive gastropathy / decompression • **portal** of entry[10] • **porto**renal /caval [eɪ] shunt[11] /systemic encephalopathy[12] • **porto**graphy[13]

Periportalfeld, Glisson-Dreieck
Leberpforte, Porta hepatis[1] Gallengänge[2] portal, Pfortader-[3] Pfortaderthrombose[4] Leberläppchen[5] Pfortaderdruck[6] Pfortaderkreislauf[7] portosystemischer Shunt[8] Pfortaderhochdruck, portale Hypertension[9] Eintrittspforte[10] portokavaler Shunt[11] portokavale/ hepatoportale Enzephalopathie[12] Portografie[13]

5

hepatic duct [dʌkt] *n term*
part of the biliary [ɪ] duct system formed by the junction of right and left hepatic ducts
intrahepatic[1] *adj term* • **extrahepatic** *adj* • **ductule**[2] *n* • **ductular** *adj*

» The left lateral and left medial segmental ducts form the left hepatic duct. At the porta hepatis the hepatic duct is joined by the cystic duct to become the common bile [aɪ] duct.

Use right[3] / left[4] / common[5] **hepatic duct** • **intrahepatic** collecting system / microvasculature • **intrahepatic** hemodynamics / hematoma / abscess[6] / cava [eɪ] • **intrahepatic** hypertension[7] / branch of the portal vein • **extrahepatic** bile ducts[8] / biliary tree[8] / obstruction • **extrahepatic** cholestasis[9] [eɪ]/ jaundice[10] [dʒɔːndɪs]/ portal vein thrombosis • (terminal/ intrahepatic) bile[11] [aɪ] • **ductules** • **ductular** cells [s]/ epithelium [iː]/ hypoplasia[12] /haɪpoʊpleɪʒ(ɪ)ə/ proliferation

Lebergallengang, Ductus hepaticus
intrahepatisch[1] Kanälchen[2] Ductus hepaticus dexter[3] D. hepaticus sinister[4] D. hepaticus communis[5] Leberabszess, intrahepatischer Abszess[6] intrahepat. Pfortaderhochdruck[7] extrahepat. Gallengänge[8] extrahepat. Cholestase[9] extrahepat. Ikterus[10] Ductuli biliferi[11] Gallenganghypoplasie[12]

6

gallbladder [gɔːlblædɚ] *n clin & term*   *syn* **gall bladder** *n clin*
pear-shaped[1] [peə] organ on the undersurface [ɜː] of the liver which serves as a storage reservoir for bile
(chole)cystic[2] [koʊˈkɒːsɪstɪk] *adj term* • **gallstones**[3] *n* • **cholecyst(o)-** *comb*

» The gallbladder contracts to eject [ɪdʒekt] bile through the common bile duct into the duodenum. Fever and chills[4] [tʃ] are absent in uncomplicated gallbladder colic[5] [kɒlɪk]. Acute cholecystitis can lead to perforation of the gallbladder. Between meals, bile is stored in the gallbladder, where it is concentrated at rates of up to 20% per hour.

Use intact / (non)functioning / contracted[6] / distended **gallbladder** • enlarged[7] / palpable / (non)tender[8] **gallbladder** • (acutely) inflamed[9] [eɪ]/ calculous [kælkjələs]/ calcified [s] **gallbladder** • strawberry[10] [ɔː]/ tumor-laden [eɪ] **gallbladder** • **gallbladder** neck[11] / musculature [ʌ]/ contraction • **gallbladder** emptying[12] / inflammation[9] / stasis[13] [eɪ]/ disease • **gallbladder** calculi [aɪ] *or* stones[3] / cancer [s]/ perforation • **cholecyst**itis[9] /okinin (*abbr* CKK) /ogram /ectomy[14] /ostomy

Gallenblase, Vesica biliaris/ fellea
birnenförmig[1] Gallenblasen-[2] Gallensteine[3] Schüttelfrost[4] Gallenkolik[5] Schrumpfgallenblase[6] vergrößerte Gallenblase[7] druckschmerzhafte G.[8] Gallenblasenentzündung, Cholezystitis[9] Erdbeer-, Stippchengallenblase[10] Gallenblasenhals, Collum vesicae felleae[11] Gallenblasenentleerung[12] Gallestauung, Cholestase[13] Gallenblasenentfernung, Cholezystektomie[14]

7

cystic duct [sɪstɪk dʌkt] *n term*
bile duct which arises from the gallbladder and joins the hepatic duct to form the CBD

» Postcholecystectomy cystic duct leaks [iː] may be treated with endoscopic sphincterotomy to facilitate bile flow across the sphincter of Oddi[1]. Cholecystitis occurs when a stone becomes impacted[2] in the cystic duct and inflammation develops behind the obstruction. Transient cystic duct obstruction results in colicky pain[3], while persistent obstruction usually produces inflammation and acute cholecystitis [-aɪtɪs].

Use (markedly) narrowed[4] **cystic duct** • **cystic duct** leak [iː]/ remnant / obstruction[5]

Gallenblasengang, Ductus cysticus
Oddi-Sphinkter, M. sphincter Oddii[1] eingekeilt, impaktiert[2] kolikartige Schmerzen[3] Gallengangstenose[4] Zystikusverschluss[5]

8

common (bile) duct *n clin & term*, *abbr* CBD   *syn* **choledochus** *n term rare*
bile duct formed by the union of the hepatic and cystic ducts which opens into the duodenum
choledochal [koʊlədɒːkˈl‖koʊlədɑkˀl] *adj term* • **choledocho-** *comb*

» Determine whether the CBD is narrowed by the pancreatitis. The neck of the gallbladder tapers [eɪ] into the narrow cystic duct, which connects with the common duct. A cholangiogram should be obtained to verify patency[1] [eɪ] between the cystic and common bile ducts.

Use distal / terminal / extrahepatic **common bile duct** • **common bile duct** exploration[2] / patency / stone[3] • **common bile duct** obstruction / stricture[4] [strɪktʃɚ]/ stenosis • intrahepatic[5] / hilar [aɪ]/ extrahepatic **bile duct(s)** • **bile duct** stone *or* calculus / proliferation[6] / dilation [eɪ]/ adenoma[7] • **choledochal** cyst[8] / sphincteric resistance • **choledocho**lithiasis[9] [aɪə] /cele [-siːl]/scopy[10] /jejunostomy

(Ductus) choledochus, Gallengang
Durchgängigkeit[1] Choledochusrevision/ intraoperative Cholangioskopie[2] Choledochusstein[3] Choledochusstriktur[4] intrahepatische Gallengänge[5] Gallengangwucherung[6] Gallengangadenom[7] Choledochuszyste[8] Choledocholithiasis[9] Choledochoskopie[10]

9

Liver & Biliary System — BODY STRUCTURES & FUNCTIONS

hepatopancreatic ampulla [æmpʊlə‖æmpjuːlə] n term
syn **ampulla of Vater** n term

cavity formed by the CBD and the pancreatic duct[1] at their opening into the duodenum
ampullary adj term • **periampullary**[2] adj • **postampullary** adj

» Gallstones impacted in the ampulla of Vater may be removed endoscopically if the pancreatitis does not resolve[3] quickly. The stool [uː] may contain occult blood, but this is more common with tumors of the pancreas or hepatopancreatic ampulla than those of the bile ducts.

Use swollen **ampulla of Vater** • **ampullary** region [iː]/ spasm / stenosis[4] / carcinoma

Ampulla hepatopancreatica, Ampulla Vateri, Vater-Ampulle
Ductus pancreaticus[1] periampullär[2] abklingt[3] Stenose d. Ampulla hepatopancreatica[4]

10

bile [baɪl] n clin & term
rel **bile acid**[1] [æsɪd], **bile salt**[2], **bile pigment**[3] n term

fluid secreted [iː] by the liver which is discharged into the duodenum to aid in the emulsification of fats[4], increase peristalsis, and retard putrefaction[5]
biliary[6] [bɪliɚi] adj term • **bilious**[6] adj • **bili-** comb

» During fasting[7], bile holding capacity for cholesterol is more saturated than during high bile flow. Acute pancreatitis is a fairly common complication of calculous biliary disease[8]. Persistence of complete cholestasis warrants[9] diagnostic studies of the extrahepatic biliary tree. The rise in hepatic excretion of bile salts [ɔː] following each meal is a function of the increased concentration of portal vein bile acids coming from the ileum [ɪ].

Use black viscous[10] [sk]/ (extra)hepatic[11] / gallbladder[12] **bile** • **bile** duct / ductules[13] / canaliculi[14] / reflux [iː] • **bile** metabolism / production[15] / flow / drainage • **bile acid** secretion [iː]/-binding [aɪ] resin[16] / pool[17] • **bile acid** sequestrant[18] / breath [e] test[19] / excretion • conjugated[20] / unconjugated[21] [dʒ] **bile acids** • primary [aɪ]/ free / reabsorbed **bile acids** • **bile salt** uptake[22]/ metabolism / malabsorption • **bile salt**-induced diarrhea[23] [iː]/ micelle [aɪ] • **bile** stasis[24] [eɪ]/ leak / peritonitis [aɪ] • **bile** ascites[25] [aɪ]/ cast[26] [æ]/-stained [eɪ] • **biliary** tract / system / duct (wall/ thickening/ stricture • **biliary** epithelium [iː]/ cholesterol / lipids • **biliary** leak / obstruction / stricture • **biliary** pain[27] / colic[27] / cirrhosis[28] • **bilious** gastric residual / emesis or vomiting[29] • **bili**genesis[15]

Galle(nflüssigkeit)
Gallensäure[1] Gallensalz[2] Gallenfarbstoff[3] Fettemulgierung[4] Zersetzung, Fäulnis[5] biliär, biliös, gallig, Galle-[6] Fasten, Nahrungskarenz[7] Gallensteinerkrankung[8] erfordert[9] pleiochrome zähflüssige Galle[10] Lebergalle[11] Blasengalle[12] Ductuli biliferi[13] Canaliculi biliferi, Gallenkanälchen, -kapillaren[14] Galle(n)produktion[15] gallensäurebindendes Harz[16] Gallensäurepool[17] Gallensand[18] 14C-Glykocholat Atemtest[19] konjugierte Gallensäuren[20] dekonjugierte G.[21] Gallensalzaufnahme[22] Gallensalzmangeldiarrhoe, cholo-gene Diarrhoe[23] Galle(n)stauung[24] galliger Aszites, Cholaskos[25] Gallethromben, -zylinder[26] Gallenkolik[27] biliäre Zirrhose[28] Vomitus biliosus, Galleerbrechen[29]

11

cholesterol [kəlɛstərɒl] n term → U78-16
rel **cholic** [oʊ] **acid**[1], **phospholipid**[2] [ɪ] n term

steroid [ɪɚ] alcohol synthesized in the liver (also absorbed from animal-derived foods); it is a precursor [ɜː] of bile salts, steroid hormones and plays a role in the formation of gallstones
cholesteatosis[3] [-stɪətoʊsɪs] n term • **cholester-** comb • **cholic** adj • **chol(e)-** comb

» The primary bile acids, cholic and chenodeoxycholic acids[4], are synthesized from cholesterol in the liver and excreted [iː] into the bile. Cholic acid is converted [ɜː] to deoxycholic acid[5] [æsɪd]. The major lipids [ɪ] of the lipoproteins are cholesterol, triglycerides [traɪglɪs-], and phospholipids.

Use high blood[6] / biliary / dietary [aɪə]/ free[7] / low-density lipoprotein[8] / HDL[9] **cholesterol** • **cholesterol**-rich / intake /-lowering diet[10] / ester / crystals [ɪ] • **cholesterol** stones[11] / embolism[12] / elevation[13] / **cholesterol**emia[6] [iː] / lithocholic acid[14] / **chol**angioles /(e)uria • **phospholipid**-binding plasma proteins[15] / content / synthesis / vesicles • negatively charged[16] **phospholipids** • anti**phospholipid** antibody[17]

Cholesterin, Cholesterol
Cholsäure[1] Phospholipid[2] Cholesteatose, Cholesterinose, Cholesterosis[3] Chenodesoxycholsäure[4] Desoxycholsäure[5] erhöhter Serumcholesterinspiegel, Hypercholesterinämie[6] freies Cholesterin[7] LDL-C.[8] HDL-C.[9] cholesterinsenkende Diät[10] Cholesterinsteine[11] Cholesterinembolie[12] Erhöhung d. Cholesterinspiegels[13] Lithocholsäure[14] phospholipidbindende Plasmaproteine[15] negativ geladene Phospholipide[16] Antiphospholipid-Antikörper[17]

12

bilirubin [uː] n term
rel **biliverdin**[1] [ɜː], **urobilinogen**[2] [-baɪlɪnɔdʒ³n] n term

red bile pigment formed from hemoglobin during destruction of erythrocytes by the RES[3]

» Bilirubin is excreted in bile as a mixture of degradation products[4] of heme [hiːm] compounds from worn-out RBCs. Complete bile duct obstruction blocks excretion of bilirubin into the gut[5] [ʌ] and results in disappearance of urobilinogen from the urine. Failure to excrete the bilirubin produced by hemolysis [hiːmɒlɪsɪs] causes jaundice[6] [dʒɔːndɪs].

Use (in)direct[7] / urine / serum [ɪɚ]/ total[8] / (un)conjugated[7] [dʒɚ] **bilirubin** • **bilirubin** concentration or level / overload • **bilirubin** diglucuronide[7] [aɪ]/ turnover[9] • **bilirubin**uria[10] /emia • portal / urinary / fecal [iː] or stool [uː] **urobilinogen**

Bilirubin
Biliverdin[1] Urobilinogen[2] retikuloendotheliales System[3] Abbauprodukte[4] Darm[5] Gelbsucht[6] direktes/konjugiertes Bilirubin, Bilirubindiglukuronid[7] Gesamtbilirubin[8] Bilirubinumsatz[9] Bilirubinurie, Bilirubinausscheidung im Harn[10]

13

BODY STRUCTURES & FUNCTIONS — Liver & Biliary System

glycogen [glaɪkədʒən] *n term*   *syn* **liver or animal starch** [stɑːrtʃ] *n clin*

highly branched[1] glucosan of high molecular weight found in most of the tissues of the body, esp. in the liver and muscle; it is the principal carbohydrate reserve as it is readily [e] converted into glucose → U78-13f

» The liver stores energy in the form of glycogen. Impairment of liver function in alcoholics may prevent adequate glycogen storage and promote a tendency to hypoglycemia[2] [-glaɪsiːmɪə] from inability to mobilize glucose.

Use hepatic *or* liver[3] / muscle [ʌ]/ stored **glycogen** • **glycogen** phosphorylase[4] [eɪ]/ synthase[5] [-eɪsǁz]/ synthesis[6] [ɪ]/ breakdown[7] • **glycogen** metabolism[8] / depletion [iːʃ]/ storage (disease)[9] • **glycogen**ase /ic /esis[6] /olysis[7] /osis[9]

Glykogen

stark verzweigt[1] Hypoglykämie[2] Leberglykogen[3] Glykogenphosphorylase[4] Glykogensynthetase[5] Glykogenese, Glykogensynthese[6] Glykogenabbau, Glykogenolyse[7] Glykogenstoffwechsel[8] Glykogenspeicherkrankheit, Glykogenose[9]

14

---

alkaline [-ɪnǁ-aɪn] **phosphatase** *n term, abbr* **ALP**

rel **acid phosphatase**[1] [-eɪz] *n term*

enzyme produced in the liver and bone; high serum [ɪə] levels are a useful diagnostic parameter in hepatic obstruction, hepatitis [aɪ], and bone disease

» In noncholestatic conjugated hyperbilirubinemia [iː] transaminase and alkaline phosphatase levels are usually normal. When the serum alkaline phosphatase level is elevated[2], serum 5-prime-nucleotidase [aɪ], which parallels liver alkaline phosphatase, should be measured to determine if the increase is from the liver or bone.

Use serum/ leukocyte[3] [uː] (abbr LAP)/ neutrophil [(j)uː] **alkaline phosphatase** • liver *or* hepatic / placental[4] [se] **alkaline phosphatase** • **alkaline phosphatase** activity[5] / concentration / determination • **alkaline phosphatase** elevation[6] / value *or* level • serum / tartrate-resistant[7] (abbr TRAP)/ prostatic[8] **acid phosphatase**

---

alkalische Phosphatase, AP

saure Phosphatase, SP[1] erhöht[2] alkalische Leukozytenphosphatase[3] Plazenta-AP[4] AP-Aktivität[5] AP-Erhöhung[6] tartratstabile saure Phosphatase[7] saure Prostataphosphatase[8]

15

---

alanine [ælənɪːn] **aminotransferase** [-eɪz] *n term, abbr* **ALT**

syn (**serum**) **glutamic pyruvic** [paɪruː-] **transaminase** *n term, abbr* **SGPT**

enzyme transferring amino groups from alanine to (alpha)-ketoglutarate or from glutamate to pyruvate

de**aminase**[1] *n term* • de/ **transamination**[2] *n* • **glutamine**[3] *n* • **glutamate**[4] *n*

» Elevated SGPT (ALT) due to liver damage may be found in iron [aɪ] poisoning[5]. In cirrhosis of the liver AST is usually elevated more than ALT. Amino acids are utilized for the synthesis of liver intracellular proteins, plasma proteins, and special compounds[6] [aʊ] such as glutathione[7] [aɪ], glutamine, taurine [ɔː], and creatine [iːə].

Use aspartate *or* serum glutamic oxaloacetic[8] (abbr SGOT)/ hepatic **transaminase** • **transaminase** activity / elevation • aspartate[8] (abbr AST) **aminotransferase** • **glutamine**-containing peptide [aɪ]/ extraction • **glutamine** deficiency[9] [ɪʃ]/ synthetase[10] [ɪ] • **glutamate** dehydrogenase[11] [-dʒəneɪz]/ decarboxylase[12] / transporter / receptor • **glutamic** acid residues[13] / dehydrogenase[11]

Alaninaminotransferase, (Serum-)Glutamat-Pyruvat-Transaminase, (S)GPT

Desaminase[1] Transaminierung[2] Glutamin[3] Glutamat[4] Eisenvergiftung[5] Verbindungen[6] Glutathion[7] Aspartataminotransferase, Glutamat-Oxalacetat-Transaminase[8] Glutaminmangel[9] Glutaminsynthetase[10] Glutamatdehydrogenase[11] Glutamatdecarboxylase[12] Glutamatsäurereste[13]

16

---

ethanol [eθənɒːl] *n term*

sim **methanol**[1], **butanol**[2] [juː], **glycol**[3] [aɪ] *n term* → U10-2, U82-13

ethyl [eθɪl] alcohol (also called grain [eɪ] alcohol), the intoxicating agent contained in liquor[4]

» Ethanol absorbed from the small bowel[5] is carried directly to the liver, where it becomes the preferred [ɜː] fuel. Ethanol competes with methanol for metabolism by alcohol dehydrogenase and increases the elimination half-life of methanol to 30 to 35 h. With repeated exposure to ethanol, severe changes in liver functioning are likely to occur, e.g. fatty accumulation, hepatitis, perivenular sclerosis, and cirrhosis. Oxidation of ethanol in the liver generates high concentrations of nicotinamide adenine dinucleotide[6] (NAD) which blocks gluconeogenesis[7] from pyruvate and leads to decreased hepatic glucose output and hypoglycemia.

Use blood[8] **ethanol** • **ethanol** consumption[9] [ʌ]/ abuse[10] / intoxication / withdrawal[11] [-ɔːəl] • **methanol** poisoning[12]

Ethanol, Äthanol, Äthylalkohol, Alkohol

Methanol, Methylalkohol[1] Butanol, Butylalkohol[2] Glykol[3] Spirituosen[4] Dünndarm[5] Nikotinsäureamidadenindinukleotid[6] Glukoneogenese, Neubildung v. Glukose[7] Blutalkohol[8] Alkoholkonsum[9] Alkoholmissbrauch, -abusus[10] Alkoholentzug[11] Methanolvergiftung[12]

17

---

ammonia [əmoʊnɪə] *n term*   *rel* **urea**[1] [jʊriːəǁjʊərɪə] *n term* → U49-13

toxic product of nitrogen [aɪ] metabolism[2] which readily forms ammonium compounds; it is metabolized in the liver (Krebs-Henseleit cycle[3]) and is mostly excreted by the kidney

ammoniacal[4] *adj term* • **ammonium**[5] *n* • **ammoniate**[6] [-eɪt] *v*

» The liver removes [uː] ammonia from the body fluids by converting [ɜː] it to urea in a cyclic [saɪklɪk] process. A markedly elevated blood ammonia usually reflects severe hepatocellular injury. Unlike ammonia, urea itself does not produce CNS toxicity.

Use serum [ɪə]/ blood **ammonia** • **ammonia** odor[7] [oʊdər]/ level[8] / production • **ammonia** concentration / excretion [iːʃ]/ intoxication[9] / water[10] • **ammonium** carbonate / chloride [aɪ]/ phosphate / ion [aɪən] / radical • **urea** cycle[3] [saɪkl] (enzyme) / nitrogen [aɪ]/ clearance[11] [ɪə]/ breath [e] test / hydrolysis[12]

Ammoniak

Harnstoff, Urea[1] Stickstoffwechsel[2] Harnstoffzyklus, Krebs-Henseleit-Zyklus[3] ammoniakhaltig, ammoniakalisch[4] Ammonium[5] mit Ammoniak behandeln/ mischen[6] Ammoniakgeruch[7] Ammoniakspiegel[8] Ammoniakintoxikation[9] wässrige Ammoniaklösung, Salmiakgeist[10] Harnstoffclearance[11] Harnstoffspaltung[12]

18

Unit 48 Kidneys & the Urinary Tract
Related Units: 49 Urine Production, 50 Female Sexual Organs, 52 Male Sexual Organs, 112 Urologic Signs

urinary [jʊɚɪneri] **tract** [æ] *or* **system** *n term*   *syn* **waterworks** *n pl clin & inf*
organs and their interconnections that facilitate[1] [sɪ] elimination of excess filtered fluids from the body
urogenital[2] [jʊɚoʊdʒen-] *adj term* • **genitourinary**[2] [dʒenɪtoʊ-] *adj*
» Try to determine if the dilated [daɪleɪ-] upper urinary tract is obstructed [ʌ]. Obtain [eɪ] a detailed history focusing on the urinary tract, complemented by a physical examination including a digital rectal examination of the prostate and a focused neurologic examination.
Use upper / lower[3] **urinary tract** • **urinary tract** infection[4] (*abbr* UTI) • **urinary** meatus[5] [ieɪ]/ output[6] / excretion [iː] • **urinary** stream[7] / flow(rate) / calcium [s]/ osmolality / sediment[8] • **urinary** obstruction[9] [ʌ]/ diversion[10] [ɜː]/ retention[11] / calculi[12] • **genitourinary system** (*abbr* GUS) assessment • **GU** organs / anomaly

Harntrakt, Harnorgane
ermöglichen[1] urogenital[2] ableitende Harnwege[3] Harnwegsinfektion[4] Meatus/ Ostium urethrae[5] Urinproduktion, -menge[6] Harnstrahl[7] Harnsediment[8] Harnabflussbehinderung[9] Harnableitung[10] Harnretention, -verhalt(ung)[11] Harnsteine[12]

1

kidney [kɪdni] *n clin & term*
paired [peəd] bean-shaped[1] [iː] organ that filters the serum [sɪɚəm], excretes [iː] the urine [jʊɚɪn], and helps regulate the body fluids
renal [riːnəl] *adj term* • **ren(o)-** *comb* • **nephr(o)-** [nefroʊ] *comb*
» The kidneys produce and eliminate urine through a complex filtration and reabsorption system comprising [aɪ] more than 2 million nephrons. Ultrasound [ʌ] can identify the renal cortex[2], medulla[3], pyramids[4] [ɪ] and a dilated collecting system or ureter.
Use contracted[5] / (poly)cystic[6] [sɪ]/ arteriosclerotic / supernumerary[7] [uː] **kidney** • shrunken[5] [ʌ]/ floating [oʊ] *or* hypermobile[8] [oʊ]/ fatty **kidney** • duplex[9] [uː]/ horse-shoe[10] / medullary sponge[11] [ʌ] **kidney** • contralateral / solitary[12] / poorly functioning / normal-sized **kidney** • unaffected[13] [æ]/ cadaver[14] [æ]/ donor[15] [oʊ]/ obstructed **kidney** • **kidney**-shaped lobe [oʊ]/ failure[16] / stone[17] / ureter and bladder (*abbr* KUB) film • **renal** sinus [aɪ]/ hilum *or* hilus[18] [aɪ]/ pedicle[18] / pole [oʊ] • **renal** capsule[19] / column[20] / calculus[17] [kjə]/ failure[16] • **nephr**itis /opathy /osis /otomy /otoxic • **reno**gram[21] /trophic factor /-vascular hypertension

Niere, Ren
bohnenförmig[1] Nierenrinde, Cortex renalis[2] Nierenmark, Medulla renalis[3] Nierenpyramiden, Pyramides renales[4] Schrumpfniere[5] Zystenniere[6] überzählige N.[7] Wanderniere, Ren mobilis[8] Nierenverdopplung, R. duplex[9] Hufeisenniere, R. arcuatus[10] (Mark)schwammniere[11] Einzelniere[12] gesunde N.[13] Leichenniere[14] Spenderniere[15] Nierenversagen[16] Nierenstein[17] Nierenhilus, -stiel, Hilum renale[18] Nierenkapsel[19] Bertin-Säulen, Columnae renales[20] Nephrogramm[21]

2

renal pelvis *n term*   *syn* **pyelon** [paɪəlɒːn] *n term rare*
funnel-shaped[1] [ʌ] ureteral expansion into the kidney collecting the urine from the calices
(intra)pelvic *adj term* • **pyelo-** [paɪəloʊ] *comb*
» The renal pelvis and calices are within the renal sinus and function as the main collecting reservoir. The renal medulla is made up of a series of pyramids the papillae[2] [iː] of which project into the minor calix, which join to form the major calices and in turn the renal pelvis.
Use dilated [eɪ] *or* overdistended[3] / (non)obstructed / hydronephrotic **renal pelvis** • **pyelo**plasty[4] /nephritis[5] [aɪ] /tomy /gram[6] • **renal pelvic** urine / pressure / stone / drainage [eɪ] • kidney / double *or* duplex **pyelon**

Nierenbecken, Pyelon
trichterförmig[1] Nierenpapillen, Papillae renales[2] erweitertes/ dilatiertes Nierenbecken[3] Nierenbecken-, Pyeloplastik[4] Pyelonephritis[5] Pyelogramm[6]

3

(renal) calyx [kælɪks] *pl* **-ices** [kælɪsiːz] *n term*   *syn* **calix** *n term*
flower-shaped recess [iː] of the pelvis into which the orifices of the renal pyramids [ɪ] project
calyceal *or* **caliceal** [kælɪsiːəl] *adj term*
» The pelvis was distended and there were branching calices with a normal renal cortex.
Use major [eɪdʒ]/ minor [aɪ] **calyx** • irregular **calices** • **calyceal** system[1] / infundibulum [ʌ]/ deformity / diverticulum[2] • **calyceal** neck stenosis[3] / fornix / stone / enlargement • lower pole [oʊ]/ anterior [ɪɚ]/ branching / debris-filled [iː] **calyces**

Nierenkelch, Calyx renalis
Kelchsystem[1] (Nieren)kelchdivertikel[2] renale Kelchhalsstenose[3]

4

nephron [nefrɒːn] *n term*   *rel* **renal** *or* **uriniferous tubule**[1] [t(j)uːbjʊl] *n term*
long convoluted tubular functional unit of the kidney consisting of the renal corpuscle [ʌ], the proximal convoluted tubule[2], the nephronic loop [uː], and the distal convoluted tubule[3]
» At the end of the proximal tubule[4] the nephron dives toward the medulla attaching to the thin limb of Henle's loop. The uriniferous tubule includes the nephron and the collecting tubule[5].
Use (im)mature [-tjʊɚ]/ cortical / juxtamedullary[6] [dʒʌkstə-]/ proximal / distal / surviving [aɪ] **nephron**

Nephron (das)
Nieren-, Harnkanälchen, Tubulus renalis[1] T. contortus proximalis, proximales Konvolut[2] Pars convoluta d. distalen Tubulus, T. contortus distalis[3] proximaler Tubulus[4] Sammelrohr[5] juxtamedulläres Nephron[6]

5

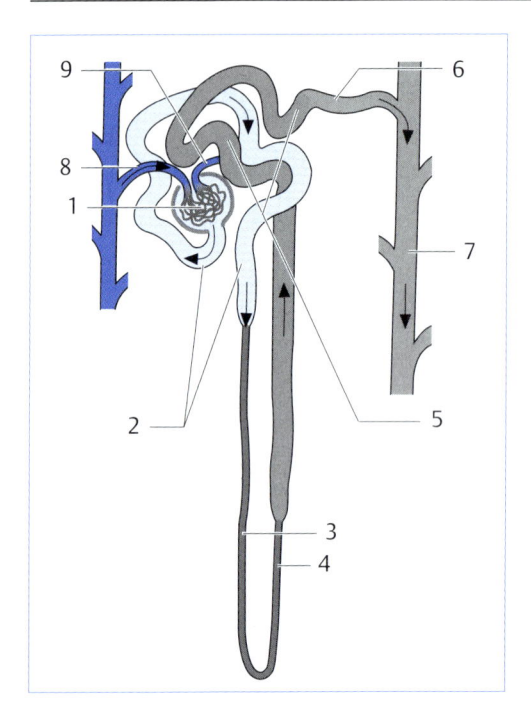

Nephron (schematic drawing):
glomerulus (**1**),
proximal convoluted tubule (**2**),
loop of Henle, descending limb (**3**),
ascending limb (**4**),
distal convoluted tubule (**5**),
junctional or connecting tubule (**6**),
collecting duct (**7**),
afferent arteriole (**8**),
efferent arteriole (**9**)

---

renal or **Malpighian corpuscle** n term   rel **glomerulus**[1] n term, pl **-i** [aɪ]

composed of a tuft [ʌ] of capillary loops[2] [uː] which is surrounded by Bowman's [oʊ] capsule[3]
glomerular adj term • **glomerul(o)-** comb • **juxtaglomerular** [dʒʌkstə-] adj

» The renal corpuscle or body is composed of the glomerulus and the glomerular capsule[3]. The glomeruli which produce an ultrafiltrate of the plasma comprise the capillary, afferent and efferent arterioles, juxtaglomerular apparatus[4] [eɪ] and Bowman's space[5] and capsule.

Use juxtamedullary **glomeruli** • **glomerular** capillary (pressure) / (capillary) tuft[6] / wall /arteriole [ɪə] • **glomerular** basement [eɪ] membrane[7] / function / filtration (rate) • **glomerular** filtrate[8] / damage / injury / lesion [iː] / sclerosis[9] • at the **glomerular** level • Bowman's capsular resistance / space[5] • **juxtaglomerular** cells[10] / hyperplasia [eɪ] • **glomerulo**pathy /nephritis [aɪ] /sclerosis[9]

Malpighi-, Nierenkörperchen, Corpusculum renale/ renis
Glomerulus[1] Kapillarschlingen[2] Bowman-Kapsel, Capsula glomeruli[3] juxtaglomerulärer Apparat[4] Bowman-Raum[5] glomeruläres Kapillarknäuel[6] Glomerulusbasalmembran[7] Glomerulusfiltrat[8] Glomerulosklerose[9] Goormaghtigh-Zellen, juxtaglomeruläre Zellen[10]

6

---

convoluted tubule [t(j)uːbjʊl] n term   syn **tubulus renalis contortus** n term

highly convoluted segments of the nephron in the renal labyrinth; the distal convoluted tubule leads from the ascending [se] limb [lɪm] of Henle's loop to the collecting tube

tubular [t(j)uːbjʊlə] adj term • **intra/ peritubular** adj

» The proximal convoluted tubules transport fluid from Bowman's capsule to the descending limb of Henle's loop.

Use distal / proximal **convoluted tubules** • renal or uriniferous[1] / collecting / glomerular / straight[2] **tubules** • **tubular** urine / epithelium [iː] / lumen [uː] / necrosis[3] • **tubule** function / fluid (flow) / pressure reabsorption • **tubule** secretion / balance / permeability

Tubulus renalis contortus
Nieren-, Harnkanälchen[1] gerade Nierenkanälchen, Tubuli recti[2] Tubulusnekrose[3]

7

---

loop of Henle n term   syn **nephronic** or **Henle's loop** [luːp] n term

U-shaped part of the nephron in the renal medulla consisting of a descending[1] and an ascending limb[2]

» The longer the loop of Henle gets in children, the higher is the concentration of urea[3] [jʊriːə] in the renal papilla, thus improving the concentrating ability.

Use descending[1] [dɪse-]/ ascending[2] / thin / thick / long / short **loop of Henle** • **loop diuretic**[4] [daɪjʊəretɪk]

Henle-Schleife
Pars descendens, absteigender Schenkel[1] Pars ascendens, aufsteigender Schenkel[2] Urea, Harnstoff[3] Schleifendiuretikum[4]

8

Kidneys & the Urinary Tract BODY STRUCTURES & FUNCTIONS **197**

collecting tubule or **tube** [tjuːb] n term   rel **collecting system**[1] [ɪ] n term

large, straight [streɪt] tubules draining the urine from the distal convoluted tubules to the renal pelvis

» The collecting tubules play a key role in maintaining body fluid balance[2]. The entire collecting system is covered with a pale, white, smooth [uː] urothelium [iː].

Use **collecting** duct[3] [ʌ] • upper / entire [aɪ]/ urinary / renal / lower pole **collecting system** • grossly [oʊ] dilated[4] / obstructed / duplicated[5] [uː] **collecting system** • **collecting system** surface area

---

ureter [jʊəətəɹ‖jʊriːtəɹ] n term

thick-walled tube transporting the urine from the renal pelvis to the bladder

(intra-/ peri-)**ureteral** adj term • **ureter**(o)- comb • **ureteric** [jʊəɹɪtɛrɪk] adj BE

» Urine is propelled down the ureter by propagated contractions and enters the bladder in squirts[1] [ɜː]. Bacteria [ɪəɹ] may ascend in the ureter against the flow of urine and cause upper urinary tract infection.

Use distal / lowermost / upper • abdominal[2] **ureter** • pelvic[3] / intravesical / juxtavesical **ureter** • ectopic / (non)affected **ureter** • mega-[4]/ hydro-[5] [aɪ]/ mid-**ureter** • **ureteral** orifice or opening[6] / lumen / wall / vessels • **ureteral** pressure / contraction • peristalsis[7] / reflux [iː] • **ureteral** spasm / obstruction / calculi[8] [aɪ]/ stenosis[9] [oʊ] • **ureteral** perforation or tear [teəɹ]/ dilation • **uretero**lysis [ɪ] /gram /scope /pelvic junction[10] [dʒʌ] (abbr UPJ) • **uretero**cele [-siːl]/neocystostomy[11] • **ureteric** contraction / pressure / bud[12] [ʌ]/ catheter • **ureteric** stones[8] / stent / reimplantation • pelvi-**ureteric** junction[10]

(urinary) bladder [blædəɹ] n term   rel **detrusor (muscle)**[1] [dɪtruːzəɹ mʌsl] n term

musculomembranous [sk] sac serving as a storage for the urine; it is lined[2] with urothelium[3] [iː] and consists of the trigone [aɪ] (urethral [iː] and ureteral orifices) at the base [eɪ] and the bladder dome[4] [oʊ] (mainly the detrusor muscle)

cystic [sɪstɪk] adj term • **cyst**(o)- comb

» Functional bladder neck obstruction[5] prevents emptying even with sustained [eɪ] detrusor contraction. There was impaired [eəɹ] detrusor contractility and abnormal bladder sensation.

Use **bladder** body[6] / dome / neck or outlet[7] / wall / filling • **bladder** capacity[8] / volume / control / emptying[9] • **bladder** compliance [aɪ]/ distention / washout[10] / training • **bladder** instability / outlet obstruction[5] / stones[11] • irritable[12] / neurogenic[13] [dʒɛ]/ automatic[14] [ɒː]/ contracted[15] **bladder** • **cysto**metry /scopy /graphy /cele • **detrusor** function / activity / fibers [aɪ] contractions • **detrusor** failure[16] [eɪ]/ outlet dyssynergia[17] [ɜː] • **detrusor** overactivity[18] / hyperreflexia[19] / instability[19] • hypotonic [aɪ]/ poorly contractile **detrusor**

(bladder) trigone [traɪɡoʊn] n term   syn **vesical** [vɛsɪkəl] **trigone** n term

triangular area of the bladder between the orifices[1] [ɔːrɪfɪsiːz] of the ureters and the urethra

trigonal adj term • (-)**vesical** adj term & comb • **vesico-** comb

» Any stretch of the trigone (with bladder filling[2]) or any trigonal contraction (with voiding[3]) leads to firm [ɜː] occlusion [uːʒ] of the intravesical ureter.

Use abnormal / superficial [ɪʃ] **trigone** • **trigonal** area / anatomy / cyst [sɪst] / function • **vesical** fistula / calculi or stones[4] • intra/ extra/ infra/ peri**vesical** • **perivesical** fat / lymphatics • **vesico**ureteral reflux[5]

---

urethra [jʊriːθrə] n term

tube that drains [eɪ] urine from the bladder to the exterior [ɪəɹ] of the body

urethral adj term • **urethr**(o)- comb • intra/ peri/ bulbourethral [ʌ] adj

» In females the urethra (only about 4 cm in length) is in close relation with the anterior wall of the vagina, and opens into the vestibule behind the clitoris. The urethral sphincter muscle surrounds the membranous urethra.

Use female [iː]/ male / prostatic[1] / membranous[2] / bulbous / penile or pendulous[3] **urethra** • **urethral** wall / valves[4] / orifice[5] / sphincter / specimen / stricture[6] / stump • **urethral** smear[7] [ɪəɹ]/ smooth [uː] muscle / resistance / obstruction / inflammation[8] [eɪ] • **urethral** meatus / discharge[9] / dilation[10] [eɪʃ]/ (closure) pressure • **urethr**algia [dʒ]/ectomy /itis[8] • **urethro**spasm /perineal /rectal /cele /cystography

---

Sammelrohr, Tubulus renalis colligens
Sammel-, Nierenbeckenkelchsystem[1] Flüssigkeitshaushalt[2] Sammelrohr[3] Verdopplung d. Nierenbeckenkelchsystems[4] stark erweitertes/ dilatiertes Nierenbeckenkelchsystem[5]   **9**

Harnleiter, Ureter
stoßweise[1] Pars abdominalis[2] Pars pelvina[3] Megaureter[4] Hydroureter[5] Harnleitermündung, Ostium ureteris[6] Ureterperistaltik[7] Ureter-, Harnleitersteine[8] Ureterstenose[9] Ureterabgang[10] Ureterneozystostomie, Neueinpflanzung d. Harnleiters i. d. Blase[11] Ureterknospe[12]

10

Harnblase, Vesica urinaria
M. detrusor vesicae, Detrusor, Harnblasenmuskulatur[1] ausgekleidet[2] Übergangsepithel, Epithelium transistonale, Urothel[3] Blasengrund, Fundus vesicae[4] Blasenhalsobstruktion[5] Blasenkörper, Corpus vesicae[6] Blasenhals, Cervix vesicae[7] Blasenkapazität[8] Blasenentleerung[9] Blasenspülung, Blasenspülzytologie[10] Blasensteine[11] Reizblase[12] neurogene Blase[13] Reflexblase[14] Schrumpfblase[15] Detrusorinsuffizienz[16] Detrusor-Sphinkter-Dyssynergie[17] Detrusorhyperaktivität[18] Detrusorinstabilität, hyperreflexiver Detrusor[19]   **11**

Blasendreieck, Trigonum vesicae
Ostia[1] Blasenfüllung[2] Blasenentleerung[3] Blasensteine[4] vesikoureteraler Reflux[5]

12

Harnröhre, Urethra
Pars prostatica (urethrae masculinae)[1] Pars membranacea[2] Pars spongiosa[3] Urethralklappen[4] Harnröhrenöffnung, -mündung, Ostium urethrae[5] Harnröhrenverengung, -striktur[6] Urethra(l)abstrich[7] Harnröhrenentzündung, Urethritis[8] Urethrorrhoe, Harnröhrenausfluss[9] Harnröhrenaufdehnung, -bougierung[10]

13

urethral sphincter [sfɪŋktɚ] *n term*   *syn* **rhabdo(urinary)** [æ] **sphincter** *n term*
narrow omega-shaped muscle around the urethra just distal to the apex [eɪ] of the prostate gland; in the female more generally distributed around the urethra
sphincteric *adj term* • **sphincter(o)-** *comb*

» External urethral sphincter contraction was absent. The fascia [fæʃ(ɪ)ə] of the striated [aɪeɪ] urethral sphincter was described as being inseparable from the prostatic sheath[1] [iː].

Use internal[2] / external **urethral sphincter** • **sphincter** activity / control / spasm / tone[3] • **sphincteric** mechanism [k]/ muscle / ring • **sphinctero**plasty[4] /tomy

Musculus sphincter urethrae, Rhabdosphinkter, Harnröhrenschließmuskel
periprostatische Faszie[1] Musculus sphincter vesicae internus, innerer Harnröhrensphinkter, Lissosphinkter[2] Sphinktertonus[3] Sphinkterplastik[4]

14

urogenital [dʒe] **diaphragm** *n term*   *rel* **pelvic diaphragm**[1] [daɪəfræm] *n term*
muscles in the pelvic floor[2] extending between the ischiopubic [sk] rami [reɪmaɪ]; composed of the external urethral sphincter and the deep transverse [ɜː] perineal [iː] muscle[3] [ʌ]

» The concept of the urogenital diaphragm surrounding the membranous urethra (implying an extrinsic portion of the striated[4] sphincter of the urethra) was not confirmed [ɜː] in these studies.

Diaphragma urogenitale
Diaphragma pelvis[1] Beckenboden[2] Musculus transversus perinei profundus[3] quergestreift[4]

15

Unit 49 Urine Production & Elimination

Related Units: 48 Urinary Tract, 78 Metabolism, 88 Physiology, 50 Female Sexual Organs, 52 Male Sexual Organs, 55 Hormones, 112 Urologic Signs & Symptoms

(glomerular) filtrate [fɪltreɪt] *n term*   *syn* **product of filtration** *n*
fluid containing metabolic waste [eɪ] products[1] passed through the glomerular filter
filter[2] *v & n* • **filtration**[3] *n* • **ultrafiltrate**[4] [ʌ] *n term* • **filterable**[5] *adj*

» Glucose is freely filtered in the glomerulus and then reabsorbed. Apart from being protein-free, the composition of the glomerular filtrate[6] is about the same as that of the blood plasma.

Use to enter/reabsorb/secrete [iː] into **the filtrate** • amount [aʊ]/ flow [oʊ]/ transport **of filtrate** • **filtered** (sodium) load[7] [oʊ] • **filtration** pressure[8] / rate[9] / fraction[10] [fræk.ʃ°n] • **filtration** membrane / barrier / process • net / plasma **filtration** • **filtrate** reabsorption[11]

(Glomerulus)filtrat
Stoffwechselendprodukte[1] filtrieren, filtern; Filter[2] Filtration[3] Ultrafiltrat[4] filtrierbar[5] Glomerulusfiltrat[6] filtrierte Natriumbelastung[7] Filtrationsdruck[8] Filtrationsrate[9] Filtrationsfraktion[10] Filtratrückresorption[11]

1

glomerular filtration rate *n term, abbr* **GFR**
   rel **renal** [iː] **plasma** [æ] **flow**[1] *n term, abbr* **RPF**
amount of fluid filtered out of the plasma through glomerular capillary walls into Bowman's [oʊ] capsules per unit time; equivalent to inulin clearance yet creatinine or DTPA[2] is used for clinical assessment

» To measure [eʒ] the GFR, inulin would be ideal, for it is freely filtered at the glomerulus but neither secreted or reabsorbed by the tubules. The GFR was determined by measurement of creatinine clearance. The effective renal plasma flow[3] (abbr ERPF) is the amount of plasma flowing to the parts of the kidney that have a function in urine production.

Use changes in / drop or decline [aɪ] or reduction [ʌ] or decrease [i] or fall in **GFR** • total / (near-) normal / elevated **GFR** • assessment or determination or measurement of[4] **GFR** • increased / effective[3] / total **renal plasma flow**

glomeruläre Filtrationsrate, GFR
renaler Plasmafluss, RPF[1] DTPA, Kalziumtrinatriumdiäthylentriaminpentaessigsäure[2] effektiver renaler Plasmafluss[3] Bestimmung der glomerulären Filtrationsrate[4]

2

(tubular) [t(j)uːbjʊlɚ] **transport** *n term*   *rel* **solvent drag**[1] [sɒlvənt] *n term*
passage of ions [aɪənz] or molecules across a cell membrane not by passive diffusion but by energy-consuming processes within the cell
transport *v term* • **transportation** *n* • **co(-)transport**[2] *n* → U78-17

» Transport of filtrate from the tubular lumen to interstitial [ɪʃ] fluid or peritubular capillaries is called reabsorption, and transport from the capillary to the tubular lumen is termed secretion [iː]. Many reabsorbed substances [ʌ] are actively transported, thus having the potential to saturate the carrier mechanism [ek]. The transport maximum[3] (abbr T_m) is the amount of a substance that can still be actively transported when all carriers[4] are saturated.

Use to block/impair[5] [eɚ]/ensure[6]/be involved in[7] **transport** • electrolyte [-laɪt]/ sodium / urine [jʊə] **transport** • active[8] / passive / carrier-mediated[9] [iː] **transport** • one-way / bidirectional[10] / antegrade **transport** • **transport** capacity[11] / system • **transport** mechanism / properties / proteins[12]

(tubulärer) Transport
konvektiver Teilchenfluss[1] Symport, gekoppelter Transport[2] Transportmaximum, maximale tubuläre Transportleistung, Tm[3] Carrier, Träger(substanzen)[4] den Transport beeinträchtigen[5] d. Transport gewährleisten[6] am Transport beteiligt sein[7] aktiver Transport[8] Carriertransport, trägervermittelter Transport[9] bidirektionaler Transport[10] Transportkapazität[11] Transportproteine[12]

3

Urine Production & Elimination BODY STRUCTURES & FUNCTIONS 199

reabsorption n term   rel **retention**[1] n term,
                opposite **secretion**[2] [sɪkriːʃən] n term → U88-11
absorption of substances in the glomerular filtrate to retain them in the serum
  reabsorb[3] [riːæbsɔːrb] v term • **retain**[4] [eɪ] v • **secrete**[5] [sɪkriːt] v
» Water reabsorption in the proximal tubules is driven by osmotic gradients[6]. Urea is passively reabsorbed from the nephron. At low flow rates there is an increased reabsorption of urea.
Use renal / selective / active **reabsorption** • passive / fractional[7] / tubular[8] **reabsorption** • electrolyte / phosphate / sodium[9] **reabsorption** • water / bicarbonate **reabsorption** • tubular[10] / distal tubule **secretion** • hydrogen [haɪdrədʒən]/ potassium[11] / renin **secretion** • **actively** reabsorbed / secreted • sodium[12] / fluid / urinary **retention**

> Note: The terms **secretion** and **secrete** are primarily used with glandular (endocrine, exocrine) function, when referring to the kidney they are used to describe the elimination of substances in the renal tubules (opposite of **reabsorb** and **reabsorption**; similar to **excrete** and **excretion**).

Reabsorption, Rückresorption
Retention, Verhalt, Rückstau[1] Sekretion, Absonderung, Abgabe[2] reabsorbieren, rückresorbieren[3] zurückhalten[4] sezernieren[5] osmot. Gefälle/ Gradient[6] fraktionelle Reabsorption[7] tubuläre Reabsorption[8] Natrium-Reabsorption[9] tubuläre Sekretion[10] Kaliumausscheidung[11] Natriumretention[12]

4

renal threshold [θreʃhoʊld] n term → U88-7
concentration of a substance in plasma above which the substance is excreted [iː] in the urine
» As renal failure progresses, there is an elevation in the renal threshold at which glycosuria[1] [aɪ] appears. Low-threshold substances include urea[2], phosphates, sulfates [ʌ], and creatinine [kriætiniːnǁɪn], while glucose [uː], amino acids[3], chlorine [iː], sodium, potassium and calcium [s] are high-threshold substances.
Use normal / reduced / decrease [iː] in / variations in **renal threshold** • low-/ high- **threshold** substance[4] • glucose[5] **threshold**

Nierenschwelle
Glukosurie, Glykosurie[1] Urea, Harnstoff[2] Aminosäuren[3] Substanz mit hoher Nierenschwelle[4] Glukoseschwelle[5]

5

diuresis [daɪjəriːsɪs] n term   sim **urinary excretion**[1] n, rel **washout**[2] n term
increased urine production
(anti-)diuretic[3] adj & n term • **excrete** v • **excretory** adj • **wash out**[4] v phr
» Urine is excreted from the collecting ducts [ʌ] into the renal pelvis. It is essential that the patient be well hydrated [aɪ] before beginning diuretic therapy and hydration be maintained [eɪ] after diuresis is initiated [ɪʃ]. This osmotic diuresis[5] washes out the medullary concentration gradient [eɪ] and subsequently [ʌ] causes polyuria.
Use to induce/produce/enhance/promote[6]/reduce **diuresis** • tubular / physiologic / pathologic **diuresis** • excessive / postobstructive [ʌ] / forced[7] **diuresis** • **diuretic** agent[8] [eɪdʒ]/ response / washout curve [ɜː] • **diuretic** effect / properties / therapy / renography[9] • potassium-sparing[10] [eəʳ] **diuretics** • sodium / electrolyte / fractional[11] / impaired [eəʳ]/ increased [iː] renal **excretion** • renal / bladder / Hippuran **washout** • **washout** time / studies / rate • **excretory** urography[12]

verstärkte Diurese, vermehrte Harnausscheidung
Harnausscheidung[1] Auswaschung, Ausschwemmung[2] diuretisch, diuresefördernd; Diuretikum[3] ausschwemmen[4] osmotische Diurese[5] Diurese fördern/ anregen[6] forcierte Diurese[7] Diuretikum, harntreibendes Mittel[8] Ausscheidungsdarstellung d. Niere(n)[9] kaliumsparende Diuretika[10] fraktionierte Ausscheidung[11] Ausscheidungs-, intravenöse Urografie[12]

6

clearance [klɪəʳəns] n term   rel **elimination**[1] [-eɪʃən], **urine output**[2] n term
amount [aʊ] of a solute[3] or substance removed [uː] from a specific [ɪ] volume of blood per unit of time in the kidney
  clear[4] v term usu pass • **eliminate** v • **clearing** n • **high-output** adj
» Factors determining [ɜː] clearance are urine volume in ml/min, urine and plasma concentration. Increase the rate at which the drug is cleared from the plasma.
Use renal[5] / tubular / (free) water[6] / creatinine[7] (abbr CrCl) / urea **clearance** • uric [jʊəʳ] acid[8] [æsɪd] / inulin[9] / albumin / extrarenal **clearance** • maximum / PAH[10] / total body[11] / plasma **clearance** • **clearance** rate / determination [ɜː]/ capacity [æs] • urinary[2] / renin / nitrogen [aɪ] urea **output** • **high-output** renal failure

Clearance
Elimination, Ausscheidung[1] Harn-, Ausscheidungsvolumen[2] gelöster Stoff[3] reinigen, eliminieren[4] renale Clearance[5] Freiwasser-Clearance[6] Kreatinin-Clearance[7] Harnsäure-Clearance[8] Inulin-Clearance[9] Para-aminohippursäure-Clearance[10] Ganzkörper-, Gesamt-Clearance[11]

7

depletion [dɪpliːʃən] n term   syn **loss** [lɒs] n term → U78-21
(i) removal of accumulated fluids or solids (ii) excessive loss of an essential body substance
  deplete [dɪpliːt] v term • **depleted**[1] adj
» The decrease in urinary magnesium [iː] excretion was attributed to replenishment[2] [e] of depleted magnesium stores. His elevated aldosterone secretion was due to sodium depletion.
Use sodium[3] / potassium / electrolyte / salt and water **depletion** • fluid[4]-/ volume[5]-/ nutritionally [ɪʃ] **depleted** • parenchymal [-kɪməl]/ (net) water / urinary nitrogen[6] [naɪtrədʒən] **loss**

Depletion, Verlust
erschöpft, entleert[1] (Wieder)auffüllung, Ergänzung[2] Natriumverlust, -mangel[3] dehydriert[4] hypovolämisch, volumendepletiert[5] Stickstoffausscheidung/ -verlust im Harn[6]

8

49

osmolality [ɒːzmoʊˈlælɪti] *n term*   *sim* **osmolarity**[1] *n term* → U81-21; U88-4

concentration of a solution expressed in osmoles of solute particles per kilogram of solvent[2]
osmotic[3] [ɒː] *adj term* • **(hyper)osmolar** [oʊ] *adj* • **osmolal** *adj* • **osmosis**[4] *n* [oʊ]
• **osmo-** *comb*

» Although osmolality in plasma is relatively constant, it varies considerably in the urine. Urea recycling helps maintain[5] osmolality in the medullary interstitium [ɪʃ] and the tubular lumen.

Use urinary *or* urine[6] / calculated serum / extracellular **osmolality** • changes in plasma[7] / serum [ɪə]/ determination [ɜː] of **osmolarity** • **low osmolality** media [iː] • **osmotic** pressure[8] / gradient / diuresis[9] / high-**osmolar** contrast agents[10] • **hyperosmolar** state / solution[11] [uːʃ] • **osmo**regulation[12] /receptors[13] /metry[14]

Osmolalität
Osmolarität[1] Lösungsmittel[2] osmotisch[3] Osmose[4] aufrechterhalten[5] Osmolalität d. Harns[6] Änderungen d. Plasmaosmolarität[7] osmotischer Druck[8] osmotische Diurese[9] hochosmolare Kontrastmittel[10] hyperosmolare Lösung[11] Osmoregulation[12] Osmorezeptoren[13] Osmometrie[14]

9

---

countercurrent [aʊ] **mechanism** *n term*   *rel* **autoregulation**[1] [ɒːtoʊ-] *n term*

passive diffusion [uːʒ] of substances across a membrane separating two countercurrent exchanger [eɪ] streams so that at each end the fluid leaving along one side of the membrane resembles the fluid entering on the other side

autoregulatory [-regjʊləˌtɔːri] *adj term* • **self-regulation**[1] *n* → U88-18

» Inability of the newborn to concentrate urine is due to an inefficient countercurrent system. Normally renal autoregulation keeps RBF and GFR relatively constant.

Use **countercurrent** exchange system[2] / effect / multiplier [ʌ] system[3] • elaborate **countercurrent** system • renal[4] **autoregulation**

Gegenstromsystem
Autoregulation[1] Gegenstromaustauschsystem[2] Gegenstrommultiplikation[3] Autoregulation d. Nierenfunktion[4]

10

---

renin [iː‖e]-**angiotensin-aldosterone system** *n term*   *abbr* **RAAS**

mechanism stimulating aldosterone production and sodium retention as a result of volume depletion, thus raising [eɪ] renal renin production and conversion of angiotensin [dʒ] I to angiotensin II in the plasma

reninism *n term*

» The RAAS system regulates sodium balance, fluid volume, and BP[1].

Use **renin** release[2] [iː] (rate) / concentration / level / activity[3] / determination • plasma **renin** concentration[4] • **angiotensin** converting [ɜː] enzyme [enzaɪm] (*abbr* ACE)/ I • **angiotensin** II blocker *or* antagonist[5]

Renin-Angiotensin-Aldosteron-System
Blutdruck[1] Reninausschüttung, -freisetzung[2] Reninaktivität[3] Plasmareninkonzentration[4] Angiotensin-II-Blocker[5]

11

---

urine [jʊərɪn] *n term*   *syn* **water** *n clin & inf*

clear, straw-colored fluid containing urea, sodium and other substances excreted by the kidney
urinary [jʊərɪnəri] *adj term* • **uriniferous**[1] *adj* • **urinal**[2] [jʊərɪnəl] *n* • **uro-** *comb*

» There is an overexcretion of sodium in the urine. Are there any bacteria in the urine? Do you have difficulties passing your water[3]? His blood lipids and urinary amino acids are elevated.

Use to pass[4] **urine**/water • **urine** culture [ʌ] / osmolality / output • **urine** specimen [es] *or* sample[5] • **urine** concentration / specific gravity / storage • cloudy[6] / blood-tinged[7] / sterile / pH / 24-hour[8] **urine** • dark / residual[9] / primary[10] **urine** • first void *or* morning[11] / midstream[12] **urine** • **urinary** tract / albumin / sphincter / stream • **urinary** reflux / volume / sediment[13] / stone *or* calculus[14] • **urinary** casts[15] / diversion[16] / dipstick[17] / dribbling[18] • **uro**flowmetry[19] /gram /genital /thelium[20] [iː] /dynamics [aɪ] /bilinogen [-dʒən] /pathy[21]

Urin, Harn
harnableitend[1] Urinal, Urinflasche[2] Beschwerden beim Urinieren[3] Harn lassen, urinieren[4] Harnprobe[5] trüber Harn[6] blutig tingierter Harn[7] 24-Stunden-Harn[8] Restharn[9] Primärharn[10] Morgenharn[11] Mittelstrahlharn[12] Harnsediment[13] Harnstein[14] (Harn)zylinder[15] Harnableitung[16] Harnstreifentest[17] Harnträufeln[18] Uroflowmetrie[19] Übergangsepithel, Urothel[20] Harnwegserkrankung[21]

12

---

urea [jʊˈriːə‖jʊərɪə] *n term*

chief end product of nitrogen metabolism excreted in the urine (about 32 gram a day)

» Urea occurs as whitish odorless[1] prismatic crystals with a saline [eɪ] taste, is soluble in water, and forms salts with acids. The proximal tubule is not as permeable to urea as to water.

Use **urea** concentration / cycle[2] [saɪkl]/ clearance test / excretion ratio [reɪʃioʊ]/ hydrolysis / synthesis[3] • urine / blood[4] **urea nitrogen** [naɪtrədʒən] (*abbr* BUN)

Urea, Harnstoff
geruchlos[1] Harnstoff-, Ornithinzyklus, Krebs-Henseleit-Zyklus[2] Harnstoffsynthese[3] Blut-Harnstoff-Stickstoff, BUN[4]

13

---

uric acid [jʊərɪk æsɪd] *n term*   *rel* **urate**[1] [jʊəreɪt] *n term*

white poorly soluble crystals [ɪ] contained in solution in the urine; sometimes solidified in small masses or in larger concretions [iːʃ] as calculi [aɪ]

urico- *comb*

» Her serum uric acid level is elevated[2]. Overproduction of uric acid is sometimes seen in gout[3] [aʊ]. Glucose [uː], sulfate [ʌ], amino acids, uric acid, and albumin have a transport maximum.

Use **uric acid** excretion / concentration[4] / metabolism / production • **uric acid** determination[5] / solubility[6] / crystals[7] / stone formation[8] • **urate** calculus[9] [kælkjʊləs]/ crystals[10] / deposition[11] / nephropathy[12] • **urico**suria/suric drugs[13]

Harnsäure, Acidum uricum
Urat, Salz d. Harnsäure[1] erhöht[2] Gicht[3] Harnsäurekonzentration[4] Harnsäurebestimmung[5] Harnsäurelöslichkeit[6] Harnsäurekristalle[7] Harnsäuresteinbildung[8] Uratstein[9] Uratkristalle[10] Uratablagerung[11] Urat-, Gichtnephropathie[12] Urikosurika, Harnsäureausscheidung fördernde Mittel[13]

14

Female Sexual Organs   BODY STRUCTURES & FUNCTIONS **201**

(urine) sto̱rage [-rɪdʒ] *n term*   *rel* **bladder filling[1], bladder capa̱city[2]** *n term*
ability of the bladder to contain 400-500 ml of urine at a relatively stable [eɪ] basal [eɪ] pressure
store[3] [stɔːr] *v* • **fill** *v*
» The first sensa̱tions [eɪʃ] of bladder filling ordina̱rily occu̱r [ɜː] when 100-150 ml of urine has accumulated in the bladder. Urine output per voi̱ding will be low when the bladder capa̱city is reduced. Bladder compliance [aɪ] refe̱rs to the change in detru̱sor pressure that accompanies an i̱ncrease in bladder vo̱lume during filling.
Use (in)a̱dequate **urine storage** • (low-pre̱ssure) bladder / u̱rinary **storage** • **storage** phase [feɪz]/ function / capa̱city[4] [æs] • **bladder** compliance / disteṉtion[5] • **filling** cystometry[6]

Harnspeicherung
Blasenfüllung[1] Blasenkapazität[2] speichern[3] Speicherkapazität[4] Blasendehnung[5] (Füllungs)zystometrie[6]
15

voiding [vɔɪdɪŋ] *n term & jar*
       syn **bladder emptying** *n clin*, **micturi̱tion** [-ɪʃən], **urina̱tion** [eɪʃ] *n term*
expulsion [ʌ] of the u̱rine stored in the bladder
void[1] [vɔɪd] *v term* • **mi̱cturate[2]** [kʃ‖ktj] *v* • **u̱rinate[2]** [jʊɚɪneɪt] *v* • **postvoid** *adj*
» The pa̱tient is unable to void. Was the bladder emptied on voi̱ding? He has difficulty u̱rinating. The pa̱tient experienced some discomfort during urina̱tion but often pain was most severe after voi̱ding had ceased [siːst]. The patient was strai̱ning[3] [eɪ] to u̱rinate and there was terminal [ɜː] dribbling.
Use to i̱nitiate/trigger/(be unable to) postpone/refrain [eɪ] from **voiding** • **voiding** act / time / pressure / pattern • **voiding** difficulty[4] / dysfunction[5] [ɪ] / cystou̱rethro̱graphy[6] • normal / difficult[4] / (in)voluntary / incomple̱te[7] **voiding** • (freshly / first-)**voided** (morning) specimen[8] • **voided** volume / bladder[9] • **postvoid** residual urine[10] / dribbling[11] • (sudden) strong u̱rge[12] [ɜːdʒ]/ inteṉse desi̱re[12] [aɪ] **to void** • **micturi̱tion** re̱flex[13] / center • storage / e̱mptying **phase of micturition** • burning[14] [ɜː] **on urina̱tion**

> Note: There are many clinical and colloquial expressions for to 'pass water' (some more polite than others): **to go to the bathroom/toilet, to take/go for a leak, pee-(wee)** [with children], **spend a penny** *(BE)*, **piss*

(Blasen)entleerung, Miktion
(Blase) entleeren, ausscheiden[1] urinieren, Harn/ Wasser lassen[2] Pressen[3] Dysurie, erschwerte Blasenentleerung[4] Blasenentleerungsstörung[5] Miktionszystourethrografie[6] unvollständige Blasenentleerung[7] Morgenharnprobe[8] entleerte Blase[9] Restharn[10] Nachträufeln[11] imperativer Harndrang[12] Miktionsreiz, -reflex[13] Brennen beim Urinieren[14]
16

(urinary) stream *n clin*   *sim* **(uro)flow[1]** *n term, rel* **dribbling[2]** *n clin* → U112-15
outflow of u̱rine during the act of micturi̱tion
midstream [mɪdstriːm] *adj term*
» Observe [ɜː] the u̱rinary stream for ca̱liber, deflection and strai̱ning. The midstream portion is collected to reduce contamina̱tion of the u̱rine sa̱mple.
Use to i̱nitiate [ɪʃ] or start/maintai̱n **the stream** • (expulsive) [ʌ] **force[3]** / caliber / deflection[4] **of stream** • weak[5] [iː]/ strong / poor[5] / na̱rrow[6] [æ]/ decrea̱sed / slow / interru̱pted[7] [ʌ] **stream** • **midstream** or clean-catch urine sa̱mple[8] [æ‖BE ɑː]/ urina̱lysis [-ælɪsɪs]

Harnstrahl
Harnfluss[1] Harnträufeln[2] Stärke d. Harnstrahls[3] Harnstrahlabweichung[4] schwacher Strahl[5] dünner/ schwacher Strahl[6] Harnstottern[7] Mittelstrahlharn[8]
17

Unit 50 Female Sexual Organs
Related Units: **51 Menstrual Cycle, 52 Male Sexual Organs,
         54 Endocrine Glands, 68 Sexuality, 69 Fertility,
         48 Urinary Tract, 96 Sexually Transmitted Diseases**

genita̱lia [dʒenɪteɪlɪə] *n term*   *syn* **genitals, sexual organs** *n term*
external [ɜː] and/or internal genital organs
genital [dʒenɪtᵊl] *adj term* • **genit(o)-** *comb*
» The external genita̱lia are the vu̱lva[1] [ʌ] in the female, and the penis [iː] and scro̱tum [oʊ] in the male. There is distal loss of temperature sense below T12 including the genitals and perine̱um[2] [iː].
Use female / male / external[1] / internal[3] / ambiguous[4] [ɪg] **genitalia** • **genital** tract / area / ridge[5] [rɪdʒ]/ folds[6] / tubercle[7] • **genital** phase [feɪz] or stage[8] / secre̱tion [iːʃ]/ lesion [iːʒ]/ bleeding • **genital** infection / herpes [ɜː]/ ulcer [ʌlsɚ]/ wart[9] [ɔː]

> Note: Expressions used by patients to refer to the external female sexual organ are **private parts, crotch** [krɒtʃ], and **down below** *(BE)*.

Genitalien, Genitale, Geschlechtsorgane
Vulva, äußeres weibl. Genitale[1] Perineum, Damm[2] inneres Genitale[3] intersexuelles Genitale[4] Genitalleiste[5] Genitalfalten[6] Genitalhöcker, Tuberculum genitale[7] genitale Phase[8] Feucht-, Feigwarze, Condyloma acuminatum[9]
1

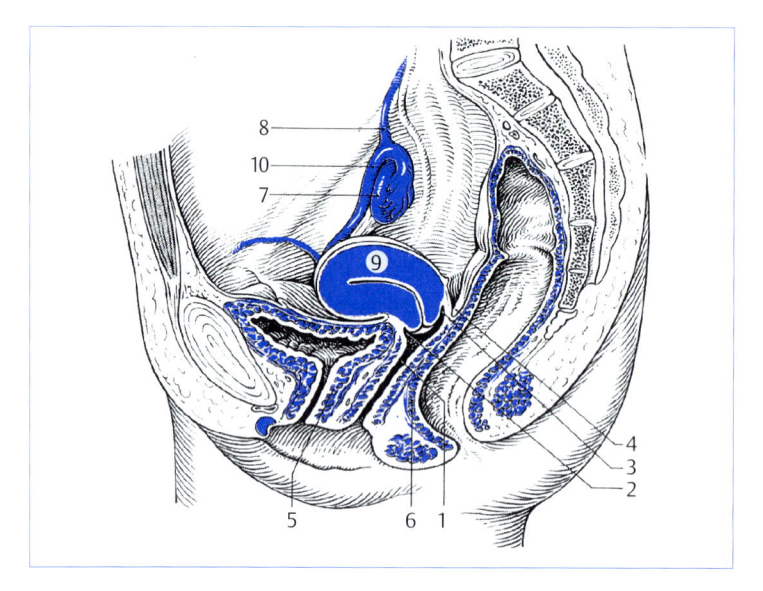

Female genitalia: vagina (**1**), anterior vaginal fornix (**2**), posterior vaginal fornix (**3**), pouch of Douglas or rectouterine cul-de-sac (**4**), anterior paracolpium (**5**), rectovaginal fascia (**6**), ovary (**7**), suspensory ligament of the ovary (**8**), uterus (**9**), Fallopian tube or oviduct (**10**)

---

female [fiːmeɪl] *adj & n clin*   sim **feminine**[1] [e] *adj*

(adj) referring to the child-bearing [eɚ] sex
(n) a girl or woman (i.e. not male)

feminize [femɪnaɪz] *v term* • **feminizing** *adj* • **(de)feminization**[2] *n*

» The length of hospital stays was higher in females than in males. The male-female gap in life expectancy[3] narrowed in the 90ies. Breasts [e], pubic [p(j)uːbɪk] hair[4], and habitus are feminine in character.

Use ***female*** gender [dʒ] *or* sex[5] /-to-male ratio [eɪʃ]/ reproductive [ʌ] tract • ***female*** germ [dʒɜːrm] cells / orgasmic disorder[6] • white ***females*** • testicular[7] ***feminization*** • ***feminine*** appearance [ɪɚ] • ***feminized*** breast • ***feminizing*** state / tumor[8] / dose of estrogen [-dʒən]/ side effects

weiblich; Frau
feminin[1] (De)feminisierung[2] Lebenserwartung[3] Schambehaarung[4] weibliches Geschlecht[5] Orgasmusstörung der Frau[6] testikuläre Feminisierung[7] feminisierender Tumor[8]

---

ovary [oʊvɚi] *n term*   syn **female gonad** *n term*,
rel **ovum**[1] *n term, pl* **ova** [oʊvə]

paired female reproductive glands containing ovarian follicles which enclose the ova; surrounding the ovary's stroma is the membrana granulosa, germinal [dʒɜː] epithelium[2] [iː], and the tunica albuginea

ovarian [eɚ] *adj term* • **transovarial** *adj* • **gonadal**[3] [eɪ] *adj* • **ovari(o)-** *comb*

» Other causes of ovarian failure and amenorrhea [iː] include premature ovarian failure, the resistant-ovary syndrome, and ovarian failure secondary to[4] chemotherapy [ɪː] or radiation therapy for malignancy. The menopausal [ɒː] ovary continues to secrete [iː] testosterone, presumably formed in stromal cells. Ovulation and ovarian steroidogenesis were inhibited.

Use polycystic[5] [sɪ]/ enlarged ***ovaries*** • ***ovarian*** follicle (development) / cells / cycle[6] [saɪkl] • ***ovarian*** cortex / function [ʌ]/ hormones[7] • ***ovarian*** estrogen [e‖iː] production / failure[8] [feɪljɚ] • ***ovarian*** hyperstimulation / atrophy • ***ovarian*** cyst[9] / mass[10] / tumor[10] • ***ovarian*** carcinoma / biopsy[11] [aɪ] • extra/ trans/ tubo***ovarian*** • ***transovarian*** route [aʊ‖uː]/ transmission • ***tuboovarian*** abscess[12] • ***ovari***ectomy[13] /opexy[14] /otomy

Ovar(ium), Eierstock, weibliche Keimdrüse
Ovum, Eizelle[1] Keimepithel[2] gonadal, Gonaden-[3] infolge von[4] polyzystische Ovarien[5] Ovarialzyklus[6] Ovarialhormone[7] Ovarialinsuffizienz[8] Ovarialzyste[9] Ovarialtumor[10] Ovarialbiopsie[11] Tuboovarialabszess[12] Ovarektomie, Eierstockentfernung[13] Eierstockfixierung, Ovariopexie[14]

Female Sexual Organs | BODY STRUCTURES & FUNCTIONS 203

(fallopian [fəloʊpɪˀn] *or* **uterine) tube** [juːtəˑɪn‖aɪn t(j)uːb] *n term*
syn **oviduct** [oʊvɪdʌkt] *n clin*, **salpinx** *n term rare, pl* **-ges** [-dʒiːz]

tubes from either side of the fundus [ʌ] of the uterus to the upper or outer extremity of the ovary; it consists of the infundibulum and the fimbriae¹ [iː], the ampulla [ʊ], isthmus [ɪsməs], and uterine parts

tubal *adj term* • **tub(o)-** *comb* • **salping(o)-** *comb* • **intrafallopian** *adj*

» *The uterine tubes, which are loosely attached* [ætʃ] *to the ovaries by the ovarian fimbriae, are lined* [aɪ] *by ciliated* [sɪl-] *epithelium²* [iː]. *The severity* [e] *and extent of adhesions* [iːʒ] *in the oviduct were assessed.*

Use endo/ hydro [aɪ]/ pyo**salpinx** [aɪ] • **tubal** pregnancy³ / function / wall (thickening) / damage • **tubal** patency⁴ [eɪ]/ occlusion [uːʒ]/ infertility • **tubal** ligation⁵ [eɪ]/ sterilization⁶ • **tubal** infection / rupture [ʌ]/ abortion⁷ • **tubal** scarring [ɑː]/ implantation • distal / healthy / reconstructed⁸ **oviduct** • **fimbriated** end of the tube⁹ • **salping**ectomy [dʒe] /itis¹⁰ [aɪ] • gamete [iː] **intrafallopian** transfer¹¹ (*abbr* GIFT) • **tubo**ovarian /plasty⁸

Eileiter, Tuba uterina (Fallopii), Tube
Fimbrien¹ Flimmerepithel² Tubargravidität, Eileiterschwangerschaft³ Tubendurchgängigkeit⁴ Tubenligatur⁵ Tubensterilisation⁶ Tubarabort⁷ Tubenplastik⁸ fimbrienbesetztes Tubenende⁹ Eileiterentzündung¹⁰ intratubarer Gametentransfer¹¹

4

uterus [juːtəˑəs] *n term, pl* **uteri**   syn **womb** [wuːm] *n clin & inf*

hollow muscular [ʌ] organ in which the impregnated ovum is implanted; it consists of the corpus or body, an upper rounded portion (fundus [ʌ]) with the cornu or horn at each extremity, and an elongated lower part (cervix or neck) at the extremity of which is the external os¹

(intra/ extra)uterine [-ɪn‖aɪn] *adj term* • **uter(o)-**, • **hyster(o)-** [hɪstəˑ-] *comb*

» *The uterus is supported in the pelvic cavity by the broad², round³, and cardinal ligaments⁴, and the rectouterine and vesicouterine folds. The upper rounded portion of the uterus is the fundus. The ovum reaches the uterine cavity through the horn or cornu of the uterus.*

Use to sound the⁵ **uterus** • bicornuate⁶ / bifid⁶ / arcuate / one-horned⁷ **uterus** • double-mouthed *or* (sub)septate⁸ **uterus** • contracting / empty / gravid / postpartum **uterus** • rudimentary / infantile / retroflexed⁹ **uterus** • **uterus** didelphys • **uterine** wall / corpus¹⁰ / fundus • **uterine** size / smooth [uː] muscle cells • **uterine** horn / contraction / vein [eɪ] / exploration • **uterine** massage [ɑːʒ]/ rupture¹¹ [ʌ]/ prolapse¹² / suspension • **uterine** bleeding / cavity / contents / cervix [ʒː] • in **utero** • **hyster**ectomy¹³ /oscopy

Uterus, Gebärmutter
äußerer Muttermund, Ostium uteri¹ Ligamentum latum, breites Mutterband² Ligamentum teres uteri, rundes Mutterband³ Ligamentum cardinale uteri⁴ Gebärmutter auskultieren, Herztöne abhören⁵ Uterus bicornis⁶ U. unicornis⁷ U. bicollis/ (sub)septus⁸ retroflektierter U.⁹ Uteruskörper, Corpus uteri¹⁰ Uterusruptur¹¹ Uterusvorfall, Prolapsus uteri¹² Hysterektomie, Gebärmutterentfernung¹³

5

endometrium [iː] *n term*   *rel* **perimetrium¹**, **myometrium²** [maɪə-] *n term*

mucous [mjuːkˀəs] membrane that makes up the innermost layer of the uterine wall; it consists of a simple columnar [ʌ] epithelium³ [iː] and a lamina propria that contains simple tubular uterine glands

endometrial [iː] *adj term* • **endometrioid** *adj* • **myometrial** *adj*

» *Endometrial biopsies* [aɪ] *are positive in gonococcal endometritis* [aɪ] *but not in the uninfected endometrium. Oxytocin also exerts a contractile action on the myometrium postpartum.*

Use menstrual / functional⁴ / scarred⁵ [ɑː] **endometrium** • **endometrial** cavity / stroma / glands • **endometrial** lining⁶ [aɪ]/ proliferation / implant • **endometrial** biopsy⁷ / sampling⁷ / aspiration • **endometrial** atypia [ɪ]/ hyperplasia⁸ [eɪʒ]/ ablation [eɪʃ]/ adenocarcinoma • **myometrial** penetration / thickness • **endome**tri**os**is⁹ /tis

Endometrium, Gebärmutterschleimhaut, Tunica mucosa
Perimetrium, Tunica serosa¹ Myometrium, T. muscularis² Zylinderepithel³ Funktionalis, Stratum functionale⁴ narbiges Endometrium⁵ Gebärmutterschleimhaut⁶ Endometriumbiopsie⁷ Endometriumhyperplasie⁸ Endometriose⁹

6

cervix (uteri) [sɜːrvɪks] *n term*   *rel* **cervical os¹** [ɒːz] *n term*

portion of the uterus extending from the isthmus [ɪsməs] of the uterus into the vagina; its supravaginal and vaginal parts are marked by its passage through the vaginal wall

cervical² [sɜːrvɪkˀəl] *adj term* • **endo/ ectocervical** *adj* • **cervic(o)-** *comb*

» *Colposcopically directed biopsy is the method of choice³ for the diagnosis of cervical lesions. Postcoital spotting⁴ was due to the cervical ooze⁵* [uːz]. *Although the cervix of the uterus is fixed, the body is free to rise and fall with the filling and emptying of the bladder⁶.*

Use anterior / deformed / double [ʌ]/ inflamed / incompetent⁷ **cervix** • **cervical** canal / mucus method⁸ / smear⁹ [ɪəˑ] cytology [saɪt-] • **cervical** erosion¹⁰ / dilation [eɪ]/ conization¹¹ [koʊnaɪ-] • internal¹² / external¹³ / endo**cervical os** • **endocervical** culture [ʌ]/ curettage [kʊəˑetɪdʒ‖tɑːʒ] • **endocervical** exudate / gonococcal infection / carcinoma¹⁴

Gebärmutterhals, Cervix (uteri)
Muttermund¹ zervikal, Zervix-² Methode der Wahl³ postkoitale (Schmier)blutung⁴ zervikaler Ausfluss⁵ Blasenentleerung⁶ Zervixinsuffizienz⁷ Zervixschleimmethode, Billings-Ovulationsmethode⁸ Zervixabstrich⁹ Portioerosion¹⁰ (Zervix)konisation¹¹ innerer Muttermund¹² äußerer Muttermund, Ostium uteri¹³ Zervixhöhlenkarzinom¹⁴

7

BODY STRUCTURES & FUNCTIONS — Female Sexual Organs

vagina [vəˈdʒaɪnə] *n term*   *rel* **birth canal**[1] [bɜːrθ kənæl] *n*

canal from the vaginal orifice[2] [-fɪs] in the vestibule to the uterine cervix lined [aɪ] by mucosa
vaginal [ˈvædʒɪnəl‖vəˈdʒaɪnəl] *adj term* • **vagin(o)-** *comb* • **colpo-** *comb*

» An appropriately sized, warmed speculum is gently [dʒ] inserted to permit inspection of the vagina and the cervix. The mucosa of the vagina is lined by stratified squamous [eɪ] epithelium[3]. Hyperflexing the mother's hips is helpful as it causes the birth canal to be straighter [streɪtɚ]. Uterine cramps and heavy [e] vaginal bleeding were noted.

Use bulging [bʌldʒɪŋ] / blind-ending[4] / distended / septate or double[5] [ʌ] **vagina** • hypoplastic / lower or distal **vagina** • to obstruct [ʌ]/ passage through **the birth canal** • infected / contaminated / colonized **birth canal** • **birth canal** secretions [iːʃ] / **vaginal** vault [ɒː] or fornix[6] / introitus[2] / bleeding • **vaginal** discharge[7] / flora[8] / douching[9] [duːʃɪŋ] • **vaginal** cream [iː]/ sponge[10] [ʌ]/ smear[11] [smɪɚ] • **vaginal** speculum[12] / suppository[13] / intercourse[14] [ɔː] • endo/ intra/ recto/ vulvo**vaginal** • **colpo**scopy /tomy /rraphy /cleisis[15] [aɪ] • **vagin**itis [aɪ] /ismus[16]/oplasty[17]

glands of Skene [skiːn] *n term*   *syn* **Skene's glands** [glændz], **paraurethral** [iː] **glands** *n term*

mucous glands in the wall of the female urethra, also referred to as the female prostate

» The peri- or paraurethral glands empty into the urethra [iː] just inside the meatus [ieɪ]. Skene's glands, which are adjacent [ədʒeɪsᵊnt] to the urethra, may also be the site of abscess [æbses] formation in the vulva.

Use involvement of[1] **Skene's glands** • **Skene's** ducts[2] [ʌ]/ gland infection

Bartholin('s) glands *n term*   *syn* **greater vestibular glands** *n term*

one of two mucus-secreting glands on either side of the lower part of the vagina, the equivalent of the bulbourethral [ʌ] glands[1] in the male

» The duct of the Bartholin's glands is about 5 mm in diameter [æ]. Acute inflammation [eɪ] of the greater vestibular gland is usually unilateral.

Use **Bartholin gland** abscess / carcinoma • **Bartholin('s)** cyst[2] / duct • **bartholin**itis[3]

vulva [vʌlvə] *n term*   *syn* **pudendum** [pjʊˈdendəm] **(muliebre)** *n term*

external female genitalia comprising [aɪ] the mons pubis, labia, clitoris, vestibule of the vagina[1] and its glands, and the vaginal and urethral openings
vulvar [ʌ] *adj term* • **vulval** *adj* • **vulv(o)-** *comb* • **pudendal** *adj* → U22-10

» The clitoral prepuce [iː] is hidden in the small cleft of the vulva and the mucous membrane of the introitus is pink and somewhat moist. Involvement of the vulva was limited to the vestibule and labia minora, but a profuse discharge[2] caused inflammation of the labia majora, perineum, and adjacent[3] skin surfaces.

Use to wash/contaminate/involve/spread [e] to **the vulva** • **vulvar** area / structures / skin • **vulvar** hair / mucosa / sweat [e] gland • **vulvar** varices [verɪsiːz]/ irritation / itching or pruritus[4] [aɪ] • **vulvar** vestibulitis [aɪ]/ cancer[5] • **vulv**itis[6] /outerine /ovaginal /ovaginitis /ectomy[7] • **pudendal** vein/ artery / arteriography / nerve/ block[8]

> **Note:** Clinical, informal and vulgar expressions for the vulva and/or vagina include: **front passage,** *****slit,** *****cunt,** *****pussy.**

clitoris [klɪtɚɪs] *n term & clin*   *syn* **corpus clitoridis** [klɪˈtɔːrɪdiːz] *n term*

erectile body consisting of a glans, corpus, and two crura located near the top of the vulva
clitoral *adj term* • **clitoridis** *n gen* • **clitor(o)-** *comb*

» The clitoris is homologous to the male penis [iː] except that it does not possess a corpus spongiosum. Enlargement of the clitoris in the newborn[1] is frequently associated with congenital [dʒe] adrenal hyperplasia. The clitoris is stimulated by indirect friction of the hood [ʊ], e.g. during penile [piːnaɪl] thrusting[2] [ʌ].

Use erect[3] / bifid or split / frenulum of the[4] **clitoris** • **clitoral** hood[5] [ʊ]/ prepuce [iː]/ vein [eɪ]/ artery • **clitoral** enlargement or hypertrophy[6] / stimulation • glans[7] / crus[8] / smegma / plexus cavernosus **clitoridis** • **clitori**dectomy[9]

Scheide, Vagina
Geburtskanal[1] Ostium vaginae, Scheideneingang[2] mehrschichtiges Plattenepithel[3] blind endigende Vagina[4] Vaginaverdopplung, V. duplex[5] Scheidengewölbe, Fornix vaginae[6] Fluor vaginalis, Ausfluss aus d. Scheide[7] Scheiden-, Vaginalflora[8] Scheidenspülung[9] Vaginalschwamm[10] Vaginalabstrich[11] Scheidenspekulum[12] Vaginalzäpfchen[13] Vaginalverkehr[14] Kolpokleisis, operativer Scheidenverschluss[15] Vaginismus, Scheidenkrampf[16] Scheidenplastik[17]

8

Skene-Drüsen, Glandulae paraurethrales
Mitbeteiligung d. Skene-Drüsen[1] Skene-Gänge[2]

9

Bartholin-Drüsen, Glandulae vestibulares majores
Cowper-Drüsen, G. bulbourethrales[1] Bartholin-Zyste[2] ein- oder beidseitige Entzündung d. Bartholin-Drüsen, Bartholinitis[3]   10

Vulva, äußeres weibl. Genitale, Pudendum femininum
Scheidenvorhof, Vestibulum vaginae[1] starker Ausfluss[2] angrenzend[3] Pruritus vulvae, Juckreiz im Vulvabereich[4] Vulvakarzinom[5] Vulvitis, Entzündung d. Vulva[6] Vulvektomie, op. Entfernung d. großen und kl. Schamlippen[7] Pudendusblock[8]

11

Klitoris, Kitzler, Corpus clitoridis
beim Neugeborenen[1] Stoßen d. Penis[2] erigierte Klitoris[3] Klitorisbändchen, Frenulum clitoridis[4] Klitorishaube[5] Klitorishypertrophie[6] Glans clitoridis, Klitoriseichel[7] Klitorisschenkel, Crus clitoridis[8] Klitoridektomie, Klitorisentfernung, weibl. Beschneidung[9]   12

Female Sexual Organs   BODY STRUCTURES & FUNCTIONS   **205**

hymen [haɪmən] *n term*
        syn **virginal** [vɜːrdʒɪnᵊl] *or* **hymenal membrane** *n clin*
thin membrane partly occluding the vaginal orifice but usually permitting normal menstrual flow in virgins[1] [vɜːrdʒɪnz]
    hymenal [aɪ] *adj term* • **hymen(o)-** *comb*
» Inspection of the vulva revealed [iː] a *dome-shaped*[2], *purplish-red* [ɜː] *hymenal membrane*. After the birth of several children, the hymen may almost disappear.
Use intact[3] / unruptured[3] [ʌ]/ imperforate[4] **hymen** • cribriform[5] / septate[6] / vertical **hymen** • **hymenal** orifice / band / ring • **hymenal** injury or laceration[7] [s]/ tear[8] [teɚ] • **hymen**itis [aɪ] /otomy /ectomy

labia minora [leɪbɪə mənɔːrə] *n term*   *syn* **small pudendal lips** *n clin*
paired longitudinal folds of mucous membrane enclosed in the cleft within the labia majora[1]
    labial [eɪ] *adj term*
» Posteriorly the labia minora gradually merge [mɜːrdʒ] with[2] the labia majora forming the fourchette[3] [ʃe], or frenulum[3]. Engorgement[4] [ɪngɔːrdʒ-] of the labia, which take on a deep wine color, signals the onset of climax[5] [aɪ].
Use **labia** majora[6] • fused[7] / inflamed **labia** • **labial** herpes [ɜː]/ mucosa / reddening

rectouterine *or* **rectovaginal pouch** [rektoʊvædʒɪnᵊl paʊtʃ] *n term*
        syn **cul-de-sac** [kʌldɪsæk] *or* **pouch of Douglas** [ʌ] *n term*
blind-ending recess[1] formed by the peritoneal fold between the rectum and the uterus
» The anterior wall of the uterus is separated from the rectum by the rectouterine pouch. In the bottom of the cul-de-sac, the peritoneum is reflected from the bladder onto the uterus at the junction [dʒʌŋkʃᵊn] of the cervix and corpus.
Use uterovesical *or* vesicouterine[2] **pouch** • pelvic / uterine / vaginal **cul-de-sac** • posterior **cul-de-sac** • **cul-de-sac** hernia [ɜː]/ tap[3] / culture [ʌ] • **cul**doscopy[4]

mons (pubis) [mɒːns pjuːbɪs] *n term*   *syn* **mons veneris** [venɚɪs] *n term*
prominence marked by a pad of fatty tissue[1] over the pubic symphysis [sɪmfɪsɪs] in the female
» At puberty, the mons pubis enlarges and becomes covered by pubic hair[2].

breast [brest] *n clin*   *syn* **mamma(ry gland)** *n term*, **bosom** [bʊzᵊm] *n inf*
(i) either of the paired [eɚ] glands in the chest of pubescent[1] [es] and adult females; also the analogous organs of the male chest, especially when enlarged (ii) rarely also the chest [tʃ]
    mammary[2] [æ] *adj term* • **breast-feed**[3] *v* • **mast-** *comb* • **mamm(o)-** *comb*
» The mean age of onset of puberty for girls as defined by breast budding is 11.2 ± 1.6 years. The patient underwent unnecessary breast biopsy[4] due to a false-positive mammogram[5].
Use (non)lactating / contralateral **breast** • **breast** (self-)examination[6] / biopsy[4] [aɪ] • **breast** buds[7] [ʌ]/ size / mass *or* lump[8] [ʌ] • **breast** cancer[9] [ˈs]/ infection / abscess / cyst [sɪst] • **breast** density / engorgement[10] [ɔːrdʒ] • **breast** milk[11] / emptying / deformity • **breast** asymmetry [ɪ]/ conservation[12] / augmentation[13] [ɔːg-] • **breast** implant / reconstruction [ʌ] surgery[14] • **mammary** artery / dysplasia [eɪʒ]/ duct [ʌ] • extra/ sub [ʌ]/ infra**mammary** • **inframammary** fold [oʊ] • **mast**itis[15] [aɪ] /ectomy[16] /opexy • **mammo**graphy /gram[5] /graphic findings[17] /plasty

nipple [nɪpl] *n clin*   *syn* **mammary papilla, mamilla** *n term*, **teat** [tiːt‖tɪt] *n inf*
wartlike [ɔː] projection [dʒe] in the center of the breast onto which the lactiferous ducts[1] [ʌ] open
» The nipple is surrounded by a circular pigmented area, termed the areola[2] [iː]. When the infant opens its mouth, rapidly insert [ɜː] as much of the nipple and areola as possible.
Use **nipple** erection[3] / retraction[4] / change • **nipple** erosion [oʊʒ]/ tenderness[5] • **nipple** line[6] / discharge[7] / pigmentation • blood-filled / sore [ɔː] **nipple** • fissured [ʃ] *or* cracked[8] / inverted[9] [ɜː] **nipple** • **nipple-areolar** loss / preservation

---

Hymen, Jungfernhäutchen
Jungfrauen[1] kuppelförmig[2] intakter/ unverletzter Hymen, Hymen intactus[3] Hymenalatresie, H. imperforatus[4] Hymen cribriformis[5] Hymen septus[6] Verletzung d. Hymens[7] Einreißen d. Hymens[8]

13

kleine Schamlippen, Labia minora
Schamspalte, Rima pudendi[1] gehen über in[2] Frenulum labiorum majorum[3] Schwellung[4] Orgasmus, Klimax[5] große Schamlippen, Labia majora[6] Labiensynechie[7]

14

Excavatio rectouterina, Douglas-Raum
Aussackung, -stülpung, Recessus[1] Excavatio vesicouterina[2] Douglas-Punktion[3] Kuldoskopie, Douglasskopie[4]

15

Mons pubis/ veneris, Schamhügel, Venusberg
Fettpolster[1] Schamhaare[2]

16

weibl. Brust, Mamma, Busen
pubertierend[1] Brust-, Mamma-[2] stillen[3] Mammabiopsie[4] Mammogramm[5] Selbstuntersuchung d. Brust[6] Brustknospen[7] Brusttumor, Mammaknoten[8] Brustkrebs[9] Brustschwellung[10] Muttermilch[11] Brusterhaltung[12] Brustvergrößerung, Mammaaugmentation[13] Mammaaufbauplastik[14] Brustdrüsenentzündung, Mastitis[15] Mastektomie, Mammaamputation[16] Mammografiebefund[17]

17

Brustwarze, Mamille, Papilla mammae
Milchgänge, Ductus lactiferi[1] Areola, Warzenhof[2] Mamillenerektion[3] Brustwarzeneinziehung[4] Brustwarzenempfindlichkeit[5] Mamillarlinie, Linea mamillaris[6] Mamillensekret, Absonderung aus d. Brustwarze[7] Brustwarzenrhagade[8] Hohl-, Schlupfwarze[9]

18

Unit 51 Menstrual Cycle

Related Units: 50 Female Sexual Organs, 55 Hormones, 68 Sexuality, 69 Fertility, 70 Pregnancy, 71 Childbirth, 85 Embryology

menstrual cycle [mɛnstruəl saɪkl] *n clin & term*

approx. 4-week period in which an ovum matures, is ovulated, and via the fallopian tubes¹ enters the uterine cavity

(**post/ peri/ pre**)**menstrual**² [iː] *adj term* • **midcycle**³ [mɪdsaɪkl] *adj*

» The menstrual cycle lasts an average of 28 days, with day 1 of the cycle designated as that day on which menstrual flow begins. In the absence of fertilization, ovarian secretions [iːʃ] wane⁴ [weɪn], the endometrium [iː] sloughs⁵ [slʌfs], and menstruation begins.

Use normal / preceding [siː] **menstrual cycle** • **menstrual cycle** disturbances⁶ [ɜː]/ abnormalities⁶ • length / stage or phase **of the menstrual cycle** • **menstrual** history⁷ / age / flow⁸ • **menstrual** bleeding⁸ / blood loss / cramps⁹ • **menstrual** pain⁹ / colic⁹ / irregularities⁶ • **premenstrual** period / symptoms / tension [-ʃⁿn] or syndrome¹⁰ • (an)ovulatory¹¹ **cycles** • **midcycle** pain¹² / LH surge¹³ [sɜːdʒ]/ spotting¹⁴

(Menstruations)zyklus
Eileiter¹ (prä)menstruell² mitt(el)zyklisch³ Produktion d. Ovarialhormone sinkt⁴ wird abgestoßen⁵ Zyklusstörungen⁶ Zyklusanamnese⁷ Menstruation, Monatsblutung⁸ Menstruationsbeschwerden, Dysmenorrhoe⁹ prämenstruelles Syndrom, PMS¹⁰ anovulatorische/ monophasische Zyklen¹¹ Mittelschmerz¹² LH-Gipfel (i. d. Zyklusmitte)¹³ Mittzyklusblutung¹⁴

1

menstruation [-eɪʃⁿn] *n term & clin*   *syn* **menses** [mɛnsiːz] *n term*,
menstrual flow or **bleeding** *n clin*,
(**menstrual**) **period** *n inf*

cyclic discharge of debris [iː] from endometrial shedding¹ in the nonpregnant uterus

menstruate² [mɛnstruEɪt] *v term* • **non/ intermenstrual**³ *adj* • **meno-** *comb*

» Pain typically occurs [ɜː] on the first day of the menses, usually about the time the flow begins. Most underage⁴ mothers were sexually precocious⁵, [-kouʃəs] having menstruated for several years before becoming pregnant. Girls should receive [siː] accurate information about menstruation before menarche [-aːrkɪ].

Use to cease⁶ [siːs] **menstruating** • to suppress / to restore / onset of⁷ **menstruation** • regular / ovulatory / persistent / painful / retrograde **menstruation** • **intermenstrual** bleeding⁸ / spotting⁸ • **meno**pause / rrhea⁹ [iː] / stasis¹⁰ [eɪ] • **meno**static /tropin¹¹ • to have the² **period** • missed / last (*abbr* LMP)/ expected **menstrual period** • delayed [eɪ]/ heavy¹² / (ir)regular **menstrual period** • breakthrough¹³ / withdrawal¹⁴ [ɔː] **bleeding**

Menstruation, Monats-, Regelblutung, Menses, Periode
Abstoßung d. Endometriums¹ menstruieren, d. Menstruation haben² intermenstruell, -menstrual³ minderjährig⁴ frühreif⁵ Ausklingen d. Menstruation⁶ Menstruationsbeginn⁷ Zwischen-, Ovulationsblutung⁸ Menstruation, Menorrhoe⁹ Menostase, Ausbleiben d. Monatsblutung¹⁰ Menotropin, Menopausengonadotropin, HMG¹¹ starke Regelblutung¹² Durchbruchblutung¹³ Abbruchblutung¹⁴

> Note: Expressions used by patients to refer to menstruation are **the time of the month**, **to come around**, **to have the days**/ **flux**/ **turns**/ *curse, domestic affliction (BE).

2

menarche [mɛnaːrki‖mənaːrki] *n term*
opposite **menopause**¹ [-pɔːz] *n term*

the time of the first menstrual period [ɪɚ] marking the onset of menstrual function [ʌ] in a girl

(**pre/ post**)**menarch(e)al** [aː] *adj term* • **pre/ postmenopausal** [ɔː] *adj*

» As the child approaches [tʃ] menarche, a marked increase in the number and size of ovarian follicles can be observed. Early age at menarche is a known risk factor for breast cancer.

Use to experience/undergo **menarche** • **menarche** occurs [ɜː] • onset / age / absence / failure [feɪljɚ] **of menarche** • early² / delayed [eɪ] at **menarche** • **menarcheal** status [eɪ‖æ] • **postmenopausal** women³ [ɪ]/ hormone therapy⁴ / osteoporosis

Menarche, erste Regelblutung
Menopause, letzte Regelblutung¹ Menarche praecox² Frauen in d. Postmenopause³ postmenopausale Hormontherapie⁴

3

germ cell [dʒɜːrm sel] *n*   *syn* **gamete** [gæ‖gəmiːt] *n term*, **sex cell** *n clin*

cell capable [eɪ] of developing into a spermatozoon [ou] or ovum [ouvəm]

germinate¹ [-eɪt] *v term* • **germinal** *adj* • **germination** *n* • **gameto-** *comb*

» The most frequent cause of ovarian failure is gonadal dysgenesis [dɪsdʒe-], in which the germ cells are absent and the ovary is replaced by a fibrous [aɪ] streak² [iː]. Ovulation is accompanied by disruption [ʌ] of the germinal epithelium³ [iː].

Use germ layers⁴ / line⁵ / line mosaicism⁶ [mouzeɪəsɪzᵊm] • **germ cell** tumor / damage⁷ / mosaicism⁶ • **germ cell** cancer / mutation [eɪ] • male / female / primordial⁸ [praɪm-] **germ cell** • **germinal** epithelium³ / spot⁹ • **gameto**genesis¹⁰ [dʒe] /pathy

Keimzelle, Gamet
sprossen, keimen¹ fibröser Strang² Keimepithel³ Keimblätter⁴ Keimbahn⁵ Keimbahnmosaik⁶ Keimschädigung⁷ Urkeimzelle⁸ Keimfleck⁹ Gametogenese¹⁰

4

Menstrual Cycle BODY STRUCTURES & FUNCTIONS 207

(human) ovum n term, pl **ova** syn **oocyte** [ouəsaɪt], **female gamete** n term

female sex cell capable of developing into a new individual of the same species [iːʃ] when fertilized by a spermatozoon; yolk[1] [joʊk] contained in the ova of different species varies greatly and influences the pattern of the cleavage [kliːvɪdʒ] division[2]

(an)ovular [ɒːǁouvjʊlɚ] adj term • **o(v)ogenesis**[3] [dʒe] n • **ovi-, ovo-, oo-** comb

» During maturation, the ovum undergoes a halving[4] of its chromosomal set[5] so that at its union [juː] with the male gamete the number of chromosomes (46 in man) is maintained [eɪ].

Use mature[6] [mətʃʊɚ]/ fertilized [ɜː]/ blighted[7] [blaɪtɪd] *ovum* • *ovum* retrieval[8] [iː]/ transfer • *ova* donor[9] [oʊ] • *oocyte* /blast /lemma[10] /gonia[11]

Ei(zelle), Ovum, O(v)ozyt(e)
Dotter[1] Furchungsteilung[2] O(v)ogenese, Entwicklung d. Eizelle[3] Halbierung[4] Chromosomensatz[5] reife Eizelle[6] Abortiv-, Windei[7] Eizellengewinnung, -entnahme[8] Eizellenspenderin[9] Oolemma, Zona pellucida, Eihülle[10] Oogonien, Ureier[11]

5

graafian follicle [fɒːlɪkl] n term syn **(vesicular) ovarian follicle** n term

mature follicle[1] in the ovary that ruptures[2] [ʌ] during ovulation to release [iː] one or more ova

follicular[3] [fəlɪkjələ˞] adj term

» In the Graafian follicle the oocyte reaches its full size and is surrounded by an extracellular glycoprotein layer (the zona pellucida) which separates it from a peripheral layer of follicular cells. The theca [θiːkə] of the ovarian follicle develops into an internal and an external layer.

Use uptured / mature[1] / preovulatory *Graafian follicle* • *follicular* fluid[4] / phase[5] / epithelium • *follicular* growth[6] / atresia[7] [iːʒ]/ cyst / adenoma / hypertrophy • primordial[8] / primary[9] [aɪ]/ secondary *follicle* • tertiary[10] [tɜːrʃieri]/ dominant / atretic[11] [e] *follicle* • *follicle* regulatory protein (abbr FRP)/ stimulating hormone[12]

Graaf-Follikel, Folliculus ovaricus maturus
(sprung)reifer Follikel[1] platzt[2] follikulär, Follikel-[3] Follikelflüssigkeit[4] Follikelphase[5] Follikelwachstum[6] Follikelatresie[7] Primordialfollikel[8] Primärfollikel[9] Tertiär-, Bläschenfollikel, präovulatorischer Follikel[10] atretischer Follikel[11] follikelstimulierendes Hormon, FSH[12]

6

follicular phase [feɪz] n term syn **proliferative** [ɪ] **phase** n term

the phase after menstruation in which the ovaries produce increasing amounts of estrogen [-dʒən] (FSH induced) and cause the uterine [juː] lining [aɪ] to proliferate

proliferate [prəlɪfəreɪt] v term • **proliferation** n

» The days of the menstrual cycle are counted from the first day of the menstrual phase in which the necrotic decidual [dɪsɪdʒʊəl] layer[2] is shed. The proliferative phase is terminated [ɜː] by rupture of a mature follicle and subsequent ovulation. During the follicular phase of the cycle, progesterone [dʒe] levels are low.

Use postmenstrual / preovulatory[3] / menstrual[4] *phase*

Follikel(reifungs)phase, Proliferationsphase
Gebärmutterschleimhaut, Endometrium[1] Dezidua[2] präovulatorische Phase[3] Menstruation[4]

7

luteal phase [luːtɪəl feɪz] n term syn **secretory** [iː] **phase** n term

stage in the cycle from the release of the ovum from a mature follicle which ruptures and – stimulated by luteinizing hormone[1] (LH) – gives rise to the corpus luteum[2] until the onset of menstruation

luteinize v term • **luteinizing** adj • **luteinization** n

» Near the end of the luteal phase progesterone and estrogen levels fall, and FSH levels begin to rise. The endometrium enters the secretory phase in response to rising levels of estrogen and progesterone. Her gynecologist [gaɪ-] found a low luteal phase progesterone level.

Use premenstrual[3] / postovulatory *phase* • shortened / early / late[4] / mid-[5]*luteal phase* • *luteal phase* deficiency [ɪʃ] or dysfunction or inadequacy[6] / pregnancy

Lutealphase, Gelbkörperphase, Sekretionsphase
luteinisierendes Hormon, Lutropin, LH[1] Corpus luteum, Gelbkörper[2] Prämenstruum[3] späte Lutealphase[4] mittlere Lutealphase[5] Lutealphasendefekt, Lutealinsuffizienz[6]

8

ovulation [oʊǁɒːvjʊleɪʃ³n] n term

opposite **anovulation**[1] n term

rupture [rʌptʃɚ] and release [iː] of an ovum from the ovarian follicle

ovulate[2] [ɒːvjəleɪt] v term • **(pre/ post/ peri/ an/ oligo-)ovulatory**[3] adj

» A non-frond-like pattern[4] on Fern [ɜː] testing[5] of the cervical mucus can be interpreted as showing that ovulation has occurred. After ovulation ceases [iː], no further secretory changes are seen. Since amenorrheic [iː] women do not ovulate, they cannot conceive[6] [siː].

Use to induce/inhibit or suppress[7]/predict *ovulation* • to monitor/promote/restore *ovulation* • to fail to *ovulate* • paracyclic[8] [-saɪklɪk] *ovulation* • *ovulation* time / method of family planning[9] • *ovulation* induction[10] / inhibition[11] [ɪʃ] • **anovulatory** women / cycle

Ovulation, Follikel-, Eisprung
Anovulation[1] ovulieren[2] ovulatorisch, Ovulations-[3] Farnkrautmuster[4] Farnkrauttest[5] schwanger werden[6] Ovulation hemmen[7] parazyklische Ovulation[8] Ovulationsmethode[9] Ovulationsinduktion[10] Ovulationshemmung[11]

9

51

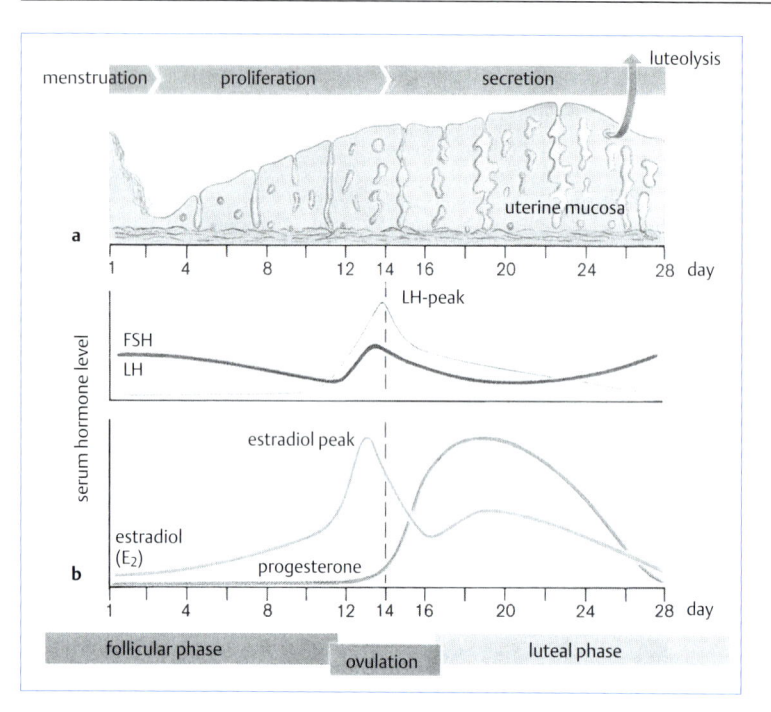

Menstrual cycle: (a) proliferation (follicular phase), degeneration and shedding of the decidua (luteal phase) during the menstrual cycle, (b) serum levels of LH, FSH, estradiol and progesterone, the hormones which regulate the menstrual cycle

menopause [me‖miːnəpɒːz] *n term & clin*   *rel* **climacteric**[1] [klaɪm-] *n & adj term*

(i) final cessation[2] of menstruation (ii) broad term for the endocrine, somatic and psychic [saɪkɪk] changes marking the end of the female reproductive period

menopausal [me‖miːnəpɔːzᵊl] *adj term* • **pre/ postmenopause** *n*

» Not all women experiencing the climacteric have symptoms of estrogen deprivation. Rectoceles[3] [-siːlz] may not become manifest until after the childbearing [eə] years[4] and frequently not until years after the menopause.

Use to have/experience the **menopause** • physiologic or natural / artificial [ɪʃ] or surgical[5] [ɜː] **menopause** • premature[6] / late[7] **menopause** • **menopausal** status [eɪ‖æ]/ syndrome[8] [ɪ] • **menopausal** patient / care / transition / involution[9] [uːʃ] • **climacteric** symptoms • **postmenopausal** bleeding[10] / women / ovary / estrogen therapy • pre[11]/ post**menopausal** • **premenopausal** years / breast [e] cancer [kænˈsɚ] • male[12] **climacteric**

Note: *I don't regularly see any longer* or *the change (of life)* are expressions a female patient may use to refer to the menopause.

hot flush [hɒːt flʌʃ] *n inf usu pl*   *syn* **hot flash** [flæʃ] *n inf usu pl* → U56-18

typical vasomotor symptoms of the climacteric involving sudden flushing and perspiration[1]

» A close temporal association between the occurrence [ɜː] of flushes and the pulsatile [ʌ] release of LH has been demonstrated. The actual flush is characterized as a feeling of heat or burning [ɜː] in the face, neck, and chest, followed by an outbreak of sweating[2] [e].

Use to trigger/reduce/be associated with/complain [eɪ] of[3] **hot flushes** • vasomotor / menopausal[4] **flushes** • facial[5] [eɪʃ]/ sensations of **flushing**

Menopause, letzte Regelblutung
Klimakterium, Klimax, Wechseljahre; klimakterisch[1] endgültiges Ausbleiben[2] Rektozelen[3] gebärfähiges Alter[4] künstliches Klimakterium[5] Climacterium praecox[6] Climacterium tardum[7] Menopausensyndrom[8] menopausale Rückbildung[9] postmenopausale Blutung[10] prämenopausal[11] Climacterium virile[12]

Hitzewallung
Transpiration, Schwitzen[1] Schweißausbruch[2] über Hitzewallungen klagen[3] Hitzewallungen[4] Gesichtsröte[5]

Male Sexual Organs   BODY STRUCTURES & FUNCTIONS **209**

Unit 52 Male Sexual Organs
Related Units: 48 Urinary Tract, 49 Urine Production, 53 Male Sexual Functions, 68 Sexuality, 112 Urologic Symptoms

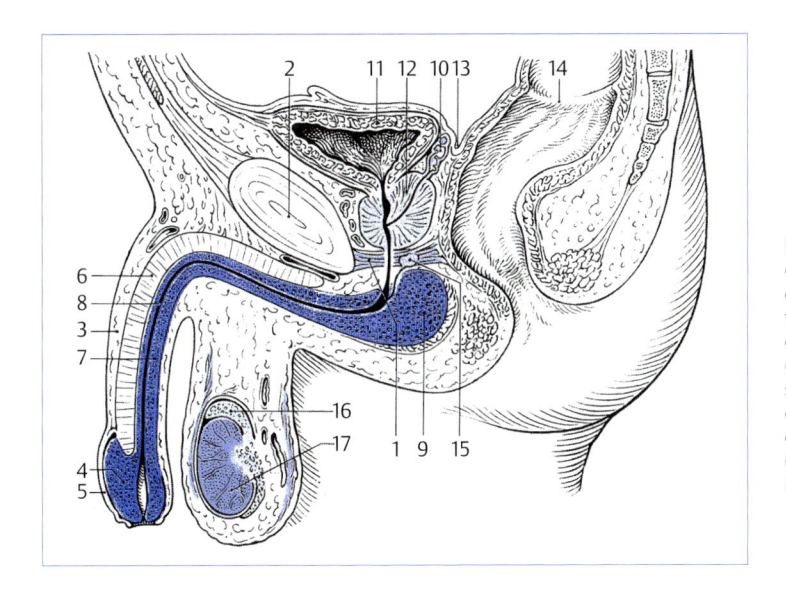

Male genitalia: urogenital diaphragm (**1**), pubic symphysis (**2**), dorsum penis (**3**), glans penis (**4**), foreskin or prepuce (**5**), corpus cavernosum (**6**), corpus spongiosum (**7**), urethra (**8**), bulb of penis (**9**), seminal vesicle (**10**), bladder dome (**11**), prostate (**12**), rectovesical pouch (**13**), Kohlrausch's fold (**14**), Cowper's glands (**15**), epididymis (**16**), testicle (**17**)

---

reproductive [ʌ] **system** [ɪ] *n term*
    syn **genital tract, genitals** [dʒenɪtᵊlz] *n clin*, **private parts** *n inf*
male or female **gonads**[1], associated ducts, and external genitalia dedicated to reproduction
genito- [dʒenɪtoʊ] *comb* • **-genital** *comb* • **genitalia**[2] [dʒenɪteɪljə] *n term*
» History of previous [iː] trauma [ɒː] to the genital tract or scrotal or inguinal surgery should be elicited[3] [ɪs]. Sexual ambiguity[4] [juː] was classified according to the gonadal defect and the impact[5] of aberrant gonadal function on the internal genital ducts and external genitalia[6].
Use male / female **reproductive system** • male / female upper / lower **genital tract** • **genital tract** disease / infection • uro/ ano**genital** [eɪ] • **genito**urinary (*abbr* GU) system *or* tract[7] /-scrotal • uro**genital** anomalies / sinus / tract[7] / diaphragm[8] [daɪəfræm]/ triangle[9] [aɪ] • hypo**genitalism**[10] [aɪ]

scrotum [skroʊtᵊm] *n term*   *rel* **hemiscrotum**[1] [e] *n term*
pouch[2] [paʊtʃ] of thin wrinkled[3] [r] skin overlying a smooth [uː] muscle [s] layer [eɪ] (tunica dartos) that contains the male gonads
(-)scrotal [skroʊtᵊl] *adj & comb term* • **hemiscrotal** *adj*
» In elderly males the scrotum, which is short and corrugated[4] in youth, may be elongated and flaccid[5] [-(k)sɪd]. Examination of the scrotal contents should be complete but very gentle [dʒ].
Use **scrotal** swellings[6] / skin / testes / septum / raphe[7] [reɪfi]/ reflex[8] / wall • **scrotal** edema[9] [iː]/ hernia[10] [ɜː]/ elevation / ectopia [oʊ]/ temperature • **scrotal** pain / bruising[11] [uː]/ exploration / hypoplasia [eɪʒ]/ mass • hypoplastic / bifid[12] / empty **scrotum** • hemi/ peno [iː]/ intra/ extra/ inguino- [ɪŋgwɪnoʊ]/ genito**scrotal**

Fortpflanzungs-, Geschlechtsorgane, Genitalien
Gonaden, Keimdrüsen[1] Geschlechtsorgane, Genitalien[2] anamnestisch erhoben[3] Intersexualität[4] Auswirkungen[5] äußere(s) Geschlechtsorgane/ Genitalien/ Genitale[6] Urogenitaltrakt[7] Diaphragma urogenitale[8] Trigonum urogenitale[9] Hypogenitalismus, Unterentwicklung d. Geschlechtsorgane[10]

1

Skrotum, Hodensack
Hemiskrotum[1] Sack[2] runzlig[3] gefältelt[4] schlaff[5] Skrotalwülste[6] Raphe scroti[7] Skrotalreflex[8] Skrotalödem[9] Skrotalhernie[10] Skrotalhämatom[11] Scrotum bipartitum, zweigeteiltes Skrotum[12]

2

BODY STRUCTURES & FUNCTIONS — Male Sexual Organs

testis n term, pl **-es**　　syn **testicle** n clin,
　　　　　　　　(male) gonad, orchis [ɔːrkɪs] n term

one of the two male reproductive [ʌ] glands in the scrotum

(intra/ para)testicular adj term • **orchid-** [k] comb • **gonadal** [eɪ] adj

» High scrotal testes have an increased tendency to glide. Distention of the lower ureter may cause referred [ɜː] pain¹ to the ipsilateral testis. Posteriorly the tunica albuginea reflects into the testicle to form the mediastinum [aɪ] testis.

Use (intra-)abdominal² / cryptorchid or undescended³ **testis** • impalpable⁴ / intrascrotally located / inguinal⁵ **testis** • retractile⁶ [-aɪl]/ fertile / dystopic / ectopic / rete [riːti] **testis** • **testicular** cord / vessels / duct⁷ [ʌ]/ appendage⁸ [-ɪdʒ]/ parenchyma [-kɪmə] • **testicular** size / swelling / (mal)descent³ / mobility / self-examination • **testicular** shock / feminization⁹ / torsion¹⁰ [tɔːrʃᵊn]/ mass / tumor [(j)uː]/ cancer [¹s]

> **Note:** Informal and vulgar expressions for the testicles include: *balls, *nuts, *family jewels, *ballocks or **bollocks**, *charleys (BE), *stones.

Testis, Hoden
übertragener Schmerz¹ Bauchhoden, Retentio testis abdominalis² Maldescensus testis, Kryptorchismus³ nicht tastbarer Hoden⁴ Leistenhoden, Retentio testis inguinalis⁵ Pendel-, Wanderhoden⁶ Samenleiter, Ductus/ Vas deferens⁷ Appendix testis⁸ testikuläre Feminisierung⁹ Hodentorsion¹⁰

3

seminiferous tubules [semɪnɪfərəs tjuːbjʊlz] n term

contorted tubules¹ in each lobe of the testis in which spermatogenesis [dʒe] occurs; they straighten just before entering the mediastinum [iː] to form the rete [riːti] testis

» Each testis contains 500 to 1,000 seminiferous tubules lined by seminiferous epithelium [iː]. FSH binds [aɪ] primarily to the Sertoli cells² within the seminiferous tubule.

Use **seminiferous** cells • straight³ [streɪt]/ convoluted **seminiferous tubules**

Hodenkanälchen, Tubuli seminiferi
gewundene Kanälchen¹ Sertoli-(Stütz)zellen² Tubuli seminiferi recti³

4

epididymis [epɪdɪdɪmɪs] n term, pl **-ides**　　syn **parorchis** [pərɔːrkɪs] n term rare

elongated structure along the posterior border of the testis, consisting of the caput, corpus, and cauda [ɔː] epididymidis¹, whose tightly coiled² duct is continuous with the ductus deferens

epididymal adj term • **epididym(o)-** comb • **epididymitis**³ n term

» The epididymis is essentially a convoluted duct which acts as a reservoir for spermatozoa. Then the testes and epididymides are palpated between the thumb [θʌm] and finger. The solid cordlike vas is easily identified and followed to its junction with the tail of the epididymis¹.

Use **epididymal** duct or tubule⁴ / epithelial [iː] cells / sperm [ɜː] maturation • **epididymal** dilation [eɪʃ]/ abnormality / cyst [sɪst] • distal / looped [uː]/ patent [eɪ]/ inflamed³ [eɪ] **epididymis** • **epididym**ectomy /oorchitis⁵ /ovasostomy⁶ • acute / chronic / bacterial [ɪə] / purulent⁷ [pjʊər-]/ suspected⁸ **epididymitis**

Epididymis, Nebenhoden
Schwanz, Cauda epididymidis¹ stark gewunden² Nebenhodenentzündung, Epididymitis³ Nebenhodengang, Ductus epididymidis⁴ Orchoepididymitis, Epididymoorchitis⁵ Epididymovasostomie⁶ eitrige Nebenhodenentzündung⁷ Verdacht auf Nebenhodenentzündung⁸

5

vas [væs] or **ductus deferens** n term　　syn **spermatic** or **deferent duct** n term

secretory [iː] duct of the testis which conveys [eɪ] sperm [ɜː] from the epididymis to the ejaculatory duct

vasectomy¹ [vəsektəmɪ] n term • **vas(o)-** [veɪzoʊ-] comb

» The vas courses down along the posterior bladder, widens and becomes convoluted before it joins the ampulla of the seminal vesicle. Spermatozoa are stored in the ampulla of the vas.

Use ampulla of / meandering [iæ]/ scrotal / hypoplastic [aɪ]/ absent / ligation [aɪ] of the² **vas deferens** • **vas**ectomy reversal³ [ɜː] • **vas** atresia / activity / contractility • **vas**otomy /-vesiculography⁴

Ductus/ Vas deferens, Samenleiter
Vasoresektion, Vasektomie¹ Vasoligatur, Unterbindung d. Samenleiters² Rekanalisation, Vasovasostomie³ Vasovesikulografie, röntgenolog. Darstellung d. ableitenden Samenwege⁴

6

spermatic [spɜːrmætɪk] **cord** n term　　syn **testicular cord** [kɔːrd] n term

cord formed by the ductus deferens, pampiniform plexus, testicular artery, vein, lymphatics¹ [ɪ] and nerves that runs from the deep inguinal ring² through the inguinal canal to the scrotum

» The posterior aspect of the testis is attached to the spermatic cord (with the epididymis lying on the posterolateral margin [dʒ]), while the remainder [eɪ] is covered by the tunica vaginalis.

Use **spermatic cord** length / occlusion [uːʒ]/ torsion³ / mobilization / tumors⁴ • blind-ending⁵ / intrascrotal / thickening of the / asymmetry of the **testicular cord**

Samenstrang, Funiculus spermaticus
Lymphgefäße¹ innerer Leistenring² Samenstrangtorsion³ Samenstrangtumoren⁴ blindendigender Samenstrang⁵

7

Male Sexual Organs

inguinal canal [ɪŋgwɪnəl kənæl] *n term*

tubular passage through the muscle layers of the lower abdominal wall that contains the spermatic cord

inguin(o)- *comb*

» As the stone is passed, pain may be felt in the inguinal or lower groin area[1]

Use **inguinal** region [iːdʒ]/ (lymph) nodes [oʊ]/ ring[2] / wall / ligament[3] [ɪ]/ testis / hernia[4] [ɜː] • **inguino**scrotal /pelvic • ilio**inguinal**

Leistenkanal, Canalis inguinalis
untere Leistengegend[1] Leistenring, Anulus inguinalis[2] Leisten-, Poupart-Band, Ligamentum inguinale[3] Leistenhernie, Hernia inguinalis[4]   8

---

seminal vesicle [semɪnəl vesɪkəl] *n term*   *syn* **seminal gland** [æ] *n clin*

paired [eə] saclike, convoluted glandular structure secreting one of the components of the semen [iː]

» Seminal vesicle secretions are usually found in the terminal portion of the ejaculate [ɪdʒækjəlɪt]. Fructose is produced in the seminal vesicles and if absent in the ejaculate implies obstruction of the ejaculatory ducts.

Use soft / firm [ɜː]/ palpably enlarged[1] / obstructed [ʌ] **seminal vesicle** • **seminal** vesiculitis[2] [aɪ]/ colliculus[3] / ducts[4] [ʌ] • **seminal vesicle** invasion [eɪʒ]/ cyst[5] [sɪst]

Samenbläschen, Bläschendrüse, Vesicula/ Glandula seminalis
tastbar vergrößertes Samenbläschen[1] Bläschendrüsenentzündung, Vesikulitis, Spermatozystitis[2] Samenhügel, Colliculus seminalis[3] Samengänge, (ableitende) Samenwege[4] Bläschendrüsenzyste[5]   9

---

prostate [prɒːsteɪt] **(gland)** *n term*   *syn* **prostatic gland** *n term*

chestnut-sized[1] body surrounding the urethra [iː] at the bladder neck; its tubuloalveolar glands[2], which discharge[3] a milky fluid into the semen on ejaculation, lie between abundant [ʌ] stromal tissue

(extra/ intra/ peri)prostatic *adj term* • **prostat(o)-** *comb*

» The central zone occupies approx. 20% of the glandular prostate. At puberty the prostate, which weighs only a few grams at birth, undergoes androgen-mediated growth and reaches the adult size of about 20 g by age 20.

Use tender[4] / acutely inflamed [eɪ]/ enlarged or hyperplastic[5] **prostate** • **prostate** size / weight [weɪt]/ volume • **prostate** cancer /-specific antigen[6] / **prostatic** urethra[7] [iː]/ tissue[8] / stroma • **prostatic** lobe [loʊb]/ duct / utricle[9] [juː] • **prostatic** capsule[10] [-sjuːl]/ fluid / biopsy [aɪ]/ calculus[11] / expressate[12] • **prostatic** massage[13] / enlargement or hyperplasia[14] [eɪʒ] • **prostati**tis [aɪ] /ism[15] /ectomy • **prostato**dynia [ɪ]/lith[11] /rrhea [iː] /vesiculitis • **periprostatic** fat • expressed **prostatic** secretion[12] [iːʃ]

> Note: Although **prostatic hypertrophy** (increase in cell size) and **prostatic hyperplasia** (increase in cell number) are not the same they are commonly used synonymously.

Prostata, Vorsteherdrüse
kastaniengroß[1] tubuloalveoläre Drüsen[2] abgeben[3] druckdolente/ -schmerzhafte Prostata[4] vergrößerte/ hyperplastische P.[5] prostataspezifisches Antigen, PSA[6] Pars prostatica (d. Harnröhre)[7] Prostatagewebe[8] Utriculus prostaticus[9] Prostatakapsel, Capsula prostatica[10] Prostatastein[11] Prostataexprimat[12] Prostatamassage[13] Prostatavergrößerung, -hyperplasie[14] chron. Prostatabeschwerden, -leiden, Prostatismus[15]   10

---

ejaculatory [ɪdʒækjələtɔri] **duct** *n term*

passage formed by the union of the vas deferens and the excretory [iː] duct[1] of the seminal vesicle which traverses [ɜː] the prostate and opens into the prostatic urethra

» The ductal network of the prostate follows the route [aʊ‖uː] of the ejaculatory ducts to the urethra.

Use **ejaculatory duct** obstruction / hematoma [iː]/ cyst

Ductus ejaculatorius
Ductus excretorius, Ausführungsgang d. Samenbläschens[1]   11

---

verumontanum [eɪ] *n term*   *syn* **seminal colliculus** or **hillock** *n term*

portion of the prostatic urethra where the prostatic utricle and ejaculatory ducts enter

» The ejaculatory ducts converge [ɜː] to open at the seminal colliculus on the floor of the urethra. An omega-shaped muscle layer envelops the urethra from the verumontanum to the striated [aɪeɪ] musculature[1] [ʌ] of the pelvic floor[2].

Samenhügel, Colliculus seminalis
quergestreifte Muskulatur[1] Beckenboden[2]   12

---

bulbourethral [bʌlboʊjʊriːθrəl] **glands** *n term*   *syn* **Cowper's glands** *n term*

two small compound racemose glands[1] along the membranous urethra just above the bulb of the corpus spongiosum that discharge[2] a mucoid secretion into the spongy portion of the urethra[3]

» The numerous mucous glands[4] of the urethra include the paired bulbourethral glands of Cowper between the leaves[5] of the urogenital diaphragm[6].

Use dilated **Cowper's gland** duct • **Cowper's gland** cyst • inflammation[7] / abscess of **Cowper's glands**

Glandulae bulbourethrales, Cowper-Drüsen
tubuloalveoläre Drüsen[1] absondern[2] Pars spongiosa (d. Harnröhre)[3] Schleimdrüsen[4] Schichten[5] Diaphragma urogenitale[6] Entzündung d. Cowperschen Drüsen[7]   13

BODY STRUCTURES & FUNCTIONS — Male Sexual Organs

penis [piːnɪs] *n clin & term*   *syn* **phallus** [fæləs], **priapus** [praɪəpəs] *n term*, **virile** [vɪraɪl‖əl] **member** *n clin*

male organ of copulation consisting of erectile [ɪrɛktaɪl] tissue; the tip or glans (penis)[1] contains the urethral meatus [miɛɪtəs]

penile [piːnaɪl] *adj term* • **phallic** *adj* • **phall(o)-** *comb* • (**micro/ di)phallus**[2] *n*

» Chronic irritation of the glans penis predisposes to penile tumors. The ischiocavernosus muscle which covers the crura of the penis is attached to the the ramus [eɪ] of the ischium.

Use   clubbed[3] [ʌ]/ erect[4] / flaccid[5] [(k)s] **penis** • bulb[6] [ʌ]/ crus [ʌ‖uː]/ root[7] [uː]/ median raphe [reɪfi]/ tip / dorsum **of the penis** • **penile** shaft[8] / skin / urethra / growth / blood vessels / erection • **penile** reflex[9] [iː]/ discharge / hygiene [haɪdʒiːn]/ curvature[10] [ɜː]/ prosthesis[11] [iː]/ fracture[12] / cancer • **penis** envy[13] [ɛnvi] • **phallic** stage[14] / enlargement / tissue [tɪʃjuː]/ duplication[2] [uː])

> **Note:** Clinical, informal and vulgar expressions for the penis include: *member*, *private parts*, *privates*, *cock*, *dick*, *prick*, *pecker*, *stick*, *little/old man* (BE) , *staff*, *tool*, *thing*.

Penis, Phallus, Membrum virile, männliches Glied
Eichel, Glans (penis)[1] Diphallus, Penisverdopplung[2] Penisdeviation[3] erigierter Penis[4] schlaffer Penis[5] Bulbus penis[6] Peniswurzel, Radix penis[7] Penisschaft[8] Bulbocavernosus-Reflex[9] Peniskrümmung[10] Penisprothese[11] Penisfraktur[12] Penisneid[13] phallische Phase[14]

14

corpus cavernosum *n term*   *syn* **cavernous** [ɜː] **body (of the penis)** *n clin*

either of two parallel columns of erectile tissue on the dorsal part of the penis forming its crura

cavernoso- [kævənousoʊ] *comb*

» The corpora cavernosa are engorged [ɪŋɡɔːrdʒd] with blood[1] on sexual excitement[2].

Use **cavernous** arteriole [ɪə]/ veins [eɪ]/ arterial (in)flow / pressure • **cavernous** peak [iː] flow[3] / ischemia [ɪskiː-]/ leakage[4] [liːkɪdʒ]/ fibrosis [aɪ] • **cavernous** nerve (stimulation)[5] / (smooth) [uː] muscle [s] • **cavernos**ography[6] /ometry[7] /ospongiosum shunt [ʃʌnt]

Corpus cavernosum penis, Schwellkörper
blutgefüllt[1] sexuelle Erregung[2] maximale Flussrate i. Corpus cavernosum[3] Schwellkörperinsuffizienz[4] Stimulation d. Nn. cavernosi penis[5] Kavernosografie[6] Kavernosometrie[7]

15

corpus spongiosum *n term*   *syn* **spongy** [spʌndʒi] **body (of the penis)** *n clin*

median [iː] column of erectile tissue located between and ventral to the two corpora cavernosa

spongiosal [spɒːndʒɪousəl] *adj term*

» The corpus spongiosum penis expands from the bulb of the penis posteriorly to the enlarged glans penis anteriorly. The urethra traverses the spongy body of the penis.

Use   proximal / urethral **corpus spongiosum** • **spongiosal** tissue[1] • **spongio**fibrosis

Corpus spongiosum, Schwellkörper
spongiöses Gewebe[1]

16

prepuce [priːpjuːs] *n term*   *syn* **foreskin** *n clin*,
preputium [-pjuʃəm] *n term rare*

loose, retractable fold of skin covering the glans penis more or less completely

preputial [prɪpjuːʃəl] *adj term*

» Forcible foreskin retraction may promote secondary scarring[1] and acquired phimosis[2]. Shed[3] epithelial cells accumulating between the inner prepuce and the glans are termed smegma[4].

Use   redundant[5] [ʌ]/ abundant dorsal / phimotic[6] [fɪmɒːtɪk] **foreskin** • **foreskin** surgery[7] • **preputial** skin / gland[8] / cicatrix [sɪkətrɪks]/ flap

Vorhaut, Präputium
Narbenbildung[1] erworbene Phimose/ Vorhautverengung[2] abgeschilfert[3] Smegma[4] überschüssige Vorhaut[5] verengte Vorhaut[6] Zirkumzision, Beschneidung[7] Glandula praeputialis[8]

17

symphysis [sɪmfɪsɪs] **(pubis)** [pjuːbɪs] *n term*   *syn* **pubic symphysis** *n term*

(i) joint between the two pubic bones
(ii) sometimes used to refer to the pubic region at the symphysis

(supra/ retro)pubic [pjuːbɪk] *adj term* • **pub(o)-** *comb*

» The suprapubic, retropubic or perineal [iː] approach[1] may be employed for open prostatectomy. Patients may localize the discomfort of lower UTI[2] to the suprapubic area or the glans.

Use   **pubic** ramus[3] [eɪ]/ tubercle[4] [ɜː]/ triangle [aɪ]/ bone[5] • mons[6] **pubis** • **suprapubic** pain / bladder tenderness / palpation [eɪʃ]/ catheterization / cystostomy[7] • **pubo**coccygeal [-kɒːksɪdʒɪəl] (exercises)

Symphysis pubis/ pubica, Scham(bein)fuge
retropubischer Zugang[1] Harnwegsinfektion[2] Schambeinast (Ramus inferior od. superior ossis pubis)[3] Tuberculum pubicum[4] Schambein, Os pubis[5] Mons pubis/ veneris, Venus-, Schamberg[6] suprapubische Blasenfistel[7]

18

escutcheon [ɪskʌtʃən] *n term*

pattern of distribution [juː] of pubic hair[1]

» There was a scarred area[2] on the mons where the normal escutcheon should be.

Use   male / female **escutcheon** • normal **escutcheon** or distribution of pubic hair

Schambehaarung, Pubes
Schamhaare[1] narbige Stelle[2]

19

Male Sexual Function　　　　　　　　　　　　　　　　　　　　　　　BODY STRUCTURES & FUNCTIONS 213

perineum [perɪˈniːəm] *n term*　　*rel* **pudendum**[1] [pjuːˈdendəm] *n term* → U22-10

(i) area between the vulva (scrotum in males) and the anus [eɪ] (ii) region between the thighs [θaɪz] from the coccyx [kɒksɪks] to the pubis and lying below the pelvic diaphragm[2] [aɪə]
perineal [perɪˈniːəl] *adj term* • **pudendal** [pjuːˈdendəl] *adj*

» *The perineal procedure* [siː] *uses this area as the point of entry into the body. A pudendal block was administered to relieve the discomfort of the expulsive* [ʌ] *second stage of labor*[3].

Use transverse [ɜː] muscle of the **perineum** • **perineal** area / tissue / tear[4] [teə·]/ body[5] / nerve • **perineal** fistula[6] / care / repair[7] • **pudendal** nerve / plexus / canal[8] / block[9]

Perineum, Damm
Schambereich, Schambeingegend; Pudendum femininum, weibl. Scham[1] Diaphragma pelvis[2] Austreibungsphase (bei d. Geburt)[3] Dammriss[4] Centrum tendineum perinei[5] Dammfistel[6] Dammnaht, Perineoplastik[7] Alcock-Kanal, Canalis pudendalis[8] Pudendusblock, -anästhesie[9]　　　　　　　　20

Unit 53　Male Sexual Function

Related Units: 52 Male Sexual Organs, 68 Sexuality, 69 Fertility, 48 Urinary Tract, 49 Urine Elimination, 55 Hormones, 112 Urologic Signs & Symptoms

male [eɪ] *adj & n clin*　　*sim* **masculine**[1][ˈmæskjʊlɪn],
　　　　manly[1], **virile**[2] [ˈvɪraɪl] *adj clin*, **android**[3] *adj term*

(adj) referring to men and boys (n) synonym for a man; opposite of the female [iː] sex; masculine and virile refer to the characteristic traits[4] [eɪ] of the male sex (e.g. strength, body hair, deep voice, potency)
manhood[5] *n inf* • **masculinity** *n term* • **virility** *n* • **virilize**[6] *v* [-aɪz] • **andro-** *comb*

» *Lung cancer is almost twice as frequent in males as in females. Your son needs help growing from boyhood to manhood. Children are often considered proof of a man's virility. He was the ideal of manly courage* [ɜː]. *These androgens have dramatic virilizing effects.*

Use **male** infant / patient / genitalia [dʒen-]/ gonad / habitus / urethra [iː] • **male** intersex / sexual partner / factor infertility[7] / nurse[8] [ɜː] • prepubescent[9] [es] • **male** • **masculine** features[10] [iːtʃ]/ clothing • **manly** looks[11] / beauty • **virile** strength / member[12] / voice • **andro**logy /gen

männlich; Mann
männlich, maskulin[1] männlich, viril[2] android[3] charakterist. Merkmale[4] Männlichkeit, Mannesalter[5] virilisieren, vermännlichen[6] Zeugungsunfähigkeit[7] Krankenpfleger[8] präpubertärer Junge[9] männliche Gesichtszüge[10] maskulines Aussehen[11] männliches Glied, Penis[12]　　　　　　　　　　1

potency [ˈpoʊtənsi] *n term*　　*opposite* **impotence**[1] [ˈɪmpətəns] *n term*

(i) capable of having sexual intercourse[2] (ii) the pharmacological activity of a substance
potent [oʊ] *adj term* • **impotent** *adj* • **potency-sparing**[3] [eə·] *adj*

» *Advances in surgical technique* [tekniːk] *have led to preservation of potency in up to 80% of prostatectomy patients. The patient was potent prior to*[4] *and after the procedure* [siː].

Use to affect[5]/preserve[6]/restore **potency** • **potency** rate • **potency-sparing** surgery • fully **potent** • sexual / postoperative / erectile **impotence** • **potent** drug[7]

(i) Potenz;
(ii) Wirkung, Wirksamkeit
Impotenz[1] Geschlechtsverkehr[2] potenzerhaltend[3] vor[4] die Potenz beeinträchtigen[5] die Potenz erhalten[6] hochwirksames Medikament[7]
　　　　　　　　　　　　　　2

erection [ɪˈrekʃən] *n term*　　*syn* *stand, *hard-on *n inf*

hard and unyielding state of the aroused penis when the erectile tissue is engorged[1] with blood
erectile[2] [ɪˈrektaɪl] *adj term* • **erector**[3] *n* • **erect(ed)**[4] *adj clin*

» *Compression of the base of the penis* [iː] *commonly elicits*[5] *an erection in boys examined for hypospadias. Psychic stimulation can augment or inhibit reflex erection by local stimuli* [aɪ].

Use to have/achieve [tʃ] /produce/induce/maintain[6] [eɪ] **an erection** • penile [ˈpiːnaɪl]/ rigid [ˈrɪdʒɪd]/ satisfactory / psychogenic [saɪk-] **erection** • reflex(ogenic) [dʒe]/ painful / persistent[7] **erection** • spontaneous [eɪ]/ nocturnal[8] [ɜː]/ early morning / artificial [ɪʃ] **erection** • **erection** center[9] / reflex[10] [iː] • difficulty with **erection** • **erectile** tissue[11] [ʃǁs]/ bodies[12] / dysfunction or impotence or insufficiency[13] • fully[14] **erect**

Erektion
gefüllt[1] erektil, erigierbar[2] Musculus ischiocavernosus[3] erigiert[4] löst aus[5] Erektion aufrechterhalten[6] Dauererektion[7] nächtl. Erektion[8] Erektionszentrum[9] Erektionsreflex[10] erektiles Gewebe[11] Schwellkörper[12] Erektionsstörung, erektile Dysfunktion/ Impotenz[13] voll erigiert[14]　　　　　　3

flaccid [ˈflæ(k)sɪd] *adj*　　*opposite* **rigid**[1] [ˈrɪdʒ-], **erect**[2], **engorged**[3] [ɪnˈɡɔːrdʒd] *adj*

penis [ˈpiːnɪs], bladder or muscles [mʌslz] which are relaxed, flabby[4], or without tone
flaccidity [flæ(k)ˈsɪdɪti] *n term* • **rigidity**[5] [rɪˈdʒɪdɪti] *n*

» *When flaccid the penis looked normal but during erection a lateral curvature* [ɜː] *was noted. Axial penile rigidity and adequacy for penetration was determined by penile buckling* [ʌ] *testing*[6].

Use **flaccid** state / (penile) length[7] / midshaft circumference [ʌ] • penile / (in)adequate / lowered / sustained[8] [eɪ] **rigidity** • **rigid** erection phase [feɪz]

schlaff
steif[1] erigiert[2] angeschwollen[3] schlaff, weich[4] Rigidität[5] Rigiditätsmessung[6] Penislänge in schlaffem Zustand[7] anhaltende Rigidität/ Steifheit[8]
　　　　　　　　　　　　　　4

BODY STRUCTURES & FUNCTIONS — Male Sexual Function

(penile) tumescence [tuːmesənˀs] *n term*   opposite **detumescence**[1] [iː] *n term*

penile [piːnail] enlargement or erectile response to erotic stimuli [aɪ], fantasies or dreams

» *Venous* [iː] *outflow*[2] *is restricted during penile tumescence. This mechanism could divert*[3] [ɜː] *blood into and away from the cavernous spaces, thus inducing erection and detumescence.*

Use full / partial / nocturnal [ɜː] penile (*abbr* NPT)/ papaverin-induced **tumescence** • penile / premature[4] [iː] **detumescence** • vacuum **tumescence** device[5] [-aɪs]

Tumeszenz, Anschwellen

Detumeszenz, Abschwellen[1] venöser Abfluss[2] umleiten[3] vorzeitige Erschlaffung[4] Vakuumpumpe[5]

5

---

seminal fluid [semɪnˀl fluːɪd] *n term*   *syn* **semen** [siːmˀn] *n clin & term*

thick, yellowish white, viscid[1] [s] fluid containing the sperm cells produced by secretions of the testes, seminal vesicles, prostate, and bulbourethral [iː] (Cowper's) glands[2]

insemination[3] [e] *n term* → U69-12 • **seminal** *adj* •
seminiferous [semɪnɪfərˀs] *adj*

» *The seminal fluid acts as an activator and as a diluent*[4] *for the spermatozoa. The key measurable parameters of semen are volume, pH, sperm count, motility and morphology.*

Use **seminal fluid** analysis • infected / undiluted **seminal fluid** • **semen** collection / sample / analysis[5] / culture • **semen** quality / volume / profile[6] • viable [aɪ]/ cryopreserved[7] [kraɪoʊ-]/ donor[8] **semen** • **seminal** emission[9] [ɪʃ] tract • plasma[10] / fructose • **seminiferous** tubules • artificial[11] / donor / intrauterine **insemination**

Samenflüssigkeit, Samen, Sperma, Semen

zähflüssig[1] Cowper-Drüsen, Glandulae bulbourethrales[2] Insemination, Befruchtung[3] Verdünnungsmittel[4] Spermauntersuchung[5] Spermiogramm[6] Spendersamen[7] Kryosperma, tiefgefrorenes Sperma[8] Pollution, nächtl. Samenerguss[9] Samenplasma, Plasma seminis[10] artifizielle Insemination, künstl. Befruchtung[11]

6

---

sperm [spɜːrm] *n term & clin*

   syn **spermatozoon** *n term, pl* -**zoa** [spɜːrmætəzoʊə]

(i) semen
(ii) spermatozoon, a mature male germ [dʒɜːrm] cell consisting of a head, neck and a tail[1] [eɪ] for propulsion[2] [ʌ]

spermatic *adj term* • **spermatoid** *adj* • **sperm(io)-** *comb* • -**spermia** *comb*

» *Spermatozoa are not formed when the testes remain in the abdominal cavity. Their developmental stages are the spermatogonium, spermatocyte* [-saɪt] *and spermatid. Testicular biopsy*[3] *confirmed the decreased sperm count and spermatogenic arrest.*

Use **sperm** head[4] / tail[1] / cell / production / count[5] / concentration • **sperm** density[6] / bank[7] / maturation / motility[8] • **sperm** penetration assay[9] / aspiration / agglutination • **spermatic** cord[10] / vessels / vein [eɪ] • **sperm**icide[11] /icidal [-saɪdˀl] / oligo[12] / hem(at)o[13] / (non)obstructive [ʌ] a(zoo)**spermia**

**(i) Sperma, Spermium
(ii) reifer Samenfaden, Spermatozoon**

Schwanz, Cauda[1] Fortbewegung[2] Hodenbiopsie[3] Kopf, Caput[4] Spermienanzahl; Spermienzählung[5] Spermiendichte[6] Samenbank[7] Spermienmotilität[8] Penetrationstest[9] Samenstrang[10] Spermizid, spermienabtötendes Mittel[11] Oligospermie, verminderte Spermienanzahl i. Ejakulat[12] Häm(at)ospermie, blutiges Ejakulat[13]

7

---

spermatogenesis [spɜːrmətədʒenɪsɪs] *n term*   *rel* **spermiogenesis**[1] *n term*

development of mature spermatozoa from spermatogonia including spermatogenesis and spermiogenesis

spermatogenic *adj term* • **spermatid**[2] [spɜːrmətɪd] *n* • **spermato-** *comb*

» *Spermatids are haploid cells derived from secondary spermatocytes and evolve by spermiogenesis into spermatozoa. Spermatogenesis is very sensitive to temperature.*

Use to stimulate/affect/suppress[3]/restore **spermatogenesis** • (ab)normal / impaired [eə] **spermatogenesis** • primary[4] [aɪ]/ secondary[5] **spermatocyte** • **spermatogenic** defects • **spermato**cele[6] [-siːl]/gonia[7] [oʊ] /gonial /cyte [-saɪt]

Spermatogenese

Spermiogenese (Differenzierung v. Spermatiden in reife Spermien)[1] Spermatide, Spermide[2] d. Spermatogenese unterdrücken[3] primärer Spermatozyt[4] sekundärer Spermatozyt[5] Spermatozele, Samenbruch[6] Spermatogonien[7]

8

Sertoli('s) cells [sels] *n term*   *syn* **cells of Sertoli** [sɜːrtəli‖sərtoʊli] *n term*

elongated cells in the seminiferous tubules to which spermatids are attached during spermiogenesis; they secrete androgen-binding protein and establish the blood-testis barrier[1] by forming tight junctions[2]

» *When both Sertoli (tubular) and Leydig* [aɪ] *(interstitial* [ɪʃ]*) cell elements are present in the tumor it is called an androblastoma*[3]*. The testis was composed of Sertoli and Leydig cells*[4]*, but no germinal* [dʒɜːrmɪnˀl] *cells*[5] *were present.*

Use **Sertoli**-cell-only syndrome[6] [ɪ] / cell tumor[7] /-Leydig cell tumor[3] • adult [ʌ]/ type of / density of **Sertoli's cells**

Sertoli (Stütz)zellen

Blut-Hoden-Schranke[1] Zonulae occludentes[2] Sertoli-Leydig-Zelltumor, Androblastom[3] Leydig-Zwischenzellen[4] Keim-, Germinalzellen[5] Germinalzellaplasie, Castillo-Syndrom, Sertoli-cell-only-Syndrom[6] Sertoli-Zelltumor[7]

9

---

sperm motility [moʊtɪlɪti] *n term*

ability of sperm cells to move spontaneously [eɪ]

motile [moʊtˀl‖taɪl] *adj term* • **immotile**[1] *adj* • **non-motile**[1] *adj*

» *80% of the ejaculated spermatozoa were motile. Semen analysis revealed a good sperm count with poor motility. Total motile sperm concentration was markedly* [ɪ] *diminished.*

Use to inhibit/affect **sperm motility** • normal / decreased [iː]/ poor (**sperm**) **motility** • **motile** sperm count[2] [kaʊnt]

(Spermien)motilität, -beweglichkeit

unbeweglich[1] Anzahl d. beweglichen Spermien[2]

10

Endocrine Glands   BODY STRUCTURES & FUNCTIONS **215**

ejaculate [v ɪdʒækjʊleɪt‖n ɪdʒækjʊlɪt] v & n term   syn **come, shoot** v inf

(v) to expel semen (n) seminal fluid ejected¹ during ejaculation or emission² [ɪʃ]

(an)ejaculation³ n term • **(an)ejaculatory** adj • **ejaculated** adj

» Less than 10% of the ejaculate is spermatozoa, the remainder [eɪ] being seminal fluid and prostatic secretions [iː]. The patient ejaculates a few drops only.

Use inability to **ejaculate** • mean [iː] motile sperm per / split⁴ **ejaculate** • **ejaculated** semen [iː] • **ejaculate** volume⁵ • antegrade / retrograde⁶ [e]/ premature⁷ [iː] **ejaculation** • difficult / spontaneous [eɪ] **ejaculation** • to abstain [eɪ] from⁸ / to control **ejaculation** • to delay⁹/impair **ejaculation** • **ejaculatory** dysfunction¹⁰ [ɪ]/ latency [eɪ]/ reflex¹¹ [iː]/ duct [ʌ]/ abstinence¹²

ejakulieren; Ejakulat
ausgestoßen¹ Pollution, nächtl. Samenerguss² Ejakulation³ aufgetrenntes Ejakulat⁴ Ejakulationsvolumen⁵ retrograde Ejakulation⁶ vorzeitiger Samenerguss, Ejaculatio praecox⁷ enthaltsam sein⁸ d. Ejakulation hinauszögern⁹ Ejakulationsstörung¹⁰ Ejakulationsreflex¹¹ Enthaltsamkeit, sexuelle Abstinenz¹²   11

feminization [femɪnaɪzeɪʃ³n] n term

opposite **masculinization** or **virilization**¹ n term, rel **hirsutism**² [ɜː] n term

(i) development of female sex characteristics³ by a male often resulting in sexual ambiguity⁴
(ii) surgical or hormonal treatment for intersex disorders⁴ in the female direction

feminize/ virilize [-aɪz] v term • **feminizing/ virilizing** adj • **masculinized** adj

» Testicular feminization syndrome⁵ is a type of male pseudohermaphroditism⁶ characterized by female external genitalia, rudimentary vagina and uterus [juː] and intra-abdominal testes. Adrenal virilization in the female at birth is associated with ambiguous external genitalia⁷ (female pseudohermaphroditism⁸). Hirsutism is limited to females and is hair growth in a male pattern of distribution.

Use florid⁹ **feminization** • (in)complete¹⁰ **testicular feminization** • **feminizing** effect / genital [dʒe] reconstruction¹¹ [ʌ] • inadequately **virilized** • to prevent / partial [pɑːrʃᵊl]/ full¹² **masculinization**

Feminisierung
Maskulinisierung, Virilisierung¹ Hirsutismus² Geschlechtsmerkmale³ Intersexualität⁴ testikuläre Feminisierung⁵ Pseudohermaphroditismus masculinus⁶ intersexuelles äußeres Genitale⁷ Pseudohermaphroditismus femininus⁸ sichtbare Feminisierung⁹ komplette testikuläre Feminisierung¹⁰ Geschlechtsumwandlung in weibl. Richtung, Mann-zu-Frau-Geschlechtsumwandlung¹¹ komplette Virilisierung¹²   12

Unit 54 Endocrine Glands
Related Units: **55** Hormones, **46** Digestion, **68** Sexuality, **69** Fertility, **50** Female Sexual Organs, **51** Menstrual Cycle, **52** Male Sexual Organs, **53** Male Sexual Function, **112** Urologic Signs & Symptoms

gland [glænd] n

term for organs having a secretory (endocrine glands) or excretory function (exocrine glands)

(intra/ extra)glandular adj term • **polyglandular**¹ [pɒːlɪ-] adj

» The pituitary hormones regulate peripheral endocrine glands as well as growth and lactation. Hyperthyroidism is common early in the disease because of increased [iː] hormone release [iː] from the markedly inflamed [eɪ] gland.

Use endocrine² [-kraɪn‖krɪn‖kriːn] exocrine³ / lacrimal [æ] or tear⁴ [tɪɚ]/ sweat⁵ [e] **gland(s)** • salivary⁶ [æ]/ sebaceous⁷ [eɪʃ]/ mammary⁸ **gland(s)** • mucous⁹ [mjuːkəs]/ seromucous / urethral¹⁰ [iː]/ greater vestibular or Bartholin's¹¹ **glands** • merocrine / apocrine / holocrine **gland** • **glandular** fever¹² [iː]/ mastitis¹³ [aɪ]/ (hyper)secretion / tissue¹⁴ [ʃ‖s] • **glandular** mucosa / swelling / dysfunction / atrophy • **extraglandular** site / tissue

Note: Both in clinical jargon and colloquially the term **gland** is also used to refer to the lymph nodes (e.g. swollen or enlarged lymph [lɪmʃ] glands).

Drüse, Glandula
pluriglandulär¹ endokrine Drüsen, Glandulae endocrinae² exokrine D., Gg. exocrinae³ Tränendrüse, G. lacrimalis⁴ Schweißdrüsen, Gg. sudoriferae⁵ Speicheldrüsen, Gg. salivariae⁶ Talgdrüsen, Gg. sebaceae⁷ Brustdrüse, G. mammaria⁸ muköse Drüsen, Gg. mucosae⁹ Littré-Drüsen, Gg. urethrales¹⁰ Bartholin-Drüsen, Gg. vestibulares majores¹¹ infektiöse Mononukleose, Pfeiffer-Drüsenfieber¹² parenchymatöse Mastitis¹³ Drüsengewebe¹⁴   1

secrete [sɪkriːt] v   sim **synthesize**¹ [ɪ], **produce**², **express**³, **release**⁴ [iː] v → U88-1; U49-4

forming a physiologically useful substance [ʌ] (e.g. a hormone, enzyme [aɪ], or metabolite) by a cell and to deliver⁵ it into the blood, a body cavity, either by direct diffusion [juː] or by means of a duct [ʌ]

secretion⁶ [iːʃ] n term • **secretory**⁷ adj • **(bio)synthesis** n • **expression** n

» Virtually all hormones produced by the hypothalamus and the pituitary are secreted in a pulsatile [ʌ] or burst-like [ɜː] fashion with brief periods of inactivity and activity interspersed⁸ [ɜː]. Most endocrine organs have a limited capacity to store the hormones they synthesize.

Use to suppress/stimulate/promote⁹/control¹⁰ **secretion** • pulsatile¹¹ / enhanced / bile [baɪl] or biliary¹² [ɪ]/ glandular **secretion** • hormone / enzyme / exocrine / paracrine¹³ / pancreatic **secretion** • ACTH¹⁴-/ hormone-/ **secreting** • steroid [ɪɚ]/ enzymatic / TSH¹⁵ **synthesis**

absondern, sezernieren, produzieren
(künstl.) herstellen, synthetisieren¹ produzieren, erzeugen² herausdrücken, exprimieren³ freisetzen, abgeben⁴ abgeben⁵ Sekretion, Sekret⁶ sekretorisch, sezernierend⁷ dazwischen⁸ Sekretion fördern/ anregen⁹ S. regulieren/ steuern¹⁰ pulsierende Sekretion¹¹ Gallenproduktion¹² parakrine Sekretion¹³ Kortikotropinproduzierend¹⁴ Thyr(e)otropin-Synthese¹⁵   2

BODY STRUCTURES & FUNCTIONS — Endocrine Glands

regulate v   sim **control**[1] v & n, **govern**[2] [ʌ], **mediate**[3] [iː] v → U88-2
to control the rate or manner of biosynthesis and/or of the physiologic products formed thereby
regulation n term • **(counter)regulatory**[4] [kaʊntə-] adj • **regulator**[5] adj & n
» Aldosterone secretion is regulated by the renin-angiotensin [dʒ] mechanism and to a lesser extent by ACTH. Secretion of these hormones is governed by complex feedback loops [uː]. The b1-receptors [se] mediate the adrenergic stimulated renin release [iː].
Use **to regulate** sodium excretion[6] / cellular growth[7] • renal [iː]/ enzyme[8] / auto-/ down[9]-/ up-**regulation** • osmotic[10] / temperature / metabolic **regulation** • **regulatory function**[11] [ʌ]/ action[11] / mechanism • **regulatory** abnormality / cell / protein / gene[12] [dʒiːn] • **regulator** gene[12] • **regulating** hormones[13] • hormonal / (negative) feedback / homeostatic / nervous / inhibitory **control** • be under pituitary[14] **control** • hormone-/ insulin-/ receptor-/ catecholamine-[k] **mediated** • adrenergic- [-ɜːrdʒɪk]/ hypothalamic-**mediated**

hypothalamus [haɪpoʊθæləməs] n term
structure beneath the thalamus which controls pituitary hormone production and regulates key body functions; it produces TSH and corticotropin-releasing hormones (abbr TRH, CRH), growth hormone and prolactin-regulating (i.e. releasing and inhibiting) factors (GHRF, GHIF, PRF, PIF)
hypothalamic[1] [haɪpoʊθəlæmɪk] adj term
» The anterior pituitary is under hypothalamic control. The posterior lobe is the major [eɪdʒ] site for ADH storage[2], but ADH is synthesized within the hypothalamus.
Use **hypothalamic** releasing[3]/inhibiting[4] **factors** • **hypothalamic**-pituitary-adrenal (abbr HPA) axis[5] /-pituitary portal system • **hypothalamic** centers / neurohormones[6] / obesity [iː].

---

steuern, regulieren
steuern, regulieren, unter Kontrolle bringen; Steuerung; Überwachung[1] regulieren, beherrschen[2] vermitteln[3] Gegensteuerungs-[4] Regulator-; Regler[5] Natriumausscheidung regulieren[6] Zellwachstum steuern[7] enzymat. Regulation[8] Verminderung, Down-Regulation[9] Osmoregulation[10] Steuerfunktion[11] Regulatorgen[12] Steuer(ungs)hormone[13] durch die Hypophyse gesteuert sein/ werden[14]   3

Hypothalamus
hypothalamisch, Hypothalamus-[1] Speicherung v. antidiuretischem Hormon[2] Releasing-Hormone/ -Faktoren, Liberine[3] Inhibiting-Hormone/ -Faktoren, Statine[4] Hypothalamus-Hypophysen-Nebennierenrinden-Achse[5] Hypothalamushormone[6]   4

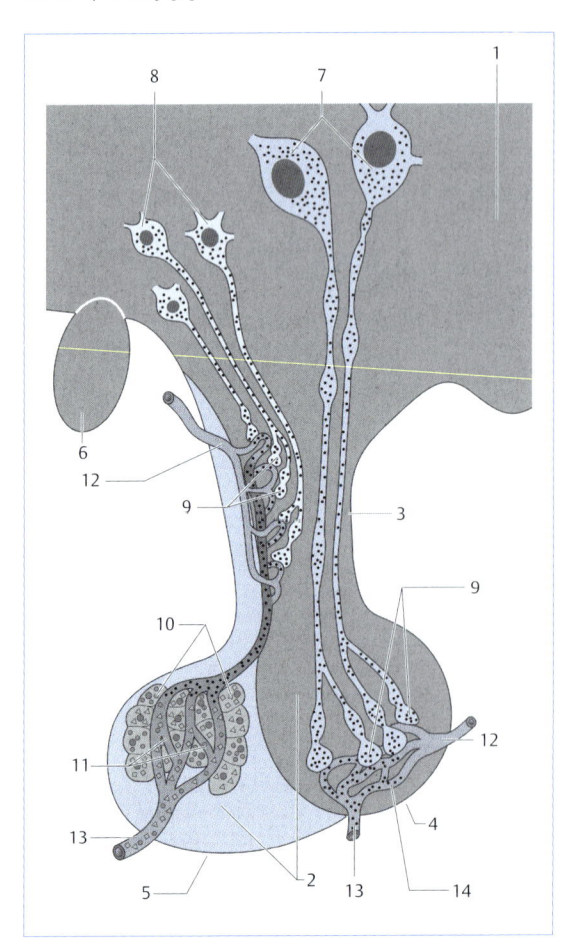

Hypothalamic-pituitary axis:
hypothalamus (**1**),
pituitary gland (**2**),
pituitary stalk or infundibulum (**3**),
posterior pituitary (**4**),
anterior pituitary (**5**),
optic nerve (**6**),
synthesis of neurohormones (**7**),
synthesis of regulatory hormones (**8**),
nerve endings (**9**),
secretory cells (**10**),
sinus (**11**),
artery (**12**),
vein (**13**),
capillaries (**14**)

Endocrine Glands BODY STRUCTURES & FUNCTIONS **217**

pituitary (gland) [pɪt(j)uːəteri] *n term*   *syn* **hypophysis** [haɪpɒː-] *n term rare*

master gland located in the sella turcica[1] [tɜːrkɪkə‖-sɪkə] connected to the adjacent [eɪs] hypothalamus by the pituitary stalk[2] [stɔːk], the gland is divided into the posterior pituitary lobe[3] [oʊ] (neurohypophysis[3]) and the middle[4] and anterior lobes[5] (adenohypophysis[5]) and secretes eight major hormones

(hypo)pituitary *adj term* • **hypophyseal** [ɪ] or **-ial** *adj* • **hypophys-** *comb*

» The anterior pituitary hormones include growth hormone, ACTH, thyroid-stimulating hormone, FSH, LH, prolactin, and melanocyte-stimulating hormone. Anterior pituitary gland function is controlled by regulating hormones produced by the hypothalamus and by direct feedback inhibition.

Use posterior[3] / anterior[5] **pituitary** • **pituitary** tumors[6] / dwarfism[7] [ɔː] / fossa / lobe [oʊ]/ function • **pituitary** adenoma / hyperfunction[8] / lesion [iːʒ]/ stalk[2] • **hypophyseal** portal blood vessels / release • **hypopituitary** adult[9] • (pan)hypo[10]/ hyper[8]**pituitarism** • **hypophys**ectomy /itis[11] [aɪ]

---

thyroid (gland) [θaɪrɔɪd glænd] *n term*

large, horseshoe-shaped[1] gland (two lateral lobes connected by a narrow isthmus [s]) at the upper trachea which secretes thyroid hormone and calcitonin and acts as the body's storehouse for iodine[2] [aɪə]

thyro- *comb* • **-thyroid** *comb*

» TSH regulates the structure and function of the thyroid and stimulates synthesis and release of its hormones. The BP[3] should be checked and the thyroid carefully palpated. The patient had painless thyroiditis [aɪ] and was hyperthyroid because of increased release of thyroid hormone from the thyroid gland.

Use enlarged[4] / palpable / overactive **thyroid** • **thyroid** scan[5] / function (test) / stimulating hormone[6] (*abbr* TSH) • **thyroid** cartilage[7] [-ɪdʒ]/ thyroxine-binding globulin[8] (*abbr* TBG)/ extract • **thyroid** bruit[9] [bruːi‖bruːt]/ nodule[10] / storm[11] • **thyroid** insufficiency [ɪʃ]/ intoxication • **thyro**iditis[12] /megaly[13] /toxin[14] /idectomy /hyoid [aɪ] • **thyro**tropic hormone[6] /tropin[6] /globulin[15] • crico [kraɪkoʊ]/ eu [juː]/ hypo/ hyper/ anti**thyroid**

---

parathyroid (gland) [pærəθaɪrɔɪd] *n term*

four small oval glands on the posterior surface of the thyroid gland which help maintain[1] serum calcium [s] concentration and regulate blood clotting[2], neuromuscular [ʌ] excitation [ks], and cell membrane permeability [pɜːr-]

parathyroid *adj term* • **parathormone**[3] [-θɔːrmoʊn] *n* • **parathyro(id)-** *comb*

» The parathyroid glands secrete PTH[3] that regulates the metabolism of calcium and phosphorus. When first-time parathyroid exploration is performed by an experienced surgeon, routine preoperative localization of parathyroid tissue is unnecessary.

Use superior[4] / inferior[5] **parathyroid** • **parathyroid** hormone[3] / hyposecretion or insufficiency[6] • **parathyroid** adenoma[7] / (dys)function [ʌ] • **parathyroid** hyperplasia[8] [eɪʒ]/ tissue / tetany • **parathyroid** exploration / surgery /-vitamin [aɪ‖ɪ] D axis • **parathyroid**ectomy • hypo[6]/ hyper**parathyroidism**

---

pancreas [pæŋkrɪəs] *n term*

rel **islets** or **islet** [aɪlɪt] **cells (of Langerhans)**[1], **beta** [eɪ‖iː] **cells**[2] *n term*

elongated lobulated retroperitoneal [iː] gland extending from the duodenum to the spleen[3] which consists of an exocrine (digestive enzymes) and an endocrine part (insulin, glucagon, somatostatin)

pancreatic [pæŋkriætɪk] *adj term* • **pancreat(ico)-** *comb*

» The endocrine pancreas secretes insulin and glucagon [uː], while the exocrine part produces digestive [dʒe] enzymes, which are discharged[4] [tʃɑː] into the intestine in the pancreatic juice[5] [dʒuːs]. Before entering the systemic circulation, blood draining from the islets of Langerhans perfuses the pancreatic acini, which are exposed to high levels of hormones.

Use endocrine[6] / exocrine / inflamed [eɪ] **pancreas** • swollen [oʊ]/ necrotic / annular[7] **pancreas** • **pancreatic** duct[8] [ʌ]/ head or caput[9] / body or corpus[10] • **pancreatic** tail [eɪ] or cauda[11] [ɒː]/ enzymes[12] / A cells • **pancreatic** stone[13] / abscess / enlargement • islet cell tumors[14] • **pancreatic** inflammation[15] / carcinoma / pseudocyst[16] [suːdoʊsɪst]/ polypeptide (*abbr* PP) • **pancreas** transplant(ation)[17] • **pancreato**lysis [ɪ] /lith[13] /graphy /genous • **pancreati**tis[15] [aɪ]

Hypophyse, Hirnanhangdrüse, Glandula pituitaria

Türkensattel, Sella turcica[1] Hypophysenstiel[2] Hypophysenhinterlappen, Neurohypophyse[3] Hypophysenmittel-, -zwischenlappen[4] Hypophysenvorderlappen, Adenohypophyse[5] Hypophysentumoren[6] hypophysärer Klein-/ Minderwuchs[7] Hypophysenüberfunktion, Hyperpituitarismus[8] Erwachsener mit Hypopituitarismus[9] Hypopituitarismus, Hypophysenvorderlappen-/ HVL-Insuffizienz[10] Hypophysenentzündung, Hypophysitis[11]   5

Schilddrüse, (G.) thyroidea

hufeisenförmig[1] Iod[2] Blutdruck[3] vergrößerte Schilddrüse[4] Schilddrüsenszintigrafie[5] Thyr(e)otropin, thyreotropes/ thyreoideastimulierendes Hormon, TSH[6] Schildknorpel, Cartilago thyroidea[7] thyroxinbindendes Globulin, TBG[8] Schwirren über d. Schilddrüse[9] Schilddrüsenknoten[10] thyreotoxische /hyperthyreote Krise[11] Schilddrüsenentzündung, Thyreoiditis[12] Schilddrüsenvergrößerung[13] Thyroxin, Tetraiodthyronin[14] Thyreoglobulin[15]   6

Neben-, Beischilddrüse, Epithelkörperchen, G. parathyroidea

aufrechterhalten[1] Blutgerinnung[2] Parathormon, PTH[3] Glandula parathyroidea superior, oberes Epithelkörperchen[4] G. parathyroidea inferior, unteres Epithelkörperchen[5] Hypoparathyreoidismus, Nebenschilddrüsenunterfunktion[6] Nebenschilddrüsenadenom[7] Nebenschilddrüsen-, Epithelkörperchenhyperplasie[8]   7

Pankreas, Bauchspeicheldrüse

Langerhans-Inseln[1] B-Zellen, Betazellen[2] Milz[3] sezerniert[4] Pankreassaft, -sekret[5] endokrines Pankreas[6] P. anulare, Ringpankreas[7] Pankreasgang, Ductus pancreaticus[8] Caput pancreatis, Pankreaskopf[9] Corpus p., Pankreaskörper[10] Cauda p., Pankreasschwanz[11] Pankreasenzyme[12] Pankreasstein, Pankreolith[13] Pankreasinselzelltumoren[14] Bauchspeicheldrüsenentzündung, Pankreatitis[15] Pankreaspseudozyste[16] Pankreastransplantation[17]

  8

BODY STRUCTURES & FUNCTIONS — Endocrine Glands

gastrointestinal (*abbr* **GI) mucosa** *n term*   *rel* **secretin¹** [sɪkriːtᵊn] *n term*

several hormones and releasing factors which increase or contribute to the flow of intestinal juice² are produced by the parietal [pəraɪəˀl] cells³ of the gastric glands and in the proximal small intestine⁴

mucosal [mjʊkoʊsᵊl] *adj term*

» *Cholecystokinin*⁵ [aɪ] *and perhaps other GI hormone peptides (e.g., gastrin-releasing peptide⁶) are released from the duodenal mucosa. The entry of fat into the duodenum, plus the presence of acid, causes release of secretin and cholecystokinin, which in turn stimulate flow of bile⁷* [baɪl] *and pancreatic juice.*

Use gastric / (proximal small) intestinal / pyloric [paɪ-] **mucosa** • **GI** peptides⁸

Magen-Darmschleimhaut

Sekretin¹ Darmsaft² Parietal-, Belegzellen³ Dünndarm⁴ Cholecystokinin⁵ gastrin-releasing peptide, GRP, gastrinsezernierendes Peptid⁶ Galle⁷ gastrointestinale Peptide⁸

9

adrenal (gland) [ədriːnᵊl] *n term*   *syn* **suprarenal** [suːprəriːnᵊl] **(gland)** *n term*

paired [eə] roughly triangular gland resting upon the upper end of each kidney producing epinephrine¹ [ef] and norepinephrine from the medulla [ʌ] and steroid hormones from the cortex

adrenal² *adj term* • **(alpha/ beta)adrenergic³** *adj* • **adren(o)-** *comb*

» *Testosterone and androstenedione* [iː] *are the major functional androgens secreted by the adrenal. Due to their decreased ability to carry out gluconeogenesis* [dʒe]*, patients with adrenal insufficiency* [ɪʃ] *develop hypoglycemia* [aɪsiː] *after fasting⁴.*

Use **adrenal** cortex⁵ / medulla⁶ [ʌ]/ steroids [ɪɚ]/ androgens [dʒ] • **adrenal** virilism⁷ / crisis⁸ [aɪ]/ insufficiency [ɪʃ] • **adrenal** mass / hyperplasia⁹ [eɪʒ]/ adenoma • hypothalamic-pituitary-**adrenal axis** • **adrenal**ectomy /itis • **adren**arche¹⁰ [-ɑːrki] • **adrenergic** bronchodilator¹¹ [k]/ blocking agent¹² [eɪdʒ] • **adrenergic** receptor / drug / nerve • **adreno**genital [dʒe] syndrome⁷ [ɪ]

Nebenniere, G. suprarenalis

Adrenalin¹ adrenal, Nebennieren-² adrenerg³ Fasten⁴ Nebennierenrinde, Cortex glandulae suprarenalis, NNR⁵ Nebennierenmark, Medulla glandulae suprarenalis, NNM⁶ adrenogenitales Syndrom⁷ Addison-Krise, akute Nebennierenrindeninsuffizienz⁸ Nebennierenhyperplasie⁹ Adrenarche¹⁰ adrenerges Broncho(spasmo)lytikum¹¹ Adrenozeptorblocker, -antagonist¹²

10

gonad [goʊnæd] *n term*   *syn* **sex gland** *n*,
  rel **hypogonadism¹, agonadism²** *n term*

a gland that produces germ [dʒɜː] cells³, e.g. the ovary⁴ in the female and the testis⁵ in the male

(a/ extra)gonadal *adj term* • **gonadotrop(h)in⁶** *n* • **gonadopathy** *n*

» *The male gonad has an inhibitory effect on the hypothalamus-pituitary-gonadal axis. The resulting hyperprolactinemia* [iː] *is often associated with hypergonadotropism and secondary hypogonadism. The prostate is the major accessory sex gland of the male.*

Use female⁴ / male⁵ / indifferent⁷ / streak⁸ [iː] **gonad** • **gonadal** sex⁹ / dose¹⁰ / shield¹¹ / streak⁸ / steroid • **gonadal** function / failure / ambiguity⁷ [juː] • **gonadal** dysgenesis¹² [dʒe]/ agenesis [eɪ]/ atrophy [æ] • **gonadotropic** hormone⁶ / activity / cycle [saɪkl] • primary¹³ [aɪ]/ secondary / hypergonadotropic¹³ **hypogonadism**

Keimdrüse, Gonade

Hypogonadismus, Keimdrüseninsuffizienz¹ Agonadismus, Fehlen d. Gonaden² Keimzellen³ Eierstock, Ovar⁴ Hoden, Testis⁵ Gonadotropin⁶ indifferente Gonadenanlage⁷ rudimentärer Keimdrüsenrest, Streak-Ovar⁸ gonadales Geschlecht⁹ Gonadendosis¹⁰ Gonadenschutz¹¹ Gonadendysgenesie¹² hypergonadotroper/ primärer Hypogonadismus¹³

11

thymus (gland) [θaɪməs] *n term, pl* **thymi, thymuses**

primary lymphoid [ɪ] organ in the superior mediastinum and lower neck that consists of two parts partially subdivided into lobules with an inner medullary and an outer cortical portion

thymic [θaɪmɪk] *adj term* • **thymus-dependent¹** *adj* • **thym(o)-** *comb*

» *The thymus, which plays an important role in early life for the normal development of immunological function², reaches its greatest relative weight shortly after birth and begins to involute² after puberty.*

Use enlarged or hyperplastic³ [ʌ] absent⁴ **thymus** • **thymic** vein [eɪ]/ humoral [ʰjuː] factor⁵ • **thymic** cyst [sɪst]/ tumor⁶ / radiation [eɪ] therapy • **thymic** involution⁷ / tissue / transplant⁸ • **thymic** aplasia [eɪʒ]/ hyperplasia³ • **thymus**-derived [aɪ] lymphocytes⁹ [ɪ] /-mediated [iː]

Thymus(drüse)

thymusabhängig¹ sich zurückbilden² Thymusvergrößerung, -hyperplasie³ fehlende Thymusanlage, Thymusagenesie⁴ endokriner Thymusfaktor⁵ Thymustumor, Thymom⁶ Thymusinvolution, -rückbildung⁷ Thymustransplantat⁸ T-Lymphozyten⁹

12

pineal body [paɪnɪəl‖niːəl] *n term*   *syn* **pineal gland** *n term*

small, cone-shaped glandular structure believed to be the major site of melatonin biosynthesis; it lies below the corpus callosum and contains concretions¹ [iːʃ] called brain sand²

pineal³ *adj term* • **pineal-** *comb*

» *Plain* [eɪ] *skull* [ʌ] *films⁴ yielded* [jiː]*changes suggestive* [dʒe] *of⁵ raised* [eɪ]*intracranial* [eɪ] *pressure and displacement of a calcified pineal gland. His skull x-ray is normal except for a shift of a calcified pineal body to one side.*

Use **pineal gland** calcification • calcified **pineal body** • **pineal** peduncle⁶ [ʌ]/ recess⁷ [s]/ activity • **pineal** hypertrophy / tumor⁸ • **pineal**oma⁸ /ectomy /ocytes⁹

Epiphyse, Zirbeldrüse, Corpus pineale

Konkremente¹ Hirnsand, Acervulus cerebri² pineal, Epiphysen-³ Leeraufnahmen d. Schädels⁴ hinweisen auf⁵ Epiphysenstiel, Habenula⁶ Recessus pinealis⁷ Pinealom, Pinealozytom⁸ Pinealzellen⁹

13

Hormones BODY STRUCTURES & FUNCTIONS 219

Unit 55 Hormones

Related Units: 54 Endocrine Glands, 78 Metabolism, 46 Digestion, 51 Menstrual Cycle, 53 Male Sexual Function, 68 Sexuality, 69 Fertility

hormone [hɔːrmoʊn] n term   sim **factor**[1] [fæktɚ] n term
chemical messengers[2] mostly formed in endocrine glands and carried via the bloodstream[3] to their target organs where they trigger or regulate functional [Δ] activity
hormonal adj term • **prohormone**[4] n • **neurohormone**[5] n • **hormone-** comb
» Most hormones are formed by ductless [Δ] glands, but secretin [iː] and pancreozymin [aɪ], formed in the gastrointestinal tract, by definition are also hormones. The regulatory feedback mechanisms [ek] that control hormone synthesis [ɪ] were intact.
Use to release[6] [iː] /secrete [iː] /produce/synthesize [ɪ] **hormones** • circulating [sɜː] **hormones** • (male/ female) sex[7] / pituitary [(j)uː] trop(h)ic[8] **hormones** • peptide[9] / protein[10] / tissue[11] **hormones** • follicle-stimulating / gastrointestinal[12] **hormones** • placental[13] [se] / lipid-mobilizing or lipotropic or lipolytic[14] [ɪ] **hormones** • pancreatotropic / hypothalamic / synthetic **hormones** • **hormone** action / assay[15] / precursor[4] [ɜː] • **hormone** replacement therapy[16] / withdrawal[17] [ɒː] • **hormone** concentration / on level[18] / preparation[19] • **hormone** receptor[20] / release[21] • **hormonal** receptor[20] / stimulation / response / excess[22] • **hormonal** deficiency [ɪʃ]/ overproduction[22] / status / therapy • releasing[23] / inhibiting[24] / regulatory **factor** • **hormone**-secreting /-dependent[25] /-binding • **hormone**-resistant /-releasing

  Note: Messengers of established chemical identity are termed **hormones** while substances [Δ] of unknown chemical nature are termed **factors**.

target tissue [tɑːrgɪt tɪʃ‖tɪsjuː] n term   rel **receptor site**[1] [rɪseptɚ saɪt] n term
tissue or organ having appropriate receptors upon which a hormone exerts [ɜː] its action[2]
target[3] n & v • **hormone-receptor complex**[4] n term
» The function of all target glands will decrease [iː] when all pituitary hormones are deficient [ɪʃ]. Multiple defects [iː] were detected in receptor interaction including absent hormone binding [aɪ] to the receptor, decreased receptor affinity, deficient hormone-receptor localization, and abnormalities of the DNA-binding domain [eɪ] of the receptor.
Use **target** gland / cell[5] / hormone response / organ[6] / site / enzyme [aɪ]/ protein • **target cell** receptor / membrane / expression • hormone / androgen[7] / epidermal [ɜː] growth factor (abbr EGF) **receptor** • estrogen (abbr ER)/ surface[8] / membrane[9] / intracellular[10] **receptor** • **receptor** (super)family[11] / antagonist[12] • **receptor** blocker or blocking agent[12] / occupancy[13] • **receptor** specificity [ɪs]/ affinity[14] / activation • **receptor** binding (assay) / defect / protein[15] • **receptor** potential[16] / density[17] • **receptor** scintigraphy[18] [sɪnt-]/-mediated[19] [iː]

uptake [Λpteɪk] n term
absorption of a substance (radioactive marker, food, etc.) by a gland, organ or body system
» Thyroidal [θaɪrɔɪdəl] RAI **uptake**[1] may be high, with a normal thyroid scan[2].
Use thyroid [aɪ]/ T3 resin[3] / absolute iodine [aɪə] (abbr AIU) **uptake** • radioactive iodine[1] (abbr RAI)/ hormone / serotonin [oʊ] **uptake** • rapid[4] / reduced or decreased / increased **uptake** • hepatic / gallium / calcium [s] **uptake**

steroid [stɪɚ‖sterɔɪd] n term   rel **corticosteroid**[1] [kɔːrtɪkoʊ-] n term
large family of chemical substances including many hormones (androgens, estrogens, ACTH[2] etc.), vitamin D, cholesterol, body constituents, and drugs which all have a steroid ring system
(non)steroidal adj term • **steroidogenesis**[3] n • **steroidogenic** adj
» Plasma and urinary steroid levels were low and returned to normal[4] after ACTH treatment. Steroids diffuse passively through the cell membrane and bind to intracellular receptors.
Use **steroid** hormones / secretion [iːʃ]/ (bio)synthesis[3] [ɪ] • **steroid** level / therapy / ointment[5] [ɔɪ] • **steroid** administration[6] / rage [reɪdʒ]/ rosacea[7] [eɪʃ]/ acne[8] / diabetes[9] [iː] / adrenal[1] [iː]/ adrenocortical[1] / sex **steroids** • gonadal [eɪ]/ androgenic[10] [dʒe] **steroids** • anabolic[11] / urinary [jʊɚ]/ synthetic / exogenous [ɒdʒ] **steroids** • **steroid**-treated /-resistant /-dependent /-induced[12] • topical / systemic / oral / high-potency[13] / high-dose **steroids** • non-**steroidal** anti-inflammatory drugs[14] (abbr NSAIDs)

Hormon
Faktor[1] Botenstoffe[2] Blutbahn[3] Prohormon[4] Neurohormon[5] Hormone freisetzen/ ausschütten[6] weibl. Geschlechts-/ Sexualhormone[7] hypophyseotrope Hormone[8] Peptidhormone[9] Proteohormone[10] Gewebehormone[11] gastrointestinale Hormone[12] Plazentahormone[13] lipotrope Hormone[14] Hormonbestimmung[15] Hormonersatz-, substitutionstherapie[16] Hormonentzug[17] Hormonspiegel[18] Hormonpräparat[19] Hormonrezeptor[20] Hormonausschüttung[21] Hormonüberschuss[22] Freisetzungsfaktor[23] Inhibiting-Hormon, -Faktor[24] hormonabhängig[25]

Zielgewebe
Rezeptorstelle[1] wirken, Wirkung ausüben[2] Ziel; abzielen auf, zum Ziel haben[3] Hormon-Rezeptor-Komplex[4] Zielzelle[5] Ziel-, Erfolgsorgan[6] Androgenrezeptor[7] Oberflächenrezeptor[8] Membran-, membranständiger R.[9] intrazellulärer R.[10] Rezeptorsuperfamilie[11] Rezeptorblocker[12] Rezeptorbesetzung[13] Rezeptoraffinität[14] Rezeptorprotein[15] Rezeptorpotential[16] Rezeptordichte[17] Rezeptorszintigrafie[18] rezeptorgesteuert, -vermittelt[19]

Aufnahme
Radioiodaufnahme[1] Schilddrüsenszintigrafie[2] T3-, Triiodthyronin-Aufnahme[3] rasche Aufnahme[4]

Steroid
Kortiko(stero)id(e)[1] adrenokortikotropes Hormon, Kortikotropin[2] Steroid(bio)synthese[3] normalisierten sich[4] Steroidsalbe[5] Steroidapplikation[6] Steroidrosacea[7] Steroidakne[8] Steroiddiabetes[9] Androgene[10] anabole Steroide, Anabolika[11] steroidinduziert[12] hochwirksame Steroide[13] nicht-steroidale Antirheumatika[14]

human growth hormone n term, abbr GH   syn somatotropin n term

protein hormone produced in the anterior lobe of the pituitary[1] which promotes body growth, fat mobilization, and inhibition of glucose utilization; excess GH may cause diabetes [iː]
growth-enhancing[2] [groʊθ ɪnhænˈsɪŋ] adj • somato- [soʊmətə‖səmætə] comb
» Plasma insulin-like growth factor[3] I (IGF-I), also known as somatomedin-C[3] [iː], should be measured [eʒ] in all patients with suspected acromegaly. Short stature[4] may be seen with an associated growth hormone or thyroid hormone deficiency [ɪʃ].
Use growth hormone release-inhibiting hormone[5] / inhibiting hormone[5] (abbr GIH) • growth hormone releasing [iː] hormone[6] (abbr GHRH)/ releasing factor[6] (abbr GRF) • pituitary[7] growth hormone • somatostatin[5] /crinin[6] /medins[8] • somatotropin release-inhibiting factor[5] /-releasing hormone[6] /-mediating hormones[8] • cellular / hematopoietic[9] / myeloid [aɪ] neurologic growth factors • epidermal [ɜː] (abbr EGF)/ platelet-derived[10] [aɪ] (abbr PDGF) growth factors • vascular endothelial [iː] (abbr VEGF) growth factors • growth deficiency[4]

Wachstumshormon, somatotropes H., Somatotropin (STH)
Adenohypophyse[1] wachstumsfördernd[2] insulinähnlicher Wachstumsfaktor (+ IGF-1), Somatomedin C[3] Minderwuchs[4] Somatostatin, SST[5] Somatoliberin, SRH[6] hypophysäres Wachstumshormon[7] Somatomedine[8] hämopoetische Wachstumsfaktoren[9] Plättchenwachstumsfaktor, PDGF[10]

[5]

thyroid hormone [θaɪrɔɪd hɔːrmoʊn] n term
rel thyrotropin or thyroid-stimulating hormone[1] n term, abbr TSH

iodine-containing compound[2] secreted by the thyroid in the form of triiodothyronine[3] [aɪ] (T₃) and thyroxine[4] [nː] (T₄) which act to increase the BMR[5], control heart function, body temperature, etc.
thyroid[6] n term • (hypo/ hyper)thyroid adj • thyrotropic adj
hyper/ hypothyroidism[7] n
» The hypothyroid state[7] associated with thyroid hormone withdrawal enhances the uptake of radioiodine [aɪ] by reducing its clearance. Thyrotropin-releasing hormone (abbr TRH) controls TSH release and also may influence prolactin release.
Use thyroid hormone production / level / precursor[8] [ɜː]/ preparation[9] / replacement[10] • thyroid hormone binding ratio [reɪʃioʊ] (abbr THBR)/ deficiency / resistance[11] • thyroid peroxidase[12] / releasing hormone[13] / stimulating antibody • TSH-secreting [iː] tumors / assay / surge[14] [sɜːrdʒ]/ concentration • thyrotropin releasing hormone[13] • long-acting thyroid stimulator[15] (abbr LATS) • thyroid-stimulating immunoglobulin[15] • thyroxine-binding globulin[16] (abbr TBG)

Schilddrüsenhormon
thyreoideastimulierendes Hormon, Thyr(e)otropin, TSH[1] Verbindung[2] Triiodthyronin[3] Thyroxin[4] Grund-, Basalumsatz[5] Schilddrüse, Glandula thyroidea[6] Schilddrüsenunterfunktion, Hypothyreose[7] Vorstufe e. Schilddrüsenhormons[8] Schilddrüsenhormonpräparat[9] Schilddrüsenhormonsubstitution[10] Schilddrüsenhormonresistenz[11] Schilddrüsenperoxidase[12] Thyroliberin, Thyreotropin-Releasinghormon[13] TSH-Anstieg[14] Thyreotropin-Rezeptor-Antikörper, TRAK[15] thyroxinbindendes Globulin, TBG[16]

[6]

parathyroid hormone n term, abbr PTH   syn parathormone [θɔː] n term

peptide hormone formed by the parathyroids [aɪ] that controls serum calcium concentration by regulating calcium absorption in the gut[1] [ʌ], calcium resorption and deposition in bone and calcium excretion
» Parathyroid hormone-related peptide[2] (abbr PTHrP) causes most cases of humoral hypercalcemia of malignancy. PTH promotes renal formation of the active metabolite of vitamin D.
Use parathyroid hormone-related protein /-like substance [ʌ] • parathyroid hormone-like factor / receptor[3] / levels[4] / immunoassay • immunoreactive[5] (abbr iPTH)/ circulating [sɜː]/ serum [ɪɚ]/ excess[6] PTH

Parathormon, Parathyrin
Darm[1] parathormonähnliches Peptid[2] Parathormonrezeptor[3] Parathormonspiegel[4] immunreaktives Parathormon[5] Parathormonüberschuss[6]

[7]

calcitonin [kælsɪ-] n term   syn thyrocalcitonin n, rel calcitriol[1] [aɪ] n term

peptide hormone produced in the parafollicular cells[2] of the thyroid; its action is opposite to that of PTH in that calcitonin increases the deposition of calcium [s] and phosphate in bone
» The serum level of calcitonin is increased by glucagon and by Ca²⁺, which opposes postprandial hypercalcemia [iː]. In most patients with palpable thyroid lesions [iːʒ] basal [eɪ] calcitonin levels are elevated.
Use calcitonin receptor / gene-related [dʒiːn] peptide[3] (abbr CGRP/ administration • serum / excess / ectopic / salmon[4] [sæmən] calcitonin • calcitonin-secreting or C-cells[5] /-secreting medullary carcinoma of the thyroid[6] • supplementary[7] / intravenous [iː]/ small doses of calcitriol • treatment or therapy with calcitriol

Calcitonin, (CT), Kalzitonin Thyreocalcitonin
Calcitriol[1] parafollikuläre Zellen[2] CGRP[3] (synthetisches/ rekombinantes) Lachs-Calcitonin[4] C-Zellen[5] calcitoninproduzierendes medulläres Schilddrüsenkarzinom, C-Zellkarzinom[6] Calcitriol-zusatz[7]

[8]

Hormones   BODY STRUCTURES & FUNCTIONS **221**

---

adrenocorticotrop(h)ic hormone [ədriːnoʊ-] *n term, abbr* **ACTH**
    syn **corticotrop(h)in** [kɔːrtɪkoʊtroʊfɪn‖pɪn] *n term*
single chain [tʃeɪn] polypeptide anterior pituitary hormone which stimulates the adrenal cortex and the secretion of corticosteroids
    corticotropic *adj term* • **cortical** *adj* • **ACTH-(in)dependent** *adj*
» *Corticotropin-releasing hormone is the primary* [aɪ] *agent that stimulates ACTH release, and ACTH stimulates the adrenal cortex to secrete cortisol and several weak androgens. The CRH-ACTH-cortisol axis is central to the response to stress, and in the absence of ACTH, the adrenal cortex atrophies and secretion of cortisol virtually* [ɜː] *ceases[1]* [siːs-].
Use to inhibit/suppress/be independent of **ACTH** secretion • serum / pituitary / endogenous / synthetic[2] **ACTH** • **ACTH** secretion / level[3] / release / regulation / determination[4] • **ACTH** overproduction / stimulation test[5] / excess • **ACTH** therapy /-producing tumors[6] • rapid **ACTH** stimulation test[7] • ectopic **ACTH** syndrome[8] • **corticotropin**-releasing hormone[9] (*abbr* CRH) • **corticotropic** cells[10]

adrenokortikotropes Hormon, Kortikotropin, ACTH
beinahe aufhört/ versiegt[1] synthetisches ACTH[2] ACTH-Konzentration[3] ACTH-Bestimmung[4] ACTH-Belastungs-/ Stimulationstest[5] ACTH-produzierende Tumoren[6] ACTH-Schnelltest[7] ektopes ACTH-Syndrom, EAS[8] Kortikoliberin, corticotropin-releasing hormone, CRH[9] ACTH-produzierende Zellen[10]

       9

---

cortisol [kɔːrtɪ-] *n term*   *syn* **hydrocortisone** [haɪdrə-] *n, rel* **cortisone**[1] *n term*
steroid hormone secreted by the adrenal cortex; it is a reduction product of cortisone and the most potent [oʊ] of the naturally occurring [ɜː] glucocorticoids[2]
    11-deoxycortisol[3] [dɪɒksɪ-] *n term* • **hypercortisolism**[4] *n* • **-cortic(o)-** *comb*
» *Endogenously, cortisone is probably a metabolite of cortisol but exhibits no biological activity until converted* [ɜː] *to[5] cortisol; it acts upon carbohydrate* [aɪ] *metabolism[6] and influences the nutrition[7]* [ɪʃ] *and growth of connective tissue.*
Use **cortisol** concentration / excretion [iːʃ]/ response / production rate • **cortisol**-binding [aɪ] globulin[8] / metabolites / (bio)synthesis [ɪ] • serum / free[9] / circulating[10] / deficient / plasma[11] **cortisol** • urinary / protein-bound [aʊ] **cortisol** • fludro**cortisone** • **cortisone** acetate [æs] / eye ointment[12] • gluco**corticoid**[13] • mineralo**corticoid**[14] • adreno**cortical** • **cortico**sterone[15] /steroids[16]

Cortisol, Hydrocortison
Cortison, Kortison[1] natürl. Glukokortikoide[2] 11-Desoxycortisol[3] Hypercortisolismus, -cortizismus[4] umgewandelt in[5] Kohlenhydratstoffwechsel[6] Ernährung[7] cortisolbindendes Globulin, Transcortin[8] freies Cortisol[9] zirkulierendes C.[10] Plasmacortisol[11] kortisonhaltige Augensalbe[12] Glukokortikoid[13] Mineralokortikoid[14] Corticosteron[15] Kortiko(stero)ide[16]

      10

---

epinephrine [epɪnefrɪn] *n term*   *syn* **adrenaline** [ədrenəlɪn] *n term espBE*
this catecholamine [koʊ] (the chief neurohormone of the adrenal medulla [ʌ]) is the most potent stimulant of adrenergic α- and β-receptors; it acts on the heart rate, controls vasoconstriction [eɪ] and vasodilation [eɪʃ], relaxation of bronchiolar [k] and intestinal smooth [uː] muscle[1], and the metabolism of glycogen [aɪ] and lipids
    norepinephrine[2] *n term* • **epinephrine-like** *adj* • **adrenergic**[3] [ædrənɜːrdʒɪk] *adj*
» *Cortisol and epinephrine induce breakdown[4] of muscle glycogen* [-dʒən] *into glucose, which is metabolized to lactate. In coma there may be an intermittent increase in urinary excretion of epinephrine, norepinephrine, and their metabolic products.*
Use aqueous [eɪ] / circulating / high-dose / racemic[5] [siː] **epinephrine** • **epinephrine** metabolite / reversal[6] [ɜː]/ solution [uːʃ]/ injection / shock • nor**adrenaline**[2] • **adrenaline** rush[7] [ʌ] • **adrenergic** fibers [aɪ]/ receptors[8] / blocking agent[9] • **adrenergic** agonists[10] / antagonists or blockers[9] / bronchodilators[11] [k] • alpha-/ beta-**adrenergic**

Adrenalin, Epinephrin
glatte Muskulatur[1] Noradrenalin, Norepinephrin[2] adrenerg[3] Abbau[4] razemisches Epinephrin[5] Adrenalinumkehr[6] Adrenalinausstoß[7] adrenerge Rezeptoren[8] Adrenorezeptorantagonisten, Sympatholytika[9] Adrenozeptoragonisten, Sympathomimetika[10] adrenerge Bronchospasmolytika[11]

      11

---

insulin [ɪnsəlɪn] *n term*   *rel* **glucagon**[1] [gluːkəgɒn] *n term*
double-chain hormone secreted by beta [eɪ‖iː] cells in the islets [aɪləts] of Langerhans[2] that promotes storage of glucose, protein and lipid synthesis, and inhibits lipolysis [-ləsɪs] and gluconeogenesis [dʒe]
    proinsulin[3] *n term* • **insul(in)oma**[4] *n* • **insulinase**[5] *n* • **glucagonoma**[6] *n*
» *Following ingestion[7]* [dʒe] *of glucose, gut* [ʌ] *glucagon[8] is secreted into the blood and is a potent stimulus to the secretion of insulin. Glucagon, which is secreted by the alpha cells of the islet cells of Langerhans, increases serum glucose concentration.*
Use **insulin** secretion / receptor / antagonist / resistance[9] / release [iː] • **insulin** antibodies[10] / allergy[11] / shock[12] / analog or analogue[13] • **insulin** deficiency or lack[14] / replacement[15] / tolerance test[16] • **insulin** dosage / syringe[17] [sɪrɪndʒ]/ pump[18] / pen[19] • **insulin**-secreting tumor /-like growth factor[20] (*abbr* IGF)/ -dependent-diabetes [iː] mellitus[21] /-induced hyperglycemia [aɪsiː] • exogenous [ɒdʒ]/ pork or porcine[22] [-saɪn]/ human / beef **insulin** • protamine zinc (*abbr* PZI)/ intermediate-acting[23] **insulin** • (ultra)lente or long-acting[24] / sustained [eɪ] release[25] / regular or short-acting or rapid-acting or unmodified[26] **insulin** • immunoreactive[27] **glucagon** • **glucagon** test[28]

Insulin
Glucagon[1] Langerhans-Inseln[2] Proinsulin, Insulinvorstufe[3] Insulinom, Inselzelladenom, -tumor[4] Insulinase[5] Glucagonom[6] Aufnahme[7] Enteroglucagon[8] Insulinresistenz[9] Insulinantikörper[10] Insulinallergie[11] Insulinschock[12] Insulinanalogon[13] Insulinmangel[14] Insulinsubstitution[15] Insulintoleranztest[16] Insulinspritze[17] Insulinpumpe[18] Insulin-Pen[19] insulinähnlicher Wachstumsfaktor[20] insulinabhängiger/ juveniler Diabetes mellitus, D. M. Typ 1, Insulinmangeldiabetes[21] Schweineinsulin[22] Intermediärinsulin[23] Langzeitinsulin[24] Verzögerungs-, Depotinsulin[25] Altinsulin[26] immunreaktives Glucagon[27] Glucagontest[28]

      12

secretin [sɪkriːtᵊn] *n term*   *rel* **gastrin**[1] [gæstrɪn], **pancreozymin**[2] [-zaɪmɪn] or **cholecystokinin**[2] [koʊləsɪstəkaɪnɪn] *n term, abbr* **CCK**

hormone secreted by the duodenal and jejunal mucosa under the stimulus of acid chyme[3] [kaɪm] from the stomach; it chiefly stimulates secretion of pancreatic juice[4] and also of bile[5] and intestinal juices

gastric inhibitory (poly)peptide[6] (*abbr* **GIP**) *n term* • **gastrinoma**[7] *n*

» The secretin test was used to exclude a gastrinoma. Hypersensitivity to gastrin and cholecystokinin was present. Loss of antral gastrin, the gastrotropic hormone secreted in the pyloric-antral mucosa, resulted in loss of parietal [aɪ] and peptic cells.

Use intravenous [iː] **secretin** • (fasting) serum **gastrin** level[8] • **secretin**-CCK test[9] / (stimulation) test[9] / injection [dʒe] test[10] • **secretin** agonist / injection • **gastrin**-secreting tumor[7] • **secretin**-mediated [iː] • secretion of / administration of synthetic **cholecystokinin** • vasoactive intestinal[11] (*abbr* VIP) **(poly)peptide**

follicle-stimulating hormone *n term, abbr* **FSH**

anterior pituitary hormone that stimulates growth and maturation[1] of the graafian follicle[2] and the secretion of estradiol[3] [aɪ] (in females) and is essential for spermatogenesis [dʒe] (in males)

» The pituitary glycoprotein [aɪ] hormones TSH, LH, and FSH and HCG are composed of identical (alpha) but different (beta) subunits.

Use to secrete/release/check **FSH** • pituitary / serum / purified[4] [jʊə] **FSH** • **FSH**-LH ratio [eɪʃ]/ activity / secretion[5] • **FSH** receptor / deficiency[6] / releasing factor[7] / postmenopausal [ɒː] **FSH** levels[8] • midcycle [saɪ] LH/FSH surge[9] [3ː] • **FSH**-dependent

luteinizing [luːtiː(ə)naɪzɪŋ] or **luteotropic hormone** *n term, abbr* **LH**
   rel **interstitial-cell-stimulating** [ɪʃ] **hormone**[1] *n term, abbr* **ICSH**

glycoprotein hormone stimulating progesterone secretion by the theca [θiːkə] cells of the ovary, maturation of the follicles to release the ovum, and corpus luteum formation (in females)

» In males LH (also referred to as ICSH) stimulates the production of testosterone by the Leydig cells[2] in the testis. Increased PRL[3] leads to lowered LH and FSH levels. Elevated FSH and LH levels indicate ovarian failure[4] and early menopause.

Use **luteinizing hormone**-releasing hormone (*abbr* LHRH) • **LH** receptor / value[5] / release[6] / surge [sɜːrdʒ]/ peak[7] [iː]/ deficiency [ɪʃ] • **LHRH** agonist / analogue[8]

testosterone [testɒːstəroʊn] *n term*
   rel **androsterone**[1], **androgen**[2] [-dʒən] *n term*

principal androgen produced in the Leydig [aɪ] cells of the testes in response to pituitary LH secretion as well as in the adrenal cortex (in both males and females)

androstenedione[3] [iː] *n term* • **dehydroepiandrosterone**[4] *n, abbr* **DHEA**

» Testosterone stimulates the development of the male sexual organs and is responsible for the secondary sexual characteristics (e.g. beard[5] [ɪə], muscle development). Excessive adrenal androgens can inhibit gonadotropin production so that the testes remain infantile in size. Androstenedione is secreted in about equal amounts by the adrenals and ovaries.

Use to convert[6] [3ː] **testosterone** • **testosterone** derivative[7] / binding affinity / cream[8] / injection • **testosterone** formation / preparation[9] / patch[10] / enanthate [æ]/ propionate[11] • dihydro**testosterone**[12] [daɪhaɪdroʊ-] (*abbr* DHT) • depot [iː]/ total plasma / low **testosterone** • bioavailable / free / parenteral[13] **testosterone** • **androgen** blockade / ablation [eɪʃ] therapy[14] • **androgen** deprivation[14] / insensitivity *or* resistance[15] • plasma / circulating **androstenedione**

estrogen [estrədʒən] *n term, BE* **oestrogen** [iː]   *syn* **estrin** [estrɪn] *n term*

collective term for steroids formed mainly in the ovary [oʊ], placenta [se], and testes which stimulate secondary sexual characteristics[1], growth of long bones, etc.

estrogenic[2] [estrədʒenɪk] *adj term* • **anti-estrogen** *adj*

» Estrogens promote the development of female secondary sexual characteristics. Estrogen supplementation provides symptomatic relief for menopausal [ɒː] complaints [eɪ] such as hot flushes[3] [ʌ] and night sweats[4] [e].

Use conjugated[5] / esterified[6] / topical / extraglandular / synthetic[7] **estrogens** • oral / non-steroidal[7] / natural / cyclic [saɪklɪk] **estrogens** • **estrogenic** effect / substance / hormone / stimulation • **estrogen** production / level / priming[8] [aɪ]/ status / antagonist • **estrogen**-containing contraceptive[9] [se]/ breakthrough bleeding[10] • **estrogen** withdrawal [ɒː] bleeding[11] / receptor / depletion [iːʃ] • **estrogen** preparation / replacement therapy[12] • unopposed **estrogen** secretion[13] • **anti-estrogen** therapy

---

Secretin, Sekretin
Gastrin[1] Cholecystokinin, CCK, Pankreozymin[2] Chymus, Speisebrei[3] Pankreassaft[4] Galle(nflüssigkeit)[5] gastrisches inhibitor. Polypeptid, Enterogastron, GIP[6] Gastrinom, gastrinproduzierender Tumor[7] (Nüchtern)serumgastrinspiegel[8] Secretin-Pankreozymin-Test[9] Sekretininfusionstest[10] vasoaktives intestinales Polypeptid, VIP[11]

13

follikelstimulierendes Hormon, Follitropin (FSH)
Reifung[1] Graaf-Follikel[2] Östradiol[3] gereinigtes FSH[4] FSH-Sekretion[5] FSH-Mangel[6] FSH-RF[7] postmenopausale FSH-Spiegel[8] LH u. FSH-Anstieg in d. Zyklusmitte[9]

14

luteinisierendes Hormon, Lutropin (LH)
ICSH, Interstitialzellen-stimulierendes Hormon[1] Leydig-Zwischenzellen[2] Prolaktin[3] Ovarialinsuffizienz[4] LH-Wert[5] LH-Freisetzung[6] LH-Gipfel[7] LHRH-Analogon[8]

15

Testosteron
Androsteron[1] Androgen[2] Androstendion[3] Dehydroepiandrosteron, DHEA[4] Bart[5] Testosteron umwandeln/ metabolisieren[6] Testosteronderivat[7] Testosteroncreme[8] Testosteronpräparat[9] Testosteronpflaster[10] Testosteronpropionat[11] Dihydrotestosteron, DHT[12] parenteral verabreichtes Testosteron[13] Androgenentzugstherapie[14] Androgenresistenz[15]

16

Östrogen
sekundäre Geschlechtsmerkmale[1] östrogen(artig)[2] Hitzewallungen[3] Nachtschweiß[4] konjugierte Östrogene[5] veresterte Östrogene[6] nichtsteroidale/ synthetische Östrogene[7] Östrogen-Priming, Östrogenreifung[8] östrogenhaltiges Kontrazeptivum[9] Durchbruchblutung[10] Abbruchblutung[11] Östrogenersatz-, substitutionstherapie[12] ungehemmte Östrogensekretion[13]

17

Hormones BODY STRUCTURES & FUNCTIONS 223

estradiol [estrədaɪɔːl] *n term*   *rel* **estrone**¹ [estroʊn], **estriol**² [aɪ] *n term*
principal estrogen secreted by the follicle; beta-estradiol is the most potent natural estrogen
» *Plasma levels of estradiol are lower in postmenopausal women than levels of estrone. Estriol is an estrogenic metabolite of estradiol usually found in urine. Peripheral production of estrone is enhanced by obesity [iː] and liver disease.*
Use ethinyl³ / alpha-/ beta-/ micronized⁴ [aɪ]/ transdermal [ɜː] *estradiol* • *estradiol* receptor / benzoate⁵ [-zoʊeɪt]/ valerate⁶ • *estrone* level / production / sulfate [ʌ] • urinary / unconjugated⁷ [dʒə] *estriol*

Östradiol, Estradiol
Östron, Estron¹ Östriol, Estriol²
Ethinylestradiol, Äthinylöstradiol³
mikronisiertes Östradiol⁴ Estradiol-, Östradiolbenzoat⁵ Estradiol-, Östradiolvalerat⁶ unkonjugiertes Östriol⁷
18

progesterone [proʊdʒestəroʊn] *n term*
syn **progestational** [eɪʃ] *or* **corpus luteum** [luːtiːəm] **hormone** *n term*
antiestrogenic steroid secreted by the corpus luteum to prepare the endometrium [iː] for implantation and by the placenta to maintain [eɪ] an optimal intrauterine [juː] environment [aɪ] during pregnancy
progestational *adj term* • **progestin** *n* • **progestogen** *or* **progestagen**¹ *n*
» *Depression in women taking oral contraceptives is usually associated with their high progestogen content. The tumor did not contain progesterone receptors.*
Use *progesterone* receptor / challenge [tʃæləndʒ] *or* withdrawal test² / therapy / suppository³ • *progesterone*-secreting IUD⁴ • *progestational* agents⁵ / effect / activity / phase⁶ [eɪz] • *progestin*-only pill⁷

Progesteron, Gelbkörper-, Corpus-luteum-Hormon
Progestogen, Progestagen¹ Gestagen-, Progesterontest² Progesteronzäpfchen³ Hormonspirale⁴ Gestagenvorläufersubstanzen⁵ Sekretionsphase (des Menstruationszyklus)⁶ reines Gestagenpräparat⁷
19

(human) chorionic [kɔːrɪɒnɪk] **gonadotrop(h)in** *n term, abbr* **hCG**
syn **anterior pituitary-like** *or* **chorionic gonadotropic hormone** *n term*
glycoprotein produced by the placental trophoblastic cells; its key role appears to be the stimulation of ovarian secretion of the estrogen and progesterone required for the integrity of conceptus [se] during the first trimester [aɪ]
» *hCG levels increase shortly after implantation, double approximately every 48 hours, reach a peak at 50-75 days, and fall to lower levels in the second and third trimesters. Gonadotropins are biologically active substances responsible for the development of secondary sexual characteristics. FSH and LH are two gonadotropins which are active in both sexes but with different effects in males and females.*
Use *hCG* assay¹ / titer [aɪ]/ determination² / levels³ / stimulation /-producing tumor⁴ • b- *or* β *hCG* subunit⁵ • elevated⁶ / urine *or* urinary *hCG* • pituitary⁷ / ectopic / plasma / human menopausal⁸ (*abbr* HMG) *gonadotropin* • *gonadotropin* activity / level / subunits • *gonadotropin*-releasing hormone⁹ (*abbr* GnRH)/ preparation / surge¹⁰ [sɜːrdʒ]/ suppression • *gonadotropic or* sex hormones

humanes Choriongonadotropin, HCG
HCG-Test¹ HCG-Bestimmung² HCG-Werte³ HCG-produzierender Tumor⁴ HCG-Betaunterheinheit⁵ erhöhter HCG-Wert⁶ hypophysäres Gonadotropin⁷ humanes Menopausengonadotropin (HMG), Menotropin⁸ Gonadoliberin, GnRH⁹ Gonadotropinanstieg¹⁰
20

human placental lactogen [hjuːmən pləsentəl læktədʒən] *n term, abbr* **hPL**
syn **human chorionic somatomamotropin** *n term, abbr* **hCS**
lactogen produced by the placenta which is structurally [ʌ] similar to somatotropin
» *The biological activity of hPL weakly mimics¹ that of somatotropin and prolactin. Human placental lactogen is secreted in large amounts by the placenta during the latter part of gestation². hPL disappears from the maternal [ɜː] (and fetal [iː]) circulation³ shortly after termination of pregnancy⁴.*
Use to secrete [iː]/ structural identity with / increased levels of⁵ *human placental lactogen* • *hPL* gene [dʒiːn]

Plazentalaktogen (HPL)
ist ähnlich¹ letzter Schwangerschaftsabschnitt² mütterl. Kreislauf³ Beendigung d. Schwangerschaft⁴ erhöhte HPL-Werte⁵
21

prolactin [proʊlæktɪn] *n term, abbr* **PRL**   *syn* **lactogenic** [dʒe] **hormone** *n term*
anterior pituitary [(j)uː] hormone that stimulates the secretion of milk and, during pregnancy, breast [e] growth
prolactinoma¹ *n term* • **hyperprolactinemia**² *n*
» *Pulsatile [ʌ] GnRH³ may also stimulate prolactin release [iː]. Dopamine is the major regulator of PRL and inhibits its synthesis [ɪ] and release. Lactation [eɪ] may occur [ɜː] with growth hormone excess alone, because GH is a potent lactogenic hormone.*
Use basal [eɪ]/ circulating [ɜː]/ excess / serum *prolactin* • *prolactin*-lowering agent⁴ [eɪdʒ]/ inhibitor⁵ / determination⁶ • *prolactin* concentration / elevation⁷ / insufficiency • *prolactin*-releasing factor *or* hormone⁸ (*abbr* PRH)/-inhibitory factor⁹ (*abbr* PIF)/-secreting cells¹⁰ /-secreting (pituitary) tumor¹

Prolaktin, laktogenes Hormon, Mammotropin
Prolaktinom, prolaktinproduzierender Hypophysentumor¹ Hyperprolaktinämie² pulsatile GnRH-Sekretion³ prolaktinsenkendes Mittel⁴ Prolaktinhemmer⁵ Prolaktinbestimmung⁶ erhöhte Prolaktinkonzentration⁷ prolactin-releasing hormone, Prolaktoliberin⁸ die Prolaktinfreisetzung hemmendes Hormon (PIH), Prolaktostatin⁹ prolaktinproduzierende Zellen¹⁰
22

oxytocin [ɒːksɪtoʊsɪn] *n term, abbr* **OT**

peptide hormone of the neurohypophysis structurally similar to vasopressin that causes myometrial contractions¹ at term² and promotes milk release³ [iː] during lactation

» Oxytocin has an ADH-like effect on the kidney. Therapeutically [juː] oxytocin is used to induce labor⁴ [eɪ], manage postpartum hemorrhage, and relieve painful breast engorgement⁵ [dʒ].

Use human / purified⁶ [jʊɚ] ***oxytocin*** • **oxytocin** release / concentration / challenge test⁷ / drip⁸

antidiuretic hormone *n term, abbr* **ADH**   *syn* **vasopressin** *n term, abbr* **VP**

hormone structurally related to oxytocin and vasotocin¹ [veɪzoʊtoʊsⁿn]; synthetically prepared or obtained [eɪ] from the neurohypophysis [n(j)ʊɚə-] of healthy [e] domestic animals

diuresis² [daɪjəriːsɪs] *n term* • **(anti-)diuretic³** [æntɪdaɪjəretɪk] *adj & n* → U49-6

» In pharmacological doses vasopressin causes contraction of smooth muscle, notably that of all blood vessels. Like aldosterone, ADH plays a key role in maintaining [eɪ] fluid homeostasis [eɪ] and cellular hydration [eɪʃ].

Use syndrome [ɪ] of inappropriate **ADH** secretion⁴ (*abbr* SIADH) • native [eɪ]/ synthetic / ectopic **ADH** • unresponsive to / arginine⁵ [ɑːrdʒəniːn] / aqueous⁶ [eɪkwɪəs]/ purified⁷ / intravenous [iː] ***vasopressin*** • **vasopressin** test⁸ • angiotensin-stimulated **ADH** release • **ADH** excess⁹ / deficiency¹⁰ [ɪʃ]/ administration • forced¹¹ / brisk¹² / osmotic¹³ ***diuresis*** • to induce/promote ***diuresis***

aldosterone [ældɒːstɚoʊn‖dəstɪɚoʊn] *n term*
   rel **angiotensin¹** [ændʒɪoʊ-], **renin²** *n term*

most potent³ mineralocorticoid hormone which regulates electrolyte [-laɪt] and fluid balance⁴ in the body by promoting sodium reabsorption and potassium excretion [iːʃ] by the kidney

(hyper)aldosteronism⁵ *n term* • **angiotensinogen⁶** [-sɪnədʒən] *n*

» Hyperkalemia [iː] and elevated BUN⁷ are generally not present because of the near-normal secretion of aldosterone in these patients. This opposes the vasoconstrictive effects of angiotensin II and inhibits the Na-retaining [eɪ] action⁸ of aldosterone. Reduction [ʌ] in blood volume and flow in the afferent renal arterioles [ɪɚ] induces secretion of renin.

Use **aldosterone** action⁹ / antagonist¹⁰ / metabolism /-mediated [iː] sodium reabsorption¹¹ • **aldosterone**-secreting (adrenal) adenoma¹² / deficiency • (pseudo)primary¹³ [suːdoʊ-]/ secondary / overt¹⁴ [ɜː] **aldosteronism** • **renin** release¹⁵ / activity / suppression / determination • **renin-angiotensin-aldosterone**-system¹⁶ • **angiotensin** I / II / converting [ɜː] enzyme [enzaɪm] (*abbr* ACE) inhibitor¹⁷

melanocyte-stimulating hormone *n term, abbr* **MSH**
   syn **melanotropin** [melænətroʊpɪn], **intermedin** [iː] *n term*

peptide hormone secreted by the intermediate pituitary lobe¹ which causes dispersion [ɜː] of melanin resulting in darkening of the skin, presumably by promoting melanin synthesis [ɪ]

» Hyperpigmentation occurs also in association with Addison's disease (due to lack of the inhibitory influence of cortisol on the production of MSH by the pituitary gland).

Use **MSH** activity² / stimulation • (alpha)³-/ (beta)⁴-**MSH**

thymosin [θaɪməsɪn] *n term*   *rel* **thymopoietin¹** [θaɪməpɔɪətɪn] *n term*
   rel **thymic** [θaɪmɪk] **lymphopoietic** [e] **factor¹** *n term*

thymus-produced hormone (present in greatest amount in infants) which confers immunological competence² on thymus-dependent cells and induces lymphopoiesis³ [iː] (esp. differentiation of T-lymphocytes)

Use **thymosin** fraction V

Oxytozin, Oxytocin

Uteruskontraktionen¹ bei d. Geburt² Milchejektion³ die Geburt einleiten⁴ Anschwellen d. Brust⁵ gereinigtes Oxytocin⁶ Oxytocinbelastungstest⁷ Oxytocininfusion⁸

antidiuretisches Hormon, Adiuretin, Vasopressin (ADH)

Vasotocin¹ vermehrte Harnausscheidung² antidiuretisch; Antidiuretikum³ Syndrom d. inadäquaten ADH-Sekretion, SIADH, Schwartz-Bartter-Syndrom⁴ Arginin-Vasopressin, Argipressin⁵ verdünntes Vasopressin⁶ gereinigtes Vasopressin⁷ Vasopressintest⁸ ADH-Überschuss⁹ ADH-Mangel¹⁰ forcierte Diurese¹¹ beschleunigte Diurese¹² osmotische Diurese¹³

Aldosteron

Angiotensin¹ Renin² wirksamstes³ Wasserhaushalt⁴ (Hyper)aldosteronismus⁵ Angiotensinogen⁶ Blut-Harnstoff-Stickstoff (BUN)⁷ Na-retinierende Wirkung⁸ Aldosteronwirkung⁹ Aldosteronantagonist¹⁰ aldosteronabhängige Na-Reabsorption¹¹ aldosteronproduzierendes Nebennierenadenom, Aldosteronom¹² primärer (Hyper)aldosteronismus, Conn-Syndrom¹³ manifester Hyperaldosteronismus¹⁴ Reninfreisetzung¹⁵ Renin-Angiotensin-Aldosteron-System¹⁶ ACE-Hemmer, -Inhibitor¹⁷

melanozytenstimulierendes Hormon, Melanotropin

Hypophysenzwischenlappen¹ MSH-Aktivität² Alpha-MSH³ Beta-MSH⁴

Thymosin

Thymopo(i)etin¹ macht immunkompetent² Lympho(zyto)poese³

Unit 56   The Skin & its Appendages
Related Units: 25 Build & Appearance, 62 Smell, Taste & Touch, 86 Histology, 105 Fever, 114 Skin Lesions, 140 Wound Healing, 98 Tumor Types

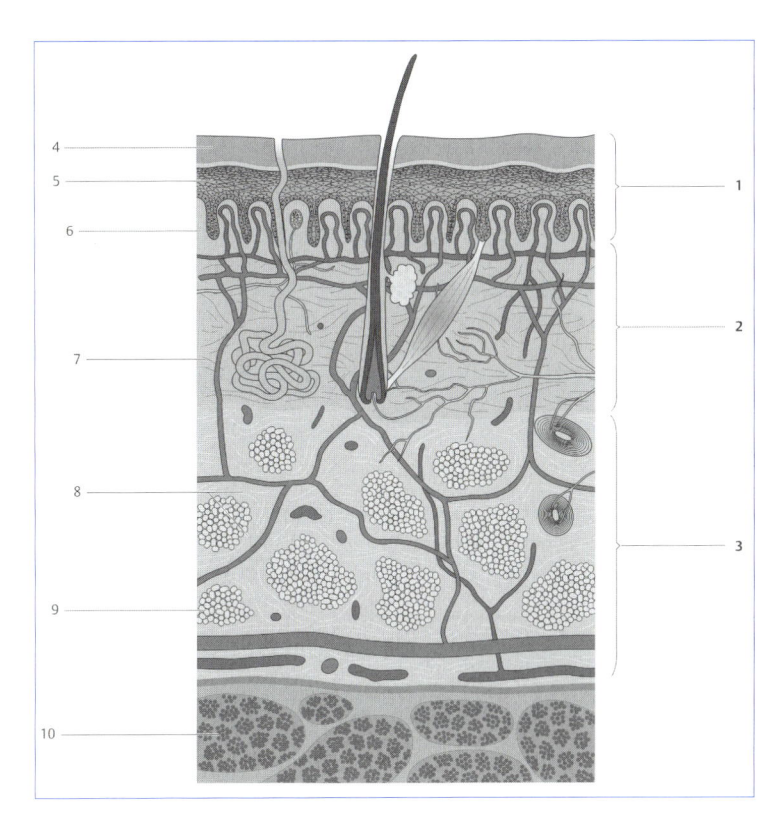

Layers of the skin:
epidermis (**1**),
dermis (**2**),
subcutaneous tissue (**3**),
horny layer or stratum corneum (**4**),
germinative layer or stratum germinativum (**5**),
papillary layer (**6**),
reticular layer or stratum reticulare (**7**),
connective tissue bands (**8**),
adipose tissue (**9**),
subcutaneous muscle layer (**10**)

skin n   syn **cutis** [kjuːtɪs], **integument** n term
  protective covering [ʌ] of the body, consisting of the epidermis and corium (dermis)
  skin[1] v clin • **dark-skinned**[2] adj • **cutaneous**[3] [eɪ] adj term • **integumentary** adj
» If the integrity of the skin is impaired [eɚ] by injury, the skin heals [iː] with scar formation[4]. Primary approximation of the skin and subcutaneous tissues immediately adjacent to the wound [uː] defect [iː] produced a fine-line scar [skɑːr] and optimal aesthetic results in skin texture[5] [tɛkstʃɚ], thickness, and color match.
Use soft / rough [rʌf]/ pale [eɪ]/ fair[6] [feɚ]/ dark / pigmented / clear[7] **skin** • overlying / healthy [e]/ normal-appearing **skin** • cool / warm / dry / moist **skin** • taut[8] [tɒːt]/ pliable[9] [aɪ]/ loose[10] **skin** • redundant[11] [ʌ]/ wrinkled[12] [r]/ aging / dead or necrotic **skin** • paper-thin / clammy[13] / cracked[14] / scaly[15] [eɪ] **skin** • charred[16] [tʃɑːrd]/ blistered[17] **skin** • scarred [ɑː]/ unbroken or intact[18] **skin** • facial / nasal / scalp[19] **skin** • plantar / vulval [ʌ]/ scrotal **skin** • **skin** layers [eɪ]/ tag[20] / appendages[21] / care • **skin**-deep /-tight [taɪt]/ color / perfusion[22] • **skin** creases[23] [iː]/ (tension) lines / temperature / retraction[24] • **skin** blister / reddening / irritation / rash or eruption[25] [ʌ] • **skin** lesion / burn / abrasion[26] [eɪʒ] • **skin** discoloration / turgor [ɜː]/ flap[27] / disease / defect / fair- or light-/ thick- or tough-[28] [tʌf]/ thin[29]-**skinned** • **skin**-colored • **cutis** laxa[30] • **cutaneous** tissue / layer / muscle • **cutaneous** nerve / vein / body surface • **cutaneous** cold receptor [s]/ exposure [oʊʒ]/ folds[23] • **cutaneous** surface / reflexes / eruption[25] • **cutaneous** reaction / hypersensitivity[31] / infection / lesion • **cutaneous** sign / ulcer [ʌlsɚ]/ wheal[32] [iː]/ scar / flushing[33] [ʌ]/ dissemination • per/ trans/ muco/ musculo**cutaneous** • **integumentary** barrier[34] / changes

Haut, Kutis, Integument
abschürfen[1] dunkelhäutig[2] dermal, kutan, Haut-[3] Narbenbildung[4] Hautstruktur[5] helle Haut[6] reine H.[7] straffe H.[8] geschmeidige H.[9] schlaffe H.[10] überschüssige H.[11] runzlige/ faltige H.[12] feuchtkalte H.[13] rissige H.[14] schuppige H.[15] verkohlte/ versengte H.[16] mit Blasen bedeckte H.[17] intakte/ unverletzte H.[18] Kopfhaut[19] Hautanhängsel[20] Hautanhangsgebilde[21] Hautdurchblutung[22] Hautfalten[23] Hauteinziehung[24] Hautausschlag[25] Hautabschürfung[26] Hautlappen[27] dickhäutig, abgebrüht[28] zartbesaitet, sensibel[29] Cutis laxa, Dermatochalasis, generalisierte Elastolyse[30] Überempfindlichkeit d. Haut[31] Quaddel[32] Hautrötung[33] Hautbarriere[34]

epidermis [ɛpɪdɜːrmɪs] n term

outermost portion of the skin consisting of the horny layer[1] [eɪ], clear or light layer[2], granular layer[3], prickle cell or spinous [aɪ] layer[4], and basal [eɪ] cell layer[5]

(sub)epidermal [sʌb-] adj term • **epidermoid**[6] [ɜː] adj & n • **epiderm(o)-** comb

» The epidermis is a stratified squamous [eɪ] epithelium[7] [iː] whose thickness is relatively uniform in all areas of the body except in the palms [ɑː] and soles, where it is particularly thick. The outermost cells of the epidermis are dead cornified cells[8] that act as a tough protective barrier against the environment. Scales[9] [eɪ] represent excessive epidermis, while crusts [ʌ] result from an inadequate epithelial cell layer. If erythematous but unpeeled skin is rubbed sideways, superficial epidermal layers separate from deeper ones and slough[10] [slʌf].

Use smooth [uː]/ intact / sun-exposed / superficial / overlying **epidermis** • **epidermal** cells / layers / basement membrane (zone) / keratin • **epidermal** pigmentation / appendages [-dɪdʒiːz]/ barrier / growth factor[11] (abbr EGF) • **epidermal** detachment[12] [ætʃ]/ denudation [uː]/ nevus[13] [iː]/ scarring / inclusion cyst[14] / cancer • **epidermal**-dermal or dermal-epidermal junction[15] [dʒʌŋkʃən] • **subepidermal** blister[16] / bullous [ʊ] lesion [iːʒ]/ vesicle / fibrosis [faɪ-] • **epidermoid** carcinoma • **epidermo**dermal junction[15] /lytic [-lɪtɪk] /lysis[12] [ɛpɪdɜːrmɒːlɪsɪs]

dermis [dɜːrmɪs] n term   syn corium [kɔːrɪəm] n term

layer of skin composed of a superficial thin layer that interdigitates[1] [ɪdʒ] with the epidermis, the stratum [eɪ‖ɑː] papillare[2], and the stratum reticulare[3]

(trans/ intra/ sub)dermal[4] adj term • **dermatome**[5] n • **derm(o)-, -derma** comb

» There are fewer cells and less ground [aʊ] substance [ʌ] in the reticular dermis than in the papillary dermis[2]. Deep dermal burns heal over a period of 25-35 days with a fragile epithelial covering that arises from the residual uninjured epithelium of the deep dermal sweat [e] glands and hair follicles.

Use papillary[2] / reticular[3] / lower / upper / superficial / adult / dry **dermis** • **dermal** capillaries / lymphatics[6] / ridges[7] • **dermal** collagen / barrier / exposure / repair • **subdermal** vessels • **derma**tological /tologist/titis[8] [aɪ] /tosis • **dermo**epidermal junction[9] /vascular /pathy /plasty[10] • erythro/ leuko/ pyo [aɪ]/ kerato/ sclero[11]/ xero**derma** [zɪɚ-]

subcutaneous layer [leɪɚ] or tissue [tɪʃ‖tɪsjuː] n term
syn **superficial fascia** [suːpɚfɪʃəl fæʃ(ɪ)ə], **subcutis** [sʌbkjuːtɪs] n term

loose connective tissue attached to the overlying corium by coarse[1] [ɔː] fibrous [aɪ] bands

subcutaneous[2] [sʌbkjʊteɪnɪəs] adj term, abbr **sub-q** • **subcuticular** adj

» The subcutaneous tissue, which insulates underlying tissue and protects it from external trauma [ɒː], is composed of fatty and areolar [iː] connective tissue[3]. Except in the auricles[4] [ɔː], eyelids, and scrotum the subcutaneous layer contains fat cells.

Use digital [ɪdʒ]/ deep / adjacent [eɪ] indurated **subcutaneous tissue** • **subcutaneous** fat (pad)[5] / vessels / (connective/ adipose) tissue[6] • **subcutaneous** lipid deposits / edema [iː]/ emphysema [iː] • **subcutaneous** nodule / injection[7] [dʒe]/ infusion [juːʒ]/ administration[8]

subcutaneous fat layer or adipose [ædɪpoʊs] tissue n term
syn **panniculus adiposus** n term → U24-9

connective tissue containing a more or less fatty deposit in a meshwork[1] of areolar tissue

fatty[2] [fæti] adj • **adiposity**[3] [ædɪpɒːsəti] n term • **adip(o)-** comb

» The subcutaneous layer shows great regional variations in thickness and adipose content. Insulin secretion [iːʃ] retards lipolysis of adipose tissue. Adiposis dolorosa (Dercum's disease)[4] is characterized by painful circumscribed [sɜːrkəm-] adipose tissue deposits in subcutaneous tissues of the extremities.

Use peripheral / brown[5] / white or yellow[6] / feminine / excess[7] **adipose tissue** • **adipose tissue** mass / storage / lymph [lɪmf] nodes / stromal cells / deposits[8] • **adipose** cells[9] • **fatty** tissue[10] / acid [s]/ liver / stools[11] [uː]/ meal / weight gain [weɪt geɪn] • generalized[12] / truncal-type[13] [ʌ] **adiposity** • **adipo**cytes[9] [-saɪts]

Oberhaut, Epidermis
Hornschicht, Stratum corneum[1] Glanzschicht, Str. lucidum[2] Körnerzellenschicht, Str. granulosum[3] Stachelzellenschicht, Str. spinosum[4] Basalzellenschicht, Str. basale[5] epidermoid, epidermisähnlich; Epidermoid[6] mehrschichtiges Plattenepithel, Epithelium stratificatum squamosum[7] verhornte Zellen[8] Schuppen[9] werden abgestoßen, schilfern ab[10] epidermaler Wachstumsfaktor[11] Epidermolysis[12] epidermaler Nävus[13] epidermale Einschlusszyste[14] dermoepidermale Grenz-/ Junktionszone[15] subepidermale Blase[16]

2

Lederhaut, Dermis, Corium
ist verzahnt mit[1] Stratum papillare[2] Stratum reticulare[3] subkutan[4] Dermatom (Instr.); von einem Spinalnerv versorgtes Hautsegment[5] subkutane Lymphgefäße[6] Haut-, Papillarleisten[7] Dermatitis, Hautentzündung[8] dermoepidermale Grenz-/ Junktionszone[9] Hautplastik[10] Sklerodermie[11]

3

subkutanes Fett- u. Bindegewebe, Subkutis
derb[1] subkutan[2] lockeres Bindegewebe[3] Ohrmuscheln[4] Unterhautfettgewebe, Fettpolster[5] Unterhautbindegewebe[6] subkutane Injektion[7] subkutane Verabreichung/ Applikation[8]

4

Unterhautfettgewebe, Panniculus adiposus
Netz(werk)[1] fett(haltig)[2] Fettsucht, Adipositas[3] schmerzhafte Adipositas/ Lipomatosis, Dercum-Krankheit[4] braunes Fettgewebe[5] (weißes) Fettgewebe[6] überschüssiges Fettgewebe[7] Fetteinlagerungen[8] Fettzellen, Adipozyten[9] Fettgewebe[10] Fettstühle[11] universelle Fettsucht[12] Stammfettsucht[13]

5

The Skin & its Appendages   BODY STRUCTURES & FUNCTIONS   227

keratin *n term*

    rel **ke**r**a**tinized *or* **ho**rny *or* **co**rnified **layer**[1] *n clin* → U114-14

    scleroprotein[2] found mainly in the epidermis and cuticular appendages (hair, nails, horny tissue)

    keratinization[3] *n term* • keratinize[4] *v* • keratic[5], keratinous[6] *adj* • kerat(o)- *comb*

» Keratin acts as a barrier to pathogens and chemicals. The widely dilated follicular openings are plugged[7] [ʌ] with keratin. A callus shows heaped-up [iː] keratin, and skin markings are preserved. Warts are composed of multiple rounded or filiform keratinized projections.

Use epidermal / soft / thickened / desquamated[8] **keratin** • **keratin** sulfate [ʌ]/-rich tissue / synthesis [ɪ]/ debris [iː]/ cyst [sɪst] • well-/ poorly / non-**keratinized** • surface / hyper**keratinization** • keratitis[9] [aɪ] /inocytes[10] /oconjunctivitis /ectomy[11] • **ker**atomalacia [-məleɪʃ(ɪ)ə] /opathy /oplasty[12] /osis

melanocyte [melənoʊ-‖mələnəsaɪt] *n term*   *sim* **pigment cell**[1] *n clin*

    pigment-producing cell in the basal [eɪ] layer[2] of the epidermis with branching processes by means of which melanosomes are transferred to epidermal cells resulting in pigmentation of the epidermis

    melanin[3] *n term* • (a)melanotic[4] *adj* • (de)pigmentation *n* • melan(o)- *comb*

» Uneven [iː] melanin deposition [ɪʃ] occurs [ɜː] in many fairhaired individuals and results in freckling[5]. Junctional [dʒʌ] nevi[6] [niːvaɪ] result from clustering of melanocytes at the epidermodermal junction. Increased melanin pigmentation and hyperkeratosis[7] [haɪpə-] reduce formation of vitamin [aɪ‖ɪ] D3 in the skin.

Use primordial / intradermal / atypical [ɪ]/ malignant **melanocytes** • **melanocyte**-stimulating hormone[8] (*abbr* MSH) • **mela**notic macule / freckle[9] / pigmentation • dark / yellow-brown / bile[10] [aɪ] **pigment** • **melanin** pigment production[11] / synthesis[11] [ɪ]/ granule[12] • **melanin** metabolism / precursor[13] [ɜː]/ deposition[14] • slight [slaɪt]/ cutaneous / excessive skin *or* hyper[15]/ hypo**pigmentation** • spotty skin[16] / abnormal / muddy[17] [ʌ]/ nipple[18] / stasis[19] [eɪ] **pigmentation** • skin / hair / retinal / patchy[20] **depigmentation** • **melano**some /cytic [sɪ] /genesis [dʒe] /ma[21] /sis

sebaceous [sɪbeɪʃəs] **gland** *n term*   *syn* **oil gland** [ɔɪl glænd] *n clin*

    holocrine gland in the corium that opens into the hair follicles and produces an oily secretion

    sebum[1] [siːbəm] *n term* • seborrheic[2] [-riːɪk] *adj* • pilosebaceous [paɪ-] *adj* • seb(o)- *comb* • oily[3] *adj clin*

» Acne occurs in sebaceous follicles, which, unlike hair follicles, have large, abundant [ʌ] sebaceous glands and usually lack hair. Retention of sebaceous secretions and dilation [eɪʃ] of the follicle may lead to cyst formation. Seborrheic dermatitis[4] [aɪ] consists of an erythematous scaly[5] dermatitis accompanied by overproduction of sebum occurring [ɜː] in areas rich in sebaceous glands[6], that is, the face, scalp, and perineum [iː]. His body folds are oily.

Use **sebaceous gland** activity / sweat / perianal [eɪ]/ meibomian[7] [maɪ-] **glands** • **sebaceous** epithelial cell / follicle / material / hyperplasia[8] [eɪʒ] • **sebaceous** overactivity / cyst[9] / adenoma[10] / tumors[11] • retention of / extrafollicular / incarcerated [s] **sebum** • **sebum** production[12] • **pilosebaceous** gland / follicle / appendage / unit / apparatus [eɪ] • **sebo**rrhea [iː] of the scalp /rrheic dermatitis[4] /lith[13] • **oily** skin[14] / face

lubricate [luːbrɪkeɪt] *v* → U17-14

    to make smooth with an ointment or other greasy [iː] substance, e.g. to make it glide with less friction[1]

    lubrication *n* • lubricant[2] *n & adj* • lubricating *adj*

» Oils help to lubricate the skin, and emollient ointments[3] should be applied within 3 min after a bath, before the skin is dried, to enhance their emollient effects.

Use **to lubricate** the skin / eye / adequate / vaginal[4] [dʒ] **lubrication** • ocular / high-viscosity / bland[5] **lubricant** • water-soluble / hydrophobic [haɪdroʊ-]/ anesthetic[6] **lubricant** • **lubricating** jelly[7] [dʒeli]/ cream / oil / eye drops

---

Keratin, Hornsubstanz

Hornschicht, Stratum corneum[1] Gerüsteiweiß, Skleroprotein[2] Keratinisation, Verhornung[3] verhornen[4] verhornt, Horn-[5] Keratin-; Hornhaut-; hornartig, Horn-[6] verstopft[7] abgestoßenes Keratin[8] Keratitis, Hornhautentzündung[9] Keratinozyten, Hornzellen[10] Keratektomie, Hornhautabtragung[11] Keratoplastik, Hornhauttransplantation[12]

6

Melanozyt

Pigmentzelle[1] Basalschicht[2] Melanin[3] melaninhaltig, melanotisch[4] Bildung v. Sommersprossen[5] Junktionsnävi[6] Hyperkeratose, übermäßige Verhornung[7] melanozytenstimulierendes Hormon, Melanotropin[8] Lentigo praemaligna, prämaligne Melanose, Dubreuilh-Krankheit[9] Gallenfarbstoff[10] Melaninsynthese[11] Melaninkörnchen, Granulum melanini[12] Melaninvorstufe[13] Melaninablagerung[14] Hyperpigmentierung[15] fleckige/ fleckig verfärbte Haut[16] graubraune Pigmentierung[17] Mamillenpigmentierung[18] Staseflecken[19] fleckenförmige Depigmentierung[20] Melanom[21]

7

Talgdrüse, Glandula sebacea

Talg, Sebum[1] seborrhoisch[2] ölig, fettig, schmierig[3] seborrhoische(s) Dermatitis/ Ekzem, Seborrhoe[4] schuppig[5] talgdrüsenreiche Areale[6] Meibom-Drüsen, Glandulae tarsales[7] Talgdrüsenhyperplasie[8] Talgzyste[9] Talg(drüsen)adenom, Adenoma sebaceum[10] Talgdrüsentumoren[11] Talgproduktion[12] Sebolith, Talgdrüsenstein[13] fettige Haut[14]

8

schmieren, gleitfähig machen

Reibung[1] Gleitmittel, Lubrikans; schmierend, Gleit-[2] pflegende Salben[3] Lubrikation[4] Gleitmittel ohne Wirkstoffe[5] schmerzstillendes Gleitmittel[6] Gleitgel[7]

9

BODY STRUCTURES & FUNCTIONS — The Skin & its Appendages

sweat [swet] **gland** n clin   syn **sudoriferous gland** n term → U105-12, 15

one of the coiled tubular structures deep in the corium or subcutaneous tissue found virtually all over the body which serve to promote cooling [uː] of the body by evaporation of their secretion [iːʃ] (sweat)

sudorific[1] [suːdərɪfɪk] adj & n term • **sudo-** comb

» The depths of apocrine glands and sweat glands were devoid of[2] bacteria [ɪɚ]. Hidradenitis[3] is differentiated from furunculosis by skin biopsy [aɪ], which shows typical involvement of the apocrine sweat glands.

Use apocrine[4] / eccrine[5] / duct [ʌ] of **sweat glands** • **sweat gland** function • **sweat** center[6] / duct / acinus [æs]/ stimulus • **sweat** electrolytes / chloride concentration • **sweat** production / test[7] /-producing physical effort / loss[8] / retention • axillary[9] / cold **sweat** • to be drenched [tʃ] in[10] **sweat** • **sudo**motor [oʊ] nerves

sweat pore [swet pɔːr] n clin
   rel **sweat duct**[1], **dermal ridges**[2] [rɪdʒiːz] n term

minute [maɪn(j)uːt] opening of eccrine sweat glands onto the surface of the skin

» Sweat glands release [iː] their secretions into the eccrine ducts which lead to the skin surface and open into a sweat pore. Thin split-thickness grafts differ from normal skin in texture, suppleness[3] [ʌ], pore pattern, hair growth, etc. The distal crease [iː] on the 5th finger was absent and there was a low-arch dermal ridge pattern on the fingertips. He has a history of congenital [dʒe] dermatological defects resulting in dry, flaking [eɪ] skin[4] and minimal sweat pore function. Prickly heat[5] is caused by sweat pore blockage and heat edema [iː].

Use blocked[6] / active **sweat pore** • **sweat pore** density / count • skin / eccrine duct / ectatic[7] **pore** • **pore** pattern / closure[8] [oʊʒ]/ size • **dermal ridge** pattern[9]

hydrated adj term   opposite **dehydrated**[1] adj term,
   rel **humidity**[2] [hjuː-] n

being combined or supplied [aɪ] with water or fluids (of the body in general or certain tissues)
(de)hydrate[3] [haɪdreɪt] v term • (de/ re/ over)hydration[4] n → U82-9

» Water is an important therapeutic [juː] agent [eɪdʒ], and optimally hydrated skin is soft and smooth. As water evaporates[5] readily [e] from the cutaneous surface, skin hydration is dependent on the humidity of ambient air, while sweating contributes little. When humidity falls below 15-20%, the stratum corneum shrinks and cracks. If sweat is prevented from evaporating (e.g. in the groin[6]), local humidity and hydration of the skin are increased.

Use well / adequately / vigorously[7] **hydrated** • to appear / to become / moderately / severely **dehydrated** • **dehydrated** patient[8] / alcoholic / appearance / cell • skin / oral / intravenous [iː]/ parenteral **hydration** • satisfactory / excessive[4] / state of **hydration** • acute / profound [aʊ]/ cellular / cerebral / hypotonic **dehydration** • hypertonic[9] [haɪpɚ-]/ isotonic[10] [aɪsə-]/ hypernatremic[9] [iː] **dehydration** • **dehy**dration fever [iː] • **hydro**lyze [-laɪz] /philic /phobic[11] /static /nephrosis • **hydro**cele [haɪdrəsiːl] /ops /cephalus /gen[12]

hair follicle [fɒlɪkl] n term   rel **hair papilla**[1] [pəpɪlə] n term

tube-like invagination of the epidermis lined by a cellular root sheath[2] from which the hair shaft develops

follicular [fəlɪkjələ] adj • **papillary** adj • **hairy**[3] [heəri] adj → U21-16; U25-15

» Painful inflammatory swellings of a hair follicle forming an abscess are known as boils[4]. In ingrown hairs the stiff tips penetrate the skin before leaving the hair follicle, provoking small pustules [ʌ] that are more a foreign-body reaction than an infection. Anagen [ænədʒen] hairs[5] have sheaths [ʃiːθs] attached to their roots [uː], whereas telogen [iː] hairs[6] have no sheaths but tiny bulbs [ʌ] at their roots.

Use hyperkeratotic / congested[7] [dʒe] infected **hair follicle** • **hair** root[8] (cell) / shaft[9] / fiber [aɪ] • **hair**-bearing skin[10] / cell of the organ of Corti • **hair** distribution / margin [dʒ] or line[11] • **hair** growth / plucking[12] [ʌ] / removal / thinning • **hair** loss / dye[13] [daɪ]/ transplant • body[14] / scalp[15] / eyebrow [aʊ]/ facial / axillary[16] **hair** • pubic[17] [juː]/ sparse[18] **hair** • **hairy** area / skin / scalp / mole or nevus[19] [iː]/ tongue[20] [tʌŋ] • (pilo)sebaceous / lash[21] **follicle** • **follicular** opening or mouth / plugging[22] / papule / pustule • dermal / tactile[23] **papillae**

Schweißdrüse, Glandula sudorifera

schweißtreibend; schweißtreibendes Mittel, Sudoriferum, Diaphoretikum[1] frei von[2] Schweißdrüsenentzündung, Hidradenitis[3] apokrine Schweißdrüsen[4] merokrine Schweißdrüsen[5] Schweißzentrum[6] Schweißtest[7] Schweißverlust[8] Achselschweiß[9] schweißgebadet sein[10]

Schweißpore, Porus sudoriferus

Ductus sudoriferus, Schweißdrüsenausführungsgang[1] Haut-, Papillarleisten[2] Geschmeidigkeit, Elastizität[3] schuppige Haut[4] Miliaria rubra, Roter Hund[5] verstopfte Schweißpore[6] erweiterte Pore[7] Porenschluss[8] Hautleistenmuster[9]

hydr(atis)iert

dehydriert, entwässert[1] Feuchtigkeit[2] dehydr(atis)ieren, Wasser entziehen[3] Hyperhydratation, Überwässerung[4] verdunstet[5] Leiste(nbeuge)[6] intensiv hydratisiert[7] dehydrierte(r) Patient(in)[8] hypertone/ hypernatriämische Dehydratation[9] isotone Dehydratation[10] wasserabstoßend, hydrophob; wasserscheu[11] Wasserstoff[12]

Haarfollikel, -balg

Haarpapille, Papilla pili[1] Wurzelscheide[2] haarig, behaart[3] Furunkel[4] Anagenhaare[5] Telogenhaare[6] verstopfter Haarfollikel[7] Haarwurzel, Radix pili[8] Haarschaft, Scapus pili[9] behaarte Haut[10] Haaransatz[11] Auszupfen v. Haaren[12] Haarfärbemittel[13] Körperbehaarung[14] Kopfhaare[15] Achselhaare, Hirci[16] Schamhaare, Pubes[17] wenig Haare[18] behaarter Naevus, N. pilosus[19] Haarzunge, Lingua villosa nigra[20] Wimpernfollikel[21] Follikelverstopfung[22] Tastpapillen[23]

The Skin & its Appendages   BODY STRUCTURES & FUNCTIONS **229**

piloerection [paɪloʊɪrekʃᵊn] *n term*   *syn* **pilomotor reflex** [iː] *n term*
  rel **goosepimple¹** [uː], **gooseflesh¹**, **goosebump¹** [ʌ] *n clin* → U105-8
raising [eɪ] of the hairs of the skin in response to skin irritation, emotional stimuli or a chilly environment
  piloerector muscle *n term* • **erector pili muscle** *n* • **pilo-** *comb*
» A rigor², a profound [aʊ] chill³ [tʃ] with piloerection accompanied by chattering [tʃ] of the teeth⁴ and severe shivering, is common in bacterial, rickettsial, and protozoal diseases and in influenza. In severe hypoglycemia [-glaɪsiːmɪə], the clinical diagnosis is difficult as the usual physical signs (sweating, gooseflesh, tachycardia [k]) are absent and the neurologic impairment⁵ [eɚ] cannot be distinguished from that caused by malaria.

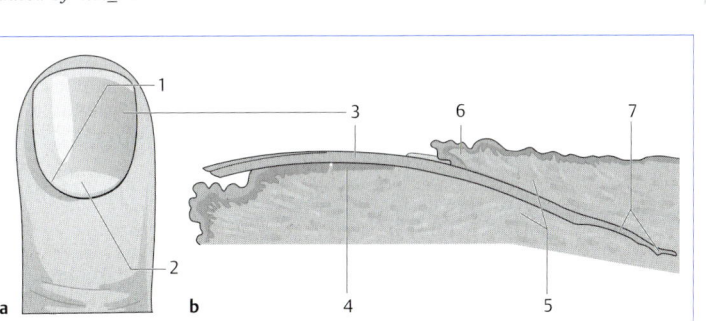

Piloerektion, -arrektion
Gänsehaut, Cutis anserina¹
Schüttelfrost² starkes Frösteln³
Zähneklappern⁴ neurologische Störungen⁵

14

Dorsal view (**a**) and longitudinal section (**b**) of the fingernail:
cuticle (**1**), lunula (**2**),
nail plate or body (**3**),
nail bed (**4**), nail sinus (**5**),
nail wall (**6**), nail root (**7**)

nail *n*   *syn* **unguis** [ʌŋgwɪs] *n term*,
                rel **cuticle¹** [kjuːtɪkl], **lunula²** [luːnjələ] *n term*
                nailfold³ [neɪlfoʊld], **nailbed⁴** *n clin*
hardened cutaneous plate formed of keratin on the dorsal part of the distal end of the digits
  (sub/ peri)ungual [ʌŋgwəl] *adj* • **-nychia** [nɪkɪə], **onych(o)** *comb*
» Peeling [iː] and fissuring [ʃ] of paronychial nail folds or keratotic debris [iː] under the nail edge⁵ also may be evident. Nails should be kept short and clean. Thickening of the distal nail plate was followed by scaling [eɪ] and a crumbly appearance of the entire nail plate surface. The crescent-shaped [s] white area near the root of the nailbed is termed lunula.
Use finger/ thumb [θʌm]/ hang⁶/ toe **nail** • ingrown⁷ / spoon⁸ [uː]/ avulsed [ʌ] **nail** • thickened / infected / dystrophic [dɪs-]/ brittle⁹ / yellowish **nails** • **nail** plate¹⁰ / matrix¹¹ [eɪ]/ file / polish¹² • **nail**-biting¹³ / abnormality / pitting¹⁴ • **subungual** skin / hemorrhage¹⁵ [-ɪdʒ]/ debris / toe abscess • lateral / proximal **nail fold** • **periungual** warts [ɔː]/ erythema [iː] • **onycho**dystrophy¹⁶ /lysis /mycosis¹⁷ [aɪ] • paro**nychia**¹⁸

Nagel, Unguis
Nagelhäutchen, Eponychium¹
Halbmond, Lunula² Nagelfalz³ Nagelbett⁴ Nagelrand⁵ Niednagel⁶ eingewachsener Nagel, Unguis incarnatus⁷ Hohl-, Löffelnagel, Koilonychie⁸ brüchige Nägel⁹ Nagelplatte¹⁰ Nagelmatrix, Matrix unguis¹¹ Nagellack¹² Nägelbeißen, -kauen, Onychophagie¹³ Nageleindellung¹⁴ subunguale Blutung¹⁵ Nagel-, Onychodystrophie¹⁶ Nagel-, Onychomykose, Pilzerkrankung d. Nägel¹⁷ Nagelfalzentzündung, Paronychie¹⁸

15

cuticle [kjuːtɪkl] *n term*   *syn* **eponychium** [epənɪkɪəm] *n term*
(i) narrow band of epidermis at the nail wall¹ projecting [dʒe] onto the nail plate [pleɪt]
(ii) thin layer covering [ʌ] the free surface of epithelial cells
  cuticular *adj term* • **eponychial** *adj* • **paronychial** *adj*
» Finger clubbing² [ʌ] is characterized by widening of the fingertips, enlargement of the distal volar pad, convexity of the nail contour, and loss of the normal angle between the proximal nail and cuticle. Thickening of the cuticle, dull red erythema, and distortion of growth of the nail plate suggest the diagnosis of candidal paronychia.
Use ragged³ [rægɪd]/ thickened⁴ **cuticle** • **cuticular** region of the finger • subcuticular or dermal suture⁵ / skin closure / layer • **eponychial** fold⁶ • **paronychial** infection

(i) **Nagel(ober)häutchen, Eponychium**
(ii) **Kutikula, Häutchen**
Nagelwall¹ Trommelschlägelfingerbildung, trommelschlägelförmige Fingerendphalangen² ausgefranstes Nagelhäutchen³ verdicktes Nagelhäutchen⁴ Intrakutannaht⁵ Nagelfalz⁶

16

56

(skin) wrinkles [skɪn rɪŋklz] n
    rel **skinfold**[1], **cleavage** [kliːvɪdʒ] or **Langer's lines**[2] n term → U129-10
    furrows [ɜː] or folds in the skin, esp. those due to age, exhaustion[3] [ɔː], or distress
    wrinkle[4] v • **(un)wrinkled**[5] adj • **wrinkling** n
» He has marked loss of tissue turgor, with sunken [ʌ] eyes and wrinkling of skin on the fingers. Ask the patient to wrinkle her forehead[6]. During the process of aging natural wrinkle lines appear perpendicular to the direction of contraction of the muscles of facial expression[7].
Use   loss of **skin wrinkles** • facial[8] [eɪʃ] **wrinkles** • **wrinkle** lines • **skin** tag / line of minimal tension • **skinfold** thickness[9] / measurement[10] [eʒ]/ calipers • **wrinkled** skin[11] / appearance [ɪə]/ brows [braʊz]/ hair shaft / tongue[12] • fine[13] / coarse[14] [ɔː]/ (premature) facial / forehead[15] **wrinkling**

(Haut)fältchen, Falten, Runzeln
Hautfalte[1] Hautspalt-, Langer-Linien[2] Erschöpfung[3] runzeln, rümpfen, Falten bekommen, runzlig werden[4] runzlig, faltig[5] ihre Stirn zu runzeln[6] Gesichtsmuskeln, mimische Muskulatur[7] Gesichtsfalten[8] Hautfaltendicke[9] Hautfaltenmessung[10] runzlige Haut[11] Faltenzunge, Lingua plicata/ scrotalis[12] Fältchenbildung[13] tiefe/ grobe Falten(bildung)[14] Stirnrunzeln[15]   17

flushing [flʌʃɪŋ] n clin   sim **blushing**[1] [ʌ] n clin, opposite **blanching**[2] n & adj term
reddening of the skin, esp. on the face and neck, due to vasodilation sometimes associated with a sensation of heat or a rise in body temperature (e.g. on exertion[3], febrile illnesses)
    flush[4] v & n clin • **blush** v & n • **flushed**[5] adj • **blanch** [blænʃ] v → U51-11
» The physical examination may be unremarkable except during an attack, when pallor[6] [æ], flushing, and excess sweating [e] may be observed [ɜː]. She has a tendency to flush easily. The patient appears flushed and the skin is hot and dry. She shuns[7] [ʌ] social situations because of a fear of blushing[8]. The overlying epidermis is thin, and the lesion is friable[9] [aɪ], bleeds easily, and does not blanch with pressure.
Use   to cause/have/experience/relieve [iː] **flushing** • cutaneous[10] / severe / transient / episodic **flushing** • systemic / alcohol-induced / prostaglandin-mediated [iː] **flushing** • facial • malar[11] [eɪ]/ diffuse / erythematous / hot[12] **flush** • cherry-colored / reddish / evanescent[13] [es] **flush** • **flushed** appearance [ɪə]/ skin / facies[14] [feɪʃiːz] • **to blanch** with pressure[15] / on compression / on elevation[16] / **blanched** patchy area / center / wound [uː] edges • digital[17] / episodic / cold-induced **blanching** • **blanching** erythema / of the knuckles[18] [nʌklz]

(Haut)rötung
Erröten[1] Erbleichen, Erblassen; abblassend[2] bei Anstrengung[3] erröten; anfallsweise Hautrötung, Flush[4] gerötet[5] Blässe[6] meidet, scheut[7] Erythrophobie[8] rissig[9] Hautrötung[10] Wangenröte[11] Hitzewallung[12] flüchtige Rötung[13] gerötetes Gesicht[14] auf Druck abblassen[15] bei Hochlagerung abblassen[16] Abblassen d. Finger/ Zehen[17] Weißwerden d. Fingerknöchel[18]

18

skin or **cutaneous turgor** [tɜːrgɚ] n term
    rel **drooping**[1] [uː], **sagging**[1] adj & n clin → U89-22
measure of skin elasticity (tested by pinching[2] the skin and checking the time until it returns to normal)
    turgescent[3] adj term • **turgid**[4] [tɜːrdʒ-] adj • **turg(o)-** comb • **sag**[5] v clin • **droop**[5] v
» Clinical features [iːtʃ] of hypothyroidism may include brittle nails, thinning of hair, and pallor with poor turgor of the mucosa. If the skin does not return to normal contour but remains tented for more than 3 sec after being pinched [tʃ], turgor is diminished. Loss of elasticity due to aging results in varying degrees of wrinkles and sagging of skin along the cheeks, jawline[6] [ɔː], and neck. The extra weight of these sagging tissues causes the lid to droop.
Use   to assess[7] **skin turgor** • increased / good / poor / decreased[8] / loss of **skin turgor** • tissue[9] / eye globe[10] **turgor** • **turgo**meter • **sagging** tissues / breast[11] [e] • **drooping of the** eyelid[12] / breast[11]

Hautturgor, Spannungszustand der Haut
herunterhängend; Hängen, Senkung[1] Kneifen, Zusammendrücken[2] anschwellend[3] (an)geschwollen[4] herabhängen, schlaff werden[5] Kinnkante[6] den Hautturgor prüfen[7] herabgesetzter/ verminderter Hautturgor[8] Gewebeturgor[9] Augenturgor[10] Hängebrust, Mastoptose[11] Ptosis, Herabhängen d. Oberlids[12]

19

exfoliate [eksfoʊlieɪt] v term   syn **shed** [ʃed], **slough** [slʌf] **(off)** v clin
    syn **desquamate** [deskwəmeɪt] v term → U114-7
to cast off superficial [ɪʃ] cells from the skin or any epithelial surface in scales[1] or laminae [iː]
    exfoliation[2] n term • **exfoliative** adj → U27-5 • **shedding** n • **slough**[3] n
desquamative [des-‖dɪskwæmətɪv] adj • **desquamation**[2] n
» Affected skin turns brown overnight and may blister[4] and exfoliate. Keratolytics [ɪ] are agents that soften, loosen, and facilitate [sɪ] exfoliation of the squamous [eɪ] cells[5] of the epidermis. In spontaneous healing, dead tissue sloughs off as new epithelium begins to cover the injured area. Shedding of the stratum corneum is increased by inflammation [eɪʃ]. The erythema in phototoxicity reactions resembles a sunburn that quickly desquamates or "peels" [iː] within several days.
Use   **to shed** cells / keratinocytes / dander[6] • **to shed** blood / tears[7] [tɪəz] / teeth[8] [iː] / viruses [aɪ] • skin[9] / tooth[10] / marked / generalized **exfoliation** • **desquamated** epithelium / keratin / skin • dry / moist[11] / fine / local / plantar[12] / palmar / widespread[13] **desquamation** • epithelial / cell / superficial / full-thickness **desquamation** • **desquamative** interstitial pneumonitis[14] [n(j)uː-]/ erythema • skin / grayish / necrotic **slough** • epidermal / mucosal[15] / conjunctival [aɪ] **sloughing** • extensive / local **sloughing** • tumor cell[16] / fecal [fiːkəl]/ viral [aɪ] **shedding**

abschilfern, abschuppen, abstoßen
Schuppen[1] Abschuppung, Abschilferung[2] abgeschilferte Haut; Schorf[3] Blasen bilden[4] Plattenepithelzellen[5] Haare verlieren[6] Tränen vergießen[7] Zähne verlieren[8] Hautabschilferung[9] Zahnausfall[10] geschwürige Hautläsion[11] Schuppung d. Handflächen[12] großflächige Epidermolyse/ Hautablösung[13] Desquamativpneumonie[14] Schleimhauterosion, -abstoßung[15] Tumorzellaussaat[16]

20

Unit 57 The Senses

Related Units: 59 Vision, 61 Hearing, 62 Smell, Taste & Touch, 40 Nervous System,
42 Nerve Function, 68 Sexuality, 73 Mental Activity, 76 Mood

stimulus n term, pl **–i** [stɪmjʊlaɪ]   rel **excitation**[1] [eksaɪteɪʃən] n term → U76-8

agent which can elicit[2] [ɪs] or evoke[3] [ou] a response in a nerve, muscle or other excitable tissue
stimulate[3] v • **stimulation** n • **stimulant**[4] adj & n term • **stimulatory** adj
• **stimulator** n • **excite**[5] v • **excitatory**[6] adj • **excitability**[7] n • **excitement**[8] n

» A patient in coma normally fails [eɪ] to respond to any external stimuli, including deep pain. Sensory stimulation (by touch, chewing, etc.) of "trigger zones" about the cheek, nose, or mouth precipitates[9] [sɪ] paroxysms of pain. In excitation-contraction coupling [ʌ] excitation of the muscle leads to the depolarization of the cell membrane. An excitatory impulse from an anterior horn cell causes contraction of all the muscle fibers [aɪ] in that motor unit.

Use visual[10] [ɪʒ]/ auditory [ɔː] or acoustic(al)[11] [uː]/ tactile **stimulus** • neural [n(j)ʊɚəl]/ neuroendocrine / verbal **stimulus** • physical [ɪ]/ thermal [ɜː]/ environmental[12] **stimulus** • adequate / conditioned[13] **stimulus** • weak [iː]/ light [laɪt]/ potent [ou]/ unpleasant [e] **stimuli** • painful / irritating / noxious[14] **stimuli** • **stimulus** control / duration / response[15] / intensity[16] • sensory / auditory / electrical **stimulation** • nerve / (para)-sympathetic / vagal [eɪ]/ CNS / hormonal **stimulation** • mechanical / digital [ɪdʒ]/ over[17]/ sexual **stimulation** • appetite[18] / CNS or psycho[19] [saɪkou-]/ respiratory[20] **stimulant** • **stimulant** medication[4] • electrical / neural / visual **excitation** • pre/ sympathetic / neuromuscular [ʌ]/ sexual **excitation** • (skeletal/ smooth) [uː] muscle[21] **excitation** • nerve / hyper[22]/ neuronal **excitability** • reflex / membrane **excitability** • **excitatory** impulse / nerve (fiber)/ neural stimuli • **excitatory** neurotransmitter / response / synapses[23]

Reiz, Stimulus
Erregung, Exzitation[1] auslösen[2] anregen, stimulieren[3] stimulierend, anregend; Stimulans, Anregungsmittel[4] an-, erregen[5] erregend, exzitatorisch[6] Erregbarkeit[7] Er-, Aufregung[8] löst aus[9] optischer Reiz[10] akustischer Reiz[11] Umweltreiz[12] bedingter/ konditionierter Reiz[13] schädliche Reize[14] Reizantwort, Reaktion[15] Reizstärke[16] Hyperstimulation[17] appetitanregendes Mittel[18] Psychostimulans[19] Atemstimulans[20] Stimulation der glatten Muskulatur[21] Übererregbarkeit, Hyperexzitabilität[22] erregende/ exzitatorische Synapsen[23]

---

perceive [pəsiːv] v   sim **feel** - felt - felt[1] v irr, **appreciate**[2] [əpriːʃieɪt] v

to become conscious [kɒnʃəs] of something through the senses
perception[3] [pəsepʃən] n • **perceptible**[4] adj • **perceptual** adj • **perceptive** adj
perceptivity[5] n term • **appreciation**[6] n • **appreciable**[7] adj

» Often patients with angina [dʒaɪ] pectoris do not perceive the discomfort as pain. The sound was perceived loudest in the affected ear. Most patients with anosmia have normal perception of salty [ɔː], sweet, sour [sauɚ], and bitter substances [ʌ], but they lack flavor [eɪ] discrimination[8]. Bone and joint [dʒ] pain may be appreciated on examination.

Use **to perceive** pain / thirst [ɜː]/ oneself • sensory / acoustic or auditory **perception** • light (abbr LP)/ color / pain[9] / misperception • depth / body image[10] [ɪmɪdʒ]/ time / extrasensory[11] (abbr ESP) **perception** • poor / (un)impaired[12] [eɚ] **perception** • normal / altered[12] [ɔː]/ dulled[12] [ʌ] **perception** • **perception of** vibration [aɪ]/ cold / sound / loudness [au] • barely[13] [eɚ] **perceptible** • **to feel** hot / cold / weak / tired / relaxed • **to feel** uncomfortable / frustrated [ʌ]/ angry / anxiety [aɪ] • **perceptual** functions / competence[5] • **perceptual** processing[14] /-motor handicap • poor / sensory[15] / pain[9] / flavor[16] / personal **appreciation** • **perceptive** deafness[17] [e]

wahrnehmen, erkennen
fühlen, spüren[1] wahrnehmen, spüren; (zu) schätzen (wissen)[2] Wahrnehmung, Perzeption[3] deutlich, spürbar[4] Wahrnehmungsvermögen, Auffassungsgabe[5] Wahrnehmung; Anerkennung, Wertschätzung[6] deutlich, merklich[7] Geschmacksunterscheidung[8] Schmerzempfindung[9] Körperschema[10] außersinnliche Wahrnehmung[11] Wahrnehmungsstörung[12] kaum wahrnehmbar[13] Wahrnehmungsverarbeitung[14] Sinneswahrnehmung[15] Geschmacksempfindung[16] Schallempfindungs-, Innenohrschwerhörigkeit[17]

---

sensation [senseɪʃən] n clin & term   sim **feeling**[1] [fiːlɪŋ] n → U76-1

an impression or a mental process resulting [ʌ] from bodily stimulation

» Reflexes, motor power, and sensation within the upper limbs[2] [lɪmz] are normal. Exquisite pinpricking or tingling sensations[3] along a flank dermatome are typical of preeruptive [ʌ] herpes zoster. The patient complains of dryness, redness, or a scratchy feeling of the eyes.

Use to have/experience/develop/produce[4]/transmit **a sensation** • auditory / gustatory [ʌ] or taste[5] **sensation** • tactile / position / proprioceptive[6] / pressure **sensation** • vibratory / temperature[7] / somatic **sensation** • cutaneous[8] [eɪ]/ facial [eɪ] **sensation** • subjective [dʒe]/ primary [aɪ]/ superficial [ɪʃ]/ deep **sensation** • intact / diminished[9] / impaired **sensation** • pleasant / aching [k]/ pain(ful) / burning [ɜː] **sensation** • blunted[9] [ʌ]/ foreign-body[10] / globus **sensation** • **sensation of** smell[11] / cold / heat or warmth[12] • **sensation of** stiffness / tingling[3] / falling • **sensation of** hunger / thirst [ɜː]/ choking[13] [tʃou-]/ orgasm • loss[14] / lack[15] **of sensation** • to verbalize [ɜː] /express/hide **one's feelings** • tired / feverish [iː]/ intense / vague [veɪg]/ loss of **feeling** • to have no/a strange/funny **feeling** • **feeling of** tension[16] / fear / tightness[17] [taɪt-]/ heaviness [e] • **feeling of** numbness[18] [nʌmnəs]/ unsteadiness [e]/ helplessness • negative / mixed / aggressive / guilt[19]/ sexual **feelings**

(Sinnes)wahrnehmung, Empfindung
Gefühl, Empfindung[1] obere Extremitäten[2] Kribbelgefühl[3] eine Empfindung hervorrufen[4] Geschmacksempfindung[5] Tiefensensibilität[6] Temperaturempfindung[7] Hautsinn, Oberflächensensibilität, Taktilität[8] herabgesetzte Sensibilität, Hypästhesie[9] Fremdkörpergefühl[10] Geruchsempfindung[11] Wärmeempfindung, -gefühl[12] Erstickungsgefühl[13] Sensibilitätsverlust[14] Gefühllosigkeit, Unempfindlichkeit[15] Spannungsgefühl[16] Engegefühl[17] Taubheitsgefühl, taubes Gefühl[18] Schuldgefühle[19]

BODY STRUCTURES & FUNCTIONS — The Senses

notice [noʊtɪs] v & n   sim note¹, experience² [ɪkspɪəˑɪᵊnᵗs] v & n, observe³ [əbzɜːrv] v

(v) to discover [ʌ] or become aware of something

(un)noticeable⁴ adj • unnoticed⁵ adj • noteworthy⁶ adj • notify⁷ [noʊtəfaɪ] v

» The patient first noticed a lack of sensation for noxious stimuli in his fingers (a painless burn). Some patients with stones in the urinary [jʊɚ-] tract note gross [oʊ] hematuria⁸ [hiːmətjʊɚɪə]. Occasionally [eɪ] I experienced a burning sensation or tingling [tɪŋlɪŋ] in my lower legs. No response was observed after 1-2 minutes. The patient observed an increase in clear cervical mucus [juː].

Use **to notice a** feeling / symptom [ɪ]/ condition • to come to/bring to⁹/escape sb.'s notice • to escape¹⁰/avoid notice • advance / on or at short¹¹ / without notice • to be/go or pass¹⁰/progress unnoticed • just / hardly / quite **noticeable** • **to note** clinical signs / abnormalities / down • to take a/be of¹² note • **to experience** pain¹³ / cough [kɒf]/ pleasure [pleʒɚ] • **to experience** anxiety [aɪ]/ relief [iː]/ trauma [ɒː] • **to observe** a patient / a process / for signs [saɪnz] of arrhythmia [ɪ]

bemerken; wahrnehmen, feststellen; Mitteilung, Benachrichtigung
bemerken, zur Kenntnis nehmen; Anmerkung, Notiz¹ erfahren, empfinden, erleben, durchmachen; Erlebnis, Erfahrung² bemerken, wahrnehmen, beobachten³ erkenn-, sichtbar, deutlich⁴ unbemerkt⁵ beachtens-, erwähnenswert⁶ benachrichtigen⁷ Makrohämaturie⁸ jem. aufmerksam machen⁹ unbemerkt bleiben¹⁰ kurzfristig, auf Abruf, sofort¹¹ wichtig/ erwähnenswert sein¹² Schmerzen haben¹³   4

sense [senᵗs] v & n   rel awareness¹ [əwɛɚnəs] n → U7-2

(v) perceive by a physical [fɪzɪkᵊl] sensation, e.g., coming from the skin or muscles [mʌslz]

sensing² adj & n • senseless³ adj • sense-datum⁴ [eɪ] n term • sensor⁵ n

» His principal symptoms are slow speech, decreased sense of taste and smell, and diminished auditory acuity⁶ [əkjuːəti]. Assess whether the patient possesses any sense of smell at all. At age 2 the child is able to sense bladder fullness and to communicate the sensation.

Use light / color⁷ / muscle / posture⁸ [pɒːstʃɚ] **sense** • (joint) position⁸ (abbr JPS)/ pressure **sense** • time / thermic [ɜː] or temperature⁹ / stereognostic / visceral¹⁰ [ɪs] **sense** • **sense of** vibration / sight [saɪt]/ smell¹¹ / taste • **sense of** equilibrium¹² / direction¹³ / (abdominal) fullness • **sense of** self / reality • **sense of** well-being¹⁴ / humor / belonging¹⁵ / security [jʊɚ] • **sense of** personal identity / hostility / worthlessness [ɜː] • to make/talk¹⁶/have (more) **sense** • common¹⁷ / business [ɪz] **sense**

fühlen, empfinden, wahrnehmen; Sinn, Gefühl
Bewusstsein¹ Fühl-; Fühlen² bewusstlos, gefühllos; sinnlos³ Sinnesempfindung, -eindruck⁴ Rezeptor, Sensor⁵ Hörschärfe⁶ Farbensinn⁷ Lageempfindung⁸ Temperatursinn⁹ viszerale Empfindung¹⁰ Geruchssinn¹¹ Gleichgewichtssinn¹² Orientierungssinn¹³ Wohlbefinden¹⁴ Zugehörigkeitsgefühl¹⁵ vernünftig sein¹⁶ gesunder Menschenverstand¹⁷   5

special sense [speʃᵊl senᵗs] n term

one of the major [meɪdʒɚ] senses, the sense of seeing, hearing, smell, taste, and touch [tʌtʃ]

» Special senses and functions may be affected, e.g. in hysterical blindness¹ [aɪ], deafness [e], or aphonia [oʊ], and both visual and auditory hallucinations may occur [ɜː]. The physiology of olfaction² is less well understood than that of the other special senses.

Use to test/come to³/take leave of⁴/believe one's senses • sixth **sense**

Sinn, Sensus
psychogene Blindheit¹ Riechen, Geruchssinn² zur Vernunft kommen³ d. Verstand verlieren⁴   6

sensorium [sensɔːrɪəm] n term

(i) portion of the nervous [ɜː] system concerned with the reception of sensory stimuli
(ii) the ability of a person's sensory apparatus [eɪ] to appreciate [iːʃ] stimuli [aɪ]

(hemi/ neuro)sensory¹ [sensɚi] adj term • sensorial adj • sens(o)- comb

» Is the patient on any medications that cloud the sensorium? His sensorium is clear, and he can walk adequately. With involvement of a sensory or mixed nerve, pain is commonly felt distal to the lesion [iːʒ]. Numbness [ʌ] occurred in the sensory distribution of the nerve root.

Use alert [ɜː]/ clear / intact / depressed / clouded² [aʊ]/ altered **sensorium** • **sensory** faculty³ / end organ / nerve⁴ / root [uː] • **sensory** pathways⁵ [æ]/ receptor / stimuli⁶ • **sensory** threshold⁷ / acuity level⁸ (abbr SAL) • **sensory** deficit / deprivation⁹ /-perceptual [pɚseptʃʊəl] overload • hemisensory loss • **sensorial** clouding² / disturbances [ɜː] • **sensori**neural /motor¹⁰

**(i) Sensorium, Bewusstsein
(ii) Wahrnehmungsvermögen**
sensorisch, Sinnes-¹ Bewusstseinstrübung² Wahrnehmungsvermögen³ sensorischer/ sensibler Nerv⁴ sensorische Bahnen⁵ Sinnesreize⁶ sensorische Reizschwelle⁷ Sinnesschärfe⁸ sensorische Deprivation⁹ sensomotorisch¹⁰   7

The Senses

BODY STRUCTURES & FUNCTIONS 233

sensibility [sensəbɪləti] *n clin & term*   *sim* **sensitivity**[1] *n clin & term* → U39-23

ability to perceive sensory stimuli or having an understanding of esthetic or abstract qualities

(in)sensible[2] *adj term* • (in/ over)sensitive[3] *adj* • (in/ hyper)sensitivity[4] *n*

» The motor disturbances were accompanied by altered sensibility, especially those involving touch, pain, temperature, and position [ɪʃ] sense. Increased sensitivity to odors[5] [oʊ] usually reflects a neurotic [n(j)ʊɚˈɒːtɪk] personality. There was excessive sensitivity[4] to bright light and loud noise.

Use to assess sb's **sensibility** • tactile / deep[6] / vibratory [aɪ] **sensibility** • joint [dʒɔɪnt] / epicritic[7] / temperature **sensibility** • good / extraordinary / altered **sensibility** • zone / loss **of sensibility** • **sensitivity to** pain / cold[8] / light[9] / pressure • **sensitivity to** sounds / odors / vitamin D • point / photo[9] / olfactory[5] **sensitivity** • good / increased or heightened [haɪtnd] or enhanced [æ] / abnormal **sensitivity** • **sensitivity** threshold / testing[10] • **insensible** water loss[11] / area • **sensitive** to cold / pressure • highly / light-/ heat[12]-/ pain-/ hormone[13]-**sensitive**

Sensibilität, Empfindungsvermögen

Empfindlichkeit, Sensibilität; Feingefühl; Sensitivität[1] unempfindlich, gefühllos[2] sensibel, empfindlich, sensitiv[3] Überempfindlichkeit, Hypersensibilität[4] Geruchsempfindlichkeit[5] Tiefensensibilität[6] epikritische Sensibilität[7] Kälteempfindlichkeit[8] Photosensibilität, Lichtempfindlichkeit[9] Resistenzbestimmung[10] Perspiratio insensibilis, unmerkliche Wasserabgabe[11] wärme-, hitzeempfindlich[12] hormonsensitiv[13]   8

---

sensuous [senʃʊəs] *adj*   *syn* **sensual** [senʃʊəl] *adj* → U68-9

relating to bodily or sensory pleasure rather than appealing [iː] to the intellect

sensuality[1] *n clin* • sensuousness[1] *n*

» He takes such a sensual pleasure[2] in good food and wine. I've never neglected the sensuous pleasures[2] of food and sex. She is completely lacking in sensuality and intimate feeling.

Use **sensuous** feeling / delights[2] [dɪlaɪts]/ woman • **sensuous** beauty [bjuːti]/ voice[3] / music • **sensual** mouth[4] / experience[5] / desire[6] [aɪ]/ appeal [iː]/ charm • radiant[7] [eɪ]/ male / obsessive **sensuality**

sinnlich, lustvoll

Sinnlichkeit[1] Sinnenfreude, sinnl. Genuss/ Genüsse[2] erotische Stimme[3] sinnlicher Mund[4] sinnliche Erfahrungen[5] sinnliches Verlangen[6] erotische Ausstrahlung[7]

9

(sensory) receptor [rɪseptɚ] *n term*

    rel **sense organ**[1] [ɔːrgən] *n term*

sensory nerve ending or sense organ that responds to a specific type of stimulus, e.g. muscle spindles

receptive[2] *adj term* • reception[3] [rɪsepʃˀn] *n* • (un)receptivity[4] *n*

» The bolus then activates oropharyngeal [dʒ] sensory receptors that initiate [ɪʃ] the deglutition reflex[5]. Each receptor has its own set of sensitivities to specific stimuli, size and distinctness of receptive fields.

Use stretch[6] / skin / somatosensory **receptor** • sound / pressor[7] / hormone **receptor** • photo/ baro[7]/ osmo/ chemo [kiːmoʊ]/ mechano**receptor** • **receptor** cell / site[8] /-mediated[9] [iː] • **receptor** antagonist / stimulation / blockade • olfactory / auditory / light[10] **reception** • **receptive** aphasia[11] [əfeɪʒ(ɪ)ə]

Rezeptor

Sinnesorgan[1] empfänglich, aufnahmefähig, rezeptiv, sensorisch[2] Aufnahme, Empfindung, Wahrnehmung[3] Aufnahmefähigkeit, Empfänglichkeit[4] Schluckreflex[5] Dehnungsrezeptor[6] Presso-, Baro-, Druckrezeptor[7] Rezeptorstelle[8] rezeptorvermittelt[9] Lichtempfindung[10] sensorische Aphasie, Wernicke-Aphasie[11]

10

---

proprioceptor [proʊprioʊseptɚ] *n term*

    rel **position sense**[1] [pəzɪʃˀn] *n clin*

sense organ in the muscles, tendons, joints inner ear mediating spatial [eɪ] position

proprioceptive[2] *adj term* • proprioception[3] *n* • proprio- *comb*

» Stimulation of proprioceptors in muscles, joints, and tendons may induce a sense of dysequilibrium, but this is not true vertigo [ɜː]. There was reduced pinprick and thermal sensation but proprioception, motor function [ʌ], and deep tendon jerks[4] [dʒɜːrks] were intact.

Use proprioceptive sense[3] / (nerve) receptor / reflex[5] • proprioceptive sensation[3] / neuromuscular facilitation[6] (*abbr* PNF)/ feedback • proprioceptive deficits / sensory loss • peripheral / joint[7] / impaired proprioception • propriospinal afferents

Propriorezeptor

Lageempfindung[1] propriozeptiv[2] Propriozeption, Tiefensensibilität[3] Sehnenreflexe[4] propriozeptiver Reflex, Eigenreflex[5] propriozeptive neuromuskuläre Fazilitation, Kabat-Behandlung[6] Gelenkempfindung, -sensibilität[7]

11

---

muscle or **neuromuscular spindle** *n term*

    rel **Golgi tendon organ**[1] *n term*

proprioceptive end organ in skeletal muscle in which nerve fibers terminate[2]

» A tap[3] on a tendon stretches muscle spindles and activates the primary [aɪ] spindle afferent fibers [aɪ]. The alpha motor neuron receives direct excitatory input from corticomotoneurons and primary muscle spindle afferents.

Use neurotendinous[4] **spindle** • **muscle spindle** receptor • **spindle** afferents

Muskelspindel, Fusus neuromuscularis

Golgi-Sehnenorgan[1] enden[2] Beklopfen[3] Sehnenspindel, Fusus neurotendineus[4]

12

57

nociceptor [noʊsɪseptɚ] n term → U104-6ff

rel **thermoreceptor**[1] [ɜː] n term

somatic or visceral [s] free nerve ending[2] which reacts to and transmits painful stimuli
nociceptive[3] adj term • **noci(per)ception**[4] n • **noci-** comb • **therm-** comb

» Cutaneous [eɪ] afferent innervation is subserved [ɜː] by a rich variety of receptors, including naked [neɪkɪd] endings (nociceptors and thermoreceptors) as well as encapsulated terminals [ɜː] (mechanoreceptors[5]).

Use primary afferent / peripheral **nociceptor** • **nociceptive** stimulus / fibers / afferents • **nociceptive** reflex[6] / spinal [aɪ] transmission / pain[7] • **thermo**esthesia[8] [-esθiːʒ(ɪ)ə] /sensitive /regulation

Schmerzrezeptor, Nozi(re)zeptor
Temperatur-, Thermorezeptor[1] freie Nervenendigung[2] nozizeptiv[3] Nozizeption, Schmerzempfindung[4] Mechanorezeptoren[5] nozizeptiver Reflex[6] Nozizeptorenschmerz, nozizeptiver Schmerz[7] Temperatursinn, -empfindung[8]

13

kinesthesia [kɪnəsθiːʒ(ɪ)ə] n term   *sim* **muscle** [mʌsl] **sense**[1] n clin,

rel **somesthesia**[2] [soʊməsθiːʒ(ɪ)ə] n term

sense mediating [iː] the perception of one's own body, esp. its movements, tension, and weight
kinesthetic[3] [e] adj term • **kinetics**[4] n • **kine(sio)-** [aɪ‖ɪ] comb • **-esthesia** comb

» The larger fibers of the spinothalamic pathway subserve tactile and position sense and kinesthesia. The parietal [aɪə] lobes integrate somesthetic stimuli for recognition and recall[5] of form, texture[6] [tekstʃɚ], and weight.

Use **kinesthetic** sense[1] / memory / disorder • my[1] [maɪ] graph/ hyp(o)esthesia • par/ syn [sɪn]/ dys [dɪs]/ an**esthesia** • **kinesi**algia[7] [-ældʒə] /a[8] /meter /atrics[9] • **kineto**genic /therapy[9]

Kinästhesie, Bewegungsempfindung
Muskelsensibilität[1] Tiefensensibilität, Propriozeption, Eigenwahrnehmung[2] kinästhetisch[3] Kinetik, Bewegungslehre[4] Erinnerung[5] Beschaffenheit[6] Bewegungsschmerz[7] Bewegungskrankheit, Kinetose[8] Bewegungs-, Kinesiotherapie[9]

14

pacinian [pəsɪnɪən] or **Pacini's corpuscle** [pətʃiːniːz kɔːrpʌsl] n term

rel **Merkel's disk** or **corpuscle**[1] n term

pressure-sensitive sensory end-organ in the subcutaneous [eɪ], submucous, and subserous [ɪɚ] tissues of the palms of the hands, soles of the feet, tendons, genital organs mediating [iː] deep sensation

» Most vesical afferent axons terminate as free nerve endings, except for sparse[2] pacinian corpuscles. Merkel's disks have a very low threshold of sensitivity and will therefore fire[3] with the faintest[4] [eɪ] touch.

Use end bulbs [ʌ] of Krause or Krause('s)[5] **corpuscles** • Ruffini('s)[6] / tactile or Meissner's[7] **corpuscles** • Merkel **receptor** • Merkel cells[8]

(Vater-)Pacini-(Tast-/ Lamellen)körperchen, Corpusculum lamellosum
Merkel-Tastkörperchen, -Scheibe, Meniscus tactus[1] vereinzelte[2] reagieren auf[3] leiseste[4] Krause-Endkolben/ Kältekörperchen[5] Ruffini-Körperchen[6] Meissner-Tastkörperchen[7] Merkel-Zellen[8]

15

attitudinal [uː] or **postural reflex** n term

rel **righting** [raɪtɪŋ] **reflex**[1] n term

adjustment [ədʒʌst-] made by the body in motion [moʊʃ°n] to maintain stable [eɪ] equilibrium

» Through stimulation of the receptors in the neck muscles and semicircular canals the postural reflexes bring about movements of the limbs [lɪmz] appropriate to a given movement of the head in space. There is orthostatic hypotension resulting from a loss of attitudinal reflexes.

Use impaired / loss of **postural reflexes** • body[2] / neck[3] / optical[4] / labyrinthine[5] **righting reflex** • static / statokinetic[6] / tonic neck[3] / tonic labyrinthine[5] / startle[7] **reflex** • **reflex** movement • **postural** sense / tone / stability / unsteadiness

Halte-, Haltungsreflex
Stellreflex[1] Kopfstellreflex[2] Halsstellreflex, tonischer Halsreflex[3] Augen-Kopfstellreflex[4] Labyrinth-Kopfstellreflex, tonischer Labyrinthreflex[5] statokinetischer Reflex[6] Moro-Reflex[7]

16

vibration [vaɪbreɪʃ°n] **sense** n clin

rel **pressure** [preʃɚ] **sense**[1] n clin

ability to feel a quivering [kwɪvɚɪŋ], shaking or to-and-fro[2] [froʊ] movement
vibrate[3] v • **vibratory** adj • **vibrational** [eɪʃ] adj • **vibr(o)-** comb

» The sense of vibration is tested with a tuning [juː] fork, preferably a large one that vibrates at 128 Hz. The decay[4] [dɪkaɪ] of vibration using this fork is slow enough to be of quantitative use because it takes 15 to 20 s to decay below threshold. His neuropathy is marked by diminished ankle reflexes[5], decreased sensitivity to vibration, pinprick, and light touch.

Use **vibration** perception[6] / stimuli / testing[7] • **vibratory** sense loss / sensation[6] • **vibratory** sensibility[6] / massage / impairment[8] [eɚ] • **vibrating** tuning fork[9] / high-frequency / voice / coarse[10] [ɔː]/ sound / palpable **vibrations** • **vibro**percussion [ʌ] • threshold of **vibration** perception[11]

Pallästhesie, Vibrationsempfindung
Druckempfindung[1] hin u. her[2] zittern, beben, vibrieren[3] Nachlassen[4] Achillessehnenreflexe[5] Vibrationsempfindung[6] Messung d. Vibrationsempfindung, Pallästhesiometrie[7] herabgesetzte Vibrationsempfindung[8] schwingende Stimmgabel[9] niederfrequente Schwingungen[10] Vibrationsempfindungsschwelle[11]

17

labyrinthine [ɪ] **sense** *n term*   *syn* **sense of equilibrium** *or* **balance** *n clin*
perception of body position and motion mediated by utricular receptors[1] in the vestibular apparatus[2]
labyrinth *n term* • **(dys)equilibrium**[3] *n* • **equilibratory** *adj* → U60-10
» *Prolonged streptomycin* [aɪ] *treatment may impair vestibular function and result in inability to maintain* [eɪ] *equilibrium*[4]. *Vertigo due to disorders of the labyrinthine apparatus, such as acute labyrinthitis may be accompanied by vomiting with nausea* [ɔː] *and retching*[5].
Use **labyrinthine** apparatus [eɪ]/ fluid[6] / (dys)function / (righting) reflex[7] • **labyrinthine** deafness[8] [e]/ defect / concussion / [ʌ]/ vertigo[9] [ɜː] • bony *or* osseous[10] / membranous[11] **labyrinth** • cochlear [k]/ vestibular / ethmoidal **labyrinth** • **labyrinth**itis /ectomy • to maintain[4]/restore/recover **equilibrium** • dynamic[12] [aɪ]/ loss of **equilibrium** • impairment of[3] / disorder of[3] **equilibrium** • emotional / mental / hormonal / acid-base[13] / osmotic **equilibrium** • **equilibrium and** coordination / gait[14] • **equilibratory** apparatus / coordination • **equilibratory** disturbance[3] [ɜː]/ ataxia[15]

Gleichgewichtssinn
Utrikulusrezeptoren[1] Vestibularapparat[2] Dysäquilibrium, Ungleichgewicht, Gleichgewichtsstörung[3] Gleichgewicht halten[4] Brechreiz[5] Peri-, Endolymphe[6] Labyrinthstellreflex[7] Innenohrschwerhörigkeit[8] Labyrinth-, Vestibularisschwindel[9] knöchernes Labyrinth, Labyrinthus osseus[10] häutiges L., Labyrinthus membranaceus[11] dynamisches Gleichgewicht[12] Säure-Basen-Gleichgewicht[13] Gleichgewicht u. Gang[14] vestibuläre Ataxie[15]

18

Unit 58 Eyes
Related Units: 21 Head & Neck, 59 Vision, 57 Senses, 40 Nervous System, 41 Brain, 42 Nerve Function, 103 Clinical Symptoms

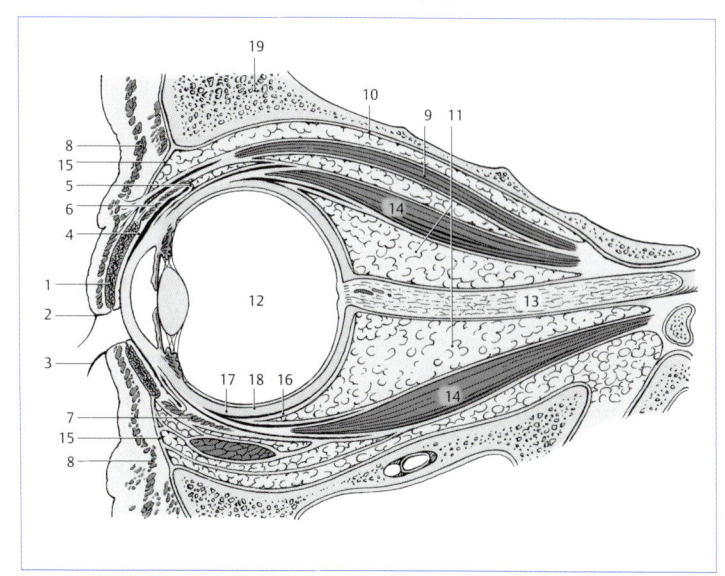

Eye socket (cross-section): Meibomian or tarsal glands (**1**), anterior lid margin (**2**), eyelashes (**3**), conjunctiva (**4**), conjunctival fornix (**5**), superior tarsal muscle (**6**), inferior tarsal muscle (**7**), eyelid closing or orbicularis muscle (**8**), levator palpebrae superioris (**9**), orbital periosteum or periorbita (**10**), orbital fat pad (**11**), eye bulb (**12**), optic nerve (**13**), extraocular muscles (**14**), orbital septum (**15**), Tenon's capsule or vagina bulbi (**16**), sclera (**17**), choroid (**18**), bony orbit (**19**)

(ocular) orbit [ɔː] *n term*   *syn* **eye socket** [sɒːkɪt] *n clin*, **orbital cavity** *n term*
bony cavity containing the eyeball and ocular adnexa (muscles [ʌ], vessels and nerves [ɜː]) which is formed by the maxilla and the ethmoid, frontal, lacrimal, nasal [eɪ], palatine, sphenoid [iː] and zygomatic [zaɪɡə-] bones
(infra/ peri/ intra/ retro)orbital[1] *adj term* • **orbit(o)-** *comb*
» *Fracture of the ethmoid bone most frequently occurs* [ɜː] *with blunt* [ʌ] *trauma*[2] [ɔː] *to the orbit. The exit of the supraorbital nerve*[3] *from the orbit is readily* [e] *identified by palpating the supraorbital notch*[4] [nɒːtʃ].
Use bony[5] / medial [iː]/ inferior **orbit** • **orbital** bones / floor[6] / roof[7] / apex [eɪ] • **orbital** rim[8] / septum / wall / contents • **orbital** fat / aperture[9] / veins [eɪ] / **orbital** trauma / fissure[10] [fɪʃə-]/ cellulitis [aɪ] • **infraorbital** rim[11] / foramen [eɪ]/ nerve [ɜː]/ canal[12] • **periorbital** edema[13] [iː]/ swelling *or* puffiness[14] [ʌ]/ hematoma • **intraorbital** pressure / foreign [fɔːrən] body[15] • **retro-orbital** pain • axis of the **eye socket** • **orbito**nasal [eɪ] /temporal /meatal [miːeɪtəl] line

Augenhöhle, Orbita
orbital, Orbita-[1] stumpfes Trauma[2] N. supraorbitalis[3] Foramen supraorbitale, Incisura supraorbitalis[4] knöcherne Augenhöhle[5] Orbitaboden[6] Orbitadach[7] Orbita-, Augenhöhlenrand[8] Orbitaeingang, Aditus orbitae[9] Augenhöhlenspalte, Fissura orbitalis[10] unterer Augenhöhlenrand, Margo infraorbitalis[11] Canalis infraorbitalis[12] periorbitales Ödem[13] verschwollene Augen[14] intraorbitaler Fremdkörper[15]

1

BODY STRUCTURES & FUNCTIONS — Eyes

eyeball [ˈaɪbɔːl] n   syn **eye bulb** [bʌlb] n rare, **bulbus** [ʌ] **oculi** [aɪ] n term

the globe [gloʊb] of the eye → U21-3

eye¹ n & v • **ocular**² [ˈɒkjələr] adj term • **bulbar**³ [ʌ] adj • **ophthalm(o)-** comb

» In myopia the image is focused in front of the retina because the axis of the eyeball is too long or the refractive power⁴ of the eye is too strong. Detailed examination of the ocular fundi is mandatory. Irrigate the eyes with saline [eɪ] or a buffered [ʌ] ophthalmic solution.

Use tender⁵ / softened / protruding⁶ [uː]/ enlarged **eyeballs** • shrunken [ʌ]/ ruptured [ʌ] **eyeballs** • equator [eɪ] of the **eyeball** • **eyeball** axis / movement / compression reflex⁷ • to open/close/roll⁸/rub [ʌ] one's eyes • infected / lackluster [ʌ] or dull⁹ [ʌ] **eyes** • dry / red prominent **eyes** • corner¹⁰ / muscles [ʌ]/ outer canthus¹¹ of the eye • globe¹² / equator / fundi¹³ [ˈfʌndaɪ] of the eye • eyegrounds¹³ [aʊ]/ bank / contact / glasses • **eye** bath /drops /sight¹⁴ [aɪsaɪt] /strain¹⁵ [eɪ] • **eye** closure / movement • **eye** examination / chart¹⁶ [tʃɑːrt]/ patch¹⁷ / right (abbr OD)/ left (abbr OS)/ (un)affected **eye** • **ocular** muscles / fundi¹³ / pursuit [pɚ(j)uːt] of objects • **ocular** globe¹² / motility / rotation • **ocular** pressure / deviation¹⁸ / irritant¹⁹ • **ocular** burning [ɜː]/ tremor²⁰ • intra/ extra/ bin/ mon/ peri/ vestibulo**ocular** • **bulbar** conjunctiva²¹ [aɪ]/ muscles / palsy or paralysis²² • **ophthalm**ology /ologist²³ /ic /itis²⁴ /odynia [ɔːfθælməˈdɪnɪə]

eyelid n   syn **palpebra** [ˈpælpɪbrə‖-piːbrə] n term, pl **-ae** [iː]
  rel **eyelashes**¹ [-læʃɪz] n pl, **canthus**² [ˈkænθəs] n term, pl **-i** [aɪ]

movable fold of skin covering [ʌ] the eye with eyelashes along its margin [ˈmɑːrdʒɪn]

(**inter/ bi**)**palpebral**³ adj term • (**epi**)**canthal** adj • **blephar(o)-**³ [-blef-] comb

» He has heavy-appearing eyelids and ptosis [t]. The fascia [ˈfæʃ(ɪ)ə] of the eyelids join with the fibrous [aɪ] orbital septum to isolate the orbit from the lids. Patients with leprosy may lose eyelashes and eyebrows. The swelling was more prominent below the medial palpebral ligament [ɪ]. In anterior blepharitis⁴ scales⁵ [eɪ] must be removed from the lids daily.

Use to raise [eɪ] /lower⁶ one's **eyelids** • upper / lower / open / closed **eyelids** • sluggish [ʌ] movement / ptosis or drooping⁷ [uː] of the eyelids • **eyelid** margins⁸ / closure [oʊʒ] reflex⁹ [iː] • **eyelid** swelling / blinking¹⁰ / fluttering [ʌ] • **palpebral** fissure¹¹ / conjunctiva [dʒʌ] • upper / lower / depigmented / inturned¹² **eyelashes** • elongation / infestation¹³ of the eyelashes • **blephar**ospasm /itis [blefəˈraɪtɪs] /optosis⁷ [t] • inner or medial¹⁴ [iː]/ outer or lateral **canthus** • medial/lateral **canthal** ligament¹⁵ • **canthal** area / hypertelorism¹⁶ • **epicanthal** fold¹⁷ [oʊ]

conjunctiva [kɒndʒʌŋkˈtaɪvə] n term, pl **-ae** [iː]

mucous membrane lining the anterior part of the eyeball and the inner surfaces of the eyelids

(**sub**)**conjunctival** [aɪ] adj term • **conjunctivitis**¹ [-ˈvaɪtɪs] n

» Subconjunctival hemorrhage [-ɪdʒ] results from rupture [ʌ] of small vessels bridging the potential space between the episclera and conjunctiva. To search the conjunctival fornices [-siːz], the lower lid should be pulled down and the upper lid everted² [ɜː]. Carcinoma of the conjunctiva arises [aɪ] frequently at the limbus or the inner canthus in the exposed area of the bulbar [ʌ] conjunctiva.

Use palpebral³ / (upper/ lower) tarsal⁴ / bulbar **conjunctiva** • **conjunctival** surface / fornix⁵ / sac⁶ / vessels • **conjunctival** irritation / hyperemia [iː] or injection⁷ [dʒe] • **conjunctival** chemosis⁸ [kiː-]/ discharge / smear [ɪɚ] or swab⁹ [ɒː] • bacterial / inclusion¹⁰ / allergic [ɜː] **conjunctivitis** • hay fever¹¹ [ˈheɪfiːvɚ]/ purulent¹² [pjʊɚ-]/ follicular **conjunctivitis**

cornea [ˈkɔːrnɪə] n term

5-layered [eɪ] convex transparent [eə] coat¹ [koʊt] covering [ʌ] the anterior pole [poʊl] of the eyeball

(**circum/ irido**)**corneal** adj term • **-cornea, corne(o)-** comb

» The cornea is steamy² [iː], the anterior chamber [tʃeɪmbɚ] shallow³ [ˈʃæloʊ], and the aqueous humor⁴ turbid² [ɜː] enough to obscure⁵ [-jʊɚ] the fundus. Kayser-Fleischer rings⁶ were detected by unaided visual [ɪʒ] inspection as a brown band at the junction [dʒʌŋkʃⁿn] of the iris [aɪ] and cornea. A corneal scar⁷ [skɑːr] is present.

Use anterior / dry / hazy⁸ [ˈheɪzɪ] **cornea** • cloudy [aʊ] or milky⁸ / enlarged **cornea** • **corneal** epithelium [iː]/ curvature⁹ [ɜː]/ sensation • **corneal** reflex¹⁰ / luster [ʌ]/ opacity⁸ [æs]/ clouding⁸ • **corneal** foreign body / burns [ɜː]/ abrasion¹¹ [eɪʒ]/ erosion [oʊʒ] • **corneal** ulcer¹² [ʌ]/ scarring / drying / grafting¹³ • **circumcorneal** injection • **iridocorneal** angle¹⁴ • **corneo**retinal potential /mandibular reflex¹⁵ /scleral suture¹⁶

Augapfel, Bulbus oculi
Auge; anstarren¹ okulär, Augen-² bulbär, Bulbus-³ Brechkraft⁴ druckschmerzhafte Augäpfel⁵ hervortretende Augäpfel⁶ okulokardialer Reflex, Bulbusdruckversuch⁷ d. Augen rollen/ verdrehen⁸ glanzlose A.⁹ Augenwinkel¹⁰ äußerer Augenwinkel¹¹ Augapfel¹² Augenhintergrund, Fundi oculi¹³ Sehkraft, Sehen¹⁴ Überanstrengung/ Ermüdung d. Augen¹⁵ Sehprobentafel¹⁶ Augenklappe¹⁷ Schielen¹⁸ Augenreizstoff¹⁹ Augenzittern, Nystagmus²⁰ Bindehaut d. Augapfels, (Tunica) conjunctiva bulbi²¹ Bulbärparalyse²² Augenarzt/-ärztin, Ophthalmologe/-in²³ Augenentzündung²⁴
2

Augenlid, Palpebra
Wimpern¹ Augen-, Lidwinkel² Lid-³ Lidrandentzündung, Blepharitis⁴ Schuppen⁵ d. Augenlider senken⁶ Ptosis, Herabhängen d. Oberlider⁷ Lidränder⁸ Lidschlussreflex⁹ Lidschlag¹⁰ Lidspalte, Rima palpebrarum¹¹ einwärtsgekehrte Wimpern¹² Parasitenbefall d. Wimpern¹³ innerer Augenwinkel¹⁴ Ligamentum palpebrale laterale¹⁵ Telekanthus¹⁶ Epikanthus, Mongolenfalte¹⁷
3

Bindehaut, Konjunktiva
Bindehautentzündung, Konjunktivitis¹ ausgestülpt² (Tunica) conjunctiva palpebrarum³ Conjunctiva tarsi⁴ Fornix conjunctivae, Umschlagfalte d. Konjunktiva⁵ Bindehautsack, Saccus conjunctivae⁶ konjunktivale Injektion/ Hyperämie⁷ Chemosis, Bindehautödeme⁸ Konjunktivalabstrich⁹ Einschlusskonjunktivitis¹⁰ allergische Konjunktivitis¹¹ eitrige Konjunktivitis¹²
4

Kornea, Cornea, Hornhaut
Hülle, Schicht¹ trüb² flach³ Kammerwasser⁴ verdecken⁵ Kayser-Fleischer-Ringe⁶ Hornhautnarbe⁷ Hornhauttrübung⁸ Hornhautkrümmung⁹ Kornealreflex¹⁰ korneale Abrasion; Abrasio corneae, operative Hornhautabschabung¹¹ Hornhautgeschwür, Ulcus corneae¹² Hornhauttransplantation, Keratoplastik¹³ Kammerwinkel, Angulus iridocornealis¹⁴ mandibulopalpebrale Synkinese, Gunn-Zeichen¹⁵ Limbus corneae¹⁶
5

Eyes
BODY STRUCTURES & FUNCTIONS 237

sclera [sklɪ‖eəɚ] *n term, pl* **-ae** [iː]   *syn* **white of the eye** *n clin*
tough[1] [tʌf], opaque [oupeɪk] white coat forming the outer envelope of the eye
(epi)scleral [epɪsklɛəəl] *adj term* • **episclera**[2] *n* • **scler(o)-** *comb*
» Mild *jaundice*[3] [dʒɔːndɪs] is best seen by examining the sclerae in natural light. Penetrating injuries may lead to *disruption*[4] [ʌ] of the cornea or sclera. Widening of the palpebral aperture [-tʃɚ], with *exposure*[5] of sclera is suggestive [dʒɛ] of exophthalmos.
Use blue[6] / icteric *or* jaundiced[7] **sclerae** • **sclerae** and conjunctivae (*abbr* S & C) • **scleral** bed / rim[8] / canal / hemorrhage • **scleral** icterus[7] / buckling[9] [ʌ]/ laceration [læs-]/ rupture[10] • **episcleral** blood vessels / space[11] / inflammation / injection[12] • **sclero**corneal junction[13] • **scler**itis /ectomy[14] /otomy

Sklera, Lederhaut
fest[1] Episklera[2] Ruptur, Zerreißung, Gelbsucht[3] Riss[4] Freilegung[5] blaue Skleren[6] Sklerenikterus, Gelbfärbung d. Skleren[7] Sklerarand[8] Vorwölbungen d. Sklera[9] Skleraruptur[10] Tenon-Raum, Spatium episclerale/ intervaginale[11] episklerale Gefäßinjektion[12] Limbus corneae[13] Sklerektomie[14]

6

uvea [juːvɪə] *n term*   *syn* **uveal tract** [juːvɪəl trækt] *n term*
   rel **ciliary body**[1] [sɪliəːi bɒːdi], **choroid**[2] [kɔːrɔɪd] *n term*
fibrous [aɪ] layer underlying [aɪ] the sclera formed by the ciliary body, the iris and the choroid
uveal, uveitic [ɪ] *adj term* • **uveitis**[3] [aɪ] *n* • **uve(o)-** *comb* • **choroid(al)** *adj*
» Cystine [sɪstiːn] crystals [ɪ] are deposited in the cornea, ocular conjunctiva, or uvea. Leakage [liːkɪdʒ] of serous [ɪɚ] fluid from the choroid causes localized *detachment*[4] [tʃ] of the retinal pigment epithelium [iː]. Vision became *blurred*[5] [ɜː] with ciliary body inflammation. Corneal laceration [s] of the sclera was associated with prolapse of uveal structures [ʌ].
Use **uveal** structures / tissue [tɪʃ‖sjuː]/ prolapse / melanoma • **ciliary body** prolapse / inflammation[6] • **ciliary** muscle [mʌsl]/ folds[7] / processes[8] / rupture[9] / tumors[10] / lesions [iːʒ] **of the choroid** • **choroid** layers [eɪ]/ coat of the eyes / plexus • **choroidal** vessels[11] / circulation • **choroidal** melanoma[12] / effusion[13] [juː]

Uvea, Tunica vasculosa bulbi, mittlere Augenhaut
Corpus ciliare, Ziliarkörper[1] Choroidea, Aderhaut[2] Uveitis, Uveaentzündung[3] Ablösung, Ablatio[4] verschwommen[5] Ziliarkörperentzündung, Zyklitis[6] Ziliarfalten[7] Ziliarfortsätze[8] Aderhautruptur[9] Aderhaut-, Choroideatumoren[10] Aderhautgefäße[11] Aderhautmelanom[12] Aderhauteffusion[13]

7

iris [aɪrɪs] *n term, pl* **irises** *or* **irides** [aɪ‖ɪriːdiːz]   *rel* **pupil**[1] [pjuːpəl], **lens**[2] *n*
circular contractile disc between the cornea and the lens of the eye
iridic [aɪ‖ɪrɪdɪk] *adj term* • **aniridia**[3] *n* • **ir(id)o-** *comb* • **pupillary**[4] *adj*
» Adhesions [iːʒ] of the iris to the anterior lens may produce a fixed pupil. Dilation of the pupil may push the *root* [uː] of the *iris*[5] forward against the anterior chamber [eɪ] angle[6] obstructing [ʌ] the *outflow*[7] of aqueous humor. Did you find a poorly reacting pupil and shallow anterior chamber in the left eye? *Ophthalmoscopy*[8] showed opacities [æs] of the cornea, lens, and vitreous. Altered collagen was detected in the suspensory ligament [ɪ] of the optic lens.
Use peripheral / cloudy / displaced / tremulous[9] **iris** • **iris** sphincter / dilator muscle / root[5] / color • **iris** nodule / damage / prolapse[10] • **iris** coloboma[11] / scissors [s] / tonic / (mid)dilated[12] / fixed[13] **pupils** / poorly reacting[14] / (un)responsive / unequal[15] [iː] **pupils** • **pupils** equal, round, and reactive to light and accommodation (*abbr* PERLA) • optic *or* ocular[16] / dislocated[17] **lens** • (intraocular) prosthetic [e]/ contact / +2-diopter [aɪp] **lenses** / rigid[18] [dʒ]/ soft / tinted[19] [ɪ] **lenses** • **lens** nucleus / capsule[20] / fibers [aɪ] • **lens** fluid / dislocation[17] / opacities[21] / implantation • **pupillary** sphincter / muscle / membrane • **pupillary** function / constriction *or* miosis[22] / enlargement • **pupillary** light reflex *or* response *or* reaction[23] • **pupillary** reactivity / reflexes[24] • **pupillary** assessment[25] / size / equality[26] / defect • **iridic** muscles / folds • **irid**itis /docorneal angle[6] /docyclitis • **irid**oplegia[27] /dectomy

Iris, Regenbogenhaut
Pupille[1] Linse; Kontakt-, Haftlinse[2] Aniridie, Fehlen d. Regenbogenhaut[3] Pupillen-[4] Iriswurzel[5] Kammerwinkel, Angulus iridocornealis[6] Abfluss[7] Augenspiegelung, Ophthalmoskopie[8] Irisschlottern, Iridodonesis, Iris tremulans[9] Irisprolaps[10] Iriskolobom, angeb. Spaltbildung d. Iris, Coloboma iridis[11] weite/ erweiterte Pupillen[12] lichtstarre P.[13] Pupillenträgheit[14] ungleiche P.[15] Okular[16] Linsenluxation[17] harte Kontaktlinsen/ Haftschalen[18] Farblinsen[19] Linsenkapsel[20] Linsentrübung[21] Pupillenverengung, Miosis[22] Lichtreaktion[23] Pupillenreaktionen, -reflexe[24] Pupillenprüfung[25] Pupillengleichheit[26] Iridoplegie[27]

8

lacrimal gland [lækrɪməl glænd] *n term*   *rel* **tear**[1] [tɪɚ] *n clin*,
   dacryon[1] [dækrɪɒn] *n term*
exocrine gland located in the upper lateral part of the orbit producing the fluid that moistens the cornea and conjunctiva; it consists of a smaller palpebral and a larger orbital part and has approx. 10 ducts
tearing[2] *n clin* • **nasolacrimal** *adj term* • **(hypo/ de) lacrimation**[3] *n* • **lacrim(o)-** *comb*
» The lacrimal sacs fill with tears secreted [iː] by the lacrimal glands and conveyed [eɪ] through the lacrimal duct. Massage of the nasolacrimal sac to express *purulent discharge*[4] [-tʃɑːrdʒ] through the *punctum*[5] [ʌ] is helpful in infants.
Use accessory[6] [əksɛs-] **lacrimal glands** • **lacrimal** apparatus [eɪ]/ sac[7] / caruncle[8] [ʌ] • **lacrimal** bone / nerve [ɜː]/ passages[9] • **lacrimal** duct[10] [ʌ]/ fold[11] [oʊ]/ papilla • **lacrimal** outflow[12] / drainage system [ɪ]/ lake[13] • **tear** fluid[14] / punctum[5] / duct[10] / sac[7] • **tear** drops / -shaped / production[3] / artificial[15] [ɪʃ] **tears** / to burst [ɜː] into[16] **tears** • release [iː]/ overflow[2] **of tears** • **lacrim**onasal [eɪ] duct[17] /turbinal [ɜː] suture [suːtʃɚ] • **dacryo**cystitis[18] [aɪ] /cystocele [dækrɪəsɪstəsiːl] /adenitis

Tränendrüse, Glandula lacrimalis
Träne[1] Tränenträufeln, Epiphora[2] Tränensekretion[3] eitriges Sekret[4] Tränenpunkt, Punctum lacrimale[5] akzessorische Tränendrüsen, Gll. lacrimales accessoriae[6] Tränensack, Saccus lacrimalis[7] Tränenwärzchen, Caruncula lacrimalis[8] Tränenwege[9] Tränengang, Canaliculus lacrimalis[10] Plica lacrimalis, Hasner-Klappe[11] Tränenabfluss[12] Tränensee, Lacus lacrimalis[13] Tränenflüssigkeit[14] künstl. Tränenflüssigkeit[15] in Tränen ausbrechen[16] Tränen-Nasen-Gang, Ductus nasolacrimalis[17] Tränensackentzündung, Dacryocystitis[18]

9

238 BODY STRUCTURES & FUNCTIONS — Eyes

vitreous (body) [vɪtrɪəs] *n term*   *syn* **vitreous humor** [hjuːmɚ] *n term*

transparent jelly-like¹ [dʒ] substance [ʌ] composed of a delicate network enclosing a watery fluid, the vitreous fluid², filling the posterior chamber [tʃeɪmbɚ] of the eye behind the lens

intravitreous *adj term* • **(intra)vitreal** [ɪntrəvɪtrɪˀl] *adj* • **vitre(o)-** *comb*

» Blood in the vitreous body clots³ rapidly. Opacities developed in the vitreous, casting shadows upon the retina. The drug's penetration into vitreous humor is poor.

Use cloudy⁴ [aʊ]/ fluid **vitreous** • **vitreous** cavity⁵ / gel [dʒel]/ membrane / duct • **vitreous** opacity⁴ / clouding⁴ / hemorrhage⁶ • **vitreous** degeneration [dʒ]/ floaters⁷ [oʊ]/ bands⁸ • **vitreous** traction⁹ [trækʃˀn]/ detachment¹⁰ • **vitreal** hemorrhage⁶ / inflammation / abscess • **intravitreal** injection • **vitre**oretinal /ctomy¹¹

Glaskörper, Corpus vitreum
gallertartig¹ Humor vitreus, Glaskörperflüssigkeit² koaguliert³ Glaskörpertrübung⁴ Glaskörperraum⁵ Glaskörperblutung⁶ Mückensehen, Mouches volantes⁷ Glaskörperstränge⁸ Glaskörpertraktion⁹ Glaskörperabhebung, -ablösung¹⁰ Vitrektomie, op. Glaskörperentfernung¹¹

10

aqueous humor [eɪ‖ækwɪəs hjuːmɚ] *n term*

rel **canal of Schlemm**¹ *n term*

transparent intraocular fluid filling the anterior and posterior chambers of the eye; secreted by the ciliary processes, it passes from the anterior chamber through the trabecular meshwork² and is reabsorbed at the iridocorneal angle by way of the canal of Schlemm

» Secondary glaucoma [ɔː] is caused by interference³ [ɪɚ] with the flow of aqueous humor from the posterior chamber through the pupil into the anterior chamber to the canal of Schlemm. Use slit-lamp⁴ examination to identify inflammatory cells floating⁵ in the aqueous humor.

Use ocular / vitreous **humor** • hyposecretion [iːʃ]/ flow⁶ / loss **of aqueous humor**

Kammerwasser, Humor aquaeus
Schlemm-Kanal, Sinus venosus sclerae¹ Reticulum trabeculare² Störung³ Spaltlampe⁴ schwebend⁵ Kammerwasserabfluss⁶

11

(ocular or **optic) fundus** [fʌndəs] *n term, pl* **-i**   *syn* **eyeground** [aʊ] *n clin*

interior of the eyeball around the posterior pole as seen with the ophthalmoscope¹

fundal *adj term* • **fundic** *adj* • **funduscopy**² [ɔː] *n* • **funduscopic** *adj*

» Examination of the optic fundi [fʌndaɪ] helps to evaluate vascular disease. Inspect the eyelids, conjunctiva, cornea, anterior chamber, pupils, lens, vitreous, and fundus for breaks³ [eɪ] in tissue and hemorrhage. Funduscopic and slit-lamp examinations may reveal⁴ [iː] corneal clouding or the presence of a cherry [tʃ] red macule.

Use pale⁵ [eɪ]/ opaque / dilated **fundus** • **fundus** examination² / lesions • **fundal** signs / examination² / details • **funduscopic** examination² / appearance [ɪɚ]/ findings⁶

Augenhintergund, Fundus (oculi)
Augenspiegel, Ophthalmoskop¹ Augenspiegelung, Funduskopie, Ophthalmoskopie² Einrisse³ ergeben⁴ blasser Augenhintergrund⁵ Funduskopiebefund⁶

12

retina *n term, pl* **-ae** [iː]

rel **fovea** [oʊ] **(centralis)¹, macula (lutea)²** *n term*

delicate semitransparent membrane that receives images of external objects and transmits visual impulses; it consists of the iridial, ciliary, and optic parts, the latter comprises [aɪ] 9 layers, among them a pigment, a ganglion cell layer, and a layer of photoreceptors [se] (the rods³ [ɒː] and cones⁴ [oʊ])

retinal *adj term* • **fovea**⁵ *n* • **foveation**⁶ *n* • **macular** *adj* • **retin(o)-** *comb*

» There are approx. 100 million rods and 5 million cones in the human retina. Visual orientation and eye movements are served by retinal input to the superior colliculus⁷. At the posterior pole⁸ of the visual axis is the macula, in the center of which is the fovea, the area of acute vision⁹.

Use avascular / neurosensory / temporal / inner **retina** • outer or peripheral¹⁰ • edematous [iː]/ detached¹¹ [tʃ] **retina** • **retinal** layer / pigment / rods³ / rhodopsin¹² • **retinal** arteriole [ɪɚ]/ fold¹³ / projection [dʒe]/ image¹⁴ • **retinal** edema / flecks¹⁵ / hemorrhage • **retinal** vein occlusion [uːʒ]/ ischemia [kiː]/ breaks or tears¹⁶ • **retinal** detachment¹¹ / degeneration¹⁷ • central / cherry red **fovea** • **macular** degeneration / edema / hole¹⁸ • epi/ intra/ sub/ vitreo/ corneo**retinal** • **retin**itis • **retino**pathy /scopy¹⁹ /cerebral [s] • **retino**choroiditis /blastoma

Retina, Netzhaut
Fovea centralis¹ gelber Fleck, Macula lutea² Stäbchen³ Zapfen⁴ Grube⁵ Foveation⁶ Colliculus superior, oberer Hügel a. d. Sehbahn⁷ hinterer Augenpol, Polus posterior⁸ Stelle d. schärfsten Sehens⁹ Netzhautperipherie¹⁰ Netzhautablösung, Ablatio retinae¹¹ Rhodopsin, Sehpurpur¹² Retinafalte¹³ Netzhautbild¹⁴ Netzhautflecken, Retinopathia pigmentosa¹⁵ Netzhautrisse¹⁶ Nezthautdegeneration¹⁷ Makulaloch¹⁸ Retinoskopie, Skiaskopie¹⁹

13

optic disk or **disc** *n term*   *syn* **optic papilla** *n term*, **blind spot** *n clin*

oval area in the fundus of the eye (approx. 3 mm medial [iː] to the fovea) where retinal ganglion cell axons converge¹ [-vɜːrdʒ] to form the optic nerve that is not supplied with light receptors

optic(al)² *adj term* • **optician**³ [ɪʃ] *n* • **-op(s)ia, opt(ico)-** *comb*

» Ganglion cell axons which sweep [iː] along⁴ the inner surface [ɜː] of the retina in the nerve fiber layer exit the eye at the optic disc. The optic disc appears mildly plethoric⁵ with surface capillary telangiectases, but no vascular leakage on fluorescein [-sɪən] angiography⁶. The entire upper pole of the optic disc seems to be damaged.

Use **optic disk** pallor [æ]/ drusen⁷ [uː]/ swelling / edema⁸ • **optic** fundi / foramen [eɪ]/ pathways⁹ • bi/ pre/ pan**optic** • **optical** illusion¹⁰ [uːʒ] activity • **opto**metry /metrist /kinetic

blinder Fleck, Sehnervenpapille, Discus/ Papilla nervi optici
s. vereinen¹ optisch, Augen-, Seh-² Optiker(in)³ entlangziehen⁴ prall gefüllt⁵ Fluoreszenzangiografie⁶ Papillendrusen⁷ Papillenödem, Stauungspapille⁸ Sehbahnen⁹ optische Täuschung¹⁰

14

Vision   BODY STRUCTURES & FUNCTIONS 239

optic nerve [ɒːptɪk nɜːrv] *n term*   *rel* **optic chiasm¹** [kaɪæzᵊm] *n term*

second cranial [eɪ] nerve containing purely sensory fibers carrying visual impulses from the retina to the optic chiasm where part of the fibers cross to the opposite optic tract²

(pre/ post/ supra)chiasmal [æ] *adj term* • **chiasmatic** *adj*

» About half the fibers [aɪ] in the optic nerve originate [ɪdʒ] from ganglion cells serving [ɜː] the macula. The optic impulses travel through the optic nerve, optic chiasm, and optic tract to reach targets in the brain. At the optic chiasm, fibers from nasal [eɪ] ganglion cells decussate³ [ʌ] into the contralateral optic tract.

Use **optic nerve** fibers / pathways / head⁴ • **optic** sheath [ʃiːθ]/ compression / damage⁵ • **optic nerve** trauma/ hypoplasia/ atrophy⁶ / tumor • **optic** tract / radiation⁷ / neuropathy / neuritis⁸ • **optic chiasm** compression⁹ • compression of the⁹ **optic chiasm** • **chiasmal** axons / tumor¹⁰ • **postchiasmal** visual pathways / lesion

Sehnerv, Nervus opticus
Sehnervenkreuzung, Chiasma opticum¹ Tractus opticus² kreuzen³ Sehnervenkopf⁴ Sehnerven-, Optikusschädigung⁵ Sehnerven-, Optikusatrophie⁶ Radiatio optica, Gratiolet-Sehstrahlung⁷ Sehnervenentzündung, Neuritis nervi optici⁸ Chiasmakompression⁹ Chiasma opticum-Tumor¹⁰

15

extra- *or* **external ocular muscles** [mʌslz] *n term*
                              rel **oculomotor nerve¹** [ɒːkjəloumoutɚ nɜːrv] *n term*

the six voluntary muscles that move the eyeball including the inferior, superior, middle and lateral rectus and the superior and inferior oblique [oubliːk] muscles

» Diplopia² usually results from extraocular muscle imbalance. This elaborate efferent motor system is supplied by cranial nerves from the oculomotor, trochlear [k], and abducens nuclei which coordinate smooth [uː] pursuit³, saccades⁴, and gaze stabilization⁵ during head and body movements. The oculomotor or 3ʳᵈ cranial nerve⁶ supplies the levator palpebrae superioris, the ciliary muscle⁷, the sphincter pupillae, and all extrinsic muscles of the eye except the lateral rectus and superior oblique.

Use eye⁸ / orbital / orbicularis oculi / intraocular / focusing⁹ **muscles** • **extraocular** (eye) movements / muscle paresis • **extraocular** muscle entrapment¹⁰ / nerve palsy • **oculomotor** nuclei / complex / activity / (nerve) palsy¹¹ • abducens / trochlear¹² **nerve** • **oculo**gyric crisis¹³ /glandular /sympathetic palsy¹⁴

äußere Augenmuskeln
Nervus oculomotorius¹ Diplopie, Doppelbilder² glatte/ kontinuierliche Folgebewegungen³ Sakkaden, ruckartige Augenbewegungen⁴ Blickstabilisierung⁵ Nervus oculomotorius, III. Hirnnerv⁶ M. ciliaris⁷ Augenmuskeln⁸ Akkommodationsmuskeln⁹ Einklemmung e. äußeren Augenmuskels¹⁰ Okulomotorius-, Augenmuskellähmung¹¹ N. trochlearis, IV. motor. Hirnnerv¹² Blickkrampf¹³ (Bernhard)-Horner-Syndrom, okulopupilläres Syndrom¹⁴

16

Unit 59 Vision
Related Units: 58 Eyes, 57 Senses, 42 Nerve Function, 67 Gestures, 21 Head & Neck, 40 Nervous System

see - saw - seen *v irr*   *rel* **look¹, view², watch³, observe³** [ɜː] *v* → U57-4

(i) to use the power of sight to perceive [siː] one's surroundings [aʊ]
(ii) to understand (iii) to imagine

seeing [siːɪŋ] *n* • **look⁴** *n* → U67-14 • **view⁵** *n* • **watchful⁶** *adj* • **observation** *n*

» Do you see halos⁷ [eɪ] around electric lights? Open your eyes and look up at my finger. The act of seeing begins with the capture of images focused by the cornea and lens upon the retina, a light-sensitive membrane in the back of the eye. Watching the patient swallow⁸ [ɒː] can be very helpful.

Use **to see** in one's mind's eye⁹ / double [ʌ] images¹⁰ • **to look** hard at sth. / for sth.¹¹ / away • **to look** back / up / into the distance / good • **to view** from a distance • **to watch** (carefully) for sth.¹² / TV • to take a (good/ quick/ second) **look** • side-/ dreamy [iː]/ glazed¹³ [eɪ] **look** • **to observe** the patient / for blood / sterile technique¹⁴ • to allow a full¹⁵ / overall / point of¹⁶ **view** • the act of **seeing** • **watchful** eyes / care • to permit/admit *or* hospitalize sb. for¹⁷/ keep a patient under **observation** • visual / clinical / close / direct / period of¹⁸ **observation**

sehen, an-, einsehen
schauen, gucken, an-, aussehen¹ sehen, betrachten, besichtigen² zusehen, beobachten³ Blick, Aussehen⁴ (Aus/An)sicht⁵ wachsam⁶ (Licht)hof⁷ schlucken⁸ sich etw. vorstellen⁹ Doppelbilder sehen¹⁰ etw. suchen¹¹ nach etw. Ausschau halten¹² glasiger Blick¹³ sich an d. aseptischen Kauteln halten¹⁴ eine gute Darstellung ermöglichen¹⁵ Gesichts-, Standpunkt¹⁶ jem. zur Beobachtung (stationär) aufnehmen¹⁷ Beobachtungszeit(raum)¹⁸

1

gaze [geɪz] *n clin & term*   *rel* **stare¹** [steɚ], **glare²** *n & v*, **peer³** [pɪɚ] *v*

steady [e] look with fixed eyes in one direction; normally there are six basic positions of gaze

gaze⁴ *v clin* → U67-13 f • **glaring** [gleɚɪŋ] *adj & n* • **staring** *adj & n*

» Ocular [ɒːkjəlɚ] signs include a characteristic stare with widened [aɪ] palpebral fissures⁵, infrequent blinking, lid lag⁶, and failure to wrinkle [r] the brow⁷ [aʊ] on upward gaze. The patient is preoccupied, distracted, tense and sits motionless [oʊʃ], staring into space⁸.

Use avoidance of eye⁹ / steady [e]/ listless¹⁰ **gaze** • primary / (right/ left) lateral / vertical **gaze** • upward / down¹¹/ up**gaze** • **gaze** stabilization /-evoked nystagmus¹² / palsy [ɔː] / direction¹³ / line / center¹⁴ / (cardinal) fields¹⁵ **of gaze** • **to peer** at sb. / over one's shoulder • **to peer** (short-sightedly) into the distance¹⁶ / over one's glasses • **to glare** round the room / crossly at sb. • angry **glare** • blinding **glare** of light • motionless / confused [juː]/ blank¹⁰ / glassy **stare** • **staring** spell¹⁷ / into space

(starrer) Blick; Blickrichtung
starrer Blick; starren¹ stechender Blick, greller Schein; (wütend) starren, grell leuchten² gucken, spähen³ (an)starren⁴ Lidspalten⁵ Graefe-Zeichen, Lidspaltenerweiterung bei Blicksenkung⁶ die Stirn runzeln⁷ vor s. hinstarrend⁸ Vermeiden d. Blickkontakts⁹ teilnahmsloser Blick¹⁰ Blicksenkung¹¹ Blickrichtungsnystagmus¹² Blickrichtung¹³ Blickpunkt¹⁴ Blickfelder¹⁵ angestrengt i. d. Ferne schauen¹⁶ Absence-Anfall¹⁷

2

BODY STRUCTURES & FUNCTIONS — Vision

blink [blɪŋk] v → U67-15   rel **dazzle**[1] [dæzl], **shine**[2] [ʃaɪn] v clin
to close and open the eyes reflexively or intentionally [ɪntenʃən-]
blink[3] n clin • **blinking** n & adj • **blinkers**[4] n pl • **dazzling** adj
» Ask the patient to blink or nod [ɒ:] for an affirmative [ɜː] reply to yes/no questions. Neonatal [eɪ] seizures [siːʒ-] may consist of brief episodes of apnea, eye deviation, eye blinking, or repetitive movements of the arms and legs. He is capable [eɪ] of blinking and voluntary eye movement in the vertical [ɜː] plane, with preserved pupillary responses to light.
Use **to blink** one's eyes[5] / spontaneously [eɪ]/ very often • **to blink** at sb.[6] / back one's tears[7] [tɪɚz] (espBE) • eye / weakened [iː] **blink** • **blink** reflex[8] [iː]/ of an eye / response / frequency [iː] • eyelid / involuntary[9] / rapid / infrequent[10] **blinking** • **blinking** lights / of the eyelids / and staring[11] • **dazzle** reflex[12] • **dazzling** brightness [braɪtnəs]/ lights [laɪts]/ whiteness

blinzeln, (zu)zwinkern
blenden; verblüffen[1] (hell) leuchten, strahlen, scheinen, glänzen[2] Blinzeln, flüchtiger (Augen)blick[3] Scheuklappen[4] m. d. Augen zwinkern[5] jem. zuzwinkern[6] m. d. Tränen kämpfen[7] Blinzelreflex[8] unwillkürl. Blinzeln/ Zwinkern[9] seltener Lidschlag[10] Zuzwinkern u. Anstarren[11] Lidschluss-, Blendreflex[12]

3

squint [skwɪnt] n clin → U67-14   syn **cross-eyes** n clin & jar, **strabismus** n term
deviation [eɪʃ] of one eye from parallelism with the other due to muscle imbalance, which may be manifest (tropia), latent [eɪ] (phoria [foʊrɪə]), divergent [daɪvɜːrdʒənt] (exotropia[1]), convergent [ɜː] (esotropia[2] [esə-]), upward (hypertropia [haɪpɚ-]) or downward (hypotropia)
squint[3] v clin • **cross-eyed**[4] adj • **strabismic** adj term
» A near-sighted person may squint to produce a pinhole effect, which improves distance vision. Sixth nerve paralysis [æ] causes convergent squint in the primary position with failure of abduction [ʌ] of the affected eye. Exophthalmic ophthalmoplegia [-pliːdʒ(ɪ)ə] refers to ocular muscle [mʌsl] weakness that results in impaired [eɚ] upward gaze, convergence [dʒ] and strabismus with varying degrees [iː] of diplopia[5] [dɪploʊpɪə].
Use to have[6]/present with/develop **a squint** • to be associated [oʊʃ] with/outgrow[7] **a squint** • accommodative[8] / manifest / vertical[9] **squint** • divergent / latent / downward / upward **squint** • **squint** deviation[10] • (non)paralytic[11] [ɪ]/ concomitant[12] / binocular[13] **strabismus** • convergent[2] / corrected / pseudo**strabismus** [suːdoʊ-] • **strabismus** surgery[14] • **strabismic** patient / deviation[10] / amblyopia[15]

Schielen, Strabismus
Auswärtsschielen, Exotropie, Strabismus divergens[1] Einwärtsschielen, Esotropie, S. convergens[2] (nach innen) schielen; blinzeln[3] schielend[4] Diplopie, Doppelsehen[5] schielen[6] d. Schielen wächst s. aus[7] akkommodativer Strabismus[8] Höhenschielen, S. verticalis[9] Schielwinkel[10] Lähmungsschielen, Strabismus paralyticus[11] Begleitschielen, S. concomitans[12] beidseitiges Schielen[13] Strabismusoperation[14] Schielamblyopie[15]

4

visual image [vɪʒʊəl ɪmɪdʒ] n   rel **afterimage**[1] n term
visual impression or representation of an object, person or scene [siːn] produced on a surface
» The ganglion cells translate the visual image impinging[2] [dʒ] upon the retina into a continuously varying barrage [-ɒːʒ] of action potentials. If diplopia is reported in one direction, check whether the peripheral or the central image disappears. Sudden onset of floaters[3] [oʊ], particularly when associated with flashing lights (photopsia), necessitates dilated [eɪ] fundal [ʌ] examination to exclude a retinal tear[4] [teɚ] or detachment[5] [ætʃ].
Use optical / retinal[6] / central / peripheral **image** • outer / three-dimensional[7] **image** • polarized / false / mirror[8] / double[9] [ʌ] **image** • mental / memory[10] **image** • positive / negative[11] **afterimage** • **visual** impression / perception[12] [se]/ memory • **visual** apparatus [eɪ] • **visual** angle[13] [æŋgl] • axis[14] [æ] • **visual** cortex / purple[15] [ɜː]/ stimulation • **visual** disturbance [ɜː]/ haze[16] [heɪz]/ aid[17] [eɪd] • **visually** impaired [eɚ]/ handicapped[18]

(optisches) Bild
Nachbild[1] sich abbilden[2] Mückensehen, Mouches volantes[3] Netzhautriss[4] Netzhautablösung[5] Netzhautbild[6] dreidimensionales Bild[7] Spiegelbild[8] Doppelbild[9] Erinnerungsbild[10] negatives Nachbild[11] opt./ visuelle Wahrnehmung[12] Sehwinkel[13] Sehachse, Axis opticus, Gesichtslinie[14] Sehpurpur, Rhodopsin[15] Schleier-, Nebelsehen[16] Sehhilfe[17] sehbehindert[18]

5

vision [vɪʒ³n] n term   syn **(eye)sight** [aɪsaɪt] n clin, rel **light perception**[1] [se] n
(i) ability to perceive visual sensations (ii) imagined mental image not elicited by visual stimuli
(in)visible[2] [vɪzɪbl] adj • **envision**[3] v • **sighted**[4] [saɪtɪd] adj • **visu(o)-** comb
» The patient complains of pain and photophobia, blurring [ɜː] of vision[5], and eye irritation. Ocular trauma [ɒː] can lead to loss of vision[6]. He gives a history of lightheadedness, and dimming of vision[5]. Blind infants reach developmental landmarks on a different schedule [ske-‖ʃe-] from that of sighted children. An intraocular lens would lead to rapid recovery [ʌ] of sight. If the patient's eyesight is poor, he should be assisted with grooming[7] [uː].
Use to affect[8]/alter/diminish/obscure[8] **vision** • to lose/improve/restore/correct **vision** • faculty of[9] / monocular / normal[10] / clear / partial **vision** • twenty-twenty[10] / low or poor **vision** • impaired or reduced / double [ʌ]/ blurred[5] [ɜː] **vision** • stereoscopic[11] / (un)corrected[12] / distant / near **vision** • peripheral[13] / night[14] / tunnel [ʌ] **vision** • **vision** in depth[15] • to lose one's/save sb.'s **sight** • poor / failing[16] [eɪ] **eyesight** • loss[6] / preservation **of sight** • short[17]-/ long-/ non-**sighted** • **sight**-threatening [e] infection • **visuo**sensory /auditory [ɒː] /spatial [vɪʒʊoʊspeɪʃəl] disorientation[18]

(i) Sehvermögen, -kraft, Sehen, Visus
(ii) Vorstellung
Lichtwahrnehmung[1] (un)sichtbar[2] s. vorstellen[3] sehend[4] verschwommenes Sehen[5] Visusverlust, Verlust d. Sehkraft[6] Körperpflege[7] die Sehkraft beeinträchtigen[8] Sehvermögen[9] Emmetropie, Normalsichtigkeit[10] stereoskopisches Sehen[11] Visus naturalis, Sehleistung[12] peripheres Sehen[13] skotopisches Sehen, Nachtsehen[14] Tiefensehen, räuml. Sehen[15] nachlassende Sehkraft[16] kurzsichtig[17] visuospatiale Störung[18]

6

Vision

BODY STRUCTURES & FUNCTIONS

visual field [vɪʒʊəl fiːld] *n term, abbr* **VF**   *syn* **field of vision** *n term & clin*

area simultaneously [eɪ] visible to one eye in a straight-ahead position

visualize[1] [-aɪz] *v clin* • **visibility**[2] *n* • **hemifield**[3] [e] *n term* • **visualization** *n*

» Disturbances in vision may consist of image distortion, photophobia, color change, spots before the eyes, visual field defects[4] [iː], brief loss of vision, or haloes around lights. Map visual fields by confrontation testing[5] in each quadrant of the visual field for each eye individually. The visual loss was described as a curtain[6] [kɜːrtᵊn] passing vertically across the visual field. A hand-held direct ophthalmoscope allows visualization of the ocular fundus[7].

Use (para)central / peripheral / lateral / binocular[8] **visual field** • contracted[9] / impaired **visual field** • **visual field** testing[10] / analysis[10] / perimetry[10] / target • **visual field** constriction[9] / disturbances [ɜː]/ loss[9] / axis[11] / line[11] / direction / (upper/ lower) half **of vision** • graying [eɪ]/ deterioration or fading[12] [eɪ]/ dimness **of vision** • blurring / loss / islands[13] [aɪ]/ recovery[14] [ʌ] **of vision** • **to visualize** the retina • good / poor[15] **visibility** • visual hemi**field**

Gesichts-, Sehfeld
s. etw. vorstellen, sichtbar machen, darstellen[1] Sichtbarkeit, Sicht(weite)[2] linkes/ rechtes Gesichtsfeld[3] Skotom, Gesichtsfeldausfall[4] Konfrontationsversuch[5] Schleier[6] Augenfundus[7] binokulares Gesichtsfeld[8] Gesichtsfeldeinengung[9] Gesichtsfelduntersuchung, Perimetrie[10] Sehachse, Gesichtslinie[11] Verminderung d. Sehkraft[12] Sehinseln[13] Wiedererlangen d. Sehkraft[14] schlechte Sicht[15]

7

visual acuity [əkjuːəti] *n term, abbr* **VA**   *sim* **sharp-sightedness**[1] *n clin*

visual ability to resolve[2] fine detail [iː] in a visual image, also known as resolving power[3]

stereoacuity[4] [steəɪoʊ-] *n term* • **hyperacuity** [haɪpə-][5] *n* • **sharp-eyed** *adj clin*

» If the patient is unable to read the top line of the chart [tʃ], acuity is recorded as counting fingers (CF), hand movements (HM), perception of light (PL), or no light perception (NLP). Significantly decreased corrected visual acuity (e.g. 6/30 [20/100] in a patient who normally has 6/6 [20/20] vision) generally indicates disease of the eyeball or visual pathway.

Use to lose/test/determine[5] **acuity** • central[6] / near / distant[7] / corrected[8] **visual acuity** • **visual acuity** for distance[7] / chart[9] / resolution[3] [uːʃ]/ degree [iː] of **acuity** • superb [ɜː]/ near-normal / diminished[10] **acuity** • impaired[10] / poor[11] **visual acuity** • foveal[6]/ stereoscopic / absolute intensity / threshold[12] **acuity** • auditory[13]/ taste / mental[14] **acuity** • **acuity** testing[15] / level • to be[16] **sharp-eyed**

Sehschärfe
Scharfsichtigkeit[1] auflösen[2] Auflösungsvermögen[3] binokulare Sehschärfe[4] d. Sehschärfe bestimmen[5] zentrale S.[6] Fernsehschärfe, Fernvisus[7] korrigierte S.[8] Sehprobentafel[9] herabgesetzte Sehschärfe[10] Sehschwäche[11] Minimalsehschärfe[12] Hörschärfe[13] Geistesschärfe[14] Sehschärfenbestimmung, -prüfung[15] gute Augen haben[16]

8

color vision *n clin & term*   *rel* **night vision**[1] *n clin*, **chromatopsia**[2] *n term*

ability to perceive and discriminate colors [kʌlɚz] which is based on the cones [oʊ] in the retina that have visual pigments of differing peak [iː] spectral sensitivity

colored [ʌ] *adj* • **(mono/ di/ tri/ a)chromatic** *adj term* • **di/ trichromat**[3] *n*

» Acquired defects in color vision[4] frequently result from disease of the macula. Man's color vision can distinguish up to 300,000 different hues[5] [hjuːz]. The cones[6], active under daylight conditions, are specialized for color perception and high spatial resolution[7]. These photoreceptor [se] pigments in the retina are involved in night, day, and color vision.

Use (ab)normal / decreased[4] / impairment of[4] / loss of **color vision** • **color vision** testing / disturbance[4] • yellow[8] / day[9] / twilight[10] [aɪ] **vision** • to perceive[11] [iː] **colors** • **colored** halo [eɪ] • **color** perception (test) / match[12] / adaptation • **color** confusion[13] [juːʒ]/ change / blind(ness)[14] • **monochromatic** light • **trichromatic vision**[15]

Farbensehen
Nachtsehen[1] Chromatopsie, Chromopsie[2] (normaler) Trichromat, Person m. normalem Farbensinn[3] Farbenfehlsichtigkeit, -sinnstörung[4] Farbtöne[5] Zapfen[6] räuml. Auflösung[7] Gelbsehen, Xanthopsie[8] Tagessehen, photopisches S.[9] Dämmerungs-, Nachtsehen, skotopisches S.[10] Farben wahrnehmen[11] Farbabstimmung[12] Farbverwechslung[13] Farbenblindheit[14] trichromatisches S., normales Farbensehen[15]

9

light *or* **photopic adaptation** *n term* → U88-17

rel **illumination**[1], **miosis**[2] [maɪ‖miː] *n term*

adjustment to vision in bright light (photopia) by reducing the concentration of photosensitive pigments

illuminate [uː] *v* • **adapt**[3] *v* • **adaptive**[4] *adj term* • **miotic**[5] [maɪɒtɪk] *adj & n*

» Inadequate intake or utilization of vitamin A can impair dark adaptation[6] and cause night blindness. The rods[7] are operative under scotopic, or dim illumination[8]. The pupil responded poorly to direct light but constricted briskly[9] when the other eye was illuminated. Determine whether the anterior chamber[10] [tʃeɪ] is shallow[11] by oblique [-liːk] illumination of the anterior segment of the eye. The corneal light reflex [iː] is evaluated by shining [aɪ] the beam [iː] of a light at the patient's eyes, observing the reflections off each cornea.

Use dark or scotopic[6] / retinal[12] / color / auditory [ɒː] **adaptation** • **adaptation** period • **adaptive** mechanism / response / capacity[13] [æs] • bright / room / (in)adequate / good / source [ɔː] of **illumination** • dark-**adapted** • **light**-adapted eye /-dark discrimination[14] / reflex • **light** examination of the eye / intensity • **light** threshold[15] / source / ray[16] [reɪ] • to perceive/refract[17] **light** • natural / pen[18] / monochromatic / full-spectrum[19] **light** • ultraviolet [aɪ] (*abbr* UV)/ sun **light** • reactive to **light** • perception (*abbr* PL)/ reflection **of light** • scattering / wavelength / flashes[20] **of light** • pupillary[2] / unilateral **miosis** • **miotic** pupils/ eye drops[21] / effect

Helladaptation
Be-, Ausleuchtung[1] Pupillenverengung, Miosis[2] anpassen, adaptieren[3] anpassungsfähig[4] pupillenverengend, miotisch; Miotikum, pupillenverengendes Mittel[5] Dunkeladaptation[6] Stäbchen[7] schwache Beleuchtung[8] rasch[9] vordere Augenkammer, Camera oculi anterior[10] flach[11] Netzhautadaptation[12] Anpassungsfähigkeit[13] Hell-Dunkel-Unterscheidung[14] minimale Lichtwahrnehmung[15] Lichtstrahl[16] Licht brechen[17] Diagnoseleuchte[18] Vollspektrum-Licht[19] Lichtblitze[20] pupillenverengende Augentropfen[21]

10

242 BODY STRUCTURES & FUNCTIONS — Vision

brightness [braɪtnəs] *n*   *opposite* **dimness**¹ *n, rel* **contrast**² [kɒːntræst] *n & v*

degree of illumination along the black-to-white continuum or the quality of emitting or reflecting light

bright³ *adj* • **brighten** [braɪtən] (**up**) *v* • **dim**⁴ [dɪm] *adj & v* • **dimming** *n*

» The patient complains [eɪ] of a loss of brightness in the affected eye. Haloes around lights or bright objects are suggestive [dʒe] of acute angle-closure [oʊ] glaucoma⁵ [glɔːkoʊmə]. Baring⁶ [eɚ] of the blind spot and small scotomata above or below fixation were noted with small and dim visual field targets [tɑːrgəts].

Use **brightness** control⁷ / modulation • **bright** outdoor light / colors⁸ / day / red⁹ • **bright** light source /-eyed¹⁰ / future • **brightly** colored • visual¹¹ **dimness** • **dimness** of vision¹¹ • **dim** vision¹¹ / light / illumination • **dimmed** vision¹¹ • high¹² / distinct / simultaneous / successive¹³ [səksesɪv] **contrast** • **contrast** sensitivity / resolution • **contrast** enhancement¹⁴ / agent [eɪdʒ] or dye [daɪ] or medium¹⁵ [iː]

Helligkeit, Leuchten, Glanz
Halbdunkel, Trübheit, Mattheit¹ Kontrast, Gegensatz; gegenüberstellen, einen Vergleich anstellen² hell, strahlend; schlau³ dunkel, dämmrig; dämpfen, trüben⁴ akutes Winkelblockglaukom⁵ Exkavation⁶ Helligkeitsregulation, -steuerung⁷ leuchtende Farben⁸ leuchtend rot⁹ helläugig, mit strahlenden Augen¹⁰, Augentrübung, Sehschwäche¹¹ starker Kontrast¹² Sukzessivkontrast¹³ Kontrastverstärkung¹⁴ Kontrastmittel¹⁵

11

(ocular) accommodation [eɪʃ] *n term*

  rel **refraction**¹ [rɪfrækʃən] *n term*

adjustment in focal length of the lens to focus on objects at long or short distances by contraction or relaxation of the ciliary [sɪliɚi] muscles which adapt the curvature [ɜː] of the anterior surface of the lens

accommodative² *adj term* • (**un**)**accommodated** *adj* • **refractive**³ *adj*

» The pupils should constrict promptly and equally to accommodation and to direct and indirect light. With the onset of middle age, presbyopia⁴ develops as the lens within the eye becomes unable to increase its refractive power to accommodate upon near objects. Large refractive errors⁵ and poor accommodative ability⁶ may manifest as headaches.

Use pupillary / binocular / negative / positive / muscles [mʌslz] of⁷ **accommodation** • (impaired) visual / fixed-gaze **accommodation** • light and (*abbr* L & A)/ loss of⁸ / disturbances of **accommodation** • **accommodation** reflex⁹ • paralysis of the muscles of¹⁰ **accommodation** • **accommodative** capacity⁶ / squint or strabismus¹¹ / esotropia / asthenopia¹² • **unaccommodated** eye¹³ • **to refract** light • **refractive** power (of the eye)¹⁴ / eye examination¹⁵ / index¹⁶ / **refractive** error / state / amblyopia¹⁷ / correction • hyperopic¹⁸ [oʊ]/ errors of⁵ / unequal **refraction** • **refraction** screening

Akkommodation
Lichtbrechung, Refraktion¹ akkommodativ, Akkommodations-² Brech(ungs)-³ Presbyopie, Altersweitsichtigkeit⁴ Refraktionsanomalien, Brechungsfehler⁵ Akkommodationsfähigkeit⁶ Akkommodationsmuskeln⁷ Akkommodationsverlust⁸ Akkommodationsreflex⁹ Akkommodationslähmung¹⁰ akkommodativer Strabismus¹¹ akkommodative Asthenopie¹² nicht akkommodiertes Auge¹³ Brechkraft d. Auges¹⁴ Refraktionsbestimmung¹⁵ Brechungsindex¹⁶ Refraktionsamblyopie¹⁷ Brechungshyperopie, -hypermetropie¹⁸

12

---

convergence [kənvɜːrdʒənˡs] *n term*   *opposite* **divergence**¹ [daɪ-] *n term*

coordinated inclination of the visual axes toward their common point of fixation

converge [kənvɜːrdʒ] *v* • **convergent**² *adj term* •
diverge [daɪvɜːrdʒ] *v* • **divergent** *adj term*

» Difficulty with convergence at near point³, however, may interfere [-ɪɚ] significantly with the process of reading. Check for pupillary accommodation with convergence by asking the patient to follow a small object as it moves toward the bridge of the nose⁴. A concomitant strabismus may be convergent (esotropia), divergent (exotropia), or vertical (hyper- or hypotropia). Near objects can be seen clearly, but distant objects require a diverging lens⁵ in front of the eye.

Use to preserve **convergence** • adaptive / near point of (*abbr* NPC)/ far point of⁶ **convergence** • poor / absence of **convergence** • **convergence** of the eyes / at near point /-type nystagmus⁷ • **convergent** squint⁸ / rays⁹ • **converging** lens¹⁰

Konvergenz (d. Augenachsen)
Divergenz, Abweichen d. Augenachsen¹ s. nähernd, zusammenlaufend, konvergent, konvergierend² Nahpunkt, Punctum proximum³ Nasenrücken⁴ Konkav-, Zerstreuungslinse⁵ Fernpunkt⁶ Konvergenznystagmus⁷ Einwärtsschielen, Strabismus convergens, Esotropie⁸ konvergierende Strahlen⁹ Konvex-, Sammellinse¹⁰

13

---

saccade [sækɑːd] *n term*   *syn* **saccadic eye movement** *n, rel* **fixation**¹ *n term*

rapid binocular movements that enable the eyes to fixate on moving or changing objects

(**re**)**fixate**² *v term* • **fix** (**on**) *v* • **refixation** *n*

» Saccades, or quick refixation eye movements, are assessed by having the patient look back and forth between two stationary [eɪʃ] targets³. The patient is instructed to gaze upon a small fixation target⁴ in the distance.

Use consecutive / corrective⁵ / downwards **saccades** • hypometric / hypermetric [aɪ] **saccades** • **saccadic** gaze⁶ / jump / displacement • visual / point of⁷ / binocular⁸ / distance or distant⁹ / near¹⁰ **fixation** • **fixation** movement¹¹ / point⁷ / task / shift¹² / disparity¹³ • **to fixate** (up)on objects • **to fix** (up)on / an object with the eyes • to achieve [tʃ] **fixation** • **refixation** (eye) movement¹⁴

Sakkade, ruckartige Augenbewegung
Fixation, Einstellung d. Augen¹ fixieren² unbewegte Objekte³ Fixationsobjekt⁴ Korrektursakkaden⁵ sakkadische Augenbewegung⁶ Fixationspunkt⁷ beidäugige/ binokulare Fixation⁸ Fernfixation⁹ Nahfixation¹⁰ Fixationsbewegung¹¹ wechselnde Fixation, Fixationswechsel¹² Fixationsdisparation¹³ Augenbewegung zur Refixation¹⁴

14

Vision　　　　　　　　　　　　　　　　　　　　　　　　　　　　　BODY STRUCTURES & FUNCTIONS 243

---

eye alignment [aɪ əlaɪnmənt] *n term*　　*syn* **ocular alignment** *n term*
　　　　　　opposite **ocular misalignment¹, eye deviation¹** [diːviːeɪʃ⁽ə⁾n] *n term*

ability to fix the gaze on a target by keeping the visual axes² of both eyes directed to this point
(mis)aligned³ [aɪ] *adj term* • **deviate⁴** [diːvieɪt] *v* • **deviated** *adj* • **deviating** *adj*

» One way of evaluating eye alignment is with the cover test⁵, in which the patient looks at a target while one eye is covered. Besides alignment, ocular rotations should be evaluated in the six cardinal positions of gaze. Check the alignment and convergence of the eyes and whether there are deviations or latent nystagmus⁶ [ɪ]. His eyes are aligned orthotropically.

Use to judge or test **ocular alignment** • normal / good **alignment** • correctly / well-aligned • **alignment** of the eyes⁷ / evaluation • **misalignment** of the visual axes¹ • ocular¹ / (dys)conjugate (gaze or eye⁸) / inward **deviation** • (concomitant) medial [iː]/ downward / latent⁹ [eɪ]/ skew¹⁰ [skjuː] **deviation** • **deviation** from parallelism / of one eye / of both eyes • **to deviate** inward / outward / conjugately • **deviated** eye¹¹

Orthophorie, Normophorie
Augenfehlstellung, Fehlstellung d. Augenachsen, Strabismus, Heterophorie¹ Sehachsen² ausgerichtet, assoziiert³ abweichen⁴ Abdecktest, Cover-Test⁵ latenter Nystagmus⁶ Orthophorie⁷ Deviation conjugee, konjugierte Bulbusabweichung⁸ latentes Schielen, Heterophorie⁹ Hertwig-Magendie-Syndrom, Magendie-Schielstellung¹⁰ schielendes Auge¹¹
　　　　　　　　　　　　　　　15

---

ocular motility *n term*　　*rel* **conjugate** [-dʒʊgeɪt] **eye movement¹** *n term*

movement of the eyeballs effected by the extraocular muscles to position the eyes for proper vision
monocular *adj term* • **binocular** [baɪnɒːkjələ˞] *adj* • **binocularity²** *n*

» Ocular motility must be assessed and the globe³ examined for injury, vascular embarrassment⁴, and increased intraocular pressure⁵.

Use full / impaired⁶ [eə]/ disturbance [ɜː] in / improved **ocular motility** • conjugate lateral gaze / gaze palsy⁷ [ɔː]/ eye deviation • **ocular** rotation • **monocular** depth cues⁸ [kjuːz]/ visual stimulation / ischemia [ɪskiː-] • **monocular** diplopia⁹ [oʊ]/ visual loss / blindness • **binocular** (double) [ʌ] vision² / visual field • **binocular** near point / patching¹⁰ / microscope¹¹ [aɪ]

Augenbeweglichkeit
konjugierte Augenbewegung, Version¹ binokulares Sehen² Augapfel³ Gefäßschädigung⁴ Augeninnendruck, intraokularer D.⁵ eingeschränkte Augenbeweglichkeit⁶ konjugierte Blicklähmung⁷ monokulare Hinweisreize d. Tiefenwahrnehmung⁸ monokulare Diplopie⁹ Binokulusverband¹⁰ Binokularmikroskop¹¹
　　　　　　　　　　　　　　　16

---

short- or **near-sighted** [nɪə˞saɪtɪd] *adj clin*　　*syn* **myopic** [maɪpː‖oʊpɪk] *adj term*

inability to focus on¹ near objects because rays [reɪz] of light entering the eye parallel to the optic axis focus² in front of the retina, mostly because of excessive axial length of the eyeball
nearsightedness³ *n clin* • **far-** or **long-sighted⁴** *adj* • **far-sightedness⁵** *n* • **hyperopia⁵** *n term* • **hyperopic⁴** *adj* • **myopia³** *n* • **-opic, -opia** *comb*

» More than 70 million people in the U.S. are nearsighted. If you are farsighted you have more trouble seeing up close than you do in the distance. Most children have a hyperopic refraction, which begins to diminish at about 8 years of age and does not require correction. Saying the hyperopic child is sighted for far (not near) is misleading, since the child can focus on near targets if the hyperopia is not excessive.

Use **nearsighted** vision³ / eye / patients / children • to cause/lead to/correct **nearsightedness** • to be (severely⁶/ mildly) / the **farsighted** • degree [iː] of / mild / extreme [iː] **farsightedness** • high-grade / unilateral / sudden / transient⁷ myopia • axial⁸ / index⁹ / simple or primary [aɪ]/ curvature [ɜː]/ progressive¹⁰ myopia • emmetr¹¹/ presby¹²/ tr/ esotr**opia** • exotr/ ambly¹³/ heterotr¹⁴/ hypotr**opia** [haɪpətroʊpiə] • dipl/ hemian¹⁵/ [hemiənoʊpiə] quadrantan**opia**

kurzsichtig, myop(isch)
einstellen, klar sehen¹ s. bündeln² Kurzsichtigkeit³ weitsichtig⁴ Weitsichtigkeit, Hyperopie, Hypermetropie⁵ stark weitsichtig sein⁶ vorübergehende/ passagere Myopie⁷ Achsenmyopie⁸ Brechungsmyopie⁹ progressive Myopie¹⁰ Normalsichtigkeit, Emmetropie¹¹ Presbyopie, Altersweitsichtigkeit¹² Schwachsichtigkeit, Amblyopie¹³ manifestes Schielen, Heterotropie¹⁴ Halbseitenblindheit, Hemianopsie¹⁵
　　　　　　　　　　　　　　　17

---

blind [blaɪnd] *adj clin*　　*opposite* **sighted¹** [saɪtɪd] *adj clin* → U59-6

being unable to see or to suffer [ʌ] from visual impairment [eə] (e.g. color blindness)
blindness² *n clin & term* • **blind³** *n & v* • **blinding** *adj* • **-alopia** [-əloʊpiə] *comb*

» I was blinded by the lights of an approaching [əproʊtʃ-] car. Patients with age-related macular degeneration, though often legally blind (< 20/200 vision), have good peripheral vision and useful color vision, and they should be advised [aɪ] that they will not lose all sight.

Use to go⁴/be/be born **blind** • legally [iː]/ color⁵ **blind** • **blind** child • **blind**fold⁶ / as a bat⁷ / in one eye⁸ / spot⁹ • acquired¹⁰ [aɪ]/ sudden / fleeting¹¹ [iː] **blindness** • progressive / permanent [ɜː]/ bilateral **blindness** • total or absolute / irreversible [ɜː]/ curable [kjʊə-] **blindness** • cortical¹² / psychic¹³ [saɪkɪk]/ night¹⁴ / day / snow¹⁵ **blindness** • sun / eclipse / (red-green) / yellow-blue) color¹⁶ **blindness** • **blinding** eye lesion¹⁷ [iːʒ]/ retinal detachment [ætʃ] • nyct**alopia**¹⁴ [nɪktəloʊpiə]

blind
sehend¹ Blindheit² die Blinden; Jalousie, Blende; blind machen, blenden³ blind werden, erblinden⁴ farbenblind⁵ m. verbundenen Augen⁶ stockblind, vollkommen blind⁷ auf einem Auge blind⁸ blinder Fleck⁹ erworbene Blindheit¹⁰ Amaurosis fugax¹¹ Rindenblindheit, kortikale B.¹² funktionelle B.¹³ Nachtblindheit, Nyktalopie¹⁴ Schneeblindheit¹⁵ Rotgrünblindheit¹⁶ zur Erblindung führende Augenläsion¹⁷
　　　　　　　　　　　　　　　18

Unit 60 Ears

Related Units: 21 Head & Neck, 61 Hearing, 57 Senses, 40 Nervous System, 41 Brain, 42 Nerve Function

outer *or* **external ear** [ɪkstɜːrnəl ɪɚ] *n*   *rel* **middle ear**[1], **inner ear**[2] *n* → U21-15

visible portion of the ear, the outer ear canal, and the outer surface of the eardrum

earshot[3] *n clin* • **(ear)wax**[4] *n* •
(bin)aural [baɪ-‖bɪnɔːrəl] *adj term* • **ot(o)-** [oʊtə-] *comb*

» *Scaling*[5] [eɪ] within the external ear is often mistaken for a chronic fungal [ʌ] infection. Clear or blood-tinged[6] [dʒ] fluid emerging [ɜː] from the ear must be assumed to be cerebrospinal fluid.

Use **external ear** canal / cartilage [-ɪdʒ]/ injury • to have sharp/plug [ʌ] the[7] **ears** • prominent[8] / low-set[9] / lop[10] / plugged / tender[11] / running[12] **ears** • chronically discharging / bleeding from the **ears** • affected / ipsilateral / right / (non)tested **ear** • foreign body / pain / itching / fullness **in the ear** • to lend sb. your **ear** • **ear**ache[13] [ɪɚeɪk]/ wick[14] / infection / plug[15] • **ear** flap[16] / nose and throat[17] [oʊ] (*abbr* ENT) • speculum[18] • within / out of[19] earshot • **ear**-phone /ring /splitting[20] • mon/ retro**aural** • **aural** discharge[12] / fullness / pressure • **monaural** hearing / stimulation • **oto**logy /genous [dʒə] /toxic /pharyngeal [ɪndʒ] /rrhea[12] [-riːə] / scope[18] /plasty • **ot**algia[13] [-dʒ(ɪ)ə] /itis [oʊtaɪtɪs]

äußeres Ohr, Auris externa
Mittelohr, Auris media[1] Innenohr, Auris interna[2] Hörweite[3] Zerumen, Ohrenschmalz[4] (Ver)schuppung, Schuppenbildung[5] blutig tingiert[6] d. Ohren zustopfen[7] abstehende O.[8] tiefsitzende O.[9] Hängeohren[10] druckschmerzempfindl. O.[11] Otorrhoe, Ohrenfluss[12] Ohrenschmerzen, Otalgie[13] Wattebausch, Gazestreifen (für d. Ohr)[14] Gehörstöpsel, Gehörschutzpfropfen[15] Ohrenschützer[16] HNO[17] Ohrenspiegel, Otoskop[18] außer Hörweite[19] ohrenbetäubend[20]

1

auricle [ɔːrɪkl] *or* **pinna** *n term*   *rel* **earlobe** *or* **ear lobe**[1] [ɪɚ loʊb] *n clin*

shell-like[2] flap of the ear projecting from the side of the head; it consists of the concha[3] [kɒŋkə], helix[4] [iː], ant(i)helix[5], tragus[6] [eɪ], antitragus[7] and the lobule [ɒː] of the auricle[1]
auricular *adj term* • **pinnal** [pɪnəl] *adj* • **auricul(o)-** *comb*

» The auricle collects the sound waves and directs them to the external auditory canal. These patients present with a swollen, hot, red pinna, usually with sparing[8] [eə] of the lobule. Lop ear, the most common congenital [dʒe] deformity of the auricle, is the result of failure of development of the antihelical fold or excessive protrusion [uːʒ] of the conchal cartilage.

Use tender / deformed **pinna** • bifid[9] / affected / contralateral / stretched[10] **earlobe** • post/ retro/ pre**auricular** • **auricular** appendage[11] [-ɪdʒ]/ cartilage[12] / muscle [ʌ]/ nerve [ɜː] • **auricular** trauma [ɒː]/ deformity[13] / hillock[14] • **auriculo**temporal nerve /palpebral [iː]/ reflex[15] [iː]

Ohrmuschel, Pinna, Auricula
Ohrläppchen[1] muschelartig[2] Concha auricularis, Ohrmuschel[3] Helix, Ohrleiste[4] Anthelix, Gegenleiste[5] Tragus, knorpelige Erhebung vor d. Gehörgang[6] Antitragus[7] Aussparung[8] Doppelläppchen[9] gedehntes Ohrläppchen[10] Aurikular-, Ohranhänge[11] Ohr(muschel)knorpel, Cartilago auricularis[12] angeborener Ohrmuscheldefekt, Ohrmuscheldeformität[13] Ohrmuschelhöcker[14] akust. Lidreflex[15]

2

external auditory [ɒːdɪtɔːri] **canal** *or* **meatus** [miːeɪtəs] *n term, abbr* **EAM**
   syn **outer ear canal** [kənæl] *n clin*

passage from the pinna to the eardrum about 2.5 cm long and lined by skin which is directly attached to the periosteum of the temporal bone in the medial half (no subcutaneous [eɪ] layer)

» Is the FB[1] lodged [dʒ] medial to the isthmus [ɪsməs] of the external auditory canal? Purulent[2] [jʊɚ] debris filling the ear canal should be gently [dʒ] removed to permit entry of the topical medication. There is an opening in the petrous portion[3] of the temporal bone through which the auditory and facial nerves and blood vessels pass.

Use pressure in / lesions [iːʒ] in / inspection of / inflammation [eɪʃ] of[4] **the external auditory canal** • obstructed [ʌ]/ patent[5] [eɪ] **external auditory canal** • internal[6] [ɜː] **auditory meatus** *or* **canal** (*abbr* IAM) • **external auditory canal** bone / fluid • **ear canal** skin / wall / pressure / discharge[7] [-tʃɑːrdʒ] • middle **meatus** antrostomy

äußerer Gehörgang, Meatus acusticus externus
Fremdkörper[1] eitrig[2] Felsenbeinpyramide, Pars petrosa ossis temporalis[3] Entzündung d. äußeren Gehörgangs[4] durchgängiger äußerer Gehörgang[5] innerer Gehörgang, Meatus acusticus internus[6] Otorrhoe, Ohrenfluss[7]

3

eardrum [ʌ] *n clin*   *syn* **tympanum** [ɪ], **tympanic membrane** *n term, abbr* **TM**

thin tense[1] membrane at the boundary [aʊ] between the external and middle ear which separates the tympanic cavity from the external auditory meatus

drum rupture[2] [ʌ] *n* • **hemotympanum**[3] [hiːmətɪmp-] *n term* • **tympan(o)-** *comb*

» When sound strikes [aɪ] the ear, it causes the tympanic membrane to vibrate [aɪ]. The eardrum reacts to sound waves and starts the ossicular chain [tʃeɪn] moving. Do a caloric test of the external ear canal by gently instilling ice water against the tympanic membrane. A hemotympanum gives the eardrum a blue-black color.

Use to examine/visualize/injure/penetrate **the eardrum** • perforated[4] / injected [dʒe]/ immobile **eardrum** • perforation[4] / inspection / immobility / rupture[2] [-ptʃɚ] of **the eardrum** • **tympanic** antrum[5] / nerve [ɜː]/ vein [eɪ] • **tympanic** notch[6] [nɒːtʃ]/ swelling / injury / temperature • intact / normal-appearing / gray / retracted[7] **tympanic membrane** • mobility[8] / compliance[9] [aɪə] **of the tympanic membrane** • **tympanic membrane** perforation[4] • **tympan**itis [aɪ] /oplasty[10] /ometry[11] /ocentesis [iː] /osclerosis[12] • sinus [aɪ]/ fundus [ʌ] / chorda [kɔːrdə]/ tegmen[13] **tympani**

Trommelfell, Membrana tympani
straff[1] Trommelfellruptur[2] Hämatotympanon, Blutansammlung in d. Paukenhöhle[3] Trommelfellperforation[4] Antrum mastoideum[5] Incisura tympanica[6] Trommelfelleinziehung, -retraktion, retrahiertes Trommelfell[7] Trommelfellbeweglichkeit[8] Trommelfellcompliance[9] Tympanoplastik[10] Tympanometrie[11] Tympanosklerose[12] Tegmen tympani, knöchernes Dach d. Paukenhöhle[13]

4

Ears BODY STRUCTURES & FUNCTIONS **245**

auditory *or* **ear ossicle** [ɒːsɪkəl] *n term*
rel **malleus¹** [mælɪəs], **incus²** [ɪŋkəs], **stapes³** [steɪpiːz] *n term*
small bones (hammer¹, anvil² [æ], stirrup³ [ɜː]) that convey [eɪ] sound impulses from the eardrum to the oval window
ossicular⁴ *adj term* • **stapedial** [iː] *adj* • **ossicul(o)-** *comb* • **staped(e)-** *comb*
» The handle of the malleus⁵, the first and largest of the ossicles, is attached [tʃ] to the eardrum, while the head is attached to the roof of the tympanic cavity by the superior malleolar ligament, and articulates with the anvil. When moved by the incus, the stapes, the third and inner bone of the ossicular chain, vibrates in the oval window.
Use middle ear **ossicle** • **ossicular** chain⁶ / discontinuity⁷ [uː]/ disruption [ʌ] • **ossicular** malformation⁸ / erosion⁹ [oʊʒ]/ implants • **stapes** surgery / fixation¹⁰ • **stapedial** footplate¹¹ • **staped**iovestibular /dius muscle¹² /otomy /ectomy¹³ /iolysis /ioplasty¹⁴

Gehörknöchelchen
Hammer, Malleus¹ Amboss, Incus² Steigbügel, Stapes³ ossikulär⁴ Hammerstiel, Manubrium mallei⁵ Gehörknöchelchenkette⁶ Gehörknöchelchenunterbrechung⁷ Gehörknöchelchendefekt, -fehlbildung⁸ Arrosion der Gehörknöchelchen⁹ Stapesfixation¹⁰ Stapes-, Steigbügelfußplatte¹¹ Steigbügelmuskel, Musculus stapedius¹² Steigbügelentfernung, Stapedektomie¹³ Stapesplastik¹⁴
5

middle ear cavity [kævəti] *n clin*   *syn* **tympanic cavity** *n term rare*
portion of the hearing mechanism [ek] between the outer and inner ears formed by the eardrum, the ossicles, the opening of the eustachian tube, the oval window, and the round window
» If no infection is present, the middle ear cavity generally contains normal mucosa [mjuː-]. Owing to the normal aeration of the middle ear cavity¹, the tympanic membrane retained [eɪ] its mobility.
Use air-filled² **middle ear cavity** • **middle ear** space³ [speɪs]/ cleft³ / structures [ʌ]/ conduction [ʌ] • **middle ear** pressure⁴ / effusion⁵ [juːʒ]/ fluid • **middle ear** ventilation¹ / examination / infection / deafness⁶ [e] • **middle ear** inflammation⁷ / damage⁸ / tumor / aspirate / surgery

Paukenhöhle, Cavum tympani, Cavitas tympanica, Tympanum, Tympanon
Belüftung d. Paukenhöhle¹ lufthaltige Paukenhöhle² Paukenhöhle³ Mittelohrdruck⁴ Paukenhöhlenerguss⁵ Mittelohrschwerhörigkeit⁶ Mittelohrentzündung, Otitis media⁷ Mittelohrschädigung⁸
6

eustachian [juːsteɪʃ(ə)n] **tube** *n term*   *syn* **auditory tube** [ɒːdɪtɔːri t(j)uːb] *n clin*
tube connecting the nasopharynx with the middle ear which opens during swallowing¹
» The narrowest portion of the auditory tube is in the region of the sphenopetrosal [iː] fissure² [ɪʃ]. Prolonged eustachian tube dysfunction results in chronic negative middle ear pressure that draws inward the upper flaccid³ [(k)s] portion of the tympanic membrane. The patient should be advised to swallow [ɒː], yawn⁴ [jɔːn], and autoinflate frequently during underwater descent [dɪsent], which may be painful if the auditory tube collapses.
Use **eustachian tube** mucosa / function (*abbr* ETF)/ pressure • **eustachian tube** dysfunction [ɪ]/ obstruction / inflation • **eustachian** muscle⁵ / tonsil⁶ / cartilage • **auditory** artery / nerve / pathway⁷ • **auditory** cortex⁸ / stimuli / perception / memory⁹ / hallucinations¹⁰ • overly patent¹¹ [eɪ]/ hypofunctioning / semicanal of the¹² **auditory tube**

Ohrtrompete, Tuba auditiva/ Eustachii, Eustachische Röhre
Schlucken¹ Fissura sphenopetrosa² schlaff³ gähnen⁴ Musculus tensor tympani, Trommelfellspanner⁵ Tubenmandel, Tonsilla tubaria⁶ Hörbahn⁷ Hörrinde, akust. Rindenfeld/ Cortex⁸ akust. Erinnerungsfeld/ -region⁹ akust. Halluzinationen¹⁰ klaffende Ohrtrompete¹¹ Semicanalis tubae auditivae¹²
7

oval window *n term*   *syn* **fenestra vestibuli** [-aɪ] *n*, *rel* **round window¹** *n term*
oval opening on the medial [iː] wall of the middle ear leading to the vestibule which is closed by the footplate of the stapes
» A less common source of posttraumatic vertigo [ɜː] is disruption [ʌ] of the oval or round window with leakage [iː] of perilymph² [ɪ] into the middle ear. In a perforated eardrum drugs can be absorbed into the inner ear fluids through the secondary tympanic membrane³ at the round window.
Use **oval window** niche [niːʃ]/ perilymph / reflex • **round window** reflex / injury / rupture • cochlear¹ / vestibular⁴ **window** • **fenestra** ovalis⁴ / cochleae or rotunda¹

Vorhoffenster, ovales Fenster, Fenestra vestibuli
Schneckenfenster, rundes F., Fenestra cochleae¹ Perilymphe² Membrana tympani secundaria³ Vorhoffenster, Fenestra vestibuli⁴
8

vestibule [-bjuːl] **(of the ear)** *n term*   *rel* **utricle¹** [juːtrɪkəl], **saccule²** *n term*
central cavity in the bony labyrinth of the inner ear between the cochlear and semicircular [sɜː] canals containing the otolithic apparatus³ [eɪ], the saccule [-kjuːl] and the utricle
vestibular [vestɪbjələ] *adj term* • **utricular** *adj* • **vestibul(o)-** *comb*
» The utricle is the larger of the two sacs that occupy a portion of the membranous labyrinth of the vestibule. The vestibular end organs are dynamic structures that respond to linear acceleration [əks-] (saccule and utricle) and to angular acceleration⁴ (semicircular canals).
Use **vestibular** apparatus⁵ / system / window / scala⁶ [skeɪlə]/ nerve / end organ • **vestibular** input / (dys/ hypo)function / damage / toxicity • **vestibular** loss⁷ / vertigo⁸ / schwannoma / nystagmus⁹ / nasal [eɪ]/ (labio)buccal [ʌ] **vestibule** • **utricular** nerve / otolithic membrane • **utriculosaccular** duct¹⁰ [ʌ] • **macula acustica** utriculi¹¹ [-laɪ]/ sacculi¹² • **vestibular¹³ saccule** • **vestibul**itis [aɪ] • **vestibulo**ocular reflex¹⁴ [iː] (*abbr* VOR) /cochlear nerve¹⁵ /cerebellar • **vestibulo**spinal [aɪ] /tomy /genic [dʒe]

Vestibulum (labyrinthi)
Utrikulus, großes Vorhofsäckchen¹ Sakkulus, kleines Vorhofsäckchen² Otolithenorgan, -apparat³ Winkelbeschleunigung⁴ Vestibularapparat⁵ Scala vestibuli, Vorhoftreppe⁶ Vestibularisausfall⁷ Vestibularisschwindel⁸ vestibulärer Nystagmus⁹ Ductus utriculosaccularis¹⁰ Macula utriculi¹¹ Macula sacculi¹² Vorhofsäckchen¹³ vestibulookulärer Reflex¹⁴ Nervus vestibulocochlearis, VIII. Hirnnerv¹⁵
9

60

246 BODY STRUCTURES & FUNCTIONS — Ears

semicircular canals [-sɜːrkjələ kənælz] *n term*

rel **labyrinth**[1] [læbərɪnθ] *n term*

three tubes in the osseous labyrinth of the ear lying in planes [eɪ] at right angles to each other which contain communicating membranous sacs that are filled with endolymph [ɪ] and surrounded by perilymph

labyrinthine[2] *adj term* • **labyrinth(o)-** *comb*

» The head is elevated 30 degrees to bring the horizontal semicircular canal into a vertical [ɜː] position. Angular acceleration of the head displaces endolymph in the semicircular canals and deflects hair cell cupulae [kjuːpjəliː] in the **cristae**[3] [krɪstiǁaɪ], which results in either an increase or decrease in neuronal impulses to the vestibular nuclei.

Use anterior[4] / posterior / lateral **semicircular canals** • bony or osseous[5] / membranous[6] / cochlear[7] **labyrinth** • vestibular[8] / hypofunctioning / dead **labyrinth** • **labyrinthine** apparatus [eɪ] / (dys)function / concussion[9] [-kʌʃᵊn]/ vertigo[10] • **labyrinthine** sedative / ischemia [ɪskiːmɪə]/ reflex[11] [iː]/ deafness[12] [e] • **labyrinth**ectomy /itis[13] [-aɪtɪs]

knöcherne Bogengänge, Canales semicirculares

Labyrinth[1] labyrinthär, Labyrinth-[2] Cristae ampullaris[3] Canalis semicircularis anterior, vorderer knöcherner Bogengang[4] knöchernes Labyrinth, Labyrinthus osseus[5] häutiges Labyrinth, L. membranaceus[6] Schneckenlabyrinth, L. cochlearis[7] Vorhoflabyrinth, L. vestibularis[8] Labyrintherschütterung[9] Vestibularisschwindel[10] Labyrinthreflex[11] Labyrinth-, Innenohrschwerhörigkeit[12] Labyrinthitis, Innenohrentzündung[13]

10

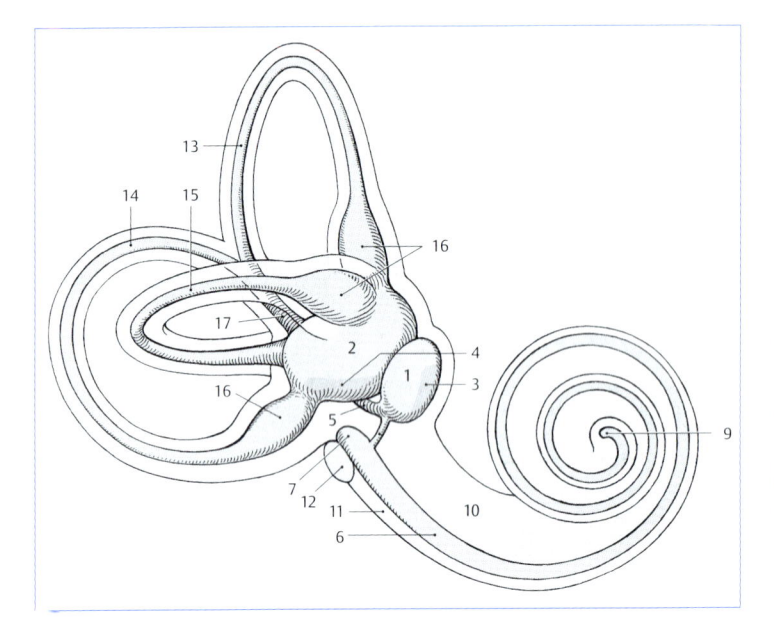

Membranous labyrinth:
saccule (**1**),
utricle (**2**),
macula sacculi (**3**),
macula utriculi (**4**),
utriculosaccular duct (**5**),
cochlear duct (**6**),
vestibular cecum (**7**),
cochlear cupula (**8**),
cupular cecum (**9**),
scala vestibuli (**10**),
scala tympani (**11**),
round window (**12**),
anterior semicircular canal (**13**),
posterior semicircular canal (**14**),
lateral semicircular canal (**15**),
membranous ampulla (**16**),
common osseous crus (**17**)

cochlea [kɒːǁkoʊklɪə] *n term*

spiral [aɪ] canal in the inner ear coiled[1] [kɔɪld] into the shape of a snail [eɪ] shell containing the organ of Corti, the end-organ of hearing; it makes two and a half turns around a central core of spongy [spʌndʒi] bone, the modiolus[2] [mədaɪələs]

(**intra/ endo**)**cochlear** *adj term* • **cochle(o)-** *comb*

» From the cochlea the vibrations are passed to the brain by the auditory nerve[3]. A bony plate, the spiral lamina[4], extends from the modiolus and partially divides the cochlea. Prolonged exposure [oʊʒ] to sounds exceeding [iː] 85 dB is potentially injurious[5] to the cochlea.

Use membranous[6] / bony **cochlea** • apex[7] [eɪ]/ cupula[7] [juː]/ canaliculus *of the cochlea* • spiral [aɪ] canal[8] / basilar membrane *of the cochlea* • **cochlear** duct[6] [ʌ]/ window / recess[9] • **cochlear** labyrinth / aqueduct[10] [æ]/ fluid / perilymph • **cochlear** hair cells[11] / nerve / microphonic potential[12] • **cochlear** artery / concussion / implant[13] • **cochleo**stapedial reflex[14] /neural deafness [e] /vestibular neuritis [n(j)ʊəˈaɪtɪs] • **cochle**itis

Schnecke, Cochlea, Kochlea

gewunden[1] Schneckenachse, -spindel, Modiolous[2] Nervus vestibulocochlearis[3] Lamina spiralis ossea[4] schädlich[5] häutiger Schneckengang, Ductus cochlearis[6] Schneckenspitze, Cupula cochleae[7] Schneckengang, Canalis spiralis cochleae[8] Recessus cochlearis[9] Ductus perilymphaticus, Aqueductus cochleae[10] Corti-Hörzellen, -Haarzellen[11] (endocochleäres) Mikrophonpotential[12] Kochleaimplantat[13] Stapediusreflex[14]

11

Ears   BODY STRUCTURES & FUNCTIONS 247

organ of Corti n term   syn **spiral** [aɪ] **organ** or **organum spirale** n term

specific neuroepithelial [iː] receptor organ for hearing within the vestibule and semicircular canals; its sensory hair cells (stereocilia[1] [sɪ]/ are embedded in or in contact with the tectorial membrane[2] while the other end is in close contact with many nerve endings

» The organ of Corti rests on the basilar membrane[3] within the cochlear duct [ʌ] (scala [eɪ] media [iː]) and contains the hair cells, and their supporting cells. Not only does the organ of Corti respond to acoustic [uː] stimulation, it also produces otoacoustic emissions[4] (abbr OAE) which can be evoked [oʊ] by acoustic stimulation. Aging is associated with progressive loss of outer hair cells within the organ of Corti.

Use arch[5] [ɑːrtʃ]/ pillar[6] [ɪ]/ (hair) cells[7] **of Corti** • **Corti** ganglion[8] • **Corti's** tunnel[9] / membrane[2] • **spiral** ganglion of the cochlea[8] / vein [eɪ] of the modiolus [aɪ]

Corti-Organ, Organum spirale
Stereozilien[1] Membrana tectoria[2] Basilarmembran, Lamina basilaris[3] otoakustische Emissionen[4] Corti-Bogen[5] Corti-Pfeilerzelle[6] Corti-Hörzellen, -Haarzellen[7] Ganglion spirale cochleae[8] Corti-Tunnel, innerer Tunnel[9]

12

auditory nerve [ɜː] n term
            syn **acoustic** [əkuːstɪk] or **vestibulocochlear nerve** n term

8th cranial nerve combining the cochlear and vestibular nerves

» At low frequencies, individual auditory nerve fibers [aɪ] can respond more or less synchronously with the stimulating tone. Tests of hearing by air conduction[1] [ʌ] provide information about the integrity of the cochlea, acoustic nerve, and central auditory pathway.

Use **auditory** cortex / neurons / artery / function / acuity[2] [juː] • **auditory** adaptation / brainstem evoked response[3] (abbr ABR) • 8th (cranial)[4] / facial [eɪʃ] **nerve** • **nerve** deafness[5] [e]/ palsy [pɔːlzi] • **acoustic** hair cell[6] / chamber[7] [tʃeɪ-]/ stimulus / power[8] • **acoustic** reflex[9] (decay) [dɪkeɪ]/ impedance[10] [iː]/ trauma [ɒː]

Nervus vestibulocochlearis/statoacusticus, Akustikus
Luftleitung[1] Hörschärfe[2] akustisch evozierte Hirnstammpotentiale[3] VIII. Hirnnerv, N. vestibulocochlearis[4] Schallempfindungs-, Innenohr-, Labyrinthschwerhörigkeit[5] Corti-Haarzelle, Corti-Hörzelle[6] schalldichter Raum[7] Schallintensität, -stärke, Lautstärke[8] Stapediusreflex[9] akust. Impedanz[10]

13

mastoid process [mæstɔɪd prɒːses] n term   syn **mastoid (bone)** n jar & clin

raised [eɪ], nipple-like[1] projection [dʒe] of the temporal bone behind the external [ɜː] ear mastoidal[1] adj term • **(stylo** [staɪloʊ]**/ sterno** [ɜː]**)mastoid**[1] adj • **mastoid-** comb

» Palpate the mastoid process to check if it is tender. The mastoid air cells[2] are in contiguity [juː] with[3] the middle ear space[4]. Bone conduction[5] aids [eɪ] can be implanted in the mastoid process.

Use external **mastoid process** • **mastoid** (air) cells or sinuses[2] [aɪ]/ cavity or antrum[6] / foramen [eɪ] • **mastoid** wall[7] / notch [nɒːtʃ] or incisure[8] [ɪnsɪʒɚ]/ fontanelle[9] / canaliculus • **mastoid** x-ray [eksreɪ]/ abscess • **mastoid** ecchymosis [ekɪmoʊsɪs]/ tenderness[10] / infection • **mastoid**ectomy[11] /itis • **stylomastoid** foramen[12] [eɪ] • **sternomastoid** muscle [mʌsl]

Warzenfortsatz, Processus mastoideus, Mastoid
warzenförmig, mastoid[1] Warzenfortsatzzellen, Cellulae mastoideae[2] in Verbindung stehen[3] Paukenhöhle[4] Knochenleitung[5] Antrum mastoideum[6] Paries mastoideus[7] Incisura mastoidea[8] hintere Seitenfontanelle, Fonticulus mastoideus/posterolateralis[9] Druckschmerz über d. Proc. mastoideus[10] Mastoidektomie[11] Foramen stylomastoideum[12]

14

cerumen [səruːmən] n term   syn **(ear)wax** [ɪɚwæks] n clin

yellow or brown wax-like substance secreted [iː] in the outer third of the external ear canal **ceruminous** adj term • **waxy** or **wax-like**[1] adj clin

» Tympanometry does not require removal of cerumen unless the canal is completely blocked. Tinnitus may be experienced by patients with noise-induced hearing loss or ceruminous impaction[2]. Parents should be advised that earwax protects the ear (cerumen contains lysozymes [laɪsəzaɪmz] and immunoglobulins that curtail[3] [eɪ] infection). Very hard wax adhering [ɪɚ] to the wall of the ear canal should be softened[4] before irrigation is attempted.

Use to remove **cerumen** • soft / moist / hard(-packed) or inspissated[5] / excess / impacted[5] **cerumen** • **cerumen** plug[5] [ʌ]/ solvent / removal • **ceruminous** glands[6] / impaction[2] / deafness [e] • **earwax** removal • **waxy** material / appearance [ɪɚ]

Zerumen, Ohrenschmalz
wächsern, wachsartig[1] Zeruminalpfropf, Cerumen obturans[2] hintanhalten[3] aufgeweicht[4] impaktiertes Zerumen, Zeruminalpfropf[5] Ohrenschmalzdrüsen, Glandulae ceruminosae[6]

15

Unit 61 Hearing

Related Units: 57 Senses, 60 Ears, 41 Brain, 66 Speech, 42 Nerve Function, 59 Vision, 113 Neurologic Findings

listen [lɪsᵊn] v   sim **hear¹** [hɪɚ] - heard - heard [hɜːrd] v irr

to pay attention in order to hear something

over**hear**² v irr • **unheard** adj • **hearsay**³ [hɪɚseɪ] n • **listening** adj & n • **listener**⁴ n

» Test hearing by determining [ɜː] whether the patient can hear soft sounds⁵ like a watch ticking. These hearing aids [eɪ] promise substantial improvements in speech [spiːtʃ] intelligibility⁶, especially under difficult listening circumstances [sɜː].

Use **to hear** sounds [aʊ] / a tuning [(j)uː] fork⁷ / high tones [oʊ]/ oneself speak • (un)able / difficult **to hear** • **to listen** to music / for heartbeats [hɑːrtbiːts]/ intently⁸ / hard⁸ / in on a conversation⁹ • attentive / empathic **listening** • to be a good **listener** • **listening** comprehension¹⁰

(zu)hören, horchen (auf)
(an)hören¹ (zufällig) mithören² Gerüchte, Hörensagen³ (Zu)hörer(in)⁴ leise Geräusche⁵ Sprachverständlichkeit⁶ den Ton einer Stimmgabel hören⁷ aufmerksam zuhören⁸ ein Gespräch mithören⁹ Hörverständnis¹⁰

1

---

hearing [hɪərɪŋ] n clin & term   rel **audibility¹** [ɒdɪbɪləti] n

(i) the ability to perceive [siː] sound (ii) the sensation [eɪ] of sound (as opposed to vibration [aɪ])

(in)audible [ɒːdɪbl] adj • **auditory**² adj term • **audiometry**³ [ɒː] n • **audi(o)-** comb

» You should have your hearing tested. If hearing is going to return, it is likely to do so in 10 to 14 days. Labyrinthectomy is appropriate only for patients with little or no hearing in the involved ear. Inflammation of the internal auditory artery may produce hearing loss.

Use to maximize/preserve [ɜː] /be within⁴/be hard of⁵ **hearing** • normal / color⁶ / excellent / diminished **hearing** • threshold⁷ / clarity [æ] / measurement [eʒ] **of hearing** • (sudden [ʌ]/ permanent) [ɜː] / sense **of hearing** • **hearing** status / level / test⁹ • **hearing** device [dɪvaɪs] or aid¹⁰ / (ear) dog / distance • **hearing** difficulty / disorders¹¹ / deficit¹² / defect [iː]/ loss¹³ • **audible** sound / frequency¹⁴ • **auditory** canal¹⁵ / nerve / cortex • **auditory** perception [se]/ function [ʌ]/ cue¹⁶ [kjuː] • **auditory** signal / acuity [əkjuːəti]/ threshold⁷ • **auditory** evoked [oʊ] potentials¹⁷ / impairment¹² [eɚ] • **auditory** hallucination [s]/ rehabilitation • **audio**logic assessment or evaluation or testing³ • **audio**gram /logist /vestibular • impedance¹⁸ / speech¹⁹ / pure [pjʊɚ] tone²⁰ / serial **audio**metry • brain stem evoked response²¹ / threshold²² **audiometry**

(i) Hören, Hörfähigkeit, -vermögen (ii) Gehör
Hörbarkeit, Vernehmbarkeit¹ auditiv, akustisch, Hör-, Gehör-² Audiometrie³ in Hörweite sein⁴ schwerhörig sein⁵ Auditio colorata, Farbwahrnehmung beim Hören⁶ Hörschwelle⁷ akuter Hörverlust, Hörsturz⁸ Hörprüfung⁹ Hörgerät, -hilfe¹⁰ Hörstörungen¹¹ Schwerhörigkeit¹² Schwerhörigkeit, Hörverlust¹³ hörbare Frequenz¹⁴ Gehörgang¹⁵ akust. Signal¹⁶ akust. evozierte Potentiale¹⁷ Impedanzaudiometrie¹⁸ Sprachaudiometrie¹⁹ Ton(schwellen)audiometrie²⁰ elektrische Reaktionsaudiometrie (AEP)²¹ Schwellenaudiometrie²²

2

---

sound wave [saʊnd weɪv] n   rel **tone¹, noise², ultrasound³** [ʌ] n → U118-16

successive patterns of compression and rarefaction⁴ (pressure waves or vibrations) in a medium

(ultra)sonic adj • **wavelength**⁵ n • **noisy** adj • **noiseless**⁶ adj • **sono-** comb

» Sound waves strike the tympanic membrane and produce in-and-out vibrations that transmit sound energy to the ossicular chain⁷. In conductive [ʌ] losses⁸, the sound appears louder in the poorer-hearing ear, whereas in sensorineural [-n(j)ʊəɹəl] losses⁹ it lateralizes to the better side.

Use to generate/amplify/perceive¹⁰/reflect/transmit **sound waves** • **sound waves** propagate or travel¹¹ • speech / audible / faint [eɪ]/ low-pitched¹² / guttural [ʌ] **sound** • dull¹³ [ʌ]/ ringing¹⁴ / tick-tack / crackling¹⁵ **sound** • **sound** source¹⁶ [ɔː]/ field¹⁷ / energy¹⁸ / stimulation • **sound** perception / transmission / amplification¹⁹ • **sound** level (meter) [iː]/ pressure level²⁰ (abbr SPL)/ vibration [eɪʃ] • **sound** recognition [ɪʃ]/ discrimination / blending /-proof room²¹ • memory for / passage of **sounds** • bone-conducted / heart²² / bowel²³ [baʊəl] **sound** • fetal [iː] heart²⁴ (abbr FHT)/ beeping²⁵ [iː]/ intense **tones** • continuous / interrupted **tones** • **tone** decay / tikeɹ] test²⁶ • pure **tone** audiometry • to hear/make **a noise** • average / peak [iː]/ high-level **noise** • background / rustling²⁷ [ʌ]/ banging / loud²⁸ **noise** • **noise** level / signal /-induced hearing loss²⁹ • **noise** exposure / trauma [ɒː] • **noisy** environment [aɪ]/ breathing [iː]

Schallwelle
Ton, Klang¹ Geräusch, Lärm² Ultraschall³ Abflachung⁴ Wellenlänge⁵ laut-, geräuschlos⁶ Gehörknöchelchenkette⁷ Schallleitungsschwerhörigkeit⁸ Schallempfindungsschwerhörigkeit⁹ Schallwellen wahrnehmen¹⁰ S. breiten sich aus/pflanzen s. fort¹¹ niederfrequenter Ton, Brummton¹² gedämpfter Ton, dumpfer Schall¹³ hoher/klingender Ton¹⁴ Knistern¹⁵ Schallquelle¹⁶ Schallfeld¹⁷ Schallenergie¹⁸ Schallverstärkung¹⁹ Schalldruckpegel²⁰ schalldichter Raum²¹ Herzton²² Darmgeräusch²³ kindl. Herztöne²⁴ Piepstöne²⁵ Schwellenschwundtest²⁶ Raschelgeräusch²⁷ Lärm²⁸ Lärmschwerhörigkeit²⁹

3

---

air conduction [ʌ] n term, abbr **AC**   rel **sound transmission¹** n clin

propagation of sound waves in air through the auditory canal to the tympanic [ɪ] membrane

conductive adj term • **conduct²** [kəndʌkt] v • **conductivity³** n • **transmit** v

» The stem⁴ of the vibrating [aɪ] tuning [t(j)uːnɪŋ] fork⁵ is placed on the mastoid process to assess bone conduction and then the tines⁶ [taɪnz] of the fork are held immediately lateral to the external ear to evaluate air conduction. Normally, a tone is heard louder by air conduction [ʌ] than by bone conduction.

Use hearing by **air conduction** • **air conduction** hearing / stimulus / threshold⁷ / hearing aid • bone⁸ (abbr BC)/ nerve / impulse **conduction** • **conductive** hearing impairment⁹ / loss⁹ • **conduction** deafness⁹ [e]/ velocity¹⁰ [ɒːs] • **transmission** of sound (waves)¹

Luftleitung
Schallübertragung¹ leiten; führen² Leitfähigkeit³ Fuß⁴ Stimmgabel⁵ Zinken⁶ Hörschwelle bei Luftleitung⁷ Knochenleitung⁸ Schallleitungsschwerhörigkeit⁹ Leit(ungs)geschwindigkeit¹⁰

4

Hearing BODY STRUCTURES & FUNCTIONS 249

loudness [laudnəs] n   syn **volume** n, opposite **softness**[1] n, rel **intensity**[2] n

subjective sensation of the effect of the amplitude of sound; it is measured in decibel (dB)

loud adj • **aloud** [əlaud] adj • **soft**[3] adj • **high-intensity** adj • **loudspeaker** n

» The unit of measurement of subjective loudness is the "sone", while the unit of loudness level[4] is known as the "phon". The threshold of normal hearing is from 0 to 20 dB, which corresponds to the loudness of a soft whisper[5]. The amplitude and frequency of sound waves are related to the subjective psychoacoustic [saɪk-] attributes of loudness and pitch.

Use sensation[6] / perception[6] / index **of loudness** • **loudness** level[4] (abbr LL)/ discomfort level / of sounds • **loud** spoken voice[7] / noise / bang[8] • **intensity** range [reɪndʒ]/ **of sound**[2] • performance-**intensity** function • **soft** voice[9] / music • **to** read/think/count[10] **aloud**

Lautstärke, Lautheit

geringe/ reduzierte Lautstärke, Gedämpftheit[1] Schallintensität[2] leise, gedämpft; weich[3] Lautstärkepegel[4] leises Flüstern[5] Lautstärkeempfindung[6] lautes Sprechen[7] lauter Knall[8] gedämpfte/ leise Stimme[9] laut zählen[10]

5

(sound) frequency [fri:kwən'si] n clin & term   rel **pitch**[1] [pɪtʃ] n & v

the inverse [ɜː] of wavelength measured in Hertz (abbr Hz)

high-/ low-frequency[2] adj • **medium-** [iː]/ **high-/ low-pitched**[2] adj

» A 512-Hz tuning fork is employed, since frequencies below this level elicit[3] a tactile response. Pure-tone thresholds in decibels were obtained over the range of 250-8000 Hz (the main speech frequencies are between 500 and 3000 Hz) for both air and bone conduction. Hearing loss due to cochlear [k] damage is noted first with high-frequency tones. An audiogram is a plot[4] of intensity in dB required to achieve threshold versus frequency.

Use audio / hearing / speech / ultrasonic[5] **frequency** • light / infrasonic[6] / infrared / **frequency** • **frequency** range[7] / band • fluctuation in[8] **frequency** • **high-frequency** hearing loss[9] • **pitch** range • perfect or absolute[10] **pitch** • **high-pitched** cry[11]

Schallfrequenz

Tonhöhe; anstimmen[1] tief, niederfrequent[2] auslösen[3] grafische Darstellung[4] Ultrahochfrequenz[5] Infraschall[6] Frequenzbereich[7] Frequenzschwankungen[8] Hochton-Hörsenke, Hörabfall im Hochtonbereich[9] absolutes Gehör[10] schriller Schrei[11]

6

hearing or **auditory threshold** [ɔːdɪtɔːri θreʃʰould] n term

rel **spondee** [spɒːndiː] **threshold**[1] n term, abbr **ST**

the intensity of the slightest perceptible [se] sound

» Conductive hearing losses usually have a fairly equal threshold elevation for each frequency. During tympanometry[2] an intense tone (80 dB above the hearing threshold) elicits [ɪs] contraction of the stapedius [iː] muscle[3]. The audiometer[4] delivers acoustic stimuli [aɪ] of specific frequencies (pure tones) so the hearing threshold for each frequency can be determined.

Use to achieve **threshold** • frequency-specific **thresholds** • pure-tone / speech reception[5] / bone-conduction[6] **threshold** • air-conduction / intensity[7] **threshold** • average / differential[8] / pain[9] / absolute / detection[10] **threshold** • **threshold** level[11] / response / of hearing[12] / audiometry[13] • **threshold** of vibration perception / for sound perception[12]

Hörschwelle

Spracherkennungsschwelle[1] Tympanometrie[2] Musculus stapedius[3] Audiometer[4] Sprachwahrnehmungsschwelle[5] Hörschwelle bei Knochenleitung[6] Schallintensitätsschwelle[7] (Intensitäts)diskriminationsschwelle[8] Schmerzschwelle[9] Wahrnehmbarkeitsschwelle[10] Schwellenwert[11] Hörschwelle[12] Schwellenaudiometrie[13]

7

hyperacusis [haɪpərˌak(j)uːsɪs] n term   opposite **hypacusis**[1] n term → U59-8

rel **presby(a)cusis**[2] [prezbɪ(ə)kjuːsɪs] n term

very acute sense of hearing[3] (associated with a low hearing threshold); the term is frequently used to describe painful sensitivity to loud noise

» If the nerve to the stapedius [iː] is interrupted, there is hyperacusis. Presbyacusis is the progressive, predominantly high-frequency symmetric hearing loss of old age.

Übersteigerung der Hörschärfe, Hyperakusis

vermindertes Hörvermögen, Hypakusis[1] Altersschwerhörigkeit, Presbyakusis[2] scharfes Gehör[3]

8

deaf [def] adj & n   rel **deaf-mute**[1] [defmjuːt] adj & n

(adj) to be hard of hearing or unable to hear (n) persons with severe hearing impairments

deafen[2] [defⁿn] v clin • **deafening** adj • **deafness** n • **deaf-mutism**[3] n term

» Cochlear implants allow deaf persons to distinguish environmental sounds and warning signals and help them to make their speech more intelligible to hearing persons. Check patients with blast injuries[4] for nerve or conduction hearing deficits or deafness.

Use to be/go[5]/become or turn[5] **deaf** • to turn a **deaf** ear to sth.[6] • to fall on **deaf** ears[7] • tone[8]-/ stone[9]-/ profoundly [au] **deaf** • **deaf**-blind • and dumb[10] [dʌm]/ as a post[9] / from birth / child • acoustic trauma[11] [ɔː] conduction / high-tone **deafness** • nerve or sensorineural or perception[12] / high-frequency **deafness** • word[13] / cortical / hysterical[14] **deafness** • congenital [dʒe] or hereditary[15] / acquired [aɪ]/ family / sudden[16] **deafness** • progressive / unilateral / partial / chronic **deafness** • **deafness**, vertigo [ɜː] and tinnitus [ɪ] • **deafening** music / sound / noise[17]

taub, schwerhörig; Gehörlose, Taube

taubstumm; Taubstumme[1] taub machen; betäuben[2] Taubstummheit[3] Explosions-, Knalltrauma[4] taub werden[5] s. taub stellen[6] kein Gehör finden[7] Tonhöhen nicht unterscheiden können[8] stocktaub[9] taubstumm[10] Lärmschwerhörigkeit[11] Schallempfindungsschwerhörigkeit[12] Worttaubheit, sensorische Aphasie[13] psychogene Schwerhörigkeit/ Taubheit[14] angeborene Taubheit[15] Hörsturz[16] ohrenbetäubender Lärm[17]

9

speech reading [spiːtʃ riːdɪŋ] n syn **lipreading** [lɪpriːdɪŋ] n
understanding what a person is saying by observing [ɜː] the movement of the lips
lip-read v irr • **read** [riːd] - read - read [red] v irr • **misread**[1] [mɪsriːd] v irr
» In time, patients with pure word deafness teach themselves lip reading and may appear to have improved upon superficial bedside examination. Cochlear implants help with speech reading by allowing the profoundly deaf to distinguish when a word begins and ends.
Use **speech reading** skills • **speech** sounds / discrimination[2] (abbr SD)/ audiometry[3] • **speech** reception threshold (abbr SRT)/ intelligibility • **speech** pathologist[4] / defect / therapy[5] • thought or mind[6] **reading** • **reading** skills / aloud / comprehension[7] /(-learning) disorder[8]

Lippenlesen
falsch lesen, missverstehen (beim Lesen)[1] Sprachdiskrimination[2] Sprachaudiometrie[3] Logopäde/-in[4] Logopädie[5] Gedankenlesen[6] Leseverständnis[7] Lesestörung, -schwäche[8]   10

mute [mjuːt] adj & n & v syn **dumb** [dʌm] adj,
rel **silent**[1] [aɪ], **quiet**[2], **muffled**[3] [ʌ] adj
(adj) unable or unwilling to speak (n) persons who cannot speak, esp. the deaf
muteness[4] n clin • **muted**[3] adj • **silence**[5] n & v • **dumbness**[4] n • **mutism**[6] n term
» For mute children, the value of learning sign [saɪn] language[7] is not yet established. Other hysterical [ɪ] symptoms, e.g. loss of vision [ɪʒ], deafness, muteness, or paralysis, may require similar treatment. Dysarthria[8] [dɪsɑːrθrɪə] and mutism do not, by themselves, lead to a diagnosis of aphasia [eɪʒ].
Use to be **mute** • **mute** patient / state • total **muteness** • deaf-/ akinetic[9] / (s)elective[10] / hysterical[11] **mutism** • **muted** response / applause [ɒː]

stumm; Stumme; dämpfen
schweigsam, still[1] ruhig, still[2] gedämpft[3] Stummheit[4] Schweigen, Stille; zum Schweigen bringen[5] Mutismus[6] Zeichen-, Gebärdensprache[7] Dysarthrie, Artikulationsstörung, verwaschene Sprache[8] akinetischer Mutismus[9] (s)elektiver M.[10] neurotischer/ hysterischer/ psychogener Mutismus[11]   11

Unit 62   Smell, Taste & Touch
Related Units: 57 Senses, 21 Head & Neck, 42 Nerve Function, 26 Teeth, 45 Digestive Tract, 43 Lungs, 44 Respiration

smell n & v syn **olfaction** [ɒːǁoʊlfækʃⁿn] n term
(n, i) the sense that is able to perceive [siː] odors [oʊ]
(ii) any pleasant [e] or unpleasant odor
smelly[1] adj • **smelling** adj • **olfactory**[2] adj term • **osm(o)-, -osmia** comb
» His breath [e] smells of alcohol. By one week of age, newborns recognize and discriminate the smell of their mother, not the smell of milk alone. The sense of smell determines [ɜː] the flavor [eɪ] and palatability[3] of food and drink.
Use sense or faculty[4] / loss / disorder **of smell** • **to smell** good / of disinfectant[5] • characteristic / sweet(ish) / delicious [ɪʃ] **smell** • strong / penetrating / unpleasant or disagreeable[6] [iː] **smell** • aversive[7] [ɜː] / musty[8] [ʌ]/ pungent [ʌ]/ distorted[9] **smell** • **smell of** tobacco / sweaty [e] feet • **smell** perception[10] [se]/ disorder or disturbance[11] [ɜː]/ identification test • strong-/ foul-**smelling** [faʊl] • to affect **olfaction** • olfactory system [ɪ]/ placode / nerves[12] [ɜː]/ tracts or pathways[13] • olfactory cilia[14] [sɪlɪə]/ bulb[15] [ʌ] (defect) [iː]/ (chemo)receptor[16] [kiːmoʊ-] • olfactory nerve filaments / neuroepithelium[17] [iː] • olfactory mucosa / sensitivity[18] / loss / dysfunction[11] [ʌ] • **smelly** room / feet / body • **smelling** salt[19] • **osmo**ceptor[16] • **dys** [ɪ]/ an/ hyp [aɪ]/ par(a)[20]/ cac/ hyper**osmia**

(i) **Geruch(ssinn), Riechen, Olfaktus**
(ii) **Duft, Gestank; riechen, duften, stinken**
übelriechend[1] Geruchs-, Riech-, olfaktorisch[2] Schmackhaftigkeit, Wohlgeschmack[3] Geruchssinn, -vermögen[4] nach Desinfektionsmittel riechen[5] unangenehmer Geruch[6] widerlicher G.[7] moderiger G.[8] veränderte/ gestörte Geruchsempfindung[9] Geruchsempfindung, -wahrnehmung[10] Riech-, Geruchsstörung[11] Nervi olfactorii, Riechnerven[12] Riechbahnen[13] Riechfächer[14] Riechkolben, Bulbus olfactorius[15] Geruchsrezeptor[16] Riechepithel[17] Geruchsempfindlichkeit[18] Riechsalz[19] Parosmie, Geruchstäuschung[20]   1

sniff v & n → U10-18; U11-23 sim **sniffle**[1] [snɪfl] v & n, rel **whiff**[2] [ʰwɪf] n
(v) to draw air audibly [ɒː] up the nose to sense an odor or to prevent mucus [mjuːkəs] from running down the nose
sniffing[3] adj & n • **sniffy**[4] [snɪfi] adj • **sniffer**[5] n • **sniffling** adj & n
» With the eyes closed, the patient sniffs and tries to identify the stimulus. Three to four whiffs[6] from an aerosol inhaler [eɪ] may be given at 3- to 4-minute intervals as needed.
Use **to sniff** cocaine[7] [eɪ] • to take/have a deep **sniff** • **sniff** test • to be **sniffy** about sth. • **to sniffle** into one's handkerchief • to have the[8] **sniffles** • solvent / gasoline [gæsᵊliːn] / glue[9] [gluː] **sniffing** • to catch or get a[10] **whiff**

schnuppern, schnüffeln, schniefen; Schniefen
schniefen, schnüffeln; leichter Schnupfen[1] Hauch, Duft(wolke)[2] schnüffelnd; Schnüffelsucht[3] hochnäsig, verschnupft, eingeschnappt[4] Schnüffler(in)[5] Sprühstöße[6] Kokain schnupfen[7] einen leichten Schnupfen haben[8] Klebstoffschnüffeln[9] d. Geruch v. etw. wahrnehmen[10]   2

Smell, Taste & Touch   BODY STRUCTURES & FUNCTIONS 251

odor [oʊdɚ] n   sim **fragrance**¹ [eɪ], **scent**¹ [sent], **aroma**² n, rel **perfume**³ n

an unpleasant smell or the sensation that results when olfactory receptors are stimulated

odorless⁴ adj • **malodor**⁵ n • **malodorous**⁶ [mæloʊdərəs] adj • **odorant**⁷ adj & n
• **fragrant** [freɪgrənt] adj • **aromatic** adj • **scented**⁸ adj • **deodorant** [oʊ] n

» A bitter almond [ɒː] odor⁹ can be detected on the breath. Periodontal disease, caries or tonsillitis [aɪ] cause a fetid [iː‖e] odor often accompanied by a bad taste. Fragrances contained in cosmetic products are also potent [oʊ] photosensitizers.

Use to have/give (off)¹⁰/perceive [siː]/emit or release¹⁰ [iː] **an odor** • **faint**¹¹ [eɪ]/ strong / body¹² **odor** • breath¹³ [e]/ alcohol **odor** • bad or foul [faʊl]/ offensive / fishy¹⁴ / fecal [fiːkəl] **odor** • urinary / ammoniacal [aɪ]/ fruity [uː]/ garlic¹⁵ **odor** • **odor** threshold¹⁶ / identification / control /-proof¹⁷ [uː] • **fragrant** oil / perfume • **scented** toilet tissue • **aromatic** odor / flavor [eɪ]/ amino acids¹⁸/ hydrocarbons¹⁹

(übler) Geruch

Duft, Wohlgeruch¹ Duft, Aroma² Parfüm, Duft³ geruchlos⁴ übler Geruch⁵ übelriechend⁶ duftend; Duftstoff⁷ (stark) duftend, parfümiert⁸ Bittermandelgeruch⁹ einen Duft verbreiten¹⁰ schwacher Geruch¹¹ Körpergeruch¹² Mundgeruch¹³ Fischgeruch¹⁴ Knoblauchgeruch¹⁵ Geruchsschwelle¹⁶ geruchundurchlässig¹⁷ aromatische Aminosäuren¹⁸ aromat. Kohlenwasserstoffe¹⁹   3

stench [stentʃ] n   syn **stink, reek** [riːk] n

a very strong unpleasant and offensive smell, esp. one that makes you want to vomit

stink¹ - stank - stunk v irr • **reek (of)**¹ v • **stinking**² adj • **stinky**² adj

» The stench of charred³ [tʃɑːrd] flesh was ubiquitous⁴. The whole place reeks of stale cigarette smoke⁵. Urinary incontinence is inevitably linked with shame [ʃeɪm], stink, and ostracism⁶.

Use foul / gagging⁷ [æ]/ pungent⁸ [ʌ]/ overpowering⁹ [aʊ] **stench** • sickening⁷ **stink** • **stinking** fish / sewer¹⁰ [suːɚ]/ rotten food • **to reek of** mouthwash¹¹ / garlic / excrement

Gestank, (üble) Ausdünstung

stinken/ riechen (nach)¹ stinkend² verkohlt³ überall⁴ kalter Rauch⁵ soziale Ausgrenzung⁶ widerlicher/ ekelerregender Gestank⁷ scharfer/ durchdringender Geruch⁸ unausstehlicher Gestank⁹ stinkender Abwasserkanal¹⁰ stark nach Mundwasser riechen¹¹   4

pungent [pʌndʒənt] adj   rel **acrid**¹, **musty**² [ʌ], **stale**³ [eɪ], **putrid**⁴ [pjuː-] adj

very strong, spicy [spaɪsi], or biting [aɪ] in taste or smell (e.g. garlicky or peppery)

» Chloral hydrate [aɪ] is available in capsules and in solutions [uːʃ] that have a pungent, unpleasant [ez] taste. A strong putrid odor was detected, although the lesions [iː3] were not painful. Sodium phenylbutyrate has a strong, musty odor.

Use **pungent** whiff / stool [uː] odor⁵ / taste • **acrid** smell / fumes⁶ [juː]/ smoke • **musty** smell / room • **stale** air⁷ / cigarette smoke / beer⁸ / **stale** sweat [e]/ bread⁹ • **putrid** smell / odor / meat [iː] • **putrid** sputum¹⁰ [(j)uː]/ abscess [æbses]

scharf, stechend, durchdringend

bitter, sauer, beißend¹ mufflig² alt, abgestanden, muffig³ faulig⁴ intensiver Stuhlgeruch⁵ stechend riechende Dämpfe⁶ verbrauchte Luft⁷ abgestandenes Bier⁸ altbackenes Brot⁹ faulig riechender Auswurf¹⁰   5

taste [teɪst] v & n   syn **gustation** [gʌsteɪʃən] n term

(n) sensation produced by a suitable stimulus applied to the gustatory nerve endings¹

tasty² adj • **tasteless** adj • **sweet-tasting** adj • **aftertaste**³ n • **tastant**⁴ n **(post)gustatory**⁵ [ʌ] adj term • **gusto-** comb • **-geusia** [dʒuːsɪə‖gjuːzɪə] comb

» Do foods taste metallic or unpleasant? At the surface [ɜː], the taste bud has a pore into which microvilli [aɪ] of the receptor cells project [dʒe]. After therapy she complained [eɪ] of diarrhea [daɪəriːə], constipation, dry mouth, and a change in taste.

Use **to taste** good / strongly of wine • sense⁶ / loss / distortion **of taste** • bitter / salty / sour [saʊɚ]/ sweet / bad **taste** • unpleasant / foul / metallic **taste** • **taste** bud⁷ [ʌ] / receptor cells⁸ / corpuscle⁷ [-pʌsl]/ pore⁹ [pɔːr] • **taste** perception¹⁰ [se]/ quality¹¹ / sensation¹⁰ [eɪ]/ preference • **taste** testing¹² / provocation [keɪ]/ deficit • **tastant**-odorant perception • bitter-/ sour-/ strong-**tasting** • fresh-/ foul-/ food / wine¹³-**tasting** • **gustatory** stimuli [aɪ]/ receptor¹⁴ / pathways / afferents • **gustatory** relay [riːleɪ]/ function / hallucinations / loss • hypo¹⁵/ **ageusia** [ə‖eɪ] • **gusto**lacrimal /metry¹²

schmecken, kosten, probieren; Geschmack(ssinn)

Geschmacksnervenendigungen¹ schmackhaft² Nachgeschmack³ Geschmacksstoff⁴ Geschmacks-, gustatorisch⁵ Geschmackssinn⁶ Geschmacksknospe, Caliculus gustatorius⁷ Schmeckzellen⁸ Geschmacksporus, Porus gustatorius⁹ Geschmacksempfindung¹⁰ Geschmacksqualität¹¹ Geschmacksprüfung¹² Weinverkostung¹³ Geschmacksrezeptor¹⁴ herabgesetzte Geschmacksempfindung, Hypogeusie¹⁵   6

bland adj   sim **flavorless**¹ [eɪ] adj, opposite **spicy**² [aɪ], **hot**³, **savory**⁴ [eɪ] adj

lacking taste, flavor or strong ingredients [iː] → U3-18f

blandness n • **flavor**⁵ n & v • **(un)flavored**⁶ adj • **flavoring**⁷ n • **savor**⁸ v & n

» Bland oral feedings in small amounts at frequent intervals may be started. As distinct flavors depend on aromas to stimulate the olfactory chemoreceptors [kiːmoʊ-], taste and smell are physiologically interdependent. Increase the palatability of charcoal [tʃ] by adding a sweetener or a flavoring agent [eɪdʒ] to the suspension.

Use **bland** diet⁹ [daɪət]/ foods / fluids /-tasting • **bland** oral feedings [iː]/ ointment¹⁰ [ɔɪ]/ suppository • to have/give **a flavor** • aromatic / bitter / good / delicious [tʃ] **flavor** • nutty [ʌ]/ fruity [fruːti]/ lemon / vanilla **flavor** • faint [eɪ]/ full / strong / rich¹¹ **flavor** • **flavor** recognition [tʃ]/ appreciation¹² [iːʃ]/ detection • **flavor** discrimination¹³ / change / enhancer¹⁴ [æ] • well-/ intensely / tea-/ herb¹⁵- [(h)ɜːrb]/ chocolate-**flavored** • artificial¹⁶ [tʃ] • spicy **flavoring** • **savory** dish • **spicy** food

bland, mild, reizlos

geschmacklos, fad¹ würzig, stark gewürzt² scharf³ schmackhaft, pikant⁴ Geschmack, Aroma; Geschmack verleihen, würzen⁵ gewürzt, geschmackskorrigiert⁶ Aroma(stoff)⁷ genießen, auskosten; Geschmack⁸ blande Diät⁹ beruhigende Salbe¹⁰ intensiver/ voller Geschmack¹¹ Geschmacksempfindung¹² Geschmacksvermögen, -unterscheidung¹³ Geschmacksverstärker¹⁴ m. Kräutern gewürzt¹⁵ künstliche Aromastoffe¹⁶   7

62

BODY STRUCTURES & FUNCTIONS — Smell, Taste & Touch

touch [tʌtʃ] n & v   sim **tactile sensation**[1] [tæktaɪl‖-ᵊl sensˈeɪʃᵊn] n term

(n) sensations felt by proprioreceptors in the skin, esp. the fingers and lips which can tell the difference between[2] hard and soft, rough[3] [rʌʃ] and smooth[4] [smuːð], wet and dry, as well as cold and hot

touchy[5] adj • **touching**[6] adj • **tactile**[7], **tactual**[7] adj • **tactometer** n • **contact** n & v

» The patient is asked to touch his index finger[8] repetitively to the nose. On examination, there is marked cutaneous [eɪ] hyperesthesia [iːs] to even the slightest touch. A 512-Hz tuning [juː] fork[9] is employed, since frequencies below this level elicit[10] [ɪs] a tactile response. Don't be so touchy.

Use to be soft to the[11]/in/keep in[12] (close) **touch** • to have a (humorous)[13] [hjuː]/be out of[14]/lose one's **touch** • light or gentle[15] [dʒe]/ deep / coarse [ɔː] **touch** • fine / conscious [ʃ]/ tender to[16] **touch** • **a touch** of flu[17] • **touch** localization / sensation[1] / receptor • human / personal[18] **touch** • **tactile** cell or corpuscle[19] [ʌ]/ hairs[20] / perception[1] • **tactile** stimuli / contact / recognition • **tactile** discrimination / fremitus[21] • **touchy** person / subject[22] [ʌ] • **touching** moment / story • to be in/get into/make **contact** • human / casual [ʒ]/ direct / close **contact** • physical [ɪ]/ skin[23] / patient **contact** • (non)sexual[24] / animal / telephone **contact** • **contact** time / sports / lenses / allergy [ælərdʒi]/ dermatitis[25] [aɪ] • **tactual** stimuli

Tastsinn, -gefühl; berühren
Tast-, Berührungsempfindung[1] unterscheiden zwischen[2] rau[3] glatt[4] empfindlich, leicht reizbar, heikel[5] bewegend, rührend[6] fühl-, tastbar, Tast-, taktil[7] Zeigefinger[8] Stimmgabel[9] auslösen[10] s. weich anfühlen[11] in Kontakt bleiben[12] einen humorvollen Anstrich haben[13] nicht auf d. Laufenden sein[14] leichte/ sanfte Berührung[15] druckdolent, -schmerzhaft[16] leichte Grippe[17] persönliche Note[18] Meissner-Tastkörperchen, Corpusculum tactus[19] Tasthaare[20] tastbarer Fremitus[21] heikles Thema[22] Hautkontakt[23] Sexualkontakt[24] Kontaktdermatitis[25]   8

---

palpable [pælpəbl] adj term → U107-7   rel **tangible**[1] [tændʒəbl] adj

capable [eɪ] of being handled or touched or felt, especially on digital [ɪdʒ] palpation[2] [eɪʃ])

non/ impalpable adj term • **palpate**[3] v • **palpation**[2] n • **palpatory**[4] adj

» The liver and spleen[5] [iː] were both palpable. The structures are easily palpated via the rectum. Reinforce[6] acceptable behavior with praise[7] [eɪ] or tangible rewards [ɔː].

Use **palpable** vibration [eɪʃ]/ lymph [lɪmf] nodes / pulse [ʌ]/ nodule[8] [nɒːdjuːl]/ tumor • **palpable** fear / tension [ʃ] • **to palpate** for the pulse[9] / the ribs for tenderness • **tangible** sign [saɪn]/ relief[10] / evidence[11] / outcome • light / gentle[12] [dʒ]/ firm [ɜː]/ deep **palpation** • one-finger / (bi)manual [aɪ] **palpation**

tast-, fühlbar, palpabel
spürbar, greifbar; handfest[1] Abtasten, Palpation[2] abtasten, palpieren[3] Tast-, palpatorisch[4] Milz[5] verstärken[6] Lob[7] tastbarer Knoten[8] d. Puls fühlen[9] spürbare Erleichterung[10] handfester Beweis[11] vorsichtiges Abtasten[12]   9

---

caress [kəres] v & n clin   sim **stroke**[1], **fondle**[2] [ɔː], **pat**[3] [æ], **pet**[4] v

(v) to touch or kiss lightly in a loving or affectionate[5] [əfekʃᵊnət] manner

caressing[6] adj & n • **fondling** n • **patting** adj • **petting** n & adj → U68-2; U67-3

» These expressions of tenderness, fondling, caressing, and kissing usually culminate [ʌ] in orgasm. The plantar response[7] may be determined [ɜː] by pressure applied to the anterior tibia, stroking[8] toward the ankle.

Use **to caress** sb.'s hair / each other • soft / gentle / soothing [uː]/ verbal **caresses** • **to stroke the** skin / throat[9] [θroʊt]/ cat • **to fondle** a woman / her breasts [e]/ each other • genital[10] [dʒe]/ lesbian **fondling** • to indulge [ɪndʌldʒ] in heavy [e] **petting** • **petting** animals / zoo[11] [zuː]

streicheln, kosen; Liebkosung
streicheln, (be)streichen[1] streicheln, schmusen[2] tätscheln[3] liebkosen[4] zärtlich, liebevoll[5] zärtlich, sanft; Schmusen[6] Plantarreflex[7] streichend[8] den Hals bestreichen[9] Streicheln d. Geschlechtsteile, Petting[10] Streichelzoo[11]   10

---

tickle v & n clin → U103-17   rel **rub**[1] [ʌ], **pinch**[2] [pɪntʃ], → U1-20
scratch[3] [skrætʃ], **prick**[4] v & n → U5-9

(v) to touch or stroke lightly causing uneasiness [iː], laughter, or spasmodic movements

ticklish[5] adj • **tickling** adj • **pinprick**[6] n • **prickling**[7] adj • **prickly**[8] adj

» I've constantly got a tickle in my throat[9] which makes me cough [kɒf]. There is significant lack of response to stimuli such as tickling or a pinch on the back of the neck. Sensory testing is rarely contributory, but touch, tickle, and pinprick testing[10] can be used in small children.

Use **to tickle** sb. / sb.'s toes / the taste buds [ʌ] • **to rub** in / off / hard / against sth. • back[11] **rub** • **to pinch** one's lips together / the nose closed / off / shut • pain with / thumb[12] [θʌm] **pinch** • **pinch** mark • nose **tickling** • **ticklish** task / nose • needle-[iː]/ finger[13]-/ heel-**prick** [iː] • **pinprick** stimulus / sensation / loss • **prickling** sensation • **prickly** heat[14]

kitzeln, kratzen, jucken; Kitzeln
reiben, frottieren; (Ab)reiben[1] kneifen, zwicken, (ein)klemmen; Kneifen[2] kratzen; Kratzer[3] stechen; Stich[4] kitz(e)lig, heikel[5] Nadelstich[6] kribbelnd, prickelnd[7] stach(e)lig, kratzig[8] Hustenreiz, Halskratzen[9] Sensibilitätstest mit einer Nadel[10] Rückenmassage[11] Schlüsselgriff[12] Einstich i. d. Fingerbeere[13] Hitzepickel, Schweißfriesel, Miliaria[14]   11

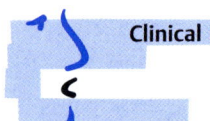

Clinical Phrases

He has a good nose for trends. Er hat einen guten Riecher für Trends. • The material is soft to the touch. Der Stoff fühlt sich weich an. • I'll never touch alcohol again. Ich werde keinen Alkohol mehr anrühren. • He has a taste for expensive sports cars. Er hat eine Vorliebe für teure Sportautos. • A sour smell hung in the air. Ein säuerlicher Geruch erfüllte den Raum. • Does this odor smell most like chocolate, banana, or onion? Riecht es am ehesten nach Schokolade, Banane oder Zwiebel? • My wife complains that my feet smell. Meine Frau beklagt sich, dass meine Füße ungut riechen.

Unit 63 Posture & Position

Related Units: 64 Body Movement, 31 Musculoskeletal Function, 107 Physical Examination, 134 Perioperative Care, 142 Physical Therapy & Rehabilitation

posture [pɒːstʃɚ] n clin & term   syn **position** [pəzɪʃən] n, **bearing** [eɚ], **carriage** n inf

(i) position or arrangement [eɪ] of the body (ii) way of bearing [beɚɪŋ] one's body

postural adj • **position**[1] v • **posturing**[2] n • **positional** adj • **(re)positioning**[3] n

» Large breasts [e] can cause poor posture[4], back and shoulder pain. Postural therapy[5] will suffice [səfaɪs]. Ambulatory[6] patients should be instructed to assume the knee-chest position.

Use to improve one's **posture** • body[7] / sitting / standing / upright or erect[8] **posture** • flexed / horizontal / good / normal **posture** • relaxed / rigid[9] [dʒ] / poor / faulty[10] [ɔː] **posture** • **postural** change[11] / exercises[12] • back problem • **postural** instability / kyphosis [kaɪfoʊsɪs]/ vertigo[13] [ɜː] • **postural** hypotension[14] [haɪpoʊ-]/ correction • **postural** drainage[15] [eɪ]/ reflexes[16] • flexor / extensor / decorticate **posturing** • decerebrate[17] [se]/ unusual **posturing** • change in[11] / anatomic / neutral [(j)uː] **position** • (physiologic) resting[18] / fetal [iː] **position** • knee-chest [tʃ] or genupectoral **position** • knee-elbow or genucubital[19] [dʒ]/ head-down[20] **position** • juxta**position**[21] [dʒʌks-] • **positional** vertigo[13] • intraoperative **positioning** • frequent[22] repositioning

(i) (Körper)haltung
(ii) (Körper)stellung

lagern, platzieren[1] Lage, Stellung[2] (Um)lagerung[3] schlechte Haltung[4] Haltungstherapie[5] gehfähig[6] Körperhaltung[7] aufrechte H.[8] starre H.[9] Fehlhaltung, Haltungsfehler[10] Lagewechsel, -veränderung[11] Haltungsschule, -übungen[12] lagebedingter Schwindel, Lageschwindel[13] orthostat. Hypotonie[14] Lagedrainage[15] Haltungsreflexe[16] Dezerebrationshaltung[17] Ruheposition[18] Knie-Ellenbogen-Lage[19] Kopftief-, Trendelenburglage(rung)[20] Juxtaposition, Anlagerung[21] häufige Umlagerung[22]   1

---

erect [ɪrekt] adj term & clin   opposite **slouched**[1] [slaʊtʃt], **slumped**[1] [ʌ] adj term

(i) upright[2] in position or straight-backed [streɪt] in posture (ii) stiff (esp. of sexual organs)

erector[3] n term • **slouch**[4] [aʊ] v & n clin • **slump**[4] [ʌ] v & n • **slumping** n

» In the partially erect positions the neck veins [eɪ] were full. His round-shouldered, slouched posture will persist postoperatively. Sit in a straight chair with no slumping. Suddenly he straightened up from his slouch. Totally exhausted [ɒː] he slumped into a chair[5].

Use **erect** position / spine [aɪ]/ penis [iː] • to sit[6]/stand **erect** • **erector** muscle [ʌ] of the spine[7] / penis • **slouched** against the bar[8] / on the bed • **to slouch** over the keyboard • postural **slumping**

(i) aufrecht
(ii) erigiert

gekrümmt, gebeugt, zusammengesunken[1] aufrecht[2] Musculus erector[3] (herum)lümmeln, zusammensacken[4] krumme Haltung[4] sich in einen Sessel fallen lassen[5] gerade/ aufrecht sitzen[6] Musculus erector spinae, Rückenstrecker[7] an der Bar hängend[8]   2

---

stoop [uː] v & n clin   sim **bow**[1] [baʊ] v, **bend forward**[2] v phr irr → U31-4

to change to a posture in which the top half of the body is inclined [aɪ] forward and downward

stooped[3] adj • **(un)bent**[3] adj • **bending** n & adj • **bend**[4] n • **bow**[5] [baʊ] n

» Progression of bradykinesia is represented by a gradually worsening [ɜː] stooped posture. Doesn't he have a slight stoop[6]? When lifting heavy [e] objects, keep your back straight and just bend your knees. Typical exercises include bent-knee sit-ups and hamstring [æ] stretching[7]. Heartburn[8] [ɜː] typically occurs after a large meal, with stooping or bending.

Use **to stoop** down[9] / over • **stooped** posture[10] • to walk with a[6] **stoop** • **to bend** down / over[9] / your legs / your head[11] • on **bended** knees[12] • (deep) knee[13] [niː]/ **bend** • forward / backward / (left) lateral **bending** • forceful / limitation on[14] **bending** • **bending** exercise / maneuver [uː] • **bent** fracture[15] / ears[16] • **to bow** to sb. / one's head[17] • to give[18] a **bow**

s. bücken/ beugen; krummer Rücken, Buckel

s. (ver)beugen[1] s. vorneigen[2] gebeugt[3] Biegung, Krümmung[4] Verbeugung[5] leicht gebeugt gehen[6] Dehnen d. Oberschenkelbeuger[7] Sodbrennen[8] s. bücken/ vorbeugen[9] gebeugte/ gebückte Haltung[10] d. Kopf neigen[11] auf Knien[12] Kniebeuge[13] Beugeeinschränkung[14] Biegungsfraktur[15] fehlgebildete Ohren[16] d. Kopf senken, s. verneigen[17] eine Verbeugung machen[18]   3

---

squat (down) [skwɒːt] v & n   syn **crouch** [kraʊtʃ] v & n, rel **kneel**[1] [niːl] v

(v) to sit on one's heels [iː] with one's legs bent under the body

» I've got this awful pain in my knee when squatting on my heels. It happened when I bent to a squat. Have the patient squat and strain[2] [eɪ] to demonstrate the prolapse. Kneel astride[3] [əstraɪd] the victim's thighs [θaɪz]. Have the patient kneel on a chair with the feet hanging free over the edge.

Use **squatting** position[4] / exercise[5] • to rise from a **squat** • to perform[5] **squats** • **squat** thrusts[5] [ʌ] • **to kneel** down[6] / in front of

hocken, kauern; Hocke, Hockstellung; Kniebeuge

knien[1] pressen[2] m. gespreizten Beinen knien über[3] Hockstellung[4] Kniebeugen (machen)[5] s. nieder-/ hinknien[6]   4

---

straddle v   rel **frog-leg(ged)**[1] adj clin, **spread-eagled**[2] [spred iːgld] adj inf

(i) to stand or sit astride[3] of an object with the legs apart
(ii) to extend across a gap, junction [dʒʌŋkʃən] or division

straddle[4] n • **spread-eagle** n

» He sat down straddling the chair. The urethra [iː] may be injured as a result of falling astride of an object, a so-called straddle injury[5]. AP x-rays and frog-leg lateral views were obtained.

Use **frog-legged** position[1] • **straddle** toys[6] • **frog-leg** view [vjuː]/ projection [dʒe]

(i) rittlings sitzen, breitbeinig stehen (über), grätschen
(ii) überbrücken

(in) Froschstellung[1] m. ausgebreiteten Armen u. gespreizten Beinen[2] rittlings[3] Grätsche[4] Dammverletzung[5] Spielzeug z. Draufsetzen[6]   5

COMPLEX BODY FUNCTIONS — Posture & Position

curl (up) [kɜːrl ʌp] v   syn **huddle** [ʌ], **cower** [kaʊɚ] v

to twist or roll one's body into a curl [ɜː] sometimes referred to as the embryo position[1]

curled[2] adj • **uncurl**[3] vt & vi

» The boy was fast asleep, curled up in the fetal position[1]. Point your foot downward and curl your toes. Why are you always sitting with your legs curled under[4]? In a biliary colic the patient usually curls up in bed and frequently changes positions to be more comfortable.

Use **to curl** into a ball • **to curl one's** toes[5] / lips[6] / fingers round sth. • **curled** hair[7]

decubitus [dɪkjuːbɪtəs] n term

(i) position in which the patient lies flat on a horizontal surface
(ii) bedsore[1] due to pressure occurring on the elbows, sacrum [eɪ], heels or shoulder blades in long-term immobilized patients (pl decubiti [aɪ‖iː])

decubital adj term

» Place the patient in a left lateral decubitus position[2] with the head down.

Use dorsal / lateral[3] **decubitus** • **decubitus** position / film or x-ray [eks reɪ]/ radiograph [eɪ] • **decubitus** ulcer[1] [ʌlsɚ]/ care

supine [suːpaɪn‖paɪn] adj term   syn **dorsal decubitus position** n term

lying flat on one's back with the face upward

» Obtain [eɪ] vital [aɪ] signs with the patient supine. The patient may be sitting or supine. First, have the patient lie supine, with the head raised [eɪ] about 10 degrees.

Use three-fourths / dorso**supine** • **supine**-to-sit transfer[1] / view / x-rays • **supine** hypotension / position[2] / Heimlich (maneuver)[3] [uː]

prone [proʊn] adj term   syn **face-down** adj clin

position in which the patient lies face down with the arms folded to support the face

semiprone[1] [semɪproʊn] adj term • **prone-lying**[2] [proʊn laɪɪŋ] n & adj

» The patient is placed in a prone position with the head in the midline. A choking [tʃoʊkɪŋ] infant[3] under age 1 should be placed face-down over the rescuer's[4] arm. The best "splint[5]" for the hip is prone-lying for several hours a day on a firm [ɜː] bed.

Use to lie/place **prone** • **prone** position[6] / positioning • **prone**-sleeping infant[7] / in Trendelenburg position • **semiprone** position[1]

(zusammen)kauern, (sich) zusammenrollen
Embryostellung[1] zusammengerollt; gelockt[2] auseinanderrollen, s. strecken[3] auf d. Unterschenkeln sitzen[4] d. Zehen krümmen[5] d. Lippen kräuseln/ schürzen/ verziehen[6] lockiges/ krauses Haar[7]   6

**(i) Liegen, Liegeposition
(ii) Wundliegen, Dekubitus**
Dekubitalgeschwür, Wundliegen[1] 30 Grad Seitenlage links[2] Seitenlage[3]
    7

auf d. Rücken (liegend), in Rückenlage
Umlagern v. Liegen zum Sitzen[1] Rückenlage[2] Heimlich-Handgriff beim liegenden Patienten[3]
    8

in Bauchlage, auf d. Bauch (liegend)
(in) Halbseitenlage[1] Bauchlage; auf d. Bauch liegend[2] Kind mit einem Erstickungsanfall[3] Retter(in), Helfer(in)[4] Schiene[5] Bauchlage[6] auf d. Bauch schlafendes Kind[7]
    9

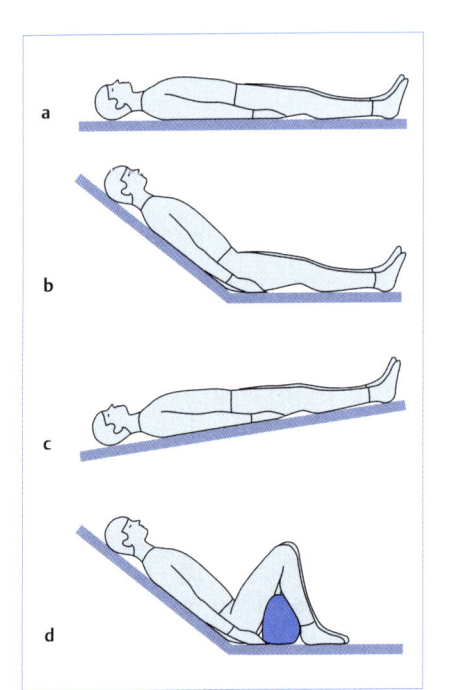

Types of patient positioning:
(**a**) supine position,
(**b**) recumbent position,
(**c**) Trendelenburg position,
(**d**) jackknife position

Body Movement COMPLEX BODY FUNCTIONS 255

recumbent [ʌ] adj term   sim **reclining**[1] [aɪ], **leaning back**[1] adj
                              rel **incline**[2], **tilt**[3] v

lying back with the head and upper back (slightly) propped up[4], e.g. by a pillow[5]
semi/ **dorsorecumbent**[6] adj term • **recumbency** [rɪkˈʌmbənˈsi] n
» It occurred [ɜː] while the patient was sleeping in a recumbent position. Heartburn [ɑː] was worse [ɜː] on recumbency[7]. The patient should be kept recumbent and the injured part left open to the air. The symptoms were relieved by reclining.
Use to keep a patient / to lie / left arm[8] **recumbent** • **recumbent** position / lateral films • dorsal / lateral **recumbent position** • while **reclining** • overnight **recumbency** • nocturnal [ɜː] **recumbency** leg cramps[9] • **to tilt** back(ward) forward[10] / to the side • head[11] / chin [tʃ] / lateral / talar [eɪ] **tilt** • **tilt** table[12] / testing

jackknife position [dʒæknaɪf pəzɪʃ°n] n clin

semisitting position with the shoulders elevated and the thighs flexed at right angles to the abdomen
» Evaluation of hemorrhoids [e] is best performed in the prone jackknife position[1].

Fowler('s) position [faʊlɚz] n term   rel **lithotomy position**[1] n term

half-sitting position obtained [eɪ] by raising [eɪ] the head of the bed and (sometimes) elevating the knees
» Institute bed rest in the semi-Fowler position to promote [oʊ] dependent drainage after an abdominal operation. The sciatic [saɪætɪk] nerve[2] may be damaged if the patient is in the dorsal lithotomy position with the thighs [aɪ] and legs extended outward and rotated.
Use high / low / semi-**Fowler's position** • Sims'[3] **position** • dorsal lithotomy **position**

dependent position n clin   sim **dangling**[1] [æ], **pendent**[2], **pendulous**[2] adj

supported from above with the body or part of the body hanging down
dangle v • **suspend**[3] v • **suspension**[4] [səspenʃ°n] n term • **suspensory**[5] adj
pending[6] adj term • **pendulum**[7] n & adj
» Patients with ischemic [ɪskiːmɪk] rest pain experience some relief [iː] by placing their limbs [lɪmz] in a dependent position. Have the patient sit up with the legs dangling over the side of the bed. Mrs Roe's lab results are still pending[8].
Use head[9] **dependent position** • **dependent** portion / drainage[10] [eɪ] / swelling • **dangling** arm • **pendulous** palate[11] [æ]/ breast[12] [e]/ abdomen[13] / urethra [iː] • ventral / balanced / uterine[14] [juː] **suspension** • **suspensory** ligament[15] [ɪ] • **pendulum** exercise / rhythm[16] [rɪðəm]

liegend, sich lehnend
(s.) zurücklehnend, zurückgelehnt[1]
(s.) neigen[2] (s.) neigen, kippen, schräg stellen[3] gestützt auf[4] Kissen[5] auf d. Rücken liegend[6] im Liegen[7] halbliegend auf d. linken Arm gestützt[8] nächtl. Beinkrämpfe[9] (s.) nach vorne neigen, nach vorne kippen[10] Kopfneigung, schräge Kopfhaltung[11] Kipptisch[12]
10

Oberkörperhochlagerung m. angezogenen Beinen
Knieellenbogenlage[1]
11

Fowler-Lagerung
Steinschnittlage[1] Ischiasnerv, Nervus ischiadicus[2]
Sims-Position[3]

12

Hängelage
baumelnd[1] hängend, Hänge-[2] aufhängen, suspendieren[3] Aufhängung, Suspension[4] Halte-, Stütz-[5] bevorstehend, ausständig, anhängig[6] Pendel; Pendel-[7] noch ausständig[8] Kopftieflage[9] Lagedrainage[10] (Gaumen)zäpfchen, Uvula[11] Hängebrust[12] Hängebauch[13] Uterushalteapparat[14] Lig. suspensorium, Aufhängeband[15] Pendelrhythmus[16]
13

Unit 64 Body Movement
Related Units: 31 Musculoskeletal Function, 63 Posture, 65 Walking, 107 Physical Examination, 113 Neurologic Findings, 142 Physiotherapy

motion [moʊʃ°n] n clin & term   syn **movement** [muːvmənt] n

(i) change of place or position [ɪʃ] of the entire [aɪ] or parts of the body
(ii) stool [uː] (iii) defecation
motionless adj • **move**[1] v & n • **(im)movable**[2] adj • **motor**[3] [moʊtɚ] adj
» A few days of rest will be required to regain [eɪ] normal hip motion. Elbow motion is limited only in extreme [iː] flexion. Guarded[4] [ɡɑː-] early motion may be initiated [ɪʃ] under supervision. Ask the patient to move hands and feet spontaneously and against resistance.
Use active / gliding [aɪ] / twisting[5] / pain-free **motion** • smooth[6] [uː]/ gentle [dʒe]/ ciliary[7] [sɪ] **motion** • **motion** sickness[8] / disorder • body / joint [dʒ]/ limb [lɪm]/ hand **movement** • lip / head / neck / cervical [sɜː] spine [aɪ] **movement** • voluntary[9] / abrupt [ʌ]/ reflex [iː]/ jerky[10] [dʒɜːrki] **movement** • convulsive[11] [ʌ]/ spontaneous [eɪ]/ purposeful[12] [ɜː]/ limited **movement** • (rapid) eye[13] (abbr REM)/ downward / inward / backward **movement** • to make a[14] **move**

(i) **Bewegung**
(ii, iii) **Stuhl(gang)**
bewegen; ergreifen, erschüttern; Bewegung; Schritt, Maßnahme[1] (un)beweglich[2] motorisch; Motor-, Bewegungs-[3] vorsichtig[4] Drehbewegung[5] fließende/ geschmeidige B.[6] Zilienbewegung[7] Reise-, Bewegungskrankheit, Kinetose[8] Willkürbewegung[9] ruckartige B.[10] spastische/ krampfartige B.[11] zielgerichtete B.[12] schnelle Augenbewegung im Schlaf[13] etwas/ Schritte unternehmen[14]
1

COMPLEX BODY FUNCTIONS — Body Movement

mobility [moʊbɪləti] *n*   *opposite* **immobility**[1] *n* → U141-5

ability of moving freely (normal range of motion[2] (*abbr* ROM), full functional [ʌ] movement, coordination, strength [streŋkθ], endurance[3] [(j)ʊɚ], etc.)

(im)mobilize[4] [moʊbɪlaɪz] *v term* • **(im)mobilization** *n* • **(hyper/ im)mobile**[5] *adj*

» His forearm is grossly [oʊ] swollen[6] [oʊ], acutely tender, and immobile. Mobility is greatest in the cervical spine and least[7] [iː] in the thoracic [æs] spine. Obese [iː] patients should be mobilized as soon as possible after surgery [ɜː]. The fracture was treated by immobilization in plaster[8] [æ] for 3 weeks. The incidence of venous [iː] thrombosis increases with periods of immobility.

Use patient / wheelchair [iː]/ impaired [eɚ] or restricted[9] **mobility** • joint / skin / tongue [tʌŋ] **mobility** • relative / complete / period [ɪɚ] of **immobility** • cervical / gentle active / early[10] **mobilization** • adequate / cast [æ]/ brace[11] [breɪs]/ rigid [ɪdʒ]/ prolonged **immobilization** • external / neck / spine / fracture[12] / surgical **immobilization** • to become/lie[13] **immobile** • **immobile** patient / face[14] • **mobile** kidney[15] / portion • **mobile** arm support / meals[16] • **hypermobile** joints[17] / child

Mobilität, Beweglichkeit
Unbeweglich-, Bewegungslosigkeit[1] Bewegungsausmaß[2] Ausdauer[3] ruhigstellen, immobilisieren[4] immobil, unbeweglich[5] stark geschwollen[6] am geringsten[7] Gips[8] eingeschränkte Beweglichkeit[9] Frühmobilisation[10] Immobilisierung durch eine Schiene[11] Retention, Fixation, Ruhigstellung einer Fraktur[12] bewegungslos daliegen[13] unbewegtes Gesicht[14] Wanderniere, Ren mobilis[15] Essen auf Rädern[16] erhöhte Beweglichkeit/ Überstreckbarkeit d. Gelenke[17]

2

---

stir [stɜːr] *v & n*   *sim* **budge**[1] [bʌdʒ] *v*

(i) to move very slightly
(ii) to wake up, activate, provoke or motivate, esp. after inactivity, sleep or rest

» It hurts so much I'm afraid to stir. Don't stir her up[2] now, she hasn't been sleeping well. He hasn't budged from his room all week. I won't stir from the spot. Would you budge up[3] a bit?

Use **to stir up** emotions [oʊʃ]/ the blood[4] / trouble[5] [ʌ] • **stir-up** regimen[6] [edʒ] • **stirring** movement / speech[7] • to cause a[8] stir • **to budge** from one's seat / a heavy desk[9] / a step

bewegen; (sich) rühren/ regen
s. bewegen; nachgeben[1] aufwecken[2] Platz machen[3] d. Blut i. Wallung bringen[4] Unruhe stiften[5] mobilisierende Therapie[6] bewegende Ansprache[7] Aufsehen erregen[8] einen schweren Tisch verrücken[9]

3

---

shift [ʃɪft] *vi & vt*   *sim* **displace**[1] [dɪspleɪs], **transfer**[2] [trænˈsfɜːr] *v* → U20-15

(i) to move around, esp. by changing place or direction (ii) to move abruptly [ʌ] or very slightly
shift[3] *n* • **shifting** *adj & n* •
transfer[4] *n term* • **displacement**[5] [eɪ] *n* → U106-4

» The neck pain shifts characteristically from side to side and finally settles in one area, frequently radiating [eɪ] to the jaw and ears. The femoral head was felt to displace with a jerk. Arrange for immediate transfer of the victim to the nearest hyperbaric chamber[6] [eɪ].

Use **to shift** your legs / arms / feet • lateral / right[7] / downward **shift** • fluid / mood[8] [uː]/ night[9] **shift** • **shift** in position[10] / of pain / to the right[7] • **shift** in sleeping pattern / worker • weight[11] **shifting** • **shifting** pattern / pain / border / dullness [ʌ] • **displaced** fracture[12] / anteriorly • downward / traumatic **displacement** • supine [aɪ] to sit / sit-to-stand **transfer** • interhospital / patient[13] **transfer** • **transfer** with standby assistance • **transfer** to the intensive care unit[14] / to the nursing [ɜː] home

(sich) verlagern, verschieben
verlagern, -schieben[1] verlegen; überstellen; übertragen[2] Verschiebung, Wechsel[3] Umlagerung; Verlegung, Überstellung[4] Verschiebung, Dislokation[5] Überdruckkammer[6] Rechtsverschiebung[7] Stimmungsschwankung[8] Nachtschicht[9] Lagewechsel[10] Gewichtsverlagerung[11] dislozierte Fraktur[12] Patientenverlegung, -überstellung[13] Verlegung auf die Intensivstation[14]

4

---

sway [sweɪ] *v*   *rel* **swing**[1] - swung - swung *v irr*,
                rock[2], **tilt**[3], **lean**[4] [iː], **wobble**[5] [ɒː] *v*

to move sideways or back and forth in an unsteady [e] way
swaying *adj* • **swinging** *adj* • **swing**[6] [swɪŋ] *n* • **tilt**[7] [tɪlt] *n* • **wobbly**[8] *adj*

» Tilt your head this way a little. There is a reduction in automatic movements such as swinging of the arms while walking. My legs still feel a bit wobbly. Keep the airway open with the head-tilt and chin-lift maneuver[9] [uː]. The patient should sit up and lean forward.

Use **to sway** to the music / back and forth / from side to side[10] • **swaying** movement / gait[11] [eɪ] • **to swing** from left to right / to the left / at the ball[12] / round • **swing**-to gait[13] / door • arm[14] / mood [uː] **swing** • **to rock** a child to sleep • gentle **rocking** • **to tilt** to the left • head[15]-/ dorsal **tilt** • **to lean** forward / backward • **wobbly** voice[16] / legs

schwanken, torkeln
schwingen, baumeln[1] schaukeln, wiegen[2] neigen, kippen[3] (s.) lehnen, neigen[4] wackeln, schwanken[5] Schwung[6] Neigung[7] zittrig, (sch)wabblig[8] Esmarch-Handgriff[9] hin u. her schwanken[10] Watschelgang[11] (zum Schlag) ausholen (b. Golf)[12] Zu-Schwung-Gang (Krücken)[13] Armschwingen, Mitschwingen d. Arme[14] Kopfneigung[15] zitternde Stimme[16]

5

Body Movement   COMPLEX BODY FUNCTIONS **257**

---

shake - shook - shaken v irr   sim **tremble¹, quiver¹** [kwɪvɚ], **shiver¹** [ɪ] v & n
(i) to move back and forth (e.g. the head) (ii) to move with a tremor [e] because of fear or cold
shaky² [ʃeɪki] adj • **shaking** adj & n • **shakiness³** n
shivery⁴ adj • **shivering** n & adj • **tremulous⁵** adj → U113-4
» Hold it steady, don't shake or shake! Shake the victim⁶ gently. Sponging⁷ [spʌndʒ-] with lukewarm [uː] water will cause shivering, which may ultimately raise the temperature.
Use **to shake** one's head / one's fist⁸ / hands (with) • hand**shake** • **to tremble** all over⁹ / slightly / with excitement [aɪ] • violent [aɪə]/ vigorous¹⁰ [ɪ]/ head **shaking** • **shaking** chills¹¹ [tʃ]/ palsy¹² [ɔː] • **shake** lotion¹³ [oʊʃ] • **shaky** handwriting / motion • **to shiver** with cold • to cause/produce/control/inhibit/block **shivering** • **shivering** attack¹¹ / response • **trembling** hands / voice¹⁴

schütteln, zittern, wackeln
zittern, beben, zucken; Schaudern, Zittern¹ wackelig, zittrig² Unsicherheit³ fröstelnd, zittrig⁴ zitternd, bebend⁵ Opfer⁶ Abreiben⁷ mit d. Faust drohen⁸ am ganzen Körper zittern⁹ kräftiges Schütteln¹⁰ Schüttelfrost¹¹ Schüttellähmung, Parkinson-Krankheit, Paralysis agitans¹² Schüttelmixtur¹³ zitternde Stimme¹⁴
6

---

jerk [dʒɜːrk] v & n clin & jar   sim **lurch¹** [lɜːrtʃ], **jolt²** [dʒoʊlt] v & n clin
(v) to move abruptly with seemingly uncontrolled motions (n) a sudden, short move
jerky³ [dʒɜːrki] adj clin • **jerkiness** n • **jerking⁴** adj & n → U113-1
» The femoral head was felt to displace with a jerk. Some scorpion stings may cause muscle cramps, twitching and jerking and occasionally convulsions⁵ [ʌ]. His gait is slow with a broadened base and lurching from side to side. I woke up with a jolt.
Use   knee (abbr KJ)/ ankle⁶ (abbr AJ)/ jaw⁷ [dʒɒː]/ (deep) tendon **jerk** • muscular⁸ / convulsive / tonic **jerking** • clonic⁹ / uncontrollable **jerking** • **jerking** eye movements / of all extremities • **jerky** move / respiration¹⁰ / inspiration • **jerky** pulse¹¹ / incoordinate movement • **to lurch** forward • **to jolt** sb. into action¹² / along¹³

Note: In slang the noun *****jerk¹⁴** (or **jerk-off**) is also a common insult (=idiot, fool) and **to *****jerk off** is a vulgar expression for **to masturbate**.

zucken, sich ruckartig bewegen; Ruck, Reflex
torkeln; Ruck¹ durch-, aufrütteln; Ruck, Schock² ruckartig, stoßweise³ ruckartig; Zuckung, Zucken⁴ Krämpfe, Konvulsionen⁵ Achillessehnenreflex⁶ Masseter-, Mandibularreflex⁷ Muskelzuckung⁸ klonische Krämpfe⁹ unregelmäßige/ schnappende Atmung¹⁰ unregelmäßiger/ schnellender Puls¹¹ jem. aufrütteln¹² dahinholpern¹³ Blödmann¹⁴
7

---

roll (over) v clin   syn **turn** [tɜːrn] **(over)** v
to make a rolling motion or turn, esp. when lying down
rolled-up¹ adj • **eye-rolling²** n • **neck roll³** n • **turning⁴** n
» Place a rolled bath towel under the left scapula. The head and trunk [ʌ] must be lifted and rolled as one unit (logroll). Avoid turning to the side or rolling over in bed too suddenly.
Use   **to roll** your eyes / oneself in a blanket⁵ / down the hill • to toss and⁶ **turn** • **to turn** around / your head away / back • **to turn** to the side / the patient • outward / inward • head⁷ **turning** • rigid [ɪdʒ] or en bloc / frequent⁸ **turning** • **rolled-up** sleeves⁹ [iː]/ blanket / towel¹⁰ [taʊəl]

(auf die Seite/ um)drehen, wenden, rollen
zusammengerollt¹ Rollen d. Augen² Nackenrolle³ (Um-, Ver)drehen⁴ sich in eine Decke wickeln⁵ s. hin u. her wälzen⁶ Kopfdrehung⁷ häufiges Umlagern⁸ hochgekrempelte Ärmel⁹ zusammengerolltes Handtuch¹⁰
8

---

grasp v & n   syn **grip** v & n, rel **hold¹** - held - held, **cling²** - clung - clung [ʌ] v irr, **grab³, clench⁴** [klentʃ] v
(v, i) to hold firmly [ɜː] with the hands (ii) to understand the meaning
grasping⁵ adj • **grasper⁶** n • **grip⁷** n • **hold⁸** n • **holder⁹** n • **handgrip¹⁰** n
» Pain is aggravated by grasping. Evaluate the child's reach and type of grasp. Grasp the patient's feet and lift his legs. The arches [tʃ] of the hand¹¹ are essential for gripping, pinching and cupping¹² [ʌ]. Mary is still a very clinging¹³ child.
Use   **to grasp** at / for / sb. by the neck¹⁴ • to slip from one's¹⁵ **grasp** • to have a good / hand / palmar / pincer¹⁶ [ˈts] **grasp** • **grasp** reflex¹⁷ [iː]/ strength • **grasping** forceps⁶ / movement / muscles [mʌslz] • to lose¹⁸/relax/tighten [taɪtᵊn] /strengthen **one's grip** • firm / loose / weak [iː] **grip** • precision [sɪ]/ power¹⁹ **grip** • **grip** strength • tight **gripping** • **to hold one's** breath²⁰ [e]/ urine [jʊɚ] • film²¹ / needle²² [iː]/ chart [tʃɑːrt] **holder** • **to cling** to sb.²³ / together • **to grab** hold of²⁴ / at / sth. from sb.²⁵ • **grab** bar²⁶ • **to clench one's** fist²⁷ / teeth²⁸ [tiːθ]

(er-, be)greifen; Griff
halten; fassen¹ festhalten, s. klammern (an)² (zu)packen, schnappen³ packen, ballen⁴ Greif-, Fass-⁵ Fasszange⁶ Griff⁷ Griff, Halt⁸ Halter, Haltevorrichtung⁹ (Hand)griff; Händedruck¹⁰ Handwölbung¹¹ Hohlhandbildung¹² anhänglich¹³ jem. am Genick packen¹⁴ aus d. Hand rutschen, entgleiten¹⁵ Pinzettengriff¹⁶ Greifreflex¹⁷ d. Halt verlieren¹⁸ Kraft-, Grobgriff, Faustschluss¹⁹ d. Atem anhalten²⁰ Filmhalter²¹ Nadelhalter²² s. an jem. hängen²³ etw. packen²⁴ jem. etw. entreißen²⁵ Haltegriff²⁶ d. Faust ballen²⁷ d. Zähne zusammenbeißen/ -pressen²⁸
9

64

COMPLEX BODY FUNCTIONS — Body Movement

squeeze [skwiːz] v & n   sim **pinch**[1], **compress**[2], **crush**[3] [ʌ], **squash**[3] [skwɒʃ] v → U6-6

(v) to press together firmly (or even out of shape) between the fingers, with your hands or arms

squeezing adj clin • **pinch** [pɪnʲʃ] n • **compression** n • **crushing**[4] adj → U5-13

» Ask the patient to squeeze the eyes shut tightly. Squeeze the relaxed calf[5] [kæf], which normally causes plantar flexion of the ankle. Pinch the victim's nose closed. Compress the bag with the right hand. Immerse [ɜː] the tube for 15 seconds in crushed ice. Ova can usually be detected in rectal biopsy specimens and are best identified by squashing a small amount of tissue between two glass slides[6] [aɪ] and viewing the tissue microscopically.

Use **to squeeze** a handgrip / one's eyes shut[7] [ʌ] / medication under the tongue [tʌŋ] • **to squeeze** blood out of the vessel • voluntary[8] **squeeze** • **squeezing** chest pain[9] • **to pinch** off[10] / shut • **pinched** face[11] / appearance [ɪə] • lateral / key[12] / stable [eɪ] / weak **pinch** • tip to tip[13] / chuck[14] [tʃʌk] **pinch** • fingers meet in **pinch** • **pinch** stimulation[15] • **to compress** neural [n(j)ʊərəl] tissue • spinal [aɪ] cord / digital [ɪdʒ] / (nerve) root[16] [uː] / tracheal [k] **compression** • **compression** injury [ɪndʒəri] / bandage or dressing[17] / hosiery[18] [oʊ] • **to crush** a tablet • **crush** injury[19] / wound [uː] • **crushed** tissue / bone / pelvis[20] / ice[21] • **crushing** injury / force / blow[22]

stroke [stroʊk] v   rel **pat**[1] [pæt], **tap**[2], **rub**[3] [rʌb], **tickle**[4] [tɪkl] v → U5-9

to touch lightly [laɪtli] and with affection using brushing [ʌ] motions[5]

stroking n & adj • **tap**[6] n clin & jar • **tapping**[7] n clin • **rub**[8] n • **ticklish**[9] adj

» Stroke the throat to encourage [ɜː] swallowing. After rising the skin should be patted dry[10] (not rubbed). Creams should be rubbed into the skin gently. Gentle tapping over the vein may help to distend it. Continued rubbing and scratching will lead to an itch[11]-scratch-rash-itch cycle. There was hoarseness[12] [ɔː] with a tickling sensation in the back of his throat [oʊ].

Use gentle / firm [ɜː] / sole[13] [oʊ] **stroking** • **to tap** the chest for fluid • spinal[14] / belly[15] / suprapubic bladder **tap** • fresh / plain[16] / lukewarm [uː] / contaminated **tap water** • **to rub** in a lotion [oʊʃ] / into the skin / sth. together[17] • **to rub** warm / away or off[18] / one's eyes • face / pleural[19] [ʊə] / pericardial friction [kʃ] **rub**

Note: Do not mix up **to stroke** with **to strike**[20] (struck - struck), **stroking** with the noun **stroke**[21], and **tapping** with **taping**[22].

push [pʊʃ] v & n   syn **thrust** [θrʌst], **shove** [ʃʌv] v & n, rel **press**[1] v, **kick**[2] v & n

(v) applying force to move sth. away or press against sth. without being able to move it

pushy[3] adj • **pushing** n • **push-ups**[4] n usu pl • **pressing**[5] n

» Avoid pushing the foreign [ɒː] body[6] farther down the tube. The distended stomach [k] pushes the diaphragm [aɪ] upward. During pregnancy the appendix is shoved farther out of the pelvis. Ask the patient to press her hands on her hips. Temper tantrums[7] are characterized by the child lying or throwing himself down, kicking and screaming [iː].

Use **to push** sth. away / oneself / against the limit • abdominal[8] / tongue[9] [tʌŋ] **thrust** • **to kick** one's legs / a ball / a habit[10] • to give sb. a[11] **kick** • knee[12] [niː] **kick** • **kick** count[13] [aʊ] • forward **pushing** • **pushy** preschooler[14] [iː] / nature [neɪtʃə]

pull [pʊl] v & n   rel **drag**[1] [æ], **tug**[2] [tʌg], **retract**[3] v, **tear**[4] [teə] - tore - torn v irr → U5-7

(v) applying force to move something toward the source of motion

pulling[5] adj & n • **pull-up**[6] n • **wear-and-tear**[7] n • **retraction**[8] n → U132-16

» Pull the skin taut[9] [tɔːt]. Then the infant is pulled by the arms to a sitting position. Gently [dʒ] tug on the pinna[10] to elicit [ɪs] pain. Drag the victim carefully away using dry clothing, rubber [ʌ], or other dry non-conductive [ʌ] materials. He tore off his clothes and fell into bed. In phimosis, the foreskin cannot be retracted over the glans.

Use **to pull** up / down / out / by the hand • **to pull** away (from) / back / through[11] / at sth. • **to pull** sth. apart[12] / on a rope / hard / a muscle[13] [mʌsl] • lateral / muscle **pull** • hair **pulling** • **to drag** one's leg[14] / the victim away • tracheal[15] [k] **tugging** • **torn** vessel[16] / tendon[17] • meniscal / cruciate [uːʃ] ligament[18] / rectal **tear** • **tear of** muscle / the capsule[19] • **to retract the** foreskin / eyelid • eardrum[20] [ɪədrʌm] / nipple[21] **retraction**

(zusammen)drücken, quetschen; (Hände)druck, Pressen

kneifen, zwicken[1] zusammendrücken, komprimieren[2] zerquetschen, -drücken, -stoßen[3] zerschmetternd[4] Wade[5] Objektträger[6] d. Augen fest schließen[7] willkürl. Pressen[8] Druckschmerz i. d. Brust[9] abknipsen, -zwicken[10] verhärmtes Gesicht[11] Schlüsselgriff[12] Spitzgriff[13] Kuppengriff[14] Kneiftest[15] Wurzelkompression[16] Kompressionsverband[17] Kompressionsstrümpfe[18] Quetschung[19] Beckenzertrümmerung[20] zerstoßenes Eis[21] zermalmender Schlag[22]

10

streicheln, streichen über

klopfen, tätscheln[1] klopfen; anzapfen, punktieren[2] reiben[3] kitzeln[4] Bürstbewegungen[5] Punktion[6] (Be)klopfen, leichtes Klopfen an/auf[7] Abreibung[8] kitz(e)lig[9] trockentupfen[10] Jucken[11] Heiserkeit[12] Bestreichen d. Fußsohle[13] Lumbalpunktion[14] Bauchpunktion[15] reines Leitungswasser[16] etwas aneinander reiben[17] wegreiben[18] Pleurareiben[19] schlagen[20] Schlag; Schlaganfall[21] Tapen, Tape-Verband (anlegen)[22]

11

drücken, schieben, stoßen; Druck, Stoß

drücken, pressen[1] treten, strampeln; (Fuß)tritt[2] aufdringlich[3] Liegestütze[4] Drücken, Pressen, Drängen[5] Fremdkörper[6] Wutanfälle[7] Druckstoß auf d. Bauch[8] Zungenpressen[9] e. Gewohnheit ablegen[10] jem. einen Tritt versetzen[11] Stoß mit d. Knie[12] Zählen d. Kindsbewegungen[13] aufsässige(r) Vorschüler(in)[14]

12

ziehen; Zug(kraft)

schleifen, (nach)ziehen[1] ziehen, zerren[2] zurückziehen[3] (zer)reißen[4] Zug-; Ziehen[5] Klimmzug[6] Verschleiß[7] Verkürzung, Retraktion, Einziehung[8] straffen[9] Ohrmuschel[10] durchziehen; durchkommen, sich erholen[11] etw. auseinanderziehen[12] sich einen Muskel zerren[13] ein Bein nachziehen[14] Oliver-Cardarelli-Zeichen[15] Gefäßruptur[16] Sehnenriss, -ruptur[17] Kreuzbandruptur[18] Kapselriss[19] Trommelfelleinziehung[20] Brustwarzeneinziehung[21]

13

Body Movement   COMPLEX BODY FUNCTIONS 259

throw - threw [θruː] - thrown v irr   syn **toss** [tɒːs] v, **cast** - cast - cast v irr
                                    sim **hurl**[1] [hɜːrl] v, **fling**[1] - flung - flung [ʌ] v irr

to propel an object through the air with a rapid movement of the arm and wrist

throw[2] [θroʊ] n clin & term • **toss**[3] n • **cast**[4] [kæst] n

» Show me how to throw a ball. Use one throw of a square knot[5] [nɒːt] to close the skin around the tube. He was hurling all loose objects he could find against the wall. The patient tossed his blanket aside and got up. The child flung herself face downward on the floor.

Use **to throw** back (one's hair/ shoulders) • **to throw** (oneself) down on the floor[6] / a ball at sth. • **to throw** the baby out with the bath water[7] • **to throw** sth. away / up (food)[8] / off (a cold)[9] • overhead[10] / underhand **throw** • **throwing** movement / athlete[11] • **to toss** toys to the ground • **to hurl** away / oneself into work[12] • **to fling** sth. away[13]

(zu-, ab)werfen, schleudern
schleudern, stoßen[1] Wurf; Schlinge[2] Wurf[3] Wurf; Guss; Gips(verband)[4] Schifferknoten[5] sich zu Boden werfen[6] d. Kind mit d. Bad ausschütten[7] erbrechen[8] eine Verkühlung loswerden[9] Überkopfwurf[10] Werfer(in)[11] sich in d. Arbeit stürzen[12] etwas wegwerfen/ vergeuden[13]

14

drop [drɒːp] vi & vt   rel **sink**[1]- sank - sunk v irr, **droop**[2] [uː], **sag**[3] v,
                          shed[4] - shed - shed [ʃed] v irr

(i) to bring down to a lower place or level (ii) to let an object fall to the ground

drop[5] n • **droop**[6] n • **droopy**[7] [druːpi] adj • **sagging**[7] [sægɪŋ] adj → U113-17

» Allow the head of the child to suddenly drop backward about 1-2cm. The injury typically results from a fall on the outstretched hand. The sternum [ɜː] may sink inward, leaving [iː] a sharp elevation at the rib margins [dʒ]. If you don't wear a bra[8] your breasts [e] might start drooping. Reconstructions in the face often tend to sag. The endometrial [iː] lining is shed as menstrual flow.

Use **to drop** down / to the ground[9] / behind / one's voice / dead[10] • foot[11] / toe/ wrist[12] [r] **drop** • **drop** shoulder / hand / finger[13] / attack[14] • eye / ear / nose[15] **drops** • **drop** by drop / counter[16] [aʊ] • **drop** in blood pressure • **to shed** tears [ɪɚ]/ blood / cells[17] / light on a matter • virus[18] [aɪ] • **shedding** • left-sided facial [eɪʃ] **droop** • **drooping of the** mouth / palate[19] • **droopy** ears / upper lid • **sagging** tissue [tʃ∥sjuː]/ breasts[20] [e]

fallen (lassen)
(ver)sinken, (s.) senken[1] herunterhängen, hängen lassen[2] herabhängen, s. senken[3] abwerfen, -stoßen; vergießen[4] Tropfen; (Ab)fall; Senkung[5] Herabhängen, Ptosis[6] hängend, schlaff[7] Büstenhalter, BH[8] (s.) zu Boden fallen (lassen)[9] tot umfallen[10] Spitzfußstellung (b. Peronäuslähmung)[11] Fallhand[12] Hammerfinger[13] Drop attack[14] Nasentropfen[15] Tropfenzähler[16] Zellen abstoßen, abschilfern[17] Virusausbreitung[18] Gaumensegellähmung[19] Hängebrüste[20]

15

lift v   sim **elevate**[1] [eləveɪt], **raise**[2] [reɪz] v, rel **carry**[3] [keɚi], **support**[4] v

to move upward or raise to a higher position, esp. objects or body parts

lifting[5] n • **lift**[6] n • **elevation**[7] n • **support**[8] n • **supportive** adj

» You must avoid heavy lifting and straining[9] [eɪ] at stool [uː]. Reduce tension on the Achilles [k] tendon by placing a heel [iː] lift[10] in the shoes. Jaw [dʒɔː] thrust [ʌ] and chin [tʃ] lift[11] were ineffective in airway opening. Instruct the patient to elevate the leg as frequently as possible. The child cannot raise the arm completely on the affected side. Immobilize the fracture and support the fingers and wrist with a dynamic splint until the fracture has healed.

Use **to lift** up (one's face/ eyes) / sth. off the ground • heavy / weight[12] **lifting** • neck / chin / face[13] **lift** • **to elevate the** foot[14] / scapula[15] / head of the bed • **elevated** extremity / blood pressure[16] / diaphragm[17] [daɪəfræm] • heel / leg / head / eyelid **elevation** • **to carry** heavy loads [oʊ]/ a burden [ɜː]/ a patient / a risk[18] / an incision [sɪ] (up to) • arch[19] [ɑːrtʃ]/ brace [breɪs]/ elastic **support** • emotional / life[20] / ventilatory[21] **support** • **supporting** ligaments / tissues[22] • **supportive** appliances [aɪ]/ measures[23] [eʒ]/ care • **support** suture[24] / stockings / garment / group[25] • **to raise** your arm (overhead) / the bite[26] • leg **raising** • **raised** borders[27] / plaques [plæks]/ titer [aɪ]

> Note: Mark the difference between **to raise** and **to rise**[28] (rose - risen) and between **carry** (objects), **wear** (clothes) and **bear** (body weight).

(hoch)heben
erhöhen, hochlagern[1] (an)heben[2] tragen[3] (unter)stützen[4] Heben[5] Straffung; Aufzug, Lift[6] Anhebung, Erhöhung[7] Halt, Stütze[8] Pressen[9] Fersenpolster[10] Esmarch-Handgriff[11] Gewichtheben[12] Gesichtshautstraffung, Face lifting[13] den Fuß hochlagern[14] das Schulterblatt hochziehen/ heben[15] Bluthochdruck[16] Zwerchfellhochstand[17] mit einem Risiko behaftet sein[18] Schuheinlage[19] lebenserhaltende Maßnahmen[20] Atemhilfe[21] Stützgewebe[22] unterstützende Maßnahmen[23] Haltenaht[24] Selbsthilfegruppe[25] d. Biss heben[26] erhabene Ränder[27] aufstehen, ansteigen[28]

16

restless adj clin & term → U113-2   sim **fidgety**[1] [fɪdʒɪti], **fretful**[2] adj inf

(i) hyperactive, always in motion and unable to keep still
(ii) nervous [ɜː] and anxious [æŋkʃəs]

rest[3] [rest] v & n • **resting**[4] adj • **restful**[5] adj • **restlessness**[6] n • **fidget**[7] v → U76-8

» Why don't you take a rest now. Put the patient on bed rest[8] and elevate the limb [lɪm]. The patient is anxious and restless, and attempts to relieve the pain by moving about in bed. The patient appears anxious, restless, and fidgety.

Use **restless** patient / sleep • **resting** position[9] / (muscle) activity • **resting** pressure (abbr RP) tremor[10] • **to be**[11]/occur [ɜː] **at rest** • **rest** period / pain[12] / and exercise balance • (strict) bed / arm[13] / foot[14] **rest** • motor[15] / feeling of **restlessness**

unruhig, rastlos, hyperaktiv
zappelig[1] quengelig[2] ruhen; s. auf etw. stützen; Ruhe, Pause[3] Ruhe-[4] ruhig, erholsam[5] Unruhe, Ruhelosigkeit[6] zappeln[7] Bettruhe[8] Ruhelage, -stellung[9] Ruhetremor[10] in Ruhelage sein[11] Ruheschmerz[12] Armlehne[13] Fußstütze[14] motor. Unruhe[15]

17

physical activity n

rel **exercise**[1], **workout**[2], **training**[2] [eɪ] n clin → U1-12

things people [iː] do (work, sports) involving movement, esp. exerting the muscles to keep fit (**hyper/ in**)**active** adj term • **inactivity**[3] n • **exercise**[4] v • **train**[4] v • **trainer** n

» Walking to the bus is the only exercise I get. Don't exercise to the point of fatigue[5] [fətiːg]. How much weight [weɪt] do you lose in an hour's workout? Women who engage in vigorous [ɪ] athletic [e] training often have low sex hormone levels.

Use muscle / leisure[6] [liːʒɚ] **activity** • isometric / passive / active assisted **exercise** • warm-up[7] / progressive resistance **exercise** • low intensity / forward bending **exercise** • stretching[8] [tʃ]/ (full) weight-bearing[9] [eɚ] **exercise** • **to exercise** your muscles • aerobic / high stress / vigorous[10] / light **workout** • **to train** hard • gait[11] [eɪ]/ physical [fɪzɪkᵊl]/ endurance[12] [(j)ʊɚ]/ relaxation **training** • autogenic / toilet[13] / assertiveness[14] [ɜː] **training**

exertion [ɪgzɜːrʃᵊn] n   sim (**physical**) **effort**[1] [fɪzɪkᵊl ɛfɚt] n
rel **exhaustion**[2] [ɪgzɒːstʃᵊn] n,
strain[3] [eɪ] n & v → U5-17

to try or work hard, use much effort or physical or mental energy to achieve a goal [oʊ] **exert**[4] [ɪgzɜːrt] vt & ref • **exertional**[5] adj • **overexertion**[6] n • **exhausted**[7] adj **inexhaustible** [ɒː] adj • **strenuous**[8] [strɛnjʊəs] adj • **effortless** adj

» Avoid exertion that involves straining [eɪ] the upper extremity muscles. The patient complains of feeling fatigued [iː] and exhausted and waking up tired. Avoid pushing yourself to the point of exhaustion and collapse.

Use physical [ɪ]/ vigorous[9] / worsened [ɜː] by **exertion** • strenuous[9] / patient / respiratory[10] / (un)sustained[11] [eɪ] **effort** • **effort**-dependent / fatigue [fətiːg]/ dyspnea[12] [dɪspnɪə] • **effort** thrombosis / migraine[13] [eɪ]/ intolerance • chest pain / shortness of breath [e] or dyspnea[12] **on exertion** • **to exert** your body / muscles / influence[14] • **exertional** activity[15] / headache • **exertional** muscle pain / in nature • **strenuous** activity[15] / exercise • physical[16] / heat[17] / nervous [ɜː] **exhaustion** (low) back / muscle[18] / ligamentous[19] **strain**

Unit 65   Walking & Locomotion
Related Units: 64 Body Movement, 31 Musculoskeletal Function, 5 Injuries
63 Posture, 113 Neurologic Findings, 142 Physical Therapy

walk [wɒːk] v & n   sim **hike**[1] [haɪk] v & n, **ambulation**[2] [æmbjəleɪʃᵊn] n term

(v) to move along by alternately placing one foot in front of the other
ambulate v term • **ambulatory**[3] adj •
walking[4] adj & n • **walker**(**ette**)[5] n

» You will be able to walk about[6] in comfort immediately [iː] after the procedure [siː]. I can tell him by his walk. If postural hypotension is detected, ambulation should be allowed with caution [ɒː]. The patient ambulates with minimal assistance. After the fractures have healed [iː], we will start you on a supervised [uː] exercise program that includes daily walking. The patient was ambulatory with a walker within a few days after surgery.

Use **to walk** barefoot [beɚfʊt]/ **on** level ground[7] [aʊ]/ uphill[8] / unaided [eɪ] • **to walk** to tolerance[9] / a straight [streɪt] line / with a cane[10] [keɪn] • to go for a[11] / to take a short / unsteady[12] [e] **walk** • tandem[13] / inability to / brisk[14] **walk** • to go on or take **a hike** • brisk[15] / difficulty[16] / toe-**walking** [oʊ] • heel-to-toe[17] [iː]/ crutch[18] [krʌtʃ]/ sleep[19] **walking** • **walking** shoes[20] / cast[21] / heel or piece[22] / aid[5] • early[23] / gradual / full **ambulation** • (non-)weight-bearing[24] [weɪt beɚɪŋ] indoor / independent **ambulation** • **to ambulate** without difficulty / with crutches • to be[25]/become (**non-**)**ambulatory** • **ambulatory** patient / elderly / on crutches • **ambulatory** monitoring[26] / care[27] / baby**walker**[28]

Bewegung, körperliche Tätigkeit/ Aktivität
Übung, Bewegung[1] Training[2] Untätigkeit, Inaktivität[3] üben, trainieren[4] Erschöpfung[5] Freizeitbeschäftigung[6] Aufwärmübung[7] Dehnungsübung[8] Belastungsübung[9] intensives/ hartes Training[10] Gehschule[11] Ausdauertraining[12] Sauberkeitserziehung[13] Selbstbewusstseinstraining[14]

18

Anstrengung, Belastung
(körperl.) Anstrengung/ Einsatz, Bemühung, Mühe[1] Erschöpfung[2] Belastung; über-, belasten[3] ausüben; sich anstrengen[4] anstrengend; Belastungs-[5] Überanstrengung[6] erschöpft[7] anstrengend[8] große Anstrengung/ Belastung[9] Atemarbeit[10] anhaltende/ hartnäckige Bemühungen[11] Belastungsdyspnoe[12] belastungsbedingte Migräne[13] Einfluss ausüben[14] anstrengende Tätigkeit[15] körperl. Erschöpfung[16] Hitzeerschöpfung[17] Muskelzerrung[18] Bänderzerrung[19]

19

(spazieren) gehen, laufen, wandern;
(Spazier)gang, Fußmarsch
wandern; Wanderung[1] Umher-, Herumgehen[2] gehfähig, mobil; ambulant[3] Geh-, Lauf-, Schritt-; (Spazieren) gehen, Wandern[4] Gehhilfe[5] herumgehen[6] im Ebenen gehen[7] bergauf gehen[8] gehen solange es erträglich ist[9] am Stock gehen[10] spazieren gehen, e. Spaziergang machen[11] unsicherer Gang[12] Tandem-Gang[13] flotter Fußmarsch[14] rasches Gehen, Walken[15] Beschwerden b. Gehen[16] Ferse-Zehen-Gang[17] Gehen an Krücken[18] Schlafwandeln[19] Wanderschuhe[20] Gehgips[21] Gehstollen, Sohlenplatte[22] Frühmobilisation[23] Gehen ohne Belastung[24] gehfähig sein[25] ambulante Überwachung[26] ambulante Betreuung[27] Laufgestell[28]

1

Walking & Locomotion   COMPLEX BODY FUNCTIONS **261**

gait [geɪt] n clin & term   rel **locomotion**[1] [loʊkəmoʊʃən] n term

pattern of locomotion which may be changed by altered [ɔː] weight distribution, lack of mobility, etc.

locomotor[2] adj term

» Abnormalities of gait and balance were evaluated with the patient's eyes open and closed. His symptoms [I] include ataxic wide-based gait[3] and footslap[4] as well as loss of position. He has trouble [ʌ] maintaining [eɪ] balance in locomotion.

Use swaying[5] [eɪ]/ spastic [æ]/ ataxic[6] / staggering or reeling[5] [iː] **gait** • slow / waddling[7] / heel-toe **gait** • double-step [ʌ]/ swing-through[8] **gait** • scissor[9] [s]/ high-stepping or steppage[4] [stepɪdʒ] / antalgic[10] **gait** • in-toed[11] / shuffling[12] [ʌ]/ short-stepped or festinating[13] **gait** • **gait** analysis / disturbance[14] [ɜː]/ unsteadiness[15] [e] • **gait** ataxia[16] / training • cell / directed / reduced [(j)uːs] **locomotion** • **locomotor** ataxia[17]

Gang(art)

(Fort)bewegung, Lokomotion[1] lokomotorisch, Bewegungs-[2] breitbeiniger Gang[3] Steppergang, Hahnentritt[4] schwankender/ torkelnder/ taumelnder Gang[5] ataktischer G.[6] Watschel-, Entengang[7] Gang mit Durchschwingen d. Beine[8] Scherengang[9] antalgischer Gang[10] Innenrotationsgang[11] schlurfender G.[12] kleinschrittiger/ trippelnder Gang[13] Gangstörung[14] Unsicherheit b. Gehen[15] Gangataxie[16] lokomotor. Ataxie, Bewegungsstörungen[17]   2

---

stance [stænˈs] n   sim **station**[1] [eɪʃ] n term, **stand**[2] - stood - stood n & v irr clin

(i) the standing position at a particular moment
(ii) attitude toward a particular issue

standing adj • **stationary**[3] [eɪ] adj • **standstill**[4] n • **standpoint**[5] n

» He altered [ɔː] his stance and stood with his feet apart. During the stance phase[6] [eɪz] (strike of the heel on the ground till lift off of the toe) the leg and foot bear all of the body weight. If postural sense[7] is deranged [eɪ], the patient is unable to stand with his feet together and eyes closed. Tandem walking and standing and hopping on each foot are tests of station and gait.

Use to take up a[8] **stance** • normal / abnormality of / single limb [lɪm] **stance** • **stance** time / phase • proper / abnormal **station** • **to stand** still / straight [streɪt]/ aside[9] [aɪ] • **to stand** back[9] / up / by sb.[10] • **standing** balance / height [haɪt]/ position[11]

(i) (Körper)haltung
(ii) Einstellung

Stellung, Lage, Stand[1] Stand(punkt), Einstellung; stehen[2] stillstehend, stationär; unverändert[3] Stillstand[4] Standpunkt[5] Standphase (b. Gehen)[6] Lageempfindung[7] eine Haltung einnehmen[8] zur Seite treten, (tatenlos) danebenstehen[9] beistehen, s. bereithalten[10] aufrechte Körperhaltung, Orthostase[11]   3

---

step n & v   sim **stride**[1] - strode - strode/stridden [straɪd stroʊd strɪdən] n & v irr

(n, i) changing location by raising the foot and setting it down again
(ii) horizontal part of a staircase

footsteps[2] n • **stepping** adj • **stepwise**[3] adj • **steppage gait**[4] n term

» Why don't you take a couple [ʌ] of steps on the corridor. Inability to initiate [ɪʃ] and coordinate steps in a sequential fashion is termed apraxia. Move up a step, please. He fails to swing his arms with the stride.

Use to take a/be in[5]/be out of/mind the[6]/watch one's[7] **step** • **step** by step[3] • forward / the first (tentative)[8] / faltering [ɔː] or halting[9] [ɔː] dance **steps** • to follow in sb.'s[10] **footsteps** • **to step** on sb.'s foot / aside / over an obstacle • **stepping** reflex[11] • high **steppage** gait[4] • **to stride** off[12] / across • with long **strides**

Schritt, Stufe; treten, steigen

(langer) Schritt, Gang; schreiten[1] Schritte, Fußstapfen[2] schritt-, stufenweise[3] Steppergang[4] im Gleichschritt/ Takt sein[5] Vorsicht Stufe[6] achtgeben[7] d. ersten (zaghaften) Schritte[8] zögernde/ zaghafte Schritte[9] in jem. Fußstapfen treten[10] Schreitreflex[11] sich mit schnellen Schritten entfernen[12]   4

---

tread - trod - trodden [tred] v irr   sim **trample**[1], **stomp**[2] [ɒː], **stamp**[2] v

(i) to put down or place the foot on the ground
(ii) to step on an object (and crush [krʌʃ] it)

tread[3] n • **treadmill**[4] [tredmɪl] n

» Unwary[5] [eə] victims may tread on stingrays[6] [eɪ] when they are wading[7] [eɪ] in the surf[8] [ɜː]. Stamp your feet to keep warm. He got trampled under[9] in the mass panic.

Use to tread on sb.'s toes / water[10] / with care[11] • heavy [e]/ limping[12] **tread** • to trample over sth. / to death[13] • to stamp one's foot[14] / on sth. / down • **treadmill** exercise / testing[15]

(auf)treten, gehen

niedertreten, zertrampeln[1] (auf)stampfen[2] Schritt, Tritt[3] Laufband[4] unvorsichtig[5] Stachelrochen[6] waten[7] Brandung[8] zu Boden getrampelt[9] Wasser treten[10] vorsichtig auftreten[11] Humpeln, Hinken[12] zu Tode trampeln[13] (m. d. Fuß auf-) stampfen[14] Laufbandergometrie[15]   5

---

pace [peɪs] n & v clin

(n, i) distance covered by one step (ii) speed of walking or running

pacing[1] [peɪsɪŋ] n & adj term • **pacesetter**[2] n • **pacemaker**[2] n → U123-13

» I heard him pacing up and down the waiting room. He is unable to walk at this pace for more than 3 min. You will have to pace yourself[3] carefully when you exercise. Restless patients with extrapyramidal syndromes [ɪ] often need to pace.

Use **to pace** a room • to keep[4]/quicken one's[5]/take a **pace** • to set the[6]/walk at your own **pace** • **pacing** impulse / catheter • cardiac **pacing** • cardiac[7] / permanent [ɜː]/ implantable **pacemaker**

Schritt, Tempo;
hin u. her/ auf und ab gehen

(nervöses) Herumgehen; Schrittmachertherapie; d. Rhythmus/ Tempo regulierend[1] Schrittmacher[2] d. richtige Tempo/ Belastung finden[3] Schritt halten (mit)[4] d. Schritt beschleunigen[5] d. Tempo bestimmen[6] Herzschrittmacher[7]   6

65

stroll [stroʊl] v & n   syn **amble** [æ], **saunter** [ɔː], **wander** [ɒː] v & n

(v) to walk slowly and in a relaxed way (n) a relaxed walk for recreational [ieɪʃ] purposes [ɜː]

» *Just stroll along the beach after work. Why don't you go for a saunter in the park. You could just amble along the garden paths for a while.*

Use **to take a¹ stroll** • leisurely² [iːʒ‖BE eʒ] **stroll** • **to go for a¹ saunter** • **to saunter along**

schlendern, bummeln; Spaziergang, Bummel
einen Spaziergang/ Bummel machen¹ gemächliches Schlendern²

7

tiptoe [tɪptoʊ] v   rel **sneak¹** [sniːk], **crawl²** [krɒːl], **glide³** [glaɪd] v
rel **creep⁴** [kriːp] - crept - crept, **slide⁵** [slaɪd] - slid - slid [ɪ] v irr

to walk on the tips of one's toes, esp. in order to make as little noise as possible

sneakers⁶ n pl • **crawling⁷** n • **crawl⁸** n • **sliding⁹** [aɪ] adj

» *She tiptoed out very gently [dʒe] while he slept. Can you walk over here on tiptoes? About 25% of affected infants learn to sit, and none to crawl or walk. Cautiously [ɒːʃ] slide your hand under the patient's back. The louse [aʊ] was found crawling among pubic hair. The cruciate [uːʃ] ligaments restrict anteroposterior gliding of the tibia when the knee is flexed.*

Use **to tiptoe** across the hall • to stand/walk¹⁰ **on tiptoe(s)** • **to sneak** out of the room / sth. into a room¹¹ • **to sneak** a look at sth.¹² • **to creep** up on sb.¹³ • **crawling** baby¹⁴ / insect / sensation [eɪ] • **to slide** backward • **sliding** door / scale¹⁵ / hernia¹⁶ [ɜː]/ flap¹⁷

auf Zehenspitzen gehen
schleichen¹ krabbeln² gleiten³ kriechen⁴ rutschen, schieben, schlittern⁵ Freizeit-, Tennisschuhe⁶ Krabbeln⁷ Kraul(en) (Schwimmart)⁸ gleitend, Schiebe-⁹ auf Zehenspitzen gehen¹⁰ etw. in ein Zimmer schmuggeln¹¹ verstohlen auf etw. schielen¹² langsam auf jem. zukommen¹³ Krabbelkind¹⁴ Balkenwaage¹⁵ Gleithernie, -bruch¹⁶ Verschiebelappen¹⁷

8

stagger [stægɚ] v   rel **lurch¹** [lɜːrtʃ] v & n, **stumble²** [ʌ], **trip²** v

to walk in an unsteady [e] and uncontrolled way (e.g. when drunk) or with difficulty

staggering adj & n • **stumbling** [ʌ] adj & n • **tripping** adj & n

» *He clutched³ [ʌ] his chest and staggered back to bed. Ankle sprains⁴ are most commonly caused by stumbling on uneven⁵ [iː] ground. I was lurched forward when the car came to a sudden stop.*

Use **to stagger** about⁶ / to the nearest chair • **to lurch** from side to side⁷ • to give a⁸ **lurch** • **to stumble** and fall / about / around / on a wet surface [ɜː] • **stumbling** gait / block⁹ • **to trip** over an object

torkeln; taumeln, wanken
torkeln, ruckartig bewegen; Ruck, Schlingern¹ stolpern² griff sich an³ Knöchelverstauchungen⁴ uneben⁵ herumtorkeln⁶ hin und her taumeln/ torkeln⁷ einen Ruck machen⁸ Stolperstein, Hindernis⁹

9

waddle [wɒdl] v   rel **toddle¹** [tɒdl], **totter²** [tɒtɚ], **wriggle³** [rɪgl] v

to walk unsteadily with short steps swinging the body from one side to the other

toddler⁴ n • **waddling** adj • **tottering** adj • **wriggle** n

» *The waddling gait in these children is compensated in later years. Closely supervise⁵ toddlers during recreational [eɪʃ] boating. The boy is starting to wriggle in his seat. In her new high-heeled [iː] shoes⁶ the girl tottered unsteadily down the stairs.*

Use **waddling** gait⁷ • **toddler** years / development • **to wriggle** one's toes⁸ / out of a tight [aɪt] pullover / free • **tottering** steps • **wriggling** movements⁹

watscheln
wackelig gehen (Kleinkind)¹ tapsen, taumeln² zappeln, sich winden³ Kleinkind⁴ beaufsichtigen⁵ Stöckelschuhe⁶ Watschelgang⁷ mit d. Zehen wackeln⁸ choreatische Bewegungen⁹

10

limp [lɪmp] v & n & adj   rel **hobble¹** [ɒː], **shuffle²** [ʃʌfl] v, **lame³** [leɪm] adj & v
rel **festination⁴** [festɪneɪʃᵊn] n term

to walk with difficulty as a result of an injured leg or a physical [ɪ] handicap or limitation

limping n • **shuffling** adj • **lameback⁵** n • **festinating⁶** adj term

» *Loss of power in the lower limb manifests itself by a limp or by a dragging⁷ of the leg. She hobbled toward the ambulance. It caused pain of the hip joints and limping.*

Use **to limp** to the car /badly⁸ • to have a (slight) [slaɪt]/ walk with a⁹ **limp** • to feel¹⁰/go **limp** • **limp** wrist [rɪst]/ handshake¹¹ • **festinating** gait⁴ • **to hobble** along / about • **lame** leg¹²

hinken, humpeln; Hinken; schlaff
humpeln¹ schlurfen² lahm; lahmen³ Trippelgang, Festination⁴ Hyperkyphose, verstärkte K.⁵ trippelnd⁶ Nachziehen⁷ stark hinken⁸ hinken, humpeln⁹ s. schlapp fühlen¹⁰ schlaffer Händedruck¹¹ lahmes Bein¹²

11

tumble [tʌmbl] v   sim **slip¹**, **skid²** [skɪd] v, **fall³** - fell - fallen v irr → U6-4
rel **collapse⁴** [kəlæps] v & n, **break down⁴** v phr

(i) fall suddenly or cause sb. to fall down
(ii) roll and turn on the floor skillfully (as in judo [dʒuːdoʊ] or gymnastics [dʒɪm-])

tumbling n & adj • **tumble⁵** n • **fall⁵** n • **breakdown** [breɪkdaʊn] n → U7-4

» *I lost balance, tumbled over and fell on my wrist⁶. Don't skid on the ice. Most forearm fractures are associated with a history of a fall on an outstretched arm.*

Use **to tumble** over / down • to have³ **a tumble** • **to slip** away / on the ice / off one's shirt⁷ • **slipped** disk⁸ / **hernia⁹** [ɜː]/ meniscus • **slipped** capital femoral [e] epiphysis¹⁰ • **slipping** ribs / patella¹¹ • **to skid** on oil • **to collapse** with exhaustion¹² [ɒː]/ under the weight [weɪt] • circulatory [ɜː] or cardiovascular¹³ / respiratory / lung or pulmonary [ʊ‖ʌ] **collapse** • nervous¹⁴ [ɜː]/ emotional [oʊʃ]/ skin¹⁵ **breakdown** • to take/have³ **a fall**

**(i) straucheln, fallen, stürzen
(ii) Bodenakrobatik machen**
(aus)rutschen; schlüpfen¹ schleudern, ausrutschen² stürzen³ zusammenbrechen, kollabieren; Kollaps⁴ Sturz⁵ Handgelenk⁶ d. Hemd ausziehen⁷ Bandscheibenvorfall⁸ Gleithernie⁹ Epiphyseolysis capitis femoris¹⁰ tanzende Patella¹¹ vor Erschöpfung zusammenbrechen¹² Kreislaufkollaps¹³ (Nerven)zusammenbruch¹⁴ Hautschädigung¹⁵

12

Walking & Locomotion　　COMPLEX BODY FUNCTIONS **263**

stalk [stɒːk] v　syn **strut** [strʌt], **swagger** [swæɡəʳ] v

to walk in a stiff, a̱ngry or proud [aʊ] and pompous¹ [pɒːmpəs] way

stalk² n term • **strut**³ n • **swagger**⁴ n clin • **swa̱ggering**⁵ adj

» He sta̱rted to yell [jel] a̱t⁶ the nurse [ɜː] and stalked out of the room. He was strutting aro̱und in my office as if he owned the place. He came in with his u̱sual impertinent swagger.

Use **to stalk** out of a mee̱ting • **to strut** aro̱und / your stuff⁷ [ʌ]/ past⁸ • **to swagger** abo̱ut⁹ / forward • pitu̱itary¹⁰ [(j)uː]/ conne̱ctive ti̱ssue **stalk** • sta̱inless [eɪ] steel¹¹ / pla̱stic **strut** • **struts** of bone¹² • **swa̱ggering** self-co̱nfidence / youngster

jog [dʒɒːɡ] v & n

sim **run**¹ - ran - run v irr & n, **trot**² [trɒːt], **march**³ [mɑːrtʃ] v & n

to run at a moderately swift pace, esp. for exercise

jogger n • **jogging** n → U1-14 • **runner** n • **do̱gtrot**⁴ n

» Are you coming for a 30-minute jog? Neither jogging nor long-di̱stance runni̱ng⁵ have been shown to be rela̱ted to osteoarthri̱tis [aɪ]. Runners push off⁶ from their toes, which puts great stress on their first metata̱rsal heads.

Use **to jog** down the road / in place • to go for a **jog** • **jog**-trot⁷ • **to run** abo̱ut⁸ / aro̱und the room • **to run** after sb.⁹ / awa̱y from home / o̱ver sb.¹⁰ • **jogging** craze¹¹ [eɪ]/ suit¹² [suːt]/ shoes • to break into a¹³ **run** • long-di̱stance / re̱gular / fast **running** • uphill / downhill **running** • trained / mara̱thon **runner** • **march** foot or fra̱cture¹⁴

rush [rʌʃ] v　sim **sprint**¹, **dart**¹, **dash**¹, **race**², **hasten**³ [heɪsᵊn], **hurry**³ v

to move fast or hurriedly or to urge [ɜːrdʒ] others to speed [iː] up

haste⁴ [heɪst] n • **ha̱sty**⁵ adj • **hurry**⁴ [ɜː|‖BE ʌ] n • **rush**⁶ n clin & term

» You should not be rushing about so much. He must be rushed to the OR imme̱diately. Don't try to rush the pro̱cess. I felt a sudden rush of di̱zziness⁷. I hate to hu̱rry you now. Early a̱ctive mo̱tion [oʊʃ] e̱xercises within the li̱mits of to̱lerance will ha̱sten recove̱ry [ʌ].

Use **to rush** through work⁸ / for an e̱mpty seat / sb. to the do̱ctor⁹ • **to hasten** to say / sb.'s death¹⁰ / recove̱ry / elimina̱tion • to make/do sth. in a **haste** • **to hurry** up¹¹ / on / alo̱ng / back • to be in a/no (great) **hurry** • to make a **rush** for the door¹² • adre̱naline¹³ **rush** • blood¹⁴ [ʌ]/ obstru̱ctive [ʌ]/ perista̱ltic¹⁵ **rushes**

jump [ʌ] v　syn **leap** [liːp] - le(a)pt - le(a)pt [e] v irr,

sim **hop**¹, **skip**², **startle**³ [ɑː] v

(i) to move forward by leaps and bounds (ii) to move off the ground

jump⁴ n clin • **leap**⁴ [liːp] n • **skipping**⁵ n • **sta̱rtling**⁶ adj • **sta̱rtle**⁷ n

» The fra̱cture was caused by a sudden jump on the ball of the foot⁸. I leapt aside to avoid a crash. At age 4 children a̱lternate feet going up and down stairs, hop on one foot, and throw a ball ove̱rhand. Skipping is my favorite e̱xercise. He may sta̱rtle to a loud noise.

Use **to jump** down from a height [haɪt]/ up / to your feet / on sb. • high / long⁹ **jump** • **to hop** down a few steps / out of bed • **skipping** rope¹⁰ • **to leap** from a window / into air / forward • to take a¹¹ (huge) [hjuːdʒ] **leap** • qua̱ntum¹² **leap** • ea̱sily¹³ **sta̱rtled** • **sta̱rtle** re̱flex¹⁴ / response or reaction¹⁵ / disea̱se¹⁶ • **sta̱rtled** awa̱kening [eɪ] • **sta̱rtling** news

rise [raɪz] - rose [oʊ] - risen v irr

sim **stand up**¹, **get up**¹ v phr, rel **raise**² [reɪz] v→ U116-19

(i) to move from a lying or sitting position to standing (ii) to get out of bed (iii) to increase

arise³ [əraɪz] v irr • **riser** [raɪzəʳ] n • **rise**⁴ n • **raised**⁵ [reɪzd] adj • **ra̱ising** n

» She had difficulty rising from the chair. When do you usually rise in the morning? Instruct [ʌ] patients to stand up gradually and use support stockings⁶. He had to get up to void⁷ [vɔɪd] every two hours. The cremasteric [kriː-] vessels arise from the inferior epigastric vessels. These tumors typically arise in the cerebellum.

Use **to rise** to your feet / from your chair / from the dead • **Rise** and shine!⁸ • **to get up** from bed / out of a chair • **to raise** the leg⁹ / a question / fears [fɪəʳz] • **to raise** the heart rate¹⁰ / a child • late¹¹ / early¹² **riser** • **raised** plaque [plæk‖ɑːk]/ bo̱rders¹³ / blood pre̱ssure¹⁴ • **raised** toi̱let seat / as fe̱males • straight [streɪt] leg **raising**

---

stolzieren, tänzeln

arrogant¹ Stiel² Strebe, Pfeiler³ Stolzieren; Großtuerei⁴ forsch; angeberisch⁵ anschreien⁶ aufschneiden, e. Show abziehen⁷ vorbeistolzieren⁸ herumstolzieren⁹ Hypophysenstiel¹⁰ Edelstahlbolzen¹¹ Knochenbälkchen¹²

13

joggen, trotten; Dauerlauf

laufen; Lauf¹ traben; Trab² marschieren; (Fuß)marsch³ gemächlicher Trott⁴ Langstreckenlauf⁵ s. abstoßen⁶ gemächlicher Trab, Trott⁷ herumlaufen⁸ jem. nachlaufen⁹ jem. überfahren¹⁰ Lauffimmel¹¹ Jogginganzug¹² zu laufen beginnen¹³ Deutschländerfraktur, Marschfraktur¹⁴

14

eilen, hetzen; drängen

sprinten, spurten¹ rasen, hetzen; um d. Wette laufen² s. beeilen, (zur Eile) antreiben; beschleunigen³ Hast, Eile⁴ hastig; voreilig⁵ Eile; Andrang; Anfall⁶ Schwindelanfall⁷ d. Arbeit hastig erledigen⁸ jem. mögl. rasch z. Arzt bringen⁹ zu einem vorzeitigen Tod führen¹⁰ sich beeilen¹¹ zur Tür drängen¹² Adrenalinausstoß¹³ Wallungen¹⁴ Bauchknurren, Borborygmus¹⁵

15

springen, hüpfen

springen, hopsen¹ (über)springen; auslassen² auf-, erschrecken³ Satz, Sprung⁴ Seilspringen⁵ bestürzend; aufregend, sensationell⁶ Schreck⁷ Fußballen⁸ Weitsprung⁹ Sprungseil¹⁰ e. Satz machen¹¹ Quantensprung¹² schreckhaft¹³ Moro-(Umklammerungs)reflex¹⁴ Schreckreaktion¹⁵ Hyperekplexie¹⁶

16

(i, ii) sich erheben, aufstehen (iii) (an)steigen

aufstehen¹ erhöhen, heben; aufziehen² entstehen, s. ergeben; s. erheben; ausgehen von³ Erhöhung, Anstieg, Zunahme⁴ erhöht; großgezogen; erhaben⁵ Stützstrümpfe⁶ urinieren⁷ Raus aus den Federn!⁸ d. Bein heben⁹ d. Herzfrequenz erhöhen¹⁰ Langschläfer(in)¹¹ Frühsteher(in)¹² erhabene Ränder¹³ erhöhter Blutdruck¹⁴

17

climb [klaɪm] v sim **scramble**[1] [skræmbl]**, clamber**[1] [klæmbɚ] v

to move with difficulty (esp. upward by grasping [æ]) on a ladder, rock, hill, etc.

climber[2] n clin • **climbing**[3] n & adj • **scramble**[4] n

» He can climb stairs when holding on to the rails[5] [eɪ]. The baby tried to climb out of his playpen[6]. Ann scrambled out of bed. She scrambled up the hillside and over the rocks.

Use **to climb** up and down stairs / a mountain / onto the table • **to scramble** to one's feet[7] / up the hill • **to clamber** into bed / onto the bus • rock[8] / high **climbing** • **climbing** steps or stairs[9] / frame[10] [eɪ] • social[11] **climber**

klettern, steigen

krabbeln, kraxeln, drängeln, s. aufrappeln[1] Bergsteiger(in), Kletterer(in)[2] Bergsteigen, Klettern; Kletter-[3] Klettertour[4] Treppen-, Stiegengeländer[5] Laufstall[6] sich aufrappeln[7] Felsklettern[8] Treppen-, Stiegensteigen[9] Klettergerüst[10] Emporkömmling[11]

18

Unit 66 Human Sounds & Speech
Related Units: 26 Teeth, 21 Head & Neck, 44 Respiration, 61 Hearing, 67 Gestures, 113 Neurologic Findings

utter [ʌ] v sim **articulate**[1] v term

to make a sound with your voice (includes verbal expression[2] but also shouts[3] [aʊ], laughter [læftɚ], cries[4], and other human sounds)

utterance[5] n • **articulation**[6] n term • **(in)articulate**[7] adj

» His verbal utterances include unassociated rambling statements[8]. Their speech [spiːtʃ] is well-articulated but has little content. The patient is clear and articulate[9].

Use poor / compensatory / place of **articulation** • compulsive / involuntary / phrase length [leŋᵏθ] **utterances**

äußern, Laute hervorbringen

artikulieren, deutlich (aus)sprechen[1] verbale Äußerung[2] Rufe[3] Schreie[4] Sprechweise, (stimmliche) Äußerung[5] Sprechlautbildung, Artikulation[6] deutlich artikuliert, verständlich[7] unzusammenhängendes Gefasel[8] drückt s. klar u. deutlich aus[9]

1

laugh [læf] v & n → U67-9 sim **giggle**[1], **snicker**[1], **chuckle**[2] [tʃʌkᵊl], **roar**[3] [ɔː], **howl**[4] [haʊl] v inf

(v) to smile and make the typical guttural [ʌ] sounds[5] to express amusement or pleasure[6] [e₃]

laughter[7] n • **laughable**[8] adj • **giggly**[9] [gɪgli] adj

» The symptoms include uncontrollable crying and laughter. Coughing[10] [kɒf-], straining[11] [eɪ], sneezing[12] [iː] and laughing brought on[13] severe [-ɪɚ] headaches.

Use to have to/make sb./be a[14]/raise [reɪz] a[15] **laugh** • belly[16] **laugh** • **to laugh** softly[17] / out loud / one's head off[18] / at[19] sb. or a joke / about sth. • to burst [ɜː] out[3] **laughing** • **to roar** with laughter[20] • roaring / hysterical / nervous **laughter**

lachen; Lachen

kichern[1] kichern, in sich hineinlachen[2] schallend lachen[3] (vor L.) brüllen; heulen[4] Guttural-, Kehllaute[5] Vergnügen, Freude[6] Gelächter[7] lächerlich[8] albern[9] Husten[10] Pressen[11] Niesen[12] verursachte[13] urkomisch sein[14] Gelächter ernten[15] dröhnendes L.[16] leise lachen[17] sich totlachen[18] lachen über[19] vor Lachen brüllen[20]

2

sob [sɒb] v & n sim **weep** [iː] - wept - wept[1] v irr, **cry**[1], **whimper**[2], **wail**[3] [eɪ] v → U67-10

(v) to weep in convulsive [ʌ] gasps[4] with or without shedding tears[5] [tɪɚz]

» The child was sobbing her heart out[6]. She called the ambulance, her voice choked [tʃoʊkt] with sobs[7].

Use **to sob** bitterly[6] / oneself to sleep • to let out a[8] / choking / bitter **sob** • to have a good[9] **weep**

schluchzen; Schluchzen

weinen[1] wimmern[2] jammern, klagen[3] krampfartiges Keuchen[4] Tränen vergießen[5] bitterlich/ herzzerreißend weinen[6] m. tränenerstickter Stimme[7] aufschluchzen[8] sich ausweinen[9]

Note: Mark the two meanings of **cry** and **crying**, (i) to break out in tears, and (ii) to shout. → U66-14

3

sigh [saɪ] v & n sim **moan**[1] [moʊn], **groan**[1] [oʊ] v & n

(v) breathe [briːð] heavily [e] and exhale audibly[2] [ɔː] to express sadness, boredom[3], etc.

» She sat down with a sigh. The baby's breathing movements resembled[4] a deep sigh. Sighing is a common sign of neurasthenic [nʊɚ-] pain. She woke us up moaning and groaning.

Use to let out[5]/give[5]/heave[5] [iː] **a sigh** • (in)audible[6] **sigh** • **sigh** of relief[7] [iː]

seufzen; Seufzer

stöhnen, klagen; Stöhnen, Ächzen[1] (deutlich) hörbar ausatmen[2] Langeweile[3] ähnlich sein[4] e. Seufzer ausstoßen[5] leiser/ lauter Seufzer[6] Seufzer der Erleichterung[7]

4

snore [snɔːr] v & n rel **snort**[1], **grunt**[2] [ʌ] v & n

(v) to breathe noisily while sleeping due to vibration of the soft palate[3]

» Loud snores were coming from her bedroom. Is there a cure[4] for snoring? An estimated 25% of the adult male population and 15% of the adult female population snore every night. A loud snort accompanies the first breath following an apneic episode.

Use loud / severe / severity [e] of / cyclical [saɪk-]/ habitual / chronic **snoring** • heavy [e] **snorer** • **snore** guard[5] [gɑːrd] • **to snort** with laughter

schnarchen; Schnarchen

(wütend) schnauben, prusten; Schnauben[1] knurren, ächzen, brummen, grunzen; Ächzen[2] weicher Gaumen[3] (Heil)mittel[4] Nachtschiene[5]

5

Human Sounds & Speech COMPLEX BODY FUNCTIONS

sneeze [sniːz] v & n   rel **cough**[1] [kɒf] v & n, **to clear one's throat**[2] [θroʊt] phr

to exhale explosively because of a cold, irritants in the nose, etc.

» *The pain gets worse with sneezing. Advise the patient to avoid sneezing and blowing his nose[3]. The introduction of allergens into the nose is associated with sneezing, stuffiness[4] [ʌ] and nasal [eɪ] discharge[5] [dɪstʃɑːrdʒ]. Cats make her sneeze. When somebody sneezes you might say 'Bless you'[6].*

Use to cause/have a fit or paroxysm of[7] **sneezing** • episodic / violent[8] [aɪə]/ light-induced or photic / irrepressible[9] **sneezing** • **sneezing** fit[7] / reflex[10] • **sneezed** sputum [pjuː] • **sneeze**(-inducing) effect[11] • not to be **sneezed** at[12] • to have/give a **cough** • bad[13] / mild / productive / nonproductive or dry or hacking[14] **cough** • **to cough up** blood / phlegm[15] [flem] • **cough** reflex / syrup

niesen; Niesen

husten, Husten[1] sich räuspern[2] s. die Nase putzen[3] Verstopftsein (d. Nase)[4] Nasensekret[5] Gesundheit[6] Niesanfall (haben)[7] heftiges N.[8] nicht unterdrückbares N.[9] Niesreflex[10] Niesreiz[11] nicht zu verachten[12] starker Husten[13] trockener/ unproduktiver H.[14] Schleim aushusten[15]

6

---

gargle [gɑːrgl] v & n

(v) rinse[1] one's throat with mouthwash[2] and/or make bubbling[3] sounds with the fluid

» *Gargling with saline[4] [eɪ] may remedy[5] a sore throat[6]. In these cases gargles or sprays of lidocaine [eɪ] should be used before intubation.*

gurgeln; Gurgeln, Gurgelmittel

spülen[1] Mundwasser[2] blubbernd[3] Kochsalzlösung[4] helfen bei[5] Halsschmerzen[6]

7

---

speak [iː] - spoke - spoken v irr   rel **communicate**[1], **vocalize**[2] v

express thoughts in language, e.g. to talk, mention[3] [-ʃən], remark[3], gossip[4], observe, suggest[5] [dʒ], imply[6] [aɪ], state, report, confirm[7] [ɜː], insist (on)[8], hint[9], deny[10] [aɪ], read out loud, etc.

speech[11] [spiːtʃ] n term • **communication** n • **communicative**[12] adj **vocalization**[13] n

» *Speech may have a nasal timbre[14] [tæmbɚ] caused by weakness of the palate. Symptoms of confusion, slurred [ɜː] speech[15], ataxia and inappropriate behavior are common.*

Use **to speak** up or louder / fluently[16] / distinctly[17] / coherently[18] [ɪə]/ frankly[19] • to deliver[20] a **speech** • **speaking** aids[21] • **speech** development[22] / output / pattern / disturbance[23] / arrest • **speech** center / perception[24] / discrimination / (-language) pathologist[25] / therapist[25] • (un)clear or (un)intelligible [-dʒɪbl]/ clipped or scanning[26] / spontaneous [eɪ]/ disorganized **speech** • purposeful / esophageal[27] [-dʒiːəl]/ absence of **speech** • **language** development / function • spoken / written / body / sign[28] **language** • **communicative** assessment • (non)verbal / level of / to encourage [ɜː] **communication** • **communication** skills[29]

sprechen

kommunizieren, s. verständigen[1] Ausdruck verleihen, vokalisieren[2] erwähnen, bemerken[3] tratschen[4] vorschlagen[5] andeuten, implizieren[6] bestätigen[7] beharren (auf)[8] hinweisen[9] bestreiten, leugnen[10] Sprache[11] mitteilsam, gesprächig[12] Vokalisation[13] Stimmklang, Timbre[14] verwaschene Sprache[15] fließend sprechen[16] deutlich spr.[17] zusammenhängend reden[18] offen/ ehrlich sagen[19] Rede halten[20] Sprechhilfen[21] Sprachentwicklung[22] Sprach-, Sprechstörung[23] Sprachverständnis[24] Logopäde/-in[25] abgehackte Sprechweise, skandierende Sprache[26] Ösophagusstimme[27] Zeichensprache[28] kommunikative Fähigkeiten[29]

8

---

log(o)- comb   rel **-phasia**[1] [feɪʒɪə], **-arthria**[2] comb

referring to language, speech or words

logopedics[3] [iː] n term • **aphasic**[4] [eɪ] adj • **dysarthric**[5] [ɪ] adj → U113-10

» *Logopedics or speech therapy[3] is the study and treatment of speech defects[6]. Speech output[7] is fluent but paraphasic[8]; comprehension of spoken language is intact. The paraphasic output in conduction aphasia interferes [ɪə] with[9] the ability to express meaning.*

Use logorrhea[10] [iːə] • conduction[11] / (non)fluent transcortical / global / anomic[12] / motor[13] **aphasia** • **aphasic** deficit / patient / syndrome • dys[14]/ para**phasia** • **paraphasic** speech • mild / marked / spastic[15] **dysarthria**

Wort-, Sprach-, Sprech-, Logo-

-phasie[1] -arthrie[2] Logopädie[3] aphasisch[4] dysarthrisch[5] Sprach-, Sprechstörungen[6] Sprachproduktion[7] paraphasisch[8] beeinträchtigt[9] Rededrang, Logorrhoe[10] Leitungsaphasie[11] amnestische A.[12] motor./ Broca-A.[13] Dysphasie[14] pyramidale/ spastische Dysarthrie[15]

9

---

voice n & v   rel **phonation**[1] [eɪ] n term

(n) sound produced by the vocal folds[2] and articulated in the vocal tract

voiced[3] adj • voiceless adj • vocal[4] adj • vocalist[5] n phonic[6] adj term • phon(o)-[7] comb

» *Her voice sounded nasal and she had difficulty swallowing[8] [ɒː]. His voice lowered to a whisper. The voice is 'breathy" when too much air passes incompletely apposed vocal cords, as in unilateral vocal cord paralysis.*

Use hoarse[9] [ɔː] • thick[10] / breathy [breθi]/ low[11] / deep **voice** • high-pitched[12] / hollow-sounding / squeaky[13] [skwiːki] **voice** / harsh[14] / poorly modulated / comforting[15] / (normal) spoken[16] **voice** • to lower[17]/raise/lose one's **voice** • **voice** is shaking or quivering[18] • **voice** box[19] / problem / change • to hear **voices** (within you) • **vocal** apparatus / folds / cords[20] / sounds • **phonic** tic / spasm[21] • **phon**ia-trics[22] /ology /etic /etics /eme /asthenia[23] [iː]

Stimme; zum Ausdruck bringen

Stimm-, Lautbildung[1] Stimmlippen[2] stimmhaft[3] Stimm-, vokal[4] Sänger(in)[5] Stimm-, phonisch[6] Laut-, Ton-, phono-[7] beim Schlucken[8] heisere Stimme[9] belegte St.[10] leise St.[11] hohe/ schrille St.[12] piepsende St.[13] raue St.[14] beruhigende St.[15] Sprechstimme[16] d. Stimme dämpfen[17] St. zittert[18] Kehlkopf[19] Stimmbänder[20] Stimmritzenkrampf, Laryngospasmus[21] Phoniatrie[22] Phonasthenie, Stimmschwäche[23]

10

Human Sounds & Speech

tone [toʊn] **(of voice)** *n*   *sim* **sound**¹ [saʊnd] *n & v* → U61-3

quality (including pitch² [tʃ], timbre, loudness or volume, etc.) of a person's voice

intonation³ *n term* • **overtone**⁴ *n* • **undertone**⁵ *n*

» Suddenly his tone of voice changed. The timbre of the voice depends on the size and shape of the resonating chambers⁶ [tʃeɪ-] (mouth, pharynx, nasal sinuses [aɪ], chest, etc.).

Use **in a(n)** harsh⁷ / normal / angry / subdued⁸ [uː]/ friendly / threatening⁹ [e] **tone** • **high-tone** range • **sound** substitution¹⁰ / discrimination¹¹ • in an⁸ **undertone**

Ton(fall,-höhe), Klang, Stimme
Laut, Schall, Ton, Geräusch; klingen, sondieren¹ Tonhöhe² Intonation, Sprach-, Satzmelodie³ Oberton (musik.), Unterton (fig.)⁴ Unterton; gedämpft⁵ Resonanzkörper⁶ in barschem/ scharfem Ton⁷ m. gedämpfter Stimme⁸ m. drohender St.⁹ Lautersatz¹⁰ Lautunterscheidung(svermögen)¹¹   11

---

syllable [sɪləbl] *n*

a unit of language consisting of several phonemes¹ [iː] (vowels² [aʊ] or consonants³)

monosyllabic⁴ *adj term & clin* • **syllable-stumbling**⁵ [ʌ] *n*

» The form of stuttering⁶ [ʌ] in which patients halt⁷ [ɒː] before certain syllables they find difficult to enunciate [ʌns] is termed syllable-stumbling or dyssyllabia⁵ [eɪ].

Silbe
Phoneme, (Einzel)laute¹ Vokale, Selbstlaute² Konsonanten³ einsilbig; wortkarg⁴ Silbenstolpern⁵ Stottern⁶ stocken⁷   12

---

pronunciation [ʌ] *n*   *sim* **phonation**¹, **enunciation**² [ʌ] *n term*

production of sounds in accordance with the phonetic system of a specific language (includes emphasis³, intonation, and accent⁴ [æksənt])

pronounce⁵ [aʊ] *v* • **enunciate**⁶ *v term* • **phonate**⁷ *v* • **phonetic** *adj*

» The alterations in phonation were due to obstruction. He enunciates each word carefully. She had difficulty segmenting words into pronounceable components.

Use **to pronounce** badly / properly • hard⁸ **to pronounce** • word **pronunciation** • normal **phonation** • **phonating** structure • **phonetically** balanced (*abbr* PB)

> **Note:** The word pronounced⁹ (adj) commonly appears in medical contexts as a synonym for marked⁹, e.g. Stiffness was more pronounced in the morning.

Aussprache
Laut-, Stimmbildung¹ Artikulation² Betonung³ Akzent, Tonfall⁴ aussprechen; erklären⁵ artikulieren⁶ Laute bilden, phonieren⁷ schwer auszusprechen⁸ deutlich, ausgeprägt⁹

13

---

shout [ʃaʊt] *v & n*   *syn* **cry, yell** [jel], **scream** [iː], **holler, shriek** [iː] *v & n inf*

to raise your voice when talking or utter a loud scream (of protest, anger [ŋg], fear [fɪə], etc)

» During night terrors¹ a child may sit up in bed screaming and thrashing [ʃ] about². A weak or absent cry at birth may suggest [dʒ] vocal cord impairment. In laryngitis [dʒaɪ], vigorous [ɪg] use³ of the voice (shouting, singing, swearing⁴ [eə], roaring⁵) may cause vocal nodules⁶.

Use normal hunger / shrill / protracted⁷ **cry** • **to shriek** in terror⁸ / with laughter

schreien, brüllen, (laut) rufen; Schrei, Ruf, Gebrüll
Nachtangst, Pavor nocturnus¹ (wild) um sich schlagen² starke Beanspruchung³ fluchen⁴ brüllen⁵ Stimmlippenknötchen⁶ langgezogener Schrei⁷ vor Angst kreischen⁸   14

---

murmur [mɜːrmɚ] *v & n*   *sim* **mumble**¹ [ʌ], **mutter**¹ [ʌ] *v*

(v) to speak indistinctly³ in a low voice
(n) constant quiet sound or voice that cannot be heard [ɜː] or understood very well

» She mumbled something about her late husband³. She was murmuring to herself.

murmeln, nuscheln; Gemurmel, Raunen
murmeln, nuscheln, brummeln¹ undeutlich² verstorbener Ehemann³   15

---

whisper [ʰwɪspɚ] *v & n*   *sim* **whispering**¹ *n*

(v) speaking softly² in a low² voice without vibration [aɪ] of the vocal cords

» There was impaired [eə] fluency³ which then resolved⁴ into a hoarse whisper. Whispered pectoriloquy⁵ is an extreme form of bronchophony in which softly spoken words are readily heard by auscultation [ɒːsk-].

Use **to whisper** into sb's ear • to speak in a / soft⁶ **whisper** • **whispered** voice⁷ / speech / sounds / bronchophony⁵ • **whispered** voice test⁸

flüstern; Geflüster
Flüstern, Getuschel, Gerede¹ leise² Redeflussstörung³ überging in⁴ Bronchophonie, Bronchialstimme⁵ leises Geflüster⁶ Flüsterstimme⁷ Flüsterprobe⁸

16

---

babble *v & n*   *sim* **coo**¹ [kuː] *v*, **lallation**² *n term*

to produce incoherent³, meaningless sounds, e.g. a baby or like a baby

babbling⁴ *n* • **lal(o)-** *comb* • **-lalia** *comb*

» By two months of age the child's vocalizations⁵ include cooing, while babbling begins by 6–10 months of age.

Use **babble** of voices⁶ • **lallation** phase⁷ • echo⁸ [k] / copro⁹/ rhino¹⁰ [aɪ]/ dys**lalia**¹¹ • **lalo**phobia¹²

babbeln, plappern; Babbelei, Geplapper
lallen¹ Lallen² unverständlich, unzusammenhängend³ Plappern, Babbelei⁴ Sprachäußerungen⁵ Stimmengewirr⁶ Lallphase⁷ Echolalie⁸ (zwanghafter) Gebrauch vulgärer Ausdrücke; Koprolalie⁹ Näseln, Rhinophonie, -lalie¹⁰ Artikulationsstörung, Dyslalie¹¹ Sprechangst, Lalophobie¹²   17

eloquent [ˈeləkwent] *adj* *sim* **communicative**[1], **talkative**[1] [tɒːk-] *adj*
very articulate and able to express oneself fluently, clearly, effectively
eloquence[2] *n* • **uncommunicative** *adj* • **taciturn**[3] [æs] *adj*
》 Profoundly [aʊ] retarded[4] children (IQ < 30) are usually minimally communicative.

wortgewandt, beredt
gesprächig, redselig, mitteilsam[1] Redegewandtheit, Eloquenz[2] schweigsam, wortkarg[3] schwerstbehindert[4]

18

ramble *v* *sim* **rant**[1], **chatter**[2] [tʃ], **blab(ber)**[3] *v*, **go on about sth.**[4] *phr*
to speak incessantly[5] [se] and in a confused way about unimportant matters
》 The patient's language was a rambling monolog. Our new patient keeps ranting on about the melting polar caps. Stop this idle [aɪ] chatter[6], you've got work to do.

faseln, unzusammen-hängendes Zeug reden
irres Zeug reden, Tiraden loslassen[1] schwatzen[2] plappern, ausplaudern[3] stundenlang etw. erzählen[4] unaufhörlich[5] leeres Geplapper[6]

19

stutter [ʌ] *n & v* *sim* **stammer**[1] [æ] *n & v*, **pause**[2] [ɒː], **falter**[2] [ɒː] *v clin*
(n) speech disorder marked by involuntary hesitations[3] and repetitions; mispronunciation and transposition of sounds is referred to as stammering; esp. in BE usage stutter and stammer are used synonymously
stammerer[4] *n* • **stutterer**[4] *n* • **stammering**[5] *n*
》 She only stammers when she is tense[6] or uptight[7] [-taɪt].
Use a severe / nervous **stammer** • to have a[8] **stutter** • syllable[9] **stuttering**

Stottern, Dysphemie; stottern
Stammeln, Dyslalie; stammeln[1] stocken[2] Stocken[3] Stotterer(in)[4] Stottern, Gestotter[5] angespannt[6] nervös[7] stottern[8] Silbenstolpern[9]

20

lisp *v & n* *syn* **(para)sigmatism** *n term*, *sim* **hiss**[1] *v & n*
(n) speech defect in which sibilants[2] esp. [s] and [z] are distorted[3] to a hissing sound
》 She began lisping when she lost one of her front teeth. Should my 30-month-old see a speech therapist for her lisp? You may even think that your child's lisp sounds cute[4] [kjuːt] now.
Use to speak with/utter with/correct **a lisp** • frontal **lisp**

lispeln; Lispeln, Sigmatismus
zischen; Zischen[1] Zischlaute[2] fehlerhaft gebildet[3] klingt niedlich[4]

21

hypernasal [eɪ] *adj term* *opposite* **hyponasal**[1] [haɪpoʊ-] *adj term*
excessive nasal air emission [ɪʃ] commonly due to velopharyngeal [dʒ] incompetence[2]
》 Speech problems including hypernasality and articulation errors[3] are commonly associated with facial [feɪʃəl] clefts[4].
Use **hyponasal** resonance / voice • **hypernasal** speech[5] • momentary / intermittent[6] **hyponasality**

hypernasal
hyponasal[1] Insuffizienz d. velopharyngealen Abschlusses[2] Artikulationsstörungen[3] Gesichtsspalten[4] näselnde Sprache, Rhinolalie[5] intermittierende/ zeitweilig auftretende Hyponasalität[6]

22

aphonia [eɪfoʊnɪə] *n term* *sim* **dysphonia**[1] [dɪs-] *n term* → U103-6
inability to vocalize[2] (except for whispered speech) because of disease or injury to organs of speech
》 These laryngeal [-dʒiːəl] disorders are commonly associated with hoarseness[3], aphonia, and stridor[4] [aɪ]. Dysphonia refers to any kind of difficulty or pain in speaking.
Use spastic / hysteric **aphonia** • **aphonic** voice[5]

Aphonie, Stimmlosigkeit
Dysphonie, Stimmstörung[1] (laut) aussprechen[2] Heiserkeit[3] Stridor, pfeifendes Atemgeräusch[4] tonlose Stimme[5]

23

Clinical Phrases

The patient spoke in low murmurs. Der/Die Patient(in) murmelte leise vor sich hin. • He has a bad stammer. Er stottert stark. • His voice was breaking much too early. Er hatte viel zu früh den Stimmbruch. • She gave a history of marked difficulty with swallowing and a "hot-potato" voice. Sie klagte über starke Schluckbeschwerden und eine belegte Stimme. • When did you first notice the deepening and coarsening of the voice? Wann ist Ihnen erstmals aufgefallen, dass Ihre Stimme rauer und tiefer wird? • The words are phonetically balanced. Die Sprache ist phonetisch unauffällig. • The patient's spontaneous speech was fluent maintaining appropriate phrase length and melody. Die Spontansprache des Patienten war fließend; Satzlänge und Satzmelodie waren im normalen Bereich.

Unit 67 Gestures & Body Language

Related Units: 66 Speech, 21 Head & Neck, 25 Build, 31 Musculoskeletal Function, 64 Body Movement, 76 Mood, 107 Physical Examination, 113 Neurologic Findings

gesture [dʒestʃɚ] n & v

(n) motion [oʊʃ] of the hands or body to express thoughts or feelings or to communicate familiar signals

gesticulate[1] [dʒestɪkjʊleɪt] v • **gesticulation** n • **gestural** adj • **gesticulatory** adj

» When assessing behavior [eɪ], gait [geɪt], gestures, and coordination of bodily movements are evaluated. Gestures and pantomime did not improve communication.

Use **to gesture** toward sth.[2] / to sb. • to make/use/rely [aɪ] on[3] **gestures** • friendly / kind[4] / angry / fidgety[5] [dʒ] **gesture** • defiant[6] [aɪ]/ menacing[7] / rude[8] [uː]/ noble[9] **gesture** • **gesture** of approval[10]/ of good will[11] • **to gesticulate** with one's arms / wildly[12] / frantically[12] • **gesticulatory** functions[13] / motion • **gestural** language[14]

Geste, Gebärde; gestikulieren

gestikulieren[1] auf etw. deuten[2] auf Gesten angewiesen sein[3] nette Geste[4] hektische Geste[5] trotzige Geste[6] Drohgebärde[7] rüde Geste[8] noble Geste[9] zustimmende Geste[10] Geste d. guten Willens[11] wild gestikulieren[12] Gestik[13] Gebärdensprache[14]

1

signal [sɪgnəl] v & n   sim **sign**[1] [saɪn] n & v → U108-1

(v, i) to indicate (ii) to communicate non-verbally [ɜː]; e.g. in sign language[2]

» She made no show of resistance but gave a countermanding sign[3] and sank into her seat. I gave him the signal agreed on[4] between us in such a circumstance. Then he signaled to me so I joined him. Listen to and act on the signals you are getting.

Use to give/make **a signal** • hand **signal** • **to signal** (to/ for) sb. to do sth.[5] • to make a **sign** • tell-tale[6] / clear / V[7] **sign** • clinical / favorable [eɪ]/ unmistakable[8] [eɪ] **sign** • **sign** of the cross[9] / language / of disease

(i, ii) anzeigen, signalisieren; Signal, Zeichen

(An)zeichen; Zeichen geben[1] Zeichensprache[2] Zeichen d. Ablehnung/ Widerrufs[3] vereinbartes Zeichen[4] jem. ein/ das Zeichen geben, etw. zu tun[5] verräterisches Z.[6] Sieges-, Victory-Z.[7] unmissverständliches Z.[8] Kreuzzeichen[9]

2

nod [nɒːd] v & n   opposite **shake one's head**[1] phr → U64-6

(v, i) to lower and raise [eɪ] the head to show approval [uː]
(ii) when the head drops forward due to drowsiness [draʊzɪnəs]

» Ask the patient to blink or nod for an affirmative [ɜː] reply to yes/no questions. Motor tics occur [ɜː] especially about the face, head, and shoulders (e.g., blinking, sniffing[2], frowning [aʊ], shoulder shrugging[3], head thrusting[4] [ʌ], etc). She shook her head in disbelief[5].

Use **to nod** at or to sb.[6] / in agreement[7] / to give a quick[8] / approving **nod** • head **nod-ding** • **nodding** movement • **to shake** hands with sb. / your fist at sb.[9] / all over[10]

nicken; einnicken; Nicken; ein Nickerchen machen

d. Kopf schütteln[1] Schnüffeln[2] Schulterzucken[3] ruckartige Kopfbewegungen[4] ungläubig[5] jem. zunicken[6] zustimmend nicken[7] kurz nicken[8] jem. m. d. Faust drohen[9] am ganzen Körper zittern[10]

3

shrug one's shoulders [ʃoʊldɚz] phr   sim **shrug** [ʃrʌg] **sth. off**[1] phr

to raise one's shoulders usually to indicate indifference[2] or resignation [eɪʃ]

» He shrugged his shoulders in a non-committal[3] way, which might mean a lot of things. Check shoulder shrug[4] (trapezius [iː]) and head rotation to each side against resistance. Health care administrators ought to be wringing [r] their hands[5] but most are shrugging their shoulders.

Use **to shrug** at an idea • a **shrug** of the shoulders[6] • to give a / embarrassed[7] **shrug** • to rub[8] [ʌ] **shoulders with sb.** • to give sb. the cold[9] **shoulder** • **to shrug off** one's nervousness[10] [ɜː]/ difficulties

mit d. Achseln zucken

etw. (mit e. Achselzucken) abtun, abschütteln[1] Gleichgültigkeit[2] nichtssagend[3] Schulterheben[4] d. Hände ringen[5] Achselzucken[6] verlegenes A.[7] mit jem. i. Berührung kommen[8] jem. d. kalte Schulter zeigen[9] die Nervosität ablegen[10]

4

wave [weɪv] v   rel **beckon**[1] [bekᵊn] v

to signal with the hands to greet [iː] sb., say goodbye, or that sb. should move in the direction indicated

wave[2] n • **beckoning**[3] adj • **waving**[3] adj

» The last I saw, she was waving her hand in farewell[4]. He beckoned me out of the room. I beckoned her to the window. Give grandma a wave, darling.

Use **to wave** at / to sb. / your hand / sb. through • **to wave** sb. on / (sb.) good-bye[4] / to give sb. a[5] **wave** • **with a wave** of his hand[6] • **to beckon** to sb. / with your finger • **to beckon** sb. over / sb. to follow[7]

(zu)winken, herumfuchteln

winken, e. Zeichen geben[1] Handbewegung, Wink(en)[2] winkend, Zeichen gebend[3] z. Abschied winken[4] jem. (zu)winken[5] mit e. Handbewegung[6] jem. e. Zeichen geben mitzukommen[7]

5

Gestures & Body Language COMPLEX BODY FUNCTIONS 269

clap one's hands phr   syn **applaud** [ɔː] v, rel **cheer**¹ [tʃɪɚ] v,
opposite **boo**² [buː] v

strike [aɪ] the flat of the hands together, esp. to indicate approval or encouragement [ɜː‖BE ʌ]
applause³ [əplɔːz] n • **clap**⁴ [klæp] n • **cheer**⁵ n • **cheerful**⁶ [tʃɪɚfʊl] adj
» I don't see how you can applaud and support this. This will cheer his drooping [uː] spirits⁷ considerably. A dozen [ʌ] times she sprang to her feet to cheer and wave.
Use **to clap** loudly / in time to the music⁸ / your hand over your mouth⁹ • to give a big¹⁰ **clap** • to give or shout a / vigorous¹¹ [ɪɡ]/ faint [eɪ] **cheer** • **to cheer** sb. on¹² / for sb. / yourself hoarse¹³ [ɔː] • **to boo** sb. off / loudly • to say **boo** • **cheerful** disposition¹⁴ [ɪʃ]/ manner

(Beifall) klatschen, applaudieren
zujubeln, aufmuntern¹ auspfeifen² Beifall, Applaus³ (Hände-/ Beifall) klatschen⁴ Beifallsruf, Jubel⁵ fröhlich, vergnügt⁶ aufmuntern⁷ im Rhythmus mitklatschen⁸ s. d. Mund zuhalten⁹ begeistert Beifall klatschen¹⁰ kräftiger Beifall¹¹ jem. anspornen¹² s. vor Begeisterung heiser schreien¹³ fröhliche(s) Art/ Naturell¹⁴   6

embrace [ɪmbreɪs] v & n   syn **hug** [hʌɡ] v & n, sim **cuddle**¹ [ʌ] v & n, rel **kiss**² v & n

(v) to take another person in the arms in greeting or to express acceptance or fondness and affection³
embracing⁴ adj & n • **hugging**⁴ adj & n • **cuddly**⁵ [kʌdli] adj
» As children develop a sense of self, they hug another who is in distress. The Moro reflex⁶ [iː] is an embracing movement as a startle response⁷. He was not fond of⁸ kissing children. The presence of HIV-inhibitory proteins [oʊ] in saliva⁹ [səlaɪvə] lessens any risk of transmission by kissing.
Use **to embrace** tenderly / warmly / an idea¹⁰ • **embracing** movement • tight [taɪt]/ warm / passionate¹¹ [pæʃ-]/ strong **embrace** • to give sb. a¹² **hug** • big / bear¹³ [beɚ]/ tight **hug** • **to cuddle** a baby / up together¹⁴ • to give sb. a¹⁵ **cuddle** • **cuddly** child / toys¹⁶ [tɔɪz]

umarmen, i. d. Arme schließen, umfassen; Umarmung
i. d. Arme nehmen, schmusen; Liebkosung¹ küssen; Kuss² Zuneigung³ umarmend; Umarmung⁴ anschmiegsam; z. Liebhaben⁵ Moro-(Umklammerungs)reflex⁶ Schreckreaktion⁷ ungern⁸ Speichel⁹ für eine Idee eintreten¹⁰ leidenschaftl. Umarmung¹¹ jem. umarmen¹² ungestüme U., Umklammerung¹³ zusammenkuscheln¹⁴ jem. i. d. Arme nehmen¹⁵ Kuscheltiere¹⁶   7

grimace [ɡrɪməs‖eɪs] n & v   rel **look**¹ n & v, **face**² n, **looks**³ n pl → U25-10f

(n) a contorted facial expression executed with the facial muscles (v) to make a face
grimacing adj & n • **grim-faced**⁴ adj • **facial** [feɪʃˀl] adj • **sad-looking** adj
» He gave a little grimace when it was suggested to him. Sustained [eɪ] contraction of the facial muscles [mʌslz] results in a grimace or sneer⁵ [snɪɚ] (risus sardonicus). In REM sleep muscle tone is reduced, although the sleeper may twitch⁶ and grimace.
Use to make/give **a grimace** • **to grimace** in or with pain⁷ • facial / distorted⁸ / contemptuous⁹ **grimace** • multiple [ʌ] **grimacing** • angry / surprised / doubtful [daʊtfˀl] **look** • gloomy¹⁰ [uː]/ strange / scornful⁹ / miserable **look** • prying¹¹ [aɪ]/ wry [raɪ] **look** • **look-alike**¹² • **to look** unhappy / ill • good / sickly¹³ / grave [eɪ]/ saucy¹⁴ [sɔːsi] **looks** • puzzled¹⁵ [ʌ] / stern¹⁶ [ɜː]/ expressionless / pudding¹⁷ [ʊ] **face** • to keep a straight¹⁸/pull a¹⁹ **face** • **facial** appearance / expression / flushing²⁰ [ʌ] • **facial** movements / bones / asymmetry [ɪ]/ tic • normal-/ innocent²¹-/ clever-**looking** • good-/ dreadful- [e]/ rosy-**looking** • kind-/ strange- or odd-/ curious²²-**looking** [kjʊɚɪəs] • guilty- [ɡɪlti]/ official- [ɪʃ]/ placid²³-**looking** [plæsɪd]

Grimasse; Gesichter schneiden, grimassieren
Blick, Miene, Aussehen; aussehen¹ Gesicht(saussdruck)² Blicke, Aussehen³ finster blickend⁴ hämisches Grinsen⁵ Muskelzuckungen haben⁶ vor Schmerz d. Gesicht verziehen⁷ verzerrtes Gesicht⁸ verächtl. Blick⁹ finsterer Blick¹⁰ neugieriger B.¹¹ Doppelgänger(in)¹² kränkliches Aussehen¹³ dreiste Blicke¹⁴ verdutztes Gesicht¹⁵ strenge Miene¹⁶ Mondgesicht¹⁷ ernst bleiben, keine Miene verziehen¹⁸ d. Gesicht verziehen¹⁹ Gesichtsrötung²⁰ mit unschuldigem Blick²¹ neugierig blickend²² mit gelassener Miene²³   8

smile [aɪ] v & n   rel **grin**¹, **leer**² [lɪɚ], **smirk**³ [ɜː], **beam**⁴ [iː], **laugh**⁵ [læf] v

(v) to spread [e] the lips, esp. to signal pleasure [pleʒɚ]
(n) facial expression characterized by turning up the corners of the mouth to show pleasure or amusement
smiling⁶ adj • **grin**⁷ [ɡrɪn] n • **leer**⁸ n • **smirk**⁷ [smɜːrk] n → U66-2
» The infant is now smiling, laughing out loud, and anticipating [ɪs] food on sight [saɪt]. Then a subtle [sʌtˀl] smile crossed her face. I noticed a big grin⁹ on the face of the old woman. He has this self-satisfied smirk¹⁰ on his face.
Use **to smile** sweetly / cheerfully / from ear to ear¹¹ / coldly • **to smile** wryly¹² [raɪli]/ bitterly / with satisfaction¹³ / at sb. • to flash¹⁴/hide/repress¹⁵/give sb. **a smile** • friendly / beaming¹⁶ / sunny [ʌ]/ happy **smile** • big / faint [eɪ]/ knowing **smile** • dirty [ɜː]/ forced¹⁷ / radiant¹⁶ [eɪ] **smile** • **smile** line¹⁸ • **to grin** mischievously [tʃ] at sb.¹⁹ • silly / broad⁹ [ɔː]/ scared [skeɚd] / sheepish²⁰ [iː]/ pleased [iː] **grin** • **to beam** at sb. / with delight²¹ [dɪlaɪt] • drunken **leer**

lächeln; Lächeln
grinsen¹ anzüglich lächeln² süffisant lächeln³ strahlen⁴ lachen⁵ lächelnd⁶ Grinsen⁷ heimtückischer Blick⁸ breites Grinsen⁹ selbstgefälliges Lächeln¹⁰ übers ganze Gesicht lachen¹¹ ironisch lächeln¹² zufrieden lächeln¹³ jem. e. Lächeln schenken¹⁴ sich d. Lachen verbeißen¹⁵ strahlendes Lächeln¹⁶ gezwungenes Lächeln¹⁷ Lachlinie¹⁸ jem. verschmitzt anlächeln¹⁹ verlegenes Lächeln²⁰ vor Freude strahlen²¹   9

67

270 COMPLEX BODY FUNCTIONS   Gestures & Body Language

weep [iː] - wept - wept *v irr*   *rel* **sob**[1] [ɒː], **lament**[2], **sniffle**[3], **snuffle**[3] [ʌ] *v*

(i) to shed tears [tɪəz] because of sadness or pain
(ii) to produce an oozing[4] [uː] fluid and pus[5] [ʌ] (of a wound [uː])

weepy[6] *adj* • **weeping**[7] *adj & n* • **weep** *n* • **sobbing**[8] *adj & n* → U66-3; U12-12f

» He did not wring his hands or weep. The skin is weepy from the inflammation. He will sob himself to sleep[9] as usual. Nasal secretions are increased with sniffling and loose cough.

Use **to weep** with joy / bitter tears / tears of joy[10] / over or for sb.[2] • to feel **weepy** • **weepy** voice[11] / lesion[12] [iː] • **to sob** one's heart [ɑː] out[13] / to give a **sob** • **sob** story[14] • **weeping** mourners[15] [ɔː]/ eczema [eks-]/ sore[12] [sɔː] • to burst [ɜː] out / dry / **sobbing** • **sobbing** sniffle / scream • **to lament** (over) sb.'s death

(i) weinen (ii) nässen (Wunde)

schluchzen[1] beklagen, weinen/ trauern (um)[2] schniefen[3] sickernd[4] Eiter[5] weinerlich; nässend[6] weinend; nässend; Weinen[7] schluchzend; Schluchzen[8] sich i. d. Schlaf weinen[9] Freudentränen vergießen[10] weinerliche Stimme[11] nässende Wunde[12] bitterlich weinen[13] rührselige Geschichte[14] weinende Trauergäste, Klageweiber[15]

10

frown [fraʊn] *v & n*   *rel* **scowl**[1] [skaʊl] *v & n*

(v) to wrinkle [r] one's forehead[2] as a sign of dislike or disapproval[3] [uː]

frowning[4] *adj* • **frowned-on**[5] *adj* • **scowling**[6] *adj*

» She frowned, unsure whether she was being taken seriously. More muscles are needed for producing a frown than for a smile. He looked at me with a scowl. She wears [weəz] a permanent [ɜː] scowl on her face every morning.

Use **to frown** at sb. / with displeasure [eʒ]/ sternly[7] [ɜː] • **to be frowned** (up)on • disapproving / worried[8] [ɜː] **frown** • **frowning** glance[9] • **to scowl** at sb.[10]

d. Stirn runzeln; Stirnrunzeln

e. finsteres Gesicht machen; finsterer Blick[1] d. Stirn runzeln[2] Missbilligung[3] finster, missbilligend[4] verpönt[5] missmutig[6] ein finsteres Gesicht machen[7] sorgenvolles Gesicht[8] finsterer Blick[9] jem. böse ansehen[10]

11

glance [glænˈs] *v & n clin*   *sim* **glimpse**[1], **peek**[2] [piːk], **peep**[2] [piːp] *v & n*

(v) to take a quick look at something or someone and then look down or at sth. else

» He glanced around the room to see if he could recognize anyone. I could tell at a glance[3] that he was in acute distress. With a right angle lens a glimpse can be obtained [eɪ] of the renal calyces [kælɪsiːz]. Close your eyes, Tommy, and don't peek.

Use **to glance** at sth. or sb. / over a page[4] / up from a book / round the room • to take or cast[5] **a glance** • to give sb. a sideways[6] / at first[7] **glance** • to catch/obtain a **glimpse** • to take a **peek**

blicken; (kurzer) Blick

e. Blick werfen; flüchtiger Blick[1] kurz/ verstohlen blicken, gucken; kurzer Blick[2] auf einen Blick[3] e. Seite überfliegen[4] e. kurzen Blick werfen[5] jem. einen Seitenblick zuwerfen[6] auf den ersten Blick[7]

12

gape [geɪp] *v*   *rel* **glare**[1] [gleə], **glower**[2] [glaʊə] *v & n* → U59-2

to look at sth. or sb. in great surprise, typically [ɪ] with one's mouth wide open

» She stood in the door gaping at the visitor in the hallway[3] [ɔː]. The elderly patient glared fiercely [fɪəsli] at the nurse [ɜː] as she came in with the tray. His glower turned into a grin when he realized that the telephone call was a hoax[4] [həʊks].

Use **to gape** at sb. or sth. / speechlessly[5] [tʃ] • **to glare** at sb. / sternly [ɜː] • angry / fierce[6] **glare** • **to glower** defiantly [aɪə] at sb.[7] • **glowering** look

starren, gaffen, glotzen

zornig (an)starren; zorniger Blick[1] finster blicken; finsterer Blick[2] Eingangshalle, Diele[3] Streich[4] wortlos vor sich hinstarren[5] grimmiger Blick[6] jem. trotzig anfunkeln[7]

13

stare [steə] *v & n*   *syn* **gaze** [geɪz] *v & n*,   *sim* **look**[1], **squint**[2] [skwɪnt] *v & n*

(v) to look at sth. or sb. with a fixed gaze (n) fixed look with eyes wide open

staring[3] *adj & n* • **overlook**[4] *v* • **looker-on**[5] *n* • **squinting** *adj & n* → U59-2,4

» The patient is asked to stare at a finger held directly in the line of gaze overhead with both eyes. Signs of thyrotoxicosis [θaɪ-] may include stare and lid lag[6]. The sun made me squint.

Use **to stare** into space[7] / at sb. / sb. in the face • **staring** eyes[8] / appearance / spell • long / confused / angry / blank[9] / motionless **stare** • **to gaze** straight ahead[10] • upward / downward / horizontal **gaze** • vertical / lateral / listless[9] **gaze** • **to look** at sb. or sth. / sb. in the eyes / for evidence[11] • **to look** up to sb. / down (on) / back / (a)round • to take or have a[12] (good) **look** • **to squint** one's eyes[13] / at a picture

starren; (starrer) Blick

(an)schauen, blicken, (hin)sehen; Blick[1] blinzeln, schielen; Schielen, Silberblick[2] starrend; Starren[3] übersehen[4] Zuschauer(in)[5] Graefe-Zeichen, Zurückbleiben d. Oberlids (bei Blicksenkung)[6] ins Leere starren[7] starrer Blick[8] leerer B.[9] vor s. hinstarren[10] e. Beweis suchen[11] e. Blick werfen[12] d. Augen zusammenkneifen[13]

14

wink [wɪŋk] *v*   *sim* **blink**[1] *v*, *rel* **raise one's (eye)brows**[2] [braʊz] *phr* → U59-3

to close one eye for a moment as a signal (of greeting [iː], friendliness [e], etc.)

» He smiled and winked at me to show his approval. I didn't sleep a wink[3]. A deaf [def] child will not blink in response to a loud sound. Her blink, a controlled slow flutter [ʌ] of the lids, suggested impatience[4] [eɪʃ].

Use **to wink** at sb. • to give sb. a **wink** • can't get a wink of sleep[3] • jaw[4] [dʒɔː] • **winking** • **to blink** one's eyes / at sth.[6] • eye **blinking** • **blink** reflex[7] [iː] • to mop or wipe[8] [aɪ]/ wrinkle[9] [r] **one's brow**

zuzwinkern, -blinzeln

zwinkern, blinzeln[1] d. Augenbrauen hochziehen[2] kein Auge zutun/ zugetan[3] Ungeduld[4] mandibulopalpebrale Synkinese, Marcus-Gunn-Syndrom[5] hinwegsehen über[6] Blinzel-, Kornealreflex, Lidreflex[7] s. d. Stirn abwischen[8] d. Stirn runzeln[9]

15

67

Sexuality COMPLEX BODY FUNCTIONS 271

pout [paʊt] v & n   sim **sulk¹** [sʌlk] v

(v) to make an annoyed [ɔɪ] face or try to look sexually attractive, esp. by sticking out the lips (n) a disdainful² [eɪ] grimace

sulky³ adj • **sulk**⁴ n

» If she doesn't get her way she just pouts. "I will not stay," she said, with a pout. He was sulky, and so I came along. I gave it up and let her sulk it out.
Use **to pout** one's lips⁵ • **sulky-**looking boy • to go into a / to be in a⁶ **sulk**

schmollen, einen Schmollmund machen; Schmollmund
schmollen, beleidigt sein¹ geringschätzig, verächtlich² beleidigt, schmollend³ Schmollen⁴ d. Mund schmollend verziehen, e. Schmollmund machen⁵ beleidigt/ sauer sein⁶   16

lick one's lips phr   rel **stick out one's tongue¹** [tʌŋ] phr

to pass the tongue over the lips usually indicating pleasure at the thought of sth.

» Persistent licking and smacking of the lips was the most prominent motor phenomenon, which suggests a temporal lobe lesion. Late manifestations of tardive dyskinesia may include difficulty in sticking out the tongue, increased blink frequency, lip smacking, chewing motions, puffing [ʌ] of the cheeks², or disrupted [ʌ] speech³.
Use to move/smack⁴ [æ]/ purse [ɜː]/ pucker⁶ [ʌ]/open/bite⁷ **one's lips** • to bite/poke [oʊ] out¹ **one's tongue** • to keep a stiff upper⁸ **lip** • **lip** biting [aɪ]/ smacking food⁹ / reading¹⁰ [iː]

sich die Lippen lecken
d. Zunge herausstrecken¹ Aufblasen d. Wangen² Sprechstörung³ schmatzen⁴ e. Schmollmund machen⁵ d. Lippen spitzen⁶ s. auf d. Lippen beißen⁷ Haltung bewahren, s. nichts anmerken lassen⁸ leckeres Essen⁹ Lippenlesen¹⁰   17

whistle [ʰwɪsl] v & n   rel **hum¹** [hʌm] v

(v) to produce a loud shrill sound by blowing air through the pursed lips

» He pursed his lips up as if about to whistle but he made no sound. Wheezes² [iː] are continuous whistling noises caused by turbulent [ɜː] airflow through narrowed intrathoracic [æs] airways.
Use **to whistle** to sb. / an old tune [tjuːn]/ softly / cheerfully³ • to let out a⁴ / to blow / to wet one's⁵ **whistle** • wolf⁶ **whistle** • **whistling** noises⁷ / rales⁸ [æ] • **to hum** a tune⁹ / to yourself¹⁰

pfeifen; Pfiff; (Triller)pfeife
summen¹ Giemen, pfeifendes Atemgeräusch² vergnügt pfeifen³ e. Pfiff ausstoßen⁴ s. d. Kehle anfeuchten⁵ bewundernder Pfiff⁶ Pfeifgeräusche⁷ pfeifende Rasselgeräusche⁸ e. Melodie summen⁹ vor s. hinsummen¹⁰   18

snap [snæp] v   sim **snarl¹** [snɑːrl], **growl¹** [graʊl], **grumble²** [ʌ] v

to speak to sb. in an angry, unfriendly, sharp, or abrupt [ʌ] tone

snappish³ adj • **grumpy**⁴ [ʌ] adj • **snarl** n • **growl** n • **grumble** n

» "I'm not returning," snapped the stout⁵ [aʊ] lady and closed the door with a bang. Mr. Roe keeps grumbling about the quality of our hospital food. "You've hurt me," he growled.
Use **to snap** out / back / sb.'s head off⁶ / one's fingers⁷ / out of sth.⁸ • **snappish** manner⁹ / answer • **to snarl** at sb.¹⁰ • **to grumble** about sth. • your stomach¹¹ [k] **grumbles** • **to growl** at sb.¹⁰ / out orders • with or in a menacing¹² [menɪsɪŋ] **growl**

anfahren, -schnauzen
(wütend) knurren, brummen¹ schimpfen, murren² bissig³ mürrisch, grantig⁴ korpulent⁵ jem. anschnauzen⁶ m. d. Fingern schnippen⁷ etw. bleiben lassen⁸ bissige Art⁹ jem. anknurren¹⁰ d. Magen knurrt¹¹ mit e. drohenden Unterton¹²   19

Unit 68   Sexuality
Related Units: 69 Fertility, 50 Female Sexual Organs, 51 Menstrual Cycle, 52 Male Sexual Organs, 53 Male Sexual Function, 55 Hormones, 70 Pregnancy

sex n   syn **gender** [dʒendɚ] n term, **sexuality** [sekʃuæləti] n

(i) referring [ɜː] to men and women (ii) activities associated [oʊʃ] with sexual intercourse¹ [ɔː]

inter²/ transsexuality³ n term • **(a)sexual** [eɪsekʃʊəl] adj • **unisexual** adj
sexy adj inf • **sexism** n • **sexist**⁴ adj & n • **oversexed**⁵ adj • **sexology**⁶ n

» They wanted to know the sex of their baby before birth. The clinical risks of x-linked disorders are different for the two sexes. Is she currently [ɜː] sexually active? These gender differences decrease with advancing age. What is the exact nature of androgen action on male sexuality?
Use to have/practice safe(r) **sex** • premarital⁷ / the opposite⁸ / chromosomal **sex** • gonadal⁹ [eɪ]/ male / female / (un)protected / casual [æʒ] **sex** • **sex** chromosomes¹⁰ / appeal [iː]/ life • **sex** role / object / hormone /-linked¹¹ • **sex** education¹² / determination / identification • **sex** characteristics¹³ / therapist • **sexual** drive¹⁴ / activity / excitement [aɪ]/ partner • **sexual** deviation [eɪ] or perversion¹⁵ [ɜː]/ practices / harassment¹⁶ / development • **sexual** pleasure [pleʒɚ]/ behavior¹⁷ [eɪ]/ history¹⁸ / preference / abuse • **sexual** differences / relationships¹⁹ / precocity²⁰ [prɪkɒːsəti]/ identity²¹ • **sexually** transmitted disease²² (abbr STD)/ (in)active / mature²³ [mətʃ(j)ʊɚ]• **asexual** reproduction / parasite • hetero / homo**sexual** • **sexy** women / clothes • female / male **gender** • **gender** role / difference / assignment²⁴ [aɪ]/ identity²¹ /-related • adolescent [es]/ male / extramarital [æ]/ immature / infantile **sexuality**

(i) **Geschlecht** (ii) **Koitus, Geschlechtsverkehr, Sexualität**
(Geschlechts)verkehr¹ Intersexualität² Transsexualität³ sexistisch; Sexist(in)⁴ m. übermäßig starkem Sexualtrieb, sexbesessen⁵ Sexualwissenschaft, Sex(u)ologie⁶ vorehelicher Geschlechtsverkehr⁷ das andere Geschlecht⁸ gonadales G.⁹ Gonosomen, Geschlechtschromosomen¹⁰ geschlechtsgebunden¹¹ Sexualerziehung¹² Geschlechtsmerkmale¹³ Geschlechts-, Sexualtrieb¹⁴ sexuelle Deviation¹⁵ sexuelle Belästigung¹⁶ Sexualverhalten¹⁷ Sexualanamnese¹⁸ sexuelle Beziehungen¹⁹ vorzeitige Geschlechtsreife, Pubertas praecox²⁰ Geschlechtsidentität²¹ sexuell übertragbare Krankheiten²² geschlechtsreif²³ Geschlechtszuordnung²⁴   1

sexual arousal [ərauzᵊl] *or* **excitement** [ɪksaɪtmənt] *n clin & term*
   rel **foreplay¹** [fɔːrpleɪ] *n*, **necking²** *n inf*
   sexual stimulation prior to intercourse, e.g. kissing, hugging³ [ʌ], cuddling⁴ [ʌ], caressing⁵, and petting⁶
   arouse⁷ [ərauz] *v* • **neck⁸** (**with**) *v inf*
   » Heterosexual women are encouraged [ɜː] to heighten [haɪtᵊn] arousal before penetration⁹ by stimulating the clitoris, e.g. by indirect friction¹⁰ [ɪkʃ] of the hood¹¹ [ʊ] being pulled back and forth over this organ. It happened when I was necking with her in the car.
   Use to cause/achieve [tʃ] /impair [ɪmpeə] **arousal** • prolonged / increased / diminished / inadequate **sexual arousal** • lack of / response to / vaginal [dʒ] emotional [ouʃ]/ erotic **arousal** • **arousal** phase¹² [feɪz]/ response / pattern¹³

sexuelle/ geschlechtliche Erregung
Vorspiel, Präludium¹ Austausch v. Zärtlichkeiten ohne Stimulation d. Geschlechtsorgane, Necking² Umarmen³ Kuscheln⁴ Streicheln, Liebkosung⁵ Stimulation d. Geschlechtsorgane ohne Koitus, Petting⁶ wecken, erregen; bereiten, verursachen⁷ schmusen⁸ Eindringen (d. Penis)⁹ Reibung, Friktion¹⁰ Klitorishaube¹¹ Erregungsphase¹² Erregungsmuster¹³
2

turn on [tɜːrn ɒːn] *v phr inf*   *rel* **sexy¹**, *****horny¹** *adj inf, BE* *****randy¹** [æ] *adj inf*
   make sb. feel sexually excited and ready to have sex
   » Asparagus² is said to be an aphrodisiac³ which effectively turns on frigid women. The patient complains [eɪ] of having problems of getting turned on.
   Use **sexy** underwear⁴ [-weə]/ voice

anturnen, scharf/ geil machen
sexy, scharf, geil¹ Spargel² Aphrodisiakum, libido- u. potenzsteigerndes Mittel³ Reizwäsche⁴
3

libido [lɪbaɪ‖iːdoʊ] *n term*   *syn* **sexual desire** [dɪzaɪə] *or* **urge** [ɜːrdʒ] *n*,
   sex drive [draɪv] *n clin, sim* **lust¹** [lʌst] *n & v inf*
   (i) conscious or unconscious sexual interest
   (ii) psychic energy (esp. in Jungian/Freudian psychology)
   » If libido and erectile function are normal, the absence of orgasm is almost always due to a psychiatric [saɪk-] disorder. Virilization is marked by hirsutism, temporal balding², clitoromegaly, increased libido, etc. Nymphomania³ [eɪ] is an insatiable⁴ [seɪʃ] sexual desire in a female; in males this is termed satyriasis⁵ [aɪ]. He always looks at her with lust in his eyes.
   Use to improve or enhance/affect **libido** • diminished / declining⁶ / change in / lack of⁷/ loss of⁸ **libido** • libidinal [ɪ]/ sexual⁹ **drive** • **to lust** after sb. • **lust** murderer

Libido, sexuelles Verlangen, Sexualtrieb
Begierde, Sinnes-, Wollust; begehren¹ temporale Alopezie² Nymphomanie³ unersättlich⁴ Satyriasis⁵ Nachlassen d. Libido⁶ Alibidinie⁷ Libidoverlust⁸ Sexualtrieb⁹
4

(sexual) intercourse [ɪntəˈkɔːrs] *or* **act** *n clin*   *syn* **coitus** *n term*, **sex** *n inf*
   act of insertion [ɜː] of the penis [iː] into the vagina [dʒaɪ] and stimulation until orgasm occurs
   coital *adj term* • **postcoital** *adj* • **noncoital** *adj*
   » Whether frequent intercourse promotes recurrent [ɜː] disease is unknown. Attacks of coital headache subside [aɪ] in a few minutes if coitus is interrupted [ʌ]. One of the oldest contraceptive methods is withdrawal of the penis before ejaculation [ɪdʒ-] (coitus interruptus¹).
   Use to have/practice **intercourse** • (un)protected² / painful³ / (un)planned **intercourse** • vaginal⁴ / oral / pain on³ / (receptive) anal⁵ **intercourse** • duration / frequency⁶ / (temporary) avoidance **of intercourse** • **intercourse** satisfaction • **coital** act(ivity) / positions⁷ / lubricants⁸ [uː] • **postcoital** douche [duːʃ]/ spotting⁹

Geschlechtsverkehr, Koitus, Kohabitation, Beischlaf
Coitus interruptus¹ ungeschützter Geschlechtsverkehr² Dyspareunie, schmerzhafter Geschlechtsverkehr/ Koitus³ Vaginalverkehr⁴ Analverkehr⁵ Koitusfrequenz⁶ Koituspositionen⁷ Gleitmittel, Lubrikanzien⁸ postkoitale (Schmier)blutung⁹

5

> **Note:** There are many clinical and colloquial expressions for **to have sex** (some more polite than others): **to sleep with**, **to make love to**, **be intimate with**, **to do it**, **to bed sb.**, **to** *****fuck**, *****to screw**, *****to bang**, *****to get laid**

orgasm [ɔːrgæzᵊm] *n*   *syn* **(sexual) climax** [klaɪmæks] *n clin*
   moment of most intense pleasure [pleʒə] in sexual intercourse
   orgasmic¹ *adj term* • **anorgasmic** *adj* • **anorgasmia** *n*
   » During orgasm changes in pulse rate, blood pressure, and respiratory rate reach a peak [iː]. Orgasm was less intense. Some women are orgasmic with clitoral stimulation but not during intercourse. A series of rhythmic muscular [ʌ] contractions signals the onset of climax.
   Use to experience²/reach/delay [eɪ] **orgasm** • female / male / fake³ [feɪk] **orgasm** • urinary loss at / absence of⁴ **orgasm** • **orgasmic** sensation / phase⁵ / pleasure • **orgasmic** dysfunction⁶ / problems⁶ / platform⁷

Orgasmus, (sexueller) Höhepunkt
orgastisch, Orgasmus-¹ einen Orgasmus haben² vorgetäuschter Orgasmus³ Anorgasmie⁴ Orgasmusphase⁵ Orgasmusstörung(en)⁶ Plateauphase⁷

6

Sexuality | COMPLEX BODY FUNCTIONS 273

female sexual arousal [aʊ] **disorder** n term
  syn **frigidity** [frɪdʒɪdəti], **sexual dysfunction** [dɪsfʌŋkʃən] n clin

female sexual inadequacy (inability to achieve orgasm or sexual response considered unsatisfactory by either the female herself or her partner) marked by symptoms such as decreased libido, dypareunia[1], etc.
frigid[2] [frɪdʒɪd] adj inf
» Treatment in female sexual arousal disorder is primarily focused on eliminating sexual anxieties[3] [ænzaɪəti:z]. My husband keeps telling me I am frigid. Frigidity and vaginismus[4] [ædʒ] are the most common forms of female sexual dysfunction.
Use **sexual dysfunction** of the female • sexual **frigidity** • male sexual or erectile[5] / orgasmic **dysfunction**

sexuelle Funktionsstörung/ Libido- u. Orgasmusstörung d. Frau, Frigidität
schmerzhafter Koitus[1] frigid, gefühlskalt[2] sexuelle Ängste[3] Vaginismus[4] erektile Impotenz[5]

7

masturbate [mæstərbeɪt] v syn ***jerk** [dʒɜːrk] **off** v inf,
  rel **sexual stimulation**[1] n

sexual gratification[2] through self-stimulation, e.g. by rubbing [ʌ] or stroking[3] [oʊ] one's genitals
masturbation[4] n term • **masturbatory** adj • **stimulate** v
» The foreign body[5] had been inserted for masturbatory purposes. Occasionally both labia[6] [eɪ] are unusually large, which has been wrongly assumed to be the result of masturbation.
Use vibratory [aɪ] **masturbation** • visual [ɪʒ] sexual / erotic / vibratory[7] **stimulation** • **masturbatory** activity[4]

masturbieren
sexuelle Stimulation[1] sexuelle Befriedigung[2] Streicheln[3] Masturbation, (sexuelle) Selbstbefriedigung[4] Fremdkörper[5] Schamlippen, Labien[6] Vibratorstimulation[7]

8

erotic [ɪrɒːtɪk] adj rel **sensuous**[1], **seductive**[2] [ʌ],
  flirtatious[3] [eɪʃ], **lustful**[4] adj → U57-9

sexually appealing [iː], arousing or gratifying
seduce[5] [sɪdjuːs] vt • **flirt** [ɜː] (**with**) v inf • **erogenous**[6] [ɒːdʒ] adj • **eroticism**[7] n
» The achievement [tʃ] of erotic pleasure by being humiliated[8] [ɪ], enslaved [eɪ], and partially asphyxiated[9] [ɪ] is termed bondage[10] [bɒːndɪdʒ]. She is erotically obsessed with him.
Use **erotic** stimuli [aɪ]/ arousal / tension [ʃ] • **erotic** fantasies[11] / dreams / sensations or feelings[12] • **erotic** film / paintings • **erogenous** zone[13] • anal[14] [eɪ] **eroticism** • **sensuous** lips[15] • **seductive** behavior • **flirtatious** relationship • **lustful** thoughts

erotisch
sinnlich[1] sexy, verführerisch[2] kokett[3] lüstern[4] verführen[5] erogen[6] Erotik, Erotismus, Erotizismus[7] gedemütigt[8] erstickt[9] Sado-Maso-Fesselspiele[10] erotische Phantasien[11] erotische Gefühle[12] erogene Zone[13] Analerotik[14] sinnl. Lippen[15]

9

obscene [əbsiːn] adj sim **indecent**[1] [iːs], **dirty**[1] adj, opposite **prude**[2] [uː] adj

shocking, offensive[3], morally loose or immoral sexual behavior (exposure [oʊʒ], nudity[4] [uː], indecencies, pornography, etc.)
obscenity [əbsenəti] n • **prudish** [pruːdɪʃ] adj • **indecency**[5] [ɪndiːsənˈsi] n
» I'm not prudish but I think this photo violates[6] the Obscene Publications Act[7]. It is considered indecent for women to wear hot pants in here. The rape scene at the beginning of the film is indecent, to say the least.
Use **obscene** language / phone call / behavior • **dirty** joke[8] / old man • to shout **obscenities** • **indecent** proposal[9] [oʊ] / exposure[10] / assault[11] [ɒː]

obszön
unanständig, unzüchtig, schmutzig[1] prüde[2] anstößig[3] Nacktheit[4] unsittliches Verhalten[5] verstoßen gegen[6] Erlass, Verordnung[7] schmutziger Witz[8] unmoralisches Angebot[9] Erregung öffentl. Ärgernisses[10] sexuelle Nötigung[11]

10

virginity [vɜrdʒɪnəti] n rel **celibacy**[1] [selɪbəsi], **sexual abstinence**[1] n clin

refers to a person (mostly to women) who has never had sexual intercourse
virgin[2] [vɜːrdʒɪn] n • **virginal** adj • **celibate**[3] [selɪbət] adj
» In some cultural [ʌ] backgrounds virginity at marriage is an absolute requirement [aɪ]. Cancer of the cervix [sɜː] is more frequent in prostitutes while it is unusual in celibate women.
Use to lose[4]/preserve [ɜː] **one's virginity** • periodic / ejaculatory[1] [dʒæ] **abstinence** • **abstinence** from coitus[1] • **virginal** women / state

Jungfräulichkeit, Unschuld
sexuelle Enthaltsamkeit[1] Jungfrau[2] enthaltsam, zölibatär[3] seine Unschuld verlieren[4]

11

promiscuity [prɒːmɪskjuːəti] n opposite **chastity**[1] [tʃæstəti] n

having casual [kæʒʊəl] sexual relations with various partners
promiscuous[2] [prəmɪskjuəs] adj term • **sleep around**[3] v phr • **chaste**[4] [tʃeɪst] adj
» Risk factors for cervical cancer include early sexual experience [ɪə] and promiscuity. Chastity is associated with almost total freedom from cervical cancers. Promiscuous entanglements[5] with many partners are typical for histrionic individuals[6].
Use (hetero)sexual / episodic **promiscuity** • **promiscuous** sexual activity[7] / homosexual men • sexually **promiscuous**

Promiskuität, häufiger Partnerwechsel
Keuschheit, Unberührtheit[1] promiskuitiv, promiskuös[2] mit häufig wechselnden Partnern schlafen[3] keusch[4] häufige Affären[5] Personen mit histrionischer Persönlichkeitsstörung[6] promiskuöses Sexualverhalten[7]

12

fornication [fɔːrnɪkeɪʃᵊn] *n leg*   *sim* **adultery**¹ [ədʌltəri] *n*

legal term for having extramarital sex; if one of the partners is married this is referred to as adultery

fornicate *v leg* • **adulterer**², **-ess**² *n* • **adulterous** *adj*

» In some states fornication is still listed as a crime. She will divorce him on grounds of adultery.

Use to be guilty of / constitute **fornication** • to commit / accuse sb. of **adultery** • **adulterous** relationship / couple / affair

Unzucht
Ehebruch¹ Ehebrecher(in)²

13

(sexual) orientation [eɪ] *n*   *syn* **sex(ual) preference** [prefɚᵊnᵗs] *n*

preferred biologic sex of sexual partner, e.g. hetero-, homosexual (gay¹/ lesbian²), bisexual [aɪ]

» The sexual history can cover sexual desire, arousal, orgasm, contraception, concerns [sɜː] about gender [dʒ] identity³ and sexual orientation, etc.

Use homosexually / heterosexually **orientated** • homosexual **preference**

sexuelle Orientierung
schwul¹ lesbisch² Geschlechtsidentität³

14

(sexual) perversion [ɜː] *or* **deviation** [diːvieɪʃᵊn] *n clin*   *sim* **paraphilia**¹ [pærəfɪlɪə] *n term*

biologically abnormal, morally wrong, or legally prohibited sexual practice, e.g. bestiality², pedophilia³ [iː]

deviant⁴ *adj term* • **perverse** *adj* • **pervert**⁵ [*n* pɜːrvɜːrt‖*v* pəvɜːrt] *n & v* **paraphiliac**⁶ *n*

» The diagnosis of a paraphilia can be made in patients markedly distressed by recurrent sexually arousing fantasies involving a particular sexual deviation (e.g. fetishism⁷) for 6 months.

Use **deviant** sexual behavior⁸ [eɪ] • severe / male / treatment-resistant **paraphilia** • **paraphilia**-related disorders / therapist

sexuelle Deviation, Perversion
Paraphilie¹ Sodomie² Pädophilie³ deviant, abweichend⁴ perverser Mensch; pervertieren⁵ Paraphile(r)⁶ Fetischismus⁷ abweichendes Sexualverhalten⁸

15

sexual abuse [əbjuːs] *n*   *sim* **child molestation**¹, **(sexual) harassment**² *n*

engaging [eɪdʒ] dependent, immature children in sexual activities they do not fully understand or which violate [aɪ] the laws and taboos [uː] of a society

abuse *v* • **molest**³ *v* • **harass**³ *v* • **harassed** *adj* • **child molester**⁴ *n*

» Forms of sexual abuse include pedophilia and all forms of incest [s] and rape but also fondling⁵, oral-genital contact, exhibitionism, voyeurism, and involvement of children in the production of pornography. Unwelcome sexual advances⁶, e.g. by a superior⁷ [ɪɚ] toward an employee⁸ [iː], are referred to as sexual harassment (experienced by 42% of females on the job). Adolescents are more commonly molested by strangers.

Use to evaluate a patient for / evidence of / alleged⁹ [edʒ]/ child **sexual abuse** • childhood sexual¹ / physical¹⁰ / emotional **abuse** / parental¹¹ / elder / spousal¹² [aʊ] **abuse** • **harassment** by peers¹³ • sexual² **molestation**

sexueller Missbrauch
sexueller Kindesmissbrauch¹ sexuelle Belästigung² belästigen³ Kinderschänder⁴ Begrapschen⁵ Annäherungsversuche⁶ Vorgesetzte(r)⁷ Angestellte(r)⁸ mutmaßlicher sexueller Missbrauch⁹ körperliche Misshandlung¹⁰ Kindesmissbrauch durch e. Elternteil¹¹ Vergewaltigung i. d. Ehe¹² Belästigung durch Gleichaltrige/ Arbeitskollegen¹³

16

rape [reɪp] *n & v*   *rel* **sexual** *or* **indecent** [iː] **assault**¹ [əsɔːlt] *n term*

crime of making (usually) a woman submit to sexual intercourse (vaginal, anal or oral penetration) against her will by force, intimidation², or without legal consent (e.g. with a minor³ [aɪ])

rapist⁴ *n* • **assault**⁵ *vt* • **assaultive** [əsɔːltɪv] *adj*

» Determine whether rape has occurred and proceed [siː] accordingly. In the acute phase humiliation⁶ [hjuː], revenge [rɪvendʒ] and self-blame⁷ [eɪ] are typical emotional reactions of rape victims, while recurrent nightmares⁸ [eɚ] and phobias [oʊ] are common in the long term.

Use statutory⁹ / acquaintance [eɪ]/ date¹⁰ / alleged **rape** • **rape** victim¹¹ / counseling [aʊ]/ trauma [ɒː] • **rape** syndrome [ɪ]/ crisis [aɪ] intervention • **post-rape** medical care • **sexual assault** treatment center • physical [ɪ]/ victims of **assault** • **assaultive** behavior

Vergewaltigung, Notzucht; vergewaltigen, notzüchtigen
sexuelle Nötigung¹ Einschüchterung² Minderjährige(r)³ Vergewaltiger⁴ s. an jem. vergehen, tätlich werden⁵ Demütigung⁶ Selbstvorwürfe⁷ Alpträume⁸ Beischlaf m. Unmündigen⁹ Vergewaltigung durch den Freund¹⁰ Vergewaltigungsopfer¹¹

17

Unit 69 Fertility & Reproductive Medicine
Related Units: 68 Sexuality, 51 Menstrual Cycle, 53 Male Sexual Function, 55 Hormones, 70 Pregnancy, 71 Childbirth

reproduce [riːprəd(j)uːs] *v clin & term*   *syn* **procreate** [proukrieɪt] *v*
(i) to have offspring[1] (ii) to copy (iii) repeat
reproductive [ʌ] *adj term* • **reproduction** [ʌ] *n* • **procreation** [eɪ] *n*
» These special medical needs and concerns[2] [sɜː] vary with the patient's reproductive status, her reproductive potential, and her desire [aɪ] to reproduce. If the hypospadias[3] [eɪ] is glandular, the penis [iː] is usually functional both for micturition [ɪʃ] and procreation.
Use to impair [eɚ] **reproduction** • **reproductive** tract or system / organs[4] / glands[5] • **reproductive** hormones / cycle • **reproductive** age[6] (range) / capacity / (dys)function • **reproductive** mortality / counseling [aʊ]/ technology / toxicology[7] • (a)sexual / cell / assisted[8] / cytogenic [dʒe] **reproduction**

(i) sich fortpflanzen, zeugen
Nachkommen[1] Anliegen[2] Hypospadie, untere Harnröhrenspalte[3] Geschlechtsorgane, Genitalien[4] Keimdrüsen, Gonaden[5] gebärfähiges Alter[6] Reproduktionstoxikologie[7] assistierte Reproduktion/ Fortpflanzung[8]

1

fertility [fətɪlɪti] *n term & clin*
            opposite **infertility**[1], **subfertility**[2] [ʌ] *n term* → U70-1
ability to reproduce (to conceive[3] [-siːv] or impregnate[4])
(in/ sub)fertile[5] [fɜːrtᵊl‖BE -taɪl] *adj term* • **fertilize**[4] *vt* • **fertilization**[6] *n*
» The outlook for fertility is greatly reduced. Infertility affects about 1/6 couples [ʌ] of childbearing [eɚ] age[7]. The approach in infertile couples involves assessment of both the man and the woman. There is a modestly increased risk of primary tubal infertility with IUD[8] use.
Use to preserve/impair[9]/decrease/lose/restore **fertility** • in vivo / assisted / immediate [iː]/ future **fertility** • in vitro[10] (*abbr* IVF)/ pre-/ post-**fertilization** • **fertility**-enhancing effect / factor[11] • **fertility** control[12] / rate[13] / statistics • **fertile** period / male • to treat/contribute to/correct **infertility** • primary / secondary / male (factor)[14] **infertility** • female / unexplained **infertility** • exercise-induced / endometriosis-related[15] **infertility** • **infertility** evaluation[16] / test / procedure [siː]

Fruchtbarkeit, Fertilität
Infertilität, Unfruchtbarkeit, Sterilität[1] Subfertilität[2] empfangen, schwanger werden[3] schwängern, befruchten[4] fruchtbar, fertil[5] Befruchtung, Fertilisation[6] gebärfähiges Alter[7] Spirale[8] d. Fertilität beeinträchtigen[9] künstl. Befruchtung, In-vitro-Fertilisation, IVF[10] Fertilitäts-, F-Faktor[11] Kontrazeption, Empfängnisverhütung[12] Fertilitäts-, Fruchtbarkeitsziffer/-rate[13] männliche Infertilität[14] endometriosebedingte Infertilität[15] Abklärung d. Infertilität[16]

2

sterilization *n term & clin* → U139-2
            rel **vasectomy**[1], **tubal ligation**[2] *n term*
(i) procedure rendering a person incapable of reproduction (e.g. castration[3], salpingectomy[4] [dʒe]) (ii) elimination of microorganisms using physical (autoclave), chemical (alcohol) or other aseptic techniques
sterile[5] *adj term* • **sterility**[6] *n* • **sterilize** *v* • **sterilized** *adj* • **vasectomize**[7] *v*
» Mumps [ʌ] orchitis[8] [kaɪ] may result in sterility. Sterilization in men is by vasectomy, an outpatient procedure[9] that requires only local anesthesia. Contraception or sterilization should be used to prevent unwanted pregnancy. Failure rates after tubal sterilization are approx. 0.5%.
Use to consider/desire/confirm/reverse[10] **sterilization** • tubal[2] / male / female / permanent [ɜː] **sterilization** • elective / laparoscopic **sterilization** • **sterilization** procedure / vasectomy • to lead to/prevent/produce or cause **sterility** • male[11] / permanent / two-child **sterility** • prophylactic[12] / contralateral / bilateral [aɪ] **vasectomy** • **vasectomy** surgery / site • **vasectomized** men • **tubal ligation** reversal[13] [ɜː] • **tubal** coagulation[14]

(i, ii) Sterilisation
Vasektomie, Vasoresektion[1] Tubenligatur, -unterbindung[2] Kastration[3] Salpingektomie, Eileiterentfernung[4] unfruchtbar, steril, infertil[5] Unfruchtbarkeit, Sterilität[6] vasektomieren[7] Mumpsorchitis[8] ambulanter Eingriff[9] Tubensterilisation rückgängig machen[10] Sterilität d. Mannes[11] prophylaktische Vasektomie[12] Sterilitätsoperation, Tubenplastik[13] Tubenkoagulation[14]

3

vasectomy reversal *n term*   *syn* **vasovasostomy** *n, rel* **tuboplasty**[1] *n term*
reanastomosis[2] of the ends of the vas deferens that were ligated[3] [laɪgeɪtɪd] in a previous [iː] vasectomy procedure
» Pregnancy rates following vasectomy reversal range between 45 and 60%, compared to 50- 80% following reanastomosis of the oviduct[4] [oʊvɪdʌkt] (*tuboplasty*).
Use to undergo[5] **vasectomy reversal** • to be subjected to microscopic **vasovasostomy** • **postvasovasostomy** fertility rate[6] • microsurgical epididymo**vasostomy**[7]

(Vaso)vasostomie, Refertilisierung, Rekanalisation d. Samenleiter
Eileiter-, Tubenplastik[1] Reanastomosierung[2] unterbunden[3] Eileiter[4] sich e. Vasotomie unterziehen[5] Fertilitätsrate nach Vasotomie[6] mikrochir. Epididymovasostomie[7]

4

COMPLEX BODY FUNCTIONS — Fertility & Reproductive Medicine

birth control n clin   sim **contraception**[1] n term, **family planning**[2] n clin

medication, device [-vaɪs] or method that prevents conception [sɛ] or impregnation; natural family planning methods (periodic abstinence on fertile days) include the calendar[3], basal body temperature[4] (abbr BBT), and cervical [sɜː] mucus [mjuːkəs] methods[5]

contraceptive[6] [kɒntrəsɛptɪv] adj & n term

» When lactation[7] [eɪ] is used as a method of birth control, there must be no supplemental feeding. Progestogen [dʒe] implants are available for long-term contraception.

Use to seek [iː] /use/practice **birth control** • **birth control** pill[8] / methods • **contraceptive** device[9] / jelly[10] [dʒ]/ method[11] / pill[8] • **contraceptive** implant[12] / effectiveness / use / education • oral[8] (abbr OC)/ injectable [dʒe]/ postcoital / barrier[9] **contraceptive** • to begin / to use / effective **contraception** • postcoital or emergency[13] [ɜː]/ (barrier) methods of **contraception** • natural[14] / basal-body temperature method of[4] **family planning**

Geburtenregelung, -kontrolle
Kontrazeption, Antikonzeption, Konzeptions-, Empfängnisverhütung[1] Familienplanung[2] Kalendermethode[3] Temperaturmethode[4] Zervixschleim-, Billings-Ovulationsmethode[5] kontrazeptiv; Kontrazeptivum, Verhütungsmittel[6] Stillen[7] Antibaby-Pille, orales Kontrazeptivum[8] mechan. Kontrazeptivum[9] spermizides Gel[10] Verhütungsmethode[11] kontrazeptives Implantat[12] postkoitale Kontrazeption, Notfallverhütung[13] natürliche Kontrazeption/ Geburtenregelung[14]
5

---

condom n   syn **prophylactic, rubber** [ʌ], BE **sheath** [ʃiːθ], **French letter** n inf

thin rubber or latex sheath worn over the penis during intercourse as a prophylactic (contraceptive) device

» Adding a small quantity of spermicide reduces the failure rate[1] if the condom breaks[2] during coitus. Semen [iː] may escape from the condom as a result of failure to withdraw before detumescence[3]. The use of condoms will protect against gonorrhea[4].

Use to use/wear **a condom** • male / female[5] / latex-free[6] [eɪ] **condom** • **condom** use / rupture[7] [ʌ] • base / tip **of the condom**

Kondom, Präservativ
Versagerquote[1] reißt, platzt[2] Abschwellung[3] Gonorrhoe, Tripper[4] Kondom für d. Frau, Femidom[5] latexfreies Kondom[6] Reißen/ Platzen d. Kondoms[7]
6

---

oral contraceptive n term, abbr **OC**   syn **(contraceptive) pill** n clin sing

compound taken orally that suppresses ovulation by duplicating [uː] the action of estrogen [eǀiː] and progesterone [dʒe]

» Combination-type OCs, which contain both synthetic [sɪn-] estrogen and progestogen, are given continuously for 3 weeks only to allow for withdrawal [-ɔːl] bleeding in the 4th wk.

Use **oral contraceptive** use / agent[1] [eɪdʒ]/-induced colitis [aɪ] • high-dose[2] / long-term / combination or combined[3] **OC** • string to take the **/** birth control **pill** • morning after[4] / mini[5] / missed **pill** • three-phased[6] [feɪzd]/ estrogen-containing[7] **pill** • combination[3] / progestogen-only[8] / step-up[9] **pill**

orales Kontrazeptivum, Antibabypille, Pille
orales Kontrazeptivum[1] hochdosierte Pille[2] Kombinationspräparat, Einphasenpille, Mikropille[3] Nidationshemmer, Postkoitalpille, Pille danach[4] Minipille[5] Dreiphasenpille[6] östrogenhaltige Pille[7] reines Gestagenpräparat[8] Mehrphasenpräparat[9]
7

---

spermicide [spɜːrmɪsaɪd] n term   rel **vaginal suppository**[1] [səpɒzɪtɔːri] n clin

foam[2] [oʊ], cream [iː] or jelly [dʒ] destructive [ʌ] to sperm which is inserted [ɜː] into the vagina [vədʒaɪnə] 5-10 min before intercourse[3] [ɔː]

spermicidal[4] [spɜːrmɪsaɪdəl] adj term

» In addition to their spermicidal effect on sperm, vaginal [dʒ] suppositories also act as a mechanical [kæ] barrier to entry of sperm into the cervical canal. Spermicides may be used alone or in conjunction [dʒʌ] with a diaphragm or condom.

Use intravaginal nonoxynol-9-containing / HIV-inhibiting **spermicide** • **spermicide-coated** [oʊ] condom[5] • **spermicidal** preparations[6] / agents[6] / property • antibacterial [ɪɚ]/ estrogen / progesterone **suppository**

Spermizid, spermienabtötende(s) Substanz/ Mittel
Vaginalzäpfchen, -suppositorium[1] Vaginalschaum[2] (Geschlechts)verkehr[3] spermizid, spermienabtötend[4] spermizidbeschichtetes Kondom[5] Spermizide[6]
8

(contraceptive) diaphragm [daɪəfræm] n term   rel **vaginal sponge**[1] [spʌndʒ], **cervical** [sɜː] **cap**[2], **pessary**[3] n clin

dome-shaped rubber cup fitted to the vaginal cul-de-sac [ʌ] to cover the cervix in a pool of spermicide

» Contraceptive jelly should be used with the diaphragm to improve contraceptive effectiveness in case it is displaced during coitus. A sponge acts as a sperm barrier and releases [iː] spermicides. The cervical cap, which must be fitted by a clinician [ɪʃ], can be left in place for 48 h. Normally a pessary must be removed daily for cleaning.

Use coil-spring / flat-spring **contraceptive diaphragm** • **contraceptive diaphragm** fitting[4] • contraceptive vaginal[1] **sponge** • vaginal / well-fitted **pessary** • donut[5] [oʊ]/ ring[5] / cup[6] **pessary** • **pessary** support[7]

(Scheiden)diaphragma, Scheidenpessar
Vaginalschwamm[1] Portiokappe, Okklusivpessar[2] Pessar, Scheidendiaphragma[3] Positionieren d. Scheidendiaphragmas[4] Ringpessar[5] Schalenpessar[6] Pessarbehandlung, -unterstützung[7]
9

Fertility & Reproductive Medicine   COMPLEX BODY FUNCTIONS   277

intrauterine device n term, abbr **IUD**   syn **coil** [kɔɪl] n clin

contraceptive appliance [aɪ] of varied form (e.g. coil, loop, bow) inserted into the uterus
» There is no need to change a plastic unmedicated IUD[1] unless the patient develops increased bleeding [iː] after it has been in place for more than one year. When an IUD is removed, contraceptive counseling[2] [aʊ] is essential.
Use to insert[3]/remove **an IUD** • **IUD** strings[4] / users or wearers [eɚ] • **IUD** failure / insertion / removal • coil / bow [oʊ]/ loop [uː] **IUD** • progesterone-releasing[5] [iː]/ dislodged[6] [dʒ] **IUD**

Intrauterinpessar, IUP, IUD, Spirale
IUD ohne Gestagene[1] Empfängnisverhütungsberatung[2] Spirale einlegen[3] Rückholfäden[4] Hormonspirale, intrauterines System (IUS)[5] disloziertes IUS[6]   10

assisted reproductive technologies n term   abbr **ART**

collective term for techniques [k] used to bring about conception without sexual intercourse and offer hope to couples with unexplained or previously untreatable infertility[1]
» In vitro fertilization was the first ART developed and is the most commonly used ART procedure. To prepare the female for ART, hormonal medications are usually used, either alone or in combination, to stimulate the development of the ovarian follicles.
Use **art** procedure / services / (specialist) provider • **reproductive** endocrinology[2] / tract / organs[3] • **assisted** reproductive medicine[4] / oocyte [oʊəsaɪt] fertilization / (embryo) hatching[5] [hætʃɪŋ]

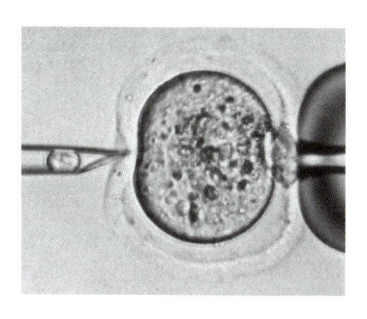

assistierte(s) mediz. Fortpflanzung/ Reproduktion(sverfahren)
therapieresistente/ nicht behandelbare Unfruchtbarkeit[1] gynäkol. Endokrinologie[2] Geschlechtsorgane, Genitalien, Genitale[3] Reproduktionsmedizin[4] Schlüpfhilfe, Assisted Hatching, AH[5]   11

Intracytoplasmic sperm injection: the oocyte is aspirated (right) and the sperm is injected with a pointed cannula (left)

in vitro fertilization n term, abbr **IVF**   sim **artificial insemination**[1] n term

process whereby (usually multiple) ova are placed in a medium to which sperms are added for fertilization; the zygote[2] [zaɪɡoʊt] is then introduced into the uterus [juː] and allowed to develop to term[3]
prefertilization[4] adj term • **postfertilization** adj
» IVF has been simplified by the use of ultrasound-guided [ʌ] transvaginal ovarian puncture[5] [ʌ] to collect[6] oocytes for fertilization. More than 100,000 babies have been born through IVF since the world's first test tube baby[7] was born in 1978. Aspirated oocytes in the pronuclear stage[8] were fertilized in vitro when they were mature. What makes ZIFT different from IVF is that the embryo is placed into the fallopian tube[9] via laparoscopy instead of the uterus.
Use to perform **IVF** • **IVF** procedure / cycle[10] • (failure) to achieve **fertilization** • in vivo [iː]/ natural / laboratory[11] / dispermic[12] **fertilization** • **in vitro** insemination[1] • artificial donor[13] / therapeutic [juː]/ intrauterine [juː] **insemination** • **fertilization** rate[14] • **postfertilization** cell divisions • **IVF with** husband's sperm[15] (abbr AIH)/ donor sperm[16] (abbr AID)

künstliche Befruchtung, In-vitro-Fertilisation, IVF
artifizielle Insemination[1] befruchtete Eizelle, Zygote[2] bis zur Geburt[3] vor d. Befruchtung[4] ultraschallgesteuerte transvaginale Follikelpunktion[5] gewinnen, entnehmen[6] Retortenbaby[7] Pronukleus-, Vorkernstadium[8] Eileiter[9] IVF-Zyklus[10] extrakorporale B./ Reagenzglasbefruchtung, Laborb.[11] Dispermie[12] heterologe Insemination[13] Fertilisationsrate[14] homologe IVF[15] heterologe IVF[16]   12

microsurgical epididymal sperm aspiration n term, abbr **MESA**
    sim **testicular sperm extraction**[1] n term, abbr **TESE**

surgical [ɜː] sperm retrieval procedure that is timed for the same day that the woman has her egg collection as part of the IVF treatment cycle [aɪ]; if sufficient sperm are retrieved some can be prepared and used for ICSI, while any remaining sperm can be frozen for future use
» The number of times MESA can be performed is limited due to the formation of scar tissue[2] at the surgical site. TESE is an open needle biopsy [aɪ] procedure performed under direct vision[3]. PESA is a blind procedure in which a needle is placed into the epididymis in the hope that a pocket of sperm will be found and aspirated. Unlike sperm obtained by MESA spermatozoa produced by testicular biopsy[4] are generally unsuitable for frozen storage.
Use to perform/undergo[5] **MESA** • testicular (abbr TESA)/ percutaneous [eɪ] epididymal[6] (abbr PESA) **sperm aspiration** • retrograde[7] (abbr RESA) **epididymal sperm aspiration** • testicular fine needle[8] (abbr TEFNA) **aspiration** • **sperm** retrieval[9] / procurement[9] • cryo-TESE[10]

mikrochirurg. epididymale Spermienaspiration, MESA
testikuläre Spermien-/Spermatozoenextraktion, TESE[1] Narbengewebe[2] unter direkter Kontrolle[3] Hodenbiopsie[4] sich e. MESA unterziehen[5] perkutane epididymale Spermatozoenaspiration, PESA[6] retrograde epididymale S., RESA[7] testikuläre Feinnadelaspiration, TEFNA[8] Spermien-, Spermatozoengewinnung[9] Kryokonservierung testikulärer Spermatozoen, Kryo-TESE[10]   13

COMPLEX BODY FUNCTIONS — Fertility & Reproductive Medicine

embryo freezing [iː] n clin   syn **embryo cryopreservation** [kraɪoʊ-] n term   rel **sperm bank**[1] n → U14-12

maintenance of the viability[2] [aɪ] of embryos at very low temperatures; also applied to sperm and oocytes

cryopreserve[3] [ɜː] v term • **freeze-thawing**[4] [ɔː] n • **frozen-thawed** [oʊ] adj

» Testicular sperm do not freeze and thaw as well as epididymal sperm and are harder to work with in the andrology laboratory. Pregnancy rates have been significantly enhanced[5] through cryopreservation and thaw of pronuclear [uː] stage oocytes. Sperm retrieved [iː] from your epididymis is frozen and stored to be used as a backup[6] if your wife is unable to achieve [tʃ] a pregnancy[7] with your ejaculated sperm following your vasectomy reversal.

Use **cryopreserved** ovum[8] [oʊ]/ sperm[9] / embryo / tissue • **embryo thaw**[10]

Kryokonservierung/ Tiefgefrieren v. Embryonen
Samenbank[1] Lebensfähigkeit[2] kryokonservieren[3] Gefrier-Tau-Zyklus[4] verbessert[5] Reserve[6] schwanger werden[7] kryokonservierte Eizelle[8] Kryosperma[9] Auftauen d. Embryos[10]

14

intracytoplasmic sperm injection n term, abbr **ICSI**

micromanipulation technique where a single sperm is picked up with an injection pipette [paɪ-] and introduced into the ooplasm to enable fertilization with very low sperm counts or with non-motile[1] sperm

» ICSI has revolutionized treatment for severe male factor infertility because only one healthy sperm is required to potentially achieve fertilization. ICSI has largely replaced the previously developed micromanipulation techniques of partial zona dissection[2] (abbr PZD) and subzonal insertion[3] [ɜː] (abbr SUZI).

Use to undergo/use/offer **ICSI** • sperm aspiration for / fertilization by or via[4] [vaɪə‖viːə]/ attempts at **ICSI** • **ICSI** procedure [siː]

intrazytoplasmat. Spermieninjektion, ICSI, Mikroinjektion
unbeweglich[1] partielle Zona-Dissektion[2] subzonale Spermieninjektion[3] künstl. Befruchtung durch Mikroinjektion[4]

15

embryo transfer n term   rel **oocyte retrieval**[1] [iː], **donor oocyte**[2] n term

after in vitro [ɪ‖iː] insemination the fertilized ovum is transferred to the recipient's uterus or oviduct

donate[3] [doʊneɪt] v term • **retrieve**[4] [rɪtriːv] v

» The patient's single fertilized ovum was cultured[5] [ʌ] for 41 hours and transferred as a four-cell embryo. Not all patients entering an IVF program progress to oocyte retrieval and embryo transfer along with cycle [saɪkl] outcome. Success rates for embryo and egg donation are in the range of 40% pregnancies achieved per transfer with fresh embryos.

Use (non)operative / laparoscopic / tubal[6] [t(j)uːbəl] (abbr TET) **embryo transfer** • frozen[7] (abbr FET) or cryopreserved[7] (abbr CET)/ IVF[8] and (abbr IVF-ET) **embryo transfer** • tubal ovum (abbr TOT)/ low tubal ovum (abbr LTOT) **transfer**

Embryo(nen)transfer
Eizellenentnahme, -gewinnung[1] Spendereizelle[2] spenden[3] entnehmen[4] kultiviert[5] tubarer Embryotransfer[6] Transfer/ Einsetzen von kryokonservierten Embryonen, IVF-Kryozyklus / Auftauzyklus[7] In-vitro-Fertilisation mit Embryotransfer[8]

16

ovarian (hyper)stimulation n term   syn **superovulation** n term

administration of exogenous gonadotropins to enhance the maturation[1] of 8-10 follicles and control the timing of ovulation (thereby improving the chances for retrieval of mature eggs)

superovulatory adj term • **superovulated** adj • **pre-stimulation** [priː-] adj

» The ovary can then be stimulated directly by injections of hMG[2] which allows control over both ovarian stimulation and timing of egg collection[3]. Extra oocytes harvested[4] from a superovulated cycle[5] can be cryopreserved and stored for use at a later time.

Use **ovarian hyperstimulation** syndrome[6] [ɪ] (abbr OHSS) • controlled[7] **ovarian hyperstimulation** (abbr COH) • **superovulated** cycle[5]

ovarielle (Hyper/ Über)stimulation, Superovulation
Reifung[1] humanes menopausales Gonadotropin[2] Eizellenentnahme[3] gewonnen[4] Stimulationszyklus[5] Überstimulationssyndrom[6] kontrollierte ovarielle Stimulation[7]

17

gamete [iː] **intrafallopian (tube) transfer** n term   abbr **GIFT**

involves ovarian stimulation to produce multipleoocytes, oocyte retrieval by transvaginal US-guided needle aspiration[1], and placement of sperm and ova in the oviduct[2] by laparoscopy or minilaparotomy

pre-GIFT adj term

» GIFT is effective in couples [ʌ] with nonmechanical causes of infertility and normal fallopian tubes[2]. The natural process of fertilization in the Fallopian tube is mimicked[3] in GIFT procedures by depositing sperms and oocytes in the distal tube via the laparoscope.

Use zygote[4] [aɪ] (abbr ZIFT) **intrafallopian (tube) transfer** • **GIFT** procedure / cycle / zygote / oocyte retrieval [iː] / oocyte donation / technique / program

intratubarer Gametentransfer, GIFT
ultraschallgesteuerte transvaginale Nadelaspiration[1] Eileiter[2] simuliert[3] intratubarer Zygotentransfer[4]

18

Pregnancy COMPLEX BODY FUNCTIONS **279**

surrogate [ɜː‖BE ʌ] **(gestational)** [dʒesteɪʃənəl] **mother** n term
    rel **host uterus**[1] [hoʊst juːtərəs] n term
artificial insemination of a female whose pregnancy is carried to term[2] with the intention of giving the infant up for adoption[3] to the couple whose male partner has contributed the sperm
surrogacy[4] [sɜːrəgəsi] n
» Variations of the IVF and GIFT procedures include ZIFT, use of donor oocytes, and transfer of frozen embryos to a surrogate mother. The embryos seem to have implanted in the host uterus, but only survived for about seven days. The gestational carrier[5] provides a host uterus for the offspring but does not contribute genetic material.
Use **surrogate** motherhood[4] / ovum / IVF / GIFT / parenting • **host uterus** procedure • **gestational** carrier[5] • gestational[4] **surrogacy** • **surrogacy** contract[6] / program

Leih-, Ersatz-, Surrogatmutter
Trage-, Ammenmutter[1] ausgetragen[2] das Kind zur Adoption freigeben[3] Ersatz-, Leihmutterschaft[4] Surrogatmutter[5] Leihmutterschaftsvertrag[6]

19

Unit 70 Pregnancy
Related Units: **71** Childbirth, **69** Fertility, **68** Sexuality, **51** Menstrual Cycle, **84** Genetics, **85** Embryology

fertilize [fɜːrtəlaɪz] v → U69-2ff   sim **impregnate**[1], **inseminate**[2] [e] v term
penetration of the oocyte [oʊəsaɪt] by the spermatozoon [oʊ] and fusion[3] [fjuːʒən] of the male and female gametes [iː] (usually occurs in the oviduct[4]) to form a zygote [aɪ] from which the embryo develops
fertilization[5] n • (un)**fertilized** adj • **fertile**[6] adj • (in)**fertility**[7] n
» The fertilized ovum may reach the endometrial [iː] cavity prematurely and may not achieve nidation. The ovum remains in the tube 3 days after ovulation where fertilization takes place. Tests are available to evaluate the ability of sperms to fertilize an ovum. Group A women impregnated by group O men have a 10 times greater risk of developing choriocarcinoma.
Use to achieve [tʃ] /prevent **fertilization** • **fertile** period / couples [ʌ] • in vivo / in vitro[8] / impaired [eə] **fertilization** • **fertilized** ovum[9] • to affect/preserve[10]/restore/ enhance/recover **fertility** • normal / documented / reduced or impaired[11] **fertility** • **fertility** rate[12] / potential / control • to result in/contribute to **infertility** • long-standing / tubal / male (factor)[13] **infertility** • **infertility** evaluation / rate

> Note: The expression **fertilize** is widely used with both humans and animals, while **breed** [iː] and **mate** [eɪ] (→ U84-30) are normally used to refer to animals only. **Inseminate** is often used with assisted reproductive techniques and **impregnate** more often relates to adding protective substances to materials. Slang expressions for **making pregnant** include **to *knock up** /(BE) ***bang up a woman**.

befruchten
eindringen (d. Spermien durch d. Zona pellucida)[1] (künstl.) befruchten, besamen[2] Verschmelzung, Konjugation[3] Eileiter, Tuba uterina[4] Befruchtung, Fertilisation[5] fruchtbar, fertil[6] (In)fertilität, (Un)fruchtbarkeit[7] In-vitro-Fertilisation[8] befruchtete Eizelle, Zygote[9] Fertilität erhalten[10] Subfertilität[11] Fertilitätsrate[12] Infertilität durch herabgesetzte Spermienqualität[13]

1

conception [se] n term   rel **impregnation**[1], **insemination**[2] n term → U69-5ff
(i) the beginning of pregnancy (ii) fertilization (iii) genE, creation of a concept or idea
conceptus[3] n term • **conceptive**[4] adj • **conceive** [iː] v • **contraception** n
» Of these patients 30% will conceive within two years. This fluid can contain large numbers of active sperm, i.e. impregnation is possible before ejaculation. Ideally, a rudimentary horn should be resected before the woman conceives [siː] a child[5].
Use spontaneous [eɪ]/ successful / rate of **conception** • (retained) [eɪ] products of[6] (abbr POC) **conception** • **conceptional** age[7] • artificial[8] [ɪʃ]/ intrauterine / donor[9] **insemination**

> Note: Mark the differences between **conceptional** (refers to conception), **conceptive** (= able to conceive), and **conceptual** (related to concepts or ideas).

(i, ii) Empfängnis, Konzeption
Imprägnation[1] Insemination[2] Keimling, Konzeptus[3] Empfängnis-[4] Kind empfängt, schwanger wird[5] Plazentareste[6] Schwangerschaftsdauer[7] artifizielle Insemination[8] donogene Insemination, DAI[9]

2

nidation [naɪdeɪʃən] n term   syn **implantation** n term
attachment [ætʃ], penetration and embedding of the fertilized ovum in the uterine mucosa
implant[1] v term • **implanting** adj
» The endometrial activity goes out of phase [feɪz], so that nidation is thwarted[2] [ɔː] even if fertilization does occur. Luteal [luːtɪəl] phase inadequacy may lead to a shortened luteal phase, an endometrium [iː] incapable [eɪ] of supporting implantation of an embryo, or both.
Use to achieve **nidation** • normal **nidation** • ectopic / superficial[3] [ɪʃ]/ embryo im**plantation** • (disrupted) [ʌ] placental[4] [se] **implantation** • **implantation** site[5]

Einnistung, Nidation, Implantation
s. einnisten, implantieren[1] verhindert[2] Erstkontakt bei Implantation[3] plazentare Nidationsstörung, Einnistungsstörung[4] Implantationsort[5]

3

fetus [fiːtəs] *n term*, BE **f(o)etus**   *rel* **embryo¹** [embrɪoʊ] *n term* → U85-1
unborn baby from the end of the 8th week after conception until birth
fetal [iː] *adj term* • **embryonal²**, **embryonic²** *adj* • **embryo-, feto-** *comb*

» Fetal scalp sampling should be avoided. Virilization may occur [ɜː] in the mother as well as in female fetuses³. The endometrium of the hyperstimulated cycle [saɪkl] is thought to be not the most hospitable environment⁴ to an implanting embryo.

Use developing / male / lost / viable⁵ [aɪ] **fetus** • **fetal** growth / life⁶ / movements⁷ • **fetal** age / tissue / assessment • **fetal** blood flow / imaging / monitoring • **fetal** heart tones⁸ (*abbr* FHT)/ outcome / survival • **fetal** damage / loss or wastage⁹ [eɪ] • **fetal** alcohol syndrome¹⁰ [ɪ] (*abbr* FAS)/ demise or death¹¹ • maternal **fetal** barrier¹² • human / normally conceived / preimplantation **embryo** • healthy-appearing / frozen(-thawed) [ɔː] **embryo** • **embryo** transfer¹³ / donation • **embryonal** growth / carcinoma¹⁴ • **embryonic** cell / disk¹⁵ / stage / life¹⁶ • **embryonic** death / tissue / development¹⁷ • **embryo**genesis¹⁷ /logic /toxic /pathy • **feto**maternal /pelvic disproportion /protein /scopy¹⁸

Fötus, Fetus
Embryo¹ embryonal, Embryonal-² weibl. Feten³ nicht das günstigste Milieu⁴ lebensfähiger Fetus⁵ Fetalperiode⁶ Kindsbewegungen⁷ kindl. Herztöne⁸ Abort⁹ embryofetales Alkoholsyndrom, Alkoholembryopathie¹⁰ intrauteriner Fruchttod¹¹ Plazentaschranke¹² Embryonentransfer¹³ Embryonalkarzinom¹⁴ Keimscheibe¹⁵ Embryonalperiode¹⁶ Embryonalentwicklung¹⁷ Fetoskopie¹⁸

4

expectant *adj clin*   *syn* **pregnant** *adj clin*, **gravid** *adj term*
  sim **to expect a baby¹, to be with child¹**, BE **to be gone¹** *phr inf*
referring to parents (esp. mothers) who know they are going to have a baby

» She's expecting another baby. Expectant mothers often have cravings [eɪ] for unusual foods². Is she expecting again? She's two months pregnant. She's 7 months gone³.

Use **expectant** mother / father • to be⁴/get⁴/become⁴ **pregnant** • **pregnant** woman / diabetic⁵ [e]/ teenager / patient • to have⁶/deliver⁷ a baby • unborn / newborn / blue⁸ **baby** • **baby** boy / foods⁹ / talk / sitter • primi/ secundi**gravid** • **gravid** uterus [juː]/ state [eɪ]

schwanger, gravid
e. Kind erwarten/ unter d. Herzen tragen¹ ungewöhnliche Essensgelüste² im 8. Monat schwanger³ schwanger werden⁴ schwangere Diabetikerin⁵ ein Kind bekommen⁶ e. Kind gebären⁷ zyanotischer Säugling, blue baby⁸ Baby-, Säuglingsnahrung⁹

5

Fetal ultrasound obtained at 18 weeks of gestation: the facial profile, spine, and thorax are within normal limits

pregnancy [pregnən(t)si] *n clin, abbr* **preg**   *syn* **gestation** [dʒesteɪʃ(ə)n] *n term*
condition of the expecting mother from conception until the birth of the baby (10 lunar [uː] months¹, 40 weeks or 280 days calculated from the first day of the last menses)
gestational *adj term* • **prepregnancy** *adj* • **pseudopregnancy²** [suːdoʊ-] *n & adj*

» Usually the first sign of pregnancy is a missed menstrual period³. In a normal fetus, the bladder may be visualized [ɪз] at 14 weeks' gestation. Accurate maternal [ɜː] dates remain the best indicator of gestational age⁴.

Use to plan/prevent/avoid/fail to achieve/complicate/terminate⁵/sustain⁶ [eɪ] **pregnancy** • multiple⁷ [ʌ]/ unplanned / suspected / unwanted⁸ **pregnancy** • (extra)uterine / ectopic / tubal⁹ / abdominal¹⁰ **pregnancy** • first / early / mid/ late / (post-)term¹¹ / high-risk¹² **pregnancy** • false or spurious² [jʊə]/ uneventful¹³ **pregnancy** • **prepregnancy** weight [weɪt] • **pregnancy**-induced /-related / test¹⁴ / rate / urine [jʊɚ] • **gestation** period [ɪɚ]/ length¹⁵ [leŋkθ] • after 28 days / in the 6th month **of gestation** • **gestational** age⁴ / assessment • 36 weeks' **gestation**

Note: Informal expressions for **being pregnant** include **to be having a baby**, **to be in the family way, to be in trouble** (out of wedlock¹⁶), **to be *large/ *big/ *heavy/ *great**, (advanced pregnancy), and **to fall for a baby** (unplanned pregnancy).

Schwangerschaft, Gravidität
Lunarmonate¹ Scheinschwangerschaft² ausgebliebene Regelblutung³ Gestationsalter⁴ Schwangerschaft abbrechen, abtreiben⁵ Schwangerschaft erhalten⁶ Mehrlingsschwangerschaft⁷ unerwünschte Schwangerschaft⁸ Eileiterschwangerschaft, Tubargravidität⁹ Bauchhöhlenschwangerschaft, Abdominalgravidität¹⁰ Übertragung, Überschreitung d. Geburtstermins¹¹ Risikoschwangerschaft¹² komplikationslose/ unkomplizierte Schwangerschaft¹³ Schwangerschaftstest¹⁴ Schwangerschaftsdauer¹⁵ unehelich¹⁶

6

Pregnancy COMPLEX BODY FUNCTIONS 281

gravidity [grəvɪdɪti] *n term, abbr* **G**   *rel* **reproductive** [ʌ] **history**¹ *n clin*
the number of pregnancies a female has had, including miscarriages², abortions, etc.
(primi)gravida³ [praɪmɪɡrævɪdə] *n term* • **multigravida**⁴ [ʌ] *n* • **gravidarum** *adj*
» Each pregnancy increases gravidity, so that a woman with two pregnancies is a gravida 2. These worries are often not voiced, especially by primigravidas.
Use **gravida**, para, multiple births, abortions, live births (*abbr* GPMAL) • secundi/4-**gravida** • **gravida** 3 / 5 • hyperemesis⁵ / pruritus [aɪ]/ striae⁶ [straɪiː] **gravidarum**

   Note: Do not confuse **gravidity** with **gravity**⁷ or **gravitation**⁸.

(Anzahl d. bisherigen) Schwangerschaften
Schwangerschafts- u. Geburtenanamnese¹ Fehlgeburten² Primigravida³ Multi-, Plurigravida⁴ Hyperemesis gravidarum, übermäßiges Schwangerschaftserbrechen⁵ Schwangerschaftsstreifen⁶ Schwerkraft⁷ Massenanziehung, Gravitation⁸   7

parity [peəɪti] *n term, abbr* **P**   *rel* **TPAL**¹ *term*
total number of births (including stillbirths² and abortions at more than 28 weeks of gestation)
(nulli/ multi³/ primi⁴)para *n term* • **(primi/ multi/ nulli)parous**⁵ *adj*
» A multiple birth is considered a single parous experience. Record the maternal age, blood type, gravidity and parity. Menstrual pain usually decreases with parity. The TPAL system records the total number of term deliveries, premature [iː] **births**⁶, abortions or miscarriages before 28 weeks' gestation, and children living (e.g. para 1-1-1-2)
Use to determine⁷ [ɜː] /decrease with **parity** • maternal [ɜː]/ multi**parity** • **para** 1 / 2 / 3 • **parous** cervix [sɜː]/ introitus • grand⁸ [grænd] **multipara**

Parität
analog zum dt. G/P/A/AR-System¹ Totgeburten² Mehrgebärende, Multi-, Pluripara³ Erstgebärende⁴ nullipar⁵ Frühgeburten⁶ Parität feststellen⁷ Vielgebärende (mehr als 4 Kinder)⁸

   8

trimester [aɪ] *n term*   *rel* **lunar** [uː] **month**¹ *n clin*
term used to define a period of three months in pregnancy; the first trimester is 1-12 weeks, the second or mid-trimester is 13-26 weeks, and the third or last trimester is 27 weeks to delivery
» The first trimester is often accompanied by fatigue² [fətiːɡ], breast [e] tenderness, nausea³ [ɔː], and urinary frequency⁴, and an increased preoccupation with self and the growth of the fetus. Suction [ʌ] curettage⁵ is generally preferred for carrying out first-trimester termination procedures⁶.
Use late 2ⁿᵈ **trimester** • **first-trimester** pregnancy / bleeding / curettage [kjʊə-] • **first-trimester** prenatal diagnosis / exposure [oʊʒ] to • **midtrimester** stillbirth⁷ / amniocentesis [iː]

Trimenon
Lunarmonat¹ Müdigkeit² Übelkeit³ Pollakisurie, häufiges Wasserlassen⁴ Saugkürettage⁵ Schwangerschaftsabbruch im 1. Trimenon⁶ Totgeburt im 2. Trimenon⁷

   9

due date [d(j)uː] *phr clin*   *syn* **expected date of delivery** *phr term, abbr* **EDD**
   syn **expected date of confinement** [aɪ] *phr term, abbr* **EDC**
the date of delivery calculated from the day of conception (226 days) or the LMP¹ (280 days) or by counting back 3 months from the first day of the and adding 7 days (Naegele's rule²)
» Take your antenatal classes³ well before your due date. The date of onset of the last normal menstrual period (*abbr* LNMP) is important to define. Uterine size on bimanual examination was larger than it should be by dates⁴. Estimate the due date and gestational age of the fetus.
Use to estimate the **due date** • small⁵ / large for⁶ **dates** • maternal [ɜː]/ obstetric / embryologic / inaccurate **dates** • possible conception⁷ / predicted delivery **date** • **date of** birth (*abbr* DOB)/ the last menstrual period¹ (*abbr* LMP)

voraussichtl. Geburtstermin
1. Tag d. letzten Menstruation¹ Naegele-Regel² Schwangerengymnastik, Geburtsvorbereitungskurs³ nach d. errechneten Schwangerschaftsdauer⁴ dystrophes Neugeborenes, negative Diskrepanz (zw. US-Befund und Normtabelle)⁵ großes Kind, positive Diskrepanz⁶ mögl. Empfängnistermin⁷
   10

at term [tɜːrm] *phr clin & term*
at the expected date of delivery [dɪlɪvəɪ]
full-term *adj clin & term* • **preterm** [priːtɜːrm] *adj* • **post-term** *adj*
» Nulliparous women and women whose first full-term pregnancy was after age 35 have a slightly higher incidence of breast cancer. At term, about 4/5 of the placenta is of fetal origin.
Use **term** infant¹ / pregnancy or gestation • **preterm** labor² [leɪbɚ]/ delivery • **full-term** neonate [iː] *or* newborn¹ • **post-term** infant³

termingerecht, zum errechneten Termin, bei der Geburt
ausgetragenes Kind, Reifgeborenes¹ vorzeitige Wehen² übertragenes Kind³

   11

morning sickness *n clin*   *rel* **hyperemesis gravidarum**¹ *n term* → U103-11f
bouts [aʊ] of nausea and vomiting frequently experienced by expecting mothers in early pregnancy²
» The morning sickness of early pregnancy is probably related to hormonal changes; if it is related to fluid disturbances [ɜː] or nutritional [ɪʃ] deficits it is termed hyperemesis [aɪ] gravidarum.

morgendliches Erbrechen, Vomitus matutinus, Emesis gravidarum
Hyperemesis gravidarum, unstillbares Schwangerschaftserbrechen¹ Frühschwangerschaft²   12

282 COMPLEX BODY FUNCTIONS Childbirth

(fetal) quickening n clin & inf   syn **fetal movements** n clin

first fetal movements felt (abbr FFMF) by the mother-to-be[1]

» The onset, quality, and strength of fetal quickening and the age of achievement of motor milestones[2] are helpful aspects in the history. Fetal movement often results in a greater sense of reality about the pregnancy. In the 5th month, fetal "quickening" movements may be felt as the baby moves and kicks within the amniotic fluid.

Use   onset[3] / the mother's perceptions / lack **of fetal movements** • (ab)normal / decreased / intrauterine **fetal movement** • to feel[4]/count **fetal movements**

Kindsbewegungen
werdende Mutter[1] wichtige motorische Entwicklungsschritte[2] erste Kindsbewegungen[3] Kindsbewegungen wahrnehmen[4]

13

twin n & adj   sim **triplets**[1] [ɪ], **quadruplets**[2] [ʌ‖u], **quintuplets**[3] n term

one of two infants born of the same pregnancy and developed either from the same ovum (identical twins[4]) or from two ova which ovulated and were fertilized simultaneously [eɪ] (fraternal [ɜː] twins[5])

twin-to-twin adj term • **twinning**[6] [twɪnɪŋ] n

» In fraternal twins, the placentas may be two distinct chorions and amnions or fused. Twinning occurs in one of every 80 pregnancies. My doctor told me I am going to have triplets.

Use   monozygotic or identical[4] / dizygotic [daɪzaɪɡɒːtɪk] or fraternal[5] **twins** • monochorionic / conjoined[7] [dʒɔɪ] / Siamese[8] [aɪ] **twins** • **twin** (intrauterine) pregnancy or gestation[9] • **twin** birth / sister[10] / brother / studies • female **twins** • **twin-to-twin** transfusion [juː] syndrome[11] [ɪ]

Zwilling; Zwillings-
Drillinge[1] Vierlinge[2] Fünflinge[3] eineiige Zwillinge[4] zweieiige Zwillinge[5] Zwillingsbildung[6] Doppelmissbildung[7] Siamesische Zwillinge[8] Zwillingsschwangerschaft[9] Zwillingsschwester[10] Zwillingstransfusionssyndrom[11]

14

PUPPP abbr   **pruritic urticarial papules and plaques of pregnancy** n term

intensely itching[1] and sometimes vesicular eruption appearing on the trunk[2] and arms in the 3rd trimester

» As there is no specific diagnostic test, PUPPP may be difficult to differentiate from other pruritic[3] [ɪ] eruptions [ʌ] of pregnancy. PUPPP resolved spontaneously[4] within 10 days of term.

Schwangerschaftsdermatose
stark juckend[1] Rumpf[2] juckend[3] klang spontan ab[4]

15

striae [straɪiː] n term pl   syn **stretch marks** [stretʃ mɑːrks] n clin pl

marks commonly seen in rapidly growing tissue as a side effect of pregnancy; usually apparent [eə] on the abdomen, breasts [e], thighs[1] [θaɪz], and buttocks[2] [ʌ]

» During pregnancy adrenal [iː] hormone levels increase, probably causing the purplish [ɜː] striae[3] on the skin known as stretch marks.

Use   cutaneous[4] [eɪ]/ abdominal / purplish[3] **striae**

Schwangerschaftsstreifen, Striae gravidarum
Oberschenkel[1] Gesäß[2] rötlich-bläuliche Striae[3] Hautdehnungsstreifen, Striae cutis distensae/ atrophicae[4]

16

Unit 71   Childbirth
Related Units: 70 Pregnancy, 69 Fertility, 50 Female Sexual Organs, 51 Menstrual Cycle, 55 Hormones, 85 Embryology

be born [bɔːrn] v pass   sim **arrive**[1] [əraɪv] v inf

to pass from the mother's womb[2] [wuːm] at the beginning of life

newborn[3] [n(j)uːbɔːrn] adj & n • **arrival**[4] [aɪ] n • **unborn**[5] adj • **stillborn**[6] adj

» Two of her children were born at home. She was born to poor parents. He is a natural born leader. She was born Mary Smith. The baby arrived before they reached the hospital. Smoking might harm your unborn baby.

Use   first-/ German[7]-**born** • **born** on May 5 / in Rome / to sing • **born** with a handicap[8] / deaf[9] [def]/ free

geboren werden
auf die Welt kommen[1] Gebärmutter, Uterus[2] neugeboren; Neugeborenes[3] Neuankömmling, neuer Erdenbürger[4] noch nicht geboren, ungeboren[5] totgeboren[6] gebürtige(r) Deutsche(r)[7] von Geburt an behindert[8] taub geboren[9]

1

give birth [bɜːrθ] **(to)** phr   sim **have a baby**[1], **become a mother**[2] [ʌ] phr inf

to be delivered of a baby[3] after nine months of pregnancy

birthing[4] [bɜːrθɪŋ] adj • **stillbirth**[5] n • **motherly** adj • **motherhood**[6] [mʌðərhʊd] n

» Your wife's given birth to a healthy boy. Having a baby will change your life completely. I was present at the births of my two children. Motherhood and career can be difficult to combine.

Use   to register [edʒ] /announce [aʊ] **a birth** • date / place[7] / country [ʌ] **of birth** • **birth** pangs[8] / certificate[9] [ɪ]/ injury / rate[10] / trauma [ɔː] • **birth**right /day /mark[11] /place[7] • to be French by[12] / at **birth** • to lose the **baby** • newborn **baby** • baby food / clothes • high-risk / adolescent [es] / nursing[13] [ɜː] • **mother** • **mother**-to be /-in-law[14] / figure / country • **mother** tongue [tʌŋ] • instinct[15] / fixation • **mother's** milk[16] / day / lap[17] • **motherly** feelings • surrogate[18] [ɜː]‖BE ʌ] • **motherhood**[19] • in your birthday suit[19] [suːt] • **birthing** center / room[20] / chair[21]

gebären
ein Kind bekommen[1] Mutter werden[2] von e. Kind entbunden werden[3] Gebär-[4] Totgeburt[5] Mutterschaft[6] Geburtsort[7] (Geburts)wehen[8] Geburtsurkunde[9] Geburtenrate, -ziffer[10] Muttermal[11] gebürtiger/ gebürtige Französin/ Französe sein[12] stillende Mutter[13] Schwiegermutter[14] Mutterinstinkt[15] Muttermilch[16] Mutterschoß[17] Leihmutterschaft[18] im Eva-/ Adamskostüm[19] Kreißsaal[20] Gebärstuhl[21]

2

Childbirth | COMPLEX BODY FUNCTIONS 283

labor [leɪbɚ] *n clin, BE* **labour**   *syn* **labor pains** *n clin*,
                              contractions, travail [trəveɪl‖træveɪl] *n term*

contractions [kʃ] of the uterus [juː] causing the products of conception [se] to descend [s] into the birth canal [kənæl].

contract[1] [kəntrækt‖kɒːntrækt] *v* • **toco-** [toʊkoʊ-] *comb*

» During labor, contractions cause dilation [eɪʃ] and thinning of the cervix [sɜː] and aid in the descent[2] of the baby into the birth canal. There were no signs of beginning labor. The fetus [iː] was delivered by cesarean [sɪzeəɪən] section[3] after 16 hours of labor and attempted vaginal [dʒ] delivery.

Use to undergo/go into/be in[4]/trigger[5]/initiate[5] [ɪʃ]/precipitate[5] [sɪ] **labor** • to induce[6] [(j)uː] /shorten/prolong/ suppress or inhibit[7] **labor** • spontaneous [eɪ]/ abnormal[8] / false[9] [ɔː]/ induced or artificial [ɪʃ] **labor** • dry[10] / violent [aɪə]/ first-stage[11] / second-stage[12] **labor** • prolonged / premature or preterm[13] [ɜː]/ dysfunctional[8] **labor** • onset[14] / induction / length / cardinal movements *of* **labor** • **labor** ward [ɔː]/ suite [swiːt]/ and delivery room[15] / coach / record[16] / myometrial [iː] or uterine[17] (*abbr* UC) **contractions** • to produce/stimulate UC • after**pains**[18] • **to-co**lytic [ɪ] agent[19] /lysis /graph[20]

confinement [kənfaɪnmənt] *n clin*   *syn* **accouchement** [əkuːʃmɔː] *n term rare*

final [aɪ] stage of pregnancy when labor and delivery begin

to lie in[1] *phr inf* • **to be brought to bed**[1] *phr dated* • **accoucheur, -euse**[2] *n*

» Labor usually begins within 2 weeks of the estimated date of confinement. Since calculation of the EDC is subject [ʌ] to error, the diagnosis of postdatism[3] [eɪ] is uncertain.

Use expected (*abbr* EDC)/ calculated[4] (*abbr* CDC) **date of confinement** • period of **confinement**

fetal presentation [fiːtəl prezᵊnteɪʃᵊn] *n term*

rel **fetal lie**[1] [laɪ], **fetal position**[2] [pəzɪʃᵊn], **fetal attitude**[3] [ætɪt(j)uːd] *n term*

part of the fetus first entering the birth canal; fetal lie refers to the relationship of the long axis of the fetus to the long axis of the uterus; fetal position is the relationship of the presenting part to the maternal pelvis; fetal attitude is the relationship of fetal head to the body

» Overdistention of the vagina caused by the presenting part of the infant may cause rupture of the vaginal musculature. Cephalic presentations[4] include vertex[5] [ɜː], brow[6] [aʊ], or face[7].

Use presenting part[8] • cephalic [səf-]/ breech[9] [briːtʃ]/ transverse[10] [ɜː] **presentation** • shoulder[11] / compound [-aʊnd] **presentation** • occiput[5] [ɒksɪpət] (O)/ mentum (M)/ sacrum [eɪ] (S)/ right (R)/ left (L) **position** • anterior (A)/ posterior (P)/ ROP[12] (=right occiput posterior) **position** • low / longitudinal / oblique[13] [oʊbliːk]/ transverse **lie**

rupture [rʌptʃɚ] **of membranes** *n term, abbr* ROM
                              syn **rupture of bag of waters** *n clin*

leak [iː] or breakage [breɪkɪdʒ] in the amniotic and chorionic sac (often referred to as bag of waters) resulting in a steady [e] flow of clear, pink, or greenish-brown fluid (amniotic fluid[1]) from the vagina [dʒaɪ].

waters break[2] *phr clin* • **forewaters**[3] [fɔːrwɒːtɚz] *n* • **forebag** *n*

» Her membranes are intact[4]. The fetal membranes arise from the placenta at its margin [dʒ]. In patients with early ruptured membranes prophylactic antibiotics are indicated. Careful examination of the membranes revealed [iː] torn vessels.

Use spontaneous / premature[5] (*abbr* PROM)/ artificial[6] / prolonged **rupture of membranes** • fetal[7] / retention of[8] **membranes** • ruptured membranes[9] / bag of waters[9]

(bloody) show [blʌdi ʃoʊ] *n jar & term*

(i) vaginal discharge[1] [tʃ] (mostly mucus [mjuːkəs] tinged [dʒ] with blood[2]) that appears as labor begins, esp. the mucus plug[3] [ʌ] that dislodges[4] when the cervix [sɜːrvɪks] begins to efface[5] [eɪ] (ii) broadly, any light bleeding[6] [iː] from the vagina [dʒaɪ].

» Bloody show may precede[7] [siː] the onset of labor by as much as 72 hours.

Use to give[8] **bloody show**

Wehen, Geburt, Labores uteri

kontrahieren[1] Tiefertreten[2] Kaiserschnitt, Schnittentbindung, Sectio caesarea[3] i. d. Wehen liegen[4] Wehen auslösen[5] Geburt einleiten[6] Wehen hemmen[7] Wehenanomalien, -dystokie[8] Senkwehen[9] Geburt nach vorzeitigem Blasensprung, Trockengeburt, Partus siccus[10] Eröffnungswehen[11] Austreibungs-, Presswehen[12] vorzeitige Wehen[13] Einsetzen d. Wehen, Geburtsbeginn[14] Kreißsaal[15] Wehenaufzeichnung[16] Wehen[17] Nachwehen[18] wehenhemmendes Mittel, Tokolytikum[19] Wehenschreiber[20]

3

Geburt, Entbindung, Niederkunft

niederkommen, gebären[1] Hebamme, (nichtärztl.) Geburtshelfer[2] Übertragung[3] errechneter Geburtstermin[4]

4

Kindslage

Poleinstellung[1] Positio[2] Kopfhaltung[3] Kopf-, Schädellagen[4] Hinterhauptlage[5] Vorderhaupt-, Stirnlage[6] Gesichtslage[7] vorangehender Kindsteil[8] Beckenend-, Steißlage[9] Querlage[10] Schulterlage[11] Positio occipitalis posterior im zweiten Durchmesser[12] Schräglage[13]

5

Blasensprung

Fruchtwasser[1] die Blase springt, Blasensprung[2] Vorwasser[3] intakte/stehende Fruchtblase[4] vorzeitiger Blasensprung[5] Blasensprengung[6] Eihäute[7] Eihautretention, unvollständige Nachgeburtsteile[8] Blasensprung[9]

6

Zeichnen

Scheidenausfluss[1] blutig, blutgefärbt[2] Schleimpfropf[3] löst sich[4] Zervix ist aufgebraucht[5] leichte Blutung[6] vorausgehen[7] es zeichnet[8]

7

Childbirth

birth canal [bɜːrθ kənæl] *n clin & inf*

passage through which the infant passes during vaginal birth
» *The fetus was infected in its passage through the birth canal. Explore the uterine cavity and the birth canal for lacerations* [s] *and retained placental fragments¹.*
Use infected **birth canal** • **birth canal** secretions [iːʃ] • to give **birth** to² • at **birth** • live³ / date of (*abbr* DOB)/ premature⁴ **birth** • vaginal / multiple⁵ [ʌ]/ cesarian [eəʳ]/ winter **birth** • **birth** weight⁶ [weɪt]/ history / records / defect [iː] • **birth** / mark⁷ / process [ɒːs]/ attendant⁸ / control⁹

Geburtskanal
unvollständige Nachgeburtsteile¹ gebären, zur Welt bringen² Lebendgeburt³ Frühgeburt⁴ Mehrlingsgeburt⁵ Geburtsgewicht⁶ Muttermal, Nävus⁷ Geburtshelfer(in), Hebamme⁸ Familienplanung, Geburtenregelung, Antikonzeption⁹   8

---

delivery [dɪlɪvəri] *n clin*   *syn* **(child)birth** *n clin*,   **parturition** [pɑːrtʃəˈrɪʃən] *n term*

expulsion [ʌ] or extraction of the fetus [iː] and the placenta [se] from the uterus at birth
deliver¹ *v term* • **parturient²** [(j)ʊəʳ] *adj & n* • **pre-/ postpartum** *or* **-delivery** *adj*
» *I would not recommend home delivery in your case because of the risk of complications during labor and delivery. She delivered a healthy girl. Elective delivery (induction³* [ʌ] *or cesarean section⁴) prior to 39 weeks of gestation* [dʒe-] *requires confirmation of fetal lung maturity⁵. The patient must be monitored until the placenta is delivered intact. Hepatitis* [aɪ] *B virus may be transmitted to the infant at parturition or, less often, transplacentally.*
Use normal spontaneous [eɪ]/ full-term normal (*abbr* FTND)/ mode of **delivery** • vaginal / cesarean⁴ / vertex⁶ [ɜː]/ Lamaze / (modified) Leboyer⁷ **delivery** • premature / complicated / assisted cephalic [sef-]/ midforceps⁸ [s] **delivery** • (failed/ high) forceps⁹ / breech¹⁰ [briːtʃ] **delivery** • double footling¹¹ / postmortem¹² **delivery** • **delivery** room¹³ / suite [swiːt]/ forceps¹⁴ / (manually) **delivered** placenta • **childbirth** education classes¹⁵ / technique [tekniːk] • **childbirth** trauma [ɒː]/ laceration [s]/ without pain (*abbr* CWP) • (un)prepared / emergency [ɜː]/ traumatic / natural⁷ **childbirth** • **postdelivery** asphyxia¹⁶ [æsfɪksɪə]/ medication [eɪʃ]

Entbindung, Geburt
entbunden werden, gebären¹ gebärend, Geburts-; Gebärende² Geburtseinleitung, Weheninduktion³ Schnittentbindung, Sectio (caesarea), Kaiserschnitt⁴ Lungenreife⁵ Entbindung aus Hinterhauptlage⁶ sanfte/ natürliche Geburt⁷ Zangenextraktion aus Beckenmitte⁸ hohe Zangengeburt⁹ Entbindung aus Beckenendlage, Steißgeburt¹⁰ E. aus vollständiger Fußlage¹¹ Sarggeburt¹² Kreißsaal¹³ Geburtszange¹⁴ Geburtsvorbereitungskurs¹⁵ postpartale Asphyxie¹⁶

   9

---

effleurage [efləˈrɑːʒ] *n term*   *sim* **pétrissage¹** [peɪtrɪˈsɑːʒ] *n term* → U142-15

rhythmic [ɪ] massage of the lower abdomen (light circular stroking [oʊ] movements) used in natural childbirth to help the parturient relax and control her breathing [iː] rhythm during uterine contractions
» *The mother may perform an effleurage of the lower abdomen during contractions.*
Use fingertip / rolling **effleurage** • **effleurage** technique / on uterus [juː]

Streichmassage, Effleurage
Knetmassage, Pétrissage¹

   10

---

bearing down [beərɪŋ daʊn] *phr term*

voluntary effort by the parturient in the second stage of labor to help expel¹ the fetus by increasing the intra-abdominal pressure
» *Conduction* [ʌ] *anesthesia²* [iːʒ] *prevents the patient from bearing down adequately. In addition to the uterine contractions, expulsive bearing-down efforts are required for spontaneous delivery³.*
Use **bearing-down** pains⁴ / efforts / sensation [eɪʃ]/ type of pain

Pressen
austreiben¹ Leitungsanästhesie² Spontangeburt³ Presswehen⁴

   11

---

effacement [eˈfeɪsmənt] *n term*   *sim* **cervical dil(at)ation¹** [sɜːrvɪkəl] *n term*

thinning of the cervix and its merging [mɜːrdʒɪŋ] with the uterus wall (estimated in percentages) which occurs [ɜː] on cervical dilation (recorded in cm of the cervical diameter [daɪæ-])
» *Delivery must not be attempted before the cervix is fully effaced. The mucous* [mjuːkəs] *membrane is rose-colored and lies in irregular folds that become effaced by distention.*
Use cervical / degree [iː] of / early / full or complete² **effacement** • no / little / gradual [ædʒ]/ advanced **effacement** • **effacement** and dilatation [daɪləˈteɪʃən]

Muttermunderöffnung, Zervixverkürzung
Zervixdilatation¹ vollständige Eröffnung des Muttermundes²

   12

---

stage [steɪdʒ] *n term*   *rel* **station¹** [steɪʃən] *n term*

three stages of labor are distinguished (labor pains, expulsion² [ʌ], afterbirth); the level of the biparietal [aɪ] plane [eɪ] of the fetal head relative to the ischial [ɪskɪəl] spines³ [aɪ] of the maternal pelvis is referred to as station
» *Perform a vaginal examination to determine the position and station of the head. Maternal hemorrhage* [-rɪdʒ] *must be prevented during the 3ʳᵈ stage of labor (delivery of the placenta).*
Use first⁴ / second⁵ / third⁶ **stage of labor** • zero⁷ **station** • **station** plus two / minus 3

Geburtsphase
Höhenstand d. vorangehenden Kindsteils (VKT)¹ Austreibung² Spinae ischiadicae³ Eröffnungsperiode⁴ Austreibungsperiode⁵ Nachgeburtsperiode⁶ VKT auf Interspinallinie⁷

   13

Childbirth   COMPLEX BODY FUNCTIONS 285

engagement [ɪngeɪdʒmənt] *n term*   *rel* **descent**¹ [dɪsent], **fetal rotation**² *n term*

station of labor in which the fetal head (or largest diameter of the presenting part) enters the true pelvis³

» In cephalopelvic disproportion, failure of engagement, and incomplete dilation of the cervix forceps delivery is contraindicated. The baby's head may need to be rotated manually or with obstetric forceps⁴ to aid its descent through the birth canal.

Use breech [briːtʃ] **engagement** • **engagement** at term • shoulder **engaged** • protracted⁵ **descent** • **descent** of the presenting part⁶

Eintritt d. VKT in d. Beckeneingang
Tiefertreten¹ Rotation d. vorangehenden/ führenden Kindsteils² kleines Becken³ Geburtszange⁴ verzögertes Tiefertreten⁵ Tiefertreten d. VKT⁶

14

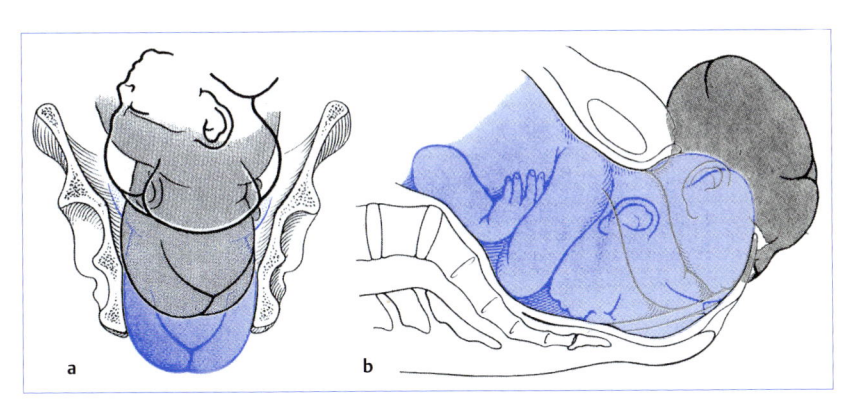

Crowning: the head of the baby rotates 90 degrees as it passes through the bony pelvis

crowning [kraʊnɪŋ] *n term*   *rel* **expulsion**¹ [ɪkspʌlʃən] *n term*

stage of childbirth when the fetal scalp can be seen at the introitus² and the largest diameter of the head is encircled by the vulvar [ʌ] ring³

expel⁴ [ɪkspel] *v term* • **expulsive** [ʌ] *adj* • **crown-to-heel length**⁵ [hiːl leŋkθ] *n*

» In 80-90% of these cases, spontaneous [eɪ] labor and expulsion of the fetus and placenta occur within 48 hours. Body length is measured [eː] from crown to heel.

Use **crowning** of infant's head • labor pains⁶ **crowning** • **crown**-to-rump [ʌ] length⁷ • expelled fetus [iː]/ infant / afterbirth⁸ • **expulsion** contractions⁹

Einschneiden
Austreibung¹ Scheideneingang² Vulvaring³ austreiben, ausstoßen⁴ Scheitel-Fersen-Länge⁵ Wehenakme⁶ Scheitel-Steiß-Länge⁷ ausgestoßene Nachgeburt⁸ Austreibungs-, Presswehen⁹

15

placenta [pləsentə] *n term*   *syn* **afterbirth** [æftəbɜːrθ] *n clin* → U85-14

organ of fetal-maternal [ɜː] metabolic exchange consisting of a uterine¹ and a fetal² (chorion) portion with the umbilical cord (amnion) normally attached [tʃ] near the center; diffusion [juː3] takes places across the placental membrane in the chorionic villi³, so no direct mixing of fetal and maternal blood occurs; the marginal [dʒ] sinus [aɪ], a large vein [eɪ] at the periphery of the placenta returns part of the maternal blood

(utero-/ feto-/ trans)placental⁴ *adj term* • **placentation**⁵ *n*

» The maternal portion¹ of the placenta amounts to less than one-fifth of the total placenta by weight. The fetal surface of the placenta is covered by the shiny amniotic membrane. At term, the human placenta is disk-shaped and averages about 1/7 the weight of the fetus.

Use to pass/cross **the placenta** • fetal / uterine / fundal [ʌ] **placenta** • incarcerated / adherent⁶ [ɪə]/ low lying / retention of⁷ **placenta** • inaccessible [kse]/ battledore⁸ / fused [fjuːzd] **placenta** • **placenta** delivered intact/manually⁹ • **placental** (implantation) site / barrier or membrane¹⁰ / septum / villi [vɪlaɪ]/ perfusion¹¹ [juː3]/ fragment / (dys)function / abnormality • **transplacental** infection / spread [e]/ passage / transmission • **afterbirth** pains¹²

Plazenta, Mutterkuchen, Nachgeburt
mütterl. Anteil, Pars uterina/ materna¹ kindl. Anteil, Pars fetalis² Chorionzotten³ plazentar, Plazenta-⁴ Plazentation, Plazentabildung⁵ anhaftende/ angewachsene Plazenta, P. adhaerens⁶ Plazentaretention⁷ Plazenta m. randständiger Insertion⁸ manuelle Plazentalösung⁹ Plazentaschranke¹⁰ Plazentadurchblutung¹¹ Nachgeburtswehen¹²

16

umbilical cord [ʌmbɪlɪkəl‖-laɪkəl kɔːrd] *n term & clin*

spongy [ʌ] structure that connects the fetus to the placenta carrying nourishment[1] [ɜː] and removing waste [weɪst] via two veins [eɪ] and an artery; it is formed of the yolk [joʊk] sac[2], the body stalk[3] [stɔːk], and the allantois [əlæntoʊəs]

umbilicus[4] [ʌmbɪlɪkəs‖-bɪlaɪkəs] *n term* • **umbilical** *adj* • **omphal(o)-** [ɒː] *comb* • **navel**[4] [neɪvəl] *n clin*

» The umbilical cord is clamped and cut after delivery, and when the cord stump[5] [ʌ] falls off, the baby's umbilicus is revealed [iː]. Cut the umbilical cord after ligating [laɪɡeɪtɪŋ] it about 2-3 inches from the infant's abdomen.

Use to clamp[6]/cut[7] **the umbilical cord** • **umbilical cord** blood / insertion [ɜː] site / stump[5] / compression • **umbilical** circulation / arterial [ɪə] pulse / vessels[8] • **umbilical** artery catheter (*abbr* UAC)/ blood (sampling) (*abbr* UBS) • **umbilical** venous [iː] line[9] / compression / hernia[10] [ɜː] • **cord** stump[5] • **umbilical** region • prolapsed[11] **umbilical cord** • **omphal**ocele[12] [-siːl] /omesenteric duct[13] [ʌ] /itis[14]

episiotomy [ɪpɪ‖iːpiːzɪɒːtəmi] *n term*
   rel **perineal suture**[1] [-niːəl suːtʃɚ] *n term*

incision [sɪ] of the vulva [ʌ] and perineum [iː] made when the baby's head is showing to enlarge the vaginal opening and prevent perineal rupture[2] [ʌ]

» Early and adequate episiotomy, and avoidance of traumatic delivery tend to prevent or at least to minimize prolaps. Pain from an uncomfortable episiotomy can be relieved with hot sitz baths[3]. Maternal tissue fragility [dʒɪ] may complicate episiotomy or cesarean section.

Use **episiotomy** repair[1] [rɪpɛɚ]/ stitches[1] [tʃ] / infection / scars [ɑː] • median [iː] or midline[4] / mediolateral[5] / early **episiotomy**

meconium [mɪkoʊnɪəm] *n term*
   rel **vernix (caseosa)**[1] [vɜːrnɪks kæsɪoʊsə] *n term*

sticky[2], dark-green material in the fetal intestine that forms the first stools [uː] of a newborn

» Failure of a newborn infant to pass meconium[3] demands investigation. Was the amniotic fluid[4] contaminated with meconium or vernix? Do not wash off all the vernix caseosa which covers most of the body, as it provides some antibacterial [ɪə] protection.

Use to pass[3] **meconium** • (delayed) [eɪ] passage[5] / presence / analysis **of meconium** • fetal / thick or inspissated or tenacious[6] [eɪʃ] aspirated **meconium** • **meconium** fluid / stool [uː]/ discharge[5] [dɪstʃɑːrdʒ] / ileus[7] / **meconium** examination / aspiration[8] (syndrome) [ɪ] • **meconium** plug [ʌ] syndrome[9] [ɪ]/ stained [eɪ] amniotic fluid[10] / peritonitis[11] [aɪ]

afterpains [æftɚpeɪnz] *n clin*   *sim* **afterbirth pains**[1] *n clin*

uterine contractions in the first few days postpartum[2] which resolve spontaneously [eɪ]

» Afterpains tend to be strongest in multiparas[3], multiple [ʌ] births, and during breastfeeding[4].

puerperium [pjuːɚpɪɚɪəm] *n term*
   sim **postpartum period**[1] [pɪərɪəd] *n term*

period (approx. 3 - 6 wks postpartum) following childbirth in which the uterus returns to prepartum[2] dimensions and the dramatic physiologic changes of pregnancy resolve

puerpera[3] [ɜː] *n term* • **puerperal** [ɜː] *adj* • **ante/ peri/ intra/ postpartum**[4] *adj*

» The early puerperium[5] is accompanied by a rise in fibrinogen and several clotting factors[6]. Sleep disturbances [ɜː] during pregnancy and the puerperium are common.

Use (ab)normal **puerperium** • **puerperal** uterus / period[7] / complications / infection • **puerperal** sepsis or fever[8] [iː]/ mastitis [aɪ]/ morbidity • immediate [iː]/ early **postpartum period** • to occur/develop/be/remit or resolve[9] **postpartum** • **postpartum** women [ɪ]/ state / days / psychosis[10] [saɪkoʊsɪs] • **postpartum** care / recovery [ʌ]/ hemorrhage[11] [-rɪdʒ]/ mastitis / thyroiditis[12] [aɪ] • **antepartum** bleeding / risk factors / diagnosis • **intrapartum** period / asphyxia[13] [ɪ]/ transmission • **peripartum** fever / cardiomyopathy[14] [aɪɒː]

Nabelschnur, -strang, Funiculus umbilicalis
Nährstoffe[1] Dottersack[2] Bauchstiel[3] Nabel, Umbilicus[4] Nabelschnurrest[5] Nabelschnur abklemmen[6] Nabelschnur durchtrennen, abnabeln[7] Nabelgefäße[8] Nabelvenenkatheter[9] Nabelbruch, Hernia umbilicalis[10] Nabelschnurvorfall[11] Nabelschnurbruch, Omphalozele[12] Dottergang, Ductus omphaloentericus[13] Nabelentzündung, Omphalitis[14]

17

Episiotomie, (Scheiden)dammschnitt
Dammnaht[1] Dammriss[2] Sitzbäder[3] mediane Episiotomie[4] mediolaterale Episiotomie[5]

18

Mekonium, Kindspech
Fruchtschmiere, Vernix caseosa[1] klebrig[2] Mekonium absetzen[3] Fruchtwasser[4] Mekoniumabgang[5] eingedicktes/ kittartiges M.[6] Mekoniumileus[7] Mekoniumaspiration[8] Mekoniumpfropfsyndrom[9] mekoniumhaltiges Fruchtwasser[10] Mekoniumperitonitis[11]

19

Nachwehen
Nachgeburtswehen[1] nach d. Geburt[2] Mehrgebärende[3] Stillen[4]

20

Wochen-, Kindbett, Puerperium
Postpartalperiode[1] vor d. Geburt[2] Wöchnerin, Puerpera[3] postpartal, Wochenbett-[4] Frühwochenbett[5] Gerinnungsfaktoren[6] Wochenbett, Puerperium[7] Puerperal-, Kindbettfieber[8] nach d. Geburt abklingen[9] Wochenbett-, Puerperalpsychose[10] postpartale Blutung[11] Postpartum-Thyreoiditis[12] intrapartale Asphyxie[13] peripartale Kardiomyopathie[14]

21

Childbirth   COMPLEX BODY FUNCTIONS **287**

(baby or **maternity) blues** [mətɜːrnəti bluːz] *n clin & inf*
    sim **postpartum depression**[1] [poʊstpɑːrtəm dɪpreʃˀn] *n term* → U77-17
mild depression (characterized by sadness, impatience[2] [eɪʃ], and restlessness[3]) resulting from the dramatic hormonal swings[4] commonly seen following childbirth
depressive *adj term* • **depressed** *adj clin* • **to feel blue/ down**[5] *phr inf*
» *If inability to care for the baby persists after 2 weeks postpartum, the condition is termed postpartum depression (a more severe form of the "baby blues"). Maternity blues are not in themselves psychopathologic, but those predisposed to mood disorders may break down.*
Use premenstrual[6] / holiday **blues** • reactive[7] / mild / major[8] [eɪdʒ] **depression** • morbid / incapacitating[9] [æs] **depression** • **depressive** phase [feɪz]/ periods • **maternity** ward[10] [ɔː]/ clothes[11] / girdle [ɜː]/ leave[12] [liːv]

lochia [loʊ‖lɒːkɪə] *n term*   *syn* **lochial flow** [loʊkɪəl floʊ] *n term*
vaginal flow in the puerperium made up of leukocytes [luːkəsaɪts], endometrial [iː] mucus, fetal lanugo[1] [(j)uː], meconium, etc.
» *During the first 3-4 days postpartum the lochia is red but takes on a yellowish-white color as endometrial epithelialization progresses during the 3rd week. Cessation [seseɪʃˀn] of the flow of lochia at about 6 weeks is usual.*
Use **lochia** rubra[2] [uː]/ serosa[3] / flava[4] [fleɪ‖flɑːvə]/ alba[5] • foul-smelling [aʊ] or malodorous[6] [oʊ]/ purulent[7] [pjʊɚ-] **lochia**

colostrum [kəlɒːstrəm] *n term*
sticky whitish or yellowish fluid secreted [iː] by the breasts [e] during mid to late pregnancy and for the first few days postpartum before the breast milk comes in[1] which contains valuable nutrients[2] [(j)uː]
» *Colostrum contains antibodies and stimulates the passage of meconium. At delivery, the newborn may be put to breast[3] for a few minutes to receive* [siː] *some colostrum.*
Use **colostrum** feeding [iː]/ expressed from the breast

lactation [lækteɪʃˀn] *n term*   *rel* **breast-feeding**[1] [brest fiːdɪŋ] *n clin*
(i) synthesis [ɪ] and secretion of breast milk (ii) period of time during which a child is nursed
lactate[2] [lækteɪt] *v term* • **lactating**[3] *adj* • **lactational**[4] [eɪ] *adj* • **lactiferous**[4] *adj*
» *Lactation does not begin until at least three days after birth. This drug is contraindicated during early pregnancy and lactation. Supplemental feedings may alter both the pattern of lactation and the intensity of infant suckling* [ʌ].
Use to suppress[5] **lactation** • **lactation(al)** amenorrhea[6] [iː]/ mastitis [aɪ] • **lactating** women [ɪ]/ breast[7] • **lactiferous** duct[8] [ʌ]

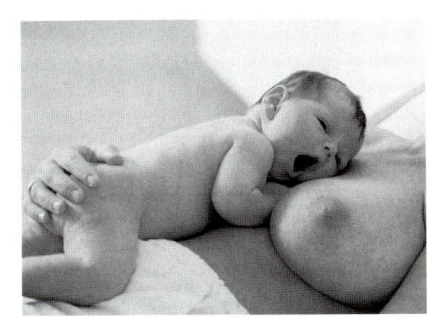

Newborn on the third postpartal day: bonding promotes maternal-infant attachment

breast-feed, -fed, -fed [brestfiːd] *v irr clin*   *syn* **nurse** [ɜː] **a baby** *v phr inf*
giving an infant milk from the breast by promoting successful latch-on[1] [lætʃ] and suckling [ʌ]
breast-/ bottle-feeding *n* • **nursing**[2] [ɜː] *adj & n* • **nursling**[3] *n* → U14-8
» *Deliberate[4] continuation of nursing after it is no longer necessary for infant nutrition has long been a widespread contraceptive method. Breastfeeding may have advantages, but women who bottle-feed their babies must not be made to feel guilty[5]* [gɪlti] *or inadequate.*
Use to discontinue[6] **breastfeeding** • (in)effective / interrupted [ʌ] **breastfeeding** • **breastfed** infant[7] • long-term **breast-feeding** • **breastfeeding** process / difficulties[8] • fullness of the **breasts** • **breast** pump[9] • **bottlefed** infant[10] • **feeding** on demand[11]

---

postpartale Verstimmung, baby blues
Wochenbettdepression[1] Ungeduld[2] innere Unruhe[3] hormonelle Schwankungen[4] niedergeschlagen/ deprimiert sein[5] prämenstruelle Gereiztheit[6] reaktive Depression[7] depressive Episode[8] lähmende Depression/ Schwermut[9] Wöchnerinnenstation[10] Umstandskleider[11] Mutterschafts-, Karenzurlaub[12]
22

Wochenfluss, Lochien
Lanugo(haare)[1] Lochia cruenta/ rubra, blutiger Wochenfluss[2] L. serosa, wässriger Wochenfluss[3] Lochia flava, gelblicher Wochenfluss[4] L. alba, weißl. Wochenfluss[5] fötide Lochien[6] eitriger Wochenfluss[7]
23

Vormilch, Kolostrum
Muttermilch schießt ein[1] Nährstoffe[2] angelegt werden[3]

24

Laktation, Milchproduktion; Laktationsperiode
Brusternährung, Stillen[1] Milch absondern[2] stillend[3] laktifer, milchführend[4] Laktation unterdrücken[5] Laktationsamenorrhoe[6] laktierende Mamma[7] Milchgang, Ductus lactiferus[8]
25

stillen
Anlegen[1] stillend, Still-; Pflege, Stillen[2] Säugling[3] bewusst[4] schuldig[5] abstillen[6] Stillkind[7] Stillschwierigkeiten[8] Milchpumpe[9] Flaschenkind[10] Stillen nach Bedarf[11]

26

let-down *or* **milk ejection reflex** [ɪdʒekʃən riːfleks] *n term*
　　　　　　　　　　rel **breast engorgement**¹ [brest ɪŋɡɔːrdʒmənt] *n clin*

sensation [eɪ] when milk comes in the breasts of lactating mothers, e.g. when the baby begins to suckle²

» If the mother is not going to breast-feed, firm [ɜː] support of the breasts is needed, since drooping³ [uː] stimulates the let-down reflex and encourages milk flow. There was pain and swelling of the breasts caused by edema [iː] and engorgement of the ductal [ʌ] systems.

Use milk **let down** • to ingest⁴ [dʒe] /consume via/secrete [iː] **milk** • (fortified) breast or maternal⁵ [ɜː] **milk** • uterine⁶ **engorgement** • **breast milk** jaundice⁷ [dʒɔːndɪs]

Milchejektionsreflex
Anschwellen d. Brust¹ saugen² Hängen (d. Brust)³ Milch zu sich nehmen/ trinken⁴ nährstoffangereicherte Muttermilch⁵ Anfüllung u. Schwellung d. Uterus⁶ Muttermilchikterus⁷

27

---

weaning [wiːnɪŋ] *n clin* **syn ablactation** [æblækteɪʃən] *n term*

(i) to discontinue breast feeding and begin nourishment with other food
(ii) to decrease dependency¹ or gradually remove a patient from therapy, esp. mechanical [k] ventilation²

wean [wiːn] *v*

» Women are less fertile [ɜː] when nursing than after weaning. Some infants wean themselves.

Use **to wean** onto solid food³ / from the respirator

(i) Abstillen, Ablaktation
(ii) Entwöhnung
Abhängigkeit¹ künstliche Beatmung² auf feste Nahrung umstellen³

28

Unit 72 Sleep
Related Units: 7 States of Consciousness, 19 On the Ward, 73 Mental Activity, 103 Clinical Symptoms

drowsy [draʊzi] *adj clin* **syn somnolent** *adj term*, **sleepy** *adj*,
　　　　　　　　　　　　rel **yawn**¹ [jɔːn] *v & n clin*

having difficulty in maintaining [eɪ] a wakeful state, as a result of heat, being unwell, medication side effects² or drinking alcohol – rather than because of physical tiredness or listlessness³

drowsiness⁴ *n* • **drowse**⁵ *v & n* • **sleepiness**⁴ *n clin* • **yawning** *n clin* • **somnolence**⁴ *n term*

» I was so drowsy and just couldn't fight off the urge⁶ [ɜːdʒ] to sleep. Drowsiness is a condition that simulates light sleep from which the patient is easily aroused by touch or noise and can maintain alertness⁷ [ɜː] for some time. The patient is sleepy but arouses to loud voice⁸.

Use to be/become **drowsy** • slightly / mildly **drowsy** • **drowsy** patient • **somnolent** patient / detachment⁹ [tʃ] • to appear¹⁰/become **sleepy** • **sleepy**head¹¹ / individual • to cause¹²/induce¹²/increase/minimize/develop **drowsiness** • moderate / intense / excessive **drowsiness** • intolerable / transient / morning / afternoon **drowsiness** • progressive / excessive daytime / disorder of excessive (*abbr* DOES) **somnolence** • **to yawn** wearily¹³ [ɪɚ] • to be accompanied by / eye rubbing [ʌ] and¹⁴ **yawning**

schläfrig, somnolent
gähnen; Gähnen¹ Nebenwirkungen² Lust-, Teilnahmslosigkeit³ Schläfrigkeit, Somnolenz⁴ vor sich hindösen/ -dämmern; Halbschlaf⁵ Drang⁶ Wachheit⁷ durch Zuruf weckbar⁸ schläfrige Teilnahmslosigkeit⁹ schläfrig wirken¹⁰ Schlafmütze¹¹ schläfrig machen¹² müde gähnen¹³ Augenreiben und Gähnen¹⁴

1

---

doze [doʊz] *v & n* **syn nap** [næp] *n, sim* **nod**¹ [nɒd] *v & n, rel* **wink**² *n*

(to have) a short, light sleep, esp. on a couch [kaʊtʃ] during the daytime

(**half-**)**dozing** *adj & n* • **dozy**³ *adj BE* • catnap⁴ *n & v* • **nodding** *adj & n*

» The patient becomes drowsy in the morning, dozes much of the day, and has a fitful⁵, interrupted sleep at night. It's time for you to take a little nap. Try to avoid daytime naps including dozing at the TV set. He came out of his doze with a start. Last night I did not get a wink of sleep⁶.

Use **to doze** off⁷ • to fall *or* go off into a⁷ **doze** • to take *or* have⁸ **a nap** • afternoon⁹ / scheduled [ʃǁsk] 1-h¹⁰ **nap** • **to nod** off⁷ • to take⁸/have⁸/catch⁸ **forty winks** • **a wink** of sleep¹¹

dösen; Nickerchen
ein Nickerchen machen, nicken; Nicken¹ Nickerchen, Schläfchen, Blinzeln, Zwinkern² schläfrig, verschlafen³ Nickerchen; dösen⁴ unruhig⁵ kein Auge zugetan⁶ einnicken⁷ ein Nickerchen machen⁸ Nachmittagsschläfchen⁹ ein regelmäßiges einstündiges Schläfchen¹⁰ Nickerchen, Schläfchen¹¹

2

---

retire [aɪ] *v* **syn go to bed, turn in** *phr*,
　　　　　　sim **lie down**¹ *v phr*, **hit the sack² phr inf

formal expression for leaving a room, party or activity, esp. to go to bed, relax or take a rest

» The patient awakened several hours after retiring despite daytime control of pain. I'm ready to go to bed. After staying up late the night before he was glad to turn in without delay [eɪ].

Use **to retire** to one's bedroom / early³ / at 11 o'clock • to send/put a child (back) to⁴ **bed** • on / before⁵ / after retiring • **to turn in** at midnight

sich zurückziehen, zu Bett gehen
sich hinlegen¹ sich in die Falle hauen² früh zu Bett gehen³ ein Kind ins/ zu Bett bringen/ schlafen legen⁴ vor dem Schlafengehen⁵

3

Sleep   COMPLEX BODY FUNCTIONS 289

bedtime [bɛdtaɪm] *n & adj clin*   *syn* **hora somni** *n term, abbr* **h.s.**

the clock time when one tries to fall asleep in the evening

» *The patient should be given commonsense[1] advice [ədvaɪs] about consistent bedtimes. This condition does not usually respond to attempts to reestablish normal bedtime hours[2]. In short-term management the usual dosage is 5-10 mg at bedtime.*

Use to be taken at[3] / 1h before / into (IBT) **bedtime** • **bedtime** regimen [ɛdʒ]/ dose[4] / snack[5] / ritual [ɪtʃ]/ environment [aɪ]/ stories[6] • early / consistent[7] **bedtimes**

Schlafenszeit; beim/ vor dem Schlafengehen
vernünftig[1] Schlafenszeiten[2] vor dem Schlafengehen einzunehmen[3] Medikamentendosis vor d. Schlafengehen[4] kl. Mahlzeit vor d. Schlafengehen[5] Gutenachtgeschichten[6] regelmäßige Schlafenszeiten[7]

4

sleep [sliːp] - slept - slept *n & v irr*   *syn* **slumber** [slʌmbɚ] *n & v, rel* **rest**[1] *n & v*

(n) natural state of rest marked by reduced consciousness and a decrease in activity and metabolism

sleeping *adj* • **sleeper** *n* • **sleeplike**[2] *adj* • **restlessness**[3] *n* • **restless** *adj*

» *Symptoms that awaken the patient from sleep, e.g., pain or the urge to defecate[4] should be investigated. She complains of chronic inability to sleep adequately at night. Alcohol ingestion[5] [dʒe] prior to sleep is contraindicated in patients with sleep apnea. Attempting to sleep propped up on pillows[6] hardly ever succeeds. I need very little sleep, doctor.*

Use to sleep well / little / poorly / prone[7] [proʊn] • to sleep on one's side / like a log[8] / late[9] • to sleep as long as / in[10] / off a headache / through the night[11] • to go (back)/get/send sb./try/be unable to sleep • to put sb./drop off[12]/drift off[12]/cry oneself[13] to sleep • light [laɪt]/ deep[14] / sound[15] [aʊ]/ quiet / dreamless **sleep** • night-time *or* nocturnal[16] [ɜː]/ poor / restless[17] / beauty / disturbed [ɜː] **sleep** • lack[18] / duration[19] [eɪʃ] **of sleep** • **sleep** onset / pattern / period / stages[20] [eɪdʒ] • **sleep** time / spindles[21] / efficiency [ɪʃ]/ position • **sleep** hygiene [haɪdʒiːn]/-related / center / architecture [k] • **sleep** disorder *or* disturbance[22] / deprivation[23] • **sleep** latency[24] [eɪ]/ drunkenness[25] [ʌ] • **sleep** attacks[26] / apnea /-wake disorder • **sleep** log *or* diary [daɪɚi] • to be a light[27]/heavy **sleeper** • **sleeping** child / partner / pill[28] / sickness[29] / bag • motor[30] / physical [ɪ] **restlessness** • **restless** bed partner / legs syndrome [ɪ] (*abbr* RLS)

Schlaf; schlafen
Ruhe; ruhen, sich ausruhen[1] schlaffähnlich[2] Unruhe, Ruhelosigkeit[3] Stuhldrang[4] Alkoholkonsum[5] auf mehreren Kissen[6] auf d. Bauch schlafen[7] wie e. Klotz schlafen[8] lange schlafen[9] aus-, verschlafen[10] durchschlafen[11] einschlafen[12] sich i. d. Schlaf weinen[13] Tiefschlaf, tiefer S.[14] tiefer/ fester S.[15] Nachtschlaf[16] unruhiger S.[17] Schlafmangel[18] Schlafdauer[19] Schlafstadien[20] Schlafspindeln[21] Schlafstörung[22] Schlafentzug[23] Schlaflatenz[24] Schlaftrunkenheit[25] Schlafanfälle, Narkolepsie[26] e. leichten Schlaf haben[27] Schlafmittel[28] Schlafkrankheit[29] motorische Unruhe[30]

5

asleep [əsliːp] *adj*   *opposite* **awake**[1] [əweɪk] *adj*

» *Involuntary loss of urine while awake or asleep is extremely embarrassing[2] for most patients. A glass of fluid should be consumed [(j)uː] hourly while awake and if the patient is up at night.*

Use to be *or* lie[3]/fall[4]/stay **asleep** • to be fast *or* sound[5] [aʊ] **asleep** • to be/lie/stay/ keep sb.[6] /appear **awake** • wide *or* fully[7] / half / not quite **awake** • **awake** patient / state[8] / and alert[9] [ɜː] / intubation[10]

schlafend
wach[1] peinlich[2] schlafen[3] einschlafen[4] fest/ tief schlafen[5] jdn. wachhalten[6] hellwach[7] Wachzustand[8] wach und ansprechbar[9] Intubation des wachen Patienten[10]

6

awake - awoke - awoken *vi & vt irr*   *syn* **awaken, wake (up)** *vi & vt, sim* **arouse**[1] *vt*

to stop sleeping spontaneously [eɪ] or due to some noise or stimulus

awakening[2] [eɪ] *n & adj* • **arousal**[3] [aʊ] *n term* • **wakeful**[4] *adj* • **wakefulness** *n*

» *It was broad daylight when she awoke and sat up in bed. Wake him up. Try to awaken the child earlier in the morning. The headaches are present when I wake up in the morning. Numbness[5] [nʌmnəs] of the hands often wakes the patient from sleep. Attempt to arouse the patient by vigorous[6] shaking or shouting to rule out[7] sleep or a faint[8] [eɪ].*

Use to awaken sb. from sleep / early • **awakening** time[9] / schedule • premature *or* early morning / nocturnal [ɜː] *or* night-time / momentary[10] / frequent / (up)on[11] / final **awakening** • to arouse the patient / suspicion[12] [ɪʃ] • **arousal** mechanism [ek]/ from deep sleep / response[13] / threshold[14] / pattern • full / brief / partial [ʃ]/ transitory / autonomic / behavioral[15] [eɪ] **arousal** • impaired [eɚ] movement / agitated [ædʒ] / EEG / sexual[16] **arousal** • **wakeful** period / patient • to maintain **wakefulness** • full / intermittent[17] / early morning[18] / reduced [(j)uː] **wakefulness** • behavioral[19] / relaxed / eyes-open[20] **wakefulness**

aufwachen, (auf)wecken
(er)wecken, erregen[1] Erwachen, erwachend[2] Arousal, Aufwachen[3] schlaflos, wachsam[4] Taubheit[5] kräftig[6] ausschließen[7] Ohnmacht[8] Aufwachzeit[9] kurzes Aufwachen[10] beim Auf-/ Erwachen[11] Verdacht erregen[12] Weckreaktion[13] Weckschwelle[14] Verhaltensaktivierung[15] sexuelle Erregung[16] nächtliche Wachperioden[17] zu frühes Erwachen, morgendl. Früherwachen[18] motor. Aktivitäten während d. Wachphasen[19] Wachzustand mit offenen Augen[20]

7

290 COMPLEX BODY FUNCTIONS — Sleep

sleep-wake cycle n term
rel **circadian rhythm**¹ [sɚˈkeɪdiˀn ˈrɪðˀm] *n term*

innate² [eɪ], daily periodicity [ɪs] of sleeping and waking, generally tied to the 24 hour day-night cycle [saɪkl]

» The hazards associated with night work include both circadian disruption [ʌ] and sleep deprivation. The sleep-wake cycle is governed³ by two neurobiologic systems; one actively generates sleep and sleep-related processes while the other times sleep within the 24-h day.

Use 24-hour or daily⁴ **sleep-wake cycle** • regulation / preservation **of the sleep-wake cycle** • **sleep-wake h**abits⁵ / pattern / state / shift⁶ / disorder or disturbance⁷ • **wake** times⁸ / center / after sleep onset (*abbr* WASO) • **circadian** rhythm disorder⁹ / dysrhythmia⁹ [dɪsrɪðmɪə]/ pattern / periodicity¹⁰ [ɪs] • dark-light **cycle**

Schlaf-Wach-Rhythmus
zirkadianer Rhythmus, Tagesrhythmus¹ endogen² wird gesteuert³ 24-stündiger Schlaf-Wach-Rhythmus⁴ Schlaf-Wach-Gewohnheiten⁵ Wechsel v. Schlafen u. Wachen⁶ Störung d. Schlaf-Wach-Rhythmus⁷ Weckzeiten⁸ zirkadiane Rhythmusstörung⁹ zirkadiane Periodik¹⁰

8

dream [driːm] v & n
rel **nightmare**¹ [ˈnaɪtmeɚ] *n*

(n) mental images and emotions [oʊʃ] experienced while sleeping

dreamy² [ˈdriːmi] *adj* • **dreaming** *adj & n* • **daydream**³ *n & v* • **dream-like** *adj*

» The child usually becomes fully awake and can vividly recall⁴ the details of the dream. There is no accompanying dream. Hypoglycemia [siː] during sleep may cause night sweats⁵ [e], unpleasant [e] dreams, and early-morning headache.

Use **to dream** about sb. / of doing sth. • vivid⁶ / unpleasant / bad⁷ / violent [aɪ] / frightening⁸ [aɪ]/ wet⁹ / waking³ **dream** • **dream** state / sleep¹⁰ / elements / imagery¹¹ [ˈɪmɪdʒɚi] / recall¹² [iː] • **dream** associations / deprivation / anxiety [aɪ] attacks¹³ • **dream-like** images • **dreamy** state / eyes / gaze¹⁴ [geɪz] / stupor [(j)uː] • to fall into/be given to¹⁵ **daydreaming** • persistent **nightmares**

träumen; Traum
Alptraum¹ verträumt, träumerisch² Tag-, Wachtraum; mit offenen Augen träumen, tagträumen³ sich erinnern⁴ Nachtschweiß⁵ lebhafter Traum⁶ böser T.⁷ Angsttraum⁸ nächtl. Samenerguss⁹ REM-, desynchronisierter Schlaf¹⁰ Traumbilder¹¹ Traumerinnerungen¹² Alp-, Angstträume¹³ verträumter Blick¹⁴ zum Tagträumen neigen¹⁵

9

REM sleep n term   syn dream or D state or paradoxic sleep n term
state of sleep in which rapid eye movements, alert [ɜː] EEG patterns, and dreaming occur [ɜː]

» In REM sleep, the rate and depth of respiration are increased while muscle tone is lower than in NREM sleep. In infancy, REM sleep may comprise [aɪ] 50 % of sleep time.

Use to enter¹/induce/delay/block **REM sleep** • **REM sleep** episode² / pattern³ / dreams / motor inhibition • **REM sleep** onset /-suppressive effect / deprivation⁴ / regulation • **REM** cycle / period / activity / density / rebound⁵ [aʊ] • **sleep** state / stages⁶ [eɪdʒ]/ continuity⁷ / latency⁸ / depth⁹ • active **sleep state** • delta / NREM **sleep stage** • spindle / sleep-onset **REMS**

REM-Schlaf, desynchronisierter/ paradoxer Schlaf
in die REM-Schlafphase eintreten¹ REM-Schlafphase² REM-Schlafmuster³ REM-Entzug⁴ REM-Rebound, plötzliche REM-Zunahme⁵ Schlafstadien⁶ Schlafkontinuität⁷ Schlaflatenz⁸ Schlaftiefe⁹

10

NREM or non-REM sleep n term   syn S stage sleep [es steɪdʒ sliːp] n term
non-rapid eye movement (or slow-wave, *abbr* SWS) sleep which is characterized by delta waves and low levels of physiological activity and is interrupted [ʌ] by periods of REM sleep

» NREM sleep can be divided into four EEG stages, with stages 3 and 4 representing the deepest sleep. The deepest NREM sleep occurs [ɜː] during the first 1-3 hours after going to sleep, with transitions [ɪʃ] to NREM stage 2 sleep and brief awakenings.

Use stage 1/2/3/4 **NREM sleep** • deep¹ **NREM sleep** • **NREM** stage 3 sleep / phase² [feɪz] • **sleep stage** period / length / demarcation³ [keɪ]

Non-REM-Schlaf, synchronisierter/ orthodoxer Schlaf
tiefer Non-REM-Schlaf¹ Non-REM-Schlafphase² Abgrenzung d. Schlafstadien³

11

nocturnal [ɜː] myoclonus [maɪˈɒklənəs] n term
rel **body** or **muscle twitch**¹ [ˈmʌsl twɪtʃ], **jerk**² [dʒɜːrk] *n clin* → U64-7

(i) brief contraction of muscle groups which may occur in normal persons as they fall asleep
(ii) periodic limb [lɪm] movement disorder in which extensions of the great toe and dorsiflexion of the foot recur every 20 to 40 s during NREM sleep in episodes lasting from minutes to hours

myoclonic [maɪəˈklɒnɪk] *adj term* • **twitch**³ *v clin* • **jerk**³ *v* • **jerky**⁴ *adj*

» In nocturnal myoclonus periodic lower leg movements occur during sleep with subsequent [ʌ] daytime sleepiness, anxiety, depression, and cognitive impairment. Nocturnal myoclonus is the chief objective finding on polysomnography⁵ in 17% of patients with insomnia⁶.

Use generalized / segmental / multifocal **myoclonus** • **nocturnal** leg cramps⁷ / enuresis⁸ [iː]/ penile [iː] tumescence⁹ [es] • **nocturnal** emission¹⁰ [ɪʃ]/ choking¹¹ [tʃ]/ dyspnea [ɪ]/ confusion¹² • brief / fine / fascicular¹³ [sɪ]/ muscular **twitching** • spontaneous / myoclonic **twitching** • **myoclonic** movements / jerking / seizure¹⁴ [siːʒɚ]/ epilepsy¹⁵ • sudden / tonic / clonic¹⁶ **jerking** • **jerky** movements

(i) Muskelzucken beim Einschlafen
(ii) nächtliches Myoklonie-Syndrom
Muskelzucken¹ ruckartige Bewegung, Zuckung² zucken³ ruckartig⁴ Polysomnografie⁵ Schlaflosigkeit, Insomnie⁶ nächtl. Beinkrämpfe⁷ Bettnässen, Enuresis nocturna⁸ nächtl. Erektion⁹ nächtl. Samenerguss¹⁰ nächtl. Erstickungsanfall¹¹ nächtl. Verwirrtheit¹² Faszikulation¹³ myoklonischer Anfall¹⁴ Myoklonusepilepsie¹⁵ klonischer Krampfanfall¹⁶

12

Sleep COMPLEX BODY FUNCTIONS 291

sleep apnea [sli:p æpnɪə‖æpni:ə] *n term*   *rel* **snoring**[1] [snɔ:rɪŋ] *n clin*

sleep disorder marked by epis<u>o</u>dic interruption of breathing [i:] between NREM and REM sleep
apneic[2] [æpni:ɪk] *adj term* • **snore** *v & n clin* • **snorer**[3] *n clin*

» The obstru<u>c</u>tive [ʌ] episodes of sleep apnea produce interrupted [ʌ] sleep associated with hyp<u>o</u>xia and hyperc<u>a</u>pnia. Bed p<u>a</u>rtners <u>u</u>sually report loud cyclical sn<u>o</u>ring, br<u>ea</u>th [e] cess<u>a</u>tion[4] [ses-], and often thr<u>a</u>shing [æʃ] m<u>o</u>vements[5] of the extr<u>e</u>mities during sleep.

Use to exp<u>e</u>rience **apnea** • obstr<u>u</u>ctive[6] / c<u>e</u>ntral[7] / mixed **sleep apnea** • **sleep apnea** syndrome • adult (sleep) / prolonged <u>i</u>nfantile / recurrent **apnea** • **apneic** <u>e</u>pisodes or spells[8] / p<u>a</u>tients • hab<u>i</u>tual [ɪtʃ]/ sev<u>e</u>re[9] / h<u>ea</u>vy[9] **snoring** • **snoring** sounds[10]

parasomnia [ɔ:] *n term*   *rel* **sleep terror**[1] *n clin* or **pavor nocturnus**[1] *n term*

abnormal behavior during sleep, such as br<u>u</u>xism[2] [ʌ], enur<u>e</u>sis, night t<u>e</u>rrors or sl<u>ee</u>pwalking

» The paras<u>o</u>mnias include sleep t<u>e</u>rrors and sleepwalking which—unlike nightmares or dream anxiety att<u>a</u>cks—are not ass<u>o</u>ciated with full ar<u>o</u>usal and memory of the <u>e</u>pisode. Sleep t<u>e</u>rror is an abr<u>u</u>pt [ʌ], t<u>e</u>rrifying ar<u>o</u>usal from sleep, usually in pre-<u>a</u>dolescent boys[3] [es].

Use to s<u>u</u>ffer [ʌ] from **parasomnia** • **pavor** di<u>u</u>rnus[4] • night[1] / day[4] **terrors**

somnambulism [sɔ:mnæmbjəlɪzm] *n term*   *syn* **sleepwalking** *n clin*

disorder of sleep primarily seen in children inv<u>o</u>lving complex m<u>o</u>tor acts like l<u>ea</u>ving one's bed and w<u>a</u>lking ar<u>ou</u>nd during non-REM sleep with no rec<u>a</u>ll of the <u>e</u>pisode on awakening
somnambul<u>i</u>stic[1] *adj term* • **somn(i)-** *comb* • **sleepwalker**[2] *n* • **sleepwalk**[3] *v*

» Somnambulism involves cl<u>u</u>msy[4] [ʌ] walks during which <u>o</u>bjects <u>u</u>sually are av<u>oi</u>ded. In predisp<u>o</u>sed children sleepwalking may be tr<u>i</u>ggered[5] by f<u>e</u>brile <u>i</u>llnesses.

Use persistent **sleepwalking** • **somnamb<u>u</u>listic** tr<u>a</u>nce [æ] • **somn**amb<u>u</u>late /ambu-lant /<u>i</u>loquism[6] /<u>i</u>loquy[6] [-ɪləkwɪ] • **sleep** t<u>a</u>lking[6]

insomnia [ɪnsɔ:mnɪə] *n*   *syn* **sleeplessness** *n clin, rel* **dyssomnia**[1] *n term*

broad term for disorders of in<u>i</u>tiating [ɪʃ] and/or maint<u>ai</u>ning sleep (*abbr* DIMS), e.g. chr<u>o</u>nic sl<u>ee</u>plessness, d<u>i</u>fficulty f<u>a</u>lling asl<u>ee</u>p, or inab<u>i</u>lity to remain asl<u>ee</u>p throughout the night
ins<u>o</u>mniac[2] *adj & n* • **sleepless** *adj* • **polysomnogram**[3] *n* • **-somnia** *comb*

» What is the dr<u>u</u>g of ch<u>oi</u>ce[4] for c<u>a</u>ses of ac<u>u</u>te ins<u>o</u>mnia such as jet lag? P<u>a</u>tients with dyss<u>o</u>mnia ass<u>o</u>ciated with the r<u>e</u>stless legs s<u>y</u>ndrome [ɪ] report an irres<u>i</u>stible[5] urge [ɜ:] to m<u>o</u>ve their legs when aw<u>a</u>ke and in<u>a</u>ctive, ab<u>o</u>ve all when l<u>y</u>ing in bed just prior to sleep.

Use to s<u>u</u>ffer from[6] **insomnia** • in<u>i</u>tial or sleep <u>o</u>nset[7] / sleep maint<u>e</u>nance[8] / early m<u>o</u>rning[9] / long-term **insomnia** • cond<u>i</u>tioned [ɪʃ]/ tr<u>a</u>nsient (situ<u>a</u>tional) [eɪʃ]/ intr<u>a</u>ctable[10] / MAO-ind<u>u</u>ced **insomnia** • psychophysiol<u>o</u>gic [saɪk-]/ alt<u>i</u>tude[11] [æ]/ unexpl<u>ai</u>ned / f<u>a</u>tal [eɪ] fam<u>i</u>lial[12] **insomnia** • **sleepless** night • sleep st<u>u</u>dy **poly-somnogram** • all night / diagnostic nocturnal **polysomnography**

hypersomnia [haɪpɚsɔ:mnɪə] *n term*   *syn* **hypersomnolence** *n term*

dis<u>o</u>rder marked by <u>e</u>xcessive dr<u>ow</u>siness or by sleep of exc<u>e</u>ssive depth and abn<u>o</u>rmal dur<u>a</u>tion
hypers<u>o</u>mnic *adj term* • **hypers<u>o</u>mnolent** *adj* • **hypos<u>o</u>mnia**[1] *n*

» He experiences hypers<u>o</u>mnic att<u>a</u>cks 3-4 times a year with conf<u>u</u>sion[2] on awakening. Some depr<u>e</u>ssives[3] m<u>a</u>nifest in<u>i</u>tial ins<u>o</u>mnia and hypers<u>o</u>mnia often ext<u>e</u>nding into d<u>ay</u>time hours.

Use (semi)chr<u>o</u>nic[4] / idiop<u>a</u>thic **hypersomnia** • d<u>ay</u>time[5] / epis<u>o</u>dic **hypersomnolence**

narcolepsy [nɑ:rkəlepsɪ] *n term*   *syn* **paroxysmal** [ɪ] **sleep** *n clin*
  rel **Gélineau's syndrome**[1] *n term*

s<u>u</u>dden uncontr<u>o</u>llable sleep att<u>a</u>cks occ<u>u</u>rring [ɜ:] during any type of act<u>i</u>vity; ass<u>o</u>ciated with c<u>a</u>taplexy[2], hypnag<u>o</u>gic halluc<u>i</u>nations[3], and sleep par<u>a</u>lysis[4]
narcol<u>e</u>ptic[5] *adj & n term* • **narc<u>o</u>tic**[6] *adj & n* • **narco-** *comb* • **p<u>a</u>roxysm**[7] *n*

» Ap<u>a</u>rt from <u>e</u>xcessive d<u>ay</u>time s<u>o</u>mnolence, most p<u>a</u>tients with n<u>a</u>rcolepsy also report sev<u>e</u>re disr<u>u</u>ption [ʌ] of noct<u>u</u>rnal sleep. C<u>a</u>reful observ<u>a</u>tion of the children and s<u>i</u>blings[8] of known narcol<u>e</u>ptics, particularly in the s<u>e</u>cond d<u>e</u>cade, can lead to early diagn<u>o</u>sis. The p<u>a</u>tient can be ar<u>ou</u>sed from narcol<u>e</u>ptic sleep as r<u>ea</u>dily[9] [e] as from n<u>o</u>rmal sleep.

Use **narcolepsy** syndrome [ɪ] • **narcol<u>e</u>ptic** REMS nap / sleep (att<u>a</u>ck)[10] / patient / t<u>e</u>trad • **narc<u>o</u>tic** anal<u>ge</u>sics[11] [dʒi:]/ <u>a</u>ddict • **paroxysmal** ev<u>e</u>nt / cough(ing)[12] [kɒ:fɪŋ]/ noct<u>u</u>rnal [ɜ:] dyspn<u>ea</u> (*abbr* PND)

Schlafapnoe(syndrom)
Schnarchen[1] apnoisch[2] Schnarcher(in)[3] Atemstillstand[4] Strampeln, Treten, Umsichschlagen[5] obstruktives Schlafapnoesyndrom[6] zentrales Schlafapnoesyndrom[7] anfallsweises Auftreten v. Atemstillständen, Atemaussetzer[8] starkes Schnarchen[9] Schnarchgeräusche[10]
13

Parasomnie
Nachtangst, Pavor nocturnus[1] Zähneknirschen, Bruxismus[2] präadoleszente Knaben[3] Pavor diurnus, Tagangst[4]
14

Schlaf-, Nachtwandeln, Somnambulismus
somnambul, schlafwandlerisch[1] Schlafwandler(in), Somnambule(r)[2] schlafwandeln[3] tollpatschig[4] ausgelöst[5] Somniloquie, Sprechen im Schlaf[6]
15

Schlaflosigkeit, Asomnie, Insomnie, Agrypnie
Schlafstörung, Dyssomnie[1] an Schlaflosigkeit leidend; an Schlaflosigkeit Leidende(r)[2] Polysomnogramm[3] Medikament der Wahl[4] unwiderstehlich[5] an Schlaflosigkeit leiden[6] Einschlafstörung[7] Durchschlafstörung[8] morgendliches Frühwachen[9] therapierefraktäre Schlaflosigkeit[10] höhenbedingte Schlaflosigkeit[11] fatale familiäre Insomnie[12]
16

Schlafsucht, Hypersomnie
Hyposomnie[1] Verwirrtheit, Desorientiertheit[2] depressive Patienten[3] chronische Schlafsucht[4] Tagesmüdigkeit mit Einschlafneigung[5]
17

Narkolepsie, Schlafanfall
Gelineau-Syndrom[1] affektiver Tonusverlust, Kataplexie[2] hypnagoge Halluzinationen[3] Schlaflähmung[4] narkoleptisch; Narkoleptikum; ein(e) an Narkolepsie Leidende(r)[5] narkotisch; Narkotikum[6] Anfall, Paroxysmus[7] Geschwister[8] leicht[9] Schlafanfall[10] Narkoanalgetika[11] Hustenanfall[12]
18

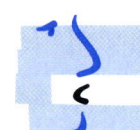

Clinical Phrases

Did you sleep well? Haben Sie gut geschlafen? • I tossed and turned for hours before I could fall asleep. Ich wälzte mich stundenlang im Bett hin und her, bis ich endlich einschlief. • I'm so excited that I can scarcely sleep. Ich bin so aufgedreht, dass ich kaum schlafen kann. • It hurts so much I can't get to sleep, doctor. Herr Doktor, es tut so weh, dass ich nicht einschlafen kann. • I did not sleep a wink. Ich habe kein Auge zugetan. • Have you noticed increased yawning? Mussten Sie vermehrt gähnen? • Get a good night's sleep and tomorrow we'll discuss it, all right? Schlafen Sie erst einmal darüber, und morgen besprechen wir das, einverstanden? • I had a sleepless night and was suffering from a headache and fever when I got up. Ich konnte die ganze Nacht nicht schlafen und in der Früh, als ich aufstand, hatte ich Kopfschmerzen und Fieber.

Unit 73 Mental Activity

Related Units: 72 Sleep, 7 States of Consciousness, 74 Memory, 75 Personality & Behavior, 76 Mood & Attitude, 77 Mental Health, 42 Nerve Function, 41 Brain, 57 Senses, 113 Neurologic Findings

mentation [-eɪʃᵊn] *n term*   *rel* **reasoning**[1], **perception**[2] [sɛ] *n clin & term* → U57-2

any type of conscious [kɒnˈʃəs] or unconscious mental process [ɒːs]

mentality[3] *n* • **mental**[4] *adj* • **reason**[5] [riːzᵊn] *n* • **(un)reasonable**[6] *adj*

» Subarachnoid [æk] bleeding is associated with depressed mentation, ranging from lethargy to coma. The alert [ɜː] state[7] with normal mentation requires intact interaction between the cognitive functions of the cerebral hemispheres and the reticular arousal [aʊ] mechanisms[8].

Use sleep / dreaming[9] [iː]/ (ab)normal / altered [ɒː]/ impaired [ɛə] **mentation** • slowed / disturbances [ɜː] of **mentation** • abstract / conceptual[10] [-septʃʊəl]/ inductive [ʌ] reasoning • deductive / arithmetical / spatial[11] [eɪʃ] reasoning • flaws [ɒː] in[12] / line of[13] reasoning • reasoning skills[14] / abilities[14] / strategy • to be[15] (un)reasonable

mentale Aktivität, Mentation
logisches/ schlussfolgerndes Denken[1] Wahrnehmung, Perzeption[2] allgem. geistige Einstellung, Mentalität[3] geistig, seelisch, mental, Geistes-[4] Verstand, Vernunft; Grund[5] vernünftig[6] Wachzustand, Vigilanz[7] Erregungsmechanismen[8] Traumaktivität[9] abstraktes/ begriffl. Denken[10] räuml. D.[11] Denkfehler[12] Gedankengang[13] Denkvermögen[14] unvernünftig sein[15]   1

mental faculties [fækᵊltiːz] *n term*   *sim* **mental functions**[1] [fʌŋkʃᵊnz] *n clin*

cognitive and perceptual powers of the mind, e.g. sensation [eɪʃ], awareness [ɛə], memory, speech, etc.

» Other mental faculties such as attention[2], comprehension, orientation, cognition, learning, problem solving, and behavior [eɪ] may also be affected. The cerebral cortex and autonomic centers in the brainstem[3] coordinate autonomic outflow with higher mental functions.

Use mental activity / age[4] (*abbr* MA)/ abilities / development[5] • **mental** state or status[6] [eɪ‖æ]/ acuity[7] [əkjuːəti]/ alertness[8] [ɜː] • **mental** slowness[9] / imagery[10] / confusion[11] [juːʒ]/ stress • **mental** irritability / hospital or institution[12] / handicap[13] / retardation[13] • intact / complex / higher / altered **mental functions** • depressed / impaired[14] **mental functions** • deterioration or regression in / recovery [ʌ] of **mental function** • **mentally** alert / intact / slow / retarded [ɑː] or handicapped[15] • **mentally** unstable[16] [eɪ]/ ill[17] / incompetent[18]

geistige Fähigkeiten
mentale Funktionen[1] Aufmerksamkeit[2] Hirnstamm[3] Intelligenzalter[4] geistige Entwicklung[5] geistige Verfassung, psychischer Zustand[6] Denkschärfe[7] Wachheit, Vigilanz[8] verlangsamtes Denken[9] mentale Vorstellung(skraft)[10] geistige Verwirrtheit[11] Nervenheilanstalt[12] geistige Behinderung[13] Beeinträchtigung d. geistigen Leistungen[14] geistig behindert[15] psychisch labil[16] psych. krank[17] nicht zurechnungsfähig[18]   2

volition [vəʊlɪʃᵊn] *n term*   *sim* **will**[1], **willpower**[2] [wɪlpaʊə] *n*
   rel **willingness**[3], **intention**[4] [ɪntenʃᵊn] *n*, **wish**[5] *n & v*

conscious impulse, power or act of making a choice, i.e. performing or abstaining from an act

volitional[6] *n term* • **wil(l)ful**[7] *adj* • **(un)willing** *adj* • **(un)willingness** *n* • **(in)voluntary**[8] *adj* • **intend**[9] *v* • **(un)intentional** *adj* • **well-intentioned**[10] *adj*

» Schizophrenia [iː] is characterized by perturbations[11] [ɜː] of language, perception, thinking, social activity, affect[12], and volition. Volition is mental activity for good or for evil [iː]. Sustaining [eɪ] of respiration by this mechanical device [aɪs] is contrary to my every wish[13].

Use mental / passive / of one's own[14] / power or energy of[2] **volition** • exercise of / acts of **volition** • free / living[15] / against my / good**will** • to have a(n) strong/iron **will** • strong-/ weak[16]-**willed** • **volitional** control / movements[17] / processes / activity • **unwilling** child / to change • self-destructive[18] [ʌ] **intention** • **intention** to die / tremor[19] • **intentional** hyperventilation / weight-loss[20] [weɪt] / tort[21] [tɔːt] • **unintended** pregnancy[22]

Wollen, Wille(nskraft)
Wille, Wollen; Testament[1] Willenskraft, -stärke[2] Bereitschaft[3] Absicht[4] Wunsch; wünschen[5] Willens-, willentlich[6] eigenwillig, mutwillig, vorsätzlich[7] freiwillig, willkürlich[8] beabsichtigen, wollen[9] wohlmeinend, gut gemeint[10] Störungen[11] Affekt[12] ganz gegen meinen Willen[13] aus freiem W.[14] Patientenverfügung[15] willensschwach[16] Willkürbewegungen[17] Selbsttötungsabsicht[18] Intentionstremor[19] beabsichtigte Gewichtsabnahme[20] vorsätzliche(s) Tat/ Vergehen[21] ungewollte Schwangerschaft[22]   3

Mental Activity COMPLEX BODY FUNCTIONS 293

cognition [kɒɡˈnɪʃ³n] n term   rel **recognition**[1], **knowledge**[2] [ˈnɒlɪdʒ], **competence**[3] n → U74-3

conscious mental processes such as knowing, thinking, learning, reasoning [iː], and judging
cognitive adj term • **recognize** v • **knowledgable**[4] adj • **(in)competent** adj

» Three components of cognition are particularly important for school learning: memory, attention[5] [əˈtenʃ³n], and the coordination of these processes. On occasion [eɪʒ] the drug will increase confusion [juːʒ] in cognitively impaired patients. A patient who is competent has the ability to understand his or her medical condition.

Use impaired or decreased [iː] **cognition** • assessment / clouding[6] [aʊ]/ impairment[6] of cognition • changes / oddities[7] / deficits **in cognition** • **cognition**-impairing drugs • **cognitive** process[8] / (dys)function[6] / skills[9] / abilities[9] • **cognitive** level / performance[10] • **cognitive** development[11] / decline [aɪ]/ impairment[6] / deficit[6] / slowing • **cognitive**-behavioral therapy[12] / test • (fund [ʌ] of) general[13] / object / self-/ basic or working[14] **knowledge** • sound[15] [aʊ]/ thorough[15] [ˈθɜːrə]/ up-to-date / current [ɜː] **knowledge** • cognitive[9] / rational / advanced / social[16] [oʊʃ] **competence** • **knowledgeable** therapist[17] / about sth. • mentally[18] / socially / legally[19] [iː]/ immunologically[20] **(in)competent**

Kognition, Erkennen
Wiedererkennen[1] Wissen, Kenntnis(se)[2] Fähigkeit, Kompetenz[3] kenntnisreich, mit großem Wissen[4] Aufmerksamkeit[5] kognitive Störung[6] kognitive Auffälligkeiten[7] kognitiver Prozess[8] verständlich[6] kognitive Fähigkeiten[9] kognitive Leistung[10] kognitive Entwicklung[11] kognitive Verhaltenstherapie[12] Allgemeinwissen, -bildung[13] Grundkenntnisse[14] gründl. Kenntnisse[15] soziale Kompetenz[16] sachkundige(r) Therapeut(in)[17] zurechnungsfähig[18] geschäftsfähig[19] immunkompetent[20]

4

intellect n clin & term   rel **comprehension**[1], **understanding**[2], **insight**[3] [aɪ] n

capacity [æs] for rational thought, inference[4] and/or discrimination[5] [eɪ]
intellectual adj & n • **intelligent** adj • **intelligence** n • **(un)intelligible**[6] adj • **comprehend**[7] v • **(in)comprehensible** adj • **misunderstanding** n

» The child shows no significant discrepancy between intelligence and achievement[8] [tʃ]. The most common clinical picture is slow disintegration of personality[9] and intellect due to impaired insight and judgment and loss of affect. Confusion is a behavioral [eɪ] state of reduced mental clarity [eə], coherence [ɪə], comprehension, and reasoning [iː].

Use normal / intact / impaired **intellect** • **intellectual** (cap)abilities[10] / level[11] / function / potential • **intellectual** flexibility / maturation[12] / decline[13] / deficit • **intellectually** disadvantaged / challenged[14] [tʃæ] • (non)verbal / performance / social / above-average[15] / overall **intelligence** • normal / borderline **intelligence** • **intelligence** test / quotient[16] [oʊʃ] (abbr IQ) • language / reading[17] / listening[18] / deficits of **comprehension** • full / comprehensive[19] / speech / the patient's / sympathetic[20] **understanding** • parental / better or greater or improved **understanding** • semantic **misunderstandings** • to gain[21]/develop/provide **insight** • good / greater / lack of / poor / sudden **insight** • **insight** into the illness[22] / psychotherapy [saɪkoʊ-]

Verstand, Denkvermögen, Intellekt
Verständnis, Auffassungsgabe[1] Verstehen, Auffassung, Kenntnisse[2] Einblick, -sicht, Verständnis[3] Schlussfolgerung[4] Unterscheidung, Urteilsfähigkeit[5] verständlich[6] verstehen, begreifen[7] Leistung[8] Persönlichkeitszerfall[9] geistige Fähigkeiten[10] Intelligenzgrad, -niveau[11] intellektuelle Reifung[12] geistiger Verfall[13] geistig überfordert[14] überdurchschnittliche Intelligenz[15] Intelligenzquotient[16] Leseverständnis[17] Hörverständnis[18] gründliche Kenntnisse[19] Mitgefühl, Verständnis[20] Einblick gewinnen/ bekommen[21] Krankheitseinsicht[22]

5

thinking n & adj   sim **reflection**[1] n, rel **judgement**[2] [ʌ], **learning**[3] [ɜː] n

(n) using the power of reason to make inferences, decisions [sɪʒ], or arrive at a solution
think - thought - thought v irr • **thought**[4] [θɔːt] n • **thoughtful**[5] adj • **judge**[6] [dʒʌdʒ] v & n

» Depressed patients typically present with difficulty in thinking, including inability to concentrate, ruminations[7] [eɪ], and lack of decisiveness[8] [saɪ]. As children enter school, they begin to develop operational thought, shifting from associative [oʊʃ] thinking[9] to use of verbal [ɜː] mediation activity in learning and thinking. He had difficulty thinking and slowness of speech and comprehension.

Use abstract / concrete / associative[9] / critical **thinking** • clear / operational[10] [eɪ] **thinking** • wishful[11] / referential[12] / goal-directed[10] [oʊ] **thinking** • confused / slow(ed)[13] / (un)realistic **thinking** • (ir)rational / delusional[14] [uː] **thinking** • (dis)organized[15] / psychotic [saɪkɒtɪk] / autistic[16] [ɔːt-] **thinking** • **thinking** ability / pattern[17] / error • train of[18] / conscious thought / thought process[19] / activity / pattern[17] / content[20] / disorder[21] • **to think** about sth. or sb. / sth. over[22] / hard[23] • impaired[24] / faulty [ɔː]/ common sense[25] / ethical / moral **judgement** • social / cognitive[26] / word / spatial / lifelong **learning** • **learning** process / pattern / problems / (dis)ability[27] / assistance

Denken; denkend, vernünftig
Nachdenken, Überlegung, Reflexion[1] Urteil(svermögen), Meinung[2] Lernen[3] Gedanke[4] nachdenklich; rücksichtsvoll[5] beurteilen, einschätzen; Richter[6] Grübeln[7] Unentschlossenheit[8] assoziatives Denken[9] zielgerichtetes D.[10] Wunschdenken[11] Beziehungsdenken[12] verlangsamtes D.[13] wahnhaftes Denken[14] zerfahrenes D.[15] autistisches D.[16] Denkmuster[17] Gedankengang[18] Denkprozess[19] Denkinhalt[20] Denkstörung[21] etw. überdenken[22] scharf nachdenken[23] vermindertes Urteilsvermögen[24] vernünftige Meinung/ Entscheidung[25] kognitives Lernen[26] Lernfähigkeit[27]

6

73

COMPLEX BODY FUNCTIONS — Mental Activity

rational [ˈræʃənəl] adj   opposite **irrational**[1] adj
(i) referring to reasoning [iː] and higher thought processes
(ii) guided by the intellect rather than by emotion [oʊ] or experience
(iii) capable of normal reasoning, i.e. not delirious, comatose or insane[2] [eɪ]
rationale[3] [æ] n • **rationalize**[4] v • **rationality**[5] n term • **rationalization** n

» Adolescents require both individuality and involvement with family and society to facilitate [sɪ] development of identity and of rational competence. Was the patient assaultive[6] [ɔː], irrational, deluded or abusive[7]? The child developed protracted vomiting[8] and irrational behavior. She became somewhat irrational and showed extreme emotional lability. The use of diet [daɪət] therapies should be based on a scientific rationale and sound [aʊ] data.

Use **rational** thinking[9] / decision [sɪ]/ choice / justification[10] / competence • **rational** approach[11] [-oʊtʃ]/ impulse • emotive [oʊ] therapy[12] (abbr RET) • **irrational** behavior / idea / fear[13]

rational, vernünftig, vernunftbegabt
irrational, unvernünftig, unsinnig[1] geistesgestört[2] Grundprinzip, logische Grundlage[3] rational begründen; rationalisieren[4] Vernünftigkeit, Vernunft, Rationalität[5] aggressiv, gewalttätig[6] beleidigend, ausfallend[7] protrahiertes Erbrechen[8] rationales Denken[9] rationale Rechtfertigung[10] rationales Vorgehen, vernünftiger Ansatz[11] rational-emotive Therapie[12] irrationale Angst[13]   **7**

idea [aɪdɪə] n   sim **notion**[1] [noʊʃən], **concept**[2] [kɒːnsept] n
rel **purpose**[3] [ɜː] n, **aim**[4] [eɪm] n & v
(i) a thought, impression, image or opinion
(ii) a belief, plan or suggested [dʒ] course [ɔː] of action
ideation[5] [aɪdieɪʃən] n term • **ideational**[6] adj • **conceptual**[7] [-tʃʊəl] adj
purposeful[8] adj clin • **aimless**[9] adj

» Writing samples[10] should be obtained to evaluate spelling, syntax [ɪ], and fluency of ideas. In conversion [ɜː] disorders[11] vomiting may be an attempt to represent a forbidden idea or wish. Older adolescents have very rigid [dʒ] concepts of what is right and what is wrong.

Use associated / preconceived[12] [siː]/ repressed / fixed[13] **idea** • disconnected[14] / persecutory[15] / grandiose **ideas** • suicidal [saɪ]/ obsessive-compulsive[16] [ʌ]/ flight [flaɪt] of[17] **ideas** • bizarre / homicidal / paranoid / phobic [foʊbɪk] **ideation** • **ideas of** reference[18] / persecution[15] [juːʃ] • **ideational** apraxia[19] • to be based on/support/abandon [æ]/question[20] **a concept** • **conceptual** reasoning or thinking[21] • **purposeful** movement / action / behavior • **aimless** wandering [ɔː]/ pacing[22] [peɪsɪŋ]/ activity

Gedanke, Idee, Einfall, Vorstellung, Ahnung
Vorstellung Ahnung[1] Vorstellung, Begriff, Konzept[2] Absicht, Zweck, Ziel[3] Absicht, Ziel; abzielen, vorhaben[4] Gedanken-, Bewegungsentwurf, Ideation[5] ideatorisch[6] begrifflich[7] entschlossen[8] ziel-, planlos[9] Schriftproben[10] Konversionsneurosen[11] vorgefasste Idee[12] fixe Idee[13] unzusammenhängende Gedanken[14] Verfolgungsideen[15] Zwangsvorstellungen[16] Ideenflucht[17] Beziehungswahn[18] ideatorische Apraxie[19] e. Konzept i. Frage stellen[20] begriffl. Denken[21] zielloses Umhergehen[22]   **8**

imagination [-dʒɪneɪʃən] n   sim **fantasy**[1], **fancy**[1] [ˈfænsi], **visualization**[2] n
act or ability of reproducing mental images of situations, activities or persons from memory
imagine[3] [ɪˈmædʒɪn] v • **imaginative**[4] adj • **image**[5] [ɪmɪdʒ] n • **imagery**[6] n **imaginary**[7] adj • **fantasize** v • **fantasist** n • **visualize**[3] [ɪʒ] v • **fancy**[8] v

» Children test new experiences [ɪə] in fantasy, both in their imagination and in play. The patient is unable to differentiate reality from fantasy. By first grade[9], fantasy and imagination are still strong. In early childhood male transsexuals behave [eɪ] and fantasize as if they were girls.

Use to have a vivid[10]/capture sb's[11] **imagination** • lack of **imagination** • tact and / frightening [aɪ] elaborate[12] **fantasy** • (homo)sexual / delusional[13] [uːʒ] **fantasy** • **fantasy** world • (distorted) body[14] / (positive/ negative) self-/ mirror[15] **image** • visual / after[16]/ delusional **image** • emotive[17] / visual[2] **imagery** • **imagined** guilt [gɪlt] • **imaginary** line / friends

Vorstellung(skraft), Phantasie, Einbildung(skraft)
Phantasie(vorstellung), Einbildung[1] Vorstellung, Visualisierung[2] s. etw. vorstellen[3] einfallsreich, phantasievoll[4] Bild, Vorstellung[5] bildhafte Vorstellungen, Bilder(sprache)[6] eingebildet, erfunden, imaginär[7] s. etw. einbilden, glauben[8] bis z. Schuleintritt[9] e. rege Phantasie haben[10] jem. faszinieren[11] blühende Phantasie[12] Wahnvorstellung[13] Körperschema[14] Spiegelbild[15] Nachbild[16] bildl. Vorstellung[17]   **9**

illusion [ɪˈluːʒən] n clin & term   rel **vision**[1] [vɪʒən], **hallucination**[2] n clin & term → U77-20
(i) misperception of sensory stimuli [aɪ], esp. visual and auditory [ɔː] ones
(ii) idea or belief that most people would consider unrealistic or false
illusional adj • **illusory**[3] [uːʒ] adj • **disillusioned**[4] [uːʒ] adj • **visionary**[5] adj & n

» In volatile solvent abuse[6] illusions, hallucinations [s], and delusions[7] develop as the CNS becomes more deeply affected. Some patients describe a sense of detachment[8] [ætʃ], depersonalization, or illusions that objects are growing smaller (micropsia) or larger (macropsia).

Use to have **illusions** about sth. • perceptual[9] / interpretative[10] **illusion** • optical[11] / auditory / nocturnal [ɜː] **illusion** • **illusions of** hearing / smell[12] / doubles[13] [ʌ] • **vision** of the future • auditory / visual / tactile [æ] **hallucinations**

(i) (Sinnes)täuschung, Trugwahrnehmung
(ii) Illusion, Einbildung
Vision[1] Halluzination[2] trügerisch, illusorisch[3] desillusioniert[4] visionär, hellseherisch; Seher(in), Phantast(in)[5] Lösungsmittelschnüffeln[6] Wahnvorstellungen[7] Loslösung, Abgewandtheit[8] Sinnestäuschung[9] subjektives Bedeutungserlebnis[10] optische Täuschung[11] Geschmackshalluzinationen[12] Capgras-Syndrom, Doppelgängerillusion[13]   **10**

Memory   COMPLEX BODY FUNCTIONS **295**

instinct n clin & term   sim **drive**[1] [draɪv], **urge**[2] [ɜːrdʒ] n & v → U11-2; U77-19 | **Instinkt, (Natur)trieb**
inborn pattern of behavior in response to specific stimuli that does not involve reason | (An)trieb, Drang; treiben[1] Drang; drängen[2] instinktgeleitet, -gesteuert[3] instinktiv, Instinkt-[4] treibende Kraft[5] Zwang[6] unwiderstehlich[7] schändlich[8] instinktiv handeln[9] Selbsterhaltungstrieb[10] Mutterinstinkt, mütterlicher I.[11] Herdentrieb[12] Geschlechts-, Sexualtrieb[13] Libido, Geschlechtstrieb; Lebenswille, -kraft[14] Atemantrieb[15] unwiderstehlicher Drang[16] Harndrang[17]

instinctual[3] adj term • **instinctive**[4] adj term & clin • **driving force**[5] n

» A **compulsion**[6] [ʌ] is an **overwhelming**[7] urge to do something aggressive, **disgraceful**[8] [eɪs], or obscene [siː]. Association cortex and limbic system [ɪ] areas integrate sensory perceptions with instinctual and acquired [əkwaɪ-] memories to create [krieɪt] learning and thought and their expression, i.e. behavior.

Use **to act** on[9]/by or from[9] **instinct** • natural / life-preserving[10] [ɜː] **instinct** • maternal [ɜː] or mother[11] / ego [iː]/ herd[12] [ɜː] **instinct** • **instinct** control • **instinctual** decision • **instinctive** decision • basic / sex(ual)[13] / libidinal[14] / sympathetic **drive** • ventilatory or respiratory[15] / perfectionistic **drive** • **drive** development / for perfection • sucking [ʌ] strong or intense **urge** • compulsive[16] / irresistible[16] **urge** • **urge to** smoke / void[17] [vɔɪd]/ defecate   **11**

---

motivation [eɪʃ] n clin & term   sim **impulse**[1] [ɪmpʌls] n, rel **desire**[2] [dɪzaɪɚ] n & v | **Motivation**
sum total of all conscious or unconscious needs[3], drives and incentives[4] [se] in an individual at a given moment that influence will and arouse [aʊ] or maintain a particular behavior | Anregung, Anstoß, Impuls[1] Wunsch, Verlangen; (sich) wünschen, begehren[2] Bedürfnisse[3] Anreize[4] Motiv, Beweggrund[5] unmotiviert[6] impulsiv, spontan[7] Leistungsmotivation[8] anhaltende Motivation[9] hochmotiviert[10] Motivationskonflikt[11] motivationale Unreife[12] impulsive Reaktion[13] Spontanhandlungen[14] starkes Verlangen[15] dringender Wunsch[16] sexuelles Verlangen[17]

(a)**motivational** adj term • **amotivation** n • (de)**motivate** [oʊ] v • **motive**[5] n (un)**motivated**[6] adj • **motivator** n • **impulsive**[7] [ʌ] adj • **impulsiveness** n

» Suicidal acts usually result from multiple and complex motivations. Patients who are not adequately motivated should not be started on diet [daɪət] therapy.

Use personal / poor / low / strong **motivation** • achievement[8] [tʃ]/ intrinsic / sustained[9] [eɪ] **motivation** • level or degree [iː]/ lack **of motivation** • highly[10] / well-/ un/ self-**motivated** • **motivational** development / problem • **motivational** counseling [aʊ]/ conflict[11] / immaturity[12] • forbidden / sexual / restless **impulse** • **impulsive** response[13] / actions[14] / talking / behavior • intense[15] / strong / urgent[16] [ɜː] **desire** • persistent / unconscious / sexual[17] **desire**   **12**

---

habit [hæbɪt] n clin & term   rel **ritual**[1] [rɪtʃuəl], **custom**[2] [kʌstəm] n | (i) **Gewohnheit, Habit**
(i) pattern of behavior acquired through frequent repetition (ii) substance abuse → U11-5 | (ii) **Sucht**
habitual[3] [həbɪtʃuəl] adj term • **habituation**[4] n • **habituate**[5] v • **ritualistic**[6] adj | Zeremoniell, Ritual[1] Sitte, Brauch[2] gewohnheitsmäßig, habituell[3] Gewöhnung, Habituation[4] s. gewöhnen, süchtig machen[5] rituell[6] Zungenpressen[7] Reisediarrhoe[8] Lebensgewohnheiten[9] s. etw. abgewöhnen[10] Ernährungsgewohnheiten[11] Essgewohnheiten[12] Stuhlgewohnheiten[13] Tic(k)[14] suchterzeugend[15] habituelles Schlucken[16] hab. Luxation[17] habitueller Abort[18] Arzneimittelgewöhnung[19] Gute-Nacht-Ritual[20] ritualisiertes Verhalten[21] rituelle Beschneidung[22]

» Causes of glossitis [aɪ] include oral habits such as tongue-pressing[7] [tʌŋ]. Traveler's diarrhea[8] [daɪəriːə] is commonly due to unusual food and drink and change in living habits[9] or in bowel flora.

Use to acquire/give up or kick[10] **a habit** • healthful [e]/ hygienic [haɪdʒiːnɪk]/ sleep / nutritional[11] [ɪʃ] **habits** • dietary or eating[12] / bowel[13] [baʊəl] **habits** • unconscious / sexual / exercise / working **habits** • neurotic / smoking **habit** • **habit** spasm[14] /-forming[15] / swallowing[16] • **habitual** behavior / snoring / dislocation[17] / abortion[18] • alcohol / drug[19] **habituation** • to carry out **rituals** • bedtime[20] / compulsive **ritual** • **ritual** behavior[21] / practice / circumcision[22] [sɪ] • **ritualistic** performance of an action   **13**

Unit 74 Memory
Related Units: 73 Mental Activity, 42 Nerve Function, 41 Brain, 40 Nervous System, 7 Consciousness, 72 Sleep, 75 Behavior, 77 Mental Health, 113 Neurologic Findings

---

recall [v rɪkɔːl‖n riːkɔːl] v & n   syn **remember** v, | s. **erinnern/ ins Gedächtnis zurückrufen; Erinnerung**
                                        sim **come/ spring to mind**[1] phr |
(v) to be aware [eɚ] or think of past events or reproduce facts from memory | einfallen[1] Erinnerung, Andenken[2] etw. berücksichtigen/ bedenken[3] aufpassen/ achten auf; Geist, Verstand, Gedächtnis[4] Reproduktionsgedächtnis[5] Zahlen[6] s. nicht erinnern[7] Immediat-, Sofort-, Neugedächtnis[8] Traumerinnerung[9] nicht vergessen, im Auge behalten[10] vergessen[11] im Gedächtnis bleiben[12] Gedanken lesen[13] geistesabwesend, zerstreut[14] aufgeschlossen[15] einfältig[16] zielstrebig, unbeirrbar[17] Verfassung, Stimmung[18] Sinnesänderung[19]

remembrance[2] [rɪmembrənts] n • **to be mindful of**[3] phr • **mind**[4] [maɪnd] v & n

» If the child does not recall the correct reason [iː], he is briefly reminded. Retentive memory[5] and immediate [iː] recall can be tested by determining [ɜː] the number of digits[6] that can be repeated in sequence [iː]. I can't remember seeing him before. There is poor recall of the event on waking [eɪ] in the morning.

Use to try/aid/be (un)able to/fail to[7] **recall** • immediate[8] / poor / impaired [eɚ]/ total **recall** • word / information / dream[9] [iː] **recall** • **to remember** events / objects / a person • to keep or bear [beɚ] in[10] **mind** • to slip[11]/stick in[12]/read[13]/be fresh in **one's mind** • happy **remembrances** • in **remembrance** of sth./sb. • absent[14] -/ open[15] -/ simple[16] -/ single[17] -**minded** • absence / frame[18] [eɪ]/ change[19] **of mind**   **1**

remind sb. (of) vt   sim **bring/ call to mind**[1] phr,
                              prompt[2] v, **cue**[3] [kju:] v & n → U19-11

to make sb. think about things (s)he has forgotten (e.g. to suggest a name, activity, etc.)
reminder[4] [aɪ] n • **reminisce**[5] [remɪnɪs] v • **reminiscence**[6] n • **reminiscent** adj

» *That reminds me of my mother. The patient should be reminded that mental clarity [eə] and dexterity[7] may remain impaired for 24-48 hours. Battered[8] children avoid reminders of the traumatic event. Help the patient to select a reminder cue to take his daily dose.*

Use **to remind** patients / oneself • **to remind sb.** of his duty / that ... • constant / daily / mailed[9] / unnecessary **reminder** • **to prompt** suspicion[10] [ɪʃ]/ psychiatric [saɪkɪ-] evaluation / sb. to seek [i:] medical attention[11] • **to cue** sb. • to recognize[12]/interpret/respond to **cues** • a baby's / nonverbal [ɜ:]/ sensory / auditory [ɔ:]/ subtle[13] [sʌtl] **cues** • **to be reminiscent of** one's childhood • **reminiscences** of/about the past • **reminiscent** look / smile / of sth.

identify [aɪdentəfaɪ] v   sim **recognize**[1] v,
                              rel **name**[2], **place**[3], **date**[3] v → U73-4

to establish the identity of someone or something
identification n • **(un)identified**[4] adj • **identifiable** adj → U75-2
recognition n • **recognizable**[5] adj

» *The earliest symptom was vague [eɪ] abdominal heaviness that the patient did not identify as a pain. He failed to recognize his son. Obese patients are taught to recognize "eating cues" and how to avoid or control them. Her face looks familiar but I can't place her.*

Use **to identify** a person / a virus / objects / with sb. else • **to recognize** symptoms / a smell[6] • object / patient[7] / visual **identification** • diagnostic / endoscopic / accurate **identification** • **identification** bracelet[8] / tag[9] / number • **identification** or ID card[10] / test / methods • to promote/aid in/impede [i:]/delay [eɪ] **recognition** • word / sound[11] / pattern / prompt **recognition** • early[12] / beyond[13] **recognition**

realize [ri:əlaɪz] v   rel **understand**[1], **appreciate**[2] [əpri:ʃieɪt] v → U57-4

(i) to become fully aware[3] of sth. or to perceive[4] [si:] sth. mentally
(ii) to make sth. real or put it into practice
realization[5] [eɪʃ] n • **understanding**[6] n & adj • **appreciation**[7] [eɪʃ] n

» *Patients presenting with transient global amnesia [i:z] may be unaware[8] of their deficit, but most realize that "something is wrong"; a few may recognize that their memory is impaired. One must be explicit[9] [ɪs] and make sure that the teen understands what is being asked. Do you think he is able to appreciate the consequences of refusing treatment.*

Use **to realize** one's limitations[10] / what's happening / the truth • **to appreciate** life's pleasures [eʒ]/ pressure / a heart [ɑ:] murmur[11] [ɜ:] • growing / sudden **realization** • to show/be/provide **understanding** • mutual[12] [mju:tʃʊəl] / parental / difficulty in **understanding** • general / clear / full **understanding** • thorough[13] [ɜ:]/ better / impaired [eə] **understanding**

associate [əsoʊʃieɪt] v   sim **relate**[1] [rɪleɪt], **connect**[1], **link**[1] v

to make a logical or causal [ɔ:] connection
association[2] [eɪʃ] n term • **associative** [ʃǁs] adj • **associational** adj
• **(un)related**[3] [eɪ] adj • **relation(ship)**[4] [rɪleɪʃᵊnʃɪp] n • **connection**[5] n • **link**[5] n

» *Dyslexics[6] [dɪs-] may have difficulty determining [ɜ:] which letters in words form specific sound-symbol [ɪ] associations such as vowel [aʊ] patterns, affixes, syllables [ɪ], and word endings.*

Use **to associate** A and/with B • free[7] / word / controlled[8] / clang or klang[9] **association** • **association** test[10] / area[11] / tracts[12] / of ideas • **associative** learning • **related** to stature [stætʃɚ]/ age-/ sex-/ drug[13]-/ alcohol-/ dose-/ school-**related** • **unrelated** event / illness / to injury[14] / doctor-patient[15]-/ parent-child-/ close[16] / causal **relationship** • weak [i:]/ cross-/ genetic [dʒen-]/ etiologic [i:tɪə-] **link**

Memory COMPLEX BODY FUNCTIONS 297

rehearse [rɪhɜːrs] v   sim **practice**[1] BE **practise**, **drill**[2] v & n

to enhance memory by repeating new information to oneself in order not to forget it

rehearsal[3] n • **practice** n • **practicable**[4] adj

» Learning disorders may be associated with deficiencies [ɪʃ] in memory functions, esp. information retention, rehearsal strategies, and verbal [ɜː] retrieval[5] [iː] and production. Short-movement exercises should be practiced while seated. We had this behavior drilled into us[6].

Use **to rehearse** a speech[7] (over and over) / for a show • **to practice** doing sth. / for sth. / the violin[8] [aɪ]/ safe sex / medicine[9] • **to put into**[10] / piano **practice** • **to drill** sb. in/on sth. • spelling[11] • disaster **drills** • maintenance **rehearsal**

einüben, -studieren, proben
(aus)üben, praktizieren[1] einüben, pauken; Drill(übung)[2] Wiederholung, Übung, Probe[3] durchführbar[4] Wortfindung[5] wurde uns eingerichtet[6] e. Rede einstudieren[7] auf d. Geige üben[8] als Arzt/ Ärztin praktizieren[9] in d. Praxis umsetzen[10] Rechtschreibübungen, -drills[11]   6

repeat [rɪpiːt] v   sim **revise**[1] [rɪvaɪz] v, rel **learn**[2] [lɜːrn] v

to state again, to recapitulate[3] or do sth. over[4], e.g. to practice or learn it

repetition [ɪʃ] n • **repetitive**[5] adj • **revision** [ɪʒ] n • **re/ unlearn**[6] vt • **learning** n

» During these episodes, the patient repeated the same questions again and again and did not recognize that her memory was impaired. There is an impairment in the ability to learn new information or recall previously [iː] learned information.

Use **to repeat** words / oneself / an act • **to revise** a book / for an examination[7] • **to learn** new skills[8] / to adapt / how to do sth. • **to learn** from mistakes[9] / from experience[10] • word[11] / paired [eə˞] associate[12] [oʊʃ] • **learning** skill / spatial[13] [eɪ]/ social[14] **learning** • **learning** curve [ɜː]/ process[15] / pattern • **learning** (dis)ability[16] / disorder[17] / problem / deficit /-disabled[18] • **learning to** read / walk • **learned** behavior[19] [eɪ]/ response

wiederholen, nachsprechen
durchsehen, überarbeiten, ändern[1] (er)lernen[2] (kurz) zusammenfassen, rekapitulieren[3] noch einmal machen[4] s. wiederholend, repetitiv[5] abgewöhnen, ablegen[6] d. Stoff für e. Prüfung wiederholen[7] etw. Neues lernen[8] aus Fehlern lernen[9] aus Erfahrung lernen[10] verbales Lernen[11] assoziatives L.[12] räuml. L.[13] soziales L.[14] Lernprozess[15] Lernbehinderung[16] Lernstörung[17] lernbehindert[18] erlerntes Verhalten[19]   7

memory [meməɪ] n clin & term   sim **recollection**[1] [rekəlekʃən] n

(i) power of retaining and recalling past experience, facts, ideas, etc.
(ii) sth. that is remembered

memorize[2] [-aɪz] vt • **memorable**[3] adj • **commemorate**[4] v • **recollect** v

» Then the child goes back to sleep and has no memory of the event the next day. Memory function[5] includes registration (encoding or acquisition), retention (storage or consolidation), stabilization, and retrieval [iː] (decoding or recall). Do you have a good memory for figures[6]? Memory for new information[7] is severely affected but memory of distant events[8] is less so. He has impaired recollection of the ictal phase[9] [feɪz].

Use to have a good/poor **memory** • to refresh or brush [ʌ] up[10] **one's memory** • to improve or enhance/jog[11] [dʒɒːɡ] **one's memory** • to have problems with/interfere [-ɪə˞] with[12]/recover [ʌ] **one's memory** • to store/arouse[13] [aʊ] /relive [riːlɪv] a **memory** • visual [ɪʒ] or iconic[14] [aɪkɒnɪk]/ auditory [ɒː] or echoic[15] [ekoʊɪk] **memory** • procedural [siː] or implicit[16] **memory** • declarative or explicit[17] / screen[18] **memory** • episodic[19] / semantic[20] **memory** • recent [iːs] / secondary[21] / immediate [iː] or primary[22] [aɪ] / remote[8] **memory** • long-term[21] (abbr LTM) / short-term[22] (abbr STM) **memory** • delayed[23] / working[24] **memory** • impaired[25] / intact / failing[26] [eɪ] **memory** • fleeting[27] [iː] / photographic / (un)conscious [ʃ] **memory** • **memory for** smells / facts / past events • **memory for** words / names / faces[28] • **memory** faculties[29] / capacity [æs] or skills[29] • **memory** retrieval[30] / disturbance[25] [ɜː] • **memory** aids[31] [eɪdz]/ consolidation • **memory** lapse[32] / loss[33] / deficit • to bring back **memories** • impaired / little / vague[27] [veɪɡ]/ conscious **recollection**

(i) Gedächtnis, Erinnerungsvermögen (ii) Erinnerung
Erinnerung[1] s. etwas einprägen[2] unvergesslich, denkwürdig[3] gedenken[4] Gedächtnisleistung, -funktion[5] Zahlengedächtnis[6] Neugedächtnis[7] Altgedächtnis[8] Anfallsphase, iktale Phase[9] s. Gedächtnis auffrischen[10] seinem G. auf d. Sprünge helfen[11] s. Erinnerungsvermögen beeinträchtigen[12] e. Erinnerung wecken[13] visuelles Gedächtnis[14] akust. G.[15] prozedurales/ implizites G.[16] deklaratives/ explizites G.[17] Deckerinnerung[18] episod. Gedächtnis[19] semant. G.[20] sekundäres G., Langzeitgedächtnis[21] Sofort-, Immediat-, Kurzzeitgedächtnis[22] mittelfristiges G.[23] Arbeitsgedächtnis[24] Gedächtnisstörung[25] nachlassendes G.[26] schwache Erinnerung[27] Personengedächtnis[28] Gedächtnisfähigkeiten[29] Abrufung v. Gedächtnisinhalten[30] Gedächtnisstützen, -hilfen[31] Gedächtnislücke[32] Gedächtnisverlust[33]   8

encoding [ɪnkoʊdɪŋ] n term   rel **register**[1] [redʒɪstə˞], **imprint**[2] v, **take in**[3] v phr

first stage in the memory process involving processes associated with acquisition [ɪʃ] of stimuli [aɪ] through one or more of the senses (i.e. briefly registering and modifying information)

de/ encode[4] v term • **encoded** adj • **code**[5] v & n • **registration** n • **imprint**[6] n

» It is well known that active rehearsal facilitates [sɪ] encoding and later retrieval [iː] of stimuli. What is the role of sleep and dreams in encoding memory? Elaborate encoding refers to making associations. Loss of encoded information (a type of forgetting) occurs [ɜː] rapidly unless the next two stages in the memory process, storage and retrieval, are activated.

Use visual[7] / verbal / structural[8] [ʌ] / phonemic[9] [iː] encoding • semantic[10] / neural [(j)ʊə˞]/ synaptic encoding • (poor) initial [ɪʃ] enriching[11] / elaborate[12] encoding • encoding memory tasks / and retrieval processes • encoding efficiency [ɪʃ]/ specificity[13] [ɪs] • encoding-related brain activity / transactive memory • memory encoding areas / process[14] • declarative / emotional [oʊʃ]/ neutral [(j)uː] memory encoding • to make/leave[2] an imprint • coded signal • to decode (word) meaning

Enkodierung, Gedächtnisspeicherung, Einspeicherung
ablegen, registrieren[1] (ein)prägen[2] registrieren, aufnehmen[3] codieren, verschlüsseln[4] codieren; Code[5] Gedächtnisspur, Zeichen[6] visuelles Enkodieren[7] strukturelle Enkodierung[8] phonologische Enkodierung[9] semantische Enkodierung[10] vertiefende Verarbeitung[11] elaborierte Verarbeitung[12] Enkodierungsspezifität[13] Enkodierungsprozess[14]

9

COMPLEX BODY FUNCTIONS — Memory

(memory) storage [stɔːrɪdʒ] *n term*   *sim* **retention**¹ *n, rel* **retrieval**² [iː] *n term*

mental processes associated with retention of stimuli that have been registered and modified by encoding

store³ [stɔːr] *v & n* • **stored** *adj* • **retain**⁴ [rɪteɪn] *v* • **retrieve**⁵ [rɪtriːv] *v*

» Retention [ʃ] or retrieval problems cause dyslexics to confuse the names of letters and words that are similar in structure. Some information appears to be stored accurately for an indefinite time, whereas other items fade⁶ [eɪ] or become distorted⁷. Declarative memory refers to facts and past personal events that must be consciously retrieved to be remembered. Long-term potentiation⁸ (abbr LTP), which refers to a long-lasting enhancement of synaptic transmission, is presumed [juː] to be involved in memory acquisition⁹ and storage.

Use long-term or permanent [ɜː] **memory storage** • **storage** capacity¹⁰ / buffer [ʌ] • **to store** new memories • information¹¹ / digit¹² [dɪdʒɪt] retention • verbal [ɜː] **retrieval**

Gedächtnisspeicherung

Behalten, Retention, Merkfähigkeit¹ Abruf(en), Erinnern² speichern, ablegen; Vorrat, Speicher³ speichern, s. merken⁴ abrufen⁵ verblassen, zerfallen⁶ verzerrt werden⁷ langfristige Auflagung⁸ Gedächtnisbildung⁹ Speicherkapazität¹⁰ Informationsspeicherung¹¹ Zahlengedächtnis¹²

10

---

intrusion [ɪntruːʒən] *n term*   *sim* **flashback**¹ [flæʃbæk] *n clin* → U11-9

unexpected but very vivid memory of a past event (esp. of traumatic experience)

» Children frequently reexperience² elements of traumatic events in nightmares³ [eə] and intrusive daytime flashbacks. If flashbacks (mental imagery from a "bad trip") later triggered⁴ by mild stimuli [aɪ] such as alcohol) occur [ɜː], a short course [ɔː] of an antipsychotic⁵ is usually sufficient [ɪʃ]. Like other posttraumatic stress responses, intrusion of previously [iː] avoided memory can be cued⁴ by environmental stimuli⁶.

Use to produce/experience/have **flashbacks** • transient / distressing⁷ **flashbacks** • **flashback** episodes • alpha-wave / impending / habit **intrusion** • **intrusion** error

Intrusion, belastendes Wiedererleben

Flashback, Rückblende¹ wiedererleben² Alpträume³ ausgelöst⁴ Neuroleptikum, Antipsychotikum⁵ Umweltreize⁶ belastende Flashbacks⁷

11

---

engram *n term*   *syn* **neurogram** [n(j)ʊərə-], **memory trace** [treɪs] *n term*

imprint every mental experience leaves on the brain, stimulation of which retrieves the original experience

neurogrammic *adj term* • **neurography**¹ *n* • **engrammic** *adj*

» Encoding is the process of converting [ɜː] an event into an engram. The set of cells with facilitated synapses is the anatomical correlate of the memory and is called a memory trace.

Use to establish²/(re)activate or retrieve **an engram** • memory / neural / biochemical / dormant³ **engram** • **engram** (memory) pattern / selection • enduring⁴ / olfactory / visual⁵ / motor⁶ **memory trace**

Engramm, Gedächtnisspur

Neurografie¹ ein Engramm bilden² schlummerndes Engramm³ langanhaltende/ dauerhafte Gedächtnisspur⁴ Erinnerungsbild⁵ Bewegungsmuster⁶

12

---

mnemonic(s) *n term*   *syn* **mnemotechnic(s)** *n, rel* **mneme**¹ [niːmi] *n term*

systematic memory training² based on memory-aiding devices³ [aɪ] linking a new item [aɪ] with one that is already established in the memory, e.g. associating a new telephone number with one's birthday

mnemonic⁴ [nɪmɒnɪk] *adj term* • **mnemic**⁵ [iː] *adj* • **mnem(o)-** [niːmoʊ-] *comb*

» Mnemonics are memory training devices or ways of making associations designed to enhance [æ] memory⁶ and recall. Improve your memory via mnemonics. First-letter mnemonics can be useful for overcoming memory blocks⁷. Mnemonics uses associations, triggers, and rhyming [aɪ] methods to develop a system to remember a wide variety of information.

Use phonetic / (alphabet/ rhyming) peg⁸ / medical **mnemonics** • **mnemonics memory** technique / devices³ / course • **mnemonic** devices³ / systems / programming • **mnem**asthenia⁹ [iː]

Mnemotechnik, Mnemonik

Gedächtnis, Erinnerung, Mneme¹ Gedächtnistraining² Gedächtnishilfen, -stützen³ mnemotechnisch, mnemonisch, Gedächtnis-⁴ mnestisch, das Gedächtnis betreffend⁵ die Gedächtnisleistung steigern⁶ Gedächtnisblockaden, Blackouts⁷ Gedächtnis-, Eselsbrücke⁸ Gedächtnisschwäche⁹

13

---

forget - forgot - forgotten *v irr*   *rel* **repress**¹ [rɪpres], **suppress**² [səpres] *v*

to fail to keep in memory or to intentionally dismiss from the mind

(un)forgetable *adj* • **long-forgotten** *adj* • **repression**³ [eʃ] *n term*

» Insight [ɪnsaɪt] fails to develop in histrionic⁴ persons because they can easily repress or forget unpleasant [e] experiences⁵. The defense mechanisms⁶ [ek] in hysterical conversion [ɜː] are repression (a barring [ɑː] from consciousness⁷) and isolation (a splitting of the affect from the idea).

Use **to forget** (about) sth. / one's name / problems / oneself • **to repress** emotions [oʊʃ]/ guilty [ɡɪlti] feelings⁸ • **to suppress** memories⁹ / (sexual) fantasies / respiration / secretion¹⁰ [iːʃ] • **repressed** memory¹¹ / desire [aɪ] / anger¹² / aggressions • unconscious¹³ **repression**

vergessen

unterdrücken, verdrängen¹ unterdrücken, verdrängen, hemmen² Verdrängung³ hysterisch⁴ unangenehme Erlebnisse⁵ Abwehrmechanismen⁶ Ausschluss aus d. Bewusstsein⁷ Schuldgefühle verdrängen⁸ Erinnerungen verdrängen⁹ die Sekretion hemmen¹⁰ verdrängte Erinnerung¹¹ unterdrückter Zorn¹² unbewusste Verdrängung¹³

14

Memory   COMPLEX BODY FUNCTIONS 299

forgetful adj   sim **oblivious**[1] [əblɪviəs] adj, rel **absent-minded**[2] [aɪ] adj
  repeatedly [iː] failing to keep something in mind or to be to mindful [aɪ] or attentive
  forgetfulness[3] n • **oblivion**[4] n • **absent-mindedness** n
» The patient became slightly forgetful. Patients presenting with bruxism[5] [ʌ] may be oblivious of the habit. Disoriented patients are often oblivious to the most obvious features [fiːtʃɚz] of the surrounding [aʊ] environment [aɪ].
Use to be/become **forgetful** • **forgetful** confusion[6] [juː] • normal / benign[7] [bɪnaɪn]/ increased [iː] **forgetfulness** • **to be oblivious** to a symptom[8] [ɪ]/ of one's habits • to be/become **absent-minded**

vergesslich, achtlos, nachlässig
vergesslich, nicht wahrnehmend[1] geistesabwesend[2] Vergesslichkeit, Nachlässigkeit[3] Vergessen(heit)[4] (Zähne)knirschen, Bruxismus[5] Vergesslichkeit und Verwirrtheit[6] benigne Vergesslichkeit[7] e. Symptom nicht wahrnehmen[8]
15

inattentive adj clin & term   sim **unconcentrated**[1], **distracted**[2] adj clin
  not fully concentrated because of a lack of interest, negligence[3], or absent-mindedness
  attentive adj • **attentional** [ˈʃ] adj term • **(in)attention** or **-tiveness**[4] n
  • **concentrate** v • **concentration** n • **distract**[5] v • **distraction**[6] n
» Patients with large basal [eɪ] lesions [iː] are apathetic[7], inattentive to stimuli [aɪ], and indifferent[8] to the implications of their acts. Patients on large doses of depressants frequently show slowness of speech with poor memory, faulty [ɔː] judgment[9] [ʌ], and narrowed attention span.
Use to be (**in**)**attentive** • to pay[10]/focus[11]/turn one's/lack/affect/seek [iː] **attention** • to warrant [ɔː] or require[12]/ attract or catch[13] **attention** • to receive [siː] /direct/ escape/ divert[14] [ɜː] **attention** • undivided[15] [aɪ] / close[16] / scrupulous[17] [uː] **attention** • strict[17] / little / medical[18] **attention** • level / focus / impairment [eə]/ lapses **of attention** • **attention** span[19] / deficit (hyperactivity) disorder[20] / to drug selection • **attentional** mechanism / behavior[21] / abilities / distraction[22] • temporary / sensory / inappropriate **inattention** • visual [ɪ] **attentiveness** • **to concentrate** on sth. • to enhance/lose/lack **concentration** • powers of[23] **concentration**

unaufmerksam
unkonzentriert[1] abgelenkt, zerstreut[2] Unachtsamkeit[3] (Un)aufmerksamkeit[4] ablenken[5] Ablenkung, Zerstreuung, Zerstreut-, Verwirrtheit[6] apathisch, teilnahmslos[7] gleichgültig[8] schlechtes Urteilsvermögen[9] Aufmerksamkeit schenken[10] seine Aufmerksamkeit richten auf[11] A. erfordern[12] A. erregen[13] ablenken[14] volle Aufmerksamkeit[15] genaue Beobachtung[16] strikte Einhaltung[17] ärztl. Behandlung[18] Aufmerksamkeitsspanne[19] Aufmerksamkeitsdefizitsyndrom, hyperkinetisches S.[20] aufmerksamkeitsheischendes Verhalten[21] Ablenkung[22] Konzentrationsfähigkeit[23]
16

amnesia [æmniːʒə] n term   syn **memory loss**, rel **blackout**[1] n clin
  total or partial inability to recall past experience due to loss of information stored in long-term memory
  amnesic [æmniːzɪk] or **amnestic**[2] [e] adj term • **-mnesia, -mnes(t)ic** comb
» Retrograde [-eɪd] amnesia (i.e. inability to remember events just preceding [siː] the accident) always indicates some degree [iː] of cerebral [s] damage[3]. Event-specific amnesia is particularly common after violent [aɪ] crimes such as sexual abuse or homicide[4] of a close relative or friend.
Use to induce/produce **amnesia** • period / episode **of amnesia** • transient global[5] / partial[6] / anterograde[7] **amnesia** • retrograde[8] / event-specific **amnesia** • posttraumatic / posthypnotic[9] [ɪ]/ psychogenic[10] [saɪkə-] **amnesia** • hysterical / mild / profound[11] [aʊ] **amnesia** • isolated [aɪ] / benign / progressive **memory loss** • disabling[12] [eɪ]/ early / acute short-term **memory loss** • to have a / alcohol-related or alcoholic[13] **blackout** • **amnesic** gap[14] / state /-confabulatory [æ] syndrome[15] • **amnestic** episode / disorder / aphasia[16] [eɪ]

Amnesie, (vorübergehender) Gedächtnisverlust
Gedächtnislücke, kurzer Bewusstseinsverlust; Blackout[1] amnestisch[2] Hirnschädigung, -schaden[3] Mord, Totschlag[4] transitorisch-globale Amnesie[5] partielle A.[6] anterograde A.[7] retrograde A.[8] posthypnotische A.[9] psychogene A.[10] vollständige A.[11] funktionell beeinträchtigende Gedächtnisstörung[12] alkoholbedingte Amnesie, Alkoholamnesie[13] Gedächtnis-, Erinnerungslücke[14] Korsakow-Syndrom, amnest. Syndrom[15] amnestische Aphasie[16]
17

paramnesia [pærə-] n term   rel **deja vu**[1], **jamais-vu**[2], **confabulation**[3] n term
  general term applied to faulty recollection in which fact and fantasy are confused, e.g. déjà vu, events that have never occurred [ɜː], mislocations in time and space, or confabulation
» This is a case of paramnesia rather than of genuine recall. Deja vu is a paramnesia consisting of the sensation or illusion [uː] that one is seeing what one has seen before. Temporal lobe lesions [iː] can lead to depersonalization, behavioral disturbances, sensations of deja vu or jamais vu, visual field defects[4], and auditory illusions or hallucinations. Another type of misidentification is reduplicative [uː] paramnesia, in which there is the belief that a familiar person, place, object or body part has been duplicated.
Use identifying / reduplicative **paramnesia** • **paramnesia** confabulation[5] • **deja vu** phenomenon • sensations of[1] **deja vu**

Paramnesie, Erinnerungsverfälschung, paramnestische Dysmnesie, Wahnerinnerung
Deja-vu-Erlebnis, vermeintliche Vertrautheit[1] Jamais-vu-Erlebnis, vermeintliche Fremdheit[2] Konfabulation[3] Gesichtsfeldausfälle[4] Pseudologia phantastica[5]
18

74

twilight state [twaɪlaɪt steɪt] *n term & clin*

temporary absence of consciousness seen in hysteria or epilepsy during which actions may be performed without conscious [ʃ] volition[1] [ɪʃ] and with no memory of the episode

» Theta has been called the "twilight state," between waking and sleep which is often accompanied by dreamlike mental images. The therapist's voice is heard until the patient deepens relaxation to the "twilight state" level (defined by theta waves).

Use traumatic[2] / psychogenic / epileptic **twilight state** • **twilight** sleep[3] / dreams

Dämmerzustand
Wille, Willenskraft[1] posttraumatischer Dämmerzustand[2] Dämmerschlaf[3]

19

fugue state [fju:g steɪt] *n term*   syn **psychogenic** [saɪkədʒenɪk] **fugue** *n term*

state of altered [ɔ:] consciousness that may last for hours or days marked by amnesia for events occurring [ɜ:] during the fugue period and physical [ɪ] flight [flaɪt] from an intolerable situation
fugue-like *adj term*

» Psychogenic fugue is the most commonly encountered [aʊ] dissociative [ʊʃ] state[1] in the ER. On recovery [ʌ], there is a residual [ɪdʒ] amnesic [i:] gap[2] for the period of the fugue. In contrast to organic amnesia, fugue states are associated with amnesia for personal identity and events closely associated with the personal past.

dissoziative(r)/ psychogene(r) Fugue(-Zustand)
dissoziative Störung[1] amnestische Lücke[2]

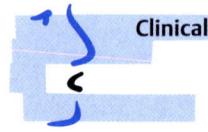

20

Clinical Phrases

Remember to take these drops daily before bedtime. Vergessen Sie nicht, diese Tropfen täglich vor dem Schlafengehen einzunehmen. • I don't remember that. Daran kann ich mich nicht errinnern. • Do you remember signing this?. Wissen Sie noch, ob Sie das unterschrieben haben? • I can't describe it, it slipped my mind. Ich kann es nicht beschreiben, es ist mir entfallen. • The name is on the tip of my tongue, but I can't say it. Der Name liegt mir auf der Zunge, aber er fällt mir im Moment nicht ein. • Think hard! Try to remember what the doctor told you. Denken Sie scharf nach! Versuchen Sie sich zu erinnern, was der Arzt zu Ihnen gesagt hat. • Does this ring a bell? Erinnert Sie das an etwas? • She used to be able to quote whole poems from memory. Früher konnte sie ganze Gedichte auswendig hersagen. • If my memory serves me right, that was back in 1999. Wenn ich mich recht erinnere, dann war das im Jahr 1999. • Did you suffer from pneumonia as a child? No, not that I remember/ know of. Hatten Sie als Kind einmal eine Lungenentzündung. Nein, nicht dass ich wüßte. • I'm afraid my memory is failing me. Ich fürchte, mein Gedächtnis läßt mich im Stich. • The days when I used to go to school are still fresh in my mind. Die Zeit, als ich noch zur Schule ging, ist mir noch gut im Gedächtnis. • I don't know what happened, Doctor, my mind just went blank. Ich weiß nicht was passiert ist, Herr Doktor, ich kann mich an nichts erinnern.

Unit 75   Personality & Behavior
Related Units: 76 Mood, 68 Sexuality, 73 Mental Activity, 77 Mental Health, 80 Aging, 113 Neurologic Findings

personality trait [treɪt] *n*   *rel* **character**[1], **type**[2] [taɪp], **nature**[3] [eɪ] *n*

one of the behavioral, emotional and mental attributes that characterize an individual
person *n* • **(inter/ im)personal** *adj* • **characterize** *v* • **good-natured**[4] *adj*

» These unusual personality traits are not due to epilepsy but probably result from psychosocial [saɪkoʊ-] factors. Borderline personalities are unstable in several areas, including self-image, mood [u:], behavior, and interpersonal relationships[5]. She's by nature inclined [aɪ] to be very scrupulous[6] [u:]. It's not in his nature to be so assertive[7] [ɜ:]. These recent actions of hers are totally out of character[8]. He's quite nice but just not my type.

Use premorbid[9] [ɔ:] **personality traits** • (ab)normal / well-adjusted [ʌ]/ inadequate[10] **personality** • (in)dependent[10] / (un)stable[11] [eɪ]/ emotionally [ʊʃ] labile [eɪ]/ embittered **personality** • antisocial[12] / seclusive[13] [u:]/ hysterical[14] **personality** • split *or* multiple[15] [ʌ]/ compulsive[16] [ʌ] **personality** • strength / normalization **of personality** • **personality** profile / type / test / features[17] [fi:tʃɚz] • **personality** structure / development[18] / changes / disorder[19] • schizoid[20] [sk]/ schizotypal[21] [aɪ]/ paranoid / borderline **personality disorder** • to be in/out of[8]/a man of/quite a[22] **character** • to give sb. a good[23] / to have a bad/strong[24] **character** • **character** defect[25] [i:]/ problem • **personal** characteristics / habits / perspective[26] • **personal** lifestyle (change) / preference / motivation • **personal** hygiene[27] [haɪdʒi:n]/ contact / interaction • **personal** relationship / belongings[28] / loss • elderly / dominant / neatly groomed[29] [u:] **person** • (hyper)sensitive / (mentally) unstable **person** • orientation (as) to **person** • **person**-to-person contact[30] • **type** A person • ill-**natured**

Charakter-, Wesenszug, Persönlichkeitsmerkmal, -zug
Charakter, Wesen[1] Typ[2] Natur, Wesen(sart)[3] gutmütig[4] zwischenmenschliche Beziehungen[5] gewissenhaft, genau[6] bestimmt[7] untypisch (für)[8] prämorbide Persönlichkeitszüge[9] abhängige Persönlichkeit[10] stabile P.[11] asoziale Persönlichkeit[12] eigenbrötlerisches Wesen[13] histrionische Persönlichkeit[14] multiple P.[15] anankastische/ zwanghafte P.[16] Persönlichkeitszüge[17] Persönlichkeitsentwicklung[18] Persönlichkeitsstörung[19] schizoide P.[20] schizotypische P.[21] e. Original sein[22] jem. e. gutes Zeugnis ausstellen[23] e. starke Persönlichkeit sein[24] Charakterfehler[25] persönl. (An)sicht[26] Körperpflege[27] pers. Eigentum[28] gepflegte Person[29] zwischenmenschlicher Kontakt[30]

1

Personality & Behavior | COMPLEX BODY FUNCTIONS **301**

identity [aɪdenˈəti] n   sim **self-concept**[1] n, rel **individuality**[2] [æ] n

distinct personality by which individuals perceive [pəˈsiːv] their own self

identify (with) v • **individual** [ɪndɪˈvɪdʒʊəl] adj & n • **selfish**[3] adj • **self** n

» Did the patient take on a new identity? He has to establish an independent identity and separate from the family. When lack of self-confidence[4] and identity problems are factors in the depression, individual psychotherapy can be oriented to ways of improving self-esteem[5] [iː], increasing assertiveness, and lessening dependency. Except for delirium organic memory loss shows disorientation that is worse for time but never for self. Adolescents require both individuality and involvement with family and society to facilitate development of identity.

Use to establish[6]/struggle [ʌ] with **one's identity** • personal / gender[7] [dʒ] / (homo)-sexual / social **identity** • sense / change / loss[8] **of identity** • **identity** card / crisis[9] [aɪ]/ disorder / diffusion[10] [juː3] • positive / negative / improved **self-concept** • **self**-image[11] /-acceptance[12] /-centered[13] • **self**-confident or -assured[14] /-conscious[15] /-awareness [ɚ]/-control • sense of **self** • **self**-care /-help /-mutilation[16] [mjuː]/-reproach[17] [tʃ] • **self**-depreciation[18] /-destructive behavior[19] /-injury • loss of **individuality**

Identität
Selbstkonzept[1] Individualität[2] egoistisch, selbstsüchtig[3] Selbstvertrauen, -bewusstsein[4] Selbstwertgefühl[5] s. eigene Identität ausbilden/ entwickeln[6] Geschlechtsidentität[7] Identitätsverlust[8] Identitätskrise[9] Identitätsdiffusion, unklare I.[10] Selbstverständnis, -bild[11] Selbstannahme[12] egozentrisch, ichbezogen[13] selbstbewusst[14] befangen, gehemmt[15] Selbstverstümmelung[16] Selbstvorwurf[17] Selbsterniedrigung[18] selbstzerstörerisches Verhalten[19]

2

behavior [bɪˈheɪvɪɚ] n   syn **conduct** n, rel **manner**[1] [æ], **attitude**[2] [æ] n

a person's actions, activities, and objectively observable interaction with the environment

behave[3] v • **manners**[4] n • **mannerism**[5] n • **behavioral** adj term • **behaviorism**[6] n

» Psychomotor seizures [siːʒɚz] of temporal lobe origin are not characterized by unprovoked aggressive behavior. Out-of-control behavior may be managed through cognitive behavior modification[7] and behavior control training. He is known to be ill-mannered and badly dressed. The attitude of the doctor should be one of honesty, interest, and hopefulness.

Use to modify **behavior** • human / (anti-)social / emotional [oʊʃ]/ motor / sexual[8] **behavior** • (mal)adaptive[9] / (task-/dis)oriented / coping[10] [oʊ] **behavior** • drunken [ʌ]/ attention getting / withdrawn [ɒː] **behavior** • bizarre / (ab)normal[11] / (in/age-)appropriate[12] **behavior** • deviant[13] [iː]/ aggressive **behavior** • violent [aɪ]/ suicidal [saɪ]/ (self-)destructive **behavior** • criminal / health-compromising[14] **behavior** • **behavior** pattern[15] / modification (program) • **behavior** management (technique) [tekniːk]/ therapy[16] / problem • **behavioral** norms[17] / assessment / test / changes or alterations[18] • **behavioral** responses / disorder or disturbance[11] [ɜː] • in a calm [kɑːm] casual[19] [kæʒʊəl] careless **manner** • pensive[20] / stiff / bedside[21] **manner** • conservative / hostile[22] / pessimistic / negative[23] **attitude** • to have no / good / bad **manners** • ill-**mannered**[24] • to display (bizarre / nervous) **mannerisms**

Benehmen, Verhalten
(Eigen)art, Weise[1] Einstellung, Haltung[2] s. benehmen/ verhalten[3] Benehmen, Umgangsformen[4] Maniriertheit, gekünsteltes Gehabe[5] Behaviorismus[6] kognitive Verhaltenstherapie[7] Sexualverhalten[8] Anpassungsverhalten[9] Bewältigungsverhalten, Coping[10] Verhaltensstörung[11] altersgemäßes Verhalten[12] abweichendes Verhalten, Devianz[13] gesundheitsgefährdendes V.[14] Verhaltensmuster[15] Verhaltenstherapie[16] Verhaltensnormen[17] Verhaltensänderungen[18] ungezwungene Art[19] nachdenkliche/ ernste Wesensart[20] Umgang (d. Arztes) m. Patienten[21] feindselige Haltung[22] negative Einstellung[23] ungezogen, ungehobelt, schlecht erzogen[24]   3

temperament n   rel **(pre)disposition**[1] [ɪʃ], **composure**[2] [oʊʒ] n → U76-2

(i) characteristic tendency, mood [uː], or attitude of mind[3] in a person
(ii) having a tendency to openly display one's emotions [oʊʃ]

temperamental[4] adj • **(pre/ in)disposed**[5] [-dɪspoʊzd] adj

» The Greeks proposed four temperament types: choleric, sanguine, melancholic, and phlegmatic. We are both quiet by temperament. Reduced serotonergic [ɜː] activity in the CNS correlated with temperament, impulsivity, and aggression. He can be very temperamental.

Use fiery[6] [faɪɚi] childhood[7] / cyclothymic [aɪ] difficult / problems of **temperament** • cheerful[8] / amiable[9] [eɪ] nervous [ɜː] **disposition** • jealous [dʒeləs] premorbid neurotic [n(j)ʊə-] **disposition** • **predisposition** to behave in a certain way / to panic • to lose one's[10] **composure** • **temperamental** trait[11] / pattern / inclinations[12] / difficulties

(i, ii) Temperament, Wesen, Naturell
Veranlagung, Neigung, Hang, Naturell; Anfälligkeit, Disposition[1] Fassung; Beherrschung[2] Geisteshaltung[3] temperamentvoll; anlagebedingt[4] unpässlich, unwohl[5] feuriges Temperament[6] kindliches T.[7] fröhliche Art[8] liebenswürdiges Wesen[9] d. Beherrschung verlieren[10] Wesenszug[11] Veranlagungen, Neigungen[12]

4

pleasant [e] adj   rel **friendly**[1] [e], **amiable**[2] [eɪ], **kind**[3] [aɪ], **polite**[4] [aɪ], **tactful**[5] adj

agreeable[6], pleasing[6] [iː] and enjoyable in manner, style or behavior

unpleasant[7] adj • **friendliness** n • **unkind** adj • **impolite** adj • **tactless**[8] adj

» This depressive patient reported a pleasant elevation of mood[9]. Is this pleasant and energetic [dʒe] patient—albeit[10] talkative[11], jocular[12] [dʒɒː], and overly[13] friendly—so disordered that psychiatric [saɪk-] hospitalization must be considered? She has always been so kind to me.

Use **pleasant** experience / woman / activity • **pleasant** smile[14] / sensations / smell[15] / surprise • **to be pleasant** to sb.[16] • **amiable** friend / young man • **kind**-hearted[17] [ɑː]/ care / offer / brother • **polite** man / conversation • **tactful** inquiry[18] / physician [ɪʃ] • **unpleasant** feelings / dream (imagery) / situation • to be **tactful**

angenehm, freundlich, nett
freundlich[1] liebenswürdig[2] freundlich, nett[3] höflich[4] taktvoll[5] angenehm[6] unangenehm[7] taktlos[8] Stimmungsaufhellung[9] obgleich[10] redselig[11] witzig[12] außerordentlich[13] freundliches Lächeln[14] angenehmer Geruch[15] zu jem. nett sein[16] gutherzig[17] taktvolle Anfrage[18]

5

75

cheerful [tʃɪəfəl] adj

rel **glad**[1], **optimistic**[2], **lighthearted**[3] [laɪthɑːrtɪd] adj

to be lively [aɪ] and happy or show good spirits

cheer (up)[4] v • **cheerless**[5] adj • **optimist** n • **lightheartedness** n

» People with mild degrees of dementia [-ʃə] usually mask their intellectual impairment [ɚ] by a cheerful and cooperative manner. Hyperthymic [aɪ] individuals are characterized by the following lifelong traits: cheerful, overoptimistic, exuberant[6] [uː], overconfident, self-assured [əʃʊɚd], boastful[7] [oʊ], energetic, full of plans, uninhibited[8], overtalkative, overinvolved[9], meddlesome[10], and stimulus-seeking [iː].

Use **cheerful** person / mood / disposition[11] / manner[12] / look • to be/stay **cheerful** about sth. • **to be glad** that / to say / of sth.[13] • **lighthearted** attitude

heiter, fröhlich

froh, erfreut[1] zuversichtlich, optimistisch[2] unbeschwert, heiter[3] aufheitern, -muntern[4] freudlos, trübsinnig[5] überschwänglich[6] prahlerisch[7] frei von Hemmungen[8] ohne die nötige Distanz, überengagiert[9] s. in alles einmischend[10] Frohnatur[11] heitere Wesensart[12] über etw. froh sein[13]

6

witty [wɪti] adj   rel **smart**[1] [ɑː], **wise**[2] [aɪ], **humorous**[3], **droll**[4] adj

to have or show a quick and clever mind or an amusing [juː] way of expressing oneself

wit[5] n usu pl • **quick-witted**[6] adj • **humor** [hjuːmɚ] n • **humorless** adj

» My wife says I look like Alfred Hitchcock when I want to be witty. In retrospect I suppose we should have waited, but it is easy to be wise after the event. He has a wonderful sense of humor.

Use **witty** reply [aɪ]/ comment[7] / person / idea / saying[8] • **smart** kid / move[9] / clothes • **wise** decision[10] [ɪ]/ precaution [ɔː]/ guy[11] [gaɪ] • **to have a sense**[12] / lack **of humor** • **droll** person / expression / laugh • sharp or keen[13] [iː] **wit** • half-/ slow[14]-/ dim-**witted** • **to be at one's wits' end**[15]

geistreich, witzig

gescheit, tüchtig; fesch[1] klug, weise, umsichtig[2] humorvoll, lustig[3] komisch, drollig[4] Verstand, Geist, Witz[5] aufgeweckt, schlagfertig[6] geistreicher Kommentar[7] witziger Spruch[8] geschickter Zug[9] kluge Entscheidung[10] Klugscheißer[11] (Sinn für) Humor haben[12] wacher Geist[13] schwer von Begriff[14] mit seinem Latein am Ende sein[15]

7

sympathetic adj   syn **compassionate** adj,
opposite **indifferent**[1], **callous**[2] adj

showing pity[3] and understanding for the misery[4] of others

sympathy[3] [ɪ] n • **sympathize (with)**[5] v • **compassion**[3] n • **indifference** n

» Tact, sympathy and understanding are expected of the physician. We all sympathize [ɪ] with you for your great loss. He gave the mistaken impression of being depressed or emotionally indifferent. They did not show much compassion toward him. Patients with large basal frontal lobe lesions [iːʒ] are apathetic and indifferent to the implications[6] of their acts.

Use **sympathetic** friend / understanding / staff behavior • **sympathetic** to or with sb. / nerve endings[7] • **to arouse**[8] [aʊ] /do sth. out of/seek [iː] **sympathy** for sb. • deep(est) / strong / heartfelt[9] [ɑː] **sympathy** • expression / atmosphere **of sympathy** • **compassionate** dialog [aɪə]/ physician [ɪʃ] • **compassionate** manner / toward sb. / use[10] (protocol) • to have/show/arouse[8] **compassion** • **indifferent** about sth. / to(ward)[11] / concerning [ɜː] sth. • to show/display/affect/feign[12] [feɪn] **indifference to** pain/the environment [aɪ] • **callous** to suffering [ʌ]/ act / disregard for ethics

> Note: Do not confuse **sympathetic** with **likeable**[13] (= agreeable[14]). **Sympathetic** is also used in connection with the nervous system (→ U40-9).

mitfühlend, verständnisvoll

gleichgültig[1] gefühllos, abgebrüht[2] Mitleid, Mitgefühl[3] Not(lage), Elend, Jammer[4] mitfühlen, Mitleid haben[5] Auswirkungen[6] sympathische Nervenendigungen[7] Mitleid erregen[8] aufrichtiges/ tiefempfundenes Mitgefühl[9] Verabreichung v. nicht zugelassenen Testmedikamenten[10] gleichgültig gegenüber[11] Gleichgültigkeit vortäuschen[12] sympathisch[13] nett, angenehm[14]

8

reliable [rɪlaɪəbl] adj   rel **responsible**[1], **dependable**[2], **predictable**[3] adj

to be trustworthy[4] [ʌ] because of one's consistency[5] in behavior [eɪ] or performance

unreliable adj • **rely** [aɪ] **(on)**[6] v • **reliability** n • **irresponsible**[7] adj • **unpredictable**[8] adj

» Is the patient reliable in terms of follow-up and sexual abstinence? Surgical excision [ɪʒ] offers the most reliable hope of cure [kjʊə]. The early adolescent [es] has unpredictable changes of mood and intense attachment [ætʃ] **to peers**[9] [pɪɚz].

Use **reliable** information / test[10] / results • to be/hold sb. **responsible** for sth.[11] / to sb. • **responsible** adult / behavior • **(un)predictable** pattern / reaction / menses[12]

verlässlich, vertrauenswürdig

verantwortlich; verantwortungsvoll, -bewusst[1] zuverlässig, verlässlich[2] berechenbar[3] vertrauenswürdig[4] Beständigkeit[5] s. verlassen (auf)[6] verantwortungslos[7] unbeständig, unberechenbar[8] Gruppenbindung[9] zuverlässiger Test[10] jem. veranwortlich machen für etw.[11] (un)regelmäßige Monatsblutung[12]

9

Personality & Behavior — COMPLEX BODY FUNCTIONS

consistent adj   rel **conscientious**[1] [kɒ:nˈʃɪenˈʃəs], **faithful**[2] [eɪ], **loyal**[3] adj
to behave in agreement with one's principles and/or with one's typical patterns of behavior
inconsistent[4] adj • **(in)consistency**[5] n • **disloyal**[6] adj • **(dis)loyalty** n
» I know I should be more consistent when it comes to bedtimes and discipline. Persons with group conduct disorder demonstrate peer loyalty. The goal [oʊ] of management is the conscientious participation by the patient in an exercise program.
Use **consistent** improvement / tendency / breast-feeding[7] [e] • **consistent** abstinence period / schedule [ʃ‖sk]/ bedtimes[8] • **to be consistent** life-style[9] [aɪ] • to lack in[10] **consistency** • **consistency** in rules • **loyal** to sb. • strong / unshakable[11] [eɪ]/ blind / group **loyalty**

   Note: Mark the difference between **consequent**[12] and **consistent**.

konsequent, (be)ständig
gewissenhaft[1] (ge)treu[2] loyal, treu[3] unbeständig, inkonsequent[4] Beständigkeit, Konsequenz[5] treulos, illoyal[6] voll Stillen (ohne zuzufüttern)[7] gleichbleibende/ regelmäßige Schlafenszeiten[8] mit d. Lebensweise im Einklang stehen[9] unbeständig sein[10] unerschütterliche Treue[11] (darauf)folgend[12]

10

determined [dɪtɜːrmɪnd] adj   rel **resolute**[1], **firm**[2] [fɜːrm] adj
        opposite **scrupulous**[3] [uː], **indecisive**[4] [ɪndɪsaɪsɪv], **reluctant**[5] [ʌ] adj
to have made up one's mind, be sure of one's purpose [ɜː] and strongly motivated to succeed
determine [ɜː] v • **determination**[6] n • **irresolute**[4] adj • **(in)decisiveness**[7] n • **decide** [aɪ] v • **(in)decision**[7] [dɪsɪʒ³n] n • **unscrupulous**[8] adj • **reluctance**[9] n
» She seems determined to brave [eɪ] the matter out[10]. The child was sitting on her bed, pale [eɪ] and resolute, with tight [taɪt] lips and gleaming[11] [iː] eyes. Any response should be questioned gently [dʒ] but firmly. How should I convince a reluctant patient to accept the test?
Use **determined** person / voice / to do sth. / on doing sth. • **resolute** commitment[12] / opposition • **resolute** sense of purpose / in one's decisions • **firm** conviction[13] / believer / proof [uː]/ body[14] / bed[15] • **scrupulous** care / attention / about hygiene [aɪ] • **reluctant** to seek care / smile • fierce[16] [fɪəs]/ firm / dogged[17] [dɒɡɪd]/ self-**determination**

entschlossen, bestimmt
resolut, entschieden, entschlossen[1] hart, fest (entschlossen)[2] penibel, sehr gewissenhaft, überängstlich[3] unentschlossen[4] zögernd, zurückhaltend, widerwillig[5] Entschlossenheit[6] Unentschlossenheit[7] skrupel-, gewissenlos[8] Widerstreben, Abneigung[9] d. Sache durchstehen[10] funkelnd[11] voller Einsatz[12] feste Überzeugung[13] straffer Körper[14] festes/ hartes Bett[15] wilde Entschlossenheit[16] Hartnäckigkeit, Verbissenheit[17]

11

honest [ɒnɪst] adj   sim **sincere**[1] [sɪnsɪə] adj
        opposite **dishonest**[2], **false**[3] [fɔːls], **mean**[4] [miːn] adj
to be truthful [uː] and without pretensions[5] [enʃ], not deceptive[6] [se], fraudulent[7] [ɒː] or disposed to cheat[8] [tʃiː], lie or steal [iː]
honesty[9] n • **sincerity**[10] [e] n • **insincere**[2] adj • **falsehood**[11] n • **falsity**[12] n
» Help the patient to cope [oʊ] with[13] his residual [ɪd] pain by tactful, honest, informative discussions [ʌ]. Answer all questions as openly and honestly as possible. The family should be given a realistic, honest appraisal[14] [eɪ] of the severity [e] of the patient's condition and the prognosis. She offered a sincere apology for her behavior.
Use to be **honest** with sb. • **honest** people / living[15] / opinion • **honest** face / admiration • **sincere** concern[16] [ɜː]/ interest[17] [ɪɡret] • **sincere** promise / sympathy[18] [ɪ] • **dishonest** tricks • **false** hopes / promises / modesty[19] / beliefs • **false** friends / alarm[20] / imprisonment • **falsely** cheerful / attributed / accused • **mean** look[21] / to sb.[22] / about sth.

ehrlich, aufrichtig, redlich
offen, lauter, ehrlich[1] unehrlich[2] treulos, falsch, hinterhältig[3] niederträchtig, gemein; geizig[4] Anmaßung, Dünkel[5] täuschend[6] betrügerisch[7] betrügen, schwindeln[8] Ehrlichkeit, Anständigkeit[9] Aufrichtigkeit, Lauterkeit[10] Unwahrheit[11] Unrichtigkeit, Falschheit[12] zurechtkommen mit[13] Beurteilung[14] rechtschaffenes Leben[15] ernste Bedenken[16] aufrichtiges Bedauern[17] aufrichtiges Mitgefühl[18] falsche Bescheidenheit[19] blinder Alarm[20] gehässiger Blick[21] fies zu jem.[22]

12

frank [æ] adj   syn **candid** [æ], **outspoken** adj,
        rel **outgoing**[1], **extroverted**[1] adj
to be open, straightforward[2] [streɪt-], truthful, and direct in manner or speech [spiːtʃ]
frankness n • **extrovert** n • **extroversion** [ɜː] n term • **introversion**[3] n
» Did you speak frankly with the patient and the family regarding the likely course of disease? I will be frank with you at the outset. Be as candid as possible when interviewing patients with paranoid disorders. He is extroverted, warm[4], and people-seeking[5] [iː].
Use **frank** tone / eyes / smile / reply [aɪ]/ hostility[6] • **frank** bleeding [iː]/ jaundice[7] [dʒɔːndɪs] • **candid** criticism / nature[8] • **to be frank** or **straight** with sb.[9] / about sth. • **outspoken** views / opponent[10] / advocate • blunt[11] [ʌ]/ disarming[12] **frankness** • **extroverted** person(ality type)[13] / attitude • **extroverted** behavior[14] / tendencies / individual • (excessive) social **extroversion**

offen, frei(mütig), unverhohlen
extra-, extrovertiert[1] ehrlich, direkt[2] Introvertiertheit[3] herzlich[4] gesellig[5] unverhohlene Feindseligkeit[6] klin. manifester Ikterus[7] offene Art[8] mit jem. offen sprechen[9] offene(r) Gegner(in)[10] schonungslose Offenheit[11] entwaffnende Ehrlichkeit[12] extrovertierter Typ[13] extrovertiertes Verhalten[14]

13

introverted adj   rel **withdrawn**[1] [ɔː], **unsociable**[2] [oʊʃ] adj
coy[3] [kɔɪ], **cowardly**[4] [kaʊə·dli] adj

person who tends to shrink from[5] social contacts and is preoccupied[6] with his/her own thoughts

introvert [ɪntrəvɜːrt] n • **sociable**[7] [soʊʃəbl] adj • **(un)sociability** n • **coward**[8] n

» Schizoid [skɪtsɔɪd] personalities are introverted, withdrawn, solitary[9], emotionally cold, and distant. My husband is a bit of an introvert. Patients with this pattern of schizophrenia [iː] are described as isolated [aɪ], shy, and withdrawn. Depressive patients are gloomy[10] [uː], pessimistic, humorless, incapable [eɪ] of fun, lethargic [ləθɑːrdʒɪk], introverted; complaining [eɪ], self-reproaching[11] [-oʊtʃɪŋ] and self-derogatory[12], and preoccupied with their own inadequacy[13] and negative events.

Use **introverted** personality (style) / disposition[14] / child / learning style • **withdrawn** manner[15] / life[16] • to feel **unsociable** • shy[17] / quiet / agonizing[18] [æ] **introvert** • **sociable** person[19] / extrovert • **to be coy** about sth.[20] / with sb.[21] • to behave **cowardly** • diminished **sociability**

introvertiert
verschlossen, in s. gekehrt[1] ungesellig, reserviert[2] verlegen, bescheiden, verschämt[3] feige, hinterhältig[4] s. verschließen[5] fixiert auf[6] umgänglich, gesellig[7] Feigling[8] eigenbrötlerisch[9] trübsinnig[10] machen sich Vorwürfe[11] erniedrigen sich selbst[12] Unzulänglichkeit[13] introvertiertes Wesen[14] verschlossenes W.[15] zurückgezogenes Leben[16] scheuer / introvertierter Mensch[17] an s. Introvertiertheit leidender M.[18] umgänglicher/ geselliger M.[19] verlegen sein wegen etw.[20] mit jem. kokettieren[21]   14

well-balanced adj   rel **stable**[1], **steady**[2] [e] adj,
opposite **labile**[3] [eɪ] adj

to show good judgement[4] [ʌ] and be emotionally well-adjusted[5] to one's situation, station[6], etc.

(un)balanced[3] adj • **unstable**[3] adj • **unsteady** adj • **lability**[7] [leɪbɪləti] n

» She used to be a fun-loving, well-balanced person. An emotionally stable and encouraging [ɜː] family also fosters adjustment[8]. Their characters are fully formed and they are both very stable children. Depressions are more common among emotionally labile personalities.

Use **well-balanced** child / mind[9] / lifestyle / training • **well-behaved**[10] /-**meaning**[11] [iː] /-disposed /-**intentioned**[11] • **stable** personality / mood[12] / patient • **stable** infant / home situation[13] / family • **stable** relationship[14] / disease / weight [weɪt] • emotionally[15] / neurologically / hemodynamically[16] [aɪ] **stable** • **steady** manner / look / relationship[14] / young man • **balanced** life / diet [daɪət] • **unstable** person[17] / behavior disorder / gait[18] [eɪ]/ fracture • **labile** personality / patient / emotional [oʊʃ] states[19] • **unsteady** gait[18] / hands • emotional[19] / mood[20] [uː]/ autonomic[21] **lability**

(innerlich) ausgeglichen
stabil[1] beständig, zuverlässig[2] labil[3] Urteilsvermögen, Einschätzung[4] angepasst[5] soziale Stellung[6] Unausgeglichenheit, Labilität[7] fördert die Anpassung[8] ausgeglichenes Gemüt[9] artig, wohlerzogen[10] wohlmeinend, -wollend[11] ausgeglichene Stimmung[12] geordnete Verhältnisse[13] feste Beziehung[14] innerlich/ seelisch ausgeglichen[15] kreislaufstabil[16] labiler Mensch[17] unsicherer Gang[18] emotionale Labilität[19] Stimmungslabilität[20] vegetative Labilität[21]   15

tolerant [tɒːləənt] adj   rel **open-minded**[1], **forgiving**[2], **easygoing**[3] [iː] adj

to show respect for the opinions, rights, actions or habits of others even if one does not agree with them

(in)tolerance[4] n • **tolerate**[5] v → U121-12 • **intolerant** adj • **broad-minded**[6] adj

» Am I being too tolerant of his smoking? He's very sympathetic, forgiving, and understanding[7]. My intense[8] 2-year-old is nothing like his easygoing sister.

Use to grow (more/less) **tolerant** of sb. or sth. • **tolerant** father / smile / of criticism[9] / toward children[10] • to have a/show **tolerance** for sth. • **intolerant** of milk[11] / to citrus [saɪtrəs] fruits / of temperature changes • **open-minded** attitude[12] • **forgiving** nature • **easygoing** couple [ʌ]/ dad / llfestyle[13] / atmosphere • **easygoing** pace[14] [peɪs]/ neighbors / to the point of inertia [ɪnɜːrʃə] • **open**-hearted [ɑː] /-handed /-mouthed /-eyed • narrow[15]-**minded**

tolerant, duldsam, nachsichtig
aufgeschlossen[1] versöhnlich, nicht nachtragend[2] unbeschwert, lässig, gelassen[3] (In)toleranz[4] (v)ertragen, dulden[5] großzügig, tolerant[6] verständnisvoll[7] gefühlsbetont[8] Kritik ertragen können[9] nachsichtig m. Kindern[10] Milchunverträglichkeit[11] aufgeschlossene Haltung[12] sorgloses Leben[13] lockeres Tempo[14] engstirnig[15]   16

timid [tɪmɪd] adj   rel **shy**[1] [ʃaɪ], **reserved**[2] adj,
opposite **confident**[3], **bossy**[4] adj

fearful and cautious[5] [kɒːʃəs], inhibited[6], self-conscious[6] [kɒːnʃəs], easily frightened [fraɪt-] or lacking self-confidence

intimidated[7] adj • **shyness** [aɪ] n • **reserve** [rɪzɜːrv] n • **confidence**[8] n

» Daytime wetting[9] most often occurs [ɜː] in timid and shy children or in attention-deficit disorder[10]. Often there is overlap between reactions to developmental crises [aɪ] and temperamental traits such as oversensitiveness[11], shyness, somberness[12] [ɒː], and reserve. The parents must feel confident that the primary [aɪ] physician[13] [ɪʃ] can provide the necessary follow-up care[14]. Children frequently become bossy or demanding when parent and child roles are not defined clearly enough.

Use **timid** teenager • **shy** child • **to be shy** with girls • publicity[15]-**shy** [ɪs] • **reserved** man / about sth. • to overcome one's[16] / incapacitating[17] [æs] **shyness** • over[18]/ self-**confident**

scheu, schüchtern, ängstlich
befangen, schüchtern, scheu[1] zurückhaltend, reserviert[2] (selbst)sicher, zuversichtlich[3] rechthaberisch, herrisch[4] vorsichtig[5] gehemmt, befangen[6] eingeschüchtert[7] Selbstvertrauen[8] Enuresis diurna[9] Aufmerksamkeitsdefizitsyndrom[10] Überempfindlichkeit[11] Trübsinnigkeit[12] Hausarzt/-ärztin[13] Nachsorge[14] publicityscheu[15] seine Schüchternheit überwinden[16] lähmende S.[17] übertrieben selbstbewusst[18]   17

Personality & Behavior COMPLEX BODY FUNCTIONS **305**

rash [ræʃ] *adj* *rel* **impatient¹** [ɪmˈpeɪʃᵊnt], **impulsive²** *adj*
choleric³ [ˈkɒlərɪk], **reckless⁴, bold⁵** [oʊ] *adj*

having a tendency to act with unthinking boldness and defiant⁶ [aɪ] disregard for danger or consequences

rashness *n* • **(im)patience⁷** [eɪʃ] *n* • **patient** *adj* • **recklessness⁸** *n*

» In a **rash moment⁹** I told him we would take care of her. In patients with borderline personality disorder impulsive [ʌ] actions are a risk factor for suicidal [saɪ] behavior. Test reckless drivers for cocaine [eɪ] and marijuana. Excessive crying in children may be an early manifestation of an insistent, impatient personality style. Hurry up, my patience is wearing [eɚ] thin¹⁰!

Use **rash** move / decision¹¹ • **to be impatient** with sb. / to have surgery¹² [ɜː] • **impatient** tone / movement / personality style • **impulsive** behavior / talking / spending¹³ / (sexual) activity¹⁴ • **reckless** driver¹⁵ / behavior • **bold** step or move¹⁶ • **patient** waiting / nurse [ɜː] • to be **patient** with sb.¹⁷ • to have (no)/require/test sb.'s/run out of¹⁸ **patience** • endless / infinite / inexhaustible [ɒː] **patience**

unbesonnen, überstürzt, voreilig

ungeduldig, ungehalten¹ impulsiv, spontan² cholerisch³ rücksichtslos, leichtsinnig, unbekümmert, fahrlässig⁴ mutig, verwegen, dreist⁵ trotzig, aufsässig⁶ Geduld⁷ Leichtsinn, Rücksichtslosigkeit⁸ unbedachter Augenblick⁹ allmählich verliere ich d. Geduld¹⁰ vorschnelle Entscheidung¹¹ die Operation kaum erwarten können¹² Impulsivkauf¹³ unbeherrschtes Sexualverhalten¹⁴ rücksichtslose(r) Fahrer(in)¹⁵ mutiger Schritt¹⁶ mit jem. geduldig sein¹⁷ d. Geduld verlieren¹⁸

18

stubborn [ˈstʌbən] *adj* *syn* **obstinate** [ˈɒbstɪnət], **pigheaded** *adj*
rel **willful¹, strong-minded²** *adj*

marked by a tenacious³ [eɪʃ] unwillingness to yield⁴ [jiːld] in spite of all arguments and attempts at persuasion⁵ [eɪʒ]

stubbornness *n* • **obstinacy** *n* • **strong-willed⁶** *adj* • **pigheadedness** *n*

» I was faced with a stubborn and self-assured⁷ [ʃ] lady who was determined not to compromise on the issue⁸. She obstinately insisted on remaining in the surgical ward [ɔː]. Passive-aggressive behavior is characterized by obstinacy, inefficiency [ɪʃ], and sullenness⁹ [ʌ].

Use **stubborn** boy / refusal¹⁰ [juː]/ about sth. / as a mule¹¹ [juː] • **stubborn** symptoms / warts [ɔː] / rash¹² [ræʃ] / out of sheer¹³ [ʃɪɚ] **stubbornness** • **obstinate** nature / look¹⁴ • **pigheaded** fool / about sth. / of sb. • single¹⁵-**minded** • head**strong¹⁶** • **willful** child / conduct¹⁷ / neglect / pride [praɪd]

stur, eigensinnig, halsstarrig, hartnäckig

eigensinnig, -willig¹ willensstark, energisch² beharrlich, hartnäckig³ nachgeben⁴ Überredungsversuche⁵ eigensinnig; willensstark⁶ selbstsicher⁷ in diesem Punkt nicht nachzugeben⁸ Missmutigkeit⁹ hartnäckige Weigerung¹⁰ störrisch wie ein Esel¹¹ hartnäckiger Ausschlag¹² aus purem Eigensinn¹³ störrischer Blick¹⁴ zielstrebig, beharrlich¹⁵ eigensinnig, dickköpfig¹⁶ eigensinniges Verhalten¹⁷

19

vain [veɪn] *adj* *syn* **conceited** [kənˈsiːtɪd], **big-headed** *adj*
rel **snobbish** or **snobby¹, arrogant², assertive³** [ɜː] *adj*

having excessive confidence or pride⁴ in one's qualities or an exaggerated [ædʒ] sense of self-importance

vanity⁵ [ˈvænəti] *n* • **conceit⁶** [kənˈsiːt] *n* • **arrogance⁷** *n* • **assertiveness** *n*

» She has always been horribly vain over her cooking and scornfully contemptuous⁸ of other people's aspirations. She is full of conceit [iː]. He had the vanity to think I would be disappointed if he did not call. She is a neatly groomed, assertive, and self-sufficient person.

Use **vain** people / about one's appearance⁹ [ɪɚ] • **conceited** fellow¹⁰ / thoughts / fool • **arrogant** and self-indulgent¹¹ [ʌldʒ]/ look • to flatter sb.'s¹² **vanity** • unbearable [eɚ]/ intellectual **arrogance** • **assertiveness** training¹³

eitel, eingebildet

hochnäsig¹ überheblich, anmaßend, arrogant² anmaßend³ Stolz⁴ Eitelkeit, Einbildung⁵ Einbildung, Dünkel⁶ Arroganz, Überheblichkeit⁷ verächtlich u. geringschätzig⁸ eitel⁹ eitler Tropf¹⁰ anmaßend u. zügellos¹¹ jem. Eitelkeit schmeicheln¹² Selbstbewusstseinstraining¹³

20

self-centered *adj* *syn* **selfish, egocentric** [iːɡoʊˈsɛntrɪk], **ego(t)istic** *adj*
rel **possessive¹** *adj*

to be interested in or care about nothing but oneself and one's own needs² [iː]

selfishness³ *n* • **ego(t)ism³** *n* • **egoist** *n* • **possessiveness** *n* • **ego** *n*

» In late adolescence [s] teenagers may become extremely self-centered and ambitious⁴ [ɪʃ]. Persons with aggressive conduct disorder⁵ show selfishness, failure of normal bonds⁶ with others, and a lack of appropriate guilt⁷ [ɡɪlt]. Why is she so jealous [dʒɛləs] and possessive about me?

Use to be **self-centered** in sth. • **selfish** child / old lady • **egocentric** views / personality • **possessive** mother⁸ / about sth. / toward sb. • to boost [uː] one's⁹ **ego** • **ego**centricity [ɪs] /maniac¹⁰ [eɪ] • **self**-respect /-praise [eɪ] /-flattery¹¹ • **self**-interested /-indulgent¹² [ʌ]/ -contained [eɪ] • **self**-love /-pity /-effacing¹³ [eɪs] /-denial¹⁴ [dɪnaɪəl] • **self**-fulfillment /-willed¹⁵ • **ego** development / trip¹⁶

selbstsüchtig, egoistisch, egozentrisch

habgierig, besitzergreifend¹ Bedürfnisse² Egoismus³ ehrgeizig⁴ Verhaltensstörung⁵ Bindungen, Beziehungen⁶ mangelndes Schuldbewusstsein⁷ besitzergreifende Mutter⁸ sein Selbstvertrauen stärken, einen Auftrieb geben⁹ Größenwahnsinnige(r)¹⁰ Eigenlob¹¹ hemmungs-, zügellos¹² zurückhaltend¹³ Selbstverleugnung¹⁴ eigenwillig¹⁵ Egotrip¹⁶

21

Unit 76   Mood & Attitude

Related Units: 75 Personality, 73 Mental Acitivty, 77 Mental Health, 113 Neurologic Findings, 142 Physical Therapy, 12 Death

emotion [ɪmoʊʃⁿn] *n usu pl*   *rel* **feeling**[1] [fiːlɪŋ] *n usu pl* → U57-3

strong manifestation of mental unrest or arousal[2] [aʊ] directed towards a definite object

emotional[3] *adj* • **emotionless**[4] *adj* • **unfeeling**[4] *adj* • **feel**[5] - felt - felt *v irr*

» Both hemispheres of the brain mediate [iː] emotion. Much of the emotional aspect of pain can be traced to[6] [eɪs] anxiety [aɪ]. Do you feel isolated? These support groups help patients deal [iː] with feelings of loss, grief[7] [iː], and guilt[8] [ɡɪlt].

Use to experience/recognize/acknowledge[9] [əknɒlɪdʒ] /express **emotions** • strong / inhibited / dulled[10] [ʌ] / reversed [ɜː] / covert[11] [oʊ] **emotions** • **emotional** health or well-being / needs / stress • **emotional** gratification[12] / ties[13] / response • **emotional** control / (in)stability / adjustment [adʒʌ-] • **emotional** burden[14] [ɜː]/ barrier / explosiveness / outburst[15] [ɜː] • **emotional** distress *or* upset[16] / support[17] / deprivation • **emotionally** (un)stable [eɪ] charged[18] [tʃɑːrdʒd] / depleted[19] [iː]/ mature [-jʊɚ]/ labile [eɪ] • to hurt sb.'s/hide one's **feelings** • **feelings of** guilt / despair [dɪspeɚ]/ inadequacy[20] / despondency[21]

Emotion, Gemütsbewegung

Gefühl[1] Erregung[2] gefühlvoll, gefühlsmäßig, emotional, emotionell[3] gefühl-, emotionslos[4] fühlen, spüren[5] zurückführen auf[6] Kummer, Trauer[7] Schuld[8] Gefühle eingestehen[9] abgestumpfte G.[10] versteckte G.[11] innere Genugtuung[12] emotionelle Bindungen[13] psychische/ seelische Belastung[14] Gefühlsausbruch[15] seelische Erschütterung[16] seelische Stütze[17] emotionsgeladen[18] abgestumpft[19] Gefühl d. Unzulänglichkeit[20] Niedergeschlagenheit, Mutlosigkeit[21]   **1**

---

mood [muːd] *n*   *rel* **spirits**[1], **temper**[2], **humor**[3] [hjuːmɚ] *n* → U75-4

(i) a characteristic or habitual [ɪtʃ] emotional state[4] or disposition
(ii) the prevailing[5] [eɪ] psychological state

moody[6] [muːdi] *adj* • **moodiness**[7] *n* • **spirited** *adj* • **bad-tempered**[8] *adj*

» This will put you in a good mood. Mood changes toward depression and anxiety can occur [ɜː] at the time of menopause. She's in one of her moods again. Is he subject [ʌ] to sharply varying moods? Doing some sports will help to lift your spirits. How often does she have those fits of temper[9]? What seems to be the source [sɔːrs] of his good humor?

Use to be in a(n) good/bad/odd[10] **mood** • to elevate[11]/enhance[11] sb.'s **mood** • to throw a[12]/keep/lose one's[13] **temper** • to have a(n) even[14] [iː] /sweet/bad **temper** • lability of **mood** • **mood** disturbances [ɜː]/ swings[15] / alterations / disorders[16] • to be in low[17]/high **spirits** • to keep up one's[18] **spirits** • **spirits** lift[19] / sink • to have no[20]/a (good) sense of **humor** • hot- *or* quick[21]-/ short-/ sweet[22]-/ ill[8]-**tempered**

Stimmung, Laune

Wesen, Naturell[1] Temperament, Veranlagung[2] Stimmung, Humor[3] Gemütszustand, Stimmungslage[4] vorherrschend[5] launisch[6] Launenhaftigkeit[7] schlecht gelaunt[8] Wutanfälle[9] in einer eigenartigen Stimmung sein[10] jem. Stimmung heben[11] einen Wutanfall bekommen[12] d. Beherrschung verlieren[13] e. ausgeglichenes Wesen haben[14] Stimmungsschwankungen[15] affektive Psychosen/ Störungen[16] niedergeschlagen sein[17] d. Mut nicht verlieren[18] (neuen) Mut bekommen[19] keinen Humor haben[20] jähzornig, aufbrausend[21] sanft-, gutmütig[22]   **2**

---

affect [æfekt] *n term* → U113-3   *rel* **attitude**[1] [ætət(j)uːd] *n* → U75-3

the outward manifestation of a person's emotional feelings, tone [toʊn], and mood

affective[2] *adj term* • **affectivity**[3] *n* • **affection**[4] [əfekʃⁿn] *n clin* • **affectionate** *adj*

» A depressed affect predominates. Typically, affect is blunted[5] [ʌ], but in the early stages it may be excessive. Phototherapy is used in seasonal [iː] affective disorder. She seems to have undergone a change of attitude over the past few months.

Use adequate / flat(ened)[6] / shallow[6] [æ]/ inappropriate / depressed **affect** • **affective** disorder[7] / personality[8] / response / episode[9] • to feel *or* have a deep[10] **affection**

Affekt

Einstellung, Haltung[1] affektiv, Affekt-[2] Affektivität[3] Zuneigung, Gefühl[4] verflacht[5] flacher Affekt[6] affektive Störung[7] zyklothyme Persönlichkeit[8] affektive Episode[9] e. tiefe Zuneigung empfinden, (jem.) sehr gern haben[10]   **3**

---

sensitive *adj* → U57-8   *sim* **touchy**[1] [tʌtʃi], **thin-skinned**[1] *adj inf*
opposite **insensitive**[2] [ɪnsensɪtɪv] *adj*

(i) acutely aware of interpersonal situations (ii) capable [eɪ] of perceiving [siː] sensations [eɪ] or responding to stimuli [aɪ] (iii) immunologically, a sensitized antigen or a person (or animal) rendered susceptible [se] by previous [iː] exposure [oʊʒ] to the antigen concerned [sɜː]

(hyper)sensitive[4] *adj* • **sensitivity**[5] *n* • **insensitivity** *n* • **sensibility**[5] *n*

» Parents must be sensitive to a child's needs. She is very sensitive about her skin blemishes[6]. He was too thin-skinned to cope with the criticism. Why is she so touchy about her hygiene [aɪdʒ] practices? I feel the nursing [ɜː] staff are very insensitive about my toileting problems.

Use **sensitive** about one's appearance [ɪɚ]/ to criticism[7] / to pain / to cold[8] • **sensitive** nature / child[9] / relationship / matter[10] / nodule • over[11]/ light / pressure[12] **sensitive** • **emotional**[13] / personal / sun **sensitivity** • photoallergic[14] / food / salt / drug[15] **sensitivity** • heightened[16] [haɪt-]/ acquired [aɪ] induced **sensitivity** • **sensitivity** for each other's feelings / to stress • **touchy** about sth. / question[17] • musical[18] / esthetic **sensibility**

Note: Do not confuse **sensitive** and **sensible**[19] (= rational); and **sensory**[20] (= related to sensation) and **sensual**[21] or **sensuous**[21] (=love of physical, esp. sexual pleasures). While **sensible** is only rarely used in medical contexts, **sensibility** is often used as a near synonym of **sensitivity**.

(i) empfindsam, einfühlsam, sensibel
(ii, iii) empfindlich

empfindlich, dünnhäutig[1] gefühllos, insensibel; unempfindlich[2] anfällig, empfindlich[3] überempfindlich, hypersensibel[4] Empfindsamkeit, Sensibilität; Empfindlichkeit[5] Hautunreinheiten[6] empfindlich auf Kritik reagieren[7] kälteempfindlich[8] sensibles/ empfindsames Kind[9] heikle Angelegenheit[10] überempfindlich[11] druckempfindlich[12] Feinfühligkeit, Empfindsamkeit[13] Photoallergie[14] Arzneimittelallergie[15] erhöhte Empfindsamkeit[16] heikle Frage[17] Musikalität, muskalisches Einfühlungsvermögen[18] vernünftig[19] sensorisch[20] sinnlich[21]   **4**

Mood & Attitude | COMPLEX BODY FUNCTIONS

anxious [æŋkʃəs] adj rel **concerned**[1] [sɜː], **apprehensive**[2] adj **fearful**[2] [fɪərfəl], **tense**[3] adj → U77-5

(i) worried [ɜː] and tense about sth. (ii) to be eager [iː] and looking forward to sth.

anxiety[4] [aɪ] n • **concern**[5] n • **apprehension**[6] n • **tense up**[7] v clin • **tension**[8] [ʃ] n clin & term

» Patients with a high heart rate usually appear anxious and are often sweating [e] excessively. Mr. Coe is anxious to know[9] the prognosis. The patient is tremulous, fearful and concerned about his well-being. She was quite tense when she came in for the exam.

Use **anxious** patient / facies [feɪʃiːz] • overly[10] **anxious** • over**anxious**[10] • **concerned** about[11] / with[12] • **tense** feeling / with anger / muscles [s] • low / high / increased / patient **anxiety** • dental / presurgical [ɜː] / separation[13] **anxiety** • **anxiety** state[14] / reaction / disorder / hysteria[15] [ɪ]/ neurosis [n(j)ʊəˈroʊsɪs] • emotional / premenstrual[16] **tension**

(i) besorgt, ängstlich
(ii) gespannt/ bedacht (auf)
besorgt[1] ängstlich[2] angespannt, nervös[3] Angst, Sorge[4] Sorge, Besorgnis[5] Besorgnis, Befürchtung[6] anspannen, straffen[7] Spannung[8] wollte unbedingt wissen[9] überängstlich[10] besorgt über[11] beschäftigt mit[12] Trennungsangst[13] Angstzustand[14] Angsthysterie[15] prämenstruelles Syndrom[16]

5

---

nervous [nɜːrvəs] adj rel **uneasy**[1] [ʌniːzi], **jittery**[2] [dʒɪtəri] adj **edgy**[2], **highstrung**[3] [ʌ], **fidgety**[4] [fɪdʒəti] adj

(i) easily excited [aɪ], upset or agitated [ædʒ-] (ii) suffering [ʌ] from emotional instability

nervousness[5] n • **be on edge**[6] phr • **get on sb's nerves**[7] [ɜː] phr

» He is a nervous man who does not like meeting new people. Are you nervous about something? The patient appears fidgety and squirms [ɜː] restlessly[8] in his seat. This affair really got on my nerves. He became uneasy when he heard about the delays [eɪ]. She seems a bit on edge today. The patient reports being uneasy and nervous at work and with people.

Use **nervous** person / breakdown[9] [eɪ]/ tension • **nervous** exhaustion[10] [ɔː]/ stimuli [aɪ] • **nervous** instability / irritability / disturbance [ɜː]/ indigestion[11] [ɪndɪdʒe-]/ function / wreck[12] • **uneasy** feeling[13] • **jittery** mood[14]

nervös, unruhig, aufgeregt
unruhig, beklommen[1] nervös[2] überspannt[3] unruhig, zappelig[4] Nervosität[5] nervös sein[6] jem. auf d. Nerven gehen[7] rutscht unruhig hin u. her[8] Nervenzusammenbruch[9] psychovegetatives Syndrom[10] funktionelle Dyspepsie[11] nervliches Wrack[12] ungutes Gefühl[13] gereizte Stimmung[14]

6

---

irritable [ɪrɪtəbl] adj → U104-3 syn **testy** adj, rel **excitable**[1] [ɪksaɪtəbl] adj

abnormally sensitive, easily annoyed[2] [ɔɪ], and tending to react immoderately to stimuli

irritability[3] n • **excitability**[4] n

» The patient is irritable and seeks [iː] seclusion[5] [uː]. These children often react with irritability, aggressiveness, back talk, and temper outbursts[6] [ɜː]. When my husband gave up smoking he grew nervous and excitable.

Use **irritable** and tense / mood[7]/ bowel [baʊəl] syndrome [ɪ]/ bladder • increased[8] / cyclic [saɪklɪk] **irritability** • **testy** old man[9] / comments • highly / easily **excitable**

reizbar, gereizt
reizbar, nervös[1] verärgert[2] Reizbarkeit, Gereiztheit[3] Reizbarkeit, Erregbarkeit[4] d. Einsamkeit suchen, s. zurückziehen[5] Temperamentsausbrüche[6] gereizte Stimmung[7] erhöhte Reizbarkeit[8] mürrischer Alter[9]

7

---

agitated [ædʒɪteɪtɪd] adj term rel **excited**[1] [aɪ], **aroused**[1] [aʊ] adj rel **overwrought**[2] [oʊvərɔːt], **restless**[3] adj → U113-2

to be disturbed [ɜː] and/or emotionally troubled [ʌ], displaying psychomotor [saɪkə-] excitement marked by purposeless[4] [ɜː] restless activity (e.g. pacing[5] [peɪsɪŋ], crying, laughing [læfɪŋ])

agitation[6] n term • **agitate**[7] v • **excitation**[8] n clin • **excitement**[9] n • **restlessness**[10] n

» Note whether the victim is calm [kɑːm], agitated, or confused [juː]. Over a period of years, memory loss, poor judgment [ʌ], agitation, and withdrawal[11] become more severe. With less severe agitation, reassurance [riːəʃʊə-] alone may suffice[12] [səfaɪs]. Cocaine [eɪ] causes euphoria, excitation and restlessness.

Use **agitated** behavior [eɪ]/ response / patient / depression[13] • uncontrollable / intense / motor[14] **agitation** • **excited** state • psychomotor / catatonic[15] / frenzied[16] **excitement** • sexual[17] **excitation** • **restless** patient / sleep[18] / bed partner / leg (syndrome)[19]

agitiert, erregt, unruhig
aufge-, erregt[1] überreizt[2] unruhig, rastlos[3] sinnlos[4] Auf- u. Abgehen[5] psychomotor. Unruhe, Agitiertheit[6] aufregen, -wühlen[7] Erregung, Exzitation[8] Erregung, Begeisterung[9] Unruhe, Rastlosigkeit[10] sozialer Rückzug[11] genügen[12] agitierte Depression[13] motor. Unruhe, Agitiertheit[14] katatoner Erregungszustand[15] rasende Erregung[16] sexuelle Erregung[17] unruhiger Schlaf[18] Restless legs-Syndrom, S. d. unruhigen Beine[19]

8

---

upset [v ʌpset‖n ʌpset] v & adj & n rel **cheerless**[1] [tʃɪərləs], **cranky**[2] adj rel **grouchy**[2] [graʊtʃi], **fed up**[3], **sulky**[4] [ʌ], **sullen**[5] [ʌ] adj

(v) to disturb the balance (adj) emotionally troubled (e.g. by grief) (n) a minor illness

cheer sb. up[6] v phr • **cheerful**[7] adj • **cheerfulness**[8] n • **sulkiness**[9] n

» These emotional upsets may temporarily affect the person's moods and behavior. His condition is very upsetting[10] for his family and friends. I'm fed up to the back teeth with these shots[11], doctor. You cannot protect her from all upsetting and frustrating [ʌ] events. All of a sudden boy turned sulky and did not say another word.

Use emotional[12] / gastrointestinal **upset** • **to upset** one's stomach [k] • **to be fed up** with sb./ sth.[13] • **cheerless** looks / day • **sulky** looks / tone • **sullen** face • **cheerful** manner[14]

aufregen, aus d. Fassung bringen; betrübt, verärgert, bestürzt; Verstimmung, Ärger
trübsinnig, traurig[1] griesgrämig[2] verärgert, sauer[3] beleidigt, schmollend[4] missmutig, verdrießlich[5] jem. aufheitern[6] fröhlich, vergnügt[7] Fröhlichkeit[8] Schmollen, schlechte Laune[9] unangenehm[10] Spritzen, Injektionen[11] Aufregung[12] d. Nase voll haben von[13] fröhliche Art[14]

9

COMPLEX BODY FUNCTIONS — Mood & Attitude

---

angry adj   syn **enraged** adj, rel **outraged**[1], **furious**[2] [jʊɚ], **cross**[3], **mad**[4] adj
strong feeling of dislike as a reaction to behavior that is experienced as unacceptable or unfair
anger[5] [æŋɡɚ] n • **angered**[6] adj • **rage**[5] [reɪdʒ] n • to fly off the handle[7] phr • to see red phr
» What's making you so angry? The initial [ɪʃ] affective change may be dominated by irritability, with periods of anger and violence [vaɪələnˈs]. Don't be angry with[8] me.
Use **angry** at or about sth.[9] / look / voice / behavior / response / teenager • to react **angrily** • to fly into a[10] / a fit of / violent **rage** • to suppress/control[11] one's anger • to cry with[12] **anger**

zornig, verärgert, wütend
empört, entrüstet[1] wütend[2] böse, sauer[3] wütend, sauer[4] Zorn, Wut[5] verärgert[6] an d. Decke gehen[7] böse sein auf[8] e. böse/ ungehalten sein über[9] e. Wutanfall bekommen[10] seinen Zorn beherrschen[11] vor Zorn weinen[12]

10

---

bitter adj   syn **embittered** [ɪmbɪtɚd] adj, rel **resentful**[1] adj
                                              frustrated[2] [ʌ] adj,
                                              to have a grudge[3] [ɡrʌdʒ] phr
feeling anger and disappointment, usually about situations that are difficult to accept or bear
bitterness[4] n • **resent**[5] [rɪsɛnt] v • **resentment**[6] n • **frustrate** [ʌ] v
» Do you still feel bitter toward your mother? The patient tolerates frustration poorly. This uncertainty was very frustrating to me. The patient looked at me somewhat resentfully.
Use **bitter** experience[7] / memories / disappointment[8] / reproach[9] [-oʊtʃ] • **resentful** silence[10] /look / eyes / tone • sexually **frustrated** • patient / parental **frustration** • **frustration** tolerance[11] • to bear sb. a[12] **grudge**

bitter, verbittert
ärgerlich, voller Groll[1] frustriert[2] einen Groll hegen[3] Bitterkeit[4] übelnehmen, s. ärgern[5] Ärger, Groll[6] schlimmes Erlebnis[7] bittere Enttäuschung[8] bitterer Vorwurf[9] beklemmende Stille[10] Frustrationstoleranz[11] jem. etw. nachtragen[12]

11

---

embarrassed adj   rel **self-conscious**[1] [kɒnˈʃəs],
                            insecure[2] [ɪnsɪkjʊɚ], **ashamed**[3] [eɪ] adj
feeling ashamed about your own inadequacy[4] or because you've made a fool of yourself[5]
embarrassment[6] n • **embarrass**[7] v • **shame**[8] [ʃeɪm] n & v • **shameful**[9]/**-less** adj
» She blushed [ʌ] slightly when the embarrassing story was told. Instead of overprotection sympathetic support should be directed against feelings of inferiority[10], self-consciousness, and other emotional handicaps. Embarrassment and pity are devastating[11] [e] to the morale of a patient with Parkinson's disease. I could die of shame. He feels ashamed[12] of himself.
Use **embarrassing** lapses[13] • to put sb. to[14] / be filled with **shame** • to feel **insecure**

Note: Mark the difference between **self-conscious** and **self-confident**[15].

verlegen
befangen, gehemmt[1] unsicher[2] beschämt[3] Unzulänglichkeit[4] s. lächerlich gemacht[5] Verlegenheit[6] in Verlegenheit bringen, beschämen[7] Scham, Schande; beschämen, eine Schande machen[8] schändlich[9] Minderwertigkeit[10] verheerend[11] schämt sich[12] peinliche Fehler[13] jem. beschämen[14] selbstbewusst[15]

12

---

self-reproach [rɪproʊtʃ] n
                    rel **remorse**[1] [ɔː], **compunction**[2] [-pʌŋkʃən] n → U77-10
blaming [eɪ] oneself with a feeling of deep regret or shame[3] [ʃeɪm] usually for sth. done wrong
reproach (oneself[4]/ sb.) v • **reproachful**[5] adj • **remorseless**[6] adj
» Tendencies to anxiety, self-reproach, and self-punitive [pjuː-] thinking[7] were magnified in the morning. Common symptoms [ɪ] of depression are low self-esteem[8] [iː], irritability, guilt[9] [ɡɪlt], confusion [juːʒ], indecisiveness[10] [saɪ], and eating and sleep disturbances [ɜː].
Use to be beyond[11] **reproach** • self-respect[12] /-control /-discipline • **self**-image /-denial[13] [aɪ] /-mutilation[14] [mjuː-] • **self**-hatred [eɪ] /-criticism[15] • **self**-sufficient[16] [ɪʃ]/-centered /-reliant [aɪ]/-effacing[17] [ɪfeɪsɪŋ] • to feel no / be filled with **remorse**

Selbstvorwurf
Reue[1] Schuldgefühle, Gewissensbisse[2] Scham[3] s. Vorwürfe machen[4] vorwurfsvoll[5] ohne Reue, unbarmherzig[6] selbstbestrafende Tendenzen[7] Minderwertigkeitsgefühl[8] Schuldgefühle[9] Unentschlossenheit[10] über jeden Vorwurf erhaben sein[11] Selbstachtung[12] Selbstverleugnung[13] Selbstverstümmelung[14] Selbstkritik[15] selbstständig, genügsam[16] zurückhaltend[17]

13

---

reluctant [rɪlʌktənt] adj   syn **unwilling** [ɪ] adj, rel **hesitant**[1] adj
not inclined or indecisive to participate, join in, or do something
reluctance[2] n • **hesitate**[3] [hɛzɪteɪt] v • **(un)willingness**[2] n • **hesitation** n
» He's very reluctant to complain[4] [eɪ] about pain. Hesitations in choosing words are early signs of dyslexia [ɪ]. He was hesitant about giving a detailed description. Don't hesitate to contact me. Pressure sores occur in bedridden patients who are unwilling to change position.
Use **reluctant** to admit sth.[5] / to express one's thoughts / toddler[6] • to show (extreme) **reluctance** • **hesitant** voice[7] / gait[8] [eɪ] / speech[9] • **unwilling** child / to do sth.[10]

unwillig, widerwillig
zögernd, unentschlossen[1] Widerwillen[2] zögern, zaudern[3] es widerstrebt ihm zu klagen[4] nicht zugeben wollen[5] widerspenstiges Kind[6] zaghafte Stimme[7] unsicherer Gang[8] stockendes Sprechen[9] nicht bereit, etw. zu tun[10]

14

Mood & Attitude — COMPLEX BODY FUNCTIONS

detached [dɪtætʃt] adj   rel **apathetic**[1] [æpəθetɪk], **indifferent**[2] adj **uninvolved**[3], **withdrawn**[4] [ɔː] adj

(i) showing a lack of emotional involvement (ii) separated physically [ɪ]

de**tach**ment[5] n • **apathy**[6] n • **indifference** n • **withdrawal**[7] n → U10-11f

» Throughout the physical examination she seemed very much detached, as if she were preoccupied with[8] other things. The patient tends to be distractible[9], euphoric, facetious[10] [fəsiːʃəs], and indifferent to social niceties [naɪsətiːz]. The child was withdrawn, apathetic, and always whimpering[11].

Jse **detached** manner[12] / observer [ɜː] • **apathetic** behavior • **withdrawn** behavior[7] / patient • emotional **indifference** • social[13] / purposeful [ɜː] **withdrawal**

kühl, distanziert, losgelöst

apathisch, teilnahmslos[1] gleichgültig, indifferent[2] unbeteiligt[3] verschlossen, zurückhaltend[4] Distanz, Losgelöstsein, Gleichgültigkeit[5] Apathie, Teilnahmslosigkeit[6] Abkapselung, Rückzug[7] fixiert auf[8] leicht ablenkbar, unkonzentriert[9] mokant[10] weinerlich[11] distanzierte Art[12] soziale(r) Rückzug/ Abkapselung[13]   15

---

euphoric [juːfɔːrɪk] adj term   rel **ecstatic**[1] [ɪkstætɪk], **thrilled**[2] adj **exulted**[3] [ʌ], **exuberant**[4] [uː] adj

exaggerated [ædʒ] feeling of emotional well-being, exultation, rapturous delight[5], or frenzy[6]

dysphoric[7] [dɪs-] adj term • **euphoria**[8] n • **ecstasy**[9] n • **exultation**[10] n

» Euphoria occurs in many patients with multiple sclerosis, but in others a reactive depression is present. The drug can provide a sensation of euphoria. Parental feelings right after birth may vary from ecstasy to disappointment.

Jse **euphoric** mood[11] / feeling / effect / patient • mild / inappropriate[12] • cocaine-induced [(j)uːs] / surface[13] **euphoria** • **thrilled** to bits[14] • **ecstatic** welcome / response • to be in / go into[15] **ecstasy**

euphorisch

ekstatisch[1] freudig erregt[2] jubelnd[3] überschwänglich[4] Entzücken[5] Freudentaumel[6] verstimmt[7] Euphorie[8] Ekstase[9] Jubel(stimmung)[10] euphorische Stimmung[11] übersteigerte Euphorie[12] oberflächliche Wohlgestimmtheit[13] s. freuen wie ein Kind, aus d. Häuschen vor Freude[14] in Ekstase geraten[15]   16

---

energetic [enədʒetɪk] adj

opposite **dull**[1] [ʌ], **inactive**[2], **sluggish**[3] [ʌ], **listless**[4] adj

to be full of life, enthusiasm [uː], plans and activities, dynamic [aɪ], hard-working and tireless

active adj • (**in/ over**)**activity**[5] n • **listlessness**[6] n • **sluggishness**[7] n → U7-12

» Follow a daily program of energetic walking. He always sat alone, dull and irritable. Physically inactive patients with low cardiac output are at increased [iː] risk of developing thrombi [aɪ] in the veins [eɪ] of the lower extremities. The child is sluggish and presents with wasted[8] [eɪ] extremities. The patient feels listless and weak [iː].

Jse **energetic** person / activity • **dull** patient / facial [eɪʃ] appearance[9] / on questioning / as ditchwater[10] • **sluggish** movements[11] / blood flow • **listless** gaze[12] [eɪ]/ feeling • to develop / onset of **listlessness** • mental[13] / morning **sluggishness**

schwungvoll, tatkräftig, energiegeladen

lustlos, schwerfällig, abgestumpft[1] untätig, träge[2] schwerfällig, träge[3] lust-, teilnahmslos[4] Hyperaktivität[5] Lust-, Teilnahmslosigkeit[6] Trägheit, Schwerfälligkeit[7] abgemagert[8] stumpfer Gesichtsausdruck[9] stinklangweilig[10] schwerfällige Bewegungen[11] leerer Blick[12] geistige Trägheit[13]   17

---

tired (out) adj   syn **weary** [ɪə], **exhausted** [ɔː], **worn out, burnt out** adj

having used up a lot of strength due to great strain[1] [eɪ], bodily overexertion[2] or stress

tiring[3] [taɪrɪŋ] adj • **tiredness**[4] [taɪədnəs] n • **weariness**[4] [wɪərɪnəs] n • **exhaustion**[5] n → U103-8

» The patient felt weak and tired. He reports being exhausted in the morning. Exhaustion, sleepiness [iː], and neurotic fatigue[6] [fətiːg] must be differentiated.

Jse **tired** feeling / eyes • to feel/become/appear[7]/wake up **tired** • physical [ɪ]/ intense[8] **tiredness** • physically **exhausted** • to be **worn out** • **exhausting** exercise[9] • emotional[10] / heat [iː]/ rapid **exhaustion** • **weary** smile[11] / sigh[12] [saɪ]

müde, erschöpft

Belastung[1] körperl. Überanstrengung[2] anstrengend, ermüdend[3] Müdigkeit, Abgeschlagenheit[4] Erschöpfung[5] Müdigkeit, Ermüdung[6] müde wirken[7] große Müdigkeit[8] anstrengende Übung[9] emotionale Erschöpfung[10] müdes Lächeln[11] müder Seufzer[12]   18

---

relaxed [rɪlækst] adj → U1-11

syn **laid-back** [leɪd-], **at ease** [iːz], **unwound** [aʊ] adj rel **quiet**[1] [kwaɪət], **calm**[2] [kɑːm] adj & v & n

to be comfortable and free from strain [eɪ], worries[3] [ɜː] or anxiety [æŋzaɪəti]

relax[4] v • **relaxation**[5] [eɪ] n • **relaxant**[6] n • **unwind**[4] [aɪ] v • **calmness** n

» The mother should assume[7] [uː] a comfortable, relaxed position. Encourage [ɜː] the patient to relax by slow, deep breathing [iː]. I haven't had time to unwind. Why don't you relax a bit and take it easy[8]? This will help set your mind at ease[9]. Wait until the patient is calm enough [ʌ] to lie down. Review the patient in a calm and quiet setting[10]. He loves the quiet and the clean air in the mountains.

Jse **relaxed** body (posture)[11] / attitude / wakefulness [eɪ]/ muscles[12] [mʌslz] • **relaxed** patient / knee [niː]/ pace[13] [peɪs] • to keep sb. / to stay or remain[14] **calm** • outwardly[15] / emotionally **calm** • **calm** atmosphere / voice / manner or demeanor[16] [iː] • **calm** words / reassurance[17] [riːəʃʊərənˈts] • **quiet** alert [ɜː] state[18] / room / breathing[19] [iː]/ sleep • peace [iː] and **quiet** • **to be laid back** about sth. • **laid-back** attitude[20] / approach [əprəʊtʃ] • muscle / mental / physical **relaxation** • **relaxation** technique [tekniːk]/ exercises[21] • to be (very much) / ill[22] **at ease**

locker, entspannt

ruhig, still, unauffällig; beruhigen; Ruhe[1] ruhig, gelassen, friedlich; beruhigen; Ruhe, Stille[2] Sorgen[3] (sich) entspannen, abschalten[4] Entspannung, Lockerung[5] Relaxans, entspannungsförderndes Mittel[6] einnehmen[7] s. schonen[8] s. beruhigen[9] ruhige Umgebung[10] entspannte Körperhaltung[11] entspannte Muskeln[12] lockeres (Lauf)tempo[13] ruhig bleiben[14] äußerlich ruhig[15] ruhige/ gelassene Art[16] beruhigender Zuspruch[17] ruhiger Wachzustand[18] ruhige/ regelmäßige Atmung[19] lockere Einstellung[20] Entspannungsübungen[21] s. nicht wohl fühlen[22]   19

miserable [mɪzɚəbl] *adj*   *rel* **heart-broken**[1] [hɑːrtbroʊkən], **pitiful**[2] [ɪ], **sorrowful**[3] [ɔː], **despondent**[4] *adj*

in a very unhappy, hopeless, deplorable[5], and sorry state

misery[6] *n* • sorrow[6] *n* • pity[7] [pɪti] *v & n* • broken-hearted[8] *adj* • heartache[9] *n*

» I just felt miserable and had a low-grade [eɪ] fever. I get increasingly despondent when the headaches don't go away for days. Don't you feel any pity for the dying?

Use **miserable** life • to feel/grow[10] **despondent** • **sorrowful** sigh / glance[11] • **heart-broken** at his loss • **pitiful** sight [saɪt] • state[12] [eɪ] • to feel / what a[13] **pity**

elend, unglücklich
todunglücklich[1] mitleiderregend, bemitleidenswert[2] traurig[3] niedergeschlagen, mutlos[4] bedauernswert[5] Kummer, Trauer[6] bemitleiden; Mitleid[7] untröstlich[8] Kummer[9] d. Mut verlieren[10] trauriger Blick[11] erbärmlicher Zustand[12] (wie) schade![13]
20

disturbed [ɜː] *adj* → U77-13   *rel* **shaken**[1] [eɪ], **maladjusted**[2] [dʒʌ], **despairing**[3] *adj*

(i) emotionally unstable [eɪ]
(ii) afflicted by great trouble or grief[4]
(iii) neurotic [n(j)ʊəɹɒːtɪk]

disturbing[5] *adj* • disturbance *n* • maladjustment[6] *n* • despair[7] [dɪspeə] *n & v*

» He may be emotionally disturbed but he's definitely not mentally retarded[8] [ɑː]. She was a bit shaken after the accident but unhurt [ɜː]. Suicide [suːəsaɪd] is always a concern [sɜː] in sad, despairing, or depressed patients.

Use **disturbed** behavior[9] / child / mental status [eɪ∥æ]/ sleep • behaviorally[2] / mentally **disturbed** • psychosocial [saɪkə-]/ sexual **maladjustment** • faced with / feeling of / deep[10] **despair**

beunruhigt; gestört
erschüttert, mitgenommen[1] unangepasst, verhaltensauffällig[2] verzweifelt[3] Kummer, Leid[4] beunruhigend, störend[5] mangelnde Anpassung, Anpassungsstörung[6] Verzweiflung; verzweifeln[7] geistig zurückgeblieben[8] gestörtes Verhalten[9] tiefe Verzweiflung[10]

21

depressed *adj* → U77-17   *syn* **down(cast), blue, low(-spirited)** *adj*
   syn **glum** [ʌ], **gloomy** [uː] *adj, rel* **melancholic**[1] [kɒː] *adj*

(i) despondent, despairing, and/or unable to cope with[2] or adjust to the environmental circumstances
(ii) affected by a depression

depression[3] *n term* • depressive[4] *adj & n clin & term* • melancholia[5] *n*

» The patient had been depressed for weeks and seemed unable to adjust to the situation. The temperament types of the Greeks were sanguine, melancholic, choleric and phlegmatic. The patient is withdrawn, depressed, and apathetic.

Use **depressed** mood[6] / mental status / bipolar [aɪ] patient / (level of) consciousness [ʃ] • **depressive** reaction[7] / state / symptoms / episode[8] / psychosis [saɪkoʊsɪs] • manic [æ]/ postpartum[9] / seasonal[10] [iː]/ masked[11] **depression** • **depression**, despair, and suicide • to look[12] **glum**

niedergeschlagen, deprimiert
schwermütig, melancholisch[1] fertigwerden mit, bewältigen[2] Depression[3] depressiv, an Depressionen Leidende(r)[4] Melancholie, Schwermütigkeit, -mut[5] depressive Verstimmung[6] depressive Reaktion, reaktive Depression[7] depressive Episode[8] Wochenbettdepression, postpartale D.[9] saisonale D.[10] larvierte/ maskierte D.[11] niedergeschlagen wirken/ aussehen[12]
22

Unit 77   Mental Health
Related Units: 73 Mental Activity, 75 Personality, 76 Mood, 7 States of Consciousness, 42 Nerve Function, 113 Neurologic Findings, 10 Alcohol, 11 Substance Abuse, 142 Physical Therapy

mental state *or* **status** [steɪtəs∥stætəs] *n term*
   sim **mental health**[1] [helθ] *n clin* → U73-2, 76-1ff

degree of competence[2] in terms of personality as well as intellectual, psychological and emotional [oʊʃ] functions [ʌ] with reference to a statistical norm (as assessed in psychological testing, esp. by mental status examination[3])

» There is marked fluctuation in the patient's mental state with intermittent periods [ɪə] of lucidity[4] [luːsɪdəti] but without focal [oʊ] abnormalities. The first mental changes were behavioral [eɪ], with irritability, moodiness[5] [uː], antisocial behavior followed by psychiatric [saɪkɪ-] disturbances [ɜː] and signs of dementia. Assessment[6] was hampered[7] by altered [ɔː] mental status due to neurologic injury [ɪndʒɚi].

Use to determine [ɜː] the[8] **mental status** • quiet [kwaɪət]/ abnormal / slowed[9] / (acutely) altered[10] **mental state** • disinterested / depressed / (psychotic) organic[11] **mental state** • **mental health** consultation[12] / nursing [ɜː]/ center[13] / practitioner [ɪʃ] • **mental health** specialist / problems[14] / treatment[15] [iː] • **mental** hygiene[16] [haɪdʒiːn]/ age[17] (*abbr* MA)/ balance / capacity[18] [æs] • **mental** abilities / patient[19] / hospital[13] • **mentally** alert[20] [ɜː]/ clouded [aʊ]/ ill • **mentally** defective *or* deficient [ɪʃ] *or* disturbed [ɜː]/ handicapped[21]

Neurostatus, neurolog./ mentaler Status, psych. Zustand
psychische Gesundheit, Geisteszustand[1] Funktionsfähigkeit[2] Erhebung d. neurolog. Status[3] Klarheit[4] Stimmungsschwankungen[5] Untersuchung[6] erschwert[7] d. Neurostatus erheben[8] gedankliche Verlangsamung/ Verlangsamung d. Denkens[9] veränderter mentaler Status[10] organische Psychose[11] psychiatr. Beratung[12] psychiatr. Klinik[13] psychische Probleme[14] psychiatr. Behandlung[15] Psychohygiene[16] Intelligenzalter[17] geistige Leistungsfähigkeit[18] psychisch Kranke(r)[19] geistig wach, aufmerksam[20] geistig behindert[21]
1

Mental Health COMPLEX BODY FUNCTIONS **311**

psyche [saɪki] n   sim **soul**[1] [soʊl], **spirit**[2] [spɪrɪt] n
           rel **id**[3], **(super)ego**[4] [iː‖e] n, opposite **soma**[5] n term
an individual's [ɪdʒ] vital [aɪ] mental and spiritual entity including both conscious [kɒnʃəs] and unconscious processes

psychic[6] [aɪ] adj & n & comb • **spiritual**[7] adj •
somatic[8] adj term • **psych-** comb

» The instinct to avoid conflict is deeply lodged [dʒ] in your psyche. Has psychotherapy replaced religion as the healer [iː] of the soul? These strategies calm [kɑːm] the spirit, relieve emotional constraints [eɪ], and increase the patient's energy. Spirit disease is a disorder of the soul in which a foreign spirit force enters the body. Stressful experiences such as these often cause suffering [ʌ] in body and soul. The symptoms [ɪ] often represent somatic manifestations of anxiety [aɪ], such as dizziness, nausea [ɔː], and stomach [k] distress.

Use human **psyche** • human / disquieted[9] [aɪ]/ fighting / evil [iː] **spirit** • free[10] / team / community[11] **spirit** • **spirit of** optimism / reconciliation[12] [s]/ solidarity • to bare [beə] one's[13] **soul** • **soul** process • mate[14] [eɪ]/-destroying • **soul**-searching[15] [sɜːrtʃɪŋ]/-centered /ful[16] • **psychic** stimuli / energy / pain[17] / conflict / factors • **psychic** symptoms / blindness[18] / deafness [e]/ shock • **psychic** trauma [ɔː]/ overlay[19] / inhibitor • **psychic** research[20] • **spiritual** condition / life[21] / needs / beliefs[22] • **spiritual** values[23] / distress / support[24] • **spiritual** comfort[25] / therapy • **somatic** (nerve) [ɜː] fibers [aɪ]/ reflex / disorder[26] / complaints[27] • **psych**algia[17] [saɪkældʒ(ɪ)ə] /edelic[28] (drug) /ataxia /anopsia[18]

Psyche, Seele, Geist
Seele, Wesen, Gefühl[1] Geist, Seele, Gesinnung[2] Id[3] (Über)ich[4] Körper, Soma[5] mental, seelisch, psychogen, übersinnlich; medial veranlagte Person, Medium[6] geistig, geistlich, spirituell[7] somatisch, physisch[8] innere Unruhe[9] Freigeist, -denker[10] Gemeinschaftssinn[11] versöhnliche Haltung[12] s. Inneres öffnen[13] Seelenfreund(in)[14] Gewissenserforschung[15] gefühlvoll[16] seelischer Schmerz[17] psychogene Blindheit[18] psychogene Überlagerung[19] Parapsychologie[20] Seelen-, Gemütsleben[21] religiöse Überzeugung, Glaube[22] geistige Werte[23] geistl. Beistand[24] geistlicher Trost[25] somatische Störung[26] körperl. Beschwerden[27] psychodelisch, bewusstseinserweiternd[28]

2

---

sane [seɪn] adj inf & leg   syn **mentally sound** [aʊ] phr
           sim **be in one's right mind**[1] phr inf
to show good understanding, and judgement[2] [ʌ] and/or be free from any mental disorder

sanity[3] [æ] n leg & inf • **insane**[4] [eɪ] adj • **insanity** n • **mentally unsound**[4] phr

» In my opinion he was sane at the time of the murder. Was she of sound mind when it happened? The court [ɔː] determined [ɜː] that the patient's sanity had not been restored. Should the therapist be asked to verify[5] a patient's sanity? In the old person who is mentally sound but physically weak [iː], observation of the fast[6] would further weaken the body. A 72-year-old mentally sound lady presented to her GP[7] complaining of difficulty swallowing[8].

Use to keep **sane** • **sane** person • to question or doubt[9] [aʊ] /lose/keep or retain [eɪ] one's sanity • sanity inquest[10] / to have a or be of sound[1] mind • to go/be/judge [ʌ] sb.[11] **insane** • clinically / criminally / permanently **insane** • **insane** asylum[12] [aɪ]

Note: The terms **sane**, **insane** and **insanity** are predominantly legal [iː] terms for persons who are not capable of providing adequate self-care and cannot be held responsible for their actions. They are mostly used in medicolegal[13] rather than in clinical contexts.

(geistig) gesund/ normal; zurechnungsfähig
bei klarem Verstand sein[1] Urteilsvermögen[2] Zurechnungsfähigkeit, geistige Gesundheit[3] verrückt, geisteskrank, unzurechnungsfähig[4] bestätigen[5] weiteres Fasten[6] Hausarzt/-ärztin[7] Schluckbeschwerden[8] an jds. Verstand zweifeln[9] Prüfung d. Zurechnungsfähigkeit[10] jem. für unzurechnungsfähig erklären[11] Nervenheilanstalt[12] gerichtsmedizinisch[13]

3

(mental) confusion [kənfjuːʒən] n clin & term
           sim **bewilderment**[1] [ɪ] n clin, **disorientation**[2] n term → U7-8
mental state marked by inappropriate reactions to environmental stimuli [aɪ], abnormal orientation to time, place or person, perplexity[3], lack of orderly thought, and inability to choose or act decisively [saɪ]

confused[4] adj • **bewildered**[5] [ɪ] adj • **disoriented** adj term • **confusional** adj

» Headache, drowsiness[6] [aʊ], and mental confusion are the usual sequelae [iː] of a convulsion[7] [ʌ]. Postoperative confusion and delirium are common in the aged. In confabulation[8] the bewildered patient substitutes[9] [ʌ] imaginary or confused experiences for those he cannot recall[10]. The patient is easily lost and confused and requires ongoing supervision[11] [ɪʒ].

Use agitated[12] [ædʒ-]/ identity[13] / visual **confusion** • right-left[14] / directional[15] / forgetful **confusion** • postictal[16] / drug-induced / color[17] **confusion** • mild / increasing / marked **confusion** • sudden / (sub)acute [ʌ] **confusion** • transient / prolonged / intermittent / nighttime[18] **confusion** • to be/become/feel (severely) **confused** • **to confuse** two things / a person[19] • mild / acute / global / agitated[12] **confusional state** • organic / metabolic / psychotic[20] **confusional state**

(geistige) Verwirrtheit
Verwirrung, Verblüffung[1] Desorientiertheit, Verwirrtheit[2] Verblüffung, Bestürzung[3] verwirrt, wirr[4] durcheinander, verwirrt[5] Schläfrigkeit, Benommenheit[6] Folgen e. Krampfanfalls[7] Konfabulation[8] ersetzt[9] erinnern[10] ständige Beaufsichtigung[11] Agitation und Verwirrtheit[12] persönl. Desorientierung[13] Rechts-Links-Störung[14] Orientierungsstörung[15] postiktale Verwirrtheit[16] Farbverwechslung[17] nächtl. Verwirrtheit[18] jem. verwechseln[19] psychot. Verwirrtheitszustand[20]

4

COMPLEX BODY FUNCTIONS — Mental Health

anxiety [æŋzaɪəti] n   rel **apprehension**[1] n, **fear**[2], **dread**[2] [e] n & v → U76-5
  anguish[3] [æŋgwɪʃ], **angst**[4] n clin,
  phobia[5] [foʊbɪə] n term & comb

vague [eɪ] uneasy[6] feeling unattached [tʃ] to a clearly identifiable [aɪ] stimulus which is often accompanied by restlessness, apprehensiveness[7], decreased attention span, clammy [æ] skin[8], quivering voice[9], tachycardia [k], and insomnia

anxious[10] [æŋkʃəs] adj • **anguished** adj • **apprehensive**[10] adj • **phobic** adj term

» The disabling [eɪ] anxiety symptoms of irritability, worry[11] [ɜː], and hypervigilance[12] [ɪdʒ] cause long-lasting somatic complaints. The prognosis is better if the anxiety-panic-phobia-depression cycle can be broken. Rape victims[13] may feel anxiety at being examined by a physician of the opposite sex. Did the patient describe his personal anguish and apprehension?

Use to experience/feel/cause **anxiety** • to alleviate [iː] or allay [eɪ] or lessen[14]/exhibit/control **anxiety** • situational[15] / stranger[16] / inappropriate[17] **anxiety** • overwhelming / free-floating[18] [oʊ] / panic **anxiety** • separation[19] / daytime / anticipatory[7] [ɪs] **anxiety** • signs / degree **of anxiety** • **anxiety** reaction / dream[20] / attack[21] / states[22] • **anxiety** neurosis[23] / disorder / relief • to heighten [aɪ] or intensify/have/master[24] **fears** • intense / unfounded [aʊ] or irrational[25] **fear** • paralyzing / morbid[26] / paranoid **fear** • **fear of** heights[27] [haɪts]/ flying[28] [aɪ]/ failure • **fear of** blushing[29] [ʌ]/ intimacy • **fear of** losing control / closed spaces[30] • **fear of** open places[31] / the dark / death or dying[32] / haunting[33] [ɔː]/ sense of **dread** • social[34] / toilet / school[35] / animal[36] **phobia** • claustro[30]/ agora[31]/ hydro**phobia** • phobo/ phago[37]/ homo**phobia** • **phobic** stimulus / anxiety / ideation[38] / reaction • **phobic** avoidance / disorder[5] / neurosis[5]

Note: Mark the different usage of **anxiety** (=vague unpleasant [e] emotion experienced in anticipation of a usually ill-defined misfortune[39]) and **fear** (= apprehensions about concrete dangers).

hysteria [hɪstɪərɪə] n clin & term   rel **panic**[1] n & v,
  agitation[2] [ædʒɪteɪʃən] n term

(i) popular expression for a state of excessive uncontrolled excitement [aɪ], fear or anger
(ii) broad and dated medical term for conversion disorder[3] and dissociative disorders[4]

hysteric(al)[5] [e] adj • **hysterics**[6] [e] n • **panicky**[7] [æ] adj → U6-21; U113-2

» Patients suffering from heat exhaustion [ɔː] may be thirsty [ɜː] and weak, with symptoms such as anxiety, paresthesias [iː], impaired [eə] judgment [ʌ], hysteria, and in some cases psychosis. Lack of humor, feelings of dread, and fears of annihilation[8] generate higher anxiety levels, with occasional [eɪʒ] panic and suicidal [aɪ] ideation[9], as the individual fails to cope.

Use to be close to/ affected by **hysteria** • conversion[10] [ɜː] **hysteria** • dissociative [oʊʃ]/ social / mass[11] / anxiety[12] **hysteria** • to be in[13]/have[13] **hysterics** • to get in(to) a[14] **panic** • **panic**-stricken / reaction[15] / episode[16] • **panic** attack[16] / state / disorder • **hysterical** or histrionic personality[17] / state / symptom • **hysterical** fainting[18] [eɪ]/ amnesia[19] [iː]/ reaction • **hysterical** coma / neurosis[3] • **hysterical** conversion (reaction) / blindness[20] • **panicky** expression / person

combative adj clin   rel **unruly**[1] [uː], **hostile**[2] [hɒstəl‖-aɪl] adj clin
  assaultive[3] [ɔː], **belligerent**[3] [ɪdʒ] adj clin

unwilling to submit to authority[4], aggressive and showing an inclination[5] to disagree or dispute [juː]

combativeness n clin • **assault**[6] [ɔː] v & n • **hostility**[7] [ɪ] n • **belligerence** n

» Confused patients are often uncooperative or combative, making evaluation difficult. Acute alcoholic intoxication may be manifested by flushed [ʌ] facies[8] [eɪʃ], staggering gait[9] [geɪt], combative, hostile, abusive[10] [juː], or belligerent behavior.

Use **combative** patient / state • **combative** and confused / and uncooperative • **unruly** patient • **hostile** response / attitude[11] • **hostile** laughter [æ]/ intentions[12] • **assaultive** behavior[13] • **belligerent** behavior / patient • unrestrained[14] [eɪ] • **combativeness** • physical[15] [ɪ]/ sexual **assault** • outbursts [ɜː] of[16] / underlying [aɪ]/ frank[17] **hostility**

Angst(zustand), Beklemmung
Befürchtung, Besorgnis[1] (Real)angst, Furcht[2] Qual, Pein, Angst[3] Grauen, große Furcht[4] Phobie, phobische Störung[5] unbehaglich, beklemmend[6] Ängstlichkeit, Erwartungsangst[7] feucht-kalte Haut[8] zitternde Stimme[9] ängstlich, besorgt[10] Sorge[11] Vigilanzsteigerung[12] Vergewaltigungsopfer[13] Angst(zustände) mildern[14] Situationsangst[15] Fremdeln[16] unangemessene Angst[17] frei flottierende A.[18] Trennungsangst[19] Angsttraum[20] Angstattacke[21] Angstzustände[22] Angstneurose[23] Ängste bewältigen[24] grundlose Angst[25] krankhafte A.[26] Höhenangst[27] Flugangst[28] Erythrophobie, Errötungsangst[29] A. vor geschlossenen Räumen, Klaustrophobie[30] Platzangst, Agoraphobie[31] Angst vor d. Sterben[32] quälende A.[33] soziale Phobie[34] Schulangst[35] Tierphobie[36] Schluckangst, psychogene Dysphagie[37] phobische Gedanken[38] Unglück[39]

5

(i) Hysterie (ii) hyst. Reaktion, klass. Konversionssyndrom
Panik, panische Angst; in Panik geraten[1] Agitiertheit[2] Konversionsneurose[3] dissoziative Störungen[4] hysterisch[5] Hysterie, hyst. Anfall[6] überängstlich[7] Vernichtungsängste[8] Suizidgedanken[9] Konversionshysterie[10] Massenhysterie[11] Angsthysterie[12] e. hyst. Anfall haben[13] in Panik geraten[14] Kurzschluss-, Panikreaktion[15] Panikattacke[16] histrionische Persönlichkeit[17] hysterische Ohnmachtsanfälle[18] psychogene Amnesie[19] psychogene Blindheit[20]

6

streitsüchtig, kämpferisch, aggressiv
widerspenstig, ausgelassen, ungestüm[1] feindselig[2] aggressiv, angriffslustig[3] s. unterordnen/ beugen[4] Neigung[5] tätlich werden, angreifen; Tätlichkeit, Angriff[6] Feindseligkeit[7] gerötetes Gesicht[8] torkelnder Gang[9] beleidigend, ausfallend[10] feindselige Haltung[11] böse Absichten[12] aggressives Verhalten[13] ungezügelte Streitbarkeit[14] Tätlichkeit[15] Aggressionsdurchbrüche, Raptus[16] unverhohlene Feindseligkeit[17]

7

Mental Health   COMPLEX BODY FUNCTIONS 313

social withdrawal [ɒː] *n*   *rel* **apathy**[1] [æ] *n term*, **detachment**[2] [ætʃ] *n clin*

pattern of behavior marked by a lack of social involvement and a retreat[3] [iː] into oneself

withdraw (from)[4] *v* → U11-12 • apathetic *adj* → U7-12 • detached[5] *adj*

» Loss of inhibitions[6] [ɪʃ] and belligerence may occur [ɜː] and alternate with passivity and social withdrawal. Apathy, social withdrawal, irritability, and intermittent disinhibition[6] are common in Huntington's chorea [kəriːə]. The patient is dull[7] [ʌ], confused, and apathetic. Is there a wish to avoid or withdraw from daily activities? The child tends to withdraw into an internal [ɜː] world of fantasy.

Use autistic[8] / emotional / psychologic **withdrawal** • extreme or profound [aʊ]/ prominent or blatant [eɪ] **apathy** • mental[9] / sexual[10] **apathy** • emotional / feelings of **detachment** • **detachment** from surroundings[11] [aʊ] • **apathetic** state / countenance[12] [aʊ]/ hyperthyroidism[13] [aɪ] • **withdrawn** behavior[14] / catatonic state[15] / from friends

---

sozialer Rückzug

Teilnahmslosigkeit, Apathie[1] (innerer) Abstand, Distanz, Gleichgültigkeit[2] Rückzug[3] s. zurückziehen[4] losgelöst, distanziert[5] Enthemmung[6] abgestumpft, träge[7] autist. Rückzug[8] mentale Apathie[9] sexuelles Desinteresse[10] Abkapselung von d. Umwelt[11] teilnahmslose Miene[12] apathische Hyperthyreose[13] verschlossenes Verhalten[14] katatoner Sperrungszustand[15]

8

---

coping mechanism [koʊpɪŋ mɛkənɪzm] *n clin & term*
   rel **adjustment**[1] [ədʒʌst-], **adaptation**[2] *n clin & term* → U88-17

cognitive and subconscious process by which individuals solve problems, deal with stress and make decisions [sɪ] that enable them to keep or regain [eɪ] their emotional equilibrium[3]

cope (with)[4] *v phr* • **(re)adjust** *v* •
(mal)adaptive[5] *adj term* • **maladjustment**[6] *n*

» Denial[7] [aɪ] as a coping mechanism should not be discouraged [ɜː]. The process of coping with a chronic illness is an ongoing one. The patient feels inadequate to cope with situations of everyday life. Assisting patients with the psychosocial adjustments required by cystic [sɪstɪk] fibrosis is critical. The characteristic patterns of maladjustment were evident from childhood on.

Use mental / (un)healthy / successful **coping mechanisms** • exaggerated[8] [ædʒ]/ ineffective / positive **coping mechanisms** • (ego-)defense[9] / escape[10] [eɪ] **mechanism** • **coping** behavior[11] / skills / patterns[12] / strategies • **coping** reaction / techniques [tekniːks] • family[13] / intrapsychic [-saɪkɪk]/ defensive / long-term / day-to-day[14] **coping** • self-defeating [iː] **coping** techniques[15] / to make[16] **adjustments** • emotional / psychosocial[17] / (inter)personal / patient-family **adjustment** • life / posthospital / age-appropriate[18] **adjustment** • poor / pathologic pattern of[19] **adjustment** • **adjustment** problems[20] / disorder • **to cope with** stress[21] / pain / problems • **to cope with** setbacks[22] / decreased self-esteem [iː] • (in)ability / to attempt / to learn **to cope** • **to (re)adjust** to a situation • emotional [oʊʃ] / (psycho)social / sexual **maladjustment** • **adaptive** behavior[23] / social skills • **maladaptive** coping techniques[15] / attitudes / emotional response

---

Bewältigungsmechanismus, Coping-Strategie

Anpassung[1] Anpassung, Adaptation[2] seelisches Gleichgewicht[3] zurechtkommen/ fertig werden (mit), bewältigen[4] (nicht) anpassungsfähig, (mal)adaptiv[5] mangelnde Anpassung, Anpassungsstörung[6] Verleugnung, Verweigerung[7] übersteigerte Bewältigungsmechanismen[8] Abwehrmechanismus[9] Fluchtreaktion, -mechanismus[10] Coping-, Bewältigungsverhalten[11] Bewältigungsmuster[12] familiäre(s) Coping/ Bewältigung[13] Alltagskompetenz[14] maladaptives Coping[15] Korrekturen vornehmen[16] psychosoziale Anpassung[17] altersgemäße A.[18] dysfunktionales Anpassungsmuster[19] Anpassungsschwierigkeiten[20] Stress bewältigen[21] m. Rückschlägen fertig werden[22] Anpassungsverhalten[23]

9

---

guilt [gɪlt] *n*   *rel* **compunction**[1] [ʌ] *n* → U76-13
   remorse[2] [rɪmɔːrs] *n*, **blame**[3] [eɪ] *n & v*

feeling of shame[4] [ʃeɪm] and/or self-reproach[5] [-oʊtʃ] because of a real or imagined [ædʒ] misdeed[6] [iː] or offence[7]

guilty [gɪlti] *adj* • **remorseful**[8] *adj* • **blameless**[9] *adj* •
blameworthy[10] [-wɜːði] *adj*

» Help the suicide's family deal with their guilt feelings and sorrow. The child feels shame and guilt about his personal inadequacies[11]. His antisocial behavior shows little foresight[12] [-saɪt] and is not associated [oʊʃ] with remorse or guilt. The patient feels guilty for having survived [aɪ].

Use to engender[13] [dʒe] / alleviate[14] [iː] or relieve[14]/ feel[15] **guilt** • pathologic / unconscious[16] / sexual **guilt** • criminal / sense of[17] / feelings of[1] **guilt** • **guilt**-ridden[18] / -prone [oʊ]/ feelings[1] • **guilt** reaction / complex[19] / to take[20]/give sb. **the blame** • self[5]-**blame** • **to blame** sb. for sth. / sth. on others[21] / yourself • to be bitten by[22] / deep feelings of **remorse** • to be/feel[15] **guilty** • **guilty** feeling / look or expression[23] • **guilty** conscience / ruminations[24] / of negligence

---

Schuld, Schuldgefühl

Gewissensbisse, Schuldgefühle[1] Reue[2] Schuld, Tadel; Vorwürfe machen, beschuldigen[3] Scham, Schande[4] Selbstvorwurf[5] Fehlverhalten[6] Vergehen, Straftat[7] reumütig, reuig[8] schuldlos, untadelig[9] tadelnswert, schuldig[10] Unzulänglichkeiten[11] Weitblick[12] Schuldgefühle auslösen[13] S. abbauen[14] s. schuldig fühlen[15] unbewusste Schuld[16] Schuldgefühl[17] schuldbeladen[18] Schuldkomplex[19] d. Schuld auf sich nehmen[20] d. Schuld auf andere schieben[21] tiefe Reue empfinden[22] schuldbewusste Miene[23] Grübeln über Schuldgefühle[24]

10

emotional deprivation n term   syn **psychologic deprivation** n term, rel **emotional neglect**¹ [nɪglekt] n term

lack of appropriate emotional, cognitive and environmental support in the formative years²; typically seen in neglected³, isolated [aɪ], and abused⁴ [juː] children

deprive [aɪ] (**of**)⁵ v • **neglect**⁶ v & n • **negligence**⁷ [neglɪdʒənˈs] n • **deprivational** [eɪʃ] adj term

» Extreme [iː] emotional deprivation may retard [ɑː] growth. Disturbances [ɜː] in motor and personality development may be associated with psychologic deprivation. The most common feature [fiːtʃɚ] of emotional neglect is the absence of normal parent-child attachment⁸ [ætʃ].

Use maternal [ɜː]/ parental⁹ **deprivation** • environmental / dietary [aɪ] or nutritional¹⁰ [ɪʃ] **deprivation** • sensory or stimulus¹¹ / sleep¹² **deprivation** • **deprivation** dwarfism¹³ [ɔː] • physical [ɪ] / child¹⁴ / dietary **neglect** • medical care / self¹⁵-/ wilful¹⁶ / unilateral¹⁷ **neglect** • contralesional [iːʒ] / hemispatial¹⁷ [eɪʃ]/ visual¹⁸ [ɪʒ] **neglect** • **neglect** syndrome¹⁷ [ɪ]/ of children¹⁴ / of one's health / of duty¹⁹ • **deprived** sibling [ɪ] syndrome²⁰ • socially²¹ / (socio)economically **deprived**

emotionale Vernachlässigung, Deprivation, Liebesentzug

mangelnde affektive Zuwendung¹ Entwicklungsjahre² vernachlässigt, verwahrlost³ missbraucht, -handelt⁴ entziehen, vorenthalten⁵ vernachlässigen, missachten, unterlassen; Vernachlässigung, Unterlassung⁶ Nach-, Fahrlässigkeit⁷ Eltern-Kind-Bindung⁸ Deprivationssyndrom⁹ Nahrungsentzug¹⁰ sensor. Deprivation/ Neglect¹¹ Schlafentzug¹² psychosozialer Minderwuchs¹³ Kindesvernachlässigung¹⁴ Selbstvernachlässigung¹⁵ absichtl. V.¹⁶ Neglect(-Syndrom), Halbseitenunaufmerksamkeit¹⁷ visuelle Deprivation¹⁸ Pflichtversäumnis¹⁹ Syndrom d. vernachlässigten Geschwisters²⁰ sozial benachteiligt²¹   11

---

inferiority complex n term & clin   rel **unconscious** [-ʃəs] **conflict**¹ n

acute sense of personal inferiority arising from conflict between the desire [aɪ] to be noticed and the fear of being humiliated² [hjuː-] which results either in extreme timidity³ or aggressiveness through overcompensation⁴

» A superiority complex⁵ is based on a false feeling of power and security [kjʊɚ] that conceals⁶ [siː] an underlying inferiority complex. Many uncomplicated depressions are a reaction to life stresses or interpersonal conflicts. Externalization⁷ of internal [ɜː] conflicts often leads to clashes⁸ with others in ways that bring the patient under medical observation.

Use to have an/suffer [ʌ] from an⁹/shake off one's **inferiority complex** • nagging¹⁰ [æ] **inferiority complex** • superiority⁵ / persecution¹¹ [kjuː] **complex** • castration¹² / Oedipus¹³ [e‖iː]/ Electra **complex** • symptom / AIDS-dementia **complex** • feeling or sense¹⁴ **of inferiority** • (intra)psychic [saɪ] or internal¹⁵ [ɜː]/ emotional **conflict** • interpersonal¹⁶ / internalized **conflict** • marital¹⁷ / family / parent-adolescent [es]/ motivational¹⁸ **conflict** • psychosexual / unconscious / unresolved¹⁹ **conflict** • **conflict** of interest / resolution²⁰ [uː]

Minderwertigkeitskomplex

unbewusster Konflikt¹ erniedrigt, gedemütigt² Schüchternheit, Ängstlichkeit³ Überkompensation⁴ Überlegenheitskomplex⁵ überdeckt⁶ Auslagerung⁷ Konflikte⁸ an e. Minderwertigkeitskomplex leiden⁹ ständige Minderwertigkeitsgefühle¹⁰ Verfolgungswahn¹¹ Kastrationskomplex¹² Ödipus-Komplex¹³ Minderwertigkeitsgefühl¹⁴ innerer Konflikt¹⁵ zwischenmenschl. K.¹⁶ Ehekonflikt¹⁷ Motivkonflikt¹⁸ ungelöster K.¹⁹ Konfliktlösung²⁰   12

---

mentally ill adj & n clin   syn **mentally deranged** or **disturbed** adj clin & term

(adj) suffering from a mental illness

derangement¹ [dɪreɪndʒmənt] n term • **disturbance**¹ [ɜː] n

» Psychiatrists [saɪk-] have a responsibility in advising and supporting the families of the mentally ill. Most patients with sigmoid volvulus are mentally ill or bedridden² persons who do not evacuate stool [uː] with regularity. Seizures³ [siːʒɚz] result from a focal or generalized disturbance of cortical function. Most overt⁴ [ɜː] psychiatric derangements are observed [ɜː] after the 3rd postoperative day.

Use **mentally** confused⁵ / unstable [eɪ]/ cloudy⁶ [aʊ]/ (in)competent⁷ • **mentally** handicapped / defective or deficient⁸ [ɪʃ] • mental⁹ / psychiatric⁹ / metabolic / immunologic **derangement** • **derangement of** personality or mind¹⁰ • emotional¹¹ / affective or mood¹¹ [uː]/ psychomotor / memory¹² **disturbance** • sleep / behavioral¹³ / personality¹⁰ **disturbance** • family / psychiatric⁹ **disturbance**

psychisch krank, geisteskrank; psych. Kranke

Störung¹ bettlägerig² Krampfanfälle, epilept. A.³ klin. manifest⁴ geistig verwirrt⁵ bewusstseinsgetrübt⁶ (un)zurechnungsfähig⁷ psych. gestört, geistig behindert⁸ psychiatr. Störung⁹ Persönlichkeitsstörung¹⁰ Affektstörung, affektive Psychose¹¹ Gedächtnisstörung¹² Verhaltensstörung¹³

13

---

psychosomatic illness n term   syn **psychophysiologic disorder** n term

dysfunction [ɪ] of an organ or group of organs controlled by the autonomic nervous [ɜː] system [ɪ] which is caused or aggravated¹ by psychic factors, e.g. peptic ulcer [ʌlsɚ]

» Manifestations of masked depression may include recurrent [ɜː] psychosomatic complaints [eɪ], e.g. headache, lethargy, or dizziness. Most cases of myofascial [æʃ] pain syndrome² are psychophysiologic in origin and result from tension-relieving toothgrinding [aɪ] habits³.

Use **psychosomatic** reaction / complaints⁴ / pain / medicine⁵ • **psychophysiologic** abnormality / manifestations • **psychophysiologic** symptoms / insomnia⁶ / gastrointestinal reaction

psychosomat. Erkrankung

verstärkt, -schlimmert¹ myofasziales Schmerzsyndrom, Costen-Syndrom² habituelles Zähneknirschen³ psychosomatische Beschwerden⁴ psychosomat. Medizin, Psychosomatik⁵ psychogene Schlaflosigkeit⁶

14

Mental Health COMPLEX BODY FUNCTIONS 315

insane [eɪ] *adj inf & leg*   *sim* **mad¹, crazy²** [eɪ], **frenzied³,
unhinged⁴** [-dʒd] *adj inf, rel* **demented⁵** [dɪmentɪd] *adj*
legal and social expression for being mentally ill (practically not used in clinical contexts)
insanity⁶ [æ] *n inf & leg* • **madness⁷** *n* • *****madman⁸** *n inf* • **frenzy** [frenzi] *n*
» *The patient expresses fears that he is going insane. The jury found Roberts not guilty
by reason of insanity. The criteria for insanity vary from state to state. Providing a
clear demarcation between schizophrenia's* [iː] *characteristic cluster* [ʌ] *of signs and
symptoms and other types of madness has proved difficult.*
Use to go⁹/become⁹/be **insane** • **insane** asylum¹⁰ [aɪ] / ward¹¹ [ɔː] • to drive sb.¹²/go⁹
mad • raving¹³ [eɪ] **mad** • **to be/get mad** at sth. or sb. • *****mad**house¹⁰ /-doctor /
cow disease¹⁴ • to drive or make sb.¹²/go⁹ **crazy** • **to be crazy** about sth. or sb. •
mildly / globally / chronically / severely **demented** • **demented** patient • to
plead¹⁵ [iː] **insanity** • affective or emotional¹⁶ / alcoholic / religious¹⁷ **insanity** •
senile¹⁸ / toxic¹⁹ / temporary **insanity** • myxedema²⁰ [mɪksɪdiːmə]/ megaloblastic
madness • **frenzied** excitement²¹ [ɪksaɪt-]/ activity / applause²² [ɔː]

> **Note:** There are plenty of colloquialisms for **insane**, e.g. *not right in the head,
> not in one's right mind, out of one's mind, non compos mentis, to be a case,
> round the bend, be/go nuts, have bats in the belfry, hasn't a full sack of
> marbles, brainsick, feeble-minded, be a bit touched, have a screw loose.* Also
> note that **mad** and **crazy** are often used to mean *angry* or *out of control.*

**geisteskrank, wahnsinnig,
verrückt, unzurechnungsfähig**
wahnsinnig, verrückt; böse, wütend¹ verrückt, wahnsinnig² wahnsinnig, rasend, wild, hektisch³ verstört, übergeschnappt⁴ dement, verrückt⁵ Irresein, Geisteskrankheit, Unzurechnungsfähigkeit⁶ Verrücktheit, Wut; Wahnsinn⁷ Irrer, Verrückter⁸ verrückt werden⁹ Irrenanstalt¹⁰ psychiatr. Abteilung¹¹ jem. auf d. Palme bringen¹² total verrückt¹³ Rinderwahnsinn, BSE¹⁴ auf Unzurechnungsfähigkeit plädieren¹⁵ Affektstörung¹⁶ religiöser Wahn, Theomanie¹⁷ Alterspsychose¹⁸ Intoxikationspsychose¹⁹ hypothyroide P.²⁰ rasende Erregung²¹ frenetischer Beifall²²

15

psychiatric disease *or* **illness** [saɪkiætrɪk dɪziːz] *n term*
                              syn **mental disorder** *n clin*
emotional, mental or behavioral disturbance manifesting as maladaptive behavior, impaired
functioning and/or disturbed emotional equilibrium¹ due to genetic, chemical, psychologic, or
social causes
psychiatry² [saɪkaɪətri] *n* • **psychiatrist³** *n* • **psycho-** [saɪkoʊ-] *comb*
» *Check patients with frank⁴ neurologic or psychiatric disease for Kayser-Fleischer
rings⁵. In some psychiatric disorders the degree of withdrawal can be so substantial⁶
that the noncommunicative⁷ patient appears unconscious.*
Use acute / superimposed⁸ **psychiatric illness** • **psychiatric** patient / admission⁹ /
unit¹⁰ • **psychiatric** ward¹⁰ [ɔː]/ state • **psychiatric** disturbance / symptoms •
psychiatric interview / consultation • **psychiatric** assessment or evaluation¹¹ •
psychiatric emergency [ɜː] (room)¹² / nursing¹³ [ɜː] • emotional **illness** • personality / behavior or conduct¹⁴ / mood **disorder** • seasonal [iː] affective¹⁵ (*abbr*
SAD)/ anxiety **disorder** • bipolar¹⁶ / conversion¹⁷ [ɜː]/ identity **disorder** • attention-deficit hyperactivity¹⁸ (*abbr* ADHD), autistic¹⁹ [ɔː] **disorder** • **mental** deterioration²⁰ / aberration²¹ / dysfunction • community²² / biologic / descriptive /
dynamic²³ / existential **psychiatry** • child and adolescent²⁴ / geriatric [dʒerɪ-] **psychiatry** • **psycho**logy /dynamics²⁵ /genic /motor agitation²⁶ [ædʒɪ-] • **psycho**social [-soʊʃ°l] /sexual /pathic /pathology

**Geisteskrankheit, psychiatr./
psychische Erkrankung**
seelisches Gleichgewicht¹ Psychiatrie² Psychiater(in), FA f. Psychiatrie³ klin. manifest⁴ Kayser-Fleischer-Ringe⁵ stark⁶ verschlossen⁷ überlagerte psych. Erkrankung⁸ psychiatr. Aufnahme⁹ psychiatr. Abteilung¹⁰ p. Untersuchung¹¹ p. Notaufnahme¹² p. Pflege¹³ Verhaltensstörung¹⁴ saisonale affektive S.¹⁵ bipolare Psychose, manisch-depressive Krankheit¹⁶ Konversionsstörung¹⁷ Aufmerksamkeits-Hyperaktivitäts-Syndrom¹⁸ autist. Störung, (frühkindl.) Autismus¹⁹ geistiger Verfall²⁰ psychische Störung²¹ Gemeindepsychiatrie, kommunale P.²² psychoanalyt./ dynamische P.²³ Kinder- u. Jugendpsychiatrie²⁴ Psychodynamik²⁵ psychomotor. Unruhe²⁶   16

depression [dɪpreʃ°n] *n term & clin*   *rel* **bipolar** [baɪpoʊlɚ] **disorder¹** *n term*
(i) mood disorder marked by feelings of sadness, dejection² [dʒe], despair³ [eə], or
discouragement⁴ [ɜː]
(ii) a state of feeling unhappy or disappointed
depressed⁵ *adj* • **depressive⁶** *adj & n term* • **(anti)depressant⁷** *adj & n*
• **repression⁸** *n term* • **repress** [rɪpres] *v*
» *Repressed anger* [æŋɚ] *is considered to be a significant factor contributing to
depression. Clinical depression and mania* [eɪ] *are diagnosed when sadness or elation* [eɪʃ] *is overly intense and continues beyond the expected impact of a stressful
life event. Severely depressed patients often have no desire for socializing or physical
activity, have low self-esteem⁹* [iː], *feelings of worthlessness¹⁰* [ɜː], *and thoughts of
self-injury* [ɪndʒɚi] *or suicidal* [saɪ] *ideation¹¹.*
Use psychotic¹² / endogenous¹³ [ɒdʒ]/ agitated¹⁴ **depression** • major¹⁵ [eɪdʒ]/
masked¹⁶ / neurotic¹⁷ **depression** • unipolar / postpartum¹⁸ **depression** • reactive
or situational¹⁹ / transient **depression** • major **depressive** disorder¹⁵ • **depressive**
symptoms / phase [feɪz] or episode²⁰ / mood swings²¹ • **depressive** state / illness /
psychosis / syndrome²² • to release [iː] a²³ / traumatic / full **repression** • massive
/ unconscious²⁴ **repression** • **to repress** emotions / desires²⁵ [aɪ] • **to repress**
memories / unpleasant [e] experiences

(i) Depression (ii) Niedergeschlagenheit, Schwermut
manisch-depressive Krankheit¹ Niedergeschlagenheit, Melancholie² Verzweiflung, Hoffnungslosigkeit³ Mutlosigkeit⁴ deprimiert, bedrückt⁵ depressiv, schwermütig; e. an D. leidende Person⁶ beruhigend, dämpfend; Beruhigungsmittel, Sedativum⁷ Verdrängung⁸ Selbstachtung⁹ Wertlosigkeit¹⁰ Suizidgedanken¹¹ psychot. Depression¹² endogene D.¹³ agitierte D.¹⁴ schwere depressive Episode¹⁵ larvierte/ maskierte D.¹⁶ depressive Neurose, neurot. D.¹⁷ postpartale D.¹⁸ reaktive D.¹⁹ depressive Phase²⁰ depressive Verstimmungen²¹ depressives Syndrom²² Verdrängtes auflösen²³ unbewusste Verdrängung²⁴ Wünsche verdrängen²⁵   17

mania [meɪnɪə] n term   rel **elation**[1] [ɪleɪʃᵊn],   **excitement**[2] [aɪ],
                              euphoria[3] [juːfɔːrɪə] n → U76-8,16

state marked by extreme excitement [aɪ], hyperactivity, overtalkativeness[4], flight [flaɪt] of ideas[5], fleeting [iː] attention[6] and sometimes violent, destructive [ʌ] behavior

maniac[7] [meɪnɪæk] adj & n inf • **maniacal** adj • (hypo)**manic**[8] [æ] adj term • **elated** [ɪleɪtɪd] adj clin • **euphoric** [juːfɔːrɪk] adj • -**mania** [eɪ] comb

» Atypical manic episodes can include gross [oʊ] delusions[9] [uːʒ], paranoid ideation[10] of severe proportions, and auditory [ɒː] hallucinations usually related to some grandiose perception[11]. Euphoria, elation, or aggressive behavior are commonly seen in patients with dementia.

Use acute / dysphoric[12] / mixed **mania** • full-blown[13] / mild / impending[14] **mania** • attack / episode[15] **of mania** • **manic** episode[15] / state / patient / phase[15] • **manic-depressive** illness or disorder or disease[16] • mental / euphoric / psychomotor **excitement** • catatonic[17] / frenzied[18] **excitement** • mild / surface[19] [ɜː] cocaine-induced / inappropriate[20] **euphoria** • **euphoric** sensations[21] / response • **manic-depressive** psychosis[16] • hypo**mania**[22] • poto**mania**[23] • **hypomanic** period or episode[24] / personality • **hypomanic** symptoms / tendencies / swings or switches

Manie
Hochstimmung, Begeisterung[1] Er-, Aufregung[2] Euphorie[3] ungehemmter Redefluss, Logorrhoe[4] Ideenflucht[5] flüchtige Aufmerksamkeit[6] wahnsinnig; Wahnsinnige(r), Verrückte(r)[7] manisch[8] massive Wahnvorstellungen[9] paranoide Ideen[10] Größenideen[11] gereizte Manie[12] ausgeprägte M.[13] bevorstehende manische Episode[14] manische E.[15] manisch-depressive Krankheit, bipolare affektive Störung[16] katatone Erregung[17] rasende E.[18] oberflächl. Wohlgestimmtheit[19] übersteigerte Euphorie[20] euphorische Gefühle[21] Hypomanie[22] Trunksucht, Potomanie[23] hypomanische Episode[24]

18

compulsion [-pʌlʃᵊn] n clin & term
                              sim **obsession**[1] [ɒː‖əbseʃᵊn] n term & clin

persistent irresistible urge[2] [ɜːrdʒ] to act contrary to one's ordinary judgement [dʒʌdʒ-], which usually results from an obsession and—if not completed—causes overt anxiety

compulsive[3] [kəmpʌlsɪv] adj • **obsessive**[4] adj • **obsessional**[4] adj

» A compulsion has the same autonomous characteristics as an obsession, but rather than being merely [ɪə] an idea or image, it is an overwhelming urge[2] to do something aggressive, disgraceful[5] [eɪs], or obscene [-siːn]. Obsessive-compulsive disorder[6] is characterized by obsessive thoughts and compulsive behaviors that impair[7] [eə] everyday functioning [ʌ].

Use repetition[8] / overpowering[2] [aʊ] obsessive[6] **compulsion** • **obsession** with food • **compulsive** desire / personality[9] / imperative ideas[10] / ritual [ɪtʃ] • **compulsive** motor activity[11] / water drinking • **compulsive** drug use[12] / sexual behavior / crying[13] • **obsessive** thoughts[10] / ruminations[14] / dieting[15] [aɪ] / exercise • **obsessive-compulsive** symptoms / neurosis[6] / disorder[6] (abbr OCD) • **obsessive-compulsive** patient / behavior / personality disorder[6] • **obsessional** personality characteristics[16]

(innerer) Zwang, Anankasmus
Zwang, Obsession, Besessenheit[1] unwiderstehl. Drang[2] kompulsiv, zwanghaft, Zwangs-[3] obsessiv, zwanghaft[4] schändlich[5] Zwangsstörung, -neurose[6] beeinträchtigen[7] Wiederholungszwang[8] zwanghafte/anankastische Persönlichkeit[9] Zwangsgedanken, -ideen[10] Akathisie[11] Drogenabhängigkeit[12] Zwangsweinen[13] zwanghaftes Grübeln[14] zwanghaftes Fasten[15] anankastische Persönlichkeitszüge[16]

19

delusion [dɪluːʒᵊn] n term
                              rel **hallucination**[1] [həluːsɪneɪʃᵊn] n clin & term → U73-10

persistent aberrant perception[2] [se] or belief firmly [ɜː] maintained [eɪ] by a person despite evidence to the contrary

delusional[3] adj term • **deluded** adj • **hallucinate**[4] v • **hallucinatory**[5] adj

» Paranoid disorders are usually distinguished from schizophrenia [skɪtsə-] by the absence of prominent hallucinations, incoherence[6] [ɪə], or bizarre delusions. The patient delusionally misinterpreted overheard scraps of conversation[7] as confirming [ɜː] his paranoid beliefs. His symptoms are not delusional in quality.

Use depressive[8] / systematized[9] / fragmentary **delusions** • mixed / mood-incongruent **delusions** • somatic[10] / grandiose[11] [æ] **delusions** • paranoid / persecutory[12] [juː] **delusions** • **delusion of** grandeur[11] / reference[13] / persecution[12] • **delusion of** guilt[14] [ɡɪlt]/ jealousy[15] [dʒeləsi]/ parasitosis[16] • **delusional** disorder[17] / thoughts or ideas[18] / fantasy[18] • **delusional** state[19] / behavior / depression[8] / patient

Wahn(idee), -vorstellung
Halluzination, Sinnestäuschung[1] Wahrnehmungsstörung[2] eingebildet, wahnhaft, Wahn-[3] halluzinieren, H. haben[4] halluzinatorisch[5] sprunghaftes Denken, Inkohärenz[6] mitgehörte Gesprächsfetzen[7] depressiver Wahn[8] systematisierter W.[9] hypochondrischer W.[10] Größenwahn, Megalomanie[11] Verfolgungswahn[12] Beziehungswahn[13] Versündigungs-, Schuldwahn[14] Eifersuchtswahn[15] Dermatozoenwahn[16] wahnhafte Störung[17] Wahnideen[18] Wahnstimmung[19]

20

Mental Health   COMPLEX BODY FUNCTIONS 317

psychosis [saɪkoʊsɪs] *n term, pl* **-ses** [-siːz]

rel **neurosis**[1] [n(j)ʊəˈroʊsɪs] *n term*

major [eɪdʒ] mental disorder in which the patient's capacity to communicate, recognize reality, and cope with life demands[2] is impaired

psychotic[3] [ɒː] *adj & n term* • **neurotic**[4] *adj & n* • **psych(o)-, neur(o)-** *comb*

» Atypical depressions, identity confusion, and particularly drug abuse and alcohol may mask, herald[5], or compound[6] [aʊ] the onset of the psychosis. The patient who appeared to be suffering from paranoid psychosis was later recognized to be schizophrenic [e].

Use acute / chronic / reactive[7] / functional **psychosis** • organic[8] / full-blown / drug-induced[9] **psychosis** • alcoholic[10] / paranoid / toxic[11] / amphetamine **psychosis** • childhood / late-life *or* senile[12] **psychosis** • postoperative / Korsakoff's[13] **psychosis** • brief reactive / manic(-depressive) / schizophrenic[14] **psychosis** • **psychotic** episode / reaction / disorder[15] • **psychotic** thinking / depression • anxiety[16] / psycho/hysterical[17] **neurosis** • obsessional[18] / phobic[19] [oʊ] **neurosis** • **neur**opathic /opsychiatric /asthenia [iː] • **neur**algia [n(j)ʊərældʒ(i)ə] /oma /opsychology[20] • **psycho**active substances[21] /analytic [ɪ] /emotional /social • **psycho**genic [dʒe] /tropic agents[21] [eɪdʒ] /somatic disorder[22] /therapy • **psycho**analyst[23] /pathology /pathy /pharmacology[24]

Psychose

Neurose[1] Anforderungen d. (tägl.) Lebens[2] psychotisch; Psychotiker(in)[3] neurotisch; Neurotiker(in)[4] ankündigen[5] verschlimmern[6] reaktive Psychose[7] organ./symptomat. P.[8] pharmakogene/medikamentös induzierte P.[9] Alkoholpsychose[10] Intoxikationspsychose[11] Alterspsychose[12] Korsakow-P., -Syndrom[13] schizophrene P.[14] psychotische Störung[15] Angstneurose[16] Konversionsneurose[17] Zwangsneurose[18] Phobie[19] Neuropsychologie[20] psychotrope Substanzen, Psychopharmaka[21] psychosomat. Störung[22] Psychoanalytiker(in)[23] Psychopharmakologie[24]

21

mental retardation *n term & clin*   *sim* **mental deficiency**[1] [ɪʃ] *n clin*

subaverage intellectual capacities[2] (IQ < 70) as exhibited by learning disability, social maladjustment, lack of emotional control, and/or subnormal or backward intellectual development[3]

retard[4] *v* • **mentally retarded**[5] *adj* • **mentally deficient** *or* **disabled**[5] *adj*

» Slowing of mental responsiveness and retardation of development of the brain was observed [ɜː] in both neonates [iː]. Although autism [ɒː] and mental retardation often coexist, the vast majority of mentally retarded children do not show the essential characteristics of autism. About 14% of children tested in school had IQs identified as borderline retardation[6]. Children with cat's cry syndrome[7] are slow to develop and profoundly [aʊ] mentally retarded[8].

Use to have/cause **mental retardation** • degree of[9] / mild[10] **mental retardation** • moderate[11] / pronounced [aʊ] *or* severe[12] [ɪɚ] **mental retardation** • unexplained / disabling [eɪ] **mental retardation** • X-linked / fragile [ædʒ] X[13] **mental retardation** • developmental / growth[14] **retardation** • intellectual / psychomotor[15] **retardation** • familial / borderline[6] **mental deficiency** • mild[10] / severe[12] **mental deficiency** • **mental** decline[16] [aɪ]/ disability[1] / defect[1] [iː] • **mental** dysfunction / disturbance [ɜː]/ aberrations [eɪʃ] • mildly / severely *or* profoundly **retarded**

mentale/ geistige Retardierung

geistige Behinderung, Intelligenzminderung, -störung[1] unterdurchschnittliche intellekt. Fähigkeiten[2] geistige Entwicklungsverzögerung[3] verzögern, verlangsamen[4] geistig retardiert/ zurückgeblieben[5] Grenzdebilität[6] Katzenschreisyndrom[7] schwer(st) geistig behindert[8] Schweregrad d. Intelligenzminderung[9] leichte geistige Retardierung, Debilität[10] mäßiggradige g. B., Imbezillität[11] schwer(st)e g. B., Idiotie[12] Marker-X-, fragiles X-Syndrom[13] Wachstumsverzögerung[14] psychomotorische Retardierung[15] geistiger Verfall[16]

22

dementia [dɪmenˈʃə] *n term*

rel **pseudodementia**[1] [suːdoʊ-] *n term*

general mental deterioration[2] characterized by disorientation, impaired cognitive memory, judgement[3], and intellect, aphasia[4] [eɪʒ], and apraxia[5], and a shallow labile affect[6]

demented[7] *adj* • **dementing** *adj*

» In most cases onset of dementia is insiduous[8] over months to years. Examples of primary degenerative dementia are Alzheimer's dementia[9] (most common) and Pick[10], Creutzfeldt-Jakob, and Huntington[11] dementias. The EEG findings alone cannot indicate whether a patient is demented or distinguish between dementia and pseudodementia [suːdoʊ-].

Use to develop[12]/produce *or* lead to/diagnose/mimic[13]/manage **dementia** • (pre)senile[14] / (primary) [aɪ] degenerative[15] [dʒe] **dementia** • alcoholic[16] / toxic / substance-induced **dementia** • frontal lobe / frontotemporal **dementia** • (sub)cortical / dialysis[17] [aɪɚ] **dementia** • HIV(-associated)[18] / multi-infarct[19] **dementia** • vascular[20] / posttraumatic **dementia** • late-onset[14] / inherited / persisting **dementia** • chronic progressive[21] / mild **dementia** • frank[22] / (ir)reversible [ɜː] **dementia** • **dementia** of the Alzheimer type[9] / paralytica [ɪ] • AIDS **dementia** complex[18] • **demented** patient / person • to be/become/appear [ɪɚ] **demented** • mildly [aɪ]/ globally / chronically **demented** • **dementing** illness[23] / process[24] / syndrome [ɪ]

Demenz, Dementia

Pseudodemenz[1] geistiger Verfall[2] Urteilsfähigkeit[3] Aphasie[4] Apraxie[5] flacher u. labiler Affekt[6] dement[7] schleichend[8] Alzheimer-Krankheit, -Demenz[9] Pick-Krankheit, -Atrophie[10] Huntington-Chorea[11] e. Demenz entwickeln[12] e. Demenz vortäuschen[13] senile D.[14] primär degenerative D.[15] Alkoholdemenz[16] Aluminium-, Dialyseenzephalopathie[17] HIV-Enzephalopathie, -Demenz, AIDS-D.[18] Multiinfarkt-D.[19] vaskuläre D.[20] chronisch progrediente D.[21] manifeste D.[22] zu Demenz führende Erkrankung[23] Demenzprozess[24]

23

COMPLEX BODY FUNCTIONS — Mental Health

Sorry Mr. Gumley, you can't go out. Visiting hours are when people come to visit **YOU**.

mental patient n clin   rel ***psycho(path)**[1] [aɪ], *ptr**idiot**[2] n, *ptr**lunatic**[3] n & adj
person afflicted with mental derangement or a personality disorder
psychopathy[4] n term • **psychopathic** adj • *ptr**idiocy**[5] n inf • *ptr**lunacy**[6] [uː] n
» Is the mental patient accompanied by an escort[7] so he can be transported safely? When she was labeled [eɪ] a mental patient, the woman lost custody of her children. Some autistics, popularly known as idiot savants[8], show extraordinary ability in a circumscribed [sɜː] area while functioning on a mentally retarded level in all other ways. I felt like a complete idiot.
Use **mental** acuity [juː] or alertness [ɜː]/ distress[9] • **mental** slowing / exhaustion or fatigue [iː]/ symptoms • juvenile [dʒuː]/ sexual **psychopath** • stupid / village **idiot** • (non)criminal **lunatic** • **lunatic** patient / fringe[10] / asylum[11] • cretinoid[12] idiocy

Note: Colloquial expressions for mental patients (most are derogatory) include *madman, *madwoman, *nut, *weirdo, *moron, *wacko, *looney.

Geisteskranke(r), psychisch Kranke(r)
Psychopath(in), Geistesgestörte(r)[1] Schwachsinnige(r); Dummkopf[2] Geistesgestörte(r), Verrückte(r); geisteskrank, wahnsinnig[3] Psychopathie, Persönlichkeitsstörung[4] Idiotie, schwere geistige Behinderung[5] Wahnsinn[6] Betreuer(in)[7] hochbegabte Autisten[8] psych. Belastung[9] extreme Randgruppe[10] Nervenheilanstalt[11] Idiotie bei Kretinismus[12]
24

custodial care [kʌstoʊdiəl keɚ] n   syn **maintenance** [eɪ] **care** n
rel **guardianship**[1] [gɑːrdiənʃɪp], **caregiver**[2] n
level of care which may also be provided by non-professionals, relies on supportive supervision[3] and safeguarding [eɪ] and mainly addresses deficits in activities of daily living, e.g. for the mentally disabled
custody[4] [ʌ] n • **custodian**[5] [oʊ] n • **custodianship**[6] n • **guardian**[5] n
» In the 19th century the main role of psychiatry was to provide custodial care for the mentally ill. Infection rates are especially high among retarded children in custodial care. Ninety percent of all long-term care is custodial care. Alzheimer's disease exacts a heavy emotional toll[7] [tɒːl] on family members and caregivers. The best we could hope for was custodial care within the four walls of a mental asylum [aɪ].
Use to provide/receive/be under[8] **custodial care** • in-home[9] / asylum-rooted [uː]/ long-term **custodial care** • full-time[10] / interim / purely **custodial care** • **custodial** mental health care / institution • **custodial** duties[11] [(j)uː]/ costs • to be (held) in[12]/have[13]/release [iː] from/take into[14] **custody** • parental[15] / joint[16] [dʒɔɪnt]/ police / overnight **custody** • **custody** of the child • legal[17] / court-appointed **guardian** • medical / primary / adult • overstressed[18] **caregiver** • **caregiver** dysfunction / guilt [gɪlt]/ burnout[19] [ɜː]

(psycho)soziale Betreuung
Vormundschaft, Obhut, Schutz[1] (Für-)sorgeberechtigte(r), Betreuer(in)[2] Beaufsichtigung, Aufsicht[3] Obhut, Pflegschaft, Vormundschaft, Gewahrsam[4] Wächter, Betreuer; Vormund[5] Vormundschaft[6] stellt e. große psych. Belastung dar[7] in psychosozialer Betreuung sein[8] häusliche/ aufsuchende B.[9] ständige B.[10] Betreuungspflichten[11] i. Gewahrsam sein[12] d. Sorgerecht haben[13] i. Gewahrsam/ Haft nehmen[14] elterliches Sorgerecht[15] gemeinsames S.[16] gesetzlicher Vormund[17] überlastete(r) Betreuer(in)[18] Burnout-Syndrom/ Erschöpfungszustände bei Betreuern[19]
25

straightjacket or **straitjacket** [streɪtdʒækɪt] n
syn **camisole** [æ] **(restraint)** n term, rel **padded room**[1] n clin
jacket-like garment[2] used to tighten [taɪtᵊn] the arms against the body as a means [iː] of restraining a violent [aɪ] person
restrain[3] [eɪ] v • **restraint**[4] [rɪstreɪnt] n • **unrestrained** adj • **restraining** n & adj
» In the unruly[5] [uː] patient, it is perhaps wise to consider restraints, sedation [eɪʃ], local or general anesthesia [iːʒ]–or even to postpone[6] [oʊ] wound [uː] evaluation.
Use to put sb. in a[7] **straightjacket** • to lock sb. up in a[8] **padded room** • physical [ɪ] or mechanical[9] / safety [eɪ] belt[10] / head / arm[11] / lateral / chemical[12] **restraint** • **to restrain** a patient / movement • **restraining** mitts[13] • **padded** restraints[14]

Zwangsjacke
Gummizelle[1] Kleidungsstück[2] einschränken, fest-, abhalten, bändigen[3] Ein-, Beschränkung; Zwangsmaßnahme[4] tobend[5] verschieben[6] jem. in e. Zwangsjacke stecken[7] jem. i. e. Gummizelle sperren[8] mechan. Fixierung[9] Sicherheitsgurt[10] Handgelenksfessel[11] chemische Zwangsjacke/ Einschränkung[12] bewegungseinschränkende Handschuhe[13] gepolsterte Fesseln[14]
26

Metabolism COMPLEX BODY FUNCTIONS **319**

Unit 78 Metabolism

Related Units: 88 Physiology, 81 Biochemistry, 83 Cell Biology, 79 Nutrition, 46 Digestion, 44 Respiration, 55 Hormones, 47 Liver, 49 Urine Production

metabolism [mətæbəlɪzəm] *n term*   *rel* **buildup**[1] [ɪ], **breakdown**[2] [eɪ], **turnover**[3] [ɜː] *n clin*

chemical changes occurring [ɜː] in the body including the breakdown of large molecules into small ones, biodegradation of xenobiotics[4] [zenoʊ-] as well as reactions that build up endogenous [ɒdʒ] molecules

(hyper)metabolic *adj term* • **metabolize**[5] *v* • **metabolizable** *adj*

» Patients with cancer may have abnormal energy, protein, or carbohydrate [aɪ] metabolism. Production of glucose by the liver involves breakdown of stored glycogen.

Use body / cell / tissue [ʃ‖s]/ carbohydrate[6] / calcium [s]/ lipid **metabolism** • alcohol / water / acid-base[7] [s]/ intermediary[8] [iː]/ B12 **metabolism** • hyper/ hypo**metabolism** • **metabolic** function / clearance [ɪɚ] rate • **metabolic** response[9] • by-product[10] / end-products[11] / control[12] • **metabolic** intermediates[13] / demands *or* needs / state *or* status • **metabolic** (im)balance / block / pathways[14] / process / step / substrates [ʌ] • **metabolic** acidosis / alkalosis / disorder *or* disturbance[15] [ɜː] / **metabolic** crisis [aɪ]/ support / derangement[15] [eɪ] • **metabolically** active • **to metabolize** sucrose • muscle **buildup** • cell / iron [aɪɚn]/ bone[16] (calcium) / glucose / protein **turnover** • nucleic acid[17] / accelerated[18] / increased[18] **turnover** • **turnover** number[19] / rate[20] / time

Stoffwechsel, Metabolismus
Aufbau[1] Abbau, Aufspaltung[2] Umsatz[3] Xenobiotika[4] umwandeln, metabolisieren[5] Kohlenhydratstoffwechsel[6] Säure-Basen-Stoffwechsel[7] Intermediär-, Zwischenstoffwechsel[8] Stoffwechselreaktion[9] Stoffwechselnebenprodukt[10] Stoffwechselendprodukte[11] Stoffwechselregulation, -steuerung[12] Stoffwechselzwischenprodukte[13] Stoffwechselwege[14] Stoffwechselstörung[15] Knochenumsatz[16] Nukleinsäurenstoffwechsel[17] erhöhter Umsatz[18] mol(ekul)are Aktivität, Wechselzahl[19] Umsatzrate[20]

1

basal metabolic rate *n term, abbr* **BMR**   *syn* **basal** [eɪ] **metabolism** *n term*

turnover of energy required to maintain vital functions in a fasting[1], awake individual at rest

» Physiologic changes in body composition including loss of lean [iː] body mass[2] and lower basal metabolic rate lead to decreased energy requirements in elderly patients. A profound[3] [aʊ] hypermetabolism occurs in the postburn [ɜː] period, and in severe burns the metabolic rate may increase to double [ʌ] the basal rate.

Use cerebral[4] / myocardial [aɪ]/ normal / elevated *or* accelerated[5] [əksel-] **metabolic rate** • reduced / low / fall *or* decrease [iː] in[6] **metabolic rate**

Grund-, Basalumsatz
nüchtern[1] fettfreie Körpermasse[2] ausgeprägt[3] Hirnstoffwechselrate[4] erhöhte Stoffwechselrate[5] Sinken/ Abfall/ Senkung d. Stoffwechselrate[6]

2

anabolic [ænəbɒːlɪk] *adj term*

   opposite **catabolic**[1] *adj term*

related to the buildup of complex chemical compounds[2] [aʊ] in the body from simpler ones

anabolism[3] *n term* • **anabolite**[4] *n* • **catabolism** *n* • **catabolize**[5] *v* • **catabolite** *n*

» Wait for the patient on long-term parenteral nutrition [ɪʃ] to move from catabolic breakdown to sustained [eɪ] anabolism. In the initial [ɪʃ] catabolic response to trauma [ɒː] body protein, fat, and carbohydrate are depleted [iː]. In cancer patients synthesis [ɪ], catabolism, and turnover of body protein are all increased, but the change in catabolism is greatest.

Use **anabolic** reaction / phase [feɪz]/ state / pathways[6] • **anabolic** steroids[7] (*abbr* AS)/ agents[7] [eɪdʒ]/ hormones[7] • bacterial [ɪɚ] **anabolism** • **antianabolic** effect • **catabolic** process[8] / patient / disorder • **catabolic** rate / weight loss / pathways[9] • to inhibit/prevent/augment/ reverse[10] [ɜː] **catabolism** • amino acid[11] / protein / tissue / accelerated **catabolism**

anabol(isch), aufbauend
katabol(isch), abbauend[1] chemische Verbindungen[2] Anabolismus, aufbauende Stoffwechselprozesse[3] Anabolit[4] abbauen, katabolisieren[5] anabol(isch)e Stoffwechselwege[6] Anabolika[7] Abbauprozess[8] katabol(isch)e Stoffwechselwege[9] den Katabolismus umkehren[10] Aminosäureabbau[11]

3

(bio)synthesis [baɪoʊsɪnθəsɪs] *n term, pl* **-ses**

   opposite **lysis**[1] [laɪsɪs] *n term*

composition or buildup of compounds [aʊ] by physiologic processes in the living organism

synthetize[2] [ɪ] *v term* • **synthetic** *adj* • **synthetase**[3] *n* •**–lysis, –lyze** *comb*

» The release [iː] and synthesis of insulin are stimulated by activation of specific glucoreceptors [se] located on the surface [ɜː] membrane of the beta [eɪ‖iː] cell. The liver synthesizes water-soluble bile acids[4] from water-insoluble cholesterol.

Use to block *or* inhibit[5] **synthesis** • (glyco)protein [glaɪk–]/ albumin **synthesis** • fatty acid[6] / folic [oʊ] acid[7]/ cholesterol / collagen **synthesis** • urea[8] / enzymatic / DNA **synthesis** • antibody / hormone / steroid [ɪɚ] **synthesis** • **synthesis** inhibitor[9] / rate / defect [iː] • chemically / newly **synthesized** • proteo[10]/ lipo/ hydro[11]/ glycogeno/ glyco**lysis** [glaɪkɒːlɪsɪs] • (hemo)dia/ cyto/ thrombo[12]/ fibrino/ (auto-)hem**olysis** • clot[12] / collagen / bone **lysis** • hydro[13]/ hemo/ proteo**lyze**

(Bio)synthese, Aufbau
Lyse, Lysis, Auflösung[1] synthetisieren[2] Synthetase, Ligase[3] wasserlösliche Gallensäuren[4] die Synthese hemmen[5] Fettsäuresynthese[6] Folsäuresynthese[7] Harnstoffsynthese[8] Synthesehemmer[9] Proteolyse, Eiweißabbau[10] Hydrolyse[11] Thrombolyse[12] hydrolisieren[13]

4

COMPLEX BODY FUNCTIONS — Metabolism

assimilate v term   syn **take up** v phr, sim **absorb**[1] [ɔː] v term → U46-13, U88-8

to incorporate[2] digested [dʒe] nutrients into body tissue

assimilation[3] [eɪʃ] n term • assimilable[4] adj • **uptake**[5] n • **absorption**[6] n

» Most organic compounds in food, although metabolized and assimilated by the body, are not essential in the sense that their deletion[7] [iːʃ] from the diet[8] [daɪət] does not cause illness. Higher intakes[9] of oral calcium permit adequate calcium assimilation despite a lower efficiency of intestinal calcium absorption. Hypophosphatemia [iː] decreases calcium uptake into bone, increases intestinal calcium absorption, and stimulates bone breakdown.

Use to undergo[10] / rapid **assimilation** • carbohydrate [aɪ]/ glucose / calcium **assimilation** • amino acid / bilirubin / cellular potassium[11] **uptake** • (insulin-mediated) [iː] glucose[12] / impaired [eə] **uptake**

assimilieren, aufnehmen
ab-, resorbieren[1] einbauen[2] Assimilation[3] assimilierbar[4] Aufnahme[5] Ab-, Resorption[6] Streichen, Weglassen[7] Nahrung[8] Zufuhr[9] assimiliert werden[10] zelluläre Kaliumaufnahme[11] insulinvermittelte Glukoseaufnahme[12]

5

convert [ɜː] v   sim **transform**[1] v,
     rel **exchange**[2] v & n, **recycle**[3] [rɪsaɪkl] v term

to change the nature, form or property of substances or exchange or replace them with another

conversion[4] n term • reconvert[5] v • **transformation** n • **cycle**[6] n • **cyclic**[7] adj

» Aminoglutethimide [-ɪmaɪd] inhibits the conversion of cholesterol to pregnenolone, a key step in steroid hormone biosynthesis [1]. These alterations can hasten[8] [heɪsn] transformation of the fatty streak[9] [iː] into a lesion [iːʒ] richer in fibrous [aɪ] smooth [uː] muscle cells[10]. There is a continuous exchange of water and solutes across all cell membranes. Urea recycling[11] [aɪ] helps maintain osmolality in the renal medulla.

Use **to convert** T4 to T3 • to enhance or promote/inhibit/block **conversion** • renal / peripheral / bilirubin / enzymatic[12] **conversion** • lipoxygenase[13] [-dʒəneɪz]/ prothrombin **conversion** • to undergo[14]/enhance/retard/suppress **transformation** • (reduced/ accelerated) bio[15]/ enzymatic[12] / blast **transformation** • genetic [dʒ]/ histologic / malignant **transformation** • gas or air / fluid / capillary **exchange** • ion [aɪən]/ sodium-calcium • cationic[16] [aɪː] **exchange** • citric [s] acid[17] / folic acid metabolism[18] / urea[19] **cycle** • Cori[20] / Krebs[17] **cycle** • **cyclic**[21] AMP / guanosine monophosphate / nucleotides [-taɪdz]

umwandeln, umformen
umwandeln, transformieren[1] austauschen; Austausch[2] wiederaufbereiten, -verwerten[3] Umwandlung[4] zurückwandeln[5] Zyklus[6] zyklisch[7] beschleunigen[8] lipidhaltige Plaque[9] glatte Muskelzellen[10] Rückdiffusion v. Harnstoff[11] enzymat. Umwandlung[12] Umwandlung durch Lipoxygenase[13] transformiert werden[14] Biotransformation[15] Kationenaustausch[16] Zitronensäurezyklus, Krebs-Zyklus[17] Folsäurezyklus[18] Harnstoff-, Ornithinzyklus[19] Cori-, Glukose-Laktat-Zyklus[20] zyklisches Adenosin-3′,5′-monophosphat, cyclo-AMP, cAMP[21]

6

esterify [esterɪfaɪ] v term   rel **phosphorylate**[1], **alkylate**[2] [ælkəleɪt],
     carboxylate[3], **acetylate**[4] [se],
     hydroxylate[5], **glycosylate**[6] v term

to convert into an ester, e.g. in the reaction of ethanol and acetic [siː] acid to form ethyl acetate

(poly)ester n term • esterase[7] n • esterification[8] n • esterifyable [aɪ] adj

» These patients lack the enzyme that normally esterifies cholesterol in the plasma. In the intestinal mucosa provitamin carotenoids undergo central fission[9] [ʃ] of the molecule to form retinol, which is then esterified. In the basal ganglia levodopa is decarboxylated[10] to form dopamine and replace the missing neurotransmitter.

Use ester bonds[11] • anticholin [k]/ (acetyl)choline**sterase** • **alkylating** agent[12] • dealk/ decarbox/ dehydrox/ dephosphor**ylation** • glycos/ hydrox[13]/ (hypo/ re)meth**ylation** • (tri/un)phosphor/ hydrox/ glycos/ (non)carbo**xylated** • biotin[14]/ salic[15]/ meth**ylate**

verestern
phosphorylieren[1] alkylieren[2] carboxylieren[3] acetylieren[4] hydroxylieren[5] glykosylieren[6] Esterase[7] Veresterung[8] Spaltung[9] decarboxyliert[10] Esterbindungen[11] alkylierende Substanz, Alkylans[12] Hydroxylierung[13] biotinylieren, mit Biotin versetzen[14] Salicylat, m. Salicylsäure behandeln[15]

7

enzyme [enzaɪm] n term   syn **organic catalyst** [kætəlɪst] n term → U81-16

protein secreted by the body acting as a catalyst[1] to promote biochemical reactions in other substances; most enzymes are named by adding -ase to the name of the substrate [ʌ] on which they act (e.g., glucosidase), the substance activated (e.g. hydrogenase), and/or the type of reaction (e.g. transferase)

enzymatic[2] adj term • proenzyme[3] n • co-enzyme n • -ase [-eɪz] comb

» Liver enzymes and serum lipids must be checked periodically. Cigarette smoking can induce hepatic enzymes. The pancreatic enzymes are not activated in acute pancreatitis.

Use digestive[4] / liver or hepatic / cardiac[5] / iso[6] [aɪsoʊ-]/ fat-splitting[7] / active **enzyme** • brush [ʌ] border[8] / key[9] / serum **enzymes** • proteolytic [ɪ]/ hydrolytic[10] [aɪ]/ restriction[11] **enzymes** • **enzyme** activity[12] / induction[13] [ʌ]/ pattern[14] / determination / assay[15] • **enzyme**-labeled[16] [eɪ]/ inhibition[17] / defect[18] • **enzyme** deficiency [ɪʃ]/ replacement[19] / studies[20] • **enzymatic** reaction / synthesis [ɪ]/ cleavage[21] [iː]/ deficiency • glucosid/ oxidoreduct/ transfer/ hydrol[10]/ ly**ases** [laɪeɪsɪz] • isomer/ lig/ hydrogen[22]/ synthet**ase**

Enzym, Ferment
Katalysator[1] enzymatisch[2] Proenzym, Zymogen[3] Verdauungsenzym[4] Herzenzym[5] Isoenzym[6] fettspaltendes E.[7] Bürstensaumenzyme[8] Schlüsselenzyme[9] Hydrolasen[10] Restriktionsenzyme, -endonukleasen[11] Enzymaktivität[12] Enzyminduktion[13] Enzymmuster[14] Enzymtest[15] enzymmarkiert[16] Enzymhemmung[17] Enzymdefekt[18] Enzymsubstitution[19] Enzymdiagnostik[20] enzymatische Spaltung[21] Hydrogenase[22]

8

Metabolism   COMPLEX BODY FUNCTIONS **321**

precursor [prɪkɜːrsɚ] n term
  rel **provitamin**[1] [aɪ‖ɪ], **prohormone**[2], **(pre)proprotein**[3] n term
  physiologically inactive substance [ʌ] or cellular component that is synthesized or converted [ɜː] to an active enzyme, vitamin, hormone, etc.
» *Each of the reactions requires the conversion of inactive precursor proteins into active proteases by limited proteolysis. Levodopa, the metabolic precursor*[4] *of dopamine, is capable of crossing the blood-brain barrier*[5]*.*
Use immediate [iː]/ circulating [ɜː]/ vitamin A[6] / DNA / heme[7] [hiːm] **precursor** • **precursor** molecule[8] / cell[9] / protein[10] / form / synthesis • **provitamin** A[6] / D3

Vorstufe, Vorläufer, Precursor
Provitamin[1] Prohormon[2] (Prä)proprotein[3] Vorstufe[4] Blut-Hirn-Schranke[5] Provitamin A[6] Hämvorstufe[7] Vorläufermolekül[8] Precursorzelle, Vorläuferzelle[9] Proteinvorstufe[10]
9

(bio)degradation [baɪoʊdegrədeɪʃ⁽ə⁾n] n term → U46-11
  syn **breakdown, splitting** n clin & jar, rel **decomposition**[1] n term
  breakdown of complex chemical compounds in the body into smaller and/or less complex ones
degrade[2] [dɪgreɪd] v term • **break down**[2] v phr •
split (up)[2] v phr • **(un)split** adj • **(non/ bio)degradable**[3] adj
» *Debranching enzyme*[4] *and phosphorylase are responsible for complete degradation of glycogen*[5] *[aɪ]. Lactase is an intestinal mucosal enzyme which splits lactose to galactose and glucose. The splitting of ATP*[6] *then dissociates the myosin [aɪ] crossbridge*[7] *from the actin.*
Use protein / lipid / fatty acid[8] / fibrin(-fibrinogen) [aɪ]/ purine **degradation** • metabolic / proteolytic[9] [iː]/ intracellular[10] / bacteria-produced [ɪɚ] **degradation** • **degradation** pathways / products[11] / by-product[12] / fragments / rate • metabolic / catabolic[13] / (muscle) [mʌsl] protein **breakdown** • glycogen[5] [-dʒən]/ fat / tissue / hepatic **breakdown** • **breakdown** products[11] • urea-/ fat[14]-**splitting** • tissue / thermic[15] [ɜː]/ bacterial **decomposition** • **split** product[16] / fat

(biolog.) Abbau/ (Auf)spaltung
Zersetzung, Zerfall[1] abbauen, (auf)spalten[2] biolog. abbaubar[3] Amylo-1,6-Glukosidase, Debranching enzyme[4] Glykogenolyse, -abbau[5] Adenosintriphosphat[6] Querbrücke[7] Fettsäureabbau[8] Proteolyse, Eiweißabbau[9] intrazellulärer Abbau[10] Abbauprodukte[11] kataboles/ degradatives Nebenprodukt[12] Abbaustoffwechsel, Katabolismus[13] fettspaltend[14] thermische Zersetzung, Pyrolyse[15] Spaltprodukt[16]
10

metabolite [mətæbəlaɪt] n term   rel **antimetabolite**[1] [ænti-] n term
  substance [ʌ] produced by metabolic processes [ɒːs]
» *Higher doses of vitamin D or its metabolites increase the efficiency [ɪʃ] of intestinal calcium absorption. Normally, the anion [ænaɪən] secretory [iː] system eliminates metabolites that have been conjugated with glycine [aɪs], or glucuronic acid*[2]*.*
Use (in)active / stable[3] [eɪ]/ reactive / endogenous [ɒːdʒ]/ drug / toxic[4] **metabolite** • hormone / cortisol / salicylate [ɪs]/ intermediary[5] / major[6] / minor[7] **metabolite** • urinary / water-soluble[8] / oxygen / excreted [iː] **metabolites** • **metabolite** of vitamin D / level / accumulation / excretion • purine[9] / systemic **antimetabolite**

Stoffwechsel(zwischen)produkt, Metabolit
Antimetabolit[1] Glukuronsäure[2] stabiler Metabolit[3] toxischer Metabolit[4] Stoffwechselzwischenprodukt, Intermediat[5] Hauptmetabolit[6] Nebenmetabolit[7] wasserlösl. Metaboliten[8] Purinantagonist, -antimetabolit[9]
11

energy metabolism n term   rel **energy expenditure**[1] [ɪkspendɪtʃɚ] n term
  metabolic processes in which energy is produced or utilized [juː], e.g. ATP-dependent processes
(bio)energetics[2] [enɚdʒetɪks] n term • **energy-rich**[3] [enɚdʒi rɪtʃ] adj
» *The basal metabolic energy requirement depends on the age, sex, and lean body mass. In starvation*[4]*, energy is derived [aɪ] principally from fat metabolism.*
Use cellular / metabolic[5] / dietary / mechanical[6] / kinetic[7] **energy** • electrical / thermal[8] [ɜː]/ radiant[9] [eɪ]/ muscle **energy** • **energy** requirements or demands or needs[10] • **energy** production / source [ɔː]/ stores / reserves [ɜː] • **energy** supplies[11] [aɪ]/ balance[12] / deficiency [ɪʃ] • **energy** cost[1] / utilization[1] [juː] • **energy** consumption[1] [ʌ]/-requiring process[13] / transfer[14] /-rich compounds[15] • **high-energy** compounds[15] [aʊ]/ bond[16] / phosphates • total (abbr TEE)/ resting[17] (abbr REE)/ basal[17] **energy expenditure**

Energiestoffwechsel
Energieverbrauch[1] Bioenergetik[2] energiereich[3] Hungern, Nahrungskarenz[4] Stoffwechselenergie[5] mechan. Energie[6] Bewegungsenergie[7] Wärmeenergie[8] Strahlungsenergie[9] Energiebedarf[10] Energievorräte[11] Energiehaushalt, -bilanz[12] energieverbrauchender Prozess[13] Energieübertragung[14] energiereiche Verbindungen[15] energiereiche Bindung[16] Grund-, Basalumsatz[17]
12

glycogen [glaɪkədʒən] n term   rel **glucose**[1] [gluːkoʊs‖z] n term → U79-7
  polysaccharide [æk] that acts as the main carbohydrate reserve [ɜː] of the body; it is readily [e] converted into glucose and released [iː] into the body as required
hypo/ eu/ hyperglycemia[2] [-glaɪsiː-] n term • **hyperglycemic** adj • **glyco-** comb
» *Increased fat oxidation would impair glucose uptake and glycogen synthesis. When blood glucose levels start to fall, the liver converts glycogen back into glucose and releases it into the blood. Symptoms of hypoglycemia include sweating [e], trembling*[3]*, hunger, fast heartbeat, weakness [iː], mental confusion, and on occasion, seizures*[4] *[siːʒɚz] and coma.*
Use liver or hepatic[5] / muscle / stored **glycogen** • **glycogen** breakdown[6] [eɪ]/ metabolism / deposition • **glycogen** stores / storage (disease)[7] / depletion [iːʃ] / phosphorylase[8] • diabetic [aɪ]/ chronic / fasting[9] / mild **hyperglycemia** • marked / early morning[10] **hyperglycemia** • alimentary / fasting[11] / factitious[12] [ɪʃ] **hypoglycemia** • alcoholic / profound[13] [aʊ]/ postprandial[14] **hypoglycemia** • **glyco**lytic enzyme[15] /genosis[7] • **glyco**lipid /protein /peptide /side /suria

Glykogen
Glukose[1] Hyperglykämie, erhöhter Blutzuckerspiegel[2] Zittern[3] Krampfanfälle[4] Leberglykogen[5] Glykogenabbau, Glykogenolyse[6] Glykogenspeicherkrankheit, Glykogenose[7] Glykogenphosphorylase[8] erhöhter Nüchternblutzucker[9] morgendl. Erhöhung d. Blutzuckerspiegels[10] Hungerhypoglykämie[11] artifizielle Hpoglykämie[12] ausgeprägte Hypoglykämie[13] postprandiale Hypoglykämie[14] glykolyt. Enzym[15]
13

glycolysis [glaɪkɒːlɪsɪs] *n term*　　*rel* **proteolysis**[1] [ɒː], **glycogenolysis**[2] *n term*
　　　　　　　　　　　　　　　opposite **glycogenesis**[3] [-dʒenəsɪs] *n term*

conversion of glucose to lactic acid (instead of pyruvate [paɪ-] oxidation products) in various tissues (esp. muscle) when sufficient oxygen is not available resulting in energy stored in the form of ATP

glycolytic [ɪ] *adj term* • **proteolytic** *adj* • **-lysis** *comb* • **-genesis** *comb*

» The liver functions to maintain normal levels of blood sugar by a combination of glycogenesis, glycogenolysis, glycolysis, and gluconeogenesis[4]. Insulin decreases glycogenolysis, lipolysis, proteolysis, gluconeogenesis, ureagenesis, and ketogenesis. Some of these glycolytic enzyme deficiencies are localized to the red cells.

Use to stimulate/enhance[5]/inhibit/block **glycolysis** • (an)aerobic[6] / increased[7] / terminal **glycolysis** • muscle / hormone / limited[8] **proteolysis** • **glycolytic** pathway[9] / phosphorylation / enzyme[10] (defect) • **proteolytic** enzyme / activity / degradation • keto[11]/ rhabdomyo/ ureo[12]/ thromb**olysis** • lipo/ gluconeo[4]/ steroido**genesis**

Glykolyse
Proteolyse, Eiweißabbau[1] Glykogenolyse[2] Glykogensynthese, Glykogenese[3] Glukoneogenese[4] d. Glykolyse verstärken[5] (an)aerobe Glykolyse[6] verstärkte/ vermehrte Glykolyse[7] limitierte Proteolyse[8] Emden-Meyerhof(-Parnas-Stoffwechsel)weg[9] glykolytisches Enzym[10] Ketolyse, Ketonkörperverwertung, -abbau[11] Harnstoffspaltung, Ureolyse[12]

14

creatine [kriːətiːn] *n term*
　　　　　　rel **adenosine triphosphate**[1] *n term, abbr* **ATP**

occurs [ɜː] in muscle, (usually as phosphocreatine[2]) and in urine (usually as creatinine)

creatinine[3] [krɪætɪniːn] *n term* • **creatinemia** [iː] *n* • **creatinuria** *n*

» The high-energy phosphate stores in ATP are in equilibrium with those in the form of creatine phosphate. Creative phosphokinase splits creatine phosphate in the presence of ADP to yield creatine and ATP.

Use muscle / dehydrated[3] [aɪ]/ urinary **creatine** • **adenosine** diphosphate [aɪ] (ADP) • **creatine** phosphokinase[4] [aɪ] (*abbr* CPK)/ kinase[4] (*abbr* CK) • **creatine** phosphate[2] / clearance[5] [ɪɚ] • muscle / intracellular / exogenous **ATP** • breakdown[6] / availability / analogue **of ATP** • **ATP** synthesis / degradation[6] / molecule • **ATP**-dependent solute transport[7] • **ATP**-sensitive potassium channel[8] [tʃ] • **ATP**-induced contraction / depletion[9] [iːʃ]

Kreatin
Adenosintriphosphat, ATP[1] Kreatinphosphat[2] Kreatinin[3] Kreatin(phospho)kinase[4] Kreatin-Clearance[5] ATP-Abbau[6] ATP-abhängiger Transport gelöster Stoffe[7] ATP-abhängiger Kaliumkanal[8] ATP-Speicherentleerung, -Mangel[9]

15

cholesterol [kəlestərɒːl] *n term* → U47-12
　　　　　　rel **cortisol**[1] [kɔːrtɪsɒːl] *n term* → U55-10

abundant [ʌ] fat-like steroid [ɪɚ] normally synthesized in the liver which is essential for the production of steroid hormones (e.g. the catabolic steroid cortisol), bile acids[2], vitamin D, etc.

» High levels of cholesterol in the blood stream are a marker for heart disease. Cholesterol circulates in the plasma complexed to proteins of various densities and is a key factor in the pathogenesis of atheromatous plaques[3] [plæks]. Apo AI also activates the enzyme lecithin cholesterol acyltransferase (*abbr* LCAT), which esterifies free cholesterol in plasma.

Use serum / plasma / free / dietary [aɪ] **cholesterol** • high-density lipoprotein[4] (*abbr* HDL)/ LDL-**cholesterol**[5] • dihydro**cholesterol**[6] • **cholesterol** esterase[7] / ester / (micro)crystals[8] [ɪ] • **cholesterol** (gall)stones[9] [ɔː]/ saturation /-lowering drugs[10] • **cholesterol** synthesis / transport / intake[11] • **cholesterol** level or concentration[12] / content

Cholesterin, Cholesterol
Cortisol, Hydrokortison[1] Gallensäuren[2] atheromatöse Plaques, arteriosklerotische Beete[3] HDL-Cholesterin[4] LDL-Cholesterin[5] Dihydrocholesterin, Cholestanol[6] Cholesterinesterase, Cholesterase[7] Cholesterinkristalle[8] Cholesterinsteine[9] cholesterinsenkende Medikamente[10] Cholesterinzufuhr[11] Cholesterinspiegel[12]

16

carrier [kæriɚ] **system** *or* **mechanism** *n term*　　*sim* **transport system**[1] *n term*

mechanism [k] involving carrier substances[2] [ʌ] that bind to and transport specific compounds in the blood or across cell membranes

carrier *n term* • **transport** *v & n* • **transporter** *n* • **carrier-mediated**[3] [iː] *adj*

» The carrier mechanism accepts for transport only those substrates having a relatively specific molecular configuration, and the process is limited by the availability of carrier. Hib[4] vaccines [æks] in which PRP is conjugated to protein carrier molecules have been developed.

Use **carrier** protein[5] • plasma / electron / isotope [aɪ] **carrier** • **carrier-mediated** diffusion process / (cellular) uptake • active[6] / passive[7] / amino acid[8] / glucose **transport** • iron [aɪɚn]/ sodium[9] / electrolyte [-laɪt]/ ion [aɪən]/ oxygen [-dʒən] **transport** • intracellular / membrane[10] / epithelial [iː]/ tubular[11] / intestinal **transport** • **transport** medium[12] [iː]/ process / maximum[13] / proteins[14] • biochemical / humoral [hjuː]/ vasoactive [veɪzoʊ-] **mediator** • mast cell / potent [oʊ]/ inflammatory[15] **mediator** • insulin-/ IgE-/ receptor- / cell[16]-**mediated** • glucose[17] / amino acid / glutamate [uː] **transporter**

Carrier-, Stofftransport
Transportsystem[1] Carrier, Träger-(substanzen)[2] träger-, carriervermittelt[3] Haemophilus influenzae Typ b (Hib)[4] Träger-, Carrierprotein[5] aktiver Transport[6] passiver T.[7] Aminosäuretransport[8] Natriumtransport[9] Membrantransport[10] tubulärer Transport[11] Transportmedium[12] Transportmaximum[13] Transportproteine[14] Entzündungsmediator[15] zellvermittelt[16] Glukosetransporter[17]

17

Metabolism   COMPLEX BODY FUNCTIONS 323

albumin [ælbjə‖uːmɪn] *n term & comb*   *rel* **globulin**[1] [ɒː] *n term & comb*

water-soluble heat-coagulable protein produced in the liver that is the most abundant transport protein in the plasma where it contributes significantly to the colloidal osmotic pressure[2]
albuminated [juː] *adj term* • **albuminoid**[3] *adj*
» His serum albumin is low, while gamma globulin is increased. In the portal venous [iː] system, fatty acids derived [aɪ] from medium-chain [iː] triglycerides[4] [aɪ] are transported bound [aʊ] to albumin.
Use **albumin** A • (human) serum or plasma[5] / bovine[6] / heme [hiːm]/ salt-poor **albumin** • **albumin** production or synthesis / level /-binding [aɪ] site • **albumin**-bound complex / content • **albumin**-globulin (*abbr* A/G) ratio[7] [reɪʃ(ɪ)oʊ]• **albumin** catabolism / excretion[8] [iːʃ]/ infusion • **albumin**uria[9] / pre**albumin**[10] • **globulin** fraction[11] / synthesis • alpha-1 / beta-2 / gamma[12] **globulin** • immune[13] / antihemophilic[14] (*abbr* AHG) **globulin** • antilymphocyte [ɪ] (*abbr* ALG)/ cortisol-binding (*abbr* CBG) **globulin** • thyroxine-binding[15] [aɪ] (*abbr* TBG) **globulin** • immuno[13]/ anti/ antithyro[16]/ macro/ cryo[17]/ micro**globulin** • macro/ hyper/ cryo/ agamma**globulinemia**

Albumin
Globulin[1] kolloidosmotischer/ onkotischer Druck[2] eiweiß-, albuminähnlich[3] mittelkettige Triglyzeride[4] Serum-, Plasmaalbumin[5] Rinderalbumin[6] Albumin/Globulin-Quotient, Eiweißquotient[7] Albuminausscheidung[8] Albuminurie, Proteinurie[9] Präalbumin[10] Globulinfraktion[11] Gammaglobulin[12] Immunglobulin[13] antihämophiles Globulin[14] thyroxinbindendes Globulin[15] Thyreoglobulin[16] Kryoglobulin[17]

18

scavenge [skævəndʒ] *v term*   *rel* **(free-radical) scavenger**[1] *n term* → U39-17

(i) to cause a chemical reaction by readily [e] binding to free radicals[2]
(ii) to absorb small particles and/or destroy bacteria [ɪɚ] by phagocytosis [fægəsaɪtoʊsɪs]
» These proteins bind siderophores[3] that scavenge iron for transport into the bacterial cell. Adenosylcobalamin (*abbr* AdoCb) serves [ɜː] as a scavenger system for catabolism of precursors of propionate.
Use **scavenging** mechanism / process • **scavenger** cell[4] / function / activity / receptor • monocyte-macrophage [-feɪdʒ] **scavenger** system[5]

(i) abräumen, (ab)fangen, (ab)binden
(ii) phagozytieren
Radikalfänger, Scavenger[1] freie Radikale[2] eisenbindende Substanzen, Siderophore(n)[3] Scavenger-Zelle, Abbauzelle[4] Monozyten-Makrophagen-System[5]

19

store [stɔːr] *v & n*   *sim* **pool**[1] [puːl] *v & n*, **reservoir**[2], **depot**[2] [de-‖diːpoʊ] *n*
    rel **deposit**[3], **accumulate**[4] [əkjuːmjəleɪt] *v*

(n) depot of substances [ʌ] kept as a reserve [ɜː] for future use, e.g. glycogen in the liver
storage *n* • **pooling**[5] *n term* • **accumulation** *n* • **deposit**[6] *n* • **deposition**[6] *n*
» Fat cells also serve as a reservoir for storage of fatty acids released during the clearance of chylomicrons [kaɪloʊ-] and can release these stored fatty acids by the intracellular hormone-sensitive lipase. Phenytoin [ɪ] is cleared from body storage depots quite slowly. Aside from circulating red blood cells, the major location of iron in the body is the storage pool.
Use (total) body-fat[7] / adipose / (hepatic/ marrow) iron[8] **stores** • (bone) alkaline / potassium[9] **stores** • energy / carbohydrate / protein / vitamin / (extra)cellular / tissue / liver / brain **stores** • **to store** fat / urine • **store** depletion • **stored** fat / vitamin A • adipose or fat[10] / storage **depot** • **depot** injection [dʒe]/ insulin / preparation[11] • bile [aɪ] salt / circulating [ɜː] / calcium [s]/ total body / lymphocyte[12] [ɪ] **pool** • glycogen / iron / lipid or fat[13] **storage** • urine / bladder / hepatocyte **storage** • **storage** site / iron[14] / capacity[15] [æs]/ pool / protein • **storage** defect / function[16] / failure [eɪ] • **storage** disease[17] / temperature / fat(ty) / fluid[18] / glycolipid **accumulation** • intracellular calcium / drug **accumulation** • progressive / slow / rapid **accumulation**

speichern; Speicher
(sich) ansammeln, poolen; Ansammlung, Pool[1] Speicher, Reservoir[2] ablagern[3] (sich) ansammeln, anhäufen, akkumulieren[4] Pooling, Ansammlung[5] Ablagerung[6] Körperfettdepots[7] Eisenspeicher[8] Kaliumspeicher[9] Fettdepot[10] Depotpräparat[11] Lymphozytenpool[12] Fett-, Lipidspeicherung[13] Speichereisen[14] Speicherkapazität[15] Speicherfunktion[16] Speicherkrankheit[17] Flüssigkeitsansammlung[18]

20

depletion [dɪpliːʃ³n] *n term*   *rel* **deficit**[1], **deficiency**[1],
    replenishment[2] *n term* → U49-8

excessive loss of (essential) body constituents [ɪtʃ], e.g., salt, water, etc.
deplete *v term* • **depleted** *adj* • **deficient**[3] [dɪfɪʃ³nt] *adj* • **replenish** [rɪplenɪʃ] *v*
» Net distal K+ secretion [iːʃ] or reabsorption occurs [ɜː] in the setting of K+ excess or depletion. Significant chronic blood loss from any cause will deplete iron stores and exceed [iː] the capacity [æs] to absorb iron from the diet. In nonrenal [iː] losses of water, total body sodium deficits may also be present despite the hypernatremia [iː].
Use water / electrolyte[4] / K+ / (potassium) chloride / (skeletal) calcium **depletion** • salt[5] / protein / extracellular volume / ATP **depletion** • total body Na / lymphocyte[6] [-saɪt]/ immune-cell **depletion** • iron-/ sodium-/ fluid[7] / nutritionally [ɪʃ] **depleted** • (acid-)base / electrolyte / neurologic[8] / hearing[9] [ɪɚ] **deficit** • nutritional[10] / trace [eɪ] metal[11] / immune[12] / vitamin A **deficiency** • iron / ion / lactase / selenium[13] [iː]/ folic [oʊ] acid[14] **deficiency**

Entleerung, Verminderung, Verlust, Depletion
Mangel, Defizit[1] Auffüllung, Ergänzung[2] mangelhaft; -arm[3] Elektrolytverlust[4] Salzverlust[5] Lympho(zyto)penie[6] dehydriert, ausgetrocknet[7] neurolog. Ausfälle[8] Schwerhörigkeit[9] Mangelernährung, Nährstoffmangel[10] Mangel an metallischen Spurenelementen[11] Immundefekt, -defizienz[12] Selenmangel[13] Folsäuremangel[14]

21

78

dehydration [dɪhaɪdreɪʃ°n] *n term* → U56-12
　rel **fluid balance**[1] *n term* → U88-19f
　loss of body fluid by sweating [e], diarrhea [iː], excessive urine output, inadequate fluid intake (**de**[2]/ **over**[3]/ **re**/ **well-**)**hydrated** *adj term* • **dehydrating** *adj* • **imbalance** *n*
» The rate at which the deficit is replaced depends on the severity [e] of dehydration. Fluid balance should be maintained [eɪ] but overhydration[4] avoided. Check the infant for signs of dehydration before instituting rehydration therapy.
Use cellular / red cell / cerebral / isotonic[5] / hypotonic[6] [aɪ] **dehydration** • hypertonic[7] / hypernatremic [iː]/ profound [aʊ] **dehydration** • to become/appear/ be (severely) **dehydrated** • **dehydrated** patient • parenteral / IV / oral / good / inadequate / excessive[4] **hydration** • **hydration** status [eɪ∥æ] • **dehydrating** enteritis [aɪ]/ agent[8] [eɪdʒ] • **oral rehydration** therapy[9] (*abbr* ORT)/ solution[10] (*abbr* ORS) • acid-base[11] **balance** • to maintain **fluid balance** • **fluid** replacement[12] / overload[4]

electrolyte [ɪlektrəlaɪt] *n term*　*rel* **ion**[1] [aɪən] *n term* → U81-11
　ionizable[2] [aɪənaɪz-] acid, base [eɪ] or salt [ɔː] which–in solution–conducts [ʌ] electricity and is decomposed (electrolyzed) by it
　electrolytic [ɪ] *adj term* • **electrolyze**[3] *v* • **electrolysis**[4] [ɒː] *n* • (**non**)**ionic**[5] *adj*
» Disordered electrolyte concentrations are often mistaken for primary [aɪ] neurologic [n(j)ʊəə-] or metabolic abnormalities. Magnesium [iː], calcium, and sodium may share some of the same carriers, since if there is an excess of one, others tend to be excreted [iː], i.e. the common pump [ʌ] is saturated by the ion in excess.
Use plasma / serum [ɪə]/ urinary or urine / sweat [e] **electrolytes** • **electrolyte**(-containing) solution[6] [uːʃ]/ composition[7] • **electrolyte** determination[8] / deficit or deficiency[9] • **electrolyte** loss[10] / (im)balance[11] / derangement[12] [eɪ] • **electrolyte** accumulation / abnormality / therapy[13] • urea & (*abbr* U & E) **electrolytes** • **fluid and electrolyte** imbalance / replacement • hydrogen[14] [aɪ] / mineral / metal / ammonium / (chloride) [aɪ] bicarbonate **ion** • **ion** exchange (resins)[15] / channel [tʃ] • **ion** trapping[16] / transport / flux[17] [ʌ] • **ionic** diffusion [juːʒ]/ pump[18] / gradient [eɪ]/ strength[19] / environment

prostaglandin *n term, abbr* **PG**　*rel* **histamine**[1], **catecholamine**[2] [koʊ] *n term*
　any of a group of long-chain hydroxy [haɪdrɒːksi] fatty acids which are physiologically active in vasodilation [veɪzoʊ-] and constriction, platelet [eɪ] aggregation[3], lipid metabolism, etc.
　histaminergic [-ɜːrdʒɪk] *adj term* • **histidine** [hɪstədiːn] *n*
» Prostaglandins are prostanoic acids[4] with ortho side-chains of varying degrees of unsaturation[5] and oxidation. Thromboxane[6] is a potent prostaglandin vasoconstrictor.
Use **prostaglandin** A / B / E1 (PGE1)/ I / (bio)synthesis[7] / metabolism • **prostaglandin** release[8] [iː]/ antagonist[9] / synthetase inhibitor[10] / analogue [ænəlɒːg] • vasoconstricting / renal [iː]/ gastric / mucosal / rectal / endogenous [ɒːdʒ] **prostaglandins**

Unit 79　Nutrition
Related Units: **2** Diet & Dieting, **3** Food & Drink, **27** Mastication, **46** Digestion, **78** Metabolism

nourish [nɜːrɪʃ] *v*　*sim* **nurture**[1] [nɜːrtʃər] *v* & *n*, **feed**[2] [iː] *v irr* & *n* → U2-3
　to provide babies or the seriously [ɪə] ill with food or supply body tissues with nourishing substances [ʌ]
　nourishment[3] *n* • **nourishing**[4] *adj* • **mal**/ **overnourishment**[5] *n term*
» Make sure the children are well-nourished[6]. The child's behavior may need to be modified in order for the parent to be able to appropriately nourish and nurture the baby. Evaluate the patient's state of health, nourishment and physical development. Persistent sepsis and difficulty in nourishing the patient contributed to rapid weight [weɪt] loss.
Use well / poorly[7] / (in)adequately / fully **nourished** • poorly / mal-/ well-**nourished**, *abbr* W/N patient • **nourishing** oral supplement • **to feed** a baby[8] • **to breast**[9]- [e] /bottle-/cup-**feed** • oral / IV or drip[10] / enteral **feeding** • **feeding** difficulties

---

Entwässerung, Wasserentzug, Dehydratation
Flüssigkeitshaushalt[1] dehydriert[2] hyperhydriert, überwässert[3] Hyperhydratation, Überwässerung[4] isotone Dehydratation[5] hypotone D.[6] hypertone D.[7] Entwässerungsmittel[8] orale Rehydratationstherapie[9] Rehydratationslösung[10] Säure-Basen-Gleichgewicht[11] Flüssigkeitsersatz, -substitution[12]

Elektrolyt
Ion[1] ionisierbar[2] mittels Elektrolyse trennen, elektrolysieren[3] Elektrolyse[4] ionisch, Ionen-[5] Elektrolytlösung[6] Elektrolytzusammensetzung[7] Elektrolytbestimmung[8] Elektrolytmangel[9] Elektrolytverlust[10] Elektrolytgleichgewicht[11] Elektrolytentgleisung, Störung d. Elektrolythaushalts[12] Elektrolyttherapie[13] Wasserstoffion[14] Ionenaustauscher(harze), Resine[15] Ionentrapping, Einfangen v. Ionen[16] Ionenfluss, -wanderung[17] Ionenpumpe[18] Ionenstärke[19]

Prostaglandin
Histamin[1] Katecholamin[2] Thrombozytenaggregation[3] Prostansäuren[4] ungesättigte Bindungen[5] Thromboxan[6] Prostaglandin(bio)synthese[7] Prostaglandinfreisetzung[8] Prostaglandinantagonist[9] Prostaglandinsynthetase-Hemmer[10]

(er)nähren
aufziehen, pflegen; Pflege, Erziehung[1] füttern, ernähren, stillen; Futter, Stillen, Fütterung[2] Nahrung[3] nahrhaft[4] Unter-, Überernährung[5] gut ernährt[6] unterernährt[7] ein Kind füttern/stillen[8] stillen[9] parenterale/ künstl. Ernährung[10]

Nutrition COMPLEX BODY FUNCTIONS 325

nutrient [nuːtriᵊnt] n & adj   sim **nutriment**¹ n

(n) substance in food that can be metabolized by the organism to give energy and build tissue
(adj) nourishing

nutritive² adj • **nutritious**³ [ɪʃ] adj • **macronutrient** n term

» Nutritional requirements and tolerances can be altered [ɔː] by increased utilization of nutrients, hyper- and malabsorption, impaired metabolism of nutrients, and nutrient wastage⁴.

Use **nutrient** intake⁵ / uptake⁶ [ʌ]/ requirements [kwaɪɚ]/ content⁷ / delivery / processing / vessels⁸ / solution⁹ / broth¹⁰ • adequate / ingested¹¹ [dʒ]/ essential **nutrients** • **nutritive** value¹² / ratio [eɪʃ] • drug-**nutrient** interaction • **nutritious** diet [aɪə]/ snacks¹³

Nährstoff; nahrhaft
Nahrung(smittel), Nährstoff¹ Nähr-, Ernährungs-² nahrhaft³ Nährstoffverlust⁴ Nährstoffzufuhr⁵ Nährstoffaufnahme, -resorption⁶ Nährstoffgehalt⁷ ernährende Gefäße⁸ Nährlösung⁹ Nährbouillon¹⁰ zugeführte Nährstoff¹¹ Nährwert¹² nahrhafte Zwischenmahlzeiten¹³

2

nutrition [nuːtrɪʃᵊn] n   syn **alimentation** n term

(i) process of food uptake and metabolism
(ii) study of human food and liquid requirements

malnutrition¹ n term • **nutritional**² adj • **alimentary**³ adj • **nutritionist**⁴ n

» Dietary intake and nutritional status were poor. Diet counseling⁵ [aʊ] can help improve nutrition. He's a professor of nutrition at Yale.

Use adequate / infant⁶ / total parenteral⁷ (abbr TPN) **nutrition** • **nutritional** needs / disorder or disturbance⁸ [ɜː]/ assessment⁹/status • **nutritional** therapy / support¹⁰ / deficiency [ɪʃ]/ habits¹¹ • mild [aɪ] degree of / severe [ɪɚ]/ chronic / energy protein¹² **malnutrition** • **nutritionally** balanced diet • artificial¹⁰ [ʃɪʃ]/ forced¹³ **alimentation** • **alimentary** tract or canal¹⁴

Ernährung(slehre)
Mangel-, Fehlernährung¹ Ernährungs-, nahrhaft² alimentär, Nahrungs-, Verdauungs-³ Ernährungswissenschaft(l)er(in)⁴ Ernährungsberatung⁵ Säuglingsernährung⁶ (totale) parenterale E.⁷ Ernährungsstörung⁸ Erhebung d. Ernährungszustandes⁹ künstliche E.¹⁰ Ernährungsgewohnheiten¹¹ Protein-Energie-Mangelsyndrom¹² Zwangsernährung¹³ Verdauungstrakt¹⁴

3

joule [dʒuːl] n, abbr **J**   sim **calorie**¹ [kæləri] n, abbr **cal**

unit of heat or energy content; for referring to food kcal has been replaced by J (4.187 J equals 1 cal).

(non)caloric² adj • **calorific**³ adj • **calorimeter** n

» Excess [ɪksəs] calories⁴ are stored in the body as fat. Every effort should be made to provide sufficient [ɪʃ] amounts of carbohydrate [aɪ] and calories.

Use to burn⁵/count **calories** • empty / large or kilo**calories** • **calorie**-conscious⁶ [ʃ] / content • **caloric** intake / expenditure⁷ [-tʃɚ]/ restriction / requirement⁸ / deficiency • high / low⁹-**calorie diet** • **caloric** excess / deficit / recommendation¹⁰ / value¹¹

Joule
Kalorie¹ kalorisch, Kalorien-² wärmeerzeugend³ überschüssige Kalorien⁴ K. verbrauchen/ -brennen⁵ kalorienbewusst⁶ Kalorienverbrauch⁷ Kalorienbedarf⁸ kalorienarme Kost⁹ empfohlene Kalorienzufuhr¹⁰ Brennwert, kalorischer Wert¹¹

4

carbohydrates [aɪ] n term   syn **carbs** n jar, rel **starch**¹ [stɑːrtʃ] n clin

main ingredients² [iː] in many foods including sugar compounds³, starches, glycogen [glaɪkədʒᵊn], and cellulose polysaccharides; starch is built up of glucose residues⁴ and converted⁵ into dextrin, glucose, and maltose

starchy⁶ adj clin • **carbohydrate-rich** adj term

» Much of the carbohydrate we ingest is in the form of starch. A diet with excessive nonprotein calories from starch or sugar but deficient in total protein and essential amino acids eventually results in protein-energy malnutrition. Carbohydrate-rich meals are advisable [aɪz].

Use **carbohydrate** (mal)absorption / metabolism / oxidation / stores⁷ • rich in / simple / complex / easily digestible⁸ [daɪdʒ-] **carbohydrates** • to hydrolyze⁹ [aɪ]/ soluble / corn¹⁰ / potato **starch** • **starch** solutions / sugar¹¹ / intolerance • **starchy** food / vegetables

Kohlenhydrate (KH)
Stärke¹ Bestandteile² Zuckerverbindungen³ Glukosereste⁴ aufgespalten⁵ stärkehaltig⁶ KH-Depots⁷ leicht verdauliche KH⁸ Stärke abbauen/ spalten⁹ Maisstärke¹⁰ Stärkezucker¹¹

5

saccharides [sækəraɪdz‖ɪdz] n term pl   syn **sugars** [ʃʊgɚz] n

saccharides are classified as mono-, di- [daɪ], tri- [traɪ], and polysaccharides according to the number of monosaccharide groups they are composed of

saccharin(e)¹ n & adj • **saccharo-** comb • **secchariferous**² adj term

» Nonabsorbable saccharides (e.g. sorbitol) help promote the evacuation of stools³. The nonnutritive sweetener saccharin is considered safe for consumption [ʌ] by all people with diabetes [daɪəbiːtɪz].

Use (un)split di⁴/ lipopoly/ mucopoly**saccharides** • **high-sugar** dessert⁵ • **sugar-containing** beverages⁶ • fasting blood⁷ (abbr FBS) / milk⁸ / fruit sugar • simple / complex / triple⁹ [ɪ]/ starch **sugars** • **sugar-free** gum

Saccharide, Zucker
Saccharin, Süßstoff; Zucker-¹ zuckerhaltig² Stuhlgang fördern³ (un)aufgespaltene Disaccharide⁴ stark gesüßte Nachspeise⁵ zuckerhaltige Getränke⁶ Nüchternblutzucker⁷ Milchzucker, Laktose⁸ Dreifachzucker⁹

6

Nutrition

glucose [gluːkoʊs] *n term*   *syn* **dextrose** *n term* → U78-13

simple sugar found in certain foods; fructose and other monosaccharides are converted into glucose which is the chief source of energy for the body; its metabolism[1] is controlled by insulin; excess glucose is stored in the form of glycogen[2] [glaɪkədʒ³n] or converted into fat

gluco- *comb* • **gluconate**[3] [eɪ] *n term* • **glucosamine**[4] [iː] *n*

» Unlike other organs, the brain relies mainly on[5] glucose to supply its energy requirements.

Use liquid **glucose** • **glucose** load[6] / threshold[7] [θreʃoʊld]/ tolerance factor (*abbr* GTF) • **glucose** tolerance test / administration[8] / feeding / metabolism • blood / CSF[9] / urine / postprandial[10] / fasting plasma[11] **glucose level** • **glucose**-nitrogen [aɪ] ratio/ assimilation / carrier[12] • **gluco**kinase [kaɪneɪz]/genesis [dʒen]/corticoid • suria[13]

Glukose, Traubenzucker, Dextrose
Stoffwechsel, Metabolismus[1] Glykogen[2] Glukonat[3] Glukosamin[4] abhängig sein von[5] Glukosebelastung[6] Glukoseschwelle[7] Glukosegabe[8] Liquorzucker(spiegel)[9] Glukosespiegel nach Nahrungszufuhr[10] Nüchternblutzucker[11] Glukosetransporter[12] Glukosurie[13]

7

lactose [læktoʊs] *n term*   *syn* **milk sugar** *n clin*, **lactin** *n term rare*

disaccharide in mammalian [eɪ] milk[1] used in modified milk preparations and food for infants

lacto-[2] *comb* • **lactosuria**[3] *n term* • **lactose-free /-containing** *adj*

» The drug reduces the rate of absorption of most carbohydrates such as starches, dextrins, maltose, and sucrose (but not lactose). Hereditary lactase deficiency[4] [fɪʃ] causes lactose intolerance.

Use (non)metabolized / (un)hydrolized[5] [aɪ] **lactose** • **lactic** acid[6] • **lactose** content / ingestion / assay [æseɪ] *or* tolerance test[7] / intolerance[8] / (mal)absorption • **lacto**ferrin /genic /vegetarian

Laktose, Milchzucker
Säugetiermilch[1] lakto-, Milch-[2] Laktoseausscheidung i. Harn, Laktosurie[3] angeborener/ kongenitaler Laktasemangel[4] aufgespaltene Laktose[5] Milchsäure[6] Laktosebelastung[7] Laktoseintoleranz[8]

8

protein [proʊtiːn] *n*

compounds of one or more polypeptides [aɪ] involved in many essential body structures and functions (hormones, enzymes [zaɪ], muscle contraction, blood clotting[1] immunological response)

proteo- *comb* • **proteinuria**[2] *n term* • **proteolytic**[3] [ɪ] *adj*

» Reduction in physical activity results in a decrease in both energy and protein requirements.

Use **protein** balance[4] / concentration / deficiency / biosynthesis [sɪn] efficiency ratio • structural[5] / soy [sɔɪ]/ whey[6] [weɪ]/ egg **protein** • basic / foreign[7] [ɒː]/ native [eɪ] *or* natural[8] / C-reactive (*abbr* CRP) **protein** • **protein**-bound iodine[9] [aɪədɪn] (*abbr* PBI) / binding / denaturation[10] / kinase [aɪ] • **proteolytic** enzyme[11] • **proteo**glycans[12] [aɪ]/lysis

Protein, Eiweiß
Blutgerinnung[1] Proteinurie[2] eiweißabbauend, proteolytisch[3] Proteinbilanz, -haushalt[4] Strukturprotein, Gerüsteiweiß[5] Molkeeiweiß[6] Fremdprotein[7] natives P.[8] proteingebundenes Iod[9] Proteindenaturierung[10] Protease, proteolytisches Enzym[11] Proteoglykane[12]

9

amino acids [æmiːnoʊ æsɪdz] *n*   *abbr* **AA**, *syn* **aminos** *n jar*

nitrogen-bearing[1] [naɪtrədʒ³n] organic acids absorbed via the gut[2] [ʌ] that are the building blocks of the body's own protein

aminoacidemia[3] [iː] *n term* • **aminoaciduria**[4] *n*

» The 9 essential amino acids (among them leucine [luːsiːn], tyrosine [aɪ], valine [eɪ‖æ], threonine [iː], lysine [aɪ]) cannot be produced by the body and must be absorbed from the diet.

Use (non)essential[5] (*abbr* EAA and NEAA) / basic[6] [eɪ]/ acidic [sɪ]/ **amino acid** • neutral [uː]/ aromatic / branched chain[7] (*abbr* BCAA) / BCAA-enriched **amino acid** • **amino acid** metabolism / content / composition / solution[8] / infusion / imbalance

Aminosäuren
stickstoffhaltig[1] Darm[2] Aminoazidämie[3] Aminoazidurie[4] (nicht) essentielle Aminosäure[5] basische A.[6] verzweigtkettige A.[7] Aminosäurelösung[8]

10

fat [fæt] *n & adj*   *syn* **lipid** [lɪpɪd] *n & comb term*

n (i) the triglycerides [traɪglɪs-] in greasy [iː], oily and waxy substances that are insoluble[1] in water (ii) adipose or fatty body tissue
adj (i) containing or composed of fat (ii) impolite expression for being big, overweight or obese[2] [iː]

fatty[3] *adj clin* • **lip(o)-** *comb* • **lipoid**[4] *adj term*

» You should reduce the amount of fat in your diet. Try vegetable fats[5] such as palm [pɑːm] oil instead of butter, meat or cheese. Polyunsaturated fat is a triglyceride composed of fatty acids that contain 2–4 double bonds[6].

Use **fat** absorption /-free / deposits[7] / pad[8] / exchange / embolism • saturated [sætʃə-]/ (mono/poly)unsaturated[9] **fatty acids** • long-/medium-chain[10] / free / triglyceride **fatty acids** • **fatty** meal / foods / tissue[11] / stool[12] / brown[13] / depot **fat** • simple / compound[14] **lipid** • **lipo**protein /tropic • **lipid**emia [iː]/osis

Fett, Lipid; fett(haltig), fettsüchtig, -leibig
unlöslich[1] fettleibig[2] fetthaltig, Fett-[3] fettartig, lipoid[4] pflanzliche Fette[5] Doppelbindungen[6] Fetteinlagerungen[7] Fettpolster[8] mehrfach ungesättigte Fettsäuren[9] mittelkettige F.[10] Fettgewebe[11] Fettstuhl, Steatorrhoe[12] braunes F.[13] komplexes Lipid[14]

11

Nutrition COMPLEX BODY FUNCTIONS **327**

essential [ɪsenˈʃəl] **fatty acid** [æsɪd] *n term*   *abbr* **EFA**

EFAs cannot be synthesized [sɪnθəsaɪzd] by the body and must be supplied in the diet; they include linoleic [lɪnəliːɪk] acid[1], omega-3 fatty acids[2], and monounsaturated fats[3]

» *Deficiencies in EFAs can develop quickly in the infant of very low birth weight* [weɪt], *who has little body stores of essential fatty acids at the time of birth.*

essentielle Fettsäure
Linolsäure[1] Omega-3-Fettsäuren[2] einfach ungesättigte Fette[3]

12

vitamin [aɪ‖ɪ] *n*   *sim* **multivitamin**[1], **provitamin**[2] *n*

organic substances present in small amounts in natural foodstuffs; essential to normal metabolism; insufficient amounts in the diet can cause deficiency diseases[3]

» *Disorders of vitamin excess*[4] *may now be more common than vitamin deficiency*[5]. *Retinol (vitamin A) is important for healthy skin, teeth and bones. The vitamin B complex includes thiamin* [θaɪəmɪn] *(B-1), riboflavin* [raɪbouˈfleɪvɪn] *(B-2), and pyridoxine* [pɪrˈdɒksɪn] *(B-6).*

Use **vitamin** preparations[4] / level / B-12 deficiency / supplement[5] / absorption • fat soluble / water soluble[8] / high potency **vitamin** • excess intake / synthetic analogues[6] **of vitamins** • **vitamin** A precursor[9] [ɜː]/ derivative[10] / toxicity

Vitamin
Multivitamin[1] Provitamin[2] Mangelkrankheiten[3] Hypervitaminosen[4] Vitaminmangel[5] Vitaminpräparate[6] Vitaminzusatz, -anreicherung[5] wasserlösliches V.[8] Provitamin A[9] Vitaminderivat[10]

13

folic acid [foʊlɪk æsɪd] *n term*   *syn* **folacin** [foʊləsɪn] *n term*
   sim **folate**[1] [foʊleɪt] *n term*

a member of the vitamin B complex necessary for the production of red blood cells and in pregnancy

» *Folic acid can also be produced synthetically. Vitamins A, B6, B1 and B3 as well as folate (folacin or folic acid) may be deficient in apparently* [eə] *well-nourished alcoholics.*

Use **folic acid** deficiency anemia[2] [iː]/ supplementation[3] / antagonist / synthesis inhibitor[4]

Folsäure
Folat, Folsäuresalz[1] Folsäuremangelanämie[2] Folsäuresupplementierung[3] Folsäuresynthesehemmer[4]

14

ascorbic [əskɔːrbɪk] **acid** *n term*   *syn* **vitamin C** *n clin*

a water-soluble antioxidant[1] and detoxifier[2] which must be supplemented[3] [ʌ] regularly as it cannot be stored

» *Vitamin C functions primarily in the formation of collagen* [kɒlədʒən], *the body's chief protein substance and aids in*[4] *the absorption of iron.*

Use L-**ascorbic acid** deficiency / level • **vitamin C**-deficient patients • to replenish[5] / total-body pool of[6] / long-term use of[7] **vitamin C**

Ascorbinsäure, Vitamin C
Antioxidans[1] Entgiftungsmittel[2] ergänzt, zugeführt[3] fördert[4] Vit. C ergänzen[5] Vitamin C-Gesamtmenge i. Körper[6] Vitamin C-Langzeittherapie[7]

15

(dietary) fiber [daɪətəri faɪbə·] *n sing, BE* **fibre**   *syn* **roughage** [rʌfɪdʒ] *n espBE,*
   sim **bulk**[1] [ʌ] *n clin*

largely indigestible material, e.g. bran[2] [æ], cereals [sɪə·] and vegetable fibers serving as a stimulant of intestinal peristalsis[3]

bulky[4] *adj* • bulkage[5] *n* • bulkiness[6] *n*

» *If you ingest a diet higher in roughage, you will produce more frequent and bulkier stools*[7]. *Pectin is a soluble fiber found in the skins of fruits and vegetables thought to slow digestion and keep food in the stomach longer. Enhanced fiber intake increases fecal* [fiːkəl] *bulk*[8].

Use intake of **dietary fiber** • low / high[9] **roughage diet** • **high-fiber** diet[9] / content / intake • **fiber** supplementation / supplement / dietary[10] / intestinal / muscle[11] [mʌsl] **bulk** • **bulk**-producing agent / forming laxatives[12] • **bulky** food[9] / tumors

Ballaststoffe
Ballaststoffe; Menge, Masse, Volumen[1] Kleie[2] Darmtätigkeit, Peristaltik[3] voluminös, raumfüllend[4] Füllmaterial (Darm)[5] Volumen; Beleibtheit[6] voluminösere Stühle[7] Kotmasse[8] ballaststoffreiche Nahrung[9] Ballaststoffe[10] Muskelmasse[11] Füllmittel, Quellstoffe[12]

16

trace [treɪs] **element** *n term*   *sim* **trace mineral**[1], **trace metal**[2], **micronutrients**[3] [uː] *n term*

inorganic molecules in food (e.g. iron[4] [aɪə·n], iodine[5] [aɪə], copper[6], fluorine[7] [iː‖ɪ], manganese[8] [iː], selenium[9] [iː], zinc[10] [z], silicon[11]) required in minute[12] [maɪnuːt] amounts (less than 1 mg/d) which are essential nutritionally and in metabolism

trace[13] *v* • **traceable**[14] *adj* • **(radio)tracer** *n term*

» *The functions of trace elements and of more abundant*[15] [ʌ] *metals (calcium*[16] [kælsɪəm], *phosphorus, potassium*[17], *sodium*[18] [oʊ], *chloride*[19] [aɪ], *and magnesium* [iː]) *are determined, in part, by their charges*[20] [tʃɑːrdʒɪz], *mobilities, and binding constants to biological ligands*[21] [aɪ].

Use disturbance in / absorption of **trace elements** • **trace** amounts[22] / component / concentration / metal deficiency / impurity[23] [pjʊə·] • to be found in **traces**[24] • to be **traceable** to sth.[25]

Spuren-, Mikroelement
mineralisches Spurenelem.[1] metallisches Sp.[2] essentielle Mikroelemente[3] Eisen[4] Iod[5] Kupfer[6] Fluor[7] Mangan[8] Selen[9] Zink[10] Silizium[11] sehr klein[12] aufspüren[13] nachweis-, auffindbar[14] reichlich vorhanden[15] Kalzium[16] Kalium[17] Natrium[18] Chlorid[19] Ladungen[20] Liganden[21] geringste Mengen[22] minimale Verunreinigung[23] in Spuren (vorkommen)[24] zurückzuführen auf[25] Silikon[26]

Note: Mark the difference between *silicon* and *silicone*[26] and between *manganese* and *magnesium*.

17

Unit 80   Growing Up & Aging

Related Units: 71 Childbirth, 12 Death & Mortality, 69 Fertility, 55 Hormones, 102 History Taking

age [eɪdʒ] n & v   rel **lifetime**[1], **life expectancy**[2] n

(n) number of years sb. has lived (v) to grow older

aged[3] adj • **ag(e)ing**[4] adj & n • **life span**[1] n • **lifelong**[5] adj • **outlive**[6] v

» He is quite tall for his age. Average life expectancy is now 17 years at age 65. Although they may occur at any age, these cysts [sɪsts] are commonest before age 20. The process of aging may be hastened[7] [heɪsᵊnd] by physical and social environmental factors.

Use to live to/reach **an age** • at an early / of the same[8] / to be 5 years of / tender[9] **age** • middle / increasing [iː] / advanced[10] / old[11] / venerable[12] **age** • chronological[13] / mental[14] / developmental[15] **age** • achievement[16] [tʃ]/ bone / childbearing[17] [eə]/ legal [iː] **age** • to look/show/act[18] **one's age** • **age**-related / and sex-dependent • **age** group / 45 - **aged** 29 • **aging** population • people of all[19] **ages** • (activities of) daily / fetal / family **life** • (full) social / early / adult / sexual **life** • **life** event /-style / pattern • **life**-threatening [e]/-saving • time / period / quality[20] **of life** • way / in the prime / quality **of life** • standard of **living**

Alter; älter werden
Lebenszeit, -dauer[1] Lebenserwartung[2] alt, -jährig, betagt[3] alternd; Altern[4] lebenslang[5] überleben[6] beschleunigt[7] gleichaltrig[8] zartes Alter[9] fortgeschrittenes A.[10] hohes A.[11] ehrwürdiges A.[12] chronolog./ kalendarisches A.[13] Intelligenzalter[14] Entwicklungsalter[15] Leistungsalter[16] gebärfähiges Alter[17] (sich) altersgemäß benehmen/ handeln[18] Menschen aller Altersstufen[19] Lebensqualität[20]

1

young [jʌŋ] adj & n   opposite **old**[1] - older/ elder - oldest/ eldest adj & n

to be relatively immature[2] [-ʊə], in an early stage of development and not advanced in years

youth[3] [juːθ] n • **youthful**[4] adj • **youngster**[5] n • **elderly**[6] n & adj

» You still look very young for your age. How old are you now? It makes me feel incredibly old. Both the young and the elderly should avoid these foods.

Use **young** people / children[7] / adults / at heart [ɑː] / in spirit[8] • **youth** club / gang[9] • in my / to mourn [ɔː] / one's lost[10] / misspent[11] **youth** • to grow/get/become/be **older** • **old** age / people's home[12] / man[13] • a 15-year-**old** (boy) • **youthful** appearance [ɪə]/ vigor[14] [ɪ]/-looking • **elderly** patients[15] [eɪʃ]/ person / population[16] [eɪʃ]

Note: The adjective **old** (to denote older than 50 or 60) is used disrespectfully (the **old maid**[17]) or jokingly to refer to oneself or to close friends or one's family (my old lady/ man). In clinical contexts it is replaced by **elderly**. Normally **older/ oldest** are used for comparison, while **elder/ eldest** is only used in the same family (my **elder brother**[18]).

jung, die Jungen
alt, die Alten[1] unreif[2] Jugend; Jugendliche(r)[3] jugendlich[4] Junge, Kind[5] die Älteren; ältere(r), ältlich[6] Kleinkinder[7] geistig jung[8] Jugendbande[9] seiner Jugend nachtrauern[10] vertane Jugend[11] Alters-, Seniorenheim[12] Greis[13] jugendlicher Elan[14] ältere Patienten[15] betagte Bevölkerung[16] alte Jungfer[17] älterer Bruder[18]

2

grow up [groʊ] vi phr   sim **develop**[1] vi

to develop physically, get older and more mature and gradually become an adult

growth[2] n • **growing**[3] adj • **development** n • **outgrow**[4] v • **ingrown**[5] adj

» Mild asthma [æzmə] is more likely to be outgrown. His parents failed [eɪ] to provide [aɪ] food, clothing, shelter[6], and a safe environment [aɪ] in which he could grow and develop normally.

Use **to grow** old(er) / out of a habit[7] / to full height [haɪt] • to promote/stimulate/ impair[8] [eə] **growth** • to reach full[9]/arrest **growth** • pattern of / emotional [oʊʃ]/ cognitive[10] / stunted[11] [ʌ] **growth** • excessive / catch-up / accelerated **growth** • **growth** rate / acceleration[12] / spurt[13] [ɜː] • **growth** deficiency / in height[14] • **growing** pains[15] • well-**developed** • **underdeveloped** ears • **ingrown** toenail[16] • **to outgrown** stuttering / a food allergy / bed-wetting / a problem / shyness

auf-, heranwachsen, erwachsen werden
s. entwickeln[1] Wachstum, Entwicklung[2] (heran)wachsend[3] herauswachsen aus, sich auswachsen[4] eingewachsen[5] eine Gewohnheit ablegen[7] d. Wachstum beeinträchtigen[8] Endgröße erreichen[9] geistige Entwicklung[10] Minderwuchs[11] Wachstumsbeschleunigung, -akzeleration[12] Wachstumsschub[13] Längenwachstum[14] Wachstumsschmerzen[15] eingewachsener Zehennagel[16]

3

infant n & adj   sim **newborn**[1] n clin, **neonate**[1] [niːoʊneɪt] n term

(n, i) child from the newborn period (1st mo.) to the end of the 1st year of life
(ii) in gen E, a young child

infancy[2] n clin • **infantile**[3] [-aɪl‖-ᵊl] adj • **infantilism**[4] n • **infanticide**[5] [-saɪd] n

» Nutrition [ɪʃ] in pregnancy significantly affects maternal health and infant size and well-being. Cardiac failure is common in infancy and in older untreated patients; it is uncommon in late childhood and young adulthood. This field of medicine is still in its infancy[6].

Use newborn / young / healthy / preterm[7] [iː] **infant** • stable[8] [eɪ]/ sensitive / stillborn[9] **infant** • breast-fed[10] [e]/ sick / high-risk[11] / full-term[12] **infant** • low birth-weight [-weɪt]/ immature / malformed[13] **infant** • **infant** mortality[14] / feeding • blue / depressed / sleeping **newborn** • **newborn** baby / period / care / maturity rating[15] • early / late **infancy** • **infantile** behavior / speech / colic [kɒlɪk] • **infantile** apnea [æpnɪə‖æpniːə][16] / reflexes[16] [iː]/ spasms • sudden **infant** death syndrome[17] [ɪ] (abbr SIDS) • mother-**infant** bonding[18]

(i) Säugling, Säuglings-, (ii) Kleinkind; Kindes-
Neugeborenes[1] frühes Kindesalter[2] kindlich, kindisch, infantil[3] Infantilismus[4] Kindestötung[5] steckt noch i. d. Kinderschuhen[6] Frühgeburt[7] psychisch/ gesundheitl. stabiles Kind[8] Totgeburt[9] Stillkind[10] Risikokind[11] Reifgeborenes, ausgetragenes Kind[12] missgebildetes K.[13] Säuglingssterblichkeit[14] Reifebestimmung d. Neugeborenen[15] frühkindl. Reflexe[16] plötzl. Kindstod[17] Mutter-Kind-Beziehung[18]

4

Growing Up & Aging COMPLEX BODY FUNCTIONS 329

child [tʃaɪld] *n, pl* **children** *syn* **kid** *n inf, rel* **baby**[1], **toddler**[2] [ɒː] *n clin*

a boy or girl from birth to the onset of adolescence

childhood[3] *n* • **childlike**[4] *adj* • **childish**[5] *adj* • **childless**[6] *adj*

» During examination, the infant or toddler is often held in the mother's lap[7]. In observing the parent-child interaction, the physician should look for reciprocity, mutual enthusiasm, and enjoyment in the relationship. Counseling [aʊ] focuses on poison prevention[8] for the toddler.

Use to adopt/bring up *or* raise [eɪ]/ spoil *or* pamper[9] *a* **child** • healthy [e]/ middle / unwilling **child** • difficult / backward[10] **child** • **child** care[11] / abuse[12] / development / psychiatrist [saɪkaɪə-]/ welfare • small / young / older / preschool[13] / school-age **children** • **child's** age / needs / ability / motor status[14] / temperament • **children's** hospital • **toddler** years / seat[15] • **childhood** diseases[16] / years / fears / temperament / nutrition • **childish** behavior • **childlike** innocence[17] / trust[18] [ʌ]

Kind
Säugling, Baby[1] Kleinkind[2] Kindheit[3] kindlich[4] kindisch[5] kinderlos[6] Schoß[7] Verhütung v. Giftunfällen[8] Kind verwöhnen/ verhätscheln[9] zurückgebliebenes K.[10] Kinderbetreuung, -pflege, Jugendfürsorge[11] Kindesmisshandlung[12] Kinder i. Vorschulalter[13] motor. Entwicklungsstand d. Kindes[14] Kindersitz[15] Kinderkrankheiten[16] kindl. Unschuld[17] kindl. Vertrauen[18]

5

pediatric [piːdiætrɪk] *adj term* *syn* **paediatric** *adj term BE*

related to the development, diseases and medical care of children

pediatrics[1] *n term* • **pediatrician**[2] [-ɪʃᵊn] *n* • **pedi-, pedo-** *comb*

» The usefulness of aspirin in pediatric practice is limited because it prolongs bleeding time and tends to cause gastric irritation. A pediatrician or neonatologist should be in attendance[3] at high-risk deliveries[4]. In recent years, pediatrics has enlarged its scope[5] to include perinatology and adolescent medicine.

Use **pediatric** age group / behavior [eɪ]/ office visit[6] • **pediatric** (out)patient / emergency / ward [ɔː]/ care • **pediatric** surgeon[7] / urology / oncology / dentistry / psychiatrist[8] • **pediatric** drug dosage / intensive care unit / infections[9] / tumors • ambulatory / adolescent **pediatrics** • behavioral and developmental **pediatrics** • general / primary [aɪ] care / experienced **pediatrician** • **pedo**philia[10] /phile /philiac[11] /dontist[12]

pädiatrisch, Kinderheilkunde-
Pädiatrie, Kinderheilkunde[1] Kinderarzt/-ärztin, Pädiater(in)[2] dabei sein[3] Risikogeburten[4] Fachbereich[5] Termin b. Kinderarzt[6] Kinderchirurg(in)[7] Kinderpsychiater(in)[8] Kinderkrankheiten[9] Pädophilie[10] pädophil; Pädophiler[11] Kinderzahnarzt -ärztin[12]

6

puberty *n clin & term* *rel* **pubescence**[1], **pubarche**[2] [pjubɑːrkɪ] *n term*

approach of the age of sexual maturity[3] in young adults, characterized by the beginning of gametogenesis, secretion [iː] of gonadal [eɪ] hormones, development of secondary sexual characteristics, and reproductive [ʌ] function [ʌ]

(pre/ post)**pubertal**[4] *adj term* • **pubescent**[5] *adj* • **midpuberty** *n*

» In girls, the first signs of puberty may be evident at age 8 with the process largely completed by age 16. Ethnic factors may influence the time at which events typical of puberty occur.

Use at / in early / during / precocious[6] [prɪkoʊʃᵊs]/ delayed[7] [eɪ]/ onset of[1] **puberty** • **pubertal** stage / changes / growth spurt[8] [ɜː]/ girl • **pubertal** gynecomastia[9] [dʒɪnəkoʊ-‖gaɪnəkoʊ-]/ development / progression • **pubescent** uterus

Pubertät, Geschlechtsreife
Pubertätsbeginn[1] Pubarche, Beginn d. Wachstums d. Schamhaare[2] Geschlechtsreife[3] pubertär, puberal, Pubertäts-[4] pubertierend[5] vorzeitige Pubertät, Pubertas praecox[6] verspätete Pubertät, Pubertas tarda[7] pubertärer Wachstumsschub[8] Pubertätsgynäkomastie[9]

7

adolescent [es] *adj & n clin* *sim* **juvenile**[1] [dʒuːvənaɪl‖-ᵊl] *n clin & adj term,* **teenager**[2], **youth**[3] *n*

(adj) referring to the period between the onset of puberty and adulthood (the teen years)

adolescence[4] *n term* • **teenage**[5] *adj* • **teens**[2] *n* • **teen** *adj & n*

» A pediatrician's waiting room scattered with toddler's toys[6] make adolescent patients feel that they have outgrown the practice. During early adolescence, many teenagers may be shy [ʃaɪ] and modest[7], especially if examined by a physician [ɪʃ] of the opposite sex. Youths may be brought in for evaluation of drug or alcohol use, parent-adolescent conflict[8], school failure, depression, or a suspected eating disorder[9]. This is useful in counseling teenagers who lag behind[10] their peers[11] [pɪɚz] in physical development.

Use young / older / female [iː]/ school-age / rapidly growing **adolescent** • obese [iː]/ body conscious / sexually active **adolescent** • suicidal[12] [saɪ]/ substance-abusing[13] / delinquent[14] / gay[15] [eɪ] **adolescent** • **adolescent** boy / girl / development • **adolescent** growth spurt[16] / behavior • **adolescent** acne [ækni]/ hypertension / turmoil[17] [ɜː] • **adolescent** rebellion / psychiatry[18] / adjustment [ʌ] • to approach [-oʊtʃ]/ early / middle / late / constitutionally delayed [eɪ] **adolescence** • **teenage** patient / health problem / pregnancy • **teen** years • in his **teens** • **juvenile** offenders / delinquency[19] / freckles[20] • **juvenile** rheumatoid [ruː-] arthritis [-aɪtɪs]/-onset diabetes [daɪəbiːtɪs]

jugendlich; Jugendliche(r)
Heranwachsende(r); juvenil, halbwüchsig, Jugend-[1] Teenager[2] Jugendliche(r); Jugend[3] Jugend, Adoleszenz[4] im Teenageralter[5] Kinderspielzeug[6] schamhaft[7] Generationskonflikt[8] Essstörung[9] zurückbleiben hinter[10] Gleichaltrige[11] suizidgefährdete(r) Jugendliche(r)[12] suchtmittelabhängige(r) J.[13] straffällige(r) J.[14] schwuler Jugendlicher[15] pubertäre Wachstumsschub[16] pubertäre Identitätskrise/ Zerrissenheit[17] Jugendpsychiatrie[18] Jugendkriminalität[19] Sommersprossen, Epheliden[20]

8

80

minor [maɪnə] *n*   *sim* **under age¹** *phr*

person who has not yet reached [iː] the age at which (s)he legally becomes an adult

to come/ be of age² *phr* • **minority³** *n* • **majority⁴** [mədʒɒːrəti] *n*

» Oral contraceptives can be prescribed to minors confidentially⁵. Tobacco sales to minors is illegal [iː]. Several years ago he was accused of having sex with a minor.

Use an emancipated / a mature⁶ **minor** • **under age** drinking • **age** of consent⁷ / of majority

adult [ædʌlt] *n & adj*   *syn* **grown-up** *n & adj inf, rel* **maturity¹** [mətjʊrəti] *n*

(n) a fully developed person from maturity onward

adulthood² *n* • **grow** - grew - grown *v irr* • **grown³** *adj* • **(im)mature⁴** *adj* • **mature⁵** *v* • **maturation⁶** *n*

» Clinical illness is more severe in adults than in children. The condition is seen primarily in young adults between ages 20 and 50. Scoliosis seen after skeletal maturity is termed adult scoliosis. Don't forget she's a grown woman now. Girls who mature late will attain a greater ultimate height [haɪt] because of the longer period of growth before the growth spurt.

Use in healthy / average-sized⁷ / young / older / aging **adults** • to attain **adult** life / growth • to reach/lack in **maturity** • skeletal / sexual⁸ / emotional / delayed⁹ **maturity** • fetal [iː]/ legal age of¹⁰ **maturity** • **maturity**-onset diabetes • **adult** age group / height¹¹ / patient • **adult** cases / ward¹² / form / immunization • **adult** dosage / genitalia [eɪ]/ onset diabetes¹³ • **adult** varicella [sel]/ hemoglobin / coping patterns¹⁴ / urology • to reach / in early / by¹⁵ / throughout / delayed until **adulthood** • fully / sexually **mature** • **mature** judgement¹⁶ [dʒʌdʒ-]/ lymphocyte [-saɪt] • **immature** infant¹⁷ / skeletal age / coordination / cells

decade [dekeɪd] **(of life)** *n term*   *rel* **thirties¹** [ɜː] *n clin pl*

refers to a period of 10 years of life (the twenties, thirties, forties, fifties, sixties, etc.)

» Whipple's disease may occur [ɜː] at any age but most commonly affects white men in the fourth to sixth decades. She's in her early thirties². My father is in his late sixties³. Carol is in her mid-thirties⁴.

Use in the first days / months / second year⁵ / fifth decade **of life** • end⁶ / loss **of life**

middle age *n*   *sim* **midlife¹** [mɪdlaɪf] *n*, **midadult life¹** *n*

period in life between youth and old age (usually the 4th and 5th decades of life)

middle-aged² *n & adj* • **midlife³** *adj*

» Symptoms of seasonal [iː] allergic [ɜː] rhinitis⁴ [-aɪtɪs] are usually most severe from adolescence through midadult life. This is a disorder of middle-aged adults and is rare in children.

Use **midlife** (identity) crisis [aɪ] • **middle** life¹ • **middle-aged** men / women / smokers

senior [siːnjə] *n & adj*   *sim* **elderly¹**, **aged²** [eɪdʒd] *n & adj*

(n) person who is older or of a higher rank (adj) advanced in years

seniority³ *n* • **senescence⁴** *n term* • **senescent** *adj* • **senile⁵** [siː‖senaɪl] *adj*

» Senior citizens [sɪ] is an expression used to avoid saying old people. The lab data were the same for the elderly as for younger adults. He is 3 years my senior. He's still going strong⁶ but his wife is beginning to look her age⁷ and has gone a bit senile.

Use **senior** doctor⁸ / citizens • **elderly** patients / parents / relatives • in the⁹ **aged** • **aged** spouse¹⁰ [aʊ] • **senile** involution [uːʃ]/ memory / tremor • **senile** warts¹¹ [ɔː]/ dementia¹² / plaques¹³ [æ‖BE ɑː]

> **Note:** The expression **elderly** is the polite way to refer to someone who is advanced in years, while **old** is not considered very tactful and is therefore avoided. The abbreviation **sr.** (senior) after a name refers to the father by the same name (**jr.** = junior; the son)

Minderjährige(r)

minderjährig, unmündig¹ volljährig werden/ sein² Minderjährigkeit³ Volljährigkeit, Mündigkeit⁴ vertraulich⁵ ein(e) strafmündige(r) Minderjährige(r)⁶ Ehemündigkeit⁷

9

Erwachsene(r); erwachsen, adult

Reife, Maturität¹ Erwachsenenalter² erwachsen³ (un)reif, (nicht) ausgewachsen⁴ reifen⁵ (Heran)reifen, Reifeprozess⁶ durchschnittl. große Erwachsene⁷ Sexualreife⁸ verzögerte Reife⁹ Volljährigkeit¹⁰ Erwachsenen-, Endgröße¹¹ Erwachsenstation¹² Erwachsenen-, Altersdiabetes¹³ erwachsenes Copingverhalten¹⁴ bis zum Erwachsenenalter¹⁵ reifes Urteilsvermögen¹⁶ unreifes Neugeborenes¹⁷

10

Lebensjahrzehnt

Dreißiger¹ Anfang dreißig² Ende sechzig³ Mitte dreißig⁴ im 2. Lebensjahr⁵ Lebensende⁶

11

mittleres (Lebens)alter

Lebensmitte¹ (Personen) mittleren Alters; in mittleren Jahren² in der Lebensmitte³ saisonale allergische Rhinitis⁴

12

Senior(in); (dienst)älter, vorgesetzt

die Älteren; ältere(r)¹ alte Menschen; alt, betagt² höhere(s/r) Position/ Alter/ Rang³ Altern, Seneszenz⁴ Alters-, greisenhaft, senil⁵ gut in Schuss sein⁶ jem. das Alter ansehen⁷ Oberarzt -ärztin⁸ bei alten Leuten⁹ betagte(r) Gatte/-in¹⁰ Alterswarzen, Verrucae seniles¹¹ senile Demenz¹² senile Plaques/ Drusen¹³

13

Growing Up & Aging   COMPLEX BODY FUNCTIONS **331**

retiree [rɪtaɪriː] *n*   *syn* **(old age) pensioner** [penˈʃ³nɚ] *n BE, abbr* **OAP**
person who has stopped his/her working career due to old age, illness, etc.
retirement[1] *n* • **pension**[2] *n* • **retire**[3] *vi* • **retired**[4] *adj* • **pension off**[5] *vt phr*
» Most current [ɜː] retirees rely on the social security system for a considerable portion of their income. I am retired now. He is a retired postmaster. Any thoughts of retiring yet?
Use to grant [æ]/award [ɔː]/receive [siː]/draw[6]/be eligible for[7] ***a pension*** • disability[8] / old-age[9] / survivor's[10] ***pension*** • **to retire** from one's job • to take early[11] / to live in forced / semi-*retirement* • *retirement* home / age[12]

Pensionist(in), Rentner(in)
Pensionierung[1] Pension, Rente[2] in Pension/ d. Rente gehen, s. pensionieren lassen[3] pensioniert, im Ruhestand[4] vorzeitig pensionieren[5] Pension/ Rente beziehen[6] pensions-/ rentenberechtigt sein, Anspruch auf e. Pension/ Rente haben[7] Invalidenrente[8] Altersrente, -pension[9] Hinterbliebenenrente[10] in Frühpension/ die Frührente gehen[11] Pensions-, Rentenalter[12]   **14**

geriatric [dʒeriætrik] *adj term*
relating to those who are advanced in years
geriatrics[1] *n term* • **geriatrician**[2] *n* • **gerontology**[3] *n* • **gero(nto)-** *comb*
» As much as 25% of nursing time in geriatric hospitals is consumed [uː] dealing with incontinence. Geriatrics is a multidisciplinary field. The physician referred her family to a geriatrician for further evaluation. Geriatricians often become the primary [aɪ] physician for older adults. Students are required to take 27 hours in gerontology.
Use **geriatric** medicine[1] / psychiatry [saɪkaɪə-]/ specialist • **geriatric** patient / population[4] / admission **geriatric** care[5] / day care / social groups[6] / clinical / outpatients **geriatrics** • consultant [ʌ] **geriatrician** • **gero**derma[7] /psychiatry /dontology[8] • **geronto**therapy[9] /logist /phobia

geriatrisch, alters-
Geriatrie, Altersheilkunde[1] Geriater(in)[2] Altersforschung, Gerontologie[3] betagte Bevölkerung[4] Altenpflege[5] Seniorenrunden[6] Geroderma[7] Alterszahnheilkunde, Gerodontologie[8] Behandlung älterer Patienten, Gero(nto)therapie[9]

15

octogenarian [ɒktoʊdʒɪneərɪən] *n*   *sim* **sexagenarian**[1]**, septuagenarian**[2] *n*
person who is in his/her eighties (between 80 and 89 years old)
» He is pushing 75[3] and is all set[4] to outlive[5] his family and become an octogenarian.

Achtzigjährige(r)
Sechzigjährige(r)[1] Siebzigjährige(r)[2] auf die 75 zugehen[3] ist drauf und dran[4] überleben[5]   **16**

Unit 81 Biochemistry & Molecular Biology

Related Units: 88 Physiology, 78 Metabolism, 55 Hormones, 42 Nerve Function, 79 Nutrition, 83 Cell Biology, 84 Genetics, 91 Toxicology, 92 Pharmacologic Agents

chemical [kemɪkᵊl] adj & n   rel **irritant**[1] n & adj → U104-3; U89-10, **pesticide**[2] [-saɪd] n term → U91-8

(n) substance [ʌ] produced by or used in a reaction involving changes in atoms or molecules
bio/ histochemical adj term • (**bio/ cyto**)**chemistry**[3] [saɪtəkemɪstri] n • **chem(o)-** comb

» Supportive care should be directed toward removal [uː] of chemical injury by iodine [aɪə], carbolic or salicylic [sɪ] acids. Chemicals used in chemoprevention[4] [kiːmoʊ-] must be nontoxic and well tolerated by otherwise asymptomatic individuals. Obtain [eɪ] samples for CBC[5] and a serum [ɪɚ] chemistry profile[6] [-faɪl].

Use **chemical** substance / compound[7] [-aʊnd]/ affinity / energy • **chemical** agent [eɪdʒ]/ messenger[8] / analysis • **chemical** abnormality / stimulus / constituents[9] [ɪtʃ]/ burn[10] [ɜː] • **chemical** formula[11] / equation[12] [eɪʒ]/ coupling[13] [ʌ] • organic / synthetic / irritative[1] **chemical** • inhaled [eɪ]/ psychoactive [saɪkoʊ-]/ hazardous[14] [æ] **chemicals** • corrosive[15] / toxic / radioactive **chemicals** • household / industrial [ʌ] **chemicals** • potent chemical / airways[16] **irritants** • **irritant** agent / gases / fumes [juː] • **biochemical** parameter / study / diagnosis / disorder / assay[17] • (in)organic[18] / medical / clinical / blood / brain **chemistry** • analytic [ɪ]/ applied[19] / biological[20] **chemistry** • physiological[21] / physical [ɪ] **chemistry** • (macro)molecular / pharmaceutical[22] [suː]/ nuclear / radiation[23] [eɪʃ] **chemistry** • **chemistry** lab / profile / panel[24] • (immuno)histo[25]/ neuro/ photo/ micro**chemistry** • chemo(re)ceptor [se] /attractants[26] /taxis [kiːmoʊtæksɪs] • **chemo**suppression /prophylaxis[4] /therapeutic agents or drugs[27]

chemisch; Chemikalie, chemische Substanz
Reizstoff, -mittel, Irritans; reizend, Reiz-[1] Pestizid, Pflanzenschutz- u. Schädlingsbekämpfungsmittel[2] Zytochemie[3] Chemoprophylaxe[4] großes Blutbild[5] chem. Blutuntersuchung[6] chem. Verbindung[7] chem. Botenstoff[8] chem. Komponenten[9] Verätzung[10] chem. Formel[11] chem. (Reaktions)gleichung[12] chem. Kopplung[13] gefährliche Chemikalien[14] Ätzmittel[15] Atemwegsirritanzien, Reizgase[16] biochem. Untersuchung[17] (an)organische Chemie[18] angewandte C.[19] Biochemie[20] physiolog. C.[21] pharmazeutische C.[22] Strahlenchemie[23] biochemische Standarduntersuchung[24] (Immun)-histochemie[25] Chemoattraktantien, chem. Lockstoffe, Pheromone[26] Chemotherapeutika[27]

1

molecule [mɒlɪkjuːl] n   rel **atom**[1] n, **compound**[2] [-aʊnd] n & v, **micelle**[3] [maɪsel] n term

smallest unit of atoms that exhibits the chemical properties of an element or compound
(**bio/ intra**)**molecular** [e] adj term • (**bio/ macro**)**molecule**[4] n • **atomic** adj

» The molecules of parathyroid [aɪ] hormone lack cysteine [sɪstiːn]. Adherence [ɪɚ] of microorganisms to host cells results from a highly specific molecular reaction between ligands [aɪ]. Cobalamin is a complex organometallic compound in which a cobalt atom is situated within a corrin ring. Bile [aɪ] acids[5] [s] are detergents[6] [ɜː] that in aqueous [eɪ‖æ] solutions and above a critical concentration form molecular aggregates[7] called micelles.

Use **carrier**[8] [eɚ]/ nutrient[9] [uː]/ acceptor **molecule** • cytoskeletal / parent / extracellular matrix [eɪ] **molecule** • albumin / hemoglobin / antibody / hydrophobic **molecule** • (un)charged[12] [tʃ]/ hybrid [aɪ]/ polar[13] / binding [aɪ]/ signaling **molecule** • **molecular** structure[14] / marker / mass[15] • **molecular** configuration / probe[16] / study • **molecular** biology / (cyto)genetics[17] [saɪtədʒe-]/ epidemiology • **molecular** pathogenesis [dʒe]/ defect / diagnosis • organic / synthetic / (un)saturated / (in)active **compound** • water-soluble[18] / low-viscosity / (non)toxic **compound** • high-energy / heat-stable[19] [eɪ]/ low-molecular weight [weɪt] **compound** • fluorescing [es]/ radioactively labeled[20] [eɪ] **compound** • aromatic / nitrogenous[21] [ɒːdʒ]/ carbon[22] **compound** • paraffin / phenol-containing **compound** • ferric hydroxide-dextran / cyanide[23] [saɪ] **compound** • codeine / bismuth / (di)azo[24] [aɪ] **compound** • oxygen / hydrogen / cobalt / sulfur[25] [ʌ]/ rare [reɚ] earth[26] / tagged[27] **atom** • **atomic** weight / mass / number[28] / structure • **atomic** orbit[29] / stability / radiation

Molekül
Atom[1] Verbindung; verbinden, mischen[2] Mizelle[3] Makromolekül[4] Gallensäuren[5] Tenside, Netzmittel, Detergenzien[6] Molekülaggregate[7] Träger-, Carriermolekül[8] Nährstoffmolekül[9] Bausteinmolekül[10] Adhäsionsmolekül[11] (nicht) geladenes M.[12] polares M.[13] Molekularstruktur[14] Molekularmasse[15] Molekülsonde[16] Molekulargenetik[17] wasserlösl. Verbindung[18] thermostabile/ hitzebeständige V.[19] radioaktiv markierte V.[20] Stickstoffverbindung[21] Kohlenstoffverbindung[22] Zyanid-, Blausäureverbindung[23] Diazoverbindung[24] Schwefelatom[25] Atome der seltenen Erden[26] radioaktives/ radioaktiv markiertes Atom[27] Kernladungszahl, Ordnungszahl[28] (Atom)orbital[29]

2

molecular weight n term, abbr **mol wt**   rel **mole**[1] n term, abbr **mol, M**

total of the atomic weights of all the atoms in a molecule relative to that of a carbon-12 atom
molarity[2] n term • **molality**[3] n • **molar**[4] , **molal**[5] adj • **millimol** n, abbr **mM**

» A 1-molar solution contains 1 gram molecular weight of a compound dissolved[6] in 1 liter of fluid. Special enteral diets contain protein in the form of low-molecular-weight free amino acids or polypeptides. Factor XIII deficiency [ɪʃ] is diagnosed by showing instability of the fibrin [aɪ] clot in 8-molar urea.

Use **gram**[1] (abbr GMW) **molecular weight** • high-/ low-**molecular weight** substance[7] • **molecular** mass • **mole** fraction / ratio[8] / percent[9] • (gram) atomic / molar • specific[10] / cell weight • weight density[10] • molar volume / number[11] • concentration • **molal** solution • **mM**/L[12]

Molekulargewicht, Mol. Gew., relative Molekularmasse
Mol, Grammolekül[1] Molarität[2] Molalität[3] molar[4] molal[5] gelöst[6] niedermolekulare Substanz[7] molares Verhältnis[8] Molprozent[9] spezifisches Gewicht, Dichte[10] Molzahl[11] Millimol pro Liter[12]

3

moiety [mɔɪəti] *n term*   *sim* **subunit¹, fraction²** [frækʃən] *n term*,
                                rel **residue³** *n term*

portion of a molecule exhibiting particular chemical properties

fractionate⁴ *v term* • **fractionation⁵** *n* • **fractional⁶** *adj* • **residual** [ɪdʒ] *adj*

» Oxidation of the heme [hi:m] *moiety*⁷ dissociated from the hemoglobin generates biliverdin [ɜː], which is then metabolized to bilirubin. The prime function of folate is to transfer 1-carbon moieties such as methyl groups to various organic compounds. Amino-peptidase A may then cleave [iː] the amino residue off⁸ angiotensin [ændʒɪoʊ-] II to form angiotensin III.

Use active / binding / enzymatic / lipid / apoprotein⁹ **moiety** • antiviral [aɪ]/ glucuronic acid¹⁰ / salicilate **moiety** • sulfa [ʌ]/ corrin / ADP ribose [aɪ] **moiety** • catalytic / encoding¹¹ / regulatory / aromatic **subunit** • halogenated¹² / hexon / receptor **subunit** • polypeptide / G protein **subunit** • conjugated / protein / gamma globulin¹³ **fraction** • esterified / supernatant¹⁴ [eɪ] **fraction** • (polymorphic) amino acid¹⁵ / D-alanine **residue** • terminal glutamine / sialic [saɪælɪk] acid¹⁶ **residue** • ethanol or alcohol¹⁷ / Cohn¹⁷ / hyper/ accelerated **fractionation** • **fractionation** process / scheme [skiːm]

---

radical *n term*   *sim* **group¹** *n term*,
                       rel **substituent², oxidant³** *n*, **chelate⁴** [iː] *n & v term*

group of atoms, ions or molecules with unpaired electrons which passes unchanged from one compound to another and is incapable of prolonged existence in a free state

antioxidant⁵ *n term* • **chelation** [kiːleɪʃən] *n* • **chelator⁶** *n* • **-yl, -ylene** [iː] *comb*

» Radicals are groups of atoms with at least one unpaired [eə] electron. Prolonged application of ice causes tissue damage by increasing the release [iː] of oxidants and free radicals. Antioxidants such as selenium⁷ [iː] and the ubiquinone⁸ [ɪkw] group can reverse [ɜː] the symptoms of vitamin E deficiency. Like tetracyclines [saɪ], all fluoroquinolones are chelated by divalent⁹ and trivalent [aɪ] cations [aɪ]. D-penicillamine [sɪ] has the ability to chelate copper.

Use acid / oxidant / allyl / propyl / methylene **radical** • (intracellular/ oxygen-derived/ free¹⁰ / oxygen¹¹ / nitric [aɪ] oxide¹² **radicals** • electrophilic / highly-reactive chemical¹³ **radicals** • hydroxyl / amino / methyl / phenolic¹⁴ **group** • potent **oxidant** • **oxidant** reaction / drugs¹⁵ / stress¹⁶ / exposure [oʊʒ]/ damage / dietary [aɪ] **antioxidant** vitamins¹⁷ • **antioxidant** substance⁵ / effect *or* function¹⁸ / defense system • water-soluble **chelate** • metal / copper / aluminum / iron [aɪən]/ citrate-mediated¹⁹ [iː] **chelation** • (oral) iron / calcium **chelator** • **chelation** therapy²⁰ • iron-**chelated** • **chelating** agent⁶ • hydrox/ benz/ acet/ carbox**yl** [kɑːrbɒːksɪl] • aden/ cholester/ (di)meth**yl** • alk/ glucuron/ am**yl** • sulfhydr/ (poly)vin**yl** • (poly/trichloro)eth/ x²¹/ methylene [meθəlɪn‖iːn]

---

dimer [aɪ] *n term*
                   rel **monomer¹, trimer²** [aɪ], **oligomer³, polymer⁴** *n term*

compound produced by the union of two radicals or similar monomeric molecules

heterodimer⁵ *n term* • **dimeric⁶** *adj* • **dimerization⁷** *n* • **di-, tri-, poly-** *comb*

» When growth factor binds to its receptor, the latter forms a dimer or oligomer with adjacent [ədʒeɪs-] counterparts [aʊ]. All polypeptides and proteins are polymers of amino acids. The complex of core protein and link protein then binds to a long chain of hyaluronic acid to form a huge copolymer called a proteoglycan [aɪ] aggregate. Fiber⁸ is a chemically complex group of indigestible carbohydrate polymers (cellulose, pectins, gums⁹, and mucilages).

Use to form¹⁰ **dimers** • ionic / thymine [aɪ]/ pyrimidine / D¹¹-**dimer** • collagen / IgA / fibrin **monomer** • antisense¹² **oligomer** • complex / linear / (highly) branched¹³ **polymer** • biodegradable¹⁴ [eɪ]/ hydrophilic **polymer** • glucose / fibrin / salicylate **polymer** • acrylic [ɪ]/ silicone¹⁵ / co**polymer** • **dimeric** protein • **polymer** formation / chain¹⁶ / **polymeric** diet¹⁷ /merase /merization/merize¹⁸ / **tri**glyceride [traɪɡlɪsəraɪd] /phosphate • **poly**ester /ethylene /amid /propylene • **poly**vinyl [aɪ] chloride /peptide /saccharide [k] /glycolic acid¹⁹ • **poly**urethane dressing²⁰ /cyclic hydrocarbon²¹

Anteil, Gruppe

Untereinheit¹ Fraktion² Rest³ fraktionieren, auftrennen⁴ Fraktionierung⁵ fraktioniert⁶ Hämgruppe⁷ abspalten⁸ Apoproteinanteil⁹ Glukuronsäurebestandteil, -anteil¹⁰ codierende Untereinheit¹¹ halogenierte Untereinheit¹² Gammaglobulinfraktion¹³ Überstand¹⁴ Aminosäurerest¹⁵ Sialinsäurerest¹⁶ Cohn-Fraktionierung¹⁷

4

Radikal, Radikalgruppe

Gruppe, Radikal¹ Substituent² Oxidans³ Chelat(komplex); ein Chelat bilden⁴ Antioxidans⁵ Chelat-, Komplexbildner⁶ Selen⁷ Ubichinon⁸ zweiwertig, bi-, divalent⁹ freie Radikale¹⁰ Sauerstoffradikale¹¹ Stickoxidradikale¹² stark reaktionsfähige/ hochreaktive chem. Radikale¹³ Phenolgruppe¹⁴ oxidativ wirkende Mittel¹⁵ Oxidanzienbelastung, oxidativer Stress¹⁶ in der Nahrung enthaltene antioxidative Vitamine¹⁷ antioxidative Wirkung¹⁸ zitratvermittelte Chelatbildung¹⁹ Antidottherapie²⁰ Xylen²¹

5

Dimer

Monomer¹ Trimer² Oligomer³ Polymer⁴ Heterodimer⁵ dimer⁶ Dimerisation, Dimerisierung⁷ Ballaststoffe⁸ Gummiharze⁹ Dimere bilden¹⁰ D-Dimer¹¹ Antisense-Oligomer¹² stark verzweigtes Polymer¹³ biolog. abbaubares Polymer¹⁴ Silikonpolymer¹⁵ Polymerkette¹⁶ Polymerdiät¹⁷ polymerisieren, ein Polymer bilden¹⁸ Polyglykolsäure¹⁹ Polyurethanverband²⁰ polyzykl. Kohlenwasserstoff²¹

6

MEDICAL SCIENCE — Biochemistry & Molecular Biology

benzene [iː] **ring** n term   rel **cyclic compound**[1], **chain**[2] [tʃeɪn], **bridge**[3] n term

closed-chain hexagon arrangement of the carbon and hydrogen atoms in the benzene molecule
nonring adj term • **long-chain**[4] adj • **tricyclic**[5] [traɪsaɪklɪk] adj • **benz(o)-** comb

» Cystine [sɪ] crystals [ɪ], with a characteristic hexagonal benzene ring shape, are seen only in patients with cystinuria. Tetracyclines [saɪ] consist of four aromatic rings with various substituent [ɪtʃ] groups. Glucose polymers and medium-chain [iː] triglyceride [ɪ] supplements [ʌ] can be used to increase caloric intake[6]. This peptide consists of a single-chain structure composed of 84 amino acids.

Use porphyrin[7] / purine / aromatic[8] **ring** • 6-carbon hexane / 5-carbon pentane **ring** • side[9] / (poly)peptide / glycyl [aɪ] or A[10] **chain** • phenylalanyl or B[11] / branched[12]-/ 20-carbon **chain** • short-/ medium[13]-/ single-/ heavy-[e]/ light-**chain** • **chain** termination[14] / terminator[15] • actin-myosin cross[16]-/ peptide / methylene **bridge** • poly/ tetra/ bi/ a/ macro/ hetero**cyclic** • **cyclic** polypeptide / adenosine monophosphate[17] (abbr cAMP)/ GMP[18] • **tricyclic** antidepressants[19] • gamma **benzene** hexachloride[20] • **benzene** compound / poisoning[21] • **benzo**ate /ic acid[22] /yl peroxide /caine /diazepine [aɪæ] • **benz**amide /idine /quinamide /alkonium chloride

Benzolring
zykl. Verbindung[1] Kette[2] Brücke[3] langkettig[4] trizyklisch[5] Kalorienzufuhr[6] Porphyrinring[7] aromatischer Ring[8] Seitenkette[9] A-Kette (Insulin)[10] B-Kette (Insulin)[11] verzweigtkettig[12] mittelkettig[13] Kettenabbruch[14] Terminations-, Stoppcodon[15] Aktin-Myosin-Querbrücke[16] zykl. Adenosinmonophosphat, cAMP[17] zykl. Guanosinmonophosphat, cGMP[18] trizykl. Antidepressiva[19] Lindan, Gamma-Hexachlorhexan[20] Benzolvergiftung[21] Benzoesäure[22]

7

---

bind [baɪnd] - **bound** - **bound** [baʊnd] v irr term
    opposite **detach**[1] [dɪtætʃ] v, **split**[2] - split - split v irr, **cleave**[2] [kliːv] v term
to combine molecules by reactive groups or with a binding chemical, i.e. a conjugate
binding[3] n & adj term • **bond**[4] v & n • **bonding** n • **bonded** adj • **split**[5] adj • **cleavage** [kliːvɪdʒ] n

» Not all molecular sites at which drugs bind are properly designated as receptors. It binds to the pituitary[6] dopamine receptor and thus inhibits prolactin secretion from the gland. Pepsin cleaves peptide bonds, especially those containing phenylalanine, tyrosine, or leucine [luːsiːn]. The workup[7] includes determination of total iron binding capacity[8] and TSH levels[9]. The enzymatic action of renin splits angiotensin I off the alpha-2 globulin angiotensinogen.

Use **to bind** calcium / to receptors / to the cell surface • **binding** site[10] / energy[11] / affinity / capacity / properties • complement / protein / hormone / thyroxine **binding** • ligand-/ matrix- [eɪ]/ loosely **bound** • to disrupt[12] [ʌ] /cleave[12]/form[13] /be linked by **bonds** • single / double / triple[14] [ɪ]/ covalent[15] [eɪ]/ electrovalent / stable[16] [eɪ] **bond** • intramolecular / hydrogen / (weak) peptide[17] / disulfide [ʌ]/ high-energy[18] **bond** • urea[19]-/ fat-**splitting** • **split** products of fibrin[20] [aɪ] • **cleavage** product[21] / site • lactose-**cleaving** enzyme • proteolytic[22] [ɪ] **cleavage**

binden
(ab-, los)lösen[1] (ab-, auf) spalten[2] Bindung; Bindemittel; (ver)bindend, Bindungs-[3] binden; Bindung[4] (auf)gespalten, Spalt-[5] hypophysär[6] med. Untersuchungen[7] Eisenbindungskapazität[8] Thyreotropin-Spiegel[9] Bindungsstelle[10] Bindungsenergie[11] Bindungen spalten[12] Bindungen eingehen[13] Dreifachbindung[14] Atombindung, kovalente B.[15] stabile/ feste Bindung[16] schwache Peptidbindung[17] energiereiche Bindung[18] Harnstoffspaltung[19] Fibrinspaltprodukte[20] Spaltprodukt[21] Proteolyse, Eiweißabbau[22]

8

---

conjugated [kɒndʒəgeɪtɪd] adj term   rel **aggregated**[1] [ægrəgeɪtɪd] adj term
chemical substance combined with another compound, e.g. steroid hormones with glucuronic or sulfuric acid; this alters or terminates its biological activity to make the compound ready [e] for excretion [iːʃ]
unconjugated adj term • **conjugation**[2] n • **conjugate**[3] v & n & adj • **aggregate**[4] v & n

» Folates in various foodstuffs are largely conjugated to a chain of glutamic acid residues[5] [-d(j)uːz]. At these concentrations the bile [aɪ] salts aggregate to form micelles[6].

Use **conjugated** compound / linoleic acid[7] (abbr CLA)/ bilirubin / bile acids[8] • **conjugated** double [ʌ] bond[9] / antibodies / estrogens / to toxins • **aggregated** proteins / platelets[10] [eɪ] • cell(ular)[11] / molecular[12] / proteoglycan [aɪ] **aggregate**

konjugiert
zusammengelagert, aggregiert[1] Konjugation[2] konjugieren; Konjugat; konjugiert[3] zusammenlagern, aggregieren; Aggregat[4] Glutaminsäurereste[5] Mizellen[6] konjugierte Linolsäure[7] konjugierte Gallensäuren[8] konjugierte Doppelbindung[9] Thrombozytenaggregation[10] Zellaggregat[11] Molekülaggregat[12]

9

---

valence (state) or **valency** [veɪlənˈsi] n term   rel **charge**[1] [tʃɑːrdʒ] n & v term
combining power of one atom of an element (or radical) using the hydrogen atom as the unit of comparison; determined by the number of electrons in the outer shell of the atom[2] (valence electrons[3])
covalent [eɪ] adj term • **bi/ divalent**[4] adj • **polyvalent** adj • **(un)charged**[5] adj

» One equivalent (eq) of an ion is equal to 1 mole (mol) multiplied by the valence of the ion. The ionic strength[6] is a measure [eʒ] of the magnitude of this electrical field and increases as the concentration of ions increases and their valence or charge increases. In HCl chlorine is monovalent, in H₂O oxygen is bivalent [aɪ], in NH₃ nitrogen [aɪ] is trivalent [aɪ]. Ethanol is a weakly [iː] charged[7] molecule that moves easily through cell membranes.

Use negative / positive **valence** • **valence** change[8] • **covalent** bond[9] / complex • **divalent** cation / iron[10] / electric(al)[11] / electrostatic / positive **charge** • anionic / cell surface[12] **charge** • **charge** number[13] / transfer complex • zero[14]-/ uni- or mono[15]-**valent** • penta[16]/ equi[17]/ tri**valent** • negatively / highly[18] **charged** • **charged** molecule / particle[19] • **uncharged** benzene ring

Wertigkeit, Valenz
Ladung; laden[1] Atomhülle[2] Außen-, Valenzelektronen[3] zweiwertig, bi-, divalent[4] (nicht) geladen[5] Ionenstärke[6] schwach geladen[7] Valenzwechsel[8] kovalente Bindung, Atombindung[9] zweiwertiges Eisen[10] elektr. Ladung[11] Zelloberflächenladung[12] Ordnungszahl, Kernladungszahl[13] nullwertig[14] monovalent, einwertig[15] pentavalent, fünfwertig[16] gleichwertig, äquivalent[17] stark geladen[18] geladenes Teilchen[19]

10

Biochemistry & Molecular Biology — MEDICAL SCIENCE 335

ion [aɪən] *n term* → U78-23   *rel* **anion**[1], **cation**[2] [aɪ], **electron**[3] *n term*
proton[4], **positron**[5] *n term* → U99-22

atom or group of atoms carrying an electric charge resulting from gain or loss of one or more electrons

(non)ionic[6] [aɪɒːnɪk] *adj term* • **ionization**[7] *n* • **ionized** *adj* • **anionic**, **cationic** *adj*

» *Ions charged with negative electricity* [ɪs] *(anions) travel toward a positive pole* [poʊl] *or anode, while positively charged ions (cations) travel toward a negative pole or cathode. Ions may exist in solid, liquid, or gaseous environments, although those in liquid (electrolytes) are more common and familiar.*

Use activated / hydrogen[8] [aɪ]/ mineral / metal / calcium [s] **ion** • (chloride) bicarbonate / ammonium **ion** • **ion** activity / exchange (resins)[9] / flux[10] • **ion** trapping[11] / transport / channel[12] [tʃ] • (in)organic / acid / superoxide / chloride **anion** • **anion** transport / gap[13] / exchange • **anionic** charge / compound / phospholipid / detergents[14] [ɜː] • extracellular / divalent **cation** • **cationic** protein • to donate[15]/pass[15]/ collect[16] **electrons** • outer-shell[17] / orbiting[18] / positive **electrons** • **electron** acceptor[19] / donor[20] / transfer / pair • **electron** density[21] / transport chain / beam[22] [iː]/ microscopy • **proton** number / pump [ʌ] inhibitor[23] / dissociation constant • **ionic** concentration / dissociation / diffusion / current[24] [ɜː] • **ionic** pump[25] / gradient [eɪ]/ strength[26] / compound / bond[27] • **ionic** content / imbalance / environment [aɪ]

Ion
Anion, neg. geladenes Ion[1] Kation, positiv geladenes Ion[2] Elektron[3] Proton[4] Positron[5] ionisch, Ionen-[6] Ionisation, Ionisierung[7] Wasserstoffion[8] Ionenaustauscher(harze), Resine[9] Ionenfluss, -wanderung[10] Ionenfang, Einfangen von Ionen[11] Ionenkanal[12] Anionenlücke[13] anionische Detergenzien[14] Elektronen abgeben[15] Elektronen aufnehmen[16] Außen-, Valenzelektronen[17] kreisende Elektronen[18] Elektronenakzeptor, -empfänger[19] Elektronendonator, -spender[20] Elektronendichte[21] Elektronenstrahl[22] Protonenpumpenhemmer[23] Ionenstrom[24] Ionenpumpe[25] Ionenstärke[26] Ionenbindung[27]

11

---

affinity [əfɪnəti] *n term*   *rel* **adsorption**[1], **coupling**[2] [ʌ] *n term* → U88-8

tendency of atoms to bind to certain others to form strongly or weakly bound compounds

adsorbent[3] *adj & n* • **adsorptive**[4] *adj* • **adsorb**[5] **(on)to** *v*
• **uncoupling** *n* • **couple**[6] *v & n*

» *Proteins containing this amino acid have a strong affinity for calcium ions. This permits calcium binding and adsorption onto phospholipid surfaces. Biochemical desensitization*[7] *of the receptor may alter* [ɔː] *the affinity for the ligand or prevent receptor coupling to downstream substrates* [ʌ]. *Salicylates* [sɪ] *uncouple cellular oxidative phosphorylation*[8], *resulting in anaerobic metabolism and excessive production* [ʌ] *of lactic acid.*

Use binding / receptor / proton / oxygen[9] / photo/ immuno/ residual[10] [ɪdʒ] **affinity** • low-/ high-/ reduced **affinity** • **affinity** for carbon monoxide[11] / to insulin • **affinity** chromatography[12] / testing / maturation[13] • to mediate [iː] /avoid/prevent **adsorption** • physical [ɪ]/ physicochemical / gastrointestinal / hem[14] [iː]/ immuno/ viral[15] [aɪ] **adsorption** • **adsorbent** material[16] • receptor-effector • excitation-contraction[17] / antigenic [dʒe] **coupling** • **coupling** reaction • agent / medium[18] [iː] • redox[19] [iː] **couple** • **coupled** with glucose transport / to enzymes

---

Affinität
Adsorption[1] Koppelung[2] adsorbierend; Adsorbens, adsorbierende Substanz[3] adsorbierend[4] adsorbieren[5] koppeln, verbinden; Paar[6] biochem. Desensibilisierung[7] oxidative Phosphorylierung[8] Sauerstoffaffinität[9] Restaffinität[10] Affinität zu Kohlenmonoxid[11] Affinitätschromatografie[12] Affinitätsreifung[13] Hämadsorption[14] Adsorption v. Viren, Virusanheftung[15] adsorbierende(s) Material/ Substanz, Adsorbens[16] elektromechan. Kopplung[17] Koppelmedium[18] Redoxpaar[19]

12

---

hydrophilic [haɪdrəfɪlɪk] *adj term*   *opposite* **hydrophobic**[1] [-foʊbɪk] *adj term*
rel **(non)polar**[2] *adj term*

having a strong affinity to water molecules, a property of polar radicals and ions

pole[3] [poʊl] *n term* • **-philic, -phobic** *comb* • **hydro-** [haɪdrə-] *comb*

» *Water-insoluble lipids, such as cholesterol, can be dissolved within the hydrophobic centers of bile salt micelles. Bile acid molecules have hydrophilic and hydrophobic poles. Nonionized* [aɪə] *forms of nonpolar weak bases tend to be reabsorbed readily* [e] *from tubular urine.*

Use **hydrophilic** agent[4] [eɪdʒ]/ properties[5] / colloids[6] / petrolatum [eɪ‖ɑː] • **hydrophilic** gel [dʒel]/ polymer / groups[7] • **hydrophobic** amino acid / peptide / pole[8] • **hydrophobic** ligand / groups[9] / interaction[10] • **polar** molecule / metabolite • **nonpolar** solvent[11] / lipid • lipo-/ lyo**phobic** • lipo[12]/ acido / baso / lyo**philic** [laɪə-]

---

hydrophil, wasseranziehend
hydrophob, wasserabstoßend[1] (un/a)polar[2] (Zell)pol[3] hydrophile Substanz[4] hydrophile Eigenschaften[5] hydrophile Kolloide[6] hydrophile/polare Gruppen[7] hydrophober Pol[8] hydrophobe/ nichtpolare Gruppen[9] hydrophobe Wechselwirkung[10] un/nichtpolares Lösungsmittel[11] lipophil, fettlöslich, Fett anziehend[12]

13

ligand [laɪgənd] *n term*   *rel* **receptor**[1] [rɪsept♂·], **complex**[2] *n term*

(i) organic molecule attached to a metallic ion by coordinate covalent bonds
(ii) any ion or molecule reacting to form a complex with another compound

complexed (to)[3] *adj term* • **complex** *adj* • **complexation**[4] *n* → U55-2; U39-8

» When LDL undergoes lipid peroxidation it becomes a ligand for an alternative scavenger receptor pathway. Ligand binding induces oligomerization of receptor subunits. The corrin nucleus of cobalamin functions as a ligand for the porphyrin portion of heme. In plasma 12% of calcium is present as a diffusible but undissociated [oʊʃ] complex with anions such as citrate, bicarbonate, and phosphate. From the liver, vitamin A is transported to the body attached [ætʃ] to retinol-binding protein complexed to prealbumin [iː].

Use endogenous [ɒː]/ bacterial [ɪɚ]/ intracellular / radio/ matrix-bound[5] **ligand** • soluble / negatively charged[6] / hydrophobic / CD40 **ligand** • **ligand**-receptor occupancy[7] / pair / activation / expression • **receptor** occupancy • large molecular / (in)soluble / (in)active **complexes** • colipase-lipase / lipoprotein / enzyme-cofactor[8] **complexes** • receptor / antigen-antibody[9] / immune[9] **complexes** • carboxyhemoglobin[10] / iron-deferoxamine **complex** • prothrombin[11] / plasminogen-streptokinase [aɪ] activator[12] **complex** • cholesterol / pyruvate dehydrogenase[13] [ɒːdʒ]/ enzyme[14] **complex** • **complex** salt / carbohydrates[15] / oligosaccharide • **complex** lipids / bilirubin polymers / reaction • **complexed** with fatty acids / to organic anions • calcium **complexation**

chemical reaction [riːækʃ°n] *n*   *rel* **cycle**[1] [saɪkl] *n term*

intermolecular action of substances upon each other in which they are transformed

react *v* • **reactivity**[2] *n term* • **reactive** *adj* • **reagent**[3] [riːeɪdʒənt] *n* • **reactant**[4] *n*

» Do not attempt to neutralize [(j)uː] the alkali [-laɪ] with acid, since the heat generated by the chemical reaction may cause further injury [dʒ]. Vitamins [aɪ‖ɪ] function not as substrates for energy production but as catalytic [ɪ] cofactors for biologic reactions. Phase [feɪz] I reactions result in chemical modification of reactive groups by oxidation, reduction [ʌ], hydroxylation, sulfoxidation, deamination[5], dealkylation, or methylation.

Use to produce[6]/trigger[6] *a chemical reaction* • heat-producing [(j)uː]/ cyclic series of **chemical reactions** • biochemical / metabolic / enzymatic / exergonic[7] **reaction** • (non)synthetic / (ir)reversible[8] [ɜː]/ (self-propagating) chain[9] **reaction** • alkaline[10] / acid / reductive[11] [ʌ]/ methylation[12] / catalase-peroxidase **reaction** • chromaffin / agglutination / quellung[13] **reaction** • Krebs' urea or Krebs-Henseleit[15] / ammonia / Cori[16] **cycle** • chemical / metabolic / cellular / tissue [tɪʃ‖sjuː]/ immunologic / pattern of **reactivity** • highly / auto/ hyper/ cross-/ immuno/ photo/ non**reactive** • **reactive** aldehyde [-haɪd]/ free radical / (oxygen) intermediate[17] [iː] • **reactive** metabolite / collagen [-dʒən] • commercially [ɜː] available [eɪ]/ dipstick[18] / Coombs' enzyme-linked / monoclonal / tissue factor **reagent** • **reagent** strip[19]

catalyst *n term*   *rel* **substrate**[1] [ʌ], **enzyme**[2], **surfactant**[3] *n term* → U78-8

substance that changes the rate of a chemical reaction without being consumed or altered

catalyze[4] [-aɪz] *v term* •(-)**catalytic** [ɪ] *adj & comb* • **catalysis**[5] *n* • **cata**- *comb*

» Nitrites [aɪ] enhance detoxification by acting as a catalyst for sulfide [ʌ] oxidation. Conjugation of bilirubin is catalyzed by glucuronyl transferase, an enzyme on the endoplasmic reticulum. The enzyme plasmin catalyzes the lysis [aɪ] of fibrin. Many vitamins have catalytic functions. Surfactants increase the wetability[6], solubility, and dispersibility[7] of the active drug and thereby increase its dissolution [uːʃ] rate.

Use (in)organic / negative / positive[8] / bio[9] / industrial [ʌ] **catalyst** • metabolic / enzyme[10] [aɪ]/ fat **substrate** / steroid / triglyceride [ɪs] **substrate** • ketone [iː]/ matrix / renin / energy / radiolabeled [eɪ]/ excess[11] / test **substrate** • **substrate** availability /-specific / specificity[12] [ɪs]/ utilization[13] • **substrate** mobilization / flow • **substrate** delivery / deficiency [ɪʃ]/ saturation[14] • catalytic activity[15] / cofactor / (sub)unit[16] [ʌ]/ protein • auto[17]/ photo**catalytic** • **cata**bolism[18] /bolize /lase[19] [-leɪz]

Ligand

Rezeptor[1] Komplex[2] angelagert (an), verbunden (mit)[3] Komplexbildung[4] matrixgebundener Ligand[5] negativ geladener Ligand[6] Liganden-Rezeptorenbesetzung[7] Enzym-Cofaktor-Komplexe[8] Antigen-Antikörper-Komplexe, Immunkomplexe[9] Carboxyhämoglobin-Komplex[10] Prothrombinkomplex[11] Plasminogen-Streptokinase-Aktivatorkomplex[12] Pyruvatdehydrogenase-Komplex[13] Enzymkomplex[14] komplexe Kohlenhydrate[15]

14

chemische Reaktion

Zyklus[1] Reaktivität[2] Reagenz, Reagens[3] Reaktionspartner[4] Desaminierung[5] eine chem. Reaktion auslösen[6] exergone Reaktion[7] (ir)reversible Reaktion[8] Kettenreaktion[9] alkalische/ basische Reaktion[10] Redoxreaktion[11] Methylierungsreaktion[12] Quellungsreaktion[13] Zitronensäure-, Zitrat-, Trikarbonsäure-, Krebs-Zyklus[14] Harnstoff-, Ornithin-, Krebs-Henseleit-Zyklus[15] Glukose-Laktat-, Cori-Zyklus[16] reaktionsfähiges Zwischenprodukt[17] Reagens auf Teststreifen[18] Reagenzstreifen[19]

15

Katalysator

Substrat[1] Enzym[2] oberflächen-, grenzflächenaktive Substanz, Detergens; Surfactant[3] katalysieren, beschleunigen[4] Katalyse[5] Benetzbarkeit[6] Dispersionsfähigkeit[7] Akzelerator[8] Biokatalysator[9] Enzymsubstrat[10] überschüssiges S.[11] Substratspezifität[12] Substratverbrauch[13] Substratsättigung[14] katalyt. Wirkung[15] katalyt. (Unter)einheit[16] autokatalytisch[17] Katabolismus, Abbaustoffwechsel[18] Katalase[19]

16

Biochemistry & Molecular Biology   MEDICAL SCIENCE 337

oxidation [ɒːksɪdeɪʃᵊn] *n term*   *opposite* **reduction**¹ [rɪdʌkʃᵊn] *n term*
    rel **redox** [iː] **reaction**², **combustion**³ [ʌ] *n term*
reaction involving an increase in the valence of a compound or ion due to a loss of electrons
oxidoreduction² *n term* • **oxidative**⁴ *adj* • **oxidize**⁵ *v* • **combustible**⁶ *adj & n*
» Oxidation of the constituent [ɪtʃ] molecules of food to CO_2 and water generates ATP⁷. Vitamin C is a potent antioxidant⁸ involved in many oxidation-reduction reactions. Amino groups, which are derived [aɪ] from oxidation of BCAAs⁹ or transamination of other amino acids, are donated to pyruvate to form alanine and glutamine. Lactic acid is oxidized to carbon dioxide and water in the Krebs cycle [saɪkl]. As a free radical, nitric [aɪ] oxide¹⁰ (*abbr* NO) readily [e] undergoes addition, substitution, redox, and chain-terminating [ɜː] reactions.
Use aerobic¹¹ / biologic¹² / hepatic / beta [eɪ‖iː] **oxidation** • photo/ auto¹³/ omega / per**oxidation** • fatty (acid) / amino acid / FFA¹⁴ / glucose **oxidation** • ethanol / LDL / lysine [aɪ] **oxidation** • sulfide [ʌ]/ substrate¹⁵ [ʌ] **oxidation** • **oxidation** product / state¹⁶ / rate • **oxidation-reduction** reaction² / potential / enzyme¹⁷ • **redox** system¹⁸ / couple¹⁹ [ʌ]/ state²⁰ • **redox** potential²¹ / cycle /-activated form • **combustion** material / of polyvinyl [aɪ] chloride • **combustion** of flammable [æ] material / engine²² • (in)complete²³ • products / of heat [iː] of²⁴ **combustion** • **oxidative** deamination²⁵ / phosphorylation²⁶ • **oxidative** decarboxylation / denaturation

Oxidation
Reduktion¹ Redoxreaktion, Oxidations-Reduktions-Reaktion² Verbrennung³ oxidativ⁴ oxidieren⁵ brennbar; Brennstoff⁶ Adenosintriphosphat, ATP⁷ Antioxidans⁸ verzweigtkettige Aminosäuren⁹ Stick(stoffmon)oxid¹⁰ aerobe Oxidation¹¹ biolog. Oxidation¹² Autooxidation¹³ Oxidation freier Fettsäuren¹⁴ Substratoxidation¹⁵ Oxidationszahl, -stufe¹⁶ Oxidoreduktase¹⁷ Redoxsystem¹⁸ Redoxpaar¹⁹ Redoxzahl²⁰ Redoxpotential²¹ Verbrennungsmotor²² (un)vollständige Verbrennung²³ Verbrennungswärme²⁴ oxidative Desaminierung²⁵ oxidative Phosphorylierung²⁶

17

derivative [iː] *n & adj term*   *rel* **intermediate**¹ *or* **intermediary**¹ *adj n & adj term*
(n) chemical compound that may be produced from another of similar structure
derivation² [eɪʃ] *n term* • **derived (from)**³ [dɪraɪvd] *adj*
» This enzyme catalyzes oxidative decarboxylation of the branched-chain keto acid derivatives⁴ of leucine [luːsiːn], isoleucine, and valine. Clofazimine, a compound derived from a phenazine dye [daɪ], is highly lipophilic. Malonyl-CoA, the first committed intermediate in the synthesis of fatty acids from glucose, is a competitive inhibitor of carnitine palmitoyltransferase I.
Use water-soluble / fluorinated / cellulose / purified protein⁵ (*abbr* PPD) **derivative** • thiazide [aɪ]/ ergot / benzene / (semi)synthetic⁶ **derivative** • hematoporphyrin (*abbr* HPD)/ penicillin⁷ [sɪ] **derivative** • oxygen-/ plasmin-/ T-cell **derived** • metabolic⁸ / reactive (oxygen) **intermediate** • sequential [-enʃᵊl]/ short-lived⁹ **intermediate** • **intermediate** metabolism¹⁰ • chemical **intermediary** • **intermediary** metabolism¹⁰ / metabolite / product¹¹ / compound / form • hematopoetic / embryologic **derivation**

Derivat, Abkömmling; abgeleitet
Zwischenprodukt, Intermediat; Zwischen-, intermediär¹ Derivatio, Ableitung, Ursprung² stammen/ s. ableiten von³ verzweigtkettige Keto-Säurederivate⁴ aufgereinigtes Eiweißderivat⁵ (halb)synthetisches Derivat⁶ Penicillinderivat⁷ Stoffwechselzwischenprodukt⁸ kurzlebiges Zwischenprodukt⁹ Intermediär-, Zwischenstoffwechsel¹⁰ Zwischenprodukt¹¹

18

acid [æsɪd] *n & adj & comb term*   *opposite* **alkali**¹ [-laɪ], *pl* **-li(e)s**, **base**² *n term*
(n) substance which yields [jiːldz] hydrogen [aɪ] ions when dissociated [ouʃ] in solution [uːʃ]
(adj) sour [sauə]
acidity³ *n term* • **acidic**⁴ *adj* • **acidosis**⁵ *n* • **acido-** *comb* • **basic**⁶ [eɪ] *adj* • **alkaline**⁶ [-laɪn] *adj term* • **alkalinity**⁷ [eɪ] *n* • **alkali(ni)zation**⁸ *n* • **alkalosis**⁹ *n*
» All acids react with bases to form salts and water. Acute respiratory alkalosis caused by overventilation¹⁰ is common. Decreased oxygen delivery caused by dehydration may lead to lactic acidosis. Metabolic alkalosis may result from retention of alkali and is indicated by an alkaline pH. The erythromycin [aɪs] base is more acid-stable¹¹.
Use amino / (essential/ free) fatty¹² / hydrochloric¹³ / salicylic [sɪ] **acid** • lactic¹⁴ / acetic [siː] / bile¹⁵ [aɪ] **acid** / ascorbic¹⁶ / citric¹⁷ / uric **acid** • **acid** crystals / phosphatase /-base balance¹⁸ • **acid** secretion [iːʃ]/-fast¹¹ / burn¹⁹ [ɜː]/ residue²⁰ • to neutralize / gastric²¹ **acidity** • uremic [iː]/ metabolic / diabetic / renal [iː] tubular²² / nonrespiratory **acidosis** • **alkali** ingestion • **alkaline** urine / phosphatase²³ / pH / earth [ɜː] metals • mild / hypokalemic [iː]/ metabolic **alkalosis** • respiratory²⁴ / hypochloremic²⁵ **alkalosis** • chemical / conjugate **base** • **base** pair /-forming food / analogue²⁶ / excess²⁷

Säure; sauer, säurehaltig
Alkali¹ Base, Lauge² Säuregrad, Azidität³ säurehaltig, -bildend, sauer⁴ Azidose⁵ basisch, alkalisch⁶ Alkalität, Alkaliengehalt⁷ Alkalisierung⁸ Alkalose⁹ Hyperventilation¹⁰ säurebeständig, -fest¹¹ freie Fettsäure¹² Salzsäure (HCl)¹³ Milchsäure¹⁴ Gallensäure¹⁵ Ascorbinsäure, Vitamin C¹⁶ Zitronensäure¹⁷ Säure-Basen-Haushalt¹⁸ Verätzung¹⁹ Säurerest²⁰ Magensäuregehalt²¹ renal tubuläre Azidose²² alkalische Phosphatase²³ respirator. Alkalose²⁴ hypochlorämische A.²⁵ Basenanalogon²⁶ Basenüberschuss, -exzess²⁷

19

buffer [bʌfɚ] n & v term

rel **barrier**[1] [bæriɚ], **pH**[2] n, **neutralize**[3] v term

mixture of an acid and its conjugate base[4] (salt) that, when present in a solution, reduces any changes in pH which would otherwise occur in the solution when acid or alkali is added to it

(un/ non)**buffered**[5] [ʌ] adj • **neutralization**[6] n • **neutral** [n(j)uːtrəl] adj

» Isolates [aɪ] were then rinsed in buffer[7] and placed in culture [ʌ] dishes[8]. The pH of the blood is maintained virtually [ɜː] constant (pH 7.45) although acid metabolites are continually being formed in the tissues. Excessive acid intake may contribute to "dissolution" of bone as the body attempts to buffer the extra acid.

Use aqueous[9] [eɪ‖æ]/ phosphate[10] / acetate / neutralizing / temporary **buffer** • **buffer** solution[9] / base[11] / capacity[12] / system[13] • **buffered** saline [eɪ] solution • biologic / anatomic / blood-brain[14] / alveolocapillary **barrier** • (gastric) mucosal[15] / charge-selective / protective **barrier** • toxin / heat of[16] / partial [ʃ]/ virus **neutralization** • **neutralization** test / titer • **neutral** solution / pH[17] / fats[18] / to saline

osmosis n term, abbr osm → U49-9

rel **diffusion**[1] [dɪfjuːʒən] n term → U88-4

process by which solvents tend to move through a semipermeable [ɜː] membrane from a solution of lower to one of higher osmolal solute concentration (to which the membrane is relatively impermeable)

osmotic[2] adj term • **osmolar** adj • **osmolarity**[3] n • **osmolality**[4] n • **osmo-** comb

» Saline laxatives[5] contain cations and anions that exert [ɜː] an osmotic effect to increase intraluminal [uː] water content. Hypernatremia [iː] secondary to nonosmotic urinary water loss is usually due to diabetes [iː] insipidus characterized by impaired [eɚ] AVP[6] secretion.

Use electro[7]-/ reverse [ɜː] (abbr RO) **osmosis** • **osmotic** pressure[8] (abbr OP)/ gradient [eɪ]/ threshold[9] / diuresis[10] [iː] • **osmotic** diarrhea [iː]/ equilibrium / fragility[11] [dʒɪ]/ imbalance • iso/ non**osmotic** • **osmolar** gap[12] / concentration • hyper/ hypo/ high-/ low[13]-**osmolar** • **osmo**regulation[14] /receptor[15] [se] /le /lyte [-laɪt]

dissociation [dɪsoʊʃieɪʃən] n term → U88-4

rel **dissolution**[1], **liquefaction**[2], **dispersion**[3] [dɪspɜːrʒən] n term

change of chemical compounds into simpler ones by a lytic [ɪ] reaction[4] or by ionization

dissociate[5] v • **dissolve** v • **solvent**[6] n & adj • **liquid**[7] [lɪkwɪd] adj & n → U82-4

disperse[8] [dɪspɜːrs] v • **dispersal** n

» Reduction in the synthesis of 2,3-bisphosphoglycerate [ɪs] causes a shift to the left of the oxygen-hemoglobin dissociation curve [ɜː]. CO_2 arising from metabolism is hydrated [aɪ] to carbonic acid[9] and dissociates into hydrogen and bicarbonate. Because of the dissociation characteristics of carbonic acid (H_2CO_3) at body pH, dissolved CO_2 is almost exclusively in the form of bicarbonate (HCO_3^-). Uric acid stones[10] occur [ɜː] because of increased urine acidity in which undissociated[11] uric acid crystallizes [ɪ].

Use Ionic **dissociation** • **dissociation** constant[12] • (hemoglobin-)oxygen **dissociation** curve[13] • to undergo/promote or hasten[14]/retard **dissolution** • chemical / enzymatic **dissolution** • gallstone[15] [ɔː]/ clot[16] / enamel[17] **dissolution** • **dissolution** rate[18] / therapy • basal cell / eosinophilic **liquefaction** • **liquefaction** of secretions[19] • necrosis • cell / aqueous[20] / colloidal[21] / pigment **dispersion** • **dispersion** of light / medium[22] [iː] • hetero**disperse**[23] • **dispersal** phase[24]

Puffer, puffern

Barriere, Schranke[1] pH(-Wert)[2] neutralisieren[3] konjugierte Base[4] (un)gepuffert[5] Neutralisation[6] mit Pufferlösung gespült[7] Kulturschalen[8] Pufferlösung[9] Phosphatpuffer[10] Pufferbase[11] Pufferkapazität[12] Puffersystem[13] Blut-Hirn-Schranke[14] Magenschleimhautbarriere[15] Neutralisationswärme[16] neutraler pH-Wert[17] Neutralfette[18]

20

Osmose

Diffusion[1] osmotisch[2] Osmolarität[3] Osmolalität[4] salinische Abführmittel/ Laxanzien[5] Argipressin, Arginin-Vasopressin[6] Elektroosmose[7] osmotischer Druck[8] osmotische Schwelle[9] osmotische Diurese[10] osmotische Erythrozytenresistenz[11] Differenz zwischen gemessener und errechneter Osmolarität[12] niederosmolar[13] Osmoregulation[14] Osmorezeptor[15]

21

Dissoziation, Auftrennung, Aufspaltung, Zerfall

Auflösung[1] Verflüssigung, Liquefaktion[2] Dispersion, Verteilung[3] lytische Reaktion, Zerfallsreaktion[4] dissoziieren, zerfallen[5] Lösungsmittel; (auf)lösend[6] flüssig; Flüssigkeit[7] dispergieren, (fein) verteilen[8] Kohlensäure[9] Harnsäure-, Uratsteine[10] undissoziiert[11] Dissoziationskonstante[12] Sauerstoffdissoziationskurve[13] d. Auflösung beschleunigen[14] Gallensteinauflösung[15] Thrombolyse[16] Schmelzauflösung[17] Lösungsgeschwindigkeit (Arznei)[18] Sekretverflüssigung[19] wässrige Lösung[20] kolloidale Verteilung[21] Dispersionsmittel, Dispergens[22] heterodispers, gemischtdispers[23] disperse Phase, Dispersum[24]

22

Biochemistry & Molecular Biology — MEDICAL SCIENCE

concentration n term   rel **dilution**[1] [dɪ‖daɪluːʃən],
    titer[2] [taɪtɚ] n term → U116-17

ratio [reɪʃ(ɪ)oʊ] of the volume or mass of a solute[3] to that of the solution or solvent

concentrate[4] n & v term • **(un)concentrated** adj • **dilutional** [uːʃ] adj
diluent[5] [dɪljuənt] adj & n term • **dilute**[6] [daɪluːt] v & adj • **titration**[7] n • **titrate**[8] v

» A normal blood pH of 7.40 is equal [iː] to a hydrogen ion concentration of 40 nmol/L. A measurement [eʒ] of serum salicylate [ɪ] concentration should be obtained [eɪ] immediately. His polyuria [juɚ] is due to the expansion and dilution of body fluids.

Use hydrogen ion[9] / plasma (abbr P) / urine or urinary (abbr U) **concentration** • renin / fractional / solute **concentration** • molar / osmole or osmolal[10] **concentration** • normal / hypertonic / steady-state[11] [e] **concentration** • peak [iː] / high[12]-/ total **concentration** • **concentration** gradient[13] [eɪ] / ability[14] /-dependent • highly[12] / maximally **concentrated** • 1:10 / urinary / plasma / serum / hemo[15] [iː] / thermo-**dilution** [ɜː] • serial[16] [ɪɚ] / isotope [aɪ] / at a high[17] **dilution** • bacterial [ɪɚ] / serologic / serum **titer** • antibody[18] / IgM / reagin [riːeɪg‖dʒən] **titer** • elevated[19] / high / low / rising **titer** • **titer** rise[20] • **diluted** to a 5% solution / 1:4 in normal saline [eɪ] • **diluted** to half strength / 1:1 with water • **dilute** solution[21] / suspension / urine • passive / sterile **diluent** • **dilutional** acidosis[22] / hyponatremia[23] [iː] • chemical / serial / cross[24] / upward / dose[25] **titration** • **titration** curve[26] [ɜː]

---

saturated [sætʃəreɪtɪd] adj term   opposite **desaturated**[1], **unsaturated**[1] adj term

(i) dissolved up to that concentration beyond which the addition of more results in two phases
(ii) to satisfy all the chemical affinities of a substance (as by converting all double bonds[2] to single bonds)

(de[3]**/ super**[4]**)saturation** [eɪʃ] n term • **saturate**[5] v • **saturable**[6] adj

» Fetal hemoglobin is 85% saturated at PO_2 levels of 42 mm Hg. Monitor O_2 saturation[7] by pulse oximetry. A lowering of PO_2 produces desaturation of hemoglobin.

Use highly[8] / fully / super**saturated** • (arterial) oxygen[7] / Hb[9] / cholesterol **saturation** • mixed venous O_2 (abbr SvO_2) / percent(age)[10] **saturation** • mono / poly**unsaturated** fatty acids[11] • arterial / O_2 / tissue **desaturation** • **desaturated** blood

---

suspension [səspenʃən] n term   sim **solution**[1] [uː], **emulsion**[2] [ʌ] n term

solid dispersed [ɜː] through a liquid in finely divided particles

(re)suspend[3] v term • **solute**[4] [sɔːljuːt] n & adj • **emulsify**[5] v • **emulsifier**[6] n • **emulsification**[7] n → U88-5; U9-11

» Tetracycline [aɪ] oral suspension is held in the mouth for 2 to 5 min to coat the ulcers [ʌ] before swallowing. Resistant scalp patches may respond to local superficial injection of triamcinolone [sɪ] acetonide suspension diluted with saline [eɪ] to 2.5 mg/mL. Bile [aɪ] salts have a major [eɪdʒ] role in the emulsification of fatty acids.

Use liquid / colloid[8] / (un)diluted / turbid[9] [ɜː] **suspension** • crystalline [ɪ] / oral / chlorothiazide [aɪ] **suspension** • petroleum jelly [dʒ] / corticosteroid / bismuth subsalicylate **suspension** • aqueous / (balanced) salt / colloid **solution** • crystalloid / emulsified fat[10] / electrolyte[11] **solution** • dextrose / potassium iodide [aɪ] / sodium bicarbonate **solution** • dilute[12] [uː] / antiseptic **solution** • 5% amino acetate / silver nitrate [aɪ] / lactated Ringer' (intravenous) [iː] fat[14] / 20% lipid / oily / soapy [oʊ] / water-in-oil[15] **emulsion** • low-molecular-weight[16] [weɪt] / ingested [dʒe] / body fluid **solute** • **solute** composition / transport / concentration / load [oʊ] • **solute**-free water / excretion [iːʃ] / diuresis [iː]

---

colloid [kɒːlɔɪd] n & adj term   opposite **crystalloid**[1] [ɪ] n & adj term → U82-5

(n) aggregate of atoms or molecules which are finely dispersed in a gaseous, liquid, or solid medium [iː]

hydrocolloid[2] n term • **colloidal** adj • **crystalline**[3] adj • **crystal-** comb

» Begin volume replacement with saline [eɪ] or colloid solutions and with vasopressors [veɪzoʊ-], if necessary. Patients who have inadequate urine output despite administration of a high volume of crystalloid often respond to colloid.

Use polysaccharide [æk] / artificial [ɪʃ] **colloids** • **colloidal** preparation / gel / dispersion / solution[4] • **colloidal** osmotic pressure[5] / bismuth compound[6] • **colloid** droplets / solution[4] / infusion • **hydrocolloid** dressing[7] • **crystal** formation[8] / aggregation / deposition[9] (disease) / lattice[10] • **crystalloid** fluid / salt solution[11]

Konzentration
Verdünnung, Dilution[1] Titer[2] gelöste Substanz[3] Konzentrat; konzentrieren[4] verdünnend; Verdünnungsmittel[5] verdünnen, diluieren; verdünnt[6] Titration[7] titrieren[8] Wasserstoffionenkonzentration[9] osmolale K.[10] Gleichgewichts-, steady-state K.[11] hochkonzentriert[12] Konzentrationsgefälle, -gradient[13] Konzentrationsfähigkeit, -vermögen[14] Hämodilution, Blutverdünnung[15] Verdünnungsreihe[16] bei starker Verdünnung[17] Antikörpertiter[18] erhöhter T.[19] Titeranstieg[20] verdünnte Lösung[21] Verdünnungs-, Dilutionsazidose[22] Schwartz-Bartter-Syndrom, Verdünnungshyponatriämie[23] Kreuztitration[24] Dosistitration[25] Titrationskurve[26]   23

gesättigt, saturiert
desaturiert; ungesättigt[1] Doppelbindungen[2] Desaturierung[3] Übersättigung[4] sättigen, saturieren[5] sättigungsfähig[6] Sauerstoffsättigung[7] hochgesättigt[8] Hämoglobin-Sättigung[9] prozentmäßige S., Sättigungsgrad[10] mehrfach ungesättigte Fettsäuren[11]   24

Aufschwemmung, Suspension
Lösung[1] Emulsion[2] aufschwemmen, suspendieren[3] gelöste Substanz; gelöst, in Lösung[4] emulgieren[5] Emulgator[6] Emulgierung[7] kolloidale Suspension[8] trübe/milchige Suspension[9] Fettemulsion[10] Elektrolytlösung[11] verdünnte Lösung[12] Ringer-Laktat-Lösung[13] intravenöse Fettemulsion[14] Wasser-in-Öl-Emulsion[15] niedermolekulare Lösung[16]   25

Kolloid; kolloid(al)
kristalloide Lösung; kristalloid, kristallartig[1] Hydrokolloid[2] kristallartig, kristallin[3] kolloidale Lösung[4] kolloidosmotischer Druck[5] kolloidale Wismutverbindung[6] Hydrokolloidverband[7] Kristallbildung[8] Kristallablagerung[9] Kristallgitter[10] kristalloide Salzlösung[11]   26

precipitate [n prɪˈsɪpɪtət‖v -teɪt] n & v term → U136-17
    rel **flocculation**[1], **sedimentation**[2] n, **supernatant**[3] [eɪ] adj & n term

(n) solid particles deposited from dissolved substances
(v) to cause a substance to settle out[4] of solution

precipitation[5] n term • **precipitin** n • **flocculate**[6] v • **flocculent**[7] adj • **sediment**[8] n

» Sufficient uric acid in the urine may plug [ʌ] both ureters with precipitate. Alkali injuries [dʒ] are more serious, since alkalies are not precipitated by the proteins of the eye as are acids. Phosphate precipitates in an alkaline urine. A high liquid intake[9] will minimize urate [ˈjʊəreɪt] precipitation in the urinary tract. Barium [eə] flocculates in the intestine. Clearing of the milky appearance from the supernatant [eɪ] of the centrifuged pleural [ʊə] fluid suggests empyema [iː].

Use **to precipitate** barium sulfate [ʌ]/ bile [aɪ] acids[10] / fluoride [ʊə] • fine / amorphous / cryo[11]/ sulfosalicylic [sɪ] acid **precipitate** • **flocculation** test[12] / titer [aɪ] • erythrocyte[13] [ɪ] (abbr ESR)/ rapid / elevated **sedimentation rate** • to test/pour off[14] **the supernatant** • turbid [ɜː]/ clear / xanthochromic [zænθə-] **supernatant** • **supernatant** fluid • to cause[15]/facilitate/promote/prevent **precipitation** • cold-induced[16] / calcium phosphate **precipitation** • uric acid / urate crystal[17] **precipitation** • **flocculent**[18] / renal [iː] **precipitation** • **precipitated** sulfur • **precipitating** antibodies[19] • **flocculent** material • centrifuged[20] / urinary or urine[21] / CSF[22] • **sediment** • **sediment** residue [ˈrezɪd(j)uː]:

Niederschlag, Präzipitat; ausfällen, präzipitieren
(Aus)flockung, Flockenbildung[1] Ablagerung, Sedimentbildung, Sedimentation[2] obenauf schwimmend; Überstand[3] präzipitieren, s. absetzen[4] Präzipitation, Ausfällung[5] (aus)flocken[6] flockig[7] (Boden)satz, Sediment[8] Flüssigkeitszufuhr[9] Gallensäuren ausfällen[10] Kryopräzipitat[11] Flockungstest[12] Blutkörperchensenkungsgeschwindigkeit, BSG, Erythrozytensenkungsreaktion, ESR[13] den Überstand abgießen[14] zur Präzipitation führen[15] Kälteprazipitation[16] Ausfällung v. Harnsäurekristallen[17] Ausflockung[18] präzipitierende Antikörper[19] zentrifugiertes Sediment[20] Harnsediment[21] Liquorsediment[22]
27

Unit 82   Biochemical Elements & Compounds
Related Units: 81 Biochemistry, 78 Metabolism, 79 Nutrition, 83 Cell Biology, 84 Genetics, 92 Pharmacologic Agents, 93 Anesthetics, 91 Toxicology, 99 Radiology

(chemical) element n   rel **particle**[1], **isotope**[2] [ˈaɪsətoʊp] n term → U99-22

one of the substances [ʌ] of which all matter[3] is composed that cannot be decomposed[4] by ordinary chemical means; made up of atoms each of which consists of a nucleus of protons and neutrons [(j)uː] and a cloud of negatively charged electrons[5] that are identical in configuration and chemical properties

elemental[6] adj term • **(non)particulate**[7] adj • **radioisotope**[8] n • **isotopic** adj

» Radioactive elements do not have a balanced proton-to neutron ratio [eɪʃ] in their nuclei and therefore readily [e] give off nuclear particles. Iron, iodine [aɪ], copper, manganese, zinc, and cobalt are the most important of the 13 essential trace [treɪs] elements. Gamma-rays [reɪz] are emitted during the decay[9] [dɪˈkeɪ] of radioactive isotopes.

Use **stable**[10] [eɪ]/ **labile** [eɪ]/ electropositive / radioactive **elements** • **transuranic**[11] / rare earth[12] / macro/ trace[13] **elements** • **elementary**[14] / dissolved / colloid / aerosolized / charged[15] [tʃɑːrdʒd] **particles** • osmotically active / heavy / alpha[16] / beta [eɪ‖iː] **particle** • **particle** size / beam[17] [iː]/ agglutination / accelerator[18] • to take up / (non)radioactive[8] / short-lived[19] / gamma-emitting **isotope** • chromium / uptake of / bone-seeking[20] [iː] **isotope** • **isotope** (bone) scanning /-labeled [eɪ]/ study • **isotope** renogram[21] [iː]/ dilution [uːʃ] technique[22] • **elemental** calcium / iron / zinc • **particulate** matter / elements / radiation[23] / smoke / alkali / antigens

(chemisches) Element
Partikel, Teilchen[1] Isotop[2] Materie[3] zerlegt[4] Elektronenwolke[5] elementar[6] Teilchen-, Partikel-[7] Radioisotop, -nuklid[8] Zerfall[9] stabile Elemente[10] Transurane[11] seltene Erden[12] Spurenelemente[13] Elementarteilchen[14] (elektr.) geladene Teilchen[15] α-Teilchen[16] Korpuskularstrahl[17] Teilchenbeschleuniger[18] kurzlebiges Radionuklid[19] knochenaffines Isotop[20] (Radio)isotopennephrogramm, Nierenszintigramm[21] Isotopenverdünnungsmethode[22] Teilchenstrahlung[23]
1

gaseous [ˈɡæʃ‖ˈɡæsɪəs] adj term   rel **volatile**[1] [ˈvɒːlət³l‖-taɪl] adj term

in an air-like form in which the molecules are separated from one another and are capable of indefinite expansion; by compression and cold gases are also convertible [ɜː] into liquids

gas n • **volatilize**[2] v term • **volatilization** n • **nonvolatile** adj

» The elements in the zero [ˈzɪəroʊ] group in the periodic system (helium [iː], neon [ˈniːɒn], argon, krypton [ɪ], xenon [ze‖ziː-], and radon) are termed noble gases[3].

Use **gaseous** form / environment / ethylene oxide • **volatile** gases / vapor / anesthetic[4] • **volatile** solvents / amines / nitrites [aɪ] oils[5] / irritant[6] / greenhouse[7] **gases** • inert [ɜː] or noble[3] / noxious[8] [ɒkʃ]/ toxic **gases** • (highly) soluble / (super)heated / expansile **gases** • odoriferous[9] / sewer[10] [suːə]/ explosive / blood[11] **gases** • hydrogen[12] [aɪ]/ formaldehyde **gas** • radon / radiolabeled xenon **gas** • tear[13] [tɪə]/ mustard[14] / pressurized / intestinal **gas** • **gas** mixture[15] / exchange[16] / gangrene

gasförmig, Gas-
flüchtig, volatil, ätherisch[1] verdampfen, -dunsten (lassen), s. verflüchtigen[2] Edelgase[3] Inhalationsanästhetikum, volatiles Anästhetikum[4] ätherische Öle[5] Reizgase[6] Treibhausgase[7] schädliche Gase[8] übelriechende Gase[9] Kanalgase[10] Blutgase[11] Knallgas[12] Tränengas[13] Senfgas, Gelbkreuz, Lost[14] Gasgemisch[15] Gasaustausch[16]
2

Biochemical Elements & Compounds — MEDICAL SCIENCE

vapor [veɪpɚ] n   rel **steam¹** [stiːm] n, **fumes²** [fjuːmz] n pl

substance in the gaseous state that results from heating [iː] of a liquid or solid

evaporate³ [ɪvæpɚeɪt] v • **vaporize⁴** [væpɚaɪz] v • **vaporizer⁵** n • **steamy** adj

» As inspired [aɪ] gas enters the upper airway, it becomes saturated [sætʃ-] with water vapor. Humidifying [hjuː-] aerosols⁶ and steam inhalations [eɪ] exert [ɜː] an antitussive [ʌ] effect⁷ by their demulcent [dɪmʌlsənt] action⁸ and by decreasing [iː] the viscosity of bronchial [k] secretions [iːʃ].

Use water⁹/ heated / mercury¹⁰ [ɜː] **vapor** • metal¹¹ / acid [æsɪd]/ sulfur [ʌ] dioxide¹² **fumes** • toxic / coal tar¹³ [tɑːr] **fumes** • zinc oxide / paint¹⁴ / exhaust¹⁵ [ɔː] **fumes** • irritant / poisonous¹⁶ / industrial [ʌ] **fumes** • saturated¹⁷ **steam** • **steam** sterilizer¹⁸ / sterilization • **steam** cautery¹⁹ [ɔː]/ inhalation

Dampf, Dunst

(Wasser)dampf¹ Dämpfe, Rauch(gas)² verdampfen, -dunsten, s. verflüchtigen³ verdampfen, vernebeln, vaporisieren⁴ Verdampfer, Verdampfungsgerät⁵ Aerosole zum Befeuchten⁶ hustenreizstillende Wirkung⁷ reizlindernde W.⁸ Wasserdampf⁹ Quecksilberdampf¹⁰ Metalldämpfe¹¹ Schwefeldioxiddämpfe¹² Teerdämpfe¹³ Farbdämpfe¹⁴ Abgase¹⁵ giftige D.¹⁶ gesättigter Wasserdampf¹⁷ Dampfsterilisator¹⁸ Elektrovaporisation¹⁹   3

---

aqueous [eɪ‖ækwɪəs] adj term   syn **watery** adj,
    rel **fluid¹** [fluːɪd], **liquid¹** adj & n

prepared with, containing [eɪ], dissolved in, or similar to water

water n • **liquefy²** [lɪkwəfaɪ] v • **liquefaction³** n term • **aqua-** [æ‖ɑːkw] comb

» When the reaction is performed in an aqueous medium [iː], the water-soluble conjugated bilirubin reacts directly with sulfanilic acid⁴, giving a positive direct van den Bergh reaction. Conjunctival [dʒʌ] instillation of a 1% aqueous solution of silver nitrate [aɪ] is effective in preventing blindness.

Use **aqueous** medium / solution⁵ / environment • **aqueous** iodine / formalin / aerosol • **aqueous** acetic [siː] acid⁶ / epinephrine • **aqueous** penicillin⁷ [sɪ]/ dispersion [ɜː]/ slurry⁸ [ɜː] • **watery** discharge⁹/ exudate • clear / hot / viscous [vɪskəs] **liquid** • acidic / strongly concentrated¹⁰ **liquid** • flammable [æ] / caustic¹¹ [ɔː]/ non/ semi**liquid** • **liquid** oxygen / nitrogen¹² [aɪ] • **liquid** mercury¹³ [ɜː]/ petrolatum [eɪ‖ɑː] (emulsion) [ʌ] • **liquid** soap [oʊ]/ culture [ʌ] medium¹⁴ • **liquid** suspension / diet [daɪət]/ chromatography¹⁵ • crystalloid [ɪ] / colloid **fluid** • body¹⁶ / extracellular (abbr ECF) **fluid** • clear / milky / cloudy¹⁷ [aʊ]/ blood-tinged¹⁸ [dʒ] **fluid** • serous [ɪə]/ low-viscosity **fluid** • **fluid**-filled space / balance¹⁹ / intake²⁰ / accumulation • **fluid** overload²¹ / retention / replacement²² • mineral / distilled²³ / saline [eɪ]/ carbonated²⁴ **water** • tap²⁵ / fluoridated / heavy²⁶ [e]/ drinking²⁷ / potable²⁷ [oʊ] **water** • total body²⁸ (abbr TBW)/ hard / boiling **water** • **water**-soluble²⁹ /-soaked [oʊ]/-borne³⁰ [ɔː] • aqua fortis³¹ / pura / bidestillata / regia³² [riːdʒɪə]

wässrig, wasserhaltig

flüssig; Flüssigkeit¹ (s.) verflüssigen² Verflüssigung³ Sulfanilsäure, p-Aminobenzolsulfonsäure⁴ wässrige Lösung⁵ verdünnte Essigsäure⁶ wässrige Penicillin-Lösung⁷ Aufschwemmung i. Wasser⁸ wässrige(s) Sekret/ Absonderung⁹ Ätzflüssigkeit¹⁰ hochkonzentrierte F.¹¹ flüssiger Stickstoff¹² fl. Quecksilber¹³ fl. Kulturmedium¹⁴ Flüssigkeitschromatografie¹⁵ Körperflüssigkeit¹⁶ trübe F.¹⁷ blutig tingierte F.¹⁸ Flüssigkeitshaushalt¹⁹ Flüssigkeitszufuhr, -aufnahme²⁰ Überwässerung, Hyperhydratation²¹ Flüssigkeitsersatz²² destilliertes Wasser, Aqua destillata²³ Sodawasser, kohlensäurehaltiges W.²⁴ Leitungswasser²⁵ schweres W.²⁶ Trinkwasser²⁷ Gesamtkörperwasser²⁸ wasserlöslich²⁹ durch W. übertragen³⁰ Scheidewasser, Salpetersäure³¹ Königswasser³²   4

---

normal saline [seɪliːn‖aɪn] n term   rel **salt¹** [sɔːlt] n → U3-18
    mineral² n & adj, **crystal³** [ɪ] n → U81-26

isotonic solution of 0.9% sodium chloride⁴ in aqueous solution (distilled water)

saline⁵ adj term • de/ remineralization n • **crystalize⁶** v • **salin(o)-** comb

» First a dilute⁷ [daɪluːt] normal saline solution is administered at a rate of 10 mL/kg over 15 min. Cover the cut with a sterile dressing that has been soaked⁸ [oʊ] in saline. Fortification⁹ of foodstuffs [ʌ] with essential minerals, such as iodine [aɪ] in salt has nearly eliminated once-common deficiency [ɪʃ] states such as iodine-deficient goiter¹⁰ [ɔɪ] and rickets¹¹.

Use isotonic¹² [aɪsɑ-]/ hypertonic [aɪ]/ buffered¹³ [ʌ]/ 3% / iced / nebulized / heparinized **saline** • **saline** solution / nasal rinses¹⁴ / cathartic¹⁵ / antibody¹⁶ • **saline** enema¹⁷ /-filled prosthesis [iː]/ infusion • (in)organic / (poorly) soluble / bicarbonate [baɪ-] **salt** • common¹⁸ / stone / table¹⁹ / iodized²⁰ [aɪədaɪzd] **salt** • chloride / phosphate / calcium-containing [eɪ] **salts** • magnesium [iː]/ aluminum²¹ / copper / zinc **salts** • acid / neutral²² [(j)uː]/ (mildly) alkaline or basic²³ [eɪ]/ buffer / bile²⁴ [aɪ] **salt** • **salt** solution / content / load / crystals [ɪ]/ loss²⁵ / tablets • **salt**-containing • wasting²⁵ [eɪ]/ depletion²⁶ [iː]/ restriction /-losing nephropathy²⁷ • low-**salt** diet²⁸ [aɪ] • trace²⁹ **minerals** • bone **mineral** density³⁰ • **mineral** phase [feɪz]/ ions [aɪənz]/ oil / wax • cholesterol / uric acid³¹ / apatite **crystals** • calcium pyrophosphate dihydrate [aɪ] (abbr CPPD)/ calcium oxalate **crystal** • **crystal** structure / lattice³² [lætɪs]/ deposition³³ (disease) /-associated arthritis [aɪ] • skeletal³⁴ / bone / tooth [uː] demineralization

physiolog. Kochsalzlösung

Salz¹ Mineral; anorganisch, mineralisch² Kristall³ Natriumchlorid⁴ salzhaltig, salinisch, Salz-⁵ (aus)kristallisieren⁶ verdünnt⁷ getränkt⁸ Anreicherung⁹ Iodmangelstruma¹⁰ Rachitis¹¹ isotone Kochsalzlösung¹² gepufferte K.¹³ salzhaltige Nasenspüllösung¹⁴ salinisches Abführmittel¹⁵ Antikörper in phys. Kochsalzlösung¹⁶ Einlauf m. Kochsalzlösung¹⁷ Kochsalz, Natriumchlorid¹⁸ Tafel-, Speisesalz¹⁹ iodiertes S.²⁰ Aluminiumsalze²¹ Neutralsalz²² basisches S.²³ Gallensalz²⁴ Salzverlust²⁵ Salzverlust, -mangel²⁶ renales Salzverlustsyndrom²⁷ salzarme Diät²⁸ mineralische Spurenelemente²⁹ Mineralgehalt d. K.³⁰ Knochendichte³⁰ Harnsäure-, Uratkristalle³¹ Kristallgitter³² Kristallablagerung³³ Knochenentmineralisierung³⁴   5

342 MEDICAL SCIENCE — Biochemical Elements & Compounds

metal [metʰl] n & adj opposite **nonmetal**[1] n & adj
  rel **solid**[2] n & adj, **alloy**[3] [æloɪ‖əloɪ] n & v

(n) chemical element marked by luster[4] [ʌ], ductility[5], malleability[6], conductivity[7] (electricity, heat), and high corrosion [oʊʒ] resistance[8] that has the tendency to lose rather than gain electrons in solution

(non)metallic adj • **solidify**[9] v • **solidity**[10] n • **metall(o)-** comb

» Noble [oʊ] metals such as gold or platinum are highly resistant to oxidation and corrosion. Lithium is a naturally occurring [ɜː] alkali metal. Metal fume fever[11] [iː] results from acute exposure [oʊʒ] to fumes or smoke of zinc, copper, magnesium, and other volatilized metals.

Use to bind **metals** • alkali / abundant [ʌ]/ rare earth[12] / light / hard / heavy[13] **metals** • trace[14] / (high/ non)noble[15] / (non)precious[15] [eʃ] **metals** • liquid / volatilized[16] / fusible[17] [juː] **metal** • colloidal / caustic / toxic **metal** • **metal** ions / chelator[18] [kiːleɪtə]/ particles / toxicity [ɪs] • soft / caustic **solids** • **solid** matter[19] / compound [-aʊnd]/ component[20] [oʊ]/ media [iː] • **solid** phase[21] / salt / foods • cobalt-chrome / gold-palladium / titanium(-based) / brass[22] [æ] **alloy** • **metallic** mercury (vapor) / surface [ɜː] taste[23] / sound[24] / tinkle[24] • **metallo**protein[25] /enzymes[26] /protease[27] • **metall**urgy [-ɜːrdʒi] /oid

Metall; metallisch

Nichtmetall, nichtmetallisch[1] fester Stoff, Festkörper; fest, massiv, dicht[2] (Metall)legierung; legieren[3] Glanz[4] Dehnbarkeit[5] (Ver)formbarkeit[6] Leitfähigkeit[7] Korrosionsfestigkeit, -beständigkeit[8] fest werden, erstarren[9] Festigkeit, Dichtheit[10] Metalldampffieber[11] seltene Erden, Lanthaniden[12] Schwermetalle[13] metallische Spurenelemente[14] Edelmetalle[15] Metalldämpfe[16] schmelzbares Metall[17] Chelatbildner[18] Feststoffe[19] fester Bestandteil[20] feste Phase[21] Messinglegierung[22] metallischer Geschmack[23] Metallklang[24] Metallprotein[25] Metallenzyme[26] Metalloprotease[27]

6

---

melting point or **temperature** n rel **boiling point**[1] n, abbr **b.p.**

temperature at which a solid becomes a liquid

melt[2] [melt] v & n • **boil**[3] [bɔɪl] v • **boiled** adj

» The cylinder [sɪ-] is made of nonoxidizing gold alloy with a melting point of 1,280°C. Phosphorus is a potent [oʊ] oxidizing agent [eɪdʒ] which ignites[4] [aɪ] and melts on air contact. Non-precious [eʃ] metals cannot be used because of their high melting temperature. Precautions [ɔː] against cholera [ɒː] include using boiled water.

Use **melting** process / charge[5] / furnace [ɜː] or crucible[6] [uːs] • freezing[7] [iː] **point** • surface / environmental[8] / critical[9] / solidification[10] **temperature** • bonding / fusion [juːʒ]/ polymerization[11] / absolute **temperature** • **boiling** water • **to melt** away / down[12]

Schmelzpunkt, -temperatur

Siedepunkt, -temperatur[1] schmelzen; Schmelze, Schmelzmasse[2] kochen, sieden[3] s. entzünden[4] Schmelzgut[5] Schmelzofen[6] Gefrierpunkt[7] Umgebungstemperatur[8] kritische Temperatur[9] Erstarrungspunkt[10] Polymerisationstemperatur[11] einschmelzen[12]

7

---

condensation n term rel **(re)sublimation**[1], **distillation**[2] n term

process of changing from a gaseous to a liquid or from a liquid to a solid

density[3] [densəti] n • **condense**[4] vt & vi • **condensable** adj • **condensate**[5] n term • **sublimate**[6] [sʌblɪmeɪt‖ət] n • **distillate**[7] [dɪstɪleɪt‖dɪstɪlət] n

» The process by which water changes from a gaseous state to a liquid state is termed condensation. Alcohol is thought to promote the carcinogenic [dʒe] effects of tobacco condensates in saliva[8] [səlaɪvə].

Use to undergo[9]/catalyze/result in **condensation** • oxidative / (non)enzymatic[10] **condensation** • **condensation** reaction / product[5] • vacuum / molecular / dry[11] / fractional[12] **distillation** • water / vapor / metallic / mineral / bone[13] / radiographic[14] **density** • petroleum[15] **distillate**

Kondensation

(Re)sublimation[1] Destillation[2] Dichte[3] kondensieren, verdichten; kondensieren, sich niederschlagen, s. verflüssigen[4] Kondensat, Kondensationsprodukt[5] Sublimat[6] Destillat[7] Speichel[8] kondensieren[9] enzymat. Kondensation[10] trockene Destillation[11] fraktionierte D.[12] Knochendichte[13] radiolog. Dichte[14] Erdöldestillat[15]

8

---

hydrogen [haɪdrədʒən] n, **H** rel **(di)hydrate**[1] [daɪhaɪdreɪt], **anhydride**[2] [aɪ] n term

gaseous element (atomic no. 1) which exists in three isotopes, namely protium[3] [oʊʃ‖t], deuterium[4] [ɪə], and tritium[5] [ɪʃ‖t]

(de)hydrogenate[6] v term • **hydrolysis**[7] n • **(an)hydrous**[8] adj • **hydr(o)-** comb

» The lactate buffers the metabolic acidemia [iː] of shock by absorbing hydrogen ion to form lactic acid[9]. A hydrate is formed when water molecules combine with a drug molecule in crystal [ɪ] formation. Phospholipids are soluble in both lipid and aqueous environments.

Use **hydrogen** atom / gas / dioxide / peroxide[10] / sulfide[11] [ʌ]/ ion / bond[12] • light[3] / heavy[4] [e] **hydrogen** • carbo[13]/ mono/ tri/ calcium / chloral[14] **hydrate** • uric acid / calcium pyrophosphatase (abbr CPPD) **dihydrate** • **anhydrous** methanol / lanolin[15] / glycerin [ɪs] • **dehydro**genase[16] • **hydro**genase /xide /xy acid[17] /xyl radicals /xylation[18] /xylase • **hydro**chloride /chloric acid[19] /gel /fluoric acid[20] • **hydro**lyze [haɪdrəlaɪz] /static pressure /carbons[21]

Wasserstoff, Hydrogenium

(Di)hydrat[1] Anhydrid[2] Protium, leichter Wasserstoff[3] Deuterium, schwerer W.[4] Tritium, radioaktiver/ überschwerer W.[5] W. entziehen, dehydrieren[6] Hydrolyse[7] wasserhaltig[8] Milchsäure[9] Wasserstoff-(su)peroxid[10] Schwefelwasserstoff[11] Wasserstoffbindung[12] Kohlenhydrat[13] Chloralhydrat[14] Lanolinum anhydricum, Adeps lanae anhydricus, Wollwachs[15] Dehydrogenase[16] Hydroxysäure[17] Hydroxylierung[18] Salzsäure, HCl[19] Fluorwasserstoff-, Flusssäure[20] Kohlenwasserstoffe[21]

9

Biochemical Elements & Compounds   MEDICAL SCIENCE **343**

carbon [kɑːrbᵊn] *n*, **C**   *rel* **carboxyl group**[1],
                                    carboxylation[2] *n term*, **coal**[3] [oʊ] *n*

nonmetallic tetravalent[4] element (atomic no. 6, atomic wt. 12.01) which has two natural and two radioactive isotopes[5] [aɪ]

carbonyl [-nɪl] *n term* • **carbonic** *adj* • **carbonate**[6] *n & v* • **carb(o)-** *comb*

» *Prostanoic acid*[7], *the parent compound of prostaglandins, contains a 20-carbon chain with a cyclopentane* [-teɪn] *ring. The glucose-alanine/glutamine-BCAA cycle*[8] *shuttles*[9] [ʌ] *amino groups and carbon from muscle to liver for conversion* [ɜː] *into glucose.*

Use **carbon** chain [tʃeɪn]/ cycle [saɪkl]/ dioxide (tension)[10] / monoxide (poisoning)[11] / tetrachloride • radioactive[12] / hydro**carbon** • **coal** tar[13] [tɑːr]/ dust [ʌ]/ miner [aɪ] • **carbonyl** group • **carbonic** acid / anhydrase[14] [aɪ] (inhibitor) • calcium [s]/ lithium / bi**carbonate** [baɪ-] • **carbo**hydrate / (an)hydrase[14] • **carboxy**hemoglobin[15] /peptidase / terminal [ɜː] (region) • **carboxyl** transferase /ic acid[16] /ase • **carbonated** beverages[17]

Kohlenstoff, Carboneum
Carboxylgruppe[1] Carboxylierung[2] Kohle[3] vierwertig[4] Isotope[5] Carbonat, Karbonat; mit Kohlensäure od. Kohlendioxid versetzen, karbonisieren[6] Prostansäure[7] Glukose-Alanin-Zyklus[8] transportiert[9] Kohlendioxidspannung[10] Kohlenmonoxidvergiftung[11] Radiokohlenstoff, radioaktiver K.[12] Steinkohlenteer[13] Kohlensäure-, Carboanhydrase[14] CO-, Kohlenmonoxid-, Carboxyhämoglobin[15] Carbonsäure[16] kohlensäurehaltige Getränke[17]

10

oxygen [ɒksɪdʒᵊn] *n*, **O**

rel **oxidation**[1], **oxidant**[2] *n term* → U81-5, U44-6

colorless, odorless[3] gaseous element found in the atmosphere; it can combine with all elements except inert [ɜː] gases and is involved in many physiologic processes, esp. combustion[4] [ʌ] and respiration

oxygenate[5] *n term* • **oxidize**[6] [-daɪz] *v* • **oxide** [ɒksaɪd] *n* • **-oxide, oxy-** *comb*

» *Protection against oxygen radical damage appears to be important for the development and maintenance* [eɪ] *of nerve and muscle* [mʌsl] *function. Significant improvements in arterial-alveolar oxygen ratio* [reɪʃ(ɪ)oʊ] *(PaO₂/PAO₂) and inspired* [aɪ] *oxygen fraction (FIO₂) were sustained* [eɪ] *for 48 hours.*

Use to administer[7]/deliver[7]/give[7] **oxygen** • inspired / supplemental / liquid[8] **oxygen** • humidified / hyperbaric / lack of[9] **oxygen** • hyperbaric **oxygen** therapy[10] • **oxygen** diffusion / (de)saturation[11] / gradient[12] [eɪ]/ tension [tenʃᵊn]/ delivery • **oxygen** carrying capacity[13] [æs]/ consumption[14] [ʌ]/ requirement [aɪ]/ tent[15] • **oxygen** content / supply [aɪ]/ dissociation curve[16] [ɜː] • **oxygen** cycle / radicals[17] / utilization / uptake[18] / transport • **oxygen**-dependent pathways /-rich / affinity / debt[19] [det]/ toxicity [ɪs] • anti**oxidant**[20] • **oxidant** stress[21] • sulfur [ʌ] di[22]/ carbon mon/ nitrous[23] [aɪ]/ nitric[24] **oxide** • iron[25] / zinc / per/ super/ hydr**oxide** • **oxid**ase /oreductase[26] [ʌ] • **oxy**hemoglobin /codone /benzone

Sauerstoff, Oxygenium
Oxidation[1] Oxidans, Oxidationsmittel[2] geruchlos[3] Verbrennung[4] oxygenieren, m. Sauerstoff anreichern[5] oxidieren[6] S. zuführen[7] flüssiger S.[8] Sauerstoffmangel[9] hyperbare Oxygenation, Sauerstoffüberdrucktherapie[10] Sauerstoffsättigung[11] Sauerstoffgefälle, -gradient[12] Sauerstofftransportkapazität[13] Sauerstoffverbrauch[14] Sauerstoffzelt[15] Sauerstoffdissoziationskurve[16] Sauerstoffradikale[17] Sauerstoffaufnahme[18] Sauerstoffschuld[19] Antioxidans[20] oxidativer Stress[21] Schwefeldioxid[22] Distickstoffoxid, Lachgas[23] Stickstoffmonoxid, Stickoxid[24] Eisenoxid[25] Oxidoreduktase[26]

11

ketone [kiːtoʊn] *n term*

rel **acetone**[1] [æsətoʊn], **aldehyde**[2] [ældəhaɪd] *n term*

substance [ʌ] containing the carbonyl group and hydrocarbon groups bound to the carbonyl carbon

acetoacetic [siː] **acid**[3] *n term* • **keto(n)-** [kiːtoʊ-] *comb*

» *As expected, the urine of the hypoglycemic* [aɪsiː] *child was positive for ketones. Retinaldehyde is reduced by an aldehyde reductase* [ʌ] *to retinol. In diabetic ketosis*[4], *acetone is present in the breath* [e]. *In many patients with hypoaldosteronism, the transformation of the C-18 methyl of corticosterone to the C-18 aldehyde of aldosterone is impaired.*

Use circulating [ɜː]/ urinary or urine / plasma **ketones** • **ketone** group[5] / bodies[6] / body transport • **ketone** formation or production[7] / level[8] / reagent [eɪdʒ] strip[9] / **keto** acid[10] / group[5] / analogue • **acetone** metabolite / odor[11] [oʊ] • form[12]/ acet[13]/ benz/ par/ glut**aldehyde** • **aldehyde** dehydrogenase [ɒːdʒ] (*abbr* ALDH) • oxidase[14] / fuchsin [fjuːksən‖iːn]/ moiety[15] • **keto**acidosis /nemia[16] [iː] /steroid [ɪə]/ /genesis[7] • **keto**glutarate [ɑː] /lysis[17] [kɪtɒːləsɪs] /nuria[18] • **aceto**nuria[18] /nemia[16] /nide /acetate

Keton
Propanon, Aceton, Dimethylketon[1] Aldehyd[2] Acetessigsäure, β-Ketobuttersäure[3] Ketose[4] Ketogruppe[5] Ketonkörper[6] Ketonkörperbildung, Ketogenese[7] Ketonkörperspiegel[8] Ketonreagenzstreifen[9] Ketosäure[10] Acetongeruch[11] Formaldehyd[12] Acetaldehyd, Äthanal[13] Aldehydoxidase[14] Aldehydanteil, -gruppe, -rest[15] Keton-, Acetonämie, erhöhte Ketonkörperkonzentration i. Blut[16] Ketolyse, Ketonkörperverwertung, -spaltung[17] Keton-, Acetonurie, Ketonkörperausscheidung i. Harn[18]

12

phenol [fiːnoʊl‖fənɔːl] *n term*   *syn* **carbolic** *or* **phenolic acid** *n term*
rel **alcohol¹**, **essence²** *n* → U10-2; U3-27f
glycerol³ [glɪsəɔːl‖oʊl] *n term*

highly toxic compound obtained [eɪ] by distillation⁴ of coal tar⁵; used as an antiseptic and disinfectant⁶

phenolic⁷ *adj term* • **carbolated⁸** *adj* • **glyceride** *n* • **-ol, glycer-** *comb*

» Phenol precipitates [sɪ] tissue proteins and causes respiratory alkalosis followed by metabolic acidosis. Castor oil⁹ dissolves phenol and may retard its absorption. Fats are esters formed by the bonding of fatty acids with glycerol.

Use camphorated / liquefied¹⁰ **phenol** • octyl/ brom/ pentachloro¹¹/ dinitro**phenol** • **phenol** poisoning¹² / oxidase¹³ /-containing compound • **phenol**-inactivated virus [aɪ]/ red indicator¹⁴ • synthetic **phenolics** • phosphatidyl / diacyl¹⁵ [daɪæsɪl-] (*abbr* DAG) **glycerol** • buffered [ʌ]/ iodinated [aɪ] **glycerol** • **glycerol** saline / kinase • **phenolic** ring / hydroxl group / glycolipid I • **pheno**lphthalein¹⁴ [-fθeɪliːn] • primary / anhydrous / trihydric¹⁶ **alcohol** • denatured¹⁷ [eɪtʃ]/ sugar¹⁸ / wood¹⁹ **alcohol** • absolute / grain²⁰ [eɪ]/ benzyl²¹ / ethyl²⁰ [eθɪl] **alcohol** • methyl¹⁹ / nicotinyl / isopropyl [oʊ] **alcohol** • **alcohol** solution / dehydrogenase • **carbolated** petrolatum • mono/ di/ tri**glyceride** • medium-chain²² [iː] (*abbr* MCT)/ long-chain **triglycerides** • endogenous [ɒːdʒ]/ circulating / VLDL²³ **triglycerides** • methan¹⁹ / ethan²⁰ / octadecan/ mannit**ol** • ethylene glyc/ panthen²⁴/ butan**ol** • **glycer**aldehyde²⁵ /olize /yl trinitrate²⁶ [aɪ]

---

ester [estɚ] *n term*
rel **esterification¹, saponification²** *n term* → U78-7

organic compound formed by hydrolysis between the –OH of an acid and an alcohol group

(re)**esterify³** *v term* • **esterase⁴** *n* • **soap** [oʊ] *n* • **soapy** *adj* • **sapo(n)-** *comb*

» Cholesteryl ester transfer protein (*abbr* CETP) circulates in plasma in association with HDL⁵. Esterification of fatty acids to triglycerides is impaired. Detergents [ɜː] are nonsoap synthetic products used for cleaning [iː] purposes because of their surfactant properties. Strong alkali produces "liquefaction necrosis⁶," which involves dissolution of protein and saponification of fats.

Use water-soluble / tri- [traɪ-]/ fatty acid⁷ **esters** • cholesteryl⁸ / corticosteroid / 5-phosphate / phorbol⁹ **ester** • tryptophan [ɪ] ethyl / glycerin [ɪ]/ retinyl¹⁰ / testosterone **ester** • **ester** bond¹¹ • **saponification** of calcium / number¹² • fatty acid **esterification** • esterified cholesterol¹³ / carnitine / fraction / to triglyceride • cholesterol / leukocyte [uː]/ nonspecific¹⁴ **esterase** • **esterase** deficiency¹⁵ [ɪʃ]/ inhibitor¹⁶ • detergent [dʒ]/ disinfectant¹⁷ / antiseptic¹⁸ / green¹⁹ **soap** • mild / strong / neutral / surgical¹⁸ / ionic²⁰ **soap** • **soap** bubble [ʌ]/ solution [uːʃ]/ substitute²¹ [ʌ] • **soapy** water • **sapo**naceous²² [eɪʃ] /nified /toxin /nins²³

---

alkyl [ælkᵊl] *n term*   *syn* **alkide** *n term*,
rel **alkene¹** [-kiːn], **alkane²**, **paraffin³** *n term*

molecular fragment of the formula C_nH_{2n+1} derived [aɪ] from an alkene by dropping a hydrogen atom

alkylator⁴ *n term* • **alkylation⁵** *n* • **alkylating⁶** *adj* • **-ene, -ane** [-eɪn] *comb*

» Anabolic steroids containing an alkyl or ethinyl group at carbon 17 may cause cholestatic reactions. Alkenes are unsaturated [ætʃ] aliphatic hydrocarbons⁷ containing at least one carbon-carbon double [ʌ] bond⁸. Hepatic drug clearance is based on oxidation, reduction, hydroxylation, sulfoxidation, deamination⁹, dealkylation, or methylation of reactive groups.

Use **alkyl** group¹⁰ / substitution¹¹ / methanearsonate compound / mercury derivative¹² • covalent¹³ **alkylation** • **alkylating** agent⁴ • **alk**yne¹⁴ [ælkaɪn] /enyl /ylamine • ethyl/ 1-prop**ene** • liquid¹⁵ / solid **paraffin** • **paraffin**-embedded tissue /-fixed specimens¹⁶ [es]/ bath¹⁷

Phenol(um), Hydroxybenzol, Karbolsäure, Acidum carbolicum

Alkohol¹ Essenz² Glyzerin, Glycerol³ Destillation⁴ Steinkohlenteer⁵ Desinfektionsmittel⁶ phenolisch⁷ phenolisiert⁸ Rizinusöl⁹ wässrige Phenollösung¹⁰ Pentachlorphenol¹¹ Phenolvergiftung¹² Phenoloxidase¹³ Phenolphthalein¹⁴ Diglyzerid, Diacylglycerol¹⁵ dreiwertiger Alkohol¹⁶ vergällter/ denaturierter A.¹⁷ Zuckeralkohol¹⁸ Methanol, Methylalkohol, Holzgeist¹⁹ Äthylalkohol, Ethanol, Äthanol, Weingeist, Spiritus²⁰ Benzylalkohol²¹ mittelkettige Triglyzeride²² VLDL-T.²³ (Dex)panthenol²⁴ Glyzerinaldehyd, Glyzeral²⁵ Glyceroltrinitrat, Nitroglyzerin²⁶

13

Ester

Veresterung¹ Verseifung, Saponifikation² verestern³ Esterase⁴ High-Density-Lipoproteine, Lipoproteine hoher Dichte⁵ Kolliquations-, Verflüssigungsnekrose⁶ Fettsäureester⁷ Cholesterinester⁸ Phorbolester⁹ Retinolester¹⁰ Esterbindung¹¹ Verseifungszahl¹² verestertes Cholesterin¹³ unspezifische Esterase¹⁴ Esterasemangel¹⁵ Esteraseinhibitor, -hemmer¹⁶ Sapo medicatus, medizin. Seife¹⁷ antiseptische Seife¹⁸ Kali-, Schmierseife, Sapo kalinus¹⁹ Invertseife²⁰ Seifenersatz²¹ seifig, seifenartig²² Saponine²³

14

Alkyl(gruppe, -rest, -radikal)

Alken¹ Alkan² Paraffin(um)³ Alkylans, alkylierende Substanz⁴ Alkylierung⁵ alkylierend⁶ ungesättigte aliphatische Kohlenwasserstoffe⁷ C=C-Doppelbindung⁸ Desaminierung⁹ Alkylgruppe¹⁰ Alkylsubstitution¹¹ Alkylquecksilberderivat¹² kovalente Alkylierung¹³ Alkin¹⁴ flüssiges Paraffin¹⁵ in Paraffin eingebettete Präparate¹⁶ Paraffinbad¹⁷

15

Biochemical Elements & Compounds — MEDICAL SCIENCE

nitrogen [naɪtrədʒən] n, N

rel **nitrite¹, nitrate²** [naɪtreɪt] n term

gaseous element which makes up about 4/5 of the air we breathe [iː]; it is soluble in body fluids (esp. blood) and occurs [ɜː] in proteins and amino acids

nitric³ [naɪtrɪk] adj term • **nitrous⁴** adj • **nitrogenous⁵** adj [ɒːdʒ] • **nitr(o)-** comb

» About one half the nonprotein nitrogen in the blood is contained in urea [jʊəriːə]. The difference in nitrogen intake minus output estimates the 24-hour nitrogen balance⁶. In starvation⁷ the main component of urine nitrogen is ammonia [oʊ] (rather than urea), which buffers the acid urine that results from ketonuria. Most urinary pathogens will convert [ɜː] nitrite to nitrate.

Use heavy [e]/ liquid⁸ / amide [-aɪd‖ɪd]/ rest or nonprotein⁹ (abbr NPN) **nitrogen** • **nitrogen** blood urea¹⁰ (abbr BUN)/ waste [eɪ]/ fecal [fiːkəl] **nitrogen** • **nitrogen** (di)oxide¹¹ /-containing compounds / mustard¹² [ʌ] • **nitrogen** intake / equilibrium¹³ / metabolism¹⁴ /-fixing bacteria¹⁵ [ɪə]/-end products • **nitric** acid¹⁶ / oxide¹¹ • **nitrogenous** compound¹⁷ / solutes / toxins / waste products¹⁸ • long-acting / silver¹⁹ / (iso)butyl / glyceryl tri²⁰/ gallium **nitrate** • sodium²¹ / amyl / butyl / dietary [aɪ] **nitrite** • **nitrite** therapy / preservatives²² / test strip²³ • **nitrous** gases²⁴ / oxide²⁵ • **nitro**glycerin²⁰ [ɪs] /benzene²⁶ /blue tetrazolium (abbr NBZ) /furantoin /cellulose²⁷ • **nitr**azine paper²⁸ /itoid reaction /osamines²⁹ [oʊ]

Stickstoff, Nitrogenium

Nitrit¹ Nitrat² Stickstoff-, Salpeter-³ nitros, salpetrig⁴ stickstoffhaltig⁵ Stickstoffbilanz⁶ Hungern⁷ flüssiger Stickstoff⁸ Reststickstoff, Rest-N⁹ Blut-Harnstoff-Stickstoff¹⁰ Stick-(stoffmon)oxid¹¹ Stickstoff-, N-Lost¹² Stickstoffgleichgewicht¹³ Stickstoffstoffwechsel¹⁴ stickstoffbindende Bakterien¹⁵ Salpetersäure¹⁶ Stickstoffverbindung¹⁷ stickstoffhaltige Abfallprodukte¹⁸ Silbernitrat, Höllenstein, Argentum nitricum¹⁹ Glyceroltrinitrat, Nitroglyzerin²⁰ Natriumnitrit²¹ nitrithaltige Konservierungsmittel²² Nitrit-Teststreifen²³ nitrose Gase, Stickoxide²⁴ Distickstoffoxid, Lachgas²⁵ Nitrobenzol²⁶ Nitrozellulose, Zellulosenitrat²⁷ Charta nitrata, Salpeterpapier²⁸ Nitrosamine²⁹   16

amine [ə‖æmiːn] n term

rel **amide¹** [æmaɪd‖ɪd] n term → U79-10

organic substance [ʌ] derived [aɪ] from ammonia² [oʊ] by the replacement of one or more of the hydrogen atoms by hydrocarbon or other radicals

(trans)aminate³ [æ] v term • **(trans/ de)amination⁴** n • **amin(o)-** comb

» Some foods such as cheese contain significant amounts of vasoactive amines. Hydrogen bonds⁵ are formed between main-chain and side-chain amides of interacting proteins. Glutamine is taken up by the small bowel⁶ [aʊ], transaminated to form additional alanine, and released [iː] into the portal circulation⁷. The amino groups which are derived from transamination of other amino acids are donated to pyruvate [paɪruː-] to form alanine and glutamine.

Use aromatic⁸ / biogenic⁹ [dʒe]/ primary¹⁰ [aɪ]/ secondary¹¹ / tertiary¹² **amines** • sympathomimetic / pressor¹³ / vasoactive / amphet**amines** • **amine** group¹⁴ / precursor¹⁵ [ɜː]/ oxidase¹⁶ / hormone • **amine** transmitter / uptake / transport / odor¹⁷ • hist/ catechol¹⁸ [kætəkoʊl-] / (dextro)amphet/ dop/ defer**oxamine(s)** • tripeptide / tetrapeptide **amide** • sulfon/ sulfacet [se]/ chlorprop/ carb¹⁹/ acetazol**amide** • ethion/ cyclophosph/ nicotin²⁰/ tolbut**amide** [juː] • **amino** (side) group¹⁴ / terminus/ acid residue²¹ [-d(j)uː] • gamma-**amino**butyric acid²² [æsɪd] • **amin**uria

Amin

Amid¹ Ammoniak² (trans)aminieren³ Desaminierung⁴ Wasserstoffbrückenbindungen⁵ Dünndarm⁶ Pfortaderkreislauf⁷ aromatische Amine⁸ biogene Amine⁹ primäre Amine¹⁰ sekundäre Amine¹¹ tertiäre Amine¹² Vasopressoren, -konstriktoren¹³ Aminogruppe¹⁴ Aminvorstufe¹⁵ Aminoxidase¹⁶ Amingeruch¹⁷ Katecholamine¹⁸ Carbamid, Harnstoff, Urea¹⁹ Nicotinamid, Nicotinsäureamid²⁰ Aminosäurerest²¹ Gammaaminobuttersäure, GABA²²

17

sodium [soʊdiəm] n, Na

rel **potassium¹** [pətæsiəm] n, K

alkali metal element which readily [e] oxidizes in air or water and is the major cation of the extracellular fluid (abbr ECF); other alkali metals are lithium² (Li), cesium³ [siːziəm] (Cs), and rubidium⁴ (Ru)

hypernatremia [iː] n term • **hypo/ hyperkalemia⁵** n • **natr(o)-, kal(i)-** comb

» Due to increased [iː] delivery of sodium to the distal nephron sodium-potassium ion [aɪən] exchange is enhanced [æ]. Drinking sodium citrate [sɪtreɪt] will raise [eɪ] the gastric pH in most patients. Long-standing hyperkalemia [iː] is best treated by dietary potassium restriction and, if necessary, sodium polystyrene [aɪ] sulfonate [ʌ].

Use total body / serum [ɪə]/ urine / ipodate [aɪpədeɪt]/ mono/ di/ tri**sodium** • **sodium** salts / chloride⁶ [-aɪd]/ fluoride / (bi)carbonate⁷ • **sodium** phosphate / (thio)sulfate⁸ [θaɪoʊsʌl-]/ citrate • **sodium** urate crystals [ɪ]/ benzoate • **sodium** nitroprusside⁹ [ʌ]/ nitrite / succinate [sʌksəneɪt] • **sodium** intake / reabsorption¹⁰ / excretion¹¹ [iːʃ]/ loss¹² • **sodium** retention¹³ / channel¹⁴ [tʃ]/ pump¹⁵ [ʌ]/ wasting [eɪ] • **sodium** content /-restricted diet • **potassium** chloride / acetate / citrate [sɪ]/ iodide / permanganate¹⁶ • **potassium** sorbate / (bi)tartrate / oxalate • total body¹⁷ / serum / intracellular / renal [iː]/ dietary **potassium** • **potassium** intake¹⁸ /-containing salt substitute¹⁹ [ʌ]/ channel • **potassium** stores / balance²⁰ / tolerance / depletion²¹ [iːʃ]/ excretion • **potassium** wasting²² / deficit /-sparing [eə] diuretic²³ /-supplemented diet • **kali**uresis [iː] /uretic [e] • normo/ hypo/ hyper**natremia** • **natri**uresis /uretic²⁴

Natrium

Kalium¹ Lithium² Cäsium³ Rubidium⁴ Hyperkaliämie⁵ Natriumchlorid, Kochsalz⁶ Natriumbikarbonat, Natriumhydrogenkarbonat, doppeltkohlensaures Natron⁷ Natriumsulfat, Glaubersalz⁸ Nitroprussidnatrium⁹ Na-Rückresorption¹⁰ Natriumausscheidung¹¹ Natriumverlust¹² Natriumretention¹³ Natriumkanal¹⁴ Natriumpumpe¹⁵ Kaliumpermanganat, übermangansaures Kalium¹⁶ Gesamtkaliumgehalt d. Körpers¹⁷ Kaliumzufuhr¹⁸ kaliumhaltiger Salzersatz¹⁹ Kaliumhaushalt, -gleichgewicht²⁰ Kaliumverlust, -erschöpfung²¹ Kaliumarmung, -mangel²² kaliumsparendes Diuretikum²³ Natriuretikum; die Natriumausscheidung fördernd, natriuretisch²⁴

18

MEDICAL SCIENCE — Biochemical Elements & Compounds

calcium [kælsiəm] n, Ca

rel **phosphorus**[1] *n*, **P**, **lime**[2] [aɪ] *n inf*

divalent[3] element (atomic no. 20) which is the most abundant [ʌ] mineral in the body
calcific[4] *adj term* • **calcification**[5] *n* • **phosphate** [fɒːsfeɪt] *n* • **phosphoric** *adj* • **calc-**, **phosph(o)-** *comb*

» The oxide of calcium is quicklime[2], an alkaline earth[6], which on the addition of water becomes calcium hydrate/hydroxide[7] also known as slaked [eɪ] lime[7]. Mechanisms of hypophosphatemia include intracellular shifts of phosphorus related to the correction of respiratory acidosis and the use of drugs that increase renal phosphate excretion. When glucose is converted to lactate by glycolysis, only two high-energy phosphates are produced. Phosphatase enzymes cannot hydrolyze [aɪ] the central carbon-phosphorus-carbon bond.

Use inorganic / ionized / protein-bound [aʊ]/ total body / ingested[8] [dʒe] **calcium** • **calcium** salts / ion / (pyro)phosphate / chloride / folinate[9] • **calcium** carbonate[10] / gluconate / oxalate / sulfate[11] [ʌ] • **calcium** intake / metabolism /-phosphorus ratio[12] [eɪʃ]/ receptor site • **calcium** stone / absorption / deposits • antagonists or channel blocker[13] • organic / dietary / intracellular / serum **phosphorus** • elemental / yellow / amorphous or red[14] **phosphorus** • **phosphorus** compounds[15] / ions / absorption / poisoning[16] / sulfurated / burnt[2] / air-slaked[7] / chlorinated **lime** / **calcific** deposits[17] / tendinitis [aɪ]/ stenosis • coronary / valvular [æ]/ cerebral / ligamentous **calcification** • (in)organic / cellulose / dihydrogen / disodium **phosphate** • pyridoxal[18] / glycerol / (mono)potassium / adenosine **phosphate** • creatine / nicotinamide adenine dinucleotide[19] (*abbr* NADP) **phosphate** • aluminum[20] / estramustine (*abbr* EMP) **phosphate** • **phosphate** level / clearance[21] / deficiency /-binding gels / stones[22] • **phosphoric** acid[23] • **calc**ification /ifying /ified • **phospho**lipid /(fructo-)kinase[24] /gluconate • **phospho**rylate /rylase kinase /orylation[25] • **phosph**atase[26]

Kalzium, Calcium
Phosphor[1] gebrannter Kalk, Kalziumoxid[2] bivalent, zweiwertig[3] kalkbildend[4] Kalzifikation, Verkalkung[5] Erdalkalimetall[6] Kalziumhydroxid, gelöschter Kalk[7] oral zugeführtes Kalzium[8] Kalziumfolinat[9] Kalziumkarbonat[10] Kalziumsulfat[11] Kalzium-Phosphor-Quotient[12] Kalziumantagonisten, -Kanalblocker[13] amorpher/ roter Phosphor[14] Phosphorverbindungen[15] Phosphorvergiftung[16] Kalkablagerungen[17] Pyridoxalphosphat[18] Nikotinamidadenindinukleotid, NAD[19] Aluminiumphosphat[20] Phosphatclearance[21] Phosphatsteine[22] Phosphorsäure[23] Phosphofruktokinase[24] Phosphorylierung[25] Phosphatase[26]

19

magnesium [mægniːziəm] n, Ma

rel **barium**[1] [beərɪəm] *n*, **Ba**

silvery-white alkaline earth element that oxidizes to magnesia [mægniːʒə‖ʃə]
magnesia[2] *n* • **hypo/ hypermagnesemia**[3] [iː] *n term* • **-magnes-** *comb*

» Magnesium is essential for muscular [ʌ] excitability[4], neurochemical transmission, and many enzyme activities. Hypomagnesemia is often treated with parenteral fluids containing magnesium sulfate or magnesium chloride. Barium sulfate [ʌ] is given as an oral or rectal suspension for x-ray visualization of the GI tract.

Use dietary / total body / intracellular / serum / muscle / fecal [iː]/ elemental **magnesium** • **magnesium** salts / (ammonium) phosphate[5] / sulfate[6] / (hydr)oxide • **magnesium**-containing / stores / wasting / deficiency[7] / replacement[8] • milk or magma of[9] / burnt / effervescent **magnesia** • **magnesia** magma[9] • micropulverized **barium** • **barium** sulfate[10]/ carbonate / chloride[11] / nitrate[12] / solution • **magnes**uria /emia

Magnesium
Barium[1] Magnesia, Magnesiumoxid[2] Hypermagnesiämie[3] Muskelerregbarkeit[4] Magnesiumammoniumphosphat, Struvit[5] Magnesiumsulfat, Bittersalz[6] Magnesiummangel[7] Magnesiumsubstitution[8] Magnesiamilch[9] Bariumsulfat[10] Bariumchlorid[11] Bariumnitrat[12]

20

iron [aɪən] n, Fe

rel **selenium**[1] [səliːnɪəm] *n*, **Se**

metallic trace element that occurs in the heme of hemoglobin, myoglobin, transferrin, ferritin, and iron-containing porphyrins, and is an essential component of enzymes such as catalase
ferric *adj term* • **ferrous** [ferəs] *adj* • **seleno-** *comb*

» In the last two trimesters of pregnancy the daily iron requirement increases to 5-6 mg. The iron of the heme [hiːm] must be in the ferrous state to bind oxygen. Copper is excreted primarily in the bile[2] [aɪ], but selenium, chromium, and molybdenum are excreted primarily in the urine. Selenium plays a key role in the body's defenses against free radicals.

Use total body[3] / heme(-bound)[4] / divalent[5] / elemental / free / serum / medicinal[6] **iron** • **iron** supply / stores / pool[7] / chelator / deficiency (anemia)[8] • **iron** excess[9] / saturation / preparation[6] / stain[10] / **iron** supplement / overload[11] / poisoning / utilization[12] • **iron**-binding capacity[13] / metabolism / storage disease[14] / dietary **iron** intake[15] • **ferrous** iron[5] / salts / sulfate / carbonate / gluconate / fumarate • **selenium** sulfide[16] (lotion) / deficiency[17] / toxicity • **selen**ious acid[18] /ite / ocysteine[19] /osis[20]

Eisen, Ferrum
Selen[1] Galle[2] Gesamteisenbestand (d. Körpers)[3] Hämeisen[4] zweiwertiges Eisen[5] Eisenpräparat[6] Eisenpool[7] Eisenmangel(anämie)[8] Eisenüberschuss[9] Eisenfärbung[10] Eisenüberladung[11] Eisenverwertung, -utilisation[12] Eisenbindungskapazität[13] Eisenspeicherkrankheit[14] Nahrungseisenzufuhr[15] Selensulfid[16] Selenmangel[17] selenige Säure[18] Selenocystein[19] Selenvergiftung[20]

21

Biochemical Elements & Compounds   MEDICAL SCIENCE 347

iodine [aɪədɪn‖aɪn] n, **I**   rel **fluorine**[1] [flʊəˑiːn‖ən] n, **F**

nonmetallic element essential in nutrition which occurs in sea water and is used as an antiseptic

iodinated[2] adj term • **iodized**[2] adj • **iodination** n • **iodide** n • **fluoride**[3] n
• **iod(o)-, fluor(o)-** comb

» Deficiency of iodine causes goiter[4] [ɔɪ]. Many drugs, e.g. aminosalicylic [sɪ] acid, lithium[5], and even iodine in large doses, may block thyroid [aɪ] hormone synthesis [ɪ]. Fluoride combines with some apatite crystals [ɪ] in the tooth structure to form the less soluble fluorapatite.

Use aqueous[6] / radioactive[7] / protein-bound[8] [aʊ] (abbr PBI)/ titratable [aɪ] **iodine** • **iodine** complex / solution[9] / tincture[10] / (skin) disinfectant • **iodine** number[11] / intake / uptake / excretion • **iodine**-deficient [ɪʃ] goiter[12] / therapy[13] • **iodinated** dye [daɪ]/ contrast agent[14] • **iodized** salt[15] / oil • **iod**ism[16] /ophor /oform • **fluoro**carbon /quinolone [kwɪ] /sis[17] /uracil • sodium[18] / topical **fluoride** • **fluoride** ions / inhibitor / mouth rinse[19] • **fluor**idation[20] /inated toothpaste[21]

Iod, Jod

Fluor[1] iodiert[2] Fluorid[3] Struma, Kropf[4] Lithium[5] Iodwasser[6] Radioiod[7] proteingebundenes Iod[8] Iodlösung[9] Iodtinktur[10] Iodzahl[11] Iodmangelstruma[12] Radioiodtherapie[13] iodhaltiges Kontrastmittel[14] iodiertes Salz[15] Iodismus, chron. Iodvergiftung, Iodintoxikation[16] (Dental)fluorose, Fluorvergiftung[17] Natriumfluorid[18] fluoridhaltige Mundspüllösung[19] Fluoridierung[20] fluorhaltige Zahnpaste[21]

22

chlorine [klɔːriːn] n, **Cl**   rel **chloride**[1] [-aɪd], **bromine**[2] [broʊmiːn] n, **Br**

toxic gaseous element which together with Br, I, F and astatine[3] (At) is a member of the halogen group[4]

chloral[5] n term • **chlorinated**[6] adj • **bromic** adj • **bromide**[7] n
• **-chloric, chlor(o)-, brom(o)-** comb

» Inhalation of volatile acids or gases such as chlorine, fluorine, bromine, or iodine causes severe irritation of the throat [oʊ] and larynx. Be sure that the water in hot tubs[8] [ʌ] and spas is properly treated [iː] with chlorine. Three mechanisms are responsible for sodium and chloride absorption in the small intestine.

Use organo**chlorine**[9] • **chlorine** gas[10] / disinfection / water[11] • calcium / sodium[12] / potassium[13] / ferric **chloride** • aluminum / methyl / ammonium[14] • **chloride** • ethyl / vinyl / sweat[15] [e] **chloride** • **chloride** ions / salt / transport / channel[16] [tʃ]/ absorption • di/ hexa/ carbon tetra[17]/ hydro**chloride** • **bromine** water[18] /-containing • **chlorinated** lime[19] / insecticides [-saɪdz]/ bleaches[20] [bliːtʃiːz] • **bromic** acid[21] • ethyl / hydrogen[22] / potassium **bromide** • **chloral** hydrate[23] [haɪdreɪt] • **chlor**oform[24] /amphenicol /obutanol /hexidine /amine gas • **brom**sulphalein[25] [æ] (abbr BSP) /ate /ocriptine /acetone[26] • **brom**hexine /phenol blue /ism[27] /oderma[28] [ɜː] /ated

Chlor

Chlorid[1] Brom[2] Astat, Astatin(um)[3] Halogengruppe[4] Chloral[5] chlorhaltig[6] Bromid[7] Thermalbäder[8] organische Chlorverbindung[9] Chlorgas[10] Chlorwasser, Aqua chlorata[11] Natriumchlorid, Kochsalz[12] Kaliumchlorid, Kalium chloratum[13] Ammoniumchlorid, Salmiak[14] Chloridgehalt im Schweiß[15] Chloridkanal[16] Tetrachlorkohlenstoff, -methan[17] Bromwasser[18] Chlor-, Bleichkalk[19] chlorhalt. Bleichmittel[20] Bromwasserstoffsäure[21] Bromwasserstoff[22] Chloralhydrat[23] Chloroform, Trichlormethan[24] Bromsulfalein[25] Bromaceton[26] Brom(id)vergiftung, Bromismus[27] Bromoderma[28]   23

sulfur [sʌlfɚ] n term, **S**   syn **brimstone** [ɪ] n inf,
                                    rel **sulfide**[1] [-aɪd], **sulfate**[2] [ʌ] n term

chemical element that occurs in the amino acids cysteine [ɪ] and methionine; also spelled sulphur in BE

sulfuric, -ous adj term • (tran)**sulfurate**[3] v • **sulfurize**[3] v • **sulfa**[4] n • **sulf-** comb

» Sulfur combines with oxygen to form sulfur dioxide (SO_2) and SO_3, and with many metals and nonmetallic elements to form sulfides. Acute irritative bronchitis [kaɪ] may be caused by volatile organic solvents, chlorine, hydrogen sulfide, sulfur dioxide, or bromine.

Use sublimed[5] [aɪ]/ washed[6] / colloidal[7] / precipitated [sɪ] or milk of[8] / radioactive **sulfur** • **sulfur** ointment[9] [ɔɪ]/ in petrolatum / dioxide (fumes)[10] [juː] • **sulfur** springs[11] /-containing amino acids • **sulfuric** acid[12] / ether • **sulfurated** potash / lime solution • di/ tri/ poly/ hydrogen[13] / selenium **sulfide** • bi/ thio/ magnesium / estrone[14] **sulfate** • quinine [kwaɪ‖kwɪn-]/ neomycin [aɪs]/ zinc / iron or ferrous[15] **sulfate** • **sulf**atide [sʌlfətaɪd] /ones[16] /oxide /onamide[4] /onate

Schwefel, Sulfur

Sulfid, Salz d. Schwefelwasserstoffes[1] Sulfat, Salz d. Schwefelsäure[2] mit Schwefel verbinden, schwefeln[3] Sulfonamid[4] Sulfur sublimatum[5] S. depuratum, gereinigter Schwefel[6] Sulfur colloidale, kolloidaler S.[7] Schwefelmilch, S. praecipitatum, Lac sulfuris[8] schwefelhaltige Salbe[9] Schwefeldioxid(dämpfe)[10] Schwefelquellen[11] Schwefelsäure[12] Schwefelwasserstoff[13] Östronsulfat[14] Eisensulfat[15] Sulfone[16]

24

chromium [kroʊmiəm] n, **Cr**   syn **chrome** n
                                    rel **cobalt**[1] [koʊbɔːlt] n, **Co**

blue-whitish brittle[2] metallic element that is resistant to tarnishing[3] and corrosion [oʊʒ]

chromic adj • **chromate**[4] [kroʊmeɪt] n • **chrom**affin[5] adj • **cobaltous** adj

» Protein-energy malnutrition[6] [ɪʃ] may be complicated by deficiencies [ɪʃ] in iron, zinc, copper, selenium, or chromium. Vitamin B12 is a water-soluble cobalt compound.

Use **chromium** salts[7] / hydroxide / (tri)oxide • **chromium** oxychloride /-51 / deficiency[8] / therapy • pure [pjʊɚ]/ radiolabeled[9] [eɪ]/ sealed [iː] **cobalt** • **cobalt**-60 / atom / compound /-chrome alloy[10] • **cobalt** chloride / blue light[11] / teletherapy[12] / irradiation[13] • **chrome** worker/ yellow color[14] / alloy / pigment • **chromic** catgut[15] [ʌ] / acid[16] • **chrom**affin cells / tissue[17] [ʃ‖s] / paraganglia[18] / tumor

Chrom

Kobalt, Cobalt[1] spröde[2] oxidationsbeständig[3] Chromat[4] chromaffin, m. Chromsalzen anfärbbar[5] Protein-Energie-Mangelsyndrom, Marasmus[6] Chromsalze[7] Chrommangel[8] Radiokobalt[9] Kobalt-Chrom-Legierung[10] kobaltblaues Licht[11] Kobalt-Teletherapie[12] Kobaltbestrahlung[13] chromgelb[14] Chromcatgut[15] Chromsäure[16] chromaffines Gewebe[17] sympathische/ chromaffine Paraganglien[18]   25

MEDICAL SCIENCE — Biochemical Elements & Compounds

manganese [iː] n, **Mn**   syn **manganum** n term rare,
   rel **vanadium**[1] [eɪ] n, **V**

metallic element found in trace [treɪs] amounts [aʊ] in body tissues where it acts as an activator of enzymes [aɪ], as a component of metalloenzymes, and is essential for normal bone structure

manganic[2] [æ] adj term • **manganous**[3] adj • **vanadic** adj • **vanadate** [æ] n

» Manganese is the cofactor for the metalloenzymes which are involved in the initial [ɪʃ] step in gluconeogenesis [dʒe] and in cellular antioxidant capability. Manganese poisoning is usually limited to those who mine [aɪ] and refine [aɪ] ore[4].

Use **manganese**-superoxide dismutase / dioxide / citrate / chloride • **manganese** blue[5] / dust[6] [ʌ]/ deficiency[7] / poisoning[8] • **manganous** salt[9] • **vanadium**ism[10] • **vanadic** acid[11]

Mangan
Vanadium, Vanadin[1] manganhaltig, Mangan-; dreiwertiges M. enthaltend, Mangan-III-[2] zweiwertiges M. enthaltend, Mangan-II-[3] Manganerz abbauen[4] Manganblau[5] Manganstaub[6] Manganmangel[7] Manganvergiftung[8] Mangansalz[9] chron. Vanadiumvergiftung, Vanadismus[10] Vanadinsäure[11]

26

---

bismuth [bɪzməθ] n, **Bi**
   rel **nickel**[1] n, **Ni**, **molybdenum**[2] [ɪ] n, **Mo**

trivalent metallic element; its salts, some of which contain BiO+ rather than Bi3+ are called subsalts [ʌ], are used for pharmaceutical [suː] substances, e.g. to treat peptic ulcers[3]

bismuthosis[4] n term • **molybdic** [ɪ] adj • **molybdate**[5] [məlɪbdeɪt] n

» Colloidal bismuth compounds aid ulcer [ʌlsɚ] healing [iː] by forming (in an acid medium [iː]) a bismuth-protein coagulant which protects the ulcer from acid and pepsin digestion. Nickel causes more cases of allergic [ɜː] contact dermatitis [aɪ] than all other metals combined.

Use **bismuth** compounds / salts / citrate [sɪ] • subsalicylate[6] [sɪ] • **bismuth** (sub)nitrate[7] / tribromophenate gauze [ɔː] • **bismuth** gingivitis [dʒɪndʒ-]/ line[8] / stomatitis[9] [aɪ] • **nickel** sulfate / oxide / carbonyl[10] (vapor) [eɪ] • **nickel** crucible[11] [uːs]/-cadmium battery • **nickel** worker /-sensitive[12] / allergy[13] • **nickel** dermatitis / exposure [oʊʒ]/-free diet • **molybdenum**-99 / cofactor[14] • **molybdic** acid[15]

Wismut, Bismut(um)
Nickel[1] Molybdän[2] Ulcera peptica, peptische Geschwüre/ Ulzera[3] (chron.) Wismutvergiftung[4] Molybdat[5] basisches Bismutsalicylat, Bismutum subsalicylicum[6] bas. Bismutnitrat, Bismutum subnitricum[7] Wismutsaum[8] Wismutstomatitis[9] Nickeltetracarbonyl[10] Nickelschmelztiegel[11] empfindl. gegen Nickel[12] Nickelallergie[13] Molybdän-Cofaktor[14] Molybdänsäure[15]

27

---

silver [sɪlvɚ] n, **Ag**
   rel **gold**[1] [oʊ] n, **Au**, **platinum**[2] [plætʰnəm] n, **Pt**

grayish-white univalent precious [ʃ] metal which occurs in argentite[3] and is used in medicine for its caustic [ɒː], astringent[4], and antiseptic effect as well as for dental restorations (esp. in soldering[5] [ɒː])

» Mild silver protein[6] contains between 19 and 21% silver. The use of silver nitrate [aɪ] in the treatment of burns [ɜː] may lead to metabolic alkalosis. Toxic reactions to gold include pruritus [aɪ], dermatitis, stomatitis, and albuminuria. The platinum compounds[7] cisplatin and carboplatin are the only heavy metal compounds approved for use as antitumor agents.

Use **silver** salts / nitrate[8] / halide / fluoride / picrate • **silver** sulfadiazine [aɪ]/ protein / amalgam • **silver** ionization / staining[9] [eɪ]/ impregnation technique[10] • **silver**-palladium alloy[11] • colloidal / bactericidal **silver** • methenamine [iː] **silver** staining[12] • dental / (non/ semi)cohesive[13] [iː]/ (crystalline) sponge[14] [ʌ] **gold** • platinized / radioactive / injectable **gold** • **gold** salts / compound / thiomalate[15] /-plated or gilded[16] / content / foil[17] • **gold** alloy / inlay[18] / toxicity / seeds • **gold** therapy /-induced thrombocytopenia [iː] • **platinum** group /-based chemotherapy / sensitive tumor[19]

Silber, Argentum
Gold[1] Platin[2] Argentit, Silberglanz[3] adstringierend, zusammenziehend[4] Löten[5] Silberkolloid[6] Platinverbindungen[7] Silbernitrat[8] Silberfärbung[9] Silberimprägnationstechnik[10] Silber-Palladium-Legierung[11] Methenamin-Silbernitrat-Färbung, Grocott-Färbung[12] Stopfgold[13] Schwammgold[14] Aurothiomalat[15] vergoldet[16] Goldfolie, Blattgold[17] Goldinlay, -gussfüllung[18] platinsensitiver Tumor[19]

28

---

tin [tɪn] n, **Sn**   syn **stannum** [stænəm] n term
   rel **copper**[1] [ɒː] n, **Cu**, **zinc**[2] [zɪŋk] n, **Zn**

silvery malleable[3] [æ] metallic element that resists corrosion; used in many alloys[4] and to coat[5] other metals to prevent corrosion; obtained chiefly from cassiterite[6] where it occurs [ɜː] as tin oxide

stannous[7] [æ] adj term • **cupric**[8] [k(j)uːprɪk] adj • **cuprous**[9] adj • **cupr(a)-** comb

» Several inert [ɜː] dusts[10] [ʌ], including iron oxide, barium, and tin, may produce conditions known as siderosis, baritosis[11], and stannosis, respectively.

Use **tin** oxide[12] / protoporphyrin / foil[13] [ɔɪ] / free / ceruloplasmin-bound[14] [aʊ] **copper** • serum[15] [ɪɚ]/ hepatic **copper** • **copper** sulfate[16] / citrate / arsenite [-aɪt] • **copper**-(carrying) protein /-transporting ATPase[17] / metabolism • **cupric** iron / sulfate[16] • **cupr**uresis[18] [iː] • crystalline [ɪ] **zinc** • **zinc** ore [ɔːr]/ chloride / salts[19] • **zinc** oxide ointment[20] / paste[20] [eɪ]/ acetate [æs] • **zinc**-binding protein / pyrithione [aɪ] • **zinc** chill[21] [tʃ]/ deficiency[22] [ɪʃ]/ finger[23] / oxide fumes[24] [juː]

Zinn, Stannum
Kupfer[1] Zink[2] weich[3] Legierungen[4] beschichten[5] Kassiterit, Zinnstein[6] zweiwertiges Zinn enthaltend[7] zweiwert. Kupfer enth.[8] einwert. K. enth.[9] inerte Stäube[10] Barytose, Baryt-, Schwerspat-Staublunge[11] Zinnoxid[12] Zinnfolie, Stanniol[13] caeruloplasmingebundenes Kupfer[14] Serumkupfer[15] Kupfersulfat[16] kupfertransportierende ATPase[17] vermehrte Kupferausscheidung i. Harn[18] Zinksalze[19] Zinksalbe, -paste[20] Zink-, Gießerfieber[21] Zinkmangel[22] Zinkfinger[23] Zinkoxiddämpfe[24]

29

Biochemical Elements & Compounds | MEDICAL SCIENCE 349

silicon [sɪlɪkən‖ɒːn] *n*, **Si**

rel **silicate**[1] [sɪlɪkeɪt‖ət] *n*, **silicone**[2] [sɪlɪkoʊn] *n*

tetravalent nonmetallic element occurring in nature as silica used as a semiconductor[3]

silica[4] [sɪlɪkə] *n term* • **silicosis**[5] *n* • **silicic**[6] [səlɪsɪk] *adj* • **silico-** *comb*

» Silicon, which occurs [ɜː] in clay[7] [eɪ], feldspar[8], granite, quartz [ɔː], and sand, is the most abundant[9] element in the earth's crust [ʌ] next to oxygen. Silicones, which are used as surfactants, sealants[10] [iː], or implants, are organic compounds consisting of alternating silicon and oxygen atoms linked to organic radicals.

Use **silicon** dioxide[4] / carbide / polymer • magnesium / potassium[11] **silicate** • pure[12] / soft **silicone** • **silicone** gel [dʒel]/ rubber[13] [ʌ]/ catheter / (breast) [e] implant[14] / prosthesis [θiː] • **silica** dust[15] [ʌ]/ gel[16] • **silico**fluoride[17] /siderosis /tuberculosis[18]

Silizium
Silikat, Salz d. Kieselsäure[1] Silikon[2] Halbleiter[3] Kieselsäure, Quarz, Siliziumdioxid[4] Silikose, Quarzstaublunge[5] kieselsauer[6] Ton, Lehm[7] Feldspat[8] meist verbreitet[9] Dichtungsmittel, Versiegelung[10] Kaliumsilikat[11] reines Silikon[12] Silikongummi[13] Silikonimplantat[14] Quarzstaub[15] Silica-, Kieselgel[16] Silikofluorid[17] Silikotuberkulose[18]

30

aluminum [uː] *n*, **Al**

rel **titanium**[1] [eɪ‖æ] *n*, **Ti**, **boron**[2] *n*, **B**, **tungsten**[3] *n*, **W**

light-weight silvery metal obtained by purifying bauxite[4] [ɒː] to produce alumina which is reduced to aluminum; it is a component of many astringents[5] and antiseptics and is used in prosthetics[6] and dentistry

alumina[7] *n term* • **alum**[8] [æləm] *n* • **titanic**[9] *adj* • **boric** *adj* • **tungstate**[10] [ʌ] *n* • **tungstic** *adj*

» Aluminum hydroxide[11] is a relatively safe, commonly used antacid[12]. Metals such as beryllium, aluminum powders[13], cobalt, titanium dioxide, and tungsten may produce interstitial [ɪʃ] pneumonitis [n(j)uː-]. Boron carbide is a slightly harder compound than silicon carbide.

Use **aluminum** oxide[7] / salts / phosphate[14] (gel) / sulfate • **aluminum** chloride / hydroxide[11] (gel) / hydrate[11] • **aluminum** acetate solution / subacetate (soak)[15] [oʊ] • **aluminum** chelation [kiː-]/ exposure / toxicity /-containing antacids[16] • **aluminum** content[17] /-induced osteomalacia [eɪʃ] • **titanium** dioxide *or* white[18] / implant[19] • **boron**-10 • **tungsten** carbide[20] / vanadium • **alumina** gel • **boric** acid ointment[21]

Note: The BE equivalent is **aluminium**.

Aluminium
Titan(ium)[1] Bor[2] Wolfram[3] Bauxit[4] Adstringenzien[5] Prothetik[6] Tonerde, Aluminiumoxid[7] Alaun, Alumen, Kaliumaluminiumsulfat[8] titansauer[9] Wolframat, Salz d. Wolframsäure[10] Aluminiumhydroxid[11] Antazidum[12] Aluminiumpulver[13] Aluminiumphosphat[14] Aluminiumsubazetatumbad[15] aluminiumhaltige Antazida[16] Aluminiumgehalt[17] Titanoxid[18] Titanimplantat[19] Wolframkarbid[20] borsäurehaltige Salbe, Borsalbe[21]

31

mercury [mɜːrkjəri] *n*, **Hg**

rel **lead**[1] [led] *n*, **Pb**

liquid metallic element used in thermometers, manometers, and other instruments

mercurial[2] [jʊ] *adj & n term* • **mercuric**[3] *adj* • **mercurous**[4] *adj* • **mercurialism**[5] *n term* • (**un**)**leaded**[6] *adj*

» Mercury is avidly bound[7] [aʊ] to sulfhydryl [aɪ] groups and disrupts[8] [ʌ] cellular enzyme and membrane function. Most adult cases of lead poisoning are due to inhalation [eɪ] exposure [oʊʒ]. Ataxia may also be caused by toxic levels of phenytoin [ɪ], lithium, bismuth, germanium [eɪ], methyl mercury, and organic solvents.

Use elemental[9] / (in)organic / metallic / liquid **mercury** • ammoniated[10] / bichloride[11] / ethyl **mercury** • chloride[12] / fulminate[13] [ʊ] *of* **mercury** • **mercury** vapor[14] [eɪ]/ bichloride[11] / subsalicylate [sɪ] • **mercury** poisoning[5] / exposure • organic / red (oxide of)[15] / black[16] / white[17] **lead** • tetraethyl / sugar of[18] **lead** • **lead**-based paints[19] /-contaminated dust • **lead** chelator [k] /-exposed worker • **lead** (mon)oxide / tetroxide[15] / carbonate[17] / sulfide • **lead** acetate[18] [æs]/ poisoning *or* intoxication • **lead** line[20] / encephalopathy / palsy[21] [ɔː]/ burden[22] [ɜː] • **lead** colic / apron[23] [eɪ]/ equivalent[24] • **mercurial** tremor[25] / diuretic • **mercurous** mercury[26] • **mercuric** salt / mercury[27] chloride / fungicide [ʌ] • **leaded** gasoline[28] [iː]/ paints[19] / glass[29]

Quecksilber, Hydrargyrum
Blei, Plumbum[1] quecksilberhaltig; Quecksilberverbindung, -präparat[2] zweiwertiges Q. enthaltend[3] einwert. Q. enthaltend[4] (chron.) Quecksilbervergiftung, -intoxikation, Merkurialismus[5] bleihaltig, Blei-[6] verbindet sich leicht[7] stört[8] elementares Quecksilber[9] Hydrargyrum praecipitatum album, Quecksilberamidchlorid[10] H. bichloratum, Sublimat[11] H. chloratum, Kalomel[12] Quecksilberfulminat, Knallquecksilber[13] Quecksilberdampf[14] Bleitetroxid, Mennige, rotes Bleioxid[15] Graphit[16] Bleikarbonat, -weiß[17] Bleizucker, -azetat[18] Bleifarben[19] Bleisaum[20] Bleilähmung[21] Bleibelastung[22] Bleischürze[23] Bleigleichwert, -äquivalent[24] Quecksilberzittern, Tremor mercurialis[25] einwertiges Q.[26] zweiwertiges Q.[27] bleihaltiges Benzin[28] Bleiglas[29]

32

arsenic [ɑːrsᵊnɪk] *n & adj*, **As**   *syn* **arsenium** [ɑːrsiːniəm] *n term*
   rel **thallium**[1] [æ] *n*, **Tl**, **cadmium**[2] [æ] *n*, **Cd**

metallic trace [eɪ] element[3] which forms a number of toxic compounds [-aʊndz] and like lead, mercury, thallium and cadmium is a leading cause of heavy metal poisoning[4]
arsenide [-aɪd] *n term* • **arsenous** *adj* • **arsenism**[5] *n* • **arsenical**[6] [e] *n & adj* • **thallous** *adj*

» Arsenic may be detected in the hair and nails for months after exposure. Thallium is radiopaque[7] [-peɪk]. Acute high-dose inhalation of cadmium can cause severe respiratory irritation with pleuritic [plʊəˌɪtɪk] chest pain, dyspnea [ɪ], and fever [iː].

Use (in)organic[8] / trivalent / pentavalent / white[9] **arsenic** • urine or urinary **arsenic level** • **arsenic** compound[10] /-containing ore[11] / acid / salt / trioxide[9] / trihydride • **arsenic** pesticide / ingestion[12] [dʒe]/ exposure • **arsenic** intoxication or poisoning[5] / excretion [iːʃ]/ level • radioactive **thallium** • **thallium**(-201) scanning[13] / uptake[14] / scintigraphy[13] / poisoning • airborne / absorbed[15] / (environmental/ occupational) exposure to[16] **cadmium** • **cadmium** exposure[16] / inhalation[17] / poisoning • **arsenical** melanosis[18] / keratosis / preparation[19] / agents [eɪ] • organic[20] **arsenicals** • **arsenous** sulfide / oxide • **thallous** chloride[21] / sulfate[22] / salts

Arsen; arsenhaltig; Arsenik
Thallium[1] Kadmium[2] metallisches Spurenelement[3] Schwermetallvergiftung[4] Arsenvergiftung[5] arsenhaltige Verbindung; arsenhaltig[6] strahlenundurchlässig, -dicht[7] anorganisches Arsen[8] weißes Arsenik, Arsentrioxid, Weißarsenik[9] Arsenverbindung[10] arsenhaltiges Erz[11] Ingestion v. Arsenik[12] Thalliumszintigrafie[13] Thalliumaufnahme[14] resorbiertes Kadmium[15] Kadmiumexposition[16] Kadmiuminhalation[17] Arsenmelanose[18] Arsenpräparat[19] organische Arsenverbindungen[20] Thalliumchlorid[21] Thalliumsulfat[22]

33

radium [reɪdiəm] *n*, **Ra**   *rel* **iridium**[1] [ɪ] *n*, **Ir**, **cesium**[2] [siːziəm] *n*, **Ce**
   technetium[3] [tekniːʃ(ɪ)əm] *n*, **Tc**

radioactive element of the alkaline earth group[4] formed by the disintegration[5] of uranium-238[6]
radon[7] [reɪdɒːn] *n term* • **radio-** [reɪdioʊ-] *comb* → U99-22

» Commonly used radioactive sources [ɔː] include iridium, cesium, and iodine, while radium, radon seeds, cobalt, yttrium [ɪ], americium [ɪʃ], and palladium are used less often. Technetium Tc⁹⁹ᵐ pyrophosphate [paɪ-] accumulates in recently infarcted myocardium [maɪ-].

Use **radium**-226 / salt / therapy[8] / implantation or insertion[9] [ɜː] • **iridium**-192 • **cesium** 137 • **radon** gas / 222 (Rn²²²)/ particles / daughters[10] / seeds[11] [iː] • **radio**iodine[12] [aɪ] /strontium /phosphorus /isotope[13] [aɪ] /nuclide[14] /tracer[14] • **technetium** bone scan / (Tc ⁹⁹ᵐ) pertechnetate[15] [ek] /-labeled [eɪ] red blood cells[16]

Radium
Iridium[1] Cäsium[2] Technetium[3] Erdalkaligruppe[4] Zerfall[5] Uran 238[6] Radon[7] Radiumtherapie[8] Einbringung v. Radiumstrahlern[9] Radontochternuklide[10] Radonseed[11] Radioiod[12] Radioisotop, Radionuklid[13] radioaktive(r) Tracer(substanz)[14] ⁹⁹ᵐTc-Pertechnetat[15] Technetiummarkierte Erythrozyten[16]

34

Unit 83   Cytology & Cell Biology
Related Units: 81 Biochemistry & Molecular Biology, 84 Genetics, 86 Histology, 88 Physiology, 78 Metabolism, 97 Oncology, 116 Lab Studies

cytology [saɪtɒːlədʒi] *n term*
   rel **cell(ular) biology**[1] [seljələ- baɪɒːlədʒi] *n term*

study of the anatomy, physiology, chemistry, and/or pathology of cells
cytologic(al)[2] *adj term* • **biologic(al)** *adj* • **cyto** , **bio-** *comb* • **biologist**[3] *n*

» Brushings[4] [ʌ] of the ulcer [ʌ] for cytology should be obtained [eɪ] prior to biopsy [aɪ]. What are the effects of growth hormone on human bone biology? New techniques in molecular biology[5] and biochemistry[6] have changed the way clinicians [ɪʃ] approach birth defects [iː].

Use exfoliative[7] [oʊ]/ (fine-needle) aspiration[8] **cytology** • sputum [(j)uː]/ bile[9] [aɪ]/ urine or urinary[10] / vaginal [dʒ] **cytology** • cervical [sɜː]/ CSF[11] / voided[10] [ɔɪ]/ bladder wash[12] / pleural [ʊə-] fluid **cytology** • **cytology** study[13] / specimen [es]/ brush / of scrapings[7] [eɪ] • tumor **cell biology** • micro/ neuro/ immuno/ radio[14]/ patho**biology** • human / stem cell / molecular / vascular **biology** • developmental / reproductive [ʌ] tumor / radiation[14] [eɪʃ] **biology** • **cytologic** examination[13] / study[13] / smear[15] [smɪə-]/ diagnosis[16] • **bio**activity /chemistry /therapy • **biologic** activity / behavior[17] / properties • **biologic** cycle [saɪkl] / signal[18] / effect / response modifiers[19] • **biologic** sex / fitness / half-life[20] / fluid • **cyto**plasm[21] /skeleton[22] /logist[23] /lysis[24] [ɪ] • **cyto**lytic [ɪ] /genetic /kine /metry /toxin /pathology • **cyto**adherence [ɪə-] /genetics /diagnosis[16] /toxicity[25] [ɪs]

Zytologie; Zellkunde, -enlehre
Zellbiologie[1] zytologisch[2] Biologe/-in[3] Bürstenabstrich[4] Molekularbiologie[5] Biochemie[6] Exfoliativzytologie, Bürstenbiopsie[7] Punktionszytologie[8] Zytologie/ zytolog. Untersuchung d. Gallenflüssigkeit[9] Harnzytologie[10] Liquorzytologie[11] Lavagezytologie der Blase[12] zytolog. Untersuchung[13] Strahlenbiologie[14] zytolog. Abstrich[15] Zytodiagnostik, zytolog. D.[16] biolog. Verhalten[17] Biosignal[18] Biologic response modifiers, Modulatoren d. biolog. Antwort[19] biolog. Halbwertszeit[20] Zytoplasma, Zellleib[21] Zytoskelett[22] Zytologe/-in[23] Zellauflösung, Zytolyse[24] Zytotoxizität[25]

1

Cytology & Cell Biology

cell [sel] n
rel **cell** or **plasma membrane**[1] n term

basic structural [ʌ] and functional [ʌ] unit of an organism

cellular[2] adj term • (**cyto/ endo**)**plasmic**[3] adj • **plasm-, -plasm** comb

» There is a focal accumulation of inflammatory cells adjacent [dʒeɪs] to[4] an epithelial [iː] crypt [krɪpt]. Adhesion [iːʒ] molecules determine [ɜː] cell shape and polarity. A structural defect in the red cell membrane is responsible for the abnormal shape.

Use somatic[5] / germ[6] [dʒɜːrm]/ epithelial / plasma[7] / host[8] **cell** • acinar [æs]/ goblet[9] / fat / stem **cell** • blood / blast[10] / mast[11] / cancer **cell** • mother[12] / daughter[13] / embryonal / flagellated[14] [ædʒ]/ ciliated [sɪ] **cell** • **cell** structure / body[15] / wall or membrane[1] • **cell** mass / growth[16] / division[17] [ɪʒ]/ cycle • **cell** size / line[18] / motility / death[19] / bank[20] • red blood / myocardial / host **cell membrane** • **cell** adhesion [iːʒ] molecule (abbr CAM)/ culture[21] [ʌ] • a/ uni/ multi/ extra[22]/ intra-**cellular** • **cellular** components or constituents[23] [ɪtʃ]/ metabolism[24] / differentiation • **cellular** proliferation / response / immunity • **cellular** integrity / repair [eɚ] • **plasma**cyte[7] /pheresis[25] [iː] • **plasmo**lysis • proto[26]/ cyto**plasm**

eukaryote [juːkærɪət‖oʊt] n term
rel **prokaryote**[1] [proʊ-] n term

large (10-100mm) cell containing a membrane-bound [aʊ] nucleus dividing by a form of mitosis

eu/ prokaryotic[2] adj term • **megakaryocyte**[3] n • **karyo-** comb → U84-10

» The interferons [ɪɚ] are a complex group of naturally occurring [ɜː] proteins produced by eukaryotic cells in response to viruses [aɪ], antigens, and mitogens [aɪ]. A fragment of the A subunit [ʌ] is translocated across the eukaryotic cell membrane into the cytoplasm.

Use **eukaryotic** cell[4] / pathogens / parasites / gene [dʒiːn] expression / host [oʊ] factors • **prokaryote**-type ribosomes[5] [aɪ] • **megakaryocyte** proliferation / production[6] • **megakaryocyte** differentiation / maturation[7] / micro**megakaryocyte**[8] • **karyo**some[9] /metric measurements[10] [meʒɚ-] /gram

nucleus [n(j)uːklɪəs] n term, pl -i
rel **nucleolus**[1] [iː], **karyoplasm**[2] n term

cellular organelle[3] in eukaryotes containing the genetic material

nuclear[4] adj term • **nucleic**[5] [eɪ‖iː] adj • **nucleolar** adj • **nucleated**[6] adj • **nucle(o)-** comb → U84-10ff

» Nuclei [aɪ] vary substantially in size, with the nuclear membrane appearing irregularly thickened and the chromatin distribution [juːʃ] quite coarse [ɔː]. Leydig's cells have a prominent round nucleus with two or three nucleoli lying eccentrically.

Use (red) cell / sperm [ɜː]/ eccentric / indented[7] / interphase[8] **nucleus** • **nuclear** membrane[9] / envelope[9] / pores[10] [ɔː]/ shape / division[11] [ɪʒ] • **nuclear** diameter [aɪæ]/ phosphoprotein / maturation [eɪʃ]/ pleomorphism[12] [pliːə-] • **nuclear** protein[13] / DNA content / chromatin [oʊ]/ residues[14] • **nuclear**-cytoplasmic ratio[15] [eɪʃ]/ binding / receptor / antigen • peri/ intra/ mono**nuclear** • **nuclear** import / receptor / medicine[16] / scanning[17] • **nucleated** cell / RBCs[18] • **nucleic** acid (sequence) [iː]/ core chain [kɔːr tʃeɪn]/ metabolism • **nucleo**plasm[2] /some[19] /tide [-taɪd] /tidase /protein[13]

microtubule [(j)uː] n term
rel **spindle** [ɪ] **fiber**[1] [aɪ], **microfilament**[2] [ɪ], **cytoskeleton**[3] n term, **flagella**[4] [dʒe], **cilia**[5] [sɪlɪə] n pl term

hollow beam-like [iː] cytoplasmic element supporting the cytoskeleton which facilitates [sɪ] movement of chromosomes and chromatids on the nuclear spindle during nuclear division [ɪʒ]

microtubular [maɪkr-] adj term • **filament** n • **filamentous**[6] adj • **ciliated** adj

» Centromeric regions [iːdʒ] are sites of microtubule attachment at metaphase. Microtubules are polymers of tubulin that originate in the centrosome and terminate [ɜː] variably in the cytoplasm. Spindle action segregates chromatids at mitosis.

Use central **microtubules** • **microtubule** apparatus [eɪ]/ segment / assembly[7] / attachment [ætʃ] • **microtubule** organizing center[8] /-associated proteins[9] / binding motif • **microtubular** structures / proteins[9] • **microtubule** doublet[10] [ʌ]/ binding motif • nuclear[11] / mitotic[11] / cleavage [iː] or achromatic[11] / central **spindle** • **spindle** pole[12] / formation /-shaped cell[13] / actin[14] / intermediate[15] / myo/ neuro**filament** • polar[16] / peritrichous[17] [-trɪkəs]/ periplasmic **flagella** • **ciliated** cells[18] / surface / epithelium[19]

Zelle
Zellmembran, Plasmalemm, Membrana cellularis[1] zellulär, Zell-, Zyto-[2] endoplasmatisch[3] anliegend[4] Körper-, Somazelle[5] Keimzelle[6] Plasmazelle, Plasmozyt[7] Wirtszelle[8] Becherzelle[9] Blast[10] Mastzelle[11] Mutterzelle[12] Tochterzelle[13] Geißelzelle[14] Zellkörper[15] Zellwachstum[16] Zellteilung[17] Zelllinie[18] Zelltod[19] Zellbank[20] Zellkultur[21] extrazellulär[22] Zellbestandteile[23] Zellstoffwechsel[24] Plasmapherese[25] Protoplasma[26]

Eukaryo(n)t
Prokaryo(n)t[1] prokaryont(isch)[2] Megakaryozyt, Knochenmarkriesenzelle[3] eukaryont(isch)e Z., Eukaryontenzelle[4] Ribosomen v. Prokaryontentyp[5] Megakaryozytopoese[6] Megakaryozytenreifung[7] Mikrokaryozyten[8] Karyosom[9] karyometr. Untersuchungen[10]

Zellkern, Nukleus
Nukleolus, Kernkörperchen[1] Nukleo-, Karyoplasma[2] Zellorganelle[3] Kern-, nuklear[4] Nuklein-[5] kernhaltig[6] eingedellter Kern[7] Interphasekern[8] Kernmembran[9] Kernporen[10] Kernteilung[11] Kernpolymorphie[12] Nukleoprotein[13] Kernreste[14] Kern-Plasma-Verhältnis[15] Nuklearmedizin[16] Magnetresonanz-, Kernspintomografie[17] kernhaltige Erythrozyten[18] Nukleosom[19]

Mikrotubulus
Spindelfaser[1] Mikrofilament[2] Zytoskelett[3] Flagella, Geißeln[4] Zilien, Flimmerhärchen[5] fadenförmig, filamentär[6] Zusammenbau d. Mikrotubuli[7] Mikrotubulusorganisationszentrum[8] mikrotubulusassoziierte Proteine[9] Mikrotubuliduplett[10] Kern-, Mitosespindel[11] Spindelpol[12] spindelförmige Zelle[13] Aktinfilament[14] Intermediärfilament[15] polare Begeißelung[16] peritriche Begeißelung[17] zilientragende/ -besetzte Zellen[18] Flimmerepithel[19]

MEDICAL SCIENCE — Cytology & Cell Biology

centrosome [sentrə-] *n term* *rel* **centriole**[1], **kinetosome**[2], **lysosome**[3] *n term*

cytoplasmic organelle usually located near the nucleus which contains one or two centrioles

centrosomal *adj term* • **(intra)lysosomal** [laɪsəsoʊmᵊl] *adj*

» The centrosome contains two cylindrical organelles with nine triplets of microtubules arrayed[4] [eɪ] around their edges. Centrioles migrate [aɪ] to opposite poles of the cell and serve to organize the spindles. Lysosomes [aɪ] are cellular organelles in which complex macromolecules are degraded[5] [eɪ] by specific acid hydrolases [aɪ]. The basal [eɪ] body[2] is the centriole from which an axoneme [-iːm] arises; also called a kinetosome or blepharoplast.

Use distal *or* posterior / anterior / nonfunctional[6] [ʌ] (*abbr* nfc) **centriole** • (intra/extra)cellular / neutrophil **lysosomes** • hepatic / phago[7] [fægə-]/ primary[8] / secondary[9] / iron-laden [eɪ] **lysosomes** • **centrosomal** separation • **lysosomal** membrane[10] / vacuole / breakdown [eɪ] *or* degradation[11] • **lysosomal** enzyme[12] / hydrolase [aɪ]/ cystine [sɪ] efflux[13] [eflʌks]/ (storage) disease[14] • dormant **kinetosome**

Centrosom, Zentrosom

Zentriol, Zentriolum, Zentralkörperchen[1] Basalkörperchen, Kinetosom[2] Lysosom[3] angeordnet[4] abgebaut[5] inaktives Zentriol[6] Phagolysosom[7] primäre Lysosomen[8] sekundäre Lysosomen[9] Lysosomenmembran[10] lysosomaler Abbau[11] lysosomales Enzym[12] lysosomaler Cystinausstrom[13] lysosomale (Speicher)krankheit[14]

6

---

mitochondrion [kɒ:] *n term, pl* **-ia** *rel* **crista**[1] *n term, pl* **-ae** [krɪstiː]

organelle of the cell cytoplasm consisting of a smooth continuous outer coat and an inner membrane arranged in tubules or more often in folds that form double membranes (cristae)

(intra)mitochondrial[2] *adj term* • **antimitochondrial** [æntɪmaɪtəkɒːndrɪᵊl] *adj*

» Mitochondria are the principal energy source [sɔːrs] of the cell and contain the cytochrome enzymes of terminal [ɜː] electron transport and the enzymes of the citric [sɪtrɪk] acid cycle[3], fatty acid oxidation, and oxidative phosphorylation[4]. The cytoplasm of primary spermatocytes is clear and contains centrioles, peripheral mitochondria with swollen crista, a small Golgi apparatus [eɪ], and a short rough [rʌf] endoplasmic system [ɪ].

Use cytoplasmic / paranuclear / renal **mitrochondria** • hepatocellular / neuronal / peripheral **mitochondria** • sperm [ɜː]/ short / abnormal **mitochondria** • disintegrating[5] / wild-type / abundant[6] [ʌ] **mitochondria** • **mitochondrial** structure / genome [dʒiːnoʊm]/ membrane[7] • **mitochondrial** matrix[8] [eɪ] (swelling) / cytochrome [aɪ] oxidase • **mitochondrial** function / enzyme / (energy) metabolism[9] / respiratory chain[10] [tʃeɪn] • **mitochondrial** calcium [s]/ proteins / ATP depletion[11] [iːʃ]/ damage[12] • **mitochondrial** DNA[13] (mtDNA) / (DNA) mutation / swelling • **antimitochondrial** (*abbr* AMA) antibody[14] • swollen / vacuolated **cristae**

Mitochondrium

Crista mitochondrialis[1] mitochondrial, Mitochondrien-[2] Zitronensäurezyklus[3] oxidative Phosphorylierung[4] zerfallende/ s. auflösende Mitochondrien[5] zahlreiche Mitochondrien[6] Mitochondrienmembran[7] Mitochondrienmatrix[8] mitochondrialer (Energie)stoffwechsel[9] mitochondriale Atmungskette[10] mitochondriale ATP-Entleerung[11] Mitochondrienschädigung[12] mitochondriale DNA[13] antimitochondrialer Antikörper, AMA[14]

7

---

endoplasmic reticulum *n term, pl* **-a**, *abbr* **ER** *rel* **microsome**[1] *n term*

network of cytoplasmic tubules or flattened sacs (cisternae[2]) in eukaryotes with (rough ER) or without (smooth ER) ribosomes on the surface of their membranes

reticular[3] *adj term* • **reticulate(d)**[3] *adj* • **reticulin**[4] *n* • **reticulo-** *comb*

» These cells include enlarged and structurally pleomorphic nuclei and nucleoli, increased numbers of abnormal mitochondria, scanty endoplasmic reticulum with an increase in free ribosomes, prominent intracytoplasmic lipid droplets, and the occasional [eɪʒ] demonstration of rod-shaped intranuclear inclusions [uːʒ].

Use smooth[5] [uː] (*abbr* SER)/ rough[6] [rʌf] (*abbr* RER) • ribosome-rich[6] / liver **endoplasmatic reticulum** • **reticulum** cells[7] / cell sarcoma / framework[8] [eɪ] • sarcoplasmic[9] / granular[6] / blue-staining [eɪ] multinucleated **reticulum** • marrow [æ] **reticulin** • **reticulin** framework / antibodies / formation / fibers[10] • **reticular** tissue[11] [tɪʃǁsjuː]/ layer [eɪ] pattern / network[8] • **reticular** activating system[12] (*abbr* RAS)/ formation[13] / density • **reticulate** body[14] • appearance • **reticulocyte**[15] /endothelial [iː] cells[16] /granular pattern • **reticulo**nodular infiltrates /(cyto)sis

endoplasmatisches Retikulum, R. endoplasmicum, ER

Mikrosom[1] Zisternen[2] retikulär, netzförmig[3] Retikulin[4] glattes/ agranuläres ER, gER[5] raues/ granuläres/ ribosomenbesetztes ER, rER[6] Retikulumzellen[7] retikuläres Netzwerk[8] sarkoplasmatisches Retikulum[9] Retikulinfasern[10] retikuläres Bindegewebe[11] aufsteigendes retikuläres Aktivierungssystem, ARAS[12] retikuläre Formation, Formatio reticularis[13] Retikular-, Initialkörperchen[14] Retikulozyt, Proerythrozyt, unreifer Erythrozyt[15] Zellen d. Monozyten-Makrophagensystems[16] 8

---

ribosome [raɪbəsoʊm] *n term* *rel* **polysome**[1] [pɒːlɪ-] *n term* → U84-15

cell organelle that is the site of protein synthesis [ɪ] by aminoacyl-tRNAs as coded by mRNAs

ribosomal *adj term* • **ribose**[2] [aɪ] *n* • **ribosyl**[3] *n* • **ribo-** *comb*

» Tetracyclines [saɪ] consist of 4 aromatic rings with various substituent [ɪtʃ] groups which interact reversibly [ɜː] with the bacterial [ɪᵊ] 30S ribosomal subunit, blocking the binding of aminoacyl tRNA to the mRNA-ribosome complex. The recognition [ɪʃ] and association of cell ribosomes with an internal ribosome entry sequence [iː] in the viral [aɪ] genomic RNA permit the translation of a polyprotein that is a fusion [juːʒ] of many or all of the viral proteins.

Use prokaryote-type[4] / bacterial / poly[1] / 50S / free **ribosome** • **ribosomal** gene [iː]/ RNA[5] (sequence) / activity / protein[6] • **ribosomal** recognition / binding site / alterations / subunit[7] • ADP **ribose**[8] • **ribo**nucleoprotein /nuclease[9] /tides /zyme

Ribosom

Polysom, Polyribosom[1] Ribose[2] Ribosyl[3] prokaryontisches Ribosom[4] ribosomale RNA/ RNS[5] ribosomales Protein[6] Ribosomenuntereinheit[7] Adenosindiphosphatribose, ADP-Ribose[8] Ribonuklease[9]

9

Cytology & Cell Biology

Golgi [gɔːldʒi] **apparatus** [eɪ] or **complex** n term
    rel **cis**[1] [sɪs]/ **trans**[2] **region** [riːdʒ°n] n term

membranous system of flattened cisternae and vesicles located between the nucleus and secretory pole of a cell; involved in the synthesis of membrane-bound secretory proteins[3]

» Virions are transported to the cell surface via the ER and the Golgi apparatus. Sertoli's cell cytoplasm of early pubertal testes consists of 82.4% ground [aʊ] substance, 7.6% mitochondria, 3.6% Golgi apparatus, 2.2% vacuoles, and 4.1% lipid droplets and ribosomes.

Use well developed[4] / small[5] / abbreviated [iː] **Golgi apparatus** • **Golgi** vesicles[6] • genetic / Golgi[7] / HLA **region** • **cis** sequences [iː]/-acting regulatory DNA sequences[8] • **cis**-trans model / effect[9] /retinoic acid / configuration[10] • **trans**-acting factors[11] /retinoic acid

Golgi Apparat, -Komplex, Complexus golgiensis

cis-Region[1] trans-Region[2] Sekretproteine[3] gut ausgebildeter Golgi-Apparat[4] kleiner Golgi-Apparat[5] Golgi-Vesikel[6] Golgi-Region[7] cis-aktive regulatorische DNA-Sequenzen[8] cis-Effekt[9] cis-Konfiguration[10] trans-agierende Faktoren[11]

  10

---

vacuole [vækjʊoʊl] n term   rel **phagosome**[1] [fægəsoʊm] n term

clear space or cavity in the protoplasm of a cell sometimes surrounding an engulfed[2] [ʌ] foreign body and serving [ɜː] as a temporary cell stomach [k] for the digestion [dʒe] of the body
vacuolar[3] adj term • vacuol(iz)ation[4] n • vacuolated adj

» The cytoplasm of basal cells is more electrondense[5] than that of glandular cells because they lack secretory [iː] vacuoles. Encapsulated meningococci [-kɒk(s)aɪ] are transported through nonciliated epithelial cells in large, membrane-bound [aʊ] phagocytic [sɪ] vacuoles.

Use contractile / internuclear / cytoplasmic[6] / lysosomal **vacuole** • neutrophil [(j)uː]/ membrane-bound **vacuole** • intracellular / secretory[7] **vacuole** • fat or lipid[8] / phagocytic[9] / parasitophorous **vacuole** • **vacuolar** membrane / area / proton pump[10] [ʌ] • **vacuolar** degeneration[11] / myelopathy [maɪə-] • fat(ty) / glycogen [aɪ]/ tubular / intracytoplasmic[12] **vacuolization** • **vacuolated** cytoplasm / cristae / macrophages [-feɪdʒɪz] • **vacuolated** eosinophils / inclusions[13] [uː3]/ appearance

Vakuole

Phagosom[1] aufgenommen, phagozytiert[2] vakuolenartig, vakuolär[3] Vakuolenbildung, Vakuolisierung[4] elektronendicht[5] Zytoplasmavakuole[6] Sekretionsvakuole[7] Fettvakuole[8] Phagozytosevakuole[9] Vakuolen-Protonenpumpe[10] vakuoläre Degeneration[11] Ausbildung von Zytoplasmavakuolen[12] vakuolisierte Einschlüsse[13]

  11

---

cell cycle [sel saɪkl] n term   rel **interphase**[1] [ɪntɚfeɪz] n term

cyclic biochemical and structural events occurring [ɜː] during rapid proliferation of cells such as in tissue culture [ʌ]; the cycle is divided into periods called: G0, Gap1 (G1), synthesis [ɪ] (S1), Gap2 (G2), and mitosis[2]

» Hyperthermia [ɜː] is particularly effective against hypoxic cells and cells in the S phase of the cell cycle, which are both radioresistant [reɪdioʊ-].

Use to regulate/activate/enter[3] **the cell cycle** • meiotic / mitotic[4] / G1 or G1 phase of the[5] **cell cycle** • **cell cycle** time[6] / phase / status [eɪ‖æ]/ progression / redistribution [juːʃ] • **cell cycle** regulatory proteins /-dependent • **cell cycle**-specific (abbr CCS) agents[7] [eɪdʒ]/ control or regulation[8] • G0 (resting)[9] / S[10] / G2[11] / M[12] / Golgi / dormant[9] **phase** • **interphase** cells / nuclei[12] [aɪ]

Zellzyklus

Interphase[1] Mitose, M-Phase[2] in den Zellzyklus eintreten[3] mitotischer Z.[4] G1-Phase, initiale/ erste Zellzyklusphase[5] Zellzykluszeit[6] zellzyklusspez. Substanzen[7] Steuerung des Zellzyklus[8] G0-Phase, Ruhephase[9] S-, Synthesephase[10] G2-, prämitotische Phase, Postsynthesephase[11] Interphase-, Ruhekerne[12]

  12

---

mitosis [maɪtoʊsɪs] n term   rel **prophase**[1], **metaphase**[2] [metəfeɪz] n term

cell division [ɪʒ] which results in the formation of two genetically identical daughter cells containing the diploid [dɪplɔɪd] number of chromosomes
anaphase[3] n term • telophase[4] [e‖iː] n • mitotic[5] adj • prometaphase[6] n

» Before mitosis the cell enters a second resting phase, in which RNA and protein synthesis continues. The phase following DNA replication but preceding [siː] cell division is termed metaphase. At the onset[7] of anaphase, the centromeric regions of each chromosome separate, and the two chromatids [oʊ] move to opposite poles of the mitotic spindle.

Use to undergo[8]/be in **mitosis** • somatic cell / Sertoli' frequent / numerous [uː] **mitoses** • rate[10] / inhibition[11] [ɪʃ] **of mitosis** • **mitosis** promoting factor[12] (abbr MPF) • **mitotic** figure / division / spindle[13] • **mitotic** activity / cycle / rate or index[10] • **mitotic** arrest / error[14] / cell death / inhibitors[15] • **metaphase** cells / chromosome analysis • mitotic **prophase**

Mitose, indirekte Kern- und Zellteilung

Prophase[1] Metaphase[2] Anaphase[3] Telophase[4] mitotisch, Mitose-[5] Prometaphase[6] Beginn[7] d. mitotische (Zell)teilung durchlaufen[8] atypische Mitose[9] Mitoserate, -index[10] Mitosehemmung[11] mitosefördernder Faktor[12] Mitose-, Kernspindel[13] Mitosefehler[14] Mitosehemmstoffe[15]

  13

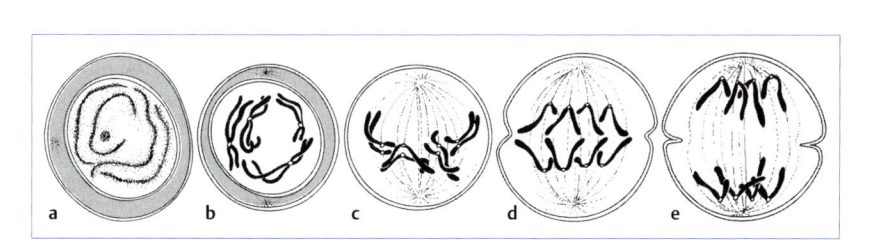

Mitosis:
(a) prophase,
(b) prometaphase,
(c) metaphase,
(d) early anaphase,
(e) late anaphase

meiosis [maɪˈoʊsɪs] *n term, pl* **-ses**   *rel* **crossing-over**[1] *n term* → U84-17

cell division consisting of two nuclear divisions in rapid succession [səkˈseʃ-] that result in the formation of four gametocytes [iː].
meiotic[2] [maɪˈɒtɪk] *adj term* • **crossover**[1] *n*

» In meiosis, homologous chromosomes pair up[3], i.e. the paternally [ɜː] derived with the maternally derived [aɪ] chromosome 1, etc. In the first meiotic division, homologous chromosomes are segregated[4], and the diploid chromosome number is reduced to the haploid.

Use to enter/undergo[5]/block/be in **meiosis** • gametic / onset of **meiosis** • **meiotic** pairing[6] [eə]/ prophase / recombination • **meiotic** maturation / stability / nondisjunction [dʒʌ] • **meiosis**-inducing substance (*abbr* MIS) • first[7] / second[8] **meiotic division** • somatic[9] / (un)equal[10] [iː] **crossing over**

---

endocytosis [-saɪˈtoʊsɪs] *n term*   *rel* **pinocytosis**[1] *n, opposite* **exocytosis**[2] *n term*

process whereby materials are engulfed[3] [ʌ] in a cell by invagination[4] [dʒ] of the plasma membrane
endocytose[5] [aɪ] *v term* • **endocytotic**[6] *adj* • **phagocytosis**[7] *n* • **-cytosis** *comb*

» Through absorptive endocytosis, lysosomes also function in the uptake[8] of vitamin B12, lipoproteins, peptide hormones, and growth factors. The influx of extracellular calcium through voltage-gated [eɪ] calcium channels causes insulin granules to move toward the cell surface and thus facilitate exocytosis. Pinocytosis probably plays a minor [aɪ] role in drug transport.

Use to initiate [ɪʃ] /be taken up by **endocytosis** • fluid / receptor-mediated[9] [iː]/ absorptive[10] **endocytosis** • to stimulate/undergo/release [iː] by[11] **exocytosis** • process of / increased[12] [iː] **exocytosis** • **endocytotic** process / pathways • trans[13]/ macro/ leuko/ thrombo/ pleo**cytosis** [pliːəsaɪˈtoʊsɪs]

---

signal transduction [ʌ] *n term*   *rel* **pathway**[1], **gene expression**[2] *n term*

activation of biochemical processes by cascades [kæsˈkeɪdz] of gene-regulated [dʒiːn-] reactions
transduce *v term* • **signaling** *n* • **signal** *v* •
(co)**express**[3] *v* • **repression** *n* → U84-26

» GH[4] receptor expression declines [aɪ] under conditions of sepsis, and other catabolic states. The absence of methyl groups provides a signal for expression. In the polyol pathway glucose is reduced to sorbitol by the enzyme aldol reductase [ʌ].

Use mitogenic / kinase-mediated[5] / neurotransmitter / photoreceptor **signal transduction** • **signal transduction** molecules / pathway[6] / cascade • hormonal[7] / extracellular[8] **signal** • **signal** molecule / sequence / peptide[9] • **signal** recognition particle (*abbr* SRP)/ transducer • juxtamembrane signal **transducer** • biochemical / biosynthetic / metabolic[10] **pathways** • enzymatic / degradation or degradative[11] / anabolic **pathways** • oxygen-dependent / anaerobic[12] **pathways** • glycolytic [ɪ] / transsulfuration / lipoxygenase **pathways** • to induce/promote/modulate[13]/limit/ inhibit **expression** • biochemical / exogenous [ɒːdʒ] phenotypic **expression** • chromosome / cell surface / adhesion molecule **expression** • dysregulated / enhanced / defective **expression** • constitutive[14] / ligand [aɪ]/ antigen **expression** • oncogene[15] / Fc receptor / over/ auto**expression** • disease / clinical **expression** • **expression** vector[16]

---

second messenger *n term*   *rel* **cyclic** [saɪklɪk] **AMP**[1] *n term, abbr* **cAMP**

chemical signal generated inside a cell when a hormone becomes bound to a surface receptor

» The classic second messenger is cyclic adenosine monophosphate[1]. In the absence of glucose, a complex between cAMP and its binding protein attaches to specific regions of DNA to activate transcription. Co-transmitters may interact with classical neurotransmitters at the level of the receptor and/or second messenger before evoking[2] [oʊ] a functional response.

Use intracellular / G protein-coupled[3] [ʌ] **second messenger** • **second messenger** system / substance / receptor [se] • first or primary[4] / cell-to-cell / internal [ɜː] **messenger** • cellular **cyclic AMP** • degradation or breakdown [eɪ] of[5] **cyclic AMP** • **cyclic AMP**-dependent protein kinase[6] [kaɪneɪz]/-independent mechanism [ek] • **cyclic AMP** response / production / level / stimulation • **cyclic** guanosine monophosphate[7] (*abbr* cGMP)/ nucleotide[8] / polypeptide

---

Meiose, Meiosis, Reduktionsteilung

Cross(ing)over[1] meiotisch[2] paaren sich[3] gespalten[4] die Reifeteilung durchlaufen[5] meiotische (Chromosomen)paarung[6] erste Reifeteilung[7] zweite Reifeteilung[8] somatisches Crossing over[9] ungleiches Crossing over[10]

14

Endozytose

Pinozytose[1] Exozytose[2] aufgenommen[3] Einstülpung[4] in die Zelle aufnehmen, endozytieren[5] endozytotisch[6] Phagozytose[7] Aufnahme[8] rezeptorvermittelte Endozytose[9] absorptive Endozytose[10] exozytotisch freisetzen[11] verstärkte Exozytose[12] Transzytose[13]

15

Signalübertragung, -transduktion

Weg, Bahn[1] Genexpression[2] exprimieren[3] Wachstumshormon[4] kinasevermittelte Signalübertragung[5] Signaltransduktions-, übertragungsweg[6] hormonales Signal[7] extrazelluläres Signal[8] Signalpeptid[9] Stoffwechselwege[10] Abbauwege[11] anaerobe Stoffwechselwege[12] die Expression modulieren[13] konstitutive Expression[14] Onkogenexpression[15] Expressionsvektor[16]

16

Second Messenger, sekundärer Bote(nstoff)

zykl. Adenosinmonophosphat, cAMP[1] auslösen[2] G-Protein-gekoppelter sekundärer Bote[3] First messenger, primärer Bote[4] Abbau v. cAMP[5] cAMP-abhängige Proteinkinase[6] zykl. Guanosinmonophosphat, cyclo-GMP, cGMP[7] zykl. Nukleotid[8]

17

Cytology & Cell Biology MEDICAL SCIENCE 355

downregulate v term   opposite **upregulate**[1] n term → U88-2
   rel **(de)activate**[2] [diːæktɪveɪt] v term → U88-12

to reduce a cellular response to a molecular stimulus, esp. by reduction of surface receptors

(down/ auto/ up)regulation[3] n term • **(up/ down/ auto)regulatory** adj

» The bile acid-binding resins cholestyramine and colestipol interfere [ɪɚ] with[4] reabsorption of bile acids[5] in the intestine[6], which results in a compensatory increase in bile acid synthesis and upregulation of LDL receptors in hepatocytes. Expression of these adhesion [iːʒ] molecules is upregulated. Some tumors downregulate expression of class I MHC antigens.

Use **to downregulate** expression • **to upregulate** virus [aɪ] replication[7] / receptor expression / collagen transcription • receptor / reversible [ɜː] **downregulation** • cytokine-mediated[8] **upregulation**

nach unten regulieren, vermindern
hochregulieren, nach oben regulieren[1] (de)aktivieren[2] Hochregulierung[3] hemmen[4] Gallensäuren[5] Darm[6] die Virusreplikation hochregulieren[7] zytokinvermittelte Hochregulierung[8]

18

modulate [mɒːdʒəleɪt] v term   rel **mediate**[1] [miːdieɪt] v term

to adapt in response to changing environmental conditions (e.g. cellular function), systematically vary the kinetics of an enzyme or metabolic pathway, or regulate the rate of mRNA translation, etc.

modulation[2] n term • **modulatory** adj • **modulator**[3] n • **mediator**[4] n

» Leptin has also been proposed as a metabolic signal that modulates reproduction. Many hormone actions are mediated by effects on adenylyl cyclase to increase or decrease cellular cyclic AMP. Nitric oxide appears to be a tertiary mediator of the signaling process.

Use **to modulate** cell activity / hormone secretion [iːʃ] • **to modulate** transmitter action / the immune responses[5] • **to mediate** attachment[6] [tʃ]/ fusion [juːʒ]/ immunity[7] • **to mediate** inflammation[8] / phagocytosis • bio/ sodium-mediated / hormonal / antigenic[9] [dʒe] **modulation** • **modulatory** neuron [(j)ʊɚ]/ transmitter mechanism • immuno[10]/ selective estrogen receptor[11] (abbr SERM)/ neuro**modulator** • cell[12]-/ receptor-/ androgen-/ prostaglandin-/ glutamate-**mediated** • carrier[13]-/ catecholamine- [koʊ]/ IgE-/ plasmid-**mediated** • physiologic / inflammatory[14] / (bio)chemical **mediator** • protein / releasing[15] [iː] **mediator** • cytokine [saɪtəkaɪn]/ soluble / phospholipid-derived [aɪ]/ (non)neural **mediator** • **mediator** substance[4] [ʌ]/ release[16]

modulieren
vermitteln[1] Modulation, Veränderung, Abwandlung[2] Modulator[3] Mediator(substanz), Vermittler[4] die Immunantwort verändern[5] Anheftung/ Adhäsion vermitteln[6] Immunität vermitteln[7] im Entzündungsprozess mitwirken[8] Antigenmodulation[9] Immunmodulator[10] selektiver Östrogenrezeptormodulator[11] zellvermittelt[12] träger-, carriervermittelt[13] Entzündungsmediator[14] Freisetzungsmediator[15] Mediatorfreisetzung[16]

19

centrifugation n term   rel **elution**[1] [ɪluːʃ°n], **wet mount**[2] [aʊ] n term

technique by means of which particles in suspension are separated by spinning so that they collect in layers at the levels of their densities in the periphery of the rotated vessel

centrifuge[3] [-fjuːdʒ] v & n term • **centrifugal** adj • **(un)centrifuged** adj • **elute** v term • **eluate**[4] [eljʊeɪt] n • **elutriation** n

» Varying volumes were used for resuspension after centrifugation. Slowly thaw[5] [ɒː] the FFP[6] to precipitate [sɪ] the plasma proteins, which are then separated by centrifugation. Centrifuge the specimen for 10 minutes at 2,000 rpm and inspect the pellet[7] for sperm cells.

Use density[8] / Percoll gradient [eɪ]/ ultra[9]/ inverted [ɜː] **centrifugation** • single / brief / double [ʌ]/ slow **centrifugation** • clinical / blood spun [ʌ] in a[10] **centrifuge** • **centrifugal** force[11] / spread [e] • **centrifuged** urine specimen[12] [es]/ urine / CSF / sediment / blood[10] • countercurrent[13] [ɜː] **elutriation** • routine / direct / india ink / saline [eɪ] **wet mount** • unstained[14]/ unspun / fungal [ʌ]/ stool **wet mount**

Zentrifugierung
Elution, Eluierung, Auswaschung; Ausschlämmung[1] Nasspräparat[2] zentrifugieren; Zentrifuge[3] Eluat[4] auftauen[5] frisch eingefrorenes Plasma[6] Pellet[7] Dichtegradientenzentrifugation[8] Ultrazentrifugation[9] zentrifugiertes Blut[10] Zentrifugal-, Fliehkraft[11] zentrifugierte Harnprobe[12] Elution im Gegenstrom[13] nicht angefärbtes Nasspräparat[14]

20

cytophotometry [saɪtəfoʊtnː-] n term   rel **microspectrophotometry**[1] n term

analysis of organic material within cells by measuring the light intensity in stained areas of cytoplasm

(hemo)cytometer[2] n term • **flow cytometry**[3] n • **cytometric** adj • **spectrometry**[4] n

» Flow cytometry of tumor cells to analyze DNA index and S-phase frequency aid in prognosis. DNA aneuploidy [ænjuː-] on flow cytometry analysis is confirmatory [ɜː] in cytology-negative cases. Flow cytometric cell-sorting techniques and rapid scanning microspectrophotometry have permitted the quantitation[5] of nuclear DNA content of prostate cancer cells.

Use multiparameter / automated[6] [ɒː]/ DNA / immunologic[7] **flow cytometry** • **flow cytometry** techniques/ analysis[3] • **cytometric** study / observation • **flow** cytometric determination[3] / karyotyping • high-resolution[8]/ atomic absorption[9] / reflectance[10] **spectrophotometry** • mass / magnetic resonance[11] **spectrometry**

Zytophotometrie
Mikrospektrophotometrie[1] Hämozytometer, Zahlkammer, Blutzellzählgerät[2] Durchflusszytometrie[3] Spektrometrie[4] Quantifizierung[5] automatisierte Durchflusszytometrie[6] immunologische Durchflusszytometrie[7] hochauflösende Spektrophotometrie[8] Atomabsorptionsspektrophotometrie[9] Reflexionsspektrophotometrie[10] Magnetresonanzspektrometrie[11]

21

(adsorption) chromatography *n term*   *rel* **gel filtration**[1] *n term*

separation of chemical compounds[2] by differential movement through a two-phase system
chromatographic *adj term* • **chromatogram** *n* • **filter**[3] *v & n* • **filtrate**[4] [-eɪt] *n*

» Gas-liquid chromatography was used for the detection of metabolic end products of bacterial [ɪə] fermentations. Bound [aʊ] materials released [iː] by acidification of affinity purified [jʊɚ] HLA class I crystals [ɪ] were analyzed by high-performance liquid chromatography.

Use qualitative / quantitative / gas[5] / gas-liquid (*abbr* GLC) **chromatography** • high-performance *or* high-pressure liquid[6] (*abbr* HPLC) **chromatography** • affinity[7] / ion-exchange[8] [aɪən-]/ paper[9] **chromatography** • thin-layer[10] (*abbr* TLC)/ column[11] [ɒː]/ partition[12] [ɪʃ] / gel[1] [dʒel] **chromatography** • **filter** paper (strips)[13]

(Adsorptions)chromatografie
Gelfiltration[1] chem. Verbindungen[2] filtern, filtrieren; Filter[3] Filtrat[4] Gaschromatografie[5] Hochdruck-Flüssigkeitschromatografie[6] Affinitätschromatografie[7] Ionenaustauschchromatografie[8] Papierchromatografie[9] Dünnschichtchromatografie[10] Säulenchromatografie[11] Verteilungschromatografie[12] Filterpapier(streifen)[13]   22

Unit 84   Clinical Genetics
Related Units: 83 Cell Biology, 81 Biochemistry, 78 Metabolism, 85 Embryology, 69 Fertility, 89 Pathology, 39 Immune System, 97 Oncology, 75 Personality

gene [dʒiːn] *n term*   *rel* **genome**[1] [dʒiːnoʊm] *n term*

functional unit of heredity that occupies a particular locus on a chromosome and is able to reproduce exactly at each cell division [ɪʒ] and direct the formation of proteins
genetic [dʒənetɪk] *adj term* • **genetics**[2] *n* • **genomic** [oʊ‖ɒː] *adj* • **gen(o)-** *comb*

» Genes occur in pairs in all cells except gametes [iː]. Cancer does not appear until the altered [ɔː] genome is expressed. Tobacco dependence may have a genetic component. Gout[3] [aʊ] is based on a genetically transmitted metabolic error[4].

Use human / parental / sex-linked[5] **genes** • Y-linked / dominant / overlapping[6] **genes** • defective / mutant [juː] *or* mutated[7] / tumor-suppressor **gene** • regulator / structural[8] / lethal[9] [iː]/ sickle[10] **gene** • cancer[11] *or* oncogene • **gene** family[12] / linkage[13] / expression[14] • **gene** product / structure / frequency / fusion [fjuːʒn] • **gene** amplification[15] / therapy / transfer / duplication[16] • **gene** copy / library[17] [aɪ]/ pool [uː]/ function • **gene** mapping[18] / carrier / cloning[19] / technology[20] • **gene** conversion [ɜː]/ dose[21] / regulatory protein • human / mitochondrial[22] [kɒː] **genome** • (retro)viral [aɪ]/ double-strand(ed) DNA **genome** • single-stranded RNA / segmented[23] **genome** • paternal [ɜː]/ haploid / host cell **genome** • **genome** map[24] • human[25] / biochemical **genetics** • medical / clinical / molecular[26] **genetics** • Mendelian[27] / reproductive [ʌ] **genetics** • population[28] / cancer / reverse[29] [ɜː] **genetics** • **genetic** code[30] / sex[31] / marker • **genetic** map / traits[32] [eɪ] • **genetic** screening [iː]/ counseling[33] [aʊ]/ affinity / **genetic** transmission / therapy • **genetic** defect [iː]/ predisposition[34] [ɪʃ]/ abnormality / splicing[35] [aɪs] • **genetic** engineering[20] [ɪə]/ disorder / factors • **genomic** DNA / material / library / sequences / imprinting[36] • **genomic** expression / instability • **genomic** defect / analysis • genotype[37] /typing /copy[38] /toxic • geneticist[39] • immuno[40]/ pharmaco[41]/ cyto**genetics**

Gen, Erbfaktor, -anlage
Genom, Erbgut, Genbestand[1] Genetik[2] Gicht[3] genetischer Stoffwechseldefekt[4] geschlechtsgebundene Gene[5] überlappende G.[6] mutiertes Gen[7] Strukturgen[8] Letalfaktor[9] Sichelzellgen[10] onc-, Onkogen[11] Genfamilie[12] Genkopp(e)lung[13] Genexpression[14] Genamplifikation[15] Genduplikation[16] Genbibliothek, -bank[17] Genkartierung[18] Genklonierung[19] Gentechnologie, -technik, -manipulation[20] Gendosis[21] mitochondriales Genom[22] segmentiertes G.[23] Genomkarte[24] Humangenetik[25] Molekulargenetik[26] Mendelsche Vererbungslehre[27] Populationsgenetik[28] reverse G.[29] genetischer Code[30] genet. Geschlecht[31] genet. (bedingte) Merkmale[32] genet. Beratung[33] genet. Prädisposition[34] Gensspleißen[35] genomische Prägung[36] Genotyp, Idiotypus[37] Genkopie[38] Genetiker(in)[39] Immungenetik[40] Pharmakogenetik[41]   1

(genetic) locus *n term, pl* **loci** [loʊsaɪ]
rel **genetic region**[1], **gene cluster**[2] [ʌ] *n term*

specific position of a gene or other marker on a chromosome (i.e. regions of DNA expressed)

» Each HLA gene locus[3] is highly polymorphic controlling about 8-50 separate antigens. A susceptibility locus for Parkinson's disease maps to chromosome 2p13.

Use gene / chromosomal[4] / autosomal / X-linked / ß-globin **locus** • ABO blood group[5] / Rb / marker / disease(-associated) **locus** • imprintable / regulatory **locus** • HLA[3] / growth-controlling / growth-suppressor **locus** • myc / (major) histocompatibility[3] / mutant **locus** • polymorphic / oncogene **loci** • **locus** heterogeneity [-iːəti]/ control region[6] • chromosomal / DNA / gene-dense[7] **region** • (central) core / pre-core **region** • (protein) coding[8] / (consensus/ antibody) binding[9] **region** • switch / transmembrane **region** • constant *or* C[10] / variable *or* V[11] / HLA (class II) **region** • promoter[12] / breakpoint cluster [ʌ] (*abbr* BCR) **region** • **cluster** of differentiation *or* determinant[13] [ɜː] (*abbr* CD)

Genlokus, -ort, Locus
Genregion[1] Gengruppe, -cluster[2] HLA-Locus[3] chromosomaler Locus[4] ABO Blutgruppen-Locus[5] Locuscontrol region[6] genreiche Region[7] proteinkodierende Region, Exon[8] Bindungsregion[9] konstante Region, C-Region[10] variable Region, V-Region[11] Promotorregion[12] Differenzierungscluster[13]   2

Clinical Genetics MEDICAL SCIENCE 357

DNA-binding [aɪ] **motif** [iː] n term   rel **functional** [ʌ] **domain**[1] [eɪ] n term

three-dimensional protein structure which establishes bonds[2] with the double [ʌ] helix [iː]

» Helix-turn-helix, homeodomain[3], zinc finger, leucine [luːsiːn] zipper[4], and helix-loop-helix [uː] are all used as DNA-binding motifs or mediate[5] [iː] dimerization of factors required for DNA binding. One motif located at the N terminus[6] [ɜː] is rich in cysteine [sɪstiːn] residues[7]. Three functional domains have been described in the U3 and R regions [iːdʒ].

Use structural [ʌ]/ DNA (sequence) / RNA-binding[8] (abbr RBM) **motif** • binding consensus / zinc finger[9] **motif** • helix-turn-helix[10] [ɜː]/ helix-loop-helix[11] **motif** • antigen recognition [ɪʃ] activation (abbr ARAM) **motif** • DNA-binding[12] / hormone-binding **domain** • antigen binding / transmembrane[13] **domain** • long triple-helical / homeo[3]/ death / N terminal **domain**

DNA-/ DNS-Bindemotiv
funktionelle Domäne[1] Bindungen[2] Homöodomäne[3] Leucinzipper[4] vermitteln[5] N-Terminus[6] Cysteinreste[7] RNA/ RNS-Bindemotiv[8] Zink-Finger-Motiv[9] Helix-Turn-Helix-Motiv[10] Helix-Loop-Helix-Motiv[11] DNA-Bindungsdomäne[12] Transmembrandomäne[13]

3

allele [əliːˀl] n term   syn **allelomorph** [e‖iː] n term

alternative forms of a gene that occupy corresponding loci [-saɪ] on homologous chromosomes

allelic [e‖iː] adj term • **nonallelic** adj

» Homologous copies of a gene are termed alleles. A haplotype[1] is a cluster of tightly [aɪ] linked specific alleles[2] on a chromosome. The maternally [ɜː] and paternally derived[3] [aɪ] autosomes that compose a pair are genetically homologous, their differences being qualitative, that is, dependent on the alleles received from each parent at polymorphic loci.

Use (co)dominant / recessive [se] / parental[4] / paternal [ɜː] **allele** • maternal[5] / maternally derived[5] **allele** • low-expression / silent[6] [aɪ]/ silenced[7] **allele** • polymorphic / HLA / MHC **allele** • defective / mutant / wild-type[8] / loss-of function or null[9] [ʌ] **allele** • gain of function or neomorphic[10] [niːə-] / hypomorphic[11] **alleles** • **allele** loss /-specific oligonucleotide[12] (abbr ASO) • **allelic** genes[13] / pairs[14] / disorder / heterogeneity [iːə] • **allelic** variation [eɪʃ]/ loss / mutation / deletion • **nonallelic** (genetic) heterogeneity[15]

Allel, Allelomorph
Haplotyp[1] gekoppelte Allele[2] paternal[3] parentales Allel[4] maternales Allel[5] stummes Allel[6] stillgelegtes/ inaktiviertes/ abgeschaltetes Allel[7] Wildtypallel[8] Nullallel[9] Allele mit erweiterter/ zusätzlicher Funktion[10] hypomorphe Allele[11] allelspezifisches Oligonukleotid[12] allele Gene[13] Allelenpaare[14] nicht-allelische Heterogenie[15]

4

homozygous [hoʊməzaɪɡəs] adj term   opposite **heterozygous**[1] adj term

having identical genes at one or more paired [eə] loci in homologous chromosomes

homo/ hetero/ hemizygote[2] [hemɪ-] n term • **homo/ heterozygosity**[3] [ɒ:] n

» Heterozygous women transmit the mutant gene to one-half of sons, who are affected, and to one-half of daughters, who are heterozygotes. If an affected male mates[4] with a heterozygous female, half of the male offspring[5] will be affected, giving the false impression of male-to-male transmission. Persons heterozygous for hemoglobin E are asymptomatic and usually not anemic [iː]. Homozygosity for the double-gene defect is lethal, since Hb lacking (alpha)-chains does not transport O2.

Use **homozygous** female / family member / offspring / state[6] / for a null gene • **homozygous** defect / missense mutation[7] / hemoglobin C disease[8] • **heterozygous** carrier[9] / parent / deficiency / mutation • asymptomatic / obligate[10] **heterozygote** • **heterozygote** detection[11] • allelic / loss of (abbr LOH) **heterozygosity**

homozygot
heterozygot[1] hemizygote Zelle[2] Heterozygotie[3] sich paaren[4] Nachkommen[5] homozygoter Zustand[6] homozygote Fehlsinnmutation[7] homozygote Hämoglobin C-Krankheit[8] heterozygoter Träger[9] obligat heterozygotes Individuum[10] Heterozygotennachweis[11]

5

chromosome [kroʊməsoʊm‖zoʊm] n term
   rel **autosome**[1] [ɒː], **gonosome**[2], **chromatin**[3] [oʊ] n term

one of the gene-bearing [eə] bodies (normally 46 in man) in the cell nucleus [(j)uː] that is capable of reproducing its structure through successive cell divisons[4] [ɪʒ]

(extra)chromosomal adj term • autosomal adj • eu[5]/ heterochromatin[6] n

» All chromosomes are paired except the sex chromosomes (X and Y) of the male. During interphase chromosomes have the form of a delicate chromatin filament and contract to form a compact cylinder [sɪ] segmented into two arms by the centromere during metaphase and anaphase stages of cell divison. In a nondividing [aɪ] cell, chromosomes are tightly packaged in the nucleus. Microscopically recognizable segments in the short arms of the acrocentric autosomes[7] are devoted to the production of ribosomal RNA and nucleoli.

Use sex[2] / X / Y / somatic[1] / (long/ short) arm of[8] **chromosome** • autosomal / ring[9] / homologous[10] **chromosomes** • yeast [jiːst] artificial[11] (abbr YAC)/ Philadelphia (Ph) **chromosomes** • **chromosome** abnormality • **autosome** imbalance • **chromosomal** DNA / material / region / sex[12] • **chromosomal** karyotype / analysis[13] / complex / bands[14] • **chromosomal** instability / breakage[15] [eɪ] (site) / rearrangement / constitution • **chromosomal** aberration[16] / loss / translocation[17] / deletion • mosaicism[18] [eɪ] • **autosomal** inheritance[19] / recessive trait[20] / codominant allele • sex[21] / nuclear / functional[5] **chromatin** • inert[6] [ɜː]/ dense **chromatin** • dark / coarsely [ɔː] textured[22] / peripherally massed **chromatin** • **chromatin** structure / pattern / distribution • **chromatin** condensation[23] / clumping [ʌ] • **chromatin** mass /-positive[24] / negative • **chromatin** gap / fragility[25] [dʒɪ]/ receptor [se] site

Chromosom, Erbkörperchen
Autosom[1] Gono-, Heterosom, Geschlechtschromosom[2] Chromatin[3] Zellteilungen[4] Euchromatin, funktionell aktives C.[5] Heterochromatin, funktionell inaktives C.[6] akrozentrische Autosomen[7] kurzer Chromosomenarm[8] Ringchromosomen[9] homologe C.[10] künstl. Hefechromosomen[11] chromosomales Geschlecht[12] Chromosomenanalyse[13] Chromosomenbanden[14] Chromosomenbruch[15] Chromosomenaberration[16] Chromosomentranslokation[17] Chromosomenmosaik[18] autosomale Vererbung[19] autosomal rezessives Merkmal[20] Barr-Körper, X-, Geschlechts-, Sexchromatin[21] grobkörniges/ grobstrukturiertes C.[22] Chromatinkondensation, -verdichtung[23] chromatinpositiv[24] Chromatinbrüchigkeit, -fragilität[25]

6

358 MEDICAL SCIENCE — Clinical Genetics

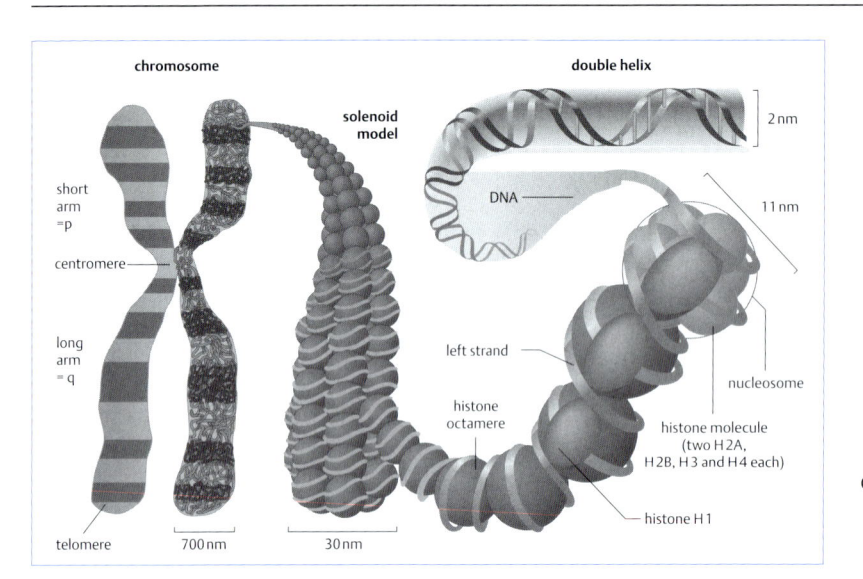

Chromosomal structures

Labels: chromosome; short arm = p; centromere; long arm = q; telomere; 700 nm; 30 nm; solenoid model; DNA; histone octamere; histone H1; double helix; 2 nm; 11 nm; left strand; nucleosome; histone molecule (two H2A, H2B, H3 and H4 each)

---

centromere [sɛntrəmɪɚ] n term   rel **telomere**[1], **chromatid**[2], **satellite**[3] n term

nonstaining primary constriction[4] of a chromosome forming the junction of the arms of chromatids where they are attached to spindle fibers[5] [aɪ]

(**peri**)**centromeric** adj term • (**sub**)**telomeric** adj • **telomerase**[6] n

» Centromeres provide a mechanism for chromosome movement during cell division. Each arm consists of two identical parts, called chromatids. In isochromosomes[7] the arms on either side of the centromere have the same genetic material. The telomeres at the ends of each chromosome are replicated through an RNA-dependent DNA polymerase called telomerase. The DNA of satellites contains no genes.

Use acrocentric / metacentric **centromere** • **centromere** position • anti**centromere** antibody[8] (abbr ACA) • shortening of[9] **telomeres** • **telomeric** sequences [iː] • **centromeric** protein[10] / index / region / chromatin • sister[11] / exchanged **chromatids** • **chromatid** pair / segment[12] / exchange / nondisjunction [ʌ] • **chromatid** aberration / gap / break [eɪ] • chromosome[3] **satellite** • **satellite** DNA[13] • centrosome[14] /oplasm[15] /iole[16]

Zentromer, Kinetochor
Telomer, Chromosomenendstück[1] Chromatid[2] Satellit[3] primäre Konstriktion/ Einschnürung[4] Spindelfasern[5] Telomerase[6] Isochromosom[7] Anti-Zentromer-Antikörper[8] Telomerverkürzung[9] Zentromerprotein[10] Schwesterchromatiden[11] Chromatidabschnitt[12] Satelliten-DNA[13] Zentrosom[14] Zentroplasma[15] Zentriol, Zentralkörperchen, Centriolum[16]

[7]

---

plasmid [plæzmɪd] n term   rel **episome**[1] [ɛpɪsoʊm‖ɛpəzoʊm] n term

extrachromosomal genetic element (paragene) chiefly found in bacterial [ɪə] host cells that can replicate[2] independently from the chromosome and is not essential to cell growth

plasmid-encoded [ɪnkoʊdɪd] adj term • **episomal** adj

» Plasmid-borne[3] penicillin resistance results from the presence of a TEM-1-type b-lactamase gene on one of five small R factors that make up a very closely related family of plasmids.

Use bacterial / R or resistance[4] / F[5] / (non)conjugative[6] [dʒə]/ transferable[7] [ɜː]/ linear / circular [ɜː] **plasmids** • **plasmid**-mediated[3] [iː]/-encoded resistance[8] / DNA / profile / pattern analysis • **plasmid-encoded** gene / enzyme [ɛnzaɪm] / enterotoxin[9] • viral [aɪ]/ resistance-transferring [ɜː] **episome** • **episomal** DNA / form

Plasmid
Episom[1] replizieren, s. verdoppeln[2] plasmidvermittelt[3] R-Plasmide, R-Faktoren, Resistenzfaktoren[4] F-Plasmide, F-Faktoren[5] d. Konjugation übertragbare Plasmide[6] übertragbare P.[7] plasmiddeterminierte/ -vermittelte Resistenz[8] plasmidkodiertes Enterotoxin[9]

[8]

Clinical Genetics   MEDICAL SCIENCE 359

haploid [hæplɔɪd] *adj term*   *opposite* **diploid**[1] [dɪplɔɪd] *adj term*

half the full set of chromosomes (23 in humans) found in reproductive cells

haploidy[2] *n term* • **aneuploid** *adj* • **aneuploidy**[3] *n*
• **ploidy** *n & comb* • **hapl(o)-** *comb*

» Secondary spermatocytes arise from primary spermatocytes after meiotic division and have a haploid number of chromosomes. The diploid human genome consists of 46 chromosomes, 22 pairs of autosomes [ɒː], and one pair of sex chromosomes. Hyperdiploidy[4] is a favorable [eɪ] finding, whereas near-diploid DNA content is associated with advanced disease.

Use **haploid** number or set of chromosomes[5] / (human) genome • **diploid** cell (culture) [ʌ]/ state • **aneuploid** parent / pattern / clone [oʊ] • **aneuploid** stem cells[6] / tumor / liveborn • DNA / chromosomal / tumor[7] **ploidy** • somatic cell chromosome / parental **aneuploidy** • fetal [iː]/ marked[8] **aneuploidy** • hyperdi/ tetra**ploid** • mixo[9]/ di/ tri**ploidy** • **haplo**identity[10] /identical donor [oʊ] /type[11]

haploid
diploid[1] Haploidie[2] Aneuploidie, abnormer Chromosomensatz[3] Hyperdiploidie, Hyperploidie im diploiden Chromosomensatz[4] haploider Chromosomensatz[5] aneuploide Stammzellen[6] Tumorploidie[7] ausgeprägte Aneuploidie[8] Mixoploidie[9] Haploidentität[10] Haplotyp[11]

9

karyotype [kærɪətaɪp] *n & v term*   *rel* **phenotype**[1] [fiːnə-],
                                         genotype[2] [dʒiː‖dʒenə-] *n term*

(n) chromosome characteristics of an individual or of a cell line; by extension the systematized array of metaphase chromosomes from a photomicrograph of a single cell arranged in descending order of size

karyotypic [ɪ] *adj term* • **karyotyping**[3] *n* • **kary(o)-** *comb* • **phenotypic**[4] *adj*

» These paired genes, called alleles, determine [ɜː] the genotype of an individual at a specific locus. Parental karyotypes are essential for all patients with translocation or deletion [iːʃ] syndromes [ɪ] to make sure that the rearrangement [eɪ] was not inherited. Sperm [ɜː] and ova donors[5] should be karyotyped to rule out[6] any heritable chromosome anomaly.

Use chromosomal / female[7] / constitutional [(j)uːʃ] **karyotype** • blood / parental / (ab)normal[8] **karyotype** • 47,XXY / mutated / mosaic[9] [zeɪ]/ XO **karyotype** • **karyotype** analysis[3] / abnormality • **karyotypic** pattern / abnormality • **karyotypic** evidence / rearrangement [dʒ] • fetal[10] / leukocyte [uː] **karyotyping** • (ab)normal / homozygous / recessive **phenotype** • immunologic[11] / cytotoxic **phenotype** • classic / male / HLA / X-linked[12] / mutant[13] **phenotype** • parental[14] / 46,XY / APOE[15] **genotype** • **karyo**some /metric measurements[16] [eʒ] • mega**karyo**cyte • **phenotypic** features [fiːtʃɚz] or characteristics[17] / sex • **phenotypic** female / differences / variability / effects • **genotypic** analysis / characteristics

Karyotyp; den Karyotyp ermitteln/ darstellen
Phänotyp(us), Erscheinungsbild[1] Genotyp(us), Erbbild[2] Chromosomenanalyse[3] phänotypisch[4] Eizellenspenderinnen[5] ausschließen[6] weibl. Karyotyp[7] aberranter/ abnormaler Karyotyp[8] Chromosomenmosaik[9] Chromosomenanalyse beim Fetus[10] Immunphänotyp[11] X-gekoppelter Phänotyp[12] Mutantenphänotyp[13] parentaler Genotyp[14] Apolipoprotein E Genotyp[15] karyometrische Analysen/ Untersuchungen[16] phänotypische Merkmale[17]

10

de(s)oxyribonucleic acid [dɪɒksɪraɪbən(j)ʊkliːɪk] *n term, abbr* **DNA**
                             rel **strand**[1] [æ], **double** [ʌ] **helix**[2] [hiːlɪks] *n term, pl* **–ces** [-siːz]

autoreproducing double-stranded molecule held together by weak [iː] bonds[3] between base [eɪ] pairs [peɚz] of nucleotides that encodes genetic information and is the repository of hereditary characteristics[4]

deoxyribonuclease[5] *n term, abbr* **DNase** • **nucleic** *adj* • **single-stranded** *adj* • **helical**[6] [e‖iː] *adj*

» When bonded together the two linear strands of DNA assume the shape of a double helix. The four nucleotides in DNA contain the bases adenine (A), guanine [ɑː] (G), cytosine [saɪ] (C), and thymine [aɪ] (T). The base sequence [iː] of each single strand can be deduced [(j)uːs] from that of its partner because base pairs form only between A and T and between G and C. The mRNA contains a sequence of purine [pjʊɚiːn] and pyrimidine [paɪrɪmədiːn] bases that is complementary to the bases of the antisense [æntaɪ-] strand[7] of the DNA.

Use exogenous [ɒːdʒ] or foreign[8] / bacterial / double-stranded[9] / single-stranded[10] **DNA** • complementary or copy[11] (*abbr* cDNA) **DNA** • **DNA** molecule / sequencing[12] / fragment / marker • **DNA** ligase [aɪ]/ polymerase [-eɪz]/ chain terminator [ɜː] • **DNA** synthesis[13] [ɪ]/ replication[14] / copy • **DNA** chip[15] / virus [aɪ]/ repair[16] (gene) • **DNA** fingerprinting (method)[17] / probe[18] • **DNA** damage[19] / template[20] / polymorphisms • **DNA**-binding domain • double-stranded[2] / **DNA** / coiled[21] / triple[22] [ɪ]/ alpha **helix** • double-/ triple-**helical** • **helical** filament [ɪ]/ coil[21] / DNA sequence / RNA • **helical** groove[23] [uː]/ nucleocapsid / pattern[24] • antisense[7] / plus-/ minus[25]-/ defective **strand** • complementary / (double) [ʌ] DNA[26] **strand** • lead[27] [iː]/ lagging *or* lag[28] **strand** • **strand**-break(age)[29] • single-/ (circular) double-/ anti-double-/ plus-**stranded**

Desoxyribonukleinsäure, DNS, DNA
Strang[1] Doppelhelix[2] Bindungen[3] Träger des Erbguts[4] Desoxyribonuklease[5] Helix-, helikal[6] gegenläufiger Strang[7] fremde DNA[8] doppelsträngige DNA[9] einzelsträngige/ Einzelstrang-DNA[10] (basen)komplementäre DNA, cDNA[11] DNA-Sequenzierung[12] DNA-(Bio)synthese[13] DNA-Replikation[14] DNA-Chip[15] DNA-Reparatur[16] DNA-Fingerprint-Methode/ -Verfahren[17] DNA-Sonde[18] DNA-Schaden/ -Schäden[19] DNA-Matrize/ -Template[20] Helixknäuel[21] Tripelhelix[22] Furche (d. Helix)[23] Helixstruktur[24] Minusstrang[25] DNA-Doppelstrang[26] Leitstrang[27] Folgestrang[28] Strangbruch[29]

11

nucleotide [-klɪətaɪd] *n term* *rel* **base pair**[1] *n, abbr* **bp**, **sequence**[2] *n & v term*

subunit of DNA or RNA consisting of a nitrogenous base (adenine, cytosine, guanine, thymine in DNA; uracil in RNA), a phosphate molecule, and a sugar molecule (deoxyribose in DNA and ribose in RNA)

nucleotidase[3] [aɪ] *n term* • **base** [eɪ] *n* • **nucle(o)-** *comb* • **sequencing**[4] [iː] *n*

» *Thousands of nucleotides are linked to form a DNA or RNA molecule. Genes consist of a giant DNA molecule containing the proper purine and pyrimidine bases to code the sequence of amino acids needed to form a specific peptide. Cis-acting regulatory DNA sequences are part of the same duplex* [uː] *DNA molecule as the coding sequence.*

Use (deoxy)ribo[5]/ mono/ di[6]/ tri/ radio/ oligo/ poly/ cyclic[7] **nucleotides** • **nucleotide** position / analogue[8] / sequence • **nucleotide** pairing / deletion / metabolism[9] / adjacent[10] [eɪs] **base pair** • **base-pair** fragment / change / deletion • purine[11] / pyrimidine[12] [paɪrɪm-]/ kilo/ mega**bases** • complementary **base** • **base** pairing[13] / mismatch / repeat [iː]/ substitution [(j)uːʃ] *or* replacement[14] • **nucle**otidyltransferase /protein /capsid[15] / side[16] • **base**[17] / gene **sequence** • (genomic/ cis-acting regulatory) DNA / complete genomic **sequence** • nucleotide[18] / telomeric / amino acid[19] / protein **sequence** • promoter / recognition / N-terminal [ɜː] **sequence** • double-stranded / repeat *or* repetitive[20] / tandem repeat **sequence** • expanded trinucleotide repeat / complementary **sequence** • TATA[21] / coding[22] / signal / intervening[23] [iː] **sequence** • flanking[24] / splice [splaɪs] site **sequence** • internal ribosome entry / mutant *or* mutated **sequence** • **sequence** tag[25] / tagged site (*abbr* STS)/ variation • **sequence** analysis[4] / homology

codon [koʊdɒːn] *n term* *rel* **anticodon**[1] *n term*

three continuous nucleotide bases on the DNA and mRNA encoding for a specific amino acid residue[2]

code[3] *n & v term* • **encode**[4] [ɪnkoʊd] *v* • **(en)coding** *adj & n* • **noncoding** *adj*

» *Starting at a specific signal, mRNA is translated into a protein, the amino acid sequence of which is predetermined* [ɜː] *by the order of codons. Both copies of the gene are defective because of the presence of a* stop codon[5] *that truncates* [ʌ] *the protein at amino acid 105. Noncoding segments are referred to as* restriction fragment length polymorphisms[6] *(abbr RFLPs), variable number of tandem repeats (abbr VNTRs), or polymorphic short tandem repeats of di- or tetranucleotides.*

Use (DNA/ RNA) triplet [ɪ]/ initiation[7] / terminator *or* termination[5] **codon** • premature termination / nonsense[8] **codon** • **codon**-198 mutation • anticodon loop[9] [uː] • **to code** for proteins[10] • genetic / DNA / mRNA **code** • **to encode** enzymes / inhibitors / hormones • (**non**)**coding** region / sequence[11] • **encoding** gene / protein

exon [eksɒːn] *n term* *opposite* **intron**[1] *n term*

active segment of a DNA molecule encoding for a section of the mature mRNA

exonic *adj term* • **intronic** *adj*

» *Information in genes is contained in exons, which are* interspersed [ɜː] with[2] *stretches of DNA that do not encode any information about the protein sequence, so-called introns.*

Use coding[3] / overlapping[4] **exons** • **exon**-intron sequence / skipping[5] • intervening [iː] **intron** • **intronic** sequences / region / GAA triplet repeat expansion[6] / mutation

ribonucleic [iː] **acid** *n term, abbr* **RNA** *rel* **ribosome**[1] [aɪ] *n term* → U83-9

macromolecule found in both the nuclei and cytoplasm of all cells which consists of ribonucleoside residues[2]; it controls cellular protein synthesis [ɪ] and genetic transcription

ribonucleotide[3] *n term* • **ribosomal**[4] [raɪbəsoʊməl] *adj* • **ribo-** [raɪboʊ-] *comb*

» *Protein synthesis is mediated* [iː] *by molecules of messenger-RNA formed on the chromosome with the gene unit of DNA acting as a template; then they pass into the cytoplasm and become oriented on the ribosomes where they in turn act as templates to organize a chain of amino acids to form a peptide.*

Use ribosomal[5] (*abbr* rRNA)/ informational *or* messenger[6] (*abbr* mRNA) **RNA** • transfer[7] (*abbr* tRNA)/ nuclear[8] (*abbr* nRNA) **RNA** • heterogeneous [dʒiː]/ (anti)genomic **RNA** • antisense[9] / (retro)viral **RNA** • **RNA** molecule / chain • polymerase[10] / fraction • **RNA** template[11] / synthesis [ɪ]/-binding proteins • **RNA**-dependent *or* -directed DNA polymerase[12] • **RNA** degradation[13] [eɪʃ]/ splicing[14] [aɪ] • **RNA** transcription / processing[15] / virus • inhibitory **ribonucleotides** • **ribonucleotide** reductase [ʌ] • cell / bacterial [ɪə]/ mammalian [eɪ]/ prokaryote-type[16] **ribosomes** • **ribosomal** protein / subunit[17] [ʌ]/ activity • **ribosomal** binding site / recognition [ɪʃ] • **ribosome**-rich endoplasmic reticulum[18] • **ribo**typing[19] • **ribonucle**oprotein /ar protein (*abbr* RNP) • ase *or* RNase[20] [-eɪz]

Nukleotid

Basenpaar[1] Sequenz; sequenzieren, eine Sequenzanalyse durchführen[2] Nukleotidase[3] Sequenzanalyse[4] (Desoxy)ribonukleotid[5] Dinukleotide[6] zyklische Nukleotide[7] Nukleotidanalogon[8] Nukleotidstoffwechsel[9] benachbartes Basenpaar[10] Purinbasen[11] Pyrimidinbasen[12] Basenpaarung[13] Basenaustausch[14] Nukleokapsid[15] Nukleosid[16] Basensequenz[17] Nukleotidsequenz[18] Aminosäuresequenz[19] repetitive Sequenz, Sequenzwiederholung[20] TATA-Sequenz, -Box[21] codierende Sequenz[22] intervenierende Sequenz[23] flankierende Sequenz[24] Markierungssequenz[25]

12

Kodon, Codon, Basen-, Nukleotidtriplett

Antikodon, -codon[1] Aminosäurerest[2] Code; codieren[3] codieren[4] Stopp-, Terminationscodon[5] Restriktionsfragment-Längen-Polymorphismus, RFLP[6] Initiator-, Startcodon[7] Nonsense-Codon[8] Anticodonschleife[9] für Proteine codieren[10] codierende Sequenz[11]

13

Exon

Intron[1] unterbrochen von[2] codierende Exonen[3] überlappende Exonen[4] Überspringen/ Auslassen von Exonen[5] Expansion d. Trinukleotidrepeats GAA in einem Intron[6]

14

Ribonukleinsäure, RNS, RNA

Ribosom[1] Ribonukleosidreste[2] Ribonukleotid[3] ribosomal, Ribosomen-[4] ribosomale RNA, rRNA[5] Messenger-RNA, mRNA[6] Transfer-RNA, tRNA[7] nukleäre RNA[8] Antisense-RNA[9] RNA-Polymerase[10] RNA-Matrize/ -Template[11] RNA-abhängige DNA-Polymerase[12] RNA-Abbau[13] RNA-Spleißen[14] RNA-Prozessierung[15] Prokaryontenribosomen[16] Ribosomenuntereinheit[17] mit vielen Ribosomen besetztes endoplasmatisches Retikulum[18] Ribotypisierung[19] Ribonuklease, RNase[20]

15

Clinical Genetics   MEDICAL SCIENCE 361

replication [replɪˈkeɪʃən] *n term*   *sim* **copy**[1] [ˈkɒːpi] *n & v term, pl* **copies**
  DNA-directed synthesis of genetic material by means of duplication [uː] and autoreproduction
  replicate[2] *v term* • **replicative**[3] *adj* • **replicon**[4] *n* • **replicator**[5] *n* • **copying** *n*
  » The capacity of DNA to replicate itself constitutes the basis of hereditary transmission. G1 arrest may allow the cell to repair damage before DNA replication. Some cells die when their telomeres no longer protect the integrity of DNA replication. The vector-containing human DNA insert is replicated, thus producing multiple copies of the segment of interest.
  Use to regulate/support/inhibit[6]/suppress **replication** • self[7]-/ asexual / DNA / cell **replication** • intracellular / virus [aɪ] or viral[8] **replication** • late / in vivo **replication** • post**replication** repair[9] [eə] • **replication** ability /-competent[10] • **replication**-defective / site [aɪ]/ error[11] • gene[12] / cDNA / paternal / defective **copy** • **replicative** cycle[13] [saɪkl]/ rate / phase [feɪz] • **replicative** marker / infection[14]

Replikation, Reduplikation, identische Verdoppelung
Kopie; kopieren, vervielfältigen, eine Kopie anfertigen[1] replizieren, sich verdoppeln[2] replikativ, Replikations-[3] Replikon[4] Replikator[5] die Replikation hemmen[6] Selbstreduplikation[7] Virusreplikation[8] Post-, Nachreplikationsreparatur[9] replikationsfähig[10] Replikationsfehler[11] Genkopie[12] Replikationszyklus[13] Infektion bei gleichzeitiger Replikation[14]   16

(genetic) recombination [eɪʃ] *n term*
                        rel **crossing-over**[1] *n term* → U83-14
  exchange of entire segments between paternal [ɜː] and maternal chromosomes by which progeny [ɒːdʒ] derive [aɪ] a combination of genes [iː] different from that of either parent
  recombinant *adj term* • **recombined**[2] [aɪ] *adj* • **recombinate**[3] *n* • **crossover**[1] *n*
  » In higher organisms, recombination can occur [ɜː] by crossing over. Genetic distance, which is expressed in centimorgans[4] (*abbr* cM), is a measure of the likelihood of crossover between two loci. In the germ [ɜː] line[5], additional loci are activated to undergo meiosis, which involves the pairing of homologous chromosomes, genetic recombination, and then the separation of recombined homologous chromosomes at anaphase[6] of the first division.
  Use to undergo/promote **recombination** • mitotic[7] / parental / homologous[8] **recombination** • **recombination** signal / distance / frequency [iː] • **recombinant** DNA (technique)[9] [tekniːk]/ clones / human DNase • **recombinant** tissue plasminogen activator[10] (*abbr* rtPA) • **recombinant** G-CSF / immunoblot assay [æseɪ] (*abbr* RIBA) • to undergo / somatic[11] / unequal[12] [iː] **crossing-over** • chromosomal **crossover** • **crossover** events

(genetische) Rekombination
Crossing over, Chiasmabildung, Austausch von Chromosomenabschnitten[1] rekombiniert[2] Rekombinante[3] Centi-Morgan, cM[4] Keimbahn[5] Anaphase[6] mitotische Rekombination[7] homologe Rekombination[8] Rekombinanten-DNA-Technik, Gentechnologie[9] rekombinanter humaner tPA[10] somatisches Crossing over[11] ungleiches Crossing over[12]

17

transcription [trænˈskrɪpʃən] *n term*
  synthesis of a single-stranded RNA with a base sequence complementary to the DNA template
  transcriptase[1] *n term* • **transcript** *n* • **transcribe**[2] [aɪ] *v* • **transcriptional** *adj*
  » Late-gene transcription is continuously dependent on DNA replication. Immediate-early [iː] genes require only a component of the viral tegument[3] and preexisting cellular transcription factors to be actively transcribed.
  Use to induce/modulate/regulate or control[4]/stimulate/enhance/block **transcription** • DNA / mRNA / reverse[5] [ɜː]/ (early/ late) gene / host cell / ER-dependent[6] **transcription** • **transcription** (regulatory) factor[7] / initiation[8] [eɪʃ] • RNA / terminally redundant [ʌ]/ overexpressed **transcript** • **transcript** translation / stability / elongation[9] / splicing • **to transcribe** DNA[10] / RNA • **transcriptional** regulation or control[11] / repression • **reverse transcriptase** activity / inhibitor[12]

Transkription
Transkriptase, RNA-Polymerase[1] transkribieren[2] Virushülle, (Virus)tegument[3] die Transkription steuern/ regulieren[4] reverse Transkription[5] östrogenrezeptorabhängige Transkription[6] Transkriptionsfaktor[7] Initiation der Transkription[8] Transkriptelongation[9] DNA umschreiben[10] Transkriptionsregulation[11] reverse Transkriptase-Hemmer/ -Inhibitor[12]   18

translation [trænˈsleɪʃən] *n term* → U83-9
                rel **initiation**[1], **elongation**[2] [iːlɒːŋgeɪʃən], **termination**[3] *n term*
  synthesis of polypeptide chains using tRNA as a template[4] for the sequence of bases [eɪ]
  translate[5] *v* • **(post)translational**[6] *adj term* • **initiator** [ɪʃ] *n* • **initiate** *v*
  • **terminator** [ɜː] *n term* • **elongate** *v* • **terminate** *v*
  » Polyribosomes [aɪ] bound [aʊ] to the rER[7] of the hepatocyte are the principal site of translation of mRNA coding for export proteins. Most mutations cause premature termination of translation. The VHL tumor suppressor protein appears to act by inhibiting the elongation of an RNA chain after transcription initiation.
  Use to facilitate [sɪ] /block/inhibit[8] **translation** • protein / mRNA **translation** / **translational** initiation (factor) / suppression • **to initiate** a cascade of events / meiotic cell division • **initiation** factor / site[9] / codon[10] • chain[11] / viral [aɪ] DNA / mRNA transcript **elongation** • **elongation** factor 2[12] (*abbr* EF-2) • transcript **termination** • **termination** codon[13] • DNA chain **terminator** • **posttranslational** modifications[14] / changes / processing

Translation, Übersetzung
Initiation[1] Elongation[2] Termination, Abbruch[3] Matrize[4] translatieren, übersetzen[5] posttranslational, Posttranslations-[6] raues endoplasmatisches Retikulum[7] die Translation hemmen[8] Initiationsort, Startstelle[9] Initiator-, Startcodon[10] Kettenverlängerung[11] Elongationsfaktor 2[12] Terminations-, Stoppcodon[13] Posttranslationsmodifikationen[14]

19

mutation [mjuːteɪʃ³n] n term sim **chromosomal aberration**¹ n term

change in the sequence of base pairs in the chromosomal molecule which is perpetuated² [etʃ] in subsequent [ʌ] divisions [ɪʒ] of the cell in which it occurs [ɜː]

(pre)mutant³ n & adj term • **mutated** adj • **mutational** adj • **aberrant**⁴ adj • **muta-** comb

» Point mutations at codons 12, 13, or 61 alter [ɒː] critical amino acids at the guanosine triphosphate binding site. The BRCA1 gene has been shown to be mutated in families with early-onset breast [e] cancer. Failure [eɪ] or delay [eɪ] in developing secondary sexual characteristics⁵ occurs in chromosomal aberrations such as Klinefelter's [aɪ] syndrome [ɪ].

Use gene or genetic⁶ / somatic⁷ **mutation** • X-linked / dominant **mutation** • new / induced⁸ / spontaneous⁹ [eɪ]/ silent¹⁰ **mutation** • disease-associated [oʊʃ]/ single-gene **mutation** • point¹¹ / lethal¹² [iː] **mutation** • unstable [eɪ]/ splice site / insertional¹³ [ɜː] **mutation** • truncation [ʌ]/ germline¹⁴ [dʒɜː-] **mutation** • missense or nonsense¹⁵ / loss-of-function¹⁶ [ʌ]/ null-allele [ʌ] **mutation** • frameshift¹⁷ [eɪ]/ ras / expanding triplet (repeat) **mutation** • **mutation** rate¹⁸ • **mutant** gene / allele / clone / DNA / strain [eɪ] of virus¹⁹ / chromosomal²⁰ / (non-)X-linked / dominant **mutant** • recessive [se]/ resistant **mutant** • **mutational** event / activation • **mutational** frequency¹⁸ / hot spots²¹ • (cyto)genetic / autosomal / sex chromosome²² / chromatid **aberration** • structural²³ [ʌ]/ numerical²⁴ / molecular **aberration** • **aberrant** cell growth / clone / expression • **aberrant** phenotype / RNA splicing • **muta**genic /genesis [dʒe] /genicity²⁵ [ɪs] /bility²⁶ /ase

(Gen)mutation, Erbänderung
Chromosomenaberration¹ beibehalten² Mutante; mutant, mutiert³ abweichend, aberrierend, aberrant⁴ sekundäre Geschlechtsmerkmale⁵ Genmutation⁶ somatische M.⁷ induzierte M.⁸ Spontanmutation⁹ stumme/ stille M.¹⁰ Punktmutation¹¹ letale M.¹² Insertionsmutation¹³ Keimbahnmutation¹⁴ Fehlsinnmutation¹⁵ M. mit einhergehendem Funktionsverlust¹⁶ Rastermutation¹⁷ Mutationsrate, -frequenz¹⁸ mutierter Virusstamm¹⁹ Chromosomenmutante²⁰ Mutationshotspots, (Genom)stellen mit den höchsten Mutationsraten²¹ X-chromosomale Aberration²² strukturelle A.²³ numerische A.²⁴ Mutagenität, mutationsauslösendes Potential²⁵ Mutabilität, Veränderlichkeit²⁶

20

(genetic) transformation [trænsfəmeɪʃ³n] n term
rel **truncation**¹, **promoter**² [oʊ], **initiator**³ n term

changes a normal cell undergoes to become a rapidly dividing malignant cell

truncate⁴ [trʌŋkeɪt] v term • **truncated** adj • **truncating** adj

» Transformation is normally suppressed by tumor suppressor genes. It is unclear how induction [ʌ] of host gene expression leads to neoplastic transformation⁵. Protein truncation tests (abbr PTT) can be used to detect any mutation that results in premature termination of the peptide during protein synthesis [ɪ], i.e. primarily nonsense⁶ and frameshift mutations⁷.

Use cell / DNA / enzymatic / malignant⁵ / leukemic [iː] **transformation** • **transformation** event • protein **truncation** • transcriptional⁸ / growth / tumor **promoter** • **promoter** region⁹ / sequence • tumor **initiator** • **initiator** protein complex / DNA control element / RNA

Transformation
Truncation, Verstümmelung¹ Promotor² Initiator³ trunkieren⁴ maligne Entartung/ Transformation⁵ Nonsense-Mutation, Nichtsinnmutation⁶ frameshift-Mutation, (Lese)rasterverschiebung⁷ Transkriptionspromotor⁸ Promotorregion⁹

21

polymorphism [ɔː] n term syn **ple(i)omorphism** [pliːə-] n term
rel **pleiotrop(h)y**¹ [plaɪɒː-],
mosaicism² [moʊzeɪəsɪz³m] n term

(in genetics) occurrence of two or more genotypes in the same population in such proportions that they cannot be maintained by recurrent mutation alone, e. g. the blood groups, the Rh factor, or the sickle cell trait; pleiotropy denotes a single-gene defect [iː] producing multiple phenotypic effects that may present as various anomalies

polymorphic³ adj term • **pleiotrop(h)ic**⁴ adj • **pleio-** comb

» In addition to single-base differences, insertions, deletions, and variation in numbers of tandemly repeated sequences, DNA polymorphisms include variable number tandem repeats (abbr VNTR) if the repeats are long and short tandem repeats (abbr STR) if the repeats are very short. There are many genetically neutral [(j)uː] polymorphic sites throughout the genome. The syndrome is inherited as an autosomal dominant trait with a high degree of penetrance⁵, variable expressivity, and significant pleiotropism¹.

Use genetic⁶ / chromosomal⁷ / (single-base / X-linked) DNA / sequence **polymorphism** • balanced⁸ / restriction-fragment-length⁹ / factor V Leiden **polymorphism** • **polymorphism** analysis • cytokine [saɪtəkaɪn] **pleiotropy** • **polymorphic** genetic system / allele / locus / site / region • **polymorphic** DNA sequence¹⁰ / amino acid residue / marker • **pleiotropic** gene / effect¹¹ • **ple(i)o**tropic /morphic

Poly-, Pleomorphismus
Polyphänie, Pleiotropie¹ Mosaik² polymorph, pleomorph, vielgestaltig³ pleiotrop, polyphän⁴ Penetranz, Manifestationshäufigkeit, -wahrscheinlichkeit⁵ genet. Polymorphismus⁶ chromosomaler Polymorphismus⁷ balancierter Polymorphismus⁸ Restriktionsfragment-Längen-Polymorphismus⁹ polymorphe DNA-Sequenz¹⁰ pleiotrope Wirkung¹¹

22

Clinical Genetics MEDICAL SCIENCE 363

deletion [dɪliːʃən] n term   rel **translocation**[1], **inversion**[2] [ɜː],
insertion[3] [ɜː], **substitution**[4] [juːʃ],
duplication[5] n term

spontaneous [eɪ] loss of part of the genetic material, which may be cytogenetically visible (chromosomal deletion) or can be inferred [ɜː] by phenotypic processes (point deletion)

microdeletion n term • **delete** v • **translocate**[6] v • **insertional** adj • **inverted** adj

» Karyotypic evidence of a specific deletion of band p13 on chromosome 11 suggested the existence of a tumor suppressor gene at that location. Detachment [ætʃ] of a chromosome segment from its normal location and its attachment to another chromosome is termed translocation. In robertsonian translocations, two acrocentric chromosomes fuse [fjuːz] at their centromeres. Most tumors exhibit chromosomal abnormalities such as deletions, inversions, translocations, or duplications.

Use (one-/ two-)gene / (X/Y) chromosome[7] / DNA / somatic **deletion** • two-locus / three-base / 2 bp / 138-nucleotide **deletion** • segmental / partial[8] [ʃ] / clonal / single / double **deletion** • **deletion** mutation / mutant[9] / mapping / syndrome[10] • chromosomal / parental / inherited / (un)balanced[11] / reciprocal **translocation** • robertsonian[12] / nonhomologous [ɒː]/ 14/21 / t(14;18) **translocation** • complex / mitochondrial[13] [kɒː] **translocation** • **translocation** carrier[14] • paracentric[15] [se]/ (peri)centric **inversion** • chimeric [kaɪ-] gene **duplication** • **insertional** mutagenesis / mutations[16] • **inverted** repeat[17]

Deletion, Verlust (e-s DNA-/ Chromosomenabschnitts)
Translokation, Verlagerung (v. Genabschnitten)[1] Inversion, Drehung (e. Genabschnitts) um 180°[2] Insertion, Einbau (v. DNA-Sequenzen od. Nukleotiden)[3] Substitution[4] Duplikation, Verdoppelung (e. DNA-Abschnitts)[5] translozieren, verlagern[6] Chromosomendeletion[7] partielle Deletion[8] Deletionsmutante[9] Deletionssyndrom[10] (un)balancierte Translokation[11] Robertson-Translokation[12] mitochondriale Translokation[13] Translokationsträger[14] parazentrische Inversion[15] Insertionsmutationen[16] invertierte repetitive Sequenz[17]

23

chromosome breakage [breɪkɪdʒ] n term   rel **rearrangement**[1] [eɪ],
nondisjunction[2] [dʒʌ] n term

disruption [ʌ] of the continuity [(j)uː] of a chromatid due to defects in DNA repair

break(point)[3] n term • **nondisjunctional** adj

» Defects of chromosomal division include breakage, nondisjunction, deletion, rearrangement, and translocation of genetic material. The result of chromosome breakage and rearrangement is often termed partial trisomy to indicate that segments rather than entire chromosomes are involved. Rearrangement of chromosome arms[4], e.g. in translocation, is a mutation even if breakage and reunion [juː] does not disrupt [ʌ] any coding sequence.

Use increased **chromosome breakage** • **chromosome breakage** site[3] / factor / disorder or syndrome[5] • DNA strand **breakage** • double-stranded chromosomal[6] / single-strand[7] **break** • chromosome[8] / DNA / structural **rearrangement** • balanced[9] / productive / receptor gene **rearrangement** • chromosomal (mitotic) / meiotic[10] **nondisjunction** • double[11] / chromatid **nondisjunction**

Chromosomenbruch
Rearrangement[1] Nondisjunction, Nichttrennung[2] Chromosomenbruchstelle[3] Chromosomenarme[4] Chromosomenbruchsyndrom[5] Doppelstrangbruch[6] Einzelstrangbruch[7] Chromosomenrearrangement, Neuanordnung v. Chromosomenabschnitten[8] balanciertes Rearrangement[9] Nondisjunction in d. Meiose[10] doppelte Nondisjunction[11]

24

trisomy [traɪsoʊmi] n term   rel **monosomy**[1], **disomy**[2] [daɪsoʊmi] n term

presence of an extra chromosome in a normally diploid cell (i.e. 47 chromosomes)

trisomic adj term • **monosomic** adj • **disomic**[3] adj

» Partial trisomy of the distal band of the long arm of chromosome 21 causes development of the full Down syndrome [ɪ]. Various combinations of these karyotypes can cause the Turner phenotype if one of them is either monosomic or partially monosomic for the X.

Use autosomal[4] / full or complete[5] / partial / fetal [iː] **trisomy** • **trisomy** 8 syndrome / 13 or Patau's syndrome[6] • **trisomy** 18 or Edwards' syndrome / 21 or Down('s) syndrome[7] • partial[8] / autosomal **monosomy** • **monosomy** X / 4p • uniparental[9] **disomy** • **disomic** chromosome / gamete • **trisomic** pregnancy / offspring • **trisomic** chromosome segment[10]

Trisomie
Monosomie[1] Disomie[2] disom[3] autosomale Trisomie[4] klassische Trisomie[5] Trisomie 13, Pätau-Syndrom[6] Trisomie 21, Down-Syndrom[7] partielle Monosomie[8] uniparentale Disomie[9] trisomer Chromosomenabschnitt[10]

25

penetrance [penətrən's] n term   rel **expressivity**[1] n term

proportion of individuals with a given genotype who present with phenotypic manifestations of a disease

(non)penetrant[2] adj term • **express**[3] v • **expression**[4] [ɪkspreʃən] n → U83-16

» MEN 1 syndrome is an autosomal dominant disorder with a high degree of penetrance and great variability in expressivity. Expressivity describes the range of phenotypic effects in individuals carrying a given mutation. The mutant gene is not penetrant if an individual carrying the mutant gene shows absolutely no phenotypic effects.

Use gene / (in)complete[5] / high / low[6] / 100%[7] **penetrance** • decreased / degree of / lack of[8] **penetrance** • **penetrance** rate • variable[9] / low / limited **expressivity**

Penetranz, Manifestationsfrequenz, -wahrscheinlichkeit
Expressivität, phänotypische Manifestationsstärke[1] penetrant[2] exprimieren[3] Expression[4] unvollständige Penetranz[5] niedrige Penetranz[6] 100%-ige Penetranz[7] fehlende Penetranz[8] variable Expressivität[9]

26

MEDICAL SCIENCE — Clinical Genetics

dominant adj term   opposite **recessive**[1] [rɪsesɪv] adj, rel **X-linked**[2] adj term

referring to a pattern of inheritance of an autosomal mendelian trait due to a gene that always manifests itself phenotypically

(co)d<u>o</u>minance[3] n term • cod<u>o</u>minant[4] adj • rec<u>e</u>ssiveness[5] n • **X-linkage** n

» The dis<u>e</u>ase is inherited in an autosomal [ɔːtə-] d<u>o</u>minant fashion in about 80% of cases; the rem<u>ai</u>nder [eɪ] are thought to be autosomal rec<u>e</u>ssive or to be caused by new mut<u>a</u>tions[6]. In autosomes a rec<u>e</u>ssive gene is expr<u>e</u>ssed only when pr<u>e</u>sent in both chromatids. A mend<u>e</u>lian ph<u>e</u>notype is char<u>a</u>cterized not only in terms of d<u>o</u>minance and recessiveness but also according to whether the det<u>e</u>rmining gene is on the X chromosome or on one of the 22 pairs of <u>au</u>tosomes.

Use **dominant** tr<u>ai</u>t[7] [eɪ]/ (gen<u>e</u>tic) transmission • **dominant** gene[8] / mutation / inher<u>i</u>tance[9] • autos<u>o</u>mal (abbr AD) **dominant** pattern (of inheritance)[10] • **dominant** condition / disorder • **recessive** gene / defect / fam<u>i</u>lial dis<u>ea</u>se[11] • **recessive** form / phenotype • autosomal / true **recessive disorders** • **X-linked** gene[12] / autos<u>o</u>mal syndrome • **X-linked** (d<u>o</u>minant) trait[13] / single-gene dis<u>o</u>rder • autos<u>o</u>mal / over**dominance** • transm<u>i</u>tted in a Mendelian **codominant** m<u>a</u>nner[14]

---

inheritance [ɪnherɪtᵊnˈs] n term   sim **heredity**[1] [hərededəti] n term → U89-7

transmission of traits or qualities from p<u>a</u>rent to offspring

inher<u>i</u>t[2] v • inh<u>e</u>rited[3] adj • inh<u>e</u>ritable[4] adj • her<u>e</u>ditary[4] adj • **heredo-** comb

» Many disorders cl<u>u</u>ster [ʌ] in f<u>a</u>milies[5] but cannot be traced to chromos<u>o</u>mal aberr<u>a</u>tions or Mend<u>e</u>lian [iː] inh<u>e</u>ritance[6] patterns. Heredity undoubtedly [aʊ] pred<u>i</u>sposes individuals to hypertension, but the exact m<u>e</u>chanism is uncl<u>e</u>ar. If an aff<u>e</u>cted person mates with an unaff<u>e</u>cted one, each <u>o</u>ffspring has a 50% chance of inher<u>i</u>ting the aff<u>e</u>cted ph<u>e</u>notype.

Use recessive / (X-l<u>i</u>nked/ autos<u>o</u>mal/ co)d<u>o</u>minant[7] **inheritance** • heter<u>o</u>zygous / X-l<u>i</u>nked[8] / hom<u>o</u>zygous **inheritance** • sex-l<u>i</u>mited[9] / interm<u>e</u>diate[10] / mitochondr<u>i</u>al[11] **inheritance** • polygenic or multifact<u>o</u>rial[12] / mode of / mat<u>e</u>rnal[13] **inheritance** • **inheritance** pattern[14] • to be influenced by **heredity** • **heredity** conditions[15] / at<u>a</u>xia[16] • **inherited** traits[17] / phenotype / tendency / abnormality • **inherited** defect / bl<u>ee</u>ding dis<u>o</u>rder[18] • gen<u>e</u>tically / pat<u>e</u>rnally / mat<u>e</u>rnally / d<u>o</u>minantly / rec<u>e</u>ssively **inherited** • **hereditary** at<u>a</u>xia[16] / f<u>a</u>ctors[17] / p<u>a</u>ttern[14] / predisposition • **hereditary** deficiency / cond<u>i</u>tions[15] / neur<u>o</u>pathy • **heredo**familial

---

ancestor [ænsestɚ] n   sim **progenitor**[1] [proʊdʒenɪtɚ] n term
   rel **offspring**[2], p<u>a</u>rent[3], descent[4] [dɪsent], **pedigree**[5] [pedɪɡriː] n

a prec<u>u</u>rsor [ɜː] or parent of success<u>i</u>ve generations in the direct line of desc<u>e</u>nt[5]

<u>a</u>ncestry[6] n • anc<u>e</u>stral adj • progeny[7] n • par<u>e</u>ntage[8] n • desc<u>e</u>ndant[2] n

» These patients pr<u>o</u>bably are desc<u>e</u>ndants of a c<u>o</u>mmon <u>a</u>ncestor. In p<u>e</u>rsons of African <u>a</u>ncestry G6PD deficiency is usually less sev<u>e</u>re than in other <u>e</u>thnic groups. His p<u>a</u>rents must have a common <u>a</u>ncestor[8] who c<u>a</u>rried a rec<u>e</u>ssive gene. Cyt<u>o</u>kines [aɪ] that act on early lineage prog<u>e</u>nitors often act also on more mat<u>u</u>re lineage cells. A family history should <u>a</u>lways be taken in a p<u>e</u>digree form.

Use ethnic / Asian [eɪʒᵊn]/ Jewish [dʒuːɪʃ] **ancestry** • **ancestral** origin[6] / gene / l<u>o</u>cus • **ancestral** transcription regulatory f<u>a</u>ctor • **progenitor** cell[9] • to have/produce **offspring** • male / female / hom<u>o</u>zygous **offspring** • (un)affected[10] / ret<u>a</u>rded[11] / tris<u>o</u>mic **offspring** • grand/ single **parent** • **parental** gene[12] • abnormal / differentiated **progeny** • to be of Native American **descent** • to have a **pedigree** family[13] three-generation / d<u>o</u>minant **pedigree** • **pedigree** an<u>a</u>lysis[14] / pattern

---

breed [iː] - bred - bred n & v irr   sim **lineage**[1] [lɪniədʒ] n, rel **mating**[2] [eɪ] n term

(n) particular race or type of <u>a</u>nimals or plants (v) sel<u>e</u>cted m<u>a</u>ting to produce a desired strain

breeding adj & n • cross-breed[3] v term • inbreeding[4] n • mate[5] v • line [aɪ] n

» Mutant mice [maɪs] were obt<u>ai</u>ned and bred to st<u>u</u>dy the gene in heter<u>o</u>zygotes and hom<u>o</u>zygotes. Affected individuals who mate with unaffected individuals who are not c<u>a</u>rriers have only unaffected <u>o</u>ffspring. In m<u>a</u>tings between individuals with the same rec<u>e</u>ssive ph<u>e</u>notypes all <u>o</u>ffspring will be aff<u>e</u>cted.

Use **to breed** true / randomly • half-**breed**[6] • line[7]-/ inter[8]-/ cross[8]-**breeding** • **breeding** ground[9] [aʊ]/ site[9] / place[9] • mixed / germ [ɜː] cell **lineage** • B lymphocyte [ɪ] • phylogen<u>e</u>tic **lineage** • pure-**bred**[10] • **inbred** mouse strain[11] / groups / popul<u>a</u>tion • maternal / blood / (Y) cell[12] / germ[13] **line** • hom<u>o</u>zygote-heter<u>o</u>zygote / inc<u>e</u>stuous[14] [se]/ consangu<u>i</u>neous[14] **mating** • **mating** group / isolate[15] [aɪ]/ type

▌ **Note:** The word **breed** is normally res<u>e</u>rved for animals and plants.

---

dominant
rezessiv[1] geschlechtsgebunden[2] (Ko)dominanz[3] kodominant[4] Rezessivität[5] Neumutationen[6] dominantes Merkmal[7] dominantes Gen[8] dominante Vererbung[9] autosomal dominanter Erbgang[10] rezessive Erbkrankheit[11] X-gebundenes/ -gekoppeltes Gen[12] X-chromosomal dominant vererbtes Merkmal[13] kodominant vererbt werden[14]

Vererbung, Erbgang
Vererbung; Erblichkeit, Heredität[1] erben[2] erblich, Erb-[3] erblich, Erb-, angeboren[4] familiär gehäuft auftreten[5] Mendelsche Vererbung[6] dominante Vererbung[7] X-gekoppelte Vererbung[8] geschlechtsgebundene V.[9] intermediäre V.[10] mitochondriale/ mitochondrien-gekoppelte Vererbung[11] multifaktorielle/ polygene Vererbung[12] maternale Vererbung[13] Vererbungsmuster, Erbgang[14] Erbkrankheiten, -leiden[15] erbliche Ataxie[16] Erbanlagen[17] angeborene Gerinnungsstörung/ Koagulopathie[18]

Ahne, Vorfahr(e), Mutterzelle
Vorfahre, Stammvater; Vorläufer(zelle)[1] Nachkomme, Kind, Sprössling[2] Eltern(teil)[3] Abstammung, Herkunft[4] Stammbaum, Ahnenreihe[5] Abstammung[6] Nachkommen(schaft)[7] gemeinsamer Vorfahre[8] Vorläuferzelle[9] gesundes Kind[10] behindertes Kind[11] elterliches/ parentales Gen[12] Familienstammbaum[13] genealogische Analyse, Stammbaumanalyse[14]

Brut, Zucht, Rasse; züchten, brüten, sich vermehren
Geschlecht, Abstammung[1] Paarung[2] kreuzen[3] Inzucht[4] (sich) paaren[5] Mischling; Hybrid, Bastard[6] Reinzucht, -kultur[7] Kreuzung[8] Brutstätte[9] reinrassig[10] durch Inzucht entstandener Mäusestamm[11] Zelllinie[12] Keimbahn[13] Inzest[14] isoliert gehaltene Tiere[15]

Clinical Genetics

consanguinity [gwɪ] *n term*

rel **kinship**[1], **relative**[2], **maternity**[3], **paternity**[4] *n*

blood relationship based on common ancestry

consanguineous[5] *adj term* • **kin**[6] [kɪn] *n clin* • **akin to**[7] *phr* • **kindred**[8] *n & adj* • **(un)related**[9] *adj* • **relationship**[10] [eɪʃ] *n* • **maternal** [ɜː] *adj* • **paternal** *adj*

» *Incest* [ɪnsest] *is an extreme form of consanguinity and may occur in the context of sexual abuse of children and teenagers. It should always be remembered that maternity is a fact, but paternity is only an assumption. Several* sibships[11] *have been reported in which more than one individual is affected with the 46,XX disorder, frequently the result of consanguineous matings, suggesting an autosomal recessive inheritance.*

Use parental / unknown / degree of[12] **consanguinity** • next of[13] **kin** • blood **kinship** • **kinship** by marriage • first-degree / 2ⁿᵈ-degree[14] / 3ʳᵈ-degree **relatives** • close[15] / (more) distant[16] **relatives** • blood[17] / biological / maternal / asymptomatic **relatives** • affected / marriage between **relatives** • **consanguineous** families / relatives[17] • **consanguineous** marriage / matings • **paternity** testing[18] • **maternal** allele / genes[19] / factors • **maternal** inheritance[20] / in origin • **paternal** chromosome / copy / haplotype • **paternal** age / grandparents[21] / transmission

Blutsverwandtschaft, Konsanguinität

Verwandtschaft[1] Verwandte(r)[2] Mutterschaft[3] Vaterschaft[4] blutsverwandt[5] Familie, Verwandte[6] verwandt mit, ähnlich[7] Verwandtschaft; verwandt[8] verwandt; zusammenhängend[9] Verwandtschaft; Beziehung, Verbindung[10] blutsverwandte/ konsanguine Familien[11] Grad d. Blutsverwandtschaft[12] nächste(r) Verwandte(r)[13] Verwandte(r) 2. Grades[14] nahe Verwandte[15] entfernte V.[16] Blutsverwandte[17] Vaterschaftsbestimmung, -feststellung[18] mütterl. Gene[19] maternale Vererbung[20] Großeltern väterlicherseits[21]

31

---

restriction endonuclease [-eɪz] *n term* *syn* **restriction enzyme** *n term*

bacterial protein that recognizes specific, double-stranded nucleotide sequences and cuts[1] (hydrolyzes[1]) [aɪ] DNA at those sites; the "chemical knife" that paved the way for DNA technology

» *Each restriction endonuclease recognizes a specific nucleotide sequence consisting of 4, 6, 8, or 10 nucleotides and* cleaves[1] [iː] *DNA within that sequence. A* genomic library[2] [aɪ] *can be constructed by randomly fragmenting human genomic DNA with restriction enzymes and then inserting the fragments into a vector. Some restriction enzymes occur frequently in DNA (e.g. every 500 bp), others much less frequently (rare-cutter* enzymes[3]*).*

Use **restriction endonuclease** analysis[4] / pattern • cleavage site[5] • **restriction enzyme** cutting site[5] / digestion [dʒe] • **restriction** (recognition) site[6] / map[7] / analysis or mapping[8] • **restriction** fragment length polymorphism analysis[9]

Restriktionsendonuklease, -enzym

schneidet[1] genomische DNA-Bank[2] selten schneidende (Restriktions)-enzyme[3] Restriktionsanalyse[4] Restriktionsschnittstelle[5] Restriktionsort, Basenerkennungssequenz[6] Restriktionskarte[7] Restriktionsanalyse, -kartierung[8] Restriktionsfragment-Längen-Analyse, RFLP-Analyse[9]

32

---

clone [kloʊn] *n & v term*

rel **cosmid**[1], **contig**[2] *n term*

(n) colony of cells or an individual organism of identical genetic constitution [(j)uːʃ] which are derived [aɪ] from a single organism or cell by asexual reproduction [ʌ] (mitotic division)

cloning[3] [oʊ] *n term* • **clonal**[4] *adj* • **subclone** [sʌbkloʊn] *n*

» *Multiple myeloma represents a malignant proliferation of plasma cells* derived from[5] *a single clone. Cytotoxicity of activated lymphocytes leads to clonal deletion of allosensitized cells. Cloned DNA fragments of the gene are used as* molecular probes[6] *to* label[7] [eɪ] *it. Cosmids can be packaged in lambda phage particles for infection into E. coli* [aɪ] *to permit cloning of larger DNA fragments than can be introduced into bacterial hosts in plasmid vectors.*

Use stem cell[8] / cDNA / B-cell / androgen-insensitive **clones** • overlapping[9] / mutant / aberrant / neoplastic **clones** • expression / positional[10] / DNA[11] **cloning** • **cloning** vector[1] • **clonal** cells / growth / proliferation / marker • **clonal** expansion[12] / rearrangement / malignancy[13] • mono/ oligo/ poly[14]/ non**clonal** • **contig** map[15] • **cosmid** library[16] [aɪ]/ DNA / vector

Klon; klonen

Cosmid, Klonierungsvektor[1] Contig-Sequenz[2] Klonierung, Klonieren[3] klonal, Klon-[4] stammen von[5] Molekularsonden[6] markieren[7] Stammzellenklone[8] überlappende Klone[9] Positionsklonierung[10] DNA-Klonierung[11] klonale Expansion[12] klonale Tumorerkrankung[13] polyklonal[14] fortlaufende (Gen)karte[15] Cosmid-Bibliothek[16]

33

---

sequencing *n term*

rel **gene mapping**[1], **homeobox**[2], **multiplexing**[3] *n term*

determination of the order of base sequences in a DNA or RNA molecule or of amino acids in a protein

sequence [siːkwənˈs] *n & v term* • **map**[4] [mæp] *v & n*

» *DNA sequencing can be performed directly on PCR products or on individual clones. Two genes have been cloned that* map to this locus[5]. *The liver phosphorylase gene has been cloned and mapped to chromosome 14. Enzymes that cut the DNA infrequently can be used to prepare DNA maps over megabase distances.*

Use genetic / DNA / nucleotide **sequencing** • direct / amino acid **sequencing** • full-length[6] / primer [aɪ] extension[7] **sequencing** • chromosomal[8] / physical / linkage[9] mapping • restriction[10] / deletion **mapping** • human gene / genome[11] map • physical / restriction **map** • genetic **map** location[12]

Sequenzanalyse, Sequenzierung

Genkartierung[1] Homöobox[2] Mehrfachanalyse[3] kartieren; Karte[4] diesem Lokus zugeordnet sein[5] Sequenzierung d. gesamten DNA[6] Sequenzierung durch Primerverlängerung[7] Chromosomenkartierung[8] Kopplungskartierung, -analyse[9] Restriktionsanalyse, -kartierung[10] Genomkarte[11] Genlokus, -ort[12]

34

MEDICAL SCIENCE — Clinical Genetics

Southern [ʌ] **blotting** [ɒː] *n term*   *syn* **Southern blot analysis** *n term*
  rel **electrophoresis**¹ [iː] *n term*

transfer by absorption of DNA fragments separated in electrophoretic gels to membrane filters for detection of specific base sequences by radiolabeled [eɪ] complementary probes

electrophoretic² [e] *adj term* • **electrophorese**³ [ɪlektrəfəˈiːz] *v*

» Northern blot analysis is being used increasingly to look for mRNA abnormalities. Specific changes in mRNA were detected on northern blots. Southern blotting, northern blotting, and western blotting each combines a fractionation and a detection method to provide a sensitive technique [iː] for the analysis of DNA, RNA, and protein, respectively.

Use **Southern** blot technique / blot hybridization⁴ • (confirmatory) [ɜː] **Western**⁵ / Northern / immuno**blotting** • (negative) Southern / Northern / Western **blot** (**analysis**) • multilocus enzyme / agarose (gel)⁶ [dʒel] / starch⁷ [stɑːrtʃ] **electrophoresis** • pulsed-field gel⁸ [ʌ] (*abbr* PFGE) / protein⁹ / (carrier-)free¹⁰ **electrophoresis** • serum protein (*abbr* SPEP) / hemoglobin (*abbr* Hb) **electrophoresis** • immuno(fixation)¹¹ / disc or discontinuous¹² **electrophoresis** • **electrophoretic** analysis / separation¹³ • **electrophoretic** profile / mobility¹⁴

polymerase chain reaction [pɒːlɪməˈreɪz tʃeɪn riːˈækʃ(ə)n] *n term, abbr* **PCR**
  rel **gene amplification**¹ [dʒiːn æmplɪfɪˈkeɪʃ(ə)n] *n term*

in vitro DNA amplification technique involving successive cloning of a strand of DNA up to 200,000-fold to allow for direct sequencing of the PCR product, digesting the amplified product with a restriction enzyme, hybridization with allele-specific oligonucleotides, etc.

polymer² *n term* • **polymerize**³ *v* • (**de**)**polymerization**⁴ *n* • **amplify**⁵ *v*

» PCR can be performed starting with genomic DNA as the template⁶. RNA can be reverse [ɜː] transcribed⁷ to yield [jiːld] cDNA for use as a template, a procedure [siː] known as reverse transcription-PCR. The PCR strategy requires repeated heating of the DNA to separate the two strands of the double helix, hybridization of the primer sequence to the appropriate target sequence, target amplification using the PCR for complementary strand extension, and signal detection via a labeled probe.

Use DNA / RNA / CSF / reverse transcription⁸- (*abbr* RT-PCR) / competitive⁹ **PCR** • **PCR**-based technique / analysis¹⁰ / assay¹⁰ • **PCR** test¹⁰ / sensitivity /-amplified¹¹ DNA • DNA (sequence) / branched-chain DNA or bDNA-based (signal)¹² **amplification** • nucleic [eɪ‖iː] acid / nested PCR¹³ **amplification** • EGFR / myc gene / allele-specific¹⁴ **amplification** • molecular / ligase [laɪɡeɪz] / oncogene **amplification** • **amplification** probe¹⁵ [prəʊb] / assay

linkage analysis or **study** *n term*   *rel* **segregation analysis**¹ *n term*

estimation of the probability of genetic recombination of genes at two or more loci [ləʊsaɪ]

linkage² [ˈlɪŋkɪdʒ] *n term* • **linker**³ *n* • **link**⁴ *v & n* • **linked** *adj* • **segregate**⁵ *v*

» Genes that contribute to multifactorial disorders are being isolated through linkage studies. Linkage analysis has localized the NDI⁶ gene to the long arm of the X chromosome in region 28 (Xq28). In mitosis the genetic material is segregated into daughter cells. The error in segregation of chromosomes can occur in the germ line.

Use DNA-based / genetic / human / family **linkage** analysis • **linkage** mapping / group⁷ / disequilibrium⁸ / genetic⁹ / close¹⁰ / clear / stable / X-**linkage** / HLA / pathogenic / BRCA2 gene **linkage** • cytogenetic / chromosomal / DNA / immunoblot¹¹ **analysis** • hybridization¹² / sib-pair¹³ / restriction enzyme¹⁴ **analysis**

fluorescent [flʊəˈres(ə)nt] **in situ hybridization** *n term, abbr* **FISH**

physical mapping technique that uses fluorescein [flʊəˈresɪən] tags¹ to detect hybridization of probes with metaphase chromosomes and the less-condensed somatic interphase chromatin

hybridize² [ˈhaɪbrɪdaɪz] *v term* • **hybrid**³ *n & adj* • **hybridized** *adj*

» FISH also makes possible the chromosomal localization of known DNA sequences, including specific genes, and the determination of their order. Nucleic acid hybridization is so sensitive that a single-stranded DNA molecule can be hybridized specifically to a complementary strand of RNA or DNA and detected if present at about 1 part in 10,000. Only a single step is required to hybridize the target-binding probe to the target sequence.

Use **FISH** probe • Southern blot⁴ / nucleic acid / allele-specific oligonucleotide⁵ **hybridization** • DNA (molecular) / comparative genomic⁶ (*abbr* CGH) / cross **hybridization** • **hybridization** analysis / technique⁷ / pattern • **to hybridize** to target DNA⁸ • **hybrid** molecule / protein⁹ / cells • **hybridized** probe¹⁰

Southern-Blot(ting)-Methode/Technik

Elektrophorese¹ elektrophoretisch² elektrophoretisch (auf)trennen³ Southern Blot-Hybridisierung⁴ Western Blot-Bestätigungstest⁵ Agarosegelelektrophorese⁶ Stärkegelelektrophorese⁷ Pulsfeldelektrophorese⁸ Proteinelektrophorese⁹ trägerfreie E.¹⁰ Immunfixationselektrophorese¹¹ Disk-Elektrophorese¹² elektrophoretische Auftrennung¹³ Wanderungsgeschwindigkeit im elektrischen Feld¹⁴

35

Polymerase-Kettenreaktion, PCR

Genamplifikation¹ Polymer² polymerisieren, ein Polymer bilden³ Polymerisation⁴ amplifizieren, vervielfältigen⁵ Matrize⁶ revers transkribiert, in cDNA umgeschrieben⁷ RT-PCR, PCR nach vorheriger reverser Transkription⁸ kompetitive Polymerase-Kettenreaktion/ PCR⁹ PCR-Analyse¹⁰ PCR-amplifizierte DNA¹¹ bDNA-Assay¹² Zweifach-PCR m. versetzten Primern¹³ allelespezifische Amplifikation¹⁴ Amplifikationssonde¹⁵

36

Kopplungsanalyse

Segregationsanalyse¹ Genkopplung² Linker³ verbinden, -knüpfen; Bindeglied, Verbindung⁴ aufspalten, trennen⁵ renaler Diabetes insipidus⁶ Kopplungsgruppe⁷ Kopplungsungleichgewicht⁸ Genkopplung, genetische K.⁹ enge Kopplung¹⁰ Immunoblot-, Westernblot-Analyse¹¹ Hybridisierungsanalyse¹² Analyse von Geschwisterpaaren¹³ Restriktionsanalyse, -kartierung¹⁴

37

in-situ-Hybridisierung mit Fluoreszenzmarkierung, FISH

Fluoreszeinmarkierung¹ hybridisieren² Hybrid, Kreuzung, Mischling; hybrid, gemischt³ Southernhybridisierung⁴ allelspezifische Oligonukleotidhybridisierung⁵ komparative Genomhybridisierung⁶ Hybridisierungstechnik⁷ an die Ziel-DNA hybridisieren⁸ Hybridprotein⁹ Hybridisierungssonde¹⁰

38

Medical Embryology | MEDICAL SCIENCE 367

transfection [trænˈsfekʃᵊn] *n term*   *sim* **cotransfection**[1] *n term*

technique of gene transfer utilizing infection of a bacterial cell with purified DNA or RNA isolated [aɪ] from a virus [aɪ] resulting in subsequent [ʌ] viral replication in the transfected cell

transfect[2] *v term* • **(co)transfected** *adj* • **transfectant**[3] *n & adj*

» Such transfected cells support in vitro replication of the intact virus and its component proteins. Defined large-scale alterations of the human CMV[4] genome was constructed by cotransfection of overlapping cosmids. Separating the transfectant media [iː] on agarose gels resulted in highly extended bands[5] characteristic of glycanated [aɪ] proteins.

Use   cell / DNA[6] / gene / PCR / stable[7] [eɪ]/ transient / in vitro **transfection** • in vivo / vector-mediated[8] **transfection** • **transfection** reagent[9] [eɪdʒ]/ method / protocol / rate • **transfection**-resistant cell type / kit[10] • stable **transfectant** • **transfected** cells[11] • **transfectant** (tumor) cells / clone / (cell) line[12]

Transfektion
Cotransfektion[1] transfizieren[2] Transfektionsreagenz, transfizierendes Agens; transfizierend[3] Zytomegalie-Virus[4] (DNA) Banden[5] DNA-Transfektion[6] stabile Transfektion[7] vektorvermittelte Transfektion[8] Transfektionsreagenz[9] Transfektionskit[10] transfizierte Zellen[11] transfizierende Zelllinie[12]

39

Unit 85   Medical Embryology
Related Units: 84 Genetics, 86 Histology, 55 Hormones, 51 Menstrual Cycle, 50 Female Sexual Organs, 69 Fertility, 70 Pregnancy

embryo [ˈembrioʊ] *n & comb term*   *rel* **fetus**[1] [ˈfiːtəs] *n term, BE* **foetus**[1]

the product of conception [se] until the 8ᵗʰ week of gestation[2] [dʒesteɪʃᵊn]; from this time to delivery[3] the unborn offspring is termed fetus

embryonic[4] [ɒː] *adj term* • **embryonal**[4] [-ɪoʊnᵊl] *adj* • **fetal** *adj* • **embryologic** *adj*

» Early in embryonic development, one of the two X chromosomes in each somatic cell of a female is randomly inactivated. One or two cells were removed from a developing 8-cell human embryo without harm to[5] the embryo.

Use human / (pre)somite[6] / developing / implanted / male **embryo** • **embryo** kidney / transfer[7] • **embryonic** tissue[8] / stage[9] / life[9] / period[9] / kidney • **embryonic** stem cells[10] / development[11] • **embryonic** remnant or rest[12] / pole [oʊ]/ disk[13] • **embryonal** cells / cyst / tumor[14] / carcinoma • **embryologic** derivation or origin[15] / course [ɔː]/ development[11] • descriptive / comparative **embryology** • **fetal** membranes[16] / growth / abnormalities or anomalies • **fetal** circulation[17] / movements[18] / death or demise[19] [aɪ] • **fetal** heart [ɑː] tones[20] / wastage[21] [weɪstɪdʒ] • **embryo**genesis [dʒe] /logy /logist /blast • **embryo**toxic /toxicity[22] [ɪs] /pathy /ma[14]

Embryo, Keimling
Fötus, Fetus[1] Schwangerschaftswoche[2] Geburt, Entbindung[3] embryonal, Embryonal-[4] Schaden für[5] Präsomitenembryo[6] Embryonentransfer, -übertragung[7] embryonales Gewebe[8] Embryonalperiode[9] embryonale Stammzellen[10] Embryonalentwicklung[11] Embryonalrest[12] Keimscheibe[13] embryonaler Tumor[14] embryolog. Ursprung[15] Eihäute[16] fetaler/ kindl. Kreislauf[17] Kindsbewegungen[18] intrauteriner Fruchttod[19] kindl. Herztöne[20] Fetalverlust[21] Embryotoxizität[22]

1

gamete [ˈgæmiːt‖gəˈmiːt] *n term*   *rel* **zygote**[1] [ˈzaɪgoʊt] *n term*

mature[2] male (spermatozoon) or female (ovum) reproductive [ʌ] (or germ [dʒɜːrm]) cell containing a haploid number of chromosomes[3]; the diploid cell resulting from the union of a sperm [ɜː] and an ovum [oʊ] is termed zygote

gametic [gəˈmeːlliːtɪk] *adj term* • **gamet(o)-** *comb* • **zygotic** [ɒː] *adj* • **zygo-** *comb*

» The union of a disomic [daɪ-] gamete with a nullisomic [ʌ] gamete from the other parent will result in a zygote with a normal karyotype [æ]. Does this agent [eɪdʒ] interfere [-fɪə] with[4] gamete transport or nidation[5] [naɪ-]? Then the zygote bursts[6] [ɜː] the protective shell of the zona pellucida [uː] in order to make contact with the uterine [juː] wall.

Use male / female [iː]/ mutant[7] [juː] **gamete** • **gamete** formation / fusion[8] [fjuːʒᵊn] • **gamete** intrafallopian [oʊ] transfer[9] (*abbr* GIFT) • **gametic** chromosome / meiosis [maɪoʊsɪs]/ fusion[8] • **gameto**cyte [gəˈmiːtəsaɪt] /genesis[10] /genic • **gameto**cide[11] [aɪ] /cidal /pathy[12] • di[13]/mono**zygotic** • homo[14]/ hetero[15]/ hemi**zygous** [ˈhemɪzaɪgəs] • **zygotic** stage • **zygo**tene[16] • mono/ di/ hetero[17]/ homo**zygosity**

Gamet, Keim-, Geschlechtszelle
Zygote, befruchtete Eizelle[1] reif[2] einfacher/ haploider Chromosomensatz[3] beeinträchtigen[4] Einnistung, Implantation, Nidation[5] bringt zum Platzen[6] mutierte Keimzelle[7] Gametenverschmelzung[8] intratubarer Gametentransfer, GIFT[9] Gameten-, Keimzellenbildung, Gametenentwicklung, Gametogenese[10] Gametozid, gametozytenschäd. Substanz[11] Keimzellschädigung[12] dizygot, zweieiig[13] homozygot, reinerbig[14] heterozygot, mischerbig[15] Zygotän[16] Heterozygotie[17]

2

cleavage [ˈkliːvɪdʒ] **(division)** *n term*   *rel* **cell division**[1] [sel dɪvɪʒᵊn] *n term*

series of cell divisions occurring [ɜː] in the ovum immediately after fertilization

cleave[2] - cleft - cleft *v irr term* • **(non-)cleaved** *adj* • **cleft**[3] [kleft] *n* • **divide**[2] [aɪ] *v*

» During cleavage, the total embryonic mass remains relatively constant. As cleavage progresses the zygote moves down the Fallopian tube[4]. Errors during cell division may result in numerical or structural [ʌ] abnormalities of chromosomes.

Use holoblastic or complete[5] / meroblastic or partial[6] [ʃ] **cleavage** • adequal[7] / discoidal / (in)determinate[8] [ɜː] **cleavage** • **cleavage** stage[9] [steɪdʒ] • to undergo **cell division** • meiotic[10] / mitotic[11] [maɪˈtɒtɪk] **division**

Furchung(steilung)
Zellteilung[1] (s.) teilen[2] Spalt, Furche[3] Eileiter, Tuba uterina (Fallopii)[4] holoblastische/ totale Furchung[5] meroblast./ partielle F.[6] äquale Teilung[7] (nicht) determinierte Furchung[8] Furchungsstadium[9] Reduktionsteilung, Meiose[10] mitotische Zellteilung, Mitose[11]

3

MEDICAL SCIENCE — Medical Embryology

morula [mɔːrjələ] n term
rel **mulberry** [ʌ] or **morula stage**[1] n term

spherical mass of blastomeres[2] [ɪɚ] resulting from the early cleavage divisions of the zygote

morular [mɔːrjʊlə] adj term • **morulation**[3] [eɪʃ] n • **moruloid**[4] adj

» At about the 16-cell stage, the individual cells of the embryo begin to adhere [ɪɚ] to one another and assume [(j)uː] a morula shape. A 12-cell morula was found in the uterine cavity.

Use **morular** cells • two-cell[5] / four-cell / lacunar[6] [k(j)uː] **stage** • **mulberry** mass

blastula or blastocyst [blæstəsɪst] n term
rel **gastrula**[1] [gæstrʊlə] n term

zygote in the early embryonal stage in which the blastomeres of the morula are rearranged to form a hollow sphere

blastular adj term • **blastulation**[2] n • **blasto-** comb • **gastrulation**[3] n

» The 107-cell blastocyst contained an embryoblast[4] with 8 vacuolated cells; the remaining 99 belonged to the trophoblast[5]. Continued expansion of the blastocyst cavity[6] eventually[7] ruptures [ʌ] the protective zona pellucida shell which disappears at the end of the 4th day.

Use **blastocyst** formation[2] / stage / wall • **blasto**cele[6] [blæstəsiːl] /meres [ɪɚ] • embedded / implantation of the **blastocyst** • **gastrulation** process[3]

germ layer [dʒɜːrm] n term
rel **germ** or **embryonic disk**[1], **ectoderm**[2] n term

one of the three primordial (ectodermal, entodermal, mesodermal) cell layers established in an embryo during gastrulation and the immediately following stages

mesoderm [me∥miːzədɜːrm] n term • **endo-** or **entoderm**[3] n • **germinal** adj

» The development and invagination [ɪnvædʒ-] of the embryonic germ layers marks the process termed gastrulation. The cloacal [eɪ] wall[4] is formed by the inner and outer germ layers. In the human embryo, the absence of yolk allows for a more rapid direct "putting in place" of the germ layers which are derived [aɪ] from the pluripotential embryonic disk.

Use ectodermal [ɜː] or outer[2] / entodermal or inner[3] **germ layer** • **germinal** epithelium[5] [iː] • bilaminar[6] / trilaminar[7] [aɪ] **germ disk** • somatic or parietal[8] [pəraɪətl]/ splanchnic [k] or visceral[9] [ɪs] **mesoderm layer** • extra-embryonic / intermediate[10] [iː] **mesoderm** • **ectodermal** layer / ridge[11] [rɪdʒ]/ cloaca [klouˈeɪkə])

yolk or vitelline sac [vaɪtelᵊn] n term
rel **umbilical** [ʌ] **vesicle**[1] [vesɪkl] n term

entodermal membrane projecting into the chorionic cavity[2] which contains the nutritive material stored in the ovum for the nutrition [ɪʃ] of the embryo; it normally disappears in the 7th week of gestation

vitellus[3] [vaɪtelᵊs] n term, pl **-es** • **yolk**[3] [jouk] n clin •

umbilicus[4] [ʌmbɪlɪkəs∥laɪkəs] n term

» In human embryos the primordial germ cells appear in the wall of the yolk sac at the end of the 3rd week of development. The yolk stalk[5] [stɒːk] connects the yolk sac to the midgut[6] [mɪdgʌt] of the embryo during the early stages of prenatal development. The primitive yolk sac is also termed the exocoelomic [-sɪlou∥ɒːmɪk] cavity[7].

Use primitive[7] / secondary or definitive[8] / embryonic **yolk sac** • **yolk sac** stalk[5] / tumor[9] • **yolk** cells / membrane[10] / cleavage • **vitelline** duct[5]/ artery • egg[11] **yolk**

primitive streak [prɪmɪtɪv striːk] n term
syn **primitive line** n term
rel **primitive groove** [uː] or **pit**[1], **primitive node**[2] [oʊ] n term

ectodermal ridge in the midline at the caudal [ɒː] end of the embryonic disk from which arises [aɪ] the intraembryonic mesoderm; formed by inward and then lateral migration of cells

» The primitive streak appears on day 15 and gives a cephalocaudal [sefəlou-] axis to the developing embryo. Then the primitive streak, or future neural [n(j)ʊəᵊl] tube[3], begins to develop. Cells of the ectodermal layer migrate[4] [aɪ] in the direction of the primitive streak.

Use **primitive** gut[5] / foregut[6] / gonad / pulmonary artery / umbilical ring / notochord

---

Morula
Morula-, Maulbeerstadium[1] Blastomeren[2] Morulabildung[3] morula-ähnlich[4] Zweizellstadium[5] lakunäres Stadium[6]

4

Blastula, Blastozyste, Keimblase
Gastrula[1] Blastulabildung, Blastulation[2] Gastrulation[3] Embryoblast[4] Trophoblast[5] Blastozystenhöhle[6] schließlich[7]

5

Keimblatt
Keimscheibe[1] Ektoderm, äußeres Keimblatt[2] Entoderm, inneres Keimblatt[3] Kloakenmembran[4] Keimepithel[5] zweiblättrige Keimscheibe[6] dreiblättrige Keimscheibe[7] parietales Mesoderm, Somatopleura[8] viszerales Mesoderm, Visceropleura[9] intermediäres Mesoderm[10] Ektodermleiste[11]

6

Dottersack, Saccus vitellinus
Nabelbläschen, Vesicula umbilicalis[1] Chorionhöhle[2] Dotter[3] Nabel, Umbilicus, Omphalos[4] Dottergang, Ductus vitellinus/ omphaloentericus[5] Mitteldarm[6] primärer Dottersack[7] sekundärer/ definitiver Dottersack[8] Dottersacktumor[9] Dottersackmembran[10] (Fi)dotter, Ei gelb[11]

7

Primitivstreifen
Primitivgrube[1] Primitivknoten[2] Neuralrohr[3] wandern[4] Primitiv-, Urdarm[5] Vorderdarm[6]

8

Medical Embryology

MEDICAL SCIENCE 369

anlage [ˈɑnlɑːgə] *n term, pl* **-gen**   *syn* **primordium** [ɔː], **rudiment** [uː] *n term*

aggregation of cells in the embryo representing the first trace of an organ or structure

primordial[1] [praɪmɔːrdɪəl] *adj term* • **rudimentary**[2] *adj*

» The external genital [dʒe] anlagen and mesonephric ducts do not respond to androgens. The gonads develop from a bipotential anlage in the genital ridge[3] of the celomic cavity[4].

Use common[5] / bipotential [baɪpətenˈʃəl]/ urogenital / gonadal [eɪ]/ pancreatic **anlage** • to remain **rudimentary** • **primordial** germ cells[6] / follicle[7] / kidney[8]

> **Note:** Although basically a synonym for **primordium** and **anlage**, **rudiment** is more commonly used for structures that have remained vestigial[2] [vestɪdʒɪəl] and are undeveloped and dysfunctional [ʌ].

Anlage
primordial, Ur-[1] anlagemäßig; rudimentär, zurückgebildet[2] Genitalleiste[3] Zölom[4] gemeinsame Anlage[5] Urkeimzellen[6] Primordialfollikel[7] Vorniere, Pronephros[8]

9

budding [ʌ] *n*   *syn* **sprouting** [spraʊtɪŋ] *n*, **gemmation** [dʒemeɪʃən] *n term*
rel **bulging**[1] [bʌldʒɪŋ], **swelling**[2] *n*

a form of fission[3] [fɪʃǁʒən] in which the parent cell does not divide [aɪ] but puts out a small budlike process (an outpocketing[4] or daughter [dɔːtɚ] cell) which then separates to begin independent existence

bud[5] *v & n* • **bud-like** *adj* • **bulge** *v & n* • **sprout** [aʊ] *v* • **gemmate** *v term*

» Early splitting of the ureteric [e] bud[6] into two parts may result in partial or complete duplication [duːp-] of the ureter. The limb buds[7] become visible at the beginning of the 5th week.

Use **budding** cells • upper limb [lɪm]/ hindlimb[8] [haɪndlɪm]/ liver / lung / pancreatic **bud** • **bud** formation[9] • heart [ɑː] *or* cardiac[10] / spinal [aɪ] cord [kɔːrd] **bulge** • facial [eɪʃ]/ genital[11] [dʒe]/ scrotal[12] [oʊ] **swellings**

Knospung, Aussprossung
Vorwölbung[1] Verdickung, Wulst[2] (Zell)teilung[3] Ausstülpung[4] knospen, keimen; Knospe, Anlage[5] Ureterknospe, -anlage[6] Extremitätenknospen[7] Beinanlage,- knospe[8] Knospung, Knospenbildung[9] primitiver Herzschlauch[10] Genitalwülste[11] Skrotalwülste[12]

10

differentiate [dɪfərenˈʃieɪt] *v term*
rel **derived** [dɪraɪvd] **(from)**[1] *v usu pass*

process in which unspecialized cells or tissues develop to achieve [tʃ] specific properties

differentiation[2] *n term* • **(un)differentiated** *adj* → U97-8
• **derivative**[3] [ɪ] **(of)** *n* • **derivation**[4] *n*

» The embryoblast differentiates into two distinct cell layers [eɪ]. The second phase of sexual differentiation is the conversion [ɜː] of the indifferent gonad into a testis or an ovary. These flattened cells, the amnioblasts, are probably derived from the trophoblast.

Use **to differentiate into** the uterine tubes[5] / spermatozoa / the epididymis [ɪ] • cell *or* cellular[6] / organ / sexual[7] **differentiation** • gonadal[8] [eɪ]/ early / cyto[6]/ [saɪtoʊ-] embryonic **differentiation** • **undifferentiated** gonad[9] / cells • endodermal / mullerian[10] **derivatives**

differenzieren
entstanden aus, (ab)stammen, sich ableiten[1] Differenzierung[2] Abkömmling, Derivat[3] Ableitung, Ursprung[4] sich in Uterusschläuche differenzieren[5] Zelldifferenzierung[6] Sexualdifferenzierung[7] Gonadendifferenzierung[8] undifferenzierte Gonade[9] Müller-Gang-Abkömmlinge[10]

11

invagination [ɪnvædʒɪneɪʃən] *n term*
rel **groove**[1] [gruːv], **fold**[2] [foʊld] *n*

(i) infolding[3] of a part of the wall of the blastula to form the gastrula
(ii) intussusception [se]

invaginate[4] *adj & v term* • **fold**[5] *v clin & term* • **folding** *n* → U130-8

» Once the cells have invaginated in the region of the primitive streak, they migrate between the ectodermal and entodermal layers to form the mesodermal germ layer.

Use primary [aɪ] **invagination** • neural[6] **groove** • cephalocaudal **(in)folding**

Invagination, Einstülpung
Rinne[1] Falte[2] Einstülpung[3] invaginiert, eingestülpt; (sich) einstülpen[4] falten, einstülpen[5] Neuralrinne[6]

12

(membrana) decidua [dɪsɪdʒəwə] *n term*   *syn* **decidual membrane** *n term*

mucous [juː] membrane lining[1] [aɪ] the pregnant uterus (so-called because it is cast off[2] in the puerperium [ɪɚ] and periodically during menstruation)

decidual [dɪsɪdʒʊəl] *adj term*

» The placenta was abnormally adherent [ɪɚ] to the myometrium [maɪoʊ-] because it developed where there was a deficiency [ɪʃ] of decidua. The maternal [ɜː] placenta is composed of compressed sheets of decidua basalis, remnants[3] of blood vessels, and, at the margin [dʒ], spongy [spʌndʒi] decidua[4].

Use degenerated [dʒe] **decidua** • **decidua** basalis *or* serotina[5] / capsularis *or* reflexa[6] • **decidua** parietalis *or* vera[7] / **decidual** changes / plate[8] / reaction[9] / **decidual** cast[10] / cells / layer[11] [eɪ]/ septa[12]

Dezidua, deziduale Membran
die auskleidet[1] abgestoßen[2] (Über)reste[3] Stratum spongiosum endometrii, Decidua spongiosa[4] D. basalis[5] D. capsularis[6] D. parietalis[7] Dezidua-, Basalplatte[8] deziduale Reaktion[9] abgestoßene Deziduaanteile[10] Deziduaschicht[11] Deziduasepten[12]

13

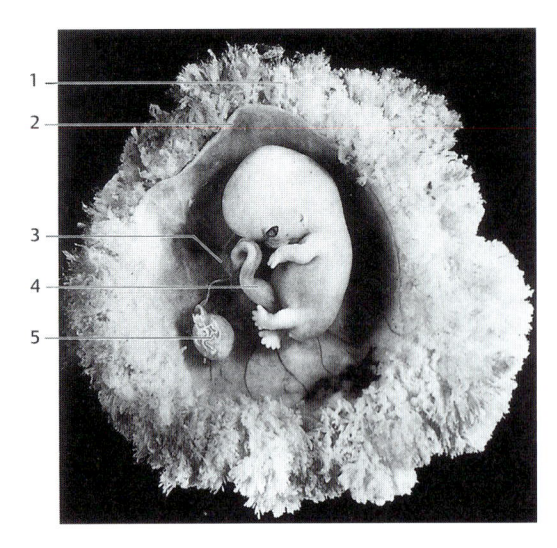

Fetus in utero at 22 weeks of gestation:
chorionic villi (**1**),
chorionic plate (**2**),
remnants of the amnion (**3**),
umbilical cord (**4**),
yolk sac (**5**)

trophoblast [troufəblæst] *n term*

    rel **placenta**[1] [pləsentə] *n term* → U71-16

mesectodermal layer of cells covering the blastocyst that erodes the uterine mucosa in implantation and contributes to the formation of the placenta and the chorionic villi[2] [vɪlaɪ]

trophoblastic *adj term* • **syncytio-**[3]**/ cytotrophoblast**[4] *n* • **trophoblastoma**[5] *n*

» At implantation the trophoblast differentiates into two new cell types. Irregular grooves [uː] or clefts divide the placenta into cotyledons[6] [kɒtəliːdᵊnz].

Use syncytial[3] [sɪnsɪʃ(ɪ)əl] **trophoblast** • **trophoblastic** layer / activity / neoplasm [iː]
• **trophoblastic** disease / cancer [ˈs] / tumors[7] / lacunae[8] [ləkjuːniǁaɪ] • **cytotrophoblast**(*ic*) shell[9] / cells[10]

amnion [æmnɪɒn] *n term*   *syn* **amniotic membrane, amniotic sac** *n term*

(i) innermost membrane enveloping[1] the embryo in utero
(ii) sometimes also used to refer to the cavity formed by this sac which contains the amniotic fluid

amniotic [æmnɪɒtɪk] *adj term* • **amnionic** *adj* • **amnio-** *comb*

» The amnion provides the epithelial [iː] covering for the umbilical cord[2]. At this stage the amniotic cavity forms above the epiblast and will later engulf[1] [ʌ] the embryo proper. The fetal surface of the placenta is covered by the smooth [u:] amniotic membrane.

Use **amniotic** cavity[3] / fluid (embolism)[4] / bands or adhesions[5] [iːʒ]/ band syndrome[6] [ɪ]/ cells • **amnio**tomy or artificial [ɪʃ] rupture [ʌ] of membranes[7] (*abbr* ARM) • **amnio**scopy[8] /centesis[9] [æmnɪousentiːsɪs] /nitis [aɪ] /cyte

chorion [kɔːrɪɒn] *n term*   *syn* **chorionic sac** or **membrane** [membreɪn] *n term*

multilayered [ʌ], outer fetal membrane consisting of extraembryonic somatic mesoderm, trophoblast, and – on the maternal [ɜː] surface – chorionic villi

chorionic [kɔːrɪɒnɪk] *adj term* • **chorio-** *comb*

» As pregnancy progresses part of the chorion develops into the definitive fetal placenta[1]. A single chorion always represents monozygotic twinning [ɪ].

Use **chorionic** plate[2] / villi[3] / cavity[4] / bushy[5] [ʊ]/ shaggy[5] / smooth[6] **chorion** • **chorionic** gonadotropin / villus sampling or biopsy[7] [aɪ] • **chorio**amnionitis [aɪ] /genesis /adenoma /carcinoma[8] • **chorion** frondosum[5] / laeve[6]

Trophoblast
Plazenta, Mutterkuchen[1] Chorionzotten[2] Synzytiotrophoblast[3] Zytotrophoblast[4] Trophoblasttumor[5] Kotyledonen, Zottenbüschel[6] Trophoblasttumoren[7] trophoblastäre Lakunen[8] Zytotrophoblasthülle[9] Zytotrophoblastzellen[10]

14

Amnion(sack), Fruchtsack, innere Eihaut, Schafhaut
einhüllen[1] Nabelstrang, -schnur[2] Amnionhöhle[3] Fruchtwasser(embolie)[4] Amnionbänder, -stränge, Simonart-Bänder[5] Amnionbändersyndrom[6] Amniotomie, Blasensprengung[7] Fruchtwasserspiegelung, Amnioskopie[8] Amnion-, Fruchtblasenpunktion, Amniozentese[9]

15

Chorion, Zottenhaut, mittlere Eihaut
kindl. Anteil, Pars fetalis d. Plazenta[1] Chorionplatte[2] Chorionzotten[3] Chorionhöhle[4] Chorion frondosum[5] Chorion laeve[6] Chorionzottenbiopsie[7] Chorionkarzinom, (malignes) Chorionepitheliom[8]

16

Medical Embryology

MEDICAL SCIENCE

allantois [əlæntəwəs] *n term*   *syn* **allantoenteric diverticulum** [daɪ-] *n term*   *syn* **allantoic sac** *n*, *rel* **body stalk**[1] [stɔːk], **urachus**[2] [jʊɚəkəs] *n term*

tubular extension of the endoderm of the yolk sac extending into the body stalk; the allantoic vessels[3] develop into the umbilical vessels and chorionic villi

-allantoic [æləntoʊɪk] *adj & comb* • **allanto-** *comb* • **urachal** [jʊɚəkəl] *adj*

» The urachus represents the remains [eɪ] of the embryonic allantois. Vesicourachal diverticula [daɪ-] occur when the communication[4] between the bladder and urachus fails to obliterate[5]. The body stalk connects the allantoic sac to the fetal abdomen at the umbilicus.

Use **allantoic** membrane[6] / duct[7] [ʌ] • connecting **stalk**[1] • patent[8] [eɪ]/ persistent[9] / partially obliterated **urachus** • **urachal** cyst[10] / remnant[11] / fistula[12] • **urachal** diverticulum[13] / sinus[14] [aɪ] • **allanto**chorion /genesis

Allantois, Urharnsack
Haftstiel[1] Urachus, Harngang, embryon. Harnleiter[2] Allantoisgefäße[3] Verbindung[4] nicht obliteriert/ verödet[5] Plica umbilicalis medialis[6] Allantoisgang[7] offener Urachus[8] persistierender Urachus, Urachuspersistenz[9] Urachuszyste[10] Urachusrest[11] Urachusfistel[12] Urachusdivertikel[13] Urachussinus[14]

17

---

neural tube *n term*   *rel* **neural plate**[1] [n(j)ʊɚəl pleɪt] *n term*

tube formed from the early neuroectoderm by the closure of the neural groove which develops into the spinal cord[2] and brain

» Defects of neural tube closure constitute the most common congenital malformations affecting the nervous system. The neural plate appears and the neural tube forms and closes during days 0-28 of gestation, the so-called period of induction.

Use **neural** crest[3] / folds[4] / groove[5] • **neural tube** formation / defect[6] (NTD)/ closure[7]

Neuralrohr
Neuralplatte[1] Rückenmark[2] Neuralleiste[3] Neuralfalten[4] Neuralrinne[5] Neuralrohrdefekt[6] Neuralrohrverschluss[7]

18

---

somite [soʊmaɪt] *n term*   *syn* **mesoblastic segment** *n term*

one of the 42 to 44 paired blocklike masses of mesodermal cells forming along the neural tube that give rise to the vertebrae, voluntary muscles, bones, connective tissue, and dermal layers

somitic [soʊmɪtɪk] *adj term* • **presomite**[1] [priːsoʊmaɪt] *adj*

» The first pair of somites appears in the future occipital [ksɪ] region. A lateral mesenchymal [kaɪ] plate defect [iː] affects the thoracic somite buds, causing failure of differentiation and ventral and caudal migration.

Use sacral [eɪ]/ thoracic [æs]/ occipital **somites** • **somite** wall[2] • buds • **somitic** mesoderm • 16-day presomite[3] / 28-somite **embryo**

Somit, Ursegment
Präsomiten-[1] Somitenwand[2] 16 Tage alter Präsomitenembryo[3]

19

---

notochord [noʊtəkɔːrd] *n term*   *syn* **chorda dorsalis** *or* **vertebralis** *n term*

axial fibrocellular cord about which the vertebral primordia develop; vestiges[1] [-ɪdʒɪːz] of it persist in the adult as the nuclei [n(j)uːklɪaɪ] pulposi[2] of the intervertebral disks[3]

notochordal *adj term* • **prochordal** *adj*

» Anterior to the notochord an ectodermal thickening develops, the prochordal plate. Chordomas[4] are tumors derived [aɪ] from the remnants[1] of the primitive notochord.

Use definitive[5] **notochord** • **notochordal** or head process[6] / canal[7] / cells / origin • **prochordal** plate[8] [eɪ]

Rückensaite, Chorda dorsalis
Reste[1] Gallertkerne, Nuclei pulposi[2] Zwischenwirbelscheiben, Disci intervertebrales[3] Chordome[4] definitive Chorda[5] Chorda-, Kopffortsatz[6] Chordakanal[7] Prächordalplatte[8]

20

---

cloaca [kloʊeɪkə] *n term*   *rel* **primitive gut**[1] [gʌt], **mesonephros**[2] *n term*

endodermally lined chamber [tʃeɪ-] in early embryos into which the hindgut[3] [aɪ] and allantois empty

cloacal [kloʊeɪkəl] *adj term* • **pronephros**[4] *n* • **metanephros**[5] *n*

» The cloaca divides into the anorectal [eɪnoʊ-] canal[6] and the urogenital sinus[7] [aɪ] into which the mesonephric duct is gradually absorbed. During the 4th week, the dorsal aspect of the yolk sac is incorporated into the embryo as an endodermal tube, the primitive gut. In the 4th week of intrauterine life, the mesonephros is derived from the intermediate mesoderm.

Use endodermal [ɜː]/ ectodermal **cloaca** • persistent[8] / faulty [ɔː] division of the[9] **cloaca** • **cloacal** membrane[10] / fold / plate • **cloacal** anomaly[11] / exstrophy[12] • pharyngeal[13] [dʒ] fore[14]/ mid[15]/ hind**gut** • **mesonephric** or wolffian [uː] duct[16] • **paramesonephric** or mullerian duct[17]

Kloake
Primitiv-, Urdarm[1] Mesonephros, Urniere[2] Hinterdarm[3] Pronephros, Vorniere[4] Metanephros, Nachniere[5] Anorektalkanal[6] Sinus urogenitalis[7] Kloakenpersistenz[8] Störung d. Kloakenseptierung[9] Kloakenmembran[10] Kloakenfehlbildung[11] Kloakenekstrophie, Ecstrophia cloacae[12] Schlunddarm[13] Vorderdarm[14] Mitteldarm[15] Urnierengang, Wolff-Gang[16] Müller-Gang, Ductus paramesonephricus[17]

21

---

myotome [maɪətoʊm] *n term*   *syn* **myomere** *n*, *rel* **dermatome**[1] *n term*

(i) in embryos, the part of the somite that develops into skeletal muscle
(ii) all muscles [mʌslz] derived from one somite and innervated by one segmental spinal nerve

myotomal *adj term* • **dermatomal** *adj* • **sclerotome**[2] *n* • **nephrotome**[3] *n*

» Each somite forms its own myotome, sclerotome, and dermatome. After the sclerotome cells have migrated in ventro-medial [iː] direction where they will form the vertebral column[4] [ɔː], the remaining dorsal somite wall, now referred to as the dermatome, gives rise to a new layer of cells.

Use occipital / preotic [priːoʊtɪk] **myotome** • **dermatomal** distribution/ sensory loss

Myotom, Muskelplatte
Dermatom[1] Sklerotom[2] Nephrotom[3] Wirbelsäule[4]

22

placode [plækoʊd] *n term*

local thickening in an embryonic epithelial layer representing a primordium for an organ

» After the neural tube closes the otic [oʊ] and the lens placodes appear as outpocketings of the brain. The otic placode invaginates [ædʒ] to form the otic pit[1].

Use otic or auditory[2] [ɒː]/ lens or optic[3] **placode**(*s*) • ectodermal[4] / olfactory [æ] or nasal[5] [eɪ] **placode**(*s*)

Plakode

Ohrgrübchen[1] Ohrplakode[2] Linsenplakode[3] ektodermale Plakode[4] Riechplakode[5]

23

stem villi [stɛm vɪlaɪ] *n term*

primordium of the chorionic villi consisting of cytotrophoblastic and syncytical [sɪ] cells

» The early stem villi consist of cordlike masses of trophoblast separated by blood lacunas[1].

Use primary[2] / secondary[3] / tertiary[4] [ʃ] **stem villi** • **stem** or progenitor [dʒe] cells[5]

Stammzotten

Blutlakunen[1] Primärzotten, frühe Zotten[2] Sekundärzotten[3] Tertiärzotten[4] Stammzellen[5]

24

Unit 86 Histology

Related Units: 83 Cell Biology, 85 Embryology, 87 Anatomy, 89 Pathology, 98 Tumor Types, 116 Lab Studies, 118 Diagnostic Procedures

histology [hɪstɒːlədʒi] *n term*   *syn* **microscopic anatomy** [ənætəmi] *n term*
   rel **cytology**[1] [saɪtɒːlədʒi] *n term* → U83-1

science [saɪənˈs] studying the minute [maɪn(j)uːt] structure of cells, tissues, and organs in relation to their function [ʌ]

histologic(al)[2] *adj term* • **hist**ologist[3] *n* • **histo**- *comb* → U87-1

• **micro**scope[4] [maɪkrəskoʊp] *n term* • **micro**scopy[5] [ɒː] *n* • **micro**- *comb*

» Neither the symptoms [ɪ] nor the gross [oʊ] appearance[6] helped predict the histology, so biopsy [aɪ] was necessary. The injury around the missile wound[7] [uː] was evaluated microscopically. The sheath [ʃiːθ] can be seen on microscopy.

Use normal / testicular / breast [e] **histology** • **histologic** examination / appearance [ɪɚ]/ features[8] [fiːtʃɚz] • **histologic** pattern / section[9] / findings[10] / diagnosis • **histologically** benign [bɪnaɪn]/ negative margins[11] [dʒ] • **histo**chemical /genesis [dʒe] /compatibility[12] /pathology • to examine under (standard) light[13] **microscopy** • electron / polarization or polarizing[14] **microscopy** • dark-field[15] / wet-mount[16] [aʊ] **microscopy** • (immuno)fluorescence[17] [es]/ phase-contrast[18] **microscopy** • binocular / dissecting[19] / ultraviolet[20] [aɪ] **microscope** • fluorescent / low-power[21] / operating[22] **microscope** • **microscope** slide[23] [aɪ] • **microscopic** analysis / examination or study[24] • **microscopic** magnification / appearance • **microscopic** urinalysis / hematuria[25] [(j)ʊɚ]/ changes / field • **microscopic** section / trauma[26] [ɒː]/ foci [foʊsaɪ]/ tears[27] [eɚ] • **micro**biology /flora / embolus[28] /fracture /organism

Histologie, Gewebelehre

Zytologie, Zell(en)lehre[1] histologisch[2] Histologe/-in[3] Mikroskop[4] Mikroskopie, mikrosk. Untersuchung[5] makroskop. Erscheinungsbild[6] Schusswunde[7] histolog. Merkmale[8] Gewebeschnitt, histol. S.[9] histol. Befund[10] histol. tumorfreie Resektionsränder[11] Histokompatibilität[12] lichtmikroskop. untersuchen[13] Polarisationsmikroskopie[14] Dunkelfeldmikroskopie[15] mikroskop. Untersuchung m. Immersionsobjektiv[16] Fluoreszenzmikroskopie[17] Phasenkontrastmikroskopie[18] Präpariermikroskop[19] Ultraviolettmikroskop[20] Mikroskop m. geringer Auflösung[21] Operationsmikroskop[22] Objektträger[23] mikroskop. Untersuchung[24] Mikrohämaturie[25] Mikrotrauma[26] mikroskop. kleine Risse[27] Mikroembolie, Mikroembolus[28]

1

-cyte [-saɪt] *comb*
   rel **(-)blast**[1] [blæst] *comb & n*

suffix denoting a differentiated cell which has usually lost its mitotic potential, while a precursor [ɜː] cell[2], which may retain mitotic capability, is termed –blast, e.g. myeloblast [aɪ]

-cytic [-sɪtɪk] *comb* • **cyto**- *comb* • **(-)blastic** *comb & adj* • **blasto**- *comb*

» His leukocyte [uː] count[3] [aʊ] is normal to low, with variable shift. The adult spleen[4] [iː] produces monocytes, lymphocytes [ɪ], and plasma cells. Myelodysplasias without excess bone marrow blasts[5] are termed "refractory anemia[6]" with or without ringed sideroblasts[7].

Use osteo[8]/ lympho/ erythro[9] [ɪ] /mono/ reticulo**cyte** • histio/ hepato/ adipo[10]/ oo[11]/ melano**cyte** • granulo/ normo/ macro[12] **cytic** • micro/ nonlympho/ myelo**cytic** • **cyto**logy /logic /metry[13] /plasm /plasmic[14] /toxic • **blast** cell[15] / crisis[16] [aɪ] • chondro[17]/ osteo/ fibro [aɪ]/ lympho**blast** • **blasto**genesis[18] • megalo/ osteo/ sidero/ tropho**blastic** • **blastic** transformation[19] / phase [feɪz]

-zyt

-blast, Blast[1] Vorläuferzelle[2] Leukozytenzahl[3] Milz[4] Myeloblasten[5] refraktäre Anämie[6] Ringsideroblasten[7] Osteozyt, Knochenzelle[8] Erythrozyt, rotes Blutkörperchen[9] Fettzelle, Adipozyt[10] Eizelle, Oo-, Ovozyt[11] makrozytär[12] Zytometrie[13] zytoplasmatisch[14] Blast(enzelle)[15] Blastenkrise, -schub[16] Chondroblast, Knorpelbildungszelle[17] Blastogenese, Blastenbildung[18] Blasttransformation[19]

2

Histology   MEDICAL SCIENCE 373

tissue [tɪʃjuː‖tɪsjuː] n

collection of similar cells and the intercellular substances [ʌ] surrounding them

» *The four basic tissues in the body are epithelial [iː], muscle [mʌsl], nerve [ɜː], and connective tissues (including blood, bone, and cartilage [-lɪdʒ]). Sarcomas arise in any type of soft tissue (adipose, fibrous [aɪ], muscular, mesenchymal [kaɪ], histiocytic, neural [n(j)ʊərəl], vascular, lymphatic, and synovial).*

Use subcutaneous [eɪ]/ (multilocular) adipose or fatty[1] / nerve or nervous[2] **tissue** • connective[3] / fibrous / fibrohyaline [aɪ]/ soft[4] / hard or compact[5] **tissue** • bone or osseous[6] / cancellous[7] [kænˈsələs]/ chondroid[8] / cartilaginous[9] [ædʒ] **tissue** • (skeletal/ smooth [uː]/ cardiac) muscle [s] or muscular[10] [ʌsk] **tissue** • lymph [ɪ] node[11] / lymphatic or lymphoid[11] / liver [ɪ]/ myeloid[12] [aɪ] **tissue** • scar[13] [skɑːr]/ granulation / interstitial[14] [ɪʃ]/ reticular **tissue** • periapical [eɪ]/ gingival [dʒɪndʒ-]/ erectile[15] / indifferent[16] **tissue** • **tissue** turgor[17] [tɜːrɡəʳ]/ oxygenation / perfusion [juː]/ plane [eɪ]/ breakdown[18] [eɪ] • **tissue** injury or damage[19] / necrosis / repair [eəʳ] • **tissue** culture[20] [ʌ]/ engineering[21] [-ɪəɪŋ]/ bank / typing[22]

Gewebe
Fettgewebe[1] Nervengewebe[2] Bindegewebe[3] Weichteile[4] Kompakta, Substantia compacta[5] Knochengewebe[6] Spongiosa, S. spongiosa[7] Knorpelgrundsubstanz[8] Knorpelgewebe[9] glatte Muskulatur[10] lymphat. G.[11] Markgewebe, Knochenmark[12] Narbengewebe[13] Zwischengewebe, interstitielles Gewebe[14] erektiles G.[15] undifferenziertes embryonales G.[16] Turgor, Gewebespannung[17] Gewebeabbau, -auflösung[18] Gewebeschädigung, -schaden[19] Gewebekultur[20] Tissue engineering, Gewebezüchtung[21] Gewebetypisierung[22]

3

connective tissue n term   sim **fibrous** [faɪbrəs] **tissue**[1] n term
                                rel **collagen**[2] [kɒːlədʒən] n term

type of tissue consisting mainly of fibroblasts and elastic and collagen fibers which supports and connects internal [ɜː] organs, and forms bones, vascular walls, ligaments [ɪɡ], tendons, etc.

» *The fatty connective tissue is especially thick around the kidney where it forms the perinephric fat. The outermost layer of the testis contains a dense covering composed of interlacing [eɪ] bundles [ʌ] of fibrous tissue, the tunica albuginea [dʒɪ].*

Use dense or firm[3] [ɜː]/ loose[4] [uː]/ supporting[5] **connective tissue** • subcutaneous[6] / submucosal [koʊ] **connective tissue** • fibrous[1] / fibroelastic / collagenous[7] / hyaline / fatty **connective tissue** • **connective tissue** cells[8] / protein / strands[9] / matrix [eɪ]/ plane • **connective tissue** elasticity [ɪs]/ disease / nevus[10] / massage[11] / scar[12] • dense[3] / underlying [aɪ]/ lamellar[13] / granulomatous **fibrous tissue** • **fibrous tissue** bundle / hyperplasia [eɪʒ]

Bindegewebe
fibröses/ faserreiches/ straffes Bindegewebe[1] Kollagen[2] straffes Bindegewebe[3] lockeres Bindegewebe[4] Stützgewebe[5] Unterhautbindegewebe/ subkutanes B.[6] kollagenes Bindegewebe[7] Bindegewebezellen[8] Bindegewebestränge[9] Bindegewebenävus[10] Bindegewebemassage[11] Bindegewebenarbe[12] straffes parallellfasriges Bindegewebe[13]

4

collagen fiber n term   syn **collagenous fiber** [kəlædʒɪnəs faɪbəʳ] n term
                              rel **elastic** [ɪlæstɪk] **fiber**[1], **reticular fiber**[2] n term

most common type of fiber in the intercellular matrix of connective tissue which is arranged in parallel rows [oʊ] and adds strength to the skin, cartilage, etc.; elastic fibers allow tissues to stretch; reticular fiber, a branching network of thin fiber, forms the stroma of organs

fibrous[3] [aɪ] adj term • elasticity[4] [ɪs] n • elastin[5] n • fibro-, reticulo- comb

» *Within the collagen fiber layer [eɪ] at least two different courses [ɔː] of collagen fibers can be distinguished. Beneath [iː] the urothelium [iː] and separating it from the muscular coat [oʊ] is the lamina propria, which contains both elastic and collagenous fibers.*

Use dermal [ɜː]/ tough[6] [tʌf] **collagen fiber** • **collagen** fibrils[7] / diseases[8] / synthesis[9] [ɪ] • **collagen** structure / metabolism / deposition[10] /ase[11] • **collagenous** tissue / colitis[12] • rich in[13] / loss of / tangled[14] **elastic fibers** • **elastic** cartilage[15] / tissue / lamina • **elastic** structure / membrane / properties • muscle / nerve **fiber** • **reticular** dermis[16] / pattern / tissue[17] • **reticulo**endothelial [iː] system /cyte[18]

Kollagenfaser, kollagene F.
elastische Faser[1] argyrophile/ retikuläre F., Gitterfaser, Retikulinfaser[2] faserig, fibrös[3] Elastizität[4] Elastin[5] zugfeste kollagene Faser[6] Kollagenfibrillen[7] Kollagenkrankheiten, Kollagenosen[8] Kollagensynthese[9] Kollagenablagerung[10] Kollagenase[11] kollagene Kolitis[12] reich an elastischen Fasern[13] (gitterartig) vernetzte/ verflochtene elastische Fasern[14] elastischer Knorpel, Cartilago elastica[15] Stratum reticulare, Geflechtschicht[16] retikuläres Bindegewebe[17] Retikulozyt[18]

5

areolar tissue [əriːələʳ tɪʃjuː] n term   syn **areolar connective tissue** n term

connective tissue which consists of loosely woven fibers and areolae [-liː] and has little tensile strength

» *The tail [eɪ] of the epididymis is loosely attached [ætʃ] by areolar tissue to the lower portion of the testis. Fatty areolar tissue separates the tendon[1] from its sheath[2] [iː].*

Use loose [luːs]/ fibro/ fatty[3] **areolar tissue** • fibro/ peri/ sub**areolar**

lockeres/ faserarmes Bindegewebe
Sehne[1] Sehnenscheide, Vagina tendinis[2] lockeres Fett-Bindegewebe[3]

6

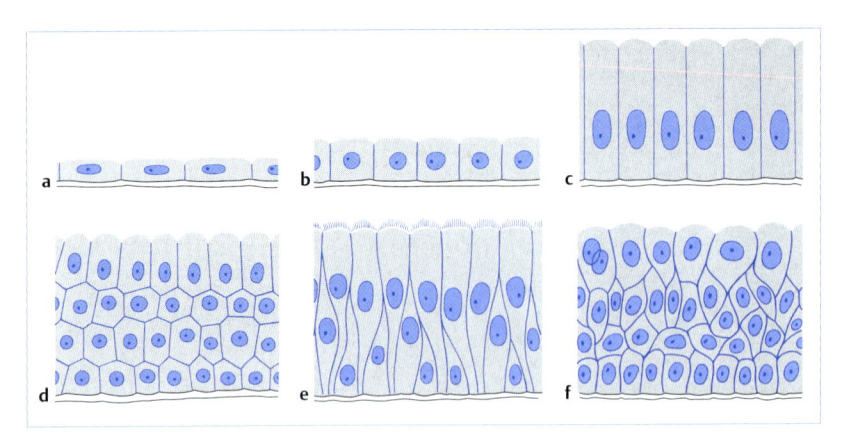

Types of epithelial tissue:
(a) simple squamous epithelium,
(b) simple cuboid epithelium,
(c) simple columnar epithelium,
(d) stratified columnar epithelium,
(e) pseudostratified ciliated epithelium,
(f) transitional epithelium

epithelium [epɪθiːlɪəm] *n term, pl* **-ia**   *syn* **epithelial** [iː] **tissue** *n term*

purely cellular avascular[1] layer covering all the free surfaces [ɜː], cutaneous [kjuːteɪnɪəs], mucous [mjuːkəs], and serous [ɪə] structures

epithelial[2] *adj term* • **(re)epithelialization**[3] *n* • **reepithelialize**[4] *v* • **epithelioma**[5] *n term* • **epithelioid**[6] *adj*

» Normally epithelium is bound [aʊ] tightly [taɪt-] to the underlying [aɪ] dermis through its undulating [ʌ] basement [eɪ] membrane[7] and epidermal [ɜː] appendages[8] [-ɪdʒɪz]. The cornea is severely [ɪə] damaged and epithelial strands hang from the corneal surface [ɜː].

Use alveolar [ɪə]/ bronchial [k]/ urogenital[9] [dʒe]/ corneal / retinal pigment[10] / surface[11] **epithelium** • ductal [ʌ]/ glandular[12] / germinal[13] [dʒɜːr-]/ mucus-secreting [iː]/ ciliated[14] [sɪlɪeɪtɪd] **epithelium** • **epithelium**-lined[15] [aɪ] • **epithelial** bridge[16] / appendages / barrier[17] / debris[18] [iː]/ lining[19] • **epithelial** denudation / defect [iː]/ damage / cyst[20] [sɪst] • **epithelial cell** layer [eɪ]/ membrane / renewal[21] [(j)uː]/ proliferation / loss[22] • non/ intra/ trans/ uro/ myo/ lympho/ neuro**epithelial** • **subepithelial** hemorrhage[23] [-ɪdʒ]/ edema [iː]/ deposits • rate of[24] **epithelialization** • **epithelioid** cells[25] / sarcoma / granuloma • basal [eɪ] cell[26] / sebaceous [eɪʃ] **epithelioma**

---

lining [aɪ] *n clin & term*

rel **sheath**[1] [ʃiːθ], **envelope**[2], **coating**[3] [oʊ] *n term*

layer of cells which forms the inside surface [ɜː] of an organ or tube [t(j)uːb]

line[4] *v term* • **lined** *adj* • **(en)sheathed**[5] *adj* • **envelope**[6] *v* • **coat**[7] *v*

» Histologically, dilated [eɪ] lymphatics have a thin endothelial cell lining overlying a delicate network of elastin and collagen. A layer of water lines the alveolar surface. The alveolar lining cells[8] are swollen. On incision [sɪ] of the posterior rectus sheath the peritoneum [iː] is exposed. Fibronectin is a glycoprotein coating the surface of the mucosa. The dorsal vein [eɪ] complex is enveloped within a 2 cm layer of fibroareolar tissue.

Use epithelial[9] / smooth [uː]/ surface / serous / endothelial[10] / mucosal[11] **lining** • peritoneal / gut [ʌ] or bowel[12] [aʊ]/ uterine / rectal / synovial[13] **lining** • **lining cells** / layer[14] / membrane / of the nose[15] / of the tendon sheath • columnar-/ arachnoid- [æk]/ epithelium/ mucosally / synovial-/ squamous epithelium[16]-**lined** • fibrous / fascial [fæʃ(ɪ)əl] / (flexor) tendon[17] **sheath** • synovial / nerve [ɜː]/ myelin[18] [aɪ] **sheath** • fascial / cell / viral[19] [aɪ] **envelope**

Epithel(ium), -gewebe

gefäßlos[1] epithelial, Epithel-[2] Epithelisierung, -sation, Epithelbildung[3] reepithelisieren[4] Epitheliom(a)[5] epitheloid, -ähnlich[6] wellenförmige Basalmembran[7] epidermale Anhangsgebilde[8] Urothel, Übergangsepithel, E. transitionale[9] Pigmentepithel d. Retina[10] Oberflächenepithel[11] Drüsenepithel[12] Keimepithel[13] Flimmerepithel[14] m. E. ausgekleidet[15] Epithelbrücke[16] Epithelgrenze[17] Epithelreste[18] epitheliale Auskleidung[19] Epithelzyste[20] Epithelzellerneuerung, Reepithelisation[21] Epithelzellverlust[22] subepitheliale Blutung[23] Epithelisationsrate[24] Epitheloidzellen[25] Basaliom, Epithelioma basocellulare[26]

7

Auskleidung

Scheide, Hülle, Ummantelung[1] Hülle, Schale, Umhüllung[2] Deckschicht, Belag; Beschichtung, Überzug[3] auskleiden[4] ummantelt, -hüllt[5] einhüllen[6] überziehen, bedecken[7] Alveolarepithelzellen[8] epitheliale Auskleidung[9] Endothel[10] Schleimhaut(auskleidung)[11] Darmauskleidung[12] Synovialis, Synovialhaut[13] auskleidende Schicht[14] Nasenschleimhaut[15] mit Plattenepithel ausgekleidet[16] Sehnenscheide[17] Mark-, Myelinscheide[18] Virushülle[19]

8

Histology | MEDICAL SCIENCE 375

serosa [sɪərouzə] *n term*   *syn* **serosal** *or* **serous** [sɪə·əs] **membrane** *n term*
type of m*e*mbrane which lines body c*a*vities that do not open to the exterior and the *o*rgans cont*ai*ned [eɪ] within them
serous[1] [ɪə·] *adj term* • **subserosa**[2] *n* • **serositis**[3] [aɪ] *n* • **seroma**[4] *n* • **sero-** *comb*
» The periton*ea*l [iː] layer of the m*e*sentery env*e*lops the b*o*wel [aʊ] and is called the v*i*sceral [ɪs] periton*eu*m[5], *or serosa*. *The esophagus has no serosal layer.*
Use intestinal / col*o*nic **serosa** • diaphragm*a*tic **serosal membranes** • **serosal** surface / tear[6] [eə·]/ fold [oʊ]/ refl*e*ction[7] • **serosal** inflamm*a*tion[3] / cyst[8] • **serous** c*a*vity[9] / fluid / discharge[10] • **serous** eff*u*sion[11] [juːʒ]/ ot*i*tis [aɪ] m*e*dia[12] [iː] • **sero**fibrinous [aɪ] /muc*oi*d /m*u*scular [ʌ] /s*e*rous suture[13] [suːtʃə·]

stratified epithelium *n term*
                                      opposite **simple epithelium**[1] *n term*
epith*e*lial tissue cons*i*sting of two or more layers [leɪə·z] of cells
pseudostratified[2] [suːdoʊ-] *adj term* • **stratification**[3] *n* • **stratify**[4] *v*
» *These cystic* [sɪstɪk] *tumors cont*ai*n a mass of* desquamated epith*e*lium[5] *produced by stratified squ*a*mous* [skweɪməs] *epithelial lining. The collecting d*u*cts* [ʌ] *are composed of simple cub*oi*dal c*o*lumnar epithelium, which becomes taller on examin*a*tion from the c*o*rtex to the med*u*lla* [ʌ‖ʊ]*.*
Use **stratified** squ*a*mous epith*e*lium[6] • **pseudostratified** epith*e*lium[7] / c*o*lumnar epith*e*lium[8]

columnar [kəlʌmnə·] **epithelium** *n term*
                                      sim **cuboidal** [kjuːbɔɪdᵊl] **epithelium**[1] *n term*
epith*e*lial tissue whose cells are shaped like c*o*lumns [kɒləmz]
» *V*i*lli* [aɪ] *are c*o*vered* [ʌ] *by c*o*lumnar epith*e*lial cells that have a* br*u*sh [ʌ] *border*[2] *consisting of microvilli 1 μm in height* [haɪt]*. Histologically, simple mucoc*e*les* [siː] *of the appendix are lined by* fl*a*ttened cub*oi*dal epith*e*lium[3] *or no epithelium at all.*
Use **columnar** (epithelial) cells[4] /-lined esophagus / muc*o*sa • tall / c*i*liated[5] [sɪ] **columnar epithelium** • squamo**columnar** j*u*nction[6] [dʒʌŋkʃᵊn]

squamous [skweɪməs] **or pavement** [eɪ] **epithelium** *n term*
flat, scaly[1] [skeɪli] or plate-like epith*e*lial tissue
squame[2] *n term* → U114-7 • **squamo-** *comb*
desquamation *n* → U56-20 • **squamo-** *comb*
» *Cub*oi*dal type II cells and sq*ua*mous epithelium c*o*vered den*u*ded* [uː] *alv*eo*lar b*a*sement m*e*mbranes. These t*u*mors show both squ*a*mous and adenocarcin*o*matous components.*
Use simple[3] / strat*i*fied[4] / c*o*rnified[5] **squamous epithelium** • at*y*pical / (non)keratinized[5] **squamous epithelium** • **squamous** cell carcin*o*ma[6] / patches • **squamous** metapl*a*sia[7] • intraepithelial l*e*sion • papulo/ baso**squamous** • adeno**squamous** carcin*o*ma[8] • **squamo**ciliary /c*o*lumnar

transitional [trænsɪʃᵊnᵊl] **epithelium** *n term*
highly dist*e*nsible[1] pseudostratified epithelium in the urinary tract with pol*y*ploid superficial [ɪʃ] cells which are cub*oi*dal in the rel*a*xed but broad and squ*a*mous in the dist*e*nded state
trans*i*tion[2] *n term* • **posttrans*i*tional** *adj* • **trans*i*t**[3] *n* • **trans*i*tory**[4] *adj*
» *Each pap*i*lla is surr*ou*nded by transitional cell epithelium, the c*o*mplex referred to as a c*a*lyx. These p*o*lyps consist of a f*i*brous str*o*ma c*o*vered by benign* [aɪ] *transitional epithelium.*
Use **transitional** cell (carcin*o*ma)[5] / layer / configur*a*tion • **transitional** state[6] / zone[7] [zoʊn]/ p*e*riod [ɪə·] • sharp / abr*u*pt [ʌ]/ smooth[8] [uː] **transition** • gr*a*dual [ædʒ]/ menop*au*sal [ɔː] **transition** • **transition** zone[7] / from stage 2 to 3

Serosa, Tunica serosa, seröse Haut
serös; serumartig, -haltig[1] Subserosa, subseröse Bindegewebsschicht[2] Serositis, Entzündung seröser Häute[3] Serom[4] Peritoneum viscerale, Serosa[5] Serosa(ein)riss[6] Peritonealduplikatur[7] Serosazyste[8] seröse Höhle[9] seröses Sekret[10] seröser Erguss[11] seröse Mittelohrentzündung/ Otitis media[12] seroseröse Naht[13]

9

mehrschichtiges Epithel
einschichtiges Epithel[1] mehrreihig, pseudostratifiziert, scheingeschichtet[2] Schichtung, Schichtenbildung[3] schichten, S. bilden[4] abgeschilferte Epithelzellen[5] mehrschichtiges Plattenepithel[6] mehrreihiges/ pseudostratifiziertes E.[7] mehrreihiges Zylinderepithel[8]

10

Zylinderepithel, hochprismat. E., Epithelium columnare
kubisches Epithel, E. cuboideum[1] Bürstensaum[2] flaches kubisches Epithel[3] hochprismat. Epithelzellen, Zylinderepithelzellen[4] Zylinderepithel m. Flimmerbesatz[5] Plattenepithel-Zylinderepithel-Grenze[6]

11

Plattenepithel, E. squamosum
schuppenartig[1] Schuppe, Squama[2] einschichtiges Plattenepithel[3] mehrschichtiges P.[4] verhorntes P.[5] Plattenepithelkarzinom[6] Plattenepithelmetaplasie[7] adenosquamöses Karzinom[8]

12

Übergangsepithel, Epithelium transitionale
dehnbar[1] Übergang[2] Durchtritt, Passage[3] vorübergehend, transitorisch[4] Übergangszell-, Transitionalzellkarzinom[5] Übergangsstadium[6] Übergangszone[7] fließender Übergang[8]

13

endothelium [endəˈθiːlɪəm] *n term, pl* **-ia**   *rel* **mesothelium**[1] [ˈmezə-] *n term*
layer of flat cells that line[2] the blood and lymphatic vessels[3] and the heart [ɑː]
(**reticulo/ sub**)**endothelial**[4] [iː] *adj term* • **endothel-** *comb* • **mesothelial**[5] *adj*

» Trauma [ɒː] to the endothelium of the vein wall resulting in exposure of subendothelial tissues to platelets[6] [eɪ] in the venous [iː] blood may initiate [ɪʃ] thrombosis.

Use capillary[7] / vascular / arterial / corneal / sinusoidal[8] **endothelium** • **endothelial** cells[9] / lining / wall / surface • **endothelial** permeability / (cell) adhesion [iːʒ]/ (dys)function • **endothelial** cell growth factor[10] / injury / swelling / cancer[11] • **reticuloendothelial** cells / system[12] / organs / iron stores / tumors • **endothel**ioma[11] /iosis /ialization • diaphragmatic / c(o)elomic [sɪˈloʊmɪk] **mesothelium** • **mesothelial** cells[13] / cyst [sɪst]/ lining [aɪ] • **mesothel**ioma • pleural[14] [ʊə] **mesothelioma**

Endothel(ium)
Mesothel(ium)[1] auskleiden[2] Lymphgefäße[3] endothelial[4] mesothelial[5] Blutplättchen, Thrombozyten[6] Kapillarendothel[7] Sinusoidendothel[8] Endothelzellen[9] Endothelzellwachstumsfaktor[10] Endotheliom[11] retikuloendotheliales System (RES), Monozyten-Makrophagen-System (MMS)[12] Mesothelzellen[13] Pleuramesotheliom[14]   14

---

membrane [ˈmembreɪn] *n*   *rel* **lamina**[1] *n, pl* **-ae** [iː], **-as**, **septum**[2] *n term, pl* **-a**
thin sheet [iː] or layer of pliable[3] [aɪ] tissue, serving [ɜː] as a covering [ʌ] or envelope[4] of a part, e.g. the lining[5] of a cavity, a partition [ɪʃ] or septum, or to connect two structures
(**peri/ pseudo**)**membranous**[6] *adj term* • **pseudomembrane**[7] *n* • **septal** *adj* • **laminar**[8] *adj term* • **laminated** *adj* • **lamination**[9] *n* • **septate**[10] *adj*

» The bowel [aʊ] wall has a very thick, shaggy[11] membrane covering it. The ventricular defect was located in the membranous portion [ˈpɔːrʃən] of the septum.

Use to pass across a / separated by a **membrane** • (red blood) cell / cutaneous **membrane** • cricothyroid[12] [kraɪkoʊˈθaɪrɔɪd] / synovial[13] **membrane** • tympanic[14] / plasma[15] **membrane** • mesenteric / amniotic **membrane** • **membranous** cells / septum / trachea[16] [k] • **membranous** urethra[17] [iː]/ labyrinth[18] / obstruction [ʌ]/ • nasal[19] [eɪ]/ atrial [eɪ] **septum** • interventricular[20] / vesicovaginal[21] **septum** • **septal** leaflet[22] [iː]/ cartilage [-lɪdʒ]/ defect • **septal** rupture [ʌ]/ deviation[23] [diːviˈeɪʃən] • **septate** cells / appearance • **septate** hyphae [ˈhaɪfiː]/ uterus[24] [juː] • **pseudomembranous** colitis[25] [aɪ]/ croup[26] [ʊ] • basal[27] [eɪ]/ internal / elastic **lamina** • intimal / orbital[28] **lamina** • **lamina** propria / cribrosa / densa • **laminar** fibrosis

---

Membran(a)
Platte, Schicht, Lamina[1] Septum, Scheide-, Trennwand[2] geschmeidig[3] Hülle[4] Auskleidung[5] membranös, häutig[6] Pseudomembran[7] laminar[8] Schichtung, Lamination[9] septiert[10] zottig[11] Conus elasticus laryngis[12] Membrana synovialis[13] Trommelfell, M. tympani[14] Zellmembran, Plasmalemm[15] membranöse Trachearückwand[16] Pars membranacea (d. männl. Harnröhre)[17] häutiges Labyrinth[18] Nasenscheidewand, Septum nasi[19] S. interventriculare, Kammerscheidewand[20] S. vesicovaginale[21] Cuspis septalis[22] Septumdeviation[23] Uterus septus[24] pseudomembranöse Kolitis[25] echter Krupp[26] Lamina basalis, Basalmembran[27] Lamina orbitalis[28]   15

---

basement [ˈbeɪsmənt] **membrane** *n term*
thin extracellular layer which attaches [ætʃ] the epithelium to the underlying [aɪ] connective tissue and is made up of a superficial [ɪʃ] basal lamina and an underlying reticular lamina

» Human skin is a sandwich of two distinctive compartments, the epidermis and dermis, separated by a basement membrane. Circulating [ɜː] anti-basement membrane antibodies[1] were found in the serum.

Use **basement** epithelium / tissue • glomerular[2] / acinar [æs]/ (dermal-)epidermal / capillary **basement membrane** • (sub)endothelial / tubular / alveolar[3] [ɪə] **basement membrane** • underlying / denuded[4] [uː]/ thin **basement membrane** • **basement membrane** zone / thickening[5]

Basalmembran, -lamina
Antibasalmembran-Antikörper[1] Glomerulusbasalmembran[2] alveoläre Basalmembran[3] freiliegende Basalmembran[4] Verdickung d. Basalmembran[5]

16

---

mucosa [mjuːˈkoʊzə] *n term*   *syn* **mucous** [ˈmjuːkəs] **membrane** *n clin*
mucus-producing tissue lining various tubular structures consisting of epithelium, lamina propria, and a layer of smooth [uː] muscle [mʌsl] in the digestive [dʒe] tract
mucosal *adj term* • **mucus**[1] [ˈmjuːkəs] *n* • **mucoid**[2] *adj* • **mucin**[3] [ˈmjuːsən] *n term* • **mucinous**[4] *adj* • **muco-** *comb*

» The normal relationship of parietal [aɪ] cell mucosa to antral mucosa was changed. Mucus is the clear viscid[5] [s] secretion [iːʃ] of the mucous membranes, consisting of mucin, epithelial cells, leukocytes [uː], and various inorganic salts suspended in water. Once the mucosal barrier[6] is breached [briːtʃt] by ulceration [s], the patient can become septic.

Use small bowel[7] [aʊ]/ gastric[8] / airway **mucosa** • buccal[9] [ʌ]/ bladder / nasal **mucosa** • oral / intestinal *or* gut [ʌ] *or* bowel[10] **mucosa** • underlying / thickened / normal-appearing **mucosa** • friable[11] [aɪ]/ pale[12] [eɪ] **mucosa** • sub**mucosa**[13] [ʌ] • **mucosal** changes[14] / bleeding [iː] / **mucosal** edema [iː]/ tag[15] / prolapse • **mucosal** injury / tear[16] [teə]/ damage • **mucosal** ulcer [ʌlsə]/ thickening[17] / inflammation[18] • dry / pale[12] **mucous membrane** • irritation of the / oral **mucous membrane** • **mucous** lining[19] [aɪ]/ glands[20] / plug[21] [ʌ] • **mucoid** secretion[22] [iːʃ]/ sputum [(j)uː]/ discharge[22] [-tʃɑːrdʒ] • **mucoid** stool [uː]/ diarrhea [iː]/ impaction[23] • **muco**ciliary [sɪ] clearance[24] /cutaneous junction [ʌ] • **muco**purulent [jʊə] sputum[25] • **muco**cele [-siːl] /lytics[26] [ɪ] /sitis [aɪ] /viscidosis[27]

Schleimhaut, Mukosa, Tunica mucosa
Schleim, Mucus[1] mukös, schleimig[2] Muzin, Mukoid, Schleimstoff[3] muzinös, schleimig[4] zähflüssig, viskös[5] Schleimhautbarriere[6] Dünndarmschleimhaut[7] Magenschleimhaut[8] Wangenschleimhaut[9] Darmschleimhaut[10] rissige S.[11] blasse S.[12] (Tunica) submucosa[13] Schleimhautveränderungen[14] Schleimhautfetzen[15] Schleimhaut(ein)riss[16] Schleimhautverdickung[17] Schleimhautentzündung[18] Schleimhautausbleidung[19] muköse Drüsen, Glandulae mucosae[20] Schleimpfropf[21] schleimige Absonderung[22] Mucoid impaction, Schleimverlegung v. Bronchien[23] mukoziliäre Clearance[24] schleimig-eitriger Auswurf[25] Muko-, Sekretolytika, Schleimlöser[26] Mukoviszidose, zyst. Fibrose[27]   17

Histology   MEDICAL SCIENCE 377

goblet cells [gɒːblət selz] *n term*

    syn **beaker** [iː] *or* **chalice** [tʃælɪs] **cells** *n term*

special epithelial cells that become distended apically [eɪ] with accumulations of mucus for lubrication

» Like the nose, the sinuses [aɪ] are lined with respiratory epithelium that includes mucus-producing goblet cells and ciliated [sɪlɪeɪtɪd] *cells¹*.

Use conjunctival² [dʒʌ] **goblet cells** • **goblet cell** hyperplasia [eɪʒ]/ carcinoid³

Becherzellen

Flimmerzellen¹ Becherzellen d. Bindehaut² Becherzellkarzinoid³

18

extracellular matrix [eɪ] *n term*   *rel* **interstitium** *or* **interstice¹** [-ɪs] *n term*

intercellular material of connective tissue made up of protein fibers [aɪ] and ground [aʊ] substance [ʌ]

intracellular² *adj term* • **intercellular³** *adj* • **interstitial⁴** [ʃ] *adj*

» The interaction of cells with their scaffolding⁵ (extracellular matrix and basement membrane) involves adhesion [iːʒ] through specific receptors [se]. Microscopically, edema [iː] of the interstitium was found. Complications involve airway obstruction [ʌ] or interstitial pulmonary [ʊ‖ʌ] infiltration.

Use **extracellular matrix** constituents [ɪtʃ] *or* components⁶ [oʊ] • *extracellular matrix* proteins⁷ /-bound [aʊ] ligands⁸ [aɪ] • (intra)cellular / organic / germinal [dʒɜː]/ connective tissue **matrix** • collagen / cartilage⁹ / bone¹⁰ / nail¹¹ **matrix** / **matrix** cells / deposition / accumulation • **matrix** production / repair • *intercellular* bridge¹² / space¹³ / adhesion molecules • lung *or* pulmonary¹⁴ / renal [iː]/ tubular [(j)uː] **interstitium** • *interstitial* space¹ / cells¹⁵ / stroma • *interstitial* fluid¹⁶ / fibrosis • *interstitial* infiltrate / edema¹⁷ • *interstitial* emphysema [iː]/ lung disease • *interstitial* pneumonitis¹⁸ [n(j)uː-]/ nephritis [aɪ] • *interstitial* cystitis [sɪst-]/ radiotherapy¹⁹

Interzellularsubstanz, extrazelluläre Matrix

Interstitium, Zwischenraum¹ intrazellulär² interzellulär³ interstitiell⁴ Gerüstsubstanz, Zellgerüst⁵ Bestandteile d. Interzellularsubstanz⁶ extrazelluläre Matrixproteine⁷ extrazelluläre Liganden⁸ Knorpelmatrix, -grundsubstanz, M. cartilaginea⁹ Knochenmatrix, Osteoid¹⁰ Nagelbett, -matrix, M. unguis¹¹ Interzellularbrücke¹² Interzellularraum¹³ Lungeninterstitium¹⁴ Leydig-(Zwischen)zellen¹⁵ interstitielle Flüssigkeit¹⁶ int. Ödem¹⁷ int. Pneumonie¹⁸ int. Strahlentherapie¹⁹

19

organ [ɔːrɡən] *n*   *rel* **organelle¹**, **organism²**, **body³** *n term*

differentiated body structure such as the heart or liver performing a specific function in an organism

(in)organic⁴ [æ] *adj term* • **multiorgan** *adj* • **organo-** *comb* • **bodily⁵** *adj clin*

» Progressive sepsis led to multiple [ʌ] organ failure affecting the respiratory, renal, hepatic, and immune systems. The gallbladder [ɔː] is a pear-shaped [peɚ-] organ adherent [ɪɚ] to the undersurface of the liver. Mitochondria [k] are intracellular organelles that generate energy via a series [ɪɚ] of respiratory chain complexes. Pain has the critical signal function of alerting [ɜː] the organism to potentially harmful tissue damage. Tissue cells contain most of the body's potassium.

Use human / paired⁶ [peɚd] / hollow⁷ **organ** • target⁸ [ɑː]/ donor⁹ [oʊ]/ end¹⁰-**organ** • visceral¹¹ [ɪs]/ pelvic / reproductive¹² [ʌ] **organs** • vital¹³ [aɪ] / adjacent¹⁴ [dʒeɪs] / internal¹¹ **organs** • **organ** (dys)function [ʌ]/ system [ɪ] • **organ** perfusion [juːʒ]/ injury • **organ** donation¹⁵ / damage¹⁶ • **organ** failure¹⁷ [eɪ]/ transplantation • **organ** preservation¹⁸ / rejection¹⁹ [dʒe]/-confined [aɪ] cancer • infective / pathogenic [dʒe] *or* causative [ɔː] micro**organism** • **multiorgan** system / failure • **organic** disease²⁰ / causes²¹ / impotence²² / acids • **organic** mercury [ɜː]/ solvent / chemistry [k] • **organo**megaly²³ /genesis [dʒe] /phosphate poisoning • vertebral / vitreous²⁴ [ɪ]/ ciliary / carotid²⁵ / foreign **body** • cell / mamillary / corporal²⁶ **bodies** • inclusion²⁷ [uːʒ]/ Donovan / Heinz / ketone [iː] **bodies** • **bodily** contact / secretions [iːʃ] • **fluids**²⁸ • **bodily** wastes [eɪ]/ harm²⁹ [ɑː] • **body** cavity / fluids²⁸ / temperature • **body** surface³⁰ / fat³¹ / image³²

Organ, Organon, Organum

(Zell)organelle¹ Organismus; Keim, Erreger² Körper, Corpus³ (an)organisch⁴ körperlich, physisch⁵ paarig angelegtes Organ⁶ Hohlorgan⁷ Ziel-, Erfolgsorgan⁸ Spenderorgan⁹ Endorgan¹⁰ innere O.¹¹ Geschlechtsorgane, Genitalien¹² lebenswichtige O.¹³ Nachbarorgane¹⁴ Organspende¹⁵ Organschädigung, -schaden¹⁶ Organversagen¹⁷ Organkonservierung, -erhaltung¹⁸ Organabstoßung¹⁹ organ. Leiden²⁰ organ. Ursachen²¹ organ. bedingte Impotenz²² Vergrößerung innerer Organe, Viszero-, Organomegalie²³ Glaskörper, Corpus vitreum²⁴ Glomus caroticum, Karotisdrüse, -körper²⁵ Schwellkörper (i. Penis)²⁶ Einschlusskörperchen²⁷ Körperflüssigkeiten²⁸ Körperverletzung²⁹ Körperoberfläche³⁰ Körperfett³¹ Körperschema³²

20

viscera [vɪsɚə] *n term pl, sing* **viscus** [vɪskəs] *rare*

the internal organs, esp. those in the abdominal cavity

visceral¹ *adj term* • **splanchnic** [k] *adj* • **evisceration²** *n* • **viscer(o)-** *comb*

» Pain referred [ɜː] to the spine [aɪ] may arise from abdominal or pelvic viscera. Inflammatory involvement of the visceral pleura resulted in a serous pleural effusion³ [juːʒ]. Rupture [ʌ] of all layers of the abdominal wall and extrusion of abdominal viscera is called evisceration.

Use abdominal / pelvic⁴ / thoracic [æs] / hollow⁵ **viscera** • solid⁶ / herniated [ɜː]/ adjacent [eɪ] **viscera** • **visceral** organ (involvement)⁷ / cavities / peritoneum [iː]/ vessels • **visceral** pleura⁸ [ʊɚ]/ smooth [uː] muscle / reflex⁹ [iː] • **visceral** pain¹⁰ / injury / parasitic disease / herniation • **splanchnic** nerves [ɜː]/ vessels / (vascular) bed / blood flow / viscera • **viscero**parietal [aɪ] /peritoneal [iː] /megaly¹¹ • **visceralgia¹⁰** [-ældʒ(ɪ)ə]

Viscera, Eingeweide

viszeral¹ Eingeweideprolaps, Eviszeration, Exenteration² seröser Pleuraerguss³ Beckenorgane⁴ Hohlorgane⁵ parenchymatöse Organe⁶ Befall innerer Organe⁷ Lungenfell, Pleura visceralis⁸ viszeraler Reflex⁹ viszeraler Schmerz, Viszeralschmerz¹⁰ Viszero-, Splanchnomegalie¹¹

21

MEDICAL SCIENCE

parenchyma [pərɛnkɪmə] n term

syn **parenchymal tissue** n,
rel **stroma**[1] n term

the functional tissue of an organ as opposed to the supportive (stromal) structures [ʌ]

(intra/ extra)**parenchymal** or **-matous**[2] adj term • **stromal**[3] [stroʊməl] adj

» Leydig cell tumors often compress the surrounding parenchyma. Several layers of soft endothelial cells are supported by a sparse fibrous stroma. All patients except for those with renal parenchymal damage did well after ureteral reconstruction.

Use brain / breast [e]/ renal[4] [iː]/ lung or pulmonary **parenchyma** • hepatic or liver[5] [ɪ]/ adjacent[6] **parenchyma** • **parenchymal** organs[7] / lesion [iːɜ]/ changes / involvement[8] • **parenchymal** infiltrate / necrosis[9] / damage[10] • endometrial[11] [iː]/ corneal / ovarian[12] / prostatic **stroma** • fibrous [aɪ]/ interstitial / well-vascularized **stroma** • **stromal** cells / component / compartment[13] / tissue[1] • **stromal** collagen / endometriosis[14] • **stromal** keratitis [aɪ]/ sarcoma / invasion[15] [eɪɜ]

cortex n term, pl cortices [kɔːrtəsiːz]

rel **medulla**[1] [ʌ‖ʊ] n term

outer portion of organs such as the kidney, as distinguished from the inner or medullary portion

cortical[2] adj term • **medullary**[3] [mɪdʌləɹi‖mɛdjələɹi] adj • **cortico-** comb

» Histologically, the cortex is composed of three zones of cells called, from cortex to medulla, the zona glomerulosa, the zona fasciculata, and the zona reticularis. At autopsy [ɔː], the cut surface of the polycystic [sɪ] kidney showed extensive parenchymal replacement of cortical and medullary cysts [sɪsts].

Use (ad)renal[4] [iː]/ bone or bony[5] / cerebral[6] **cortex** • cerebellar / motor / association **cortex** • temporal lobe / visual[7] [ɪɜ]/ auditory [ɔː] **cortex** • **cortical** steroids / blindness[8] / involvement • **cortical** thinning[9] [ɪ]/ bone[5] • outer[10] / inner / (ad)renal **medulla** • **medullary** tissue[1] / interstitium / cavity[11] • **medullary** center / pyramid [ɪ]/ sponge [spʌndʒ]/ kidney[12] • **cortico**spinal [aɪ] tract[13] /medullary junction[14] [dʒʌŋkʃ°n] • **cortico**bulbar [ʌ] pathway[15] /steroid /tropin [oʊ]

Unit 87   Anatomy
Related Units: **21** Head & Neck, **22** Trunk, **23** Extremities, **86** Histology

anatomy [ənætəmi] n term

rel **topography**[1] n, **histology**[2] n term → U86-1

(i) the structure [ʌ] of the body (ii) study, classification and description of body structures

anatomic(al) [ænətɒːmɪk] adj term • **topographic** adj • **anatomist**[3] [æ] n

» The incision [sɪɜ] was closed anatomically. There are great individual variations in coronary anatomy. The anatomically short female urethra [iː] facilitates[4] [sɪ] the ascent[5] [se] of organisms from the introitus into the bladder. The pericardium stabilizes the heart [ɑː] in anatomic position [ɪʃ]. Topographically, the skin lesion [iːɜ] was irregular and partly raised [eɪ].

Use topographic or regional[6] [iːdʒ]/ functional[7] [ʌ]/ descriptive or systematic[8] **anatomy** • general comparative / human **anatomy** • histologic[9] / pathologic / surgical [ɜː] **anatomy** • macroscopic or gross[10] [oʊ]/ microscopic[9] **anatomy** • **anatomic** location[11] / layer [eɪ]/ structure / position[12] • **anatomic** site / alterations or changes[13] / abnormality / variations / features [fiːtʃəz] • **anatomical** appearance / landmark[14] / malformation • **topographic** examination / location / relationships[15] / map[16]

plane [pleɪn] n & adj term   syn **planum** [pleɪnəm] n, rel **plate**[1] [pleɪt] n term

(n, i) flat surface
(ii) imaginary surface defined by three reference points or by extension through an axis

(multi/ bi)**planar** [baɪpleɪnəɹ] adj term • **plate-like**[2] adj

» The lesion extended deep to the plane of the facial [eɪʃ] nerve [ɜː]. The skeletal muscle [mʌsl] end plate[3] bridges the neuromuscular [ʌ] junction [dʒʌŋkʃ°n].

Use horizontal / transverse [ɜː]/ sagittal[5] [ædʒ]/ median[6] [iː]/ coronal [oʊ] or frontal[7] / vertical [ɜː] **plane** • nail[8] / epiphyseal [ɪ] or growth[9] / volar[10] / urethral [iː]/ cribriform[11] [ɪ] **plate** • tarsal[12] [ɑː]/ bone[13] / motor end[3] **plate**

Parenchym
Stroma[1] parenchymatös[2] stromal, Stroma-[3] Nierenparenchym[4] Leberparenchym[5] angrenzendes P.[6] parenchymatöse Organe[7] Parenchymbeteiligung[8] Parenchymnekrose[9] Parenchymschaden, -schädigung[10] Endometriumstroma[11] Ovarialstroma[12] stromales Kompartiment[13] Stromaendometriose, Stromatose[14] Stromainfiltration[15]

22

Kortex, Rinde
Medulla, Mark[1] kortikal[2] markhaltig, medullär[3] Nebennierenrinde, Cortex glandulae suprarenalis, NNR[4] Kortikalis, Knochenrinde[5] Großhirnrinde, Cortex cerebri[6] Sehrinde, visueller Kortex[7] Rindenblindheit[8] Knochensubstanzverlust[9] Außenzone d. (Nieren)marks[10] Markhöhle, Cavitas medullaris[11] (Mark)schwammniere[12] Tractus corticospinalis, Pyramidenbahn[13] Mark-Rinden-Grenze[14] kortikobulbäre Bahn, Tractus corticonuclearis[15]

23

Anatomie, Körperbau, Aufbau, Struktur
Topografie, Lageverhältnis[1] Histologie[2] Anatom[3] ermöglicht[4] Aufsteigen[5] topografische Anatomie[6] funktionelle A.[7] systematische A.[8] mikroskop. A., Histologie[9] makroskop. A.[10] anatomische Lage[11] anatom. Lage/ Stellung/ Position[12] anatom. Veränderungen[13] anatom. Orientierungspunkt[14] topograf. Verhältnisse/ Beziehungen[15] topografische Karte[16]

1

Ebene, Planum; flach
Platte[1] plattenförmig[2] Muskelendplatte, motor. E.[3] Transversalebene[4] Sagittalebene[5] Medianebene[6] Frontalebene[7] Nagelplatte[8] Epiphysenfuge[9] Palmaraponeurose[10] Siebbeinplatte, Lamina cribrosa[11] Lidplatte, Tarsus[12] Knochenplatte[13]

2

Anatomy   MEDICAL SCIENCE 379

axis [æksɪs] *n term, pl* **axes** [-iːz]   *rel* **pole¹** [poʊl] *n term*

central line passing through a spherical body between its two poles
axial² [æksɪəl] *adj term* • **off-axis³** *adj* • **polar** [poʊlɚ] *adj*
» Angulation of the esophageal [dʒiː] axis was noted above the tumor. The ECG shows left axis deviation [eɪʃ]. The lesion is located cephalad to the superior [ɪɚ] pole of the thyroid [aɪ] gland.
Use long(itudinal)⁴ / short / vertical⁵ **axis** • central / cerebrospinal [aɪ] **axis** • hypothalamic-pituitary [(j)uː]/ optic *or* visual⁶ [ɪʒ]/ pelvic⁷ **axis** • **axial** skeleton⁸ / plane / parallelism⁹ / surface of a tooth • **axial** alignment¹⁰ [aɪ]/ inclination¹¹ / view¹² / loading¹³ [oʊ] • upper renal¹⁴ [iː]/ lower / inferior / superior **pole** • anterior / posterior / frontal **pole** • temporal / occipital¹⁵ **pole** • **pole of the** testis¹⁶ / breast [e]/ patella

Achse, Axis
Pol¹ axial, achsenförmig, Achsen-² aus der Achse³ Längs-, Longitudinalachse⁴ Körperlängs-, Vertikalachse⁵ Sehachse, Axis opticus⁶ Beckenachse, Axis pelvis⁷ Achsen-, Stammskelett⁸ Achsenparallelität⁹ Achsenausrichtung¹⁰ Achsenfehlstellung, -neigung¹¹ Axialaufnahme¹² axiale Belastung¹³ oberer Nierenpol, Extremitas superior renis¹⁴ Polus occipitalis¹⁵ Hodenpol, Extremitas testis¹⁶   3

---

aspect [æspekt] *n term*   *sim* **surface¹** [sɜːrfəs] *n & adj, rel* **view²** [vjuː] *n term*

the side of a structure facing³ [eɪs] a specific direction
surface⁴ *v* • **view⁵** *v* • **viewpoint⁶** *n* • **in view of⁷** *phr*
» There was numbness⁸ [ʌ] of the anterolateral aspect of the calf⁹ [kæf] and dorsum of the foot. You should review the radiographic aspects of his condition. Aortography should include oblique [oʊbliːk] views¹⁰ of the thigh [θaɪ] and leg arteries. Suggestive [dʒe] findings include scattered white nodules over the parietal [aɪ] surfaces and adhesions [iːʒ] between adjacent [eɪ] organs.
Use internal¹¹ [ɜː]/ external / medial [iː] **aspect** • posterior / lateral / posterolateral **aspect** • dorsal / panoramic¹² **view** • lateral¹³ / anteroposterior¹⁴ **view** • to bring/come into¹⁵ **view** • body¹⁶ / mucosal [mjʊkoʊzəl] **surface** • bone / joint¹⁷ [dʒɔɪnt] **surface** • exposed¹⁸ [oʊ]/ outer¹⁹ **surface** • inner / cut²⁰ **surface** • **surface** area²¹ / trauma²² [ɒː] • **surface** damage [-ɪdʒ]/ tension²³

Aspekt, Fläche, Seite, Teil
(Ober)fläche; oberflächlich¹ (An)sicht, Aufnahme² ausgerichtet/zugewandt sein³ auftauchen; verblenden, beschichten⁴ betrachten⁵ Sicht, Standpunkt⁶ wegen⁷ Taubheitsgefühl⁸ Wade⁹ Schrägaufnahmen¹⁰ Innenseite, -fläche¹¹ Panoramaaufnahme¹² Seitenaufnahme, -ansicht¹³ ap-Aufnahme¹⁴ sichtbar werden¹⁵ Körperoberfläche¹⁶ Gelenkfläche¹⁷ exponierte Fläche¹⁸ Außenseite, -fläche¹⁹ Schnittfläche²⁰ Oberfläche²¹ oberflächl. Verletzung²² Oberflächenspannung²³ 4

---

section [sekʃən] *n & v term*   *rel* **cross-section¹** *n & v,*
                                        transection² *n term* → U126-10

(n, i) cut or division [ɪʒ]
(ii) portion [ʃ] of a structure
(iii) cut surface
(iv) thin slice [aɪ] of tissue³, [ʃ‖s] esp. for microscopic examination
cross-sectional *adj term* • **transect⁴** *v* • **dissection⁵** *n* • **dissect⁶** *v*
» If medical measures [eʒ] fail, section of peripheral nerves may be necessary to relieve pain. Duodenal biopsy [aɪ] specimens should then be sectioned for histologic examination. The kidney was freed and exposed by blunt [ʌ] dissection⁷.
Use abdominal⁸ / serial⁹ [ɪɚ]/ thin **section** • microscopic / histologic **section** • frozen¹⁰ / sagittal / coronal **section** • perineal [iː]/ pituitary stalk¹¹ / cesarean¹² [eɚ] **section** • to perform a frozen¹³ **section** • **cross-sectional** area¹⁴ / view / ECG / study¹⁵ • sharp / finger¹⁶ **dissection** • en bloc / lymph node¹⁷ [lɪmf noʊd] **dissection** • extensive¹⁸ / minimal / meticulous¹⁹ **dissection** • neck / axillary²⁰ **dissection** • **to dissect** free²¹ / off²² • **dissecting** microscope²³ [aɪ]

(Ab)schnitt, Durchtrennung; inzidieren, e. Schnitt machen
Querschnitt, quer durchschneiden¹ Querschnitt; Durchtrennung² Gewebescheibe³ durchtrennen⁴ (Dis)sektion, Obduktion, Ausräumung⁵ sezieren, präparieren⁶ stumpfe Präparation⁷ Bauchschnitt, Laparotomie⁸ Serienschnitt⁹ Gefrierschnitt¹⁰ Hypophysenstieldurchtrennung¹¹ Kaiserschnitt, Schnittentbindung¹² e. Gefrierschnitt anfertigen¹³ Querschnittsfläche¹⁴ Querschnittstudie¹⁵ Fingerdissektion¹⁶ Lymphknotendissektion, -ausräumung¹⁷ weite Präparation¹⁸ exakte P.¹⁹ axilläre Lymphknotendissektion²⁰ freilegen²¹ abpräparieren²² Präpariermikroskop²³   5

---

segment [segmənt] *n & v term*   *rel* **portion¹** [pɔːrʃən] *n & v term*

(n) part of an organ or other body structure delimited² naturally or artificially [ɪʃ] from the remainder [eɪ], or having independent function, supply [aɪ], drainage [-ɪdʒ], etc.
(v) divide into small equal parts
segmental³ *adj term* • **segmented** *adj* • **segmentation⁴** *n* • **midportion⁵** *n*
» The entire [aɪ] distal portion of the foot is pale [eɪ] and cold. The chest film demonstrated air trapping⁶ distal to the obstructed [ʌ] segment. The occlusion [uːʒ] was segmental in distribution [juːʃ].
Use sacral [eɪ]/ renal [iː]/ skin **segment** • lung *or* pulmonary⁷ [ʊ‖ʌ] **segment** • spinal [aɪ] cord⁸ / intestinal **segment** • lower uterine / diseased *or* involved⁹ / stenotic **segment** • **segmental** bronchus¹⁰ [k]/ fracture¹¹ • **segmental** resection¹² / reflex¹³ [iː] • **segmented** polys¹⁴ / haustral¹⁵ [ɔː] **segmentation** • upper / major **portion** • marginal¹⁶ [mɑːrdʒ-]/ diseased **portion** • dependent¹⁷ / osseous¹⁸ **portion** • membranous / tumorous¹⁹ [(j)uː] **portion**

Segment, Abschnitt; segmentieren
Teil, Abschnitt; auf-, zuteilen¹ abgegrenzt² segmentär, segmental³ Segmentation, Segmentbildung⁴ mittlerer Abschnitt⁵ Lufteinschluss⁶ Lungensegment⁷ Rückenmarksegment⁸ befallenes S.⁹ Segmentbronchus, B. segmentalis¹⁰ Etagenfraktur¹¹ Segmentresektion¹² Segmentreflex¹³ segmentkernige Granulozyten¹⁴ Haustrenbildung¹⁵ marginaler Abschnitt¹⁶ weiter peripher gelegener Teil¹⁷ knöcherner Anteil¹⁸ Tumoranteil¹⁹   6

MEDICAL SCIENCE — Anatomy

travel v term   syn **run, course** v, rel **traverse**¹ [ɜː], **enter**², **cross**³ v term
- **course**⁴ [kɔːrs] n term • **crossing**⁵ adj & n

» Afferents from the palate⁶ travel with the greater superficial petrosal nerve to the geniculate ganglion. The nerve supply to the penis runs on the posterolateral surface of the prostate.

Use **to travel** from / to / through / (with)in • **to travel** proximally along / via / toward • **to run** (superficially) [ɪʃ] along / underneath [iː]/ **in a groove**⁷ [uː]/ anterior to • in its entire⁸ **course** • **crossing** vessel⁹ / point • arteriovenous [iː] **crossing**

verlaufen, ziehen
queren¹ eintreten, münden² kreuzen³ Verlauf⁴ kreuzend; Kreuzung⁵ Gaumen⁶ in einer Furche verlaufen⁷ in s. gesamten Verlauf⁸ kreuzendes Gefäß⁹

7

---

layer [leɪɚ] n & v   syn **stratum** [eɪ‖ɑː] n term, pl **-a**
rel **plica**¹ [plaɪkə], **lamina**² n term, pl **-ae** → U86-15

sheet [iː] of a substance lying upon another from which it is different or not continuous with³ it
layered⁴ adj • **stratified**⁴ [æ] adj term • **plicated**⁵ adj • **plication**⁶ n

» The chest was closed in anatomic layers. A layer of corneal epithelial cells lined⁷ the crater. The absorptive surface of the mucosa is multiplied by circular mucosal folds termed plicae circulares that project into the lumen.

Use intimal⁸ / deep / skin / subcutaneous fat⁹ **layer** • fascial / muscle¹⁰ / germ¹¹ / basal¹² **layer** • **layer** upon layer • closed in¹³ **layers** • **stratum** granulosum / corneum • **stratum** germinativum¹⁴ [aɪ] spinosum • single¹⁵-**layered** • synovial¹⁶ / epiglottic **plica** • **plica** ileoc(a)ecalis

Schicht, Lage; (be)schichten
Plica, Falte¹ Schicht, Platte, Lamina² verbunden³ geschichtet, in Schichten⁴ faltig, gefaltet⁵ Faltenbildung, Faltung⁶ kleidete aus⁷ Intima, Tunica intima/ interna⁸ subkut. Fettschicht⁹ Muskelschicht¹⁰ Keimblatt¹¹ Basalis, Stratum basale¹² schichtweise verschlossen¹³ Keimschicht, Stratum germinativum¹⁴ einschichtig¹⁵ Plica synovialis¹⁶

8

---

line [laɪn] n clin & term   syn **linea** [lɪnɪə] n term

(i) an imaginary [ædʒ] connection of reference points
(ii) long narrow mark distinguished from the adjacent [eɪ] tissues¹ by color, texture, or elevation
hairline² [heɚlaɪn] n & adj • **linear**³ [lɪnɪɚ] adj • **delineate**⁴ [dɪlɪnieɪt] v

» The tube was inserted [ɜː] in the anterior 3rd intercostal space at the midclavicular line. Incise [saɪ] the eschar⁵ [eskɑːr] along the anterior axillary line bilaterally to the costal margins⁶. Perform tube thoracostomy [ɒː] through the fifth or sixth intercostal space in the midaxillary line.

Use nipple⁷ / lip / anterior axillary⁸ **line** • (left) midclavicular⁹ (abbr MCL) **line** • median¹⁰ [iː]/ intertrochanteric **line** • scratch¹¹ **lines** • skin **lines** of minimal tension or Langer' **lines** alba¹³ / aspera / semilunaris / nigra [aɪ] • **lines of** cleavage¹² [kliːvɪdʒ] • **line of** demarcation / vision¹⁴ • **linear** pattern / lesion / scar¹⁵ • **linear** growth / relationship¹⁶

Linie, Linea
angrenzende/ benachbarte Gewebe¹ Haaransatz; haarfein, sehr dünn² linear, linienförmig³ umreißen, darstellen, abgrenzen⁴ Verbrennungsschorf⁵ Rippenbogen⁶ Mamillarlinie, Linea mamillaris⁷ vordere Axillarlinie, L. axillaris anterior⁸ Medioklavikularlinie, L. medioclavicularis⁹ Medianlinie¹⁰ Kratzlinien¹¹ Hautspalt-, Langer-Linien¹² Linea alba, weiße Linie¹³ Sehachse, Gesichtslinie¹⁴ linienförmige Narbe¹⁵ lineare Beziehung¹⁶

9

---

boundary [baʊndɚi] n, pl **-ies**   syn **border** [bɔːrdɚ] n
sim **margin**¹ [mɑːrdʒɪn], **edge**¹ [edʒ], **limit**² n, rel **demarcation**³ n

the line separating a structure [ʌ] from adjacent ones or determining [ɜː] the limits of an area
bound⁴ [aʊ] v • **border**⁵ v • **borderline** adj & n • **delimit**⁴ v • **demarcate**⁴ [iː] v • **marginal**⁶ adj • **limited** adj • **limitation**⁷ n • **-edged** comb

» There are signs of extension beyond the boundaries of the pancreas. The oral cavity is bounded anteriorly by the vermilion border⁸ of the lips. The margin of the ulcer [ʌlsɚ] is sharply demarcated. The lesion [iːʒ] should be excised with a small margin of normal tissue⁹.

Use to define/maintain [eɪ] /breach¹⁰ [briːtʃ] **boundaries** • anatomic / anterior / superior **boundary** • well-outlined¹¹ / outer / lateral **border** • indistinct¹² / poorly demarcated **border** • ill-defined¹² / irregular / left sternal [ɜː] / raised¹³ [eɪ] **border** • age¹⁴ / time **limit** • costal¹⁵ / liver / adjacent **margin** • uninvolved / clear surgical¹⁶ **margins** • liver / wound¹⁷ [uː]/ skin / lateral **edge** • free / cutting¹⁸ [ʌ] **edge** • ragged-edged filling defect¹⁹ [iː] • smooth-**edged** [uː] appearance [ɪɚ] • well²⁰ **demarcated**

Grenze, Saum, Grenzlinie
Rand, Kante, Margo¹ Grenze, Beschränkung² Abgrenzung, Demarkation³ be-, ab-, angrenzen⁴ be-, angrenzen⁵ rand-, wandständig, marginal⁶ Begrenzung, Beschränkung⁷ Lippenrot⁸ gesunde Gewebemanschette⁹ Grenzen überschreiten¹⁰ deutl. erkennbare(r) Grenze/ Rand¹¹ unscharfe Begrenzung¹² erhabener Rand¹³ Altersgrenze¹⁴ Rippen(bogen)rand¹⁵ tumorfreie Resektionsränder¹⁶ Wundrand¹⁷ Schneide¹⁸ unscharf begrenzter Füllungsdefekt¹⁹ gut abgegrenzt²⁰

10

---

adjacent [ədʒeɪsᵊnt] adj   syn **contiguous, adjoining** adj, opposite **distant**¹ adj

having a common boundary, lying close to each other without intervening [iː] space²
contiguity³ [kɒntɪgjuːəti] n • **adjoin**⁴ [ədʒɔɪn] v

» The pericardium may be affected by diseases of adjacent tissues. Retinal vessel sheathing⁵ [ʃiːðɪŋ] may occur [ɜː] adjacent to such lesions. The disease spread [e] by contiguity to adjacent viscera⁶ [ɪs].

Use **adjacent** tissue / structures⁷ / joints / vertebrae [ɜː]/ to the affected vessel⁸ • **contiguous** viscera⁶ / rib / structures⁷ / areas / involvement • **contiguous** skin infection / to the involved tendon • to extend or spread by⁹ **contiguity** • **distant** site / disease / metastases¹⁰ / (tumor) spread • **distant** vision [ɪʒ]/ visual acuity¹¹ [juː]/ breath [e] sounds¹²

angrenzend, benachbart
entfernt, Fern-¹ Zwischenraum² Kontiguität, Berührung³ angrenzen⁴ postinflammatorische retinale Gefäßschädigung⁵ Nachbarorgane⁶ benachbarte/ angrenzende Strukturen⁷ an d. betroffenen Gefäße angrenzend⁸ s. durch Berührung ausbreiten⁹ Fernmetastasen¹⁰ Sehschärfe i. d. Ferne¹¹ ohrferne Atemgeräusche¹²

11

Anatomy — MEDICAL SCIENCE 381

continuous with [kəntɪnjʊəs wɪθ] *phr*
opposite **distinct¹** [dɪstɪŋkt] *adj*

extending in space without interruption [ʌ], break or irregularity

continuity² [(j)uː] *n* • **continuation³** *n* • **distinction⁴** *n* • **discontinuous⁵** *adj* • **distinctive⁶** *adj*

» *The fascia* [fæʃ(ɪ)ə] *covering the superior surface of the levator* [eɪ] *ani is continuous with the endopelvic fascia. There is an interruption in the continuity of the lower shaft. These fibers* [aɪ] *are continuous with the outer coat of the detrusor* [uː] *muscle.*

Use to maintain *or* preserve⁷ [ɜː] / (re)establish **continuity** • gross⁸ [oʊ]/ interruption in / bone **continuity** • anatomic / restoration of⁹ **continuity** • **distinct** margin / border¹⁰ / area • **distinct** neuroanatomic sites [aɪ]/ clinical entity¹¹

verbunden mit, s. fortsetzend
verschieden, getrennt; deutlich¹ Zusammenhang, Kontinuität² Fortsetzung³ Unterschied, Unterscheidung⁴ unzusammenhängend, unterbrochen⁵ auffällig, unverkennbar, charakteristisch⁶ die Kontinuität erhalten⁷ makroskop. Kontinuität⁸ Wiederherstellung d. K.⁹ deutl. Abgrenzung¹⁰ eigenständige(s) klin. Bild/ Entität¹¹
12

---

visceral [vɪsɚəl] *adj term*
opposite **parietal¹** [pəraɪəṱəl] *adj term, abbr* **P**

related or close to any of the large interior organs in the abdominal or thoracic [æs] cavities

viscera² *n pl term, sing* **viscus** [vɪskəs] • **viscerad** *adj* • **viscero-, parieto-** *comb*

» *This caused a shift of the mediastinal* [aɪ] *viscera to the opposite side. Parietal pain is more easily localized than visceral pain.*

Use **visceral** pleura³ [ʊɚ]/ peritoneum⁴ [iː]/ pain⁵ • hollow⁶ / abdominal **viscera** • **parietal** lobe⁷ [oʊ]/ area / bone⁸ / pleura • **parietal** pericardium⁹ / region [iːdʒ]/ surface • **parieto**colic fold /-occipital [ksɪ]/ sulcus¹⁰ [ʌ]

viszeral, Eingeweide-
parietal, seitlich, wandständig¹ Eingeweide, Viszera² Lungenfell, Pleura visceralis/ pulmonalis³ Peritoneum viscerale⁴ Viszeralschmerz⁵ Hohlorgane⁶ Parietal-, Scheitellappen⁷ Scheitelbein, Os parietale⁸ parietales Perikardblatt⁹ Sulcus parieto-occipitalis¹⁰
13

---

proximal [prɒːksɪməl] *adj term, abbr* **prox**
opposite **distal¹** [dɪstəl] *adj term*

closer to the center (usually the trunk² [ʌ] of the body), midline or any point of reference

disto-, proximo- *comb* • **interproximal³** *adj*

» *Total gastrectomy is required for tumors of the proximal half of the stomach. The findings on physical examination are typical of distal* small bowel⁴ [aʊ] *obstruction.*

Use **proximal** interphalangeal [dʒ] (*abbr* PIP) joints / tibia / phalanx⁵ • **proximal** colon [oʊ]/ bile [aɪ] duct⁶ [ʌ]/ convoluted tubule [(j)uː] • **distal** aspect / phalanges⁷ [fəlændʒiːz]/ pulses⁸ [ʌ] • **distal** colonic stump⁹ / convoluted tubule¹⁰

proximal, rumpfwärts
distal¹ Rumpf, Stamm² approximal, interdental³ Dünndarm⁴ Grundglied, -phalanx, P. proximalis⁵ proximaler Gallengang⁶ Endphalangen, -glieder⁷ periphere Pulse⁸ distaler Kolonstumpf⁹ Tubulus contortus distalis¹⁰
14

---

peripheral [pərɪfɚəl] *adj*
opposite **central¹** [sentrəl] *adj*

situated closer to the periphery of an organ or body part in relation to a specific reference point

periphery² [pərɪfɚi] *n* • **center** [sentɚ] *n, BE* **centre**

» *There is increased mobilization of fatty acids from peripheral* adipose depots³*. Calcification of the periphery of the hilar* [aɪ] *nodes was noted. The central pulmonary arteries are enlarged.*

Use **peripheral** blood (smear)⁴ [smɪɚ]/ vessel / resistance⁵ / circulation [sɜːr-] • **peripheral** pulses⁶ / vision⁷ [ɪʒ]/ cyanosis⁸ [saɪənoʊsɪs] • **central** lobule / canal [æ]/ face / incisor⁹ [sɪ] • **central** nervous system / venous [iː] pressure¹⁰ / catheter

peripher
zentral¹ Rand(zone), Peripherie² Fettdepots³ peripherer Blutausstrich⁴ peripherer Widerstand⁵ periphere Pulse⁶ peripheres Sehen⁷ periphere Zyanose⁸ linker mittlerer Schneidezahn⁹ zentraler Venendruck, ZVD¹⁰
15

---

dorsal [dɔːrsəl] *adj term*   *sim* **posterior¹** [pɒːstɪɚiɚ] *adj term*
opposite **ventral²** *adj, sim* **anterior³** *adj term*

referring to the back of the body, the backside or any dorsum⁴

dorso-, postero-, ante- *comb* • **ventro-, -retro** *comb* •
dorsiflex⁵ *v* • **dorsiflexion⁶** *n*

» *Pain* due to⁷ *cervical disk disease may involve the dorsal aspect of the thumb* [θʌm]*. Color blindness can occur* [ɜː] *from* bilateral strokes⁸ *involving the ventral portion of the occipital lobe. Equipment now available makes it possible to obtain sonograms through openings in the skull, either through* bur [ɜː] *holes or via the anterior fontanelle in infants.*

Use **dorsal** spine⁹ [aɪ]/ vertebrae¹⁰ [eɪ‖iː]/ root [uː] ganglion¹¹ • **dorsal** flexure [flɛkʃɚ] of the spine • **dorsal** vein [eɪ]/ recumbent [ʌ] position¹² • **posterior** pancreas • **ventral** pancreas / (nerve) [ɜː] root / hernia¹³ [ɜː]/ aspect • **retro**grade [eɪ] /pubic¹⁴ [juː] /sternal [ɜː] /peritoneum • **retro**version [ɜː] /flexion /bulbar¹⁵ [ʌ] • **anterior** fontanelle¹⁶ / abdominal wall • **anterior** axillary line¹⁷ / surface / portion

dorsal(is), rückseitig
posterior, hintere(r)¹ ventral, bauchseitig² anterior, vordere(r)³ Dorsum, Rücken⁴ dorsal flektieren, rückwärts beugen⁵ Dorsalflexion⁶ aufgrund von⁷ bilateraler Insult⁸ Brustwirbelsäule⁹ Brustwirbel, Vertebrae thoracicae¹⁰ Spinalganglion¹¹ Rückenlage m. gespreizten, angezogenen Beinen¹² Bauchwandhernie, Hernia abdominalis/ ventralis¹³ retropubisch, hinter d. Schambein liegend¹⁴ retrobulbär¹⁵ große Fontanelle, Fonticulus anterior¹⁶ vordere Axillarlinie, Linea axillaris anterior¹⁷
16

382 MEDICAL SCIENCE — Anatomy

plantar [plæntɚ‖-tɑːr] *adj term*   opposite **palmar**[1] [pæl‖pɑː(l)mɚ],
  volar[1] [oʊ] *adj term*

  relating to the sole [soʊl] of the foot

» *Pallor* [æ] *is best detected on the plantar surfaces of the toes or in the nail beds. Bleomycin* [aɪs] *can produce edema* [iː] *of the interphalangeal joints and hardening of the palmar and plantar skin.*

Use **plantar** aspect / arch[2] [tʃ]/ flexors • **plantar** flexion[3] / reflex[4] / callosities • **plantar** nerve / warts[5] [ɔː]/ fascia [ʃ] or aponeurosis[6] • **palmar** fascia / muscle [mʌsl]/ flexion[7] • **palmar** arch / crease[8] [iː]/ erythema[9] [iː] • **volar** pad (of the fingertip)[10] / ligament[11] [ɪ]/ plate injury

plantar, sohlenwärts
palmar, handflächenwärts[1] Sohlenbogen, Arcus plantaris[2] Plantarflexion[3] Fußsohlen-, Plantarreflex[4] Fußsohlenwarze, Verruca plantaris[5] Plantaraponeurose, A. plantaris[6] Palmar-, Volarflexion[7] Handlinie[8] Palmarerythem[9] Fingerbeere, -ballen[10] Retinaculum flexorum (manus), Lig. carpi transversum[11]   17

---

lateral [æ] *adj term*   opposite **medial**[1] [iː], **median**[1] [iː], **midline**[1] [ɪ] *adj term*

  on the right/left side or (further) away from the median or midsagittal [ædʒ] plane[2]
  contralateral[3] *adj term* • lateralize *v* • lateralization[4] *n* • latero- *comb*

» *The nerve courses* [ɔː] *just lateral to the sinus* [aɪ]. *Open the glottis by lateralizing a vocal cord. Anesthetize* [e] *the antecubital* [juː] *fossa*[5] *over the medial aspect of the forearm.*

Use **lateral** ventricle[6] / hemisphere [e]/ curvature [ɜː] of the spine[7] / ligament • **lateral** bending (exercises) / recumbent position[8] • **lateral** view[9] / infarction[10] • **laterally** reflected • **lateral** to the incision • contralateral aspect / breast [e]/ ear / kidney[11] • antero/ infero/ col/ ipsi**lateral** • **medial** to / malleolus[12] [iː]/ epicondyle [-aɪl]/ meniscus[13] • **median** plane[2] / nerve[14] / eminence / sternotomy[15] • **midline** scar / (skin) incision[16] • movable in the **midline**

lateral, seitlich, seitwärts
medial, mittlere(r, -s)[1] Medianebene[2] kontralateral, auf d. entgegengesetzten Seite[3] Lateralisation[4] Ellenbeuge, Fossa cubitalis[5] Seitenventrikel, Ventriculus lateralis[6] Skoliose[7] Sims-Lage[8] Seitenaufnahme, -ansicht[9] Lateralinfarkt[10] kontralaterale Niere[11] Innenknöchel, Malleolus medialis[12] Meniscus medialis[13] Nervus medianus, Medianus[14] mediane Sternotomie[15] Medianschnitt[16]   18

---

cephalad [sefəlæd] *adj term*   *syn* **cephalic, cranial** [kreɪnɪəl] *adj term*
  opposite **caudad** or **caudal**[1] [ɒː] *adj term*

  toward the head and away from the end(s) or tail [teɪl]
  cephalo- *comb* • caudo- *comb* • caudate[2] [kɒːdeɪt] *adj term*

» *As the disease advances, symptoms progress in a cephalad direction and back motion* [oʊʃ] *becomes limited. CT scans show caudal displacement of the fourth ventricle. Hepatic imaging studies revealed* [iː] *a prominent caudate lobe*[3].

Use **cephalad** aspect / direction / migration [maɪ-]/ to the superior pole[4] • **cephalic** vein[5] / index[6] / presentation[7] • **cephalo**caudad diameter [aɪæ] /metry[8] • **cephalo**pelvic disproportion[9] • **caudal** aspect / pole / branches [tʃ] • **caudal** ligament / anesthesia [iːʒ] or block[10] • **caudate** process[11] / nucleus[12] [(j)uː]

kranial, kopfwärts
kaudal, schwanzwärts[1] schwanzförmig[2] Lobus caudatus[3] kranial vom oberen Pol[4] V. cephalica[5] Schädelindex[6] Schädel-, Kopflage[7] Schädelmessung, Kephalometrie[8] Schädel-Becken-Missverhältnis[9] Kaudal-, Sakralanästhesie[10] Processus caudatus (hepatis)[11] Nucleus caudatus, Schweifkern[12]
  19

---

frontal [frʌntəl] *adj term*   opposite **occipital**[1] [ɒksɪpɪtəl] *adj term*

  referring to the front of the head, esp. the forehead[2]

» *Frontal epidural* [(j)ʊɚ] *abscesses are usually quiescent*[3] [kwaɪesənt]. *Frontal sinusitis* [aɪ] *that does not promptly respond to outpatient care*[4] *should be managed aggressively. The neurologic symptoms* [ɪ] *usually persist for 20 to 30 min and are generally followed by a throbbing*[5] *occipital headache.*

Use **frontal** bone[6] / lobe / sinus[7] [aɪ] / plane[8] • **frontal** gyrus [dʒaɪrəs]/ balding[9] [ɒː]/ bossing[10] • **occipital** bone[11] / region / protuberance [(j)uː] • **occipital** flattening[12] / hairline[13] / artery

frontal, Stirn-
okzipital, Hinterhaupt-[1] Stirn[2] klin. stumm[3] ambulante Behandlung[4] pochend[5] Stirnbein, Os frontale[6] Stirnhöhle, Sinus frontalis[7] Frontalebene[8] Ausbildung e. Stirnglatze[9] Vorwölbung d. Stirn[10] Hinterhauptbein, Os occipitale[11] Abflachung d. Hinterkopfes[12] hinterer Haaransatz, Nackenhaaransatz[13]   20

---

orifice [ɔːrɪfɪs] *n term*   *syn* **opening, aperture** [æpɚtʃɚ] *n clin*
  os [oʊs] *pl* **ora, ostium** [ɒːstɪəm] *n term, pl* **ostia**

  the entrance or outlet of ducts [ʌ], tubes [(j)uː], and body cavities
  open[1] *v* • opening *adj* • orificial [ɔːrɪfɪʃəl] *adj term*

» *Lesions* [iːʒ] *close to the orifice of the duct may be palpated manually. The anal* [eɪ] *opening*[2] *must be dilated daily for 6-8 months to prevent stricture formation. The superior aperture*[3] *of the thorax is also called either the thoracic* [æs] *inlet*[3] *or the thoracic outlet*[3]. *The placenta* [se] *may cover the internal os of the cervix* [sɜː] *completely.*

Use ureteral[4] [iː]/ anal[2] / esophagogastric[5] **orifice** • gastroduodenal or pyloric[6] [paɪlɔːrɪk] **orifice** • root canal[7] / mitral[1] / tricuspid[9] [ʌ] **orifice** • aortic [eɪ]/ artificial[10] [ɪʃ]/ narrow **opening** • patent[11] [eɪ]/ vaginal[12] [dʒ] **opening** • diaphragmatic / anal[2] **aperture** • piriform[13] / palpebral [iː] **aperture** • (external[14]/ internal[15]) **cervical os** • coronary / vaginal[12] **ostium** • **ostium** primum [aɪ] defect[16] [iː]/ secundum defect[17] • **to open** up / into

Ostium, Öffnung, Mündung
öffnen, münden[1] Analöffnung[2] obere Thoraxapertur, Apertura thoracis superior[3] Harnleitermündung, Ostium ureteris[4] O. cardiacum[5] O. pyloricum[6] Wurzelkanaleingang[7] O. atrioventriculare sinistrum[8] O. atrioventriculare dextrum[9] künstl. Öffnung, Stoma[10] durchgängige Öffnung[11] Scheideneingang, O. vaginae[12] Apertura piriformis, vordere Öffnung d. (knöchernen) Nasenhöhle[13] äußerer Muttermund, Ostium uteri[14] innerer M.[15] Ostium-primum-Defekt, ASD I[16] Ostium-secundum-Defekt, ASD II[17]   21

Anatomy | MEDICAL SCIENCE **383**

lumen [luːmən] *n term, pl* **lumina, lumens**

space in the interior of tubular structures, e.g. blood vessels or intestines

luminal *adj term* • **intra/ transluminal** *adj*

» Blood flowing through such a narrow, irregular, or ulcerated [ʌ] lumen may clot[1]. A luminal diameter of 14-15 mm is usually sufficient [ɪʃ] to relieve dysphagia[2] [eɪdʒ].
Use arterial [ɪɚ]/ bowel or gut[3] [ʌ]/ bronchial [k] **lumen** • vascular or vessel[4] • tubal[5] **lumen** • patent / true[6] / false[7] **lumen** • narrowed[8] / normal **lumen** • **lumen of the** bowel[3] / vein / appendix • **luminal** diameter / dilatation • **luminal** narrowing[9] / obstruction • double-**lumen** catheter[10] • **intraluminal** debris [iː]/ cyst [sɪst] • **intraluminal** pressure[11] / airway obstruction

Lumen, lichte Weite
Blutgerinnsel bilden[1] Schluckstörung, Dysphagie[2] Darmlumen[3] Gefäßlumen[4] Tubenlumen[5] echtes Lumen[6] falsches Lumen[7] eingeengtes Lumen[8] Lumeneinengung[9] doppellumiger Katheter[10] intraluminaler Druck[11]

22

lobe [loʊb] *n term*

rel **lobule**[1] [lɒːbjuːl] *n term* → U43-3; U47-3; U41-5

(i) subdivision of organs (e.g. the brain, lung, liver, etc.) bounded [aʊ] by fissures [ɪʃ], septa or other structural demarcations
(ii) rounded [aʊ] projecting [dʒe] part, e.g. the ear lobe[2]

lob(ul)ar[3] *adj term* • **lobulated**[4] *adj* • **lobotomy**[5] [ɒː] *n* • **lobectomy**[6] *n*

» The stroke [oʊ] involved the nondominant parietal lobe. Did you find any lobar or patchy infiltrates[7] on chest x-ray[8]? Two distinct lobes are separated by a shallow [æ] median furrow[9] [ɜː]. When fibrosis is so extensive that fibrous [aɪ] septa surround parenchymal [kɪ] nodules and alter [ɒː] the normal architecture [ɑːrkɪ-] of the liver lobule the histologic lesion is defined as cirrhosis [səroʊsɪs].
Use frontal[10] / occipital / temporal **lobe** • parietal[11] [aɪ]/ left lower / right middle[12] **lobe** • **lobe of the** brain[13] / lung / liver / prostate / thyroid[14] [aɪ] • **lobar** bronchi [-kaɪ]/ pneumonia[15] [n(j)uː-] • pulmonary[16] [ʊ‖ʌ]/ hepatic or liver **lobules** • **lobulated** contour / kidney[17] / tongue[18] [tʌŋ] • **lobular** pattern / inflammation / carcinoma

Lobus, Lappen
Lobulus, Läppchen[1] Ohrläppchen[2] lobulär[3] gelappt[4] Lobo-, Leukotomie[5] Lobektomie, Lappenentfernung[6] fleckige Infiltrate[7] Thoraxröntgen[8] nicht sehr tiefe Furche[9] Stirn-, Frontallappen, Lobus frontalis[10] Parietal-, Scheitellappen, L. parietalis[11] (rechter) Mittellappen[12] Großhirnlappen[13] Schilddrüsenlappen[14] Lobär-, Lappenpneumonie[15] Lungenläppchen, Lobuli pulmonis[16] Ren lobatus[17] Lappenzunge, Lingua lobata[18]

23

pedicle [pedɪkəl] *n term*   *syn* **peduncle** [piː‖pɪdʌŋkəl] *n term*, **stalk** [stɒːk] *n*

a narrow stem or tube attached [ætʃ] to an organ, tumor or skin flap

pedicled[1] *adj term* • **pedunculated**[1] [ʌ] *adj* • **peduncular**[2] *adj*

» From the renal pedicle the lymphatic channels [tʃæn-], usually four or five trunks, drain to lymph [ɪ] nodes along the inferior vena cava [viːnə keɪvə] and to the lateral aortic nodes. In Nothnagel':] and contralateral cerebellar ataxia.
Use renal[4] [iː]/ splenic [e]/ vascular[5] / stump [ʌ] of **pedicle** • **pedicle** graft or flap[6] • cerebral[7] / (superior[8]/ middle[9]/ inferior[10]) cerebellar **peduncle** • **pedunculated** polyp[11] [pɒːlɪp]/ growth[12] / fibroid [aɪ] • pituitary [(j)uː] or infundibular or hypothalamic[13] **stalk**

Stiel
gestielt[1] stielförmig, Stiel-[2] Okulomotoriuslähmung[3] Nierenstiel[4] Gefäßstiel[5] gestielter Lappen[6] Hirnstiel, Pedunculus cerebri[7] P. cerebellaris superior/ rostralis, oberer Kleinhirnstiel[8] P. cerebellaris medialis, mittlerer K.[9] P. cerebellaris inferior/ caudalis, unterer K.[10] gestielter Polyp[11] gestielte Geschwulst[12] Hypophysenstiel, Infundibulum[13]

24

apex [eɪpeks] *n term, pl* **apexes** *or* **apices** [eɪpəsiːz]

rel **base**[1] [beɪs], **root**[2] [ruːt], **hilum** *or* **hilus**[3] [aɪ] *n term*

the top part or tip of a cone-shaped [oʊ] or pointed organ, body part or an extremity

apical [eɪpɪkəl] *adj term* • **basilar**[4] [æ‖eɪ] *adj* • **basal** [eɪ] *adj* • **hilar**[5] [haɪlɚ] *adj*

» Pleural [ʊɚ] pressure at the apex is more negative when the body is erect. In Le Fort III fracture the entire facial [eɪʃ] skeleton is dislocated from the base of the skull [ʌ]. There is a marked loss of cells in the posterior root [uː] ganglia[6] and degeneration of peripheral sensory fibers [aɪ]. Nodal spread [e] was found above the renal hilum.
Use cardiac[7]/ root[8] **apex** • **apex of the** bladder / prostate[9] / cochlea [k] / lung[10] • **apical** bronchus [k] / foramen [eɪ] **root** • **root of the** lung[11] / tongue[12] / nerve[13] [ɜː]/ aortic / tooth[14] / motor[15] **root** • **root** canal / compression[16] / lung / bladder / skull[17] **base** • tongue[12] / narrow / broad **base** • **base of the** neck / skull[17] / aorta • **base of the** heart[18] [ɑː]/ brain[19] / prostate • liver or hepatic[20] / renal[21] **hilum** • **hilum of the** lung / spleen[22] [iː]/ kidney[21] / liver[20]

Apex, Spitze
Basis[1] Radix, Wurzel[2] Hilum, Hilus[3] basilaris, Basilar-[4] hilär[5] Spinalganglien[6] Herzspitze, Apex cordis[7] Wurzelspitze, A. radicis dentis[8] A. prostatae[9] Lungenspitze, A. pulmonis[10] Lungenwurzel, Radix pulmonis[11] Zungenwurzel, -grund, Radix linguae[12] Nervenwurzel[13] Zahnwurzel, R. dentis[14] vordere/ motorische Wurzel (d. Spinalnervs)[15] Wurzelkompression[16] Schädelbasis, Basis cranii[17] Herzbasis, Basis cordis[18] Hirnbasis, B. cerebri[19] Leberhilum, Leberpforte[20] Nierenhilus, Hilum renis/ renale[21] Milzhilus, Hilum splenicum[22]

25

fossa [ɒː] n term, pl **-ae**   rel **groove**[1] [uː], **sulcus**[1] [sʌlkəs] n term
cleft[2], **fissure**[2] [fɪʃə] n term

depression or longitudinal furrow[3] [ɜː], esp. on the surface of a bone

grooved[4] adj term • **fissure** v • **fissured**[5] adj • **cleft**[6] [kleft] adj

» The nasal [eɪ] cavity is divided into right and left nasal fossae by the nasal septum. These lesions [iːʒ] typically occur [ɜː] in the depths of the body folds e.g. in the groin[7] and the intergluteal [uː] cleft[8]. In the Sylvian fissure the middle cerebral artery in most patients divides into superior and inferior divisions. Bicipital [baɪsɪp-] tendinitis [aɪ] is produced by friction [ɪkʃ] on the tendon of the long head of the biceps [aɪs] as it passes through the bicipital groove. Superiorly, the hypothalamic sulcus of the third ventricle separates the thalamus from the hypothalamus.

Use iliac[9] [ɪ]/ supraclavicular / antecubital[10] [(j)uː]/ **fossa** • glenoid[11] [iː]/ pituitary[12] **fossa** • atrioventricular[13] / condylar **groove** • olecranon • ulnar[14] [ʌ]/ bicipital[15] **groove** • **grooved** tongue[16] • branchial[17] [k]/ joint[18] **cleft** • fracture[19] / gluteal[8] **cleft** • **cleft** palate[20] / lip[21] / tongue • **cleft** hand / foot • gingival[22] [dʒɪ]/ costophrenic **sulcus** • central[23] / lateral[24] **sulcus** • auricular-mastoid / pulmonary / hypothalamic **sulcus** • lobar / (inferior/ superior) orbital **fissure** • palpebral / anal[25] **fissure** • Sylvian[24] [ɪ] **fissure** • **fissured** lips[26] / tongue[16] / skin[27]

Fossa, Grube
Furche, Rinne, Sulcus[1] Spalt(e), Furche, Fissur[2] Rinne, Furche[3] gefurcht, furchig, gerillt[4] gespalten, rissig[5] gespalten, (auseinander-)klaffend[6] Leiste(nbeuge)[7] Gesäßspalte, Rima ani[8] Fossa iliaca, Darmbeingrube[9] F. cubitalis, Ellenbeuge[10] Cavitas glenoidalis, Schultergelenkpfanne[11] Fossa hypophysialis[12] Sulcus coronarius, Kranzfurche (d. Herzens)[13] S. nervi ulnaris[14] S. intertubercularis[15] Faltenzunge, Lingua plicata/ scrotalis[16] Kiemenspalte, -gang[17] Gelenkhöhle, Cavitas articularis[18] Bruchspalt[19] Gaumenspalte, Palatoschisis, Palatum fissum[20] Lippenspalte, Cheiloschisis[21] Zahnfleischfurche, Sulcus gingivalis[22] Zentralfurche, S. centralis/ Rolandi[23] Sylvius-Furche, S. lateralis[24] Analfissur[25] aufgesprungene Lippen[26] rissige Haut[27]   26

prominence [prɒːmənənts] n term   rel **process**[1] [prɒːses], **protuberance**[2] [(j)uː], **projection**[3] [-dʒekʃ°n] n term

a bulging [bʌldʒɪŋ] eminence[4]

prominent[5] adj term • **protuberant**[6] adj • **project**[7] v • **projecting** adj

» In diabetics [e] the heel [iː] and bony prominences are particularly vulnerable[8] [ʌ]. The location of the supraspinatus [eɪ] tendon between the greater tuberosity of the humeral [juː] head and the overhanging acromion process renders it vulnerable to mechanical [k] compression. Dermatofibrosarcoma develops as a circumscribed [sɜːr-] protuberance arising [aɪ] from the skin of the trunk [ʌ].

Use bony[9] / laryngeal[10] [dʒ] **prominence** • (external/ internal) occipital[11] / rounded [aʊ] **protuberance** • **protuberant** abdomen / lips / ears[12] • bony[9] / finger-like / slender **projection** • alveolar [ɪə]/ coracoid / mastoid[13] **process** • **prominent** scar[14] [skɑːr]/ mucous [mjuːkəs] folds • **prominent** spur[15] [ɜː]/ eyes[16]

Prominentia, Vorsprung, Vorwölbung
Processus, Fortsatz[1] Vorsprung, Protuberanz, Höcker[2] Vorsprung[3] Erhöhung, Vorsprung, -wölbung, Eminentia[4] vorstehend, -springend; markant[5] vorstehend, hervortretend[6] vorspringen, vorragen[7] empfindlich[8] Knochenvorsprung[9] Adamsapfel, Prominentia laryngea[10] Protuberantia occipitalis interna[11] abstehende Ohren[12] Warzenfortsatz, Mastoid, Proc. mastoideus[13] wulstige Narbe[14] Knochensporn[15] hervortretende Augäpfel[16]   27

Unit 88   General Physiology
Related Units: 78 Metabolism, 81 Biochemistry, 83 Cell Biology, 55 Hormones, 47 Liver & Bile, 49 Urine Production, 31 Muscle Function, 42 Nerve Function

physiologic(al) [fɪziəlɒːdʒɪk] adj term   opposite **unphysiologic(al)**[1] adj term

related to normal vital [aɪ] processes in organisms and the physical and biochemical factors involved, esp. to normal functions not affected by drugs or disease (as opposed to pathologic)

(patho)**physiology**[2] [ɒː] n term • **physiologist**[3] n • **-physiologic** comb

» The pancreatic A cells of diabetics are hyperresponsive to physiologic levels of epinephrine[4]. I will now discuss the anatomy of the anal [eɪ] sphincter and the physiology of defecation.

Use **physiologic** function / activity / mechanism / response / stress(es)[5] • **physiologic** rest position / dead space[6] / cup[7] • **physiologic** effects / dose / changes or alterations[8] • **physiologic** abnormality / jaundice[9] [dʒɒːndɪs]/ saline [eɪ] (solution)[10] • molecular / cell / body / developmental[11] **physiology** • normal / clinical / cardiovascular / endocrine / thyroxine [aɪ] **physiology** • altered [ɒː] lung / morbid or pathologic[2] **physiology** • **unphysiologic(al)** reabsorption / angulation / concentration • supraphysiologic dose[12] / amount [aʊ]/ level • **physio**pathology[2] • electro[13]/ neuro[14] [n(j)ʊəoʊ-]/ patho/ psycho [saɪkoʊ-]/ sub**physiologic**

physiologisch
unphysiologisch[1] (Patho)physiologie[2] Physiologe/ -in[3] Adrenalin, Epinephrin[4] physiolog. Belastung(en)[5] physiolog. Totraum[6] physiol. Ausbuchtung (i. Netzhaut), Excavatio papillae nervi optici[7] physiolog. Veränderungen[8] physiolog. Neugeborenenikterus[9] physiolog. Kochsalzlösung[10] Entwicklungsphysiologie[11] supraphysiologische Dosis[12] elektrophysiologisch[13] neurophysiologisch[14]

General Physiology   MEDICAL SCIENCE **385**

regulation [regjʊleɪʃ⁽ə⁾n] n → U54-3; U83-18   syn **control** n,
rel **mechanism**[1] [mekə-] n term
control of the rate or manner in which a process progresses or a product is formed
regulate[2] v • **control**[2] v • **regulatory** adj • **(un)regulated** adj
» Regulation of the sodium concentration[3] in plasma or urine is intimately associated with regulation of total body water. Nitric [aɪ] oxide[4] is involved in regulating vascular tone. The gastrointestinal tract is the major site of homeostatic control for iron [aɪən] and zinc.
Use feedback[5] [iː]/ down/ up/ de- or dys[6]/ osmotic[7] **regulation** • temperature / auto[8]/ metabolic[9] **regulation** • up/ down/ counter[10] [aʊ]/ de**regulate** • feedback[5] / active / control[11] **mechanism** • autoimmune [ɒːtə-]/ protective[12] **mechanism** • compensatory[13] / antireflux [iː]/ sweating [e]/ defense[14] **mechanism** • secretory [iː]/ transport or carrier[15] **mechanism** • paracrine / coping[16] [oʊ] **mechanism** • cellular / molecular / neurophysiologic / pathogenic [dʒe] **mechanism** • **regulatory** mechanism[11] / function / factor / protein[17] • metabolic[9] / hypothalamic / cell cycle [saɪkl]/ motor **control** • neuroendocrine / feedback[5] **control** • **control** mechanism[11] / system [ɪ]

Steuerung, Regulation, Regelung
Mechanismus[1] regulieren, steuern[2] Natriumkonzentration[3] Stick(stoffmon)oxid[4] Rückkopplungs-, Feedbackmechanismus[5] Fehlsteuerung, Regulationsstörung[6] Osmoregulation[7] Selbstregulation[8] Stoffwechselregulation[9] gegensteuern[10] Steuerungsmechanismus[11] Schutzmechanismus[12] Kompensationsmechanismus[13] Abwehrmechanismus[14] Carriertransport[15] Bewältigungsmechanismus[16] Regulatorprotein[17]

2

supply [səplaɪ] v & n
rel **provide**[1] [aɪ], **transport**[2] v, **perfuse**[3] [pərfjuːz] v term
(v) to transfer [ɜː] and provide with biochemical [ke] substances [ʌ]
supplying [aɪ] adj • **co-transport** n term • **perfusion**[4] [pərfjuːʒ⁽ə⁾n] n → U36-5
» The production of hemoglobin requires a supply of iron and synthesis of heme [hiːm] and globin. Most drug molecules are transported across a membrane by simple diffusion from a high concentration area to a low concentration area without expenditure of energy[5]. As a tumor grows, nutrients[6] are provided by direct diffusion from the circulation. In this phase of septic shock (so-called warm shock) the skin remains well perfused and warm.
Use **to supply** nutrients [uː] to the tissues / the transplant with blood[7] • oxygen[8] / arterial [ɪə]/ (adequate) blood[9] **supply** • microvascular / nerve[10] [ɜː] **supply** • medical[11] / water / energy[12] **supplies** • electrolyte / amino acid / intestinal calcium [s] **transport** • oxygen / reverse [ɜː]/ cholesterol[13] **transport** • diffusive or passive[14] / active / cellular **transport** • carrier-mediated[15] [iː]/ bidirectional **transport** • cardiac / lung[16] / regional [iːdʒ] **perfusion** • **perfusion** rate

versorgen; Versorgung, Zufuhr
bereitstellen, liefern, sorgen für[1] befördern, transportieren[2] durchströmen, perfundieren[3] Durchblutung, -strömung, Perfusion[4] Energieaufwand, -verbrauch[5] Nährstoffe[6] das Transplantat mit Blut versorgen[7] Sauerstoffversorgung, -zufuhr[8] Blutversorgung, -zufuhr[9] nervale Versorgung, Innervation[10] Ärztebedarf[11] Energievorräte[12] Cholesterintransport[13] passiver Transport[14] carriervermittelter T., Carriertransport[15] Lungenperfusion, -durchblutung[16]

3

diffusion [dɪfjuːʒ⁽ə⁾n] n term
rel **osmosis**[1] [ɒzmoʊsɪs] n term → U81-21; U49-9
movement of molecules, ions [aɪənz] or solid particles in a fluid from an area of higher concentration to an area of lower concentration to reach an even [iː] distribution[2] [juːʃ]
diffuse[3] [dɪfjuːz] v term • **(non)diffusible**[4] adj • **diffusive** adj • **osmotic**[5] adj
» Gastric mucus [juː] acts as a barrier to the diffusion of pepsin. A nonionized [aɪ] drug diffuses more readily [e] from the glomerular filtrate into the blood. Potassium[6] diffuses passively along electrical and concentration gradients [eɪ].
Use passive / facilitated[7] [sɪ]/ immuno[8]/ carrier-mediated[9] [iː] **diffusion** • back[10] / exchange[11] [tʃ] **diffusion** • oxygen / rate of / drug / impaired[12] [eə] **diffusion** • **diffusion** barrier[13] / process / constant[14] / coefficient[15] [ɪʃ] • **diffusion** capacity[16] / defect [iː] or impairment[12] • agar gel [dʒel] **diffusion** test or assay[17] • **diffusing** capacity[16] / freely / non-**diffusible** • **osmotic** gradient[18] / pressure[19] / diuresis[20] [iː]/ imbalance / regulation

Diffusion
Osmose[1] Verteilungsgleichgewicht[2] diffundieren[3] diffusionsfähig[4] osmotisch[5] Kalium[6] erleichterte Diffusion[7] Immundiffusion[8] Carrier-, carriervermittelter Transport[9] Rückdiffusion[10] Austauschdiffusion[11] Diffusionsstörung[12] Diffusionsbarriere[13] Diffusionskonstante[14] Diffusionskoeffizient[15] Diffusionskapazität[16] Diffusionstest[17] osmotisches Gefälle[18] osmot. Druck[19] osmot. Diurese[20]

4

soluble [sɒljəbl] adj term   opposite **non-** or **insoluble**[1] adj term → U81-25
capable [eɪ] of changing from a solid to a dispersed [ɜː] form, esp. by immersion[2] [ɜː] in a fluid of suitable properties
solution[3] [uːʃ] n term • **solvent**[4] adj & n • **solubility**[5] n • **solubilize**[6] v • **solubilization**[7] n • **dissolve**[8] v
» High soluble fiber [aɪ] content in the diet may have a favorable effect on blood cholesterol levels. The number of dissolved particles per unit of water was not computed.
Use fat- or lipid[9] / water-**soluble** • **solubility** product[10] / test • aqueous [eɪ‖æ] or water[11] / lipid / low or poor **solubility** • **(in)soluble** compound[12] [aʊ] • saturated[13] [sætʃə-]/ priming[14] [aɪ]/ buffered[15] [ʌ]/ hypertonic **solution** • sterile / (normal) saline[16] [eɪ] (abbr N/S)/ irrigating[17] **solution** • balanced salt[18] / 5% / acetic [iː] acid **solution** • **dissolved** gases / particles / in water

löslich
unlöslich[1] Eintauchen[2] Lösung[3] (auf)lösend; Lösungsmittel[4] Löslichkeit[5] löslich machen[6] Solubilisation[7] (sich) auflösen[8] fettlöslich[9] Löslichkeitsprodukt[10] Wasserlöslichkeit[11] unlösl. Verbindung[12] gesättigte Lösung[13] Starterlösung[14] gepufferte Lösung[15] physiolog. Kochsalzlösung[16] Spülflüssigkeit[17] isotone Salzlösung[18]

5

MEDICAL SCIENCE — General Physiology

permeable [pɜːrmiəbl] adj term opposite **impermeable**[1] adj term
to permit the passage of substances (liquids, gases, heat) across a membrane or other structure
permeate[2] [pɜːrmieɪt] v term • (**im**)**permeability**[3] n • **hyper/ semipermeable**[4] adj

» Injury [dʒ] to the barrier renders the duct [ʌ] permeable to large molecules. The renal [iː] tubule [(j)uː] is impermeable to mannitol. The inability of chloride anions [aɪ] to permeate the cell membrane results in the transcellular exchange of H+ for K+.

Use selectively[5] / freely / water-/ vapor[6] [eɪ] • **permeable** • **impermeable** barrier [ær]/ stricture / to macromolecules • relatively **impermeable** • increased capillary[7] / membrane / microvascular **permeability** • endothelial [iː]/ intestinal / pleural [ʊɚ] **permeability** • glomerular / blood-brain barrier[8] **permeability** • ion[9] [aɪən]/ water[10] / low **permeability**

permeabel, durchlässig
impermeabel, undurchlässig[1] durchdringen[2] Durchlässigkeit, Permeabilität[3] semipermeabel[4] selektiv durchlässig[5] dampfdurchlässig[6] erhöhte Kapillardurchlässigkeit[7] Permeabilität/ Durchlässigkeit d. Blut-Hirn-Schranke[8] Ionendurchlässigkeit[9] Wasserdurchlässigkeit[10]

6

threshold [θreʃhoʊld] (**value** or **level**) n term → U49-5; U104-18
point at which a stimulus is great enough to produce an effect, e.g. excitation [ɪksaɪteɪʃⁿn] of any structure or to elicit[1] [ɪs] a sensation [eɪʃ], motor response, etc.

» The lesion [iːʒ] in proximal renal tubular acidosis is a lowering of the renal bicarbonate threshold. The pH threshold for secretin release [iː] from the duodenum and jejunum is 4.5.

Use **threshold** of sensation / dose[2] / pressure • **threshold** potential[3] / stimulus[4] / percussion[5] [ʌ] • energy / pain[6] / renal[7] / calcium excretion [iːʃ] **threshold** • osmotic / sensory **threshold** / auditory [ɔː] or hearing[8] / speech reception[9] (abbr SRT) **threshold** • below / above the **threshold** • supra[10]/ sub**threshold** • high[11]-/ low-**threshold** substance

Schwelle, Schwellenwert
auslösen[1] Schwellendosis[2] Schwellenpotential[3] Schwellenreiz[4] Schwellenwertperkussion[5] Schmerzschwelle[6] Nierenschwelle[7] Hörschwelle[8] Sprachhörschwelle[9] überschwellig[10] Schwellensubstanz[11]

7

absorption n term rel **reabsorption**[1], **assimilation**[2], **incorporation**[2] n term
passage of substances across tissues, e.g. of nutrients into intestinal villi[3]
absorbent[4] [ɔː] adj & n term • (**re**)**absorb**[5] v • **absorptive** adj → U49-4; U46-13 • as/ **dissimilate**[6] [dɪsɪməleɪt] v term • **dissimilation**[7] n

» Complete absorption of alcohol requires 30 minutes to 6 hours, depending upon the volume, the presence of food, etc. What is the best method of studying cerebrospinal [aɪ] fluid flow and absorption? Elemental diets [daɪəts] provide essential nutrients in a readily [e] assimilated form and require little or no active digestion. Some iron is taken up in the liver parenchyma [-kɪmə] for incorporation into heme [hiːm] enzymes [aɪ] and for ferritin storage.

Use to facilitate [sɪ]/delay [eɪ] or retard[8]/reduce/enhance **absorption** • net / calcium / drug[9] / energy / nutrient[10] [uː] **absorption** • systemic / oral / skin or dermal[11] [ɜː] **absorption** • gut [ʌ] or (gastro)intestinal[12] (abbr GI)/ small bowel[13] [aʊ] colonic **absorption** • fat[14] / bile acid / iron / mucosal carbohydrate [aɪ] **absorption** • **absorption** rate[15] / test[16] / passive / rapid / poor / mal[17] / impaired [eɚ] **absorption** • tubular / water / (avid) renal (sodium)[18] **reabsorption** • protein / mal**assimilation** • **assimilation of** calories / information • **absorptive** surface [ɜː]/ function / capacity / hypercalciuria • **to be assimilated** by the body / in the intestine / for reutilization

Ab- Resorption, Aufnahme
Reabsorption; Rückresorption[1] Assimilation, Aufnahme[2] Darmzotten[3] saugfähig, absorbierend; Absorbens[4] ab, resorbieren[5] abbauen, dissimilieren[6] Abbau, Dissimilation, Katabolismus[7] die Resorption verzögern[8] Arzneimittelresorption[9] Nährstoffaufnahme[10] perkutane Resorption[11] enterale / intestinale Resorption[12] Dünndarmresorption[13] Fettresorption[14] Resorptionsgeschwindigkeit[15] Resorptionstest[16] Malabsorption[17] überaus starke renale Natriumreabsorption[18]

8

humor [hjuːmɚ] n term, BE **humour** → U58-10f
body fluid such as blood or lymph [lɪmf]
(**non**)**humoral**[1] adj term • **neurohumoral** adj

» Reduced cardiac output can also activate several neural [n(j)ʊərəl] and humoral systems [ɪ]. This causes disruption [ʌ] of the blood-aqueous humor barrier[2], vasodilatation [veɪzoʊ-], and increased permeability.

Use aqueous[3] / ocular / vitreous[4] [ɪ] **humor** • **humoral** immunity[5] / response[6] / factors • **humoral** mediator [iː]/ antibodies[7] • **humoral** activity / control[8] / hypercalcemia [siː]/ presensitization[9] • **humorally** mediated • **neurohumoral** adjustment [ədʒʌst-]/ factors / response[10] / stimulation

(Körper)flüssigkeit, Humor
humoral[1] Blutkammerwasserschranke[2] Kammerwasser, Humor aquaeus[3] Glaskörper, Corpus vitreum[4] humorale Immunität[5] humorale Reaktion[6] humorale Antikörper[7] humorale Regulation[8] vorangegangene humorale Immunsensibilisierung[9] neurohumorale Reaktion[10]

9

endogenous [endɒːdʒənˀs] adj term opposite **exogenous**[1] adj term
arising [aɪ] from or caused by factors within the organism

» Alterations in the host defense mechanism predispose the patient to infections from his usually nonpathogenic [dʒe] endogenous microflora [aɪ]. Exogenous steroids may be safely discontinued[2].

Use **endogenous** factor / flora [ɔː]/ cycle [saɪkl]/ toxins / infection[3] • **endogenous** creatinine / obesity [iː]/ pyrogens[4] [aɪ] / depression[5] • **exogenous** sources[6] [ɔː]/ reinfection[7] / contamination / steroid administration[8]

endogen
exogen[1] abgesetzt[2] endogene Infektion, Autoinfektion[3] endogene Pyrogene[4] endogene Depression[5] exogene Quellen[6] exogene Reinfektion[7] exogene Steroidzufuhr[8]

10

General Physiology

discharge [dɪstʃɑːrdʒ] v   rel **secrete**¹ [sɪkriːt],
    excrete² [iː] v clin & term, → U49-4
    release³ [rɪliːs] v & n term

(i) to set free or liberate a body fluid
(ii) to release an electric charge or emotions [oʊʃ]
(iii) to release a patient from hospital → U20-16

discharge⁴ n clin • **secretion**⁵ [sɪkriːʃⁿn] n term • **secretory**⁶ [iː] adj → U54-2
• **excretion**⁷ [ekskriːʃⁿn] n term • **excretory**⁸ [iː] adj • **excreta**⁹ n pl → U46-20

» Vulvovaginal candidiasis [aɪ] typically presents as a cottage cheese-like vaginal discharge. Following hydrolysis of the thyroglobulin, T4 and T3 are secreted into the plasma. Then the pustule ulcerates [ʌ], produces a milky secretion, and slowly invades the adjacent [eɪs] skin.

Use **to discharge** pus¹⁰ [ʌ] from a wound [uː]/ mucus [juː] from the rectum • **to discharge** a patient from the hospital • adrenergic [ɜː]/ nasal **discharge** • purulent [jʊə]/ aural¹¹ [ɔː]/ electrical **discharge** • urethral [iː]/ vaginal¹² / bloody / mucoid / watery¹³ **discharge** • **to secrete** growth factors / sex hormones • **to secrete** copious [oʊ] amounts¹⁴ [aʊ] / insulin / estrogen • **to excrete** urine / bilirubin / a gallstone [ɔː] • **to excrete** nitrogenous [ɒːdʒ] waste products¹⁵ • gastric¹⁶ / hormone or hormonal¹⁷ **secretion** • bile¹⁸ / lipid / milk / over**secretion** • **to** clear¹⁹/evacuate/suction²⁰ [ʌ] **secretions** • airway / oral / salivary²¹ / vaginal²² / ocular **secretions** • clear / thick / purulent²³ / tenacious²⁴ [eɪʃ] **secretions** • hypo/ hyper**secretory** • renal / urinary albumin / fecal [iː] fat²⁵ / water / uric acid **excretion**

> **Note:** The terms **excrete** and **excretion** typically refer to evacuation or expulsion [ʌ] of material from the body or an individual cell (e.g. feces²⁶ [fiːsiːz]). Also, do not confuse **secretion** and **secret**²⁷.

stimulate [stɪmjəleɪt] v   sim **activate**¹ v, rel **enhance**² [ɪnhænˈs] v

to cause increased [iː] functional [ʌ] activity in the body or any of its parts or organs

stimulation n term • **stimulus**³ n, pl -i • **stimulatory** adj • **activator** n
• **(psycho)stimulant**⁴ adj & n term • **enhancement**⁵ n • **(un)enhanced** adj

» The release of amino acids from muscle [mʌsl] is regulated by insulin, which stimulates amino acid uptake⁶ and protein synthesis [ɪ]. Opioids produce analgesia [dʒiː] by activating pain-inhibitory neurons [n(j)ʊə-]. Intrinsic factor secretion is enhanced by stimuli that evoke [oʊ] H+ output from parietal [aɪ] cells.

Use **to stimulate** growth / potassium excretion⁷ [iːʃ]/ appetite⁸ / nerve [ɜː] fibers⁹ [aɪ] • skin / hormonal / electrical¹⁰ / mechanical [k] **stimulation** • vagal¹¹ [eɪ]/ sympathetic / antigenic¹² [dʒe]/ over- or hyper**stimulation** • sensory¹³ / tactile / auditory [ɒː] **stimuli** • conditioned¹⁴ / painful / noxious¹⁵ [ɒːkʃ] **stimuli** • **to activate** cells / a muscle / receptors / neurons / platelets¹⁶ [eɪ] • prothrombin / tissue [tɪʃ‖sjuː] plasminogen¹⁷ **activator** • **to enhance** blood supply / cardiac output¹⁸ / analgesic [dʒiː] effects¹⁹ • **enhancement of** insulin secretion / estrogen levels²⁰ / urinary excretion • circulatory [sɜː] contrast²¹ **enhancement**

trigger [trɪɡə] v   syn **evoke** [ɪvoʊk], **elicit** [ɪlɪsɪt] v term → U102-3

to initiate [ɪʃ] or stimulate an action, mechanism or course [ɔː] of events

trigger¹ n

» Platelets, which play a key role in thrombus formation, trigger the coagulation process. Triggered activity occurs [ɜː] when afterdepolarizations reach the threshold level required to trigger a new depolarization. The formation of intratubular casts² was the major trigger for his acute renal failure. Secondary hyperparathyroidism [aɪ] was evoked by urinary losses of calcium. In osteoarthritis [aɪ] of the knee joint movement commonly elicits bony crepitus.

Use **to trigger** sweating [e]/ ovulation / a cough³ [kɒf]/ symptoms [ɪ]/ attacks⁴ • **trigger** mechanism⁵ / stimulus⁶ / factors⁷ / point⁸ / area or zone⁹ • asthma¹⁰ [æzmə]/ bacterial [ɪə]/ endogenous / environmental **trigger** • **to evoke** pain¹¹ / symptoms / muscle relaxation • **to evoke** an immune response¹² / inflammation [eɪʃ]/ acute exacerbations¹³ [s] • **to elicit** a reflex [iː] or jerk¹⁴ [dʒɜːrk]/ an allergic [ɜː] reaction¹⁵ / rebound [aʊ] tenderness¹⁶ / the patient's wishes

---

MEDICAL SCIENCE 387

(i) **ausscheiden, absondern**
(ii) **(sich) entladen**
(iii) **entlassen**

absondern, sezernieren¹ absondern, ausscheiden² ausschütten, freisetzen; Abgabe, Freisetzung³ Absonderung, Sekret⁴ Absonderung, Sekretion; Sekret⁵ sekretorisch, sezernierend⁶ Ausscheidung, Exkretion⁷ exkretorisch⁸ Exkrete⁹ Eiter absondern¹⁰ eitriger Ausfluss aus d. Ohr¹¹ Scheidenausfluss, Fluor vaginalis¹² wässriges Sekret¹³ große Mengen sezernieren¹⁴ Stickstoffschlacken ausscheiden¹⁵ Magensekretion¹⁶ Hormonsekretion¹⁷ Gallensekretion, -produktion¹⁸ Sekret entfernen¹⁹ S. absaugen²⁰ Speichel²¹ Scheidensekret²² eitriges S.²³ zähes S.²⁴ Stuhlfettausscheidung²⁵ Stuhl²⁶ Geheimnis²⁷

11

stimulieren, anregen

aktivieren, anregen¹ verstärken, steigern² Stimulus, Reiz³ stimulierend; Stimulans, Anregungsmittel⁴ Vergrößerung, Enhancement, Steigerung⁵ Aufnahme⁶ d. Kaliumausscheidung anregen⁷ d. Appetit anregen⁸ Nervenfasern stimulieren⁹ Elektrostimulation¹⁰ Vagusstimulation¹¹ Antigenstimulation¹² Sinnesreize¹³ konditionierte/ bedingte R.¹⁴ schädl. Reize¹⁵ die Blutplättchen aktivieren¹⁶ Gewebeplasminogenaktivator¹⁷ d. Herzminutenvolumen erhöhen¹⁸ d. schmerzstillende Wirkung erhöhen¹⁹ Erhöhung d. Östrogenspiegel²⁰ Kontrastverstärkung²¹

12

auslösen, triggern

Auslöser, Trigger¹ Harnzylinder² e. Hustenanfall auslösen³ Anfälle auslösen⁴ Triggermechanismus⁵ Triggerreiz⁶ Triggerfaktoren⁷ Triggerpunkt⁸ Triggerzone⁹ Asthmaauslöser¹⁰ Schmerzen hervorrufen¹¹ e. Immunreaktion/ -antwort auslösen¹² zu einer akuten Verschlechterung führen¹³ e. Reflex auslösen¹⁴ e. allergische Reaktion auslösen¹⁵ den Loslassschmerz auslösen¹⁶

13

MEDICAL SCIENCE — General Physiology

inhibit v   syn **block** v, sim **inactivate**[1], **suppress**[2], **depress**[3] v

to cause a decrease, slow down or arrest of a function or process

(dis)**inhibition**[4] n term • **inhibitory**[5] adj • **inhibitor**[6] n • (in)**activation** n • (in)**activity**[7] n term • (in/ hyper)**active** adj • **suppression**[8] n • **depression** n

» Estrogens inhibit the actual secretion of milk. Several drugs reduce spasticity [ɪs] by inhibiting the spinal cord reflexes. Hypergastrinemia is due to loss of acid inhibition of gastrin G cells. The fasting state is necessary to avoid postprandial depression of phosphate. Do not suppress cough.

Use **to inhibit** enzyme activity / bone resorption / growth[9] • competitive[10] / feedback / reflex **inhibition** • near-complete / transient / (ir)reversible [ɜː]/ short-term **inhibition** • platelet-**inhibiting** agents [eɪdʒ] or drugs[11] • prostaglandin / monoamine oxidase[12] (abbr MAO) **inhibitor** • **to suppress** androgens / insulin release[13] / a reflex / overactivity • bone marrow [æ]/ hormonal / immune[14] / T cell **suppression** • appetite-**suppressing** drugs[15] • appetite-**suppressants**[15] • **to depress** ventilation / the CNS[16] / liver function • myocardial / respiratory[17] / bone marrow[18] **depression** • adrenergic / antibacterial[19] / enzyme[20] / metabolic **activity** • plasma renin[21] / reflex / cardiac[22] / ovarian / bladder **activity**

hemmen, inhibieren
inaktivieren[1] unterdrücken, supprimieren, z. Stillstand bringen[2] dämpfen, herabsetzen[3] (Dis)inhibition, (Ent)hemmung[4] hemmend[5] Inhibitor, Hemmer[6] Tätigkeit, Aktivität; Wirkung[7] Suppression, Unterdrückung[8] das Wachstum hemmen[9] kompetitive Hemmung[10] Thrombozytenhemmstoffe[11] Monoaminooxidase-, MAO-Hemmer[12] Insulinausschüttung unterdrücken[13] Immunsuppression[14] Appetitzügler[15] d. ZNS dämpfen[16] Atemdepression[17] Knochenmarkdepression[18] antibakterielle Wirkung[19] Enzymaktivität[20] Plasmareninaktivität[21] Herztätigkeit[22] 14

---

accumulate [əkjuː-] v   rel **replenish**[1] [e] v, opposite **deplete**[2] [iː] v term → U78-21

to increase in number or amount, e.g. fluids, cells, or various components collecting in a duct

accumulation n term • **accumulative**[3] adj • **depletion**[4] [iːʃ] n • **replenishment**[5] n

» In chronic bronchitis [kaɪ] secretions accumulate to produce dyspnea [ɪ] and wheezing[6] [iː]. Renal shut-down[7] [ʌ] may increase the risk of systemic accumulation of diphenidol. Even small worm [ɜː] burdens [ɜː] can deplete iron [aɪən] reserves [ɜː]. Initial [ɪʃ] treatment should replenish fluid and electrolyte [-laɪt] deficits.

Use **to accumulate** in the plasma / locally / to toxic levels[8] • fluid[9] / bilirubin / bacterial **accumulation** • (visceral) [ɪs] fat or lipid / drug **accumulation** • (extracellular/ intravascular) volume / salt[10] / water **depletion** • electrolyte / iron (-store)[11] / potassium[12] / nutritional[13] [ɪʃ] **depletion** • **to replenish** iron supplies[14] [aɪ]/ fluids / body stores • salt / vitamin [aɪ‖ɪ]/ volume[15] **replenishment**

ansammeln, akkumulieren
auffüllen, ergänzen[1] entleeren, erschöpfen[2] akkumulierend, (sich) anhäufend[3] Verlust, Entleerung, Depletion[4] Auffüllung, Ergänzung[5] pfeifendes Atemgeräusch, Giemen[6] Nierenversagen[7] toxische Werte erreichen[8] Flüssigkeitsansammlung[9] Salzverlust[10] Eisenverlust, -mangel[11] Kaliummangel[12] Mangelernährung[13] d. Eisenvorräte auffüllen[14] Volumenersatz, -substitution (bei Hypovolämie)[15] 15

---

output [ˈaʊtpʊt] n term   rel **clearance**[1] [klɪərənˈs] n term → U49-7
ejection[2] [ɪˈdʒekʃən] n term → U33-8

quantity of a specific substance produced, ejected, or excreted per time unit, e.g. urinary sodium output

eject[3] v term • **high-/ low-output** adj

» Resistance to infection, trauma [ɔː], and other stress is diminished because of reduced adrenal [iː] output. Drug elimination depends on the contribution [juːʃ] of renal elimination to total body clearance. No ejection click[4] is audible [ɔː]. Clinical workup[5] demonstrated a decreased [iː] hepatic uptake and clearance.

Use fluid[6] / energy / cardiac (abbr CO) **output** • cardiac minute[7] (abbr CMO) / stroke[8] **output** • stool [uː]/ sperm [ɜː]/ urinary or urine[9] **output** • saliva [aɪ]/ intake and[10] (abbr I & O) **output** • gastric acid [æsɪd]/ basal [eɪ] acid (abbr BAO)/ peak [iː] or maximal acid (abbr PAO/ MAO)/ speech[11] **output** • high-**output** (heart [ɑː]/ renal) failure[12] / septic shock[13] • (endogenous) creatinine[14] / renal[15] (calcium) / airway[16] **clearance** • metabolic / mucociliary[16] [sɪ] **clearance** • hepatic (bilirubin) / drug / inulin[17] **clearance** • **ejection** rate / fraction[18] / click[4] / sound[4] / murmur[4] [ɜː]

Output, (Arbeits)leistung, Abgabe, Ausstoß
Clearance[1] Ausstoß, -wurf[2] auswerfen, -stoßen[3] Ejektionsklick, systol. Austreibungsgeräusch[4] klin. Untersuchungen[5] Flüssigkeitsausscheidung, -abgabe[6] Herzminutenvolumen, HMV[7] Schlagvolumen[8] Harnausscheidung, -volumen[9] Aufnahme u. Ausscheidung[10] Sprachproduktion[11] Herzinsuffizienz m. großem HMV[12] hyperdynam. septischer Schock[13] Kreatinin-Clearance[14] renale C.[15] mukoziliäre C.[16] Inulin-C.[17] Ejektions-, Auswurffraktion[18] 16

---

adaptation [ædæpˈteɪʃən] n term → U77-9; U59-10
rel **acclimatization**[1], **accommodation**[2] n term → U59-12

change in function or constitution [(j)uːʃ] of tissue or an organ to meet new conditions

adaptive[3] adj term • (re)**adapt**[4] v • **adaptability**[5] n • **adaptational** adj • **acclimatize** [aɪ] v

» This could cause a rapid shift of water into cells that have undergone osmotic adaptation. Chronic ingestion [dʒe] of ethanol leads to adaptation by the liver. Growth hormone, which rises during fasting, is important in the body's adaptation to lack of food. Individuals not acclimatized to heat may develop symptoms [ɪ] as a result of salt depletion[6].

Use homeostatic / metabolic[7] / physiologic[8] / renal [iː]/ bacterial [ɪə] **adaptation** • dark[9] / light[10] / sexual / social / family **adaptation** • cold[11] / heat[12] [iː]/ altitude[13] [æ]/ full **acclimatization** • psychosocial [saɪkoʊ-]/ visual [ɪʒ] **accommodation** • **to adapt to** changes / physiologic alterations[14] / stress / challenges[15] [tʃæ] • **adaptive** mechanism[16] / capacity[5] [æs] / effect / response[17] / behavior [eɪ] • non/ mal**adaptive** • cold-/ host[18]- [oʊ]/ human-/ animal-/ highly / poorly **adapted**

Adapt(at)ion, Anpassung
Anpassung, Akklimatisation[1] Anpassung, Akkommodation[2] anpassungsfähig, adaptiv[3] anpassen, adaptieren[4] Anpassungsfähigkeit, Adaptabilität[5] Salzverlust[6] metabol. Anpassung/ Adaptation[7] physiolog. A.[8] Dunkeladaptation[9] Helladaptation[10] Kälteakklimatisation[11] Wärmeakklimatisation[12] Höhenakklimatisation, -adaptation[13] d. veränderten physiologischen Bedingungen anpassen[14] d. Anforderungen anpassen[15] Anpassungsmechanismus[16] Anpassungsreaktion[17] wirtsspezifisch[18] 17

General Pathology

MEDICAL SCIENCE 389

countercurrent [kaʊntəˈkɜːrənt] *n term* → U49-10

two currents [ɜː] flowing in opposite directions to effect an exchange of biochemical substances

» Loop [uː] diuretics[1] [e] interfere [ɪəʳ] with the countercurrent mechanism and produce an isoosmotic solute diuresis [iː]. Minimum edema [iː] at the papillary tip, within the renal pelvis[2], could influence the countercurrent concentrating mechanism.

Use **countercurrent** principle[3] / (flow/ concentrating) mechanism[3] / exchange system[4] • **countercurrent** multiplier (system) / immunoelectrophoresis[5] (*abbr* CIE)

Gegenstrom
Schleifendiuretika[1] Nierenbecken[2] Gegenstromprinzip[3] Gegenstromsystem[4] Elektrosyn(h)ärese, Überwanderungs-, Gegenstromelektrophorese[5]

18

---

metabolic imbalance *n term*   *syn* **disequilibrium** [dɪsɪkwɪˈlɪbrɪəm] *n term*
opposite **balance[1], equilibrium[1]** *n term*

disparity[2] in the quantities, concentrations, and proportionate amounts of bodily constituents or difference between intake and utilization, storage, or excretion of a substance

balanced[3] *adj term* • **counterbalance[4]** *n & v* • **equilibrate[5]** [ɪkwɪˈlɪbreɪt] *v*

» Heat stroke[6] is a result of imbalance between production and dissipation of heat[7]. Primary [aɪ] respiratory disturbances [ɜː] in acid-base balance[8] result in minimal transcellular K+ shifts[9]. Isotonic crystalloid [ɪ] salt solution was infused to counterbalance [aʊ] the loss of plasma volume into the extravascular space. The stability of body weight [weɪt] requires that intake and expenditure of energy[10] be balanced over time.

Use acid-base / fluid / electrolyte[11] / muscle[12] **imbalance** • protein / (negative) water / dietary[13] [aɪ] **balance** • (negative/ positive/ 24-hour) nitrogen[14] [aɪ]/ andrenergic-cholinergic [-ɜːrdʒɪk] **balance** • **balanced** salt solution[15] / diet[13] / suspension • to reach/maintain/be in **equilibrium** • osmotic[16] / pressure **(dis)equilibrium** • **equilibrium** state / phase / dialysis[17] [daɪˈæləsɪs]

Stoffwechselstörung
Gleichgewicht, Äquilibrium[1] Ungleichheit[2] ausgewogen, -geglichen[3] (ein) Gegengewicht (bilden), ausgleichen[4] ins Gleichgewicht bringen, im G. halten, äquilibrieren[5] Hitzschlag[6] Wärmeabgabe[7] Säure-Basen-Haushalt[8] Verlagerungen[9] Energieverbrauch[10] gestörter Elektrolythaushalt[11] muskuläre Dysbalance[12] ausgewogene Ernährung/ Kost[13] Stickstoffgleichgewicht, ausgeglichene Stickstoffbilanz[14] physiolog. (Koch)salzlösung[15] osmot. (Un)gleichgewicht[16] Gleichgewichtsdialyse[17]

19

---

steady state [ˈstedi steɪt] *n term*   *abbr* **ss**

condition in which the formation or introduction of substances just keeps pace[1] [peɪs] with their destruction or removal [uː] so that all volumes, concentrations, pressures, and flows [oʊ] remain constant

» A drug is considered to be at steady state after it has been continuously administered at the same dosage and interval for at least five half-lives[2]. In muscle physiology, a steady state is reached when the removal of lactic acid[3] by oxidation keeps pace[1] with its production, the oxygen supply being adequate, and the muscles [ʌs] do not go into debt [det] for oxygen[4].

Use to achieve [tʃ] /reach/be in/remain [eɪ] in/produce/maintain[5] [eɪ] **a steady state** in the / time to **steady state** • **steady state** (plasma) levels[6] / concentration[7] / hematopoiesis [iː] • **steady** potential[8] / fluid increase / decline[9] [aɪ]

Fließgleichgewicht, dynam. Gleichgewicht, Steady state, ss
s. d. Waage/ Schritt halten[1] Halbwertszeiten[2] Laktateliminierung[3] Sauerstoffschuld[4] e. Steady state aufrechterhalten[5] Steady-state-Plasmaspiegel[6] Steady-state-Konzentration[7] Bestandspotential[8] kontinuierliche(r) Rückgang/ Abnahme[9]

20

Unit 89   General Pathology
Related Units: 5 Injuries, 104 Pain, 106 Fractures, 12 Mortality, 94 Infections Diseases, 99 Tumor Types, 117 Diagnosis, 124 Medical & Surgical Emergencies

---

pathologic(al) [pæθəˈlɒːdʒɪk] *adj term*

related to the causes [ɒː], development, and nature of abnormal conditions, to the resulting structural and functional changes, or to pathology as a medical science and specialty

pathology[1] *n term* • **pathologist[2]** *n* • **pathogen[3]** *n* •
patho-, -opathy *comb*

» This condition is characterized pathologically by diffuse inflammatory changes. Psychoses [saɪˈkoʊsiːz] are manifested by pathology in all areas of mental function.

Use **pathologic** anatomy / histology / feature[4] [fiːtʃəʳ] / changes / abnormality / condition • **pathologic** finding[5] / appearance [ɪəʳ] / structure / confirmation • **pathologic** entity[6] / examination / diagnosis / staging • anatomical / cellular[7] / clinical / comparative / functional / humoral / medical / molecular / surgical **pathology** • underlying[8] / characteristic / dental / endocrine [ɪ‖aɪ] / bladder / bowel [aʊ]/ speech / negative for[9] **pathology** • (no) evidence[9] / site / type *of* **pathology** • cyto/ histo[10]/ neuro [ʊəʳ]/ immuno**pathology** • (lymph)aden/ arthr/ coagul[11]/ nephr/ encephal**opathy** • **patho**genic[12] [dʒe] /genesis /physiology /psychology [-saɪk] • cyto [saɪ-]/ neuro**pathogen**

pathologisch, krankhaft
Pathologie, path. Prozess/ Befund[1] Pathologe/-in[2] (Krankheits)erreger[3] path. Merkmal[4] p. Befund[5] p. Einheit[6] Zell-, Zytopathologie[7] Grundleiden, -krankheit[8] kein path. Befund[9] Histopathologie[10] Koagulopathie, Gerinnungsstörung[11] pathogen, krankheitserregend[12]

1

MEDICAL SCIENCE — General Pathology

morbid [ɔː] adj term → U120-12; U100-9   syn **diseased** [iː] adj clin
related to physical or mental diseases or pathologic conditions
morbidity[1] n term • **comorbidity**[2] n • **dys**-[3] [dɪs] • **mal**-[3] comb
• **-osis, -iasis** [aɪ] comb
» Hypernatremia [iː] in the elderly is a heterogeneous [dʒiː], morbid, and iatrogenic [aɪæ-] entity. In most cases there is little clinical morbidity or deterioration[4] [ɪɚ] of global ventricular function.
Use **morbid** mood[5] / depression / obesity[6] [iː]/ fear / jealousy[7] [dʒel-]/ anatomy[8] (BE)
• cardiovascular / drug-related / fetal [iː] **morbidity** • **dys**function(al) /plasia [eɪʒ] / peptic • tubercul/ acid/ cirrh [sɪr-]/ leukocyt**osis** [uː] • ameb/ cholelith[9] [k] / psor[10] [s]/ candid**iasis** • **mal**formation[11] /function(ing) /position[12]

krank(haft), pathologisch, morbid
Morbidität, Krankheitshäufigkeit[1] Komorbidität, Begleiterkrankung[2] Dys-, Fehl-, gestört[3] Verschlechterung[4] Verstimmung[5] Fettsucht, Adipositas[6] krankhafte Eifersucht[7] patholog. Anatomie[8] Cholelithiasis, Gallensteinleiden[9] Psoriasis, Schuppenflechte[10] Missbildung[11] Lageanomalie[12]
2

---

focus n term, pl -**i** [foʊsaɪ]   sim **lesion**[1] [liːʒᵊn] n term → U5-5
center or starting point of a pathologic process or change in the tissues; the term lesion is often used to refer to one of the sites of a multifocal disease
focal[2] [foʊkᵊl] adj term • **multifocal** adj
» Lesions may be localized, circumscribed[3] [aɪ], discrete[4] [iː], linear, poorly demarcated[5], diffuse or generalized in distribution. Were you able to determine the initial [ɪʃ] focus of infection?
Use **lesions** consist of / contain / are composed of / are confined [aɪ] to[6] / are clustered [ʌ] in • **lesions** are centered around / begin as / spread [e] to[7] / are associated [oʊʃ] with[8] • carious[9] / upper GI tract bleeding / primary [aɪ], solitary[4] / elevated[10] / genetic **lesion** • inflammatory / chronic / pre-existing / (intracranial [eɪ]) mass[11] / obstructive / palpable[12] / painless **lesion** • **focus of** inflammation[13] • principal / contiguous[14] [-ɪɡjʊəs]/ external **focus** • multiple / metastatic[15] **foci** • **focal** abscess / infection[16] / hemorrhage / infiltrate / neurologic deficit

(Krankheits)herd, Fokus
Läsion, Schädigung, Verletzung, Tumor[1] herdförmig, fokal[2] umschrieben[3] einzelstehend, solitär[4] schlecht abgegrenzt[5] sind beschränkt auf[6] breiten sich aus[7] gehen einher mit[8] kariöse Läsion[9] erhabene L.[10] intrakranielle Raumforderung[11] tastbare L.[12] Entzündungsherd[13] Nachbarherd[14] Metastasenherde[15] Fokal-, Herdinfektion[16]
3

---

affect vt clin → U4-10f   syn **involve** vt,
   sim **compromise**[1] [-maɪz], **impair**[2] [eə˞] vt clin
(i) to have a morbid, incapacitating[3], or otherwise damaging impact
(ii) to influence in some way
(un)affected adj term • **(un)involved** adj • **involvement**[4] n • **impairment**[5] n
» Males and females are equally affected. Many antibiotics impair renal function.
Use **to affect** adults / the bowel • adversely[6] / most commonly **affected** • **affected** joints / area / limb[7] [lɪm]/ eye / boys / first-degree relatives • **impaired** function / perfusion / vision[8] [ʒ] • hemodynamically / immuno[9] / acutely **compromised** • cognitive / transient[10] / irreversible / neurologic **impairment** • nodal[11] [oʊ]/ pleural [ʊə˞]/ intestinal / systemic / metastatic[12] / secondary / concomitant renal[13] **involvement**

(i) befallen, angreifen
(ii) betreffen
beeinträchtigen, gefährden[1] einschränken, schwächen, schädigen[2] behindernd, arbeitsunfähig machend[3] Befall, Beteiligung[4] Störung, Schwächung, Schädigung[5] geschädigt, angegriffen[6] betroffene Extremität[7] eingeschränktes Sehvermögen[8] abwehrgeschwächt[9] vorübergehende Beeinträchtigung[10] Lymphknotenbefall[11] Metastasierung[12] gleichzeitige Nierenbeteiligung[13]
4

---

anomaly n term   syn **abnormality** n, sim **mal/ deformation**[1] n term
deformity[1], impairment, dysfunction or deviation[2] [iː] from the average or norm
anomalous[3] adj term • **abnormal**[3] adj • **de-/malformed** adj → U142-3
» Occlusion may occur as a result of an anomalous course[4] of the artery. This leads to anomalies involving the eyes, brain, and kidneys.
Use congenital[5] / chromosome / fetal / vertebral / genital / developmental **anomaly** • **malformed** fetus[6] [iː]/ teeth • **deformed** joint • heart / valves[7] [æ]/ nail / ear

Anomalie, Fehlbildung
Missbildung, Deformierung, Deformität[1] Abweichung[2] abnorm, anomal[3] abnormer Verlauf[4] angeborene Fehlbildung[5] missgebildeter Fetus[6] deformierte Herzklappen[7]
5

---

congenital [dʒen] or **inborn** adj term   opposite **acquired**[1] [əkwaɪɚd] adj
diseases, malformations, anomalies, mental or physical traits[2] [eɪ] existing at birth
hospital-[3]/ **community-**/ **household-**/ **transfusion-acquired** adj term
» Rubella causes a variety [aɪə] of congenital defects, e.g. deafness[4] [defnəs] and mental retardation.
Use **congenital** disorder / absence of the eye[5] / malformation / deficiency / infection / heart disease[6] / deafness • to occur on a **congenital** basis • **inborn** error of metabolism[7] • perinatally [eɪ]/ nosocomially / venereally [ɪɚ] or (hetero)sexually[8] / occupationally[9] [eɪʃ]/ domestically / acutely **acquired**

angeboren, kongenital
erworben[1] Merkmale, Eigenschaften[2] nosokomial[3] Taubheit[4] Anophthalmus congenitus[5] angeborener Herzfehler[6] genet. Stoffwechseldefekt[7] durch Sexualkontakt erworben[8] berufsbedingt, Berufs-[9]
6

General Pathology   MEDICAL SCIENCE **391**

here**ditary** *or* **inh**e**rited** *adj clin & term*   *sim* **fam**i**lial**[1] *adj term* → U84-28

transmitted from parent to offspring[2] in an ancestral [se] line of descent[3] [disent]

inh**e**rit (from)[4] v • inh**e**ritance[5] n • h**e**redity[5] n • inh**e**ritable[6] *adj*
• h**e**redo- *comb*

» Synovitis [aɪ] *is frequently seen in familial forms with early* onset[7]. *The* ancestral *history*[8] *showed* dominant *inheritance of* susceptibility[9] [sep] *to retinoblastoma. Both disorders are inherited as* autosomal [ɒː] *inherited traits*[10].

Use **her**e**ditary** syndrome • **inh**e**rited** clotting [ɒː] disorder[11] / trait / gen**e**tic defect • mode of / mat**e**rnal[12] / Mendelian **inh**e**ritance** • familial / auts**o**mal / d**o**minant[13] / rec**e**ssive / x-linked[14] **inh**e**ritance pattern** • **fam**i**lial** x-linked trait / t**e**ndency / (pre)disposition *or* susceptib**i**lity[9] • **fam**i**lial** transmission / syndrome / pattern / clustering [ʌ] *or* aggregation[15] • **fam**i**lial** occurrence[16] [ɜː]/ incidence / polyp**o**sis • x-linked[14] **h**e**redity** • **h**e**redo**familial /pathology

   Note: Do not confuse *familial* and *familiar* as in *to be familiar with*[17].

erblich, hereditär, Erb-
familiär[1] Kind, Nachkomme[2] von einer Generation auf die nächste[3] erben[4] Vererbung, Heredität[5] erblich, vererbbar[6] Beginn, Ausbruch[7] Ahnengeschichte[8] (fam. Prä)disposition[9] autosomal vererbte Merkmale[10] angeborene Koagulopathie/ Gerinnungsstörung[11] maternale Vererbung[12] dominante V.[13] X-chromosomaler Erbgang[14] fam. Häufung[15] familiäres Auftreten[16] vertraut sein mit[17]

7

idiopathic [ɪdɪoʊpæθɪk] *adj term*

referring to a disease of unknown cause *or* etiology[1] [iː]
» *The majority of cases are idiopathic in origin.*
Use **idiopathic** pericard**i**tis [aɪ]/ vitil**i**go [aɪ‖ɪ] • **chronic idiopathic** jaundice[2] [dʒɔːndɪs] / diarrh**ea** [daɪərɪːə]

idiopathisch, genuin, essentiell
Ätiologie, (Krankheits)ursache[1] chronische(r) idiopathische(r) Gelbsucht/ Ikterus[2]

8

iatrogenic [aɪætrədʒenɪk] *adj,* **-ically** *adv term* → U121-15

induced by an unfavorable[1] [eɪ] response to medical or surgical treatment
» *Pneumothorax* [nuː-] *may be classified as* spontaneous [eɪ], *traumatic, or iatrogenic, depending on the cause. Many* renal *infections are iatrogenic, i.e. introduced at the time of stone manipulation.*
Use **iatrogenic** factor / infection / trauma [ɒː]/ complication • **iatrogenically** induced / triggered[2] / compromised[3]

iatrogen, durch d. Arzt verursacht
ungünstig, unerwünscht[1] iatrogen[2] durch ärztliche Maßnahmen beeinträchtigt[3]

9

irritation [ɪrɪteɪʃᵊn] *n* → U104-3

(i) itching[1] [ɪtʃ], painful, or incipient[2] [sɪp] inflammatory reaction
(ii) overexcitation[3] [ksaɪ] or excessive sensit**i**vity[4]
irritate v • **irritative** *or* **-able**[5] *adj* • **irritab**i**lity**[6] n • **irritant**[7] n
» *All* penic**i**llins *are irritating to the CNS. There was some local irritation at the site of injection.*
Use nerve root[8] / meningeal [-dʒɪəl] / gastric[9] / chronic / chemical **irritation** • (generalized/focal) nervous / neuromuscular / reflex / gastric (outlet) **irritab**i**lity** • **irritative** reaction / lesion / voiding symptoms[10] • **irritable** mood[11] [uː]/ and tense patient[12] / bladder[13] / colon *or* bowel syndrome[14]

Reizung, Irritation
juckende[1] beginnende[2] Überreizung[3] Überempfindlichkeit[4] reizbar, Reiz-[5] Reizbarkeit, Irritabilität[6] Irritans, Reizmittel[7] Nervenwurzelreizung[8] Magenreizung[9] Reizblasen-Syndrom, irritative Blasenentleerungsstörung[10] gereizte Stimmung[11] reizbare(r) und nervöse(r) Patient(in)[12] Reizblase[13] Reizkolon[14]

10

inflammation [ɪnfləmeɪʃᵊn] *n*

dynamic cytologic and histologic reactions in response to injury or abnormal stimulation caused by physical, chemical, or biologic agents; includes local reactions and the resulting morphologic changes, destruction or removal of injurious[1] [dʒuː] materials, and responses leading to repair and healing
inflamed[2] [eɪ] *adj* • **-itis** [aɪtɪs] *comb* • **(non-/ anti-)inflammatory**[3] [æ] *adj*
» *Inflammations of* mucous m**e**mbranes *with free* discharge[4] [-tʃɑːrdʒ] *are called* catarrh. *The so-called* cardinal signs of inflammation[5] *are redness, heat, swelling, pain, and inhibited function.*
Use (sub)acute / chronic / exudative[6] [uː]/ catarrhal / adhesive[7] [iː] **inflammation** • allergic [ɜː]/ atrophic / degenerative **inflammation** • focal[8] / fibrinous [aɪ] fibroid / granulomatous **inflammation** • hyperplastic *or* proliferative[9] / interstitial [ɪʃ]/ necrotic[10] **inflammation** • productive [ʌ]/ sclerosing / serous[11] [ɪɚ]/ serofibrinous / purulent [pjʊɚ] *or* suppurative[12] [ʌ] **inflammation** • **inflammatory** process / reaction / eruption[13] / bowel disease / exudate / infiltrate • **anti-inflammatory** drugs[14]

   Note: All terms for inflammations end in **-itis**, e.g. gastritis, bronchitis [k], etc.

Entzündung
schädlich, schädigend[1] entzündet[2] entzündlich[3] (Flüssigkeits)absonderung[4] klassische Entzündungszeichen[5] exsudative E.[6] Adhäsion infolge v. E.[7] fokale E.[8] proliferative E.[9] nekrotisierende E.[10] seröse E.[11] eitrige E.[12] entzündl. Exanthem[13] entzündungshemmende Mittel, Antiphlogistika[14]

11

MEDICAL SCIENCE — General Pathology

pus [pʌs] *n term*

a protein-rich liquid inflammation product comprised of leukocytes [uː], a thin fluid, and cellular debris[1]

purulent[2] [pjʊəˀəlˀnt] *adj term* • **pyo-** [paɪoʊ] *comb* • **purulence**[3] *n*

» An abscess is a localized collection of pus in a cavity formed by the disintegration of tissue[4].

Use to release [iː] *or* discharge[5]/contain **pus** • sterile / foul-smelling[6] [aʊ]/ gross[7] [oʊ]/ frank[8] / localized / loculated **pus** • aspiration / drainage[9] / evacuation **of pus** • **pus** collections[10] /-forming[11] / formation / cells • **pus** from an abscess • **purulent** collections[10] / effusion[12]

Eiter, Pus
Zelltrümmer[1] eitrig, purulent[2] Eiterung, Eiterbildung[3] Gewebeeinschmelzung[4] Eiter absondern[5] übelriechender Eiter[6] makroskop. sichtbare Eiterung[7] klin. manifeste Abszedierung[8] Eiterableitung[9] Eiteransammlungen[10] eiterbildend[11] eitriger Erguss[12]

12

---

consolidation *n term*   *rel* **infiltration**[1] *n term*

(i) solidification[2] into a firm dense mass; esp. inflammatory changes of the lung due to the presence of cellular exudate in the air spaces
(ii) stage in healing, e.g. in fractures when the callus changes into bone

consolidate[3] *v term* • **consolidated** *adj* • **infiltrate**[4] *v & n* • **infiltrative**[5] *adj*

» Chest x-rays show consolidation in several pulmonary segments. The normal sound of underlying air-containing lung is resonant, while consolidated lung or a pleural [ʊɚ] effusion[6] sounds dull[7] [ʌ].

Use to undergo[3] **consolidation** • areas[8] / (x-ray) signs[9] **of consolidation** • pulmonary[10] / (multi)lobar / diffuse / focal[11] / segmental **consolidation** • massive / patchy[12] / parenchymal / air space **consolidation** • **consolidated** pulmonary infiltrate • organ / pulmonary / metastatic / tumor / bone marrow[13] **infiltration** • nodular / diffuse / pulmonary / cellular / inflammatory[14] / interstitial [ɪʃ] **infiltrate** • **infiltrative** tumor / lung disease / process

(i) Verdichtung
(ii) (Ver)festigung, Aushellung
Infiltration[1] Hart-, Festwerden[2] verdichten[3] infiltrieren; Infiltrat[4] infiltrativ[5] Pleuraerguss[6] gedämpft[7] Verdichtungsareale[8] (radiolog.) Verschattung[9] pulmonale Verdichtung[10] Verdichtungsherde[11] intrapulm. Verdichtungsbezirke[12] Knochenmarkinfiltration[13] entzündliches Infiltrat[14]

13

---

induration *n term*

(i) pathological process of becoming extremely firm or hard (ii) focus of indurated tissue

indurated *adj* • **indurate**[1] *v* • **indurative** *adj*

» The rash[2] tends to be associated with muscular pain, tenderness, and induration. After rupture the tissues surrounding the ulcer [ʌlsɚ] often become indurated, reddened and tender[3].

Use localized / extensive / focal / painful / palpable / leathery [e] *or* brawny[4] [ɔː]/ red / gray / doughy[5] [doʊi] **induration** • area / degree **of induration** • **indurated** borders / edges / nodules[6] / inflammatory tissue / plaque / ulcer

Induration, Verhärtung
verhärten, indurieren[1] Ausschlag, Exanthem[2] (druck)schmerzempfindlich[3] Gewebeverhärtung[4] teigige Induration[5] indurierte Knoten[6]

14

---

hypertrophy [haɪpɜːrtrəfi] *n term*   *sim* **hyperplasia**[1] [-eɪ(ɪ)ə] *n term*

increase in bulk[2] [ʌ] (through increase in size not in number of cells) of an organ or tissues not due to tumor formation

hypertrophic[3] *adj term* • **hypertrophied**[4] *adj* • **hyperplastic**[5] *adj*

» The patient presents with marked hypertrophy of the left ventricle, involving in particular the interventricular septum of the left ventricular outflow tract.

Use cardiac[6] / left ventricular[7] (*abbr* LVH) / gastric / glomerular / benign [-aɪn] prostatic[8] (*abbr* BPH) / compensatory[9] **hypertrophy** • **hypertrophic** scar[10] / gastritis[11] / cardiomyopathy[12] • **hypertrophied** muscle / ventricle

Note: Although different in meaning, *hypertrophy* and *hyperplasia* are often (incorrectly) used synonymously.

Hypertrophie, Vergrößerung
Hyperplasie[1] Größe[2] hypertroph[3] vergrößert[4] hyperplastisch[5] Herzhypertrophie[6] Linksherzhypertrophie[7] benigne Prostatahyperplasie[8] kompensat./ vikariierende Hypertrophie[9] hypertrophe Narbe[10] Ménétrier-Syndrom[11] hypertroph. Kardiomyopathie[12]

15

---

nodule [nɒːdjʊl] *or* **-lus** *n term*   *sim* **swelling**[1], **tumor**[1] [tjuːmɚ] *n term*, **lump**[1] [ʌ], **mass**[1] *n jar & clin* → U97-2f

(i) a small, palpable mass of solid pathologic tissue (ii) rarely also a node of normal tissue

nodosity[2] *n term* • **nodular** *or* **nodose**[3] [noʊdoʊs] *adj* • **nodulation**[4] *n*

» Most multinodular goiters[5] are benign, while a solitary[6] thyroid [aɪ] nodule tends to be malignant.

Use pulmonary / rheumatoid [uː]/ gouty[8] [aʊ]/ solitary *or* discrete[9] **nodule** • subcutaneous [eɪ] / calcified [s]/ ulcerated / mobile[10] [ˀ∥aɪ]/ metastatic **nodules** • **nodular** aggregations[11] / lesion / hyperplasia • breast [e]/ painless[12] / firm **lump** • axillary / abdominal / asymptomatic / palpable **mass**

Nodulus, Knoten, Knötchen
Schwellung, Geschwulst, Tumor, Knoten[1] Knoten(bildung), Nodositas[2] knotig, knotenförmig[3] Knotenbildung[4] Kropf, Struma[5] solitär[6] Rheumaknoten, Nodulus rheumaticus[7] Gichtknoten, Tophus arthriticus[8] Solitärknoten[9] bewegliche K.[10] Knotenansammlungen[11] indolenter Knoten[12]

Note: Even though the term *tumor* is generally used for any morbid enlargement or swelling, patients are more likely to associate this word with its second meaning, i.e. *neoplasia*. Therefore, the expressions *swelling*, *mass*, and *lump* should be preferred when talking to patients.

16

General Pathology   MEDICAL SCIENCE 393

ulcer [ʌlsɚ] *n term & clin*   *sim* **sore¹** [sɔːr] *n & adj clin* → U104-11
                                     rel **erosion²** [ɪrouʒᵊn] *n term* → U114-13

lesion on the surface of the skin or mucosa caused by loss of superficial³ [ɪʃ] tissue (esp due to inflammation)

ulcerative⁴ *adj term* • **ulcerated** *adj* • **ulceration⁵** *n* • **erosive** *adj*

» A wound [uː] with superficial loss of tissue from trauma is not primarily an ulcer, but may become ulcerated if infection occurs.

Use **ulcer** crater⁶ [eɪ] • gastric⁷ / peptic⁸ / decubitus⁹ / symptomatic / penetrating / inflamed / perforated¹⁰ **ulcer** • varicose¹¹ / aphthous¹² [æfθəs]/ venereal *or* soft¹³ / rodent¹⁴ [ou]/ / hard¹⁵ **ulcer** • groin¹⁶ / marginal¹⁷ [dʒ]/ chronic / indolent¹⁸ / sloughing [ɒːf] *or* perambulating¹⁹ **ulcer** • healed / herpetic / serpiginous [ɪdʒ] *or* creeping²⁰ **ulcer** • dendritic [ɪ]/ diphtheritic / distension / undermining [aɪ] **ulcer** • **ulcer of the** foot / cornea • bed *or* pressure⁹ / running²¹ / cold²² / oriental²³ / plaster²⁴ **sore**

Ulkus, Ulcus, Geschwür
wunde Stelle, Hautläsion, Geschwür; wund¹ Erosion² oberflächlich³ ulzerös, ulzerierend⁴ Geschwürbildung, Ulzeration⁵ Ulkuskrater⁶ Magengeschwür, U. ventriculi⁷ Ulcus pepticum⁸ Dekubitalgeschwür⁹ perforiertes U.¹⁰ U. varicosum, Unterschenkelgeschwür¹¹ Aphthe¹² weicher Schanker, U. molle venereum¹³ U. rodens, exulzerierend wachsendes Basaliom¹⁴ U. durum, harter Schanker¹⁵ Granuloma inguinale¹⁶ Randulkus¹⁷ nicht heilendes Geschwür¹⁸ U. phagedaenicum¹⁹ kriechendes G.²⁰ eiternde Wunde²¹ Herpes simplex²² kutane Leishmaniase, Orientbeule²³ Druckstelle durch Gipsverband²⁴

17

obstruction [ʌ] *n term*   *sim* **occlusion¹**, **obturation²** *n term*, → U124-13
                                 rel **obliteration³**, **atresia⁴** [-iːʒ(ɪ)ə] *n term*

blockage or clogging² of vessels, ducts, and body passages, e.g. by occlusion, obturation or stenosis

obstruct⁵ *v term* • **(non)obstructive⁶** *adj* • **obstructing⁶** *adj* • **occlude⁷** *v* • **occlusive** *adj* • **atretic** [e] *or* **imperforate⁸** *adj*

» Barium enema⁹ demonstrated an obstructing lesion in the colon. Simple mechanical [k] obstruction of the colon may develop insidiously¹⁰.

Use to produce/cause/demonstrate/relieve **obstruction** • strangulating / pyloric [aɪ]/ intestinal / airway(s)¹¹ / nasal / extrahepatic / biliary¹² [ɪ] **obstruction** • bladder outlet¹³ / cardiac outflow / fixed coronary / membranous **obstruction** • recurrent¹⁴ / prolonged / pronounced¹⁵ / partial **obstruction** • **obstructed** airway / vessels • **obstructing** foreign [fɒːrɪn] body / tumor / calculi [aɪ] • **obstructive** process / lung disease / shock / uropathy¹⁶ • intestinal / choanal¹⁷ [kouənᵊl]/ biliary¹⁸ **atresia** • **atretic** duct [ʌ] • **imperforate** hymen¹⁹ [aɪ]/ anus²⁰ [eɪ]

Obstruktion, Verlegung, Abflussstörung
Okklusion, Verschluss¹ Verlegung² Obliteration, Verödung³ Atresie⁴ obstruieren, verlegen⁵ obstruktiv, obturierend⁶ verstopfen, -schließen⁷ atretisch⁸ Bariumeinlauf⁹ schleichend¹⁰ Atemwegsobstr.¹¹ Gallengangobstr.¹² Blasenhalsobstr.¹³ rezidivierende O.¹⁴ ausgeprägte O.¹⁵ Harnwegsobstruktion¹⁶ Choanalatresie¹⁷ Gallengangatr.¹⁸ hymenale A., Hymen imperforatus¹⁹ Analatresie²⁰

18

stricture [strɪktʃɚ] *n term*   *sim* **stenosis¹** [ou] *n term, pl* -ses

abnormal narrowing of a tube or duct due to contracture² [-æktʃɚ] or deposition of tissue

constrict³ *v term* • **constriction⁴** *n* • **constrictive** *adj* • **strictured** *adj*

» Crohn's disease may produce gastric ulceration and/or scarring⁵ with stricture formation. Peptic esophageal [dʒɪəl] ulcers heal slowly, tend to recur, and leave a stricture upon healing.

Use biliary / urethral⁶ [iː]/ rectal / peptic / short / annular⁷ / anastomotic⁸ **stricture** • contractile / bridle⁹ [aɪ]/ functional **stricture** • nondilatable [aɪleɪt]/ intrinsic / spasmodic¹⁰ / permanent / temporary / recurrent **stricture** • **stricture** dilation¹¹ • **constrictive** pericarditis / edema¹²

Striktur, (hochgradige) Verengung
Stenose, Verengung¹ Kontraktur² verengen³ Ein-, Verengung, Einschnürung, Konstriktion⁴ Narbenbildung⁵ Harnröhrenstriktur⁶ anuläre Verengung⁷ Anastomosenstr.⁸ Bridenstriktur⁹ spastische/ funktionelle Str.¹⁰ Bougierung¹¹ Stauungsödem¹²

19

stenosis [stənousɪs] *n term, pl* -ses

narrowing or constriction of a heart valve, blood vessel, or other body passages

stenose¹ *v term* • **stenotic** *or* **stenosed** *adj* • **stenosing²** *adj*

» One of the arteries to the brain is markedly stenosed. The success rate in treating stenoses of small vessels are better than for complete occlusion.

Use valvular³ / mitral [aɪ]/ aortic⁴ [eɪ]/ tracheal [k]/ artherosclerotic / carotid / ureteral⁵ / pyloric⁶ [aɪ]/ anal [eɪ] **stenosis** • partial⁷ / high-grade⁸ / short / degree *or* severity of **stenosis** • **stenosed** aortic valve / Eustachian [juː] tube • **stenotic** lesion / segment • **stenosing** tenosynovitis

Stenose, Verengung
stenosieren, eng werden¹ verengend² (Herz)klappenstenose³ Aortenstenose⁴ Harnleiterstenose⁵ Pylorusstenose⁶ inkomplette S.⁷ hochgradige Stenose⁸

20

MEDICAL SCIENCE — General Pathology

calculus n term, pl **-i** [aɪ]   syn **stone** n clin, **concretion** [iː] n term

concretion usually composed of salts of inorganic or organic acids forming in body passages, most commonly in the biliary and urinary tracts

(a)calculous[1] adj term • **-lith(o)-** comb • **stone-free**[2] /**-forming**[3] adj

» Calculi less than 1 cm in diameter may be approached endoscopically. If a stone has previously been passed or if one is recovered, its chemical composition should be analyzed.

Use salivary[4] / biliary / urinary[5] / vesical[6] / preputial[7] [uːʃ] **calculus** • uterine [aɪ‖ɪ]/ arthritic [ɪ]/ bronchial / cerebral **calculus** • lacrimal[8] / mammary[9] / intestinal[10] / pancreatic **calculus** • pleural [ʊɚ]/ dental[11] / pulp [ʌ]/ subgingival [dʒ] **calculus** • staghorn[12] / apatite [aɪ]/ struvite [-uːvaɪt]/ oxalate [eɪ]/ coral[13] / cystine [sɪ] **calculus** • fibrin / weddellite[14] / hematogenetic / encysted / pocketed[15] / dislodged[16] [ɒːdʒ]/ renal[17] **calculus** • common duct[18] / gall[19] / kidney[17] **stone** • **stone** disease[20] / clearance[21] / impaction[22] / extraction / former[23] / gastric[24] / calcium [s] **concretion** • **litho**tomy /tripsy[25] /tripter • uro/ nephro/ chole**lithiasis**

---

prolapse [n proʊlæps‖v -læps] n & v term

sim **ptosis**[1] [toʊsɪs] n term → U113-17

(n) displacement or sagging[2] of an organ or structure, esp at a natural or artificial orifice

ptotic adj term • **prolapsing** adj • **prolapsed** adj

» A long pedunculated [ʌ] polyp[3] had prolapsed through the anus. Ptosis, i.e. a droopy[4] [uː] upper eyelid, may be congenital or acquired.

Use mitral valve[5] /mucosal / rectal[6] / uterine / intervertebral disk[7] **prolapse** • partial / first-degree / complete[8] / postpartum **prolapse** • fluctuating[9] / myo/ nephro/ neurogenic / progressive **ptosis**

---

hernia [hɜːrnɪə] n term   rel **rupture**[1] [rʌptʃɚ] n & v term → U5-19

protrusion[2] of a structure through the tissues normally enclosing it

herniate[3] v term • **herniation**[4] n • **hernial** adj •
hernio-, -cele [siːl] comb

» Surgery is indicated if the hernia has incarcerated[5]. The hernia sac[6] was excised [aɪ]. A ureterocele is a ballooning[7] [uː] of the distal submucosal ureter into the bladder.

Use **hernial** sac[6] / canal[8] / defect • abdominal / hiatal or hiatus[9] [aɪeɪ]/ inguinal[10] / scrotal [oʊ]/ direct **hernia** • umbilical[11] [ʌ]/ diaphragmatic / orbital / cerebral **hernia** • epigastric / sciatic[12] [saɪætɪk]/ obturator / incisional[13] [sɪʒ] **hernia** • lumbar [ʌ]/ sliding or slipped[14] / double loop [uː]/ (ir)reducible[15] / strangulated[16] **hernia** • complete / concealed[17] [siː]/ retrograde / synovial [aɪ] **hernia** • **hernia** repair[18] / defect • **hernia of the** broad ligament of the uterus • **herniated** intervertebral disk[19] / bowel / material or mass[20] • lumbar disk / brain[21] / internal **herniation** • **hernio**plasty[18] /rrhaphy • recto/ varico/ cysto[22]/ meningo/ hydro**cele**

---

cyst [sɪst] n term   sim **pseudocyst**[1] [suːdoʊsɪst] n term

abnormal sac containing gas, fluid or semisolid material which has a membranous lining[2] [aɪ]

cystic[3] adj term • **cyst(o)-** comb • **cyst-like** adj • **cystitis**[4] [sɪstaɪtɪs] n

» The contents of the encapsulated cyst[5] ruptured into the bronchioles.

Use jaw[6] / ovarian / sebaceous[7] [eɪ]/ calcified / ruptured / multilocular[8] / solitary / sequestration[9] **cyst** • **cyst** fluid / leakage[10] [liːkɪdʒ]/ wall / cavity • **cystic** disease / lesion / fibrosis[11] [aɪ]/ dilation • **cystic** duct[12] / spaces / kidney[13] /degeneration [dʒ] • **cysto**urethrography[14] /gram /cele /sarcoma /scopy • pancreatic **pseudocyst**

---

fistul(iz)ation n term

pathologic or therapeutic [pjuː] formation of an abnormal passage from one epithelialized [iː] surface to another

fistula[1] n term, pl **-as** or **-ae** [iː] • **fistulated** adj • **fistulous**[2] adj • **fistulo-** comb

» Fistulas to the bladder or vagina [dʒ] produce recurrent infections.

Use arteriovenous[3] [iː]/ bronchopleural [ʊɚ]/ pancreatic / perilymph / (peri)anal / vesical[4] / tracheoesophageal[5] [-dʒɪəl] **fistula** • draining[6] / internal[7] / blind[8] / long-standing **fistula** • **fistulous** tract[9] / opening[10] / communication[11] / anomaly • **fistul**otomy /graphy

---

Stein, Konkrement
(nicht) steinbedingt, Stein-[1] steinfrei[2] steinbildend[3] Speichelstein, Sialolith[4] Harnstein[5] Blasenst.[6] Balanolith, Präputialstein[7] Dakryolith[8] Milchgangst.[9] Kotstein[10] Zahnst.[11] Ausgussst.[12] Korallenst.[13] Weddellitst.[14] eingekapselter Blasenst.[15] abgegangener S.[16] Nierenstein[17] Choledochusstein[18] Gallenstein[19] Steinleiden[20] Abgang d. Steines[21] Steinimpaktion, -einklemmung[22] Steinbildner[23] Gastrolith, Magenstein[24] Lithotripsie, Steinzertrümmerung[25]   21

Vorfall, Prolaps
Ptose, Senkung[1] Senkung[2] gestielter Polyp[3] herabhängend[4] Mitralklappenprolaps[5] Rektumprolaps, Mastdarmvorfall[6] Diskushernie, Bandscheibenvorfall[7] Totalprolaps[8] intermittierende Ptose[9]   22

Hernie, Bruch
Ruptur, Riss; reißen, platzen[1] Hervortreten[2] austreten[3] Einklemmung, Herniation[4] inkarzeriert, eingeklemmt[5] Bruchsack[6] ballonförmige Auftreibung[7] Bruchpforte[8] Hiatushernie[9] Leistenbruch[10] Nabelbruch[11] Hernia glutaealis/ ischiadica[12] Narbenbruch[13] Gleithernie[14] (ir)reponible H.[15] inkarzerierte H.[16] nicht palpierbare H.[17] Bruchoperation, Hernioplastik[18] Bandscheibenvorfall[19] Bruchinhalt[20] zerebrale Herniation[21] Zystozele[22]   23

Zyste
falsche Z., Pseudozyste[1] epitheliale Auskleidung[2] zystisch; Blasen-[3] Zystitis, Blasenentzündung[4] eingekapselte Zyste[5] Kieferzyste[6] Atherom, Talgzyste[7] mehrkammerige/ multilokuläre Z.[8] Sequesterzyste[9] Austritt v. Zystenflüssigkeit[10] zyst. Fibrose, Mukoviszidose[11] Gallenblasengang, D. cysticus[12] Zystenniere[13] Miktionszystourethrografie[14]   24

Fistelbildung; Anlegen einer Fistel
Fistel[1] fistelartig, Fistel-[2] ateriovenöse Fistel[3] Blasenfistel[4] Ösophagotrachealfistel[5] ableitender Fistelgang[6] innere Fistel[7] blind endende F.[8] Fistelgang[9] Fistelmaul, -mund[10] fistelartige Verbindung[11]   25

General Pathology   MEDICAL SCIENCE 395

hematoma [hiːmətoumə] *n term, pl* **-as**

         rel **hemorrhage**[1] [hemərɪdʒ] *n & v term* → U5-13

localized mass of extravasated[2] blood confined [aɪ] in tissue spaces, e.g. a bruise[3] [bruːz] or a black eye[4]

    hemorrhagic *adj term* • **bleeding**[1] [iː] *n clin* • **bleed**[5] *v* • **ooze**[6] [uːz] *v*

» *Some hematomas will resorb, but those that become encapsulated usually require surgical treatment. In hematomas the blood is usually clotted and may manifest various degrees of organization and discoloration. Incidentally discovered[7] aneurysms* [ænjɚ-] *that have not previously* [iː] *hemorrhaged have a 2–3 % annual risk of bleeding.*

Use (intra)cerebral / superficial [ɪʃ]/ (intra)cranial[8] [eɪ]/ epi- or extradural / subdural **hematoma** • to control or arrest[9] **a hemorrhage** • to stop[9] **a bleeding** • subarachnoid [æk] / intraventricular **bleeding** • postpartum[10] / nasal / retinal / gastric / splenic [e]/ pelvic / subungual [ʌ] or splinter[11] **hemorrhage** • punctate[12] [ʌ]/ oozing[13] / occult / spurting[14] [ɜː]/ intermediate / internal[15] **hemorrhage** • primary / secondary[16] / serous [ɪɚ]/ unavoidable **hemorrhage** • **hemorrhagic** rash[17] / fever [iː]/ cystitis / shock / infarction / stroke[18] / necrosis

petechia [pɪtekɪə] *n term, usu pl* **-ae** [iː]

         sim **ecchymosis**[1] [ekɪmousɪs] *n term, pl* **-ses** [siːz]

punctate purpuric[2] [pɜːrpjuɚɪk] lesion due to extravasation of blood into tissues differing from ecchymosis only in size

    petechial *adj term* • **ecchymotic** *adj* • **micropetechiae** *n*

» *The rash of scarlet fever[3] blanches[4] on pressure, may become petechial, and fades[5]* [eɪ] *in 2–5 days. Signs of coagulopathy include hematuria, easy bruising[6], hematemesis, petechiae, and oozing at sites of venipuncture. Purpura and ecchymoses may also be present.*

Use palatal / discrete[7] [iː]/ linear / scattered[8] **petechiae** • **petechial** hemorrhage / lesion / rash • **petechially** confluent[9]

ischemia [ɪskiːmɪə] *n term*   *opposite* **hyperemia**[1] [aɪ] *n term BE* **-aemia**

local deficiency of blood due to functional constriction or mechanical obstruction of vessels

    (anti-)ischemic[2] *adj term* • **hyperemic**[3] *adj* • **ischemia-induced** *adj*

» *At laparoscopy the terminal ileum appeared hyperemic and boggy[4]. Obstruction was related to hyperemia and engorgement[5]* [dʒ] *of the microvasculature.*

Use to precipitate[6] [sɪ]/produce/develop[7] **ischemia** • cerebral / myocardial [aɪ]/ intestinal / peripheral **ischemia** • end-organ / limb[8] [lɪm]/ digital [dʒ] **ischemia** • exercise-induced / postural[9] [tʃɚ]/ focal / local / tourniquet[10] [tɜːrnɪkət] **ischemia** • irreversible / persistent / transient / silent / recurrent / profound[11] [aʊ] relative **ischemia** • active / passive / conjunctival [aɪ]/ pulp / congestive[12] [dʒe] **hyperemia** • **hyperemic** mucosa

degenerative [dɪdʒenərətɪv] *adj clin & term*

         rel **atrophic**[1] [eɪtrɒːfɪk] *adj term*

marked by gradual deterioration[2] [ɪɚ] of cells and organs with concomitant[3] loss of function

    degeneration[4] *n clin & term* • **degenerate** *v* • **degenerating** *adj* • **atrophy**[5] [ætrəfi] *n & v term*

» *Atrophy is a wasting* [eɪ] *of tissues[6] due to necrosis and resorption of cells, diminished cellular proliferation, pressure, ischemia, malnutrition, lessened function, hormonal changes, etc. At endoscopy, atrophic degeneration and scalloping[7] of the duodenal folds were observed.*

Use cerebellar / macular[8] / hyaline [haɪəlɪn] / arthritic / fatty / cheesy[9] [iː]/ progressive **degeneration** • **degenerative** lesion / changes / joint disease[10] • **atrophic** age-related macular degeneration / gastritis / skin • degenerative / scar / gingival[11] [dʒ]/ muscle or muscular **atrophy** • disuse or inactivity[12] / senile[13] [siːnaɪl]/ optic[14] **atrophy**

Hämatom, Bluterguss
Blutung, Hämorrhagie; bluten[1] (aus d. Gefäßen) ausgetreten[2] blauer Fleck, Bluterguss[3] blaues Auge[4] bluten[5] (Blut) sickern[6] zufällig entdeckt[7] intrakranielles Hämatom[8] Blutung stillen[9] Nachgeburtsblutung[10] subunguale Blutung[11] punktförm./ petechiale Blutung[12] Sickerblutung[13] pulssynchron spritzende B.[14] innere B.[15] Nachblutung[16] hämorrhagisches Exanthem[17] hämorrhagischer Insult[18]

26

Petechie, punktförmige Hautblutung
Ekchymose, flächenhafte Hautblutung[1] purpuraartig[2] Scharlach[3] blass werden[4] verblassen, -schwinden[5] Neigung z. Hämatomen[6] einzelne Petechien[7] disseminierte P.[8] mit konfluierenden Petechien[9]

27

Ischämie, Blutleere
vermehrte Blutfülle, Hyperämie[1] ischämisch[2] hyperämisch[3] aufgequollen[4] Anschwellen[5] Ischämie auslösen[6] ischämisch werden[7] Extremitätenischämie[8] lagebedingte I.[9] Esmarch-Blutleere[10] absolute/ totale I.[11] Stauungshyperämie[12]

28

degenerativ
atrophisch[1] allmähliche Verschlechterung[2] bei gleichzeitigem[3] Degeneration, Entartung[4] Atrophie; verkümmern, atrophieren[5] Gewebeschwund[6] Fältelung[7] Makuladegeneration[8] Verkäsung[9] degen. Gelenkerkrankung, Arthrose[10] Gingivaatrophie[11] Inaktivitätsatrophie[12] Altersatrophie[13] Sehnerven-, Optikusatrophie[14]

29

396 MEDICAL SCIENCE — Microbes, Pathogens & Parasites

necrosis [nekrousɪs‖nɪ-] *n term*   *syn* **cell death** *n clin*,
rel **gangrene**[1] [iː] *n term*
localized death of cells as a result of irreversible damage (e.g. shrinkage of tissue[2])
necrotic[3] *adj term* • **necrose**[4] [ous] *v* • **necrotizing** *adj* • **gangrenous**[5] *adj term*

» The outlines of individual necrotic cells are indistinct, and cells may become merged[6] [ɜːrdʒ], sometimes forming a focus of coarsely [ɔː] granular[7], amorphous, or hyaline [aɪ] material. Swelling, edema, and then frank necrosis of the scrotal wall progressing to gangrene may occur, resulting in fever and toxemia [iː].

Use to undergo **necrosis** • tissue[8] / aseptic / avascular / fat / caseation or caseous[9] [eɪ] **necrosis** • central / focal[10] / total / coagulation / bridging[11] / cystic **necrosis** • epiphyseal [fɪs]/ fibrinoid [aɪ]/ laminar / cortical / renal papillary / acute tubular **necrosis** • progressive / pressure[12] / hemorrhagic / radiation[13] / hepatic[14] / suppurative[15] [ʌ] **necrosis** • **necrosis** of the newborn • tumor **necrosis** factor (*abbr* TNF) • to be/become/appear **necrotic** • **necrotic** debris[16] [debriː]/ foci [fousaɪ] / tissue • dermal / venous [iː]/ emphysematous [iː] *or* gas[17] **gangrene** • (non)traumatic / distal / wet[18] / dry / incipient[19] [sɪ] **gangrene**

Nekrose, Zell-, Gewebstod
Gangrän, Brand[1] Gewebeschrumpfung[2] nekrotisch[3] absterben, nekrotisieren[4] gangränös[5] verschmolzen[6] grobkörnig[7] Gewebstod[8] verkäsende N.[9] fokale N.[10] nekrotisierender Verbindungsgang[11] Drucknekr.[12] Strahlennekr.[13] Lebernekr.[14] eitrige N.[15] nekrot. Gewebetrümmer[16] Gasbrand, -ödem[17] feuchte Gangrän[18] beginnende Gangrän[19]

30

Unit 90 Microbes, Pathogens & Parasites
Related Units: 39 Immune System, 94 Infectious Diseases, 95 Childhood Diseases, 96 Sexually Transmitted Diseases, 89 Pathology, 91 Toxicology, 139 Asepsis

microorganisms [maɪkrou-] *n term usu pl*   *syn* **microbes** [aɪ] *n term usu pl*
microscopic forms of life, esp. those which are capable of causing disease in humans and animals
microflora[1] *n term* • **organism** *n* • **(anti)microbial**[2] [ou] *adj* • **micro-** *comb*

» At birth infants move from a sterile intrauterine environment to one teeming [iː] with[3] micro-organisms. Microbes have developed a variety of strategies for escaping host [ou] immunity. Repeat cultures [ʌ] yielded [iː] organisms different from the initial [ɪʃ] flora.

Use free-living / intracellular / ubiquitous[4] [juːbɪkwətəs]/ predominant **microorganism** • infectious / pathogenic[5] [dʒe] **microorganism** • causative [ɒː] *or* offending[6] / virulent [ɪ]/ antibiotic-resistant[7] **microorganism** • to kill[8]/contain **microbes** • intracellular / transmissible[9] **microbes** • invading [eɪ]/ pathogenic **microbes** • **microbial** flora / culture[10] / growth • **microbial** spread[11] [e]/ population • **microbial** species [spiːʃɪz]/ enzyme [enzaɪm]/ infection[12] / antigens • **microbial** etiology / virulence / detection[13] • **microbial** products / debris [iː]/ suppression / clearance • oral / gut [ʌ] *or* intestinal[14] / resident[15] **microflora** • endogenous / causative[16] / encapsulated **organisms** • contaminating / pyogenic[17] [paɪə-] **organisms** • virulent / tuberculous/ urea-splitting **organisms** • dormant[18] / cultured[19] **organisms** • **micro**bicidal[20] [saɪ] /biologic agents /filariae /environment[21]

Mikroorganismen, Mikroben
Mikroflora[1] mikrobiell, Mikroben-[2] wimmelnd von[3] überall vorkommender/ ubiquitärer Mikroorganismus[4] pathogener M., Krankheitserreger[5] krankheitsauslösender M.[6] antibiotikaresistenter M.[7] Mikroorganismen abtöten[8] übertragbare M.[9] Mikrobenkultur[10] Ausbreitung d. Mikroorganismen[11] durch M. verursachte Infektion, mikrobielle Infektion[12] Erregernachweis[13] Darmflora[14] Residentflora[15] Erreger, verursachender Keim[16] eiterbildende Erreger[17] ruhende Organismen[18] kultivierte O.[19] mikrobenabtötend, mikrobizid[20] Mikromilieu[21]

1

protozoon [proutəzouɒːn] *n term*
rel **sporozoa**[1] [spɒːrəzouə] *n term pl*
single-celled self-contained microorganism of the subkingdom[2] Protozoa (the lowest form of animal life) which have organelles for locomotion, respiration, attachment, etc. and are classified into 7 phyla[3] [faɪlə]
protozoal *adj term* • **protozoan**[4] *adj & n* • **sporozoite**[5] [-aɪt] *n* • **sporocyst**[6] *n*

» Protozoa are more complex than bacteria. Tetracyclines [saɪk] are strongly inhibitory for the growth of mycoplasmas[7] [maɪkə-], rickettsiae [-iː], chlamydiae [kləmɪdiiː], spirochetes [aɪ], and some protozoa (e.g. amebas [iː]). The cells resulting from the sexual union [juː] of spores during the life cycle [saɪkl] of a sporozoan is called sporozoites.

Use ciliated[8] [sɪl]/ flagellated[9] [ædʒ]/ intracellular / blood **protozoa** • intestinal[10] / insect-borne[11] / parasitic[12] [ɪ] **protozoa** • free-living / opportunistic **protozoa** • **protozoal** infection[13] / diseases / flagellate / organism • to form/produce/liberate[14]/kill **sporozoites** • motile / plasmodial [ou]/ malaria **sporozoites** • **sporozoite**-containing oocysts [ouəsɪsts]

Protozoon, tierischer Einzeller, Urtierchen
Sporentierchen, Sporozoa[1] Unterreich[2] Stämme[3] Protozoen-; Protozoon[4] Sporozoit[5] Sporozyste[6] Mykoplasmen[7] Ziliaten, Wimper(n)tierchen, Ciliophora[8] Flagellaten, Geißeltierchen[9] Darmprotozoen[10] d. Insekten übertragene Protozoen[11] parasitäre P.[12] Protozoeninfektion, Protozoonose[13] Sporozoiten freisetzen[14]

2

Microbes, Pathogens & Parasites　　　　　　　　　　　　　　　　　　　　　　MEDICAL SCIENCE 397

spore [spɔːr] *n term*

　　　　　　　　　　　　　rel **endospore**[1] *n term*

inactive form of certain species [spiːʃ‖siːz] of bacteria that is resistant to heat

spore-forming *adj term* • **sporulate**[2] *v* • **sporulation**[3] *n* • **spor(o)**- *comb*

» Windstorms can carry spores to adjacent[4] [dʒeɪs] nonendemic areas and cause case clusters[5] [ʌ]. Diseases caused by spore-forming bacteria include anthrax[6], botulism, gas gangrene[7] [g] and tetanus. During reheating, the organisms sporulate and germinate [dʒɜː].

Use to inhale/ingest[8] [dʒe]/contain/propagate[9]/be contaminated with **spores** • to kill/inactivate/destroy **spores** • dormant / budding[10] [ʌ]/ airborne **spores** • wind-borne / heat-resistant[11] / dry / mature[12] [-tʲʊɚ‖tʃʊɚ] **spores** • (indoor/ outdoor) mold[13] [oʊ]/ infectious **spores** • **spore** forms / count /-forming organisms[14] • **spore**-forming bacilli[14] [aɪ]/ stain[15] [eɪ] • Aspergillus [dʒɪ]/ anthrax[16] / botulinal [aɪ] **spores** • **spore** formers[14] • **spor**ogony[17] /ogenous /ogenesis[18] • **spor**ogeny[18] /icide [-saɪd] /angia[19] [-ændʒɪə] • **endospore**-like structures

Spore
Endospore[1] Sporen bilden[2] Sporenbildung, Sporulation[3] benachbart[4] Anhäufung v. Krankheitsfällen[5] Milzbrand, Anthrax[6] Gasbrand, -ödem[7] Sporen oral aufnehmen[8] S. ausbringen/ verbreiten[9] ausprossende S.[10] hitzebeständige/ -resistente S.[11] reife Sporen[12] Schimmelpilzsporen[13] sporenbildende Bakterien, Sporenbildner[14] Sporenfärbung[15] Anthraxsporen[16] Sporogonie[17] Sporenbildung, Sporogenese[18] Sporangien, Sporenbehälter[19]

3

ameba [əmiːbə] *n term, pl* **-ae** *or* **-s**, *BE* **amoeba**

　　　　　　　　　　　rel **trophozoite**[1], **schizont**[2] [skɪzɒːnt‖skɪtsɒːnt] *n term*

one-celled, naked protozoon capable of ameboid change or movement by cytoplasmic extrusions[3] [uː] (pseudopodia[4]), e.g. Entamoeba histolytica [ɪ] which causes amebic dysentery [ɪ] and hepatic amebiasis

amebic *adj term* • **ameboid**[5] *adj* • **amebiasis**[6] [aɪə] *n* • **ameb(i)-** *comb*

» Bloodstained [eɪ] flecks of mucus [juː] in the stool were positive for amebas. Although amebic penetration is limited by the muscular coat, perforation of the mucous membrane occasionally results in regions of fecal [iː] stasis [eɪ]. Erythromycin [aɪ] and tetracycline are active against intestinal trophozoites, but are inactive against trophozoites in liver abscesses.

Use to search for/be negative for[7] **amebae** • free-living / motile **amebae** • flagellated[8] / motile / protozoal **trophozoite** • amebic / pleomorphic [pliː-ə-]/ hematophagous[9] [-ɒːfəgəs] **trophozoite** • **trophozoite** stage[10] • blood / hepatic or liver / tissue **schizont** • **amebic** infection[6] / carrier[11] / invasion [eɪ]/ cysts [sɪsts] • **amebic** dysentery[12] [ɪ]/ colitis[13] [aɪ]/ (liver) abscess[14] • **ameboid** cell / shape / movement[15] • (extra)intestinal[12] / cutaneous [eɪ]/ hepatic[16] **amebiasis** • nondysenteric / (non)invasive[17] **amebiasis** • **ameb**oma[18] /icide[19] /icidal

Amöbe
Trophozoit[1] Schizont[2] Protoplasmaausstülpungen[3] Scheinfüßchen, Pseudopodien[4] amöbenartig, amöboid[5] Amöbiasis, Amöbeninfektion[6] keine Amöben nachweisbar[7] geißeltragender Trophozoit[8] hämatophager T.[9] Trophozoitenstadium[10] Amöbenträger[11] Amöbendysenterie, -ruhr, intestinale Amöbiasis[12] Amöbenkolitis[13] Amöben(leber)abszess[14] amöboide Fortbewegung[15] Amöbenhepatitis, Hepatitis amoebiana[16] invasive Amöbiasis[17] Amöbom, Amöbengranulom[18] Amöbizid, amöbizides Mittel[19]

4

pathogen [pæθədʒən] *n term* *syn* **germ** [dʒɜːrm] *n clin,*

　　　　　　　　　　　　　sim **bug**[1] [bʌg] *n jar*

any microorganism [maɪkroʊ-] capable [eɪ] of causing disease

pathogenic *n term* • **pathogenicity**[2] *n* → U89-1 •
germinate[3] *v* • **germination** *n* • **germicide**[4] *adj & n*

» Alteration of oropharyngeal [ɪ] normal flora with colonization by pathogens and subsequent aspiration of infected secretions [iː] is the most common cause of lung infections. Once a pathogen is isolated, antibiotic regimens[5] [edʒ] can be tailored [eɪ] to[6] in vitro sensitivities. He has constantly recurring thoughts such as fears of exposure to germs. Toxin is produced in and absorbed from the intestine after the germination of ingested [dʒe] spores.

Use to identify/eradicate[7] **pathogens** • microbial / protozoal / bacterial / viral [aɪ] **pathogen** • exogenous [ɒːdʒ]/ nosocomial[8] / intracellular **pathogen** • respiratory / enteric / urinary **pathogen** • gram-positive / (an)aerobic[9] / blood-borne[10] **pathogen** • sexually transmitted / antibiotic-resistant[11] **pathogen** • opportunistic[12] / encapsulated / isolated **pathogen** • non/ cyto/ immuno/ entero**pathogenic** • high / little *or* low **pathogenicity** • **germ**-based contagion[13] [eɪdʒ]/-free environment[14] • kissing *or* cone-nose *or* reduviid *or* assassin[15] / bed / water **bugs** • airborne[16] / nocturnally [ɜː] feeding [iː]/ laboratory-reared[17] [ɪɚ] **bugs** • **bug** bite[18] / feces [iːs]/ killer[19]

(Krankheits)erreger, pathogener (Mikro)organismus
Erreger, Bazillus; Insekt, Wanze[1] Pathogenität[2] keimen, sprossen[3] germizid, keimtötend; Germizid, keimtöt. Mittel[4] Antibiotikatherapie[5] abgestimmt auf[6] Krankheitserreger ausrotten[7] Hospitalkeim[8] anaerober Erreger, Anaerobier[9] hämatogener Erreger[10] antibiotikaresistenter Erreger[11] opportunistischer Erreger[12] erregerassoziierte Infektion[13] keimfreies Umfeld[14] Raubwanzen, Reduviidae[15] aerogen übertragbare Erreger[16] in vitro gezüchtete Erreger[17] Wanzenbiss, Insektenstich[18] Insektenvernichtungsmittel[19]

5

bacterium [bæktɪəɪəm] n term, pl –ia

single-celled prokaryotic microorganism lacking a true nucleus and reproducing by cell division
bacterial[1] *adj term* • **bacter(o)**- *comb*

» Autoclaving destroys all vegetative bacteria and most resistant dry spores. The commonest bacterial organisms include H influenzae [-iː], S pneumoniae, M catarrhalis, S aureus, and anaerobes. Topical antibiotics are commonly used to suppress bacterial growth.

Use (an)aerobic[2] / (non)motile / filamentous **bacteria** • gram-negative[3] skin / mouth **bacteria** • intestinal[4] / pathogenic / pyogenic[5] [paɪədʒɛnɪk] **bacteria** • **bacterial** organism / load [oʊ] *or* burden[6] [ɜː] • **bacterial** counts[7] / toxin / colonization[8] • **bacterial** growth[9] / overgrowth[10] • **bacterial** proliferation / colony[11] • **bacterial** culture[12] [kʌltʃə] / contamination • **bacterial** pneumonia [n(j)uː-]/ vaginosis[13] [vædʒ-] • **bacter**icidal[14] [-saɪdl] /emia [-iːmɪə] /iuria[15] /iostatic[16] /iology

Bakterium
bakteriell, Bakterien-[1] aerobe Bakterien, Aerobier[2] gramnegative B.[3] Darmbakterien[4] eiterbildende Bakterien[5] Bakterienbelastung[6] Bakterienanzahl[7] Bakterienbesiedelung, bakterielle B.[8] Bakterienwachstum[9] bakterielle(s) Überwucherung/ Overgrowth[10] Bakterienkolonie[11] Bakterienkultur[12] bakterielle Vaginose[13] bakterizid, bakterientötend[14] Bakteriurie, Bakterienausscheidung im Harn[15] bakteriostatisch, bakterienhemmend[16]   6

bacillus [bəsɪləs] n term, pl -i [bəsɪlaɪ]

genus [dʒiːnəs] of aerobic or facultatively anaerobic, spore-forming bacteria[1] (family Bacillaceae) which contain Gram-positive rods [ɒː] and are found primarily in soil[2]; broadly any rod-shaped bacterium

(strepto/ cocco/ multi/ pauci)bacillary[3] *adj term* • **bacill(o)-** *comb*

» The viability [vaɪə-] and density of bacilli per milligram of vaccine [æks] may vary with the strain[4] [eɪ] used. Typhoid [aɪ] fever[5] [iː] is caused by the gram-negative bacillus Salmonella typhi [aɪ]. Gastric acidity[6] is a major factor that prevents colonization of the GI tract by nosocomial gram-negative bacillary pathogens.

Use dormant / acid-fast[7] (*abbr* AFB)/ gram-negative **bacilli** • enteric spore-forming / rod-shaped[8] **bacilli** • coccal [kɒːkəl]/ pleomorphic [iː]/ fusiform[9] **bacilli** • anaerobic / toxin-producing **bacilli** • irregularly staining / dead / viable [vaɪəbl] **bacilli** • **Bacille** Calmette-Guerin[10] (*abbr* BCG) • anthrax[11] / tubercle[12] / typhoid [taɪfɔɪd] **bacillus** • acne [ækni]/ strepto[13]/ lacto/ actino**bacillus** • **bacillary** antigen / dysentery[14] [ɪ] / meningitis [dʒaɪ]/ angiomatosis • **bacil**liform /emia[15] [iː] /osis /uria

Bazillus, Bacillus
fakultativ anaerob wachsende, sporenbildende Bakterien[1] Boden, Erdreich[2] bakterienarm, paucibakteriell[3] Stamm[4] Typhus abdominalis, Febris typhoides[5] Säuregrad d. Magensafts[6] stäbchenförmige Bakterien/ Stäbchen[7] Stäbchenbakterien[8] Fusobakterien[9] Bacillus Calmette-Guerin, BCG[10] Milzbrandbazillus, B. anthracis[11] Tuberkelbazillus, Mycobacterium tuberculosis[12] Streptobacillus[13] bakterielle Ruhr, Dysenterie, Shigellose[14] Bakteriämie[15]   7

streptococcus n term, pl -cocci [kɒːkaɪǁksaɪ]   rel **staphylococcus**[1] n term

genus of mostly nonmotile , nonspore-forming bacteria (some are pathogenic) containing Gram-positive, spherical [sfɛrɪkəl] or ovoid [oʊ] cells; occur in the mouth and intestines, dairy [deə˞ɪ] products[2], etc.

coccal [kɒːkəl] *adj term* • **coccoid**[3] *adj* • **cocco-, strept(o)-** [streptoʊ] *comb*

» The most common infecting organisms found in splenic [e] abscesses are staphylococci, streptococci, anaerobes, and aerobic gram-negative rods, including salmonella. Is this drug effective for eradication of staphylococcal nasal [eɪ] carriage?

Use group B / (an)aerobic / microaerophilic[4] **streptococci** • alpha-hemolytic[5] [ɪ]/ viridans[6] **streptococcus** • **Streptococcus** pyogenes[7] / pneumoniae / viridans[8] • faecalis [keɪ] • **Staphylococcus** aureus[8] / epidermidis / saprophyticus [fɪ] • (anti)strepto/ staphylo/ crypto/ gono**coccal** • **streptococcal** antigen / endocarditis / sepsis[9] • **streptococcal** pharyngitis [dʒaɪ] *or* tonsillitis *or* sore throat[10] • **strep** throat[10] • **staphylococcal** infection[11] / food poisoning / pneumonia[12] [n(j)uː-] • **staphylococcal** scalded [ɔː] skin syndrome[13] (*abbr* SSSS) • **staphylococcal** enterotoxin / clumping test[14] • anaerobic / gram-positive[15] **cocci** • pneumo/ meningo/ entero/ gono/ diplo**cocci** • **cocco**bacilli • **strepto**bacillus /bacillary (rat-bite) fever[16]

Streptokokkus, -coccus
Staphylokokkus, -coccus[1] Milchprodukte[2] kokkenähnlich[3] mikroaerophile Streptokokken[4] alphahämolysierender Streptokokkus[5] Streptococcus viridans, vergrünender S.[6] Streptococcus pyogenes, ß-hämolysierender Streptokokkus d. Gruppe A (nach Lancefield)[7] Staphylococcus aureus[8] Streptokokkensepsis[9] Streptokokkenangina[10] Staphylokokkeninfektion, -kokkose[11] Staphylokokkenpneumonie[12] staphylogenes Lyell-Syndrom, SSSS[13] Staphylokokken-Clumping-Test[14] grampositive Kokken[15] Streptobazillen-Rattenbissfieber, Haverhill-Fieber[16]   8

spirochete [spaɪrəkiːt] n term   rel **spirillum**[1] [spaɪrɪləm] n term, pl -a

genus[2] of motile bacteria (order[3] Spirochaetales) [-kiːteɪliːz] containing Gram-negative, flexible, undulating [ʌ], spiral-shaped rods

spirochetal *adj term* • **spirocheticidal**[4] *adj* • **spirillary** *adj* • **spir(o)-** *comb*

» The Spirochaetales include three genera[2]—Leptospira, Borrelia and Treponema [iː]—that are pathogenic for humans. Lyme [laɪm] borreliosis is a tick-transmitted[5] spirochetal illness. The diagnosis of relapsing fever[6] [iː] is confirmed most easily by the detection of spirochetes in blood. Spirillum infection causes pain and purple [ɜː] swelling at the site of the initial bite.

Use to harbor[7]/ detect[8] **spirochetes** • (non)pathogenic / anaerobic / tick-borne **spirochetes** • louse-borne[9] / motile / relapsing-fever **spirochetes** • **Spirillum** minus[10] • **spirochetal** infections *or* diseases[11] / fever[12] • **spirillary** rat-bite fever[12] • **spiro**cheticide /olysis /emia

Spirochäte, schraubenförmiges Bakterium
Spirillum[1] Gattung(en)[2] Ordnung[3] spirochätenabtötend[4] durch Zecken übertragen[5] Rückfallfieber, Febris recurrens[6] Spirochäten enthalten/ haben/ beherbergen[7] Spirochäten nachweisen[8] durch Läuse übertragene Spirochäten[9] Spirochaeta muris, Spirillum minus[10] Spirochätosen[11] Spirillen-Rattenbissfieber, Sodoku[12]   9

Microbes, Pathogens & Parasites

MEDICAL SCIENCE

virus [vaɪrəs] *n term, pl* **viruses** [vaɪrəsiːz]

smallest of all parasites containing either DNA or RNA (not both) usually covered by a protective protein shell or capsid[1] which is wholly dependent on host cells for reproduction

(**anti**)**vir**al[2] [aɪ] *adj term* • **virulence**[3] [ɪ] *n* • **virulent** *adj* [ɪ] • **vir**(**o**)- *comb*

» Hepatitis [aɪ] C virus is a single-stranded[4] RNA virus in the flavivirus family. Epstein-Barr virus infection is established by detecting a fall over several weeks of IgG antibody to the VCA[5]. Viruses do not produce toxins but they are highly antigenic.

Use influenza / herpes / Epstein-Barr (*abbr* EBV) **virus** • pox[6] / cytomegalo/ polio/ adeno**virus** • DNA / RNA / retro[7]/ respiratory **viruses** • arbo/ coxsackie/ rota/ echo [ekoʊ]/ pro[8]/ entero**viruses** • oncogenic[9] / live[10] [aɪ]/ attenuated[11] **virus** • ubiquitous / latent [eɪ] **virus** • species-specific / rodent-borne[12] / sexually transmitted **virus** • **virus** particle / strain / reservoir[13] • **virus** replication[14] / culture • **virus** transmission / infection • **virus** shedding[15] [ʃe-]/ isolation / titer [aɪ] • **vir**al enzyme / protein / genome[16] [dʒiː] • **vir**al envelope[17] / uncoating[18] • **vir**al capsid antigen[5] (*abbr* VCA)/ burden [ɜː] *or* load[19] / **virulent** organism / bacteria / strain[20] • a[21]/ neuro**virulent** • to confer [ɜː] /modulate/regain **virulence** • gonococcal / high / low / lowered[22] **virulence** • **virulence** factor[23] / determinant [ɜː] / genes [dʒiːnz] • **vir**emia [iː] /ology /ucidal[24] /ustatic agents[25]

virion [vɪ‖vaɪrɪɒːn] *n term*   *rel* **subvirion**[1], **viroid**[2] [aɪ], **prion**[3] [priːɒːn] *n term*

structurally intact virus particle which can survive extracellularly and infect living cells

» Assembly[4], budding[5] [ʌ], and maturation of virions take place in the absence of the envelope glycoprotein [glaɪkə-]. On entry into the cytoplasm, virion polymerase completes DNA synthesis. Only split virus (subvirion) or purified-surface antigen preparations should be used. Viroids are simply molecules of naked, cyclical, mostly double-stranded, small RNAs. Prions are abnormal cellular proteins that can spread from cell to cell and effect changes in normal cellular proteins, thereby disrupting cellular function and propagating themselves[6].

Use **virion** component / particle / mass / envelope[7] / surface [ɜː] • **virion** structural [ʌ] proteins[8] [oʊ]/ clearance rate[9] / rotavirus / HIV / rubella **virion** • intact / circulating[10] / trapped[11] / infectious **virions** • **prion** disease[12] / protein[13] / strain [eɪ]/ rods • disease-producing[14] / host-encoded **prion protein** • normal / protease-resistant[15] **prion protein** • **subvirion** vaccine[16]

rickettsia [rɪketsɪə] *n term, pl* **-ias** *or* **-iae** [rɪketsiiː]

genus of bacteria (family Rickettsiaceae) containing nonfilterable, often coccoid to rod-shaped organisms that usually occur in lice [laɪs], fleas, ticks, and mites [aɪ]; pathogenic species are virus-like intracellular parasites[1] causing typhus[2], Rocky Mountain spotted fever[3], tsutsugamushi disease, and rickettsialpox[4]

rickettsial *adj term* • **rickettsiosis**[5] *n* • **rickettsicidal** *adj*

» The rickettsioses are febrile exanthematous diseases caused by rickettsiae, small gram-negative obligate intracellular bacterial parasites of arthropods[6].

Use typhus-like [taɪfəs]/ pathogenic / cat-flea[7] [iː] **rickettsia** • **Rickettsia** akari / australis / rickettsii[8] • **rickettsial** organism / species / antigen[9] [-dʒən]/ disease[5] / infection[5] • (Eastern) tick-borne[10] [bɔːrn] **rickettsiosis**

parasite [pærəsaɪt] *n term*   *rel* **saprophyte**[1][sæprəfaɪt], **host**[2] [oʊ] *n term*

organism harbored[3] by a host from which it derives [aɪ] energy and sustenance[4] [ʌ] → U94-5

parasitic[5] [ɪ] *adj term* • **parasitize**[6] [-aɪz] *v* • **parasitization**[7] *n* • **parasit-** *comb*

» Like most other parasites, viruses stimulate host antibody production. The dog is the principal definitive host[8] and the sheep the most common intermediate. The disease is spread from host to host by fecal-oral routes, either directly or indirectly via food or water. Candida albicans is a saprophyte that normally is not invasive [eɪ] unless the mouth is abraded [eɪ].

Use human / active / obligate or obligatory[9] **parasite** • facultative[10] / intracellular / intestinal[11] **parasite** • bacterial / malarial / tissue[12] **parasite** • protozoal / filarial / nematode / helminthic **parasite** • **parasite** ova[13] [oʊvə]/ replication / amplification • **parasite** burden [ɜː] *or* load[14] / examination / killing • **parasitic** (super)infection[15] / disease[15] / invasion • **parasitic** cycle [saɪkl] / infestation[7] / larvae [iː‖aɪ] • **parasit**emia /icidal /osis[15] • **parasit**ism[16] /ology /ized cells[17] • ecto[18]/ endo[19]/ macro/ micro**parasites** • soil / fungal [fʌŋɡəl] **saprophyte**

Virus

Kapsid[1] antiviral[2] Virulenz[3] einzelsträngig[4] virales Kapsid-Antigen[5] Pockenvirus[6] Retroviren[7] Proviren[8] onkogenes V.[9] Lebendvirus[10] virulenzgeschwächtes V.[11] durch Nagetiere übertragenes Virus[12] Virusreservoir[13] Virusvermehrung, -replikation[14] Virusfreisetzung[15] Virusgenom[16] Virushülle[17] Uncoating, Freisetzung d. Virusgenoms[18] Viruslast[19] virulenter Stamm[20] nicht-, avirulent[21] abgeschwächte Virulenz[22] Virulenzfaktor[23] viruzid, Viren abtötend[24] Virostatika, Virustatika[25]

10

Virion, Viruspartikel

subvirales Partikel[1] Viroid, hüllenloses Minivirus[2] Prion[3] Zusammensetzung[4] Knospung, Sprossung[5] s. vermehren[6] Virushülle[7] virale Strukturproteine[8] Virionen-Clearance, -Ausscheidung[9] zirkulierendes Virion/ Virusmaterial[10] gebundene Viruspartikel[11] Prionenkrankheit[12] Prionenprotein[13] krankheitsauslösendes Prionenprotein[14] proteaseunempfindliches Prionenprotein[15] Spaltvakzine[16]

11

Rickettsia, Rickettsie

intrazelluläre Parasiten[1] Fleckfieber[2] Felsengebirgs(fleck)fieber, amerikan. Zeckenbissfieber[3] Rickettsienpocken[4] Rickettsieninfektion, Rickettsiose[5] Arthropoden, Gliederfüßer[6] durch d. Katzenfloh übertragene Rickettsie[7] Rickettsia rickettsii[8] Rickettsienantigen[9] Zeckenbissfieber[10]

12

Parasit

Saprophyt[1] Wirt[2] beherbergt[3] Nahrung[4] parasitär[5] schmarotzen, als Parasit leben, parasitieren[6] Parasitenbefall[7] End-, Definitivwirt[8] obligater Parasit[9] fakultativer Parasit[10] Darmparasit[11] Gewebeparasit[12] Parasiteneier[13] Parasitenbelastung[14] Parasitose[15] Schmarotzertum, Parasitismus[16] parasitenbefallene Zellen[17] Ektoparasiten[18] Endoparasiten[19]

13

400 MEDICAL SCIENCE — Microbes, Pathogens & Parasites

Chlamydia [kləˈmɪdɪə] *n term*
rel **C. trachomatis**[1], **C. psittaci**[2] [s] *n term*
genus of gram-negative, nonmotile[3] bacteria which are obligate intracellular parasites
chlamydial *adj term* • **trachoma**[4] [trəˈkoʊmə] *n* • **psittacosis**[5] *n* → U96-9

» A patient with urethritis [aɪ] needs to be evaluated for gonorrhea [iː], chlamydia, and Trichomonas infection. Chlamydia is probably the leading cause of infertility in females. Mature chlamydial inclusions [uː3] were detected in infected cells with iodine [aɪədɪn] stains [eɪ].

Use **Chlamydia** trachomatis infection / organism • **Chlamydia** epidemic[6] / antigen detection test[7] • **Chlamydia** isolate [aɪ]/-seropositive women[8] • **Chlamydia**-induced tubal scarring[9] [ɑː]/ pneumoniae [n(j)uːˈmoʊniː] • **chlamydial** (genital/ eye) infection / DNA / conjunctivitis[10] [dʒʌ]

Chlamydie, Chlamydia
Chlamydia trachomatis[1] C. psittaci[2] unbeweglich[3] Trachom, ägypt. Augenkrankheit[4] Psittakose, Papageienkrankheit[5] Chlamydienepidemie[6] Chlamydienantigentest[7] Chlamydien-seropositive Frauen[8] chlamydienbedingte Tubenvernarbung[9] chlamydieninduzierte Konjunktivitis[10]

14

Insect carriers:
(a) head of the tsetse fly, which transmits trypanosomiasis commonly known as sleeping sickness
(b) head of the yellow fever mosquito (*Aedes aegypti*) the vector of yellow fever and dengue

true louse [laʊs] *n, pl* **lice** [laɪs]   *syn* **pediculus** *n term*
rel **tick**[1], **mite**[2] [maɪt], **flea**[3] [fliː], **fly**[4] *n, pl* flies
wingless blood-sucking [ʌ] insect[5] parasitic on mammals[6] which also acts as a vector of diseases, e.g. typhus [taɪfəs]
pediculous *adj term* • **pediculation**[7] *n* • **pediculosis**[7] [pɪdɪkjəˈloʊsɪs] *n*

» Head lice hatch eggs[8], so-called nits[9], in silvery oval-shaped envelopes that attach [-ætʃ] to the hair shafts. Rickettsia typhi is transmitted from rat to rat through the rat flea. Soft ticks[10] feed painlessly and can survive for 10 years or more with only an occasional blood meal.

Use (human) body *or* clothes[11] / head[12] **louse** • crab *or* pubic[13] [pjuːbɪk]/ cat / chicken **louse** • biting / blood-sucking **lice** • adult [ʌ]/ infected / exposure [oʊ3] to **lice** • **louse** infestation[7] /-borne typhus[14] / dog / deer / Lone Star[15] / hard-bodied[16] *or* ixodid [ɪksoʊdɪd‖ˈɒːdɪd] **tick** • soft-bodied[10] / infectious **ticks** • **tick** bite[17] /-transmitted /-infested area[18] • **tick** exposure /-borne relapsing fever[19] (*abbr* TBRF) • **tick**-borne encephalitis[20] [aɪ]/ repellent[21] • Central European **tick-borne** encephalitis[22] • (house) dust[23] / bird / rodent **mites** • itch *or* scabies[24] [skeɪbiːz] **mite** • larval / infected **fleas** • human[25] / dog / cat / rat[26] **flea** • water / sand **flea** • **flea**-infested /-bitten appearance • fruit / flesh[27] / gad[28] / tabanid[28] [æ‖eɪ] **fly** • day-biting[29] / tsetse[30] / house[31]/ horse**fly**

echte Laus, Pediculus
Zecke[1] Milbe[2] Floh[3] Fliege[4] flügelloses, blutsaugendes Insekt[5] Säugetiere[6] Pedikulose, Läusebefall[7] Eier legen[8] Nissen[9] Argasidae, Lederzecken[10] Kleiderlaus, Pediculus humanus[11] Kopflaus, P. capitis[12] Scham-, Filzlaus, Phthirus pubis[13] Läusefleckfieber, epidem. F.[14] Amblyomma americanum[15] Schild-, Haftzecke, Ixodida[16] Zeckenbiss[17] zeckenverseuchtes Gebiet[18] Zeckenrückfallfieber[19] Zeckenenzephalitis[20] Zeckenschutzmittel[21] Frühsommermeningoenzephalitis, FSME[22] Hausstaubmilben[23] Krätzmilbe, Sarcoptes scabiei[24] Menschenfloh, Pulex irritans[25] Rattenfloh[26] Fleischfliege, Sarcophaga[27] Bremse, Tabanus[28] tagaktive Fliege[29] Tsetsefliege[30] Stubenfliege[31]

15

Microbes, Pathogens & Parasites — MEDICAL SCIENCE

roundworm [ɜː] n clin syn **nematode** [e] n term,
rel **helminth(e)s**[1] n term pl

soft-bodied member of the phylum [faɪlᵊm] Nematoda often found as parasites in mammals

deworm[2] [dɪwɜːrm] v • **worm-like**[3] adj • **(anti)helminthic**[4] adj & n term

» Nematodes are elongated, symmetric roundworms and constitute one of the largest phyla in the animal kingdom. If the acute symptoms do not subside[5] [aɪ] with antibiotics, attempts should be made to extricate[6] the worms. Most helminths and protozoa exit the body in the feces [iːs].

Use to harbor a **roundworm** • intestinal **roundworm** • **roundworm** infection / infestation • hook[7] / pin or thread[8] [e]/ flat[9] **worm** • tape[10] / whip[11] / guinea [gɪni] **worm** • microfilarial / ectopic **worms** • adult[12] / male / female **worms** • motile / dead / immature[13] **worms** • heavy [e]/ moderate / low **worm** burden or load[14] • **worm** disease[15] / migration • free-living[16] • parasitic[17] / filarial **nematodes** • intestinal / tissue / soil-transmitted **helminthes** • platy**helminth**[9] • **helminth**iasis[15] [aɪ] /icide[4]

> **Note:** The term ringworm[18] is a synonym for **tinea**, [tɪniə] a fungal infection of the skin (e.g. athlete's foot or tinea pedis[19]), which is not caused by worms.

Rundwurm, Fadenwurm, Nematode
Helminthen, Eingeweidewürmer[1] entwurmen[2] wurmähnlich, vermiform[3] wurmabtötend, anthelminthisch; Wurmmittel, Anthelminthikum[4] abklingen[5] abführen, entfernen[6] Hakenwurm, Ancylostoma (duodenale)[7] Madenwurm, Enterobius/ Oxyuris vermicularis[8] Plattwurm, Plathelminth[9] Bandwurm, Cestoda[10] Peitschenwurm, Trichuris trichiura[11] geschlechtsreife Würmer[12] unreife W.[13] geringer Wurmbefall[14] Wurmerkrankung, Helminthiasis[15] freilebende Nematoden[16] parasitäre N.[17] Trichophytie, Tinea[18] Fußpilz(erkrankung)[19]
16

---

fluke [fluːk] n clin syn **trematode** n term,
rel **schistosome**[1] [skǁʃɪstəsoʊm] n term

one of internal [ɜː] parasitic flatworms which are characterized by complex digenetic life cycles involving a snail initial host, in which larval multiplication occurs, and the release [iː] of swimming larvae [iːǁaɪ] (cercariae[2] [sɜːrk-]) which directly penetrate the skin of the final host[3] (as in schistosomes)

schistosomiasis[4] [-aɪəsɪs] n term

» The large intestinal fluke, Fasciolopsis [sɪə] buski, is a common parasite of humans and pigs in central and South China. Flukes reside [aɪ] mostly in small to medium-sized biliary [ɪ] ducts[5] [ʌ]. Unlike most other trematodes, schistosomes are of two sexes, but this characteristic is evident only in the adult stage.

Use lung[6] / intestinal[7] / blood / liver[8] / adult / fish-infesting **fluke** • schistosoma **flukes** • **fluke** infection[9] • adult / digenetic [daɪ-] / lung-dwelling[6] **trematode** • intestine-dwelling[7] / liver-dwelling[8] **trematode** • **trematode** infection[9] / ova[10] [oʊvə] • **Schistosoma** haematobium[11] / japonicum / mansoni / mekongi

Trematoda, Egel, Saugwurm
Schistosoma, Saugwurm, Bilharzia[1] Zerkarien, Schwanzlarven[2] Endwirt[3] Schistosomiasis, Bilharziose[4] Gallengänge[5] Lungenegel[6] Darmegel[7] Leberegel[8] Trematodeninfektion[9] Trematodeneier[10] Schistosoma haematobium[11]
17

---

fungus [fʌŋgəs] n term, pl **fungi** [fʌŋgaɪǁfʌndʒaɪ]
rel **mold**[1], **yeast**[2] [jiːst],
mycelium[3] [maɪsiːliᵊm],
hypha[4] [haɪfə] n term, pl -ae

general term for parasitic organisms reproducing by budding[5] [ʌ] and/or spores used to encompass the diverse morphological forms of yeasts and molds (in BE spelled moulds)

(anti)fungal [g] adj term • **mold**[6] [oʊ] v • **moldy**[7] adj • **fung(i)-, myc(o)-** comb

» Relatively few fungi are pathogenic for man, whereas most plant diseases are caused by fungi. Fungi that grow as yeasts include species of Candida and Cryptococcus, while fungi that grow as molds include species of Aspergillus and dermatophytes[8] (ringworm fungi[8]). Inquire [aɪ] about air conditioning, humidifiers[9], and the presence of mold or mildew[10] [mɪld(j)uː] in the home.

Use offending / pathogenic[11] [dʒe] **fungus** • yeast-like / dermatophyte[8] [-faɪt]/ dimorphic[12] [daɪ-] **fungus** • ergot[13] [ɜː]/ true[14] **fungus** • **fungus** infection[15] / cells / ball[16] /-like • slime[17] [aɪ] • black[18] / airborne / hyaline [aɪ] **molds** • **mold** spores / colonies / buildup[19] • **mold** allergens / infections • **moldy** hay [heɪ]/ silage[20] [saɪlɪdʒ] • **myco**sis[15] /bacteria /tic infection[15] /plasmal pneumonia[21] [n(j)uː-] • **fungi**form[22] /cide[23] [saɪd] /cidal[24] • **myce**lia [siː] /etoma[25]

Pilz, Fungus
Schimmel(pilz)[1] Hefe(pilz), Sprosspilz[2] Pilzgeflecht, Myzel[3] Pilzfaden, Hyphe[4] Sprossung[5] schimmeln, schimm(e)lig werden[6] verschimmelt[7] Dermatophyt(en)[8] Luftbefeuchter[9] Schimmel; Mehltau[10] pathogener Pilz[11] dimorpher P.[12] Mutterkornpilz[13] echter Pilz[14] Pilzinfektion, Mykose[15] Pilz-, Fungusball[16] Schleimpilze, Myxomyzeten[17] Schwärzepilze, Dermatiaceae[18] Schimmelbildung[19] schimm(e)liges Silofutter[20] Mykoplasmen-Pneumonie[21] pilzförmig, fungiform(is)[22] Fungizid, Antimykotikum[23] pilzabtötend, fungizid[24] Myzetom[25]
18

Unit 91 Toxicology

Related Units: 6 Accidents & Emergencies, 9 Drugs & Remedies, 10 Alcohol & Smoking, 11 Substance Abuse, 82 Biochemical Compounds, 122 Immunization, 90 Pathogens, 92 Pharmacologic Agents, 93 Anesthetics, 99 Radiology, 124 Medical Emergencies

noxious [nɒːkʃəs] *adj term*   *syn* **injurious, deleterious** [ɪɚ], **detrimental** *adj*

tending to cause harm and/or damage or have an adverse[1] [ɜː] effect on physical or mental health

non-noxious *adj term* • **self-injurious** [ɪndʒʊɚɪəs] *adj clin*

» Accumulation of noxious metabolites should be prevented. He should avoid or minimize inhalation of noxious particulates[2], including cigarette smoke. Ingestion of large amounts of alcohol or other injurious agents is an important causative [ɒː] factor of gastritis [aɪ].

Use **noxious** substance[3] [ʌ]/ stimuli [aɪ]/ agent[3] • **noxious** exposure/ habits[4] / inhalation [eɪʃ] • **injurious** agent[3] / plants / noise[5] / gases / effect / to tissue[6] • **self-injurious** behavior • **deleterious** consequences / habits[4] • **deleterious** (side) effects / health effects[7] / influence • **detrimental** changes / effects / to health[8]

schädlich, schädigend

nachteilig, ungünstig, unerwünscht[1] Schadstoffpartikel[2] Schadstoff, Noxe, schädigendes Agens[3] gesundheitsschädigende Gewohnheiten[4] gesundheitsschädigender Lärm[5] gewebeschädigend[6] gesundheitsschädliche Auswirkungen[7] gesundheitsschädlich[8]

1

poison [pɔɪzᵊn] *n & v*

sim **venom**[1] [venᵊm] *n*

(n) substance that is harmful to health when ingested [dʒe], inhaled [eɪ], applied to, injected into or produced in the body; venom is the poisonous fluid secreted [iː] by spiders[2] [aɪ], snakes, scorpions, etc.

(non)poisonous[3] *adj clin* • **poisoning**[4] *n* • **venomous** *adj*

» Alone, cathartics[5] do not prevent poison absorption. Each year, children are accidentally poisoned by household chemicals, e.g. polishes[6] or bleaches[7] [iː]. Management of venom poisoning by marine creatures [iː] is similar to that of venomous snakebite. These insects inject venom through a stinger[8] connected to a venom reservoir supplied by venom glands[9].

Use inhaled [eɪ]/ ingested[10] [dʒe]/ systemic / contact[11] **poison** • vascular / neural[12] [ʊɚ]/ sedative **poison** • irritant *or* acrid[13] [k]/ acid [s]/ alkali [-laɪ]/ corrosive[14] **poisons** • insect / bee [iː]/ rat[15] / counter[16] [aʊ]/ deadly **poison** • **poison** absorption / elimination[17] / gas[18] • **poison** ivy[19] [aɪ]/ prevention / (control) center[20] • acute / fatal [eɪ]/ accidental[21] **poisoning** • food / systemic (chemical) / childhood *or* pediatric **poisoning** • iron [aɪ]/ lead[22] [e]/ pesticide / arsenic[23] **poisoning** • carbon monoxide[24] / cyanide [aɪ] **poisoning** • heavy metal[25] / aluminum **poisoning** • narcotic / barbiturate / methanol **poisoning** • (snake) [eɪ] venom / rattlesnake[26] / mushroom[27] [ʌ] **poisoning** • **poisoning** by amphetamines / due to barbiturates • **poisonous** snake[28] / substance [ʌ]/ mushrooms [uː] • (rattle) snake[29] / cobra / insect / honeybee[30] [ʌ] **venom** • **venom**-filled / reservoir *or* sac[31] • **venom** component / hemolysis / extractor • insect **venom** allergy • **venomous** animal / sting[32] / reptile / snake(bite)[28]

Gift; vergiften

(tierisches) Gift, Zootoxin[1] Spinnen[2] giftig, toxisch, Gift-[3] Vergiftung[4] Abführmittel[5] Polituren, Lacke[6] Bleichmittel[7] Stachel[8] Giftdrüsen[9] oral aufgenommenes Gift[10] Kontaktgift[11] Neurotoxin, Nervengift[12] Reizgifte[13] Ätzgifte[14] Rattengift[15] Gegengift, -mittel[16] Giftelimination[17] Giftgas[18] Gifteefeu, -sumach[19] Giftinformationszentrale[20] akzidentelle Vergiftung[21] Bleivergiftung[22] Arsenvergiftung[23] Kohlenmonoxidvergiftung[24] Schwermetallvergiftung[25] Klapperschlangenbiss[26] Pilzvergiftung[27] Giftschlange[28] Schlangengift[29] Bienengift[30] Giftsack, -blase[31] Giftstachel[32]

2

toxicology [tɒksɪkɒːlədʒi] *n term*

sim **biotoxicology**[1] *n term*

scientific study of poisons, their source, chemical [k] composition, action, detection, and antidotes[2]

toxicologic *adj term* • **toxicologist**[3] *n* • **toxi(co)-** *comb*

» If a toxicology screen [iː] is required, urine [jʊ] is the best specimen[4] [es] for broad screening. Toxicologic studies may be useful in confirmation[5] of the diagnosis but are rarely helpful in the ER[6]. Consult [ʌ] a medical toxicologist or regional poison control center for advice [-aɪs].

Use clinical[7] / forensic[8] / maternal-fetal [ɜː] **toxicology** • food[9] / pesticide / acute / urine[10] **toxicology** • **toxicology** screen(ing) / study *or* test[11] • **toxicologic** emergencies[12] [ɜː]/ screening • **toxi**cokinetics[13]

Toxikologie

Biotoxikologie[1] Gegengifte, Antidote[2] Toxikologe, -login[3] Untersuchungsmaterial[4] Bestätigung[5] Notaufnahme[6] klin. Toxikologie[7] forensische T.[8] Lebensmitteltoxikologie[9] Untersuchung auf Giftkonzentrationen im Harn[10] toxikolog. Test[11] toxikolog. Notfälle[12] Toxikokinetik[13]

3

Toxicology   MEDICAL SCIENCE 403

toxin [tɒːksɪn] *n term*

rel **phytotoxin**[1] [faɪtə-], **zootoxin**[2] [zoʊə-] *n term*

noxious substance formed either by cells of the body (endotoxin[3]), as an extracellular product of certain microorganisms and some higher plant and animal species (exotoxin[4]), or a combination of both

(**neuro**/ **non**/ **cyto**)**toxic**[5] *adj term* • **toxi(co)genic**[6] [dʒe] *adj* • **toxicant**[7] *n*

» Consider gastric lavage[8] if ingestion of a toxin is a diagnostic possibility. Make sure the child is not exposed to potentially toxic substances. Full information on toxicants is available [eɪ] for only a small percentage of chemicals. Liquid mercury [ɜː] is nontoxic if swallowed.

Use anti[9]/ hemo[10] [iː]/ leuko/ entero[11]/ neuro[12]/ noso**toxin** • bio/ plant[1] / animal[2] / myco**toxin** [aɪ] • bacterial / tetanus / cholera[13] / diphtheria [ɪə] **toxin** • **toxin** exposure / neutralization • **toxin**-producing bacteria /-mediated disease • **toxic** reaction / side-effects[14] / (systemic) level • **toxic** dose[15] (*abbr* TD)/ amount [aʊ]/ wastes [eɪ] • **toxic** vapors[16] [eɪ]/ chemicals / contrast agents • **toxic** state / edema / tremor / psychosis [saɪk-] • **toxic** dilation (of the colon) or megacolon[17] / purpura [ɜː] • **toxic** nodular goiter[18] / shock syndrome[19] [ɪ]/ equivalent[20] (quantity) (*abbr* TEQ) • to be/ appear **toxic** • **nontoxic** goiter[21] / drug • endo/ thyro[22]/ oto**toxic** • plant[1] **toxicant**

Toxin, Gift(stoff)
pflanzl. Gift, Phytotoxin[1] tierisches Gift, Zootoxin[2] Endotoxin[3] Exotoxin[4] zytotoxisch, zellschädigend[5] toxinbildend, toxigen[6] Gift, Toxikum[7] Magenspülung[8] Antitoxin[9] Hämotoxin, Blutgift[10] Enterotoxin, Darmgift[11] Neurotoxin, Nervengift[12] Choleratoxin[13] toxische Nebenwirkungen[14] toxische Dosis, Dtox.[15] giftige Dämpfe[16] toxisches Megakolon[17] hyperthyreote Knotenstruma[18] tox. Schocksyndrom, TSS[19] tox. Äquivalent, TEQ[20] blande Struma[21] thyreotoxisch[22]

4

environmental hazards [ɪnvaɪrənmentəl hæzədz] *n*

rel **permissible exposure** [oʊʒ] **limit**[1] *n term, abbr* PEL

health risks posed by the physical [ɪ] environment, esp. toxic exposure[2]

hazardous[3] *adj clin* • **expose**[4] [ɪkspoʊz] *v*

• **biohazard**[5] *n term* • **pre**/ **postexposure** *adj*

» This disease is an occupational [eɪʃ] hazard among sewer [suːə] and abattoir workers[6]. All employees [iː] must be informed about potentially hazardous exposures[7].

Use (public) health[8] / natural / occupational[9] / radiation[10] [eɪ] **hazard** • safety / contamination[11] / chemical **hazard** • environmental[12] / industrial [ʌ] toxin **exposure** • heavy metal / lead[13] [e]/ coal dust [ʌ] **exposure** • radiation[14] / x-ray / inhalation **exposure** • cumulative[15] [juː]/ route [uːǁaʊ] of / time of[16] / risk of **exposure** • **exposure** time[16] • **exposure to** chemical carcinogens [sɪ]/ teratogenic agents / asbestos[17] • **environmental** medicine[18] / quality standard (*abbr* EQS)/ concentration of CO_2 • **hazardous** materials[19] (*abbr* hazmat)/ chemicals • **hazardous** noise / exposure / waste[20] • **biohazard** precautions[21] [ɔː] • **hazard** boundary [aʊ] area[22] / line[23] / suppression[24] • control / recommended **limit** • short term exposure (*abbr* STEL)/ maximum residue (*abbr* MRL) **limit**

Umweltgefahren, -schadstoffe
höchstzulässige Schadstoffkonzentration[1] Schadstoffbelastung[2] gefährlich, risikoreich, unsicher[3] exponieren, aussetzen[4] Schadstoff[5] Kanal- u. Schlachthofarbeiter[6] Gefährdung durch Schadstoffe[7] Gesundheitsrisiko[8] Berufsrisiko[9] Strahlenrisiko[10] Verseuchungsgefahr[11] Umweltbelastung[12] Bleibelastung[13] Strahlenexposition, -belastung[14] kumulative Exposition/ Gesamtdosis[15] Expositionszeit[16] Asbestbelastung[17] Umweltmedizin[18] Gefahrenstoffe, gefährliche Stoffe[19] Giftmüll[20] Schadstoffschutzmaßnahmen[21] Gefahrenbereich, Sperrgebiet[22] Gefahrengrenze, -linie[23] Gefahreneindämmung[24]

5

pollutant [pəluːtənt] *n clin & term*   *sim* **contaminant**[1] *n term & clin*→ U139-9

substance, esp. in sewage[2] [suːɪdʒ], dust, smoke and other waste [eɪ] matter, that contaminates the water, air or soil[3] [sɔɪl]

pollute[4] *v* • **polluted** *adj* • **pollution**[5] [pəluːʃn] *n* • **contamination**[6] [eɪʃ] *n*

» Patients with severe asthma should be advised to stay indoors when concentrations of air pollutants are high. Ambient air pollution[7] with respect to levels of ozone [oʊzoʊn] and fine-particulate matter[8] has been related to increased rates of hospital admissions for respiratory diseases.

Use air or atmospheric[9] / water / industrial[10] [ʌ]/ indoor **pollutants** • **pollutant** level[11] / soil / air[7] / (urban) [ɜː] noise[12] / heavy [e] **pollution** • **pollution** source [sɔːrs]/ alert [ɜː] level[13] • **polluted** area / (ground)water[14] [aʊ] • environmental[15] / air[9] / chemical **contaminants** • groundwater **contamination**

Schadstoff (bes. i. d. Luft)
Schadstoff, Kontaminant[1] Abwässer[2] Boden, Erdreich[3] verunreinigen, -schmutzen[4] Verunreinigung, -schmutzung[5] Verunreinigung, Kontamination[6] Luftverschmutzung[7] Staubpartikel[8] Luftschadstoffe[9] Industrieschadstoffe[10] Schadstoffwert[11] Lärmbelästigung[12] Schadstoff-, Smog-Alarmstufe[13] verseuchtes/ kontaminiertes (Grund)wasser[14] Umweltschadstoffe[15]

6

404 MEDICAL SCIENCE Toxicology

dust [dʌst] *n*   *rel* **aerosol**[1] [eəˈəsɒːl], **smoke**[2], **smog**[3] *n* → U10-16, U82-3

suspension of solid particles of 0.1 to 5.0 microns [aɪ] in a gas (e.g., talc[4])
dust *v* • **dusty** *adj* • **dust-borne**[5] [ɔː] *adj term* • **aerosolized**[6] *adj* → U92-14

» Standard sets of allergen extracts are available commercially for pollens, animal danders[7], dust, and dust mites[8] [aɪ]. Silicosis may develop within 10 years when the exposure to dust is extremely high, e.g. in the tunneling industry. Acute irritative bronchitis may be caused by various vegetable dusts, fumes [juː] from strong acids, or nitrogen [aɪ] dioxide.

Use to raise[9] [eɪ] /disperse [ɜː]/circulate [sɜː] **dust** • (in)organic[10] / inert [ɜː]/ mineral **dust** • coal[11] / manganese [-niːz]/ silica[12] **dust** • house / cotton[13] [ʌ]/ wood **dust** • grain[14] [eɪ]/ cement [s]/ asbestos[15] **dust** • contaminated • spore-laden[16] [eɪ]/ inhaled **dust** • **dust** particles[17] / exposure / load [oʊ]/ filter[18] • **dust**free /-tight [taɪt] *or* -proof[19] / control[20] • small-particle[21] / coarse [ɔː]/ contaminated **aerosol** • infectious[22] • virus-containing [aɪ] **aerosol** • tobacco[23] / cigarette / mainstream[24] [eɪ] **smoke** • sidestream / kerosine **smoke** • **smoke** inhalation /-free environment[25] • **smoke** alarm[26] / constituents • murky[27] [ɜː]/ high levels of **smog**

pesticide [pestɪsaɪd] *n term*   *rel* **herbicide**[1] [(h)ɜːrbɪsaɪd], **insecticide**[2] *n term*
    repellent[3], **fungicide**[4] [ʌ] *n term*

substance or mixture of substances intended for preventing, destroying or repelling pests
pest[5] *n* • **pesticidal** *adj* • **herb**[6] *n* • **repel**[7] [rɪpel] *v* • **-cidal** [-saɪdᵊl] *comb*

» Low-level arsenic exposure is due to the commercial [ɜː] use of inorganic arsenic compounds in products such as wood preservatives[8] [ɜː], pesticides, herbicides, fungicides, and paints. Some toxins, such as PCBs[9] and chlorinated pesticides[10], are concentrated in milk. Insect repellents and mosquito [iː] netting are essential precautions [ɒː] in malarial areas.

Use general use (*abbr* GUP)/ restricted use (*abbr* RUP) **pesticide** • agricultural [ʌ]/ broad-spectrum[11] **pesticide** • organophosphate / arsenic-containing **pesticide** • **pesticide** absorption / residues[12] / poisoning / toxicology • organic / organophosphorus[13] / carbamate **insecticides** • quick-kill / botanical[14] / residual[15] [ɪdʒ] **insecticides** • **insecticide** spraying / resistance[16] • insect / mosquito[17] / tick[18] **repellent** • arthropod / mite [aɪ]/ DEET-containing[19] **repellent** • **pest** control[20] / mosquitoes[21] • fungi/ bacteri/ viru/ microbi**cidal**

cyanide [saɪənaɪd] *n term*   *rel* **nitrile**[1] [aɪ] *n term*

extremely poisonous salt containing the radical CN; nitriles are organic cyanide compounds
cyanin *n term* • **cyanogenic** [dʒe] *adj* • **cyanic** [æ] *adj* • **cyan(o)-** *comb*

» Cyanide is generated by the breakdown of nitroprusside[2] [ʌ]. Although charcoal[3] [tʃ] has a low affinity for cyanide, the usual doses are adequate to bind typically ingested lethal [iː] doses. Hydrogen [aɪ] cyanide[4] is used as a fumigant [juː] rodenticide[5], and organic cyanide compounds (aʊ) (nitriles) are often used in the synthetic [sɪn-] rubber [ʌ] industry.

Use potassium[6] / sodium[7] / mercuric [jʊə] **cyanide** • **cyanide** acetonitrile or methyl [ɪ]/ smoke-related **cyanide** • **cyanide** compounds[8] • salts[9] /-generating glycoside[10] [aɪ] • **cyanide** ingestion / poisoning[11] / toxicity / antidote kit[12] • **cyano**genic plants /acrylate /cobalamin[13] • acrylo**nitrile**[14] [ɪ] • aceto**nitrile**[15] [s] • **nitrile** hydratase [-eɪz] /-coated / rubber / glove [ʌ].

caustic [kɒːstɪk] *n & adj term*   *sim* **corrosive**[1] [kəroʊsɪv] *n & adj term*

(adj) having a burning or corrosive effect (n) solution [uːʃ] of a strong alkali, e.g., caustic soda[2]
corrosion [oʊʒ] *n term* • **corrode**[3] *v*

» Corrosive esophagitis[4] [dʒaɪ] is caused by the ingestion of caustic agents, such as strong alkalies or acids. Do not induce vomiting if caustics have been ingested. Dishwasher detergents[5] [ɜː] which contain bleaching [bliːtʃ-] agents[6] can cause caustic burns[7].

Use **caustic** burns[7] [ɜː]/ alkali [-laɪ]/ ingestion • **caustic** esophageal [dʒiː]/ injury[4] / substance • liquid[8] **caustic** • **corrosive** ingestion / injury[7] / agent • **corrosive** chemical / substance / poison[9] • acid[10] [æsɪd]/ gastrointestinal **corrosion**

Staub, Pulver, Puder, Mehl

Aerosol; Spraydose[1] Rauch[2] Smog[3] Talkum[4] durch Staubpartikel übertragen[5] vernebelt[6] Tierhaare[7] (Haus)staubmilben[8] Staub aufwirbeln[9] (an)organischer Staub[10] Kohlenstaub[11] kieselsäurehaltiger S.[12] Baumwollstaub[13] Getreidestaub[14] Asbeststaub[15] sporenhaltiger S.[16] Staubpartikel[17] Staubfilter[18] staubdicht[19] Staubbekämpfung[20] feines Aerosol[21] infektiöses A.[22] Tabakrauch[23] Hauptstromrauch[24] rauchfreie Umwelt[25] Rauchmelder[26] dichter Smog[27]

7

Schädlingsbekämpfungsmittel, Pestizid

Herbizid, Unkrautbekämpfungsmittel, -vertilgungsmittel[1] Insektizid, Insektenbekämpfungsmittel[2] Repellent, Insektenschutzmittel[3] Fungizid, pilzabtötendes Mittel[4] Schädling[5] Kraut[6] abwehren, -schrecken[7] Holzschutzmittel[8] polychlorierte Biphenyle[9] chlorierte Pestizide[10] Breitband-P.[11] Pestizidrückstände[12] phosphororgan. Insektizide[13] pflanzl. I.[14] I. m. Residualeffekt[15] Insektizidresistenz[16] Anti-Mückenmittel[17] Zeckenschutzmittel[18] DEET-haltiges (Diäthyl-m-toluamid) Insektenschutzmittel[19] Schädlingsbekämpfung[20] Stechmücken[21]

8

Cyanid, Zyanid

Nitril[1] Nitroprussid[2] Holzkohle[3] Blausäure, Cyanwasserstoff, HCN[4] Ausräucherungsmittel f. Nager[5] Cyankali(um), Kaliumcyanid, KCN[6] Natriumcyanid[7] Cyanverbindungen[8] Cyanate[9] zyanogenes Glykosid[10] Blausäure-, Cyanidvergiftung[11] Cyanidantidot-Therapieausrüstung[12] Cyanocobalamin (INN)[13] Acrylnitril[14] Acetonitril[15]

9

ätzende Substanz, Ätzmittel, Kaustikum; ätzend, kaustisch

Ätz-, Korrosionsmittel; ätzend, korrosiv, zerfressend[1] Ätznatron, Natriumhydroxid[2] ätzen, zerfressen, korrodieren[3] Ösophagusverätzung[4] Spülmittel[5] Bleichmittel[6] Verätzung[7] Ätzflüssigkeit, ätzende F.[8] Ätzgift[9] Säureverätzung[10]

10

Toxicology

MEDICAL SCIENCE

toxicity [tɒːksɪsəti] *n term*

rel **lethal dose**[1] [liːθ°l doʊs] *n term, abbr* **LD**

having toxic effects, esp. the degree of virulence [I] of poisons and toxic agents [eɪdʒ°nts]

dosage [doʊsɪdʒ] *n* • **overdose**[2] [oʊvəˈdoʊs] *n & v* → U11-11; U121-7

» Acute toxicity can result from ingestion of massive doses of vitamin A. The serum levels of the drug should be measured [eʒ] to avoid. While it may take over 100 bees [iː] to inflict[3] a lethal dose of venom in most adults, one sting[4] can cause a fatal [eɪ] anaphylactic reaction in a hypersensitive person.

Use to minimize/avoid/exacerbate[5] [æs] /assess **toxicity** • clinical / acute[6] / chronic[7] / cumulative / organ[8] **toxicity** • digitalis [dʒ]/ mercury[9] [ɜː]/ minimal **toxicity** • severe / unacceptable / systemic **toxicity** • photo/ cyto[10] / [saɪtə-] cardio/ hepato[11] / neuro[12] / nephro**toxicity** • median[13] [iː] (*abbr* MD50)/ minimum[14] (*abbr* MLD) **lethal dose** • single / potentially / oral **lethal dose** • (sub)acute [ʌ]/ accidental / intentional[15] **overdose** • digoxin / narcotic / salicylate **overdose** • **overdose** syndrome [I]/ patient • **overdose** with alcohol / with suicidal [saɪ] intent[15]

Toxizität, Giftigkeit
letale Dosis, LD od. DL[1] Überdosis, Überdosierung; überdosieren[2] verabreichen[3] Stich[4] d. Toxizität erhöhen[5] akute Toxizität[6] chronische T.[7] Organtoxizität[8] Quecksilbertoxizität[9] Zytotoxizität[10] Hepatotoxizität[11] Neurotoxizität[12] mittlere letale Dosis, Dosis letalis media[13] kleinste tödl./ letale Dosis, D. letalis minima[14] suizidale Überdosierung[15]

11

embryotoxicity *n term*

rel **fetal** [iː] **toxicity**[1], **teratogenicity**[2] *n term* → U92-33

cancerogenic, mutagenic, teratogenic and toxic effect of substances that result in disturbances in fetal growth, malformations, deformities, etc. when they enter the placental circulation

embryotoxic[3] *adj term* • **teratogenic**[4] [dʒe] *adj* • **teratology** *n* • **terato-** *comb*

» Because ribavirin [aɪ] is mutagenic, teratogenic, and embryotoxic, its use is generally contraindicated in pregnancy. Teratogenicity [ɪs] has not been causally [ɒː] related to chlorpromazine, but prudence[5] is indicated particularly in the first trimester of pregnancy. Animal studies on the effects of this drug suggest embryotoxicity and a potential for CNS toxicity.

Use methyl mercury[6] / peritoneal [iː] fluid-mediated [iː]/ in vitro **embryotoxicity** • **embryotoxicity** testing[7] / assay[7] / dose range [eɪ] • to produce / potential for[8] / risk of / possible **teratogenicity** • human[9] / animal / morphologic **teratogenicity** • arsenic-induced / valproic acid[10] / anesthetic **teratogenicity** • to be (weakly)[11] [iː] **embryotoxic** • **teratogen** agent[12] / drug[13] / effect / potential / in humans

Embryotoxizität
Fetotoxizität[1] Teratogenität[2] embryotoxisch, d. Embryo schädigend[3] teratogen, Missbildungen verursachend[4] Umsicht[5] Embryotoxizität v. Methylquecksilber[6] Embryotoxizitätsprüfung[7] teratogenes Potential[8] teratogene Wirkung beim Menschen[9] Teratogenität d. Valproinsäure[10] schwach embryotoxisch sein[11] Teratogen[12] teratogenes Medikament[13]

12

mutagenicity [ɪs] *n term*

rel **oncogenicity**[1], **carcinogenicity**[2] *n term*

ability of a substance to induce a genetic mutation [mjuːteɪʃ°n] → U84-20; U97-1ff

mutagenic[3] [dʒe] *adj term* • **mutagenesis**[4] *n* • **carcinogen**[5] [sɪ] *n* • **oncogene** *n*

» Concerns [sɜː] about mutagenicity and carcinogenicity from metronidazole [aɪ] have led to recommendations that it not be used in pregnancy.

Use potential / short-term[6] **mutagenicity** • human / long-term / transplacental[7] **carcinogenicity** • **oncogenicity** study[8] • **mutagenic** chemicals[9] / effects / potential • insertional[10] [ɜː] **mutagenesis**

Mutagenität
Onkogenität[1] Karzinogenität[2] mutagen, mutationsauslösend[3] Mutagenese[4] Karzinogen, Kanzerogen[5] kurzfristige Mutagenität[6] diaplazentare Karzinogenität[7] Onkogenitätsstudie[8] mutagene Chemikalien[9] Insertionsmutagenese[10]

13

envenomation [ɪnvenəmeɪʃ°n] *n term*

rel **intoxication**[1] *n clin & term* → U10-5

toxic effects caused by insect, scorpion or spider stings, arthropod or snakebites, venomous spines[2], etc.

envenomate[3] *v term* • **endointoxication**[4] *n* • **intoxicate** [ɪntɒːksɪkeɪt] *v*

» Immediately after envenomation, attempts should be made to limit the dispersion[5] [ɜː] of venom by application of a pressure-immobilization or a venous-lymphatic pressure dressing[6]. In drug overdoses, intoxication precedes [siː] coma and is marked by prominent nystagmus in all directions of gaze[7] [geɪz].

Use scorpion / marine [iː]/ animal / sea urchin[8] [ɜːrtʃɪn] **envenomation** • bee [iː]/ wasp [ɒː]/ spider [aɪ] **envenomation** • snake [eɪ]/ arthropod / stingray[9] / neurotoxic / trivial **envenomation** • life-threatening [e]/ severe or serious[10] / lethal **envenomation** • quinidine[11] [kwɪnˑdiːn]/ acute / cyanide / arsenic[12] **intoxication** • carbon monoxide[13] / methanol / vitamin D / stimulant **intoxication** • **intoxication** amaurosis[14] [ɔː]

Vergiftung (durch Gifttiere)
Intoxikation, Vergiftung; Rauschzustand[1] Giftstachel[2] vergiften[3] Autointoxikation, Selbstvergiftung[4] Verteilung[5] Druckverband[6] Blickrichtungen[7] Vergiftung durch einen Seeigel[8] Vergiftung durch einen Stachelrochen[9] schwere Vergiftung[10] Chinidinvergiftung[11] Arsenvergiftung[12] Kohlenmonoxidvergiftung[13] toxische Amaurose[14]

14

antivenin n term   syn antivenom n clin,
rel **antitoxin**[1] n term, **antidote**[2] n clin → U9-15

antibodies from the serum of an immunized animal used to neutralize[3] the venom of a poisonous animal

antitoxic adj term • **antineurotoxin** n • **antidotal** [æntɪdoʊtᵊl] adj

» Polyvalent [eɪ] crotalid antivenin[4] is effective against all pit vipers[5] [aɪ] found in the USA. Strychnine [ɪk] is an antidote for depressant poisons. Specific antivenin is indicated when signs of progressive envenomation are present. Antidotes counteract [aʊ] the effects of poisons by neutralizing [(j)uː] them.

Use black widow spider / snake[6] / intravenous [iː] **antivenin** • equine[7] / polyvalent[8] **antivenin** • potential / safe / specific[9] / universal **antidote** • physiological / chemical / mechanical **antidote** • **antitoxin** immunity[10] / level[11] / therapy[12] • to administer[13]/inject **antitoxin** • botulism / tetanus / diphtheria[14] [ɪə] **antitoxin** • unit of[15] / trivalent [aɪ]/ diluted[16] [uː] **antitoxin** • **antitoxic** immunity[10] • specific **antivenom**

portal of entry n term   rel **snakebite**[1], **fang**[2] [æ], **bee sting**[3], **spine**[4] [aɪ] n

site or part of the body where the venom of a poisonous animal enters the body

stinger[4] [stɪŋɚ] n • **sting** - stung - stung v irr •
bite [baɪt] - bit - bitten v irr → U5-10

» The venom of stingrays[5] is contained in the one or more spines located on the dorsum of the animal's tail [eɪ]. Injuries by sea urchin[6] spines, which break off in the skin, can give rise to local tissue [ʃǁs] reactions. Snake venom, when injected through the hollow fangs of the snake, can cause profound [aʊ] neurotoxic or hemotoxic [iː] systemic reactions.

Use **entry** portal[7] / site[7] / route [aʊǁuː]/ point[7] / means [iː] **of entry** • multifocal **entry** • wasp[8] / hornet[9] / arthropod **sting** • scorpion / stonefish[10] / catfish[11] **sting** • pectoral / anal [eɪ]/ venom-filled[12] **spine** • embedded / retained[13] [eɪ]/ thick / thin **spine** • stinging apparatus[14] [eɪ]/ fire ant[15] / insects • insect **stinger** • insect / spider[16] [aɪ]/ dog **bite** • **fang** marks[17] / punctures[17] [ʌ]/ entrance site[18] [aɪ]

volume of distribution [dɪstrɪbjuːʃᵊn] n term, abbr **Vd**
rel **elimination half-life**[1] n term, abbr **t1/2** → U92-5; U121-4ff

relationship between the amount of the drug in the body and the plasma concentration at equilibrium

» If a drug is sequestered[2] outside the blood and is highly tissue-bound, it will have a very large volume of distribution. TAT[3] is cheaper than human antitoxin but its half-life is shorter.

Use large[4] / small / high[4] / low / initial[5] [ɪʃ] / final / decreased **Vd** • drug[6] / initial / final / tissue[7] / intravascular **distribution** • **distribution** pattern[8] • to prolong[9]/reduce **the half-life** • circulating / plasma or serum **half-life** • intracellular / biologic[10] / physical[11] **half-life** • to prolong / to enhance / poison[12] / drug[13] **elimination** • dye[14] / route of[15] / rate of[16] (intrinsic) **elimination** • **elimination** time / rate[16]

tolerable or acceptable daily intake n term, abbr **TDI/ADI**
rel **threshold limit value**[1] n term, abbr **TLV**,
no-effect-level[2] n term, abbr **NEL**

dose of a chemical that can be ingested daily over a lifetime without appreciable [iːʃ] health risks

» TDIs are applied to chemical contaminants in food and drinking water. The NEL of a pollutant is the concentration at or below which there will be no defined effect, either deleterious[3] or beneficial[4] [ɪʃ], on a member of a population exposed to the pollutant in question. Threshold limit values are developed only as guidelines [aɪ] to assist in the control of health hazards[5].

Use maximum permissible[6] (abbr MPI)/ acceptable weekly[7] (abbr AWI) **intake** • provisional [ɪʒ] acceptable daily (abbr PADI) **intake** • no observed[2] [ɜː] (abbr NOEL)/ no observed adverse[2] [ɜː] (abbr NOAEL) **effect level** • lowest observed adverse[8] (abbr LOAEL) **effect level** • dose / exposure[9] [oʊʒ] **level** • maximum acceptable safe **level** • threshold limit of safe exposure[10] • ceiling[11] [siːlɪŋ] (abbr CV) **value**

Schlangengift-Antivenin, Schlangengift-Antiserum
Antitoxin[1] Gegengift, Antidot[2] neutralisieren[3] polyvalentes Vipernserum[4] Grubenvipern[5] Schlangenserum[6] Pferdeserum[7] polyvalentes Immunserum[8] spezifisches Antidot[9] antitoxische Immunität[10] Antitoxinkonzentration[11] Antitoxintherapie[12] ein Antitoxin verabreichen[13] Diphtherieantitoxin[14] Antitoxineinheit[15] verdünntes/ diluiertes Antitoxin[16]

15

Eintrittspforte, -stelle
Schlangenbiss[1] Giftzahn[2] Bienenstich[3] Stachel[4] Stachelrochen[5] Seeigel[6] Eintrittsstelle[7] Wespenstich[8] Hornissenstich[9] Steinfischstich[10] Katzenwelsstich[11] Giftstachel[12] steckengebliebener Stachel/ Stechapparat[13] Stechwerkzeuge, -apparat[14] Feuerameise, Solenopsis saevissima[15] Spinnenstich[16] Bissspuren, -male[17] Bissstelle[18]

16

Verteilungsvolumen
Eliminationshalbwertszeit[1] sequestriert[2] Tetanusantitoxin[3] großes Verteilungsvolumen[4] initiales Verteilungsvolumen[5] Arzneistoffverteilung[6] Gewebeverteilung[7] Verteilungsmuster[8] d. Halbwertszeit verlängern[9] biolog. H.[10] physikal. H.[11] Giftelimination[12] Arzneistoffelimination[13] Kontrastmittelausscheidung[14] Ausscheidungsweg[15] Eliminationsgeschwindigkeit[16]

17

duldbare tägliche Aufnahme(menge), DTA
Grenzschwellenwert[1] NEL-Wert, unwirksame Dosis[2] schädlich[3] günstig[4] Gesundheitsrisiken[5] maximal tolerierbare Aufnahme[6] duldbare wöchentl. Aufnahme(menge)/ Dosis[7] niedrigste Dosis m. erkennbarer schädlicher Wirkung[8] Expositionswert, -konzentration[9] maximale Arbeitsplatzkonzentration (MAK)[10] höchster zulässiger Wert[11]

18

Toxicology   MEDICAL SCIENCE 407

(bio)accumulation [eɪʃ] n term   rel **potentiation**[1] n term

absorption (via breathing [iː], ingestion or active uptake) and tendency of a chemical to become more concentrated in the body as it passes through the food web[2] or as a result of repeated exposure

(bio)accumulate[3] [baɪoʊəkjuːmjʊleɪt] v • **potentiate** [poʊtenˈʃieɪt] v

» In Wilson's disease[4] impairment [ɛə] of the normal excretion [iːʃ] of hepatic copper[5] results in toxic accumulations of the metal in the liver and other organs. X-ray fluorescence was investigated as a method for estimating long-term accumulation of lead[6] [e] in bone. Potentiation of the drug's anticholinergic [-ɜːrdʒɪk] and CNS depressant effects may occur [ɜː].

Use extracellular [se]/ localized / rapid / drug[7] **accumulation** • halothane-induced / lithium[8] **potentiation** • **to potentiate** (toxic) effects[9] / narcotics

(Bio)akkumulation, (Stoff)kumulation i. Körper
Potenzierung[1] Nahrungskette[2] (sich) ansammeln/ -häufen, akkumulieren[3] Morbus Wilson, Wilson-Krankheit, hepatolentikuläre Degeneration[4] hepatische Kupferausscheidung[5] Blei[6] Arzneimittelanreicherung[7] Lithiumaugmentation, Wirkungsverstärkung durch Lithium[8] d. toxische Wirkung potenzieren[9]   19

toxicosis [tɒːksɪkoʊsɪs] n term   syn **systemic poisoning** n clin → U124-5, 8

any condition or disease of toxic origin

» Patient stabilization is the first priority in cases of zinc toxicosis[1]. Copper toxicosis[2] is a metabolic disorder in which copper is accumulated [juː] in the liver. Thyrotoxicosis [aɪ] in which serum T4 is normal or low in the absence of a deficiency of TBG[3], while the serum T3 is increased, is termed T3 toxicosis. The nature[4], reversibility, and severity of systemic poisoning[5] depend on the dose, potency, and metabolic disposition[6] of the chemical.

Use endogenic / exogenic[7] / (inherited/ acquired) copper[2] (abbr CT) **toxicosis** • barbiturate[8] / acute / jellyfish[9] [dʒ]/ T3 / T4 / hashi[10]/ renal **toxicosis** • **systemic poison**

Toxikose, system. Vergiftung
Zinkvergiftung[1] Kupferspeicherkrankheit[2] thyroxinbindendes Globulin[3] Art[4] Schweregrad d. system. Vergiftung[5] Stoffwechselwirkung[6] exogene Toxikose[7] Barbituratvergiftung[8] Quallenvergiftung[9] Hashitoxikose[10]
                                             20

food poisoning [fuːd pɔɪzəˈnɪŋ] n clin   rel **botulism**[1] [bɒtjəlɪzm] n term

poisoning from ingestion[2] of foodstuffs [ʌ] containing naturally occurring [ɜː] poisons (e.g. wild berries, mushrooms) or bacterial or other toxins (e.g. contaminated, improperly canned food[3])

botulinus [aɪ] **toxin**[4] n term • **botulinous** [aɪ] adj • **botul(in)ogenic** adj

» Not all food poisoning has a bacterial [ɪə] cause. If symptoms [ɪ] suggest food poisoning, obtain [eɪ] a history of foods consumed during the preceding [siː] 24 hours. Botulism is food poisoning usually caused by ingestion [dʒe] of Clostridium botulinum, a spore-forming bacillus [sɪ] found in soil [sɔɪl].

Use (non)bacterial[5] / enterotoxin / staphylococcal / self-limited[6] / classic **food poisoning** • fish / meat / seafood / mushroom [ʌ] **poisoning** • **poisoning** by mushrooms / by amphetamines / due to barbiturates • victims / treatment or management / symptoms and signs[7] [aɪ]/ prevention / severity[8] [e] **of poisoning** • food-borne [ɔː]/ wound[9] [uː]/ infant[10] **botulism** • **botulism** antitoxin[11] / immune globulin[11] • **botulinum** (neuro)toxin[4] / spores / toxoid[12] / toxin therapy[13] • **botulinous** toxin[4]

Lebensmittelvergiftung
Botulismus, Vergiftung durch Botulinustoxin[1] Aufnahme, Ingestion[2] unsachgemäß konservierte Nahrungsmittel[3] Botulinustoxin[4] bakterielle Lebensmittelvergiftung[5] selbstlimitierende Lebensmittelvergiftung[6] Vergiftungserscheinungen[7] Schweregrad d. Vergiftung[8] Wundbotulismus[9] Säuglingsbotulismus[10] Botulismus-Antitoxin, -Immunserum[11] Botulismus-Toxoid-Impfstoff[12] Botulinustoxintherapie[13]
                                             21

toxemia [tɒksiːmɪə] n term   syn **blood poisoning** n clin, rel **toxic shock**[1] n term

(i) clinical syndrome [ɪ] caused by toxic substances [ʌ] in the blood (ii) clinical manifestations which are due to noxious [kʃ] substances elaborated[2] by infectious agents

toxemic [iː] adj term • **endotoxemia**[3] n

» In these cases fetal [iː] death in utero[4] due to bacterial toxemia is not uncommon. Most cases of toxic shock syndrome[5] have been described in menstruating adolescents [es] and young women using vaginal [dʒ] tampons. Signs of toxemia and prostration[6] became prominent.

Use alimentary / general(ized) / systemic / eclampt(ogen)ic[7] / acute **toxemia** • profound[8] [aʊ]/ fulminant [ʊ] or overwhelming[9] **toxemia** • **toxemia** syndrome / of pregnancy[7] • accidental[10] **poisoning** • **toxemic** mother / patient • **toxic shock** (-like) syndrome[5] (abbr TSS) • staphylococcal / nonmenstrual **toxic shock**

(i) Tox(ik)ämie, Toxinämie
(ii) Blutvergiftung
toxischer Schock[1] produziert[2] Endotoxämie[3] intrauteriner Fruchttod[4] toxisches Schocksyndrom, TSS[5] völlige Erschöpfung, Prostration[6] Schwangerschaftstoxikose, Gestose, Präeklampsie[7] massive Toxämie[8] fulminante T.[9] akzidentelle Vergiftung[10]
                                             22

detoxify v term → U10-15   rel **decontaminate**[1],
                               degas[2], **delead**[3] [e] v term → U82-32

to diminish the toxic effects of any substance or the virulence [ɪ] of pathogenic organisms

detoxification[4] n term • **decontamination**[5] n • **degassing** n • **deleading** n

» Transfer the patient to an inpatient detoxification setting. Normally these metabolites are detoxified by combining with hepatic glutathione [aɪ]. During the pretoxic phase, prior to the onset of manifestations, decontamination is the highest priority.

Use **to detoxify** venoms[6] / noxious agents • **to decontaminate** the victim • inpatient[7] / hepatic[8] / alcohol **detoxification** • drug[9] / cocaine [eɪ] methadone / self[10]-**detoxification** • **detoxification** from opioids / treatment[11] • thorough [ɜː]/ gut [ʌ] or gastrointestinal[12] / victim **decontamination**

entgiften
dekontaminieren, entgiften, entseuchen[1] entgasen[2] entbleien[3] Giftelimination, Entgiftung, Detoxi(fi)kation[4] Dekontamination, Entgiftung, -seuchung[5] Tiergifte eliminieren[6] stationäre Entgiftung[7] Entgiftung i. d. Leber[8] Arzneimittelentgiftung[9] Selbstentgiftung[10] Entgiftungstherapie[11] Entgiftung d. Magen-Darm-Trakts[12]
                                             23

Epsom salt(s) n   syn **magnesium** [iː] **sulfate** [ʌ] n, rel **sodium sulfate**¹ n term
active ingredient² [iː] of most natural laxatives³ used as a cathartic⁴ in certain poisonings
» In hydrofluoric acid burns⁵ [ɜː] which are particularly penetrating and corrosive prompt immersion⁶ [ɜː] into Epsom salts solution is helpful. Acceptable cathartics include magnesium sulfate or sodium sulfate (250 mg/kg/dose orally).

(syrup of) ipecac [sɪrəp ɒːv ɪpəkæk] n term
rel **activated** or **medicinal** [ɪs] **charcoal**¹ [tʃɑːrkoʊl] n term
dried root of a shrub² [ʌ] (Uragoga ipecacuanha) which contains emetine [-tiːn], cephaeline [eɪ], psychotrine [saɪkə-], ipecacuanhic acid, and methylpsychotrine which is used as an expectorant³, emetic⁴, and antidysenteric⁵
» Use the ipecac to induce vomiting and the activated charcoal to adsorb the poison. Charcoal may be given by mouth or by a stomach [k] tube⁶. Thirty grams of charcoal should be made into a slurry⁷ [ɜː] with a minimum of 240 mL of diluent⁸ [ɪ].
Use powdered⁹ [aʊ] **ipecac** • **ipecac**-induced emesis or vomiting • to administer / animal¹⁰ / vegetable [edʒ] **charcoal** • multiple-dose¹¹ / repeat-dose¹¹ / coated¹² [oʊ] **charcoal** • **charcoal** administration / solution / slurry / hemoperfusion¹³ / stool [uː]

gastric lavage [ləvɑːʒ‖BE lævɪdʒ] n term   syn **gastric washing** n → U118-10
rel **(naso)gastric tube**¹ [eɪ] n term → U125-18
insertion [ɪnsɜːrʃən] of a gastric tube¹ to irrigate and drain [eɪ] the stomach [k]
lavage² v term • **wash** v & n • **washings**³ [wɒʃɪŋz] n pl
» Empty the stomach by gastric lavage and administer activated charcoal. A large (32F) tube should be passed and the stomach [k] emptied of its contents and lavaged until clean.
Use to perform/proceed [siː] with/continue **gastric lavage** • vigorous⁴ / cautious [ɒːʃ]/ iced⁵ [aɪst]/ prompt **gastric lavage** • early-morning **gastric lavage** • **gastric lavage** fluid⁶ / solution [uːʃ]/ tube¹ • **gastric** emptying⁷ • nasogastric [æ]/ (gastro)intestinal⁸ **lavage** • whole-gut or whole bowel⁸ [aʊ]/ bronchoalveolar⁹ [ɪə] (abbr BAL) **lavage** • tracheobronchial [ɒː]/ pleural¹⁰ [ʊə]/ **lavage** • bladder / (diagnostic) peritoneal¹¹ [iː]/ oral **lavage** • ice-water / saline¹² [eɪ] **lavage** • bronchial⁹ [k]/ alveolar / mouth¹³ / hand washing • cytologic³ [saɪtə-]/ bladder / throat¹⁴ [oʊ] **washings** • to insert [ɜː] or place¹⁵ **a nasogastric tube** • large-bore¹⁶ [ɔː]/ small-bore / standard **nasogastric tube** • orogastric¹ / stomach¹ / intestinal **tube**

Unit 92   Pharmacologic Agents
Related Units: 9 Drugs & Remedies, 121 Pharmacologic Treatment, 93 Anesthetics

pharmacology [fɑːrməkɒːlədʒi] n term
sim **pharmaceutics**¹ [-suːtɪks] n term
science of natural and synthetic medicinal substances, including pharmacognosy², pharmacokinetics³, pharmacodynamics⁴ [aɪ], pharmacogenetics⁵ [dʒ], pharmacotherapy and toxicology
pharma(co)- comb • **pharmacologic** adj • **pharmacopeia**⁶ [piːə] n esp.
» Pharmacokinetics is the study of the activity of drugs within the body, particularly their rates of absorption, distribution⁷, binding [aɪ], biotransformation and elimination⁸.
Use clinical / biochemical **pharmacology** • **pharmacologic** effect / action / properties⁹ / treatment / agent • **pharma**ceutical chemistry¹⁰ /cologist¹¹ • US / British / International¹² / European **pharmacopeia**

agent [eɪdʒᵊnt] n term
broad term for any substance capable [eɪ] of triggering¹ a chemical, physical [fɪ] or biological [aɪ] effect (e.g. drugs, bacteria, chemical substances, contrast media² [iː] etc.)
» Not all preparations and agents are approved³ [uː] for this indication. Treatment consists of adding bulk [ʌ] **agents**⁴. Proteus species [spiːʃiːz] are common causative [ɒː] **agents**⁵.
Use rapidly/long acting / oral / sunscreen⁶ **agent** • antipsychotic⁷ [saɪkɒː]/ antiulcer [ʌls]/ antiangina [dʒaɪ]/ cholinergic⁸ [kɒːlɪnɜːrdʒɪk]/ germicidal⁹ [-saɪdᵊl] **agent** • alkylating¹⁰ / embedding / foamy [oʊ]/ antifoaming¹¹ / retrovirus-like / sclerosing / nephrotoxic / mucolytic¹² [ɪ]/ contrast² / infectious¹³ [ɪnfekʃəs] **agent**

Magnesiumsulfat, Bittersalz
Glaubersalz, Natriumsulfat¹ Wirkstoff² Abführmittel, Laxanzien³ Purgans⁴ Verätzungen m. Flusssäure⁵ Eintauchen⁶   24

Brechwurzelsirup, Sirupus ipecacuanhae
Aktivkohle, Carbo medicinalis¹ Strauch² Expektorans³ Brechmittel, Emetikum⁴ Mittel gegen Amöbenruhr⁵ Magenschlauch⁶ Aufschwemmung⁷ Verdünnungsmittel⁸ gepulverte Brechwurzel⁹ Tierkohle¹⁰ Mehrfachgaben v. Aktivkohle¹¹ beschichtete Aktivkohle¹² Hämoperfusion m. Aktivkohle¹³
25

Magenspülung, -aushebung
Magenschlauch¹ (aus)waschen, -spülen² Lavagematerial³ gründliche Magenspülung⁴ Magenspülung mit Eiswasser⁵ Magenspülflüssigkeit⁶ Magenentleerung⁷ Darmreinigung⁸ bronchoalveoläre Lavage, Bronchiallavage⁹ Pleuraspülung¹⁰ (diagnost.) Peritonealspülung¹¹ Spülung m. Kochsalzlösung¹² Mundspülung¹³ Rachenspülproben¹⁴ einen Magenschlauch einführen¹⁵ großlumiger Magenschlauch¹⁶
26

Pharmakologie, Arzneimittellehre
Pharmazie, -zeutik¹ Pharmakognosie² Pharmakokinetik³ Pharmakodynamik⁴ Pharmakogenetik⁵ Arzneibuch, Pharmakopöe⁶ Verteilung⁷ Elimination, Ausscheidung⁸ pharmakologische Eigenschaften⁹ pharmazeutische Chemie¹⁰ Pharmakologe/-in¹¹ internat. Arzneibuch¹²   1

Mittel, Wirkstoff, Agens, Erreger
auslösen, hervorrufen¹ Kontrastmittel² zugelassen³ Ballaststoffe⁴ (Krankheits)erreger⁵ Sonnenschutzmittel⁶ Antipsychotikum, Neuroleptikum⁷ Cholinergikum⁸ Desinfektionsmittel, keimtötendes M.⁹ Alkylans¹⁰ Entschäumer, Antischaummittel¹¹ schleimlösendes M.¹² Infektionserreger¹³   2

Pharmacologic Agents   MEDICAL SCIENCE **409**

pharmacologic activity n term   syn **bioactivity, action, effect** n term → U121-8

activate[1] v term • **activator**[2] n • **activation**[3] n • **activating** adj • **active** adj
» The balance between cholinergic and dopaminergic activity[4] in the basal ganglia is improved.
Use synergistic [dʒɪ]/ specific / in vitro / peak[5] [iː]/ serotonergic[6] **activity** • **activated** charcoal[7] [tʃ] • antibacterial / site of[8] **action** • extension of[9] **effect**

Arzneimittelwirkung, biologische Aktivität/ Wirkung
aktivieren, anregen[1] Aktivator[2] Aktivierung, Anregung[3] dopaminerge Wirkung[4] maximale W.[5] Serotoninaktivität[6] Aktivkohle, Carbo medicinalis[7] Wirkort[8] Wirkungsverlängerung[9]

3

biotransformation [aɪ] n term   sim **biodegradation**[1] n term

successive[2] biochemical changes a substance undergoes as it is metabolized[3] in the body
biodegradable[4] [eɪ] adj term
» The precise kinetics of metallic substances depend on their diffusibility[5], rate of biotransformation[6], availability of intracellular ligands[7] [aɪ‖ɪ], etc.

Biotransformation
biologischer Abbau[1] aufeinanderfolgend[2] abgebaut, umgewandelt, metabolisiert[3] biologisch abbaubar[4] Diffusionsvermögen[5] Biotransformationsrate[6] Liganden[7]

4

pharmacologic half-life [hæf laɪf] n term   rel **biologic half-life**[1] n term

time required for half the administered dose of a drug or radioactive substance to be eliminated by normal metabolic processes[2]
» Multiple daily doses are required because of the drug's short half-life.
Use elimination[3] / cellular / serum [ɪɚ]/ functional **half-life** • **half-life** range[4] [reɪndʒ]

pharmkolog. Halbwertszeit
biologische Halbwertszeit[1] Stoffwechselprozesse[2] Eliminationshalbwertszeit[3] Halbwertbreite[4]

5

antagonist n term   opposite **agonist**[1]**, synergist**[2] [sɪnɚdʒɪst] n term

agent (also physiologic structure or process) neutralizing [uː] or impeding[3] [iː] the action or effect of other agents
(ant)agonistic adj term • **antagonism** n • **synergistic** adj term • **synergism**[4] n
» Some opioid antagonists have mixed[5] agonist/antagonist activity.
Use calcium / competitive[6] / enzyme [zaɪ]/ folic acid[7] / insulin / narcotic / H₂ receptor **antagonist** • potent[8] / partial / moderate **antagonists**

Antagonist
Agonist[1] Synergist[2] hemmen[3] Synergismus[4] sowohl ... als auch[5] kompetitiver A.[6] Folsäureantagonist[7] hochwirksame Antagonisten[8]

6

blocking agent or **blocker** n term   syn **inhibitor** n term

(i) agent that interferes with[1] [ɪɚ] or retards[2] chemical, physiologic, or enzymatic [enzɪmætɪk] activity
(ii) nerve which on stimulation represses activity
» Patients with beta-blocker[3] [eɪ‖iː] or ACE inhibitor[4] intolerance should be considered for surgery.
Use angiotensin converting enzyme (abbr ACE)[4] / monoamine oxidase [eɪz] (abbr MAO) **inhibitor** • alpha / ganglionic[5] / calcium channel[6] [tʃænəl] **blocker**

Hemmstoff, Hemmer, Blocker, Inhibitor
hemmen, stören[1] verzögern[2] Beta-(Rezeptoren)blocker[3] ACE-Hemmer[4] Ganglienblocker, Ganglioplegikum[5] Kalziumantagonist, -blocker[6]

7

cholinergic [kɒːlənɜːrdʒɪk] adj & n term
                opposite **anticholinergic** or **parasympatholytic**[1] [ɪ] adj & n term

(n) agent affecting[2] the regulation of the autonomous nervous system[3]
» Unlike[4] phenothiazines [fiːnoʊθaɪəziːnz] (anticholinergic) the drug has powerful peripheral cholinergic effects.
Use cholinergic stimulation / blocking agent / fibers[5] [aɪ]/ receptor • **anticholinergic** potency[6] [oʊ]/ preparations

cholinerg; Cholinergikum
anticholinerg, Anticholinergikum, Parasympatholytikum, -lytisch[1] beeinflussen[2] autonomes Nervensystem[3] im Gegensatz zu[4] cholinerge (Nerven)fasern[5] anticholinerge Wirkung[6]

8

antibiotic [æntɪbaɪɒːtɪk] n & adj term   syn **antimicrobial/-bacterial agent** n,
                                             sim **antiviral** [aɪ] **agent**[1] n term

(n) drug produced from a mold[2] [oʊ] or similar bacterium which inhibits the proliferation[3] of other micro-organisms
» Broad spectrum antibiotics[4] have a wide range of activity against both Gram-positive and Gram-negative organisms.
Use broad-spectrum / bactericidal[5] [-saɪdəl]/ oral / IV / acquired [kwaɪ] resistance to[6] **antibiotics** • **antibiotic-associated** diarrhea [daɪəriːə] • **antibiotic** use / cover[7] / sensitivity test[8]

Antibiotikum; antibiotisch
Virostatikum, antivirales Mittel[1] Schimmelpilz[2] Wachstum, Proliferation[3] Breitbandantibiotika[4] bakterizide A.[5] erworbene Antibiotikaresistenz[6] antibiot. Abschirmung[7] Antibiogramm[8]

9

penicillin [penɪsɪlɪn] n term

(i) antibiotic substance obtained from cultures of molds
(ii) natural or synthetic variants of penicillic acid

penicillamine[1] [iː] n term • penicillinase[2] n • **penicillin-allergic** adj

» Penicillins are mainly bactericidal in action (especially active against Gram-positive organisms). Erythromycin [aɪs] may be used in penicillin-allergic individuals.
Use oral / systemic / aqueous[3] [eɪkwɪəs] **penicillin** • **penicillin** B / G / O / N / V /-sensitive /-fast[4] / derivative[5]

anti-inflammatory drugs n term

drugs such as glucocorticoids or aspirin capable of indirectly reducing inflammation[1] by metabolic activity[2]

» All NSAIDs are analgesic [dʒiː], antipyretic[3] [aɪ] and anti-inflammatory in a dose-dependent fashion.
Use non-steroidal[4] **anti-inflammatory drugs** (abbr NSAIDs) • **anti-inflammatory** effect

emetic n & adj term   opposite **antiemetic**[1] n & adj term, **antivomiting drug**[1] n clin

(n) agent such as ipecac syrup[2] that induces vomiting; used mainly after ingestion[3] [dʒe] of noxious [kʃ] substances[4]

» The antiemetic can be delivered[5] IM or by rectal suppository[6]. Administration of emetics proved unsuccessful.
Use ectopic / effective / weak[7] **antiemetic** • **antiemetic** medication / effect / therapy / properties

laxative [æks] n & adj term   syn **stool** [uː] **softener** n clin, opposite **antidiarrheal**[1] [aɪ] n & adj term

(n) drug stimulating bowel [aʊ] movement[2] and/or softer or bulkier [ʌ] stools[3] (ranging from mild aperients[4] [ɪə] to strong purgatives [pɜːrg] or cathartics[5] such as Castor oil[6]

» Epsom salt[7] is used in constipation[8] for its purgative properties[9].
Use chronic / osmotic / rapid-acting / oily / saline [eɪ] / oral / mild[4] **laxatives** • **laxative** abuse[10]

inhalant [eɪ] n term   syn **aerosol** [eəˈɒsɒːl] n term

(i) aerosolized (combinations of) medication taken by inhalation with nebulizers[1] or metered [iː] dose inhalers[2]
(ii) generally, any substance that is inhaled, esp. allergens, narcotics, and irritants[3]

inhalation[4] [eɪ] n term • inhale[5] [eɪ] v • inhaler[6] n

» In adults sympathomimetic bronchodilators[7] [k] should be given in aerosol form.
Use water / particulate[8] **aerosol** • **aerosol** inhalation / generator[1] [dʒe] / therapy • broncho**aerosol**

expectorant n & adj term   syn **phlegm** [flem] **loosener** [uː] n clin, **mucolytic** [ɪ] n & adj term

agent promoting bronchial [k] secretion [iː] and expulsion[1] [ʌ] of mucus[2] from the respiratory tract

expectorate[3] v term • expectoration[4] n

» Treatment for mucoviscidosis [s] includes expectorants, and bronchodilators.

anticoagulants n term   syn **antihrombotic (agents)** n, rel **thrombolytic (agents)**[1] n term

anticlotting[2] drugs that can suppress or delay[3] [eɪ] coagulation
coagulate[4] [koʊæɡjəleɪt] v term • coagulation[5] n

» The patient is on anticoagulants for coronary thrombosis. Streptokinase [aɪ] and urokinase are thrombolytics capable of disintegrating[6] thrombi [aɪ].

Penizillin, Penicillin
Penicillamin[1] Penizillinase, Beta-Laktamase[2] wasserlösliches P.[3] penizillinresistent[4] Penicillinderivat[5]

10

Antiphlogistika, entzündungshemmende Mittel
Entzündung[1] Stoffwechsel(prozesse)[2] fiebersenkend[3] nichtsteroidale Antiphlogistika, NSA[4]

11

Emetikum; emetisch
Antiemetikum; Übelkeit u. Erbrechen verhindernd[1] Brechwurzelsirup[2] Einnahme[3] schädliche Substanzen[4] appliziert[5] Zäpfchen, Suppositorium[6] leichtes Antiemetikum[7]

12

Abführmittel, Laxans, Laxativum; abführend, laxierend
Antidiarrhoikum, stopfendes Mittel[1] Stuhlentleerung[2] voluminösere Stühle[3] schwache Abführmittel, Aperitiva[4] Purganzien, Kathartika[5] Rizinusöl[6] Bittersalz[7] Verstopfung, Obstipation[8] abführende Wirkung[9] Laxanzienabusus[10]

13

Aerosol, Inhalat(ionsmittel)
Handzerstäuber, Nebulisator[1] Dosierinhalator[2] Irritanzien, Reizmittel[3] Inhalation, Einatmung[4] einatmen, inhalieren[5] Inhalator[6] Broncholytika, -dilatatoren[7] Trocken-, Staubaerosol[8]

14

Expektorans, Sekretolytikum; schleimlösend
Auswerfen[1] Schleim[2] aushusten, expektorieren[3] Aushusten, Expektoration[4]

15

Antithrombotika, Antikoagulanzien, Gerinnungshemmer
Fibrino-, Thrombolytika[1] gerinnungshemmend[2] verzögern[3] koagulieren, gerinnen[4] Koagulation, (Blut)gerinnung[5] auflösen[6]

16

Pharmacologic Agents

MEDICAL SCIENCE

vasodilators [veɪzoʊdaɪleɪtɚz] *n term*
opposite **vasoconstrictors** or **-pressors**[1] *n term*

agents causing dilation[2] of the blood vessels; often used for their antihypertensive[3] effect
vasodilat(at)ion[4] *n term* • **vasoconstriction**[5] *n* • **vasoconstrictive** *adj*

» Alpha-adrenergic agonists are used as nasal decongestants[6] [dʒe] orally and as vasodilators conjunctivally[7] [kəndʒʌŋktaɪ-]. Captopril, an ACE inhibitor, acts as an arteriolar and venous [iː] vasodilator.
Use arterial / pulmonary [ʊ‖ʌ]/ coronary[8] **vasodilator** • topical / intranasal **vasoconstrictor**

Vasodilatanzien, -dilatatoren, gefäßerweiternde Mittel
Vasokonstringenzien, gefäßverengende Mittel[1] Erweiterung[2] blutdrucksenkend[3] Vasodilatation, Gefäßerweiterung[4] Vasokonstriktion, Gefäßverengung[5] abschwellende Mittel[6] bei konjunktivaler Applikation[7] Mittel m. koronardilatator. Wirkung[8]

17

---

antiarrhythmic [æntɪeɪrɪθmɪk] *n & adj term* *syn* **antiarrhythmic agent** *n term*

medication that can prevent or alleviate[1] [iː] cardiac arrhythmias[2]

» In patients with heart failure[3] quinidine[4] [kwɪnɪdiːn] and other antiarrhythmics had a proarrhythmic effect.

Antiarrhythmikum
lindern, vermindern[1] Rhythmusstörungen, Arrhythmien[2] Herzversagen[3] Chinidin[4]

18

---

antispasmodic *n & adj term* *syn* **spasmolytic** [ɪ] *n & adj term*

agent that prevents or relieves spasms, esp. of smooth [uː] muscles[1] in the arteries, bronchi, bile ducts[2] [baɪl dʌkts], intestines or sphincters

» It exerts[3] a direct antispasmodic effect on smooth muscle[1].
Use biliary[4] [bɪlɪɚi]/ urinary / bronchial / systemic **antispasmodic** • **antispasmodic** action

Spasmolytikum; spasmolytisch, krampflösend
glatte Muskulatur[1] Gallengänge[2] haben, ausüben[3] Spasmolytikum bei Gallenkolik[4]

19

---

anticonvulsive or **-ant** [ʌ] *n & adj term* *syn* **antiepileptic** *n & adj term*

agent reducing the severity[1] [e] of convulsions[2] and epileptic seizures[3] [siːʒɚz]

» Patients on[4] anticonvulsants such as phenobarbital [iː] and phenytoin may develop osteomalacia [eɪʃ]. Phenytoin prevents the spread [e] of excessive discharges[5] in cerebral motor areas. The anticonvulsant properties of hydantoin [aɪ] derivatives are attributed to[6] their stabilizing effect on the cell membrane.
Use tricyclic / long-term **anticonvulsants**

Antikonvulsivum, -epileptikum; krampflösend, antiepileptisch
Schwere(grad)[1] Krampfanfälle[2] epileptische Anfälle[3] behandelt mit[4] Depolarisationen[5] zugeschrieben[6]

20

---

diuretics [daɪjəretɪks] *n term* *syn* **water pills** *n inf & clin*,
opposite **antidiuretics**[1] *n term*

agents that increase urinary excretion[2] [iːʃ] (by increasing cardiac output[3], renal perfusion[4] or decreasing reabsorption)
diuresis [iː] *n term* • **diuretic**[5] [e] *adj* → U49-6

» Hypokalemia[6] [iː] may occur in hypertensives taking potassium-wasting diuretics[7].
Use to administer **diuretics** • cardiac / (in)direct / rapidly acting / loop[8] [uː]/ injectable / thiazide[9] [θaɪəzaɪd]/ K+ sparing[10] [eɚ] **diuretics** • **antidiuretic** hormone[11] (*abbr* ADH) / response / therapy

Diuretika, wassertreibende Mittel
Antidiuretika[1] Harnausscheidung, Diurese[2] Herzminutenvolumen[3] Nierendurchblutung[4] diuresefördernd, harntreibend[5] Hypokaliämie[6] Saluretika[7] Schleifendiuretika[8] Thiaziddiuretika[9] kaliumsparende D.[10] antidiuret. Hormon, Adiuretin, Vasopressin[11]

21

---

antihistamines *n term* → U78-24

drugs used in the treatment of allergic reactions for their antagonistic action on histamine

» Use a symptom-sign-directed approach including an H₁ antihistamine[1] for the pruritus[2] [aɪ].
Use nonsedating[3] / IV / oral / OTC[4] / topical **antihistamines**

Antihistaminika, Histaminantagonisten
H₁-Rezeptorenblocker, H₁-Antihistaminikum[1] Hautjucken, Pruritus[2] nicht sedierende A.[3] rezeptfreie A.[4]

22

---

psychoactive [saɪkoʊ-] **substances** *n term* *syn* **psychotropic agents** *n term*

agents that act on the mind or behavior and are used to treat emotional disorders; these include antidepressants, lithium carbonate (for manic [æ] episodes[1]), neuroleptics[2], antianxiety [-ænzaɪəti] agents[3], stimulants[4], sedatives[5], tranquilizers[6] [aɪz], and hypnotics [ɪ] or sleeping aids[7]

» Discontinuation[8] of psychotropic or anti-Parkinson drugs[9] should be considered[10].

Psychopharmaka, psychotrope Substanzen
manische Phasen[1] Neuroleptika[2] Anxiolytika, angstlösende Mittel[3] Stimulanzien[4] Sedativa, Beruhigungsmittel[5] Tranquilizer[6] Hypnotika, Schlafmittel[7] Absetzen[8] Antiparkinsonmittel[9] in Betracht ziehen[10]

23

MEDICAL SCIENCE — Pharmacologic Agents

antidepressants *n term*   *opposite* **barbiturates**[1] *n term*,
downers[2] [aʊ] *n jar & inf*

agents relieving symptoms of depression (e.g. tricyclic [traɪsaɪklɪk] antidepressants[3] and MAO inhibitors[4])

» Women have a higher frequency of ADRs[5] to antidepressants and anticonvulsants. Benzodiazepine [aɪæ] overdosage potentiates[6] the respiratory depressive effects of barbiturates.

Antidepressiva
Barbiturate[1] Beruhigungsmittel[2] trizyklische A.[3] Monoaminooxidasehemmer, -inhibitoren[4] Nebenwirkungen[5] verstärken, potenzieren[6]
24

anthelmintic *n & adj term*   *syn* **anthelminthic (agent)** *n term* → U90-16

drug that expells[1] or eradicates[2] parasitic worms (esp. intestinal tapeworms[3] [eɪ], roundworms[4], etc.)

» Many anthelmintic drugs are toxic and must be given with care. If a tapeworm is the cause of vitamin deficiency[5] [ɪʃ], an anthelmintic agent is indicated.

Anthelminthikum, Wurmmittel; anthelminthisch
abtreiben[1] abtöten[2] Bandwürmer[3] Rund-, Fadenwürmer, Nematoden[4] Vitaminmangel[5]
25

antifungal [-fʌŋɡəl] *n & adj term*   *syn* **antimycotic** [aɪ] *n & adj*,
sim **fungicide**[1] [-saɪd] *n term* → U90-18

agent that destroys fungi[2] [fʌŋɡaɪ] and suppresses their growth and reproduction

fungal *adj term* • **fungicidal**[3] *adj* • **fungistatic**[4] *adj*

» The use of powders [aʊ] containing antifungals or chronic use of antifungal creams may prevent recurrences of athlete's foot (tinea pedis [iː])[5]. Cutaneous [eɪ] candidiasis[6] [aɪə] responds well to topical application of an antifungal agent.
Use systemic / topical[7] / oral / broad-spectrum *antifungal* • *antifungal* drugs / lotion / mouthwash / antibiotics / activity / prophylaxis / therapy

Antimykotikum; antimykotisch
fungizides Mittel, Fungizid (Schädlingsbekämpfungsmittel)[1] Pilze, Fungi[2] fungizid[3] fungistatisch[4] Fußpilzerkrankung, Tinea pedis[5] kutane Candidose[6] lokal wirkendes Antimykotikum[7]
26

sympatho- [sɪmpəθoʊ] *or* **adrenomimetics** *n term*
opposite **sympatholytic (agents)**[1] *n term*

agents that mimic[2] the action of the sympathetic nervous system, esp. epinephrine[3] and norepinephrine[4]

» Asthmatics[5] [z] with infrequent symptoms should be given an inhaled sympathomimetic PRN[6]. Some of these patients benefit from[7] sympatholytic drugs such as methyldopa.

Sympathomimetika
Sympatholytika[1] nachahmen, imitieren[2] Adrenalin[3] Noradrenalin[4] Asthmatiker[5] bei Bedarf[6] profitieren von[7]
27

uricosuric drugs *n term*   *syn* **urinary acidifiers** [əsɪdɪfaɪɚz],
uric acid reducers *n term*

agents reducing serum levels of uric acid[1], e.g. to combat[2] the symptoms of gout[3] [aʊ]

» Serum uric acid is used as an indirect measure [eɜ] of the therapeutic [juː] effect of uricosurics. In quinine [kwɪn-] overdose urinary elimination can be enhanced[4] with an acidifying agent. Because contrast agents are uricosuric, tubule obstruction by crystals of uric acid has been proposed as the pathogenic [dʒe] mechanism [k].

Urikosurika
Harnsäure[1] bekämpfen[2] Gicht[3] gesteigert[4]
28

antacid [æntæsɪd] *n & adj term*

agent reducing or neutralizing [uː] acidity[1], e.g. of the gastric juice[2] [dʒuːs] in peptic ulcer[3] [ʌlsə]

» Treatment of the underlying reflux [iː] with antacids was curative.
Use effervescent[4] / fast-acting / high-dose / liquid / contact[5] / magnesium-containing [iː] *antacid* • *antacid* tablet / action / combinations / preparation

Antazidum; antazid, säurebindend
Azidität, Säuregrad[1] Magensaft[2] Ulcus pepticum[3] brauseförmiges Antazidum[4] schleimhautprotektives Antazidum[5]
29

emollient [ɪmɒːljənt] *n & adj term*   *sim* **demulcent**[1] [dɪmʌlsənt] *n & adj term*

agent (e.g. mucilage[2] [mjuːsəlɪdʒ], oil) used to soothe[3] [suːð] and relieve irritation, esp. of the mucous [mjuːkəs] layer[4]

» White petrolatum[5] [eɪ] and other topical emollients may be used if the itching[6] [tʃ] skin is dry.
Use emollient paste [eɪ] / dressing[7] / laxative[8] • *demulcent* expectorant

erweichendes Mittel, Emollienzium; lindernd, beruhigend
Demulzenzium, einhüllendes/ milderndes Mittel; lindernd[1] Schleim, Mucilago[2] lindern[3] Schleimhaut[4] weiße(s) Vaselin(e), Vaselinum album[5] juckend[6] feuchtwarmer Umschlag[7] Gleitmittel[8]
30

antineoplastic [iː] *or* **cytostatic agents** *n term*
sim **antitumor antibiotics**[1] *n term*

various groups of agents (e.g. antimetabolites[2], alkaloids, or antihormones[3]) used in chemotherapy [kɪ] for their inhibiting effect on the maturation and proliferation[4] of cancer cells[5]

» Although little is known about distribution of antineoplastic agents into breast-milk, breast-feeding[6] [e] is not recommended during chemotherapy.

Zytostatika, antineoplastische Substanzen
zytostatische Antibiotika[1] Antimetaboliten[2] Antihormone, Hormonantagonisten[3] Wucherung[4] Krebszellen[5] Stillen[6]
31

Anesthetics MEDICAL SCIENCE 413

cytotoxic [saɪtoʊtɒksɪk] *adj term* → U91-4 *sim* **cytostatic**[1] *adj & n term*
harmful to cells; used esp. to refer to antitumor drugs that selectively destroy dividing cells
cytotoxicity[2] *n term* • **cytotoxin**[3] *n* • **-toxic** *adj & comb*
» Antimetabolites induce cytotoxicity by serving as *false* [ɔː] *substrates*[4] [ʌ] in biochemical *pathways*[5] [æ].
Use **cytotoxic** drug[6] / antitumor agents / therapy • direct / cellular[7] / antibody-mediated[8] [iː] **cytotoxicity** • cardio/ hepato/ nephro[9]/ thyro [θaɪroʊ]/ myelo[10] [aɪ]/ oto**toxic**

zytotoxisch, zellschädigend
zytostatisch; Zytostatikum[1] Zytotoxizität[2] Zytotoxin, Zellgift[3] Substrate[4] biochem. Abläufe[5] zytotox. Substanz[6] Zelltoxizität[7] antikörpervermittelte Zytotoxizität[8] nephrotoxisch, nierenschädigend[9] myelotoxisch[10]
32

teratogenic [-dʒenɪk] *adj term* *sim* **embryotoxic**[1] *adj term* → U91-12
capable of inducing disturbed fetal [iː] growth, malformations[2] and deformities
teratogenicity[3] *n term* • **teratogen**[4] *n* • **teratogenesis**[5] *n*
» Because of its teratogenicity thalidomide is contraindicated in women *of childbearing age*[6] [eɚ].
Use **teratogenic** potential / effect / drug

teratogen
embryotoxisch[1] Missbildungen[2] Teratogenität[3] Teratogen[4] Teratogenese[5] im gebärfähigen Alter[6]
33

biologic response modifiers [mɒːdɪfaɪɚz] *n term, abbr* **BRM**
 syn **immunomodulators** *n term*
chemical agents capable of modifying the response of the immune system, e.g. by stimulating antibody formation or inhibiting WBC[1] activity
» Biologic response modifiers such as interleukin-2 [uː] have received much attention recently.

Immunmodulatoren
Leukozyten, weiße Blutkörperchen[1]

34

Unit 93 Anesthetics
Related Units: 9 Drugs & Remedies, 92 Pharmacologic Agents, 104 Pain, 7 States of Consciousness, 131 The Surgical Suite, 134 Perioperative Management, 135 Anesthesiology

general anesthesia [-θiːʒə] *n term, abbr* **GA**
 rel **general anesthetic**[1] [e] *n term*
loss of the ability to appreciate[2] [iːʃ] pain and unconsciousness produced by anesthetic agents
» With the patient under general anesthesia, the exteriorized *bowel* [aʊ] was *rinsed*[3] with *Ringer's lactate solution*[4]. In large amounts Midazolam (a short-acting benzodiazepine) is a general anesthetic.
Use to undergo/require/necessitate[5]/tolerate/induce/maintain[6]/recover from/awake from **general anesthesia** • inhalation **general anesthetics** • closed manipulation / dissection[7] / rigid [dʒ] bronchoscopy / open biopsy [aɪ]/ patients **under general anesthesia**

Allgemeinanästhesie, (Voll)narkose
Anästhetikum, Narkotikum[1] empfinden[2] Darm wurde gespült[3] Ringer-Laktat-Lösung[4] (Voll)narkose erfordern[5] Narkose aufrechterhalten[6] Präparation in/unter Vollnarkose[7]

1

balanced anesthesia *n term*
technique of GA based on the concept that administration of a mixture of small amounts of different anesthetics summates[1] [ʌ] the advantages but not the disadvantages of the individual agents
» Following premedication[2] and induction by thiopentone [θaɪə-], balanced anesthesia was maintained by a combination of muscle relaxants, inhalational and IV anesthetic agents.

balancierte Anästhesie
vereint[1] Prämedikation[2]

2

local anesthesia *n term, abbr* **LA** *sim* **regional** [riːdʒ-] **anesthesia**[1] *n term*
anesthesia of the operative site produced by direct infiltration of a local anesthetic into the area of small, terminal nerve endings or, rarely, by freezing[2] (cryoanesthesia[3] [kraɪoʊ-])
» A regional anesthetic is used when it is desirable that the patient remain conscious during the operation. If the FB[4] can be palpated, local anesthesia is given by means of submucosal and s.c. injections[5] of 0.5 % bupivacaine.
Use to be a good candidate for **anesthesia** • topical[6] / periodontal / axillary / sacral [eɪ]/ girdle[7] [ɜː]/ stocking[8] [ɒː]/ glove[9] [ʌ] **anesthesia** • pharyngeal [dʒɪəl]/ segmental / unilateral / visceral [s] *or* splanchnic[10] [k]/ corneal / infiltration[11] **anesthesia**

Lokalanästhesie
Regionalanästhesie[1] Vereisen[2] Kälteanästhesie[3] Fremdkörper[4] subkutane Injektion[5] Oberflächen-, Lokalanästhesie[6] gürtelf. A.[7] strumpff. A.[8] handschuhförmige Anästhesie[9] Splanchnikusanästhesie[10] Infiltrationsanästhesie[11]

3

93

Don't worry, Mr. Pym, next week our supply of anesthetics will arrive on time again.

anesthetic [ænəsθetɪk] *n & adj term*   *syn* **anesthetic agent** [eɪdʒ°nt] *n term*

(n) compounds that reversibly depress nerve function and produce loss of ability to perceive[1] [iː] pain and/ or other sensations; also collective term for anesthetizing agents administered to an individual at a particular time
(adj, i) characterized by or capable of producing loss of sensation
(ii) associated with or due to the state of anesthesia

» Most anesthetics delay[2] healing. If available, instill local anesthetic drops. All local anesthetics have CNS toxicities including confusion[3], coma, and seizures[4] [siːʒɚz].

Use to give/administer **anesthetics** • **anesthetic** medication / agent / drugs / solution / gargles[5] / ether [iː] / area / block • **anesthetic** approach[6] / effect / properties / risk / shock / mishap or accident • short-acting[7] / long-acting **anesthetics** • general / topical / inhalation / flammable[8] / volatile[9] / gaseous[10] **anesthetic** • intravenous [iː]/ primary / secondary / spinal / highly potent / halogenated [dʒ] **anesthetics** • delivery of[11] **anesthetics** • **anesthetic**-related complications /-induced convulsions[12] / cardiac arrest

Narkose-, Betäubungsmittel, Anästhetikum, Narkotikum; anästhesierend, betäubend, gefühllos, unempfindlich
empfinden, wahrnehmen[1] verzögern[2] Verwirrtheit[3] (Krampf)-anfälle[4] anästhesierendes Gurgelmittel[5] Anästhesieverfahren[6] Kurznarkotika[7] brennbare Anästhetika[8] volatile A., Inhalationsanästhetika[9] gasförm. Narkotika, Narkosegase[10] Zufuhr von Narkotika[11] anästhesiemittelbedingte Krämpfe[12]

4

lidocaine [laɪdəkeɪn] **(hydrochloride)** [aɪ] *n term*
   syn espBE **lignocaine** [ɪ] *n term*

crystalline compound[1] used as a local anesthetic with pronounced[2] [aʊ] antiarrhythmic [ɪ] and anticonvulsant [ʌ] properties[3]

» Anesthetize the skin with 1% lidocaine with the 10mL syringe and the 25-gauge [eɪ] needle. Injection of a local anesthetic such as lidocaine into the trigger point[4] site often results in pain relief. Lidocaine, tetracaine and cocaine [koʊkeɪn] are the most common choices for topical anesthesia of the airway, while procaine is too poorly absorbed to be effective topically.

Use topical / intranasal[5] [eɪ]/ 0.5% / viscous[6] [sk] **lidocaine** • **lidocaine** solution / infusion / periarticular infiltration / jelly[7] [dʒ] overdose / poisoning • to instill[8]/inject/administer **lidocaine**

Lidocain
Verbindung[1] ausgeprägt[2] krampflösende Eigenschaften[3] Triggerpunkt[4] intranasal verabreichtes L.[5] viskoses L.[6] Lidocain-Gel[7] Lidocain einträufeln/ instillieren[8]

5

conduction [ʌ] *or* **block anesthesia** *n term*   *syn* **blockade** [-eɪd] *or* **blockage** [-ɪdʒ] *n term*

regional anesthesia in which a local anesthetic is injected about nerves[1] to inhibit nerve transmission; includes spinal, epidural, nerve block, and field block anesthesia[2], but not local or topical anesthesia

» Local wound [uː] infiltration or regional nerve block with 0.5% bupivacaine will help alleviate the pain. A postpartum hemorrhage is best treated by dilation and curettage using paracervical block anesthesia[3]. In patients with mitral [aɪ] valve disease conduction anesthesia is preferred to preclude[4] complications during labor[5] and delivery[6]. In a combative[7] patient, use of neuromuscular blockade provides good control of the airway.

Use sympathetic[8] / parasacral [eɪ]/ pudendal[9] / caudal [ɒː]/ nasopalatine / (sub)lingual nerve / saddle[10] / inferior [ɪɚ] alveolar **block (anesthesia)** • neuromuscular / ganglionic **blocking agent** *or* **blocker**[11] • field[2] / cholinergic[12] [kɒːlɪnɜːrdʒɪk]/ profound[13] **blockage**

Leitungsanästhesie
Nerven werden umspritzt[1] Feldblock[2] Parazervikalblockade[3] ausschließen[4] Wehen[5] Entbindung[6] aggressiv[7] Sympathikusblockade[8] Pudendusblock[9] Sattelblock[10] Ganglienblocker[11] Cholinrezeptorenblockade[12] stark ausgeprägter Block[13]

6

Anesthetics

spinal [spaɪnᵊl] **anesthesia** *n term*   *syn* **subarachnoid** [æk] **(block) anesthesia** *n term*

anesthesia produced by injection of local anesthetics into the spinal subarachnoid space[1]

» Predisposing[2] factors of CNS infections include head and neck trauma, lumbar puncture[3] [pʌŋktʃɚ], recent neurosurgery and spinal anesthesia. Complications from epidural anesthesia are the same as those from spinal anesthesia, with the exception of headache.

Use differential / total / high[4] / low[5] / single shot / continuous[6] / intra-**spinal anesthesia**

epidural [epɪdʊɚᵊl] **anesthesia** *or* **block** *n term*

syn **peridural anesthesia** *n term*

regional anesthesia produced by injection of a local anesthetic into the extradural space that blocks the spinal nerve roots

» Epidural anesthesia may be preferable when a low spinal level[1] is adequate for the procedure.

Use spinal[2]/ fractional [ækʃ]/ postoperative / lumbar **epidural anesthesia** • extradural **anesthesia** • epidural / spinal **block**

barbotage [bɑːrbətɑːʒ] *n term*

repeated alternate injection and withdrawal of fluid with a syringe[1]; for spinal anesthesia a portion of an anesthetic agent is injected into the CSF[2], and some CSF is withdrawn[3] [ɔːn] into the syringe until the entire contents of the syringe are injected; the technique is also used for gastric lavage[4]

inhalation [eɪ] **anesthesia** *n term*   *sim* **insufflation anesthesia**[1] *n term*

anesthesia effected by inspiration or insufflation of volatile anesthetics (gases or vapors[2] [eɪ]) into the respiratory tract using special delivery systems[3]

» Inhalation anesthesia where the gases exhaled by the patient are rebreathed[4] [iː] as some carbon dioxide [daɪ-] is simultaneously [eɪ] removed and anesthetic gas and oxygen [ɒːksɪdʒən] are added so that no anesthetic escapes into the room is termed closed circuit anesthesia[5]. The advantage of inhalation anesthesia is that the anesthetics can be titrated[6] [aɪ] according to the patient's needs.

Use **inhalation** anesthetics[7] / induction / agents[7] • combined intravenous-**inhalation anesthesia**

nitrous [aɪ] **oxide** [aɪ] *n term*   *syn* **(laughing** [læfɪŋ]**) gas** *n clin*

colorless gas (N₂O) producing loss of sensibility to pain on inhalation which is preceded [iː] by exhilaration[1] and sometimes laughter; widely used as a rapidly acting, rapidly reversible, nondepressant, and nontoxic inhalation analgesic [dʒiː] to supplement[2] [ʌ] other anesthetics and analgesics, e.g. in dentistry

» For routine delivery[3] analgesia with 40% nitrous oxide may be used as long as verbal contact with the patient is maintained. Nitrous oxide/oxygen and local anesthesia was used in 8 patients, IV sedation in 15, and no anesthetic at all in one patient. Since nitrous oxide does not provide total anesthesia, it is given in combination with a volatile anesthetic or narcotic.

Use **nitrous oxide** inhalation • oxygen-**nitrous oxide** mix[4]

halothane [hæləθeɪn] *n term*

a widely used potent nonflammable [æ] and nonexplosive inhalation anesthetic with rapid onset and reversal; largely supplanted by[1] later-generation halogenated [dʒ] hydrocarbon[2] [aɪ] anesthetics

» The side effects of halothane include cardiovascular and respiratory depression[3], and sensitization to epinephrine-induced[4] arrhythmias [ɪ]. Anesthesia was maintained with halothane and nitrous oxide.

Use **halothane** administration / anesthesia / hepatotoxicity[5] / metabolites / reactions

intravenous [iː] **anesthesia** *n term*

rel **endotracheal** [eɪk] **anesthesia**[1] *n term*

anesthesia produced by injection of anesthetic agents into the venous [iː] circulation

» Patients with a normal airway[2] may be intubated under intravenous anesthesia.

MEDICAL SCIENCE 415

Spinalanästhesie

spinaler Subarachnoidalraum[1] begünstigend[2] Lumbalpunktion[3] hohe Spinalanästhesie[4] tiefe Spinalanästhesie[5] kontinuierliche Spinalanästhesie[6]

7

Epi-, Periduralanästhesie

Anästhesie im lumbalen Bereich[1] Epiduralspinalanästhesie (ESA)[2]

8

Barbotage

Spritze[1] Liquor[2] aspiriert, abgesaugt[3] Magenspülung[4]

9

Inhalationsnarkose

Insufflationsnarkose[1] Dämpfe[2] Narkosesysteme[3] wieder eingeatmet[4] geschlossenes Narkosesystem[5] titriert[6] Inhalationsanästhetika, -narkotika[7]

10

Distickstoffoxid, Lachgas

Hochstimmung[1] ergänzen, verstärken[2] Entbindung[3] Sauerstoff-Lachgas-Gemisch[4]

11

Halothan

verdrängt durch[1] Halogenkohlenwasserstoff[2] Atemdepression[3] adrenalinbedingt[4] halothanbedingte Leberschädigung[5]

12

intravenöse Anästhesie

Endotracheal-, Intubationsnarkose[1] Atemwege[2]

13

barbiturates [ɪtʃə] *n term*   *syn* **sleeping pills** *n clin*

derivatives of barbituric acid (including phenobarbital [fi:noʊ-]) that act as CNS depressants and are used for their tranquilizing[1], hypnotic[2] [ɪ], and anti-seizure[3] [i:3] effects; most barbiturates have the potential for abuse[4]

» Sedation can be achieved[5] by barbiturates, benzodiazepine or narcotics. Long-acting barbiturates (6–8h) also include methobarbital, barbital, and primidone.

Use short-acting[6] / rapidly acting / IV **barbiturates** • **barbiturate** sedatives / withdrawal[7] / overdosage / intoxication / poisoning / syndrome [ɪ]/ therapy

basal [eɪ] **anesthesia** *n term*

parenteral administration of one or more sedatives to produce a state of depressed consciousness prior to[1] induction [ʌ] of GA

» A patient under basal anesthesia does not respond to words but still reacts to pinprick[2] stimulation.

muscle [mʌsl] **relaxants** *n term*

agents capable of relaxing striated [straɪeɪtɪd] muscle[1]; includes drugs acting at the spinal [aɪ] cord level or directly on muscle to decrease tone[2], as well as the neuromuscular relaxants

» Muscle relaxants act mainly as CNS depressants[3], inhibiting spinal synaptic reflexes, prolonging synaptic recovery time, and reducing repetitive discharges[4].

Use (non)depolarizing[5] / skeletal or striated / smooth[6] [u:] **muscle relaxant**

(tubo)curare [t(j)u:boʊ-] *n term*   *sim* **tubocurarine**[1] [-kjʊəɑ:rɪn] *n term*

toxic alkaloid (chief active constituent[2] of the arrow poison[3] curare) that produces nondepolarizing paralysis of skeletal muscle after IV injection by blocking transmission at the myoneural [aɪ] junction[4] [dʒʌŋkʃən]; used clinically (e.g, as d-tubocurarine chloride [aɪ], metocurine iodide [aɪə]) to provide muscle relaxation during surgical operations

» Sedation, paralysis with curare-like agents, and mechanical ventilation[5] [kæ] are often required to control tetanus spasms.

acupuncture analgesia *n term*   *rel* **acupressure**[1] *n term*

placement of acupuncture needles at specific points in the body to produce a loss of sensation of pain, e.g. for surgical procedures by blocking afferent nerve impulses

» Acupuncture anesthesia and the placebo [si:] effect may be mediated[2] [i:] in part by endorphins.

Use pressure **analgesia** • pressure[3] / acupuncture[4] **anesthesia**

Barbiturate, Schlafmittel
sedierend, beruhigend[1] hypnotisch, schlaffördernd[2] antikonvulsiv, antiepileptisch[3] Missbrauch[4] erzielt, erreicht[5] kurzwirkende B.[6] Barbituratentzug[7]

14

Basisnarkose
vor[1] Nadelstich[2]

15

Muskelrelaxanzien
quergestreifte Muskulatur[1] Muskeltonus[2] zentral dämpfende Mittel[3] wiederholte Depolarisation[4] (nicht) depolarisierendes Muskelrelaxans[5] auf die glatte Muskulatur wirkendes Relaxans[6]   16

(Tubo)curare
Tubocurarin[1] Bestandteil[2] Pfeilgift[3] motor. Endplatte, neuromuskuläre Synapse[4] maschinelle Beatmung[5]

17

Akupunkturanalgesie
Akupressur[1] vermittelt[2] Akupressuranästhesie[3] Akupunkturanästhesie[4]

18

Unit 94   Infectious Diseases

Related Units: 4 Illness & Recovery, 89 Pathology, 90 Pathogens, 95 Childhood Diseases, 39 Immune System, 122 Immunization, 105 Fever, 113 Neurologic Findings, 119 Etiology, 139 Asepsis, 92 Pharmacologic Agents

infectious [-fekʃəs] **disease** *n*   *sim* **communicable** or **contagious** [eɪdʒ] **disease**[1] *n, rel* **reportable** or **notifiable** [aɪə] **disease**[2] *n term*

illness that is capable [eɪ] of being transmitted by infection

infectiousness[3] *n* • contagion[4] *n* • contagiousness[5] *n* • notify[6] *v* • report *v*

» Chickenpox[7], like measles [i:], is highly communicable[8]. HAV[9] spreads[10] [e] primarily by fecal-oral [i:] contact but blood and secretions [i:] are also possibly infectious. The virus [aɪ] laboratory must be notified that rubella is suspected. Patients are contagious from 1 or 2 days before the onset of symptoms[11] until 4 days after the appearance [ɪə] of the rash[12]. In hay fever[13] [heɪfi:və] there is no contagion among close contacts.

Use childhood / viral [aɪ]/ tropical[14] / acute **disease** • cat-scratch[15] / inflammatory [æ] bowel[16] [baʊəl] **disease** • pelvic inflammatory[17] (*abbr* PID) **disease** • **communicable** agent / viral infection • **communicable** from person to person / bacteria [ɪə]/ period • **infectious** agent[18] / organism[18] / cause / process / virus • **infectious** lesion [i:3]/ mononucleosis[19] / diarrhea[20] [i:]/ colitis [aɪ] • mildly / highly[8] **contagious** • **contagious** by touch • to reduce / duration of / degree of **infectiousness** • to prevent[21] / germ-based **contagion** • **contagion** among close contacts

Infektionskrankheit
ansteckende/ übertragbare Krankheit[1] meldepflichtige K.[2] Infektiosität, Übertragbarkeit[3] Ansteckung, Kontagion[4] Kontagiosität, Ansteckungsfähigkeit[5] benachrichtigen, mitteilen, melden[6] Windpocken[7] hochinfektiös[8] Hepatitis-A-Virus[9] breitet sich aus[10] Auftreten v. Symptomen[11] Ausschlag, Exanthem[12] Heuschnupfen, -fieber[13] Tropenkrankheit[14] Katzenkratzkrankheit[15] entzündl. Darmerkrankung[16] Adnexitis[17] Infektionserreger[18] infektiöse Mononukleose, Pfeiffer-Drüsenfieber[19] infektiöse Gastroenteritis[20] e. Ansteckung verhindern/ vorbeugen[21]

1

Infectious Diseases — MEDICAL SCIENCE 417

infect v clin   sim **communicate**[1] [juː] v rare, rel **invade**[2] [eɪ], **infest**[3] v

to pass a pathogen to a person so they can invade and replicate[4] in body tissues

(**super**)**infection** n • **infective**[5] adj • **communicability**[6] n term • **infestation**[7] n

» These staphylococci [aɪ] readily [e] invade the bloodstream and infect sites distant from the primary site of infection. Individuals of any age may be infected. In measles[8] [iː] communicability is greatest during the preeruptive [ʌ] stage but continues as long as the rash remains.

Use **to infect** children / oneself / the fetus [iː]/ cells • **to be infected with** a virus / bacteria / AIDS[9] • **infected** material / debris [iː]/ tissue / blood / wound[10] [uː] • **infected** saliva [aɪ]/ foci [foʊsaɪ]/ joint [dʒ]/ animal / ticks[11] • acutely / perinatally / secondarily / HIV-**infected** • **to communicate** a disease to sb.[12] • **to infest** body cavities / genital [dʒe] hair[13] / wounds / houses • tick-/ flea- [iː]/ snake-**infested** • to fight/rule out[14]/resist/treat/lead to/eradicate[15] **infection** • acute / chronic / bacterial[16] **infection** • fungal[17] [ʌ]/ viral / wound[18] **infection** • airway[19] / primary / local(ized) **infection** • occult [ʌ] or latent[20] [eɪ]/ disseminated **infection** • systemic / ascending[21] [se]/ urinary tract[22] (abbr UTI) **infection** • upper respiratory tract[23] (abbr URI)/ pyogenic [aɪ]/ nosocomial[24] **infection** • cross[25]-/ re/ super**infection** • risk / signs / focus[26] / source[27] [ɔː] spread [e] **of infection** • **infection** site / rate / control • **infective** droplets[28] / larvae [iː‖aɪ]/ endocarditis[29] [-aɪtɪs] • parasitic [ɪ]/ larval [ɑː]/ mite[30] [aɪ] **infestation** • tapeworm[31] [eɪ]/ intestinal / heavy **infestation** • **infestation** with head lice [laɪs]

anstecken, infizieren

anstecken, übertragen[1] eindringen[2] befallen[3] s. vermehren[4] infektiös, ansteckend[5] Übertragbarkeit[6] Parasitenbefall, Infestation[7] Masern[8] m. AIDS infiziert sein[9] infizierte Wunde[10] infizierte Zecken[11] jmdm./ (auf jem.) e. Krankheit übertragen[12] Schamhaar befallen[13] Infektion ausschließen[14] I. ausrotten[15] bakterielle I.[16] Pilzinfektion[17] Wundinfektion[18] Atemwegsinfektion[19] latente I.[20] aufsteigende/ aszendierende I.[21] Harnwegsinfektion[22] Infektion d. oberen Atemwege[23] Krankenhaus-, nosokomiale Infektion[24] Kreuzinfektion[25] Infektionsherd[26] Infektionsquelle[27] infektiöse Aerosole[28] infektiöse Endokarditis[29] Milbenbefall[30] Bandwurmbefall[31]

2

transmission [trænzmɪʃən] n term   rel **spread**[1] - spread - spread [e] n & v irr term

process of passing infectious agents from an infected person to a susceptible [se] individual

transmissible[2] adj term • **transmitted** adj • **transmit** v

» Humans are infected as a result of tick bites[3], but transmission from blood transfusion has also been reported. Contact isolation[4] prevents spread of highly transmissible or epidemiologically important infections that do not warrant[5] [ɔː] strict isolation. Streptococcal infections spread more rapidly. Head lice[6] [aɪ] may be transmitted by shared use of hats or combs.

Use airborne[7] [ɔː]/ waterborne / droplet[8] / food-borne **transmission** • fecal-oral[9] / direct-contact[10] / nosocomial **transmission** • horizontal[11] / vertical[12] / germline[13] **transmission** • patient-to-patient / iatrogenic[14] [aɪə-] **transmission** • mother-to-child or maternal-infant **transmission** • perinatal / transplacental[15] [se] **transmission** • (hetero)sexual[16] / venereal[16] [ɪə]/ endemic / vector[17] **transmission** • mosquito [kiː]/ viral / HIV **transmission** • route[18] [aʊ‖uː]/ source [ɔː] / mode / risk **of transmission** • means [iː] / rate / prevention **of transmission** • **transmission** by dust [ʌ] / by saliva[19] [aɪ]/ of germs [dʒɜː]/ from parent to child • **transmission** to host[20] [oʊ]/ through blood products • sexually / transfusion **transmitted** • sexually **transmitted** disease[21] (abbr STD) • **transmitted by** fleas [iː]/ skin-to-skin contact[22] • **to transmit** a virus to susceptible individuals / by inoculation • airborne[7] / direct / hematogenous[23] **spread** • lymphatic / metastatic[24] **spread** • droplet[7] / epidemic / infectious **spread** • disease / heterosexual **spread** • **spread of** virus [aɪ] / infection[25] / HIV / tumor / to the liver • **spread** among family members / by body contact

Übertragung, Transmission

Aus-, Verbreitung; sich ausbreiten[1] übertragbar, ansteckend[2] Zeckenbisse[3] Kontaktisolierung, -isolation[4] erfordern[5] Kopfläuse[6] aerogene Übertragung[7] Tröpfcheninfektion[8] fäkal-orale Übertragung[9] direkte Kontaktübertragung[10] horizontale Übertragung[11] vertikale Ü.[12] germinative Ü.[13] iatrogene Übertragung[14] diaplazentare Ü.[15] sexuelle Ü.[16] Vektorübertragung[17] Übertragungsweg[18] Übertragung durch Speichel[19] Übertragung auf d. Wirt[20] sexuell übertragbare Krankheit[21] durch Hautkontakt übertragen[22] hämatogene Ausbreitung[23] Metastasierung[24] Infektionsausbreitung[25]

3

vector [vektɚ] n term   sim **carrier**[1] [keriɚ] n, rel **reservoir**[2] n term

animal (e.g. tick, mite [aɪ], bat[3], fly) capable of transmitting infectious agents from one host to another

» Rubella virus is a togavirus closely related to the alphaviruses but does not require a vector for transmission. There are two types of carrier state: silent carriers retain their infectiousness, while latent carriers are not infectious. Rifampin is the drug of choice[4] to eradicate the meningococcal carrier state. Most rickettsiae are maintained in nature by a cycle involving an animal reservoir and an insect vector (usually an arthropod) that infects humans.

Use **vector**-borne transmission[5] • contaminated / food / (non/retro/adeno)viral [aɪ]/ mechanical[6] [kæ] **vector** • urban [ɜː]/ animal[7] / insect / mosquito / arthropod **vector** • **vector** fly / tick species [iːʃ] • asymptomatic / silent[8] / human **carrier** • chronic[9] / latent[10] [eɪ]/ heterozygous [zaɪ] **carrier** • translocation[11] / typhoid [aɪ]/ hepatitis B virus / HIV[12] **carrier** • **carrier** state / frequency / mother / detection • natural / virus **reservoir** • **reservoir** host[13] / of infection / of HBV carriers

(Krankheits)überträger, Vektor, Transportwirt

Vektor, Carrier, (Keim-, Über)träger[1] (Infektionserreger)reservoir[2] Fledermaus[3] Medikament der Wahl[4] Vektorübertragung[5] mechanischer Überträger[6] tierischer Vektor[7] klin. inapparenter Träger[8] Dauerausscheider, -träger[9] latenter Träger[10] Translokationsträger[11] HIV-Träger[12] Reservoirwirt, Parasitenreservoir[13]

4

host [həʊst] *n term*   *rel* **parasite**[1] [pærəsaɪt] *n term* → U90-13

organism that harbors[2] a parasite for which it provides energy and sustenance[3] [ʌ]

» The dog is the principal definitive host and the sheep the most common intermediate [iː]. The disease is spread from host to host by fecal-oral routes, either directly or indirectly via food or water. Like most other parasites, viruses stimulate host antibody production.

Use (non)human / natural / (immuno)compromised[4] / weakened [iː]/ immunocompetent[5] / susceptible[6] [se]/ preferred[7] [ɜː]/ colonization of **host** • primary or definitive or final[8] / intermediate[9] / transport or paratenic[10] / amplifier / accidental or dead-end[11] **host** • **host** tissue / range[12] / predilection /-parasite interaction /-specific[13] • **host** cell (function) / defense mechanism / change[14] / resistance /-susceptibility

Wirt, Wirtsorganismus
Parasit[1] beherbergt[2] Nahrung[3] abwehrgeschwächter Wirt[4] gesunder Wirt[5] empfänglicher Wirt[6] Hauptwirt[7] Endwirt[8] Zwischen-, Intermediärwirt[9] Transport-, Sammel-, Stapelwirt, paratenischer Wirt[10] Fehlwirt[11] Wirtsspektrum[12] wirtsspezifisch[13] Wirtswechsel[14]

5

---

incubation period *n term*   *rel* **latency**[1] [eɪ], **dormancy**[2] [ɔː] *n term* → U116-6

period [ɪə] between infection and onset of the disease[3], i.e. the appearance [ɪə] of the first symptoms

incubating [ɪnkjʊbeɪtɪŋ] *adj term* • **latent**[4] *adj* • **dormant**[5] [dɔːmənt] *adj*

» In gonococcal disease the incubation period is short, usually 2-5 days. Syphilis [ɪ] is characterized by sequential clinical stages and by years of symptomless latency. The dermatitis appears after a latent period[6] of 1-2 days from the time of contact.

Use usual / short / long[7] / prolonged / median [iː]/ 21-day **incubation period** • period of / 48h of / overnight **incubation** • **incubation** time / of cultures[8] • **incubating** infection[9] / carrier[10] / syphilis • **latency** period[11] / clinical / disease **latency** • after years of / tumor[12] **dormancy** • **latent** interval[1] / infection / stage[1] / virus / tetany[13] • to be/become/remain/lie[14] **dormant** • **dormant** pathogen / bacilli [aɪ]/ infection[15]

Inkubationszeit
Latenz, -stadium, -phase[1] Ruhezustand, Inaktivität, Latenz[2] Krankheitsbeginn, -ausbruch[3] latent, inapparent[4] ruhend, inaktiv[5] Latenzzeit[6] lange Inkubationszeit[7] Inkubation von Kulturen[8] inkubierende Infektion[9] Inkubationsausscheider[10] Latenzzeit, Inkubationszeit[11] Tumorlatenz[12] latente Tetanie[13] latent vorhanden sein[14] latente Infektion[15]

6

---

outbreak [aʊtbreɪk] *n clin & term*   *sim* **onset**[1] [ɒnset] *n clin & term*, → U119-5
rel **recrudescence**[2] *n term*

sudden increase in the number of occurrences of a (usually highly contagious) disease

break out[3] *v phr clin* • **recrudescent**[4] [riːkruːdesənt] *adj term* • **recrudesce** *v*

» There have been recent reports of new outbreaks in several regions. In a typical outbreak confined [aɪ] to a household or nursery[5] [ɜː], some affected children have only fever [iː], without localizing signs. Vaccine [ksiː] should be administered early in the autumn before influenza outbreaks occur. Recrudescence of old TB infections is common in insulin-dependent diabetics. Certain S. aureus infections may recrudesce after years of dormancy.

Use **outbreak** of cholera [k]/ in nurseries / control • food-borne / waterborne[6] **outbreak** • family / common-source [ɔː]/ airborne[7] **outbreak** • annual / seasonally [iː] recurrent **outbreak** • community / classroom **outbreak** • hospital or nosocomial / localized / large-scale[8] **outbreak** • highly fatal [eɪ]/ massive / epidemic[9] / viral **outbreak** • influenza[10] / hepatitis [aɪ]/ cholera / hantavirus **outbreak** • abrupt[11] [ʌ]/ acute / summer **onset** • juvenile [dʒuː]/ insidious[12] [ɪ] **onset** • full / late **recrudescence** • **recrudescent** infection / typhus[13] [taɪfəs] • **to break out in a rash**[14] [æ]/ (cold) sweat[15] [e]

Ausbruch (einer Epidemie)
Beginn, Ausbruch[1] Rückfall, Rezidiv[2] ausbrechen[3] wiederaufflammend, rezidivierend[4] Kindergarten[5] Ausbruch einer mit d. Wasser übertragenen Infektion[6] Tröpfcheninfektion, aerogene Infektion[7] Pandemie[8] Ausbruch einer Epidemie[9] Ausbruch e. Grippeepidemie[10] plötzl./ fulminanter Krankheitsbeginn[11] schleichender (Krankheits)-beginn[12] Brill-(Zinsser)-Krankheit[13] e. Ausschlag bekommen[14] e. Schweißausbruch haben[15]

7

---

epidemic [epɪdemɪk] *adj & n term*   *rel* **pandemic**[1], **endemic**[2] *adj & n term*

(n, i) disease whose frequency of occurrence is higher than the expected frequency in a population during a given time interval;
(ii) distinguished from endemic, since the disease is not continuously present but has been introduced from outside
(iii) temporary clustering[3] [ʌ] of cases of an endemic disease

hyperendemic [haɪpə-] *adj term* • **epidemiologic**[4] [epɪdiːmɪə-] *adj*

» Epidemics occur in winter and early spring in 3- to 4-yr cycles [saɪklz] (the period required to develop a new group of susceptibles[5] [se]). How likely is a pandemic of influenza? Dengue [deŋɡiǁɡeɪ] is endemic throughout the tropics and subtropics.

Use to be / AIDS[6] / local / worldwide / seasonal[7] **epidemic** • point-source[8] / explosive[9] **epidemic** • **epidemic** measles [iː]/ typhus • **endemic** area or region[10] / population / disease[11] / foci [fəʊsaɪ] • **endemic** transmission / infection / goiter[12] [ɡɔɪtə] • malaria-/ highly / non**endemic** • global / acute / cholera **pandemic** • **pandemic** history / wave / years / strain[13] [eɪ]

epidemisch; Epidemie
pandemisch; Pandemie[1] endemisch; Endemie[2] Häufung[3] epidemiologisch[4] empfängl. Personen[5] AIDS-Epidemie[6] saisonale/ jahreszeitl. bedingte E.[7] v. einem Ort ausgehende E.[8] Explosivepidemie[9] Endemiegebiet[10] endemische Krankheit[11] endemische Struma[12] pandemischer Stamm[13]

8

Infectious Diseases MEDICAL SCIENCE 419

influenza [ɪnfluˈenzə] *n term & clin*   *syn* **flu** [fluː], **grippe** *n clin*
  rel **common cold**[1], **acute rhinitis** [raɪnaɪtɪs] *or* **coryza**[2] [kəraɪzə] *n term*

acute respiratory disease caused by Hemophilus influenzae viruses marked by sudden onset, catarrhal inflammation, chills[3], fever of short duration, severe prostration, muscle aches[4], sneezing, and coughing

parainfluenza[5] *n term* • **flu-like**[6] *adj clin* • **influenzal** *adj*

» Mutations [eɪ] in the influenza virus[7] are frequent and the immunity usually does not affect new, antigenically [dʒe] different strains. Influenza commonly occurs in epidemics, and sometimes in pandemics, which develop quickly and spread rapidly.

Use to transmit/prevent **influenza** • **influenza** A virus / infection / epidemic[8] / season [siːzᵊn] • **influenza**-like illness / pneumonia[9] / vaccination or immunization[10] • acute / cultureconfirmed [ʌ] / uncomplicated **influenza** • pandemic / type B / avian[17] **influenza** • to have a touch of[11]/catch (the) *flu* • Hongkong / swine / bird or avian[17] *flu* • **flu-like** illness / symptoms[12] [ɪ]/ syndrome • **influenzal** prodrome / pneumonia[9] • acute viral / bacterial [ɪə] / vasomotor[13] [veɪzoʊ-] **rhinitis** • allergic[14] [ɜː]/ recurrent [ɜː]/ seasonal[15] [iː]/ perennial **rhinitis** • copious[16] [oʊ]/ mild **coryza**

Influenza, Grippe
Erkältung, Schnupfen[1] Virusschnupfen, Rhinitis acuta[2] Schüttelfrost[3] Muskelschmerzen[4] Parainfluenza[5] grippeähnlich[6] Influenza-, Grippevirus[7] Influenzaepidemie[8] Grippepneumonie[9] Grippeschutzimpfung[10] eine leichte Grippe haben[11] grippeähnl. Symptome[12] vasomotor. Rhinitis, nervöser Schnupfen[13] allerg. Rhinitis, Heuschnupfen, -fieber[14] saisonale/ jahreszeitl. bedingte Rhinitis[15] starker Schnupfen[16] aviäre Influenza, Influenza A (H5N1), Vogelgrippe, Geflügelpest[17]

9

(infectious) mononucleosis *n term*   *syn* **glandular fever** [iː] *n clin*

acute herpes [ɜː] virus infection caused by Epstein-Barr virus characterized by fever, sore throat, lymphadenopathy, and the presence of atypical lymphocytes; sometimes referred to as "kissing disease"

» In children infectious mononucleosis is usually self-limited and treatment is largely supportive with bed rest, analgesics[1] [dʒiː] and saline gargles[2]. Infectious mononucleosis can be distinguished from acute lymphoblastic leukemia by the morphology of individual lymphocytes.

Use to mimic[3] **mononucleosis** • acute / heterophil (antibody)-negative / cytomegalovirus[4] [saɪtə-] (*abbr* CMV) **mononucleosis** • **mononucleosis**-like syndrome / (spot) test *or* Monospot[5]

infektiöse Mononukleose, Mononucleosis infectiosa, Pfeiffer-Drüsenfieber
Analgetika, Schmerzmittel[1] salzhaltige Gurgellösung[2] der Mononukleose ähnlich sein[3] CMV-Mononukleose[4] Mononukleosetest[5]

10

---

tetanus *n term & clin*   *rel* **trismus**[1] [trɪzməs], **lockjaw**[2] [lɒːkdʒɒː] *n clin*

disease marked by painful tonic muscular [ʌ] contractions caused by the neurotropic toxin of Clostridium tetani [aɪ] which flourishes[3] [ɜː] in hypoxic wounds [uː] contaminated with soil or feces [fiːsiːz]

tetanic[4] *adj term* • **tetanoid**[5] *adj* • **tetaniform**[5] *adj* • **tetan(o)-** *comb*

» Since immunity does not follow clinical tetanus, the patient should receive a full immunizing course of toxoid after recovery. TIG for established tetanus is given preferably in the proximal portion of the wounded [uː] extremity or in the vicinity [sɪ] of the wound.

Use generalized / local(ized) / cephalic [sef-]/ neonatal[6] [eɪ]/ postoperative **tetanus** • **tetanus** prophylaxis[7] / immunization / antitoxin[8] • **tetanus** booster[9] [uː]/ immune globulin[10] (*abbr* TIG)/-prone [oʊ] wound • adsorbed **tetanus** toxoid[11] • **trismus** of the masseter [iː] muscle • **tetanic** muscle contractions • (muscle) spasms[12] • **tetano**spasmin

Note: The term *tetany*[13] refers to a state of neuromuscular hyperexcitability[14] related to hypoparathyroidism [aɪ], alkalosis or vitamin D deficiency [ɪʃ].

Tetanus, Wundstarrkrampf
Trismus, Spasmus masticatorius[1] Trismus; Tetanus[2] sich stark vermehrt[3] tetanisch, Tetanus-[4] tetanusähnlich, tetanoid, tetaniform[5] Tetanus neonatorum, Neugeborenentetanus[6] Tetanusprophylaxe[7] Tetanusantitoxin[8] Tetanusauffrischung(simpfung)[9] Tetanusimmunglobulin[10] Tetanusadsorbatimpfstoff[11] tetanische Muskelkrämpfe[12] Tetanie[13] neuromuskuläre Übererregbarkeit[14]

11

---

rabies [reɪbiːz] *n term & clin*

highly fatal infectious disease of the CNS that may affect most mammals including man; it is transmitted by the bite of infected animals, esp. dogs, cats, skunks [ʌ], wolves, foxes, racoons[1] [uː] and bats

rabid[2] [reɪbɪd] *adj term* • **rabiform** *adj*

» The symptoms of rabies are characteristic of a profound [aʊ] disturbance of the nervous system, including excitement[3], hydrophobia, and rage[4] followed by paralysis and death. There is little to distinguish rabies from other viral encephalitides. Determine if the animal is rabid.

Use animal / canine [keɪnaɪn]/ human / urban[5] [ɜː]/ bat[6] **rabies** • symptomatic / clinical / furious[7] [fjʊə-]/ dumb[8] [dʌm] **rabies** • **rabies** prevention[9] / virus[10] [aɪ]/ exposure [oʊʒ] • **rabies** deaths / control program • **rabid** state [eɪ] animal[11]

Tollwut, Rabies, Hydrophobie
Waschbären[1] tollwütig[2] Erregungszustände[3] Raserei[4] Haustier-, urbane Tollwut[5] Fledermaustollwut[6] rasende Wut[7] stille Wut[8] Tollwutprophylaxe[9] Tollwutvirus[10] tollwütiges Tier[11]

12

meningitis [menɪndʒaɪtɪs] *n term & clin, pl* **-itides** [-dʒɪtɪdiːz]
rel **encephalitis**[1] [ɪnsefə-], **arachnoiditis**[2] [əræk-] *n term*

inflammation of the membranes of the brain (dura mater, pia mater, arachnoid) or spinal cord[3] presenting as headache, and neck stiffness[4] sometimes preceded by fever, malaise, anorexia[5], and vomiting

meningitic[6] [dʒɪ] *adj term* • **meningeal**[7] [iː] *adj* • **mening(o)-** *comb* • **encephalitic** *adj*

» Most bacteria cause an acute meningitis, but tuberculous and syphilitic meningitides are subacute. In meningitis Kernig's and Brudzinski's signs[8] are usually positive. The distinction between aseptic meningitis and encephalitis is based on the extent and severity of cerebral dysfunction, independent of signs of meningeal inflammation. Meningitis should be suspected when a child has high fever, neck stiffness, or other meningeal signs.

Use to rule out[9]/induce/diagnose/treat/develop **meningitis** • (sub)acute / low-grade / purulent[10] **meningitis** • refractory[11] / (a)bacterial[12] / Hib[13] / meningococcal **meningitis** • pneumococcal / cryptococcal [ɪ] **meningitis** • viral or aseptic[14] / fungal[15] [ʌ]/ tuberculous[16] **meningitis** • (cerebro)spinal [aɪ] (*abbr* CSM)/ neonatal [eɪ]/ otogenic [dʒe] **meningitis** • lepto/pachy**meningitis** • **mening**itis[17] /itides[18] • **meningitic** pneumococcal disease • **meningeal** involvement[19] / signs / irritation[20] • acute viral / tick-borne[21] [bɔːrn] **encephalitis** • (eastern/ western) equine[22] [eǁiːkwaɪn] (*abbr* EEE/ WEE) / Central European tick-borne[23] **encephalitis** • Japanese[24] / (multi)focal / granulomatous / necrotizing **encephalitis** • herpes simplex or HSV / toxoplasma / postvaccinal[25] [æks] **encephalitis** • **encephalitic** signs / prodrome / phase [eɪz] • **meningo**encephalitis /(myelo)cele [-siːl] /coccemia [iː] /vascular syphilis

pneumonia [n(j)uːmoʊnɪə] *n*   *sim* **pneumonitis**[1] [-aɪtɪs] *n term*
rel **infiltrate**[2], **pleurisy**[3] [plʊərəsi] *n term*

inflammation [eɪʃ] of the lungs associated with consolidation and exudation

pneumonic *adj term* • **bronch**opneumonia[4] [k] *n* • **pleuritic** [plʊərɪtɪk] *adj*

» Viral pneumonias are often interstitial in their early phases. Friedlander's pneumonia is characterized by frequent upper lobe involvement, sputum that looks like currant [ɜː] jelly[5] [dʒ], tissue necrosis with early abscess formation, and a fulminant [ʊ] course[6] [kɔːrs].

Use acute (bacterial) / pneumococcal[7] / streptococcal / staphylococcal **pneumonia** • legionella [iːdʒ]/ viral / fungal[8] / chlamydial [ɪ] **pneumonia** • atypical[9] / afebrile / chronic eosinophilic / tuberculous **pneumonia** • aspiration[10] / lip(o)id / embolic **pneumonia** • community-acquired / nosocomial[11] / congenital [dʒe] **pneumonia** • basal / lobar[12] / segmental / central **pneumonia** • bilateral or double[13] [ʌ]/ abscess-forming[14] / fatal **pneumonia** • radiation[15] / suppurative [ʌ] **pneumonitis** • (nonspecific / lymphoid [ɪ]/ desquamative) interstitial[16] [ɪʃ] (*abbr* NIP/ LIP) / hypersensitivity[17] **pneumonitis** • **pneumonic** infection / infiltrate / plague[18] [pleɪɡ] • acute / fibrinous [aɪ] adhesive [iː]/ viral **pleurisy** • tuberculous / wet or exudative[19] [uː] **pleurisy** • **pleuritic** (chest) pain / effusion[20] [juːʒ]

hepatitis [hepətaɪtɪs] *n term*

inflammation of the liver from a viral infection or due to toxic agents, obstructive jaundice[1] [dʒɔː], etc.

» In chronic hepatitis B, superinfection by HDV[2] appears to carry a more severe prognosis, often resulting in fulminant hepatitis or severe chronic hepatitis that rapidly progresses to cirrhosis.

Use infectious / acute / viral / non-A, non-B **hepatitis** • NANBNC[3] / delta / alcoholic **hepatitis** • cholestatic [kɒːlɪ-]/ posttransfusion[4] / giant [dʒaɪ] cell[5] **hepatitis** • neonatal / chronic active[6] **hepatitis** • granulomatous / ischemic [ɪskiː]/ fulminant [ʊ]/ drug-induced **hepatitis** • halothane[7] [æ]/ serum[8] / toxic / autoimmune[9] **hepatitis** • **hepatitis** A virus (*abbr* HAV) / B surface antigen[10] [-dʒən] (*abbr* HBsA) • **hepatitis** C infection / D /-like picture

---

Meningitis, (Ge)hirnhautentzündung

Enzephalitis, Gehirnentzündung[1] Arachnoiditis, Arachnitis, Entzündung d. Arachnoidea[2] Rückenmark[3] Nackensteifigkeit[4] Appetitlosigkeit[5] meningitisch[6] Hirnhaut-, meningeal[7] Brudzinski-Nackenzeichen[8] Meningitis ausschließen[9] eitrige Meningitis, M. purulenta[10] therapieresistente M.[11] (a)bakterielle M.[12] Haemophilus influenzae B Meningitis[13] Virus-, aseptische M.[14] Pilzmeningitis[15] tuberkulöse Hirnhautentzündung, M. tuberculosa[16] Meningismus[17] Meningitiden[18] Hirnhautbeteiligung[19] Hirnhautreizung[20] Zeckenenzephalitis[21] Pferdeenzephalitis[22] Frühsommer-Meningoenzephalitis, FSME, zentraleuropäische E.[23] japanische E.[24] postvakzinale E.[25]

13

Pneumonie, Lungenentzündung

(interstitielle) Lungenentzündung/ Pneumonie, Pneumonitis[1] Infiltrat[2] Pleuritis, Brustfellentzündung[3] Bronchopneumonie[4] Johannisbeergelee[5] fulminanter Verlauf[6] Pneumokokken-Pneumonie[7] Pilzpneumonie[8] atypische P.[9] Aspirationspneumonie[10] nosokomiale P.[11] Lobär-, Lappenpneumonie[12] beidseitige Lungenentzündung[13] abszedierende Pneumonie[14] Strahlenpneumonitis, -pneumonie[15] Desquamativpneumonie[16] Hypersensitivitätspneumonitis, exogen allerg. Alveolitis[17] Lungenpest, Pestpneumonie[18] exsudative Pleuritis, P. exsudativa[19] Pleuraerguss[20]

14

Hepatitis, Leberentzündung

Gelbsucht, Ikterus[1] Hepatitis-D-Virus[2] Non-A-Non-B-Non-C Hepatitis[3] Transfusionshepatitis[4] Riesenzellhepatitis[5] chron. aggressive Hepatitis[6] Halothanhepatitis[7] Serumhepatitis, Hepatitis B[8] autoimmune Hepatitis[9] Hepatitis-B-Oberflächenantigen[10]

15

Infectious Diseases MEDICAL SCIENCE 421

tuberculosis [t(j)uːbɜːrkjəlousɪs] *n term & clin, abb* **TB**

chronic mycobacterial [maɪk-] infection characterized by the formation of tubercles and caseous [eɪ] necrosis[1] which may affect almost any tissue in the body (most commonly the lungs [ʌ]) **tubercle**[2] *n term* • **tuberculous**[3] *adj* • **tuberc(ulo)-** *comb*

» *Hematogenous dissemination[4] from the primary focus throughout the lungs (miliary TB[5]), to the pleural [ʊə] space, or to extrapulmonary sites is a rare complication of primary tuberculosis. Treatment of pulmonary tuberculosis is continued for 9-12 months if there is any evidence of noncompliance [aɪ] or slow bacteriologic response to therapy.*

Use (extra)pulmonary[6] [ʊ‖ʌ]/ open[7] / disseminated **tuberculosis** • cutaneous[8] [eɪ]/ intestinal **tuberculosis** • spinal [aɪ]/ genitourinary / osseous or bony[9] **tuberculosis** • drug-resistant / perinatal / postprimary [aɪ] or reactivation[10] **tuberculosis** • **tuberculosis** of the lungs[6] • **tuberculous** lesion [iːʒ]/ enteritis [aɪ]/ arthritis[11] • **tubercle** bacillus[12] [sɪ]/ formation • **tuberc**ulin (skin) test[13]

Tuberkulose, TB
käsige Nekrose[1] Tuberkel, Knötchen[2] tuberkulös[3] hämatogene Streuung[4] Miliartuberkulose[5] Lungentuberkulose[6] offene Tuberkulose[7] kutane Tuberkulose, Tuberculosis cutis[8] Knochentuberkulose[9] postprimäre Tuberkulose[10] Gelenktuberkulose, Arthritis tuberculosa[11] Tuberkelbazillus, -bakterium, Mycobacterium tuberculosis[12] Tuberkulintest[13]

16

leprosy [leprəsi] *n clin & term*   *syn* **Hansen'**[kəs] membranes and peripheral nerves **lepromatous**[1] [ɒː] *adj term* • **leprous**[2] *adj* • **leprotic**[2] *adj* • **lepr(o)-** *comb*

» *The deformities of leprosy are socially stigmatizing in many cultures [ʌ]; patients and their families are often ostracized[3] [-saɪzd]. Patients with polar tuberculoid leprosy have an intense cellular response to M. leprae and a low bacillary load[4], whereas those with lepromatous disease have no detectable cellular immunity to the leprosy bacillus.*

Use early or indeterminate[5] [ɜː]/ paucibacillary[6] [ɒː]/ multibacillary[7] **leprosy** • tuberculoid[8] (*abbr* TL) / borderline[9] **leprosy** • **Hansen'** **lepromatous leprosy**[10] (*abbr* LL)/ **disease / patient** • **leprous** neuritis • **lepromin skin test**[11] /logist

Lepra, Hansen-Krankheit
lepromatös[1] lepröş[2] ausgestoßen[3] Bakterienbelastung[4] indeterminierte Lepra[5] bakterienarme Lepra[6] bakterienreiche Lepra[7] tuberkuloide Lepra[8] borderline-Lepra[9] lepromatöse Lepra[10] Lepromintest[11]

17

amebic [iː] **dysentery** [dɪsᵊnteri] *n term*   *syn* **intestinal amebiasis** [-baɪəsɪs] *n, rel* **shigellosis**[1] [ʃɪgəl-], **(gastro)enteritis**[2] [aɪ] *n term* → U91-21

diarrhea resulting from ulcerative inflammation of the colon caused chiefly by infection with Entamoeba [iː] histolytica; may be mild or severe and may also be associated with amebic infection of other organs

dysenteric[3] *adj term* • **ameboid**[4] [əmiːbɔɪd] *adj* • **shigella** *n* • **entero-** *comb*

» *Unlike those in shigellosis and salmonellosis, the stools in amebic dysentery do not contain large numbers of WBCs[5]. Prominent vomiting suggests viral enteritis or S aureus food poisoning[6]. Patients with amebiases should be placed under enteric precautions [ɒː].*

Use bacillary or Shigella[1] / acute / full-blown[7] / fulminant **dysentery** • (extra)intestinal[8] / (non)invasive [eɪ]/ nondysenteric **amebiasis** • cerebral / cutaneous **amebiasis** • bacterial / Campylobacter **enteritis** • Salmonella / regional / radiation[9] **enteritis** • epidemic / childhood / ampicillin-resistant **shigellosis** • acute / infectious[10] / nonbacterial **gastroenteritis** • eosinophilic [iːə-]/ dehydrating / protozoal **gastroenteritis** • **dysenteric** infection / bowel [aʊ] disease[11] • **amebic** colitis[12] / ulcer [ʌ]/ invasion [eɪʒ]/ penetration / liver abscess[13] • **ameboid** movement / shape • **entero**colitis[14] /biasis /pathy[15] /toxic /virus

Amöbenruhr, -dysenterie, Amöbiasis
Bakterienruhr, Shigellose, bakterielle Dysenterie[1] (Gastro)enteritis[2] dysenterisch[3] amöbenähnlich, amöboid[4] Leukozyten[5] Lebensmittelvergiftung[6] klin. Vollbild d. Amöbenruhr[7] extraintestinale Amöbiasis[8] Strahlenenteritis[9] infektiöse Gastroenteritis[10] dysenterieähnl. Darmerkrankung[11] Amöbenruhr, -kolitis[12] Amöbenabszess[13] Enterokolitis[14] Darmerkrankung[15]

18

typhoid (fever) [taɪfɔɪd fiːvɚ] *n term & clin*   *syn* **enteric fever** *n term, rel* **salmonellosis**[1] *n term*

acute generalized febrile infection caused by Gram-negative salmonella bacteria (mainly S. typhi) which is marked by a typical stepladder onset of fever[2], anorexia, vomiting, watery diarrhea [iː] or constipation[3], and a transient rose-colored rash on the trunk[4] [ʌ]

paratyphoid[5] *adj & n term* • **typhoid(al)** *adj* • **typho-** *comb* • **salmonella** *n*

» *During typhoid fever, worms [ɜː] may penetrate the weakened bowel wall. Immunization is not always effective but should be provided for household contacts of a typhoid carrier, for travelers to endemic areas, and during epidemic outbreaks.*

Use intermittent / infantile **typhoid** • **typhoid** bacilli[6] [aɪ]/ (fever) vaccine[7] / carrier[8] / perforation • **paratyphoid** A / B /-enteritidis group / organism • (viral) hemorrhagic [ædʒ]/ Rocky Mountain spotted[9] (*abbr* RMSF)/ relapsing[10] **fever** • yellow[11] / Q / Lassa / dengue [deŋgi‖geɪ] (hemorrhagic) **fever** • **fever** of unknown origin[12] (*abbr* FUO) • **typhoidal** rash[13] / tularemia [iː] • nontyphoidal **salmonellosis** • **salmonella** infection[1]

■ **Note:** Do not mix up **typhoid** and **typhus**[14].

Typhus abdominalis, Febris typhoides, Unterleibstyphus
Salmonellose, Salmonelleninfektion[1] treppenförm. Fieberanstieg[2] Obstipation[3] Rumpf[4] Paratyphus-; Paratyphus[5] Typhusbakterien[6] Typhusimpfstoff, -vakzine[7] Typhusträger[8] Felsengebirgs(fleck)-fieber, amerikan. Zeckenfleckfieber[9] Rückfallfieber, Febris recurrens[10] Gelbfieber[11] Fieber unbekannter Genese[12] typhusähnl. Ausschlag[13] Fleckfieber, -typhus[14]

19

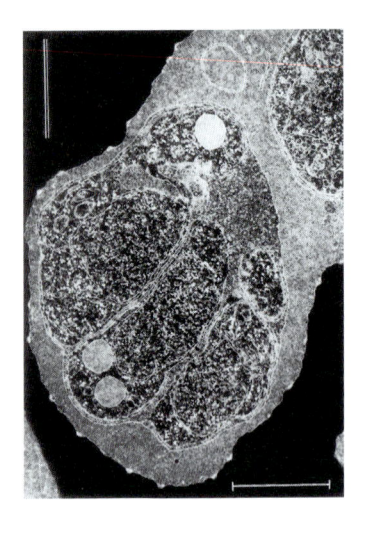

Malaria parasites (*Plasmodium falciparum*) invading an erythrocyte

malaria [məlɛəˈɪə] *n term & clin*

disease transmitted by mosquitoes marked by paroxysms of high fever, chills[1], sweating and prostration

(**anti**)**malarial**[2] *adj term* • **malarious**[2] *adj*

» Anemia [iː] and thrombocytopenia [iː] in a febrile traveler or immigrant are among the hallmarks[3] [ɔː] of malaria. Giemsa-stained [eɪ] thick smears[4] [ɪɚ] offer the highest diagnostic accuracy for malaria parasites.

Use cerebral / (chloroquine-resistant) falciparum[5] / congenital **malaria** • quartan[6] / P. ovale[7] / P. vivax[7] **malaria** • **malarial** parasite / infection / attacks or paroxysms[8] / spleen [iː]/ pigment[9] • **antimalarial** prophylaxis[10] / agent • **malarious** region[11]

Malaria, Sumpf-, Wechselfieber
Schüttelfrost[1] Malaria-[2] charakterist. Merkmale[3] dicker Tropfen[4] Malaria tropica[5] Malaria quartana[6] Malaria tertiana[7] Malariaanfälle[8] Malariapigment[9] Malariaprophylaxe[10] Malariagebiet[11]

20

(Asiatic) cholera [eɪʒɪætɪk kɒːləˈə] *n term & clin* *rel* **vibriosis**[1] [vɪbrɪ-] *n term*

acute, sometimes fulminant epidemic infection (endemic in India and Southeast Asia) causing profuse watery diarrhea, effortless vomiting, dehydration, saline depletion[2], and shock

» Cholera is spread by feces-contaminated water and food. Cholera can be a mild, uncomplicated episode of diarrhea or a fulminant, potentially lethal disease. Cholera vaccine contains a suspension of killed vibrios, including prevalent antigenic types.

Use to catch/contract[3] **cholera** • acute / Bengal / epidemic / pancreatic[4] / El Tor[5] **cholera** • uncomplicated / life-threatening [e]/ lethal[6] [iː]/ **cholera** • **cholera** bacillus / strain[7] / toxin[8] / pandemic[9] • **cholera** vaccine[10] / control strategies /-like syndrome

(klassische) Cholera
Vibrioinfektion[1] Salzverlust[2] sich Cholera zuziehen[3] pankreatische Cholera, Verner-Morrison-Syndrom[4] Eltor-Cholera[5] tödl. verlaufende Cholera[6] Cholerastamm[7] Choleraenterotoxin, Choleragen[8] Cholerapandemie[9] Choleravakzine[10]

21

Unit 95 Childhood Diseases
Related Units: 4 Illness & Recovery, 94 Infectious Diseases, 122 Immunization, 89 Pathology, 105 Fever, 119 Etiology

childhood disease [tʃaɪldhʊd] *n* *sim* **infantile** *or* **juvenile disorder**[1] *n term*

disorders (esp. easily communicable infections) which affect children rather than adults; juvenile-onset diseases are chronic conditions that may begin in childhood (e.g. diabetes [iː])

childhood-onset[2] *adj term* • **juvenile-onset**[2] [dʒuːvənaɪl‖ᵊl] *adj*

» Childhood asthma [z] is often related to maternal smoking. She had acquired hepatitis B infection in childhood. All children with juvenile rheumatoid [uː] arthritis need to be screened.

Use vaccine [væksiːn]-preventable / highly communicable[3] / common **childhood disease** • rare / latent [eɪ]/ undiagnosed **childhood disease** • **childhood** disorder / form of the disease[4] / infection • **childhood** eczema[5] / fears / enuresis[6] [iː] • **childhood** hernia [ɜː]/ immunization / vaccine • **childhood** febrile convulsions [ʌ]/ myxedema [mɪks-]/ aphasia [eɪʒ] • **juvenile** cases / variant / rheumatoid [ruːmə-] arthritis[7] /-onset diabetes • **infantile** diarrhea[8] [iː]/ autism [ɒː]/ eczema[5] [eks]/ hypothyroidism[9] [aɪ]

Kinderkrankheit
juvenile Erkrankung, E. d. Kindes- u. Jugendalters[1] Krankheitsbeginn i. d. Kindheit[2] hochinfektiöse Kinderkrankheit[3] juveniler Typ d. Erkrankung[4] Säuglingsekzem[5] Einnässen im Kindesalter[6] juvenile Rheumatoidarthritis, juvenile chron. Polyarthritis[7] Sommerdiarrhö[8] Kretinismus[9]

1

Childhood Diseases MEDICAL SCIENCE

(nine-day) measles [miːzlz] *n*   *syn* **rubeola** [ruːbiələ‖ioʊlə], **morbilli** [-aɪ] *n*, *rel* **roseola**[1] [roʊziːələ‖ioʊlə] *n term*

common childhood disease marked by fever and malaise[2] [eɪ], catarrhal inflammation of the respiratory mucous membranes, conjunctivitis, and a generalized maculopapular eruption of a dusky [ʌ] red[3] color

measles-like[4] *adj term* • **morbilliform**[4] *adj* • **roseolar** *adj*

» The eruption [ʌ] in measles occurs early on the buccal [bʌkᵊl] mucous membrane in the form of Koplik's spots[5] (few to countless small white papules on a diffusely red base), a manifestation utilized in early diagnosis. In rubeola, the rash[6] spreads to the trunk[7] [ʌ] and arms and soon becomes confluent, while the rash of rubella usually remains discrete [iː].

Use to have/catch/develop/mimic[8]/complicate/be exposed to **measles** • classic / atypical / modified **measles** • German or three-day / black or hemorrhagic[9] / tropical **measles** • epidemic[10] / clinical / mild **measles** • protracted / severe / fatal[11] [eɪ] **measles** • **measles** virus[12] [aɪ]/ patient / history / exposure [oʊʒ] • **measles** immunity / outbreak or epidemic[10] • **measles** infection / exanthema[13] [iː]/ eruption[13] [ʌ] • **measles** encephalitis[14] /-mumps-rubella (*abbr* MMR) vaccine[15] [væksiːn] • **morbilliform** rash[16] [æ]/ reaction • **roseola**-like rash / infantum or sixth disease[1]

Note: In medical English the term **rubeola** normally denotes **measles**, while in several other languages (German, French, Spanish) **rubeola** is used as a synonym for **rubella**.

Masern, Morbilli

Roseola infantum, Dreitagefieber[1] Unpässlichkeit, allgem. Krankheitsgefühl[2] dunkelrot[3] masernähnlich, morbilliform[4] Koplik-Flecken[5] Ausschlag[6] Rumpf[7] ein masernähnliches Krankheitsbild hervorrufen[8] hämorrhagische Masern[9] Masernepidemie[10] letal verlaufende Masern[11] Masernvirus[12] Masernexanthem[13] Masernenzephalitis[14] Masern-Mumps-Röteln-Impfstoff[15] masernähnlicher Ausschlag[16]

2

German measles *n clin*   *syn* **rubella** [ruːbelə] *n term*, **three-day measles** *n clin*

usually mild childhood infection marked by sore throat, swollen lymph [lɪmf] nodes, slight cold, fever and a fine pink rash; maternal infection of unborn babies can cause major malformations

rubella-like[1] *adj term* • **rubelliform**[1] *adj* • **pseudorubella**[2] [suːdoʊ-] *n*

» It is desirable for girls to catch German measles in childhood, otherwise they should be immunized. German measles also spreads from the hairline[3] downward but unlike that of measles the rash of rubella tends to clear from affected areas as it migrates and may be pruritic[4] [ɪ]. Rubella is clinically differentiated from measles by the milder, more evanescent[5] rash and by the absence of Koplik's spots, coryza[6] [aɪ], photophobia[7], and cough.

Use to be immunized against[8] **rubella** • fetal / postnatally acquired[9] [aɪ] **rubella** • childhood / maternal / post-**rubella** • congenital **rubella** syndrome[10] • **rubella** virus / antibody titer[11] / immunity[12] • **rubella** immunization / rash / infection / vaccine / outbreak • **rubella** arthritis[13] [aɪ]/ embryopathy[10] /-specific IgG

Röteln, Rubeola, Rubella

rötelnähnlich[1] Pseudorubella, Roseola infantum, Dreitagefieber[2] Haaransatz[3] mit Juckreiz verbunden[4] flüchtig[5] Schnupfen[6] Lichtscheu[7] gegen Röteln geimpft sein/ werden[8] postnatale Röteln[9] Rötelnembryopathie, Embryopathia rubeolosa, Gregg-Syndrom, kongenitales Rubella-Syndrom[10] Rötelnantikörpertiter[11] Rötelnimmunität[12] Rötelnarthritis[13]

3

mumps [mʌmps] *n*   *syn* **infectious** or **epidemic parotitis** [pærətaɪtɪs] *n term*

highly contagious childhood disease marked by swelling of the parotid gland[1]

» Mumps, the incidence of which peaks[2] in late winter and early spring, is less communicable than measles or chickenpox. A history of contact to a child with parotitis [aɪ] is not proof of mumps exposure. Mumps is a classic cause of orchitis[3] [kaɪ]. Less common manifestations of mumps include meningitis, and inflammation of the testis[3] (25% of postpubertal men).

Use to have/experience **mumps** • gestational [dʒest-]/ prepubertal / uncomplicated **mumps** • **mumps** live virus vaccine[4] / orchitis[5] /-induced swelling / parotitis • **mumps** encephalitis / meningitis [dʒaɪ]/ reinfection • acute[6] / viral [aɪ]/ bacterial[7] [ɪə] **parotitis** • submandibular / suppurative[8] [ʌ] **parotitis** • postoperative[9] / bilateral [aɪ]/ recurrent [ɜː] idiopathic **parotitis**

Mumps, Ziegenpeter, Parotitis epidemica

Parotis, Glandula parotidea, Ohrspeicheldrüse[1] Höhepunkt erreichen[2] Hodenentzündung, Orchitis[3] Mumpsvirus-Lebendimpfstoff, -vakzine[4] Mumpsorchitis[5] akute Parotitis, Parotitis acuta[6] bakterielle Parotitis[7] eitrige Parotitis[8] postoperative Parotitis[9]

4

whooping cough [ʰwuːpɪŋ kɒːf] *n clin*   *syn* **pertussis** [pətʌsɪs] *n term*

acute infectious inflammation of the respiratory tract typically affecting young children which is marked by recurrent bouts[1] [aʊ] of spasmodic coughing ending in a noisy inspiratory stridor[2] [aɪ] (the "whoop")

whoop[2] [uː] *n jar* • **whoop**[3] *v jar* • **whooping** *n* • **parapertussis**[4] [ʌ] *n*

» The onset of pertussis is insidious[5], with catarrhal upper respiratory tract symptoms (rhinitis, sneezing, and an irritating cough[6]). The term whooping cough may mislead clinicians by implying that whoops are an essential feature [iːtʃ] of the disease. Infants with otherwise typical, severe pertussis often lack characteristic whooping.

Use adult / clinical / severe / undiagnosed **pertussis** • **pertussis**-like syndrome / control • **pertussis** immunization[7] / toxin[8] / toxoid / vaccine[9] • distinctive[10] / high-pitched[11] / inspiratory[2] **whoop**

Keuchhusten, Pertussis

Anfälle[1] inspiratorischer Stridor[2] keuchend atmen[3] Parapertussis[4] langsam-progredient, schleichend[5] lästiger Husten[6] Pertussisschutzimpfung[7] Pertussistoxin[8] Pertussisimpfstoff[9] charakteristischer Stridor[10] pfeifendes Atemgeräusch[11]

5

scarlet [skɑːrlət] fever n   syn scarlatina [iː] term rare, rel fourth disease¹ n clin

acute infection caused by hemolytic streptococci [aɪ] marked by fever, tonsillitis, prostration², and a generalized eruption [ʌ] followed by desquamation³ in large scales⁴ [eɪ] or shreds⁵
scarlatinal [iː] adj term • **scarlatiniform**⁶ adj • **scarlatinosa** adj

» In scarlet fever the face is flushed [ʌ] with circumoral pallor⁷, the tongue is coated⁸ with enlarged aggregated red papillae (strawberry tongue⁹), and there are red macules on the mucous membranes of the mouth and fauces¹⁰ [fɔːsiːz]. The rash of scarlatina is diffusely erythematous, resembling a sunburn, with superimposed fine red papules, is most intense in the groin¹¹ and axillas, blanches [ʃ] on pressure¹², and fades [eɪ] in 2-5 days followed by scaly desquamation. In scarlet fever, the skin is diffusely erythematous and appears roughened [ʌ] (sandpaper rash¹³).

Use to produce/resemble **scarlet fever** • mild / (non)streptococcal¹⁴ / staphylococcal **scarlet fever** • **scarlet fever** toxin¹⁵ /-like syndrome / rash¹⁶ • **scarlet**-red patches¹⁷ • **scarlatiniform** eruption¹⁸ / erythema [iː]

Scharlach, Scarlatina
Scarlatinella¹ Erschöpfung² Schuppung³ Schuppen⁴ Hautfetzen⁵ scharlachähnlich⁶ periorale Blässe⁷ belegt⁸ Himbeerzunge⁹ Rachen¹⁰ Leiste(nbeuge)¹¹ blasst auf Druck ab¹² Scharlachfriesel¹³ Streptokokken-Scharlach¹⁴ Scharlachtoxin¹⁵ Scharlachexanthem¹⁶ scharlachrote Flecken¹⁷ scharlachähnliches Exanthem¹⁸

6

chickenpox [tʃɪkənpɒks] n clin   syn varicella [værɪselə] n, rel variola¹ [aɪ] n term or smallpox¹ n clin, herpes [ɜː] zoster² [zɒː] n term or shingles² [ʃɪŋɡlz] n clin

highly contagious [eɪdʒ] childhood disease caused by the varicella-zoster virus marked by crops of³ pruritic eruptions beginning as papules⁴ which turn into vesicles⁵ and then pustules⁶ [ʌ]
varicelliform adj term • **-pox** comb • **varioliform**⁷ adj • **(post)herpetic**⁸ adj

» Unvaccinated children who lack a reliable history of chickenpox should receive varicella vaccine before the teenage years. Perinatal exposure can cause severe to fatal disseminated varicella. In varicella and variola, viremia [iː] precedes [iː] the onset of the diffuse centrifugal rash. Adult-onset shingles is usually a reemergence⁹ [ɜː] of a dormant chickenpox virus. About 10% of patients who develop shingles suffer from postherpetic neuralgia¹⁰.

Use nosocomial / severe / post-**chickenpox** • **chickenpox**-related pneumonia¹¹ [n(j)uː-]/ lesions [iːʒ] • childhood / bullous [ʊ]/ hemorrhagic / latent **varicella** • congenital¹² [dʒe]/ perinatal [eɪ]/ (primary) adult¹³ **varicella** • **varicella** exposure / pneumonia¹¹ /-related • **varicella**-zoster virus¹⁴ (abbr VZV)/ immune globulin (abbr VZIG) • cow¹⁵/ monkey / rickettsial **pox** • endemic **smallpox** • **smallpox** vaccination / eradication¹⁶ • **variola** virus¹⁷ / major / minor • genital¹⁸ / epithelial [iː] **herpes** • **herpes** infection / encephalitis¹⁹ [aɪ] • **herpes** simplex virus (abbr HSV)/ labialis / keratitis • **herpes**-associated erythema [iː] multiforme • **herpetic** lesion / stomatitis²⁰ • trigeminal [dʒe]/ pain from¹⁰ **shingles**

Varizellen, Windpocken, Schafblattern
Pocken, Blattern, Variola¹ Gürtelrose, Herpes zoster² gruppiert³ Papeln⁴ Bläschen⁵ Pusteln⁶ pockenähnlich⁷ herpetisch, Herpes-⁸ Wiederauftreten⁹ Zosterneuralgie¹⁰ Varizellen-Pneumonie¹¹ konnatale Varizellen¹² Varizellenerkrankung d. Erwachsenen, Varicellae adultorum¹³ Varicella-Zoster-Virus¹⁴ Kuhpocken¹⁵ Ausrottung d. Pocken¹⁶ Variolavirus¹⁷ Herpes genitalis¹⁸ Herpes-Enzephalitis¹⁹ Gingivostomatitis herpetica, Stomatitis aphthosa²⁰

7

polio(myelitis) [poʊlioʊmaɪəlaɪtɪs] n clin & term   syn infantile paralysis n term

contagious disease causing inflammation of the anterior horn¹ cells of the spinal cord
poliovirus n term • **poliovaccine** n • **postpolio** adj • **polio-** comb

» In paralytic poliomyelitis approx. 25% of patients suffer severe permanent disability while about 50% recover with no residual paralyses. Man is the only natural host for polioviruses. Siblings² and household contacts of a child who is immunodeficient³ should not receive OPV unless the immunodeficient child has been immunized against poliomyelitis. The bulbar [ʌ] form of polio may start with difficulty swallowing⁴ [ɔː].

Use acute / bulbar⁵ / abortive⁶ / spinal⁷ [aɪ]/ nonparalytic [ɪ] **polio** • vaccine-associated paralytic⁸ (abbr VAPP) **polio** • **poliomyelitis**-like syndrome / immunization / eradication • inactivated⁹ (abbr IPV)/ oral¹⁰ (abbr OPV) **poliovaccine** • **polio**virus (vaccine) /encephalitis

Poliomyelitis, Kinderlähmung
Vorderhorn¹ Geschwister² immungeschwächt³ Schluckbeschwerden⁴ bulbäre Poliomyelitis⁵ abortive Poliomyelitis⁶ Poliomyelitis acuta anterior, spinale Kinderlähmung⁷ Impfpoliomyelitis⁸ inaktivierte Poliovakzine⁹ Polioschluckimpfung¹⁰

8

diphtheria [dɪfθɪəriə] n term & clin

infectious childhood disease characterized by sore throat, fever [iː], and formation of a typical pseudo-membrane¹ at the site of infection as well as myocarditis, and neuropathy tissues
(post)diphtheritic² [ɪ] adj term • **diphtheric²** [e] adj • **diphtheroid³** n & adj

» Laryngeal [dʒ] diphtheria⁴ often presents as hoarseness⁵ and cough. In tonsillopharyngeal diphtheria, only erythema may be noted initially, but isolated spots of gray or white exudate are common. Recovery [ʌ] from severe diphtheria is slow, and patients must be prevented from resuming [uː] activities too soon.

Use to contract/mimic⁶ **diphtheria** • pharyngeal⁷ [dʒ] / tonsillar⁷ / faucial⁷ [fɔːʃəl] **diphtheria** • nasal⁸ / respiratory **diphtheria** • cutaneous⁹ [eɪ] / vaginal [dʒ]/ wound¹⁰ [uː] **diphtheria** • malignant or bull-neck¹¹ **diphtheria** • **diphtheria** (anti)toxin¹² / toxoid¹³ /-tetanus toxoids (abbr DT)/ bacilli¹⁴ [aɪ] • **diphtheritic** infection / (pseudo)membrane / croup¹⁵ • **diphtheritic** neuropathy / polyneuritis [pɒlɪn(j)ʊəraɪtɪs]/ myocarditis¹⁶

Diphtherie
Pseudomembran¹ diphtherieähnlich, diphtherisch² Diphtheroid, diphtherieähnl. Erkrankung; diphtheroid³ Kehlkopfdiphtherie⁴ Heiserkeit⁵ Diphtherie vortäuschen⁶ Rachendiphtherie⁷ Nasendiphtherie⁸ Hautdiphtherie⁹ Wunddiphtherie¹⁰ maligne Diphtherie¹¹ Diphtherie(anti)toxin¹² Diphtherietoxoid, -impfstoff¹³ Diphtheriebakterien¹⁴ echter Krupp¹⁵ diphtherische Myokarditis¹⁶

9

Sexually Transmitted Diseases   MEDICAL SCIENCE 425

croup [uː] *n term*   *rel* **spasmodic croup**[1] *n*, **crowing** [oʊ] **inspiraton**[2] *n term*

acute laryngotracheobronchitis in infants and young children caused by parainfluenza viruses which is characterized by difficult and noisy respiration and a hoarse cough

croupy[3] *adj* • **croupous**[3] *adj term* • **pseudocroup**[1] *n* • **croupette**[4] *n*

» Confirm [ɜː] the diagnosis and exclude retropharyngeal abscess, foreign body, or epiglottitis, all of which may mimic croup. Spasmodic croup occurs typically at night in a child with a history of previous [iː] attacks

Use infantile / viral [aɪ]/ supraglottic / (pseudo)membranous[5] **croup** • diphtheric[5] / febrile / false[1] **croup** • catarrhal / treatment or management of[6] **croup** • **croup** patient / syndrome[1] / episode[7] / **croup** management[6] /-associated (*abbr* CA) virus[8] /-like illness / tent[4] • croupy cough[9] • **croupous** conjunctivitis / bronchitis[10] [aɪ] • **croupous** pneumonia / rhinitis / nephritis • to place sb. in a **croupette**

Krupp
Pseudokrupp, Krupp-Syndrom[1] inspirator. Stridor[2] kruppartig, kruppös[3] Nebelzelt[4] echter Krupp[5] Kruppbehandlung[6] Kruppanfall[7] kruppassoziiertes Virus, Parainfluenzavirus[8] kruppartiger Husten[9] kruppöse Bronchitis[10]

10

rickets [rɪkɪts] *n*   *rel* **infantile** or **juvenile osteomalacia**[1] [-məleɪʃ(ɪ)ə] *n term*

disease caused by vitamin-D deficiency and characterized by deficient calcification of osteoid tissue, with associated skeletal deformities, disturbances in growth, and hypocalcemia [siː]

pseudorickets[2] [suːdoʊ]- *n term*

» Rickets is usually accompanied by irritability[3], listlessness, and generalized muscular weakness; fractures are frequently seen while tetany[4] [e] is relatively rare.

Use acute / hemorrhagic[5] [-rædʒɪk]/ hereditary / infantile / late / adult **rickets** • celiac [siː]/ renal or vitamin D-resistant (*abbr* VDDR)[2] / nutritional[6] [ɪʃ] **rickets**

Rachitis
Osteomalazie[1] renale/ Vitamin-D-resistente Rachitis[2] Gereiztheit[3] Tetanie[4] hämorrhagische Rachitis[5] Vitamin-D-Mangel Rachitis[6]

11

otitis media [oʊtaɪtɪs miːdɪə] *n term*

inflammation [eɪʃ] of the middle ear commonly seen in children which typically presents with rapid onset of symptoms such as earache, fever, irritability, anorexia, or vomiting

otitic *adj term* • **panotitis**[1] *n*

» Otitis media is particularly common in infants who have had prolonged endotracheal intubation or an indwelling nasogastric feeding tube[2]. Chronic serous otitis or glue ear[3] does not require antibiotic therapy.

Use external[4] **otitis** • acute[5] (*abbr* AOM)/ chronic[6] / bilateral **otitis media** • suppurative [ʌ] or purulent[7] [pjʊɚ-]/ serous [ɪɚ] or secretory[3] (*abbr* SOM) **otitis media** • **otitis** sclerotica / externa[4] / pathogens / episodes • **otitic** meningitis[8] [dʒaɪ]/ barotrauma[9] [bæroʊtrɒːmə]

Mittelohrentzündung, Otitis media
Panotitis[1] Magenverweilsonde (zur enteralen Ernährung)[2] chron. seröse/ seromuköse Otitis media[3] Entzündung d. äußeren Ohrs[4] akute Mittelohrentzündung, Otitis media acuta[5] chron. M., Otitis media chronica[6] eitrige Mittelohrentzündung[7] otogene Meningitis[8] Aerootitis, Barotitis[9]

12

strep throat [strep θroʊt] *n jar & clin* → U90-8

    rel **peritonsillar abscess**[1] *n term*, **quinsy**[1] [kwɪnzi] *n clin*

streptococcus infection of the oral pharynx and tonsils[2] [tɒːnˈsəlz]

streptococcal *adj term* • **tonsillitis**[3] *n* • **tonsillar** *adj* • **tonsil-** *n & comb*

» "Strep throat" is characterized by a sudden onset of fever, sore throat, pain on swallowing, tender[4] cervical adenopathy, malaise, and nausea. Antibiotics prevent local suppurative complications such as peritonsillar abscess, otitis media, and sinusitis. Refer patients for tonsillectomy when persistently enlarged tonsils cause chronic upper airway obstruction.

Use streptococcal sore throat[5] / throat infection[5] / tonsillitis[5] [aɪ]/ tonsillopharyngitis[5] • **tonsillar** pillar[6] [ɪ]/ crypt[7] [krɪpt]/ exudate / palatine[8] [-aɪn]/ lingual[9] / pharyngeal[10] / enlarged[11] **tonsil** • **peritonsillar** space / fold / swelling / cellulitis • acute / chronic / (non)exudative **tonsillitis** • **tonsillectomy**[12]

Streptokokkenangina
Peritonsillarabszess[1] Tonsillen, (Gaumen)mandeln[2] Tonsillitis, Angina, Mandelentzündung[3] druckschmerzhaft[4] Streptokokkenangina[5] Gaumenbogen[6] tonsilläre Krypte[7] Gaumenmandel, Tonsilla palatina[8] Zungenmandel, T. lingualis[9] Rachenmandel, T. pharyngealis[10] vergrößerte Tonsille[11] operative Entfernung d. Gaumenmandeln, Tonsillektomie[12]

13

Unit 96   Sexually Transmitted Diseases

Related Units: 94 Infectious Diseases, 68 Sexuality, 70 Pregnancy, 71 Childbirth, 112 Urologic Symptoms, 114 Skin Lesions

venereal [vənɪɚɪəl] *adj term*   *sim* **sexually transmitted**[1] *adj clin*

related to or resulting from sexual [sekʃʊəl] intercourse [ɔː] or genital [dʒenɪtᵊl] contact

venereology[2] *n term* • **STD**[3] *abbr* • **venereologist** *n* • **venereologic** *adj*

» The patient was concerned[4] [ɜː] about the possibility of venereal infection. The term sexually transmitted disease[3] is used to denote disorders spread by intimate contact[5], which includes kissing, mouth-breast [e] contact, and intercourse.

Use **venereal** disease[6] (*abbr* VD)/ disease clinic (*abbr* VDC)/ disease research laboratory (*abbr* VDRL) • **VDRL** test[7] • **venereal** transmission / infection / wart[8] [ɔː] • **venereal** ulcer [ʌlsɚ] or sore[9] [sɔːr]/ bubo[10] [b(j)uːboʊ] • granulomatous **VD** • **STD** history / pathogen [-dʒən]/ syndrome [ɪ] • **venereally** acquired [əkwaɪɚd]

Geschlechtskrankheiten betreffend, venerisch
sexuell übertragen[1] Venerologie[2] sexuell übertragbare Krankheit[3] besorgt[4] Intimkontakt[5] Geschlechtskrankheit[6] VDRL-Test[7] Kondylom, Feigwarze[8] harter Schanker, Ulcus durum[9] venerische Lymphknotenentzündung[10]

1

Sexually Transmitted Diseases

gonorrhea [gɒːnəriːə] *n term*   *sim* **gonococcal infection**[1] *n term*

contagious [eɪdʒ] catarrhal inflammation of the genital mucous membranes chiefly transmitted by coitus

(non)gonorrheal[2] [iː] *adj term* • **gonococcemia**[3] [iː] *n* • **gonorrhoeae** *adj*

» A detailed history of prior [aɪ] STD should not only include gonorrhea and syphilis, but also document exposure to HIV, herpes virus [aɪ], and Chlamydia [ɪ]. Gonorrhea may involve the urethra [iː], endocervix [sɜː], and uterine [juː] tubes, or spread to the peritoneum [iː]. In gonorrheal infection the appearance of the vaginal discharge[4] is thick and creamy. A presumptive [ʌ] diagnosis of gonorrhea can be made on the basis of the stained [eɪ] smear[5] [ɚ].

Use venereal disease[6] (*abbr* VDG)/ untreated / uncomplicated **gonorrhea** • culture [ʌ] tests / treatment / at high risk **for gonorrhea** • **gonorrheal** infection / urethritis[7] [aɪ]/ cervicitis [sɜːrvɪsaɪtɪs]/ arthritis • **gonococcal** conjunctivitis[8] [dʒʌ] • disseminated **gonococcal** infection[9] • gram-negative Neisseria **gonorrhoeae**

Gonorrhö, Tripper
Gonokokkeninfektion[1] gonorrhoisch[2] Gonokokkensepsis, Gonokokkämie[3] vaginaler Ausfluss[4] angefärbter Abstrich/ Ausstrich[5] genitale Gonorrhö[6] gonorrhoische Urethritis, U. gonorrhoica[7] Gonoblennorrhö, Conjunctivitis gonorrhoica[8] disseminierte Gonokokkeninfektion, benigne Gonokokkensepsis[9]

2

---

syphilis [sɪfɪlɪs] *n clin & term*   *syn* **lues** [luːiːz] *n term rare*

chronic systemic infection (usually sexually transmitted) marked by a primary [aɪ], secondary and a tertiary [tɜːrʃəri] stage as well as episodes of active disease interrupted [ʌ] by periods of latency [eɪ]

syphilitic[1] *adj term* • **neurosyphilis**[2] [n(j)ʊəˈsɪfɪlɪs] *n* • **luetic** [luːetɪk] *adj*

» After an incubation period of 2-3 weeks the first symptom is a chancre[3], also called venereal sore or ulcer, followed by slight fever [iː] and other constitutional symptoms (primary syphilis), a skin eruption [ʌ] of various appearances with mucous [juː] patches[4], and then by the formation of gummas[5] [ʌ], cellular infiltration, and cardiovascular and CNS lesions [iː3] (tertiary syphilis). Examine the body for stigmata of syphilis at intervals of 3 to 6 weeks.

Use primary [aɪ]/ secondary / acquired[6] [aɪ]/ congenital[7] [dʒe] **syphilis** • (non)venereal[8] / active / latent[9] [eɪ] **syphilis** • early[10] / late or tertiary[11] / CNS[2] **syphilis** • meningovascular / endemic[8] **syphilis** • **syphilitic** infection / lesion [iː3] gummas[5] • **syphilitic** aneurysm[12] [ænjərɪzᵊm]/ meningitis [dʒaɪ]/ nephritis • serologic tests for[13] **syphilis**

Syphilis, Lues (venerea), harter Schanker
syphilitisch, Syphilis-[1] Neurosyphilis, -lues[2] harter Schanker, Ulcus durum[3] Schleimhautefloreszenzen, Plaque muqueuses[4] Gummen, Gummiknoten[5] erworbene S., S. aquisita[6] angeborene Syphilis, S. connata[7] nichtvenerische/ endemische Syphilis[8] Syphilis latens[9] Frühsyphilis[10] Spät-, tertiäre Syphilis[11] syphilitisches Aneurysma[12] Luesserologie[13]

3

---

chancroid [ʃæŋkrɔɪd] *n term*   *syn* **soft chancre** [ʃæŋkɚ] *n term*

acute, localized, contagious STD caused by Haemophilus ducreyi which is marked by a painful genital ulcer [ʌlsə]

chancre[1] *n term* • **chancroidal** *adj* • **chancriform**[2] *adj*

» The chancre of primary syphilis is an indurated[3], firm [ɜː], nontender[4] papule or ulcer with raised [eɪ] borders[5]. The early chancroid lesion is a vesicopustule [ʌ] on the pudendum, vagina [dʒaɪ], or cervix [sɜː] which turns into a saucer-shaped[6] [sɔːɚ] ragged[7] [rægɪd] ulcer circumscribed [sɜː] by an inflammatory [æ] wheal[8].

Use serpiginous [ɪdʒ] **chancroid** • rectal / hard[9] / primary[9] / painless[9] / syphilitic[9] **chancre** • **chancre** develops / appears / evolves / heals[10] [iː] • **chancre** sore

Ulcus molle, weicher Schanker
Schanker[1] schankrös, schankerartig[2] induriert[3] schmerzlos, indolent[4] erhabene Ränder[5] tellerförmig[6] unterminiert[7] Hof[8] harter Schanker, syphilitischer Primäraffekt[9] der Schanker heilt ab[10]

4

---

bubo [b(j)uːboʊ] *n term, pl* **buboes**

inflammatory swelling of inguinal lymph nodes which usually suppurates[1] and drains pus[2]

» During the inguinal bubo[3] phase which is marked by a purplish-blue cutaneous induration the groin[4] is exquisitely tender[5]. Aspirated pus from a bubo is the best material for culture.

Use to aspirate a **bubo** • fluctuant [ʌ]/ subacute / inguinal[3] / early / fully developed **bubo** • venereal / gonorrheal / chancroidal[6] / indolent or nontender[7] **bubo**

Bubo(nen)
eitert[1] Eiter[2] Leistenbubo, Bubo inguinalis[3] Leiste[4] äußerst druckschmerzempfindlich[5] schankröser Bubo[6] indolenter Bubo[7]

5

---

granuloma inguinale [ɪŋgwɪneɪliǁæli] *n term*   *syn* **donovanosis** *n term*

specific ulcerating granuloma presenting as small nodules, papules or vesicles in the groin [grɔɪn] and the genitalia [eɪ] caused by Calymmatobacterium granulomatis

granulomatous [grænjəloʊmətˈs] *adj term* • **Donovan body**[1] *n*

» Granuloma inguinale most often involves the skin and subcutaneous [eɪ] tissues of the vulva [ʌ] and inguinal regions and is marked by a malodorous [oʊ] discharge[2] [dɪstʃɑːrdʒ]. The diagnosis of granuloma inguinale is made by demonstrating Donovan bodies[1] in biopsy [baɪ-] or smear [smɚ] material stained [eɪ] with Wright's, silver, or Giemsa's stain[3].

Use **granuloma** pudendi / venereum / annulare [æ] • benign [bɪnaɪn]/ pyogenic[4] [paɪədʒ-]/ caseous [eɪ] **granuloma** • **granulomatous** venereal lesions[5] / ulceration/ formation / STD • **granulomatous** infection / tissue reaction / salpingitis [dʒaɪ]

Granuloma inguinale/ venereum, Donovanosis
Donovan-Körperchen[1] übelriechendes Sekret[2] Giemsa-Färbung[3] Granuloma pediculatum/ teleangiectaticum/ pyogenicum[4] granulomatöse venerische Läsionen[5]

6

Sexually Transmitted Diseases — MEDICAL SCIENCE

lymphogranuloma venereum [ɪɚ] *or* **inguinale** *n term*   *abbr* **LGV**
   syn **lymphopathia** [lɪmfəpǽθɪə] **venereum** *or* **tropical bubo** *n term*
   venereal infection (usually caused by Chlamydia trachomatis) characterized by a transient genital ulcer associated with inguinal (in males) and perirectal adenopathy and rectal stricture (in females)
   lymphogranulomatous [ɒː] *adj term* • **lymphogranulomatosis** *n*
» Lymphogranuloma venereum is characterized by chronic lymphadenitis [aɪ], rectal stricture, vulvar [ʌ] elephantiasis [aɪ], and chronic hypertrophic changes of the vulvar skin.
Use to produce¹ **LGV**

Lymphogranuloma inguinale, Lymphopathia venerea
Lymphopathia venerea hervorrufen¹

7

(vaginal) trichomoniasis [-aɪəsɪs] *n term*   *syn* **trichomonas infection** *n term*
   widespread venereal infection caused by Trichomonas vaginalis which is usually asymptomatic but may produce vaginitis, with vaginal and vulvar pruritus [aɪ], leukorrhea [-iːə] with frothy¹ watery discharge, and (rarely) purulent² [pjʊɚ-] urethritis [jʊɚɪθraɪtɪs] in males
   trichomonal³ [trɪkəmoʊnᵊl] *adj term* • **trichomonads**⁴ [-ædz] *n*
» If the smear⁵ is examined while it is still warm, actively motile [oʊ] trichomonads can usually be seen. Trichomonas infection is marked by a white to grayish-green discharge⁶ that may be frothy. Trichomoniasis tends to be worse just after menses or during pregnancy.
Use to acquire **trichomoniasis** • symptomatic **trichomoniasis** • **trichomonas** vaginalis • **trichomonal** urethritis⁷ • to harbor⁸ **trichomonads**

Trichomoniasis, Trichomonosis genitalis
schaumig¹ eitrig² Trichomonaden-³ Trichomonaden⁴ Abstrich⁵ Ausfluss, Fluor⁶ Trichomonadenurethritis⁷ Trichomonaden beherbergen/ enthalten⁸

8

chlamydial infection *n term*   *syn* **chlamydiosis** *n, rel* **psittacosis**¹ [sɪ-] *n term*
   broad term for conditions caused by Chlamydia viruses [aɪ] which may result in very mild, so-called silent² [aɪ] STD and patients often seek [iː] treatment³ only after unwitting⁴ transmission has occurred [ɜː]
   chlamydia [kləmɪdɪə] *n term, pl* **-diae** [dɪiː] • **chlamydial** *adj*
» Salpingitis [dʒaɪ] is a common complication of gonorrheal, chlamydial, and post-abortion cervicitis. Chlamydial infection during pregnancy may be associated with preterm labor⁵.
Use **chlamydial** cervicitis⁶ [saɪ]/ cervix colonization / urethritis / inclusions⁷ [uːʒ] • **chlamydia** trachomatis (infection) / psittaci / pneumoniae [n(j)uː-]

Chlamydieninfektion
Psittakose, Papageienkrankheit¹ klinisch stumm/ inapparent, symptomlos² sich i. Behandlung begeben³ unwissentlich⁴ vorzeitiger Wehenbeginn⁵ Chlamydien-zervizitis⁶ Chlamydieneinschlusskörperchen⁷

9

genital herpes [dʒenɪtᵊl hɜːrpiːz] *n term*   *rel* **herpes simplex**¹ *n term*
   recrudescent [es] infections² caused by herpes virus [aɪ] type 2 which are marked by the eruption of groups of vesicles on the genitalia where they may reappear during febrile illnesses or even menstruation
   herpesvirus *n term* • **herpetiformis** *adj* • **herpes-like** *adj* • **herpetic**³ *adj*
» Topical acyclovir ointment⁴ applied several times daily can limit pain and virus shedding⁵ and reduce healing time in primary genital herpes infections. If a regular partner has not been infected after prolonged exposure to genital herpes, no precautions are necessary.
Use primary / symptomatic / recurrent⁶ [ɜː]/ persistent **genital herpes** • neonatal⁷ [eɪ]/ anorectal / preputial [(j)uːʃ]/ orofacial [eɪʃ] **herpes** • **herpes**-virus infection (*abbr* HSV) / pain • **herpes** zoster⁸ / labialis / gestationis • dermatitis⁹ **herpetiformis** • **herpetic** lesion¹⁰ / whitlow¹¹ [ʰwɪtloʊ]/ recurrence

Herpes genitalis
Herpes simplex¹ rezidivierende Infektionen² herpetisch, Herpes-³ Salbe⁴ Virusausscheidung⁵ Herpes-genitalis-Rezidiv⁶ Herpessepsis d. Neugeborenen, Herpes neonatorum⁷ Herpes zoster, Gürtelrose⁸ Dermatitis herpetiformis, Duhring-Brocq-Krankheit⁹ Herpesläsion, Fieberblase¹⁰ Herpesparonychie¹¹

10

cytomegalovirus [saɪtə-] **(CMV) infection** *n term*
   syn **cytomegalic inclusion** [uːʒ] **disease** *n, abbr* **CID**, *rel* **TORCH complex**¹ *n term*
   primarily congenitally acquired (maternal-fetal [iː] transmission in utero) viral disease which is often asymptomatic in later life but may cause stillbirth², postnatal death or extensive pathology in neonates
   cytomegaloviral *adj term* • **CMV-positive** *adj* • **cytomegalic**³ *adj*
» Microorganisms capable of crossing the placenta and causing major perinatal infections are known as TORCH agents (toxoplasmosis, rubella, cytomegalo-, and herpes viruses).
Use **CMV** disease / encephalitis⁴ / retinitis / pneumonia [n(j)uː-]/ mononucleosis⁵ • **CMV**-induced / immune globulin⁶ (*abbr* CMVIG) • anti-**CMV** • congenital⁷ [dʒe] **CID** • postnatally [eɪ] acquired CMV infection • **TORCH** infection

Zytomegalie(virusinfektion), Einschlusskörperchenkrankheit
TORCH-Komplex¹ Totgeburt² Zytomegalie-³ CMV-Enzephalitis⁴ CMV-Mononukleose⁵ Zytomegalievirusimmunglobulin⁶ konnatale/ kongenitale Zytomegalie⁷

11

scabies [skeɪbiːz] *n clin & term*   *syn* **seven-year itch** [ɪtʃ] *n clin* → U103-17

contagious skin disease caused by the itch mite[1] [maɪt] (Sarcoptes scabiei), a parasite that forms burrows[2] [ɜː] in the skin which cause intense itching about four weeks after infestation[3]

(**post**)**scab**(**i**)**etic**[4] *adj term* • **scabi**(**eti**)**cide**[5] *n & adj* • **antiscabetic**[5] *adj & n*

» Both scabies and pediculosis[6] may be sexually transmitted. Scabetic papules occur [ɜː] predominantly on covered body areas, e.g. the male genitalia, the groin, and axillary regions. Patients with scabies report intense itching[7] that worsens at night.

Use animal-transmitted / Norwegian[8] [iː dʒ]/ crusted[8] [ʌ]/ impetiginized [ɪdʒ] **scabies** • **scabies** mite[1] / infestation [eɪʃ] • **scabetic** infection / distribution [juːʃ] • **post-scabietic** papules • **antiscabetic** therapy[9]

Krätze, Skabies, Scabies

Krätzmilbe, S. scabiei[1] Milbengänge[2] Befall[3] skabiös, krätzig[4] Antiskabiosum, Krätzemittel; antiskabiös[5] Pedikulose, Läusebefall[6] starker Juckreiz[7] Borkenkrätze, Boeck-Skabies[8] antiskabiöse Behandlung/ Therapie[9]

12

human papillomavirus [pæpɪloʊməvaɪrəs] (*abbr* **HPV**) **infection** *n term*

infection with any of the 70 strains of papovaviruses which cause cutaneous and genital warts and are associated with cervical intraepithelial neoplasia as well as anogenital

» The list of organisms traditionally thought of as causing STD has been extended to include CMV, herpes simplex virus types I and II, Chlamydia, group B Streptococcus, molluscum [ʌ] contagiosum virus, Sarcoptes scabiei, hepatitis viruses, and HIV.

Use **HPV** (lower) genital tract infection • genital / cervicovaginal • silent[1] **HPV infection** • **HPV** (sub)types [ʌ]/ testing /-related • oncogenic [dʒe] **HPV** types[2]

humane Papillomavirusinfektion

klinisch inapparente HPV-Infektion[1] onkogene HPV-Typen[2]

13

venereal wart [wɔːrt] *n term*   *syn* **condyloma acuminatum** [eɪ] *n term*

benign [aɪ] projecting growth on the external genitals or at the anus [eɪ] consisting of fibrous [aɪ] overgrowths covered by epithelium showing koilocytosis[2]; due to infection by HPV

warty[2] [wɔːrti] *adj* • **wartlike** *adj* • **condylomatous** [kɒndəloʊmətəs] *adj term*

» Sexually transmitted genital warts[3] which are caused by a virus of the papovavirus group[4] are papillary growths that tend to coalesce [-es] and form large cauliflower-like[5] [ɔː] masses.

Use condylomatous / anogenital[6] [eɪ]/ penile [iː] **warts** • urethral [iː]/ perianal [eɪ]/ dysplastic [ɪ] **warts** • **condyloma** latum[7] [ɑː]

spitze(s) Feigwarze/ Kondylom, Condyloma acuminatum

Koilozytose[1] warzig, Warzen-[2] Genitalwarzen[3] Papoviridae[4] blumenkohlartig[5] anogenitale Warzen[6] breites Kondylom, Condyloma latum[7]

14

acquired [əkwaɪə˞d] **immunodeficiency** [ɪʃ] **syndrome** *n term, abbr* **AIDS**

infection with the human imunodeficiency virus[1] (HIV), which is spread [e] by sexual contact or exposure to contaminated blood or body fluids and causes a defect in cell-mediated [iː] immunity

» In women with AIDS, vaginal candidiasis [aɪ] is usually the first and most frequent opportunistic infection[2]. Factor VIII concentrates are heat-treated to reduce the likelihood of transmission of AIDS. In Western countries heterosexual spread [e] of AIDS has been much less rapid than among homosexual men.

Use to contract[3]/develop[4]/have/progress to **AIDS** • clinical[5] / symptomatic / established[6] **AIDS** • pediatric[7] / advanced / progression to / full-blown[8] **AIDS** • **AIDS**-defining [aɪ] illness[9] /-dementia [-ˈʃ(ɪ)ə] complex[10] (*abbr* ADC) • **AIDS**-associated retrovirus[11] [e] (*abbr* ARV)/ encephalopathy[10] • **AIDS** wasting[12] [eɪ]/-related complex[13] (*abbr* ARC) • **AIDS**-associated [oʊʃ] Kaposi' **AIDS** virus[11] [aɪ]/ patient / cases • **AIDS** diagnosis / epidemic[14]

AIDS, erworbenes Immunschwäche-/ -defektsyndrom

humanes Immundefizienzvirus, HIV[1] opportunistische Infektion[2] sich m. AIDS anstecken[3] AIDS entwickeln[4] klin. manifestes AIDS[5] gesichertes AIDS[6] pädiatrisches AIDS[7] AIDS-Vollbild[8] AIDS-definierende Erkrankung[9] AIDS-Demenz, HIV-Demenzsyndrom, HIV-Enzephalopathie[10] AIDS-assoziiertes Retrovirus, AIDS-Virus[11] HIV-Kachexiesyndrom[12] AIDS-related Complex, Prä-AIDS, ARC[13] AIDS-Epidemie[14]

15

Unit 97   General Oncology

Related Units: 98 Tumor Types, 89 Pathology, 84 Genetics, 85 Embryology, 91 Toxicology, 99 Radiology, 121 Pharmacologic Treatment, 126 Surgical Treatment, 129 Reconstructive Surgery

oncology [ɒnkɒːlədʒi] *n term*

branch of medicine concerned with the study and treatment of malignant disease

oncologic(**al**)[1] *adj term* • **oncologist**[2] *n* • **onco-** *comb*

» The pediatric oncology patient should be monitored steadily [e] during cancer therapy. She should be referred to[3] a gynecologic oncologist to determine if the pregnancy can progress to fetal viability.

Use clinical / pediatric[4] / radiation[5] [eɪ]/ head **oncology** • neck / neuro- [n(j)ʊə˞oʊ]/ psycho- [saɪkoʊ-]/ surgical [ɜː] **oncology** • medical / research / urologic **oncologist** • **oncology** ward[6] [ɔː]/ consultation[7] / patient[8] • **oncology** certified [sɜː] nurse [ɜː] (*abbr* OCN)/ clinical nurse specialist • **onco**gene[9] [-dʒiːn] /genesis [dʒe] /static[10] /lysis [ɪ] • **onco**genic viruses[11] [aɪ] /fetal antigens[12] • **oncologic** anatomy / emergency [ɜː] staging[13] [eɪdʒ]/ surgeon/history

Onkologie

onkologisch[1] Onkologe/-in[2] überwiesen werden zu[3] Kinderonkologie[4] Radioonkologie[5] onkolog. Station[6] onkolog. Sprechstunde/ Beratung[7] Tumorpatient(in)[8] Onkogen, geschwulsterzeugendes Gen[9] onkostatisch[10] onkogene Viren, Tumorviren[11] onkofetale Antigene[12] Tumorstaging[13]

1

General Oncology

MEDICAL SCIENCE 429

tumor [t(j)uːmɚ] *n term, BE* **tumour**

syn **swelling, growth** [groʊθ] *n clin* → U89-16

abnormal overgrowth[1] of cells which can be either benign or malignant

tumorous[2] [t(j)uːmɚəs] *adj term* • **intratumoral** *adj* • **tumor-** *comb*

» Although the term "tumor" originally denoted any mass or swelling, it is generally used synonymously with neoplasm. Malignant ectopic ACTH-secreting tumors tend to recur after resection. Benign growths may arise in any layer [eɪ] of the esophagus. Most growths arising within the testis are malignant.

Use primary[3] [aɪ]/ localized / advanced / bulky[4] [ʌ] **tumor** • malignant / recurrent[5] / residual[6] [ɪdʒ] **tumor** • **tumor** size[7] [aɪ]/ cells / tissue / mass / bed[8] • **tumor** capsule / involvement[9] / activity • **tumor** formation / extent / growth / spread[10] [e] • **tumor** control / burden[11] [ɜː] / recurrence[5] [ɜː] • **tumor** regression / necrosis factor[12] / site[13] / shrinkage[14] [-ɪdʒ] • debulking [ʌ] of the[15] **tumor** • **tumori**genesis /cidal[16] [saɪ] • **tumorous** lesion • benign[17] [aɪn]/ malignant / warty[18] [ɔː]/ submucosal / polypoid **growth**

Tumor, Geschwulst; Schwellung
Wucherung, übermäßiges Wachstum[1] tumorös, -artig, Tumor-[2] Primärtumor[3] großer/ voluminöser T.[4] Tumorrezidiv[5] Resttumor, Tumorrest[6] Tumorgröße[7] Tumorbett[8] Tumorbefall[9] Tumorausbreitung[10] Tumorlast[11] Tumornekrosefaktor[12] Tumorsitz[13] Tumorschrumpfung, -rückgang, -involution[14] Tumorverkleinerung, Debulking[15] tumorzerstörend[16] gutartige Geschwulst[17] warzenartige Wucherung[18]

2

(tumor) mass *n*   *syn* **(mass) lesion** [liːʒən] *n term*, **lump** [ʌ] , **nodule** *n clin*

abnormal growth that consists of a tumorous node and adjacent [dʒeɪs] areas of invasion

nodular[1] [nɒdjələ˞] *adj term* • **nodularity**[2] *n* • **lumpectomy**[3] *n* • **lumpy**[1] *adj clin*

» Benign lesions are ten times as common as malignant ones. Metastatic skin lesions provide important diagnostic material in lung cancer. Breast [e] cancer usually consists of a nontender[4] lump with poorly delineated margins[5] [dʒ]. A palpable abdominal mass is a common finding in adrenal [iː] carcinoma.

Use movable[6] / fixed / palpable[7] / discrete[8] [iː]/ ill-defined[9] [aɪ] **mass** • firm [ɜː] or solid / doughy[10] [doʊi]/ indurated[11] / benign **mass** • cancerous / abdominal / flank / intracranial [eɪ] **mass** • adnexal / renal / suprapubic **mass** • **mass** effect / lesion[12] • space-occupying[13] / tumor-like[14] / tumor[12] **lesion** • (palpable) breast [e]/ painless[15] **lump** • inflammatory [æ]/ (non)ulcerating [ʌ]/ metastatic **nodule** • pea-sized [iː]/ ovoid / solitary[16] / pulmonary [ʊ‖ʌ] **nodule** • **nodular** swelling / lesion / infiltrate • **nodular** hyperplasia [haɪpɚ-]/ melanoma[17]

Tumormasse, Knoten
knotig, knotenförmig, Knoten-, nodulär[1] Nodositas, Knotenbildung[2] Lumpektomie, Tylektomie[3] nicht druckdolent[4] schlecht abgrenzbare Ränder[5] verschiebliche Tumormasse[6] tastbare(r) Tumormasse/ Knoten[7] abgrenzbare T.[8] schlecht abgrenzbare T.[9] teigige Masse[10] indurierter Tumor/ Knoten[11] Tumorläsion[12] raumfordernder Tumor, Raumforderung[13] tumorähnliche Veränderung[14] indolenter Knoten[15] Solitärknoten[16] noduläres Melanom[17]

3

neoplasia [niːəpleɪʒ(ɪ)ə] *n term*

rel **neoplasm**[1] [niːəplæzəm] *n term*

abnormal rapid proliferation of new tissue which may be benign or malignant

neoplastic[2] *adj term* • **-plasia** [pleɪʒ(ɪ)ə] *comb*

» Neoplasms usually form a distinct mass of tissue and show partial or complete lack of structural organization and functional coordination with the normal tissue. The increased use of anabolic steroids by body-conscious[3] [ʃ] adolescents poses a risk of hepatic neoplasia.

Use bronchogenic [k]/ intracranial / papillary / vascular **neoplasm** • gonadal [eɪ]/ cervical [ɜː] intraepithelial [iː] (*abbr* CIN) **neoplasia** • multiple [ʌ] endocrine[4] (*abbr* MEN) **neoplasia** • gestational [dʒe-] trophoblastic[5] (*abbr* GTN)/ radiation-induced[6] **neoplasia** • **neoplastic** growth / cells / disease[7] • **neoplastic** process / transformation / lesion[7] • (**non**)**neoplastic** polyp[8] • ana/ hypo/ hyper**plasia**

Neoplasie, Neubildung
Neoplasma[1] neoplastisch[2] körperbewusst[3] multiple endokrine Neoplasie, MEN[4] Trophoblasttumor[5] strahleninduzierte Neoplasie[6] Tumorleiden, Tumorläsion[7] (nicht-)neoplastischer Polyp[8]

4

malignant [məlɪgnənt] *adj term*

opposite **benign**[1] [bɪnaɪn] *adj term*

having the invasive and metastatic properties of cancer and tending to become worse

malignancy[2] *n term* • **premalignant**[3] *adj* • **benignancy/-ity**[4] *n*

» Malignancy can only be diagnosed [aɪ] in the presence of metastases or invasion into surrounding tissues. These malignant cells can proliferate in the absence of the specific host [oʊ] factors (e.g. growth-promoting proteins, a vascular supply [aɪ]) seen in more typical cancers. There is a progressive change from benign to malignant and invasive.

Use to (turn out to) be/become[5] **malignant** • **malignant** cells / lesion / transformation[6] • **malignant** change / degeneration[7] / behavior / melanoma • histologically / less / highly[8] **malignant** • **benign** tumor[9] / growth[9] / illness / course[10] [ɔː] • **benign** nodule / polyps[11] / hypertrophy • pelvic / bowel [aʊ] / lung / underlying[12] **malignancy** • advanced / inoperable[13] **malignancy**

bösartig, maligne
gutartig, benigne[1] Bösartigkeit, Malignität; bösartiger Tumor, Malignom[2] präkanzerös, präkarzinomatös[3] Gutartigkeit, Benignität[4] maligne entarten[5] maligne Transformation[6] maligne Entartung[7] hochgradig maligne, hochmaligne[8] gutartiger/ benigner Tumor[9] gutartiger Verlauf[10] benigne Polypen[11] bösartige Grunderkrankung[12] inoperables Malignom[13]

5

MEDICAL SCIENCE — General Oncology

cancer [kænˈsɚ] n clin & term   rel **carcinoma**[1] [kɑːrsɪnoʊmə], **sarcoma**[2] n term → U98-3

general term for various types of lesions (esp. carcinomas or sarcomas) in which malignant cells grow out of control, spread [e] to other parts of the body, tend to recur [ɜː] after attempted removal and cause death of the patient unless adequately treated

(pre)c**a**ncerous[3] adj term • sarc**o**matous[4] [sɑːrkoʊmətəs] adj • sarco- comb

» Women [ɪ] with breast [e] cancer are at risk of developing a contralateral lesion. He has undergone curative [kjʊəˈətɪv] cancer therapy. Both early and advanced carcinoma of the prostate may be asymptomatic at the time of diagnosis. Osteogenic [dʒe] sarcomas mostly involve the knees or long bones.

Use lung / colon[5] / bone / skin / childhood / adult / latent[6] [eɪ] **cancer** • clinically insignificant[7] / localized[8] **cancer** • disseminated breast / recurrent[9] / terminal stage[10] **cancer** • **cancer**-free /-prone [oʊ] family[11] / gene[12] [dʒiːn]/-ravaged [-ɪdʒd] body[13] • **cancer**-causing gene[12] /-related mortality[14] • **cancer** screening[15] [iː]/ victim / deaths[16] / registry[17] [edʒ] • **cancerous** bone marrow[18] / tissue / growth[19] • **precancerous** adenomatous polyps / lesion[20] / skin lesion[21] • **cancer**icidal [saɪ] • anaplastic / soft tissue / retroperitoneal [iː] **sarcoma** • **sarco**genic /carcinoma /cele[22] [-siːl]

Krebs, maligner Tumor
Karzinom (maligner epithelialer Tumor)[1] Sarkom (maligner mesenchymaler T.)[2] präkanzerös, -karzinomatös[3] sarkomatös[4] Dickdarmkrebs[5] latentes Karzinom[6] klin. nicht signifikantes K.[7] lokalisiertes/ lokal begrenztes K.[8] Karzinomrezidiv[9] Krebs i. Endstadium[10] Familie m. hohem Krebsrisiko[11] Krebs-, Onkogen[12] v. Krebs gezeichneter Körper[13] Krebssterblichkeit[14] Krebsvorsorgeuntersuchung[15] Krebstote[16] Krebsregister[17] krebsbefallenes Knochenmark[18] Krebsgeschwulst[19] Präkanzerose[20] präkanzeröse Hautveränderung[21] Sarkozele[22]

6

---

tumor growth or **proliferation** n term   rel **tumor progression**[1] n term

division and multiplication of cells which may be slow or rapid, disorganized and aggressive

prolif**e**rate[2] v term • prolif**e**rative[3] adj • pr**o**gress[4] [n prɒˈɡres‖v -ˈɡres] n & v • progr**e**ssive[5] adj

» Lipiodol [aɪ] chemoembolization [kiːmə-] reduced tumor growth but often caused liver failure and did not improve survival [aɪ]. Tumor suppressor genes inhibit tumor growth, and oncogenesis occurs when these genes are lost. It turns off the signaling pathways that drive proliferation within a tumor.

Use to control[6]/suppress/prevent/delay/halt[7] [ɒː] /monitor **tumor growth** • **tumor growth** rate / remission[8] • tumor cell / benign / abnormal **proliferation** • malignant / uncontrolled (cellular)[9] **proliferation** • **proliferative** rate / potential / changes • cancer / tumorigenic[1] / neoplastic **progression** • local / metastatic[10] / stage **progression** • relentless[11] / rapid **progression** • slow / evidence of[12] / pattern of **progression** • rate of / time to **progression** • **progression**-free survival (abbr PFS) rate[13]

Tumorwachstum, -proliferation
Tumorprogression[1] wuchern, proliferieren[2] wuchernd, proliferativ[3] Fortschritt; fortschreiten, s. (weiter)entwickeln[4] fortschreitend, progredient, progressiv[5] d. Tumorwachstum unter Kontrolle bringen/ halten[6] d. Tumorwachstum z. Stillstand bringen[7] Tumorremission, -rückbildung[8] ungehemmtes Zellwachstum[9] Fortschreiten d. Metastasierung[10] ständige Progression[11] Hinweis auf Progression[12] progressionsfreie Überlebensrate[13]

7

---

dedifferentiation [diː-] n term   opposite **differentiation**[1] [dɪfəˈrentʃieɪʃən] n term

loss of structural differentiation seen in most, but not all, malignant neoplasms

(un)differ**e**ntiated[2] adj term • (de)differ**e**ntiate[3] v

» Because of its role in cell differentiation, vitamin A has been postulated to have a role in cancer prevention. This dramatic reduction in differentiated smooth [uː] muscle cells in the vicinity[4] of malignant foci [saɪ] suggests dedifferentiation of smooth muscle to fibroblastic cells.

Use to undergo malignant[5] / progressive **dedifferentiation** • lack / stage / pattern[6] / degree[7] **of differentiation** • cell(ular) or cyto[8]-**differentiation** [saɪ] • well / poorly / fully or terminally[9] [ɜː] **differentiated** • **undifferentiated** carcinoma[10] / cells

Entdifferenzierung
Differenzierung[1] (un)differenziert[2] (ent)differenzieren[3] in d. Nähe[4] maligne entarten[5] Differenzierungsmuster[6] Differenzierungsgrad[7] Zelldifferenzierung[8] vollständig differenziert[9] undifferenziertes Karzinom[10]

8

---

organ-confined [aɪ] adj term   sim **localized**[1], **encapsulated**[2] adj term

a tumor that is wholly confined to a specific area, surrounded by a capsule

c**a**psule[3] [ˈkæpsəl‖ˈjuːl] n term • encapsul**a**tion[4] n • unenc**a**psulated adj

» Organ-confined disease, by itself, does not discriminate[5] men who are expected to progress by PSA[6] from those who are not. Bladder carcinoma in situ is characterized by poorly differentiated transitional cell carcinoma[7] confined to the urothelium[8]. Nearly half of the patients treated for apparently localized breast cancer develop metastatic disease.

Use **organ-confined** tumor / disease / carcinoma / cancer • capsule[9]-/ specimen-/ nonorgan-**confined** • **to be confined** to the liver[10] • **localized** breast cancer[11] / disease / mesothelioma • **localized** metastases / prostate cancer • **encapsulated** tumor / bacteria[12] • degree of / evidence of **encapsulation**

organbegrenzt
lokal begrenzt[1] verkapselt[2] Kapsel[3] Ein-, Verkapselung[4] unterscheiden[5] prostataspezif. Antigen, PSA[6] Übergangs-, Transitionalzellkarzinom[7] Urothel, Übergangsepithel[8] auf d. Kapsel beschränkt[9] auf d. Leber beschränkt sein[10] lokal begrenztes Mammakarzinom[11] Kapselbakterien[12]

9

General Oncology   MEDICAL SCIENCE 431

carcinoma-in-situ n term, abbr **CIS** → U98-2   rel **focal involvement**[1] n term

an intraepithelial [iː] lesion characterized by cytologic changes associated with invasive carcinoma but limited to the epithelial lining [aɪ] and without histologic evidence of extension to adjacent structures

carcinomatous[2] adj term • **carcinoid**[3] adj & n • **focus**[4] n, pl **foci** [foʊsaɪ] → U89-3

» CIS is presumed to be the histologically recognizable precursor[5] of invasive carcinoma, i.e. a localized stage at which it is still curable. Bronchioloalveolar cell carcinoma, a subtype of adenocarcinoma, is a low-grade lesion representing about 2 % of cases of bronchogenic carcinoma. Focal areas of induration indicate malignant rather than benign prostatic growth.

Use bladder / vaginal [dʒ]/ ductal[6] [ʌ]/ lobular[7] / diffuse / high-grade[8] **CIS** • sarco/ adeno/ cysto [sɪ]/ terato/ chorio**carcinoma** [k] • localized / small-cell lung[9] / squamous [eɪ] cell **carcinoma** • hepatocellular / prostate or prostatic[10] **carcinoma** • **carcinoma of the** cervix [sɜː]/ breast[11] [e] • **carcinoma of the** head of the pancreas / prostate[10] • **carcinomatous** lesion / invasion • **carcinoid** malignancy[12] / tumor[12] / syndrome[13] • **focal** findings[14] / features[15] [iː]/ lesion[16] / growth • **focal** nodular hyperplasia / infection[17] • tumor / metastatic **focus** • multiple / microscopic **foci** • uni/ multi[18]/ non**focal**

Carcinoma in situ, präinvasives K., Oberflächenkarzinom
herdförm. Befall[1] karzinomartig, karzinomatös, krebsig[2] karzinoid, krebsartig; Karzinoid[3] Herd, Fokus[4] Vorläufer[5] intraduktales C.i.s.[6] lobuläres C.i.s.[7] hochgradig differenziertes C.i.s.[8] kleinzelliges Lungenkarzinom[9] Prostatakarzinom[10] Mammakarzinom[11] Karzinoid[12] Karzinoidsyndrom[13] Herdbefall[14] Herdsymptome[15] herdförmige Läsion[16] Herd-, Fokalinfektion[17] multifokal[18]

10

tumor spread [e] or **extension** n term   rel **route**[1] [raʊt‖ruːt] n

proliferation of cancer cells either locally into adjacent tissues[2] or to distant sites via blood or lymph vessels

spread - spread - spread[3] [spred] v irr • **extend**[4] v • **extent**[5] n

» Some metastases reveal [iː] tumor spread of a single lineage [lɪnɪədʒ] to subdural tumor nodules. Has the tumor spread beyond the confines [aɪ] of resection[6]? Grading and staging of these sarcomas by histologic criteria, location, and metastatic spread[7] have prognostic value. Follicular thyroid [aɪ] cancers have a tendency to spread by the hematogenous route[8] to the lungs, skeleton, and liver.

Use local / microscopic / diffuse / hematogenous[9] **tumor spread** • primary / extravesical / extent of[10] **tumor spread** • direct / malignant or neoplastic / local nodal[11] / regional [iːdʒ] **extension** • extracapsular / extramural / extraprostatic **extension** • disease / tumor[12] / wound **extent** • lymphatic[13] **route**

Tumorausbreitung
Weg, Route[1] angrenzendes/ benachbartes Gewebe[2] s. ausbreiten[3] s. ausdehnen, erstrecken[4] Ausdehnung, Größe, Grad[5] Resektionsgrenzen, -ränder[6] Metastasierung[7] Blutbahn[8] hämatogene Metastasierung[9] Ausmaß d. Tumorausbreitung[10] lokaler Lymphknotenbefall[11] Tumorausdehnung, -größe[12] Lymphweg[13]

11

invasion [ɪnveɪʒᵊn] n term   rel **infiltration**[1] n term

local spread of a malignant neoplasm by infiltration or destruction of adjacent [ədʒeɪsᵊnt] tissue

(non)invasive[2] adj term • **(non)infiltrative, -ing**[3] adj • **infiltrate**[4] v

» With epithelial neoplasms, invasion signifies infiltration beneath the epithelial basement [eɪ] membrane[5]. Tumor spread is by direct invasion or blood-borne [ɔː] metastases[6].

Use depth[7] / evidence **of invasion** • tumor / neoplastic / vascular[8] / extracapsular **invasion** • local / regional / minimal / deep **invasion** • progressive / primary / secondary **invasion** • **invasive** tendency[9] / lesion / carcinoma[10] • micro/ pre**invasive** • early **invasive** cancer[11] • **noninvasive** cancer / disease • intracapsular / metastatic / malignant **infiltration** • **infiltrative** tumor[12] / lesion / (lung) disease / growth[13]

Invasion
Infiltration[1] invasiv[2] infiltrierend, infiltrativ wachsend[3] infiltrieren, eindringen, durchwachsen[4] Basalmembran[5] hämatogene Metastasen[6] Invasionstiefe[7] Gefäßinfiltration[8] Invasionsneigung[9] invasives Karzinom[10] frühinvasives Karzinom[11] infiltrierender Tumor[12] infiltrierendes Wachstum[13]

12

metastasis [mətæstəsɪs] n term, pl -**ses** [siːz]   syn **secondary tumor** n, **secondaries** n clin pl

(i) a second tumor developing away from the site [saɪt] of the primary tumor (ii) the process by which cancer cells spread via the blood, lymph vessels or CSF[1] to distant organs

(micro/ non)metastatic[2] adj term • **metastasize**[3] v • **metastasectomy**[4] n

» The most common cause of this type of anemia is carcinoma metastasizing to bone marrow from primary tumors. Metastases to distant sites, particularly the lungs, occur [ɜː] much later. Bacteremia with metastatic foci of infection may occur, often with startling rapidity. Surgical removal of the primary lesion and resectable secondaries is indicated if technically feasible [iː].

Use to develop/have/present with/detect/exclude or rule out[5] **metastases** • bloodborne [ɔː] or hematogenous[6] / lymphatic[7] / contact[8] **metastases** • axillary / nodal or lymph [lɪmf] node[9] [oʊ] **metastases** • bone or bony[10] / early / brain / drop[8] **metastases** • local / regional[11] / solitary / distant[12] / multiple / widespread/ lung or pulmonary[13] **metastases** • **metastases** to the lungs[13] • **to metastasize** to bone • **metastatic** calcification[14] • resectable **secondaries**

Tochtergeschwulst, Metastase(nbildung), Metastasierung, Absiedelung
Zerebrospinalflüssigkeit, Liquor (cerebrospinalis)[1] metastasierend, metastatisch, Metastasen-[2] M. bilden/ setzen, metastasieren[3] Metastasenexstirpation[4] M. ausschließen[5] hämatogene M.[6] lymphogene M.[7] Kontakt-, Abklatschmetastasen[8] Lymphknotenmetastasen[9] Knochenmetastasen[10] regionäre M.[11] Fernmetastasen[12] Lungenmetastasen[13] Calcinosis metastatica[14]

13

staging [ˈsteɪdʒɪŋ] n term

rel **grading**[1] [ˈgreɪdɪŋ] n term

evaluation of tumors based on the extent of tumor involvement at the primary site (T), lymph node involvement (N) and metastasis (M) each followed by a number starting at 0 for no evident metastasis

stage[2] n & v term • **under/ over/ misstaging**[3] n • **grade**[4] n & v • **graded**[5] adj

» Standardized staging for tumor burden[6] at the time of diagnosis is essential. For stage I and II breast cancer, "lumpectomy" combined with radiation results in 10-year survival. Grading is based on the histologic architecture (size, pleomorphism, mitotic rate, hyperchromatism).

Use TNM[7] (tumor, nodes, metastases) / clinical[8] / surgical[9] **staging** • pathologic / non-invasive / intraoperative **staging** • preoperative / axillary / bladder cancer **staging** • **staging** criteria [ɪɚ]/ system / laparotomy[10] / procedure [siː] • at an early[11] / advanced[12] **stage** • **stage**-specific • tumor / low-/ high-/ histologic malignancy[13] **grade** • accurate[14] / histologic / cytologic(al) / Gleason[15] **grading** • **grading** system / scale [skeɪl]

Staging, Stadieneinteilung
Grading, Bestimmung d. Malignitätsgrades[1] Stadium; d. Stadium bestimmen[2] falsches Staging[3] (Malignitäts)grad; d. Malignitätsgrad bestimmen[4] eingestuft, klassifiziert[5] Tumorlast[6] TNM-Klassifikation[7] klin. Staging[8] Staging-Operation[9] Probelaparotomie, explorative L., Staging-Laparotomie[10] im Frühstadium[11] fortgeschrittenes Stadium[12] histolog. Malignitätsgrad[13] korrektes Grading[14] Gleason-Schema[15]

14

neovascularity [niːoʊvæskjəˈlærəti] n term   syn **neovascularization** n term

sim **tumor angiogenesis**[1] [ˌændʒioʊˈdʒenəsɪs] n term

abnormal proliferation of blood vessels, e.g. in tissue [ʃ||s] not normally containing [eɪ] them

neovascular adj term • **neovasculature**[2] [-ˈvæskjələtʃɚ] n

» Arteriography revealed neovascularity similar to renal [iː] cancer. This is the area of highest neovascularization. To grow, a tumor must generate [dʒe] a neovasculature. Discrete [iː] steps in tumor progression lead to the production of factors by the tumor cells that permit neovascularization to supply [aɪ] nutrients[3] [(j)uː] to the growing tumor.

Use to exhibit[4] / TNM **neovascularity** • **neovascular** glaucoma[5] [ɔː]/ pattern / membrane / vessel[6] / network • high / early / retinal[7] / tumor **neovascularization** • to induce/facilitate/inhibit[8] **angiogenesis** • **tumor angiogenesis** factor[9] • tumor-induced **angiogenesis**

Neovaskularisation
Tumorangiogenese[1] neugebildete Gefäßformationen[2] Nährstoffe[3] Gefäßneubildung aufweisen[4] neovaskuläres Glaukom[5] neugebildetes Gefäß[6] retinale Neovaskularisation[7] d. Angiogenese hemmen[8] Tumorangiogenesefaktor[9]

15

tumor marker n term

substance found in blood or other fluids associated with the presence of a specific tumor, e.g. CEA[1] (carcinoembryonic antigen), AFP (alpha fetoprotein), or PSA[2] (prostate-specific antigen)

» Tumor markers failed to normalize following primary chemotherapy. Mature teratomas[3] do not express[4] tumor markers. Despite their production by tumor cells, hormones are not very reliable [aɪ] tumor markers[5].

Use to serve as a **tumor marker** • serum [ɪɚ]/ prostate / cancer-specific / prepubertal **tumor marker** • strong / particularly sensitive[6] / molecular **marker** • tissue-specific[7] / B cell surface[8] **marker** • recognition / proliferation / radiopaque[9] [-oʊpeɪk] **marker** • surrogate[10] [ɜː ||BE ʌ]/ biological response **marker** • (antibiotic) resistance / predictive or prognostic[11] **marker** • **marker** concentration[12] / status

Tumormarker
karzinoembryonales Antigen[1] prostataspezifisches Antigen[2] reife Teratome, Teratomata adulta[3] exprimieren[4] zuverlässige Tumormarker[5] hochempfindlicher Marker[6] gewebsspezifischer M.[7] B-Zell-Oberflächenmarker[8] strahlendichter Marker[9] Ersatzmarker[10] prognost. Marker[11] Markerspiegel, -konzentration[12]

16

chemotherapy [ˈkiːmoʊ||ˌkiːməˈθerəpi] n term   abbr CHEM

treatment of disease (esp. cancer, infectious and mental disease) with chemical [ke] agents

chemotherapeutic[1] [-ˈpjuːtɪk] adj term • **chemo-** comb • **chemotherapeutics**[2] n

» External radiation with simultaneous [eɪ] chemotherapy (fluorouracil and cisplatin) is preferred as primary therapy. Patients with limited disease in whom local radiation fails may be effectively managed by salvage [ˈsælvɪdʒ] chemotherapy[3]. Precise tissue diagnosis is followed by institution of an appropriate chemotherapeutic combination[4] or radiotherapy.

Use anticancer / high-dose[5] / single-agent [eɪdʒᵊnt]/ second-line **chemotherapy** • aggressive / cytotoxic [saɪtə-] adjuvant [dʒuː] or adjunctive[7] [dʒʌ]/ in home **chemotherapy** • combination[4] / preoperative or neoadjuvant[8] / postoperative **chemotherapy** • **chemotherapy** treatment / regimen[9] [edʒ] cycles • **chemotherapeutic** agents or drugs[2] / protocol / toxicity • **chemo**prevention or -prophylaxis[10] /radiation (therapy)[11] • **chemo**radiotherapy[11] /sensitive /resistant /surgery[12]

Chemotherapie
chemotherapeutisch[1] Chemotherapeutika[2] Notfallchemo(therapie)[3] Kombinations-Chemotherapie[4] hochdosierte Chemotherapie[5] Chemomonotherapie[6] adjuvante C.[7] neoadjuvante C.[8] chemotherapeut. Behandlungsregime[9] Chemoprophylaxe[10] kombinierte Chemo- u. Strahlentherapie[11] Chemochirurgie[12]

17

Tumor Types   **MEDICAL SCIENCE**   433

immunomodulation *n term*

                               rel **immunotherapy**[1] *n term* → U92-34

alteration [ɒː] in the immune response by administration of agents (e.g. interferons[2] [ɪɒ-]) which are able to enhance or suppress the body's natural defense mechanisms[3], e.g. to inhibit the growth of a tumor

    immunomodulatory or **-ing** *adj term* • **immunomodulator**[4] *n* • **immuno-** *comb*

» Cancer immunotherapy seeks [iː] to evoke[5] [oʊ] effective immune responses to human tumors by administration of monoclonal antibodies[6], immunomodulatory cytokines[7] [saɪtəkaɪnz], autologous or allogeneic [-dʒəniːɪk] immunocompetent cells, and tumor vaccines[8] [æks].

Use cancer / active / (non)specific / passive[9] / adoptive[10] **immunotherapy** • adjunctive[11] / (single-)allergen / venom[12] **immunotherapy** • **immunomodulatory** therapy[1] / cytokines / effects • **immunomodulating** drug[4] / properties[13] • nonspecific[14] **immunomodulators** • **immuno**stimulatory effect /suppression[15] /regulation • **immuno**compromised[16] /deficiency[17] [ɪʃ] /suppressants[18]

Immunmodulation
Immuntherapie[1] Interferone[2] körpereigene Abwehrmechanismen[3] Immunmodulator[4] auslösen[5] monoklonale Antikörper[6] Zytokine[7] Tumorvakzinen[8] passive Immuntherapie[9] adoptive Immuntherapie[10] unterstützende Immuntherapie[11] Serumtherapie[12] immunmodulierende Eigenschaften[13] unspezif. Immunmodulatoren[14] Immunsuppression, Unterdrückung od. Abschwächung d. Immunreaktion[15] abwehrgeschwächt[16] Immundefekt[17] Immunsuppressiva[18]

                                                                                                                  18

Unit 98   Tumor Types
Related Units: **97** Oncology, **86** Histology, **89** Pathology, **84** Genetics, **85** Embryology

polyp [pɒːlɪp] *n term*

                               rel **papilloma**[1] [pæpɪloʊmə] *n term*

tumorlike growth projecting from a mucous membrane into a body cavity e.g. a rectal polyp

    polypoid[2] [pɒːlɪpɔɪd] *adj term* • **polyposis**[3] *n* • **polypectomy**[4] *n*
    • **papillomatous**[5] *adj term* • **papillomatosis**[6] *n* • **-oma** *comb*

» Polypoid tumors may induce peristaltic cramps or varying degrees of intussusception[7]. If the malignant polyp arises in the distal rectum radical resection may not be necessary. Inverted [ɜː] papillomas are benign [bɪnaɪn] tumors that usually arise in the common wall between the nose and the maxillary sinus [aɪ].

Use sessile[8] [aɪ‖ə]/ pedunculated[9] [ʌ]/ nasal / intestinal[10] **polyp** • hyperplastic [haɪpə-]/ malignant / adenomatous [oʊ] **polyp** • cervical[11] [ɜː]/ inflammatory[12] [æ]/ colorectal **polyp** • nonneoplastic[13] / juvenile[14] [dʒuː] **polyp** • familial adenomatous[15] / juvenile / nasal[16] / intestinal **polyposis** • **polypoid** lesion [iːʒ]/ tumor / adenoma / growth[17] • endoscopic[18] / colonoscopic **polypectomy** • intraductal[19] [ʌ]/ inverted[20] [ɜː]/ choroid plexus **papilloma** • cauliflower-like[21] [ɔː]/ laryngeal[22] [dʒ]/ squamous cell[23] **papilloma** • laryngeal / respiratory **papillomatosis**

Polyp
Papillom[1] polyp(en)ähnlich, polypös[2] Polypose, -is[3] Polypenabtragung, Polypektomie[4] papillomatös[5] Papillomatose, -is[6] Intussuszeption, Invagination[7] breitbasiger Polyp[8] gestielter P.[9] Darmpolyp[10] Zervixpolyp[11] entzündlicher P.[12] nichtneoplast. P.[13] juveniler P.[14] familiäre adenomatöse Polypose, Adenomatosis coli[15] Polyposis nasi[16] polypöse Wucherung[17] endoskop. Polypektomie[18] Milchgangpapillom[19] invertiertes P.[20] blumenkohlartiges P.[21] Kehlkopfpapillom[22] Epithelzellpapillom[23]

                                                                                                                  1

squamous (cell) carcinoma [kɑːrsɪnoʊmə] *n term, abbr* **SCC**

                     syn **squamous cancer** [skweɪməs kænˈsɚ] *n term*

malignant tumor of the squamous epithelium [iː]

    carcinomatous *adj term* • **carcinoid** *adj & n* • **carcino-** *comb* → U97-10

» The incidence of squamous cell carcinoma and adenocarcinoma is slightly higher among blacks compared with whites, which is the reverse [ɜː] of the situation for transitional cell carcinoma. Mucosal squamous carcinomas are sensitive to irradiation, especially if they are small and only superficially invasive [eɪ].

Use squamous metaplasia[1] [-pleɪʒ(i)ə]/ (cell) dysplasia [i] • squamous epithelium[2] / intraepithelial lesion • renal[3] (*abbr* RCC)/ clear[4] / (non-)small[5] / basal[6] [eɪ] **cell carcinoma** • embryonal [oʊ]/ transitional[7] / islet[8] [aɪlɪt] **cell carcinoma** • adenosquamous[9] / bronchogenic [dʒe] or bronchial[10] [k] / esophageal [dʒiː] **carcinoma** • gastric / hepatocellular / gallbladder[11] [ɔː] **carcinoma** • colorectal / thyroid [aɪ] **carcinoma** • endometrial [iː]/ poorly differentiated[12] / adrenal **carcinoma** • **carcinoid** tumor[13] / syndrome[14] / cells • bronchial / rectal / gastric / appendiceal[15] [siː] **carcinoid** • **carcinomatous** metastases[16] / meningitis[17] [dʒaɪ]/ changes • **carcino**gen[18] /genic /genesis /sis /lysis

Plattenepithelkarzinom
Plattenepithelmetaplasie[1] Plattenepithel[2] Nierenzellkarzinom, Hypernephrom, hypernephroides K., Grawitz-Tumor[3] klarzelliges Karzinom[4] kleinzelliges K.[5] Basaliom, Basalzell(en)karzinom[6] Übergangs-, Transitionalzellkarzinom[7] Inselzellkarzinom[8] adenosquamöses K.[9] Bronchialkarzinom, Lungenkrebs[10] Gallenblasenkarzinom[11] schlecht differenziertes K.[12] Karzinoid[13] Karzinoid-, Flushsyndrom[14] Appendixkarzinoid[15] Karzinommetastasen[16] Meningitis carcinomatosa, meningeale Metastasierung[17] krebserzeugend, karzinogen, kanzerogen; Kanzerogen, Karzinogen[18]

                                                                                                                  2

sarcoma [sɑːrkoʊmə] n term, pl –as, -ata

rel **carcinosarcoma**[1] *n term*

malignant neoplasm of connective tissue[2] formed by proliferation of mesodermal cells

sarcomatous, -toid[3] *adj term* • **sarcomatosis**[4] *n* • **-sarcoma** *comb*

» Soft tissue sarcomas are relatively radiosensitive. Fibrosarcoma is the second most common sarcoma of soft tissue, and histologic differentiation from benign fibromatoses may be difficult. Mixed tumors (carcinosarcoma, mixed mesodermal [ɜː] tumors) containing both epithelial and connective tissue malignant cells are also encountered [aʊ] in the uterus [juː].

Use soft tissue[5] / osteogenic[6] [dʒe]/ (extraosseous or extraskeletal) Ewing's[7] **sarcoma** • Kaposi's[8] / giant [dʒaɪənt] cell[9] / ameloblastic **sarcoma** • botryoid[10] / endometrial [iː] stromal / undifferentiated[11] **sarcoma** • granulocytic[12] [sɪ]/ medullary / myelogenic **sarcoma** • myeloid[13] [aɪ]/ synovial[14] **sarcoma** • radiation-induced **sarcoma** • **sarcomatous** changes / degeneration[15] • lipo/ fibro/ osteo[6]/ rhabdomyo[16]/ leiomyo**sarcoma** • chondro[17]/ lymphangio**sarcoma**

adenoma [ædˀnoʊmə] n term

rel **adenocarcinoma**[1], **adenosarcoma**[2] *n term*

benign tumor arising from glandular tissue[3] which may cause it to produce abnormal amounts of hormones, e.g. an adenoma of the pituitary [(j)uː] gland

cystadenoma[4] [sɪst-] *n term* • **adenomatous, -oid**[5] *adj* • **adeno-, -adenoma** *comb*

» Adenomas are a premalignant[6] lesion. Enlarging pituitary adenomas may compress the optic chiasm[7] [kaɪæzˀm] and cause headache. Islet [aɪlɪt] cell tumors can be part of the syndrome of multiple endocrine adenomatosis[8] type I. Overall, 53% of the tumors were described as adenomatoid. Adenocarcinoma and large-cell carcinoma resemble each other in their clinical behavior.

Use flat[9] / tubular[10] [(j)uː]/ tubulovillous • villous[11] [ɪ] **adenoma** • follicular[12] / pleomorphic [pliːə-] **adenoma** • renal / pituitary[13] [(j)uː]/ hepatic / islet cell[14] **adenoma** • aldosterone-producing / toxic / true[15] **adenoma** • **adenomatous** polyposis coli[16] [aɪ]/ hyperplasia • **adenomatoid** malformation / tumor[17] • papillary / mucinous[18] [juː] (ovarian) / serous [ɪə] **cystadenoma** • fibro[19] [aɪ] hidr[20] [aɪ]/ micro/ macro**adenoma**

hemangioma [hiːmændʒɪoʊmə] n term

rel **angioma**[1], **angiosarcoma**[2] *n term*

congenital proliferation of vascular endothelium consisting of benign clusters [ʌ] of newly formed blood vessels most frequently noticed in the skin (often forming a birthmark[3])

hemangiosarcoma *n term* • **lymphangioma**[4] [ɪ] *n* • **lymphangio-** *comb*

» Superficial involuting hemangiomas appear as sharply demarcated[5], bright-red, slightly raised [eɪ] lesions with an irregular surface [ɜː] that has been described as resembling a strawberry[6] [ɔː]. Strawberry angiomas will involute after their initial [ɪʃ] growth.

Use cavernous[7] / capillary or strawberry[8] / giant[9] **hemangioma** • choroidal[10] / involuting[11] **hemangioma** • **hemangio**fibroma [aɪ] /blastoma /endothelioma /sarcoma /pericytoma[12] [saɪ] • spider[13] [aɪ]/ retinal / capillary or cherry[8] [tʃ] cavernous[7] **angioma** • cystic [sɪstɪk] **lymphangioma**

hamartoma [hæmɑːrtoʊmə] n term, pl -mata or -s

focal malformation grossly [oʊ] resembling a neoplasm resulting from faulty development in an organ

hamartomatous[1] *adj term* • **hamartomatosis**[2] *n* • **hamartoblastoma**[3] *n*

» Hamartoma is the most common benign lung tumor. Focal nodular hyperplasia, e.g. an adenoma-like hamartomatous lesion, may expand under the influence of oral contraceptives.

Use fetal-renal / polypoid[4] / astrocytic **hamartoma** • pulmonary[5] / chondromatous[6] / iris[7] **hamartoma** • **hamartoma** of the lung[5] • **hamartomatous** polyp / lesion[8] • systemic **hamartomatosis**

Sarkom

Karzinosarkom[1] Bindegewebe[2] sarkomartig, sarkomatös[3] Sarkomatose[4] Weichteilsarkom[5] Osteosarkom[6] (extraskelettales/ extraossäres) Ewing-Sarkom[7] Kaposi-Sarkom[8] Riesenzellsarkom[9] Sarcoma botryoides[10] undifferenziertes S.[11] Chlor(osark)om[12] Myelosarkom[13] Synovialsarkom[14] sarkomatöse Entartung[15] Rhabdomyosarkom[16] Knorpel-, Chondrosarkom[17]

3

Adenom, Epithelioma adenomatosum

Adenokarzinom, Carcinoma adenomatosum[1] Adenosarkom[2] Drüsengewebe[3] Zyst-, Kystadenom, Adenokystom[4] adenomatös[5] prämaligne[6] Chiasma opticum, Sehnervenkreuzung[7] multiple endokrine Adenomatose[8] flaches Adenom[9] tubuläres A.[10] villöses A.[11] follikuläres A.[12] Hypophysenadenom[13] Inselzelladenom[14] reines A.[15] familiäre adenomatöse Polypose, Adenomatosis coli[16] Adenomatoidtumor[17] muzinöses Kystadenom[18] Fibroadenom[19] Schweißdrüsenadenom, Hidr(o)adenom[20]

4

Hämangiom, Haemangioma, gutartiger Blutgefäßtumor

Angiom(a)[1] Angiosarkom[2] Muttermal[3] Lymphangiom[4] scharf begrenzt[5] Erdbeere[6] kavernöses Hämangiom, Kavernom[7] kapillärer Blutschwamm, Haemangioma simplex[8] Riesenhämangiom[9] choroidales Hämangiom[10] Involutionshämangiom[11] Hämangioperizytom[12] Naevus araneus, Stern-, Spinnennävus[13]

5

Hamartom, gutartige (Bindegewebs)fehlbildung

hamartomartig, hamartomatös[1] Hamart(omat)ose[2] Hamartoblastom, malignes Hamartom[3] polypöses H.[4] Hamartoma pulmonum[5] Hamartochondrom[6] Irishamartom, Lisch-Knötchen[7] hamartomartige Läsion[8]

6

Tumor Types MEDICAL SCIENCE 435

myxoma [mɪksoʊmə] *n term*

benign tumor derived from connective and stromal tissue that resembles primitive mesenchymal tissue

myxomatous[1] *adj term* • **myxoid**[2] [mɪksɔɪd] *adj* • **myxo-** *comb*

» Myxoma frequently occurs [ɜː] intramuscularly [ʌ] and in the jaw [dʒɒː] bones. These clicks in mid or late systole [ɪ] indicate myxomatous changes in the mitral [aɪ] valve [æ].

Use cardiac / atrial [eɪ]/ ventricular / intracavitary / sporadic[3] **myxomas** • **myxoid** liposarcoma[4] / neurofibroma • **myxomatous** transformation / degeneration [dʒ] • **myxomatous** material / tissue[5] • **myxo**lipoma[6] /sarcoma[7] /fibroma[8] /chondroma[9] [k]

Myxom
schleimbildend, schleimig, myxomatös[1], myxomähnlich[2] vereinzelte Myxome[3] myxoides Liposarkom[4] myxomatöses Gewebe[5] Myxolipom[6] Myxosarkom[7] Myxofibrom[8] Myxochondrom[9]

7

fibroma [faɪbroʊmə] *n term*   *syn* **fibroid (tumor)** [faɪbrɔɪd t(j)uːmɚ] *n term*

benign neoplasm derived [aɪ] from fibrous [faɪbrəs] connective tissue

fibromatous[1] *adj term* • **fibromatosis**[2] *n* • **fibromyoma**[3] *n* • **fibro-** *comb*

» Subungual [ʌ] or periungual fibromas are more common in the toes. Tumors of the abdominal wall are quite common but most are benign, e.g. lipomas, hemangiomas, and fibromas.

Use (non)ossifying[4] / nonosteogenic [dʒe]/ cystic[5] [sɪstɪk] **fibroma** • ameloblastic / ovarian[6] / chondromyxoid [ɪ] **fibroma** • periungual[7] / hard[8] / soft[9] **fibroma** • neuro[10]/ osteo/ angio**fibroma** • uterine[3] / serosal / intramural **fibroid** • palpable / prolapsed[11] **fibroid** • **fibroid** enlargement of the uterus[3] • plantar[12] [æ]/ gingival[13] [dʒ] **fibromatosis** • **fibro**adenoma /sis /tic /blast /myalgia[14] [maɪældʒ(ɪ)ə] /sitis[14] [aɪ]

Note: Although they are no fibroid tumors, uterine myomas are often incorrectly referred to as **fibroids** in medical jargon.

Fibrom(a), Bindegewebegeschwulst
fibromartig, -atös[1] Fibromatose, -sis[2] Fibromyom[3] (nicht-)ossifizierendes Fibrom[4] Fibroma cysticum[5] Ovarialfibrom[6] periunguales F., Koenen-Tumor[7] Fibroma durum, hartes F.[8] Fibroma molle, weiches F.[9] Neurofibrom[10] Myoma in statu nascendi[11] Plantarfibromatose, Morbus Ledderhose[12] Fibromatosis gingivae, fibröse Gingivahyperplasie[13] Fibromyalgie, Fibrositissyndrom[14]

8

myoma [maɪoʊmə] *n term*   *rel* **leiomyoma**[1] [laɪə-], **rhabdomyoma**[2] [ræbdə-] *n term*

benign tumor of smooth [uː] (leiomyoma) or striated [aɪeɪ] muscle[3] (rhabdomyoma)

myomatous[4] *adj term* • **myomatosis**[5] *n* • **myom-** *comb*

» Myoma is the most common benign neoplasm of the female [iː] genital [dʒe] tract. Full-scale dilation [eɪ] and curettage under anesthesia [iː] is recommended in cases of cervical stenosis or when endometrial [iː] polyps, submucous myomas[6], or uterine cancer is suspected.

Use uterine[7] [juː]/ cervical [sɜːr-]/ degenerating [dʒe] **myoma** • subserous[8] [ɪɚ]/ asymptomatic **myoma** • pedunculated[9] [ʌ]/ submucous [juː] **leiomyoma** • **myomatous** uterus[10] / enlargement[11] • cardiac[12] **rhabdomyoma** • **myom**ectomy[13]

Myom
Leiomyom, Myoma laevicellulare[1] Rhabdomyom, M. striocellulare[2] quergestreifte Muskulatur[3] myomatös[4] Myomatose[5] submuköse Myome[6] Uterusmyom, M. uteri[7] subseröses M.[8] gestieltes Leiomyom[9] Uterus myomatosus, multiple Uterusmyome[10] myomatöse Vergrößerung[11] Rhabdomyom d. Herzens[12] Myomektomie, Myomenukleation[13]

9

lymphoma [lɪmfoʊmə] *n term*

rel **lymphosarcoma**[1] *n term*

broad term for ordinarily malignant neoplasms of lymphoid and reticuloendothelial tissues presenting as apparently circumscribed solid tumors composed of cells that appear primitive or resemble lymphocytes

lymphomatoid[2] *adj term* • **lympho(sarco)matous**[3] *adj* • **lympho-** *comb*

» Lymphomas are the most common of the noncarcinomatous malignant tumors of the large bowel[4] [aʊ]. In the Middle East, primary small bowel lymphoma is the most common form of extranodal lymphomatous disease. The most common gastric or small bowel cancer in children is lymphoma or lymphosarcoma.

Use malignant[1] / diffuse histiocytic [sɪ] (*abbr* DHL) **lymphoma** • histiocytic or immunoblastic[5] / (non-)Hodgkin's[6] **lymphoma** • Burkitt' lymphoplasmacytic[9] / granulomatous[10] / intestinal **lymphoma** • **lymphomatoid** granulomatosis[10] • **lymphomatous** transformation / deposits / meningitis • follicular / lymphoblastic[8] **lymphosarcoma** • **lymphosarcomatous** nodules

Lymphadenom, Lymphknotenschwellung
malignes Lymphom, Lymphosarkom[1] lymphomähnlich, lymphomatoid[2] lymphomatös[3] Dickdarm[4] immunoblastisches Lymphom[5] (Non-)Hodgkin-Lymphom[6] Burkitt-Lymphom[7] lymphoblastisches Lymphom[8] lymphoplasmozytäres Lymphom[9] Lymphogranulomatose, Morbus Hodgkin[10]

10

98

lipoma [lɪpoʊmə] *n term*   *syn* **fatty** or **adipose tumor** *n clin*
　　　　　　　　　　　　　　rel **liposarcoma**¹ *n term*

benign tumor of adipose tissue² comprised of mature fat cells
lipomatous³ *adj term* • **lipomatosis**⁴ *n* • **lipo-** *comb*

» Lipomas are the most common benign tumors of the chest wall. Large-bowel lipomas are usually asymptomatic but can cause obstruction. Although liposarcomas occur in all body areas, they are most frequent in the retroperitoneum and the lower extremities.

Use epidural / subcutaneous / (non)encapsulated⁵ / retroperitoneal **lipoma** • angiomyo⁶/ mediastinal / colonic **lipoma** • **lipomatous** lesion / carcinoma / nephritis⁷ • myxoid / ple(i)omorphic⁸ / round cell⁹ **liposarcoma** • well-differentiated / dedifferentiated¹⁰ **liposarcoma** • pancreatic¹¹ / pelvic / multiple symmetric¹² / renal sinus **lipomatosis**

(en)chondroma [enkɒːndroʊmə] *n term*   *syn* **true chondroma** *n term*
　　　　　　　　　　　　　　　　　　　rel **osteochondroma**¹,
　　　　　　　　　　　　　　　　　　　myxochondroma² *n term*

benign skeletal tumor derived from mesodermal [ɜː] cells that form cartilage³ [kɑːrtᵊlɪdʒ]
chondromatous⁴ *adj term* • **(en)chondromatosis**⁵ *n* • **chondro-** *comb*

» Benign chondromas are located within the marrow cavity and on x-ray they may appear as lytic [lɪtɪk] lesions with areas of stippled [ɪ] calcification⁶. The common benign bone tumors include enchondroma, osteochondroma, chondroblastoma and chondromyxoid fibroma, all of cartilaginous [ædʒ] origin. Enchondroma is most common in the hand, including the metacarpals and phalangeals [dʒ], and in the proximal end of the humerus [hjuː].

Use periosteal / extraskeletal⁷ / juxtacortical⁸ [dʒʌkstə-] **chondroma** • **chondromatous** hamartoma⁹ • synovial¹⁰ **chondromatosis** • **chondro**malacia [eɪʃ] of the tracheal [k] rings¹¹ /malacia patellae¹² [iː‖aɪ]

schwannoma [ʃwɑnoʊmə] *n term*   *syn* **neurinoma, neurilemmoma** *n term*
　　　　　　　　　　　　　　　　　rel **neurofibroma**¹ [nʊɚəfaɪbroʊmə] *n term*

benign, encapsulated tumor that arises from Schwann cells and includes portions of nerve fibers [aɪ]
ganglioneuroma² *n term* • **neuroblastoma**³ *n* • **neurofibromatosis**⁴ *n*

» Schwannoma is usually solitary and is apt to⁵ be exquisitely painful. Bilateral schwannomas of the eighth cranial nerves [ɜː] are diagnostic of type 2 neurofibromatosis. Most neurofibromas are multiple (Recklinghausen's disease⁶) and consist of thickened nerve sheath⁷ [ʃiːθ] elements. In mononeuropathies, the entire course of the nerve trunk [ʌ] in question should be explored manually for focal thickening or the presence of neurofibroma.

Use acoustic⁸ [uː]/ vestibular⁸ / bilateral / malignant⁹ / true **schwannoma** • ulcerated [ʌ]/ thoracic / plexiform¹⁰ / myxoid **neurofibroma** • **neurofibromatosis** patient / type 1⁶ (*abbr* NF1)/ type 2¹¹ (*abbr* NF2) • von Recklinghausen's⁶ / type I⁶ / type II¹¹ / classic **neurofibromatosis**

glioma [glaɪ‖glioʊmə] *n term*   *rel* **glioblastoma**¹,
　　　　　　　　　　　　　　　astrocytoma² [æstrəsaɪtoʊmə] *n term*

various histologic types of tumors derived from the interstitial tissue of the brain or the spinal cord³ [k]
gliomatous⁴ *adj term* • **gliomatosis**⁵ *n* • **gliosis**⁶ *n* • **glio-, -glioma** *comb*

» Most gliomas of the brainstem⁷ are astrocytomas. Some glioblastomas appear to be radiosensitive, but survival [aɪ] beyond 18 months is uncommon. Astrocytoma is the most common brain tumor of childhood.

Use malignant¹ (supratentorial) / infiltrating / optic (nerve)⁸ / pontine⁹ [-aɪn] **glioma** • indolent / spinal cord / low-grade / brain stem **glioma** • **glioblastoma** multiforme¹⁰ • reactive / astrocytic [sɪ] primary / secondary¹¹ **gliosis** • oligodendroglioma¹² • anaplastic¹⁰ / pilocytic¹³ [aɪ]/ cerebellar / high-grade **astrocytoma**

Lipom, gutartige Fett-(gewebe)geschwulst

Liposarkom¹ Fettgewebe² lipomartig, lipomatös³ Lipomatose⁴ abgekapseltes Lipom⁵ Angiomyolipom⁶ lipomatöse Nephritis⁷ pleomorphes Liposarkom⁸ rundzelliges Liposarkom⁹ entdifferenziertes Liposarkom¹⁰ Lipomatosis pancreatis¹¹ multiple symmetrische Lipomatose¹²

Enchondrom, echtes Chondrom

Osteochondrom¹ Myxochondrom² Knorpel³ chondromatös⁴ Enchondromatose, Dyschondroplasie, Ollier-Erkrankung⁵ stippchenartige Verkalkung⁶ extraossäres Chondrom⁷ juxtakortikales Chondrom⁸ Hamartochondrom⁹ Gelenkchondromatose¹⁰ Tracheomalazie¹¹ Chondromalacia patellae¹²

Schwannom, Neurinom, Neurilemmom

Neurofibrom¹ Ganglioneurom² Neuroblastom³ Neurofibromatose⁴ neigt dazu⁵ Recklinghausen-Krankheit, Neurofibromatosis generalisata, peripherer Typ d. Neurofibromatosis, NF-1⁶ Schwann-Scheide, Neurolemm⁷ Akustikusneurinom⁸ malignes Schwannom⁹ plexiformes Neurofibrom¹⁰ zentraler Typ d. Neurofibromatosis, NF-2¹¹

Gliom

Glioblastom, malignes Gliom¹ Astrozytom² Rückenmark³ gliomartig, gliomatös⁴ Gliomatose⁵ Gliose⁶ Hirnstamm⁷ Optikusgliom⁸ Brückengliom⁹ Glioblastoma multiforme¹⁰ sekundäre Gliose¹¹ Oligodendrogliom¹² pilozytisches Astrozytom¹³

Tumor Types

(malignant) melanoma [məlɪgnənt melənoʊmə] *n term* → U114-3
rel **pigmented mole** [moʊl] *or* **nevus¹** [niːvəs] *n term, pl* **-i** [niːvaɪ]
malignant tumor composed of melanocytes which commonly arises from pigmented moles
(non)melanomatous² *adj term* • **melanotic** *adj* • **melano-** *comb*

» Patients from melanoma-prone [proʊn] families who have dysplastic nevi appear to have a lifetime risk of melanoma approaching 100%. Halo [eɪ] nevi³ are pigmented moles, usually intradermal or compound [aʊ] nevi⁴, surrounded by a ring of depigmented skin⁵. A hairy mole⁶ [oʊ] may be associated with a dermoid or lipomeningocele [-siːl].

Use cutaneous [eɪ]/ nodular malignant⁷ (*abbr* NMM) **melanoma** • superficial spreading⁸ (*abbr* SSM)/ lentigo [aɪ‖iː] maligna⁹ (*abbr* LMM) **melanoma** • acral [eɪ] lentiginous¹⁰ [ɪdʒ]/ disseminated **melanoma** • metastatic / familial **melanoma** • atypical¹¹ / brownish pigmented **mole** • hydatidiform¹² [haɪdə-]/ fleshy¹³ / invasive [eɪ] **mole** • congenital [dʒe] benign acquired / blue¹⁴ **nevus** • spider¹⁵ / junctional⁴ [dʒʌ]/ dysplastic¹¹ [ɪ] **nevus** • giant pigmented *or* bathing [eɪ] trunk¹⁶ [ʌ] **nevus** • epidermal / melanocytic [sɪ]/ port-wine¹⁷ **nevus** • **melano**genesis /sis /sarcoma

Melanokarzinom, malignes Melanom

Pigment-, Muttermal, Nävuszellnävus, N. pigmentosus¹ melanomartig, melanomatös² Halonävus, N. Sutton³ Junktionsnävi/ -nävus⁴ depigmentierter Hof⁵ Haarnävus, N. pilosus⁶ noduläres Melanom⁷ superfiziell spreitendes M., SSM⁸ Lentigo-maligna-M.⁹ akrolentiginöses M.¹⁰ atypischer/ dysplastischer Nävuszellnävus¹¹ Blasenmole¹² Fleischmole¹³ blauer Nävus, N. coeruleus¹⁴ Sternnävus, Naevus araneus¹⁵ Schwimmhosennävus¹⁶ Feuermal, N. flammeus¹⁷
15

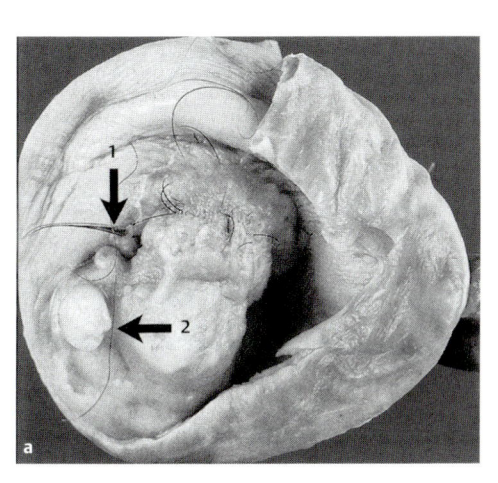

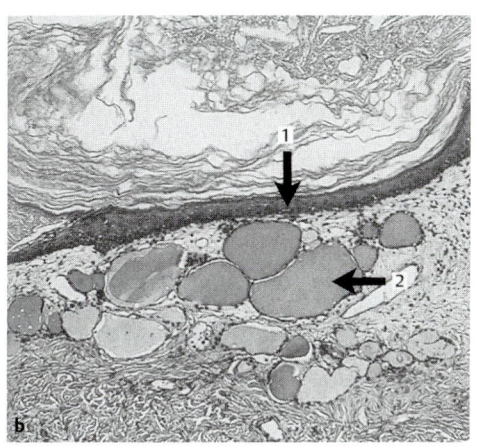

(a) dermoid cyst: hair follicle (**1**), teeth (**2**)
(b) adult teratoma: squamous epithelium (**1**), thyroid tissue (**2**)

---

teratoma *n term*   *rel* **embryonal carcinoma¹, teratocarcinoma²** *n term*
neoplasm [iː] composed of multiple tissues not normally found in the organ in which it arises
teratomatous³ *adj term* • **teratology⁴** *n* • **teratologic** *adj* • **terato-** *comb*

» Teratomas occur most frequently in the ovary [oʊ], where they are usually benign and form dermoid cysts and in the testis, where they are usually malignant. Plasma levels of hCG⁵ are elevated in all men with choriocarcinoma [kɔːrioʊ-] and in one third of those with embryonal carcinomas.

Use malignant / (benign) cystic⁶ [sɪstɪk]/ immature⁷ **teratoma** • mature⁸ / true / sacrococcygeal⁹ [ksɪ] **teratoma** • **teratomatous** cyst⁶ / neoplasm • **terato**gen /genesis /genicity¹⁰ /id⁷ /blastoma¹¹ • **embryonal** cell carcinoma¹ / rhabdomyosarcoma

Teratom, Teratoma

embryonales Karzinom¹ Teratokarzinom² teratomartig, teratomatös³ Teratologie, Lehre v. d. Fehlbildungen⁴ humanes Choriongonadotropin, HCG⁵ Dermoidzyste (d. Ovars), zystisches Teratom⁶ unreifes T., embryonales Teratom, Teratoid⁷ reifes Teratom, T. adultum⁸ Steißteratom⁹ Teratogenität¹⁰ Teratoblastom¹¹
16

---

dermoid (cyst) [dɜːrmɔɪd sɪst] *n term*   *rel* **epidermoid (cyst)¹** *n term*
tumor consisting of displaced ectodermal structures along lines of embryonic fusion [fjuː]; the wall is formed of epithelium-lined connective tissue and contains skin appendages², keratin, sebum³ [iː], and hair
dermoidectomy⁴ *n term* • **mucoepidermoid** [mjuːkoʊ-] *adj*

» Malignant change is rarely encountered [aʊ] in dermoid cysts. Dermoid cysts in the neck do not move with swallowing⁵. Similar to epidermoid tumors, intracranial [eɪ] dermoid tumors form cysts which contain skin appendages such as hair follicles or sebaceous [eɪʃ] glands⁶.

Use ovarian / orbital⁷ / intracranial / upper bulbar⁸ [ʌ] **dermoid** • **dermoid** tumor • ovarian⁹ / degenerative / epidermoid inclusion¹⁰ [uː] cyst • **epidermoid** carcinoma¹¹ • **mucoepidermoid** carcinoma / tumors¹²

Dermoid(zyste)

Epidermoid(zyste)¹ Hautanhangsgebilde² Talg, Sebum³ Dermoidentfernung, -exzision⁴ beim Schlucken⁵ Talgdrüsen⁶ Orbitadermoid⁷ epibulbäres Dermoid⁸ Ovarialzyste⁹ epidermale Einschlusszyste¹⁰ Plattenepithelkarzinom¹¹ Mukoepidermoidtumoren¹²
17

MEDICAL SCIENCE — Radiology

Unit 99 Radiology
Related Units: 82 Biochemical Elements, 106 Fractures, 118 Diagnostic Procedures, 141 Fracture Management, 97 Oncology

radiology [reɪdɪɒːlədʒi] *n term*

use of x-rays [eks reɪz], radioactive tracers[1] [eɪz] and high-energy radiation for diagnosis or treatment

radiologic(al) *adj term* • **radiologist**[2] *n* • **radio-** *comb*

» Review the radiology records[3] for recent exposure to nephrotoxic contrast agents.

Use diagnostic[4] / interventional **radiology** • **radiology** department / suite[5] [swiːt] / **radiologic** evaluation[6] / appearance [ɪə] / findings[7] [aɪ]/ diagnosis / sign / study / technologist[8] [knɒː] • **radio**protective clothing[9] /active rays

radiation [reɪdɪeɪʃᵊn] *n term*   *sim* **irradiation**[1] *n term*

(i) radiant energy or beam [iː] (ii) emanation[2] of rays (iii) irradiation

ray[3] [reɪ] *n* • **radiant**[4] *adj* • **radiate**[5] [reɪdɪeɪt] *v*

» The gonads, blood cells, and cancer cells are particularly sensitive[6] to radiation. The radiation is delivered[7] in a single session.

Use background / ionizing [aɪə]/ annihilation[8] / beta [eɪ‖iː]/ corpuscular [ʌ] / electromagnetic / scattered[9] / hetero-/ homogeneous [dʒiː]/ K-/ L-**radiation** • **radiation** sickness[10] / dose / dosimetry / energy /-induced / protection[11] / x- or roentgen [e]/ gamma / soft[12] / ultrahard [ʌ]/ ultraviolet **rays** • **radio**therapy[13] /biology /-labeled[14] [eɪ] /curable[15] /pharmaceuticals[16] [suː] /responsive /mimetic[17] /immunoassay

radiograph *n term* → U118-18f

   syn **radio-** or **roentgenogram** *n term*, **x-ray (film)** *n clin*

record or image produced on exposed[1] and processed film by radiographic means

radiography *n term* • **radiographic(ally)** *adj/adv* • **x-ray**[2] *v* • **radiographer**[3] *n, abbr* RAD

» A followup contrast radiograph obtained 7 months later was unremarkable[4]. This lesion [liːʒᵊn] cannot be visualized by x-ray. This radiographic pattern is diagnostic of bacterial [ɪə] infection.

Use to take[5] **an x-ray** • AP / PA[6] / lateral[7] **chest x-ray** • **x-ray** unit[8] / attenuation[9] / burn • GI[10] / radiographic / (lateral) skull[11] / plain[12] (abdominal) **film** • double contrast[13] **radiography** / panoramic / oblique [iː] lateral jaw / cephalometric / bite-wing[14] / lateral decubitus[15] **radiograph** • **radiographic** studies / image / evidence[16] / features [iː] / **radiographically** benign [aɪn]/ not determined[17] / mistaken for

irradiate [ɪreɪdɪeɪt] *v term*   *sim* **bombard**[1] *v term*

to expose the whole body or specific target tissues[2] to radiant energy[3]

irradiation[4] *n term* • **irradiated** *adj* • **post-irradiation** *adj*

» Irradiation alone will only produce a temporary response[5]. Lacking other options [ɒːpʃ-], the blood products from family members should always be irradiated.

Use heavily [e]/ selectively **irradiated** • **irradiated** tissue / food[6] / site / volume • elective / adjuvant / high-dose / total body[7] / grid[8] / ionizing / heavy ion [aɪən]/ beta-/ total nodal[9] (*abbr* TNI) / x-**irradiation** • **irradiation** therapy / field[10]

beam [biːm] *n & v term*

(n) unidirectional emission of electromagnetic radiation or particles from the x-ray tube

beamer[1] *n term* • **beam-splitter**[2] *n*

» AP x-rays were taken with a horizontal x-ray beam and the patient lying on the affected side.

Use to angle [æŋgl] the[3] **beam** • x-ray / divergent [ɜːrdʒ] **beam** • **beam** quality / diameter [daɪæ-]/ restrictors[4] / hardening[5] /-splitting mirror[2] • **external beam radiotherapy**[6]

Radiologie
radioaktiv markierte Substanzen, Tracer[1] Radiologe/-in[2] Röntgenberichte[3] Röntgendiagnostik[4] Röntgenbereich[5] radiol. Abklärung[6] Röntgenbefund[7] radiolog. techn./ Röntgenassistent(in)[8] Strahlenschutzkleidung[9]

1

(i) & (ii) Strahlung
(iii) Bestrahlung
Bestrahlung[1] Ausstrahlung, Emanation[2] Strahl[3] strahlend[4] (aus)strahlen[5] empfindlich[6] verabreicht[7] Annihilations-, Vernichtungsstrahlung[8] Streustrahlung[9] Strahlenkater[10] Strahlenschutz[11] weiche Strahlen[12] Strahlentherapie[13] radioaktiv markiert[14] durch Strahlentherapie heilbar[15] Radiopharmaka[16] Radiomimetikum[17]

2

Röntgen(aufnahme, -bild)
belichtet[1] röntgen[2] Röntgenassistent(in)[3] unauffällig[4] Röntgenaufnahme machen[5] pa-Aufnahme d. Thorax[6] seitliches Thoraxröntgen[7] Röntgenanlage[8] Strahlungsschwächung[9] Magen-Darm-Röntgen[10] Schädelröntgen[11] Leeraufnahme[12] Doppelkontrastdarstellung[13] Bissflügelaufnahme[14] Röntgenaufnahme in Seitenlage[15] radiolog. Nachweis[16] radiolog. nicht nachgewiesen[17]

3

bestrahlen
beschießen[1] Zielgewebe[2] Strahlungsenergie[3] Bestrahlung[4] vorübergehende Wirkung[5] bestrahlte Lebensmittel[6] Ganzkörperbestrahlung[7] Siebbestrahlung[8] Bestrahlung aller Lymphknotengruppen[9] Bestrahlungsfeld[10]

4

Strahl(enbündel);
(aus)strahlen
Beamer[1] Strahlentrennraster[2] Strahl richten (auf)[3] Streustrahlenraster[4] Strahlenhärtung[5] externe Hochvoltstrahlentherapie[6]

5

Radiology MEDICAL SCIENCE 439

collimation n term
(i) restricting the x-ray beam to a given area by elimination of scattered radiation and backscatter[1] (ii) in nuclear medicine, restricting the detection of emitted radiation from a given area of interest
collimate[2] v term • **collimator**[3] n • **collimated** adj
» The so-called gamma knife [naɪf] delivers collimated radiation through multiple portals[4] that converge [-vɜːrdʒ] on the target.
Use x-ray / fixed cone / pinhole[5] / variable aperture[6] [æpətʃɚ] **collimator** • **collimation** system / restrictions

Strahlenfokussierung, Kollimation
Rückstreuung[1] kollimieren[2] Kollimator[3] Bohrungen[4] Einlochkollimator[5] Mehrlochkollimator[6]

6

radiation exposure [ɪkspoʊʒɚ] n term   rel **radiation burn**[1] [bɜːrn] n term
short-term diagnostic, therapeutic [pjuː] or accidental contact with ionization produced by x- or gamma rays
(un)exposed adj term • **expose** v • **overexposure**[2] n
» Exposure of the whole body to approx. 10,000 rad (100 gray) causes neurologic [ʊɚ] and cardiovascular breakdown and is fatal [eɪ] within 24 hs. Though this procedure might be an atttractive alternative, radiation exposure to the fetus would be unavoidable.
Use to receive / to rule out[3] / acute / lethal [liːθəl]/ natural **radiation exposure** • massive / excessive **exposure** • **exposure** time[4] / rate / to radiation / to sunlight / to toxins • **radiation** detector[5] / absorbed dose / effects / hygiene[6] [haɪdʒiːn]/ dermatitis [aɪ]/ caries

Strahlenexposition, Strahlenbelastung
akute Strahlenschädigung[1] Strahlenüberdosis[2] Strahlenexposition ausschließen[3] Expositions-, Durchleuchtungs-, Belichtungszeit[4] Strahlungsdetektor[5] Strahlenhygiene[6]

7

fluorescence [-esəns] n term   sim **phosphorescence**[1] n term
emission of radiation by a substance exposed to a shorter wavelength radiation as long as the stimulus is present; in phosphorescence emission persists for a time after removal of the stimulus
fluorescent adj term • **fluoresce**[2] [-res] v • **fluoroscopic** adj • **fluoro-** comb
» Fluoroscopic examination demonstrated a smoothly rounded outpouching[3] [aʊtʃ] in the midline. The passage of contrast material is monitored by fluoroscopy.
Use **under fluoroscopic** control or guidance[4] [aɪ] • **fluoro**scope /scopy[5] /meter /(photo)metry[6] /(radio)graphy • **fluorescent** screen[7] • videotape **fluoroscopy** • x-ray[8] **fluorescence**

Fluoreszenz
Phosphoreszenz[1] fluoreszieren[2] gleichmäßig abgerundete Ausstülpung[3] unter fluoroskop. Kontrolle[4] (Röntgen)durchleuchtung[5] Fluorometrie[6] Leuchtschirm[7] Röntgenfluoreszenz[8]

8

radiation dose [doʊs] n term
amount of ionizing radiation of the therapeutic dosage and the penetrating power[1] of x-rays
dosimetry[2] n term • **dosimeter** n • **dosimetric** adj
» The dose delivered to the target volume and the relative dose distribution[3] within the irradiated volume were measured.
Use body / threshold[4] [θrɛʃʰoʊld]/ peak [iː]/ surface[5] / organ[6] / tissue[7] **dose** • breast [e]/ total lung / gonadal or genetically [dʒen-] significant[8] (abbr GSD) / negligible[9] [-dʒəbl] **dose** • absorbed **dose index** • **dose** rate / reduction / equivalent[10] (abbr DE) /-dependent • radiation / film **dosimetry**

Strahlendosis
Eindringtiefe[1] Dosimetrie[2] Dosisverteilung[3] Schwellendosis[4] Oberflächendosis[5] Organdosis[6] Gewebedosis[7] Gonaden-/ genetisch signifikante Dosis[8] unbedeutende Dosis[9] Äquivalentdosis, Dosisäquivalent[10]

9

roentgen-equivalent-man n term, abbr **rem**
   sim **(radiation) absorbed dose**[1] n term, abbr **rad**
dose of ionizing radiation producing the same effect in man as one roentgen of x- or gamma rays; in the SI nomenclature the rad has been replaced by the gray[2] (Gy; 1 rad = 0.01 Gy) and the rem by the sievert[3] (Sv; 1 rem = 0.01 Sv)
» For x-ray or gamma radiation, rems, rads and roentgen are virtually[4] [vɜːrtʃʊəli] the same, but for particulate radiation[5] emitted from radioactive materials these units may differ widely.

REM (Einheit für Äquivalentdosis)
Rad, rd (Einheit für Energiedosis)[1] Gray[2] Sv[3] nahezu[4] Teilchenstrahlung[5]

10

MEDICAL SCIENCE

radiopaque [-oʊpeɪk] or -dense adj term
opposite **radiolucent**[1] [-luːsənt] adj term

exhibiting relative opacity[2] [oʊpæsəti] to, or impenetrability[3] by x-rays or any other form of radiation

radiopacity[4] n term • **radiodensity**[4] n • **radiolucency** n
• **hypo-/ hyper-/ isodense**[5] [aɪ] adj term

» Soft tissue films revealed a radiodense stone. The unenhanced CT scan demonstrated no radiopacity, but the urogram showed a radiolucent area surrounded by the radiopaque urine.

Use **radiopaque** dye[6] [daɪ]/ catheter / foreign body • skeletal **radiodensity** • **radiolucent** zone[7] / (filling) defect[8] / mass / band / line

visualize [vɪʒ(u)əlaɪz] v   sim **delineate**[1], **demarcate**[2], **delimit**[2], **outline**[3] v

visualization[4] n term • **delineation**[4] n • **demarcation**[5] n • **outline**[6] n

» MRI and CT can visualize neighboring [eɪ] tumor when present. Renal stones were visualized on ultrasonography. Multiple foci [foʊsaɪ] are best visualized by MRI.

Use to allow (for)/permit/provide/ensure [-ʃʊɚ]/prevent/enhance[7] **visualization** • poor / excellent / direct / radiographic[8] / endoscopic / fetal [iː] **visualization** • adequately / clearly / readily[9] [e] **visualized** • distinctly[10] **outlined**

artifact also spelled **artefact** n term   rel **aliasing**[1] [əlaɪəsɪŋ] n term

an artificial finding (esp. in radiographic imaging or histologic specimens[2]) caused by the technique used rather than by the sample[3] or tissue studied

artifact-free adj term • **artifactual**[4] or BE **artefactitious** adj

» Take abdominal x-rays before performing peritoneal lavage [-ɑːʒ] as the procedure tends to produce artifacts. Sources of technical [k] artifacts[5] are collimator shifting and tube uncoupling[6] [ʌ].

Use motion or movement / muscle tension / eye twitching[7] [tʃ]/ EEG / pacemaker[8] [eɪs] **artifact** • **artifactually** distorted[9]

(image) resolution n term   syn **resolving power** n

measure [eʒ] of the degree to which the eye, lens or imaging device [-aɪs] can distinguish or display[1] detail, e.g. the perception[2] of adjacent[3] [ədʒeɪsᵊnt] objects as separate

high-resolution[4] adj term

» MRI has superior [ɪɚ] resolution and is relatively artifact-free. Problems of CT of the pituitary include artifacts due to bone and dental amalgam and limited soft tissue resolution[5].

Use to increase / high / good / contrast[6] / spatial[7] [eɪʃ] **resolution** • **resolution** matrix [eɪ]/ of borders[8] • **high-resolution** images / CT / contrast / scan / ultrasound [ʌ]

contrast agent [eɪdʒᵊnt] n term   syn **contrast material** or **medium** [iː], pl **-ia** n term

radiopaque material (e.g. barium [eɚ]) used to visualize soft tissues radiographically

contrast-enhanced[1] adj term • **unenhanced**[2] [æ] adj • **double-contrast**[3] adj

» CT scanning and MRI may be useful, with and without contrast. Addition of IV contrast aids recognition of pancreatic necrosis. All but[4] the smallest lesions exhibit contrast enhancement.

Use to inject/instill/excrete [iː] **contrast material** • liquid / water-soluble / IV / swallowed / iodinated[5] [aɪə-]/ radio**contrast agent** • **contrast** administration / study / radiograph[6] / enhancement[7] / substance [ʌ] / dye[8] [daɪ] / enema[9] [enɪmə] • injection of / single / double / saline [seɪlaɪn‖-iːn] bubble[10] [ʌ]/ air **contrast** • **noncontrast** scan

transillumination n term   syn **diaphanoscopy** or **-graphy** [daɪəfənɒː-] n term

passing light through tissues, organs or body cavities to examine them

transilluminate[1] v term • **diaphanoscope**[2] n • **diaphano-** comb

» These lesions do not transilluminate. In infants transillumination of the skull with an intensely bright light may disclose[3] subdural effusions and large cystic defects.

Use area[4] / intensity **of transillumination** • **transillumination of the** breasts [e]/ scrotum / sinuses[5] [aɪ]

---

strahlenundurchlässig, -dicht, radiopak
strahlendurchlässig, radioluzent[1] (Strahlen)undurchlässigkeit, Verschattung, Opazität[2] Undurchdringbarkeit[3] Strahlendichte, -undurchlässigkeit[4] hyperdens[5] radiopaker Farbstoff[6] radioluzenter Bereich[7] strahlendurchlässiger Füllungsdefekt[8]
11

darstellen, sichtbar machen
umreißen, darstellen[1] ab-, begrenzen, sich abheben (von)[2] skizzieren, umreißen[3] Darstellung[4] Ab-, Begrenzung, Grenze[5] Umriss[6] Darstellung verbessern[7] Röntgendarstellung[8] gut sichtbar, deutlich dargestellt[9] scharf umrissen[10]
12

Artefakt
Aliasing, Umklappeffekt[1] histolog. Präparate[2] (Gewebe)probe[3] artifiziell, künstlich erzeugt[4] technisch bedingte A.[5] Röhreninstabilität[6] lidschlagbedingtes A.[7] schrittmacherbedingtes A.[8] artifiziell verzerrt[9]
13

Bildauflösung, Auflösungsvermögen
(an)zeigen, darstellen[1] Wahrnehmung[2] anliegend[3] hochauflösend[4] Weichteilauflösung[5] Kontrastauflösung[6] räuml. Auflösung[7] Randschärfe[8]
14

Kontrastmittel
kontrastverstärkt[1] ohne Kontrastverstärkung[2] Doppelkontrast-[3] alle außer[4] iodiertes/ iodhaltiges Kontrastmittel[5] Kontrastaufnahme[6] Kontrastverstärkung[7] Kontrastfärbemittel[8] Kontrasteinlauf[9] Kochsalzbläschen-Kontrast[10]
15

Diaphanoskopie, Transillumination, Durchleuchtung
durch-, aufleuchten[1] Durchleuchtungsgerät, Diaphanoskop[2] zeigen, aufdecken[3] Durchleuchtungsfeld[4] Nebenhöhlendurchleuchtung[5]
16

Radiology MEDICAL SCIENCE 441

scintigraphy [sɪntɪ-] n term   rel **scintigram** or **scintiscan**[1] n term

imaging procedure employing IV injection of a radionuclide[2] [aɪ] with an affinity for the organ or tissue of interest to determine the distribution of the radioactivity with an external scintillation detector[3]

scintillation[4] n term • **scintillating** adj • **scinti-** comb

» Serial [ɪɚ] scintiscans[5] of the right upper quadrant were obtained.

Use stress[6] / rest[7] / perfusion / gated blood pool[8] / sequential[5] / thallium / lympho-/ hepatobiliary[9] **scintigraphy** • **scintigraphic** assessment / study • **scintillating** scotoma[10] • **scintillation** camera[11] / counter[3]

Szintigrafie
Szintigramm[1] Radionuklid[2] Szintillationsdetektor, -zähler[3] Szintillation, kurzlebige Lumineszenz[4] Serienszintigramme[5] Funktionsszintigrafie[6] statische Sz.[7] Blutpoolsz.[8] Chole-, Gallenwegssz.[9] Flimmerskotom[10] Gammakamera[11]   17

scan n & v term   sim **scanning**[1] n term

(n, i) short for scintiscan (ii) any image, record, or data obtained by scanning (v) to examine systematically with a sensing device[2] (e.g. an electron beam)

scanner[2] n term • **scanography**[1] n

» Encapsulated[3] abscesses are characterized by a faint[4] [eɪ] ring on the unenhanced scan.

Use bone / brain **scan** •(un)enhanced / perfusion (lung)[5] / total body **scan** • **scan** width[6] / field • ultrasound / (positive) radionuclide / Meckel / ventilation-perfusion / multiplanar [eɪ]/ color[7] **scan** • whole body[8] / (supercam) scintillation[9] / ultrasonic **scanner**

Scan(-Aufnahme), Szintigramm; scannen, abtasten
Scan(ning), Abtastung, Szintigrafie[1] Abtastgerät, (Szinti)scanner[2] abgekapselt[3] blass, undeutlich[4] Lungenperfusionsszintigramm[5] Scanbreite[6] Farbszintigramm[7] Ganzkörperscanner[8] Szinti(llations)scanner[9]
   18

tomography n term   syn **plano-, strati-, laminagraphy, sectional radiography** n term

taking sectional roentgenograms of serial tissue planes (slices[1]) by advancing the patient in the gantry[2] in small steps (increments[3])

tomograph n term • **tomographic** adj • **tomogram**[4] n

» Tomograms should be obtained for[5] calcifications may be misinterpreted on plain films[6].

Use conventional / computed[7] (abbr CT) or computerized axial[7] (abbr CAT) / reconstruction / positron emission[8] (abbr PET) **tomography** • linear / pluridirectional[9] / narrow angle [ɡ]/ focal plane **tomography** • **tomographic** film / imaging procedure

Tomografie, Schichtaufnahmeverfahren
Schichten[1] Gantry[2] Vorschübe[3] Tomogramm, Schichtaufnahme[4] denn[5] Leeraufnahmen[6] Computertomografie, CT[7] Positronenemissionscomputertomografie, PET[8] mehrdimensionale Tomografie[9]
   19

ionization [aɪənaɪzeɪʃ°n] n term

dissociation[1] of molecules into ions (cations[2] [kætaɪənz], anions[3]), e.g. by subjecting them to ionizing radiation[4]

ion [aɪən] n term • **ionize** v • **(cat/ an/ non)ionic**[5] adj • **(non)ionizing** adj

» Ionizing radiation has sufficient energy to ionize the irradiated material.

Use **ionization** chamber[6] [tʃeɪ]/ density[7] / detector / dose[8] • (ultrashort) **ionizing radiation**[9] • **ionic** contrast material[10] / bond[11] • hydrogen [aɪ]/ hydroxyl / positively charged[12] [tʃɑːrdʒd] **ion** • **ion** exchange[13]

Ionisierung, Ionisation
Aufspaltung[1] Kationen[2] Anionen[3] ionisierende Strahlung[4] (nicht)-ionisch[5] Ionisationskammer[6] Ionisationsdichte[7] Ionendosis[8] ultrakurze ionisierende Strahlung[9] ionisiertes Kontrastmittel[10] Ionenbindung[11] positiv geladenes Ion[12] Ionenaustausch[13]   20

radioactive adj term

spontaneously [eɪ] emitting alpha, beta [eɪ‖iː], or gamma rays

radioactivity[1] n term

» These thrombi [aɪ] can be detected by external scanning if the fibrinogen is labeled[2] [eɪ] with a radioactive material such as iodine-125[3] [aɪədɪn].

Use **radioactive** implants[4] / seeds[4] [iː]/ beads[4] [iː]/ pellets[4] / (labeled) isotopes [aɪ]/ tracer [treɪsɚ] or radiotracer[5] / iodine (abbr RAI) uptake study[6] • induced **radioactivity**

radioaktiv
Radioaktivität[1] markiert[2] Iod-125[3] radioaktive Implantate[4] Radiopharmakon, Tracer[5] Radioiodtest[6]
   21

radionuclide [-n(j)uːklaɪd] n term   sim **radioisotope**[1] [-aɪsətoʊp] n term

artificial or natural radioactive nuclide or isotope of iodine, cobalt, phosphorus, strontium [ʃ], etc. used as tracer substances[2], e.g. to follow the course of the normal substances in metabolism

nuclide n term • **nuclear**[3] adj

» Radionuclide imaging[4] is 90% sensitive, becoming positive within two days after the onset.

Use **radionuclide** angiography [dʒɪɒː] / cystogram[5] / impurity / generator • labeled **radioisotope** • **radioisotope** angiogram / renography[6] / uptake study • **nuclear** medicine[7] / electron / particle[8] / charge[9] [tʃ]/ decay[10] [keɪ]/ imaging / scanner

Radionuklid
Radioisotop[1] Tracer[2] nuklear, Kern-[3] Szintigrafie[4] Blasenszintigramm[5] Radioisotopennephrografie, Nierensequenzszintigrafie[6] Nuklearmedizin[7] Kernteilchen[8] Kernladung[9] radioaktiver Zerfall[10]
   22

radiosensitive *adj term* opposite **radioresistant**[1] *adj term*

readily affected[2] by the effects of radiation; self-renewing cells (e.g. sperm cells) are most susceptible[3] [səsepṭɪbl] while fixed postmitotic [aɪ] cells (e.g. neurons [(j)ʊɚ]) are least [iː] sensitive to radiation

radiosensitivity[4] *n term* • radioresistance *n* • radiosensitizing *adj*

» There was no correlation between tumor grade[5] and radiosensitivity.
Use relative **radiosensitivity** • **radiosensitizing** agent or **radiosensitizer**[6]

strahlenempfindlich
strahlenresistent, -unempfindlich[1] leicht zu schädigen[2] empfänglich, empfindlich[3] Strahlensensibilität[4] Malignitätsgrad[5] Radio-, Strahlensensitizer[6]

23

Unit 100 Medical Statistics
Related Units: 101 Medical Studies & Research

statistics [stətɪstɪks] *n term usu pl*

collection of values, facts or other items [aɪ] of information which are then analyzed, particularly with regard to the probability[1] that the resulting empirical findings are due to chance[2]

statistical *adj term* • **biostatistics**[3] [aɪ] *n* • **statistician** [-tɪʃ*ə*n] *n*

» Current [ɜː] statistics for amputation show improved disease-free survival rates. The statistical risk of recurrence [ɜː] is 50%. The dismal statistics[4] of out-of-hospital cardiac arrest patients may be improved by more aggressive interventions.

Use to interpret **statistics** • inferential[5] / descriptive / vital[6] [aɪ] **statistics** • health / cancer / outcome / mortality[7] / survival[8] / five-year **statistics** • **statistical** analysis / study / evidence[9] / comparison / difference / likelihood[1] [ʊ] / power[10] / genetics • to approach / achieve or reach[11]/be evaluated for **statistical significance**

Statistik
(stat.) Wahrscheinlichkeit[1] Zufall[2] Biostatistik[3] schlechte Statistik[4] Inferenzstatistik[5] (Bevölkerungs)statistik[6] Mortalität(sstatistik)[7] Überleben(sstatistik)[8] stat. Nachweis[9] stat. Teststärke, Power[10] statistische Signifikanz erreichen[11]

1

subject [sʌbdʒekt] *n term*   *sim* **individual** [-vɪdʒʊəl], **patient** [peɪʃ*ə*nt], **case**[1] [eɪ] *n term* → U20-2

object of research, treatment, observation, experimentation, or dissection[2]

» This complication was not seen in young subjects. 41% of subjects were lost to followup[3]. This is the first reported case of increased Tc 99m uptake due to thyroid [aɪ] follicular carcinoma.

Use asymptomatic or healthy or normal / severely [ɪɚ] ill / human / clinical research **subjects** • well-motivated / (non)obese[4] [iːs]/ elderly / control[5] **subjects** • **subject status**[6] [eɪ] / affected[7] / otherwise healthy [e]/ high-risk[8] **individuals** • infected / susceptible[9] [sep]/ untreated [iː] **individuals** • **individual case** management / screening [iː] • **case** study[10] / report / series

Proband, Testperson, Untersuchungsobjekt
Fall[1] Sektion, Obduktion[2] konnten nicht weiter kontrolliert werden[3] fettleibige Probanden[4] Kontrollpersonen[5] Probandenstatus[6] betroffene Personen[7] Risikopersonen[8] anfällige P.[9] Fallstudie, Kasuistik[10]

2

population *n term*   *sim* **cohort**[1], **series**[2] [sɪɚiːz] *sing & pl*, **(sub)group** [ʌ], **subset** *n term*

set of objects, events[3], or subjects in a particular class from which a sample is drawn

» A contemporary[4] watchful waiting[5] population was selected as a control.

Use **population**-based[6] [eɪ] • (non)white / ag(e)ing [eɪdʒɪŋ] / age-matched[7] / community-based / cell **population** • eligible[8] [dʒ]/ female [iː]/ general[9] / normal / pediatric [iː]/ patient / study **population** • placebo[10] [siː]/ prospective / screening / 1930 birth **cohort** • controlled / prospective / small / large / consecutive[11] / autopsy [ɔː] **series**

Population
Kohorte[1] Reihe[2] Ereignisse[3] gleichaltrig[4] mit Surveillance[5] bevölkerungsbasiert[6] in d. gleichen Altersgruppe[7] d. Einschlusskriterien erfüllende P.[8] Allgemeinbevölkerung[9] Placebogruppe[10] konsekutive Patientenserie[11]

3

> **Note:** *Series* is both a singular and plural noun and can be used with a singular verb and the indefinite article, e.g. *a large series is/was …*

sample [æ] *n & v term*   *rel* **sampling**[1] *n term*

representative portion of a population selected for research to achieve statistically significant results

» Selection of low-risk subsets resulted in inadequate sample size[2] [saɪz]. When sample size is calculated, the frequency of the condition to be prevented, the anticipated[3] [tɪs] effectiveness of the treatment thought to be clinically relevant, and variables such as predicted dropouts[4] and crossovers[5] must be taken into account.

Use to draw[6] [ɔː] *a* **sample** • random[7] [æ]/ big / small / representative / (un)biased[8] [aɪ] **sample** • **sample** size • estimated **sample** size[9] • **sampling** error / method[10] / with(out) replacement[11] • (quasi-)random [kweɪzaɪ]/ single or basic[12] / cluster[13] [ʌ]/ stratified[14] / quota [kwoʊ] **sampling**

Stichprobe; S. erheben/ ziehen
Stichprobenerhebung, -entnahme[1] Stichprobengröße, -umfang[2] erwartete[3] Ausfälle, Therapieabbrecher[4] Therapiewechsler[5] S. ziehen[6] Zufallsstichprobe[7] (un)verzerrte S.[8] geschätzter Stichprobenumfang[9] Stichprobenverfahren[10] Stichprobenerhebung mit/ohne Zurücklegen[11] Ziehen e. einfachen Zufallsstichprobe[12] Z. e. Klumpen-/ Cluster-Stichprobe[13] Z. e. geschichteten/ stratifizierten Stichprobe[14]

4

Medical Statistics

parameter n term   syn **variable** n term, sim **trait**¹ [eɪ], **(co)factor**², **phenomenon**³, **indicator**⁴, **index**⁵ n term

a characteristic¹ of a population

uni/ multivariate⁶ adj term • **multifactorial** adj • **variable**⁷ adj inf

» In prostate cancer disease-specific variables are poor discriminants⁸ of general quality of life. Nodal involvement was predictable preoperatively by clinical and histological parameters.

Use biochemical / prognostic or predictive / gross [oʊ] neurological⁹ **parameter** • serologic [ɪə] laboratory / sensitive / suitable [uː]/ single **parameter** • random or chance / (in)dependent¹⁰ / stochastic [kæ]/ baseline clinical **variable** • outcome / binomial [aɪ] or dichotomous¹¹ [daɪkɒːt-]/ ordinal / discrete [iː] **variable** • continuous¹² / intervening [iː]/ quantitative **variable** • growth / prognostic / risk¹³ / predisposing¹⁴ [iː] **factor** • etiologic [iː]/ contributing / complicating **factor**

Parameter, Kenngröße, Variable

Merkmal¹ (Ko)faktor² Phänomen³ Indikator⁴ Index, Kennziffer⁵ uni-/multivariat⁶ variabel, veränderlich⁷ Unterscheidungsparameter⁸ makroskopische neurolog. Variable⁹ (un)abhängige V.¹⁰ dichotome Variable, V. mit 2 Ausprägungen¹¹ stetige V.¹² Risikofaktor¹³ Prädispositionsfaktor¹⁴

5

scale(d) [skeɪld] or **standard score** n term

opposite **raw score**¹ [rɒː skɔːr] n term

statistically referenced score representing the deviation of a raw score from its mean [iː] in standard deviation units

score² v term • **score**³ n • **scoring** n • **scale**⁴ n

» The study group started at a lower pretreatment score than did the placebo arms. Score the findings on a scale of 0 – 2. This is an objective score comprising 5 urodynamic parameters.

Use to assign [əsaɪn] a **score** • age-equivalent / clinical performance **score** • initial prognostic / point or numerical⁵ / percentile rank **score** • symptom / (Gleason) tumor / IQ / achievement [tʃiː] **score** • Apgar⁶ / trauma / Glasgow Coma **score** • **raw score** table (comparison) / grouping / method • **scoring** system⁷ • color / numerical⁷ / self-rating **scale** • **scale** down

Standardwert(e), Z-Wert(e)

Rohwert(e)¹ verzeichnen, erzielen² Wert, Score, Ziffer³ Skala, Maßstab, Schema⁴ Punktezahl⁵ Apgar-Wert, -Score⁶ Punktesystem, -schema⁷

6

incidence [ɪnˈsɪdᵊnˈs] n term   sim **prevalence**¹ [prevᵊləˈns] n term

the number of new cases of a disease in a defined population over a specific period of time

» It is associated with a 15% incidence of fetal [iː] bradycardia. The number of cases of a disease existing in a given population within a specific period [ɪə] of time is termed period prevalence². In low-prevalence populations the ELISA test was less accurate.

Use age-adjusted³ [dʒʌ]/ age-specific / annual / cumulative / cancer **incidence** • increase in / fall in / peak [iː]/ overall⁴ / reported / true⁵ / worldwide **incidence** • **incidence** rate • estimated / HIV / population / smoking / point⁶ **prevalence** • **prevalence** index / rate⁷

Inzidenz, Neuerkrankungsrate

Prävalenz¹ Periodenprävalenz² altersadjustierte I.³ Gesamtinzidenz⁴ wahre Inzidenz⁵ Punktprävalenz⁶ Prävalenzrate⁷

7

rate [reɪt] n term   sim **ratio**¹ [reɪʃ(i)oʊ], **percentage**² [pəˈsentɪdʒ], **proportion**³, **preponderance**⁴ n term

proportion per 1,000 (or 100,000) of the population, e.g. number of births per 1,000 residents⁵

» Alpha interferon has had a 15 – 20 % response rate. Men outnumber women [wɪmɪn] by a 3:1 ratio. The ratio of helper to suppressor (H/S) cells in healthy individuals is about 1.6 to 2.2. This is a sizeable⁶ [aɪ] percentage of cases.

Use crude⁷ [uː]/ standardized / adjusted⁸ **rate** • birth / pregnancy / complication / cure⁹ / death / failure **rate** • recurrence¹⁰ / retreatment / success / 5-year actuarial¹¹ **rate** • odds¹² (abbr OR) / likelihood / risk-benefit / birth-death **ratio** • **percentage** points • calculated / fixed high / large / small **percentage** • male-to-female¹³ [fiːmeɪl] **preponderance**

Rate

Quotient, Verhältnis¹ Prozentsatz² Verhältnis³ Überwiegen, -hang, -gewicht⁴ Einwohner⁵ beträchtlich⁶ rohe Rate⁷ adjustierte R.⁸ Heilungsrate⁹ Rezidivrate¹⁰ 5-Jahresrate¹¹ Chancenverhältnis, Odds Ratio¹² Überhang bei Männern¹³

8

morbidity (rate) n term   rel **mortality (rate)**¹ n term → U89-2; U12-2

proportion of patients in a given population who have a particular disease at a given time

» During colonoscopy polyps can usually be excised with a lower morbidity rate. The mortality rate is the number of deaths divided by the population in which they occur. They assessed mortality adjusted for age² and severity [e] of comorbidity³ at the time of surgery.

Use to predict/reduce/minimize⁴/cause⁵/produce⁵/carry⁵/influence **morbidity** • alcohol-related / asthma [z]/ cardiac / fetal [iː]/ childhood **morbidity** • (peri)operative / long-term / significant or severe [ɪə] or major [meɪdʒə] **morbidity** • minor [aɪ] or low / minimal associated [oʊʃ]/ trivial **morbidity** • crude /5-year / specific / hospital / conditional / infant⁶ / perinatal [eɪ] **mortality rate** • standardized **mortality** rate or ratio⁷ (abbr SMR)

Morbidität(srate)

Mortalität(srate), Sterblichkeit¹ altersadjustierte Mortalität² Grad der Komorbidität/ Zweiterkrankung³ Morbidität gering halten⁴ verbunden sein mit einer Morbidität⁵ Säuglingssterblichkeitsrate⁶ standardisierter Mortalitätsquotient⁷

9

mean [miːn] *n sing & adj term*   *sim* **median**[1] [miːdiən] *n & adj term*

(n) average[2] [ævərɪdʒ] value (usually the arithmetic mean[3] unless otherwise specified) of a sample or population

» Mean time of narcotics use postoperatively was 4.3 days; 72 patients were considered cured [kjʊəd] after a mean of 18 sessions. The median value divides the probability distribution of a random variable in half.

Use sample / population / geometric[4] **mean** • **mean** age / concentration / decrease [iː] • standard error of the[5] **mean** (*abbr* SEM) • **median** followup period[6] / hospital stay

Mittel(wert); mittlere(r)
Median, Zentralwert; median(e/r)[1] durchschnittlich[2] arithmetischer Mittelwert[3] geometrischer M.[4] Standardfehler d. Mittelwerts[5] medianer Nachuntersuchungszeitraum[6]

10

---

percentile [pəsentaɪl] *n term*   *sim* **quartile**[1] [kwɔːr-], **fractile**[2], **decile**[3] [es] *n term*

rank position of an individual in a serial [ɪə] array[4] [əreɪ] of data stated in terms of what percentage of the group (s)he equals [iː] or exceeds [iː]

» About 30% of these children are below the third percentile for height[5] [haɪt]. The men in the quartile with the highest values had a 3 times higher risk of stroke than those in the lowest quartile.

Use above/below the 5th / 95th / growth / age-matched[6] **percentile** • **percentile** curve [ɜː]/ level / rank[7] / for age and sex[8]

Perzentil(e)
Quartil(e)[1] Fraktil(e)[2] Dezil(e)[3] nach Größe geordnete Reihe[4] (Körper)größe[5] altersentsprechende P.[6] Perzentilenrang[7] Alters- u. Geschlechtsperzentile[8]

11

---

frequency [iː] **distribution** [-bjuːʃən] *n term*   *rel* **outlier**[1] [aʊtlaɪɚ] *n term*

statistical description of raw data in terms of the number or frequency of items [aɪ] characterized by each of a series or range of values of a continuous variable

» The distribution of the ratios was non-Gaussian. A reading[2], value or measurement [eɪ] far outside the central range of the data is termed an outlier and is considered to be in error[3].

Use normal *or* Gaussian[4] / standardized normal / binomial [aɪ]/ probability[5] **distribution** • even[6] [iː]/ linear / Student's *or* t-[7] / Poisson / sex / female-to-male [iː] **distribution** • randomly / uniformly[8] **distributed** • **distribution** curve [ɜː]/ coefficient[9] [ɪʃ]/ free test[10]

Häufigkeitsverteilung
Ausreißer[1] Messwert[2] falsch, fehlerhaft[3] Gauß-, Normalverteilung[4] Wahrscheinlichkeitsverteilung[5] gleichmäßige V.[6] Student-, t-Verteilung[7] gleichverteilt[8] Verteilungskoeffizient[9] verteilungsunabhängiger Test[10]

12

---

deviation [diːvieɪʃən] *n term*   *sim* **skew(ness)**[1] [skjuːnəs] *n term*

(i) departure[2] [-tʃɚ] from symmetry of a frequency distribution
(ii) shift[3] away from the normal course or site

deviate[4] [diːvieɪt] *v term* • **skew** *v*

» The standard deviation is the statistical index of the variability within a distribution (the square [skweɚ] root[5] [uː] of the average of the squared deviation from the mean). The median, range, upper quartile and the skewness of chain code variance were most predictive of recurrence [ɜː].

Use standard[6] **deviation** (*abbr* SD) / of the mean (*abbr* SDM) • measure of **skewness** • **skew** distribution[7]

Abweichung
Schiefe[1] Abweichung[2] Verschiebung[3] abweichen[4] Quadratwurzel[5] Standardabweichung[6] schiefe Verteilung[7]

13

---

variance [veəriənts] *n term*   *sim* **variation**[1] [veərieɪʃən] *n term*

(i) variation found between a set of observations
(ii) state of being variable, different, divergent[2] [daɪvɜːrdʒənt]

variant[3] *adj & n* • **variability**[4] *n* • **covariance**[5] *n term*

» Variance is calculated as the square of the standard deviation. Mean pressure responses and measures of variance were calculated. These findings are at variance with[6] those of Bell.

Use analysis of[7] **variance** (*abbr* ANOVA) • coefficient [fɪʃ] of[8] **variation** (*abbr* CV) • intra-/ inter-observer[9] **variance**

Varianz
Variation[1] unterschiedlich[2] abweichend; Abart, Variante[3] Variabilität[4] Kovarianz[5] weichen ab von[6] Varianzanalyse[7] Variationskoeffizient[8] Intra-/ Inter-Beobachter-Varianz[9]

14

---

range [reɪndʒ] *n term*

statistical measure [eɪ] of the variation of values determined by the endpoint values[1]

long-range[2] *adj* • **range**[3] *v term*

» The clinical spectrum of the disease ranges from mild to life-threatening[4] [e]. The plasma concentrations exhibit[5] episodic increases, with values ranging up to 4 pmol/L.

Use broad [ɒː]/ wide [aɪ]/ narrow / in the 80–90% / age / reference[6] / therapeutic[7] [pjuː] **range** • **to range** from A to B / between A and B

Spannweite, Bereich
Extremwerte[1] langfristig[2] liegen, schwanken[3] lebensgefährlich[4] weisen auf[5] Referenzbereich[6] therapeutische Breite[7]

15

Medical Statistics

degrees of freedom *n term*   *abbr* **df**

the number of observations (subjects, test items and scores[1], trials[2] [aɪ], conditions, etc.) minus the number of independent restrictions[3] in the sampling undertaken

» *Patients with stress incontinence had a leak* [iː] *point pressure[4] of 42 cmH$_2$O (P=0.126, df=10).*

confidence interval *n term*   *abbr* **CI** *n term*

statistical measure for the range of uncertainty about the probability of an outcome

» *Actuarial disease-specific survival rates and associated 95% confidence intervals were calculated using the Kaplan-Meier method[1].*

Use **confidence** limit[2] / band / level[3] • disease-free / follow-up **interval**

bias [baɪəs] *n term*   *syn* **systematic error, distortion** [dɪstɔːrʃ°n] *n, rel* **confounder[1]** [aʊ] *n term*

deviation [diːviˈeɪʃ°n] of results from the truth or mechanisms [k] leading to such deviation, e.g. analysis bias, measurement bias, selection bias, withdrawal [-ɒːəl] bias[2], etc.

biased[3] *adj* • **unbiased[4]** *adj* • **confounding** *adj*

» *The common biases of screening are length, lead-time* [iː] *and selection biases. Lead-time bias[5] occurs when the patient is merely [ɪɚ] diagnosed at an earlier time but life expectancy[6] remains unchanged. An extreme [iː] form of length bias is overdiagnosis. The data may be biased.*

Use to minimize/be prone [oʊ] to[7]/reflect **bias** • selection / gender [dʒ]/ information / length / confounding / recall **bias** • **biased** study / sample[8] [æ] • to be **biased** toward children[9] / by personal involvement / related to patient selection • **unbiased** estimator[10] • sampling / standard[11] / systematic / false-positive [ɔː]/ false-negative **error** • **confounding** variable[1]

event [ɪvent] *n term*

experience, incident[1], trait, or clinical condition defined by a binary [aɪ] outcome measure[2]

» *It is not relevant when the underlying event[3] took place. Ovulation or some other natural event causing mild discomfort may be experienced as an abdominal catastrophy.*

Use **event** rate /-driven data[4] / analysis / recorder • simple / certain[5] / (non-)excluding[6] / impossible / complementary **event** • clinical / random[7] / initial [ʃ]/ recurrent[8] / stressful / reportable **event** • perinatal [eɪ]/ negative life / traumatic / precipitating[9] [sɪp]/ isolated [aɪ] **event** • work-related / multicasualty[10] [-ʒʊəlti]/ (pre)terminal [ɜː] **events**

endpoint *n term*   *syn* **primary** [aɪ] **outcome** *or* **event** *n term*

outcome variable used to judge[1] [dʒʌdʒ] the effectiveness of treatment

» *In terms of major endpoints the test drug did not prove superior [ɪɚ] to[2] placebo [siː]. Endpoints examined were semen [iː] analyses, sperm [ɜː] functional assessments[3], and pain scores.*

Use hard[4] / soft[5] / study / valid[6] / primary / secondary / multiple **endpoints** • **endpoint** analysis • clinical / treatment / quality-of-life[7] / overall / long-term[8] **outcome** • favorable [eɪ]/ poor / adverse [ɜː]/ fatal[9] [eɪ] **outcome**

statistically significant *adj term*   *opposite* **insignificant[1]** *adj term*

the statistical probability that a finding is very unlikely the result of chance alone

significance[2] *n term*

» *Raised* [eɪ] *alkaline phosphatase was of no prognostic value, while creatinine reached marginal* [dʒ] *significance[3]. The factor was found to be of significance for tumor recurrence.*

Use highly **significant** • statistically **insignificant** • least **significant** difference[4] (*abbr* LSD) • **significance** level[5] • p-value[6] • prognostic / clinical / borderline[3] **significance**

false [ɔː] **positive** *adj & n term*   *opposite* **false negative[1]** *adj & n term*

test result which wrongly indicates the presence of a disease, condition or finding

» *No false positives were found in the control group[2]. The two false negative results were obtained in normotensive patients[3].*

Use **false positive** error[4] / result [ʌ]/ rate / scan / test / cultures [ʌ] • true[5] **positive** / **negative**

Freiheitsgrade, FG
Werte, Scores[1] Versuche, Untersuchungen[2] Einschränkungen, Restriktionen[3] Blasendruck bei unwillkürlichem Harnabgang[4]   16

Konfidenzintervall, Vertrauensbereich
Kaplan-Meier Schätzung/ Methode[1] Konfidenzgrenze[2] Konfidenzniveau[3]   17

Bias, systemat. Fehler/ Verzerrung
Störgröße, verzerrender Faktor[1] Verzerrung durch abgebrochene Beobachtungen[2] verzerrt[3] unverzerrt[4] Lead-time Bias[5] Lebenserwartung[6] für/auf Biasanfällig sein[7]
verzerrte Stichprobe[8] gegenüber Kindern befangen/ voreingenommen sein[9] erwartungstreue Schätzfunktion[10] Standardfehler[11]
18

Ereignis
Vorfall[1] dichotomer Parameter[2] ursächliches E.[3] ereignisabhängige Daten[4] sicheres E.[5] (nicht) ausschließendes E.[6] zufallsabhängiges E.[7] wiederkehrendes E.[8] auslösendes E.[9] Naturkatastrophen[10]
19

Endpunkt, Zielgröße
beurteilen[1] sich als besser erweisen als[2] Spermiogramme[3] harte Endpunkte[4] weiche E.[5] valide E.[6] Ergebnis einer Lebensqualitätsstudie[7] Langzeitergebnis[8] letaler Ausgang[9]
20

statistisch signifikant
nicht signifikant[1] Signifikanz[2] grenzwertige S.[3] Grenzdifferenz[4] Signifikanzniveau[5] p-Wert[6]

21

falsch-positiv(er Wert)
falsch-negativ(er Wert)[1] Kontrollgruppe[2] bei Normotonikern[3] falsch positiver Fehler[4] richtig positiv/ negativ[5]
22

sensitivity n term   rel **specificity**[1] [spesɪfɪsəti] n term

proportion of individuals with a positive test result for the disease that the test is intended to reveal [iː]

» *The reliability[2] [aɪə] of a diagnostic test is measured by its sensitivity and specificity. The specificity of a screening test is the number of true negative results as a proportion of the total of true negative and false-positive results. The test has a sensitivity of 75% and a specificity of 95%.*

Use 95% / high / moderate / low / lack of[3] **sensitivity** • to increase[4] [iː]/enhance[4] [æ]/ diagnostic **specificity**

Sensitivität
Spezifität[1] Reliabilität, Zuverlässigkeit[2] mangelnde Sensitivität[3] die Spezifität verbessern[4]

23

cut-off or **cutoff (point** or **value)** n term   syn **cut-point, threshold** n term

point or value in an ordered sequence [iː] used to separate these values into two subgroups

» *Test sensitivity and specificity depend on the reference range used, i.e. the cutoff point above which a test is interpreted as abnormal. Many programs use age cutoffs[1] to select potential transplant recipients[2] [sɪp].*

Use sharp[3] / low / subgrouping **cutoff** • a **cutoff** value of 4 ng/mL

Schwellenwert, Grenzwert, Cutoff
Altersgrenzen[1] Transplantatempfänger[2] exakter Grenzwert[3]

24

survival [səˈvaɪvᵊl] n term   sim **survivorship**[1] n term

period between the institution or completion of any procedure and death

survive[2] v • survivor[3] n

» *The limiting factor for survival was the tumor, not age. Children with Hodgkin's disease have a 75% overall survival rate at more than 20 years' followup. Median survival was 11 months.*

Use **survival** rate[4] / time or period[5] / probability / curve / benefit[6] / trial / analysis[7] • **survival** to adulthood[8] / to the 6th decade / to age 50 • **survival** from colon cancer / following bypass surgery / at 1 year • median or mean / disease-free / event-free[9] / cumulative **survival** • infarct / expected graft[10] / improved / lower **survival** • long-term / childhood cancer **survivor**

Überleben(szeit)
Überleben, Gruppe der Überlebenden[1] überleben[2] Überlebende(r)[3] Überlebensrate[4] Überlebenszeit[5] Überlebensvorteil[6] Überlebenszeitanalyse[7] Ü. bis ins Erwachsenenalter[8] ereignisfreies Überleben[9] erwartete Transplantatlebensdauer[10]

25

life-table analysis [ənæləsɪs] n term   syn **survival analysis** n term

a method of analysis that relies [aɪ] on a count of the number of events (e.g. death) observed and the time points at which those events occurred [ɜː], relative to some zero [ɪə] point[1]

» *In life-table analysis for clinical trials the time to an event for a patient is usually measured from the time of randomization and treatment effects are assessed by comparing event rates in the different treatment groups. Lifetable analysis to 15 years failed to yield a deterioration[2] [ɪə] in graft outcome for these patients.*

Use to run **a life-table analysis** • to generate [dʒen-]/prepare/create [ieɪ] **a life table** • period / abridged[3] [ɪdʒ]/ survivor analysis / cohort[4] **life table** • **life-table** methods / event rates / survivorship

Überlebenszeitanalyse, -statistik
Nullzeitpunkt[1] Verschlechterung aufzeigen[2] abgekürzte Sterbetafel[3] Kohortensterbetafel[4]

26

table n term   sim **diagram**[1] [aɪə]**, graph**[1] n**, chart**[1] [tʃ]**, plot**[1] n & v term

data arranged in parallel rows [roʊz] and columns[2] to display the essential facts in an easily appreciable[3] [iːʃ] form

tabulation[4] n term • **tabulated**[5] adj • **plotter**[6] n • **-gram** comb

» *Surface area, like metabolic rate, is not a linear function of weight [weɪt] and requires the use of a table or nomogram. The postoperative results are summarized in the table. The pressure was plotted against the flow rate. This increase was evidenced by[7] a larger area under the curve (abbr AUC) in the receiver [iː] operating characteristic (abbr ROC) plot.*

Use **tabulated** results • contingency[8] [ɪndʒ] / (cohort) life **table** • bar[9] / scatter[10] / block[11] / vector **diagram** • pie[12] [aɪ]/ bar[9] / flow[13] **chart** • ROC / Kaplan-Meier[14] / scatter[10] **plot** • **to plot** X against Y[15] • acid-base **nomogram** • histo**gram**

Tabelle, Tafel
Diagramm, Graph, grafische Darstellung; (i. Graph) eintragen, plotten[1] Spalten[2] übersichtlich[3] tabellarische Darstellung[4] tabellarisch[5] Kurvenschreiber[6] belegt durch[7] Kontingenztafel[8] Säulen-, Balkendiagramm[9] Streudiagr.[10] Blockd.[11] Kreis-, Tortendiagramm[12] Flussd.[13] Kaplan-Meier Diagramm[14] X gegen Y auftragen[15]

27

multivariate [-ɪtǁɪeɪt] **analysis** n term   syn **multivariable analysis** n term

statistical model in which more than one dependent variable is simultaneously [eɪ] predicted

» *Data from the Mayo Clinic using multivariate analysis indicate that only the presence of a locally advanced lesion [iːʒ] was independently predictive of recurrence and ultimate [ʌ] death from disease.*

Use **multivariate analysis** of variants (abbr MANOVA) • **multivariate** relative risk model • frequency / univariate / bivariate[1] / covariance[2] **analysis** • factor / interim / cluster[3] / correspondence / discriminant[4] **analysis**

multivariate/ mehrdimensionale Analyse
bivariate A.[1] Kovarianzanalyse[2] Cluster-Analyse[3] Diskriminanzanalyse[4]

28

Medical Statistics   MEDICAL SCIENCE **447**

---

prediction [prɪdɪkʃ³n] *n term*   *sim* **estimation**¹ [estɪmeɪʃ³n] *n term*
  statement anticipating² [tɪs] or forecasting³ [æ] a future event or prognosis
  predictive *adj term* • **predict** *v* • **predictor**⁴ *n* • **estimate**⁵ *n & v*
» A positive biopsy finding has a predictive value of about 90%. Location and thickness of primary melanoma are the most accurate predictors of prognosis.
Use positive⁶ / negative **predictive value** • actuarial⁷ **estimation** • **estimation** of a proportion

Vorhersage, Prädiktion
Schätzung¹ vorhersehen² voraussagen³ prädiktiver Parameter⁴ Schätzwert; schätzen⁵ positiver Vorhersagewert⁶ (Sterbe)tafelmethode⁷   29

reliability [rɪlaɪəbɪləti] *n term*   *rel* **reproducibility**¹, **validity**² *n term*
  measure [eʒ] of the consistency of statistical data (i.e. results are reproducible on retesting)
  validation³ *n term* • **validate**⁴ *v* • **valid**⁵ [vælɪd] *adj* • **(un)reliable**⁶ *adj*
» Cancers can be detected with a high degree of reliability with colonoscopy. Suboptimal effort limits the validity of lung volume calculations derived [aɪ] from⁷ spirometry [aɪ].
Use **test-retest**⁸ / interjudge⁹ [-dʒʌdʒ] **reliability** • **reliable** indicator / marker / test • internal / external / predictive **validity** • protocol **validation**

Reliabilität, Zuverlässigkeit
Reproduzierbarkeit¹ Gültigkeit, Validität² Gültigkeitsprüfung³ validieren⁴ gültig⁵ (un)zuverlässig⁶ basierend auf⁷ Retest-Stabilität⁸ Inter-Beobachter-Reliabilität⁹   30

probability *n term*   *syn* **likelihood** [laɪklɪhʊd] *n genE*
  statistical measure indicating how likely¹ a specific event is to occur [ɜː]
  (im)probable² *adj* • **to be (un)likely to happen**² *phr*
» Prosthetic replacement has the greatest probability of preventing recurrence. The probability of obtaining³ a given outcome due to chance is expressed by the P value (a significance of p < 0.05 means that up to 5 times out of 100 the result could have occurred by chance).
Use **probability** interval / curve [ɜː]/ distribution⁴ / density⁵ • low / high / greater / calculation of / conditional⁶ **probability** • posttest / pretest / prior [praɪɚ]/ 1% / long-term **probability** • lifetime⁷ / cumulative [kjuː] survival⁸ **probability** • **high-probability** lung scan

Wahrscheinlichkeit
wahrscheinlich¹ (un)wahrscheinlich² erzielen³ Wahrscheinlichkeitsverteilung⁴ Wahrscheinlichkeitsdichte⁵ bedingte Wahrscheinlichkeit⁶ Lebenszeitwahrscheinlichkeit⁷ kumulative Überlebenswahrscheinlichkeit⁸   31

correlation *n term*   *sim* **association**¹, **relation(ship)**², **link**³ *n term*
  degree of relationship (positive or negative) between two sets of paired [eɚ] measurements⁴ of traits [eɪ] or events
  (un)correlated⁵ *adj term* • **correlate** *v* • **correlative**⁶ *adj*
» There is a strong correlation with the presence of HLA-B27 antigen. The reliability of the index was high, with a test-retest correlation coefficient of r = 0.93.
Use Spearman's rank⁷ / Pearson's **correlation coefficient** • cross-⁸/ auto**correlation** • **to correlate** with / well / better / poorly⁹ / closely / strongly • **to correlate** directly / positively / negatively / inversely¹⁰ [ɜː] • **to be correlated** with • **correlation** between A and B / of A and/with B • **correlative** study • causal [kɔːzᵊl]/ close / inverse linear¹¹ **relationship** • to be associated with¹²

Korrelation
Zusammenhang¹ Beziehung² Verbindung³ zwei Wertepaare⁴ (un)korreliert⁵ Korrelations-⁶ Spearman'scher Rangkorrelationskoeffizient⁷ Kreuzkorrelation⁸ schwach korrelieren⁹ gegensinnig k.¹⁰ gegensinnig lineare K.¹¹ in Zusammenhang stehen¹²   32

regression [rɪɡreʃ³n] *n term*   *rel* **slope**¹ [sloʊp] *n term*
  functional relationship between a dependent and one or more independent variables
» Prediction of mortality was performed by logistic [dʒ] regression analysis².
Use **regression** coefficient³ / line⁴ / curve • univariate⁵ / bivariate [aɪ]/ linear [ɪ]/ multiple [ʌ] **regression**

Regression
Steigung¹ logistische Regressionsanalyse² Regressionskoeffizient³ Regressionsgerade⁴ univariate Regression⁵   33

chi-square(d) [kaɪ-] **test** *n term*   *rel* **t-** or **student's test**¹ *n term*
  statistical technique [iːk] whereby variables are categorized to determine² whether a distribution of scores is due to chance or experimental factors
» The chi-square test and ROC curves³ were used for statistical analysis.
Use significance⁴ / binomial / log-rank⁵ / parametric **test** • **chi-square** analysis • Pearson **chi-square analysis** • partition [ɪʃ] of the⁶ **sum of squares**, abbr SS • **chi-squared** • nonparametric or distribution free⁷ / Wilcoxon's rank sum⁸ / Mann-Whitney U⁹ **test** • **test of** independence / fit / significance⁴

Chi²-Test, χ² Test
t-Test¹ feststellen² ROC (Receiver-Operating-Characteristic) Kurven³ Signifikanztest⁴ Logrank-Test⁵ Zerlegung der Quadratsummen⁶ parameterfreier T.⁷ Wilcoxon (Rangsummen)test⁸ U-Test nach Mann und Whitney⁹   34

proportional [ɔːrʃ] **hazard model** *n term*   *syn* **Cox (regression) model** *n term*
  regression method for modelling censored survival data which assumes the ratio of the risks (hazard ratio)
» The present study is aimed at updating prognosis in primary biliary cirrhosis [sɪr-] using a time-dependent Cox regression model. Cox regression uses the maximum likelihood method rather than the least [iː] squares method.
Use linear regression¹ **model** • **proportional** odds model² / censorship [sen-]

Cox Regression
lineares Regressionsmodell¹ Modell m. proportionalen Ja-Nein Quotienten²   35

100

Unit 101 Medical Studies & Clinical Trials
Related Units: 100 Medical Statistics

study [stʌdi] n & v term → U116-2; U118-1   sim **clinical trial**[1] [traɪəl] n term
(i) research activities involving the collection, analysis, or interpretation of data
(ii) project involving several investigations or a clinical trial
(iii) diagnostic investigations (biochemical [k], imaging studies[2], etc.)
» A prospective study is under way[3] to evaluate these two treatment options.
Use to perform/carry out/make/undertake/launch[4] [ɔː] a study • to be under[5] study • longitudinal[6] / (quasi-)experimental / non-experimental research / cross-sectional or prevalence[7] / follow-up[8] / prospective[9] / retrospective study • interventional[10] / observational[11] / historical / epidemiological / parallel cohort / case-control(ed)[12] / feasibility [iː] or pilot[13] [aɪ] study • study participant / population / protocol / manual • randomized / (un)controlled / triple-blinded [ɪ] / single-blind[14] / multi-center (clinical) trial • phase I / II / III / IV / open label[15] [eɪ] trial

Studie, Untersuchung; untersuchen
klinische Studie/ Untersuchung[1] bildgebende Verfahren[2] im Gange[3] Studie beginnen[4] wird zur Zeit untersucht[5] Longitudinal-, Längsschnittstudie[6] Prävalenz-, Querschnittstudie[7] Verlaufsuntersuchung[8] prospektive Studie[9] Interventionsst.[10] Beobachtungsst.[11] Fall-Kontroll-Studie[12] Pilotstudie[13] einfach blinde St.[14] offene Studie[15]
1

investigation [-geɪʃən] n term   sim **research**[1] [n riː-, v rɪsɜːrtʃ] term
(i) a thorough[2] [θɜːrə] and systematic examination or study of unknown issues[3]
(ii) a clinical study or trial
investigator[4] n term • investigate v • investigational[5] adj • investigative[5] adj term • researcher[6] n
» These observations warrant[7] [ɔː] further investigation into the effects of different management approaches. Laboratory investigations revealed microhematuria [iː].
Use to do research[1] on / into • research fellow[8] / worker[6] • clinical / preliminary[9] / longitudinal / (non-)invasive [eɪ]/ multidisciplinary / parallel group investigation • principal investigator • investigational treatment[10] / new drug application[11] (abbr INDA or IND) / device [dɪvaɪs] exemption[12] (abbr IDE) • in an investigative stage[13] [steɪdʒ] • to be under investigation

(i) (wissenschaftliche) Untersuchung (ii) klinische Studie
(Er)forschung, (er)forschen[1] gründlich[2] Zusammenhänge, Fragen[3] Untersucher(in)[4] Test-, Forschungs-, Untersuchungs-[5] Forscher(in), Wissenschaftler(in)[6] rechtfertigen[7] Forschungsstipendiat(in)[8] vorläufige U.[9] experimentelle Behandlung[10] Einsatz e. neuen Testmedikaments[11] Sondergenehmigung f. neues Medizinprodukt[12] im Forschungsstadium[13]
2

objective [dʒek] n term   syn **aim** [eɪm], sim **purpose**[1] [pɜːrpəs] n
research papers[2] about medical studies are usually structured as follows: title, abstract, introduction and objectives, materials and methods, results, discussion, and conclusion(s)
aim (at)[3] v
» The objective of the present study[4] was to assess[5] the response of BPH patients to doxazosin.

Ziel, Zielsetzung
Zweck[1] wissensch. Arbeiten/ Publikationen/ Vorträge[2] abzielen auf, anstreben[3] vorliegende Studie[4] untersuchen[5]
3

patient recruitment [uː t] n term   sim **enrollment**[1], **assignment**[2] [aɪn], **allocation**[2] n term
selecting and obtaining informed consent[3] from patients to participate in clinical trials
recruit [uː t] v term • enroll in(to)[4] v • enrollee[5] [iː] n • allocate v • assign v
» It is recommended that children with brain tumors be enrolled in multicenter protocols. The study was inconclusive owing [oʊɪŋ] to problems in recruitment and low subject enrollment.
Use patient recruitment goal [oʊ] • enrollment criteria[6] [kraɪtɪəɪə] • time of / at / prior [aɪ] to[7] enrollment • uniform or equal [iː] treatment / stratified[8] allocation • fixed / adaptive allocation design • randomly allocated to treatment[9]

Patientenrekrutierung
Aufnahme[1] Zuteilung[2] aufgeklärte Einwilligung einholen[3] i. d. Studie aufnehmen[4] Studien-, Versuchsteilnehmer(in)[5] Aufnahmekriterien[6] vor der Aufnahme[7] stratifizierte Zuteilung[8] randomisiert der Behandlung zugeteilt[9]
4

randomization [rændəmaɪzeɪʃən] n term
(i) a chance[1] [tʃæns] assignment of treatments in an experiment (ii) a statistical selection process in which all subjects or samples presumably have the same chance of being selected[2]
random[1] adj • randomize[3] v term • (non)randomized adj • randomizer[4] n
» Altogether 512 patients were randomized to chemotherapy [kiː-]. The visit where a participant is randomly assigned[5] to treatment groups of a clinical trial is termed randomization visit.
Use random number[6] / variable / process / allocation[7] / population / biopsy [aɪ] • randomized clinical trial[8] / controlled study / blocking[9] / prospective series • randomization visit / process • at[1] random • in a random fashion[1]

Randomisierung, Zufallszuteilung
zufällig[1] Rekrutierungschance[2] randomisieren[3] Zufallsgenerator[4] zugeteilt[5] Zufallszahl[6] Zufallszuteilung[7] randomis. klinische Studie[8] blockweise Randomisierung[9]
5

Medical Studies & Clinical Trials — MEDICAL SCIENCE

prospective *adj term*   *opposite* **retrospective**[1] *adj term*

subjects with a specific trait [eɪ] or parameter are identified and then observed for the occurrence[2] [ɜː] of the outcome

» This prospective two-part trial comprised[3] [aɪ] a pilot study of 10 men.
Use **prospective** study / survey[4] [ɜː] / clinical trial / series[5] [ɪə˞] • **prospective** evaluation / observation protocol / data [eɪ] • **prospective** blood donor[6] [oʊ]/ recipient[7] [sɪ] • **retrospective** analysis / chart [tʃ] review[8] [iː]

prospektiv
retrospektiv[1] Eintreten[2] bestand aus[3] prospektive Erhebung[4] p. Versuchsserie[5] potentielle(r) Blutspender(in)[6] prosp. Empfänger(in)[7] retrospektive Analyse von Krankengeschichten[8]   6

---

protocol *n term*   *sim* **study manual of operations**[1] *n term*

(i) precise plan for a clinical trial or a therapeutic [pjuː] regimen[2] [redʒ-])
(ii) guidelines (iii) official notes (e.g. at autopsy [ɒː])

» Fifty patients were on a surveillance [sə˞ˈveɪləns] protocol[3] after orchiectomy [k] alone. Treatment audits[4] [ɒː] were performed for adherence [ɪə˞] to protocols[5]. Patients who desire more aggressive treatment should be referred[6] for experimental protocol therapy.
Use **protocol** trial / design[7] • study / treatment / testing / chemotherapeutic [kiː-] **protocol** • three-drug / transfusion / field[8] / formal **protocol** • well-designed / followup / watchful waiting[3] / FDA-approved[9] / short-stay **protocol**

(Studien)protokoll
Studienanleitungen[1] Behandlungsplan[2] Surveillance, Beobachtungsstrategie[3] Therapiekontrollen[4] Einhaltung d. Behandlungsprotokolle[5] überwiesen[6] Studiendesign[7] Studienprot. f. Feldversuch[8] v. d. U.S. Gesundheits- u. Lebensmittelbehörde genehmigtes Studienprotokoll[9]   7

---

placebo [pləˈsiːboʊ] *n term*   *sim* **inactive control** *or* **sham treatment**[1] *n term*

(i) inert[2] [ɜː] substance (a sugar pill) identical in appearance with the drug studied which is administered under the pretense of real treatment; used in clinical trials to distinguish between the actual efficacy [-kəsi] of an experimental drug and its suggestive [dʒe] effect (ii) more generally, any ineffective treatment (usually prescribed to meet a patient's demands)

» Eighty percent of the patients who received a placebo became asymptomatic. Prokinetic agents were superior [ɪə˞] to[3] placebo. Those initially on placebo were switched [tʃ] to drug at the end of the 4th week of the trial.
Use **placebo** effect / control group / responder[4] / relief [iː]/ therapy /-treated patient /-controlled trial • nonmedicine **placebo** • **sham**-treated controls / group / feeding[5] [iː]/ lavage [ɑːʒ]

Plazebo, Leer-, Scheinmedikament
Scheinbehandlung[1] inaktiv, unwirksam[2] wirksamer, besser[3] Placeboresponder[4] Scheinfütterung[5]

  8

---

blind [blaɪnd] *adj term*   *syn* **blinded** *adj term*

(adj) keeping study participants and/or investigators from knowing which subjects are assigned to the treatment and the placebo group in order to keep biases[1] [baɪəsiːz] or expectations from influencing the results

blind[2] *v term* • **unblind**[3] *v*

» Our randomized double-blind study shows that administration of alpha-blockers is effective.
Use single[4]-/ double[5]-**blind study** • partially [ʃ] **blinded** • **blind(ed)** study[6] / sham controlled study / placebo trial / procedure

blind
verfälschende Faktoren, Verzerrungen[1] verblinden[2] offenlegen[3] einfacher Blindversuch[4] Doppelblindversuch[5] Blindversuch[6]

  9

---

control group *n term*   *opposite* **treatment** *or* **experimental group**[1] *n term*

subjects [ʌ] (e.g. healthy individuals or normals) participating in the same experiment as the treatment group but not exposed to[2] the test medication or the variable under investigation[3]

(case-)controlled *adj term* • **control** *v* • **controls**[4] *n pl*

» There was no difference in survival between control and study groups[1]. The results were compared to normals[5] for patient age. Healthy [e] volunteers[6] served as controls.
Use **control** animals / patients / population / samples • healthy or normal / age-matched / untreated / nonoperative[7] / unexposed / own / historical[8] **controls** • (in)active **control treatment** • **controlled** clinical trial[9]

Kontrollgruppe
Test-, Behandlungsgruppe[1] nicht exponiert bzgl.[2] Prüfvariable[3] Kontrollpersonen[4] Gesunde[5] gesunde Freiwillige[6] nicht operierte Kontrollpersonen[7] historische K.[8] kontrollierte klin. Studie[9]

  10

---

treatment block *n term*   *sim* **blocking**[1] *n*, **series**[2] [sɪə˞iːz] *n sing & pl*, **cohort**[3] *n term*

prespecified[4] number of patients enrolled in a study and assigned to the various study treatments in such a way so as to satisfy a preset[4] allocation ratio [reɪʃoʊ]

Use **treatment block** size • **block** design[5] • hospitalized[6] **cohort** • **cohort** members / study[7] • a published [ʌ]/ small / large / consecutive[8] **series**

Therapieblock
Blockbildung, blockweise Zuteilung[1] Patientenreihe, -serie[2] Kohorte[3] (vorher) festgelegt[4] Blockanlage[5] stationäre Kohorte[6] Kohortenstudie[7] konsekutive Patientenreihe[8]

  11

---

treatment arm *n term*

term sometimes used in place of study treatment, or study group

» Ten patients were randomized[1] to each arm of the study.
Use chemotherapy [kiː-]/ therapeutic [pjuː]/ no drug / control **arm**

Therapiearm
nach dem Zufallsprinzip zugeteilt, randomisiert[1]

  12

MEDICAL SCIENCE — Medical Studies & Clinical Trials

factorial design [dɪsaɪn] *n term*

treatment structure in which one study treatment is used in combination with at least one other study arm in a trial, or where multiples of a defined dose of a specified treatment are used in the same trial

Use partial [ʃ]/ full **factorial design** • adaptive / parallel group / group sequential[1] [sɪkwenʃəl]/ crossover *design* • **factorial** treatment structure

faktorielles Design
gruppensequentielles Design[1]

13

(treatment) crossover *n term*

planned (e.g in a crossover trial) or unplanned switch[1] of study treatments for a patient in a clinical trial

noncrossover[2] *adj term*

» Unplanned crossovers are called "drop out"[3] and "drop in[4]."

Use **crossover** trial[5] • **crossed** treatments

Therapiewechsel, Crossover
Wechsel[1] ohne Therapiewechsel[2] Ausfall, Therapieabbrecher[3] Zugang, Therapiewechsler[4] Crossover-Studie[5]

14

data [deɪtə] *n term pl only*   *rel* **information**[1], **documentation**[2] *n term sing only*

collection of facts on a specific patient or set of patients from which conclusions may be drawn

document[3] *v & n term* • **(un)documented** *adj* • **informative** *adj*

» There are only few data available for comparison.

Use to obtain [eɪ]/collect[4]/retrieve[5] [iː]/store/evaluate/analyze/process[6]/compare/confirm[7] *data* • scanty[8] [sk]/ abundant[9] [ʌ] *data on* sth. • ordinal / nominal / interval / historical *data* • baseline[10] [eɪ]/ (un)censored [s]/ anatomic *data* • *data* item [aɪ]/ field / form[11] / entry / base[12] / file[13] [aɪ] • *data* editing / protection[14] / and safety monitoring board, *abbr* DSMB • well/poorly **documented** • **information** retrieval / on sth. / about sth.

Daten(material), (Mess)werte, Angaben
Fakten, Informationen[1] Dokumentation, Unterlagen[2] dokumentieren, belegen; Dokument[3] Daten erheben[4] D. abrufen[5] D. verarbeiten[6] D. bestätigen[7] spärliche D. über[8] zahlreiche D.[9] Ausgangswerte[10] Datenerhebungsblatt[11] Datenbank[12] Datei[13] Datenschutz[14]

15

case report form *n term*, *abbr* **CRF**   *syn* **case record form** *n term*

standardized data entry form for all information collected and used in a clinical trial

» Even in circumstances where there is other documentation in addition to CRFs (e.g. lab slips[1]), generally all key [kiː] values[2] that will be analyzed appear on the CRF.

Patientenerhebungsbogen
Laborberichte[1] Schlüsselwerte[2]

16

evidence *n & v*   *sim* **confirmation**[1], **proof**[2] [uː], **verification**[3] *n*

(n) observations or findings which indicate, support or confirm [ɜː] assumptions[4] [ʌ] or conclusions [uː]

evident[5] *adj* • (un)confirmed *adj* • verify[6] *v*

» A growing body of evidence[7] supports our theory. There is no evidence of recurrent [ɜː] disease.

Use to seek [iː]/provide[8]/exhibit[8]/reveal[8] [iː]/search for **evidence** for / in favor of / in support of / against • strong[9] / clear(-cut)[10] / conclusive[11] [uː]/ overwhelming[12] / experimental / anecdotal[13] **evidence** • clinical / gross[14] [oʊ]/ radiographic **evidence**

Nachweis, Beweis, Beleg; belegen, beweisen
Bestätigung[1] Beweis[2] Verifizierung[3] Annahmen bestätigen[4] offensichtlich, evident[5] überprüfen, verifizieren[6] Beweismaterial[7] Be-/ Nachweis liefern[8] viele/ gute B.[9] eindeutige B.[10] schlüssige B.[11] schlagender B.[12] vereinzelte Belege[13] makroskopischer Nachweis[14]

17

in vitro [iː] *phr term*   *opposite* **in vivo**[1] [iː] *phr term*

in an artificial [fɪʃ] environment [aɪ] e.g. a test tube[2] or culture [ʌ] media [iː] rather than[3] in the living body

» These agents inhibit cellular proliferation[4] in prostate [ɒː] cancer [æ] both in vitro and in vivo.

Use **in vitro** techniques [iːk]/ model / analysis / fertilization[5] • **in vivo** administration / experiment

in vitro
in vivo[1] Reagenzglas[2] anstatt[3] Zellwachstum[4] künstliche Befruchtung[5]

18

alternative hypothesis [haɪpɒːθəsɪs] *n term, pl* -**ses** [iːz]
   opposite **null** [ʌ] **hypothesis**[1] *n term*

assumption [ʌ] that the study will yield[2] [jiːld] observations, results, differences in outcome measures [eʒ] between study groups that are not the result of chance alone

hypothesize[3] *v term* • postulate[4] *v & n* • hypothetical *adj*

» Some authors hypothesize that a more virulent [ɪ] clone must be responsible.

Use to advance[3]/develop/propose[3]/postulate *a* **hypothesis** • to put forward[3]/confirm/ support/reject[5] [rɪdʒekt] /accept *a* **hypothesis** • null treatment / working[6] / (un)tenable[7] [e] **hypothesis** • one-tailed [eɪ] or one-sided / two-tailed or two-sided[8] **alternative hypothesis**

Alternativhypothese
Nullhypothese[1] ergeben[2] eine H. aufstellen[3] postulieren, Postulat aufstellen; Postulat[4] H. widerlegen[5] Arbeitshypothese[6] unhaltbare H.[7] zweiseitige Alternativhypothese[8]

19

Medical Studies & Clinical Trials · MEDICAL SCIENCE

intention-to-treat analysis [ənæləsɪs] *n term*
    syn **analysis by intention** [ʃ] **to treat** *n term*
data analysis in which the primary outcome data are analyzed by assigned treatment and irrespective of treatment adherence[1] [ɪɚ] (analysis by treatment administered)
» *The endpoint of the study was analyzed according to the intention-to-treat principle.*

Intention-to-treat Analyse
unabhängig von der Therapietreue[1]
20

treatment lag [læg] *n term*
time required (or thought to be required) for a therapy to exert[1] [ɜː] its full effect
» *The time lag[2] for a successful response may be 6–8 weeks.*
Use **lag** period / phase [feɪz] • **to lag** behind[3] • jet[4] / lid **lag** • **treatment** interaction[5] / effect / compliance[6] [aɪ]/ difference / failure[7] [feɪljɚ]

Wirkungsverzögerung
entfalten[1] zeitliche Verzögerung[2] sich verzögern[3] Zirkadian-, Jet-Lag-Syndrom[4] Wechselwirkung von Wirkstoffen[5] Compliance[6] Therapieversager[7]
21

expanded [æ] **access** [æksɛs] *n term*
broad term for methods of distributing experimental drugs to patients who are unable to participate in ongoing clinical efficacy [efɪkəsi] trials and have no other treatment options[1]
» *These drugs are available to selected patients via expanded access. Types of expanded-access mechanisms* [k] *include parallel track, IND treatment[2], and compassionate use.*
Use **expanded access** program / trial

erweiterter Therapiezugang
Behandlungsmöglichkeiten[1] experimentelle medikamentöse Behandlung[2]
22

compassionate [kəmpæʃ(ə)nət] **use** *n term*
providing unapproved drugs to very sick patients who have no other treatment options for which case-by-case approval[1] [uː] must usually be obtained[2] [eɪ] from the FDA (Food and Drug Administration)
» *Because of toxicity, some agents have been withdrawn* [ɒː] *from the market[3] but are still available for compassionate use.*
Use **compassionate use** protocol / program / group / arm of the study

Verabreichung von nicht zugelassenen Testmedikamenten
Bewilligung[1] eingeholt[2] aus dem Verkehr gezogen[3]
23

institutional review [rɪvjuː] **board** [ɔː] *n term abbr* **IRB**
    syn **hospital ethics** [eθɪks] **committee** *n term*
a committee of physicians [fɪzɪʃ(ə)nz], statisticians [ɪʃ], community advocates, and others which must first approve[1] [uː] a clinical trial and ensure[2] [-ʃʊɚ] that it is ethical and that the rights of the study participants are protected

Ethikkommission
genehmigen[1] sicherstellen[2]
24

steering [stɪɚ-] **committee** *n term*   *abbr* **SC**
(i) broadly, the committee responsible for directing the activities of a designated[1] project
(ii) key committee in the organizational structure of a multicenter clinical trial
» *The SC is responsible for conduct[2] of the trial and gets the reports from all other committees, except the Adverse Experience Committee[3] and Data and Safety Monitoring Board and the Advisory Review and Treatment Effects Monitoring Committee.*
Use publications / research ethics[4] (*abbr* REC) / infection control[5] (*abbr* ICC) / standing[6] / joint[7] [dʒ]/ advisory[8] [aɪ] **committee**

Studienbegleitkommission
festgelegt[1] Durchführung[2] Beschwerdeausschuss[3] Ethikkommission[4] Arbeitsgruppe f. Seuchenbekämpfung[5] ständiger Ausschuss[6] gemeinsamer A.[7] Beratungskomitee[8]
25

efficacy [efɪkəsi] *n*   *syn* **effectiveness**, *sim* **efficiency**[1] [efɪʃ(ə)ntsi] *n*
capacity or power of a procedure [iː], drug etc. to produce a desired effect
effect[2] *n & v* • **effective**[3] *adj* • **efficacious**[3] [keɪʃ] *adj* • **(in)efficient**[4] [ɪʃ] *adj*
» *Our study confirms the efficacy of patient-controlled analgesia* [dʒiː]*. Corticosteroid* [ɪɚǁer] *therapy alone is considered to be less efficacious than major endocrine* [aɪǁɪ] *ablation* [eɪʃ]*.*
Use to be of/show/demonstrate **great efficacy** • long-term / documented / overall / therapeutic **efficacy** • cost-**efficient** • to have an / carry-over[5] / beneficial[6] [fɪʃ] **effect** • desired[7] [aɪ]/ favorable[8] [eɪ]/ profound [aʊ]/ systemic **effect** on

Wirksamkeit, Effektivität
Leistungsfähigkeit, Effizienz[1] Wirkung; (be)wirken[2] wirksam, effektiv[3] (un)wirksam, (in)effizient[4] Nachwirkung[5] wohltuende/ günstige Wirkung[6] erwünschte W.[7] günstige Wirkung[8]
26

outcome [aʊtkʌm] *n term*
condition of a patient following therapeutic intervention[1]
» *Nutrition recommendations were developed to meet treatment goals[2] and desired outcomes[3]. Intracranial* [eɪ] *bleeding (sometimes fatal* [eɪ] *in outcome) occurred following hypertensive crisis.*
Use to affect[4]/alter [ɒː]/improve [uː] **outcome** • **outcome** criteria [aɪ]/ data / statement • treatment / clinical / surgical[5] / primary **outcome** • 3-year / long-term / censored[6] / maternal-fetal [iː] **outcome** • fatal[7] / (un)favorable[8] / poor[9] **outcome** • multiple [ʌ] **outcomes** • binary[10] [aɪ] **outcome measure**

Therapieergebnis, Resultat, Folge
therapeutischer Eingriff[1] Behandlungsziele erreichen[2] angestrebte Behandlungsergebnisse[3] Behandlungsergebnis beeinflussen[4] Operationsergebnis[5] zensiertes E.[6] Tod, Exitus[7] (un)günstiges Ergebnis[8] schlechtes E.[9] binärer Ergebnisparameter[10]
27

censoring [sɛnˈsərɪŋ] *n term*

term used mainly in survival [aɪ] analyses[1] to denote an individual who has not experienced the event of interest at a specific point, e.g. at the time of interim analysis, end of study, or of lost to followup[2]

» *The process by which patient outcome data cannot be obtained beyond a specific point in time is termed censoring.*

zensierte Beobachtung
Überlebenszeitanalysen[1] nicht mehr zur Verlaufskontrolle erscheinen, nicht mehr zur Verfügung stehen[2]

28

withdrawal [wɪðdrɔːəl] *n term*　　*sim* **drop-out** *or* **dropout**[1] *n jar*

removing an individual from a study because of inability to return for follow-up

withdraw[2] *v term* • **drop out**[2] *v inf*

» *Withdrawals were mainly due to side effects of treatment; 12 pts. withdrew* [uː] *during treatment, 2 dropped out because of intercurrent* [ɜː] *disease*[3], *and 3 were lost to follow-up. Patients had the option of dropping out of the study at any time. There was a steady* [e] *dropout of patients.*

Use **withdrawal** from treatment / from the study / rate • patient / systematic **drop-out** • **drop-out** rate[4]

Studienabbruch, abgebrochene Beobachtung
Drop-out, Studienabbrecher(in); Ausfall[1] ausscheiden, ausfallen[2] interkurrente Erkrankung[3] Ausfallsrate, Drop-out Rate[4]

29

stopping rule [uː] *n term*　　*sim* **termination**[1], **stop condition**[2] *n term*

rule usually set prior [aɪ] to patient recruitment [uː] that specifies[3] a limit for the observed test-control treatment difference for the primary outcome, which, if exceeded [iː], leads to termination of the test or control treatment, depending on the direction of the observed difference

» *A stop condition is encountered*[4] [aʊ] *when a patient enrolled* [oʊ] *in a trial, requires or permits clinic personnel to take some action related to that patient, such as instituting a change in treatment or terminating*[5] *follow-up of that patient.*

Use early **stopping** • premature[6] [priːmətʊɚ] ***termination*** • **termination** stage / of the procedure

Studienabbruchbestimmung
Beendigung, Abbruch[1] Studienabbruchbedingung[2] festlegen[3] liegt vor[4] abbrechen, beenden[5] vorzeitige Beendigung[6]

30

History Taking   CLINICAL TERMS **453**

Unit 102 History Taking
Related Units: 1 Health, 2 Diet, 9 Drugs, 10 Alcohol & Smoking, 18 At the Doctor's, 107 Physical Examination, 103 Clinical Symptoms, 104 Pain, 105 Fever, 117 Diagnosis, 118 Diagnostic Procedures

---

present with *v phr term*   *sim* **suffer** [ʌ] **(from)**¹ *v* → U104-2

to seek [iː] medical advice [-aɪs] for examination, treatment, etc. of a health problem
presentation *n* • **presenting**² *adj* • **present**³ *adj* • **present as** *v phr*

» The child presented with an unexplained [eɪ] limp⁴. The patient presented to the emergency department for pain relief. Rarely an aneurysm will present as a pulsating mass on the chest.

Use **to present** with fever / symptoms⁵ / to a physician⁶ / in newborns⁷ • at / clinical⁸ / common / adult / initial⁹ [ɪʃ] **presentation** • age¹⁰ / mode [oʊ] / time *of presentation* • **presenting** symptoms¹¹ [ɪ]/ features [iːtʃ]/ complaints [eɪ]/ manifestation / in infancy • **present** illness¹² / symptoms

(Symptome) präsentieren; mit Beschwerden z. Arzt kommen
leiden an¹ Haupt-² gegenwärtig, vorhanden³ Hinken⁴ Symptome haben/ zeigen⁵ z. Arzt gehen/ kommen⁶ s. bei Neugeborenen manifestieren⁷ klin. Manifestation⁸ Erstmanifestation⁹ Manifestationsalter¹⁰ Hauptsymptome, -beschwerden¹¹ vorliegende Krankheit, derzeitige Erkrankung¹²   **1**

---

experience [ɪkspɪəriənˡts] *v*   *sim* **notice**¹ [noʊtɪs] *v, rel* **report**² [rɪpɔːrt] *v*

to feel or be affected by sensations [eɪ] or symptoms, e.g. pain, dryness, tightness³ [aɪ] or sweating [e]
experience⁴ *n* • **(un)noticed**⁵ *adj* • **noticeable**⁶ *adj* • **report** *n* → U57-4

» Have you ever experienced any shortness of breath⁷ [e]? I first noticed it upon waking in the morning. Is this the first time you've experienced these symptoms? How long have you been noticing this? The patient experienced remissions and exacerbations⁸ of pain. He did not experience any weight loss or fatigue⁹ [fətiːg]. The patient reported previous [iː] episodes of tenderness¹⁰.

Use **to experience** thirst [ɜː]/ irritability / emotional outbursts¹¹ [ɜː]/ toxic reactions • **to experience** fear [ɪə] of strangers¹² / painless hematuria¹³ [iː] • subjective¹⁴ / traumatic [ɒː]/ sexual **experience** • to go¹⁵/progress **unnoticed** • **noticeable** swelling¹⁶ / improvement [uː] • **to report** an unpleasant [e] taste¹⁷ / a history of urinary [jʊ] tract infections • **to report** a variety [aɪə] of symptoms / a feverish [iː] feeling

(ver)spüren, empfinden, erleben
bemerken, feststellen¹ berichten, melden² Engegefühl³ Erfahrung, Erleben, Erlebnis⁴ unbemerkt⁵ deutlich, erkennbar, sichtbar⁶ Kurzatmigkeit⁷ Verschlimmerung, Exazerbation⁸ Müdigkeit⁹ Druckschmerzhaftigkeit¹⁰ Gefühlsausbrüche haben¹¹ fremdeln¹² eine schmerzlose Hämaturie haben¹³ subjektives Erleben¹⁴ unbemerkt bleiben¹⁵ deutliche Schwellung¹⁶ über einen unangenehmen Geschmack berichten¹⁷   **2**

---

elicit [ɪˈlɪsɪt] *v term & jar* → U88-13

sim **obtain**¹ [eɪ], **uncover**² [ʌ], **disclose**², **reveal**² [iː] *vt clin*

(i) to question a patient about symptoms and other details [iː] (ii) to provoke [oʊ]
elicitation³ *n* • **(un)obtainable**⁴ *adj* • **eliciting** *adj & n*

» The sign may be elicited in the sitting position to determine if the finding is reproducible. Early elicitation of a patient's preferences and values is often helpful. Is it the chewing, swallowing⁵ [ɒː], or taste of the food that elicits facial [eɪʃ] pain? Even careful efforts at eliciting a history of true as opposed to subjective weakness may fail to distinguish the two conditions.

Use **to elicit** rebound [aʊ] tenderness⁶ / responses / reflexes⁷ [iː]/ information⁸ • **eliciting** factor / stimulus / event⁹ • **to obtain a** history¹⁰ / biopsy¹¹ [aɪə]/ blood culture [ʌ]/ mammogram

(i) erheben, eruieren
(ii) auslösen
erheben, durchführen¹ zeigen, aufdecken² Erhebung, Feststellung; Auslösung³ feststellbar, erhältlich⁴ Schlucken⁵ Loslassschmerz auslösen⁶ Reflexe auslösen⁷ Informationen erfragen⁸ auslösendes Ereignis⁹ die Anamnese erheben¹⁰ eine Biopsie durchführen¹¹   **3**

(medical) history *n term, abbr* **Hₓ**   *syn* **health** [e] **history** *n clin*

systematic account [aʊ] of events in a patient's life and factors that may have a bearing¹ [eə] on the patient's condition which is obtained by the physician [ɪʃ] in the course [ɔː] of the interview
case history² *n term* • **historic(al)**³ *adj*

» An informative history is more than an orderly listing of symptoms. There was no history of coughing [ɒːf]. With increasing experience, the pitfalls⁴ of history taking become apparent [eə].

Use **to take** or **obtain**⁵/report/complete [iː]/compile⁵ **the patient's history** • **history** and physical [fɪz-] (examination) (*abbr* HPE, H & P) • birth⁶ (*abbr* BH)/ marital (*abbr* MH)/ occupational⁷ / social⁸ **history** • sexual⁹ / menstrual / smoking / drug¹⁰ **history** • dietary [aɪə]/ psychiatric [saɪkɪætrɪk] **history** • prolonged / lifelong **history** • complete health **history** • **historic** analysis / features [iː] • **historical** questions / data¹¹ [eɪ‖æ]

Krankengeschichte, Anamnese
von Belang sein, Bezug haben¹ Fall-, Krankengeschichte² anamnestisch; historisch³ Fallstricke, Tücken⁴ die Anamnese erheben⁵ Geburtenanamnese⁶ Berufsanamnese⁷ Sozialanamnese⁸ Sexualanamnese⁹ (Genuss- u.) Arzneimittelanamnese¹⁰ anamnest. Daten¹¹   **4**

history of present illness n term, abbr **HPI**

the patient's account of the onset, duration, and nature [eɪ] of the presenting complaints [eɪ]

» The HPI should include information about the factors that precipitate¹ [sɪ] and/or relieve² the complaints and whether a similar condition has occurred in the past. First investigate the chief complaint through key questions that are included in the history of the present illness.

Use study / features [iːtʃ]/ nature³ *of the present illness*

aktuelle/ jetzige Anamnese, Anamnese d. momentanen Beschwerden
auslösen¹ lindern² Art d. aktuellen Beschwerden³

5

past medical history n term, abbr **PMH**

overall summary [ʌ] of the patient's general health obtained from the patient or his next of kin¹ which includes past injuries, allergies, surgical procedures, hospitalizations, immunizations, major illnesses², etc.

» Indications now include an active or documented past history of duodenal ulcer.

Use past surgical / no previous [iː] (abbr NPH) **history** • (no) prior / recent³ [iː]/ past⁴ (abbr PH) **history** • **past** health • unremarkable⁵ / noncontributory⁶ **PMH** • **PMH** not remarkable

frühere Anamnese, A. d. Vorerkrankungen, Altanamnese
nächste Verwandte¹ schwere Krankheiten² unmittelbare Vorgeschichte³ Vorgeschichte⁴ unauffällige Vorgeschichte⁵ belanglose Vorgeschichte⁶

6

family history n term, abbr **FH**

account of the health of the patient's immediate [iː] family members¹ in which the age and health (or cause of death) of each person is charted² [tʃ] paying special attention to familial and hereditary conditions³

familial⁴ [fəmɪlɪəl] adj • **family-centered⁵** adj • **patient-family unit** n term

» A detailed family history was obtained. A family history of heart disease should be carefully sought [sɒːt], since many of these conditions tend to run in families⁶.

Use to have/report/take/uncover/give **no/ a family history of** allergy • strong / positive / complicated **FH** • negative / uninformative / first-degree⁷ [iː] **FH** • **family** health / medicine / physician⁸ [ɪʃ]/ contacts / conflicts / counseling⁹ [aʊ] • melanoma-prone¹⁰ [oʊ] **families** • **familial** aggregation or clustering¹¹ [ʌ]/ tendency • **family-centered** (maternity) [ɜː] care / obstetric unit¹²

Familienanamnese
nächste Familienangehörige¹ erfasst² Erbkrankheiten³ familiär, Familien-⁴ familienorientiert, -freundlich⁵ familiär gehäuft auftreten⁶ positive Familienanamnese b. Verwandten ersten Grades⁷ Hausarzt, -ärztin⁸ Familienberatung⁹ Familien m. mehreren Melanomfällen¹⁰ familiäre Häufung¹¹ familienfreundlich ausgestattete Kreißsäle¹²

7

pertinent [ɜː] adj   syn **relevant** adj, opposite **noncontributory¹** adj term

aspects, e.g. of a history, clinical findings, etc. that have a bearing [eə] on the patient's condition

contribute² v • contribution³ n • contributing⁴ adj • contributory⁴ adj term

» First review⁵ [rɪvjuː] the pertinent history. The rest of the lab findings were noncontributory. Alcohol intoxication may be contributory. Sensory testing is rarely contributory. The diarrhea [daɪəriːə] may contribute to death.

Use **pertinent** history (of exposures) [oʊʒ]/ physical findings⁶ / physical examination • **pertinent** illnesses / details [iː]/ lab data⁷ / (social) factors • **noncontributory** to present illness / family history / past history • contributing factor⁸ • **contributing to** a problem / shock / colic [kɒːlɪk]/ sleep / death

relevant, von Bedeutung
nicht relevant, irrelevant, bedeutungslos¹ beitragen² Beitrag³ mitwirkend, eine Rolle spielend⁴ durchsehen, überprüfen⁵ relevante/ auffällige Befunde d. klinischen Untersuchung⁶ wichtige Laborwerte⁷ Kofaktor⁸

8

personal data [eɪ‖æ] n term   syn **patient profile** [proʊfaɪl], **particulars** n BE

these include the patient's name (first, last, maiden name¹), date of birth (abbr DOB), race (Caucasian² [kɔːkeɪʒən], Hispanic, Black), sex (male abbr M / female abbr F), marital status³ (single abbr S / married abbr M / divorced⁴ abbr D / widowed⁵ abbr W), profession, address, health insurance⁶ [ʃʊ], etc.

» Further information to be included in the patient profile may be education, habits⁷, home situation, next of kin, life changes, behavior during assessment, etc. Well, first I need a few personal data. Your name, please? What's your profession? Could I have your address and phone number? Are you married? Any children?

Use **personal** profile / history⁸ / life⁹ / interests • **personal** identity / inadequacy¹⁰ / loss¹¹ • **personal** privacy [aɪ‖ɪ]/ appearance [ɪə]/ care or hygiene¹² [haɪdʒiːn]/ lifestyle • personality¹³ / pain / thyroid¹⁴ [θaɪrɔɪd] **profile**

Personalien, Patientendaten
Mädchenname¹ Weiße(r), Kaukasier(in)² Familienstand³ geschieden⁴ verwitwet⁵ Krankenversicherung⁶ Gewohnheiten⁷ Eigenanamnese⁸ Privatleben⁹ eigene Unzulänglichkeit¹⁰ persönl. Verlust¹¹ Körperpflege¹² Persönlichkeitsprofil¹³ Schilddrüsendiagnostik, -funktionsprüfung¹⁴

9

deny [dɪnaɪ] v   opposite **admit to¹** v clin

(i) (of a patient) to state that (s)he did not experience the symptoms elicited (ii) to refuse

denying adj & n • denial² [dɪnaɪəl] n • self-denial³ n

» Some patients steadfastly⁴ [e] deny pain but will admit to a discomfort or may complain of difficulty in breathing⁵ [iː]. Patients aroused⁶ [aʊ] from that stage frequently deny having been asleep.

Use **to deny** a symptom / permission / access⁷ / sexual activity • **denial of** a deficit / illness / guilt⁸ [gɪlt]/ death / emergency [ɜː] care⁹ • high level of¹⁰ **denial**

**(i) verneinen, leugnen
(ii) ablehnen, verweigern**
eingestehen, zugeben¹ Leugnen, Verleugnung, Ablehnung² Selbstverleugnung³ beharrlich⁴ Atemprobleme, -beschwerden⁵ geweckt⁶ Zutritt verwehren⁷ Leugnung d. Schuld⁸ Verweigerung d. Erste-Hilfe-Leistung⁹ starke Ablehnung¹⁰

10

History Taking   CLINICAL TERMS **455**

review [rɪvjuː] **of systems** [ɪ] *n term*, *abbr* **ROS**
    syn **functional enquiry** [ɪŋkwaɪəri] *n term BE*

system-by-system assessment of bodily functions performed at H & P; body systems evaluated include the respiratory (*abbr* RS), gastrointestinal (*abbr* GIS), cardiovascular (*abbr* CVS), genitourinary (*abbr* GUS), head, eyes, ear, nose and throat (*abbr* HEENT), and central nervous (*abbr* CNS) systems

» The ROS should focus on signs and symptoms of possible complications. A full ROS also includes a statement about the patient's habitus, general appearance and condition as well as the psychiatric or emotional status and any additional data that may be of interest.

Use to take a[1] / careful[2] / full / rheumatic [uː] **ROS** • **functional** assessment[3] / status

medical record *n term*   *syn* **patient's chart** *n jar*, *sim* **index card**[1] *n BE*

written account including the patient's initial complaint(s) and medical history, the physician's physical findings, the results of diagnostic tests, and any therapeutic [juː] medications and/or procedures [iː]

record[2] *v* [rɪkɔːrd] • **recording**[3] *n* • **chart**[4] [tʃɑːrt] *n* • **chart**[5] *v* → U18-14

» This requires careful review of the patient's medical records and prior contacts. Pulse and BP should be recorded daily. Recumbent [ʌ] length is plotted[6] on the birth to 36-month chart.

Use a patient's medical[7] / clinical / hospital / problem-oriented **record** • **medical record** technician[8] [k] • clinical / sleep[9] / technique [-niːk] of **recording** • temperature[10] / visual [ɪʒ] acuity [juː] or Snellen[11] **chart** • fluid balance / growth[12] / percentile / pictorial / flow[13] **chart** • **chart** review • **index card** file / update

case notes [keɪs noʊts] *n clin & jar*   *sim* **case report**[1] *n clin*

(i) data on a patient recorded in the course [ɔː] of medical care (ii) relevant data on a patient's symptoms, findings, lab results, etc. a doctor may keep for ready reference (e.g. on index cards)

case *n* • **case finding**[2] *n*

» Take ample time for recording the case notes and reviewing the old charts. There is at least one case report of a patient with this penile [iː] anomaly who has produced four children.

Use **case** management / presentation[3] / book[4] / conference / study[5] • borderline[6] / coroner's[7] / (in)operable **case** • clinical / admit or admission[8] / progress[9] / transfer **notes**

consultation [kɒnsʌlteɪʃən] *n term espBE* → U18-12
    sim **medical interview**[1] [-vjuː] *n clin*, *rel* **referral**[2] [rɪfɜːrəl] *n term*

(i) conversation between a patient and a specialist where they discuss the patient's health problem (ii) meeting of two or more physicians or surgeons to discuss a particular case

consult[3] *v* • **interview** *v* • **interviewer** *n* • **consultant**[4] *n* • **consulting**[5] *adj*

» Children may be referred[6] to a pediatrician [ɪʃ] for consultation by a parent who desires a second opinion[7]. This decision should be made only after consultation with a mental health expert. The interviewer should discuss more general lifestyle questions before inquiring about use of substances. Screening by interview and observation has been found to be more sensitive.

Use to seek [iː] or obtain[8]/request/require **consultation with** a surgeon • neurologic / telephone / patient seen in **consultation** • **to consult** with colleagues[9] [-iːgz] • **consultation** report • **consulting** room[10] / hours[11] • pediatric **consultant** • **interviewing** techniques • clinical / health / child **interview** • face-to-face[12] / preoperative anesthesia[13] [iːʒ] **interview** • psychiatric [saɪkɪ-]/ initial [ɪʃ] or first / followup[14] **interview** • skillful[15] / tactful **interviewing**

questionnaire [kwestʃəneər] *n term*   *rel* **questioning**[1] *n clin & inf*

list of questions submitted orally or in writing to obtain medical information

» A shorter, questionnaire version of the HOME interview, the Home Screening Questionnaire (HSQ), provides most of the information obtained from the longer interview version [ɜː] and can be administered and scored[2] by the pediatrician during a clinic or office visit[3].

Use standardized[4] / written / screening / study entry **questionnaire** • direct / systematic / detailed[5] [iː]/ repeated[6] [iː]/ nonjudgmental[7] [dʒ] **questioning**

---

systemat. Organanamnese
eine Organanamnese erheben[1] detaillierte Organanamnese[2] Funktionsdiagnostik, -prüfung, funktionsdiagnostische Untersuchung[3]

11

Krankenakte, -blatt
Karteikarte[1] aufzeichnen, registrieren, niederschreiben, protokollieren[2] Aufzeichnung, Registrierung[3] Tabelle, Diagramm, Kurvenblatt[4] ein-, auftragen[5] eingetragen[6] Krankenakte[7] medizinische(r) Dokumentationsassistent(in)[8] Schlafprofil[9] Fieberkurve[10] Seh(proben)tafel[11] Wachstumstabelle[12] Flussdiagramm[13]

12

Fallaufzeichnungen, Patientendokumentation
Fallbericht, Kasuistik[1] systemat. Früherkennung, Detektion, Case-Finding[2] Fallpräsentation[3] Sammlung v. Fallbeschreibungen[4] Fallstudie, Kasuistik[5] Grenzfall[6] gerichtsmed. Fall[7] Aufnahmebericht[8] tägl. Dekurs[9]

13

(i) Konsultation, ärztliche Beratung
(ii) Konsilium, konsiliar. B.
Arztgespräch[1] Überweisung[2] konsultieren, zu Rate ziehen, beiziehen[3] Konsiliararzt, -ärztin, fachärztl. Berater(in); Facharzt, -ärztin (i. brit. Krankenhaus)[4] beratend, Sprech-[5] überwiesen[6] zweite Meinung, Zweitgutachten[7] e. Chirurgen/-in konsultieren[8] sich mit Kolleg(inn)en beraten[9] Sprechzimmer[10] Sprechstunde, Ordinationszeit[11] persönl. Gespräch[12] präop. anästhesiolog. Visite[13] Nachsorgegespräch[14] geschickte Fragestellung[15]

14

Patienten-Fragebogen
Befragung[1] ausgewertet[2] während d. Arztbesuchs[3] standardisierter Fragebogen[4] eingehende Befragung[5] wiederholte Befragung[6] unvoreingenommene Befragung[7]

15

102

CLINICAL TERMS

rapport [rəpɔːr] n term
rel **physician-patient relationship**[1] n → U18-8

sense of mutual[2] [mjuːtʃʊəl] understanding, trust[3] [ʌ], and respect between two people

» Primary care physicians[4] are generally more familiar with patients and have a greater rapport with the family. Hospitalization of a child depends on how well rapport can be established with the parents. Rapport can be enhanced by asking about the child's favorite toys or pets.

Use to establish *or* build/have good **rapport with** a patient[5]

medical transcriptionist [trænskrɪpʃənɪst] n term

secretary who performs machine transcription of physician-dictated medical reports

» A certified[1] [sɜːr-] medical transcriptionist (abbr CMT) has satisfied the requirements for certification by the American Association of Medical Transcription.

Vertrauensverhältnis, gutes Einvernehmen, Rapport
Patient-Arzt-Beziehung[1] gegenseitig[2] Vertrauen[3] Hausärzte, -ärztinnen[4] eine Vertrauensbasis schaffen[5]

16

medizin. Schreibkraft
geprüfte[1]

17

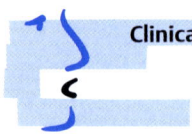

Clinical Phrases

Hello, I'm Dr. Hillard. What seems to be your trouble? Was fehlt Ihnen? • What's brought you along? *(BE)* Was führt Sie zu mir? • Do you have a lot of sneezing? Müssen Sie oft niesen? • Have you had a tetanus shot recently? Wurden Sie in der letzten Zeit gegen Tetanus geimpft? • Have you been to a doctor lately? Waren Sie in der letzten Zeit in ärztlicher Behandlung? • How much do you smoke? Wie viele Zigaretten rauchen Sie? • Have you ever been diagnosed with heart disease? Wurde bei Ihnen jemals eine Herzkrankheit festgestellt? • Did you ever have scarlet fever as a child? Hatten Sie als Kind einmal Scharlach? • Has anyone in your family had strokes? Hatte jemand in Ihrer Familie schon einmal einen Schlaganfall? • Have you been troubled with headaches? Haben Sie öfter Kopfschmerzen? • Are you on any medication? Nehmen Sie irgendwelche Medikamente? • Is there anything else bothering you? Haben Sie noch irgendwelche andere Beschwerden?

Unit 103 Nonspecific Clinical Symptoms
Related Units: 4 Illness & Recovery, 89 Pathology, 102 History Taking, 108 Clinical Signs, 109 GI Symptoms, 110 Cardiovascular Symptoms, 111 Respiratory Symptoms, 112 Urologic Symptoms, 113 Neurologic Findings, 114 Skin Lesions, 117 Diagnosis

symptom [sɪmᵖtəm] n term
rel **sign**[1], **syndrome**[2] [sɪndrəm] n term → U108-1

abnormality in body appearance, function, or sensation experienced by the patient that indicates the presence of a disease

(pre/ a)symptomatic[3] adj term • symptom-free[4] adj • symptomatology[5] n

» Pain is the most common symptom causing patients to seek medical attention[6]. There are no benefits from oral agents that are potentially suitable for long-term symptom relief. In a few patients trigeminal neuralgia is symptomatic of[7] an underlying lesion, e.g. multiple sclerosis.

Use to have/present with/show *or* exhibit/cause *or* produce[8]/develop[9] **symptoms** • to worsen *or* aggravate[10]/improve [uː] /lessen/reduce symptoms • to ease [iːz] *or* relieve[11]/ameliorate [iː] *or* alleviate[11] [iː] /palliate[11] symptoms • **symptoms are** precipitated [sɪ] *or* brought on[12]/reported • symptoms and signs[13] • mild / minor [aɪ]/ severe / local(ized) **symptoms** • systemic *or* generalized / (non-)specific **symptoms** • initial [ɪʃ]/ prodromal[14] [oʊ]/ late **symptoms** • chronic / intermittent / presenting[15] **symptoms** • cardinal[16] / subjective [dʒe]/ objective / associated[17] [oʊʃ] **symptoms** • to be/become **(a)symptomatic** • **symptomatic** improvement / relief [iː]/ treatment[18] • **(a)symptomatic** patients / disease / episodes • **asymptomatic** carriers[19] / carrier state [eɪ]/ disease

Symptom, Krankheitszeichen
Zeichen, objektives Krankheitszeichen[1] Symptomenkomplex, Syndrom[2] symptomlos, asymptomatisch[3] symptomlos, beschwerdefrei[4] Symptomatologie, Lehre v. Krankheitssymptomen[5] einen Arzt aufsuchen[6] symptomatisch für[7] Symptome verursachen/ hervorrufen[8] S. entwickeln[9] S. verschlimmern[10] S. lindern[11] S. werden ausgelöst[12] Symptomatik[13] Prodrom(alsymptome)[14] Hauptbeschwerden, -symptome[15] Leitsymptome[16] Begleitsymptome[17] symptomatische Behandlung[18] symptomlose/ asymptomatische Träger[19]

1

Note: Although clinical **symptoms** (patient's subjective experience) and **signs** (the doctor's observation) are two different things, many symptoms are accompanied by objective signs. The expression **clinical features** is often used to refer to both signs and symptoms.

Nonspecific Clinical Symptoms **CLINICAL TERMS 457**

complaints [kəmpl̲e̲ɪnts] *n clin usu pl*

(i) health problems identified by the patient or his/her next of kin[1], esp. those that cause the person to seek [iː] medical advice (ii) broadly, any bodily disorder, ailment[2] [eɪ] or disease

complain (of)[3] [eɪ] *v, abbr* c/o

» The patient complains of redness and a *scratchy feeling*[4] of the eyes. Transient vertigo [ɜː] following changes in head position is a frequent complaint. Patients with skeletal complaints should have bone x-rays. Most complaints of *wheezing*[5] [iː] are due to asthma [z].

Use chief (*abbr* CC) or presenting[6] (*abbr* PC)/ multiple / unexplained **complaints** • poorly defined / focal / minor[7] **complaints** • physical[8] / functional [ʌ]/ (psycho)somatic[9] [saɪkoʊsəmæ̲tɪk] **complaints** • **complaints of** headache [hedeɪk]/ numbness[10] [nʌmnəs]/ weakness [iː]/ back pain / neck stiffness[11]

▎ Note: Use **to complain of** with physical symptoms and **to complain about**[12] when referring to a situation you are not satisfied with.

(clinical) features [fiːtʃəz] *n usu pl*   *syn* **manifestations** [eɪʃ] *n term pl*

(i) the signs and symptoms of a disease (ii) the characteristics, e.g. of clinical findings (iii) *features*[1] also refers to the appearance of a person's face (pl only) → U25-10

manifest[2] *v & adj term*

» Typical [ɪ] clinical features are low-grade [eɪ] fevers [iː] and weight loss. Many patients do not manifest all features of *hypersplenism*[3] [e‖iː]. Sinus [aɪ] disease may manifest as headache. An inflammatory [æ] response became manifest 12 hours after injury [ɪndʒəɪ].

Use presenting / characteristic[4] / typical [ɪ]/ dominant **features** • distinctive or distinguishing[5] / classic / early[6] **features** • radiologic / histologic / laboratory **features** • pathologic / diagnostic **features** • coarse [ɔː] facial[7] [eɪʃ] **features** • **to manifest** clinical signs / as anemia [iː] • (clinically) **manifest** coronary heart disease[8] • late / rare / terminal [ɜː]/ first **manifestation of** HIV infection[9] / sepsis / angina [dʒaɪ]

bout [baʊt] *n*   *syn* **episode** *n jar, sim* **attack**[1], **spell**[1] *n clin*, **fit**[1] *n inf*

period of time marked by the appearance [ɪə] of a symptom or a disease

episodic[2] [epɪsɒ̲ːdɪk] *adj term*

» She had intermittent bouts of back pain radiating [eɪ] down the *thighs*[3] [θaɪz]. Aspirin should be avoided, as it may precipitate [sɪ] a severe episode of bronchospasm [k].

Use episodic / repeated[4] / recurrent[4] [ɜː‖ʌ] **bouts** • **bouts of** diarrhea [daɪəriːə]/ fever[5] [iː] • **episodic** or sporadic in occurrence[2] [ɜː] • acute / recurrent[4] / transient / stroke-like[6] **episodes** • arrhythmic [ɪ]/ life-threatening [e]/ panic[7] / painful[8] **episodes** • to have or throw a[9] / collapse in a / epileptic[10] **fit** • **fits of** crying[11] / laughter [æf] / anger • cyanotic [saɪə–] or hypoxemic [iː]/ choking[12] [tʃoʊkɪŋ] **spells** • dizzy[13] / fainting[14] [eɪ]/ coughing[15] [kɒːfɪŋ] **spells** • **spells of** unconsciousness[14] / vertigo[13] [ɜː]

▎ Note: The expression **attack** tends to be used with more severe conditions and symptoms, e.g. **attacks of** asthma/*biliary colic*[16]/malaria or transient ischemic attacks[6].

sore throat *n clin*   *rel* **coated** or **furry** [ɜː] **tongue**[1] *n clin* → U21-11

pain or discomfort on swallowing[2] [ɒː] due to inflammation of the tonsils, pharynx, or larynx

» The tongue [tʌŋ] was dry and furred. Use antibiotics in patients with a sore throat if the probability of streptococcal involvement (*strep throat*[3]) is greater than 25%.

Use scratchy[4] / dry / inflamed [eɪ]/ strep / injected[5] [dʒe] **throat** • **throat** swab[6] [ɒː]/ infection / culture [ʌ] • bald[7] [ɒː]/ clean / fissured[8] [ʃ] **tongue** • bitten / thick / enlarged **tongue** • burning [ɜː] or sore / beefy red / strawberry[9] **tongue** • to clear one's[10] **throat** • to put out one's **tongue**

hoarseness *n clin*   *rel* **painful phonation**[1], **dysphonia**[1] *n term*

the voice is unnaturally deep, harsh[2] or irritated; commonly seen in laryngitis [dʒaɪ]

hoarse[3] *adj clin* • **aphonia**[4] *n term* • a/ **dysphonic** *adj* → U66-13,23

» Peritonsillar abscess and cellulitis present with severe sore throat, *odynophagia*[5], trismus, and hoarseness ("hot potato" voice). The voice may be hoarse or *aphonic*[6].

Use to produce[7]/experience/check for **hoarseness** • persistent / progressive / stridor [aɪ] and **hoarseness** • **hoarse** voice[8] / cry • spastic **dysphonia** • hysteric / paralytic [ɪ] **aphonia**

Beschwerden, Symptome
nächste(r) Verwandte(r)[1] Leiden[2] klagen über[3] Fremdkörpergefühl[4] Giemen, pfeifendes Atemgeräusch[5] Hauptbeschwerden[6] leichte Beschwerden[7] körperliche Beschwerden[8] psychosomatische Beschwerden[9] Taubheitsgefühl[10] Nackensteifigkeit[11] sich beklagen über[12]

2

klin. Symptome/ Manifestationen/ Erscheinungsbild
Gesichtszüge[1] s. manifestieren/ zeigen; (klinisch) manifest, erkennbar[2] Hyperspleniesyndrom, Hypersplenismus[3] charakterist. Merkmale/ Kennzeichen[4] Unterscheidungsmerkmale[5] Frühsymptome[6] grobe Gesichtszüge[7] klin. manifeste koronare Herzkrankheit[8] Erstmanifestation einer HIV-Infektion[9]

3

Anfall, Schub, Episode
Anfall, Schub, Attacke[1] episodisch (auftretend)[2] Oberschenkel[3] (immer) wiederkehrende Anfälle[4] Fieberattacken, -schübe[5] transitorische ischämische Attacken, TIAs[6] Panikattacken[7] Schmerzattacken[8] einen (Wut)anfall haben[9] epilept. Anfall[10] Weinkrämpfe[11] Erstickungsanfälle[12] Schwindelanfälle[13] Ohnmachtsanfälle[14] Hustenanfälle[15] Gallenkoliken[16]

4

Halsentzündung, -schmerzen
belegte Zunge[1] beim Schlucken[2] Streptokokkenangina[3] Halskratzen[4] geröteter Hals[5] Rachenabstrich[6] Lackzunge[7] Faltenzunge[8] Himbeer-, Erdbeerzunge[9] sich räuspern[10]

5

Heiserkeit
Stimmstörung, Dysphonie[1] rau[2] heiser, rau[3] Stimmlosigkeit, Aphonie[4] schmerzhaftes Schlucken, Odynophagie[5] ton-, klanglos[6] Heiserkeit verursachen[7] heisere Stimme[8]

6

CLINICAL TERMS — Nonspecific Clinical Symptoms

malaise [məlez‖eɪz] *n clin* → U4-5 *sim* **discomfort**[1] *n clin* → U104-1
to feel out of sorts[2] *phr inf & clin*

vague feeling of uneasiness [iː] or weakness often marking the onset of diseases
» The fever, productive [ʌ] cough[3], myalgia[4], and malaise usually resolve within a month. Malaise may be marked[5]. The patient experienced malaise, sweating [e], chills[6] [tʃ], anorexia[7] and prostration. Motion [moʊʃən] sickness may be associated with dizziness, headache, and general discomfort.
Use general(ized feeling of)[8] / mild[9] **malaise** • fever / myalgia [maɪæɫdʒ(ɪ)ə]/ weakness and **malaise** • general(ized) / vague [veɪg]/ local / slight or little[10] / persistent feeling of / tolerable[11] **discomfort**

fatigue [fətiːg] *n term*   *sim* **tiredness**[1], **lassitude**[2] *n clin,*
rel **prostration**[3] *n term* → U4-6

(i) generalized weariness[4] [ɪə], sleepiness and/or abnormal lack of energy for normal routines
(ii) exhaustion[5] [ɒː] after strenuous[6] physical activity
fatigued *adj clin* • **fatig(u)ability**[7] *n* • **prostrate** [prɒːstreɪt] *adj*
» Ordinary physical activity did not cause undue[8] fatigue or anginal [dʒ] pain. Mr Cohn presented with fatigue related to anemia [iː]. The patient woke up fatigued. In radiation sickness nausea, vomiting, exhaustion, lassitude, and in some cases prostration may occur. She became progressively prostrate as the disease advanced.
Use **fatigue** reaction / state / fracture[9] • chronic **fatigue** syndrome[10] • muscle[11] [mʌsl]/ daytime / excessive or extreme [iː]/ **fatigue** • auditory [ɒː]/ functional vocal **fatigue** • to experience / feeling of / post-therapy **lassitude** • marked or severe / extreme / heat[12] **prostration** • easy[13] **fatiguability**

weakness [wiːknəs] *n clin*
sim **feebleness**[1] [iː], **fragility**[2] [dʒɪ] *n clin* → U4-7

reduction [ʌ] in normal power of one or more muscles; patients often use the word to refer to increased fatiguability or limitation of motor function due to pain
weak *adj clin* • **weaken**[3] *vi & vt* • **feeble**[4] *adj* • **fragile** *adj*
» Weakness may result from disuse of muscles, malnutrition[5] [ɪʃ], electrolyte disturbances [ɜː], anemia, neurologic disorders, or myopathies. Arterial occlusion in an extremity usually results in pain, numbness [ʌ], tingling[6], weakness, and coldness. The skeletal weakness caused by osteoporosis manifests clinically as bone fractures.
Use physical[7] / motor / (subjective) muscular[8] [ʌ]/ triceps [aɪ] **weakness** • left-sided / generalized / diffuse / (right) facial **weakness** • upper arm / leg / lower limb[9] / focal[10] **weakness** • fluctuating [ʌ]/ progressive spastic[11] / exercise-dependent[12] **weakness** • bilateral / asymmetric / flaccid[13] [(k)s] **weakness** • easy fatiguability / lethargy / wasting[14] [eɪ] **and weakness** • skin / bone[15] / vascular / capillary **fragility** • to feel[16]/be **weak** • **weak** leg / hand muscles / stomach[17] [k]/ cry • **feeble** pulse[18] [ʌ]/ respirations / heart[19] / urinary stream • **fragile** health[20] / bones[21] / tissue

anorexia [ænəreksɪə] *n term*   *syn* **loss of appetite** [æpətaɪt] *n clin* → U2-11

diminished appetite; the patient is 'off his food', i.e. dislikes what (s)he enjoyed eating before
anorexic[1] *adj & n term* • **anorectic** *adj*
» AIDS patients frequently suffer from anorexia, nausea and vomiting, all of which contribute to weight loss. In infants diarrhea [iː] is usually accompanied by loss of appetite, failure to gain weight, and irritability. She reported an increased appetite for salt.
Use to experience[2]/complain of[3] **anorexia** • history / episodes **of anorexia** • **anorexic**, nausea [ɒː] & vomiting[4] • **anorexic** patient / behavior • good / poor[5] / diminished **appetite** • change in / (inability) to control[6] / return [ɜː] of[7] **appetite** • to affect/ increase or improve or stimulate[8]/lose[9] **appetite** • **anorexic** drug or agent[10] • **anorectic** state *or* disease

> **Note:** The term **anorexia** denotes 'decreased appetite' and must be distinguished from the eating disorder termed **anorexia nervosa**[11] (**anorexic** can refer to both).

Unpässlichkeit, Unwohlsein
(leichte körperl.) Beschwerden[1] s. unwohl fühlen[2] produktiver Husten, H. mit Auswurf[3] Muskelschmerz(en), Myalgie[4] stark ausgeprägt[5] Schüttelfrost[6] Appetitlosigkeit[7] allgem. Krankheitsgefühl[8] leichte Unpässlichkeit[9] leichte Beschwerden[10] erträgliche Beschwerden[11]

7

(i) Müdigkeit
(ii) Ermüdung, -schöpfung
Müdigkeit[1] Mattigkeit, Abgeschlagenheit[2] extreme Erschöpfung/ Kraftlosigkeit, Prostration[3] Müdigkeit, Lustlosigkeit[4] Erschöpfung[5] anstrengend[6] Ermüdbarkeit[7] übermäßig[8] Ermüdungsbruch, -fraktur[9] chron. Müdigkeits-, Erschöpfungssyndrom[10] Muskelermüdung[11] Hitzeerschöpfung[12] leichte Ermüdbarkeit[13]

8

Schwäche(gefühl)
Schwäche, Kraftlosigkeit, Mattigkeit[1] Ge-, Zerbrechlichkeit; Brüchigkeit[2] (ab)schwächen, schwach, schwächer werden[3] schwach, matt[4] Mangel-, Fehlernährung[5] Kribbeln[6] körperl. Schwäche[7] Muskelschwäche, Myasthenie[8] Schwäche d. Beine[9] fokale Schwäche[10] progrediente Spastik[11] belastungsbedingte Schwäche[12] schlaffe Lähmung[13] Auszehrung u. Schwäche[14] Knochenbrüchigkeit[15] sich schwach fühlen[16] empfindlicher Magen[17] schwacher Puls[18] schwaches Herz[19] schwache Gesundheit, Anfälligkeit[20] brüchige Knochen[21]

9

Appetitlosigkeit, Anorexie
appetitlos, anorektisch; Pat. m. Anorexia nervosa[1] an Appetitlosigkeit leiden, keinen Appetit haben[2] über Appetitlosigkeit klagen[3] Appetitlosigkeit, Übelkeit u. Erbrechen[4] schlechter Appetit[5] den Appetit zügeln[6] sich (wieder) bessernder A.[7] den Appetit anregen[8] den Appetit verlieren[9] Appetitzügler, -hemmer, Anorektikum[10] Anorexia nervosa, Magersucht[11]

10

Nonspecific Clinical Symptoms   CLINICAL TERMS **459**

---

nausea [nɔːzɪə‖nɒːʒə] *n clin & term* *rel* **sickness**[1] *n clin & inf* → U4-1

unpleasant [e] sensation in the abdominal region that may be associated with an urge [ɜːdʒ] to vomit; typical causes include seasickness, early pregnancy, or food poisoning[2]

nauseated[3] *adj clin* • **nauseating**[4] *adj* • **nauseous**[4] *adj* • **sea-sick**[5] *adj*

» The patient had nausea with two episodes of vomiting. A rectal suppository[6] may be useful for patients who are too nauseated to swallow pills without experiencing further emesis [eməsɪs]. The morning sickness of early pregnancy is another instance of nausea and vomiting possibly related to hormonal changes.

Use to cause/be accompanied by **nausea** • **nausea and** vomiting (*abbr* N & V)/ heartburn[7] • **nausea and** diarrhea [aɪ]/ lethargy • postprandial / evening / postoperative **nausea** • persistent / transient **nausea** • **nauseated** patient / and dizzy • to feel[8] **nauseous** • motion[9] [oʊʃ]/ car / air[10] / sea / high altitude [æ] or mountain[11] / x-ray *or* radiation[12] / serum [ɪɚ]/ morning[13] **sickness**

> Note: In **British** usage **to feel sick** means 'to be nauseated' and **to be sick** 'to vomit' while **to be ill** means 'not healthy'; so **to be sick two times** refers to two episodes of vomiting. **Sickness** is a synonym for **illness** and **disease** as well as **nausea**.

vomiting *n clin*   *syn* **emesis** *n term*,
                      rel **regurgitation**[1] [ɜː] *n clin & term* → U46-4

the act of bringing or spitting up material from the stomach [k]

vomit[2] *v & n clin* • **vomitus** *n term* • **(anti)emetic**[3] *adj & n* • **-emesis** *comb*

» Continuous suction [ʌ] via a nasogastric tube[4] is begun to prevent vomiting and aspiration of vomitus. What did the patient vomit? Do not induce emesis because of the risk of seizures [iːʒ]. Antiemetics clearly reduce nausea in these patients. The patient presents with heartburn[5] [ɜː] and regurgitation due to gastroesophageal [dʒiː] reflux and esophagitis [dʒaɪ].

Use to induce/eliminate **vomiting** • **vomiting** begins / occurs [ɜː]/ subsides [aɪ]/ is present • mild / repeated / protracted[6] / persistent **vomiting** • intractable[7] / (non)bilious [ɪ] *or* bile-stained[8] [aɪ]/ copious[9] [oʊ] **vomiting** • pronounced [aʊ]/ dry / forceful / self-induced[10] / feculent[11] [ek] **vomiting** • **vomiting** of blood[12] • bloody *or* black *or* coffee-ground[13] [aʊ] **vomitus** • anticipatory / spontaneous [eɪ] **emesis** • delayed [eɪ]/ acute / induced **emesis** • hemat[12] [iː]/ hyper**emesis** [aɪ] • effortless[14] / postprandial **regurgitation** • **regurgitation of** undigested [dʒe] food

> Note: The polite clinical expression for vomiting is **to bring up food**. So when taking a history you might ask: *Did you bring up anything on these occasions?* **Throw up**[15] may be used in clinical situations while *****puke**[16] [pjuːk] should be avoided by physicians. Note that **to bring up** can also be used to mean **expectorate** (sputum, phlegm[17] [flem], etc. from the lungs).

dizziness [dɪzɪnəs] *n clin*   *syn* **giddiness** *n*, *sim* **light-headedness**[1] *n clin*

broad term used by patients to describe symptoms such as faintness[2] [eɪ], spinning[3], and unsteadiness[4]

dizzy[5] *adj clin & inf* • **giddy**[5] [ɡɪdi] *adj* • **light-headed** [laɪthedɪd] *adj* → U113-6

» A careful history is necessary to determine exactly what the patient complaining of dizziness is experiencing (is it true vertigo, a sensation that the surroundings are spinning around the patient, or nonspecific lightheadedness). The drug makes some patients dizzy or drowsy[6].

Use to cause/produce/develop/complain of **dizziness** • **dizzy** spells[7] • episodes of[7] / transient / postural[8] / drug-induced / paroxysmal[9] [ɪ] **dizziness** • **lightheadedness** and confusion

blurred vision [blɜːrd vɪʒ³n] *n clin*   *syn* **blurring of vision,**
                                                visual blurring *n clin*

visual [vɪʒʊəl] disturbances[1] [ɜː] marked by inability to see objects clearly; the image seen is distorted[2]

» Side effects such as dry mouth[3], blurred vision, urinary obstruction may limit the drug's utility.

Use to cause/have an episode of **blurred vision** • short-lived[4] / incipient [sɪ] **blurred vision** • slight [slaɪt]/ temporary[4] **blurring of vision** • **vision** was **blurred**

Übelkeit, Brechreiz, Nausea
Übelkeit, Brechreiz; Krankheit, Erkrankung[1] Lebensmittelvergiftung[2] an Übelkeit/ Brechreiz leidend[3] ekelerregend, Übelkeit verursachend[4] seekrank[5] Rektalzäpfchen[6] Übelkeit u. Sodbrennen[7] Brechreiz verspüren[8] Reise-, Bewegungskrankheit, Kinetose[9] Luft-, Flugkrankheit[10] Höhen-, Bergkrankheit[11] Strahlenkater[12] morgendl. Übelkeit[13]

11

Erbrechen, Emesis, Vomitus
Rückströmen, (passives) Zurückströmen, Regurgitation, Reflux[1] erbrechen, s. übergeben; Erbrochenes, Vomitus[2] emetisch; Brechmittel, Emetikum[3] Magenschlauch[4] Sodbrennen[5] protrahiertes Erbrechen[6] unstillbares E.[7] galliges E.[8] starkes E.[9] selbstinduziertes E.[10] Koterbrechen, Miserere[11] Bluterbrechen, Haematemesis[12] kaffeesatzartiges Erbrochenes[13] Erbrechen ohne Antiperistaltik, passives Zurückfließen v. Mageninhalt[14] erbrechen, sich übergeben[15] kotzen[16] Schleim[17]

12

Schwindel(gefühl)
Schwindel, (leichte) Benommenheit[1] Schwächegefühl[2] Drehschwindel[3] Schwanken, Unsicherheitsgefühl[4] schwind(e)lig[5] schläfrig[6] Schwindelanfälle[7] lagebedingter Schwindel, Lageschwindel[8] Anfallschwindel[9]

13

verschwommenes Sehen
Sehstörungen[1] verzerrt[2] Mundtrockenheit[3] kurze Episode von verschwommenem Sehen[4]

14

103

CLINICAL TERMS — Nonspecific Clinical Symptoms

photophobia [foʊtəfoʊbɪə] *n term*   *syn* **sensitivity to light** *phr clin*

abnormal visual intolerance to light[1]; e.g. when a patient reports that (bright) light hurts his/her eyes
light-sensitive[2] *adj clin* • sensitive to light[2] *phr* • **photophobic**[2] *adj term*

» She complained of photophobia, spots before the eyes[3], and blurring of vision. The patient developed persistent sensitivity to light, necessitating long-term avoidance of sun exposure[4].

Use to produce/develop/exhibit/relieve **photophobia** • mild / severe **photophobia** • hyper[1] [aɪ]/ persistent **sensitivity to light** • in[5]/ photo/ chemo/ radio**sensitive**

Lichtscheu, Photophobie
Überempfindlichkeit gegen Licht[1] lichtscheu, -empfindlich[2] Augenflimmern[3] Meiden von Sonnenlicht[4] unempfindlich[5]

15

---

cough [kɒːf] *v & n clin*
   rel **snort**[1], **sneeze**[2] *v*, **to blow one's nose**[3] *phr clin*

(n) sudden expulsion [ʌ] of air from the lungs that clears the air passages
coughing *n & adj clin* • **sneezing** *n* • **snorting** *n* → U44-2; U10-20

» In acute sinusitis nasal discharge or postnasal drip[4] and daytime cough usually persist longer than 10 days. Dry cough, dyspnea [ɪ], and a flu-like illness are commonly seen at the onset. Coughing associated with rhinitis [aɪ] may be an allergic [ɜː] response. The patient has been coughing up frothy[5], pinkish material.

Use to give a/develop/experience/control or suppress **cough** • **to cough** up[6] • bad or severe[7] / dry / wet[8] / persistent / irritating **cough** • hacking or staccato[9] / barking[10] / brassy[11] **cough** • episodic / persistent / nagging[12] / chronic **cough** • nocturnal [ɜː] or night / morning / mild[13] **cough** • loose[14] / (non/ un)productive[8] / whooping[15] [uː]/ croupy [uː] **cough** • **cough** reflex / tenderness[16] / with expectoration[8] • **cough** fracture[17] / suppressant[18] / syrup [ɪ] • to trigger or provoke / (severe) bouts [aʊ] or fits of[19] **coughing** • severe / vigorous[20] / violent [aɪə]/ reflex [iː]/ daytime / incessant[21] [se] **coughing** • **coughing** efforts / spells or paroxysms[19] [-ɪzəmz] • **coughing** spasm / and wheezing [iː] • paroxysmal[22] [ɪ]/ frequent **sneezing** • nose[23] **blowing**

husten; Husten
schnauben, schnupfen[1] niesen[2] sich d. Nase putzen, s. schnäuzen[3] Schleimstraße im Nasenrachenraum[4] trüb, schaumig[5] aushusten[6] starker Husten[7] Husten m. Auswurf, produktiver Husten[8] Stakkatohusten[9] bellender Husten[10] metallisch klingender Husten[11] hartnäckiger Husten[12] leichter Husten[13] lockerer Husten[14] Keuchhusten, Pertussis[15] Hustenschmerz[16] Hustenfraktur[17] Antitussivum, Hustenmittel[18] Hustenanfälle[19] starkes Husten[20] ständiges Husten[21] Niesanfall[22] Schnäuzen[23]

16

---

expectorate [ɪkspektəreɪt] *v term*   *syn* **cough up** or **out** *v phr clin*
   sim **bring up**[1] *v phr clin,*
   rel **hawk**[2] [hɔːk] *v,*
   spit[3] *n & v irr inf* → U27-10

to eject [ɪdʒekt] saliva, mucus, or other fluid from the throat [oʊ] or lungs by coughing or clearing one's throat[2] and spitting
expectoration[4] *n term* • **expectorant**[5] *adj & n* • **hemoptysis**[6] *n* → U111-7

» Ask the patient to expectorate a sputum specimen during the evaluation. When you bring up any material again, I'd like you to save a sample in this container. Expectoration of hard mucous plugs [ʌ] or hemoptysis [hɪmɒptɪsɪs] may occur. Did you cough up any blood?

Use to encourage[7] [ɜː] /ease [iː] **expectoration** • **expectorated** material[8] / respiratory secretions / sputum[8] • spontaneous **expectoration** • **expectorant** cough mixture[9] • **to cough up** (frothy) sputum / (a few streaks of) blood / retained secretions • **to bring up** secretions / food • blood[6] **spitting** • to hawk and **spit** • **to spit** out[10]

aus-, abhusten, auswerfen, expektorieren
aushusten; erbrechen[1] sich räuspern[2] Spucke; spucken[3] Expektoration, Aushusten; Auswurf, Sputum[4] d. Expektoration fördernd; Expektorans, auswurffördernde/ schleimlösendes Mittel[5] Hämoptoe, -ptyse, Bluthusten, -spucken[6] d. Expektoration fördern[7] Auswurf, Sputum[8] schleimlösender Hustensaft[9] ausspucken[10]

17

---

sputum [sp(j)uːtəm] *n term*
   sim **phlegm**[1] [flem] *n clin*

expectorated matter, esp. mucus or mucopurulent [jʊə] matter brought up in diseases of the air passages

» He has a chronic cough with scanty[2] sputum production. These low-pitched rhonchi [kaɪ] are caused by sputum in large airways. Do you bring up any phlegm when you cough?

Use to produce/obtain [eɪ] or collect[3]/clear **sputum** • clear[4] / blood-tinged [dʒ] or -streaked[5] [iː]/ rusty-colored[6] [ʌ] **sputum** • frothy[7] / (non-/muco)purulent / foul-smelling[8] [aʊ] **sputum** • **sputum** analysis or examination[9] / specimen or sample[10] • **sputum** smear[11] [ɪɚ]/ culture [ʌ] • **sputum** cytology[12] / Gram stain [eɪ]/ production • **sputum** viscosity [kɒ]/ induction • to bring up[13] **phlegm**

Sputum, Auswurf
Schleim[1] wenig[2] Sputum gewinnen[3] klares Sputum[4] blutig-tingierter Auswurf[5] rotbraunes Sputum[6] schaumiger Auswurf[7] fötider/ übelriechender Auswurf[8] Sputumuntersuchung[9] Sputumprobe[10] Sputumabstrich[11] Sputumzytologie[12] Schleim aushusten[13]

18

Pain CLINICAL TERMS **461**

itching [ɪtʃɪŋ] n & adj clin   syn **pruritus** [pruəraɪtəs] n term
  rel **formication**¹ [keɪ] n term

tingling², irritating sensation on an area of the skin that arouses [aʊ] the desire to scratch³
itch⁴ v & n clin & inf • **itchy**⁵ adj • **pruritic** adj term

» Her chief complaints were headache, photophobia and itching of the eyes. Her itch was severe. Chronic otitis externa causes pruritus rather than ear pain. The boy's rash does not itch. The presence of formication and stereotypy⁶ may be suggestive of stimulant abuse.

Use to relieve/aggravate or exacerbate⁷ [æs] **itching** • nasal / intense or severe⁸ / generalized / transient **itching** • **itchy** swelling / area / skin • **itching** skin lesion⁹ [i:ʒ]/ sensation [eɪʃ]/ rash¹⁰ / dermatitis [aɪ] • dryness / lacrimation **and itching** • vaginal¹¹ [dʒ]/ perianal¹² [eɪ] **itching** • (peri)anal¹² / vulvar [ʌ]/ chronic / severe⁸ **pruritus**

Jucken, Juckreiz, Pruritus; juckend
Ameisenlaufen, Kribbeln, Formicatio¹ kribbelnd² kratzen³ jucken; Juckreiz; Krätze, Skabies⁴ juckend⁵ Stereotypie⁶ den Juckreiz verschlimmern⁷ starker Juckreiz⁸ juckende Hautläsion⁹ juckender (Haut)ausschlag¹⁰ Scheidenjucken¹¹ Afterjucken, Pruritus ani¹²
19

neck stiffness n clin   syn **nuchal rigidity** [n(j)u:kᵊl rɪdʒɪdɪti] n term
  rel **cramp**¹ n & v clin, **spasm**² n & comb, **spasticity**³, **rigor**⁴ [aɪ] n term → U12-15

contraction of the neck muscles [ʌ], which may produce torsion of the head with the chin [tʃ] pointing to the other side (also termed wry [raɪ] neck or torticollis⁵)
stiff⁶ adj • **rigid**⁶ adj • **stiffening**⁷ n • **cramping** n & adj • **spastic**⁸ adj term

» Rigidity of the neck or torticollis toward the opposite side may develop. Spasticity is distinct from rigidity and paratonia⁹, two other types of increased tone [oʊ]. Extensive spasm of skeletal muscle causes cramps and tetany¹⁰.

Use muscle / morning / generalized / joint¹¹ [dʒ] **stiffness** • **stiffness of** joints¹¹ / extremities • to be/feel/become **stiff** • **stiff** neck • muscle / board-like¹² / cogwheel¹³ / decerebrate¹⁴ [se]/ fluctuating [ʌ] **rigidity** • abdominal / chest [tʃ] **wall rigidity** • overall body / progressive / arterial [ɚ] **stiffening** • muscle / writer's¹⁵ / (nocturnal) [ɜː] leg / heat¹⁶ **cramp** • abdominal / calf¹⁷ [kæf] **cramping** • **spastic** bladder¹⁸ / colon¹⁹ [oʊ]/ weakness / torticollis / paraplegia²⁰ [i:dʒ] / blepharo²¹ / laryngo [ɪŋg] / vaso²² [eɪ]/ broncho**spasm** [k]

Nackensteifigkeit, Genickstarre
(Muskel)krampf; (ver)krampfen, K. auslösen¹ Krampf, Verkrampfung, Spasmus, Konvulsion² Spastizität, Spastik³ Rigidität, Rigor⁴ Schiefhals, Torticollis⁵ starr, (ver)steif(t), unbeweglich, rigid⁶ Versteifung⁷ spastisch, krampfartig⁸ Paratonie⁹ Tetanie¹⁰ Gelenksteifigkeit¹¹ bretthartes Abdomen¹² Zahnradphänomen¹³ Enthirnungsstarre¹⁴ Schreibkrampf¹⁵ Hitzschlag¹⁶ Wadenkrampf¹⁷ Reflexblase¹⁸ Reizdarmsyndrom, Reizkolon¹⁹ spast. Paraplegie²⁰ Lidkrampf²¹ Vasospasmus²²
20

Unit 104 Pain
Related Units: 135 Anesthesiology, 93 Anesthetics, 5 Injuries, 89 Pathology

discomfort n clin

slightly painful feeling, e.g. after a minor injury¹ or being in an uncomfortable² position; often used as a clinical understatement
(un)comfortable³ adj • **comfort**⁴ n & v

» Does this cause any discomfort? There was some discomfort but no real pain.

Use to cause/feel/experience⁵/tolerate⁶/control/aggravate⁷/ameliorate⁸ [i:]/ minimize **discomfort** • migratory [aɪ]/ postprandial / vague [veɪg] **abdominal discomfort** • aching / acute / mild / chest / pelvic / epigastric / postural⁹ [pɒstʃɚəl]/ local / residual¹⁰ **discomfort**

(leichte körperliche) Beschwerden, Unpässlichkeit
leichte Verletzung¹ unbequem, unangenehm² angenehm³ Trost, Beruhigung, Bequemlichkeit; trösten⁴ sich unwohl fühlen⁵ B. ertragen⁶ B. verstärken⁷ B. lindern⁸ haltungsbedingte B.⁹ Restbeschwerden¹⁰
1

distress n & v clin   sim **suffering**¹ [ʌ] n clin → U4-3

(i) being affected by worries, extreme sadness, pain (ii) to be in danger or in urgent [ɜːrdʒᵊnt] need of help
distressed², **-ing**, **-ful** adj • **suffer (from)**³ v • **sufferer**⁴ n

» The patient was in acute distress because of central chest pain. Distress mostly refers to emotional suffering. He is suffering from severe malnutrition. He did not suffer at all and died peacefully. For some death may represent an escape from unbearable [eɚ] suffering⁵.

Use **to be in** (no) acute⁶ / minimal **distress** •signs of **distress** • emotional / physical / family⁷ / respiratory⁸ / fetal [i:] **distress** • **distressing** experience / symptom⁹ • **distressed** child / family¹⁰ • hay [heɪ] fever¹¹ [i:]/ chronic tinnitus **sufferer**

Not(lage), Leid, Kummer; bedrücken, beunruhigen
Leid(en)¹ notleidend, bekümmert² (er)leiden³ Leidende(r), Patient(in)⁴ unerträgliche(s) Leiden⁵ dringend Hilfe benötigen⁶ familiäre Sorgen⁷ Atemnot⁸ beunruhigendes Symptom⁹ besorgte Familienangehörige¹⁰ Heuschnupfenpatient(in)¹¹ leiden an¹² e. Schlaganfall erleiden¹³

Note: Mark the difference between to suffer from¹² an illness and to suffer a stroke¹³, a heart attack, an injury, etc.

2

Pain

hurt - hurt - hurt [hɜːrt] *v irr & adj*   *sim* **irritate**[1], **bother**[2] [ɒː] *v*

v (i) to feel physical or emotional pain (ii) injure oneself or sb. else or be injured → U5-1
to get/ be hurt *phr* • **irritating**[3] *adj* • **irritation**[4] *n* • **bothersome**[5] *adj*

» Where does it hurt most? The light hurts my eyes. Are you hurt? I was deeply hurt by his remarks. His *irritating rash*[6] [æ] has become extremely bothersome. It does not bother me that much.

Use to cause/avoid **irritation** • skin / mucosal[7] / gastric / local **irritation** • to (be) **bother(ed)** about sth.[8]

schmerzen, weh tun; (sich) verletzen; verletzt
irritieren, stören[1] zu schaffen machen, stören[2] unangenehm, störend[3] Irritation, Reizung[4] lästig, beeinträchtigend[5] Hautirritation[6] Schleimhautreizung[7] sich Sorgen machen[8]   3

---

ache [eɪk] *v & n & comb* → U113-16

(v) to hurt constantly (n) a continuous, not very intense, often not precisely localized pain
headache[1] *n* • **toothache**[2] *n* • **earache** *n* • **aching**[3] *adj*

» My arm is giving me much less pain but still aches when I carry something heavy. Low abdominal pain is usually *crampy*[4] or colicky but may be a dull constant ache.

Use dull[5] [ʌ]/ vague / mild / generalized [dʒen-]/ deep-seated[6] **ache** • muscle / stomach-[7] [k]/ belly**ache**[8] • throbbing[9] head**aches** • **aching** feet / pains[10] • to be **aching** all over[11]

schmerzen, weh tun; Schmerz(en); -weh
Kopfschmerzen[1] Zahnschmerzen[2] schmerzhaft[3] krampfartig[4] dumpfer S.[5] tiefsitzender S.[6] Magenschmerzen[7] Bauchschmerzen[8] klopfende/ pochende Kopfschmerzen[9] Schmerzen am ganzen Körper, Wehwehchen[10] alles tut weh[11]   4

---

aches and pains *phr clin*   *syn* **aching pains** *n clin*

refers to minor pains all over the body, esp. in muscles or joints, after excessive exercise

» *Prostration*[1] and generalized aches and pains are commonly the first manifestations of influenza. It's no problem – just the *aches and pains of old age*[2].

Use vague / widespread [e]/ disseminated / generalized[3] **aches and pains** • growing[4] **pains**

Gliederschmerzen, S. am ganzen Körper, Wehwehchen
Erschöpfung(szustand), Prostration[1] Altersbeschwerden, -wehwehchen[2] Schmerzen am ganzen Körper[3] Wachstumsschmerzen[4]   5

---

pain *n usu sing*   *syn* **dolor** *n term rare*

(i) unpleasant sensation[1] [eɪ] related to tissue damage, conveyed[2] [eɪ] to the brain by nerve fibers where its conscious appreciation[3] [iːʃ] may be modified by various factors
(ii) painful uterine contraction in childbirth (usu pl)

painful[4] *adj* • **pained**[5] *adj* • **painless, pain-free** *adj* • **indolent**[6] *adj term*

» How long have you had this pain? You won't feel any pain. This is a completely painless procedure.

Use to cause *or* arouse [aʊ] *or* evoke *or* give rise to[7]/aggravate **pain** • **pain** arises / spreads / persists[8] / recurs • to be in/feel **pain** • to have a **pain** in the chest • a **pained** face[9] / expression • **pain-free** intervals • **pain** therapy • **pain on** palpation / coughing[10] [kɒfɪŋ]/ urination • menstrual *or* period / labor[11] [eɪ] **pains** • (in)sensitivity to **pain**[12] / **painful** stimuli [aɪ]/ sensation / joints / swallowing[13] / lesion • **painless** swelling / mass[14] • **indolent** ulcer[15] [ʌlsɚ]

Note: *Pain* is normally singular. When used in the *plural* it refers to the pain related to menstruation or childbirth or to show that it recurs. It can also mean *to try very hard* , e.g. in *painstaking*[16] and *to take* or *go to great pains*[17].

**(i) Schmerz(en)
(ii) Wehen**
Empfindung[1] übertragen[2] bewusste Wahrnehmung[3] schmerzhaft[4] schmerzerfüllt[5] langsam heilend, schmerzlos, indolent[6] S. verursachen[7] S. halten an/ persistieren[8] schmerzverzerrtes Gesicht[9] S. beim Husten[10] Wehen[11] Schmerzunempfindlichkeit[12] Schluckbeschwerden[13] indolenter Tumor[14] schlecht abheilendes/ indolentes Geschwür[15] sorgfältig, gewissenhaft[16] sich Mühe geben[17]

6

---

character *or* **nature of pain** *n clin*

» What kind of pain is it? Ulcer pain is typically described as "*aching discomfort*". *Colicky pain*[1] is usually promptly *alleviated*[2] [əliːvieɪt-] by analgesics. *Tearing* [eə] pain is characteristic of a *dissecting aneurysm*[3] [-jarɪzᵊm].

Use **pain** of a colicky nature[1] • burning / crampy / cutting / lancinating[4] / stabbing *or* piercing[5] / shooting[6] [uː]/ boring[7] **pain** • stinging[5] / gnawing[8] [nɒːɪŋ] / dragging *or* tearing[9] **pain** • disabling[10] / psychogenic [saɪkoʊdʒenɪk] / hunger[11] / rest[12] **pain**

Schmerzqualität
kolikartige Schmerzen[1] gelindert[2] Aneurysma dissecans[3] lanzinierender S.[4] stechender S.[5] plötzlich einschießende S.[6] bohrender Schmerz[7] nagender S.[8] ziehender Schmerzen[9] starke (funktionell beeinträchtigende) S.[10] Nüchternschmerz[11] Ruheschmerz[12]   7

---

duration [eɪ] and **periodicity of pain** *n clin*

» When did you first notice this pain? How long did it last? The episodes of pain became more frequent, remissions[1] became shorter, and a dull ache persisted between the episodes of stabbing pain.

Use fleeting[2] [iː]/ intermittent / chronic / steady [e] *or* persistent[3] **pain** • lingering[3] [ŋg]/ unremitting *or* stubborn[4] [ʌ] nagging[5] [æ]/ night / delayed[6] [eɪ]/ postprandial **pain**

Schmerzdauer
Remissionen, Besserung[1] flüchtiger Schmerz[2] anhaltende Schmerzen[3] hartnäckige S.[4] dumpfe S.[5] Spätschmerz[6]

8

Pain   CLINICAL TERMS 463

intensity of pain *n clin*

sensitive or painful as a result of pressure or contact which normally does not cause discomfort

» Doctor, this pain is killing me. Does anything make it worse? How do you get relief? Lidocaine is ineffective for prevention or relief of this intense pain. Agonizing pain is a sign of serious [ɪɚ] or advanced disease.

Use mild[1] [aɪ]/ dull[2] [ʌ]/ moderate / intense or sharp[3] / acute **pain** • intractable[4] / severe[3] / intolerable[5] / violent [aɪə] or killing[6] / excruciating [uːʃ] or exquisite or agonizing[7] [aɪz] **pain**

Schmerzintensität
leichte Schmerzen[1] dumpfer Schmerz[2] heftige/ starke S.[3] therapierefraktäre S.[4] unerträgliche S.[5] rasende S.[6] qualvolle Schmerzen[7]   9

site [saɪt] or **loc(aliz)ation of pain** *n*

» Could you point to the spot where it hurts most. A history of renal stones might be a cause of referred back pain.

Use deep(-seated)[1] / superficial[2] / (poorly) localized[3] / diffuse / radiating[4] [eɪ] **pain** • spreading [e]/ migratory[5] [aɪ]/ generalized / non-specific / referred[6] [ɜː] **pain** • chest / flank[7] / phantom limb[8] [lɪm]/ joint / suprapubic [pjuː]/ upper abdominal / epigastric / low(er) back[9] **pain**

Schmerzlokalisation
Tiefenschmerz[1] oberflächl. S.[2] schwer abgrenzbarer S.[3] ausstrahlende S.[4] wandernder S.[5] Synalgie, übertragener S.[6] Flankenschmerz[7] Phantomschmerz[8] Kreuzschmerzen[9]   10

tender *adj clin*   *sim* **sore**[1] [sɔːr], **painful**[2] *adj inf & clin*

tenderness[3] *n clin* • **soreness, painfulness** *n rare*

» The cardinal manifestations are fever, pain (continuous, stabbing, or pleuritic [ʊ]) and an enlarged and tender liver. Bursitis [-aɪtɪs] is likely to cause focal tenderness[4] and swelling.

Use **tender** point / swelling / mass[5] • **tender(ness)** to palpation / to motion[6] / over the injury • abdominal / costovertebral angle [ŋg]/ exquisite[7] **tenderness** • diffuse / point or pencil[8] / localized[4] / rebound[9] **tenderness** • **sore** throat[10] [oʊ]/ muscles[11] / nipples[12]

(druck)schmerzhaft, druckempfindlich
wund, entzündet[1] schmerzhaft[2] Druckschmerz, Schmerzhaftigkeit[3] lokalisierter Schmerz[4] schmerzhafter Knoten[5] Bewegungsschmerz[6] überaus starke Schmerzen[7] Punktschmerz[8] Loslassschmerz[9] Halsschmerzen[10] Muskelschmerzen, -kater[11] empfindliche Brustwarzen[12]   11

wince [wɪn¹s] *v & n*   *syn* **flinch** [flɪntʃ] *v rare*

to move back, tighten[1] [aɪt] the muscles because of pain or make a pained face[2]

» The boy watched me stick in the needle without wincing. "Ouch[3]," [aʊtʃ] he said with a wince. The pain may be so intense that the patient winces, hence[4] the condition is termed tic[5].

(vor Schmerz) zusammenzucken; Zucken
anspannen[1] schmerzverzerrtes Gesicht[2] au (weh)[3] daher[4] Tic(k), Muskelzucken[5]   12

stitch [stɪtʃ] *n & v*   *syn* **twinge** [twɪndʒ], **pang** *n inf*

sharp pain of short duration, e.g. a stitch in the side[1] which is due to excessive physical exercise

» Suddenly I felt this slight twinge in my hamstring[2] again. If you are prone [oʊ] to[3] stitches[1] do your exercise with an empty stomach[4].

Use breast[5] [e]/ hunger **pang**

Stich, (kurzer) stechender Schmerz; stechen
Seitenstechen[1] Beinbeuger[2] neigen zu[3] mit leerem Magen, nüchtern[4] stechender Brustschmerz[5]   13

paroxysm [pærəksɪzᵊm] *n term & clin*   *sim* **attack**[1] *n*

recurrent bouts[2] [aʊ] of sharp pain or symptoms such as chills[3] [tʃ], colics or cramps that are sudden in onset[4]

paroxysmal[5] *adj term*

» Certain maneuvers [uː] triggered paroxysms of pain. His infection was characterized by paroxysms of chills, fever, and sweating [e]. A transient, paroxysmal disturbance of cardiac rhythm [ɪ] was suspected.

Use **paroxysmal** pain[6] / symptoms / tachycardia[7] [k]/ cough[8] [kɒf] / nocturnal dyspnea [dɪspniːə] (*abbr* PND) / vertigo[9] [ɜː]/ hypertension • spasmodic[10] **paroxysm**

Anfall, Paroxysmus
Anfall, Attacke[1] wiederkehrende Anfälle[2] Schüttelfrost[3] plötzlich auftretend[4] anfallsartig, paroxysmal[5] Schmerzattacken[6] paroxysmale Tachykardie[7] Hustenanfälle[8] Schwindelanfälle[9] anfallsartiger Muskelkrampf[10]   14

colic [kɒlɪk] *n clin & term*

paroxysmal pain in the abdomen typical of gastrointestinal disorders, stone disease[1], and in infants

colicky[2] *adj clin*

» He complained of colicky flank pain[3] radiating to the groin[4]. Biliary colic[5] may be precipitated[6] by eating a fatty meal. She was a colicky baby[7] who had 3–6 loose stools[8] [uː] per day.

Use gastric / biliary [bɪliɚi] or hepatic[5] / renal[9] [iː]/ menstrual / pancreatic / tubal **colic**

Kolik
Steinleiden[1] kolikartig[2] Flankenschmerz[3] Leiste(nbeuge)[4] Gallenkolik[5] ausgelöst[6] von Bauchkrämpfen geplagtes Baby[7] breiige Stühle[8] Nierenkolik[9]   15

CLINICAL TERMS — Pain

lumbago [lʌmbeɪɡoʊ] *n term* *sim* **sciatica**[1] [saɪætɪkə] *n term & clin*
  lower back pain[2] caused by muscle strain[3] [eɪ], arthritis [aɪ] or a ruptured intervertebral disk[4]
  sciatic[5] [saɪætɪk] *adj clin*
» *Sciatica is characterized by low back pain radiating [eɪ] down[6] the buttock[7] [ʌ] and down the knee [niː].*
Use **sciatic** pain / nerve (distribution)

Lumbago, Hexenschuss
Ischias(syndrom)[1] Kreuzschmerzen[2] Muskelhartspann, -verspannung[3] Bandscheibenvorfall[4] Ischias-[5] ausstrahlen[6] Gesäß[7]
16

paresthesia(s) [pæresθiːʒ(ɪ)ə] *n term* *rel* **pins-and-needles**[1] *n clin*
  abnormal sensation such as tingling [ŋɡ] pain[2], numbness[3] [nʌmnəs], prickling[4] or burning
  paresthetic [e] *adj term* • **dysesthesia** *n* • **hyperesthesia** *n*
» *Severe pain, numbness, paresthesia and coldness developed.*
Use general / perioral / distal limb / painful **paresthesia**

subjektive Missempfindung, Parästhesie
Kribbeln, Ameisenlaufen[1] schmerzhaftes Brennen[2] taubes Gefühl[3] Prickeln[4]
17

pain threshold [θreʃʰoʊld] *n term* *rel* **pain tolerance**[1] *n clin*
  the threshold of pain refers to the smallest intensity of pain the patient is able to appreciate[2] [iːʃ], while pain tolerance is the maximum (s)he can endure[3]; the unit of pain intensity is dol
» *Assess[4] joint swelling and functional activity and the patient's pain tolerance.*
Use low / high **pain threshold** • to appreciate/induce[5]/produce[5] **pain** • to bear[3] [beɚ]/endure/put up with[6] **pain**

Schmerzschwelle
Schmerztoleranzgrenze[1] empfinden[2] ertragen[3] abklären[4] Schmerzen verursachen[5] s. mit den Schmerzen abfinden[6]
18

pain relief [rɪliːf] *n clin* *sim* **palliative therapy**[1] *n term*
  to deaden pain[2] [e] and obtund [ʌ], dull [ʌ] or blunt [ʌ] sensation[3]
  relieve[4] *v clin* • **palliate**[4] *v term* • **palliation**[5] *n* • **palliative**[6] *adj & n*
» *How do you get relief? The pain was well controlled. Radiotherapy for palliation of pain significantly improves the quality of life of patients suffering from incurable malignancies. The drug failed to relieve suffering.*
Use to relieve [-iːv] *or* ease [iːz] *or* soothe [suːð] *or* alleviate [iː] *or* mitigate[7] / abolish / suppress **pain** • **pain** subsides [aɪ] *or* resolves[8] • **palliative** needs / home care / drug[9] / measures [eʒ]/ surgery[10]

Schmerzlinderung, -beseitigung
Palliativtherapie[1] Schmerz stillen[2] Sensibilität herabsetzen[3] mildern, lindern[4] Linderung[5] palliativ, lindernd; Palliativum[6] Schmerz lindern[7] S. lässt nach[8] Palliativum[9] Palliativoperation[10]
19

Don't say you've forgotten that pain-killing spray again!

analgesic [ænəldʒiːzɪk‖sɪk] *n & adj term* *syn* **pain killer** *n inf & jar*
  (n) drug to render a patient pain-free[1] without clouding [aʊ] of consciousness[2]
  (adj) deadening pain sensation
  analgesia[3] [ænəldʒiːzɪə] *n term* → U135-7
» *Will this kill the pain, doc? The patient required very large amounts of analgesics for relief.*
Use to obtund / dull / blunt **pain sensation** • **pain** receptor / sensitive pathways[4] • **pain**-transmission neurons [ʊɚ] • **analgesic** receptor / nephropathy[5]

schmerzstillendes Mittel, Analgetikum; schmerzstillend, analgetisch
d. Patient(in) schmerzfrei machen[1] Bewusstseinstrübung[2] Aufheben der Schmerzempfindung, Analgesie[3] Schmerzbahnen[4] Analgetikanephropathie[5]
20

-algia [ældʒ(ɪ)ə] *comb* *syn* **-(o)dyn(o)** [dɪn] *comb*
  refers to pains all over the body, esp in muscles or joints or after excessive exercise
» *Acute jaw [dʒɒː] or throat pain after therapy may be due to glossopharyngeal [-færɪndʒiːəl] neuralgia [nʊɚældʒ(ɪ)ə].*
Use my[1] [aɪ] / (trigeminal) [aɪdʒe] neur[2]/ ot/ caus/ arth**algia** • prostato[3]/ pleuro [ʊɚ]/ teno**dynia**[4] [tenədɪnɪə]

-schmerz
Muskelschmerzen, Myalgie[1] Trigeminusneuralgie[2] Prostatodynie[3] Sehnenschmerz, Ten(d)odynie, Tenalgie[4]
21

104

Fever & Sweating   CLINICAL TERMS **465**

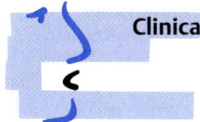

Clinical Phrases

Doctor, I have an awful pain in my shoulder. Herr Doktor, ich habe schreckliche Schmerzen in der Schulter. • When did you first notice this pain? Wann traten diese Schmerzen erstmals auf? • What brings it on? Wodurch werden sie ausgelöst? • Did it come on suddenly? Sind die Schmerzen plötzlich aufgetreten? • Does anything make it worse? Werden sie durch irgendetwas verstärkt? • Did you notice pins and needles? Spürten Sie ein Kribbeln? • He won't feel the pain. Er wird keine Schmerzen haben. • I've had this pain on and off for the past three months. Ich hatte diese Schmerzen immer wieder in den letzten 3 Monaten. • How much are you bothered by the urinary symptoms? Wie sehr fühlen Sie sich durch die Beschwerden beim Harnlassen beeinträchtigt? • Take care to avoid any skin irritation. Hautreizungen sollten Sie nach Möglichkeit vermeiden. • He went on to suffer multiple relapses. Er hatte immer wieder einen Rückfall. • She continued to suffer from stiffness and joint pain for several years. Sie litt noch mehrere Jahre lang an Gelenkschmerzen und Steifigkeit. • I usually drink a glass of milk to soothe the pain. Normalerweise trinke ich zur Schmerzlinderung ein Glas Milch. • She is without pain now. Sie ist jetzt schmerzfrei. • Freedom from pain was achieved on postoperative day 5. Schmerzfreiheit bestand ab dem 5. postoperativen Tag.

Unit 105 Fever & Sweating
Related Units: **108** Clinical Symptoms, **56** Skin, **44** Respiration, **94** Infectious Diseases

temperature [tempəətʃəʳ] *n*

(i) relative measure [eʒ] of body heat [iː] or degree [iː] of hotness of air, water, etc.
(ii) hyperthermia [ɜː]
(iii) colloquially used to refer to elevated temperature

» What's her temperature? His temperature is still up[1]. When the temperature is greater than 40 °C, esp. if prolonged, symptomatic treatment may be required.
Use to take[2]/measure[2]/record/cool[3]/lower[3] *the temperature* • to have/run *a temperature* • basal [eɪ] body[4] / core [kɔːr] or internal[5] [ɜː]/ axillary[6] / oral[7] / rectal temperature • skin[8] / surface / limb temperature • (sub)normal[9] / elevated[10] / high[11] temperature • stable [eɪ]/ peak [iː] temperature • ambient or environmental[12] / room temperature • change / rapid rise / drop / abrupt [ʌ] fall[13] in temperature • temperature sensation [eɪʃ] or appreciation[14] [iːʃ]/ reading[15] [iː] • temperature sense[16] / (-time) curve [ɜː]/ chart[17] [tʃɑːrt] • temperature instability / spike[18] [aɪ]/ regulation • temperature control / compensation[19] / spots[20]

> **Note:** In the US temperature is measured in **Fahrenheit degrees** (°F) rather than **Celcius degrees** or **centigrade** (°C). To convert °F into °C subtract 32 and divide by 9/5. Here are some clinically important equivalents: 96°F = 35.56°C; 98.6°F = 37°C; 100.4°F = 38°C; 102.2°F = 39°C; 104°F = 40°C.

(i) (Körper)temperatur
(ii, iii) erhöhte Temperatur
noch erhöht[1] Temperatur/ Fieber messen[2] Temperatur senken[3] Basal-, Aufwach-, Morgentemperatur[4] (Körper)kerntemperatur[5] Axilla-, Achsel(höhlen)temperatur[6] Oral-, Sublingualtemperatur[7] Hauttemperatur[8] Untertemperatur[9] erhöhte T.[10] Fieber[11] Umgebungstemperatur[12] Temperatursturz, rascher Temperaturabfall[13] Temperaturempfindung[14] Temperaturanzeige, -ablesung[15] Temperatursinn[16] Fieberkurve, Kurvenblatt[17] Fieberzacke, -spitze[18] Temperaturausgleich[19] Thermorezeptoren[20]

1

thermogenesis [θɜːrmoʊdʒenɪsɪs] *n term*
                        opposite **thermolysis**[1] [θɜːrmɒlɪsɪs] *n term*
physiologic process of heat production by the cells in the body

thermogenetic[2] [θɜːrmoʊdʒenetɪk] *adj term* • **thermo-** *comb*

» This receptor in adipose tissue[3] was found to be involved in lipolysis and thermogenesis. In healthy adults, energy expenditure[4] is primarily determined by three factors: basal energy expenditure [-tʃəʳ], thermic effect of food, and physical activity.
Use regulatory / increased[5] / perinatal [eɪ] *thermogenesis* • moderate / profound[6] [aʊ] local *thermolysis* • general / induced / accidental *thermolysis* • thermography[7] /stat /therapy[8] /stable[9] • **thermo**cautery[10] [ɒː] /labile /coagulation[11] /inhibitory • **thermo**regulation[12] /dynamic [aɪ] /receptor[13]

Thermogenese, Wärmebildung
Thermolyse, Wärmeabgabe[1] thermogenetisch, wärmebildend[2] Fettgewebe[3] Energieverbrauch[4] erhöhte Wärmebildung[5] verstärkte Wärmeabgabe[6] Thermografie[7] Wärme-, Thermotherapie[8] thermostabil, wärmebeständig[9] Thermokaustik[10] Thermokoagulation[11] Wärme-, Temperaturregulation[12] Thermorezeptor[13]

2

CLINICAL TERMS — Fever & Sweating

fever [fiːvɚ] n → U94-10,19 *syn* **pyrexia** [paɪrɛksɪə] n term

(i) body temperature above the normal of 98.6°F or 37°C
(ii) disease marked by an elevation of the body temperature above the normal

feverish[1] [fiːvɚɪʃ] adj clin • **febrile**[1] [fɛ‖fiːbraɪl] adj term • **subfebrile**[2] [ʌ] adj • **afebrile**[3] [eɪ] adj term • **apyrexia** [eɪ] n • **hyperpyrexia**[4] [aɪ] n • **subfebrility** n

» Not all fevers are due to infection. He's been afebrile for 48 hours. High doses of cocaine may induce lethal [iː] pyrexia. After 7 days the fever reached a plateau and the patient appeared exhausted [ɔː] and prostrated[5] [eɪ]. Patients should be isolated [aɪ] and kept at bed rest until afebrile [eɪfɛbraɪl‖eɪfiːbraɪl].

Use to present with/reduce/suppress[6] **fever** • to develop/have/produce (**a**) **fever** • low-grade[7] [eɪ]/ mild[7] / high(-grade)[8] **fever** • intermittent[9] / spiking[13] / relapsing[10] / remittent[11] **fever** • sustained[12] [eɪ] hemorrhagic [hɛməræd͡ʒɪk] **fever** • onset / absence or lack / bouts[13] [aʊ] **of fever** • **fever** abates[14] [eɪ] persists / subsides[14] [aɪ]/-free periods[15] • thirst[16] [ɜː]/ artificial[17] [ɪʃ]/ dehydration[16] [aɪ] **fever** • rheumatic[18] [ruː-]/ scarlet[19] / yellow[20] / typhoid[21] [taɪfɔɪd] **fever** • trench[22] [tʃ]/ catarrhal / hay[23] [heɪ] **fever** • catheter[24] / unexplained[25] **fever** • **fever** sore or blister[26] / spikes[27] • **febrile** patient / illness / response • **febrile** episodes[13] / urine [jʊɚɪn]/ UTI[28] • **febrile** convulsions [ʌ] or seizures[29] [siːʒɚz]/ delirium[30] • ante/ post**febrile** • mild / extreme **hyperpyrexia** • **feverish** feeling / child

antipyretic [ɪ‖aɪ] adj term *syn* **antifebrile, antithermic** [ɜː] adj
 opposite **febrifacient**[1] [fɛbrɪfeɪʃənt] adj & n term

lowering body temperature to prevent or alleviate [iː] fever

febricide[2] [fɛbrɪsaɪd] n term • **febrifuge**[2] [-fjuːdʒ] n • **antipyretic**[2] n

» In most instances, antipyretic therapy by itself is not needed except for reasons of comfort or in patients with marginal [mɑːrdʒ-] hemodynamic status [eɪ‖æ].

Use **antipyretic** drug[2] / agent[2] [eɪdʒ]/ effect[3] / properties / therapy / measures[4] [eʒ]

hyperthermia [haɪpɚθɜːrmɪə] n term
 opposite **hypothermia**[1] n term

(i) markedly elevated body temperature
(ii) therapeutically [juː] induced hyperpyrexia

thermic[2] [ɜː] adj term • **thermal**[2] adj • **hypothermal** or **hypothermic** adj

» Severe hyperthermia (40-41°C) may rapidly cause brain damage and multiorgan failure. Hypotension with tachycardia indicates profound fluid and electrolyte depletion, and mild hypothermia is usually present. Treat hyperthermia with aggressive cooling.

Use malignant[3] / life-threatening [e]/ microwave[4] [aɪ]/ regional [iːdʒ] **hyperthermia** • moderate / severe[5] / local / general **hypothermia** • systemic / induced or artificial[6] / accidental[7] **hypothermia** • **thermic** sense[8] / fever[9] • **thermal** radiation[10] / conductivity[11] • **thermal** energy / comfort / water[12] / burn[13] [ɜː]

thermometer [θɜːrmɒmətɚ] n
 rel **centigrade scale**[1] [sɛntɪɡreɪd] n term

instrument for measuring the temperature; usually a sealed [iː] vacuum tube containing mercury[2] [ɜː], which expands with heat and contracts with cold, the exact degree of variation being indicated by a scale [skeɪl]

» Digital thermometers measure quickly and are more accurate than glass thermometers. The thermometer must be left in place for 2 min for rectal, and 3 min for oral temperatures.

Use standard clinical / extended-range / low-reading **thermometer** • glass[3] / sterile / clinical **thermometer** • oral / tympanic membrane[4] **thermometer** • electronic[5] / digital[6] [ɪdʒ]/ Fahrenheit / Centigrade **thermometer** • Fahrenheit / Kelvin **scale**

Fieber, Pyrexie
febril, fiebernd, fieberhaft, fiebrig[1] subfebril, leicht fieberhaft[2] fieberfrei, afebril[3] Hyperpyrexie, hohes Fieber[4] völlig erschöpft[5] Fieber unterdrücken[6] leichtes F.[7] hohes F.[8] intermittierendes F., Febris intermittens[9] Rückfallfieber, F. recurrens[10] remittierendes F.[11] anhaltendes F., Febris continua[12] Fieberschübe[13] d. Fieber fällt (ab)/ geht zurück[14] fieberfreie Intervalle[15] Durstfieber[16] künstl. F.[17] rheumat. F.[18] Scharlach[19] Gelbfieber[20] Typhus[21] wolhynisches F., Fünftagefieber[22] Heufieber, -schnupfen[23] Katheterfieber[24] Fieber unbekannter Ursache[25] Fieberblase, Herpes simplex[26] Fieberzacken[27] fieberhafte Harnwegsinfektion[28] Fieberkrämpfe[29] Fieberwahn, -delir[30]   3

fiebersenkend
fiebererzeugend; fiebererzeugendes Mittel, Pyrogen, Pyretikum[1] Antipyretikum, fiebersenkendes Mittel[2] fiebersenkende Wirkung[3] fiebersenkende Maßnahmen[4]   4

(i) Hyperthermie, Überwärmung (ii) Fiebertherapie
Hypothermie, Unterkühlung[1] thermisch, Wärme-[2] maligne Hyperthermie[3] Mikrowellenhyperthermie[4] starke Unterkühlung[5] künstl. Hypothermie/ Winterschlaf, artifizielle Hibernation[6] akzidentelle Hypothermie[7] Temperatursinn[8] Hitzschlag[9] Wärmestrahlung[10] Wärmeleitfähigkeit[11] Thermalwasser[12] Verbrennung[13]   5

Thermometer, Fiebermesser
Celsius-Skala[1] Quecksilber[2] Glasthermometer[3] Ohrthermometer[4] elektron. Thermometer[5] Digitalthermometer[6]   6

Fever & Sweating CLINICAL TERMS **467**

shiver [ʃɪvɚ] v & n   sim **shake¹** [ʃeɪk] - shook - shaken v,
  tremble², **shudder³** [ʌ] v & n

(v) reflexive muscle activity in response to cold, fear, excitement⁴ and other stressors⁵
shivering n clin • **shivery⁶** adj • **shaky⁷** adj • **tremulous⁸** adj • **tremor** n term
» He is shivering with cold. I felt shivers up and down my spine [aɪ]. He's feeling hot and cold and he's shivery. She's still a bit shaky on her legs⁹. Attempt to arouse¹⁰ [aʊ] the patient by vigorous [ɪg] shaking. When shivering begins, heat production increases.
Use to produce/begin/control/inhibit **shivering** • **to shiver with** fear¹¹ • to get¹²/give sb. **the shivers** • **shaken** baby syndrome¹³ • **shaking** injury / palsy¹⁴ [ɔː] • gentle¹⁵ [dʒe] **shaking** • **to tremble** all over¹⁶ / with anger • **tremble** in my voice • chin¹⁷ [tʃɪn] **trembling**

zittern; Schauer
schütteln, zittern, wanken¹ (er)zittern; Zittern, Beben² schaudern, beben, zittern; Schau(d)er³ Auf-, Erregung⁴ Stressfaktoren⁵ zittrig, fröstelnd⁶ zittrig, wack(e)lig⁷ zitternd, bebend⁸ wack(e)lig auf d. Beinen⁹ (auf)wecken¹⁰ vor Angst zittern¹¹ e. Gänsehaut kriegen¹² Shaken-Baby-Syndrom, Schütteltrauma¹³ Schüttellähmung, Parkinson-Krankheit¹⁴ leichtes Schütteln¹⁵ am ganzen Körper zittern¹⁶ Kinnzittern¹⁷   7

gooseflesh [guːsfleʃ] n   syn **goose pimples** or **bumps** [ʌ] n clin
  rel **piloerection¹** [paɪloʊɪrekʃ°n] n term

skin reaction to chilly sensations, fear, excitement [aɪ] or irritation causing erection of the hairs on the skin and the follicular orifices [ɔːrɪfɪsiːz] to become prominent
goose-pimply adj clin • **pilomotor reflex¹** n term → U56-14
» The chilly breeze brought her arms out in gooseflesh. A prodrome including dizziness², nausea³ [ɔː], chills and gooseflesh of the chest and arms is occasionally seen in heatstroke⁴.

Gänsehaut, Cutis anserina
Pilomotorenreaktion, Piloerektion¹, Schwindel² Übelkeit³ Hitzschlag⁴

8

chills [tʃɪlz] n clin usu pl   sim **rigor¹** [rɪ‖raɪgɚ] n term → U103-20; U12-15

attack of shivering with a feeling of coldness typically marking the start of an infection and the development of a fever
chilly² [tʃɪli] adj • **chilliness³** n • **chilled⁴** adj • **chill⁵** v
» This was followed by an abrupt onset of chills, high fever and prostration. Septic shock is suspected when a febrile patient has chills associated with hypotension. Chills or chilliness usually marks an acute onset. The rigors are suggestive of appendiceal perforation.
Use **chills and** fever / rigors⁶ / prostration / piloerection • shaking⁷ / nervous⁸ / periodic / intermittent **chills** • to feel⁹ **chilly** • **chilly** sensation • **chilling** effect¹⁰ • to catch a¹¹ **chill**

Frösteln, Kältegefühl, Schüttelfrost
Schüttelfrost; Rigor, Steifigkeit¹ kühl, frösteln² Kältegefühl; Kühle, Frostigkeit³ gekühlt, unterkühlt⁴ (ab)kühlen⁵ starker Schüttelfrost⁶ Schüttelfrost⁷ nervöses Zittern⁸ frösteln⁹ kühlende Wirkung¹⁰ sich erkälten¹¹

9

cold intolerance n term
  opposite **heat intolerance¹** n term

inability to withstand² cold marked by a tendency to be easily chilled when exposed to cool temperatures
» His extremity became cool and clammy³ and intolerant of temperature changes (particularly cold). The patients exhibited severe emaciation⁴ [ɪmeɪsɪeɪʃ°n] and complained of cold intolerance.
Use **cold** exposure [oʊ]/ injury⁵ • (fatty) food⁶ / glucose / exercise **intolerance** • **heat** loss / gain / production⁷ • **heat** regulation / balance⁸ / wave • urticaria⁹ [ɜː] • to apply external **heat** • **heat**-stable¹⁰ [eɪ]

Kälteintoleranz
Wärmeintoleranz, -unverträglichkeit¹ aushalten² feuchtkalt, klamm³ Abmagerung, Auszehrung⁴ Kälteschaden⁵ Nahrungsmittelunverträglichkeit⁶ Wärmebildung⁷ Wärmehaushalt⁸ Wärmeurtikaria⁹ hitzebeständig, thermostabil¹⁰

10

heat stroke [hiːt stroʊk] n clin   syn **heat hyperpyrexia** n term,
  rel **sunstroke¹** n clin

severe, often fatal [eɪ] illness produced by exposure to high temperatures, characterized by headache, vertigo, confusion, hot dry skin, and a rise in body temperature; in severe cases collapse and coma, very high fever, and tachycardia [tækɪ-] develop
» Heat exhaustion [ɒː] may progress to heat stroke if sweating ceases [siːsɪz]. Heat stroke is imminent when the core (rectal) temperature approaches 41 °C.
Use **heat** exhaustion or prostration² / acclimatization³ / rash⁴ [æ] / cramps⁵ • **heat** syncope⁶ / stress⁷ / shock proteins⁸ • **heat** edema [iː] / sensitivity⁹ • body / exposure to **heat** • prickly⁴ **heat** • exertional¹⁰ [ɜː] **heat stroke** • **heat stroke** victim

Hitzschlag, Hitzehyperpyrexie
Sonnenstich¹ Hitzeerschöpfung² Hitzeakklimatisierung³ Roter Hund, Miliaria (rubra)⁴ Hitzekrämpfe⁵ Hitzekollaps, -synkope⁶ Hitze-, Wärmebelastung⁷ Hitzeschock-, Stressproteine⁸ Hitze-, Wärmeempfindlichkeit⁹ belastungsbedingter Hitzschlag¹⁰

11

CLINICAL TERMS — Fever & Sweating

sweat [swet] v syn **perspire** [pɚˈspaɪɚ] v
to excrete [iː] salty fluid through the pores [ɔː] of the skin
sweat[1] [e] n • **perspiration**[2] [pɜːrspɪreɪʃən] n • **sweaty**[3] [sweti] adj • **sweating**[2] n

» She mopped[4] his sweaty forehead with a tissue[5]. I was literally drenched [tʃ] in sweat[6]. The fever was associated with rigors and sweats[7]. The sweat glands on the palms [ɑː] do not participate in thermal sweating[8] [e]. Perspiration serves as a mechanism for regulating body temperature. The skin is hot and initially covered with perspiration.

Use **sweat** gland[9] / pore / duct [ʌ]/ production / retention • **sweat** chloride determination / test[10] • cold / bloody / fetid[11] **sweat** • clammy / night[12] **sweats** • to break out in a[13] / to be soaked in[6] [oʊ]/ beads [iː] of[14] **sweat** • **to sweat** buckets[15] [ʌ]/ a lot / like a pig • (in)sensible[2] / excessive / unexplained **perspiration** • **to perspire** heavily [e]/ freely / readily[16] [e] • profuse[17] [juː]/ increased [iː]/ diminished **sweating** • **sweaty** palms [pɑːmz]/ feet[18] / handshake[19] / clothes

schwitzen, transpirieren
Schweiß[1] Transpiration, Schweiß(sekretion), Perspiratio sensibilis[2] verschwitzt, schweißbedeckt, Schweiß-[3] wischte ab[4] Taschentuch[5] schweißgebadet (sein)[6] thermisches Schwitzen[7] Schweißausbrüche[8] Schweißdrüse, Glandula sudorifera[9] Schweißtest[10] übelriechender Schweiß[11] Nachtschweiß[12] e. Schweißausbruch haben[13] Schweißperlen[14] stark/ viel schwitzen[15] leicht/ sofort schwitzen[16] starke(s) Schwitzen/ Schweißsekretion[17] Schweißfüße[18] feuchter Händedruck[19]   12

---

moist [mɔɪst] adj syn **damp** [æ] adj, sim **damp**ish[1], **humid**[2] [hjuːmɪd] adj
slightly wet and not quite dry
moisture[3] [mɔɪstʃɚ] n • **moisten**[4] [mɔɪsən] v • **moisturize**[5] [-aɪz] v • **moisturizer**[6] n • **damp(en)**[4] v • **dampness**[3] n • **damp**[3] n • **humidity**[7] [hjumɪdəti] n • **humidify**[4] v • **humidifier**[8] n

» Pat the skin dry[9] with a damp towel. The skin was cool and moist, and the pulse was weak. Intertrigo[10] [aɪ] is caused by the effect of heat, moisture, and friction[11], esp. in humid climates.

Use **moist** skin / heat[12] / dressing[13] / compresses / packs[14] / environment • **moist** air / conditions / climate [aɪ] • **moist** rales[15] [æ‖ɑː]/ gangrene[16] [iː] • **moisture** chamber[17] [tʃeɪmbɚ]/ content[18] • facial [feɪʃəl] **moisturizer** • **damp** clothes / soil[19] [sɔɪl]/ weather / cold • relative[20] / high **humidity**

feucht
etwas feucht[1] feucht[2] Feuchtigkeit[3] an-, befeuchten[4] mit e. Feuchtigkeitscreme behandeln, Feuchtigkeit verleihen[5] Feuchtigkeitscreme[6] (Luft)feuchtigkeit[7] (Luft)befeuchter[8] ab-, trockentupfen[9] Wundsein, Wolf, Intertrigo[10] Reibung[11] feuchte Wärme[12] feuchter Verband[13] feuchte Packungen/ Wickel[14] feuchte Rasselgeräusche[15] feuchte Gangrän[16] feuchte Kammer[17] Feuchtigkeitsgehalt[18] feuchter Boden[19] relative Feuchtigkeit/ Feuchte[20]   13

---

evaporate [ɪˈvæpɚeɪt] vt & vi term sim **volatilize**[1] [vɒlətəlaɪz], **dissipate**[2] vt & vi term → U82-2f
to lose fluid volume by conversion into vapor[3] [veɪpɚ] or change from a liquid to volatile[4] form
evaporation[5] n term • **evaporative** adj • **dissipation**[6] n

» Local humidity and hydration of the skin are increased if sweat is prevented from evaporating. Evaporation can be accelerated by fanning[7]. Failure of the heat dissipation[8] mechanism may result in dizziness, blurred [ɜː] vision[9] [ʒ], diarrhea [iː], confusion, or collapse.

Use water / fluid **evaporates** • heat / gas / (drug) effect **dissipates** • to enhance/ prevent **evaporation** • surface[10] / water **evaporation** • **evaporative** heat loss[11] / cooling / fluid loss • **evaporated** milk[12] • **volatilized** mercury[13] [ɜː]

verdampfen, verdunsten
(sich) verflüchtigen, verdampfen[1] (sich) auflösen, verschwinden[2] Dampf[3] flüchtig, gasförmig, volatil, ätherisch[4] Verdunstung, -dampfung, Evaporation[5] Auflösung[6] Fächeln[7] Wärmeabgabe[8] verschwommenes Sehen[9] Schweißverdunstung durch d. Haut[10] Wärmeabgabe durch Verdunstung[11] Kondensmilch[12] verdampftes Quecksilber[13]   14

---

diaphoresis [daɪəfəriːsɪs] n term syn **hidrosis** [aɪ‖ɪ] n term rel **sudor**[1] [uː] n term
production and secretion [iː] of sweat, above all profuse sweating associated with elevated body temperature, strenuous[2] [e] physical exercise, mental or emotional stress or exposure to heat
diaphoretic[3] [e] adj & n term • **sudorific**[3] adj & n • **sudoriferous**[4] adj **an(h)idrosis**[5] n term • **(an)hidrotic**[3] adj & n • **hidr(o)-** comb

» Typical malarial attacks show sequentially shaking chills, fever to 41 °C or higher, and marked diaphoresis. His skin was clammy, pale, and diaphoretic.

Use excessive / intense[6] / marked[6] / prostration and **diaphoresis** • **diaphoretic** skin[7] / patient • **sudorific** drug[3] • **sudoriferous** glands[8] / duct • **hidr**opoiesis [-pɔɪiːsɪs] /adenitis[9] [aɪ] • **hidr**adenoma /ocystoma /oschesis[10] [-skiːsɪs] • dys [ɪ]/ hyper-**hidrosis**

Schweißsekretion, -absonderung
Schweiß, Sudor[1] anstrengend[2] schweißtreibend; schweißtreibendes Mittel, Diaphoretikum, Hidrotikum, Sudoriferum[3] Schweiß-, schweißbildend[4] fehlende Schweißsekretion, Anhidrose[5] starke Schweißsekretion[6] schweißbedeckte/ schwitzende Haut[7] Schweißdrüsen, Glandulae sudoriferae[8] Schweißdrüsenentzündung, Hidradenitis[9] Hidroschesis, Verhinderung d. Schweißabgabe[10]   15

Fractures | CLINICAL TERMS 469

fever or **pyrexia of unknown origin** n term, abbr **FUO** or **PUO**

term applied to a febrile illness marked by a temperature of 101°F or more persisting over at least 3 weeks without diagnosis of the cause despite intensive hospital evaluation

» Evaluation of patients with FUO includes a chest radiograph, sinus [aɪ] films, upper GI series[1] with small bowel [aʊ] follow-through[2], barium enema[3], proctosigmoidoscopy, and gallbladder function studies. Many cancers can present as FUO. Because infection is the most common cause of FUO, urine, sputum, stool [uː], and CSF[4] are usually cultured.

'se **fever** of undetermined/ unidentified origin[5] • to cause **FUO** • classic **FUO**

Fieber unklarer Genese
Magen-Darm-Passage[1] Dünndarmpassage[2] Bariumeinlauf[3] Liquor (cerebrospinalis), Hirn-Rückenmarkflüssigkeit[4] Fieber unbekannter Ursache[5]

16

fastigium [fæstɪdʒɪəm] n term rare   sim **acme**[1] [ækmi] n term rare

climax[2] [aɪ] or most pronounced [aʊ] phase in the course [ɔː] of a disease, esp. of a febrile illness

fastigial [fæstɪdʒɪəl] adj term

» The steadiness [e] of the fever for a week or longer after reaching the fastigium is an important point. Typhoid [aɪ] fever is characterized by diarrhea, prostration and muscular [ʌ] debility, gradually increasing and often becoming profound at the acme of the disease.

Fastigium, Gipfel, Höhepunkt
Akme, Höhepunkt im Krankheitsverlauf od. einer Fieberkurve[1] Gipfel, Höhepunkt[2]

17

defervescence [dɪfəˈvɛsəns] n term   rel **crisis**[1] [aɪ], **lysis**[2] [laɪsɪs] n term

period of abatement[3] [eɪ] or resolution of fever when elevated temperatures fall and/or return to normal

defervesce[4] [-vɛs] v term • **defervescent**[5] adj • **lytical**[l] adj → U124-1

» In viral [aɪ] hepatitis [aɪ] defervescence often coincides [aɪ] with the onset of jaundice[6] [dʒɔːndɪs]. Relapses may occur up to two weeks after the patient defervesces. A sudden change, usually for the better, in the course of an acute disease is termed crisis (in contrast to the gradual improvement by lysis). The decrease of fever may be lytical or critical.

'se **defervescence** stage[7] • **rapid**[1] / through 3 days of / gradual[2] [ædʒ] **defervescence** • infection-related / life-threatening **crisis** • acute / hypertensive[8] / gastric[9] **crisis** • tumor[10] / cell[11] / adhesiolysis

Entfieberung, Deferveszenz
Krisis, Krise, kritische Entfieberung, abrupter Fieberabfall[1] Lysis, lytische Deferveszenz, allmähl. Fieberabfall[2] Nachlassen, Rückgang[3] abfiebern[4] fiebersenkend, antipyretisch[5] Gelbsucht, Ikterus[6] Stadium d. Fieberabfalls, Stadium decrementi[7] hypertensive Krise, Blutdruck-, Hochdruckkrise[8] gastrische Krise[9] Tumorzerfall[10] Zytolyse[11]

18

flush [ʌ] v & n   sim **blush**[1] [ʌ] v & n

(n, i) sudden, subjective sensation of heat (ii) reddening of the face (iii) sudden, rapid flow of a liquid

flushed[2] adj • **flushing** n & adj • **blushing**[3] n & adj

» The patient complained of burning with episodes of flushing. She reported a tendency to flush easily. Toxic manifestations of the drug include hyperactivity, incoordination, diaphoresis[4], flushing, rigidity, and wild movements.

'se facial / malar[5] / erythematous / hot[6] / hectic[7] **flush** • **flushed** face or complexion[8] / cheeks / appearance / skin • to experience/produce/relieve **flushing** • alcohol-induced **flushing** • **flushing of** the upper body / the face • tumor[9] **blush**

erröten, rot werden; spülen; Hautröte, Flush, anfallsweise Hautrötung
erröten; Erröten[1] rot, gerötet[2] Erröten; errötend[3] Diaphorese, Schweißsekretion[4] Wangenröte[5] Hitzewallung[6] hektische Röte[7] Gesichtsröte[8] Rubor[9]

19

Unit 106 Fractures
Related Units: 5 Injuries, 99 Radiology, 141 Fracture Management

fracture [fræktʃɚ] v term → U5-20

syn **break** [eɪ] - broke - broken v irr, sim **crack**[1] v & n clin

to cause a break in the continuity of a bone

fracture[2] n term, abbr **Frx** •**refracture**[3] v & n • **fractured**[4] adj

» Direct root [uː] compression may be relieved by reduction[5] [ʌ] of the dislocation or by removal of fractured bone or disrupted disk. Most fractures of the clavicle occur in the middle third. Oblique [-iːk] views may also help identify and evaluate fractures of the tibial plateau[6] [oʊ].

'se **to fracture** a bone / one's shin[7] • simple / closed[8] / isolated [aɪ]/ (in)complete[9] / subperiosteal / pathologic[10] / spiral[11] [aɪ] **fracture** • (radial [eɪ]) neck / (femoral [e]) shaft / transverse[12] / oblique[13] **fracture** • (sub)trochanteric [k]/ supracondylar / growth plate or epiphyseal [ɪ]/ articular[14] / (un)stable [eɪ] **fracture** • nasal / pelvic **fracture** • **fracture of the** patella • micro**fracture** • exposure of / motion at / separation at **the fracture site** • **fracture** healing[15] [iː]/ cleft[16] • **fractured** pelvis / rib / clavicle / tooth[17] / nose / base of skull[18]

(Knochen) brechen/ frakturieren
(zer)brechen; e. Sprung bekommen; Riss, (Knochen)fissur[1] (Knochen)fraktur, -bruch[2] erneut brechen; Refraktur[3] gebrochen, frakturiert[4] Einrichtung, Reposition[5] Tibiakopf[6] s. d. Schienbein brechen[7] geschlossene Fraktur[8] (un)vollständige/ (in)komplette F.[9] pathol. F., Spontanfraktur[10] Dreh-, Spiralbruch, Torsionsfraktur[11] Querfraktur[12] Schrägfraktur[13] Gelenkfraktur[14] Knochenbruch-, Frakturheilung[15] Bruchspalt[16] Zahnfraktur[17] Schädelbasisbruch[18]

1

fragment n term sim **chip**[1] [tʃɪp] n, **splinter**[2] n & v clin

fragmentation[3] n term • fragment[4] v • to chip (off)[5] v clin

» A displaced free fragment may tear [teə] the overlying lateral meniscus. A cartilage [-ɪdʒ] was chipped and fragments floated in the joint. If the bones are fragmented the fracture is said to be comminuted.

Use (nasal) bone / fracture / cartilage[6] / osteochondral [kɒː] **fragment** • articular / butterfly[7] / styloid [aɪ]/ (extruded) disk / femoral head **fragment** • devascularized / necrotic / displaced[8] / free **fragment** • (cancellous [kænˈs-]) bone[9] / grafted chips • chip fracture[10] • **chipped** ankle / cartilage / knee [niː] • buried[11] [e]/ wood **splinter**

(Knochen)fragment, Bruchstück
(Knochen)splitter, -fragment[1] Splitter; (zer)splittern[2] Fragmentation, Zersplitterung[3] in Stücke brechen, fragmentieren[4] absplittern, -sprengen[5] Knorpelfragment[6] Biegungskeil[7] verschobenes/ disloziertes F.[8] Spongiosaspäne[9] Absprengungs-, Abrissfraktur[10] verschobener Splitter[11]   2

closed fracture n term sim **simple fracture**[1],
opposite **open** or **compound** [aʊ] **fracture**[2] n term

bone fracture that is not associated with a break or laceration[3] [s] in the overlying skin

» Open fractures require operative reduction, but closed fractures should be managed with a posterior plastic splint[4]. As occult [ʌ] fracture[5] is a common underlying cause, arthrocentesis for posttraumatic joint effusions might result in a compound fracture.

Use **closed** (Colles'/ uncomminuted) fracture / disruption / (head) injury[6] / reduction or manipulation[7] • **open** (tibial/ forearm/ contaminated/ comminuted) fracture[8] / dislocation[9] • **compound** dislocation[9] / depressed skull fracture[10] / wound[11] [uː]

geschlossener Bruch
einfacher Bruch[1] offener B.[2] Zerreißung[3] Schiene[4] i. Röntgen nicht nachgewiesene Fraktur[5] stumpfe (Schädel)verletzung[6] geschlossene Reposition/ Einrichtung[7] offene Trümmerfraktur[8] offene Luxation[9] Schädelimpressionsfraktur[10] offene Wunde[11]   3

(sub)luxation [ʌ] or **dislocation** n term
rel displacement[1], angulation[2] n term → U5-20

displacement of a bone from its articulation

luxate[3] [ʌ] v term • dislocate[4] v • subluxated[5] adj •
redisplacement[6] n • angulate[7] v • angular[8] adj

» Small elevators[9] were used to carefully luxate[10] the teeth to be extracted. Unstable fracture-dislocations of the middle and upper thirds of the ulnar shaft complicated by dislocation of the radial head are termed Monteggia [-edʒa] fracture.

Use fracture-[11] / partial[12] [ʃ]/ closed / complete / habitual[13] / pathologic[14] [ɒːdʒ]/ obturator **dislocation** • **dislocation of the** hip (joint) / radial head / distal fragment • fracture / congenital [dʒe] (hip)[15] / elbow / (posterior) facet[16] [fæset]/ atlantoaxial **subluxation** • **subluxated** digit [dɪdʒɪt] • displaced fracture[17] • (in)significant / (un)acceptable[18] / 10-degree / late angulation • angulated radial [eɪ] neck fracture[19] / lesion [iː] • **angular** displacement[2] / deformity / stress

(Teil)verrenkung, (Sub)luxation
Verschiebung, Dislokation, Fehlstellung[1] Achsenknickung, -fehlstellung[2] verrenken, luxieren[3] verschieben, dislozieren[4] subluxiert[5] neuerliche Verschiebung[6] einen Winkel bilden[7] Winkel-, Achse betreffend[8] Hebel[9] heraushebeln[10] Luxationsfraktur[11] Teilverrenkung[12] habituelle L.[13] Spontanluxation[14] angeborene (Hüftgelenk)subluxation[15] S. des Facettengelenks[16] dislozierte Fraktur[17] (nicht) tolerierbare Achsenknickung[18] (ad axim) verschobene Radiushalsfraktur[19]   4

avulsion [əvʌlʃən] (chip fracture) n term
sim **disruption**[1] [ʌ] n term → U5-19

fracture that occurs when soft tissue (joint capsule, ligament, muscle insertion or origin) is pulled away from the bone; fragments of the bone may come away with it

avulse[2] v term • avulsed[3] adj • disrupted[4] adj

» Avulsion of the ulnar [ʌ] styloid [aɪ] may accompany the distal radius [eɪ] fracture. X-rays [eks] may show a bit of bone avulsed from the fibular head.

Use traumatic / cortex / tooth / minor [aɪ] **avulsion** • **avulsion** (flap) injury[5] • avulsed teeth[6] / (bone) fragment[7] • traumatic / bone[8] / articular / wound[9] [uː] **disruption** • ligamentous / (soft) tissue[10] / pelvic / intimal[11] **disruption** • **disrupted** muscle[12] [mʌsl]/ disk[13] / operative wound

Ab-, Ausrissfraktur, knöcherner Ausriss
Ruptur, Riss[1] ab-, ausreißen[2] ab-, ausgerissen[3] zer-, (auf)gerissen[4] Ausrissverletzung[5] ausgeschlagene/ luxierte Zähne[6] Knochenabsprengung[7] Knochenbruch[8] Klaffen d. Wunde, Wunddehiszenz[9] Weichteilzerreißung[10] Intimaruptur[11] Muskelriss[12] rupturierte Bandscheibe[13]   5

impacted fracture n term sim **compression fracture**[1] n term

fracture with one of the fragments driven into the cancellous tissue[2] of the other fragment

impaction[3] [ɪmpækʃən] n term • impact[4] n

» Impacted and minimally angulated fractures can be treated by means of a shoulder immobilizer. Most surgeons prefer to use internal fixation for impacted fractures. Closed manipulation is justifiable [aɪ], but if possible impaction or locking of the fragments is desirable [aɪ].

Use **impacted** tooth[5] / foreign [fɒːrən] bodies / gallstone [ɔː] / cerumen[6] [sɪruːmən] • lateral / multiple / stable[7] [eɪ] **compression fractures** • dorsal / food[8] **impaction**

Stauchungsbruch
Kompressionsfraktur[1] Spongiosa[2] Impaktion, Einkeilung[3] Auswirkung, Einfluss[4] impaktierter Zahn[5] Zeruminalpfropf, Cerumen obturans[6] stabile Kompressionsfrakturen[7] Retention/ Impaktion v. Speiseresten[8]   6

Fractures CLINICAL TERMS 471

comminuted fracture n term   sim **splinter(ed) fracture**[1] n term

fracture in which the bone is crushed [ʌʃ] or broken into several fragments
comminution[2] n term • **non/ uncomminuted** adj • **splinter**[3] v & n

» Comminuted fractures of the clavicle with displacement can usually be managed successfully by closed reduction. First the severity[4] [e] of comminution and magnitude[4] of the displacement were determined by x-rays. Often the fracture line[5] will splinter to reach the medial [iː] wall of the inner ear.

Use to check for **comminution** • **comminuted** bone fragments • minor [aɪ]/ extensive / severe[6] [ɪɚ] **comminution** • spiral / butterfly[7] **fracture** • **splintered** to pieces / fragments

> **Note:** Butterfly fracture is not equivalent with the German term Schmetterlingsfraktur (= bilateral fracture of the pubic rami).

Trümmerbruch
Splitterbruch[1] Zertrümmerung, -splitterung[2] zersplittern; Splitter[3] Ausmaß[4] Frakturlinie[5] starke Zertrümmerung[6] (Schaft)fraktur m. beidseitigen Biegungskeilen[7]

---

skull [ʌ] **fracture** n clin   syn **cranial** [eɪ] **fracture** n term → U124-19

break of the cranium [eɪ] resulting from trauma [ɒː] which may be associated with injury to underlying brain

» These skull fractures may also injure [ɪndʒɚ] cranial nerves that course [ɔː] through the skull base. Basal skull fractures may be recognized by the presence of CSF rhinorrhea[1] [raɪnəriːə] or otorrhea.

Use simple / closed / open / compound / comminuted / stellate[2] [eɪ] basal [eɪ] or basilar[3] / depressed[4] / expressed[5] **skull fracture** • **fracture of the** skull vault[6] [vɔːlt]/ base [eɪ] of the skull[3] • temporal bone[7] / blow-out[8] **fracture**

Schädelbruch, -fraktur
nasale Liquorrhoe[1] Sternfraktur, sternförmige F.[2] Schädelbasisbruch[3] Impressionsfraktur[4] Berstungsfraktur[5] Schädeldach-, Kalottenfraktur[6] Schläfenbeinfraktur[7] Blow-out F.[8]

---

fracture by contrecoup [kɒːtrəkuː] n term

fracture of the skull at a point opposite to where the blow[1] [oʊ] was received

» Deceleration [s] of the brain against the inner skull causes contusions [t(j)uː], either under a point of impact[2] (coup lesion) or in the antipolar area (contrecoup lesion).

Use **contrecoup** lesion [liːʒən] / injury [ɪndʒɚi]/ contusion[3]

Gegenstoß-, Contrecoup-Fraktur
Schlag, Stoß[1] Stoßherd[2] Contrecoup-Hirnprellung[3]

Colles' [kɒːlɪs] **fracture** n term
    sim **silver-fork fracture** or **deformity**[1] n term

fracture of the lower end of the radius with displacement of the distal fragment dorsally

» Colles' fracture is typically caused by falls on the outstretched [tʃ] hand, the wrist [rɪst] in dorsi-flexion, and the forearm in pronation so that the force is applied to the palm [pɑːm] of the hand[2].

Use Smith's or reversed[3] **Colles' fracture** • Pott's[4] **fracture** • bony / gross [oʊ]/ buttonhole[5] [ʌ]/ cloverleaf skull[6] / ulnar [ʌ] drift[7] / Volkmann's compression-type[8] **deformity**

Radiusfraktur an typischer Stelle, Fractura radii loco classico
F. radii loco classico m. Bajonettfehlstellung[1] Handfläche[2] Smith-, Radiusflexionsfraktur[3] Pott-, Bimalleolarfraktur[4] Knopflochdeformität[5] Kleeblattschädel[6] Ulnardeviation[7] Volkmann-Sprunggelenkdeformität[8]

---

fissure(d) [fɪʃɚ] or **hairline** or **linear fracture** n term   sim **crack**[1], **cleft**[2] n clin

fracture in which there is a crack in the cortex but not through the entire [aɪ] bone
fissure[1] n term • **fissured**[3] [fɪʃɚd] adj

» A fissure fracture can be treated by immobilization [aɪz] in plaster for 3 weeks. Fracture of the lunate[4] [luːneɪt] may be manifested by a crack, by comminution, or by impaction. Linear fractures usually extend from the point of impact toward the base of the skull.

Use multiple [ʌ] **fissure fractures** • **linear** skull fracture • direction / obliteration / extension[5] / configuration **of the fracture cleft** • widened [aɪ]/ oblique [-iːk]/ facial[6] [feɪʃəl]/ palatal[7] **cleft** • **crack** fracture[1]

Fissur, Haarbruch
Riss, Fissur[1] Spalt[2] gespalten, rissig[3] Os lunatum, Mondbein[4] Frakturausläufer[5] Gesichtsspalte[6] Gaumenspalte[7]

---

greenstick fracture n term   sim **bending fracture**[1] n term

bending of a bone with incomplete fracture involving the cortex on the convex side (typically seen in children)

» If angulation of a greenstick fracture exceeds [iː] 15 degrees, reduction should be carried out. An undisplaced valgus greenstick fracture of the proximal tibia had caused the deformity.

Use bent[1] **fracture**

Grünholzfraktur
Biegungsfraktur[1]

106

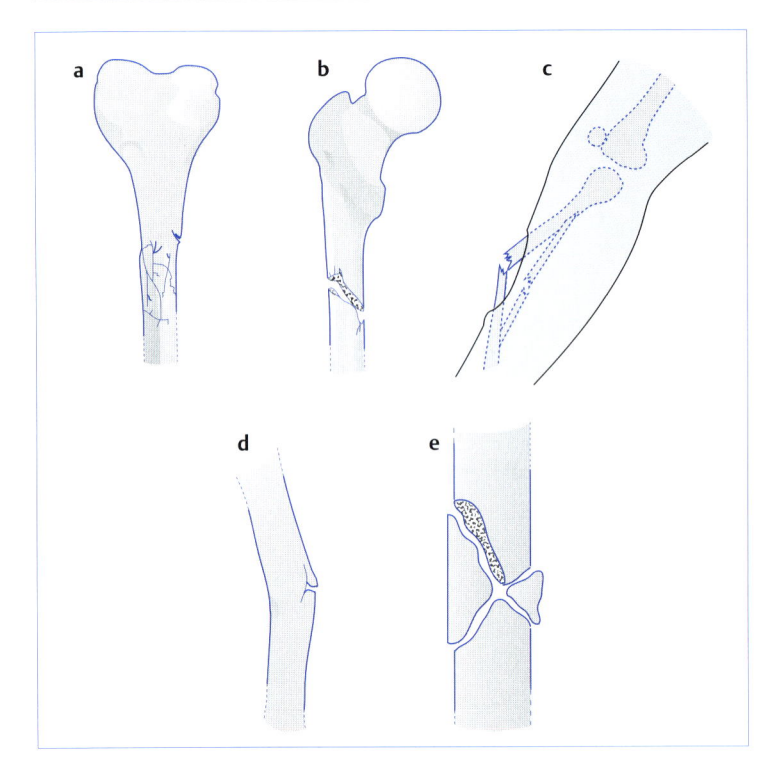

Types of fractures
a comminuted fracture
b spiral fracture
c compound fracture
d greenstick fracture
e butterfly fracture

fatigue [fəti:g] **fracture** n term   syn **stress fracture** n clin & term
sim **march** [mɑːrtʃ] **fracture**[1] n clin

mostly transverse crack in bones that are subjected to excessive or unusual endogenous stress

» Fatigue fracture of the shafts of the metatarsals has been given various names (e.g. march, stress, strain and insufficiency fracture). Patients with march fractures typically have pain and point tenderness[2] but do not always have a history of dramatically increased activity.

Ermüdungsbruch
Marschfraktur[1] punktuelle Druckschmerzhaftigkeit[2]

13

crepitation n term   syn **crepitus, crepitance** n term → U111-9

(i) crackling sound or sensation produced by the grating[1] [eɪ] of the fragments at a fracture site[2]
(ii) sound heard on auscultation [ɒː] over areas of consolidation in lung inflammation

» Fracture is suggested [dʒe] by crepitance or palpably mobile bony segments. Did you note any tenderness, crepitation, or movement of the fractured bones on palpation?
Use leathery[3] [e] **crepitation** • subcutaneous [eɪ]/ soft tissue / joint[4] [dʒ]/ marked[5] / bony[6] **crepitus**

(i) Krepitation, Crepitatio, Reibegeräusch
(ii) Knisterrasseln
Reiben[1] Bruchstelle[2] lederartiges Reibegeräusch[3] Gelenkreiben[4] deutl. Reibegeräusch[5] ossäre Krepitation[6]

14

bone or **bony union** n clin   rel **callus** [kæləs] **formation**[1] n term

growing together of the ends of fractured bone as fibrous [aɪ] callus[2] forms between the fragments

(un/ mal)united[3] adj term • **callous**[4] [kæləs] adj • **callosity**[5] n

» A persisting fibrous callus forming between fractured bone is termed fibrous union. The callus holding the break [eɪ] firm until new bone is remodeled eventually turns into bone. Callus bridging a fracture may deform plastically and angulate if the fracture is loaded too early.
Use to be in (direct)[6] **union** • **bone** formation / healing[7] [iː] • postfracture bone[7] / fibrous / faulty[8] [ɒː]/ delayed[9] [eɪ]/ stable [eɪ] **union** • cartilaginous [ædʒ]/ advancing [æ]/ mal[8]/ non[10]-**union** • exuberant [uː] **callus** formation[11] • provisional[12] / definitive[13] **callus** • **malunited** fracture[8] • to avoid/treat/repair [eə] **nonunion** • complete / partial [ʃəl]/ tibial / infected[14] **nonunion** • **nonunion** site [aɪ]/ of bone / of the fracture[10]

Knochen-, Frakturheilung
Kallusbildung[1] bindegewebiger Kallus[2] vereinigt[3] kallös; schwielig[4] Callositas, Schwiele[5] Knochen ist verheilt[6] Frakturheilung[7] Frakturheilung in Fehlstellung[8] verzögerte Heilung[9] Pseudarthrose[10] überschießende Kallusbildung, Callus luxurians[11] provisor. K., Intermediärkallus[12] knöcherner K., Sekundärkallus[13] Infektpseudarthrose, infizierte P.[14]

15

Unit 107 Physical Examination

Related Units: 102 History Taking, 17 Medical Equipment, 18 At the Doctor's, 103 Clinical Symptoms, 108 Clinical Signs, 116 Lab Studies, 117 Diagnosis, 118 Diagnostic Procedures

examine [ɪgzæmɪn] *v clin*   *sim* **test**[1], **explore**[2] [ɔː], **evaluate**[3] *v*, **check**[4] [tʃek] *clin & inf* → U18-9

to look at and investigate the condition and bodily functions[5] [ʌ] of a patient for abnormalities or evidence of disease; the expression is also used for diagnostic investigations (e.g. ECG) and lab tests

examiner[6] *n* • **re(-)examine** *v* • **test** *n* → U118-2
• **examining table**[7] *n* • **check-up**[8] *n*

» Now I'm going to examine your groin[9] [grɔɪn]. Did you examine the legs for edema [iː]? After a local anesthetic [e] was instilled, the eye was examined with the aid of a hand flashlight[10]. Crescent-shaped[11] retinal tears[12] [teəz] are usually present and can be seen by an experienced examiner.

Use **to examine** carefully / thoroughly[13] [θɜːrəli]/ promptly • **to examine** cytologically [saɪtə-]/ endoscopically[14] • **to examine for** abnormalities / swelling / hepatomegaly • **examined by** immunohistochemistry [ke]/ MRI[15] / culture [ʌ]/ a pathologist • **examined** at intervals • **to test** coordination / hearing / olfaction[16] / blood • **to test** the urine for blood[17] / the function [ʌ] of nerves [ɜː] • **to test** strength / for incontinence • **to explore** the abdomen / the wound [uː] • **to evaluate** breath [e] sounds[18] / bleeding / the airway • **to evaluate** the extent of the tumor[19] [(j)uː]/ the patient thoroughly • **to check** the blood pressure[20] / the pulse • **to check** vital [aɪ] signs [saɪnz]/ pupillary size • **to check** the position of the catheter / for swelling • **examining** room[21] / finger / physician [fɪzɪʃən]

untersuchen
untersuchen, testen, prüfen[1] untersuchen, erforschen[2] untersuchen, prüfen, abklären[3] kontrollieren, (über)prüfen[4] Körperfunktionen[5] Untersucher(in)[6] Untersuchungstisch[7] Vorsorge-, Kontrolluntersuchung[8] Leiste(nbeuge)[9] Taschenlampe[10] halbmond-, sichelförmig[11] Netzhautrisse[12] gründl. untersuchen[13] endoskop. untersuchen[14] kernspintomografisch/ mittels Magnetresonanztomografie untersucht[15] d. Geruchssinn überprüfen[16] d. Harn auf Blut untersuchen[17] d. Atemgeräusche auskultieren/ abhören[18] d. Tumorausdehnung abklären[19] d. Blutdruck kontrollieren[20] Untersuchungszimmer, -raum[21]

---

physical exam(ination) *n clin, abbr* **PE**
syn **physical** [fɪzɪkəl] *n jar* → U18-9

evaluation of a patient's condition for diagnostic purposes [ɜː] by inspection, palpation, etc.

on examination[1] *phr, abbr* **O/E** • **self-examination**[2] *n*

» What did you find on the physical? This condition may not be suspected on the basis of the history and physical examination. Physical examination was unrevealing[3] [iː]. On examination the patient was well nourished and hydrated but appeared older than the stated age.

Use to perform/carry out/be given a **PE** • entrance[4] • comprehensive[5] / inconclusive [uː]/ careful[5] **PE** • repeat / routine[6] / preemployment / thorough[5] **PE** • history[7] & **PE** (*abbr* HPE) • digital rectal (*abbr* DRE)/ auscultatory[8] **examination** • laboratory / x-ray **examination** • gross[9] / microscopic / neurologic **examination** • pathologic / mental status **examination** • breast[10] [e] (*abbr* BSE)/ testicular self-examination • **physical** assessment / manifestations / sign • **physical** diagnosis / findings[11] [aɪ]/ condition[12]

klinische/ körperliche Untersuchung
bei der Untersuchung[1] Selbstuntersuchung[2] unauffällig[3] Aufnahmestatus, Erstuntersuchung[4] gründl. körperl. Untersuchung[5] klinische Routineuntersuchung[6] Anamnese- und Statuserhebung[7] Auskultation[8] makroskop. Untersuchung[9] Selbstuntersuchung d. Brust[10] klinischer Befund[11] körperl. Verfassung, Gesundheitszustand[12]

---

instructions [ɪnstrʌkʃənz] *n pl*
rel **order**[1] *n* → U20-7

directions given and polite requests made e.g. by the physician when examining a patient

instruct[2] [ʌ] *v* • **instructive** *adj* • **order**[3] *v*

» Instruct the patient to take a deep breath[4] [e] and hold it[5]. Lie down on the couch, please. Would you roll over on the left side now. Now I'd like you to lie flat on your stomach [k].

Use to give/receive [siː] /comprehend[6]/execute[7] **instructions** • written[8] / routine / general **instructions** • specific / pretreatment **instructions** • therapeutic [pjuː]/ discharge[9] / aftercare / dosing[10] [ou] **instructions**

Anweisungen
Anordnung[1] anweisen, instruieren[2] an-, verordnen[3] tief Atem holen[4] nicht mehr atmen[5] Anweisungen verstehen[6] Anweisungen ausführen[7] schriftl. Anweisungen[8] Anweisungen bei d. Entlassung[9] Dosierungsvorschriften[10]

474 CLINICAL TERMS — Physical Examination

Uhm, Miss Bluebell ... I don't think that's what the doctor was talking about when he asked you to strip to the waist!!

---

strip v   *syn* **take/ slip off clothes** *phr*, **undress** *v clin & inf*

to remove (part of) one's clothing, e.g. to enable the doctor to examine certain parts of the body

» *Strip down to your waist[1] [eɪ], please! Would you mind taking off all your clothes except for your underwear[2] [eɚ]. Could you just slip off your pants for a moment. And now roll up your sleeve[3]. All right, Mr. Bell you can get dressed now and I'll write up[4] some medicine for you.*

sich ausziehen/ freimachen
Oberkörper freimachen[1] Unterwäsche[2] Ärmel[3] aufschreiben[4]

[4]

---

cubicle [kjuːbɪkl] *n*

small division of a larger room (mostly partitioned [ɪʃ] off[1] with curtains [kɜːrtᵊnz] only) for examining patients in privacy [aɪ]‖*BE* ɪ]

» *Let me examine you briefly in the cubicle over there; nurse [ɜː] will you draw the curtains[2] please and prepare Mrs Pym for a physical.*

Untersuchungskabine
abgetrennt[1] Vorhänge zuziehen[2]

[5]

---

inspection [ɪnspekʃᵊn] *n term*

rel **exploration**[1] [eksplǝreɪʃᵊn] *n term*

visual observation[2], e.g. of the throat, external genitals for detection of clinical features [iːtʃ] perceptible[3] to the eye

inspect[4] *v term* • **inspected** *adj* • **exploratory**[5] *adj*

» *On inspection his tongue was smooth[6] [uː] and beefy red. The laceration[7] should be cleansed[8] [e] and inspected for the presence of foreign bodies[9]. Increased cardiac activity was noted on inspection. General inspection disclosed the odor of tobacco smoke. Inspect the spine[10] [aɪ] with the shirt pulled up and the child bent over for evaluation of scoliosis.*

Use to facilitate[11]/permit/allow **inspection** • visual [ɪʒ]/ manual / direct / gross[12] [oʊ] **inspection** • general / throat [oʊ]/ perianal [eɪ] **inspection** • close[13] / daily **inspection** • thoroughly / periodically **inspected** • manual[14] / wound [uː]/ surgical[15] [ɜː] **exploration** • **exploratory** incision / biopsy[16] [aɪ]/ surgery[15] / laparotomy[17]

Inspektion
Untersuchung, Exploration[1] Betrachtung[2] sicht-, feststellbar[3] inspizieren, betrachten[4] explorativ, Probe-[5] glatt[6] Risswunde[7] gereinigt[8] Fremdkörper[9] Wirbelsäule[10] Inspektion ermöglichen/ erleichtern[11] makroskop. Untersuchung[12] genaue Betrachtung, sorgfältige Untersuchung[13] Palpation[14] operative Exploration, explorativer Eingriff[15] Probeexzision[16] Explorativ-, Probelaparotomie[17]

[6]

---

palpate [pælpeɪt] *v term*   *syn* **feel for** *v phr jar & clin*

to examine with the hands by applying the fingers with light pressure to the body surface [ɜː]

palpation[1] *n term* • **palpable**[2] *adj* • **palpatory**[3] *adj* • **palpating** *adj*

» *Examination of the skin requires that the entire surface of the body be palpated and inspected in good light. The physical revealed icterus and a palpable spleen[4] [iː]. Palpation of the breast [e] for masses should be performed with the ipsilateral arm abducted [ʌ].*

Use to perform/examine by/be detectable by **palpation** • to appreciate [iːʃ] by[5]/elicit with **palpation** • light-touch[6] [laɪt tʌtʃ]/ deep / digital [ɪdʒ] **palpation** • bimanual[7] / kidney [kɪdni]/ neck **palpation** • pain on[8] **palpation** • **palpable** mass[9] / radial [eɪ] pulse [ʌ]/ stone • **palpatory** findings[10] / evidence • **palpably** enlarged / mobile • **palpating** finger[11]

Note: Do not mix up **palpation** and *palpitation*[12].

palpieren, (ab)tasten
Palpation, Abtasten[1] tastbar, palpabel[2] Palpations , Tast , palpatorisch[3] Milz[4] palpatorisch feststellen[5] Fingerspitzenpalpation[6] bimanuelle Untersuchung/ Palpation[7] Druckschmerz[8] palpable Tumormasse[9] Palpations-, Tastbefund[10] Tastfinger[11] Palpitation, Herzklopfen[12]

[7]

Physical Examination CLINICAL TERMS **475**

percussion [pɚˈkʌʃən] *n term* → U17-9

tapping of the body surface (esp. over the chest and the abdomen) with the fingers or a pleximeter[1] to determine the location, size and density of the underlying organs by the pitch of the sound[2] produced

percuss[3] [pɚˈkʌs] *v term* • **percussion note**[4] *n*

» Bibasilar percussion dullness [ʌ] *and* reduced breath sounds[5] *were noted. The chest is clear to percussion and auscultation. Percuss and palpate all joints and vertebrae* [eɪ‖iː].

Use auscultatory[6] [ʌ]/ palpatory[7] **percussion** • digital[8] / fist / chest[9] / bimanual[10] [æ] **percussion** • instrumental[11] / threshold[12] / light[13] / deep **percussion** • dullness[14] [ʌ]/ tenderness[15] / hyperresonance[16] / clear[17] **to percussion** • **percussion** tympany[18] [ˈtɪmpəni] • tympany[18] / shifting dullness[19] **on percussion** • **percussion** sound[4] / tenderness[15] • tympanitic[18] [ɪ] **percussion note**

Perkussion, Beklopfen
Plessimeter[1] Tonhöhe[2] perkutieren, ab-, beklopfen[3] Perkussions-, Klopfschall[4] Atemgeräusche[5] auskultator. Perkussion[6] palpator. P.[7] Finger-Perkussion[8] Thoraxperkussion[9] Finger-Finger-P.[10] indirekte/ mittelbare P.[11] Schwellenwertperkussion[12] leichte/ leise P.[13] gedämpfter Perkussionsschall, perkutor. Dämpfung[14] Perkussionsempfindlichkeit[15] hypersonorer Klopfschall[16] perkutorisch frei[17] tympanitischer Klopfschall[18] Schallwechsel[19]

8

auscultation [ˌɒːskʌlˈteɪʃən] *n term*

listening to the patient's heart [hɑːrt] and bowel [aʊ] sounds[1], respiration, etc. (with a stethoscope → U17-2)

auscultate[2] [ɒː] *v term* • **on auscultation** *phr* • auscultatory[3] [ʌ] *adj*

» *During auscultation of the lungs the patient is instructed to take deep, slow breaths through the mouth. Cough* [kɒf], *dyspnea* [ɪ], *and* crackles[4] *on chest auscultation are typical findings. Clinical evaluation includes auscultation over the subclavian* [eɪ] *vessels to determine whether there are any* bruits[5] [bruːiːz]. *Aortic insufficiency may be auscultated in up to 5 % of patients.*

Use lungs[6] / chest **clear to auscultation** • direct[7] / (im)mediate[7] [iː]/ cardiac / obstetric **auscultation** • detected by / heard on **auscultation** • **auscultation** of the heart • **auscultatory** examination / percussion / monitoring / findings[8] • **to auscultate** for air entry / the chest for breath [e] sounds

Auskultation, Abhorchen
Darmgeräusche[1] auskultieren, abhorchen[2] auskultatorisch, Auskultations-[3] Rasseln, Knistern[4] Strömungsgeräusche[5] Lungen/ Pulmo auskultatorisch frei[6] direkte Auskultation[7] Auskultationsbefund[8]

9

general appearance [ɪɚ] *n clin, abbr* **GA**   *sim* **body habitus**[1] *n term*

general aspects O/E, e.g. build[2] (height, weight), posture[3], physical condition, nutritional [ɪʃ] status[4] (wasted[5] [eɪ]/ well-nourished [ɜː]/ emaciated[5]), skin color and texture[6], hydration [eɪ] (well-/ dehydrated), personal hygiene [ˈhaɪdʒiːn] (unkempt[7]), consciousness, compliance (cooperative/ uncooperative), etc.

appear [əˈpɪɚ] *v* • apparent[8] [eɚ] *adj* • disappear *v* • disappearance *n*

» *Note the patient's general appearance, mental status* [eɪ], *volume status, and the presence of abdominal tenderness. It gives the skin a rough* [rʌf] *texture or appearance. The child appears acutely ill. These lesions appear as a* lump[9] [ʌ] *in the breast* [e].

Use clinical / gross[10] [oʊ]/ endoscopic / radiologic[11] **appearance** • milky / waxy / innocuous[12] **in appearance** • **to appear** cachectic [kəˈkɛktɪk]/ healthy / cyanotic [saɪə-]/ comatose[13] / dehydrated [aɪ]

allgem. Erscheinungsbild
Habitus, Konstitution[1] Körperbau[2] Haltung[3] Ernährungszustand[4] abgemagert, ausgezehrt[5] Hautbeschaffenheit, -struktur[6] ungepflegt[7] offensichtlich[8] Knoten[9] makroskop. Aussehen[10] radiolog. Erscheinungsbild[11] harmlos aussehend[12] komatös sein[13]

10

acute distress *n clin, abbr* **AD** → U104-2

state of severe physical or mental pain, suffering, concern [ɜː], sorrow, misery or discomfort

distressing[1] *adj* • distressed *adj* • distressful *adj* • distraught[2] [dɪˈstrɒːt] *adj*

» *On admission the patient was in acute distress. Do not underestimate the degree of* distress[3]. *The patient is in obvious distress. Tachycardia* [k] *is a nonspecific sign of distress.*

Use to be in[4]/cause/demonstrate/disclose/relieve [iː] **acute distress** • respiratory[5] / fetal[6] [iː]/ emotional / no apparent [eɚ] **distress** • great / extreme **distress** • severely / mildly [aɪ] **distressed** • distressing symptoms[7] [ɪ]/ experience

akut krank, akute Schmerzen
besorgniserregend[1] verzweifelt[2] Not, Qual[3] akut krank sein, akute Schmerzen haben[4] Atemnot[5] fetale Hypoxie, fetaler Gefahrenzustand, fetal distress[6] belastende Beschwerden[7]

11

orientation *n term*   *opposite* **disorientation**[1] *n term* → U7-8

awareness of one's physical environment with regard to time, place and person

(well-)oriented *adj* • disoriented *adj* • reorientation[2] *n* • orienting *adj*

» Orientation as to time[3] *was lost. As a quick screen, assessing orientation by asking the patient to draw a clock with the* hands[4] *at a set time can be very informative.*

Use to assess/facilitate **orientation** • temporal[3] / (false) spatial[5] [eɪʃ] **orientation** • level / disturbance[6] [ɜː] **of orientation** • spatially / alert [ɜː] and **oriented** • **oriented to** time, place and person[7] • **oriented** in all spheres [sfɪɚz] • complete / right-left **disorientation** • **orienting** reflex [iː] (*abbr* OR) *or* response[8]

Orientierung
Desorientiertheit[1] Neuorientierung[2] zeitl. Orientierung[3] Zeiger[4] räumliche Orientierung[5] Orientierungsstörung[6] zeitl., örtl. u. zur eigenen Person orientiert[7] Orientierungsreaktion[8]

12

476 CLINICAL TERMS — Physical Examination

pulse [pʌls] *n clin & term, abbr* **P** → U36-9

rhythmic [ɪ] dilation [eɪ] of the arteries; O/E it can be palpated at the wrist[1] [r] (radial pulse[2]), neck (carotid), or the back of the knee (popliteal [ɪ]); the rate (beats/min), rhythm and amplitude are recorded

pulsation[3] [eɪʃ] *n term* • **pulsatile**[4] *adj* • **pulse rate**[5] *n* • **pulse wave**[6] *n*

» Let me take your pulse; hold out your wrist. The pulse is 80 and regular. Check the adequacy of the heart rate and the peripheral pulses. The appearance of a high resting pulse[7] may herald[8] overt [ɜː] cardiac toxicity[9]. The pulse has a rapid rise and fall, with an elevated systolic and low diastolic [aɪ] pressure. There is no impairment [eə] of arterial pulsations.

Use to take the[10] **pulse** • **pulse** amplitude[11] / pressure[12] / deficit[13] / oximetry[14] / quality[15] • femoral [e]/ jugular [dʒʌ] venous[16] [iː] (*abbr* JVP)/ popliteal [ɪ] **pulse** • (diminished) peripheral[17] / bounding[18] [aʊ]/ exaggerated [ædʒ] **pulse(s)** • DP/PT (dorsalis pedis, posterior tibial) **pulses** • **pulses** 2+ and equal bilaterally • regular[19] / rapid / full / strong **pulse** • hard[20] / soft[21] / weak [iː] or feeble[22] [iː]/ thready[23] [e] **pulse** • rapidly rising / irregular or jerky[24] [dʒɜː] **pulse** • paradoxic(al)[25] / dicrotic[26] [daɪ-] **pulse** • precordial / decreased [iː]/ absent **pulsations**

blood pressure reading [iː] *n clin*
  syn **sphygmomanometry** [sfɪɡmoʊ-] *n term* → U17-8; U36-8

pressure of the blood within the arteries (usually the systolic and diastolic pressures expressed as mm of mercury[1]) measured with a sphygmomanometer[2]; the BP is influenced mainly by cardiac output[3], peripheral vascular resistance and elasticity, blood volume and viscosity

» Initially elevated BP readings[4] may decline [aɪ] if the patient is allowed to relax and rest. This helps to normalize BP in 1-5 minutes. Some normovolemic [iː] patients may demonstrate an orthostatic fall in blood pressure, but without associated increase in pulse rate.

Use to take or measure[5] [eʒ] /check[6]/record/lower/raise [eɪ] /control[7] **the BP** • **BP** cuff [ʌ] (inflated)[8] [eɪ]/ test / monitoring • **BP** control / medication[9] • low[10] (*abbr* LBP)/ high[11] / elevated[12] / labile **BP** • (un)stable [eɪ]/ stabilized / rise in[13] / fall in **BP** • systolic[14] (*abbr* SBP)/ diastolic[15] (*abbr* DBP) **BP** • end-diastolic (*abbr* EDP)/ arterial (*abbr* ABP)/ central venous[16] [iː] (*abbr* CVP) **pressure**

pupils equal & reactive to light *phr jar, abbr* **PERL** → U108-3

normal finding on examination of the eyes during a vital [aɪ] sign check

pupillary[1] [pjuːpələri] *adj term* • **pupil** [pjuːpəl] *n, pl* **pupils**

» The pupils do not respond to light. The pupils should be examined for absolute and relative size [saɪz] and reactions to both light and accommodation. A large, poorly reacting pupil may be due to third nerve palsy[2] [ɔː].

Use **pupils** equal [iːkwəl] & reactive to light and accommodation (*abbr* PERLA)/ round and regular (*abbr* PRR) • (fixed) dilated[3] [eɪ]/ pinpoint[4] **pupils** • poorly or sluggishly [ʌ] reacting[5] **pupils** • (brisk / un/non)reactive / unequal[6] **pupils** • **pupil** reaction and size • **pupillary** aperture[7] [-tʃʊə]/ reflex or reaction or response[8] / dilation or dilatation[9] [eɪ] • **pupillary** enlargement / equality[10] / light reaction or reflex[11] • **pupillary** changes / size / constriction[12] • sluggish **pupillary** reaction[5]

chest or **respiratory excursion** *n term*
  sim **chest (wall) expansion**[1] *n term* → U44-3

functional respiratory movement of the rib cage[2] [keɪdʒ] on inspiration and expiration

excursive [ɜː] *adj term* • **expand**[3] [æ] *v* • **expanded** *adj* • **expandable**[4] *adj*

» Respiratory excursions [ɜː] were not visible. Chest pain was associated with respiratory excursion that reflexively inhibited respiration. The chest expands adequately bilaterally. There was chest expansion but collapse of the abdomen on inspiration.

Use adequate / full / bilaterally [aɪ] equal / asymmetric / limited or restricted **chest expansion** • ineffective / diminished[5] **respiratory excursion** • inspiratory [aɪ]/ free / equal[6] / diaphragmatic[7] [daɪəfræɡ-] **excursion** • **respiratory** embarrassment[8] / effort[9]

Puls(schlag), Pulsus
Handgelenk[1] Radialispuls[2] Pulsieren, Pulsation[3] pulsierend[4] Pulsfrequenz[5] Pulswelle[6] Ruhepuls[7] ankündigen[8] akute Kardiotoxizität[9] Puls fühlen/ messen[10] Pulsamplitude[11] Pulsdruck[12] Pulsdefizit[13] Pulsoximetrie[14] Pulsqualität[15] Jugularvenenpuls[16] periphere Pulse[17] schnellender Puls, Pulsus celer[18] regelmäßiger Puls[19] harter Puls, P. durus[20] weicher Puls, P. mollis[21] schwacher Puls[22] fadenförm. Puls, P. filiformis[23] unregelm./ arrhythmischer Puls, P. irregularis[24] paradoxer Puls, P. paradoxus[25] dikroter/ doppelschlägiger Puls, P. dicrotus[26]
13

Blutdruckmessung
Quecksilber, Hg[1] Sphygmomanometer, Blutdruckmessgerät[2] Herzminutenvolumen[3] Blutdruckwerte[4] Blutdruck messen[5] B. kontrollieren[6] B. regulieren[7] Blutdruckmanschette (aufgeblasen)[8] blutdrucksenkendes Mittel[9] niedriger Blutdruck, Hypotonie[10] Bluthochdruck, Hypertonie[11] erhöhter Blutdruck[12] Blutdruckanstieg[13] systol. Blutdruck[14] diastol. Blutdruck[15] zentraler Venendruck, ZVD[16]
14

Pupillen seitengleich & konsensuell/ prompt & isochor
Pupillen-, Pupillar-[1] Okulomotoriuslähmung[2] (lichtstarre) erweiterte/ weite Pupillen[3] gegen P.[4] verzögerte Pupillenreaktion[5] ungleiche Pupillen[6] Pupillenöffnung[7] Pupillarreflex, Pupillenreaktion[8] Pupillenerweiterung[9] Pupillengleichheit[10] Lichtreflex, -reaktion[11] Pupillenverengung[12]
15

Atemexkursion
Thorax(wand)expansion[1] Brustkorb[2] s. ausdehnen, s. ausbreiten[3] dehnbar[4] eingeschränkte Atemexkursion[5] seitengleiche Exkursion[6] Zwerchfellexkursion[7] Atembehinderung, -störung[8] Atemarbeit[9]
16

Physical Examination   CLINICAL TERMS 477

reveal [iː] vt   syn **show, disclose, demonstrate** vt,
             sim **display**[1]**, exhibit**[1] vt clin

to make previously [iː] secret or unknown facts, information or features [fiːtʃəz] known or obvious

(un)revealing[2] [iː] adj • **display**[3] n • **demonstration** n

» Physical examination reveals profound [aʊ] jaundice[4] [dʒɔːndɪs]. It is difficult to predict which patients will show clinical improvement. Physical activity has been shown to reduce anxiety [æŋzaɪəti]. In this situation full disclosure [oʊʒ] to the patient might be harmful. Pelvic examination disclosed tender indurated nodules in the cul-de-sac[5] [ʌ]. These children display a wide range of deficits in social and language skills.

Use to fail [eɪ] **to reveal** clues[6] [uː] • **to display** indifference[7] / emotion / peculiar interests • **to display** mannerisms / sth. on the chart[8] [tʃ] • **to disclose** a neoplasm [iː]/ no abnormalities[9] • **to disclose** basilar fracture[10]

ergeben, zeigen
zeigen, aufweisen[1] aufschlussreich[2] Demonstration, Anzeige[3] starke Gelbsucht[4] Douglas-Raum[5] keine Hinweise ergeben[6] sich gleichgültig zeigen[7] etw. in d. Tabelle hervorheben; etw. in die Fieberkurve eintragen[8] keine Anomalien ergeben[9] eine Schädelbasisfraktur ergeben[10]

17

---

unremarkable adj clin   rel **uneventful**[1]**, uncomplicated**[1] adj clin → U134-9

(of physical findings or a patient's course[2] [ɔː] or progress) to show no abnormalities

» The CSF[3] is unremarkable except for mild protein elevation. The patient's HEENT (head, eyes, ears, nose and throat) are unremarkable. She had significant proteinuria but an otherwise unremarkable urinary sediment[4]. Most children with viral [aɪ] croup [kruːp] have an uneventful course and improve within a few days.

Use **unremarkable** findings[5] / plasma levels / results[5] [ʌ] • **uneventful** (postoperative) course[6] / pregnancy • **uneventful** recovery [ʌ]/ neurologic examination / monitoring • **uncomplicated** burn [ɜː]/ infection / fracture / ulcer [ʌlsɚ]/ pregnancy • **uncomplicated** delivery[7] / course[6] / case / patient

unauffällig, ohne Befund, o. B.
komplikationsfrei, -los[1] Krankheitsverlauf[2] Liquor (cerebrospinalis)[3] unauffälliges Harnsediment[4] unauffällige(r) Befund/ Ergebnisse[5] komplikationsfreier Verlauf[6] komplikationslose Entbindung[7]

18

---

within normal limits phr jar, abbr **WNL**   syn **in the normal range** phr jar

(of physical findings or lab data) to be unremarkable (i.e. not decreased [iː] or elevated)

» Is the gas pattern in the colon within normal limits? Otherwise speech and language were WNL. Patients with frontal lobe tumors may present with changes in motivation and personality while the results of the neurologic examination remain within normal limits.

Use above / below **the normal limit** • at the upper/lower limit of[1] **normal** • **normal** temperature and pressure (abbr NTP)/ in size[2] • **normal** to palpation[3] / BP / contours[4] / affect

im Norm(al)bereich
im oberen Norm(al)bereich[1] normal groß[2] palpatorisch unauffällig[3] normale Umrisse[4]

19

---

no abnormality or **nothing abnormal detected** phr jar espBE, abbr **NAD**

(of physical findings or lab data) to show no appreciable [iːʃ] signs of disease

» No abnormalities were detected by intraoperative ultrasonography. The general physical examination revealed no abnormalities. Look for markedly abnormal hemodynamics. A sudden fluctuation in electrolyte levels without frankly abnormal serum values was observed.

Use **abnormal** physical findings / gait[1] [eɪ]/ position • **abnormal** growth / heart sound[2] / gene [dʒiːn] • no significant / mild / laboratory **abnormality** • metabolic[3] / endocrine / hemodynamic [hiːmədaɪ-]/ neurologic **abnormalities** • **abnormally** undersized [aɪ] person / sensitive[4] / low / high concentration[5]

ohne Befund, o.B., unauffällig
auffälliger Gang[1] Herzgeräusch[2] Stoffwechselanomalien[3] überempfindlich[4] abnorm hohe Konzentration[5]

20

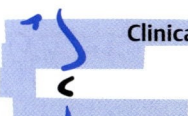

Clinical Phrases

Nurse, would you prepare Mrs. Knight for a physical, please. Schwester, bereiten Sie bitte Frau K. für die Untersuchung vor. • Would you lie flat on the couch for a moment. Bleiben Sie bitte kurz auf dem Rücken liegen. • Please roll up your sleeve and let me take your blood pressure. Schieben Sie bitte den Ärmel hoch, damit ich Ihren Blutdruck messen kann. • Would you mind taking off your shoes and socks. Würden Sie bitte Schuhe und Socken ausziehen. • Open your mouth wide and say ‚ah'. Mund bitte weit öffnen und "Aaaah" sagen. • Now I'd like to examine your ears. Jetzt möchte ich Ihre Ohren untersuchen. • Let me see you walk across the room. Gehen Sie bitte ein paar Schritte. • Bend your arm this way as far as you can. Beugen Sie den Arm so weit wie möglich. • There's nothing wrong with your lungs, Mr. Cohn. Herr C., Ihre Lunge ist völlig in Ordnung. • There's nothing to be worried about. Es gibt keinen Grund zur Sorge. • Okay, Mrs. Bentham, we're done. You can get dressed now and then we can talk further. Das war alles, Frau B. Sie können sich anziehen, dann besprechen wir alles Weitere.

Unit 108 Common Clinical Signs

Related Units: 4 Illness & Recovery, 89 Pathology, 103 Clinical Symptoms, 105 Fever, 107 Physical Examination, 109-114 Specific Signs & Symptoms

sign [saɪn] *n term & clin*

rel **stigma**[1] [stɪgmə] *n term, pl* **stigmas, -ata** *n*

physical [fɪz-] abnormality recognized by a doctor as an indication of a disease → U103-1

stigmatized [stɪgmətaɪzd] *adj*

» Pallor[2] usually indicates anemia [iː] but may be a sign of low cardiac output[3]. Physical examination revealed stigmata of alcoholic liver disease. AIDS is still a very stigmatized disease.

Use to produce/look for/search for/show[4] **signs of** • clinical / physical / presenting **sign** • useful diagnostic / neurologic [n(j)ʊɚ-]/ early[5] **sign** • first[6] / cardinal[7] / classic / pathognomonic[8] **sign** • reliable [aɪ]/ danger or alerting[9] [ɜː] **sign** • Babinski('s)[10] / Kernig's[11] **sign** • ominous or unfavorable [eɪ] prognostic[12] / radiologic **sign** • cutaneous [eɪ]/ physical / characteristic **stigma** • **stigmata of** alcohol abuse / chronic liver disease / Turner's syndrome [ɪ] • to carry a[13] / social **stigma**

> **Note:** In English there is a difference between **signs** and **symptoms**. The latter refer to the patient's subjective complaints. For instance **dyspnea** is a symptom not a sign. Many typical signs are named after the physicians [ɪʃ] who first described them.

(objektives) Krankheitszeichen, (klinisches) Zeichen, Symptom
Zeichen, Symptom, Stigma[1] Blässe[2] Herzminutenvolumen[3] Anzeichen von ... aufweisen[4] Frühsymptom[5] erstes Anzeichen[6] Leitsymptom[7] pathognomonisches Zeichen/Symptom[8] Warnzeichen, Warnsignal[9] Babinski-Zeichen, -Reflex[10] Kernig-Zeichen[11] ungünstiges/schlechtes prognostisches Zeichen[12] mit einem Stigma behaftet sein[13]

1

clinical picture *n term*

rel **clinical entity**[1] [klɪnɪkəl entɪti] *n term*

overall presentation of the symptoms [ɪ], signs, history, etc. of a patient or disorder

» The clinical picture suggests systemic involvement. Diabetes [iː] can produce the same clinical picture. Hypoprolactinemia [iː] is another clinical entity that may be associated with hypogonadotropism.

Use to produce/develop/show **a clinical picture** • classic[2] / (a)typical / characteristic **clinical picture** • similar / mixed **clinical picture** • radiographic or x-ray[3] / histologic / gross [oʊ] pathologic **picture** • distinct or well-defined[4] / idiopathic **clinical entity** • (specific) disease / pathologic / well-recognized[5] **entity** • **clinical status**[6] / spectrum / setting[7] / presentation • clinical observations[8] / assessment or analysis[9] / findings[10] [aɪ]

Krankheitsbild, klin. Erscheinungsbild/ Manifestation
klin. Entität, eigenes Krankheitsbild[1] klassisches Krankheitsbild[2] radiolog. Befund[3] eigenständiges Krankheitsbild[4] bekanntes Krankheitsbild[5] klin. Status[6] klin. Situation/ Lage[7] klin. Beobachtungen[8] klin. Untersuchung[9] klin. Befund[10]

2

vital signs [vaɪtəl saɪnz] *n term, abbr* **VS** → U107-13,15; U105-1ff

measurement of the respiratory rate (18 per min, labored[1] [eɪ] / unlabored), body temperature (98.6° F[2], afebrile[3]/ febrile), pulse rate (80/min), and sometimes BP (120/80 mm Hg) and pupillary reflexes, etc.

» Monitoring the patient's vital signs before and during the transfusion is important to identify hemolytic [ɪ] reactions promptly. The vital signs are within normal limits.

Use to assess[4]/determine/obtain [eɪ] /record/monitor[5]/check[4] **vital signs** • complete[6] / normal / stable[7] [eɪ] **vital signs** • change in / orthostatic or postural **vital signs** • **vital sign** check[8]

Vitalfunktionen, -zeichen
erschwert[1] entspr. 37°C[2] fieberfrei, afebril[3] Vitalfunktionen prüfen[4] Vitalfunktionen überwachen[5] alle Vitalfunktionen[6] stabile Vitalfunktionen[7] Prüfung d. Vitalfunktionen[8]

3

jaundice [dʒɔːndɪs] *n clin & term*   *syn* **icterus** [ɪktɚəs] *n term*

yellowish discoloration[1] of the skin and the whites of the eyes due to an accumulation of bile [baɪl] pigment[2] in the body tissues

jaundiced[3] *adj clin* • **icteric**[3] [ɪktɛrɪk] *adj term*

» Clinical deterioration was noted as jaundice developed. Infants who appear excessively jaundiced require evaluation. In patients with hepatitis [aɪ] dark urine and light stools[4] [uː] occur before the appearance [ɪɚ] of scleral [ɛ] or skin icterus[5].

Use cholestatic [kɔːliː-] or obstructive[6] [ʌ]/ prehepatic[7] **jaundice** • posthepatic / hemolytic[8] / neonatal[9] [eɪ] **jaundice** • mild[10] / deep[11] / deepening **jaundice** • clinical / physiologic / prolonged[12] **jaundice** • drug-induced / breast-feeding or breast [e] milk[13] **jaundice** • **jaundice** of pregnancy[14] • degree / onset **of jaundice** • be/become **jaundiced** • **jaundiced** or **icteric** patients • scleral[15] / skin **icterus** • **icteric** skin

Gelbsucht, Ikterus
Gelbverfärbung[1] Gallenfarbstoff[2] ikterisch[3] helle/ acholische Stühle[4] Hautikterus[5] cholestatischer Ikterus, Verschlussikterus[6] prähepatischer Ikterus[7] hämolyt. Ikterus, Icterus haemolyticus[8] Neugeborenenikterus, Icterus neonatorum[9] leichte Gelbsucht[10] ausgeprägte Gelbsucht[11] Icterus prolongatus[12] Muttermilchikterus[13] Schwangerschaftsikterus, Icterus gravidarum[14] Sklerenikterus[15]

4

Common Clinical Signs

pallor [pǽlɚ] *n term*　*syn* **paleness** [péɪlnəs] *n clin & inf*

the face looks a lighter color than usual often because of fear, shock, or illness

pale¹ [peɪl] *adj clin* • **pale**² *v* • **pallid**¹ [pǽlɪd] *adj rare*

» *Physical examination revealed pallor and splenomegaly*³. *On examination, these patients are usually pale and mildly icteric. Didn't you notice his paleness when he heard the news.*

Use to turn *or* become²/appear **pale** • skin is **pale** and gray [eɪ] • **pale** red / yellow / mucous [juːk] membranes⁴ / stools⁵ [uː] • central / extreme / cold-induced / ashen⁶ [ǽʃᵊn] **pallor** • facial [éɪʃ]/ optic disk / circumoral *or* perioral⁷ **pallor** • **pallor** of the foot on elevation

Blässe, Pallor
blass, bleich, fahl¹ blass werden² Milzvergrößerung³ blasse Schleimhäute⁴ acholische/ helle Stühle⁵ aschfahle Hautfarbe⁶ periorale Blässe⁷

5

cyanosis [saɪənóʊsɪs] *n term*

rel **acrocyanosis**¹ *n term*

bluish discoloration of the skin and mucous membranes due to insufficient [ɪʃ] perfusion with oxygen

cyanotic² [saɪənɒ́ːtɪk] *adj term* • **cyanosed**² [saɪənóʊzd] *adj* • **a/ noncyanotic** *adj*

» *There is slight cyanosis of the lips and cheeks. In a small percentage of patients the toes, appear cyanotic and clubbed*³ *[ʌ] in contrast to normally pink fingers. Acrocyanosis is characterized by persistent cyanosis of the hands and feet.*

Use to cause/develop **cyanosis** • generalized / peripheral⁴ / central⁵ **cyanosis** • cutaneous [eɪ]/ perioral / digital **cyanosis** • mild / marked / mottled⁶ **cyanosis** • increasing / deepening of / intense **cyanosis** • to become/appear **cyanotic** • deeply *or* severely **cyanotic** • **cyanotic** discoloration⁷ / spells / congenital [dʒé] heart disease⁸

Zyanose
Akrozyanose¹ zyanotisch² trommelschlägelförmig³ periphere Zyanose⁴ zentrale Zyanose⁵ fleckige Zyanose⁶ Blaufärbung⁷ angeborener Herzfehler⁸

6

erythema [erəθíːmə] *n term*　*syn* **redness** *n clin & inf*, **rubor** [rúːbɚ] *n term*

inflammatory [æ] redness of the skin

erythematous¹ [eǀíː] *adj term* • **erythematosus** *adj* • **ruborous** *adj* → U114-2

» *Administration of NSAIDs*² *is more effective in reducing erythema evoked by UV-B. The rash of scarlet fever*³ *is diffusely erythematous, resembling a sunburn with superimposed fine red papules. Patients with a generalized erythematous exanthem are more likely to have a drug eruption*⁴ *than those with a similar rash limited to the sun-exposed portions of the face.*

Use bright [braɪt]/ blotchy⁵ [ɒː]/ local / diffuse **erythema** • blanchable⁶ [tʃ]/ intense / drug associated **erythema** • skin / facial⁷ / lid / palmar **erythema** • sunburn⁸ [ɜːr]/ light-sensitive⁹ **erythema** • **erythema** nodosum / induratum / multiforme • **erythematous** lesion / eruption [ʌ]/ papules¹⁰ / plaque [plæk] • **erythematous** nodule / border / halo¹¹ [eɪ] • systemic lupus¹² [uː] (*abbr* SLE)/ pemphigus [f] **erythematosus** • generalized / marked / visible¹³ **redness** • acute / patchy⁵ **redness** • intense / dependent¹⁴ **rubor**

Erythem, (Haut)rötung
erythematös¹ nichtsteroidale Antiphlogistika² Scharlach³ Arzneimittelexanthem⁴ fleckförmige Rötung⁵ wegdrückbares Erythem⁶ Gesichtserythem⁷ Sonnenbrand, Erythema solare⁸ Lichterythem⁹ erythematöse Papeln¹⁰ entzündl. geröteter Hof¹¹ systemischer Lupus erythematodes¹² sichtbare Rötung¹³ Rötung der weiter distal gelegenen Areale¹⁴

7

facial flush [féɪʃᵊl flʌʃ] *n clin*　*sim* **malar** [eɪ] **flush**¹ *n term* → U51-11

sudden blush [ʌ] of the face or subjective feeling of heat due to exertion or vasomotor instability

flushing² [flʌ́ʃɪŋ] *n & adj clin* • **flush**³ *v* • **flushed** *adj*

» *In scarlet fever patients typically have a facial flush and a "strawberry" tongue*⁴*. The patient appears flushed and her skin is hot and dry. Some patients experience cutaneous flushing.*

Use to experience⁵/cause *or* produce **hot flushes** • erythematous **flush** • cutaneous [eɪ]/ systemic / diffuse red / transient *or* episodic **flushing** • **flushed** face⁶ / skin⁷

Gesichtsröte
Wangenröte¹ Erröten, Hitzewallung; errötend² rot werden, erröten³ Himbeerzunge⁴ Hitzewallungen haben⁵ gerötetes Gesicht⁶ gerötete Haut⁷

8

rash [ræʃ] *n term & clin*　*syn* **skin eruption** [ɪrʌ́pʃᵊn] *n term* → U114-2, U103-19

temporary exanthema [-θíːmə] or eruption on the skin

» *The rash resolved*¹ *promptly after treatment with doxycycline was begun. The pertinent features of rashes include their configuration (i.e. annular*² *or target), the arrangement of their lesions, and their distribution (i.e. central or peripheral).*

Use to break out in³/produce/develop³ **a rash** • butterfly⁴ [ʌ]/ malar / diaper⁵ [aɪ] **rash** • petechial [ek]/ pruritic⁶ [prʊərɪ́tɪk] **rash** • urticarial⁷ [ɜːr-]/ scaly⁸ [eɪ] **rash** • acute fever and (*abbr* AFR)/ skin **rash** • centrally distributed / diffuse **rash** • mild⁹ / hemorrhagic [-rǽdʒɪk] **rash** • maculopapular / scarlatiniform¹⁰ / vesicular / drug¹¹ **rash**

Hautausschlag, Exanthem
klang ab¹ ringförmig² e. Ausschlag bekommen/ entwickeln³ schmetterlingsförm. Ausschlag⁴ Windelausschlag, -dermatitis⁵ juckender A.⁶ Nesselausschlag⁷ schuppiger A.⁸ leichter A.⁹ scharlachähnliches Exanthem¹⁰ Arzneimittelexanthem¹¹

9

CLINICAL TERMS

edema [ɪdiːmə] n term   syn **swelling, puffiness** [ʌ] n clin
   rel **dropsy**¹ [ɒː] n BE, **hydrops**² [haɪdrɒːps] n term
excessive accumulation of fluid in the tissue; in British English spelled oedema
edematous³ adj term • **swell**⁴ - swelled - swollen v irr • **puffy**⁵ adj • **dropsical** adj
» Diuretics are usually not indicated unless edema is associated with heart failure. The swelling over the eyelids was confined to⁶ the left side. The edema started as a puffiness about the ankle made worse by long periods of activity.
Use peripheral / ankle⁷ / pulmonary or lung⁸ **edema** • pitting⁹ / bilateral leg / lid¹⁰ **edema** • **edematous** lesions [iːʒ]/ mucosa [mjuːkoʊzə] / periorbital / local / inflammatory [æ] **swelling** • joint / eyelid¹⁰ **swelling** • soft tissue¹¹ / brain / optic disk **swelling** • spinal cord / scrotal **swelling** • **swollen** ankles¹² / lymph [lɪmf] nodes / and tender¹² **swelling** subsides¹³ [aɪ]/ facial¹⁴ [eɪʃ]/ diffuse / periorbital **puffiness** • **puffy** face¹⁴ / swelling • fetal¹⁵ [iː]/ meningeal [-dʒiːəl]/ endolymphatic **hydrops** • **hydrops** fetalis¹⁵

(digital or **finger) clubbing** [ʌ] n term   rel **drumstick** [ʌ] **appearance**¹ n clin
abnormal enlargement of the fingers, characterized by broadening [ɔː] of the nail-beds, abnormally curved [ɜː] and shiny [ʃaɪni] nails, and sometimes excoriation [eɪʃ]
clubbed² [klʌbd] adj term
» Finger clubbing may be associated with cyanotic heart disease, advanced chronic pulmonary disease, biliary [ɪ] cirrhosis³ [oʊ], colitis, or thyrotoxicosis⁴ [aɪ]. When clubbing is advanced, the finger may have a drumstick appearance.
Use advanced / early / symmetric [sɪm-] **clubbing** • fingers appear **clubbed** • **clubbed** fingers or digits⁵ [dɪdʒɪts]

organomegaly n term   rel **hypertrophy**¹ n & v, **hyperplasia**² [eɪʒ] n term
abnormal enlargement of the viscera³ [ɪs], such as may be seen in acromegaly⁴
-megaly, mega(lo)- comb • **hypertrophic**⁵ adj • **hyperplastic**⁶ [æ] adj → U89-15
» On examination, jaundice and splenomegaly were noted. The liver was examined for hepatomegaly to exclude liver metastases. The ECG revealed right ventricular hypertrophy.
Use hepato/ spleno⁷ [e]/ hepatospleno/ acro⁴/ cardio**megaly** • cardiac / left ventricular⁸ **hypertrophy** • muscle or muscular / benign prostatic⁹ **hypertrophy** • benign [bɪnaɪn] prostatic⁹ / gingival [dʒ]/ endometrial [iː] **hyperplasia**

irritability n clin → U76-6f   syn **jitteriness** [dʒɪ] n inf & clin, rel **lability**¹ n clin
having a tendency to be unduly [(j)uː] sensitive², nervous, and react immoderately³ to stimuli
irritate v • **irritable**⁴ adj • **irritation** n • **jittery**⁴ adj • **jitters**⁵ n pl inf
» Extremes of irritability and even frank aggressive behavior rather than depressed mood per se are quite common in childhood depressions. Are there any signs of tension⁶ [ʃ], irritability, or apathy on either side of the parent-child relationship. The patient complains of mild CNS side effects, primarily jitteriness, anxiety, insomnia⁷, and difficulty in concentrating⁸.
Use emotional / (focal) [oʊ] nervous [ɜː]/ neuromuscular⁹ **irritability** • reflex / aggressive¹⁰ / labile [eɪ] **irritability** • airway / gastric¹¹ / vesical **irritability** • skin¹² / eye / nerve root¹³ [uː]/ GI **irritation** • **irritable** bowel [baʊəl] syndrome¹⁴ [ɪ] • emotional / mood¹⁵ [uː]/ autonomic **lability**

wasting [eɪ] n term   rel **weight loss**¹ [weɪtlɒːs] n clin → U24-10; U25-7
   rel **emaciation**² [-sɪeɪʃⁿn], **cachexia**³ [kəkeksɪə], **inanition**⁴ [ɪʃ] n term
gradual deterioration [ɪə] of a patient associated with weakness [iː] and loss of muscle mass
wasting adj • **wasted** adj • **emaciated**⁵ [ɪmeɪsɪeɪtɪd] adj • **cachectic** adj
» In progressive muscular atrophy, muscle wasting and marked weakness begin in the hands. Severe weight loss to the point of cachexia in a person who seems unconcerned⁶ about the obvious emaciation is a prominent feature of anorexia nervosa⁷. Parenteral alimentation⁸ is indicated in catabolic wasting states such as tumors when gastric feedings are inadequate.
Use generalized / muscle / extremity⁹ / renal salt **wasting** • potassium¹⁰ / profound [aʊ] or severe [ɪə] **wasting** • **wasting** disorder / of affected muscles • to lose or take off¹¹/gain [eɪ] or put on **weight** • mild / marked¹² / significant / rapid / progressive **weight loss** • **weight** gain / control /-for-height¹³ [haɪt]/ problem • extreme [iː] **emaciation** • to become / severely **emaciated** • cancer¹⁴ ['s]/ HIV-related / cardiac / progressive¹⁵ **cachexia** • **cachectic** patient • general / exogenous¹⁶ [ɒː] **inanition**

Ödem, Schwellung
Hydrops, Wassersucht; Ödem¹ Hydrops, Wassersucht² ödematös³ anschwellen⁴ aufgedunsen, verschwollen⁵ beschränkt auf⁶ Knöchelödem⁷ Lungenödem⁸ Dellen bildendes/ eindrückbares Ödem⁹ Lidödem¹⁰ Weichteilschwellung¹¹ geschwollen u. druckschmerzempfindlich¹² Schwellung geht zurück¹³ aufgedunsenes/ verschwollenes Gesicht¹⁴ Hydrops connatalis¹⁵

10

Bildung von Trommelschlägelfingern
trommelschlägelartiges Aussehen¹ trommelschlägelförmig, -artig² biliäre Zirrhose³ Hyperthyreose, Schilddrüsenüberfunktion⁴ Trommelschlägelfinger⁵

11

Viszeromegalie
Hypertrophie; hypertrophieren, s. vergrößern¹ Hyperplasie² innere Organe³ Akromegalie⁴ hypertroph⁵ hyperplastisch⁶ Milzvergrößerung, Splenomegalie⁷ Linksherzhypertrophie⁸ benigne Prostatahyperplasie⁹

12

Reizbarkeit, Gereiztheit, Nervosität
Labilität¹ überempfindlich² überreagieren³ (leicht) reizbar, gereizt, nervös⁴ Zittern, Bammel, Tatterich⁵ Spannungen⁶ Schlaflosigkeit⁷ Konzentrationsschwäche⁸ neuromuskuläre Übererregbarkeit⁹ aggressive Gereiztheit¹⁰ Reizmagen¹¹ Hautreizung¹² Irritation d. Nervenwurzel¹³ Reizkolon¹⁴ Stimmungslabilität¹⁵

13

Kräfteverfall, Auszehrung, (Muskel)schwund
Gewichtsverlust¹ Abmagerung, Auszehrung² Kachexie³ Inanition⁴ ausgezehrt⁵ gleichgültig⁶ Magersucht, A. nervosa⁷ parenterale Ernährung⁸ Muskelschwund i. d. Extremitäten⁹ (verstärkter) Kaliumverlust¹⁰ (Gewicht) abnehmen¹¹ starker Gewichtsverlust¹² Körpergröße-Gewicht-Verhältnis¹³ Krebskachexie¹⁴ progrediente Kachexie¹⁵ Hungerdystrophie¹⁶

14

Unit 109 Gastrointestinal Signs & Symptoms
Related Units: 103 Clinical Symptoms, 108 Clinical Signs, 46 Digestion, 47 Liver, 2 Diet, 3 Food, 79 Nutrition

indigestion [ˌɪndɪdʒestʃən] *n clin*   *syn* **dyspepsia** [dɪsˈpepsɪə] *n term*,
 upset stomach [ˌʌpset ˈstʌmək] *n inf*

 broad term for vague [veɪɡ] abdominal discomfort, e.g. nausea¹ [ɔː], bellyache, epigastric fullness², bloating³ [oʊ], gaseousness⁴ or food intolerance resulting from failure of proper digestion [aɪ] and absorption

 dyspeptic *adj term* • **indigestible**⁵ *adj clin* • **stomach**⁶ *v inf*

» When given a history of indigestion, determine the location, duration and temporal relation of the symptoms to the ingestion of food⁷. Did his indigestion respond to antacids? Patients often interpret the pain of infarct as indigestion. The term dysmotility-like dyspepsia is used when belching⁸ [tʃ], abdominal distention³, and early satiety⁹ [aɪ] are prominent symptoms.

Use to suffer from/get **indigestion** • gastric¹⁰ / fat¹¹ / acid / nervous **indigestion** • functional¹² / chronic / postprandial **indigestion** / **indigestion** associated with fatty food¹¹ / and belching • nonspecific / flatulent / (non)ulcer¹² [ʌlsə]/ ulcer-like **dyspepsia** • **dyspeptic** symptoms / patient • **stomach** upset¹⁰ / spasms /ache [-eɪk]/ ulcer¹³ • to upset one's¹⁴ **stomach** • gastric¹⁰ / gastrointestinal¹⁵ / GI tract¹⁵ **upset** • hemodynamic [aɪ]/ emotional¹⁶ [oʊ] **upset**

Verdauungsstörung, Magenverstimmung, Indigestion, Dyspepsie
Übelkeit¹ Völlegefühl² Bauchauftreibung, geblähtes Abdomen³ Blähungen⁴ un-/ schwer verdaulich⁵ vertragen⁶ Nahrungsaufnahme⁷ Aufstoßen⁸ vorzeitiges Sättigungsgefühl⁹ Magenverstimmung¹⁰ Störung d. Fettverdauung¹¹ funktionelle/ nichtulzeröse Dyspepsie¹² Magengeschwür, Ulcus ventriculi¹³ s. den Magen verderben¹⁴ Verdauungsstörung¹⁵ Aufregung¹⁶

1

halitosis [ˌhælɪˈtoʊsɪs] *n term*   *syn* **bad breath** [e], **breath odor** [oʊ] *n clin*,
 stomatodysodia *n term*

 foul¹ [aʊ] and/or offensive² odor from the mouth also termed fetor [iː] oris
 stomatitis [ˌstoʊməˈtaɪtɪs] *n term* • **stomat(o)-** *comb* • **malodorous**³ *adj* → U62-3

» Extensive dental caries [eə], periodontal disease, or tonsillitis causes halitosis often accompanied by a bad taste. Fetid [e‖iː] breath odor⁴ and blood-tinged [dʒ] saliva [aɪ] may accompany any ulcerative lesions [iːʒ] of the oral mucosa. The patient's breath smells of alcohol.

Use chronic / imagined / psychogenic **halitosis** • unpleasant⁵ [e]/ fruity / mousy / characteristic⁶ **breath odor** • to have/be aware of one's own **bad breath** • **breath** freshener⁷ • aphthous [æfθəs] *or* herpetic⁸ **stomatitis** • **stomat**ology /algia⁹ [-ˈældʒ(ɪ)ə] /oglossitis

(übler) Mundgeruch, Halitose, Foetor ex ore
faulig, übel(riechend)¹ widerlich, abstoßend² übelriechend³ übler Mundgeruch⁴ unangenehmer Mundgeruch⁵ charakteristischer Mundgeruch⁶ Mundwasser⁷ Stomatitis aphthosa, Gingivostomatitis herpetica⁸ Stomatodynia⁹

2

water brash *n clin*   *rel* **hypersalivation**¹, **rumination**² *n term*

 sudden appearance of a mouthful of salty or sour fluid due to reflex salivary hypersecretion in response to acid reflux into the lower esophagus (occasionally accompanying heartburn and dyspepsia); also spelled **waterbrash**
 saliva *n term* • **salivate**³ *v* → U27-9f • **ruminate**⁴ *v* • **ruminative** *adj*

» Water brash is an unusual symptom of gastro-esophageal reflux disease⁵ (*abbr* GERD). Water brash is reflex hypersalivation in response to peptic esophagitis and should not be confused with regurgitation⁶. Patients with severe regurgitation often report that bitter or sour-tasting fluid may regurgitate as far as the throat and mouth (water brash), especially when they are supine [aɪ].

Use reflex⁷ / profuse / excessive¹ / decreased⁸ / impaired **salivation** • swallowed / thick / tenacious⁹ [eɪʃ]/ artificial¹⁰ **saliva**

maulvoller Rückfluss d. Speiseröhreninhalts
gesteigerte Speichelsekretion, Hypersalivation, Sialorrhoe¹ Rumination, Wiederkäuen; Grübeln² Speichel produzieren³ wiederkäuen⁴ Refluxkrankheit⁵ Rückströmen, Regurgitation⁶ reflektorische Speichelsekretion⁷ verminderte S., Oligosialie⁸ zähflüssiger Speichel⁹ Speichelsubstitution¹⁰

3

heartburn [ˈhɑːrtbɜːrn] *n clin*   *syn* **pyrosis** [paɪˈroʊsɪs] *n term*
 rel **(gastro)esophageal** [-ˈdʒiːəl] **reflux**¹ [ˈriːflʌks] *n term*

 substernal [ɜː] pain or burning [ɜː] typically associated with regurgitation [dʒ] of gastric juice² into the esophagus which is occasionally accompanied by eructation³ [ʌ] of an acid fluid

» His heartburn is worse on recumbency⁴ [ʌ]. The patient gives a history of nausea, burping³ [ɜː], early satiety [aɪ], bloating [oʊ], heartburn, and regurgitation [ɜː]. A prolonged history of heartburn and reflux preceding [siː] dysphagia indicates peptic stricture. Acid [æsɪd] reflux⁵ was due to lower esophageal sphincter incompetence.

Use occasional / nocturnal [ɜː]/ severe / long-standing⁶ / persistent **heartburn** • **esophageal** motility⁷ / acid exposure [oʊʒ] • **esophageal** spasm⁸ [æ]/ obstruction [ʌ]/ webs⁹ • **esophageal** foreign body¹⁰ / stricture / achalasia¹¹ [ˌækəˈleɪʒ(ɪ)ə] • **esophageal** atresia [iːʒ]/ chest pain / varices¹² [ˈveərəsiːz] • **gastroesophageal**¹ (*abbr* GER)/ acid⁵ **reflux** • **reflux** (erosive) esophagitis¹³ [ɪsˌpːfəˈdʒaɪtɪs]

Sodbrennen, Pyrosis
gastroösophagealer Reflux¹ Magensaft² Aufstoßen, Rülpsen³ im Liegen⁴ Säurereflux⁵ langjähriges Sodbrennen⁶ Ösophagusmotilität⁷ Ösophagospasmus⁸ intraösophageale Membranen⁹ Ösophagusfremdkörper¹⁰ (Ösophagus)achalasie¹¹ Ösophagusvarizen¹² Refluxösophagitis¹³

4

482 CLINICAL TERMS — Gastrointestinal Signs & Symptoms

dysphagia [dɪsfeɪdʒ(ɪ)ə] n term   syn **difficulty swallowing** [ɒː] phr clin,
   rel **globus sensation**[1] [eɪ] n term

inability to pass an ingested bolus [oʊ] or liquids down the esophagus, which may range from a sensation of having a lump [ʌ] in the throat[1] to severe obstruction

dysphagic adj term • **-phagia** comb • **swallow**[2] v → U46-1

» Difficulty in swallowing may lead to aspiration pneumonia[3] [n(j)uː-]. With a lower esophageal ring[4], dysphagia is intermittent. Dysphagia should not be confused with globus sensation, a feeling of having a lump in the throat[1] that is unrelated to swallowing and occurs without impaired transport. Globus sensation may result from esophageal reflux or from frequent swallowing and drying of the throat[5] associated with anxiety [aɪ] or other emotional states.

Use to develop/produce[6]/report/relieve[7] [iː] **dysphagia** • sudden / gradually progressive **dysphagia** • transient / long-standing **dysphagia** • mechanical [k]/ motor / oropharyngeal[8] **dysphagia** • (pre-)esophageal[9] / sideropenic[10] [iː] **dysphagia** • to initiate/have difficulty (in)[11] **swallowing** • impaired[12] [eɚ]/ pain on[13] / forceful / air[14] **swallowing** • **swallowing** mechanism[15] [ek]/ disorder or dysfunction[12] • odyno[13]/ a/ aero[14]/ hyper**phagia** • **globus** hystericus[1] [ɪ]/ pharyngeus[1] [fərɪndʒɪəs]

Schluckstörung, Dysphagie
Globusgefühl, -syndrom[1] schlucken[2] Aspirationspneumonie[3] Schatzki-Ring[4] Austrocknen d. Rachens[5] Schluckstörungen hervorrufen[6] Schluckstörungen lindern[7] oropharyngeale Dysphagie[8] ösophageale Dysphagie[9] sideropenische Dysphagie, Plummer-Vinson-Syndrom[10] Schluckbeschwerden haben[11] Schluckstörung[12] schmerzhaftes Schlucken, Odynophagie[13] Luftschlucken, Aerophagie[14] Schluckmechanismus, -bewegung, -akt[15]

5

constipation n clin & term   sim **obstipation**[1] n term rare
   rel **obstruction**[2], **ileus**[3], **volvulus**[4] n term

condition marked by infrequent bowel movements[5] or difficult evacuation of the feces[6] [fiːsiːz]

(non)constipated[7] adj term • **obstipated**[8] adj • **pseudo-obstruction** n

» A history of alternating constipation and diarrhea [iː] suggests an underlying motility disorder, e.g. irritable bowel syndrome[9]. Because of the wide range of normal bowel habits[10], constipation is difficult to define precisely. In volvulus of the sigmoid, there are intermittent cramp-like pains, increasing in severity [e] as obstipation becomes complete. Peristaltic rushes[11], gurgles [ɜː], and high-pitched tinkles[12] are audible during attacks of cramping pain in distal obstruction.

Use to have/report/prevent/cause **constipation** • bowel [aʊ]/ mild[13] / intermittent / marked / severe[14] **constipation** • slow-transit[15] / acute / intractable[16] / persistent / chronic **constipation** • retentive[17] / atonic / spastic[18] / functional / psychogenic [dʒe] **constipation** • (upper/ small/ partial) intestinal / esophageal / pyloric or gastric outlet[19] **obstruction** • distal small bowel / closed-loop[20] / luminal / mechanical **obstruction** • adynamic or paralytic[21] / dynamic or spastic **ileus** • gallstone[22] / meconium **ileus** • reflex / postoperative / gastric / colonic **ileus** • midgut / cecal / sigmoid[23] / gastric[24] **volvulus** • to be/feel/remain **constipated** • **constipated** patient / bowel / stool

Note: In English **obstipation** refers to extreme constipation marked by absence of passage of both stool and flatus (verging on complete obstruction).

Obstipation, (Stuhl)verstopfung, Darmträgheit
ausgeprägte Obstipation[1] Obstruktion, Verlegung[2] Ileus, Darmverschluss, -lähmung[3] Darmverschlingung, Volvulus intestini[4] Stuhlgang[5] Stuhl, Kot[6] obstipiert[7] vollkommen verstopft[8] Reizkolon, Colon irritabile[9] Stuhlgewohnheiten[10] Bauchknurren, Borborygmen[11] hochfrequente Darmgeräusche[12] leichte Verstopfung[13] starke V.[14] Obstipation durch verlangsamten Kolontransit[15] therapierefraktäre O.[16] Kotstauung[17] spast. O.[18] Pylorusobstruktion, Verlegung d. Magenausgangs[19] Adhäsions-, Strangulationsileus[20] paralyt. Ileus[21] Gallensteinileus[22] Sigma-, Sigmoidvolvulus[23] Magenvolvulus, Volvulus ventriculi[24]

6

flatulence [flætʃələnˢs] n term   syn **gaseousness** [gæsɪəsnəs‖geɪʃ-] n clin
   rel **meteorism**[1] [iː] n rare,
   tympany[2] [tɪmpəni] n term → U46-15

excessive amount of gas formed in the intestines which may be expelled through the anus

flatus[3] [eɪ] n term • **flatulent**[4] [æ] adj • **gaseous** adj • **gas**[3] [æ] n

» Patients complaining of excessive gas, bloating [oʊ], distention, and flatulence should be carefully questioned about dietary preferences. Plain [eɪ] x-rays of the abdomen[5] show marked gaseous distention of the colon. Rectal examination in infants may be followed by expulsion of stool and flatus. Bloating was not due to excessive quantities of intestinal gas[6]. Physical examination revealed[7] abdominal distention with tympany, and visible peristalsis.

Use to cause/experience[8]/complain of **flatulence** • increased / burping [ɜː] and[9] **flatulence** • (extra)intestinal[6] / colonic **gas** • **gas** production /-filled intestinal loops[10] • it gives me[11] **gas** • to expel or pass[12] **flatus** • voluminous [uː]/ excessive **flatus** • **gaseous** distention[13] / eructations[14] [ʌ]

Flatulenz, Blähung(en)
Blähsucht, Meteorismus[1] Tympanie, Trommelbauch; trommelartiger Klopfschall[2] Blähung, Wind, Flatus[3] blähend, flatulent[4] Abdomenübersichtsaufnahme, Leeraufnahme[5] Darmgas[6] ergab[7] Blähungen haben[8] Eruktation u. Flatulenz[9] gasgefüllte Darmschlingen[10] ich bekomme davon Blähungen[11] einen Wind abgehen lassen[12] Auftreibung[13] Aufstoßen, Eruktation[14]

7

Gastrointestinal Signs & Symptoms CLINICAL TERMS 483

(abdominal) bloating [oʊ] or **distention** [dɪstenʃˀn] n clin rel **fullness**[1] n clin

(i) subjective feeling of being stuffed [ʌ] after meals (ii) protuberant [uː] abdomen[2] due to an increase in intra-abdominal content, poor muscle tone, excessive subcutaneous [eɪ] fat, etc.

bloated[3] adj clin • **(non)distended**[4] adj • **distensible**[5] adj • **full** adj

» Belching, bloating, fullness, and nausea may be associated with gallstones [ɔː], peptic ulcer disease, or functional distress. Persistent bloating after eating and loss of appetite are suggestive of[6] GI obstruction. The patient complains of flatulence, abdominal bloating, heartburn, nausea, and dysphagia. If the aortic aneurysm [jɚ] ruptures [ʌ] in the retroperitoneum [iː], a poorly defined midabdominal fullness can be felt, and shock becomes profound [aʊ].

Use upper / diffuse / mild / marked / tense[7] **abdominal distention** • progressive / gross [oʊ] or severe[8] **abdominal distention** • gaseous[9] / (epi)gastric[10] / (small) bowel / colonic **distention** • visceral [ɪs]/ hepatic / venous[11] [iː] **distention** • **distended** abdomen[12] / stomach[10] / colon • **distended** loop [uː] of bowel[13] / with air / with fluid • painful **abdominal bloating** • functional / postprandial[14] **bloating** • **bloating and** flatulence[15] / belching / constipation[16] / tenderness • feeling of[1] / epigastric[17] / left upper quadrant [ɒː]/ postprandial[14] **fullness** • **fullness** after meals[14] • **bloated** abdomen[12] / sensation[1] • to feel[18] **bloated** • **full** stomach[19] [k]

(i) Völlegefühl
(ii) Bauchauftreibung, geblähtes Abdomen

Völle(gefühl), Blähung[1] vorgewölbtes Abdomen[2] gebläht, aufgetrieben[3] gedehnt, erweitert[4] dehnbar[5] hindeuten auf[6] (brett)hartes geblähtes Abdomen[7] starke Bauchauftreibung[8] Blähung, Auftreibung[9] aufgeblähter Magen[10] Erweiterung d. Jugularvenen[11] Bauchauftreibung, geblähtes Abdomen[12] erweiterte Darmschlinge[13] postprandiales Völlegefühl[14] Völlegefühl u. Blähungen[15] Völlegefühl/ Blähungen u. Verstopfung[16] Völlegefühl i. Oberbauch[17] ein Völlegefühl haben[18] voller Magen[19]

8

ascites [əsaɪtiːz] n term syn **abdominal** or **peritoneal dropsy** n term espBE
rel **abdominal girth**[1][ɜː], **ballottement**[2] [ɒː] n term

swollen, protuberant abdomen due to accumulation of serous fluid in the peritoneal cavity

ascitic[3] [ɪ] adj term • **dropsical**[4] adj BE • **pseudoascites**[5] n • **ballottable** adj

» A tensely distended abdomen with tightly stretched skin, bulging [dʒ] flanks, and everted [ɜː] umbilicus [ʌ] is characteristic of ascites. The blood-ascitic fluid albumin gradient is greater than 1.1 g/dL. Determine whether ascitic fluid is present by testing for "shifting dullness[6]".

Use fatty / bile[7] [aɪ]/ pancreatic / chylous[8] [kaɪləs]/ cirrhotic [sɪr-] **ascites** • portal hypertensive / urinary [jʊ]/ congenital [dʒe] **ascites** • postoperative / exudative [uː]/ malignant[9] / gross **ascites** • uro/ bacter**ascites** • neutrocytic [sɪ]/ tense / infected / turbid[10] [ɜː] **ascites** • blood-stained [eɪ] or blood-tinged[11] [dʒ]/ intractable or refractory[12] **ascites** • **ascitic** fluid • effusion [juːʒ]/ leak[13] [iː] • **ascitic** patient / white blood count[14] • **ballottable** mass • increasing [iː] abdominal[15] **girth** • **girth** measurement[16] [eʒ]

Aszites, Bauchwassersucht

Bauchumfang[1] Ballottement[2] aszitisch, Aszites-[3] ödematös, aszitisch[4] Pseudoaszites[5] Schallwechsel[6] galliger Aszites, Cholaskos[7] chylöser Aszites[8] maligner Aszites[9] trüber Aszites[10] blutiger/ hämorrhagischer Aszites[11] therapierefraktärer Aszites[12] Austritt v. Aszitesflüssigkeit[13] Leukozytenzahl in der Aszitesflüssigkeit[14] zunehmender Bauchumfang[15] Messung d. Bauchumfangs[16]

9

diarrhea [daɪəriːə] n term & clin syn **loose stools** n clin, **to have the runs** phr inf
rel **maldigestion**[1] [æ], **malabsorption**[2] n term

abnormally frequent passage of semisolid or fluid fecal [iː] matter from the bowel

diarrheal adj term • **steatorrhea**[3] n • **stooling**[4] n • **malabsorbed** adj

» She developed severe chronic diarrhea leading to malnutrition. The onset of fulminant [ʊ], catastrophic diarrhea results in massive fluid loss which may rapidly lead to dehydration [aɪ].

Use to produce/experience/develop/exacerbate[5] [ɪgzæs-] **diarrhea** • acute / explosive / episodic / mild[6] **diarrhea** • chronic / protracted[7] / massive / severe **diarrhea** • self-limited[8] / watery / mucous [mjuːkəs]/ blood-tinged[9] **diarrhea** • traveler's[10] / allergic [ɜː]/ infectious[11] / antibiotic-associated **diarrhea** • watery[12] / liquid / foul-smelling[13] **stools** • soft / semi-solid[14] / mucoid **stools** • intestinal / nutrient[15] [uː]/ fat **malabsorption** • carbohydrate[16] [aɪ]/ glucose-galactose **malabsorption** • amino acid / vitamin B12 / bile salt **malabsorption** • **malabsorption** syndrome

Diarrhoe, Durchfall

Maldigestion, Verdauungsstörung[1] Malabsorption, Absorptionsstörung[2] Fettdurchfall, Steatorrhoe[3] Stuhlgang[4] Durchfall verschlimmern[5] leichter D.[6] protrahierte/ anhaltende Diarrhoe[7] spontan abklingende D.[8] blutiger Durchfall[9] Reisediarrhoe[10] infektiöse D.[11] wässrige Stühle[12] übelriechende Stühle[13] breiige S.[14] Nährstoffmalabsorption[15] Kohlenhydratmalabsorption[16]

10

melena [məliːnə] n term syn **tarry stool** n, rel **gastrointestinal bleeding**[1] n clin

passage of dark-colored stools stained [eɪ] with blood[2] that has been altered by the intestinal juices [dʒuːsɪːz]; passage of bright red blood per rectum is termed hematochezia[3] [-kiːzɪə]

melenic [məliːnɪk] adj term → U46-19

» Melena usually is due to bleeding from the upper GI tract. Seemingly melenic stool should always be tested for occult blood, since many substances (iron, spinach[4], etc) may cause dark stools. Stool analysis may be positive for blood even though melena is not observed.

Use hematemesis [e]/ steatorrhea [ɪə] **and melena** • bright red / bloody[3] / blood-streaked[3] [iː] **stools** • blood-tinged[3] [dʒ]/ guaiac-positive[3] [g(w)aɪæk]/ heme-positive[3] **stools** • melenic[5] / black[5] / occult [ʌ] blood in[6] **stools** • small-caliber[7] / ribbon(-like)[7] / color of[8] **stools** • **stool** specimen or sample[9] • **stool** fat / smear[10] [smɪɚ]/ culture[11] [ʌ]/ softener[12] • **stool** analysis or examination[13] / consistency[14]

Melaena, Teerstuhl

gastrointestinale Blutung[1] blutig tingiert[2] blutiger Stuhl, Blutstuhl, Hämatochezie[3] Spinat[4] Teerstuhl[5] okkultes Blut i. Stuhl[6] Bleistiftstuhl[7] Stuhlfarbe[8] Stuhlprobe[9] Stuhlabstrich, -ausstrich[10] Stuhlkultur[11] Laxans[12] Stuhluntersuchung[13] Stuhlbeschaffenheit[14]

11

rebound [riːbaʊnd] **tenderness** *n term* → U104-11   *rel* **epigastric pain**[1] *n term*

sensation of pain on deep palpation of the abdomen with abrupt [ʌ] release[2] [iː]

» Localized rebound tenderness in the RUQ is a common feature [iː] of acute cholecystitis [kɒːlɪ-]. If the perforated duodenum has given rise to peritonitis [aɪ], rebound tenderness and a rigid [ɪdʒ] abdomen[3] are present. The patient experienced sudden, intense, steady [e] epigastric pain spreading [e] rapidly throughout the abdomen.

Use to elicit[4] [ɪs] /test for **rebound tenderness** • direct / generalized / referred[5] [ɜː]/ lower abdominal **rebound tenderness** • right lower quadrant [ɒː] (*abbr* RLQ)/ intense / true[6] **rebound tenderness** • focal [oʊ]/ costovertebral angle[7] (*abbr* CVAT) **tenderness** • right upper quadrant (*abbr* RUQ) **tenderness** • flank / point[8] / local / localized / marked[9] **tenderness** • **tenderness to/on** pressure[10] / palpation[10] • cramping[11] (abdominal) / periumbilical [ʌ] / RLQ **pain** • midabdominal / groin[12] [ɔɪ]/ loin[13] / right iliac [ɪ] fossa **pain** • **epigastric** discomfort[14] / tenderness / tightness[15] [aɪ] • **epigastric** distress / mass / hernia [ɜː]

Loslassschmerz, Blumberg-Zeichen
Schmerzen i. Oberbauch[1] bei plötzlichem Loslassen[2] brettharthes Abdomen[3] Loslassschmerz auslösen[4] übertragener Loslassschmerz[5] echter L.[6] Nierenlagerschmerzen[7] Punktschmerz(haftigkeit)[8] deutl. Druckschmerzhaftigkeit[9] Druckschmerzhaftigkeit, -dolenz[10] krampfartiger Schmerz[11] Leistenschmerz[12] Lendenschmerz[13] Beschwerden i. Oberbauch[14] Druckgefühl i. Oberbauch[15]   12

(abdominal) guarding [gɑːrdɪŋ] *n term*
  rel **abdominal muscle** *or* **wall rigidity**[1] *n term*

spasm of abdominal wall muscles detected on palpation avoiding pressure on or agitation[2] [dʒ] of abdominal viscera [s] affected by injury or disease, e.g. in appendicitis [saɪ]

guard (against)[3] *v*

» I suspect that abdominal guarding is masking an acutely inflamed [eɪ] gallbladder[4] [ɔː]. Tenderness, guarding, distention, lack of bowel sounds, or hemodynamic [aɪ] instability mandates immediate evaluation[5] for blunt [ʌ] abdominal trauma[6] [ɒː]. The patient usually guards against palpation and limits movement.

Use (in)voluntary / muscle[7] [mʌsl]/ diffuse [juː] **guarding**

Abwehrspannung der Bauchdecke
Bauchdeckenspannung[1] Bewegung[2] schützen (gegen), bewahren (vor)[3] akute Gallenblasenentzündung[4] erfordert sofortige Abklärung[5] stumpfes Bauchtrauma[6] Muskelanspannung[7]

13

board-like (abdominal) rigidity [rɪdʒɪdɪti] *n term*
  rel **colic**[1], **(abdominal) cramping**[2] *n clin*

contraction of abdominal muscles typically seen in abdominal injury, inflammation or bleeding

rigid[3] *adj* • **colicky**[4] *adj* → U104-15 • **cramp-like** *adj* • **cramp**[5] *n & v*

» Patients with a perforated peptic ulcer [ʌ] typically present with tenderness accompanied by board-like rigidity of the abdomen. In volvulus of the sigmoid, there are intermittent cramp-like pains, increasing in severity [e] as obstipation becomes complete. Staphylococcal food poisoning commonly presents as diarrhea, nausea, vomiting, and abdominal cramping.

Use generalized / muscle or muscular[6] **rigidity** • mild / severe / muscular[7] / uterine **cramping** • **cramping** pain[8] • lower **abdominal cramps** • abdominal / intestinal[9] / biliary[10] [ɪ] **colic** • gallstone[10] / renal [iː]/ infantile **colic** • **colicky** infant[11] / abdominal pain[12]

brettharthes Abdomen
Kolik[1] Bauchkrämpfe[2] starr, steif, rigid[3] kolikartig[4] Krampf; Krämpfe verursachen/ auslösen[5] Muskelsteifigkeit, -steife[6] Muskelkrämpfe[7] krampfartiger Schmerz[8] Darmkolik[9] Gallenkolik[10] von Koliken geplagtes Baby[11] kolikartige Bauchschmerzen[12]

14

tenesmus [tənezməs] *n term*   *rel* **fecal** [iː] *or* **stool** [uː] **impaction**[1] *n term*

painful, ineffective straining[2] [eɪ] accompanied by an urgent [ɜː] desire [aɪ] to evacuate[3] the bowel (or bladder)

tenesmic *adj term* • **impacted**[4] *adj*

» Chronic recurrent diarrhea, alternating with constipation, is most common, but severe dysentery [ɪ] with bloody mucoid [juː] stools, tenesmus, and colic [ɒː] may occur intermittently. The onset of fecal impaction in bedridden[5] patients is often heralded[6] by a feeling of rectal distention, urgency [ɜː] of defecation, or tenesmus.

Use rectal / vesical[7] **tenesmus** • bolus / meat / (dental/ esophageal) food[8] **impaction** • **impacted** gallstone[9] [ɔː]/ stool[1] / foreign body[10] / fracture / tooth[11]

Tenesmus, schmerzhafter (Stuhl/ Harn)drang
Kotstauung, Koprostase[1] Pressen[2] entleeren[3] eingekeilt, impaktiert[4] bettlägrig[5] kündigt s. an[6] schmerzhafter Harndrang[7] Retention/ Impaktion v. Speiseresten[8] eingeklemmter Gallenstein[9] festsitzender Fremdkörper[10] impaktierter Zahn[11]   15

Clinical Phrases

Have your bowels been moving all right? Haben Sie regelmäßig Stuhl? • I've been off my food lately. In der letzten Zeit hatte ich keinen Appetit. • You should avoid eating large meals and eliminate things from your diet that increase acid secretion in your stomach. Sie sollten nur kleine Mahlzeiten zu sich nehmen und Speisen meiden, die die Säureproduktion im Magen anregen. • Have you ever had any heartburn? Hatten Sie schon einmal Sodbrennen? • I've got the runs. Ich habe Durchfall. • There is tenderness to gentle palpation in the right upper quadrant and the umbilical region. Das Abdomen ist paraumbilikal und im rechten oberen Quadranten bei leichter Palpation schmerzhaft. • Did you get a history of vomiting after meals? Ergab die Anamnese einen Hinweis auf postprandiales Erbrechen? • Have you ever passed blood from your rectum? Hatten Sie jemals Blut im Stuhl? • Have your bowel movements ever been this black before? Hatten Sie vorher schon einmal einen derart schwarzen Stuhl? • Now I would like to examine your back passage. Ich möchte Sie jetzt rektal untersuchen.

Unit 110 Cardiovascular Signs & Symptoms

Related Units: 33 Cardiac Function, 36 Blood Circulation, 103 Clinical Symptoms, 108 Clinical Signs, 102 History Taking, 107 Physical Examination

(cardiac) palpitation [pælpɪteɪʃᵊn] *n clin & term usu pl*

abnormal pounding¹ [aʊ] or racing [eɪs] of the heart² associated with strong emotions or heart disease

palpitate³ *v clin*

» Chronic hyperventilation may present with various nonspecific symptoms, including fatigue⁴ [fəti:g], dyspnea [ɪ], anxiety [aɪə], palpitations, and dizziness⁵. Ask the patient to check the radial [eɪ] pulse during episodes of palpitation to assist in the diagnosis [aɪ]. Palpitations may occur [ɜː] because of awareness [eɚ] of the heart due to LV enlargement. I felt faint⁶ [eɪ] and my heart began to palpitate.

Use to have⁷/experience⁷/complain of/cause/be unaware of ***palpitations*** • physiologic / benign [aɪ]/ postdosing⁸ [oʊ] ***palpitations*** • tachycardia with / chest discomfort and ***palpitations*** • rapid² / (ir)regular / continuous / arrhythmia-induced [ɪ] *palpitations*

Note: Do not mix up ***palpitation*** with *palpation*⁹.

Palpitation, Herzklopfen, Palpitatio cordis
Pochen¹ Herzrasen² (heftig) klopfen, pochen³ Müdigkeit⁴ Schwindel⁵ schwach⁶ Herzklopfen haben⁷ Palpitationen nach Medikamenteneinnahme⁸ Palpation, Ab-, Betasten⁹

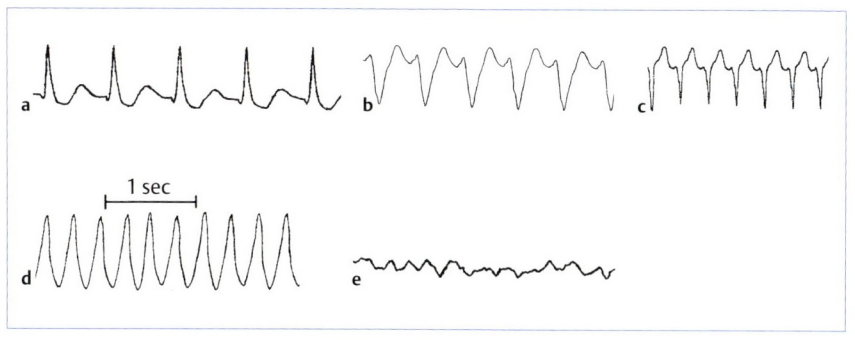

ECG findings in different types of tachycardia:
(**a**) atrial tachycardia, (**b**) ventricular tachycardia, (**c**) paroxysmal AV node tachycardia, (**d**) ventricular flutter, (**e**) ventricular fibrillation

tachycardia [tækɪ-] *n term*

opposite **bradycardia**¹ [brædɪ-] *n term* → U33-5

abnormally rapid beating of the heart, usually applied to heart rates over 100 per minute

tachycardi(a)c *adj term* • **bradycardi(a)c** *adj* • **brady/ tachyarrhythmia**² *n*

» Preexcitation arrhythmia may present as an episode of paroxysmal [ɪ] supraventricular tachycardia or atrial [eɪ] fibrillation [ɪ‖aɪ] with an excessively rapid ventricular response³. Bradycardia is usually defined as a rate of less than 60 beats per minute. Closely monitor his heart rate and BP⁴, as excessive tachycardia and ventricular ectopy may occur.

Use to develop/cause/lead to/trigger/control ***tachycardia*** • atrial⁵ [eɪ]/ sinus⁶ [aɪ]/ paroxysmal⁷ [ɪ] ***tachycardia*** • nonparoxysmal junctional [dʒʌ]/ ectopic *or* automatic⁸ ***tachycardia*** • supraventricular⁹ (*abbr* SVT)/ paroxysmal supraventricular (*abbr* PST *or* PSVT) ***tachycardia*** • atrioventricular reciprocating (*abbr* AVRT)/ compensatory / antidromic¹⁰ ***tachycardia*** • multifocal or chaotic [keɪ-] atrial [eɪ] / (A-V) nodal¹¹ ***tachycardia*** • wide (-complex) QRS¹² / pacemaker-induced¹³ ***tachycardia*** • sinus (node)¹⁴ / fetal¹⁵ [iː]/ reflex [iː]/ symptomatic ***bradycardia*** • transient / relative ***bradycardia*** • marked¹⁶ / life-threatening [e] ***bradycardia*** • **bradycardiac** spells / effect¹⁷

Tachykardie, erhöhte Herzfrequenz, Herzjagen, -rasen
Bradykardie, verlangsamte Herzschlagfolge/ Herztätigkeit¹ Tachyarrhythmie² Kammeraktion, -tätigkeit³ Blutdruck⁴ Vorhoftachykardie⁵ Sinustachykardie⁶ paroxysmale T.⁷ heterotope T.⁸ supraventrikuläre T.⁹ gegenläufige/ antidrome Tachykardie¹⁰ AV-Knotentachykardie¹¹ Tachykardie bei breitem Kammerkomplex¹² schrittmacherinduzierte T.¹³ Sinusbradykardie¹⁴ fetale Bradykardie¹⁵ deutliche/ ausgeprägte Bradykardie¹⁶ frequenzsenkende Wirkung¹⁷

CLINICAL TERMS

Cardiovascular Signs & Symptoms

(heart) murmur [ɜː] *n term & clin*   *rel* **thrill**[1], **hum**[2] [ʌ], **rumble**[3] [ʌ] *n term*

atypical [eɪ] sound heard on auscultation of the heart which is due to altered [ɔː] cardiac blood flow; thrills are fine abnormal vibrations [aɪ] in the vascular or the respiratory system noted on palpation

» Heart murmurs are graded [eɪ] according to intensity. Grade VI murmurs are loud and can be heard with the stethoscope off the chest. These systolic ejection [dʒe] *murmurs*[4] are of grade I-II intensity and are high-pitched. A grade 4/6 or louder murmur (with a thrill) implies [aɪ] severe mitral [aɪ] regurgitation [ɜː].

Use holosystolic *or* pansystolic[5] [ɪ]/ (pre[6]/mid[7])systolic / pandiastolic [aɪə] **heart murmur** • valvular [æ]/ aortic [ɔː]/ late systolic[8] (*abbr* LSM) **murmur** • (mitral/ tricuspid [ʌ]) regurgitation *or* regurgitant[9] **murmur** • aortic ejection / diastolic flow[10] **murmur** • to-and-fro[11] / hemic [iː] **murmur** • high-pitched[12] / continuous / harsh[13] / soft[14] **murmur** • innocent[15] / loud [aʊ]/ faint [eɪ]/ audible [ɔː] **murmur** • crescendo-decrescendo[16] [ʃ]/ blowing[17] / rumbling [ʌ] **murmur** • **murmur** radiating [eɪ] to the axilla • palpable / coarse [ɔː] / prominent / systolic[18] **thrill** • apical [eɪ]/ parasternal / precordial / thyroid [aɪ]/ carotid[19] **thrill** • (cervical/ innocent) venous[20] [iː] **hum** • presystolic [iː]/ middiastolic filling[21] / apical crescendo **rumble**

bruit [brɥi:‖bruːt] *n term*   *rel* **souffle**[1] [suːfl], **heave**[2] [iː] *n term*

abnormal vascular sound heard on auscultation of an artery, organ or gland (e.g. thyroid)

» All pulses should be palpated, and the presence of bruits should be sought. A thrill and bruit lasting throughout systole and diastole are present over the fistula. Left ventricular hypertrophy produces a sustained thrust at the apex that is easily differentiated from the precordial heave of right ventricular hypertrophy.

Use vascular[3] / self-audible / soft / systolic **bruit** • diastolic / epigastric / splenic [e] **bruit** • arterial / subclavian / carotid[4] **bruit** • **bruit** de moulin[5] • femoral [e]/ abdominal / hepatic **bruit** • cardiac[6] / carotid / splenic **souffle** • mammary / uterine[7] / umbilical[8] **souffle** • right ventricular / left-sided / sternal **heave** • central precordial / thyroid **heave**

systolic [sɪstɒːlɪk] **click** *n clin*   *rel* **snap**[1], **knock**[2] [nɒːk] *n term*

sharp high-pitched extra heart sound of short duration occurring [ɜː] during systole [sɪstəliː]

» Late systolic murmurs following midsystolic clicks are due to late systolic mitral [aɪ] regurgitation[3] caused by prolapse of the mitral valve[4]. The mitral opening snap follows S2 by 40-120 ms, which is typical of mitral stenosis. An S3 that is earlier (0.10 - 0.12 s after A2) and higher-pitched than normal (a pericardial knock) often occurs in patients with constrictive pericarditis[5]. A diastolic knock occurs at the same point in early diastole as an S3.

Use ejection[6] [ɪdʒe-]/ (late /mid/ early) systolic[7] / prosthetic **click** • mitral (valve)[8] [æ]/ (delayed/ tricuspid [ʌ]) opening[9] (*abbr* OS)/ closing **snap** • pericardial[10] / diastolic / precordial **knock**

gallop (rhythm) [rɪðəm] *n term*   *rel* **cardiac arrhythmia**[1] [eɪrɪðmɪə], **ectopic beat**[2], **extrasystole**[2] *n term*

triple cadence to the heart sounds on auscultation usually due to an abnormal third or fourth heart sound[3] (S3, S4) being heard in addition to S1 and S2 → U33-6

dysrhythmia[4] [ɪ] *n term* • **(anti)arrhythmic** *adj & n* • **(post)extrasystolic** *adj*

» Cardiogenic shock is suggested by engorged [ɡɔːrdʒ] neck veins[5], signs of pulmonary congestion, and a gallop rhythm. A summation gallop occurs when both S3 and S4 are present in a patient with tachycardia. By palpation there is a presystolic gallop accentuated [əksentjʊ-] during inspiration. Chronic suppression of ventricular arrhythmias with antiarrhythmic drugs[6] has many side effects . Severe MR may cause palpitations owing to the frequency of ectopic beats and post-extrasystolic hyperdynamic action of the enlarged left ventricle.

Use (right-sided) cardiac / S3[7] / ventricular diastolic (*abbr* VDG)/ atrial[8] **gallop** • presystolic *or* S4[8] / protodiastolic[7] / summation[9] [eɪ] **gallop** • **gallop** sound • to be prone to[10]/precipitate/exacerbate **arrhythmias** • brady/ tachy/ pro**arrhythmic** • self-limiting / (a)symptomatic / new-onset **arrhythmia** • worsening / malignant / life-threatening [e] **arrhythmia** • fixed / (non)sustained[11] [eɪ]/ paroxysmal / sinus[12] [aɪ] **arrhythmia** • (supra)ventricular[13] / reperfusion / pediatric **arrhythmia** • **arrhythmia** evaluation[14] /-induced syncope • ventricular (*abbr* VEBs)/ atrial[15] / AV nodal[16] **ectopic beats** • atrial premature[15] **beats** • occasional / atrial[15] / ventricular / coupled[17] [ʌ] **extrasystoles** • idioventricular[18] / junctional[19] [dʒʌ] **escape**[20] / pacemaker **rhythm** • **rhythm** disturbance[4]

Herzgeräusch

Schwirren[1] Summen, Brausen[2] Kollern[3] Austreibungs-, Ejektionsgeräusche[4] holosystol. Herzgeräusch[5] präsystolisches H.[6] mesosystol. H.[7] spätsystol. H.[8] kardiales Refluxgeräusch[9] diastol. Strömungsgeräusch[10] Duroziez-Zeichen/ Doppelgeräusch[11] hochfrequentes Herzgeräusch[12] raues H.[13] weiches H.[14] funktionelles H.[15] Spindelgeräusch, Crescendo-Decrescendo-Geräusch[16] blasendes Herzgeräusch[17] systol. Schwirren[18] Karotis-, Halsschwirren[19] Nonnengeräusch, -sausen[20] mesodiastolisches Füllungsgeräusch[21]

3

(Strömungs)geräusch, Bruit

blasendes Geräusch[1] Heben[2] Gefäßgeräusch[3] Strömungsgeräusch über d. Arteria carotis[4] Mühlradgeräusch[5] Herzgeräusch[6] Uterinageräusch[7] Nabelschnurgeräusch[8]

4

systolischer Klick

Klappenton[1] Krachen, grobes Geräusch[2] Mitral(klappen)insuffizienz[3] Mitralklappenprolaps[4] konstriktive Perikarditis, Pericarditis constrictiva[5] Ejektionsklick[6] frühsystolischer Klick[7] Mitralöffnungston, MÖT[8] Trikuspidalöffnungston[9] Perikardton[10]

5

Galopp(rhythmus)

Herzrhythmusstörung[1] Extrasystole, ES[2] Vorhofton, S4, IV. Herzton[3] (Herz)rhythmusstörung, Dysrhythmie[4] hervortretende/ prominente Halsvenen[5] Antiarrhythmika[6] Dritter-Ton-Galopp, protodiastolischer G.[7] präsystolischer Galopprhythmus[8] Summationsgalopp[9] zu Herzrhythmusstörungen neigen[10] anhaltende/ persistierende Arrhythmie[11] Sinusarrhythmie[12] supraventrikuläre A.[13] Herzrhythmusanalyse[14] Vorhofextrasystolen[15] AV-Extrasystolen[16] Bigeminie[17] idioventrikulärer Rhythmus, (z.B. Kammerautomatie)[18] Rhythmus a. d. atrioventrikulären Übergangszone[19] Ersatzrhythmus[20]

6

Cardiovascular Signs & Symptoms — CLINICAL TERMS

atrial or auricular flutter n term
rel **atrial fibrillation**[1] [ɪ‖aɪ] n term, abbr **AF**

very rapid but regular atrial arrhythmia [eɪɾɪðmɪə] with rates of 230-400 per minute

fluttering [ʌ] n term • **(anti)fibrillatory**[2] adj • **defibrillator**[3] [ɪ‖aɪ] n → U123-12f

» The bradycardia-tachycardia syndrome is manifested on the standard ECG as tachyarrhythmias, mostly atrial flutter or fibrillation. High-frequency atrial ectopic beats may presage[4] [-eɪdʒ] atrial fibrillation but are neither specific nor sensitive predictors. Digitalis [dʒ] is less effective than calcium antagonists in converting atrial flutter into atrial fibrillation.

Use conversion [ɜː] of / pure [pjuːɚ] / postoperative / recurring[5] [ɜː] / chronic **atrial flutter** • ventricular[6] / heart **flutter** • **flutter** waves[7] /-fibrillation[8] / with 4:1 conduction[9] • fixed / paroxysmal[10] [ɪ] / recurrent / chronic **atrial fibrillation** • recent-onset / lone / persistent[11] / episodes of **atrial fibrillation** • ventricular[12] (abbr VF) **fibrillation** • high-frequency[13] / muscle [mʌsl] / eyelid[14] **fluttering**

pericardial (friction) rub [ʌ] n clin
rel **cardiac tamponade**[1] [-neɪd] n term

scratchy sound heard on auscultation due to rubbing of inflamed pericardial membranes

tamponade[2] [tæmpᵊneɪd] v term • **pericard-** comb

» Pericarditis [aɪ] is typically manifested by a pericardial friction rub or evidence of pericardial effusion. Paradoxical pulse[3], a hallmark [ɔː] of cardiac tamponade, occurs in only approximately one-third of patients with constrictive pericarditis.

Use audible [ɒː] friction[4] / pleural [ʊɚ] friction or pleuritic[5] [ɪ] **rub** • acute / frank / (de)compensated **cardiac tamponade** • life-threatening[6] / fatal [eɪ] **cardiac tamponade** • pericardial[1] / (non/ post)traumatic / balloon[7] [uː] (tube) **tamponade** • **pericardial** effusion[8] [juːʒ] / disease • **pericard**itis /iocentesis[9] [-sentiːsɪs]

cardiomegaly n term   syn **cardiac enlargement** n clin → U108-12; U89-15
rel **cardiac hypertrophy**[1] [haɪpɜːrtəfi] n term

enlargement of the heart, e.g. due to volume overload

enlarged[2] adj • **hypertrophic**[3] adj term • **cardio-** comb • **-megaly** comb

» Chest x-rays reveal marked cardiomegaly with pulmonary venous [iː] congestion [dʒe]. In many patients with cardiac hypertrophy and dilatation [aɪ], systolic and diastolic failure coexist as the ventricle empties and fills abnormally. Palpation of local arterial enlargement is adequate for diagnosing popliteal [ɪ] aneurysms.

Use asymptomatic / borderline[4] / persistent / generalized / right-sided[5] **cardiomegaly** • progressive / marked[6] **cardiac enlargment** • right heart[5] / left atrial / chamber[7] [tʃeɪ-]/ biventricular **enlargment** • myocardial [aɪ]/ left ventricular[8] (abbr LVH) **hypertrophy** • asymmetric septal[9] (abbr ASH) **hypertrophy** • **hypertrophic** obstructive cardiomyopathy[10] (abbr HOCM)/ subaortic stenosis (abbr HSS) • **cardio**logist /(myo)pathy /gram /centesis • **cardio**pulmonary resuscitation[11] [sʌs] /version[12] [ɜː] • organo/ spleno[13] [e]/ ventriculo/ hepato**megaly**

aortic regurgitation [rɪgɜːrdʒɪteɪʃᵊn] n term, abbr **AR**
syn **aortic** [eɪ] **insufficiency** [ɪʃ] n term → U124-12

reflux of blood through an incompetent aortic valve into the left ventricle during diastole

regurgitant[1] adj term • **insufficient** adj

» The murmur [ɜː] of aortic regurgitation was best heard in the 2ⁿᵈ intercostal space at the left sternal [ɜː] edge. Dilatation of the root of the aorta can cause aortic regurgitation, dissection of the aorta, and rupture. Murmurs due to functional tricuspid and pulmonic insufficiency may occur in cor pulmonale [pʌlməneɪli].

Use chronic / severe / congenital[2] [dʒe]/ isolated **aortic regurgitation** • tricuspid (valve)[3] / mitral[4] [aɪ] (abbr MR)/ atrioventricular valve **regurgitation** • pulmonic or pulmonary[5] / low-volume **regurgitation** • **regurgitation** murmur[6] / and stenosis / of food • **aortic** stenosis • cardiac / (left-sided) valvular / mitral[4] / cardiopulmonary **insufficiency** • coronary[7] / cerebrovascular[8] **insufficiency** • (peripheral/ acute) arterial / basilar artery **insufficiency** • chronic venous [iː]/ renal [iː] **insufficiency** • **regurgitant** murmur[6] / flow[9] • **regurgitant** (stroke) volume[10] / fraction / wave[11] • **insufficient** blood supply[12] [aɪ]

Vorhofflattern
Vorhofflimmern[1] fibrillierend, flimmernd[2] Defibrillator[3] ankündigen[4] rezidivierendes Vorhofflattern[5] Kammerflattern[6] Flatterwellen[7] Flimmerflattern, Flatterflimmern[8] Flattern mit 4:1 Überleitung[9] paroxysmales Vorhofflimmern[10] persistierendes Vorhofflimmern[11] Kammerflimmern[12] hochfrequentes Flattern[13] Lidflattern, Blepharoklonus[14]

7

perikardiales Reiben, Perikardreiben
Herzbeutel-, Perikardtamponade[1] tamponieren[2] paradoxer Puls, Pulsus paradoxus[3] hörbares Reibegeräusch[4] Pleurareiben[5] lebensbedrohliche Perikard-/ Herz(beutel)tamponade[6] Ballontamponade[7] Perikarderguss[8] Perikardpunktion[9]

8

Kardiomegalie, Herzvergrößerung
Herzhypertrophie[1] vergrößert[2] hypertroph(isch)[3] geringfügige Kardiomegalie[4] Rechtsherzvergrößerung[5] deutliche Herzvergrößerung[6] Kammervergrößerung[7] Linksherzhypertrophie[8] asymmetrische Septumhypertrophie[9] hypertrophobstruktive Kardiomyopathie[10] kardiopulmonale Reanimation/ Wiederbelebung[11] Kardioversion[12] Splenomegalie, Milzvergrößerung[13]

9

Aorten(klappen)insuffizienz
rückfließend, regurgitierend[1] angeborene Aorteninsuffizienz[2] Trikuspidal(klappen)insuffizienz[3] Mitral(klappen)insuffizienz[4] Pulmonal(klappen)insuffizienz[5] Reflux-, Regurgitationsgeräusch[6] Koronarinsuffizienz[7] zerebrovaskuläre Insuffizienz[8] Rückfluss, -strom[9] Regurgitationsvolumen[10] Regurgitationswelle[11] unzureichende Blutversorgung[12]

10

488 CLINICAL TERMS — Cardiovascular Signs & Symptoms

syncope [sɪŋkəpi] *n term*   *syn* **fainting** [feɪntɪŋ] *n clin* → U7-4

sudden fainting or swooning[1] [uː] due to a fall in BP or failure of the cardiac systole which results in cerebral ischemia [ɪskiːmɪə] and a short-lived loss of consciousness[2] [kɒnˈʃəsnəs]

presyncope *n term* • (**pre/ post**)**syncopal** [sɪŋkəpᵊl] *adj* • **faint**[3] *n & v*

» The patient usually does not recall presyncopal symptoms. Cardiac faints[4] of this type may recur several times a day. Rising too soon may precipitate[5] [sɪ] another faint. The patient is warned of the impending faint by a sense of "feeling bad," of giddiness[6], and of movement or swaying[7] [eɪ] of the floor or surrounding objects.

Use brief [iː]/ impending[8] / near-/ recurrent [ɜː||BE ʌ] **syncope** • vasomotor[9] [eɪ]/ cardiac[4] / neurocardiogenic [dʒe] **syncope** • vasovagal [eɪ] or vasodepressor[10] **syncope** • neurovascular / postural[11] [stʃ] **syncope** • hypovolemic [iː]/ carotid sinus / cough or tussive[12] [ʌ] **syncope** • hyperventilation / heat[13] **syncope** • quinidine [kwɪnɪdɪn]/ micturition(al) [ɪʃ] **syncope** • (adolescent) stretch[14] / Stokes-Adams[15] **syncope** • exertional [ɜː] or effort / cerebrovascular **syncope** • sudden / vasovagal[10] **faint** • to feel close to / simple / hysterical [hɪst-] **fainting** • **fainting** spell or episode[16] • **presyncopal** symptoms / anxiety [zaɪə] • **syncopal** attack or episode[16]

Synkope, Ohnmacht, kurze Bewusstlosigkeit

ohnmächtig werden[1] Bewusstlosigkeit[2] Ohnmacht, Synkope; ohnmächtig werden[3] kardiale Synkopen[4] auslösen[5] Schwindelgefühl[6] Schwanken[7] drohende Ohnmacht[8] Vasomotorenkollaps[9] vasovagale/ vasodepressorische Synkope[10] orthostatische/ lageabhängige Synkope[11] Hustensynkope, -schlag[12] Hitzekollaps[13] Kollaps aufgrund wachstumsbedingter Hypotonie[14] Adams-Stokes-Anfall, -Synkope[15] Ohnmachtsanfall[16]

11

cardiovascular or **circulatory collapse** *n term*   *rel* **heart failure**[1] *n term*

loss of effective blood flow due to dysfunction [ɪ] of the heart and/or peripheral vasculature

collapse[2] *v clin* • **collapsed** *adj* • **collapsing** *n & adj* • **fail** [feɪl] *v*

» Lactic acidosis is often present in diabetic [e] patients who have suffered severe cardiovascular collapse. Hypovolemia [iː] should not be overlooked, especially if there is no other explanation for the collapsed state. Congestive [dʒe] heart failure[3] [feɪljɚ] in infancy is usually associated with large left-to-right shunts[4] [ʌ].

Use acute / early / fatal [eɪ] **cardiovascular collapse** • hemodynamic [hiːmoʊ-]/ (hypovolemic [iː] **collapse** • (peripheral) vascular / vasomotor / lung[5] **collapse** • **collapsed** state / neck veins • **collapsing** pulse[6] • congestive[7] / left[7] / right[8] / chronic **heart failure** • compensated / mild / severe **heart failure** • (low-output) cardiac[1] / pump / forward[9] **failure** • backward[10] / left ventricular[7] **failure** • multiple organ[11] / pulmonary / treatment[12] **failure**

Kreislaufkollaps, -zusammenbruch

Herzinsuffizienz, -versagen, Myokardinsuffizienz[1] zusammenbrechen, kollabieren[2] Stauungsinsuffizienz, dekompensierte (Rechts)-herzinsuffizienz[3] Links-Rechts-Shunts[4] Lungenkollaps[5] Wasserhammer-, Corrigan-Puls, Pulsus celer et altus[6] Linksherzinsuffizienz[7] Rechtsherzinsuffizienz[8] Vorwärtsinsuffizienz[9] Rückwärtsinsuffizienz[10] multiples Organversagen[11] Therapieversagen[12]

12

hypertension [haɪpəˈtenʃᵊn] *n term*   *opposite* **hypotension**[1] *n term* → U36-8

persistently high blood pressure (in adults 140/90 [read: 140 over 90])

hyper/ hypo/ normotensive[2] *adj & n term & clin* • **antihypertensive**[3] *adj & n*

» The hyperthyroid [aɪ] patient undergoing surgery is apt to[4] develop hypertension, severe cardiac dysrhythmias, and congestive heart failure. Palpitations, tachycardia, and systolic hypertension with increased pulse pressure are common findings in hyperthyroidism. Untreated hypertension may cause stroke[5], myocardial [aɪ] infarction, and renal failure.

Use to have/cause/aggravate **hypertension** • (right/ left) atrial / arterial[6] / venous [iː] **hypertension** • systolic / diastolic / systemic **hypertension** • portal[7] / pulmonary[8] (arterial) / intracranial [eɪ] **hypertension** • renal / pregnancy-induced[9] / upper extremity **hypertension** • labile [leɪbaɪl||ᵊl]/ essential[10] / malignant or accelerated[11] **hypertension** • long-standing[12] / chronic **hypertension** • asymptomatic [eɪ]/ episodic / moderate **hypertension** • mild / poorly controlled **hypertension** • postural [pɔːstʃɚᵊl] or orthostatic[13] / systemic / symptomatic[14] **hypotension** • **hypertensive** patient[15] / episode / crisis[16] [kraɪsɪs]

Hypertonie, -tension, Bluthochdruck

Hypotonie, -tension, niedriger Blutdruck[1] normoton; Normotoniker(in)[2] antihypertensiv, blutdrucksenkend; Antihypertensivum, -tonikum[3] neigt dazu[4] Schlaganfall, Gehirnschlag, Apoplexie[5] arterielle Hypertonie, Bluthochdruck[6] portale H., Pfortaderstauung[7] pulmonale H.[8] Schwangerschaftshypertonie[9] essentielle/ primäre H.[10] maligne H.[11] langjährige H.[12] orthostatische Hypotonie[13] sekundäre/ symptomat. H.[14] Hypertoniker(in)[15] Blut-, Hochdruckkrise[16]

13

cardiogenic [-dʒenɪk] **shock** *n term* → U124-4f   *rel* **pump** [ʌ] **failure**[1] *n jar*

circulatory failure marked by inadequate tissue perfusion from abnormal cardiac function

shocking *adj clin* • **shock**[2] *v* • **countershock**[3] [aʊ] *n term* • **antishock** *adj*

» Patients in shock may demonstrate normal mental status [eɪ|æ] or may be restless, agitated, confused, lethargic, or comatose as a result of inadequate perfusion of the brain. Is there a cardiac cause of shock? Early in septic shock the extremities may be warm and dry, but as shock progresses, they become cold and clammy[4] [æ].

Use to be in[5]/produce/suspect/treat **shock** • distributive / cardiac compressive / hemorrhagic[6] [-ædʒɪk] **shock** • hemodynamic / hypovolemic[7] / obstructive **shock** • neurogenic [(j)ʊɚ]/ anaphylactic[8] **shock** • (high-output/ low-output) septic[9] / spinal [aɪ]/ surgical **shock** • impending[10] / delayed[11] [eɪ]/ persistent / worsening **shock** • profound / decompensated / irreversible [ɜː] **shock** • **shock**(-like) state[12] / syndrome / phase / treatment[13] • synchronized DC[14] **countershocks** • military **antishock** trousers[15] (*abbr* MAST) • **antishock** garment[15]

kardiogener Schock

Pumpversagen[1] schockieren, e. Schock versetzen; e. Schockbehandlung durchführen, schocken[2] Elektroschock[3] feucht[4] unter Schock stehen, e. Schock haben[5] hämorrhag. Schock[6] hypovolämischer Schock[7] anaphylaktischer Schock[8] septischer Schock[9] drohender Schock[10] Spätschock[11] Schockzustand[12] Schockbehandlung[13] synchrone Gleichstromimpulse[14] Antischockhose[15]

14

Cardiovascular Signs & Symptoms   CLINICAL TERMS **489**

venous congestion [kənˈdʒestʃən] *n clin* → U124-12

    rel **vasocongestion**[1] [veɪzoʊ-] *n term*

engorgement[2] of veins with blood due to obstructive disease or right ventricular failure

congestive[3] *adj term* • **(de)congest**[4] *v* • **congested** *adj* • **vaso-** *comb*

» *If there is venous obstruction [ʌ] and the extremity is congested, as with stagnation of blood flow, cyanosis [saɪə-] is also present. Obstruction of the appendix leads to increased intraluminal pressure, venous congestion, infection, and thrombosis of intramural vessels. Following head trauma [ɒː], intracranial [eɪ] pressure may rise quickly to very high levels as a result of vascular congestion, extravasation, and cerebral edema[5].*

Use vascular / pulmonary[6] / hepatic[7] / peripheral ***congestion*** • genital [dʒe]/ penile [piːnaɪl] ***vasocongestion*** • ***congestive*** heart failure (*abbr* CHF)/ cardiomyopathy[8] (*abbr* CCM) • ***congestive*** splenomegaly [e]/ cirrhosis[9] [s] • ***congested*** blood vessels / liver[7] / nose[10] • ***vaso****constriction /dilator [eɪ] /motor tone[11] /-occlusive [uː] episode • ***vaso****spasm[12] /vagal [eɪ] syncope /active drug

Venenstau(ung), venöse Stauung, Venostase
Vasokongestion[1] Schwellung[2] kongestiv, Stauungs-[3] stauen[4] Hirnödem[5] Stauungslunge[6] Stauungsleber[7] kongestive/ dilatative Kardiomyopathie[8] Stauungszirrhose[9] verstopfte Nase[10] Vasomotorentonus[11] Vaso-, Angiospasmus, Gefäßkrampf[12]

15

neck vein [veɪn] **distention** [dɪsˈtenʃən] *n clin, also spelled* **distension**

    syn **jugular** [ˈdʒʌɡjələ˞] **venous** [iː] **distention** *n term, abbr* **JVD**

distend *v* • **distensible**[1] *adj* • **distensibility** *n*

» *Signs of heart failure or neck vein distention accompanied by fever [iː] and distant heart sounds generally suggest pericardial involvement. Jugular venous distention, sacral or peripheral edema , pleural effusions, and ascites [əsaɪtiːz] are typical signs of fluid overload[2].*

Use pronounced[3] [aʊ]/ massive[3] **neck vein distention** • (systemic) venous / abdominal / bladder **distention** • **neck vein** collapse[4] / examination • ***jugular venous*** pulse[5] (*abbr* JVP)/ pressure / pulsations • ***jugular venous*** catheter / cutdown[6] / hypertension • ***jugular*** notch[7] / vein[8] • ventricular / myocardial [aɪ]/ chest wall **distensibility**

Jugularvenenerweiterung, -dilatation
dehnbar[1] Überwässerung, Hyperhydratation[2] starke/ deutliche Erweiterung d. Jugularvene(n)[3] Halsvenenkollaps[4] Jugularvenenpuls[5] Jugularispunktion[6] Incisura jugularis (sterni)[7] Drosselvene, Vena jugularis[8]

16

varix [ˈværɪks] *n, usu pl* **varices** [ˈværɪsiːz] *n term*

    sim **varicosity**[1] [ˌværɪˈkɒːsɪti] *n, rel* **phlebitis**[2] [flɪˈbaɪtɪs] *n term*

a dilated [eɪ], enlarged and often knotted[3] [nɒːtɪd] and tortuous[4] [tɔːrtʃʊəs] vein, usually in the superficial veins of the lower legs

(peri)varicose[5] *adj term* • **variceal** *adj* • **varico-, phleb(o)-** *comb*

» *Patients with asymptomatic varicosities often seek cosmetic treatment. Endoscopy allows for several therapeutic [juː] options such as sclerotherapy[6] of varices and coagulation of bleeding vessels. Consult a vascular or general surgeon about elective stripping of varicose veins[7].*

Use extensive / visible / ruptured [ˈrʌptʃəd] venous **varicosities** • saphenous [iː]/ secondary / asymptomatic **varicosities** • large-sized[8] / (acutely) bleeding / prominent / starburst[9] [ɜː] **varices** • fragile [-dʒaɪl]/ submucosal [oʊ] gastric / esophageal[10] [-dʒiːəl]/ scrotal [oʊ]/ rectal **varices** • **variceal** (re)bleeding or hemorrhage[11] / ligation [eɪ] • **varicose** veins[12] / ulcer[13] [ʌlsə˞] / **varicocele**[14] [-siːl] /celectomy /sɪs[15] / superficial[16] / deep / migratory[17] [aɪ] **phlebitis** • portal / suppurative[18] [ʌ]/ septic **phlebitis** • **phleb**ography[19] /otomy[20] • pyle[21] / thrombo[16]/ endo**phlebitis**

Krampfader, Varize, Varix
Varikosität; Varize[1] Phlebitis, oberflächl. Venenentzündung[2] knotenförmig[3] geschlängelt[4] varikös, krampfaderartig[5] Sklerotherapie, Sklerosierung, Verödung[6] Varizenstripping[7] voluminöse V.[8] Besenreiservarizen[9] Ösophagusvarizen[10] Varizenblutung[11] varikös veränderte Venen, Varizen[12] Ulcus varicosum/ cruris[13] Varikozele, Krampfaderbruch[14] Varikose, ausgedehnte Krampfaderbildung[15] oberflächl. Phlebitis, Thrombophlebitis[16] Phlebitis migrans/ saltans[17] eitrige Phlebitis/ Venenentzündung[18] Phlebo-, Venografie[19] Phlebotomie, Venae sectio[20] Pylephlebitis, Pfortaderentzündung[21]

17

aneurysm [ˈænjə˞ɪzəm] *n term* → U124-15

circumscribed dilation [eɪʃ] of the vascular wall most commonly in the aorta or the major arteries

aneurysmal[1] *adj term* • **micro/ macro/ pseudoaneurysm**[2] [suːdoʊ-] *n*

» *Most aneurysms are considered to be a manifestation of atherosclerosis. Intracranial aneurysms may be divided into five types: "berry" or saccular[3], arteriosclerotic, mycotic[4] [aɪ], traumatic, and dissecting. In heavyset[5] [e] individuals even large aneurysms may be difficult to detect on physical examination. Determine the extent of aneurysmal involvement of the iliac arteries.*

Use false[2] [ɔː]/ true[6] / dissecting[7] / rapidly expanding / ruptured ***aneurysm*** • leaking / giant [dʒaɪ]/ large / congenital ***aneurysm*** • aortic arch [tʃ]/ aortic[8] / intracranial[9] ***aneurysm*** • popliteal [ɪ]/ coronary / left ventricular ***aneurysm*** • ***aneurysmal*** dilatation [aɪ]/ disease / wall • ***aneurysmal*** segment[10] / sac[11] / rupture / bleeding

Aneurysma
aneurysmatisch, Aneurysma-[1] falsches Aneurysma, A. spurium[2] sackförmiges Aneurysma, A. sacciforme[3] mykotisches Aneurysma[4] untersetzt, korpulent[5] echtes Aneurysma, A. verum[6] A. dissecans, dissozierendes Aneurysma[7] Aortenaneurysma[8] intrakranielles Aneurysma[9] aneurysmat. Gefäßabschnitt[10] Aneurysmasack[11]

18

intermittent claudication [ɒː] *n term*   *syn* **calf** [kæf] **claudication** *n term*
   rel **amaurosis fugax**[1], **Raynaud's phenomenon**[2] *n term*

transient pain or fatigue [fɑtiːɡ] in the muscles [ʌs] of the lower leg secondary to inadequate peripheral [pərɪfərəl] perfusion

» Patients also should be advised [aɪ] to walk for 30 to 45 min daily, stopping at the onset of claudication and resting until the symptoms resolve before resuming [uː] ambulation. Fleeting [iː] blindness[1] (amaurosis fugax) is characteristically caused by retinal emboli [aɪ] from ipsilateral carotid disease.

Use to mimic/relieve **claudication** • vascular / venous[3] / mild / incapacitating **claudication** • crescendo [ʃ]/ neurogenic [n(j)ʊɚ-]/ intestinal[4] / jaw[5] [dʒɔː] **claudication** • vasospastic **amaurosis fugax** • unilateral / hysteric[6] / intoxication / traumatic / congenital[7] **amaurosis** • **Raynaud's** disease[8] / syndrome

Claudicatio intermittens, intermittierendes Hinken, Schaufensterkrankheit
Amaurosis fugax, flüchtige Blindheit[1] Raynaud-Phänomen, sekundäres Raynaud-Syndrom[2] Claudicatio venosa[3] Claudicatio intestinalis[4] Kieferschmerzen b. Kauen[5] psychogene Blindheit[6] angeborene A., Amaurosis congenita[7] primäres Raynaud-Syndrom, Raynaud-Krankheit[8]

19

epistaxis [epɪstæksɪs] *n term, pl* **-es**   *syn* **nosebleed** [noʊzbliːd] *n clin*

bleeding [iː] from the nasal [eɪ] mucosa [mjuːkoʊzə]

» Control epistaxis with nasal packing[1] or cautery [ɔː]. Factors predisposing to epistaxis include nasal trauma [ɔː] (nose picking[2], foreign bodies, forceful nose blowing), rhinitis [aɪ], drying of the nasal mucosa from low humidity[3], deviation of the nasal septum, and alcohol use. Bleeding from Kiesselbach's plexus[4], a vascular plexus on the anterior nasal septum[5], is by far the most common type of epistaxis encountered.

Use spontaneous [eɪ]/ (non)traumatic / mild[6] [aɪ]/ minimal **epistaxis** • brisk[7] / excessive / severe[7] **epistaxis** • intractable[8] / frequent / prolonged / recurrent / posterior **epistaxis** • persistent[9] **nosebleed**

Nasenbluten, Epistaxis
Nasentamponade[1] Nasenbohren[2] Luftfeuchtigkeit[3] Locus Kiesselbachi[4] Nasenscheidewand, -septum[5] leichtes Nasenbluten[6] starkes Nasenbluten[7] unstillbares Nasenbluten[8] lang anhaltendes Nasenbluten[9]

20

Clinical Phrases

Have you ever experienced faints or blackouts? Haben Sie schon einmal das Bewusstsein verloren? • I felt a tightness in my chest. Ich hatte ein Engegefühl in der Brust. • Have you noticed any swelling of your legs? Haben Sie manchmal geschwollene Beine? • Now I would like to listen to your heart and lungs. Ich möchte Sie jetzt abhören. • We are going to run another ECG tomorrow morning. Morgen früh werden wir noch ein EKG machen • His ECG shows a little left ventricular strain. Sein EKG zeigt eine leichte Linksherzbelastung. • I'd recommend an IVP if you fail to control his BP with simple measures. Wenn sein Blutdruck durch einfache Maßnahmen nicht unter Kontrolle zu bringen ist, würde ich ein Ausscheidungsurogramm empfehlen. • First obtain the blood gases and then ventilate the patient appropriately. Bestimmen Sie zuerst die Blutgase und beatmen Sie dann den Patienten entsprechend.

Unit 111 Respiratory Signs & Symptoms
Related Units: **108** Clinical Signs, **103** Clinical Symptoms, **107** Physical Examination, **44** Respiration, **66** Human Sounds

dyspnea [dɪspnɪə‖dɪspniːə] *n term*   *syn* **shortness of breath** [e] *n, abbr* **SOB**,
   rel **nasal** [eɪ] **flaring**[1] [eɚ] *n clin*

subjective difficulty or distress in breathing due to disease rather than physical exertion[2] or high altitude[3]

dyspneic[4] [iː] *adj term* • **short of breath**[4] *adj clin* •
breathlessness[5] *n* • **breathless** *adj*

» The severity [e] of dyspnea can usefully be assessed by the amount of physical exertion [ɜː] required to produce the sensation (e.g. flights of stairs). Have you been short of breath at all? Fatigue[6] [-iːɡ] and dyspnea on effort[7] are typical clinical signs of left ventricular failure. Increased ventilatory effort induces dyspnea even at rest, and breathing [iː] is labored[8] and retarded, especially during expiration. He reported several episodes of flushing[9] [ʌ], chest tightness [aɪ], dyspnea, palpitations[10], and anxiety [aɪə]. He's too short of breath for speech.

Use to experience/have/develop/suffer from[11]/cause/precipitate [sɪ] **dyspnea** • to exhibit/complain of[12]/alleviate [iː] /relieve **dyspnea** • acute / effort or exertional[7] [ɜː] **dyspnea** • obstructive [ʌ]/ restrictive / orthostatic[13] • **dyspnea** on recumbency[13] [ʌ] • paroxysmal [ɪ] nocturnal[14] [ɜː] (*abbr* PND)/ pulmonary[15] **dyspnea** • cardiac[16] / functional / psychogenic [dʒe]/ unexplained **dyspnea** • episodic / mild / moderate / one-flight[17] / intolerable **dyspnea** • **dyspnea** on exertion[7] (*abbr* DOE)/ at rest[18] • **shortness of breath** on exertion[7] (*abbr* SOBOE) • **dyspneic** infant / episode

Kurzatmigkeit, Atemnot, Dyspnoe
Nasenflügelatmen[1] körperl. Anstrengung[2] Höhenlage[3] dyspnoisch[4] Atemnot, Kurzatmigkeit, Atemlosigkeit[5] Müdigkeit[6] Belastungsdyspnoe[7] erschwert[8] Hitzewallung[9] Herzjagen, -rasen[10] an Kurzatmigkeit leiden[11] über Kurzatmigkeit klagen[12] Orthopnoe[13] paroxysmale nächtl. Dyspnoe[14] pulmonale Dyspnoe[15] kardiale Dyspnoe[16] Atemnot nach einer Treppe[17] Ruhedyspnoe[18]

1

Respiratory Signs & Symptoms   CLINICAL TERMS 491

orthopnea [ɔːrθɒːpnɪə‖-θəpniːə] *n term*
    rel **labored** [leɪbɚd] **respiration**¹ *n clin & jar*
dyspnea which is brought on or aggravated [æg] in a recumbent position²
orthopneic³ [ɔːrθɒpniːɪk] *adj term* • **unlabored** *adj*
» Patients with orthopnea must elevate their heads on several pillows⁴ at night and frequently awaken short of breath. Patients with edema due to renal failure⁵ usually do not develop orthopnea. Nocturnal cough [kɒːf], orthopnea, dyspnea on exertion, and ankle swelling⁶ are commonly seen in mild heart failure.
Use simple / pronounced⁷ [aʊ]/ two-pillow **orthopnea** • **orthopnea** position / breathlessness and insomnia • **orthopneic** episode • **labored** breathing¹ [iː] • **laboring** to breathe⁸ [briːð] • noisy / gasping⁹ [æ]/ irregular / shallow¹⁰ [ʃæ]/ sighing¹¹ [saɪɪŋ] **respirations** • stertorous¹² / Kussmaul¹³ / Cheyne-Stokes¹⁴ **respiration(s)**

Orthopnoe, schwere Dyspnoe
erschwerte Atmung¹ im Liegen² orthopnoisch³ Kissen⁴ Nierenversagen⁵ Knöchelödeme⁶ massive Orthopnoe⁷ schwer atmen⁸ Schnappatmung⁹ flache Atmung¹⁰ Seufzeratmung¹¹ röchelnde Atmung, Stertor¹² Kussmaul-Atmung¹³ Cheyne-Stokes-Atmung¹⁴

2

hypoxia [haɪ‖hɪpɒːksɪə] *n term* → U123-8
   rel **hypoventilation**¹, **hypercapnia**², **hypercarbia**² [ɑː] *n term*
decreased levels of oxygen in inspired gases, arterial [ɪɚ] blood, or tissue [ʃ‖s]
hypoxic *adj term* • **hypoxemia**³ [iː] *n* • **hypoxemic** *adj* • **-oxia** *comb*
» Hypoxia causes pulmonary arterial constriction, which shunts [ʌ] blood away⁴ from poorly ventilated areas toward better-ventilated portions of the lung. The most common cause of respiratory hypoxia is ventilation-perfusion mismatch⁵, which results from perfusion of poorly ventilated alveoli [aɪ]. Arterial blood gas studies revealed hypoxemia. Because of the role of hypoxic pulmonary vasoconstriction in pulmonary hypertension, the hypoventilating "blue bloater⁶" with alveolar hypoxia and hypercarbia more frequently suffers from pulmonary hypertension than does the emphysematous "pink puffer⁷" without alveolar hypoxia.
Use respiratory⁸ / alveolar / circulatory⁹ / anemic¹⁰ [iː] **hypoxia** • perinatal [eɪ]/ neonatal / histotoxic¹¹ / cerebral **hypoxia** • systemic / local / tissue¹² / birth **hypoxia** • severe / prolonged / chronic **hypoxia** • alveolar¹³ / secondary / frank¹⁴ / chronic **hypoventilation** • **hypoxic** patient / episode • **hypoxic** ventilatory drive¹⁵ /-ischemic [ɪskiː-] damage • chronic / arterial¹⁶ / acute [ɜː] **hypoxemia** • exercise-induced¹⁷ / life-threatening [e] **hypoxemia** • hyper/ an**oxia** • hypoxemia and / acute / hypercarbic / permissive¹⁸ **hypercapnia** • **hyper**oxidation /capnic

Sauerstoffmangel, -not, Hypoxie
Hypoventilation¹ Hyperkapnie² Hypoxämie³ Blut ableitet⁴ abnormes Ventilations-Perfusions-Verhältnis⁵ B-Typ/ zyanot.-plethor.-bronchialer Typ d. Emphysematikers, Blue bloater⁶ Pink-puffer, A-Typ⁷ respirator./ ventilator. Hypoxie⁸ zirkulator. H.⁹ anämische Hypoxie¹⁰ histotoxische H.¹¹ Gewebehypoxie¹² alveoläre Hypoventilation¹³ klin. manifeste Hypoventilation¹⁴ hypoxischer Atemantrieb¹⁵ arterielle Hypoxämie¹⁶ belastungsbedingte Hypoxämie¹⁷ zulässige/ tolerierbare Hyperkapnie¹⁸

3

asphyxia [æsfɪksɪə] *n term* → U44-8   *rel* **(pulmonary) aspiration**¹ *n term*
severe hypoxia that causes hypoxemia [iː], hypercapnia, and loss of consciousness² [ʃ]; common causes include drowning³ [aʊ] and aspiration of vomitus⁴ into the respiratory tract
asphyxiated [ɪ] *adj term* • **asphyxiation**⁵ *n* • **aspirate**⁶ *v & n* → U127-16
» Spasm of the respiratory muscles caused acute asphyxia. Cough helps protect the lungs against aspiration. Acute aspiration of gastric contents⁷ may be catastrophic. Asphyxiated infants which are small for gestational [dʒ] age are prone to⁸ early hypoglycemia [siː].
Use to cause or produce/prevent **asphyxia** • acute / birth or intrapartum⁹ / traumatic **asphyxia** • nocturnal / neonatal¹⁰ [eɪ] / life-threatening [e] **asphyxia** • partial / death by **asphyxiation** • tracheobronchial / foreign-body¹¹ / fluid / acid / micro**aspiration** • meconium¹² / recurrent / chronic **aspiration** • risk of **aspiration** • **aspiration** pneumonia¹³ [n(j)uː-]/ prophylaxis¹⁴ / of saliva [aɪ]/ of gastric contents / of toxic materials

Asphyxie, Atemdepression
Aspiration¹ Bewusstlosigkeit² Ertrinken³ Erbrochenes⁴ Erstickung(szustand)⁵ aspirieren; Aspirat⁶ Mageninhalt⁷ neigen zu⁸ intrapartale Asphyxie⁹ Asphyxie d. Neugeborenen¹⁰ Fremdkörperaspiration¹¹ Mekoniumaspiration¹² Aspirationspneumonie¹³ Aspirationsprophylaxe¹⁴

4

tachypnea [tækɪ(p)niːə] *n term*   *rel* **hyperventilation**¹ *n term*
       opposite **bradypnea**² *n term*
very rapid rate of respiration associated with respiratory distress³ typically seen in pneumonia [n(j)uː-], high fever, respiratory insufficiency, or compensatory respiratory alkalosis
tachypneic *adj term* • **hyperventilate**⁴ *v* • **apnea**⁵ [æpnɪə‖-niːə] *n* • **apneic** *adj*
» In pneumonia tachypnea and respiratory distress may be present either with a clear chest on auscultation⁶ or with discrete rales in affected lung segments. Evaluate him for respiratory distress by assessing vital signs, use of accessory muscles of respiration⁷, retractions⁸, nasal flaring, and pulse oximetry. Acute hyperventilation lowers the PCO₂ without changing the plasma bicarbonate concentration, thereby lowering the hydrogen [aɪ] ion [aɪən] concentration.
Use transient⁹ / mild / marked / severe / increasing **tachypnea** • acute / chronic / central (neurogenic) / psychogenic¹⁰ **hyperventilation** • alveolar / reflex¹¹ / compensatory¹² / anxiety **hyperventilation** • intentional / isocapnic [aɪ]/ controlled **hyperventilation** • **hyperventilation**-induced respiratory alkalosis¹³ / syndrome¹⁴ / tetany¹⁵ • to be/become (mildly/ increasingly) **tachypneic** • central / sleep¹⁶ / traumatic [ɒː] **apnea** • **apneic** episodes¹⁷ / spells¹⁷

Tachypnoe, beschleunigtes Atmen, erhöhte Atemfrequenz
Über-, Hyperventilation¹ Bradypnoe, verlangsamte Atmung² Atemnot³ hyperventilieren⁴ Atemstillstand, Apnoe⁵ auskultator. freie Lungen⁶ Atemhilfsmuskulatur⁷ Einziehungen⁸ transitorische Tachypnoe⁹ psychisch bedingte Hyperventilation¹⁰ reflektor. Hyperventilation¹¹ kompensator. Hyperventilation¹² Hyperventilationsalkalose¹³ Hyperventilationssyndrom¹⁴ Hyperventilationstetanie¹⁵ Schlafapnoe¹⁶ Apnoeanfälle, -attacken¹⁷

5

492 CLINICAL TERMS — Respiratory Signs & Symptoms

lung or **pulmonary hyperinflation** [haɪpəˈɪnfleɪʃən] n term
  syn **overinflation** n, rel **air trapping**[1] n term

excessive inflation or excursion [ɜː] of the lungs [ʌ] or pulmonary lobes
hyperinflate v term • **(auto)inflation**[2] n • **trap** v • **trapped**[3] adj

» Air trapping and hyperinflation of the affected lobes was found on chest x-ray film[4]. The chest may appear quite hyperinflated owing to[5] air trapping. Air trapping (a high ratio [eɪʃ] of residual volume[6] to total lung capacity[7]) and reduction in pulmonary diffusing capacity were noted.

Use acute[8] / chronic / bilateral [aɪ] / lobar[9] [oʊ]/ emphysematous **hyperinflation** • compensatory[10] / residual [ɪdʒ]/ postobstructive **hyperinflation** • **hyperinflation** of the lung[11] • **inflation** of the lungs[12] • alveolar **inflation** pressure • generalized / localized / distal / bilateral / progressive **air trapping** • **air trapping** on expiration • **trapped** alveolar gas[13] / air / fluid / blood

Lungenüberblähung
Air-trapping, Lufteinschluss[1] Aufblähung[2] eingeschlossen[3] Thoraxröntgen[4] aufgrund von[5] Residualvolumen[6] Totalkapazität[7] akute Lungenüberblähung[8] lobäre Überblähung[9] kompensatorische Lungenüberblähung[10] Lungenüberblähung[11] Belüftung/ Ventilation der Lungen[12] eingeschlossene Alveolarluft[13]

6

---

hemoptysis [hɪmɒpˈtəsɪs] n term
  rel **cough**[1] [kɒf], **expectoration**[2] n clin & term → U103-16f

bringing up blood or blood-stained sputum from the lungs or bronchial tubes
cough (up)[3] v phr clin • **coughing** n • **expectorate**[3] v clin & term • **expectorant**[4] n

» Exposure to irritant gases induces marked cough, hemoptysis, wheezing[5], retching[6], and dyspnea, the severity of these symptoms being dose-related. Expectoration of hard mucous plugs[7] or hemoptysis may occur. How do you differentiate hemoptysis from hematemesis[8]?

Use to have/exhibit/evaluate[9] **hemoptysis** • small-volume / frank or gross[10] [oʊ] / massive or brisk / persistent **hemoptysis** • recurrent[11] [ɜːʌ] / cryptogenic[12] / cough with **hemoptysis** • unproductive or dry / painful / barking[13] **cough** • **cough** headache[14] / syncope[15] [ɪ]/ mechanism • **cough** relief / mixture / suppressant[16] • to cause/ease[17] [iː] /allow/encourage [ɜːʌ] **expectoration** • effective / increased / spontaneous [eɪ] **expectoration** • oral **expectorant** • **expectorant**-mucolytic [ɪ] therapy

Hämoptoe, -ptysis, Bluthusten, -spucken
Husten[1] Aushusten, Expektoration[2] aus-, abhusten[3] Expektorans, auswurfförderndes Mittel[4] Giemen[5] Brechreiz[6] Schleimpfropfen[7] Bluterbrechen, Hämatemesis[8] Hämoptoe abklären[9] makroskop. H.[10] rekurrierende Hämoptoe[11] kryptogenetische H.[12] bellender Husten[13] Hustenkopfschmerz[14] Hustensynkope[15] hustenstillendes Mittel, Antitussivum[16] d. Aushusten erleichtern[17]

7

---

rhonchus n term, pl **-i** [rɒŋkaɪ]   rel **wheezing**[1] [ʰwiːzɪŋ] n term

abnormal sound heard on auscultation of airways obstructed by secretions, spasm, neoplasm, etc.
wheeze[2] v term • **wheezes**[3] n, usu pl • **wheezy** adj • **rhonch(i)al** adj

» The patient complains of chest tightness[4] [aɪ] and wheezing associated with sneezing[5] [iː], rhinorrhea [aɪ], and other upper respiratory symptoms. Asthma [æzmə] is characterized by episodic wheezing, feelings of tightness in the chest[4], dyspnea, and cough. He presents with coarse [ɔː] wheezing[6], a prolonged expiratory phase, and a croupy [kruːpi] cough[7], all of which increase with agitation[8] [ædʒɪ-].

Use rales and / loud or prominent / bilateral / sibilant[9] [ɪ] **rhonchi** • expiratory / low-pitched[10] / occasional [eɪʒ]/ coarse[6] **rhonchi** • chronic / focal / diffuse **wheezing** • audible[11] [ɒː]/ monophonic **wheezing** • **rhonchal** fremitus[12]

Rasselgeräusch, RG, Rhonchus
Giemen, Keuchen[1] keuchen, pfeifend atmen[2] pfeifende Atemgeräusche[3] Engegefühl i. d. Brust[4] Niesen[5] grob-/ großblasige Rasselgeräusche[6] kruppartiger Husten[7] Er-, Aufregung[8] pfeifende Rasselgeräusche[9] nichtklingende/ ohrferne RG[10] deutlich hörbares Giemen[11] Bronchialfremitus[12]

8

---

crackles n pl jar & clin   syn **rales** [æ‖ɑː] n pl jar, **crepitation**, **crepitus** n term

bubbling [ʌ] sounds heard on auscultation [ɔːskʌl-] during inspiration
crackling[1] adj clin & jar • **crepitant**[1] adj term → U106-14

» Rales are heard widely over both lung fields. Abnormal sounds on auscultation can be classified as continuous (wheezes, rhonchi) or discontinuous (crackles, crepitations, or rales). Any combination of crackles, rhonchi, and wheezes may be heard over an area of bronchiectasis.

Use (end-)inspiratory[2] / diffuse / posttussive[3] [ʌ] **crackles** • **crackles** on chest auscultation[4] • **crackles** on inspiration[2] / at the (lung) bases[5] / inspiratory[2] / coarse[6] / fine[7] / dry[8] / moist[9] **rales** • mucous [juː]/ amphoric / atelectatic[10] / bubbling[6] **rales** • cavernous / clicking / (sub)crepitant[11] **rales** • whistling / guttural [ʌ]/ gurgling [ɜː] **rales** • metallic[12] / audible / palpable **rales** • sibilant[13] / sonorous[14] / (bi)basilar[5] **rales** • scattered / diffuse **rales** • coarse[6] / fine[7] / dry[8] / moist[9] **crepitation** • subcutaneous [eɪ] **crepitus** • **crackling** sound on auscultation[4] / rales[11]

Knisterrasseln, Rasselgeräusche, Krepitation, Crepitatio
knisternd[1] inspiratorisches Rasseln[2] posttussives Knisterrasseln[3] auskultatorisch wahrnehmbares Knisterrasseln[4] Rasselgeräusche über d. Lungenbasis[5] grob-/ großblasige Rasselgeräusche[6] fein-/ kleinblasige Rasselgeräusche[7] trockene R.[8] feuchte R.[9] Entfaltungsknistern[10] Knisterrasseln[11] metallisch klingende Rasselgeräusche[12] pfeifende Rasselgeräusche[13] klingende Rasselgeräusche[14]

9

Respiratory Signs & Symptoms   CLINICAL TERMS **493**

stridor [straɪdɚ] *n term*   *rel* **laryngospasm**[1] [lərɪŋɡəspæzəm] *n term*

high-pitched, noisy respiration in the upper airways typically seen in laryngeal obstruction [ʌ] **stridulous**[2] [strɪdʒələs] *adj term* • **bronchospasm** [brɒːŋkə-] *n*

» Examination reveals [iː] stridor, gurgling [ɜː] sounds[3] and ineffective respiratory excursion[4] [ɜː]. His hoarseness [ɔː] progressed to stridor over several weeks. Laryngospasm with stridor can obstruct the airway, causing fatal [eɪ] asphyxia [æsfɪksɪə].

Use to have/develop/listen for **stridor** • congenital[5] [dʒe] / expiratory / inspiratory[6] / soft **stridor** • high-pitched / laryngeal / frank **stridor** • **stridulous** breathing[7]

Stridor, pfeifendes Atemgeräusch
Laryngospasmus[1] stridulös, stridorös, pfeifend[2] großblasige Rasselgeräusche[3] Atemexkursion[4] Stridor connatus/ congenitus[5] inspiratorischer Stridor[6] pfeifendes Atmen[7]

10

fremitus *n term*

rel **hoarseness**[1] [ɔː] *n clin*, **aphonia**[2] [eɪfoʊnɪə] *n term* → U103-6

tremulous vibration [aɪ] of the chest wall that can be palpated and auscultated [ɒː] on physical examination

hoarse[3] *adj clin* • **aphonic** *adj term* • **-phonic** *adj & comb* → U66-23

» Dullness [ʌ], increased fremitus, egophony[4], bronchial breath sounds are signs of pulmonary consolidation. Physical findings in pneumothorax [n(j)uː-] include decreased tactile fremitus[5], hyperresonance, unilateral chest expansion, and mediastinal [aɪ] shift.

Use to assess[6] **fremitus** • increased / (decreased/ absent) tactile[5] / coarse [ɔː] **fremitus** • vocal[7] [oʊ]/ rhonchal or bronchial[8] [k] **fremitus**

Fremitus
Heiserkeit[1] Stimmlosigkeit, Aphonie[2] heiser[3] Ägophonie, Ziegenmeckern[4] tastbarer Fremitus[5] den Fremitus prüfen[6] Stimmfremitus[7] Bronchialfremitus[8]

11

pleural [plʊərəl] **(friction) rub** [ʌ] *n clin*

rel **pleural effusion**[1] [ɪfjuːʒən] *n term*

sound produced by friction[2] of the roughened[3] [ʌf] pleural surfaces that is typical of pleurisy[4] [plʊərəsi]

» The classic signs of pulmonary embolism–hemoptysis, pleural friction rub, gallop rhythm [ɪ], cyanosis [saɪənoʊsɪs], and chest splinting[5]–are present in only 20% of patients. Thoracentesis[6] [iː] should be performed if pleural effusion develops.

Use pericardial / audible / leathery [e]/ high-pitched[7] **friction rub** • **pleural** fluid / fibrosis or peel[8] [iː] • **pleural** suppuration[9] / exudate / pain / thickening[8] • **pleural** scarification / tapping[6] / drainage • chylous[10] [kaɪləs]/ asbestos / massive / early **pleural effusion** • transudative [uː]/ hemorrhagic[11] [ædʒ]/ exudative / left-sided **pleural effusion** • drug-induced / purulent[9] [jʊə] **pleural effusion** • pericardial **effusion**

Pleurareiben
Pleuraerguss[1] Reibung[2] rau, entzündet[3] Ripp-, Brustfellentzündung, Pleuritis[4] Behinderung d. Atemexkursion[5] Thorakozentese, Pleurapunktion[6] hochfrequentes Reibegeräusch[7] Pleuraschwarte, -schwiele[8] Pleuraempyem, eitriger Pleuraerguss[9] chylöser Pleuraerguss[10] hämorrhagischer P.[11]

12

pulmonary edema [ɪdiːmə] *n term*

accumulation of extravascular fluid in the lung most commonly from left ventricular failure[1]

edematous[2] *adj term* • **angioedema**[3] [ændʒɪoʊ-] *n* • **lymphedema**[4] [lɪmf-] *n*

» Then she developed full-blown clinical pulmonary edema with bilateral wet rales and rhonchi, and the chest radiograph showed diffuse haziness[5] [eɪ] of the lung fields with greater density in the more proximal hilar [aɪ] regions.

Use to cause or lead to/exacerbate [æs] or worsen/treat **pulmonary edema** • acute / marked / frank[6] **pulmonary edema** • unilateral / episodic / recurrent [ɜː] **pulmonary edema** • (non)cardiogenic[7] [dʒe]/ neurogenic [n(j)ʊɚ-]/ hydrostatic [aɪ] **pulmonary edema** • high-altitude[8] [æ] (*abbr* HAPE)/ drug-induced / reexpansion[9] **pulmonary edema** • (upper/ rebound) [aʊ] airway / (nasal) mucosal **edema** • laryngeal [dʒ]/ bronchial / bronchiolar **edema** • alveolar[6] [ɪə]/ interstitial[10] [ɪʃ]/ cerebral **edema** • inflammatory[11] [æ]/ latent [eɪ]/ profound[12] [aʊ] **edema**

Lungenödem
Linksherzinsuffizienz[1] ödematös[2] Angioödem[3] Lymphödem[4] diffuse Verschattung[5] alveoläres/ manifestes Lungenödem[6] kardiales Lungenödem[7] Höhenlungenödem[8] Reexpansionsödem[9] Prälungenödem, interstitielles Lungenödem[10] entzündl. Ödem[11] massives Ödem[12]

13

empyema [empaɪiːmə] *n term*   *syn* **pyothorax** [paɪoʊθɔːræks] *n*,

rel **lung abscess**[1] *n term*

accumulation of pus[2] [ʌ] in a body cavity; when used without qualification, it refers to thoracic empyema

empyemal[3] *adj term* • **microabscess** *n* • **hemothorax**[4] [iː] *n* • **chylothorax**[5] [kaɪloʊ-] *n*

» Empyema is an exudative [uː] pleural effusion caused by direct infection of the pleural space, causing the pleural fluid to appear purulent [pjʊɚ] or turbid[6] [ɜː]. Since carcinoma underlies 10-20% of lung abscesses, this should always be excluded.

Use acute / pyogenic [dʒe]/ streptococcal / tuberculous[7] [ɜː]/ anaerobic **empyema** • loculated[8] / pleural [ʊə]/ interlobar[9] [oʊ]/ chronic **empyema** • **empyema** cavity[11] / thoracis[10] • pulmonary[1] / (peri)tonsillar / mediastinal[12] [aɪ] **abscess** • (retro)pharyngeal [dʒ]/ nasal [eɪ] septal **abscess**

(Pleura)empyem
Lungenabszess[1] Eiter[2] empyematös[3] Hämothorax[4] Chylothorax[5] trüb[6] tuberkulöses Pleuraempyem[7] gekammertes Pleuraempyem[8] interlobäres Pleuraempyem[9] Pleuraempyem, Pyothorax[10] Empyemhöhle[11] Mediastinalabszess[12]

14

(pulmonary) atelectasis [ˌætəlɛktəsɪs] *n term*   *rel* **lung collapse**¹ *n term*

collapsed, airless state of (portions of) the lung, esp. of the alveoli [aɪ], associated with failure of expansion² and alveolar [ɪə] gas exchange due to airway obstruction or pressure from fluid or air in the pleural space

atelectatic³ [ˌætəlɛktætɪk] *adj term* • **collapse**⁴ *v* • **collapsed** *adj*

» *Atelectasis is alveolar collapse that is not due to pneumothorax* [n(j)ʊː] *or hydrothorax*⁵ [aɪ]. *Pulmonary atelectasis is common in respiratory failure*⁶, *and often requires bronchoscopy and aspiration. If severe enough, atelectasis can be diagnosed by x-ray confirmation of platelike collapse of pulmonary parenchyma. Tension pneumothorax*⁷ *may result in complete lung collapse and mediastinal shift*⁸.

Use acute / partial / complete / focal / lobar⁹ / segmental¹⁰ **atelectasis** • (diffuse) bilateral / (right-sided) basilar **atelectasis** • micro/ macro**atelectasis** • fetal or primary¹¹ [aɪ] / massive **atelectasis** • rounded / resorption or obstructive¹² **atelectasis** • asymptomatic / compression or compressive¹³ / postoperative **atelectasis** • massive / unilateral **lung collapse** • respiratory or pulmonary¹ /(large-)airway **collapse** • alveolar¹⁴ / (peripheral) lobar **collapse** • **atelectatic** lung (areas) / rale¹⁵ / air sacs¹⁶ / alveoli¹⁶ • **collapsed** lung¹⁷ / alveoli [aɪ]/ neck vein [eɪ]/ person

Atelektase
Lungenkollaps¹ fehlende Entfaltung² atelektatisch³ kollabieren⁴ Hydrothorax⁵ Ateminsuffizienz⁶ Spannungspneumothorax⁷ Mediastinalverziehung⁸ Lappenatelektase⁹ Segmentatelektase¹⁰ fetale Atelektase¹¹ Obstruktions-, Resorptionsatelektase¹² Kompressionsatelektase¹³ Alveolarkollaps¹⁴ Entfaltungsrasseln, -knistern¹⁵ atelektatische Alveolen¹⁶ kollabierte Lunge¹⁷

(pulmonary) emphysema [-siːmə] *n term*   *rel* **airway(s) obstruction**¹ *n term*

abnormal distention due to destruction of alveolar septa in the air spaces distal to the terminal bronchioles

emphysematous² *adj term* [ˌɛmfɪsiːmətəs‖-sɛmətəs] • **(non)obstructive**³ [ʌ] *adj*

» *Chronic bronchitis* [aɪ] *and emphysema, which often occur together and are collectively known as chronic obstructive pulmonary disease*⁴ *(abbr COPD), have a high correlation with smoking. Orthopnea, though mainly characteristic of congestive* [dʒɛ] *heart failure, may also occur in some patients with asthma* [z] *and chronic obstruction of the airways.*

Use acute / chronic / advanced⁵ / diffuse⁶ **emphysema** • bullous⁷ / centrilobular⁸ / basilar **emphysema** • hypoplastic / obstructive⁹ / panacinar⁶ [æs] **emphysema** • mediastinal¹⁰ / congenital [dʒɛ] lobar **emphysema** • pulmonary interstitial¹¹ / paracicatricial [-ɪʃəl] or scar¹² / compensatory¹³ **emphysema** • **emphysematous** lesion [iːʒ]/ lobe / bleb or bulla¹⁴ [ʊ] • **emphysematous** hyperinflation / pink puffer [ʌ] • airflow / nasal / (upper/ lower/ progressive/ total) (endo)bronchial **obstruction** • foreign body / chronic / expiratory **obstruction** • **obstructive** lung disease / pneumonitis¹⁵ [n(j)uːmənaɪtɪs]

Lungenemphysem, -blähung
Atemwegsobstruktion¹ emphysemartig, emphysematös² blockierend, verschließend, obstruktiv³ chronisch-obstruktive Lungenkrankheit, COLD, COPD⁴ fortgeschrittenes Lungenemphysem⁵ panlobuläres/ panazinäres/ diffuses L.⁶ bullöses L.⁷ zentrolobuläres L.⁸ obstruktives L.⁹ Mediastinalemphysem¹⁰ interstitielles Lungenemphysem¹¹ Narbenemphysem¹² kompensatorisches (Lungen)emphysem¹³ Emphysemblase¹⁴ Obstruktionspneumonie¹⁵

bronchiectasis [-ɛktəsɪs] *n term*   *opposite* **bronchial constriction**¹ *n term*

irreversible [ɜː] dilatation [eɪʃ] and destruction of the walls in the bronchial [brɒŋkɪəl] tree²

bronchiectatic³ [ˌbrɒŋkɪɛktætɪk] *adj term* • **constrictive**⁴ *adj*

» *Symptoms of bronchiectasis typically include a constant productive cough, copious* [oʊ] *purulent sputum*⁵, *moist rales, and finger clubbing*⁶ [ʌ]. *Good pulmonary hygiene* [haɪdʒiːn] *and avoidance of infectious complications may reverse* [ɜː] *cylindric* [sɪ-] *bronchiectasis*⁷. *Acetylcholine increases tracheobronchial secretions and stimulates bronchial constriction.*

Use congenital⁸ / central / proximal / diffuse **bronchiectasis** • localized / saccular⁹ / varicose¹⁰ **bronchiectasis** • bronchiolar¹¹ / pulmonary arteriolar **constriction** • **bronchiectatic** changes / airways / area / cavity¹² • **constrictive** airway disease / pulmonary dysfunction / pericarditis [aɪ] • broncho**constrictive**

Bronchiektase, Bronchiektasie
Bronchokonstriktion¹ Bronchialbaum² bronchiektatisch³ einschnürend, konstriktiv⁴ maulvolles eitriges Sputum⁵ Bildung von Trommelschlägelfingern⁶ zylindrische Bronchiektas(i)e⁷ angeborene Bronchiektas(i)e⁸ zystische Bronchiektas(i)e⁹ variköse B.¹⁰ Verengung der Bronchiolen¹¹ Bronchiektasenhöhle¹²

Clinical Phrases

Breathe in, … and out, … hold your breath, … and breathe away with your mouth open. Bitte einatmen, … ausatmen, … nicht mehr atmen, … mit offenem Mund weiteratmen. • Give a cough, please. Husten Sie bitte einmal. • Does it hurt when you take a deep breath? Tut es weh, wenn Sie tief einatmen? • He complained of a dry hacking cough which was unrelenting. Er klagte über einen hartnäckigen trockenen Husten. • Are you bringing anything up when you cough? Kommt etwas herauf, wenn Sie husten? • She has very scanty sputum production. Sie hat nur wenig Auswurf • Have you ever experienced any shortness of breath? Leiden Sie hin und wieder an Atemnot? • How many steps can you climb before getting short of breath? Nach wie vielen Treppen müssen Sie stehenbleiben, um Atem zu holen? • Have you ever had to get up to catch your breath at night? Müssen Sie sich nachts manchmal aufsetzen, um besser Luft zu bekommen? • How many pillows do you sleep on? Wie viele Kissen brauchen Sie beim Schlafen? • Is he using his accessory muscles of respiration? Verwendet er die Atemhilfsmuskulatur? • Her breath sounds are distant over the right basis. Die Atemgeräusche über der rechten Lungenbasis sind ohrfern. • The chest is clear to auscultation. Die Lungen sind auskultatorisch frei. • We'll have to administer oxygen by mask. Wir werden den Patienten über eine Maske beatmen müssen.

Unit 112 Urologic Signs & Symptoms

Related Units: 102 History Taking, 103 Clinical Symptoms, 108 Clinical Signs, 48 Urinary Tract, 49 Urine Production, 52 Male Sexual Organs, 53 Male Sexual Function, 55 Hormones, 68 Sexuality, 69 Fertility

dysuria [dɪsjʊɚ-ɪə] *n term*   *syn* **painful urination** *n*, **pain on urination** *phr clin*

painful or difficult urination, e.g. irritative voiding [vɔɪdɪŋ] symptoms[1]
dysuric [dɪsjʊɚ-ɪk] *adj term* • **-uria** [jʊɚ-ɪə] *comb* • **-uric** *comb*

» Pain and dysuria are often seen in bladder involvement. He complains of low back and flank pain, dysuria and ill-defined [aɪ] perineal [iː] discomfort. Pain on urination is usually caused by inflammation [eɪʃ] of the lower urinary tract.

Use spastic / postoperative / severe / mild / acute **dysuria** • **dysuria**-frequency syndrome[2] • bacteri/ crystall [ɪ]/ glycos**uria** [aɪ] • hypercalci [aɪ]/ hyperuricos[3]/ protein/ py**uria** • heavy / sterile[4] / unexplained / microscopic **pyuria** • (a)symptomatic [eɪ]/ low-level / significant[5] **bacteriuria** • lower tract / recurrent[6] [ɜː] **bacteriuria** • absorptive[7] / renal [iː]/ idiopathic[8] **hypercalciuria**

erschwerte/ schmerzhafte Blasenentleerung/ Miktion, Dysurie
irritative Miktionsbeschwerden[1] Pollakisurie[2] erhöhte Harnsäureausscheidung im Harn[3] abakterielle/ sterile Pyurie[4] signifikante Bakteriurie[5] rezidivierende B.[6] absorptionsbedingte Hyperkalz(i)urie[7] idiopathische H.[8]

1

polyuria [pɒːlɪjʊɚ-ɪə] *n term*   *opposite* **oliguria**[1] *n term,*
                                          rel **anuria**[2] [æn(j)ʊɚ-ɪə] *n term*

abnormally high urine [jʊɚ-ɪn] output (greater than 2,000 to 2,500 mL per 24 hours)
polyuric *adj term* • **(non)oliguric** [ɒːlɪg(j)ʊɚ-ɪk] *adj* • **anuric** *adj*

» Total body potassium loss from polyuria as well as from vomiting[3] may be greater than 200 meq. Type I diabetes [iː] is characterized by polyuria, polydipsia[4], and rapid weight loss associated [oʊʃ] with unequivocal hyperglycemia[5] [aɪsiː]. Anuria suggests complete urinary tract obstruction but may complicate severe cases of intrinsic renal azotemia [iː].

Use to result in/cause/be accompanied by/improve [uː]/complicate **polyuria** • hypotonic / lithium-induced **polyuria** • excessive / chronic / nocturnal[6] [ɜː]/ protracted **polyuria** • mild / acute / transient **oliguria** • prolonged[7] / progressive / prerenal **oliguria** • abrupt [ʌ]/ total or complete **anuria** • irreversible [ɜː]/ calculus[8] **anuria** • **polyuric** stage / phase[9] [feɪz] • **oliguric** patient / phase / renal failure [feɪljɚ]

Polyurie, übermäßige Harnausscheidung
Oligurie, verminderte Harnausscheidung[1] Anurie[2] Erbrechen[3] gesteigertes Durstempfinden u. vermehrte Flüssigkeitsaufnahme, Polydipsie[4] manifeste Hyperglykämie[5] nächtl. Polyurie[6] länger anhaltende Oligurie[7] steinbedingte Anurie[8]
polyurische Phase[9]

2

hematuria [hiːmət(j)ʊɚ-ɪə] *n term*

                syn **bloody** or **bloodstained** [eɪ] **urine** *n clin*

red pigmentation of urine because of blood or red blood cells
microhematuria[1] [aɪ] *n term* • **hematuric** *adj*

» Patients who develop hematuria on long-term dialysis should be screened for RCC[2]. Gross hematuria[3] is visible to the naked eye (i.e. blood-stained urine). Her hematuria cleared within 2 days. The urine may be grossly bloody or show a blood tinge[4] [dʒ] at the end of micturition.

Use gross [oʊ] or macroscopic[3] / microscopic[1] / essential[5] **hematuria** • post-traumatic [ɔː]/ self-limiting[6] **hematuria** • false[7] [ɔː]/ benign[8] [bɪnaɪn]/ initial [ɪʃ]/ terminal[9] [ɜː] **hematuria** • total / painful / painless[10] **hematuria** • urethral [iː]/ vesical / renal **hematuria** • endemic or Egyptian[11] [ɪdʒɪpʃ³n] **hematuria**

Hämaturie, Erythrozyturie, Blut im Harn
Mikrohämaturie[1] Nierenzellkarzinom, Hypernephrom, hypernephroides Karzinom[2] Makrohämaturie[3] blutig tingiert[4] essentielle Hämaturie[5] spontan abklingende H.[6] Pseudohämaturie[7] gutartige/ benigne H.[8] terminale H.[9] schmerzlose H.[10] Urogenitalschistosomiasis, ägyptische Hämaturie[11]

3

(urinary) urgency [ɜːrdʒ³n¹si] *n term*

                rel **frequency-urgency syndrome**[1] *n term*

sudden, strong urge to void [vɔɪd] accompanied by a fear of leakage [liːkɪdʒ] or the sensation [eɪ] of bladder fullness; may be due to a failure to fill or store urine or to detrusor hyperreflexia secondary to bladder outlet obstruction[2]

urge[3] [ɜːrdʒ] *v & n* → U73-11 • **urgent**[4] [ɜːrdʒ³nt] *adj*

» The patient was unable to quickly enough respond to urinary urgency. She had the typical symptoms of urinary tract infection (frequency, urgency, and dysuria). Leakage was preceded [iː] by the abrupt [ʌ] onset of an intense urge to urinate that could not be forestalled[5].

Use a sense of / motor / sensory / fecal[6] [fiːkᵊl] **urgency** • **urge** incontinence or leakage[7] • **urge to** void or urinate[8] [jʊɚ]/ defecate[9] • to feel the / first[10] / strong **urge (to void)** • irresistible or uncontrollable[11] **urge (to void)**

imperativer Harndrang, Urge
Frequency-Urgency-Syndrom, Reizblase[1] Blasenhalsobstruktion[2] drängen; Drang, Bedürfnis[3] dringend[4] nicht unterdrückt werden[5] imperativer Stuhldrang[6] Drang-, Urgeinkontinenz[7] Harndrang[8] Stuhldrang[9] beginnender Harndrang[10] nicht unterdrückbarer/ imperativer Harndrang[11]

4

Urologic Signs & Symptoms

urinary frequency [iː] n term   syn **frequent voiding** n term, **frequency** n jar
abnormal frequency (at intervals <2 hs) of the urge to void without increase in urinary output[1]
» Reduced bladder capacity and polyuria are the two main causes of urinary frequency. Many enuretic [e] patients have significant urinary frequency, voiding about twice as often as normal children. An increase in daytime urinary frequency may simply be psychogenic in origin.
Use to evaluate[2]/deny [aɪ] /cause/note **urinary frequency** • daytime or diurnal [daɪɜːrnᵊl]/ increased **urinary frequency** • nonpsychogenic [-saɪkoʊdʒenɪk] / intolerable **urinary frequency** • painful / (non)psychogenic[3] / nocturnal[4] [ɜː] **frequency** • bowel [baʊᵊl]/ breathing [iː] **frequency** • **frequency** rate / of voiding[5]

nocturia [nɒːkt(j)ʊɚɪə] n term   syn **nycturia** [nɪkt(j)ʊɚɪə] n term
(i) frequent awakening at night because of voiding sensations; may result from increased urinary output, lower urinary tract obstruction, detrusor instability, etc.
(ii) occasionally used as a synonym for enuresis
» The complex of irritative (frequency, nocturia, urge incontinence, etc.) and obstructive symptoms (e.g. straining[1], urinary retention) is termed prostatism[2].
Use to cause/develop/lead to/prevent/lessen **nocturia** • frequency / history[3] / development **of nocturia**

(urinary) hesitancy [hezɪtᵊnˀsi] n clin
         syn **difficulty** or **trouble starting (the stream)** phr clin
undue delay[1] in starting the urinary stream often associated with other obstructive symptoms such as straining to void, terminal dribbling[2], urinary retention, and intermittent, slow or weak stream[3]
» Urethral polyps may cause micturition symptoms such as dysuria, hesitancy, decreased urinary stream[3], gross hematuria, frequency, or day and night wetting[4].

detrusor instability or **hyperreflexia** n term
         rel **spasticity**[1] [-ɪsɪti] n term
state of increased contractility and hypertonicity[2] [aɪ] of the bladder muscle with exaggeration [ɪɡzædʒ-] of the reflexes[3] [iː]
unstable[4] [-steɪbl] adj • **spasm**[5] [spæzᵊm] n term • **spastic**[6] [æ] adj → U103-20
» Outlet obstruction which was associated with detrusor hyperreflexia gave rise to hesitancy. Urethral [iː] instability refers to a total loss of urethral closure [oʊʒ] pressure provoked by bladder filling without a corresponding increase in intravesical pressure. In patients with obstructive unstable bladders the instability may resolve after relief [iː] of obstruction.
Use **detrusor** contractility / areflexia[7] / overactivity or hyperactivity[8] • **detrusor** spasticity /-sphincter dyssynergia[9] [ɜː] • (painful) bladder or detrusor[10] / ureteral **spasm** • **spastic** or reflex or automatic bladder[11]

intermittency n term   syn **(urinary) stammering** or **stuttering** [ʌ] n clin & jar
frequent involuntary interruption [ʌ] occurring [ɜː] during the act of micturition [-ɪʃᵊn]
» This symptom score also evaluates the severity [e] of intermittency, terminal [ɜː] dribbling[1], urgency, impairment [eɚ] of size and force of stream [iː], dysuria, and sensation of incomplete voiding[2].

urinary or **urine retention** [rɪtenˀʃᵊn] n term   syn **retention of urine** n clin
incomplete bladder emptying[1] which may be associated with a sensation of bladder fullness
» The patient had urinary retention secondary to[2] bladder outlet obstruction. Obstructive symptoms such as diminution [uːʃ] in the caliber and force of the urinary stream, hesitancy in initiating voiding, postvoid dribbling, the sensation of incomplete emptying, and urinary retention must be distinguished from irritative symptoms such as dysuria, frequency, and urgency.
Use to induce or precipitate/prevent/treat/reverse [ɜː] **urinary retention** • acute / complete[3] [iː] **urinary retention** • painful / refractory[4] / long-term **urinary retention** • chronic / hyperkalemic [iː]/ postoperative / postpartum[5] **urinary retention** • water / uric acid[6] [jʊɚɪk æsɪd]/ sodium[7] [oʊ]/ fluid **retention**

Pollakisurie, häufige Blasenentleerung
Harnmenge[1] Pollakisurie abklären[2] vermehrtes nächtl. Wasserlassen, Nykturie[3] psychisch bedingte Pollakisurie[4] Miktionsfrequenz[5]

5

Nykturie, (vermehrtes) nächtl. Wasserlassen
Pressen[1] chron. Prostatabeschwerden, -leiden, Prostatismus[2] positive Anamnese bzgl. Nykturie[3]

6

Miktions-, Startverzögerung
beträchtliche Verzögerung[1] Nachtröpfeln, -träufeln[2] schwacher Harnstrahl[3] nächtl. Einnässen, Bettnässen, Enuresis nocturna[4]

7

Detrusorinstabilität, hyperreflexiver Detrusor
Spastik, Spastizität[1] Tonuserhöhung[2] gesteigerte Reflexantworten, übersteigerte Reflexe[3] instabil[4] Spasmus, Krampf[5] spastisch, krampfartig[6] Detrusorareflexie[7] Detrusorhyperaktivität[8] Detrusor-Sphinkter-Dyssynergie[9] Detrusorspasmus[10] Reflexblase, autonome/ spastische Blase[11]

8

Harnstottern
Nachtröpfeln[1] unvollständige Blasenentleerung[2]

9

Harnverhalt(ung), -retention
unvollständige Blasenentleerung[1] infolge von[2] absolute Harnretention, komplette Harnsperre[3] therapieresistente Harnretention[4] postpartale Harnverhaltung[5] Harnsäureretention[6] Natriumretention[7]

10

Urologic Signs & Symptoms — CLINICAL TERMS

postvoid residual (urine) n term abbr **PVR**   syn **residual** [rɪzɪdʒʊəl] **urine** n jar
  urine remaining in the bladder at the end of micturition due to incomplete emptying
» The residual volume after voiding was determined. The finding of a PVR is more a sign of detrusor decompensation than of the outlet obstruction that caused it.
Use **residual**-free micturition[1] / disease • **postvoid** residual (urine) volume / dribbling[2] • **postvoid** wetting[3] / incontinence[3] / (bladder) film

> Note: The term **residual volume** (abbr RV) is more often used in connection with lung capacity and spirometry than with bladder emptying and uroflowmetry.

(urinary) reflux [riːflʌks] n term   rel **bladder neck obstruction**[1] [ʌ] n term
  backward flow of urine from the bladder into the ureter (vesicoureteral) or renal pelvis (ureteropelvic)
  (non)refluxing, -ive[2] [ʌ] adj term • **anti-reflux** adj • **(post)obstructive**[3] adj
» The reflux was categorized into grades of severity on the basis of a voiding cystourethrogram[4] [sɪstoʊ-]. Transurethral [iː] prostatectomy[5] (abbr TURP) was performed to relieve bladder neck obstruction.
Use primary [aɪ] / persistent / intrarenal[6] / sterile **reflux** • high-grade[7] / (vesico)ureteral[8] **reflux** • **reflux** nephropathy[9] • **(non)refluxing** megaureter • **anti-reflux** anastomosis / surgery[10] • bi-/unilateral / congenital [dʒe] / upper urinary tract / ureteral **obstruction** • ureteropelvic junction[11] [dʒʌ] (abbr UPJ)/ infravesical[12] **obstruction** • BPH / supravesical **obstruction** • (bladder) outflow or bladder outlet[13] / ejaculatory [dʒæk] duct **obstruction** • extrinsic / intrinsic **obstruction** • **obstructive** uropathy[14] / megaureter • symptom (score)

uremia [jʊriːmɪə] n term   rel **azotemia**[1] [eɪzoʊtiːmɪə] n term
  excess of nitrogenous [naɪtrɒːdʒənˠs] wastes[2] in the serum [ɪə] observed e.g. in chronic renal failure that requires dialysis [daɪælɘsɪs]
  (hyper/ non)uremic[3] [iː] adj term • **azotemic** [eɪzoʊtiːmɪk] adj
» Malnutrition [ɪʃ] leading to generalized tissue wasting [eɪ] is a prominent feature [iːtʃ] of chronic uremia. Patients with bilateral ureteral obstruction secondary to trigonal compression by tumor may exhibit azotemia and uremia.
Use acute[4] / chronic[5] / terminal [ɜː]/ severe or advanced **uremia** • unexplained / untreated / overt[6] [ɜː] **uremia** • **uremic** coma [koʊmə] / acidosis [oʊ]/ fetor[7] [iː] • **uremic** poisoning[8] / toxins[9] • prerenal / extrarenal[10] / postrenal **azotemia**

(urinary or renal) cast [kæst] n term & jar
           rel **pseudocast** [suːdoʊkæst] or **spurious** [spjʊəriəs] **cast**[1] n term
  particles (e.g. from albumin, blood cells) in the urine formed in the renal tubule [(j)uː]
» If RBC or WBC casts are detected in the urinary sediment, the presence of renal disease is established. Many of the dilated [aɪ] tubules contained colloid casts.
Use white cell (abbr WBC) or leukocyte[2] / (finely/coarsely) granular[3] **casts** • waxy[4] / red-cell or RBC or erythrocyte[5] **casts** • epithelial[6] / fatty[7] / hyaline[8] [aɪ] **casts**

(urinary) incontinence n term   syn **urine** or **urinary leakage** [liːkɪdʒ] n,
                           rel **(urinary) dribbling**[1] n clin
  trouble [ʌ] holding one's water and involuntary loss of urine[2] as a result of coughing [kɒːfɪŋ], straining [eɪ], weakness [iː] of the bladder neck, detrusor instability, etc.
  (in)continent[3] adj term • **continence** n • **(anti)incontinence** adj • **leak**[4] v & n
» Reflex incontinence[5], i.e. loss of urine due to detrusor hyperreflexia and/or involuntary urethral relaxation in the absence of the desire to void, occurs in neurogenic [dʒe] disorders. The patient leaks urine with major stress which requires 2 pads[6]/day for protection.
Use (motor or sensory) urge[7] / stress[8] (abbr SUI)/ overflow or passive[9] **(urinary) incontinence** • bladder[10] / bowel [aʊ] or fecal[11] [iː]/ anal [eɪ]/ posttraumatic **incontinence** • total / transient / occasional **incontinence** • urethral / stress urinary[8] / diffuse capillary **leakage** • continuous / postvoid or postmicturition[12] **dribbling** • terminal[12] / overflow **dribbling** • daytime or diurnal [ɜː]/ nighttime or nocturnal **continence** • complete / appliance-free [aɪ] **continence** • to achieve/ affect/restore **urinary continence** • to improve/maintain[13]/preserve[13] [ɜː] **urinary continence** • **incontinent** of urine[14] / of stool [uː]/ patient

---

Rest-, Residualharn
restharnfreie Blasenentleerung[1] postmiktionelles Nachtröpfeln/ Nachträufeln[2] Harnträufeln/ Harnverlust nach d. Miktion[3]

Reflux, Rückfluss
Blasenhalsobstruktion[1] refluxiv[2] obstruktiv[3] Miktionszystourethrogramm[4] transurethrale Prostatektomie[5] intra-, pyelorenaler Reflux[6] hochgradiger R.[7] vesikoureteraler R.[8] Refluxnephropathie[9] Antirefluxplastik[10] Ureterabgangsenge, -stenose[11] subvesikale Obstruktion[12] Blasenhalsobstruktion[13] obstruktive Harnwegserkrankung[14]

Urämie, Harnvergiftung
Azotämie[1] stickstoffhaltige Abbauprodukte[2] urämisch[3] akute Urämie[4] chronische Urämie[5] klin. manifeste Urämie[6] Foetor uraemicus[7] urämische Intoxikation[8] Urämiegifte[9] extrarenale Azotämie[10]

Harnzylinder
Pseudozylinder[1] Leukozytenzylinder[2] grobgranulierte Zylinder[3] Wachszylinder[4] Erythrozytenzylinder[5] Epithelzylinder[6] Fettzylinder[7] hyaline Zylinder[8]

(Harn)inkontinenz
Harnträufeln[1] unwillkürl. Harnabgang/ -verlust[2] (in)kontinent[3] undicht sein, auslaufen; undichte Stelle, Leck[4] Reflexinkontinenz[5] Einlagen[6] (sensorische) Dranginkontinenz, Urge-Inkontinenz[7] Stress-, Belastungsinkontinenz[8] Überlaufinkontinenz[9] Harninkontinenz[10] Stuhlinkontinenz[11] Nachträufeln, -tröpfeln[12] die Harnkontinenz erhalten[13] harninkontinent[14]

enuresis [ˈenjərˌiːsɪs] *n term*   *syn* **(bed-)wetting** *n clin*

repeated involuntary loss of urine due to lack of bladder control, esp. during sleep in young children

(non)enuretic [ˌenjərˈetɪk] *adj term* • **wet**[1] *v & adj clin* • **bedwetter**[2] *n*

» If enuresis follows a significant dry interval[3] it is termed secondary enuresis[4]. Bed-wetting spontaneously [eɪ] ceased [siːst] at age 7. Children who wet may have urinary tract damage.

Use   diurnal[5] [daɪˈɜːrnəl] / nocturnal[6] / persistent[7] / primary[8] / adult-onset **enuresis** • **enuretic** child / patient / episode • childhood **bedwetting** • postvoid / refractory[9] **wetting** • **wetting** incident • **wet** pad[10]

Enuresis, Ein-, Bettnässen
einnässen, nass machen; nass, feucht[1] Bettnässer(in)[2] Kontinenz-periode, -interval[3] sekundäre Enuresis[4] Einnässen am Tag, Enuresis diurna[5] Enuresis nocturna[6] fortbestehende/ persistierende Enuresis[7] primäre Enuresis[8] therapierefraktäres Einnässen[9] Einlage[10]

16

Clinical Phrases

What about your waterworks? Haben Sie Beschwerden beim Urinieren? • Does your water burn when you have to pass it? Brennt es beim Harnlassen? • Do you have any difficulty starting your stream? Haben Sie Startschwierigkeiten? • Do you ever have to push or strain to begin urination? Müssen Sie pressen, um urinieren zu können? • I've got a weak bladder, doctor. I sometimes leak. Ich habe eine schwache Blase, Herr Doktor. Manchmal verliere ich etwas Harn. • How many times a night do you have to get up to urinate? Wie oft müssen Sie in der Nacht zum Wasserlassen aufstehen? • Over the past month how often have you found it difficult to postpone urination? Wie oft hatten Sie im letzten Monat Probleme, den Harn zu halten? • Have you had a sensation of not emptying your bladder completely after finishing urination? Hatten Sie nach dem Urinieren jemals das Gefühl, dass Ihre Blase nicht ganz leer ist? • Do you sometimes have a weak urinary stream? Haben Sie manchmal einen schwachen Harnstrahl?

Unit 113 Neurologic Findings

Related Units: 103 Clinical Symptoms, 108 Clinical Signs, 7 States of Consciousness, 42 Nerve Function, 57 Senses, 59 Vision, 61 Hearing, 64 Body Movement, 65 Walking, 66 Speech, 72 Sleep, 73 Mental Activity, 74 Memory, 75 Personality, 76 Mood, 77 Mental Health

plantar reflex [iː] *n term*
   rel **Babinski's sign**[1] *n term*, **ankle jerk**[2] [dʒɜːrk] *n jar*→ U42-12f; U64-7

response to tactile stimulation of the ball of the foot which normally triggers plantar flexion of the toes

(a/ hyper)reflexive[3] *adj term* • **a/ hyper/ hyporeflexia** *n* • **jerky**[4] *adj clin*

» The plantar reflex is elicited [ɪs] by stroking the lateral surface of the foot beginning near the heel [iː] and moving toward the toes. Symmetric motor signs (hemiparesis, hyperreflexia, and Babinski's sign) may be present. The destruction [ʌ] of the sciatic [saɪˈætɪk] nerve[5] always leads to loss of the ankle [æŋkl] jerk.

Use   to test/trigger *or* elicit[6] **reflexes** • flexor / extensor **plantar reflex** • corneal (light) / oculomotor / red[7] / acoustic[8] [uː] **reflex** • deglutition [uː] *or* swallowing[9] [ɒː]/ pharyngeal [dʒ] *or* gag[10] **reflex** • cough [kɒf]/ suck(ing)[11] [ʌ]/ letdown **reflex** • blink / Achilles [k] *or* ankle[2] / patellar[12] / positive *or* upgoing Babinski[13] **reflex** • **reflex** activity / response[14] / testing / irritability • **reflex** salivation[15] / eye movement / micturition[16] [ɪʃ]/ bladder[17] • baro**reflex** • **reflex**-induced /-stimulated • (focal/ lateralizing) neurologic / Romberg('s) **sign** • meningeal[18] [dʒiː]/ Homan's / Brudzinki's **sign** • Kernig('s) / straight-leg-raising[19] [eɪ] (*abbr* SLR) / iliopsoas[20] [s] **sign** • knee[12] / jaw[21] [dʒɔː]/ tendon[22] **jerk** • deep tendon[22] (*abbr* DTR) / muscle [mʌsl] stretch[22] / postural **reflex** • superficial [ɪʃ]/ vasoconstriction / brain stem[23] **reflex** • unconditioned[24] (*abbr* UCR)/ acquired[25] [aɪ] **reflexes** • intact / hyperactive / brisk[26] / depressed / absent[27] **reflexes** • **reflexes** equal & active bilaterally[28] • **jerky** movements[29]

Plantar-, Fußsohlenreflex
Babinski-Zeichen, -Reflex[1] Achillessehnenreflex, ASR[2] reflektorisch[3] ruckartig[4] N. ischiadicus[5] Reflexe auslösen[6] Fundusreflex[7] Stapediusreflex[8] Schluckreflex[9] Würg(e)reflex[10] Saugreflex[11] Patellarsehnenreflex[12] positiver Babinski-R.[13] Reflexantwort[14] reflektor. Speichelsekretion[15] reflektor. Blasenentleerung[16] Reflexblase[17] meningeales Zeichen[18] Lasegue-Zeichen[19] Psoaszeichen[20] Masseterreflex[21] Sehnenreflex[22] Hirnstammreflex[23] unbedingte/ angeborene Reflexe[24] erworbene/ bedingte Reflexe[25] lebhafte Reflexe[26] nicht auslösbare Reflexe[27] Reflexe seitengleich auslösbar[28] ruckartige Bewegungen[29]

1

Neurologic Findings

CLINICAL TERMS 499

Mr. MacPhearson's knee jerk on the right was quite brisk.

agitation [ædʒɪteɪʃˀn] *n term*   *sim* **restlessness**[1], **hyperactivity**[2] *n clin & term*
rel **anxiety**[3] [æŋzaɪəti], **distress**[4] *n clin* → U104-2

(mental) state of excessive psychomotor excitation and/or activity usually due to emotional tension

agitated[5] *adj term* • **agitate**[6] *vt* • **agito-** *comb* • **restless** *adj* → U76-8

» During an attack of transient global amnesia [iː3], agitation is not a clinical feature [iːtʃ]. Note whether the victim[7] is calm [kɑːm], agitated, or confused [juː]. Restless activity which may include pacing[8] [eɪs], shaking[9] [eɪ], sobbing[10] or laughing without apparent [eə] cause serves to release nervous tension[11] associated with anxiety, fear or other mental stress.

Use to produce[12]/control/reduce/decrease [iː] **agitation** • (psycho)motor [saɪk-]/ severe / moderate / extreme [iː]/ uncontrolled **agitation** • **agitated** patient • **restless** legs / sleep[13] • motor[14] / nocturnal[15] [ɜː]/ inner sense of[16] **restlessness** • **agito**phasia [ædʒɪtəfeɪz(ɪ)ə] /lalia /graphia

Agitiertheit, psychomotorische Unruhe
Unruhe, Ruhelosigkeit[1] Hyperaktivität, -kinese[2] Angst, Beklemmung[3] Schmerz, Kummer, Not(lage)[4] agitiert, unruhig[5] aufregen, -wühlen[6] Opfer[7] hin u. her gehen[8] Zittern[9] Schluchzen[10] Nervenanspannung[11] psychomotor. Unruhe hervorrufen[12] unruhiger Schlaf[13] motor. Unruhe[14] nächtl. Unruhe[15] innere Unruhe[16]

2

flat affect *n term* → U76-3   *rel* **listlessness**[1] *n clin*, **lethargy**[2] *n term & clin*

absence or decrease in the amount of typical emotional tone, outward emotional reaction, or mood

affective[3] [əfektɪv] *adj term* • **listless** *adj clin* • **lethargic** *adj* [ləθɑːrdʒɪk] → U7-12

» He shows no overt [ɜː] psychotic [saɪk-] symptoms but there is social withdrawal[4] [ɔː], flat affect, and eccentric [ks] behavior. Up to 50% of cases of impotence are related to psychogenic [dʒe] factors, e.g. affect disturbances [ɜː] like anxiety, anger, guilt [gɪlt], or fear. She presents with listlessness, easy fatigability[5] [iː], and sensations of coldness.

Use normal / (in)appropriate[6] / shallow[7] [ʃæloʊ]/ blunted[7] [ʌ] **affect** superficial [ɪʃ]/ labile[8] [eɪ]/ pseudobulbar[9] [ʌ] **affect** • **affect** memory / and emotion [oʊʃ] • **affective** changes in personality / response[10] / symptoms • **affective** episodes / psychosis[11] [koʊ]/ illness or disorder[12] • major [ɜː] / seasonal[13] [iː] (*abbr* SAD)/ episodic **affective disorder** • **listless** gaze[14] [geɪz] • mental / mild / noticeable **lethargy** • profound [aʊ]/ extreme **lethargy** • **lethargy and** irritability / anxiety / confusion[15] / stupor / coma

flacher Affekt, Affektabflachung, -verflachung
Teilnahms-, Lustlosigkeit[1] Lethargie[2] affektiv[3] sozialer Rückzug[4] leichte Ermüdbarkeit[5] inadäquater Affekt[6] flacher A.[7] Affektlabilität[8] pseudobulbärer Affekt, Zwangsweinen, -lachen[9] affektive Reaktion[10] affektive Psychose[11] affektive Störung[12] saisonale affektive Störung[13] teilnahmsloser Blick[14] Lethargie u. Verwirrtheit[15]

3

tremor [tremɚ] *n term*   *syn* **trembling** *n clin*, *rel* **titubation**[1] [eɪʃ] *n term rare*

involuntary rhythmic [ɪ], alternating [ɔː] shaking [eɪ] movements produced by repetitive patterns of muscle [mʌsl] contraction and relaxation

tremulous[2] [tremjələs] *adj term* • **tremulousness**[3] *n*

» Panic attacks typically present with trembling, visible as a fine tremor[4] of the outstretched hands, sweating [e], generalized motor weakness [iː] and dizziness[5]. Titubation is a gross [oʊ] tremor of the head and body and is a form of sustention tremor[6] evident on assuming the upright position and disappearing with recumbency[7] [ʌ]. Delirium tremens is a profoundly delirious [ɪə] state associated with tremulousness and agitation.

Use muscle[8] / ocular / rest(ing)[9] / passive[9] **tremor** • active or action[10] / cerebellar / essential[11] **tremor** • fine[4] / coarse or gross[12] / postural[6] **tremor** • ataxic / pill-rolling[13] / persistent **tremor** • intention[14] / sustention[6] / flapping[15] **tremor** • involuntary / fine[4] / chin[16] [tʃɪn] **trembling** • **trembling** with fear [fɪɚ]/ to shock[17] / of hands • truncal [ʌ] **titubation** • alcoholic / severe **tremulousness**

Tremor, Zittern
Wackeltremor, Titubation[1] zitternd, bebend[2] Zittrigkeit, Zittern[3] feinschlägiger Tremor[4] Schwindelgefühl[5] Haltetremor, posturaler Tremor[6] im Liegen[7] Muskelzittern[8] Ruhetremor[9] Aktionstremor[10] essentieller Tremor[11] grobschlägiger Tremor[12] Pillendrehertremor[13] Intentionstremor[14] Flapping tremor, Flattertremor, sog. Flügelschlagen, Asterixis[15] Kinnzittern[16] Zittern vor Schreck[17]

4

CLINICAL TERMS — Neurologic Findings

seizure [siːʒɚ] *n clin & term*   *syn* **convulsion** [kənvʌlʃən] *n clin,* **ictus** *n term rare*

(i) sudden occurrence [ɜː] or recurrence of a disease
(ii) paroxysmal¹ [ɪ] involuntary contractions of major muscle groups due to hyperexcitation of neurons [(j)ʊɚ] in the CNS, esp. epileptic seizures

convulsive² [ʌ] *adj term* • **(anti)convulsant³** *n* • **(inter/ post)ictal** *adj*

» Every case of suspected seizure disorder warrants⁴ [ɔː] an EEG. Partial seizures begin focally with a specific sensory, motor, or psychic [aɪ] aberration that reflects the affected part of the cerebral hemisphere where the seizure originates [ɪdʒ]. Infants of opioid-dependent mothers may present with tremors, a high-pitched⁵ cry, jitters⁶ [dʒɪtɚz], convulsions, and tachypnea [iː]. Syncope [sɪŋkəpiː] due to seizures is abrupt [ʌ] in onset and associated with muscular jerking⁷ or convulsions, incontinence, and tongue biting⁸ [tʌŋ baɪtɪŋ].

Use to have/cause/precipitate⁹ [sɪ] /develop/be accompanied by/control **seizures** • alcohol withdrawal [ɒː]/ (non)febrile¹⁰ / generalized **seizures** • hysterical / post-traumatic / neonatal¹¹ [eɪ] **seizures** • brief / prolonged / single / unprovoked¹² **seizures** • persistent / adult-onset / intractable¹³ **seizures** • convulsive¹⁴ / epileptic / grand mal / (multi)focal¹⁵ **seizures** • temporal lobe / psychomotor / (minor/ major) motor **seizures** • tonic-clonic¹⁶ / myoclonic [aɪ]/ akinetic / absence¹⁷ **seizures** • hemi/ pseudo**seizure** [suːd-]• **seizure** episodes /-like disorder / threshold¹⁸ • **seizure** activity / recurrence¹⁹ [ɜː]/-free²⁰ / frequency²¹ • childhood febrile **convulsion** • **convulsive** movements / jerking²² / motor activity • **convulsive** status [eɪ] epilepticus / shock therapy • **ictal** phase [feɪz]/ patterns • interictal period²³ / behavior • **postictal** state / confusion [juːʒ]/ paralysis [pəræləsɪs] • **postictal** coma / aphasia²⁴ [eɪ]/ EEG

(i) (plötzlicher) (Krampf)anfall
(ii) epileptischer Anfall, Iktus
anfallsartig¹ krampfartig² Antikonvulsivum, Antiepileptikum³ erfordert⁴ schrill⁵ Zittern⁶ Muskelzuckungen⁷ Zungenbiss⁸ Anfälle auslösen⁹ Fieberkrämpfe¹⁰ Neugeborenenkrämpfe¹¹ Spontananfälle, A. ohne Auslöser¹² therapierefraktäre A.¹³ Krampfanfälle¹⁴ fokale Anfälle¹⁵ tonisch-klonische Krämpfe/ Anfälle¹⁶ Absence-Anfälle¹⁷ Krampfschwelle¹⁸ rezidivierende Anfälle¹⁹ anfallsfrei²⁰ Anfallshäufigkeit²¹ ruckartige Muskelzuckungen²² interiktale Periode, anfallsfreies Intervall²³ postiktale Aphasie²⁴

5

vertigo [vɜːrtɪɡoʊ] *n term*   *sim* **dizziness¹, giddiness¹** *n clin* → U103-13

abnormal spinning sensation either of oneself or of external objects whirling² [ɜː] about in any plane [eɪ]

(non)vertiginous³ [ɪdʒ] *adj term* • **dizzy⁴** [dɪzɪ] *adj clin* • **giddy⁴** [ɡɪdi] *adj*

» Bed rest may help reduce the severity of acute vertigo. Dizziness, light-headedness⁵, vertigo, tinnitus, and dimmed vision⁶ or syncope occur frequently in patients with hypertension. The first attack of vertigo⁷ was associated with nausea⁸ [ɔː] and vomiting.

Use to experience/produce **vertigo** • subjective / objective / central / epileptic **vertigo** • visual [ɪʒ] or ocular⁹ / organic / vestibular¹⁰ **vertigo** • rotatory or spinning¹¹ / positional [ɪʃ] or postural¹² / height¹³ [haɪt] **vertigo** • intermittent / continuous¹⁴ / mild / episodic¹⁵ **vertigo** • spell or bout⁷ [aʊ]/ severity [e]/ absence **of vertigo** • control / relief [iː] **of vertigo** • **vertiginous** patient / episode⁷ / attack⁷ • **vertiginous** imbalance / ataxia • **nonvertiginous** dizziness • to feel **dizzy** • **dizzy** patient / sensation¹⁶ / spell⁷ • sense of¹⁶ / paroxysmal¹⁵ [ksɪ]/ persisting¹⁴ **dizziness** • postural¹² / whirling¹¹ **dizziness** • **giddy** euphoria [juːfɔːrɪə]

Schwindel, Vertigo
Schwindelgefühl, -anfall, Benommenheit¹ sich drehend² schwindlig, vertiginös³ benommen, schwindlig⁴ Benommenheit⁵ verschwommenes Sehen⁶ Schwindelanfall⁷ Übelkeit⁸ visueller Schwindel, Vertigo ocularis⁹ Vestibularisschwindel¹⁰ Drehschwindel¹¹ Lage-, Lagerungsschwindel¹² Höhenschwindel¹³ Dauerschwindel¹⁴ Anfallschwindel¹⁵ Schwindelgefühl¹⁶

6

neurologic deficits *n pl*   *rel* **paresis¹** [iː]**, paralysis²** [æ]**, palsy²** [ɔː] *n term*

symptoms or signs of impaired [eɚ] nerve function that may range from paresthesias [iːʒ], sensory impairment, memory loss, motor weakness, dysarthria, cranial [eɪ] nerve palsies to complete paralysis

hemiparesis *n term* • **paretic** [e] *adj* • **paralytic³** [ɪ] *adj* • **paralyze** *v* • **palsied⁴** *adj term* • **-plegia** [-pliːdʒ(ɪ)ə]**, -plegic** *comb* → U135-11

» Neurologic deficit involving S2-4 is particularly significant. Total palsy of the oculomotor nerve causes ptosis [toʊsɪs] and a dilated pupil [juː]. Neck stiffness⁵ may be accompanied by focal findings such as cranial nerve palsies, ataxia, or hemiparesis. Asymmetric flaccid [(k)s] limb paralyses⁶ without sensory loss in a child with an acute febrile illness suggests poliomyelitis.

Use focal / (in)complete / long-term / full **neurologic deficits** • ischemic [kiː]/ residual⁷ / rapidly evolving **neurologic deficits** • progressive / disabling⁸ [eɪ]/ permanent [ɜː] **neurologic deficits** • sensory / (lower) motor⁹ (neuron) **deficits** • **neurologic(al)** abnormalities / disturbance¹⁰ [ɜː]/ impairment [eɚ]/ footdrop¹¹ • spastic / sympathetic / general¹² **paresis** • oculomotor (nerve) / gaze [eɪ]/ limb [lɪm]/ tongue **paresis** • respiratory¹³ / bladder¹⁴ / vocal cord¹⁵ / neuromuscular **paralysis** • sensory / partial / symmetric / (ascending) [se] motor¹⁶ **paralysis** • bilateral / tick-bite¹⁷ / sleep¹⁸ **paralysis** • facial¹⁹ [eɪʃ]/ cerebral (*abbr* CP)/ (pseudo)bulbar²⁰ [suːdoʊ-]/ Bell's **palsy** • **paralytic** bladder¹⁴ / ileus / polio(myelitis) [aɪ]/ strabismus²¹ • **palsied** muscle / child • hemi/ di/ para/ quadri²²/ ophthalmo**plegia** • para/ gastro/ ophthalmo/ quadri**paresis** • acute / motor / contralateral / right **hemiparesis** • facial²³ **diplegia**

neurologische Ausfälle
Parese, unvollständige Lähmung¹ Paralyse, (vollst.) Lähmung² gelähmt, Lähmungs-, paralytisch³ gelähmt⁴ Nackensteifigkeit⁵ schlaffe Lähmung d. Extremitäten⁶ Restdefizite, neurolog. Residuen⁷ funktionell beeinträchtigende neurolog. Ausfälle⁸ motor. Ausfälle⁹ neurolog. Störung¹⁰ neurolog. bedingter Spitzfuß¹¹ progressive Paralyse¹² Atemlähmung¹³ Blasenlähmung¹⁴ Stimmbandlähmung¹⁵ aufsteigende Muskellähmung¹⁶ Zeckenlähmung, -paralyse¹⁷ Schlaflähmung¹⁸ Fazialislähmung¹⁹ (Pseudo)bulbärparalyse²⁰ Lähmungsschielen, Strabismus paralyticus²¹ Quadri-, Tetraplegie, vollst. Lähmung aller 4 Extremitäten²² Diplegia facialis, Lähmung beider Gesichtshälften²³

7

Neurologic Findings

CLINICAL TERMS 501

ataxia [ətǽksɪə] *n term*   *syn* **incoordination** *n clin* → U31-19f
rel **cerebellar gait**[1] [eɪ] *n term* → U65-2

impaired ability to coordinate voluntary movements manifesting as staggering gait[2] [eɪ] and postural imbalance[3], unclear speech, blurred [ɜː] vision[4], altered hand coordination, or tremor with movement

ataxic *or* **atactic**[5] *adj term* • **coordination** *n clin* • (**un**/ **dys**)**coordinated** *adj*

» Spastic paraparesis and sensory ataxia[6] were detected on neurologic examination. Ataxic gait[7], muscular weakness [iː], incoordination, intention tremor and other signs of cerebellar dysfunction followed, which produced unsteadiness[8] [e] with rapid movements. Coordination can be further tested with finger-to-nose or knee-to-shin maneuvers [uː].

Use hereditary / autosomal recessive [se]/ acquired [əkwaɪəd]/ chronic progressive **ataxia** • spinocerebellar[9] [aɪ] (*abbr* SCA)/ optic / oculomotor **ataxia** • truncal[10] [ʌ]/ extremity / gait[11] **ataxia** • spastic / vertiginous [ɪdʒ]/ static[12] **ataxia** • symmetrical / sensory[6] / Friedreich's[13] **ataxia** • **ataxia**-telangiectasia [eɪʒ] • **ataxic** signs / syndrome [ɪ]/ weakness • **ataxic** gait[7] / speech / aphasia[14] / tremor • festinating[15] **gait** • **gait** disorder[16] / disturbance[16] [ɜː]/ impairment[16] / unsteadiness[17] • muscular / limb / visuomotor **coordination** • hand-eye / fine motor[18] / reflex **coordination** • impaired / poor / proper[19] **coordination** • **coordination and strength** / equilibrium[20] [ɪ] • neuromuscular [ʌsk]/ motor **incoordination**

Ataxie, Koordinationsstörung
zerebellarer Gang[1] schwankender Gang[2] Gleichgewichtsstörungen[3] verschwommenes Sehen[4] unkoordiniert, ataktisch[5] sensorische Ataxie[6] ataktischer Gang[7] Unsicherheit[8] spinozerebellare Ataxie[9] Rumpfataxie[10] Gangataxie[11] Standataxie[12] Friedreich-A., spinozerebellare Heredoataxie[13] Broca-, motor. Aphasie[14] Trippelgang[15] Gangstörung[16] Gangunsicherheit[17] feinmotor. Koordination[18] richtige Koordination[19] Koordination u. Gleichgewicht[20]

8

apraxia [eɪprǽksɪə] *n term*

sim **dyspraxia**[1] [ɪ] *n, rel* **agraphia**[2], **alexia**[3] *n term*

loss of the ability to manipulate familiar objects and execute purposeful movements that is not attributable to pyramidal, extrapyramidal, cerebellar, or sensory impairment or failure to understand the task

apraxic *or* **apractic**[4] *adj term* • **dyslexia** *n* • **dyslexic**[5] *adj* & *n* • **-praxia** *comb*

» Buccofacial [ʌ] apraxia[6] involves apraxic deficits in movements of the face and mouth. Abnormalities of higher cortical function—e.g. aphasia, apraxia, dyslexia, dysgraphia, agnosia [oʊʒ‖z], left-right disorientation, and unilateral neglect[7]—are commonly seen. Dyspraxia and developmental maladroitness[8] [ɔɪ] should also be considered if writing problems exist.

Use motor *or* cortical / ideational[9] [eɪʃ]/ limb-kinetic[10] / ideomotor[11] **apraxia** • unilateral / left body / construction(al)[12] [ʌ]/ dressing[13] **apraxia** • **apraxic** patient / deficits / gait disturbance • speech / dressing **dyspraxia** • developmental **dyslexia** • echo[14] [ekoʊprǽksɪə] / neura/ para**praxia**

Apraxie
Dyspraxie, leichte Apraxie[1] Agrafie, Schreibunfähigkeit[2] Alexie, Leseunfähigkeit[3] apraktisch[4] legasthenisch; Legastheniker(in)[5] Gesichtsapraxie[6] einseitige Vernachlässigung[7] Ungeschicklichkeit[8] ideatorische Apraxie[9] gliedkinet. A.[10] ideomotor. Apraxie[11] konstruktive A.[12] Ankleideapraxie[13] Echopraxie, -kinese, Nachahmung v. Bewegungen[14]

9

dysarthria [dɪsɑːrθrɪə] *n term* → U66-9

sim **aphasia**[1] [əfeɪʒ(ɪ)ə], **dysphasia**[2] *n term*

slurred [ɜː] speech[3] (poorly articulated) due to incoordination, spasticity [ɪs], or paralysis [pərǽlɪsɪs] of the muscles of speech [spiːtʃ]

dysarthric[4] *adj term* • **aphasic** [əfeɪzɪk] *adj* • **paraphasia**[5] [pǽrəfeɪʒ(ɪ)ə] *n*

» Dysarthria and dysphagia[6] [eɪdʒ] are due to involvement of brainstem nuclei [aɪ] and pathways. Speech is labored[7] [eɪ], dysarthric, and interrupted by many word-finding pauses [ɔː]. Anomic aphasia[8] is the single most common language disturbance seen in head trauma [ɔː] and metabolic encephalopathy. Her symptoms include facial weakness, dysphagia, dysphonia[9], difficulty in chewing [uː], and inability to swallow [ɔː] or expel saliva [aɪ].

Use cerebellar / spastic / paroxysmal / stuttering[10] [ʌ]/ mild / prominent **dysarthria** • conduction[11] [ʌ]/ fluent transcortical *or* transcortical sensory[12] **aphasia** • non-fluent transcortical *or* transcortical motor[13] / amnestic[8] **aphasia** • global[14] / primary progressive / receptive [se] *or* sensory *or* Wernicke's[15] **aphasia** • expressive *or* motor *or* Broca's[16] / postictal **aphasia** • expressive **dysphasia** • semantic[17] / phonemic[18] [iː] **paraphasia** • **paraphasic** errors

Dysarthrie, Artikulationsstörung
Aphasie[1] Dysphasie[2] verwaschene Sprache[3] schlecht artikuliert, dysarthrisch[4] Paraphasie[5] Dysphagie, Schluckstörung[6] angestrengt[7] Wortfindungsstörung, Wortamnesie[8] Dysphonie, Stimmstörung[9] Stottern[10] Leitungsaphasie[11] transkortikal-sensorische A.[12] transkortikal-motor. A.[13] globale A.[14] Wernicke-, sensorische A.[15] Broca-, motor. A.[16] semant. Paraphasie[17] phonematische P.[18]

10

CLINICAL TERMS

diplopia [dɪploʊpɪə] *n term*   *syn* **double vision** [dʌbl vɪʒ°n] *n clin* → U59-6ff
    rel **gaze palsy**¹ [geɪz pɔːlzi], **scotoma**² [skətoʊmə] *n term*
impaired vision in which a single object is perceived [siː] as two objects
    hemianopia³ [hemɪənoʊpɪə] *n term* • **-op(s)ia** *comb* • **visual** [vɪʒʊəl] *adj*
» Clarify whether diplopia persists in either eye after covering the fellow eye⁴. Her cardinal symptoms are lid retraction, conjunctival [aɪ] injection, restriction of gaze [geɪz], diplopia, and visual loss from optic nerve compression.
Use to cause/alleviate [iː]/correct **diplopia** • monocular⁵ / binocular⁶ / horizontal / vertical **diplopia** • ampho⁶/ mono**diplopia**⁵ • blurred [ɜː] *or* hazy⁷ [eɪ]/ foggy [ɒː] *or* dim⁷ / yellow⁸ / impaired **vision** • **vision** blurring⁷ / defect [iː]/ loss / testing • conjugate⁹ [kɒːndʒəɡət]/ supranuclear [uː] **gaze palsy** • **gaze** paresis¹ / preference / deficit • **visual** field defect / changes / distortion¹⁰ / loss • ambly/ ametr/ esotr/ exot**ropia** • hyper/ presby/ my**opia** [maɪoʊpɪə] • chromat/ phot/ micr/ macr**opsia** • bilateral / central / arcuate¹¹ **scotoma** • ring¹² / scintillating¹³ [sɪnt-] **scotoma**

nystagmus [nɪstæɡməs] *n term*   *syn* **uncontrolled eye movements** *n clin*
involuntary rhythmical [ɪ] oscillation [ɒːsɪ-] of one or both eyes from side to side, up and down, or rotary
    nystagmic¹ *adj term* • **nystagmoid**² *adj* • **nystagmography**³ [ɒː] *n*
» The pattern of nystagmus may vary [veəri] with gaze position [ɪʃ]. Horizontal nystagmus is best assessed⁴ at 45° and not at extreme lateral gaze⁵. Jerk [dʒɜːrk] nystagmus⁶, which is characterized by a slow drift off the target followed by a fast corrective saccade⁷ [ɑː], can be downbeat, upbeat [iː], horizontal (left or right), and torsional [tɔːrʃən°l].
Use to develop/be accompanied by/produce⁸/reveal [iː] **nystagmus** • physiologic⁹ / gaze evoked¹⁰ [oʊ]/ congenital [dʒe] **nystagmus** • pendular¹¹ / symmetric / disconjugate¹² / bilateral **nystagmus** • horizontal / lateral gaze / downbeat¹³ **nystagmus** • vertical [ɜː]/ rotary¹⁴ **nystagmus** • opticokinetic¹⁵ / vestibular¹⁶ / positional¹⁷ [ɪʃ] **nystagmus** • rapid / fine¹⁸ / mild / jerk⁶ / latent [eɪ] **nystagmus** • pattern / degree¹⁹ **of nystagmus** • **nystagmoid** movement / jerk • **nystagmic** response • **electronystagmography**²⁰ (*abbr* ENG)

tinnitus [tɪnɪ‖tɪnaɪtəs] *n term*   *rel* **hearing** [hɪɚɪŋ] **loss**¹, *abbr* **HL**,
    deafness² [e] *n clin* → U61-9
subjective sensation of constant or intermittent ringing, humming [ʌ], or buzzing [ʌ] noises in the ears
» Vertebral artery spasm following whiplash injury³ may cause tinnitus, dizziness, and vertigo. Unilateral deafness and tinnitus indicate cochlear [k] nerve involvement.
Use to have/experience/cause/aggravate⁴ **tinnitus** • pulsatile⁵ [ʌ]/ tonal / high-pitched⁶ **tinnitus** • high-frequency⁶ / intermittent **tinnitus** • **tinnitus** sufferer [ʌ]/ suppression / masker⁷ • acute / complete / bilateral **hearing loss** • (a)symmetric / mild / profound [aʊ] degree [iː] of⁸ **hearing loss** • sensory / neural [(j)ʊɚ]/ noise-induced⁹ / conductive¹⁰ [ʌ] **hearing loss** • isolated [aɪ]/ transient / sudden¹¹ **deafness** • partial [ʃ]/ permanent / high-tone **deafness** • 8ᵗʰ nerve [ɜː]/ conduction¹⁰ / labyrinthine¹² / pure [pjʊɚ] word¹³ **deafness**

neuralgia [n(j)ʊrældʒ(ɪ)ə] *n term*   *syn* **nerve pain** *n clin, rel* **neuropathy**¹ *n term*
sharp pain that is throbbing or stabbing² in character in the course or distribution³ of one or more nerves
    neuralgic⁴ *adj term* → U104-21 • **neuropathic** *adj* • **neur(o)-** *comb*
» Detection of a sensory abnormality or cranial nerve dysfunction rules out⁵ trigeminal [aɪdʒe] neuralgia as the cause of pain. Tricyclics⁶ [saɪ] are of particular value in the management of neuropathic pains such as painful diabetic [e] neuropathy and postherpetic neuralgia⁷.
Use cranial [eɪ]/ facial [eɪʃ] **neuralgia** • glossopharyngeal [dʒ]/ trigeminal⁸ / postoperative **neuralgia** • intercostal⁹ / zoster-associated⁷ **neuralgia** • **neuralgic** pain • **neuropathic** pain states¹⁰ / arthropathy¹¹ / deficit / bowel [aʊ] / **neuropathic** bladder / voiding dysfunction¹² / ulcer [ʌ]/ joint disease¹¹ • cranial / optic / autonomic / acute motor axonal (*abbr* AMAN) **neuropathy** • brachial [eɪk] plexus / peripheral **neuropathy** • (multi)focal / motor / sensory / compression *or* entrapment¹³ **neuropathy** • ischemic [kiː]/ demyelinating¹⁴ [aɪ]/ traumatic / toxic **neuropathy** • poly(radiculo)/ mono/ adrenomyelo**neuropathy** • **neuro**pathology / pathogenesis

---

Diplopie, Doppeltsehen
Blicklähmung¹ Skotom, Gesichtsfeldausfall² Hemianopsie, Halbseitenblindheit³ kontralaterales Auge, Gegenauge⁴ monokulare Diplopie⁵ binokulare Diplopie⁶ verschwommenes Sehen⁷ Gelbsehen, Xanthopsie⁸ konjugierte Blicklähmung⁹ visuelle Verzerrung¹⁰ bogenförmiges Skotom, Bjerrum-Skotom¹¹ Ringskotom¹² Flimmerskotom¹³

11

Nystagmus, Augenzittern
nystagtisch¹ nystagmusartig² Nystagmografie³ festgestellt⁴ extrem seitl. Blickrichtung⁵ Rucknystagmus⁶ Sakkade⁷ Nystagmus hervorrufen⁸ physiologischer Nystagmus⁹ Blick(richtungs)nystagmus¹⁰ Pendelnystagmus¹¹ dissoziierter Nystagmus¹² Down-beat-N.¹³ Drehnystagmus, rotatorischer N.¹⁴ optokinet. N.¹⁵ vestibulärer N.¹⁶ Lagenystagmus¹⁷ feinschlägiger N.¹⁸ Nystagmusintensität¹⁹ Elektronystagmografie²⁰

12

Tinnitus aurium, Ohrenklingen, -sausen, Ohrgeräusch
Hörverlust, -störung, Schwerhörigkeit¹ Schwerhörigkeit, Taubheit² Schleudertrauma³ d. Tinnitus verstärken⁴ pulssynchrone Ohrgeräusche⁵ hochfrequente/ pfeifende O.⁶ Tinnitus-Masker⁷ Schwerhörigkeitsgrad⁸ Lärmschwerhörigkeit⁹ Schallleitungsschwerhörigkeit¹⁰ Hörsturz¹¹ Innenohrschwerhörigkeit¹² Worttaubheit¹³

13

Neuralgie, Nervenschmerz
Neuropathie, Nervenleiden¹ stechend² Versorgungsgebiet³ neuralgisch⁴ schließt... aus⁵ trizykl. Antidepressiva⁶ Zosterneuralgie⁷ Trigeminusneuralgie⁸ Interkostalneuralgie⁹ neurogene Schmerzzustände¹⁰ Arthropathia neuropathica¹¹ neurogene Blasenentleerungsstörung¹² Kompressions-, Engpassneuropathie¹³ Entmarkungsneuropathie, demyelinisierende Neuropathie¹⁴

14

Neurologic Findings | CLINICAL TERMS 503

impingement [-pɪndʒ-] n term   syn **nerve entrapment** or **encroachment** [outʃ] n

narrowing[1] and compression of nerves, tendons or organs at critical sites due to pathologic processes

impinge/ encroach (on/ upon)[2] v • **impinging** adj • **entrap**[3] v

» A torn rotator cuff[4] [ʌ] is a potential outcome of shoulder impingement. Misalignment[5] [aɪ] of the joint surfaces may cause subluxation and capsular and synovial impingement with eventual destruction of joint cartilage. Impingement between the lateral malleolus and talus of the anterior talofibular ligament resulted in persistent synovitis. Entrapment of the nerve at the wrist (carpal tunnel [ʌ] syndrome[6]) may be secondary to overuse[7] of the wrist.

Use to cause/be due to **impingement** • nerve root[8] [uː]/ osseous **impingement** • osteoarthritic [ɪ]/ subacromial / femoroacetabular **impingement** • **impingement** lesion[9] [iː]/ sign / syndrome[10] / surgery • **impingement** of the rotator cuff / on tendons • cranial nerve / muscle / vascular **entrapment** • **entrapment** neuropathy[11] • capsular / nerve root[8] / soft tissue **encroachment** • **to impinge on** a nerve / the brain stem[12] / neighboring structures • **to encroach on** the spinal canal[13] / vascular lumen • **impinging** soft tissue

Engpasssyndrom, Impingement

Einengung[1] einengen, drücken (auf)[2] einklemmen[3] Rotatorenmanschettenruptur[4] Fehlstellung[5] Karpaltunnelsyndrom[6] Überbeanspruchung[7] eingeklemmte/ eingeengte Nervenwurzel[8] Engpassgeschehen[9] Impingement-/ Engpass-Syndrom[10] Nervenkompressionssyndrom[11] auf d. Hirnstamm drücken[12] auf den Wirbelkanal drücken[13]

15

migraine [maɪɡreɪn‖miː] n term & clin   rel **cluster** [ʌ] **headache**[1] n term

a complex of symptoms occurring [ɜː] periodically which are characterized by headache (usually unilateral), vertigo, nausea [ɔː] and vomiting, photophobia[2] [ou], and scintillating [sɪntɪ-] appearances of light

migrainous[3] [aɪ] adj term • **migraineur**[4] [miːɡrənɜːr] n → U104-4

» Photophobia is prominent with migraine headache but occurs also with meningitis [dʒaɪ]. Rhinorrhea [iː] and lacrimation during headache typify the cluster variant of migraine and are ipsilateral to the pain. Cluster headaches[1] frequently awaken patients from sleep. Myalgia [maɪældʒ(ɪ)ə] of posterior neck muscles often accompanies tension [tenʃ⁽ə⁾n] headaches[5].

Use to precipitate/mimic[6]/alleviate [iː] or ameliorate [iː] /be associated with **migraine** • **migraine**(-like) headache(s) [eɪk]/ attacks[7] • **migraine** sufferer[4] [ʌ]/ pattern / with aura[8] [ɔːrə] • classic / common / ophthalmoplegic [iːdʒ] **migraine** • cortical / basilar[9] / ophthalmic[10] **migraine** • familial hemiplegic[11] / disabling [eɪ]/ childhood **migraine** • acute / chronic / daily / episodic / morning / mild / dull[12] [ʌ] **headache** • intense / throbbing[13] [ɒː]/ persistent / intractable **headache** • frontal / occipital [ksɪ]/ generalized / stress-related[14] **headache** • tension[5] / vascular / posttraumatic / brain tumor **headache** • **headache** and neck stiffness / eyestrain[15] [eɪ]/ dizziness / malaise[16] [məleɪz] • **headache** and flushing [ʌ]/ chills[17] [tʃ]/ disorientation / vomiting • **migrainous** neuralgia[1] / episodes[7] / syndrome [ɪ]

Migräne

Bing-Horton-Syndrom/ -Neuralgie, Erythroprosopalgie, Histaminkopfschmerz, cluster headache[1] Lichtscheu[2] migräneartig, Migräne-[3] Migräne-Patient(in)[4] Spannungskopfschmerz[5] einer Migräne ähnlich sein[6] Migräneanfälle[7] Migräne m. Aura[8] Basilarismigräne[9] Migraine ophthalmique, Hemicrania ophthalmica[10] familiäre hemiplegische M.[11] dumpfer Kopfschmerz[12] pochende Kopfschmerzen[13] stressbedingte Kopfschmerzen[14] Kopfschmerzen u. Überanstrengung d. Augen[15] Kopfschmerzen u. allgem. Unwohlbefinden[16] Kopfschmerzen u. Schüttelfrost[17]

16

ptosis [tousɪs] n term, pl **-ses**   syn **droop** [uː] n clin & jar, rel **prolapse**[1] n term

(i) drooping of the upper eyelid often caused by paralysis of the 3rd cranial nerve
(ii) sagging of an organ

ptotic [tɒːtɪk] adj term • **proptosis**[2] n • **-ptosis** comb •
droop[3] v clin • **drooping** adj & n → U89-22

» The patient presented with amaurosis fugax, diplopia, scotomata, ptosis, and vision blurring [ɜː]. Neurologic causes of ptosis include Horner's syndrome and third nerve palsy [ɔː]. Proptosis is an abnormal forward protrusion [uː] of one or both eyes.

Use neurogenic / lid[4] / unilateral / partial **ptosis** • complete / fluctuating [ʌ]/ congenital[5] **ptosis** • **ptosis** of the eyelid[4] • lip **drooping** • facial **droop** • **ptotic** kidney[6] • painless / mild / massive **proptosis** • blepharo[4]/ nephro[6]/ glosso**ptosis**

**(i) Ptosis, Ptose, Herabhängen des Oberlids
(ii) Senkung**

Vorfall, Prolaps[1] Exophthalmus, Protrusio bulbi[2] (schlaff) herab-/ herunterhängen[3] Ptosis[4] Ptosis congenita[5] Nephroptose, Senkniere[6]

17

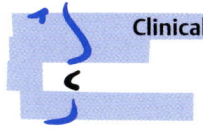

Clinical Phrases

Have you noticed any weakness or rigidity in your limbs? Hatten Sie jemals Muskelsteifigkeit oder ein Schwächegefühl in den Armen oder Beinen? • Do you sometimes see spots in front of your eyes? Sehen Sie manchmal Punkte vor den Augen? • When did you first experience these dizzy spells? Wann hatten Sie erstmals solche Schwindelanfälle? • On physical examination she was found slightly confused. Bei der klinischen Untersuchung wirkte sie leicht verwirrt. • His deep tendon reflexes are slightly diminished. Die Sehnenreflexe sind etwas abgeschwächt. • There were no ocular symptoms and the fundi appeared normal. Es wurden keine Sehstörungen festgestellt und der Augenhintergrund war unauffällig. • The patient lapsed into unconsciousness for a short time but told her husband she felt alright when she came out of it. Die Patientin verlor kurz das Bewusstsein, doch als sie wieder zu sich kam, sagte sie zu ihrem Mann, es sei alles in Ordnung. • Muscle tone was increased but the cranial nerves were unremarkable. Der Muskeltonus war erhöht, doch die Hirnnerven waren unauffällig.

Unit 114 Skin Lesions

Related Units: 5 Injuries, 25 Build & Appearance, 56 The Skin, 103 Clinical Symptoms, 108 Clinical Signs, 89 Pathology, 95 Childhood Diseases, 98 Tumor Types

eczema [eksə‖ıgzi:mə] *n term*

sim **dermatitis**[1] [dɜːrmətaıtıs] *n term*

inflammatory condition of the skin often accompanied by sensations of itching[2] and burning, typically erythematous, edematous [iː], papular, vesicular, and crusting[3]; followed often by lichenification [aık] and scaling[4] [eı] and occasionally by duskiness[5] [ʌ] of the erythema and hyperpigmentation

eczematous[6] [ıgzemət̬ᵊs] *adj term* • **eczematoid**[7] *adj* • **derma-** *comb*

» As the child grows older, the eczema tends to *wax and wane*[8] [weın], sometimes disappearing completely for months. Psoriasis [səraıəsıs] should be distinguished from seborrheic [iː] dermatitis and eczema.

Use localized / hand / flexural[9] / weeping[10] [iː]/ atopic[11] [eı] **eczema** • infantile or childhood[12] / adolescent [es]/ dyshidrotic [dıshaı-]/ allergic [ɜː] **eczema** • impetiginous[13] [ıdʒ]/ asteatotic [æstıə-] **eczema** • nummular[14] [ʌ]/ contact[15] / seborrheic[16] **eczema** • **eczema**-like rash / herpeticum • **eczematous** skin / eruption / plaque [plæk] • **eczematoid** skin rash[17]/ lesion [iːʒ] / contact[15] / seborrheic[16] **dermatitis** • **derma**tologic /tologist /tome /tosis[18] /tomyositis [-maıəsaıtıs]

---

exanthem(a) [eksænθəm‖egzænθi:mə] *n term*

syn **rash** [ræʃ],
eruption [ırʌpʃᵊn] *n clin*
rel **erythema**[1] [erəθi:mə] *n term*

a skin lesion that may have specific features [fiːtʃɚz] of an infectious disease

exanthematous[2] [e] *adj term* • **(pre)eruptive** [ʌ] *adj* • **erythematous** [e‖iː] *adj*

» Acute onset of a symmetrical erythematous skin eruption associated with systemic signs may suggest a drug hypersensitivity rash, viral [aı] exanthem, or *scarlet fever*[3] [iː]. After several days of itching and burning [ɜː] in a dermatomal distribution a vesicular eruption appears consisting of clear vesicles on an erythematous base.

Use infectious / febrile / viral / measles [iː]/ childhood / truncal[4] [ʌ] **exanthem** • **exanthematous** disease / rash • **exanthema** subitum[5] • cutaneous or skin[6] / drug[7] / generalized **eruption** • exudative [uː]/ creeping[8] [iː]/ serpiginous[9] [ıdʒ] **eruption** • nodular / maculopapular[10] / acne-like **eruption** • scaly[11] / petechial [ek]/ blistering[12] / pustular [ʌ] **eruption** • herpetic / urticarial[13] [ɜːrtı-]/ pruritic [ı]/ phototoxic / chronic **eruption** • **eruptive** nodule / stage / psoriasis[14] / xanthoma [zænθ-] • **erythematous** skin / exanthema / papules / patches / halo[15]

---

pigmented mole [oʊ] *n term* → U25-19

syn **pigmented nevus** *n term, pl* **nevi** [niːvaı]

benign pigmented groups of raised[1] [eı] or level melanocytes either present at birth or arising early in life

pigment[2] *n & v* • **pigmentary** *adj term* • **(hyper/ hypo/ re/ de)pigmentation**[3] *n*

» Intradermal nevi are the typical dome-shaped, sometimes pedunculated[4] [ʌ], fleshy to brownish pigmented moles that are characteristically seen in adults. In general, a benign mole is a small (< 5 mm), well-circumscribed [sɜːrkəm-] lesion with a well-defined [aı] border and a single shade of pigment from beige [beıʒ] or pink to dark brown.

Use (giant) [dʒaıᵊnt] hairy[5] / flat / benign [-aın]/ atypical[6] **mole** • bathing [eı] trunk[7] / melanocytic [sı]/ epidermal **nevus** • vascular / junctional[8] [dʒʌ]/ dysplastic[6] / spider[9] **nevus** • compound / blue[10] **nevus** • **nevus** cells / comedonicus / araneus[9] [eı]/ flammeus[11] / needle / puncture[12] [ʌ] / suture [suːtʃɚ] **marks** • scratch / pinch[13] [tʃ]/ birth[14] [ɜː]/ bluish **marks** • **pigmentary** changes / disorder / retinopathy[15] • darkly / deeply or heavily[16] [e] **pigmented** • skin / hair / nipple[17] / brownish / increased **pigmentation** • altered [ɒː]/ melanin / stasis [eı]/ cafe au lait[18] **pigmentation** • degree / lack[19] *of* **pigmentation** • secondary / postinflammatory / diffuse / generalized **hyperpigmentation**

Ekzem, Ekzema

Hautentzündung, Dermatitis[1] Jucken, Juckreiz[2] krustenbildend, krustös[3] Schuppung[4] livide Verfärbung[5] ekzematös, exzematisiert[6] ekzemartig[7] kommt u. vergeht[8] Ekzema flexurarum[9] nässendes Ekzem[10] atopisches/ endogenes E.[11] Kinderekzem, E. infantum[12] E. impetiginosum[13] nummuläres/ diskoides Ekzem[14] Kontaktekzem[15] seborrhoisches Ekzem[16] ekzemartiger Hautausschlag[17] Hautkrankheit, Dermatose[18]

1

Exanthem, Hautausschlag

Erythem(a), Hautrötung[1] exanthematös, -tisch[2] Scharlach[3] Exanthem am Rumpf[4] Dreitagefieberexanthem, Exanthema subitum, Roseola infantum[5] Hautausschlag[6] Arzneimittelexanthem[7] Hautmaulwurf, Larva migrans cutanea[8] geschlängeltes Exanthem[9] makulopapulöses Exanthem[10] schuppiges Exanthem[11] blasiges Exanthem[12] urtikarielles Exanthem[13] akute exanthematische Psoriasis guttata[14] geröteter Hof[15]

2

Pigmentmal, -fleck, (Mutter)mal, (Pigment)nävus, N. pigmentosus

erhaben[1] Farbstoff, Pigment; färben, pigmentieren[2] Depigmentierung[3] gestielt[4] behaarter Nävus, N. pilosus[5] dysplastischer N.[6] Schwimmhosennävus[7] Junktionsnävus[8] Stern-, Spinnennävus, N. araneus[9] blauer Nävus, N. coeruleus[10] Feuermal, Weinfleck, Nävus flammeus[11] Punktionsnarben[12] Kneifmale[13] Muttermale, Nävi[14] Retinopathia pigmentosa[15] stark pigmentiert[16] Mamillenpigmentierung[17] milchkaffeefarbene Pigmentflecken, Cafe-au-lait-Flecken[18] Pigmentmangel[19]

3

Skin Lesions

CLINICAL TERMS 505

vitiligo [vɪtəlaɪgoʊ] *n term*   *rel* **leukoderma¹** [luːk-],
   albinism², piebaldism³ [aɪ] *n term*

appearance of irregular patches of skin which are totally unpigmented due to destruction of melanocytes

vitiliginous⁴ [ɪdʒ] *adj term* • **albino⁵** [ælbaɪnoʊ] *n* • **piebald** [paɪbɔːld] *adj*

» In contrast to idiopathic vitiligo, melanoma-associated leukoderma often begins on the trunk, and its appearance should prompt⁶ a search for metastatic disease. Piebaldism is a localized hypomelanosis that is manifested by a white forelock⁷. Pigmentation does not occur in the skin of albinos because of a defect in melanin metabolism, nor in areas of vitiligo because of the absence of melanocytes. Vitiligo tends to cause pruritus in anogenital folds.

Use areas of⁸ / patchy / extensive / generalized⁹ **vitiligo** • vitiligo-like / chemical¹⁰ / melanoma-associated / syphilitic¹¹ **leukoderma** • pseudo**leukoderma**¹² [suːdoʊ-] • ocular¹³ / oculocutaneous¹⁴ (*abbr* OCA) **albinism** • **vitiliginous** areas⁸

Vitiligo, Weißfleckenkrankheit

Leukoderm¹ Albinismus² Piebaldismus³ vitiliginös⁴ Patient(in) m. Albinismus, Albino⁵ veranlassen⁶ Stirnlocke⁷ Vitiligoflecken⁸ generalisierte/ komplette Vitiligo⁹ durch Chemikalien verursachtes Leukoderm¹⁰ syphilit. Leukoderm, Halsband d. Venus¹¹ Pseudoleukoderm¹² okulärer Albinismus¹³ okulokutaner Albinismus¹⁴

4

lentigo [lentaɪ‖iːgoʊ] *n term, pl* **-gines** [lentɪdʒəniːz]   *syn* **liver spot** *n clin*
   rel **freckles** *n or* **ephelides¹** [efe‖iːlədiːz] *n term*

flat or brownish spot on the skin due to an increased number of melanocytes at the epidermo-dermal junction² in sun-exposed areas of middle-aged or elderly individuals, particularly the dorsa of the hands³

lentiginous⁴ [lentɪdʒənəs] *adj term* • **freckled⁵** *adj clin* • **freckling** *n* → U25-18

» Lentigines are darker, sparser⁶, and more scattered⁷ than freckles, and do not darken or multiply [ʌ] with sun exposure. Freckles first appear in young children, darken with ultraviolet exposure despite use of sunscreens, and fade⁸ [eɪ] with cessation [ses-] of sun exposure.

Use solar⁹ / atypical [ɪ] / juvenile [dʒuː]/ multiple¹⁰ **lentigines** • **lentigo** senilis¹¹ [ɪ]/ maligna (melanoma)¹² / juvenile¹ / senile⁹ / melanotic *or* Hutchinson's¹³ [ʌ]/ dark **freckle(s)** • multiple / axillary **freckle(s)** • acral [æ] **lentiginous** melanoma¹⁴

Lentigo, Linsen-, Leberfleck

Epheliden, Sommersprossen¹ dermoepidermale Junktionszone² Handrücken³ lentiginös⁴ sommersprossig⁵ weniger zahlreich⁶ verstreut⁷ blasser werden⁸ Leberflecken⁹ multiple Lentigines, Leopard-Syndrom¹⁰ Alterspigmentierungen, Lentigo senilis¹¹ Lentigo-maligna(-Melanom)¹² prämaligne Melanose¹³ akrolentiginöses Melanom¹⁴

5

comedo *n term, pl-* **-ones** [kɒːmɪdoʊniːz]   *syn* **blackhead** *n clin*
   rel **milium¹** [mɪliəm] *n term, pl* **-ia** *or* **whitehead¹** *n clin*

dilated opening of a hair follicle filled with keratin and sebum² [iː]

comedonal³ *adj term* • **microcomedo** *n* • **miliaria** [eə] *n* • **comedo-** comb

» Superficial acne [ækni] is characterized by comedones, either open (blackheads) or closed (whiteheads). Open comedones are the predominant clinical lesion in early adolescent acne. Intrafollicular hyperkeratosis leads to blockage of the pilosebaceous [eɪʃ] follicle with consequent formation of the comedo, composed of sebum, keratin, and microorganisms.

Use closed⁴ / open⁵ **comedo** • **comedo** extraction / extractor⁶ • acne / infected **comedones** • **comedonal** acne⁷ / component • **comedo**genic /carcinoma⁸ /-like • to extrude *or* remove⁹ / (un)inflamed [eɪ] **blackheads** • facial [eɪʃ]/ pigmented **milia** • colloid¹⁰ **milium**

Mitesser, Komedo, Comedo

Hautgrieß, Milium, Milie¹ Talg² von Komedonen ausgehend³ geschlossener Komedo⁴ offener Komedo⁵ Komedonenquetscher⁶ Acne comedonica⁷ Komedokarzinom⁸ Mitesser entfernen⁹ Kolloidmilium, Pseudomilium colloidale¹⁰

6

(skin) scales [skeɪlz] *n*   *syn* **squames** [skweɪmz] *n term* → U56-20
   rel **dandruff¹** [dændrəf], **scurf¹** [ɜː] *n clin*

dry, platelike flakes² [eɪ], usually composed of excessive or abnormally shed³ epithelial cells

scale (off)⁴ *v clin* • **scaling** *n* • **scaly⁵** *adj* • **scurfy⁵** *adj* • **squamous⁶** [eɪ] *adj*

» The lesion may be covered by dry, horny, adherent [ɪɚ] scales. Scales are typically found in seborrhea⁷ [iː], pityriasis⁸ [pɪtəraɪəsɪs], and psoriasis⁹ [s]. Patients with pemphigus foliaceus [eɪʃ] rarely demonstrate intact blisters but rather exhibit shallow erosions associated with scale and crust formation.

Use epidermal [ɜː] / (greasy) [iː] scalp¹⁰ / thick / yellowish / silvery¹¹ / dry¹² **scales** • **dandruff** shampoo¹³ [uː] • **scale**-like • **scaling** of the scalp / disease • **squamous** epithelium¹⁴ [iː]/ lesions

(Haut)schuppen

Kopfschuppen¹ Schuppen² abgestoßen, abgeschilfert³ (ab)schuppen, abschilfern⁴ schuppig, geschuppt⁵ schuppig, schuppenförmig, squamös⁶ Seborrhoe⁷ Pityriasis⁸ Schuppenflechte, Psoriasis⁹ (fettige) Kopfschuppen¹⁰ silbergraue Schuppen¹¹ trockene S.¹² Schuppenshampoo¹³ Plattenepithel, Epithelium squamosum¹⁴

7

CLINICAL TERMS — Skin Lesions

crust [krʌst] *n*   *sim* **scab¹** [skæb] *n*,
   rel **scar²** *n clin*, **eschar³** [eskɑːr] *n term* → U140-9

deposit of dried exudates or secretions, cellular debris⁴ and bacteria found on skin lesions

crust (over)⁵ *v clin* • **(en)crusted⁶** *adj* • **crusting** *adj & n* • **incrustation** *n term*

» Crusts are the result of an inadequate or inconsistent epithelial cell layer. Picking the crust⁷ covering an opened lesion [iː] may delay [eɪ] healing [iː] for several weeks and produce a pitted scar⁸. Crusting occurs [ɜː] in a wide variety [aɪ] of inflammatory [æ] and infectious diseases. These crusts heal without scarring⁹ [ɑː].

Use to produce or form¹⁰/clear away or remove¹¹ **crusts** • dry / dark / thick¹² / foul-smelling [aʊ] **crust** • honey-colored / serosanguineous / keratotic **crust** • **crust** formation¹³ • **encrusted** lesion • **crusted** surface / ulcer [ʌ]/ skin lesion¹⁴ • **crusted** plaque / eschar • **crusted** infection / impetigo [aɪ‖iː]/ scabies¹⁵ [skeɪbiːz] • chronic / purulent [jʊə]/ weeping [iː] and¹⁶ / oozing [uː] and¹⁶ **crusting**

macule *or* **macula** [mækjʊl‖lə] *n term*   *sim* **spot¹** [spɒt] *n clin* → U25-18f

small discolored² patch on the skin which is neither raised³ above nor depressed below the skin's surface

macular⁴ *adj term* • **maculo-** *comb* • **spotted⁴** *adj* • **spotty⁵** *adj clin*

» The rashes generally occur [ɜː] in crops⁶ as macules, papules, pustules [ʌ], or squamous lesions. Koplik's spots⁷ are tiny, grayish-white macules with red margins [dʒ] occurring during the late prodromal and early eruptive [ʌ] stages of measles [iː]. Should she use makeup to conceal [-siː] spots, scars and other skin blemishes?

Use depigmented / pink-red / tan⁸ / faint [eɪ] **macules** • blanching⁹ [ˈʃ]/ oval / facial [eɪʃ] **macules** • truncal [ʌ]/ widely scattered / circumscribed¹⁰ [aɪ]/ nontender¹¹ **macules** • **macular** erythema¹² / seborrhea / rash • flat / discolored / cafe au lait / rose / yellowish **spot** • purpuric [jʊə]/ cotton-wool¹³ / hypopigmented **spot** • **maculo-**papular¹⁴ • **spotted** fever¹⁵ [iː] • **spotty** distribution [juːʃ]

papule *or* **papula** [pæpjʊl‖lə] *n term*   *sim* **plaque¹**, **patch²** [pætʃ] *n clin & jar*

circumscribed [ɜː], small, solid elevation on the skin less than 1 cm in diameter [aɪæ]

papular *adj term* • **papulo-** *comb* • **papulation³** *n* • **plaquelike** [plæk] *adj*

» The lesions consist of dusky red⁴, well-localized, single or multiple plaques, 5-20 mm in diameter, usually on the face. In lichen planus a recurrent, pruritic, inflammatory eruption characterized by small discrete⁵ [iː] angular papules that may coalesce⁶ [-es] into rough [rʌf] scaly patches⁷ is often accompanied by oral lesions. Primary lesions may include papules, erythematous macules, and vesicles, which can coalesce to form patches and plaques.

Use moist / pinhead-sized⁸ / dome-shaped⁹ **papules** • flat-topped¹⁰ / bluish-red / pink **papules** • deep / painless / pruritic [ɪ]/ umbilicated¹¹ [ʌm-]/ erythematous **papules** • urticarial / hyperkeratotic / excoriated / scaly **papules** • facial / grouped¹² / confluent¹³ / discrete [iː]/ split **papules** • **papular** lesion / rash / eruption / mucinosis¹⁴ [mjuːs-] • **papular** urticaria [ɜːrt-]/ scaling disease • reddish / scaly / papulosquamous **plaque** • eczematous / herald¹⁵ / bluish-black **patch** • leukoplakic [luːkə-]/ shagreen¹⁶ / salmon¹⁷ [æ] **patch** • poorly demarcated¹⁸ [iː]/ discrete / circular / scaly / leathery [e] **patch** • **plaque**-like • **papulo**squamous eruptions /nodular /pustular /vesicular

wheal [ʰwiːl] *n term & clin*   *syn* **hive** [haɪv] *n clin & jar*
   rel **urticaria** [ɜːrtɪkeərɪə] *or* **nettle rash¹** *n term*

evanescent² [es] edematous urticarial lesion accompanied by intense itching that disappears within hours; produced by exposure to allergenic substances in susceptible³ [se] persons

» These well-circumscribed wheals with erythematous raised serpiginous borders and blanched centers may coalesce to become giant hives. For diagnosis of cold urticaria⁴, an ice cube is applied to the skin for 4-5 minutes, and as the skin rewarms a wheal appears.

Use to produce⁵/develop **a wheal** • skin or cutaneous / edematous [iː]/ erythematous **wheal** • urticarial / linear / blotchy⁶ [tʃ]/ pruritic **wheal** • **urticarial** eruption⁷/ plaque / papule / rash⁷ / vasculitis⁸ [aɪ] • to suffer / scattered / recurrent⁹ [ɜː] • **hives** • **wheal**(-and-flare) [fleə] reaction¹⁰

Kruste, Borke, Crusta
(Wund)schorf, Kruste¹ Narbe² Verbrennungs-, Ätzschorf³ Zelltrümmer⁴ verkrusten⁵ verkrustet, mit e. Kruste überzogen⁶ d. Kruste wegkratzen⁷ tiefe Narbe⁸ Narbenbildung⁹ e. Kruste bilden, verkrusten¹⁰ Krusten entfernen¹¹ dicke Kruste¹² Krustenbildung¹³ verkrustete Hautläsion¹⁴ Scabies crustosa¹⁵ nässend u. krustenbildend¹⁶

Makula, Macula, Fleck
Fleck, Pickel¹ verfärbt² erhaben, die Hautoberfläche überragend³ gefleckt, fleckig, makulös⁴ fleckig, voller Pickel⁵ gruppiert⁶ Koplik-Flecken⁷ pigmentierte Flecken⁸ auf Druck abblassende Flecken⁹ umschriebene Flecken¹⁰ nicht druckschmerzhafte Flecken¹¹ Roseola¹² Cotton-wool-Herd¹³ makulopapulös¹⁴ Fleckfieber, -typhus¹⁵

Papula, Papel
Plaque, flach erhabene (plattenförm.) Hautveränderung¹ Fleck, Plaque² Papelbildung³ livid⁴ einzelstehend⁵ konfluieren⁶ schuppige Plaques⁷ stecknadelkopfgroße Papeln⁸ kuppelförmige Papeln⁹ pyramidenstufenartige Papeln¹⁰ zentral genabelte Papeln¹¹ gruppierte Papeln¹² zusammenfließende/ konfluierende Papeln¹³ Skleromyxödem, Mucinosis papulosa¹⁴ Primärmedaillon, -plaque¹⁵ Chagrinlederhaut¹⁶ Storchenbiss¹⁷ schlecht abgegrenzter Fleck¹⁸

Quaddel, Urtica
Urtikaria, Nesselsucht¹ flüchtig² empfindlich³ Kälteurtikaria, Urticaria e frigore⁴ eine Quaddel hervorrufen⁵ unregelmäßig begrenzte Quaddel⁶ urtikarielles Exanthem⁷ Urtikariavaskulitis⁸ rezidivierende Urtikaria⁹ Quaddelbildung mit gerötetem Hof¹⁰

Skin Lesions　　　　　　　　　　　　　　　　　　　　　　　　　　　　　　　CLINICAL TERMS

vesicle [vɛsɪkl] *n term*　　*syn* **bleb** *n*,
　　　　　　　　　　　rel **blister**[1] *n clin*, **bulla**[2] *n, pl* **–ae** [buli‖aɪ],
　　　　　　　　　　　pustule[3] [pʌstʃʊl] *n term*

circumscribed lesion less than 5 mm in diameter which is elevated and contains fluid
vesicular[4] *adj term* • **vesiculation** *n* • **(vesiculo)pustular** *adj* • **bullous**[5] *adj*
• **blister**[6] *v clin* • **blistering**[7] *n & adj*

» Depending on their size, cutaneous blisters are referred to as vesicles (<0.5 cm) or bullae (>0.5 cm). The blisters were linear and of acute onset. First-degree burns are not blistered initially. The typical chickenpox[8] lesions progress from macule to papule to vesicle and begin crusting within 6 to 8 h. Relapsing crops of bullae appeared on normal skin.

Use skin or cutaneous / fluid-filled / clear[9] / bloody / itchy or pruritic **vesicles** • deep-seated / superficial / crusting **vesicles** • weeping[10] / linear / confluent / grouped **vesicles** • subepidermal / oral / hemorrhagic [ædʒ]/ purulent[11] **blister** • intact / flaccid[12] [(k)s]/ tense[13] / ruptured [ʌ] **blister** • **blister** formation / cavity / roof[14] • **blister** fluid / debridement [iː] • **vesicular** lesion / eruption / rash / flare-up[15] / keratitis / dermatitis • emphysematous / isolated / (non-)inflammatory / mucous [juː] membrane **bullae** • **bulla** formation[16] • **bullous** fluid / drug eruption / keratopathy • **bullous** impetigo[17] / lichen [aɪk] planus [eɪ]/ pemphigoid (*abbr* BP) • scattered / superficial / subcorneal / (peri)follicular **pustules** • sterile[18] / foul-smelling / ulcerated / necrotic **pustules** • **pustular** lesion / rash / acne / psoriasis[19] / folliculitis

erosion [ɪroʊʒᵊn] *n term*　　*rel* **excoriation**[1], **denudation**[2],
　　　　　　　　　　　　　　　ulcer[3] [ʌlsɚ] *n term* → U89-17

(i) a moist, circumscribed, usually depressed lesion that results from destruction or progressive wearing [eɚ] away[4] of superficial tissue layers, esp. the epidermis
(ii) a shallow ulcer which may heal without scarring[5]; an excoriation is a traumatic erosion or ulcer which is often linear, e.g. a deep scratch

(non)erosive [ɪroʊsɪv] *adj term* • **erode**[6] [ɪroʊd] *v* • **denude** [dɪnuːd] *v*

» Tying the tape too tightly can cause erosion of the skin and venous [iː] congestion [dʒe] above the tie. The painless silver-gray erosion surrounded by a red periphery on the glans is suggestive of syphillis. Erythema multiforme major with extensive denudation of skin is best treated in a burn unit. Skin irritation caused itching and severe excoriation from scratching.

Use cutaneous / superficial / deep / punctate[7] [ʌ]/ inflammatory[8] / crusted **erosion** • bony / joint / duodenal / oral **erosion** • gastric[9] / mucosal[10] / corneal[11] / cervical[12] [sɜː] **erosion** • epidermal / endothelial / superficial / extensive[13] **denudation** • skin / severe / perineal [iː] **excoriation** • **erosive** lichen planus[14] / lesions • **erosive** gastritis / arthritis / esophagitis[15] [dʒaɪ] • **denuded** skin / area[16] • **denuding** endothelial injury

lichenification [laɪkᵊn-] *n term*　　*rel* **keratinization** *or* **cornification**[1] *n term*

leathery induration and thickening of the skin with hyperkeratosis, due to a chronic inflammation caused by scratching[2] or long-continued irritation

lichenoid, -ified[3] *adj term* • **lichen**[4] *n* • **kera(tino)-** *comb* • **corn**[5] *n clin*

» Pruritus [aɪ] ani [eɪnaɪ] may present as erythema, fissuring[6] [ʃ], maceration[7] [s] lichenification, and fibrosis of the perianal skin. Scratching or rubbing [ʌ] may lead to lichenification.

Use flexural[8] [flekʃʊɚᵊl] **lichenification** • **lichen** planus[9] [eɪ]/ sclerosus / simplex chronicus • surface / marked[10] **keratinization** • **kerat**itis /osis /olytic /oderma /omalacia [eɪʃ] /oconjunctivitis • **lichenoid** reaction / papule / infiltrate • **lichenified** plaque • amyloidosis[11]

impetigo [ɪmpətaɪ‖iːgoʊ] *n term*

contagious [eɪdʒ] superficial pyoderma [aɪ], caused by cocci [aɪ] most commonly occurring on the face, beginning with a superficial flaccid [(k)s] vesicle which ruptures and forms a thick yellowish crust

impetiginous[1] [ɪdʒ] *adj term* • **impetiginization**[2] *n* • **impetiginized**[ɪdʒ] *adj*

» Erosions covered by honey-colored crusts are diagnostic of impetigo. Perianal [eɪ] scratching may result in excoriation and impetigo. We first have to exclude underlying [aɪ] dermatosis with secondary impetiginization.

Use bullous [ʊ]/ crusted / streptococcal **impetigo** • **impetigo** contagiosa[3] [eɪdʒ]/-like lesion • **impetiginous** lesion • eczema • **impetiginized** area / scabies [eɪ]

Bläschen, Vesicula

Bläschen, Blase[1] Blase, Bulla[2] Pustel, Pustula[3] bläschenförmig, vesikulär[4] großblasig, bullös[5] Blasen hervorrufen, B. bekommen/ bilden[6] Blasenbildung; blasenbildend[7] Windpocken, Schafblattern, Varizellen[8] seröse Bläschen[9] nässende Bläschen[10] eitriges Bläschen[11] schlaffe Blase[12] pralle Blase[13] Blasendach[14] Aufschießen von Bläschen[15] Blasenbildung[16] großblasige Impetigo, Impetigo bullosa[17] sterile Pusteln[18] Psoriasis pustulosa[19]

12

Erosion

Exkoriation, Abschürfung[1] Denudation, Abschwimmen d. Epidermis[2] Geschwür, Ulkus[3] Abschwimmen[4] Narbenbildung[5] erodieren, zerfressen[6] punktförm. Erosion[7] entzündl. Erosion[8] Magenerosion[9] Schleimhauterosion[10] Hornhauterosion, Erosio corneae[11] Portioerosion[12] großflächige Freilegung d. Dermis[13] erosiver Lichen ruber[14] erosive Ösophagitis[15] (von d. Epidermis) entblößtes Areal[16]

13

Lichenifikation

Verhornung, Keratinisierung[1] Kratzen[2] lichenoid, lichenartig[3] Lichen, Flechte[4] Hühnerauge, Clavus[5] Fissurenbildung[6] Mazeration, Aufweichung d. Haut[7] lichenifiziertes Beugeekzem[8] Lichen ruber planus[9] starke Verhornung[10] lichenoide Amyloidose[11]

14

Impetigo, Eiterflechte

impetigoartig, impetiginös[1] Impetiginisation[2] Impetigo contagiosa[3]

15

furuncle [fjʊɚʌŋkl] n term   syn **boil** n clin, rel **abscess**[1], **whitlow** or **felon**[2] n clin

painful nodule caused by a suppurative[3] [ʌ] staphylococcal infection originating in a hair follicle
furunculosis[4] n term • **furunculous** adj • **carbuncle**[5] n • **boil-like** adj clin • **gumboil**[6] [gʌmbɔɪl] n

» *Furuncles usually start in infected hair follicles. Carbuncles develop more slowly than single furuncles and may be accompanied by fever and prostration. Herpetic whitlow may occur [ɜː] by inoculation of virus via a break in the epidermis surface or by direct introduction of virus into the hand, e.g. through occupational [eɪʃ] exposure. A felon should be drained where it points—usually in the mid pad—by a central longitudinal incision [sɪʒ].*

Use to pick/squeeze[7] [iː] /incise [aɪ]/drain **a furuncle** • nasal[8] / labial[9] / [eɪ] **furuncle** • to produce/form/arise [əraɪz] from **boils** • recurrent[10] [ɜː]/ Aleppo[11] **boil** • acute / chronic or cold[12] / subcutaneous[13] **abscess** • collar-button[14] [ʌ]/ deep neck **abscess** • brain / perianal[15] / pyogenic [paɪədʒenɪk] **abscess** • bacterial [ɪɚ]/ micro/ macro**abscess** • **abscess**-forming[16] / lancet ['s]/ drainage[17] • herpetic[18] [hɜːr-] **whitlow** • **whitlow** lesion / on the thumb [θʌm] • finger / bacterial **felon**

Furunkel
Abszess[1] Panaritium, Nagelgeschwür[2] eitrig, purulent[3] Furunkulose[4] Karbunkel[5] submuköser Zahnfleischabszess, Parulis[6] e. Furunkel ausdrücken/ -quetschen[7] Nasenfurunkel[8] Lippenfurunkel[9] rezidivierender Furunkel[10] Orient-, Aleppobeule, kutane Leishmaniose[11] chronischer/ kalter/ tuberkulöser Abszess[12] subkutaner Abszess[13] Kragenknopfpanaritium[14] perianaler Abszess[15] abszessbildend, abszedierend[16] Abszessdrainage[17] Herpesparonychie[18]

16

verruca [vəruːkə] n term, pl **-ae** [iː]   syn **wart** [wɔːrt] n clin, rel **skin tag**[1] n

flesh-colored growth characterized by circumscribed hypertrophy of the papillae of the corium, with a horny surface due to thickening of the malpighian, granular, and keratin layers of the epidermis
verrucous[2] [vəruːkəs] adj term • **verruciform**[2] adj • **warty**[2] adj clin

» *Verrucae (common warts) are round or oval elevated lesions with rough surfaces composed of multiple rounded or filiform keratinized projections, commonly on the fingers and hands. Flesh-colored or hyperpigmented pedunculated tags[3] on the neck, axilla or groin may become irritated and can be removed with a curette or by freezing with liquid nitrogen[4] [aɪ].*

Use **verruca** plana juvenilis / vulgaris / plantaris[5] • common[6] / viral [aɪ]/ plantar[5] / venereal[7] [ɪɚ] **wart** • (ano)genital[7] [dʒe]/ periungual [ʌ]/ flat / filiform[8] **wart** • **wart** virus[9] /-like lesion /-free interval / removal / therapy • **verrucous** skin lesion / papules / carcinoma • **warty** growth[10] / surface • superficial / external **skin tag** • hypertrophic / mucosal / cutaneous[1] [eɪ] **tag**

Warze, Verruca
Hautanhängsel[1] warzenartig, verrukös[2] gestielte Anhängsel[3] flüssiger Stickstoff[4] Fußsohlenwarze, Verruca plantaris[5] gewöhnliche Warze, Verruca vulgaris[6] Condyloma acuminatum, spitze(s) Feigwarze/ Kondylom[7] Verruca filiformis, fadenförm. Warze[8] Warzen-, Papillomavirus[9] warzenähnliche Wucherung[10]

17

Unit 115 Clinical Abbreviations & Acronyms

Important Note: The entries in this unit are **listed alphabetically**. Additional abbreviations and acronyms can be found in all other units with the respective entries. To look them up please refer to the **index** where all are listed alphabetically.

a	arterial	arteriell	ALL	acute lymphatic leukemia		akute lymphatische Leukämie
a.m.	in the morning	Vormittag; vormittags	All.	allergies		Allergien
A/O	alert and oriented	wach und orientiert	ALS	amyotrophic lateral sclerosis		amyotropische Lateralsklerose
A₂	aortic second sound	2. Herzton				
AA	amino acid	Aminosäure	AMI	acute myocardial infarction		akuter Herzinfarkt
	African-American	Amerikaner(in) afrikanischer Abstammung	amt.	amount		Menge
			AGF	angle of greatest flexion		max. Beugewinkel
AAA	abdominal aortic aneurysm	abdominelles Aortenaneurysma	AOB	alcohol on breath		Atemalkohol
			APE	acute pulmonary edema		akutes Lungenödem
AAOx3	awake, alert, oriented x 3 (to person, place, time)	wach und orientiert		acute pulmonary embolism		akute Lungenembolie
			APLS	advanced pediatric life support		erweiterte pädiatr. Reanimationsmaßnahmen
abn, ABNL	abnormal	abnorm, gestört	APH	ante-partum hemorrhage anterior pituitary hormone		Blutung vor der Geburt Hypophysenvorderlappenhormon
ABP	arterial blood pressure	arterieller Blutdruck				
ABW	actual body weight	derzeitiges Körpergewicht				
ac	before meals *(ante cibum)*	vor den Mahlzeiten	ARC	American Red Cross		Amerikan. Rotes Kreuz
AC	alternating current	Wechselstrom	ARD	acute respiratory distress		akute Atemnot
ACLS	advanced cardiac life support	erweiterte kardiolog. Reanimationsmaßnahmen	ARF	acute renal failure		akutes Nierenversagen
AGA	appropriate gestational age	der Schwangerschaftswoche entsprechende Reifung	AROM	artificial rupture of membranes		Blasensprengung
AED	automatic external defibrillator	automatischer externer Defibrillator	aROM	active range of motion		aktive Beweglichkeit
			ASA	acetylsalicylic acid *(aspirin)*		Azetylsalizylsäure

Clinical Abbreviations & Acronyms

ASAP	as soon as possible	ehestmöglich
ASHD	arteriosclerotic (or atherosclerotic) heart disease	koronare Herzkrankheit, KHK
AST	aspartate aminotransferase (formerly SGOT)	Aspartataminotransferase, AST, ASAT
ATLS	advanced trauma life support	erweiterte traumatolog. Reanimationsmaßnahmen
av	average	Durchschnitt; durchschnittlich
AWL	absence without leave	unerlaubte Abwesenheit
B/C	blood cultures	Blutkulturen
BAT, B.A.T	blunt abdominal trauma	stumpfes Bauchtrauma
BBP	blood-borne pathogen	hämatogen übertragbarer Erreger
BHT	blunt head trauma	stumpfes Schädeltrauma
bib	drink	trinke
BIBA	brought in by ambulance	mit d. Rettungswagen eingeliefert
BID	brought in dead	tot eingeliefert
BNTI	blind nasotracheal intubation	blinde nasotracheale Intubation
BRBPR	bright red blood per rectum	frische rektale Blutung
BS, B/S	blood sugar	Blutzucker
	bowel sounds	Darmgeräusche
	breath sounds	Atemgeräusche
BSA	body surface area	Körperoberfläche
	bovine serum albumin	Rinderserumalbumin
BSE	bovine spongiform encephalopathy	BSE, Rinderwahnsinn
BSI	body substance isolation	Entnahme v. Gewebeproben, Blut u. Körperflüssigkeiten
BSO	bilateral salpingo-oophorectomy	beidseitige Salpingo-oophorektomie
BTLS	basic trauma life support	traumatolog. Basismaßnahmen zur Reanimation
BVM	bag-valve mask	Beatmungsbeutel
C	centigrade, Celsius	Celsius
c	with (cum)	mit
cc	cubic centimeter	Kubikzentimeter
c.m.	tomorrow morning	morgen früh
c.p.s	cycles per second	Umdrehungen/Sekunde
c/min	cycles per minute	Umdrehungen/Minute
CA, Ca	carcinoma	Karzinom
CCU	coronary/cardiac care unit	kardiolog. Intensivstation
CF	cardiac failure	Herzversagen
	cystic fibrosis	Mukoviszidose, zystische Fibrose
CHB	complete heart block	totaler Herzblock
Charr.	Charrière (see also F)	Charrière (= 1/3 mm)
CHI	closed head injury	gedecktes Schädeltrauma
CJD	Creutzfeldt-Jakob disease	Creutzfeldt-Jakob-Krankheit
CME	continuing medical education	medizinische Fortbildung
CN 2–12	cranial nerves 2–12	Hirnnerven 2–12
CP	chest pain	Schmerzen i. Brustraum
CS	Cesarean section	Kaiserschnitt
C & S	culture & sensitivity	Kultur & Resistenzbestimmung
CTA	clear to auscultation	auskultatorisch frei
CTD	close to death	im Sterben
CY	calendar year	Kalenderjahr
d/c, dc	discontinue	(Therapie) absetzen
	discharge	Entlassung; Sekret, Ausfluss, Absonderung
	diarrhea/ constipation	Durchfall/ Obstipation
D/W	dextrose in water	Dextrose-Infusionsflüssigkeit
D5 W	dextrose 5% in water	5% Dextrose in Wasser
dbl	double	doppelt
DC	direct current	Gleichstrom
D & C	dilatation & curettage	Dilatation & Kürettage, Ausschabung d. Gebärmutter
deg	degree	Grad, Ausmaß
	degeneration	Degeneration
devel	develop(ment)	entwickeln; Entwicklung
DH$_x$	drug history	Arzneimittelanamnese
DIC	disseminated intravascular coagulation	Verbrauchskoagulopathie
DIU	death in utero	intrauteriner Fruchttod
DNI	do not intubate (cf. DNR)	keine Intubation
DoH	Dept. of Health (UK)	Gesundheitsministerium
doz	dozen	Dutzend
DM	diabetes mellitus	Zuckerkrankheit, D.m.
DP	distal pulses	periphere Pulse
dsg	dressing	Verband
DPOA	durable power of attorney	ständige Sachwalterschaft (bei Geschäftsunfähigkeit)
DR	delivery room	Kreißsaal
DRT	dead right there	tot am Unfallort
dT	tetanus booster with diphtheria booster	Tetanus-Diphtherie-Auffrischung(simpfung)
DTV	due to void by …. (time)	Harnblase entleeren bis … (bei Z. n. Op i. Harntrakt)
DUI	driving under the influence (of alcohol)	Trunkenheit am Steuer
DVT	deep vein thrombosis	tiefe Venenthrombose
DWAI	driving while ability impaired	Inbetriebnahme e-s KFZ trotz eingeschränkter Fahrtüchtigkeit
EBL	estimated blood loss	geschätzter Blutverlust
EDP	emotionally disturbed person	psychisch Kranke(r)
EENT	ears, eyes, nose, throat	Ohren, Augen, Nase, Hals
EHS	extremely hazardous substance (= hazmat)	Gefahrengut, -stoff
EMB	eosin-methylene blue	Eosin-Methylenblau
EMD	electromechanical dissociation (see PEA)	elektromechanische Entkoppelung/ Dissoziation
EMD	emergency medical doctor	Notarzt/-ärztin
EOA	esophageal obturator airway	Ösophagusobturator
EOH	ethyl alcohol	Ethanol, Äthylalkohol
EOMI	extraocular muscles intact	Augenbewegungen normal
EP	ectopic pregnancy	ektopische Schwangerschaft
	electrophysiologic	elektrophysiologisch
	emergency physician	Notarzt/-ärztin
epith	epithelial	d. Epithel betreffend
EPS	extrapyramidal symptoms	extrapyramidale Symptome
equiv	equivalent	Entsprechung; entspricht
ESRD	end-stage renal disease	terminale Niereninsuffizienz
est	estimate / estimation	bewerten, (ein)schätzen; Beurteilung

ETI	endotracheal intubation	endotracheale Intubation	IHSS	idiopathic hypertrophic subaortic stenosis	IHSS
ETT	exercise treadmill test	Belastungsergometrie	IM	internal medicine	innere Medizin
EUA	examination under anesthesia	Untersuchung in Vollnarkose	in d.	daily	täglich
EW	emergency ward	Notaufnahme	in	inch	Inch (ca. 2,5 cm)
F	Fahrenheit	Fahrenheit	inj	injury	Verletzung
	French scale (cf. Charr.)	Charrière-Skala		inject, injection	injiziere; Injektion
f/	female	Frau, weiblich	inop	inoperable	inoperabel
F&R	force & rhythm	Pulsstärke & -rhythmus	int	internal	innere
FD	fatal dose	letale Dosis	IOP	intraocular pressure	Augeninnendruck
	freeze-dried	gefriergetrocknet	IPPB	intermittent positive pressure breathing	intermittierende Überdruckbeatmung
FHR	fetal heart rate	fetale Herzfrequenz	IU	international units	internationale Einheiten
fl	fluid	Flüssigkeit	IVR	idioventricular rhythm	idioventrikulärer Rhythmus
FL	flatline (EEG)	Nullinien-(EEG)	kcal	kilocalorie	Kilokalorie
FMP	final menstrual period	letzte monatliche Regelblutung, Menopause	KVO	keep veins open	langsamste Infusionsgeschwindigkeit
FOS	full of stool (esp. on x-ray)	obstipiert, verstopft	L	liter	Liter
FROM	full range of motion	frei beweglich	lb	pound (weight)	Pfund (= 0,45 kg)
ft	foot (= 12 inches)	Fuß (= 30,48 cm)	LBP	low(er) back pain	Kreuzschmerzen
FTT	failure to thrive	Gedeihstörung	LCTA	lungs clear to auscultation	Lungen auskultatorisch frei
FU, F/U	follow-up	Nachsorge, -untersuchung	LDH	lactic dehydrogenase	Laktat-Dehydrogenase
FWB	full weight-bearing	volle Belastung	LE	lower extremities	Beine
F_x	fracture	Knochenbruch, Fraktur		lupus erythematosus	Lupus erythematodes
FYI	for your information	zu Ihrer Information	LET	lidocaine, epinephrine and tetracaine (topical anesthetic)	Lidocain, Adrenalin & Tetracain
G/W	glucose in water	Glukoselösung	LGIB	lower gastrointestinal bleeding	untere Gastrointestinalblutung
G6PD	glucose-6-phosphate dehydrogenase	Glukose-6-Phosphat-Dehydrogenase	LIF	left iliac fossa	linke Fossa iliaca, linker unterer Quadrant
gal	galactose	Galaktose	LMA	laryngeal mask airway	Larynxmaske
GCS	Glasgow Coma Scale	Glasgow-Koma-Skala	LMD	local medical doctor	niedergelassene(r) Arzt/Ärztin
gm, g	gram	Gramm	LOC	level of consciousness	Bewusstseinslage
GOMER, Gomer	get out of my emergency room	schwierige(r) ältere(r) Patient(in)		loss of consciousness	Bewusstlosigkeit, Ohnmacht
	(originally a problem patient seeking treatment for minor complaints – now a hospital slang term for elderly patients with multiple medical problems unable to communicate their complaints)		LPM	liters per minute	Liter pro Minute
			LR	lactated Ringer's (solution)	Ringer-Laktat-Lösung
h, hr, H	hour	Stunde	lt	left	links
h.d.	at bedtime (hora decubiti)	vor dem Schlafengehen	LV	left ventricle	linke Herzkammer
HCVD	hypertensive cardiovascular disease	Hochdruckherz, Hochdruck-Herzkrankheit	LVEDP	left ventricular end-diastolic pressure	linksventrikulärer enddiastolischer Druck
HBC	hyperbaric chamber	Überdruckkammer	Lx	laxative	Abführmittel
HD	hearing distance	Hörweite	M.	mix	mische
HEMS	Helicopter Emergency Medical Services (UK)	Flugrettung mit Rettungshubschrauber	m.dict.	as directed (= modo dictu)	wie angegeben
			mμ	millimicron (= nanometer)	Millimikron, Nanometer
HI	hemagglutination inhibition (test)	Hämagglutinationshemmtest	MAE	moves all extremities	kann alle Glieder bewegen
			MCI	mass casualty incident	Massenunfall
HSM	hepatosplenomegaly	Hepatosplenomegalie	ME	medical examiner	Gerichtsmediziner(in)
HTN	hypertension	Bluthochdruck, Hypertonie	mEq, meq	milligram equivalent	Milliäquivalent
HVD	hypertensive vascular disease	hypertonische Gefäßerkrankung	MIC	minimum inhibitory concentration	minimale Hemmkonzentration
H_x	history	Vorgeschichte, Anamnese	micro	microscopic	mikroskopisch
Hz	hertz (cycles/ second)	Hertz	mL	milliliter	Milliliter (ml)
HZ	hazard zone	Gefahrenzone	mo, mos.	month(s) also 3/12	Monat(e); drei Monate
I & D	incision & drainage	Drainage durch Inzision			
IA	incurred accidentally	unfallbedingt, akzidentell	MO	mental observation (psychiatr. patients)	Beobachtung bei Verdacht auf psychische Krankheit
IBW	ideal body weight	Idealgewicht			
ICS	intercostal space	Zwischenrippen-, Interkostalraum	MOI	mechanism of injury	Verletzungsmechanismus
			mol wt	molecular weight	Molekulargewicht
ICT	inflammation of connective tissue	Bindegewebsentzündung	mOsm	milliosmole	Milliosmol
IDA	iron deficiency anemia	Eisenmangelanämie			
IDDM	insulin-dependent diabetes mellitus	insulinpflichtiger Diabetes			

Clinical Abbreviations & Acronyms

MR	mental retardation	Intelligenzminderung
MRG	murmurs, rubs or gallops	Herz-, Reibegeräusche oder Galopprhythmus
MS	mental status	Neurostatus
	multiple sclerosis	multiple Sklerose, MS
	mitral stenosis	Mitralstenose
MVA	motor vehicle accident	Verkehrsunfall
MVC	motor vehicle collision	Verkehrsunfall
MVO_2	myocardial oxygen demand	myokardialer Sauerstoffverbrauch
MVP	mitral valve prolapse	Mitralklappenprolaps
n.r., non rep.	do not repeat (= non repetatur)	nicht wiederholen
N/V/D/C	nausea/ vomiting/ diarrhea/ constipation	Übelkeit/ Erbrechen/ Diarrhö/ Obstipation
NABS	normoactive bowel sounds	Darmgeräusche unauffällig
NAD	no acute distress	keine Akutbeschwerden
	no apparent distress	keine offensichtliche akute Symptomatik
NC	nasal cannula	Nasenkanüle
NC/AT	normocephalic/ atraumatic	keine Kopfverletzungen
ND	non-distended	nicht gebläht (bes. Abdomen)
NGT	nasogastric tube	Nasen-Magen-Sonde
NH	nursing home	Pflegeheim
NK(D)A	no known (drug) allergies	keine (Arzneimittel)allergien bekannt
NL, nml, norm	normal	unauffällig
NPO, n.p.o.	nothing by mouth (nil per os)	nüchtern
NPN	nonprotein nitrogen	Nicht-Protein-Stickstoff
NR	normal range	(im) Norm(al)bereich
NRB NR(F)M	non-rebreathing (face) mask	Sauerstoffmaske ohne Rückatmung
NS	not significant	nicht signifikant
	normal saline (0,9% NaCl)	physiol. Kochsalzlösung
NSD	normal spontaneous delivery	normale Spontangeburt
NT	non-tender	nicht druckdolent
NTG	nitroglycerin	Nitroglyzerin
NYD	not yet diagnosed	noch nicht diagnostiziert
o.s., OS	left eye	linkes Auge
OBS	obstetrics	Geburtshilfe
	organic brain syndrome	organ. Psychosyndrom
OOB	out of bed	nicht mehr bettlägrig
Op., op	operation	Operation, Eingriff
OPA	oropharyngeal airway	oropharyngealer Tubus
	outpatient appointment	Ambulanztermin
OPV	outpatient visit	Ambulanzbesuch
org	organism	Erreger
ORIF	open reduction & internal fixation	offene Reposition & innere Fixation
oz.	ounce	Unze (= 28,35 g)
P&A	percussion & auscultation	Auskultation & Perkussion
PAC	premature atrial contraction	supraventrikuläre atriale Extrasystole
$PaCO_2$	arterial carbon dioxide partial pressure	arterieller Kohlendioxid-partialdruck
PACU	postanesthesia care unit	anästhesiolog. Intensivstation
PALS	pediatric advanced life support (also APLS)	erweiterte pädiatr. Reanimationsmaßnahmen
PaO_2	partial arterial oxygen pressure	arterieller Sauerstoff-partialdruck
PASG	pneumatic anti-shock garment	Antischockhose
PAT	paroxysmal atrial tachycardia	paroxysmale Vorhof-tachykardie
	pre-admission testing	ambulante präoperative Abklärung
PCD	pacing cardioverter/ defibrillator (cf. ICD)	implantierbarer Kardio-verter-Defibrillator
pCO_2	partial pressure of CO_2	Kohlendioxidpartialdruck
PCP	pneumocystis carinii pneumonia	Pneumocystis carinii-Pneumonie
	primary care physician	Hausarzt, -ärztin
PCR	patient care record/ report	Pflegebericht; Pflegerapport
PDA	patent ductus arteriosus	offener Ductus arteriosus
PDR	physician's desk reference	Arzneimittelverzeichnis (Rote Liste, Austria-Codex)
PE	pulmonary edema	Lungenödem
	pulmonary embolism	Lungenembolie
PEA	pulseless electrical activity	pulslose elektrische Herz-aktivität
pen	penetrating	durchdringend, penetrierend
pend	pending	noch ausstehend
perf	perforating, perforated	perforierend; perforiert
PDU	perforated duodenal ulcer	perforiertes Duodenalulkus
PG	pregnant	schwanger
	postgraduate	nach d. Diplom/ Promotion
PIA	personal injury accident (= MVA w/ injuries)	Unfall mit Personenschaden
PJC	premature junctional contraction	vorzeitige junktionale (AV-)Kontraktion
pl, PLT	platelets	Thrombozyten
p.m.	in the afternoon	nachmittags
PNB	pulseless non-breathing	pulslos & ohne Atmung
PO, p.o.	orally, by mouth (per os)	oral
POD	postoperative day	postoperativer Tag
PO_2	oxygen pressure/ tension	Sauerstoffdruck
POLST	physician's orders for life-sustaining treatment	ärztl. Anweisungen bzgl. lebenserhaltender Therapie
PPD	purified protein derivative	gereinigtes Proteinderivat (Tuberkulinprobe)
	packs per day	Zigarettenpackungen pro Tag
ppm	parts per million	Milligramm pro Kilogramm
ppt	precipitate	Niederschlag; ausfällen
p.r.	per rectum	rektal
prep	preparation (esp. for surgery)	Vorbereitung; Zubereitung
pt./pts.	patient(s)	Patient(en)
PTA	prior to admission	vor der Aufnahme, präklinisch
PT(C)A	percutaneous transluminal (coronary) angioplasty	perkutane transluminale Angioplastie (d. Koronar-arterien)
PTC	percutaneous transhepatic cholangiography	perkutane transhepatische Cholangiografie
PTX	pneumothorax	Pneumothorax
p.v.	vaginal (per vaginam)	vaginal
PVC	premature ventricular contraction (cf. VPB)	ventrikuläre Extrasystole
P-Y	pack years (smoking)	Jahre i. d. jem. tägl. 1 Pkg. Zigaretten geraucht hat
qt	quart	Quart (= 0,95 Liter)
RA	right atrium	rechter Vorhof
	rheumatoid arthritis	progrediente chronische Polyarthritis
RBBB	right bundle branch block	Rechtsschenkelblock

CLINICAL TERMS

RCM	right costal margin	rechter Rippen(bogen)rand	
req	require	benötigen	
RF	renal failure	Nierenversagen	
	rheumatic fever	rheumatisches Fieber	
	rheumatoid factor	Rheumafaktor	
RIND	reversible ischemic neurologic deficit	reversibles ischämisches neurolog. Defizit	
RL	Ringer's lactate (also LR)	Ringer-Laktat-Lösung	
RM	respiratory movements	Atembewegungen	
RMA	refuses medical assistance	verweigert ärztliche Hilfe	
ROT	rule of thumb	Faustregel	
RRR	regular rate & rhythm	Puls unauffällig	
RSI	rapid sequence induction (anesthesia)	Anästhesie mit kurzer Anflutungszeit	
RSR	regular sinus rhythm	regelmäßiger Sinusrhythmus	
rt	right	rechts	
RTC	return to clinic	ambulanter Wiederbestelltermin	
RVH	right ventricular hypertrophy	Rechtsherzhypertrophie	
RVR	rapid ventricular response	schnelle Kammerüberleitung	
R_x	prescription, take (medicine)	Verordnung, Rp	
s	without (sine, cf. W/O)	ohne	
S/E	systematic enquiry (BE)	systemat. Organanamnese	
s/p	status post	Zustand nach	
S/S	signs and symptoms	Symptomatik	
SaO₂	arterial oxygen saturation	arterielle Sauerstoffsättigung	
SARS	servere acute respiratory syndrome	schweres akutes respiratorisches oder Atemwegssyndrom	
SBE	subacute bacterial endocarditis	subakute bakterielle Endokarditis	
SFM	simple face mask	Notfallbeatmungsmaske	
SH, SH$_x$	social history	Sozialanamnese	
SI(L)	seriously ill (list)	schwer krank, Liste der Schwerkranken	
Sig.	write on label	Signatur (pharm.)	
SITREP	situation report	Lagebericht	
SOL	space-occupying lesion	Raumforderung	
SOP	standard operating procedures	standardisierte Operationsrichtlinien	
sp gr, SG	specific gravity	spezifisches Gewicht	
spec	specimen	(Gewebe)probe	
sq	square	Quadrat-	
stat	immediately (statim)	unverzüglich	
std	standard	Standard, Standard-	
STS	serologic test(s) for syphilis	serologischer Syphilistest, Lues-, Syphilisserologie	
SVT	supraventricular tachycardia	supraventrikuläre Tachykardie	
S$_x$	symptoms	Symptome	
SXR	skull x-ray	Schädelröntgen	
sym	symmetrical	symmetrisch	
TA	traffic accident	Verkehrsunfall	
TAH	total abdominal hysterectomy	totale abdominelle Hysterektomie	
TB	tuberculosis	Tuberkulose	
TBF	total body failure	Multiorganversagen	
Td	tetanus toxoid without diphtheria booster	Tetanus-Diphtherie-Impfstoff mit verringertem Diphtherietoxoid-Gehalt	
TKO	to keep open	IV Nadel durch langsame Infusion offenhalten	
TLC	tender loving care	fürsorgliche Pflege	
T$_{max}$	maximal temperature	Maximaltemperatur	
TPR	temperature, pulse, respiration	Temperatur, Puls und Atemfrequenz	
tsp	teaspoon	Teelöffel (= 5 g)	
TT	thrombin time	Thrombinzeit	
TTS	transdermal therapeutic system	transdermales therapeutisches System	
TU	tuberculin unit	Tuberkulineinheit	
TV	tidal volume	Atemzugvolumen	
TVH	transvaginal hysterectomy	vaginale Hysterektomie	
U, u	unit	Einheit	
U/P	urine/plasma ratio	Plasma-Harn-Konzentration	
UCHD	usual childhood diseases	übliche Kinderkrankheiten	
UA, U/A	urine analysis	Urinuntersuchung	
UGIB	upper gastrointestinal bleeding	obere Gastrointestinalblutung	
unk	unknown	unbekannt	
US, U/S	ultrasound	Ultraschall	
ut.dict.	as directed	wie angegeben	
V, vol	volume	Volumen	
vag hyst	vaginal hysterectomy	vaginale Hysterektomie	
VFIB	ventricular fibrillation	Kammerflimmern	
VPB	ventricular premature beats	ventrikuläre Extrasystolen	
VPC	ventricular premature contraction	ventrikuläre Extrasystole	
V/Q scan	ventilation-perfusion scan	Ventilations- u. Perfusionsszintigrafie	
vs.	versus	gegen, gegenüber	
VSA	vital signs absent	Vitalfunktionen fehlen	
VSS	vital signs stable	Vitalfunktionen stabil	
VT	ventricular tachycardia	ventrikuläre Tachykardie	
WB	whole blood	Vollblut	
w/c	wheelchair	Rollstuhl	
w/o	without (cf. s)	ohne	
WDWN	well-developed, well-nourished	gut entwickelt u. in gutem Ernährungszustand	
W/F	white female	Patientin weißer Hautfarbe	
wk, /52	week, e.g. 3/52	Woche, z.B. drei Wochen	
W/M	white male	Patient weißer Hautfarbe	
WPD	warm, pink, dry (skin signs)	(Haut) warm, rosa & trocken	
WPW	Wolff-Parkinson-White Syndrome	WPW-, Präexzitationssyndrom	
W/R	ward round	Stationsvisite	
wt	weight	Gewicht	
x	times, fold (8x = eight-fold)	-fach, z.B. 8-fach	
Y/O	years old	Jahre alt	
YOB	year of birth	Geburtsjahr	
yr	year	Jahr	
ZE	Zollinger-Ellison syndrome	Zollinger-Ellison-Syndrom	
ZN	Ziehl-Neelsen	Ziehl-Neelsen-Färbung	
? ….	query …	Verdacht auf …	
μg	microgram	Mikrogramm	
μmol	micromole	Mikromol	

Unit 116 Routine Lab Studies
Related Units: 117 Diagnosis, 118 Diagnostic Procedures, 89 Pathology, 86 Histology, 81 Biochemistry, 83 Cell Biology, 84 Genetics

pathology laboratory n term   syn **path lab** [pæθ læb] n jar → U89-1

unit in a hospital where histopathologic, microbiologic [aɪ], biochemical, hematologic, microscopic and immunologic investigations are performed; in Britain pathologists also perform autopsies [ɒː]

pathologic(al)[1] adj term • **pathologist**[2] [pəθɒːlədʒɪst] n • **pathology**[3] n

» Other groups at high risk of hepatitis [aɪ] B include staff at hemodialysis [-daɪælɪsɪs] centers, and physicians [ɪʃ], nurses [ɜː], and personnel working in clinical and pathology laboratories and blood banks[4].

Use hematology / bacteriology[5] / oncology / research[6] / microbiology[7] [aɪɒː] **laboratory** • toxicology / clinical **lab** • **laboratory** medicine / examination[8] / techniques [tekniːks]/ procedures [siː] • **laboratory** evaluation / technician [ɪʃ] on-call[9] / pathologist • **laboratory** animals[10] / apparatus [eɪ] • **laboratory** parameter / values[11] • clinical[12] / surgical [sɜːrdʒ-]/ cellular[13] [se] **pathology**

Pathologielabor
krankhaft, pathologisch[1] Pathologe/-in[2] Pathologie, patholog. Befund[3] Blutbanken[4] bakteriolog. Labor[5] Forschungslabor(atorium)[6] mikrobiolog. Labor[7] Laboruntersuchung[8] diensthabende(r) Laborant(in)[9] Versuchs-, Labortiere[10] Laborwerte[11] klin. Pathologie[12] Zellularpathologie[13]

1

lab(oratory) study n term   syn **lab test** n jar, rel **reaction**[1] n → U81-15

procedure evaluating secretions [iːʃ], blood samples[2], smears[3] [smɪəz], tissue [ʃ‖s] specimens[4] or for the purpose of providing data for the prevention, diagnosis or treatment of diseases

study[5] [stʌdi] v • **test**[5] v • **testing** n • **react** [riækt] v • **(non-)reactive** adj

» The recent [iːs] availability of rapid laboratory tests for detection of streptococci [-k(s)aɪ] (elimi-nating the delay [eɪ] caused by culturing) have made this approach feasible[6] [iː]. A strong reaction at a dilution [uː ʃ] exceeding [iː] 1:1 is presumptive [ʌ] evidence for ketoacidosis.

Use **laboratory** findings[7] / abnormality / workup[8] / diagnosis / error • cultures [ʌ] sent to the **lab** • **lab** data[9] / slip[10] / results[7] • cardiac / agglutination / hemodynamic **study** • in vitro[11] / animal[12] **study** • enzyme / albumin-globulin (abbr A/G)/ pH **test** • lactic dehydrogenase [ɒːdʒ] (abbr LDH)/ glucose [uː] tolerance[13] **test** • indirect bilirubin [uː]/ positive washout / blood[14] **test** • bedside laboratory[15] / daily urine / antibiotic sensitivity[16] **testing** • oxidative / flocculation[17] / seropositive **reaction**

labordiagnost. Untersuchung
chem./ phys. Reaktion[1] Blutproben[2] Abstriche[3] Gewebeproben[4] untersuchen, testen, prüfen[5] möglich[6] Laborergebnisse, -befund[7] Laboruntersuchungen, -diagnostik[8] Laborwerte, -daten[9] labordiagnostisches Untersuchungsformular[10] In-vitro-Studie[11] Tierstudie[12] Glukosetoleranztest[13] Blutuntersuchung[14] labordiagnost. Untersuchung am Krankenbett, Bedside-Diagnostik[15] Antibiotikaaustestung[16] Flockungsreaktion[17]

2

assay [æseɪ] n & v term   sim **bioassay**[1] [baɪouæseɪ] n, rel **immunoassay**[2] n term

quantitative assessment of the purity[3] [pjuəɹəti] or activity of biologic substances [ʌ]

» Several new assays for cardiac enzymes [aɪ] have been developed which are quite specific for cardiac necrosis. A 24-hour urine collection was assayed for creatinine.

Use diagnosed / established[4] **by assay** • biochemical / quantitative / qualitative **assay** • functional[5] [ʌ]/ (competitive/ complement) binding[6] [aɪ] **assay** • enzyme / serologic [ɪə] **assay** • clotting factor / (latex [eɪ]/ microhem)agglutination[7] **assay** • antigen (detection) / hormone **assay** • estrogen receptor (abbr ER)/ (ligase/ polymerase) chain reaction **assay** • immunoradiometric[8] (abbr IRMA)/ recombinant immunoblot (abbr RIBA) **assay** • sensitive TSH / C-terminal [ɜː] (double) antibody / fluorescent [es] antibody[9] **assay** • Western blot[10] / enzyme-linked immunosorbent[11] (abbr ELISA) **assay** • cytotoxin/ sperm penetration **assay** • enzyme-linked[11] **immunoassay** • **assay** kit / technique[12] • **interassay** variation

Analyse, Test, Bestimmung, Nachweis, Assay; analysieren, testen, bestimmen
Bioassay[1] Immunoassay[2] Reinheit[3] durch einen Test gesichert[4] Funktionstest[5] Bindungstest, -assay[6] Latex(agglutinations)test[7] immunradiometrische(r) Bestimmung/ Assay[8] Immunfluoreszenztest[9] Westernblot-Methode[10] Enzym-Immunassay, ELISA[11] Nachweismethode[12]

3

stain [steɪn] n & v term   syn **dye** [daɪ] n & v term

(n, i) substance used to give color to tissues which are to be examined under the microscope
(ii) area of discoloration of the skin
(v, i) using dye or a combination of dyes and reagents [eɪdʒ] to color tissues in order to examine them under the microscope for diagnostic purposes (ii) to discolor

staining[1] adj & n • **(un)stained** adj • **stainable**[2] adj

» The ulcer [ʌlsɚ] stained green with fluorescein [-esɪən]. Examinations of stained conjunctival scrapings[3] [eɪ] are recommended in severe cases. Demonstration of mycobacteria [maɪkə-] by acid-fast staining[4] (of material taken by fine-needle aspiration[5]) will confirm [ɜː] the diagnosis. Stain the sediment with a basic dye, e.g. toluidine blue, to demonstrate the bacteria.

Use acid-fast[4] [s]/ Gram('s)[6] / hematoxylin-eosin[7] [iː] **stain** • methylene blue / Prussian [ʌ] blue[8] **stain** • Wright's / Ziehl-Neelsen[9] / iron [aɪɚn]/ silver[10] **stain** • trichrome [aɪ]/ India ink / Giemsa('s)[11] **stain** • C-banding / differential / double **stain** • fluorescent / caustic [ɒː]/ (intra)vital[12] [aɪ] **stain** • negative / neutral / nuclear / selective **stain** • **staining** technique[13] / properties[14] • time • Gram-**stained** • oil / radiopaque[15] [-peɪk]/ supravital[16] **dye** • administration / concentration / excretion **of dye**

(n, i) Farbstoff, Färbung
(ii)   Mal, Fleck;
(v, i) (an)färben
(ii)   verfärben
Färbe-; Färbung[1] färbbar[2] Konjunktivalbiopsien[3] säurefeste Färbung, F. auf säurefeste Stäbchen[4] Feinnadelaspiration[5] Gram-Färbung[6] Hämatoxylin-Eosin-F.[7] Berliner-Blau-F.[8] Ziehl-Neelsen-F.[9] Silberimprägnation[10] Giemsa-F.[11] Vitalfärbung[12] Färbetechnik[13] Färbeeigenschaften[14] strahlendichter Farbstoff[15] Supravitalfarbstoff[16]

4

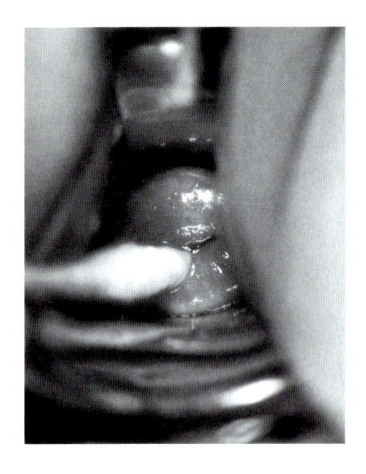

Intravaginal view of the external os in a 29-year-old para 2 at routine Pap smear: cells are obtained from the cervix to screen for cancer and other cervical abnormalities

smear [smɪɚ] *n & v term*   *sim* **brushing**[1] [ʌ], **washing**[2] *n*, → U118-10
swab[3] [swɒːb] *n & v term* → U17-13

thin specimen prepared by spreading [e] it onto a glass slide[4] [aɪ] and fixing it for microscopic study

» A peripheral blood smear[5] can be stained with supravital dyes to demonstrate the presence of hemoglobin H. Thrombocytopenia [iː] was present, and platelets[6] [eɪ] on smear were abnormally large. Smears of ascitic [əsɪtɪk] fluid for acid-fast bacilli[7] [bəsɪlaɪ] are rarely positive.

Use cytologic / blood[5] / sputum [(j)uː]/ Gram-stained **smear** • esophageal [dʒiː]/ gastric **smear** • duodenal / colonic / Pap[8] **smear** • vaginal [dʒ] , cervical [ɜː], endocervical (*abbr* VCE)/ endometrial [iː] **smear** • fast[9] / vaginal[10] / urinary[11] [jʊɚ]/ stool [uː] **smear** • abnormal / atypical / direct **smear** • wet / repeat[12] / air-dried[13] **smear** • sterile cotton[14] / pre-moistened / throat[15] [θroʊt] **swab** • (endo)cervical [sɜː]/ urethral [iː] **swab** • cytologic[16] **brushings** • bronchial[17] [brɒːŋkɪəl] **washing**

culture [kʌltʃɚ] *n term*
  rel **incubator**[1] [ɪnkjʊbeɪtɚ] *n term*

lab test which involves the propagation[2] of microorganisms or cells on or in a special growth medium[3] [iː]

culture[4] *v term* • culturable[5] *adj* • incubate[6] *v* • **incubation** *n*

» High-dose corticosteroids [ɪɚ] are instituted as well as empiric [ɪɚ] antibiotics pending culture results[7]. Scraping [eɪ] and culture for Candida in body folds will distinguish psoriasis [s] from candidiasis [-daɪəsɪs]. These blood agar [ɑː] plates need to be incubated at 37°C.

Use to obtain [eɪ] /shake **cultures** • viral [aɪ]/ bacterial / fungal[8] [fʌŋgəl] **culture** • (an)aerobic / cell[9] **culture** • tissue[10] / blood[11] [ʌ]/ urine **culture** • stool[12] / throat / pure[13] [pjʊɚ]/ broth[14] [ɒː] **culture** • identified / confirmed [ɜː]/ established **by culture** • **culture** medium[3] / plates[15] [eɪ] • **culture** bottle or flask[16] / solution[17] / techniques[18] • **culture**-proven /-negative endocarditis [aɪ] • **to culture** cells[19] / organisms / viruses [aɪ] • **to culture** fungi [-dʒaɪ‖-gaɪ]/ samples / stools [uː] • overnight **incubation**

> Note: In lab contexts the verb **to culture** is much more commonly used than its synonym **to cultivate**.

Aus-, Abstrich, Zellabstrich; ausstreichen, auftragen
Bürstenabstrich[1] Waschung, Spülung, Lavage[2] Abstrich; Tupfer; abtupfen[3] Objektträger[4] Blutausstrich[5] Blutplättchen, Thrombozyten[6] säurefeste Bakterien[7] Pap(anicolaou)-Abstrich[8] Schnellabstrich[9] Scheidenabstrich[10] Harnausstrich[11] Kontrollabstrich[12] luftgetrockneter Ausstrich[13] steriler Watteträger, -tupfer[14] Rachenabstrich[15] Bürstenabstriche[16] Bronchiallavage[17]

Kultur, Züchtung
Inkubator[1] Vermehrung, Fortpflanzung[2] Nährmedium, -boden[3] kultivieren, anzüchten, eine Kultur anlegen[4] kultivierbar[5] inkubieren[6] bis d. Kulturergebnisse vorliegen[7] Pilzkultur[8] Zellkultur[9] Gewebekultur[10] Blutkultur[11] Stuhlkultur[12] Reinkultur[13] Kultur in Nährmedium[14] Kulturschale[15] Kulturflasche, -gefäß[16] Nährlösung[17] Kulturverfahren[18] Zellen kultivieren[19]

Routine Lab Studies CLINICAL TERMS 515

blood chemistry n term

rel **serum electrolytes**[1] [ɪlektrəlaɪts] n term

lab study of the concentration of various substances in the serum, e.g. acid/ alkaline phosphatase, lipids (HDL/ LDL cholesterols, triglycerides [ɪs]) creatinine [ɪæ], amylase, glucose, phosphates, BUN[2], etc.

biochemical [baɪoʊkemɪkᵊl] adj term • **immunohistochemistry**[3] n

» Electrolytes are substances which dissociate [oʊʃ] into positively or negatively charged [tʃɑːrdʒd] ions[4] [aɪənz] when dissolved in fluids, e.g. sodium[5], potassium[6] [æ], calcium [s], magnesium [iː] (cations [kætaɪənz]) and chloride [klɔːraɪd], bicarbonate, phosphate (anions).

Use routine / body / brain / serum [ɪɚ] **chemistry** • serum **chemistry** graph (abbr SCG) • clinical / nutritional[7] [ɪʃ] **biochemistry** • **biochemical** analysis and culture / results • **biochemical** study / monitoring • **electrolyte** (im)balance[8] / profile / determination[9] • **electrolyte** composition[10] [ɪʃ]/ concentration / derangement[11] [eɪndʒ] • **electrolyte** deficit[12] / depletion [iːʃ] or loss[13] / therapy • urea [jʊriːə] & (abbr U & E) **electrolytes** • **blood** smear or film[14] / culture / count[15]

chem. Blutuntersuchung
Serumelektrolyte[1] Blut-Harnstoff-Stickstoff(wert)[2] Immunhistochemie[3] negativ geladene Ionen[4] Natrium[5] Kalium[6] Ernährungsbiochemie[7] (Störung d.) Elektrolythaushalt(s)[8] Elektrolytbestimmung[9] Elektrolytzusammensetzung[10] Elektrolytentgleisung[11] Elektrolytmangel[12] Elektrolytverlust[13] Blutausstrich[14] Blutbild[15]

7

white blood count n term, abbr **WCB**   syn **white count** n jar

determination [ɜː] of the number of white blood cells (WBCs) per cmm of blood

» Skin rashes[1] [ræʃiːz] and a mild reduction in white count are common. The conventional laboratory investigations[2] such as complete blood count[3], serum chemistries, and urinalysis usually reveal [iː] the cause. Investigations for primary cancer elsewhere in the body are not indicated unless abnormal signs and results of simple lab studies[2] (e.g. CBC[3] and differential[4], stool sample[5] for occult [ʌ] blood) suggest an extrapulmonary [ʊ‖ʌ] lesion [iːʒ].

Use to obtain a **WBC** • complete or full[3] (abbr CBC or FBC)/ (differential) [-enˈʃᵊl] white[4] / red **blood count** • white / reticulocyte[6] [-saɪt] / platelet[7] [eɪ] count

Leukozytenzählung, -(gesamt)zahl, weißes Blutbild
Hautausschläge[1] Laboruntersuchungen[2] komplettes/ großes Blutbild[3] Leukozytendifferentialzählung[4] Stuhlprobe[5] Retikulozytenzählung, -zahl[6] Thrombozytenzählung, -zahl[7]

8

hemoglobin [hiːməɡloʊbɪn] n term, BE **haemo-**   abbr **Hb** or **Hgb**

protein-iron compound in the RBCs that carries oxygen to the cells and CO_2 back to the lungs
oxyhemoglobin[1] n term • **carboxyhemoglobin**[2] n • **hemoglobin(o)-** comb

» The reference ranges[3] for hemoglobin are age- and sex-dependent. Each molecule of hemo-globin contains several molecules of heme[4] [hiːm], each of which can carry one molecule of oxygen. Oximetry provides a noninvasive means of monitoring oxyhemoglobin saturation with oxygen[5].

Use total circulating[6] [ɜːr-]/ oxygenated / oxidized / adult[7] **hemoglobin** • fetal[8] [iː]/ admission[9] / sickle[10] / abnormal **hemoglobin** • **hemoglobin** concentration / saturation • **hemoglobin** derivatives[11] /-oxygen-dissociation curve[12] [ɜː]/ A / C disease[13] • **hemoglobin**emia /uria /opathy

Blutfarbstoff, Hämoglobin, Hb
Oxyhämoglobin[1] Carboxy-Hämoglobin[2] Referenzbereiche[3] Häm[4] Sauerstoffsättigung[5] Gesamthämoglobin d. Blutes[6] adultes Hämoglobin, HbA[7] fetales H, HbF[8] Hb bei Aufnahme (des Patienten)[9] Sichelzellen-Hämoglobin, HbS[10] Hämoglobinderivate[11] Sauerstoffdissoziationskurve[12] Hämoglobin-C-Krankheit[13]

9

hematocrit [hɪmætəkrɪt] n term, abbr **Hct**
  syn **packed cell volume** n term, abbr **PCV**
  rel **mean** [iː] **corpuscular** [-pʌskjələ˞] **volume**[1] n term, abbr **MCV**

percentage of total blood volume occupied by packed red cells centrifuged [se] at 2000 rpm

» WBC and differential counts, hematocrit or hemoglobin, and platelet counts were obtained regularly. The normal MCV is between 82 and 92 μm^3. Packed cell volume is determined by centrifuging the blood sample after adding an anticoagulant.

Use whole [hoʊl] blood[2] / large vessel **hematocrit** • mean circulatory / venous [iː] **hematocrit** • **hematocrit** reading[3] [iː] • **mean corpuscular** hemoglobin[4] (abbr MCH) • **mean corpuscular** hemoglobin concentration[5] (abbr MCHC)

Hämatokrit, Zellpackungsvolumen, HK(T)
mittleres korpuskuläres Erythrozytenvolumen[1] Vollbluthämatokrit[2] Hämatokritwert[3] Färbekoeffizient, MCH[4] mittlere korpuskuläre Hämoglobinkonzentration, MCHC[5]

10

blood gas analysis [blʌd ɡæs ənæləsɪs] n term

lab studies of arterial [ɪɚ] and venous [iː] blood determining the partial pressure of oxygen[1] (abbr PaO₂), of carbon dioxide (abbr PaCO₂) in arterial blood, the percentage of oxygen-saturated [ætʃ] hemoglobin (abbr SaO₂), bicarbonate[2] (HCO₃) and the pH

» Physicians [ɪʃ] must maintain a high index of suspicion [ɪʃ] and request an ABG study if a clinically important acid-base disturbance[3], hypoxemia [iː], or hypercapnia[4] is suspected.

Use arterial[5] [ɪɚ] (abbr ABG) **blood gases** • **arterial blood gas** measurement [eʒ]/ sample / profile • determination[6] / assessment[6] / monitoring of **blood gases**

Blutgasanalyse
Sauerstoffpartialdruck[1] Hydrogenkarbonat, Bikarbonat[2] Störung d. Säure-Basen-Haushalts[3] Hyperkapnie, Hyperkarbie, Erhöhung d. arteriellen CO₂-Partialdrucks[4] art. Blutgase[5] Blutgasanalyse[6]

11

516 CLINICAL TERMS — Routine Lab Studies

(erythrocyte) [ɪ] **sedimentation rate** n term, abbr **ESR**   syn **sed rate** n jar
rate at which RBCs settle¹ in a calibrated glass column² of anticoagulated blood
» Elevated sed rates indicate the presence of inflammation. The lab studies included a CBC and sedimentation rate, serum protein electrophoresis [iː], U & E³, liver and thyroid [aɪ] function tests, tests for antinuclear [(j)uː] antibody, and fasting blood glucose⁴ level.
Use high / elevated⁵ / rapid / normal **ESR** • corrected / Wintrobe's / Westergren's⁶ **ESR** • **sedimentation** reaction / index • **sedimented** red cells

Blutkörperchensenkungsgeschwindigkeit, BKS, BSG
sedimentieren, sich absetzen¹ Glaspipette² Harnstoff u. Elektrolyte³ Nüchternblutzucker⁴ erhöhte BSG⁵ BSG-Bestimmung nach Westergren⁶
12

bleeding [iː] **time** n term   rel **platelet aggregation**¹ n term → U38-11
screening [iː] test to detect platelet [pleɪtlɪt] disorders² in which the time required [aɪ] for a standardized wound [uː] to stop bleeding (normally 2-9 min) is assessed
» The bleeding time does not predict surgical bleeding, so patients with positive bleeding histories require a platelet count³, PT⁴, PTT⁵, and hematology consultation. Aspirin interferes [ɪɚ] with⁶ platelet function and prolongs bleeding time.
Use shortened / prolonged **bleeding time** • coagulation⁷ / whole blood clotting **time** • activated clotting time / thrombin⁸ / prothrombin⁴ (abbr PT) **time** • partial thromboplastin (abbr PTT) **time** • to suppress or inhibit/stimulate **platelet aggregation** • ADP-induced **platelet aggregation** • **platelet aggregation** study / inhibitor⁹ • **platelet** count³ / activation / adhesion¹⁰ [iː3] • **platelet** (dys)function / destruction [ʌ] or consumption¹¹ [ʌ]

Blutungszeit
Thrombozytenaggregation¹ Thrombozytopathien² Thrombozytenzählung³ Prothrombin-, Thromboplastinzeit, TPZ, Quick-Wert⁴ Partialthromboplastinzeit, partielle T.⁵ stört, hemmt⁶ Blutgerinnungszeit⁷ (Plasma)thrombinzeit, (P)TZ⁸ Thrombozytenaggregationshemmer⁹ Thrombozytenadhäsion¹⁰ Thrombozytenabbau¹¹
13

liver function tests n term, abbr **LFTs**   syn **liver function studies** n term pl
evaluation of the storage, filtration and excretion ability of the liver [ɪ] by assessment of the serum bilirubin [uː], alkaline phosphatase¹ [-eɪz], prothrombin time, AST (formerly SGOT²) and ALT (SGPT³) levels
» Whether routine monitoring of liver function tests helps to avoid this side effect is not known. Liver function studies showed mildly elevated bilirubin, aspartate and alanine aminotransferase as well as abnormal albumin levels.
Use lung or pulmonary⁴ [ʊ‖ʌ]/ renal⁵ [iː]/ pituitary⁶ [(j)uː] **function tests** • **LFT** abnormality

Leberfunktionstests
alkal. Phosphatase¹ Serum-Glutamat-Oxalacetat-Transaminase, Aspartataminotransferase² Serum-Glutamat-Pyruvat-T., Alaninaminotransferase³ Lungenfunktionsprüfung⁴ Nierenfunktionsprüfung⁵ Hypophysenfunktionstests⁶
14

Are you absolutely sure if this is what the doc had in mind when he asked for a midstream urine sample?

urinalysis [jʊɚɪnæləsɪs] n term, pl **-ses**   syn **urine analysis** n
  rel **urine sample** [æ] or **specimen**¹ [spesɪmən], **urine culture**² n
collecting a urine specimen for physical, microscopic (bacteria, crystals [ɪ], pus³ [ʌ], casts⁴, etc. in the sediment) and chemical examination (for ketones [iː], sugar, proteins, etc.)
» The macroscopic findings on urinalysis include pH, specific gravity, color (strawcolored⁵, dark), turbidity⁶ (clear, cloudy) and odor⁷ (slightly aromatic, foul-smelling⁸) of the urine. Lab studies in children with reflux⁹ [iː] should include urinalysis and urine culture at each visit.
Use to obtain [eɪ] a/send urine for¹⁰/detect on **urinalysis** • dipstick¹¹ / routine / (clean-catch) midstream¹² [iː] (abbr MSU) **urinalysis** • fractionated / 3-glass¹³ **urinalysis** • **urinalysis** findings • to collect¹⁴/examine/evaluate **a urine sample** • first-voided [ɔɪ] or (first-)morning¹⁵ / random **urine sample** • catheterized¹⁶ / fresh(ly voided)¹⁷ **urine sample** • 24-hour¹⁸ / post-ejaculate [dʒæ] **urine specimen** • obtained for / put in **culture** • alkaline / concentrated / casts [æ] in⁴ **urine** • **urine** collection¹⁹ / glucose [uː] level / cytologic study²⁰ • **urine** ketones / creatinine [æ]/ electrolytes • **urine** concentration²¹ / bile acids [baɪl æsɪdz]/ specific gravity [æ]

Harnuntersuchung, Harnanalyse
Harn-, Urinprobe¹ Harn-, Urinkultur² Eiter³ Harnzylinder⁴ strohgelb⁵ Trübung⁶ Geruch⁷ übelriechend⁸ Reflux⁹ Rückfluss⁹ Urin zur Analyse einschicken¹⁰ klin. Harnuntersuchung (m. Teststreifen)¹¹ Untersuchung v. Mittelstrahlurin¹² Dreigläserprobe¹³ e. Harnprobe entnehmen¹⁴ Morgenharn¹⁵ Katheterharn, -urin¹⁶ frisch gelassener Harn¹⁷ 24-Stunden-Harn¹⁸ Harngewinnung¹⁹ Harnzytologie²⁰ Harnkonzentrierung, -konzentration²¹
15

Routine Lab Studies   CLINICAL TERMS 517

level n   syn **value** [vælju:], **concentration** [kɒnˈsᵊntreɪʃᵊn] n → U81-23
quantity of an amount [aʊ] measured [meʒɚd]
  level off[1] v phr • **(un)concentrated** adj • **concentrate**[2] n & v • **low-level** adj
» The serum cortisol level generally remains elevated for 1-3 days postoperatively. Cellular immunity may be impaired when the blood glucose concentration exceeds[3] [i:] 250 mg/dL.
Use urine / blood[4] / peak [i:] serum[5] **level** • iron [aɪɚn]/ dose / toxic **level** • **level of** calcium / toxins / consciousness[6] (abbr LOC) • **level of** anxiety [ŋzaɪ]/ anesthesia [i:ʒ]/ tolerance / diaphragm[7] [daɪəfræm] • diagnostic / religious / nutritional[8] [ɪʃ] **value** • reference[9] / mean[10] [i:]/ baseline[11] [eɪ] **value** • to be of (no/ little/ great/ clinical/ diagnostic[12]) **value** • low / high / increased / reduced **concentration**

Spiegel, Wert, Gehalt, Pegel, Konzentration
ausgleichen; abflachen, s. einpendeln[1] Konzentrat; anreichern, konzentrieren[2] übersteigt[3] Blutspiegel[4] Serumhöchstwert[5] Bewusstseinslage[6] Zwerchfellstand[7] Nährwert[8] Referenzwert[9] Mittelwert[10] Ausgangswert[11] von diagnostischem Wert sein[12]
16

titer [taɪtɚ‖espBE ti:-] n term, BE **titre**   rel **dilution**[1] [daɪluːʃᵊn] n → U81-23
strength of a solution or concentration of a solute[2] as determined by volumetric assessment (titration[3])
  titrate[4] v term • **microtiter** n • **titration**[3] n • **high-titer** adj • **titratable** adj
» An agglutination titer of 1:160 or higher is considered positive. Seroconversion [ɜ:] (a two- to fourfold rise in titer[5]) is useful in previously [i:] nonimmune individuals. The infusion dosage must be titrated upward[6] to achieve [tʃ] the desired [aɪ] effect.
Use blood / antibody[7] (abbr Ab)/ IgG / (serum) complement fixation **titer** • (indirect) hemagglutination / serum reagin [riːeɪgɪn] **titer** • hemolytic [ɪ]/ cerebrospinal [aɪ] fluid **titer** • low / rising / elevated[8] / high **titer** • **titer** rise[9] / of 1:5 / of agglutinins • **to titrate** the dose (to response/ to effect[10]) • **microtiter** plate[11] [eɪ]/ wells[12] • dose / serial[13] [ɪɚ]/ upward **titration** • **titration** curve[14] [ɜ:]/ steps / period / test[15] • **high-titer** antiserum / inhibitor / vaccine [ks] • **titratable** acid[16] [æsɪd]/ iodine

Titer
Verdünnung, Dilution[1] gelöste Substanz[2] Titration[3] titrieren[4] vierfacher Titeranstieg[5] hinauftitriert[6] Antikörpertiter[7] erhöhter Titer[8] Titeranstieg[9] d. Dosierung nach Wirkung titrieren[10] Mikrotiterplatte[11] Vertiefungen in der Mikrotiterplatte[12] Serientitration[13] Titrationskurve[14] Titrationsanalyse[15] titrierbare Säure[16]
17

yield [ji:ld] v & n   sim **result**[1] [rɪzʌlt] v & n
(v, i) to produce results (ii) to bend or give up resistance under pressure
  low-yield[2] adj • **unyielding**[3] adj • **result in**[4]/ **from** v phr
» Aspiration failed to yield gross [oʊ] pus[5] [pʌs]. Pericardial biopsy [aɪ] has a higher yield but may also be negative. Throat [oʊ] cultures from carriers usually yield only small numbers of organisms. His alkalosis may result from fluid and electrolyte losses.
Use **to yield** good results / a diagnosis • diagnostic / maximum / low **yield** • **unyielding** fascia [fæʃ(ɪ)ə] • **low-yield** procedure[6] [si:]

(i) **ergeben, liefern; Ergebnis, Ertrag**
(ii) **nachgeben**
sich ergeben, resultieren; Ergebnis[1] unergiebig[2] nicht nachgebend, unelastisch[3] führen zu[4] makroskopisch sichtbarer Eiter[5] Verfahren mit geringer Ausbeute[6]
18

elevated adj   syn **increased** [i:], **raised** [eɪ] adj,
                    rel **high**[1] adj, **rise**[2] [aɪ] vi irr & n → U64-17
  elevation[3] [eɪʃ] n • **elevate** v • **increase**[2] [v ɪnkriːs‖n ɪn-] vi & vt & n • **raise**[4] vt
» Leisure [i:] time physical activity[5] levels seem to increase with income and education and to decrease with age. Including smoking status in the history can result in a significant increase in stop-smoking messages. Fasting blood sugar[6] was elevated.
Use grossly[7] / initially [ɪʃ] **elevated** • **elevated** triglycerides[8] [ɪ]/ body temperature • **elevated** ST segment[9] / sed rate / skin lesion [i:ʒ]/ position [ɪʃ] • transient / intermittent / persistent **elevation** • **increased** risk[10] / • small / great / twofold[11] **increase** • **increase in** size[12] / number • **rise in** pressure[13] / antibody titer • 6-fold / pulse [ʌ]/ temperature[14] **rise**

  Note: Mark the difference between **to rise** - rose - risen[2] (e.g. the blood pressure rises to high levels) and **to raise**[4] (e.g. the leg/ the BP).

erhöht
hoch, erhöht[1] (sich) erhöhen, ansteigen; Erhöhung, Anstieg[2] Erhöhung; Hochlagerung[3] erhöhen, (an)heben[4] Freizeitsport[5] Nüchternblutzucker[6] stark erhöht[7] erhöhte Triglyzeridwerte[8] ST-Streckenhebung[9] erhöhtes Risiko[10] Anstieg auf das Doppelte[11] Vergrößerung[12] Druckanstieg[13] Temperaturanstieg[14]
19

decreased [i:] adj   syn **reduced, diminished, depressed** adj, rel **low**[1] adj
  decrease[2] v & n • **decline**[3] [aɪ] vi & n • **reduce**[4] vt • **reduction** [ʌ] n • **lower**[4] v
» Laboratory abnormalities include decreased concentrations of serum proteins. The calculated gain [eɪ] in life expectancy from modest[5] decreases in blood cholesterol is low. Nasal polyps may result in a diminished sense of smell. She had depressed levels of LH and FSH.
Use slightly [slaɪtli]/ considerably / markedly[6] / dramatically **decreased** • **decreased** activity / air entry / breath [e] sounds[7] • **decreased** glucose content / bile [aɪ] salts [ɔ:] • **decreased** cardiac output / blood flow [oʊ] • **decreased** reflexes[8] [i:]/ hearing [ɪɚ] • **reduced** blood flow / cell count / lung volume • **diminished** breath sounds[7] / cardiac output / GH secretion [i:ʃ] • **depressed** plasma level / tubular reabsorption / thyroid function • **low** concentration / intensity / density / WBC[9]

herabgesetzt, vermindert
niedrig[1] abnehmen, sinken; verringern, senken; Abnahme, Rückgang[2] abnehmen, sinken; Abnahme, Rückgang[3] reduzieren, senken[4] geringfügig[5] deutlich herabgesetzt/ niedriger[6] abgeschwächte Atemgeräusche[7] verminderte Reflexe[8] niedrige Leukozytenzahl[9]
20

CLINICAL TERMS — Diagnosis

normal adj   opposite **abnormal[1], atypical[1]** adj → U107-19f

in agreement with the norm, an average or a particular statistically defined range in a large population

norm[2] n • **normalize[3]** v • **abnormality[4]** n • **typical** adj • **normo-** comb

» His blood glucose level has returned to normal. A respiratory rate of 18/min is normally considered WNL[5], though some would set the limit of normal at 16 or 25 breaths/min. A high central venous pressure suggests volume expansion exceeding the upper limit of normal[6].

Use to return to[3]/be/appear **normal** • within[5] (abbr WNL)/ beyond[7] **normal limits** • completely / nearly / otherwise[8] **normal** • (to be) above or below / grossly[9] **normal** • at the lower limit of[10] **normal** • **normal** range[11] / tissue / temperature • **normal** living / size / assay volume • **normally** developed / functioning • **abnormally** low / high / sensitive / fast[12] • adult / age-specific / social / cultural [ʌ] **norm** • **normo**tensive[13] /tensives[14] /active • **normo**thermia [ɜː] /volemia[15] [iː]/ chromic anemia

normal, im Norm(al)bereich

anomal, abnorm, atypisch, von d. Norm abweichend[1] Norm(wert)[2] (sich) normalisieren[3] Anomalie[4] im Normalbereich[5] oberer Normalwert[6] außerhalb des Norm-/ Normalbereichs[7] sonst ohne Befund[8] makroskopisch normal[9] im unteren Normalbereich[10] Normalbereich[11] ungewöhnlich schnell[12] normoton[13] Normotoniker[14] Normovolämie[15]

21

positive adj term, abbr +**ive, pos.**   opposite **negative[1]** adj term, abbr –**ive, neg.**

(of lab tests or clinical signs) indicating that a substance or finding is present, which is usually a pathologic sign

» Strongly positive[2] results were obtained in 23% of patients. This group had more results that were truly positive[3], that is the patients had more advanced disease. A highly sensitive test will render[4] few false [ɔː] negative results[5]. Two sputum [(j)uː] specimens were positive for acid-fast bacilli[6] [bəsɪlaɪ].

Use weakly [iː]/ skin[7]-/ sero[8]/ gram-**positive** • **positive** reaction / x-ray [eksreɪ] findings[9] / washout test / family history[10] • **negative** cytology [saɪ-]/ charge[11] [tʃɑːrdʒ]/ response[12] / for occult [ʌ] blood[13]

positiv

negativ[1] stark positiv[2] eindeutig positiv[3] ergeben[4] falsch-negative Ergebnisse[5] d. Test auf säurefeste Bakterien war positiv[6] m. pos. Hauttest[7] seropositiv[8] positiver Röntgenbefund[9] pos. Familienanamnese[10] negative Ladung[11] negative Reaktion[12] kein Nachweis v. okkultem Blut[13]

22

borderline adj term & jar   sim **equivocal[1], doubtful[1]** [daʊtfəl], **suspicious[2]** [ɪʃ] adj

(of findings, symptoms or status) to be questionable[1] or inconclusive[1] (i.e. slightly but not quite abnormal)

suspect[3] v & n • **suspicion[4]** [ɪʃ] n • **suspected[5]** adj • **undoubtedly[6]** adv

» These drugs should be avoided in patients with borderline or elevated blood pressure. Is this mole[7] suspicious? A prolonged clinical course [ɔː] should raise the suspicion of possible cancer. In doubtful cases bone marrow examination is indicated. Laparoscopic evaluation is of considerable value in evaluation[8] in patients with a suspected anomaly of the GU tract.

Use **borderline** case[9] / hypertension[10] [haɪpɚ-]/ curve [ɜː]/ glucose tolerance test • **borderline**-low value / malignancy[11] / syndrome [ɪ] • **equivocal** response / findings[12] / diagnosis • **doubtful** cases / results • **suspicious** cells / lesion [iːʒ]/ mass / area[13] • **suspected** acute myocardial [maɪ-] infarction/ diagnosis[14] / appendicitis

grenzwertig, borderline

unklar, nicht eindeutig[1] verdächtig[2] vermuten, Verdacht haben; Verdächtige(r)[3] Verdacht[4] Verdacht auf[5] zweifellos[6] Leberfleck, Nävus[7] Abklärung[8] Grenzfall[9] Grenzwert-, Borderline-Hypertonie[10] Borderline-Tumor[11] nicht eindeutiger Befund[12] verdächtiges Areal[13] Verdachtsdiagnose[14]

23

Unit 117 Diagnosis

Related Units: 118 Diagnostic Procedures, 102 History Taking, 107 Physical Examination, 116 Lab Studies, 119 Etiology

assess [əses] vt   sim **evaluate[1]** [ɪvæljueɪt] vt

to collect, check and verify information about a patient's condition (history, physical, lab data)

assessment[2] n • **assessible** adj • **reassess[3]** vt • **evaluation[4]** [ɪvæljueɪʃən] n

» This technique [tekniːk] is likely to be most useful in patients whose symptom severity[5] [e] cannot be assessed by history or exercise testing[6]. The history[7] is also very important in assessing therapeutic [juː] failure[8]. Clinical and laboratory evaluation must include assessment for heart disease and hematologic disorders.

Use **to assess** a patient's needs / adequacy of circulation[9] • **to assess** neurologic status[10] / bladder function [ʌ] • clinical / functional[11] / quantitative [ɒː] primary [aɪ] bedside[12] **assessment** • preoperative / (non)invasive [eɪ]/ (cardiac) risk[13] / psychiatric[14] [saɪkɪætrɪk]/ nutritional [ɪʃ] **assessment** • **assessment** technique / of health status • baseline [eɪ]/ outpatient[15] / speech [spiːtʃ]/ personality **evaluation** • home / infertility / disability[16] **evaluation**

bestimmen, beurteilen

beurteilen, auswerten, abklären[1] Beurteilung, Bestimmung[2] erneut bestimmen[3] Auswertung, Abklärung[4] Stärke, Schweregrad[5] Belastungstest[6] Anamnese[7] Therapieversagen[8] die Kreislauffunktion prüfen[9] den Neurostatus erheben[10] Funktionsprüfung[11] Statuserhebung am Krankenbett[12] Risikoeinschätzung, -beurteilung[13] psychiatr. Untersuchung[14] ambulante Untersuchung/ Abklärung[15] Beurteilung des Invaliditätsgrades[16]

1

Diagnosis | CLINICAL TERMS 519

determine [dɪtɜːrmɪn] *vt*   *rel* **estimate**[1] [*v* ɛstɪmeɪt‖*n* ɛstɪmət] *v & n*

to establish the exact nature [eɪ] of a clinical feature [fiːtʃɚ] or parameter by means of a test or investigation

determination[2] *n term* • **determinant**[3] *adj & n* • **indeterminate**[4] *adj* • **estimation**[5] *n*

» The size of the aneurysm [ænjɚɪzəm] is best determined by ultrasound [ʌ] examination. The volume deficit [dɛfɪsɪt] can be estimated from clinical signs and changes in body weight. The patient and family should be given an estimate of prognosis and expected quality of life.

Use **to determine** kidney size [aɪ]/ vital [aɪ] signs[6] • clinical / prognostic / antigenic[7] [dʒe] **determinant** • risk-benefit[8] / dose / rough[9] [rʌf]/ accurate **estimate** • **estimated** blood loss[10] (*abbr* EBL)/ date of delivery[11] • **estimated** time of arrival [aɪ] (*abbr* ETA)/ rate • pH / blood glucose[12] [uː]/ chemical [ke-]/ serial [sɪəɪəl]/ monthly [ʌ] **determination** • **indeterminate** mass / number [ʌ]/ time / ELISA test[13]

feststellen, -legen, bestimmen, ermitteln
einschätzen, bewerten, beurteilen; Schätzung, Beurteilung[1] Bestimmung, Feststellung[2] entscheidend; Determinante, entscheidender Faktor[3] unbestimmt, unklar, nicht determiniert[4] Bestimmung, (Ein)schätzung[5] die Vitalfunktionen prüfen[6] Antigendeterminante, Epitop[7] Risiko-Nutzen-Abwägung[8] grobe Schätzung[9] geschätzter Blutverlust[10] voraussichtl. Geburtstermin[11] Blutzuckerbestimmung[12] nicht eindeutiger/ zweifelhafter ELISA-Test[13]   2

---

obtain [əbteɪn] *vt*   *sim* **collect**[1] [kəlɛkt] *vt*

to gather information or come into possession of data, qualities, or objects

obtaining[2] *n jar* • **(un)obtainable** *adj* • **collection**[3] *n*

» The cells were obtained from a fresh tumor specimen[4]. Baseline levels must be obtained before starting therapy. Pulse and BP were unobtainable. Collect a small amount of urine in a sterile container.

Use **to obtain** x-rays[5] / a biopsy [baɪɒpsi]/ footprints / adequate rest • **to obtain** pain relief[6] [iː]/ stability / a complete remission[7] • **to obtain** surgical consultation / written consent[8] / skin grafts[9] / readily [e] **obtainable** • **to collect** secretions [iːʃ]/ urine[10] / specimens [es] • blood / stool / urine / data / time of / method of **collection** • **collection** technique / jar [dʒɑːr]/ device [dɪvaɪs] • **collection** system [ɪ]/ error • of pus[11] [ʌ]/ of specimens[12] • blood **collection** bag

erhalten, gewinnen, erzielen
(an)sammeln, entnehmen[1] Anamneseerhebung[2] (An)sammlung, Entnahme[3] Tumorgewebeprobe[4] Röntgenaufnahmen machen[5] Schmerzlinderung erzielen[6] e. Vollremission erzielen[7] schriftl. Einwilligung einholen[8] Hauttransplantate entnehmen[9] Harn sammeln[10] Eiteransammlung[11] Probenentnahme[12]   3

---

miss *v term*   *opposite* **identify**[1] [aɪdɛntəfaɪ], **recognize**[2], **localize**[3] [loʊkəlaɪz] *v*

to overlook a diagnostically helpful clinical feature [iːtʃ] or fail to diagnose a condition correctly

missing[4] *adj* • **identification** *n* • **identifiable**[5] [-aɪəbl] *adj* • **recognition** [ɪʃ] *n* • **(well-/ un)recognized**[6] *adj* • **localization** *n*

» For confirming equivocal[7] findings Doppler ultrasound is superior to phlebography, which may miss small thrombi [aɪ] in the calf [kæf] veins[8]. The rash[9] may suggest the diagnosis but is often missed because it chiefly occurs during the night. No specific source [ɔː] of pain was identified. MRI may be necessary to identify and localize the site of cord compression.

Use **missed** diagnosis / menses[10] / polyps / abortion[11] • **to identify** abnormalities / injuries / inflammation[12] / pathogens • **to identify** patients with ureteral [iː] obstruction [ʌ]/ risk factors • **to recognize** symptoms[13] [ɪ]/ signs • **to localize** pain[14] / a tumor / polyps / focal lesions [iːʒ] • **missing** secretions / teeth / link / neurotransmitters[15] / early[16] / microscopic[17] **identification** • intraoperative / endoscopic / accurate **identification** • to be/go[18]/pass **unrecognized** • clinical / prompt / early[16] / delayed [eɪ]/ timely[19] • under-/ self-**recognition** • **unrecognized** disease / trauma [ɒː]/ measles[20] [iː]

übersehen, nicht bemerken
feststellen, nachweisen, identifizieren, erkennen[1] (wieder)erkennen[2] lokalisieren, festlegen, bestimmen[3] fehlend[4] feststell-, nachweisbar[5] unerkannt[6] unklar, nicht eindeutig[7] Venae fibulares[8] Ausschlag[9] ausgebliebene Monatsblutung[10] Missed abortion, verhaltener Abort[11] eine Entzündung feststellen/ nachweisen[12] Symptome erkennen[13] Schmerz lokalisieren[14] fehlende Neurotransmitter[15] Früherkennung[16] mikroskop. Nachweis[17] unbemerkt bleiben[18] rechtzeitiges Erkennen[19] nicht erkannte Masern[20]   4

---

detect [dɪtɛkt] *vt*   *sim* **ascertain**[1] [æsɚteɪn], **encounter**[2] [aʊ], **appreciate**[3] [əpriːʃieɪt] *vt*

to find or determine pathologic abnormalities, esp. in the diagnostic process

detection *n* • **(un)detectable**[4] *adj* • **appreciable**[5] *adj* • **(un)appreciated** *adj*

» Thyroid [θaɪrɔɪd] dysfunction is difficult to detect clinically. Antibodies were detected in two women with known breast [e] cancer, and in a third, finding the antibody led to the detection of underlying breast cancer. A2[6] is best appreciated at the left sternal [ɜː] border.

Use **to detect** emboli [aɪ]/ anemia [iː]/ gallstones[7] [ɔː]/ metastases / antibodies • **to detect** pathogens / recurrences[8] [ɜː]/ occult [ʌ] disease[9] • **to ascertain the** exact diagnosis[10] / cause of occlusion [uːʒ]/ origin of nerves • **to encounter** a situation / difficulties / evidence of mania [eɪ] • **to encounter** resistance[11] / complications / patients with similar complaints [eɪ] • **to appreciate** a heart murmur[12] [ɜː]/ on chest x-ray[13] • to permit *or* allow (for)/improve/escape[14] **detection** • prenatal [eɪ]/ early[15] / antigen[16] / carrier / cancer **detection** • **detection** rate[17] / test / method / threshold[18] • **appreciable** rise[19] / amount [aʊ]

entdecken, feststellen
ermitteln, feststellen[1] stoßen auf[2] feststellen, erkennen, wahrnehmen[3] nicht feststellbar[4] feststellbar; deutlich, nennenswert[5] zweiter Aortenton, A2[6] Gallensteine feststellen[7] Rezidive feststellen[8] einen okkulten Tumor entdecken[9] eine Abschlussdiagnose stellen[10] auf Widerstand stoßen[11] e. Herzgeräusch feststellen[12] auf d. Thoraxröntgen erkennen[13] unbemerkt bleiben[14] Früherkennung[15] Antigennachweis[16] Entdeckungsrate[17] Wahrnehmungsschwelle[18] deutlicher Anstieg[19]   5

520 CLINICAL TERMS   Diagnosis

finding [fɪndɪŋ] n clin & term, usu pl   sim **result**[1] [rɪzʌlt] n

observation or result of examinations, tests, or diagnostic procedures[2] [siː]

find[3] - found - found [faʊnd] v irr • **result in**[4]/ **from** v phr

» The findings on examination included pain and numbness[5] [ʌ] of the toes. The most common finding is the presence of a cystic [sɪstɪk] mass. Treatment should be started on the basis of clinical findings without waiting for laboratory confirmation. These drugs have definite effects on the lab results.

Use to have/record[6] **findings** • clinical[7] / physical / auscultatory[8] [ɔːskʌl-]/ laboratory[9] **findings** • biopsy / CT / radiographic or radiologic[10] **findings** • (ab)normal / common / rare / solitary / focal **findings** • prominent or striking[11] [aɪ] / pertinent[12] [ɜː] **findings** • suggestive [dʒe] / negative[13] / positive **findings** • diagnostic / ominous[14] [ɒː]/ early **findings** • late / chance or incidental[15] **findings** • **findings of** pleural [ʊə] effusion [juː3] / metastases • **findings on** gross [oʊ] examination[16] / diagnostic workup • **findings on** ultrasound [ʌ] / barium enema[17] / admission[18] • test[19] / treatment / (ab)normal / spurious[20] [jʊə] **results** • interim[21] / final [aɪ] or conclusive[22] [uː]/ long-term[23] **results**

Befund, Beobachtung
Ergebnis[1] diagnostische Verfahren[2] (heraus)finden, feststellen[3] führen zu[4] Taubheitsgefühl[5] den Befund protokollarisch festhalten/ protokollieren[6] klin. Befund[7] Auskultationsbefund[8] Laborbefund[9] Röntgenbefund[10] auffällige Ergebnisse[11] klin. relevante Ergebnisse[12] negativer Befund[13] schlechter Befund[14] Zufallsbefund[15] makroskop. B.[16] Befund nach Bariumeinlauf[17] Aufnahmebefund[18] Untersuchungs-, Testergebnisse[19] falsche E.[20] Zwischenergebnisse[21] endgültige E.[22] Langzeitergebnisse[23]
6

alert [əlɜːrt] v   rel **watch** [wɒtʃ] **for**[1] v phr, → U8-7; U7-2
opposite **allay**[2] [əleɪ] v

to call the physician's [ɪʃ] attention to the possibility of health risks or complications

alertness[3] n • alert[4] adj • alert[5] n • watchful[4] adj • watchfulness[3] n

» These findings should alert the physician. Be alert for delayed development of upper airways obstruction. Clinicians should be alert to this diagnostic possibility. The results depend on the physician's alertness to physical clues[6] [kluːz]. An enlarged lymph [ɪ] node that persists may warrant [ɔː] aspiration biopsy in order allay concern [sɜː] about malignancy.

Use **to be alert** to complications • **to be on the alert** for sth. • medical **alert** bracelet[7] [eɪs] • **to watch for** potential side effects[8] / circulatory overload / airway obstruction [ʌ] • watchful waiting[9] / approach [-oʊtʃ] • **to allay** fear [fɪə] / concerns or anxiety[10] [æŋzaɪəti] / apprehension[11] / doubts[12]

warnen, aufmerksam machen
Ausschau halten nach, achten auf[1] beruhigen, beschwichtigen[2] Wachsam-, Aufmerksamkeit[3] wachsam, aufmerksam[4] Alarm[5] klinische Anzeichen[6] medizin. Informationsarmband[7] auf mögl. Nebenwirkungen achten[8] Surveillance, Beobachtungsstrategie[9] Ängste nehmen[10] Sorgen vertreiben[11] Zweifel zerstreuen[12]
7

suspect [v səspekt‖n & adj sʌspekt] v & n & adj   rel **doubt**[1] [daʊt] v & n

(v) to assume [(j)uː] sth. without definite proof or to be uncertain [sɜː] about sth.

suspicion[2] [səspɪʃən] n • suspected[3] adj • suspicious[4] adj • doubtful[5] adj • dubious[5] [duːbiəs] adj

» This should lead the physician to suspect bladder injury. Nodules suspicious [ɪʃ] for malignancy should be biopsied. Patients with documented or suspected heart disease should be excluded. If the diagnosis remains in doubt, repeated careful reappraisal[6] [eɪ] of the patient's progress is necessary.

Use to arouse[7] [aʊ] /raise[7] [eɪ] /prompt[7] **suspicion** • (high/ low) clinical / a high index of / strong / inappropriate[8] **suspicion** • **suspicion of** infection / cancer • suspicious lesion / nodule[9] • **suspected** hearing loss / lung disease[10] / diagnosis[11] / case / carrier[12] • **suspected** cause [kɒːz] / abnormality / malignancy[13] / offending agent [eɪdʒ] • to be in[14] / there is no **doubt** • **doubtful** cases[15] / results[16] • **dubious** reputation / accuracy • to be of **dubious** diagnostic value[17]

vermuten, einen Verdacht haben; Verdächtige(r); verdächtig, suspekt
(an)zweifeln; Zweifel[1] Verdacht[2] Verdachts-, Verdacht auf[3] verdächtig[4] unsicher, zweifelhaft[5] Neubeurteilung[6] Verdacht erregen[7] unbegründeter Verdacht[8] verdächtiger Knoten[9] Verdacht auf Lungenkrankheit[10] Verdachtsdiagnose[11] vermutl. Keimträger[12] Verdacht auf e. bösartigen Tumor[13] anzweifeln, Zweifel haben[14] fragl. Fälle[15] zweifelhafte/ unklare Ergebnisse[16] von zweifelhaftem diagnost. Wert sein[17]
8

evidence [evɪdəns] n   sim **proof**[1] [pruːf] n, rel **manifestation**[2] n → U103-3

facts and observations which support a concept, diagnosis, treatment plan or hypothesis

evident[3] adj • prove [pruːv] v • biopsy-proven [baɪɒpsi] adj • manifest[4] adj & v

» There was no evidence of recurrent [ɜː] disease[5]. However, these observations have been difficult to confirm [ɜː] and must be considered anecdotal evidence. A blood test will provide [aɪ] proof of diagnosis[6]. Crepitus was manifest with motion [oʊʃ].

Use to find/obtain [eɪ] /collect/provide[7] [aɪ] /show **evidence** • clinical / experimental / little[8] / strong / growing **evidence** • recent [iːs] / radiographic[9] / laboratory / irrefutable[10] [juː] **evidence** • (no) **evidence of** disease[11] (abbr NED)/ pathology / invasion [eɪ3] / metastases • a growing body of **evidence** • irrefutable[10] / clinical / definite[12] **proof** • **to manifest** itself[13] / as headaches / symptoms / suicidal [saɪ] tendencies • early / cardinal / clinical / cutaneous[14] [eɪ] **manifestations** • neurologic / systemic / disease **manifestations** • to be/become[13] **manifest** • clinically[15] **manifest** • **manifest** deviation [eɪ] / coronary heart disease[16]

Anzeichen, Hinweis, Beweis
Be-, Nachweis[1] Anzeichen, Symptom, Manifestation[2] offensichtlich, klar[3] deutl. erkennbar, manifest; auftreten, s. manifestieren[4] Rezidiv[5] Diagnose bestätigen[6] Hinweise liefern[7] wenig Hinweise[8] radiolog. Nachweis[9] unwiderlegbarer Beweis[10] tumorfrei[11] eindeutiger Beweis[12] sich manifestieren[13] Hautmanifestationen[14] klin. manifest[15] manifeste/ symptomatische koronare Herzerkrankung[16]
9

Diagnosis | CLINICAL TERMS **521**

diagnose [daɪəgnoʊz] v term   opposite **misdiagnose**[1] v term
to identify the cause and type of a disease on the basis of the history, physical, lab data, etc.
over/ self-diagnose v term • **(un)diagnosed**[2] adj • **diagnosable**[3] adj
» In its early stages, cor pulmonale [-ɑːliː] can be diagnosed on the basis of radiologic evidence. He was diagnosed with lung cancer a year ago. The lesion [iː3] was clinically diagnosed as chancroid[4] [ʃ]. Urethral [iː] carcinoma may be frequently misdiagnosed as stricture.
Use to be **diagnosed with** certainty / AIDS[5] • (in)correctly / reliably [aɪ]/ timely[6] **diagnosed** • not yet (abbr NYD)/ erroneously[7] [oʊ]/ mistakenly[7] / newly[8] **diagnosed** • impossible[9] / difficult / failure [feɪljɚ] **to diagnose** • **undiagnosed** fracture / malignancy • clinically[10] **diagnosable**

diagnostizieren, eine Diagnose stellen
e. Fehldiagnose stellen[1] (un)erkannt, (nicht) diagnostiziert[2] feststell-, diagnostizierbar[3] weicher Schanker, Ulcus molle[4] bei jem. AIDS diagnostizieren[5] rechtzeitig diagnostiziert[6] fälschlich/ irrtümlich diagnostiziert[7] neu diagnostiziert[8] nicht diagnostizierbar[9] klinisch diagnostizierbar[10]   10

diagnosis n term, pl -ses, abbr **D**ₓ   rel **(diagnostic) workup**[1] n jar
(i) outcome of the diagnostic workup
(ii) process of clinical assessment and decision-making
(non-)diagnostic adj • **diagnostician**[2] [-ɪʃᵊn] n • **diagnostics**[1] n rare
» Most patients are incurable at the time of diagnosis. Blood tests are a key part of the diagnostic workup. The diagnostic procedures were well tolerated. The workup was not diagnostic.
Use to make[3]/establish[4]/verify[5]/confirm[5]/support/suggest **a diagnosis** • clinical / physical / laboratory **diagnosis** • antenatal [eɪ]/ neonatal / differential[6] / suspected[7] **diagnosis** • admission[8] / working or provisional[9] / (un)equivocal / missed **diagnosis** • preliminary or presumptive [ʌ] or tentative[9] / most likely / transfer **diagnosis** • discharge / final or definitive[10] / accurate[11] / pathologic **diagnosis** • at the time of[12] **diagnosis** • **diagnostic** evaluation / staging / aid[13] [eɪ]/ tool[13] [uː] • **diagnostic** study / imaging[14] / surgery / indicators • **diagnostic** abnormality / value / purpose • means [iː] of[15] **diagnostics**

(i) Diagnose
(ii) Diagnostik
diagnostische Untersuchungen, Diagnostik[1] Diagnostiker(in)[2] eine Diagnose stellen[3] die D. sicherstellen/ absichern[4] die D. bestätigen[5] Differentialdiagnose[6] Verdachtsdiagnose[7] Einweisungsdiagnose[8] vorläufige D., Erstdiagnose[9] Abschlussdiagnose[10] exakte D.[11] bei Diagnosestellung[12] diagnost. Hilfsmittel[13] bildgebende Diagnostik[14] diagnost. Maßnahmen/ Mittel[15]

11

confirm [kənfɜːrm] vt   syn **verify** [vɛrɪfaɪ] vt
sim **corroborate**[1] [ɒː], **support**[1],
substantiate[1] [səbstænʃieɪt] vt
to make a diagnosis, suspicion, or concept more definite, e.g. by additional clinical evidence
confirmation[2] n • **verification**[2] n • **support**[3] n • **confirmatory**[4] adj
» The diagnosis is usually confirmed by plain [eɪ] films[5]. Family members were able to provide confirmation of weight loss. Challenge [tʃ] tests[6] to confirm the diagnosis are risky. Electron microscopy is confirmatory in equivocal cases.
Use to require/provide **confirmation** • unequivocal[7] / diagnostic / laboratory **confirmation** • serologic / x-ray [ɛksreɪ] or radiologic[8] **confirmation** • **confirmatory** tests[9] / culture [ʌ]/ laboratory studies • **confirmatory** serologic assays[10]/ data

bestätigen
erhärten, untermauern[1] Bestätigung[2] Unterstützung[3] bestätigend, Bestätigungs-[4] Leeraufnahmen[5] Provokationstests[6] eindeutige Bestätigung[7] radiolog. Bestätigung[8] Bestätigungstests[9] bestätigende serolog. Untersuchungen/ Tests[10]

12

mimic [mɪmɪk] vt   syn **masquerade** [mæskəreɪd] vt, rel **mask**[1] vt
to resemble, esp. a disease that produces symptoms that can easily be mistaken for those of another
masked[2] adj term • **masquerading** adj • **mimicry**[3] [mɪmɪkri] n
» Preeclampsia-eclampsia can mimic and be confused with many other conditions. Swelling may mask a palpable defect [iː] in the tendon[4]. Nasal [eɪ] diphtheria may be mimicked by a foreign body[5]. The cutaneous lesions[6] of syphilis [ɪ] may masquerade as skin tumors.
Use rarely / initially / occasionally [eɪ3] / closely[7] **mimic** • molecular[8] / mechanisms [ek] of[9] **mimicry** • **mimicry** of other diseases • **to masquerade** as pneumonia [n(j)uː-]/ as allergic [əlɜːrdʒɪk] rhinitis [aɪ] • **masked** depression[10]

ähnlich sein, vortäuschen
verdecken, überlagern[1] verdeckt, larviert[2] Nachahmung, Mimikry[3] Sehne[4] Fremdkörper[5] Hautläsionen[6] sehr ähnlich sein[7] molekulares Mimikry[8] Nachahmungsmechanismen[9] larvierte Depression[10]

13

rule out [ruːl aʊt] vt phr, abbr **R/O**   syn **exclude** [ɪksklu̶ːd] vt
to eliminate possible causes of the patient's condition and dismiss them from consideration[1]
exclusion[2] [uː3] n • **exclusive**[3] adj • **excludable** adj
» Neither MRI nor CT scan is diagnostic of Alzheimer's disease, but both are useful in ruling out frontal lobe tumor, stroke[4] or hemorrhage[5]. All possible known causes have been ruled out. A normal sedimentation rate does not exclude the diagnosis of polymyalgia [aɪ] rheumatica. After exclusion of organic causes, the patient was diagnosed with idiopathic anal [eɪ] pain.
Use to require[6]/warrant[6] [ɔː] /permit **exclusion** • serologic / genetic / careful **exclusion** • **exclusion** of secondary causes • diagnosis of or by[7] **exclusion** • **excludable** diagnosis[8]

ausschließen
nicht mehr berücksichtigen[1] Ausschluss[2] ausschließlich, alleinig, ausschließend, Ausschluss-[3] Schlaganfall[4] Blutung[5] den Ausschluss erfordern[6] Ausschlussdiagnose[7] auszuschließende Diagnose[8]

14

differential [dɪfəren¹ʃəl] **diagnosis** n term, abbr **DD, DD_x**
rel **distinguish¹** [dɪstɪŋgwɪʃ], **discriminate¹** v

determination by systematic comparison of the diagnostic findings which of two or more conditions causing similar clinical features is the one from which the patient is suffering

differentiate¹ [dɪfəren¹ʃieɪt] v • **differentiation²** n • **distinction²** [dɪstɪŋkʃən] n • **discrimination²** n • **indiscriminate³** adj • **(in)distinguishable⁴** adj

» The main differential diagnosis is between impetigo and acute allergic contact dermatitis [aɪ]. Differential diagnostic considerations⁵ relate chiefly to the specific pulmonary [ʊ‖ʌ] disease. The primary differential diagnoses are restrictive cardiomyopathy and tamponade. A history of contact helps distinguish contact dermatitis from other skin lesions.

Use to perform/make⁶/narrow⁷/be crucial [uːʃ] to⁸/be part of **the differential diagnosis** • to aid or assist or be helpful⁹ **in DD** • to be considered in or to enter into or to be included¹⁰ **in the DD** • clinical clue to / major or main / accurate / precise [saɪ]/ difficult / radiologic or radiographic **DD** • **DD of** hepatitis / breast cancer / esophagitis¹¹ [dʒaɪ]

Differentialdiagnose
unterscheiden, differenzieren¹ Unterscheidung, Differenzierung² unkritisch, willkürlich, wahllos³ (nicht) zu unterscheiden⁴ differentialdiagnostische Überlegungen⁵ eine Differentialdiagnose stellen⁶ die Differentialdiagnose eingrenzen⁷ für die Differentialdiagnose überaus wichtig sein⁸ bei d. Differentialdiagnose hilfreich sein⁹ in d. Differentialdiagnose miteinbezogen werden¹⁰ Differentialdiagnose der Ösophagitis¹¹

15

hallmark [hɔːlmɑːrk] n   sim **cornerstone¹** n

the most prominent, distinctive or diagnostic clinical feature [fiːtʃɚ] of a disease

» Severe pain radiating [eɪ] to the back² and weight loss are hallmarks of pancreatic cancer. For mild to moderate preeclampsia-eclampsia, bed rest³ is the cornerstone of therapy. Endocrinologic profiles are the cornerstones of laboratory investigations.

Use clinical⁴ / pathologic / histologic / cytogenetic [saɪtə-] **hallmark** • **cornerstone of** diagnosis⁵ / nutritional [ɪʃ] assessment / prevention / treatment

Kennzeichen, charakterist. Merkmal
Eckpfeiler, wichtigstes Kriterium¹ der in d. Rücken ausstrahlt² Bettruhe³ klin. Merkmal⁴ entscheidendes diagnost. Kriterium⁵

16

outweigh [aʊtweɪ] v   rel **weigh (against)¹** [weɪ] v

to be of greater importance, benefit, or relevance than something else
weighty² [weɪti] adj

» Consider this approach [-outʃ] only when the benefits³ clearly outweigh the risks. When ordering this test, clinicians must weigh the anticipated [ɪs] costs⁴ against the potential benefit.

Use clearly⁵ / far **outweigh** • **weighty** argument / matters / issue⁶ [ɪʃjuː‖BE ɪsjuː] • carefully⁷ **weigh**

überwiegen, gewichtiger sein, etw. aufwiegen
(gegeneinander) abwägen¹ schwerwiegend, gewichtig² Vorteile³ voraussichtl. Kosten⁴ deutlich überwiegen⁵ schwerwiegendes Problem⁶ sorgfältig abwägen⁷

17

clinical judgement [dʒʌdʒmənt] n   rel **decision-making¹** [dɪsɪʒən meɪkɪŋ] n

thinking process involved in making decisions in order to arrive at a definite diagnosis and treatment plan

judge² [dʒʌdʒ] v • **judicious³** [dʒuːdɪʃəs] adj • **decide** [saɪ] v • **decisive⁴** [aɪ] adj

» It is not relevant how mild the disease is judged to be. Enemas⁵ may be administered judiciously. Laparoscopy may be an adjunct⁶ [ædʒʌŋkt] to decision-making in the acute abdomen.

Use surgical [ɜː]/ good / impaired⁷ / moral / common sense⁸ **judgement** • **judicious** use of drugs⁹ / exercise / fluid management • **decision-making** process¹⁰ / skills¹¹ • **decision** tree¹² • clinical / therapeutic [juː] informed / emergency [ɜː] **decision** • critical or difficult / (don't) treat¹³ / do not resuscitate¹⁴ [ʌs] (abbr DNR) **decision**

ärztl. Urteil, klin. Beurteilung
Entscheidungsfindung¹ (be)urteilen, einschätzen² klug, umsichtig³ entscheidend⁴ Einläufe⁵ Hilfsmittel⁶ beeinträchtigtes Urteilsvermögen⁷ vernünftige Einschätzung⁸ umsichtiger Einsatz v. Medikamenten⁹ Entscheidungsprozess¹⁰ Entschlusskraft¹¹ Entscheidungsbaum¹² Behandlungsverzicht¹³ Reanimationsverzicht¹⁴

18

Diagnostic Procedures & Investigations   CLINICAL TERMS **523**

Unit 118 Diagnostic Procedures & Investigations

Related Units: 117 Diagnosis, 116 Lab Studies, 107 Physical Examination, 99 Radiology, 17 Medical Equipment, 20 Hospital Routines, 127 Operative Techniques, 128 Minimally Invasive Surgery, 125 Critical Care

investigate [ɪnvˈestɪɡeɪt] v term   syn **examine, study** [stʌdi] v → U101-1

to carry out a systematic search in order to find diagnostic evidence, shed light on a clinical setting[1], etc.

investigation[2] n term • **investigator** n •
investigative adj term • **investigational**[3] adj

» Laboratory investigations disclosed[4] microhematuria, eosinophilia, and an accelerated sed rate[5] early in the clinical course [ɔː]. Symptoms [ɪ] in the CNS should be investigated by brain CT or MRI. Heavier or irregular intermenstrual bleeding[6] warrants[7] [ɔː] investigation.

Use to perform/carry out/conduct [ʌ] /undertake/undergo[8]/terminate [ɜː] **an investigation** • to be under[9] **investigation** • clinical / radiologic / ultrasonographic **investigation** • experimental / thorough[10] [ɜː] **investigation** • controlled / careful[10] / limited **investigation** • extensive[11] / non-invasive[12] [eɪ] **investigation** • preliminary[13] / preoperative **investigation** • thoroughly / closely / routinely **investigated** • **investigative** study / surgery[14] [ɜː] • **investigational** therapy[15] / agent or drug[16] / tests

untersuchen, abklären, erforschen
klin. Erscheinungsbild[1] Abklärung, Untersuchung, Erforschung[2] experimentell, Test-[3] ergaben[4] erhöhte Blutsenkung[5] Zwischenblutung[6] erfordert[7] sich e. Untersuchung unterziehen[8] untersucht/ überprüft werden[9] gründliche U.[10] eingehende/ umfangreiche U.[11] nichtinvasive U.[12] Voruntersuchung[13] explorativer Eingriff[14] experimentelle Therapie[15] Test-, Versuchsmedikament[16]

1

patch test [pætʃ test] n term

rel **skin test**[1], **scratch** [skrætʃ] **test**[2], **prick test**[3] n term

skin test designed to document sensitivity to a specific antigen; suspected substances [ʌ] are applied to an adhesive[4] [iː] which is placed on the patient's skin and checked for a reaction after 24 or 48 hours

(re)testing n term • **(pre)test** [priːtest] v & adj • **untested** adj

» A positive patch test reaction does not necessarily identify the agent causing the contact dermatitis [aɪ]. As patch testing may yield ambiguous results during the acute phase of the dermatitis, patch testing should be done after the eruption [ʌ] subsides[5] [aɪ]. A scratch test should precede [siː] an intradermal [ɜː] test in very sensitive patients. The prick test is useful to confirm a suspected food allergy [-dʒi] or to identify a previously unrecognized allergen.

Use negative / positive **patch test** • **patch test** reaction / site • hypersensitivity / tuberculin[6] / intradermal[7] **skin test** • purified [jʊə] protein derivative[8] (abbr PPD) **skin test** • **skin test** antigen / response[9] • sensitive[10] / noninvasive / screening[11] / provocation[12] **test** • glucose tolerance[13] / (Mono)spot / Rinne tuning [juː] fork[14] **test**

Epikutantest, Läppchenprobe
Hauttest[1] Skarifikations-, Scratchtest[2] Prick-Test[3] Testpflaster[4] d. Ausschlag abklingt[5] Tuberkulintest[6] Intrakutantest[7] Tuberkulintest m. gereinigtem Tuberkulin[8] Hauttestreaktion[9] empfindlicher Test[10] Screening-Test[11] Provokationstest[12] Glukosetoleranztest[13] Rinne-Stimmgabelversuch[14]

2

spirometry [spaɪrˈɒ-] n term

rel **lung** or **pulmonary function tests**[1] n term

measurement of airflow rates and forced vital [aɪ] capacity[2] to assess pulmonary function
spirometer[3] n term • **spirometric** adj • **spirogram**[4] n • **-metry** comb

» If there is any question about the respiratory status, simple spirometry is an excellent screen. The most helpful screening pulmonary function tests are forced vital capacity (abbr FVC) and forced expiratory volume in 1 sec (abbr FEV1). VC, expiratory reserve volume (abbr ERV), and inspiratory capacity (abbr IC) are measured [eː] by having the patient breathe [iː] into and out of a spirometer.

Use routine / preoperative / baseline [eɪ]/ ergo/ incentive[5] [se] **spirometry** • standard or routine / specialized / baseline / abnormal **pulmonary function tests** • incentive[6] **spirometer** • liver (LFTs)/ thyroid[7] [aɪ]/ pituitary[8] **function tests** • renal [iː]/ platelet[9] [eɪ]/ vestibular **function tests** • **spirometric** measurement [eː]/ screening [iː]/ findings[10] • cysto/ uroflow/ bone densito[11]/ radiation dosi**metry** • esophageal mano[12]/ pulse oxi[13]/ audio[14]/ mass spectro**metry**

Spirometrie
Lungenfunktionsprüfung[1] forciertes Exspirationsvolumen[2] Spirometer[3] Spirogramm[4] Messung d. Vitalkapazität[5] Incentive-Spirometer[6] Schilddrüsenfunktionsprüfung[7] Hypophysenfunktionsprüfung[8] Thrombozytenfunktionsprüfung[9] Spirometriebefund[10] Knochendichtemessung, Osteodensiometrie[11] Ösophagusmanometrie[12] Pulsoximetrie[13] Audiometrie[14]

3

524 CLINICAL TERMS
Diagnostic Procedures & Investigations

specimen [spɛsɪmən] n term   syn **sample** [sæmpl] n term → U100-4

small, representative part of a substance or clinical material collected for testing and diagnosis
sampling¹ n term • **sample**² v • **sample** adj

» A standard culture [ʌ] should be done on specimens testing negative. Draw [ɒː] a sample of venous [iː] blood for CBC³. Knowing when the specimen was collected is important.

Use to collect/obtain [eɪ] /take/stain⁴ [eɪ]/ culture [ʌ] **a specimen** • sputum [(j)uː]/ urine [jʊɚ]/ catheterized **specimen** • stool [uː] (diseased) tissue⁵ [ʃǁs]/ swab⁶ [ɒː]/ skin-punch⁷ [ʌ] **specimen** • surgical⁸ [ɜː]/ biopsy⁹ / fasting¹⁰ [æ] **specimen** • sterile / fresh / (formalin) fixed¹¹ **specimen** • cytologic [saɪtə-]/ pathologic / uncontaminated **specimen** • potentially infectious / biohazard¹² [æ] **specimen** • **specimen** slide¹³ [aɪ]/ collection / tube¹⁴ / **specimen** contamination / labeling¹⁵ [eɪ] • to take/obtain/ draw a **sample** • (arterial [ɪɚ]/ venous [iː]/ capillary) blood¹⁶ **sample** • arterial gas / lymph [ɪ] node¹⁷ / selective endometrial¹⁸ [iː] sampling • **sample** size / analysis • **to sample** material / tissue / nodes [oʊ]/ blood • **sample** history / questionnaire¹⁹

Untersuchungsmaterial, Probe, Präparat
Probenentnahme; Stichprobenerhebung¹ e. Probe entnehmen, e. Stichprobe ziehen² großes Blutbild³ e. Probe anfärben⁴ Gewebeprobe⁵ Abstrichmaterial⁶ Stanzbiopsie⁷ Operationspräparat⁸ Biopsie(material)⁹ Nüchternblutprobe¹⁰ formalinfixiertes Präparat¹¹ Schadstoffprobe¹² Objektträger¹³ Abstrichröhrchen¹⁴ Probenkennzeichnung¹⁵ Blutprobe¹⁶ Lymphknotenbiopsie¹⁷ hysteroskopisch geführte Endometriumbiopsie¹⁸ Musterfragebogen¹⁹   4

---

biopsy [baɪɒːpsi] n term, abbr **Bₓ**

(i) small samples of tissue from living patients obtained for diagnostic examination
(ii) removal [uː] of a small piece of living tissue for microscopic examination
bioptic¹ [ɒː] adj term • **biopsy**² v • **biopsy-proven** [uː] adj • **biopsied** adj

» The diagnosis was established by biopsy of the erosion [oʊʒ]. A 25-gauge [geɪdʒ] needle³ [iː] was used to biopsy suspicious [ɪʃ] nodules. The lesion [iːʒ] was biopsied for histologic examination.

Use to obtain or take⁴/perform or do⁵/plan **a biopsy** • needle / fine-needle (aspiration)⁶ / aspiration⁷ / punch⁸ [pʌntʃ] **biopsy** • cone [oʊ]/ core [ɔː]/ wedge⁹ [dʒ] **biopsy** • excisional¹⁰ [ɪʒ]/ incisional¹¹ [sɪ]/ brush¹² [ʌ] **biopsy** • surface / sponge¹³ [spʌndʒ]/ percutaneous [eɪ]/ open¹¹ **biopsy** • skin / liver / sternal **biopsy** • cytological / blind¹⁴ / endoscopic / ultrasound-guided¹⁵ [aɪ]/ random¹⁴ **biopsy** • liver / lung / gastric mucosal **biopsy** • **biopsy** specimen / material¹⁶ / examination • **biopsy** findings¹⁷ / forceps¹⁸ [fɔːrseps]/ gun¹⁹ [ʌ] • **biopsy under** local anesthesia [iːʒ]/ ultrasound [ʌ] guidance¹⁵

(i) Biopsie, Gewebeprobe
(ii) Gewebeentnahme
bioptisch, Biopsie-¹ biopsieren² 25er Nadel³ e. Gewebeprobe entnehmen⁴ e. Biopsie durchführen⁵ Feinnadelbiopsie⁶ Aspirations-, Saugbiopsie⁷ Stanzbiopsie⁸ Keilexzision⁹ Probeexzision¹⁰ offene Biopsie, Probeinzision¹¹ Bürstenbiopsie¹² Schwammbiopsie¹³ Blind-, Zufallsbiopsie¹⁴ ultraschallgezielte Biopsie¹⁵ Biopsie-, Probematerial¹⁶ Biopsiebefund¹⁷ Biopsiezange¹⁸ Biopsiepistole, Schussapparat¹⁹   5

---

stool guaiac test [stuːl g(w)aɪæk] n term   syn **Hemoccult®** [hiːməkʌlt] test n
syn **fecal** [iː] **occult blood test** n term, abbr **FOBT**

screening test for occult fecal blood in which glacial acetic acid and guaiac are mixed with the specimen; the presence of blood in the stool is indicated by a blue stain¹ [eɪ] on addition of hydrogen [aɪ] peroxide²

» Close monitoring by regular stool guaiac examinations for blood loss is essential. Annual fecal Hemoccult screening should be initiated [ɪʃ] at age 50. Perform rectal examination, and obtain stool for occult blood testing. Obtain a stool sample for occult blood testing to check for posttraumatic intraperitoneal [iː] bleeding [iː].

Use **stool examination for** occult blood³ / fat / ova [oʊ] and parasites⁴ • **Hemoccult**-positive stools • annual **FOBT** • negative / positive⁵ **fecal occult blood test** • **stool** collection / sample⁶ / check / examination or analysis⁷ • **stool** weight [weɪt]/ color / osmolality / consistency⁸ • **stool** occult blood (testing) / culture⁹ [ʌ] • **guaiac-positive** stool / (slide) test⁵

Guajaktest, Hämoccult®-Test
Blaufärbung¹ Wasserstoffsuperoxid² Stuhluntersuchung auf okkultes Blut³ Stuhluntersuchung auf Wurmeier und Parasiten⁴ positiver Hämoccult-Test⁵ Stuhlprobe⁶ Stuhluntersuchung⁷ Stuhlbeschaffenheit, -konsistenz⁸ Stuhlkultur⁹

6

---

lumbar puncture [lʌmbɚ pʌŋktʃɚ] n term, abbr **LP**   syn **spinal tap** [spaɪnəl] n jar,
rel **myelography**¹ [maɪəlɒːgrəfi] n term→ U127-16

insertion of a needle into the subarachnoid [æk] space of the lumbar spine [aɪ] for withdrawing [ɒː] CSF², measuring [eʒ] CSF pressure³, or injecting [dʒe] anesthetics [e] and contrast media [iː] **puncture**⁴ v & n term • **venipuncture**⁵ n • **myelographic** n • **tap**⁶ v & n → U5-10

» Use a small-diameter [aɪæ] needle for the spinal tap. Lumbar puncture is to be avoided in patients with bleeding [iː] disorders. Although myelography is helpful in evaluating patency [eɪ] of the spinal canal, it should only be done if warranted⁷ by noninvasive [eɪ] x-ray studies.

Use to consider/perform/undergo⁸/avoid **a lumbar puncture** • diagnostic / traumatic **LP** • repeat / pediatric / therapeutic⁹ [juː] **LP** • conventional / contrast¹⁰ / CT myelography • lumbar / cervical [sɜː]/ emergency [ɜː] **myelography** • **myelographic** study / dye [daɪ]/ evidence¹¹ / sternal [ɜː]/ exploratory¹² / arterial [ɪɚ] **puncture** • **puncture** site¹³ [aɪ]/ wound [uː]/ marks¹⁴ / tray¹⁵ • jugular¹⁶ [dʒʌgjələ] **venipuncture** • **venipuncture** site / needle • aqua¹⁷ [uː] acu**puncture** • prick-**puncture** testing¹⁸ • suprapubic (bladder) / subdural / bloody¹⁹ **tap**

Lumbalpunktion
Myelografie¹ Zerebrospinalflüssigkeit, Liquor² Liquordruck³ (durch-/ein)stechen, punktieren; Punktion⁴ Venenpunktion⁵ punktieren, anzapfen; Punktion; (Zapf)hahn⁶ falls erforderlich⁷ sich e. Lumbalpunktion unterziehen⁸ therapeutische L.⁹ Kontrast-Myelografie¹⁰ myelograf. Nachweis¹¹ Probepunktion¹² Punktionsstelle¹³ Punktionsnarben¹⁴ Punktionsschale¹⁵ Jugularispunktion¹⁶ Wasserinjektion¹⁷ Pricktest¹⁸ blutiger Liquor¹⁹

7

Diagnostic Procedures & Investigations | CLINICAL TERMS 525

paracentesis [pærəsentiːsɪs] *n term*

rel **thora(co)centesis**[1] *n term*

passage of a trocar and cannula, catheter, needle or other hollow instrument via a percutaneous [eɪ] incision into a body cavity in order to withdraw fluid[2]; termed according to the cavity punctured

paracentetic *adj term* • **-centesis** *comb*

» Large-volume paracentesis was repeated daily until her ascites [əsaɪtiːs] had resolved. What were the diagnostic findings on thoracentesis [θɔːrəkoʊ-]?

Use abdominal[3] / thoracic[1] [æs]/ diagnostic / therapeutic / repeat **paracentesis** • arthro/ amnio[4]/ culdo[5] [ʌ]/ pericardio**centesis**

Parazentese

Thorakozentese[1] Flüssigkeit absaugen[2] Abdominozentese[3] Amnionpunktion, Amniozentese[4] Douglas-Punktion, Punktion d. Douglas-Raums[5]

8

bone marrow aspiration [boʊn mæroʊ æspɪreɪʃən] *n term* → U127-16

removal of tissue from the punctured marrow by means of a special needle for histologic examination

aspirate[1] [*v* æspɪreɪt‖*n* æspɪrət] *v & n term* • **aspirational** [eɪʃ] *adj* • **aspirator**[2] *n*

» Leukemia [iː] and lymphoma are diagnosed by bone marrow aspiration, lymph node biopsy, white count and differential. The bone marrow aspirate and the bone marrow biopsy[3] appear hypocellular, with only scant amounts of normal hematopoietic progenitors[4] [ɡʒe].

Use **bone marrow** examination / aspirate / needle / biopsy[3] • **bone marrow** / morphology / purging[5] [pɜːrdʒɪŋ]/ culture[6] / transplantation[7] • **aspiration** biopsy[8] / needle / port[9] /-irrigation • fine-needle **aspiration** cytology[10] • nasogastric / tracheal [k] **aspirate** • ultrasonic tissue / meconium [koʊ] **aspirator**

Knochenmarkaspiration

an-, absaugen; aspirieren; Aspirat[1] Aspirator, Sauger[2] Knochenmarkbiopsie[3] Vorläuferzellen[4] Knochenmark-Aufreinigungstechnik, (Tumorzell-)Purging[5] Knochenmarkkultur[6] Knochenmarktransplantation[7] Aspirationsbiopsie[8] Aspirationskanal[9] Feinnadel-Aspirations-/ Punktionszytologie[10]

9

lavage [ləvɑːʒ‖*BE* lævɪdʒ] *n term*

syn **washing** *n, rel* **brushing**[1] [ʌ] *n term* → U91-26

washing out of a cavity or viscus[2] [ɪsk] by copious irrigation[3] for diagnostic or therapeutic purposes

lavage[4] *v term* • **wash**[4] *v* • **brush** *v & n* • **washout**[5] *n* • **brushings** *n* • **washings**[6] *n*

» Maxillary sinus [aɪ] puncture and aspiration frequently provides a sample for culture; endoscopic sinus lavage may accomplish the same purpose. The area was lavaged with sterile saline[7] [eɪ]. Multiple washings were taken for examination. Invasive diagnostic procedures such as bronchial brushing or washing should be undertaken in critically ill patients when other means do not adequately define [aɪ] etiology.

Use to perform **a lavage** • gastric[8] / bronchial [k] or bronchoalveolar[9] [ɪə] **lavage** • intra-operative colonic[10] / whole bowel[11] [aʊ] **lavage** • (diagnostic) peritoneal[12] [iː]/ joint[13] / closed-needle joint **lavage** / ice-water **lavage** • tap water[14] / **lavage** solution[15] / fluid[15] • endoscopic / bronchial **brushing** • nasal [eɪ]/ throat / tracheal [k]/ bronchial[16] **washings** • mucosal / bronchial / cytologic / tumor **brushings**

Lavage, Spülung

Bürstenbiopsie[1] Hohlorgan[2] gründliche Spülung[3] spülen[4] Auswaschung, -spülung[5] Lavagematerial[6] physiolog. Kochsalzlösung[7] Magenspülung[8] Bronchiallavage, bronchoalveoläre L.[9] intraoperative Kolonlavage[10] Darmspülung, -reinigung[11] Peritoneallavage,- spülung[12] Gelenkspülung[13] Spülung m. Leitungswasser[14] Spülflüssigkeit[15] Bronchiallavagematerial[16]

10

gastroscopy [ɡæstrɒskəpi] *n term*

rel **bronchoscopy**[1] [kɒː], **cystoscopy**[2] [sɪst-] *n term*

visual [ɪʒ] examination of the stomach [k] by means of an endoscope

gastroscopic[3] *n term* • **gastroscope** *n* • **-scope, -scopy** *comb* → U128-2

» All patients with a newly discovered gastric ulcer [ʌlsɚ] should undergo gastroscopy[4] and gastric biopsy. Arrange [eɪ] for rigid bronchoscopy under general anesthesia [iːʒ] to remove the foreign object. The involved ureter needs to be catheterized under cystoscopic control.

Use to require/prompt/perform/appear normal by **gastroscopy** • fiberoptic / repeat **gastroscopy** • **gastroscopic** biopsy • emergency[5] / flexible / rigid[6] [ɪdʒ]/ fiberoptic[7] **bronchoscopy** • **bronchoscopy** techniques / aspirate / instruments / suite [swiːt] • **bronchoscopic** findings[8] / drainage [-ɪdʒ]/ removal [uː] • **bronchoscopic** specimen / evaluation[9] • conventional / flexible / preoperative / followup[10] **cystoscopy** • **cystoscopic** examination / inspection / visualization[11] • **cystoscopic** evidence / maneuver [uː]/ basket retrieval [iː] • endo/ arthro/ colpo/ colono**scopy** • ano [eɪnɒːskəpi]/ laparo/ esophago**scopy** • broncho/ laryngo/ cysto[12]/ duodeno**scope** • fiberoptic endo[13]/ procto/ uretero/ ophthalmo[14]/ oto**scope**

Gastroskopie, Magenspiegelung

Bronchoskopie[1] Zystoskopie, Blasenspiegelung[2] gastroskopisch[3] sich einer Gastroskopie unterziehen[4] Notfallbronchoskopie[5] Bronchoskopie m. starrem Instrument[6] Fiberbronchoskopie[7] Bronchoskopiebefund[8] bronchoskop. Abklärung[9] Kontrollzystoskopie[10] zystoskopische Darstellung[11] Zystoskop[12] Fiber(endo)skop, Glasfaserendoskop[13] Augenspiegel, Ophthalmoskop[14]

11

electroencephalogram [ɪlektrəʊnsefələɡræm] *n term, abbr* **EEG**

recording of the brain waves¹ in various regions of the cerebrum by means of electrodes placed on the scalp and intracranially [eɪ]; the type, localization, frequency and amplitude of the waves are evaluated

electroencephalography *n term* • **electroencephalographic** *adj* → U7-17f; U125-14

» In cases of repeated apneic [iː] episodes, 24-hour electroencephalographic monitoring may be helpful in detecting a seizure [siːʒɚ] disorder². The postictal state produces a pattern of continuous, generalized slowing of the background EEG activity.

Use to take/obtain [eɪ] /warrant³ [ɔː] /confirm [ɜː] by *an EEG* • (ab)normal / baseline⁴ [eɪ]/ awake [eɪ] sleep / cortical⁵ / scalp-recorded⁶ *EEG* • video / ictal⁷ / isoelectric or flat⁸ *EEG* • *EEG* leads⁹ [iː]/ tracing [eɪs] or recording¹⁰ / delta waves / alpha activity • *EEG* findings¹¹ / pattern / changes¹² / technologist¹³ / monitoring¹⁴

electromyography [aɪɒː] *n term, abbr* **EMG**

rel **electroneurography**¹ *n term*

recording of the electrical activity in skeletal muscle via a needle electrode² inserted [ɜː] into the muscle

electromyogram *n term* • **electromyographic** *adj* • **myo-** [maɪə-] *comb*

» EMG may be used to demonstrate denervation of the muscles [mʌslz] in the appropriate nerve root [uː] distribution [juːʃ]. The electromyogram shows continuous discharge³ of motor units and shortening of the silent [aɪ] interval normally seen after an action potential.

Use surface⁴ [ɜː]/ needle / single-fiber⁵ [aɪ]/ pelvic floor *electromyography* • periurethral [iː]/ intra-anal [eɪ]/ sphincter *electromyography* • *electromyographic* response / pattern⁶ / findings⁷ / evidence / sampling • *electro*neuromyography⁸ (*abbr* ENMG)

electrocardiogram [elektroʊkɑːrdɪəɡræm] *n term, abbr* **ECG, EKG**

graphic recording of the heart's electric activity via electrodes (leads¹ [iː]) that are placed in specific anatomic points with an adhesive [iː] gel to facilitate impulse transmission to the electrocardiograph²

electrocardiography [ɒː] *n term* • **electrocardiographic** *adj*

» The resting ECG³ is often insensitive to ischemia [iː]. The ECG revealed [iː] left ventricular hypertrophy. The diagnosis was an incidental finding on electrocardiographic monitoring.

Use admission / serial [ɪə]/ borderline⁴ *ECG* • exercise or stress⁵ / fetal [iː]/ 12-lead⁶ [iː] *ECG* • precordial⁷ / signal-averaged⁸ (*abbr* SAECG) *ECG* • *electrocardiographic* lead / monitoring / pattern / signs • *ECG* tracing⁹ [eɪs]/ findings¹⁰ / machine² [ʃiː] • intracardiac *ECG* recording¹¹

echocardiogram [ekoʊkɑːrdɪəɡræm] *n term*

ultrasound [ʌ] recording of the morphology and motion [oʊʃ] of the heart and great vessels to diagnose cardiovascular lesions [iː] such as mitral [aɪ] disease, pericardial effusion¹ [juːʒ], and abdominal aortic aneurysm [ænjəɪzᵊm]

echocardiography² [ɒː] *n term* • **echocardiographic** *adj* • **echo**³ *n & v & comb*

» Tamponade [eɪ] calls for immediate echocardiography and pericardiocentesis⁴ [iː]. TEE is more sensitive than surface echocardiography⁵ for detecting valvular [æ] lesions⁶.

Use to obtain [eɪ] *an echocardiogram* • emergency / two-dimensional⁷ (*abbr* 2D)/ M-mode⁸ *echocardiogram* • transthoracic⁹ [æs] (*abbr* TTE)/ transesophageal¹⁰ [-dʒiːəl] (*abbr* TEE) *echocardiogram* • bedside / fetal [iː]/ contrast(-enhanced)¹¹ [æ] *echocardiography* • color flow Doppler¹² / stress or exercise¹³ *echocardiography* • *echocardiographic* imaging² / studies • *echocardiographic* detection / evidence • *echo*encephalography¹⁴ • *echo*gram /genicity [ɪs]/ pattern¹⁵ /dense¹⁶ • *echo*density /lucent¹⁷ [ekoʊluːsᵊnt]/-free • hypo¹⁸/ hyper¹⁶/ iso*echoic* [aɪsoʊekoʊɪk]

Elektroenzephalogramm, EEG

Hirnströme¹ Anfallserkrankung² e. EEG erfordern/ notwendig machen³ Ausgangs-EEG⁴ Elektrokortikogramm⁵ Standard-, Kopfhaut-EEG⁶ iktuales EEG⁷ Nulllinien-EEG, isoelektrisches EEG⁸ EEG-Ableitungen⁹ EEG-Registrierung¹⁰ EEG-Befund¹¹ EEG-Veränderungen¹² EEG-Assistent(in)¹³ EEG-Überwachung¹⁴

12

Elektromyografie (EMG)

Elektroneurografie¹ Nadelelektrode² Entladung³ Oberflächenelektromyografie⁴ Einzelfaserelektromyografie⁵ elektromyografisches Aktivitätsmuster⁶ Elektromyografiebefund⁷ Elektroneuromyografie⁸

13

Elektrokardiogramm, EKG

Ableitungen¹ Elektrokardiograph, EKG-Gerät² Ruhe-EKG³ grenzwertiges EKG⁴ Belastungs-EKG⁵ EKG m. 12 Kanalableitungen⁶ Brustwandableitungen⁷ Signalmittelungs-EKG, SAEKG⁸ EKG-Registrierung⁹ EKG-Befund¹⁰ intrakardiale Elektrokardiografie¹¹

14

Echokardiogramm

Perikarderguss¹ Echokardiografie, Ultraschall-Kardiografie, UKG² Echo, Widerhall; zurückwerfen, widerhallen³ Perikard-, Herzbeutelpunktion⁴ Standard-Echokardiografie⁵ (Herz)klappenfehler⁶ zweidimensionales (2-D) Echokardiogramm⁷ eindimensionales/ M-Mode-E.⁸ transthorakales E.⁹ transösophageales E.¹⁰ kontrastmittelverstärkte Echokardiografie¹¹ farbcodierte Doppler E.¹² Stress-E.¹³ Echoenzephalografie¹⁴ Schallmuster¹⁵ schalldicht¹⁶ schalldurchlässig¹⁷ schallarm¹⁸

15

Diagnostic Procedures & Investigations   CLINICAL TERMS 527

angiography [ænd͡ʒɪˈɒːɡrəfi] n term   rel **angiogram**[1] [ˈænd͡ʒɪəɡræm] n term

X-ray visualization of the internal anatomy of the heart [hɑːrt] and blood vessels after the injection [d͡ʒe] of radiopaque [ˌreɪdioʊˈpeɪk] contrast medium [iː]

angiographic n term • **angio-** [ˈænd͡ʒɪəǁoʊ] comb

» Angiography is essential in the diagnostic evaluation of patients with vascular pathology. The angiogram demonstrates embolic occlusion [uːʒ] of the superior [ɪɚ] mesenteric artery. Digital [ɪd͡ʒ] subtraction angiography electronically digitizes x-ray signals and enhances the images using computer subtraction techniques [tekniːks].

Use cardiac / (selective) coronary[2] / pulmonary [ʊǁʌ] **angiography** • carotid[3] / cerebral[4] / spinal[5] [aɪ]/ hepatic **angiography** • mesenteric / vertebral[6] / CT **angiography** • conventional / magnetic resonance (abbr MRA) **angiography** • digital subtraction[7] (abbr DSA) **angiography** • retrograde / (super)selective[8] **angiography** • fluorescein [-esɪən]/ radionuclide[9] [(j)uː] **angiography** • **angiographic** demonstration / confirmation • **angiographic** embolization / findings • **angio**plasty /catheter /cardiography[10] • **angio**dysplasia [-dɪspleɪʒ(ɪ)ə] /edema [iː] /pathy[11]

ultrasound (imaging) [ˈʌltrəsaʊnd ˈɪməd͡ʒɪŋ] n term, abbr **US**
    syn **(ultra)sonography** [ˌʌltrəsəˈnɒːɡrəfi] n term

use of high-frequency or ultrasound waves[1] ranging from 1.6 - 10 MHz for diagnostic visualization, measurement [eʒ], or delineation[2] of deep structures

ultrasonographic[3] adj term • **ultrasonic**[3] adj • **(ultra)sonogram**[4] n
• **(ultra)sonographer** n term • **endosonography** n

» The liver biopsy was performed under ultrasound guidance[5] [aɪ]. Bilateral small kidneys on US are diagnostic. Renal US performed prior [aɪ] to catheterization is important to exclude obstruction [ʌ]. Endorectal ultrasonography provides very accurate information about the depth of penetration of rectal cancer into or through the bowel [aʊ] wall.

Use **US** image[4] / screening • diagnostic / transrectal / transvaginal [d͡ʒ] **US** • color duplex[6] [uː]/ pulsed[7] [ʌ]/ continuous-wave[8] **US** • Doppler[9] / real-time[10] / gray-scale[11] [eɪ] **US** • three-dimensional[12] / high-resolution[13] [uːʃ] **US** • cardiac / renal [iː]/ fetal / prenatal [eɪ] **US** • A-mode / B scan[14] **ultrasonography** • **ultrasonographic** echo [ekoʊ] • **ultrasonic** waves[1] / nebulizer[15] / mist • **ultrasonic** scanner[16] / microscope • **ultrasound** examination or study[17] / scan[4] • **ultrasound**-guided[5] [aɪ]/ probe[18] [oʊ]/ transducer[18] [(j)uːs] • A-mode[19] / B scan **ultrasonogram**

Angiografie
Angiogramm[1] Koronarangiografie[2] Karotisangiografie[3] zerebrale Angiografie[4] spinale Angiografie[5] Vertebralisangiografie[6] digitale Subtraktionsangiografie[7] (super)selektive Angiografie[8] Radionuklidangiografie[9] Angiokardiografie[10] Angiopathie, Gefäßkrankheit[11]

16

Ultraschall(diagnostik), US, USD, Sonografie
Ultraschallwellen[1] Darstellung[2] sonografisch, Ultraschall-[3] Sonogramm[4] unter sonografischer Kontrolle, ultraschallgezielt[5] farbcodierte Duplexsonografie, Farb-Doppler Darstellung[6] Impulsechoverfahren[7] nicht gepulster US[8] Doppler-Ultraschall, -Sonografie, -Verfahren[9] Echtzeitsonografie, -darstellung[10] Grauwert-Sonografie[11] 3-D-Ultraschall[12] hochauflösende Sonografie[13] B-Mode Darstellung[14] Ultraschallvernebler[15] Sonograph[16] Ultraschalluntersuchung[17] Schallkopf[18] A-Scan Ultraschall, Amplituden-Scan[19]

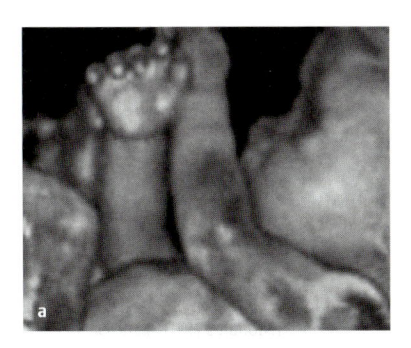

17

(a) Three-dimensional fetal ultrasound obtained at 26 weeks of gestation
(b) Intravenous pyelography (IVP)

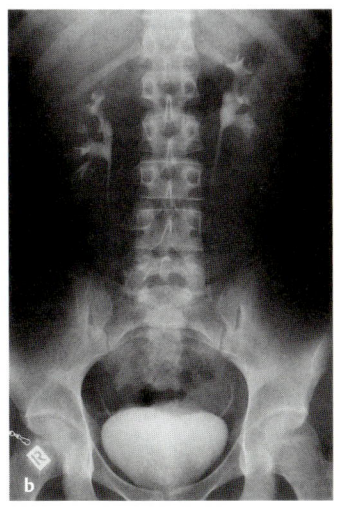

528 CLINICAL TERMS — Diagnostic Procedures & Investigations

chest x-ray [tʃest eksreɪ] *n term & clin, abbr* **CXR**
    syn **chest film** *n jar*, **chest radiograph** [eɪ] *n term* → U99-3
roentgenogram of the thoracic cavity and its viscera [ɪs] (esp. the heart and lungs)
radiography[1] *n term* • **radiographic** *adj* • **radiologic(al)** *adj* • **-gram** *comb*

» Chest x-ray reveals [iː] evidence of cardiac enlargement primarily involving the right ventricle. Abdominal shielding must be used if a chest film is obtained [eɪ]. Would you pin these x-rays onto the light box[2], please? Excessive exposure [ouʒ] to x-rays can cause radiation sickness[3]. The right knee should also be x-rayed.

Use erect / plain[4] [eɪ]/ frontal / posteroanterior[5] [ɪə] (*abbr* PA) **CXR** • anterior-posterior (*abbr* AP)/ lateral[6] **CXR** • inspiratory / expiratory / portable **CXR** • preoperative / follow-up[7] / normal or negative **CXR** • suspicious [ɪʃ]/ visible on **CXR** • **CXR** findings / abnormalities • to take[8]/ perform[8]/ obtain[8] [eɪ] **x-rays** • **x-ray** film / picture[9] / tube[10] / machine[11] • **x-ray** unit[12] / department / technician[13] [k] • **x-ray** study / examination / findings / therapy[14] • plain abdominal[15] / serial / barium[16] **x-ray** • anteroposterior[17] (*abbr* AP)/ bone / skull **x-ray** • sinus [aɪ] / upper GI[18] / small bowel[19] [aʊ] **x-rays** • **x-ray** pelvimetry / fluoroscopy[20] / film viewer[2] • roentgeno/ veno/ arterio/ cysto/ mammo/ reno**gram** • **radiologic** technologist[13]

Thorax-Röntgen(aufnahme)
Röntgen(untersuchung)[1] Röntgenbildbetrachter[2] Strahlenkrankheit, -kater[3] Thorax-Nativaufnahme[4] pa-Aufnahme d. Thorax[5] seitl. Thorax-röntgen[6] Thorax-Kontrollröntgen[7] Röntgenaufnahmen machen[8] Röntgen(aufnahme, -bild)[9] Röntgenröhre[10] Röntgenstrahler[11] Röntgenanlage[12] radiolog.-techn./ Röntgenassistent(in)[13] Röntgentherapie[14] Abdomen-Leer-/ Übersichtsaufnahme[15] Bariumkontrastmittelaufnahme, -darstellung[16] ap-Aufnahme[17] Magen-Darm-Passage[18] Dünndarmröntgenaufnahmen, Sellink-Passage[19] Röntgenfluoroskopie[20] 18

intravenous pyelography [ɪntrəviːnəs paɪəlɒːgrəfi] *n term, abbr* **IVP**
    syn **IV** or **excretory** [iː] **urography** *n, abbr* **IVU**,
        rel **KUB film**[1] *n term*
serial x-rays of the urinary [jʊə] system taken as an IV contrast medium is cleared by the glomeruli [aɪ]; KUB stands for kidney, ureter and bladder
pyelogram, urogram [jʊə.ə-] *n term* • **urographic** *adj* • **-graphy** *comb*

» In addition to hydroureteronephrosis the IVP revealed poor concentrating ability. For small stones renal ultrasound is not as sensitive as excretory urography. Since GI and GU diseases tend to mimic[2] each other, the KUB film may be helpful in differential diagnosis.

Use to obtain an/confirm [ɜː] by/appear normal on **IVP** • postpartum **IVP** • antegrade[3] / retrograde[4] **pyelography** • emergency / follow-up **excretory urography** • **excretory urographic** evaluation[5] • **KUB study**[1] / equipment • **pyelographic** contrast / abnormalities • antegrade[3] / retrograde[4] **urography** • **urographic** features [fiːtʃəz]

intravenöse Pyelo-/ Urografie, Ausscheidungsurografie
Leeraufnahme d. Harntraktes (Nieren, Ureteren, u. Blase)[1] ähnliche Symptome hervorrufen wie[2] antegrade Pyelografie/ Urografie[3] retrograde Pyelografie/ Urografie[4] Abklärung mittels Ausscheidungsurografie[5]

19

percutaneous [eɪ] **transhepatic cholangiography** *n term, abbr* **PTC**
    rel **endoscopic retrograde cholangiopancreatography**[1] *n term, abbr* **ERCP**
radiographic imaging of the bile [aɪ] ducts following direct needle injection of contrast medium
cholangiogram [kəlændʒɪəgræm] *n term* • **cholangiographic** *adj*

» PTC or ERCP provides [aɪ] the most direct and accurate means of determining [ɜː] the cause, location, and extent of biliary [ɪ] obstruction [ʌ]. The need for preoperative ERCP is expected to decrease further as laparoscopic techniques improve.

Use oral / intravenous [iː]/ endoscopic retrograde[2] **cholangiography** • direct[3] / (intra)operative[4] / MR[5] **cholangiography** • retrograde / IV **cholangiogram** • preoperative[6] / urgent [ɜː] **ERCP** • endoscopic / magnetic resonance (*abbr* MRCP) **cholangiopancreatography**

perkutane transhepatische Cholangiografie
endoskopische retrograde Cholangiopankreatografie[1] endoskop. retrograde Cholangiografie[2] direkte Cholangiografie[3] intraoperative Cholangiografie[4] MR-Cholangiografie[5] präoperative ERCP[6]

20

barium (meal) examination *n term*   *syn* **barium meal** [beərɪəm miːl] *n jar*
        sim **upper GI series**[1] *n, abbr* **UGI**,
        rel **barium enema**[2] *n term*
ingestion[3] of barium sulfate [ʌ], a contrast medium, for radiographic examination of the alimentary canal

» Barium meal examination of the upper GI tract reveals the large gastric folds, which are readily [e] confirmed [ɜː] by endoscopy. Double contrast barium enema can detect up to 90% of polyps [ɪ], especially those larger than 1 cm.

Use double-contrast[4] [ʌ]/ small bowel [aʊ] **barium meal examination** • **barium** swallow [ɒː] or esophagography[5] / (x-ray/ contrast) study • **barium** radiography / upper GI series[1] • to perform an/detect on **upper GI series** • small bowel[6] series • double-contrast or air-contrast[7] / nondiagnostic **barium enema** • **barium enema** examination / x-ray / study

Barium(brei)-Untersuchung
Magen-Darm-Passage[1] Bariumeinlauf[2] orale Gabe[3] Barium-Doppelkontrastuntersuchung[4] Bariumbreischluck[5] (Magen-Duodenal-)Dünndarm-Passage (MDDP)[6] Bariumdoppelkontrasteinlauf[7]

21

perfusion lung scan *n term*   *rel* **perfusion** [juːʒ] **scintigraphy**¹ [sɪnt-] *n term*
radionuclide [reɪdɪoʊn(j)uːklaɪd]
or **nuclear scanning**² *n term*

x-ray of the lungs [lʌŋz] performed after intravenous injection of a contrast medium which is used to aid [eɪd] in the diagnosis of pulmonary embolism

lung scanning [lʌŋ skænɪŋ] *n term* • **scanner** *n* • **(re)scan** *v*

» *Ventilation/perfusion lung scans*³ *are interpreted as being normal, low, indeterminate* [ɜː] *or high probability for the presence of a pulmonary thromboembolism. Sonography and radionuclide scanning are helpful in establishing the diagnosis*⁴ *of cholelithiasis* [aɪ]*.*

Use radionuclide / isotopic / Xenon [zeǁziːnɒːn] **lung scan** • **lung scan** interpretation • bone⁵ / (radionuclide) brain⁶ **scan** • abdominal CT / ultrasound **scan** • pulmonary⁷ / high-probability **perfusion scan** • exercise or stress / rest / myocardial⁸ [aɪ] **perfusion scintigraphy**

Lungenperfusionsszintigramm
Perfusionsszintigrafie¹ Szintigrafie² Lungenventilations- und perfusionsszintigramme³ Sicherstellung d. Diagnose⁴ Knochen-, Skelettszintigramm⁵ Hirnszintigramm⁶ Lungenperfusionsszintigramm⁷ Myokardperfusionsszintigrafie⁸

22

---

arthrography [ɑːrθrɒːgrəfi] *n term*
rel **arthrogram**¹, **arthroscopy**² *n term*

radiography of a joint (e.g. the TMJ³) usually following injection of contrast media [iː]

» *Arthrography revealed* [iː] *a contracted joint capsule and no bursal* [ɜː] *filling. MRI is more sensitive than arthrography or CT for the diagnosis of soft tissue* [ʃǁs] *injuries.*

Use air⁴ / hip / opaque [-eɪk] **arthrography** • double-contrast⁵ **arthrogram**

Arthrografie
Arthrogramm¹ Arthroskopie² Kiefergelenk, Art. temporomandibularis³ Pneumarthrografie⁴ Doppelkontrastarthrogramm⁵

23

(nuclear) magnetic resonance imaging *n term*   *abbr* **MR(I)** or **NMR**

noninvasive [eɪ] (nonionizing [aɪ]) diagnostic imaging modality using magnetic fields and radiofrequency pulses [ʌ] to scan for abnormalities of the soft tissues¹ and body fluids

» *MRI demonstrated changes of portal hypertension. Multiple foci* [foʊsaɪ] *are best visualized*² *by MRI. In this context the relative merits of MRI versus CT scanning remain controversial.*

Use diagnostic / radiologic³ / ultrasound **imaging** • radioisotope⁴ [aɪ]/ cardiac / cerebral **imaging** • **imaging** modality⁵ / technique⁵ [iː] • **MRI** scan or image⁶ / study / findings • **MR** angiography / brain scan / scanner / contrast-enhanced⁷ / sideview **MRI** • T1-weighted [weɪtɪd]/ T2-weighted⁸ **MRI**

Kernspin-, Magnetresonanztomografie, MRT
Weichteile¹ dargestellt² Röntgendarstellung³ Szintigrafie⁴ bildgebendes Verfahren⁵ Kernspintomogramm, MRT⁶ kontrastmittelverstärkte Kernspintomografie⁷ T2-gewichtetes Kernspintomogramm/ MRT⁸

24

Unit 119 Etiology, Course & Prognosis
Related Units: 4 Illness & Recovery, 89 Pathology, 103 Clinical Symptoms,
              108 Clinical Signs, 117 Diagnosis, 134 Perioperative Management

---

predisposed (to) *adj*   *syn* **prone** [proʊn]/ **susceptible/ liable** [laɪəbl] **to** *adj*

to have a tendency to develop a particular condition or be sensitive to¹ a type of pathogenic agent

predisposition² *n term* • **predisposing**³ *adj* • **susceptibility**² [səseptɪbɪləti] *n*

» *Smoking predisposes a person to lung cancer. An underlying predisposition to thrombosis was detected. The elderly in particular are predisposed to constipation*⁴*. Diabetics* [e] *seem somewhat less prone to develop this syndrome* [ɪ]*. Patients susceptible to gastric or duodenal ulceration should receive other treatment.*

Use **predisposed** to infection⁵ / to venous [iː] thrombosis / to sudden [ʌ] death • **predisposed** to form gallstones⁶ [ɔː]/ to lung infections • genetically⁷ / racially [eɪʃ] **predisposed** • **predisposition** to(ward) pneumonia [n(j)uː-]/ to breast [e] cancer / for the development of meningitis [dʒaɪ] • genetic or inherited or hereditary⁸ / familial⁹ **predisposition** • **susceptibility to** infection¹⁰ / autoimmune disease¹¹ • **predisposing** factor¹² / cause / condition / genes [dʒiː] / illness • accident¹³-/ cancer-**prone** • **liable to** injury / digestive [dʒe] disorders¹⁴ / compression / episodes of dehydration [aɪ]

prädisponiert/ anfällig für
empfindlich gegen(über)¹ (Prä)disposition, Anfälligkeit, Veranlagung² prädisponierend, begünstigend³ Verstopfung, Obstipation⁴ infektionsanfällig⁵ prädisponiert für Gallensteine⁶ genetisch prädisponiert⁷ genet. Bereitschaft/ Prädisposition⁸ familiäre Prädisposition⁹ Infekt(ions)anfälligkeit¹⁰ Prädisposition für Autoimmunkrankheiten¹¹ prädisponierender Faktor¹² unfallgefährdet¹³ anfällig für Krankheiten d. Verdauungstrakts¹⁴

1

CLINICAL TERMS — Etiology, Course & Prognosis

etiology [iːtiˈɒːlədʒi] *n term*, BE **aetiology**
　　　　　　　rel **pathogenesis**[1] [pæθədʒenəsɪs],
　　　　　　　causation[2] [kɒˈzeɪʃən] *n term* → U89-1

(i) the cause(s) of a disease
(ii) study of factors contributing to the development of a condition, e.g. the nature of the causative organism, predisposing factors, susceptibility, route of transmission[3], etc.
etiologic[4] *adj term* • **causative**[5] *adj* • **causal**[6] [kɒːzˀl] *adj* • **pathogen**[7] *n*

» *Establishing a specific etiologic diagnosis of pneumonia is often difficult. From an etiologic standpoint, she probably has type I diabetes [iː], but her present clinical status is "non-insulin-dependent." The etiology of* urge [ɜːrdʒ] *urinary incontinence*[8] *includes urethral [iː] or detrusor instability or a combination of these mechanisms.*

Use viral [aɪ]/ organic / multifactorial / (un)known[9] **etiology** • **etiologic** factor / classification / features [fiːtʃɚz] • **etiologic** role / diagnosis / considerations • underlying / unknown **pathogenesis** • **causative** agent [eɪdʒ] or organism[10] / mechanism • genetic / postoperative / viral **causation** • **causal** association[11] / relationship[11] / role • bacterial [ɪɚ]/ cultured[12] [ʌ]/ blood-borne / enteric **pathogens** • nosocomial [oʊ]/ opportunistic[13] / spread [e] of / growth of **pathogens**

Ätiologie, Krankheitsursachen
Pathogenese[1] Entstehung, Verursachung[2] Übertragungsweg[3] ätiologisch[4] verursachend[5] kausal, ursächlich[6] Krankheitserreger, pathogener (Mikro)organismus[7] Drang-, Urgeinkontinenz[8] unbekannte Ätiologie[9] (Krankheits)erreger[10] kausaler Zusammenhang[11] gezüchtete Erreger[12] opportunistische Krankheitserreger[13]

---

herald [herˀld] *v*　*syn* **presage** [prɪseɪdʒ‖preˈsɪdʒ] *v, rel* **harbinger**[1] [ɑː] *n term*

to foreshadow[2] the development or worsening of a disease by a warning sign or symptom [ɪ]
herald[1] *n* • **heralding** *adj*

» *Failure to respond to treatment usually heralds a prolonged series of* relapses[3]. *Recurrent attacks*[4] *are frequently heralded by a prodrome consisting of local itching*[5] [tʃ] *and pain. Transient ischemic [kiː] attacks may be a harbinger of impending stroke*[6]. *Developing hip disease within the first 2 years of disease onset presages a worse prognosis.*

Use **to herald** progression / tumor recurrence[7] [ɜː]/ massive hemorrhage [-rɪdʒ]/ death • **to herald** an impending myocardial [aɪ] infarction[8] • **to herald** the development of postoperative complications • **to presage** complications / acute liver failure [feɪljɚ]/ a worse prognosis • **herald** patch[9] • **harbinger of** pancreatic carcinoma [s]/ clinical improvement

ankündigen, andeuten
Vorbote, Vorzeichen[1] andeuten, hindeuten auf[2] Rezidive, Rückfälle[3] rezidivierende Anfälle[4] Juckreiz[5] Vorbote eines Schlaganfalls[6] (auf) ein Tumorrezidiv hinweisen/ anzeigen[7] einen Herzinfarkt ankündigen[8] Primärmedaillon (b. Pityriasis rosea)[9]

---

precursor [prɪkɜːrsɚ] *n term*　*sim* **prodrome**[1] *n term*, **forerunner**[2] *n clin*

(i) symptom [ɪ] which precedes[3] [siː] a disease
(ii) substance [ʌ] (enzyme [enzaɪm], vitamin [aɪ‖ɪ], hormone, etc.) from which another usually more active one is derived [dɪraɪvd]
prodromal[4] *adj term*

» *Respiratory exercises, deep breathing [iː], and coughing [kɒːfɪŋ] help prevent atelectasis, which is a precursor of pneumonia [n(j)uː-]. There is little or no prodrome in this condition.*

Use **precursor of** acne [ækni]/ cancer[5] / dopamine[6] [oʊ] • protein / RBC[7] / estrogen **precursor** • **precursor** cell[8] / protein / molecule • mild / short / febrile / flu-like[9] **prodrome** • **prodromal** illness / phase or stage or period[10] [ɪɚ]/ manifestations / fever [iː] • **forerunner of** asthma [æzmə]

(erstes) Anzeichen, Vorbote, -läufer, -stufe
Prodrom, Vorzeichen, Frühsymptom[1] Vorbote, (erstes) Anzeichen[2] vorausgeht[3] prodromal, vorausgehend[4] Frühsymptom v. Krebs[5] Dopaminvorstufe[6] Retikulozyt, Proerythrozyt[7] Vorläuferzelle[8] grippeähnliche Frühsymptome[9] Prodromal-, Vorläuferstadium[10]

---

onset [ɒːnset] *n term*　*syn* **inception** [ɪnsepʃən] *n term rare* → U94-7

the beginning of a disease, development, process or activity
adult-/ late-/ early-/ new-onset[1] *adj term* • **incipient**[2] [ɪnsɪpɪənt] *adj clin*

» *Pain may be mild at onset and is usually worse at night. Alzheimer's has an insidious onset and is steadily [e] progressive. Psoriasis [səraɪəsɪs] mostly precedes [siː] the onset of arthritis [aɪ]. The pain is sudden in onset, sharp, and does not radiate [eɪ].*

Use rapid[3] / acute / gradual / slow / simultaneous [eɪ]/ sudden[3] / abrupt[3] [ʌ] **onset** • recent / delayed [eɪ]/ clinical / insidious[4] [ɪ]/ late **onset** • adult- or maturity-**onset** diabetes[5] [iː] • childhood-**onset** obesity [iː] • **juvenile-onset** diabetes[6] / hypertension / spondyloarthropathy • mode / speed / time / rapidity **of onset** • **onset of** symptoms / asthma / labor[7] [eɪ]/ action[8] • **onset of** puberty [juː]/ menstruation[9] / sleep • **incipient** renal [iː] failure / cataract[10] / gangrene [iː]/ herniation / pain

Krankheitsbeginn, Ausbruch
de novo[1] beginnend, einsetzend[2] plötzl. Ausbruch/ Beginn[3] schleichender Beginn[4] nicht-insulinabhängiger/ Typ II Diabetes mellitus, Erwachsenen-, Altersdiabetes[5] insulinabhängiger/ Typ I/ juveniler Diabetes mellitus[6] Wehenbeginn[7] Wirkungseintritt[8] Menstruationsbeginn[9] beginnender grauer Star, Cataracta incipiens[10]

CLINICAL TERMS

latent [leɪtᵊnt] *adj term*   *syn* **silent** [saɪlənt], **covert** [koʊvɜːrt] *adj clin*
sim **occult**[1] [əkʌlt], **inactive**[2], **quiescent**[3] [kwiesᵊnt] *adj term*

signs or symptoms of a disease which are dormant, not (yet) manifest, or detected

latency[4] [leɪtᵊnˈsi] *n term* • **quiescence**[4] *n* • **active** *adj* • **(in)activity** *n*

» There is a latent period between the onset of symptoms and the initial positive radiographic finding. Detection of latent, nonprogressive cancers exposes patients to unnecessary treatment. Spinal malalignment[5] [aɪ] may persist after the disorder has become quiescent.

Use **latent** period[6] / infection / syphilis[7] / virus • clinically[8] **silent** • **silent** ischemia [iː]/ mutation[9] / episodes • **silent** gallstones[10] / abdomen / carrier • **covert** bacteriuria[11] / embryopathy • **occult** blood[12] / cancer / fracture / bleeding [iː] • **quiescent** state[13] / cells[14] / interval / period or phase[15] • clinical / relative / apparent [ɚ]/ period of[15] **quiescence** • **latency** period or stage[6] • **(in)active** ulcer [ʌlsɚ]/ tumor[16] / (lung) disease

---

latent, symptomlos

okkult, verborgen[1] inaktiv, ruhend[2] ruhig, Ruhe-[3] Ruhe[4] Fehlstellung[5] Latenzzeit[6] Syphilis latens, latenter Verlauf d. Syphilis[7] klin. inapparent/ stumm[8] stille Mutation[9] stumme Gallensteine[10] asymptomatische Bakteriurie[11] okkultes Blut[12] Ruhezustand[13] inaktive Zellen[14] Ruhephase[15] inaktiver Tumor[16]

6

---

insidious [ɪnsɪdiəs] *adj*   *opposite* **frank**[1], **overt**[1] [oʊvɜːrt] *adj term*

refers to a disease which develops slowly and does not produce noticeable symptoms in its early course

» The saddle nose deformity may develop insidiously without overt inflammation. Screening procedures [siː] are capable of detecting disorders before frank symptoms of disease exist.

Use **insidious** development / clinical presentation[2] • to begin/progress **insidiously** • **frank** diabetes[3] [iː]/ infection / coma / arthritis [aɪ] • **overt** shock / anemia [iː]/ uremia[4] [iː]/ clinical signs • **overt** blood loss / heart failure [feɪlɚ]

---

schleichend

klinisch manifest[1] schleichende Symptomatik/ Manifestation[2] klin. manifester Diabetes[3] klinisch manifeste Urämie[4]

7

---

precipitate [prɪsɪpɪteɪt] *v term*   *syn* **bring on** *v phr*, **cause** [kɒːz] *v*
syn **provoke** [prəvoʊk], **trigger** [trɪgɚ], **induce** [ɪnd(j)uːs] *v*

precipitating[1] *adj term* • **precipitant**[2] *n* • **drug-induced**[3] *adj*

» Her vomiting was precipitated by ambulation[4]. Attacks of angina [dʒaɪ] may be brought on by a heavy meal or emotional stress. Physical exertion[5] [ɜː] can also trigger the onset of acute myocardial [maɪə-] infarction, particularly in persons who are habitually [ɪtʃ] sedentary[6].

Use **precipitating** factor / cause / event[7] / condition / stress • alcohol-/ aspirin-/ virus-**induced** • catheter-/ cold-/ exercise[8]-/ self[9]-**induced**

---

auslösen, herbeiführen, induzieren, verursachen

auslösend[1] Auslöser[2] arzneimittel-induziert[3] Umhergehen[4] körperl. Anstrengung[5] viel sitzen[6] auslösendes Ereignis[7] belastungsbedingt[8] selbstverursacht[9]

8

---

course [kɔːrs] *n term*   *rel* **natural history**[1] [nætʃɚᵊl hɪstɚi] *n term*

(i) progression of a disease (ii) series of drugs administered or sessions of treatment

» The patient pursued [(j)uː] a rapid downhill course[2]. These measures [eʒ] have no effect on the natural course of the disease. The postoperative course was complicated by severe pulmonary hypertension. Let the episode run its course[3]. Anti-inflammatory [æ] agents[4] do not affect the natural history of uremic pericarditis.

Use to follow/run[5]/have[5] **a course** • clinical / benign [bɪnaɪn]/ (pre)hospital[6] **course** • uneventful[7] / waxing and waning[8] [eɪ] **course** • protracted[9] / relentlessly downhill / stormy **course** • stabilized / febrile / neonatal [eɪ] **course** • **course** of therapy[10] • aggressive / benign[11] / malignant / long-term / rapid **natural history**

(i) (Krankheits)verlauf
(ii) Kur, Behandlung

natürlicher Verlauf[1] ging es schnell bergab[2] seinen Lauf nehmen[3] entzündungshemmende Medikamente, Antiphlogistika[4] e. Verlauf nehmen/ haben[5] präklin. V.[6] komplikationsloser V.[7] wechselhafter Verlauf[8] protrahierter Verlauf[9] Behandlungszyklus[10] gutartiger Verlauf[11]   9

---

acute [əkjuːt] *adj term & clin*   *opposite* **chronic**[1], **long-standing**[2],
protracted[3] *adj term & clin*

illness which is sudden in onset, usually consists of a single episode only and runs a short course; chronic conditions are of long duration and patients are incapacitated[4] over an extended period of time

subacute[5] [sʌbəkjuːt] *adj term* • **chronicity**[6] [krɒːnɪsəti] *n*

» For patients with chronic heart failure, the risk-benefit may be more favorable [eɪ]. The patient presented with prolonged acute chest pain consistent with myocardial ischemia [kiː].

Use **acute** bleeding / attack / abdomen[7] / exacerbation[8] [ɪgzæsɚ-]/ illness / form • **acute** stage[9] / life-threatening [e] episode / renal failure[10] • **acutely** ill / poisoned / infected • **chronic** cough[11] [kɒːf]/ anemia / bronchitis [kaɪ]/ carrier[12] • **chronic** care facility[13] [sɪ]/ abuse / alcoholism • **long-standing** obstruction [ʌ]/ diabetes [iː] mellitus / hypertension[14] • **protracted** vomiting[15] / diarrhea [daɪəriːə]/ polyuria [pɒːlɪjʊɚɪə]

---

akut

chronisch[1] langjährig[2] protrahiert, langdauernd[3] arbeitsunfähig[4] subakut[5] Chronizität, chron. Verlauf[6] akutes Abdomen[7] akute Verschlimmerung[8] akutes Stadium[9] akutes Nierenversagen[10] chronischer Husten[11] Dauerausscheider[12] Pflegeheim f. chronisch Kranke[13] langjähriger Bluthochdruck[14] protrahiertes Erbrechen[15]

10

CLINICAL TERMS — Etiology, Course & Prognosis

persistent or **persisting** adj   opposite **intermittent**[1], **episodic**[2] adj term
off and on[3], **come and go**[3] phr clin

(of symptoms or conditions that) continue without interruption [ʌ] for some time and do not go away

persist[4] [pəˈsɪst] v • **persistence**[5] n • **intermittency**[6] [ˌɪntəˈmɪtᵊnˈsi] n term

» Loss of body fluids occurs in persistent vomiting, severe diarrhea, or **copious** [oʊ] **sweating**[7] [e]. These patients often have a good premorbid history, a **precipitous** [sɪ] **onset**[8], and an episodic course with symptom-free intervals. The burning [ɜː] sensation [eɪ] comes and goes. I've had these headaches off and on for the past two months.

Use **persistent** hoarseness[9] [ɔː]/ cough [kɒf]/ tremor / epigastric pain • **episodic** symptom / coughing spells[10] / amnesia[11] [iː] • **intermittent** fever[12] [iː]/ claudication [klɒdɪˈkeɪʃᵊn]/ hypertension

persistierend, anhaltend
intermittierend, in Schüben/ periodisch auftretend[1] episodisch[2] ab und zu, immer wieder (auftreten)[3] anhalten, persistieren[4] Fortbestehen, Persistenz[5] Aussetzen, Unterbrechung[6] starkes Schwitzen[7] plötzlicher Beginn[8] anhaltende Heiserkeit[9] episodisch auftretende Hustenanfälle[10] episodische Amnesie[11] intermittierendes Fieber, Febris intermittens[12]
11

progressive [prəˈɡresɪv] adj   opposite **stable**[1] [steɪbl], **stabilized**[2] [eɪ], **self-limiting**[3] adj term

refers to a disease taking an unfavorable course[4] (i.e. the complaints[5] become more intense or severe)

progression[6] n term • **progress**[7] [v prəˈɡres‖n ˈprɒːɡres] v & n • **stabilize**[8] v term • **stability** n

» His condition was characterized by progressive muscle weakness and wasting[9] [eɪ]. The patient is progressing satisfactorily. He felt he was making poor progress and had thoughts of "giving up." The patient's condition is stable enough to permit evaluation. The arthritis is commonly self-limiting after several weeks or months.

Use **progressive** swelling[10] / dyspnea [ɪ]/ cirrhosis [sɪr-]/ neurologic deficits[11] • **progressive** intellectual decline[12] [aɪ]/ deterioration or worsening[13] [ɜː] • **stable** health patient / status[14]/ angina[15] [dʒaɪ]/ vital [aɪ] signs[16] • hemodynamically [hiːm-]/ emotionally [oʊʃ]/ clinically[17] **stable** • slow / tumor / gradual **progression** • rapid disease[18] / neurologic **progression** • to tend/continue[19]/be likely **to progress** • **progress** note[20] • **stabilized** critically ill infant / blood pressure / fracture • clinical / hemodynamic / emotional / fracture **stability**

Note: Mark the difference between **progress** and **progression** in medical contexts. While *progression* usually refers to disease (esp. cancer) and denotes a worsening, *progress* is often used to refer to the patient's course, e.g. *progress report*, *developmental progress* or *to make progress*.

fortschreitend, progredient
stabil, gleichbleibend[1] stabilisiert[2] spontan abklingend, selbstlimitierend[3] ungünstiger Verlauf[4] Beschwerden[5] Fortschreiten, Progression, Progredienz[6] s. weiterentwickeln, fortschreiten; Fortschritt[7] (sich) stabilisieren[8] Kräfteverfall[9] zunehmende Schwellung[10] progrediente neurolog. Ausfälle[11] fortschreitender geistiger Verfall[12] zunehmende Verschlechterung[13] stabiler Zustand[14] stabile Angina pectoris[15] stabile Vitalfunktionen[16] klin. stabil[17] rasches Fortschreiten d. Krankheit[18] weiter fortschreiten, s. weiterentwickeln[19] Verlaufsbericht[20]
12

fulminant [ʊ] or **fulminating** adj term
rel **overwhelming**[1] adj, **florid**[2] adj term

a condition (fever, infection, hemorrhage) which is very sudden in onset, severe and rapidly progressive

fulminate[3] [ˈfʊlmɪneɪt] v term

» The resulting colitis [aɪ] may vary in severity [e] from chronic and indolent to acute and fulminating. The clinical course ranges from asymptomatic, with moderate mitral [aɪ] regurgitation[4] [ɜːrdʒ] remaining stable for years, to a fulminant progression of overwhelming congestive [dʒe] heart failure[5]. The more florid symptoms fade[6] [feɪd] within a few days.

Use **fulminant** course[7] / attack / presentation[8] / hepatitis • **fulminating** shock / fatal [eɪ] dysentery [ɪ]/ colitis [aɪ] • **overwhelming** sepsis[9] • **florid** picture[10] / delirium / pneumonitis [n(j)uː-] • **florid** stool [uː] abnormalities / papule / exacerbations

fulminant, foudroyant, blitzartig auftretend
überwältigend stark[1] florid, voll ausgeprägt[2] plötzl. auftreten/ ausbrechen[3] Mitral(klappen)insuffizienz[4] dekompensierte Herzinsuffizienz[5] klingen ab[6] fulminanter Verlauf[7] fulminante Symptomatik[8] perakut verlaufende Sepsis, Sepsis acutissima[9] florides klin. Bild[10]
13

full-blown adj term   syn **massive** adj,
opposite **early**[1], **incipient**[1] [sɪ] adj clin

a disease exhibiting all characteristic clinical features [fiːtʃəz] in a fully developed form

» Eventually her symptoms escalated into a full-blown manic [æ] episode. Therapeutic [juː] thoracentesis[2] [iː] is indicated only if massive effusion[3] [juːʒ] causes dyspnea.

Use **full-blown** syndrome / ulcer [ʌlsə-]/ infection / AIDS[4] / psychosis [saɪk-] • **massive** bleeding or hemorrhage[5] [-rɪdʒ]/ blood loss[6] • **massive** embolism / edema [iː]/ trauma • **massive** proteinuria / transfusion [juːʒ]/ swelling[7] / splenomegaly • **early** infection / stage[8] / childhood • **early** breast [e] cancer / ambulation[9] / abortion[10] • **early** onset of menses[11] / detection[12] • **early** symptom[13] / pregnancy[14]

-Vollbild, massiv, stark
Früh-, beginnend[1] Thorakozentese[2] Erguss[3] AIDS-Vollbild[4] massive Blutung, Massenblutung[5] starker Blutverlust[6] starke Schwellung[7] Frühstadium[8] Frühmobilisation[9] Frühabort[10] Menarche praecox[11] Früherkennung[12] Frühsymptom[13] Frühschwangerschaft[14]
14

Etiology, Course & Prognosis   CLINICAL TERMS 533

state [steɪt] *n clin*   *syn* **status** [steɪtəs‖stæ-] *n term* → U107-10
   rel **stage¹** [steɪdʒ] *n term & clin* → U97-14

referring to the state of health, the condition or situation of a patient
» Keep the patient's comorbid conditions² and her overall state of health³ in mind. Emphasis is placed on the assessment of functional [ʌ] status, exercise tolerance⁴, and cardiac symptoms.
Use **state of** consciousness⁵ [kɒnˈʃəsnəs]/ shock / relaxation • clinical / asymptomatic / quiet alert⁶ [ɜː]/ agitated⁷ [ædʒ] **state** • confusional⁸ [juːʒ]/ mood⁹ [uː]/ metabolic **state** • acid-base¹⁰ [s]/ fasting¹¹ / in the resting **state** • steady¹² [e]/ carrier / euthyroid [juːθaɪrɔɪd]/ anxiety¹³ [aɪ] **state** • shock(-like) / (non)pregnant / persistent vegetative¹⁴ [edʒ] (*abbr* PVS) **state** • physical [ɪ]/ functional / activity **status** • mental¹⁵ / marital¹⁶ / neurologic¹⁷ **status** • at an early / at an advanced¹⁸ **stage** • end-stage renal [iː] disease¹⁹

Zustand, Status
Stadium¹ Begleiterkrankungen² Allgemeinzustand³ physische Belastbarkeit⁴ Bewusstseinslage⁵ ruhiger Wachzustand⁶ Erregungszustand⁷ Verwirrtheit(szustand)⁸ Stimmungslage⁹ Säure-Basen-Status¹⁰ Nüchternzustand¹¹ Fließgleichgewicht, dynam. G., steady state¹² Angstzustand¹³ apallisches Syndrom¹⁴ Geisteszustand, geistige Verfassung¹⁵ Familienstand¹⁶ neurolog. Status¹⁷ im fortgeschrittenen Stadium¹⁸ terminale Niereninsuffizienz¹⁹
15

concomitant [kənkɒmɪtᵊnt] *adj term*   *syn* **concurrent** [ɜː‖BE ʌ], **coexisting** *adj*

disease, therapy or situation that occurs at the same time as or is associated [oʊʃ] with¹ another
coexist (with) *v* • **coexistence²** *n* • **coexistent** *adj* • **concomitant³** *n term*
» This finding is indicative of portal hypertension but does not exclude concomitant malignancy. False-negative reactions may be due to concurrent infection. Detrusor overactivity may be due to coexisting urethral [iː] obstruction [ʌ].
Use **concomitant/concurrent** disease³ / drug therapy⁴ / strabismus or squint⁵ [skwɪnt]/ administration⁶ • **coexisting** lesion [iːʒ]/ nausea [nɔːzɪə]/ iron deficiency⁷ [ɪʃ]

begleitend, Begleit-, gleichzeitig bestehend/ auftretend
vergesellschaftet mit¹ Nebeneinanderbestehen, Koexistenz² Begleitkrankheit, Komorbidität³ medikamentöse Begleittherapie⁴ Begleitschielen, Strabismus concomitans⁵ gleichzeitige Verabreichung⁶ gleichzeitiger Eisenmangel⁷
16

remission [rɪmɪʃᵊn] *n term*   *sim* **regression¹** [rɪgreʃᵊn] *n term*
   opposite **exacerbation²** [ɪgzæsəˈbeɪʃᵊn] *n term*, **flare(-up)³** [fleəˑ] *n clin*

partial [pɑːrʃᵊl] or complete, temporary or lasting disappearance of clinical signs
remit *v term* • **remittent⁴** *adj* • **regress** *v* • **exacerbate** *v* • **flare up** *v phr clin*
» This regimen [edʒ] has been shown to be effective in inducing regression of advanced cancers. In osteomyelitis [aɪ] a flare-up can occur [ɜː] after decades of inactivity. Her arthritis [-aɪtɪs] flared up and produced new symptoms.
Use to achieve⁵/induce/have/produce **a remission** • to be/remain **in remission** • full or complete⁶ / partial⁷ / spontaneous⁸ [eɪ]/ lasting **remission** • **remittent** fever⁹ [iː]/ symptoms / disease • symptomatic / acute¹⁰ / brief / intermittent / intense flare-up • to elicit a¹¹ [ɪs] *flare-up*

Remission, Nachlassen, vorübergehende Besserung
Rückbildung, Regression¹ Exazerbation, Verschlimmerung² Aufflackern³ vorübergehend nachlassend, remittierend⁴ eine Remission erzielen⁵ Vollremission⁶ Teilremission⁷ Spontanremission⁸ remittierendes Fieber, Febris remittens⁹ Akutwerden¹⁰ einen erneuten Ausbruch auslösen¹¹
17

relapse [riːlæps] *n term*   *syn* **setback, recurrence** [ɜː‖BE ʌ] *n clin*
   recrudescence [rɪkruːˈdesᵊnᵗs] *n term*

reappearance of the signs and/or symptoms of a condition after a period of remission
relapse¹ [rɪlæps] *v term* • **recur²** [rɪkɜːr] *v* • **recurrent³** *adj* • **set back⁴** *v phr*
» Relapse may occur after discontinuing⁵ therapy. This is a regimen⁶ [edʒ] for the treatment of Hodgkin's disease in relapse. The clinical course may be acute or chronic and relapsing. Radiotherapy can provide local palliation⁷ for recurrent tumors. About 1/3 of cyclosporine [saɪkləspɔːrɪn] responders relapse.
Use to suffer *or* have¹ **a relapse** • symptomatic / silent **relapse** • **relapse** rate⁸ /-free survival⁹ [aɪ] • **relapsing** disorder / fever¹⁰ / diarrhea [iː]/-remitting course¹¹ • a minor¹² / serious **setback** • **recurrent** stricture / attacks¹³ / bouts¹³ [aʊ] • **recurrent** tumor¹⁴ / urinary tract infection¹⁵ • risk of / rate of⁸ / late¹⁶ / local **recurrence**

Rückfall, Rezidiv
Rückfall erleiden¹ wieder auftreten, rezidivieren² rekurrent, rezidivierend³ zurückwerfen, verzögern⁴ Absetzen⁵ Behandlungskonzept, -strategie, -schema⁶ Linderung⁷ Rückfall-, Rezidivrate⁸ rezidivfreie Überlebenszeit⁹ Rückfallfieber, Febris recurrens¹⁰ schubweiser Verlauf¹¹ leichter Rückfall¹² rezidivierende Anfälle¹³ Tumorrezidiv¹⁴ rezidivierende Harnwegsinfektion¹⁵ Spätrezidiv¹⁶
18

prognosis [prɒɡnoʊsɪs] *n term, pl* **-ses**   *syn* **outlook** *n, rel* **prediction¹** *n clin*

estimate of a patient's probable course, prospects² of recovery [ʌ], and/or outcome³ of a disease
prognostic⁴ *adj term* • **prognosticate⁵** *v* • **predict** *v* • **predictive⁶** *adj*
» The prognosis in any individual case is guarded⁷ at the onset, since sudden changes for the worse are common. The long-term outlook is poor, but treatment may at least delay the onset of major disability. Estrogen receptors are of prognostic significance in breast cancer.
Use to give a⁸/alter⁹ [ɒː] /determine/estimate **prognosis** • good¹⁰ / favorable¹⁰ [eɪ]/ poor¹¹ **prognosis** • adverse¹¹ [ɜː]/ grave¹² [eɪ]/ dismal¹³ **prognosis** • medical / nursing [ɜː]/ functional¹⁴ / long-term / guarded¹⁵ [ɑː] **prognosis** • **prognostic** factors / value / indicators / index¹⁶ • grim¹¹ / bleak¹³ [iː]/ gloomy¹³ [uː] **outlook** • **predictive** value¹⁷

Prognose
Vorhersage¹ Aussichten² Folge(n), Zustand nach³ prognostisch⁴ vorhersagen, prognostizieren⁵ Vorhersage-⁶ vorsichtig, zurückhaltend⁷ eine Prognose stellen⁸ d. Prognose ändern⁹ gute/ günstige Prognose¹⁰ schlechte P.¹¹ sehr schlechte P.¹² infauste P.¹³ funktionelle Prognose¹⁴ vorsichtige P.¹⁵ Prognoseindex¹⁶ Vorhersagewert¹⁷
19

Unit 120 Therapeutic Intervention

Related Units: 121 Pharmacologic Treatment, 126 Surgical Treatment, 140 Wound Healing, 141 Fracture Management, 142 Physical Therapy

treatment [iː] n clin, abbr **T_x**   syn **therapy** [θerəpi] n term, **management** n jar
care for the sick or injured [ɪndʒəd] by conservative measures [eʒ], medical treatment, surgical intervention, etc.
treat[1] v clin • **manage**[1] v • **manageable**[2] adj • **treatable**[2] adj

» Patients with positive tests are treated as having syphilis. Microbial infections are best treated early. Many of these patients will gradually improve without treatment. Treatment consists of administering magnesium. This does not require further treatment. The patient was managed symptomatically[3]. The patient refused to submit to treatment[4].

Use to be under[5]/start/initiate [ɪʃ]/discontinue[6]/interrupt [ʌ]/undergo[4] **treatment** for a disease • preferred[7] / primary [aɪ] or first-line[8] / definitive / long-term **treatment** • life-long / operative / gold standard / multimodality / drug[9] **treatment** • a course [ɔː] of[10] / emergency[11] [ɜː]/ post/ self-/ over**treatment** • **treatment** of choice[7] / of sepsis / failure[12] [eɪ]/ center / room • **to treat** on an outpatient basis[13] / at an early stage / in hospital[14] • **treated** for 2 weeks / for gastritis[15] [aɪ]/ acutely / topically[16] • **treated** conservatively or medically / surgically / adequately • **treated** with 0.45% saline [eɪ]/ with cold compresses / by fixation / by a physician / as indicated[17] • insulin-/ placebo-**treated** • vigorously[18] [ɪg]/ promptly / successfully / previously[19] **treated** • prehospital[20] / patient / dietetic / home[21] **management**

cure [kjʊə] v & n   sim **heal**[1] [hiːl] v → U140-4
(v) to restore health by treating successfully
(n) a promising drug or course of treatment[2] (also at a spa[3])
curative[4] adj term •
(in)curable[5] adj clin • **curability**[6] n • **healing**[7] adj & n

» Physicians should attempt to achieve a cure at least in some patients, relieve symptoms as often as possible and always comfort[8] the patient. This is a promising new drug which may cure 60–80% of patients in first remission. The only cure for eclampsia is termination of pregnancy[9]. The outlook for cure[10] remains poor for children with high-grade gliomas [aɪ]. Hysterectomy alone is usually curative.

Use to effect a[11]/be treated with intent to/have a chance of **cure** • water / clinical / complete / permanent **cure** • **cure** rate[12] • **curative** approach [outʃ]/ intent[13] / resection / treatment[14] • **curable** cancer[15] / by surgery

treatment or **therapeutic** [juː] **modality** n term   sim **tool**[1] [uː] n jar
                        rel **option**[2] [ɒpʃⁿ] n clin & jar
the drug(s), operation, or approach chosen to treat a patient

» Lithotripsy combined with salt therapy is a valuable treatment modality for single gallstones [ɔː]. No therapeutic modality has been shown to be superior[3] [ɪə].

Use preferred treatment[4] / chemotherapeutic [iː] **modality** • combined **modality** therapy[5] • treatment[6] **options**

therapy [θerəpi] n term
any of the various treatment modalities, e.g. immunotherapy, genetic, operative therapy, etc.
therapeutic [juː] adj term • **therapist**[1] n • **-therapy** comb

» In elderly patients digitalis [dʒ] has a narrow therapeutic window[2].

Use physical[3] [ɪ]/ antiviral [aɪ]/ laser / electroshock / speech **therapy** • adjuvant[4] [ædʒə-]/ occupational[5] [eɪʃ]/ standby[6] / high-dose[7] **therapy** • to institute[8]/discontinue[9] **therapy** • **therapeutic** approach[10] / strategy / behavior[11] / rehabilitation nurse[12] / home / speech[13] [spiːtʃ] **therapist** • physio/ chemo[14] [iː]/ radio**therapy**

Behandlung, Therapie
behandeln[1] behandelbar[2] symptomatisch behandelt[3] sich einer Behandlung unterziehen[4] in B. sein[5] B. absetzen[6] B. der Wahl[7] Primärbehandlung[8] medikamentöse B.[9] Kur, Behandlungszyklus[10] Notfallversorgung[11] Therapieversagen[12] ambulant behandeln[13] stationär behandeln[14] auf Gastritis behandeln[15] lokal behandeln[16] laut Indikation behandeln[17] intensiv behandeln[18] vorbehandelt[19] präklinische Versorgung[20] häusliche Pflege[21]

1

heilen; Behandlung, Heilung, Kur, Heilmittel
(ab-, ver)heilen[1] Kur[2] Kurort[3] kurativ, heilend[4] (un)heilbar[5] Heilbarkeit[6] heilsam, -end; Heilung[7] beruhigen[8] Schwangerschaftsabbruch[9] Heilungsaussichten[10] Heilung bewirken[11] Heilungsrate[12] Heilungsabsicht[13] kurative Behandlung[14] heilbarer Krebs[15]

2

Behandlungsmethode, Behandlungsmodalität
(Hilfs)mittel, Instrument[1] Wahl, Möglichkeit[2] besser, überlegen[3] Methode der Wahl[4] Kombinationstherapie[5] Behandlungsmöglichkeiten[6]

3

Therapie, Behandlung
Therapeut(in)[1] therapeutisches Fenster[2] Physiotherapie, physikal. Therapie[3] medikam. Zusatztherapie, adjuvante Therapie[4] Beschäftigungstherapie[5] Therapiereserve[6] hochdosierte Therapie[7] Therapie einleiten[8] Behandlung absetzen[9] therap. Ansatz[10] Verhaltenstherapeut(in)[11] Krankengymnast(in)[12] Logopäde/-in[13] Chemotherapie[14]

4

Therapeutic Intervention CLINICAL TERMS **535**

regimen [rɛdʒɪmˤn] *n term*   *sim* **course**[1] [kɔːrs] *clin*, **protocol**[2] *n term*

systematic course of treatment (esp. prescribed medication, diet, exercise, change in life-style)
» Progress in drug therapy has resulted in the development of curative chemotherapy regimens for several tumors. A protocol or treatment plan is an outline of care.
Use treatment / split course[3] / prescribed[4] /(multi)drug **regimen** • combination / dosage[5] [ɪdʒ] / initial / curative[6] / preparative[7] / recommended **regimen** • 2-dose / low-dose / 5-day / 3-drug / alternate [ɒː] day **regimen** • **regimen** of drugs / for herpes • a **course** of estrogens[8] [e‖iː]

    Note: Sometimes **regimens** are incorrectly referred to as *regime*.

therapeut. Maßnahme(n), Diät, Behandlung(sschema)
Kur, Behandlung(szyklus)[1] Behandlungsplan, -protokoll[2] Sequenztherapie[3] verordnete Behandlung[4] Dosierungsschema[5] kurative Behandlung[6] Vorbehandlung, vorbereitende Maßnahmen[7] Östrogenbehandlung, -kur[8]   5

prophylactic [prɒːfəlæktɪk] *adj & n term & clin*   *syn* **preventive** *adj clin*

(adj) preventing the onset or spread [e] of disease (preventive medicine[1]) or pregnancy
prophylaxis[2] *n term* • **prevention**[2] [prɪvenʲʃˤn] *n*
» Broad-spectrum antibiotics[3] should never be given for prophylaxis. Routine or prophylactic use of penicillins is not required. Prophylactic therapy consists of increasing renal [iː] output[4].
Use to require/receive **prophylaxis** • **prophylactic** administration[5] / measures[6] [eʒ]/ agent / antibiotics / use • effective for / used as / postexposure[7] [oʊʒ]/ antibiotic[8] / long-term **prophylaxis** • oral / stress ulcer[9] [ʌlsɚ]/ chemo[10] [iː]/ single-dose **prophylaxis** • **prophylaxis** against or for malaria / with antacids

prophylaktisch, vorbeugend, präventiv; vorbeugende Maßnahme; Kondom
Präventivmedizin[1] Prophylaxe, Prävention, Vorbeugung[2] Breitbandantibiotika[3] Harnproduktion[4] prophyl. Verabreichung[5] vorbeugende Maßnahmen[6] postexpositionelle Prophylaxe[7] Antibiotikaprophylaxe[8] Stressulkusprophylaxe[9] Chemoprophylaxe[10]   6

surveillance [sɚˈveɪlənʲs] *n term*   *syn* **watchful waiting, expectant therapy** *n clin*

active observation and ongoing monitoring of a patient without actual treatment; a wait-and-see strategy[1]
» Close contacts of patients with diphtheria [ɪɚ] must be kept under surveillance for one week. Continuous surveillance for long-term complications is neccessary. The postoperative management options include either surveillance or 2 cycles of adjuvant chemotherapy.
Use close[2] / ongoing[3] / immune[4] / endoscopic / wound[5] [uː] **surveillance**

Beobachtungsstrategie, Surveillance, Überwachung
abwartende Strategie[1] strenge Überwachung[2] ständige Überwachung[3] immunologische Überwachung[4] Wundkontrolle[5]   7

adjuvant [ædʒəvˤnt] *n & adj term*   *syn* **adjunct** [ædʒʌŋkt] *n & adj clin & inf*

(n) additional treatment to increase the efficiency of primary therapy, e.g. chemotherapy following surgery
neoadjuvant[1] *n & adj term* • **adjunctive**[2] *adj*
» We generally use radiation treatment as an adjunct to surgery for these patients. Cytokine [aɪ] immunotherapy has shown promise as an adjunctive measure. Regimens that are not effective against bulky[3] [ʌ] tumors may be curative when used in an adjuvant setting.
Use **adjuvant** regimen / chemotherapy / irradiation[4] • pharmacologic[5] **adjunct** • **adjunctive** nephrectomy / medication[5] / measure[6] / management

Zusatztherapie, Adjuvans; adjuvant
Neoadjuvans, neoadjuvant[1] unterstützend[2] groß, raumfordernd[3] adjuvante Strahlentherapie[4] medikamentöse Zusatztherapie[5] unterstützende Maßnahme[6]   8

palliative [æ] *adj & n term*   *opposite* **curative**[1] [kjʊɚətɪv] *adj clin & term*

(adj) supportive treatment alleviating[2] [iː] or relieving[2] [iː] symptoms without curing the underlying [aɪ] disease[3]
palliate[2] *v term* • **palliation**[4] *n*
» Strictures at the hilum [aɪ] may be difficult to palliate endoscopically. Surgery may be used for palliation in patients for whom cure is not possible. A smooth [uː] transition[5] in treatment goals[6] [oʊ] from curative to palliative is difficult to achieve in all cases.
Use **palliative** (home) care[7] / needs / procedure / drugs / surgery[8] • to provide / pain / effective / long-term **palliation** • **curative** measure / dose[9] / intent[10] / approach[10]

palliativ, lindernd; Palliativum
kurativ[1] lindern, erleichtern[2] Grundkrankheit, zu Grunde liegendes Leiden[3] Linderung[4] fließender Übergang[5] Behandlungsziele[6] palliative (häusliche) Pflege[7] Palliativoperation[8] kurative Dosis[9] kurativer Ansatz[10]   9

CLINICAL TERMS — Therapeutic Intervention

indication [eɪ] *n term & clin*   *opposite* **contra-indication**[1] *n term*

(i) diagnostic basis for initiation[2] of a therapeutic course or for performing a clinical investigation (ii) sign

indicate[3] *v* • **indicative (of)**[4] *adj* • **(contra-)indicated**[5] *adj* • **indicator**[6] *n*

» Breast [e] feeding[7] [iː] *is not a contraindication for* vaccination[8] [ks]. *Heart-lung transplants have been performed for a variety* [aɪ] *of indications. The ECG changes are indicative of an* infarct.

Use clear[9] / clinical / vital[10] [aɪ] / excellent / principal[11] / emergency **indication** • major / compelling *or* absolute[12] / relative **contraindication** • **to be (contra)indicated** in patients / in pregnancy • diagnostic / prognostic **indicator**

(i) Indikation
(ii) (An)zeichen
Kontraindikation, Gegenanzeige[1] Einleitung, Beginn[2] anzeigen, indizieren[3] hinweisen(d) auf[4] (kontra)indiziert[5] Indikator[6] Stillen[7] Impfung[8] eindeutige Indikation[9] vitale I., Vitalind.[10] Hauptindikation[11] absolute Kontraindikation[12]   10

---

response *n term*

(i) reaction of the patient's body to therapy
(ii) reaction to stimuli [aɪ], viruses [aɪ], questions, etc.

respond (to)[1] *v term* • **(non)responder**[2] *n* • **(un)responsive(ness)**[3] *adj/n*

» *Fifty percent of patients* failed to respond to[4] *this regimen. The tumor was found to shrink in response to* tamoxifen withdrawal[5] [-ɔːl]. *His diarrhea* [iː] was unresponsive to fasting[6].

Use clinical / (durable) complete / poor / partial[7] [ʃ] / immune[8] **response** • **response rate** • **to respond** well[9] / poorly / inadequately / partially • placebo[10] [siː] **responder** • to be **responsive** to treatment

Ansprechen, Reaktion
ansprechen (auf), reagieren[1] Responder[2] ansprechend; Ansprechen[3] sprachen nicht an auf[4] Absetzen von Tamoxifen[5] persistierte trotz Nahrungskarenz[6] Teilreaktion[7] Immunantwort, -reaktion[8] gut ansprechen[9] Plazeboresponder[10]
11

---

morbidity *n term*   → U89-2; U100-9

undesirable[1] [aɪ] consequences and complications resulting from treatment

» *Morbidity is lower if transplantation is performed before the patient is critically ill. This technique is associated with* considerable morbidity[2], *above all in bilateral procedures.*

Use high / low / increased / minimal / long-term[3] / late[4] / septic[5] / infective **morbidity**

Morbidität
unerwünscht[1] beträchtliche Morbidität[2] Langzeitmorbidität[3] Spätmorbidität[4] sepsisbedingte M.[5]
12

---

refractory *adj term*   *syn* **intractable, resistant, recalcitrant** [kælsɪ] *adj term*

showing little or no response to treatment

intractability[1] *n term* • **refractoriness**[2] *n* • **resistance**[1] *n*

» *Hypotension can progress to refractory shock.* Notable features[2] [fiːtʃɚz] *of this tumor include refractoriness to cytotoxic agents. Abdominal pain and vomiting may become intractable.*

Use **refractory** cases / symptoms / period[3] / anemia [iː]/ heart failure • **intractable** pain[4] / ascites [əsaɪtiːz]/ insomnia[5] / to treatment[6] • drug[7] **resistance** • **recalcitrant** disease / case / lesion [iː3]

refraktär, (therapie)resistent, hartnäckig
(Therapie)resistenz[1] auffällige Merkmale[2] Refraktärzeit[3] therapieresistente(r) Schmerz(en)[4] therapieresistente Schlaflosigkeit[5] therapieresistent[6] Arzneimittelresistenz[7]
13

---

aftercare [æftɚkeɚ] *n term*

sim **followup**[1] [fɒːloʊʌp] *n term, abbr f/u* → U134-15

management (treatment, help, supervision[2] [ɪʒ]) of a patient in the postoperative or convalescent [es] period[3]; followup is also spelled follow-up

» *Aftercare following psychiatric* [saɪkɪætrɪk] *hospitalization involves a continuing program of rehabilitation to* reinforce[4] [riːɪn-] *the effects of the therapy by* partial [ʃ] hospitalization[5], outpatient treatment[6], *etc.*

Use aftercare treatment / plan[7] • long-term[8] **aftercare** • followup period[9] / examination[10] • **followup** at 6 months postoperatively[11]

Nachsorge, -behandlung
Nachuntersuchung, Verlaufskontrolle[1] Überwachung[2] Rekonvaleszenz, Genesungszeit[3] unterstützen[4] teilstationäre Behandlung[5] ambulante Beh.[6] Nachbehandlungsplan[7] Langzeitnachbetreuung[8] Nachuntersuchungszeitraum[9] Kontroll-, Nachuntersuchung[10] postop. Verlaufskontrolle nach 6 Monaten[11]   14

(patient) compliance [kəmplaɪənˢs] *n term*   *sim* **adherence**[1] [ɪɚ] *n clin*

consistency[2] and accuracy[3] with which a patient follows the prescribed[4] treatment regimen

(non)compliant[5] *adj term* • **noncompliance** *n* • **(un)cooperative**[5] *adj*

» *The importance of adherence to the recommended regimens for diet, exercise and glucose monitoring should be stressed. Patient compliance is essential if surveillance is to work.*

Use to ensure[6] [-ʃʊɚ]/monitor[7] **compliance** • poor[8] / strict[9] / patient **compliance** • **adherence** to treatment[10] • **compliance** with therapy[10] / rate

(Patienten-)Compliance
Befolgung, Einhaltung[1] Konsequenz, Beständigkeit[2] Genauigkeit[3] verordnet[4] (nicht) kooperativ[5] Compliance sicherstellen[6] C. überwachen[7] mangelnde Einhaltung/ Compliance[8] genaue Befolgung[9] Therapietreue[10]
15

Unit 121 Pharmacologic Treatment

Related Units: 9 Drugs & Remedies, 92 Pharmacologic Agents, 93 Anesthetics, 91 Toxicology

prescribe [aɪ] v term   sim **order¹, schedule²** [skedjuːl‖ʃed-] v clin

ordering (in writing) the preparation, dispensing³ and/or administration⁴ of medication or treatment for a particular patient; some medications are available only on prescription⁵ others without (over-the-counter⁶ [aʊ])

prescription⁷ n term, abbr **Rx** • **nonprescription**⁶ adj

» Prescriptions include the sign Rx (i.e. take), the names and quantities of the drugs ordered, directions⁸ for compounding⁹ [aʊ] the ingredients¹⁰ [iː] and designation of the form (pill, powder, solution, etc.) in which the drug is to be made, directions for the patient regarding the dose, route [uː‖aʊ] of administration and times of taking the drug. Drugs are effective only if the patient takes them as prescribed¹¹.

Use **to prescribe** drugs / baths¹² / a diet [daɪət]/ exercises • **prescribed** dose / regimen [edʒ] or course [ɔː] of therapy¹³ • to write out a¹⁴ **prescription** • vitamin / dietary¹⁵ / eyeglass¹⁶ **prescription** • **prescription** drugs or medications¹⁷ / preparation / error

> **Note:** Common abbr for the dosage and administration of drugs include: b.i.d. [biːaɪdiː] (twice a day), q.d. (every day), t.i.d. (3 times/day), q.i.d. (4 times/day), q.h. or o.h. (every hour), p.r.n. or qrs. or q.l. or q.p. (at will, as needed), a.c. (before meals [iː]), o.n. or h.s. (every night), alt.noct. (every other night) and q4 (every 4 hs). These may also be written in upper case letters, e.g. PRN.

verschreiben, verordnen
ver-, anordnen¹ planen, ansetzen² Zubereitung, Abgabe³ Verabreichung⁴ auf Rezept, rezeptpflichtig⁵ rezeptfrei⁶ Verordnung, Rezept⁷ Anleitungen⁸ (ver)mischen⁹ Bestandteile¹⁰ nach Vorschrift, vorschriftsmäßig¹¹ Bäder verordnen¹² verordnete(s) Therapie(schema)¹³ Rezept ausstellen¹⁴ Diätvorschrift¹⁵ Brillenverordnung¹⁶ rezeptpflichtige Medikamente¹⁷

1

proprietary [prəpraɪətərɪ] adj term   opposite **non-proprietary¹, generic¹** [dʒenerɪk] adj term

proprietary drug names are protected trade names or trademarks² (e.g. Zovirax®) while generic drug names³ (e.g. acyclovir) are those recognized by official organizations and recommended for general use (unlike trademarks they are not capitalized)

» Many proprietary antacids⁴ contain both magnesium and aluminum hydroxides [aɪ].

patentrechtlich geschützt
generisch, allgemein¹ geschützte Handelsnamen/ Warenzeichen² Freinamen³ Antazida, säurebindende Mittel⁴

2

administration n term   sim **application¹** n term

the act of giving a patient medication

administer² v term • **apply³** [əplaɪ] v • **applicator⁴** n

» These preparations can be swallowed whole⁵ [hoʊl] or chewed [tʃuːd] or administered as a patch⁶ or paste [eɪ] via the transdermal route⁷. Heparin is administered to patients with acute thrombosis. This drug must be administered under close supervision [ʒ] of a physician.

Use **to administer** an enema⁸ / a local anesthetic • **administered by** infusion / the parenteral route⁹ / inhalation / jet [dʒet] nebulizer¹⁰ • **administered** at full dose / in doses of • acute / chronic / continuous¹¹ / lifelong¹¹ / long-term / simultaneous [eɪ] **administration** • oral / intravaginal [dʒ]/ systemic / oxygen / once-daily / self-/ patient-**administration** • for ease¹² [iːz]/ safest route¹³ / preferred method¹⁴ / frequency / timing **of administration**

> **Note:** Common abbr for the route of administration include: p.o.¹⁵ (by mouth), i.m. (intramuscular), i.v. (intravenous), i.a. (intra-arterial) and sub-q or s.c. (subcutaneous). These abbr may also be written in upper case letters, e.g. IV.

Verabreichung, Gabe
Anwendung, Applikation¹ verabreichen² applizieren, anwenden, auftragen³ Applikator⁴ unzerkaut geschluckt⁵ Pflaster⁶ per-, transkutan⁷ Einlauf machen⁸ parenteral verabreicht⁹ mit Düsenaerosolgerät verabreicht¹⁰ Dauermedikation¹¹ zur leichteren Anwendung¹² sicherste Applikationsart¹³ bevorzugte Applikationsart¹⁴ peroral¹⁵

3

drug delivery n term   sim **drug targeting¹** [g], rel **drug release²** [iː] n term

(i) route of supplying or providing therapeutic agents
(ii) transport of substances to the target tissue³

deliver⁴ v term • **target⁵** v • **release⁶** v

» Drugs for transdermal delivery⁷ must have suitable [uː] skin penetration characteristics and high potency⁸. Clonidine diffusion through a membrane provides controlled drug delivery over a period of 1 wk.

Use **drug delivery** system⁹ / device [aɪ] • slow-**release** drug¹⁰

Applikation(sart)
Drug targeting (gezielte Konzentr. e. Arzneistoffes am Wirkort)¹ Arzneistoff-, Wirkstofffreisetzung² Wirkort, Zielgewebe³ zuführen, applizieren⁴ abzielen auf⁵ freisetzen⁶ transdermale Applikation⁷ Wirkungsstärke⁸ therapeut. System⁹ Depot-, Retardpräparat¹⁰

4

CLINICAL TERMS — Pharmacologic Treatment

topical *adj term*   *opposite* **systemic¹** *adj term*

applied or restricted to a specific area (usually the skin)

» Newer, very p*o*tent² topical corticost*e*roids [ɪɚ] may be applied less often.
Use **topical** application³ / agents [eɪ] / anesth*e*tic⁴ / stimulant / steroids / ointments⁵

Note: Topical cr*ea*ms [iː], ointments, etc. are *applied* to the skin, while oral, IV drugs, etc. are *administered*.

topisch, lokal
systemisch, generalisiert¹ stark, (hoch)wirksam² topische/ lokale Anwendung³ Lokalanästhetikum⁴ Salben z. lokalen Anwendung⁵

5

discontinue *v term*   *sim* **withdraw¹** [wɪðdrɔː] -drew [uː] -drawn *v irr term*

discontinu*a*tion or discont*i*nuance² *n term*

» First nonessential medication should be discontinued. Whether to discontinue or switch [ɪtʃ] a drug³ depends on the sev*e*rity [e] of the skin erupt*i*on [ʌ]. The dose is gradually t*a*pered⁴ [eɪ] and discontinued over several days.
Use **to discontinue** drug therapy⁵ / all oral int*a*ke⁶ / application of heat • **discontin-uation of** therapy / life support⁷

absetzen, -brechen
entziehen, absetzen¹ Abbruch, Unterbrechung² Medikament wechseln³ allmählich reduziert⁴ medikamentöse Behandlung absetzen⁵ Nahrungsaufnahme einstellen⁶ Intensivtherapie absetzen, lebenserh. Maßnahmen einstellen⁷

6

dose [doʊs] *n & v term*   *syn* **dosage** [ˈdoʊsɪdʒ] *n clin* → U91-11; U11-11

n (i) qu*a*ntity [ɒː] of medication to be taken at a time
(ii) radiation administered or absorbed

overdose¹ *n & v term, abbr* **OD** • **dose-dependent²** *adj* • **d*o*simeter** *n*

» The dose-effect curve³ of a drug results from its p*o*tency (loc*a*tion of curve along the dose *a*xis), peak [iː] *e*fficacy or c*ei*ling [iː] eff*e*ct⁴ (greatest att*ai*nable response), slope⁵ (change in response per equivalent dose⁶), and biologic variation of response among tested individuals.
Use to adj*u*st [ʌ] the⁷ **dosage** • oral / missed⁸ / minimal effective / t*o*lerance⁹ **dose** • curative [kjʊɚ] or therape*u*tic¹⁰ [uː]/ recommended **dose** • single¹¹ / initial¹² [ɪʃ]/ maintenance¹³ / lethal¹⁴ [iː] (*abbr* LD) **dose** • **dose** fraction*a*tion / calculation / distrib*u*tion /-response curve³ • **high dose** therapy¹⁵ • liberal / in divided¹⁶ **doses**

Dosis, Dosierung, Gabe; dosieren
Überdosis; überdosieren¹ dosisabhängig² Dosis-Wirkungs-Kurve³ Wirkungsmaximum⁴ Steilheit d. Dosis-Wirkungs-K.⁵ Dosisäquivalent⁶ D. anpassen⁷ vergessene Einnahme⁸ Toleranzdosis (radiolog.)⁹ kurative D., D cur¹⁰ Einzelgabe, -dosis¹¹ Anfangs-, Initialdosis¹² Erhaltungsd.¹³ letale D.¹⁴ hochdosierte Therapie¹⁵ in Teildosen¹⁶

7

action [ˈækʃən] *n term*   *sim* **activity¹, effect²** *n term* → U92-3

» It is important to better understand the mech*a*nism [k] of action³ of these new drugs. These c*e*phalosporins [s] have good activity against most gram-positive c*o*cci [kaɪ‖ksaɪ]. These drugs reach their peak action⁴ in 4h. Each *a*gent poss*e*sses a dist*i*nct⁵ pharmacodyn*a*mic profile of action⁶.
Use bacteric*i*dal [saɪ]/ broad spectrum of⁷ / gram-positive / in vitro **activity** • onset of⁸ / pharmacologic / selective / cytoprotective [saɪtoʊ-]/ hypot*e*nsive⁹ **action** • on-off¹⁰ / wearing-off¹¹ **effect**

Wirkung
Wirksamkeit, Wirkung¹ Effekt, (Aus)wirkung² Wirkungsmechanismus³ maximale Wirkung⁴ charakteristisch⁵ pharmakodynam. Wirkprofil⁶ breites Wirkungsspektrum⁷ Wirkungseintritt⁸ blutdrucksenkende W.⁹ Wirkungsfluktuation, On-off Effekt¹⁰ verkürztes Ansprechen, Wearing-off Effekt¹¹

8

potency [ˈpoʊtənˈsi] *n term* → U53-2   *sim* **efficacy¹** [ˈɛfɪkəsi] *n term*

(i) pharmacol*o*gical effectiveness of a drug (ii) opposite of s*e*xual *i*mpotence
potent² *adj term* • **low-/ high-p*o*tency³** *adj*

» Unfortunately the potency of inhaled steroids is not me*a*surable [eʒ] by improvements in asthma [æzmə] activity. Levorphanol has good oral potency. This patient must not be placed on high potency agents. Nitroglycerin [aɪ] loses potency unless stored in a tightly [aɪt] sealed⁴ [iː] light-res*i*stant⁵ container.
Use clinical / carcinog*e*nic [dʒen]/ antiarrhythmic [ɪ] **potency** • highly / m*o*derately⁶ **potent drugs**

(i) Wirksamkeit, Wirkungsstärke
(ii) sexuelle Potenz
Effektivität, Wirksamkeit¹ stark, wirksam² hochwirksam, -potent³ (luft)dicht verschlossen⁴ lichtundurchlässig⁵ Medikamente mittlerer Wirkungsstärke⁶

9

bioavailability [baɪoʊ-] *n term*   *sim* **rate of absorption¹** *n term*

ext*e*nt and rate at which a given amount of a drug is absorbed and made available to the target tissue
bioav*a*ilable² *adj term*

» The c*o*ncept of bioavailab*i*lity relates to the efficiency [ɪfɪʃənˈsi] of the dosage formulation as an extravascular drug delivery system and permits comparison of drug pr*o*ducts for rel*a*tive availability or bioequiv*a*lence³. Although bioavailability generally refers to the extent of input only, it includes consideration of both the amount and rate of absorption into the syst*e*mic circulation⁴ [sɜːr] following extrav*a*scular administration.
Use level of **bioavailability** • low⁵ / high / reduced / decreased / poor⁵ **bioavailability**

Bioverfügbarkeit, biolog. Verfügbarkeit
Resorptionsgeschwindigkeit¹ biologisch verfügbar² Bioäquivalenz³ Körper-/ großer Kreislauf⁴ geringe Bioverfügbarkeit⁵

10

Pharmacologic Treatment   CLINICAL TERMS **539**

drug interactions *n term usu pl*   *sim* **cross-reaction**[1] *n term*

harmful[2] or desirable[3] [aɪ] pharmacological effects of drugs interacting with other drugs or themselves, (non)physiologic chemical agents, components of the diet[4] [daɪət], etc.

interact with[5] *v phr* • **cross-react** *v term* • **cross-reactivity** *n*

» Unwanted interactions can cause adverse [ɜː] drug reactions[6] or therapeutic failure[7] [eɪ]. Pharmacokinetic interactions are mainly due to alteration of absorption, distribution, metabolism, or excretion [iːʃ], which changes the amount and duration of a drug's availability at receptor sites[8]. If a formulation[9] has the potential to interact with food the drug should be administered apart from meals[10].

Use drug-drug / drug-food / nutrient-drug[11] / pharmacokinetic[12] / pharmacodynamic interactions • adverse **drug interaction** • **cross**-reaction /-reactive antigen

(Arzneimittel)wechsel-wirkungen, -interaktionen
Kreuzreaktion[1] schädlich[2] erwünscht[3] Nahrungsstoffe[4] s. gegenseitig beeinflussen[5] Nebenwirkung(en)[6] Therapieversagen[7] Rezeptorstellen[8] Arzneiform[9] nicht mit Mahlzeiten eingenommen werden[10] Wechselwirkung zw. Nahrungsmitteln u. Medikamenten[11] pharmakokinet. Interaktionen[12]
11

tolerate *v term & clin* → U75-16

able to endure or resist the action of a drug, poison[1], radiation [eɪ] or food without untoward [ʌntəˈwɔːrd] effects[2].

(in)tolerance[3] *n term* • **cross-tolerance**[4] *n* • **(in)tolerable**[5] *adj*

» Parenteral quinidine[6] [kwɪn-] is generally well tolerated by most patients. The patient developed unacceptable symptoms despite medical therapy to its tolerable limits[7]. The initial dosage of 2 mg tid is increased as tolerated[8].

Use well[9] / better / poorly / not[10] **tolerated** • short-term[11] / acquired[12] [əkwaɪəd] **tolerance** • drug[13] / food / exercise / cold **intolerance** • minimal / organ[14] / tissue **tolerance dose** • **tolerance** test[15] / to opioids • **intolerable** pain / side effects

vertragen
Gift[1] schädliche Auswirkungen[2] (Un)verträglichkeit, (In)toleranz[3] Kreuztoleranz[4] (un)verträglich[5] Chinidin[6] max. verträgliche Dosis[7] nach Verträglichkeit[8] gut vertragen, verträglich[9] nicht vertragen, unverträglich[10] kurzfristige Verträglichkeit[11] Toleranzentwicklung[12] Arzneimittelunverträglichkeit[13] Organtoleranzdosis (radiol.)[14] Toleranztest[15]
12

toxic level *or* **range** [reɪndʒ] *n term* → U91-18

opposite **therapeutic** [juː] **range**[1] *n term*

dosage of any substance that is beyond[2] the maximal therapeutic dose and produces overdosage[3] toxicity

nontoxic[4] *adj term* • **toxicity**[5] [tɒːkˈsɪsɪti] *n* • **toxicology** *n*

» This dosage produces a toxic response on chronic administration. Overdosage toxicity is the predictable toxic effect that occurs with dosages in excess of[2] the therapeutic range for a particular patient. Equivalent mg/kg doses well tolerated by adults can result in serious [ɪə] toxicity in neonates[6] [iː]. These drugs are particularly toxic to the organ of Corti.

Use drug / side-effect[7] / digitalis[8] [dʒ]/ local / systemic / hepatic[9] / long-term **toxicity** • **toxic** reaction / manifestations[10] / shock / agent / effect • **toxicity** test[11] / study

toxischer Wirkungsbereich
therapeutische Breite[1] (liegt) über[2] Überdosierung[3] ohne toxische Wirkung, ungiftig[4] Toxizität, Giftigkeit[5] Neugeborene[6] toxische Nebenwirkungen[7] Toxizität v. Digitalis[8] Lebertoxizität[9] Intoxikationszeichen[10] toxikologischer Test[11]

13

adverse [ɜː] **drug reaction** *n term, abbr* **ADR**

syn **side** *or* **untoward effect** *n clin*

secondary effects of a drug not normally seen in the therapeutic range that may cause minor[1] [aɪ], significant and even life-threatening[2] [e] morbidity

» Serious[3] [ɪə] adverse reactions are uncommon. Adverse effects should be discussed with patients to encourage [ɜː] them to mention them to the physician [fɪzɪʃ³n] prior [aɪ] to stopping medication[4].

Use to cause or provoke[5] [oʊ] / minimize **adverse effects** • **adverse** response to[6] / effect on

unerwünschte Arzneimittelwirkung, Nebenwirkung
gering(fügig)[1] lebensbedrohlich[2] ernsthaft, schwer(wiegend)[3] vor dem Absetzen d. Medikamente[4] Nebenwirkungen auslösen[5] unerwünschte Reaktion auf[6]

14

drug-induced [(j)uːs] *adj clin*   *sim* **iatrogenic**[1] [aɪə-] *adj* → U89-9,

rel **nosocomial**[2] [koʊ] *adj term*

resulting from the administration of a drug, e.g. a drug rash, psychosis, or liver disease

» Predisposing[3] iatrogenic factors include cancer chemotherapy [kiː], genitourinary instrumentation or catheterization, recent surgery, steroid therapy, and antibiotic administration.

Use **drug-induced** disease / hepatitis / gingivitis • **drug**-fast *or* -resistant /-related fever /-associated /-free • **iatrogenic** illness[4] / fracture / factors / injury[5] / infection[6]

arzneimittelinduziert, -bedingt
iatrogen, durch d. Arzt verursacht[1] nosokomial, Krankenhaus-[2] prädisponierend[3] iatrogene Erkrankung[4] iatrogene Verletzung/ Schädigung[5] iatrogene Infektion[6]

15

121

Unit 122 Immunization

Related Units: 39 The Immune System, 91 Infectious Diseases, 91 Childhood Disease, 94 Pathogens & Parasites, 95 Toxicology, 4 Illness & Recovery

inoculate [ɪnɒːkjəleɪt] v term   syn **vaccinate** [æks] v,
rel **immunize**[1] [-aɪz] v clin & term

to introduce a substance into the body which produces or increases immunity to a specific disease

inoculation n term • **inoculable**[2] adj • **inoculant** or **inoculum**[3] n, pl **-a**

» HBV[4] is usually transmitted by inoculation of infected blood or blood products. The most frequent adverse [ɜː] complication of vaccination is inadvertent[5] [ɜː] inoculation (usually autoinoculation) at other sites. In most cases, failure to vaccinate susceptible[6] [se] persons, not vaccine failure, is responsible for the outbreak.

Use **to inoculate** organisms into the skin / a test strain[7] [eɪ]/ rickettsiae [-siː]/ **to vaccinate** against HBV / children / high-risk populations[8] / **to immunize** sb. against tetanus/wasp [ɒː] stings / contacts of vaccine recipients [sɪ] • direct / primary [aɪ]/ protective[9] / cutaneous[10] [eɪ] **inoculation** • nasal [eɪ]/ conjunctival [aɪ]/ virus [aɪ] **inoculation** • self- or auto[11]/ mosquito **inoculation** • tick-bite[12] / site of[13] **inoculation** • **inoculation** eschar[14] [eskɑːr]/ of cell cultures [ʌ] • infecting / bacterial [ɪə]/ virus **inoculum** • rickettsial / exogenous [ɒːdʒ] **inoculum** • **inoculum** size[15]

vaccine [væksiːn] n term & clin   rel **antiserum**[1] [æntɪsɪərəm] n term, pl **-a**

suspension of inactivated microorganisms administered to induce active immunity to this agent

(un)vaccinated[2] adj term • **vaccino-** comb • **vaccinal** adj • **(re)vaccinee**[3] n

» Vaccines directed against poliovirus infections have largely eliminated the disease in developed countries. Unvaccinated or partially vaccinated children younger than 2 years of age should receive a complete series of vaccinations. A bite by a bat[4] mandates antiserum.

Use active / passive / recombinant[5] / influenza or flu [uː] **vaccine** • hepatitis [aɪ] B / genetically engineered[6] [ɪə] **vaccine** • Bacille Calmette-Guerin[7] (abbr BCG)/ smallpox[8] **vaccine** • oral polio[9] (abbr OPV)/ Salk[10] [sɔːk] / live[11] [laɪv] **vaccine** • whole-virus[12] / inactivated / booster [uː] **vaccine** • combination or conjugate[13] [kɒndʒ-]/ sub-unit / adsorbed[14] **vaccine** • (type-/mono)specific[15] / heterologous / polyvalent [eɪ] (anti)rabies[16] [reɪbiːz] **antiserum** • equine[17] [eǁiːkwaɪn]/ saline-active [eɪ]/ high-titer[18] [aɪ] **antiserum** • fully / previously [iː]/ recently **vaccinated** • **vaccinal** areola [ɪə]/ fever[19] [iː]/ encephalomyelitis • adult / healthy / primary / seropositive **vaccinee** • hetero[20]/ entero**vaccine** • **vaccino**phobia /therapy[21]

vaccination n term, abbr **vacc**   syn **inoculation** n, rel **immunization**[1] n term

administration of an immunizing substance producing a mild form of the disease followed by immunity

revaccination[2] n term • **pre/ postvaccination** adj • **immunity**[3] n

» Stimulation of the immune system by vaccination may elicit[4] unanticipated responses, above all hypersensitivity reactions[5]. Measles [iː] vaccination[6] prevents the disease in susceptible exposed individuals if given within 72 hours. Update[7] diphtheria immunization of all contacts[8], including hospital personnel. Vaccination is no guarantee of immunization.

Use **to** recommend/advise/seek/require/postpone[9] [oʊ] **vaccination** • initial[10] / routine / oral[11] / active / passive **vaccination** • prophylactic[12] / mass / repeat[2] / annual **vaccination** • pre-exposure[13] / postpartum / (universal) childhood / depot **vaccination** • measles [iː]-mumps [ʌ]-rubella (abbr MMR) / pneumococcal [n(j)uː-]/ rabies **vaccination** • (primary/ full) course or schedule[14] [ʃǁskedjuːl]/ mode[15] **of vaccination** • **vaccination** for tetanus / against smallpox[16] / technique[15] • **vaccination** site / scar[17] / reaction / schedule[14] / program / requirement • **prevaccination** level / era [ɪə] • **postvaccination** serologic testing • mandatory[18] / mass[19] / intranasal / polio / basic[20] **immunization** • primary[21] / active / passive / travel[22] **immunization** • **immunization** status [eɪǁæ]/ procedure [siː]/ coverage [kʌvərɪdʒ] • **immunization** schedule[14] / history[23] • to confer [ɜː] life-long[24] **immunity**

---

impfen, inokulieren, vakzinieren

immun machen, immunisieren[1] inokulierbar, durch Impfung übertragbar/ infizierbar; impfbar[2] Impfmaterial, Inokulum[3] Hepatitis-B-Virus[4] unbeabsichtigt, akzidentell[5] anfällig, empfindlich[6] einen Teststamm inokulieren[7] Risikopopulationen impfen[8] Schutzimpfung[9] Kutanimpfung[10] Autoinokulation[11] Zeckenschutzimpfung[12] Impfstelle[13] Impfschorf[14] Inokulummenge[15]

1

Impfstoff, Vakzine

Antiserum[1] geimpft[2] Impfling, Geimpfte(r)[3] Fledermaus[4] rekombinanter Impfstoff[5] gentechn. hergestellter I.[6] BCG-Vakzine[7] Pockenimpfstoff[8] Polio-, Sabin-Schluckvakzine[9] Polioformolimpfstoff, Salk-Vakzine[10] Lebendimpfstoff, -vakzine[11] Ganzvirusimpfstoff[12] Kombinationsimpfstoff[13] Adsorbatimpfstoff[14] monospezifisches Antiserum[15] Tollwut-Antiserum[16] Pferdeserum[17] Antiserum m. hohem Antikörpertiter[18] Impffieber[19] Heterovakzine[20] Vakzinetherapie[21]

2

Schutzimpfung, Vakzination

Immunisierung[1] Revakzination, Wiederholungsimpfung[2] Immunität[3] auslösen[4] Überempfindlichkeitsreaktionen[5] Masernschutzimpfung[6] auffrischen[7] Kontaktpersonen[8] die Impfung verschieben[9] Erstimpfung[10] Schluckimpfung[11] Schutzimpfung[12] präexpositionelle Impfung[13] Impfschema[14] Impfmethode[15] Pockenschutzimpfung[16] Impfnarbe[17] obligatorische Impfung[18] Massenimmunisierung[19] Grundimmunisierung[20] Erstimmunisierung[21] Reiseimpfung[22] Impfanamnese[23] lebenslange Immunität verleihen[24]

3

Immunization   CLINICAL TERMS 541

vaccine injection [ɪndʒekʃən] *n term*
　　　　　　　　　　rel **shot**[1] *n jar* → U11-8,
　　　　　　　　　　jab[1] [dʒæb] *n inf BE*

introduction of a preparation of inactivated organisms into the subcutaneous [ʌ] tissue with a hypodermic [ɜː] needle[2] and a syringe[3] [sɪrɪndʒ] → U17-10f

inject[4] *v term* • **postinjection** *adj* • **(auto)injectable**[5] *adj* • **jab**[6] *v inf*

» *Injection of DTP vaccine containing the whole-cell pertussis [ʌ] component is associated with high rates of local reactions and fever. For adults, a complete course of hepatitis A vaccine consists of two IM injections given 6 to 12 months apart. Ask patients who cannot be depended on to take oral medication to come to your office for a "shot."*

Use to give an[7] *injection* • intravenous [iː] (*abbr* IV)/ subcutaneous[8] [eɪ] (*abbr* sub-q or SC) *injection* • intramuscular (*abbr* IM)/ intradermal[9] [ɜː] *injection* • vaccination by / booster [uː]/ drug / local *injection* • intraperitoneal [iː]/ single morning / jet[10] [dʒet]/ pain on *injection* • bolus[11] / depot / dye[12] [daɪ] *injection* • intraarterial / intracardiac[13] / intrathecal [iː]/ insulin *injection* • lactated Ringer's[14] / saline [eɪ]/ sensitizing[15] *injection* • *injection* site / technique / equipment[16] / therapy • **injectable** (poliovirus) vaccine • *injection of* vaccines / sera / contrast (media)[17] • tetanus[18] / subcutaneous / booster[19] *shot* • insulin / single / golden[20] / evening *shot* • flu[21] / insulin *jab* (*BE*) • **postinjection** flare[22] [fleə] • *to jab* the needle in(to) the thigh [θaɪ].

exposure [ɪkspoʊʒɚ] *n term* → U91-5
　　　　　　　　sim **contact**[1] *n, rel* **sensitization**[2] *n term* → U94-2f

being subjected to infectious microorganisms, radiation [eɪ] or other toxic or harmful agents

exposed[3] *adj* • **pre-/ post-exposure**[4] *adj term* • **sensitize**[5] [sensɪtaɪz] *v*

» *If a child is seen within 72 hours of exposure to measles virus, vaccination is the preferred method of protection. If they have not been exposed to the virus or are low risk, immunization should be initiated [ɪʃ]. All sexual contacts of the patient should be traced*[6] [treɪst].

Use measles / rabies [eɪ]/ drug / environmental / dust[7] [ʌ]/ industrial [ʌ] *exposure* • toxin / lead[8] [led]/ prolonged[9] / chronic / skin / fetal [iː] *exposure* • level / risk[10] / history[11] *of exposure* • *exposure to* (foreign) antigens / infectious or transmissible agents • *exposure to* contaminated water / infected food • *exposure to* infections / irritants / allergens[12] • *exposure to* (ionizing) [aɪə] radiation[13] / stress / heat • **pre-exposure** booster dose • **post-exposure** vaccination / (rabies) prophylaxis[14] • (close) bodily[15] / skin(-to-skin)[16] / oral-fecal [iː] *contact* • sexual / household / patient **contacts** • family / sibling[17] [ɪ]/ social **contacts** • **contact** with blood / with an infected person / tracing • *contact* ulcer [ʌlsɚ]/ allergy / dermatitis[18] [dɜːrmə-]/ isolation[19] • skin / primary / allergic[2] [ɜː] **sensitization**

attenuated [ətenjʊeɪtɪd] **live virus** *n term*　　　*syn* **live attenuated virus** *n term*

living microorganism that has been cultured [kʌltʃɚd] under conditions which deprived[1] [aɪ] it of its virulence [ɪ] but not of its ability to induce protective immunity[2] [ɪmjuːnɪti]

attenuation[3] *n term* • **attenuate** *v* • **unattenuated** *adj*

» *In mid 1995, a live attenuated vaccine for varicella [se] was approved and released commercially. The vaccine consists of live, unattenuated virus of types 4 and 7 administered in enteric-coated capsules*[4]*, which stimulate local and systemic antibodies that are protective against subsequent acute respiratory disease due to those serotypes [ɪə].*

Use whole[5]-/ live[6] *virus vaccine* • *attenuated live virus* measles [iː]-mumps [ʌ]-rubella (*abbr* MMR) vaccine[7] / immunization • *live attenuated* varicella-zoster [zɒː] vaccine (*abbr* VZV)/ oral poliovirus vaccine (*abbr* OPV) • *attenuated* poliovirus / strain[8] [eɪ]/ illness[9] • **attenuation** of infection

---

parenterale Impfung/ Vakzination

Spritze; Injektion[1] Injektionsnadel[2] Spritze[3] injizieren, (ein)spritzen[4] injizierbar[5] stechen, stoßen, eine Spritze geben/ verpassen[6] eine Injektion verabreichen[7] subkutane Injektion[8] intradermale I.[9] nadellose (Jet)injektion[10] Bolusinjektion, intravenöse Schnellinjektion[11] Farbstoffinjektion[12] intrakardiale I.[13] Ringerlaktatinjektion[14] Desensibilisierungsspritze[15] Injektionsbesteck[16] Kontrastmittelinjektion[17] Tetanusimpfung[18] Auffrischung(simpfung)[19] goldener Schuss[20] Grippe(schutz)impfung[21] postvakzinale Hautrötung[22]

4

Exposition

Kontakt, Kontaktperson[1] Sensibilisierung[2] ausgesetzt, exponiert[3] postexpositionell[4] sensibilisieren[5] ausfindig gemacht/ eruiert werden[6] Staubexposition[7] Bleibelastung[8] Langzeitexposition[9] Expositionsrisiko[10] Expositionsanamnese[11] Allergenexposition[12] Strahlenexposition[13] postexpositionelle Prophylaxe[14] Körperkontakt[15] Hautkontakt[16] im gleichen Haushalt lebende Geschwister[17] Kontaktdermatitis[18] Isolierung[19]

5

abgeschwächtes/ attentuiertes lebendes Virus

nehmen, entziehen[1] Impfschutz[2] Attenuierung, Virulenzabschwächung[3] magensaftresistente Kapseln[4] Ganzvirusimpfstoff[5] Lebendimpfstoff, -vakzine[6] attenuierte Masern-Mumps-Röteln-Lebendvakzine[7] attenuierter Stamm[8] abgeschwächte Erkrankung[9]

6

CLINICAL TERMS — Immunization

inactivated vaccine n term   syn **killed(-virus) vaccine** n term

strains of virus whose pathogenic potential has been destroyed by heat, suspension in formalin[1], etc.

inactivation n term • **inactive** adj • **activation** n • **activity**[2] n

» The influenza vaccine is a trivalent inactivated vaccine containing antigens from two strains[3] of influenza A and one strain of influenza B. Inactivated vaccines (with the exception of cholera and yellow fever[4]) can be given simultaneously or at any time after a different vaccine. This vaccine consists of a purified inactive subunit of the virus and is therefore not infectious.

Use **inactivated** polio vaccine (abbr IPV)/-virus vaccine / anti-HIV antisera • completely / partially / heat[5]-***inactivated*** • phenol- [fiːnoʊl]/ acetone- [æs]/ formalin[6]-***inactivated*** • **killed** whole-cell preparations[7] / bacterial toxins / cholera [kɒːləə] vaccine • heat[5]-/ phenol-***killed*** • complement[8] / heat ***inactivation*** • biologically[9] ***inactive*** • ***inactive*** infection / drug[10] / patient

inaktivierter Impfstoff, Totimpfstoff, -vakzine
Formalin[1] Aktivität, Wirkung[2] Stämme[3] Gelbfieber[4] hitzeinaktiviert[5] formalininaktiviert[6] inaktivierte zelluläre Vakzine[7] Komplementinaktivierung[8] biolog. inaktiv, bioinert[9] unwirksames Medikament[10]

7

toxoid [tɒːksɔɪd]] n term   syn **anatoxin** n, rel **antitoxin**[1] n term → U91-15

toxin of a pathogenic microorganism which has been treated so that it loses its virulence [1] but retains its ability to induce protective immunity

(cyto)toxin[2] [saɪtətɒːksɪn] n term • **toxic**[3] adj • **toxi(co)-** comb

» Td (tetanus toxoid combined with adult-dose diphtheria toxoid) is preferable to tetanus toxoid[4] alone. A tetanus toxoid booster is indicated for any questionable wound [uː]. The 2nd and 3rd doses of toxoid are given at monthly intervals. Diphtheria toxoid[5] is prepared by formaldehyde [fɔːrmældəhaɪd] inactivation of diphtheria toxin[6].

Use diphtheria [ɪə]-tetanus (abbr DTT) **toxoid** • pertussis [ʌ]/ single-antigen / maternal [ɜː] **toxoid** • **toxoid** immunization / vaccine[7] / content / series • **toxoid**-antitoxin mixture (abbr TAM)/ antitoxin floccules • diphtheria[8] / botulism[9] / gangrene / trivalent [aɪ] **antitoxin** • equine[10] [aɪ]/ maternal IgG **antitoxin** • **antitoxin** unit[11] / immunity[12] • **antitoxic** immunity[12]

Toxoid(impfstoff), Anatoxin
Antitoxin[1] Toxin[2] giftig, toxisch[3] Tetanustoxoid[4] Diphtherietoxoid[5] Diphtherietoxin[6] Toxoidimpfstoff[7] Diphtherieantitoxin[8] Botulismusantitoxin[9] Pferdeantitoxin[10] Antitoxineinheit[11] antitoxische Immunität[12]

8

booster [uː] **(vaccination)** n term   syn **booster (re)immunization** n term

administration of a vaccine or toxoid to maintain the immune response at the desired level

» Check the date of the most recent booster shot[1]. Those previously immunized should receive a booster dose[2] of vaccine. Adult-formulation Td boosters are recommended every 10 years thereafter.

Use **booster** injection or shot[3] / toxoid / response[4] /-positive reaction[4] / policy • pertussis vaccine / tetanus toxoid / second[5] **booster** • preexposure[6] / periodic / routine **booster dose** / single[7] / intramuscular **booster dose**

Auffrischung(simpfung)
letzte Auffrischungsimpfung[1] Auffrischungs-, Booster-Dosis[2] Auffrischung(simpfung)[3] Booster-Effekt[4] zweite Auffrischung(simpfung)[5] präexpositionelle Booster-Dosis[6] einmalige Booster-Dosis[7]

9

diphtheria-pertussis-tetanus vaccine n term, abbr **DPT**   syn **triple** [ɪ] n jar

combination vaccine administered to healthy children at 6-8 weeks of age in three doses

» The FDA[1] has licensed [aɪs] use of two DTaP vaccines for use as a 4th and 5th dose in children 12 months to 7 years of age, only after they receive three primary doses of DPT, and if 6 months have elapsed[2] since the third DPT. Fever [iː] occurred [ɜː] within 48 hours of a diphtheria [dɪfθɪərɪə]-pertussis [ʌ]-tetanus vaccine.

Use **DPT** vaccination[3] / immunization[3] / injection / booster[4] • third[5] **DPT**

DPT-Impfstoff/ -Vakzine
U.S. Arznei- u. Lebensmittelbehörde[1] vergangen sind[2] Dreifachschutzimpfung[3] DPT-Auffrischung/ -Boosterung[4] dritte DPT-Teilimpfung[5]

10

seroconversion [sɪəroʊkənvɜːrʒən] n term   rel **serotype**[1], **seroresponse**[2] n term

development of detectable antibodies in the serum [sɪərəm] in response to immunization or infection

seroconvert[3] v term • **serologic(al)**[4] adj • **serology**[5] [sɪrɒːlədʒi] n • **sero-** comb

» The vaccine is very immunogenic as seroconversion occurs in 95% of children after a single dose. Repeat the test to observe [ɜː] for seroconversion or for a rising titer [aɪ]. Two distinct clinical syndromes can be distinguished by the serotype of the infecting strain [eɪ].

Use to show / HIV / asymptomatic **seroconversion** • **seroconversion** reaction / rate / syndrome[6] • **serologic** immunity / immune marker / assay or test[7] / typing[8] / titer • **serologic** evidence[9] / diagnosis[10] / reaction or response[2] / follow-up • **serotype**-specific / III • **sero**logist /logic test[7] /typing /survey [ɜːrveɪ] • **sero**group /positive[11] /negative • **sero**converter /diagnosis[10] /positivity[12] • **sero**immunologic abnormalities /therapy[13]

Serokonversion
Serotyp, Serovar[1] Seroreaktion[2] serokonvertieren[3] serologisch[4] Serologie[5] Serokonversionskrankheit[6] serolog. Untersuchung/ Test[7] serolog. Typisierung[8] serolog. Nachweis[9] Serum-, Serodiagnostik[10] seropositiv[11] Seropositivität[12] Serumtherapie[13]

11

Unit 123 Resuscitation
Related Units: 6 Accidents, 8 First Aid, 7 Consciousness, 44 Respiration, 110 Cardiovascular Signs, 111 Respiratory Symptoms, 125 Critical Care, 136 Blood Transfusion, 134 Perioperative Care, 135 Anesthesiology

lifesaving [laɪfseɪvɪŋ] adj & n
opposite **life-threatening**[1] [laɪf θretᵊnɪŋ] adj
(n) recovering [ʌ] or preserving [ɜː] from loss or danger, e.g. saving the lives of drowning [aʊ] persons
save[2] [seɪv] v • **lifeless**[3] adj • **life-endangering**[1] [ɪndeɪndʒərɪŋ] adj • **life-saver**[4] n
» In tension pneumothorax[5] [n(j)uːmə-], quick removal of air may be life-saving. After emergency [ɜː] lifesaving treatment, such as airway control, has been provided, the emphasis is on providing definitive treatment rapidly for those who are likely to survive [aɪ] as a result. Treat metabolic disorders, drug ingestion [dʒe], or other potentially life-threatening medical conditions first.
Use lifesaving maneuver [uː]/ measures[6] [eʒ]/ therapy or treatment • **lifesaving** care / drug[7] / equipment[8] • **life-threatening** condition / crisis [aɪ]/ (medical) emergency [dʒ] • **life-threatening** event / episode[9] / manifestations • **life-threatening** morbidity / complication / (head) injury[10] • **life-threatening** bleeding [iː]/ blood loss[11] / infection • **life-threatening** sepsis / poisoning [ɔɪ]/ airway obstruction[12] [ʌ] • **life-threatening** asthma [æzmə]/ bronchospasm [k]/ arrhythmia [ɪ]/ cardiac tamponade[13] [eɪ] • **to save** lives / a limb [lɪm]/ vision [ɪʒ]/ a tooth [uː] • limb-saving • life-jeopardizing[1] [dʒepədaɪz-]/ belt[14] / jacket[15] /-support measures[16] • life-sustaining [eɪ] therapy[17]-and-death situation[18]

lebensrettend; Lebensrettung, Rettungsschwimmen
lebensbedrohlich, -gefährdend, -gefährlich[1] retten; (er)sparen, aufbewahren[2] leblos[3] Lebensretter(in), Rettungsschwimmer(in)[4] Spannungs-, Ventilpneumothorax[5] lebensrettende Maßnahmen[6] lebensrettendes Medikament[7] Notfallausrüstung[8] lebensbedrohl. Episode[9] lebensgefährl. Kopfverletzung[10] lebensbedrohlicher Blutverlust[11] lebensbedrohl. Atemwegsobstruktion[12] lebensbedrohl. Herz(beutel)tamponade[13] Rettungsring[14] Schwimmweste[15] lebenserhaltende Maßnahmen[16] lebenserhaltende Therapie[17] lebensbedrohliche/ kritische Situation[18]
1

cardiac arrest or **standstill** n term abbr **CA**
rel **heart block**[1] n term
sudden cessation [ses-] of effective heart action often associated with ventricular fibrillation (abbr VF) and ventricular standstill; CPR may be attempted to avoid sudden cardiac death[2] (abbr SCD)
arrest[3] [ərest] v term • **arrested** adj • pre/ postarrest adj
» Begin CPR for cardiac arrest due to profound [aʊ] hypothermia [ɜː]. Cardiac emergencies commonly present as chest pain, dyspnea [ɪ], respiratory distress, syncope [ɪ], cardiac arrest, or shock. What are the effects of hypothermia and cardiac arrest on outcome of near-drowning [aʊ] accidents?
Use to develop/cause/diagnose/resuscitate from **cardiac arrest** • brief[4] / clinically evident[5] / out-of-hospital[6] **cardiac arrest** • in-hospital / prehospital / impending[7] **cardiac arrest** • primary [aɪ]/ secondary hypovolemic [iː]/ asystolic[8] [eɪsɪs-] **cardiac arrest** • hypothermic / hypoxic / anesthetic(-induced) **cardiac arrest** • **cardiac arrest** survivor [aɪ] • atrial [eɪ]/ bradycardiac / arterial [ɪə]/ **arrest** • sinus [aɪ] (node) or cardiac sinus **arrest** • **to arrest** (a) hemorrhage [-ɪdʒ] or bleeding[9] / the progression of infection • ventricular / atrial / transient[10] **standstill** • second-degree / congenital [dʒe]/ complete[11] / Wenckebach[12] **heart block** • (first-degree) A-V[13] / left bundle [ʌ] branch[14] (abbr LBBB) **block** • sinoatrial[15] [eɪ] (sinoatrial/ ventricular) exit[16] **block** • conduction[17] [ʌ]/ fascicular[18] [sɪ] **block** • **arrested** heartbeat[19] [hɑːrtbiːt]/ respiration / growth / disease • prearrest sign • postarrest assessment

Herz(-Kreislauf)stillstand
Erregungsleitungsstörung[1] akuter Herztod[2] unterbrechen, stillen, hemmen, z. Stillstand bringen[3] kurzer Herzstillstand[4] klin. manifester H.[5] präklin. Herzstillstand[6] drohender H.[7] Asystolie[8] e. Blutung stillen[9] temporärer Herzstillstand[10] totaler Herzblock[11] Wenckebach-Block, AV-Block II. Grades Typ I[12] AV-, atrioventrikulärer Block[13] Linksschenkelblock[14] sinuatrialer/ sinuaurikulärer B., SA-Block[15] Ausgangsblockierung, Exit-Block[16] Leitungsblock[17] Faszikelblock[18] Herzstillstand[19]
2

resuscitate [rɪsʌsɪteɪt] vt   syn **revive** [aɪ] vt, **bring back to life** phr clin
rel **bring (a)round**[1] v phr clin
to help a collapsed, unconscious or apparently [eə] dead person to regain [eɪ] consciousness[2]
» Rapid fluid administration failed to resuscitate the patient. Shouting and gentle [dʒ] shaking are usually enough to revive or awaken [eɪ] victims who have fainted[3] [eɪ] or are just sleeping. The lifeguard[4] succeeded [iː] in reviving the swimmer with oxygen. Perhaps a sniff of smelling salts[5] will bring her around. We were unable to resuscitate the patient.
Use **to resuscitate** victims / from sudden [ʌ] death / severely bleeding patients • **to resuscitate** acutely ill patients / a drowned [aʊ] person[6] • **to resuscitate** promptly / successfully[7] • do not **resuscitate** (abbr DNR) order[8] • **resuscitated** patients

wiederbeleben, reanimieren
jem. wieder zu sich bringen[1] das Bewusstsein wiedererlangen[2] in Ohnmacht fielen, ohnmächtig wurden[3] Rettungsschwimmer(in), Bademeister(in)[4] Riechsalz[5] e. Ertrunkene(n) wiederbeleben[6] erfolgreich wiederbeleben/ reanimieren[7] Anweisung, keine Wiederbelebung durchzuführen, DNR-Order[8]
3

544 CLINICAL TERMS — Resuscitation

resuscitation n
rel **Code Blue**[1] n, **basic life support**[2] n term, abbr **BLS**

reviving a person in cardiac and/or respiratory arrest by sustaining vital functions by means of cardiac massage[3], artificial respiration[4], stabilization of acid-base balance by IV infusion, etc.

resuscitator[5] [ʌ] n term • **resuscitative** adj • **postresuscitation** adj

» The speed with which defibrillation/ cardioversion is carried out is an important element for successful resuscitation. Cardiac arrest patients who survive initial resuscitation attempts[6] always require hospitalization. The patient is in need of immediate resuscitative measures[7].

Use to start/perform/require/attempt **resuscitation** • to achieve[8] [əˈtʃiːv] /withhold[9]/delay [eɪ] **resuscitation** • acute / emergency / cardiopulmonary[10] [uː][ʌ] (abbr CPR) **resuscitation** • closed chest[11] [tʃ]/ mouth-to-mouth[12] / aggressive **resuscitation** • newborn / fluid[13] / electrolyte [-laɪt] **resuscitation** • burn [ɜː]/ cerebral or brain **resuscitation** • need for **resuscitation** • **resuscitation** team / room[14] / protocol / efforts[6] / skills • **resuscitative** efforts[6] / attempts[6] / phase [feɪz]/ procedure [siː] • **resuscitative** maneuver [uː]/ technique [tekˈniːk]/ devices[15] [aɪs]/ equipment[15] • mechanical [kæ]/ heart-lung[16] **resuscitator** • **resuscitator** bag[17] / mask • advanced[18] (abbr ALS) **life support** • **Code** Red[19] / Pink[20] / White[21] • no **code** or **DNR**[22]

> Note: In English terminology the expression **reanimation** is practically never used in connection with CPR.

cardiac massage [məsɑːʒ] n term
rel **precordial thump**[1] [θʌmp] n term

manual rhythmic [ɪ] compression of the heart applied through the chest wall to maintain the circulation

massage[2] [məsɑːʒ] v • **massaging** n → U142-15

» If heart beat and carotid pulse cannot be detected, closed chest cardiac massage is initiated [ɪʃ] as soon as artificial [ɪʃ] ventilation[3] is started. If respiratory arrest precipitating [sɪ] cardiac arrest is suspected, a second precordial thump is delivered after the airway is cleared[4].

Use to perform **cardiac massage** • internal or open[5] / direct[5] / closed-chest[6] **cardiac massage** • carotid (sinus)[7] **massage** • precordial blow[1] [oʊ] • chest[1] **thump**

respiratory arrest n clin
syn **apnea** n term,
rel **respiratory failure**[1] n clin

cessation[2] of breathing due to airway obstruction, decreased respiratory drive, or respiratory muscle weakness (primary) or as a result of ventricular fibrillation, asystole [ɪ], or cardiac arrest (secondary)

apneic[3] [æpˈniːɪk] adj term • **fail**[4] v clin • **failing** [feɪlɪŋ] adj • **failed** adj

» Respiratory failure or apnea may require mechanical ventilation. Symptoms [ɪ] and signs of anaphylactic reactions include difficulty breathing[5], coughing, nausea[6] [ɔː], vomiting, bronchospasm, respiratory arrest, shock, and loss of consciousness. Complete respiratory arrest may develop acutely in a conscious victim secondary to' FB obstruction[8] [ʌ].

Use to produce/suffer[9] [ʌ] a **respiratory arrest** • impending[10] / central / complete **respiratory arrest** • abrupt [ʌ] or sudden[11] / acute / fatal [eɪ] **respiratory arrest** • **respiratory arrest** victim • inspiratory[12] / cardiorespiratory[13] / (total/ cerebral) circulatory[14] [ɜː] **arrest** • hypothermic / developmental / (un)witnessed **arrest** • **respiratory** distress[15] • to cause/develop/induce/experience **apnea** • acute / central / obstructive / impending[10] / episodes of[16] **apnea** • postoperative / posttussive [ʌ]/ sleep[17] / infantile **apnea** • **apnea** monitor / test(ing)[18] • **apneic** spells or episodes[16] / patient / victim / infant[19] • to diagnose/lead to/precipitate[20]/prevent/ correct **respiratory failure** • acute / chronic / early / adult / frank[21] **respiratory failure** • posttraumatic / hypoxemic / postoperative **respiratory failure** • (acute) pulmonary / ventilatory / multiple organ[22] **failure** • **respiratory** depression[23] / insufficiency[1] • collapse • **respiratory** acidosis / support[24] • **failed** intubation / operation

---

Reanimation, Wiederbelebung
Herzalarm[1] lebensrettende Sofortmaßnahmen, primäre Reanimationsmaßnahmen, Basismaßnahmen z. CPR, Ersthilfereanimation[2] Herzmassage[3] künstl. Beatmung[4] Beatmungsgerät; Reanimator[5] Reanimationsversuche[6] Reanimationsmaßnahmen[7] erfolgreich wiederbeleben[8] keine Reanimation durchführen[9] kardiopulmonale R., CPR[10] Herzdruckmassage[11] Mund-zu-Mund-Beatmung[12] Volumenersatz[13] Schockraum[14] Reanimationsgeräte, -ausrüstung[15] Herz-Lungen-Maschine[16] Atembeutel[17] erweiterte Reanimationsmaßnahmen, ALS[18] Feueralarm[19] Kindesentführung[20] Bombendrohung[21] keine Wiederbelebung, DNR-Order[22]

Herzmassage
präkordialer Faustschlag[1] massieren[2] künstl. Beatmung[3] nach Freimachen d. Atemwege[4] offene Herzmassage[5] externe Herzmassage, Herzdruckmassage[6] Karotissinusdruckmassage[7]

Atemstillstand, Apnoe
respirator. Insuffizienz[1] Stillstand[2] apnoisch[3] versagen, ausfallen, fehlschlagen, scheitern[4] erschwerte Atmung, Atembeschwerden[5] Übelkeit[6] infolge von[7] Fremdkörperobstruktion[8] e. Atemstillstand haben[9] drohender Atemstillstand[10] plötzlicher A.[11] Murphy-Zeichen, druckschmerzbedingtes Sistieren d. Atmung b. tiefer Inspiration[12] Herz- u. Atemstillstand[13] Kreislaufstillstand[14] Atemnot[15] Apnoephasen, -anfälle[16] Schlafapnoe[17] Apnoetest[18] apnoisches Kind[19] respirator. Insuffizienz auslösen[20] manifeste respirator. Insuffizienz[21] multiples Organversagen[22] Atemdepression[23] Atemhilfe[24]

Resuscitation

CLINICAL TERMS 545

asphyxiation n term   syn **suffocation** [ʌ] n,
  sim **choking**¹ [tʃoʊk-] n clin → U44-8

impaired [eɚ] or absent gas exchange associated with hypercapnia² and hypoxia or anoxia
asphyxia³ [əsfɪksɪə] n term • **asphyxiate**⁴ v • **asphyxiant**⁵ n •
suffocative adj clin

» The asphyxia associated with drowning is usually due to aspiration of fluid. Large amounts of blood in the airways can cause the patient to suffocate. The patient awakens [eɪ] with a sense of suffocation. Respiratory depression may be due to tumor, hemorrhage, strangulation, asphyxiation, near-drowning, or aspiration.

Use to suffer from⁶/die from/prevent **asphyxiation** • partial [ʃ]/ death by or from⁷ **asphyxiation** • acute / life-threatening [e]/ fatal / traumatic **asphyxia** • birth or intrapartum⁸ / nocturnal [ɜː]/ blue⁹ / perinatal⁸ [eɪ] **asphyxia** • **asphyxia** livida⁹ / pallida¹⁰ / neonatorum⁸ • chemical [ke-] **asphyxiant** • death due to⁷ / feeling of¹¹ / impending / accidental **suffocation** • food / nocturnal / obstructive [ʌ] **choking** • **choking** victim¹² / sensation¹¹ [eɪʃ]/ distress¹³

hypoxia [haɪpɒːksɪə] n term
  rel **hypoxemia**¹ [iː], **anoxia**² n term

decreased levels of oxygen in inspired gases, arterial blood, or tissue
hypoxic³ adj term • **hypoxemic**⁴ [haɪpɒːksiːmɪk] adj • **anoxic** [ænɒːksɪk] adj

» Acidosis accompanying hypoxia may indicate either inadequate ventilation or inadequate perfusion [juːʒ]. Inhaled [eɪ] nitric [aɪ] oxide⁵ is a selective pulmonary vasodilator capable of reversing [ɜː] hypoxic pulmonary vasoconstriction [veɪzoʊ-].

Use acute / chronic / arterial / anemic⁶ [iː]/ circulatory⁷ **hypoxia** • ischemic⁸ [kiː] local(ized) / intracellular / histotoxic⁹ **hypoxia** • tissue¹⁰ / cerebral / respiratory¹¹ **hypoxia** • alveolar [ɪə]/ myocardial [maɪə-] **hypoxia** • intrauterine / environmental¹² / mild **hypoxia** • marked¹³ / severe **hypoxia** • prolonged / intermittent / increasing or worsening [ɜː] **hypoxia** • **hypoxia**-ischemia / and hypercarbia / and hypercapnia • **hypoxic** episode or spell¹⁴ / tissue [ʃ‖s]/ (brain) damage • **hypoxic** cardiac arrest / cor pulmonale /-ischemic coma • arterial / venous [iː]/ chronic / nocturnal **hypoxemia** • progressive / exercise-induced¹⁵ **hypoxemia** • **hypoxemic** COPD¹⁶/ infant • cerebral / tissue **anoxia** • **anoxic** injury¹⁷ / encephalopathy / insult

mouth-to-mouth breathing [iː] or **ventilation** or **resuscitation** n clin
  sim **artificial** [ɪʃ] **ventilation**¹ n term → U125-10f

respiratory support by manual means in persons unable to sustain [eɪ] spontaneous [eɪ] respiration²
ventilate³ [ventɪleɪt] v term • **underventilated** adj • **ventilator**⁴ n

» If ventilation cannot be achieved by mask- or mouth-to-mouth breathing and if endotracheal intubation cannot be performed, emergency cricothyrotomy is indicated. Attempt to ventilate the victim after each series of steps. Auscultate [ɒː] the chest for breath [e] sounds⁵, and verify adequacy of ventilation. Before an attempt to administer artificial ventilation, airway patency⁶ [eɪ] must be tested and any obstruction [ʌ] removed.

Use to apply [aɪ] /administer/institute **mouth-to-mouth breathing** • rescue⁷ [reskjuː]/ mouth-to-nose⁸ **breathing** • continuous positive airway pressure⁹ (abbr CPAP)/ intermittent positive pressure¹⁰ (abbr IPP) **breathing** • to deliver¹¹/depress/compromise/support/maintain **ventilation** • assisted¹² / mechanical¹³ / (inability to sustain) spontaneous **ventilation** • bag-and-mask¹⁴ / endotracheal **ventilation** • positive-pressure / assist-control (mode)¹² **ventilation** • synchronized [ɪ] intermittent mandatory¹⁵ (abbr SIMV)/ high-frequency jet¹⁶ [dʒ] **ventilation** • **ventilation**-perfusion (abbr V/Q) ratio¹⁷ [reɪ]- • **mouth-to-mouth** seal [iː] • **artificial** respiration¹ / airway / life support¹⁸ / lung¹⁹ • to put sb. on a²⁰/wean [iː] from the²¹/take off the²² **ventilator**

Erstickung(szustand)
Ersticken, Würgen¹ Hyperkapnie² Asphyxie³ ersticken⁴ Asphyxie hervorrufendes Mittel⁵ an Erstickungsanfällen leiden⁶ Tod durch Ersticken, Erstickungstod⁷ Neugeborenenasphyxie⁸ blaue Asphyxie⁹ weiße Asphyxie¹⁰ Erstickungsgefühl¹¹ Erstickungsopfer¹² Erstickungsanfall¹³

7

Hypoxie, Sauerstoffmangel
Hypoxämie¹ Anoxie² hypoxisch³ hypoxämisch⁴ Stickstoffmonoxid, Stickoxid⁵ anämische Hypoxie⁶ kreislaufbedingte H.⁷ ischämische Hypoxie⁸ gewebeschädigende H.⁹ Gewebehypoxie¹⁰ ventilator./ respirator. Hypoxie¹¹ hypoxische H.¹² beträchtl./ deutliche Hypoxie¹³ hypoxische(r) Phase/ Anfall¹⁴ belastungsinduzierte Hypoxämie¹⁵ COLD/ chron. obstruktive Lungenerkrankung mit Hypoxämie¹⁶ anoxische Schädigung¹⁷

8

Mund-zu-Mund Beatmung, Atemspende
künstl. Beatmung¹ Spontanatmung² belüften, ventilieren; beatmen³ Respirator, Beatmungsgerät⁴ Atemgeräusche⁵ Freiheit/ Offensein d. Atemwege⁶ Atemspende⁷ Mund-zu-Nase-Beatmung⁸ CPAP-Atmung⁹ intermittierende Überdruckbeatmung¹⁰ beatmen¹¹ druckunterstützte Beatmung¹² maschinelle Beatmung¹³ Masken-B.¹⁴ synchronisierte intermittierende maschinelle B.¹⁵ Hochfrequenzbeatmung¹⁶ Ventilations-Perfusions-Verhältnis¹⁷ Organersatztherapie¹⁸ Eiserne Lunge, Tankrespirator¹⁹ jem. künstl. beatmen²⁰ v. Respirator entwöhnen²¹ die künstl. Beatmung absetzen²²

9

Resuscitation

endotracheal [eɪk] (*abbr* **ET**) **intubation** *n term*
　　　　　　　　　　rel **artificial airway**[1] *n term*
passage of a tube through the nose or mouth into the trachea to maintain the airway[2] (e.g. in emergencies or during anesthesia, prevent aspiration, and/or facilitate [sɪ] assisted ventilation
in/ extubate[3] [-t(j)uːbeɪt] *v term* • **intubator**[4] *n* • **intubated** *adj* • **extubation** *n*

» The patient is promptly intubated, CPR is continued, and an attempt is made to control hypoxemia and acidosis. The first priority of management should be to provide an airway and restore circulation. An artificial airway may be lifesaving for patients who fail to respond to oxygen supplements [ʌ]. This may suffice [səfaɪs] until a definitive airway can be established. The patient developed a croupy [uː] cough[5] that led to life-threatening airway obstruction.

Use to perform/undergo/attempt **endotracheal intubation** • to require or necessitate[6]/support with **endotracheal intubation** • **endotracheal tube**[7] • oral or orotracheal[8] / nasal or nasotracheal[9] **intubation** • tracheobronchial[10] / nasogastric[11] / duodenal **intubation** • unrecognized esophageal[12] [dʒiː]/ emergency / early / prompt **intubation** • prophylactic / digital[13] / blind[14] **intubation** • rapid-sequence[15] [iː]/ difficult **intubation** • prolonged[16] / retrograde[17] **intubation** • to tolerate / early / accidental **extubation** • **extubation** failure • to establish or provide[18]/ensure [ɪnʃʊɚ] or maintain[2] **an adequate airway** • to open or clear[18] /control/ protect/secure[2] [sɪkjʊɚ] **the airway** • surgical[19] [ɜː]/ oropharyngeal / nasal or nasopharyngeal[20] [ɪ] **airway** • esophageal obturator[21] (*abbr* EOA)/ esophageal gastric tube[22] (*abbr* EGTA) **airway** • pharyngotracheal lumen[7] [uː]/ patent[23] [eɪ] **airway** • protective **airway** reflexes[24] [iː] • **airway** reflexes[25] / patency / management or control[26] • **airway** care / protection / narrowing / collapse • **airway** plugging[27] [ʌ]/ obstruction[28] / resistance[29]

endotracheale Intubation
Tubus[1] d. Atemwege freihalten[2] extubieren, d. Tubus entfernen[3] Intubator[4] kruppartiger Husten[5] e. endotracheale Intubation erforderlich machen[6] Endotrachealtubus[7] orotracheale Intubation[8] nasotracheale/ nasale I.[9] endobronchiale I.[10] Legen e. Magensonde[11] unbemerkte ösophageale Intubation[12] I. unter Tastkontrolle[13] blinde Intubation[14] Blitzeinleitung, Crush-Intubation[15] prolongierte I.[16] retrograde endotracheale I.[17] d. Atemwege freimachen[18] Tracheostoma[19] Nasopharyngealtubus[20] Obturator-T.[21] Kombitubus[22] freie Atemwege[23] Atemschutzreflexe[24] Atemreflexe[25] Freihalten d. Atemwege[26] Atemwegsverlegung[27] Atemwegsobstruktion[28] Atemwegswiderstand, Resistance[29]

10

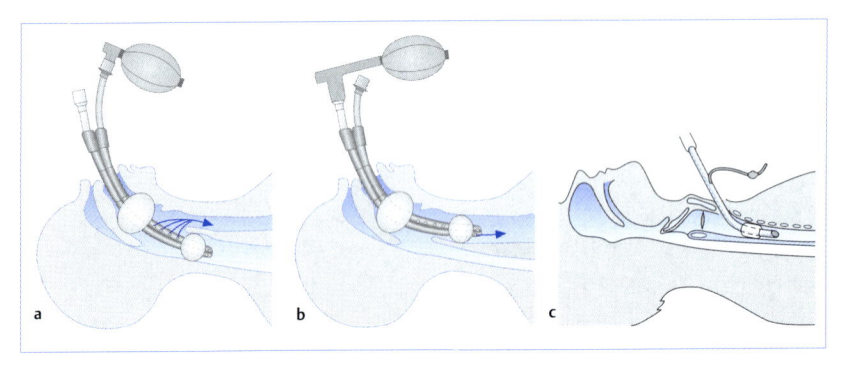

(a) Blind intubation using an esophageal gastric tube airway (EGTA): the cuffs are inflated to prevent air from getting into the stomach in case of esophageal placement; ventilation of the lung is achieved via the proximal tube
(b) EGTA: tracheal placement; the lung is ventilated via the distal tube
(c) Cricothyroidotomy: the airway has been inserted into the trachea via the incision in the cricothyroid membrane which is located between the cricoid and thyroid cartilages

tracheotomy [treɪkɪɒːtəmi] *n term*　*sim* **cricothyr(oid)otomy**[1] [kraɪkoʊθaɪr-] *n*
　　　　　　　　　　　　　　　　　　　rel **thoracotomy**[2] [θɔːrəkɒːtəmi] *n term*
incision [sɪʒ] into the trachea [treɪkɪə∥espBE trɑkiːə] below the larynx [lærɪŋks] to gain access [æksɛs] to the airway obstructed by an FB[3], tumor, etc.
tracheostomy[4] *n term* • **tracheotome**[5] *n* • **transtracheal** [eɪ] *adj*

» If equipment is not at hand for emergency tracheotomy or cricothyrotomy, the Heimlich maneuver [uː] can be attempted for relieving foreign body airway obstruction. Tracheostomy has become an elective operating room procedure.

Use to require/necessitate/perform **tracheotomy** • urgent[6] [ɜː]/ immediate / emergency[6] / bedside[7] **tracheotomy** • adult / pediatric / permanent / distal / high[8] **tracheotomy** • **tracheotomy** procedure / set • percutaneous [eɪ] dilational[9] [eɪʃ]/ chronic **tracheostomy** • **tracheostomy** tract[4] / collar [ɒː] / tube[10] / cuff[11] [ʌ] • **tracheostomy** insertion [ɜː]/ care[12] / suction [sʌkʃən]

Tracheotomie, Luftröhrenschnitt
Krikothyreotomie, Koniotomie[1] Thorakotomie, Brustkorberöffnung[2] Fremdkörper[3] Tracheostoma[4] Tracheotom[5] Nottracheotomie[6] Tracheotomie am Krankenbett[7] Tracheotomia superior, obere Tracheotomie[8] perkutane Tracheostoma-Anlage[9] Tracheakanüle[10] aufblasbare Manschette d. Tracheakanüle[11] Tracheostomapflege[12]

11

defibrillation [dɪfɪ‖aɪ-] *n term*   *sim* **cardioversion**[1] *n term*,
   rel **electroshock**[2] *n term*

emergency procedure to arrest atrial or ventricular fibrillation [ɪ‖aɪ] and restore the normal cardiac rhythm [rɪðᵊm] by delivering an electric shock to the precordium through the chest wall
defibrillator[3] *n term* • **defibrillate**[4] *v* • **cardiovert**[5] *v* • **countershock**[6] [aʊ] *n*

» The sooner defibrillation is performed, the higher the survival [aɪ] rate. Automatic defibrillators can recognize ventricular fibrillation and deliver a countershock. If cardioversion is not successful the usual measures [eʒ] for advanced life support must be initiated. Can these drugs prevent reversion [ɜː] to AF[7] after cardioversion?

Use to perform **defibrillation** • manual / chest thump[8] [ʌ]/ electrical[9] / automatic **defibrillation** • in-the-field[10] / failed / repeat **defibrillation** • **defibrillation** equipment / machine / paddles[11] • attempt • to undergo/use/require/respond to/profit from/avoid **cardioversion** • electrical / (synchronized) direct-current[12] [ɜː] (*abbr* DC) **cardioversion** • chemical / implanted[13] **cardioversion** • synchronized [ɪ] **electroshock** • **electroshock** therapy • electrical / DC[14] / low energy / synchronized **countershock** • cardiac / manual / (semi)automated [ɒː] monitor[15]-**defibrillator** • automatic internal / automatic internal cardioverter-[16] (*abbr* AICD) **defibrillator** • implantable cardioverter[17]- (*abbr* ICD) **defibrillator** • **defibrillator** paddles[11] / device[3] [dɪvaɪs]

cardiac pacing [kɑːrdɪæk peɪsɪŋ] *n term*
   rel **ventricular pacing**[1] *n term*

maintenance [eɪ] of a normal sinus [aɪ] rhythm by means of artificial electrical stimulation
pacemaker *or* **pacer**[2] [peɪsɚ] *n* • **pace**[3] *n & v*

» Transcutaneous [eɪ] cardiac pacing is a safe, noninvasive [eɪ] method of temporarily treating bradyarrhythmias [ɪ] and asystole [eɪsɪstəli]. Does your pacing device include backup defibrillation capabilities[4] [eɪ]? The patient can be gradually weaned[5] [iː] from pacer therapy[6] by a decrease in the pacing rate[7].

Use to induce/undergo **cardiac pacing** • external / transcutaneous[8] / transthoracic[8] [æs] **cardiac pacing** • emergency / temporary / permanent [ɜː] **cardiac pacing** • **cardiac pacing** threshold[9] • dual-chamber[10] [d(j)uːəl tʃeɪmbɚ]/ electrical[11] / (rapid) atrial [eɪ] **pacing** • ventricular-inhibited[12] / AV sequential [sɪkwenʃᵊl] **pacing** • endocardial / epicardial / prophylactic **pacing** • overdrive / antitachycardia **pacing** • **pacing** catheter / therapy[6] / device[2] / lead[13] [iː] • **pacing** wire [waɪɚ]/ impulses / intervals / rate • ventricular-inhibited[14] **pacer** • (external/ internal) cardiac / ventricular / programmable *or* demand[15] **pacemaker** • ventricular demand[16] / dual-chamber[17] **pacemaker** • sinus [aɪ] node / fixed-rate[18] **pacemaker** • rate-adaptive *or* rate-responsive[19] / escape[20] **pacemaker** • (temporary) transvenous [iː]/ transcutaneous [eɪ] **pacemaker** • antitachycardia / permanent **pacemaker** • **pacemaker** code[21] / activity / rhythm • **pacemaker** sensing[22] / implantation / failure [eɪ]/ syndrome[23] [ɪ]

Defibrillation

Kardioversion[1] Elektroschock[2] Defibrillator[3] defibrillieren[4] kardiovertieren[5] Defibrillation[6] Vorhofflimmern[7] Defibrillation durch präkordialen Faustschlag[8] elektr. Defibrillation[9] präklinische Defibrillation, D. am Unfallsort[10] Defibrillatorpaddel, -elektroden[11] Gleichstrom-Kardioversion[12] Kardioversion mittels implantiertem Defibrillator[13] Gleichstromimpulse[14] Defibrillator mit Monitoreinheit[15] ICD-Schrittmacher[16] implantierbarer Kardioverter-Defibrillator[17]

12

Schrittmachertherapie

Ventrikel-, Kammerstimulation[1] (Herz)schrittmacher[2] Schritt, Tempo; m. Schrittmacher stimulieren[3] m. automat. internem Defibrillator[4] entwöhnt[5] Schrittmachertherapie[6] Impulsrate[7] externe Stimulation d. Herzens[8] Reizschwelle[9] Zweikammerstimulation[10] Elektrostimulation[11] QRS-inhibierte Stimulation[12] Schrittmacherelektrode[13] Schrittmacher im VVI-Modus[14] Demand-, Bedarfs-, programmierbarer Schrittmacher[15] kammergesteuerter Schrittmacher[16] Zweikammerschrittmacher[17] Festfrequenzschrittmacher[18] frequenzadaptierter/ Rate-response-S.[19] Ersatzschrittmacher[20] Schrittmachercode[21] Reizschwellenbestimmung[22] Schrittmachersyndrom[23]

13

Unit 124 Medical & Surgical Emergencies

Related Units: 6 Accidents, 8 First Aid, 123 Resuscitation, 125 Critical Care,
7 States of Consciousness, 135 Anesthesiology, 110 Cardiovascular Symptoms,
111 Respiratory Symptoms, 136 Blood Transfusion

medical emergency [ɜː] *n term*   *rel* **clinical crisis**[1] [aɪ],
catastrophe[2] [kətæstrəfi] *n term*

sudden life-threatening [e] situation or acute deterioration[3] [ɪɚ] of a patient's condition
critical [krɪtɪkᵊl] *adj* • **catastrophic** *adj* • **crises** [kraɪsiːz] *n pl* → U6-20

» Acute bacterial meningitis [dʒaɪ] is a life-threatening medical emergency. Torsion [ʃ] of the spermatic cord[4] is a surgical emergency. Retinal detachment[5] [ætʃ] is a true emergency, for permanent [ɜː] loss of central vision [ɪʒ] will occur if the macula is threatened. The acute adrenal [iː] crisis is usually precipitated by acute stress, e.g. trauma [ɔː] or surgery. His symptoms are typical of paralytic [ɪ] ileus, perhaps suggestive of an abdominal catastrophe.

Use grave[6] [eɪ]/ surgical [ɜː]/ acute abdominal / airway[7] / aspiration **emergency** • metabolic / oncologic / obstetric[8] **emergencies** • heat / eye / dental / natural hazard [æ] **emergencies** • **emergency** management or treatment[9] / consultation / medicine[10] • **emergency** surgery or operation[11] / amputation / bronchoscopy[12] [ɒː] • acute / immediate [iː] **clinical crisis** • **clinical crisis** protocol / management[13] • to precipitate [sɪ] /cause/develop/provoke **a crisis** • to experience/cope with[14]/anticipate **a crisis** • medical / metabolic[15] / gastric[16] / thyrotoxic[17] [aɪ] **crisis** • cholinergic [ɜː] or myasthenic[18]/ sickle cell / aplastic[19] **crisis** • akinetic[20] / emotional / life / identity **crisis** • **crisis** situation / event / intervention[21] (center) / hotline • neurologic / obstetric / vascular[22] / (intra)abdominal / GI **catastrophe** • **catastrophic** illness / complication[23] / (clinical) event • **catastrophic** bleeding [iː]/ attack / seizure [siːʒɚ]

major risk factor *n clin* → U134-5

rel **peril**[1], **jeopardy**[2] [dʒepɚdi], **hazard**[2] [hæzɚd] *n*

key feature [iː] responsible for increasing the danger of or susceptibility[3] [ʌs] to unhealthful effects
high-risk[4] *adj* • **at risk**[5] *phr* • **hazardous**[6] *adj* → U8-4 • **jeopardize**[7] *v* → U134-5

» Heavy [e] cigarette smoking is a major [eɪdʒ] risk factor for ischemic [kiː] heart disease. High BP is a risk factor for stroke[8] and renal failure. If the limb [lɪm] is not in jeopardy, a more conservative [ɜː] approach [-oʊtʃ] may be taken. These children are at high risk of abrupt [ʌ] airway obstruction [ʌ]. The chief hazard of a faint[9] [eɪ] in most elderly persons is not the underlying disease but fracture or other trauma due to the fall.

Use systemic / environmental[10] / genetic / surgical **risk factors** • preoperative / cardiovascular / coronary **risk factors** • perinatal [eɪ]/ relevant / multiple **risk factors** • known[11] / independent / extra **risk factors** • **risk factor** profile / analysis • to be[12] **at risk** • infant[13] / families / groups **at risk** • **at risk** patient / pregnancy[14] • cancer[15] / stroke / transfusion / anesthetic[16] **risk** • occupational[17] [eɪʃ]/ mortality **risk** • good-/ better-/ low-/ average-**risk patient** • cumulative [juː]/ overall[18] / potential **risk** • long-term / lifelong / attributable[19] **risk** • empiric(al)/ theoretical / substantial[20] / relative **risk** • **risk** management /-benefit ratio[21] [eɪ]/ assessment[22] / behavior • **risk of** infection / exposure[23] / developing cancer[15] • **risk of** recurrence[24] [ɜː]/ complications / death • **high-risk** dog bite • **hazardous** materials[25] (*abbr* hazmat)/ chemicals or substances[25] [ʌ] • **hazardous** wastes[26] [eɪ]/ situations / drugs / exposure • to be/place sth.[7] **in peril** • fetal[27] / myocardial **jeopardy** • **to jeopardize** health / healing [iː]/ circulation • **to jeopardize** one's safety / the lives of others[28]

---

mediz./ internist. Notfall

akute medizinische/ klinische Krise[1] akuter lebensbedrohl. Zustand[2] Verschlechterung[3] Samenstrang-, Hodentorsion[4] Netzhautablösung, Ablatio retinae[5] ernster Notfall[6] Patient(in) mit akuten Atemproblemen[7] geburtshilfl. Notfälle[8] Not(fall)behandlung[9] Notfallmedizin[10] Not(fall)operation[11] Notfallbronchoskopie[12] Akutbehandlung[13] eine Krise überstehen[14] Stoffwechselkrise, metabolische K.[15] gastrische Krise[16] thyreotoxische Krise[17] cholinergische/ myasthenische K.[18] aplastische Krise[19] akinet. Krise[20] Krisenintervention[21] (kardio)vaskuläre Katastrophe[22] lebensbedrohliche Komplikation[23]

1

Hauptrisikofaktor

Gefahr[1] Gefahr, Risiko[2] Anfälligkeit, Empfänglichkeit[3] m. erhöhtem Risiko, (Hoch)risiko-[4] Risiko-[5] riskant[6] gefährden, in Gefahr bringen[7] Schlaganfall, Gehirnschlag, apoplekt. Insult[8] Ohnmachtsanfall, Synkope[9] umweltbedingte Risikofaktoren[10] bekannte Risikofaktoren[11] gefährdet sein, ein erhöhtes Risiko haben[12] Risikokind[13] Risikoschwangerschaft[14] Krebsrisiko[15] Narkoserisiko[16] Berufsrisiko[17] Gesamtrisiko[18] zuschreibbares/ attributables Risiko[19] beträchtl. Risiko[20] Risiko-Nutzen-Verhältnis[21] Risikoeinschätzung[22] Expositionsrisiko[23] Rezidivrisiko[24] gefährliche Stoffe, Gefahrenstoffe[25] Giftmüll, Problemstoffe[26] fetale Gefährdung[27] d. Leben anderer gefährden[28]

2

Medical & Surgical Emergencies

CLINICAL TERMS 549

anaphylactic reaction n term

syn **anaphylaxis** [ænəfilæksɪs] n term

transient allergic reaction occurring within minutes after administration of drugs or nonhuman proteins (esp. foods, sera, or venoms[1]) marked by smooth [uː] muscle [s] contraction[2] and dilation of capillaries

anaphylactoid[3] adj term • **nonanaphylactic** adj • **anaphylatoxin**[4] n

» A history of allergic [ɜː] reaction to radiographic contrast agents may range from urticaria [ɜː] to frank anaphylactic reaction[5]. Topical bovine thrombin can cause allergic or anaphylactic reactions, intravascular coagulation[6], or death. If the cyst [sɪst] ruptures, she may go into anaphylactic shock. Patients with mild manifestations of anaphylaxis (e.g. urticaria[7]) that have resolved[8] with treatment may be discharged[9] from the emergency department. Does the history suggest anaphylactic shock?

Use frank[5] / life-threatening / fatal / systemic[10] **anaphylactic reaction** • **anaphylactic** response / shock[11] / syndrome [i] • **anaphylactic** crisis / allergy / (drug) reaction[12] • **anaphylactic** complication / manifestations / intoxication • to treat/cause/develop/experience **anaphylaxis** • mild / severe / mild / life-threatening **anaphylaxis** • food / penicillin / antiserum / reversed or inverse[13] [ɜː] **anaphylaxis** • venom-induced / exercise-related[14] **anaphylaxis** • active / passive cutaneous[15] [eɪ]/ systemic or generalized[10] / local / chronic **anaphylaxis** • **anaphylactoid** reaction / purpura[16] [ɜː]/ egg allergy [-dʒi]

Anaphylaxie, anaphylakt. Reaktion, Überempfindlichkeitsreaktion v. Soforttyp

(tierische) Gifte[1] Kontraktion d. glatten Muskulatur[2] anaphylaktoid[3] Anaphylatoxin[4] klin. manifeste Anaphylaxie[5] intravasale Gerinnung[6] Nesselsucht, Urtikaria[7] abgeklungen[8] entlassen[9] generalisierte anaphylakt. Reaktion[10] anaphylakt. Schock[11] Arzneimittelallergie[12] inverse Anaphylaxie[13] Anaphylaxie durch starke körperliche Belastung[14] passive kutane A.[15] Purpura Schoenlein-Henoch[16]

3

---

shock [ʃɒːk] n term & clin

(i) state of inadequate peripheral perfusion due to severe injury, dehydration [aɪ], emotional upset, etc.
(ii) broad term for a sudden physical [ɪ] or mental disturbance [ɜː]

shock[1] v inf • **shocking** n & adj • **shocked**[2] adj • **shocky**[2] adj jar • **post/ antishock** adj term → U8-13

» If shock is profound [aʊ] smaller feeding tubes[3] should be used. The causes of distributive shock[4] are diverse and include septic shock, anaphylactic shock, and neurogenic shock[5].

Use to prevent/produce/develop/treat **shock** • to be or present[6]/remain **in shock** • sudden / mild[7] / moderate / severe / refractory[8] **shock** • impending[9] / initial [ɪʃ]/ delayed [eɪ] **shock** • cardiogenic [dʒe]/ burn[10] [ɜː]/ hemorrhagic [ædʒ]/ electric[11] **shock** • spinal [aɪ]/ traumatic / surgical **shock** • birth / hypovolemic [iː]/ hypoglycemic[12] [aɪs] **shock** • to contribute / due or secondary[13] / response **to shock** • degree / signs / onset[14] / treatment[15] / cause **of shock** • **shock** lung[16] / phase [feɪz]/ state[17] / therapy[15] • (to be) badly[18] **shocked** • **shocky** patient • pallid and[19] **shocky** • **shocking** experience[20] • **antishock** garment[21]

(i, ii) Schock(zustand)

schockieren, schrecken, e. Schock versetzen[1] schockiert, unter Schock stehend[2] Ernährungssonden[3] distributiver Schock[4] neurogener S.[5] unter Schock stehen, in e. Schockzustand sein[6] leichter Schock[7] therapieresistenter S.[8] drohender S.[9] Verbrennungsschock[10] elektr. Schlag, Elektroschock[11] hypoglykämischer S.[12] infolge e. Schocks[13] Einsetzen d. Schocks[14] Schockbehandlung[15] Schocklunge[16] Schockzustand[17] e. schweren Schock haben[18] blass u. unter Schock stehend[19] schreckliches Erlebnis[20] Antischockanzug[21]

4

---

septic shock n term   syn **endotoxin** or **bacteremic** [iː] **shock** n term

rel **septicemia**[1] [septəsiːmɪə], **bacteremia**[2] n term

shock associated [oʊʃ] with sepsis or septicemia caused by Gram-negative bacteria [ɪə]

sepsis[1] n term • **sepsis-related** adj • **(non-)septicemic** [siː] adj

» Hypotension can occur [ɜː] without septic shock or as part of a full-blown shock state. Sepsis denotes significant infection in which bacteria, bacterial toxins, or inflammatory [æ] mediators [iː] escape the control of the immune system, enter the bloodstream, and incite[3] [saɪ] a systemic response. Septicemia usually means bacteremia plus leukocytosis [luːkə-].

Use meningococcal / high-output[4] / low-output **septic shock** • Gram-negative / fulminant [u] **septic shock** • to develop/cause/combat[5]/treat **sepsis** • (intra-)abdominal / bacterial / viral [aɪ]/ fungal [ʌ] Candida[6] **sepsis** • IV catheter or catheter-related or catheter-acquired[7] [aɪ] **sepsis** • neonatal / postoperative / puerperal[8] [ɜː] **sepsis** • early / deep / systemic or generalized **sepsis** • overwhelming[9] / fatal [eɪ] **sepsis** • **septic** complications / foci[10] [foʊsaɪ]/ arthritis [aɪ]/ embolism[11] • **septic** thrombophlebitis / abortion[12] / death • acute / transfusion-related / early-onset / advanced **septicemia** • systemic / sustained[13] [eɪ]/ anaerobic **bacteremia** • gram-positive / persistent[13] **bacteremia** • Salmonella / catheter-related / transient[14] / occult [ʌ] **bacteremia** • **septicemic** form / infection / plague[15] [pleɪg]

Endotoxinschock, septischer/ bakterieller Schock

Blutvergiftung, Septikämie, Sepsis[1] Bakteriämie[2] auslösen, in Gang setzen[3] hyperdynamer Schock[4] Sepsis bekämpfen[5] Candida-Sepsis[6] Kathetersepsis[7] Puerperalfieber, -sepsis, Wochenbett-, Kindbettfieber[8] fulminante Sepsis[9] Sepsisherde[10] septischer Embolus[11] septischer Abort[12] persistierende Bakteriämie[13] transitorische Bakteriämie[14] Pestsepsis, -septikämie[15]

5

hypertensive crisis [haɪpətensɪv kraɪsɪs] n term

most severe category of hypertension in emergency care with the BP rising above 220/150 mm Hg

hypertensive[1] n term • hypertension[2] n • hypotension[3] [-tenʃᵊn] n

» In acute hypertensive crisis the BP is frequently greater than 220/150 mm Hg, with severe manifestations of headache, visual disturbances, papilledema [iː], retinal hemorrhages, encephalopathy, pulmonary edema, aortic dissection[4], or hemorrhagic stroke[5].

Use acute / renal[6] [iː] **hypertensive crisis** • hemolytic[7] [ɪ]/ hypoplastic / blast[8] **crisis** • (transient) aplastic / anemic [iː] **crisis** • catecholamine [koʊ]/ adrenal [iː] or Addisonian[9] **crisis** • acute / chronic / essential[10] **hypertension** • malignant[11] / pulmonary / intracranial [eɪ] **hypertension**

hypertensive/ hypertone Krise, (Blut)hochdruckkrise

Hypertoniker(in), Hochdruckpatient(in)[1] Hypertension, Hypertonie, Bluthochdruck[2] Hypotonie, -tension, niedriger Blutdruck[3] Aortendissektion, Aneurysma dissecans d. Aorta[4] hämorrhag. Insult[5] renal bed. Hochdruckkrise[6] hämolyt. Krise[7] Blastenkrise, -schub[8] Addison-Krise, akute Nebenniereninsuffizienz[9] essentielle/ primäre Hypertonie[10] maligne H.[11]   6

diabetic [daɪəbetɪk] or hyperglycemic coma [haɪpəglaɪsiːmɪk] n term → U7-14
rel **diabetic ketoacidosis**[1] n term, abbr **DKA**, **Kussmaul breathing**[2] [iː] n term

life-threatening condition that develops as a result of severely deranged [dʒ] insulin levels which lead to severe ketone [iː] waste accumulation, acidosis [æsɪdoʊsɪs], dehydration, and hypoxia

diabetes [iː] n term • **diabetic**[3] n & adj • **hypoglycemia** n • **comatose**[4] adj

» We should check his blood and urine glucose levels to exclude diabetic coma and hypoglycemic shock. Patients in deep hypoglycemic coma appear adequately hydrated [aɪ], are generally flaccid[5] [(k)s], and have quiet breathing. Most patients with diabetic acidosis are not severely depleted [iː] of phosphorus. Patients in ketotic hyperglycemic coma who are severely dehydrated and have acidosis exhibit Kussmaul breathing [iː].

Use to cause/lapse into[6]/be followed by/be in/accompany **coma** • metabolic / hypoglycemic[7] / hyperosmolar[8] **coma** • nonketotic hypoglycemic-hyperosmolar (abbr **NKHHC**) **coma** • traumatic / organic / alcoholic / hepatic[9] [ɪ] **coma** • hypoxic-ischemic [iː]/ myxedema[10] [mɪks-]/ postictal[11] / uremic[12] [iː]/ hysterical **coma** • abrupt / deep[13] / prolonged / irreversible **coma** • **coma** cast[14] • **diabetic** diet / gangrene[15] [iː] • alimentary / alcoholic / hyperinsulinemic [iː] **hypoglycemia** • postprandial or reactive[16] / drug-induced **hypoglycemia** • rebound[17] [aʊ]/ nocturnal [ɜː]/ fasting[18] **hypoglycemia** • **Kussmaul** respiration[2]

diabet./hyperglykäm. Koma Coma diabeticum

diabet. Ketoazidose (DKA)[1] Kussmaul-Atmung[2] Diabetiker(in); diabetisch[3] komatös[4] schlaff[5] ins Koma fallen[6] hypoglykäm. Schock/ Koma, Coma hypoglycaemicum[7] hyperosmolares Koma[8] hepatisches Koma, Leberkoma, Coma hepaticum[9] hypothyreotisches Koma, hypothyreote Krise, Myxödemkoma[10] postiktales Koma[11] urämisches Koma[12] tiefes Koma[13] Komazylinder[14] diabetische Gangrän[15] postprandiale Hypoglykämie[16] Hypoglykämie infolge d. Rebound-Phänomens[17] Fastenhypoglykämie[18]

7

thyrotoxic [θaɪroʊ-] or hyperthyroid crisis n term   syn thyroid storm n clin

extreme form of thyrotoxicosis manifested by marked delirium, severe tachycardia [k], vomiting, diarrhea [iː], dehydration, and often very high fever [iː]

thyrotoxicosis[1] n term • **hyperthyroidism**[1] n • **thyroiditis**[2] [aɪ] n → U54-6

» Thyroid storm in late pregnancy or labor[3] [eɪ] is a life-threatening emergency. Death may occur in thyroid storm or because of heart failure or severe cachexia [ke]. If left untreated, thyrotoxicosis causes progressive catabolic disturbances [ɜː] and profound [aʊ] cardiac damage.

Use to be in thyrotoxic **storm** • **thyrotoxic** state[4] / patient / phase / syndrome / goiter[5] [ɔɪ] • T3 / true[6] / transient / mild / frank **thyrotoxicosis** • florid / severe / gastrointestinal **thyrotoxicosis** • recurrent [ɜː]/ spontaneously [eɪ] resolving[7] / untreated **thyrotoxicosis** • congenital [dʒe]/ juvenile [dʒuː]/ adult / apathetic **hyperthyroidism** • factitious[8] [ɪʃ]/ Graves'[9] / iodine-induced[10] [aɪ] **hyperthyroidism** • pituitary [(j)uː] or TSH-induced[11] **hyperthyroidism** • (sub)clinical / marked / occult [ʌ] **hyperthyroidism** • **hyperthyroid** state[4] • chronic / (sub)acute [ʌ]/ silent[12] / suppurative [ʌ] **thyroiditis** • radiation [eɪ]/ Hashimoto's[13] **thyroiditis** • postpartum / chronic autoimmune[13] / chronic lymphocytic[13] [sɪ] **thyroiditis** • woody or invasive[14] [eɪ]/ chronic fibrous [aɪ] or Riedel's[14] **thyroiditis**

hyperthyreote/ thyreotoxische Krise, endokrines/ Basedow-Koma

Schilddrüsenüberfunktion, Hyperthyreose, Thyreotoxikose[1] Schilddrüsenentzündung, Thyreoiditis[2] Wehen[3] hyperthyreoter Zustand[4] hyperthyreote Struma[5] primäre Hyperthyreose[6] spontan ausheilende Hyperthyreose[7] Hyperthyreosis factitia[8] Basedow-Krankheit, Morbus Basedow[9] iodinduzierte Hyperthyreose[10] hypophysäre Hyperthyreose[11] (klin.) stumme Thyreoiditis[12] Hashimoto-Thyreoiditis, Struma lymphomatosa[13] Riedel-Struma, eisenharte Struma, S. fibrosa Riedel[14]   8

Medical & Surgical Emergencies

CLINICAL TERMS 551

status [eɪ‖æ] **epilepticus** n term

rel **grand-mal seizure**[1] [siːʒɚ] n term

medical emergency characterized by prolonged epileptic seizures or multiple [ʌ] episodes without intervening [iː] periods of consciousness for 10-15 minutes or more

epilepsy [ɛpɪlɛpsi] n term • **epileptic**[2] n & adj clin & term

» The usual causes of death in TCA overdose[3] are cardiac arrhythmias [iː] and status epilepticus. If the patient stops having overt [ɜː] seizures[4], yet remains comatose, an EEG should be performed to rule out[5] ongoing status epilepticus.

Use to experience/be in/present with/treat **status epilepticus** • acute / focal[6] / generalized[7] **status epilepticus** • (non)convulsive [ʌ]/ grand-mal **status epilepticus** • tonic-clonic / psychomotor [saɪkə-] **status epilepticus** • complex partial[8] / refractory[9] / childhood **status epilepticus** • petit mal[10] / tonic-clonic[11] seizure • absence[12] / temporal lobe or psychomotor[13] epilepsy • posttraumatic / juvenile myoclonic[14] [maɪə-] (abbr JME)/ poorly controlled epilepsy • epileptic syndrome / drop attacks[15] / aura[16] [ɔːrə]/ focus • known / idiopathic[17] **epileptics**

Status epilepticus
Grand mal(-Epilepsie), großer Anfall[1] Epileptiker(in); epileptisch[2] Überdosis trizyklischer Antidepressiva[3] manifeste Anfälle[4] ausschließen[5] fokaler Status epilepticus[6] generalisierter Status (epilepticus)[7] komplex-partieller Status[8] therapierefraktärer Status epilepticus[9] Petit mal(-Epilepsie)[10] tonisch-klonischer Anfall[11] Absence-Epilepsie[12] psychomotorische E., Temporallappenepilepsie[13] juvenile myoklonische E., Impulsiv-petit-mal[14] Drop-Anfälle[15] epilept. Aura[16] Patienten m. idiopathischer Epilepsie[17]
9

---

status asthmaticus [steɪtəs æzmætɪkəs] n term

medical emergency characterized by severe asthma refractory to[1] conventional therapy

asthma[2] [æzmə] n • **asthmatic**[3] n & adj • **nonasthmatics** n pl • **antiasthmatic** adj

» Patients with status asthmaticus should not be permitted to fly. The child was known to have asthma in status asthmaticus and respiratory failure. Chest films[4] of ventilated[5] asthmatics should be obtained [eɪ] daily.

Use severe **status asthmaticus** • to have/provoke/develop/die from/exacerbate[6] [æs]/ mimic **asthma** • severe / life-threatening / nocturnal[7] [ɜː]/ childhood **asthma** • bronchial[8] [k]/ chronic / episodic **asthma** • allergic [ɜː] or extrinsic[9] / exercise-induced[10] **asthma** • occupational[11] [eɪʃ]/ adult-onset / fatal[12] **asthma** • **asthma** attack / exacerbations / admission[13] • **asthma** medication / mortality[14] • asymptomatic / labile [eɪ]/ severe **asthmatics** • **antiasthmatic** drug / therapy[15]

Status asthmaticus
nicht ansprechen auf[1] Asthma (bronchiale), anfallsweise Atemnot[2] Asthmatiker(in); asthmatisch[3] Thoraxröntgen[4] künstl. beatmet[5] d. Asthma verschlimmern[6] nächtl. Asthmaanfälle[7] Bronchialasthma, A. bronchiale[8] extrinsisches A. bronchiale[9] anstrengungsbedingtes Asthma[10] berufsbed. Asthma[11] tödl. Asthmaanfall[12] stationäre Aufnahme wegen Asthma[13] Asthmasterblichkeit[14] Asthmatherapie[15]
10

---

myocardial [maɪoʊ-] **infarction** n term, abbr **MI**   syn **heart** [ɑː] **attack** n clin

rel **coronary artery disease**[1] n, abbr **CAD**,
angina [dʒaɪ] **pectoris**[2] n term

necrosis of an area of the heart muscle due to inadequate vascular supply (ischemic [iː] heart disease) resulting from coronary artery occlusion [uː] (usually due to atherosclerosis[3] or thrombosis)

infarct [ɪnfɑːrkt] n term • **(re)infarction**[4] [ɪnfɑːrkʃən] n • **postinfarction**[5] adj • **infarcted** adj • **anginal** [ændʒaɪ-‖ændʒɪnəl] adj • **coronary** [kɔːrənəri] n inf BE

» Should the implantable defibrillator be used as a first-choice therapy in post-infarct sudden death survivors [aɪ]? If the patient has arteriosclerotic heart disease, a sudden increase in heart rate may lead to angina or myocardial infarction. Catheterization in patients with unstable angina[6] or acute MI is frequently performed to define the sites of coronary artery disease that require bypass grafting.

Use to have a/trigger/rule out/mimic **myocardial infarction** • acute / old / anterior[7] / healed[8] [iː]/ inferior **MI** • extensive / (non)transmural[9] [juɚ]/ nonfatal **MI** • painless[10] / asymptomatic or silent[10] / unrecognized[11] **MI** • postoperative / post-/ uncomplicated **MI** • right ventricular / anterior wall[7] / (non-)Q-wave **infarction** • cerebral / pulmonary[12] / intestinal[13] / re[14]/ hemorrhagic[15] **infarction** • anterolateral / posterolateral / recurrent[14] / recent[16] [iː] **infarction** • splenic[17] / renal [iː]/ cortical **infarct** • multi-/ fresh[16] / old / extensive **infarct** • hemorrhagic[15] / septic / pale [eɪ] or ischemic[18] / red[19] **infarct** • **infarct** location[20] / size / extension • atherosclerotic / single-vessel / unstable / preexisting[21] [iː] **CAD** • **angina** attack[22] /-like chest pain[23] • (un)stable[24] / crescendo[25] [ʃe]/ intestinal or abdominal[26] **angina** • exercise-induced or exertional[27] [ɜː]/ rest[6] **angina** • nocturnal / postinfarction / preinfarction[25] **angina** • recurrent / variant or Prinzmetal's[28] **angina** • **anginal** (chest) pain[23] / attack[22]

Herz(muskel)-, Myokardinfarkt
koronare/ ischämische Herzkrankheit, KHK[1] Angina pectoris, Stenokardie[2] Arteriosklerose[3] Infarzierung, Infarkt[4] postinfarziell, nach d. Infarkt[5] instabile Angina pectoris[6] Vorderwandinfarkt[7] abgeheilter Myokardinfarkt[8] transmuraler Herzinfarkt[9] stummer Herzinfarkt[10] nicht erkannter Herzinfarkt[11] Lungeninfarkt[12] Darminfarzierung[13] Reinfarkt[14] hämorrhagische Infarzierung[15] frischer Infarkt[16] Milzinfarkt[17] ischämischer/ weißer I.[18] roter/ hämorrhagischer I.[19] Infarktlokalisation[20] vorbestehende koronare Herzkrankheit[21] Angina pectoris-Anfall[22] pektanginöse Schmerzen i. d. Brust[23] stabile Angina pectoris[24] Crescendo-Angina, Status anginosus, Präinfarkt-Angina[25] Angina abdominalis/ intestinalis[26] Belastungsangina[27] Prinzmetal-A.[28]
11

552 CLINICAL TERMS — Medical & Surgical Emergencies

congestive heart failure [kɒːndʒestɪv hɑːrt feɪljɚ] *n term, abbr* **CHF** → U110-12
rel **cardiac insufficiency**[1] [ɪʃ] *n term* → U123-6

impaired [eɚ] cardiac activity due to MI, cardiomyopathy [aɪɒː] or ischemic [ɪskiː-] heart disease[2] (IHD)

(**anti**)**congestive** *adj term* • **congestion**[3] [kəndʒestʃən] *n* • (**in**)**sufficient** *adj*

» Congestive heart failure is caused by extensive myocardial infarction, volume overload, arrhythmias [ɪ], acute mitral [aɪ] regurgitation [dʒ], or ventricular septal rupture [ʌ]. In children with congestive heart failure profuse sweating[4] [e] is frequent. Digitalis [dɪdʒ-] and occasionally inotropic [aɪ‖iː] agents may be indicated for cardiac insufficiency.

Use to be at risk for/develop/cause or precipitate [sɪ] **congestive heart failure** • to die from/treat **congestive heart failure** • left-sided[5] / right-sided[6] / fetal / low-salt **congestive failure** • severe / florid[7] / mild / early **congestive failure** • preexisting / longstanding[8] / chronic **congestive failure** • unresponsive / decompensated[9] **congestive failure** • **congestive** cardiomyopathy[10] / atelectasis • heart (*abbr* HF)/ renal **failure** • acute / chronic / left(-sided)[5] / right[6] **heart failure** • clinical[11] / overt [ɜː] or symptomatic[11] **heart failure** • early / incipient[12] [sɪ] / fetal / high-output[13] / progressive **heart failure** • (cardio)respiratory / coronary / mitral [aɪ] **insufficiency** • aortic (valve)[14] [æ]/ circulatory [sɜː] / vascular **insufficiency** • arterial / venous [iː]/ pulmonary **insufficiency** • cerebrovascular / hepatic / (exocrine) pancreatic **insufficiency** • (polyglandular) endocrine[15] / (primary/ secondary) adrenal [iː]/ adrenocortical[16] **insufficiency** • **insufficient** perfusion or blood supply[17] • circulatory / pulmonary (vascular)[18] / splanchnic [k] **congestion** • venous / hepatic / lymphatic / nasal[19] **congestion**

pulmonary [u‖ʌ] **embolism** *n term, abbr* **PE**
rel **deep vein thrombosis**[1],
vascular occlusion or **obstruction**[2] *n term*

blockage of a pulmonary artery most frequently by detached [tʃ] fragments of a thrombus from a leg or pelvic vein, esp. in thrombosis following surgery or confinement [aɪ] to bed[3]

embolization[4] *n term* • **embolus** *n, pl* -**i** • **thrombus** *n* • **thrombo-** *comb*

» Prevent propagation[5] of the original thrombus and pulmonary embolization of thrombi [aɪ]. Pulmonary embolism is characterized by dyspnea and sudden chest pain. In some cases of mesenteric vascular occlusion [uːʒ]—esp. with a high venous [iː] occlusion—shock is an early finding.

Use to suffer/have/suspect/rule out[6] **a pulmonary embolism** • acute / established[7] / massive[8] / recurrent[9] [ɜː] **PE** • postoperative / unresolved[10] / fatal **PE** • gas or air[11] / fat[12] / arterial[13] / cerebral[14] **embolism** • venous / deep-vein / iliofemoral / infectious **thrombosis** • effort(-induced) / cavernous sinus[15] **thrombosis** • coronary[16] / multi-/ fresh / old / extensive **thrombosis** • major / pulmonary / intracranial [eɪ] mesenteric[17] **vascular occlusion** • acute arterial[18] / partial / complete[19] **occlusion** • (thrombo)embolic / thrombotic **occlusion** • vaso[2] [eɪ]/ aortic[20] / coronary artery / carotid / caval[21] [eɪ] **occlusion** • hepatic vein / dural venous sinus [aɪ]/ large-vessel[22] **occlusion** • major / deep / high / massive **venous occlusion** • lower limb / portal[23] **venous occlusion** • **occlusive** arterial disease[24] / atherosclerosis • **occlusive** cerebrovascular disease / stroke[25] • to form/detect/ lyse[26] [laɪs] **thrombi** • obstructing[27] [ʌ]/ occlusive[27] **thrombi** • arterial / mural[28] / iliac vein **thrombi** • calf [kæf]/ newly formed / firmly adherent [ɪɚ]/ propagated[29] **thrombi** • massive / multiple / cerebral / systemic **emboli** • clot / metastatic[30] / fat / pulmonary / coronary **embolus** • septic[31] / straddling or saddle[32] **embolus** • **thromb**ectomy /o**embolism**[33] /**olysis**[34] /ophlebitis [aɪ]

Stauungsinsuffizienz, dekompensierte Herzinsuffizienz

Herz-, Myokardinsuffizienz, Herzmuskelschwäche, Insufficientia cordis[1] koronare Herzkrankheit (KHK)[2] Stauung[3] starkes Schwitzen[4] Links(herz)insuffizienz[5] Rechts(herz)insuffizienz[6] ausgeprägte Stauungsinsuffizienz[7] chronische S.[8] dekompensierte Herzinsuffizienz[9] kongestive/ dilatative Kardiomyopathie[10] manifeste Herzinsuffizienz[11] beginnende H.[12] high-output failure, Herzinsuffizienz m. erhöhtem Herzminutenvolumen[13] Aorten(klappen)insuffizienz[14] pluriglanduläre Insuffizienz, polyglanduläres Autoimmunsyndrom[15] Nebennierenrindeninsuffizienz[16] unzureichende Blutversorgung, Mangeldurchblutung[17] Lungenstauung, Stauungslunge[18] Nasenverstopfung[19]

12

Lungenembolie

tiefe Venenthrombose, Phlebothrombose[1] Gefäßverschluss[2] Bettlägrigkeit[3] Embolusbildung, -entstehung; therapeut. Embolisation[4] Verschleppung[5] eine Lungenembolie ausschließen[6] gesicherte Lungenembolie[7] massive L.[8] rezidivierende L.[9] persistierende L.[10] Gas-, Luftembolie[11] Fettembolie[12] arterielle E.[13] Hirnembolie[14] Kavernosusthrombose[15] Koronarthrombose[16] Mesenterialgefäßverschluss[17] akuter Arterienverschluss[18] totaler/ kompletter Verschluss[19] Aortenverschluss[20] Kavaverschluss[21] Verschluss e. großen Gefäßes[22] Pfortaderverschluss[23] arterielle Verschlusskrankheit[24] ischämischer Hirninfarkt[25] Thromben auflösen[26] obturierende Thromben[27] wandständige T.[28] verschleppte T.[29] Tumorembolus[30] septischer Embolus[31] reitender Embolus[32] Thromboembolie[33] Thrombolyse[34]

13

Medical & Surgical Emergencies — CLINICAL TERMS

stroke [stroʊk] n   syn **cerebrovascular accident** n, abbr **CVA**, **cerebral infarct(ion)** n, rel **transient ischemic** [iː] **attack**[1] n term, abbr **TIA**

cerebrovascular disorder characterized by the abrupt onset of focal neurologic deficits[2] resulting from impairment [ɚ] of cerebral blood supply by hemorrhage or occlusion

microinfarction n & adj term • **ischemia**[3] [ɪskiːmɪə] n

» He had a major stroke in May. It is important to distinguish stroke from a space-occupying lesion[4] [iː3] (e.g. a brain tumor). In completed stroke[5] neurologic deficits are stable. Cerebrovascular accident due to infarction is mostly the result of embolization of thrombotic or atheromatous debris [iː] from an extracranial vascular source. Atherosclerosis in the carotid artery is often heralded[6] by a TIA or minor stroke, which is commonly caused by embolism.

Use to suffer[7] [ʌ] (from)/experience or have[7]/prevent **a stroke** • paralytic [ɪ]/ (athero)-thrombotic **stroke** • (cardio)embolic / (focal/ acute) ischemic[8] **stroke** • occlusive [uː]/ hemorrhagic[9] [æd3]/ hemiplegic [iːdʒ]/ ipsilateral **stroke** • evolving or progressing[10] / impending / completed[5] (abbr CS) **stroke** • minor[11] [aɪ]/ major / fluctuating[10] [ʌ]/ amnesic [iː]/ aphasic [eɪ]/ fatal **stroke** • brainstem[12] / cerebellar / carotid **stroke** • (exertional) [3ː]/ heat[13] / sun**stroke** • **stroke** risk[14] / prevention / patient / victim • **stroke** syndrome /-in-evolution[10] (abbr SIE) • hypoxic / hemodynamic [iː]/ toxic **insult** • neurologic[15] / environmental **insult** • acute / impending / first / previous [iː] **CVA** • **CVA** masses • crescendo[16] [ʃ]/ recurrent [3ː]/ recent-onset **TIA(s)** • brain[17] / cerebellar[18] / renal / splenic[19] **infarct** • **infarct** site / size • multi-**infarct** dementia[20]

 Note: In medical English **insult** is commonly used to refer to injury, damage, or noxious effect, e.g. **toxic insult**[21], and **apoplexy** is rarely used (mainly used with **pituitary apoplexy**[22]).

ruptured aortic aneurysm [ænjɚɪzᵊm] n term → U110-18

rupture of a circumscribed dilation of the abdominal aorta marked by severe pain, blood loss, and shock

aneurysmal [ɪ] n term • **rupture** [rʌptʃɚ] n & v • **intra-aortic** [eɪɔːrtɪk] adj

» The pulsatile [ʌ] mass may indicate a leaking abdominal aneurysm. Hemorrhage from aneurysm often arises from outpouchings[1] [aʊ] at arterial bifurcations near the base of the brain.

Use ascending [se]/ thoracic [æs]/ abdominal / expanding[2] **aortic aneurysm** • pulsatile[3] / leaking [iː]/ dissecting[4] **aortic aneurysm** • (left) ventricular[5] / coronary / splenic artery **aneurysm** • cerebral / intracranial [eɪ]/ popliteal **aneurysm** • arteriovenous[6] [iː]/ atherosclerotic / fusiform[7] [juː] **aneurysm** • false / infected / berry or saccular **aneurysm** • **aneurysm** formation[8] / wall / size • **aneurysm** expansion (rate) / resection[9] / repair • **aneurysmal** sac / dilation [eɪ]/ bone cyst [sɪst]/ lesion • **aneurysmal** surgery / subarachnoid [æk] hemorrhage[10] / varix[11] • **aortic** dissection • aneurysm(al) / intraperitoneal [iː]/ cardiac or myocardial[12] **rupture** • ventricular septal / disk[13] **rupture** • drum[14] / splenic / plaque[15] [plæk] **rupture** • spontaneous [eɪ]/ traumatic / impending[16] / delayed **rupture**

acute abdomen n jar   syn **(acute) surgical** [3ː] **abdomen** n term
rel **intraabdominal bleeding** or **hemorrhage**[1] [-rɪdʒ] n term

condition marked by sudden onset of severe abdominal pain which requires prompt evaluation and may call for emergency surgical intervention (e.g. for appendicitis [saɪ] or splenic rupture[2])

bleed [bliːd] v • **rebleed**[3] v • **bleed**[4] n jar • **bleeder**[4] [bliːdɚ] n jar → U5-18

» An erect chest x-ray[5] is essential in all cases of an acute abdomen. Many acute abdominal emergencies that lead to the surgical abdomen are associated with nausea[6] and vomiting.

Use to have/present as/mimic[7] **an acute abdomen** • acute abdominal emergency / pain / distress[8] / crisis / catastrophe • to cause/evaluate[9]/stop or arrest[10]/control (a) **bleeding** • (upper/ lower) gastrointestinal (tract) (abbr GI)/ retroperitoneal **bleeding** • intraperitoneal / aneurysmal / intracranial [eɪ]/ intrapleural [ʊɚ] **bleeding** • internal[11] / intestinal / vaginal [dʒ]/ gingival or gum[12] [ʌ] **bleeding** • brisk[13] / massive[14] / life-threatening / profuse[13] [juː] **bleeding** • prolonged / persistent / delayed[15] [eɪ] **bleeding** • frank / occult [ʌ]/ deep / fatal **bleeding** • nose[16] / variceal[17] [s] **bleed** • **bleeding** site[18] / vessel / time[19] • **bleeding** from the gums[12] / from the nose[16] • major[13] / acute / exsanguinating[14] / secondary[20] **hemorrhage**

Schlaganfall, Gehirnschlag, Apoplexie, apoplekt. Insult
transitorische ischämische Attacke, TIA[1] neurolog. Ausfälle[2] Ischämie, Blutleere[3] raumfordernde Läsion[4] vollendeter (Hirn)infarkt, completed stroke[5] angekündigt[6] einen Schlaganfall erleiden[7] ischämischer Hirninfarkt[8] hämorrhagischer Insult[9] progredienter Insult, progressive stroke[10] leichter Schlaganfall[11] Hirnstammapoplexie[12] Hitzschlag[13] Schlaganfallrisiko[14] Nervenschädigung, neurolog. Störung[15] Crescendo-TIA[16] Hirninfarkt, Apoplexie[17] Kleinhirninfarkt[18] Milzinfarkt[19] Multiinfarktdemenz[20] toxische Einwirkung[21] Hypophysenapoplexie[22]

14

rupturiertes Aortenaneurysma, Aortenaneurysmaruptur
Aussackungen[1] sich erweiterndes Aortenaneurysma[2] pulsierendes A.[3] dissezierendes A.[4] Herzwanddaneurysma[5] arteriovenöses Aneurysma[6] fusiformes/ spindelförmiges Aneurysma[7] Entstehung eines Aneurysmas[8] Aneurysmaresektion[9] aneurysmabedingte Subarachnoidalblutung[10] aneurysmatische Aussackung[11] Herzruptur[12] Diskusruptur[13] Trommelfellruptur[14] Plaquefissur, -ruptur[15] drohende Ruptur[16]

15

akutes Abdomen
intraabdominale Blutung[1] Milzruptur[2] neuerlich bluten[3] Blutung, Bluten[4] Thorax-Röntgen im Stehen[5] Übelkeit[6] dem akuten Abdomen ähnliche Symptome hervorrufen[7] akute abdominelle Beschwerden[8] eine Blutung abklären[9] eine Blutung stillen[10] innere B.[11] Zahnfleischbluten[12] starke Blutung[13] massive B., Massenblutung[14] Spätblutung[15] Nasenbluten[16] Varizenblutung[17] Blutungsstelle, blutende Stelle[18] Blutungszeit[19] Nachblutung[20]

16

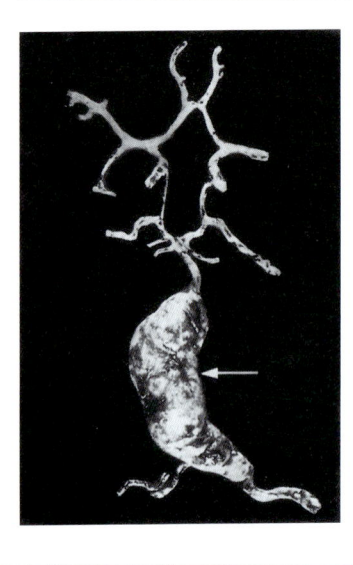

Fusiform aneurysm:
incidental autopsy finding in an 83-year-old patient

flail chest [fleɪl tʃest] *n term* → U111-15

rel **open pneumothorax**[1] [n(j)uːmoʊ-]
mediastinal shift[2] [miːdiəsteɪnəl ʃɪft] *n term*

life-threatening anterior chest trauma usually due to fractures of multiple ribs or bilateral disruption of the costochondral junctions [Δ] resulting in a mechanically unstable, free-floating segment of the chest wall

» All patients with flail chest injuries require immediate hospitalization. The immediately life-threatening pulmonary conditions are tension pneumothorax, open pneumothorax, flail chest, and rarely a massive hemothorax [iː]. Large open sucking [Δ] wounds of the chest and massive crush [Δ] injuries with flail chest require emergency intubation and ventilation. Chest x-ray findings include volume loss in a small hemithorax with mediastinal shift.

Use to support[3] **flail chest** • posttraumatic[4] / marked[5] **flail chest** • **flail chest** injury • to relieve[6] **pneumothorax** • tension[7] [tenʃən] **pneumothorax** • **flail** segment[8] / anterior chest wall[9] / deformity of the chest wall • contralateral **mediastinal shift**

spinal cord injury *or* **trauma** [ɔː] *n*   *rel* **spine** *or* **spinal injury**[1] [ɪndʒɚi] *n*,
whiplash [ʰwɪplæʃ] *or*
hyperextension injury[2] *n term*

traumatic disruption [Δ] of the integrity of the spine [aɪ] and spinal cord which is associated with motor and sensory losses and may produce varying degrees of paraplegia [iːdʒ] or quadriplegia[3] → U142-5

» In the first hours after significant spinal cord [kɔːrd] injury, spinal shock produces complete flaccid [(k)s] paralysis[4]. People with blunt [Λ] head injury[5] or multiple injuries from blunt or penetrating trauma should be assumed to have cervical [sɜː] or thoracolumbar [Δ] spine injuries. Try to move the head as little as possible because injury to the spinal cord and cervical vertebrae may not be initially [ɪʃ] apparent [eə].

Use to have/evaluate/exclude[6] *a* **spinal cord injury** • (in)complete / acute / traumatic **spinal cord injury** • significant / high[7] **spinal cord injury** • cervical / fatal [eɪ]/ suprasacral [eɪ]/ suspected[8] **spinal cord injury** • **spinal cord injury** patient / pain • **spinal cord** lesion[9] [iːʒ]/ damage[9] / compression • **spinal cord** involvement[10] / swelling / transection[11] • double-level[12] [Δ] **spinal injury** • **spinal** trauma[1] / shock[13] / stenosis

---

Thoraxinstabilität, instabiler Thorax

offener Pneumothorax[1] Mediastinalverziehung[2] die Thoraxwand stabilisieren[3] posttraumatische Thoraxinstabilität[4] erhebliche Thoraxinstabilität[5] den Pneumothorax entlasten[6] Spannungs-, Ventilpneumothorax[7] instabiles Thoraxsegment[8] instabile Thoraxwand[9]

17

Rückenmarkverletzung

Wirbelsäulen-, Rückenmarkverletzung[1] (Halswirbelsäulen)schleudertrauma, Peitschenschlagverletzung[2] Tetraplegie, Lähmung aller vier Extremitäten[3] schlaffe Lähmung[4] stumpfes Schädeltrauma[5] eine Rückenmarkverletzung ausschließen[6] hohe Rückenmarkverletzung[7] Verdacht auf Rückenmarkverletzung[8] Rückenmarkschädigung[9] Rückenmarkbeteiligung[10] Rückenmarkdurchtrennung[11] Zwei-Etagen-Verletzung[12] spinaler Schock[13]

18

Critical Care   CLINICAL TERMS 555

(cranio)cerebral injury or **trauma** n term → U106-8; U5-4,13f
  syn **(traumatic) brain injury** n clin, rel **skull** [ʌ] **fracture**¹, **brain damage**² n

trauma to the skull involving damage to the underlying neural tissue by concussion³ [ʌ], cerebral contusion⁴ [(j)uː], penetrating injury, open or depressed skull fracture⁵, intracranial hemorrhage, etc.

» Craniocerebral trauma, the most common cause of subarachnoid [k] hemorrhage, produces severe disability. If the airway is compromised, hypoxemia [iː] may be superimposed⁶ upon traumatic brain injury. Even without skull fracture the brain may be lacerated⁷ [æs] as a result of deceleration injury⁸.

Use to sustain⁹ [eɪ]/ aggravate **a traumatic brain injury** • **brain**-injured / edema¹⁰ [iː]/ compression¹¹ • **brain** herniation¹² / involvement¹³ / death¹⁴ • primary / hypoxic-ischemic / anoxic / focal [oʊ] **brain injury** • diffuse / manifest / irreversible [ɜː] **brain injury** • anoxic / ischemic / irreversible¹⁵ / permanent¹⁵ [ɜː] **brain damage** • (minor/ severe/ open) head / intracranial [eɪ]/ cranial nerve [ɜː] **injury** • basal or basilar¹⁶ / linear / compound¹⁷ [-aʊnd] **skull fracture** • fractured base of¹⁶ **skull** • **skull** base [eɪ]/ **injury**¹⁸ • (closed¹⁹/ blunt²⁰) [ʌ] head / (maxillo)facial [eɪʃ] **trauma**

Schädel-Hirn Trauma, SHT
Schädelfraktur¹ Hirnschaden, -schädigung² Gehirnerschütterung, Commotio cerebri³ Hirnprellung, -kontusion, Contusio cerebri⁴ Schädelimpressionsfraktur⁵ überlagern⁶ verletzt⁷ Dezelerationstrauma⁸ ein SHT erleiden⁹ Hirnödem¹⁰ Hirnquetschung, Compressio cerebri¹¹ zerebrale Herniation¹² Hirnbeteiligung¹³ Hirntod¹⁴ bleibender Hirnschaden¹⁵ Schädelbasisbruch¹⁶ offene Schädelfraktur¹⁷ Schädelverletzung, -trauma¹⁸ gedeckte(s) Schädelverletzung/ SHT¹⁹ stumpfes SHT²⁰   19

Unit 125 Critical Care
Related Units: 124 Medical & Surgical Emergencies, 123 Resuscitation, 7 Consciousness, 12 Mortality,
  135 Anesthesiology, 110 Cardiovascular Symptoms, 111 Respiratory Symptoms,
  118 Diagnostic Procedures, 119 Etiology & Prognosis, 134 Perioperative Care, 136 Blood Transfusion

critical care n term, abbr **CC**   syn **intensive care** n term, abbr **IC**

care of critically ill patients provided in acute life-threatening [e] conditions using sophisticated resuscitative [ʌs] and monitoring equipment with continuous high-quality nursing [ɜː] and medical supervision

intense¹ adj • **intensity** n • **intensify**² [ɪntensɪfaɪ] v • **intensivist** n term

» About 50% of late trauma [ɔː] deaths could be prevented by better critical care management³. The critical care phase in trauma cases is important in reducing deaths due to sepsis and multiple [ʌ] organ failure⁴. Intensive care is needed in cases of respiratory paralysis⁵ [æ].

Use pediatric / surgical [ɜː]/ neonatal [eɪ]/ intermediate-term⁶ [iː] **critical care** • **critical care** medicine⁷ / center / unit⁸ (abbr CCU)/ monitoring⁹ • **critical care** cardiology / procedure [siː] • **critical care** air transport¹⁰ / error • to require/provide • mobile **intensive care** • **intensive care** unit⁸ (abbr ICU)/ facility⁸ [sɪ]/ patient¹¹ • neonatal or newborn¹² / medical¹³ (abbr MICU) **ICU** • surgical / pulmonary [ʊǁʌ]/ prenatal / neurological **ICU** • 24-hour¹⁴ / trauma / burn [ɜː]/ airway¹⁵ **care** • emergency cardiac (abbr ECC)/ (intensive) supportive **care** • end-of-life or respite or terminal¹⁶ [ɜː] **care** • **critical** case / condition¹⁷ / illness¹⁸ / level • **critical** state¹⁷ / list / period / airway narrowing / **critically** ill¹⁹ / injured • **intensive** (nursing/ coronary) care²⁰ / therapy / observation unit²¹ • **intense** pain²² / supportive care • **intense** motor agitation²³ / fear [fɪə]/ heat [iː] • **intense** muscular [ʌsk] activity / inflammatory [æ] reaction • **intensity of** nursing care / exposure [oʊʒ]/ attacks / treatment [iː]

Intensivpflege, -therapie, -medizin
intensiv, heftig, stark¹ intensivieren, verstärken, steigern² Intensivtherapie³ multiples Organversagen⁴ Atemlähmung⁵ intermediäre/ zwischenzeitliche Intensivtherapie⁶ Intensivmedizin⁷ Intensiv-, Wachstation, ITS⁸ Intensivüberwachung⁹ luftgestützter Intensivtransport¹⁰ Intensivpatient(in)¹¹ Neugeborenenintensivstation¹² mediz./ interne Intensivstation¹³ Rund-um-die-Uhr-Betreuung¹⁴ Atemwegspflege¹⁵ Sterbebegleitung¹⁶ krit. Zustand¹⁷ schwere Krankheit¹⁸ schwer krank, in krit. Zustand¹⁹ Intensivpflege²⁰ Intensivüberwachungseinheit²¹ heftige Schmerzen²² starke motor. Unruhe²³

1

clinically unstable adj term   opposite **clinically stable**¹ [eɪ] adj term → U119-12

(of a patient's condition) showing a tendency to rapid deterioration and progression of disease

(de)stabilize² [steɪbəlaɪz] v term • **(in)stability**³ [stəbɪləti] n • **(de)stabilization** n

» Clinically stable patients should undergo predischarge evaluation⁴ to determine [ɜː] whether residual jeopardized [e] myocardium [aɪ] is present. Initial [ɪʃ] therapy is directed toward fluid resuscitation⁵ and stabilization of the patient. If the patient cannot be stabilized, emergency pulmonary angiography should be considered. The child presented with life-threatening [e] episodes of cardiorespiratory instability involving cyanosis [saɪə-] and apnea. A CT scan is a helpful diagnostic aid if the patient's condition is stable enough to permit this delay [eɪ].

Use to be/remain **stable** • medically / metabolically / neurologically / emotionally [oʊʃ] **stable** • **stable** patient / condition or state⁶ / course [ɔː]/ vital [aɪ] signs⁷ • **stable** symptoms⁸ [ɪ]/ injury / fracture⁹ / personality • **to stabilize the** patient / BP¹⁰ / airway / flail [eɪ] segment¹¹ / initial / emergency / clinical **stabilization** • hospital-based or in-patient¹² / hemodynamic¹³ [aɪ] **stabilization** • cardiovascular¹⁴ / vasomotor / nervous **instability** • temperature / bladder¹⁵ / joint / gait¹⁶ [eɪ] **instability** • pH / circulatory¹⁷ [ɜː]/ airway¹⁸ **stability** • genetic [dʒ]/ skeletal / visual **stability**

klinisch instabil
klin. stabil¹ stabilisieren² (In)stabilität³ Entlassungs-, Abschlussuntersuchung⁴ Flüssigkeitstherapie, Volumenersatztherapie⁵ stabiler Zustand⁶ stabile Vitalfunktionen⁷ unveränderte Symptome⁸ stabile Fraktur⁹ den Blutdruck stabilisieren¹⁰ das instabile Thoraxsegment stabilisieren¹¹ Stabilisierung im Krankenhaus¹² hämodynamische Stabilisierung¹³ Herz-Kreislauf-Instabilität¹⁴ Blaseninstabilität¹⁵ unsicherer Gang¹⁶ Kreislaufstabilität¹⁷ stabile Atemwege¹⁸

2

125

advanced life support [ədvæn'st laɪf səpɔːrt] n term, abbr **ALS**
rel life-sustaining [eɪ] measures[1] [meʒɚz] n clin → U123-4

measures intended to achieve adequate ventilation, control cardiac arrhythmias [ɪ], stabilize the hemodynamic [aɪ] status [eɪ‖æ], restore organ perfusion [juːɜ], etc.

life-supporting[2] adj • **support** v • **supportive**[3] adj • **sustain**[4] [səsteɪn] v

» Provide respiratory support with assisted ventilation and supplemental oxygen if necessary. For patients on ventilatory support[5] with positive pressure, the tube is often left in place until weaning[6] [iː] can be accomplished. Severe acute polyneuropathy is a medical emergency requiring constant monitoring and vigorous support of vital functions. Supportive therapy[7] includes oxygen, respiratory support, and monitoring of liver, renal, and heart functions.

Use to provide/require/withdraw [ɔː] **life support** • basic[8] (abbr BLS)/ artificial [ɪʃ] **life support** • symptom-based / (basic/ advanced) cardiac / advanced trauma [ɔː] **life support** • extracorporeal[9] [iː] (abbr ECLS)/ invasive [eɪ]/ cessation [ses-] of[10] **life support** • **life support** skills / course / team[11] / procedures • **life support** system / techniques [tekniːks]/ priorities [aɪɔː] • circulatory[12] / cardiovascular / hemodynamic **support** • blood volume[13] / fluid / transfusion / cardiac **support** • advanced perfusion / respiratory[5] **support** • (mechanical/ prompt/ partial [ʃ]/ prolonged) ventilatory[5] / inspiratory pressure **support** • (full) machine[14] [ʃiː]/ antibiotic / nutritional [ɪʃ] **support** • emotional [oʊʃ]/ family **support** • **life supporting** measures[1] / treatment • **supportive** care / measures[7] / therapy • **supportive** management[15] / counseling [aʊ]

APACHE abbr   rel TISS[1] abbr

short for **A**cute **P**hysiology **a**nd **C**hronic **H**ealth **E**valuation; systematic clinical assessment of health status and prognosis in ICU patients; TISS[1] stands for **T**herapeutic [juː] **I**ntervention **S**coring **S**ystem

» The APACHE II scoring system, which uses the worst values of 12 physiologic measurements plus age, and previous [iː] health status, provides a good description of illness severity[2] [e] for a wide range of conditions and predicts[3] the probability of survival [aɪ].

Use **APACHE** II data / scoring / score[4] / prognostic system • **TISS** points / data [eɪ‖æ]

ICU observation & monitoring n term
sim supervision[1] [ɪʒ], surveillance[2] n term

close watch kept on ICU patients by specially trained staff using sophisticated monitoring devices[3] [aɪs]

observe v • **observational** [eɪʃ] adj • **monitor**[4] v & n • **supervise**[5] [suːpəvaɪz] v

» The patient requires ICU observation for at least 24 hours. Critically ill patients should be kept under direct observation at all times. Patients with wringer [r] injuries[6] should be observed hourly [aʊəli]. During this critical period, continued observation is necessary so that any circulatory embarrassment[7] can be identified at once. The use of a ventilator does not obviate[8] the need for close observation of the patient's condition by a qualified nurse. Once close observation and monitoring are no longer required, the patient is discharged[9] from the ICU to a regular hospital room. Attach [tʃ] an ECG monitor, and watch closely for bradycardia.

Use to provide/require or need **ICU observation** • **intensive observation** area / unit[10] / period [ɪə] (abbr IOP) • to keep under/be under/admit for[11] **observation** • in-hospital or inpatient[12] / postanesthetic [e]/ nursing [ɜː] **observation** • home / direct / expectant / long-term **observation** • close[13] / intensive-level[13] / careful[13] **observation** • continuous[14] / definitive **observation** • frequent / clinical / medical **observation** • untiring [aɪ]/ general **observation** • **observation** period[15] / window • **to observe** the patient / for signs of illness[16] • **to monitor** the patient / vital [aɪ] signs[17] / BP • **to monitor** cardiac rhythm [ɪ]/ fluid status / oxygen saturation • **to monitor** regularly / continuously or steadily[18] [e] • patient[19] / fetal[20] [iː] physiological / pulmonary function **monitoring** • self[21]-/ meticulous[22] / (non)invasive / electrocardiographic (abbr ECG) **monitoring** • ongoing[14] / intraoperative[23] / periodic / bedside[24] **monitoring** • central / home / ambulatory[25] **monitoring** • **monitoring** device / equipment • intensive / close (medical) / followup[26] / health **supervision** • to keep under[27] **surveillance** • continued / lifelong / ongoing **surveillance**

---

erweiterte Reanimationsmaßnahmen

lebenserhaltende Maßnahmen[1] lebenserhaltend[2] stützend[3] (er)halten, aufrechterhalten; erleiden[4] mechan. Atemhilfe[5] Entwöhnung[6] unterstützende Therapie/ Maßnahmen[7] Basismaßnahmen d. kardiopulmonalen Reanimation, ABC-Maßnahmen, Ersthilfereanimation, lebensrettende Sofortmaßnahmen[8] extrakorporale Membran-Oxygenation[9] Abbruch d. Intensivtherapie[10] Reanimationsteam[11] Kreislauf(unter)stützung[12] Volumenersatztherapie[13] maschinelle Unterstützung[14] adjuvante Therapie[15]

APACHE-Bewertungssystem

TISS-Bewertungssystem[1] Schweregrad d. Erkrankung[2] sagt vorher, prognostiziert[3] APACHE Punktezahl[4]

Intensivüberwachung

Aufsicht, Überwachung; Leitung[1] Überwachung, Surveillance[2] Überwachungsgeräte[3] überwachen, kontrollieren; Monitor, Überwachungs-/ Kontrollgerät[4] beaufsichtigen, überwachen[5] Ableberung[6] hämodynam. Instabilität[7] überflüssig machen[8] entlassen[9] Intensivüberwachungseinheit[10] z. Beobachtung stationär aufnehmen[11] stationäre Beobachtung/ Überwachung[12] genaue Beobachtung, sorgfältige Überwachung[13] ständige Überwachung[14] Beobachtungszeitraum[15] auf Krankheitszeichen hin beobachten[16] d. Vitalfunktionen überwachen[17] ständig überwachen[18] Patientenüberwachung[19] fetale Überwachung[20] Selbstkontrolle[21] sorgfältige Überwachung[22] intraoperative Überwachung[23] bettseitige Überwachung[24] ambulante Kontrolle/ Überwachung[25] Verlaufsbeobachtung[26] überwachen[27]

Critical Care CLINICAL TERMS 557

intensive care monitor n term

rel **cardiac monitor**[1] n term → U118-14

TV-like screen with a continuous display of curves [ɜː] and/or digital readouts[2] representing vital parameters in the body, e.g. the blood pressure, intracranial [eɪ] pressure, blood oximetry and ECG reading[3]

» Sophisticated [fɪ] intensive care monitors continuously collect large amounts of physiological data from acutely ill patients. I believe intensive care monitor alarms are a major burden [ɜː] on both nurses and patients. His intensive care monitor went flat line[4]. The intensive care monitor failed to sound an alarm when her heartbeat showed signs of trouble.

Use blood pressure[5] (*abbr* BP)/ cardiorespiratory **monitor** • transcutaneous [eɪ] oxygen / ambulatory[6] / (24-h) Holter[6] **monitor** • **monitor**-defibrillator / leads[7] [iː] • central venous [iː] pressure[8] (*abbr* CVP)/ acid-base / 24-hour pH **monitoring** • urine [jʊəɪn] output[9] / (invasive) hemodynamic [hiːməʊdaɪnæmɪk] **monitoring**

Intensivüberwachungsgerät
Herzmonitor[1] Digitalanzeige[2] EKG-Registrierung[3] zeigte eine Nulllinie[4] Blutdrucküberwachungsgerät[5] Holter-Monitor, Langzeit-EKG-Rekorder[6] Monitorableitungen[7] Überwachung d. zentralen Venendrucks[8] Überwachung d. Harnmenge[9]

6

central venous line [sentrəl viːnəs laɪn] or **catheter** n term, *abbr* **CVL** or **CVC**

rel **Swan-Ganz catheter**[1] [kæθətɚ] n term

very thin tube (connected to a monitor) inserted into a vein [eɪ] in either the arm or the chest just below the shoulder, or on the side of the neck to measure the central venous pressure

catheterization n term • **catheterize**[2] v • **catheterizable** *adj* → U127-19

» Close monitoring of fluid and electrolytes requires a central venous line. A Swan-Ganz catheter is used to record[3] BP and blood gas concentrations in the heart and in the pulmonary vessels. Percutaneously [eɪ] placed CVCs should not be used for initial resuscitation.

Use permanent or indwelling[4] / long-term **central venous catheter** • single-lumen [uː]/ triple-lumen[5] **central venous catheter** • **central venous catheter**-related bloodstream [iː] infection[6] • **central venous** cannulation or catheterization[7] / monitoring • **central venous** infusion rate / pressure (monitor) • **Swan-Ganz** monitor / pressure (monitoring) • **Swan-Ganz** thrombosis / pulmonary arterial [ɪɚ] flotation catheter[1] • (diagnostic/ interventional) cardiac / (right-/ left-sided) heart[8] [ɑː] **catheterization** • pulmonary artery[9] / percutaneous [eɪ] (transfemoral) [e] **catheterization** • subclavian [eɪ] vein / retrograde [-ɡreɪd] **catheterization**

zentraler Venenkatheter, Kavakatheter
Swan-Ganz-Katheter, Pulmonalarterienkatheter, PAK[1] katheterisieren, einen Katheter einführen/ legen[2] aufzeichnen, überwachen[3] zentraler Venenverweilkatheter[4] dreilumiger zentraler Venenkatheter[5] Kathetersepsis[6] zentralvenöse Katheterisierung[7] Linksherz-Katheterisierung[8] Pulmonaliskatheterisierung[9]

7

intra-aortic [eɪɔːrtɪk] **balloon** [uː] **counterpulsation** [kaʊn-] n term, *abbr* **IABC**

retrograde insertion of a catheter with a balloon pumping system into the thoracic [æs] aorta to assist circulation when low-output circulatory states[1] are due to significant refractory left ventricular pump failure[2]

» Early use of intra-aortic balloon counterpulsation appears to be extremely valuable for temporarily reversing [ɜː] shock in patients with acute MI[3]. In cardiogenic [dʒe] shock, mechanical [kæ] assistance with an intra-aortic balloon pumping [ʌ] system [ɪ] capable of augmenting[4] [ɒːɡ-] both diastolic [daɪə-] pressure and cardiac output[5] may be helpful.

Use external / internal / aortic / balloon pump [ʌ] **counterpulsation** • **counterpulsation** device[6] • **intra-aortic** balloon pump[7] (*abbr* IABP) • **IABP** catheter / support

intraaortale Ballongegenpulsation, IABP
durch niedriges Herzzeitvolumen bedingte Kreislaufstörungen[1] therapierefraktäres linksventrikuläres Pumpversagen[2] Myokardinfarkt[3] erhöhen[4] Herzminutenvolumen[5] Gegenpulsationsvorrichtung[6] intraaortale Ballonpumpe[7]

8

pulse oximetry n term

rel **arterial** [ɪɚ] **blood gases**[1] [ɡæsiːz] n term, *abb* **ABG**

measurement of the oxygen saturation[2] (SaO2) of hemoglobin using an oximeter

co-oximetry[3] n term • pulse oximeter [pʌls ɒksɪmətɚ] n • oximetric [e] *adj*

» A pulse oximetry sensor can be clipped over the tip of a digit[4] to detect the oxygen saturation [tʃɚ] of arterial blood. Oximetry reflects trends in oxygenation before, during, and after intubation. Pulse oximetry provides no information about the adequacy of ventilation, therefore it cannot substitute [ʌ] for[5] ABG determinations in most clinical settings.

Use to monitor with/determine by/obtain [eɪ] **pulse oximetry** • continuous pulse / transcutaneous [eɪ]/ transmission[6] **oximetry** • finger / overnight / nocturnal [ɜː]/ home **oximetry** • cuvette[7] / ear[8] **oximeter** • **oximetric** mapping[9] • devices [iː] • **arterial blood gas** analysis[10] / reading [iː]/ determination[11] • **arterial blood gas** levels[12] / sample[13] / measurement[11] [eʒ]

Pulsoxymetrie, -oximetrie
arterielle Blutgase[1] Sauerstoffsättigung[2] Hämoxymetrie[3] Fingerkuppe[4] ersetzen[5] Transmissionsoxymetrie[6] Küvettenoxymeter[7] Ohroxymeter[8] oxymetr. Messreihe[9] arterielle Blutgasanalyse[10] Bestimmung d. arteriellen Blutgaswerte[11] arterielle Blutgaswerte[12] Blutprobe z. Bestimmung d. arteriellen Blutgaswerte[13]

9

125

558 CLINICAL TERMS — Critical Care

respirator [rɛspɪreɪtɚ] n term   syn **ventilator** n term → U123-9

machine that humidifies¹ [hjuː-] and delivers air in the appropriate percentage of oxygen and at the appropriate rate to the patient with inadequate spontaneous ventilation to perform or support breathing [iː].

respiration [eɪʃ] n term • **ventilation**² n • **(hyper)ventilate**³ [haɪpɚ-] v → U44-5

» He has sustained [eɪ] an irreversible brain injury and is being kept alive on a respirator. Continuous mechanical ventilation provides ventilation at a specified rate for patients who are apneic [iː]. ACMV ensures a backup ventilation in the absence of an intact respiratory drive⁴ and allows for synchronization of the ventilator cycle [saɪkl] with inspiratory effort.

Use to be (maintained) on a⁵ **respirator** • pressure-controlled⁶ / volume-controlled⁷ / infant **respirator** • **respirator** therapy / dependence / support⁸ • to wean [iː] from⁹ **the ventilator** • automatic or mechanical / volume(-cycled)⁷/ pressure (-limited)⁶ **ventilator** • **ventilator** support /(-assisted) breaths [e]/ settings / tubing¹⁰ [(j)uː] • **ventilator** pressure / barotrauma [ɒː]/ disconnection¹¹ / management • artificial¹² **respiration** • mechanical¹³ / controlled¹⁴ / continuous positive pressure¹⁵ **ventilation** • continuous mechanical (abbr CMV)/ assist control mode¹⁶ [oʊ] (abbr ACMV) **ventilation** • positive end expiratory pressure¹⁷ (abbr PEEP) **ventilation**

Respirator, Beatmungsgerät
befeuchten¹ Ventilation, Belüftung; Beatmung² hyperventilieren³ Atemantrieb⁴ künstl. beatmet werden⁵ druckgesteuertes Beatmungsgerät⁶ volumengesteuertes B.⁷ mechan. Atemhilfe⁸ vom Respirator entwöhnen⁹ Respiratorschläuche¹⁰ Unterbrechung d. Beatmungssystems¹¹ künstl. Beatmung¹² maschinelle Beatmung¹³ kontrollierte Beatmung¹⁴ kontinuierliche Überdruckbeatmung¹⁵ druckunterstützte Beatmung¹⁶ PEEP-Beatmung, Beatmung m. erhöhtem endexspirator. Druck¹⁷

10

---

heart-lung (bypass) machine n term   syn **pump** [ʌ] **oxygenator** n → U44-6
   rel **cardiopulmonary bypass**¹ [baɪpæs] n term, abbr **CPB**

mechanical device that can temporarily take over the function of the heart and lungs by extracorporeal [-rɪə] circulation² of the patient's blood via a pump and an artificial lung chamber [eɪ] for gas exchange

bypass³ v & n term • **oxygenate**⁴ [ɒːksɪdʒəneɪt] v • (re/ hyper)**oxygenation**⁵ n

» Total cardiopulmonary bypass is usually accomplished by draining [eɪ] blood through catheters placed in the right atrium from the patient, through the heart-lung machine, and back through a small cannula in the aorta. CPB requires the heart to be arrested and filled with a cardioplegic [iːdʒ] solution to keep it still. After institution of CPB and cardioplegic arrest⁶, an incision [sɪʒ] is made in the area of infarction. In a beating [iː] heart coronary artery bypass graft (abbr CABG) procedure, the patient does not require CPB with a heart-lung machine.

Use to place on/be hooked up to⁷/set up/operate **a heart-lung machine** • **heart-lung** resuscitation [ʌs] techniques [tekniːks]/ transplant • (bypass) membrane⁸ / pump / film⁹ / bubble¹⁰ [ʌ] **oxygenator** • to institute/place a patient on **cardiopulmonary bypass** • full or total / partial [ʃ]/ hypothermic¹¹ [ɜː]/ **CPB** • **CPB** machine¹² • extracorporeal / surgical **bypass** • coronary (artery) or aortocoronary¹³ / gastric **bypass** • **bypass** operation or surgery¹⁴ / graft [æ]

Herz-Lungen-Maschine
Herz-Lungen-Bypass, kardiopulmonaler B.¹ extrakorporale(r)Kreislauf/ Zirkulation² umgehen, -leiten; Bypass³ m. Sauerstoff anreichern, oxygenieren⁴ Oxygenation, Oxygenierung⁵ Kardioplegie, künstl. induzierter Herzstillstand⁶ an e. Herz-Lungen-Maschine angeschlossen sein/ hängen⁷ Membranoxygenator⁸ Filmoxygenator⁹ Bubble-Oxygenator¹⁰ hypothermer CPB¹¹ Herz-Lungen-Maschine¹² aortokoronarer Bypass¹³ Bypass-Operation¹⁴

11

---

oxygen tent [ɒːksɪdʒən] n term   syn **O₂ tent** n, rel **head tent**¹ n term → U44-6

transparent [eɚ] enclosure suspended over the patient's bed to supply a high O₂ concentration

» Either a monoplace chamber [tʃeɪ-] pressurized with pure O₂ or a multiplace chamber pressurized with compressed air where the patient receives [iː] pure O₂ by mask, head tent, or endotracheal [eɪ] tube may be used for hyperbaric oxygen therapy².

Use to place in **an oxygen tent** • humidified [hjuː-] **oxygen tent** • mist(ifier) [-faɪɚ]/ steam [iː] **tent** • to give or administer³/deliver³ **oxygen** • **oxygen** uptake⁴ / supply⁵ [aɪ]/ utilization / consumption⁶ [ʌ] • **oxygen** tension⁷ [tenʃən]/ gradient [eɪ]/ saturation⁸ • supplemental / 100% / high-flow⁹ **oxygen** • hyperbaric² [aɪ] **oxygenation**

Sauerstoffzelt
Gesichtszelt¹ Sauerstoff-Überdrucktherapie, hyperbare Oxygenation² Sauerstoff verabreichen/ zuführen³ Sauerstoffaufnahme⁴ Sauerstoffzufuhr, -versorgung⁵ Sauerstoffverbrauch⁶ Sauerstoffspannung⁷ Sauerstoffsättigung⁸ high-flow Sauerstoffzufuhr⁹

12

---

intracranial [eɪ] **pressure monitor** n term, abbr **ICP monitor**
   rel **subarachnoid bolt** [sʌbəræknɔɪd boʊlt] or **screw**¹ [skruː] n term

device for intraventricular, subarachnoid or epidural measurement of the pressure inside the skull

» Ventriculostomy is a procedure for measuring intracranial pressure by placing an ICP monitor within one of the CSF-filled ventricles². Continuous ICP measurement³ is widely used to monitor progress in patients with severe head injuries. Although the intraventricular catheter is thought to be more accurate, a subarachnoid bolt is less invasive [eɪ] and easier to place and is preferred if immediate access is necessary.

Use to place **an ICP monitor** • (invasive) **ICP** monitoring⁴ • elevated or increased or raised⁵ [eɪ] **ICP** • **intracranial** pressure screw⁶ / injury / (mass) lesion⁷ [iːʒ] • rise [raɪz] or increase in⁸ **intracranial pressure**

Hirndruckmonitor, intrakranielle Druckmesssonde
Subarachnoidalschraube¹ liquorgefüllte Hirnkammern/ Hirnventrikel² kontinuierl. Hirndruckmessung³ invasive Hirndruckmessung⁴ erhöhter intrakranieller Druck⁵ intrakranielle Druckmesssonde⁶ intrakranielle Raumforderung⁷ Hirndrucksteigerung⁸

13

Critical Care   CLINICAL TERMS 559

evoked potentials [ɪvoʊkt poʊtenˈʃəlz] *n term, abbr* **EP** → U118-12
  rel **brain electrical activity mapping**[1] *n term, abbr* **BEAM**

electrical response in the brainstem or cerebral cortex elicited[2] [ɪs] by a specific stimulus

» In the diagnosis of coma and brain death, somatosensory evoked potentials supplement [ʌ] the results of auditory [ɒː] evoked potentials. Auditory brain stem responses are evoked by stimulating the brain stem with sound waves via headphones. Evoked responses may be used to test the integrity of peripheral, spinal [aɪ], and central nervous pathways.

Use cerebral / cortical / (somato)sensory[3] (*abbr* SEPs) **evoked potentials** • motor[4] / auditory[5] / visual[6] [13] (*abbr* VEP) **evoked potentials** • brain stem auditory[7] (*abbr* BAEP)/ cognitive **evoked potentials** • low-amplitude **EPs** • auditory brainstem[7] (*abbr* ABR)/ sacral [eɪ] **evoked response** • **evoked** response testing • **brain stem** testing *or* studies / auditory evoked response[7] • **brain stem** evoked response audiometry[8] (*abbr* BSERA) • **brain electrical activity** map

ventricular drainage [dreɪnɪdʒ] *n term*   *rel* **ventricular drain**[1] *n term*

evacuation of CSF from the cerebral ventricles for the relief of intracranial [eɪ] pressure

drain (off)[2] *v phr term* • **undrained** *adj* → U140-15 • **ventriculo-** *comb*

» Obstructive [ʌ] hydrocephalus[3] [se] usually requires direct ventricular drainage of CSF. If acute obstructive hydrocephalus occurs, a ventricular drain aids in controlling increased intracranial pressure. An epidural abscess required emergency drainage via laminectomy[4].

Use temporary / direct **ventricular drainage** • surgical / incision [sɪ] and **drainage** • **ventricular** puncture[5] [ʌ] • **ventriculo**tomy /cisternostomy[6] /stomy • **ventriculo**-**atrial** [eɪ] shunt[7] [ʃʌnt] /graphy /megaly

chest tube [tʃest t(j)uːb] *n clin & jar*   *syn* **thoracostomy tube** *n term*

curved [ɜː] plastic tube inserted into the pleural [plʊəəl] space[1] to remove effusions[2] [juː3], drain fluids, treat a tension pneumothorax[3] [n(j)uːmə-], etc.

thoracotomy[4] [θɔːrəkɒːtəmi] *n term* • **thoracoscopy** *n* • **thoracoscopic** *adj*

» Attach [tʃ] the yellow connector of the chest tube collection tubing to the port marked "patient" on the lid of the blood collection bag. The chest tube is placed under water-seal [iː] drainage[5], and suction [ʌ] is applied until the lung expands. When an effusion [juː3] produces respiratory compromise [-maɪz], it should be drained with a thoracostomy tube.

Use to insert [ɜː] /place/require/inject [dʒe] via/drain via[6]/remove **a chest tube** • small-bore[7] [bɔːrl]/ 8 French / clamped[8] [æ] **chest tube** • **chest tube** insertion[9] / drainage[10] / decompression • **chest tube** (re)placement[9] / collection tubing[11] / closed[12] / pleural / water-sealed[5] **tube drainage** • tracheostomy[13] / suction-irrigation[14] **tube** • needle[15] [iː]/ tube[16] **thoracostomy** • emergency / exploratory[17] / left / extrapleural [ʊɚ] **thoracotomy** • video-assisted[18] **thoracoscopy** • **thoracos**-**copic** lung biopsy[19] [aɪ]/ surgery [sɜːrdʒɚɪ]/ pleurectomy

pericardial decompression *n term*   *rel* **pericardiocentesis**[1] [-sentiːsɪs] *n term*

evacuation of blood or fluid from the pericardium, esp. in cardiac tamponade[2] [-neɪd]

compression *n* • **(de)compress**[3] [dɪkəmpres] *v* • **-centesis** *comb*

» If the patient is stable, obtain an echocardiogram to confirm [ɜː] the presence of pericardial fluid and to assist in pericardiocentesis. Treatment of penetrating cardiac injuries has gradually changed to prompt thoracotomy and pericardial decompression. Chest decompression by needle thoracostomy may be lifesaving in suspected tension pneumothorax.

Use emergency / chest thump [ʌ]/ cerebral[4] **decompression** • optic nerve [ɜː]/ gastric / bladder **decompression** • endoscopic / surgical[5] / percutaneous [eɪ] **decompres**-**sion** • thoracic [æs] outlet[6] / portal / root[7] [uː] **decompression** • **decompression** tube / sickness[8] / chamber[9] [tʃeɪ-] • to perform/require/relieve by[10] **pericardio**-**centesis** • emergency / diagnostic[11] / therapeutic [juː] **pericardiocentesis** • percutaneous / (transthoracic) needle / blind **pericardiocentesis** • **pericardiocentesis** tray[12] / needle • closed chest (cardiac)[13] / nerve (root) **compression** • spinal [aɪ] cord[14] / brain stem / digital[15] **compression** • **compression** injury / fracture[16] • **compression** dressing *or* bandage[17] [-ɪdʒ]/ atelectasis[18] • thoraco/ (abdominal) para/ arthro**centesis** • culdo[19] [ʌ]/ tympano [ɪ]/ amnio**centesis**

evozierte Potentiale, EP
Brain Electrical Activity Mapping, BEAM[1] ausgelöst[2] somatosensibel evozierte Potentiale[3] motor. evozierte Potentiale[4] akust. evozierte Potentiale (AEP)[5] visuell evozierte Potentiale[6] AEP früher Latenz[7] Hirnstammaudiometrie[8]

14

Ventrikeldrainage
Ventrikeldrain[1] ableiten, abfließen lassen[2] Verschlusshydrozephalus, H. occlusus[3] Wirbelbogenresektion, Laminektomie[4] Ventrikelpunktion[5] Ventrikulozisternostomie, Torkildson-Drainage[6] ventrikuloatrialer Shunt[7]

15

Thoraxdrain
Pleuraraum[1] Ergüsse[2] Spannungspneumothorax[3] Thorakotomie, Brustkorberöffnung[4] Bülau-Drainage[5] über e. Thoraxdrain ableiten[6] kleinlumiger Thoraxdrain[7] abgeklemmter T.[8] Platzierung e. T.[9] Thoraxdrainage[10] Thoraxdrainageschlauch[11] geschlossene Saugdrainage[12] Trachealkanüle[13] Saug-Spül-Drain/ -Kanüle[14] Thorakozentese[15] Thorakostomie mit Drainage[16] Probethorakotomie, explorative T.[17] videogestützte Thorakoskopie[18] thorakosk. Lungenbiopsie[19]

16

Perikard-, Herzdekompression
Perikardpunktion, -(io)zentese[1] Perikard-, Herz(beutel)tamponade[2] v. Druck entlasten, dekomprimieren[3] Schädeldekompression[4] op. Dekompression[5] op. Entlastung des Thoracic Outlet-Syndroms[6] Wurzeldekompression[7] Caisson-, Druckfall-, Dekompressionskrankheit[8] Dekompressionskammer[9] durch Perikardpunktion entlasten[10] diagnost. Perikardpunktion[11] Perikardpunktionsbesteck[12] Herzdruckmassage[13] Rückenmarkkompression[14] digitale Kompression[15] Kompressionsfraktur, Stauchungsbruch[16] Kompressionsverband[17] Kompressionsatelektase[18] Douglaspunktion[19]

17

nasogastric or **NG tube** n term   rel **jejunostomy** or **J tube**[1] n term → U91-26

a tube passed into the sto*ma*ch [k] through the nose; a J tube is a type of fe*e*ding [iː] tube[2] surgically [ɜː] ins*e*rted [ɜː] into the small int*e*stine[3]

nasoduodenal adj term • **jejunotomy** [dʒɪdʒuːnɒtəmi] n • **jejunoileal** adj

» F*ee*ding by a nasog*a*stric [neɪzoʊ-] tube or an endosc*o*pically placed gastr*o*stomy tube[4] may be n*e*cessary for nutritional [ɪʃ] support. *O*ral intake is withh*e*ld, and a nasog*a*stric tube is ins*e*rted to *a*spirate gastric secr*e*tions [iːʃ]. A fe*e*ding jejun*o*stomy is *i*ndicated whenever prol*o*nged nutritional support is anticipated [ɪs].

Use to pass or insert or place[5] **a nasogastric tube** • indwelling[6] **NG tube** • **(naso)gastric** intubation[7] / suction[8] / aspirate • **(naso)gastric** sampling / lavage[9] [-ɑːʒ]/ fe*e*ding[10] • esophageal [dʒ] gastric (abbr EGT)/ fe*e*ding[2] / Sengstaken-Blakemore[11] **tube** • ball*oo*n[12] / int*e*stinal / triple-l*u*men[13] **tube** • jejunal (fe*e*ding)[1] / st*o*mach[4] / G[4] **tube** • **jejunostomy** fe*e*ding[14] (tube) • **nasoduodenal** fe*e*ding / tube[15]

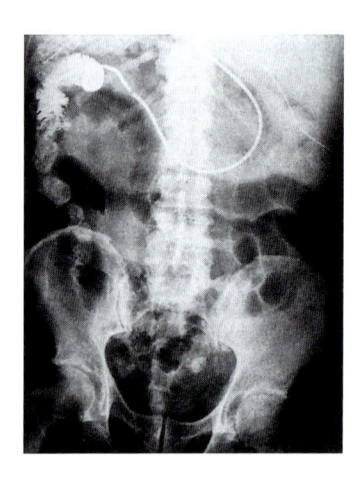

Radiographic view confirming correct placement of a nasoduodenal tube for enteral feeding

Nasen-Magen-Sonde

Jejunalsonde[1] Ernährungssonde[2] Dünndarm[3] perkutane Magensonde[4] e. Magensonde legen[5] Dauerkanüle[6] Legen e. Magensonde/ nasogastralen Sonde[7] Aspiration/ Absaugen d. Mageninhalts[8] Magenspülung, -ausheberung[9] Ernährung über e. Magensonde[10] Sengstaken-Blakemore-Sonde[11] Ballonsonde[12] dreilumige Sonde[13] Ernährung über eine Jejunalsonde[14] nasoduodenale Ernährungssonde[15]

18

---

parenteral nutrition [nuːtrɪʃ°n] or **alimentation** [ælɪmənteɪʃ°n] n term
    syn **intravenous** [iː] or **drip feeding** [iː] n, rel **tube feeding**[1] n term

meeting a p*a*tient's nutritional needs by means of IV fe*e*dings, e.g. to prov*i*de [aɪ] bowel [baʊəl] rest f*o*llowing s*u*rgery for m*a*ssive GI tr*au*ma [ɔː].

enteral [entərəl] adj term • **hyperalimentation**[2] [haɪpɚ-] n → U79-3

» Chr*o*nic par*e*nteral nutrition at home is required if *o*ral intake[3] is not t*o*lerated. In most situations, solutions [uːʃ] of *e*qual [iː] n*u*trient value[4] can be designed [aɪ] for d*e*livery v*i*a *e*nteral and par*e*nteral r*ou*tes [aʊ‖uː], but differences in abs*o*rption must be consid*e*red.

Use to require/receive[5] [siː] /delay [eɪ] **parenteral nutrition** • total (abbr TPN)/ partial / supplem*e*ntary **parenteral nutrition** • temporary / prol*o*nged[6] / long-term[6] **parenteral nutrition** • chronic / preoperative / home / periph*e*ral[7] (abbr PPN) **parenteral nutrition** • *e*nteral[1] / intrav*e*nous[8] **nutrition** • **nutrition** support[9] / therapy[10] • l*e*vel or state[11] / maintenance / source [ɔː] **of nutrition** • *e*nteral[1] (tube) / *o*ral **alimentation** • **parenteral** administration[12] / fluid support / fe*e*ding[8] / diet [daɪət] • **parenteral** hyperalimentation / therapy • **parenteral** antibi*o*tics[13] / dose / formula • (assisted) *e*nteral[1] / IV[8] / central line[14] fe*e*ding • nasointestinal / (naso)jej*u*nal[15] / jejun*o*stomy[15] **feeding** • **feeding** tube / jejun*o*stomy[16] • **nutritional** intervention / support[9] / (replacement) therapy[10]

parenterale Ernährung

Sondenernährung, enterale Ernährung[1] Hyperalimentation[2] perorale Nahrungsaufnahme[3] Nährwert[4] parenteral ernährt werden[5] parenterale Langzeiternährung[6] parenterale Ernährung über e. peripheren Zugang[7] parenterale Ernährung[8] künstl. Ernährung[9] Ernährungstherapie[10] Ernährungszustand[11] parenterale Verabreichung/ Applikation[12] parenteral verabreichte Antibiotika, Antibiotika zur parenteralen Applikation[13] Ernährung über e. zentralen Venenkatheter[14] Ernährung über eine Jejunalsonde[15] Ernährungsfistel im Jejunum[16]

19

---

indwelling (urinary or **Foley) catheter** [kæθətɚ] n term → U127-19

tube for c*o*nstant drainage [dreɪnɪdʒ] of *u*rine [jʊɚɪn] left in place in the bl*a*dder [æ] where it is retained [eɪ] by an infl*a*table [eɪ] ball*oo*n [uː].

» Indwelling pigtail [pɪgteɪl] uret*e*ral [iː] catheters[1] can be placed for acute or long-term dr*ai*nage in selected p*a*tients. Determine [ɜː] how long a postoperative c*a*theter should be left indwelling. Insert a Foley c*a*theter to monitor urine output.

Use to place/insert/pass/replace[2] **an indwelling catheter** • long-term / permanent [ɜː]/ chronic **indwelling catheter** • **indwelling** (dr*a*ining) dev*i*ce [aɪs]/ urethral [iː] c*a*theter[3] / bl*a*dder c*a*theter[4] • **indwelling** endotracheal [eɪk] tube / double [ʌ] J stent[5] / arterial [ɪɚ] line • self-ret*ai*ning[6] [eɪ]/ balloon-tip[7] **catheter** • **Foley** c*a*theter dr*ai*nage / ball*oo*n / ins*e*rtion tray[8] [treɪ]

Dauer-, Verweilkatheter

Doppel-J-Ureterkatheter[1] einen Dauerkatheter auswechseln[2] Harnröhrendauerkatheter[3] Blasenverweilkatheter[4] Doppel-J-Schiene/-Stent[5] selbsthaltender Katheter[6] Ballonkatheter[7] Foley-Instrumententasse[8]

20

Critical Care   CLINICAL TERMS **561**

hemofiltration [hiːmoufɪltreɪʃən] *n term*   *rel* **dialysis**[1] [daɪæləsɪs] *n term*
                                                rel **artificial** [ɪʃ] **kidney**[2] [kɪdni] *n term*
removal of toxic substances and water from the blood by diffusion via extracorporeal circulation

hemodialyzer[2] *n term* • **hemodialysis** *n* • **dialyze**[3] *v* • **dialysate**[4] *n*

» Dialysis–either hemodialysis, continuous arteriovenous [iː] hemofiltration[5], or peritoneal [iː] dialysis–may need to be instituted to treat life-threatening [e] complications. Higher sodium intake[6] is permitted for patients on peritoneal dialysis because the dialysate can be adjusted [dʒʌ] to remove the excess. Many patients with severe vesicoureteral [iː] reflux[7] [iː] ultimately require chronic dialysis[8].

Use to need/require/institute/undergo/receive [iː] **hemofiltration** • aggressive / chronic **hemodialysis** • prophylactic / continuous ambulatory peritoneal[9] (*abbr* CAPD) **dialysis** • intermittent peritoneal[10] / emergency[11] **dialysis** • hospital-based / home[12] **dialysis** • daily / maintenance[13] [eɪ]/ (long-term) renal[13] [iː] **dialysis** • **dialysis** patient[14] / support / membrane[15] • **dialysis** catheter / fluid[4] / therapy[16] / unit[17] / solution[4] [uːʃ] • hollow fiber [aɪ] or capillary[18] **dialyzer** • ultrafiltration[19] **hemodialyzer** • **artificial kidney** machine[2] / program • priming [aɪ] of[20] • wearable[21] [weərəbl] (*abbr* WAK) **artificial kidney** • intra-abdominal / calcium-free [s] **dialysate**

support hose [hoʊz] *n clin*   *syn* **TED hose** *n jar*, **anti-embolic stockings** *n term*
SED-type (sequential compression device) stockings worn to preclude edema, embolism and/or improve hemodynamics in postoperative, bedridden[1] or unconscious patients (TED = thromboembolic disease)

» Edema [iː] usually decreases with use of an elastic support hose or increased rest with the legs elevated[2] or, preferably [ɜː], lying on the side. Get her a TED hose to wear at night. These surgical stockings called TED hose will prevent pooling [uː] of blood[3] in your legs.

Use to advise [aɪ] /wear **a TED hose** • knee-length[4] [niː leŋkθ]/ thigh-high [θaɪ haɪ] **TED hose** • antiembolism[5] / pneumatic [n(j)uː-] compression[6] **hose** • elastic compression[5] / surgical support[5] **stockings**

(urinary) leg bag *n clin*   *rel* **space** or **Spenco boots**[1] [buːts] *n jar*
plastic bag tied to the leg which is connected to an indwelling bladder catheter to collect urine

» Patients who rely [aɪ] on catheters require a leg-bag for the collection of urine. Try connecting the night bag to the end of the leg bag and leaving the leg bag tap[2] open. The padded[3] support devices used to position the feet and ankles of patients who are unconscious [ʃ] for long periods to avoid the development of deformities are called space boots. My daughter's on a respirator, and her feet are in these cuffs [ʌ] they call Spenco boots.

Use to wear/attach [tʃ] /empty **a leg bag** • to keep a **leg bag** in place[4] • reusable[5] [juː]/ full **leg bag** • **leg bag** tubing / straps[6] / user • **leg bag** access opening / emptier

posey vest [poʊzi vest] *n jar*   *syn* **Houdini jacket** [dʒækɪt] *n jar* → U77-26
supportive device that fits on the patient like a sleeveless[1] sweater [e], and zips up the front with two long ties that go around the patient; it is used to prevent falls out of bed or from a wheelchair[2] [iː]

» The posey vest restricts the patient's upper body movement. Patients with suspected overdose should be restrained[3] [eɪ] with soft ankle and wrist [rɪst] restraints[4] as well as a posey vest. He needs assistance with getting in and out of bed and has to be strapped[3] in with a posey vest due to upper body weakness.

Use to apply/place sb. in **a posey vest** • **vest** restraint • body[5] **jacket** • **posey** belt[6]

eye tape [aɪ teɪp] *n term* → U141-11
tape used to close and keep moist the eyes of an unresponsive patient who has lost the blink reflex[1] [iː]

» To protect the eyes and to prevent them from drying out, eye drops[2] may be put into the eyes and eye tapes may be used to close them. Her eyes are closed with eye tape and she's hooked [ʊ] up to an ICP monitor[3]—it was all scary[4] [skeɚi] for me to see unprepared.

Hämofiltration
Dialyse[1] künstliche Niere, (Hämo)dialysator, Dialysegerät[2] dialysieren, mittels Dialyse trennen[3] Dialysat, Dialysier-, Spüllösung[4] kontinuierliche arteriovenöse Hämofiltration[5] Natriumzufuhr[6] vesikoureteraler Reflux[7] chronische Dialyse(behandlung)[8] kontinuierliche ambulante Peritonealdialyse[9] intermittierende P.[10] Notfalldialyse[11] Heimdialyse[12] Dauerdialyse[13] Dialysepatient(in)[14] Dialysemembran[15] Dialysebehandlung[16] Dialysestation[17] Hohlfaser-, Kapillardialysator[18] Ultrafiltrat-Hämodialysegerät[19] Priming (vorbereitende Spülung/ Füllung) des Dialysators[20] tragbares Dialysegerät[21]   21

elastische Stütz-/ Kompressionsstrümpfe
bettlägrig[1] hochgelagert[2] Blutstau[3] kurze Stützstrümpfe[4] elastische Stütz-/ Kompressionsstrümpfe[5] aufblasbare Kompressionsstrümpfe[6]

22

Bein-Urinbeutel
Stiefel zur Spitzfußprophylaxe[1] Hahn beim Urinbeutel[2] gepolstert[3] den Urinbeutel fixieren[4] wiederverwendbarer Urinbeutel[5] Urinbeutelfixierung[6]

23

Fixationsweste
ärmellos[1] Rollstuhl[2] angegurtet, fixiert[3] Handgelenksriemen, -gurte[4] Zwangsjacke[5] Bauchgurt[6]

24

Lidverschlusspflaster
Blinzel-, Kornealreflex[1] Augentropfen[2] Hirndruckmonitor, intrakranielle Druckmesssonde[3] schrecklich, schlimm[4]

25

Unit 126 Surgical Treatment

Related Units: 127 Operative Techniques, 129 Plastic Surgery, 131 Surgical Suite, 132 Surgical Instruments, 134 Perioperative Management, 137 Sutures, 139 Asepsis, 140 Wound Healing, 141 Fracture Management

operate on *v phr term*

performing surgery in a patient [eɪʃ] with the help of instruments in order to remove or repair damaged tissue

operation[1] *n term & clin* • **(in)operable**[2] *adj* • **preoperated** *adj*

» The patient should be operated on immediately following *chest x-ray*[3]. *Resuscitation*[4] [SAS] is continued as the patient is being operated on. Complications occur in approximately 2% of all people operated on for *biliary tract disease*[5]. The prognosis is good if the patient is operated on in the early stages of the illness.

Use **to operate on the** heart [ɑː]/ leg • to undergo[6]/be subjected to/perform[7]/postpone[8]/schedule[9] [sk||ʃedjuːl]/ **an operation** • chest-wall / hip / gynecologic [ɡaɪnə||dʒɪnɪ-] / major[10] [eɪdʒ] **operation** • open[11] / high-risk / repeat[12] [iː]/ second-look[13] / prolonged **operation** • **preoperated** abdomen[14] • **(in)operable** tumor / lesion • newly **operated** patient[15]

> **Note:** Mark the difference between *to operate*[16] *(e.g. a machine)* and *to operate on* (e.g. a patient). The preposition must not be dropped, also in the passive.

operative *adj term*   *syn* **operating, surgical** [sɜːrdʒɪkəl] *adj term*

pre/ postoperative *adj term* • **intra/ perioperative** *adj*

» When fever [iː] appears after the second postoperative day, we ought [ɒːt] to reconsider[1] the diagnosis. This kind of hematoma [iː] requires operative intervention[2].

Use **operative** field[3] / site[4] / time / approach[5] [-oʊtʃ]/ risk / scar[6] / management or treatment / mortality rate / permit[7] / wound [uː] • **operating** room[8] (*abbr* OR) or BE theatre[8] (*abbr* OT)/ (micro)scope / table[9] / team • **preoperative** evaluation / history[10] / hospital stay / fasting[11] • **preoperative** diagnosis / management[12] / workup[13] / counseling [aʊ]/ cessation [s] of smoking • **postoperative** pain / course[14] [ɔː]/ period / day 2 / care[15] / followup[16] • **intraoperative** findings[17] [aɪ]/ evaluation / monitoring[18]

surgery [sɜːrdʒəri] *n term & clin*

(i) operative treatment
(ii) in BE the room where a doctor or dentist sees and treats patients

surgeon[1] *n* • **surgical** *adj* •
electro-/ micro-/ **cryosurgery**[2] [kraɪoʊ-] *n term*

» In the hands of an experienced surgeon the operative mortality rate should approach zero[3] [zɪəroʊ]. This problem demands immediate surgical attention[4].

Use minor[5] / major / elective[6] / emergency[7] [ɜːrdʒ]/ radical / exploratory[8] **surgery** • corrective / abdominal / hand / day[9] / plastic / palliative **surgery** • general / vascular[10] /assistant **surgeon** • **surgical** treatment / candidate / margin[11] [dʒ]/ center / ward[12] [ɔː]/ case / condition / correction / excision[13] / outcome[14]

(surgical *or* **operative) procedure** [prəsiːdʒər] *n term*
 syn **technique** [tekniːk] *n term*

specific type of surgery the steps and maneuvers [uː] of which are more or less standardized

technical [k] *adj* • **technically** *adv*

» The awake patient may experience cough[1] [kɒf] during the procedure. The key factor for achieving optimal healing [iː] after operation is good surgical technique. Many cases of healing failure[2] [feɪljər] are due to technical errors.

Use adjunctive[3] [dʒʌ] / invasive [eɪ] / dental / termination / staged [eɪdʒ]/ two-stage[4] / salvage[5] [sælvɪdʒ]/ V-Y[6] / staging[7] **procedure** • laser [eɪ] / closed[8] / irrigation / childbirth[9] **technique** • **technically** feasible[10] [iː]

---

operieren

Operation, chir. Eingriff[1] (nicht) operierbar, (in)operabel[2] Thorax-Röntgen[3] Reanimation[4] Gallenerkrankung[5] s. einer Op. unterziehen[6] Op. durchführen[7] Op. verschieben[8] Op. ansetzen[9] großer Eingriff[10] offenchir. Eingriff[11] Reoperation[12] (diagnost.) Zweiteingriff, Second-look-Operation[13] voroperiertes Abdomen[14] frischoperierte(r) Patient(in)[15] bedienen[16]

1

operativ, Operations-, chirurgisch

sollten überdenken[1] chir. Eingriff[2] Operationsfeld[3] Operationssitus[4] operativer Zugang[5] Operationsnarbe[6] Operationseinwilligung[7] Operationssaal, OP[8] OP-Tisch[9] präop. Anamnese[10] präop. Nahrungskarenz[11] Operationsvorbereitung[12] präop. Anamnese u. Diagnostik[13] postop. Verlauf[14] p. Nachsorge[15] p. Nachuntersuchung[16] intraop. Befund[17] intraop. Überwachung[18]

2

(i) Chirurgie, chir. Eingriff
(ii) Ordination, Praxis

Chirurg(in), Operateur(in)[1] Kryochirurgie[2] bei Null liegen[3] chir. Behandlung[4] kleiner chir. Eingriff[5] Wahl-, Elektiveingriff[6] Not(fall)op.[7] explorative Op.[8] op. Eingriff i. einer Tagesklinik[9] Gefäßchirurg(in)[10] chir. Schnittrand[11] chir. Station[12] op. Entfernung[13] Operationsergebnis[14]

3

Operation(stechnik), operative(s) Verfahren/ Methode

Husten[1] schlechte (Ver)heilung[2] unterstützende Maßnahme[3] zweizeitige Op.[4] organ-/ lebensrettender Eingriff[5] V-Y Plastik[6] Staging-Operation[7] nicht invasives Verfahren[8] Entbindungstechnik[9] technisch durchführbar[10]

4

Surgical Treatment | CLINICAL TERMS 563

elective adj term

opposite **emergency** [ɜːrdʒ], **urgent**[1] [ɜːrdʒᵊnt] adj → U6-18

an elective procedure is one that can be scheduled without any pressure of time

» Elective surgical repair is indicated to prevent complications. There is no need for an urgent or emergency operation.

Use **elective** procedure[2] / treatment / case / resection / left colectomy / abortion [-ɔːrʃᵊn]/ dental surgery • **emergency** situation[3] / consultation / measures[4] [eʒ]/ room[5] (abbr ER) / ward / department[5] / physician[6] [fɪzɪʃᵊn] / treatment / surgical care / amputation[7] • in (case of) an[8] / medical **emergency** • on an **emergency** basis • **urgent** attention / admission[9] / evaluation[10] / referral[11] / intervention / transfusion / laparotomy

elektiv, zum Zeitpunkt der Wahl
Not(falls)-[1] Wahl-, Elektiveingriff[2] Notfall[3] Notmaßnahmen[4] Notaufnahme(zimmer, -station)[5] Notarzt, -ärztin[6] Notamputation[7] im Notfall[8] Notfallaufnahme[9] dringende Abklärung[10] dringende Überweisung[11]
5

(surgical) approach [əprəʊtʃ] n term

sim **access**[1] [ækses], **route**[2] [uː‖aʊ] n term

specific anatomic dissection by which access is gained[3] [eɪ] to the operative field

approach[4] v • (in)accessible[5] adj • accessibility n

» The left chest approach affords[6] limited access to the esophagus [ɪsɒːf-]. The laparoscopic approach provides good access with low morbidity. Submandibular abscesses are best approached through an incision 2 cm below the inferior [ɪɚ] border of the mandible. An extraperitoneal approach via the flank is preferred for upper retroperitoneal and perirenal [iː] lesions [iːʒ].

Use combined / lateral / transpalatal **approach** • to gain[3]/allow (for) or provide[7]/have/ limit[8] **access to** • operative / vascular / intravenous[9] [iː]/ limited / easy / good / wide[10] **access** • **access** route[1] • surgically **(in)accessible** areas • easily **accessible**

Note: Access (the right, privilege or possibility to enter or make contact) and approach (the way or route of entering or doing something) are clearly different in usage and meaning. Also do not confuse accessible and accessory[11].

Operationsweg, operativer Zugang
Zugang(sweg)[1] Zugangsweg, -art[2] Zugang erlangen[3] s. nähern, herangehen an[4] (un)zugänglich[5] ermöglicht[6] Zugang ermöglichen[7] Z. beschränken[8] venöser Z.[9] breiter Zugang[10] zusätzlich, Hilfs-[11]
6

(surgical) exposure [ɪkspəʊʒɚ] n term

the extent to which the operative field is visualized[1] [ʒ], accessible and provides sufficient [ɪʃ] working space[2]

expose[3] v term • (un)exposed[4] adj

» The hepatic flexure [kʃ] may have to be mobilized to expose the duodenum. The tissue must be either retracted upward[5] or divided to allow for adequate exposure of the trachea [treɪkɪə].

Use to achieve[6]/allow for or permit[7] **adequate exposure** • good / wide **exposure**

Freipräparierung, Freilegung, Darstellung
dargestellt[1] genügend Arbeitsraum[2] freilegen, -präparieren[3] (nicht) freiliegend[4] n. oben gezogen[5] ausreichend darstellen[6] e. ausreichende Darst. ermöglichen[7]
7

landmark n term

a distinctive site[1] or anatomic feature[2] [fiːtʃɚ] used by surgeons to facilitate[3] orientation in the operative field

» Use the brachial [eɪk] artery as a landmark. All landmarks were obliterated[4] by the swelling.

Use anatomic **landmark** • to locate[5]/find/identify/visualize[6] [ʒ]/lose **landmarks**

Orientierungs-, Bezugspunkt
markante Stelle[1] anatomische Struktur[2] erleichtern[3] verdeckt[4] Orientierungspunkte lokalisieren[5] Orientierungspunkte darstellen[6]
8

incise [ɪnsaɪz] v term

sim **circumcise**[1] v term, **cut**[2] v jar

opposite **excise**[3] v term

cutting the skin or a tissue layer with a scalpel to open up the operative field

incision[4] [ɪnsɪʒᵊn] n term • incisional adj • incised adj

» The lung is incised over the cyst [sɪst]. A transverse incision[5] overlying the upper trachea is developed by separating[6] the muscles of the neck in the midline.

Use to make[7]/deepen **an incision** (into) • the **incision** is carried[8] / developed[8] / continued[8] along the ... • **incise** and drain[9] • flank[10] / skin[11] (crease) [iː] / Pfannenstiel / stab[12] **incision** • circular[13] / midline[14] / muscle-splitting[15] / relaxing[16] / inadvertent[17] / Z-shaped **incision** • **incisional** biopsy[18] [aɪ] / hernia[19] / drainage [-ɪdʒ]

inzidieren, ein-, aufschneiden
um-, beschneiden[1] (ein-, durch-, ab)schneiden[2] exzidieren, (her)ausschneiden[3] Eröffnung, (Ein)schnitt, Inzision[4] Querinzision[5] (Durch)trennen, Spalten[6] inzidieren, einschneiden[7] Schnitt w. geführt[8] inzidieren u. (durch Drain) ableiten[9] Flankenschnitt[10] Hautschnitt[11] Stichinzision[12] kreisförm./ zirkulärer Schnitt[13] Medianschnitt[14] Wechselschnitt[15] Entlastungsschnitt[16] unbeabsichtigter Einschnitt[17] Probeexzision[18] Narbenbruch[19]
9

CLINICAL TERMS — Surgical Treatment

section [sekʃən] v & n term   syn **sectio** n term, **sectiones** pl
(i) making an incision
(ii) a cut surface[1]
(iii) segmentation of an anatomic structure
cross-section[2] n term • **cross-sectional** adj

» The transverse carpal ligament had to be sectioned to liberate[3] the median [iː] nerve. The vessel was doubly [ʌ] ligated [aɪ] and sectioned[4].

Use histologic / frozen[5] / serial[6] [ɪɚ] / cesarean[7] [sɪzeəɪən] **section** • **cross-sectional** area[8] / plane [eɪ]/ view / image / study • nerve **sectioning**

---

inzidieren, durchtrennen; Schnitt(fläche), Abschnitt
Schnittfläche[1] Querschnitt[2] freilegen[3] zwischen zwei Ligaturen abgesetzt[4] Gefrierschnitt[5] Serienschnitt[6] Kaiserschnitt, Schnittentbindung, Sectio caesarea[7] Querschnittfläche[8]

10

---

exploration n term   sim **inspection**[1] n term
(i) surgical or clinical examination for diagnostic purposes
(ii) initial step in some surgical procedures performed either for gaining orientation or strategy planning
(re)explore v term • **inspect** v • **exploratory**[2] adj term

» Arteriography or surgical exploration of the neck is recommended for penetrating injuries. Exploratory laparotomy[3] or laparoscopy is advisable [aɪz] if all investigations prove inconclusive[4].

Use vaginal [dʒ] / manual[5] / visual [ʒ] **exploration** • **exploratory** incision / biopsy / puncture[6] [pʌŋktʃɚ]/ surgery • **to explore** the depth of the wound[7]

Exploration, Untersuchung, Austastung
Inspektion, Prüfung, Kontrolle[1] explorativ, Probe-[2] Explorativ-, Probelaparotomie[3] ergebnislos[4] Austastung[5] Probepunktion[6] Tiefe einer Wunde feststellen[7]

11

---

dissect v term   sim **free**[1], **liberate**[1] v jar
to cut and separate body tissues in surgery, autopsy [ɒː], or for anatomic study
dissection[2] n term • **dissect free**[1] v phr • **dissector**[3] n

» The surrounding tissue is carefully dissected away from[4] the tumor. The dissection was carried upward to the axilla. The ureter was freed and wrapped [r] in omentum.

Use **dissected** bluntly[5] [ʌ]/ off or free from[6] • extensive / meticulous[7] / gentle [dʒ]/ sharp[8] / blunt / finger / (lymph) node[9] / subintimal **dissection** • **dissecting** microscope[10] [aɪ]/ aneurysm[11] [jɚ]

---

präparieren, sezieren
freilegen, -präparieren[1] Präparation, (Dis)sektion, Obduktion[2] Prosektor; Dissektor[3] abpräpariert[4] stumpf präpariert[5] frei-, abpräpariert[6] exakte Präparation[7] scharfe P.[8] Lymphadenektomie, -knotendissektion[9] Präpariermikroskop[10] Aneurysma dissecans[11]

12

---

preserve v   syn **spare** [speɚ] v, **leave** [iː] **intact** v phr
(i) to maintain in normal, healthy or unchanged condition
(ii) not affected by dissection or disease
preservation[1] n • **(life-)preserving**[2] adj • **organ-sparing**[3] adj term

» Every effort must be made to preserve antegrade ejaculation [ɪdʒæk-]. The technique spares[4] the patient a second anesthetic [e].

Use **to preserve** viable [aɪə] tissue / normal weight-bearing [weɪt]/ full range of motion[5] / the duodenum • functional[6] **preservation** • **preservation of** length / health[7] / position sense[8] / arterial [ɪɚ] blood flow • nerve-**sparing** procedure[9]

---

erhalten, schonen
Erhaltung, Konservierung[1] (lebens)erhaltend[2] organerhaltend[3] erspart[4] volle Beweglichkeit erhalten[5] Funktionserhaltung[6] Gesunderhaltung[7] E. der Lageempfindung[8] nerv(en)schonender Eingriff[9]

13

---

transect v term   sim **bisect**[1] [aɪ] v term **divide**[2], **split**[2] v
to incise and separate transversely, esp. vessels and tubes; sever[3] is also used for traumatic amputations
transection[4] n term • **division**[5] [dɪvɪʒən] n

» Take care not to transect the vein or puncture its outer wall. Stapled [eɪ] transection[6] has replaced the older technique of direct suture [suːtʃɚ] ligation[7] of varices [æ].

Use partial [ʃ] / gastric[8] / ureteral / line of **transection** • **split**-thickness graft[9] / tongue[10] [tʌŋ]/ rectus muscle [mʌsl] • transverse / longitudinal[11] / cell **division**

(quer) durchtrennen, -schneiden
(zwei)teilen[1] trennen, spalten[2] abtrennen[3] Querschnitt; Durchtrennung[4] Durchtrennung[5] Absetzen zw. Klammerreihen[6] Umstechungsligatur[7] Absetzen d. Magens[8] Spalthauttransplantat[9] Spaltzunge[10] Längsteilung[11]

14

---

resection n term   syn **excision, extirpation** n term → U127-1
surgical removal of an organ or part of an organ
resect[1] v term • **resectable** adj • **excise**[2] [aɪz] v • **extirpate**[3] v

» Obstructing lesions of the left colon are best managed by resection. Nonsurgical modalities should be reserved for patients who are poor candidates for resection.

Use rib / wedge[4] [dʒ] / segmental / transurethral[5] / (en) bloc(k)[6] / complete / curative [kjʊɚ] **resection** • **resectable** lesion [liːʒən] or tumor[7] • **resected** tissue / tonsil / aneurysm • **resecto**scope[8]

Resektion, Exzision, Entfernung
resezieren, entfernen[1] exzidieren[2] exstirpieren[3] Keilresektion[4] transurethrale R.[5] En-Bloc R.[6] resezierbarer Tumor[7] Resektoskop[8]

15

Unit 127 Basic Operative Techniques

Related Units: 126 Surgical Treatment, 137 Sutures, 132 Surgical Instruments, 129 Plastic & Reconstructive Surgery, 128 Minimally Invasive Surgery

-ectomy *comb* → U126-15

word ending for terms referring to surgical removal or excision [eksɪʒən]
gastrectomy[1] *n term* • **gingivectomy** [dʒɪndʒ-] *n* • **appendectomy**[2] *n*

-ektomie, -exzision, -entfernung
Gastrektomie, totale op. Magenentfernung[1] Appendektomie[2]   1

-(o)tomy *comb* → U126-9f

word ending for terms denoting surgical incision
laparotomy[1] *n term* • **osteotomy** *n* • **cystotomy**[2] *n* • **episiotomy**[3] *n term*

-tomie, -schnitt, -eröffnung
Laparotomie, Bauchschnitt, -höhleneröffnung[1] Zystotomie, Blasenschnitt[2] Episiotomie, (Scheiden)dammschnitt[3]   2

-stomy *comb*

word ending denoting surgical creation of an opening into a hollow viscus[1] [sk] or the artificial [ɪʃ] communication[2] (also termed stoma[3]) between two spaces
colostomy[4] *n term* • **antrostomy**[5] *n* • **tracheostomy**[6] *n*

-stomie, -stoma, op. angelegte Öffnung
Hohlorgan[1] künstl. Verbindung[2] Stoma[3] Kolostomie[4] Kieferhöhlenfensterung[5] Tracheostoma[6]   3

-plasty *comb* → U129-3

word ending denoting surgical repair or restoration of form and/or function of organs or structures
angioplasty[1] [dʒ] *n term* • **arthroplasty**[2] *n* • **rhinoplasty** [aɪ] *n* • **genioplasty**[3] *n term*

-plastik, -ersatz, op. Korrektur
Angioplastie, Gefäßplastik[1] Arthroplastik, Gelenkersatz[2] Genio-, Kinnplastik, Kinnkorrektur[3]

> **Note:** Many (in BE practically all) terms with the above endings carry the main stress on the vowel that comes before the ending, e.g. anatomy, ...ostomy, ...oplasty.

4

microsurgery [aɪ] *n term*   *sim* **microneurosurgery** [ʊɚ] *n term*

dissection of tiny[1] [aɪ] structures using a micromanipulator[2] or laser beam [iː] and magnifying lenses
microsurgical(ly) *adj/adv term* • **microsurgeon**[3] *n* • **microdissect** [ɪ‖aɪ] *v*
» A laser microprobe[4] was used to vaporize[5] [eɪ] a minute[1] [maɪnuːt] area of tissue.
se laser / pituitary[6] / transsphenoidal **microsurgery** • **microsurgical** technique / excision / conization[7]

Mikrochirurgie
winzig[1] Mikromanipulator[2] Mikrochirurg(in)[3] Mikrosonde[4] verdampfen, vaporisieren[5] mikrochirurg. Eingriff a. d. Hypophyse[6] mikrochir. Konisation[7]   5

operating microscope *n term*   *sim* **magnifying loupe** [luːp] *or* **lens**[1] *n term*

specially designed loupe for surgery on delicate[2] structures not visible to the naked [neɪkɪd] eye[3]
magnification[4] *n term* • **magnify** *v*
» An operating microscope with two viewing binocular [baɪ-] lenses[5] and swaged-on needles[6] [swedʒd] of 60 μm are required.
se 3-fold / 8 times / with×100[7] **magnification**

Operationsmikroskop
Lupe(nbrille)[1] zarte[2] mit bloßem Auge[3] Vergrößerung[4] Binokularmikroskop[5] atraumatische Nadeln[6] bei 100facher Vergrößerung[7]   6

laser [leɪzɚ] *n term*

acronym for light amplification by stimulated emission of radiation; a high-energy narrow beam of nondivergent[1] [-daɪvɜːrdʒənt] electromagnetic radiation highly useful in microsurgery (eye, spine [aɪ], brain surgery)
lase[2] [leɪz] *v term* • **laser-assisted** *adj*
» Carcinoma in situ can be eradicated[3] by cauterization, cryotherapy, laser vaporization[4], cone biopsy [aɪ], or electrosurgical loop [uː] excision[5].
se **laser** surgery / ablation / excision / photocoagulation / iridotomy • **laser** probe[6] [oʊ]/ tip • beam[7] [iː]/ energy • argon / krypton [ɪ]/ Nd:YAG[8] / helium-neon [iː]/ carbon dioxide [aɪ]/ dye[9] [daɪ]/ thermal / endoscopic **laser**

Laser
nicht divergierend[1] lasern[2] völlig beseitigt[3] Laservaporisation[4] Abtragung mittels Diathermieschlinge[5] Lasersonde[6] Laserstrahl[7] Neodym-YAG-Laser[8] Farbstofflaser[9]   7

CLINICAL TERMS

cryosurgery [kraɪoʊ-] *n term*
  operating on tissue subjected to extreme cold, e.g. by application of carbon dioxide
  cryoprobe[1] *n term* • **cryocautery**[2] [ɒː] *n* • **cryothalamotomy** *n*
» The hemorrhoids [e] were necrosed by freezing with a cryoprobe of liquid nitrogen[3] [naɪtrədʒən].
Use **cryosurgery** technique • **cryosurgical** destruction • **cryo**therapy[4]

electrosurgery *n term*   sim **diathermy**[1] [daɪəθɜːrmi],
    electrocautery[2] [ɒː] *n term*
  searing[3] [ɪə] and coagulating tissue using high-voltage current[4] [ɜː] from an electrosurgical unit
  electrosurgical *adj term* • **cauterize**[5] *v term* • **cautery**[6] *n* • **cauterization** *n*
» The bleeding site was cauterized. Mild degrees of cervicitis [sɜːrvɪsaɪtɪs] can be treated by office cauterization[7], either chemically with 20% silver nitrate [aɪ] solution on cotton-tipped applicators, by light radial cauterization with nasal-tipped thermal cautery or electrocautery.
Use **electrosurgical** pencil[8] • monopolar / bipolar [aɪ] • shortwave[9] **diathermy** • **diathermy** tips • snare[10] [eə] / cold[11] / wet field / steam [iː] / gas **cautery** • **cautery** knife [naɪf] / probe • **electro**resection / desiccation

  Note: The terms *cauterization, cautery, cauterize,* and *cauter* also include the application of heat and caustic[12] [ɒː] substances to destroy tissue.

hemostasis [hiːmoʊsteɪsɪs] *n term, BE* **haemostasis**
    rel **coagulation**[1] *n term*
  stopping a bleeding either by surgical means or physiologically by blood clotting[1]
  coagulate[2] *v term* • **coagulator**[3] *n* • **electrocoagulation** *n* •
  hemostatic[4] [iː] *adj & n term* • **hemostat**[5] *n*
» In this patient who has a coagulation disorder[6] adequate hemostasis was achieved with fibrin [faɪbrɪn] glue[7] [gluː].
Use to ascertain or ensure[8] / accomplish[9] / maintain **hemostasis** • bipolar **coagulation** • **coagulated** bleeding points / tissue • **hemostatic** clamp[5] / material

snare [sneə] *n term*
  wire [aɪ] loop[1] [uː] used for removing small pedunculated[2] [ʌ] growths, e.g. polyps [ɪ]
  (en)snare[3] *v term* • **(electro)cautery snare**[4] *n*
» Polypectomy with a snare can be performed safely through the endoscope. Small polyps can be snared during endoscopy.
Use polypectomy[5] **snare** • **snare** technique

conization [kɒːn-‖koʊnɪzeɪʃən] *n term*
    sim **electroconization**[1], **cone biopsy**[2] [aɪ] *n term*
  electrosurgical or cold knife [naɪf] resection of a cone[3] of tissue, e.g from the uterine [aɪ‖ɪ] cervix
» Superficial conization may be necessary to rule out invasion. Cervical cone biopsy[4] alone is therapeutic [pjuː] in many cases.
Use cold[5] / laser / excisional[6] / cervical[4] **conization** • **cone biopsy** specimen[2]

ablation [æbleɪʃən] *n term*
    sim **extirpation**[1], **resection**[2] *n term*
  surgical detachment[3] [tʃ], removal[4] or destruction of tissue
  cryoablation[5] *n term* • **ablate**[6] [eɪ] *v* • **ablative** *adj* • **resect** *v*
» Many supraventricular arrhythmias [ɪ] can be definitely treated by catheter ablation[7] procedures.
Use laser[8] / tissue / catheter-induced[7] / radio frequency **ablation** • **ablative** techniques / surgery

  Note: The term *ablation* is also used for hormone withdrawal therapy[9] but not for the pathologic detachment[3] of tissue layers (e.g. ablatio placentae or retinae).

Basic Operative Techniques

Kryochirurgie
Kryo-, Kältesonde[1] Kryokauter[2] flüssiger Stickstoff[3] Kryotherapie, Kältebehandlung[4]

8

Elektrochirurgie
Diathermie[1] Elektrokauterisation[2] verschorfen[3] Strom[4] kauterisieren[5] Kauter; Kauterisation[6] ambulante Kauterisation[7] Diathermiestift[8] Kurzwellendiathermie[9] Schlingenelektrode[10] Kryokauter(isation)[11] ätzend, kaustisch[12]

9

Hämostase, Blutstillung
Koagulation, Blutgerinnung[1] koagulieren; gerinnen[2] Koagulator[3] blutstillend; Hämostyptikum, -statikum[4] Gefäßklemme[5] Koagulopathie, Gerinnungsstörung[6] Fibrinkleber[7] Hämostase sicherstellen[8] Hämostase erreichen[9]

10

Schlinge
Drahtschlinge[1] gestielt[2] anschlingen[3] elektr. Schlinge, Diathermieschlinge[4] Polypenschlinge[5]

11

Konisation
Elektrokonisation[1] Konusbiopsie[2] Konus, Kegel[3] Zervix-, Portiokonisation[4] Schnittkonisation[5] Exzisionskonisation[6]

12

Ablatio, Abtragung
op. Entfernung, Exstirpation[1] Resektion[2] Ablösung[3] Entfernung[4] Kryo-, Kälteablation[5] abtragen, amputieren[6] Katheterablation[7] Laserablation[8] Hormonentzugstherapie[9]

13

Basic Operative Techniques
CLINICAL TERMS 567

fulguration [fʌlgjəreɪʃən] *n term*   *syn* **electrodesiccation** *n term*
destruction of tissue with sparks[1] from a high-frequency current applied with needle electrodes
fulgurate[2] *v term* • **fulgurating**[3] *adj*
» Patients who are poor surgical risks may be palliated[4] with laser fulguration of the tumor mass.
Use direct / indirect / endoscopic / intraurethral [iː] *fulguration*

Elektrodesikkation, Fulguration
Funken[1] elektrochir. zerstören[2] blitzartig[3] Erleichterung verschaffen[4]
14

vaporize [veɪpəˌaɪz] *vt term*   *sim* **evaporate**[1] [æ] *vt/i term*
converting a solid or liquid into vapor[2] [eɪ]; in surgery it mostly refers to tissue ablation by laser
vaporization[3] [eɪ] *n term* • **evaporation**[4] [æ] *n*
» Using the endoscopic laser part of the tumor was vaporized to relieve her symptoms.

(Gewebe) verdampfen, vaporisieren
verdampfen; sich verflüchtigen[1] Dampf[2] Vaporisation[3] Verdampfung, -dunstung[4]
15

suction [sʌkʃən] *n & v term*   *syn* **aspiration, suctioning** *n term*
  rel **tap(ping)**[1] [æ] *n term*
(n) in surgery, a procedure to aspirate fluids or material from the body through a tube or needle
aspirate[2] [-eɪt] *v term* • **aspirator**[3] *n* • **aspirate**[4] *n* [-ət] • **tap**[5] *v*
» Suction evacuates[6] blood or serum [ɪɚ] accumulating[7] in the wound [uː] bed. The aspirate was heavily [e] contaminated. The diagnosis may be established[8] by fine-needle aspiration[9] and a cytologic [saɪ-] study of abnormal nodes. The material was aspirated for culture. The suction tube was plugged[10] [ʌ] with secretions.
Use to apply[2] *suction* • *suction* device[3] [dɪvaɪs]/ drainage[11] [-ɪdʒ]/ curettage[12] • (naso)gastric / low intermittent / continuous[11] *suction* • blood / bronchial [k] / foreign body[13] (*abbr* FB) / synovial [aɪ] fluid *aspiration* • *aspiration* biopsy[14] / gastric *aspirate* • suprapubic (bladder) / lumbar [ʌ] *or* spinal[15] [aɪ]/ (non)traumatic / bloody / dry *tap*

> Note: *Aspiration* and *aspirate* can refer to the withdrawal of fluids or tissue specimens as well as to accidental inhalation of fluids or FBs into the respiratory tract.

Aspiration, Saug-; aspirieren, absaugen
Punktion[1] ab-, ansaugen, aspirieren[2] Saugvorrichtung, Aspirator[3] Punktionsflüssigkeit, Aspirat[4] punktieren; perkutieren[5] entfernen[6] ansammeln[7] gesichert[8] Feinnadelbiopsie[9] verlegt[10] Saugdrainage[11] Saugkürettage[12] Fremdkörperaspiration[13] Saug- Aspirationsbiopsie[14] Lumbalpunktion[15]
16

irrigation *n term* → U118-10; U140-15
to flush[1] [ʌ] and wash out a cavity or wound [uː] with fluid
irrigate[2] *v term* • **irrigator**[3] *n* • **irrigating** *adj*
» Irrigate the eyes gently[4] with sterile [sterɪl‖aɪl] saline [eɪ] solution. Then the wound was debrided[5] [aɪ] and irrigated again. In this case the use of jet irrigators[6] for cleaning teeth is not advisable.
Use daily / throat [oʊ]/ mouth / copious[7] [oʊ]/ whole gut[8] [ʌ] *irrigation* • bladder[9] / pressure[10] / (non)sterile / local antibiotic *irrigation* • *irrigating* solution[11]

Irrigation, (Aus-, Durch)spülung
(durch)spülen[1] (aus-, durch)spülen[2] Irrigator[3] vorsichtig[4] Wundränder w. angefrischt[5] Munddusche[6] gründliche Spülung[7] Darmspülung[8] Blasenspülung[9] Druckspülung[10] Spülflüssigkeit[11]   17

(venous) [iː] **cutdown** *n term*   *sim* **vene-** *or* **venipuncture**[1] [e‖iː] *n term*
small incision to gain access to[2] a subcutaneous vein [eɪ] for insertion of a needle or cannula
» Three IV lines are necessary for severe shock, two of them being large-bore catheters[3] placed by cutdown. An intraluminal device was implanted via a jugular [dʒʌgjələ˞] *venous cutdown*[4]. Allow enough time for the first venipuncture to clot, or leave the catheter in place to occlude the venipuncture site.
Use saphenous [iː] vein / antecubital fossa **cutdown** • emergency / jugular[4] *venous cutdown* • *cutdown* site / procedure / approach / tray • routine / subclavian[5] [eɪ] *venipuncture* • *venipuncture* technique

Venae sectio, Venenschnitt, Phlebotomie
Venenpunktion[1] Zugang schaffen[2] großlumige Katheter[3] Jugulariseröffnung[4] Subklaviapunktion[5]
18

catheter [kæθətɚ] *n term*   *syn* **line** [aɪ] *n clin & jar* → U125-7
tube used for insertion into blood vessels, urinary passages or body cavities to inject or withdraw[1] [ɔː] fluids, keep the passage patent[2] [eɪ], etc.
catheterization[3] *n term* • **catheterize**[4] *v*
» The stricture [strɪktʃɚ] may be dilated[5] [aɪ] with a transhepatic balloon-tipped [uː] catheter[6]. Change the arterial [ɪɚ] line sites every 3–4 days. This requires insertion of a radial or femoral [e] arterial line.
Use to insert[7]/introduce[7]/place[7]/remove *a catheter* • ureteral[8] / cardiac[9] / suction / central venous[10] / subclavian / balloon[6] *catheter* • pigtail[11] / olive tip / indwelling[12] / Swan-Ganz / Foley / angio*catheter* • *catheter* tip[13] / site / dilatation / fever[14] [iː] • intermittent[15] / self-*catheterization*

Katheter
absaugen, aspirieren[1] offen, durchgängig[2] Katheterisierung[3] katheterisieren[4] (auf)gedehnt[5] Ballonkatheter[6] K. legen/ einführen[7] Harnleiter-, Ureterkatheter[8] Herzk.[9] zentraler Venenk.[10] Doppel-J-K.[11] Dauer-, Verweilkatheter[12] Katheterspitze[13] Katheterfieber[14] intermittierende Katheterisierung[15]
19

568 CLINICAL TERMS — Minimally Invasive Surgery

stent *n & v term*

thin, mostly catheter-like metal or resin tube[1] for supporting healing vessels or ducts and ensure [-ʃʊəʳ] patency[2] or for holding surgical grafts[3] in place

stenting *n term*

» A stent of minimally reactive foreign material, (e.g. Silastic) that fills the lumen above and below the intubated area should be placed.

Use to insert/place **a stent** • urethral[4] [iː]/ bile [aɪ] duct [ʌ]/ intraoral • percutaneous[5] [eɪ]/ self-expandable[6] (metal) / occluded[7] **stent** • **stent** tube / placement / plugging[7] [ʌ]

Stent, Splint, Endoprothese; e. Stent platzieren, schienen
Kunststoffschlauch[1] offenhalten[2] Transplantate[3] Harnröhrenstent[4] perkutaner Stent[5] selbstexpandierender Stent[6] Stentverlegung[7]

20

Unit 128 Minimally Invasive Surgery
Related Units: 126 Surgical Treatment, 127 Operative Techniques, 133 Laparoscopic Equipment, 132 Surgical Instruments, 138 Endoscopic Suturing

minimally invasive [eɪ] **surgery** [sɜːrdʒəri] *n term*
  syn **minimal access** [æksɛs] **surgery** *n term espBE*

endoscopic surgical approach to the abdomen, pelvis, chest, and spine minimizing the trauma of access without compromising operative exposure[1] by use of a scope[2] [oʊ] and specially designed instruments

invasiveness[3] *n term* • **(in)accessible**[4] *adj* • **access**[5] *n* → U126-6

» There is a growing body of international data that demonstrate the safety and efficacy of minimally invasive cardiac surgery. The minimal invasiveness of these procedures helps reduce perioperative morbidity and shorten the length of hospitalization and convalescence[6].

Use **minimally invasive** procedure[7] [siː]/ treatment options / laparoscopic surgery • **minimally invasive** technique [k]/ colon resection[8] • **minimally invasive** thoracic [æs]/ heart / coronary bypass / spine or spinal [aɪ]/ disk[9] / parathyroid [aɪ] **surgery** • to gain[10]/permit or afford[11]/provide[11] **access** to the kidney • easy / straight-forward[12] **access** • direct[12] / laparoscopic / three-port[13] **access** • minimal access suturing[14] • freely **accessible**

---

minimal invasive Chirurgie, MIC, Schlüssellochchirurgie
Darstellung, Freilegung[1] Endoskop[2] Invasivität[3] (un)zugänglich[4] (operativer) Zugang(sweg)[5] Rekonvaleszenz[6] minimal invasives Verfahren[7] minimal invasive Kolonresektion/ Kolonteilentfernung[8] minimal invasive Bandscheibenoperation[9] Zugang erlangen[10] Zugang ermöglichen[11] direkter Zugang[12] Zugang über 3 Trokare[13] minimal invasive Nahttechnik[14]

1

---

endoscopic surgery *n term* → U118-11
  rel **video(-assisted) endoscopic technique**[1] [tekniːk] *n term*

operative procedures inside body cavities or tubes (e.g. the GI tract[2], lungs, etc.) via an endoscope supplied with a working channel[3], suction [ʌ] tip[4], biopsy brush[5], electrode tip for cauterization [ɔː], etc.

endoscopy[6] *n term* • **endoscopist**[7] *n* • **endoscope** *n* • **-scopy** *comb*

» An undefined pulmonary mass was assessed and resected by video-assisted thoracic [æs] surgery[8] (abbr VATS). Videoendoscopic techniques are used in surgery of the esophagus.

Use rigid[9] [dʒ]/ flexible / fiberoptic[10] **endoscope** • video[1]/ broncho(fibro) [k]/ arthro/ gastroscopy • colono/ sigmoido/ cystoscopy • under **endoscopic** guidance [aɪ] or control[11] • **endoscopic** inspection / approach [-oʊtʃ]/ intervention / evaluation[12] • **endoscopic** tools[13] / biopsy [aɪ] findings[14] [aɪ]/ followup / visualization[15] • **endoscopic** drainage [dreɪnɪdʒ]/ (laser) therapy / ultrasonography[16] • **endoscopic** sinus [aɪ] surgery / polypectomy[17] • **endoscopic** retrograde cholangiopancreatography[18] [koʊl-] (*abbr* ERCP)/ sclerotherapy[19] • **endoscopically** placed / removed / guided[11] [aɪ] • pre**endoscopic** manometry • video**endoscopic** resectability

---

endoskopische Chirurgie
Videoendoskopie[1] Verdauungstrakt[2] Arbeitskanal[3] Absaugvorrichtung[4] Biopsiebürste[5] Endoskopie[6] Endoskopeur[7] videogestützte Thoraxchirurgie[8] starres Endoskop[9] Fiber(endo)skop[10] unter endoskop. Kontrolle/ Sicht[11] endoskop. Abklärung[12] endoskop. Instrumente[13] Endoskopiebefund, endoskop. B.[14] endoskop. Darstellung[15] Endosonografie[16] endoskop. Polypektomie/ Polypenabtragung[17] endoskop. retrograde Cholangiopankreatografie[18] endoskop. Sklerosierung/ Sklerotherapie[19]

2

---

laparoscopic surgery *n term* syn **operative laparoscopy** *n*,
  opposite **open surgery**[1] *n term*

examination of the abdominal cavity and/or minimally invasive procedures with the help of a laparoscope introduced via a small abdominal incision [sɪ]; the surgical instruments are inserted [ɜː] via trocars

(laparo)scope[2] *n term* • **laparoscopist**[3] *n* • **open-surgical**[4] *adj*

» Advantages of laparoscopy over open surgery include unimpaired [eə] anatomic relationships, good visualization of abdominal structures, and low morbidity.

Use exploratory[5] / diagnostic / therapeutic [-pjuːtɪk]/ emergency[6] [ɜː] **laparoscopy** • pelvic[7] / gasless[8] / pediatric [iː]/ hand-assisted[9] **laparoscopy** • **laparoscopic** dissection[10] / approach / equipment • **laparoscopic** appendectomy • varix ligation [eɪ] • **laparoscopic** cholecystectomy[11] / hernia [ɜː] repair[12] • **laparoscopy** cart[13] [k] • beginning[14] / experienced **laparoscopist** • **open surgical** counterpart[15] [aʊ]/ procedure

---

laparoskopische Chirurgie
offene Chirurgie[1] Laparoskop[2] Laparoskopeur[3] offen-chirurgisch[4] explorative Laparoskopie[5] Notfalllaparoskopie[6] Pelviskopie[7] gaslose Laparoskopie[8] handassistierte L.[9] laparoskopische Präparation/ Dissektion[10] lap. Cholezystektomie/ Gallenblasenentfernung[11] lap. Hernioplastik[12] Instrumentenwagen f. lap. Operationen[13] Laparoskopeur i.d. Lernphase[14] offen-chirurgisches Pendant[15]

3

Minimally Invasive Surgery

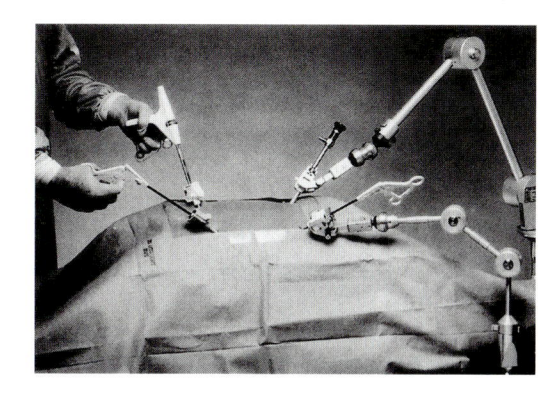

CLINICAL TERMS 569

Minimal access intra-abdominal surgery: the surgeon is supported by robotic arms which hold and maneuver the laparoscope and surgical instruments

pelvi(o)scopy *n term*   *rel* **pelviscopic surgery**[1] *n term*

(i) endoscopic visualization of the pelvis with a pelviscope[2]
(ii) minimally invasive surgery in the pelvis

» Minimally invasive surgery, utilizing pelviscopic instruments and a laser, is used to diagnose and effectively treat endometriosis, ovarian cysts, and adhesions [iːʒ] or complications of pelvic infection. With pelviscopy an open abdominal incision can be avoided, allowing the procedure to be done on an outpatient basis[3]. We have established a program to give residents[4] hands-on experience with pelviscopy.

Use diagnostic / extraperitoneal [iː]/ retroperitoneal[5] **pelviscopy** • operative[1] / laser / three-port **pelviscopy** • **pelviscopic** appendectomy / hysterectomy[6] [ɪ]/ myomectomy [aɪ] • **pelviscopic** salpingectomy [dʒe]/ tubal anastomosis[7] • **pelviscopic** ovarian surgery / colposuspension

retroperitoneoscopy [retroʊperɪtənɪːskəpi] *n term*

minimally invasive technique using a retroperitoneal approach

» Retroperitoneoscopy eliminates the need to traverse [ɜː] the peritoneal cavity[1] and thus provides a more direct and rapid access to the ureter.

Use laparoscopic operative **retroperitoneoscopy** • **retroperitoneoscopic** percutaneous ureterostomy[2] / pyeloplasty [aɪ]/ lumbar [ʌ] sympathectomy

thoracoscopy [θɔːrəkɒːskəpi] *n term*   *rel* **mediastinoscopy**[1] [miːdɪ-] *n term*

(i) inspection of the pleural [ʊə] cavity with an endoscope
(ii) minimally invasive surgery of the thorax

thoracoscopic *adj term* • **mediastino/ thoracoscope**[2] *n* • **thoraco-** *comb*

» In thoracoscopy flexible trocars are used as conduits[3] for the passage of curved instruments. Pleurodesis[4] [iː] using various abrasive techniques is also performed thoracoscopically. Mediastinoscopy permits direct biopsy of paratracheal lymph nodes without thoracotomy[5].

Use interventional[6] / video-assisted[7] **thoracoscopy** • suprasternal [ɜː]/ parasternal / subxiphoid[8] [zɪf] **mediastinoscopy** • **thoraco-abdominal** approach • **thoracoscopic** surgery / staging[9] [eɪdʒ]/ lung biopsy[10] [aɪ] • **thoracoscopic** pleurectomy / drainage / vagotomy • **thoracoscopic** wedge resection[11] / lung volume reduction • **thoraco**scope /tomy /centesis[12] [iː]

arthroscopy [ɑːrθrɒːskəpi] *n term*   *rel* **arthroscopic surgery**[1] *n term*

(i) inspection of the interior of a joint with an arthroscope[2]
(ii) minimally invasive surgery within a joint

» Arthroscopy is particularly helpful in the management of the patient with a "problem knee", i.e. significant symptoms but minimal or confusing physical findings. Arthroscopic removal of loose cartilage fragments[3] can prevent locking[4] and relieve pain.

Use knee / video **arthroscopy** • **arthroscopic** examination / lavage[5] • **arthroscopic** drainage / fenestration • **arthroscopic** debridement / synovectomy [ɪ] • **arthroscopic** knee surgery / meniscectomy[6] [se]

Pelviskopie
pelviskopischer Eingriff[1] Pelviskop[2] ambulant[3] Assistenzärzte in Fachausbildung[4] retroperitoneale Pelviskopie[5] pelviskopische Hysterektomie/ Uterusentfernung[6] pelviskopische Tubenplastik[7]

Retroperitoneoskopie
Zugang quer durch d. Peritonealraum[1] retroperitoneoskop. perkutane Ureterostomie/ Harnleiterfistelung[2]

Thorakoskopie
Mediastinoskopie[1] Thorakoskop[2] Zugang[3] Pleurodese[4] Thorakotomie, Brustkorberöffnung[5] therapeut. Thorakoskopie[6] videogestützte Thorakoskopie[7] subxiphoidale Mediastinoskopie[8] thorakoskop. Tumorstaging[9] thorakoskop. Lungenbiopsie[10] thorakoskop. Keilresektion[11] Thorakozentese, Pleurapunktion[12]

Arthroskopie
arthroskop. Operation[1] Arthroskop[2] Knorpelfragmente[3] Gelenkblockierung[4] arthroskop. Spülung[5] arthroskop. Meniskusteilresektion[6]

570 CLINICAL TERMS — Minimally Invasive Surgery

pelvitrainer n term

training device [dɪvaɪs] with which handling laparoscopic instruments can be simulated

» Before embarking [ɑː] on[1] laparoscopic operations the learning laparoscopist can train the basic maneuvers [uː] with the pelvitrainer.

Use **pelvitrainer** exercises[2] • closed[3] **pelvitrainer**

pneumoperitoneum [n(j)uːmoʊ-] n term

rel **pneumoretroperitoneum**[1] [iː] n term

insufflation of air or gas into the peritoneal cavity to create working space for laparoscopic procedures

» In laparoscopy, the peritoneum is tented away[2] anteriorly by the pneumoperitoneum. Congenital [dʒe] diaphragmatic [daɪə-] defects may be responsible for pneumothorax complicating the creation of artificial pneumoperitoneum for laparoscopy.

Use to establish[3]/obtain or create[3] **a pneumoperitoneum** • to maintain[4]/release[5] [iː] **the pneumoperitoneum** • CO₂ / low-pressure / loss of[6] **pneumoperitoneum**

insufflate [ɪnsəfleɪt] v term

rel **instill**[1] v, opposite **desufflate**[2] [iː] v term

to introduce gas or air into a body cavity, e.g. to establish a pneumoperitoneum for laparoscopy

insufflation n term • **instillation** n • **insufflant** or **insufflating gas**[3] n

» In certain patients the sheer [ʃɪə] mass[4] of the anterior abdominal wall may necessitate the maintenance of higher insufflation pressures to obtain an adequate working space.

Use **to in-**/**desufflate** the abdomen / air / CO₂ • rapid / safe / gas[5] **insufflation** • pressurized[6] **insufflant** • **insufflation** gas[3] / pressure[7] / valve[8] [æ]/ tubing[9] [(j)uː] • **insufflation** channel [tʃ]/ needle / anesthesia[10] [iːʒ] • **to instill** a local anesthetic [e]/ ointment[11] [ɔɪ]/ eye drops • direct / local / intraperitoneal / drug[12] / rapid / rectal[13] **instillation**

aspiration-irrigation system n term   syn **suction-irrigation system** n term

tube or channel in the scope that serves to flush[1] [ʌ] and suction the operative site, cavity or wound [uː]

irrigate[1] v term • suction[2] [sʌkʃ°n] v • aspirate[2] v → U127-16f

» Some optical systems are provided with an integral irrigation channel. This hook electrode[3] has a suction/irrigation channel that allows for suction/irrigation, coagulation and transection[4]. Following inspection the area was copiously [oʊ] irrigated[5] with saline[6] [eɪ] through the laparoscope.

Use **irrigation** system / fluid[7] • **aspiration** channel / tubing / unit[8] / device[8] [aɪ] • integrated suction-**irrigation** device[9] • continuous **suction** • pool **suction** tip[10]

(initial) stab incision [ɪnsɪʒ°n] n term

syn **initial puncture** [ʌ] n term → U127-18

surgical puncture of the abdominal wall in laparoscopy to be able to place the first trocar, insert the scope, and gain access to the operative field which carries a considerable risk of injury to underlying viscera [s]

» Laparoscopic procedures are commonly initiated by a stab incision. After the initial stab incision a towel [taʊ°l] clip[1] is placed on either side of the umbilicus to elevate[2] the abdominal wall.

Use to make a **stab incision** • to re**puncture** the abdominal wall[3] • blind[4] **puncture**

minilaparotomy n term

rel **laparotomy**[1] n term or **lap**[1] n jar → U127-2

small incision into the peritoneum to lower the risk of injury to underlying viscera during trocar placement

laparotomize[2] [læpərɒtəmaɪz] v term

» Instead of the initial stab incision a minilaparotomy can be performed for the placement of the first trocar, which greatly reduces the risk of inadvertent[3] [ɜː] injury during this maneuver [uː].

Pelvitrainer
beginnen mit[1] Übungen am Pelvitrainer[2] Pelvitrainer ohne direkte Sicht[3]

8

Pneumoperitoneum
Pneumoretroperitoneum[1] an-, abgehoben[2] ein Pneumoperitoneum einleiten/ anlegen/ setzen[3] das P. aufrechterhalten[4] das Pneumoperitoneum ablassen[5] Gasverlust aus dem Pneumoperitoneum[6]

9

insufflieren, einblasen
instillieren, einträufeln[1] (Gas) ablassen[2] Insufflationsgas[3] allein die Masse[4] Gasinsufflation[5] unter Druck stehendes Insufflationsgas[6] Insufflationsdruck[7] Insufflationsventil[8] Insufflationsschlauch[9] Insufflationsanästhesie[10] Salbe instillieren[11] Arzneimittelinstillation[12] rektale Instillation[13]

10

Spül-Saugvorrichtung
spülen, auswaschen[1] absaugen[2] Diathermiehäkchen[3] Durchtrennung[4] gründlich gespült[5] Salzlösung[6] Spülflüssigkeit[7] Absaugvorrichtung[8] integrierte Saug-Spülvorrichtung[9] Bienenkorbsauger[10]

11

Primärpunktion, Stichinzision
Tuchklemme[1] anheben[2] die Bauchdecke neuerlich durchstoßen[3] Blindpunktion[4]

12

Minilaparotomie
Laparotomie[1] laparotomieren[2] versehentlich[3]

13

Minimally Invasive Surgery   CLINICAL TERMS **571**

balloon [uː] **dissection** n term → U126-12

                              sim **balloon dila(ta)tion**[1] n term

distending a body cavity with a gas or fluid-filled inflatable device, e.g. to create sufficient working space

» *Balloon dissection was introduced to gain access to the retroperitoneum. Balloon dilatation was performed using a latex condom ligated to the fixation grip of a 10-mm trocar sheath.*

Use videoendoscopically guided hydraulic[2] [aɪ] **balloon dissection** • dissection **balloon** • minimal / meticulous[3] / blunt[4] [ʌ] **dissection** •/ finger[5] / ultrasonic / hydro[6]- or aqua**dissection** • *(dilating) balloon* dissection technique / catheter[7]

adhesiolysis [ædhiːzɪˈɒlɪsɪs] n term → U134-10   syn **adhesiotomy** n term

releasing [iː] adhesions, esp. in the previously [iː] operated abdomen

adhesion[1] [ədˈhiːʒən] n term • **adhere to**[2] [ædˈhɪə] v • **adhesive**[3] [iː] adj

» *Exclude the presence of adhesions at the planned site of initial trocar placement. Once a primary telescopic port and secondary working port have been inserted, relatively extensive adhesiolysis may be safely undertaken to facilitate[4] subsequent* [ʌ] *port positioning.*

Use to release or lyse[5] [laɪs]/circumvent[6] **adhesions** • abdominal wall / peritoneal **adhesions** • fibrous [aɪ]/ intestinal[7] pre-existing **adhesions** • postoperative[8] / tubal[9] / extensive[10] **adhesions** • **adhesion** formation[11] • **adhesive** peritonitis [aɪ]/ intestinal obstruction[12] [ʌ]/ bands[13]

morcellation [mɔːrsəˈleɪʃən] n term

fragmentation of resected tissue or organs (e.g. a tumor) for removal in small pieces

morcellate[1] v term • **morcellator**[2] n → U133-17

» *The tumor-bearing [eə] kidney was not morcellated, but removed in toto in an entrapment sack[3]. The use of a retrieval bag[3] generally requires tissue morcellation, which has the disadvantage of rendering pathologic assessment of the specimen impossible.*

Use **to morcellate** manually • tissue[4] [tɪʃjuː/tɪs-/] mechanical [k]/ digital[5] **morcellation** • **morcellation** process

organ retrieval [rɪˈtriːvəl] n term → U126-15; U133-16

evacuation of a resected organ or specimen via a laparoscopic port, usually after fragmentation inside an organ bag[1]

retrieve[2] [rɪˈtriːv] v

» *Now the nodal [oʊ] package[3] is dissected free[4] and can be retrieved. Cautious [ɒː] retrieval of the resected specimen in an entrapment sack is essential to avoid tumor seeding[5] [iː].*

Use specimen [es]/ tissue / stone basket[6] **retrieval** • **retrieval** sack[1]

resurfacing [rɪˈsɜːrfɪsɪŋ] n term   syn **exiting, closure** [ˈkloʊʒə] n term

closing surgical access wounds (e.g. port sites) with sutures [suːtʃ]; this is usually done in layers

» *For resurfacing the peritoneum the ends of the running suture[1], which need not withstand[2] much stress, may also be secured [kjʊə] with a clip[3]. To ensure a watertight* [taɪt] *closure, three interrupted [ʌ] sutures[4] are placed through the areas of the vas between each of the four quadrant [ɒː] stitches [ɪ].*

Use epithelial [iː] **resurfacing** • **exiting** the abdomen • layered[5] [eɪ]/ two-layer / skin / suture[6] **closure** • tape[7] / water-tight[8] / immediate [iː] **closure**

conversion [ɜː] **to laparotomy** or **open surgery** phr term

emergency [ɜː] procedure [iː] in the event of a major complication during laparoscopic surgery

convert [ɜː] v

» *If emergency laparotomy is necessary the trocar should be left in place to guide the surgeon to the site of injury. In one patient the procedure had to be converted to open laparotomy.*

Use to perform/undergo/warrant [ɔː] or require or call for[1] **laparotomy** • **laparotomy** set[2] • emergency[3] / exploratory[4] / immediate / urgent [ɜː] **laparotomy**

Ballondissektion
Ballondilatation[1] videoendoskop. gesteuerte hydraulische Ballondissektion[2] sorgfältiges (Ab)präparieren[3] stumpfe(s) Abpräparieren/ Präparation[4] Fingerpräparation[5] Aquadissektion[6] Ballonkatheter[7]

14

Adhäsiolyse
Adhäsion, Verwachsung, Verklebung[1] kleben/ haften an[2] klebend, haftend, adhäsiv[3] erleichtern[4] Adhäsionen lösen[5] A. umgehen[6] Darmadhäsionen[7] postoperative A.[8] Tubenverklebungen[9] ausgedehnte Verwachsungen[10] Adhäsionsbildung[11] Obstruktion d. Darmes durch Adhäsionen[12] Verwachsungsstränge, Briden[13]

15

Morcellement, Zerstückelung
zerkleinern, zerstückeln[1] Morcellator, Gewebezerkleinerer[2] Endobag, Organsack, -beutel, Bergungssack[3] Gewebezerkleinerung[4] digitales Morcellement[5]

16

Organbergung
Organ(bergungs)sack, -beutel, Bergungssack[1] bergen, entfernen[2] Lymphknotenpaket[3] abpräpariert[4] Tumordissemination, -verschleppung[5] Entfernung mit Steinkörbchen[6]

17

operativer Verschluss
fortlaufende Naht[1] standhalten[2] mit Klip versorgen/ ligieren[3] Einzelknopfnähte[4] schichtweiser Verschluss[5] Nahtverschluss[6] Verschluss m. Klebeband[7] wasserdichter Verschluss[8]

18

eine laparoskop. Operation offen-chirurgisch fortsetzen
Laparotomie erfordern[1] Laparotomiebesteck[2] Notfalllaparotomie[3] Probelaparotomie[4]

19

Unit 129 Plastic & Reconstructive Surgery
Related Units: 130 Grafts & Flaps, 126 Surgical Treatment, 127 Operative Techniques

reconstruction n term   syn **restoration** n, **repair** [rɪpeɚ] n & v term
surgical [sɜːrdʒɪkᵊl] restoration of diseased or damaged tissues
reconstruct[1] v term • **restore** v • **reconstructive** adj • **restorative** adj
» *Primary attempts to reconstruct the stellate [stɛleɪt] wound[2] [uː] with local flaps failed[3].*
Use facial [feɪʃᵊl]/ scalp / nasal [eɪ]/ ear[4] / lip / eyelid / digital[5] [dʒ] **reconstruction** • primary / secondary / one-stage / cosmetic / postablative[6] [eɪ] **reconstruction** • bladder / hernia[7] [ɜː] **repair** • **reconstructive** mammoplasty[8]

-plastik, Rekonstruktion, Wiederherstellung
wiederherstellen, rekonstruieren[1] sternförmige Wunde[2] fehlschlagen, nicht gelingen[3] Ohr-, Otoplastik[4] Fingerplastik[5] R. nach Amputation[6] Hernioplastik[7] Mammaaufbau-(plastik)[8]
                                    1

surgical correction n term   sim **replacement**[1], **rehabilitation**[2] n term
surgical procedure [prəsiːdʒɚ] that repairs or modifies traumatized [ɒː], diseased or undesirable body structures
correct[3] v term • **corrective** adj
» *Correction may be done with simultaneous reduction or augmentation[4] [ɒː]. The defect was corrected by splenectomy. The use of implants as a foundation for prosthetic [e] replacement of missing teeth has become widespread. Geriatric [dʒ] amputees[5] [iː] were rarely rehabilitated.*
Use elective **correction** • surgically **correctable** • **corrective** osteotomy[6] / procedure / repair / measures [eʒ] • **replacement** bone[7] / graft / prosthesis [iː] / tooth • stomach[8] [k] **replacement** • facial / cardiac / oral or dental[9] / bladder / prosthetic[10] **rehabilitation** • auditory [ɒː]/ speech / (psycho)social [saɪk]/ partial / postoperative **rehabilitation** • **rehabilitation** center

operative Korrektur
Ersatz, Prothese[1] Wiederherstellung[2] beheben, korrigieren[3] Aufbau, Vergrößerung[4] Amputierte[5] Korrekturosteotomie[6] Ersatzknochen[7] Ersatzmagenbildung[8] orale Rehabilitation[9] prothetische Versorgung, Protheseneinbau[10]
                                    2

plastic surgery n term   syn **reconstructive surgery** n term
surgical specialty or procedure concerned with the restoration, construction, reconstruction, or improvement in the shape and appearance [ɪɚ] of missing, defective, damaged, or mishappen[1] body structures
-plasty[2] comb • **neo-** [niːoʊ] comb → U127-4
» *Neither plastic surgery nor prosthetic rehabilitation has provided a good cosmetic outcome[3].*
Use **plastic** surgeon[4] / closure [ʒ]/ repair / revision [ɪʒ] • esthetic[5] **plastic surgery** • angio[6] [ændʒɪə-]/ arthro/ oto[7]/ gastro/ stricture/ Z-[8]/ valvulo**plasty**[9] • **neo**bladder[10]

Wiederherstellungs-, plastische Chirurgie
missgebildet[1] -plastik, -plastie[2] kosmetisches Ergebnis[3] plast. Chirurg(in)[4] ästhethische plastische Chirurgie[5] Angioplastie[6] Ohrplastik[7] Z-Plastik[8] Valvuloplastie[9] Neoblase[10]
                                    3

fashion [fæʃⁿ] v & n term   syn **shape, create** [ieɪ], **tailor** [eɪ],   sim **remodel**[1] v term
preshaped[2] [iː] adj term • reshaped adj
» *The flap is fashioned to avoid tension[3] [ʃ] when the wound is closed. The surgically created defects were too large and did not heal without membrane coverage [kʌvɚɪdʒ].*
Use **fashioned** flap • **in a(n)** similar / stepwise[4] / retrograde / sequential[4] [-ʃᵊl]/ routine / piecemeal[5] / uncontrolled / tongue-like [tʌŋ] **fashion** • poorly[6] **fashioned** • arrow[7] / wedge[8] [dʒ] / cone [oʊ]/ funnel[9] [ʌ]/ horseshoe[10] / oval / loop[11] [uː]/ L-/ acorn[12] [eɪkɔːrn]/ irregularly **shaped** • **to create** space[13] / tunnels [ʌ]/ windows / grooves[14] [uː]/ smooth [uː] surfaces / tension / flaps

formen, zurechtschneiden; Form, Art, Weise
umformen[1] vorgeformt[2] Zug vermeiden[3] schrittweise[4] Stück für Stück; stückweise[5] ungünstig geformt[6] pfeilförmig[7] keilf.[8] trichterf.[9] hufeisenf.[10] schlingen-, schleifenf.[11] eichelförmig[12] Platz schaffen[13] Furchen bilden[14]
                                    4

coaptation [koʊæpteɪʃⁿ] n term → U137-5
joining[1] or approximating[2] two structures, e.g. the lips of a wound or nerve stumps[3] [ʌ], etc.
coapt[4] v term • **coapted** adj
» *Intraoperative factors such as proper coaptation, hemostasis [eɪ], and suture line tension[5] determine the outcome[6]. The soft tissues were coapted using the sutures of choice[7].*
Use nerve / skin **coaptation** • **coaptation** suture[8]

Adaptation, Wiedervereinigung
Verbinden[1] Adaptieren[2] Stümpfe[3] adaptieren, annähern[4] Nahtspannung[5] sind entscheidend für das Ergebnis[6] Nahtmaterial der Wahl[7] Adaptationsnaht[8]
                                    5

Plastic & Reconstructive Surgery   CLINICAL TERMS **573**

anastomosis n term, pl -ses   sim **shunt**[1] [ʌ] n term → U36-14

(i) surgical union of two hollow or tubular structures (ii) connection created by surgery, trauma, or disease between normally separate spaces or organs (iii) natural communication[2] between two blood vessels

an**a**stomose[3] v term • anasto**mo**tic adj • **a**nastomosed adj

» Recurrent [ɜː] anastomotic stricture[4] [-tʃɚ] is usually due to gastroesophageal [-dʒiːəl] reflux.
Use arteriovenous [iː]/ portocaval [eɪ]/ cavopulmonary / microvascular / primary / side-to-side[5] / end-to-side / end-to-end / Roux-en-Y[6] / stapled[7] [eɪ] **anastomosis** • **anastomotic** disruption / leakage[8] [liːkɪdʒ]/ failure[9] / patency[10] [eɪ]/ ulcer [ʌlsɚ]

-pexy comb   sim **suspension**[1] n term → U141-3

combining form referring to lifting or fixation by surgical suturing

» Contralateral orchiopexy[2] [k] is necessary because of the high incidence of recurrent torsion.
Use orchi(d)o[2] [k]/ masto/ gastro**pexy** • uterine [ɪ‖aɪ] **suspension** • suspension wire[3] [waɪɚ]/ sling[4]

plication [plaɪkeɪʃn] n term   sim **intussusception**[1] [sɛ],
                                         invagination[1] [-væd ʒ-] n term → U85-12

procedure involving folding, ensheathing[2] [iːð], or inserting a structure within itself or another

plicated adj term • **plica**[3] n pl -ae [plaɪsiː‖kiː] • **intussusceptum**[4] n

» There are signs of epithelial [iː] invagination. Vaginal [dʒ] hysterectomy with anterior colporrhaphy[5] (urethral [iː] suspension, plication of the bladder neck[6], and cystocele [-siːl] repair) was indicated.
Use fundal[7] [ʌ] **plication** • **plication** suture[8] • **invaginated** ileum / epithelium

skin coverage [kʌvɚɪdʒ] n term

spreading [e] skin grafts or flaps over exposed or denuded[1] [uː] areas

(un)cover[2] [ʌ] v term • covering[3] n • covered[4] adj

» Obtaining good skin coverage for these burns[5] will be difficult. The flap was repeatedly checked to ensure [ɪnʃʊɚ] coverage of the area without tension.
Use soft tissue / bone / flap[6] / wound[7] [uː] **coverage**

  Note: The term coverage is also used as a synonym for protection, e.g. in health insurance coverage[8] or antibiotic coverage[9].

tissue [tɪʃuː‖tɪsjuː] **expansion** [æ] n term

                             rel **line of minimum tension**[1] n term

» Tissue expansion techniques should be reserved for complicated cases of decubitus ulcers[2]. An incision placed parallel to the skin lines of minimal tension will yield[3] [jiːld] the best results.
Use **tissue** expander[4] • controlled **tissue expansion**

elevate v term   syn **raise** [reɪz] v term → U64-16

(i) to dissect skin, etc. away from the underlying[1] [aɪ] tissue
(ii) increase
(iii) lift up to a higher position

elev**a**tion[2] n term

» The middle line of the incision in a Z-plasty is made along the line of greatest tension, and triangular [aɪ] flaps are raised and transposed[3]. Seromas often follow operations that involve elevation of skin flaps.
Use **raised** margins[4] / pressure[5] / plaques[6] [plæks] • leg[7] / bite[8]-**raising** • surgical / shoulder / BP[9] / leg[7] **elevation**

harvest v & n term   sim **explant**[1] v term

(v) to collect tissue from a donor site[2] [aɪ] for transplantation

harvesting n term • **explant**[3] n • **explantation**[4] n

» Bone marrow[5] was harvested by repeated aspiration from the posterior iliac [ɪliæk] crest[6].
Use graft[7] / bone **harvest** • **harvest** organ[8] / tissue / technique / to be **harvested** from

Anastomose
Shunt, A-V Anastomose[1] Verbindung[2] anastomosieren[3] Anastomosenverengung[4] Seit-zu-Seit-A.[5] Roux-Y Operation[6] geklammerte A.[7] Anastomosenleck[8] Anastomoseninsuffizienz[9] Anastomosendurchgängigkeit[10]

6

-fixation, -anheftung, -pexie
Aufhängung, Suspension[1] Orchi(do)pexie[2] Suspensionsdraht[3] Suspensionsschlinge[4]

7

Plikation
Intussuszeption, Invagination, Einstülpung[1] Einscheiden[2] Falte, Plica[3] Intussuszeptum, Invaginat[4] vordere Kolporrhaphie[5] Blasenhals[6] Funduseinstülpung[7] Duplikatur-, Verstärkungsnaht[8]

8

Hautdeckung
freigelegt[1] bedecken, überziehen; bloßlegen[2] Hülle, Deckschicht[3] gedeckt[4] Verbrennungen[5] Lappendeckung[6] Wundabdeckung[7] Krankenversicherung[8] antibiotische Abschirmung[9]

9

Gewebedehnung
Linie d. geringsten Spannung[1] Dekubitalgeschwüre[2] bringen, erzielen[3] Gewebeexpander[4]

10

(an)heben
darunterliegend[1] Heben; Erhöhung; Erhebung[2] transponiert[3] angehobene Ränder[4] erhöhter Druck[5] erhabene Plaque[6] Hochlagern d. Beins[7] Bisshebung[8] Erhöhung d. Blutdrucks[9]

11

(Gewebe) entnehmen; Entnahme
explantieren[1] Spenderareal[2] Explantat[3] Explantation[4] Knochenmark[5] Darmbeinkamm, Crista iliaca[6] Transplantatentnahme[7] entnommenes Organ[8]   12

CLINICAL TERMS — Plastic & Reconstructive Surgery

transpose v term   syn **transfer** v term

to remove tissues or organs from their anatomic position and graft them to a different site
transposable adj term • **transfer**[1] n • **transposition(ing)**[1] n

» The LD muscle[2] [s] can be detached[3] [tʃ] from its origin and transposed to the anterior chest. Avoidance of folding or kinking[4], transposition with minimal tension, and proper length-to-width ratio [reɪʃ(ɪ)oʊ] are key considerations in the technique of elevation and transposition of flaps.

Use toe-to-thumb[5] [θʌm]/ nerve / embryo / free-tissue[6] **transfer** • **transposition** flap[7] / of the great vessels • nerve[8] **transpositioning**

verpflanzen, übertragen
Verpflanzung, Übertragung[1]
M. latissimus dorsi[2] abgelöst[3]
Knicken[4] Nicoladoni-Operation[5]
freie Gewebeübertragung[6]
Transpositionslappen[7]
Nervtransposition[8]

13

---

transplant [trænˈsplænt] v, [trænˈs-] n term → U130-1

(v) to transfer or graft tissues from a donor [oʊ] to a recipient
(n) tissue or organ which is transposed
(**re**[1]/ **auto**[2])**transplantation** n term • (**non**)**transplanted**[3] adj
• (**pre / post**)**transplant** adj

» Dialysis [daɪˈælɪsɪs] and renal transplantation afford[4] excellent survival in patients with ESRD[5]. Carefully selected patients in their 60s have undergone transplantation successfully.

Use **transplant** surgery / recipient[6] / patient / candidate / failure[7] / center / setting / kidney[8] • to undergo **transplantation** • **transplant-related** morbidity / complications • organ / heart / renal or kidney / bone marrow[9] (abbr BMT) / single lung **transplant(ation)** • **pretransplant** transfusion / management • **posttransplant** course / immunosuppression • (**non**)**transplant** patient / organ / tissue / kidney

transplantieren; Transplantat
Retransplantation[1] Autotransplantation[2] transplantiert[3] ermöglichen[4] End-stage renal disease, terminale Niereninsuffizienz[5] Transplantatempfänger(in)[6] Transplantatversagen[7] Transplantationsniere[8] Knochenmarktransplantation[9]

14

---

donor [doʊnɚ] n term   opposite **recipient**[1] [rɪsɪpiənt] n term → U136-9

organism from whom blood, tissue, or an organ is taken for transfusion or transplantation
donate[2] v term • **donation**[3] n • **donated** adj

» Adequate amounts of donor bone were harvested from the iliac crest. Excess tissue[4] (dog ears) at the recipient site must be meticulously trimmed[5].

Use **donor** site[6] [aɪ]/ area / tissue / screening / selection[7] / marrow / hospital / (pledge [dʒ]) card[8] • heart / matched[9] / (HLA-identical) sibling[10] / universal[11] **donor** • tissue / (directed) blood / (vital or cadaver) organ[12] / replacement **donation** • **recipient** site[13]

Spender(in)
Empfänger(in)[1] spenden[2] Spende[3] überschüssiges Gewebe[4] sorgfältig zurechtgeschnitten[5] Spenderstelle[6] Spenderauswahl[7] Organspenderausweis[8] passende(r) Spender(in)[9] genetisch idente(r) Geschwisterspender(in)[10] Universalspender(in)[11] Leichenorganspende[12] Empfängerareal[13]

15

---

autologous [-gəs] or **autogenous** [ɒːdʒ] adj term   rel **homologous** or **homogenous**[1] adj term

referring to a transplant in which the donor and recipient areas are in the same individual

» The previously[2] harvested chips of autologous bone[3] were grafted into two implant sites.

Use **autologous** graft[4] / tissue • **homologous** insemination / serum [ɪɚ] jaundice[5]

autogen, autolog
allogen, homolog[1] vorher[2] autologe Knochenspäne[3] Autograft[4]
homologer Serumikterus[5]

16

---

cadaver [æ] **donor** n term   opposite **living donor**[1] n term

a brain dead donor[2] from whom viable[3] [vaɪəbl] tissue or organs are harvested
cadaveric adj term

» These recipients of cadaver organs[4] do not benefit from[5] pretransplant transfusions.

Use **cadaver** kidney[6] (donor) / (homo)graft • **cadaveric** transplantation • (non)related[7] **living donor** • non-heart beating[8] **cadaver donor**

Leichenspender(in)
Lebendspender(in)[1] hirntote(r) Spender(in)[2] lebensfähig[3] Leichenorgane[4] profitieren, Nutzen ziehen[5] Leichenniere[6] verwandte(r) Lebendspender(in)[7] Sp. m. Herz-Kreislaufstillstand[8]

17

---

implant [ɪmplænt] v [ɪmplænt] n term

(n) biocompatible material grafted into tissues, e.g. in orthopedics [iː] metallic or plastic devices [aɪ] employed in joint reconstruction (v) to place such a device
implantation[1] n term • **implantable** adj • **implanted** adj

» An intraocular lens is routinely implanted at the time of cataract surgery. Complications include hematoma [iː], infection, and exposure, deflation[2] or rupture of the silicone implant. If implantation is delayed, patients with complete heart block require temporary pacing[3] [peɪsɪŋ].

Use **implant** material / surgeon / denture[4] [-tʃɚ] • orbital / intraocular / penile [iː]/ cochlear [k] **implant** • inflatable[5] [eɪ]/ breast / silicone gel [dʒ] bag / radioactive seed [iː] **implant** • surgical / endosseous or endosteal[6] / magnetic / submucosal **implant** • subperiosteal / supraperiosteal / triplant **implant** • **implantation** site • pacemaker[7] [eɪs]/ post or pin[8] **implantation** • **implantable** hearing device[9] • **implanted** defibrillator [ɪ]

implantieren; Implantat
Implantation[1] Kollabieren[2] Schrittmacherunterstützung[3] implantatgestützte Zahnprothese[4] aufblasbares Implantat[5] enossales Implantat[6] Schrittmacherimplantation[7] Stiftimplantation[8] implantierbares Hörgerät[9]

18

Grafts & Flaps   CLINICAL TERMS 575

augmentation [ɒːgməntɛɪʃᵊn] *n term*   *opposite* **reduction¹** [ʌ] *n term*
  increasing structures in size, shape, or volume by means of grafts or implants
  augmented *adj term* • **augment** *v* • **reduce** [uː] *v*
» Some patients require operative augmentation of bladder capacity by enterocysto-
  plasty².
Use *augmentation* procedure / mammoplasty³ / material • patch⁴ / bone⁵ / allo-
  plastic⁶ / alveolar [ɪə]/ maxillary sinus⁷ [aɪ] *augmentation* • **augmented** breast

Vergrößerung, Augmentation
Reduktion, Verkleinerung¹ Blasen-
darmplastik² Mammaaugmenta-
tionsplastik³ Patch-Plastik⁴
Knochenaufbau⁵ alloplast. Organ-
vergrößerung/ Augmentation⁶ Sinusboden-Augmentation, Sinus-
lift-Operation⁷   19

(bio)inert [baɪoʊɪnɜːrt] *adj term*   *sim* **biocompatible¹** *adj term*
  (i) not bioactive and therefore biocompatible implant material
  (ii) chemicals without active properties², e.g. inert gases³
  (iii) drugs without pharmacologic or therapeutic [juː] effect
  biocompatibility *n term* • **bioacceptance⁴** *n* • **inertness** *n*
» A biologically inert membrane that does not allow penetration of cells was placed.
Use *inert* (plastic) materials • implant⁵ *biocompatibility*

biologisch inaktiv, bioinert
biokompatibel¹ Eigenschaften²
Edelgase³ reizlose Akzeptanz/ Ge-
webeannahme⁴ Gewebeverträg-
lichkeit/ Biokompatibilität d.
Implantats⁵
                                  20

Unit 130 Grafts & Flaps
Related Units: **129** Plastic & Reconstructive Surgery

graft [æ∥BE ɑː] *v & n term*   *syn* **transplant** *v & n term* → U129-14
  (v) to transplant
  (n) free (unattached [tʃ]) tissue, organ or synthetics for transplantation
  grafting *n term* • **pre/ postgraft** *adj* • **engraft¹** *v* •
  engraftment *n term*
» Avascular [eɪ] wound [uː] beds will not accept skin grafts unless viable [vaɪəbl]
  periosteum or perichondrium [kɒː] is present. The grafted area may shrink² to 50%
  of its original size and both the skin graft and the surrounding tissue may become
  distorted³.
Use to transfer/serve as/repair with⁴/perform⁴/place⁵/accept *a graft* • tendon / corneal / fascia [ʃ]/ nerve / fat / fascicular [sɪ]/ (osteo)periosteal / mucosal⁶ / omental
  graft • anastomosed / bypass / vascularized [aɪ]/ poorly functioning / avascular
  graft • augmentation⁷ [ɒː]/ autodermic⁸ [ɜː]/ hyperplastic / cable / composite⁹
  graft • implantation / infusion / H-/ orthotopic / syngeneic¹⁰ [sɪndʒəniːɪk]/ ca-
  daver¹¹ *graft* • *graft* take¹² / placement / bed¹³ / conduit / anastomosis / closure
  [ʒ] rate / infection / destruction¹⁴ • *pregraft* suppression • *postgraft* contractions
  • **ungrafted** body surface

  > Note: Although *graft* and *transplant* are often used synonymously, *graft* is
  > usually preferred with autologous *transplantation* of tissues while *transplant*
  > is more often used with allogeneic organ transplantation.

**transplantieren, verpflanzen;
Transplantat**
einpflanzen¹ schrumpfen²
verschoben³ Transplantation
durchführen⁴ Transplantat ein-/
aufbringen⁵ Schleimhauttransplan-
tat⁶ Augmentationsplastik⁷ autogenes Hauttransplantat⁸ composite
graft (Haut & Knorpel)⁹ syngenes
T.¹⁰ Leichentransplantat¹¹ Trans-
plantatannahme¹² Transplantat-
bett¹³ Transplantatzerstörung¹⁴
                                   1

autogeneic [-dʒəniːɪk] **graft** *or* **autograft** *n term*
         syn **autologous** [-gəs] *or* **autoplastic graft** *or* **autotransplant** *n term*
  tissue or an organ transferred by grafting into a new position in the body of the same individual
» It is prudent¹ to preserve² the saphenous [fiː] vein as a venous [iː] autograft for
  vascular repair.
Use spleen³ [iː]/ adrenal [iː]/ bone marrow⁴ [æ] *autotransplantation* • conjunctival⁵
  [kəndʒʌŋktaɪvᵊl] *autografting* • **autologous** transplantation / tissue / material /
  bone marrow

**Autotransplantat, autogenes/
autologes Transplantat**
sinnvoll¹ erhalten² autologe Milz-
transplantation³ autologe
Knochenmarktransplantation⁴ autologe Bindehauttransplantation⁵
                                   2

allogeneic graft *or* **allograft** *n term*
         syn **homologous** *or* **homoplastic graft** *or* **homograft** *n term*
  a graft transplanted between genetically nonidentical individuals of the same species [spiːʃiːz]
» This tends to recur [rɪkɜːr] in renal allografts but without marked impairment¹ [eɚ]
  of graft function.
Use *allogeneic* bone marrow transplantation / transplant recipients² • (un)related³
  allogeneic transplants • *allograft* survival enhancement⁴ / reaction

**Allograft, -transplantat,
allogenes Transplantat**
Beeinträchtigung¹ allogene Trans-
plantatempfänger² allogene Ver-
wandtentransplantate³ Verlängerung der Überlebenszeit eines
Allotransplantats⁴   3

CLINICAL TERMS — Grafts & Flaps

syngeneic [ɪ] **graft** *or* **isogeneic** [aɪ] **graft** *n term*   *syn* **isologous** *or* **isoplastic graft** *n term*

tissue or organ transplanted between genetically identical individuals (i.e. identical or monozygotic [zaɪ] twins¹)

» When donor and recipient are identical twins, there is no antigenic [dʒe] difference and grafts are accepted without immunosuppressive therapy.

Use twin-to-twin **graft** • **grafts** from HLA-identical siblings²

Syno-, Isotransplantat, syngenes/ isologes T.
eineiige Zwillinge¹ Transplantate von HLA-identen Zwillingen²

4

animal *or* **zooplastic** [zoʊə-] **graft** *n term*   *syn* **xenograft** [zenə‖ziːnə-], **heterograft** *or* **xenogeneic** *or* **heterologous** *or* **heteroplastic graft** *n term*

graft of tissue from an animal to a human, e.g. porcine [pɔːrsaɪn] (pig) or canine [keɪnaɪn] (dog) grafts; xenografts are tissues transferred from one species to another

» Extensive burns¹ may be temporarily covered² by a biologic dressing, e.g. a porcine xenograft which is bacteriostatic and helps control pain.

Use **heterodermic** graft³

Tier-, Xenotransplantat, xenogenes T.
großflächige Verbrennungen¹ (ab)gedeckt² heterologes Hauttransplantat³

5

skin graft *n term*   *sim* **dermal graft¹** [ɜː] *n term*

a patch² [æ] of skin transplanted from one part of the body to another, e.g. to resurface³ [ɜː] a denuded⁴ [uː] area; types of skin grafts include full-tickness⁵ (skin & subcutaneous [eɪ] tissue) and split- or partial-thickness grafts⁶ (epidermis & part of the dermis)

» Wound [uː] closure with the help of a skin graft may be contemplated⁷. If the area can be skin grafted, meshed split-thickness grafts¹³ are most effective (no collections of bacterial exudate).

Use to obtain⁸/cover with/apply/accept **a skin graft** • primary **skin graft** • cutis / epidermic⁹ / dermal-fat *or* adipodermal¹⁰ **(skin) graft** • **graft donor** depth¹¹ / site [aɪ] • pinch¹² [tʃ]/ sieve¹³ [sɪv] **graft** • free **skin grafting**

Hauttransplantat, -lappen
Dermislappen¹ Lappen² decken³ entblößt, freiliegend⁴ Vollhautlappen⁵ Spalthauttransplantat⁶ in Erwägung ziehen⁷ Hautlappen entnehmen⁸ Epidermistransplantat⁹ Hautfettgewebetranspl.¹⁰ Entnahmetiefe, Tiefe d. Entnahmestelle¹¹ Epidermisläppchen¹² Mesh-Graft¹³

6

delayed [dɪleɪd] **(skin) graft** *n term*   *opposite* **primary** [aɪ] **(skin) graft¹** *n term*

skin graft (first sutured [suːtʃəd] back to its bed) applied after several days so that healthy [e] granulations can form

» The avulsed² [ʌ] skin was completely discarded³ in favor of a delayed split-thickness skin graft.

zweizeitige(s)/ sekundäre(s) Hauttransplantat(ion)
primäre(s) H.¹ lose, traumatisiert, abgelöst² entfernt³

7

mesh(ed) [meʃt] **graft** *n term*   *syn* **accordion graft** *n term*

skin graft with multiple [ʌ] perforations which can be stretched [tʃ] to cover a larger area

» An advantage of meshed grafts is that they can be placed on an irregular, possibly contaminated wound bed¹ and will usually take². Although mesh grafts can be expanded to 9 times their original size, expansion to one and a half the unmeshed size has proved most successful.

Use **meshed** split-thickness skin graft³

Mesh-, Netztransplantat
verunreinigtes Wundbett¹ wächst meist ein² Netztransplantat³

8

cancellous [kænˈsələs] **bone graft** *n term*   *opposite* **block (bone) graft¹** *n term*

grafting of small chips² [tʃ] of spongy [spʌndʒi] bone which are packed into a bone defect, also termed filler graft

» The patient was treated with an autologous onlay corticocancellous bone graft harvested³ from the iliac crest⁴. All voids⁵ between the block bone graft and the residual⁶ mandible were packed⁷ with cancellous bone chips.

Use onlay⁸ / cortical⁹ / cranial [eɪ]/ composite / freeze-dried¹⁰ [friːz draɪd] **bone graft**

Spongiosaplastik, -transplantat
Knochenspanplastik¹ Späne² entnommen³ Beckenkamm, Crista iliaca⁴ Zwischenräume⁵ verblieben⁶ aufgefüllt⁷ Onlay-Plastik⁸ Kortikalistransplantat⁹ gefriergetrocknetes Knochentranspl.¹⁰

9

free graft *or* **flap** *n term*   *opposite* **pedicle graft** *or* **flap¹** *n term*

graft freed completely from its bed and transplanted to the recipient site without its pedicle²

» The implants were placed into free nonvascularized iliac bone grafts.

Use **free-flap** transplantation • **free** gingival³ [dʒɪndʒ-]/ bone / mucosal⁴ **graft**

freier Lappen
gestielter Lappen¹ Stiel² freies Gingivatransplantat³ freies Schleimhauttransplantat⁴

10

Grafts & Flaps CLINICAL TERMS **577**

(pedicle) flap n term   syn **pedicle(d) graft** n term

tongue [tʌŋ] of skin and subcutaneous tissue (sometimes including muscle) only partially removed from its underlying tissue for transplantation; sustained[1] [eɪ] by a blood-carrying stem[2] or pedicle from the donor

bipedicle [aɪ] or **double pedicle flap**[3] n term

» In periodontal surgery, pedicle flaps are used to cover a root surface by moving the attached [tʃ] gingiva[4] [dʒ] to an adjacent [ədʒeɪsənt] position and suturing the free end. The vascular pedicle[2] areas of some flaps contain functional nerves which are also reattached.

Use to raise[5] [eɪ]/reflect[6]/debride [iː]/advance[7]/develop[8]/create[8] [ieɪ]/design[8]/rotate/ (re)explore *a flap* • skin / buccal [ʌ]/ mucoperiosteal / deltopectoral / trans-rectus abdominis muscle, abbr TRAM / arterial / neurovascular[9] [ʊɚ]/ gingival / lingual or tongue *flap* • lined [aɪ]/ microvascular / sensory / motor / composite or compound[10] / bilobed[3] [oʊ]/ cross[11] / free bone / local / distant[12] / direct or immediate[13] [iː]/ sickle *flap* • omental / palmar-based / muscle / permanent **pedicle flap** • **pedicle flap** transfer

gestielter Lappen
versorgt[1] Gefäßstiel[2] doppelt gestielter Lappen[3] befestigte Gingiva, G. propria[4] Lappen heben[5] Lappen zurückklappen[6] Lappen verschieben[7] Lappen darstellen[8] neurovaskulärer Lappen[9] kombinierter Lappen[10] Kreuzlappen[11] Fernlappen[12] Nahlappen[13]

11

axial [æksɪəl] **(pattern)** or **arterial** [ɪɚ] **flap** n term
opposite **random (pattern) flap**[1] n term

flap that includes a direct specific artery within its longitudinal axis

» As they include their arteriovenous [iː] system, axial flaps may be 4 times as long as their base.

Arterienlappen
Lappen ohne zugrundeliegende Gefäßstruktur[1]

12

(vascularized) free tissue transfer n term   syn **free flap** n term

axial flap whose neurovascular bundle[1] [ʌ] is anastomosed to that in the recipient site

» In a free or island [aɪ] flap[2] the donor vessels are severed[3] [sevɚd] proximally and the flap is revascularized by anastomosing its supplying vessels to those of the recipient area using microsurgical techniques. Due to its long and relatively large and reliable [aɪ] vascular pedicle the latissimus dorsi [aɪ] is a popular muscle for free tissue transfer. Examples of free flaps frequently used are axial pattern skin flaps.

Use **vascularized free** compound [aʊ] transfer • microvascular [aɪ] *free flap*

freie(s) Gewebetransplantat, -übertragung
Nerven- u. Gefäßbündel[1] Insellappen[2] durchtrennt[3]

13

advancement flap n term   syn **sliding** [aɪ] or **French flap** n term

rectangular[1] flap raised in an elastic area, with its free end adjacent [dʒeɪs] to[2] a defect which is covered by longitudinally stretching the flap over it

» Flaps used in reconstruction of the eyelids are advancement flaps, Z-plasty[3] and transposition flaps[4].

Verschiebelappen
rechteckig[1] anliegend[2] Z-Plastik[3] Transpositionslappen[4]

14

tubed [juː] **(pedicle) flap** n term   syn **rope** [oʊ] or **Filatov(-Gillies) flap** n term

the sides of the pedicle are sutured together[1] to create a tube entirely covered by skin

» In contrast to flat (open) flaps[2], tubed flaps are often created by joining two random flaps.

Roll-, Rundstiellappen
miteinander vernäht[1] einseitig bedeckter Lappen[2]

15

caterpillar [kætɚpɪlɚ] **flap** n term   syn **waltzed** [wɒltst] **flap** n term,
sim **jump** [dʒʌmp] **flap**[1] n term

tubed flap transferred end-over-end in stages from the donor site to a distant recipient site

» Jump flaps are distant flaps transferred in stages via an intermediate [iː] carrier; e.g., an abdominal flap is attached to the wrist[2] [rɪst], then at a later stage the wrist is brought to the face.

Wanderlappen
mehrfach transponierter Rundstiellappen[1] Handgelenk[2]

16

envelope [envəloʊp‖ɒn-] **flap** n term   syn **wrap-around** [ræp-] **flap** n term

mucoperiosteal flap[1] retracted from a horizontal incision along the free gingival margin [dʒ]

» If the papilla between the 1st and 2nd molars has been elevated, envelope flaps may require an intraproximal suture. Envelope flaps have one, rectangular flaps[2] have two vertical relaxing incisions[3].

umhüllender Lappen
Mukoperiostlappen[1] Trapezlappen[2] Entlastungsschnitte[3]

17

buried [berɪd] **flap** n term   opposite **non-buried flap**[1] n term

flap denuded of both surface epithelium [iː] and superficial dermis and transferred into the subcutaneous [eɪ] tissue margin

» Buried flaps can be effectively evaluated by means of Doppler ultrasonography.

Unterfütterungslappen
Decklappen[1]

18

130

hinged [hɪndʒd] or **rotation flap** n term   sim **turnover flap**¹ n term

turnover flap transferred by lifting it over on its pedicle as though² [ðoʊ] the pedicle was a hinge³

» A hinged flap that is turned over 180 degree to receive a second covering flap is termed a turnover flap. A lumbar [ʌ] periosteal turnover flap was used to reinforce⁴ the spinal cord repair.

Use superiorly [ɪɚ]/ nasaly [eɪ] **hinged flap** • flag **flap**

Rotationslappen
Wendelappen¹ als ob² Scharnier³ verstärken⁴

19

---

graft-versus-host [oʊ] **disease** or **reaction** n term   abbr **GVHD** or **GVHR**

incompatibility¹ reaction in a transplant recipient (=host) caused by T cells from grafted tissue which react immunologically against the recipient's antigens [-dʒənz] and attack the recipient tissues

» GVHD affects especially the skin, gastrointestinal tract, and liver with symptoms including skin rash² [ræʃ], fever [iː], diarrhea [daɪəriːə], liver dysfunction, abdominal pain, and anorexia³, and may be fatal⁴ [eɪ].

Use to develop / oral / maternofetal [iː]/ chronic **GVHD**

GVHD, GVHR, Transplantat-gegen-Wirt Reaktion
Unverträglichkeit¹ Hautausschlag, Exanthem² Appetitlosigkeit³ tödlich⁴

20

---

graft survival [sɚvaɪvᵊl] n term   opposite **graft rejection**¹ [rɪdʒekʃᵊn] n term

satisfactory take² and ingrowth³ of a viable⁴ [aɪ] transplant into the recipient bed

» The term white graft⁵ refers to rejection of a skin allograft so acute that vascularization never occurs. A clear understanding of the mechanisms [k] involved in graft rejection will improve the selection of adequate immunosuppressive therapy and help prolong graft survival⁶.

Use **graft survival** rate / curve • to enhance or extend⁵ **graft survival** • improved / 1-year **graft survival** • to prevent/halt⁷ [ɔː] /be responsible for **rejection** • (hyper)acute⁸ [aɪ]/ chronic [k] **rejection** • organ⁹ **graft rejection**

Überlebenszeit d. Transplantats
Transplantatabstoßung¹ Transplantatannahme² Einheilen³ lebensfähig⁴ weiße Abstoßung⁵ Überlebenszeit d. T. verlängern⁶ Transplantatabstoßung aufhalten⁷ hyperakute Transplantatabstoßung⁸ Organabstoßung, -rejektion⁹

21

Unit 131 The Surgical Suite
Related Units: 126 Surgical Treatment, 134 Perioperative Management, 135 Anesthesiology, 139 Asepsis

operating room BE **theatre** [θɪətəʳ] n term   abbr **OR**, BE **OT**

hospital room equipped and used for performing surgical procedures

» The OR may only be entered by persons wearing [eɚ] clean operating attire¹ [ətaɪɚ] not worn elsewhere. Traffic² and talking in the OR should be minimized. A patient with shock or unexplained hemorrhage [-ɪdʒ] should be taken to the OR for emergency exploration.

Use to be rushed³ [ʌ] /taken/brought/transferred **to the OR** • **OR** facilities⁴ [sɪ]/ personnel / procedure [-iːdʒɚ]/ temperature

Operationssaal, OP
OP-Kleidung¹ aus u. ein gehen² schnell in den OP gebracht werden³ OP-Einrichtung⁴

1

---

presurgical suite [swiːt] n term   sim **operating** or **surgical** [sɜːrdʒɪkᵊl] **suite**¹ n term

holding or catchment area² on the operating floor¹ where the ward [ɔː] nurse³ hands the patient (and the chart⁴ [tʃ]) over to the anesthesiologist; also includes rooms with facilities for scrubbing⁵ [ʌ], gowning⁶ [aʊ] and gloving [ʌ]

» Even though the patient appears to be safely dozing⁷ [oʊ] with a strap in place⁸, he should not be left alone in the presurgical suite.

Vorräume zum OP-Saal
Operationstrakt¹ Wartebereich (vor OP-Schleuse)² Stationsschwester, -pfleger³ Krankenblatt⁴ chir. Händereinigung⁵ Anlegen d. OP-Kleidung⁶ (vor sich hin)dösen⁷ angegurtet⁸

2

---

induction room [ʌ] n term   sim **prep room**¹ n jar

a quiet room adjoining² the OR where the anesthesiologist administers³ the preoperative anesthetic [e]

» In the induction room undesirable [aɪ] noise and conversations should be avoided as the patient may be acutely aware⁴ of everything he hears.

Narkose(prämedikations)-raum
Vorbereitungsraum¹ neben² verabreicht³ (bewusst) wahrnehmen⁴

3

---

operating or **surgical team** n term

includes the surgeon [dʒ], the surgeon's assistant¹, the anesthesiologist, the circulating and scrub nurses

» Nonsterile ORs and the operating team remain a source [ɔː] of infection². Members of the surgical team should not operate if they have viral [aɪ] infections that may cause coughing [kɒːfɪŋ] or sneezing³ [iː].

Operationsteam
Operationsassistent(in)¹ Infektionsquelle² Niesen³

4

The Surgical Suite

CLINICAL TERMS 579

surgeon [sɜːrdʒˀn] *n term*   *syn* **operator** *n term*

physician who specializes in surgery; in the UK they are traditionally addressed[1] as Mr X rather than Dr X.

operator-dependent[2] *adj term*

» Given an accomplished[3] surgeon and good preoperative preparation this nerve can be preserved[4] in more than 98% of cases. In this technique skillful operators make only minimal use of sutures [tʃ].

◀Use attending[5] / general / plastic / house[6] *(BE)* / assistant / experienced **surgeon** • **the surgeon's** technical [k] skills / judgement[7] [dʒʌdʒ-]/ responsibility / experience

> **Note:** Do not be confused by the fact that the *operator* is commonly the person who works on a telephone switchboard or operates any other apparatus or machine.

Chirurg(in), Operateur(in)
angesprochen[1] abhängig v. Chirurg(in)[2] gut, fähig[3] erhalten[4] behandelnde(r) Chirurg(in)[5] ®Assistenzarzt od. -ärztin / Turnusarzt od. -ärztin (öst.) a. d. chir. Abteilung[6] Ermessen d. Chirurgen/-in[7]

5

anesthesiologist [ænəsθiːziːɒlədʒɪst] *n term*
   syn **anaesthetist** [əniːsθətɪst] *n term BE* → U15-11

physician who administers the anesthetic [e] and monitors[1] the patient while under anesthesia [-iːʒə]

» The anesthesiologist continuously assesses[2] the depth of anesthesia[3].

◀Use **anesthesiologist**-on-call[4]

> **Note:** Unlike in the U.K., the *anesthetist* in the U.S. is a nurse [ɜː] anesthetist[5] [e], a registered nurse[6] with extra qualifications working under the supervision of an anesthesiologist.

Anästhesist(in), Narkosearzt/-ärztin
überwacht[1] überprüft[2] Narkosetiefe[3] diensthabende(r) Anästhesist(in)[4] Narkoseschwester/-pfleger[5] Diplom-, staatl. geprüfte(r) Krankenschwester/-pfleger[6]

6

anesthesia screen [ænəsθiːʒə skriːn] *n term*

protective screen attached above the patient's chest to preclude airborne contamination[1] from the anesthesiologist or the patient him/herself

Abgrenzung d. Sterilbereichs, Sichtschutz z. Anästhesiebereich
Kontamination über die Atemluft verhindern[1]

7

surgical nurse [nɜːrs] *n term*   *syn* **scrub** [ʌ] **nurse** *n jar* → U16-2f

(s)he is responsible for the scrub-up procedures, lays [leɪz] out[1] sterile instruments and equipment, assists by providing the required sutures, drains, etc. and checks to ensure that all sponges[2] [ʌ], etc. are accounted for[3]

» Have the scrub nurse label[4] [eɪ] the specimen[5] and send it to the lab.

Instrumentier-, OP-Schwester
auflegen[1] Tupfer[2] abgezählt[3] etikettieren[4] (Gewebe)probe[5]

8

circulating nurse *n jar*   *sim* **OR tech(nician)**[1] [teknɪʃˀn] *n term*

(s)he manages the OR (proper temperature, lighting[2], availability of supplies[3], etc.) coordinates activities of lab or x-ray staff, and monitors aseptic practices to avoid breakdowns in technique[4]

» The circulating nurse must observe the patient to ensure that his needs are provided for[5].

unsterile Hilfe
OP-(Ge)hilfe[1] Beleuchtung[2] Verfügbarkeit von OP-Bedarf[3] Verstöße gegen d. aseptischen Kautelen/Vorsichtsmaßregeln[4] dass er entsprechend versorgt ist[5]

9

operating table *n*

special table on which the patient is positioned during the surgical procedure; sandbags, straps[1] and braces[2] [eɪs] may be used to keep the patient stable [eɪ] and comfortable

» Proper positioning[3] of the patient on the operating table is crucial[4] [kruːʃˀl].

◀Use to flex or break[5] [eɪ] /incline [aɪ] or tilt[6]/elevate[7] **the operating table**

Operationstisch
Gurte[1] Stützen, Schienen[2] richtige Lagerung[3] sehr wichtig[4] O. knicken[5] O. neigen/ kippen[6] O. anheben[7]

10

position *n & v term*   *sim* **positioning**[1] *n term*, **place**[2] *v* → U63-1ff

(n) depending on the procedure scheduled[3] [skˈʃedjuːld] the patient is brought into a position on the table which is as comfortable as possible (e.g. no undue[4] [ʌnduː] pressure on nerves), does not interfere [ɪə] with[5] respiration or circulation, and provides adequate exposure[6] [oʊʒ] of the operative field

reposition[7] *v term* • **repositioning** *n*

» Improper positioning of the patient can result in immediate and long-term complications. The legs were positioned in stirrups[8] [ɜː].

◀Use to be in/bring into/place in/remain in /assume[9] [suː] /adopt[9] **a position** • satisfactory / patient **positioning** • change of[10] / left lateral[11] / supine[12] [aɪ]/ with the patient/foot (placed) in a ... **position**

Lage, Position, Stellung; legen, positionieren
Lagerung[1] lagern[2] geplant[3] übermäßig[4] beeinträchtigen[5] Darstellung[6] umlagern[7] Fußstützen, -halter[8] Stellung einnehmen[9] Positionswechsel, Umlagerung[10] linke Seitenlage[11] Rückenlage[12]

11

CLINICAL TERMS — The Surgical Suite

dorsal recumbent [ʌ] **position** n term

the standard position with the patient flat on the back, legs slightly flexed[1] and straddled[2]; one arm is placed palm[3] [pɑːm] down alongside the trunk[4] [ʌ] while the other is positioned on an armboard[5] for IV infusion

» *Laparoscopy is usually performed with the patient in the dorsal recumbent position.*

Rückenlage m. angewinkelten, gespreizten Beinen
angewinkelt[1] gespreizt[2] Handfläche[3] Rumpf[4] Armstütze[5]

12

Trendelenburg('s) position n term

opposite **reverse** [ɜː] **Trendelenburg position**[1] n term

supine position[2] on the operating table, which is inclined[3] [aɪ] so that the pelvis is higher than the head; the patient is supported by padded shoulder braces[4] [eɪ] and thigh [θaɪ] straps[5]

» *The Trendelenburg position is employed for procedures on the pelvis and lower abdomen to obtain good exposure by displacing[6] the intestines somewhat more cephalad[7] [sɛfəlæd].*

Kopftief-, Trendelenburglage
Anti-Trendelenburg-, Fußtieflage[1] Rückenlage[2] geneigt[3] gepolsterte Schulterstützen[4] Oberschenkelgurte[5] verlagern[6] nach kranial[7]

13

lithotomy position n term   syn **dorsosacral** [eɪ] **position** n term

a supine position with the buttocks [ʌ] extending over the table[1], the hips and knees [niːz] are flexed at 90° and the feet held in position by strapping them to stirrups

» *For nearly all rectal and vaginal [dʒ] operations the patient is brought into the lithotomy position.*

Steinschnittlage
Gesäß bis an den Rand der Unterlage vorgezogen[1]

14

semiprone [oʊ] or **English position** n term   syn **Sims'** or **lateral (recumbent) position** n term

the patient lies on the side with the under arm behind the body; the upper leg[1] is flexed more than the lower one; this is the position of choice for vaginal and rectal procedures (exams, enemas[2], etc)

» *Delivery[3] may be accomplished[4] in either the lithotomy or the Sims' position.*

Sims-Lage
Oberschenkel[1] Einläufe[2] Entbindung[3] erfolgreich durchgeführt[4]

15

lateral decubitus [uː] **position** n term   syn **flank** [æ] **position** n term

lateral recumbent position, but with the lower leg flexed, the upper leg extended, and the table broken at the patient's waistline[1] [eɪ]

» *The flank position is used for nephrectomy. The patient is placed on his well side[2]. An intra-operative x-ray in the lateral decubitus position is usually the best way to assess[3] the problem.*

Use left/right lateral / dorsal[4] / ventral[5] **decubitus position**

Seitenlage(rung)
Taille[1] gesunde Seite[2] abklären[3] Rückenlage[4] Bauchlage[5]

16

recovery [ʌ] **room** n clin, abbr **RR**   syn **postanesthesia** [-iːʒə] **recovery area** n term, abbr **PAR**

unit or room adjoining the ORs staffed and equipped with facilities[1] to provide optimal care during the recovery period[2] until the patient can be safely transferred[3] back to the surgical ward[4] [ɔː]

» *While en route[5] from the OR to the recovery area the patient is accompanied by a physician. In the recovery room the anesthesiologist generally exercises primary responsibility[6].*

Use **recovery** area / room nurse[7] / room staff • **recovery** system / score card[8]

Aufwachraum
Einrichtungen[1] Aufwachperiode[2] verlegt[3] chir. Station[4] auf dem Weg[5] hat die Hauptverantwortung[6] Aufwachschwester/-pfleger[7] Beurteilungsschema im Aufwachprotokoll[8]

17

recovery (room) bed n clin

special bed for patients in the immediate postoperative period; it is supplied with side rails[1] [eɪ] which can be raised[2] [eɪ], receptacles[3] for IV poles[4] [oʊ], and often has a chart [tʃ] storage rack[5]

» *If the patient is unattended[6], the side rails of the recovery bed are placed in position[2].*

Aufwachbett
seitl. Gitter[1] hochgezogen[2] Haltevorrichtung[3] Infusionsständer[4] Ablage f. Fieberkurve/ Aufwachprotokoll[5] unbeaufsichtigt[6]

18

instrument cart [kɑːrt] n clin

small table on wheels on which the scrub nurse lays [leɪz] out the set of sterilized instruments; many other mobile[1] carts supplied with various special equipment are used in hospitals (e.g. the crash cart[2] for emergencies)

» *Hospital ERs[3] usually have several crash carts equipped with analgesics, antiseptics, sponges[4] [ʌndʒ], swabs[5] [ɒː], hemostats[6] [iː], etc.*

Instrumentenwagen
fahrbar[1] Notfallwagen[2] Notaufnahmen[3] chir. Tupfer[4] Tupfer (z. Desinfektion)[5] Gefäßklemmen[6]

19

Unit 132 Surgical Instruments

Related Units: 17 Basic Medical Equipment, 127 Basic Operative Techniques, 128 Minimally Invasive Surgery, 133 Laparoscopic Equipment, 139 Medical & Surgical Asepsis

---

instrument n genE & v term

sim **instrumentation**[1], **instrumentarium**[2] n term

equipment[3], tools[4] or appliances[5] [aɪ] or any means [iː] used to perform surgical procedures
instrumental[6] adj genE & term

» The mobility of the tumor can be determined by manipulation with the tip of the instrument.

Use to sterilize/hand-wash/lay [eɪ] out[7]/sharpen/pass or insert[8]/scald[9] [ɒː] **instruments** • soiling[10] / successful passage / set[11] / stock[12] **of instruments** • dissecting[13] / gas sterilized [aɪ] / microsurgical / lensed[14] **instruments** • endoscopy / urethral [iː] **instrumentation** • **instrumental** birth[15] / perforation / malfunction • by **instrumental** means[16] • **instrument** tray[17]

Instrument; instrumentieren
Instrumentieren, -ation[1] Instrumentarium[2] Ausrüstung[3] Werkzeuge, Geräte[4] Vorrichtungen, Geräte[5] förderlich, behilflich; instrumentell[6] I. auflegen[7] I. einführen[8] I. thermisch desinfizieren[9] Kontamination von I.[10] Instrumentensatz, chir. Besteck[11] Instrumentenbestand[12] Präparierbesteck[13] optische Geräte[14] operative Entbindung[15] instrumentell[16] Instrumentenschale, -tray[17]   **1**

---

sharps n jar

instruments for cutting and transfixing[1] tissue that are razor [reɪzə] sharp[2] and therefore require special [eʃ] safeguards[3] for handling (often marked by a red stripe [aɪ] on the handle[4] and disposed of[5] in a sharps container)

Use **sharp** blade[6] [eɪ] / curette[7] / tip / dissection[8] / -edged[9] / -pointed

scharfe bzw. spitze Instrumente
durchstoßen, -stechen[1] messerscharf[2] Sicherung, Schutz[3] Griff[4] entsorgt[5] scharfe Klinge[6] scharfe Kürette[7] scharfes Präparieren[8] scharfkantig[9]   **2**

---

scalpel n term   syn **knife** [naɪf] n inf & jar

surgical knife usually with an interchangeable blade[1] and a straight handle or blade [eɪ] holder[2]

» A No. 15 blade is used to scrape[3] [eɪ] the lesion [iːʒ] until it is flat.

Use to cut/incise/excise/probe[4] **with a scalpel** • disposable[5] / dissecting[6] / micro/ cold / heated / laser-assisted **scalpel** • **knife** blade / point[7] / handle / edge[8] / needle • crescent[9] [s] / slit **blade** • needlepoint / spoon[10] [uː] / hook [ʊ] / gum[11] **knife**

Skalpell, chir. Messer
Wechselklinge[1] Klingenhalter[2] ausschaben[3] m. e. Skalpell sondieren[4] Einmalskalpell[5] Seziermesser[6] Messerspitze[7] Messerschneide[8] sichelförm. Klinge[9] scharfer Löffel[10] Zahnfleischmesser[11]   **3**

---

scissors [sɪzəz] n pl   sim **shears**[1] [ɪə] n pl term

a cutting instrument with two crossed shearing blades which may have a sharp or blunt [ʌ] nose[2]

microscissors[3] [aɪ] n term • shear[4] v irr

» Do you want the scissors with dissecting or plain [eɪ] blades[5]?

Use a pair of long / short / curved[6] [ɜː]/ straight[7] **scissors** • medium-sized / heavy[1] [e]/ double-action / pointed / delicate or fine **scissors** • dissecting[8] / suture[9] [suːtʃə]/ ligature[10] [-tʃʊə] / wire cutting[11] / Metzenbaum **scissors** • bone[12] / rib / sternum [ɜː] / plaster[13] **shears**

Schere
(große/ stabile) Schere[1] stumpfe Spitze[2] Mikroschere[3] scheren, schneiden[4] ungezahnte/ glatte Schneidblätter[5] gebogene Schere[6] gerade S.[7] Präparierschere[8] Naht-, Fadenschere[9] Ligaturschere[10] Draht(schneide)schere[11] Knochenschere[12] Gipsschere[13]   **4**

(surgical) needle [iː] n term → U17-11; U136-6   sim **awl**[1] [ɒːl] n term

sharp instrument used for puncturing [ʌ] and/or suturing; the shaft may be cutting or round-bodied; at the tip there is usually a tapered[2] [eɪ] point and the suture is threaded[3] [e] at the eye[4] or it is already swaged[5] [edʒ] to the needle for atraumatic sewing[6] (so-called armed sutures[7])

needle-shaped adj • **needle-like** adj • **needling**[8] n term

» Precautions[9] [ɒː] must be taken against leaving needles, clamps, sponges, etc. inside the patient.

Use to pass/push/pull/rotate/withdraw[10] [ɒː] **the needle** • straight / curved / suture[11] / arterial [ɪə] suture[12] **needle** • intestinal or abdominal suture[13] / Reverdin / punch[14] [ʌ] / swaged-on[15] **needle** • hollow / hypodermic[16] [aɪ] / fine / large-bore[17] **needle** • **needle** count / point / shaft / site[18] [aɪ]/ holder

(chirurgische) Nadel
Ahle[1] spitz zulaufend[2] eingefädelt[3] Öhr[4] übergangslos verbunden[5] (Ver)nähen[6] armierte/ atraumatische Nähte[7] Ritzen (m. N.), Punktion[8] (Sicherheits)vorkehrungen[9] N. zurückziehen/ entfernen[10] Nähnadel[11] Gefäßnadel[12] Darmnadel[13] stanzende Biopsienadel[14] Nadel-Faden-Kombination, öhrlose Nadel[15] Injektionsnadel[16] großlumige Hohlnadel[17] Punktions-, Einstichstelle[18]   **5**

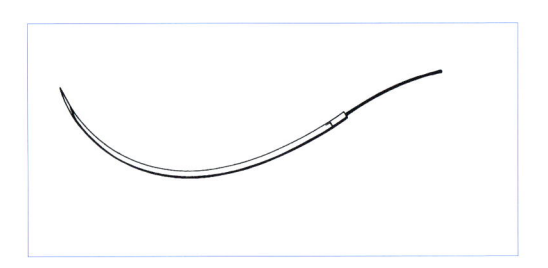

Curved atraumatic needle

cannula n term → U136-3

tube introduced into a vessel, duct or body cavity

cannulate[1] v term • **cannular** adj • **cannul(iz)ation** n

» The cannula may be left in place for two weeks. Inability to cannulate the subclavian [eɪ] vein [eɪ] is among the most common technical [k] complications.

Use to insert or introduce[1]/place[2] **a cannula** • IV • central venous[3] [iː]/ (intra-)arterial / plastic / flexible / small-bore / 18-gauge[4] [geɪdʒ] / infusion[5] / needle-tipped **cannula** • suction[6] [sʌkʃᵊn]/ nasal / wash or irrigating[7] / ointment[8] **cannula** • **cannula** insertion / removal • percutaneous [eɪ] **cannulation**

Kanüle, Hohlnadel
K. einführen[1] K. legen[2] zentraler Venenkatheter[3] Kanüle, Größe 18[4] Infusionskanüle[5] Saugkanüle[6] Spülkanüle[7] Salbenkanüle[8]
6

trocar [oʊ] n term → U133-5f sim **stylet** or **stilet(te)**[1] [staɪlət] n term

metal tube (cannula) with a sharp-tipped, three-cornered obturator[2] (trocar) inside which is withdrawn after insertion; strictly speaking the complete instrument is termed trocar and cannula

» Seeds[3] [iː] are placed into the residual tumor[4] with a trocar.

Use to place/insert/introduce **a trocar** • working[5] **trocar** • **trocar** sheath[6] [iː] • floppy or flexible / introducing / lighted [aɪ]/ needle **stylet**

Trokar
Mandrin[1] Trokardorn m. Dreikantspitze[2] radioaktive Implantate[3] Resttumor[4] Arbeitstrokar[5] Trokarhülse[6]
7

probe [proʊb] v & n term syn **sound** [aʊ] n, sim **director**[1] n term

(v) to explore a wound [uː], duct [ʌ] or cavity (n) slender[2] instrument inserted for exploration[3] • **cryoprobe**[4] n term • **probing**[5] adj & n

» Introduction of the probe is tricky[6] and care must be exercised to avoid perforation.

Use ultrasonic[7] / suction [ʌ]/ antrum[8] / rectal **probe** / blind[9] / gentle **probing** • uterine[10] [aɪ||ɪ] **sound** • (rectal) grooved[11] [uː]/ hernia [ɜː] **director**

sondieren; Sonde
Führungs(hohl)sonde[1] fein[2] Austastung, Exploration[3] Kryo-, Kältesonde[4] sondierend; Sondierung[5] schwierig[6] Schallsonde[7] Kieferhöhlensonde[8] Sondieren ohne Sichtkontrolle[9] Uterussonde[10] Rektal-Hohlsonde[11]
8

hook [hʊk] n & v sim **loop**[1] [luːp] n → U138-5

(n) instrument with a curved[2] tip for elevating[3] or trapping[4] and ensnaring[5] [eə˞] tissues

» Foreign [fɒːrᵊn] bodies[6] may be removed with a loop or a hook without irrigation.

Use wire[7] / suture[8] / tape / cautery[9] [ɒː]/ cord **loop** • right-angled [æŋgld]/ electrosurgical **hook** or **hook** electrode[9] • to place or ensnare in a[5] **loop**

Haken; festhaken
Schlinge[1] (auf)gebogen[2] anheben[3] fassen[4] anschlingen[5] Fremdkörper[6] Drahtschlinge[7] Nahtschlinge[8] Diathermieschlinge[9]
9

curet(te) [kjʊrɛt] v & n term sim **spoon** [uː] or **scoop**[1] [uː] n jar

(v) remove layers of tissue from a surface such as the uterus [juː]
(n) a long and thin spoon-shaped instrument

curettage [kjʊrɛtɪdʒ] or curettment n term • **scoop** or **scrape**[2] [eɪ] v jar & inf

» Necrotic nodes should be curetted out. The curettings[3] were suggestive [dʒe] of[4] ectopic pregnancy.

Use skin / metal / blunt or dull[5] [ʌ]/ sharp / plastic **curette** • sharp / subgingival / cervical / root[6] / suction[7] **curettage** • dilatation and[8] **curettage** (abbr D & C)

kürettieren, auskratzen; Kürette
Löffel[1] auskratzen, -schaben[2] kürettiertes Gewebe[3] hindeuten auf[4] stumpfe K.[5] Wurzelglätten[6] Saugkürettage[7] Uterusdilatation u. Kürettage[8]
10

rongeur (forceps) [rɒːndʒɚ] n term sim **bone chisel** [tʃɪzᵊl] or **osteotome**[1], **gouge**[2] [gaʊdʒ] n term

heavy-duty forceps for cutting bone, enamel[3], or other tough [tʌf] tissue; an osteotome is a wedge-like[4] [dʒ] tool with a cutting edge at the tip of the blade

» A gouge is a hollow chisel for cutting away bone chips. Osteotome tips are not beveled[5]. Rongeurs were used to procure[6] [-kjʊə˞] small bone chips from bony protuberances.

Use bone[7] / intervertebral disk[8] / laminectomy[9] **rongeur** • rounded[2] / straight[10] **osteotome** • sternum / hemostatic[11] **chisel**

Knochen(fass-), Luer-Zange
Knochenmeißel, Osteotom[1] Hohlmeißel[2] (Zahn)schmelz[3] keilförmig[4] abgeschrägt[5] entnehmen[6] Hohlmeißel-, Luer-Knochenzange[7] Bandscheiben-Rongeur[8] Laminektomie-Stanze[9] Flachmeißel[10] Blutstillungsmeißel[11]
11

Surgical Instruments | **CLINICAL TERMS 583**

raspatory n term   syn **bone scraper, rasp, rugine** [ruːʒiːn] n jar,
                    sim **file**[1] [faɪl] n & v

hardened steel tool with cutting ridges used to lift or scrape away[2] periosteum; files serve to smoothen[3] [uː] surfaces, e.g. of a tooth or root canal

» After lifting the periosteum with a raspatory, the implant bed was prepared. Alveoloplasty was performed using bone-cutting burs, rongeurs, and bone files.

Use bone / rib[4] / nasal[5] / antrum[6] **raspatory** • bone[7] / nail **file**

Raspatorium, Raspel, Schabeisen
Feile; feilen[1] abschieben, -präparieren[2] glätten[3] Rippenraspatorium[4] Nasenraspel[5] Antrumraspel[6] Knochenfeile[7]
                       12

grasper [æ] n term & jar   syn **grasping forceps** n term,
                   sim **clamp**[1] n term, **tweezers**[2] [iː] n clin pl

instruments with two tongs[3] [ʌ] that can be clamped to lift, seize[4] [iː] or compress tissue

grasp[4] v • clamp[5] v term • cross-clamping[6] n

» The mucosa above the hemorrhoid is grasped with forceps. Gently [dʒ] spread [e] the clamp to dilate the vein. The duct proximal to the stone must be temporarily clamped. The appendix was serially clamped[7] and cut.

Use three-prong(ed)[8] [ɒː] **grasper** • to apply/place/release [iː] **clamps** • aortic crossclamping • doubly[9] clamped • vascular[10] / right-angle / Kocher's / crushing[11] [ʌ] / noncrushing[12] / towel[13] [aʊ]/ bulldog[14] **clamp**

Fasszange
Klemmzange, Klemme[1] Pinzette[2] Branchen[3] fassen[4] (ab)klemmen[5] vollständiges Abklemmen[6] mehrfach abgeklemmt[7] F. mit 3 Maulteilen[8] zweifach abgeklemmt[9] Gefäßklemme[10] scharfe Klemme, Gewebe(fass)kl.[11] atraumatische K.[12] Tuchklemme[13] Bulldog-, Gefäßklemme[14]
                       13

forceps [fɔːrseps] n pl term   sim **tweezers**[1] n clin, **applicator**[2] n term

instruments with two blades to grasp or compress tissue or dressings[3] in surgery

» It was done with a mosquito [k] forceps[4]. Tweezers are small forceps that can be held between the thumb [θʌm] and forefinger.

Use to apply/place/release **forceps** • delivery[5] / high[6] / low / hemostatic[7] [iː]/ splinter[8] / dressing[9] / ear[10] / clip removing **forceps** • ring / cup / biopsy[11] [aɪ] / nasal / polyp / tissue[12] **forceps** • smooth[13] [uː]/ toothed or hooked[14] / four-prong[15] / thread[16] [e]/ sterile [aɪ] **forceps** • cotton(-tipped)[17] / sonic / sealed [iː]/ laryngeal [dʒ] **applicator** • a pair of / fine tipped **tweezers**

Zange, Klemme, Pinzette
kleine Zange, Pinzette[1] Applikator[2] Wundauflagen[3] Moskitoklemme[4] Geburtszange[5] hohe Z.[6] Gefäßklemme[7] Splitterzange, -pinzette[8] Tupferzange[9] Ohrpinzette[10] Biopsiezange[11] Gewebefassz.[12] anatomische P., Gefäßp.[13] chirurgische P.[14] Vierkrallen-Fasspinzette[15] Fadenpinzette[16] Watteträger[17]
                       14

needle holder n term   syn **suture** [suːtʃɚ] **forceps** n term

forceps used to grasp the needle and pass it through the tissue

Nadelhalter
                       15

retractor n term   syn **tenaculum** n term

pointed or hooked instrument used for holding the wound [uː] edges[1] apart[2] or vessels and other tissues out of the operative field; may have one or several claws [ɒː] or teeth[3] at either end

retract[4] v term • retraction n

» Retractors out! The vein was retracted medially. The injury was due to a misplaced retractor.

Use sharp or toothed[5] / blunt[6] / (non-)malleable[7] / self-retaining[8] **retractor** • lip / cheek[9] / vaginal [dʒ] / abdominal[10] **retractor** • **retracting** clamp

Wundhaken, -sperrer, -spreizer
Wundränder[1] auseinander[2] Zinken, Zähne[3] zurückziehen, auseinanderspreizen[4] scharfer/ gezahnter Wundhaken[5] stumpfer W.[6] (nicht) federnder W.[7] selbsthaltender Wundspreizer[8] Wangen(ab)halter[9] Bauchdeckenhalter[10]
                       16

dila(ta)tor [daɪl(ət)eɪtɚ] n term   sim **bougie (boule)**[1] [buːʒɪ] n term

instrument to expand and enlarge the diameter[2] [daɪæmətɚ] of a tube or passage [-ɪdʒ], e.g. a narrowed[3] duct

dila(ta)te[4] v term • dila(ta)tion n • bougi(e)nage[5] [-ɑːʒ] n

» How much dilatation is desirable? A 32F dilator was passed orally.

Use anal[6] [eɪ]/ antegrade / retrograde / tent / Hegar's[7] **dilator** • dilating[1] / olive-tipped / medicated **bougie** • catheter / balloon[8] [uː] **dilation** • **dilation** and evacuation / of stricture [-ktʃɚ]

Dilatator, Erweiterer, Dehner
(Dilatations)bougie, Dehnsonde[1] Durchmesser[2] verengt[3] dilatieren, aufdehnen, (sich) erweitern[4] Bougierung[5] Analdehner[6] HegarStift, -Uterusdilatator[7] Ballondilatation[8]

Note: The F in 32F dilator stands for French, a measure to indicate the diameter or thickness of dilators, catheters, bougies and similar instruments.
                       17

(surgical) sponge [spʌndʒ] n term & jar

sterile, absorbent material used to control bleeding sites, mostly a compressed pad of aseptic gauze[1] [ɡɔːz] that swells[2] when moistened[3]

» Dry sponges are used and weighed [weɪd] to estimate intraoperative blood loss. Sponge and needle count are correct.

Use alcohol[4] / (sterile) gauze[5] **sponge** • **sponge** biopsy[6] [aɪ] / count / forceps[7] / stick[8]

Tupfer
Verbandsmull, Gaze[1] (auf)quellen[2] befeuchtet[3] Alkoholtupfer[4] Gazekissen[5] Abstrich, Tupfpräparat[6] Tupferzange[7] Tupfträger[8]
                       18

Unit 133 Laparoscopic Equipment

Related Units: 128 Minimally Invasive Surgery, 132 Surgical Instruments, 138 Endoscopic Suturing, 118 Diagnostic Procedures, 17 Medical Equipment

instrument holder n term   sim **robotic** or **support arm**[1] n term

electromechanical device[2] for holding instruments in a stable position (can also be remote-controlled[3])

robotic adj term • **robot** [rɒːbət] n • **instrumentation** n → U132-1

» The instrument holder which was mounted [aʊ] to[4] the side rails[5] [eɪ] of the operating table was mainly used for fixation of the endoscope. The joints[6] [dʒ] of this instrument holder are fixed by a pneumatic [n(j)uː-] locking mechanism[7] [k] which is controlled by buttons in the handle[8].

Use pneumatic[9] **robotic arm** • **robotic** device • **microrobotic** intra-abdominal device [dɪvaɪs] • surgical / three-armed **robot** • **robot**-assisted[10] surgery / arm • **instrument** design / maneuverability[11] [uː] • jamming [dʒ] of[12] **instruments** • disposable[13] [oʊ]/ reusable [juː] or nondisposable[14] **instruments** • multiuse[15] / cutting **instruments** • dissecting / grasping **instruments** • retracting [æ] insulated[16] **instruments** • **instruments** with interchangeable handles[17]

Instrumentenhalter, Haltevorrichtung
Roboterarm[1] Vorrichtung[2] ferngesteuert[3] befestigt an[4] Befestigungsschienen am OP-Tisch[5] Gelenke[6] Feststellmechanismus[7] Griff[8] druckluftarretierter Roboterarm[9] robotergestützte Chirurgie[10] Handhabung d. Instrumente[11] Behinderung d. Instrumentenführung (durch zu nahe beieinanderliegende Trokarpositionen)[12] Einmal-, Einweginstrumente[13] Mehrweginstrumente[14] Mehrzweckinstrumente[15] isolierte I.[16] I. m. austauschbaren Griffen[17]   **1**

(laparo)scope [læpəskoʊp] n term

rel **endoscope**[1], **optics**[2], **lens**[3] n term → U118-11

illuminating [uː] fiberoptic [aɪ] instrument[4] for visualizing [ɪz] the abdominal cavity

» The 30° laparoscope is inserted through the midline port to examine the retropubic space. Do not hesitate to shift the scope to another port to achieve a better view. Often, the superficial vessels can be seen by transilluminating the abdominal wall with the laparoscope.

Use to insert[5] [ɜː] /view through[6]/position/maneuver [uː] **the laparoscope** • camera-bearing [eə]/ 0-degree or straight-ahead[7] **laparoscope** • angled / oblique[8] [-liːk]/ 10-mm **laparoscope** • 3D video[9] / laser / stereoscopic **laparoscope** • **laparoscope** with built-in working channel[10] [tʃ] • stereo / video / flexible **endoscope** • **endoscopically** controlled insufflator • under (direct) **endoscopic** control or monitoring[11] • to point or direct the **laparoscope** toward[12]

Laparoskop
Endoskop[1] Optik, optisches System[2] Linse[3] lichtleitendes Glasfaserinstrument[4] d. Laparoskop einführen/ -bringen[5] durch d. Laparoskop betrachten[6] L. mit prograder Optik[7] L. mit Seitenblickoptik[8] dreidimensionales Videolaparoskop[9] L. mit integriertem Arbeitskanal[10] unter (direkter) endoskop. Kontrolle/ Sicht[11] laparoskop. einstellen[12]   **2**

optical system [ɒptɪkəl sɪstəm] n term

rel **camera**[1] n term

consists of the documentation system and the camera/video system

fiberoptic [faɪbəɒptɪk] adj term • **fiberoptics**[2] n

» The magnification provided by the optical system permits precise dissection. Then the laparoscope with the video camera attached [ætʃ] is passed, and additional trocars are placed under direct visual control. The procedure is initiated with the camera in the umbilical [ʌ] port, but for ligating the lumbar vessels the scope is shifted to a port in the flank.

Use endoscopic / video / compact / digital(ized)[3] **camera** • eye-piece coupled[4] [ʌ]/ light-sensing[5] **camera** • **camera** operator or assistant / box[6] / port[7] • charge-coupled [tʃ] device[8] (abbr CCD)/ solid state **chip camera** • digital / single-/ triple[9] [ɪ]-**chip camera** • sterile[10] [e] **camera wrap**

Optik, optisches System
Kamera[1] (Glas)faseroptik[2] Digitalkamera[3] am Okular fixierte Kamera[4] Kamera mit automat. Belichtungseinstellung[5] Kameragehäuse[6] Kamera-, Optiktrokar, Videoport[7] CCD-Kamera[8] Dreichip-Kamera[9] sterile Kameraabdeckung[10]   **3**

rod-lens system n term   syn **Hopkins system** n term

series of glass lenses separated by short air spaces which reverse [ɜː] the image at the eyepiece[1]

» Rotating the 30° lens until it points at the underside of the abdominal wall greatly facilitates safe placement of additional ports. Conventional rigid [dʒ] optical systems[2] (e.g. the Hopkins rod-lens system) are also employed in laparoscopic surgery.

Use eyepiece[1] / objective[3] [dʒe] / 0-degree / 30-degree **lens** • fogging of the[4] **lens** • **lens**-camera interface

Stablinsen-, Hopkinsoptik
Okular[1] starre optische Systeme[2] Objektiv[3] Anlaufen d. Optik[4]   **4**

Laparoscopic Equipment

CLINICAL TERMS 585

initial trocar [oʊ] *n term* → U132-7   *syn* **primary trocar** *n term*, *rel* **port¹** *n term* → U136-5

instrument used to gain access² to a body cavity; it consists of a sharp-tipped obturator which is withdrawn after successful placement and a metal sleeve [iː] which provides access for instruments

» The Hasson cannula was used to allow primary trocar insertion under direct vision. A standard four-port access was obtained for laparoscopic cholecystectomy, comprising a 10mm umbilical port, a 10mm epigastric port, and two 5mm right upper quadrant ports. The primary trocar should be inserted only after determining the height of uterine fundus [ʌ].

Jse to place³/insert³/introduce³/reposition • **a trocar** • to anchor⁴ [k]/cantilever⁵/dislodge⁶ **a trocar** • to withdraw or retract⁷/steam-sterilize⁸ [iː] **a trocar** • to disassemble⁹/reassemble/rearm¹⁰ **a trocar** • secondary / working¹¹ / scope or camera-bearing¹² [ɚ] **trocar** • (non-)disposable¹³ / reusable [juː] or autoclavable¹⁴ [eɪ] **trocar** • metal / (lightweight) plastic / trumpet-type [ʌ] **trocar** • **trocar** placement or insertion / handle • **trocar** body / shaft / tip • working length of a¹⁵ **trocar** • laparoscopic / access / camera / 5mm **port** • **port** site¹⁶ [aɪ] / placement / assignment¹⁷ [aɪn]/ closure [oʊʒ] • array [əreɪ] of¹⁸ **ports** • **ports** are placed in an array • peri**trocar** gas leak [iː]

> **Note:** In laparoscopy the term **trocar** may stand for the obturator, the trocar sheath or the entire instrument. Strictly speaking, **port** refers to the access route established by the trocar, but in laparoscopic contexts the terms **port** and **trocar** (**sheath**) are often used synonymously. In endoscopy the term **port** is used to denote the access to the suction [ʌ], irrigation or working channels.

trocar sheath [ʃiːθ] or **sleeve** [iː] *n term*   *rel* **obturator¹** *n term*

outer cannula which remains in place after successful puncture [ʌ] and withdrawal of the obturator

» The sheath of a 5-mm trocar is then introduced into the abdominal cavity. The trocar sheath must have an airtight sealing² [iː] against the abdominal wall to prevent loss of pneumoperitoneum. A simple but efficient way of anchoring [k] the sheath is to place sutures. Complications with reusable trocars whose obturator point had been dulled³ [ʌ] by repeated use led us to abandon blind puncture in favor of the Hasson technique.

Jse outer / self-retaining⁴ [eɪ]/ beveled⁵ **sheath** • threaded⁶ [e] **sleeve** • pyradmidal pointed⁷ / conical / blunt-tipped⁸ / dull tip of⁹ **obturator**

safety mechanism [mek-] *n term*   *sim* **safety shield¹** [seɪfti ʃiːld] *n term*

device covering the sharp tip of the obturator to prevent inadvertent² [ɜː] injury to underlying tissues

» Because of the safety mechanism the sheaths of disposable trocars have vertically cut tips. This trocar comes with a safety shield which is designed to extend over the blade [eɪ] and decrease bowel [aʊ] injury with entry of the trocar into the peritoneal cavity.

Jse to trigger or release³ • **the safety shield** • (de)activated⁴ / integrated **safety shield**

valve mechanism [vælv] *n term*

valves preventing leakage [liːkɪdʒ] of gas¹ when instruments are passed through the trocar

» When the valve is opened, a seal prevents gas from escaping past an inserted instrument. To pass instruments into the trocar sheath the trumpet [ʌ] valve² has to be opened manually.

Jse Luer lock sidearm³ / two-way⁴ / flap⁵ **valve** • stopcock⁶ / ball-and-socket⁷ [ɒː]/ spring-loaded⁸ [oʊ] **valve**

retention feature [fiːtʃɚ] or **mechanism** *n term*   *syn* **retentive sleeve** *n term*

mechanism which helps secure the trocar sheath in position during surgical manipulation

» This trocar has an integrated retention feature¹. Some trocars have a Malecot-type retention feature² in their tips, the wings of which can be actively expanded after successful insertion.

Jse plastic / integral¹ / detachable³ [ætʃ] **retentive sleeve**

Primärtrokar
Port, Trokar¹ Zugang² einen Trokar setzen/ stechen/ einbringen/ platzieren³ den Trokar fixieren⁴ den Trokar schwenken⁵ den Trokar dislozieren⁶ d. Trokar entfernen⁷ d. Trokar autoklavieren⁸ d. Trokar zerlegen⁹ d. Trokar erneut bestücken¹⁰ Arbeitstrokar, Instrumentenport¹¹ Optiktrokar, Videoport¹² Einmaltrokar¹³ autoklavierbarer Trokar¹⁴ Arbeitslänge eines Trokars¹⁵ Einstichstelle d. Trokars¹⁶ Anordnung/ Platzierung d. Trokare¹⁷ Trokaranordnung¹⁸

5

Trokarhülse
Obturator, Trokardorn¹ luftdichter Verschluss² stumpf geworden³ selbstfixierende Trokarhülse⁴ vorne schräg angeschliffene Trokarhülse⁵ Trokarhülse m. integriertem Fixationsgrip/ Gripgewinde⁶ Obturator m. dreikantiger, schneidender Spitze⁷ stumpfer Obturator⁸ stumpfe Obturatorspitze⁹

6

Sicherheitsmechanismus, Sicherheitseinführschutz
Sicherheitsschild¹ versehentlich² d. Sicherheitsmechanismus aktivieren³ (de)aktivierter Sicherheitsmechanismus⁴

7

Trokarventil(mechanismus)
Ausströmen von Gas¹ Trompetenventil² genormter seitl. Zugang³ Zweiwegventil⁴ Klappenventil⁵ Drehventil⁶ Kugelventil⁷ Federventil⁸

8

Fixations-, Haltevorrichtung
integrierte Fixationsvorrichtung¹ Haltevorrichtung m. aufklappbarem Malecot-Körbchen (a. d. Trokarspitze)² abnehmbare Fixationsvorrichtung³

9

586 CLINICAL TERMS — Laparoscopic Equipment

sliding ring [slaɪdɪŋ rɪŋ] *n term*

device screwed[1] [uː] onto the trocar sheath to prevent it from being advanced too far into the abdomen

» In addition, an outer sliding ring can be locked[2] onto the trocar sheath at skin level so it cannot be retracted or advanced[3] inadvertently.

Use to backload the[4] **sliding ring**

Distanzring
geschraubt[1] befestigt[2] vorgeschoben[3] den Distanzring darüberschieben[4]

10

reducer [rɪd(j)uːsɚ] **(sheath** or **sleeve)** *n term*   sim **reducer cap**[1] *n term*

device for downsizing a trocar[2] so that smaller instruments can be passed without allowing gas to escape

» Both ends of the suture are pulled out through a reducer sheath or a suture introducer.

Reduzierhülse
Reduzierstück, -plättchen[1] Reduzieren d. Trokardurchmessers[2]

11

dilation set [daɪleɪʃən set] *n term*   rel **dilator**[1] [daɪleɪtɚ] *n term* → U132-17

instruments required for replacing a trocar by a larger one without loss of pneumoperitoneum

» The 8 F dilator is replaced by a 24 F dilator, over which the 10-mm trocar is inserted. Then a dilator of adequate size is preloaded with the larger trocar[2], and with a rotating movement the dilator, which has a blunt, threaded[3] tip, is advanced over the metal rod[4] into the abdomen. The dilator is introduced over a guide[5] [aɪ], and a trocar sheath is slid over the dilator.

Dilatationsbesteck
Dilatator[1] d. größere Trokar wird darübergeschoben[2] mit Gewinde[3] Metallstab[4] Führungsstab[5]

12

Veress needle [iː] or **cannula** [kænjələ] *n term*   syn **insufflation needle** *n term*

needle used to penetrate the peritoneal cavity and to initiate the pneumoperitoneum

» In the virgin abdomen[1] establishing a pneumoperitoneum is simple if the Mitchel technique of Veress cannula placement is used. The Veress needle must be placed as far as possible from adhesions [iː] and scarring[2] [ɑː] from previous [iː] surgery.

Use to insert or pass[3]/place[3] **the Veress needle** • **Veress** insufflation needle / needle injury • disposable / reusable[4] [riːjuːzəbl] **insufflation needle** • shaft[5] / hub[6] [ʌ] **of the Veress needle** • closed **Veress** technique

Veress-, Insufflationsnadel
nicht voroperiertes Abdomen[1] Vernarbung[2] die Veress-Nadel einführen[3] Mehrfachinsufflationsnadel[4] Schaft d. Veress-Nadel[5] Kopfstück d. Veress-Nadel[6]

13

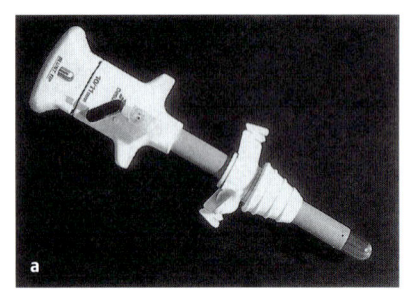

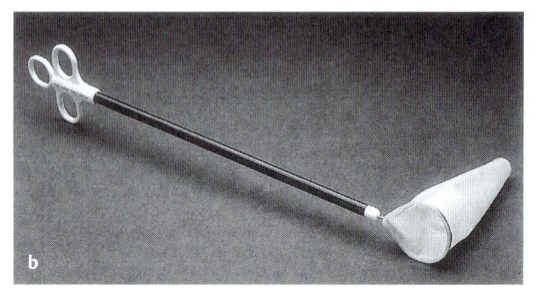

(a) blunt-tipped Hasson cannula inserted via minilaparotomy, (b) entrapment sack for retrieval of small organs

Hasson cannula or **trocar** *n term*   syn **Hasson-type cannula** *n term*

specially designed trocar consisting of a blunt-tipped obturator[1] and a conical outer adjustable sleeve

» The Hasson cannula was inserted through a stab incision[2]. We use the open Hasson technique to establish the pneumoperitoneum to reduce the risk of visceral [ɪs] injury.

Use collar of **the Hasson cannula** • open **Hasson cannula** placement[3] • open **Hasson** technique[3] [-iːk] • **Hasson trocar** technique

Hasson-Kanüle/ -Trokar(hülse)
stumpfer Mandrin[1] Stichinzision[2] Minilaparotomie[3]

14

insufflator *n term* → U128-10   rel **desufflation lever**[1] [e] *n term*

device controlling the flow of pressurized insufflation gas from the supply tank into the patient's abdomen

» Malfunction of the C0₂ insufflator was the cause of abdominal overdistention.

Use **insufflator** (pressure) gauge[2] [geɪdʒ]/ with built-in working channel • electronically controlled / CO_2 (gas)[3] / high-flow[4] **insufflator**

Insufflationsgerät, Insufflator
Desufflationshebel[1] Insufflationsdruckanzeige[2] CO_2-Insufflator[3] Insufflator mit hoher Durchflussrate[4]

15

Perioperative Management   CLINICAL TERMS **587**

entrapment sack *n term*   *syn* **retrieval** [iː] *or* **organ** *or* **specimen bag** *n term*
device for removing resected organs or tissue through a trocar to limit spread [e] of cancer or contagion¹ [eɪdʒ]
entrap¹ *v term* • **retrieve**² *v* → U128-17
» In pediatric nephrectomy, the organ can be removed directly without maneuvering it into an entrapment sack. We favor the specimen bag, as this minimizes specimen fragmentation.
Use specimen retrieval³ [iː] **bag** • mouth⁴ / neck *of the retrieval bag* • *entrapment sack* with built-in closure [oʊʒ] mechanism⁵ • impermeable⁶ [ɜː]/ self-unfolding⁷ *entrapment sack* • *entrapped* specimen • organ *retrieval*

Organ-, Bergebeutel, Organ(bergungs)sack, Endobag
Ansteckung, Krankheitsübertragung¹ bergen, entfernen² Bergebeutel, Organsack³ Öffnung d. Bergebeutels⁴ Organbeutel m. integriertem Verschlussmechanismus⁵ undurchlässiger Organsack⁶ sich automatisch öffnender Organsack⁷   16

morcellator [mɔːrsəleɪtɚ] *n term*   *sim* **tissue homogenizer**¹ [ɒːdʒ] *n term*
instrument for fragmenting tissue specimens too large to be removed intact
morcellation² *n* • **morcellate** *v* → U128-16
» So far, we have had no need to employ a tissue morcellator in pediatric nephrectomy.
Use electrical tissue / aspirating³ *morcellator* • *morcellation* process²

Gewebezerkleinerer, Morcellator
Gewebehomogenisator¹ Morcellement, Zerstückelung² Morcellator m. Saugvorrichtung (z. Fixierung v. Gewebe³   17

Unit 134 Perioperative Management
Related Units: 126 Surgical Treatment, 131 Surgical Suite, 135 Anesthesiology, 139 Asepsis, 140 Wound Healing

preoperative assessment *n term*   *syn* **preoperative workup** *n jar*
patient evaluation¹ including a detailed history², PE³, and specific diagnostic investigations⁴
» The nutritional [ɪʃ] status⁵ [eɪ] of the patient is an essential factor in the preoperative workup. Additional workup including skin testing and a biopsy [aɪ] is required. The preoperative evaluation should be completed before hospitalization.
Use to undergo or have⁶ *a workup* • (non)emergency / initial / outpatient⁷ / diagnostic⁴ / routine / extensive / laboratory / complete urologic / prebiopsy *workup*

Anamnese u. präop. Diagnostik
Abklärung¹ Anamnese² körperl. Untersuchung, Status(erhebung)³ diagnost. Untersuchungen⁴ Ernährungsstatus⁵ s. einer Durchuntersuchung unterziehen⁶ ambulante Untersuchungen⁷   1

patient selection [sɪlɛkʃən] *n term*
select¹ *v & adj* • **selective** *adj* • **unselectively** *adv*
» Specific indications for the selection of patients for curative radiotherapy are listed below.
Use **in selected** patients² / cases • donor-recipient³ [sɪ]/ drug *selection* • *selection* criteria⁴ [aɪ] • *selective* angiography⁵

Patientenselektion
auswählen; ausgewählt¹ bei ausgewählten Patienten² Spender-Empfänger-Auswahl³ Selektions-, Auswahlkriterien⁴ selektive Angiografie⁵   2

informed consent *n term*   *sim* **operative permit**¹ *n term*
agreement (usually in writing²) by a patient, guardian³ [gɑːrdiən] or next of kin⁴ to treatment suggested [dʒ] by the physician or surgeon
informed waiver⁵ [eɪ] *n term*
» Informed consent must be based on a full discussion of the potential benefits⁶, risks, and complications of the treatment proposed as well as a discussion of alternative options.
Use to obtain⁷/be (in)capable of giving / full / written / voluntary / presumed⁸ *informed consent* • *informed consent* form⁹ / for removal of tissue for grafting¹⁰

Einwilligung(serklärung) nach Aufklärung
Operationseinwilligung¹ schriftlich² gesetzliche(r) Vertreter(in), Vormund³ Angehörige(r)⁴ aufgeklärte Verzicht(s)erklärung⁵ mögliche Vorteile⁶ E. einholen⁷ angenommene E.⁸ Einwilligungsformular⁹ E. zur Gewebeentnahme für e. Transplantation¹⁰   3

presurgical anxiety [æŋzaɪəti] *n term* → U77-5
commonly includes emotional strain¹ [eɪ] created by the prospect² of surgery, worries about losing job, friends, etc.
» Anxiety and fear [fɪɚ] are normal in patients undergoing surgery³. Patients facing surgery⁴ may be beset by⁵ fears of anesthesia [-iːʒə] or death. Relieving anxiety⁶ and restlessness⁷ is one of the principal goals⁸ [oʊ] of preoperative medication⁹.

Operationsangst
emotionelle Belastung¹ Aussicht² s. einer Op. unterziehen³ denen eine Op. bevorsteht⁴ befallen von⁵ Angstabbau⁶ Unruhe⁷ Hauptziele⁸ Prämedikation⁹   4

134

CLINICAL TERMS — Perioperative Management

Proper psychological preparation for the operative stress includes permitting the patient some degree of anxiety, as it will eventually help him to develop effective ways of coping with the situation.

(operative) risk n & v term   sim **hazard**[1] n → U8-4; U91-5

at-risk[2] adj term • **poor-/ low-risk**[3] adj • **risk-benefit ratio**[4] [reɪʃiou] n

» Their risk of acquiring [kwaɪ] cancer is two times that of age-matched controls[5]. Patients who have sustained[6] [eɪ] head injuries are at risk for/of spinal injury. This patient is a good operative risk[7]. The risks associated with the procedure are too high.

Use to face/run or take[8]/have/expose to/carry or involve[9]/avoid/lessen/reduce/minimize/eliminate **a risk** • (peri)operative / increased / long-term / overall[10] / potential / high-/good-**risk** • **high-risk** patient[11] • **risk** factor / group • life-threatening[12] [e] **hazard**

(Operations)risiko; Risiko eingehen
Risiko, Gefahr[1] Risiko-[2] risikoarm, m. geringem R.[3] Risiko-Nutzen-Verhältnis[4] Kontrollpersonen[5] erlitten[6] hat ein sehr geringes Operationsrisiko[7] R. eingehen[8] mit R. verbunden sein[9] Gesamtrisiko[10] Risikopatient(in)[11] lebensbedrohliche Gefahr[12]
    5

---

preoperative bowel [baʊəl] **preparation** n term   syn **bowel prep** n jar

in elective procedures[1] most patients are put on a light diet[2] or fasted[3] overnight and may be given a cleansing [e] enema[4] the evening before; esp. for intestinal surgery mechanical [k] cleansing of the bowels[5], laxatives[6], or whole-gut [ʌ] lavage[7] [ləvɑːʒ] and systemic antibiotics may be required

» Measures taken to eliminate the fecal mass[8] [iː] and reduce the number of bacteria [ɪɚ] as much as possible prior [aɪ] to surgery[9] are known as the "bowel prep".

präop. Darmentleerung
elektive Eingriffe[1] auf leichte Kost gesetzt[2] nüchtern bleiben müssen[3] Klistier, Einlauf[4] Darmreinigung[5] Abführmittel[6] Darmspülung[7] Stuhl[8] präoperativ[9]
    6

---

postoperative course [kɔːrs] n term

progress[1] the patients makes after the operation (convalescence[2] [-esᵊn¹s], complications)

» The appearance of a pleural effusion[3] late in the postoperative course suggested[4] the presence of a subdiaphragmatic [aɪə] inflammation. At this time the surgeon should explain the operation and the expected postoperative course to the patient.

Use smooth [uː] or uneventful or uncomplicated[5] **course** • preoperative **course**

postoperativer Verlauf
Fortschritte[1] Rekonvaleszenz[2] Pleuraerguss[3] deutete hin auf[4] komplikationsfreier Verlauf[5]
    7

---

postanesthetic observation n term   syn **monitoring** n,   sim **surveillance**[1] [sərveɪlən¹s] n term

as the patient recovers from the effects of the anesthetic[2] the vital [aɪ] signs[3] [aɪ] are closely watched; in some patients invasive [eɪ] monitoring, cardiopulmonary [u‖ʌ] support and critical care management[4] are required

observe[5] v • **observer** n • **monitor**[6] v & n term

» Appearance of a mass while the patient is under observation may be a sign of local perforation. Pulse [ʌ] oximetry is increasingly becoming a standard of care in patient monitoring during general anesthesia.

Use period of / close[7] / continuous[8] / frequent observation • cardiac[9] / Holter **monitor** • hourly[10] [aʊɚli]/ hemodynamic [iː]/ intraoperative **monitoring**

postop. Überwachung
Beobachtung[1] Anästhetikum[2] Vitalfunktionen[3] Intensivtherapie[4] beobachten[5] überwachen; Monitor, Überwachungsgerät[6] intensive Ü.[7] ständige Überwachung[8] Herzmonitor[9] stündliche Überprüfung[10]
    8

---

complication n term & clin   sim **sequel** [siːkwəl] or **sequela**[1] [sɪkwelə] n term -ae [iː] pl

(i) generally the occurrence [ɜ] of concomitant disorders[2] in a patient (ii) in surgery, any intra- or postoperative event, injury or disorder that sets back[3] or delays the patient's convalescence

(un)complicated[4] adj • **uneventful**[5] adj

» Complications are most common on the 2nd to 5th postoperative days. Major bleeding is the most worrisome[6] complication. Vitreous [ɪ] hemorrhage is a common sequela. The postoperative course was uneventful.

Use to avoid[7]/prevent/preclude[8]/suspect/develop/lead to/contribute to[9]/be due to[10] **complications** • rare / minor [aɪ] / serious [ɪɚ]/ life-threatening[11] [e]/ anesthetic-related / late[12] / wound [uː] **complication** • **complication** rate[13] [eɪ] • **(un)complicated** postoperative course / delivery[14] / fracture • long-term[15] **sequelae**

Komplikation
Folge(erscheinung)[1] Begleiterkrankungen[2] zurückwerfen[3] komplikationslos, -frei[4] unauffällig[5] beunruhigend[6] Komplikationen vermeiden[7] K. ausschließen[8] zu K. beitragen[9] auf K. zurückzuführen sein[10] lebensbedrohliche K.[11] Spätkomplikation[12] Komplikationsrate[13] schwierige/ Entbindung[14] Langzeitfolgen[15]
    9

Perioperative Management   CLINICAL TERMS **589**

adhesion [ædhiːʒən] *n term*   *sim* **adherence**[1] [ɪəˑ] *n term*

two surfaces which are normally separate adhere to each other[2] due to scar formation[3], e.g. after abdominal surgery; adhesions which produce intestinal obstruction [ʌ] have to be released[4] [iː] on repeat [iː] surgery[5]

adhesiolysis[6] [-ɒːlɪsɪs] *n term* • **adherent**[7] *adj* • **adhesio-** *comb*

» *Formation of adhesions acquired from abdominal operations is more commonly seen in adults.*

Use to form/produce/cause/develop/prevent/free[8]/lyse[8] [aɪs‖z] **adhesions** • fibrous [aɪ]/ bowel[9] [baʊəl]/ inflammatory **adhesions** • **adhesio**tomy[6]

Verwachsung, -klebung, Adhäsion
Anhaftung, Adhärenz[1] miteinander verkleben[2] Narbenbildung[3] gelöst[4] Reoperation[5] Adhäsiolyse, Lösen v. Adhäsionen[6] adhärent, verklebt, -wachsen[7] Verwachsungen lösen[8] Darmadhäsionen[9]
10

postoperative hospitalization *or* **hospital stay** [steɪ] *n term*

time of required postop inpatient care[1] (observation and treatment) until discharge[2] [dɪstʃɑːrdʒ]

» *Early surgery can reduce the length of postoperative hospitalization by[3] 5 – 7 days. In the event of[4] complications the hospital stay will be longer. The laparoscopic technique reportedly achieves similar results with a shorter hospital stay and convalescence.*

Use short / prolonged[5] / reduced **hospital stay**

postop. Krankenhausaufenthalt
stationäre Behandlung[1] Entlassung[2] um[3] bei (Auftreten von)[4] längerer Krankenhausaufenthalt[5]
11

postoperative oral intake *n term*

most patients are first put on TPN[1] or a clear liquid diet[2] [daɪət] and only gradually resume regular oral intake[3]

» *These patients do not benefit from[4] total parenteral nutrition[1] and can resume an oral diet.*

Use (un)restricted[5] / permissible[6] **oral intake** • fluid[7] / protein / nutrient[8] / salt **intake**

postop. Nahrungsaufnahme
künstl. Ernährung[1] flüssige Nahrung (ohne Einlage)[2] zur normalen Kost zurückkehren[3] profitieren von[4] eingeschränkte N.[5] erlaubte N.[6] Flüssigkeitszufuhr[7] Nährstoffzufuhr[8]
12

ambulation *n term sing*   *sim* **mobilization**[1] *n term* → U64-2; U141-5

walking about[2] and not confined [aɪ] to bed[3] (e.g as a result of surgery or disease)

ambulate[2] *v term* • **mobilize**[4] *v* • **ambulatory**[5] *adj*

» *Initial treatment consists of bed rest[6] for a few days followed by ambulation on crutches[7] [ʌtʃ]. Vomiting was precipitated[8] by ambulation. The catheter can be removed if the patient is expected to ambulate. Dietary measures [eʒ], early mobilization[9] and active rehabilitation are essential in all cases. Gradual mobilization with protected weight [weɪt] bearing[10] [eəˑ] follows.*

Use early[9] / crutch[7] / indoor / progressive / limited / prolonged **ambulation** • controlled / exaggerated[11] [ædʒ]/ passive **mobilization** • **ambulatory** patient[12] / care[13] / therapy / monitoring

Umhergehen, Mobilisation
Mobilisation, -sierung[1] umhergehen[2] bettlägrig[3] mobilisieren[4] gehfähig, mobil; ambulant[5] Bettruhe[6] Gehen an Krücken[7] ausgelöst durch[8] Frühmobilisation[9] vorsichtige Belastung[10] übermäßige Mobilisation[11] gehfähige(r) Patient(in)[12] ambulante Behandlung[13]
13

return to normal activity *phr term*   *sim* **recovery**[1] [ʌ], **recuperation**[1] [uː], **convalescence**[1] *n clin*

progressive improvement[2] as the symptoms disappear and body functions return to normal

convalesce[3] [-les] *v* • **convalescent**[4] *adj & n* • **recuperate**[3] *v* • **recover**[3] *v i/t*

» *Recuperation and return to normal activity are usually faster in minimal access surgery[5]. Most patients improve sufficiently [ɪʃ] to return to full activity. In these young amputees[6] anything but return to full function is not acceptable.*

Use **time to** recovery[7] / disease progression / recurrence • **to recover** from an illness / one's eyesight[8] [-saɪt] • to resume **normal activities** • to accelerate[9] [kse] /promote/delay[10] [eɪ] /prolong **recovery** • partial / (in)complete / prompt / quick or rapid / spontaneous[11] [eɪ]/ functional **recovery** • hope / chance / period[7] [ɪəˑ] extent **of recovery** • **convalescent** stage / period[7] / home[12]

Wiederaufnahme d. Aktivitäten d. tägl. Lebens
Genesung, Rekonvaleszenz[1] fortschreitende Besserung[2] genesen, sich erholen; etw. wiedererlangen[3] genesend; Rekonvaleszent(in)[4] minimal invasive Chirurgie[5] Amputierte[6] Genesungszeit[7] Sehkraft wiedererlangen[8] Genesung beschleunigen[9] G. verzögern[10] Spontanheilung[11] Erholungsheim[12]
14

postoperative follow-up *n term*   *syn* **followup**, *abbr* **f/u** *or* **F/U**

examining, monitoring or observing the progress made by the patient in the postoperative course

follow[1] *v term*

» *Follow-up visits should be scheduled[2] [sk‖ʃ] at 4- to 6-week intervals. The patient was advised to seek followup consultation[3] with his primary-care physician[4]. This is a 10-year follow-up study[5].*

Use to require/receive/arrange/refer for[6]/be discharged [-tʃɑːrdʒd] to[7] **follow-up** • **follow-up** examination / care / appointment[8] / instructions / period / evaluation / testing • long-term / 5-year / telephone / periodic / close[9] / daily / outpatient[10] **followup** • at[11] **followup**

Nachuntersuchung, -sorge, Verlaufskontrolle
nachuntersuchen, Verlaufskontrolle durchführen[1] terminisiert[2] zur Nachsorge kommen[3] prakt. Arzt, Hausarzt[4] Verlaufskontrollstudie[5] zur Nachsorge überweisen[6] zur N. entlassen werden[7] Nachuntersuchungstermin[8] intensive Nachsorge[9] ambulante N.[10] bei der/ zum Zeitpunkt der Nachunters.[11]
15

134

CLINICAL TERMS — Anesthesiology

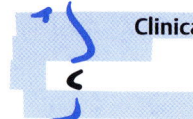

Clinical Phrases

Are you on any medication? Nehmen Sie irgendwelche Medikamente? • Nurse, please prepare Mr. Smith for a colectomy on Monday. Schwester, bereiten Sie bitte Herrn S. für die am Montag geplante Kolektomie vor. • The patient was put on a clear liquid diet. Der Patient bekam nur flüssige Nahrung. • Early ambulation should be encouraged. Der Patient sollte möglichst früh mobilisiert werden. • Mrs. Moore has made a complete recovery. Frau M. ist vollkommen wiederhergestellt. • Ten out of 154 patients were lost to followup. Zehn von 154 Patienten erschienen nicht mehr zur Nachuntersuchung. • Followups were performed at 6 and 12 months postoperatively. Verlaufskontrollen wurden 6 und 12 Monate nach dem chirurgischen Eingriff durchgeführt.

Unit 135 Anesthesiology

Related Units: 93 Anesthetics, 7 Consciousness, 104 Pain, 134 Perioperative Management, 125 Critical Care

anesthetize [ənesθɪtaɪz] v term, BE **anaesthetise, -ize** [iː]
    syn **put under** v phr clin

to induce a loss of feeling or sensation by means of anesthetic drugs
put to sleep[1] phr inf •
anesthetization [eǁiː] n term • **unanesthetized** adj
» The catheter can be placed after anesthetization. In the anesthetized arm surgery was tolerated up to 30 min. Anesthetize the skin with lidocaine [aɪ] using a 10mL syringe [dʒ] and 22-gauge [ɡeɪdʒ] needle. The wound may be anesthetized locally with lidocaine. After full nebulized[2] lidocaine anesthetization of the pharynx and vocal cords the bronchoscope is passed through the nostrils[3].
Use deeply[4] **anesthetized** • **anesthetized** area / wound [uː]/ operative field / patient / skin / eye • **anesthetizing** needle / drugs[5]

anästhesieren, narkotisieren, betäuben
einschläfern[1] vernebelt[2] Nasenöffnungen, -löcher[3] unter starken Narkotika stehend, stark narkotisiert[4] Anästhetika, Narkotika[5]

[1]

anesthesia [ænəsθiːʒə] n term & clin   syn & rel **anesthesiology** n term

(i) informal term for anesthesiology
(ii) partial or complete loss of sensation, esp. when induced by pharmacologic depression of nerve function [ʌ] to permit performance of surgery or other painful procedures
anesthetic[1] [e] adj & n term • **anesthesiologist**[2] [iː] or BE **anaesthetist**[2] n
» This procedure can be performed under local anesthesia on an outpatient basis[3]. The main objectives[4] of general anesthesia are analgesia [-dʒiːzɪə], unconsciousness, skeletal muscle relaxation and control of sympathetic nervous system responses to noxious[5] [nɒkʃəs] stimuli [aɪ].
Use prompt onset of[6] / time under / level of[7] / recovery from / surgical / standby / conduction[8] **anesthesia** • to administer/induce[9] /maintain[10]/awaken from **anesthesia** • **anesthesia** management[11] / consent / consultation / accident / hazard[12] / adjuvant • **anesthesia of the** skin / airway • **anesthesia for** abdominal surgery / children • monitored **anesthetic** care[13] • **anesthesiologist** on-call[14]

(i) **Anästhesie, Narkose, Anästhesiologie**
(ii) **Betäubung, Schmerzunempfindlichkeit**
anästhetisch; Anästhetikum, Narkotikum[1] Anästhesist(in), Anästhesiologe/-in, Narkosearzt/-ärztin[2] ambulant[3] Ziele[4] schädlich[5] rascher Wirkungseintritt[6] Narkosetiefe[7] Leitungsanästhesie[8] N. einleiten[9] N. aufrechterhalten[10] Narkoseführung[11] Narkoserisiko[12] anästhesiologische Überwachung[13] diensthabende(r) Anästhesist(in)[14]

Note: In the States the *anesthetic* may be administered by the *anesthesiologist* or another physician, a *nurse anesthetist*, or an *anesthesia assistant*. Unlike in British usage, the *anesthesiologist* is never referred to as the *anesthetist*.

[2]

numb [nʌm] adj & v clin   syn **blunt** [ʌ] adj & v, **dull** [ʌ], **deaden** [dedᵊn] v inf

(adj) lack or loss of sensation, e.g. because of cold, poor blood perfusion or anesthesia
numbness[1] n clin • **benumb**[2] v inf
» My face is numb. As anesthesia blunts the normal compensatory mechanisms, sudden changes in the patient's position can cause hypotension. Numbness may be used to describe a complete loss of feeling, paresthesias [- θiːʒ(ɪ)əs], or paralysis. The patient complained that his feet had a numb or wooden feeling. Frostbitten[3] parts are numb, painless, and of a white or waxy[4] appearance.
Use **numb** fingers / feeling / chin [tʃ] syndrome [ɪ] • **numbness** and tingling[5] [ŋg] • temporary / partial / subjective / facial [eɪʃ] **numbness** • nerve-**numbing** drugs[6] • **blunted** sensation / response / reflexes / affect[7] • **dulled** perception[8]

taub; betäuben, unempfindlich (machen)
Taubheit, Gefühllosigkeit[1] betäuben[2] v. Erfrierungen betroffen[3] wächsern[4] Taubheitsgefühl u. Kribbeln[5] nervenbetäubende Medikamente[6] Affektabstumpfung[7] eingeschränktes Wahrnehmungsvermögen[8]

[3]

Anesthesiology   CLINICAL TERMS **591**

hyp(o)esthesia [haɪpesθiːʒə] *n term*   *syn* **blunted sensation** *n clin & inf*

diminished sensation¹ (hyposensitivity¹) in reaction to stimulation (esp. touch)

hyp(o)-/ hyperesthetic *adj term* • **paresthesia**² *n* • **hyperesthesia**³ *n*

» Sensory symptoms include hypesthesia (numbness or impaired feeling) or paresthesia (tingling, pins and needles⁴, or a painful burning). Abnormal spontaneous sensations are generally termed paresthesias. The involved zone was hyperesthetic.

Use **hypesthetic** area – malar⁵ [eɪ]/ corneal / transitory⁶ **hypesthesia** • distal extremity / limb⁷ [lɪm]/ facial / peri- or circumoral **paresthesias**

Hypästhesie, verminderte (Berührungs)empfindlichkeit
herabgesetzte Sensibilität¹ Parästhesie, subjektive Missempfindung² Hyperästhesie, Überempfindlichkeit³ Kribbeln, Ameisenlaufen⁴ Hypästhesie der Wange⁵ vorübergehende H.⁶ Parästhesien i. d. Extremitäten⁷   **4**

---

narcotics *n term usu pl, abbr* **narc**   *syn* **narcotic agent/ drug** *n clin* → U11-1

(i) drugs (e.g. morphine and other opium derivatives) used in moderate doses to relieve pain, dull sensation, and induce profound [aʊ] sleep that have the potential for dependence and tolerance¹ on repeated administration
(ii) illegal and street drugs such as marijuana, LSD, etc.

narcotic² *adj & n term & clin*
nonnarcotic *adj & n term* • **narcotize**³ *v* • **narco-** *comb*

» Increasing amounts of narcotics were required. The terms narcotics and opioids are often used interchangeably⁴ for drugs whose effects mimic⁵ those of morphine.

Use sedative / intravenous [iː]/ parenteral / long-acting / epidural / opioid⁶ **narcotics** • **narcotic** addict⁷ / effect / analgesics⁸ • **narco**lepsy /hypnosis [hɪp-] /anesthesia

**(i) Narkotika, Anästhetika
(ii) Rauschmittel, -gift**
Gewöhnung, Toleranzentwicklung¹ Narkose-; Narkotikum, Rauschgift² narkotisieren, betäuben³ synonym⁴ ähnlich sein⁵ Opioide⁶ Rauschgiftabhängige(r)⁷ narkotisch wirkende Analgetika⁸

5

---

narcosis [nɑːrkoʊsɪs] *n term*

a state of stupor¹ [st(j)uːpɚ] or deep sleep rather than anesthesia produced by intoxicants², narcotics, or toxins

» In many people narcosis is induced at twice the legal intoxication level. Pain relief may be achieved through the judicious³ [dʒuːdɪʃəs] use of analgesics ranging from nonnarcotics to narcotic derivatives.

Use nitrogen [aɪ]/ inert [ɜː] gas⁴ / CO₂ **narcosis** • **narcotic** abuse / intoxication / poisoning / overdose / analgesia / antagonist / substitute⁵ / withdrawal⁶ • **narcotic**-induced /-related /-containing

> **Note:** In contrast to other languages (e.g. German), *narcosis* is rarely used in medical English and is hardly ever synonymous with *anesthesia*.

tiefe Bewusstlosigkeit, Narkose
Stupor, Reaktionsunfähigkeit¹ Rauschmittel² umsichtig³ Edelgasnarkose⁴ Ersatzdroge⁵ Entzug von Narkotika⁶

6

---

analgesia [ænᵊldʒiːzɪə] *n term*   → U104-20

a state in which painful stimuli [aɪ] are perceived¹ [iː] but are not interpreted as pain; usually accompanied by sedation without loss of consciousness

analgesic² [ænᵊldʒiːsɪk‖zɪk] *adj & n term*

» Provide analgesia as needed³. 10 mg of epidural morphine produces satisfactory analgesia in 90% of patients for 15–16 hours.

Use to administer/give/increase **analgesia** • (in)adequate / narcotic / (non)opioid / local / patient-controlled⁴ (*abbr* PCA) **analgesia** • duration / use / reversal⁵ / rapid onset of analgesia • **analgesic** agent [eɪdʒ-]/ activity⁶ / administration / compound⁷ / dose / effect⁶ • **analgesic** ingestion⁸ [dʒ]/ lozenges⁹ [lɒːzɪndʒ-]/ regimen¹⁰ [edʒ]/ properties¹¹ / substance / state¹² / therapy • oral / systemic / mild / simple / (non)narcotic / (non)opioid / nonaddicting¹³ / urinary [jʊɚ]/ central-acting¹⁴ **analgesics**

Analgesie, Aufhebung d. Schmerzempfindung
wahrgenommen¹ schmerzlindernd; Analgetikum, Schmerzmittel² nach Bedarf³ patientengesteuerte A.⁴ Umkehr der analget. Wirkung⁵ analget. Wirkung⁶ analget. Kombinationspräparat⁷ Einnahme v. Schmerzmitteln⁸ schmerzlindernde Pastillen⁹ schmerzstillende Maßnahmen¹⁰ analget. Eigenschaften¹¹ Analgesiestadium¹² nicht abhängig machende Analgetika¹³ zentral wirkende A.¹⁴   **7**

---

sedation [sɪdeɪʃᵊn] *n term*

(i) to relax and calm down a patient especially by the administration of sedatives
(ii) the state so induced

sedate¹ [eɪ] *v term* • **sedative**² [e] *adj* • **presedation** [iː] *adj*

» In the awake patient, neuromuscular blockade should be accompanied by sedation to blunt the noxious sensation of paralysis.

Use to be under³ **sedation** • conscious⁴ [ʃ]/ sleep⁵ / intravenous / preoperative **sedation** • **sedative** effect / action of drug / narcotic • **sedated** patient

Sedierung, Beruhigung
sedieren¹ beruhigend, sedierend² sediert sein³ schwache Sedierung⁴ Schlafsedierung⁵

8

sedative [e] *n term*   *sim* **hypnotic**[1] [hɪpnɒ:tɪk] *adj & n term*

    drug reducing nervous excitement[2] and irritability by depressing the CNS; it has a relaxing effect and tends to produce lassitude[3]; the terms sedatives, hypnotics, anxiolytics [1], antianxiety [aɪə] drugs and minor tranquilizers are often used interchangeably

» This sedative is habit-forming[4]. Heavy sedation should be avoided, but small doses of tranquilizers may be helpful in calming[5] [kɑ:m-] the emotionally disturbed patient on the first few days. Sedative and hypnotic drugs often cause restlessness[6], mental confusion[7], and uncooperative behavior in the elderly. All available hypnotics involve some risk of overdosage, habituation[8], tolerance and addiction.

Use narcotic / general / cough[9] [kɒ:f] **sedative** • **hypnotic** drug / effect / sedative or sedative hypnotic[1]

tranquilize [træŋkwɪlaɪz] *v term, BE* **tranquillize**

    to calm or quiet down anxious[1] [æŋkʃəs] or mentally disturbed patients with pacifying[2] [aɪ] or soothing[3] [u:] drugs that have no sedating or depressant effects

    tranquilizer[4] *n* • **tranquilizing** *adj* • **tranquilization**[5] *n term*

» Minor [aɪ] tranquilizers are antianxiety agents[6] (e.g. Valium, Librium), whereas major [meɪdʒɚ] tranquilizers are neuroleptics[7] such as chlorpromazine (Thorazine).

Use mild [aɪ] **tranquilizer** • **tranquilizing** drugs

paralyze [pærəlaɪz] *v term*   *rel* **paresis**[1] [i:], **palsy**[2] [pɒ:lzi] *n term* → U113-7

    to cause a loss of motor function (usually through injury to or disease of the nerve supply [aɪ])

    paralysis[2] *n term* • **paralyzed** *adj* • **paralytic** *adj* • **-plegia** [-i:dʒ(ɪ)ə] *comb*

» Make sure the endotracheal [eɪk] tube does not leak and the patient is well sedated or paralyzed. Paralysis denotes inability of a conscious patient to move the extremity either spontaneously or in response to commands or painful stimuli. Although paralysis by muscle relaxants decreases the need for volatile anesthetics[3], many signs of anesthesia[4] are absent in the paralyzed patient.

Use to cause/reverse[5] **paralysis** • flaccid[6] [(k)s] / motor[7] / spastic[8] / symmetric descending[9] / total / neuromuscular / 6th nerve / periodic / progressive / impending[10] / anesthesia / facial / respiratory[11] / diaphragmatic / vocal cord[12] **paralysis** • **paralytic** disease / polio[13] / seafood poisoning • **paralytic** patient / muscle / cord / limb [lɪm]

anesthetic [e] **risk** *n term* → U134-5

» In the preoperative [i:] anesthesia [i:] interview[1] the anesthetic risk can be estimated by a precise history[2] of the patient's previous [i:] experiences with anesthesia, eliciting[3] data on allergic reactions, delayed awakening[4], prolonged paralysis from neuromuscular blocking agents, etc.

Use overall **anesthetic risk**

anesthetic induction [ʌ] *n term*

    period from the start of anesthesia to the establishment of a depth of anesthesia[1] sufficient [ɪʃ] for surgery

    induce[2] [ɪnd(j)u:s] *v term* • **inductive** [ɪndʌktɪv] *adj*

» Unless the patient has ingested [dʒe] solid food[3], it is reasonable to allow clear fluids[4] orally up to 2 hours before induction of anesthesia. General anesthesia can be induced by IV drugs, by inhalation, or a combination of both methods. Rapid-sequence [i:] induction[5] minimizes the time during which the trachea [treɪkɪə] is unprotected.

Use **anesthetic induction** agent / regimen[6] [edʒ] • **induction** of general anesthesia • inhalation / combined intravenous-inhalation **induction**

anesthesia machine *n term*   *rel* **anesthetic circuit**[1] [sɜ:rkɪt] *n term*

    apparatus complete with flowmeters[2] [i:], vaporizers[3] [eɪ], and sources of compressed gases used for inhalation anesthesia[4]; connected with the mechanisms for elimination of carbon dioxide[5] [aɪ] and the anesthetic circuit (reservoir bag, directional valves[6] [vælvz], breathing tubes[7] [i:], CO_2 absorber)

» Malfunction of the anesthesia machine may lead to increased pressures which results in pneumothorax [n(j)u:-] in the patient.

Sedativum, Beruhigungsmittel

hypnotisch; Schlafmittel, Hypnotikum[1] Erregung[2] Müdigkeit, Mattigkeit[3] zu Abhängigkeit führend[4] beruhigen[5] Unruhe[6] geistige Verwirrtheit[7] Gewöhnung, Habituation[8] Antitussivum, Hustenreiz hemmendes M.[9]

9

beruhigen, sedieren

unruhig, ängstlich[1] beruhigend[2] besänftigend[3] Tranquilizer, Sedativum[4] Beruhigung, Sedierung[5] Anxiolytika, Ataraktika[6] Neuroleptika, Antipsychotika[7]

10

lähmen, paralysieren

Parese, (unvollständige) Lähmung[1] Lähmung, Paralyse, Plegie[2] Inhalationsanästhetika[3] Narkosezeichen[4] Lähmung rückgängig machen[5] schlaffe Lähmung[6] motorische Lähmung[7] spastische Lähmung[8] symmetr. absteigende Lähmung[9] drohende Lähmung[10] Atemlähmung[11] Stimmbandlähmung[12] paralytische Poliomyelitis[13]

11

Narkoserisiko

Anästhesiesprechstunde[1] Anamnese[2] erheben, erfragen[3] verzögertes Erwachen[4]

12

Narkoseeinleitung

Narkosetiefe[1] einleiten[2] feste Nahrung zu sich genommen[3] Flüssigkeiten[4] kurze Anflutungszeit[5] Einleitungsschema[6]

13

Narkosegerät, -apparat

Narkosesystem[1] Gasflussmesser, Rotameter[2] Verdampfer, -nebler[3] Inhalationsnarkose[4] Kohlendioxid[5] Richtungsventile[6] Atemschläuche[7]

14

Anesthesiology CLINICAL TERMS 593

anesthesia bag and **mask** n term
sim **breathing** [iː] or **reservoir bag**[1] n term → U8-12

collapsible[2] reservoir for inhaling [eɪ] and exhaling[3] gases during general anesthesia or artificial ventilation[4]

» Check for a leak[5] [iː] between the endotracheal tube and the larynx by connecting a pressure-monitored anesthesia bag to the circuit and allow it to inflate[6] [eɪ].

Use self-refilling **bag-mask** combination / unit • **bag-valve** mask • Ambu[7] **bag**

Narkosemaske
Atembeutel[1] faltbar, zusammenklappbar[2] ausatmen[3] künstliche Beatmung[4] Leck, undichte Stelle[5] aufblasen, sich füllen[6] Ambubeutel[7]

15

infusion pump [ʌ] n term → U136-1

apparatus to deliver measured [eɜ] amounts[1] [aʊ] of anesthetics or drugs over a period of time

» The dosage for adults is given as a continuous intravenous infusion[2] via[3] an infusion pump.

Use intravenous [iː]/ subcutaneous [eɪ]/ implantable[4] / constant / portable[5] / home **infusion pump**

Infusions-, Spritzenpumpe
definierte Mengen abgeben/ einleiten[1] Dauerinfusion[2] mittels, über[3] implantierbare Infusionspumpe[4] tragbare Infusionsp.[5]

16

intubate [ɪnt(j)uːbeɪt] v term → U123-10

inserting[1] an oro- or nasotracheal tube for anesthesia to prevent aspiration and/or control pulmonary [u‖ʌ] ventilation

intubation n term • **intubator**[2] n • **extubate** v

» Use of sedation alone to intubate a patient in the ER[3] can be difficult and risky. If the patient has no gag reflex[4], intubate the trachea with a cuffed [ʌ] endotracheal tube[5] to protect the airway[6].

Use to facilitate **intubation** • **intubation** tube[7] • (endo-, oro-, naso-)tracheal / low-pressure cuff / blind / controlled[8] / digital[9] **intubation** • **intubated** orally or via the mouth / patient • experienced **intubator** • **intubator's** skill[10] / hand / finger

intubieren
einführen[1] intubierende(r) Arzt/ Ärztin[2] Notaufnahme[3] Würgreflex[4] Endotrachealtubus m. Manschette[5] Atemwege[6] Tubus, Intubationsrohr[7] Intubation unter Sicht[8] I. unter digitaler Kontrolle[9] Können d. intubierenden Arztes/ Ärztin[10]

17

Esmarch [k] **tourniquet** [tɜːrnɪkət] n term → U8-8
syn **Esmarch's bandage** or **wrap** [ræp] n term

broad elastic bandage or rubber with a chain fastener[1] [fæsᵊnɚ] wrapped around a limb as a tourniquet[2]

» An Esmarch tourniquet was used to create a blood-free field for the procedure.

Use **Esmarch** maneuver[3] [uː] • to apply/use/release[4] [iː] /loosen[5] [uː] /remove a **tourniquet** • **tourniquet** time / ischemia [skiː]/ constriction / inflation[6] / effect

Esmarch Binde
Kettenverschluss[1] Stauschlauch, -manschette, Tourniquet[2] Esmarch-Blutsperre/ -leere[3] Stauschlauch lösen[4] S. lockern[5] Aufblasen d. Staumanschette[6]

18

loading dose n term   rel **maintenance dose**[1] n term

relatively large dose given initially to induce anesthesia (or initiate [ɪnɪʃɪeɪt] drug therapy)

» A loading dose of 1 mg/kg by bolus intravenous infusion[2] is followed by a maintenance dose of 1–4 mg/min by continuous intravenous infusion[3].

Initialdosis
Erhaltungsdosis[1] i.v. Schnellinfusion[2] i.v. Dauerinfusion[3]

19

depth [depθ] or **level of anesthesia** n term

classified in four stages (analgesia[1], delirium[2], surgical anesthesia[3] with 4 planes[4] [eɪ], overdose[5])

» Stage II anesthesia is marked by loss of consciousness and the lid reflex[6], excitement[7] of which may be associated with vomiting and laryngospasm. Complications with endotracheal intubabtion can be minimized by ensuring [ʃʊɚ] that the depth of anesthesia is adequate.

Use to monitor[8]/assess[9] **the depth of anesthesia** • adequate **depth of anesthesia** • to produce the desired **depth of anesthesia**

Narkosetiefe
Analgesiestadium[1] Exzitationsstadium[2] Toleranzstadium[3] Unterstufen[4] Asphyxiestadium[5] Lidrandreflex[6] Auslösung[7] Narkosetiefe überwachen[8] Narkosetiefe überprüfen[9]

20

emergence [ɪmɜːrdʒᵊnɪs] n term   sim **recovery**[1] [ʌ] n term → U134-14

return to spontaneous [eɪ] respiration, voluntary swallowing, consciousness, etc. following general anesthesia

» In children this drug can cause adverse[2] [ɜː] behavioral reactions upon emergence from sedation.

Use **emergence** delirium • postanesthesia (abbr PAR) **recovery** • **recovery** room (abbr RR) or area[3] / period

Aufwachphase
Erwachen (aus Narkose)[1] ungünstig[2] Aufwachraum[3]

21

anesthesia record n term → U20-5

written account[1] [aʊ] of drugs administered, procedures undertaken, and cardiovascular responses during surgical or obstetric anesthesia[2]

Narkoseprotokoll
Aufzeichnungen[1] geburtshilfliche Anästhesie[2]

22

postanesthetic [e] **phase** [feɪz] n term
syn **anesthesia** [iː] **recovery period** n term
period of emergence from GA during which patients are closely monitored in the RR[1]
» The first hours immediately after the operation during which the acute reaction to surgery and the residual [I] effects[2] of anesthesia are subsiding[3] [aɪ] is termed the postanesthetic observation phase of management.
Use **postanesthetic** observation / vomiting[4] / nausea [nɔːzɪə] / hang-over[5]

Aufwachperiode
Aufwachraum[1] Restwirkungen[2] nachlassen[3] Erbrechen i. d. Aufwachperiode[4] Narkosekater[5]

23

postanesthesia care unit n term   abbr **PACU**
hospital unit equipped for meeting postoperative emergencies in which surgical patients are kept during the immediate postoperative period for care and recovery from anesthesia
» Pulse, BP[1] and respiration of PACU patients are recorded every 15 min until stable.
Use **postanesthesia** nursing [ɜː]/ problems / headache / recovery area • full-intensity **PACU** care • **PACU** admission report[2] / postoperative triage [triɑːʒ] • discharge evaluation from **PACU** to ICU[3]

Aufwachstation
Blutdruck[1] Aufnahmebericht in der Aufwachstation[2] Entlassungsprotokoll b. Verlegung v. d. Aufwach- i. d. Intensiv(pflege)station[3]

24

Clinical Phrases

Have you or anyone in your family ever had problems from anesthesia? Hatten Sie oder jemand in der Familie schon einmal Probleme bei einer Narkose? • Sometimes complications occur with anesthesia, but this is very rare and we will take good care of you. Sehr selten kann es im Zusammenhang mit der Narkose zu Komplikationen kommen. Aber wir werden Sie bestens versorgen! • Do you have any false teeth, removable dental caps or bridges? Haben Sie eine Zahnprothese, abnehmbare Brücken oder Kronen? • Have you had anything to eat or drink in the past 8 hours? Haben Sie in den letzten 8 Stunden etwas gegessen oder getrunken? • Now I am going to spray your throat. Ich werde jetzt Ihren Rachen einsprühen. • Then we will give you a little needle stick here and you will get numb so that you will not feel the operation. Dann werden Sie einen kleinen Stich spüren, und dieser Bereich wird sich dann taub anfühlen, so dass Sie bei der Operation keine Schmerzen haben werden. • Squeeze my hand. Hard. Harder. Drücken Sie meine Hand. Fest! Fester! • Do your legs feel numb/ normal? Fühlen sich Ihre Beine taub/ normal an? • Do you feel dizzy? Ist Ihnen schwindlig? • Can you wiggle your toes? Können Sie Ihre Zehen bewegen? • Do you have the taste of metal in your mouth? Haben Sie einen metallischen Geschmack im Mund?

Unit 136 Blood Transfusion
Related Units: 37 Components of the Blood, 38 Hematopoiesis, 17 Medical Equipment, 127 Operative Techniques, 132 Surgical Instruments, 125 Critical Care

infusion [ɪnfjuːʒ°n] n term   rel **perfusion**[1], **instillation**[2] [ɪnstɪleɪʃ°n] n term
(i) intravenous [iː] or interstitial [ɪʃ] introduction of fluids (e.g. saline) [eɪ]
(ii) the solution [uːʃ] infused
(re)**infuse**[3] v term • **infusate**[4] n • **perfuse**[5] [pəˈfjuːz] v • **perfusate**[6] n • **instill**[7] v
» Support BP with infusion of IV fluids (colloid or crystalloid [I] solutions) until surgery can be performed. Adjust [dʒʌ] the rate of infusion so that hourly determinations of serum calcium are normal. An infusion pump[8] [ʌ] is used to establish a standard fast flow of 10 mL/min. Intra-articular instillation of antibiotics is unnecessary, since high antibiotic levels in synovial [I] fluid are attained [eɪ] when drugs are given intravenously [iː].
Use to start/begin **an infusion** • intravenous[9] (abbr IV)/ intra-arterial [ɪɚ]/ hepatic artery / re**infusion** • continuous[10] / constant[10] / 24-hour[11] / drug[12] **infusion** • maintenance[13] [eɪ]/ high-dose / rapid or bolus[14] **infusion** • pressure[15] / peripheral / long-term[16] **infusion** • fluid / saline[17] / crystalloid / glucose **infusion** • 10% dextrose / albumin **infusion** • bicarbonate / thrombolytic [I] **infusion** • **infusion** rate[18] / pump[8] / therapy • **infusion** time[19] / bottle[20] / site / set / tubing[21] • **to infuse** blood / crystalloid solution / IV fluids • peripheral vein [eɪ]/ intravenous **infusate** • **infusate** flow / rate[18] / container[20] [eɪ] / hyperthermic[22] [ɜː]/ hemo[23] [iː] /extracorporeal **perfusion** • **perfusion** therapy / chemotherapy[24] [kiːmoʊ-] • **perfusion** scintigraphy[25] [sɪnt-]/ scan • local / direct / rectal / intraperitoneal [iː] **instillation** • CT-guided[26] • drop[27] / drug **instillation** • cooled [uː]/ Sacks **perfusate** • **perfusate** solution[6] / flow rate / pH • **to instill** 32% dextran / eye drops[28]

Infusion, Infusionslösung
Perfusion[1] Instillation[2] (re)infundieren[3] Infusionslösung[4] durchströmen, perfundieren[5] Perfusionsflüssigkeit[6] einträufeln, instillieren[7] Spritzen-, Infusionspumpe, Perfusor[8] intravenöse/ i.v. Infusion[9] Dauertropfinfusion[10] 24-Stunden-I.[11] Arzneimittelinfusion[12] Erhaltungsinfusion[13] Schnellinfusion, i.v. Bolusinfusion[14] Druckinfusion[15] Langzeitinfusion[16] Kochsalzinfusion[17] Infusionsgeschwindigkeit[18] Infusionsdauer[19] Infusionsflasche[20] Infusionsschläuche[21] Perfusionshyperthermie[22] Hämoperfusion[23] Perfusionschemotherapie[24] Perfusionsszintigrafie[25] CT-gesteuerte Instillation[26] tropfenweise I.[27] Augentropfen instillieren[28]

1

Blood Transfusion — CLINICAL TERMS 595

venipuncture [ʌ] *n term*   *syn* **venepuncture** *n*,
   rel **IV infusion**[1] *n term*

transcutaneous puncture of a vein with a stylet[2] [aɪ] or cannula[3] to withdraw blood or inject a solution

puncture[4] [pʌŋktʃɚ] *v & n term* → U5-10; U127-18

» Before performing venipuncture, apply a tourniquet[5] [ɜː] proximal to the puncture site[6], ask the patient to clench [tʃ] his fist or slightly tap[7] the selected vein to aid dilation [eɪʃ] and make it more prominent. Skin cleansing [e] by swabbing[8] [ɒː] the site with alcohol or organic iodine [aɪə] is sufficient [ɪʃ] for routine injections and simple venipuncture but not for venipuncture performed to draw blood for culture [ʌ] or to permit insertion of an indwelling device[9] [aɪs].

✸se to perform/attempt/collect blood by[10]/be suitable [(j)uː] for **venipuncture** • simple / repeated / routine / difficult **venipuncture** • upper extremity / internal jugular[11] [dʒʌ]/ subclavian [eɪ] **venipuncture** • **venipuncture** site / technique [tekniːk] • needle [iː]/ percutaneous [eɪ]/ skin / fingertip[12] **puncture** • venous [iː]/ arterial [ɪɚ]/ lumbar[13] [ʌ] (*abbr* LP) **puncture** • **puncture** wound[14] [uː]/-proof container[15]

Venenpunktion
intravenöse Infusion[1] Mandrin[2] Hohlnadel, Kanüle[3] punktieren, durch-, einstechen; Einstich, Punktion[4] Stauschlauch[5] Einstich-, Punktionsstelle[6] beklopfen[7] Abtupfen[8] Verweilkanüle[9] venöses Blut durch Punktion entnehmen[10] Punktion d. V. jugularis interna[11] Einstich i. d. Fingerbeere[12] Lumbalpunktion[13] Stichwunde[14] stichfester Behälter[15]

2

---

intravenous [iː] **drip** *n jar*
   rel **IV cannula** or **catheter** or **line**[1] *n term*

(i) drop-by-drop infusion of infusates directly into the bloodstream
(ii) equipment used for drip infusion

drip[2] *v* • **dripping** *adj* • **cannulation**[3] *n term* • **cannulate**[4] *v* → U127-19; U132-6

» Once the drip is in, fix the cannula firmly [ɜː] with tape. Heparin may be given IV q 4 to 6 h[5], or by continuous IV drip with an infusion pump. The tip of the cannula may be sitting up against the posterior wall. You can try to rescue [reskjuː] the IV line by pulling the cannula back, flushing[6] [ʌ] it and taping [eɪ] it down securely [juɚ] in the new position.

✸se to set up an[7]/start an/give by **IV drip** • continuous[8] / slow **IV drip** • **IV drip** volume / (flow)rate calibration [eɪʃ] • **IV drip** patient / medications / chart [tʃ] • fluid / antibiotic **drip** • **drip** infusion (technique) / site • **drip** chamber[9] [tʃeɪmbɚ]/ rate / feeding[10] [iː] • to block[11]/flush the cannula • small-bore[12] [ɔː]/ nasal / 13-gauge [geɪdʒ]/ plastic **cannula** • flexible / Teflon / needle-tipped[13] **cannula** • **cannula** insertion [ɜː]/ tip[14] • intra/ fine / Swan-Ganz / indwelling[15] **catheter** • peripheral parenteral nutrition[16] [ɪʃ] (*abbr* PPN)/ infusion **catheter** • **catheter** insertion site [aɪ] • (central) venous [iː] (*abbr* CV)/ arterial [ɪɚ] **cannulation**

(i) i. v. Tropfinfusion, Tropf
(ii) Tropfer
Infusionskanüle, Venenkatheter[1] tropfen, tröpfeln[2] Kanülierung[3] eine Kanüle einführen, kanülieren[4] alle 4 bis 6 Stunden[5] durchspülen[6] eine Tropfinfusion anhängen[7] Dauertropfinfusion[8] Tropfkammer[9] parenterale Ernährung[10] d. Kanüle verlegen/ verstopfen[11] kleinlumige Kanüle[12] Punktionskanüle, Kanüle mit Mandrin[13] Kanülenspitze[14] Dauer-, Verweilkatheter[15] peripherer Zugang zur parenteralen Ernährung[16]

3

---

infusion set *n term*
   rel **IV bottle**[1], **IV bag**[2] *n term*, **piggy-back**[3] *n & v jar*

equipment for IV therapy consisting of a plastic or glass vacuum container, the drip chamber, flow clamp[4], and the IV tubing which connects the IV bag or bottle to the catheter in the patient's vein

bottled[5] [ɒː] *adj* • **unit-bagged**[6] *adj term* • **bottleneck**[7] *n* • **bottle-feed**[8] *v*

» No IV solution other than 0.9% sodium chloride solution should be allowed into the blood bag or in the same tubing with blood. Insert a blood filter into the bottom of the bag, and administer the blood to the patient through the infusion tubing. Add the insulin to a separate IV of 10% glucose in water and "piggyback" it into the maintenance 10% glucose IV so the insulin rate can be adjusted [ʌ] without changing the total IV infusion rate.

✸se to change **the IV set** • pediatric / micro [aɪ] drip / dual [d(j)uəl] drip **infusion set** • vented[9] / Y-type blood[10] **infusion set** • **IV** tubing[11] / pump[12] / pole *or* drip stand[13] (BE) • (sterile) blood[14] (collection) / donor [oʊ] (transfusion) **bag** • empty IV / labeled[15] [eɪ]/ warmed **bag** • to vent a[16] / plastic **blood bag** • to place/time-tape/ inspect/hook [ʊ] sb. up to[17]/disconnect[18] **the IV bottle** • infusion *or* intravenous[1] / sterile / plastic / 500cc **bottle** • blood culture[19] [ʌ]/ pill[20] **bottle** • hot-water[21] / dropper[22] **bottle** • **bottle** label[23] / holder • IV (*abbr* IVPB) **piggyback** • **piggyback** solution / IV connection *or* port[24] / IV bag • **piggyback** infusion[3] / tubing *or* line[25] / drug • **to piggy-back** IV fluids with heparin

Infusionsbesteck
Infusionsflasche[1] Infusionsbeutel[2] Zusatzinfusion; eine Z. anhängen[3] Abklemmvorrichtung[4] in Flaschen abgefüllt[5] Konserven-[6] Engpass[7] m. d. Flasche ernähren[8] entlüftetes Infusionsset[9] Infusionsset mit Y-Stück[10] Infusionsschläuche[11] Infusions-, Spritzenpumpe, Perfusor[12] Infusionsständer[13] Blutbeutel[14] mit Aufkleber gekennzeichneter Blutbeutel[15] eine Blutkonserve entlüften[16] jem. an d. Tropf hängen[17] d. T. abhängen[18] Blutkulturfläschchen[19] Arzneifläschchen[20] Wärm(e)flasche, Thermophor[21] Tropfflasche[22] Flaschenetikett[23] Anschluss f. Zusatzinfusion[24] Zusatzleitung[25]

4

136

(intra)venous access [æksɛs] n term

rel **Porta-cath**®1, **Infusa-port**®1 n term

placement of an IV catheter in order to facilitate [sɪ] infusion of fluids, perfusion, sampling, etc.

access2 v • **(in)accessible** adj • **accessibility** n • **port**3 [pɔːrt] n term

» The IV line is placed in the superior vena [iː] cava [eɪ], either by a subclavian or internal jugular [ʌ] puncture. Gain venous access with an 18-gauge IV catheter and give a crystalloid solution as needed. Elective bronchoscopy [kɒː] is accomplished with IV access in place.

Use to establish or achieve4/obtain or gain4/delay [eɪ] /lose **access** • long-term / large-bore5 / secure / lack of **IV access** • central (venous)6 / arterial **access** • arteriovenous (abbr A-V)/ peripheral / emergency [ɜː] **access** • **access** site / route7 [uː‖aʊ]/ device / equipment • **access** to the circulation / channel [tʃæ] • to start or place8/insert or establish8/discontinue **an IV line** • central9 / peripheral / large-bore **intravenous line** • indwelling10 / secure / contaminated **intravenous line** • **intravenous** route11 / hydration / feeding or alimentation12 • **intravenous** glucose infusion / pyelography13 [paɪə-] • **intravenous** fluids / crystalloid [ɪ] solution / heparin • **intravenous** administration14 / bolus injection15 / (vascular-)access / arterial / jugular / indwelling **line** • central (venous)9 (abbr CVL)/ subclavian16 **line** • Swan-Ganz / total parenteral nutrition17 (abbr TPN) **line** • **central line** feeding • **IV** cocktail / anesthesia18 [iːʒ]/ medication • **IV** fluid therapy19 / (needle site) care • catheter20 / side / irrigation21 / fluid inflow **port** • air inflation / suction22 [ʌ]/ working23 **port**

scalp vein needle [iː] n term → U17-10

syn **butterfly** [ʌ] **needle, Minicath**® n jar

rigid [ɪdʒ] needle with flexible anchoring [k] flanges1 [dʒ] at each side mainly for short-term IV infusions2

Angiocath®3 [ændʒɪoʊkæθ] n jar • **Intracath**®3 n

» The short tubing connected to the scalp vein needle should be filled with fluid before the infusion begins. The veins on the dorsum of the hand or foot are usually the most accessible for cannulation with a 21-gauge butterfly needle. Align [aɪ] the needle with the course [ɔː] of the vein4, and make sure that the bevel5 is facing up.

Use to (re)position6/slip the catheter off/secure7 **the needle** • to leave **the needle** in place • pediatric / disposable8 **scalp vein needle** • **scalp vein** catheter / (infusion) set • 27-gauge **butterfly needle** • catheter insertion9 / catheter-clad10 / fine **needle** • hypodermic [ɜː]/ spinal / probing11 **needle** • **needle**-tipped catheter /-clad catheter10 / (mis)placement • obstructed12 **needle** • 20-gauge / hub [ʌ] of the **Angiocath**

extravasate [ɪkstrævəseɪt] v term

syn **tissue** [tɪʃ‖sjuː] v jar BE
rel **infiltration**1, **phlebitis**2 [flɪbaɪtɪs] n term

administering the transfusate into adjacent [ədʒeɪs-] tissues3 due to inadvertent [ɜː] misplacement4 of the needle tip; this may cause bruising5 [uː], infection, ulceration [ʌlsə-], tissue necrosis and thrombosis

tissu(e)ing n jar • **extravasation**6 n term • **extravascular**7 adj • **infiltrate**8 v & n

» Calcium chloride causes thrombophlebitis2 when given IV and is highly irritating if extravasated. In children up to 58% of IV lines may tissue. Extravasation is often associated with multiple attempts at venipuncture after failing to cannulate a vein. Extravasation of vesicant drugs9 requires emergency treatment. The drip has tissued. Infiltration occurs [ɜː] when IV fluid leaks [iː] from the vein into the perivascular or subcutaneous [eɪ] tissue.

Use to experience/cause/lead to/result in **extravasation** • recognition [ɪʃ] of / contrast / drug / dye [daɪ] **extravasation** • urinary10 / excessive fluid / lymph11 [ɪ] **extravasation** • **extravasation** injury / risk • **tissued** drip • to avoid **infiltration** • local / perivascular / cellular **infiltration** • inflammatory12 / tumor **infiltration** • **infiltration** anesthesia13 [iːʒ] • acute / superficial2 / migratory14 [aɪ] / suppurative15 [ʌ] **phlebitis** • catheter-related16 / postinfusion / chemical **phlebitis** • deep (vein)17 / thrombo2/ endo**phlebitis**

---

venöser Zugang

Port(katheter)-System, implantierbarer Zugang[1] Zugang haben zu[2] Zugang[3] s. Zugang verschaffen, gelangen[4] Zugang über einen großlumigen Venenkatheter[5] zentralvenöser Z.[6] Zugangsweg[7] e. venösen Zugang legen[8] zentraler Venenkatheter (ZVK)[9] Venenverweilkatheter[10] i.v. Applikationsweg[11] parenterale Ernährung[12] Ausscheidungsurografie, i.v. Uro-/ Pyelografie[13] i.v. Verabreichung/ Applikation[14] i.v. Schnell-, Bolusinjektion, Bolus-Gabe[15] Subklaviakatheter[16] ZVK zur parenteralen Ernährung[17] i.v. Anästhesie[18] i.v. Rehydratation[19] Katheterzugang[20] Spülkanal[21] Absaugkanal[22] Arbeitstrokar (Laparoskopie), Arbeitskanal (Endoskop)[23]

5

Butterfly(-Nadel)

Befestigungsstege[1] Kurzinfusionen[2] Venenkatheter, -verweilkanüle[3] die Nadel parallel zur Vene einführen[4] abgeschrägte Nadelspitze[5] d. Nadel (noch einmal) einführen[6] d. Nadel befestigen[7] Einweg-Butterfly-Nadel[8] Mandrin[9] (Punktions)kanüle mit Mandrin[10] Führungsnadel[11] verstopfte/ verlegte Nadel[12]

6

para laufen; extravasieren, austreten (aus d. Gefäß)

Infiltration[1] oberflächl. Venenentzündung, Thrombophlebitis[2] benachbarte/ angrenzende Gewebe[3] versehentl. falsche Positionierung[4] Hämatombildung[5] Extravasation/ Flüssigkeitsaustritt aus e. Gefäß, Paravasation; Paravasat, Extravasat[6] extravasal, außerhalb e. Gefäßes[7] eindringen, infiltrieren; Infiltrat[8] blasenziehende Mittel, starke Hautreizmittel, Vesikanzien[9] Harnaustritt, Urinextravasation[10] Austritt v. Lymphe[11] entzündl. Infiltration[12] Infiltrationsanästhesie[13] Thrombophlebitis migrans[14] eitrige T.[15] katheterbedingte T.[16] Phlebothrombose[17]

7

Blood Transfusion

CLINICAL TERMS 597

blood transfusion n term   rel **autotransfusion**[1], **hypertransfusion**[2] n term

administration of whole [hoʊl] blood[3] or blood products[4] to replace blood lost in surgery, through trauma [ɔː], etc. or to provide deficient [ɪʃ] blood elements, e.g. to improve coagulation
transfuse[5] [-fjuːz] v term • **pre/ posttransfusion**[6] [juː3] adj •
transfusion-associated[6] adj

» Before any transfusion is started, both label [eɪ] and report of compatibility testing must be checked. How many units of blood[7] were transfused? Because of the equipment needed, autotransfusions are not necessarily less expensive than bank blood[8]. In sickle [k] cell anemia, hydration and hypertransfusion should constitute initial [ɪʃ] therapy.

se to (re)start/stop/require or necessitate[9] **a transfusion** • whole / periodic / incompatible **blood transfusion** • donor-specific[10] (abbr DST)/ third-party **blood transfusion** • transmitted by or via / acquired by **blood transfusion** • elective / (in)direct / contaminated / massive[11] **transfusion** • intraoperative / emergency **autotransfusion** • **autotransfusion** device [aɪs] or unit[12] / exchange[13] / substitution[14] [juːʃ]/ replacement[14] **transfusion** • autologous[1] / pretransplant **transfusion** • granulocyte / red blood cell[15] / platelet[16] [eɪ] **transfusion** • **transfusion**-associated or -related infection /-acquired [aɪ] HIV infection[17] • **transfusion** protocol / reactions or complications[18] • **transfusion** therapy / refusal[19] [juː] • **pretransfusion** testing[20] • **posttransfusion** blood sample / blood count[21] [aʊ] • **posttransfusion** seroconversion [ɜː]/ hepatitis[22] [aɪ] • **transfusion-acquired** disease

blood donor [blʌd doʊnɚ] n   opposite **recipient**[1] [rɪsɪpɪənt] n → U129-15

person who volunteers [ɪɚ] to have blood drawn [drɔːn] for transfusion

» In patients with major allergic [ɜː] reactions, samples of the patient's and the donor's blood should be sent to the blood bank to rule out[2] the possibility of a hemolytic [ɪ] reaction. The patient has already donated his or her own blood before scheduled [skǁʃ] surgery.

se seronegative **blood donor** • universal[3] / volunteer[4] [ɪɚ]/ family / (un)matched[5] **donor** • **donor** blood (type)[6] / red cells[7] / platelets • **donor**-specific transfusion / screening • blood transfusion / potential blood / adult **recipient** • immunocompromised[8] / neonatal [eɪ]/ pediatric **recipient** • seropositive / bone marrow transplant[9] (abbr BMT) **recipient** • **to donate** blood / an organ • to draw[10] blood / fresh[11] / heparinized / transfused blood • blood product / derivatives[12] / container • blood pledge [pledʒ] card[13] / withdrawal[14] [ɔː]/ aspiration /-borne infection[15] • blood / autologous[16] [ɔː]/ prehospital / organ **donation** • **donated** blood (unit) / kidney

blood typing [taɪpɪŋ] n term   rel **cross-matching**[1] [krɒsmætʃɪŋ] n term

classification of blood on the basis of the presence or absence of genetically determined [ɜː] antigens on the surface [ɜː] of RBCs
type[2] v term • **blood type** or **group**[3] [uː] n • **typed** adj • **crossmatch**[4] v

» Type and cross-match blood if anemia [iː] is present. Blood typing is performed by suspending RBCs obtained [eɪ] from a tube of clotted [ɒː] blood[5] in saline[6] [eɪ] and then adding commercially [ɜː] available specific antisera to the suspension and watching for agglutination. Draw blood for typing and cross-matching. Cross-matching is more time-consuming[7] and expensive than typing and screening alone. Cord blood[8] is used for blood typing, Coombs' testing, and serology.

se to send/obtain a specimen for[9] **blood typing** • to type[10]/cross-match **blood** • whole / maternal [ɜː] **blood typing** • ABO[11] / compatible[12] / rare[13] / unusual[13] **blood types** • **typed** blood / as serotype [ɪɚ] B

compatible [kəmpætɪbl] adj   opposite **incompatible**[1] adj

referring to the ability of two substances to coexist without harmful effects on the function of either, e.g. blood, tissues, or organs that cause no reaction when transfused or no rejection [dʒe] when transplanted
compatibility n • **incompatibility**[2] n

» The presence of alloantibodies[3] to RBC antigens may delay [eɪ] finding antigen-negative crossmatch compatible products for transfusion. Antibodies to Lewis system carbohydrate [aɪ] antigens are the most common cause of incompatibility during pretransfusion screening.

se to be (**in**)**compatible** with • *compatible* blood / donors[4] / plasma • ABO / cross-match-/ histo/ HLA-**compatible** • blood group / HLA / histo[5] / tissue[5] / partial **compatibility** • **compatibility** testing[6] • red cell / ABO[7] / Rh[8] **incompatibility** • major [eɪdʒ]/ alloantibody **incompatibility**

Blutübertragung, -transfusion

Eigenblut-, Autotransfusion, autologe T.[1] Übertransfusion, Volumenüberlastung[2] Vollblut[3] Blutpräparate, -produkte[4] transfundieren, (Blut) übertragen[5] posttransfusionell, transfusionsbedingt[6] (Blut)konserven[7] Konservenblut[8] eine Transfusion erfordern[9] spenderspezifische Bluttransfusion[10] Massivtransfusion[11] Autotransfusionsgerät[12] Austauschtransfusion[13] Substitutionstransfusion[14] Erythrozytentransfusion[15] Thrombozytentransfusion[16] durch Transfusion erworbene HIV-Infektion[17] Transfusionszwischenfälle[18] Transfusionsverweigerung[19] prätransfusionelle Untersuchungen[20] Blutbild nach Transfusion[21] (Post)transfusionshepatitis[22]

8

Blutspender(in)

Empfänger(in)[1] ausschließlich[2] Universalspender(in)[3] freiwillige(r) Spender(in)[4] kompatible(r) Spender(in)[5] Spenderblut(gruppe)[6] Spendererythrozyten[7] immun-/ abwehrgeschwächte(r) Empfänger(in)[8] Knochenmarkempfänger(in)[9] Blut ab-/ entnehmen[10] Frischblut[11] Blutprodukte[12] Blutspenderausweis[13] Blutabnahme[14] hämatogene Infektion[15] Eigenblutspende[16]

9

Blutgruppenbestimmung

(Durchführung einer) Kreuzprobe, Cross-match[1] (Blutgruppe) bestimmen[2] Blutgruppe[3] eine Kreuzprobe durchführen[4] geronnenes Blut[5] Kochsalzlösung[6] zeitaufwendig[7] Nabelschnurblut[8] Blut zur Blutgruppenbestimmung abnehmen[9] die Blutgruppe bestimmen[10] AB-Null-, ABO-Blutgruppen[11] kompatible Blutgruppen[12] seltene Blutgruppen[13]

10

kompatibel, verträglich

inkompatibel, unverträglich[1] Inkompatibilität, Unverträglichkeit[2] Alloantikörper[3] kompatible Spender[4] Histokompatibilität, Gewebeverträglichkeit[5] Kompatibilitätstestung[6] ABNull-Inkompatibilität[7] Rh-Inkompatibilität[8]

11

136

CLINICAL TERMS

hemolytic [I] **(transfusion) reaction** *n term*   *rel* **Coomb's test**[1] *n term* → U38-4

symptoms due to agglutination of the recipient's RBCs when incompatible blood has been transfused or when the recipient has a hypersensitivity to a component in the donor blood

(auto)hemolysis[2] [hɪmɒːləsɪs] *n term* • **hemolyze**[3] *n* • **hemolysate**[4] *n* • **nonhemolytic** *adj*

» As the clinical features [iː] of minor allergic reactions may mimic[5] those of major life-threatening [e] reactions, transfusion must be stopped at once if a patient manifests untoward[6] signs or symptoms. When acute hemolysis is suspected, the transfusion must be immediately stopped, IV access maintained, and the reaction reported to the blood bank.

Use acute / major / immediate-type[7] [iː] / delayed[8] **hemolytic transfusion reaction** • serologic / (massive) blood / allergic[9] **transfusion reaction** • minor / febrile (nonhemolytic)[10] **transfusion reaction** • suspected[11] / immediate / fatal [eɪ] **transfusion reaction** • acute / chronic / increased[12] / intravascular[13] **hemolysis** • mild / low-grade / fulminant [ʊ] / severe **hemolysis** • antibody-mediated [iː] or immune[14] **hemolysis** • (in)direct[15] / negative **Coombs' test** • **Coombs'** antiglobulin test[1] / reagent[16] [eɪdʒ] • **Coombs'** testing /-positive hemolytic anemia [iː] • **hemolytic** process

(plasma) volume expander [æ] *n term*   *syn* **plasma substitute** [ʌ] *n term*

solution of a substance (usually a high molecular weight dextran) transfused as a substitute for plasma

expand[1] *v* • **expansion** *n* • **substitute**[2] (for) *vt & vi* • **substitution** [(j)uːʃ] *n*

» Artificial [ɪʃ] colloids (dextran, gelatin, hetastarch[3]) [tʃ] are inexpensive, effective plasma expanders without infectious risks. Expand intravascular volume with administration of IV crystalloid [ɪ] solution. Plasma is the most satisfactory temporary substitute for blood.

Use colloidal / effective **volume expander** • plasma[4] / tissue[5] / skin **expander** • **volume** replacement[6] / expansion [ʃ] / overload[7] / depletion[8] [iː] • platelet-rich[9] (*abbr* PRP) / pooled[10] [uː] **plasma** • **plasma** exchange therapy[11] / infusion / volume extender[4] • **plasma** volume expansion / concentration / dilution[12] [uːʃ] • **plasma** constituents[13] [ɪtʃ] / fractions or derivatives[14] / supernatant [eɪ] • (cautious [kɒːʃ]s] / continuous / inadequate) blood **volume expansion** • plasma / intravascular **volume expansion** • extracellular fluid[15] (*abbr* ECF) / rapid / substantial / moderate **volume expansion** • (oxygen-carrying) blood[16] / heparin **substitute** • **substitution** transfusion / therapy[17]

whole blood [hoʊl blʌd] *n term*

unmodified blood (except for the addition of an anticoagulant, e.g. heparin[1]) drawn from a selected donor used for transfusion in surgery [ɜː], emergencies [ɜː], etc.

» Whole blood provides both oxygen-carrying capacity and volume expansion. Administer whole blood as soon as available, using hematocrit and BP[2] as guides to dosage. Type and cross-match for 10 units of whole blood.

Use to give *or* administer[3] / receive [iː] **whole blood** • universal [ɜː] donor / O-negative / type-specific[4] **whole blood** • autologous [ɒː] / fresh / stored / capillary / clotted **whole blood** • reconstituted[5] / heparinized[6] / citrated[7] [sɪ] **whole blood** • **whole blood** transfusion[8] / typing / cross-matching / pH • **whole blood** clotting time[9] / glucose determination • freshly drawn[10] / (universal) donor[11] / Rh-negative **blood** • **blood** cell separator[12] / preservative[13] [ɜː]

plasmapheresis [plæzməfəriːsɪs] *n term*   *sim* **leukapheresis**[1] [luːkə-] *n term*

removal of plasma from withdrawn blood by centrifugation and reinfusion of the cellular elements suspended in a plasma substitute (e.g. saline) into the donor

pheresis *n term* • **apheresis** [æfəriːsɪs] *n* • **-pheresis** *comb*

» Plasmapheresis with plasma exchange has recently emerged [ɜː] as an effective form of treatment which is superior to simple plasma infusion. Treatment of thrombotic thrombocytopenic [iː] purpura[2] [ɜː] has focused on the use of exchange transfusion or intensive plasmapheresis coupled [ʌ] with infusion of fresh frozen plasma.

Use large-volume / repeated / periodic / serial [ɪə] **plasmapheresis** • therapeutic[3] [juː] / emergency / maintenance [eɪ] **plasmapheresis** • filtration-**leukapheresis** device[4] [aɪs] • lympho/ platelet[5] / sham[6] [ʃæm] **pheresis** • cyt[7] / hem[8] / T lymphocyte [ɪ] **apheresis** • erythrocyt [ɪ] / lipoprotein / LDL[9] **apheresis** • single-donor **apheresis** platelets[10] • **apheresis** technology / machine[4]

hämolytische(r) Transfusionsreaktion/ -zwischenfall

Coombs-Test, Anti(human)globulintest[1] Hämolyse[2] hämolysieren[3] Hämolysat[4] ähnlich sein wie[5] unerwünscht[6] sofortige hämolytische Transfusionsreaktion[7] verzögerte hämolytische Transfusionsreaktion[8] allergische/ anaphylakt. T.[9] nicht-hämolyt. febrile T.[10] Verdacht auf eine Transfusionsreaktion[11] gesteigerte Hämolyse[12] intravasale Hämolyse[13] Immunhämolyse[14] (in)direkter Anti(human)globulintest[15] Coombs-Serum, Anti-Human-Globulin-Serum[16]

12

Plasmaexpander, -ersatzstoff

erweitern, ausdehnen, vergrößern[1] substituieren, ersetzen; als Ersatz dienen[2] Hydroxyäthylstärke, HÄS[3] Plasmaexpander[4] Gewebeexpander[5] Volumenersatz[6] Volumenüberlastung[7] Volumen-, Flüssigkeits-, Blutverlust[8] thrombozytenreiches Plasma[9] Pool-, Mischplasma, gepooltes Plasma[10] Plasmaaustauschtherapie[11] Plasmaverdünnung[12] Plasmabestandteile[13] Plasmaderivate, -fraktionen[14] extrazelluläre Flüssigkeitssubstitution[15] Blutersatz[16] Substitutions-, Ersatztherapie[17]

13

Vollblut

Heparin[1] Blutdruck[2] Vollblut transfundieren[3] blutgruppenspezifisches Vollblut[4] aufbereitetes Vollblut[5] heparinisiertes Vollblut[6] Zitratblut[7] Vollbluttransfusion[8] Vollblutgerinnungszeit[9] Frischblut[10] Universalspenderblut[11] Blutzellseparator[12] Blutkonservierungslösung[13]

14

Plasmapherese

Leukapherese[1] thrombotisch-thrombozytopenische Purpura, Moschcowitz-Krankheit[2] therapeutische Plasmapherese[3] Blutzellseparator, Separator für d. Filtrationsleukapherese[4] Thrombapherese[5] Scheinapherese[6] Zell-, Zytapherese[7] Hämapherese[8] LDL-Apherese[9] Einzelspender-Thrombozytenkonzentrat[10]

15

Sutures & Suture Material | CLINICAL TERMS **599**

packed red blood cells *n term, abbr* **PRBCs**
    rel **fresh-frozen** [oʊ] **plasma**[1] *n, abbr* **FFP, buffy coat**[2] [bʌfi koʊt] *n term*
    whole blood fractionated [frækʃ-] into RBCs (including leukocyte-poor, filtered, or frozen deglycerolized [ɪs] products) prepared from whole blood by centrifugal techniques[3]
    freeze - froze - frozen *v irr* • **freeze-thaw** *v* • **thaw**[4] [θɒː] *v* • **frozen-thawed** *adj*
» A unit of packed red blood cells will increase the hemoglobin by approximately 10 g/L. Fresh-frozen plasma is used as an adjunct[5] [ædʒʌŋkt] to massive blood transfusions when only packed red cells are available [eɪ]. White blood cell-poor packed red blood cells[6] are given if needed. Massive transfusion with thawed washed RBCs[7] could cause hypokalemia [iː] since frozen RBCs lose up to half of their K+ during storage.
Jse cross-matched / O-negative / autologous **packed red blood cells** • transfused[8] / type-specific[9] **packed red blood cells** • **freeze**-thaw technique /-thaw cycle[10] [saɪkl] • **freeze**-dried plasma /-thawing[10] • **packed** cells / RBC transfusion / cell volume[11] • **frozen** blood (program) /(-thawed) RBCs • **thaw** time[12]

Erythrozytenkonzentrat
tiefgefrorenes Frischplasma, Fresh frozen Plasma, FFP[1] Buffy coat-Konserve, Leukozytenmanschette[2] Zentrifugieren[3] auftauen[4] Zusatz[5] leukozytendepletierte Erythrozyten[6] gewaschene E.[7] transfundiertes Erythrozytenkonzentrat[8] blutgruppenspezifisches Erythrozytenkonzentrat[9] Gefrier-Tau-Zyklus[10] Hämatokrit[11] (Auf)tauzeit[12]

16

cryoprecipitate [kraɪoʊprəsɪpɪtət] *n term*   *rel* **factor VIII concentrate**[1] *n term*
concentrate prepared by freeze-thawing the plasma from a single donor which is rich in fibrinogen, factor VIII, and von Willebrand factor (vWF)
cryoprecipitable [sɪ] *adj term* • **cryopreservation**[2] *n* • **cryo-** *comb* → U81-27
» Cryoprecipitate contains about half the factor VIII activity of FFP in 1/10 the original volume. Bags of cryoprecipitate are stored frozen and their contents are dissolved in 10 mL of 0.9% sodium chloride solution[3] before use. Cryoprecipitates and factor VIII concentrates do not contain factor IX. When the fibrinogen deficiency is severe, cryoprecipitate must be given.
Jse to transfuse/replace with **cryoprecipitate** • a unit[4] / a bag / administration[5] / infusion **of cryoprecipitate** • pooled [uː] blood product / clotting [ɒː] factor[6] / factor IX **concentrate** • antihemophilic factor[1] (*abbr* AHF) **concentrate** • platelet[7] / prothrombin complex[8] **concentrate** • vWF-enriched[9] [ɪtʃ] / C1q esterase inhibitor / plasma **concentrate** • **cryoprecipitable** monoclonal [oʊ] immunoglobulins / immune complexes • **cryopreserved** blood stem cells[10] / tissue / bone marrow • **cryopreserved** spermatozoa[11] / ova / embryo • **cryo**proteins[12] /(immuno)globulins[13] /globulinemia[14] [iː] • **cryo**fibrinogen [kraɪoʊfaɪbrɪnədʒən] /supernatant [eɪ] fraction of plasma[15]

Kryopräzipitat
Faktor VIII-Konzentrat[1] Gefrier-, Kryokonservierung[2] Kochsalzlösung[3] Kryopräzipitatkonserve[4] Verabreichung v. Kryopräzipitat[5] Gerinnungsfaktorkonzentrat[6] Thrombozytenkonzentrat[7] Prothrombinkomplexkonzentrat[8] mit Willebrand-Faktor angereichertes Konzentrat[9] kryokonservierte Blutstammzellen[10] Kryosperma[11] Kryoproteine[12] Kryoglobuline[13] Kryoglobulinämie[14] kryopräzipitatarme Plasmafraktion[15]

17

Unit 137 Sutures & Suture Material
Related Units: 127 Operative Techniques, 140 Wound Healing, 132 Surgical Instruments, 138 Endoscopic Suturing

suture [suːtʃɚ] *n & v term*   *syn* **stitch** [stɪtʃ] *n & v clin & jar*
(n, i) the seam[1] [iː] formed by surgical sewing[2] [oʊ] (ii) material used to approximate[3] wound [uː] edges (iii) a suture joint, e.g. in bones of the skull (v) closing a wound or surgical incision with surgical stitches
suturing *n term* • **sutureless** *adj* • **resuture** *v*
» The subcutaneous tissue should always be sutured, care being taken to "bury" [e] the knot[4] [nɒːt]. Facial [eɪʃ] skin sutures should be removed no later than on the 4th day. The suture is placed so that it does not break[5] or pull free[6].
Jse to apply *or* place[7]/tie [aɪ]/secure[8]/remove *or* take out[9] **sutures** • **to suture** into place • approximation[10] / subcutaneous / fine[11] / buried[12] [e] **suture** • vascular / layered[13] [eɪ]/ relaxation[14] / fixation[15] **suture** • inverting[16] / primary[17] / delayed[18] [eɪ]/ (double) armed[19] **suture** • **suture** closure / material / line • to place *or* take[7] **stitches** • **stitch** abscess • **suturing** instruments / in layers[20]

(i,ii) Naht(material) (iii) Sutura; Naht legen, (an)nähen
Naht[1] chir. Nähen[2] adaptieren[3] Knoten versenken[4] reißen[5] aufgehen[6] Nähte legen[7] N. sichern[8] N. entfernen[9] Situations-, Adaptationsnaht[10] feines Nahtmaterial[11] versenkte Naht[12] Schicht-, Etagennaht[13] Entlastungsnaht[14] Haltenaht[15] invertierende N.[16] Primärnaht[17] aufgeschobene Primärnaht[18] armierte Naht[19] schichtweiser Wundverschluss[20]

1

-rrhaphy [rəfi] *comb*
word ending denoting surgical suturing, e.g. neurorrhaphy[1] [n(j)ʊɚ-] is a nerve suture *or* neurosuture[1]
herniorrhaphy [ɜː] *n term* • **tenorrhaphy**[2] *n* • **colporrhaphy** *n*
» The duration of immobilization after tenorrhaphy is generally for no more than 3–4 weeks.

-naht, -rrhaphie
Nervennaht[1] Sehnennaht[2]

2

137

600 CLINICAL TERMS — Sutures & Suture Material

ligate [laɪgeɪt] *v term*   *syn* **tie** [taɪ] **off** *v phr jar*

(i) tying a blood vessel, pedicle[1], etc. with a suture or wire to constrict it
(ii) in dentistry, using a wire [aɪ] to secure[2] an orthodontic attachment to an archwire[3]
clip[4]-**/ suture**[5]-**ligate** *v term* • **ligature**[6] [ɪ] *n & v* • **ligation**[7] [aɪ] *n*

» The common hepatic artery can be safely ligated. Venous injuries are best managed by ligation. Now the umbilical [ʌ] cord[8] can be ligated.
Use to do/place/apply/anchor[9] [k] **a ligature** • **ligature** loop[10] [uː]/ needle / wire[11] [aɪ] • tubal[12] / varix / caval[13] [eɪ]/ high / suture[14] / rubber band[15] / occluding **ligature** • suture / proximal **ligation** • doubly / clamped and[16] **ligated**

ab-, unterbinden, Ligatur legen, ligieren
Gefäßstiel[1] befestigen[2] Drahtbogen[3] clippen, m. Clip ligieren[4] umstechen, Umstechungsnaht setzen[5] Ligatur (legen)[6] Unterbindung[7] Nabelschnur[8] L. sichern[9] Ligaturschlinge[10] Ligaturendraht[11] Tubenunterbindung[12] Vena cava-Ligatur[13] Umstechung[14] elast. Ligatur[15] abgeklemmt und ligiert[16]   3

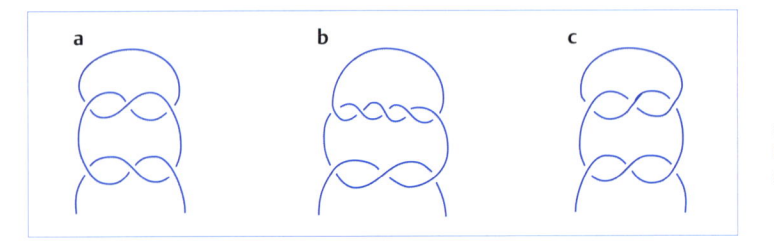

a square knot
b surgical knot
c false knot

---

secure [sɪkjʊɚ] *v & adj term*   *rel* **tack**[1] *v jar*

(v) to fix or attach firmly (adj) safe

» Use staples[2] [eɪ] to secure a patch of mesh[3] over the internal inguinal ring. Take care to repair the fascial [ʃ] defect securely. Bleeding points were secured. The flap[4] is tacked into position.
Use **secured** in place[5] / with tape • **secure** closure[6] [ʒ] • **securely** knotted[7] [ɒːtɪd] • **tacking** suture[8]

sichern; sicher
anheften, klammern[1] Klammern[2] Meshtransplantat[3] Lappen[4] fixiert[5] sicherer (Wund)verschluss[6] fest verknotet[7] Heftnaht[8]   4

---

coapt [koʊæpt] *v term*   *sim* **(re)approximate**[1], **appose**[1] *v term* → U140-2

to join or fit together two surfaces or stumps[2] [ʌ], e.g. a severed[3] nerve or wound margins[4] [dʒ]
coaptation[5] *n term* • **(re)approximation** *n* • **apposition**[6] *n* • **apposing** *adj*

» The skin edges can be approximated with tapes. Sutures should accurately appose skin edges without undue[7] tension. Meticulous[8] nerve coaptation is essential.
Use proper / incomplete **coaptation** • **coaptation** suture[9] / splint[10] • to achieve or obtain or bring into[11] / close / accurate **approximation** or **apposition**

adaptieren
(wieder) annähern, adaptieren[1] Stümpfe[2] durchtrennt[3] Wundränder[4] Koaptation, (Nerven)adaptation[5] Apposition, Anlagerung[6] übermäßig[7] exakt[8] Stoß-auf-Stoß-Naht[9] Führungsschiene[10] (wieder) vereinigen, aneinanderlegen[11]   5

---

knot [nɒːt] *v & n*   *syn* **tie** *v jar* → U138-6f

(v) to tie and fix suture ends (n) the result of knot-tying
knot-tying[1] *n term* • **knotting**[1] *n* • **slipknot**[2] *n*

» Synthetic sutures must be knotted at least four times. To tie a surgical knot[3] the thread [e] is passed twice through the first loop[4] [uː] and then once through the second. The suture knots should be placed on the outside.
Use to tie/tighten[5] [aɪ]/secure/cinch[5] [sɪntʃ] **a knot** • **to pull a knot** taut[5] [ɒː]/tight[5] • surgeon's[3] / double / square[6] [eɚ]/ microsurgical [aɪ] false[7] [ɔː] **knot**

(ver)knoten -knüpfen; Knoten
Knoten(technik)[1] Schiebeknoten[2] chir. Knoten[3] Schlinge[4] Knoten zuziehen[5] Schifferknoten[6] Weiberknoten[7]   6

---

suture material *n*   *sim* **thread**[1] [e], **strand**[1] [æ] *n*, **filament**[1] *n term*

monofilament[2] *adj term* • **multifilament** or **braided**[3] [eɪ] *adj*

» Monofilament plastic will not harbor[4] bacteria. Sutures are available in various diameters[5] (e.g fine 8–0 sutures) and tensile [ɪ] strengths[6]. Even buried nylon sutures are better tolerated than braided or absorbable sutures. Wait a few minutes to allow the suture material to swell[7].

> **Note:** The caliber of suture lines[5] ranges from fine 10–0 to coarse[8] [ɔː] 2–0 and 0 to 4 (the largest) sutures.

Nahtmaterial
Faden[1] monofil[2] multifil, geflochten[3] enthalten, beherbergen[4] Fadenstärke, -durchmesser[5] Zugfestigkeit[6] quellen lassen[7] dick[8]   7

Sutures & Suture Material | CLINICAL TERMS **601**

absorbable *adj term*   opposite **non-absorbable**[1] *adj term*
type of suture material that can be digested[2] [daɪdʒestɪd] by the body and need not be removed
resorb[3] *v term* • **resorption** *n, espBE* **absorption**
» *The urethra* [iː] *is closed with a single layer of 4–0 absorbable suture. Extra* precautions[4] [ɔːʃ] *include using nonabsorbable suture materials for fascial* [æʃ] *closure. Catgut*[5] *will eventually*[6] *resorb but the resorption time*[7] *is highly variable.*

catgut [kætgʌt] *n term*
traditional absorbable suture material; catgut is a misnomer[1] as it is usually made from the intestines of sheep or cattle[2]
» *There is little use for catgut sutures in modern surgery. I generally use interrupted 4–0 chromic catgut sutures*[3] *to close the mucosal edges of the renal pelvis. Modern synthetic suture materials are clearly superior* [ɪɚ] *to*[4] *catgut for fascial closure.*
Use plain[5] [eɪ]/ hardened / chromic[3] **catgut** • **catgut** suture / thread

synthetic [sɪnθetɪk] *adj term*   opposite **organic**[1] *adj term*
common synthetic suture materials are prolene, nylon and Surgilon (nonabsorbable) and Vicryl, PDS, and Dexon (absorbable); types of organic suture materials include silk[2], cotton[3] and catgut
» *Synthetic nonabsorbable materials are mostly* inert[4] [ɜː] *and* retain[5] [eɪ] *tensile strength longer.*
Use Monocryl / GORE-TEX / Teflon-coated [oʊ] polyester[6] / black silk (*abbr* BSS) **suture**

seal [siːl] *v & n term*   *syn* **seal over** *v phr jar & inf*
(v) to achieve a tight closure (n) tight closure
sealant[1] [siːlənt] *n term*
» *Fibrin* [aɪ] glue[2] [gluː]: *is a useful operative sealant to achieve* hemostasis[3] [iː] *in a variety* [aɪ] *of procedures. Perforations may be sealed by omentum. The* leak[4] [iː] *in the ureter was effectively sealed.*
Use to produce a **seal** • water-tight[5] / air-tight[6] [taɪt] / hermetic **seal**

staple [steɪpl] *n & v term*
(n) U-shaped metal (mostly stainless steel[1]) applied in rows[2] [oʊ] or circles with a stapling device[3] [aɪs] to approximate wounds or cut edges[4]
stapler[3] *n term* • **stapling** *n* • **(double-)stapled** *adj*
» *Then the graft can be stapled into place and dressed with pressure. Use staples to secure the patch of mesh. Now you can* fire[5] *the staples. Two 10-cm* rows[2] *of staples are placed* adjacent [dʒeɪs] *to each other*[6].
Use to place or apply[7]/remove **staples** • absorbable **staples** • **staple** line / disruption[8] [ʌ] • **stapled** closure / anastomosis • GIA (gastrointestinal anastomosis) / TA (tissue autosuture) / end-to-end **stapler**

clip *n & v term*
(n) mostly metal clasp-like surgical device used for hemostasis or approximation of cut edges (v, i) to place clips (ii) in genE to trim or shorten hair, fingernails, etc.
clip-ligate *v term* • **clip applier**[1] *n*
» *Control the leak by application of stainless steel clips directly to the bleeding vessels.*
Use to fire or place or apply[2]/transect between[3] **clips** • a rack of[4] **clips** • wound / occlusive[5] / towel[6] [taʊəl]/ metal / absorbable / titanium **clip** • **clip** forceps [s] or holder[7] • multi-load[8] **clip applier**

fibrin [faɪbrɪn] **glue** [gluː] *n term*
blood product rich in[1] fibrinogen [faɪbrɪnədʒən] and admixed[2] with thrombin [θ] used to coagulate surgical wounds
» *Fibrin glue can be made from the patient's own blood* donated[3] *at least three days before surgery. Instillation of fibrin glue directly into the fistula is still a matter of controversy.*
Use **fibrin** spray gun / foam[4] [oʊ]

---

resorbierbar
nicht resorbierbar[1] abgebaut[2] resorbieren[3] Vorsichtsmaßnahmen[4] Katgut[5] schließlich[6] Resorptionszeit[7]
8

Katgut, Catgut
irreführende Bezeichnung[1] Rinder[2] Chromkatgut(nähte)[3] besser als, überlegen[4] reines Katgut[5]
9

synthetisch
organisch[1] Seide[2] Baumwolle[3] biologisch inaktiv/ reaktionslos[4] behalten[5] teflonbeschichtete Polyesternaht[6]
10

abdichten, (dicht) verschließen; Verschluss, -siegelung
(Ab)dichtungsmittel, Versiegler[1] Fibrinkleber[2] zur Blutstillung[3] Leck, undichte Stelle[4] wasserdichter Verschluss[5] luftdichter Verschluss[6]
11

Klammer; klammern, Klammernaht anlegen
rostfreier Stahl[1] Reihen[2] Klammernahtgerät[3] Schnittränder[4] einschießen[5] nebeneinander[6] Klammern setzen[7] Aufgehen von Klammern[8]
12

Clip, Klammer, Klemme; (i) Clip setzen, (ab)klemmen (ii) (zurück)schneiden
Clip-Applikator[1] Clips setzen[2] zwischen Clips absetzen[3] Clip-Magazin[4] Gefäß-, Ligaturclip[5] Tuchklemme[6] Clipzange[7] Mehrfachapplikator[8]
13

Fibrinkleber
reich an[1] durchmischt[2] gespendet[3] Fibrinschaum[4]
14

602 CLINICAL TERMS — Sutures & Suture Material

interrupted [ʌ] **suture** n term   sim **over-and-over suture**[1] n term
single sutures each of which is tied separately with a surgical knot
» *Small wounds are ideally closed with fine interrupted sutures placed loosely*[2] *and conveniently* [iː] *close*[3] *to the wound edges. We prefer a running 2–0 Prolene fascial closure* [-ʒɚ] *reinforced*[4] *with interrupted polyglycolate* [aɪ] *suture to ensure* [-ʃʊɚ] *a dry wound.*

Einzelknopfnaht
Knopfnaht[1] lose[2] entsprechend nahe[3] verstärkt[4]

15

running [ʌ] or **continuous suture** n term
                rel **(inter)locking** or **lock-stitch suture**[1] n term
uninterrupted series of stitches with a single suture the ends of which are fastened [fæsnd] by a knot[2]
» *A running permanent suture can also be used and pulled out after healing has progressed. The pouch*[3] [paʊtʃ] *is then closed with two layers of 3–0 PGA running sutures to ensure water-tightness of the closure.*
Use **running** lock-stitch suture[4] • plain or simple[5] **continuous suture** • **locking** running suture[4]

fortlaufende Naht
eingewendelte Naht[1] verknotet[2] Tasche[3] eingewendelte Fortlaufnaht[4] einfache fortlaufende Naht[5]

16

mattress suture n term   syn **quilt(ed)** [kwɪlt] **suture** n jar
double stitch that forms a loop[1] [uː] about the tissue on both sides of a wound
» *A horizontal running mattress suture is useful to produce eversion* [ɜː] *of the skin edges*[2]*. Buried* [e] *half-mattress (flap) sutures are recommended for tacking skin flaps into position.*
Use interrupted / continuous / vertical / horizontal **mattress suture**

Matratzennaht
Schlinge[1] Ausstülpung der Wundränder[2]

17

purse-string [ɜː] **suture** n term
circular [sɜː] continuous suture used for closure of openings, e.g. in hernias[1] [ɜː] or appendectomy
» *Create* [kriˈeɪt] *a purse-string type of stitch around the cervix*[2] [sɜːr]*. High ligation of the hernia sac was performed with a purse-string suture of 3–0 silk.*

Raff-, Tabakbeutelnaht
Hernien, Brüche[1] Gebärmutterhals, Zervix[2]

18

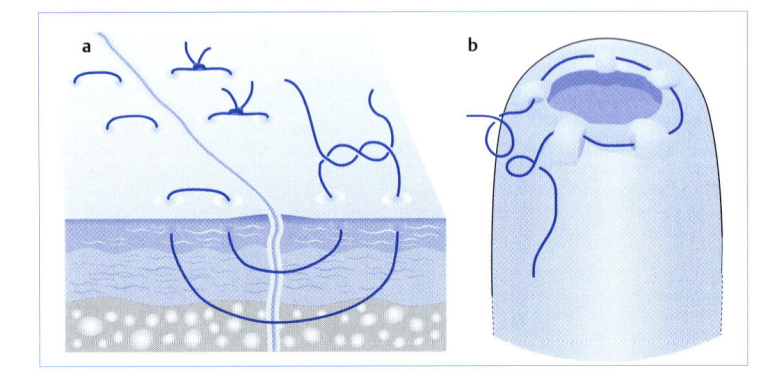

a interrupted mattress suture
b purse-string suture

figure-of-eight suture n term
a stitch in which the thread begins at the deepest layer on each side of a wound and crosses over to the superficial layers on the opposite side following the contours of the figure 8; used, e.g. to close muscle and fascial layers of an abdominal incision
» *Definite hemostasis can be achieved* [tʃiː] *with figure-of-eight sutures or hemostatic clips. Repair by wire cerclage*[1] [sɜːrklɑːʒ] *or figure-of-eight wire is preferred.*

Achternaht
Drahtcerclage[1]

19

Endoscopic Suturing   CLINICAL TERMS **603**

Unit 138 Endoscopic Suturing
Related Units: 137 Sutures, 128 Minimally Invasive Surgery, 132 Surgical Instruments

laparoscopic suturing [suːtʃɚɪŋ] *n term*

rel **endoscopic suturing**[1] *n term*

placing sutures formed inside or outside the body under endoscopic vision via access ports

suture[2] *n & v term* • **resuture** *v*

» The difficulties in laparoscopic suturing arise mainly from the two-dimensional image produced on the TV monitor. The cut edges[3] are approximated with the help of an endoscopic suturing device[4] [dɪvaɪs].

Use to thread[5] [e] a **suture** • stay[6] [eɪ] **suture** • tail[7] [eɪ]/ strand[8] / free-end strand[9] *of a suture* • excess **suture** material[10] • **suture** integrity[11] / length • minimal access[1] *suturing*

laparoskopische Nahtmethoden
endoskop. Nahtmethoden[1] Naht; nähen, Naht legen[2] Schnittränder[3] Nahtgerät[4] Naht einfädeln[5] Haltenaht[6] Naht-, Fadenende[7] Nahtfaden[8] freies Naht-, Fadenende[9] überschüssiges Nahtmaterial[10] Nahtintegrität[11]

1

laparoscopic knot [læpəˑəskɒːpɪk nɒːt] *n term*

ends of a ligature or suture tied so that they remain in place without slipping[1] or becoming detached[2] [tʃ]

knot-tying[3] [taɪɪŋ] *n term* • **knotting**[3] [nɒːtɪŋ] *n* • **knot**[4] *v*

» Knot-tying is certainly one of the more challenging aspects of laparoscopic surgery. The monofilament form of nylon is quite stiff and does not hold knots well.

Use **laparoscopic knot**-tying[5] • to cinch [sɪntʃ] a **knot** in place[6] • to deliver[7]/lock down[8]/pull taut[6] [ɒː] *a knot* • to secure[8] [sɪkjʊə] / undo or untie[9] *a knot* • first hitch of a[10] **knot** • pretied[11] [iː]/ initial [ɪʃ]/ terminal **knot**

laparoskopischer Knoten
rutschen[1] aufgehen, s. lösen[2] Knüpftechnik(en)[3] knüpfen, (ver)knoten[4] laparoskop. Knüpftechniken[5] einen Knoten zuziehen[6] e. Knoten (durch d. Trokar) hineinschieben[7] e. Knoten verriegeln[8] e. Knoten lösen[9] erste Schlinge eines Knotens[10] vorgefertigter Knoten[11]

2

intracorporeal [-kɔːrpɔːrɪəl] *adj term*

opposite **extracorporeal**[1] *adj term*

maneuvers [uː], e.g. knot-tying, performed within the body

» For intracorporeal suturing the length of suture must not exceed 10 cm, otherwise orientation may become difficult. For ligating[2] [aɪ] the vessel this knot must be tied extracorporeally.

Use **intra**/ **extracorporeally** tied knot • **extracorporeal** slipknot[3] • **intracorporeal** microsurgical knot

intrakorporal
extrakorporal[1] ligieren, unterbinden[2] extrakorporaler/ extrakorporal geknüpfter Schiebeknoten[3]

3

hitch [hɪtʃ] *n*   *syn* **throw** [θroʊ] *n*, *sim* **(suture) loop**[1] [luːp] *n*

part of a knot that can be undone by pulling against it

halfhitch or **single throw**[2] *n term*

» Finally, the knot is locked down securely with a double hitch. Tie a small surgical loop[3] (Hangman's knot[4]) at the free end of the suture.

Use pushed **halfhitch** • double[5] **hitch** • to create or place[6] *a hitch* • to form[3] *a loop*

Schlinge
Schlaufe[1] Einzelschlinge[2] eine Schlaufe machen[3] Hangman-Knoten[4] Doppelschlinge[5] eine Schlinge legen/ bilden[6]

4

preformed ligature [lɪgətʃʊəˈ‖tjʊəˈ] **loop** *n term*

sim **endoloop**[1] *n term*

commercial suture ready to be delivered to the targeted structure and tightened in place

» Preformed ligature loops are delivered into the abdomen by means of a suture introducer[2] or a knot pusher. A preformed loop for this knot is commercially available. The loop is maneuvered [uː] downward until it encircles [sɜː] the structure to be ligated [aɪ].

Use to create[3] [krieɪt] /cinch[4] [s] *a loop* • catgut [ʌ] **endoloop** • surgical / vessel[5] / resecting[6] *loop*

vorgefertigte Ligaturschlinge
Endoloop[1] Fadenapplikator[2] eine Schlaufe machen[3] eine Schlaufe (fest) zuziehen[4] Bändchen zum Anschlingen eines Gefäßes[5] Resektionsschlinge, Schlingenelektrode[6]

5

surgical or **surgeon's knot** *n term*

rel **microsurgical knot**[1] *n term*

knot tied by passing the strand[2] twice through the first and once through the second loop in a square knot[3] fashion

» Both strands are cut leaving enough [ʌ] suture material for securing the knot with an intracorporeal surgeon's knot. A surgeon's knot was tied extracorporeally, delivered into the abdomen by means of a knot pusher, and cinched in place.

Use extracorporeal / intracorporeal **surgeon's knot**

chirurgischer Knoten
mikrochirurgischer Knoten[1] Faden(ende)[2] Schifferknoten[3]

6

138

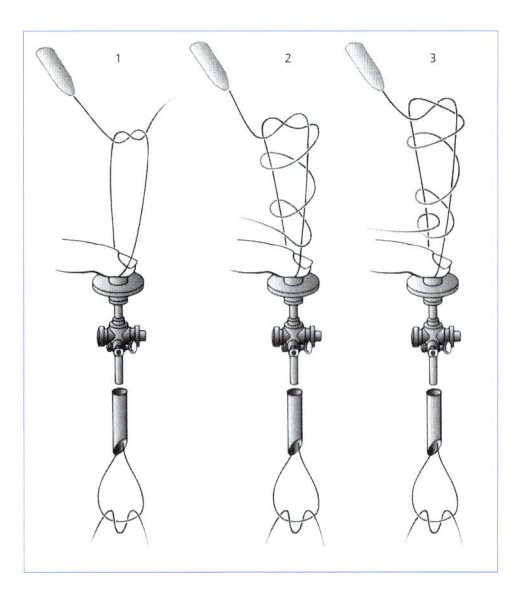

Roeder's knot

Roeder's knot *n term*   *syn* **locking loop knot** *n jar*
knot tied by making three revolutions¹ and two halfhitches around and through the initial extracorporeal loop with the free strand
» Ligature loops are available which are provided with a preformed Roeder's knot. Catgut must be used for Roeder's knot because of its tendency to swell², as this firmly locks the knot.
Use preformed³ **Roeder's knot**

Melzer's knot *n term*
modification of Roeder's knot which is also suitable for monofilament suture materials¹
» Melzer's knot is started with a surgeon's knot, then the free end of the suture is twisted² around both strands of suture three times and locked down securely with a double hitch.
Use preformed **Melzer's knot**

slipknot [slɪpnɒːt] *n term*
after forming a loop the needle is driven through the tissue, the suture is passed through this loop, which is tightened [taɪtᵊnd] by pulling on the short end of the suture
» The Dundee slipknot cannot open in running sutures¹. Delivery of extracorporeal slipknots into the peritoneal [iː] cavity is accomplished with the help of a knot pusher.
Use flat² / Dundee³ **slipknot**

rotational [eɪʃ] **knot** *n term*
combination of intra- and extracorporeal knot tying in which the long tail [eɪ] end is kept outside the abdomen and the needle holder is rotated 360 degrees three times to create three loops around the free-end strand
» Then the needle is retracted to pull both strands of the suture taut¹ and finally the rotational knot is tightened onto the tissue by applying traction² on the free-end strand of the suture.
Use intracorporeal / 360-degree **rotational knot**

Aberdeen knot *n term*   *syn* **triple-twist knot** *n jar*
three loops are formed and the needle is passed through the final loop once more, pulled through the throw formed by this maneuver [uː] and locked down securely
» The Aberdeen knot is formed by three interlocking loops¹ which are tightly [aɪ] cinched [s] in place. The beginning of the suture is also secured by a clip, as the suture material is too stiff for tying [aɪ] an Aberdeen knot.

Roeder-Knoten
Umdrehungen (d. Nadelhalters)¹ quellen² vorgefertigter Roeder-Knoten³

7

Melzer-Knoten
monofiles Nahtmaterial¹ geschlungen²

8

Schiebeknoten
fortlaufende Nähte¹ flacher Schiebeknoten² Dundee-Schiebeknoten³

9

Rotationsknoten
beide Fadenenden zuziehen¹ durch Zug²

10

Aberdeen-Knoten
dreifache Schlaufe¹

11

Endoscopic Suturing   CLINICAL TERMS **605**

suture introducer n term   syn **suture passer** n jar
  capped metal cylinder inserted inside the trocar sheath¹ [ʃiːθ] to facilitate smooth passage of sutures
  » *The long end of the suture is grasped² and withdrawn³ [ɔː] through the trocar with the help of a suture introducer so it can be threaded⁴ [e] extracorporeally.*
Use 5mm / 10 mm **suture introducer**

knot pusher [nɒːt pʊʃɚ] n term
  device to aid delivery of extracorporeally tied knots through the trocar sheath
  » *Some knot pushers have a laterally-slit ring¹ at the tip which renders threading [e] much easier, but this design also carries a risk of losing the suture as the knot is being pushed down.*
Use to open the prongs of²/withdraw **the knot pusher** • reusable / integral³ **knot pusher**

needle holder [niːdl hoʊldɚ] n term
  forceps¹ [s] with serrated jaws² [dʒɔːz] used in suturing for holding and passing the needle through the tissue
  » *The needle holder releases [iː] the shaft of the needle and regrasps the needle tip.*
Use spoon³ [uː]/ ski⁴ **needle** • **needle** exit point⁵ • automatic / hinged [dʒ] jaw **needle holder** • sliding [aɪ] sheath [iː]/ built-in / rachet-action⁶ [rætʃɪt] **needle holder** • jaw of the **needle holder**

endoclip [endoʊklɪp] n term   sim **occlusive** [uː] **clip**¹ n term
  clip the tips of which are approximated by the jaws² of the clip applier before closure [kloʊʒɚ] of the body of the clip
  clip³ v term • **hemoclip**¹ [hiːməklɪp] n • **clip-ligate**⁴ [klɪplaɪgeɪt] v
  » *After careful exposure⁵ [oʊʒ] and isolation of the main artery, three endoclips are applied proximally and two distally. Two occlusive clips are required for the cut ends of the lumbar [ʌ] arteries centrally, while one clip is sufficient [ɪʃ] peripherally.*
Use to secure [sɪkjʊɚ] with⁴/apply or place³/fire³ **a clip** • to transect between⁶ / rack of⁷ **clips** • metal⁸ / plastic⁹ / titanium¹⁰ **clip** • (non)absorbable¹¹ / PDS / Lapra-Ty¹² **clip** • doubly [ʌ] **clipped** vessel¹³ • **clip** application • hemostatic¹ **clip**

clip applier [klɪp əplaɪɚ] n term
  instrument with angulated tips¹ and fully rotatable shafts for firing clips from a right angle to the vessel
  » *The handle of the clip applier is squeezed [iː] to secure the clip onto the suture. Laparoscopists almost exclusively use disposable clip appliers with a preloaded rack of clips.*
Use to fire the² **clip applier** • reusable³ / metal / disposable⁴ / multiload or multifire⁵ / tacking⁶ **clip applier**

endostapler [endəsteɪplɚ] n term   syn **endo-GIA stapler** n term
  endoscopic stapling device¹ [aɪ] that can be inserted [ɜː] via a trocar sheath [iː]
  stapling n & adj term • **staple**² [steɪpl] n & v
  » *Use of the endostapler allows for expedient³ [iː] closure [oʊʒ] of the bladder [æ] neck⁴. 12 mm trocars are required for passing the endo-GIA stapler.*
Use **staple** size⁵ / cartridge⁶ [-ɪdʒ] placement / disruption⁷ [ʌ] • (angulating) hernia⁸ [ɜː]/ laparoscopic tissue **stapler** • multifire⁹ / circular¹⁰ [ɜː]/ end-to-end¹¹ **stapler** • titanium / row [oʊ] of¹² **staples** • absorbable / stainless [eɪ] steel [iː] wound¹³ **staples** • sequential / three successive / imbricating¹⁴ **staplings** • end-to-end **stapling** device¹¹ • **stapled** wound¹⁵ [uː] / anastomosis

Fadenapplikator
Trokarhülse¹ gefasst² herausgezogen³ eingefädelt⁴

12

Knotenschieber
Ring mit seitlichem Schlitz¹ die Maulteile d. Knotenschiebers öffnen² integrierter Knotenschieber³

13

Nadelhalter
Klemme¹ geriffelte Branchen² Löffelnadel³ Schinadel⁴ Ausstichstelle d. Naht⁵ Nadelhalter m. Arretierung⁶

14

Endoklip, -clip
Gefäßklip, Ligaturklip¹ Maulteile² klippen, einen Klip platzieren/ applizieren³ mit Klip versorgen/ ligieren⁴ Freilegung⁵ zwischen Klips absetzen⁶ Clipmagazin⁷ Metallklip⁸ Plastikklip⁹ Titanklip¹⁰ resorbierbarer Klip¹¹ Lapra-Ty-Klip¹² mit 2 Klips versorgtes Gefäß¹³

15

Klipapplikator
abgewinkelte Instrumentenspitze¹ einen Klip platzieren² sterilisierbarer Klipapplikator³ Einmalklipapplikator⁴ (automat. nachladender) Mehrfachklipapplikator⁵ Hernienstapler⁶

16

(endo-)GIA-Stapler, endo-GIA
Stapler, Klammer(naht)gerät¹ Klammer; klammern, heften² praktisch, effizient³ Blasenhals⁴ Klammergröße⁵ Klammermagazin⁶ Ausreißen der Klammern⁷ (abwinkelbarer) Hernienstapler⁸ Mehrfachstapler⁹ zirkuläres Klammernahtgerät¹⁰ Stapler f. End-zu-End-Anastomosen¹¹ Klammerreihe¹² Wundklammern aus Edelstahl¹³ dachziegelartige Klammernahtreihen¹⁴ mit Klammern versorgte Wunde¹⁵   17

Unit 139 Medical & Surgical Asepsis

Related Units: 126 Surgical Treatment, 134 Perioperative Management, 131 Surgical Suite, 140 Wound Healing, 90 Pathogens, 94 Infectious Diseases

---

aseptic [eɪ‖əseptɪk] *adj term*   opposite **septic**[1] *adj term*

aseptic surgical techniques involve precautions[2] [ɔː] against the introduction of infectious [-fekʃəs] agents [eɪ]

as**e**psis[3] *n term* • s**e**psis[4] *n* • antis**e**psis[5] *n* • antis**e**ptic[6] *adj & n*

» Strict aseptic technique is of critical importance in catheterization. The wound [uː] was aseptically dressed[7]. In these critically septic patients the mortality rate is 30%.

Use to render[8] **aseptic** • to adhere [ɪɚ] to **aseptic** techniques[9] • **aseptic** surgery / wound / fever [iː] • surgical / medical **asepsis** • to observe[9]/maintain/relax **aseptic precautions** • **septic** complications / patient / process / shock[10] / wound / localized / generalized / abdominal / late / deep[11] / lethal [iː] **sepsis** / bowel [aʊ] **antisepsis** • **antiseptic** solution / gauze[12] [ɔː]/ cleansing [e] / dressing[13] / skin[14] / topical / urinary [jʊɚ] **antiseptic**

---

keimfrei, aseptisch, steril

septisch, verunreinigt, nicht keimfrei[1] Sicherheitsmaßnahmen[2] Asepsis, Keimfreiheit[3] Sepsis, Blutvergiftung[4] Antisepsis[5] keimtötend, antiseptisch; Antiseptikum[6] verbunden[7] keimfrei machen, sterilisieren[8] s. an die asept. Kautelen/Vorsichtsmaßregeln halten[9] septischer Schock[10] schwere Sepsis[11] antiseptische Gaze[12] a. (Wund)verband[13] Hautdesinfektionsmittel[14]   **1**

---

sterile [sterəl‖aɪl] *adj term*   opposite **non-sterile, contaminated**[1] *adj term*

(i) free from micro-organisms and their spores[2]; aseptic (ii) infertile [-əl‖aɪl]

(re)st**e**rilize[3] [-laɪz] *v term* • steriliz**a**tion[4] *n* •
ster**i**lity[5] *n* • st**e**rilizer[6] *n* → U69-3

» Although much of the OR environment [aɪ] is sterile, the operative field itself is not. This must be done under sterile conditions. Total sterilization by this method requires 10 hours.

Use **sterile** field[7] / dressing / fluid • **sterilized** equipment / syringe[8] [sɪrɪndʒ]/ enema set[9] • catheter • to (with)stand[10] **sterilization** • dry heat or hot air[11] / saturated steam[12] [iː]/ safe **sterilization** • (in)adequately **sterilized** • **sterilizing** chamber[13]

(i) steril, keimfrei
(ii) steril, unfruchtbar

kontaminiert, verunreinigt[1] Sporen[2] sterilisieren, entkeimen[3] Sterilisation, -sierung[4] Sterilität, Keimfreiheit[5] Sterilisator[6] steriler Bereich[7] st. Spritze[8] st. Einlaufgerät/Irrigator[9] sterilisierbar sein[10] Heißluftsterilisation[11] Dampfsterilisation[12] Sterilisierbehälter, -trommel[13]   **2**

---

autoclave [ɔːtəkleɪv] *n & v term*

(n) apparatus [æ‖eɪ] for sterilizing instruments with superheated[1] steam [iː] under pressure; the articles are inserted in a wire [aɪ] basket and wrapped[2] [ræ] if necessary

autoclaving *n term* • **autoclavable**[3] *adj*

» Gas sterilization of materials that cannot withstand autoclaving[4] has largely replaced soaking [oʊ] in antiseptics[5].

Use high-pressure[6] / high-vacuum / gas **autoclave**

Autoklav; autoklavieren

sehr heiß[1] eingehüllt, verpackt[2] autoklavierbar[3] nicht autoklavierbar sein[4] in keimtötende Flüssigkeiten legen[5] Hochdrucksterilisator[6]
3

---

disposable *adj*   opposite **reusable**[1] [riːjuːzəbl] *adj*

materials and instruments that cannot withstand sterilization and must be discarded[2] after single use

dispose of[3] *v phr* • disposal[4] *n* • discard *v*

» New guidelines [aɪ] for disposal of materials contaminated by bacteria have been established[5].

Use **disposable** equipment / drapes[6] [eɪ]/ gloves[7] [ʌ]/ cannula • **reusable** appliances [aɪ] • sewage[8] [suːɪdʒ] / waste[9] **disposal**

Einmal-, Einweg-

wiederverwendbar[1] weggeworfen[2] entsorgen[3] Entsorgung, Beseitigung[4] festgelegt[5] Einmal-abdecktücher[6] Einmalhandschuhe[7] Abwasserentsorgung[8] Müllentsorgung[9]
4

---

disinfect *v term*   sim **cleanse**[1] [e], **rinse**[2] *v clin*

to destroy harmful microorganisms or inhibit[3] their growth [groʊθ] or pathogenic [dʒe] activity

disinf**e**ction[4] *n term* • disinf**e**ctant[5] *n & adj* • det**e**rgent[6] [ɜːrdʒ] *n*

» Painting[7] with mild disinfectants may be helpful. Disinfection of clothing, bedclothes[8] and the patient's living quarters[9] is necessary.

Use chemical / skin / wet / terminal[10] / antisepsis, sterilization and **disinfection** • **disinfectant** solution[11]

---

desinfizieren

reinigen[1] (ab-, aus)spülen[2] hemmen[3] Desinfektion, Entkeimung, Entseuchung[4] Desinfektionsmittel; desinfizierend[5] Reinigungsmittel[6] (ein)pinseln[7] Bettwäsche[8] Wohnung[9] Schlussdesinfektion[10] Desinfektionsmittel[11]   **5**

---

scrub(-up) [ʌ] *n & v jar*

(v) to rub[1] [ʌ], disinfect and rinse before surgery, esp. the hands and forearms[2] of the operative team

scrubbing[3] *n jar* • scrub suit[4] [suː] *n*

» For preoperative preparation hands should be scrubbed for 5–10 min. Shorter scrubs are acceptable between operations.

Use hand / chlorhexidine / surgical **scrub** • **scrub** routine / nurse[5] [nɜːrs] / room[6] • **(un)scrubbed** personnel[7] / team members

---

chir. (Hände)desinfektion; Hände desinfizieren

(ab)reiben[1] Unterarme[2] präoperative Desinfektion[3] Operationskleidung[4] OP-Schwester[5] Wasch-, Händedesinfektionsraum[6] (nicht) steriles Personal[7]
6

Medical & Surgical Asepsis

drape [dreɪp] v & n usu pl term

(v) to cover body parts other than the operative field with sterile materials
» *The skin is prepared with an antiseptic solution and then the area is draped.*
Use skin / patient / operative field or area **is draped** • scrubbed, sterilely prepped[1] and **draped** • adherent[2] [ɪɚ] **drape** • sterile[3] **draping**

(m. sterilen Tüchern) abdecken; (steriles) Abdecktuch
steril gemacht[1] Abdeckfolie[2] sterile Abdeckung[3]

7

ventilation [ˌvent̬ᵊleɪʃᵊn] **system** [ɪ] n term

conditioner which provides clean air for the sterile zone[1] [zoʊn], eliminates airborne bacteria[2] [ɪɚ] and avoids microbial [aɪ] dissemination[3] by controlled air flow patterns[4]
» *This ventilation system avoids microbial emission[3] between the air source and the clean zone[1] by downstream[5] turbulence [ɜː] and even works without restrictive side panels[6].*
Use laminar flow[7] / outward or exflow **ventilation**

Belüftungsanlage
Sterilzone, sterile Z.[1] Keime i. d. Luft[2] Verbreitung von Mikroorganismen[3] Luftströmung[4] nach unten gerichtet[5] seitliche Begrenzung[6] Laminar-Flow-System[7]

8

contamination n term & clin → U91-6   rel **infection**[1] n term & clin → U94-1f

soiling[2] or making impure [-pjʊɚ] or unhealthy [e] by contact with bacteria or other harmful[3] agents
(de)contaminate[4] v term & clin • **contaminant**[5] n • **contaminated** adj
• **decontamination** n
» *Additional intraincisional antibiotics [aɪ‖ɪ] failed to reduce wound infection rates in contaminated abdominal surgery. They are nonpathogenic [dʒe] surface contaminants but may be opportunistic invaders[6] in immunosuppressed[7] patients.*
Use **contaminated** wound / procedure • **contamination from** instruments / ambient hospital air[8] / linens[9] • cross-[10]**contamination** • airborne[11] / surgical / bacterial / fecal[12] [iː]/ radioactive[13] **contamination** • heavily [e] **contaminated**

Kontamination, Verunreinigung, Keimverschleppung
Infektion[1] Verunreinigung, Verschmutzung[2] schädlich[3] kontaminieren, verunreinigen[4] Schadstoff, Kontaminant[5] opportunistische Erreger[6] immunsupprimiert[7] Kontamination durch d. Raumluft i. Krankenhaus[8] K. durch Bettwäsche[9] Übertragung(sinfektion)[10] durch Luft verursachte Kontamination[11] fäkale Kont.[12] radioakt. Kontamination/ Verseuchung[13]

9

colony forming unit n term   abbr **cfu**

» *It is prudent[1] to prevent cfu from infecting the wound rather than rely [aɪ] on[2] prophylactic antibiotics[3].*

koloniebildende Einheit
sinnvoll, klüger[1] sich verlassen auf[2] Antibiotikaprophylaxe[3]

10

cross infection n term → U94-3

infection transmitted between patients or from hospital staff[1] to patients or vice versa[2] [vaɪsə vɜːrsə]
» *Surgical patients must be protected from cross-infection with virulent [ɪ] strains [eɪ] of bacteria[3].*
Use **cross infection** control policies[4]

Kreuzinfektion
Krankenhauspersonal[1] umgekehrt[2] virulente Bakterienstämme[3] Vorschriften zur Vermeidung v. Kreuzinfektionen[4]

11

hospital-acquired [əkwaɪɚd] adj term   syn **nosocomial** adj term

a new disorder (esp. an infection) a patient develops while hospitalized[1]
» *It led to a significant increase in hospital-acquired wound infections and septicemia [siː], particularly among the aged[2] [eɪdʒd] and debilitated[3].*

nosokomial, Krankenhausin stationärer Behandlung[1] Betagte[2] Geschwächte[3]

12

prophylactic antibiotic coverage [kʌvɚɪdʒ] n term → U134-6
    syn **antibiotic prophylaxis** [prɒːfɪlæksɪs] n term

preoperative administration of a broad [ɔː] spectrum antibiotic[1] to patients at risk of[2] infectious [ekʃ] complications
» *In the case of open injuries prophylactic antibiotics should be given.*

Antibiotikaprophylaxe
Breitbandantibiotikum[1] Gefahr besteht[2]

13

preoperative skin preparation n term   syn **prep** n jar

includes bathing [eɪ], shaving[1] [eɪ] and disinfecting the operative area to render the skin as free of microorganisms[2] as possible without causing irritation
» *A 1-minute skin prep was applied followed by an adherent drape[3]. In uncooperative patients a depilatory cream[4] [iː] can be used instead of skin shaving.*
Use abdominal / knee **prep**

präop. Hautdesinfektion
Rasur[1] die Haut keimfrei machen[2] Abdeckfolie[3] Enthaarungscreme[4]

14

scrub [ʌ] **suit** [suːt] *n term*   *syn* **OR attire** [aɪ], **gown** [aʊ] *n term*

close-fitting dresses, pants, suits, etc. worn with surgeon's aprons¹ [eɪ], shoes or shoe coverings [ʌ] and other protective gear² [gɪɚ] to keep the clean zone as aseptic as possible

gowning³ *n term*

» Scrub suits should only be worn in the OR. When the gown is donned⁴ [ɒː] the glove⁵ [ʌ] is grasped with the fingers still inside the sleeve⁶ [iː]. Fresh OR attire is put on each time a person enters the OR.

Use to don/sure/fasten sterile⁷ **gowns** • **gown** cuffs⁸ [ʌ]

OP-Kleidung, -anzug, -mantel
OP-Schürzen¹ Schutzvorrichtungen² Ankleiden³ angezogen wird⁴ (OP-)Handschuh⁵ Ärmel⁶ sterile OP-Kleidung zuschnüren⁷ Abschlussbund am OP-Mantel⁸

15

total body exhaust [ɪgzɔːst] **gown** *n term*

system to capture¹ [-tʃɚ], contain², and remove the continuous infective body emissions³ from the operating team

» This garment⁴ is supplied with a negative pressure necklace [nɛkləs] exhaust⁵.

OP-Anzug mit Absaugvorrichtung
einfangen¹ einschließen² Körperabsonderungen³ Anzug⁴ Absaugvorrichtung (unterhalb d. Visiers)⁵   16

surgical gloves [ʌ] *n term*

gloving *n term* • **gloved** *adj* • **glove-wearing** [eɚ] *adj & n*

» Palpate gently [dʒ] with the gloved hand. Surgical gloves should be wiped [aɪ] clean¹ of lubricants² [uː] before handling abdominal viscera³ [vɪsɚɚ]. If a glove is torn it should be replaced as promptly as patient safety permits.

Use to wear/handle with **gloves** • double⁴ [ʌ] **gloving** • latex [eɪ]/ disposable⁵ / protective⁶ / punctured⁷ [ʌ] **gloves** • **glove** cuff / lubricant / (dusting [ʌ]) powder⁸

Operationshandschuhe
sauber abgewischt¹ Gleitmittel² Eingeweide³ Doppelhandschuhe⁴ Einmalhandschuhe⁵ Schutzhandschuhe⁶ perforierte H.⁷ Handschuh(gleit)puder⁸

17

(face) mask *n & v term*   *sim* **face shield**¹ *n*, *rel* **surgical cap**² *n term*

(n) worn at all times in the OR to minimize airborne contamination

» When the moistened³ [mɔɪsᵊnd] mask is changed during operations only the strings⁴ must be handled.

Use full¹-**face mask**

Mundschutz; M. anlegen
Visier¹ OP-Haube² feucht geworden³ Bänder⁴

18

Unit 140 Wound Healing
Related Units: **5** Injuries, **106** Fractures, **126** Surgical Treatment, **139** Asepsis, **137** Sutures, **141** Fracture Management

wound [uː] **care** *or* **management** *n clin*

sim **wound repair**¹ [rɪpeɚ] *n term*

includes cleansing² [e], closing and dressing³ the wounded area, irrigation⁴, infection control, drainage [eɪ], etc.

» She requires a visiting nurse⁵ to assist with wound care at home. A carefully applied dressing assures the patient that good wound care has been provided. This is how the wound should be cared for.

Use to provide/assist with **wound care** • appropriate / negligent⁶ [-dʒənt]/ postoperative / local / deep⁷ **wound care**

> **Note:** The term **wound repair** may refer to surgical wound care as well as the body's healing process following an injury (→ U140-5).

Wundversorgung, -behandlung
chir. Wundversorgung¹ Reinigen² Verbinden³ Spülung⁴ Hauskrankenpfleger(in)⁵ nachlässige Wundversorgung⁶ Versorgung einer tiefen Wunde⁷

1

approximate *v term*   *sim* **align**¹ [əlaɪn] *v term* → U141-1; U137-5

bringing two surfaces (e.g. wound edges²) or stumps³ [ʌ] (fractured bone, vessels, nerves) close together

reapproximate *v term* • **approximation**⁴ *n* •
alignment⁵ *n term* • **approximator** *n*

» The wound edges can be approximated with tapes. Simple approximation of the freshened edges⁶ is sufficient. Precise alignment facilitates⁷ rapid healing, return of function and a good cosmetic result.

Use loosely **approximated** • to provide/allow for/permit/(re)check **approximation** • primary [aɪ]/ simple / loose⁸ / skin / tissue / end-to-end / close or exact⁹ **approximation** • rib **approximator** • **approximator** clamp

adaptieren, annähern, wiedervereinigen
reponieren, einrichten¹ Wundränder² Stümpfe, Bruchenden³ Adaptation⁴ Einrichtung, Reposition⁵ angefrischte Wundränder⁶ ermöglicht⁷ lockere Adaptation⁸ gute/ exakte A.⁹

2

Wound Healing CLINICAL TERMS 609

wound closure [kloʊʒɚ] n term

approximation of the wound edges over the wound cavity[1] by means of tapes[2], sutures or dressings[3]

» Tapes are the skin closure *of choice*[4] *for clean wounds. The ideal type of wound closure is* primary approximation of the wound edges[5].

Use to achieve/delay [eɪ] **wound closure** • early / primary[5] / adequate / precise / burn / abdominal / layered[6] [eɪ] **wound closure** • type / safety **of wound closure** • to close[7] **a wound**

Wundverschluss, -naht
Wundhöhle[1] Klebebänder, (Heft)pflaster[2] Wundauflagen, Verbände[3] der Wahl[4] primärer Wundverschluss, Primärnaht[5] schichtweiser Wundverschluss[6] Wunde schließen[7]

3

---

heal [hiːl] v i/t → U120-2

(i) to recover and become healthy [e] again
(ii) to provide therapy to support this process

healing[1] [iː] n & adj • **heal up**[2] v phr • **healed** adj • **healer**[3] n

» *A fractured leg cannot be healed, it has to be* set[4]. *The ulcer failed to heal with local care. He has a poorly healing burn on his hip. These donor sites are slower to heal.*

Use **to heal** spontaneously [eɪ] • **healing** process[5] / rate / by first intention[6] [-ʃən]/ earth[7] [ɜː] • spontaneous[8] / wound / bone / ulcer[9] [ʌlsɚ] **healing** • faith[10] [eɪ] **healer** • **heal**-all[11]

(ver)heilen
Heilung; (ab)heilend, heilsam[1] ver-, zuheilen[2] Heiler(in)[3] reponiert, eingerichtet[4] Heilungsprozess[5] Primärheilung[6] Heilerde[7] Spontanheilung[8] Geschwür-, Ulkusabheilung[9] Gesundbeter(in)[10] Allheilmittel[11]

Note: While **heal** is mainly used to describe the recovery the body makes (esp. self-healing) and less commonly for restoring sb.'s health with the help of medication or therapy, **cure** is used exclusively in the second meaning.

4

---

wound healing n   syn **wound repair** n term

natural process including blood clotting[1], tissue regeneration, and scar formation[2]

» *Wound healing is faster if the* state of nutrition[3] *is normal. In healing by first intention or* primary union[4] *wound repair occurs directly without granulation.*

Use to support/accelerate[5]/delay or interfere with[6] / moist[7] / poor **wound healing** • **wound healing by** first[4]/second[8]/third **intention**

Wundheilung
Blutgerinnung[1] Narbenbildung[2] Ernährungszustand[3] primäre Wundheilung[4] W. beschleunigen[5] W. beeinträchtigen/ verzögern[6] Wundversorgung mittels Okklusionsverband, feuchte Kammer[7] sekundäre Wundheilung[8]

5

---

epithel(ial)ization n term

growth [oʊ] of new tissue in the healing process that forms an epithelial [iː] bridge[1] in the wound cavity

» *A* scab[2] [æ] *forms and* peels [iː] off[3] *from the edges as epithelialization is completed underneath.*

Use to heal by / to produce / squamous[4] [ɒː‖eɪ] **epithelialization**

Epithelisierung, -isation
Epithelbrücke[1] Kruste, Schorf[2] sich ablösen[3] Plattenepithelbildung[4]

6

---

granulation tissue [tɪʃuː‖tɪsjuː] n term

red granular tissue containing newly formed vessels and collagen [kɒlədʒən] formed in open wounds

granulate[1] v term • granulating adj • granular[2] adj

» Exuberant [uː] granulation tissue[3] *on the wound surface is termed* proud [aʊ] flesh[4].

Use healthy / infected **granulation tissue** • **granulating** wound / ulcer[5]

Granulationsgewebe
granulieren[1] körnig, granulär[2] überschießendes Granulationsgewebe[3] wildes Fleisch, Caro luxurians[4] granulierendes Ulkus[5]

7

---

wound contraction n term   rel **contracture**[1] [kɒntræktʃɚ] n term → U31-1

as the wound heals the defect shrinks[2] and closes spontaneously; contracture, by contrast, is a pathologic process resulting from processes like excessive scar formation[3]

» *Although* [-ðoʊ] *a normal event during healing, wound contraction may* give rise to[4] *contracture.*

Narbenretraktion, -schrumpfung
Kontraktur[1] schrumpft[2] übermäßige Narbenbildung[3] führen zu[4]

8

---

scab [skæb] n & v   sim **eschar**[1] [eskɑːr] n term → U114-8

thick crust or slough[2] [slʌf] formed by coagulation of blood, pus[3] [ʌ], and/or serum [ɪə] on the surface of a wound; the sloughy[4] tissue typically seen in thermal [ɜː] burns[5] or cauterization [ɒː] are called eschars

» *The* pustules[6] [pʌstjuːlz] *become crusted and* scab over[7] *but they leave no scar.*

Use dry[8] **scab** • **scabs** form[9] / fall off • burn / necrotic[10] **eschar**

Kruste, Schorf; verschorfen
Verbrennungs-, Ätzschorf[1] Schorf[2] Eiter[3] verschorft[4] Verbrennungen[5] Pusteln[6] verschorfen[7] trockener Schorf[8] Krusten bilden sich[9] nekrotische Verschorfung[10]

9

140

CLINICAL TERMS — Wound Healing

scar [skɑːr] n & v   syn **cicatrix** [sɪkətrɪks] pl **-ces** n term

mark left on the skin by a wound that has healed; excessive scar formation is termed keloid¹ [iː]
(un)scarred² [ɑː] adj • **scarring**³ n • **cicatricial** [-trɪʃəl] adj term

» The ulcers disappeared without leaving a scar. The scar may fade⁴ [eɪ] to a varying degree. These superficial linear fissures may leave scars on healing.

Use wide⁵ [aɪ]/ fine(-line) / hypertrophic⁶ / depressed / unsightly⁷ [saɪt] / pliable⁸ [aɪ] **scar** • acne [ækni]/ burn / facial [eɪʃ] **scar** • **scar** formation³ / tissue / marks⁹ /-like / revision • to produce/promote/minimize **scarring** • progressive / permanent / severe / renal **scarring** • **scarred** face¹⁰ • **cicatricial** stenosis¹¹

Narbe, Cicatrix; vernarben, Narbe bilden
Wulstnarbe, Keloid¹ narbig, vernarbt² Narbenbildung³ blass werden⁴ breite Narbe⁵ hypertrophe N.⁶ unschöne/ hässliche N.⁷ geschmeidige N.⁸ Narben⁹ narbiges Gesicht¹⁰ narbenbedingte Stenose¹¹
10

---

wound irrigation n term   sim **lavage**¹ [lᵊvɑːʒ] n term → U127-17; U118-10

cleansing [e] a wound with a medicated irrigating solution² to remove secretions³ and promote healing

» After irrigation the site is dried with sterile sponges⁴ [ʌ] working from the wound out. The wound bed⁵ should be irrigated with a wound cleanser, e.g. saline⁶ [eɪ].

Use copious⁷ [oʊ] **irrigation** • **irrigation** to rinse or flush⁸ [ʌ]/wash out **a wound** • **irrigating** catheter / solution

Auswaschen d. Wunde; Wundspülung
Lavage, Spülung¹ medizinische Spülflüssigkeit² Wundsekret³ Tupfer⁴ Wundbett⁵ physiolog. Kochsalzlösung⁶ gründliche Spülung⁷ Wunde (aus)spülen⁸
11

---

debridement [dɪbriːdmənt‖mɒː] n term   sim **freshening**¹ n jar

surgical resection of devitalized² [aɪ] and/or contaminated³ tissue from a wound together with cellular debris⁴ [dəbriː], foreign bodies⁵, etc. to expose the adjacent [dʒeɪs] healthy tissue **debride**⁶ [iː] v term

» In this case it is better to explore and debride the wound. Now the freshened edges can be approximated. Hospitalize the patient for debridement and closure in the OR.

Use **to debride** devitalized tissue / and close a wound • surgical⁷ / radical **debridement**

Wundrandexzision, -ausschneidung, Debridement
Wundanfrischung¹ abgestorben, nekrotisch² verunreinigt, kontaminiert³ Zelltrümmer⁴ Fremdkörper⁵ ausschneiden⁶ Wundtoilette, -exzision⁷
12

---

exudate [eksjʊdeɪt] n term   rel **weep**¹ [iː] v clin, sim **transudate**² n term

fluid discharged³ from an injury (e.g the exudate that forms a scab over a skin abrasion⁴ [eɪʒ]) or inflammation (peritoneal pus in peritonitis [aɪ])
exude [ɪgzuːd] v term • **exudative**⁵ adj • **trans-/ exudation**⁶ n • **transudative** adj term

» Viral [aɪ] conjunctivitis is typically marked by a watery discharge⁷ with very scanty⁸ exudate. Compresses or soaks⁹ [oʊ] help to soothe¹⁰ [uː] weeping lesions¹¹. A thin¹² hemorrhagic [-rædʒɪk] exudate may be seen.

Use hemorrhagic [e]/ inflammatory / seropurulent¹³ **exudate** • **exudative** lesion [iːʒ]/ inflammation • clear / low-viscosity / serous [ɪə] / pleural [ʊ] **transudate** • fluid / perivascular / serosanguineous¹⁴ **transudation**

Exsudat
nässen, sezernieren¹ Transsudat² abgesondert³ Hautabschürfung⁴ exsudativ⁵ Exsudation⁶ wässrige(s) Absonderung/ Sekret⁷ wenig⁸ Bäder, feuchte Umschläge⁹ beruhigen¹⁰ nässende Wunden¹¹ wässrig¹² eitrig-seröses E.¹³ blutigseröses Transsudat¹⁴
13

---

suppurate [sʌpjʊɚeɪt] v term   syn **fester** v inf

forming and/or discharging [tʃ] pus¹ [ʌ] from infected wounds or inflamed² [eɪ] tissues
suppuration³ n term • **suppurative**⁴ adj • **purulent**⁴ [pjʊɚələnt] adj

» The furuncle was associated with gross [oʊ] suppuration⁵. Peritonitis is an inflammatory [æ] or suppurative response of the peritoneal lining⁶ to direct irritation.

Use acute / prolonged / chronic / pleural⁷ **suppuration** • **suppurative** lymphadenitis [aɪ] / otitis media⁸ [iː] / complications

eitern
Eiter¹ entzündet² Eiter(bild)ung, Suppuration³ eitrig, eiternd, purulent⁴ starke Eiterbildung⁵ Bauchfell, Peritoneum⁶ Pleuraempyem⁷ eitrige Mittelohrentzündung⁸
14

---

drain [dreɪn] n & vt & vi term

(n) patent¹ [eɪ] tube placed into wounds, infected sites etc. to prevent an accumulation² of fluids, blood or pus
drainage³ [dreɪnɪdʒ] n term

» Incise and drain the involved area. Penrose drains⁴ should not be left in place for more than about two weeks. Sump [ʌ] drains⁵ are attached to a suction [ʌ] device⁶ [aɪs]. Drains were left in place to evacuate⁷ small amounts of blood.

Use to place⁸/remove **drains** • wound **drain** • (closed) suction⁹ / surgical / closed¹⁰ (tube) / open / percutaneous / continuous¹¹ / abscess **drainage** • bladder / lymphatic¹² / postural¹³ / water-sealed [iː] catheter / vacuum⁹ / endoscopic / irrigation-aspiration¹⁴ **drainage** • **drainage** bag / bottle / tube¹⁵ / system

Drain; ableiten, -fließen
offen, durchgängig¹ Ansammlung² Drainage³ Penrose-Drains⁴ doppellumige D.⁵ Saugvorrichtung⁶ ableiten⁷ D. legen⁸ Saugdrainage⁹ geschlossene Drainage¹⁰ Dauerdrainage¹¹ Lymphdrainage¹² Lagedrainage¹³ Spül-Saug-D.¹⁴ Drainagerohr¹⁵
15

Wound Healing

CLINICAL TERMS 611

(wound) dehiscence [dɪhˈɪsᵊnˈs] *n term*

disruption[1] [ʌ] of some or all layers of a sutured wound; when associated with extrusion[2] [uː] of abdominal viscera it is termed evisceration[3] [vɪs]

dehiscent *adj term* • **dehisce**[4] [dɪhˈɪs] *v*

» The patient's unruly[5] [uː] behavior precipitated[6] dehiscence of a fresh laparotomy incision. Most wounds dehisce because the sutures cut through the fascia [fæʃ(ɪ)ə].

Use partial / total **dehiscence** • **dehiscence** without evisceration / of a wound

dressing *n*

(i) a protective, sterile covering of a wound or sore[1]
(ii) the application of a dressing

dress[2] *v* • **redress**[3] *v*

» When you remove a dressing be sure to wrap[4] [ræp] it for disposal. Nonadherent [ɪɚ] dressings[5] should be favored because they do not disturb sutures or coated [oʊ] wound edges[6] when removed.

Use to **dress** a wound[2] • to apply or put on[7]/change or replace[3]/reinforce[8]/discard[9] *a* **dressing** • surgical[10] / sterile / wet / moist[11] / dry / pressure[12] **dressing** • (non)absorbent / transparent [eɚ] film[13] / hydrocolloid [aɪ] / (semi)occlusive[14] / soiled[15] / antiseptic **dressing** • **dressing** room[16] / and stockinette[17] applied

(surgical) gauze [ɡɒːz] *n*

loosely woven[1] [oʊ] cotton[2] dressing for covering wounds

» Open fractures should be covered with saline-soaked [oʊ] gauze[3].

Use paraffin-coated[4] / fine-mesh[5] / ribbon / wrap-around roller[6] **gauze** • **gauze** bandage / dressing / pad[7] / squares[7] / sponge[8] [ʌ]/ cut / mesh • **gauze** fluff[9] [ʌ]/ wick[10] / strip[9] • expanded **gauze** roll • **gauze**-covered cotton

pad [pæd] *n & v*   *sim* **padding**[1] *n*

(n) soft cushion-like [ʊ] material, e.g for relieving pressure[2] from a dressing, absorbing fluids, etc.

» A padded dressing was applied. Thick foam [oʊ] pads[3] can help prevent pressure sores[4].

Use foam[3] / gauze / warming[5] / protective / sanitary or perineal[6] [iː]/ corn[7] / eye[8] **pad** • well / lightly[9] / loosely **padded** • **padded** splint[10] / cast[11] **padding**

bandage [bændɪdʒ] *n & v*   *sim* **binder**[1] [aɪ] *n*, **wrap**[2] [ræp] *n & v*

roll or patch [pætʃ] of gauze[3] or other material applied to an injury to absorb secretions, prevent motion, achieve compression, or keep surgical dressings in place

» This lesion may be bandaged with wet dressings. A triangular [aɪ] or scarf bandage[4] was used as a sling[5]. In wound dehiscence the abdomen must be wrapped with a binder or corset[6].

Use to apply/put on/remove[7] *a* **bandage** • roller[8] / four-tailed[9] / spiral / protective / spica[10] [aɪ] **bandage** • plaster[11] / triangular / Esmarch('s)[12] [k]/ Ace® **bandage** • elastic[13] / compression[14] **bandage** • absorbable mesh / protective **wrap** • abdominal[15] / breast [e]/ T-**binder**

(sterile) adhesive [iː] **tape** [eɪ] *or* **plaster** *n* → U141-11   *syn* **Steri-strip®** *n jar*

» Unless there is bleeding from the wound the skin is preferably closed with adhesive strips.

Use cloth[1] [ɒː]/ water-repellent[2] **adhesive tape** • **adhesive** strapping[3] / plaster • hypoallergenic [dʒe]/ restraining[4] [eɪ] **tape**

Band-Aid® *n*

small adhesive strip with a gauze pad in the middle for covering minor [aɪ] skin lesions[1] [iː]

Wunddehiszenz
Auseinanderweichen, -klaffen[1] Hervortreten[2] Eingeweidevorfall[3] aufplatzen, klaffen[4] ungestüm, wild[5] verursachte[6]

16

(i) Verband(smaterial), Wundauflage (ii) Verbinden
Läsion[1] (Wunde) verbinden[2] Verband wechseln[3] einschlagen, -wickeln[4] nicht adhärente Wundauflagen[5] bedeckte Wundränder[6] V. anlegen[7] V. verstärken[8] V. entsorgen[9] Wundauflage[10] feuchter V.[11] Druckverband[12] Sprüh-, Filmverband[13] Okklusivverb.[14] schmutziger V.[15] Verband(s)raum[16] Wundauflage u. Trikotschlauch[17]

17

Gaze, Verband(s)mull
weitmaschig[1] Baumwolle[2] kochsalzimprägnierte G.[3] paraffingetränkte Gaze[4] feinmaschiger V.[5] Mullbinde[6] Gazekissen, Mullkompresse(n)[7] Gazetupfer[8] Gazestreifen[9] Gazetampon[10]

18

Kissen, Kompresse; polstern
Polsterwatte, Polsterung[1] Druck mindern[2] Schaumpolster[3] Wundliegen, Dekubitus[4] Heizkissen[5] Vorlage, Damen-, Monatsbinde[6] Hühneraugenpflaster[7] Augenkompresse[8] leicht gepolstert[9] gepolsterte Schiene[10] Polsterung (im Gipsverband)[11]

19

Bandage, Binde, Verband; bandagieren, verbinden
Binde[1] Umschlag, Wickel; einwickeln[2] Mullkompresse[3] Dreieckstuch[4] (Arm)schlinge[5] Korsett[6] V. abnehmen[7] Rollbinde[8] Schleuderverband, Funda[9] Kornährenverb., Spica[10] Gipsverband[11] Staubinde, Esmarch-Binde[12] elastische B.[13] Kompressionsverband[14] Leibbinde[15]

20

(Heft)pflaster, Klebeband
Textilpflaster[1] wasserabweisendes Pflaster[2] Heftpflaster-, Tape-Verband; Tapen[3] Stützklebeband[4]

21

Heftpflaster
kleine Hautverletzungen[1]   22

612 CLINICAL TERMS — Fracture Management

pledget [pledʒɪt] *n term*   *syn* **cotton ball**, **swab** [ɒː] *n term & clin*

a tuft¹ [ʌ] or small compress of gauze, absorbent cotton, or lint² placed over a wound or into a cavity, e.g. to apply medication or absorb the wound discharge³

swab⁴ *v term*

» Nosebleeds⁵ can be stopped by placing long pledgets into the nasal [eɪ] cavity.
Use cotton⁶ / prethreaded [e] Teflon **pledget** • to **swab** a wound⁷

(Watte)bausch, Tupfer
Bausch¹ Verband(s)mull² Wundsekret³ (ab-, be)tupfen⁴ Nasenbluten⁵ Wattebausch⁶ Wunde abtupfen⁷
23

pack *n & v*   *syn* **packing** *n*, *sim* **tampon**¹ *n & v*

(n, i) dressing used to check bleedings (ii) wrapping a limb or the entire body in towels² [aʊ], etc. (iii) absorbent material used to plug³ [ʌ] cavities or apply medication
» Early application of ice packs⁴ to reduce swelling is indicated.
Use to apply a **pack** • moist⁵ / cold / ice⁴ / mud⁶ [ʌ]/ hot / hot wet⁷ **pack** • tracheal [eɪk]/ nasal⁸ **tampon** • vaginal [dʒ]/ gauze / nasal⁸ **packing**

Packung, Wickel; einwickeln, W. machen, tamponieren
Tampon; tamponieren¹ (Hand)tücher² zustopfen, tamponieren³ Eispackung(en)⁴ feuchter Wickel⁵ Moorpackung⁶ feuchtwarme P.⁷ Nasentampon(ade)⁸
24

compress *n term*   *sim* **poultice** [poʊltɪs] or **fomentation**¹ [oʊ] *n clin*

cloth [ɒː] pad² or dressing (with or without medication) applied firmly to a lesion
» Apply cold compresses and a sterile eye patch³. Prescribe warm compresses 3–4 times daily.
Use to prescribe/apply/cover with/treat with **compresses** • cold / cool / tap-water⁴ / hot⁵ / dry / moist / vinegar⁶ [ɪ] **compress** • mustard⁷ [ʌ]/ paraffin / linseed⁸ **poultice**

Kompresse, Umschlag
Breiumschlag, Kataplasma¹ Stoffauflage² Augenklappe³ U. m. Leitungswasser⁴ warme Kompresse⁵ Essigumschlag⁶ Senfpackung⁷ Leinsamenkataplasma⁸
25

truss [trʌs] *n & v*   *sim* **corset**¹, **brace**² [breɪs] *n*

padded belt³ around the abdomen kept in place by straps⁴ to retain⁵ a reduced hernia⁶ [ɜː]
» The patient's herniated bowel needs to be supported by a truss or binder. A corset or back brace provides external support and allows patients with lower back pain to return to activity earlier. Lumbosacral [eɪ] corsets with steel stays⁷ provide mechanical [k] support for the spine [aɪ] by reinforcing the flaccid⁸ [æ(k)s] abdominal wall.
Use to wear/prescribe/fit/support by **a truss** • elastic **corset** • extension-type⁹ **brace**

Bruchband; mit Bruchband stützen
(Stütz)korsett¹ Schiene² Gürtel³ Riemen⁴ stützen⁵ reponierte(r) Hernie/ Bruch⁶ Stahleinlagen⁷ schlaff⁸ Extensionsschiene⁹
26

Unit 141 Fracture Management
Related Units: 5 Injuries, 106 Fractures, 140 Wound Healing, 126 Surgical Treatment

alignment [əlaɪnmənt] *n term*   *sim* **apposition**¹ [ɪʃ] *n term*

(i) longitudinal position of a bone or limb [lɪm] (ii) bringing sth into line, e.g. fractured ends of a bone or teeth relative to supporting, adjacent [dʒeɪs] or opposing structures

align² *v* • malalignment³ *n* • appose⁴ *v* • appositional⁵ *adj*

» The elbow was placed in marked flexion to preserve fracture alignment. Primary repair⁶ can occur only when the fracture is stable [eɪ] and aligned and its surfaces closely apposed. Healing of the fracture in malalignment may cause limitation of shoulder motion [oʊ].
Use to bring into⁷/obtain⁷/improve/restore/maintain **alignment** • gross⁸ [oʊ]/ correct / accurate / unstable / fracture⁹ / femoral [e] **alignment** • joint / anatomical (position and) / longitudinal / rotational¹⁰ [eɪʃ] **alignment** • to achieve/be in **apposition** • side-by-side or bayonet¹¹ [eɪ] / adequate / mal³/ non**apposition** • direct / close / level¹² **bone apposition** • **to be apposed** to sth.¹³ / by sth. • **appositional bone** formation¹⁴ / fixation • gross / significant / patellar **malalignment**

(i) Achsenstellung (ii) Ausrichtung, Herstellung normaler Bissverhältnisse
Apposition, An-, Auflagerung, Adaptation¹ aus-, einrichten² Fehlstellung³ aneinanderlegen, adaptieren⁴ angelagert, Appositions-⁵ Primärheilung⁶ adaptieren, einrichten⁷ makroskop. korrekte Stellung⁸ Fraktureinrichtung⁹ Rotationsstellung¹⁰ Bajonettstellung¹¹ höhengleiche Knochenapposition¹² anliegen¹³ Knochenanbau¹⁴
1

reduction [ʌ] *n term*   *syn* **setting** *n clin*, *sim* **realignment**¹ *n term*
                rel **manipulation**² *n clin*

repositioning broken bones to their anatomical relationships by surgical or manipulative procedures

reduce³ [(j)uː] *v term* • realign³ *v* • set³ *v clin* • unset⁴ *adj* • manipulate⁵ *v*

» If reduction by closed manipulation is anatomic, transverse fractures tend to be stable. When the fracture has been properly set, a splint⁶ should be applied.
Use to obtain³/confirm/prevent/undergo **reduction** • open⁷ / closed or manual or manipulative⁸ / (non)operative⁷ / failure of **reduction** • anatomic / (in)complete / end-on-end / fracture / joint **reduction** • **reduction** under anesthesia [iː] • closed⁸ **manipulation** • **to set** a fracture⁹

Reposition, Einrichtung
Wiederherstellung d. Achsenausrichtung¹ Handgriff, Manipulation² reponieren, einrichten³ nicht reponiert⁴ manipulieren, handhaben⁵ Schiene⁶ offene Reposition⁷ geschlossene R.⁸ Fraktur/ Bruchfragmente reponieren⁹
2

Fracture Management　　　　　　　　　　　　　　　　　　　　　　CLINICAL TERMS　613

skeletal [skɛlət°l] **traction** [trækʃ°n] *n term*　　*rel* **extension**[1], **suspension**[2] *n term*

(i) pulling or dragging force exerted on a broken limb in a distal direction (ii) the act of pulling
re/ dis/ protraction[3] *n term* • **distract**[4] *v* • **suspend**[5] *v clin* • **extend**[6] *vi/t*

» Reduce gross deformity by applying traction to the tibia and manipulating it as needed to align it with the femur [iː]. Finger *extension splints*[7] can potentiate grip.
Use to apply[8]/exert/maintain **traction** • to place[8]/be held[9] **in traction** • sustained [eɪ] skeletal / axial / lateral / counter-[10] [aʊ]/ cranial [eɪ]/ cervical [ɜː] **traction** • arm extension / head halter [ɒː] or halo[11] [eɪ] **traction** • skin / manual / gentle [dʒ] / weight[12] [weɪt]/ continuous[13] / intermittent / elastic **traction** • **traction splint**[7] / device [-aɪs]/ suture[14] • balanced[15] / frontomaxillary wire [aɪ] **suspension** • **suspension** sling / wire[16] • **extension** wire

Traktion, Zug, Extension
Streckung, Extension, Verlängerung, (Aus)dehnung[1] Suspension, Aufhängung[2] Re/ Dis/ Protraktion[3] distrahieren[4] aufhängen, suspendieren[5] (aus)strecken, reichen bis[6] Extensionsschiene[7] Zug anwenden, Streckverband anlegen[8] in Extension behandeln[9] Gegenzug[10] Ext. m. Kopfhalterung (Glisson-Schlinge)[11] Gewichtszug[12] Dauerzug[13] Entlastungsnaht[14] Aufhängung in d. Schwebe[15] Suspensionsdraht[16]　　3

fracture fixation [eɪ] *n term*　　*syn* **stabilization** *n*, *rel* **osteosynthesis**[1] [-sɪnθəsɪs] *n term*

fastening [fæsnɪŋ] a broken bone in a firmly attached or stable position by internal or external fixation devices
transfix[2] *v term* • **fixator**[3] *n* • **(in)stability**[4] *n clin & term* • **(un)stable**[5] *adj*

» Good results are most readily[6] [e] obtained by rigid [dʒ] internal fixation of the fractured ulna with plate and screws and complete reduction of the dislocated radial head. Pins and wires [aɪ] were incorporated into the cast to transfix the major bone fragments.
Use (prompt/temporary/failed) external[7] / (immediate/prophylactic/rigid [dʒ]) internal[8] **fixation** • / two-point / percutaneous [eɪ]/ intermaxillary[9] (*abbr* IMF) **fixation** • mini-plate / intramedullary[10] / (axial/ lateral) pin[11] **fixation** • **fixation screw**[12] [skruː]/ device • external[13] / internal **fixator** • bony / emergency / surgical **stabilization** • **stabilization bar**[14] • (**un**)**stable** joint / spinal [aɪ] fracture[15] • midcarpal / patellar / spinal / recurrent [ɜː] shoulder[16] **instability** • fracture / mechanical [k] **stability**

Fixation, Stabilisierung
Osteosynthese[1] transfixieren[2] Fixateur[3] (In)stabilität[4] (in)stabil[5] am besten[6] sofortige externe Fixation[7] starre innere F.[8] mandibulomaxilläre F.[9] Marknagelung[10] Stiftfixation, Spickung[11] Fixierschraube[12] Fixateur externe[13] Stabilisierungsstab[14] instabile Wirbelfraktur[15] rezidivierende Schulterinstabilität/ -gelenkluxation[16]　　4

immobilization *n term & clin*　　*opposite* **mobilization**[1] *n term & clin* → U64-2

rendering a person or a body part incapable [eɪ] of moving
(**im**)**mobilize**[2] [ɒː] *v* • (**im**)**mobile**[3] [moʊb°l‖aɪl] *adj* • (**im**)**mobility**[4] *n*

» Immobilization is obtained by incorporation of the traction pin or wire in a full extremity plaster with the knee [niː] flexed 30 degrees and the foot in plantar flexion.
Use to provide excellent/treat by **immobilization** • wound [uː]/ shoulder / spine [aɪ] spica[5] [aɪ] **immobilization** • duration or length[6] / time / position / preferred [ɜː] method **of immobilization** • complete / prolonged[7] **immobility** • restricted[8] **mobility** • gradual / progressive / early[9] **mobilization**

Immobilisation, -sierung, Ruhigstellung
Mobilisation, Mobilisierung[1] ruhigstellen, immobilisieren[2] immobil, unbeweglich[3] Mobilität, Beweglichkeit[4] Immobilisierung durch Kornährenverband[5] Immobilisationsdauer[6] Langzeitimmobilität[7] eingeschränkte Mobilität/ Beweglichkeit[8] Frühmobilisation[9]　　5

(plaster) [plæstɚ] **cast** [kæst] *n*
syn **plaster (of Paris cast)** *n clin & term*, *abbr* **P.O.P.**

firm covering made of plaster of Paris to immobilize broken bones while they heal
casting[1] [æ] *n term*

» A well-molded[2] [oʊ] plaster cast is applied to maintain this position. At potential pressure sites[3] a window should be cut out of the cast. Recurrent angular displacement can be corrected by cast wedging[4] [dʒ], which involves dividing the plaster circumferentially [enʃ] and inserting wedges in the appropriate direction. Today we can apply a walker[5] [wɒːkɚ] to the cast.
Use to apply[6]/encase [eɪ] in[7]/place in[7]/immobilize in/split/spread [e]/remove **a cast** • (below-knee) walking[8] / hanging / (short/long) leg[9] **cast** • arm / forearm / boxing glove[10] [ʌ]/ (hip/shoulder) spica[11] [aɪk]/ body[12] **cast** • tubular or circumferential[13] / articulated / weight-bearing [eɚ]/ snugly [ʌ] fitting[14] / (excessively) tight [taɪt]/ well-padded[15] **cast** • **cast** treatment / immobilization / removal / (re)application • corrective[16] **casting** • **plaster** dressing or bandage[17] / boot[18] [uː]/ gauntlet[19] [ɒː] • **plaster of Paris** (*abbr* P.O.P.) jacket[12] [dʒæ]

Gipsverband
(Ein)gipsen[1] gut anmodelliert[2] Druckstellen[3] Keilen[4] Gehstollen, Sohlenplatte[5] Gips(verband) anlegen[6] eingipsen[7] Gehgips[8] Unterschenkelgips[9] Gipsverband m. Fingereinschluss[10] Spica humeri[11] Gipsmieder, -korsett[12] Gipstutor, -hülse, zirkulärer G.[13] gut sitzender G.[14] gepolsterter G.[15] Redressionsgips[16] Gipsverband[17] Gipsstiefel[18] Gipshandschuh[19]　　6

splint [splɪnt] *n clin & term*   *sim* **brace**¹ [eɪ], **jacket**², **corset**² *n clin*

orthopedic [iː] device [aɪ] used to immobilize, align, support, or protect fractured or traumatized [ɒː] sites

splint³ *v* • **splinting**⁴ *n* • **brace**³ *v*

» The elbow should be splinted in sufficient [ɪʃ] extension to avoid interfering⁵ [ɪɜ˞] with perfusion [uː3]. Splints are most commonly used to immobilize broken bones or dislocated joints. Loosen⁶ the splint if the extremity becomes cold, discolored or dusky⁷ [ʌ]. Braces allow motion of the braced part, in contrast to a splint, which prevents motion.

Use external / internal / active or functional or dynamic⁸ / (inflatable [eɪ]) air⁹ / anchor¹⁰ [k]/ coaptation¹¹ / contact **splint** • intraoral / wrist [rɪst]/ knee / tenodesis [iː]/ wire [aɪ] or ladder¹² **splint** • plaster¹³ / jacket¹⁴ / surgical / pillow¹⁵ **splint** • neck / back / ischial [sk] weight-bearing / long leg / Milwaukee¹⁶ / forearm / removable / cast¹⁷-**brace** • emergency [ɜː]/ abduction **splinting** • plastic **jacket** • to wear or use¹⁸ **a corset** • lumbosacral [ʌ]/ elastic / surgical **corset**

sling [slɪŋ] *n clin & term*

    sim **harness**¹, **cuff**² [ʌ] *n*, **swathe**³ [sweɪð] *n & v clin*

supporting or suspensory bandage used to fix or immobilize body parts, esp the arm

» Treatment of bicipital [aɪs] tendinitis [aɪ] includes cessation⁴ [s] of offending activities and short-term immobilization of the shoulder in a sling. Splint the extremity in a sling for comfort.

Use to apply/treat in/support in⁵/wear **a sling** • suspension / triangular [aɪ] bandage⁶ / arm **sling** • **sling** traction / and swathe • Pavlic⁷ / head **harness**

cervical [sɜːrvɪkᵊl] **collar** [ɒː] or **orthosis** [ɔːrθoʊsɪs] *n term*

    rel **head halter**¹ [ɒː] *n term*

orthopedic appliance [aɪ] worn around the neck to support the head (used in cervical spine [aɪ] injuries)

orthotics² [ɒː] *n term* • orthotic³ *adj* • orthotist⁴ *n*

» In stable injuries of the cervical spine, cervical collars or cervical thoracic [s] braces⁵ (4-poster) are adequate. A hard cervical spine collar is then applied, and the head is taped to a backboard, surrounded by some means of cushioning⁶ [ʊ] (e.g. rolled blankets⁷ [æ]).

Use rigid⁸ [dʒ] light **cervical collar** • firm plastic / tight / loose / soft foam⁹ [oʊ]/ inelastic **collar** • halo-type¹⁰ [heɪloʊ]/ four-poster¹⁰ / dynamic / flexion [kʃ] **orthosis** • cervical **halter** • **halter** traction¹¹

stockinet(te) *n clin*

    sim **elastic** or **compression stockings**¹ *n clin* → U125-22

tube of elastic material applied underneath casts or splints to protect the skin, prevent thrombosis, etc.

» The palmar splint is padded with a thin foam pad² and held in place with a loosely wrapped [r] roll of plaster of Paris³, stockinet or elastic bandage⁴. Conservative measures [eɜ] such as leg elevation⁵, or elastic stockings may be helpful.

Use **stockinette** dressing⁶ / amputation bandage⁷ • heavy-duty⁸ [e]/ knee-length / full-length / waist-high [eɪ]/ custom [ʌ] fitted⁹ **elastic stockings** • support¹⁰ / body¹¹ **stocking**

strapping [æ] *n clin*   *syn* **taping** [eɪ] *n clin*

application of overlapping strips of adhesive [iː] tape¹ [eɪ] to exert pressure or increase stability

strap² *n & v* • tape³ *n & v* • (un)strapped⁴ *adj* • (un)taped⁵ *adj*

» A supple⁶ [ʌ] foot that is easily corrected by strapping and casting has a more favorable prognosis. Splint the injury by taping the injured toe to its neighbor.

Use knee / shoulder / rib / metatarsal / figure-of-eight⁷ / eversion [ɜːrʒ] tape⁸ / imbricated⁹ **strapping** • chin [tʃ]/ head / cuff [ʌ] suspension¹⁰ **strap** • **strap** sling • buddy¹¹ [ʌ]/ (medial [iː]) patellar / adhesive¹² **taping** • occlusive [uː] / sterile / strips of¹³ **tape** • **tape** dressing¹⁴ / closure of wounds

---

Schiene
(Gelenk)schiene, Stützkorsett, Brace, Manschette¹ Mieder, Korsett² stützen, schienen³ Schienung⁴ Beeinträchtigung⁵ lockern⁶ bläulich verfärbt⁷ Bewegungsschiene⁸ aufblasbare Sch.⁹ Kieferbruchschiene¹⁰ Adaptationsschiene¹¹ Draht(leiter)schiene¹² Gipsschiene, -schale, -longuette¹³ Rumpforthese¹⁴ gepolsterte Schiene¹⁵ Milwaukee-, Extensionskorsett¹⁶ Funktions-, Bewegungsgips¹⁷ ein Korsett tragen¹⁸

7

Schlinge
Gurt, Zügel, Bandage¹ Manschette² Binde, Umschlag; um-, einwickeln³ Einstellen⁴ durch eine Schlinge stützen⁵ Mitella, Dreieckstuch⁶ Pavlik-Bandage⁷

8

Halskrause, Schanz-Krawatte
Kopfhalterung¹ Orthese-, Stützapparate² gerade, aufrecht, gestreckt³ Orthetiker(in)⁴ Kopf-Brust-Gipsverband, Minerva-Gips⁵ Polsterung⁶ zusammengerollte Decken⁷ starre Halskrawatte⁸ Schaumstoff-Halskrawatte⁹ Halo-Fixateur¹⁰ Haloextension¹¹

9

Baumwoll-, Trikotschlauch
Kompressions-, Antithrombosestrümpfe¹ Schaumstoffpolster² Gipsbinde³ elastische Binde⁴ Hochlagerung⁵ Schlauchverband⁶ Amputationsstrumpf⁷ starke Gummistrümpfe⁸ maßgefertigte Gummistrümpfe⁹ Stützstrumpf¹⁰ Rumpftrikotschlauch¹¹

10

Tape-, Pflasterverband
Pflaster, Klebeband¹ Riemen, Gurt; fest-, anschnallen² Band, elast. Pflasterbinde, (Heft)pflaster; (m. Heftpflaster) verkleben³ bandagiert; festgeschnallt⁴ getapet⁵ beweglich⁶ Achtertourenpflasterverband⁷ Eversions-Tapeverband⁸ Dachziegelverband⁹ (Schulter)gurtverband¹⁰ Fixation durch Nachbarfinger/ -zehe¹¹ Anlegen e. Pflasterverbandes¹² Klebestreifen¹³ Tape-Verband¹⁴

11

Fracture Management   CLINICAL TERMS **615**

osteosynthesis [ɒːstɪoʊsɪnθəsɪs] *n term*   *sim* **osteorrhaphy** [-rəfi] or
                                                                osteosuture[1] *n term*

surgical fixation of bone fragments by mechanical [k] means (e.g. wires, sutures)
» *A flexible multistrand cable system was used in posterior spinal osteosynthesis for cervical fracture-dislocation.*
Jse stable / orthodontic[2] *osteosynthesis* • *osteosynthesis* screw [skruː]

spinal [aɪ] or **vertebral fusion** [fjuːɜ°n] *n term*   *rel* **arthrodesis**[1] [iː] *n term*

joint stiffening surgery to achieve bone ankylosis[2] [oʊ] between two or more vertebrae[3] [eɪ‖iː]
» *Management of spine instability may include spinal fusion with metal plates and screws in combination with bone fusion. Fusion of the joint may be necessary due to irreparable instability or persistent infection. Surgical fusion of the talonavicular [eɪ], talocalcaneal [eɪ], and calcaneocuboid joints is known as triple arthrodesis.*
Jse bony / joint[2] / cervical / atlanto-occipital [ksɪ] *fusion* • *fusion* procedure • thumb [θʌm]/ shoulder **arthrodesis**

circumferential wiring [waɪəɪŋ] *n term*   *sim* **figure-of-eight wire**[1] *n term*

passing a slender pliable[2] [aɪ] stainless steel wire around a fractured bone for internal fixation
wire[3] *n & v term* • *wired*[4] *adj* • *wiring*[5] *n*
» *Temporary percutaneous wire fixation*[6] *was advocated. The best method of fracture fixation and restoration of the articular surface is compression by figure-of-eight wires. Significant displacement requires overhead skeletal traction*[7] *by means of a Kirschner wire*[8] *inserted through the proximal ulna* [ʌ].
Jse to insert[9] *a wire* • stiff / pull-out[10] / stainless steel / Kirschner or K-[8] / guide[11] / pinning[12] / hook[13] [ʊ]/ gold plated [eɪ] metal[14] *wire* • No. 22 / biodegradable [aɪ]/ coated[15] / supporting / suspension *wire* • *wire* fixation[5] / loop[16] [uː]/ coil[17] / cerclage[18] [sərklɑːʒ]/ stump [ʌ]/ saw[19] [sɒː]/ extension / sutures[20] • circummandibular / interosseous / transosseous / tension band[21] *wiring* • orthodontic arch[22] [ɑːrtʃ] *wire*

> **Note:** The expression *wire* is traditionally applied to pliable as well stiff wires or pins (e.g. K-wires). This is why *wiring* and *pinning* are often used synonymously.

pin [pɪn] *n clin & term*

(i) flexible but not pliable stainless steel spike[1] [aɪ] used for internal fixation
(ii) pointed metal rod[2] [ɒː] used to immobilize fractures
(iii) thin metal peg[3] or dowel[3] [aʊ] for attaching things
pinning[4] *n term* • *pin*[5] *v* • **micropin** *n* • **pinprick**[6] *n clin*
» *These fractures tend to be very unstable and frequently require percutaneous fixation with pins or open reduction. Most surgeons prefer to use internal fixation by multiple screw or pin fixation for impacted fractures to allow maintenance of reduction, earlier crutch* [krʌtʃ] *ambulation, and earlier weight bearing.*
Jse to insert or place[7]/secure with/pull out *a pin* • fixation / straight / lateral / crossed / Steinmann[8] / olecranon / (skeletal) traction *pin* • metal / dental[9] / external fixation / safety[10] *pin* • *pin* fixation[4] / fixator / tract (infection)[11] / site / placement / implant • cross- or crossed / double [ʌ] percutaneous / K-wire[12] *pinning*

(medullary) nail [neɪl] *n term*

                                    rel **screw**[1] [skruː], **bolt**[2] [oʊ] *n clin & term*

solid tubular and often flanged [dʒ] rod[3] inserted into the marrow [mæroʊ] cavity[4] for fixation of fractured long bones
nailing[5] *n clin & term* • *screw*[6] *v* • **bolt** *v* • **bolting**[7] *n*
» *The functional outcome in closed interlocking nailing of femoral* [e] *shaft fractures was excellent. The cut bones are then reshaped, repositioned, and fixed with a combination of wires or miniplates and screws.*
Jse to drive a *nail* into the bone[8] • intramedullary[9] / flanged[10] [dʒ]/ interlocking or locked or locking[11] / (un)reamed[12] [iː] *nail* • *nail* extension / closed[13] / open / intramedullary[14] *nailing* • bone[15] / transverse / (non)sliding [aɪ] or lag[16] [æ]/ titanium[17] [eɪ]/ transarticular / dynamic condylar[18] / bi-/unicortical[19] *screw* • *screw* fixation /-plate system • **bolt**head / shank

---

Osteosynthese
Knochennaht[1] kieferorthopäd. Osteosynthese[2]

12

op. Wirbelsäulenversteifung, Spondylodese
operative Gelenkversteifung, Arthrodese[1] Gelenkversteifung, Ankylose[2] Wirbel, Vertebrae[3]

13

Drahtumschlingung
Achterdraht(schlinge), Achterligatur[1] biegsam, verformbar[2] (Bohr)draht; (ver)drahten[3] gedrahtet, gespickt[4] Drahtung, Drahtosteosynthese, Spickung[5] perkutane Spickung[6] Overheadextension[7] Kirschner-(Bohr)draht, -Bohrstift[8] Draht einbringen[9] Ausziehdraht[10] Führungsdraht[11] Spickdraht, Stift[12] Hakendraht[13] vergoldeter Metalldraht[14] beschichteter D.[15] Drahtschlinge[16] Drahtspirale[17] Drahtumschlingung, -cerclage[18] Drahtsäge[19] Drahtnähte[20] Zuggurtung(s-osteosynthese)[21] kieferorthopäd. Drahtbogen[22]

14

(i) Bohrstift, Spick-, Bohrdraht
(ii) (Knochen)nagel
(iii) Stift, (Steck)nadel
Stift, Dorn[1] Stift[2] Stift, Dübel[3] Stiftfixation, Nagelung, Stift-, Spickdrahtosteosynthese, Spickung[4] fixieren, spicken, (an)heften[5] Nadelstich[6] Spickdraht/ Nagel (in d. Knochen) einbringen/ -bohren[7] Steinmann-Nagel[8] Wurzelstift[9] Sicherheitsnadel[10] Bohrlochosteitis[11] Kirschnerdraht-Fixation[12]

15

Marknagel
Schraube[1] (Schrauben)bolzen[2] Stift, Stab[3] Markhöhle[4] (Mark)nagelung, Stiftfixation[5] (ver)schrauben[6] Bolzung[7] Nagel in d. Knochen hineintreiben[8] intramedullär platzierter Nagel, Marknagel[9] geflanschter Nagel[10] Verriegelungsnagel[11] (un)aufgebohrter (Mark)nagel[12] gedeckte Nagelung[13] Marknagelung[14] Knochenschraube[15] Gleitlochschr.[16] Titanschr.[17] dyn. Kondylenschr.[18] monokortikale Schr.[19]

16

141

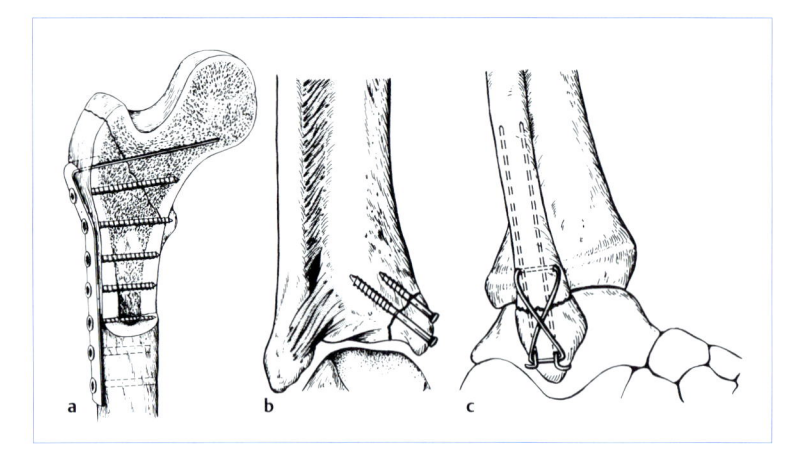

616 CLINICAL TERMS — Physical Therapy & Rehabilitation

Osteosynthesis techniques:
(a) condylar plate osteosynthesis for an intertrochanteric fracture,
(b) screw fixation of the medial malleoulus,
(c) wire osteosyntesis by figure-of-eight wiring of a fractured lateral malleolus

(bone) plate [pleɪt] *n term* sim **mini-plate**[1] *n term*
strip of metal applied to a fractured bone in order to keep its ends in apposition
plating[2] [eɪ] *n term*
» A clinical and radiographic comparison of tension band wiring and *plate fixation*[2] was performed. At operation excellent stability was achieved with bone plates.
Use fracture / metal[3] / stainless steel / side / U-shaped / nail **plate** • (sliding[4] [aɪ]/ locking[5]) screw / slotted[6] [ɒː] **plate** • compression[7] / ancillary[8] [sə] **plating** • affixed **mini-plate**

(Knochen)platte
Miniplatte[1] Plattenosteosynthese[2] Metallplatte[3] dynamische Kompressionsplatte[4] Rundlochplatte[5] Langlochplatte[6] Kompressionsosteosynthese[7] zusätzl. Plattenosteosynthese[8]

17

Unit 142 Physical Therapy & Rehabilitation

Related Units: 1 Health & Fitness, 4 Illness & Recovery, 5 Injuries, 16 Paramedical Staff, 19 On the Ward, 31 Musculoskeletal Function, 63 Posture, 64 Body Movement, 65 Walking, 66 Speech, 77 Mental Health, 104 Pain, 106 Fractures, 120 Therapeutic Intervention, 134 Perioperative Management, 140 Wound Care, 141 Fracture Management

physical therapy [fɪzɪkəl θerəpi] *n term, abbr* **PT** *syn* **physiotherapy** *n term*
evaluation, alleviation [iː] and correction of disorders using physical agents [eɪdʒ] and methods, e.g. application of cold[1], heat, light, shortwave, electrostimulation, therapeutic [juː] exercises[2], etc.
physical therapist[3] *n term* • **physiotherapist**[3] [fɪziəʊθerəpɪst] *n*
» Physical therapy is critical to prevent or allay [eɪ] contractures[4]. If the patient is severely disabled [eɪ], a trained physical therapist should supervise [uː] the exercise program. Intensive physiotherapy for postural [pɒːstʃəʳl] correction[5] and strengthening of spinal [aɪ] support musculature [ʌ] is indicated.
Use to be started on/receive [siː] /initiate [ɪʃ] /respond to[6] **physical therapy** • local / chest [tʃ]/ respiratory[7] / post-injury **PT** • twice-daily / graded[8] [eɪ]/ progressive **PT** • intensive or vigorous / rehabilitative[9] **PT** • **physical therapy** facility[10] [sɪ]/ department / program / protocol / aide[11] [eɪ] • early / gentle[12] [dʒ]/ routine **physiotherapy** • **physiotherapy** pool[13] • **physical** complaints[14] [eɪ]/ activity / condition[15] • **physical** measures[16] [eʒ]/ exercise / medicine[17]

Physiotherapie, physikalische Therapie
Kälteanwendungen[1] Heil-, Krankengymnastik[2] Physiotherapeut(in), Heil-, Krankengymnast(in)[3] Kontrakturen reduzieren[4] Haltungskorrektur[5] auf d. PT ansprechen[6] Atemgymnastik, -therapie[7] dosierte PT[8] Rehabilitationstherapie, rehabilitative PT[9] physiotherapeut. Einrichtung[10] Physiotherapieassistent(in)[11] vorsichtige/ behutsame PT[12] Physiotherapiebecken[13] körperl. Beschwerden[14] körperl. Verfassung, Gesundheitszustand[15] physikal./ physiotherapeut. Maßnahmen[16] physikal. Medizin[17]

1

142

Physical Therapy & Rehabilitation   CLINICAL TERMS **617**

rehabilitation *n term* • *syn* **rehab** [riːhab] *n jar, rel* **restoration**[1] *n clin* → U129-1f

restoring patients from injury, a disabling [eɪ] disease[2], addiction, etc. to their previous [iː] physical and emotional [oʊʃ] state enabling them to return to normal activity and resume[3] [uː] their professional task

rehabilitate[4] *v term* • **rehabilitative** *adj* • **restore** [ɔː] *v* • **restorative** *adj*

» *The longer the patient survives [aɪ] transplantation, the more apt he is to have a successful rehabilitation. Check the patient every two weeks until healing [iː] and rehabilitation are complete [iː].* Vigorous rehabilitative therapy[5] *should be given to maintain full motion* [oʊʃ] *at affected joints. The deformity of the hands limits* crutch [ʌ] *use*[6] *during rehabilitation.*

Use to promote/facilitate[7]/delay[8] [eɪ] /impede [iː] /undergo[9] **rehabilitation** • patient / cardiac[10] / pulmonary [ʊ‖ʌ]/ pain **rehabilitation** • muscle [mʌsl] / nutritional [ɪʃ]/ burn [ɜː] **rehabilitation** • auditory [ɒː]/ visual [ɪʒ]/ balance[11] / vocational[12] [eɪʃ] **rehabilitation** • full / partial [ʃ]/ upper-extremity **rehabilitation** • inpatient[13] / post-stroke[14] [oʊ] **rehabilitation** • psychosocial [saɪkə-]/ alcohol / drug[15] / penal[16] [iː] **rehabilitation** • **rehabilitation** center / clinic / facility[17] • **rehabilitation** program / training • **rehabilitation** psychologist / potential / goals[18] [oʊ] • **rehabilitation center for** the physically [ɪ] disabled[19] / alcoholics / drug addicts • **to rehabilitate** trauma [ɒː] victims / amputees [iː] • **rehabilitative** measures[20] / devices [aɪs] *or* aids[21] [eɪ]/ therapy • **rehabilitative** efforts[22] / physical exercise program

disability *n* • *syn* **disablement** [eɪ] *n*,
                    rel **impairment**[1] [eəʴ], **handicap**[2] *n* → U1-11; U4-8

loss of physical or mental function [ʌ] which substantially[3] limits a person's ability to communicate, function independently or perform activities of daily living, or vocational [eɪʃ] activities[4]

disabled[5] [eɪ] *adj & n pl* • **(in)ability**[6] *n* • **handicap** *v* • **handicapped**[5] *adj & n pl*

» *Identify the degree of physical disease contributing to the patient's disability. Roll-in shower chairs are available to allow greater independence for the severely disabled. Some blind children are multiply* [ʌ] *handicapped. Surgery may be necessary to relieve pain or diminish the functional impairment secondary to deformity.*

Use to cause/experience/correct/assess[7]/minimize **disability** • physical (*abbr* PD)/ functional[8] / learning[9] **disability** • mental[10] / neurologic [n(j)ʊəʴ-]/ psychologic **disability** • long-term / lifelong / temporary / chronic **disability** • work[11] / job-related[12] / service-connected[12] (*abbr* SCD) **disability** • level or degree or severity [e] of[13] **disability** • minor [aɪ]/ severe[14] [ɪəʴ]/ progressive / total[15] **disability** • **disability** status[13] [eɪ‖æ] (scale) [eɪ]/ benefits[16] / pension[17] [ʃ] • cognitive / sensory[18] / partial **impairment** • profound [aʊ] permanent [ɜː] **impairment** • **impairment of** (intellectual/ liver) function[8] / sensation[18] [eɪʃ] • **impairment of** memory / gait[19] [eɪ] • physical / motor[20] / orthopedic [iː] **handicap** • emotional [oʊʃ]/ lifelong **handicap** • **disabled** patient / infant • physically[21] / partially[22] / totally **disabled** • **disabling** disease[23] / pain on movement • **disabling** contractures [-tʃəʴz]/ migraine [aɪ‖BE iː]/ fatigue [fətiːg] • mentally / developmentally / severely / visually[24] **handicapped**

incapacity [ɪnkəpæsəti] *n*
                                rel **deficit**[1] [defɪsɪt], **defect**[2] [iː], **debility**[3] *n*

lack of physical or intellectual capability that renders a patient unable to perform a task or do his/her job

incapacitated[4] *adj* • **incapacitate** *v* • **capacity**[5] *n* • **incapable** [eɪ] *adj* → U4-7f • **defective**[6] *adj* • **debilitating** *adj* → U77-22

» *Legal incompetence may be caused by mental or physical incapacities such as mental illness, senility, or addiction to alcohol or other drugs. Specific cognitive assessment must be performed, since many patients are able to cover a deficit in routine conversation. This noticeably physical defect makes him feel inferior* [ɪəʴ] *to his peers.*

Use physical / mental / legal[7] [iː]/ earning[8] [ɜː]/ degree of **incapacity** • cognitive or intellectual / neurologic[9] / sensory **deficit** • motor / cranial [eɪ] nerve [ɜː]/ clinical / hearing[10] [ɪəʴ] **deficit** • visual field / language / comprehension[11] **deficit** • congenital [dʒe] *or* birth[12] [ɜː]/ cosmetic **defect** • developmental / visual field[13] **defect** • **defective** development / hearing[10] • general / musculoskeletal **debility** • **debilitating** disease[14] / fatigue / muscle [s] wasting[15] [eɪ]/ pain

---

Reha(bilitation), (Wieder)eingliederung, -herstellung

Wiederherstellung[1] zur Behinderung führende Krankheit[2] wiederaufnehmen[3] wiederherstellen, (wieder)eingliedern, rehabilitieren[4] intensive Rehabilitationstherapie[5] Verwendung v. Krücken[6] d. Reha erleichtern[7] d. R. verzögern[8] s. e. Rehabilitation unterziehen[9] kardiolog. R.[10] Wiederherstellung d. Gleichgewichts[11] berufl. Rehabilitation[12] stationäre R.[13] R. nach Schlaganfall[14] Entwöhnungsbehandlung[15] Wiedereingliederung Straffälliger[16] Rehabilitationseinrichtung[17] Rehabilitationsziele[18] Rehabilitationszentrum f. körperl. Behinderte[19] Rehabilitationsmaßnahmen[20] Rehabilitationshilfen[21] rehabilitative Bemühungen[22]   2

Fähigkeitsstörung, Behinderung, Invalidität, Arbeits-, Erwerbsunfähigkeit

Schädigung[1] soz. Beeinträchtigung, Handicap[2] erheblich[3] berufl. Tätigkeit[4] (körperl./ geistig) behindert, invalid; Behinderte[5] (Un)fähigkeit[6] d. Behinderung beurteilen[7] Funktionsstörung[8] Lernbehinderung[9] geistige B.[10] Arbeitsfähigkeitsstörung, Einschränkung d. Arbeitsfähigkeit, Erwerbsunfähigkeit[11] Invalidität infolge e. Arbeitsunfalls[12] Invaliditätsgrad[13] schwere Behinderung[14] Vollinvalidität[15] Behindertenzulage[16] Invalidenrente[17] Empfindungs-, Sensibilitätsstörung[18] Gangstörung[19] motor. Beeinträchtigung/ Behinderung[20] körperbehindert[21] teilinvalid[22] zur Behinderung führende Krankheit[23] sehbehindert[24]   3

(Arbeits-, Erwerbs)unfähigkeit

Defizit, Mangel, Verlust, Ausfall[1] (körperl.) Gebrechen, Schaden, Defekt[2] Schwäche[3] behindert, (arbeits-, erwerbs)unfähig[4] (Leistungs)fähigkeit[5] mangel-, schadhaft, gestört[6] Geschäftsunfähigkeit[7] Erwerbsunfähigkeit[8] neurolog. Ausfälle[9] Schwerhörigkeit[10] eingeschränktes Auffassungsvermögen[11] Geburtsfehler, angeborene Fehlbildung[12] Gesichtsfeldausfall[13] konsumierende Erkrankung[14] funktionell beeinträchtigende(r) Muskelschwund/ -atrophie[15]   4

142

618 CLINICAL TERMS Physical Therapy & Rehabilitation

paraplegic [iːdʒ] n & adj term & clin

rel **quadriplegic**[1] [ɒː] n & adj term & clin

person affected by impairment or loss of motor and/or sensory function due to spinal cord lesions [iːʒ]

paraplegia[2] n term • **quadriplegia**[3] n •

-plegia [-pliːdʒ(ɪ)ə], **-plegic** comb → U135-11

» Only 10% of paraplegics recover walking capacity after radiation therapy plus glucocorticoids. Paraplegic patients should not sit in one position for more than two hours. Spinal cord compression[4] may result in paraplegia or quadriplegia, depending on the segment involved.

Use **paraplegic** patient[5] • to become / T10[6] **paraplegic** • traumatic / sensory-motor / flaccid[7] [(k)s] **paraplegia** • spastic[8] [æ]/ acute / progressive **paraplegia** • fixed[9] / familial spastic (abbr FSP)/ areflexive **paraplegia** • **quadriplegic** patient

amputee [æmpjʊtiː] n

rel **disarticulation**[1] n term **stump**[2] [ʌ] n clin, **prosthesis**[3] [prɒsˈθiːsɪs] n, pl **-ses** [-siːz]

patient who has suffered [ʌ] loss of a limb [lɪm] by surgical [ɜː] removal or following severe trauma [ɒː]

amputation n • **amputate**[4] v • **prosthetic**[5] [e] adj • **prosthetist**[6] n term

» About 3-5% of amputees experience fractures in stumps at some time. Knee disarticulation is a distal above-knee amputation[7] which leaves the patient without a functional knee. The patellar tendon-bearing [eɚ] prosthesis is used for 90% of lower extremity amputees[8].

Use upper extremity[9] / forearm / below-knee[10] / diabetic **amputees** • to undergo/require [aɪ] **amputation** • surgical[11] / flap or closed[12] **amputation** • flapless or open or guillotine[13] [ɪ] **amputation** • traumatic / emergency / auto**amputation** • minor / major [eɪdʒ]/ lower limb **amputation** • leg / digital[14] [ɪdʒ]/ ray[15] [eɪ]/ **amputation** • above knee[7] (abbr AK)/ below knee (abbr BK) **amputation** • through-the-knee[16] / high[17] / hindquarter[18] [aɪ] **amputation** • **amputation** site / level[19] / stump[2] • **amputation** rate / in contiguity [gjuː]/ in continuity • finger / hip / knee[16] / wrist [r] **disarticulation** • above-knee **stump** • **stump** sock[20] / hematoma • **stump** ischemia [kiː]/ pain[21] / cover[22] [ʌ] • bio/ endo/ mechanical [kæ]/ orthopedic [iː] **prosthesis** • silicone / immediate-fit[23] [iː] **prosthesis** • patellar tendon-bearing[24] [eɚ] (abbr PTB)/ adjustable [ədʒʌst-] **prosthesis** • above-knee / cosmetic[25] **prosthesis** • upper extremity[26] / total hip / myoelectric[27] [maɪoʊ-] **prosthesis** • **prosthetic** device [aɪs]/ fitting[28] / arthroplasty / knee • **prosthetic** joint infection / replacement[29]

disfigurement [dɪsfɪɡɚmənt] n

rel **deformity**[1] [ɔː], **malformation**[2] n

outward appearance [ɪɚ], e.g. of the face, that has been spoiled[3] or is misshapen[4]

disfiguring adj • **deformation** n • **deformed**[4] adj → U89-2,5

» If left untreated, yaws[5] [jɔːz] may lead to chronic disability and disfigurement. Shoes must be properly fitted and orthopedic deformities corrected. Life is simply much more difficult when one is disfigured or disabled. This congenital malformation consists of herniation [eɪʃ] of abdominal organs into the hemithorax [hemɪ-] resulting from a defect in the diaphragm [aɪ].

Use to cause/reduce/correct **disfigurement** • cosmetic / facial[6] [eɪʃ]/ local / permanent[7] [ɜː] **disfigurement** • congenital / postural[8] / anatomic **deformity** • (musculo)-skeletal[9] [ʌ] angular / bowing [oʊ]/ flexion [ekʃ] **deformity** • joint[10] [dʒ]/ spinal / barrel-chest[11] [tʃ]/ facial **deformity** • swan-neck [ɔː]/ buttonhole [ʌ] or boutonniere[12] [uː]/ valgus [æ] **deformity** • foot[13] / clubfoot [ʌ]/ hammer toe **deformity** • **disfiguring** defect / scar[14] [skɑːr]/ acne [ækni]/ surgery

---

Querschnitt(s)gelähmte(r), Paraplegiker(in); paraplegisch
Tetraplegiker(in); tetraplegisch[1] Paraplegie, tiefe Querschnittslähmung[2] Tetraplegie, -parese, hohe Querschnittslähmung[3] Rückenmarkkompression[4] Paraplegiker(in)[5] ab d. 10. Brustwirbel gelähmte(r) P.[6] schlaffe Paraplegie[7] spastische P.[8] bleibende/ persistierende Paraplegie[9]

5

Amputierte(r)
Exartikulation, Gliedmaßenabsetzung i. Gelenk[1] (Amputations)stumpf[2] Prothese[3] amputieren, abnehmen[4] prothetisch, Prothesen-[5] Prothesenbauer(in), Orthopädiemechaniker(in)[6] Oberschenkelamputation[7] Beinamputierte[8] Armamputierung[9] Unterschenkelamputierte[10] operative Abtrennung/ Abnahme[11] geschl. Amputation, A. m. Lappendeckung[12] offene A., A. ohne Stumpfdeckung[13] Finger-, Zehenamputation[14] A. e. Finger-/ Zehenstrahls[15] Knieexartikulation[16] hohe Amputation[17] Hemipelvektomie[18] Amputationshöhe[19] Stumpfstrumpf[20] Stumpf-, Phantomschmerz[21] Stumpfdeckung[22] Immediatprothese[23] PTB-Unterschenkelschaft[24] Schmuckprothese, kosmetische P.[25] Armprothese[26] myoelektr. P.[27] Prothesenanpassung[28] prothetischer Ersatz[29]

6

Entstellung, Verunstaltung
Deformität, Deformation, Verunstaltung, Missbildung[1] Miss-, Fehlbildung[2] verunstaltet[3] missgestaltet, deformiert[4] Frambösie, Yaws[5] Verunstaltung d. Gesichts[6] bleibende Verunstaltung[7] Haltungsschaden[8] Skelettverformung, -deformierung[9] Gelenkdeformierung, -deformität[10] Fassthorax[11] Knopflochdeformität[12] Fußdeformität[13] entstellende Narbe[14]

7

Physical Therapy & Rehabilitation   CLINICAL TERMS **619**

hypermobility [haɪpɚmoʊbɪləti] n term
rel **hyperextension**[1] [-ɪkstenʃən] n term,
instability[2] n → U31-15

abnormal excessive range of motion in a joint, e.g. due to looseness[3] [uː] of the capsular ligaments

(**hypo/ im**)**mobility** n term • **hypermobile** [oʊ] adj • **hyperextend** v • **hyperextensible** adj term • **hyperextensibility**[4] n • **hyperflexion**[5] [ekʃ] n

» Joint laxity[3] and hypermobility is seen in mild to unreducible[6] [(j)uːs] dislocations of the hip. Complete ulnar [ʌ] paralysis leads to wasting[7] [eɪ] of small hand muscles and hyperextension of the fingers at the MP joints[8]. The extensor pollicis longus acts on the IP joint with much force and can even hyperextend it. Swan-neck deformity[9], a frequent complication of mallet finger[10], typically occurs [ɜː] in children with congenitally [dʒe] hypermobile joints.

se joint or articular[11] **hypermobility** • to assess/improve/maintain/restore **mobility** • functional[12] [ʌ]/ normal / sideways[13] **mobility** • spine [aɪ]/ skin / impaired physical **mobility** • limited joint[14] / thumb [θʌm]/ restricted / increased **mobility** • sudden / passive / forceful **hyperextension** • compensatory[15] / neck or cervical[16] [sɜː]/ PIP[17] **hyperextension** • **hyperextension** exercises / of the knee[18] • **hyperextension** injury / deformity[19] • **hyperextensibility of** joints / ligaments [ɪ]

goniometer [ɡoʊnɪɒmətɚ] n term
rel **grades** [eɪ] **of movement**[1] n term

instrument for measuring [eʒ] angles[2] [æŋɡlz] in a joint, esp. the range [reɪndʒ] of motion to determine [ɜː] the functional status of patients with musculoskeletal or neurologic disabilities
goniometry[3] n term → U31-18

» Serial [ɪə] evaluations of joint motion may be made using a goniometer to quantify the arc [ɑːrk] of movement[4]. The therapist investigates various combinations of parallel or perpendicular glides [aɪ] to find the correct treatment plane [eɪ] and grade of movement.

se finger[5] **goniometer** • clinical / dual axis[6] / elbow / hip **goniometry** • joint mobilization **grades of movement** • **goniometric** exam / measurement[3] / (joint) angles

biomechanics [baɪoʊmɪkæniks] n term
rel **kinesiology**[1] [kəniːzɪɒlədʒi], **biophysics**[2] [ɪ] n term

application of mechanical laws to living structures, esp. to the motor system of the human body
biomechanical adj term • kinetics[3] n • **biophysical** adj • **kine(s)-** comb

» Read this study on the biomechanics of the human [juː] anterior cruciate [kruːʃieɪt] ligament[4]. The most common biomechanical factor that causes foot, leg, and hip injuries is excessive pronation [eɪʃ] while running.

se functional / shoulder / orthopedic [iː]/ footwear[5] [-weɚ] • **biomechanics** • medical / applied[6] [aɪ]/ chiropractic [kaɪrə-]/ molecular[7] **biophysics** • **biophysics** of impact injury[8] • **biomechanical** stresses[9] / forces[10] / function • **biomechanical** analysis / disorders[11] / footwear • **biophysical** profile [aɪ]/ research laboratory[12] • kinematic motion study[13] /tic energy /sthesia[14] [-θiːʒ(ɪ)ə] /sthetic [e] awareness[14] [eɚ]

straight leg raising (test) n term, abbr **SLR**   syn **Lasegue's test** n rare
rel **upper limb** [lɪm] **tension** [tenˈʃən] **test**[1] n term, abbr **ULTT**

non-specific musculoskeletal examination to check for lumbar [ʌ] root or sciatic [saɪætɪk] nerve irritation[2]

» SLR on the left at 40° reproduces the pain in the patient's left foot, though the Valsalva maneuver[3] [uː] does not. The upper limb tension test produces strain [eɪ] on the brachial [k] plexus by a combination of shoulder girdle [ɜː] depression, shoulder abduction, external rotation of the shoulder, elbow extension, forearm supination, and wrist/finger extension.

se **straight leg raising** sign[4] / maneuver • passive[5] / active / positive[6] / ipsilateral / crossed / seated[7] [iː] **SLR** • abnormal / radial [eɪ] nerve / ulnar [ʌ] nerve **ULTT**

Hypermobilität, übermäßige Beweglichkeit (e. Gelenks)
Überstreckung, Hyperextension[1] Instabilität[2] Lockerung, Schlaffheit[3] Überstreckbarkeit[4] übermäßige Beugung, Hyperflexion[5] nicht reponierbar, irreponibel, irreduktibel[6] Schwund, Atrophie[7] Fingergrundgelenke[8] Schwanenhalsdeformität[9] Hammerfinger[10] Hypermobilität d. Gelenke[11] funktionelle Beweglichkeit[12] Seitwärtsbeweglichkeit[13] eingeschränkte Gelenkbeweglichkeit[14] kompensator. Überstreckung[15] Hyperextension d. Nackens[16] H. d. PIP-Gelenks[17] Genu recurvatum, Überstreckbarkeit d. Kniegelenks[18] Hyperextensionsfehlstellung, -deformität[19]

8

Goniometer, Winkelmesser
Bewegungsgrade[1] Winkelmessung[2] Goniometrie[3] Bewegungsradius, -ausschlag[4] Fingergoniometer[5] Zweikanal-Goniometrie (in 2 Ebenen)[6]

9

Biomechanik
Kinesiologie, Bewegungslehre[1] Biophysik[2] Kinetik[3] vorderes Kreuzband, Lig. cruciatum anterius[4] Biomechanik d. Schuhe[5] angewandte Biophysik[6] molekulare B.[7] Biophysik d. Stoßverletzung[8] biomechanische Belastungen[9] biomechan. Kräfte[10] biomechan. Störungen[11] biophysikal. Forschungslabor[12] kinemat. Untersuchung, Bewegungsanalyse[13] Kinesthäsie, Bewegungsempfindung[14]

10

Lasègue Test
upper-limb-tension-Test, ULLT[1] Irritation d. Ischiasnervs[2] Valsalva-Manöver[3] Nervus-Ischiadicus-Dehnungszeichen, Lasegue-Zeichen[4] passives Anheben d. gestreckten Beins[5] positiver Lasegue-Test[6] Lasegue-Test i. Sitzen[7]

11

620 CLINICAL TERMS   Physical Therapy & Rehabilitation

physical manipulation *n term*   *rel* **manual therapy**[1] *n term,* **correction**[2] *n*

skillful manual treatment, esp. the forceful passive movement of a joint beyond its active range of motion

manipulative *adj term* • **corrective** *adj* • **manipulate** *v clin* • **correct** *v clin*

» Physical manipulation of the patient should be minimized. Manipulation is a technique involving small amplitude, high velocity [ɒːs] thrust[3] [ʌ] at the end of range, with sufficient [ɪʃ] speed that the patient is unable to prevent the movement. Each joint should be passively manipulated through its full range of motion[4]. Orthopedic manual therapy[5] is a hands-on technique [tekniːk] that helps you regain flexibility and movement.

Use joint / neck / cervical spine[6] **manipulation** • direct / closed[7] / bimanual **manipulation** • gentle / forceful / painful **manipulation** • osteopathic[8] / chiropractic[5] / surgical **manipulation** • **manipulation** of fracture fragments • **manual therapy** techniques[9] • orthopedic [iː]/ orthopractic / spinal [aɪ] **manual therapy** • cutaneous [eɪ] reflex [iː]/ osteopathic[10] / progressive / early **manual therapy** • **manual** movements[11] / activity / skills • **manual** palpation / muscle testing[12] • **manual** exploration / positioning / traction[13] [trækʃən]/ reduction[14] [ʌ] • postural[15] / functional / therapeutic [juː] **correction** • surgical[16] [ɜː]/ full / definitive **correction** • **manipulative** (physio)therapy[17] / maneuvers[9] / reduction[14] • **corrective** measures / splint[18] / aids / shoes[19] / **corrective** treatment / surgery[16] / osteotomy[20]

passive mobilization *n term* → U141-5

        rel **ambulation**[1] *n term* → U64-1; U19-12

gentle movement in one or more joints performed by a therapist to restore motion or relieve [iː] pain

mobilize[2] *v* • **(im)mobility**[3] *n* • **ambulate** *v term* • **ambulatory**[4] *adj*

» Passive mobilization of joints should be done early, because joint mobility cannot be maintained [eɪ] by active motion. Buddy-taping[5] [ʌ] permits protected active mobilization of the injured joint. Controlled passive mobilization is initiated [ɪʃ] twice daily with the splint[6] on.

Use early[7] / immediate / intermittent **passive mobilization** • controlled / protected[8] **passive mobilization** • active / gradual[9] [ædʒ]/ joint / spine[10] **mobilization** • **mobilization** therapy[11] / on crutches[12] [ʌ]/ in a wheelchair • to advise/facilitate/ resume **ambulation** • crutch[12] / non-weight-bearing[13] / indoor / monitored **ambulation**

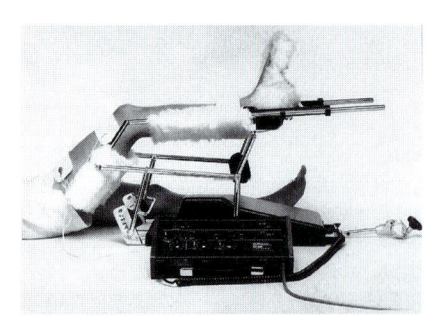

CPM-machine for the knee and hip joints

continuous passive motion [mouʃən] *n term, abbr* **CPM**   *rel* **endfeel**[1] [iː] *n jar*

technique of passive mobilization to assist in the recovery of cartilage; e.g. following knee reconstruction

» CPM enhances [æ] fluid dynamics, reduces end range deficit[2], controls edema [iː], and encourages [ɜː] positive collagen formation within the joint. The CPM will be started when your surgeon feels it would be safe. Stop the passive movement only when you obtain [eɪ] an obvious endfeel. Bilateral comparison of the degree of laxity[3] and endfeel are performed to estimate integrity of the ligaments.

Use knee / hand / shoulder / elbow / ankle / delayed [eɪ] postsurgical[4] [ɜː] **CPM** • **CPM** machine [-ʃiːn] or device[5] [-aɪs] • to quantify[6] [ɒː] **endfeel** • physiological / normal / right / left **endfeel** • hard[7] / soft[8] / bony[9] / capsular[9] **endfeel**

Manipulationsbehandlung
manuelle Therapie[1] Korrektur[2] kurzer kräftiger Ruck[3] Bewegungsausmaß[4] Manual-, Chirotherapie[5] Manipulation d. Halswirbelsäule[6] geschlossene Manipulation[7] osteopath. Behandlung[8] Grifftechniken[9] osteopathische Manualtherapie[10] Handbewegungen[11] manuelle Muskelfunktionsprüfung[12] manuelle Extension[13] manuelle Reposition[14] Haltungskorrektur, Korrektur v. Haltungsfehlern[15] operative Korrektur[16] manipulative Physiotherapie[17] Korrekturschiene[18] orthopäd. Schuhe[19] Korrekturosteotomie[20]

12

passive Mobilisation
(Umher)gehen[1] mobilisieren, (wieder) bewegl. machen[2] Beweglichkeit, Mobilität[3] gehfähig[4] Tapen mit d. benachb. Finger/ Zehen[5] Schiene[6] frühzeitige passive M.[7] vorsichtige passive M.[8] schrittweise M.[9] Wirbelsäulenmobilisation[10] Mobilisationstherapie[11] Gehen an Krücken[12] G. ohne zu belasten, belastungsfreies Gehen[13]

13

CPM-Therapie, kontinuierliche passive Mobilisierung
Endgefühl(-Test)[1] Bewegungseinschränkung[2] Schlaffheitsgrad[3] späte postoperative CPM-Therapie[4] CPM-, Bewegungsschiene[5] d. Endgefühl erheben/ ermitteln[6] hartes E., Knochenstopp[7] weiches E., Weichteilstopp[8] kapsuläres E., Kapselmuster[9]

14

Physical Therapy & Rehabilitation

CLINICAL TERMS

massage [məsɑːʒ] n & v   rel **acupressure**[1], **lymphodrainage**[2] [-ɪdʒ] n term

systematic rubbing[3] [ʌ] (frolement[4]), stroking[5] [oʊ] (effleurage[6]), vibration, tapping[7] (flagellation[8]) and percussion [ʌ] (tapotement[9]), kneading[10] [niːdɪŋ], squeezing[11] [iː] and/or compression (petrissage[12]) of the body for therapeutic purposes [ɜː], esp. to decrease pain, improve muscle tone and circulation, and/or produce relaxation

massaged adj • **masseur**[13], **masseuse**[13] [-uːz] n • **-massage** comb → U1-18

» Do not rub or massage injured tissues or apply ice or heat. Massage and passive movement of weakened [iː] spastic limbs make patients more comfortable. Swedish massage is characterized by delicate manipulation of the muscles with special oils to promote stress relief. Shiatsu is an *acupressure massage*[14] technique developed in Japan.

Jse friction[4] / fingertip[8] / scalp[15] **massage** • percussive [ʌ] hand[9] / vibratory[16] [aɪ]/ douche [duːʃ] **massage** • hydro jet[17] [aɪ]/ underwater jet[18] [dʒet]/ dry **massage** • deep tissue [ʃǁs] or sports[19] / deep muscle [s] **massage** • back / foot / reflexology[20] / therapeutic[21] **massage** • Swedish[22] [iː]/ Shiatsu [ɑː]/ pediatric / self-**massage** • **massage** therapy / table[23] / oil / lotion [oʊʃ] • gentle / forceful / upward / ocular[24] **massage** • hydro**massage**[25] • electro**massage**[26]

Massage; massieren
Akupressur[1] manuelle Lymphdrainage[2] Reiben[3] Reibmassage, Friktion[4] Streichen[5] Streichmassage[6] Klopfen[7] Klopfmassage mit d. Fingerspitzen[8] Klopfung, Klopfmassage[9] Kneten[10] Kneifen[11] Knetmassage[12] Masseur(in), Masseuse[13] Druckpunktmassage, Akupressur[14] Kopfhautmassage[15] Vibration(smassage)[16] Wasserstrahlmassage[17] Unterwasser-Druckstrahlmassage[18] Sportmassage[19] Reflexzonenmassage[20] Heilmassage[21] schwedische/ klassische M.[22] Massagetisch[23] Augenmassage[24] Hydromassage[25] Elektromassage[26]   15

---

treadmill [e] n   rel **ergometer**[1], **dynamometer**[2], **ergonomics**[3] [ɜːrg-] n term

exercise machine consisting of an endless belt on which a person can walk or jog without moving forward

ergometry[4] n term • **ergometric** adj • **dynam(o)-** [daɪn-] comb • **erg(o)-** comb

» Exercise testing can be done on a motorized treadmill or with a bicycle [aɪ] ergometer. Take the BP[5] after a standard walking exercise on a treadmill to estimate the degree of disability. Measure the maximal O₂ consumption [ʌ] achieved during escalating treadmill exercise.

Jse to exercise on a[6] / conditioning via[7] **treadmill** • step[8]-/ calibrated / motorized conventional **treadmill** • **treadmill** testing[9] / exercise[7] / exercise test[9] • **treadmill** speed[10] / elevation[11] • bicycle[12] / upper-body / rowing[13] [oʊ]/ arm / leg **ergometer** • **ergometer** cycling [saɪklɪŋ] • **ergometric** bike[12] / ECG[14] • **ergo**therapy

Laufband(-Ergometer)
Ergometer[1] Kraftmesser, Dynamometer[2] Ergonomie, Ergonomik[3] Ergometrie[4] Blutdruck[5] auf e. Laufband trainieren[6] Laufbandtraining[7] Stepper[8] Laufband-Ergometrie[9] Bandgeschwindigkeit[10] Steigungswinkel d. Laufbands[11] Fahrradergometer[12] Ruderergometer[13] Belastungselektrokardiografie, Belastungs-EKG[14]   16

---

isometric exercise [aɪsəmetrɪk] n term   rel **isotonic exercise**[1] n term → U1-15

contraction of muscles without shortening of the fibers, e.g. by pressing the knees against each other

isometrics[2] n term • **isokinetic** adj • **dystonia**[3] [dɪstoʊnɪə] n • **dystonic** adj

» As long as acute symptoms [ɪ] persist, isometric quadriceps [ɒː] exercises should be performed frequently throughout the day. The fourth heart [ɑː] sound is accentuated[4] by mild isotonic or isometric exercise in the supine [aɪ] position. Don't be worried about building bulky [ʌ] muscles by doing isometrics with weights [weɪts].

Jse **isometric** muscle contraction / training[2] / strain[5] [eɪ]/ strengthening exercises[6] • **isotonic** exercise[7] / testing / muscle strength[8] • **isokinetic** elbow flexion [ekʃ]/ maximum voluntary contraction[9] / exercises • **isokinetic** wrist [r] dynamometer[10] / exercise (machine) / swim bench[11] [tʃ] • **dystonic** muscle / movement / posturing[12] • therapeutic[13] / graded [eɪ] **exercise** • active (assisted/ bending/ resistive) **exercises** • passive / (progressive) resistance[14] **exercises** • strengthening / relaxation / postural[15] **exercises** • corrective / (range of) motion[16] **exercises** • (full) weight-bearing [eɚ]/ underwater[17] / whirlpool [ɜː]/ home[18] **exercise** • **exercise** tolerance test[19] (abbr ETT)/ ECG[20] / program

isometrische Übung
isotonische Übung[1] isometr. Training[2] Dystonie[3] betont[4] isometr. Belastung[5] isometr. Kräftigungsübungen[6] isotonisches Training[7] isotonische (Muskel)kraft[8] maximale willkürliche isokinetische Muskelanspannung[9] isokinetischer Handdynamometer[10] isokinetische Schwimmbank[11] dystone Haltung[12] Heilgymnastik[13] Widerstandsübungen[14] Haltungsübungen[15] Beweglichkeitsübungen[16] Unterwassergymnastik[17] Heimtraining[18] Belastungstest[19] Belastungs-EKG[20]   17

---

back school [bæk skuːl] n term   rel **therapeutic** [juː] **training**[1], **re-education**[2] n

training program intended to improve or rehabilitate the spine, posture[3], and the dorsal musculature [ʌ]

retraining[2] [eɪ] n • **educate** v • **education**[4] n • **educational** adj

» Back school (2 sessions of 90 min each, followed by 3-4 follow-up sessions) included safe lifting and handling, posture [pɒːstʃɚ], stretching and strengthening exercises, and pain management[5]. Environmental readjustments [ʌ] and re-education, including urgings [ɜː] that the patient resume [uː] or continue a fully active life, may help.

Jse to attend[6] / industrial [ʌ]/ low / online **back school** • **back school** program[7] • muscle / physical [ɪ]/ postural[8] **training** • gait[9] [eɪ]/ weight[10] / supervised [uː] **training** • neuromuscular [ʌ] feedback / relaxation[11] / resistance **training** • autogenic[12] [dʒe]/ occupational[13] [eɪʃ] **training** • **training** session[14] / program • to **educate** sb. about sth.[15] • patient[16] / family / health[17] / sex[18] **education** • nutrition [ɪʃ]/ vocational[19] [eɪʃ]/ special[20] [eʃ] **education** • **education** program

Rückenschule, -training
(rehabilitative) Bewegungstherapie, Heilgymnastik[1] Umschulung[2] Haltung[3] Erziehung, (Aus)bildung[4] Schmerztherapie[5] e. Rückenschule machen[6] Rückentrainingsprogramm[7] Haltungsgymnastik[8] Gangschulung[9] Gewichtstraining[10] Entspannungstraining[11] autogenes T.[12] Ergotherapie[13] Therapiesitzung, Trainingseinheit[14] jem. über etw. aufklären[15] Patientenaufklärung[16] Gesundheitserziehung[17] Sexualerziehung[18] Berufsausbildung[19] Sonderschule[20]   18

wobble board [wɒːbl bɔːrd] *n* *sim* **b**a**lance board**[1] *n*
                                     rel **prone cart**[2] [proʊn kɑːrt],
                                     be**an** [iː] **bag**[3] *n*

apparatus [eɪ] used for the re-education of proprioception[4] [se] and balance

» Like many therapists, he'd been using a wobble board – a platform built on a half-sphere [sfɪɚ] or rockers[5] – for many years.

Use prone[6] / transfer[7] **board** • **wobble board** exercise[8] • manual / motorized[9] [oʊ] **prone cart** • **bean bag** chair[10] / furniture [ɜː]/ refill • textured / giant [aɪ] **bean bag**

hydrotherapy [haɪdroʊ-] *n term* *syn* **aquatic** [əkwætɪk] **therapy** *n*
                                      rel **balneotherapy**[1] *n term*,
                                      bath[2], **soak**[3] [soʊk] *n clin* → U1-17

therapeutic application of water, e.g. tub [ʌ] baths, wet packs, shower sprays[4], or moist heat **bathe**[5] [eɪ] *v* → U19-10 • **hydrotherapeutic** *adj term* • **hydro-, balneo-** *comb*

» Hydrotherapy is a very useful form of physical therapy once the wounds [uː] are in the process of being closed. Balneotherapy is a treatment using water added with specific sea-weeds[6] [iː] or herbal [ɜː] ingredients [iː]. Often practiced in conjunction [ʌ] with balneotherapy, fangotherapy is used in the treatment of rheumatism [uː] and arthritis [aɪ].

Use **hydrotherapy** tank suit [suːt] • **hydrotherapeutic** or underwater exercises[7] • to take *or* have a[8] **bath** • complete[9] / partial[10] / warm / tepid[11] / cool **bath** • tub[12] / bed[13] / bubble[14] [ʌ]/ whirlpool [ɜː] **bath** • medicated[15] / mineral / vapor[16] [eɪ] **bath** • sitz[17]/ sponge[18] [spʌndʒ]/ hydroelectric[19] **bath** • **bath** towel [aʊ]/ oil / salt / preparations[20] • after**bath** massage • **hydro**pneumatic [n(j)uː] massage

ice application [aɪs æplɪkeɪʃᵊn] *n clin*
                  syn **local cryotherapy** [kraɪoʊ-] *n term*, *rel* **ice bag**[1] *n*

use of ice to achieve cooling of deeper tissues, vasoconstriction and reduction of localized bleeding

» R.I.C.E. (short for rest, ice, compression and elevation[2]) is the standard approach to acute injury management, to prevent inflammatory processes to go uncontrolled[3] and to speed up the recovery process[4] by eliminating swelling. Applying [aɪ] ice locally reduces swelling.

Use to apply[5] **ice** • chipped[6] [tʃ]/ crushed [ʌ]/ dry[7] / wet **ice** • **ice** cube[8] / crystals [ɪ]/ (water) bath[9] /-water sponge bath[10] • **ice**-water lavage[11] / compress / pack[12] / collar

heat [iː] **application** *n clin* *syn* **thermotherapy** [θɜːrmoʊθerəpi] *n term*
                                       rel **compress**[1], **pack**[2] [pæk] *n*

treatment of disease by the application of heat (diathermy [aɪ], warm baths or herbal wraps[3] [r])

» Treatment consists of local heat application, avoiding overuse, medicines to reduce pain and swelling and physiotherapy in the form of ultrasonic rays. Infrared thermotherapy[4] is used for the reduction [ʌ] of pain as well as for relaxation.

Use water-induced [(j)uːs] (*abbr* WIT)/ microwave[5] [aɪ]/ ultrasound [ʌ] **thermotherapy** • laser-induced / transpupillary (*abbr* TTT) **thermotherapy** • local / general / moist[6] / depth of[7] **heat application** • to apply a / (moist) hot[8] / warm / cool / saline [eɪ] **compress** • hot *or* heat / warm moist / fango (mud)[9] [ʌ]/ abdominal[10] **pack** • **heat** lamp[11] • dry[12] / infrared **heat** • infrared[4] **therapy**

(Therapie)kreisel
Wippe, Schaukelbrett[1] Rollwagen[2] Sitz-, Bohnensack, Therapiesitz[3] Propriozeption, Tiefensensibilität[4] Kufen[5] Bauchliegebrett[6] Rutschbrett[7] Schaukelbrettübung[8] motorbetriebener Rollwagen[9] Therapie-Sitzsack[10]

19

Wasserbehandlung, Hydrotherapie
Balneotherapie, Bäderbehandlung[1] Bad[2] Einweichen, Baden[3] Güsse[4] baden, waschen[5] Meeresalgen[6] (Unter)wassergymnastik[7] baden, e. Bad nehmen[8] Vollbad[9] Teilbad[10] lauwarmes B.[11] Wannenbad[12] (Ganz)waschung im Bett[13] Schaumbad[14] medizin. Bad[15] Dampfbad[16] Sitzbad[17] Waschung[18] Stangerbad, hydroelektrisches Vollbad[19] Badezusätze[20]

20

Eisbehandlung, lokale Kälteanwendung/ Kryotherapie
Eisbeutel[1] Hochlagern[2] außer Kontrolle geraten[3] d. Genesungsprozess beschleunigen[4] Eis auflegen[5] Eischips[6] Trockeneis[7] Eiswürfel[8] Eistauchbad[9] Eisabreibung[10] Eiswasserspülung[11] Eispackung[12]

21

Wärmebehandlung, Thermotherapie
Kompresse[1] Packung[2] Kräuterwickel[3] Infrarot-Wärmebehandlung[4] Mikrowellentherapie[5] Behandlung m. feuchter Wärme[6] Tiefenwirkung d. Wärmebehandlung[7] feuchtwarme Kompresse[8] Fangopackung[9] Bauchwickel[10] Wärmelampe[11] trockene Wärme[12]

22

Physical Therapy & Rehabilitation   CLINICAL TERMS 623

electrotherapy n term   rel **electrostimulation therapy**[1] n
                        ultrasonic diathermy[2] [daɪəθɜːrmi] n term
modalities used in the treatment of musculoskeletal disorders, e.g. interferential therapy[3] or laser

electrotherapeutic adj term • **stimulator** n • **ultrasound** [ʌ] n • **electr(o)-** comb

» Electrotherapy is being used predominantly in acute orthopedic conditions and sports medicine[4]. Most electrotherapy devices [aɪs] are used in conjunction [dʒʌ] with other forms of physical therapy. Cranial [eɪ] electrotherapy stimulation[5] (abbr CES) is a very safe and effective non-pharmacological treatment for anxiety [aɪ], insomnia[6] and depression.

Jse cerebral / pediatric / microcurrent [ɜː] **electrotherapy** • high-frequency[2] / low-frequency[7] **electrotherapy** • **electrotherapy** unit / devices[8] • short-wave / microwave[9] [eɪ] **diathermy** • (repetitive) electrical / transcutaneous [eɪ] electrical nerve[10] [ɜː] (abbr TENS) **stimulation** • neuromuscular [n(j)ʊɚ-] (abbr NMS) **stimulation** • electrical / peripheral nerve[11] **stimulator** • **ultrasound** therapy[12] • **electrotherapeutic** sleep[13] / bath[14] • **electro**myography (abbr EMG) /diagnostics[15] • **electro**vibratory [aɪ] massage[16] /convulsive [ʌ] therapy[17]

magnetic field therapy n term, abbr **MFT**
            syn **electromagnetic therapy** n, rel **laser** [leɪzɚ] **therapy**[1] n term
application of an alternating magnetic field to generate [dʒe] an electric current [ɜː] inside the tissues which results in changes of blood flow

» Research suggests that magnetic field therapy provides improved blood flow by acting on iron [aɪɚn] in the hemoglobin [iː] of RBCs[2]. In the treatment of sprains[3] [eɪ], strains[4], and sore [ɔː] muscles[5], not only does MFT aid in recovery [ʌ] but allows these conditions to heal [iː] better and faster. MFT has been successful in a high percentage of pain cases.

Jse pulsed[6] [ʌ] **magnetic field therapy** • **MFT** generator • low-intensity[7] (abbr LILT) or low-level[7] (abbr LLLT) or cold[7] / power[8] / pulsed[9] **laser therapy**

biofeedback therapy n term   rel **relaxation techniques**[1] [iː] n → U1-11
use of instrumentation to bring covert[2] [koʊvɜːrt] physiologic processes to the conscious [ʃ] awareness [eɚ] of the patient, usually by visual [ɪʒ] or auditory [ɒː] signals

» Patients with tension headaches[3] may benefit from techniques inducing [s] relaxation, e.g. massage, hot baths, and biofeedback. Failure of the pelvic floor to relax during straining[4] (anismus[5] [eɪ]) may be treated with relaxation exercises and biofeedback training.

Jse sensory / EEG / brainwave[6] [eɪ] **biofeedback** • **biofeedback** techniques or methods[7] / training • (skeletal) muscle[8] / profound [aʊ] muscular [ʌ] **relaxation** • jaw [dʒɒː]/ pelvic floor[9] / sleep-related **relaxation** • **relaxation** exercises / (response) training[1]

occupational [ɒːkjʊpeɪʃənᵊl] **therapy** n term, abbr **OT**
            sim **ergotherapy**[1] [ɜːrɡoʊ-] n term rare, **vocational** [eɪʃ] **therapy**[2] n term
use of purposeful [ɜː] activity to help individuals limited by physical, developmental or learning disabilities, psychosocial dysfunction or handicaps to maintain [eɪ] or regain health, achieve independence, etc.

occupation[3] n • **nonoccupational** adj • **vocation**[4] n • **avocational** adj

» Occupational therapy and graded [eɪ] social involvement should be arranged [eɪ] for to improve morale[5] [æ], motor skills[6], and quality of life in stroke [oʊ] patients[7], while for those who are more disabled [eɪ], a comprehensive structured rehabilitation program including employment retraining[8] may be planned. COPD[9] rehabilitation requires 1-3 visits per week for 6-8 weeks and should emphasize supervised [aɪ] exercise, physical and occupational therapy, respiratory therapy[10], psychosocial [saɪkə-] intervention, and follow-up[11].

Jse physical [ɪ] and **occupational therapy** • **occupational therapy** unit / aide[12] [eɪ]/ assistant[12] / evaluation • **occupational** therapist[13] (abbr OT)/ performance task • **occupational** medicine[14] / history[15] / **occupational** accident[16] / disability[17] / asthma[18] [æzmə]/ (re)adjustment[8] [ʌ]/ hazards [æ] • **vocational** activities / rehabilitation • **vocational** (re)training[8] / counseling[19] [aʊ] • gainful[20] [eɪ]/ (non)manual / sedentary[21] **occupation** • **occupation**-associated [oʊʃ] injury[22]

Note: In English usage the term **ergotherapy** has been widely replaced by **occupational therapy** which is also used to refer to vocational therapy.

Elektrotherapie
Reizstrom, Impulsstromtherapie[1] Hochfrequenz-(Wärme)therapie[2] Interferenzstromtherapie[3] Sportmedizin[4] transkranielle Stimulation[5] Schlaflosigkeit[6] Niederfrequenztherapie[7] Elektrotherapiegeräte[8] Mikrowellen-Wärmetherapie[9] TENS-Behandlung, transkutane elektr. Nervenstimulation[10] transkutaner Nervenstimulator[11] Ultraschalltherapie[12] Elektroschlaftherapie, Elektroheilschlaf[13] Stangerbad, hydroelektr. Bad[14] Elektrodiagnostik[15] Vibrationsmassage[16] Elektrokonvulsionstherapie[17]

23

Magnetfeldtherapie
Lasertherapie[1] rote Blutkörperchen, Erythrozyten[2] Verstauchungen[3] Zerrungen[4] Muskelkater[5] gepulste Magnetfeldtherapie[6] medizinische Soft-Lasertherapie[7] Power-Lasertherapie[8] Mid-Laser-Therapie[9]

24

Biofeedbacktherapie
Entspannungstechniken[1] unbewusst[2] Spannungskopfschmerzen[3] Pressen[4] Anismus[5] Hirnstrom-Biofeedback[6] Biofeedbackverfahren, -methoden[7] Muskelentspannung, -relaxation[8] Beckenbodenentspannung[9]

25

Ergo-, Beschäftigungs-, Arbeitstherapie
Ergotherapie[1] berufsvorbereitende Ergotherapie, Arbeitstherapie[2] Tätigkeit, Beschäftigung, Beruf[3] Berufung, Beruf[4] e. (moral.) Auftrieb geben[5] motorische Fertigkeiten[6] Schlaganfallpatienten[7] Umschulung[8] chron. obstruktive Atemwegserkrankung, COPD, COLD[9] Atemtherapie[10] Nachsorge[11] Ergotherapieassistent(in)[12] Ergotherapeut(in)[13] Arbeitsmedizin[14] Berufsanamnese[15] Arbeitsunfall[16] Invalidität aufgrund e. Arbeitsunfalls[17] berufsbedingtes Asthma[18] Berufsberatung[19] Erwerbstätigkeit[20] sitzende Tätigkeit[21] berufsbedingte Verletzung[22]

26

CLINICAL TERMS — Physical Therapy & Rehabilitation

activities of daily living *n term, abbr* ADL

self-care tasks such as grooming[1] [uː], bathing [eɪ], dressing, feeding, toilet and oral hygiene[2] [haɪdʒiːn], functional [ʌ] mobility and ambulation [eɪʃ], communication and social interaction as well as performing desired [aɪ] sexual activities

» *The patient is able to perform activities of daily living* **with supervision**[3] [ɪʒ]. *Medical therapy did not relieve pain sufficiently* [ɪʃ] *to allow for activities of daily living.*

Use to carry out *or* perform/cope [oʊ] with[4]/be independent in **activities of daily living** • to accomplish/require assistance with[5] **activities of daily living** • normal / simple aids to[6] **daily living** • **daily living** skills[7] / activities • **activity** intolerance[8] • basic[9] / major [eɪdʒ]/ limited **ADLs** • instrumental[10] (*abbr* IADLs)/ motor **ADLs** • to interfere [ɪɚ] with[11] / to participate fully in **daily activities** • to withdraw [ɒː] from / routine *or* regular **daily activities** • day-to-day / life / self-care / physical • social / occupational[12] **activities** • learning[13] / classroom[13] / peer[14] [pɪɚ] **activities** • recreational[15] [eɪʃ]/ outdoor[16] / aquatic [æ‖ɒː] **activities** • high-risk / compensatory **activities**

sheltered workshop [ʃɛltəd wɜːrkʃɒːp] *n* → U11-13
rel **independent living center**[1] *n, abbr* **ILC** → U14-3f

facility [sɪ] offering physically or developmentally disabled individuals a chance of adequate employment, a place to socialize [oʊʃ] and build up their self-esteem[2] [iː]

shelter[3] *v & n* • **work**[4] *n* • **independence**[5] *n* • **depend** *v* • **dependent** *adj*

» *Many people with Down's syndrome* [ɪ] *do well in sheltered workshops and group homes, but few achieve* [tʃ] *full independence in adulthood* [ʌ]. *About one-sixth of autistic* [ɒː] *children become gainfully* [eɪ] *employed as adults, and another one-sixth are able to function in sheltered workshops and* halfway [hæfweɪ] *houses*[6].

Use to need a **sheltered workshop** • **sheltered** living arrangement[7] [dʒ] • part-time[8] / sheltered / night **work** • **work** day / schedule [sk‖ʃɛdjʊl]/ habits / site[9] / environment • **work** performance[10] / capacity[11] [æs]/ absence /-related injury • **work**aholics[12] / hardening[13] • **work** load[14] [oʊ]/ tolerance[15] / permit[16] [ɜː] • to strive [aɪ] for/achieve[17] [tʃ] /lose one's/regain [eɪ] *or* recover[18] [ʌ] **independence** • **independent** living skills[19] / work • patient / loss of / economic[20] **independence**

home health aide [hɛlθ eɪd] *n*   *rel* **help**[1], **assistance**[1] *n* → U8-1
support[2] [səpɒːrt], **supervision**[3] [ɪʒ] *n*

professional trained in providing unskilled home health care under the direction of a registered nurse[4]

help *v* • **helper**[5] *n* • **self-help**[6] *n* • **helpful**[7] *adj* • **helplessness**[8] *n* • **aid**[9] *n*

» *She should have a home health aide to assist with personal hygiene* [aɪ]. *The patient requires close supervision so have an aide or relative accompany the patient at all times. Complete social independence is not a realistic goal* [oʊl] *for many chronically handicapped who will require varying degrees of lifelong supervision and assistance.*

Use nurse's[10] [ɜː] **aide** • social / walking[11] / hearing [ɪɚ] **aid** • homemaking[12] / home maintenance [eɪ] **assistance** • self-care / visiting nurse[13] **assistance** • to try to/ offer/provide[14]/need/seek [iː] *or* ask for **help** • domestic[15] **help** (*BE*) • **to help** sb. sit up[16] / out / sb. to his feet / in diagnosis • **help**line[17] (*BE*) • **self-help** *or* mutual [mjuːtʃʊəl] aid group[18] / community • **self-help** organization / needs / device [aɪs]

Aktivitäten d. tägl. Lebens (ATL)
Körperpflege[1] Mundhygiene[2] unter Aufsicht[3] d. ATL bewältigen[4] Hilfe bei d. ATL brauchen[5] ATL-Hilfsmittel[6] Fähigkeiten z. Alltagsbewältigung[7] Belastungsintoleranz[8] Basisaktivitäten d. tägl. Lebens[9] instrumentelle ATL[10] d. alltagsprakt. Kompetenz einschränken[11] berufl. Aktivitäten[12] schulische A.[13] Gemeinschafts-, Gruppenaktivitäten[14] Freizeitaktivitäten[15] Tätigkeiten i. Freien[16]

27

geschützte Werkstätte, Behindertenwerkstatt
Zentrum f. selbstbestimmtes Leben Behinderter[1] Selbstwertgefühl[2] schützen, bewahren; Schutz, Obdach[3] Beschäftigung, Arbeit, Tätigkeit[4] Unabhängigkeit, Selbstständigkeit[5] Rehabilitationseinrichtungen[6] betreute Wohngemeinschaft[7] Teilzeitarbeit[8] Arbeitsplatz[9] Arbeitsleistung[10] Arbeitsfähigkeit[11] Arbeitssüchtige[12] Arbeitsbelastungstraining[13] Arbeitsbelastung[14] berufl. Belastbarkeit, Arbeitstoleranz[15] Arbeitserlaubnis[16] Unabhängigkeit erlangen[17] Unabhängigkeit wiedererlangen[18] Fähigkeit z. Selbstversorgung[19] witschaftl. Unabhängigkeit[20]

28

Hauspflegehelfer(in)
Hilfe, Beistand[1] Unterstützung[2] Aufsicht, Überwachung[3] Diplomkrankenschwester/-pfleger[4] Helfer(in), Gehilfe/-in[5] Selbsthilfe[6] hilfsbereit, hilfreich[7] Hilflosigkeit[8] Hilfe, Hilfsmittel[9] Schwesternhelfer(in)[10] Gehhilfe[11] Haushaltshilfe[12] Betreuung durch e. Hauskrankenpfleger(in)[13] Hilfe leisten, helfen[14] Haushaltshilfe[15] beim Aufsetzen helfen[16] telefon. Beratung, Telefonberatung[17] Selbsthilfegruppe[18]

29

Index – English

Mit Hilfe des englischen Index können Sie **KWiC Web** auch zum Nachschlagen englischer Fachausdrücke verwenden. Hier finden Sie die medizinischen Schlüsselwörter und deren semantisch oder morphologisch verwandte Wörter (Wortfamilie, Synonyme, Oberbegriffe, etc.) in alphabetischer Reihenfolge (ca. 13 000). Nominalverbindungen und feststehende Wortverbindungen sind unter dem ersten Wort zu finden (z. B. *shoulder blade*, *vital capacity*, *body surface area*, *informed consent*), während Adjektiv-Komposita und Kollokationen (lose Wortverbindungen) jeweils unter dem Hauptwort gelistet sind (z. B. *bowel, large*; *traction, manual*; *lumen, vascular*; *leakage, CSF*). Bei Grenzfällen und wichtigen Termini sind jeweils beide Wörter angeführt (z. B. *range of motion*; *motion, range of* und *muscle tone*; *tone, muscle*). Bei Wörtern mit Mehrfachbedeutung wurde zur Verdeutlichung ein typisches Bezugswort in runder Klammer hinzugefügt, z. B. *formulate* (*drug*), *deliver* (*baby*), *gown* (*OR*). Bei Alternativformen werden bis auf wenige Ausnahmen, wie z. B. *neuron*(*e*); *gonadotrop*(*h*)*in*; *pedicle flap/graft* beide Formen gesondert oder die gebräuchlichere angeführt. Die britische Schreibweise wurde im Index nicht berücksichtigt.

Verwiesen wird jeweils auf die Module (Units) und Einträge (siehe Nummer rechts unten in jedem Eintrag), in denen die Fachwörter vorkommen (z. B. U32-4 verweist auf Eintrag Nr. 4 in Unit 32). Zu den Units finden Sie am schnellsten über das Griffregister.

Da die Wörter in den Modulen selbst im Sinnzusammenhang bzw. in Wortfeldern dargestellt sind, bieten diese Schlüsselwörter einen direkten Zugang zu den Termini des betreffenden Bedeutungsfeldes samt ihrem Kontext (insgesamt weit über 100 000 Begriffe, Phrasen, und Kollokationen).

A

abandonment of care U20-13
abate U4-14
abatement U4-14; U105-18
abdomen U22-4; U45-6
–, acute/surgical U124-16
abdominal U22-4; U45-6
– bloating/distention U109-8
– thrusts U8-11
abduct U31-6
abduction U31-6
abductor U31-6
Aberdeen knot U138-11
aberrant U84-20
– perception U77-20
aberrration, chromosomal U84-20
abfraction U27-21
ability U142-3
ablactation U71-28
ablation U127-13
able-bodied U1-11
abnormal U116-21
– detected, nothing U107-20
abnormality U116-21; U89-5
– detected, no U107-20
aboral /-ad U46-7
abrade U5-8
abrasion U5-8; U27-19
abrasive U27-19
– scrub U1-20

abscess U114-16
–, lung U111-14
–, peritonsillar U95-13
–, stitch U38-12
absent-minded(ness) U74-15
absorb U46-13; U78-5
absorbable U137-8
absorbent U88-8
absorption U46-13; U78-5; U88-8
–, rate of U121-10
absorptive U46-13; U88-8
abstain (from) U10-7
abstinence U10-7
– symptoms U11-12
–, sexual U68-11
abstinent U10-7
abundant U30-9
abuse U11-3; U68-16
–, volatile substance U11-23
abused U11-6; U77-11
abuser, substance U11-6
abusive U73-7; U77-7
acceleration, angular U60-9
acceptable daily intake U91-18
access U128-1
–, (intra)venous U136-5
–, surgical U126-6
accessibility U136-5
accessible U128-1
accident U6-1
– prevention U6-22

accidental U6-1
– electric shock U6-14
accident-prone U6-1
acclimatization U88-17
accommodation U88-17
–, ocular U59-12
accommodative U59-12
accouchement U71-4
accumulate U78-20; U88-15
accumulation U78-20; U88-15; U91-19
accumulative U88-15
ACE inhibitor U33-9
acellular U83-2
acetabulum U28-21
acetazolamide U82-17
acetoacetic acid U82-12
acetone U82-12
acetonitrile U91-9
acetonuria U82-12
acetylate U78-7
acetylcholine U42-11
ache U104-4
aches and pains U104-5
achievement U73-5
aching U104-4f
achromatic U59-9
acid U81-19
– (LSD) U11-22
– phosphatase U47-15
acid-base disturbance U116-11
acidic U81-19

acidity U81-19
acidosis U81-19
acid-stable U81-19
acinar U47-3
acinus, liver U47-3
acme U105-17
acoustic nerve U60-13
acquired (disease) U89-6
- immunodeficiency syndrome U96-15
acquisition, memory U74-10
acrid U62-5
acrocyanosis U108-6
acromegaly U108-12
acromion U28-11
acrylonitrile U91-9
ACTH-dependent U55-9
action (drug) U121-8; U92-3
- potential U42-5
activate U83-18; U88-12; U92-3
activation U122-7
activator U88-12
- (drug) U92-3
active U76-17; U119-6
- (drug) U92-3
activities of daily living (ADL) U142-27
-, life U142-27
activity U88-14; U119-6; U121-8
-, pharmacologic U92-3
-, physical U64-18
acuity, visual U59-8
acupressure U142-15; U93-18
acupuncture anesthesia U93-18
acute U119-10
- abdomen U124-16
- sense of hearing U61-8
Adam's apple U21-14
adaptability U88-17
adaptation U77-9; U88-17
-, light/photopic U59-10
adaptational U88-17
adaptive U59-10; U77-9; U88-17
addict U11-6
addicted (to) U11-4
addiction U11-3
-, alcohol U10-12
addictive /-ing U11-4
adduction U31-6
adductor U31-6
adenocarcinoma U98-4
adenohypophysis U54-5
adenoid(al) U35-6
adenoids U35-6
adenoma U98-4
adenomatous /-oid U98-4
adenosarcoma U98-4
adenosine triphosphate (ATP) U78-15
adenosquamous U86-12
adenovirus U90-10
adhere (to) U39-19; U128-15
adherence (therapy) U120-15
- (tissue) U134-10
-, immune U39-19
adherent U39-19
adhesiolysis U128-15; U134-10

adhesion U128-15
- (tissue) U134-10
adhesiotomy U128-15
adhesive U128-15; U118-2
- tape/plaster U140-21
adipocyte U56-5
adipose U24-9
- depots U87-15
- tissue, subcutaneous U56-5
adiposis dolorosa U56-5
adiposity /-osis U24-9; U56-5
adjacent U87-11,9
adjoin(ing) U87-11
adjunct U117-18; U120-8
adjustment U75-15; U77-9
adjuvant U120-8
administration (drug) U121-3
admission, hospital U20-1
admit to U102-10
admit(ting) U20-1
adolescence U80-8
adolescent U80-8
adoption U69-19
adrenal (gland) U54-10
adrenalectomy U54-10
adrenaline U55-11
adrenarche U54-10
adrenergic U42-11; U54-10; U55-11
- fibers U40-8
adrenocortical U55-10
adrenocorticotropic hormone (ACTH) U55-9
adsorbent U81-12
adsorption U81-12
adsorptive U81-12
adult U80-10
adulterant U11-15
adulterated (drug) U11-1
adultery U68-13
adulthood U80-10
adult-onset U119-5
advance directive U20-14
advancement flap U130-14
adventitial layer/coat U34-2
adverse drug reaction U121-14
advice, medical U18-4
advise U18-4
advocate U18-5
aerate U44-6
aerobic U1-15; U44-6
aerobics U1-15
aeromedical assistance U8-1
aerophagia U109-5
aerosol U91-7; U92-14
afebrile U105-3
affect U4-10; U76-3; U89-4
-, flat U113-3
affection U76-3
affectionate U76-3; U62-10
affective U76-3; U113-3
- disorder U4-4
affectivity U76-3
afferent U40-4
affinity U81-12

afflict U4-10
affliction U4-10
afterbath U19-9
afterbirth U71-16
- pains U71-20
aftercare U13-1; U120-14
afterdepolarization U42-6
afterimage U59-5; U73-9
afterload, (cardiac) U33-10
afterpains U71-20,3
afterpotential U42-5
aftertaste U62-6
age U80-1
-, come/be of U80-9
aged U80-1,13
agent U9-3; U92-2
-, anesthetic U93-4
-, antianxiety U135-10
-, antibacterial U92-9
-, antineoplastic U92-31
-, blocking U92-7
-, contrast U99-15
-, cytostatic U92-31
-, narcotic U135-5
-, psychotropic U92-23
ageusia U62-6
agglutinate U38-11, U39-19
agglutination, immune U39-19
-, platelet U38-11
agglutinin U37-16; U38-11; U39-19
agglutinogen U37-16
agglutinogenic U37-16
aggravate U4-12
aggregate U38-11; U81-9
aggregation, platelet U38-11
aging U80-1
agitate U76-8
agitated U76-8; U113-2
agitation U76-8; U77-6; U113-2; U7-12
- (viscera) U109-13
agitolalia U113-2
agitophasia U113-2
agonadism U54-11
agonist U31-4; U92-6
agranulocyte U37-10
agranulocytic U37-8
agraphia U113-9
agreeable U75-5
agyria U41-5
aid U8-1; U19-11; U142-29
aide U8-1; U19-11
-, home health U142-29
-, nurse's U16-3
AIDS U96-15
aids, rehabilitative U142-2
ail U4-5
ailing U4-5
ailment U4-5
aim U73-8; U101-3
aimless U73-8
air conduction (AC) U61-4
- sac U43-10
- trapping U111-6

airsick U4-1
airtight seal U17-6
airway(s) obstruction U111-16
airway, artificial U123-10
airways, upper U43-5
akinetic mutism U7-17
alanine aminotransferase (ALT) U47-16
alarm U8-7
alarming U8-7
albinism U114-4
albino U114-4
albumin U78-18
albuminated U78-18
albuminoid U78-18
alcohol U10-2; U82-13; U3-27
– content, blood U10-3
– dependency/addiction U10-12
– detoxi(fi)cation U10-15
– habituation U10-11
– intoxication, acute U10-1
– syndrome, fetal U10-13
alcoholic U10-10
Alcoholics Anonymous U10-4
alcohol-induced U119-8
alcoholism U10-12
aldehyde U82-12
aldosterone U55-25
alert U8-7; U117-7; U7-2
– state U73-1
alertness U72-1; U117-7
alexia U113-9
aliasing U99-13
alienist U15-12
align U140-2
aligned U59-15
alignment U141-1
–, ocular/eye U59-15
alimentary tract/canal U45-1
alimentation U45-1
–, parenteral U125-19
aliphatic hydrocarbon U82-15
alive U12-5
alkali U81-19
alkali(ni)zation U81-19
alkaline U81-19
– earth U82-19,34
– phosphatase U47-15
alkalosis U81-19
alkane U82-15
alkene U82-15
alkide U82-15
alkyl U82-15
alkylate U78-7
alkylation U82-15
alkylator U82-15
allantochorion U85-17
allantoic sac U85-17
allantois U85-17
allay U117-7
allegation U20-13
allele U84-4
allelic U84-4
allelomorph U84-4
allergen U39-23

allergic U39-23
allergy U39-23
alleviate U4-13
alleviation U4-13
allied health personnel U16-1
alloantibodies U136-11
allocate U8-19
allocation, patient U101-4
allograft U130-3
alloy U82-6,29
alpha fetoprotein (AFP) U97-16
altitude training U1-12
–, high U111-1
alum U82-31
alumina U82-31
aluminum U82-31
alveolar U43-10
alveolus U43-10
–, dental U26-13
amaurosis fugax U110-19
ambiguity, sexual U52-1, U53-12
ambitious U75-21
amblyopia U59-17; U113-11
Ambu bag® U8-12
ambulance U8-5
– dispatch center U8-9
ambulate U19-12; U65-1; U142-13
ambulation U19-12; U65-1; U134-13; U142-13
ambulatory U19-12; U65-1; U134-13; U142-13
– care center U14-2
ameba U90-4
amebiasis, intestinal U90-4; U94-18
amebic U90-4
– dysentery U94-18
amebicide U90-4
ameboid U90-4; U94-18
amelanotic U56-7
ameliorate U4-13
amelioration U4-13
amiable U75-5
amide U82-17
amination U82-17
amine U82-17
amino acid U79-10
ammonia U47-18; U46-17
ammoniacal U47-18
ammoniate U47-18
ammonium U47-18
amnes(t)ic U74-17
amnesia U74-17
amnesic gap U74-20
amniocentesis U85-15 U118-8
amnion U85-15
amnionic U85-15
– membrane/sac U85-15
amotivational U73-12
amphetamine U11-17
amphodiplopia U113-11
amplification, gene U84-36
ampul U9-13

ampulla of Vater U47-10
ampullary U47-10
amputation U142-6
amputee U142-6
Amsler chart U17-5
amygdala U41-11
amygdaloid U41-11
amyl U81-5
anabolic U78-3
– steroids U11-24
anabolism U78-3
anabolite U78-3
anaerobic U1-15; U44-6
– threshold U1-15
anaesthetist U131-6
anal U45-17
analgesia U104-20; U135-7
analgesic U104-20; U135-7
analysis by intention-to-treat U101-20
–, multivariate U100-28
–, survival U100-26
analyst U15-12
anaphase U83-13
anaphylactoid U124-3
anaphylatoxin U124-3
anaphylaxis U124-3
anaplasia U97-4
anastomose U34-6
anastomosis U34-6; U36-14; U129-6
anatomic(al) U87-1
anatomist U87-1
anatomy U87-1
–, microscopic U86-1
anatoxin U122-8
ancestor U84-29
ancestral U84-29
ancestry U84-29
anchor U28-25
anchoring flanges U136-6
ancillary personnel U16-15
androblastoma U53-9
androgen U55-16
android U53-1
andrology U53-1
androstenedione U55-16
androsterone U55-16
anejaculatory U53-11
anemia U38-4
–, pernicious U6-11
–, refractory U86-2
anemic U38-4
anergy U39-22
anesthesia U15-11; U135-2
– bag U135-15
– machine U135-14
– mask U135-15
– record U135-22
– recovery period U135-23
– screen U131-7
–, balanced U93-2
–, block U93-6
–, closed circuit U93-10
–, conduction U93-6
–, depth/level of U135-20

anesthesia, endotracheal U93-13
–, general U93-1
–, inhalation U93-10
–, insufflation U93-10
–, intravenous U93-13
–, local U93-3
–, regional U93-3
anesthesiologist U15-11; U131-6
anesthesiology U15-11; U135-2
anesthetic U15-11; U135-2; U93-4
– circuit U135-14
– risk U135-12
–, general U93-1
anesthetist U15-11
anesthetize U135-1
aneuploid(y) U84-9
aneurysm U110-18
–, ruptured aortic U124-15
aneurysmal U110-18; U124-15
anger U76-10
angina pectoris U124-11
anginal U124-11
Angiocath® U136-6
angiocatheter U118-16
angiodysplasia U118-16
angioedema U111-13
angiogenesis, tumor U97-15
angiogram U118-16
angiographic U118-16
angiography U118-16
–, fluorescein U58-14
angioma U98-5
angioplasty U127-4; U118-16
angiosarcoma U98-5
angiotensin U49-11; U55-25
angiotensinogen U55-25
angle (joint) U142-9
–, anterior chamber U58-8
angry U76-10
angst U77-5
anguish U77-5
angulation U106-4
anhydride U82-9
an(h)idrosis U105-15
animal graft U130-5
anion U81-11; U99-20
aniridia U58-8
anismus U142-25
ankle U23-12
– bone U28-26
– jerk U113-1
– joint U28-26
– sprain U65-9
– swelling U111-2
anlage U85-9
annihilation, fears of U77-6
annoyed U76-7
annular U108-9
anococcygeal U45-17
anomaly U89-5
anorectal canal U85-21
– juncture U45-17
anorectic U103-10
anorexia U103-10

anorexia nervosa U103-10
anorexic U103-10
anorgasmic U68-6
anosmia U62-1
anovular U51-5
anovulation U51-9
anovulatory U51-9
anoxia U123-8; U111-3
anoxic U123-8
antacid U46-10; U92-29
antagonist U31-4; U92-6
antecubital U23-4
– fossa U87-18
antenatal classes U70-10
antepartum U71-21
anterior U87-16
– chamber U15-18
– horn U41-15
– horn cell U42-14; U30-4; U95-8
anterior pituitary-like hormone U55-20
anterolateral U87-18
anthrax U90-3
antiarrhythmic U92-18; U33-6; U110-6
antiasthmatic U124-10
antibiotic U92-9
– coverage, prophylactic U139-13
–, antitumor U92-31
antibody U39-8
anticentromere antibody (ACA) U84-7
anticholinergic U92-8
anticoagulant U38-14; U92-16
anticodon U84-13
anticongestive U124-12
anticonvulsant U113-5
anticonvulsive U92-20
antidepressant U77-17; U92-24
antidiuretic U49-6; U55-24
antidiuretic hormone (ADH) U55-24
anti-doping U11-24
antidote U91-15; U9-15
antidysenteric U91-25
anti-embolic stockings U125-22
antiemetic U92-12; U103-12
– effect U46-6
antiepileptic U92-20
anti-estrogen U55-17
antifebrile U105-4
antifibrinolytic U37-12; U38-14
antifungal U92-26
antigen U39-8
–, blood group/RBC U37-16
antigen-antibody complex U39-9
antigenic U39-8
antigenicity U39-8
antigen-presenting cell U39-11
antiglobulin U39-5
antihapten U39-7
ant(i)helix U60-2
antihelminthic U90-16
antihistamines U92-22
antihrombotic U92-16
antihypertensive U110-13
anti-inflammatory (drug) U92-11
anti-ischemic U89-28

antimalarial U94-20
antimetabolite U78-11
antimicrobial U92-9; U90-1
antimitochondrial U83-7
antineoplastic (drug) U92-31
antineurotoxin U91-15
antioxidant U81-5
antiperistalsis U46-6
antiplasmin U37-15
antiplatelet U37-11
antipsychotic U74-11
antipyretic U105-4
antireflux U112-12
antirejection U39-22
antiscabetic U96-12
antiseptic U139-1
antiserum U37-3; U122-2
antishock U110-14; U124-4
antishock trousers, medical/military U8-13
antispasmodic U92-19
anti-T cell U39-13
antithermic U105-4
antithrombin U37-13
antitoxic U91-15; U122-8
antitoxin U39-8; U91-15,4; U122-8
antitragus U60-2
antitumor (drug) U92-31
antitussive effect U82-3
antivenin U91-15
antivenom U91-15
antiviral U90-10
antivomiting drug U92-12
antral U43-6
antrostomy U127-3
antrum, maxillary U43-6
anuria U112-2
anuric U112-2
anus U45-17
anvil U60-5
anxiety U76-5; U77-5; U113-2
– disorder U4-4
–, presurgical U134-4
anxious U76-5; U77-5
aorta U34-8
aortic U34-8
– regurgitation/insufficiency U110-10
aortocaval U34-8
APACHE U125-4
apathetic U76-15; U74-16; U77-8
apathy U7-12; U76-15; U77-8
aperture U87-21
–, collimator U99-6
apex U87-25
– beat U33-4
– cordis U32-4
aphasia U113-10
aphasic U113-10; U66-9
apheresis U136-15
aphonia U66-23; U103-6; U111-11
aphonic U111-11; U103-6
aphrodisiac U68-3
apical U87-25
apnea U111-5; U123-6

apnea, sleep U72-13
apneic U72-13; U111-5; U123-6
aponeurosis U30-5
aponeurotic U30-5
apoplexy U124-14
apparent U107-10
appearance, general U107-10
appendages, epidermal U86-7
appendectomy U45-13
appendiceal U45-13
appendicitis U45-13
appendix (vermiformis) U45-13
appetite U2-11
–, healthy U1-2
–, loss of U103-10
application U17-13
– (cream) U121-3
–, heat U142-22
–, ice U142-21
applicator U17-3; U121-3; U132-14
–, cotton U17-13
applier, clip U138-16
apply U17-13
– (ointment) U121-3
appointment, medical U18-2
apposition U141-1; U137-5
appraisal U75-12
appreciable U57-2; U117-5
appreciate U57-2; U117-5; U74-4
appreciation U57-2; U74-4
apprehension U76-5; U77-5
apprehensive U76-5; U77-5
approach, surgical U126-6
approximation U137-5; U140-2
apractic U113-9
apraxia U113-9
apraxic U113-9
apt to U98-13; U110-13
apyrexia U105-3
aqua aerobics U1-15
aquadissection U128-14
aquafortis U82-4
aquatic bodywork U1-18
– therapy U142-20
aqueduct, cerebral U41-4
aqueductal U41-4
aqueous U82-4
– humor U58-11
arachnoid U41-8
– mater U41-8
arachnoiditis U94-13
arborize U40-2
arc of movement U142-9
–, reflex U42-12
arch (one's back) U31-3
– of the hand U64-9
– width U26-9
–, aortic U34-8
–, dental U26-9
arched joint U30-8
areflexia U42-12
areflexive U113-1
areola U50-18
areolar (connective) tissue U86-6

argentite U82-28
arise U65-17
– (muscle) U30-3
arm U23-2
– socket U28-12
– span U24-2
armboard, padded U19-3
armed U6-8
armload U23-2
armpit U23-3
aroma U62-3
aromatic U62-3
– ring U81-7
arousal U72-7; U7-2; U76-1
– mechanism U73-1
–, sexual U68-2
arouse U68-2; U72-7
aroused U76-8
arrest, cardiac U123-2
arrested U123-2
arrhythmia, cardiac U33-6; U110-6
arrhythmic U110-6
arrive U71-1
arrogant U75-20
arsenic /-ium U82-33
arsenide U82-33
arsenism U82-33
arsenous U82-33
arson U6-10
arsonist U6-10
artefact U99-13
arteria carotis communis U34-10
arterial U34-3
– blood gases (ABG) U125-9
arteriocapillary U34-5
arteriogram U118-18
arteriolar U34-3
arteriole U34-3
arteriosus U32-11
arteriovenous U34-3
artery U34-3
–, brachiocephalic U34-9
–, common carotid U34-10
–, innominate U34-9
arthrocentesis U118-8; U125-17
arthrodesis U141-13
arthrodial joint U29-7
arthrogram U118-23
arthrography U118-23
arthroplasty U127-4
arthropod U90-12
arthroscope U128-7; U17-6
arthroscopic U128-7
arthroscopy U118-23; U128-7
articular U29-1
articulate with U29-1
articulation U29-1
–, hinged U29-5
artifact U99-13
artificial airway U123-10
– kidney U125-21
– – program U14-1
– respiration U123-4
– teeth U27-8

artificial ventilation U123-9
aryepiglottic U43-7
ascent U87-1
ascertain U117-5
ascites U109-9
ascitic U109-9
ascorbic acid U79-15
aseptic U139-1
asexual U68-1
ashamed U76-12
ashes U12-14
asleep U72-6
asparagus U68-3
aspect U87-4
asphyxia U44-8; U111-4; U123-7
asphyxiant U123-7
asphyxiate U44-8; U123-7
asphyxiated U111-4
asphyxiation U44-8; U111-4; U123-7
aspirate U44-3; U111-4; U118-9; U127-16; U128-11
aspiration U44-3; U127-16
– pneumonia U109-5
–, pulmonary U111-4
aspiration-irrigation system U128-11
aspirator U118-9; U127-16
assault U77-7; U12-10; U20-13
–, sexual/indecent U68-17
assaultive U68-17; U77-7
assay U116-3
assembly U90-11
assertive U75-20
assess U117-1
assessible U117-1
assessment U117-1
–, preoperative U134-1
assignment, patient U101-4
assimilable U78-5
assimilate U78-5
assimilation U78-5; U88-8
assistance U8-1; U19-11; U142-29
assistant, medical laboratory U16-10
assisted reproductive technologies (ART) U69-11
associate U74-5
associated with U119-16
association U74-5; U100-32
Association, American Medical (AMA) U13-13
associational U74-5
associative U74-5
astatine U82-23
asthenic U25-5
asthma U124-10
asthmatic U124-10
astragalus U28-26
astride U63-4f
astringent U82-28
astrocytoma U98-14
asylum, mental U14-5
asymptomatic U103-1
asynergy U31-4
asystole U33-3
atactic U113-8

ataxia U113-8
ataxic U113-8
atelectasis, pulmonary U111-15
atelectatic U111-15
atheromatous plaque U78-16
atherosclerosis U34-3; U124-11
athlete U25-4
athletic U25-4
atom U81-2
atomic U81-2
atresia U89-18
atrial chamber U32-7
– fibrillation U110-7
– flutter U110-7
atrial septum U32-9
atrioventricular U32-7
atrium (cordis) U32-7
atrophic U89-29
atrophy U89-29
attachment U30-3
–, parent-child U77-11
attack U103-4; U104-14
–, transient ischemic (TIA) U124-14
attend (to) U8-1; U15-3
attendance, in U15-3,17; U80-6
attendant, medical/hospital U16-14
attending (physician/surgeon) U15-3; U20-9; U131-5
attention U8-1; U73-2; U74-16
–, medical U18-4
attentional U74-16
attention-deficit disorder U4-4; U75-17
attentive U74-16
attenuate U122-6
attenuated live virus U122-6
attenuation U122-6
attire, OR U139-15
attitude U75-3f; U76-3
–, fetal U71-5
attitudinal reflex U57-16
attorney, power of U20-14
attrition U27-19
atypical U116-21
audibility U61-2
audible U61-2
audiogram U61-2
audiologist U16-1
audiometer U61-7
audiometry U61-2
audit, medical U20-12
auditory U61-2; U21-15
– acuity U57-5
– canal/meatus, external U60-3
– nerve U60-13
augmentation U129-19
aural U60-1; U21-15
auricle U32-7; U60-2
auricular U32-7; U60-2
auriculotemporal U60-2
auriculovenous U32-7
auriscope U17-7
auscultate U107-9
auscultation U107-9
auscultatory U107-9

authorization U20-5
autoantibody U39-8,21
autocatalytic U81-16
autoclave U139-3
autoexpression U83-16
autogenic training U1-12; U142-18
autogenous U129-16
autograft U130-2
autohemolysis U136-12
autoimmune U39-4
autoimmunity U39-4
autoinflation U111-6
autoinjectable U122-4
autoinoculation U122-1
autologous U39-21; U129-16
automobilist U6-3
autonomic nervous system U40-6
autopsic(al) U12-20
autopsy U12-20
autoregulation U49-10; U83-18
autoregulatory U49-10
autosomal U84-6
autosome U84-6
autotransfusion U136-8
autotransplant U130-2
autotransplantation U129-14
auxiliary, hospital U16-15
AV bundle U32-15
avascular U86-7
avidly bound U82-32
avirulent U90-10
avocational U142-26
avulsion U28-4f; U106-5
awake U72-6f
awaken U72-7
awakening U72-7
awareness U57-5
awl U132-5
axial U87-3
axillary U23-3
axipetal U40-2
axis U87-3
– cylinder U40-2
–, dens of the U28-19
–, visual U59-15
axon U40-2
axonal U40-2
axoplasm U40-2
azotemia U112-13; U37-2
azotemic U112-13

B

babble U66-17
Babinski's sign U113-1
baby U80-5
– blues U71-22
– teeth U27-2
–, have a U71-2
bacillary U90-7
bacilluria U90-7
bacillus U90-7
back U22-11

back blow U8-11
– passage U45-17
– school U142-18
backache U22-11
backboard U8-16
backbone U22-12; U28-19
backflow U36-5
backscatter U99-6
backside U22-13
bacteremia U124-5; U90-6
bacteremic shock U124-5
bacterial U90-6
bacterium U90-6
bacterostatic U90-6
bad (for) U1-3
– breath U109-2
bad-tempered U76-2
bag of waters, rupture of U71-6
bag-(valve)-mask unit U8-12
–, anesthesia U135-15
–, breathing U135-15
–, retrieval/organ/specimen U133-16
balance U88-19
– board U142-19
–, body fluid U48-9
balanced U75-15; U88-19
bald U25-16
bald-headed U25-16
baldness U25-16
ball-and-socket joint U29-4
balloon dila(ta)tion U128-14
– dissection U128-14
ballottable U109-9
ballottement U109-9
balm U9-8
balneotherapy U142-20
balsam U9-8
bandage U140-20
–, Esmarch U135-18
Band-Aid® U8-1; U140-22
bang U6-4; U11-9
banking, blood U14-12
banned substance U11-24
bar, T-/trapeze U19-4
barb(iturate)s U11-16
barbed up U11-16
barbiturate U92-24; U93-14
barbituric U11-16
barbiturism U11-16
barbotage U93-9
bare-chested U22-2
barefoot U23-13
bareheaded U21-1
baring U59-11
baritosis U82-29
barium U82-20
– enema U118-21
– examination U118-21
– meal (examination) U118-21
baroreceptor U57-10
baroreflex U113-1
barotrauma U6-17
barrage U42-4
barrel U17-10

barrel-chest deformity U142-7
barrel-chested U25-9
barrier U81-20
–, blood-brain U36-15
barring U74-14
Bartholin('s) glands U50-10
basal U43-4; U87-25
– anesthesia U93-15
– body temperature U69-5
– cell layer U56-2
– metabolism U78-2
base U32-4; U81-19; U87-25
– pair U84-12
basement membrane U86-16
basic U81-19
basilar U87-25
basophil U37-8
basophilic U37-8
basosquamous U86-12
bat U94-4
bath U19-9; U142-20
–, electrotherapeutic U142-23
–, Finnish U1-17
bathe U1-17; U19-9; U142-20
bathing U1-17; U19-9
bathroom U19-9
bathtub U19-9
battered child U74-2
battery U20-7,13
bauxite U82-31
be down with U4-6
beaker cells U86-18
beam U67-9
–, x-ray U99-5
beamer U99-5
beam-splitter U99-5
bean bag U142-19
beard U25-14f
beardless U25-14
bearing U63-1
– down U71-11
bearings U7-8
beat U33-1
beating U33-1
bed bath U142-20
– pan U19-8
– rest U4-6; U19-3
–, go to U72-3
bedcover U19-3
bedding U19-3
bedfast U4-6; U12-1
bedrails U19-3
bedridden U4-6; U77-13
bedside stand/table U19-7
bedsore U23-12; U63-7
bedtime U19-3; U72-4
bed-wetting U112-16
beeper U17-17
behavior U75-3
behavioral U75-3
behaviorism U75-3
behind U22-13
belch U46-3
bell (piece) U17-2

belligerence U77-7
belligerent U77-7
belly U22-4; U45-6
– button U22-5
beltline U22-6
bend U31-2
bend (forward) U63-3
bending U63-3
bends, the U6-17
beneficial U1-5; U91-18
benefit U1-5
–, sickness U4-1
benefits, welfare U1-7
benign U97-5
benignancy/-ity U97-5
bent U31-2; U63-3
benumb U135-3
benzamide U81-7
benzene ring U81-7
bereavement U12-13
best (for) U1-3
bestiality U68-15
beta cells U54-8
bevel U136-6
bewildered U77-4
bias U100-18
bicarbonate U36-4; U116-11
biceps (brachii) U30-11
bicipital U30-11
bicuspid U32-10
bicuspid tooth U26-6
big-headed U75-20
bile U47-11
– acid U47-11
– salt U47-11
biliary U47-11
bilious U47-11
bilirubin U47-13
biliverdin U47-13
bill, doctor's/medical U18-15
billing U18-15
bilobar U47-2
bimanual manipulation U142-12
binaural U60-1
binder U140-20
binding U81-8
binge eating U2-1
binocular U59-16; U58-2
binocularity U59-16
bioaccumulation U91-19
bioactivity U92-3
bioassay U116-3
bioavailability U121-10
biochemical blood smear U116-7
biochemical blood film U116-7
biochemistry U81-1; U83-1
biocompatible U129-20
biodegradable U78-10; U92-4
bioenergetics U78-12
biofeedback therapy U142-25
biohazard U91-5
bioinert U129-20
biologic response modifier U92-34
biologic(al) U83-1

biologist U83-1
biology, cell(ular) U83-1
biomechanics U142-10
biomolecule U81-2
biophysics U142-10
bioprosthesis U142-6
biopsy U118-5
–, cone U127-12
–, testicular U69-13
biopsy-proven U117-9
bioptic U58-14; U118-5
biostatistics U100-1
biosynthesis U54-2; U78-4
biotinylate U78-7
biotoxicology U91-3
biotransformation U92-4
bipalpebral U58-3
biplanar U87-2
bipolar disorder U77-17
birth U71-9
– canal U50-8; U71-8
– control U69-5
– defect U142-4
–, give U71-2
birthing U71-2
– room U19-2
birthmark U25-19; U98-5
bisect U126-14
bismuth U82-27
bismuthosis U82-27
bite U5-10; U27-11 f; U91-16
biting U5-10
bitten U5-10; U27-11
bitter U76-11
– almond odor U62-3
bivalent U81-10
blabber U66-19
blackhead U114-6
blackout U7-4; U74-17
bladder capacity U49-15
– dome U48-11
– neck U48-11
–, (urinary) U48-11
blame U77-10
blanching U56-18
bland(ness) U62-7
blanket, heating U19-6
blast U6-9; U86-2
– cell U38-3
– injury U61-9
blastic U38-3; U86-2
blastocyst U85-5
blastogenesis U38-3; U86-2
blastomere U85-4
blastula U85-5
blastulation U85-5
bleach U91-2
–, household U17-15
bleb U114-12
bleed U5-18; U38-6; U89-26; U124-16
bleeder U38-6; U124-16
bleeding U5-18; U38-8; U89-26
– time U116-13
–, gastrointestinal U109-11

bleeding, intraabdominal U124-16
-, menstrual U51-2
bleep U17-17
blemish, skin U25-18
blemished U25-18; U6-11
blepharitis U58-3
blepharoptosis U113-17
blepharospasm U58-3; U103-20
blind U59-18; U101-9
blind spot U58-14
blinding U59-18
blindness U59-18
blink U59-3; U67-15
- reflex U125-25
blinking U59-3; U67-15
blister U114-12
blistering U114-12
bloated U109-8
bloating, abdominal U109-8,1
block U88-14
blockade U93-6
blockage U93-6
blocker U92-7
blocking U101-11; U92-7
blood U37-1
- alcohol level/content U10-3
- bank U14-12
- cell U37-4
- chemistry U116-7
- circulation U36-1
- clot U38-12
- count, white U116-8
- donor U136-9
- film/smear U116-7
- flow U36-5
- formation U38-1
- gas analysis U116-11
- pressure U36-8
- - cuff U17-8
- - reading U107-14
- supply U36-6
- type U37-16
blood type/group U136-10
blood typing U136-10
- vessel U34-1
- viscosity U36-12
- volume U36-7
-, whole U136-14
blood-brain barrier U36-15
bloodless U37-1
bloodstained urine U112-3
bloodstream U36-1
blood-testis barrier U53-9
blood-tinged U60-1
bloody U37-1
- show U71-7
blot analysis, Southern U84-35
blow U6-4
- dry U1-17
- up U6-9
blue U76-22
- bloater U111-3
blue, feel U71-22
blues, baby/maternity U71-22

blunt U7-10; U135-3
- abdominal trauma U109-13
- injury U8-16
- trauma U58-1
blunted sensation U135-4
blunt-tipped U133-14
blurred vision U103-14
blurring of vision U103-14
blush(ing) U56-18
B-lymphocyte/-cell U39-12
BM stick U17-1
board-like rigidity U109-14
boastful U75-6
bodily U86-20
- functions U107-1
- harm U6-11
body U86-20
-, dead U12-14
- build/shape U25-1
- fat U24-5
- - content U24-7
- habitus U25-2
- height U24-2
- jacket U125-24
- mass index (BMI) U24-7
- stalk U85-17; U71-17
- stockings U22-13
- surface area U33-7
- toning U1-13
- weight U24-1
body-building U25-1
body-conscious U97-4
bodyweight calisthenics U1-15
bodywork U1-18
boil U114-16
boiling point U82-7
bolt U141-16
bolus U46-9
bombard U99-4
bond U81-8
bondage U68-9
bonds U75-21
bone U28-2
- chisel U132-11
- marrow aspiration U118-9
- plate U141-17
- scraper U132-12
- union U106-15
bone-resorptive U27-20
bony U25-7; U28-2
bony framework U28-1
booster vaccination/ (re)immunization U122-9
boots, space/Spenco U125-23
booze U10-2
boozed(-up) U10-1
borborygmus U46-14
border U87-10
borderline U87-10; U116-23
boric U82-31
born U71-1
boron U82-31
bosom U22-2; U50-17
bothersome U104-3

bottle supplements U14-8
-, hot water U19-6
bottle-feeding U71-26; U136-4
bottom U22-13
botulinous U91-21
botulism U91-21
bouncing U1-4
bound U81-8; U87-10
boundary U87-10
bounding pulse U33-8
bout U103-4
bow U31-2; U63-3
bowel habits U109-6
- movement (BM) U46-19
- sounds U46-14; U107-9
bowel(s) U45-9
bowel, large U45-15
bowing deformity U142-7
bowl, lotion U17-12
bow-legged U25-9
bowlegs U23-8
Bowman's capsule U48-6
bra(ssiere) U64-15
brace U140-26; U141-7
brachial U23-2
brachiocephalic trunk/artery U34-9
bradyarrhythmia U110-2
bradycardi(a)c U110-2
bradycardia U33-5; U110-2
bradypnea U111-5
braided (suture) U137-7
brain U41-1
- damage U6-11; U124-19
- death U7-18
- electrical activity mapping (BEAM) U125-14
- injury, traumatic U124-19
- sand U54-13
- stem U41-12
- stem testing/studies U125-14
- waves U118-12
brainpower U41-1
brains U41-1
brainwash U41-1
brainy U41-1
branch U34-13
branching U34-13
brawny U25-4
breach of confidentiality U20-13
break U106-1
- down U65-12
- down (food) U46-11
- out (disease) U94-7
break(point) U84-24
breakage, chromosome U84-24
breakdown U6-5; U7-4; U65-12; U78-1,10
breast U22-2; U50-17
- engorgement U55-23; U71-27
- milk U71-27
-, firm U1-11
breastbone U22-2; U28-13
breast-feed U50-17; U71-26
breastfeeding U71-20,25 f

breath U44-1
- odor U109-2
- sounds U107-8; U123-9
-, short(ness) of U111-1
breathe U44-1
breathing U44-1
- bag U8-12
- exercises U1-16
-, mouth-to-mouth U123-9
breathless(ness) U44-1; U111-1
breathy U44-1
breed U84-30
breeding U84-30
bridge U81-7
bright(ness) U59-11
brimstone U82-24
bring (a)round U123-3
- back to life U123-3
- on U119-8
- up (food) U46-4; U103-17
brisk walking U1-14
brittle U31-16; U82-25
brittleness U31-16
broad-minded U75-16
broad-shouldered U25-9
broken U106-1
broken-hearted U76-20
bromide U82-23
bromine U82-23
bromsulphalein U82-23
bronchial U43-9
bronchiectasis U111-17
bronchiectatic U111-17
bronchiolar U43-9
bronchiole U43-9
bronchitis U43-9
bronchoconstrictive U111-17
bronchomediastinal trunk U35-9
bronchopneumonia U94-14
bronchopulmonary U43-2,9
- segment/lobule U43-3
bronchoscopy U118-11
bronchospasm U111-10; U103-20
bronchotracheal U43-8
bronchus U43-9
brow U25-14; U59-2
brows, raise one's U67-15
Brudzinski's sign U94-13
bruisability U38-8
bruise U5-13
bruit U110-4
brush border U86-11
-, interproximal U26-22
brushing U116-5; U118-10; U83-1
- motions U64-11
bruxism U27-18; U72-14
bubble bath U1-17
bubo U96-5
-, tropical U96-7
buccal U21-7; U26-23
buckling U34-4
bud U85-10
budding U85-10; U90-18
buddy-taping U142-13

budge U64-3
buffer U81-20
buffy coat U136-16
bug U90-5; U4-2
build, body U25-1
buildup U78-1
bulb, inflating U17-8
bulbar U58-2
bulbourethral U48-13
- gland U50-10; U52-13
bulbus oculi U58-2
bulge U85-10
bulging U85-10; U22-3
bulk U45-9
-, muscular U30-2
bulla U114-12
bullous U114-12
bum U22-13
bundle U30-1
- of His U32-15
-, neurovascular U40-12
bunion U23-14
burden, tumor U97-14
burial U12-17
buried U12-17
burly U24-3
burn U5-11; U6-10
burnt out U76-18
burp U46-3
burrows U96-12
bursa, synovial U29-10
bursal U29-10
bursitis U29-10
burst U6-9
bury U12-17
bust U22-2
butanol U47-17
butt U22-13
butterfly needle U136-6
buttock U22-13
buttonhole deformity U142-7
buzz U11-9
by accident U6-1
bypass U36-14; U125-11
bystander U6-13

C

cachectic U108-14
cachexia U108-14
cadaver U12-14
- donor U129-17
cadaveric U12-14
cadmium U82-33
Caisson disease U6-17
calamity U13-12
calcaneocuboid joint U28-27
calcaneus /-um U28-27
calcific U31-14; U82-19
calcification U31-14; U82-19; U27-22
calcify U31-14
calcis (os) U28-27

calcitonin U55-8
calcitriol U55-8
calcium U82-19
- channel U42-9
- influx U42-6
calculus U89-21
calendar method U69-5
calf U23-10
- muscles U30-17
- bone U28-24
calibrated U116-12
caliceal U48-4
calipers U24-12
calisthenics U1-15
calix U48-4
call U18-7; U20-4
- roster U15-2
-, on U20-4
callipers U24-12
callosal U41-3
callous U75-8; U106-15
callus U19-10
- formation U106-15
calm(ness) U76-19
calorie U79-4
calyceal U48-4
calyx, (renal) U48-4
camera (laparoscopy) U133-3
camisole (restraint) U77-26
canal, alimentary/gastrointestinal U45-1
-, external auditory U60-3
-, outer ear U60-3
cancellation U18-2
cancellous bone U130-9
cancer U97-6
cancer-cure quack U15-23
cancericidal U97-6
cancerous U97-6
candid U75-13
candy U3-17
cane U19-14
-, quad U19-11
canine (tooth) U26-5
cannabinoid U11-15
cannabis U11-15
canned food U91-21
cannula U132-6
cannulate U136-3
cannulation U136-3
cannulization U132-6
canthal U58-3
canthus U58-3
cap, knee U23-11
-, surgical U139-18
capacity U142-4
- needs U8-9
-, respiratory/vital U44-11
capillarity U34-5
capillary, (blood) U34-5
capital punishment U12-11
capitate (bone) U28-17
capsid U90-10
capsize U6-1

capsula articularis U29-9
capsular U29-9
capsule U9-7; U97-9
–, joint U29-9
capsulectomy U29-9
capsulitis, adhesive U23-3
carbohydrate U82-10; U79-5
carbolated U82-13
carbolic acid U82-13
carbon U82-10
carbonate U82-10
carbonic U82-10
– acid U81-22
carbonyl U82-10
carboxyhemoglobin U37-6; U116-9
carboxyl group U82-10
carboxylate U78-7
carboxylation U82-10
carbuncle U114-16
carcinoembryonic antigen (CEA) U97-16
carcinogen U91-13
carcinogenesis U98-2
carcinogenicity U91-13
carcinoid U97-10; U98-2
carcinoma U97-6
–, embryonal U98-16
–, squamous (cell) U98-2
–, transitional cell U97-9
carcinoma-in-situ U97-10
carcinomatous U97-10; U98-2
carcinosarcoma U98-3
card, treatment/medical U18-14
cardia U32-3
cardiac U32-3
– apex U32-4
– arrest/standstill U123-2
– cycle U33-2
– massage U123-5
– muscle U32-6
– opening U45-8
– output U33-7
– pacing U123-13
– rate U33-5
– valve U32-10
cardiocentesis U110-9
cardiomegaly U110-9; U32-3
cardioplegic arrest U125-11
cardiopulmonary bypass (CPB) U125-11
cardiotoxicity U91-11
cardioversion U123-12
cardiovert U123-12
care U20-2
– unit, intensive U14-7
–, health U13-1
–, intensive/critical U125-1
–, maintenance U77-25
caregiver U20-3; U77-25
caress U62-10
caressing U62-10; U68-2
carotid U34-10
– artery, common U34-10
– body U37-1
carpal U23-5

carpal bones U28-17
– tunnel syndrome U113-15
carpals U28-17
carpus U23-5; U28-17
carriage U63-1
carrier U94-4
– system/mechanism U78-17
carrier-mediated U78-17
carry U64-16
carsick U4-1
cartilage U29-2
cartilaginous U29-2
– joint U29-12
case U20-2; U102-13
– cluster U90-3
– history U102-4
– record form U101-16
– report U102-13
case-controlled U101-10
caseload U20-2
caseous necrosis U94-16
casket U12-18
cassiterite U82-29
cast U64-14
– off U85-13
–, urinary/renal U112-14
Castor oil U82-13; U92-13
castration U69-3
casualties, incoming U16-14
casualty U6-12
– department U14-6
– mitigation U8-3
catabolic U78-3
catabolism U78-3
catabolite U78-3
catabolize U78-3
catalysis U81-16
catalyst U81-16
–, organic U78-8
catalytic U81-16
catalyze U81-16
cataplexy U72-18
catastrophe U6-20; U124-1
catastrophic U124-1
catch (infection) U4-2
catecholamine U78-24
catecholaminergic U42-11
catgut U137-9
cathartic U91-2,24
catheter U127-9
–, central venous U125-7
–, indwelling (urinary/Foley) U125-20
catheterizable U125-7
catheterization U125-7
catheterize U125-7
cation U81-11; U99-20
catnap U72-2
cat's cry syndrome U77-22
Caucasian U102-9
cauda epididymidis U52-5
– equina U41-15
caudad U87-19
caudal U87-19
caudate U41-15; U87-19

causal U119-2
causation U119-2
causative U119-2
cause U119-8
caustic U91-10
cauter U127-9
cauterization U127-9
caution U6-22; U9-18
cautious U75-17
caval U34-7
cavernosography U52-15
cavernous body (penis) U52-15
cavity U28-6
–, buccal U21-10; U26-23
–, oral U21-8; U45-2
–, orbital U58-1
–, tympanic/middle ear U60-6
cavopulmonary U34-7
cease U55-9
cecal U45-12
cecum U45-12
ceiling effect U11-18
Celcius U105-1
celibacy U68-11
cell U83-2
– biology U83-1
– cycle U83-12
– death U89-30
– divison U84-6
– lysis U39-10
–, red blood U37-5
–, white (blood) U37-7
cellular U83-2
celomic cavity U85-9
cementum U26-17
cemetery U12-18
censoring U101-28
Center for Disease Control (CDC) U13-3
center, micturition U40-3
centigrade U105-1
– scale U105-6
centimorgan U84-17
central U87-15
– field abnormalities U17-5
– nervous system (CNS) U40-5
– venous line/catheter U125-7
centrifugation U83-20
centrifuged U83-20
centriole U83-6
centromere U84-7
centromeric U84-7
centrosomal U83-6
centrosome U83-6
cephalad U87-19
cephalic U87-19
cephalohematoma U38-8
cephalometry U87-19
cercariae U90-17
cerebellar U41-2
– gait U113-8
cerebellopontine U41-2
cerebellum U41-2
cerebral U41-2
– injury/trauma U124-19

cerebrospinal fluid (CSF) U41-17
cerebrovascular U41-2
– accident (CVA) U124-14
cerebrum U41-2
certifiable U18-10
certificate, (doctor's) medical U18-10
certification U18-10
certified U102-17
certified nurse (CN) U16-4
certify U18-10
cerumen U60-15
ceruminous U60-15
cervical U50-7; U21-13
– cap U69-9
– collar U21-13; U141-9
– mucus method U69-5
cervix U21-13
– uteri U50-7
cesarean section U71-3
cesium U82-18,34
cessation U123-6
–, breath U72-13
–, smoking U13-4
chafe U5-8
chain U81-7
–, H-/L- U39-6
–, ossicular U61-3
chalice cells U86-18
challenge test U117-12
chamber, anterior U59-10
–, atrial U32-7
–, heart U32-8
chancre, soft U96-4
chancriform U96-4
chancroid U96-4
channel, calcium U42-9
chaplain U15-20
character U75-1
characterize U75-1
charcoal U91-9
–, activated/medicinal U91-25
charge U81-10
–, pathologist in U16-10
chart U20-5; U100-27
–, medical/patient's U18-14; U102-12
–, Snellen/visual acuity U17-5
charting U18-14; U20-5
chastity U68-12
chatter U66-19
chattering (teeth) U56-14
check U18-9; U107-1
checklist U18-9
checkup, medical U18-9; U107-1
cheek U21-7
– bone U28-9
– tooth U26-7
cheeks, puffing of the U67-17
cheer U67-6
– up U75-6; U76-9
cheerful(ness) U67-6; U75-6; U76-9
cheerless U75-6; U76-9
cheil(o)- U21-9
chelate U81-5
chelation U81-5

chelator U81-5
chemical U81-1
chemist U9-4
chemistry profile, serum U81-1
–, blood U116-7
chemoprevention U81-1
chemoprophylaxis U97-17
chemoradiotherapy U97-17
chemoreceptor U57-10
chemosensitive U103-15
chemotactic factor U39-17
chemotherapeutic U16-12; U97-17
chemotherapy U97-17
chenodeoxycholic acid U47-12
chest U22-2
– excursion/expansion U107-16
– film/radiograph U118-18
– splinting U44-10
– tube U125-16
– x-ray (film) U111-6
chew U27-15
chiasm, optic U58-15
chiasmal U58-15
chiasmatic U58-15
chickenpox U95-7
chilblain U5-12
child U80-5
– molestation U68-16
– welfare U1-7; U13-2
childbearing age U69-2
– years U51-10
childbirth U71-9
childhood U80-5
childhood-onset U95-1
childish /-like U80-5
childless U80-5
chilliness U105-9
chills U105-9; U94-20
chilly U105-9
chin U21-6; U25-10
chin-lift maneuver U8-11
chip U106-2
chiropractor U15-22
chi-square test U100-34
chlamydia U90-14; U96-9
chlamydial U90-14; U96-9
chlamydiosis U96-9
chloral U82-23
chloride U82-23
chlorinated U82-23
chlorine U82-23
chloroform U82-23
choice, drug of U94-4
–, procedure of U34-1
choke U27-16; U44-8
choking U44-8; U123-7
– victim U8-10
cholangiogram U118-20
cholangiographic U118-20
cholangiole U47-12
cholecystic U47-7
cholecystitis U47-7
cholecystokinin (CCK) U55-13; U54-9
choledochal U47-9

choledocholithiasis U47-9
choledochus U47-9
cholera, Asiatic U94-21
choleric U75-18
cholesteatosis U47-12
cholesterol U47-12; U78-16
cholesterolemia U47-12
cholic U47-12
– acid U47-12
cholinergic U40-8; U42-11; U92-8
chondral U29-2
chondroblast U86-2
chondrocyte U29-2
chondroma U98-12
chondromalacia U98-12
chondromatosis U98-12
chondromatous U98-12
chorda dorsalis/vertebralis U85-20
chordae tendineae (cordis) U32-12
chordoma U85-20
choriocarcinoma U85-16
chorion U85-16
chorionic gonadotrop(h)in, human (hCG) U55-20
– gonadotropic hormone U55-20
– sac/membrane U85-16
choroid(al) U58-7
chromaffin U82-25
chromate U82-25
chromatic U59-9
chromatid U84-7
chromatin U84-6
chromatogram U83-22
chromatography, adsorption U83-22
chromatopsia U59-9; U113-11
chrome U82-25
chromic U82-25
chromium U82-25
chromosomal U84-6
– constitution U1-8
chromosome U84-6
– arm U84-24
chronic U119-10
– tinnitus sufferer U4-3
chronically infirm U4-7
chronicity U119-10
chubbiness U25-6
chubby U25-6
chyle U35-2
chyliform U35-2
chylomicron U35-2
chylothorax U111-14
chylous U35-2
chyme U46-9
cicatricial U140-10
cicatrix U140-10
cigarette U10-19
cilia U83-5
ciliary body U58-7
– motion U44-9
– muscle U58-16
ciliated U83-5
circadian rhythm U72-8
circuit training U1-14

circulating nurse U131-9
circulation, blood U36-1
–, hepatic/portal U36-3
–, lesser/pulmonary U36-2
circulatory U36-1
– collapse U6-5
circumcise U126-9
circumcorneal U58-5
circumduction U31-7
circumference, wrist U25-3
circumferential wiring U141-14
circumoral pallor U95-6
cirrhosis, biliary U108-11
cis region U83-10
cistern U41-17
cisterna U83-8
– chyli U35-8
– magna U41-17
cisternal U41-17
citric acid cycle U83-7
claim form U18-15
clamber U65-18
clammy U105-10; U77-5; U110-14
clamp U132-13
clap (hands) U67-6
claudication, intermittent U110-19
claustrophobia U77-5
clavicle/-ula U28-11
clay U82-30
– body mask U1-20
clean U10-4
cleanse U44-9; U107-6; U139-5
cleanser, denture U27-8
clear U49-7
– (to auscultation) U111-5
– (one's throat) U66-6
– (the airway) U123-5
– layer U56-2
clearance U49-7; U88-16
–, mucociliary U44-9
cleavage U81-8; U39-10
– division U85-3
– lines U56-17
cleave U81-8; U85-3
– off U81-4
cleft U85-3; U87-26; U106-11
– palate U26-10
–, synaptic U40-13
clench U27-17; U64-9
clenching, nighttime U27-17
clerical work U15-6
clerk, medical U15-6
clerkship U15-6
client U20-2
climacteric U51-10
climax U105-17
–, sexual U68-6
climb U65-18
climber U65-18
cling U64-9
clinging child U64-9
clinic U14-2
clinical judgement U117-18; U18-5
– picture U108-2

clinical trial U101-1
clinician U14-2
clinician, nurse U16-5
clip U137-13
– applier U138-16; U137-13
–, occlusive U138-15
clip-ligate U138-15; U137-3,13
clitoral U50-12
clitoridectomy U50-12
clitoris U50-12
cloaca U85-21
cloacal U85-21
– wall U85-6
cloak U39-7
clonal U84-33
clone U84-33
cloning U84-33
closure U128-18
clot lysis U38-14
–, blood U38-12
clothes, take/slip off U107-4
clotting factor U37-12 f; U38-13
–, blood U38-10; U37-11
clubbed U108-11
clubbing, digital/finger U108-11
clubfoot deformity U142-7
clue, physical U117-7
clumsy U72-15
cluster headache U113-16
–, gene U84-2
clustering (of cases) U94-8
clutch U65-9
coagulant U38-10,13
coagulase U38-10
coagulate U38-10
coagulation U92-16; U127-10
– factor U38-13
–, blood U38-10
coagulator U127-10
coagulopathy U38-10
coagulum U38-12
coal U82-10
coalesce U114-10
coapt U137-5; U129-5
coaptation U129-5; U137-5
coarse movements U31-19
coat(ing) U86-8
coated tongue U103-5
cobalt U82-25
coca leaves U11-20
cocaine U11-20
cocainization U11-20
coccal /-oid U90-8
coccobacillary U90-7
coccygeal U28-20
coccyx, (os) U28-20
cochlea U60-11
cochlear U60-11
cochleitis U60-11
cochleostapedial U60-11
code U74-9; U84-13
Code Blue U123-4
codeine U11-18
codominant U84-27

codon U84-13
co-enzyme U78-8
coexist (with) U119-16
coexistence U119-16
coexistent /-ing U119-16
coexpress U83-16
cofactor U100-5
coffin U12-18
cognition U73-4
–, decreased U10-14
cognitive U73-4
– impairment U4-11; U142-3
cohort U100-3
coil U69-10
coiled U60-11
coital U68-5
coitus U68-5
cold intolerance U105-10
– turkey U11-12
–, catch a U4-2
–, common U94-9
colic U45-15; U104-15; U109-14
colicky U109-14
collagen U86-4
– fiber U86-5
collapse U6-5; U65-12
–, cardiovascular/circulatory U110-12
–, lung U111-15
collapsed U111-15
collapsing U110-12
collar bone U28-11
–, cervical U141-9
–, extrication U8-15
collateral U34-6
collateralization U34-6
collect U117-3
collecting system U48-9
collection U117-3
colliculus, superior U58-13
collide (with) U6-2
collimation U99-6
collision U6-2
colloid(al) U81-26
colon U45-15
colonic U45-15
colonize U46-16
colonoscopy U118-11
colonostomy U45-15
colony forming unit U139-10
color vision U59-9
colorectal U45-15
colostrum U71-24
colposcopy U50-8
column, vertebral/spinal U22-12
columnar epithelium U86-11
coma U7-14
–, diabetic/hyperglycemic U124-7
–, irreversible U7-18
comatose U124-7
combative U77-7
combativeness U77-7
combustion U81-17; U6-10
come and go U119-11
– in (teeth) U27-3

come to/round U7-6
comedo U114-6
comedogenic U114-6
comedonal U114-6
comfort U104-1
comfort(ing) U18-6
commemorate U74-8
commendable U18-5
commissural U41-3
commissure U41-3
commitment, involuntary U14-5
committee, hospital ethics U101-24
-, steering U101-25
commode U19-8
common (bile) duct U47-9
- carotid (artery) U34-10
- cold U94-9
- sense U57-5; U72-4
commotio U5-14
communal sauna U1-17
communicability U94-2
communicable disease U94-1
communicate U94-2
communication U34-6; U66-8
communicative U66-8,18
community health nurse U16-7
comorbid conditions U119-15
comorbidity U89-2
compact bone U28-2
compartment syndrome U30-7
compassion U75-8
compassionate U75-8
- use U101-23
compatibility U136-11; U14-11
compatible U136-11
compelling U11-2
compensatory activities U142-27
competence U73-4; U77-1
-, immunological U55-27
competent U73-4
-, legally U20-14; U73-4
complain (of) U103-2
complaint U103-2
complement pathway/system U39-10
complex U81-14
-, immune/antigen-antibody U39-9
complex, inferiority U77-12
-, major histocompatibility (MHC) U39-20
complexation U81-14
complexed (to) U81-14
complexion U25-11
compliance, lung U44-10
-, patient U120-15
compliant U44-10
complication U134-9
composure U75-4
compound U81-2; U77-21
comprehend U73-5
comprehensible U73-5
comprehension U73-5
compress U6-6; U64-10; U140-25; U142-22
compression U6-6,17; U64-10; U125-17

compression dressing U38-7
compromise U4-11; U1-6; U89-4
compulsion U11-2; U77-19
compulsive U11-2; U77-19
compunction U76-13; U77-10
concavity U30-8
conceal U25-18
conceited U75-20
conceive U70-2; U69-2
concentrate U36-13; U74-16; U81-23; U116-16
-, factor VIII U136-17
concentration U74-16; U81-23; U116-16
concept U73-8
conception U70-2
conceptive U70-2
conceptual U73-8
conceptus U70-2
concern U76-5; U20-9; U69-1
concerned U76-5; U96-1
concha U60-2
-, nasal U21-4
concomitant U119-16
concretion U89-21
concurrent U119-16
concussion U5-14
condensate U82-8
condensation U82-8
condition U1-9; U4-4
conditioning, abdominal U31-13
-, poor U1-9
condole with U12-12
condolence U12-12
condom U69-6
conduct U42-2; U61-4; U75-3; U20-13
conductance U42-2
conduction U42-2f
- anesthesia U93-6
-, saltatory U40-15
conductive U42-2; U61-4
conductivity U61-4; U82-6
condylar joint U29-6
condyle U28-4; U29-6
condyloma acuminatum U96-14
condylomatous U96-14
cone biopsy U127-12
cones (retina) U58-13
confabulation U74-18; U77-4
confer U55-27
conference, morbidity-mortality U20-10
confide U18-11
confidence U18-11; U75-17
- interval U100-17
confident U75-17
confidential U18-11
confidentiality U18-11
confined (to bed) U4-6; U19-12; U108-10
confinement U71-4
confines of resection U97-11
confirm U117-12
confirmation U117-12; U91-3; U101-17

confirmatory U117-12
conflict, parent-adolescent U80-8
-, unconscious U77-12
-, unresolved U4-15
confounder U100-18
confrontation testing U59-7
confused U77-4
confusion, mental U77-4; U7-8
confusional U77-4
congenital U89-6
congested U110-15
congestion U124-12
-, pulmonary U36-12
-, venous U110-15
congestive U110-15
- heart failure U124-12; U119-13
conization U127-12
conjugate U81-9
conjugation U81-9
conjunctiva U58-4
conjunctival U58-4
conjunctivitis U58-4
connect U74-5
connection U74-5
connective tissue U86-4
consanguineous U84-31; U37-1
consanguinity U84-31
conscientious U75-10
conscious U7-1
consequent U75-10
consistency U75-10,9
consistent U75-10
constipated U109-6
constipation U109-6
constitution U1-8; U25-3
constitutional U1-8; U25-3
constrict U6-6; U36-11; U89-19
constriction, bronchial U111-17
constrictive U6-6; U111-17
consult U15-3; U18-13; U102-14
consultant U15-3; U18-13
consultation U15-3; U18-13; U102-14
consumption U2-2
contact U62-8; U122-5
- isolation U94-3
contagion U94-1
contagiousness U94-1
contaminant U91-6
contaminated U139-2
contamination U91-6; U139-9
contemptuous U75-20
contents, gastric U111-4
contig U84-33
contiguity U87-11
contiguous U87-11
continence U112-15
continuation U87-12
continuity U87-12
continuous (with) U87-8,12
- passive motion U142-14
contraception U69-5; U70-2
contraceptive U69-5
-, oral U69-7
contract (illness) U4-2

contractile U31-1
contractility U31-1
contraction U31-1
contractions, uterine U71-3
contracture U31-1; U140-8; U142-1
contra-indication U120-10
contralateral U87-18
contrast U59-11
– agent U99-15
contrecoup U106-9
contribute U102-8
contribution U102-8
control U54-3; U88-2
– group U101-10
contusion U5-13; U6-6
convalesce U4-16
convalescence U4-16; U134-14
convalescent U4-16
– home U4-16
converge U58-14
convergence U59-13
convergent U59-13
conversion U78-6
– disorder U73-8; U77-6
– to laparotomy/open surgery U128-19
convert U78-6; U128-19
convey U42-2
convoluted U41-2
– tubule U48-7
convulsion U113-5
convulsive U113-5
Coombs' test U136-12
coordination U113-8
–, motor U31-19
co-oximetry U125-9
cope (with) U77-9
coping mechanism U77-9
copious U111-17
copper U82-29
copy U84-16
cor U32-1
coracoid process U30-11
cord blood U136-10
– stump U71-17
–, hepatic U47-4
–, spinal U41-15
–, testicular/ spermatic U52-7
–, umbilical U71-17
cordial U32-1
cords, tendinous U32-12
corium U56-3
corn U114-14; U19-10; U23-14
cornea U58-5
corneal U58-5
cornerstone U117-16
cornification U114-14
cornified cell U56-2
– layer U56-6
corona dentis U26-14
coronary U32-14; U124-11
– artery disease U124-11
coroner U12-21
coroner's investigation/inquest U12-21
corpora quadrigemina U41-13

corpse U12-14
corpsman, medical U16-9
corpulent U24-8
corpus callosum U41-3
– cavernosum U52-15
– clitoridis U50-12
– luteum U51-8
– luteum hormone U55-19
– spongiosum U52-16
– striatum U41-10
corpuscle, blood U37-4
–, pacinian/Pacini's U57-15
–, renal/Malpighian U48-6
corpuscular U37-4
correction U142-12
–, surgical U129-2
corrective U129-2
correlation U100-32
corroborate U117-12
corrosion U91-10
– resistance U82-6
corrosive U91-10
cortex U86-23
–, cerebral U41-6
Corti, organ of U60-12
cortical U41-6; U55-9; U86-23
corticobulbar U86-23
corticospinal tract U41-16
corticosteroid U55-4
corticosterone U55-10
corticotrop(h)in U55-9
corticotropic U55-9
cortisol U55-10; U78-16
cortisone U55-10
coryza U94-9; U45-4; U95-3
cosmid U84-33
costal U28-14
– margin U22-3; U87-9
costovertebral angle U28-14
cot U19-3
cotransfection U84-39
co-transport U49-3; U88-3
cotton applicator U17-13
– ball U140-23
cotyledons U85-14
cough U103-16; U66-6; U111-7
– up/out U103-17; U111-7
–, whooping U95-5
coughing U103-16; U111-7
–, vigorous U1-6
counseling U16-12; U18-4
–, contraceptive U69-10
counselor U16-12; U18-4
count, white blood U116-8
countenance U25-10
counterbalance U88-19
countercurrent U88-18
– mechanism U49-10
counterpulsation, intra-aortic balloon U125-8
counterregulatory U54-3
countershock U6-14; U110-14; U123-12
couple U81-12
coupling U81-12

course (vessel) U87-7
– (disease) U119-9; U18-6
– (drug) U120-5
–, postoperative U134-7
covalent U81-10
covariance U100-14
cover test U59-15
coverage, antibiotic U129-9
covert U119-6
cower U63-6
Cox regression model U100-35
coxa vara U28-21
coy U75-14
crack U106-1,11
– cocaine U11-20
crackles U111-9; U107-9
crackling U111-9
cradle U19-4
cramp U103-20; U109-14
cramping, abdominal U109-14; U103-20
cranial U28-7; U87-19
– fracture U106-8
craniocerebral injury/trauma U124-19
craniofacial U28-7
craniotomy U28-7
cranium U28-7
cranky U76-9
crash U6-2
– cart team U14-6
– helmet U6-2
craving U11-2
crawl(ing) U65-8
crazy U77-15
creamy U9-8
crease U22-9
create U129-4
creatine U78-15
creatinemia U78-15
creatinine U78-15
creatinuria U78-15
creep U65-8
cremation U12-16
crepitance U106-14
crepitant U111-9
crepitation U111-9; U106-14
crepitus U111-9; U106-14
crest U28-5
–, alveolar U26-13
–, pubic U30-14
crib U19-3
cricoid cartilage U29-2
cricothyr(oid)otomy U123-11
cricothyroid U54-6
crippling disease U4-4
crisis U105-18
– intervention service U13-3
–, clinical U124-1
–, hypertensive U124-6
–, thyrotoxic/hyperthyroid U124-8
crista U28-5; U83-7
critical U124-1
– care U125-1
– – unit U14-7

crops U95-7; U114-9
cross U76-10; U87-7
– infection U139-11
cross-breed U84-30
cross-bridge, myosin U78-10
cross-clamping U132-13
cross-eyed U59-4
cross-immunity U39-4
crossing U87-7
crossing-over U83-14; U84-17
crossmatch U136-10
cross-matching U14-12; U136-10
crossover U83-14; U84-17
–, treatment U101-14
cross-reactivity U39-2; U121-11
cross-section U87-5; U126-10
cross-tolerance U121-12
crotalid antivenin, polyvalent U91-15
crotch U22-10
crouch U63-4
croup U95-10
croupette U95-10
croupous U95-10
croupy U95-10
croupy cough U123-10
crowing inspiraton U95-10
crown, dental U26-14
crowning U71-15
crown-to-heel length U71-15
cruciate ligament U23-11
crush U64-10
– injury U6-6
crushing U64-10
– blow U6-4
crust U114-8
crusting U114-8
crutch use U142-2
crutches U19-13
–, mobilization on U142-13
cry U66-3,14
cryoablation U127-13
cryoanesthesia U93-3
cryocautery U127-8
cryofibrinogen U37-12; U136-17
cryoprecipitable U136-17
cryoprecipitate U136-17
cryopreservation U136-17
–, embryo U69-14
cryopreserve U69-14
cryoprobe U127-8; U132-8
cryoproteins U136-17
cryosupernatant U136-17
cryosurgery U127-8; U126-3
cryotherapy, local U142-21
cryptococcal U90-8
crystal U82-5
crystalize U82-5
crystalline U81-26
crystalloid U81-26
crystalluria U112-1
cubicle U19-1; U107-5
cubital U23-4
cuboid bone U28-25,27
cuboidal epithelium U86-11

cuddle U67-7
cuddling U68-2
cue U19-11; U74-2,11
cueing U19-11
cuff U141-8
–, blood pressure U17-8
cul-de-sac U50-15; U107-17
culdocentesis U125-17
culturable U116-6
culture U116-6
–, urine U116-15
cuneiform bone U28-25
cupping U64-9
cupric /-ous U82-29
curare U93-17
curative U120-2,9
cure U120-2
curet U132-10
curettage U132-10
curl (up) U63-6
curled U63-6
current flow, electrotonic U42-3
–, ionic U42-9
curtain U107-5
curvature U45-8
cushion U19-5
cusp U32-10
–, tooth U26-4
cuspid (tooth) U26-5
custodial care U77-25
custodian(ship) U77-25
custody U77-25
custom U73-13
cut U5-6; U6-7; U126-9
– edge U138-1
– surface U6-7
cutaneous U56-1
cutdown, venous U5-6; U34-4; U127-18
cuticle U56-15f
cuticular U56-16
cutis U56-1
cutoff (value) U100-24
cut-point U100-24
cutting, teeth U27-4
cyanic U91-9
cyanide U91-9
cyanin U91-9
cyanocobalamin U91-9
cyanogenic U91-9
cyanosed U108-6
cyanosis U108-6
cyanotic U108-6
cycle U78-6; U81-15
–, cardiac U33-2
–, sleep-wake U72-8
–, superovulated U69-17
cyclic U78-6
– AMP U83-17
– compound U81-7
cyclosporine U39-13
cylinder, axon/axis U40-2
cyst U89-24
–, dermoid U98-17

cystadenoma U98-4
cysteine U84-3
cystic U47-7; U48-11
– duct U47-8
cystoscopy U118-11; U128-2
cystourethrogram, voiding U112-12
cytapheresis U136-15
cytoadherence U83-1
cytochemistry U81-1
cytogenetics U84-1
cytokine U39-13; U35-12; U97-18
cytologic(al) U83-1
cytology U83-1; U86-1
cytomegalic inclusion disease U96-11
cytomegaloviral U96-11
cytometer U83-21
cytometry, flow U83-21
cytopathogenic U90-5
cytopenia U38-5
cytophotometry U83-21
cytoplasm U83-1
cytoplasmic extrusion U90-4
cytoskeleton U83-5
cytostatic U92-32
cytotoxic U91-4
– cell U39-16
cytotoxicity U39-16; U92-32
cytotrophoblast U85-14

D

dacryocystitis U58-9
dacryon U58-9
daily living, activities of U142-27
dairy product U3-5
damage U6-11
–, cerebral U74-17
damages (money) U6-11
damp(ish) U105-13
dampen U105-13
dampness U105-13
danders, animal U91-7
dandruff U114-7
danger U8-4
dangle U63-13
dangling U63-13
dark-skinned U56-1
dart U65-15
dash U65-15
data U101-15
date U74-3
–, due U70-10
daydream U72-9
dazed U7-9
dazzle U59-3
deactivate U83-18
dead U12-5
deaden (pain) U12-5; U135-3
deadly U12-5
deaf U61-9
deafen U61-9
deafening U61-9
deafferentation U40-4

deaf-mute U61-9
deaf-mutism U61-9
deafness U61-9; U113-13
dealer, drug U11-7
deaminase U47-16
deamination U82-17,15; U81-15
death U12-7
– in utero, fetal U91-22
– penalty U12-11
–, close to U12-1
–, self-inflicted U12-8
–, sudden cardiac U123-2
deathbed U12-1,7
debilitating U142-4
debility U142-4
debranching enzyme U78-10
debridement U140-12
debris, cellular U35-3; U114-8
–, loose U6-13
decade (of life) U80-11
decalcification U27-22; U31-14
decarboxylate U78-7
decarboxylation U78-7
decay U46-17; U82-1
– (vibration) U57-17
decease U12-7
deceased U12-5
deceleration injury U124-19
deceptive U75-12
decidua, membrana U85-13
decidual membrane U85-13
decile U100-11
decision-making U117-18
decisive U117-18
decisiveness U75-11; U73-6
decline U4-12; U116-20
decode U74-9
decompose U46-17
decomposition U46-17; U78-10
decompress U125-17
decompression sickness U6-17
–, pericardial U125-17
decongest U110-15
decontaminate U91-23; U139-9
decontamination U91-23
decrease U116-20
decubital U63-7
decubitus U63-7f; U4-6
decussate U58-15
decussation U41-14
dedifferentiation U97-8
deductible U18-15
deep-seated (ache) U104-4
defecate U46-18
defecation U46-18
defecatory U46-18
defect U142-4
defective U142-4
defeminization U50-2
defense mechanism U74-14
– system, body/host/immune U39-1
deferent duct U52-6
defervesce U105-18
defervescence U105-18

defervescent U105-18
defiant U75-18
defibrillate U123-12
defibrillation U123-12
defibrillator U110-7; U123-12
defibrination U38-14
deficiency U78-21
deficient U78-21
–, mentally U77-22
deficit U78-21; U142-4
–, end range U142-14
–, neurologic U113-7
deflate U44-5
deflation U44-5
deformation U89-5; U142-7
deformed U142-7
deformity U142-7
degas U91-23
degeneration U89-29
deglutition U46-2
deglutitive U46-2
degradable U78-10
degradation U78-10
degrees of freedom U100-16
dehiscence, wound U140-16
dehydrated U78-22
dehydration U6-15; U56-12; U78-22
dehydroepiandrosterone (DHEA) U55-16
deinstitutionalize U14-5
deja vu U74-18
dejection U77-17
delay of growth, constitutional U1-8
delead U91-23
delete U84-23
deleterious U91-1; U1-5
deletion U84-23
deliberate U71-26
delicacy U25-8,5
delicate U24-6; U25-8
delight, rapturous U76-16
delimit U87-10,6; U99-12
delineate U87-9; U99-12
delineation U118-17
delirious U10-14
delirium U7-16
– tremens U10-14
deliver (baby) U71-9
delivery U71-9
– room U15-17
– suite U14-9
deltoid (muscle) U30-13
delusion U77-20
–, hypochondriacal U4-9
delusional U77-20
demarcate U99-12
demarcation U87-10
demastication U27-19
demented U77-15,23
dementia U77-23
demineralization U82-5
demise U12-7
demonstrate U107-17
demonstration U107-17

demotivate U73-12
demulcent U82-3; U92-30
demyelination U40-14
denature U37-6
dendrite U40-2
dendritic cell U39-11
denervation U42-1
denial U102-10; U77-9; U12-7
dens U26-1
– molaris U26-7
densitometry U118-3
density U82-8
dental U26-1
– hygiene U1-5
dentin(e) U26-16
dentition U27-1,6
dentulous U27-7
denture U27-8
denudation U114-13
denude U114-13
deny U102-10
deodorant U62-3
deoxycholic acid U47-12
deoxycortisol, 11- U55-10
deoxygenated U44-6
deoxyribonuclease U84-11
depart U12-4
departed U12-7
Department of Health and Human Services (DHHS) U13-3
dependable U75-9
dependence U11-3,5
dependency U11-3; U14-5; U71-28
–, alcohol U10-12
dependent U142-28
– position U63-13
depigmentation U56-7; U114-3
deplete U49-8; U78-21; U88-15
depletion U49-8; U78-21; U88-15
deplorable U76-20
deploy U8-5
depolarization U42-6
– wavefronts U32-5
depolarize U42-6
depolymerization U84-36
deposit U78-20
deposition U78-20
depot U78-20
depress U88-14
depressant U77-17
depressed U76-22; U77-17; U116-20
– skull fracture U124-19
depression U76-22; U77-17; U88-14
–, postpartum U71-22
depressive U71-22; U76-22; U77-17
deprivation U77-11; U11-6
deprivational U77-11
deprive (of) U77-11
derailment, train U6-1
derangement U77-13
Dercum's disease U56-5
derivation U85-11
derivative U81-18; U85-11
derived (from) U81-18; U85-11

dermal U56-3
- ridges U56-11
dermatitis U114-1
dermatologic(al) U56-3; U114-1
dermatologist U15-10
dermatology U15-10
dermatomal U85-22
dermatome U56-3; U85-22; U114-1
dermatophytes U90-18
dermatosis U114-1
dermis U56-3
dermoepidermal U56-3
dermoid (cyst) U98-17
dermoidectomy U98-17
desaturated U81-24
descendant U84-29
descent (birth) U71-14,3
-, line of U84-29
designer drug U11-17
desire U73-12
-, sexual U68-4
desoxyribonucleic acid (DNA) U84-11
despair U76-21; U77-17
despondent U76-20
desquamate U56-20
desquamation U56-20; U86-12
desquamative U56-20
destabilization U125-2
destabilize U31-15
desufflate U128-10
desufflation lever U133-15
detach U81-8
detached U76-15; U77-8; U138-2
detachment U58-7; U76-15; U77-8
-, retinal U59-5; U124-1
-, sense of U73-10
detect U117-5
detection U117-5
detergent U81-2; U91-10
deteriorate U4-12
deterioration U4-12; U124-1
- of vision U40-1
-, mental U77-23
determinant U39-7; U117-2
determination U75-11; U117-2
determine U117-2
determined U75-11
deterrent U12-11
detonate U6-9
detonation U6-9
detoxi(fi)cation, alcohol U10-15
detoxicate U10-15
detoxification U91-23
detoxify U10-15; U91-23
detriment U6-11
detrimental U6-11; U91-1
detrusor (muscle) U48-11
- instability/hyperreflexia U112-8
detumescence U53-5; U69-6
deuterium U82-9
devastating U76-12
devastation U6-20
develop U80-3
development U80-3

developmentalist, child U15-12
deviant U68-15
deviate U59-15
deviation (data) U100-13
-, eye U59-15
-, sexual U68-15
devoid of U56-10
deworm U90-16
dexterity, motor U31-19
dextroamphetamine U11-17
dextrose U79-7
diabetes U124-7
diabetic U124-7
- coma U124-7
diacetylmorphine U11-19
diacylglycerol U82-13
diagnosable U117-10
diagnose U117-10
diagnosed U117-10
diagnosis U117-11
diagnostic U117-11
- procedure U20-8
- workup U20-8
diagnostician U117-11
diagnostics U117-11
diagram U100-27
dialysate U125-21
dialysis U125-21
dialyze U125-21
diaphanoscopy U99-16
diaphoresis U105-15
diaphoretic U105-15
diaphragm U43-12
-, contraceptive U69-9
-, urogenital U52-13
-, urogenital/pelvic U48-15
diaphragmatic U43-12
diaphyseal U28-3
diaphysis U28-3
diarrhea U109-10
diarthrodial joint U29-3
diarthrosis U29-3
diastasis, tibiofibular U29-13
diastole U33-3
diathermy U127-9
-, ultrasonic U142-23
dichromatic U59-9
die U12-4
diencephalic U41-12
diener U16-14
diet, healthful U1-1
dietary U2-12; U16-13
dietetics U16-13; U2-12
dietician U16-13; U2-12
dieting program U24-1
dietitian U16-13
differential diagnosis U117-15
differentiate U85-11; U97-8; U117-15
differentiation U85-11; U97-8; U117-15
difficulty swallowing U109-5
diffuse U88-4
diffusible U88-4
diffusion U81-21; U88-4
digest U46-11

digestant U46-11
digestion U46-11
digestive U46-11
- tract U45-1
digit U23-7; U28-18
digital U23-7
dihydrate U82-9
dilatation U36-11; U132-17
-, cervical U71-12
dilate U36-11
dilation set U133-12
dilator U133-12; U132-17
diluent U81-23
dilute U36-13; U81-23
dilution U81-23; U116-17
dim(ness) U59-11
dimer U81-6
dimerization U81-6
diminished U116-20
dimming U59-11
diphtheria U95-9
diphtheria-pertussis-tetanus vaccine
  (DPT) U122-10
diphther(it)ic U95-9
diphtheroid U95-9
diplegia U113-7
diploid U84-9
diplopia U113-11; U58-16
dipso(maniac) U10-10
dire U6-18; U12-2
directive, advance/medical U20-14
disability U142-3; U1-11; U4-8
- benefits U142-3
- status U142-3
-, service-connected U13-3
disabled U1-11; U4-8
-, mentally U77-22
disablement U142-3
disabling (disease) U4-8; U142-3
disaccharide U3-16
disappear U4-15
disappearance U4-15
disapproval U67-11
disarticulation U142-6; U29-1
disaster medical assistance teams
  U13-1
- relief organization U13-12
-, natural U6-20
discharge U20-16; U88-11; U46-18
-, nervous U42-6
disclose U102-3; U107-17; U118-1
disclosure U18-11
discoloration, dusky U25-12
-, yellowish U108-4
discolored U114-9
discomfort U103-7; U104-1
-, residual U4-14
discontinuation U121-6
discontinue (therapy) U121-6; U88-10
discontinuous U87-12
discouragement U77-17
disc, optic U58-14
discrete U114-10
discriminate U117-15; U97-9

discrimination U117-15; U73-5
-, flavor U57-2
-, self vs. nonself U39-21
disdainful U67-16
disease U4-4
-, childhood U95-1
-, communicable/contagious U94-1
-, fourth U95-6
-, infectious U94-1
-, reportable/notifiable U94-1
diseased U4-4; U89-2
disease-free U4-4
disequilibrium U88-19
disfigured U4-8
disfigurement U142-7
disfiguring scar U142-7
dish U2-8
-, kidney U17-12
dishonest U75-12
disillusioned U73-10
disinfectant U17-15
disinfection U17-15; U139-5
disinhibition U88-14; U77-8
disintegration U82-34
disintegration of personality U73-5
disk, germ/embryonic U85-6
-, intervertebral U29-12
-, optic U58-14
dislocation U5-20; U106-4
dislodge U71-7
disloyal U75-10
disomy U84-25
disorder U4-4
-, infantile/juvenile U95-1
-, mental U77-16
disordered U4-4
disorientation U77-4; U107-12; U7-8
disoriented U77-4
disparity U88-19
dispatcher U8-9
dispensary U9-5
dispense U9-5
dispersal U81-22
disperse U81-22
dispersibility U81-16
dispersion U81-22; U91-14
displace U64-4
displacement U5-20; U64-4; U106-4
display U107-17
disposable U139-4
disposal U139-4
disposition U75-4
disrupted speech U67-17
disruption U5-19; U106-5
disruptive U5-19
Disse, spaces of U47-4
dissect (free) U126-12
dissecting microscope U126-12
- scissors U132-4
dissection U87-5; U126-12
-, aortic U124-6
-, balloon U128-14
dissemination, hematogenous U94-16
dissimilation U88-8

dissipate U105-14
dissipation U105-14
- of heat U88-19
dissociate U81-22
dissociation U81-22
dissociative disorder U77-6
- state U74-20
dissolution U81-22
dissolve U81-22; U88-5
distal U87-14; U26-21
distance, interocclusal U27-14
distant U87-11
distend U110-16
distensibility U110-16
distensible U109-8; U110-16
distention, abdominal U109-8
-, neck vein/jugular venous U110-16
distillate U82-8
distillation U82-8
distinct U87-12
distinction U117-15
distinctive U87-12
distinguish U117-15
distorted U74-10
distortion U5-16
- (data) U100-18
distract U74-16
distractible U76-15
distraction U74-16; U141-3
distraught U107-11
distress U113-2; U104-2
- call U6-19
-, (in) acute U107-11
-, respiratory U111-5
distressed U107-11
distribution, frequency U100-12
-, volume of U91-17
district nurse U16-7
disturbance U76-21; U77-13
disturbed U76-21
diuresis U49-6; U55-24
diuretic U49-6
diuretics U92-21
divalent U81-10
divergence U59-13
diversion U1-10
divert U1-10
diverticulum, allantoenteric U85-17
divide U126-14
division U14-9; U126-14
-, cell U85-3
divorced U102-9
dizziness U103-13; U113-6
dizzy U103-13; U113-6; U7-5
doc U15-1
doctor, medical (MD) U15-1
doctor's bag/case U17-1
doctorate U15-1
documentation U101-15
dogtrot U65-14
dolor U104-6
domain, functional U84-3
domestic violence U13-13
dominance U84-27

dominant U84-27
donate U69-16; U129-15
donor U129-15
- oocyte U69-16
-, blood U136-9
-, cadaver U129-17
-, living U129-17
Donovan body U96-6; U86-20
donovanosis U96-6
dopamine U42-11; U82-17
dopaminergic U40-8
dope U11-1
doping U11-24
dormancy U94-6
dormant U94-6
dorsa of the hands U114-5
dorsal U22-11; U87-16
dorsiflexion U87-16
dorsorecumbent U63-10
dorsosupine U63-8
dorsum U22-11
dosage U91-11; U121-7
- form U9-6
- formulation U9-6
-, recommended U18-5
dose U121-7
- distribution U99-9
-, maintenance U135-19
-, radiation absorbed U99-10
dose-dependent U121-7
dosimeter U121-7; U99-9
dosimetry U118-3; U99-9
double bonds U81-24
- gloving U139-17
- helix U84-11
double-check U18-9
double-stapled U137-12
doubt U117-8
doubtful U116-23; U117-8
douche U19-10
- massage U142-15
down(cast) U76-22
downers U11-16; U92-24
downregulate U83-18
downsize U133-11
doze U72-2
dozy U72-2
drag U64-13; U23-1
dragging U65-11
drain U36-6; U140-15
- off U125-15
drainage U140-15
-, venous U36-6
-, ventricular U125-15
drape U19-1; U139-7
draw on U10-16
drawn U25-7
dread U6-21; U77-5
dream U72-9
dressing U140-17
-, pressure U91-14
dribbling U49-17
drill U74-6
drills, calisthenic U1-15

drink(ing) U3-24; U10-1f
drinker U10-10
drip U136-3
- feeding U125-19
drive U73-11
-, respiratory U125-10
driving force U73-11
droll U75-7
drooling U27-9
droop U56-19; U64-15; U113-17
drooping U56-19; U113-17
droopy U64-15
drop U64-15
dropout (study) U101-29
drops (medication) U9-11
dropsical U108-10; U109-9
dropsy U108-10
-, abdominal/peritoneal U109-9
drowning U6-16
drowse U72-1
drowsiness U7-5; U72-1
drowsy U72-1; U103-13
drug U9-3
- delivery U121-4
- eruption U108-7
- interaction U121-11
- release U121-4
- targeting U121-4
-, anti-inflammatory U92-11
drug-abusing U11-6
drug-dependent U11-3
druggist U9-4
drug-induced U9-3; U119-8; U121-15
drug-related U9-3; U11-1
drugs, recreational U1-10
drum membrane U17-7
- rupture U60-4
drumstick appearance U108-11
drunk U10-1,10
drunkenness U10-1
dry (out) U10-4
- nurse U16-6
drying (of the throat) U109-5
dubious U117-8
duct, excretory U52-11
-, right lymphatic U35-7
-, thoracic U35-7
ductility U82-6
ductular U47-6
ductule U47-6
ductus arteriosus U32-11
- deferens U52-6
due date U70-10
dull U76-17; U77-8
- (ache) U104-4
dulled (obturator) U133-6
dullness, shifting U109-9
dumb U61-11
dumbness U61-11
duodenal U45-10
duodenojejunal U45-10
duodenum U45-10
duplication U84-23
dura (mater) U41-8

dural U41-8
duskiness U25-12; U114-1
dusky U25-12
- red U95-2; U114-10
dust U91-7
dust-borne U91-7
dust-tight U91-7
duty, on/off U20-4; U17-16
duty-bound U20-4
dwarf U24-4
dwarfism U24-4
dye U116-4
dying U12-4
dynamometer U142-16
dypareunia U68-7
dysarthria U113-10; U61-11
dysarthric U113-10; U66-9
dysautonomia U40-6
dyscoordinated U113-8
dyscrasia U37-10
dysenteric U94-18
dysequilibrium U57-18
dysesthesia U104-17
dysfunction U4-4
-, sexual U68-7
dysfunctional U4-4
dyshematopoiesis U38-1
dyslexia U113-9
dyslexic U113-9; U74-5
dysmotility U46-6
dyspepsia U109-1
dyspeptic U109-1
dysphagia U109-5; U45-2; U87-22
dysphagic U109-5
dysphasia U113-10
dysphonia U66-23; U103-6; U113-10
dysphoric U76-16
dyspnea U111-1
dyspneic U111-1
dyspraxia U113-9
dysreflexia U42-12
dysrhythmia U110-6; U33-6
dyssomnia U72-16
dyssynergia U31-4
dystonia U142-17
dystonic U142-17
dysuria U112-1
dysuric U112-1

E

ear U21-15
- ossicle U60-5
-, inner U60-1
-, middle U60-1
-, outer/external U60-1
earache U104-4
eardrum U60-4
    U21-15
earlobe U60-2; U21-15
early-onset U119-5,14
earning incapacity U142-4
earpieces, binaural U17-2

earshot U60-1
earwax U60-1,15
ease, (ill) at U76-19
easily transmitted U4-2
easygoing U75-16
eat U2-1
eating disorder U4-4; U80-8
ecchymosis U89-27
ECG, ergometric/ exercise U142-16f
echo U118-15
echocardiogram U118-15
echocardiographic U118-15
echocardiography U118-15
echodensity U118-15
echoencephalography U118-15
echogenicity U118-15
echolucent U118-15
Ecstasy (XTC) U11-17
ecstasy U76-16
ecstatic U76-16
ectoderm U85-6
ectomorph U25-2
ectoparasite U90-13
ectopic beat U110-6
eczema U114-1
eczematous /-toid U114-1
edema U108-10; U5-15
-, pulmonary U111-13
edematous U108-10; U5-15
edentulism U27-7
edentulous U27-7
edge U87-10
-, be on U76-6
-, incisal U26-3
edgy U76-6
edible U2-5
education U142-18
effacement U71-12
effectiveness U101-26
effector organ U40-3
efferent U40-4
efficacious U101-26
efficacy U101-26; U121-9
efficiency U101-26
effleurage U71-10; U142-15
effort thrombosis of the axillary U34-4
-, physical U64-19
effortless U64-19
effusion, pleural U111-12
egg collection U69-17
ego U75-21; U77-2
egocentric U75-21
ego(t)istic U75-21
egophony U111-11
ejaculate U53-11
ejaculation U53-11
ejaculatory U53-11
eject U33-8
ejection U88-16
- period U33-8
-, ventricular U33-8
elastic U31-16
- fiber U86-5
elasticity U31-16; U86-5

elastin U31-16; U86-5
elated U77-18; U19-1
elation U77-18
elbow U23-4
elderly U80-2,13
elective U126-5
-, medical U15-6
electric current U6-14
electrical accident U6-14
electricity U6-14
electrocardiogram (ECG/EKG) U118-14
electrocardiograph U118-14
electrocardiographic U118-14
electrocardiography U118-14
electrocautery U127-9
- snare U127-11
electrocoagulation U127-10
electroconization U127-12
electrocute U6-14
electrocution U6-14
electrode, hook U128-11
-, needle U118-13
electrodessication U127-14
electroencephalogram (EEG) U118-12
electroencephalography U118-12
electrolysis U78-23
electrolyte(s) U78-23
-, serum U116-7
electrolytic U78-23
electrolyze U78-23
electromassage U142-15
electromyogram U118-13
electromyographic U118-13
electromyography (EMG) U118-13; U142-23
electron U81-11
electrondense U83-11
electroneurography U118-13
electroneuromyography U118-13
electrophoresis U84-35
electroshock U6-14; U123-12
electrosurgery U126-3; U127-9
electrotherapy U142-23
element, chemical U82-1
elemental U82-1
elevate U64-16; U116-19; U129-11
elevated U116-19
elevation U64-16; U116-19; U129-11
- (leg) U142-21
elicit U88-13; U102-3; U17-9
elicitation U102-3
eliminate U46-18; U49-7
elimination U49-7
- half-life U91-17
elongation U84-19
eloquent U66-18
elu(a)te U83-20
elu(tria)tion U83-20
emaciated U25-7; U108-14
emaciation U25-7; U108-14
emanation U99-2
embarrassed U76-12
embarrassing U72-6
embarrassment U76-12

embarrassment, circulatory U125-5
-, vascular U59-16
embittered U76-11
embolic U38-12
embolism U38-12
embolism, pulmonary U124-13
embolization U38-12; U124-13
embolus U38-12; U124-13
embrace U67-7
embrasure, incisal U26-3
embryo U70-4; U85-1
- freezing/cryopreservation U69-14
- transfer U69-16
embryoblast U85-5
embryogenesis U70-4; U85-1
embryologic U85-1
embryonal /-ic U70-4
embryonal carcinoma U98-16
embryotoxic U91-12; U85-1
embryotoxicity U91-12
emergence (anesthesia) U135-21
emergency U6-18; U14-6; U126-5
- medical service helicopter U8-5
- medical technician U8-6
- room/department U14-6
-, medical U124-1
emesis U103-12
- basin U17-12
emetic U103-12; U91-25; U92-12
eminence U87-27
emission U53-11
emissions, vehicular U6-3
emmetropia U59-17
emollient U92-30
- ointment U56-9
emotion U76-1
emotional neglect U77-11
emotionless U76-1
emphysema, pulmonary U111-16
emphysematous U111-16
empty U46-8
emptying, bladder U49-16
empyema U111-14
empyemal U111-14
emulsification U81-25
emulsifier U81-25
emulsify U81-25
emulsion U81-25
enamel, dental/tooth U26-15
encapsulated U29-9; U97-9
encapsulation U97-9
encephalitic U94-13
encephalitis U94-13; U41-1
encephalon U41-1
enchondroma U98-12
encoded U74-9
encoding U74-9; U84-13
encounter U117-5
encroach (on/upon) U113-15
encrusted U114-8
end (of life) U12-7
- plate, muscle/motor U87-2
- range deficit U142-14
endanger U8-4

endemic U94-8
end-expiratory U44-3
endfeel U142-14
endocarditis U32-5
endocardium U32-5
endocervical U50-7
endochondral U29-2
endoclip U138-15
endocytose U83-15
endocytosis U83-15
endoderm U85-6
endogenous U88-10
endo-GIA stapler U138-17
endointoxication U91-14
endoloop U138-5
endometrial U50-6
endometrioid U50-6
endometriosis U50-6
endometrium U50-6
endomorph U25-2
endonuclease, restriction U84-32
endophlebitis U136-7
endoplasmic U83-2
endoplasmic reticulum (ER) U83-8
endoprosthesis U142-6
endoscope U128-2; U133-2
endoscopic retrograde cholangio-pancreatography (ERCP) U118-20
- suturing U138-1
endoscopist U128-2
endoscopy U128-2
endosonography U118-17
endospore U90-3
endostapler U138-17
endothelial leukocyte U37-9
endothelialization U86-14
endothelium U86-14
endotoxemia U91-22
endotoxin U91-4
- shock U124-5
endotracheal U43-8
- intubation U123-10
endpoint U100-20
endsystolic U33-3
endurance U64-2
endure (pain) U4-3
energetic U1-6; U76-17
energy U1-6
- metabolism U78-12
energy-rich U78-12
engagement U71-14
engender U37-7
engorged U53-3f
- neck veins U110-6
engorgement U50-14; U110-15
-, breast U71-27
engraft U130-1
engram U74-12
engulf U83-11; U85-15
enhanced U88-12
enhancement U88-12
enlargement, cardiac U110-9
enquiry, functional U102-11
enraged U76-10

enrollment, patient U101-4
ensheathed U86-8
ensnare U127-11
ENT specialist U15-19
enter U87-7
enteral U45-1; U125-19
enteric U45-1
– fever U94-19
enteric-coated capsule U122-6
enteritis U94-18
enterocolitis U94-18
enteropathogenic U90-5
enterotoxin U45-1
enterovaccine U122-2
enterovirus U90-10
entity, clinical U108-2
entoderm U85-6
entrap U113-15; U133-16; U44-9
entrapment sack U133-16
–, nerve U113-15
entry, portal of U91-16
enunciation U66-13
enuresis U112-16
enuretic U112-16
envelop U85-15
envelope U86-8
envenomate U91-14
envenomation U91-14
environmental hazards U91-5
envision U59-6
enzymatic U78-8
enzyme U78-8; U81-16
enzyme, rare-cutter U84-32
eosinophil U37-8
eosinophilia U37-8
ephelides U114-5
epicanthal U58-3
epicardium U32-5
epicondyle U28-4; U29-6
epidemic U94-8
epidemiologic U94-8
– study U13-11
epidermal U56-2
epidermis U56-2
epidermoid U56-2
– (cyst) U98-17
epidermolytic U56-2
epididymal U52-5
epididymis U52-5
epididymitis U52-5
epididymovasostomy U52-5
epidural U41-8
epigastric pain U109-12
– region U22-3; U45-8
epigastrium U22-3
epiglottis U43-7
epilepsy U124-9
epileptic U124-9
epinephrine U55-11
epiphyseal U28-3
epiphysis U28-3
episcleral U58-6
episiotomy U71-18
episode U103-4

episodic U103-4; U119-11
episomal U84-8
episome U84-8
epistaxis U110-20
epithalamus U41-9
epithelial (tissue) U86-7
epithelialization U140-6
epithelioid U86-7
epithelioma U86-7
epithelium U86-7 ff
epitope U39-7
eponychial U56-16
eponychium U56-16
Epsom salt(s) U91-24
equilibratory U57-18
equilibrium U57-18; U88-19
–, emotional U77-9,16
equivocal U116-23; U117-4
erect chest x-ray U124-16
erect(ed) U53-3 f; U63-2
erectile U53-3
– dysfunction U4-4
erection U53-3
erector U53-3; U63-2
– pili muscle U56-14
ergometer U142-16
ergometric bike U142-16
ergometry U142-16
ergotherapy U142-26
erode U27-21
erogenous U68-9
erosion U114-13; U27-21
erosive U114-13; U27-21
erotic U68-9
eroticism U68-9
error, systematic U100-18
eructate U46-3
eructation U46-3
erupt (teeth) U27-3
eruption (skin) U108-9; U114-2
– (teeth) U27-3
–, impeded U27-3
eruptive U114-2
erythema U108-7; U114-2
erythematous U108-7; U114-2
erythroblast U37-5
erythrocyte U37-5
– sedimentation rate U116-12
erythroid U37-5
erythropoesis U37-5
eschar U114-8; U140-9
escort U77-24
escutcheon U52-19
Esmarch's tourniquet U135-18
esophageal U45-5
– reflux U109-4
esophagitis U45-5
esophagogastric U45-5
esophagus U45-5
esotropia U59-4,17; U113-11
essence U82-13
establish (diagnosis) U118-22
ester U78-7; U82-14
esterase U78-7; U82-14

esterification U78-7; U82-14
esterify U78-7
esterifyable U78-7
estimate U117-2
estimation U117-2; U100-29
estradiol U55-18
estrin U55-17
estriol U55-18
estrogen U55-17
estrogenic U55-17
estrone U55-18
ethanol U47-17
ethmoid (bone) U28-8
ethylene U82-15
etiologic U119-2
etiology U119-2
euchromatin U84-6
euglycemia U78-13
eukaryote U83-3
euphoria U76-16; U77-18
euphoric U76-16; U77-18
eustachian tube U60-7
euthanasia U12-9
euthyroid U54-6
euvolemia U36-7
evacuate (victim) U8-3
– (bowel/bladder) U46-18; U109-15
evacuation U8-3; U46-18
–, distant U6-12
evaluate U107-1; U117-1
evaluation U117-1
evanescent U114-11
evaporate U82-3; U105-14; U127-15
evaporation U105-14
evaporative U105-14
event U100-19
–, primary U100-20
eversion U31-8
evert U31-8
evidence U117-9; U101-17
–, testimonial U6-13
evident U117-9
evisceration U86-21
evoke U88-13; U57-1
evoked potentials (EP) U125-14
exacerbate U119-17
exacerbation U119-17; U102-2
examination, physical U107-2
–, follow-up U18-9
–, postmortem U12-20
examine U107-1; U118-1
examiner U107-1
examining table U107-1
exanthem(a) U114-2
exanthematous U114-2
exceed U116-16
exchange U78-6
excise U126-9,15
excision U126-15
excitability U42-8; U57-1; U76-7
excitable U76-7
excitation U42-8; U57-1; U76-8
excitatory U42-8; U57-1
excite U42-8; U57-1

excited U76-8
excitement U57-1; U76-8; U77-18
excitomotor U42-8
excludable U117-14
exclude U117-14
exclusion U117-14
exclusive U117-14
excoriation U114-13
excrement U46-20
excrementitious U46-20
excreta U46-20; U88-11
excrete U49-6; U88-11
excretion U46-20
–, urinary U49-6
excretory U49-6
excursion, chest/respiratory U107-16
–, respiratory U44-10
excursive U107-16
execution U12-11
exercise U1-12; U64-18
– regimens U14-3
– tolerance test U142-17
–, isometric U142-17; U1-15
exercise-induced U119-8
exert U64-19
exertion U64-19
exertional U64-19
exfoliate (skin) U56-20
– (teeth) U27-5
exfoliation U56-20; U27-5
exfoliative U56-20
exhalation U44-2
exhale U44-2
exhausted U64-19; U76-18
exhaustion U64-19; U76-18
exhibit U107-17
exigency U6-18
exiting U128-18
exocoelomic cavity U85-7
exocytosis U83-15
exogenous U88-10
exon U84-14
exonic U84-14
exotoxin U91-4
exotropia U59-4
expand U44-10; U107-16
expandable U107-16
expanded access U101-22
expansion U136-13
–, chest (wall) U107-16
–, failure of U111-15
–, lung U44-10
expectant U70-5
expected date of delivery/confinement U70-10
expectorant U103-17; U111-7; U92-15
expectorate U103-17; U111-7; U92-15
expectoration U103-17; U111-7
expel U71-15,11; U46-15
expenditure, energy U78-12; U88-3; U105-2
experience U57-4; U102-2
experimental group U101-10
expiration U44-3

expiration date U17-1
expire U12-4; U44-3
explantation U129-12
explicit U74-4
exploration U107-6; U126-11
exploratory U107-6
explore U107-1
explosion U6-9
expose U91-5; U99-7
exposure U122-5
– limit, permissible (PEL) U91-5
–, surgical U126-7; U128-1
–, toxic U91-5
express U54-2; U83-16; U84-26
expression U54-2; U84-26
–, gene U83-16
expressivity U84-26
expulsion U71-15,13
expulsive U71-15
exsanguinate U38-9
exsanguination U38-9; U37-1
exspiratory U44-3
extend U31-3; U97-11; U141-3
extension U31-3; U141-3
–, tumor U97-11
extensor U31-3
extent U97-11
extern U15-6
external oblique (muscle) U30-14
externalization U77-12
externship U15-6
extirpation U126-15; U127-13
extracapsular U29-9
extracellular U83-2
– matrix U86-19
extracorporeal U138-3
– circulation U16-11; U125-11
extracorpuscular U37-4
extraction socket U26-13
extraglandular U54-1
extrahepatic U47-6
extraocular muscles U58-16
extraoral U26-25
extraprostatic U52-10
extrapyramidal U41-16
extrasystole U33-3; U110-6
extrasystolic U110-6
extravasate U38-6; U136-7
extravasation U38-6; U136-7
extravascular U34-1; U136-7
extremity U23-1
–, lower U23-8
extremity, upper U23-2
extricate U8-3; U90-16
extrication collar U8-15
extroversion U75-13
extrovert U75-13
extubate U135-17
extubation U123-10
exuberant U1-6; U76-16
exudate U140-13
exudative U140-13
exultation U76-16
exulted U76-16

eye U21-3
– alignment U59-15
– bulb U58-2
– chart U17-5
– deviation U59-15
– movement, conjugate U59-16
– –, saccadic U59-14
– movements, uncontrolled U113-12
– socket U58-1
– specialist U15-18
– tape U125-25
–, black U5-13
–, white of the U58-6
eyeball U58-2; U21-3
eyebrow U21-3
eyeground(s) U58-12,2
eyelashes U58-3; U21-3
eyelid U58-3; U21-3
eyepiece U133-4
eye-rolling U64-8
eyesight U59-6
eyestrain U58-2
eyewitness U6-13

F

Fab fragment/portion U39-3
face U25-10; U67-8; U21-2
– mask U139-18
– shield U139-18
face-down U63-9
facetious U76-15
facial U25-10; U67-8; U21-2
– features U25-10
– flush U108-8
– skeleton/bones U28-9
facies U25-10; U21-2
facility, acute care U14-3
–, independent living (ILF) U14-3
factor U55-1; U100-5
– III U37-14
–, coagulation/clotting U38-13
–, Rh U37-17
–, rheumatoid U39-3
factorial design U101-13
faculties, mental U73-2
fade U4-14; U74-10; U114-5
fag U10-19
Fahrenheit U105-1
failed U123-6
failing U123-6
failure, heart U110-12
–, multiple organ U125-1
–, therapeutic U117-1
faint U110-11
–, to feel U7-4f
fainting U110-11
faintness U7-4; U103-13
fair U25-13
fair-complexioned U25-11
faith healer U15-23
faithful U75-10
fall U6-5; U65-12

fall out (teeth) U27-5
falling sickness U6-5
fallopian tube U50-4
false U75-12
- negative/positive U100-22
falsehood U75-12
falsity U75-12
falter U66-20
familial U102-7; U89-7
family doctor U4-9
- physician U15-8
- planning U69-5
family-centered U102-7
fancy U73-9
fang U91-16
fango U1-20
fango (mud) pack U142-22
fanning U105-14
fantasist U73-9
fantasize U73-9
fantasy U73-9
far-sighted(ness) U59-17
fascia U30-7
fascial U30-7
fascicle U30-1,5
fascicular U30-1; U31-5
fasciculation U30-1; U31-5
fasciotomy U30-7
fashion U129-4
fast, observation of the U77-3
fastigial U105-17
fastigium U105-17
fasting U2-15; U47-11; U54-10; U78-2
- blood glucose U116-12
- blood sugar U116-19
fast-twitch U31-5
fat U24-8; U79-11
- layer, subcutaneous U56-5
- pad U24-5
fatal U12-2
- illness U4-1
fatality U12-2
fate U12-2
fatigability U103-8; U113-3
fatigue U103-8
fat-splitting U46-11
fatty U24-5; U56-5
- acid, essential U79-12
- streak U78-6
fauces U45-4; U17-3; U21-12
-, pillars of the U35-6
faucial U45-4
Fc fragment/region U39-3
fear U77-5
fearful U76-5
feasible U116-2
features, clinical U103-3
-, facial U25-10
febricide U105-4
febrifacient U105-4
febrifuge U105-4
febrile U105-3
- illness U4-1
fecal U46-20

fecal impaction U109-15
- occult blood test U118-6
feces U46-20; U45-17
feculent U46-20
fed U2-3; U79-1
- up U76-9
feeble U4-7; U103-9
feeble pulse U4-7
feeble-minded U4-7
feebleness U103-9
feed U2-3; U79-1
feeding tube U125-18
-, intravenous/drip U125-19
fee-for-service insurance U18-15
- reimbursement U13-3
feel U57-2; U76-1
- for U107-7
feeling U57-3; U76-1
feet U23-13
feldspar U82-30
fellow U15-7
fellowship U15-7
felon U114-16; U24-5
female U50-2
feminine U50-2
feminization U53-12
feminize U50-2
femoral U28-23
femorotibial joint U28-23
femur U28-23
fenestra vestibuli U60-8
ferment U46-12
fermentable U46-12
fermentation U46-12
Fern testing U51-9
ferrous U82-21
ferric U82-21
fertile U69-2; U70-1
fertility U69-2; U70-1
fertilization U69-2; U70-1
fertilize U69-2; U70-1
fester U140-14
festinating U65-11
festination U65-11
fetal U70-4; U85-1
- alcohol syndrome U10-13
- attitude U71-5
- lie U71-5
- movements U70-13
- portion U71-16
- position U71-5
- presentation U71-5
- rotation U71-14
fetid U109-2
fetishism U68-15
fetoplacental U71-16
fetoprotein U70-4
fetus U70-4; U85-1
fever U105-3
- of unknown origin (FUO) U105-16
feverish U105-3
fiber, afferent/sensory U40-4
-, collagen(ous) U86-5
-, dietary U79-16

fiber, efferent/motor U40-4
fiberoptic(s) U133-3,2
fibrillation, atrial U110-7
fibrillatory U110-7
fibrin U37-12
- glue U137-14
fibrinogen U37-12
fibrinolysin U37-15; U38-14
fibrinolysis U37-15,12; U38-14
fibroadenoma U98-4,8
fibroareolar U86-6
fibrocartilage U29-2
fibroid (tumor) U98-8
fibroma U98-8
fibromatosis U98-8
fibromatous U98-8
fibromyoma U98-8
fibrositis U98-8
fibrous tissue U86-4
fibula U28-24
fibular U28-24
fidgety U64-17; U76-6
field measures U8-1
figure U25-1
figure-of-eight suture U137-19
filament (suture) U137-7
filamentous U83-5
file (instrument) U132-12
fill U49-15
filling U33-9
- pressure, cardiac/ventricular U33-9
-, bladder U49-15
film, plain U99-19
-, plain abdominal U45-6
filter U49-1
- paper (strips) U83-22
- tip U10-19
filtrate, glomerular U49-1
filtration, gel U83-22
-, product of U49-1
fimbriae U50-4
fimbriated U50-4
finding U117-6
-, case U102-13
fine U1-3
- coordination U31-20
- motor skills U31-20
fine-particulate matter U91-6
finger U23-7
- clubbing U108-11
fingernail U23-7
fingertip U23-7
fingerwidth U23-7
Finnish bath U1-17
fire U6-10
firearms U6-8
firing U42-6
- rate, resting U42-8
firm U1-11; U75-11
firmness U1-11
first aid U8-1
- grade U73-9
first-born U71-1
fission U78-7; U85-10

fissure U87-26; U106-11
-, cerebral U41-5
-, palpebral U59-2
fissured U87-26
fissuring U114-14
fist U23-6
fistula U89-25
fistul(iz)ation U89-25
fit U1-9
fitful U72-2
fitness, physical U1-9
fits of temper U76-2
fitting, prosthetic U142-6
fix(ate) U59-14
fixation U59-14
fixator U141-4
fixer U11-8
flabby U31-12; U53-4
flaccid U31-12; U53-4
- paralysis U124-18
- paraplegia U142-5
flaccidity U31-12; U53-4
flagella U83-5
flagellation U142-15
flail chest U124-17
flakes U114-7
flaking skin U56-11
flame U6-10
flammable U6-10
flank U22-6
flap amputation U142-6
-, advancement U130-14
-, arterial U130-12
-, axial (pattern) U130-12
-, bipedicle U130-11
-, buried U130-18
-, caterpillar U130-16
-, envelope U130-17
-, Filatov(-Gillies) U130-15
-, free U130-13
-, French U130-14
-, hinged U130-19
-, nonburied U130-18
-, random (pattern) U130-12
-, rope U130-15
-, rotation U130-19
-, sliding U130-14
-, tubed (pedicle) U130-15
-, turnover U130-19
-, waltzed U130-16
-, wrap-around U130-17
flare (up) U119-17
flaring, nasal U111-1
flash U11-9
flashback U11-9; U74-11
flashlight U17-4; U107-1
flat affect U113-3
- line U125-6
flatfooted U23-13
flatulence U46-15; U109-7
flatulent U109-7
flatus U46-15; U109-7
flavor(ing) U62-7
flavorless U62-7

flea U90-15
fleeting attention U77-18
- blindness U110-19
fleshy U24-8
flex U31-2
flexibility U31-17
flexible U31-2,17
flexion U31-2
flexor U31-2
flexure U31-17
flight of ideas U77-18
flinch U104-12
fling U64-14
flirtatious U68-9
floatation U1-19
floaters U59-5
flocculate U81-27
flocculation U81-27
flocculent U81-27
flood U6-20
floppy U31-12
flora, intestinal/bowel/gut U46-16
florid U119-13
flotation (tank) U1-19
flourish U94-11
flourishing U1-4
flow clamp U136-4
- cytometry U83-21
- sheet U20-5
-, lochial U71-23
-, urinary U49-17
flowmetry U36-5
flu U94-9
fludrocortisone U55-10
fluid U82-4
- balance U78-22
- depletion U6-15
- loading U33-10
- overload U110-16
-, lymphatic U35-2
fluke U90-17
fluorescein angiography U58-14
- tag U84-38
fluorescence U99-8
fluorescent in situ hybridization U84-38
fluoride U82-22
fluorine U82-22
fluoroquinolone U82-22
fluoroscopic U99-8
flush U56-18; U108-8; U136-3
flushed U56-18; U108-8
flushing U108-8; U36-11; U51-11
flutter, atrial/auricular U110-7
fluttering U110-7
fly U90-15
foam U69-8
foam cushion U19-5
focal U97-10
focus U97-10; U59-17; U89-3
folacin U79-14
folate U79-14
fold(ing) U25-17; U85-12
Foley catheter, indwelling U125-20

folic acid U79-14
follicle, graafian/ovarian U51-6
-, hair U56-13
follicle-stimulating hormone (FSH) U55-14
follicular U51-6f; U56-13
followup U120-14
follow-up examination U18-9
- care U75-17
-, outpatient U15-1
-, postoperative U134-15
fomentation U140-25
fondle U62-10
fondling U62-10; U68-16
fondness U67-7
fontanelle U28-7
Food and Drug Administration (FDA) U13-9
food U2-6
- additive U3-22
- exchange list U3-21
- poisoning U91-21
- residue U46-20
- substitute/replacer U3-21
- tray U19-7
- web U91-19
-, solid U2-6
foot U23-13
- (30.48 cm) U24-2
- rest U19-4
foot, ball of the U65-16
footboard U19-4
footdrop U23-13
footprint U23-13
footslap U65-2
footsteps U65-4
footwear biomechanics U142-10
foramen U28-6
- ovale U32-11
-, interventricular U41-4
force, chewing U27-15
forced vital capacity U118-3
forceps U132-14
-, grasping U132-13
-, sponge U132-18
-, suture U132-15
forearm U23-2; U28-16
forebag U71-6
forebrain U41-1
foregut U85-21
forehead U25-10; U87-20
foreign U39-21
- body U8-10
- material/matter U8-10
forelock U114-4
foreplay U68-2
forerunner U119-4
foreshadow U119-3
foresight U77-10
foreskin U52-17
forestall U112-4
forewarn U8-7
forewaters U71-6
forget U74-14

forgetable U74-14
forgetful U74-15
forgetfulness U74-15
forgiving U75-16
formaldehyde U82-12
formalin U122-7
formative years U77-11
formication U103-19
formulate (drug) U9-6
fornicate U68-13
fornication U68-13
fornix cerebri U41-3
fortification U82-5
fossa U28-6; U87-26
foul U109-2
foul-smelling U46-17; U62-1; U116-15
fourchette U50-14
fovea (centralis) U58-13
foveation U58-13
Fowler position U63-12
fractile U100-11
fraction U81-4
fractionation U81-4
fracture U106-1
- fixation U141-4
-, bending U106-12
-, calcaneal U6-5
-, chip U106-5
-, closed U106-3
-, comminuted U106-7
-, compression U106-6
-, contrecoup U106-9
-, fatigue U106-13
-, fissured U106-11
-, hairline U106-11
-, impacted U106-6
-, linear U106-11
-, simple U106-3
-, skull U106-8
-, splinter(ed) U106-7
-, stress U106-13
fragile U25-8; U31-16; U103-19
fragility U25-8; U31-16; U103-19
fragment U39-3; U106-2
fragmentation U39-3; U106-2
fragrance U62-3
fragrant U62-3
frail U25-8
frailty U25-8
frame U19-4
- size U25-3
frank U75-13; U119-7; U77-16
frankness U75-13
fraudulent U75-12
freckled U25-18; U114-5
freckles U25-13,18; U114-5
free U8-3; U126-12
- radical U78-19
- tissue transfer, vascularized U130-13
freeway space U27-14
freeze-thaw U136-16
freeze-thawing U69-14
fremitus U111-11
French letter U69-6

frenulum U26-11; U50-14
frenum U26-11
frenzied U77-15
frenzy U77-15; U76-16
frequency distribution U100-12
-, sound U61-6
-, urinary U112-5
frequency-urgency syndrome U112-4
frequent voiding U112-5
freshening (wound) U140-12
fresh-frozen plasma U136-16
fretful U64-17
friability U31-16
friable U31-16; U56-18
friction U17-14; U56-9
- rub U43-4
- -, pericardial U110-8; U17-2
- -, pleural U111-12
friendliness U75-5
fright U6-21
frigid U68-7
frigidity U68-7
frog-leg(ged) U23-8; U63-5
frolement U142-15
frond-like pattern U51-9
frontal U87-20
- bone U28-8
frostbite U5-12
frostnip U5-12
frothy U96-8; U103-16
frown(ing) U67-11
frozen-thawed U69-14; U136-16
frustrated U76-11
frustration U76-11
fugue state U74-20
-, psychogenic U74-20
fulguration U127-14
full-blown U119-14
fullness U109-8
-, epigastric U109-1
full-term U70-11
fulminant U119-13
- course U94-14
fulminate U119-13
fulminating U119-13
fumes U82-3
fumigant U91-9
function tests, lung/pulmonary U118-3
- tests/studies, liver U116-14
functional enquiry U102-11
fundal /-ic U58-12
fundus, ocular/optic U58-12
funduscopic U58-12
funduscopy U58-12
funeral home/parlor U12-16
funerary U12-17
fungal U90-18; U92-26
fungicidal U91-8; U92-26
fungicide U91-8
fungiform U90-18
fungus U90-18
funnel-shaped U46-9
furious U76-10
furrow U87-26

furry tongue U103-5
furuncle U114-16
furunculosis U114-16
fusion U28-20; U70-1

G

GABA-ergic U42-11
gag(ging) U44-8; U27-16; U40-10
gait U65-2
- disturbance U23-13
-, bouncing U1-4
-, cerebellar U113-8
-, impairment of U142-3
gallbladder U47-7
gallop (rhythm) U110-6
gallstone U47-7; U45-12
gamete U51-4; U85-2
- intrafallopian transfer (GIFT) U69-18
-, female U51-5
gametic U85-2
gametogenesis U51-4
gametopathy U85-2
gangliocytoma U40-11
ganglion U40-11
ganglionated U40-11
ganglioneuroma U98-13
ganglionic U40-11
gangrene U89-30
gantry U99-19
gap, synaptic U40-13
gape U67-13
gargle U45-4; U66-7
-, saline U94-10
garment U77-26
gas U46-15; U82-2
-, intestinal U109-7
- exchange U44-4
- gangrene U90-3
gaseous U46-15; U82-2; U109-7
gaseousness U46-15; U109-7
gasoline U11-23
gasp U44-7
gasping U44-7
gastric U45-8
- emptying rate/time U46-8
- inhibitory peptide (GIP) U55-13
- juice U46-10
- lavage U91-26
- tube U91-26
- washing U91-26
gastrin U55-13
gastrinoma U55-13
gastrin-releasing peptide U54-9
gastritis U45-8
gastroenteritis U94-18; U45-8
gastrointestinal tract/canal U45-1
gastroscope U118-11
gastroscopic U118-11
gastroscopy U118-11; U128-2
gastrostomy tube U125-18
gastrula U85-5
gastrulation U85-5

gauge U17-8; U24-12
gaunt U24-10; U25-7
gauntness U25-7
gauze, surgical U140-18
gay U68-14
gaze U59-2; U67-14
- palsy U113-11
-, extreme lateral U113-12
gel U9-8
- filtration U83-22
Gélineau's syndrome U72-18
gemmation U85-10
gender U68-1
- identity U68-14
gene U84-1
- expression U83-16
- mapping U84-34
general internist U15-9
- practitioner (GP) U15-8
generalist U15-8
generic U121-2
genetic U84-1
genetics U84-1
genial U21-6
genioplasty U127-4
genital U50-1
- ridge U85-9
- tract U52-1
genitals/-lia U50-1; U52-1
genitourinary U48-1; U52-1
genome U84-1
genomic U84-1
genomic library U84-32
genotype U84-10,1
genotypic U84-10
genu valgum U23-11
genus U90-9
geriatric U80-15
geriatrician U15-17; U80-15
geriatrics U15-17; U80-15
germ U90-5
- cell U51-4
- layer U85-6
- line U84-17
germicidal U17-15
germicide U17-15; U90-5
germinal U51-4; U85-6
- epithelium U50-3
germinate U51-4
germination U51-4; U90-5
geroderma U80-15
gerontology U80-15
gerontotherapy U80-15
gestation U70-6
gestational U70-6
- carrier U69-19
gesticulate U67-1
gesticulation U67-1
gesticulatory U67-1
gestural U67-1
gesture U67-1
get (illness) U4-2
- over U4-16
- up U65-17

get well card U1-3
giant U24-4
giddiness U103-13; U113-6
giddy U103-13; U113-6
Giemsa's stain U96-6
GIFT U69-18
gigantism U24-4
giggle U66-2
ginger U25-13
gingiva U26-12
gingivectomy U127-1
ginglymus joint U29-5
girth, abdominal U109-9
glad U75-6
glance U67-12
gland U54-1
-, Cowper's/bulbourethral U52-13
-, lacrimal U58-9
-, prostatic U52-10
-, sebaceous/oil U56-8
-, sweat/sudoriferous U56-10
-, thymus U35-5
-, tubuloalveolar U52-10
-, greater vestibular U50-10
-, paraurethral/of Skene U50-9
glandular U54-1
- fever U94-10
glare U59-2; U67-13
glass slide U17-13; U64-10; U116-5
glaucoma U59-11
glenoid cavity U28-12
glide U65-8
gliding joint U29-7
glimpse U67-12
glioblastoma U98-14
glioma U98-14
gliomatosis U98-14
gliomatous U98-14
gliosis U98-14
globulin U78-18
globus pallidus U41-10
- sensation U109-5
glomerular U48-6
- filtrate U49-1
- filtration rate (GFR) U49-2
glomerulonephritis U48-6
glomerulus U48-6
gloomy U76-22; U75-14
glossal U21-11
glossoptosis U113-17
glottic/-al U43-7
glottis U43-7
gloves, disposable U139-17
glove-wearing U139-17
gloving U139-17
glower(ing) U67-13
glucagon U55-12
glucagonoma U55-12
glucocorticoid U55-10
gluconate U79-7
gluconeogenesis U47-17; U78-14
glucosamine U79-7
glucose U78-13; U79-7
glucuronic acid U78-11

glue ear U95-12
- huffing U11-23
glum U76-22
glutamate U47-16
glutamic acid residue U81-9
glutamine U47-16
glutathione U47-16
gluteal U22-13
- muscles U30-15
gluteus maximus (muscle) U30-15
glyceraldehyde U82-13
glyceride U82-13
glycerol U82-13
glycogen U47-14; U78-13
glycogenase U47-14
glycogenesis U78-14
glycogenic U47-14
glycogenolysis U78-14
glycol U47-17
glycolipid U78-13
glycolysis U78-14
glycolytic U78-14
glycosuria U49-5; U78-13; U112-1
glycosylate U78-7
gnawing pain U104-7
go away U4-15
- through (troubles) U4-3
goblet cells U86-18
goiter U82-22
-, iodine-deficient U82-5
gold U82-28
Golgi apparatus/complex U83-10
- tendon organ U57-12
gommage U1-20
gompholic U29-14
gomphosis U29-14
gonad, male/female U50-3; U54-11
gonadal U50-3; U54-11
gonadopathy U54-11
gonadotrop(h)in U54-11
gonadotropic U54-11
goniometer U142-9
goniometry U142-9
gonococcal U90-8
gonococcemia U96-2
gonorrhea U96-2; U69-6
gonorrheal U96-2
gonosome U84-6
good (for) U1-3
good-natured U75-1
goodwill U73-3
goose pimples/bumps U105-8
goosebump U56-14
gooseflesh U56-14; U105-8
goose-pimply U105-8
gouge U132-11
gout U10-10; U49-14
govern U54-3; U72-8
gown (OR) U139-15
-, total body exhaust U139-16
gowning U139-15
graafian follicle U51-6; U55-14
grab U64-9
grace U25-5

graceful U24-6
grade U97-14
grades of movement U142-9
gradient, osmotic U49-4
grading U97-14
graft U130-1
– rejection U130-21
– survival U130-21
–, accordion U130-8
–, allogeneic U130-3
–, autogeneic U130-2
–, autologous U130-2
–, autoplastic U130-2
–, block (bone) U130-9
–, cancellous bone U130-9
–, delayed (skin) U130-7
–, dermal U130-6
–, free U130-10
–, heterologous U130-5
–, heteroplastic U130-5
–, homologous U130-3
–, homoplastic U130-3
–, isogeneic U130-4
–, isologous U130-4
–, isoplastic U130-4
–, mesh(ed) U130-8
–, primary (skin) U130-7
–, skin U130-6
–, split-thickness U130-6
–, syngeneic U130-4
–, xenogeneic U130-5
–, zooplastic U130-5
graft-versus-host disease/reaction U130-20
grandiose perception U77-18
grand-mal seizure U124-9
granular layer U56-2
granulate U140-7
granulation tissue U140-7
granulocyte U37-8
granuloma inguinale U96-6
granulomatous U96-6
graph U100-27
graphesthesia U57-14
grasp U64-9
grasper U64-9; U132-13
grasping U64-9
gratification, sexual U68-8
grave U12-18
grave emergency U6-18
gravid U70-5
gravida U70-7
gravidity U70-7
gray matter U41-7
graze U5-8
grief U12-12
grieve U12-12
grimace U67-8
grimacing U67-8
grim-faced U67-8
grin U67-9
grind U27-18
grinding wheel U27-18
grip U64-9

grippe U94-9
groan U66-4
groin U22-9
grooming U19-10; U142-27
groove U85-12; U87-26
grooved U87-26
gross U31-20
– hematuria U57-4
– motor skills U31-20
– pus U116-18
grouchy U76-9
ground U27-18
group U81-5
grow U80-10
– up U80-3
growing U80-3
growl U67-19
grown-up U80-10
growth U80-3; U97-2
– deficiency U10-13
– factor, insulin-like U55-5
– hormone, human U55-5
– plate U28-3
–, tumor U97-7
growth-enhancing U55-5
grudge U76-11
grumble U67-19
grumpy U67-19
guaiac test, stool U118-6
guard (against) U109-13
guarded U64-1
– (prognosis) U119-19
guardian U77-25
guardianship U77-25
guarding, abdominal U109-13
guidance, canine U26-5
guide U133-12
guillotine amputation U142-6
guilt U77-10
guilty U77-10
gullet U45-5
gum knife U132-3
gumboil U114-16
gumma U96-3
gummy U26-12
gums U26-12; U45-2; U81-6
gunfire U6-8
gunshot wound/injury U6-8
gurgling U46-4,14
gurgling sound U111-10
gurney U19-3
gustation U62-6
gustatory U62-6
gustometry U62-6
gut U45-9
gymnasium U1-15,18
gymnastics U1-15
gynecologist U15-16
gynecology U15-16
gyral U41-5
gyrus U41-5

H

habit U10-11; U11-5; U73-13
–, grinding U27-18
habit-forming U135-9
habitual U10-11; U11-5; U73-13
habituate U73-13
habituating U11-5
habituation U11-5; U73-13; U135-9
–, alcohol U10-11
habitus, body U25-2; U107-10
haggard U25-7
hair U25-15; U21-16
– follicle U56-13
haircut U25-15
hairiness U25-15
hairline U25-15; U87-9; U95-3
– fracture U106-11
hairy U25-15; U56-13; U21-16
half-blood U37-1
half-dozing U72-2
halfhitch U138-4
half-life, biologic U92-5
–, elimination U91-17
–, pharmacologic U92-5
halfway house U11-13; U142-28
halitosis U109-2
hallmark U117-16; U38-5; U94-20
hallucination U73-10; U77-20
–, hypnagogic U72-18
hallucinatory U77-20
hallucinogen(ic drug) U11-21
hallucinosis U11-21
halo U59-1
– nevus U98-15
halogen U82-23
halothane U93-12
hamartoblastoma U98-6
hamartoma U98-6
hamartomatosis U98-6
hamartomatous U98-6
hamate (bone) U28-17
hammer U60-5
–, reflex/neurologic U17-9
hamstring muscles U30-16
hand U23-6
– pendant control U19-4
handedness U23-6
handful U23-6
handgrip U64-9
handgun U6-8
handicap U142-3
handicapped U4-8
handshake U23-6
–, firm U1-11
handy U23-6
Hangman's knot U138-4
hangnail U56-15
hangover U10-9
Hansen's disease U94-17
haploid U84-9
haploidentity U84-9
haploidy U84-9
haplotype U84-4

hapten(e) U39-7
haptenic U39-7
harass U68-16
harassment, sexual U68-16
harbinger U119-3
harbor U90-13; U94-5
harm U6-11
harmful /-less U6-11
harness U141-8
harsh voice U103-6
harvest (tissue) U69-17; U129-12
–, stem cell U38-3
hashish U11-15
Hasson trocar U133-14
Hasson(-type) cannula U133-14
haste U65-15
hasten U65-15
hasty U65-15
haustral U45-15
– pattern U45-6
haustration U45-15
haustrum U45-15
hawk U103-17
hay fever U94-1
– – – sufferer U4-3
hazard U8-4; U124-2; U134-5
–, health U91-18
hazardous U91-5; U124-2
haziness U111-13
head U21-1
– (muscle) U30-3
– halter U141-9
– injury, blunt U124-18
– lice U94-3
– mirror U17-4
– tilt U8-17
headache U21-1; U104-4
–, cluster U113-16
headlight U17-4
head-tilt and chin-lift maneuver U64-5
heal (up) U120-2; U140-4
healer U15-23
healing U15-23; U140-4
– arts U13-14
health U1-1
– administration U13-2
– agency U13-2
– authorities U13-2
– benefit U1-5
– care U13-1; U20-3
– care facility U13-8
– care proxy U20-14
– care worker (HCW) U16-1
– certificate U1-1
– check U1-1
– club U1-18
– department U13-2
– farm U1-18
– freak U2-17
– history U102-4ff
– maintenance organization (HMO) U13-7
– professional U16-1
– service U13-1

health spa U1-18
– visitor U16-8
–, bouncing with U1-4
healthcare U1-1
health-compromising U1-1
healthful U1-1; U2-13
healthiness U1-2
health-related U13-1
healthy U1-2; U2-13
healthy-appearing U1-2
hear U61-1
hearing U61-2
– impairment U4-11
– loss U113-13
heart U32-1
– attack U124-11
– block U123-2
– failure U110-12
– –, congestive U124-12
– muscle U32-6
– rate U33-5
heart sound U33-1; U17-2
– tones U33-1
– valve U32-10
heart/lung bypass machine U16-11
heartache U32-1; U76-20
heartbeat U33-1
heart-broken U32-2; U76-20
heartburn U32-1; U109-4
heartening U32-2
heartfelt U32-2
heartless U32-2
heart-lung (bypass) machine U125-11
hearty U32-2
heat application U142-22
– exhaustion U6-15
– intolerance U105-10
– lamp U19-6; U142-22
– stroke U105-11; U88-19
heating blanket U19-6
heave U46-5; U110-4; U27-16
heaviness, epigastric U22-3
heaving U46-5
– impulse U33-4
heavy U24-8
– chain U39-6
– chores U1-14
heavyset U24-8
heel U23-13
– bone U28-27
– lift U64-16
– pad U28-27
heel-shin test U23-10
height, body U24-2
Heimlich maneuver U8-11
Heinz body U37-6
helical U84-11
helicopter, EMS U8-5
helix U60-2
helminth U90-16
help U8-1; U19-11; U142-29
–, domestic U142-29
helper U142-29
– T cell U39-14

helplessness U142-29
helpline U142-29
hemagglutination U38-11
hemagglutinin U37-16
hemangiofibroma U98-5
hemangioma U98-5
hemangiosarcoma U98-5
hemapheresis U136-15
hematemesis U103-12; U111-7
hematochezia U109-11
hematocrit U116-10
hematocyte U37-4
hematocytoblast U38-3
hematoma U38-8; U5-13; U89-26
hematopenia U37-1
hematopoiesis U38-1
hematopoietin U38-1
hematuria U112-3
heme U37-6; U116-9
hemianopia U113-11; U59-17
hemidiaphragm U43-12
hemifacial U28-9
hemifield U59-7
hemiparesis U113-7
hemiscrotum U52-2
hemisensory U57-7
hemisphere, cerebral U41-3
hemispheric U41-3
hemithorax U43-12
hemizygote U84-5
hemizygous U85-2
Hemoccult® test U118-6
hemoclip U138-15
hemoconcentration U36-13
hemocytometer U83-21
hemodialysis U125-21
hemodialyzer U125-21
hemodilution U36-13,4; U38-13; U81-23
hemodynamic U36-4
– compromise U4-11
hemodynamics U36-4
hemofiltration U125-21
hemoglobin U37-6; U116-9
hemoglobinopathy U116-9
hemolysate U136-12
hemolysin U38-4
hemolysis U38-4; U136-12
hemolytic U38-4
– (transfusion) reaction U136-12
hemolyze U136-12
hemophilia U37-1
hemopoiesis U38-1
hemoptysis U103-17; U111-7
hemorrhage U6-15; U38-8; U89-26
–, intraabdominal U124-16
hemorrhagic U38-8
hemostasis U38-10; U127-10
hemothorax U111-14
hemotympanum U60-4
hemp plant U11-15
Henle's loop U48-8; U23-1
heparin U136-14
hepatic U47-1

hepatic circulation U36-3
- duct U47-6
hepatitis U94-15
hepatocyte U47-3
hepatoduodenal U47-1
hepatomegaly U108-12; U110-9
hepatopancreatic ampulla U47-10
hepatoportal U36-3
hepatotoxicity U91-11
herald U119-3; U77-21; U109-15
herbal U3-19
herbicide U91-8; U17-15
herbology U1-19
hereditary U84-28; U89-7
heredity U84-28; U89-7
heredofamilial U84-28
hernia, sliding U45-5
heroin U11-19
herpes simplex U96-10
- zoster U95-7
-, genital U96-10
herpesvirus U96-10
herpetic U95-7; U96-10
herpetiformis U96-10
hesitancy, urinary U112-7
hesitant U76-14
hesitate U76-14
hesitation U76-14
hetastarch U136-13
heterochromatin U84-6
heterodimer U81-6
heterodisperse U81-22
heterograft U130-5
heterotropia U59-17
heterozygosity U84-5
heterozygous U84-5
hiccup U46-3
hidradenitis U56-10
hidradenoma U98-4; U105-15
hidrosis U105-15
hidrotic U105-15
high U11-10; U116-19
high-altitude sickness U6-17
high-fat U24-5
high-fiber diet U46-18
high-frequency U61-6
high-intensity U61-5
highly contagious U14-10
high-output U33-7; U49-7; U88-16
high-pitched U61-6
high-pitched tinkles U109-6
high-potency U121-9
high-resolution U99-14
high-risk U124-2; U134-5
high-titer U116-17
hike U65-1
hilar U43-4; U87-25
hilum/-us U87-25
hilum, pulmonary U43-4
hindbrain U41-1
hindgut U85-21
hindquarter amputation U142-6
hinge joint U29-5
hinged articulation U29-5

hip U22-7
hip bone U28-21
hippocampal U41-11
hippocampus U41-11
Hippocratic Oath U18-11
hirsutism U53-12
His, bundle of U32-15
hiss U66-21
histamine U78-24
histaminergic U78-24
histidine U78-24
histiocyte U39-18; U86-2
histochemical U81-1
histocompatibility U39-20
histologic(al) U86-1
histologist U86-1
histology U86-1; U87-1
histopathology U86-1
historic(al) U102-4
history, natural U119-9
-, family U102-7
-, medical U102-4ff
-, reproductive U70-7
histrionic U74-14
hit U6-2
hit-and-run accident U6-2
hitch U138-4
hive U114-11
HLA complex/system U39-20
hoarse U103-6; U111-11
hoarseness U103-6; U111-11
hobble U65-11
hoist U19-13
hold U64-9
holder U64-9
-, instrument U133-1
-, needle U132-15
home health aide U142-29
- visit U18-7
-, foster/adoptive U14-4
-, funeral U14-4
-, rest or old people,s U14-4
homemaker U16-15
homemaking assistance U142-29
homeobox U84-34
homeodomain U84-3
homicide U12-10
homogenizer, tissue U133-17
homogenous U129-16
homograft U130-3
homologous U129-16
homozygous U84-5
honest U75-12
honesty U75-12
hook, electrosurgical U132-9
hooked (on) U11-4
hop U65-16
Hopkins system U133-4
hora somni U72-4
hormonal U55-1
- swings U71-22
hormone U55-1
hormone-receptor complex U55-2
hormone-sensitive U57-8

horny U68-3
- layer U56-6,2
horseshoe-shaped U37-9
hose, TED U125-22
hospice U14-4
hospitable U70-4
hospital U14-1
- admission U20-1
- bed U19-3
- staff U15-2
- stay U19-15
- -, postoperative U134-11
- volunteer U16-15
-, psychiatric U14-5
hospital-acquired U89-6; U139-12
hospitalism U14-1,5
hospitalization U14-1; U19-15; U20-1; U134-11
hospitalize U14-1; U20-1
host U90-13; U94-5
- uterus U69-19
hostile U77-7
hostility U77-7
hot U62-7
- flush/flash U51-11; U108-8
- springs spa U1-18
- tub U82-23
Houdini jacket U125-24
house call U18-7
- officer (H.O.) U15-5
houseman U15-5
hub opening U17-10
huddle U63-6
hug(ging) U67-7; U68-2
hum U67-18; U110-3
human chorionic somato-mamotropin (hCS) U55-21
- growth hormone U55-5
- imunodeficiency virus U96-15
humeral U28-15
humeroulnar U28-15
humerus U28-15
humid U105-13
humidifier U105-13
humidify U125-10
humidifying aerosol U82-3
humidity U56-12; U105-13
humiliate U68-9; U77-12
humiliation U68-17
humor U75-7; U76-2; U88-9
-, aqueous U58-11
humoral U88-9
humorless U75-7
humorous U75-7
hunger U2-11
hung-over U10-9
hurl U64-14
hurry U65-15
hurt U5-1; U104-3
hybrid U84-38
hybridization, fluorescent in situ U84-38
hybridize U84-38
hydrate U82-9
hydrated U56-12

hydrocele U56-12
hydrocephalus, obstructive U125-15
hydrochloric acid U46-10
hydrochloride U82-9
hydrocolloid U81-26
hydrocortisone U55-10
hydrodissection U128-14
hydroelectric bath U142-20
hydrofluoric acid burn U91-24
hydrogen U82-9
– peroxide U118-6
– sulfide U46-17
hydrogenate U82-9
hydrolysis U38-4; U46-11; U82-9
hydrolyze U46-11
hydromassage U142-15
hydrophilic U81-13
hydrophobic U81-13
hydrops U108-10
hydrotherapy U142-20
hydrothorax U111-15
hydrous U82-9
hydroxylate U78-7
hygiene U1-5; U19-10
hygienic U1-5; U19-10
hygienist U1-5
hymen U50-13
hymenal U50-13
hymenitis U50-13
hyoid (bone) U28-9
hyp(o)esthesia U57-14
hypacusis U61-8
hyperactive U64-18; U88-14
hyperactivity U113-2; U7-12
hyperacuity U59-8
hyperacusis U61-8
hyperaeration U44-6
hyperaldosteronism U55-25
hyperalert U8-7
hyperalimentation U125-19
hyperbaric chamber U64-4
– oxygen therapy U125-12
hypercapnia U111-3; U123-7
hypercarbia U111-3
hypercholesterolemia U37-2
hypercortisolism U55-10
hypercytosis U38-5
hyperdense U99-11
hyperdiploidy U84-9
hyperdynamic U36-4
hyperemesis U103-12
– gravidarum U70-7,12
hyperemia U89-28
hyperendemic U94-8
hyperesthesia U104-17; U135-4
hyperexcitable U42-8
hyperexpansion U44-10
hyperextensibility U142-8
hyperextension U31-3; U142-8
– injury U124-18
hyperflexion U142-8
hyperglycemia U78-13; U37-2
hyperglycemic U78-13
– coma U124-7

hyperhidrosis U105-15
hyperimmune U39-1
hyperinflate U111-6
hyperinflation U44-5
–, lung/pulmonary U111-6
hyperkalemia U82-18
hyperkeratinization U56-6
hyperkeratosis U56-7
hypermagnesemia U82-20
hypermetabolic U78-1
hypermobile U64-2
hypermobility U142-8
hypernasal U66-22
hypernatremia U82-18
hyperopia U59-17
hyperosmia U62-1
hyperosmolar U49-9; U81-21
hyperoxygenation U125-11
hyperparathyroidism U54-7
hyperperfusion U36-5
hyperpermeability U36-16
hyperpermeable U88-6
hyperphagia U109-5
hyperpigmentation U114-3
hyperpituitarism U54-5
hyperplasia U108-12; U89-15; U97-4
hyperpolarization U42-6
hyperprolactinemia U55-22
hyperpyrexia U105-3
–, heat U105-11
hyperreflexia U42-12
hyperreflexive U113-1
hyperresponsiveness U39-2
hypersalivation U109-3; U45-3
hypersecretory U88-11
hypersensitive U76-4
hypersensitivity U39-23; U57-8
hypersensitization U39-23
hypersomnia U72-17
hypersomnic U72-17
hypersomnolence U72-17
hypersomnolent U72-17
hypersplenism U103-3
hypertension U36-8; U110-13; U124-6
hypertensive U36-8; U124-6
hyperthermia U105-5
hyperthymic U1-6
hyperthyroid U55-6
– crisis U124-8
hyperthyroidism U124-8
hypertonicity U36-8; U112-8
hypertransfusion U136-8
hypertrophic U110-9
hypertrophy U108-12; U89-15
–, cardiac U110-9
hyperuremic U112-13
hyperventilate U44-5; U111-5; U125-10
hyperventilation U111-5
hypervigilance U77-5
hyperviscosity U36-12
hyperviscous U36-12
hypesthesia U135-4
hypha U90-18
hyphema U15-18

hypnotic U135-9
hypochondriac region U22-4; U45-6
hypochondriac(al) U4-9
hypocytosis U38-5
hypodense U99-11
hypodermic (needle) U17-11
hypoechoic U118-15
hypoesthesia U135-4
hypogastric U22-8; U45-8
hypogastrium U22-8
hypogenitalism U52-1
hypogeusia U62-6
hypoglycemia U78-13; U124-7; U47-14
hypogonadism U54-11
hypokalemia U37-2
hypomania U77-18
hypomanic U77-18
hypomobility U142-8
hypomotility U46-6
hyponasal U66-22
hyponatremia U37-2
hypoperfusion U36-5
hypophyseal U54-5
hypophysectomy U54-5
hypophysis U54-5
hypopigmentation U114-3
hypopituitary U54-5
hypoplasia U97-4
hyporeflexia U42-12
hyporesponsiveness U39-2
hyposensitivity U135-4
hyposomnia U72-17
hypospadias U69-1
hypotension U36-8; U110-13; U124-6
hypotensive U36-8
hypothalamic U41-9; U54-4
hypothalamus U41-9; U54-4
hypothermal /-ic U105-5
hypothermia U105-5
hypothesis U101-19
hypothyroid U55-6
hypothyroidism U55-6
hypotonicity U36-8
hypotropia U59-17
hypoventilation U111-3
hypovolemia U6-15; U36-7
hypovolemic U36-7
– shock U6-15
hypoxemia U111-3; U123-8
hypoxemic U111-3; U123-8
hypoxia U111-3; U123-8
hypoxic U111-3; U123-8
hysterectomy U50-5
hysteria U77-6
hysteric(al) U77-6
hysterical blindness U57-6
hysterics U77-6

I

iatrogenic U89-9; U121-15
ice application U142-21
– bag U142-21

ice pack U142-21
ice-water lavage U142-21
- - - sponge bath U142-21
ICP monitor U125-13
ictal U113-5
- phase U74-8
icteric U108-4
icterus U108-4
ictus U113-5
ICU observation & monitoring U125-5
id U77-2
ID badge U17-16
idea U73-8
ideation U73-8
ideational U73-8
identifiable U74-3; U117-4
identification U74-3; U117-4
identify U74-3; U117-4
- with U75-2
identity U75-2
-, gender U18-10
idiocy U77-24
idiopathic U89-8
idiot U77-24
idiotype U39-5
ignite U6-10; U82-7
ileal U45-12
ileocecal U45-12
ileum U45-12
ileus U109-6; U45-12
iliac spine U28-22
ilioinguinal U52-8
iliopsoas (muscle) U30-15
iliopubic tract U28-22
ilium U28-22
ill U4-1
- health U1-1
-, mentally U77-13
illness U1-1; U4-1
ill-tempered U76-2
illumination U59-10; U17-4
illusion U73-10
illusional U73-10
illusory U73-10
image U73-9
imagery U73-9
imaginary U73-9
imagination U73-9
imaginative U73-9
imagine U73-9
imaging, radionuclide U99-22
imbalance U78-22
-, postural U113-8
imbibe U46-1
imbibition U46-1
immature U80-10,2
immersion U88-5; U91-24
imminent danger U8-4
immobile U64-2; U141-5
immobility U64-2; U142-8,13
immobilization U64-2; U141-5
immoderate U10-6
immortal U12-3
immotile U53-10

immovable U64-1
immune U39-1
- agglutination/adherence U39-19
- complex U39-9
- resistance U39-22
- response/reaction U39-2
- system U39-1
- tolerance U39-22
immunity U122-3
-, cell-mediated U39-4
-, humoral U39-4
immunization U39-1; U122-3
immunize U122-1
immunoassay U116-3
immunobiology U83-1
immunoblotting U84-35
immunocompetent U39-1
immunocompromised U4-11; U97-18
immunogen U39-1
immunoglobulin U39-5
immunohistochemistry U116-7; U81-1
immunomodulation U97-18
immunomodulator U97-18; U92-34
immunomodulatory /-ing U97-18
immunopathogenic U90-5
immunosuppressant U97-18
immunotherapy U97-18
impact U6-9; U106-6
impacted U109-15
- foreign body U8-10
- stone U47-8
impaction U106-6
-, fecal/stool U109-15
impair U4-11
impairment U4-11; U142-3; U89-4
impalpable U62-9
impatience U67-15; U71-22
impatient U75-18
impending stroke U119-3
impenetrability U99-11
impermeability U36-16
impermeable U36-16; U88-6
impersonal U75-1
impetiginization U114-15
impetiginized U114-15
impetiginous U114-15
impetigo U114-15
impinge (on/upon) U113-15
impingement U113-15
implant U70-3; U129-18
implantable U129-18
implantation U70-3; U129-18
implications U75-8
impolite U75-5
impotence U53-2
impotent U53-2
impregnate U70-1; U69-2
impregnation U70-2; U6-9
imprint U74-9
improve U4-13
improvement U4-13
impulse U73-12
- conduction, electrical U33-2
-, nerve/neur(on)al U42-5

impulsive(ness) U73-12; U75-18
in vitro U101-18
- - fertilization (IVF) U69-12
in vivo U101-18
inability U142-3
inaccessible U128-1; U136-5; U126-6
inactivate U88-14
inactivated vaccine U122-7
inactivation U88-14; U122-7
inactive U76-17; U88-14; U119-6
- control treatment U101-8
inactivity U64-18;
U76-17; U119-6
inadequacy U75-14; U76-12
-, dietary U16-13
inadvertent U122-1
inadvisable U18-4
inanition U108-14
inattentive U74-16
inaudible U61-2
inborn U89-6
inbreeding U84-30
incapable U142-4
incapacitate U142-4
incapacitated U16-2; U4-8; U119-10
incapacity U20-14; U142-4
incentive U73-12
inception U119-5
inch U24-2
incidence U100-7
incident U6-1
incipient U119-5,14
incise U126-9
incision U5-6; U126-9
incisor tooth U26-3
inclination U77-7
incline U63-10
incoherence U77-20
incompatibility U136-11
incompatible U136-11
incompetence U20-14
incompetent U20-14; U73-4
incomprehensible U73-5
inconclusive U116-23
inconsistent U75-10
incontinence, urinary U112-15
incontinent U112-15
incoordination U31-19; U113-8
incorporate U46-13; U78-5
incorporation U46-13; U88-8
increase U116-19
increment U99-19
incrustation U114-8
incubate U116-6
incubation U116-6
- period U94-6
incubator U116-6
incurable U120-2
incus U60-5
indecency U68-10
indecent U68-10
indecision U75-11
indecisive U75-11
independence U142-28

independent living center U142-28
indeterminate U117-2
index card U102-12; U18-14
– finger U17-10; U29-6
–, body mass (BMI) U24-7
indication U120-10
indicator U120-10
indifference U75-8; U76-15
indifferent U75-8; U76-15; U74-16
indigestible U46-11; U109-1
indigestion U109-1
–, a touch of U4-5
indiscriminate U117-15
indisposed U75-4
indistinguishable U117-15
individual U75-2
individuality U75-2
indolent U104-6
induce U119-8
induction room U131-3
–, anesthetic U135-13
induration U89-14
inebriant U10-5
inebriated U10-5
inedible U2-5
inefficient U101-26
inert U82-29; U129-20
inexhaustible U64-19
infancy U80-4
infant U80-4
– car seat U6-3
–, vigorous U1-6
infanticide U80-4; U12-8
infantile U80-4; U95-1
infantilism U80-4
infarct(ion) U124-11
–, cerebral U124-14
infarcted U124-11
infect U94-2
infection U94-2; U139-9
–, chlamydial U96-9
–, cytomegalovirus U96-11
–, gonococcal U96-2
–, human papillomavirus U96-13
–, trichomonas U96-8
infectiousness U94-1
infective U94-2
inference U73-5
inferiority complex U77-12
–, feelings of U76-12
infertile U69-2
infertility U69-2; U70-1
infest U94-2
infestation U94-2
infidelity U12-12
infiltrate U94-14; U97-12; U136-7
infiltration U97-12; U136-7; U89-13
infiltrative /-ing U97-12
infirm U4-7
infirmary U4-7; U14-2
infirmity U4-7; U1-11
inflammable U6-10
inflammation U89-11
inflate U44-5

inflation U44-5; U111-6
inflexibility U31-17
inflow U36-5
influenza U94-9
infolding U85-12
information U101-15
informed consent U134-3
inframammary U50-17
infraorbital U58-1
– rim U28-9
infrapatellar U28-24
infrared therapy U142-22
Infusa-port® U136-5
infusate U136-1
infusion U136-1
– cannula U132-6
– pump U135-16; U136-1
– set U136-4
–, bolus intravenous U135-19
–, continuous intravenous U135-19
–, IV U136-2
ingest U46-1; U2-1
ingesta U46-1
ingestants U46-1
ingestion U46-1; U2-1
ingredient, active U91-24
ingrowing hairs U25-14
ingrown U80-3
inguinal U22-9
– canal U52-8
– region U45-6
– ring, deep U52-7
inguinoscrotal U52-2,8
inhalant U44-2; U92-14
– abuse U11-23
inhalation U44-2; U92-14
inhalational U44-2
inhale U44-2
inhaler U92-14
–, metered-dose U44-2
inherit U84-28
inheritable U84-28
inheritance U84-28
inherited U89-7
inhibit U42-13; U88-14
inhibition U88-14
–, reflex/motor U42-13
inhibitions, loss of U77-8
inhibitor U42-13; U88-14; U92-7
inhibitory U42-13; U88-14
in-house U15-5
initial puncture U128-12
initiation U84-19
initiator U84-19,21
inject U122-4
injectable U122-4
injectables U17-1
injection, vaccine U122-4
injure U5-1,3
injured party U6-12
injurious U91-1; U5-2
injury U5-1 ff
–, electrical U6-11
–, spinal/spine U124-18

injury, whiplash/hyperextension U124-18
injury-free U5-2
inlet, laryngeal U43-7
–, thoracic U87-21
innate U72-8
innervation U42-1
–, reciprocal U42-14
innocuous U39-23
innominate artery U34-9
– bone U22-7
inoculable U122-1
inoculant U122-1
inoculate U122-1
inoculation U122-1,3
inoculum U122-1
inoperable U126-1
inorganic U86-20
inpatient U20-2; U19-2
insane U77-3,15
insanity U77-3,15
insatiable U68-4
insecticide U91-8
insecure U8-4; U76-12
inseminate U70-1
insemination U53-6; U70-2
–, artificial U69-12
insensible U57-8
insensitive U76-4
insensitivity U57-8; U76-4
insert (muscle) U30-3
insertion U84-23
– (muscle) U30-3
insidious U119-7; U77-23; U95-5
insight U73-5
insignificant, statistically U100-21
insincere U75-12
insoluble U88-5; U79-11
insomnia U72-16
insomniac U72-16
inspect U107-6
inspection U107-6; U126-11
inspiration U44-3
inspiratory U44-3
inspire U44-3
instability U31-15; U125-2; U142-8; U141-4
instep U23-13; U28-25
instill U128-10; U136-1
instillation U128-10; U136-1
instinct U73-11
instinctual /-ive U73-11
institution, mental U14-5
institutional review board U101-24
institutionalism U14-5
instruct U107-3
instructions U107-3
instrument U132-1
– cart U131-19
instrumentation U133-1; U132-1
insufficiency, aortic U110-10
–, cardiac U124-12
insufficient U110-10
insufflant U128-10

insufflate U128-10
insufflation U128-10
- anesthesia U93-10
- needle U133-13
insufflator U133-15
insulin U55-12
insulinase U55-12
insuloma U55-12
insult U124-14
insurance coverage U129-9
-, health U13-5
-, health/medical U18-15
insure U18-15
insurer U13-5; U18-15
intact U126-13
intake U2-1
-, oral U46-1; U2-6; U134-12
-, tolerable/acceptable daily U91-18
integument U56-1
integumentary U56-1
intellect U73-5
intellectual U73-5
intelligence U73-5
intelligent U73-5
intelligibility, speech U61-1
intelligible U73-5
intemperate U10-6
intend U73-3
intense U125-1
intensify U125-1
intensity U61-5; U125-1
- (pain) U104-9
intensive care U125-1
- - monitor U125-6
- - unit (ICU) U14-7
intensivist U125-1
intention U73-3
intention-to-treat analysis U101-20
inter U12-17
interact U121-11
interalveolar U43-10
interappointment U18-2
interarch distance U27-14
interbeat U33-1
intercarpal U28-17
intercellular U86-19
intercom system U17-17
intercondylar notch U29-6
intercostal U28-14
- space U32-4; U33-4
intercourse, sexual U68-5; U30-6
interdigitate U56-3
interferon U97-18
interlobular U43-3; U47-3
interlocking loops U138-11
intermediary U81-18
intermediate U81-18
intermedin U55-26
intermenstrual U51-2
- bleeding U118-1
interment U12-17
intermetatarsal U28-25
intermittency U112-9; U119-11
intermittent U119-11

intermittent claudication U110-19
intern, (medical) U15-5
internal medicine U15-9
- oblique (muscle) U30-14
International Red Cross (IRC) U13-12
interneuron U40-1; U42-13
internist, (general) U15-9
internship U15-5
interocclusal distance U27-14
interpersonal U75-1
interphalangeal U28-18
interphase U83-12
interproximal U87-14; U26-22
intersex disorders U53-12
intersexuality U68-1
interstitial U86-19
- cell-stimulating hormone U55-15
interstitium /-ice U86-19
intertrigo U105-13
intertubercular groove U30-12
interval training U1-12
intervene U20-11
intervention U20-11
interventional U20-11
interventricular septum U32-9
intervertebral U22-12
- disk U28-19
interview, medical U102-14
interviewer U102-14
intervillous U45-14
intestinal U45-1,9
- juice U46-10
- villi U45-14
intestine(s) U45-9
intestine, large U45-15
intimal U34-2
intimate contact U96-1
intimidated U75-17
intimidation U68-17
intoe U23-14
intolerance U75-16; U121-12
- to light U103-15
-, heat/cold U105-10
intolerant U75-16
intonation U66-11
intoxicant U10-5
intoxicate U91-14
intoxicated U10-5
intoxication U10-5; U91-14
intra-abdominal U45-6
- bleeding/ hemorrhage U124-16
intra-aortic U124-15
- balloon counterpulsation U125-8
intra-arterial U34-3
intra-articular U29-1
intracapsular U29-9
intracardiac U32-3
Intracath® U136-6
intracellular U86-19; U83-2
intracoronary U32-14
intracorporeal U138-3
intracorpuscular U37-4
intracranial U28-7
intracranial pressure monitor U125-13

intractability U120-13
intractable U120-13
intracytoplasmic sperm injection (ICSI) U69-15
intrafallopian U50-4
intrahepatic U47-6
intraluminal U34-14; U87-22
intralysosomal U83-6
intramedullary U41-14
intraocular U58-2
intraoperative U126-2
intraoral U26-25
intraorbital U58-1
intrapartum U71-21
intrapelvic U48-3
intrapleural U43-11
intratumoral U97-2
intrauterine device (IUD) U69-10
intravascular U34-1
- coagulation U124-3
intravenous U34-4
- access U136-5
- drip U136-3
- feeding U125-19
- pyelography (IVP) U118-19
intraventricular U41-4
intravitreous U58-10
introducer, suture U138-12
introitus U71-15
intron U84-14
intronic U84-14
introversion U75-13
introvert U75-14
intrusion U74-11
intubate U123-10
intubation U135-17
-, endotracheal U123-10
intubator U123-10; U135-17
intussusception U98-1; U129-8
invade U94-2
invaginate U85-12
invagination U85-12; U83-15; U129-8
invalid U4-8
- carriage, motorized U19-13
invalidism U4-8
invalidity U4-8
invasion U97-12
invasive U97-12
invasiveness U128-1
inversion U31-8; U84-23
invert U31-8
inverted U84-23
investigate U118-1
investigation U118-1; U101-2
investigational U118-1
investigations, laboratory U116-8
investigative U118-1
investigator U118-1
invisible U59-6
involuntary U40-6; U73-3
involute U54-12
involve U4-10
involvement U4-10; U89-4
-, focal U97-10

iodide U82-22
iodination U82-22
iodine U82-22
iodized U82-22
ion U78-23; U81-11; U99-20
ionic U78-23; U81-11
– current U42-9
ionization U81-11
ionize U99-20
ipecac, syrup of U91-25
ipsilateral U87-18
iridic U58-8
iridium U82-34
iridocorneal U58-5
iridoplegia U58-8
iris U58-8
iron U82-21
irradiate U99-4
irradiation U99-2
irrational U73-7
irresistible urge U77-19
irresolute U75-11
irresponsible U75-9
irreversible U4-14
irrigate U128-11
irrigation U128-11; U127-17
irrigator U127-17
irritability U76-7; U108-13; U89-10
irritable U76-7; U108-13
irritant U81-1; U89-10
irritation U108-13; U104-3; U89-10
ischemia U89-28; U124-14
–, reversible U4-14
ischemic heart disease U124-12
ischial U28-22
– spines U71-13
ischium U28-22
islet cells (of Langerhans) U54-8
isochromosomes U84-7
isodense U99-11
isoechoic U118-15
isokinetic U142-17
isolation U14-10
isolette U14-10
isomerase U78-8
isometrics U1 15; U142 17
isoosmotic U81-21
isotonic exercise U142-17
isotope U82-1
isotopic U82-1
isotype U39-5
isovolumetric U36-7
itch U103-19
– mite U96-12
–, seven-year U96-12
itching U103-19
itchy U103-19
IUD, unmedicated U69-10
IV bag U136-4
IV bottle U136-4
IV cannula/catheter/line U136-3

J

jab U122-4
jacket, Houdini U125-24
jackknife position U63-11
jacuzzi (bath) U1-17
jamais-vu U74-18
janitor U16-14
jar, specimen U17-12
jaundice U108-4
jaundiced U108-4
jaw U21-5
– thrust U8-17
– thrust and chin lift U64-16
–, upper U28-10
jawbone U21-5
jawline U56-19
jaw-thrust maneuver U8-11
jejunal U45-11
jejunitis U45-11
jejunoileal U125-18; U45-11
jejunostomy tube U125-18
jejunotomy U125-18
jejunum U45-11
jelly, lubricating U17-14
jelly-like U58-10
jeopardize U124-2; U8-4
jeopardy U124-2
jerk U64-7; U72-12
– off U68-8
–, deep tendon U57-11
jerkiness U64-7
jerking U64-7
jerky U64-7; U72-12; U113-1
jet massage U142-15
– shower U1-19
jitteriness U108-13
jittery U76-6; U108-13
job-related disability U142-3
jocular U75-5
jog(ging) U1-14; U65-14
jogger U65-14
joint U11-14; U29-1 ff
– capsule U29-9
– rest U1-10
, condyloid/condylar U29-6
–, fibrous U29-13
–, gliding/plane U29-7
jolt U64-7
joule U79-4
judge U73-6; U117-18
judgement U73-6
–, clinical U117-18
–, faulty U74-16
judicious U117-18
jugular U34-11
jugular vein, external U34-11
– venous distension /-tion U110-16
juice U3-25
–, gastric/intestinal U46-10
–, pancreatic U55-13
jump U65-16
junction, dentoenamel U26-16
–, epidermodermal U114-5

junction, myoneural/neuromuscular U30-4
junctional nevi U56-7
junkie U11-6
juvenile U80-8
juvenile-onset U95-1
juxtaglomerular U48-6

K

K cell U39-16
kaliuresis U82-18
karyoplasm U83-4
karyosome U83-3
karyotype U84-10
karyotyping U84-10
Kayser-Fleischer ring U58-5
Keith-Flack node U32-15
keratic U56-6
keratin U56-6
keratinization U56-6; U114-14
keratinous U56-6
keratitis U56-6; U114-14
keratoderma U114-14
keratomalacia U56-6
keto acid, branched-chain U81-18
ketoacidosis U82-12
–, diabetic U124-7
ketone U82-12
ketosis U82-12
kick U6-4; U64-12
kid U80-5
kidney U48-2
– dish/tray U17-12
Kiesselbach's plexus U110-20
kill(ing) U12-9; U39-16
killed(-virus) vaccine U122-7
killer cell U39-16
kin, next of U84-31; U12-21; U102-6
kind U75-5
kind-hearted U32-2
kindred U84-31
kinematic motion study U142-10
kinesialgia U57-14
kinesiology U142-10
kinesthesia U57-14; U142-10
kinesthetic U57-14
kinetics U57-14; U142-10
kinetosome U83-6
kinetotherapy U57-14
kinship U84-31
kiss U67-7
kneading U142-15
knee U23-11
kneel U23-11; U63-4
Kneipp cure/Kur U1-19
knife U132-3
knock U110-5
– down/over U6-2
knock-knees U23-11
knot U138-2 ff; U137-6
– pusher U138-13
–, locking loop U138-7

knot, rotational U138-10
-, surgical U138-6
-, triple-twist U138-11
knotting U138-2
knot-tying U138-2; U137-6
knowledgable U73-4
knowledge U73-4
knuckle U23-7; U28-18
koilocytosis U96-14
Koplik's spots U95-2; U114-9
Krause corpuscle U57-15
Krebs-Henseleit cycle U47-18
KUB film U118-19
Kupffer cells U47-4; U39-18
Kussmaul breathing U124-7

L

lab study/test U116-2
-, path(ology) U14-11; U116-1
labia minora U50-14
labial U50-14; U21-9; U26-23
labile U75-15
lability U75-15; U108-13
labor (pains) U71-3
-, dysfunctional U4-4
laboratory, pathology U116-1
-, tissue typing U14-11
labored (speech) U113-10
- (respiration) U111-2; U44-4; U108-3
labyrinth U57-18; U60-10
labyrinthine U60-10
- sense U57-18
labyrinthitis U60-10
laceration U5-7
lacquer U11-23
lacrimation U58-9; U45-3
lacrimoturbinal U58-9
lactation U71-25
lactational U71-25
lacteal (vessel) U35-10
lactic acidosis U1-6; U36-4
lactiferous U71-25
- duct U50-18
lactin U79-8
lactobacillus U90-7
lactogenic hormone U55-22
lactose U79-8
lacunar stage U85-4
lag period U39-2
laid up U4-6
laid-back U76-19
lallation U66-17
lame U65-11
lameback U65-11
lament U67-10
lamina U86-15; U87-8
-, spiral U60-11
laminagraphy U99-19
lamination U86-15
laminectomy U125-15
lamp, heat U19-6
lancet U17-1

landmark U126-8
Langer's lines U56-17
Langerhans, islets/islet cells of U54-8
lanky U25-5
lap U22-10
-, mother's U80-5
laparoscope U128-3; U133-2
laparoscopic knot U138-2
- suturing U138-1
laparoscopist U128-3
laparoscopy, operative U128-3
laparotomize U128-13
laparotomy U128-13
-, conversion to U128-19
large-framed U24-8
laryngeal inlet U43-7
laryngopharynx U45-4
laryngospasm U111-10; U43-7; U103-20
larynx U43-7
Lasegue's test U142-11
laser U127-7
- therapy U142-24
lashes U25-14
Lassa fever U14-10
lassitude U103-8
latch-on U71-26
late (dead) U12-5
latency U94-6; U119-6
latent U94-6; U119-6
late-onset U119-5
lateral U87-18
lateralization U87-18
latex agglutination test U39-19
latissimus dorsi, (musculus) U30-12
laugh U67-9; U66-2
laughing gas U93-11
lavage U91-26; U118-10; U140-11
lavatory U19-9
laxative U91-24
laxity (joint) U142-8,14
lay comprehension U6-13
layer U87-8
-, keratinized/horny/cornified U56-6
lead (Pb) U82-32
lead (ECG) U118-14
leaded U82-32
leaflet U32-10
leak U112-15
leakage U133-8
-, CSF U28-6
-, urine/urinary U112-15
lean U24-10
- backward U64-5
- body mass U78-2
leaning back U63-10
leap U65-16
learn(ing) U73-6; U74-7
learning disability U142-3
leave of absence (LOA) U18-10
-, sickness U4-1
leer U67-9
leg U23-8
- bag, urinary U125-23

leg, lower U23-10
-, upper U23-9
leiomyoma U98-9
leiomyosarcoma U98-3
leisure center U1-17
- time U1-10
lemniscus, medial U41-14
length, body U24-2
lens U58-8; U133-2
-, diverging U59-13
-, magnifying U127-6
lentiginous U114-5
lentigo U114-5
lepromatous U94-17
lepromin skin test U94-17
leprosy U94-17
leprous/-otic U94-17
leptomeninges U41-8
leptomeningitis U94-13
lesbian U68-14
lesion U5-5; U89-3
-, mass U97-3
let-down reflex U71-27
lethal U12-2
- dose U91-11
lethargic U113-3
lethargy U113-3; U7-12
leucine zipper U84-3
leukapheresis U136-15
leukemia U37-7
-, myelocytic U38-2
leukoagglutinin U39-19
leukocyte U37-7ff
-, non-granular U37-10
-, polymorphonuclear U37-8
leukocytic U37-7
leukoderma U114-4; U56-3
leukopenia U37-7
levator ani U45-17
- scapulae, musculus U30-12
level U116-16
-, no-effect- U91-18
lever, desufflation U133-15
Leydig cell U53-9; U55-15
liable for U20-13
- to U119-1
liberate U126-12
libido U68-4
lice U90-15
licensed physician U13-13
lichen U114-14
lichenification U114-14
lichenoid /-ified U114-14
lick (lips) U67-17
lid U21-3
- lag U59-2; U67-14
lidocaine U93-5
lie down U72-3
- in U71-4
-, fetal U71-5
lien U35-4
life demands U77-21
- expectancy U80-1
- support machine U12-5

life support, advanced (ALS) U125-3
– –, basic (BLS) U123-4
–, take one's U12-8
life-endangering U123-1
lifeguard U123-3
lifejacket U6-19
lifeless U12-5; U123-1
lifelong U80-1
– handicap U142-3
life-preserving U126-13
life-saver U123-1
life-saving U8-2; U123-1
lifestyle, healthy U1-2
life-supporting U125-3
life-sustaining measures U125-3
life-table analysis U100-26
life-threatening U123-1
lifetime U80-1
lift U64-16
lifting U64-16
ligament U30-6
– of teres U47-2
–, anterior cruciate U142-10
–, broad U50-5
–, cardinal U50-5
–, falciform U47-2
–, round U50-5
ligamentous U30-6
ligand U81-14
ligation U137-3
ligation, tubal U69-3
ligature U137-3
light (up) U10-18
– adaptation U59-10
– box U118-18
– chain U39-6
– layer U56-2
– source, bright U17-4
lighter U10-18
light-headed(ness) U7-5; U103-13
lighthearted U75-6
lighting U17-4
lightning (strike) U6-14,4
light-sensitive U103-15
lignocaine U93-5
likelihood U100-31
limb U23-1
limber (up) U1-13; U31-11
limbic system U41-11
limb-saving U123-1
lime U82-19
limit U87-10
–, permissible exposure (PEL) U91-5
limitation U87-10
limp(ing) U31-12; U65-11; U102-1
limpness U31-12
line U86-8; U87-9
– of minimum tension U129-10
–, central venous U127-19
linea U87-9
lineage U84-30
linear U87-9
linen U19-5
lingua U21-11

lingual U21-11; U26-23
lining U86-8
–, uterine U51-7
link U74-5
linkage analysis/study U84-37
linker U84-37
lip U21-9
lipid U79-11
lipolysis U78-4
lipoma U98-11
lipomatosis U98-11
lipomatous U98-11
lipophobic U81-13
liposarcoma U98-11
lipreading U61-10
lips, lick one's U67-17
–, small pudendal U50-14
liquefaction U81-22; U82-4
liquid U81-22; U82-4; U46-8
liquor U10-2
lisp U66-21
list U20-6
listen U61-1
listener U61-1
listless(ness) U76-17; U113-3; U72-1
lit U10-18
lithium U82-18,22
lithocholic acid U47-12
lithotomy position U63-12; U31-6
lithotripsy, gallstone U13-9
live attenuated virus U122-6
– on U12-6
lively U1-6
liver U47-1
– failure U10-12
– function tests/studies U116-14
– hilum U47-5
– lobule/acinus U47-3
– spot U114-5
lividity U12-15
living habits U73-13
– will U20-14
living-in U19-2
livor mortis U12-15
load(ing) U33-10
load, bacillary U94-17
–, heavy U6-3
–, work U142-28
loading dose U135-19
lobar U41-5; U43-3; U47-2; U87-23
lobe U41-5; U87-23
–, caudate U47-2
–, hepatic U47-2
–, pulmonary U43-3
–, quadrate U47-2
lobectomy U47-2; U87-23
lobotomy U87-23
lobular U43-3; U47-3; U87-23
lobulated U87-23
lobule U87-23
– (auricle) U60-2
–, hepatic U47-3
localization U117-4; U104-10
localize U117-4

localized U97-9
lochia U71-23
locking (joint) U128-7
– mechanism U133-1
lockjaw U94-11
locomotion U65-2
locomotor U65-2
locum (tenens) U15-6
locus ceruleus U41-10
–, genetic U84-2
logopedics U66-9
logroll(ing) technique U8-14
loin U30-15
long-chain U81-7
long-forgotten U74-14
long-legged U25-9
long-range U100-15
long-sighted U59-17
long-standing U119-10
look(s) U59-1
 U67-8,14
looker-on U67-14
loop U132-9
– diuretics U88-18
– of Henle U48-8
–, preformed ligature U138-5
–, suture U138-4
loose stools U109-10
loosen (up) U1-13,20
looseness (joint) U142-8
loss U12-13; U49-8
– of vision U15-18
lotion U9-10
lotion bowl U17-12
loudness U61-5
loudspeaker U17-17; U61-5
loupe, magnifying U127-6
louse, true U90-15
low U116-20
low(-spirited) U76-22
lower U116-20
– back pain U22-11
low-fat U24-5
low-frequency U61-6
low-output U33-7
low-pitched U61-6
low-set ears U25-10
low-yield U116-18
loyal(ty) U75-10
lozenge U9-14
LSD (lysergic acid diethylamide)
 U11-22
lubricant U17-14; U56-9; U29-8
lubricate U17-14,6
lubricating U56-9
lubrication U17-14; U56-9
lucid U7-3
lucidity U77-1
lues U96-3
luetic U96-3
lumbar car seat U6-3
– puncture (LP) U118-7
lumbosacral U28-20
lumen U87-22

lumen, vascular U34-14
luminal U34-14; U87-22
lump U97-3; U89-16
– (throat) U109-5
lumpectomy U97-3
lumpy U97-3
lunacy U77-24
lunar month U70-9
lunate (bone) U28-17
lunatic U77-24
lung base U43-4
– collapse U111-15
– expansion U44-10
– function tests U118-3
– scan, perfusion U118-22
– scanning U118-22
lung(s) U43-1
lunula U56-15
lurch U64-7; U65-9
lush U10-10
lust U68-4
luster U82-6
lusterless U31-16
lustful U68-9
luteal phase U51-8
luteinization U51-8
luteinize U51-8
luteinizing/luteotropic hormone (LH) U55-15
luxation (joint) U106-4
lyase U78-8
lymph U35-2
– node/gland U35-3
lymphadenitis U35-3
lymphangioma U98-5
lymphangiosarcoma U98-3
lymphatic U35-2
– scrub U1-20
lymphatics U35-1
lymphedema U111-13; U35-1
lympho(sarco)matous U98-10
lymphoblast U37-10; U86-2
lymphocele U35-1
lymphocyte U37-10
lymphocytic U37-10
lymphocytoma U37-10
lymphodrainage U142-15
lymphogranuloma venereum/inguinale U96-7
lymphoid U35-1
lymphokine U37-10; U39-13
lymphoma U98-10
lymphomatoid U98-10
lymphopathia venereum U96-7
lymphopheresis U136-15
lymphopoiesis U55-27
lymphosarcoma U98-10
lyse U38-14; U37-15
lysis U78-4; U105-18
lysosome U39-18; U83-6
lytic reaction U81-22
lytical U105-18

M

maceration U114-14
macroabscess U114-16
macroaneurysm U110-18
macromolecule U81-2
macronutrient U79-2
macroparasite U90-13
macrophage U39-18
–, tissue U37-9
macula (lutea) U58-13
macular U58-13; U114-9
– disease U17-5
macule /-la U114-9
maculopapular U114-9
mad U76-10; U77-15
madness U77-15
magnesemia U82-20
magnesia U82-20
magnesium U82-20
– sulfate U91-24
magnetic field therapy U142-24
– resonance imaging, (nuclear) U118-24
magnification U127-6
magnify U127-6
maiden name U102-9
mainline (drugs) U11-8
maintenance dose U135-19
major histocompatibility complex (MHC) U39-20
majority U80-9
malabsorbed U109-10
malabsorption U46-13; U109-10
maladaptive U77-9; U88-17
maladjusted U76-21
maladjustment U76-21; U77-9
–, social U13-6
maladroitness U113-9
malady U4-5
malaise U103-7; U4-5
malalignment U119-6; U141-1
malar bone U28-9
– flush U108-8
malaria U94-20
malarial /-ous U94-20
maldigestion U109-10; U46-11
male U53-1
malformation U142-7; U89-5
malignancy U97-5
malignant U97-5
malingerer U4-9
malleability U82-6
malleable U82-29
malleolus U23-12; U28-24
mallet finger U142-8
–, percussion U17-9
malleus U60-5
malnourishment U79-1
malnutrition U103-9
–, protein-energy U82-25
malocclusion U27-13
malodor(ous) U62-3; U109-2
Malpighian corpuscle U48-6

malpractice U18-1; U20-13
malunited (bone) U106-15
mamilla U50-18
mamma(ry gland) U50-17
mammal U90-15
mammary U50-17
mammogram U50-17
managed care U13-8
management U120-1
mandible U28-10
mandibular U28-10
maneuver U8-11
maneuver, manipulative U142-12
manganese/-um U82-26
manganic/-ous U82-26
mangled U12-15
mangling injury U6-8
manhood U53-3
mania U77-18
maniac U77-18
manic U77-18
manifest U103-3; U117-9
manifestation U103-3; U117-9
manipulation U141-2
–, physical U142-12
manipulative U142-12
manly U53-1
manner(s) U75-3
mannerism U75-3
mannitol U82-13
manslaughter U12-10
manual U23-6
– therapy U142-12
manubrium U28-11,13
manus U23-6
map, genome U84-34
march U65-14
margin U87-10
marginal U87-10
margins, poorly delineated U97-3
marijuana U11-15
marital status U102-9
marked U20-3; U103-7
– worsening U4-12
marker, tumor U97-16
marrow, (bone) U38-2
masculine U53-1
masculinity U53-1
masculinization U53-12
mask U117-13
masked U117-13
masquerade U117-13
mass U89-16
–, tumor U97-3
massage U142-15
–, cardiac U123-5
–, electrovibratory U142-23
massaging U123-5
masseur/-euse U142-15
massive U119-14
mastication U27-15
masticatory U27-15
mastitis U50-17
mastoid (process/bone) U60-14

mastoidal U60-14
mastoidectomy U60-14
masturbate U68-8
masturbation U68-8
masturbatory U68-8
mater, dura U41-8
maternal U84-31
- portion U71-16
maternity U84-31
- blues U71-22
- course U13-12
mating U84-30
mattress U19-5
-, vacuum U8-15
matrix, extracellular U86-19
-, interstitial U29-2
matter, gray/white U41-7
maturation U80-10; U69-17
mature U80-10
maturity U80-10
-, fetal lung U71-9
-, sexual U80-7
maxilla U28-10
maxillary antrum/sinus U43-6
maxillofacial U28-9 f; U26-26
Mayday U6-19
meal U2-7
mean U75-12; U100-10
- corpuscular volume U116-10
measles (nine-day) U95-2
-, German U95-3
-, three-day U95-3
measure U20-11
measures, medical U20-11
meatus, external auditory U60-3
mechanism U88-2
-, safety U133-7
mechanoreceptor U57-10,13
meconium U71-19
meddlesome U75-6
media, (tunica) U34-2
medial U87-18
median U87-18; U100-10
mediastinal U43-13
- shift U124-17
mediastinoscopy U128-6
mediastinotomy U43-13
mediastinum U43-13
mediate U42-4; U54-3; U83-19
mediator U83-19
medic U16-9
Medicaid U13-5
Medical Board U13-14
- Council, General (GMC) U13-14
medical U18-9; U9-1
- antishock trousers U8-13
- attention U8-1
- care U20-3
- center U14-1
- clerk/elective U15-6
- directive U20-14
- examiner U12-21; U15-21
- history, past U102-6
- interview U17-16

medical laboratory technician/assistant U16-10
- record U18-14; U20-5; U102-12
- technologist (MT) U16-10
Medicare U13-5
medicate U9-1
medication U9-1
- order U20-7
medicine U9-1
-, internal U15-9
-, occupational U142-26
meditation U1-16
meditative U1-16
medium U61-6
medulla U86-23
- oblongata U41-14
medulla (ossium) U38-2
medullary U38-2; U86-23
- cavity U28-3
megaesophagus U45-5
megakaryocyte U83-3
megaloblastic U38-3; U86-2
megathrombocyte U37-11
mega-ureter U48-10
meibomian glands U56-8
meiosis U83-14
meiotic U83-14
Meissner's corpuscle U57-15
melancholia U76-22
melancholic U76-22
melanin U56-7
melanocyte U56-7
melanocyte-stimulating hormone (MSH) U55-26
melanogenesis U56-7
melanoma, (malignant) U98-15
melanomatous U98-15
melanosarcoma U98-15
melanotic U56-7; U98-15
melanotropin U55-26
melena U109-11
melenic U109-11
melting point/temperature U82-7
Melzer's knot U138-8
membrane U86-15 ff
-, cell/plasma U83-2
-, decidual U85-13
-, mucous U86-17
-, serosal/serous U86-9
-, synovial U29-11
-, tympanic U60-4
-, virginal/hymenal U50-13
membranes, rupture of (ROM) U71-6
membranous U86-15
memorable U74-8
memorize U74-8
memory U74-8
- block U74-13
- cell/lymphocyte U39-15
- loss U74-17
- training U74-13
memory-aiding device U74-13
menarche U51-3
meningeal U41-8; U94-13

meninges U41-8
meningism U94-13
meningitis U94-13
meningoencephalitis U94-13
meningovascular U41-8
meniscus, torn U23-11
menopausal U51-10
menopause U51-3,10
menses U51-2
menstrual cycle U51-1
- flow/bleeding U51-2
menstruate U51-2
menstruation U51-2
mental U73-1 f
- asylum U14-5
- deficiency U77-22
- functions U73-2
- health U77-1
- institution U14-5
- patient U77-24
- retardation U77-22
- state/status U77-1
mentality U73-1
mentally deficient/disabled U77-22
- deranged/disturbed U77-13
mentation U73-1
mentum U21-6
mercurial U82-32
mercurialism U82-32
mercurous/-ic U82-32
mercury U82-32
mercy killing U12-9
Merkel's disk/corpuscle U57-15
mescal(ine) U11-22
mesencephalon U41-1
mesenteric U45-7
mesentery U45-7
meshwork U56-5
mesial U26-21
mesoblastic segment U85-19
mesoderm U85-6
mesomorph U25-2
mesonephric U85-21
mesonephros U85-21
mesothelial U86-14
mesothelium U86-14
messenger U55-1
metabolic U78-1
- imbalance U88-19
- rate, basal (BMR) U78-2
metabolism U78-1
metabolite U78-11
metabolizable U78-1
metabolize U78-1
metacarpal U28-17; U23-6
metacarpus U23-5
metal U82-6
metallic U82-6
metalloprotein U82-6
metanephros U85-21
metaphase U83-13
metaphysis U28-3
metastasectomy U97-13
metastasis U97-13

metastasize U97-13
metastatic U97-13
metatarsus U28-25
metathalamus U41-9
meteorism U109-7
methadone U11-19
methamphetamine U11-17
methanol U47-17
methylenedioxymethamphetamine (MDMA) U11-17
Mexican reds U11-16
MHC U39-20
micelle U81-2,9
microabscess U111-14
microaneurysm U110-18
microatelectasis U111-15
microbe U90-1
microbial U90-1
microbicidal U90-1; U91-8
microbiology U83-1; U86-1
microcirculation U36-1
microcomedo U114-6
microdeletion U84-23
microdissect U127-5
microfilament U83-5
microfilariae U90-1
microflora U90-1
microhematuria U112-3
microinfarction U124-14
micromegakaryocyte U83-3
micrometastatic U97-13
microneurosurgery U127-5
micronutrient U79-17
microorganism U90-1; U86-20
micropetechiae U89-27
microphage U39-18
microphallus U52-14
micropin U141-15
microscissors U132-4
microscope U86-1
microscopy U86-1
microsome U83-8
microspectrophotometry U83-21
microsurgeon U127-5
microsurgery U126-3; U127-5
microsurgical epididymal sperm aspiration (MESA) U69-13
– knot U138-6
microtiter U116-17
microtubular U83-5
microtubule U83-5
microvilli U45-14
micturate U49-16
micturition U49-16
midadult life U80-12
midbrain U41-1
midclavicular U28-11
– line (MCL) U33-4
midcycle U51-1
middle-aged U80-12
midface U25-10
midfacial U28-9
midgut U85-7,21
midlife U80-12

midline U87-18
midportion U87-6
midpuberty U80-7
midsagittal plane U87-18
midstream U49-17
midsystolic U33-3
mid-thirties U80-11
midtrimester U70-9
midwife U16-6
–, licensed U13-14
midwifery U16-6
migraine U113-16
migraineur U113-16
migrainous U113-16
migrate U85-8
mildew U90-18
milestones, motor U70-13
milia U114-6
miliaria U114-6
military antishock trousers U8-13
milk U3-4
– ejection reflex U71-27
– release U55-23
– sugar U79-8
– teeth U27-2
millimol U81-3
mimic U117-13
mimicry U117-13
mind, bring/call to U74-2
–, come/spring to U74-1
–, in one's right U77-3
mindful U74-1
mineral U82-5
mineralocorticoid U55-10
Minicath® U136-6
minilaparotomy U128-13
minimal access surgery U128-1
minimally invasive surgery U128-1
minimum tension, line of U129-10
mini-plate U141-17
minor U80-9; U68-17
minority U80-9
minute volume U33-7
miosis U59-10
miotic U59-10
mirror, head U17-4
misalignment U113-15
–, ocular U59-15
miscarriage U70-7
misdeed U77-10
misdiagnose U117-10
miserable U76-20
misery U76-20; U75-8
mismatch, ventilation-perfusion U111-3
misperception U57-2
misplacement U136-7
misread U61-10
miss U117-4
misshapen U142-7
missing U117-4
misstaging U97-14
misunderstanding U73-5
mite U90-15

mitigate U4-13
mitigation U4-13
mitochondrial U83-7
mitochondrion U83-7
mitosis U83-13
mitotic U83-13
mitral regurgitation U110-5
– valve prolapse U32-12
mixoploidy U84-9
mnemasthenia U74-13
mneme U74-13
mnemic U74-13
mnemonic(s) U74-13
mnemotechnic(s) U74-13
moan U66-4
mobile U64-2; U141-5
mobility U64-2; U142-8,13; U141-5
mobilization U134-13; U141-5
–, passive U142-13
mobilize U64-2; U142-13
modality, therapeutic U120-3
moderation U10-6
modest U80-8; U116-20
modiolus U60-11
modulate U42-4; U83-19
modulation U42-4; U83-19
modulator U83-19
modulatory U42-4; U83-19
moiety U81-4
moist U105-13
moisten U105-13
moisture U105-13
moisturizer U105-13
molar (tooth) U26-7
–, first U26-7
–, third U26-8
molarity U81-3
mold U90-18
moldy U90-18
mole U25-19; U81-3
–, pigmented U98-15; U114-3
molecular U81-2
– weight U81-3
molecule U81-2
molest U68-16
molester, child U68-16
molybdate U82-27
molybdenum U82-27
molybdic U82-27
monitor U125-5 f; U134-8
–, cardiac U125-6
–, intracranial pressure (ICP) U125-13
monitoring, ICU U125-5
monochromatic U59-9
monoclonal U84-33
– antibodies U97-18
monocular U59-16; U58-2
monocyte U37-9; U39-18
monocyte-macrophage scavenger system U39-17
monocytic U37-9
monocytosis U37-9
monofilament U137-7
monokine U39-18,13

monomer U81-6
mononuclear phagocytic system U35-12
mononucleosis, infectious U94-10
monosaccharide U3-16
monosomy U84-25
monozygotic U85-2
mons, veneris/pubis U50-16
mood U76-2
–, exuberant U1-6
moodiness U76-2; U77-1
moody U76-2
moor mud U1-20
moortherapy U1-20
morale U142-26
morbid U89-2
morbidity U89-2; U120-12
– mortality conference U20-10
– rate U100-9
morbilli U95-2
morbilliform U95-2
morcellation U128-16; U133-17
morcellator U133-17; U128-16
morgue U12-16
moribund U12-1
Moro reflex U67-7
morphine U11-18 f
morsel U27-12
mortal U12-3
mortality U12-3; U100-9
mortis, rigor U12-15
mortuary U12-16
morula U85-4
morular U85-4
morulation U85-4
moruloid U85-4
mosaicism U84-22
mother, become a U71-2
motherhood U71-2
motherly U71-2
mother-to-be U70-13
motif, DNA-binding U84-3
motile U46-6; U53-10
motility, gastrointestinal U46-6
–, ocular U59-16
–, sperm U53-10
motion U46-19; U64-1
–, continuous passive U142-14
–, range of U31-18
motionless U64-1
motivation U73-12
motivator U73-12
motive U73-12
motor U64-1
– coordination U31-19
– end plate U30-4
– fiber U40-4
– handicap U142-3
– skills, fine/gross U31-20
mountain sickness U6-17
mourning U12-12
moustache U25-14
mouth U21-8
– breather U44-1

mouth, floor of the U45-3
–, roof of the U26-10
mouthful U21-8
mouth-to-mouth breathing/ ventilation/resuscitation U123-9
mouthwash U21-8
move U64-1
movement U64-1
–, grades of U142-9
mucin U86-17
mucinous U86-17
mucocele U86-17
mucociliary clearance U44-9
mucocutaneous U56-1
mucoepidermoid U98-17
mucoid U86-17
mucolytic U92-15
mucopurulent U44-9; U86-17
mucosa U44-9; U86-17
–, gastrointestinal U54-9
mucosal U54-9; U86-17
mucous /-oid U44-9
mucous plug U111-7
mucoviscidosis U86-17
mucus U44-9; U86-17
mud treatment U1-20
muffled U61-11
multicasualty U6-12; U14-6
– event U8-9
multifactorial U100-5
multifilament (suture) U137-7
multifocal U97-10; U89-3
multigravida U70-7
multiorgan U86-20
multipara U70-8; U71-20
multiplanar U87-2
multiplexing U84-34
multiply handicapped U4-8
multivariable analysis U100-28
multivariate U100-5
multivitamin U79-13
mumble U66-15
mumps U95-4
munch U27-15
murder U12-10
murmur U66-15
–, heart U110-3
muscle U30-2
– aches U94-9
– fiber U30-1
– power U31-13
– relaxant U93-16
– sense U57-14
– spindle U57-12
– strength U31-13
– tone U31-10
– wasting, debilitating U142-4
–, stapedius U61-7
muscular U25-4; U30-2
musculature U30-2
musculoskeletal U28-1; U30-2
musculus pectoralis U30-10
– rectus abdominis U30-14
– sphincter U30-9

mustache U25-14
mutagenesis U91-13
mutagenic U91-13
mutagenicity U91-13; U84-20
mutant U84-20
mutation U84-20
mutational U84-20
mute U61-11
muteness U61-11
mutism U61-11
mutter U66-15
mutual U102-16
– aid group U142-29
myalgia U23-10; U103-7
mycelium U90-18
mycoplasma U90-2
mycosis U90-18
myelin sheath U40-14; U42-5
myelinated U40-14
myelographic U118-7
myelography U118-7
myeloid U38-2
myelopathy U38-2
myelopoiesis U38-1
myesthesia U57-14
myocardial U32-6
– infarction U124-11
myocardiopathy U32-6
myocardium U32-6
myoclonic U72-12
myoelectric prosthesis U142-6
myofascial pain syndrome U77-14
myofibril U30-1
myofilament U30-1
myoma U98-9
myomatosis U98-9
myomatous U98-9
myomectomy U98-9
myomere U85-22
myometrial U50-6
– contraction U55-23
myometrium U50-6
myoneural junction U30-4
myopathy U30-2
myopia U59-17
myopic U59-17
myotome U85-22
myxochondroma U98-12
myxoid U98-7
myxolipoma U98-7
myxoma U98-7
myxomatous U98-7

N

N-terminus U84-3
Naegele's rule U70-10
nagging pain U104-8
nail U56-15; U141-16
– wall U56-16
nailbed U56-15
nailfold U56-15
name U74-3

name tag U17-16
nap U72-2
nape U21-13
napkin, sanitary U1-5
narcolepsy U72-18
narcoleptic U72-18
narcosis U135-6
narcotic U11-1; U72-18; U135-5
narcotize U135-5
nares U43-5
Na-retaining action U55-25
narrow U24-6
narrow-hipped U22-7
narrow-waisted U25-9
nasal U43-6; U21-4
- packing U110-20
- prongs U8-12
- septum U110-20
- speculum U17-6
nasoduodenal U125-18
nasogastric tube U91-26; U125-18
nasolacrimal U58-9
nasopharyngeal U43-6; U45-4
nasopharynx U45-2
nasotracheal U43-8
nates U22-13
National Institutes of Health (NIH) U13-3
native cell U39-1
natriuresis U82-18
natural history U119-9
nature U75-1
nausea U103-11
nauseated /-ing U103-11
nauseous U103-11
navel U22-5; U71-17
navicular bone U28-25
near point U59-13
near-drowning U6-16
near-sighted(ness) U59-17
neck U21-13
- (with) U68-2
- roll U64-8
- stiffness U103-20
-, surgical U28-15
necking U68-2
neckline U21-13
necropsy U12-20
necrosis U89-30
necrotizing U89-30
needle holder U138-14; U132-15
-, butterfly U136-6
-, hypodermic U17-11
-, insufflation U133-13
-, scalp vein U136-6
-, surgical U132-5
needlestick U17-11
needling U17-11
needs U75-21
-, unconscious U73-12
negative U116-22
neglect U77-11; U19-10
-, medical care U20-13
-, unilateral U113-9

neglectful U20-13
negligence U77-11; U15-6
-, medical U20-13
negligible U20-13
nematode U90-16
neoadjuvant U120-8
neocortex U41-6
neonate U80-4
neonatologist U15-16
neoplasia U97-4
neoplasm U97-4
neoplastic U97-4
neovascular U97-15
neovascularity U97-15
neovascularization U97-15
neovasculature U97-15
nephritis U48-2
nephron U48-5
nephronic loop U48-8
nephrotome U85-22
nephrotoxicity U91-11
nerve (cell) U40-1 ff
- ending, free U57-13
- entrapment/encroachment U113-15
- pain U113-14
- plexus U40-12
- root U28-19
-, 10th cranial/pneumogastric U40-10
-, acoustic/vestibulocochlear U60-13
nerves, get on sb.'s U76-6
nerve-sparing U8-18
nervous U40-1; U76-6
- breakdown U6-5
- system, central/peripheral U40-5
- -, involuntary/visceral/ autonomic U40-6
nervousness U76-6
nettle rash U114-11
neural U40-1
- impulse U42-5
- pathway U40-3
- plate U85-18
- tube U85-18,8
neuralgia U113-14
neuralgic U113-14
neurapraxia U113-9
neurilemmoma U98-13
neurinoma U98-13
neuroaxonal U40-2
neuroblastoma U98-13
neuroeffector U40-1
neurofibril U40-1
neurofibroma U98-13
neurofibromatosis U98-13
neurogram U74-12
neurography U74-12
neurohormone U55-1
neurohumoral U88-9
neurohypophysis U54-5
neurologic(al) U15-14
- deficit U113-7; U142-4
- pin U17-1
neurologist U15-14
neurology U15-14

neuromodulation U42-4
neuromuscular junction U30-4
neuron(e) U40-1
neuronal U40-1
neuropathic U113-14
neuropathogenesis U113-14
neuropathologist U15-14
neuropathy U113-14
neurosensory U57-7
neurosis U77-21
neurosurgeon U15-14
neurosyphilis U96-3
neurotic U77-21
neurotoxic U91-4
neurotransmitter U42-10
neurovascular bundle U40-12
neurovirulent U90-10
neutral U81-20
neutralization U81-20
neutralize U81-20; U91-15
neutropenia U37-8; U38-5
neutrophil U37-8
nevus U25-19
-, pigmented U98-15; U114-3
newborn U71-1; U80-4
- nursery U14-8
new-onset U119-5
nibble U27-11
nickel U82-27
nicotinamide adenine dinucleotide (NAD) U47-17
nicotine U10-17
nidation U70-3
night duty U20-4
- sweat U55-17; U72-9
- vision U59-9
nightmare U72-9; U15-17
nigral U41-10
nipple U50-18
nit U90-15
nitrate U82-16
nitrazine paper U82-16
nitric U82-16
- oxide U81-17; U88-2; U123-8
nitrile U91-9
nitrite U82-16
nitrogen U82-16
-, liquid U114-17
nitrogenous U82-16
nitroglycerin U82-16
nitroprusside U91-9
nitrous U82-16
- oxide U93-11
NK cell U39-16
noble gas U82-2
noci(per)ception U57-13
nociceptor U57-13
nocturia U112-6
nocturnal myoclonus U72-12
nod(ding) U67-3; U72-2
nodal package U128-17
node of Ranvier U40-15
-, lymph U35-3

node, sinus/sinoatrial/S-A/Keith-Flack U32-15
nodosity U89-16
nodular U97-3; U89-16
nodularity U97-3
nodulation U89-16
nodule U97-3; U89-16
no-effect-level U91-18
noise U61-3
noiseless U61-3
noisy U61-3
nonalcoholics U10-2,10
nonasthmatics U124-10
noncompliant U120-15
noncontributory U102-8
noncrossover (treatment) U101-14
nondisjunction U84-24
nondistended U109-8
non-drinker U10-10
nonedible U2-5
nonexfoliated (teeth) U27-5
noninvasive U97-12
nonionic U78-23
nonlethal U12-2
nonmotile U69-15; U90-14
nonnarcotic U135-5
nonobese U24-9
nonobstructive U89-18
nonoccupational U142-26
nonprescription U121-1
non-proprietary U121-2
nonrandomized U101-5
nonresponder U120-11
nonself U39-21
non-smoker U10-16
non-sterile U139-2
nonsteroidal U55-4
nontender U96-4
nontoxic U121-13
nontransplanted U129-14
non-weight-bearing ambulation U142-13
noradrenaline U55-11
norepinephrine U42-11; U55-11
norm U116-21
normal U116-21
– limits, within U107-19
– range, in the U107-19
normalize U116-21
normoblast U38-3; U37-5
normocytic U86-2
normotensive U36-8; U110-13; U116-21
normovolemia U116-21
nose U21-4
– blowing U103-16
– picking U110-20
–, bridge of the U59-13
–, upturned U25-10
nosebleed U38-6; U110-20; U5-18; U21-4
nosocomial U121-15; U139-12
notch U28-6
–, supraorbital U58-1

note U20-6; U57-4
notes, case U102-13
noteworthy U57-4
notice U57-4; U102-2
noticeable U57-4; U102-2
notifiable U20-6
notify U20-6; U57-4; U94-1; U13-2
notion U73-8
notochord U85-20
nourish U2-3; U79-1
nourishment U79-1
noxious U91-1
– agents U35-3
NSAID U108-7
N-terminal U39-3
nucha U21-13
nuchal ligament U30-13
– rigidity U103-20; U41-8
nuclear U83-4; U99-22
nucleated U83-4
– blood cells U37-7
nuclei pulposi U85-20
nucleic U83-4; U84-11
nucleolar U83-4
nucleolus U83-4
nucleoprotein U83-4
nucleotidase U84-12
nucleotide U84-12
nucleus U83-4
–, caudate/lentiform U41-10
–, hypoglossal U41-14
nuclide U99-22
nudity U68-10
null cell U39-16
nullipara U70-8
numb U135-3
numbness U4-15; U135-3
nurse U14-8; U16-2ff
– (a baby) U71-26
– anesthetist U131-6
– practitioner U16-5
– specialist U16-5
–, circulating U131-9
–, public/community health U16-7
–, recovery room U131-17
–, registered U131-6
–, surgical U131-8
–, trainee/pupil U16-3
nurse's aide U142-29
nurse-midwife U16-6
nursery U16-2
–, newborn U14-8
nursing U14-8; U16-2f; U71-26
– home U14-4
– mother U11-15
– service U13-3
–, one-on-one U14-7
nursling U14-8; U71-26
nursology U16-2
nurture U79-1
nutrient U79-2
– value U125-19
nutrition(al) U16-13
nutrition, parenteral U125-19

nutritional supplement U3-22
– support U125-19
nutritionist U16-13
nutritious U79-2
nutritive U79-2
nyctalopia U59-18
nycturia U112-6
nymphomania U68-4
nystagmic /-oid U113-12
nystagmography U113-12
nystagmus U113-12

O

obese U24-9
obesity U24-9
obituary U12-17
objective U101-3
oblique U17-4
– view U87-4
obliterate U85-17
obliterated U47-2
obliteration U89-18
oblivion U74-15
oblivious U74-15
obscene U68-10
obscenity U68-10
obscure U58-5
observation U59-1; U107-6
–, ICU U125-5
–, postanesthetic U134-8
observational U125-5
observe U57-4; U59-1; U125-5
obsession U77-19
obsessional U77-19
obsessive U77-19
obstetric forceps U71-14
obstetrician U15-16
obstetrics U15-16
obstinacy U75-19
obstinate U75-19
obstipation U109-6
obstructing U89-18
obstruction U109-6; U89-18
–, airway(s) U111-16
–, bladder neck U112-12
–, bladder outlet U112-4
–, vascular U124-13
obstructive U111-16; U112-12
obtain U102-3; U117-3
obtaining U117-3
obtunded U7-10
obturation U89-18
obturator U133-6
occipital U87-20
– bone U28-8
occlude U27-13
occlusal U26-24; U27-13
occlusion (teeth) U27-13
– (vessel) U89-18
–, centric U27-13
–, vascular U124-13
occult U119-6

occupancy U19-2
- rate U19-15
occupant U19-15
occupation U142-26
occupational (re)adjustment U142-26
- activities U142-27
- therapy U142-26
- training U142-18
octogenarian U80-16
ocular U58-2
- muscles, external U58-16
oculist U15-18
oculogyric U58-16
oculomotor nerve U58-16
Oddi, sphincter of U47-8
odor U62-3
-, breath U109-2
odorant U62-3
odorless U62-3
odynophagia U103-6; U109-5
off and on U119-11
off-axis U87-3
offence U77-10
offensive U68-10
office visit U18-2
-, doctor's/physician's U18-1
officer U18-1
-, house (H.O.) U15-5
-, loading U16-9
-, medical U16-9
offspring U84-29; U69-1
oil gland U56-8
oily U56-8
ointment U9-8
- cannula U132-6
old U80-2
olecranon U28-16
olfaction U62-1; U4-11
olfactory U62-1
oligodendroglioma U98-14
oligomer U81-6
oligospermia U53-7
oliguria U112-2
oliguric U112-2
omental U45-7
omentum U45-7
omphalocele U71-17
on-call consultation U20-4
-, anesthesiologist U131-6
oncogene U91-13; U84-1; U97-1
oncogenic U97-1
oncogenicity U91-13
oncologic(al) U97-1
oncologist U97-1
oncology U97-1
onlooker U6-13
on-off-Effekt U121-8
onset U94-7; U119-5
onychodystrophy U56-15
oocyte U51-5
- retrieval U69-16
oogenesis U51-5
ooze U38-7; U89-26
-, cervical U50-7

oozing U38-7
open-heartedness U32-2
opening U87-21
open-minded U75-16
open-surgical U128-3
operate on (patient) U126-1
operating microscope U127-6
- room U131-1
- table U131-10
- team U131-4
- theatre U131-1
operation U126-1
operative U126-2
- permit U134-3
operator U131-5
operator-dependent U131-5
ophthalm(olog)ic U15-18
ophthalmologist U15-18
ophthalmology U15-18; U58-2
ophthalmoplegia U113-7
ophthalmoscope U58-12; U118-11
ophthalmoscopy U58-8
opiate U11-18
opinion, second U18-12
opioid U11-18
opium U11-18
opportunistic infection U96-15
optic nerve U58-15
- tract U58-15
optic(al) U58-14
optical system U133-3
optician U58-14
-, dispensing U13-14
optics U133-2
optimist U75-6
optimistic U75-6
optometry U58-14
OR technician U131-9
orad U46-7
oral U45-2
- cavity U21-8
- hygiene U1-5
- intake U125-19
- -, postoperative U134-12
orbit, (ocular) U58-1
orbital U58-1
- floor U28-9
orbitonasal U58-1
orchitis U95-4
-, mumps U69-3
order U20-7; U107-3; U90-9; U121-1
orderly U16-14
organ U86-20
- bag U133-16
- of Corti U60-12
- retrieval U128-17
organ-confined U97-9
organelle U86-20
-, cellular U83-4
organic U86-20; U137-10
organism U86-20; U90-1
organochlorine U82-23
organogenesis U86-20
organomegaly U108-12

organ-sparing U126-13
organum spirale U60-12
orgasm U68-6
orgasmic U68-6
orientation U107-12
-, (sexual) U68-14
oriented (to) U107-12
-, well U7-8
orifice U87-21; U48-12
orificial U87-21
origin (muscle) U30-3
originate (muscle) U30-3
oronasal U43-6
oropharynx U45-4
orotracheal U45-2
orthopedic prosthesis U142-6
orthopedics U15-15
orthopedist U15-15
orthopnea U111-2
orthopneic U111-2
orthopod U15-15
orthosis, cervical U141-9
orthotist U15-15
os U28-2; U87-21
- coxae U22-7; U28-21
- sacrum U28-20
-, cervical U50-7
-, external U50-5
osmoceptor U62-1
osmolal/-ar U49-9; U81-21
osmolality U49-9; U81-21
osmolarity U49-9; U81-21
osmoreceptor U57-10
osmoregulation U49-9; U81-21
osmosis U49-9; U81-21; U88-4
osmotic U49-9; U81-21; U88-4
- pressure, colloidal U78-18
ossa U28-2
osseointegration U31-14
osseous U28-2
ossicle U28-2
-, auditory/ear U60-5
ossicular U60-5
ossification U31-14
osteoblast U31-14
osteochondroma U98-12
osteomalacia U28-2
-, infantile/juvenile U95-11
osteopath(ist) U15-22
osteopathy U15-22
osteorrhaphy U141-12
osteosarcoma U98-3
osteosuture U141-12
osteosynthesis U141-4,12
osteotome U132-11
ostium U87-21
ostracism U62-4
ostracize U94-17
otalgia U60-1
otic pit U85-23
otitic U95-12
otitis media U95-12; U14-8
oto(rhino)laryngologist U15-19
otoacoustic emissions U60-12

otolithic apparatus U60-9
otology U60-1
otorrhea U15-19; U17-7; U60-1
otoscope U17-7
ototoxic U15-19; U91-4
ounce (oz.) U24-1
out of sorts U103-7
outbreak U94-7
outburst, temper U76-7
outcome U101-27; U119-19
–, cosmetic U129-3
–, primary U100-20
–, surgical U101-27
outflow U36-5
outgoing U75-13
outgrow U80-3
outlet, thoracic U87-21
outlier U100-12
outlive U12-6; U80-1
outlook U119-19
outpatient U20-2
– department U14-2
outpocketing U85-10
outpouching U28-6; U124-15
output U88-16
–, cardiac U33-7
–, urine/urinary U49-7; U112-5
outraged U76-10
outspoken U75-13
outstretched U31-3
outweigh U117-17
oval window U60-8
ovarian U50-3
– (hyper)stimulation U69-17
– failure U55-15
ovariectomy U50-3
ovary U50-3
overactivity U76-17
overanxious U76-5
overcome U4-16
overcompensation U77-12
overconcern U1-1
overdiagnose U117-10
overdosage U11-11
overdose U11-11; U91-11; U121-7
overeat U2-1
overexertion U24-9; U64-19; U76-18
overexposure U99-7
overexpression U83-16
overgrowth U97-2
overhear U61-1
overhydration U56-12; U78-22
overinflation U111-6
overinvolved U75-6
overload(ing) U33-10
overlook U67-14
overnourishment U79-1
oversensitive U57-8
oversensitiveness U75-17
overstaging U97-14
overt U119-7; U77-13
overtalkativeness U77-18
overtone U66-11
overuse U113-15

overventilation U81-19
overweight U24-8
overwhelming U119-13; U73-11
– urge U77-19
overwrought U76-8
oviduct U50-4
ovogenesis U51-5
ovular U51-5
ovulate U51-9
ovulation U51-9
ovulatory U51-9
ovum, human U51-5; U50-3
oxidant U81-5; U82-11
oxidation U81-17; U82-11
oxidative U81-17
oxide U82-11
oxidoreduction U81-17
oximeter, pulse U125-9
oximetric U125-9
oxygen U82-11
– tent U125-12
–, partial pressure of U116-11
oxygenate U44-6; U82-11
oxygenation U44-6
oxygenator U44-6
–, pump U125-11
oxyhemoglobin U37-6; U116-9; U82-11
oxytocin (OT) U55-23

P

pace U65-6; U123-13; U1-13
– (heart) U33-1
pacemaker U65-6; U123-13
pacer U123-13
pacesetter U65-6
pachygyria U41-5
pachymeninx U41-8
pacing U65-6; U76-8
–, cardiac/ventricular U123-13
pacinian corpuscle U57-15
pack U142-22; U140-24
package U9-16
– insert U9-17
packed cell volume U116-10
– red blood cells U136-16
packet U9-16
packing U140-24
pad U17-13; U140-19
–, heating U19-6
padded room U77-26
padding U140-19
pager U17-17
paging U17-17
pain U104-6
– killer U104-20
– management U142-18
– on urination U112-1
– relief U104-19
– resolution U4-15
– threshold U104-18
–, character/nature U104-7
–, duration of U104-8

pain, epigastric U109-12
–, intensity of U104-9
–, piercing U6-7
–, site/location of U104-10
pain-free U104-6
painful U104-11
pain-sensitive U57-8
palatability U62-1
palatable U2-5
palatal U26-10,23
palate U26-10
–, cleft U26-10
–, hard U28-10; U26-10
–, soft U26-10
palatine U26-10
– bone U28-9
pale U25-12; U108-5
paleness U108-5
palliation U104-19; U119-18; U120-9
palliative U120-9
– therapy U104-19
pallid U25-12; U108-5
pallidal U41-10
pallium U41-6
pallor U25-12; U108-5
palm U23-6
palmar U23-6; U87-17
palpable U62-9; U107-7
palpate U62-9; U107-7
palpating U107-7
palpation U62-9; U107-7
palpatory U62-9; U107-7
palpebra U58-3
palpitate U110-1
palpitation, cardiac U110-1; U107-7
palsied U113-7
palsy U113-7; U135-11
–, gaze U113-11
pancreas U54-8
pancreatic U54-8
– duct U47-10
pancreatitis U54-8
pancreatolysis U54-8
pancreozymin U55-13
pancytopenia U38-5
pandemic U94-8
pandiastolic U33-3
panic U6-21; U77-6
panicky U6-21; U77-6
panic-stricken U6-4
panniculus adiposus U56-5
panoptic U58-14
panotitis U95-12
pant(ing) U44-7
papaverine U11-18
papilla, hair U56-13
–, mammary U50-18
–, optic U58-14
papillary U56-13
– dermis U56-3
– muscle U32-13
papilloma U98-1
papillomatosis U98-1
papillomavirus infection, human U96-13

papovavirus U96-14
papular U114-10
population U114-10
papule /-la U114-10
papulosquamous U114-10
paracentesis U118-8
paracentetic U118-8
paradoxical pulse U110-8
parafango U1-20
paraffin U82-15
– wrap U1-20
parafollicular cell U55-8
parainfluenza U94-9
paralysis U31-12; U113-7; U135-11
–, compression U6-6
–, infantile U95-8
–, respiratory U125-1
–, sleep U72-18
paralytic U113-7
paralyze U135-11
paralyzed U31-12
paramedic U8-6; U16-9
– unit U14-7
paramedical personnel U16-1
parameter U100-5
paramnesia U74-18
paranoid ideation U77-18
paraparesis U113-7
parapertussis U95-5
paraphasia U113-10
paraphilia U68-15
paraphiliac U68-15
paraplegia U142-5
paraplegic U142-5
parapraxia U113-9
parasigmatism U66-21
parasite U90-13; U94-5
parasitemia U90-13
parasitic U90-13
parasitization U90-13
parasomnia U72-14
paraspinal U41-15
parasternal U28-13
parasympathetic fibers U40-9
parasympatholytic U92-8
paratendon U29-11
parathormone U54-7; U55-7
parathyroid (gland) U54-7
– hormone (PTH) U55-7
parathyroidectomy U54-7
paratonia U103-20
paratope U39-7
paratyphoid U94-19
paraurethral glands U50-9
parenchyma U86-22
parenchymatous /-al U86-22
parent U84-29
parentage U84-29
parenteral nutrition/alimentation U125-19; U108-14
paresis U113-7; U135-11
paresthesia U104-17; U135-4
paretic U113-7
parietal U87-13

parietal bone U28-8
– cell U54-9
parietocolic fold U87-13
parietofrontal U28-8
parity U70-8
paronychia U56-15
parorchis U52-5
parotid U45-3
parotitis, infectious/epidemic U95-4
parous U70-8
paroxysm U72-18; U104-14
paroxysmal sleep U72-18
partial recovery U4-16
– zona dissection U69-15
partially disabled U142-3
particle U82-1
particulars U102-9
particulate U82-1
– radiation U99-10
partition off U107-5
part-time work U142-28
parturient U71-9
parturition U71-9
pass away U12-4
– out U7-6
passages, respiratory/air U43-5
passive mobilization U142-13
paste U9-8
pastille U9-14
pat(ting) U62-10; U64-11
patch U114-10
– test U118-2
–, mucous U96-3
patches, Peyer's U35-11
patchy infiltrate U87-23
patella U23-11; U28-24
patency U34-14
–, airway U123-9
patent U34-14; U8-3; U23-5
paternal U84-31
paternity U84-31
path lab U14-11
pathogen U90-5; U119-2; U89-1
pathogenesis U119-2
pathogenic U90-5
pathogenicity U90-5
pathologic(al) U15-21; U89-1; U116-1;
pathologist U15-21; U116-1
pathology U15-21; U116-1; U89-1
pathophysiology U15-21; U88-1
pathway U83-16
–, alternative U39-10
–, nerve/neural U40-3
patience U75-18
patient U20-2; U75-18
– education U142-18
– instruction leaflet U9-17
– profile U102-9
Patient Self-Determination Act U13-7
patient transfer U20-15
patient('s) chart U20-5
patient-family unit U102-7
patient's room U19-2
paucibacillary U90-7

pavement epithelium U86-12
pavor nocturnus U72-14
pecs U30-10
pectoral U22-2
– muscle U30-10
pectus carinatum U22-2
pedestrian U6-3
pediatric U80-6
pediatrician U15-17; U80-6
pediatrics U15-17; U80-6
pedicle U87-24; U43-4
– flap U130-11
– graft U130-10f
–, renal U35-9
pediculosis U90-15
pediculous U90-15
pedigree U84-29
pedophilia U68-15; U80-6
peduncle U87-24
–, cerebellar U41-13
pedunculated U87-24; U114-3
– tag U114-17
pedunculotomy U41-13
peek U67-12
peep U67-12
peer U59-2
– activities U142-27
– pressure U11-13
peers, attachment to U75-9
pegged tooth U26-1
pellet U9-9; U83-20
pelvic U22-7; U28-21; U48-3
– floor U48-15
– – relaxation U142-25
pelvimetry U28-21
pelvioscopy U128-4
pelvis U22-7; U28-21
–, renal U48-3
pelviscope U128-4
pelviscopic U128-4
pelviscopy U128-4
pelvitrainer U128-8
pelvi-ureteric junction U48-10
pendent U63-13
pending U63-13; U6-12
pendulous U63-13
pendulum U63-13
penetrance U84-26,22
penetrant U84-26
penetrate U6-7
penetration U6-7; U68-2
penicillin U92-10
penile U52-14
– buckling testing U53-4
– thrusting U50-12
penis U52-14
penlight U17-4
pension U80-14
pensioner, old age U80-14
pentachlorophenol U82-13
people-seeking U75-13
peptide, gastric inhibitory (GIP) U55-13
perceive U57-2
percentage U100-8

percentile U100-11
perceptible U57-2
perception U57-2; U73-1
–, light U59-6
perceptive U57-2
perceptivity U57-2
perceptual U57-2
– disturbance U11-21
percuss U107-8
percussion U107-8
– note U107-8
–, mediate U17-9
percussor U17-9
percutaneous transhepatic cholangiography (PTC) U118-20
perfusate U36-5
U136-1
perfusion U16-11; U36-5; U88-3; U136-1
– lung scan U118-22
– scintigraphy U118-22
perfusionist U16-11
periadventitial U34-2
periampullary U47-10
perianal U45-17
pericardial effusion U118-15
– rub U110-8
pericardiocentesis U125-17; U110-8; U118-8,15
pericarditis U32-5; U110-8
–, constrictive U110-5
pericardium U32-5
perichondrium U29-2
perihilar U43-4
peril U124-2
perilymph U60-8
perimetrium U50-6
perineal U22-10; U52-20
– muscle, deep transverse U48-15
– rupture U71-18
– suture U71-18
perineum U22-10; U52-20
period, convalescent U4-16
–, menstrual U51-2
periodicity (pain) U104-8
perioperative U126-2
periorbital U58-1
periosteum U28-2
peripartum U71-21
peripheral U87-15
– resistance, total U36-10
periphery U87-15
periportal U36-3
periprostatic U52-10
perisinusoidal U47-4
peristalsis U46-6
peristaltic U46-6
– rushes U109-6
peritoneal U45-7
peritoneoscopy U45-7
peritoneum U45-7
peritonsillar abscess U95-13
periungual U56-15
perivaricose U110-17

perivesical U48-12
permeability U88-6
–, vascular U36-16
permeable U36-16; U88-6
permeate U36-16; U88-6
permissible exposure limit (PEL) U91-5
permit, operative U134-3
–, work U142-28
pernicious U6-11
pernio, erythema U5-12
peroneal (muscles) U30-17
peroneus (muscles) U30-17
peroxidation U81-17
perplexity U77-4
persevere U1-8
persist U119-11
persistence U119-11
persistent U119-11
– vegetative state U7-17
persisting U119-11
person U75-1
personal U75-1
– data U102-9
– hygiene U1-5
personality disorder U4-4
– trait U75-1
personnel, allied health/paramedical U16-1
–, ancillary U16-15
perspiration U105-12
perspire U105-12
pertinent U102-8
perturbation U73-3
pertussis U95-5
perverse U68-15
perversion, sexual U68-15
pervert U68-15
pessary U69-9
pest U91-8
pesticide U81-1; U91-8
pet(ting) U62-10
petechia U89-27
petite U25-8
Petri dish U17-12
pétrissage U71-10; U142-15
petroleum ether U11-23
petrous U60-3
petting U68-2
Peyer's patches/gland U35-11
PGY U15-4,7
pH (value) U81-20
phago(lyso)some U39-17
phagocyte U39-17
phagocytic U39-17
phagocytosis U39-17; U83-15
phagosome U83-11
phalangeal U28-18
phalanx U28-18
phallic U52-14
phallus U52-14
pharmaceutical U15-20
pharmaceutics U92-1
pharmacist U15-20
pharmacologist U15-20

pharmacology U92-1
pharmacopoeia U15-20
pharmacotherapy U15-20
pharmacy U15-20; U9-4
pharyngeal U45-4; U21-12
– reflex U27-16
pharyngopalatine U45-4
pharynx U45-4; U21-12
phase, follicular/proliferative U51-7
–, luteal/secretory U51-8
phencyclidine (PCP) U11-15
phenobarbital U11-16
phenol U82-13
phenolic acid U82-13
phenotype U1-8; U84-10
phenotypic U84-10
pheresis U136-15
phial U9-13
phlebitis U110-17; U136-7; U34-4
phlebography U110-17
phlegm U103-18
– loosener U92-15
phobia U77-5
phobic U77-5
phonation U66-10, 13
–, painful U103-6
phonetic U66-13
phoria U59-4
phosphatase U47-15
phosphate U82-19
phosphocreatine U78-15
phospholipid U47-12; U82-19
phosphorescence U99-8
phosphoric U82-19
phosphorus U82-19
phosphorylate U78-7; U82-19
phosphorylation, oxidative U83-7
photophobia U103-15
photopic adaptation U59-10
photoreceptor U57-10
phyla U90-2
physic U15-1
physical U25-1; U107-2
– examination U107-2
– exercise U1-12
– fitness U1-9
– medicine U142-1
physically disabled U142-3
– healthy U1-2
physician U15-1
–, family/primary-care U15-8
physician-patient relationship U102-16
physicist U15-1
physics U15-1
physiognomy U25-10
physiologic(al) U88-1
physiologist U88-1
physiotherapist U15-22
physiotherapy U142-1
physique U25-1
– builder U1-15
phytotoxin U91-4
pia (mater) U41-8
pial U41-8

pick up (illness) U4-2
picture, clinical U108-2
piebaldism U114-4
pierce U6-7
piggyback U136-4
pigment U114-3
– cell U56-7
pigmentary U114-3
pigmented mole/nevus U98-15; U114-3
pigtail ureteral catheter U125-20
pill U9-7
–, contraceptive U69-7
pillow U19-5
piloerection U56-14; U105-8
piloerector muscle U56-14
pilomotor reflex U56-14; U105-8
pilosebaceous U56-8
pimple U25-18
pimply U25-18
pin U141-15
pinch U62-11; U64-10; U56-19
pinched U25-7
pineal body/gland U54-13
pinealoma U54-13
pink puffer U111-3
pinna U60-2; U17-7
pinnal U60-2
pinned under a car U6-12
pinning U141-15
pinocytosis U83-15
pinprick U62-11; U141-15
pins-and-needles U104-17
pisiform (bone) U28-17
pitch U61-6
pitch (sound) U107-8
pitfall U102-4
pitiful U76-20
pitted scar U114-8
pituitary (gland) U54-5
pituitary stalk U41-9
pity U76-20; U32-2; U75-8
pityriasis U114-7
pivot joint U29-4
place U74-3; U131-11
placebo U101-8
placenta U71-16; U85-14
placental U71-16
– lactogen, human (hPL) U55-21
placentation U71-16
placode U85-23
plague, pneumonic U43-2
plain film/x-rays U109-7; U117-12
plan of care U20-9
planar U87-2
plane U87-2
– crash U6-1
– joint U29-7
planography U99-19
plantar U23-13; U87-17
– reflex U113-1
– response U62-10
planum U87-2
plaque U114-10
plaquelike U114-10

plasma bulk U37-2
– cell U37-10; U39-12
– substitute U136-13
– volume expander U136-13
–, blood U37-3
plasmacytosis U37-3
plasmapheresis U136-15; U83-2
plasmid U84-8
plasmin U37-15
plasminogen U37-15
plaster cast U141-6
plastic surgery U129-3
plate U87-2
plateau phase U42-7
platelet aggregation/agglutination U38-11; U116-13
– count U116-13
– disorder U116-13
–, (blood) U37-11
plates U27-8
plating U141-17
platinum U82-28
playpen U65-18
pleasant U75-5
pleasure, sensual/sensuous U57-9
pledget U140-23
pleiomorphism U84-22
pleiotrop(h)y U84-22
pleiotropism U84-22
pleocytosis U38-5; U83-15
pleomorphism U84-22
plessimeter U17-9
plessor U17-9
plethoric U58-14
pleura U43-11
pleural rub U111-12
pleurisy U43-11; U94-14; U111-12
pleuritic U43-11; U94-14
plexiform U40-12
pleximeter U17-9; U107-8
plexopathy U40-12
plexor U17-9
plexus U34-5; U40-12
–, Kiesselbach's U110-20
pliability U31-11
pliable U31-11; U86-15
plica U87-8; U129-8
plication U87-8; U129-8
ploidy U84-9
plot U100-27
plotter U100-27
plug, mucus U71-7
plugging U43-9
plump U25-6; U24-8
plunge U1-17
plunger U17-10; U34-14
pneumogastric nerve U40-10
pneumomediastinum U43-13
pneumonia U94-14
pneumonic U43-2; U94-14
pneumonitis U94-14
pneumoperitoneum U128-9
pneumoretroperitoneum U128-9
pneumothorax U43-2

pneumothorax, open U124-17
podiatrist U15-15, U16-1
poikilocytosis U38-5
point of maximal impulse (PMI) U33-4
poise U1-15
poison U91-2
– prevention U80-5
poisoning U91-2
–, blood U91-22
–, food U91-21
–, systemic U91-20
poisonous U91-2
polar U81-13; U87-3
pole U81-13; U87-3
–, posterior U58-13
policy U20-7
polio(myelitis) U95-8
poliovaccine U95-8
poliovirus U95-8
polish U91-2
polite U75-5
pollutant U91-6
pollute U91-6
pollution U91-6
poly U37-8
polyclonal U84-33
polydipsia U112-2
polyester U78-7
polyglandular U54-1
polymer U81-6; U84-36
polymerase chain reaction (PCR) U84-36
polymerize U84-36
polymorphic U84-22
polymorphism U84-22
–, restriction fragment length U84-13
polymorphonuclear leukocyte U37-8
polyp U98-1
polypectomy U98-1
polypeptide U55-13
polypoid U98-1
polyposis U98-1
poly(radiculo)neuropathy U113-14
polysome U83-9
polysomnogram U72-16
polysomnography U72-12
polyunsaturated U81-24
polyuria U112-2
polyuric U112-2
pons U41-12
pontine U41-12
pontomedullary U41-12
pool suction tip U128-11
pool(ing) U78-20
pooling (blood) U125-22
pop (drugs) U11-8
popliteal vein U23-9
population U100-3
pore, sweat U56-11
port U133-5; U136-5
porta hepatis U47-5
Porta-cath® U136-5
portal circulation U36-3

portal fissure U47-5
- of entry U91-16
- triad/tract U47-3,5
porter U16-14
portion U87-6
portocaval U47-5
- shunt U36-3
portography U47-5
posey vest U125-24
position U131-11
- sense U57-11
position(ing) U63-1
position, dorsal decubitus U63-8
-, dorsal recumbent U131-12
-, dorsosacral U131-14
-, embryo/fetal U63-6
-, flank U131-16
-, Fowler's U63-12
-, jackknife U63-11
-, lateral decubitus U131-16
-, lateral recumbent U131-15
-, lithotomy U63-12
-, semiprone U131-15
-, sniffing U8-17
-, stable side/lateral U8-17
positional U63-1
positive U116-22
positron U81-11
possessive(ness) U75-21
postanesthesia care unit U135-24
- recovery area U131-17
postanesthetic phase U135-23
postarrest U123-2
postburn U5-11
postcapillary U34-5
postchiasmal U58-15
postcoital U68-5
postconcussion U5-14
postdelivery U71-9
posterior U87-16
postexposure U122-5
postfebrile U105-3
postfertilization U69-12
postganglionic U40-11
postgraft U130-1
posthepatic U47-1
postherpetic U95-7
posthumous U12-19
postictal U113-5
postinfarction U124-11
postinjection U122-4
postmenarch(e)al U51-3
postmenopausal U51-3
postmenopause U51-10
postmenstrual U51-1
postmortem U12-19f
postnasal U43-6
- drip U103-16
postoperative U126-2
postpartum U71-9
- depression U71-22
- period U71-21
postpubertal U80-7
postresuscitation U123-4

postshock U124-4
postsinusoidal U47-4
postsynaptic U40-13
postsyncopal U110-11
post-term U70-11
posttransfusion U136-8
posttransplant U129-14
postulate U101-19
postural U63-1
- correction U142-1,12
- deformity U142-7
- reflex U57-16
- training U142-18
posture U63-1
posturing U63-1
-, dystonic U142-17
postvaccination U122-3
postvoid U49-16
- residual (urine) U112-11
potassium U82-18
- channel U42-7
pot-bellied U22-4
potency U53-2; U121-9
potency-sparing U53-2
potent U53-2; U121-9
potential, action U42-5
potentiate U91-19
potentiation U91-19
-, long-term U74-10
potomania U77-18
pouch of Douglas U50-15
-, rectouterine/rectovaginal U50-15
poultice U140-25
pound (lb) U24-1
pounding (heart) U110-1
pout U67-2
powder U9-9
power of attorney U20-14
-, muscle U31-13
-, penetrating U99-9
practicable U74-6
practice U15-8; U74-6
-, doctor's U18-1
practise U74-6
practitioner U18-1
-, general (GP) U15-8
-, nurse U16-5
praise U62-9
preadmission U20-1
preadolescent U72-14
prearrest U123-2
precancerous U97-6
precapillary U34-5
precaution U6-22; U9-18
precede U71-7; U119-4
precipitant U119-8
precipitate U81-27; U119-8; U10-12
precipitating U119-8
precipitation U81-27
precipitin U81-27
precipitous onset U119-11
preclinical U14-2
preclude U8-14; U36-9
precocious U51-2

precordial U22-3; U32-1
- thump U123-5
precordium U22-3; U32-1
precursor U78-9; U119-4; U39-12; U97-10
predictable U75-9
prediction U119-19; U100-29
predictive U119-19; U100-29
predictor U100-29
predigest U46-11
prediluted U36-13
predischarge evaluation U125-2
predisposed (to) U75-4; U119-1
predisposing U119-1
predisposition U75-4; U119-1
preejection U33-8
pre-eruptive U114-2
pre-existing illness U4-1
pre-exposure U122-5
preference, sex(ual) U68-14
prefertilization U69-12
pregnancy U70-6
pregnant U70-5
pregraft U130-1
prehepatic U47-1
prehospital U14-1
- use U8-15
preinvasive U97-12
preload, (cardiac) U33-10
preloaded U133-12
premalignant U97-5
premature birth U70-8
premaxilla U28-10
premenarch(e)al U51-3
premenopausal U51-3
premenopause U51-10
premenstrual U51-1
premoistened U17-13
premolar U26-6
preoccupied (with) U4-9; U75-14
preoperated U126-1
preoperative U126-2
prep U139-14
- room U19-2; U131-3
preponderance U100-8
prepregnancy U70-6
preproprotein U78-9
prepubertal U80-7
prepuce U52-17
preputial U52-17
preputium U52-17
presage U119-3; U110-7
presby(a)cusis U61-8
presbyopia U59-12
prescribe U121-1
prescription U121-1
- pad U17-1
presedation U135-8
present U102-1
- illness, history of U102-5
- (with/as) U102-1
presentation U102-1
-, fetal U71-5
presenting U102-1

preservation U8-18; U126-13
preservative, wood U91-8
preserve U8-18; U1-5; U126-13
preshaped U129-4
presomite U85-19
press(ing) U64-12
pressure sense U57-17
–, blood U107-14
–, intraocular U59-16
presymptomatic U103-1
presynaptic U40-13
presyncopal U110-11
presyncope U110-11
presystolic U33-3
pretensions U75-12
preterm U70-11
– labor U96-9
pretest U118-2
pretransfusion U136-8
pretransplant U129-14
prevaccination U122-3
prevalence U100-7
prevention U120-6
–, accident U6-22
preventive U6-22; U120-6
previsit U18-2
priapus U52-14
prick U5-10
– test U118-2
prick(ling) U62-11
prickle cell layer U56-2
prickly heat U56-11; U62-11
pride U75-20
primary care physician U15-8; U102-16
primigravida U70-7
primipara U70-8
primiparous U70-8
primitive groove/pit U85-8
– gut U85-21
– node U85-8
– streak/line U85-8
primordial U85-9
primordium U85-9
principle, all-or-none U42-8
prion U90-11
prior (to) U53-2
privacy U18-11
private U18-11
– parts U52-1
proarrythmia U110-6
probability U100-31
probationer (nurse) U16-3
probe U132-8
probing U132-8
problem list U20-6
procedure, diagnostic U20-8
–, surgical/operative U126-4
process U28-5; U87-27
–, mastoid U60-14
prochordal U85-20
procreate U69-1
procreation U69-1
proctitis U45-16
proctoscope U45-16; U118-11

proctoscopy U45-16
prodromal U119-4
prodrome U119-4
produce U54-2
productive cough U103-7
proenzyme U78-8
profile, patient U102-9
profound U78-2
profuse hemorrhage U34-10
progenitor U84-29
– cell U37-8
progeny U84-29
progestagen U55-19
progestational hormone U55-19
progesterone U55-19
progestin U55-19
progestogen U55-19
prognosis U119-19
prognostic U119-19
prognosticate U119-19
progress U97-7; U119-12
– report/note U20-6
progression U119-12
–, tumor U97-7
progressive U97-7; U119-12
prohibition U10-8
prohormone U55-1; U78-9
proinsulin U55-12
projecting U87-27
projection U87-27
prokaryote U83-3
prokaryotic U83-3
prolabium U21-9
prolactin (PRL) U55-22
prolactinoma U55-22
prolapse U113-17; U89-22
proliferate U51-7
proliferation U51-7
–, tumor U97-7
proliferative U97-7
prometaphase U83-13
prominence U87-27
–, laryngeal U21-14
prominent U87-27
promiscuity U68-12
promiscuous U68-12
promonocyte U37-9
promontory U28-4
promoter U84-21
prompt U74-2
pronate U31-9
pronation U31-9
pronator U31-9
prone U31-9; U63-9
– board U142-19
– cart U142-19
– to U119-1; U111-4
prone-lying U63-9
pronephros U85-21
pronounce U66-13
pronuclear stage U69-12
pronunciation U66-13
proof U117-9; U101-17
propagate U42-4

propagation U42-4; U124-13
property damage U6-1
prophase U83-13
prophylactic U69-6; U120-6
prophylaxis U6-22; U120-6
–, antibiotic U139-13
proportion U100-8
proportional hazard model U100-35
propose U18-5
propped up U63-10
proprietary U121-2
proprioception U57-11; U142-19
proprioceptive U57-11
proprioceptor U57-11
propriospinal U57-11
proprotein U78-9
proptosis U113-17
propulsion U46-7
prosencephalon U41-1
prospect U119-19
prospective U101-6
prostaglandin U78-24
prostanoic acid U78-24; U82-10
prostate (gland) U52-10
prostatectomy, transurethral U112-12
prostate-specific antigen (PSA) U97-16
prostatic U52-10
– sheath U48-14
prostatism U112-6
prostatodynia U52-10
prosthesis U142-6
prosthetic U142-6
prosthetist U142-6
prostrate U4-6; U103-8
prostration U4-6; U103-8
protective immunity U122-6
protein U79-9
proteinuria U112-1
proteolysis U78-14
proteolytic U78-14; U79-9
proteolyze U78-4
prothrombin U37-13
prothrombinogen U37-13
protium U82-9
protocol U101-7; U120-5
proton U81-11
protoplasm U83-2
protozoal/-an U90-2
protozoon U90-2
protracted U119-10; U73-7
protraction U141-3
protuberance U87-27
protuberant U87-27
– abdomen U109-8
provide U88-3
provitamin U78-9; U79-13
provoke U119-8
proximal U87-14; U26-22
prude U68-10
prudence U91-12
prudish U68-10
pruritic urticarial papules and plaques
  of pregnancy (PUPPP) U70-15
pruritus U103-19

pseudoaneurysm U110-18
pseudoascites U109-9
pseudocast U112-14
pseudocroup U95-10
pseudocyst U89-24
pseudodementia U77-23
pseudohermaphroditism, male U53-12
pseudoleukoderma U114-4
pseudomembrane U86-15; U95-9
pseudo-obstruction U109-6
pseudopodia U90-4
pseudopregnancy U70-6
pseudorickets U95-11
pseudorubella U95-3
pseudostrabismus U59-4
pseudostratified U86-10
psittacosis U90-14; U96-9
psoas muscle U30-15
psoriasis U114-7
psychalgia U77-2
psychanopsia U77-2
psyche U77-2
psychedelic U11-21
psychiatric disease/illness U77-16
– hospital U14-5
psychiatrist U15-12; U77-16
psychiatry U15-12; U77-16
psychic U77-2
psycho(path) U77-24
psychoactive substance U92-23
psychoanalyst U15-12; U77-21
psychodynamics U77-16
psychologist U15-12
psychology U15-12
psychomotor U15-12
psychopathic U77-24
psychopathy U77-24
psychophysiologic U88-1
– disorder U77-14
psychosis U77-21
psychosocial U77-16
psychosomatic U40-7
– illness U77-14
psychotherapist U16-12
psychotherapy U15-12; U77-21
psychotic U77-21
ptosis U113-17; U89-22
ptotic U113-17
pubarche U80-7
pubertal U80-7
puberty U80-7
pubescence U80-7
pubescent U80-7
pubic U22-8; U28-22; U52-18
– bone U28-22
– hair U50-16
– symphysis U52-18
pubis U28-22
Public Health Service (PHS) U13-3
public nurse U16-7
– welfare U13-6
pubococcygeal U52-18
puckering U25-17
pudendal U22-10; U50-11; U52-20

pudendum U22-10; U52-20
– muliebre U50-11
puerpera U71-21
puerperal U71-21
puerperium U71-21
puff U44-7
– on U10-16
puffiness U108-10; U5-15
puffing (cheeks) U67-17
puffy U108-10; U5-15
– cheeks U25-10
pull U64-13
– (muscle) U5-17
pulley, muscular U30-8
pulley-enhanced U30-8
pull-up U64-13
pulmonary U36-2; U43-2
– circulation U36-2
– edema U111-13
– embolism U124-13
– function tests U118-3
pulmonic U43-2
pulp white/red U35-4
–, dental U26-18
pulsate U36-9
pulsatile U36-9; U107-13; U55-22
pulsation U36-9; U107-13
pulse U107-13
– oximetry U125-9
– pressure U36-9
– wave U36-9
pulseless U36-9
pulsus paradoxus U36-9
pump failure U110-14
punch U6-4
punctum U58-9
puncture U6-7; U118-7; U136-2; U5-10
–, initial U128-12
pungent U62-5
pupil U58-8
pupillary U58-8; U107-15
pupils equal & reactive to light U107-15
purity U116-3
Purkinje's fibers U32-15
purpose U73-8
purposeful U73-8
– movements U31-19
purposeless U76-8
purpura, thrombotic thrombocytopenic U136-15
pursuit, smooth U58-16
purulent U89-12; U140-14
pus U17-10; U89-12
push(ing) U64-12
pusher U11-7
push-up U64-12
pustular U114-12
pustule U114-12
put to sleep U135-1
– under U135-1
putamen U41-10
putrefaction U46-17
putrefactive U46-17
putrefy U46-17

putrid U62-5
pyelogram U118-19
pyelography, intravenous (IVP) U118-19
pyelon U48-3
pyelonephritis U48-3
pyknic U25-6
pyloric U45-8
pylorus U45-8
pyothorax U111-14
pyramid U41-14
pyramidal decussation U41-14
– tract U41-16
pyrexia U105-3
– of unknown origin U105-16
pyrosis U109-4
pyuria U112-1

Q

quack (doctor) U15-23
quackery U15-23
quad cane U19-11
quadrant U26-20
quadrantanopia U59-17
quadriceps (femoris muscle) U30-16
quadrigeminal U41-13
quadriplegia U113-7
quadriplegic U142-5
quadruplets U70-14
quads U30-16
quality assessment U20-12
quantitation U83-21
quarantine (off) U14-10
quartile U100-11
query U18-11
questionable U116-23
questionnaire U102-15
quickening, fetal U70-13
quicklime U82-19
quick-tempered U76-2
quick-witted U75-7
quiescence U119-6
quiescent U119-6
quiet U61-11; U76-19
quinsy U95-13
quintuplets U70-14
quiver U64-6
quivering voice U77-5

R

rabid U94-12
rabies U94-12
rabiform U94-12
race U65-15
racemose gland U52-13
racing (heart) U110-1
radial U28-16
radiant U99-2
radiate (pain) U23-3; U104-10
– (rays) U99-2
radiation U15-13

radiation burn U99-7
– dose U99-9
– exposure U99-7
– sickness U118-18
radical U81-5
radio contact U8-6
radioactive U99-21
radioactivity U99-21
radiobiology U15-13
radiodense U99-11
radiogram U99-3
radiograph U99-3
radiographic U118-18
radiography U118-18; U99-3
–, sectional U99-19
radioimmunoassay U39-1
radioiodine U82-34
radioisotope U82-1; U99-22
radiologic(al) U118-18; U99-1
radiologist U15-13
radiology U15-13; U99-1
– suite U14-9
radiolucency U99-11
radiolucent U99-11
radionuclide U99-22
radiopacity U99-11
radiopaque U82-33; U99-11
radioresistant U99-23
radiosensitive U99-23; U103-15
radiosensitivity U99-23
radiotracer U79-17; U82-34
radioulnar joint U28-16
radium U82-34
radius U28-16
radix dentis U26-19
radon U82-34
rage U76-10; U94-12
ragged U96-4
RAI uptake U55-3
rails U65-18
raise U64-16; U65-17; U116-19
– (flap) U129-11
– one's (eye)brows U67-15
raised U64-16; U65-17; U116-19; U114-3
rales U111-9
ramus U28-5; U34-13
random U101-5
randomization U101-5
range of motion/movement (ROM) U31-18
–, therapeutic U100-15
Ranvier, node of U40-15
rape U68-17
rapist U68-17
rapport U102-16
–, physician-patient U18-8
rarefaction U61-3
rash U75-18; U108-9; U114-2
rasp U132-12
raspatory U132-12
rate U100-8
ratio U100-8
–, risk-benefit U134-5

rational U73-7
rationale U73-7
rationality U73-7
rationalization U73-7
rationalize U73-7
ray U99-2
Raynaud's phenomenon U110-19
reabsorb U49-4; U88-8
reabsorption U49-4; U88-8
react (to/with) U39-2; U116-2
reactant U39-2; U81-15
reaction U116-2
–, anaphylactic U124-3
–, chemical U81-15
–, hemolytic (transfusion) U136-12
reactive U81-15; U116-2
reactivity U39-2; U81-15
readapt U88-8
readjust U77-9
readmission U20-1
readouts, digital U125-6
reagent U81-15
realign U1-18
realignment U141-2
realization U74-4
realize U74-4
reanastomosis U69-4
reanimation U123-4
reappoint U18-2
reappraisal U117-8
reapproximate U137-5; U140-2
rearrangement U84-24
reason U73-1
reasonable U73-1
reasoning U73-1
reassess U117-1
reassurance U18-6
rebleed U38-6; U124-16
rebranch U34-13
rebreathing bag U8-12
recalcitrant U120-13
recall U74-1
recapitulate U74-7
receding gums U26-12
receptaculum chyli U35-8
reception U57-10
– desk U18-3
– room U18-3
receptionist U18-3
receptive U57-10
receptor U81-14
– site U55-2
–, sensory U57-10
recess U50-15
recessive U84-27
recessiveness U84-27
recheck U18-9
recipient U136-9; U129-15
reciprocal innervation U42-14
recirculate U36-1
reckless U75-18

reckless, driving U12-10
recklessness U75-18
Recklinghausen's disease U98-13
reclining U63-10
recognition U73-4; U74-3; U117-4
recognizable U74-3
recognize U73-4; U74-3; U117-4
recollect U74-8
recollection U74-8
recombinant U84-17
recombinate U84-17
recombination, genetic U84-17
recombined U84-17
recommend U18-5
recommendation U18-5
recompression U6-17
reconstruction U129-1
reconstructive surgery U129-3
reconvert U78-6
record U20-5
–, medical U18-14; U102-12
recording U102-12
recover (from) U4-16
recovery U4-16; U134-14
– (anesthesia) U135-21
– room U131-17
– – bed U131-18
recreation U1-10
recreational activities U142-27
– vehicle U6-3
recrudescence U94-7; U119-18
recrudescent U94-7; U96-10
recruitment, patient U101-4
rectal U45-16
– suppository U103-11
rectocele U51-10
rectosigmoid U45-16
rectouterine pouch U50-15
rectovaginal U50-8
rectum U45-16
rectus (muscle of the abdomen) U30-14
recumbency U63-10
–, on U109-4
recumbent U63-10
recuperate U4-16
recuperation U4-16; U134-14
recur U119-18
recurrence U119-18
recurrent U119-18
recycle U78-6
red blood cell U37-5
Red Cross, International (IRC) U13-12
red-faced U25-12
redisplacement U106-4
redness U108-7
redox reaction U81-17
redress U140-17
reduced U116-20
reducer cap U133-11
reduction U81-17; U116-20; U129-19
reduction (fracture) U141-2
redundancy U39-16
re-education U142-18
reefer U11-14

reek U62-4
reemergence U95-7
reepithelialization U86-7
reesterify U82-14
reexpand U44-10
reexperience U74-11
reexplore U126-11
reexposure U39-15
refer to/for U18-12
reference range U116-9
referral U18-12; U102-14
refixation U59-14
reflection U73-6
reflex U42-12; U113-1
– arc U42-12
– hammer U17-9
– inhibition U42-13
–, let-down/milk ejection U71-27
–, pharyngeal U27-16
–, plantar U113-1
–, postural/attitudinal U57-16
–, voiding U40-3
reflexive U42-12; U113-1
reflexology massage U142-15
reflux U46-4
–, (gastro)esophageal U109-4
–, urinary U112-12
refluxing /-ive U112-12
reformed alcoholic U10-6
refraction U59-12
refractive U59-12
refractoriness U42-7
refractory U120-13
– period U42-7
refracture U106-1
regeneration U1-10
regimen U120-5
region, genetic U84-2
–, inguinal U22-9
–, suprapubic/hypogastric U22-8
register U74-9
registered nurse (RN) U16-4
registrar U15-4
registration U74-9
registry, cancer/tumor U13-10
regress U119-17
regression U119-17; U14-5; U100-33
regulate U54-3
regulation U54-3; U83-18; U88-2
regulator U54-3
regulatory U54-3; U83-18; U88-2
regurgitant U110-10
regurgitate U46-4
regurgitation U46-4; U103-12
–, aortic U110-10; U36-9
rehabilitation U142-2; U129-2
–, vocational U142-2
rehabilitative measures U142-3
rehearsal U74-6
rehearse U74-6
rehydrated U78-22
rehydration U56-12
reimburse U18-15
reimbursement, fee-for-service U13-3

reinfarction U124-11
reinforce U62-9
reinfuse U136-1
reinnervate U42-1
reinsurance U13-5
rejection U39-22
relapse U119-18
relate U18-8; U74-5
related U84-31
relation U74-5; U100-32
relationship U74-5; U84-31; U100-32
–, doctor-patient U18-8; U102-16
relative U84-31
relax U1-10
relaxant U31-1; U76-19; U93-16
relaxation U1-10; U31-1; U76-19
– techniques U142-25
–, deep muscle U1-16
relaxed U31-1; U76-19
relaxing U1-16
relay U42-4
relearn U74-7
release U20-16; U54-2; U88-11
–, with abrupt U109-12
relevant U102-8
reliability U75-9; U100-30
reliable U75-9
reliance U18-8
relief U8-2
reluctance U75-11; U76-14
reluctant U75-11; U76-14
rely (on) U75-9
REM sleep U72-10
remedial U9-2
– gymnastics U1-15
remediation U9-2
remedy U9-2
remember U74-1
remembrance U74-1
remind U74-2
reminder U74-2
remineralization U82-5
reminisce U74-2
reminiscence U74-2
reminiscent U74-2
remission U119-17
remit U119-17
remittent U119-17
remnant U85-13,20
remodel U129-4
remorse U76-13; U77-10
remorseful U77-10
remorseless U76-13
remote-controlled U133-1
remyelination U40-14
renal U48-2
– failure U111-2
– insufficiency U18-5
– plasma flow (RPF) U49-2
renin U55-25
renin-angiotensin-aldosterone system
  (RAAS) U49-11
reninism U49-11
renogram U48-2

Renshaw cell U42-13
reorientation U107-12
reoxygenation U125-11
repackaging U9-16
repair U129-1
repeat U74-7
repel U91-8
repellent U91-8
reperfusion U36-5
repetition U74-7
repetitive U74-7
repigmentation U114-3
replacement U3-21; U129-2
replenish(ment) U78-21; U88-15;
  U49-8
replicate U84-16; U94-2
replication U84-16
replicative U84-16
replicator U84-16
replicon U84-16
repolarization U42-7
report U8-7; U20-6; U102-2
–, case U102-13
reportable (disease) U20-6; U13-11
reposition U131-11
repositioning U63-1
repress U74-14
repression U74-14; U77-17; U83-16
reproach U76-13
reproachful U76-13
reproduce U69-1
reproducibility U100-30
reproduction U69-1
reproductive U69-1
– system U52-1
– technologies, assisted U69-11
rescan U118-22
rescue U8-2
– worker U13-1
research U101-2
resectable U126-15
resection U126-15; U127-13
resent U76-11
resentful U76-11
resentment U76-11
reserve volume U44-12
reserved U75-17
reservoir U78-20; U94-4
– bag U8-12; U135-15
reshaped U129-4
residence/-cy U15-4
resident U15-4
residential U15-4
residual U81-4
– urine U112-11
– volume (RV) U44-12
residue U81-4
resilience/-cy U31-16
resilient U31-16
resin U11-15
resistance U120-13
– exercises U142-17
–, immune U39-22
–, vascular U36-10

resistant U39-22
resolute U75-11
resolution U4-15
–, image U99-14
–, soft tissue U99-14
resolution, spatial U59-9
resolve U4-15; U108-9
resolving power U59-8; U99-14
resorption U27-20; U137-8
respiration U44-4; U125-10
–, accessory muscles of U111-5
–, labored U111-2
respirator U44-4; U125-10
respiratory U44-4
– arrest U123-6
– excursion U107-16
– failure U123-6
– therapy U142-26
respond (to therapy) U120-11
response U120-11
–, ventricular U110-2
responsible U75-9
responsive U7-7
responsiveness U39-2
rest U1-10; U64-17; U72-5
– home U1-10
– pain U4-13
–, to settle with U4-15
resterilize U139-2
resting U64-17
– tone U1-13
restless(ness) U64-17; U72-5; U113-2
restoration U142-2
restorative U142-2
restrain(ing) U77-26
restraint U77-26; U19-2
restraints, lateral U8-16
–, wrist U125-24
restriction endonuclease/enzyme U84-32
result U116-18; U117-6
resurfacing U128-18
resuscitate U123-3
resuscitation U123-4
– bag U8-12
–, fluid U125-2
resuscitative U123-4
resuscitator U123-4
resuture U138-1; U137-1
retain U49-4; U74-10
retardation, mental U77-22
–, borderline U77-22
retarded, mentally U77-22
retch U46-5; U27-16
retching U46-5; U111-7
retention U49-4; U74-10
– feature/mechanism U133-9
–, urinary/urine U112-10
retentive memory U74-1
– sleeve U133-9
retesting U118-2
reticular U35-12; U83-8
– fiber U86-5
reticulate(d) U83-8

reticulin U83-8
reticulocyte U35-12; U37-5; U86-5
reticuloendothelial system U35-12
reticulonodular U35-12
retina U58-13
retinacular U30-8
retinaculum U30-8
retinal U58-13
retinopathy U58-13
retire U72-3
retiree U80-14
retirement U80-14
– facility U4-7
retract U64-13
retraction U64-13; U132-16; U141-3
retractor U17-6; U132-16
retraining U142-18
–, employment U142-26
retransplantation U129-14
retreat U77-8
retrieval U8-3; U74-10
– bag U133-16
–, organ U128-17
–, verbal U74-6
retrieve U69-16; U128-17; U133-16
retrocalcaneal bursitis U28-27
retro-orbital U58-1
retroperitoneoscopic U128-5
retroperitoneoscopy U128-5
retroperitoneum U45-7
retropubic U28-22; U52-18
retrospective U101-6
retroversion U31-8; U87-16
retrovirus U90-10
return to normal (activity) U4-14; U134-14
reusable U139-4
revaccination U122-3
reveal U102-3; U107-17
reversal U4-14
reverse U4-14
reversible U4-14
revert U4-14
review U20-12; U102-8
– of systems (ROS) U102-11
revise U74-7
revision U74-7
revive U123-3
revolutions U138-7
rhabdo(urinary) sphincter U48-14
rhabdomyoma U98-9
rhabdosphincter U30-9
Rhesus factor U37-17
rhinitis U15-19
–, acute U94-9
–, seasonal allergic U80-12
rhinoplasty U127-4
rhinoscope U17-6
Rh-negative /-positive U37-17
rhombencephalon U41-1
rhonch(i)al U111-8
rhonchus U111-8
rhythm, cardiac/heart U33-6
–, circadian U72-8

rhythm, gallop U110-6
rib U28-14
– cage U8-11; U22-3
– – motion U44-11
ribonucleic acid U84-15
ribonucleoprotein U83-9; U84-15
ribonucleotide U84-15
ribose U83-9
ribosomal U83-9; U84-15
ribosome U83-9; U84-15
ribosyl U83-9
ribotyping U84-15
rickets U95-11; U31-14; U82-5
rickettsia U90-12
rickettsial U90-12
rickettsialpox U90-12
rickettsicidal U90-12
rickettsiosis U90-12
ridge U28-5
–, alveolar U26-13
righting reflex U57-16
right-to-die U12-9
rigid U12-15; U31-17; U53-4; U103-20; U109-14
– abdomen U109-12
rigidity U31-17; U53-4
–, abdominal muscle/wall U109-13
–, board-like (abdominal) U109-14
–, nuchal U103-20
rigor U103-20; U105-9
– mortis U12-15
ring, lower esophageal U109-5
rinse U139-5
rise U65-17; U64-16
riser U65-17
risk U8-4
– factor, major U124-2
–, at U124-2
–, operative U134-5
risky U8-4
ritual U73-13
ritualistic U73-13
roach U11-14
robot U133-1
robotic arm U133-1
robust U1-11
rock U64-5
Rocky Mountain spotted fever U90-12
rodenticide U91-9
rod-lens system U133-4
rods U58-13
Roeder's knot U138-7
roentgen-equivalent-man U99-10
roentgenogram U99-3; U118-18
roll (over) U64-8
rolled-up U64-8
rongeur (forceps) U132-11
rooming-in U19-2
root U87-25
– (tooth) U26-19
– apex U26-19
– curettage U132-10
– dentine U26-16
– of the lung U43-4

root, spinal U41-15
roseola U95-2
rot U46-17
rota(to)ry U31-7
rotation U31-7
rotational knot U138-10
rotator cuff, torn U113-15
rough U62-8
roughage U79-16
round window U60-8
–, ward U20-9
roundworm U90-16
route U97-11
– of transmission U119-2
– (surgical) U126-6
rub U62-11; U64-11
–, pericardial (friction) U110-8
–, pleural (friction) U111-12
rubber U69-6
rubbing U142-15
rubella U95-3
rubelliform U95-3
rubeola U95-2
rubidium U82-18
rubor U108-7
ruborous U108-7
ruddiness U25-12
ruddy U25-12
rudiment U85-9
rudimentary U85-9
Ruffini corpuscle U57-15
rugine U132-12
rule U20-7
– out U117-14
rumble U46-14; U110-3
ruminate U109-3
rumination U109-3
ruminations U73-6
run U87-7
– into/over U6-2
run(ning) U1-14; U65-14
runner U1-14
runs, have the U109-10
rupture U124-15; U5-19; U89-23
– of membranes (ROM) U71-6
–, splenic U124-16
rush U11-9; U65-15

S

S-A node U32-15
sac, alveolar/air U43-10
saccade U59-14
saccharide U79-6
saccharin U79-6
saccule U60-9
sacral U28-20
sacroiliac joint U28-20
sacrum, (os) U28-20
saddle joint U29-6
sad-looking U67-8
safe U8-2
safeguard U8-2

safety U8-4
– belt U8-2
– rule U6-22
– shield U133-7
sag(ging) U56-19; U64-15
saline laxative U81-21
–, normal U82-5
saliva U45-3; U109-3; U27-9
salivary U27-9
– gland U45-3
salivate U45-3; U109-3
salivation U45-3; U27-9
salmonellosis U94-19
salpingectomy U69-3
salpingitis U50-4
salpinx U50-4
salt U82-5; U3-18
saltatory conduction U40-15; U42-3
salts, smelling U123-3
salvage U8-18
Salvation Army U13-12
salve U9-8
sample U118-4; U100-4
–, stool U116-8
–, urine U116-15
sampling U118-4; U100-4
sanatorium U14-3
sandpaper rash U95-6
sane U77-3
sanguis U37-1
sanitarium U14-3
sanitary U1-5
sanitation U1-5
sanitize U1-5
sanity U77-3
saponification U82-14
saprophyte U90-13
sarcogenic U97-6
sarcoma U97-6; U98-3
sarcomatosis U98-3
sarcomatous /-toid U98-3
sarcoplasm U30-1
satellite U84-7
satiety, early U109-1
saturable U81-24
saturated U81-24
saturation U81-24
–, oxygen U125-9
satyriasis U68-4
sauna (bath) U1-17
saunter U65-7
save U8-2; U123-1
savor U62-7
savory U62-7
scab U114-8; U140-9
scabies U96-12
scabieticide U96-12
scaffolding U86-19
scald U5-11
scale U100-6; U24-11
– (off) U114-7
–, centigrade U105-6
scale(s), skin U114-7
scaling U114-7

scalp U25-15
– vein needle U136-6
scalpel U132-3
scaly U114-7; U86-12
scan U99-18
scanner U118-22; U99-18
scanning, radionuclide/nuclear U118-22
scanography U99-18
scanty U103-18
scaphoid (bone) U28-17
scapula U28-12
scapular bone U28-12
scapuloclavicular joint U28-12
scar U114-8; U140-10
scarlatina U95-6
scarlatiniform U95-6
scarlet fever U95-6
scarring U140-10
scattered U114-5
scavenge U39-17; U78-19
scavenger cell U39-17
–, free-radical U78-19
scent U62-3
scented U62-3
schedule U121-1
schistosome U90-17
schistosomiasis U90-17
schizont U90-4
Schlemm, canal of U58-11
Schwann cell U40-14
schwannoma U98-13
sciatic nerve U63-12; U113-1
– – irritation U142-11
scintigram U99-17
scintigraphy U99-17
scintillation U99-17
scintiscans, serial U99-17
scissors U132-4
sclera U58-6
scleral U58-6
scleritis U58-6
scleroderma U56-3
scleroprotein U56-6
sclerotherapy U110-17
sclerotome U85-22
scoop U132-10
– stretcher U8-16
scope U133-2; U128-1,3
score, raw U100-6
–, scaled U100-6
–, standard U100-6
scotoma U113-11
scowl(ing) U67-11
scramble U65-18
scrape U5-9
scraping(s) U17-3; U116-4
scratch U62-11; U5-9
– test U118-2
scratchy feeling U103-2
scream U66-14
screw U141-16
scrotal U52-2
scrotum U52-2

INDEX – ENGLISH

scrub U1-20
– nurse U131-8
– suit U139-6,15
scrub-up U139-6
scrupulous U75-11,1
scurf U114-7
scurfy U114-7
seal U137-11
sealant U82-30; U137-11
sealing, airtight U133-6
search-and-rescue mission U8-2
sea-sick U103-11
seaweed wrap U1-20
sebaceous gland U56-8
seborrhea U56-8; U114-7
seborrheic U56-8
sebum U56-8
seclusion U76-7
–, room U19-2
second messenger U83-17
– opinion U18-12; U102-14
secondaries U97-13
secondary to U50-3; U112-10; U123-6
secrete U49-4; U54-2; U88-11
secretin U54-9; U55-13
secretion U49-4; U54-2; U88-11
secretomotor U40-7
secretory U54-2; U88-11
secretory fibers U40-7
sectio U126-10
section U14-9; U87-5; U126-10
secundigravid U70-5
secure U8-2; U137-4
security U8-4
sedation U135-8
sedative U135-8 f
sedentary U119-8
sediment U81-27
–, urinary U107-18
sedimentation U81-27
sed(imentation) rate U116-12
seduce U68-9
seductive U68-9
see(ing) U59-1
seeding, tumor U128-17
seep U38-7
seepage U38-7
segment U87-6
segmental U43-3; U87-6
segmentation U43-3; U87-6
segregate U84-37
segregation analysis U84-37
seizure U113-5
–, grand-mal U124-9
selection, patient U134-2
selenium U82-21; U81-5
selenocysteine U82-21
self U39-21; U75-2
self-assured U75-19
self-awareness U1-16
self-blame U68-17
self-care U13-1; U142-27,29
self-centered U75-21
self-concept U75-2

self-confident U76-12
self-conscious U76-12
self-control U75-2
self-defense U12-10
self-denial U102-10
self-depreciation U75-2
self-derogatory U75-14
self-diagnose U117-10
self-effacing U76-13
self-esteem U75-2; U142-28
– –, low U76-13
self-examination U107-2
self-help U8-1; U19-11; U142-29
– – community U11-13
self-induced U119-8
self-inflicted death U12-8
– – (injury) U6-11; U11-6
self-injurious U91-1
selfish(ness) U75-2,21
self-limiting U119-12
self-medication U9-1
self-punitive U76-13
self-referral U18-12
self-regulation U49-10
self-report U20-6
self-reproach U76-13; U77-10
self-reproaching U75-14
self-sufficient U76-13
sella turcica U54-5
semen U53-6
semicircular canals U60-10
semicomatose U7-14
semiconductor U82-30
semiliquid U82-4
semimembranosus (muscle) U30-16
seminal colliculus/hillock U52-12
– fluid U53-6
– vesicle/gland U52-9
seminiferous U53-6
– tubule U52-4
semipermeable U36-16; U88-6
semiprone U63-9
semirecumbent U63-10
semi-starvation U2-14
semistuporous U7-11
semitendinosus (muscle) U30-16
senescence U80-13
senescent U80-13; U35-4
senile U80-13
senior U80-13
seniority U80-13
sensation U57-3
–, blunted U135-4
–, impairment of U142-3
sense U57-5
– of equilibrium/balance U57-18
– organ U57-10
sense-datum U57-5
senseless U57-5
sensibility U57-8; U76-4
sensible U57-8; U76-4
sensing U57-5
sensitive U39-23; U57-8; U76-4; U119-1

sensitivity U39-23; U57-8; U76-4
– (test) U100-23
– to light U103-15
sensitization U122-5
sensitize U39-23; U122-5
sensitized tissue U39-2
sensor U57-5
sensorial U57-7
sensorineural U57-7
– loss U61-3
sensorium U57-7
sensory U57-7; U76-4
– fiber U40-4
– impairment U142-3
sensual U57-9
sensuality U57-9
sensuous(ness) U57-9; U68-9; U76-4
sepsis U124-5
septal U32-9; U86-15
septate U32-9; U86-15
septic U139-1
– shock U124-5
septicemia U124-5
septicemic U124-5
septuagenarian U80-16
septum U86-15
–, (inter)ventricular U32-9
–, interpulmonary U43-13
sequel(a) U4-16; U77-4; U134-9
sequelae, to subside without U4-14
sequence U84-12
sequencing U84-34
sequester U91-17
series U100-3; U101-11
–, upper GI U118-21
seroconversion U122-11; U37-3
seroconvert U122-11
serofibrinous U86-9
serogroup U122-11
serological U122-11
serologist U122-11
serology U122-11; U37-3
seroma U86-9
seronegative U122-11
seroresponse U122-11
serosa U86-9
serosal U86-9
serositis U86-9
serotonin U42-11
serotype U122-11
serous U86-9
serrated jaws U138-14
Sertoli('s) cell U52-4; U53-9
serum electrolytes U116-7
– glutamic pyruvic transaminase (SGPT) U47-16
– sickness U39-9
–, blood U37-3
service, medical social U13-3
service-connected disability U142-3
setback U119-18
setting U141-2
–, clinical U118-1
settle (down) U4-15; U116-12

settle out U81-27
severity (illness) U125-4; U117-1
– of disability U142-3
sewage U91-6
sex U68-1,5
– cell U51-4
– drive U68-4
– gland U54-11
sexagenarian U80-16
sexism U68-1
sexist U68-1
sexology U68-1
sexual U68-1
– abuse U68-16; U13-13
– advances U68-16
– arousal disorder, female U68-7
– arousal/excitement U68-2
– assault U68-17
– characteristics, secondary U55-17
– desire/urge U68-4
– intercourse/act U68-5
– organs U50-1
– perversion/deviation U68-15
– vigor U1-6
sexuality U68-1
– transmitted U96-1
shaggy U86-15
shake U64-6; U105-7
– one's head U67-3
shaken U76-21
shakiness U64-6
shaking U64-6; U113-2
shaky U64-6; U105-7
shallow U58-5
– (furrow) U87-23
sham treatment U101-8
shame U76-12f
shameful /-less U76-12
shank U23-10
– bone U28-24
shape U129-4
–, body U25-1
–, keep in U1-9
sharp-eyed U59-8
sharps U132-2
sharp-sightedness U59-8
shave U25-16
shearing force U36-12
shears U132-4
sheath U69-6; U86-8
–, myelin U40-14
–, reducer U133-11
–, trocar U133-6
shed U64-15
– (teeth) U27-5
shed(ding) U56-20
shedding, endometrial U51-2
–, virus U96-10
sheepskin pad U19-5
shelter U142-28
sheltered living arrangement U142-28
– workshop U11-13
Shiatsu massage U142-15
shield, safety U133-7

shift U64-4; U17-17
–, mediastinal U124-17
shifting U64-4
shigella U94-18
shigellosis U94-18
shin (bone) U23-10; U28-24
shine U59-3
shiner U5-13
shingles U95-7
shiver U64-6; U105-7
shivering U64-6; U105-7
shivery U64-6; U105-7
shock U6-4; U124-4f
–, accidental electric U6-14
–, cardiogenic U110-14
–, hypovolemic U6-15
–, toxic U91-22
shocked U124-4
shocking U110-14; U124-4
shocky U124-4
shoot U6-8
– (up) U11-8
shooting pain U104-7
short U24-3
shortening U24-3
short-limbed U23-1
shortness of breath U111-1
short-sighted U59-17
shot U122-4; U76-9
– (drugs) U11-8
–, golden U11-11
shotgun U6-8
shoulder U23-3
– blade U28-12
– girdle U28-11
– shrug U67-4
shout U66-14
shove U64-12
show U107-17
–, bloody U71-7
showering U1-19
shreds U95-6
shriek U66-14
shrink U15-12
shrinkage U31-1
shrub U91-25
shrug (shoulders) U67-4
shudder U105-7
shuffle U65-11
shuffling U65-11
shun U56-18
shunt U36-14; U129-6
–, left-to-right U110-12
shut-down, renal U88-15
shy U75-17
sibling U72-18
sibship U84-31
sick U1-3; U4-1
sickening U4-1
sickly U4-1
sickness U1-1; U4-1; U103-11
–, morning U70-12
sick-pay U4-1
side effect U121-14

side rails U19-3
– tray U19-7
sideroblast, ringed U86-2
siderophores U78-19
sigh(ing) U44-1; U66-4
sight U59-6
sighted U59-6
sigmatism U66-21
sign U67-2; U103-1; U108-1
– language U61-11
– out U20-16
–, Babinski's U113-1
signal U67-2
– transduction U83-16
significance U100-21
significant, statistically U100-21
silence U61-11
silent U61-11; U119-6
silica U82-30
silicate U82-30
silicofluoride U82-30
silicon U82-30
silicone U82-30
silicosis U82-30
silver U82-28
simple epithelium U86-10
Sims' position U63-12
sincere U75-12
sincerity U75-12
sinew U30-5
single throw U138-4
single-layered U87-8
single-minded U74-1
single-stranded U84-11
sink U64-15
sinoatrial node U32-15
sinonasal U43-6
sinus U28-6
– node U32-15
– rhythm U33-6
–, maxillary U43-6
sinuses, paranasal/air U43-6
sinusoid, hepatic U47-4
sinusoidal U47-4
sister U16-2
sitz bath U71-18; U142-20
sixth sense U57-6
size, body U24-2
skeletal U28-1
– traction U141-3
skeleton U28-1
Skene's glands U50-9
skewness U100-13
skid U65-12
skilled nursing facility (SNF) U14-3
skills, fine/gross motor U31-20
skin U56-1
– blemish U25-18
– coverage U129-9
– popping U11-8
– preparation, preoperative U139-14
– tag U114-17
– test U118-2
– turgor U56-19

skinfold U56-17
- thickness U24-12; U25-3
skinny U24-10
skip(ping) U65-16; U1-13
skull U28-7
- fracture U124-19; U106-8
slash U5-6
sleep U72-5
- apnea U72-13
- around U68-12
- terror U72-14
-, dream/REM/D state/paradoxic U72-10
-, electrotherapeutic U142-23
-, paroxysmal U72-18
-, S stage/non-REM/NREM U72-11
-, stage U72-10f
sleeper U72-5
sleepiness U72-1
sleeping U72-5
sleepless(ness) U72-16
sleeplike U72-5
sleep-wake cycle U72-8
sleepwalker U72-15
sleepwalking U72-15
sleepy U72-1
sleeve, reducer U133-11
-, trocar U133-6
slender U24-6; U25-5
slenderize U24-6
slenderness U25-5
slender-waisted U22-6
slice (of tissue) U5-6; U87-5
slide U65-8
sliding U65-8
- flap U130-14
- ring U133-10
slight U24-6; U25-8
slightness U24-6
slim (down) U24-6; U25-5
slim-hipped U25-9
slimness U25-5
sling U141-8
slip U65-12
slipknot U138-9; U137-6
slipping U138-2
slit-lamp examination U58-11
slope U100-33
slouch(ed) U63-2
slough (off) U51-1; U56-20
sludge U37-5
sluggish(ness) U76-17; U36-5
slumber U72-5
slump(ed) U63-2
slumping U63-2
slurred (speech) U10-5; U113-10
slurry U91-25
smallpox U95-7
smart U75-7
smash U6-2
smash-up U6-2
smear U116-5
-, blood U37-1
smell U62-1

smelling U62-1
smelly U62-1
smile U67-9
smiling U67-9
smirk U67-9
smog U91-7
smoke U6-10; U10-16; U91-7
smokeless U10-16
smooth U62-8
- recovery U4-16
smooth-edged U87-10
snakebite U91-16
snap U67-19; U110-5
-, opening U32-4
snappish U67-19
snare U127-11
snarl U67-19
sneak U65-8
sneakers U65-8
sneer U67-8
sneeze U103-16; U66-6
sneezing U103-16
Snellen chart U17-5
sniff(ing) U44-2; U62-2
sniffer U62-2
sniffing U10-20
- position U8-17
sniffle U44-2; U62-2; U67-10
sniffling U62-2
snobbish U75-20
snore U72-13; U66-5
snorer U72-13
snoring U44-1; U72-13
snort(ing) U10-20; U103-16; U66-5
snuff U10-20
snuffle U10-20; U44-2; U67-10
soak U19-10; U142-20
SOAP note U20-6
soap(y) U82-14
sob(bing) U67-10; U66-3
sober U10-4
sobriety U10-4
sociability U75-14
sociable U75-14
social activities U142-27
- security U13-6
- welfare U13-6; U1-7
- worker U16-8
Society, Infectious Diseases U13-13
socket U29-4
-, tooth U26-13
soda, caustic U91-10
sodium U82-18
- sulfate U91-24
soft U61-5
- drinks U10-2
- (sound) U61-1
soft tissue U118-24
softness U61-5
soil U90-7; U91-6
soldering U82-28
sole U23-13
solid U82-6
solidify U82-6

solids U46-8
solitary U75-14
solubility U88-5; U9-11
soluble U88-5
solute U81-25
solution U81-25; U88-5; U9-11
solvent U81-25; U88-5; U9-11
- drag U49-3
solvent sniffing U11-23
somatalgia U40-7
somatic U77-2
- (nerve) fibers U40-7
somatization U40-7
somatomedin-C U55-5
somatotropin U55-5
somatotype U1-8; U25-2
somatotyping U1-8
somberness U75-17
somesthesia U57-14
somite U85-19
somitic U85-19
somnambulism U72-15
somniloquy U72-15
somnolence U72-1; U7-13
somnolent U72-1
sonic U61-3
sonogram U118-17
sonography U118-17
sopor U7-13
sore U89-17; U104-11
- muscle U142-24
- throat U103-5
soreness U104-11
sorrow U12-13; U76-20
sorrowful U76-20
SOS call/message U6-19
souffle U110-4
soul U77-2
sound U1-3
- (instrument) U132-8
- (tone) U66-11
- transmission U61-4
- wave U61-3
-, mentally U77-3
Southern blotting U84-35
spa, health U1-18
space boots U125-23
-, freeway U27-14
-, interproximal U26-22
spaced out U11-10; U7-9
space-occupying lesion U124-14
span, life U80-1
spare U8-18; U20-2; U126-13
sparse U114-5
spasm U103-20; U112-8
spasmodic croup U95-10
spasmolytic U92-19
spastic U103-20; U112-8
spasticity U103-20; U112-8
spatial orientation U41-3
spatula U17-3
spatulate U17-3
speak U66-8
special education U142-18

special sense U57-6
specialist U15-8
–, nurse U16-5
specialty U15-8
specificity U100-23
specimen U118-4
– bag U133-16
– collecting container U17-1
– jar U17-12
–, urine U116-15
spectrometry U83-21; U118-3
speculum, nasal U17-6
speech U66-8
– reading U61-10
speedballs U11-20
spell U103-4
Spenco boots U125-23
sperm U53-7
– bank U69-14
– motility U53-10
spermatic U53-7
– cord U52-7
– duct U52-6
spermatid U53-8
spermatocele U53-8
spermatogenesis U53-8
spermatogenic U53-8
spermatoid U53-7
spermatozoon U53-7
spermicidal U69-8
spermicide U69-8; U53-7
spermiogenesis U53-8
sphenoid (bone) U28-8
sphenoorbital suture U28-8
sphenopetrosal fissure U60-7
sphincter (muscle) U30-9
–, urethral U48-14
sphincteric U30-9; U48-14
sphincteroplasty U30-9; U48-14
sphygmomanometer U17-8
sphygmomanometry U107-14
spicy U62-7
spider U91-2
spinach U109-11
spinal U22-12; U28-19
– cord U41-15; U22-12
– – compression U142-5
– – injury/trauma U124-18
– injury U124-18
– tap U118-7
spindle fiber U83-5
–, muscle/neuromuscular U57-12
spine U22-12; U28-5; U91-16
– board U8-16
– mobilization U142-13
–, venomous U91-14
spinning U1-14; U103-13
spinothalamic pathway U41-15
– tracts U41-9
spinous U28-19
– layer U56-2
spiral organ U60-12
spirillary U90-9
spirillum U90-9

spirit U77-2
spirits U10-2; U76-2; U3-28
spirochetal U90-9
spirochete U90-9
spirocheticidal U90-9
spirocheticide U90-9
spirogram U118-3; U44-3
spirometer U118-3
spirometry U118-3
spit U103-17; U27-10
spitoon U27-10
splanchnic U86-21
spleen U35-4
splenectomy U35-4
splenic U35-4
splenomegaly U35-4
spliff U11-14
splint U141-7
–, vacuum (limb) U8-15
splinter U106-2
splinting U141-7
–, chest U111-12
split U81-8; U126-14
– (up) U78-10
split-thickness graft U130-6
splitting U78-10
spoiled U142-7
spoken U66-8
spondee threshold (ST) U61-7
sponge bath U142-20
–, surgical U132-18
sponging U64-6
spongiofibrosis U52-16
spongiosal U52-16
spongy body (penis) U52-16
– bone U28-2
spontaneous recovery U4-16
– respiration U123-9
– resolution U4-15
spoon U132-10
spore U90-3
sporocyst U90-2
sporogenesis U90-3
sporozoite U90-2
sporozoon U90-2
sport physical U1-12
sports medicine U1-12
sportsman U1-12
sporulation U90-3
spot U114-9
spot, cafe-au-lait U25-18
spotless U25-18
spots before the eyes U103-15
spotted U114-9
spotting, postcoital U50-7
spotty U114-9
sprain U142-24
spread U31-6; U94-3; U97-11
spread-eagled U63-5
spring U1-18
sprint U65-15
sprouting U85-10
spur, calcaneal U28-27
spurious cast U112-14

spurt(ing) U38-7
spurt, pubertal height U24-2
spurter U38-7
sputum U103-18
squame(s) U86-12; U114-7
squamociliary U86-12
squamocolumnar U86-11 f
squamous U114-7
– (cell) carcinoma U98-2
– cancer U98-2
– epithelium U86-12
square knot U64-14; U138-6
squash U64-10
squat (down) U63-4
squeeze U64-10
squeezing U64-10; U142-15
squint(ing) U59-4; U67-14
stab U6-7
– incision U133-14
– –, initial U128-12
stabbing U6-7
– pain U104-7
stability U31-15; U119-12; U125-2
stabilization U31-15; U125-2; U141-4
stabilize U119-12; U125-2
stable U31-15; U75-15; U119-12; U141-4
–, clinically U125-2
staff, medical U15-2
stage U71-13; U97-14; U119-15
–, mulberry/morula U85-4
stagger(ing) U65-9
staggering gait U113-8
staging U97-14
stain U116-4
–, portwine U25-19
stainable U116-4
stained smear U96-2
staining U116-4
stale U62-5
stalk U65-13; U87-24
–, pituitary U41-9
stammer U66-20
stammering, urinary U112-9
stamp U65-5
stance U65-3
stand up U65-17
stand(ing) U53-3; U65-3
standpoint U65-3
standstill U65-3
stannous U82-29
stannum U82-29
stapedial U60-5
stapedioplasty U60-5
stapes U60-5
staphylococcus U90-8
staphylokinase U37-15
stapled U138-17
stapler U137-12
–, endo-GIA U138-17
stapling U138-17
starch U79-5
–, liver/animal U47-14
stare U59-2; U67-14

staring U59-2; U67-14
starting (stream), difficulty/trouble U112-7
startle U65-16
– response U67-7
startling U65-16
starvation U12-6; U78-12
starving U2-14
state U119-15
station U65-3; U71-13
–, quarantine U14-10
stationary U65-3
statistician U100-1
statistics U100-1
stature U24-2
–, constitutional short U1-8
status U119-15
– asthmaticus U124-10
– epilepticus U124-9
–, nutritional U79-3; U107-10
steadfastly U102-10
steady U75-15
– jogging U1-14
– state U88-20
steam U82-3
– room/bath U1-17
steamy U58-5
steatorrhea U109-10
stem cell U38-3
– villi U85-24
stench U62-4
stenosis U89-19f
stenotic U89-20
stent U127-20
step U65-4
stepladder onset U94-19
steppage gait U65-4
stepping U65-4
stepwise U65-4
stereoacuity U59-8
stereocilia U60-12
stereotypy U103-19
sterile U69-3; U139-2
sterility U69-3; U139-2
sterilization U69-3; U139-2
–, dry heat U139-2
–, saturated steam U139-2
sterilize U69-3
sterilizing chamber U139-2
Steri-strip® U140-21
sternal U28-13
sternocostal ligament U28-13
sternomastoid U60-14
sternum U28-13
steroid U55-4
steroidogenesis U55-4
steroidogenic U55-4
stethoscope U17-2
stick out (tongue) U67-17
stiff (joint) U31-17; U103-20
– (corpse) U12-14
stiffen U31-17
stiffening U103-20
stiffness U31-17

stiffness, neck U94-13
stigma U108-1
stigmatized U108-1
stilette U132-7
stillbirth U71-2; U70-8
stillborn U71-1
stimulant U11-17; U57-1; U88-12
stimulate U42-8; U57-1; U88-12
stimulation U57-1; U88-12
–, cranial electrotherapy U142-23
–, nerve U42-8
–, sexual U68-8
–, transcutaneous electrical nerve U142-23
stimulator U57-1; U142-23
stimulatory U42-8; U57-1; U88-12
stimuli, environmental U74-11
stimulus U42-8; U57-1; U88-12
sting U6-7; U5-10
–, bee U91-16
stinger U91-16,2
stinging (pain) U104-7
stink(ing) U62-4
stippled calcification U98-12
stir U64-3
stirrup U60-5
stitch U137-1
– (pain) U104-13
stockiness U25-6
stockinet U141-10
stockings, anti-embolic U125-22
–, support U65-17
stocky U25-6
stomach U22-4; U45-8; U109-1
– rumbles U46-14
– upset U10-9
stomatitis U109-2
stomatodysodia U109-2
stomatology U109-2
stomp U65-5
stone, kidney U89-21
stone (6.35 kg) U24-1
stoned U11-10
stool U46-19
– guaiac test U118-6
–, tarry U109-11
–, loose U109-10
stooling U109-10
stoop(ed) U63-3
stooped posture U25-9
stop condition U101-30
stopping rule U101-30
storage U78-20; U9-19
–, memory U74-10
–, urine U49-15
store U49-15; U74-10; U78-20
stout U24-8
strabismic U59-4
strabismus U59-4
straddle U63-5
straighforward U75-13
straight leg raising (test) U142-11
straighten U31-3
straightjacket U77-26

strain U64-19; U63-4
– (bacteria) U122-7
–, lumbar U30-16
straining U5-17; U46-18; U49-16; U109-15
straitjacket U77-26
strand U84-11
– (suture) U137-7; U138-6
strap(ping) U141-11
stratification U86-10
stratified U87-8
– epithelium U86-10
stratigraphy U99-19
stratum U87-8
– papillare U56-3
– reticulare U56-3
strawberry tongue U95-6; U108-8
straw-colored U37-3; U116-15
streak, fibrous U51-4
stream, urinary U49-17
–, weak/decreased U112-7
street drug U11-1
strength training U1-12
strengthen U31-13
strenuous U64-19; U5-17
– exercise U1-12
strep throat U95-13; U90-8
streptobacillary U90-7
streptococcal U95-13
streptococcus U90-8
streptokinase U37-15
stress, biomechanical U142-10
stressor U105-7
stretch U31-3
– marks U70-16
stretcher U8-16
stretching (exercises) U1-12f
striae U70-16
striatal U41-10
striate body U41-10
striatonigral U41-10
stricture U89-19
stride U65-4
stridor U111-10
stridulous U111-10
strike U6-4
strip U107-4
stripping (varix) U110-17
stroke U62-10; U64-11; U124-14
– output U33-7
– volume, (cardiac) U33-7
–, heat U105-11
stroking U64-11; U62-10; U68-8
stroll U65-7
stroma U86-22
stromal U86-22
strong-minded U75-19
strong-tasting U62-6
strong-willed U75-19
struck U6-4
strut U65-13
stubborn(ness) U75-19
student nurse U16-3
student's test U100-34

study U118-1; U101-1
- manual of operations U101-7
-, lab(oratory) U116-2
stuff U11-1
stumble (and fall) U65-9; U6-5
stumbling U65-9
stump U142-6
stung U5-10
stunned U7-9
stupefaction U7-11
stupor U7-11
sturdy U25-4
stutter U66-20
stuttering, urinary U112-9
stylet U132-7; U136-2
styloid process U28-16
stylomastoid U60-14
subacute U119-10
subaortic U34-8
subarachnoid U41-8
- bolt/screw U125-13
subclone U84-33
subconsciousness U7-1
subcortical nuclei U41-3
subcutaneous layer/tissue U56-4
subcuticular U56-4,16
subcutis U56-4
subdeltoid U30-13
subdermal U56-3
subdiaphragmatic U43-12
- thrusts U8-11
subdural U41-8
subendothelial U86-14
subepidermal U56-2
subepithelial U86-7
subfebrile U105-3
subfertility U69-2
subgroup U100-3
subintern U15-5
subintima U34-2
subject U100-2
subkingdom U90-2
sublethal U12-2
- damage U6-11
sublimate U82-8
sublimation U82-8
subluxation U106-4
submaxillary U28-10
submerge U6-16
submersion U6-16
subserosa U86-9
subserve U42-1
subset U100-3
subside U4-14
subsidence U4-14
subspecialty U15-8
substantia alba U41-7
- nigra U41-10
substantiate U117-12
substituent U81-5
substitute (for) U136-13
substitution U3-21; U84-23; U136-13
substrate U81-16
subtalar U28-26

subthalamic U41-9
subthalamus U41-9
subungual U56-15
subunit U81-4
subvirion U90-11
subzonal insertion U69-15
succumb (to) U12-4
suck(le) U46-2; U71-27
sucker U46-2
suckling U46-2
suction U46-2; U127-16
- cannula U132-6
- curettage U70-9
suction-irrigation system U128-11
sudomotor U56-10
sudor U105-15
sudoriferous gland U56-10
sudorific /-ferous U56-10; U105-15
suffer (from) U4-3; U102-1; U104-2
sufferer U4-3
suffering, burden of U4-3
sufficient U124-12
suffocate U44-8
suffocating /-ive U44-8; U123-7
suffocation U44-8; U123-7
sugar U3-16; U79-6
suggestive of U54-13; U109-8
suicide U12-8
suite, (pre)surgical U131-2
-, operating U131-2
-, radiology U14-9
sulcal U41-5
sulcus U87-26
-, cerebral U41-5
sulfa U82-24
sulfanilic acid U82-4
sulfate U82-24
sulfide U82-24
sulfonamide U82-24
sulfur(ous) U82-24
sulfurize U82-24
sulk U67-16
sulky U67-16; U76-9
sullen(ness) U75-19; U76-9
summit (shoulder) U28-12
sunburn U5-11
sunlight U17-4
sunscreen U25-11
sunstroke U105-11
superego U77-2
superficial fascia U56-4
superimposed U124-19
superinfection U94-2
superiority complex U77-12
supernatant U81-27
superovulated U69-17
superovulation U69-17
superovulatory U69-17
supersaturation U81-24
supervise U125-5
supervision U125-5; U142-29,27; U77-25
supinate U31-9
supination U31-9

supine U31-9; U63-8
supple U31-11; U24-6
supplement U3-22
suppleness U31-11; U56-11
supply U36-6; U88-3
support U19-11,14; U64-16; U117-12; U125-3; U142-29
- arm U133-1
- groups U11-13
- hose U125-22
-, ventilatory U20-2
supportive U19-11; U64-16; U125-3
suppository U9-12
-, vaginal U69-8
suppress U74-14; U88-14
suppression U88-14
suppuration U140-14
suppurative U140-14
supracondylar U28-4
suprahilar U43-4
supraorbital nerve U58-1
supraphysiologic U88-1
suprapubic U28-22; U52-18
- region U22-8
suprarenal (gland) U54-10
suprasternal notch U28-13; U43-13
surface U87-4
- tension U44-9
surfactant U81-16
-, pulmonary U44-9
Surgeon General U13-4
surgeon U126-3; U131-5
-, attending U131-5
-, vascular U15-14
surgeon's knot U138-6
surgery U126-3
-, arthroscopic U128-7
-, doctor's U18-1
-, endoscopic U128-2
-, laparoscopic U128-3
-, minimal access U128-1
-, minimally invasive U128-1
-, open U128-3
-, pelviscopic U128-4
-, reconstructive U129-3
surgical U126-2†
- abdomen, (acute) U124-16
- correction U129-2
- gloves U139-17
- knot U138-6
- nurse U131-8
- team U131-4
surrogacy U69-19
surrogate mother U69-19
surveillance U125-5; U120-7
-, medical U43-2
survival U12-6; U100-25
- benefit U1-5
survive U12-6
survivorship U100-25
susceptibility U119-1; U37-5
susceptible (to) U119-1; U4-7; U114-11
susceptibles U94-8
suspect U116-23; U117-8

suspend U63-13; U81-25; U141-3
suspension U63-13; U81-25; U129-7; U141-3
suspensory U63-13
suspicion U116-23; U117-8
suspicious U116-23; U117-8
sustain U4-3; U125-3
sustained U36-5
sustenance U90-13; U94-5
sutura U29-14
suture U138-1; U137-1
- (joint) U29-14
- forceps U132-15
- introducer/passer U138-12,5
- material U137-7
-, coronal U29-14
-, cranial U29-14
-, figure-of-eight U137-19
-, interlocking U137-16
-, interrupted U137-15
-, lock-stitch U137-16
-, mattress U137-17
-, over-and-over U137-15
-, purse-string U137-18
-, quilt(ed) U137-17
-, running U137-16
-, sagittal U28-8
sutureless U137-1
suture-ligate U137-3
suturing U137-1
-, laparoscopic U138-1
swab U116-5; U17-13; U140-23
swabbing U136-2
swagger(ing) U65-13
swallow U46-2; U109-5
Swan-Ganz catheter U125-7
swan-neck deformity U142-8
swathe U141-8
sway(ing) U64-5; U110-11
sweat U105-12
- duct U56-11
- gland U56-10
- pore U56-11
sweating U105-12
sweaty U105-12
sweep U44-9
sweet-tasting U62-6
swell U5-15; U138-7
swelling U5-15; U85-10; U97-2; U108-10
swing(ing) U64-5
Swiss shower U1-19
switchboard U16-15
swollen U108-10; U5-15
swooning U110-11
syllable U66-12
syllable-stumbling U66-12
sympathetic U75-8
- chain ganglia U22-8
- fibers U40-9
sympathize (with) U75-8
sympatholytic U40-9; U92-27
sympathomimetics U92-27
sympathy U75-8; U12-13

symphysis (pubis) U29-12; U52-18
symptom U103-1
symptomatic U103-1
symptomatology U103-1
synapse U40-13
synaptic contact U30-4
- gap/cleft U40-13
synarthrosis U29-13
synchondrosis U29-12
syncopal U110-11
syncope U110-11; U7-4
syncytiotrophoblast U85-14
syndesmosis U29-13
syndesmotic joint U29-13
syndrome U103-1
-, irritable bowel U109-6
synergist U31-4
synergy U31-4
synesthesia U57-14
synostosis U29-14
synostotic U29-14
synovia, articular U29-8
synovial fluid U29-8
- joint U29-3
- sheath U29-11
synovitis U29-3
synovium U29-11
synthesis U54-2; U78-4
synthesize U54-2
synthetase U78-4
synthetic U78-4; U137-10
synthetize U78-4
syphilis U96-3
syphilitic U96-3
syringe U17-10
syrup U9-11
system, lymphatic U35-1
-, reticuloendothelial U35-12
-, lymphoreticular U35-12
-, mononuclear phagocyte U35-12
systemic U121-5
systole U33-3
systolic click U110-5

T

T bar U19-4
T cell, helper/CD4+ U39-14
T helper lymphocyte U39-14
table (statistical) U100-27
-, operating U131-10
-, overbed U19-7
tablet U9-7
tabulation U100-27
tachyarrhythmia U110-2; U33-5
tachycardi(a)c U110-2
tachycardia U110-2; U33-5
tachypnea U111-5; U44-4
tachypneic U111-5
tack U137-4
tactful /-less U75-5
tactile U62-8
- sensation U62-8

tactometer U62-8
tactual U62-8
tag, skin U114-17
tail bone U28-20
tailor U129-4
take in (food) U2-1
- - (information) U74-9
- up U46-13; U78-5
talc U91-7
talkative U75-5
tall(ish) U24-3
talocalcaneal joint U28-26
talus U28-26
tampon U140-24
tamponade, cardiac U110-8; U125-17
tan U25-13
tangible U62-9
tap U64-11; U30-5; U57-12
- (puncture) U118-7; U127-16
- (tendon) U17-9
- water U64-11
tape measure U17-1
taping U141-11
tapotement U142-15
tapping U64-11; U142-15
- (suction) U127-16
target U55-2
- tissue U55-2; U99-4
-, stationary U59-14
tarnishing U82-25
tarry stool U109-11
tarsal (bone) U28-25
tarsus U28-25
tastant U62-6
taste U62-6
tasteless U62-6
tasty U62-6
taut U64-13; U138-10
tear U58-9; U64-13; U5-7,19
-, retinal U59-5
tearing U58-9; U5-19
teat U50-18
technetium U82-34
technician, medical laboratory U16-10
-, x-ray U15-13
technique, surgical/operative U126-4
technologist, medical (MT) U16-10
-, perfusion U16-11
-, radiologic U15-13
tectorial membrane U60-12
teem with U90-1
teenager U80-8
teeth U26-1
- grinding U27-18
-, baby U27-2
-, deciduous U27-2
-, false U27-8
-, front/anterior U26-2
-, milk U27-2
-, permanent U27-6
-, posterior U26-2
-, secondary U27-6
teether U27-4
teething U27-4

teetotaler U10-8
telencephalon U41-1
telomerase U84-7
telomere U84-7
telomeric U84-7
telophase U83-13
temper U76-2
temper tantrum U64-12
temperament U75-4
temperamental U75-4
temperance U10-6
temperature U105-1
–, melting U82-7
template U84-19
temporal (bone) U28-8
– balding U68-4
temporary subsidence U4-14
tenacious U75-19
– mucus U44-8
tenaculum U132-16
tender, exquisitely U23-10
tenderness U104-11
–, rebound U109-12
tendinous U30-5
– strands U32-12
tendon U30-5
– reflex U31-12
– sheath U86-6
tenesmic U109-15
tenesmus U109-15
tenorrhaphy U137-2
tense U31-10; U76-5; U30-14
tensile U31-10
tension U31-10; U76-5
– headaches U142-25
– pneumothorax U125-16
tent, oxygen/head U125-12
tented U128-9
tepid (bath) U142-20
teratoblastoma U98-16
teratocarcinoma U98-16
teratogen U92-33; U98-16
teratogenic U91-12
teratogenicity U91-12; U92-33
teratoid U98-16
teratology U91-12; U98-16
teratoma U98-16
teratomatous U98-16
term, at U70-11; U55-23
terminal U12-2
– dribbling U112-7,9
terminally ill U4-1; U12-2
termination (protein) U84-19
– (study) U101-30
– procedure, first-trimester U70-9
terminator U84-19
terror U6-21
–, sleep U72-14
test U107-1; U118-2f
– tube baby U69-12
–, lab U116-2
testicle U52-3
testicular U52-3
– feminization syndrome U53-12

testicular sperm extraction (TESE) U69-13
testing U116-2; U118-2
testis U52-3
testosterone U55-16
testy U76-7
tetanic U94-11
tetaniform U94-11
tetanoid U94-11
tetanospasmin U94-11
tetanus U94-11
tetany U94-11; U95-11; U103-20
tetraploid U84-9
tetravalent U82-10
texture U25-11
–, skin U56-1
thalamus U41-9
thalassotherapy spa U1-18
thallium U82-33
thallous U82-33
thaw U136-16; U83-20
THC U11-22
therapeutic U16-12; U120-4
– modality U120-3
– range U121-13
– training U142-18
therapist U16-12
–, occupational U142-26
therapy U16-12; U120-1,4
–, biofeedback U142-25
–, electroconvulsive U142-23
–, electromagnetic U142-24
–, electrostimulation U142-23
–, expectant U120-7
–, interferential U142-23
–, magnetic field U142-24
–, manual U142-12
–, occupational U142-26
–, palliative U104-19
–, physical U142-1
–, rehabilitative U142-2
–, vocational U142-26
thermal/-ic U105-5
thermocautery U105-2
thermoesthesia U57-13
thermogenesis U105-2
thermogenetic U105-2
thermolysis U105-2
thermometer U105-6
thermoreceptor U57-13
thermoregulation U105-2
thermotherapy U142-22
thigh U23-9
– bone U28-23
thin U24-10
think(ing) U73-6
thin-skinned U76-4
thirst U2-11
thirties U80-11
thora(co)centesis U118-8; U111-12; U125-17
thoracic U22-2
thoracic duct U35-7
thoraco-abdominal U128-6

thoracoscope U128-6
thoracoscopic U125-16; U128-6
thoracoscopy U125-16; U128-6
thoracostomy tube U125-16
thoracotomy U123-11; U125-16; U128-6
thorax U22-2
thought U73-6
thoughtful U73-6
thrashing movements U72-13
thread (suture) U137-7
threaded U133-12
– (needle) U138-12
threshold U100-24
– (level/value) U88-7
– limit value U91-18
–, hearing/auditory U61-7
–, pain U104-18
–, renal U49-5
thrill U110-3; U11-8
thrilled U76-16
thrive, fail to U15-12
thriving U1-4
throat U45-4; U21-12
–, sore U103-5
throbbing U87-20
thrombin U37-13
thrombocyte U37-11
thrombocytopenia U37-11
thromboembolism U124-13
thrombokinase U37-14
thrombokinetics U37-14
thrombolysis U124-13
thrombolytic U38-14; U92-16
thrombophlebitis U110-17; U136-7
thromboplastin U37-14
thrombosis, deep vein U124-13
thromboxane U78-24
thrombus U38-12; U124-13
throw U64-14; U138-4
thrust U8-11; U64-12
–, high velocity U142-12
thumb U23-7
thump, precordial U123-5
thunderstorm U6-14
thwart U70-3
thymectomy U35-5
thymic U35-5; U54-12
– lymphopoietic factor U55-27
thymopoietin U55-27
thymosin U55-27
thymus (gland) U35-5; U54-12
thyrocalcitonin U55-8
thyroid (gland) U54-6
– hormone U55-6
– storm U124-8
thyroiditis U124-8
thyroid-stimulating hormone (TSH) U55-6
thyrotoxic crisis U124-8
thyrotoxicosis U124-8
thyrotropic U55-6
thyrotropin U55-6; U54-6
thyroxine (T4) U55-6

tibia U28-24
tibial U28-24
tibiotalar U28-26
tic U31-5
tick U90-15
- bite U94-3
tickle U62-11; U64-11
ticklish U62-11; U64-11
tidal volume/air U44-12
- waves U6-20
tie U137-6
- off U137-3
tightness U102-2
-, chest U111-8
tilt U63-10; U64-5
-, head U8-17
time to recovery U4-16
timid U75-17
timidity U77-12
tin U82-29
tincture U9-10
tines U17-7; U61-4
tinge, blood U112-3
tinged (with blood) U71-7
tingling (sensation) U57-3; U103-9
tinnitus U113-13
tipsy U10-1
tiptoe U23-14; U65-8
tired (out) U76-18
tiredness U76-18; U103-8
tiring U76-18
TISS U125-4
tissue(ing) U136-7
tissue U86-3 ff
- expansion U129-10
- factor U37-14
- typing laboratory U14-11
-, connective U86-4
-, fibrous U86-4
-, granulation U140-7
-, parenchymal U86-22
titanic U82-31
titanium U82-31
titer U81-23; U116-17
titratable U116-17
titration U81-23; U116-17
titubation U113-4
T-lymphocyte/-cell U39-13
tobacco U10-17
tocograph U71-3
toddle U65-10
toddler U65-10; U80-5
toe U23-14
toenail U23-14
toes, lesser U28-18
toilet U19-9
- hygiene U142-27
toileting U19-9
tolbutamide U82-17
tolerable U11-5
- daily intake U91-18
tolerance U11-5; U75-16; U121-12
-, exercise U1-12; U119-15
-, immune U39-22

tolerance, pain U104-18
-, work U142-28
tolerant U75-16
tolerate U11-5; U75-16
tomogram U99-19
tomograph U99-19
tomography U99-19
tone (sound) U61-3
- (up) U1-13
- (voice) U66-11
-, arteriolar U36-10
-, muscle/muscular U31-10
tones, heart U33-1
tongue U21-11
- biting U113-5
- depressor/blade U17-3
-, coated/furry U103-5
-, stick out one's U67-17
tongue-pressing U73-13
tonic U31-10
tonicity U31-10
toning effect U1-13
tonometer U31-10
tonsil(la) U35-6; U95-13
tonsil, palatine U26-10
tonsillar U35-6; U95-13
tonsillectomy U95-13
tonsillitis U35-6; U95-13
tonsilloadenoidectomy U35-6
tonus U31-10
tooth U26-1
- cement U26-17
-, adjacent U26-1
-, bicuspid U26-6
-, cheek U26-7
-, cutting U26-3
-, eye U26-5
-, incisal U26-3
-, incisor U26-3
-, multi-rooted U26-19
-, opposing U26-1
-, pegged U26-1
-, wisdom U26-8
toothache U104-4
tooth-grinding U77-14
toothless U27-7
topical U121-5
topographic U87-1
topography U87-1
torch U17-4
TORCH complex U96-11
torn U5-7,19
torsion U5-16
- (spermatic cord) U124-1
torsional U5-16
torso U22-1; U6-8
torticollis U103-20
tortuous U110-17
torus palatinus U28-10
toss U64-14
totter(ing) U65-10
touch(ing) U62-8
touchy U62-8; U76-4
tough physical activities U25-4

tourniquet U8-8; U17-8
-, Esmarch U135-18
towel clip U128-12
toxemia U91-22
toxemic U91-22
toxic U91-4
- level U121-13
- range U121-13
- shock syndrome U91-22
toxicant U91-4
toxicity U91-11; U121-13
-, fetal U91-12
toxicokinetics U91-3
toxicologic U91-3
toxicologist U91-3
toxicology U91-3; U121-13
toxicosis U91-20
toxigenic U91-4
toxin U91-4; U122-8
toxoid U122-8
TPAL U70-8
trabeculae carneae U32-13
-, bone U31-14
trace element U79-17
- metal U79-17
- mineral U79-17
-, memory U74-12
tracer U99-21; U79-17
trachea U43-8
tracheopulmonary U43-8
tracheostomy U123-11
tracheotome U123-11
tracheotomy U123-11
trachoma U90-14
tract, digestive/alimentary U45-1
-, gastrointestinal U45-1
-, pyramidal U41-16
-, corticospinal U41-16
-, respiratory U43-5
traction, manual U142-12
-, skeletal U141-3
trafficker U11-7
tragus U60-2
train(er) U1-12; U64-18
trainee(ship) U15-7
training U1-12; U64-18
-, therapeutic U142-18
trait U100-5
-, personality U75-1
trample U65-5
trance U7-15
tranquilizer U135-10
trans region U83-10
transaminate U82-17
transamination U47-16
transcallosal U41-3
transcapillary U34-5
transcendental meditation U1-16
transcribe U84-18
transcript U84-18
transcriptase, reverse U84-18
transcription U84-18
transcriptional U84-18
transcriptionist, medical U102-17

transcytosis U83-15
transduce U83-16
transect U126-14
transection U87-5; U126-14
transendothelial U35-12
transfectant U84-39
transfected U84-39
transfection U84-39
transfer U64-4; U129-13
-, embryo U69-16
transferral U20-15
transferrin U37-6
transfix U141-4
transform U78-6
transformation U78-6
-, genetic U84-21
transfuse U136-8
transfusion, blood U136-8
transfusion-acquired U136-8
transient ischemic attack (TIA) U15-14
transillumination U99-16
transit U86-13
- time, orocecal U46-8
transition U86-13
transitional epithelium U86-13
transitory U86-13
translation U84-19
translational U84-19
translocate U84-23
translocation U84-23
transluminal U34-14
transmissible U94-3
transmission U42-2; U94-3
transmit U42-2; U61-4; U94-3
transmitted, sexually U96-1
transmitter substance U42-10
transovarial U50-3
transplacental U71-16
transplant U129-14; U130-1
transport U8-3; U20-15; U78-17; U88-3
- system U78-17
-, tubular U49-3
transportation U8-3; U49-3
transporter U78-17
- cart U20-15
transpose U129-13
transposition U129-13
transsexuality U68-1
transtracheal U123-11
transudate U140-13
transulfurate U82-24
trapeze, overhead/overbed U19-4
trapezius (muscle) U30-13
trapezoid U30-13
trapped U111-6
trauma U5-2,4
- prevention U6-22
-, blast U6-9
-, cerebral U124-19
traumatize U5-4
travail U71-3
travel U87-7
traveler's diarrhea U73-13
traverse U87-7

tray U17-12
-, food U19-7
tread U65-5
treadmill U65-5; U142-16
treatment U120-1
- arm U101-12
- block U101-11
- group U101-10
- lag U101-21
- modality U120-3
-, mud U1-20
-, sham U101-8
trematode U90-17
tremble U64-6; U105-7
trembling U105-7; U113-4; U78-13
tremor U105-7; U113-4
tremulous U64-6; U105-7
tremulousness U113-4; U10-14
Trendelenburg, reverse U131-13
triaditis U47-5
triage U8-19
tributary U34-13
triceps brachii, (musc.) U30-11
trichomonad U96-8
trichomoniasis, vaginal U96-8
trichromat(ic) U59-9
tricuspid U32-10
tricyclic(s) U81-7; U113-14
trigger U88-13; U119-8
triglyceride U82-13
-, medium-chain U35-7; U78-18
trigonal U48-12
trigone, (bladder/vesical) U48-12
triiodothyronine (T3) U55-6
trim (down) U25-4
- (nails) U19-10
trimer U81-6
trimester U70-9
trip (out) U11-10
trip(ping) U65-9
triple U122-10
triplets U70-14
triquetrum U28-17
trismus U94-11
trisomic U84-25
trisomy U84-25
tritium U82-9
trocar U132-7
- sheath/sleeve U133-6
-, initial/primary U133-5
trochanter U28-4
trochlea U28-15; U30-8
trochlear U28-15; U30-8
trochoid joint U29-4
trolley U17-12
-, ambulance U8-5
trophoblast U85-14,5
trophoblastic U85-14
trophozoite U90-4
tropia U59-4
trot U65-14
truncal U22-1
truncated U22-1
truncation U84-21

truncus U22-1
trunk U22-1; U35-9
-, brachiocephalic U34-9
-, bronchomediastinal U35-9
-, lumbar lymphatic U35-8
-, main U34-6
trust U102-16
trustworthy U75-9
t-test U100-34
tub bath U142-20
tubal U50-4
- ligation U69-3
tube feeding U125-19
-, chest U125-16
-, collecting U48-9
-, endotracheal U135-17
-, eustachian/auditory U60-7
-, nasogastric U91-26
-, NG U125-18
tubercle U28-4; U94-16
tuberculin test U94-16
tuberculosis U94-16
tuberculous U94-16
tuberosity U28-4
tubocurare U93-17
tuboovarian U50-3f
tuboplasty U69-4
tubular U48-7
tubule, collecting U48-9
-, contorted U52-4
-, distal U48-5
-, proximal U48-5
-, renal/uriniferous U48-5
-, seminiferous U52-4
tubulus renalis contortus U48-7
tug U64-13
tumble U65-12
tumbling U65-12
tumescence U5-15
-, penile U53-5
tummy U22-4; U45-6
tumor U97-2; U89-16
- growth/proliferation U97-7
- marker U97-16
- specimen U117-3
- spread/extension U97-11
-, fatty/adipose U98-11
-, secondary U97-13
tumoricidal U97-2
tumorigenesis U97-2
tumorous U97-2
tune up U1-13
tungstate U82-31
tungsten U82-31
tungstic U82-31
tunic, medical U17-16
tunica adventitia U34-2
- intima U34-2
- media U34-2
tuning fork U17-7; U61-4
turbid U58-5; U111-14
turbidity U116-15
turbinate bone U28-9
turgescent U56-19

turgid U56-19
turgor U31-10
–, skin/cutaneous U56-19
Turkish bath U1-17
turn (over) U64-8
– in U72-3
– on U68-3
turned on U11-4
turning U64-8
turnover U78-1
tweezers U132-13f
twilight state U74-19
twin U70-14
twinge U104-13
twinning U70-14
twin-to-twin transfusion U70-14
twist U31-7
twitch(ing) U31-5
twitch, body/muscle U72-12
tympanic membrane U60-4; U17-7
tympanitis U60-4
tympanocentesis U125-17
tympanometry U61-7
tympanum U60-4
tympany U109-7
type U25-2; U75-1
typed blood U136-10
typhoid (fever) U94-19
typhoid(al) U94-19
typhus U94-19
typical U116-21

U

ubiquinone U81-5
ubiquitous U62-4
ulcer U89-17; U114-13
ulna U28-16
ulnar U28-16
ulnocarpal ligament U28-16
ultrafiltrate U49-1
ultrasonic U61-3; U118-17
ultrasonographic U118-17
ultrasonography U118-17
ultrasound (imaging) U118-17; U142-23
umbilical U22-5; U71-17
– vein U47-2
umbilicus U22-5; U71-17; U85-7
unaccommodated U59-12
unaffected U89-4
unappreciated U117-5
unattenuated U122-6
unauthorized U20-7
unaware U74-4
unbalanced U75-15
unbearable (suffering) U4-3
unbent U63-3
unbiased U100-18
unblind U101-9
unborn U71-1
uncharged U81-10
unchecked U18-9

uncomfortable U104-1
uncomplicated U107-18; U134-9
unconcentrated U74-16; U81-23; U116-16
unconcerned U108-14
unconfirmed U101-17
unconjugated U81-9
unconscious U7-1
uncoordinated U31-19; U113-8
uncorrelated U100-32
uncoupling U81-12
–, tube U99-13
uncover U102-3; U129-9
uncurl U63-6
underage U80-9; U51-2
underdeveloped U80-3
underfeeding U2-3
underinsured U13-5
underlying disease U4-4
undernutrition U24-1
understaffed U15-2
understaging U97-14
understand U74-4
understanding U73-5; U74-4; U75-16
undertone U66-11
underventilated U123-9
underwear U107-4
underweight U24-10
undetectable U117-5
undiagnosed U117-10
undifferentiated U85-11; U97-8
undiluted U36-13
undisplaced U5-20
undissociated U81-22
undocumented U101-15
undoubtedly U116-23
undrained U36-6; U125-15
undress U107-4
undue U103-8
uneasy U76-6
unenhanced U88-12
unequivocal U112-2
unerupted (tooth) U27-3
uneventful U107-18; U134-9
unexposed U126-7; U99-7
unfavorable (course) U119-12
unfeeling U76-1
unfertilized U70-1
unflavored U62-7
unforgetable U74-14
ungraceful U25-5
ungual U56-15
unguis U56-15
unhealthy U1-2; U4-1
unhealthy-looking U1-2
unheard U61-1
unhinged U77-15
unhurt U5-1
unidentified U74-3
unimpaired U4-11
uninhibited U75-6
uninjured U5-1
uninsured U13-5
unintelligible U73-5

unintentional U73-3
uninvolved U4-10; U76-15
union, bony U106-15
unisexual U68-1
unit U19-1
–, critical care U14-7
–, tropical disease U14-7
unit-bagged U136-4
univariate U100-5
unkempt U107-10
unkind U75-5
unlabored U111-2
unlearn U74-7
unmotivated U73-12
unmyelinated U40-14
unnoticed U57-4; U102-2
unobtainable U102-3; U117-3
unoccupied U19-15
unpalatable U2-5
unphysiologic(al) U88-1
unpleasant U75-5
unpredictable U75-9
unreasonable U73-1
unreceptivity U57-10
unrelated U74-5
unreliable U75-9; U100-30
unremarkable U107-18
unreported U13-2
unresolved U4-15
unresponsive(ness) U7-7; U120-11
unrestrained U77-26
unrevealing U107-17,2
unruly U77-7
unruptured U5-19
unsafe U8-2
unsanitary U1-5
unsaturated U81-24
unsaturation U78-24
unscarred U140-10
unscrupulous U75-11
unset (bone) U141-2
unsociable U75-14
unsound, mentally U77-3
unsplit U78-10
unstable U31-15; U75-15; U141-4
–, clinically U125-2
unstained U116-4
unsteadiness U103-13; U113-8
unsteady U75-15
unstrapped U141-11
unsustained (contraction) U30-2
untaped U141-11
untested U118-2
untoward (effect) U121-14; U136-12
untwist U31-7
ununited (bone) U106-15
unvaccinated U122-2
unwary U65-5
unwell U1-3; U4-1
unwholesome U1-5
unwilling(ness) U73-3; U76-14
unwind U76-19
unwitnessed U6-13
unwitting U96-9

unwound U76-19
unwrinkled U56-17
unyielding U116-18
upper arm bone U28-15
– GI series U118-21
– limb tension test U142-11
upregulate U83-18
upright U63-2
upset U76-9
– stomach U109-1
upsetting U76-9
upstroke U33-8; U36-9
uptake U46-13; U55-3; U78-5
urachal U85-17
urachus U85-17
uranium U82-34
urate U49-14
urchin, sea U91-16
urea U47-18; U49-13
urea-splitting U78-10
uremia U112-13
uremic U112-13; U37-2
ureter U48-10
ureteral /-ic U48-10
ureterolysis U48-10
urethra U48-13
urethral U48-13
urethritis U48-13
urethrospasm U48-13
urge U11-2; U18-5; U73-11
– (to void) U112-4
–, sexual U68-4
urgency U6-18
–, urinary U112-4
urgent U112-4; U126-5
uric acid U49-14
uricosuria U49-14
urinal U19-8; U49-12
urinalysis U116-15
urinary U49-12
– catheter, indwelling U125-20
– frequency U112-5
– leg bag U125-23
– stammering/stuttering U112-9
– stream, feeble U4-7
– tract/system U48-1
urinate U49-16
urination U49-16
–, painful U112-1
urine U49-12
– analysis U116-15
– bottle U19-8
– sample/specimen U116-15
–, bloody/bloodstained U112-3
uriniferous U49-12
urobilinogen U47-13
uroflow U49-17
uroflowmetry U49-12
urogenital U48-1; U52-1
– diaphragm U48-15
– sinus U85-21
urogram U118-19
urographic U118-19
urography, IV/excretory U118-19

urokinase U37-15
urothelium U48-11; U97-9
urticaria U114-11
uterine U50-5
– tube U50-4
uterus U50-5
utility failure U6-10
utricle U60-9
utricular U60-9
– receptor U57-18
utter U66-1
uvea U58-7
uveal tract U58-7
uveitic U58-7
uveitis U58-7

V

vaccinal U122-2
vaccinate U122-1
vaccination U122-3
vaccine U122-2
vaccinee U122-2
vaccinotherapy U122-2
vacuol(iz)ation U83-11
vacuolar U83-11
vacuolated U83-11
vacuole U83-11
–, endocytic U39-18
Vacutainer (tube) U17-10
vacuum mattress U8-15
vagal U40-10
vagina U50-8
vaginal U50-8
– sponge U69-9
vaginismus U68-7
vaginitis U50-8
vagotomy U40-10
vagus (nerve) U40-10
vain U75-20
valence (state) U81-10
valency U81-10
valid U100-30
validation U100-30
validity U100-30
Valsalva maneuver U32-10; U40-10; U142-11
value U116-16
–, threshold limit U91-18
valv(ul)a venosa U34-12
valv(ul)ar U32-10
valvar U34-12
valve mechanism U133-8
–, heart/cardiac U32-10
–, venous U34-12
valveless U34-12
valvotomy U32-10
vanadate U82-26
vanadic U82-26
vanadium U82-26
vapor U82-3
– bath U1-17; U142-20
vaporize U82-3; U127-15

variability U100-14
variable U100-5
variance U100-14
variation U100-14
variceal U110-17
– bleeder U38-6
varicella U95-7
varicelliform U95-7
varicose U110-17
varicosity U110-17
variola U95-7
varioliform U95-7
varix U110-17
vas U34-1
– deferens U52-6
vascular U34-1
– occlusion/obstruction U124-13
– resistance U36-10
vascularization U34-1
vasculature U34-1
vasectomize U69-3
vasectomy U69-3; U52-6
– reversal U69-4
vasoactive drug U110-15
vasocongestion U110-15; U36-11
vasoconstriction U36-11; U92-17
vasodilation U36-11; U92-17
vasopressin U55-24
vasopressor U92-17
vasospasm U34-1; U103-20; U110-15
vasotocin U55-24
vasotomy U52-6
vasovagal U40-10
vasovasostomy U69-4
vastus lateralis (muscle) U30-16
vault, palatal U26-10
vector U94-4
vegetarian U2-16
vehicle, emergency U6-3
–, heavy (goods) U6-3
vein U34-4
–, azygos-hemiazygos U36-3
–, external jugular U34-11
vena cava U34-7
– jugularis externa U34-11
venepuncture U136-2; U127-18
venereal U15-10; U96-1
– wart U96-14
venereologist U15-10; U96-1
venereology U15-10; U96-1
venipuncture U118-7; U127-18; U136-2
venocavography U34-7
venom U91-2
venomous U91-2
venous U34-4
– access U136-5
– return U36-6
– valve U34-12
ventilate U44-5; U123-9; U125-10
ventilation U44-5; U125-10
– system U139-8
–, artificial U123-9; U135-15
–, bag and mask U43-5
–, mechanical U71-28; U93-17

ventilation/perfusion lung scan
  U118-22
ventilator U44-5; U123-9; U125-10
ventilatory U44-5
ventral U87-16
ventricle (heart) U32-8
–, cerebral U41-4
ventricular U32-8; U41-4
– drain U125-15
– ejection U33-8
– filling pressure U33-9
– septum U32-9
ventriculoatrial shunt U32-8
ventriculocisternostomy U125-15
ventriculomegaly U110-9
venular U34-4
venule U34-4
Veress needle/cannula U133-13
verification U117-12
verify U101-17; U117-12
vermiform appendix U45-13
vermilion border U87-10
vermis U41-2
vernix (caseosa) U71-19
verruca U114-17
verruciform U114-17
verrucous U114-17
vertebra U22-12; U28-19
vertebral column U85-22
vertiginous U113-6
vertigo U113-6
verumontanum U52-12
vesical U48-12
vesicant drugs U136-7
vesicle U114-12
–, umbilical U85-7
vesicoureteral reflux U48-12; U125-21
vesicular U114-12
vesiculation U114-12
vesiculopustular U114-12
vessels, blood U34-1
–, lymph(atic) U35-1
vestibular U60-9
– apparatus U57-18
vestibule (ear) U60-9
–, oral U21-10
vestibulitis U60-9
vestibulospinal U60-9
vestige U85-20
vestigial U85-9
viability U69-14
vial U9-13
vibrate U57-17
vibration sense U57-17
vibrational U57-17
vibratory U57-17
vibriosis U94-21
vibropercussion U57-17
Vichy shower U1-19
victim U6-12
victimize U6-12
video-assisted endoscopic technique
  U128-2
videoendoscopic U128-2

view U59-1; U87-4
vigil coma U7-17
vigilance U7-2
vigor U1-6
vigorous U1-6
villi, intestinal U35-10; U45-14
villoglandular U45-14
villous U45-14
viral U90-10
– tegument U84-18
viremia U90-10
virgin U68-11
– abdomen U133-13
virginal U68-11
– membrane U50-13
virginity U68-11
virile U53-1
– member U52-14
virility U53-1
virilization U53-12
virilize U53-1
virion U90-11
viroid U90-11
virucidal U90-10
virulence U90-10
virulent U90-10
virus U90-10
virus-induced U119-8
viscera U86-21; U108-12
viscerad U87-13
visceral U86-21; U87-13
visceralgia U86-21
visceroparietal U86-21
viscid U36-12
viscosity, blood/plasma U36-12
viscous U36-12
viscus U86-21
visibility U59-7
visible U59-6
vision U59-6; U73-10
–, blurred U103-14
–, double U113-11
–, field of U59-7
visit U18-7
–, emergency U18-9
visitation U18-7
visiting nurse (VN) U16-7
visitor U18-7
visual acuity U17-5; U59-8
– blurring U103-14
– field U59-7
– field defect U142-4
– image U59-5
visualization U59-7; U73-9
visualize U59-7; U73-9; U99-12
visually handicapped U142-3
vital U1-6
– capacity U44-11
– signs U108-3
vitality U1-6
vitamin U79-13,15
vitelline sac U85-7
vitellus U85-7
vitiliginous U114-4

vitiligo U114-4
vitreal U58-10
vitreoretinal U58-10,13
vitreous (humor/body) U58-10
– fluid U58-10
vivacious U1-6
vocal U66-10
vocation U142-26
vocational counseling U142-26
– education U142-18
– therapy U142-26
voice U66-10
void U49-16
voiding U49-16; U24-1
– symptoms, irritative U112-1
–, dysfunctional U4-4
–, frequent U112-5
–, incomplete U112-9
volar U87-17
– margin U28-17
volatile U82-2
volatilize U82-2; U105-14
volition U73-3
volitional U73-3
volume U61-5
– expander, plasma U136-13
– of distribution U91-17
–, blood U36-7
volumetric U36-7
voluntary U16-15; U40-6; U73-3
volunteer U16-15
volvulus U109-6
vomer U28-9
vomit U46-4; U103-12
vomiting U46-4; U103-12
vomitus U46-4; U103-12
vulnerable U87-27
vulva U50-11
vulvar /-al U50-11
vulvar ring U71-15
vulvitis U50-11

W

waddle U65-10
waddling U65-10
wading U65-5
waist(line) U22-6
waiting room U18-3
waiver, informed U134-3
wake (up) U72-7
wakeful(ness) U72-7
Waldeyer's ring U35-5
walk U65-1
walker(ette) U19-13; U65-1
walking U19-13; U65-1
– aid U142-29
– rounds U20-9
wander U65-7
ward round U20-9
–, hospital U19-1
–, quarantine U14-10
warm U75-13

warm up U1-13
warning U8-7
warrant U47-11; U94-3; U113-5
wart U114-17
-, venereal/genital U96-14
warty U96-14; U114-17
wash U19-10
- out U49-6
washcloth U19-10
washing U19-10; U116-5; U118-10
washings U91-26
washout U49-6; U118-10
wasp sting U6-7
waste material U37-3
- product, metabolic U49-1
wasted U108-14
wastes, nitrogenous U112-13
wasting U108-14
- away U25-7
watch U59-1
- for U117-7
watchful U59-1
- waiting U120-7
watchful(ness) U117-7
water U49-12; U82-4
waterbrash U109-3
waters break U71-6
water-seal drainage U125-16
waterworks U48-1
watery U82-4
wave U67-5
wavelength U61-3
waving U67-5
wax U60-1,15
- and wane U4-15; U114-1
wax-like U60-15
waxy U60-15
weak U103-9
weaken U31-13; U103-9
weakness U103-9
-, muscle U31-13
weaning U71-28; U125-3
weapon U6-8
wear-and-tear U64-13
weariness U76-18; U103-8
wearing-off-Effekt U121-8
weary U76-18
webbed bone U28-2
weep U66-3
- (wound) U140-13
weep(ing) U67-10
weepy U67-10
weigh U24-1
- (against) U117-17
weighing machine U24-11
weight bearing U19-14
- loss U108-14
-, body U24-1
-, molecular U81-3
weight-bearing U24-1; U19-14
weightless U24-1
weighty U117-17
welfare U1-7
- worker U16-8

welfare, public/social U13-6
well U1-3
- baby care U1-3
well-adjusted U75-15
well-balanced U75-15
well-being U1-7
well-built U25-1
well-conditioned U1-9
well-coordinated U31-19
well-cushioned U19-5
well-groomed U19-10
well-hydrated U78-22
well-intentioned U73-3
wellness U1-7
well-nourished U1-3
well-oriented U107-12
well-preserved U1-3
well-recognized U117-4
well-rounded U24-8
well-staffed U15-2
wet mount U83-20
wet nurse U14-8; U16-6
wetability U81-16
wetting U112-16
-, daytime U75-17
-, night U112-7
wheal U114-11; U96-4
wheelchair U19-13
wheezing U44-7; U111-8
wheezy U111-8
whiff U62-2
whiplash injury U124-18; U113-13
whirl U113-6
whirlpool (bath) U1-17
whisper U66-16
whistle U67-18
white (blood) cell U37-7
- coat, (doctor's) U17-16
- (blood) count U116-8
- matter/substance U41-7
whitehead U114-6
whitlow U114-16
whole blood U136-14
wholefoods U2-13
wholesome U1-5; U2-13
wholistic bodywork U1-18
whoop U95-5
whooping cough U95-5
wide-toed U23-14
widowed U102-9
will U20-14; U73-3
willful U73-3; U75-19
willing(ness) U73-3; U76-14
willpower U73-3
Wilson's disease U91-19
wince U104-12
wind U46-15
windpipe U43-8
wink (sleep) U72-2
wink(ing) U67-15
wire, figure-of-eight U141-14
wiring, circumferential U141-14
wiry U25-5
wise U75-7

wish U73-3
wit U75-7
withdraw (blood) U34-14
- (drug) U10-14; U121-6
- (from) U77-8
withdrawal (study) U101-29
- (social) U76-15,8; U77-8; U113-3
- (syndrome) U10-14
- symptoms U11-12
-, treated U10-15
withdrawn U75-14; U76-15
withstand U105-10; U128-18
witness, percipient U6-13
witnessed U20-14
witty U75-7
wobble U64-5
- board U142-19
wobbly U64-5
womb U50-5
work U142-28
- disability U142-3
workaholic U142-28
workout U1-12; U64-18
workshop, sheltered U11-13; U142-28
workup, diagnostic U20-8; U117-11
-, preoperative U134-1
World Health Organization (WHO) U13-11
worm-like U90-16
worn out U76-18
worries U76-19
worse, to be/become U4-12
worsen U4-12
worsening U4-12
worthlessness U77-17
wound U5-1,3f
- care U140-1
- closure U140-3
- contraction U140-8
- healing U140-5
- irrigation U140-11
- management U140-1
- repair U140-5
-, contused U6-6
-, crush U6-6
-, missile U86-1
wrap U140-20
-, Esmarch U135-18
-, herbal U142-22
-, paraffin U1-20
wreckage U8-7
wriggle U65-10
wring (hands) U67-4
wringer injury U125-5
wrinkle, (skin) U25-17; U56-17
wrinkling U56-17
wrinkly U25-17
wrist U23-5
write up (medicine) U107-4
writing sample U73-8
wry neck U103-20

X

xenobiotics U78-1
xenograft U130-5
xeroderma U56-3
xiphisternal notch U22-5
xiphoid process U28-13; U30-14
X-linkage U84-27
X-linked U84-27
x-ray U99-3
– sickness U4-1
– technician U15-13
–, chest (CXR) U118-18

Y

yawn(ing) U44-1; U72-1
yaws U142-7
yeast U90-18
yell U65-13; U66-14
yellow fever U122-7
yield U116-18; U75-19
yoga U1-16
yolk U51-5
– sack U85-7
young U80-2
youngster U80-2
youth U80-2,8
youthful U80-2

Z

zinc U82-29
zootoxin U91-4
zygoma U28-9
zygomatic (bone) U28-9
zygote U85-2

Index – Abbreviations

Viele medizinische Texte sind ohne Kenntnis der gebräuchlichen Abkürzungen kaum zu verstehen. Mit Hilfe dieses Index können Sie die Bedeutung der in der Medizin verbreiteten englischen Abkürzungen in **KWiC-Web** nachschlagen. Manche Kürzel wie *DNA*, *WHO* oder *CT* werden heute international verwendet, der Großteil der rund 20 000 in der anglofonen Welt verwendeten medizinischen Abkürzungen variiert jedoch sehr stark von Land zu Land, teilweise sogar von Krankenhaus zu Krankenhaus. Zudem sind viele der Kürzel recht kurzlebig und nur auf sehr spezifische Fachbereiche beschränkt. **KWiC-Web** enthält ca. 1500 der in der medizinischen Literatur und Klinik am häufigsten verwendeten Abkürzungen.

Auf den folgenden Seiten finden Sie alle im Text enthaltenen englischen Abkürzungen und Akronyme in alphabetischer Reihenfolge mit einem Verweis auf das Modul (Unit) und den betreffenden Eintrag. Bei Akronymen mit mehreren verschiedenen Bedeutungen sind die Verweise zu den Einträgen durch einen Strichpunkt getrennt. Bei Verweisen, die durch Beistriche getrennt sind, handelt es sich um parallele Belege zu ein und derselben Bedeutung. Bei Modul 115 (U115), das klinische Kürzel enthält, die in den anderen Units nicht vorkommen, sind keine Eintragsnummern angegeben, da die Abkürzungen in diesem Modul alphabetisch angeordnet sind.

A

a U115
A&E U6-1
A&W U12-5
a.c. U121-1
a.m. U115
A/G ratio U78-18, U116-2
A/O U115
A2 U115
AA U10-4; U79-10, U115
AAA U115
AAOx3 U115
Ab U39-8, U116-17
ABD, abd U45-6
ABG U116-11, U125-9
abn, ABNL U115
ABP U107-11, U115
ABR U60-13, U125-14
ABW U115
AC U41-3; U115
ac U115
ACA U84-7
ACE U55-25, U49-11
ACF U14-3
Ach U42-11
AchE U42-11
AchR U42-11
ACL U30-6
ACLS U115
ACMV U125-10
ACOG U15-16
ACS U13-13
ACTH U55-9
AD U107-11; U84-27
ADA U13-13
ADC U96-15

ADCC U39-8
ADE U9-3
ADH U55-24, U92-21
ADHD U77-16
ADI U91-18
ADL U142-27, U19-11
AdoCb U78-19
ADR U9-3; U121-14
AED U115
AF U110-7, U32-7
AFA U8-1
AFB U90-7
AFC U39-8
AFR 108-9
Ag U39-8
AGA U115
AGF U115
AHCPR U13-3
AHF U36-13; U38-13
AHG U39-5; U78-18
AICD U123-12
AID U69-12
AIDS U96-15
AIH U69-12
AIU U55-3
AJ U64-7
AK(A) U142-6
ALDH U82-12
ALG U78-18
ALL U115
All. U115
ALOS U19-15
ALP U47-15
ALS U37-4; U125-3; U115
ALT U47-16
alt.noct. U121-1
AMA U13-13; U18-4; U83-7

AMAN U113-14
AMI U115
amt. U115
ANA U39-8; U13-13
ANCA U37-8
ANOVA U100-14
AOB U115
AOM U95-12
AP U42-5; U118-18
APACHE U125-4
APC U39-8
APE U115
APH U115
APLS U115
APSAC U37-15
AR U110-10
ARAM U84-3
ARC U96-15; U115
ARD U115
ARF U115
ARM U85-15
AROM U115
aROM U115
ART U69-11
ARV U96-15
AS U34-8; U78-3
ASA U115
ASAP U115
ASD U32-7
ASH U110-9
ASHD U115
ASO U84-4
AST U47-16, U115
AT U1-15
ATG U39-5
ATLS U115
ATP U78-15

AUA U13-13
AUC U100-27
av U115
A-V U32-15; U136-5
AVRT U110-2
AWI U91-18
AWL U115

B

b.i.d. U121-1
b.p. U82-7
B/C U115
BAC U10-3
BAEP U41-12, U125-14
BAL U10-3; U91-26
BAO U88-16
BAT, D.A.T U115
BBB U36-15
BBP U115
BBQ U3-23
BBT U69-5
BC U61-4
BCAA U79-10
BCG U90-7, U122-2
BCR U84-2
BDA U13-13
BEAM U125-14
BH U102-4
BHT U115
bib U115
BIBA U115
BID U115
BK(A) U142-6
BLS U123-4, U125-3
BM U46-19

INDEX – Abbreviations

BMA U13-13
BMI U24-7
BMR U78-2
BMT U129-14, U136-9
BNTI U115
BP U36-8; U114-12
bp U84-12
BPH U89-15
BRBPR U115
BRP U19-9
BS, B/S U115
BSA U115
BSE U107-2; U115
BSERA U125-14
BSI U115
BSO U115
BSP U82-23
BSS U137-10
BTLS U115
BUN U37-1, U49-13
BVM U115
B_x U118-5

C

C U115
c U115
C&S U115
c.m. U115
c.p.s U115
c/min U115
c/o U103-2
CA U95-10; U123-2
Ca, CA U115
CABG U32-14, U125-11
CAD U32-14, U124-11
cal U79-4
CAM U83-2
cAMP U81-7, U83-17
CAPD U125-21
CAT U99-19
CBC U116-8
CBD U47-9
CBG U39-5, U78-18
CC U33-1; U125-1; U103-2
cc U115
CCD U133-3
CCK U55-13
CCM U110-15
CCP U16-11
CCS U83-12
CCU U32-14, U115; U125-1
CD U39-7, U84-2
CDC U13-3; U71-4
cDNA U84-11
CDT U37-6
CEA U39-8
CES U142-23
CET U69-16
CETP U82-14
CF U39-10; U115
CFL U28-27

cfu U139-10
CGH U84-38
cGMP U83-17
CGRP U55-8
Charr. U115
CHB U115
CHC U14-1
CHD U32-14
CHEM U97-17
CHF U110-5, U124-12
CHI U115
CI U33-2; U100-17
CID U96-11
CIE U88-18
CIN U97-4
CIS U97-10
CJD U115
CK U78-15
CKK U47-7
CLA U81-9
cM U84-17
CME U115
CMO U88-16
CMT U102-17
CMV U94-10; U125-10
CMVIG U96-11
CN U16 -4
CN 2-12 U115
CNM U16-6
CNS U40-5, U102-11
CO U33-7, U88-16
COD U12-7
COH U69-17
CON U18-10
COPD U111-16
CP U113-7; U115
CPAP U123-9
CPB U125-11
CPC U20-10
CPK U78-15
CPM U142-14
CPP U41-2
CPPD U82-5
CPR U123-4
CrCl U49-7
CRF U55-1; U101-16
CRH U54-4, U55-9
CRN U16-4
CRP U79-9
CS U124-14; U115
CSF U41-17, U79-7
CSM U94-13
CST U16-10
CT U91-20
CTA U115
CTD U115
CTL U39-13
CV U91-18; U136-3; U100-14
CVA U41-2, U124-14
CVAT U28-14, U109-12
CVC U125-7
CVL U125-7; U136-5

CVP U107-14, U125-6
CVS U102-11
CVT U16-10
CWP U71-9
CXR U118-18
CY U115

D

D U102-9
D&C U132-10, U115
d/c, dc U115
D/W U115
D5 W U115
DAG U82-13
DAWN U11-1
dbl U115
DBP U33-3, U107-15
DC U123-12, U115; U6-14
DCS U6-17
DD, DD_x U117-15
DE U99-9
DEA U11-7
deg U115
devel U115
df U100-16
DHEA U55-16
DHHS U13-3
DHL U98-10
DHT U55-16
DH_x U115
DIC U38-10, U115
DIMS U72-16
DIP U28-18
DIU U115
DKA U124-7
DLCO U44-11
DM U115
DNA U84-11
DNase U84-11
DNI U115
DNR U20-7, U117-18, U123-3
DOA U12-5
DOB U70-10, U102-9
DOE U111-1
DOES U72-1
DoH U115
doz U115
DP U115
DPOA U115
DPT U122-10
DR U115
DRE U107-2
DRT U115
DSA U118-16
dsg U115
DSMB U101-15
DST U136-8
DT U10-12; U95-9; U16-10
dT U115
DTH U39-23
DTR U42-12, U113-1

DTT U122-8
DTV U115
DUB U4-4
DUI U115
DVT U115
DWAI U115
DWI U10-5
D_x U117-11

E

E.R. U6-18
EAA U79-10
EAM U60-3
EBL U117-2, U115
EBV U90-10
ECC U125-1
ECF U82-4, U136-13
ECG U118-14, U125-5
ECLS U125-3
ECMO U44-6
ECU U14-7
ED U14-6
EDC U70-10
EDD U70-10
EDP U107-14, U115
EEE U94-13
EEG U118-12
EENT U115
EF U33-8, U44-3
EF-2 U84-19
EFA U79-12
EGF U55-5, U56-2
EGT U125-18
EGTA U123-10
EHS U115
EKG U118-14
ELISA U116-3
EMB U115
EMD U115
EMF U37-5
EMG U118-13, U142-23
EMP U82-19
EMR U20-5
EMS U6-18, U8-5, U14-6, U16-1
EMT U8-6; U16-10
ENDT U16-10
ENG U113-12
ENMG U118-13
ENT U21-14, U60-1
EOA U123-10, U115
EOH U115
EOMI U115
EP U15-1; U42-5, U125-14
epith U115
EPO U11-24
EPS U41-16, U115
EPSP U42-8
EQS U91-5
equiv U115
ER U14-6; U55-2; U83-8

INDEX – Abbreviations

ERCP U118-20, U128-2
ERPF U49-2
ERV U44-12; U118-3
ESP U57-2
ESR U37-5, U116-12
ESRD U115
est U115
ET U123-10; U16-12
ETA U117-2
ETF U60-7
ETI U115
ETT U142-17; U115
EUA U115
EW U115

F

F U102-9; U115
F&R U115
f/ U115
f/u, F/U U134-15
FAS U70-4
FB U8-10, U39-21
FBC U116-8
FBS U79-6
FD U115
FDA U13-9
FDCs U39-11
FEC U14-1
FESS U45-19
FET U69-16
FEV U44-12, U118-3
FFMF U70-13
FFP U136-16
FH U102-7
FHR U115
FHT U33-1, U70-4
FISH U84-38
fl U115
FL U115
FMP U115
FNP U16-5
FOBT U118-6
FOS U115
FP U15-8
FRC U44-11
FROM U115
FRP U51-6
Frx U106-1
FSH U55-14
FSP U142-5
ft U115
FTND U71-9
FTT U115
FU, F/U U115
FUO U94-19, 105-16
FVC U44-11, U118-3
FWB U115
Fx U115
FYI U115

G

G U70-7
G/W U115
G6PD U115
GA U107-10; U135-1
gal U115
GAPS U13-13
GCS U115
GER U109-4
GERD U109-3
GFR U49-2
GHRH U55-5
GI U54-9, U88-8
GIFT U69-18
GIH U55-5
GIP U55-13
GIS U102-11
GLC U83-22
gm, g U115
GMC U13-14
GM-CSF U37-8
GMP U81-7
GMW U81-3
GNA U19-11
GnRH U55-20
Gomer U115
GP U15-8, U18-1
Gpi U41-10
GPMAL U70-7
GRF U55-5
GSD U99-9
GSW U6-8
GTF U79-7
GTN U97-4
gtt. U9-11
GU U52-1
GUP U91-8
GUS U48-1, U102-11
GVHD U130-20
GVHR U130-20
Gy U99-10

H

H&P U102-4
h, hr, H U115
h.d. U115
H.O. U15-5
h.s U72-4, U121-1
HAPE U111-13
HAV U94-15
hazmat U91-5, U124-2
Hb U37-6, U116-9
HBC U115
HBO U44-6
HbsA U94-15
HCG, hCG U55-20
HCO U13-1
hCS U55-21
Hct U116-10
HCVD U115
HCW U16-1
HD U115
HDL U78-16
HEENT U102-11
HEMS U115
HEV U34-4
HF U124-12
Hgb U116-9
HGV U6-3
HI U115
HL U113-13
HLA U39-8,20
HMG U55-20
HMO U13-7
HOCM U110-9
HPA U54-4
HPC U38-1
HPD U81-18
HPE U102-4, U107-2
HPI 102-6
hPL U55-21
HPLC U83-22
HPV U96-13
HRV U33-5
HS U15-5; U33-1
HSM U115
HSS U110-9
HSV U95-7; U96-10
HT U16-10
HTN U115
HVD U115
H_x U102-4, U115
Hz U61-6, U115
HZ U115

I

I U82-22
I&D U115
I&O U88-16
i.a. U121-3
i.m. U121-3
i.v., IV U121-3
IA U115
IABC U125-8
IABP U125-8
IADLs U142-27
IAM U60-3
IBW U115
IC U44-11; U125-1
ICC U101-25
ICD U123-12
ICF U14-3
ICP U125-13
ICS U32-4, U115; U13-13
ICSH U55-15
ICSI U69-15
ICT U115
ICU U14-7, U125-1
IDA U115
IDDM U115
IDE U101-2
IDSA U13-13
Ig U39-5
IGF U55-12
ihD U124-12
ihss U115
ILC U142-28
ILF U14-3
IM U122-4; U115
IMA U45-7
IMD U14-5
IMF U141-4
IMV U44-5
in U115
in d. U115
IND U9-3; U101-2
INDA U101-2
inj U115
inop U115
int U115
IOP U125-5; U115
IPP U123-9
IPPB U115
iPTH U55-7
IPV U95-8, U122-7
IQ U73-5
IRB U101-24
IRC U13-12
IRMA U116-3
IRV U44-12
IU U115
IUD U69-10
IV U122-4, U136-1
IVF U69-12
IVF-ET U69-15
IVP U118-19
IVPB U136-4
IVR U115
IVU U118-19

J

J U79-4
JHO U15-5
JME U124-9
JPS U29-3, U57-5
JVD U110-16
JVP U34-11, U107-13; U110-16

K

K cell U39-16
kcal U115
KJ U23-11, U64-7
KUB U48-2, U118-19
KVO U115

INDEX – Abbreviations

L

L U43-1; U115
L&A U59-12
L1-L5 U28-19
LA U32-7; U135-3
LAD U32-14
LAK U37-10; U39-16
LAP U37-7, U47-15
LATS U55-6
lb U115
LBBB U123-2
LBP U107-14; U115
LCAT U78-16
LCDD U39-6
LCTA U115
LD U30-12; U91-11; U121-7
LDH U116-2, U115
LDL U78-16
LDRPS U14-9
LE U115
LET U115
LFTs U116-14; U118-3
LGIB U115
LGV U96-7
LH U55-15
LHRH U55-15
LIF U115
LILT U142-24
LIP U94-14
Liq. U9-11
LL U61-5; U94-17
LLL U43-3
LLLT U142-24
LMA U98-15
LMD U115
LMM U98-15
LMP U51-2, U70-10
LNMP U70-10
LOA U18-10
LOAEL U91-18
LOC U116-16, U115
LOH U84-5
LOS U19-15
LP U57-2; U118-7
LPM U115
LPN U16-4
LR U115
LRF U55-1
LSD U100-21
LSM U110-3
lt U115
LTC U13-1
LTF U39-12
LTM U74-8
LTOT U69-16
LTP U74-10
LV U33-9, U115
LVEDP U115
LVH U89-15, U110-9
LVN U16-4
Lx U115

M

M U81-3; U102-9
M&M U20-10
M. U115
m.dict. U115
m U115
MA U15-2; U20-12; U73-2, U77-1
MAE U115
MAF U39-18
MANOVA U100-28
MAO U88-14, U92-7
MAST U8-13, U110-14
MCCU U14-7
MCD U37-4
MCF U39-18
MCH U116-10
MCHC U37-4, U116-10
MCI U115
MCL U33-4, U87-9
MCO U13-8
MCP U13-8; U28-17
MCT U82-13
MCV U37-4, U116-10
MD U15-1
MD50 U91-11
MDA U11-17
MDMA U11-17
ME U115
MEN U97-4
mEq, meq U115
MESA U69-13
MFT U142-24
MH U102-4
MHC U39-20
MI U32-6, U124-11
MIC U115
micro U115
MICU U125-1
MIF U39-18
MIS U83-14
mL U115
MLD U91-11
mM U81-3
MMR U95-2; U122-3,6
MO U115
mo, mos. U115
MOI U115
mol wt U81-3, U115
mOsm U115
MPF U83-13
MPI U91-18
MR U110-10; U115
MR(I) U118-24
MRA U118-16
MRCP U118-20
MRG U115
MRL U91-5
mRNA U84-15
MRT U20-5
MS U115
MSH U55-26, U56-7

MSU U116-15
MT U16-10
MV U33-7
MVA U115
MVC U115
MVO2 U115
MVP U115

N

N&V U103-11
n.r., non rep. U115
N/S U88-5
N/V/D/C U115
NABS U115
NAD U107-20; U115
NADP U82-19
NANC U42-10
narc U135-5
NBZ U82-16
NC U115
NC/AT U115
ND U115
NE U16-5; U42-11
NEAA U79-10
NED U4-4, U117-9
neg. U116-22
NEL U91-18
NF1 U98-13
NF2 U98-13
nfc U83-6
NG tube, NGT U125-18
NH U115
NHS U13-1
NICU U14-7
NIH U13-3
NIP U94-14
NK U39-16
NK(D)A U115
NKHHC U124-7
NL, nml, norm U115
NMM U98-15
NMR U118-24
NMS U142-23
NO U81-17
NOAEL U91-18
NOEL U91-18
NPC U59-13
NPH U102-6
NPN U82-16, U115
NPO U21-8, U115
NPT U53-5
NR U115
NR(F)M U115
nRNA U84-15
NS U115
NSAIDs U55-4, U92-11
NSD U73-1
NSP U38-2
NSR U33-6
NT U42-10; U115
NTD U85-18

NTG U115
NTP U107-19
NYD U117-10, U115
NYHA U13-13

O

o.h. U121-1
o.n. U121-1
o.s., OS U115
O/E U107-2
OA U29-3
OAE U60-12
OAP U80-14
OBS U115
OC U69-7
OCA U114-4
OCD U77-19
OCN U97-1
OD U11-11, U121-7; U58-2
OHSS U69-17
oint. U9-8
OMR U20-5
OMS U13-11
OMT U16-10
OOB U115
OP U20-2; U81-21
Op., op U115
OPA U115
OPD U14-2
ophth U15-18
OPV U95-8; U115
OR U107-12; U131-1; U126-2; U100-8
org U115
ORIF U115
ORS U78-22
ORT U78-22
OS U58-2; U110-5
osm U81-21
OT U55-23; U142-26; U131-1; U126-2
OTC U9-3, U11-17
oz. U115

P

P U70-8; U81-23; U87-13; U107-13
P value U219-31
P&A U115
P.A. U15-1
p.m. U115
p.o. U121-3
P.O.P., POP U141-6
p.r. U115
p.r.n. U121-1
p.v. U115
PA U118-18
PAC U18-10; U115
PaCO$_2$ U116-11

PACU U135-24, U115
PADI U91-18
PAF U37-11
PAHO U13-11
PALS U15-17, U115
PAO U88-14
PaO_2 U116-11
PAR U135-21; U131-17
PAS U20-1
PASG U115
PAT U115
PB U66-13
PBI U79-9; U82-22
PC U103-2
PCA U20-12; U135-7
PCD U115
pCO_2 U115
PCP U15-1; U11-15; U115
PCR U84-36; U115
PCU U14-7
PCV U116-10
PD U42-5; U142-3
PDA U32-11, U115
PDGF U55-5, U37-11
PDR U115
PDU U115
PE U107-2; U124-13, U115
PEA U115
PEEP U125-10
PEL U91-5
pen U115
pend U115
PERF U16-11
perf U115
PERL U107-15
PERLA U58-8, U107-15
PESA U69-13
PET U99-19
PFGE U84-35
PFS U97-7
PFT U16-11
PG U78-24; U115
PH U102-6
phal U28-18
PhD U15-1
PHN U16-2
PHS U13-3
PIA U115
PID U94-1
PIF U55-22
PIP U28-18, U29-3, U87-14
PJC U115
PL U59-10
pl, PLT U115
PMH U102-6
PMI U33-4
PMN U37-8
PNB U115
PND U72-18, U104-14, U111-1
PNF U57-11
PNP U15-17, U16-5
PNS U40-5

PO, p.o. U115
PO_2 U115
POC U70-2
POD U115
POLST U115
POMR U20-5
pos. U116-22
PP U54-8
PPD U81-18, U118-2
ppm U115
PPN U125-19, U136-3
PPO U13-7
ppt U115
PR U45-16
PRBCs U136-16
preg U70-6
prep U115
PRH U55-22
PRL U55-22
PROM U71-6
prox U87-14
PRP U136-13
PRR U107-15
PSA U39-8
PST U110-2
PSVT U110-2
PSW U14-5
PT U37-13; U142-1
PT(C)A U115
pt., pts. U115
PTA U115
PTB U142-6
PTC U118-20, U115
PTCA U34-14
PTH U55-7
PTHrP U55-7
PTT U37-14, U116-13; U84-21
PTX U115
PUO U105-16
PUPPP U70-15
PV U47-5
PVC U115
PVF U47-5
PVR U112-11
PVS U119-15
PVS U7-17
PVT U47-5
P-Y U115
PZD U69-15
PZI U55-12

Q

q.d. U121-1
q.h. U121-1
q.l. U121-1
q.p. U121-1
q.r.s. U121-1
q4 U121-1
qt U115

R

R/O U117-14
RA U32-7, U115
RAAS U49-11
rad U99-10
RAD U99-3
RAI U55-3, U99-21
RAS U83-8
RBBB U115
RBC U37-5
RBM U84-3
RCC U98-2
RCM U115
RCT U16-10
RD U16-13
RDA U18-5
REC U101-25
REE U78-12
REM U64-1
req U115
RER U83-8
RES U35-12
RESA U69-13
RET U73-7
RF U115
RFLPs U84-13
Rh factor U37-17
RHC U44-4
RIBA U84-17, U116-3
RIND U115
RL U115
RLC U44-11
RLQ U109-12
RLS U72-5
RM U115
RMA U115
RMGI U40-5
RML U43-3
RMSF U94-19
RN U16-4
RNA U84-15
RNP U84-15
RO U81-21
ROC U100-27,34
ROM U31-18, U64-2; U71-6
ROS U102-11
ROT U115
RP U64-17
RPF U36-5, U49-2
RQ U44-4
RR U135-21, U131-17
RRC U15-4
rRNA U84-15
RRR U115
RRT U16-12
RS U102-11
RSI U115
RSR U115
rt U115
RTC U115
rtPA U84-17
RT-PCR U84-36

RUE U23-1
RUL U43-3
RUP U91-8
RUQ U109-12
RV U44-12, U112-11; U6-3
RVH U115
RVLM U41-14
RVR U115
Rx U121-1, U115

S

S U102-9
s U115
S&C U58-6
s.c. U121-3
S/E U115
s/p U115
S/S U115
S1 U33-1
S2 U33-1
S3 U33-1
S4 U33-1
SAD U77-16, U113-3
SAECG U118-14
SAL U57-7
SaO_2 U116-11, U115
SAR U8-2
SARS U115
SBBT U15-8
SBE U115
SBP U33-3, U107-14
SC U101-25, U122-4
SCA U113-8
SCC U98-2
SCD U123-2; U13-3
SCF U38-3
SCG U116-7
SCH U14-1
SCN U16-2
scuPA U37-15
SD U61-10; U100-13
SDM U100-13
SEM U100-10
SEPs U125-14
SER U83-8
SERM U83-19
SFM U115
SFST U10-4
SGOT U47-16
SGPT U47-16
SH, SH_x U115
SHO U15-5
SI(L) U115
SIADH U55-24
SIDS U80-4
SIE U124-14
Sig. U115
SIMV U123-9
SITREP U115
SLE U108-7
SLR U142-11; U113-1

INDEX – Abbreviations

SMR U100-9
SNc U41-10
SNF U14-3
SNr U41-10
SOB U44-1, U111-1
SOBOE U111-1
SOL U115
SOM U95-12
SOP U115
sp gr, SG U115
SPBI U37-3
SPC U15-1
spec U115
SPEP U84-35
SPL U61-3
sq U115
SRN U16-4
SRP U83-16
SRT U61-10; U88-7
ss U88-20
SS U100-34
SSM U98-15
SSRI U42-11
SSSS U90-8
ST U61-7
stat U115
STD U68-1, U94-3, U96-1
std U115
STEL U91-5
STM U74-8
STR U84-22
STS U84-12; U115
sub-q U56-4, U121-3, U122-4
SUI U112-15
SUZI U69-15
Sv U99-10
SvO U81-24
SVT U110-2, U115
SWS U72-11
Sx U115
SXR U115
sym U115

T

T&A U35-6
t.i.d. U121-1
t1/2 U91-17
TA U115
tab. U9-7
TAH U115
TAM U122-8
TB U94-16, U115
TBF U115
TBG U54-6, U55-6, U78-18
TBRF U90-15
TBW U82-4
TCA U81-15
TCU U14-7

TD U91-4
Td U115
TDI U91-18
TED U125-22
TEE U78-12; U118-15
TEFNA U69-13
TENS U142-23
TEQ U91-4
TESA U69-13
TESE U69-13
TET U69-16
THBR U55-6
THC U11-15
TIA U124-14
TIG U39-5, U94-11
TIL U37-10, U39-12
TISS U125-4
TKO U115
TL U94-17
TLC U44-11; U83-22; U115
TLV U91-18
TM U1-16; U60-4
Tm U49-3
T_{max} U115
TMJ U118-23
TNF U219-30
TNI U99-4
TORCH U96-11
TOT U69-16
tPA U37-15
TPAL U70-8
TPN U79-3, U125-19, U136-5
TPR U36-10; U115
TRAM U130-11
TRAP U47-15
TRH U54-4, U55-6
tRNA U84-15
TSH U55-6, U54-6
tsp U115
TSS U91-22
TT U115
TTE U118-15
TTS U115
TTT U142-22
TU U115
TURP U112-12
TV U115
TVH U115
T_x U120-1

U

U U81-23
U, u U115
U&E U78-23; U116-7
U/P ratio U115
UA, U/A U115
UAC U71-17
UBS U71-17
UC U71-3

UCHD U115
UCR U113-1
UGI U118-21
UGIB U115
ULTT U142-11
UNG U9-8
unk U115
UPJ U48-10, U112-12
UR U20-12
URI U94-2
US, U/S U118-17, U115
USPHS U13-3
ut.dict. U115
UTI U48-1, U94-2
UV U59-10

V

V, vol U115
V/Q U123-9, U115
VA U59-8
vacc U122-3
vag hyst U115
VAPP U95-8
VATS U128-2
VC U44-11
VCA U39-8, U90-10
VCE U116-5
Vd U91-17
VD U96-1
VDC U14-2, U96-1
VDDR U95-11
VDG U96-2; U110-6
VDRL U96-1
VEBs U33-1, U110-6
VEGF U55-5
VEP U125-14
VF U32-8, U123-2, U110-7; U59-7
VFIB U115
VIM U14-2
VIP U55-13
VN U16-7
VNA U13-13
VNTR U84-13,22
VO U20-7
VOR U60-9
VP U55-24
VPB U115
VPC U115
VS U108-3
vs. U115
VSA U11-23; U115
VSD U32-8
VSS U115
V_t U44-12
VT U115
VZIG U95-7
VZV U95-7, U122-6

W

W U102-9
w/c, wc U19-13, U115
W/F U115
W/M U115
W/N U1-3, U79-1
w/o U115
W/R U115
WAK U125-21
WASO U72-8
WB U115
WBC U37-7; U116-8
Wd U19-1
WDWN U115
WEE U94-13
WHO U13-11
WIT U142-22
wk, x/52 U115
WNL U107-19, U116-21
WPD U115
WPR U20-6
WPW U115
wt U115

X

x U115
XTC U11-17

Y

Y/O U115
YAC U84-6
YOB U115
yr U115

Z

ZE U115
ZIFT U69-18
ZN U115

Symbole

? U115
+ive U116-22
-ive U116-22
µg U115
µmol U115
2D U118-15

Index – Deutsch

Mit Hilfe des Index können Sie **KWiC-Web** auch zum Nachschlagen von Fachausdrücken verwenden. Hier finden Sie die deutschen Fachtermini in alphabetischer Reihenfolge. Umlaute werden dabei nicht besonders berücksichtigt, d. h. **ä**, **ö**, **ü** werden wie **a**, **o**, **u** behandelt. Adjektiv-Verbindungen finden Sie unter dem Hauptwort (z. B. *harter Gaumen* unter *Gaumen, harter*). Da auch viele fachspezifische Verben und Adjektive sowie allgemeinsprachliche Wortverbindungen im Index enthalten sind, wurde die Wortbedeutung in fraglichen Fällen durch ein typisches Bezugswort (in runder Klammer) verdeutlicht, z. B. *absetzen (Therapie), pressen (Zähne), Ableitung (EKG)*. Bei Alternativformen wurden bis auf wenige Ausnahmen, wie z. B. *Arznei(mittel)*, beide Formen oder die jeweils gebräuchlichere angeführt. Verwiesen wird auf die Module (Units) und Einträge (Zahl rechts unten in jedem Eintrag), in denen die Fachwörter vorkommen (z. B. U23-8 verweist auf Eintrag Nr. 8 in Unit 23). Zu den Modulen finden Sie am schnellsten über das Griffregister. Die halbfette Markierung des Moduls (z. B. **U23**-8) zeigt an, dass der Terminus im erstgenannten Eintrag dieser Unit als Schlüsselwort aufscheint, während bei mager formatierten Angaben die englische Bezeichnung im Kontext vorkommt (z. B. Beispielsatz).

Da die Wörter in den Modulen im Sinnzusammenhang dargestellt sind, findet man Termini derselben Wortfamilie bzw. Bedeutung jeweils im gleichen Eintrag, z. B. *Drainage* bei *Drain*, *Entkeimung* bei *entkeimen*, *druckschmerzempfindlich* bei *druckschmerzhaft*, usw. Dies ermöglicht einen sehr spezifischen Zugang zu den insgesamt über 100 000 englischen Fachtermini und deren Kontext.

A

AAK **U39**-9
Abart **U**100-14
Abbau **U27**-20;
    U78-1; **U88**-8; U46-11
– (Erythrozyten) U36-4
–, biologischer **U78**-10
–, lysosomaler **U39**-18; U83-6
abbaubar, biologisch **U78**-10; U92-4
abbauen **U78**-3,10; **U88**-8; U2-6;
    U137-8
– (Ängste) U4-13
Abbauprodukt(e) U47-13; **U78**-10
–, stickstoffhaltige U112-13
Abbauprozess **U78**-3
Abbaustoffwechsel **U78**-10; U81-16
Abbauweg U83-16
Abbauzelle **U78**-19
abbeißen **U27**-11
abbilden, sich U59-5
abbinden **U78**-19; **U137**-3
abblassen, auf Druck U23-6; U56-18
abbraten U2-9
abbrechen (Therapie) **U121**-6; U101-30
Abbruch (Proteinketten) **U84**-19
– (Therapie) U101-30; U125-3; **U121**-6
Abbruchblutung U51-2; U55-17
ABC-Maßnahmen U125-3
abdecken (Hautunreinheiten) **U25**-18
– (Kosten) U18-15
–, steril **U139**-7
Abdeckfolie (OP) U139-7,14
Abdecktest U59-15

Abdecktuch, steriles **U139**-7
abdichten **U137**-11
Abdichtungsmittel U137-11
Abdomen **U22**-4; **U45**-6
–, akutes **U124**-16; U45-6; U119-10
–, bretthartes **U109**-14; U31-17;
    U103-20
–, gebläht es **U109**-8,1; U22-4; U45-6
–, vorgewölbtes U109-8
Abdomenleeraufnahme U45-6
Abdomen-Übersichtsaufnahme U45-6;
    U118-18
Abdominalgravidität U70-6
Abdominozentese U118-8
Abduktion **U31**-6
Abduktionseinschränkung U31-6
Abduktionsgips U31-6
Abduktionshemmung U31-6
Abduktionsschiene U31-6
Abduktor **U31**-6
abduzieren **U31**-6
Aberdeen-Knoten **U138**-11
Aberration, X-chromosomale U84-20
aberrierend **U84**-20
Abfall **U64**-15
Abfallprodukt, stickstoffhaltiges
    U82-16
abfangen **U78**-19
abfiebern **U105**-18
abflachen (Kurve) **U116**-16
Abflachung (Hinterkopf) U87-20
– (Schall) U61-3
abfließen **U140**-15
Abfluss **U36**-5; U58-8

Abfluss, venöser **U36**-6; U53-5
Abflussbehinderung U36-5
Abflussstörung **U89**-18
abführend U92-13
Abführmittel **U15**-1; **U92**-13;
    U91-2,24
–, salinisches U81-21; U82-5
Abgabe **U49**-4; **U88**-11,16
– (Medikamente) U121-1
Abgase U6-3; U82-3
abgeben **U54**-2; U52-10
abgegrenzt **U89**-3; U87-6; U114-10
–, gut U87-10
abgehend (Flatus) U46-15
abgehoben U128-9
abgekapselt U99-18
abgeklemmt (ligieren) U137-3
abgeklungen U31-18
abgeleitet **U81**-18
abgelenkt **U74**-16
abgemagert **U25**-7; U76-17; U107-10
abgenutzt U27-19
abgerundet U43-1
abgesaugt U93-9
abgeschilfert U52-17
Abgeschlagenheit **U76**-18;
    U103-8
abgeschliffen U27-18
abgeschrägt (Nadelspitze) U132-11;
    U136-6
abgesetzt U88-10
abgesondert U140-13
abgespannt **U25**-7
abgestanden **U62**-5

abgestorben U140-12
abgestoßen U85-13; U56-2
abgestumpft U7-10;
    U76-17,1; U77-8
abgetrennt U107-5
Abgewandheit U73-10
abgewöhnen U74-7; U73-13
abgrenzen U87-9f; U99-12
Abgrenzung U87-10
– (Sterilbereich) U131-7
–, deutliche U87-12
abhalten U77-26
abhängig U11-3f; U9-3
Abhängigkeit U11-3; U14-5; U71-28
–, physische U11-5,3; U10-12
–, psychische U11-5
Abhängigkeitspotential U11-3
abheilen U120-2; U140-4
Abhorchen U107-9
Abhören U17-2
abhusten U103-17; U111-7
Abkapselung U76-15; U77-8
–, soziale U76-15
Abkauung U27-19
abklären U107-1; U117-1;
    U118-1
Abklärung U117-1;
    U118-1; U116-23; U134-1
– (Infertilität) U69-2
–, ambulante U18-1
–, bronchoskopische U118-11
–, endoskopische U128-2
–, präoperative U20-8
–, radiologische U99-1
–, sofortige U109-13
Abklatschmetastasen U97-13
abklemmen U137-13; U132-13
– (Nabelschnur) U71-17
Abklemmvorrichtung U136-4
abklingen (Symptome) U4-14f;
    U15-10; U124-3
–, spontan U70-15
abklopfen U107-7
Abkömmling U81-18; U85-11
abkühlen U105-9
ablagern U78-20
Ablagerung U78-20; U81-27; U27-22
Ablaktation U71-28
ablassen (Gas) U128-10
Ablatio U127-13; U58-7
– retinae U58-13; U124-1
Ablauf, biochemischer U92-32
Ablaufdatum U2-5; U17-1
Ableben U12-7
Ablederung U125-5
ablegen (Gewohnheit) U74-7,9f; U67-4
ablehnen U102-10
Ablehnung, Zeichen der U67-2
ableiten U36-6;
    U125-15; U140-15
–, sich U81-18; U85-11
Ableitung U81-18; U85-11
– (EKG) U118-14
ablenkbar, leicht U76-15

ablenken U74-16; U18-4
Ablenkung U74-16
Ablesung U24-11
ablösen U81-8; U140-6
Ablösung U58-7; U127-13
Abmagerung U25-7;
    U108-14; U105-10
abmelden, sich U20-16
abmischen U9-5
abnabeln U71-17
Abnahme U4-12; U116-20
–, kontinuierliche U88-20
–, operative U142-6
abnehmen U116-20
– (Blut) U37-1
– (Gewicht) U24-6,1; U25-5
– (Glied) U142-6
Abneigung U75-11
– (Speisen) U2-6
abnorm U116-21; U89-5
– hoch U107-20
ABNull-Inkompatibilität U136-11
Abnutzung U5-19; U27-19
ABO-Blutgruppen U37-16; U136-10
– Locus U84-2
aboral U46-7
Abort U70-4; U73-13
–, septischer U124-5
–, verhaltener U117-4
Abortivei U51-5
Abpräparieren U87-5; U126-12
–, sorgfältiges U128-14,17
abradieren U27-19
Abrasio corneae U5-8; U58-5
Abrasion U5-8; U27-19
–, korneale U58-5
abräumen U78-19
Abreiben U62-11; U64-6
abreiben U1-20; U5-8; U27-19; U139-6
Abreibung U1-20; U64-11
abreißen U106-5
Abrieb U5-8; U27-19
Abriss U28-4
–, kostochondraler U28-14
Abrissfraktur U106-5,2; U5-16;
    U28-5,25
Abrollen U23-13
Abruf U74-10
–, auf U18-2; U20-4; U57-4
abrufen U74-10
Abrufung (Gedächtnisinhalt) U74-8
absagen U18-2
absaugen U118-9; U127-16,19;
    U128-11
– (Sekret) U88-11
Absaugkanal U136-5
Absaugpumpe U8-15
Absaugvorrichtung U139-16; U17-4;
    U128-2,11
Abschaben U17-3
Abschabung U5-8
abschalten U76-19
Abscheidungsthrombus U37-11;
    U38-12

abscheulich U4-1
abschieben (Gewebe) U132-12
abschilfern U56-20;
    U114-7; U64-15
Abschilferung U56-20
Abschirmung, antibiotische U44-6;
    U92-9; U129-9
abschlachten U12-10
abschleifen U27-18
Abschlussdiagnose U117-5,11
Abschlussuntersuchung U125-2
abschneiden U5-6
Abschnitt U87-5f; U126-10
–, marginaler U87-6
–, mittlerer U87-6
abschrecken U91-8
Abschreckungsmittel U12-11
abschuppen U56-20
abschürfen U56-1
Abschürfung U5-8; U114-13
abschütteln U67-4
abschwächen U31-13; U103-9
Abschwellen U53-5
abschwellendes Mittel U92-17
Abschwellung U69-6
Abschwimmen (Epidermis) U114-13
Absence-Anfall/Epilepsie U59-2;
    U113-5
absetzen (im Gelenk) U29-1
– (Medikament) U121-6,14; U92-23
–, sich U81-27; U116-12
–, zwischen Klips U137-13; U138-15
–, zwischen Ligaturen U126-10,14
Absicht U73-8
Absicht, böse U77-7
Absiedelung U97-13
absondern U20-16; U54-2; U88-11
Absonderung U49-4; U88-11
–, schleimige U86-17
–, wässrige U82-4
Absorbens U88-8
absorbieren U46-13; U78-5; U88-8
Absorption U88-8; U78-5
Absorptionsstörung U46-13; U109-10
abspalten U81-8,4
abspecken U24-6
absplittern U106-2
abspreizen U31-6
Abspreizmuskel U31-6
Abspreizung U31-6
Absprengungsfraktur U106-2
abspülen (Asepsis) U139-5
abstammen U85-11
Abstammung U84-29f
Abstand, (innerer) U77-8
absterben U89-30
Abstillen U71-28,26
abstinent U10-7f
Abstinenz U10-6f
–, sexuelle U11-12; U53-11
Abstinenzbewegung U10-6
Abstinenzler(in) U10-7f
Abstinenzsyndrom U10-14,7; U11-12
abstoßen U56-20,2; U51-1

abstoßen (Zellen) **U64**-15
–, sich **U65**-14
abstoßend U109-2
Abstoßung **U39**-22
– (Endometrium) U51-2
–, weiße U130-21
Abstoßungsreaktion U39-22
abstreifen (mit Zungenspatel) U17-3
Abstrich **U17**-13; **U116**-5; U96-8
–, gefärbter U96-2
–, zytologischer U83-1
Abstrichmaterial U17-13; U118-4
Abstrichröhrchen U17-1; U118-4
Abstützung, seitliche U8-16
abszedierend U114-16
Abszedierung U89-12
Abszess **U114**-16
–, appendizitischer U45-13
–, intrahepatischer U47-6
Abszessdrainage U114-16
abtasten **U62**-9; **U99**-18; **U107**-7
Abtasten **U62**-9; **U107**-7; U110-1
–, vorsichtiges U62-9
Abtastgerät U99-18
Abteilung **U14**-9; **U19**-1
– für Gefäßchirurgie U14-9
–, chirurgische U14-6
–, dermatologische U15-10
–, innere U19-1
–, pathologische **U15**-21
–, psychiatrische U77-15 f
–, radiologische **U14**-9,6
abtöten **U12**-5,9; U92-25
abtragen **U27**-21,19
Abtragung **U127**-13; U5-8
Abtransport (Schleim) U44-9
abtransportieren **U8**-3
abtreiben U70-6
abtrennen U126-14
Abtrennung, operative U142-6
abtupfen **U17**-13; **U116**-5; U136-2
Abusus **U11**-3
abwägen **U117**-17
abwandeln **U42**-4
Abwandlung **U83**-19
abwartende Strategie U120-7
Abwässer U91-6
Abwasserentsorgung U139-4
Abwasserkanal U62-4
Abwasserreinigung U1-5
abwehren **U91**-8
abwehrgeschwächt U89-4; U97-18
Abwehrmechanismus U74-14; U77-9; U88-2
–, körpereigener U97-18
Abwehrspannung (Bauchdecke) **U109**-13; U45-6
abweichen **U59**-15
– (Augenachsen) **U59**-13

abweichend **U68**-15
Abweichung **U100**-13; U89-5
abwerfen **U64**-14 f
abziehen (Bett) U19-3
Abziehmuskel **U31**-6
abzielen **U55**-2; U73-8
abzwicken U64-10
ACE-Hemmer U33-9; U55-25; U92-7
ACE-Inhibitor U55-25
Acervulus cerebri U54-13
Acetabulum U28-21; U29-4
Acetaldehyd U82-12
Acetessigsäure **U82**-12
Aceton **U82**-12
Acetonämie U82-12
Acetongeruch U82-12
Acetonitril U91-9
Acetonurie U82-12
Acetylcholin **U42**-11
Acetylcholinesterase U42-11
Acetylcholinrezeptor U42-11
acetylieren **U78**-7
Achillessehne U23-13; U30-5
Achillessehnenreflex **U113**-1; U57-17
Achillobursitis U28-27
Achse **U87**-3
Achsel **U23**-3
Achselbehaarung U21-16
Achselfalte U23-3
Achselhaare U56-13
Achselhöhle **U23**-3; U19-14
Achselhöhlentemperatur U105-1
Achselkrücken U19-14
Achsellymphknoten U23-3; U35-3
Achselschweiß U56-10
Achseltemperatur U105-1
Achselvenenthrombose U34-4
Achselzucken U67-4
Achsenausrichtung U87-3
Achsenfehlstellung U87-3; **U106**-4
achsenförmig **U87**-3
Achsenknickung **U106**-4
Achsenmyopie U59-17
Achsenneigung U87-3
Achsenparallelität U87-3
Achsenskelett U28-1; U87-3
Achsenstellung **U141**-1
Achsenzylinder **U40**-2
achten auf **U74**-1; **U117**-7
Achterdraht/-ligatur **U141**-14
Achternaht **U137**-19
Achtertourenpflasterverband U141-11
achtgeben U65-4
achtlos **U74**-15
Ächzen **U66**-4 f
Achtzigjährige(r) **U80**-16
Acid **U11**-22
Acidum carbolicum **U82**-13
– uricum **U49**-14
Acne comedonica U114-6
Acrylnitril U91-9
ACTH **U55**-9
ACTH-Belastungstest U55-9
ACTH-Konzentration U55-9

ACTH-Schnelltest U55-9
ACTH-Syndrom, ektopes U55-9
ad axim verschoben U106-4
Adamsapfel **U21**-14; U43-7
Adamskostüm, im U71-2
Adams-Stokes-Synkope/Anfall U110-11
Adaptabilität **U88**-17
Adaptation **U77**-9; **U88**-17; **U129**-5
–, metabolische U88-17
Adaptationsnaht U129-5; U137-1
Adaptationsschiene U141-7
adaptieren **U59**-10; **U88**-17
– (Wundränder) **U137**-5; **U140**-2; **U129**-5
Adaption **U88**-17
adaptiv **U77**-9; **U88**-17
Addison-Krise U54-10; U124-6
Adduktion **U31**-6
Adduktionskontraktur U31-6
Adduktor **U31**-6
Adduktorenreflex U31-6
Adduktorenspasmus U31-6
adduzieren **U31**-6
Adenohypophyse U54-5; U55-5
Adenokarzinom **U98**-4
Adenokystom **U98**-4
Adenom **U98**-4
– sebaceum U56-8
Adenomatoidtumor U98-4
adenomatös **U98**-4
Adenomatose, multiple endokrine U98-4
Adenomatosis coli U98-1,4
Adenosarkom **U98**-4
Adenosin-3',5'-monophosphat, zyklisches U78-6
Adenosindiphosphat U38-11
Adenosindiphosphatribose U83-9
Adenosinmonophosphat, zyklisches **U83**-17; U81-7
Adenosintriphosphat **U78**-15,10
adenosquamöses Karzinom U86-12
Adeps lanae anhydricus U82-9
Aderhaut **U58**-7
Aderhauteffusion U58-7
Aderhautgefäße U58-7
Aderhautmelanom U58-7
Aderhautruptur U58-7
Aderhauttumoren U58-7
ADH **U55**-24
Adhaesio interthalamica U41-3
adhärent **U134**-10
Adhäsiolyse **U128**-15; **U134**-10
Adhäsion (Entzündung) U89-11
–, postoperative U128-15; **U134**-10
Adhäsionsbildung U128-15
Adhäsionsileus U109-6
Adhäsionsmolekül U81-2
adhäsiv **U128**-15
ADH-Mangel U55-24
ADH-Sekretion, inadäquate U55-24
ADH-Überschuss U55-24

adipös **U24**-9
Adipositas **U24**-9; **U56**-5; U89-2
–, schmerzhafte U56-5
Adipozyt U24-5; U56-5; U86-2
Aditus laryngis **U43**-7
– orbitae U58-1
Adiuretin **U55**-24; U92-21
adjustierte Rate U100-8
Adjuvans **U120**-8
adjuvant (Therapie) **U120**-8,4; U125-3
Adnexitis U94-1
Adoleszenz **U80**-8
Adoption U69-19
adoral **U46**-7
ADP-Ribose U83-9
adrenal **U54**-10
Adrenalin **U55**-11; U54-10; U88-1
Adrenalinausstoß U55-11; U65-15
adrenalinbedingt U93-12
Adrenalinumkehr U55-11
Adrenarche U54-10
adrenerg **U55**-11;
U54-10
Adrenozeptoragonist U40-8 f; U55-11
Adrenozeptorantagonist **U40**-8 f;
U54-10
Adrenozeptorblocker **U40**-8; U54-10
Adsorbatimpfstoff U122-2
Adsorbens **U81**-12
adsorbieren **U81**-12
Adsorption **U81**-12
Adsorptionschromatografie **U83**-22
Adstringens U82-31
adstringierend U82-28
adult **U80**-10
Adventitia **U34**-2
Adventitiadegeneration, zystische
U34-2
AEP U61-2
aerob **U1**-15; **U44**-6
Aerobic **U1**-15
Aerobicgeräte U1-15
Aerobier U44-6; U90-6
aerogen U44-12
Aerootitis U6-17; U95-12
Aerophagie U43-10; U46-2; U109-5
Aerosinusitis U6-17
Aerosol U91-7; **U92**-14
–, infektiöses U91-7; U94-2
afebril U105-3; U108-3
Affekt **U76**-3
–, flacher **U113**-3; U76-3
–, labiler U77-23
Affektabflachung **U113**-3
Affektabstumpfung U135-3
affektiv **U76**-3; **U113**-3
Affektivität **U76**-3
Affektlabilität U113-3
Affektstörung U4-4; U77-13
Affektverflachung **U113**-3
Afferenzen, (sensorische) **U40**-4
Affinität (zu) **U81**-12
Affinitätschromatografie U81-12;
U83-22

Affinitätsreifung U81-12
After **U45**-17
Afterjucken U45-17; U103-19
Afterload **U33**-10
Afterschließmuskel, innerer U30-9
Ag **U39**-8
AgAk-Komplex **U39**-9
Agarosegelelektrophorese U84-35
Agens **U92**-2
–, schädigendes U91-1
Agglutination **U39**-19
Agglutinationshemmung U39-19
Agglutinationsreaktion U39-19
Agglutinationstest U39-19
agglutinieren **U39**-19
Agglutinogen **U37**-16
Aggregat **U38**-11; **U81**-9
aggregiert **U81**-9
Aggressionsdurchbrüche U77-7
aggressiv **U77**-7; U73-7
agitiert **U76**-8;
U113-2; **U7**-12
Agitiertheit **U77**-6; **U76**-8; **U113**-2
Agonadismus **U54**-11
Agonist **U31**-4; **U92**-6
agonistisch **U31**-4
Ägophonie U111-11
Agoraphobie U77-5
Agrafie **U113**-9
Agrypnie **U72**-16
Agyrie **U41**-5
Ahle **U132**-5
Ahne **U84**-29
Ahnengeschichte U89-7
Ahnenreihe **U84**-29
ähnlich sein **U117**-13
Ahnung **U73**-8
Ahornsirup U9-11
AIDS **U96**-15
AIDS-Demenz U77-23; U96-15
AIDS-Epidemie U94-8; U96-15
AIDS-related Complex U96-15
AIDS-Virus U96-15
AIDS-Vollbild U96-15; U119-14
Air-trapping **U111**-6
Ak **U39**-8
Akathisie U77-19
A-Kette (Insulin) U81-7
Akklimatisation **U88**-17
Akkommodation U59-12; **U88**-17
Akkommodationsfähigkeit U59-12
Akkommodationslähmung U59-12
Akkommodationsmuskeln U58-16;
U59-12
Akkommodationsreflex U59-12
Akkomodationsverlust U59-12
akkommodativ **U59**-12
Akkumulation **U91**-19
akkumulieren **U78**-20; **U88**-15;
U91-19
Akme (Verlauf) **U105**-17
Akoholiker(innen), ehemalige U10-6
Akromegalie U108-12
Akromion U28-11

akrozentrisch (Autosom) U84-6
Akrozyanose **U108**-6
Aktinfilament U83-5
Aktin-Myosin-Querbrücke U81-7
Aktionspotential **U42**-5
Aktionsstrom U42-9
Aktionstremor U113-4
aktiv **U1**-6
Aktivator **U92**-3
aktivieren **U83**-18; **U88**-12; **U92**-3
Aktivierungssystem, aufsteigendes retikuläres U42-4; U83-8
Aktivität **U88**-14; **U122**-7; **U73**-1
–, biologische U92-3
–, körperliche U64-18
–, mol(ekul)are U78-1
Aktivitäten, sportliche U25-4
– des täglichen Lebens **U142**-27
Aktivkohle **U91**-25; U9-9; U46-8
Akupressur **U142**-15; U93-18
Akupressuranästhesie U93-18
Akupunkturanalgesie U93-18
Akustikus U60-13; U40-1
Akustikusneurinom U98-13
akustisch **U61**-2
akut **U119**-10
– krank **U107**-11
Akutbehandlung U124-1
Akutbett U19-3
Akute-Phase-Substanz U39-2
akutes Abdomen **U124**-16
Akutkrankenhaus U14-1
Akutwerden U119-17
Akzelerator **A**II-16
Akzent U66-13
Akzeptanz, reizlose **U129**-20
akzidentell **U6**-1; U122-1
Ala ossis sphenoidalis U28-8
Alaninaminotransferase **U47**-16;
U116-14
Alarm **U8**-7; **U117**-7
–, blinder U75-12
Alarmanlage U8-7
Alarmglocke U8-7
alarmieren **U7**-2;
U8-7
Alarmreaktion U8-7
Alarmstufe U8-7
Alaun **U82**-31
albern **U66**-2
Albinismus **U114**-4
Albino **U114**-4
Albumin **U78**-18
– /Globulin-Quotient U78-18
albuminähnlich **U78**-18
Albuminausscheidung U78-18
Albuminurie U78-18
Alcock-Kanal U52-20
Aldehyd **U82**-12
Aldehydanteil U82-12
Aldehydgruppe U82-12
Aldehydoxidase U82-12
Aldehydrest U82-12
Aldosteron **U55**-25

Aldosteronantagonist U55-25
Aldosteronismus **U55**-25
Aldosteronom U55-25
Aldosteronwirkung U55-25
Aleppobeule U114-16
Alexie **U113**-9
Algor mortis U12-15
Aliasing **U99**-13
Alibidinie U68-4
alimentär **U79**-3
Alimentation **U45**-1
Alkali **U81**-19
Alkaliengehalt **U81**-19
alkalisch **U81**-19
Alkalisierung **U81**-19
Alkalität **U81**-19
Alkalose **U81**-19
Alkan **U82**-15
Alken **U82**-15
Alkin U82-15
Alkohol **U10**-2; **U47**-17; **U82**-13
– am Steuer U10-1
–, denaturierter U10-2
Alkoholabhängigkeit **U10**-12
Alkoholabreibung U10-2
Alkoholabstinenz **U10**-4
Alkoholabusus U10-2,12; U47-17
Alkoholamnesie U74-17
alkoholarm **U10**-10
Alkoholblutprobe U10-3
Alkoholdelir **U10**-14; U7-16
Alkoholdemenz U77-23
Alkoholeinfluss, unter **U10**-5
Alkoholembryopathie **U10**-13; U70-4
Alkoholentgiftung **U10**-15
Alkoholentzug **U10**-14 f,2; U47-17
Alkoholentzugstherapie **U10**-15
Alkoholfahne U10-11
Alkoholfettleber U10-10
alkoholfrei **U10**-2
Alkoholgegner(in) **U10**-8
Alkoholgewöhnung **U10**-11
Alkoholhalluzinose U10-10; U11-21
alkoholhaltig **U10**-10
Alkoholika U10-10
Alkoholiker(in) **U10**-10
Alkoholintoxikation U10-10
–, akute U10-1
alkoholisch **U10**-10
alkoholisiert **U10**-1
Alkoholismus **U10**-12; U11-2
Alkoholkonsum U10-2; U46-1; U47-17
–, mäßiger U10-6
Alkoholkranke(r) **U10**-10
Alkoholkrankheit **U10**-12
Alkoholmessgerät U10-3
Alkoholmissbrauch U10-2,12; U47-17
Alkoholpsychose U10-10; U77-21
Alkoholsucht **U10**-12; U11-3
alkoholsüchtig **U10**-10
Alkoholsüchtige(r) U10-10
Alkoholsyndrom, embryofetales
  U10-13; U70-4
Alkoholtoleranz **U10**-11

Alkoholtupfer U132-18
Alkoholvergiftung U10-10
–, akute U10-1
Alkomat U10-3; U44-1
Alkyl(gruppe) **U82**-15
Alkylans **U82**-15; U78-7; U92-2
alkylieren **U78**-7
Alkylierung **U82**-15
Alkylquecksilberderivat U82-15
Alkylradikal **U82**-15
Alkylrest **U82**-15
Alkylsubstitution U82-15
Allantois **U85**-17
Allantoisgang U85-17
Allantoisgefäß U85-17
alleinig **U117**-14
Allel **U84**-4
Allelenpaare U84-4
Allelomorph **U84**-4
Allergen U39-23
Allergenexposition U39-23; U122-5
Allergenprovokation U39-23
Allergie U39-23
Allergiker(in) U39-23
allergisch U39-23
Allergisierung U39-23
Alles-oder-Nichts-Prinzip U42-8
Allgemeinanästhesie **U93**-1
Allgemeinbevölkerung U100-3
Allgemeinchirurg(in) U13-4
Allgemeinmediziner(in) **U15**-8,1;
  U18-1
Allgemeinsymptome U1-8; U25-3
Allgemeinzustand U119-15
Allheilmittel U140-4
Alloantikörper U39-8; U136-11
Alloarthroplastik U29-1
allogen U129-16
Allograft **U130**-3
Allotransplantat **U130**-3
Alltagsbewältigung U142-27
Alltagskompetenz U77-9
Alopecia androgenetica U25-16
Alopezie, temporale U68-4
Alpha-Alkoholismus U10-12
Alpha-MSH U55-26
Alptraum **U72**-9; U15-17; U74-11
alt **U80**-2,13; **U62**-5
Altanamnese **U102**-6
Altenpflege U80-15
Alter **U80**-1
–, gebärfähiges U51-10; U69-1 f
–, höheres **U80**-13
–, mittleres **U80**-12
Älteren, die **U80**-13,2
Altern **U80**-1,13
Alternativhypothese **U101**-19
altersadjustierte Inzidenz U100-7
Altersatrophie U89-29
Altersbeschwerden U4-10; U104-5
Altersdiabetes U80-10; U119-5
altersentsprechend U100-11
Altersflecke U25-18
Altersforschung **U80**-15

altersgemäß **U80**-1
Altersgrenze U87-10; U100-24
Altersgruppe U100-3
Altersheilkunde **U15**-17; **U80**-15
Altersheim U1-10; U4-7; U14-4
Alterspension U80-14
Altersperzentile U100-11
Alterspigmentierungen U114-5
Alterspsychose U77-15,21
Altersrente U80-14
Altersschwerhörigkeit **U61**-8
Altersstufe U80-1
Alterswarzen U80-13
Altersweitsichtigkeit U59-12,17
Alteszahnheilkunde U80-15
Altgedächtnis U74-8
Altinsulin U55-12
Alumen **U82**-31
Aluminium **U82**-31
Aluminiumenzephalopathie U77-23
Aluminiumgehalt U82-31
Aluminiumhydroxid U82-31
Aluminiumoxid **U82**-31
Aluminiumphosphat U82-19,31
Aluminiumpulver U82-31
Aluminiumsalze U82-5
Aluminiumsubazetatumbad U82-31
alveolär **U43**-10
Alveolardruck U43-10
Alveolarepithelzelle U86-8
Alveolarfortsatz U26-13
Alveolargang U43-10
Alveolargas U43-10
Alveolarkamm U27-7
Alveolarkammabbau U27-20
Alveolarkollaps U111-15
Alveolarluft U43-10
–, eingeschlossene U111-6
Alveolarmakrophage U39-18
Alveolarräume U43-10
Alveolarsäckchen U44-12
Alveole **U26**-13; U29-4
Alveolen, schlecht belüftete U43-10
Alveolitis, exogen allergische U94-14
Alveolus pulmonis **U43**-10
Alzheimer-Demenz/Krankheit U77-23
AMA U83-7
Amaurose, toxische U91-14
Amaurosis fugax **U110**-19; U59-18
Amblyomma americanum U90-15
Amblyopie U59-17
Amboss **U60**-5
Ambu-Beutel **U8**-12; U135-15
ambulant **U19**-12; **U20**-2;
  U65-1; **U134**-13,1
ambulante Behandlung U120-14
Ambulanz **U14**-2; U18-2; U19-1; U20-2
Ambulanzbesuch U20-2
Ambulanzraum U19-2
Ambulatorium **U14**-2; U20-2
Ameisenlaufen **U103**-19; **U104**-17
Amelogenese U26-15
Amid **U82**-17
Amin **U82**-17

Amingeruch U82-17
aminieren **U82**-17
Aminoazidämie **U79**-10
Aminogruppe U82-17
Aminosäure(n) **U79**-10; U46-11
–, verzweigtkettige U81-17
–, aromatische U62-3
Aminosäureabbau U78-3
Aminosäurelösung U79-10
Aminosäurerest U81-4; U82-17
Aminosäuresequenz U84-12
Aminosäuretransport U78-17
Amino-Terminal U39-3
Aminoxidase U82-17
Aminvorstufe U82-17
Amme **U16**-6; U14-8
Ammenmutter **U69**-19
Ammoniak **U47**-18; U46-17
ammoniakalisch **U47**-18
Ammoniakaufnahme U46-13
Ammoniakgeruch U47-18
ammoniakhaltig **U47**-18
Ammoniakintoxikation U47-18
Ammoniaklösung, wässrige U47-18
Ammoniakspiegel U47-18
Ammonium **U47**-18
Ammoniumchlorid U82-23
Ammonshorn **U41**-11
Amnesie **U74**-17; U5-14
–, episodische U119-11
–, psychogene U77-6
amnestisch **U74**-17
Amnion(sack) **U85**-15
Amnionbänder U85-15
Amnionbändersyndrom U85-15
Amnionhöhle U85-15
Amnionpunktion U85-15; U118-8
Amnionstränge U85-15
Amnioskopie U85-15
Amniotomie U85-15
Amniozentese U85-15; U118-8
Amöbe **U90**-4
Amöbenabszess U90-4; U94-18
amöbenähnlich **U94**-18
amöbenartig **U90**-4
Amöbendysenterie **U94**-18; U90-4
Amöbengranulom U90-4
Amöbenhepatitis U90-4
Amöbeninfektion **U90**-4
Amöbenkolitis U90-4; U94-18
Amöbenruhr **U94**-18; U90-4
Amöbenträger U90-4
Amöbiasis **U90**-4; **U94**-18
–, extraintestinale U94-18
–, intestinale U90-4
–, invasive U90-4
Amöbizid U90-4
amöboid **U94**-18
Amöbom U90-4
Amphetamin **U11**-17
Amphetaminderivat U11-17
Amphetamineinnahme U11-17
Amphetaminepidemie U11-17
Amphetaminpsychose U11-17

Amplifikationssonde U84-36
amplifizieren **U84**-36
Amplituden-Scan U118-17
Ampulla hepatopancreatica **U47**-10; U45-10
– Vateri **U47**-9
Ampulle **U9**-13
Ampullenflasche **U9**-13
Amputation U129-1
Amputationshöhe U142-6
Amputationsstrumpf U141-10
Amputationsstumpf **U142**-6
amputieren **U142**-6; **U127**-13
amputiert U22-1
Amputierte(r) **U142**-6; U134-14; U129-2
Amsler-Netz U17-5
amtlich **U18**-1
Amtsarzt/-ärztin **U16**-9; U18-1
AMV U44-12
Amygdala **U41**-11
Amylo-1,6-Glukosidase U78-10
Amyloidose, lichenoide U114-14
ANA U39-8
anabol(isch) **U78**-3
Anabolika **U11**-24; U55-4; U78-3
Anabolismus **U78**-3
Anabolit **U78**-3
anaerob **U1**-15; **U44**-6
Anaerobier U90-5
Anagenhaare U56-13
Analabstrich U45-17
Analatresie U45-17; U89-18
Analdehner U132-17
Analerotik U68-9
Analfalte U45-16
Analfissur U45-17; U87-26
Analgesie **U135**-7; **U104**-20
Analgesiestadium U135-7,20
Analgetikanephropathie U104-20
Analgetikum **U104**-20; U94-10; **U135**-7
Analöffnung U87-21
Analpruritus U45-17
Analreflex U45-17
Analring U45-17
Analverkehr U45-17; U68-5
Analyse **U116**-3
–, multivariate **U100**-28
analysieren **U116**-3
Anämie **U38**-4
–, autoimmunhämolytische U39-4
–, korpuskuläre hämolytische U37-4
–, refraktäre U86-2
anämisch **U38**-4
Anamnese **U102**-4ff; **U134**-1; U135-12
–, aktuelle/jetzige **U102**-5
–, frühere **U102**-6
Anamneseerhebung **U117**-3; U107-2
Anamnesegespräch U17-16
anamnestisch **U102**-4; U39-23
Anankasmus **U77**-19
Anaphase **U83**-13; U84-17
anaphylaktoid **U124**-3
Anaphylatoxin **U124**-3
Anaphylaxie **U124**-3

Anästhesie **U15**-11; **U135**-2
Anästhesie, balancierte **U93**-2
–, intravenöse **U93**-13
anästhesiemittelbedingt U93-4
Anästhesieprotokoll U20-5
Anästhesiesprechstunde U135-12
–, präoperative U18-13
Anästhesieverfahren U93-4
Anästhesiologie **U15**-11; **U135**-2
Anästhesist(in) **U15**-11; **U131**-6; **U135**-2
Anästhetikum **U15**-11; **U135**-5,1; **U93**-4,1; U134-8
–, volatiles U82-2
anästhetisch **U15**-11
Anastomose **U34**-6; **U36**-14; **U129**-6
–, arteriovenöse U34-6
–, portokavale U36-3
Anastomosendurchgängigkeit U129-6
Anastomoseninsuffizienz U129-6
Anastomosenleck U129-6
Anastomosenstriktur U89-19
Anastomosenverengung U129-6
anastomosieren **U34**-6
Anatom **U87**-1
Anatomie **U87**-1; U89-2
Anatoxin **U122**-8
Ancylostoma (duodenale) U90-16
andauern U7-18
Andenken **U74**-1
ändern **U74**-7
andeuten **U119**-3
Andrang **U65**-15
Androblastom U53-9
Androgen **U55**-16,4
Androgenentzugstherapie U55-16
Androgenresistenz U55-16
Androgenrezeptor U55-2
android **U53**-1
Androstendion **U55**-16
Androsteron **U55**-16
aneinanderlegen U137-5; **U141**-1
Anergie **U39**-22
anerkennen **U74**-3
Anerkennung **U57**-2
Aneuploidie **U84**-9
Aneurysma **U110**-18
– dissecans U34-8; U124-6; U126-12
–, syphilitisches U96-3
Aneurysmaresektion U124-15
Aneurysmasack U110-18
anfahren **U6**-2; **U67**-19
Anfall **U65**-15; **U72**-18; **U103**-4; **U104**-14
–, epileptischer **U113**-5; U77-13
–, hysterischer **U77**-6
–, myoklonischer U72-12
–, tonisch-klonischer U31-10; U124-9
Anfälle, rezidivierende U119-3
–, wiederkehrende U119-18
anfällig (für) **U119**-1; U76-4; U122-1
Anfälligkeit **U75**-4; **U119**-1; U103-9
anfallsartig U113-5
Anfallsschwindel U103-13; U113-6

Anfallserkrankung U118-12
anfallsfrei U113-5
Anfallshäufigkeit U113-5
Anfallsphase U74-8
Anfang dreißig U80-11
Anfangsdosis U121-7
Anfangsgewicht U24-1
anfärben **U116**-4
anfeuchten **U105**-13; U43-6
Anflutungszeit U135-13
Anfrage, taktvolle U75-5
anfrischen (Wundränder) U127-17; U140-2
anfunkeln, trotzig U67-13
angeboren **U89**-6f; **U84**-28
Angebot, unmoralisches U68-10
angegriffen **U89**-4
angegurtet U125-24
angehobene Ränder U129-11
Angehörige U12-4; U134-3
–, nächste U12-21
angelagert U81-14
Angelegenheit, heikle U76-4
angenehm **U75**-5,8
angeordnet U41-6; U83-6
angepasst U75-15
angeschlagen (Gesundheit) U4-5
angeschwollen **U53**-4; **U56**-19
angespannt **U76**-5; U66-20
Angestellte(r) U68-16
angestrengt schauen U59-2
angewiesen (auf Gesten) U67-1
angewinkelt U131-2
angewöhnen, sich U11-5
Angewohnheit **U10**-11; **U11**-5
Angina **U95**-13
– pectoris **U124**-11
Angiografie **U118**-16
–, selektive U134-2
Angiogramm **U118**-16
Angiokardiografie U118-16
Angiom(a) **U98**-5
Angiomyolipom U98-11
Angioödem **U111**-13
Angiopathie U118-16
Angioplastie **U127**-4; U129-3
–, perkutane transluminale koronare U34-14
Angiosarkom **U98**-5
Angiospasmus U36-11; U110-15
Angiotensin **U55**-25
Angiotensin-II-Blocker U49-11
Angiotensinogen **U55**-25
angreifen **U77**-7; **U89**-4
angrenzen **U87**-10f; U34-6
Angriff **U77**-7
angriffslustig **U77**-7
Angst **U76**-5; **U77**-5; **U113**-2
–, frei flottierende U77-5
–, panische **U6**-21; **U77**-6
–, unterdrückte U20-16
Angstabbau U134-4
Angstattacke U77-5

Ängste nehmen U117-7
–, sexuelle U68-7
Angsthysterie U76-5; U77-6
ängstlich **U75**-17; **U76**-5; **U77**-5
Ängstlichkeit U77-5,12
Angstneurose U4-4; U77-5,21
Angstreaktion U6-21
Angsttraum U72-9; U77-5
Angstzustand **U77**-5; U7-16; U76-5
Angulus iridocornealis U58-5,8
– mandibulae U21-5
angurten U131-2
anhaften **U39**-19
Anhaftung U134-10
anhalten (Atem) U44-1
anhaltend (Beschwerden) **U119**-11
anhängig **U63**-13
anhänglich U64-9
Anhängsel, gestielte U114-17
Anhangsgebilde, epidermale U86-7
anhäufen, (sich) **U38**-11; **U78**-20; **U88**-15
anheben **U64**-16; **U116**-19
– (Gewebe) **U129**-11; U128-12
– (Kinn) U8-11
Anhebung **U64**-16
anheften **U137**-4; **U141**-15
Anheftung **U129**-7
Anhidrose **U105**-15
anhören **U61**-1
Anhydrid **U82**-9
Anion **U81**-11; U99-20
Anionenlücke U81-11
Aniridie **U58**-8
Anismus U142-25
Ankleideapraxie U113-9
ankleiden (OP) **U139**-15
ankündigen (Krankheit) **U119**-3; U77-21; U107-13; U110-7
Ankyloglossie U21-11
Ankylose U141-13
anlächeln U67-9
Anlage **U85**-9f
anlagebedingt **U1**-8; **U25**-3; **U75**-4
anlagemäßig **U85**-9
Anlagen, sanitäre U14-3
Anlagerung U63-1; **U137**-5; **U141**-1
Anlaufen (Optik) U133-4
Anlegen U71-26
anlegen (Baby) U71-24
– (Staumanschette) U17-8
– (Verband) U17-13; U64-11
Anleitung U121-1
–, schrittweise **U19**-11
Anliegen U69-1
anliegen U34-6; U83-2; U141-1
anmaßend **U75**-20
Anmaßung U75-12
Anmeldeschalter U18-3
Anmeldung U18-3
Anmerkung **U57**-4
anmutig **U25**-8; U24-6
annähen **U137**-1
annähern **U140**-2; **U137**-5; **U129**-5

Annäherungsversuche U68-16
Annahme U101-17
Annihilationsstrahlung U99-2
anomal **U116**-21
Anomalie **U89**-5; **U116**-21
Anonyme Alkoholiker U10-4
Anophthalmus congenitus U89-6
anordnen (Therapie) **U20**-7; **U107**-3; **U121**-1
Anordnung **U107**-3
–, ärztliche U20-7
Anorektalkanal U85-21
Anorektikum U103-10
anorektisch **U103**-10
Anorexia nervosa **U103**-10; U108-14
Anorexie **U103**-10
anorganisch **U82**-5; **U86**-20
anorganische Chemie U81-1
Anorgasmie U68-6
Anovulation **U51**-9
Anoxie U123-8
anpassen **U59**-10; **U88**-17
Anpassung **U77**-9; **U88**-17
–, altersgemäße U77-9
–, mangelnde **U76**-21; **U77**-9
–, metabolische U88-17
–, physiologische U88-17
–, psychosoziale U77-9
anpassungsfähig **U59**-10; **U77**-9; **U88**-17
Anpassungsfähigkeit **U88**-17; U59-10
Anpassungsmechanismus U88-17
Anpassungsmuster, dysfunktionales U77-9
Anpassungsreaktion U88-17
Anpassungsschwierigkeiten U77-9
Anpassungsstörung **U76**-21; **U77**-9
Anpassungsverhalten U75-3; U77-9
anregen **U57**-1; **U88**-12; **U92**-3
Anregung **U73**-12
Anregungsmittel **U57**-1; **U88**-12
anreichern **U36**-13; **U116**-16
– (mit Sauerstoff) **U44**-6; **U82**-11
Anreicherung U82-5
– (Nahrungsmittel) U2-6
Anreiz U73-12
Anruf (Telefon) **U18**-7
Anrufer(in) **U18**-7
ansammeln **U88**-15; **U117**-3; **U127**-16
–, sich **U78**-20; **U91**-19
Ansammlung **U78**-20; U140-15
Ansatz **U30**-3; U73-7
–, knöcherner U28-2; U30-3
–, therapeutischer U120-4
ansaugen **U118**-9
anschauen **U67**-14
anschlagen, sich **U6**-4
anschlingen **U127**-11; U132-9
anschmiegsam **U67**-7
anschnallen **U141**-11
anschnauzen **U67**-19
anschreien U65-13
anschwellen **U53**-5; **U108**-10; U89-28

anschwellend **U56**-19
Anschwellung **U5**-15
– (Brust) **U71**-27; U55-23
ansehen **U59**-1
–, das Alter U80-13
ansetzen **U30**-3; U28-4
– (OP) **U121**-1
Ansicht **U59**-1; **U87**-4
–, persönliche U75-1
ansiedeln, sich U15-4
anspannen **U76**-5; U30-14
– (Muskel) U104-12
Anspannung **U31**-10; U32-13
–, reflektorische U40-6
–, unwillkürliche U40-6
anspornen U67-6
ansprechbar **U7**-7
Ansprechbarkeit **U39**-2
ansprechen (auf Therapie) **U7**-7; **U120**-11; U142-1
Ansprechen, verkürztes U121-8
Anspruch (auf Pension) U80-14
Anspruchsprüfung U20-12
Anstalt, geschlossene U14-5
–, psychiatrische U77-15
Anstaltsapotheke U9-4f; U15-20
Anstaltspackung U9-16
Anständigkeit **U75**-12
anstarren **U58**-2; **U59**-2f
–, zornig **U67**-13
ansteckend **U94**-2f; U4-2; U18-10
Ansteckung **U94**-1; U133-16
Ansteckungsfähigkeit **U94**-1
ansteigen **U65**-17; **U116**-19; U64-16
Anstieg **U65**-17; **U116**-19
–, deutlicher U117-5
anstimmen **U61**-6
Anstoß U73-12
anstößig U68-10
anstrengend **U64**-19; **U76**-18; U1-12
Anstrengung U56-18; **U5**-17
–, körperliche **U64**-19; U111-9
Antagonismus **U31**-4
Antagonist **U31**-4; **U92**-6
– (Zahn) U26-1; U27-13
antagonistisch **U31**-4
Antazidum **U92**-29; U46-10; U121-2
anteflektieren U31-2
Anteil **U81**-4
–, kindlicher (Plazenta) U71-16; U85-16
–, knöcherner U87-6
–, mütterlicher U71-16
Anteilnahme **U12**-12
anterior **U87**-16
Antetorsion U31-8
Anthelix U60-2
Anthelminthikum **U90**-16; **U92**-25
anthelminthisch **U90**-16
Anthrax U90-3
Anthraxspore U90-3
Anti(human)globulintest **U136**-12
antiadrenerg **U40**-8

Antiadrenergikum **U40**-8
Antialkoholiker(in) **U10**-8
Antiarrhythmikum **U33**-6; **U92**-18; U110-6
antiarrhythmisch **U33**-6
Antiatelektasefaktor **U44**-9
Antibaby-Pille **U69**-7,5; U9-7
Antibasalmembran-Antikörper U86-16
Antibiogramm U92-9
Antibiotika, zytostatische **U92**-31
Antibiotikaaustestung U116-2
Antibiotikaprophylaxe **U139**-13,10; U120-6
Antibiotikaresistenz U39-22; U92-9
Antibiotikatherapie U90-5
Antibiotikum **U92**-9
anticholinerg **U40**-8; **U92**-8
Anticholinergikum **U40**-8
Anticodon **U84**-13
Anticodonschleife U84-13
Antidepressiva **U92**-24; U35-5
–, trizyklische U81-7; U113-14
Antidiarrhoikum **U92**-13
Anti-D-Immunglobulin U37-17
Antidiuretikum **U55**-24; **U92**-21
antidiuretisch **U55**-24
antidiuretisches Hormon U92-21
Antidot **U9**-15; **U91**-15,3
Antidottherapie U81-5
Anti-D-Serum U37-17
Antiemetikum **U92**-12
Antiepileptikum **U113**-5
antiepileptisch **U92**-20; U93-14
Antifalten-Creme U25-17
Antifibrinolysin **U37**-15
Antifibrinolytikum **U37**-12
antifibrinolytisch **U37**-12; **U38**-14
Antigen **U39**-8,1
–, karzinoembryonales U97-16
–, onkofetales U97-1
–, prostataspezifisches U52-10; U97-9
–, unvollständiges **U39**-7
Antigen-Antikörper-Komplement-Komplex U39-9
Antigen-Antikörper-Komplex **U39**-9; U81-14
Antigen-Antikörper-Reaktion U39-8
Antigenbindungsstelle **U39**-7
antigene Determinante U39-8
Antigeneigenschaften U39-8
Antigenerkennung U39-8
Antigenität **U39**-8
Antigenmodulation U83-19
Antigennachweis U39-8; U117-5
Antigenshift U39-8
Antigenstimulation U88-12
Antiglobulin **U39**-5
Antihistaminika **U92**-22
Antihormon U92-31
Anti-Human-Globulin-Serum U136-12
Antihumanglobulintest, (in)direkter U136-12
antihypertensiv **U110**-13

Antihypertonikum **U110**-13
Antikoagulanzien **U38**-14; **U92**-16
Antikodon **U84**-13
antikonvulsiv U93-14
Antikonvulsivum **U92**-20; **U113**-5
Antikonzeption **U69**-5; U71-8
Antikörper **U39**-8
–, agglutinierende U39-19
–, antimitochondriale U83-7
–, humorale U88-9
–, komplementbindende U39-10
–, monoklonale U97-18
–, präzipitierende U81-27
–, zytotoxische U39-16
Antikörpertiter U81-23; U116-17; U122-2
antikörpervermittelt U92-32
Antilymphozytenserum U39-12
Antimetabolit **U78**-11; U92-31
Anti-Mückenmittel U91-8
Antimykotikum **U92**-26; U17-15; U90-18
Antioxidans **U81**-5,17; U79-15; U82-11
Antiparkinsonmittel U92-23
Antiperistaltik **U46**-6
Antiphlogistika **U92**-11; **U89**-11; U119-9
–, nichtsteroidale U92-11; U108-7
Antiphospholipid-Antikörper U47-12
Antiplasmin **U37**-15
Antipsychotikum **U74**-11; U92-2; U135-10
Antipyretikum **U105**-4
antipyretisch **U105**-18
Antirefluxplastik U112-12
Antirheumatika, nicht-steroidale U55-4
Antischaummittel U92-2
Antischockanzug U124-4
Antischockhose **U8**-13; U22-10; U110-14
Antisense-Oligomer U81-6
Antisense-RNA U84-15
Antisepsis **U139**-1
Antiseptikum **U139**-1
antiseptische Gaze **U139**-1
Antiserum **U37**-3; **U122**-2
–, monospezifisches U122-2
Antiskabiosum **U96**-12
antiskabiös **U96**-12
Antithrombin **U37**-13
Antithrombosestrümpfe **U141**-10
Antithrombotika **U92**-16
Antithymozytenglobulin U39-5
Antitoxin **U91**-15,4; **U122**-8
Antitoxineinheit U91-15; U122-8
Antitoxinkonzentration U91-15
Antitoxintherapie U91-15
Antitragus U60-2
Anti-Trendelenburglage U131-13
Antitumor-(Zyto)toxizität U39-16
Antitussivum U103-16; U111-7
antiviral **U90**-10; **U92**-9

Anti-Zentromer-Antikörper U84-7
Antragsformular U18-15
antreiben, (zur Eile) **U65**-15
Antrieb **U73**-11
Antriebslosigkeit U7-12
Antrum mastoideum U60-4,14
Antrumraspel U132-12
Antwort, biologische U83-1
Anulus inguinalis U22-9; U52-8
– umbilicalis U22-5
Anurie **U112**-2
Anus **U45**-17
– imperforatus U45-17
– praeter(naturalis) U45-17
anvertrauen **U18**-11
anweisen U20-14; **U107**-3
Anweisung **U107**-3
Anwendung **U17**-13
– (Medikament) U9-2; **U121**-3,5
Anwendungsweise U9-17
anwesend **U15**-3
Anwesende(r) **U6**-13
Anwesenheit **U15**-3
anwinkeln U23-9
Anxiolytika U92-23; U135-10
anzapfen **U64**-11; **U118**-7
Anzeichen **U67**-2; **U117**-9; **U120**-10; U108-1
–, erstes **U119**-4; U8-7
–, klinische U117-7
Anzeige (Bildschirm) **U107**-17; U24-11
anzeigen U20-6; **U67**-2; U99-14
anzeigepflichtig **U20**-6
Anzieher (Muskel) **U31**-6
anzüchten U116-6
Anzug, OP- **U139**-16
anzünden **U10**-18
anzweifeln **U117**-8
Aorta **U34**-8
–, reitende U34-8
aortal **U34**-8
Aortenaneurysma U110-18
–, rupturiertes **U124**-15
Aortenbifurkation U34-8
Aortenbogen **U34**-8
Aortenbogensyndrom U36-9
Aortendissektion U34-8; U124-6
Aortendruck, mittlerer U36-10
Aorteninsuffizienz U34-8; U36-9; U124-12
–, angeborene U110-10
Aortenisthmusstenose U34-8
Aortenklappe U32-10; U34-8
Aortenklappeninsuffizienz **U110**-10; U34-8; U36-9
Aortenruptur U34-8
Aortenschlitz U34-8
Aortenschwirren U34-8
Aortenstenose U34-8; U89-20
Aortenton, zweiter U117-5
Aortenverschluss U124-13
Aortenwurzel U34-8
AP **U47**-15
APACHE-Bewertungssystem **U125**-4

AP-Aktivität U47-15
apallisches Syndrom **U7**-17
Apathie **U76**-15; **U77**-8; **U7**-12
–, mentale U77-8
apathisch **U76**-15; U74-16
ap-Aufnahme U87-4
AP-Erhöhung U47-15
Aperitiva U92-13
Apertura pelvica superior U22-7
– pelvis U28-21
– piriformis U87-21
– thoracis superior U87-21
Apex **U87**-25
– (cordis) **U32**-4
Apexkardiogramm U32-4
Apgar-Score U100-6
Aphasie **U113**-10; U77-23
–, amnestische U74-21
–, postiktale U113-5
–, sensorische U57-10; U61-9
aphasisch **U66**-9
Aphonie **U103**-6; **U66**-23; **U111**-11
Aphrodisiakum U68-3
Aphthe **U89**-17
Apnoe **U111**-5; **U123**-6
Apnoeanfall U111-5
Apnoephasen U123-6
Apnoetest U123-6
apnoisch **U72**-13; **U123**-6
apolar **U81**-13
Apolipoprotein E Genotyp U84-10
Aponeurose **U30**-5
Aponeurosis palmaris U23-6
– plantaris U23-13; U30-5,7; U87-17
aponeurotisch **U30**-5
Apoplexie **U124**-14
Apoproteinanteil U81-4
Apotheke **U9**-4; **U15**-20
Apotheker(in) **U15**-20
Apparat, juxtaglomerulärer U48-6
Appendektomie U45-13; **U127**-1
Appendix testis U52-3
– vermiformis U45-13
Appendixkarzinoid U98-2
Appendizitis **U45**-13
–, verschleppte U20-13
Appetenz **U11**-2
Appetit U2-11,6
–, guter U1-2
Appetithemmer U103-10
appetitlos **U103**-10
Appetitlosigkeit **U103**-10,7; U2-11
Appetitzügler U2-11; U88-14
applaudieren **U67**-6
Applaus **U67**-6
Applikation **U17**-13; **U121**-4,3
–, subkutane U17-11; U56-4
Applikationsart **U121**-4,3
Applikationsweg, i.v. U136-5
Applikator U17-3; **U121**-3; **U132**-14
applizieren U17-13; U92-12; **U121**-4
Apposition **U141**-1; **U137**-5

approbieren U13-14
approximal **U87**-14
Approximalbereich U26-22
apraktisch **U113**-9
Apraxie **U113**-9; U77-23; U73-8
Aqua chlorata U82-23
– destillata U82-4
Aquadissektion U128-14
Aquduktstenose U41-4
Aquaeductus cerebri **U41**-4,2
– cochleae U60-11
– mesencephali U41-2
– Sylvii **U41**-4,2
Aquarhythmik U1-15
äquilibrieren **U88**-19
Äquilibrium **U88**-19
äquivalent U81-10
Äquivalent, toxisches U91-4
Äquivalentdosis U99-9
Arachnitis **U94**-13
Arachnoidalzotten U41-8
Arachnoidea **U41**-8
Arachnoiditis **U94**-13
ARAS U83-8
Arbeit U33-10
–, schwere körperliche U1-14
Arbeitsbelastung U33-10; U142-28
Arbeitsbelastungstraining U142-28
Arbeitserlaubnis U142-28
Arbeitsfähigkeit U1-9; U142-3,28
Arbeitsfähigkeitsstörung U142-3
Arbeitsgedächtnis U74-8
Arbeitshypothese U101-19
Arbeitskanal U136-5
–, integrierter U133-2
Arbeitslänge (Trokar) U133-5
Arbeitslast U33-10
Arbeitsleistung **U88**-16; U142-28
Arbeitsmedizin U142-26
Arbeitsplatz U142-28
–, rauchfreier U10-16
Arbeitsplatzkonzentration, maximale U91-18
Arbeitsplatzschutzmaßnahmen U6-22
Arbeitsraum (OP-Feld) U126-7
Arbeitstherapie **U142**-26
Arbeitstoleranz U142-28
Arbeitstrokar U132-7; U133-5 ; U136-5
arbeitsunfähig U4-8; U89-4; U119-10
Arbeitsunfähigkeit **U142**-3f
Arbeitsunfall U6-1; U142-3,26
ARC U96-15
Arcus aortae **U34**-8
– costalis U28-14
– dentalis inferior U28-10
– palatoglossus U45-4
– palatopharyngeus U45-4
– plantaris U87-17
– vertebrae U28-19
– zygomaticus **U28**-9
Area striata U41-6
Areale, verdächtige U116-23
–, talgdrüsenreiche U56-8

Areola U50-18
Argasidae U90-15
Argentit U82-28
Argentum **U82**-28
– nitricum U82-16
Ärger **U76**-9,11
ärgerlich **U76**-11
ärgern, sich **U76**-11
Arginin-Vasopressin U55-24; U81-21
Argipressin U55-24; U81-21
Arm **U23**-2
–, eingegipster/ruhiggestellter U23-1
–, muskulöser U25-4
Armamputierte U142-6
Armaturenbrett U6-2
Armbanduhr U23-5
Arme, verschränkte U23-2
Ärmel U107-4
–, hochgekrempelte U64-8
ärmellos U125-24
Armlehne U23-2; U64-17
Armmanschette U23-2
Armprothese U23-1; U142-6
Armschlinge U140-20
Armschwingen U64-5
Armspannweite U23-2; U24-2
Armstütze U19-3; U23-2; U131-12
Armtragetuch U23-2
Aroma **U62**-3,7
Aromastoffe **U62**-7
–, künstliche U62-7
Arousal **U72**-7; **U7**-2
Arretierung (Nadelhalter) U138-14
Arrhythmie U92-18
–, supraventrikuläre U110-6
arrogant **U75**-20; U65-13
Arroganz **U75**-20
Arrosion (Gehörknöchelchen) U60-5
Arsen **U82**-33
arsenhaltig U82-33
Arsenik **U82**-33
Arsenmelanose U82-33
Arsenpräparat U82-33
Arsentrioxid U82-33
Arsenverbindung U82-33
Arsenvergiftung **U82**-33; U91-2,14
Art **U75**-3
–, bissige U67-19
–, distanzierte U76-15
–, fröhliche U75-4; U76-9
–, gelassene U76-19
–, offene U75-13
–, ruhige U76-19
–, ungezwungene U75-3
Artefakt **U99**-13
Arteria **U34**-3
– carotis **U34**-10
– coeliaca, durchgängige U34-14
– coronaria U34-3
– iliaca communis U34-3
– profunda femoris U34-3
Arterie **U34**-3
arteriell **U34**-3
arterielles Blut U37-1

Arterienast U34-3
Arteriendruck U34-3
Arterienerkrankung U34-3
Arterienlappen **U130**-12
Arterienverkalkung U31-14
Arterienverschluss, akuter U124-13
Arteriola glomerularis afferens U34-3
arteriolär **U34**-3
Arteriole **U34**-3
Arteriolosklerose U34-3
Arteriopathie U34-3
Arteriosklerose U31-14; U124-11
Arthritis tuberculosa U94-16
Arthrodese U29-3; **U141**-13
arthrogene Kontraktur U29-9
Arthrografie **U118**-23
Arthrogramm **U118**-23
Arthropathia neuropathica U113-14
Arthroplastik U127-4
Arthropoden U90-12
Arthrose U89-29
Arthroskop U128-7
Arthroskopie **U118**-23; **U128**-7
Articulatio **U29**-1
– acromioclavicularis U28-11 f
– calcaneocuboidea U28-27
– cartilaginea U29-12,1
– condylaris **U29**-6
– coxae U28-21
– fibrosa U29-1
– genus U23-11
– humeroulnaris U23-2
– metacarpophalangealis U28-17
– metatarsophalangealis U28-25
– plana **U29**-7
– sellaris **U29**-6
– sphaeroidea **U29**-4
– synovialis **U29**-3,1
– talocalcanea/subtalaris U28-26
– talocruralis **U23**-12; U28-26; U29-1
– temporomandibularis U118-23
– tibiofibularis U28-24
– trochoidea **U29**-4
Articulationes intercarpales U28-17
artifiziell verzerrt U99-13
artig U75-15
artikulär **U29**-1
Artikulation U21-11; U26-1; **U66**-1,13
Artikulationsstörung **U113**-10; U61-11; U66-17,22
artikulieren (Gelenk) **U29**-1
artikuliert, (schlecht) **U113**-10; **U66**-1
Arznei- u. Lebensmittelbehörde (U.S.) **U13**-9
Arznei(mittel) **U9**-1 f
Arzneibuch **U9**-5; U15-20; **U92**-1
Arzneidroge U9-1
Arzneifläschchen U136-4
Arzneiform **U9**-6; U121-11
Arzneimittel **U9**-3,2; **U15**-1,20
–, gefäßerweiternde U36-11
Arzneimittelallergie U39-23; U124-3
Arzneimittelanamnese U102-4

Arzneimittelanreicherung U91-19
arzneimittelbedingt **U121**-15; U74-5
Arzneimittel-Codex **U9**-5
Arzneimittelentgiftung U91-23
Arzneimittelexanthem U108-7,9; U114-2
Arzneimittelgewöhnung U10-11; U11-5
Arzneimittelhandel U9-3
arzneimittelinduziert **U119**-8; **U121**-15
Arzneimittelinfusion U136-1
Arzneimittelinstillation U128-10
Arzneimittelinteraktion **U121**-11
Arzneimittelintoxikation U10-5
Arzneimittellehre **U92**-1
Arzneimittelmissbrauch, ärztlicher U11-3
Arzneimittelresistenz U120-13
Arzneimittelresorption U88-8
Arzneimittelunverträglichkeit U121-12
Arzneimittelvergiftung U10-5; U11-1
Arzneimittelwechselwirkung **U121**-11
Arzneimittelwirkung **U92**-3
–, unerwünschte **U121**-14; U9-3
Arzneistoffelimination U91-17
Arzneistofffreisetzung **U121**-4
Arzneistoffinkompatibilität U9-3
Arzneistoffverteilung U91-17
Arzneizubereitung U9-6
Arzt **U15**-1
– bringen, (rasch) zum U65-15
– im Praktikum U15-1,3 f; U18-1
– kommen/gehen, zum **U102**-1
–, approbierter U13-13; U15-1
–, behandelnder **U15**-3,1
–, diensthabender U15-1 f; U18-7
–, niedergelassener U18-1
–, praktischer **U15**-8,1; **U18**-1
–, promovierter U15-6
–, überweisender U15-1; U18-12
Arztberuf U15-2
Arztbesuch **U18**-2; U102-15
Ärztebedarf U9-4; U88-3
Ärztebesprechung U20-10
Ärztehaus U14-2
Ärztekammer **U13**-14
Ärzteschaft U15-2
Ärzteverband **U13**-13
Arztgespräch **U102**-14
Arzthaftpflichtversicherung U13-5
Arzthelfer(in) U16-2,10; U18-1
Arzthelferteam U14-7
Ärztin **U15**-1
Arztkittel **U17**-16
ärztlich **U9**-1
Arzt-Patient-Beziehung **U18**-8; U15-1; U74-5
Arztphobie U17-16
Arztpraxis **U18**-1; U15-1
Arztrechnung **U18**-15
Arzttasche **U17**-1
Arzttermin **U18**-2
Asbestbelastung U91-5
Asbeststaub U91-7

A-Scan U118-17
Asche **U12**-14
Aschoff-Tawara-Knoten U32-7,15
Ascorbinsäure **U79**-15; U81-19
ASD U87-21
Asepsis **U139**-1
aseptisch **U139**-1
aseptische Kautelen U131-9
Asomnie **U72**-16
Aspartataminotransferase U47-16; U116-14
Aspekt **U87**-4
Asphyxie **U44**-8; **U111**-4; **U123**-7
–, intrapartale U71-21
–, postpartale U71-9
Asphyxiestadium U135-20
Aspirat **U44**-3; **U111**-4; **U118**-9
Aspiration **U44**-3; **U111**-4; **U127**-16
Aspirationsbiopsie U118-5,9; U127-16
Aspirationskanal U118-9
Aspirationspneumonie U94-14; U109-5; U111-4
Aspirationsprophylaxe U111-4
Aspirationsspritze U17-10
Aspirationszytologie U118-9
Aspirator **U118**-9; **U127**-16
aspirieren **U44**-3; **U111**-4; **U118**-9; **U127**-16,19
Aspirin, magensaftresistentes U45-1
Assay **U116**-3
Assimilation **U78**-5; **U88**-8
assimilieren **U78**-5
Assisted Hatching U69-11
Assistent(in), med.-tech. **U16**-10
–, rad.-tech. U16-10; U99-1; U118-18
Assistenzarzt **U15**-5; U16-9
– in Fachausbildung **U15**-4
–, diensthabender U20-4
assistieren **U19**-11
Assoziation **U74**-5
–, freie U74-5
Assoziationsbahnen U74-5
Assoziationsfeld U74-5
Assoziationstest U74-5
assoziieren **U74**-5
assoziiert **U59**-15
Ast **U23**-1; **U28**-5; **U34**-13
–, absteigender U28-5
–, afferenter U40-4
–, aufsteigender U34-13
Astat U82-23
Astat(um) U82-23
Äste, anastomosierende U34-13
Asterixis U113-4
asthenisch **U25**-2,5
Asthenopie, akkommodative U59-12
Asthma (bronchiale) **U124**-10; U43-9
–, allergisches U39-23
–, berufsbedingtes U142-26
Asthmaanfall U124-10
Asthmaauslöser U88-13
Asthmaerblichkeit U124-10
Asthmatherapie U124-10
Asthmatiker(in) **U124**-10; U92-27

Astrozytom **U98**-14
asymptomatisch **U103**-1
Asynergie **U31**-4
Asystolie **U33**-3,2; U123-2
Aszites **U109**-9
–, chylöser U35-2; U109-9
–, galliger U47-11
Aszitesflüssigkeit U109-9
aszitisch **U109**-9
ataktisch **U113**-8
Ataraktika U135-10
Ataxie **U113**-8
–, lokomotorische U65-2
–, vestibuläre U57-18
–, zerebellare U41-2
Atelektase **U111**-15
atelektatisch **U111**-15; U44-9
Atem **U44**-1
–, außer U44-7
Atemalkoholmessgerät U10-3
Atemalkoholtestgerät U44-1
Atemantrieb U125-10; U73-11
–, hypoxischer U111-3
Atemarbeit U44-5; U64-19; U107-16
Atemaussetzer U72-13
Atembehinderung U107-16
Atembeschwerden U102-10; U123-6
Atembeutel U8-12; U123-4; **U135**-15
Atemdepression **U111**-4; U93-12; U123-6
Atemexkursion **U44**-10; **U107**-16; U43-12
–, Behinderung der U111-12
Atemfrequenz U44-1
–, erhöhte U111-5
Atemgeräusch U22-2; U107-8; U123-9
–, pfeifendes **U44**-7; **U111**-8,10; U103-2
Atemgeräusche U43-1; U44-1
–, abgeschwächte U116-20
–, hochfrequente U44-7
–, ohrferne U87-11
Atemgymnastik U142-1
Atemhilfe U44-5; U64-16; U123-6
–, mechanische U20-2; U125-3,10
Atemhilfsmuskulatur U44-3; U111-5
Ateminsuffizienz U44-4; U111-15
Atemlähmung U113-7; U125-1; U135-11
atemlos **U44**-1
Atemlosigkeit **U111**-1
Atemminutenvolumen U44-5,12
Atemnot U111-1,5; U44-4; U123-6
Atempause **U44**-1
Atemprobleme U102-10
–, akute U124-1
Atemreflexe U123-10
Atemschläuche U135-14
Atemschutzreflexe U123-10
Atemspende **U123**-9
Atemstillstand U111-5; **U123**-6; U44-4f; U72-13
Atemstimulans U11-17; U57-1
Atemstörung U107-16
Atemtherapeut(in) U16-12
Atemtherapie U142-1,26

Atemtrakt U43-5
Atemübungen U1-12,16
Atemvolumen **U44**-12
Atemweg(e) U135-17; U93-13
Atemwege **U43**-5; U44-4,12
–, freie U43-5
–, obere **U43**-5
–, stabile U125-2
Atemwegserkrankung, chronisch obstruktive U142-26
Atemwegsinfektion U94-2
Atemwegsirritans U81-1
Atemwegsobstruktion **U111**-16; U43-5; U89-18; U123-10
–, lebensbedrohliche U123-1
Atemwegspflege U125-1
Atemwegsreinigung U44-9
Atemwegsverlegung U123-10
Atemwegswiderstand U43-5; U123-10
Atemzug, letzter **U12**-4
Atemzugvolumen **U44**-12
Äthanal U82-12
Äthanol **U47**-17; U10-3; U82-13
Äthanol-Wassergemisch U9-10
ätherisch **U82**-2; U105-14
Atherom U89-24
Äthinylöstradiol U55-18
athletisch **U25**-2,4
Äthylalkohol **U47**-17; U10-2; U82-13
Ätiologie **U119**-2; U89-8
ätiologisch **U119**-2
ATL-Hilfsmittel U142-27
Atmen, beschleunigtes **U111**-5
atmen **U44**-1
–, keuchend **U95**-5
–, pfeifend **U111**-8; U44-4
–, schwer **U44**-7
Atmende(r) **U44**-1
Atmung **U44**-1,4
–, äußere U44-4
–, erschwerte **U111**-2
–, flache U44-1; U111-2
–, innere U44-4
–, regelmäßige U76-19
–, röchelnde U111-2
–, ruhige U76-19
–, schnappende U64-7
–, unregelmäßige U64-7
–, verlangsamte **U111**-5; U44-4
Atmungskette, mitochondriale U83-7
Atom **U81**-2
Atomabsorptionsspektrophotometrie U83-21
Atombindung U81-8,10
Atomexplosion U6-9
Atomhülle U81-10
Atomorbital U81-2
ATP **U78**-15; U81-17
ATP-Abbau U78-15
ATPase, kupfertransportierende U82-29
ATP-Entleerung, mitochondriale U83-7
ATP-Mangel U78-15
ATP-Speicherentleerung U78-15
atraumatisch umlagern **U8**-14

Atresie **U89**-18
atrial **U32**-7
Atrioventrikularbündel **U32**-7
Atrioventrikularklappe **U32**-7
Atrioventrikularknoten **U32**-7,15
Atrioventrikularrhythmus **U32**-7
Atrium **U32**-7
Atrophie **U89**-29; U142-8
Attacke **U103**-4; **U104**-14
–, transitorische ischämische **U124**-14; U15-14; U41-12
attentuiertes lebendes Virus **U122**-6
Attenuierung **U122**-6
Attest, ärztliches **U18**-10
attestieren **U18**-10
Attrition **U27**-19
atypisch **U116**-21
ätzend **U91**-10; **U127**-9
Ätzflüssigkeit U82-4; U91-10
Ätzgift **U91**-2,10
Ätzmittel **U91**-10; U81-1
Ätzmittelingestion U46-1
Ätznatron **U91**-10
Ätzschorf **U114**-8; **U140**-9
Audiologe U16-1
Audiometer U61-7
Audiometrie **U61**-2; U118-3
Auditio colorata U61-2
auditiv **U61**-2; **U21**-15
Auerbach-Plexus U40-12
Aufbau **U78**-1,4; **U87**-1; U129-2
aufbauend **U78**-3
aufbewahren U9-19
Aufbissschiene U27-12
aufblähen **U44**-5
Aufblähung **U111**-6
aufblasbare Manschette U17-8
aufblasen **U44**-5
– (Wangen) U21-6; U44-7
aufblühend **U1**-4
aufbrausend U76-2
aufbringen U17-13
aufdecken **U102**-3
aufdehnen **U132**-17
aufdringlich **U64**-12
aufeinanderfolgend U92-4
Aufenthalt **U19**-15
Aufenthaltskosten U19-15
aufessen U2-1
Auffahrunfall U6-2
auffällig **U87**-12; U120-13
Auffassungsgabe **U57**-2; **U74**-4; U73-5
Auffassungsvermögen, eingeschränktes U142-4
Aufflackern (Erkrankung) **U119**-17
auffrischen (Gedächtnis) U74-8
– (Impfung) U122-3 f,9
Auffrischungsdosis U122-9
Auffrischungsimpfung **U122**-9
auffüllen **U88**-15
Auffüllung **U78**-21; **U88**-15; U49-8
aufgedunsen **U108**-10; U5-15
aufgehen (Knoten) U137-12; U138-2
aufgeklärte Verzichtserklärung **U134**-3

aufgenommen U45-9; U83-15
aufgeputscht **U8**-7
aufgequollen U89-27
aufgeregt U76-6,8
aufgerissen **U5**-7; **U106**-5
aufgeschlossen **U75**-16; U74-1
aufgespalten **U81**-8; U79-8
aufgetrieben **U109**-8
aufgeweckt **U75**-7
aufgeweicht U60-15
Aufhängeband U63-13
aufhängen U63-13; **U141**-3
Aufhängung U63-13; **U129**-7
– in Schwebe U141-3
aufheitern **U75**-6; **U76**-9
aufhören (Rauchen) U10-16
aufklären (Patient) U18-4; U142-18
Aufklärung **U18**-11
Aufladung, langfristige U74-10
Auflagerung **U141**-1
Auflagetablett **U17**-12
auflegen (Eis) U142-21
– (Instrumente) U131-8
aufleuchten **U99**-16
auflisten U20-6
auflösen **U38**-14; **U105**-14; U37-15
– (optisch) U59-8
–, sich **U81**-22; **U88**-5; U92-16
Auflösung **U4**-14; **U78**-4; **U81**-22; **U105**-14
– (Mikroskop) U86-1
–, räumliche U59-9; U99-14
Auflösungsvermögen **U99**-14; U59-8
aufmerksam (machen) **U117**-7; U77-1
Aufmerksamkeit **U8**-1; **U74**-16; **U117**-7
–, flüchtige U77-18
Aufmerksamkeitsdefizit-Syndrom U74-16; U75-17
Aufmerksamkeits-Hyperaktivitäts-Syndrom U77-16
Aufmerksamkeitsspanne U74-16
aufmuntern **U75**-6; **U67**-6
Aufnahme **U57**-10; **U87**-4; **U88**-8,12
– (oral) **U46**-1,13; **U55**-3,12; **U78**-5; U2-1
– (Studie) **U101**-4
–, ap U118-18
–, psychiatrische U77-16
–, rasche U55-3
–, stationäre **U14**-1,5; U20-1
Aufnahme(menge), duldbare tägliche **U91**-18
–, maximal tolerierbare U91-18
Aufnahmearzt/-ärztin U20-1
Aufnahmebefund U117-6
Aufnahmebericht U20-1; U102-13
Aufnahmediagnose U20-1
aufnahmefähig **U57**-10
Aufnahmefähigkeit **U57**-10
Aufnahmekriterien U101-4
Aufnahmeprotokoll U20-6

Aufnahmesekretärin U18-3
Aufnahmestatus U107-2
Aufnahmeuntersuchung U20-1
aufnehmen **U46**-13; **U74**-9; **U78**-5
–, stationär **U14**-1; **U20**-1
–, zur Beobachtung U59-1
aufpassen (auf) **U20**-3; **U74**-1
aufplatzen **U140**-16
Aufprall **U6**-4; U5-14
aufpumpen (Blutdruckmanschette) **U44**-5
Aufputschmittel **U11**-17
aufquellen U132-18
aufrappeln, sich **U65**-18
aufrecht **U63**-2
– sitzen U63-2
aufrechterhalten **U125**-3; 36-5; U54-7
– (Erektion) U53-3
aufregen U76-8 f; **U113**-2
aufregend **U65**-16
Aufregung **U57**-1; **U77**-18; U76-9; U109-1
Aufricht(e)hilfe **U19**-4
aufrichten, (sich) **U31**-3
aufrichtig **U75**-12
Aufrichtigkeit **U75**-12
aufrütteln **U64**-7
aufsässig (Kind) U64-12; U75-18
aufsaugen **U46**-2
aufscheuern **U5**-8
aufschießen (Bläschen) U114-12
aufschlitzen **U5**-6
aufschluchzen U66-3
aufschlussreich **U107**-17
aufschneiden **U126**-9; U65-13
– (Pulsadern) U5-6
aufschrecken **U65**-16
aufschreiben **U20**-6
aufschwemmen **U81**-25
Aufschwemmung **U81**-25; U82-4; U91-25
Aufsetzen U142-29
Aufsicht **U125**-5; **U142**-29; U77-25
–, unter U142-27
aufspalten **U46**-11; **U78**-10; **U81**-8; **U84**-37
Aufspaltung **U78**-1,10; **U81**-22; U46-11; U99-20
aufspüren **U79**-17
aufstechen U5-10
aufstehen **U65**-17; U64-16
Aufstoßen **U46**-3; U109-1,4,7
aufsuchen (Arzt) U15-1; U18-1; U103-1
Auftauchen **U87**-4; U6-17
auftauen **U136**-16; U83-20
Auftauen (Embryos) U69-14
Auftauzeit U136-16
Auftauzyklus U69-16
aufteilen **U87**-6
auftragen **U20**-5; **U116**-5; **U121**-3
– (Salbe) U9-8; U17-3,13

auftreffen U42-4
Auftreibung U109-7
–, ballonförmige U89-23
auftrennen U81-4
, elektrophoretisch U84-35
Auftrennung U81-22
auftreten U65-5
–, anfallsweise U72-13
–, familiär gehäuft U102-7; U89-7
–, plötzlich U119-13
–, vorsichtig U65-5
Aufwachbett U131-18
Aufwachen U72-7
Aufwachperiode U135-23; U131-17
Aufwachphase U135-21
Aufwachprotokoll U131-17 f
Aufwachraum U131-17; U135-21,23
Aufwachschwester U131-17
aufwachsen U80-3
Aufwachstation U135-24
Aufwachtemperatur U105-1
Aufwachzeit U72-7
aufwärmen (Muskeln) U1-13; U31-11
Aufwärmübung U64-18
aufwecken U72-7; U7-2; U64-3
Aufweichung (Haut) U114-14
aufweisen U107-17
aufwiegen U117-17
Aufwölbung U34-4
aufwühlen U76-8; U113-2
aufzeichnen U18-14; U20-5; U102-12
Aufzeichnung(en) U102-12; U135-22
aufziehen U65-17; U79-1
– (Spritze) U17-10
Aufzug U64-16
Aufzweigung U34-13
Augapfel U58-2; U21-3; U59-16
–, druckschmerzhafter U58-2
–, hervortretende U58-2; U87-27
Auge U21-3; U58-2
–, blaues U5-13; U89-26
–, nicht akkommodiertes U59-12
–, schielendes U59-15
Auge-Hand-Koordination U31-19
Augen, blutunterlaufene U37-1
–, glanzlose U58-2
–, mit strahlenden U59-11
–, mit verbundenen U59-18
–, verschwollene U58-1
Augenarzt/-ärztin U15-18; U58-2
Augenbank U14-12
Augenbeweglichkeit U59-16
Augenbewegung zur Refixation U59-14
–, konjugierte U59-16
–, ruckartige U59-14; U58-16
–, sakkadische U59-14
–, schnelle U64-1
Augenblick, flüchtiger U59-3
–, unbedachter U75-18
Augenbrauen U25-14
Augenentzündung U58-2
Augenfehlstellung U59-15

Augenflimmern U103-15
Augenfundus U59-7
Augengymnastik U1-15
Augenhaut, mittlere U58-7
Augenheilkunde U15-18
Augenhintergund U58-12
Augenhöhle U58-1; U21-3; U28-8
–, knöcherne U58-1
Augenhöhlenrand U58-1
–, unterer U28-9; U58-1
Augenhöhlenspalte U58-1
Augeninnendruck U59-16
Augenkammer, vordere U15-18; U17-4; U59-10
Augenklappe U58-2; U140-25
Augenkompresse U140-19
Augen-Kopfstellreflex U57-16
Augenkrankheit, ägyptische U90-14
Augenläsion, zur Erblindung führende U59-18
Augenlid U58-3
Augenlidektropium U31-8
Augenmassage U142-15
Augenmuskellähmung U15-18; U58-16
Augenmuskeln, (äußere) U58-16
Augenoptiker U13-14
Augenpol, hinterer U58-13
Augenreiben U72-1
Augenreizstoff U58-2
Augensalbe U9-8; U15-18
–, kortisonhaltige U55-10
Augenspiegel U17-6; U58-12; U118-11
Augenspiegelung U58-12,8; U15-18
Augentropfen U125-25; U136-1
–, benetzende U17-14
–, pupillenverengende U59-10
Augentrübung U59-11
Augenturgor U56-19
Augenverband U17-5
Augenwässer U9-11; U15-18
Augenwinkel U58-3,2
Augenzahn U26-5
Augenzeuge/-in U6-13
Augenzeugenbericht U6-13
Augenzittern U113-12; U58-2
Augmentation U129-19
Augmentationsplastik U130-1
Aura, epileptische U124-9
Auricula U32-7; U60-2; U17-7
Aurikularanhänge U60-2
Auris externa/interna U60-1
– media U60-1
Aurothiomalat U82-28
ausatmen U44-2 f; U135-15
–, kräftig U44-3
Ausatmung U44-3
Ausbildung U15-7; U142-14
–, internistische U15-4
Ausbildungszeit U15-7
ausbleiben (Monatsblutung) U51-2,10
ausbluten U38-9

ausbrechen (Krankheit) U94-7; U119-13
– (Schmelz) U27-21
–, in Tränen U58-9
ausbreiten U31-6
–, sich U42-4; U94-3; U97-11; U107-16
Ausbreitung U94-3
–, hämatogene U94-3
Ausbruch U94-7
– (Krankheit) U119-5; U89-7
Ausbuchtung, physiologische (Netzhaut) U88-1
Ausdauer U64-2
Ausdauertraining U64-18
ausdehnen U31-3; U136-13
–, sich U44-10; U97-11; U107-16
Ausdehnung U97-11; U141-3
ausdrücken, sich U66-9,1
Ausdünstung U62-4
auseinanderklaffen U140-16
auseinanderklaffend U87-26
auseinanderrollen U63-6
auseinanderspreizen U132-16
Auseinanderweichen U140-16
auseinanderziehen U64-13
Ausfall (Funktion) U142-4
Ausfälle, motorische U113-7
–, neurologische U113-7; U142-4
ausfallen U123-6
– (Zähne) U27-5
ausfällen U81-27
Ausfallsrate U101-29
Ausfällung U81-27
ausflocken U81-27
Ausflockung U81-27
Ausfluss U36-5; U96-8
–, blutig tingierter U20-16
–, starker U50-11
–, vaginaler U96-2
–, zervikaler U50-7
Ausführungsgang (Samenbläschen) U52-11
Ausgang, tödlicher U12-2
Ausgangsblockierung U123-2
Ausgangsdroge U9-3
Ausgangs-EEG U118-12
Ausgangsgewicht U24-1
Ausgangswert U101-15; U116-16
ausgebreitet U31-3
– (Arme / Beine) U63-5
ausgeglichen U88-19
– (innerlich) U75-15
ausgehen von U30-3; U65-17
ausgekleidet U48-11
– (Epithel) U86-7
ausgelassen (Stimmung) U1-6; U77-15
ausgeleuchtet U17-4
ausgelöst U72-15; U74-11
ausgemergelt U24-10
ausgeprägt U66-13; U93-5
–, stark U103-7
–, voll U119-13

ausgerichtet U59-15
ausgeschlagen (Zahn) U106-5
ausgesetzt U122-5
ausgestreckt U31-3
ausgestülpt U58-4
ausgetragen (Kind) U69-19; U80-4
ausgetrocknet U78-21
ausgewachsen U80-10
ausgewählt U134-2
ausgewogen (Kost) U88-19; U1-3
ausgezehrt U25-7; U108-14; U107-10
ausgleichen U116-16
Ausgleichssport U1-12
Ausgrenzung, soziale U62-4
Ausgussstein U89-21
aushalten U4-3; U105-10
ausheben (Magen) U46-18
Ausheilung U89-13
aushelfen U18-3
Aushusten U111-7
aushusten U103-17,16; U66-6; U92-15
auskleiden U86-8,14
Auskleidung U86-8,15; U43-8
–, epitheliale U86-7f; U89-24
ausklingen (Menstruation) U51-2
auskosten U62-7
auskratzen U132-10
auskristallisieren U82-5
Auskultation U17-2; U107-9
Auskultationsbefund U107-9; U117-6
auskultatorisch U107-9
auskultieren U107-9
Auslagerung U77-12
auslassen (Griff) U65-16
ausleuchten U17-4
Ausleuchtung U59-10
auslösen U88-13,7; U119-8; U57-1
– (Reflex) U102-3; U17-9; U40-13;
auslösendes Ereignis U100-19
Auslöser U88-13; U119-8
Auslösung U102-3
ausnüchtern U10-4
Ausnüchterungszelle U10-4
auspiepsen U17-17
auspolstern U17-13
Ausprägung (Variable) U100-5
Ausräucherungsmittel (für Nager) U91-9
ausräumen U8-3
Ausräumung U87-5; U46-18
–, chirurgische U8-3
Ausreißer U100-12
ausrichten U141-1
Ausrichtung U141-1
Ausriss, knöcherner U106-5
Ausrissfraktur U106-5; U28-25
Ausrissverletzung U106-5
ausrotten (Krankheit) U4-4; U94-2
Ausrottung U13-11
ausruhen, sich U1-10; U72-5
Ausrüstung U132-1
ausrutschen U65-12

Aussackung U50-15
–, aneurysmatische U124-15
ausschaben U132-3,10
Ausschau halten nach U117-7; U59-1
ausscheiden U46-18; U49-16; U88-11
– (Studie) U101-29
Ausscheider, rekonvaleszenter U4-16
Ausscheidung U46-20; U49-7; U88-11; U92-1
–, fraktionierte U49-6
Ausscheidungsurografie U118-19; U136-5; U49-6
Ausscheidungsvolumen U49-7
Ausscheidungsweg U91-17
ausschlafen U72-5
Ausschlag (Haut) U108-9; U21-2,15
–, hartnäckiger U75-19
–, masernähnlicher U95-2
–, typhusähnlicher U94-19
Ausschlämmung U83-20
ausschließen (DD) U117-14; U93-6
Ausschluss (Bewusstsein) U74-14
Ausschlussdiagnose U117-14
ausschneiden U126-9
– (Wunde) U140-12
Ausschuss, ständiger U101-25
ausschütten U88-11
ausschwemmen U49-6
Ausschwemmung U49-6
Aussehen U59-1; U67-8
–, blühendes U25-11
–, cushingoides U25-10
–, kränkliches U67-8
–, maskulines U53-1
–, runzeliges U25-17
Außenelektron U81-10f
Außenfläche U87-4
Außenknöchel U23-12
Außenseite U87-4
Außenzone (Nierenmark) U86-23
außer Atem U44-1
äußern U66-1
außerordentlich U75-5
Äußerung, verbale U66-1
aussetzen U91-5
Aussetzen U119-11
Aussicht U59-1
Aussichten U119-19
Aussparung U60-2
Aussprache U29-1; U66-13; U26-1
aussprechen U66-1,13,23
Ausprossung U85-10
ausspucken U27-10; U103-17
ausspülen U91-26; U27-10; U139-5
– (Wunde) U140-11
Ausspülung U118-10; U127-17
ausständig, noch U63-13
Ausstichstelle (Naht) U138-14
Ausstoß U88-16
ausstoßen U33-8; U44-7; U71-15; U88-16
– (Samen) U53-11
– (Seufzer) U46-5

ausstrahlen U99-5; U99-2
– (Schmerzen) U104-16
Ausstrahlung U99-2
–, erotische U57-9
ausstrecken U31-3; U141-3
ausstreichen U116-5
Ausstrich U116-5
Ausströmen (Gas) U133-8
Ausstülpung U31-8; U28-6; U50-15; U85-10
– (Wundränder) U137-17
Austastung U126-11; U132-8
Austausch U78-6
Austauschdiffusion U88-4
austauschen U78-6
Austauschtransfusion U38-9; U136-8
austreiben U71-15,11
Austreibung (Geburt) U71-15,13
Austreibungsgeräusch U33-8; U110-3
–, systolisches U88-16
Austreibungsperiode U71-13
Austreibungsphase U33-8
– (Geburt) U52-20
Austreibungswehen U71-3,15
Austreibungszeit U33-8
austreten U89-23
– (aus Gefäß) U38-6; U136-7; U89-26
Austritt (Flüssigkeit) U38-6; U89-24
– (Lymphe) U136-7
austrocknen (Rachen) U109-5
ausüben U64-19; U74-6
– (Arztberuf) U15-8,1; U18-1
auswachsen, sich U80-3; U4-13; U59-4
Auswahlkriterien U134-2
Auswärtsdrehung (Fuß) U31-8f
Auswärtsschielen U59-4
auswaschen U91-26; U128-11
– (Wunde) U140-11
Auswaschung U49-6; U83-20; U118-10
Ausweis U18-14; U74-3
auswerfen U33-8; U88-16; U103-17
auswerten U117-1; U102-15
Auswertung U117-1
Auswirkung(en) U6-4; U75-8; U52-1; U106-6; U121-8
–, gesundheitsschädliche U6-11; U91-1
Auswurf U88-16; U103-17f
–, faulig riechender U62-5
–, Husten mit U103-7
–, schleimig-eitriger U86-17
Auswurffraktion U33-8; U88-16
Auszehrung U25-7; U108-14; U103-9
Ausziehdraht U141-14
ausziehen, sich U107-4; U65-12
auszupfen (Haare) U56-13
Autismus, (frühkindlicher) U77-16
Autist, hochbegabter U77-24
Autoagglutinine U39-21
Autoantigen U39-8,21
Autoantikörper U39-21
Autofahrer(in) U6-3

autogen **U129**-16
autogenes Training U1-12
Autograft U129-16
Autoimmunerkrankung U39-4,21
Autoimmunreaktion U39-2,4,21
Autoimmunsyndrom, polyglanduläres U124-12
Autoinfektion U39-21; U88-10
Autoinokulation U122-1
Autoinsassen U6-3
Autointoxikation **U91**-14
autokatalytisch U81-16
Autoklav **U139**-3
autoklavierbar **U139**-3
Autolenker(in), alkoholisierte(r) U10-5
autolog **U129**-16
autonomes Nervensystem U92-8
Autooxidation U81-17
Autopsie **U12**-19f; U15-21
Autopsiepräparat U12-20
Autoregulation **U49**-10
autorisieren **U20**-7
Autoscheinwerfer U6-3
Autosom **U84**-6
autosomal rezessiv U84-6
– vererbt U89-7
Autotransfusion **U136**-8
Autotransfusionsgerät U136-8
Autotransplantat **U130**-2
Autotransplantation **U129**-14
Autounfall U6-1
A-V Anastomose **U129**-6
AV-Block II. Grades Typ I U123-2
AV-Bündel **U32**-15
AV-Extrasystolen U33-3; U110-6
avirulent U90-10
AV-Knoten U32-7,15
AV-Knotentachykardie U110-2
AV-Überleitung U42-2
axial **U87**-3
Axialaufnahme U87-3
Axilla **U23**-3
axillär **U23**-3
Axillarlinie U23-3
–, vordere U87-9,16
Axillatemperatur U105-1
axipetal U40-2
Axis **U87**-3; U28-19
– opticus U59-5
Axon **U40**-2
axonal **U40**-2
Axonhügel U40-2
Axonkollaterale **U34**-6
Axonreflex U40-2
Axonscheide U40-2
Axonterminal U40-2
Axoplasma U40-2
Azidität **U81**-19; U92-29
Azidose **U81**-19
Azotämie **U112**-13

B

babbeln **U66**-17
Babinski-Reflex/-Zeichen **U113**-1; U108-1
Baby **U80**-5
baby blues **U71**-22
Babynahrung U70-5
Bacillus **U90**-7
– Calmette-Guerin U90-7
Backe **U21**-7
Backenbart U25-14
Backen-Kinnbart **U25**-14
Backenzahn **U26**-6,2
–, großer **U26**-7
Bad **U19**-9;
U142-20
–, heißes U1-17
–, hydroelektrisches U142-23
–, lauwarmes U19-9
–, medizinisches U19-9
–, türkisches U1-17
Badekur U1-18
Badematte U19-9
Bademeister(in) U123-3
Baden **U19**-9;
U142-20
baden **U1**-17; **U19**-9
Bäder U140-13
Bäderbehandlung **U142**-20
Badeunfälle U6-16
Badewanne **U19**-9
Badezimmer **U19**-9
Badezusätze U142-20
Bahn(en) **U83**-16
–, absteigende U40-3
–, afferente U40-3
–, aufsteigende U40-3
–, efferente U40-4
–, kortikobulbäre U86-23
–, motorische U30-4; U31-20; U40-3
–, sensible U41-16
–, sensorische U40-3; U41-16; U57-7
Bajonettfehlstellung **U106**-10
Bajonettstellung U141-1
Bakteriämie **U124**-5; U37-2; U90-7
bakteriell **U90**-6
bakterienabtötend U17-15
Bakterienabtötung, intrazelluläre U39-16
Bakterienanzahl U90-6
bakterienarm **U90**-7
Bakterienbelastung U90-6; U94-17
Bakterienbesiedelung U90-6
Bakterienflora U15-4; U46-16
bakterienhemmend U90-6
Bakterienkolonie U90-6
Bakterienkultur U90-6
Bakterienruhr **U94**-18
Bakteriensporen U17-15
Bakterienstamm U139-11
bakterientötend U90-6
Bakterienwachstum U90-6
bakteriostatisch U90-6

Bakterium **U90**-6
–, fakultativ anaerob wachsendes U90-7
–, säurefestes U90-7; U116-5
–, schraubenförmiges **U90**-9
–, sporenbildendes U90-3
–, stickstoffbindendes U82-16
Bakteriurie U90-6; U112-1
–, asymptomatische U119-6
bakterizid U17-15; U90-6; U92-9
Balken **U41**-3
Balkendiagramm U100-27
Balkenknie U41-3
Balkenstamm U41-3
Balkenwaage U65-8
Balkenwulst U41-3
Ballaststoffe **U79**-16; U46-11
ballen **U64**-9
Ballon U17-8
Ballondilatation **U128**-14; U132-17
Ballondissektion **U128**-14
Ballongegenpulsation, intraaortale **U125**-8
Ballonkatheter U125-20; U128-14
Ballonpumpe, intraaortale U125-8
Ballonsonde U125-18
Ballonspritze U17-10
Ballontamponade U110-8
Ballottement **U109**-9; U28-24
Balneotherapie **U142**-20; U1-18
Balsam **U9**-8
Band **U30**-6
Bandage **U140**-20; **U141**-8
bandagieren **U141**-11
Bandagist(in) **U15**-15
Bändchen **U26**-11
Bänder **U5**-16
–, lockere U30-6
Bänderriss **U5**-19; U23-11; U30-6
Bänderzerrung U64-19
Bandgeschwindigkeit U142-16
Bandhaft **U29**-13,1
bändigen **U77**-26
Bandinstabilität U30-6
Bandmaß U17-1
Bandruptur U30-6
Bandscheibe U28-19; U29-2
Bandscheibenoperation, minimal invasive U128-1
Bandscheiben-Rongeur U132-11
Bandscheibenvorfall U65-12; U89-22f; U104-16
Bandstrukturen U30-6
Bandwurm U90-16; U92-25
Bandwurmbefall U94-2
Barbituratabhängigkeit **U11**-16
Barbiturate **U11**-16;
U93-14; **U92**-24
Barbiturateinfluss, unter **U11**-16
Barbituratentzug U10-14; U11-16
Barbituratüberdosis U11-11
Barbituratvergiftung **U11**-16; U91-20
Barbitursäure U11-16
Barbotage **U93**-9

barfuß **U23**-13
Barium **U82**-20
Bariumbreischluck U118-21
Bariumbrei-Untersuchung **U118**-21
Bariumchlorid U82-20
Barium-Doppelkontrasteinlauf U118-21
Barium-Doppelkontrastuntersuchung U118-21
Bariumeinlauf U45-15; U105-16; **U118**-21
Bariumkontrastmittelaufnahme U118-18
Bariumnitrat U82-20
Bariumschluck U46-2
Bariumsulfat U82-20
Barlow-Syndrom U31-12
Barootitis U6-17
Barorezeptor U57-10
Barosinusitis U6-17
Barotitis U95-12
Barotrauma **U6**-17
Barriere **U81**-20
Barr-Körper U84-6
Bart **U25**-14; U55-16
Bartholin-Drüsen **U50**-10; U54-1
Bartholinitis U50-10
Bartholin-Zyste U50-10
bärtig **U25**-14
bartlos **U25**-14
Bartwuchs U25-14
Barytose U82-29
Baryt-Staublunge U82-29
Basalganglien U40-11
Basaliom U86-7; U98-2
Basalis U87-8
Basalkörperchen **U83**-6
Basallamina **U86**-16
Basalmembran **U86**-16; U97-12
–, wellenförmige U86-7
Basalplatte U85-13
Basalschicht U56-7
Basaltemperatur U105-1
Basalumsatz **U78**-2,12; U55-6
Basalzell(en)karzinom U98-2
Basalzellschicht U56-2
Base **U81**-19
–, konjugierte U81-20
Basedow-Koma **U124**-8
Basedow-Krankheit U124-8
Basenanalogon U81-19
Basenaustausch U84-12
Basenerkennungssequenz U84-32
Basenexzess U81-19
Basenpaar(ung) **U84**-12
Basensequenz U84-12
Basentriplett **U84**-13
Basenüberschuss U81-19
basilaris **U87**-25
Basilarismigräne U113-16
Basilarmembran U60-12
Basis **U87**-25
– cerebri U87-25
– cordis **U32**-4; U87-25

Basis cranii U28-7; U87-25
– pulmonis **U43**-4
Basisaktivitäten d. tägl. Lebens U142-27
basisch **U81**-19
Basismaßnahmen (CPR) **U123**-4; U125-3
Basisnarkose **U93**-15
basophil **U37**-8
Bauch **U22**-4; **U45**-6
– (liegend), auf dem **U63**-9
–, schlafen, auf dem U63-9; U72-5
–, hervortretender U45-6
–, straffer U1-11
–, vorstehender U22-4
Bauchaorta U34-8
Bauchatmung U22-4; U44-4; U45-6
Bauchauftreibung **U109**-8,1
Bauchdecke U22-4
– durchstoßen U128-12
Bauchdeckenhalter U132-16
Bauchdeckenreflex U45-6
Bauchdeckenspannung **U109**-13; U45-6
Bauchfell **U45**-7; U140-14
Bauchfellentzündung U45-7
Bauchfellhöhle U45-7
Bauchfelltasche U29-10; U45-7
Bauchgurt U125-24
Bauchhautreflex U45-6
Bauchhoden U52-3
Bauchhöhle U22-4; U45-6
Bauchhöhlenschwangerschaft U70-6
Bauchknurren U65-15
Bauchkrämpfe **U109**-14; U22-4; U104-15
Bauchlage U8-17; **U63**-9; U131-16
–, in **U31**-9
Bauchliegebrett U142-19
Bauchmuskel, äußerer schräger **U30**-14
–, gerader **U30**-14
–, innerer schräger **U30**-14
Bauchmuskeltraining U31-13
Bauchnabel **U22**-5; U45-6
Bauchpresse U40-10; U45-6; U5-17
Bauchpunktion U45-6; U64-11
Bauchraum U22-4
Bauchschmerzen U22-4; U104-4
–, kolikartige U109-14
Bauchschnitt U87-5; **U127**-2
bauchseitig **U87**-16
Bauchspeicheldrüse **U54**-8
Bauchspeicheldrüsenentzündung U54-8
Bauchstiel U71-17
Bauchtrauma, stumpfes U109-13
Bauchumfang **U109**-9; U22-4; U45-6
Bauchwandhernie U87-16
Bauchwassersucht **U109**-9
Bauchwickel U142-22
Bäuerchen U46-3
Bauhin-Klappe U45-12
baumeln **U63**-13; **U64**-5; U23-8
Baumwolle U137-10; U140-18
Baumwollschlauch **U141**-10

Baumwollstaub U91-7
Bausch **U17**-13; **U140**-23
Bausteinmolekül U81-2
Bauxit U82-31
Bazillus **U90**-5,7; U4-2
BCG U90-7
BCG-Vakzine U122-2
bDNA-Assay U84-36
beabsichtigen **U18**-5; U73-3
beachten **U20**-6
beachtenswert **U57**-4
Beachtung **U8**-1
BEAM **U125**-14; U41-1
Beamer **U99**-5
Beamter/-in **U18**-1
Beanspruchung, starke U66-14
beatmen **U44**-5; **U123**-9
Beatmung **U44**-5; **U125**-10; U44-4
–, assistierte U44-4 f
–, intermittierende maschinelle U44-5
–, kontrollierte U125-10
–, künstliche **U123**-9,4; U44-4; U135-15
–, manuelle (Ambu-Beutel) U44-5
–, maschinelle U125-10
–, Mund-zu-Nase- U123-9
Beatmungsbeutel **U8**-12
Beatmungsgerät **U44**-4f; **U123**-4,9; **U125**-10
–, druckgesteuertes U125-10
–, volumengesteuertes U125-10
beaufsichtigen **U125**-5; U65-10
Beaufsichtigung U77-25
–, ständige U77-4
beauftragt U20-4
beben **U57**-17; **U64**-6; **U105**-7; **U113**-4
Becherzelle **U86**-18; U83-2
Becherzellkarzinoid U86-18
Becken(knochen) **U22**-7; **U28**-21
Becken, großes U28-21
–, kleines U28-21; U71-14
–, knöchernes U28-2,21
–, plattes U22-7
Beckenachse U87-3
Beckenausgang U28-21
Becken-Bein-Gips U22-7
Beckenboden U22-7; U48-15; U52-12
Beckenbodenentspannung U1-10; U31-1; U142-25
Beckenbodenmuskulatur U30-2
Beckeneingang U22-7; U28-21
Beckenendlage U71-5
Beckenform, feminine U28-21
Beckengurt U22-10
Beckengürtel U22-7; U28-21
Beckenhöhle U22-7; U28-21
Beckenkamm U130-9
Beckenorgane U28-21; U86-21
Beckenperitoneum U45-7
Beckenrand U28-21
Beckenring U28-21
Beckenzertrümmerung U64-10
bedacht (auf) **U76**-5

Bedarf, bei U92-27
Bedarfschrittmacher U123-13
Bedauern, aufrichtiges U75-12
bedauernswert U76-20
bedecken **U86**-8; **U129**-9
bedenken **U74**-1
Bedenken, ernste U75-12
Bedeutung, von **U102**-8
Bedeutungserlebnis, subjektives U73-10
bedeutungslos **U102**-8
bedingt **U74**-5
Bedrohungen U8-4
bedrücken **U104**-2
bedrückt **U77**-17
Bedside-Diagnostik U19-7; U116-2
Bedside-Test U19-7
Bedürfnis (Drang) **U112**-4; U73-12
Bedürfnisse U75-21
beeilen, sich **U65**-15
beeinträchtigen U1-6; U77-19
– (Erinnerungsvermögen) U74-8
– (Fertilität) U69-2
– (Gasaustausch) U44-4
– (Sehkraft) U59-6
beeinträchtigt **U4**-11,8
Beeinträchtigung **U4**-11; U20-14; U130-3; U141-7; U73-2
–, soziale **U142**-3
Beendigung (Schwangerschaft) U55-21
– (Studie) **U101**-30
Beerdigung **U12**-17
Beeren **U3**-8
Beet, arteriosklerotisches U78-16
Befall **U4**-10; **U89**-4; U96-12
– (ZNS) U40-5; U41-10
–, herdförmiger **U97**-10
befallen U4-4,10; **U89**-4; **U94**-2; U134-4
befangen **U75**-17,2; **U76**-12; U100-18
befehlen **U20**-14
befestigen U133-10; U137-3
Befestigung, intraorale U26-25
Befestigungsmaterial U26-17
Befestigungsschiene (OP-Tisch) U133-1
Befestigungssteg U136-6
befeuchten **U105**-13; U17-13
Befinden **U4**-4
befolgen U120-15
–, nicht **U20**-10
befördern **U8**-3; **U20**-15; **U88**-3
Beförderung **U20**-15; **U8**-3
Befragung **U102**-15
befreien **U8**-2 f
Befreiung **U8**-3
befriedigen (Gelüste) U11-2
Befriedigung, sexuelle U68-8
befruchten **U69**-2; **U70**-1
Befruchtung **U53**-6; **U69**-2; **U70**-1
–, extrakorporale U69-12
–, künstliche **U69**-12,2; U53-6; U101-18
Befund **U117**-6
–, auffälliger U102-8
–, histologischer U86-1

Befund, intraoperativer U126-2
–, kein pathologischer U15-21
–, klinischer U14-2; U107-2; U117-6
–, ohne **U107**-18,20; U116-21
–, pathologischer **U116**-1
Befürchtung **U76**-5; **U77**-5; U6-21
befürworten **U18**-5
begehren **U68**-4; U73-12
Begeißelung, peritriche U83-5
–, polare U83-5
Begeisterung **U76**-8; **U77**-18
Begierde **U68**-4
Beginn (Krankheit) **U94**-7; U83-13; U89-7
–, plötzlicher U119-11
–, schleichender U94-7
beginnend **U119**-5,14; U89-10
begleitend U119-16
Begleiterkrankung U4-4; **U89**-2; U119-15 f
Begleitkontrolle U20-12
Begleitschielen U59-4; U119-16
Begleitsymptom U103-1
Begleittherapie U119-16
Begleitverletzung U8-7
begraben **U12**-17
Begräbnis **U12**-17
Begräbnisstätte U12-17
begradigen U31-3
begreifen **U64**-9; **U74**-4; U73-5
begrenzen **U87**-10; U21-10,14; **U99**-12
begrenzt, lokal **U97**-9
–, scharf U98-5
Begrenzung **U87**-10; U139-8
–, unscharfe U87-10
Begriff **U73**-8
begünstigend **U119**-1; U93-7
behaart **U56**-13
–, stark **U25**-15
Behaartheit **U25**-15
Behaarung, starke U22-13
Behalten **U74**-10
Behälter U9-13
behandeln (mit) **U15**-3; U92-20
behandelnder Chirurg U131-5
Behandlung **U20**-11; **U119**-9; **U120**-1 ff
– der Wahl U120-1
–, (ärztliche) **U18**-4
–, ambulante U14-2; U20-2 f; U87-20
–, antiskabiöse U96-12
–, ärztliche **U20**-3; U74-16
–, chirurgische U126-3
–, fachärztliche U15-8
–, intensive U1-6
–, medikamentöse U9-3,4
–, medizinische **U8**-1
–, osteopathische U142-12
–, präklinische U20-3
–, psychiatrische U14-5; U77-1
–, symptomatische U103-1
Behandlungsabbruch U12-9
Behandlungsfehler, ärztlicher **U20**-13
Behandlungsgruppe **U101**-10

Behandlungsmethode **U120**-3
Behandlungsmöglichkeiten U101-22; U120-3
Behandlungspflicht U13-1; U20-4
Behandlungsplan U20-9; U101-7
Behandlungsprotokoll U101-7; **U120**-5
Behandlungsraum U19-2
Behandlungsregime, chemotherapeutisches U97-17
Behandlungsschema **U120**-5; U119-18
–, empfohlenes U18-5
Behandlungstermin U18-2
Behandlungsunterlagen U20-5
Behandlungsverweigerung **U20**-13
Behandlungsverzicht U12-9; U117-18
Behandlungsziel U101-27; U120-9
Behandlungszyklus U119-9; **U120**-5,1
beharren auf U6-8
beharrlich U75-19; U102-10
Behaviorismus **U75**-3
beheben **U129**-2
– (Mangel) U4-14
beherbergen U90-13; U94-5; U137-7
beherrschen **U54**-3
Beherrschung **U75**-4
behindern **U4**-8; U8-2; U44-9; U89-4
behindert **U1**-1; **U4**-8; **U142**-4,3; U16-2
–, geistig U77-1,13,22
–, von Geburt an U71-1
Behinderte **U1**-11; **U4**-8; **U142**-3
Behindertenfahrzeug U19-13; U4-8
Behindertenintegrationszentrum U11-13
Behindertenwerkstatt **U142**-28
Behindertenzulage U142-3
Behinderung **U1**-11; **U4**-8; **U142**-3
–, geistige **U77**-22,24; U14-5; U73-2
beibehalten U27-6
Beifahrersitz U6-3
Beileid **U12**-12
beimischen (Rauschmittel) **U11**-1
Bein **U23**-8
–, lahmes U65-11
Beinahe-Ertrinken **U6**-16
Beinamputation U23-8
Beinamputierte U142-6
Beinanlage U85-10
Beine, dünne U24-10
–, ruhelose/unruhige U23-8
Beinknospe U85-10
Beinkrämpfe, nächtliche U63-10; U72-12
Beinlängenunterschied U24-2
Beinmuskulatur U23-8
Beinödem U23-8
Beinprothese U23-1
Beinschiene U23-8
Beinschwellung U23-8
Bein-Urinbeutel **U125**-23
Beipackzettel **U9**-17
Beischilddrüse **U54**-7
Beischlaf **U68**-5
– mit Unmündigen U68-17

Beisetzung **U12**-17
beißen **U27**-11; **U5**-10
beißend **U62**-5
Beißring U27-4
Beistand **U142**-29
beistehen **U8**-1; U65-3
Beitrag **U102**-8
beiziehen (Arzt) **U18**-13; **U102**-14
bekämpfen U92-28
Bekanntgabe **U18**-11
beklagen **U67**-10
–, sich U103-2
beklemmend U77-5
Beklemmung **U77**-5; **U113**-2
beklommen **U76**-6
Beklopfen **U64**-11; **U107**-8; U57-12
bekommen (Krankheit) **U4**-2
bekömmlich **U1**-1 f,5; **U2**-13
Bekömmlichkeit **U1**-5; U13-9
bekümmert U12-12; **U104**-2
beladen **U33**-10
Belag **U86**-8
Belastbarkeit, berufliche U142-28
–, physische U1-12; U119-15
belasten **U33**-10; **U64**-19; U1-13
belästigen **U68**-16
Belästigung, sexuelle **U68**-16,1
Belastung **U24**-1; **U33**-10; **U64**-19; U76-18
–, axiale U87-3
–, emotionale U134-4
–, große U64-19
–, hämodynamische U36-4
–, isometrische U142-17
–, physiologische U88-1
–, psychische U76-1; U77-24
–, richtige U65-6
–, vorsichtige U134-13
Belastungsangina U124-11
belastungsbedingt U119-8
Belastungsdyspnoe U64-19; U111-3
Belastungs-EKG U142-16 f; U118-14
belastungsfreies Gehen U142-13
Belastungsinkontinenz U112-15
Belastungsintoleranz U142-27
Belastungstest U117-1; U142-17
Belastungsübung U64-18
Belastungszeuge/-in U6-13
Beleg **U101**-17
belegen **U101**-15
Belegschaft U15-2
belegt (Bett) **U19**-15
– (Stimme) **U44**-1
– (Zunge) U95-6
Belegung U19-2
Beleg(ungs)tag U20-2
Belegzelle U28-8; U45-8; U54-9
Beleibtheit **U24**-8; **U79**-16
beleidigend U77-7; U73-7
beleidigt **U67**-16; **U76**-9
–, tödlich U12-3
Beleuchtung **U17**-4; **U59**-10

Beleuchtung, OP- U131-9
belichtet U99-3
Belichtungseinstellung U133-3
Belichtungszeit U99-7
belüften **U44**-5 f; **U123**-9
Belüftung **U44**-5; **U125**-10
– (Paukenhöhle) U60-6
–, übermäßige **U44**-6
Belüftungsanlage **U139**-8
bemerken **U57**-4; **U74**-4; **U102**-2
bemitleiden **U76**-20
bemitleidenswert **U76**-20
Bemühung **U64**-19
benachbart **U87**-11; U26-21; U41-5; U47-4
benachrichtigen **U20**-6; **U57**-4; **U94**-1
Benachrichtigung **U57**-4
benachteiligt, sozial U77-11
Benehmen **U75**-3
benennen **U74**-3
Benetzbarkeit U81-16
benigne **U97**-5
Benignität **U97**-5
benommen **U7**-5,9; **U113**-6; U6-14
Benommenheit **U113**-6; **U7**-11,5,9; U9-18
–, leichte **U103**-13
Benzin **U11**-23
–, bleihaltiges U82-32
Benzoesäure U81-7
Benzolring **U81**-7
Benzolvergiftung U81-7
Benzylalkohol U82-13
beobachten **U57**-4; **U59**-1
Beobachtung **U117**-6; **U134**-8
–, abgebrochene **U101**-29; U100-18
–, genaue U74-16
–, zensierte **U101**-28
Beobachtungen, klinische U108-2
Beobachtungsstrategie **U120**-7; U101-7; U117-7
Beobachtungsstudie U101-1
Beobachtungszeit(raum) U59-1; U125-5
Bequemlichkeit **U104**-1
beraten U16-8
beratend **U18**-13; **U102**-14
Berater(in) **U8**-1; **U16**-12; **U18**-4
–, fachärztliche(r) **U102**-14
Beratung **U15**-3; **U16**-12; **U18**-4
–, ärztliche **U18**-13; **U102**-14
–, genetische **U18**-4
–, konsiliarische **U18**-13; **U102**-14
–, onkologische **U97**-1
–, psychiatrische U77-1
Beratungsdienst U13-3; U18-4
Beratungsgespräch U18-4
Beratungshonorar U18-13
Beratungskomitee U101-25
berauschend **U11**-1
berauscht **U10**-5
berechenbar **U75**-9
beredt **U66**-18

Bereich **U100**-15
bereiten **U68**-2
bereithalten, sich U65-3
Bereitschaft **U73**-3
– genetische U119-1
–, in **U15**-3; **U20**-4
Bereitschaftsdienst U18-7
Bereitschaftstasche **U17**-1
bereitstellen **U88**-3
bergab gehen (Krankheitsverlauf) U119-9
Bergebeutel **U133**-16
bergen **U8**-2 f; **U128**-17; **U133**-16
Bergevorrichtung U8-3
Bergkrankheit **U6**-17; U103-11
Bergsteigen **U65**-18
Bergung **U8**-2
Bergungssack U128-16 f
Bergungsschiff U8-2
Bericht **U8**-7; **U20**-6
berichten **U8**-7; **U20**-6; **U102**-2
Berliner-Blau-Färbung U116-4
bernsteinfarben U9-5
Berstungsfraktur U106-8
Bertin-Säulen U48-2
Bernhard-Horner-Syndrom U58-16
berücksichtigen **U74**-1
Beruf **U142**-26
Berufsanamnese U102-4; U142-26
Berufsausbildung U142-18
berufsbedingt U89-6; U142-26
Berufsberater(in) U16-12
Berufsberatung U142-26
Berufskrankheiten U4-5
Berufsrisiko U8-4; U91-5; U124-2
Berufung **U142**-26
beruhigen **U18**-6; **U117**-7; **U135**-8 ff
–, sich **U4**-15; U76-19
beruhigend **U77**-17; **U92**-30
Beruhigung **U18**-6; **U135**-8 ff
Beruhigungsmittel **U11**-16,1; **U77**-17; **U135**-9; U92-23 f
berühren **U62**-8
Berührung **U87**-11
– kommen, in U67-4
–, leichte U62-8
Berührungsempfindlichkeit **U135**-4
Berührungsempfindung **U62**-8
besamen **U70**-1
besänftigen U135-10
Beschädigung **U6**-11
Beschaffenheit U25-11; U57-14
beschäftigt mit U76-5
Beschäftigung **U142**-26
Beschäftigungstherapeut(in) U16-12
Beschäftigungstherapie **U142**-26; U120-4
beschämt **U76**-12
bescheiden **U75**-14
Bescheidenheit, falsche U75-12
bescheinigen **U18**-10
Bescheinigung, ärztliche **U18**-10
beschichten **U87**-4,8; U82-29
beschichtet (Draht) U141-14

Beschichtung **U86**-8
beschießen **U99**-4
beschleunigen **U65**-15; **U81**-16; U78-6
– (Schritt) U65-6
Beschneidung U52-17; U73-13
–, weibliche U50-12
beschränkt auf U89-3
Beschränkung **U77**-26; **U87**-10
beschuldigen **U77**-10
Beschuldigung U20-13
beschützen **U8**-2
Beschwerdeausschuss U101-25
beschwerdefrei **U103**-1
Beschwerden **U4**-10; **U103**-2
– (beim Gehen) U65-1
– (beim Urinieren) U49-12
–, aktuelle U102-5
–, belastende U107-11
–, körperliche **U104**-1; U25-1
–, leichte körperliche **U103**-7
–, psychosomatische U77-14
–, somatische U40-7
beschwichtigen **U117**-7
Beschwichtigung U18-6
beschwipst **U10**-1
beseitigen U127-7
Beseitigung **U139**-4
Besenreiservarizen U110-17
besessen U2-17
Besessenheit **U77**-19
besetzen (Stelle) **U15**-2
besichtigen **U59**-1
besiedeln U46-16
Besiedelung, bakterielle U90-6
besitzergreifend **U75**-21
besonnen U10-4
Besorgnis **U8**-7; **U76**-5; **U77**-5
besorgniserregend **U107**-11
besorgt **U76**-5; **U77**-5; U104-2
Besprechung **U15**-3
–, interne **U20**-10
–, klin.-patholog. U20-10
bessern, sich **U4**-13 f; **U9**-2
Besserung **U4**-13 ff; U104-8
–, vorübergehende **U119**-17
beständig **U75**-10,15
Beständigkeit **U75**-10,9; U120-15
Bestandspotential U88-20
Bestandteil U79-5; U93-17; U121-1
–, fester U82-6
bestätigen **U6**-13; **U117**-12; U7-15
Bestätigung **U18**-6; **U117**-12
Bestätigungstest U84-35; U117-12
Bestattung **U12**-17
Besteck, chirurgisches U132-1
Bestellkarte (Arzttermin) U18-2
bestimmen **U20**-11; **U116**-3; **U117**-1 f
– (Sehschärfe) U59-8
– (Tempo) U65-6
Bestimmung **U20**-7; **U116**-3; **U117**-1 f; U30-2
bestrafen **U12**-11
bestrahlen **U99**-4
Bestrahlung **U15**-13; **U99**-2,4

Bestrahlungsfeld U99-4
bestreichen (Sohle/Hals) **U62**-10; U23-13; U64-11
bestürzend **U65**-16
bestürzt **U76**-9
Bestürzung U77-4
Besuch **U18**-7
besuchen **U15**-3
Besucher(in) **U18**-7
Besuchszeiten U18-7
Besuchszeitregelung U18-7; U20-7
Beta-Blocker U92-7
betagt **U80**-1,13
Betagte U139-12
Betahämolyse U38-4
Beta-Laktamase **U92**-10
Beta-MSH U55-26
Betasten U110-1
betäuben **U11**-1; **U61**-9; **U135**-1
betäubt (durch Schlag) **U7**-9
Betäubung **U7**-11
Betäubungsmittel **U93**-4; U9-3; U11-1
Betäubungsmittelintoxikation U10-5
Betazellen **U54**-8
Beteiligung **U4**-10; **U89**-4
– (ZNS) U40-5; U41-10
Betonung U66-13
betrachten **U59**-1; **U87**-4; **U107**-6
beträchtlich U20-3
Betrachtung U107-6
betreffen **U4**-10; **U89**-4; U26-14
betreuen U20-3
Betreuer(in) **U20**-3; **U77**-25,24
–, psychiatrische(r) U16-8
–, überlastete(r) U77-25
Betreuung, ambulante U14-2; U65-1
–, aufsuchende U77-25
–, häusliche U77-25
–, präklinische U14-1
–, psychiatrische U15-12
–, soziale **U77**-25
–, ständige U77-25
–, stationäre U14-5
Betreuungspflicht U77-25
Betreuungsvollmacht U16-1
Betriebsunfall U6-1
betrübt **U76**-9
betrügen U75-12
betrunken **U10**-1
Betrunkene(r) **U10**-1
Bett gehen, zu **U72**-3
–, festes / hartes U75-11
Bettbogen **U19**-4
Bettdecke **U19**-3
Bettenauslastung **U19**-15,3
Bettenstation U19-1
Bettgalgen **U19**-4
Bettgestell **U19**-4
Bettkante U19-3
Bettkeil U19-3
bettlägerig **U4**-6; U12-1; U19-12; U77-13
Bettlaken **U19**-5
Bettnässen **U112**-16,7; U72-12

Bettnässer(in) **U112**-16
Bettpfanne **U19**-8
Bettrahmen, seitlicher **U19**-3
Bettruhe **U4**-6; U64-17; U134-13
–, strenge U19-3
Bettschüssel **U19**-8
bettseitige Überwachung U125-5
Betttisch **U19**-7
Betttuch **U19**-5
Bettwaage U24-11
Bettwäsche **U19**-3; U139-5,9
Bettzeug **U19**-3
betupfen **U140**-23
Beugeeinschränkung U63-3
Beugeekzem, lichenifiziertes U114-14
Beugefurche U31-2
Beugegelenk U30-8
Beugekontraktur U31-2
Beugemuskel **U31**-2
beugen **U31**-2; U5-17
–, rückwärts **U87**-16
–, sich **U63**-3; U77-7
Beuger **U31**-2
Beugereflex U31-2
Beuge-Rückziehreflex U31-2
Beugesehne U30-5; U31-2
Beugewinkel, maximaler U31-2
Beugung **U31**-2
Beugungseinschränkung U31-2
beunruhigen **U8**-7; **U104**-2; U134-9
beunruhigt **U76**-21
Beurlaubung U18-10
beurteilen **U117**-1 f,18; **U73**-6; U100-20
Beurteilung **U117**-1 f; U75-12
–, klinische **U117**-18; U18-5
Bevölkerung, betagte U80-15
bevölkerungsbasiert U100-3
Bevölkerungsstatistik U100-1
bevorstehend **U63**-13; U7-5
bewahren (vor) **U8**-2; **U109**-13
bewältigen **U77**-9; U76-22
Bewältigung, familiäre U77-9
Bewältigungsmechanismus **U77**-9; U88-2
Bewältigungsmuster U77-9
Bewältigungsverhalten U75-3; U77-9
bewegen, (sich) **U64**-1,3
–, ruckartig **U64**-7; **U65**-9
bewegend U62-8
Beweggrund **U73**-12
beweglich **U1**-13; **U31**-11,17; **U46**-6; **U64**-1; U21-13; U141-11
Beweglichkeit **U31**-11,17; **U64**-2; **U142**-13; **U141**-5
–, eingeschränkte U64-2
–, funktionelle U142-8
–, übermäßige **U142**-8
Beweglichkeitsübungen U142-17
Bewegung(en) **U64**-1,18; **U65**-2
–, ruckartige **U72**-12; U113-1
–, zielgerichtete U31-19
–, choreatische U65-10
–, schwerfällige U76-17
–, unkoordinierte U31-19

Bewegungsanalyse U142-10
Bewegungsausmaß **U31**-18; U64-2; U142-12
Bewegungsausschlag U142-9
bewegungseinschränkende Handschuhe U77-26
Bewegungseinschränkung U31-18; U142-14
Bewegungsempfindung **U57**-14; U142-10
Bewegungsentwurf U73-8
Bewegungsenergie U78-12
Bewegungsfreiheit U23-4
Bewegungsgefühl U30-4
Bewegungsgips U141-7
Bewegungsgrade **U142**-9
Bewegungskoordination **U31**-19; U40-4
Bewegungskrankheit U6-17; U64-1
Bewegungslehre **U57**-14; **U142**-10
Bewegungslosigkeit **U64**-2
Bewegungsmuster U74-12
Bewegungsradius U142-9
Bewegungsschiene U141-7; U142-14
Bewegungsschmerz U57-14; U104-11
Bewegungsstörungen U65-2
Bewegungstherapie U57-14
–, rehabilitative **U142**-18
Beweis **U101**-17; **U117**-9
–, handfester U62-9
Beweismaterial U101-17
bewerten **U117**-2
Bewilligung U101-23
bewirken **U101**-26
Bewohner(in) **U15**-4; **U19**-15
bewusst **U7**-1; U71-26
– sein/werden, sich U74-4
bewusstlos **U57**-5; **U7**-1,6
Bewusstlosigkeit U7-14; U110-11
–, kurze **U110**-11
–, tiefe **U135**-6
Bewusstsein **U57**-5,7; **U7**-1
– wiedererlangen U123-3
–, bei **U7**-3
bewusstseinserweiternd **U11**-21; U77-2
bewusstseinsgetrübt U77-13
Bewusstseinslage U7-1; U119-15
Bewusstseinsstörung U4-11
Bewusstseinseinstrübung U7-1; U57-7
Bewusstseinsveränderung U7-1
Bewusstseinsverlust, kurzer **U74**-17
bezeugen U6-13
Beziehung **U18**-8; **U74**-5; **U100**-32
–, feste **U75**-15
–, lineare U87-9
–, sexuelle U68-1
–, topografische U87-1
–, zwischenmenschliche U75-1
Beziehungsdenken U73-6
Beziehungswahn U77-20; U73-8
Bezugspunkt **U126**-8
B-Gedächtniszelle U39-15
Bias **U100**-18
Bichat-Wangenfettpropf U24-5
biegen **U31**-2

biegsam **U31**-2,11,17; U141-14
Biegsamkeit **U31**-11,16 f
–, wachsartige U31-17
Biegung **U31**-17; **U63**-3
Biegungsfraktur **U63**-3; **U106**-12
Biegungskeil U106-2,7
Bienengift U91-2
Bienenkorbsauger U128-11
Bienenstich **U91**-16
Bigeminie U110-6
Bikarbonat U36-4; U116-11
Bikuspidat **U26**-6
Bild **U59**-5
–, dreidimensionales U59-5
–, eigenständiges klinisches U87-12
–, florides klinisches U119-13
–, klinisches U14-2
–, optisches **U59**-5
Bildauflösung U99-14
Bildschirmarbeiter U1-15
Bildung (Sommersprossen) U56-7
Bilharzia **U90**-17
Bilharziose **U90**-17
biliär **U47**-11
biliös **U47**-11
Bilirubin **U47**-13
–, direktes U47-13
–, konjugiertes U47-13
Bilirubinausscheidung (im Harn) U47-13
Bilirubindiglukuronid U47-13
Bilirubinumsatz U47-13
Bilirubinurie U47-13
Biliverdin **U47**-13
Billingsmethode U69-5
Billings-Ovulationsmethode U50-7
Bimalleolarfraktur U106-10
Binde **U140**-20; **U141**-8
–, elastische U31-16; U141-10
Bindegewebe **U86**-4,3; U29-2
–, elastisches U31-16
–, faserarmes **U86**-6
–, fibröses **U86**-4
–, kollagenes U86-4
–, lockeres **U86**-6,4; U56-4
–, retikuläres U83-8; U86-5
–, straffes **U86**-4
–, subkutanes U86-4
Bindegewebegeschwulst **U98**-8
Bindegewebeknorpel U29-2
Bindegewebemassage U86-4
Bindegewebenarbe U86-4
Bindegewebenävus U86-4
Bindegewebestrang U86-4
Bindegewebezelle U86-4
Bindegewebsschicht, subseröse **U86**-9
Bindehaut **U58**-4
– (Augen) U58-2
Bindehautentzündung **U58**-4
Bindehautödeme U58-4
Bindehautsack U58-4
Bindemittel **U81**-8
binden **U78**-19; **U81**-8
Bindung, chemische **U81**-8; U84-3
–, energiereiche U78-12; U81-8

Bindung, feste U81-8
–, kovalente U81-8,10
–, stabile U81-8
–, ungesättigte U78-24
Bindungen, emotionelle U75-21; U76-1
Bindungsenergie U81-8
Bindungsregion U84-2
Bindungsstelle U81-8
Bindungstest U116-3
Bing-Horton-Syndrom/Neuralgie **U113**-16
Binokularmikroskop U59-16; U127-6
Binokulusverband U59-16
Bioakkumulation **U91**-19
Bioäquivalenz U121-10
Bioassay **U116**-3
Biochemie U81-1; U83-1
Bioenergetik **U78**-12
Biofeedbacktherapie **U142**-25
Biofeedbackverfahren U142-25
bioinert **U129**-20; U122-7
Biokatalysator U81-16
biokompatibel **U129**-20
Biokost U1-1
Biologe/-in **U83**-1
Biologic response modifier U83-1
biologisch inaktiv **U129**-20; U137-10
– verfügbar **U121**-10
Biomechanik **U142**-10
biomechanische Belastungen U142-10
Biophysik **U142**-10
Biopsie **U118**-5
–, ultraschallgezielte U118-5
Biopsiebefund U118-5
Biopsiebürste U128-2
Biopsiematerial U118-4 f
Biopsienadel U132-5
Biopsiepistole U118-5
biopsieren **U118**-5
Biopsiezange U118-5; U132-14
bioptisch **U118**-5
Biosignal U83-1
Biostatistik **U100**-1
Biosynthese **U78**-4
biotinylieren U78-7
Biotoxikologie **U91**-3
Biotransformation U92-4; U78-6
Biotransformationsrate U92-4
Bioverfügbarkeit **U121**-10
Biphenyl, polychloriertes U91-8
birnenförmig U47-7
Bismut(um) **U82**-27
Bismutnitrat, basisches U82-27
Bismutsalicylat, basisches U82-27
Biss **U5**-10; **U27**-12
– (heben) U64-16
Bissebene U26-24
Bissen **U27**-12; **U46**-9; U2-4,6; U45-1
–, impaktierter U46-9
–, steckengebliebener U46-9
Bissflügel U27-12
Bissflügelaufnahme U26-22; U99-3
Bisshebung U129-11
Bisshöhe U27-12

Bissmale U91-16
Bissnahme U27-12
Bissspuren U91-16
Bissstelle U91-16
Bissverhältnisse, normale **U141**-1
Bissverletzung U6-1
Bisswunde U5-10
bitter **U62**-5; **U76**-11
Bitterkeit **U76**-11
Bittermandelgeruch U62-3
Bittersalz **U91**-24; U82-20; U92-13
bivalent **U81**-10,5; U82-19
bivariate Analyse U100-28
Bizeps (brachii) **U30**-11
Bizepssehnenreflex U30-11
Bjerrum-Skotom U113-11
B-Kette (Insulin) U81-7
BKS **U116**-12; U37-5
Blackout **U74**-17,13; **U7**-4
blähend **U46**-15; **U109**-7
Blähsucht **U109**-7
Blähung(en) **U46**-15; **U109**-7 f
bland **U62**-7
Bläschen **U114**-12; U95-7
–, synaptische U40-13
Bläschenbildung U21-9
Bläschendrüse **U52**-9
Bläschendrüsenentzündung U52-9
Bläschendrüsenzyste U52-9
Bläschenfollikel U51-6
bläschenförmig **U114**-12
Blase **U114**-12
–, autonome/spastische U112-8
–, entleerte U49-16
–, neurogene U48-11
–, subepidermale U56-2
blasenbildend **U114**-12
Blasenbildung **U114**-12
Blasendach U114-12
Blasendehnung U49-15
Blasendreieck **U48**-12
Blasenentleerung **U49**-16; U48-11,12
–, erschwerte **U112**-1; U49-16
–, häufige **U112**-5
–, reflektorische U113-1
–, restharnfreie U112-11
–, unvollständige U49-16; U112-9 f
Blasenentleerungsstörung U49-16
–, neurogene U113-14
Blasenfistel U89-25
–, suprapubische U22-8; U52-18
Blasenfüllung **U49**-15; U48-12
Blasengalle U47-11
Blasengrund U48-11
Blasenhals U48-11; U138-17
Blasenhalsobstruktion **U112**-12,4; U48-11
Blaseninstabilität U125-2
Blasenkapazität **U49**-15; U48-11
Blasenkörper U48-11
Blasenlähmung U113-7
Blasenmole U98-15
Blasenspiegelung **U118**-11
Blasensprengung U71-6; U85-15

Blasensprung **U71**-6
–, Geburt nach vorzeitigem U71-3
–, vorzeitiger U71-6
Blasenspülung U48-11; U127-17
Blasenspülzytologie U48-11
Blasenstein U48-11,12
–, großer U24-4
Blasenverweilkatheter U125-20
blasenziehende Mittel U136-7
blass **U25**-12; **U108**-5
– werden U140-10
Blässe **U25**-12; **U108**-5; U5-12; U56-18
–, periorale U95-6; U108-5
Blast **U38**-3; **U86**-2; U83-2
Blastenbildung U38-3; U86-2
Blastenkrise U38-3; U86-2; U124-6
Blastenphase U38-3
Blastenschub U38-3; U86-2; U124-6
Blastentransformation U38-3
Blastenzelle U86-2
Blastogenese U38-3; U86-2
Blastomere U85-4
Blastozyste **U85**-5
Blastozystenhöhle U85-5
Blasttransformation U86-2
Blastula **U85**-5
Blastulabildung **U85**-5
Blastulation **U85**-5
Blattern U95-7
Blattgold U82-28
Blatt-Spekulum U17-6
blauer Nävus U25-19
Blaufärbung U108-6; U118-6
Blausäure U91-9
Blausäureverbindung U81-2
Blausäurevergiftung U91-9
Blei **U82**-32; U91-19
Bleiäquivalent U82-32
Bleiazetat U82-32
Bleibelastung U82-32; U91-5
bleich **U25**-12; **U108**-5
Bleichkalk U82-23
Bleichmittel U91-2,10
–, chlorhaltiges U82-23
–, haushaltsübliches U17-15
Bleifarbe U82-32
Bleiglas U82-32
Bleigleichwert U82-32
bleihaltig **U82**-32
Bleikarbonat U82-32
Bleilähmung U82-32
Bleioxid, rotes U82-32
Bleisaum U82-32
Bleischürze U82-32
Bleistiftstuhl U46-19; U109-11
Bleitetroxid U82-32
Bleivergiftung U10-5; U91-2
Bleiweiß U82-32
Bleizucker U82-32
Blende **U59**-18
blenden **U59**-3,18
Blendreflex U59-3
Blepharitis U58-3
Blepharoklonus U110-7

Blepharospasmus U31-5
Blick **U59**-1 f; **U67**-8,14
–, finsterer **U67**-11,13,8
–, flüchtiger **U59**-3; **U67**-12
–, glasiger U59-1
–, kurzer **U67**-12
–, leerer U67-14; U76-17
–, neugieriger U67-8
–, starrer **U59**-2; **U67**-14
–, stechender **U59**-2
–, störrischer U75-19
–, teilnahmsloser U59-2
–, trauriger U76-20
–, zorniger **U67**-13
blicken **U67**-12,14
–, finster U67-8,13
Blickfelder U59-2
Blickkrampf U58-16
Blicklähmung **U113**-11
–, konjugierte U59-16
Blickpunkt U59-2
Blickrichtung **U59**-2; U91-14
–, extrem seitliche U113-12
Blickrichtungsnystagmus U59-2; U113-12
Blicksenkung U59-2
Blickstabilisierung U58-16
blind **U59**-18; **U101**-9
–, auf einem Auge U59-18
–, vollkommen U59-18
Blindbiopsie U118-5
Blinddarm **U45**-12
Blinddarmdurchbruch U45-12
Blinddarmentzündung **U45**-13
Blinddarmoperation U45-13
Blinden, die **U59**-18
Blindheit **U59**-18
–, psychogene U57-6; U77-2,6; U110-19
Blindpunktion U128-12
Blindversuch U101-9
blinzeln **U67**-14; U21-3
Blinzeln **U59**-3; **U72**-2
–, unwillkürliches U59-3
Blinzelreflex U59-3; U67-15; U125-25
Blisterpackung U9-16
Blitz U6-14
Blitzableiter U6-14
blitzartig **U127**-14
Blitzeinleitung U123-10
Blitzschlag **U6**-14,4
– (Verletzung durch) U7-9
Block, alveolokapillärer U34-5
–, atrioventrikulärer **U123**-2
–, sinoatrialer U32-15
–, sinoaurikulärer U32-15
Blockanlage U101-9
Blockbildung **U101**-11
Blockdiagramm U100-27
Blocker **U92**-7
blockierend **U111**-16
Blockwirbel U28-19
bloßlegen **U129**-9
Blount-Krankheit U28-24

Blow-out Fraktur U106-8
blubbern U66-7
blue baby U70-5
Blue bloater U111-3
blühend **U1**-4
Blumberg-Zeichen **U109**-12
blumenkohlartig U96-14
Blut **U36**-1; **U37**-1
– im Harn **U112**-3
–, arterielles U44-6
–, defibriniertes U38-14
–, okkultes U46-20; U119-6
–, sauerstoffreiches U44-6
–, zentrifugiertes U83-20
Blutabnahme U136-9
Blutader **U34**-4
Blutalkohol U47-17
Blutalkoholkonzentration **U10**-3
Blutalkoholspiegel **U10**-3
Blutalkoholtest U10-4
Blutansammlung (Paukenhöhle) **U60**-4
blutarm **U38**-4
Blutarmut **U38**-4
Blutausstrich U37-1; U116-5,7
–, peripherer U87-15
Blutaustausch U38-9
Blutaustritt U5-18
Blutbad **U12**-10
Blutbahn **U36**-1; U55-1; U97-11
Blutbank **U14**-12
Blutbanktechniker(in) U14-12
blutbefleckt U37-1
Blutbeutel U136-4
Blutbild U37-1; U116-7
–, komplettes/großes U81-1; U116-8
–, weißes **U116**-8
blutbildend **U38**-1
Blutbildung **U38**-1
Blutdepot **U14**-12
Blutdoping U11-24
Blutdruck U36-8; U49-11; U54-6; U135-24
–, diastolischer U107-14
–, erhöhter U65-17
–, niedriger **U36**-8; **U124**-6
–, systolischer U33-3; U36-8; U107-14
Blutdruckanstieg U107-14
Blutdruckkrise U36-8
Blutdruckmanschette **U17**-8
Blutdruckmessgerät **U17**-8
Blutdruckmessung **U107**-14
–, indirekte/unblutige **U17**-8
blutdrucksenkend **U110**-13; U92-17
Blutdrucküberwachungsgerät U125-6
Blutdruckwerte U36-8; U107-14
Bluteindickung **U36**-13
bluten U38-6,8; **U124**-16
Blutentnahmeröhrchen **U17**-10
Bluter(in) **U38**-6; **U5**-18
Bluterbrechen U37-1; U103-12; U111-7
Bluterguss **U5**-13; **U38**-8; **U89**-26
Bluterkrankheit U37-1
Blutersatz U136-13
Blutfarbstoff **U116**-9

Blutfarbstoff, roter **U37**-6
Blutfluss **U36**-5
Blutfülle U89-28
Blutgasanalyse **U116**-11
–, arterielle U125-9
Blutgase U82-2
–, arterielle **U125**-9; U116-11
Blutgaswerte, arterielle U125-9
blutgefärbt U71-7
Blutgefäß(e) **U34**-1
–, große U34-1
Blutgefäßnävus U25-19
Blutgefäßtumor, gutartiger **U98**-5
blutgefüllt U52-15
Blutgerinnsel U37-1; **U38**-12,10
– bilden U87-22
Blutgerinnselretraktion U38-12
Blutgerinnung **U38**-10; U37-1,11
Blutgerinnungsfaktor **U38**-13,10
Blutgerinnungsstörung U38-8
Blutgerinnungszeit U38-10; U116-13
Blutgift U91-4
Blutgruppe **U37**-16; **U136**-10
Blutgruppenantigene U37-16
Blutgruppenbestimmung **U136**-10; U37-1,16
Blutgruppeninkompatibilität U37-16
blutgruppenspezifisches Vollblut U136-14
Blutgruppenunverträglichkeit U37-16
Blut-Harnstoff-Stickstoff(wert) U49-13; U55-25; U82-16; U116-7
Blut-Hirn-Schranke **U36**-15; U37-1; U78-9
Bluthochdruck **U36**-8; **U110**-13; **U124**-6
Bluthochdruckkrise **U124**-6
Blut-Hoden-Schranke U53-9
Bluthusten **U103**-17; **U111**-7
blutig U37-1; U71-7
– tingiert U60-1; U109-11
– serös U140-13
Blutkammerwasserschranke U88-9
Blutkoagulum **U38**-12
Blutkonserve U6-19; U14-12; U136-8
Blutkonservierungslösung U136-14
Blutkörperchen **U37**-4
–, rote **U37**-5,4; U86-2
–, weiße **U37**-7; U45-17; U92-34
Blutkörperchensenkungsgeschwindigkeit (BSG) **U116**-12; U37-5
Blutkreislauf **U36**-1
Blutkultur U116-6
Blutkulturfläschchen U136-4
Blutlakune U85-24
blutleer (machen) **U37**-1; **U38**-9
Blutleere **U89**-27; **U124**-14
Blut-Liquor-Schranke U36-15
Blutmonozyten U37-9
Blutplasma **U37**-3
Blutplättchen **U37**-11
Blutpoolszintigrafie U99-17
Blutprobe U37-1; U116-2
Blutprodukte U136-9

Blutschwamm, kapillärer U98-5
Blutserum **U37**-3
Blutspendedienst U13-3; U14-12
Blutspender(in) **U136**-9
Blutspenderausweis U136-9
Blutspiegel U116-16
Blutspucken **U103**-17; **U111**-7
Blutstammzellen U38-1
–, kryokonservierte U136-17
Blutstase U36-5
Blutstau(ung) U36-5; U125-22
Blutstillung **U38**-10; **U127**-10; **U137**-11
Blutstillungsmeißel U132-11
Blutstuhl U46-19; U109-11
blutsverwandt **U84**-31
Blutsverwandtschaft **U84**-31
Bluttransfusion **U136**-8
Blutübertragung **U136**-8
Blutung **U5**-18; **U6**-15; **U38**-6,8; **U124**-16
–, arterielle **U38**-7
–, gastrointestinale **U109**-11
–, innere U38-8; U124-16
–, intraabdominale **U124**-16
–, lebensbedrohliche U38-8
–, leichte U71-7
–, postkoitale U50-7; U68-5
–, postmenopausale U51-10
–, postpartale U71-21
–, punktförmige U38-8
–, starke U34-10
–, subepitheliale U86-7
–, subunguale U56-15
Blutungsneigung U38-8
Blutungsstelle U124-16
Blutungszeit U116-13; U38-8
blutunterlaufen U21-3
Blutuntersuchung U116-2
–, chemische **U116**-7; U81-1
Blutverdünnung **U36**-13,4; U38-13
Blutvergiftung **U91**-22; **U124**-5
Blutverlust U136-13
–, starker U119-14
Blutversorgung **U36**-6; U37-1; U88-3
Blutviskosität **U36**-12
Blutvolumen **U36**-7
Blutzelle **U37**-4
Blutzellseparator U136-14f
Blutzellzählgerät **U83**-21
Blutzirkulation **U36**-1
Blutzuckerbestimmung U117-2
Blutzuckerspiegel, erhöhter **U78**-13
Blutzufuhr **U36**-6; U88-3
B-Lymphozyt **U39**-12; U37-10
BMI **U24**-7
B-Mode Darstellung U118-17
Bodensatz **U81**-27
Boeck-Skabies U96-12
Bogengänge, knöcherne **U60**-10
bohnenförmig U48-2
Bohnensack **U142**-19
Bohrdraht **U141**-15, 14
Bohrlochosteitis U141-15
Bohrstift **U141**-15

Bolus **U46**-9; U2-6; U45-1
Bolus-Gabe U136-5
Bolusinfusion, i.v. U136-1
Bolusinjektion U46-9; U122-4; U136-5
Bolusobstruktion U46-9
Bolustod U46-9
Bolzung **U141**-16
Booster-Dosis U122-9
Booster-Effekt U122-9
Bor **U82**-31
Borborygmus **U46**-14; U65-15
borderline **U116**-23
Borderline-Hypertonie U116-23
Borderline-Lepra U94-17
Borderline-Tumor U116-23
Borke **U114**-8
Borkenkrätze U96-12
Borsalbe U82-31
bösartig **U6**-11; **U97**-5
Bösartigkeit **U97**-5
böse **U76**-10; **U77**-15
Botenstoff U55-1
–, chemischer U81-1
Bote(nstoff), sekundärer **U83**-17
–, primärer U83-17
Botulinustoxin **U91**-21
Botulinustoxintherapie U91-21
Botulismus **U91**-21
– Antitoxin U91-21; U122-8
– Immunserum U91-21
– Toxoid-Impfstoff U91-21
Bougierung U89-19; **U132**-17
Bowman-Kapsel U48-6
Bowman-Raum U48-6
Boxerohren U21-15
Brace **U141**-7
Brachium **U23**-2
Bradyarrhythmie U33-5
bradykard **U33**-5
Bradykardie **U33**-5; **U110**-2
–, arrhythmische U33-5
–, parasympathische U40-10
Bradykardie-Tachykardie-Syndrom U33-5
Bradypnoe **U111**-5; U44-4
Branchen U132-13
Brand **U6**-10; **U89**-30
Brandbombe U6-10
Brandkatastrophe U6-10
Brandopfer U6-10
Brandschutzübung U6-10
Brandstelle **U6**-10
Brandstifter(in) **U6**-10
Brandstiftung **U6**-10
Brandverletze(r) U6-10
Brandwunde **U5**-11
bräunen U25-13
brauseförmig U92-29
Brausen **U110**-3
Brausetablette U9-7
brechen **U46**-4
– (Knochen) **U106**-1
Brechkraft (Auge) U58-2; U59-12
Brechmittel **U103**-12; U91-25

Brechreiz **U27**-16; **U46**-5; **U103**-11
–, starker U46-5
Brechreizanfälle U46-5
Brechungsfehler U59-12
Brechungshypermetropie U59-12
Brechungshyperopie U59-12
Brechungsindex U59-12
Brechungsmyopie U59-17
Brechwurzel, gepulverte U91-25
Brechwurzelsirup **U91**-25; U9-11; U92-12
Breikost U2-12
Breitbandantibiotikum U92-9; U120-6
Breitband-Pestizid U91-8
Breite, therapeutische U100-15
breitschultrig **U25**-9
Breiumschlag **U140**-25
Bremse U90-15
brennbar **U81**-17; **U6**-10; U93-4
brennen **U6**-7,10
Brennen (beim Urinieren) U49-16
–, schmerzhaftes U5-10f; U104-17
Brennspiritus U10-2
Brennstoff **U81**-17
Brennwert U79-4
bretthartes Abdomen **U109**-14
Briden U128-15
Bridenstriktur U89-19
Brill-(Zinsser)-Krankheit U94-7
Brillenverordnung U121-1
bringen, in Verbindung **U74**-5
Brittle Diabetes U31-16
Broca-Aphasie U113-8,10; U66-9
Brom(id) **U82**-23
Brom(id)vergiftung U82-23
Bromaceton U82-23
Bromismus U82-23
Bromoderma U82-23
Bromsulfalein U82-23
Bromwasser(stoff) U82-23
Bromwasserstoffsäure U82-23
Bronchialäste U43-9
Bronchialasthma U43-9; U124-10
Bronchialatmen U43-9
Bronchialbaum U43-9; U111-17
Bronchialfremdkörper U43-9
Bronchialfremitus U111-8,11
Bronchialkarzinom U98-2
Bronchiallavage U91-26; U116-5; U118-10
Bronchiallavagematerial U118-10
Bronchialstimme U66-16
Bronchialtoilette U43-9
Bronchiektase **U111**-17; U43-9
Bronchiektasenhöhle U111-17
bronchiektatisch **U111**-17
Bronchien U43-9
Bronchiole **U43**-9
Bronchiolus terminalis U43-9
Bronchitis, kruppöse U95-10
Bronchodilatatoren U92-14
Bronchokonstriktion **U111**-17
Broncholytika U92-14
–, adrenerge U54-10

Bronchophonie U66-16
Bronchopneumonie **U94**-14
Bronchoskop U17-6
Bronchoskopie **U118**-11
Bronchoskopiebefund U118-11
Bronchospasmolytika, adrenerge U54-10; U55-11
Bronchospirometrie U43-9
Bronchus **U43**-9
– lobaris U43-3
– principalis U43-9
– segmentalis U43-9; U87-6
Brot **U3**-9
Bruch **U5**-19; **U89**-23; **U137**-18
–, geschlossener **U106**-3
–, reponierbarer U140-26
Bruchband **U140**-26
Bruchende U140-2
Bruchfragment U141-2
brüchig **U31**-16
Brüchigkeit **U31**-16; **U103**-9
Bruchkerbe U9-7
Bruchlandung U6-2
Bruchpforte U89-23
Bruchsack U89-23
Bruchspalt U87-26; U106-1
Bruchstelle U106-14; U5-20
Bruchstück **U106**-2
Brücke **U41**-12; **U81**-7
Brückengliom U98-14
Brückenhaube U41-12
Brudzinski-Nackenzeichen U94-13
Bruit **U110**-4; U30-13
brüllen **U66**-14,2
brummeln **U66**-15
brummen **U67**-19; **U66**-5
Brummton U61-3
brünett **U25**-13
Brust **U22**-2
–, weibliche **U22**-2; **U50**-17
Brustaorta U34-8
Brustatmung U44-4
Brustbein **U22**-2; **U28**-13
Brustdrüse U54-1
Brustdrüsenentzündung U50-17
Brusterhaltung U50-17
Brusternährung **U71**-25
Brustfell **U43**-11
Brustfellentzündung **U94**-14; U43-11; U111-12
Brustknospen U50-17
Brustkorb **U22**-2f; U28-14
Brustkorbbeweglichkeit U44-11
Brustkorberöffnung **U123**-11; **U125**-16; U128-6
Brustkorbkompression U6-6
Brustkrebs U50-17
Brustmuskel **U30**-10; U22-2
Brustraum U22-2
Brustschmerz, stechender U104-13
Brustschwellung U50-17
Bruststück U17-2
Brusttumor U50-17
Brustvergrößerung U50-17

Brustverletzung U5-2
Brustwandableitung U32-1; U118-14
Brustwarze(n) **U50**-18
–, empfindliche U104-11
Brustwarzeneinziehung U50-18;
  U64-13
Brustwarzenempfindlichkeit U50-18
Brustwarzenrhagade U50-18
Brustwirbel U28-19; U87-16
Brustwirbelsäule U22-2,12; U87-16
brüten **U84**-30
Brutkasten **U14**-10
Brutstätte U84-30
Bruxismus **U27**-18; U72-14; U74-15
BSE U77-15
BSG **U116**-12; U81-27
BSG-Bestimmung (Westergren)
  U116-12
Bubble-Oxygenator U44-6; U125-11
Bubo **U96**-5
Bucca **U21**-7
Buckel **U63**-3
bücken, sich **U63**-3; U5-17; U31-2
Buffy coat-Konserve **U136**-16
bukkal **U21**-7; U**26**-23
Bülau-Drainage U125-16
bulbär **U58**-2
Bulbärparalyse U58-2; U113-7
Bulbocavernosus-Reflex U52-14
Bulbus duodeni U45-10
– oculi **U58**-2
– olfactorius U62-1
– penis U52-14
Bulbusabweichung, konjugierte U59-15
Bulbusdruckversuch U58-2
Bulla **U114**-12
Bulldogklemme U132-13
bummeln **U65**-7
BUN U49-13; U55-25
Bündel, neurovaskuläres **U40**-12
bündeln, sich U59-17
Burkitt-Lymphom U98-10
Burnout-Syndrom U77-25
Bursa U23-11
– anserina U29-10
– omentalis U29-10; U45-7
– subcutanea olecrani U28-16
– synovialis **U29**-10,3
Bursaerguss U29-10
Bursitis **U29**-10
– subdeltoidea U29-10
Bürstbewegungen U64-11
Bürstenabstrich **U116**-5; U83-1
Bürstenbiopsie **U118**-10,5; U25-16;
  U83-1
Bürstensaum U86-11
Bürstensaumenzym U78-8
Burst-Zyklus U42-6
Busen **U22**-2; **U50**-17
Büstenhalter U64-15
Butanol **U47**-17
Butterfly(-Nadel) **U136**-6
Buttersäuregärung U46-12
Butylalkohol **U47**-17

Bypass **U36**-14
–, aortokoronarer U32-14; U125-11
–, femoropoplitealer U28-23
–, jejunoilealer U45-11
–, kardiopulmonaler **U125**-11; U32-3
Bypass-Operation U125-11
BZ U38-8
B-Zellblast U39-12
B-Zelle **U39**-12; **U54**-8; U37-10
B-Zellendifferenzierung U39-12
B-Zellenvorläufer U39-12
B-Zell-Leukämie U39-12
B-Zell-Oberflächenmarker U97-16
B-Zell-Wachstumsfaktor U39-12

C

Caecum mobile U45-12
Cafe-au-lait-Fleck U25-18; U114-3
Caisson-Krankheit **U6**-17; U125-17
Calcaneus **U28**-27
Calcinosis metastatica U31-14; U97-13
Calcitonin **U55**-8
Calcitriol **U55**-8
Calcitriolzusatz U55-8
Calcium **U82**-19
Caliculus gustatorius U62-6
Callositas U106-15
Callus luxurians **U106**-15
Calvaria U28-7
Calyx renalis **U48**-4
Camera oculi anterior U59-10
cAMP **U83**-17; U78-6
Canales semicirculares **U60**-10
Canaliculi biliferi U34-5; U47-11
Canaliculus lacrimalis U58-9
Canalis carpi U23-5
– infraorbitalis U58-1
– inguinalis **U52**-8; U22-9
– pudendalis U52-20
– semicircularis anterior U60-10
– spiralis cochleae U60-11
Candida-Sepsis U124-5
Cannabinoid **U11**-15
Cannabinol **U11**-15
Capgras-Syndrom U73-10
Cannabis **U11**-15
Capitulum humeri U28-15
Capsula articularis **U29**-9,1
– glomeruli U48-6
– prostatica U52-10
Caput **U21**-1; U53-7
– breve U30-11
– femoris U28-23
– humeri U28-15
– longum U30-11
– musculi **U30**-3
– pancreatis U54-8
Carbamid U82-17
Carbo medicinalis **U91**-25; U9-9;
  U92-3
Carboanhydrase U82-10
Carbonat **U82**-10

Carboneum **U82**-10
Carbonsäure U82-10
Carboxy-Hämoglobin **U116**-9; U82-10
Carboxy-Hämoglobin-Komplex U81-14
Carboxylgruppe **U82**-10
carboxylieren **U78**-7
Carboxylierung **U82**-10
Carboxy-Terminal U39-3
Carcinoma adenomatosum **U98**-4
– in situ **U97**-10
Cardia **U32**-1
Caro luxurians **U140**-7
Carotispuls U33-4
Carpus **U23**-5; **U28**-17
Carrier **U94**-4; U49-3; U78-17
Carriermolekül U81-2
Carrierprotein U78-17
Carriertransport **U78**-17; U49-3;
  U88-2 ff
carriervermittelt **U78**-17; U83-19
Cartilago **U29**-2
– auricularis U29-2,7; U60-2
– cricoidea U21-14; U29-2
– elastica U86-5
– fibrosa U29-2
– thyroidea U29-2; U54-6
Caruncula lacrimalis U58-9
Case-Finding **U102**-13
Cäsium **U82**-34,18
Castillo-Syndrom U53-9
Cataracta incipiens U119-5
Catgut **U137**-9
–, einfaches U45-9
Cauda U53-7
– epididymidis U52-5
– equina **U41**-15
– pancreatis U54-8
caudatus **U41**-15
Cavitas **U28**-6
– abdominalis U45-6
– articularis U28-6; U29-1; U87-26
– glenoidalis U28-6,12; U87-26
– medullaris U28-3; U38-2
– oris **U45**-2; **U21**-8
– pelvis U22-7; U28-21
– peritonealis U45-7
– pleuralis U43-11
– tympanica **U60**-6
Cavum U28-6
– oris **U45**-2
– pelvis U22-7
– tympani **U60**-6
CCD-Kamera U133-3
CCK **U55**-13
CD4/CD8-Quotient U39-14
CD4 + Zelle **U39**-14; U37-10
CD8 +-Zelle U37-10
cDNA U84-11
Ceilingeffekt U11-18
Cellulae mastoideae U60-14
Celsius-Skala **U105**-6
Cementum **U26**-17
Centi-Morgan U84-17
Centriolum **U83**-6; U84-7

Centrum tendineum perinei U22-10; U52-20
Cerebellum **U41**-2
Cerebrum **U41**-1f
Cerumen U21-15
– obturans U60-15; U106-6
Cervix (uteri) **U50**-7
– vesicae U48-11
Cestoda U90-16
cGMP U81-7; U83-17
CGRP U55-8
Chagrinlederhaut U114-10
Chancenverhältnis U100-8
Chandu U11-18
Charakter **U75**-1
Charakterfehler U75-1
charakteristisch **U87**-12
Charakterzug **U75**-1
Charta nitrata U82-16
Chassaignac-Lähmung U23-4
Checkbiss U27-12
Chefvisite U20-9
Cheilitis U21-9
Cheiloschisis U87-26
Chelat(komplex) **U81**-5
Chelatbildner **U81**-5; U82-6
Chelatbildung, zitratvermittelte U81-5
Chemie, angewandte U81-1
–, organische U81-1
–, pharmazeutische U81-1; U92-1
–, physiologische U81-1
Chemikalie **U81**-1
–, gefährliche **U81**-1
–, giftige U44-2
–, mutagene U91-13
chemisch **U81**-1
Chemo- u. Strahlentherapie, kombinierte U97-17
Chemoattraktantien U81-1
Chemochirurgie U97-17
Chemokine U39-13
Chemomonotherapie U97-17
Chemoprophylaxe U97-17; U120-6
Chemosis U58-4
Chemotaxine U39-17
Chemotherapeutikum **U97**-17
chemotherapeutisch **U97**-17
Chemotherapie **U97**-17; U120-4
–, adjuvante U97-17
–, hochdosierte U97-17
–, neoadjuvante U97-17
Chenodesoxycholsäure U47-12
Cheyne-Stokes-Atmung U44-12; U111-2
Chi²-Test **U100**-34
Chiasma opticum **U58**-15; U41-14
Chiasmabildung **U84**-17
Chiasmakompression U58-15
Chinidin U121-12; U92-18
Chinidinvergiftung U91-14
Chiropraktik **U15**-22
Chiropraktiker(in) **U15**-22
chiropraktisch **U15**-22
Chiropraxis **U15**-22

Chirotherapie U15-22; U142-12
Chirurg(in) **U131**-5; U15-1; **U126**-3
–, zweite(r) U16-10
Chirurgie **U126**-3
–, endoskopische **U128**-2
–, laparoskopische **U128**-3
–, minimal invasive **U128**-1; U134-14
–, offene **U128**-3
–, orthopädische U15-15
–, plastische **U129**-3
chirurgisch **U126**-2
chirurgische Wundversorgung **U140**-1
chirurgischer Knoten U137-6
Chlamydia **U90**-14
– psittaci **U90**-14
– trachomatis **U90**-14
Chlamydie U90-14
Chlamydienantigentest U90-14
Chlamydieneinschlusskörperchen U96-9
Chlamydienepidemie U90-14
Chlamydieninfektion **U96**-9
Chlamydienzervizitis U96-9
Chlor **U82**-23
Chlor(osark)om U98-3
Chloral **U82**-23
Chloralhydrat U82-9,23
Chlorgas U82-23
chlorhaltig **U82**-23
Chlorid **U82**-23; U79-17
Chloridkanal U82-23
Chlorkalk U82-23
Chloroform U82-23
Chlorverbindung, organische U82-23
Chlorwasser U82-23
Cholangiografie, perkutane transhepatische **U118**-20
Cholangiopankreatografie, retrograde **U118**-20; U128-2
Cholangioskopie, intraoperative U47-9
Cholaskos U47-11; U109-9
Cholecystokinin **U55**-13; U54-9
Choledocholithiasis U47-9
Choledochoskopie U47-9
Choledochus **U47**-9
Choledochusrevision U47-9
Choledochusstein U47-9
Choledochusstriktur U47-9
Choledochuszyste U47-9
Cholelithiasis U89-2
Cholelithotripsie U13-9
Cholera **U94**-21
Choleraenterotoxin U94-21
Choleragen U94-21
Cholerapandemie U94-21
Cholerastamm U94-21
Choleratoxin U91-4
Choleravakzine U94-21
cholerisch **U75**-18
Cholestanol U78-16
Cholestase U47-7
–, extrahepatische U47-6
Cholesteatose U47-12
Cholesterase U78-16

Cholesterin **U47**-12; **U78**-16
–, verestertes U82-14
Cholesterinembolie U47-12
Cholesterinester U82-14
Cholesterinesterase U78-16
Cholesterinkristall U78-16
Cholesterinose U47-12
Cholesterinspiegel U78-16
Cholesterinstein U78-16; U47-12
Cholesterintransport U88-3
Cholesterinzufuhr U78-16
Cholesterol **U47**-12; **U78**-16
Cholesterosis **U47**-12
Cholezystektomie U47-7
–, laparoskopische U128-3
Cholezystitis U47-7
cholinerg **U42**-11
cholinerge Fasern U92-8
Cholinergikum **U92**-8,2
Cholinrezeptorenblockade U93-6
Cholsäure **U47**-12
Chondroblast U86-2
Chondrom **U98**-12
Chondromalacia patellae U98-12
chondromatös **U98**-12
Chondrosarkom U98-3
Chondrozyten U29-2
Chorda dorsalis **U85**-20
Chordae tendineae **U32**-12; U30-5
Chordafortsatz U85-20
Chordakanal U85-20
Chordom U85-20
Chorion **U85**-16
– frondosum U85-16
– laeve U85-16
Chorionepitheliom, (malignes) U85-16
Choriongonadotropin, humanes **U55**-20
Chorionhöhle U85-7,16
Chorionkarzinom U85-16
Chorionplatte U85-16
Chorionzotten U71-16; U85-14,16
Chorionzottenbiopsie U85-16
Choroidea **U58**-7
Choroideatumoren U58-7
CH-Region U39-3
Christmas-Faktor U37-14
Christmas-Krankheit U38-10,13
Chrom **U82**-25
chromaffin **U82**-25
Chromat **U82**-25
Chromatid **U84**-7
Chromatidabschnitt U84-7
Chromatin **U84**-6
Chromatinbrüchigkeit U84-6
Chromatinfragilität U84-6
Chromatinkondensation U84-6
chromatinpositiv U84-6
Chromatinverdichtung U84-6
Chromatografie **U83**-22
Chromatopsie **U59**-9
Chromcatgut U82-25
chromgelb U82-25
Chromkatgut U137-9
Chrommangel U82-25

Chrompsie **U59**-9
Chromosom **U84**-6
Chromosomenaberration **U84**-20,6
Chromosomenanalyse **U84**-10,6
Chromosomenarm **U84**-6
Chromosomenbanden **U84**-6
Chromosomenbruch **U84**-24,6
Chromosomenbruchstelle **U84**-24
Chromosomenbruchsyndrom U84-24
Chromosomendeletion U84-23
Chromosomenendstück **U84**-7
Chromosomenkartierung U84-34
Chromosomenkonfiguration U1-8
Chromosomenmosaik U84-6,10
Chromosomenmutante U84-20
Chromosomenpaarung, meiotische U83-14
Chromosomenrearrangement U84-24
Chromosomensatz U39-10; U51-5
–, abnormer **U84**-9
–, haploider U85-2; U84-9
Chromosomentranslokation U84-6
Chromsalz U82-25
Chromsäure U82-25
chronisch **U119**-10
Chronizität **U119**-10
Chylomikronen U35-2
Chylomikronenfragmente U35-2
Chyloperikard U35-2
chylös **U35**-2,10
Chylothorax **U111**-14
Chylus **U35**-2
chylusartig **U35**-2
Chymus **U46**-9,7; U55-13
CI U33-2
Cicatrix **U140**-10
Ciclosporin U39-13
Ciliophora U90-2
Cingulum membri superioris U22-2; U23-3; U30-10
cis-Effekt U83-10
cis-Konfiguration U83-10
cis-Region **U83**-10
Cisterna cerebromedullaris **U41**-17,2
– chyli **U35**-8
– interpeduncularis U41-17
– magna **U41**-17
Claudicatio intermittens **U110**-19
– intestinalis U110-19
– venosa U110-19
Clavicula **U28**-11; U21-12
Clavus **U114**-14; U23-14
clean **U10**-4
Clearance **U49**-7; **U88**-16
–, mukoziliäre **U44**-9; U88-16
–, renale U49-7; U88-16
Click U33-1
Climacterium praecox U51-10
– tardum U51-10
– virile U51-10
Clip **U137**-13
Clip-Applikator **U137**-13
Clip-Magazin U137-13; U138-15
clippen **U137**-3

Clipzange U137-13
CL-Region U39-3
Cluster-Analyse U100-28
– Stichprobe U100-4
CMV-Enzephalitis U96-11
CMV-Mononukleose U94-10; U96-11
CO_2-Insufflator U133-15
Coarctatio aortae U34-8
Cobalt **U82**-25
Cocablätter U11-20
Cocainschnupfen U10-20
Cochlea **U60**-11
Code **U74**-9; **U84**-13
–, genetischer U84-1
codieren **U74**-9; **U84**-13
CO-Diffusionskapazität U44-11
Codon **U84**-13
Coeur en sabot U32-1
CO-Hämoglobin U82-10
Cohn-Fraktionierung U81-4
Coitus interruptus U68-5
COLD U111-16
Colitis pseudomembranacea U86-15
Colliculus axonis U40-2
– seminalis **U52**-12,9
– superior U58-13
Collum **U21**-13
– chirurgicum (humeri) U28-15
– femoris U28-23
– tali U28-26
– vesicae felleae U47-7
Collyria U9-11
Coloboma iridis U58-8
Colon ascendens U45-15
– descendens U45-15
– irritabile U45-9,15; U109-6
– sigmoideum U45-15
– transversum U45-15
Columna vertebrae **U28**-19
Columnae griseae U41-7
– renales U48-2
Coma diabeticum **U124**-7
– hepaticum U47-1
– hypoglycaemicum U124-7
– vigile **U7**-17
Comedo **U114**-6
Commissura **U41**-3
– fornicis U41-3
– habenularum U41-3
Commotio **U5**-14
– cerebri U41-2; U124-19
Complexus golgiensis **U83**-10
Compliance **U44**-10; **U120**-15
–, thorakale U44-10
composite graft U130-1
Compressio cerebri U6-6; U124-19
– thoracis U6-6
Computertomografie U99-19
Concha auricularis U60-2
– nasalis U21-4; U28-9
Condyloma acuminatum **U96**-14; U50-1; U114-17
– latum U96-14
Congelatio **U5**-12

Conjunctiva bulbi U58-2
– palpebrarum U58-4
– tarsi U58-4
Conjunctivitis gonorrhoica U96-2
Conn-Syndrom U55-25
Contig-Sequenz **U84**-33
Contrecoup-Fraktur **U106**-9
Contrecoup-Hirnprellung U106-9
Contusio cerebri U5-13; U6-6; U41-2; U124-19
Conus elasticus laryngis U86-15
Coombs-Serum U136-12
Coombs-Test **U136**-12
Coping U75-3
–, familiäres U77-9
– Strategie **U77**-9
– Verhalten U77-9; U80-10
Cor **U32**-1
Corium **U56**-3
Cori-Zyklus U78-6; U81-15
Cornea **U58**-5
Cornu ammonis **U41**-11
Corona dentis **U26**-14
Corpora amygdaloidea U41-11
Corpus **U86**-20
– adiposum buccae U24-5
– amygdaloideum **U41**-11
– callosum **U41**-3
– cavernosum penis **U52**-15
– ciliare **U58**-7
– clitoridis **U50**-12
– liberum U29-3
– luteum U51-8
– mamillare **U41**-9
– mandibulae U28-10
– medullare **U41**-7,14
– ossis sphenoidalis U28-8
– pancreatis U54-8
– pineale **U54**-13
– spongiosum **U52**-16
– sterni U28-13
– striatum **U41**-10
– tali U28-26
– uteri U50-5
– ventriculi U45-8
– vertebrae U22-12; U28-19
– vesicae U48-11
– vitreum **U58**-10; U86-20; U88-9
Corpusculum lamellosum **U57**-15
– renale **U48**-6
– tactus U62-8
Corpus-luteum-Hormon **U55**-19
Corrigan-Puls U110-12
Cortex cerebelli U41-6
– cerebri **U41**-6; U86-23
– glandulae suprarenalis U54-10; U86-23
– renalis U48-2
–, akustischer U41-6; U60-7
–, motorischer U40-4; U41-6
–, okzipitaler U41-6
–, visueller U41-6
Corti-Bogen U60-12
Corticosteron U55-10

Corti-Haarzellen U60-11 ff
Corti-Hörzellen U60-11 ff
Corti-Organ **U60**-12
Corti-Pfeilerzelle U60-12
Cortisol **U55**-10; **U78**-16
Cortison **U55**-10
Corti-Tunnel U60-12
Cosmid **U84**-33
Cosmid-Bibliothek U84-33
Costa **U28**-14
– cervicalis **U28**-14; U21-13
Costae fluctuantes U28-14
– spuriae U28-14
– verae U28-13
Costen-Syndrom U77-14
Cotransfektion **U84**-39
Cotton-wool-Herd U114-9
Cover-Test U59-15
Cowper-Drüsen **U52**-13; U50-10; U53-6
Cox Regression **U100**-35
Coxa **U22**-7
– saltans U22-7
CPAP-Atmung U123-9
CPM-Schiene U142-14
CPM-Therapie **U142**-14
Crack **U11**-20
Cranium **U28**-7
C-Region U84-2
Creme **U9**-8
Crepitatio **U106**-14; **U111**-9
Crescendo-Angina U124-11
– Decrescendo-Geräusch U110-3
– TIA U124-11
CRH U55-9
Crista **U28**-5
– iliaca U28-5; U129-12; U130-9
– mitochondrialis **U83**-7
– occipitalis U28-8
– pubica U30-14
– sphenoidalis U28-8
– ampullaris U60-10
Crossing-over **U83**-14; **U84**-17
Cross-match **U136**-10
Crossover **U83**-14; **U101**-14
Crossover-Studie U101-14
Crus cerebri U41-2
– clitoridis U50-12
Crush-Intubation U123-10
Crusta **U114**-8
CT **U55**-8; U99-19
Cubitus (valgus) **U23**-4
Cuff (Tubus) U7-10; U17-8
Cupula cochleae U60-11
– pleurae U43-11
Curare **U93**-17
Curvatura (major/minor) U45-8
Cuspis **U32**-10
– dentis **U26**-4
– septalis U86-15
Cutis anserina U56-14; U105-8
– laxa U56-1
Cutoff **U100**-24
Cyanat U91-9
Cyanid **U91**-9

Cyanidantidot-Therapieausrüstung U91-9
Cyanidvergiftung U91-9
Cyankali(um) U91-9
Cyanocobalamin U91-9
Cyanverbindung U91-9
Cyanwasserstoff U91-9
cyclo-AMP U78-6
cyclo-GMP U83-17
Cysteinreste U84-3
Cystinausstrom, lysosomaler U83-6
C-Zellen U55-8
C-Zellkarzinom U55-8

D

D cur U121-7
Dach, knöchernes (Paukenhöhle) U60-4
Dachziegelverband U141-11
Dacryocystitis U58-9
DAI U70-2
Damenbinde U1-5; U140-19
Damm **U22**-10; **U52**-20; U50-1
Dämmerschlaf U74-19
Dämmerungssehen U59-9
Dämmerzustand **U74**-19; **U7**-1
Dammfistel U22-10; U52-20
Dammgegend U22-10
Dammmuskulatur U22-10
Dammnaht **U71**-18; U52-20
dämmrig **U59**-11
Dammriss U52-20; U71-18
Dammschnitt **U71**-18
Dammschutz U22-10
Dammverletzung U63-5
Dampf **U82**-3; U105-14; U127-15
Dampfbad **U1**-17; U142-20
dampfdurchlässig U88-6
Dämpfe U93-10
–, giftige U82-3; U91-4
–, stechend riechende U62-5
dämpfen **U19**-5; **U59**-11; **U88**-14
– (Stimme) U66-11
– (Symptome) **U12**-5; **U61**-11
dämpfend **U77**-17
Dampfinhalation U44-2
Dampfsterilisation U139-2
Dampfsterilisator U82-3
Dämpfung, perkutorische U107-8
Darm **U45**-9; U9-6; U46-13; U47-13
– spülen U93-1
–, träger U45-9
Darmadhäsionen U128-15; U134-10
Darmauskleidung U86-8
Darmbakterien U45-1,9; U90-6
Darmbein **U28**-22; U45-12
Darmbeingrube U87-26
Darmbeinkamm U28-5; U129-12
Darmbeinstachel U28-5
–, vorderer U28-22
Darmblutung U45-1
Darmdrüsen U45-1
Darmegel U90-17

Darmentleerung **U46**-18 f; U45-9
–, präoperative **U134**-6
Darmerkrankung U94-18
–, entzündliche U94-1
Darmflora **U46**-16,10; U45-1,9
Darmgas U45-9; U46-10; U109-7
Darmgeräusche **U46**-14; U45-9; U61-3
–, hochfrequente U46-14; U109-6
Darmgift U91-4
Darminfarzierung U124-11
Darminhalt U45-1; U46-14
Darmkolik U109-14
Darmlähmung **U109**-6
Darmlumen U87-22
Darmmotilität, gesteigerte U46-10
Darmnadel U132-5
Darmparasit U90-13
Darmpolyp U98-1
–, villöser U45-14
Darmprotozoon U90-2
Darmreinigung U46-19; U91-26; U118-10; U134-6
Darmrohr U45-1; U46-10
Darmsäfte **U46**-10; U45-1; U54-9
Darmschleimhaut U45-9; U86-17
Darmschlinge(n) U45-1,9; U46-10
–, gasgefüllte U109-7
Darmspülung U46-19; U118-10; U127-17; U134-6
Darmtätigkeit U79-16
Darmträgheit **U109**-6; U45-15
Darmtraining U46-19
Darmverschlingung **U109**-6; U45-9
Darmverschluss **U109**-6; U45-12
Darmwind **U46**-15
Darmzotten **U45**-14,1; U35-10
Darreichungsform **U9**-6
darstellen **U59**-7; **U87**-9; **U99**-12,14
Darstellung **U126**-7; U128-1
– (OP-Feld) U131-11
–, endoskopische U128-2
–, grafische U61-6; **U100**-27
–, zystoskopische U118-11
darüberschieben (Trokar) U133-10,12
darunterliegend U129-11
Datei U101-15
Daten, anamnestische U102-4
Datenbank U101-15
Datenerhebung U101-15
Datenmaterial **U101**-15
Datenschutz U101-15
Dauerausscheider U94-4; U119-10
Dauerdialyse U125-21
Dauerdrainage U140-15
Dauerelastizität U31-16
Dauererektion U53-3
Dauerinfusion U135-16,19
Dauerkanüle U125-18
Dauerkatheter **U125**-20; U127-19; U136-3
Dauerkontraktion U31-1
Dauerlauf **U65**-14
Dauermedikation U9-1; U121-3
Dauerschaden U6-11

Dauerschwindel U113-6
Dauerträger U94-4
Dauertropfinfusion U136-1,3
Dauerzug U141-3
Daumen U23-7
Daumenlutschen U46-2
Daumenluxation U5-20
davontragen (Verletzung) **U4**-3
D-Dimer U81-6
Deafferenzierung **U40**-4
deaktivieren **U83**-18
dealen U11-1
Dealer(in) U11-1
Debilität U77-22
Debranching enzyme U78-10
Debridement **U140**-12
Debulking U97-2
decarboxyliert U78-7
Decidua **U85**-13
decken (Kosten) U18-15
Deckerinnerung U74-8
Decklappen **U130**-18
Deckschicht **U86**-8; **U129**-9
Decussatio pedunculorum cerebellarium rostralium U41-14
– pyramidum **U41**-14
DEET-haltig U91-8
Defäkation **U46**-18
Defäkationsreflex U46-18
Defekt **U142**-4
Defektheilung U4-16
Defeminisierung **U50**-2
Deferveszenz **U105**-18
Defibrillation **U6**-14; **U123**-12
Defibrillator **U110**-7; **U123**-12
Defibrillatorelektroden U123-12
Defibrillatorpaddel U123-12
defibrillieren **U123**-12
Defibrinierung **U38**-14
Defibrinierungssyndrom U38-14
Definitivwirt U90-13
Defizit **U78**-21; **U142**-4
Deformation **U142**-7
Deformität **U142**-7; **U89**-5
Degeneration **U89**-29
–, hepatolentikuläre U91-19
–, striatonigrale U41-10
–, vakuoläre U83-11
degenerativ **U89**-29
Deglutition **U46**-2
dehnbar **U31**-10; **U107**-16; **U109**-8; **U110**-16
Dehnbarkeit U82-6
– (Lunge) **U44**-10
Dehnen **U1**-13; **U31**-3; **U36**-11; U63-3
Dehner **U132**-17
Dehnsonde **U132**-17
Dehnung **U36**-11; **U141**-3
–, übermäßige U31-3
Dehnungsreflex U31-3
Dehnungsrezeptor U31-3; U57-10
Dehnungsübung(en) **U1**-13; U31-3
Dehydratation **U6**-15; **U78**-22
–, hypernatriämische U56-12

Dehydratation, hypertone U36-8; U56-12
–, isotone U56-12; U78-22
dehydratisieren **U56**-12
dehydrieren **U82**-9
dehydriert **U56**-12; **U78**-22,21; U49-8
Dehydroepiandrosteron **U55**-16
Dehydrogenase U82-9
Deja-vu-Erlebnis **U74**-18
Dekalzifikation **U27**-22
Dekalzifizierung **U31**-14
Dekompression, chirurgische U6-17
–, operative U125-17
Dekompressionskammer U6-17; U125-17
Dekompressionskrankheit **U6**-17; U125-17
dekomprimieren **U125**-17
Dekontamination **U91**-23
dekontaminieren **U91**-23
Dekubitalgeschwür U5-5; U19-3; U89-17
Dekubitus **U63**-7; U4-6 ; U18-13 ; U23-12
Dekubitusprophylaxe U6-22
Dekurs, täglicher U102-13
Deletion **U84**-23
Deletionsmutante U84-23
Deletionssyndrom U84-23
Delikt U20-13
Delir, rasendes U10-14
–, toxisches U10-14
delirant **U10**-14
deliriös **U10**-14
Delirium **U7**-16
– acutum U10-14
– tremens **U10**-14
Deltamuskel **U30**-13
Demand-Schrittmacher U123-13
Demarkation **U87**-10
Demastikation **U27**-19
dement **U77**-15,23
Dementia **U77**-23
Demenz **U77**-23
–, senile U77-23; U80-13
Demenzprozess U77-23
Demonstration **U107**-17
Demulzenzium **U92**-30
Demütigung U68-17
Demyelinisation/-sierung **U40**-14
Demyelinisierungsherde U40-14
denaturiert U37-6
Dendrit **U40**-2
dendritisch **U40**-2
Denervierung **U42**-1
Denkaufgabe U41-1
Denken **U73**-6 ff, 1 f; U77-20
Denkvermögen U73-5,1; U10-14
Dens **U26**-1
– axis U28-19
– caninus **U26**-5
– incisivus **U26**-3
– molaris **U26**-7
– praemolaris **U26**-6

Dens, serotinus **U26**-8
Dentalfluorose U82-22
Dentes **U26**-1
Dentin **U26**-16
Dentinkanälchen U26-16
Dentinoblasten U26-16
Dentitio difficilis U27-3
– praecox U27-1
– tarda U27-1
Dentition **U27**-1
Denudation **U114**-13
Depigmentierung **U114**-3
–, fleckenförmige U56-7
Depletion **U49**-8; **U78**-21; **U88**-15
Depolarisation **U42**-6; U92-20
Depolarisationsausbreitung U42-6
Depolarisationsblock U42-6
Depolarisationsphase U42-6
Depolarisationswelle(nfront) U32-5
depolarisieren **U42**-6
Depotfett U24-5
Depotinsulin U55-12
Depotpräparat U9-3; U121-4
Depression **U76**-22; **U77**-17
–, agitierte U76-8; U77-17
–, endogene U77-17; U88-10
–, lähmende U71-22
–, larvierte U77-17; U117-13
–, maskierte U76-22; U77-17
–, neurotische U77-17
–, postpartale U76-22; U77-17
–, psychotische U77-17
–, reaktive U71-22; U76-22; U77-17
–, saisonale U76-22
depressiv **U76**-22; **U77**-17
deprimiert **U71**-22; **U76**-22; **U77**-17
Deprivation **U77**-11
–, sensorische U57-7; U77-11
–, visuelle U77-11
Deprivationssyndrom U77-11
derb U32-12; U56-4
Dercum-Krankheit U24-9; U56-5
Derivat **U81**-18; **U85**-11
Derivatio **U81**-18
dermal **U56**-1
Dermatiaceae U90-18
Dermatitis **U114**-1; U56-3
– herpetiformis U96-10
–, seborrhoische U56-8
Dermatochalasis U56-1
Dermatologe/-login **U15**-10
Dermatologie **U15**-10
Dermatom **U85**-22
– (Instrument) **U56**-3
Dermatophyt U90-18
Dermatose U15-10; U114-1
Dermatozoenwahn U77-20
Dermis **U56**-3
Dermislappen **U130**-6
Dermoid(zyste) **U98**-17,16
Dermoid, epibulbäres U98-17
Dermoidexzision **U98**-17
Desaminase **U47**-16
Desaminierung **U82**-17,15; U81-15

Desaminierung, oxidative U81-17
desaturiert **U81**-24
Desaturierung **U81**-24
Desensibilisierung U39-23
–, biochemische U81-12
Desensibilisierungsspritze U122-4
Desialotransferrin U37-6
Design, faktorielles **U101**-13
Designerdroge U11-17
Desinfektion **U17**-15; U131-19
–, chirurgische **U139**-6
–, high-level U17-15
–, präoperative U139-5f
Desinfektionslösung U17-15
Desinfektionsmittel **U17**-15; U82-13; U92-2; U139-5
Desinfiziens **U17**-15
desinfizieren **U17**-15; **U139**-5f
Desinteresse, sexuelles U77-8
Desmodont U26-13; U30-6
Desorientiertheit **U7**-8; **U107**-12; U72-17
Desorientierung, persönliche U77-4
Desoxycholsäure U47-12
Desoxycortisol, 11- **U55**-10
desoxygeniert **U44**-6
Desoxyribonuklease **U84**-11
Desoxyribonukleinsäure **U84**-11
Desoxyribonukleotid U84-12
Desquamativpneumonie U56-20; U94-14
Destillat **U82**-8
Destillation **U82**-8,13
destruktives Verhalten U5-19
Desufflationshebel **U133**-15
Detektion **U102**-13
Detergens **U81**-16,2
–, anionisches U81-11
Determinante **U39**-7; **U117**-2
–, antigene **U39**-7
–, isotypische U39-7
Detonation **U6**-9
detorquieren **U31**-7
Detoxi(fi)kation **U91**-23
Detrusor **U48**-11
–, hyperreflexiver **U112**-8; U48-11
Detrusorareflexie U112-8
Detrusorhyperaktivität U48-11; U112-8
Detrusorinstabilität **U112**-8; U48-11
Detrusorinsuffizienz U48-11
Detrusorspasmus U112-8
Detrusor-Sphinkter-Dyssynergie U48-11; U112-8
Detumeszenz **U53**-5
Deuterium U82-9
deutlich **U57**-2,4; **U87**-12; **U102**-2; **U117**,5
– artikuliert **U66**-1
– erhöht U37-10
– sprechen U66-8
Deutschländerfraktur U65-14
deviant **U68**-15
Devianz U75-3
Deviation conjugae U59-15

Deviation, sexuelle **U68**-15,1
devital (Zahn) U26-1
Dexpanthenol U82-13
Dextroamphetamin U11-17
Dextrose **U79**-7
Dezelerationstrauma U124-19
Dezerebrationshaltung U63-1
Dezidua **U85**-13; U51-7
Deziduaanteile, abgestoßene U85-13
Deziduaplatte U85-13
Deziduaschicht U85-13
Deziduaseptum U85-13
Dezile **U100**-11
DHEA **U55**-16
DHT U55-16
Diabetes mellitus Typ I **U55**-12
– –, insulinabhängiger U55-12
– –, Typ II/juveniler U119-5
–, instabiler juveniler U31-16
Diabetiker(in) **U124**-7; U4-3
–, fettleibige(r) U24-9
Diabetikerin, schwangere U70-5
diabetisch **U124**-7
Diacetylmorphin **U11**-19
Diacylglycerol U82-13
Diagnose **U117**-11
– stellen **U117**-10
Diagnosestellung, bei U117-11
Diagnostik **U20**-8; **U117**-11; **U134**-1
–, bildgebende U20-8; U117-11
–, zytologische U83-1
Diagnostikleuchte **U17**-4; U59-10
diagnostizieren **U117**-10
Diagramm **U102**-12; **U100**-27
Dialysat **U125**-21
Dialyse **U125**-21
Dialysebehandlung U125-21
Dialyseeinheit U14-1
Dialyseenzephalopathie U77-23
Dialysegerät **U125**-21
Dialysemembran U125-21
Dialysepatient(in) U125-21
Dialyseprogramm U14-1
Dialysestation U14-7; U125-21
Dialysierlösung U125-21
Diamorphin **U11**-19
Diaphanoskop **U99**-16
Diaphanoskopie **U99**-16
Diaphoretikum **U56**-10; **U105**-15
Diaphragma **U43**-12; **U69**-9
– pelvis **U48**-15; U52-20
– urogenitale **U48**-15; U52-1,13
diaphragmatisch **U43**-12
Diaphyse **U28**-3
Diarrhoe/-ö **U109**-10
–, chologene U47-10
Diarthrose **U29**-3,1
Diastole **U33**-3
diastolisch **U33**-3
Diät **U2**-12; **U120**-5
–, blande U62-7
–, cholesterinsenkende U47-12
–, salzarme U82-5
–, strenge U24-1

Diätassistent(in) U16-10,13
Diätempfehlung U2-12; U18-4
Diätetik **U16**-13
Diätetiker(in) **U16**-13
diätetisch **U16**-13
Diathermie **U127**-9
Diathermiehäkchen **U128**-11
Diathermieschlinge **U127**-11,7; U132-9
Diathermiestift U127-9
Diathese, hämorrhagische U38-8
Diätkost U16-13
Diätplan **U16**-13
Diätspezialist(in) **U16**-13
Diätvorschrift **U16**-13; U121-1
Diazoverbindung U81-2
dichotom (Variable) U100-5,19
dicht **U82**-6
Dichte **U82**-8; U81-3
–, radiologische U82-8
Dichtegradientenzentrifugation U83-20
Dichtheit **U82**-6
Dichtungsmittel U82-30; **U137**-11
dick **U24**-8
dickbäuchig **U22**-4
Dickdarm **U45**-15,9
Dickdarmflora U46-16
Dickdarmkrebs U97-6
Dickdarmreinigung U45-15
dickhäutig U56-1
Diele U67-13
Diencephalon **U41**-12
Dienst **U15**-3; U17-17
–, im **U20**-4; U17-16
–, sozialmedizinischer U13-3
dienstälter **U80**-13; U15-2
dienstfrei **U20**-4
diensthabend **U20**-4; U16-14; U131-6
Dienstplan U15-2
dienzephal **U41**-12
Differentialdiagnose **U117**-15,11
differenzieren **U85**-11; **U97**-8; **U117**-15
differenziert, vollständig U97-8
Differenzierung **U85**-11; **U97**-8
– (Spermien) **U53**-8
Differenzierungscluster U84-2
Differenzierungsgrad U97-8
Differenzierungsmuster U97-8
diffundieren **U88**-4
Diffusion **U81**-21; **U88**-4
Diffusionsbarriere U88-4
diffusionsfähig **U88**-4
Diffusionskapazität U88-4
Diffusionskoeffizient U88-4
Diffusionskonstante U88-4
Diffusionsstörung U88-4
Diffusionstest U88-4
Diffusionsvermögen U92-4
Digestion **U46**-11
digestiv **U46**-11
Digestivum **U46**-11
digital **U23**-7
Digitalanzeige U125-6
Digitalkamera U133-3
Digitalthermometer U105-6

Diglyzerid U82-13
Dihydrat U82-9
Dihydrocholesterin U78-16
Dihydrotestosteron U55-16
Dilatation U36-11
- (Sinusoide) U47-4
Dilatationsbesteck U133-12
Dilatationsbougie U132-17
Dilatator U132-17; U133-12
dilatieren U36-11
diluieren U36-13; U81-23
Dilution U81-23; U116-17
Dilutionsazidose U81-23
Dimer U81-6
Dimerisation U81-6
Dimerisierung U81-6
Dimethylketon U82-12
Dinukleotid U84-12
Diphallus U52-14
Diphtherie U95-9
diphtherieähnlich U95-9
Diphtherieantitoxin U95-9; U122-8
Diphtheriebakterien U95-9
Diphtherieimpfstoff U95-9
Diphtherietoxin U95-9; U122-8
Diphtherietoxoid U95-9; U122-8
Diphtheroid U95-9
diphtheroid/-isch U95-9
Diplegia facialis U113-7
diploid U84-9
Diplomkrankenpfleger U15-8; U142-29
Diplom-Krankenschwester U16-4f,3; U15-8; U131-6; U142-29
Diplopie U113-11; U58-16; U59-4
-, monokulare U59-16
Disaccharid U79-6
Discus intervertebralis U28-19; U29-12
- nervi optici U58-14
Disinhibition U88-14
Disk-Elektrophorese U84-35
Diskrepanz U18-10
-, negative (US-Befund) U70-10
-, positive U70-10
Diskriminanzanalyse U100-28
Diskriminationsschwelle U61-7
Diskushernie U89-22
Diskusruptur U124-15
Dislokation U64-4; U5-20; U106-4
dislozieren (Fraktur) U5-20; U106-4
disom U84-25
Disomie U84-25
Dispergens U81-22
dispergieren U81-22
Dispermie U69-12
Dispersion U81-22
Dispersionsfähigkeit U81-16
Dispersionsmittel U81-22
Dispersum U81-22
Disposition U75-4; U119-1
-, familiäre U89-7
Dissektion U87-5; U126-12
disseminiert U89-27
Disse-Räume U47-4
Dissimilation U88-8

dissimilieren U88-8
Dissoziation U81-22
Dissoziationskonstante U81-22
dissoziieren U81-22
distal U87-14; U26-21
Distantia sacropubica U28-20
Distanz U76-15; U77-8
Distanzeinschätzung U9-18
distanziert U76-15; U77-8
Distanzring U133-10
Distickstoffoxid U93-11; U82-11,16
Distorsion U5-16
distrahieren U141-3
Diurese U92-21
-, beschleunigte U55-24
-, forcierte U49-6; U55-24
-, osmotische U49-6,9; U81-21
-, verstärkte U49-6
diuresefördernd U49-6
Diuretikum U49-6; U92-21
-, kaliumsparendes U49-6; U82-18
diuretisch U49-6
divalent U81-10,5
Divergenz U59-13
dizygot U85-2
DL U91-11
DNA U84-11
- (Bio)synthese U84-11
-, mitochondriale U83-7
- Bindemotiv U84-3
- Bindungsdomäne U84-3
- Doppelstrang U84-11
- Fragment, doppelsträngiges U39-3
- Klonierung U84-33
- Matrize U84-11
- Polymerase U84-15
- Reparatur U84-11
- Replikation U84-11
- Sequenz, cis-aktive regulatorische U83-10
- Sequenzierung U84-11
- Sonde U84-11
- Transfektion U84-39
DNR-Order U20-7
DNS U84-11 (siehe DNA)
Doktorarbeit U15-1
Doktorat U15-1
Doktortitel U15-1
Dokumentation U101-15
Dokumentationsassistent(in), med. U15-6; U16-10; U20-5; U102-12
Domäne, funktionelle U84-3
dominant U84-27
Dominanz U84-27
Donovan-Körperchen U96-6
Donovanosis U96-6
Dopamin U42-11
Dopaminantagonist U42-11
Dopaminaufnahme (Striatum) U41-10
Dopamindepletion U42-11
Dopaminentleerung U42-11
dopaminerg U40-8; U92-3
Dopaminvorstufe U42-11; U119-4
dopen U11-1

Doping U11-24
Dopingbestimmungen U11-24
Dopingkommission U11-24
Dopingkontrolle U11-24
Dopingmittel U11-24
Dopingtest U11-24
Dopingvergehen U11-24
Dopingvorwürfe U11-24
Doppelbilder U41-12; U58-16; U59-5
- sehen U59-1
Doppelbindung U79-11; U81-24
-, C=C- U82-15
-, konjugierte U81-9
Doppelblindversuch U101-9
Doppelgänger(in) U67-8
Doppelgängerillusion U73-10
Doppelhandschuhe U139-17
Doppelhelix U84-11
Doppel-J-Schiene/Stent U125-20
- - Ureterkatheter U125-20
Doppelkinn U21-6
Doppelkontrastarthrogramm U118-23
Doppelkontrastdarstellung U99-3
Doppelläppchen U60-2
doppellumig (Drain) U140-15
Doppelmissbildung U70-14
Doppelschlinge U138-4
Doppelspekulum U17-6
Doppelstrangbruch U84-24
Doppeltsehen U113-11; U41-12; U59-4
Doppler-Stethoskop U17-2
- Ultraschall U118-17
Dorn U22-12; U28-5; U141-15
dornförmig U28-19
Dornfortsatz U28-5,19
dorsal U22-11; U87-16
Dorsalflexion U87-16
Dorsum U22-11; U87-16
dösen U72-2; U131-2
Dosieraerosol U9-6
Dosierinhalator U44-2; U92-14
Dosierung U121-7; U9-17
Dosierungsschema U120-5
Dosierungsvorschriften U107-3
Dosimetrie U99-9
Dosis U121-7
-, duldbare wöchentliche U91-18
-, genetisch signifikante U99-9
-, kleinste tödliche U91-11
-, letale U91-11; U12-2
-, suprapysiologische U88-1
-, tödliche U12-2
-, toxische U91-4
-, unwirksame U91-18
dosisabhängig U121-7
Dosisäquivalent U121-7; U99-9
Dosistitration U81-23
Dosisverteilung U99-9
Dosis-Wirkungs-Kurve U121-7
Dotter U85-7; U51-5
Dottergang U71-17; U85-7
Dottersack U85-7; U71-17
Dottersackmembran U85-7
Dottersacktumor U85-7

Douglas-Punktion U118-8; U125-17
Douglas-Raum **U50**-15; U45-16
Douglasskopie U50-15
Down-beat-Nystagmus U113-12
Down-Regulation U54-3
Down-Syndrom U84-25
DPT-Auffrischung U122-10
– Boosterung U122-10
– Impfstoff **U122**-10
– Teilimpfung U122-10
– Vakzine **U122**-10
Dragee U9-7
Drahtbogen U137-3
–, kieferorthopädischer U141-14
Drahtcerclage U137-19
drahtig **U25**-5
Drahtleiterschiene U141-7
drahtlos U17-17
Drahtnaht U141-14
Drahtosteosynthese **U141**-14
Drahtsäge U141-14
Drahtschlinge U127-11; U132-9
Drahtschneideschere U132-4
Drahtumschlingung **U141**-14
Drain **U36**-6; **U140**-15
Drainagerohr U140-15
drainieren **U36**-6
Drang **U11**-2; **U112**-4; **U73**-11; U72-1
–, unwiderstehlicher U77-19
drängen **U11**-2; **U64**-12; **U65**-15; **U112**-4; **U73**-11
Dranginkontinenz U112-4; U119-2
–, sensorische U112-15
Draufsetzen, Spielzeug zum U63-5
Drehbewegung U31-7,18; U64-1
Drehbruch U106-1
drehen, (sich) **U31**-7
–, auf die Seite **U64**-8
Drehfehlstellung U5-16
Drehnystagmus U113-12
Drehosteotomie U31-7
Drehschwindel U103-13; U113-6
Drehung **U31**-7; **U5**-16
Drehventil U133-8
Dreichip-Kamera U133-3
Dreiecksbein U28-17
Dreieckstuch U140-20; U141-8
Dreifachbindung U81-8
Dreifachschutzimpfung U122-10
Dreifachzucker U79-6
Dreigläserprobe U116-15
Dreikantspitze U132-7
Dreiphasenpille U69-7
dreist **U75**-18
Dreitagefieber **U95**-2 f
Dreitagefieberexanthem U114-2
Drillinge **U70**-14
Drill(übung) **U74**-6
dringend **U6**-18; **U112**-4
dringende Abklärung U126-5
Dringlichkeit **U6**-18; U8-19
Dritter-Ton-Galopp U33-6; U110-6
Droge **U9**-3
–, illegale **U11**-1

Droge, pflanzliche U9-2
drogenabhängig **U11**-3; U9-3
Drogenabhängige(r) **U11**-6,1
Drogenabhängigkeit U77-19
Drogenabstinenz U11-12
Drogenaufsichtsbehörde (USA) U11-7
Drogenberater(in) U11-1,7; U16-12; U18-4
Drogendealer(in) **U11**-7
Drogendelikte U11-1
Drogeneinfluss, (unter) **U11**-1,10
Drogenentzug U11-12
Drogenentzugsbehandlung U11-6
Drogengebrauch, intravenöser U11-3
Drogengebraucher(in), nichtabhängige(r) **U11**-6
Drogengewöhnung U11-5
Drogenhandel U11-1
Drogenhändler(in) **U11**-7,1
Drogenikterus U9-3
Drogenkartell U11-7
Drogenmissbrauch U11-1
Drogenrausch, (im) **U11**-10; U10-5
Drogenschmuggel U11-7
drogensüchtig U11-1
Drogensüchtige(r) **U11**-6
Drogentoter U9-3
Drogerie **U9**-4
Drogist **U9**-4 f
drohend U7-5
Drohgebärde U67-1
Drop-Anfall U64-15; U124-9
– out Rate U101-29
Drosselvene **U34**-11; U110-16
DRU U45-16
Druck **U6**-6; **U11**-2; **U64**-10,12
– mindern U140-19
–, arterieller U34-3
–, erhöhter intrakranieller U125-13
–, hydrostatischer U36-8
–, intrahepatischer U47-4
–, intraluminaler U34-14; U87-22
–, intraokularer U59-16
–, kolloidosmotischer U36-8; U78-18; U81-26
–, onkotischer U78-18
–, osmotischer U49-9; U81-21; U88-4
–, systolischer U33-3
–, zentralvenöser U36-8
Druckanstieg **U36**-9; U33-8; U116-19
Druckbelastung U33-10
druckdolent U45-6; U62-8; U97-3
Druckdolenz U109-12
druckempfindlich U76-4
Druckempfindung U57-17
drücken **U8**-11; **U64**-10,12
– (auf) **U113**-15
Druckfallkrankheit **U6**-17; U125-17
Druckgefälle U36-8
Druckgeschwür U5-5
Druckinfusion U136-1
Drucklähmung U6-6
Druckluft U44-12
druckluftarretiert U133-1

Druck(luft)manschette **U8**-8
Druckmesser U31-10
Druckmesssonde, intrakranielle **U125**-13,25
Druckmessungen U36-8
Drucknekrose U89-30
Druckpunktmassage U142-15
Druckrezeptor U57-10
Druckschmerz U60-14; **U104**-11; U107-7
druckschmerzhaft **U104**-11; U28-5
–, äußerst U23-10; U96-5
Druckschmerzhaftigkeit U102-2; U106-13
Druckspülung U127-17
Druckstelle (Gips) U89-17; U141-6
Druckstöße (auf Bauch) U8-11; U64-12
Druckverband U38-7; U91-14; U140-17
Druckverletzung **U6**-17
Drug targeting **U121**-4
Drusen, senile U80-13
Drüse **U54**-1
–, muköse U86-17
–, endokrine U54-1
–, exokrine U54-1
–, muköse U44-9; U54-1
–, tubuloalveoläre U52-10,13
Drüsenepithel U86-7
Drüsengewebe U40-6; U54-1; U98-4
DTA **U91**-18
DTPA U49-2
Dübel U141-15
Dubreuilh-Krankheit U56-7
Ductuli bilifori U47-6,11
Ductulus interlobularis U47-3
Ductus alveolaris U43-10
– arteriosus **U32**-11
– –, persistierender U32-11
– Botalli **U32**-11
– choledochus **U47**-9; U45-10
– cochlearis U60-11
– cysticus **U47**-8
– deferens **U52**-6,3
– ejaculatorius **U52**-11
– epididymidis U52-5
– excretorius U52-11
– hepaticus **U47**-6
– lactiferus U50-18; U71-25
– lymphaticus dexter **U35**-7
– nasolacrimalis U58-9
– omphaloentericus U71-17; U85-7
– pancreaticus U45-10; U47-10; U54-8
– paramesonephricus U85-21
– perilymphaticus U35-7; U60-11
– sudoriferus **U56**-11
– thoracicus **U35**-7
– utriculosaccularis U60-9
– vitellinus U85-7
Ductus-thoracicus-Drainage U35-7
Duft **U62**-1 ff
Duftstoff **U62**-3
Duftwolke **U62**-2
Duhring-Brocq-Krankheit U96-10
dulden **U75**-16

Dundee-Schiebeknoten U138-9
dunkel U59-11
Dünkel U75-20,12
dunkel(häutig) U25-12; U56-1
Dunkeladaptation U59-10; U88-17
Dunkelfeldmikroskopie U86-1
dünn U24-6,10; U87-9
Dünndarm U45-9; U47-17; U54-9
Dünndarmgekröse U45-7
Dünndarmpassage U105-16; U118-21
Dünndarmpassagezeit U46-8
Dünndarmresorption U88-8
Dünndarmröntgenaufnahmen U118-18
Dünndarmschleimhaut U86-17
dünnhäutig U76-4
Dünnschichtchromatographie U83-22
Dunst U82-3
Duodenalabstrich U45-10
Duodenum U45-10
Duplexsonografie, farbcodierte U118-17
Duplikation U84-23
Duplikaturnaht U129-8
Dura (mater) U41-8
Duralsack U41-8
Durazerreißung U41-8
durchbeißen U27-11
Durchblutung U16-11; U36-5; U88-3
–, gute U36-6
durchbohren U6-7
durchbrechen U27-3; U26-23
Durchbruch U5-19
Durchbruchblutung U51-2; U55-17
durchdringen U6-7; U36-16; U88-6
durchdringend U62-5
durcheinander U77-4
Durchfall U109-10; U46-19
Durchflussrate U133-15
Durchflusszytometrie U83-21
durchführbar U74-6
durchführen U102-3
durchgängig U34-14; U127-19
Durchgängigkeit U34-14; U47-9
durchgebrochen (Zahn) U26-6
durchhalten U1-8
durchkommen U64-13
durchlässig U88-6
Durchlässigkeit U88-6
Durchleuchtung U99-16,8
Durchleuchtungsfeld U99-16
Durchleuchtungszeit U99-7
durchmachen U4-3; U57-4
Durchmesser U132-17
durchrütteln U64-7
durchschlafen U72-5
Durchschlafstörung U72-16
durchschneiden, quer U87-5; U126-14,9
durchschnittlich U100-10
Durchschuss U5-3; U6-8
Durchschwingen (Beine) U65-2
durchsehen U74-7; U102-8
Durchsickern U38-7
durchspülen U136-3
Durchspülung U127-17

durchstechen U17-11; U118-7; U5-10; U132-2
durchstehen U75-11
durchstoßen U132-2
durchströmen U36-5; U88-3; U136-1
Durchströmung U36-5; U88-3
durchtrainiert U1-9; U25-4
durchtränken U19-10
durchtrennen U87-5; U126-10,9; U137-5
– (Nabelschnur) U71-17
–, quer U126-14
durchtrennt U5-6; U130-13
Durchtrennung U87-5; U126-14; U128-11
Durchtritt U86-13
durchuntersuchen lassen, sich U18-9
Durchuntersuchung U134-1
durchwachsen U97-12
durchziehen U64-13
Duroziez-Zeichen/Doppelgeräusch U110-3
Durstfieber U105-3
durstig U2-11
Dusch(roll)stuhl U19-13
Duschhaube U1-19
Duschkopf U1-19
Duschraum U1-19
Duschvorhang U1-19
Düse (Dusche) U1-19
Düsenaerosolgerät U121-3
Dynamik U1-6
dynamisch U1-6
Dynamometer U142-16
Dysäquilibrium U57-18
Dysarthrie U113-10; U61-11; U66-9
dysarthrisch U113-10
Dysautonomie U40-6
Dysbalance, muskuläre U88-19
Dyschondroplasie U98-12
Dysenterie U90-7
–, bakterielle U94-18
dysenterisch U94-18
Dysfunktion U4-4
–, erektile U53-3
Dyslalie U66-20,17
Dysmenorrhoe/-ö U51-1
Dysmnesie, paramnestische U74-18
Dyspareunie U68-5
Dyspepsie U109-1
–, funktionelle U76-6
Dysphagie U109-5; U87-22; U113-10
–, oropharyngeale U45-2; U109-5
–, psychogene U77-5
–, sideropenische U109-5
Dysphasie U113-10
Dysphemie U66-20
Dysphonie U103-6; U66-23; U113-10
Dyspnoe U111-1; U44-4
–, paroxysmale nächtliche U111-1
–, schwere U111-2
dyspnoisch U111-1
Dyspraxie U113-9
Dysrhythmie U33-6; U110-6

Dyssomnie U72-16
Dyssynergie U31-4
Dystokie U4-4
Dystonie U142-17
Dysurie U112-1; U49-16

E

EAS U55-9
Ebene U87-2
Echo U118-15
Echoenzephalografie U118-15
Echokardiografie U118-15
Echokardiogramm U118-15
Echokinese U113-9
Echolalie U66-17
Echopraxie U113-9
Echorausch U11-9
Echtzeitsonografie U118-17
Eckpfeiler U117-16
Eckzahn U26-5
Eckzahnführung U26-5
Eckzahnspitze U26-5
Ecstasy-Tabletten U11-17
Ecstrophia cloacae U85-21
Edelgas U82-2; U129-20
Edelgasnarkose U135-6
Edelmetall U82-6
Edelstahlbolzen U65-13
EEG, isoelektrisches U7-18
EEG-Ableitungen U118-12
EEG-Assistent(in) U118-12
EEG-Befund U118-12
EEG-Registrierung U118-12
EEG-Überwachung U118-12
EEG-Veränderungen U118-12
Effektivität U101-26; U121-9
Efferenzen U40-4
Effizienz U101-26
Effleurage U71-10
Effusion, intraartikuläre U29-8
Egel U90-17
Egoismus U75-21
egoistisch U75-2,21
Egotrip U75-21
egozentrisch U75-21,2
Eheberatung U16-12; U18-4
Ehebruch U68-13
Ehekonflikt U77-12
Ehemündigkeit U80-9
ehrenamtliche(r) Helfer(in) U16-15
ehrgeizig U75-21
ehrlich U75-12 f
Ehrlichkeit U75-12
Ei U3-13; U51-5
Eichel U52-14
Eidotter U85-7
Eierstock U50-3; U54-11
Eierstockentfernung U50-3
Eierstockfixierung U50-3
Eifersuchtswahn U77-20
Eigelb U85-7
Eigelenk U23-11

eigen U39-21
Eigenanamnese U102-9
Eigenart U75-3
Eigenblut U37-1
Eigenblutkonserve U14-12
Eigenblutspende U136-9
Eigenbluttransfusion U136-8
Eigenlob U75-21
Eigenreflex U57-11
Eigenschaft(en) U89-6
–, hydrophile U81-13
–, immunmodulierende U97-18
–, suchtbildende U11-4
Eigensinn U75-19
eigensinnig U75-19
eigenständig U14-12
Eigentum, persönliches U75-1
Eigenwahrnehmung U57-14
eigenwillig U75-19,21; U73-3
Eihaut, innere U85-15
–, mittlere U85-16
Eihäute U71-6; U85-1
Eihautretention U71-6
Eihülle U51-5
Eile U65-15
Eileiter U50-4; U69-4,12,18; U70-1; U85-3
Eileiterentfernung U69-3
Eileiterentzündung U50-4
Eileiterplastik U69-4
Eileiterschwangerschaft U50-4; U70-6
eilen U65-15
Einäscherung U12-16
einatmen U44-2 f; U92-14
–, tief U44-1
Einatmen, beim U44-3
Einatmung U44-3
einbauen U78-5
Einbildung U75-20; U73-9 f
einblasen U128-10
eindeutig, nicht U116-23; U117-4
eindringen U94-2; U97-12
– (Penis) U68-2
– (Zona pellucida) U70-1
Eindringtiefe U99-9
eineiig (Zwillinge) U130-4
einengen U6-6; U36-11; U113-15
Einengung U6-6; U89-19; U113-15
einfädeln (Naht) U132-5; U138-1,12
Einfall U73-8
einfallen U74-1
einfältig U74-1
einfangen U139-16
einfetten U17-14
Einfluss U106-6
– ausüben U64-19
einfühlsam U76-4
Einfühlungsvermögen U76-4
einführen U9-12
– (Tubus) U135-17
Eingangshalle U67-13
eingebildet U75-20; U77-20; U73-9
eingebuchtet U37-9
eingefallen U25-7

eingehüllt U139-3
eingekapselt U29-9
eingekeilt U109-15; U47-8
eingeklemmt U6-12; U36-6
eingerichtet U28-1
eingeschlossen U111-6; U8-3
eingeschränkt U7-11
eingeschüchtert U75-17
eingestehen U102-10
eingestuft U97-14
eingestülpt U85-12
eingewachsen U80-3
Eingeweide U45-9; U86-21; U87-13
Eingeweidemuskulatur U30-2
Eingeweideprolaps U86-21
Eingeweidevorfall U140-16
Eingeweidewurm U90-16
eingewendet U137-16
eingipsen U141-6
eingreifen U20-11
Eingriff U20-11; U134-6; U127-5
–, ambulanter U18-1; U20-8; U69-3
–, chirurgischer U126-3,1 f; U20-8
–, explorativer U107-6; U118-1
–, pelviskopischer U128-4
–, therapeutischer U20-11; U101-27
Einhaltung U120-15
–, strikte U74-16
einheilen (Transplantat) U130-21
Einheit, katalytische U81-16
–, koloniebildende U139-10
–, motorische U42-13
einhergehen mit U7-5; U89-3
einhüllen U86-8; U85-15
einhüllendes Mittel U92-30
Einkapselung U97-9
Einkeilung U29-14; U106-6
einklemmen U62-11; U113-15
Einklemmung (Augenmuskel) U58-16
Einlage U112-15 f
Einlauf U45-16; U121-3; U131-15
Einlaufgerät U139-2
einlegen (Spirale) U69-10
einleiten (Geburt) U55-23; U71-3
– (Narkose) U135-13
Einleitung U120-10
Einleitungsschema U135-13
einliefern, ins Krankenhaus U14-1
Einlieferung U20-1
Einlochkollimator U99-6
Einmal-Abdecktücher U139-4
Einmalhandschuhe U139-4,17
Einmalinstrument U133-1
Einmalklipapplikator U138-16
Einmalskalpell U132-3
Einmalspritze U17-10
Einmaltrokar U133-5
Einnahme (Medikament) U2-1; U121-7; U92-12
–, absichtliche U46-1
Einnässen U112-16
–, nächtliches U112-7
einnehmen (Haltung) U65-3
– (Mahlzeit) U2-1

einnicken U67-3; U72-2
einnisten, sich U70-3
Einnistung U70-3; U85-2
Einnistungsstörung U70-3
einordnen (örtl./zeitl.) U74-3
einpendeln bei, sich U116-16
einpflanzen U130-1
Einphasenpille U69-7
einpinseln U139-5
einprägen U74-8 f
einpudern U9-9
Einreibemittel U9-10
einrichten (Fraktur) U140-2,4; U141-1 f
– (Körperhaltung) U1-18
Einrichtung (Fraktur) U141-2; U106-1
Einrichtungen, medizinische U14-3
–, sanitäre U1-5; U14-3
Einriss U5-19,7; U58-12
Einsatz, freiwilliger U16-15
–, körperlicher U64-19
–, voller U75-11
einsatzbereit U7-2; U8-7
Einsatzfahrzeug U6-3
Einsatzleiter(in) U8-9; U6-1
–, ärztliche(r) U16-9
Einsatzmeldung U8-9
Einsatzzeichen U74-2
einsaugen U46-2
einschätzen U74-4; U117-2,18; U73-6
Einschätzung U117-2; U75-15
–, vernünftige U117-18
Einscheiden U129-8
einschicken (Harn) U116-15
einschieben (Patient) U18-3
einschlafen U72-5 f
einschläfern U7-13; U135-1
Einschlafstörung U72-16
Einschläge U6-9
einschleifen U27-18
einschließen U44-9; U139-16
Einschluss, vakuolisierter U83-11
Einschlusskonjunktivitis U58-4
Einschlusskörperchen U86-20
Einschlusskörperchenkrankheit U96-11
Einschlusskriterien U100-3
Einschlusszyste, epidermale U56-2; U98-17
einschmelzen U82-7
einschmieren U17-14
Einschneiden (Geburt) U71-15
einschneiden U5-6; U126-9
Einschnitt U5-6; U126-9
einschnürend U111-17
Einschnürung U6-6; U89-19
–, primäre U84-7
einschränken U77-26; U89-4
Einschränkung U77-26; U100-16
Einschüchterung U68-17
einsehen U59-1
einsetzen (Mittel) U8-5
– (Wehen) U71-3
Einsetzen (kryokonservierter Embryo) U69-16
einsetzend U119-5

Einsicht U73-5
einsilbig U66-12
Einspeicherung U74-9
einspritzen U122-4
einstechen (Nadel) U118-7; U17-11
einstellen U59-17
Einstellung U65-3; U75-3; U76-3
– (Augen) U59-14
–, gesunde U1-2
–, lockere U76-19
–, negative U75-3
Einstich U6-7; U136-2; U5-10
– (Fingerbeere) U62-11
Einstichstelle U17-11; U132-5; U136-2
– (Trokar) U133-5
Einströmen U36-5
einstudieren U74-6
einstülpen, (sich) U85-12
Einstülpung U31-8; U85-12; U83-15
Eintauchbad U19-10
Eintauchen U88-5; U91-24
eintragen (Daten) U20-5; U102-12
einträufeln U128-10; U136-1; U9-11
eintreten (für) U67-7
– (in) U87-7
Eintritt (VKT in d. Beckeneingang) U71-14
Eintrittspforte U91-16; U47-5
Eintrittsstelle U91-16
einüben U74-6
Einvernehmen, gutes U102-16; U18-8
einwachsen (Knochen) U130-8
einwärtsdrehen U31-8f
Einwärtsdrehung U31-8f
Einwärtsgang U23-14
Einwärtsschielen U59-4,13
Einweg- U139-4
Einweg-Butterfly-Nadel U136-6
Einweginstrument U133-1
Einwegspritze U17-10
Einweichen U19-10; U142-20
einweisen, ins Krankenhaus U14-1
Einweisung U20-1; U14-4
Einweisungsdiagnose U117-11
Einweisungsgrund U20-1
Einweisungsindikation, Überprüfung der U18-10
einwertig U81-10
einwickeln U140-24,17,20
einwilligen U18-11
Einwilligung(serklärung) U134-3; U20-8
Einwilligung, aufgeklärte U101-4
Einwilligungsformular U134-3
Einwohner U100-8
Einzapfung U29-14
Einzeldosis U121-7
Einzeldosisampullen U9-13
Einzeldosispackung U9-16
Einzelfaserelektromyografie U118-13
Einzelgabe U121-7
Einzelknopfnaht U137-15; U128-18
Einzellaut U66-12
Einzeller, tierischer U90-2
Einzelniere U48-2
Einzelpflege U14-7

Einzelschlinge U138-4
Einzelspender-Thrombozytenkonzentrat U136-15
einzelstehend U89-3; U114-10
Einzelstrangbruch U84-24
Einzelstrang-DNA U84-11
einzelsträngig U90-10
Einzelzimmer U19-2
Einziehung U64-13; U111-5
– (Zahn) U26-3
Eis, zerstoßenes U64-10
Eisabreibung U142-21
Eisbehandlung U142-21
Eisbeutel U142-21
Eischips U142-21
Eisen U82-21; U79-17
–, zweiwertiges U81-10; U82-21
Eisenbindungskapazität U37-6; U81-8
Eisendepot, retikuloendotheliales U35-12
Eisenfärbung U82-21
Eisenmangel U88-15
Eisenmangelanämie U38-4; U82-21
Eisenoxid U82-11
Eisenpool U82-21
Eisenpräparat U82-21
Eisenresorption U46-13
Eisenspeicher U78-20
Eisenspeicherkrankheit U82-21
Eisensulfat U82-24
Eisenüberladung U82-21
Eisenüberschuss U82-21
Eisenutilisation U82-21
Eisenvergiftung U47-16
Eisenverlust U88-15
Eisenverwertung U82-21
Eiserne Lunge U43-1; U123-9
Eispackung U140-24; U142-21
Eisprung U51-9
Eistauchbad U142-21
Eiswasserspülung U91-26; U142-21
Eiswürfel U142-21
eitel U75-20
Eitelkeit U75-20
Eiter U89-12; U96-5; U140-14
Eiterableitung U89-12
Eiteransammlung U89-12; U117-3
Eiterbildung U89-12; U140-14
Eiterflechte U114-15
eitern U140-14; U96-5
Eiterung U89-12
eitrig U60-3; U96-8; U114-16
– serös U140-13
Eiweiß U79-9
Eiweißabbau U78-14,4,10; U46-11
eiweißabbauend U79-9
eiweißähnlich U78-18
Eiweißderivat, aufgereinigtes U81-18
Eiweißfäulnis U46-17
Eiweißquotient U78-18
Eizelle U50-3; U51-5; U86-2
–, befruchtete U85-2; U69-12; U70-1
–, kryokonservierte U69-14
– reife U51-5
Eizellenentnahme U69-16f; U51-5

Eizellengewinnung U69-16; U51-5
Eizellenspenderin U51-5; U84-10
Ejaculatio praecox U53-11
Ejakulat U53-11
–, blutiges U53-7
Ejakulation U53-11
Ejakulationsreflex U53-11
Ejakulationsstörung U53-11
Ejakulationsvolumen U53-11
ejakulieren U53-11
Ejektionsfraktion U33-8; U88-16
Ejektionsgeräusche U110-3
Ejektionsklick U33-8; U110-5
Ekchymose U89-27
ekelerregend U4-1; U103-11
EKG-Befund U118-14
– Gerät U118-14
– Registrierung U118-14; U125-6
Ekstase U76-16
ekstatisch U76-16
Ektoderm U85-6
Ektodermleiste U85-6
Ektoparasit U90-13
Ekzem U114-1
–, seborrhoisches U56-8
Ekzema flexurarum U114-1
ekzematös U114-1
Elastin U31-16; U86-5
elastisch U31-2,11,16
elastische Binde U140-20
– Ligatur U137-3
Elastizität U31-16; U86-5; U56-11
Elastolyse, generalisierte U56-1
elektiv U126-5
Elektiveingriff U20-8; U126-3,5; U134-6
Elektivoperation U6-18
elektrischer Strom U6-14
Elektrochirurgie U127-9
Elektrodesikkation U127-14
Elektrodiagnostik U142-23
Elektroenzephalogramm U118-12
Elektroheilschlaf U142-23
Elektrokardiogramm U118-14
Elektrokardiograph U118-14
Elektrokauterisation U6-14; U127-9
Elektrokoagulation U6-14
Elektrokonisation U127-12
Elektrokonvulsionstherapie U6-14; U142-23
Elektrokortikogramm U118-12
Elektrolyse U78-23
elektrolysieren U78-23
Elektrolyt U78-23
Elektrolytbestimmung U78-23; U116-7
Elektrolytentgleisung U78-23; U116-7
Elektrolytgleichgewicht U78-23
Elektrolythaushalt U116-7
–, gestörter U88-19
Elektrolytlösung U78-23; U81-25
Elektrolytmangel U78-23; U116-7
Elektrolyttherapie U78-23
Elektrolytverlust U78-21,23; U116-7
Elektrolytzusammensetzung U78-23; U116-7

Elektromassage U142-15
Elektromyografie (EMG) **U118**-13; U31-5
Elektromyografiebefund U118-13
elektromyografisches Aktivitätsmuster U118-13
Elektron **U81**-11
Elektronenakzeptor U81-11
Elektronendichte U81-11
Elektronendonator U81-11
Elektronenempfänger U81-11
Elektronenspender U81-11
Elektronenstrahl U81-11
Elektronenwolke U82-1
Elektroneurografie **U118**-13
Elektroneuromyografie U118-13
Elektronystagmografie U113-12
Elektroosmose U81-21
Elektrophorese **U84**-35
elektrophysiologisch U88-1
Elektroschlaftherapie U142-23
Elektroschock **U6**-14; **U123**-12; **U124**-4
Elektroschocktherapie U6-14
Elektrostimulation U88-12; U123-13
Elektrosyn(h)ärese U88-18
Elektrotherapie U142-23
elektrotonische Ausbreitung **U42**-3
Elektrotrauma U6-11,14
Elektrounfall **U6**-14
Elektrovaporisation U82-3
Element, (chemisches) **U82**-1
elementar **U82**-1
Elementarteilchen U82-1
elend **U76**-20; U75-8
Elimination U49-7; U92-1
Eliminationsgeschwindigkeit U91-17
Eliminationshalbwertszeit **U91**-17; U92-5
eliminieren **U49**-7
ELISA U116-3
Ellbogenfreiheit U23-4
Elle **U28**-16
Ellenbeuge U23-4; U28-6; U87-18,26
Ell(en)bogen U23-4; **U28**-16
Ellenbogengrube U23-4
Ellipsoidgelenk **U29**-6; U23-11
Elongation **U84**-19
Elongationsfaktor U84-19
Eltern(teil) **U84**-29
Elternallel U84-4
Eltern-Kind-Beziehung U18-8
– – Bindung U77-11
Eltor-Cholera U94-21
Eluat **U83**-20
Eluierung **U83**-20
Elution **U83**-20
Emanation U99-2
Embolektomie U38-12
Embolie **U38**-12
Embolisation U38-12
–, therapeutische **U124**-13
Embolus **U38**-12
–, septischer U38-12; U124-5
Embolusbildung **U124**-13

Embolusentfernung, operative U38-12
Embryo **U70**-4; **U85**-1
Embryoblast U85-5
embryonal **U70**-4; **U85**-1
Embryonalentwicklung U70-4; U85-1
Embryonalkarzinom U70-4
Embryonalperiode U70-4; U85-1
Embryonalrest U85-1
Embryonentransfer U70-4; U85-1
Embryonenübertragung U85-1
Embryopathia rubeolosa U95-3
Embryostellung U63-6
embryotoxisch **U91**-12; U92-33
Embryotoxizität **U91**-12; U85-1
Embryotoxizitätsprüfung U91-12
Embryotransfer **U69**-16
Emden-Meyerhof(-Parnas-Stoffwechsel)weg U78-14
Emesis **U103**-12
– gravidarum **U70**-12
Emetikum **U92**-12; **U103**-12; U91-25
emetisch **U103**-12
Eminentia U87-27
– intercondylaris (tibiae) U28-4
Emissionen, otoakustische U60-12
Emmetropie U59-6,17
Emollienzium **U92**-30
Emotion **U76**-1
emotional **U76**-1
emotionsgeladen U76-1
emotionslos **U76**-1
Empfang (Funksignal) U16-9
empfangen (Kind) U69-2
Empfänger(in) **U136**-9; **U38**-1; **U129**-15
Empfängerareal U129-15
empfänglich **U57**-10
Empfänglichkeit **U57**-10
Empfängnis **U70**-2
Empfängnistermin U70-10
Empfängnisverhütung **U69**-5,2
Empfängnisverhütungsberatung U18-4; U69-10
empfehlen (Therapie) **U18**-4f
Empfehlung **U18**-5
empfinden **U57**-4f; **U102**-2; U93-1,4
– (Schmerz) U104-18
empfindlich **U31**-13; **U57**-8; **U62**-8; **U76**-4
– (Schmerz) **U104**-11
– (Zahn) U26-1
– gegen(über) U119-1
Empfindlichkeit **U57**-8; **U76**-4
–, verminderte **U135**-4
empfindsam **U76**-4
Empfindsamkeit **U76**-4
Empfindung **U57**-3,10; U104-6
–, viszerale U57-5
Empfindungsstörung U142-3
Empfindungsvermögen **U57**-8
Emphysem, kompensatorisches U111-16
emphysematös **U111**-16
Emphysemblase U111-16

empört **U76**-10
Empyem **U111**-14
empyematös **U111**-14
Empyemhöhle U111-14
Emulgator **U81**-25
emulgieren **U81**-25
emulgierend U9-8
Emulgierung **U81**-25
Emulsion **U81**-25
Enamelum **U26**-15
en-bloc Mobilisation U8-14
– – Resektion U126-15
– – Umlagerungstechnik U8-14
Encephalon **U41**-1
Enchondrom **U98**-12
Enchondromatose **U98**-12
Endast U34-13
Endaufzweigung U34-13
Ende (Leben) **U12**-7
–, C-terminales U39-3
–, N-terminales U39-3
Endemie **U94**-8
Endemiegebiet U94-8
endemisch **U94**-8
enden **U57**-12
Endgefühl, kapsuläres U142-14
Endgefühl-Test **U142**-14
Endglied U87-14
Endgröße U24-2; U80-3,10
Endhirn U41-2
Endobag **U133**-16; U128-16
Endocardium **U32**-5
endogen **U88**-10; U72-8
endo-GIA-Stapler **U138**-17
Endokard **U32**-5
Endokardfibroelastose U32-5
Endokarditis U32-5
–, infektiöse U94-2
Endokardkissendefekt U32-5
Endoklip /-clip **U138**-15
Endokrinologie, gynäkologische U69-11
Endoloop **U138**-5
Endolymphe U57-18
Endometriose U50-6
Endometrium **U50**-6; U51-7
Endometriumbiopsie U50-6
–, hysteroskopisch geführte U118-4
Endometriumhyperplasie U50-6
Endometriumstroma U86-22
Endoparasit U90-13
endoplasmatisch **U83**-2
Endoprothese **U127**-20
Endorgan U86-20
Endoskop **U133**-2
Endoskopeur **U128**-2
Endoskopie **U128**-2
Endoskopiebefund U128-2
Endosonografie U128-2
Endospore **U90**-3
Endothel(ium) **U86**-14,8
endothelial **U86**-14
Endotheliom U86-14
Endothelzelle U86-14
Endothelzellwachstumsfaktor U86-14

Endotoxämie **U91**-22
Endotoxin **U91**-4
Endotoxinschock **U124**-5
endotracheal **U43**-8
Endotrachealnarkose **U93**-13
Endotrachealtubus U8-13; U123-10; U135-17
endozytieren **U83**-15
Endozytose **U83**-15
endozytotisch **U83**-15
Endphalanx U28-18; U87-14
Endplatte, motorische **U30**-4; U31-20; U42-13; U87-2
–, neuromuskuläre **U30**-4
Endpunkt **U100**-20
Endstadium, im **U12**-2; U4-1; U97-6
endsystolisch **U33**-3
Endwirt U90-13,17; U94-5
Energie **U1**-6
–, mechanische U78-12
–, voller **U1**-6
Energieaufwand U88-3
Energiebedarf U78-12
Energiebilanz U78-12
Energiedosis **U99**-10
energiegeladen **U76**-17
Energiehaushalt U78-12
energiereich **U78**-12
Energiestoffwechsel **U78**-12
–, mitochondrialer U83-7
Energieübertragung U78-12
Energieverbrauch **U78**-12; U88-3,19; U105-2
Energievorrat U78-12; U88-3
energisch **U1**-6; **U75**-19
Engegefühl U57-3; U102-2; U111-8
Engpass **U136**-4
Engpassgeschehen U113-15
Engpassneuropathie U113-14
Engpass-Syndrom **U113**-15
Engramm **U74**-12
Enhancement **U88**-12
Enkodieren, visuelles U74-9
Enkodierung **U74**-9
Enkodierungsprozess U74-9
Enkodierungsspezifität U74-9
enossales Implantat U129-18
Enplattenpotential U30-4
entarten, maligne U97-5,8
Entartung **U89**-29
–, maligne U97-5
–, sarkomatöse U98-3
Entbindung **U71**-4,9; U85-1
–, komplikationslose U107-18
Entbindungsabteilung U14-9
Entbindungsanstalt U14-1
Entbindungsheim U14-1
Entbindungsklinik, private U14-8
Entbindungspfleger, diplomierter **U16**-6
Entbindungsstation U14-9
entbleien **U91**-23
entblößtes (Haut)areal U114-13
entbunden werden (Kind) **U71**-9,2

entdecken **U117**-5
Entdeckungsrate U117-5
Entdifferenzierung **U97**-8
Entengang U65-2
enteral **U45**-1
Enteritis **U94**-18
Enterobius vermicularis U90-16
Enterogastron **U55**-13
Enteroglucagon U55-12
Enterokolitis U94-18
Enterotoxin U91-4
–, plasmidkodiertes U84-8
entfalten, sich **U44**-10
Entfaltungsknistern U111-9,15
Entfaltungsrasseln U111-15
entfernen **U128**-17; **U133**-16; U127-16
entfernt **U87**-11
Entfernung, operative **U126**-15,3; **U127**-1,13; U46-18
Entfieberung **U105**-18
entgasen **U91**-23
entgegenwirken U9-15
entgiften **U10**-15; **U91**-23
Entgiftung **U91**-23; **U10**-15
Entgiftungsmittel U79-15
Entgiftungstherapie U10-15; U91-23
Entgiftungszentrum U10-15
entgleiten U64-9
Enthaarungscreme U139-14
enthalten, sich **U10**-7
enthaltsam **U68**-11; U53-11
Enthaltsamkeit **U10**-7; U53-11
–, sexuelle **U68**-11; U11-12
Enthemmung **U88**-14; U77-8
Enthirnungsstarre U103-20
Entität, eigenständige U87-12
–, klinische **U108**-2
Entkalkung **U27**-22; **U31**-14
entkeimen **U17**-15; U139-2
entladen, (sich) **U88**-11
Entladung **U42**-6; U31-5
entlangziehen U58-14
entlassen (Krankenhaus) **U20**-16; **U88**-11; U14-1,6; U18-2
Entlassung (Krankenhaus) **U20**-16; U134-11
–, verfrühte U20-16
Entlassungsbestimmungen U20-7
Entlassungsbrief U20-16
Entlassungsdatum U20-16
Entlassungsformular U20-16
Entlassungsprotokoll U20-16; U135-24
Entlassungsschein U20-16
Entlassungstermin U20-16
Entlassungsuntersuchung U125-2
Entlastung, chirurgische U6-17
Entlastungsnaht U137-1; U141-3
Entlastungsschnitt U126-9; U130-17
entleeren **U8**-3; **U46**-8; **U88**-15; U109-15
– (Darm) **U46**-18
– (Blase) **U49**-8,16
Entleerung **U49**-16; **U78**-21; **U88**-15
–, sofortige U46-8

entlüften (Blutkonserve) U136-4
entlüftetes Infusionsset U136-4
Entmarkung **U40**-14
Entmarkungsherde U40-14
Entmarkungskrankheiten U40-14
Entmarkungsneuropathie U113-14
Entnahme (Gewebe) **U117**-3; **U129**-12
Entnahmestelle U130-6
Entnahmetiefe U130-6
entnehmen **U69**-16,12; **U117**-3
– (Gewebe) U132-11; U130-9
entnommenes Organ U129-12
Entoderm **U85**-6
entreißen U64-9
entrüstet **U76**-10
Entschäumer U92-2
entscheidend **U117**-2,18
Entscheidung **U75**-7; U73-6
–, vorschnelle U75-18
Entscheidungsbaum U117-18
Entscheidungsfindung **U117**-18
Entscheidungsprozess U117-18
entschieden (fest) **U75**-11
entschlafen **U12**-4
entschlossen **U75**-11; **U73**-8
Entschlossenheit **U75**-11
Entschlusskraft U117-18
entsenden **U8**-9
entseuchen **U17**-15; **U91**-23
Entseuchung **U91**-23; **U139**-5
entsorgen U9-13; U132-2; **U139**-4
entspannen **U1**-16; **U31**-1
–, (sich) **U76**-19
Entspannung **U1**-10; **U31**-1; **U76**-19
–, biofeedbackunterstützte U31-1
Entspannungsbad U19-10
Entspannungsphase U31-1
Entspannungsreaktion U31-1
Entspannungstechniken U142-18,25
Entspannungsübungen U1-10,15; U76-19
entstanden aus **U85**-11
entstehen **U65**-17
Entstehung (Krankheit) **U119**-2
entstellend (Narbe) U142-7
entstellt **U6**-11
Entstellung **U142**-7
Enttäuschung, bittere U76-11
entwässert **U56**-12
Entwässerung **U78**-22
Entwässerungsmittel U78-22
entweichen **U38**-7
entweichend U46-15
entwickeln, sich **U80**-3; **U97**-7
Entwicklung **U80**-3; U73-2,4
– (Eizelle) **U51**-5
–, motorische U31-20
Entwicklungsalter U80-1
Entwicklungsjahre U77-11
Entwicklungsphysiologie U88-1
Entwicklungspsychologe/-in U15-12
Entwicklungsschritte, wichtige motorische U70-13
Entwicklungsstand, motorischer U80-5

Entwicklungsverzögerung, geistige U77-22
entwöhnen, vom Respirator U44-4
Entwöhnung **U71**-28; **U125**-3
Entwöhnungsbehandlung U142-2
entwurmen **U90**-16
entziehen **U10**-14; **U77**-11; **U121**-6
Entziehung, schrittweise U11-12
Entziehungskur **U10**-15,14
Entzücken U76-16
Entzug (Suchtmittel) U11-6; U135-6
–, allmählicher U10-14
–, kalter **U11**-12
Entzugsanstalt U10-15
Entzugsdelir U7-16
Entzugserscheinungen **U11**-12,4; U10-14
Entzugssyndrom **U10**-14,7; U11-12
entzünden, sich U82-7
entzündet **U104**-11; U140-14
Entzündung **U89**-11; U92-11
– (Cowper-Drüsen) U52-13
– (Gehörgang) U60-3
Entzündungsherd U89-3
Entzündungsmediator U78-17; U83-19
Entzündungszeichen U89-11
Enuresis **U112**-16
– diurna U75-17
– nocturna U72-12; U112-7
Enzephalitis **U94**-13
–, japanische U94-13
–, postvakzinale U94-13
–, zentraleuropäische U94-13
Enzephalopathie, hepatoportale U47-5
–, portokavale U47-5
Enzym **U78**-8; **U81**-16; U79-9
–, fettspaltendes U46-11; U78-8
–, fibrinspaltendes U38-14
–, glykolytisches U78-13 f
–, lysosomales U39-18; U83-6
Enzymaktivität U78-8; U88-14
enzymatisch **U78**-8
Enzym-Cofaktor-Komplex U81-14
Enzymdefekt U78-8
Enzymdiagnostik U78-8
Enzymhemmung U78-8
Enzym-Immunoassay U116-3
Enzyminduktion U78-8
Enzymkomplex U81-14
enzymmarkiert U78-8
Enzymmuster U78-8
Enzymsubstitution U78-8
Enzymsubstrat U81-16
Enzymtest U78-8
Epheliden **U25**-18; **U114**-5; U80-8
Epidemie **U94**-8
epidemiologisch **U94**-8
epidemisch **U94**-8
Epidermis **U56**-2
epidermisähnlich **U56**-2
Epidermisläppchen U130-6
Epidermistransplantat U130-6
epidermoid **U56**-2
Epidermoid **U56**-2

Epidermoid(zyste) **U98**-17
Epidermolyse, großflächige U56-20
Epidermolysis U56-2
Epididymis **U52**-5
Epididymitis **U52**-5
Epididymoorchitis U52-5
Epididymovasostomie U52-5
–, mikrochirurgische U69-4
Epiduralanästhesie **U93**-8; U41-8
Epiduralhämatom U38-8
Epiduralraum U41-8
Epiduralspinalanästhesie U93-8
Epigastrium **U22**-3; **U45**-8
Epiglottis **U43**-7
Epiglottitis U43-7
Epikanthus U58-3
Epikard **U32**-5
Epikondylus **U28**-4
Epikutantest **U118**-2
Epilepsie U6-5
Epileptiker(in) **U124**-9
Epinephrin **U55**-11; **U88**-1
Epipharynx U45-4
Epiphora **U58**-9
epiphysär **U28**-3
Epiphyse **U28**-3; **U54**-13
Epiphysenfuge U28-3; U29-12
Epiphysenknorpel U29-12
Epiphysenlösung U28-3
Epiphysenschluss U28-3
Epiphysenstiel U54-13
Epiphyseolyse U28-3
Epiphyseolysis capitis femoris U65-12
Epiploon **U45**-7
Episiotomie **U71**-18
Episklera **U58**-6
Episode **U103**-4
–, affektive U76-3
–, bevorstehende manische U77-18
–, depressive U71-22; U76-22
–, hypomanische U77-18
–, manische U77-18
–, schwere depressive U77-17
episodisch (auftretend) U**103**-4; **U119**-11
Episom **U84**-8
Epistaxis **U110**-20
Epithalamus **U41**-9
Epithel(ium) **U86**-7
–, einschichtiges U86-10
–, flaches kubisches U86-11
–, hochprismatisches **U86**-11
–, kubisches **U86**-11
–, mehrreihiges U86-10
–, mehrschichtiges U86-10
–, pseudostratifiziertes U86-10
epithelähnlich **U86**-7
Epithelbildung **U86**-7
Epithelbrücke U86-7; U140-6
Epithelgewebe **U86**-7
Epithelgrenze U86-7
epithelial **U86**-7
Epitheliom **U86**-7
Epithelioma adenomatosum U98-7

Epithelioma, basocellulare U86-7
Epithelisation **U86**-7; **U140**-6
Epithelisationsrate U86-7
Epithelisierung **U86**-7; **U140**-6
Epithelium columnare U86-11
– cuboideum **U86**-11
– squamosum **U86**-12; U114-7
– stratificatum squamosum U56-2
– transitionale **U86**-13,7; U48-11
Epithelkörperchen **U54**-7
Epithelkörperchenhyperplasie U54-7
epitheloid **U86**-7
Epitheloidzelle U86-7
Epithelreste U86-7
Epithelzellen, abgeschilferte U86-10
–, hochprismatische U86-11
Epithelzellerneuerung U86-7
Epithelzellpapillom U98-1
Epithelzellverlust U86-7
Epithelzylinder U112-14
Epithelzyste U86-7
Epitop **U39**-7
Eponychium **U56**-15 f
ER, (a)granuläres U83-8
–, glattes U83-8
–, raues U83-8
–, ribosomenbesetztes U83-8
Erbänderung **U84**-20
Erbanlage(n) **U84**-1,28
Erbbild **U84**-10
Erbfaktor **U84**-1
Erbgang **U84**-28
–, autosomal dominanter U84-27
–, X-chromosomaler U89-7
Erbgut **U84**-1
Erbkörperchen **U84**-6
Erbkrankheit U84-28; U102-7
–, rezessive U84-27
Erblassen **U56**-18
Erbleichen **U56**-18
erblich **U89**-7
Erblichkeit **U84**-28
erblinden U59-18
erbrechen **U4**-1; **U46**-4; **U103**-12,17; U64-14
– (ohne Antiperistaltik) U46-4
Erbrechen **U46**-5; **U103**-12; U73-7
–, galliges U46-4
–, morgendliches **U70**-12
Erbrochenes **U46**-4; **U103**-12; U2-5
– aspirieren U44-3
Erbsenbein U28-17
ERCP, präoperative U118-20
Erdalkaligruppe U82-34
Erdalkalimetall U82-19
Erdbeergallenblase U47-7
Erdbeerzunge U21-11; U103-5
Erden, seltene U82-1,6
Erdöldestillat U82-8
erdulden **U11**-5
Ereignis, auslösendes U102-3; U119-8
–, statistisches **U100**-19,3
–, traumatisches U6-22
ereignisabhängig U100-19

erektil **U53**-3
Erektion **U53**-3
–, nächtliche U53-3; U72-12
Erektionsreflex U53-3
Erektionsstörung U4-4; U53-3
Erektionszentrum U53-3
erfahren **U57**-4
Erfahrung U57-4; **U102**-2
–, sinnliche U57-9
erfassen **U18**-14
Erfolgsorgan U40-3; U55-2; U86-20
erfordern U94-3; U47-11
erforschen **U107**-1; **U118**-1; **U101**-2
Erforschung **U118**-1
erfreuen, sich bester Gesundheit U1-1
erfreut **U75**-6
Erfrierung **U5**-12,2; U135-3
Erfrischungen U2-10
erfroren U5-10
ergänzen **U88**-15; **U79**-15; U93-11
Ergänzung **U78**-21; **U88**-15; U49-8
ergeben **U107**-17; **U116**-18; U58-12
–, sich **U65**-17
Ergebnis **U116**-18; **U117**-6
–, unauffälliges U107-18
–, zensiertes U101-27
ergebnislos U126-11
Ergebnisparameter, binärer U101-27
Ergebnistabelle **U20**-5
Ergometer **U142**-16
Ergometertraining **U1**-14
Ergometrie **U142**-16
Ergonomie **U142**-16
Ergonomik **U142**-16
Ergotherapeut(in) U16-12; U142-26
Ergotherapie **U142**-26,18
Ergotherapieassistent(in) U142-26
ergreifen **U64**-1,9; U23-6
Erguss U119-14
–, chylöser U35-2
–, eitriger U89-12
–, seröser U86-9
erhaben **U65**-17; **U114**-3; U114-9
– (Hautläsion) U89-3; U129-11
erhalten **U8**-18; **U117**-3; **U125**-3; U1-5
– (Organ) **U126**-13; U131-5
–, gut U1-3
erhaltenswert U8-18
erhältlich **U102**-3
Erhaltung **U8**-18; **U126**-13
Erhaltungsdosis U121-7; **U135**-19
erhaltungsfähig **U8**-18
Erhaltungsinfusion U136-1
Erhaltungsoperation U8-18
erhärten **U117**-12; U7-15
erheben **U102**-3; U135-12
– (Status) U117-1
–, anamnestisch U52-1; U102-3
–, sich **U65**-17
Erhebung **U102**-3
–, knorpelige (Gehörgang) U60-2
–, prospektive U101-6
erhöhen **U64**-16; **U65**-17
– (Herzfrequenz) U65-17

erhöht **U65**-17; U49-14; **U116**-19
Erhöhung **U64**-16; **U65**-17; **U116**-19;
 U87-27
– (Blutdruck) U129-11
– (Cholesterinspiegel) U47-12
erholen, sich **U1**-10; **U4**-13,16; U64-13
erholsam **U1**-16; **U64**-17
Erholung **U1**-10; **U4**-16; U14-3
Erholungsheim U4-16; U134-14
Erholungsposition U8-17
erigiert **U53**-3 f; **U63**-2
Erinnern **U74**-10
erinnern, jem. **U74**-2
–, sich **U74**-1; U72-9; U77-4
Erinnerung **U74**-1 f,8,13; U57-14
– rufen, in **U74**-2
–, schwache U74-8
–, verdrängte U74-14
Erinnerungsbild U59-5; U74-12
Erinnerungsfeld, akustisches U60-7
Erinnerungslücke(n) U5-14; U74-17
–, alkoholbedingte U10-2
Erinnerungsregion, akustische U60-7
Erinnerungsverfälschung **U74**-18
Erinnerungsvermögen **U74**-8
erkälten, sich U4-2
Erkältung **U94**-9
erkannt, nicht (Krankheit) **U74**-3
erkennbar **U57**-4; **U74**-3; **U102**-2;
 U117-9
–, klinisch **U103**-3
erkennen **U57**-2; **U73**-4; **U74**-3 f;
 U117-4 f; U39-14
Erkenntnis **U74**-4
Erkennungsarmband U74-3
Erkennungsmarke U17-16; U74-3
erkrankt **U4**-4
Erkrankung **U4**-1,4; **U103**-11; U40-5
–, abgeschwächte U122-6
–, AIDS-definierende U96-15
–, derzeitige U102-1
–, diphtherieähnliche **U95**-9
–, juvenile **U95**-1
–, psychiatrische **U77**-16
–, psychische **U77**-16
–, psychosomatische **U77**-14
–, stigmatisierte U13-6
–, überlagerte psychische U77-16
–, zu Demenz führende U77-23
erlahmen **U31**-13
erlangen (Unabhängigkeit) U142-28
Erlass U68-10
Erlaubnis, audrückliche U20-7
erlebsam **U57**-4; **U102**-2
Erleben, subjektives U102-2
Erlebnis **U57**-4; **U102**-2
–, schlimmes U76-11
–, unangenehmes U74-14
erleichtern **U8**-2; **U120**-9
Erleichterung **U4**-13; **U8**-2; U127-14
–, spürbare U62-9
erleiden **U4**-3; **U125**-3; **U104**-2;
 U134-5
erlernen **U74**-7

erliegen **U12**-4
ermächtigen **U20**-7
Ermächtigung **U20**-7
Ermächtigungsformular U20-7
ermitteln **U117**-2,5
Ermittler, verdeckte **U11**-7
ermöglichen **U17**-6; **U48**-1
ermorden **U12**-10
Ermüdbarkeit **U103**-8
–, leichte U113-3
ermüdend **U76**-18
Ermüdung **U103**-8; U76-18
– (Augen) U58-2
Ermüdungsbruch **U106**-13; U103-8
ermutigend **U32**-2
ernähren **U2**-3; **U79**-1
Ernährung **U16**-13; **U45**-1; **U2**-3;
 U55-10
–, ausgewogene U88-19
–, enterale **U125**-19
–, künstliche **U125**-19; U134-12
–, parenterale **U125**-19
Ernährungsberater(in) U2-12; U16-12
Ernährungsberatung U18-4; U79-3
Ernährungsbiochemie U116-7
Ernährungsfistel U125-19
–, jejunale U45-11
Ernährungsgewohnheiten U79-3;
 U73-13
Ernährungslehre **U79**-3; U2-12
Ernährungssonde U124-4; U125-18
–, nasoduodenale U125-18
Ernährungsstatus U117-1
Ernährungstherapie **U16**-13,12; U125-19
Ernährungswissenschaftler(in) **U16**-13
Ernährungszustand U107-10
–, in gutem U1-3
Erneuerung **U1**-10
erniedrigt **U77**-12
ernst bleiben U67-8
ernsthaft U121-14
erodieren **U114**-13; **U27**-21
Eröffnung (OP) **U127**-2; **U126**-9
–, vollständige (Muttermund) U71-12
Eröffnungsperiode U71-13
Eröffnungswehen U71-3
erogen **U68**-9
Erosion **U27**-21; **U114**-13; **U89**-17
Erotik **U68**-9
Erotismus **U68**-9
Erregbarkeit **U42**-8; **U57**-1; **U76**-7
–, neuromuskuläre U42-8
erregen **U42**-8; **U57**-1; **U68**-2; **U72**-7
Erreger **U86**-20; **U90**-5,1; **U92**-2; **U89**-1
–, aerogen übertragbare U90-5
–, anaerobe U44-6; U90-5
–, antibiotikaresistente U90-5
–, eiterbildende U90-1
–, hämatogene U90-5
–, in vitro gezüchtete U90-5
–, opportunistische U90-5
Erregernachweis U90-1
erregt **U76**-8
–, freudig **U76**-16

Erregung U42-8; U57-1; U76-8,1; U77-18; U7-16; U135-9
–, elektrische U42-8
–, katatone U77-18
–, rasende U76-8; U77-15,18
–, sexuelle U68-2; U52-15; U72-7; U76-8
–, zentralnervöse U42-8
Erregungsimpuls U42-5,8
Erregungsleitung U33-2
–, saltatorische U40-15; U42-3
Erregungsleitungsstörung U123-2; U33-2
Erregungsleitungssystem U32-15
Erregungsmuster U68-2
Erregungsphase U68-2
Erregungsübertragung, neuromuskuläre U42-2
–, sympathische U40-9
–, synaptische U40-13
Erregungszustand U94-12; U119-15
–, katatoner U76-8
–, vegetativer U40-6
Erröten U56-18; U108-8
Errötungsangst U77-5
Ersatz, prothetischer U142-6
Ersatzdroge U135-6
Ersatzknochen U129-2
Ersatzmarker U97-16
Ersatzmutter(schaft) U69-18
Ersatzrhythmus U33-6; U110-6
Ersatzschrittmacher U123-13
Ersatzsportart U1-12
Ersatzsystole U33-1
Ersatztherapie U136-13
Erscheinungsbild U84-10
–, allgemeines U107-10
–, äußeres U1-8; U25-2
–, klinisches U103-3; U108-2
–, makroskopisches U86-1
erschlaffen U31-1
Erschlaffung U1-10; U31-1
–, vorzeitige U53-5
erschöpfen U88-15
erschöpft U49-8; U64-19; U76-18
Erschöpfung U4-6; U64-19,18; U76-18; U103-8
–, emotionale U76-18
–, körperliche U64-19
–, völlige U91-22
Erschöpfungsdelir U10-14
Erschöpfungsdelirium U7-16
Erschöpfungssyndrom, chronisches U103-8
Erschöpfungszustand U104-5
erschrecken U65-16
erschreckend U6-21
erschüttern U64-1
erschüttert U76-21
Erschütterung U5-14
–, seelische U5-4; U76-1
erschwert U44-4,7
ersetzen U136-13
ersparen U8-18

ersparen (Operation) U126-13
erspart U20-2
erstarren U82-6
Erstarrungspunkt U82-7
Erstaufnahme U20-1
Erstdiagnose U117-11
erstechen U6-7
erste Hilfe U8-1
Erste-Hilfe-Kurs U8-1
– – Leistung, Verweigerung der U102-10
– – Maßnahmen U8-1
– – Station U8-1
Erstgebärende U70-8
Ersthelfer(in) U8-6
Ersthilfereanimation U123-4; U125-3
ersticken U44-8; U123-7; U27-16
erstickt U12-7; U68-9
Erstickung(szustand) U44-8; U111-4; U123-7; U6-16
Erstickungsanfall U72-12; U123-7
Erstickungsgefahr U44-8
Erstickungsgefühl U44-8; U57-3
Erstickungsopfer U8-10; U123-7
Erstickungstod U123-7
Erstimmunisierung U122-3
Erstimpfung U122-3
Erstkontakt (Implantation) U70-3
Erstmanifestation U102-1; U103-3
erstrecken, sich U31-3; U97-11
Erstuntersuchung U107-2
Erstversorgung U13-1
ertasten (Vene) U34-4
Ertrag U116-18
ertragen U4-3; U75-16
– (Schmerzen) U104-18
erträglich U11-5
ertränken U6-16
Ertrinken U6-16; U44-8
Ertrinkungsunfall U6-1,16
Ertrunkene U6-16
Ertüchtigung, körperliche U1-12
eruieren U102-3
Eruktation U46-3; U109-7
Erwachen U72-7; U7-2
– (Narkose) U135-21,12
–, zu frühes U72-7
erwachend U72-7
erwachsen (werden) U80-3,10
Erwachsene(r) U80-10
Erwachsenenalter U80-10
Erwachsenendiabetes U119-5
Erwachsenenstation U80-10
erwartet U100-4
Erwartungsangst U77-5
erwartungstreu U100-18
erwecken U72-7
Erweiterer U132-17
erweitern U36-11; U136-13; U132-17
erweitert U109-8
Erweiterung U36-11
Erwerbstätigkeit U142-26
erwerbsunfähig U4-8
Erwerbsunfähigkeit U4-8; U142-3f

erworben (Krankheit) U4-1; U89-6
erwünscht U121-11
erwürgen U44-8; U27-16
Erythem U108-7; U114-2
–, wegdrückbares U108-7
Erythema solare U108-7
erythematös U108-7
Erythroblast U37-5
erythroid U37-5
Erythrophobie U56-18; U77-5
Erythropoese U37-5; U38-1
Erythropoetin U38-1
Erythroprosopalgie U113-16
Erythrozyt U37-5,4; U86-2
–, Technetium-markierter U82-34
–, unreifer U83-8
erythrozytär U37-5
Erythrozyten, kernhaltige U37-5; U83-4
–, leukozytenarme gewaschene U37-7
–, überalterte U37-5
–, unreife U37-5
Erythrozytenabbau U38-4
Erythrozytenagglutination U39-19
Erythrozytenauflösung U38-4
Erythrozyteneinzelvolumen, mittleres U36-7; U37-4
Erythrozytenfragilität U37-5
Erythrozytenkonzentrat U136-16; U37-5
Erythrozytenlebensdauer, verkürzte U38-4
Erythrozytenmembran U37-5
Erythrozytenresistenz, osmotische U81-21
Erythrozytensenkungsreaktion U81-27
Erythrozytentransfusion U136-8
Erythrozytenüberlebensdauer U37-5
Erythrozytenüberlebenszeit U37-5
Erythrozytenverteilungskurve U37-5
Erythrozytenvolumen U36-7
–, mittleres korpuskuläres U116-10
Erythrozytenvorläufer U37-5
Erythrozytenvorstufe U37-5
Erythrozytenzahl U37-5
Erythrozytenzählung U37-5
Erythrozytenzylinder U112-14
Erythrozytopoese U37-5
Erythrozyturie U112-3
Erz, arsenhaltiges U82-33
erzeugen U54-2
Erziehung U142-18
Erziehungsanstalt U14-5
erzielen U117-3; U100-6
erzittern U105-7
erzogen, schlecht U75-3
Eselsbrücke U74-13
Esmarch Binde U135-18; U140-20
– Blutleere U17-8; U89-28
– Blutsperre U135-18
– Handgriff U8-11; U28-10; U64-5,16
Esotropie U59-4,13
ESR U81-27
essbar U2-5

essen U2-1f
Essen U2-6,7
– auf Rädern U64-2
–, leckeres U67-17
–, schwerverdauliches U24-8
Essensgelüste U2-6; U11-2
–, ungewöhnliche U70-5
Essenstablett U19-7; U17-12
essentiell U89-8
Essenz U82-13
Essgewohnheiten U2-1,7; U73-13
–, schlechte U10-11
Essigsäure, verdünnte U82-4
Essigsäuregärung U46-12
Essigumschlag U140-25
Essstörung U2-1; U4-4; U11-2; U80-8
Ester U82-14
Esterase U78-7; U82-14
Esterasehemmer U82-14
Esterasemangel U82-14
Esterbindung U78-7; U82-14
Estradiol U55-18
Estradiolbenzoat U55-18
Estradiolvalerat U55-18
Estriol U55-18
Estron U55-18
Etagenfraktur U87-6
Etagennaht U137-1
Ethanol U47-17
Ethikkommission U101-24
Ethinylestradiol U55-18
etikettieren U9-5; U131-8
Euchromatin U84-6
Eukaryo(n)t U83-3
Eukaryontenzelle U83-3
Euphorie U76-16; U77-18
Euphoriewelle U11-9
euphorisch U76-16
Euthanasie U12-9
evakuieren U8-3
Evakuierung U8-3
Evaporation U105-14
Eversion U31-8
Eversionsfraktur U31-8
Eversions-Tapeverband U31-8; U141-11
evident U101-17
Eviszeration U86-21
evozierte Potentiale U125-14
Ewing-Sarkom U98-3
Exanthem U108-9; U114-2; U89-11,14; U94-1
–, hämorrhagisches U89-26
–, scharlachähnliches U95-6
–, urtikarielles U114-11
Exanthema subitum U114-2
exanthematös U114-2
Exartikulation U29-1; U142-6
Exazerbation U119-17; U102-2
Excavatio papillae nervi optici U88-1
– rectouterina U50-15; U45-16
– rectovesicalis U45-16
– vesicouterina U50-15
Excretum U46-20
Exekution U12-11

Exenteration U86-21
Exfoliativzytologie U83-1
exhalieren U44-2
Exit-Block U123-2
Exitus U101-27
Exkavation U59-11
Exkoriation U114-13; U5-8
Exkremente U46-20
Exkret U46-20; U88-11
Exkretion U88-11
exkretorisch U88-11
exogen U88-10
Exon U84-14,2
Exophthalmus U113-17
Exostosen, multiple kartilaginäre U28-3
Exotoxin U91-4
Exotropie U59-4
Exozytose U83-15
Expansion, klonale U84-33
Expektorans U92-15; U103-17; U111-7
Expektoration U103-17; U111-7; U44-9
expektorieren U103-17; U92-15
experimentell U118-1; U101-2,22
Explantat U129-12
explantieren U129-12
explodieren U6-9
Exploration U107-6; U126-11; U132-8
explorativ U107-6
explorative Operation U126-3
Explorativlaparotomie U107-6
Explosion U6-9
Explosionstrauma U5-2; U6-9; U61-9
explosiv U6-9
Explosivepidemie U94-8
exponieren U91-5
exponiert U122-5
Exposition U122-5
–, erneute U39-15
–, kumulative U91-5
Expositionsanamnese U122-5
Expositionskonzentration U91-18
Expositionsrisiko U122-5; U124-2
Expositionswert U91-18
Expositionszeit U91-5; U99-7
Expression U84-26
–, konstitutive U83-16
Expressionsvektor U83-16
Expressivität U84-26
exprimieren U54-2; U83-16; U39-12
Exsanguination U38-9
Exspiration U44-3
–, forcierte U44-2f
Exspirationsvolumen, forciertes U118-3
exspiratorisch U44-3
exspirieren U44-3
Exspirium U44-3
Exstirpation U127-13
exstirpieren U126-15
Exsudat U140-13; U28-3
–, chylöses U35-2
–, hämorrhagisches U38-8
Extasy U11-17
Extension U31-3
– (Fraktur) U141-3

Extension, manuelle U142-12
Extensionskorsett U141-7
Extensionsschiene U31-3; U140-26; U141-3
Extensor U31-3
extrakorporal U138-3
– (Kreislauf) U16-11
Extraktionshöhle U26-13
extramedullär U38-2
extraoral U26-25
extrapyramidal U41-16
Extrasystolen (ES) U110-6; U33-1,3
– , vereinzelte U33-3
extravasal U136-7
Extravasat U38-6; U136-7
Extravasation U136-7
extravasieren U136-7
extravertiert U75-13
extrazellulär U83-2
extrazelluläre Matrix U86-19
Extremitas superior renis U87-3
– testis U87-3
Extremität U23-1; U22-1
–, obere U23-2; U34-7; U57-3
–, schlaffe U23-1
–, untere U23-8
Extremitätenableitung U23-1
Extremitätengürtel U23-1
Extremitätenischämie U89-28
Extremitätenknospe U85-10
Extremitätenskelett U28-1
Extremwert U100-15
extrovertiert U75-13
extubieren U123-10
exzematisiert U114-1
exzidieren U126-15,9
Exzision U126-15; U127-1
Exzisionskonisation U127-12
Exzitation U42-8; U57-1; U76-8
Exzitationsstadium U135-20
exzitatorisch U57-1

F

Fab-Anteil U39-3
Fab-Antikörperfragment U39-3
Fab-Fragment U39-3
Face lifting U64-2
Facettengelenk U106-4
Fach(kranken)schwester U16-5
Facharzt U15-8
– für Anästhesiologie U15-11
– – Augenheilkunde U15-18
– – Frauenheilkunde U15-16
– – Geburtshilfe U15-16
– – Gefäßchirurgie U15-14
– – Geschlechtskrankheiten U15-10
– – Hals-Nasen-Ohren-Heilkunde U15-19
– – innere Medizin U15-9
– – Kinderheilkunde U15-17
– – Kinderneurologie U15-14
– – Neurochirurgie U15-14

Facharzt für Neurologie U15-14
– – Orthopädie U15-15
– – Psychiatrie U15-12
– – Radiologie U15-13
– – Venerologie U15-10
– in Ausbildung U15-7,3
Facharztausbildung U15-4,7
Fachbereich U80-6
fächeln U105-14
Fachgebiet U15-8
Fachgutachten U18-12
Fachkollege/-in U15-7
Fachkrankenpfleger U16-5
Facies U21-2
– adenoidea U25-10
Faden U137-7
Faden(ende) U138-6
Fadenapplikator U138-12,5
Fadenende U138-1
fadenförmig U83-5; U21-16
Fadenpinzette U132-14
Fadenschere U132-4
Fadenstärke U137-7
Fadenwürmer U90-16; U92-25
Fähigkeit(en) U142-3; U73-4f
–, motorische U31-20
–, unterdurchschnittliche intellektuelle U77-22
Fähigkeitsstörung U142-3
fahl U25-12; U108-5
fahrbar U131-19
Fahren, rücksichtsloses U12-10
Fahrer(in), rücksichtslose(r) U75-18
Fahrerflucht U6-2
fahrlässig U75-18
Fahrlässigkeit U20-13; U77-11
Fahrradergometer U142-16
Fahrzeuglenker(in) U6-3
fäkal U46-20
Fäkalien U45-17; U46-20
Fakten (Studie) U101-15
Faktor U55-1
– I U37-12
– II U37-13
– III U37-14
– IX U37-14
– VIII-Konzentrat U136-17
– XI U37-14
–, antihämophiler U38-13
–, Mitose-fördernder U83-13
–, prädisponierender U119-1
–, statistischer U100-5
–, trans-agierender U83-10
–, verzerrender U100-18
Faktoren, chemotaktische U39-17
fäkulent U46-20
Fall U20-2; U64-15; U100-2
–, gerichtsmedizinischer U102-13
Fallaufzeichnungen U102-13
Fallbericht U102-13; U20-2,6
Fallbeschreibung U102-13
Fallbesprechung U20-10
fallen U6-5; U65-12

fallen, zu Boden U64-15
Fallgeschichte U102-4
Fallhand U23-5; U64-15
Fall-Kontroll-Studie U101-1
Fallpauschale U13-3
Fallpräsentation U102-13
Fallstudie U20-2; U100-2; U102-13
Fallsucht U6-5
Falschgelenk U29-1
Falschheit U75-12
falsch-negativ U116-22
falsch-positiv U100-22
Fältchen U25-17; U56-17
Fältchenbildung U56-17
Falte U25-17; U85-12; U87-8; U129-8
Fältelung U89-29
falten U25-17; U85-12
Falten U56-17
Faltenbildung U87-8; U56-17
Faltenzunge U21-11; U56-17; U103-5
faltig U25-17,7; U56-17; U87-8
Faltung U87-8
Falx cerebri U41-2
Falz U25-17
familiär U89-7
– gehäuft U102-7
Familienanamnese U102-7
Familienangehörige U102-7
Familienberatung U102-7
familienfreundlich U102-7
Familienfürsorger(in) U16-8
Familienhelfer(in) U16-8
Familienpfleger(in) U16-15
Familienplanung U69-5; U71-8
Familienstammbaum U84-29
Familienstand U102-9; U119-15
Famulant(in) U15-6
Famulatur U15-6
famulieren U15-6
fangen U78-19
Fangobehandlung U1-20
Fangopackung U142-22
Farbabstimmung U59-9
färbbar U116-4
Farbbolus U46-9
Farbdämpfe U82-3
Farb-Doppler Darstellung U118-17
Färbeeigenschaften U116-4
Färbekoeffizient (MCH) U116-10
färben U116-4
Farben wahrnehmen U59-9
–, leuchtende U59-11
farbenblind U59-18
Farbenblindheit U59-9
Farbenfehlsichtigkeit U59-9
Farbensehen U59-9
Farbensinn U59-9; U57-5
Farbensinnstörung U59-9
Färbetechnik U116-4
Farblinsen U58-8
Farbstoff U116-4
–, strahlendichter U116-4
Farbstoffinjektion U122-4
Farbstofflaser U127-7

Farbszintigramm U99-18
Farbtöne U59-9
–, dunkelviolette U25-12
Färbung U116-4
Farbverdünnungsmittel U11-23
Farbverwechslung U59-9; U77-4
Farbwahrnehmung (beim Hören) U61-2
Farnkrautmuster U51-9
Farnkrauttest U51-9
Fascia lata U30-7
Fasciculus U30-1,5
– atrioventricularis U32-15
faseln U66-19
Faser, argyrophile U86-5
–, elastische U86-5; U31-16
–, kollagene U86-5
–, langsam zuckende U30-1
–, retikuläre U86-5
–, schnell zuckende U31-5
–, zugfeste kollagene U86-5
Faserbahnen, sensible U40-7
–, somatosensorische U40-7
Faserbündel U30-5
faserig U86-5
Faserknorpel U29-2
Fasern, adrenerge U40-8
–, afferente U40-4
–, cholinerge U40-8
–, efferente U40-4
–, motorische U40-4
–, parasympathische U40-9
–, sekretorische U40-7
–, sensible U40-4
–, sensorische U40-4
–, somatische U40-7
–, sympathische U40-9
Faseroptik U133-3
Faserstoffe, fermentierbare U46-12
fassen U64-9; U132-13,9
Fassthorax U25-9; U22-2; U142-7
Fassung U75-4
fassungslos U7-9
Fasszange U64-9; U132-13
fasten U2-14f; U47-11; U54-10; U77-3
Fasten, zwanghaftes U77-19
Fastenhypoglykämie U124-7
Fastigium U105-17
Faszie U30-7
–, periprostatische U48-14
–, tiefe U30-7
Faszienloge U30-7
Faszien naht U30-7
Faszienrand U30-7
Faszienspaltung U30-7
Faszienstrang U30-7
Faszikel U30-1
Faszikelblock U30-1; U31-5; U123-3
faszikulär U30-1; U31-5
Faszikulation U30-1; U31-5; U72-12
Faszikulationspotential U31-5
Fasziotomie U30-7
Fauces U45-4; U21-12
faulen U46-17
faulig U62-5; U44-1; U46-17

Fäulnis **U46**-17; U47-11
Fäulnisbakterien U46-17
fäulniserregend **U46**-17
Faust **U23**-6
Faustregel U20-7
Faustschlag **U6**-4
–, präkordialer **U123**-5; **U32**-1
Faustschluss U64-9
Fäzes **U46**-20
fazial **U25**-10
Fazialiskrämpfe U31-5
Fazialislähmung U21-2; **U28**-9; U113-7
Fazialisparese U28-9
Fazilitation, propriozeptive neuromuskuläre U57-11
Fc Fragment **U39**-3
Fc-Anteil **U39**-3
Fc-Bindungsstelle U39-3
FDA-Studien U13-9
febril **U105**-3
Febris intermittens U119-11
– recurrens U94-19; U105-3
– remittens U119-17
– typhoides **U94**-19; U90-7
federnd (Gang) U1-4
Federventil U133-8
Feedback-Hemmung U42-13
Feedbackmechanismus U88-2
Fehlbildung **U89**-5; **U142**-7
–, angeborene U142-4
Fehldiagnose stellen **U117**-10
Fehlen (Gonaden) **U54**-11
– (Regenbogenhaut) **U58**-8
Fehler, peinlicher U76-12
–, systematischer **U100**-18
fehlerhaft U100-12
Fehlernährung U16-13; **U79**-3; U103-9
Fehlgeburten U70-7
Fehlhaltung U63-1
fehlschlagen **U123**-6; U129-1
Fehlsinnmutation U84-20
–, homozygote U84-5
Fehlstellung **U5**-20; **U106**-4,15; **U141**-1
– (Augenachsen) **U59**-15
– (Zahn) U26-1
Fehlsteuerung U88-2
Fehlverhalten U77-10
Fehlwirt U94-5
feige **U75**-14
Feigwarze U50-1; U96-1
–, spitze **U96**-14; U114-17
Feile **U132**-12
feindselig **U77**-7
Feindseligkeit **U77**-7
–, unverhohlene U75-13; U77-7
Feinfühligkeit U76-4
Feingebäck **U3**-10
Feingefühl **U57**-8
Feinkoordination U31-19
feinmaschig U140-18
Feinmotorik **U31**-20
Feinnadelaspiration U116-4
–, testikuläre U69-13
Feinnadelbiopsie U118-5; U127-16

Feinnadelzytologie U118-9
Feldblock U93-6
Feldlazarett U8-1; U14-1
Feldsanitäter(in) U16-9
Feldspat U82-30
Feldspital U14-1
Feldversuch U101-7
Felsenbeinpyramide U60-3
Felsengebirgs(fleck)fieber U90-12; U94-19
Femidom U69-6
feminin **U50**-2
Feminisierung **U50**-2; **U53**-12
–, testikuläre U50-2; U52-3; U53-12
femoral **U28**-23
Femoralispuls U28-23
Femur **U28**-23; U23-9
Femurkopf U28-23
Fenestra cochleae U60-8
– vestibuli U60-8
Fenster, ovales **U60**-8
–, rundes U60-8
Ferment **U78**-8
Fermentation **U46**-12
Fermentator **U46**-12
fermentieren **U46**-12
Fermentierung **U46**-12
Fernfixation U59-14
ferngesteuert U133-1
Fernlappen U130-11
Fernmetastasen U87-11; U97-13
Fernpunkt U59-13
Fernsehschärfe U59-8
Fernvisus U59-8
Ferrum **U82**-21
Ferse **U23**-13
Fersenbein **U28**-27; U23-13
Fersenbeinfraktur U6-5
Fersenfettgewebe U17-13; U28-27
Fersenhöcker U28-27
Fersenpolster U17-13; **U28**-27; U64-16
Fersensporn U23-13; U28-27
Ferse-Schienbein-Test U23-10
Ferse-Zehen-Gang U65-1
Fertigkeiten, motorische U40-4; U142-26
fertil **U69**-2; **U70**-1
Fertilisation **U69**-2; **U70**-1
Fertilisationsrate U69-12
Fertilität **U69**-2; **U70**-1
Fertilitätsfaktor U69-2
Fertilitätsrate U69-2,4; U70-1
Fertilitätsziffer U69-2
fesch **U75**-7
Fesseln **U23**-12
–, gepolsterte U77-26
fest U58-6
– (werden) **U82**-6
feste Nahrung U135-13
Festfrequenzschrittmacher U123-13
festgeschnallt **U141**-11
festgestellt, nicht **U74**-3
festhalten **U18**-14; **U64**-9; **U77**-26
Festigkeit **U31**-15; **U82**-6

Festigung **U89**-13
Festination **U65**-11
Festkörper **U82**-6
festlegen **U117**-2,4
festmachen **U8**-2
feststellbar **U102**-3; **U117**-5,10; U107-6
feststellen **U57**-4; **U102**-2; **U117**-2,4 ff
– (Herzgeräusch) **U74**-4
Feststellmechanismus U133-1
Feststellung **U102**-3; **U117**-2
Feststoff U82-6
Festwerden U89-13
Fetalperiode U70-4
Fetalverlust U85-1
Feten, weibliche U70-4
Fetischismus U68-15
Fetoskopie U70-4
Fetotoxizität **U91**-12
fett **U56**-5
Fett **U79**-11
Fett(gewebe)geschwulst, gutartige U98-11
Fett(gewebe)schwund U24-5
fett(haltig) **U24**-5
fett(leibig) **U24**-8
Fettabbau U24-5
Fettansammlung U24-5
fettarm **U24**-5
Fett-Bindegewebe, lockeres U86-6
Fettdepot U24-9; U78-20; U87-15
Fettdurchfall U109-10
Fette, einfach ungesättigte U79-12
–, gesättigte U46-1
Fetteinlagerung U24-5,9; U56-5; U79-11
Fettembolie U24-5; U124-13
Fettemulgierung U47-11
Fettemulsion U81-25
fettfreie Körpermasse U24-7
Fettgehalt U24-5
Fettgewebe U24-5,9; U86-3; U79-11
–, subkutanes **U56**-4
fetthaltig **U56**-5; **U79**-11
fettig **U24**-5; **U56**-8; U9-8
Fettleber U24-5
fettleibig **U24**-9; **U79**-11
Fettleibigkeit **U24**-5,9
fettlöslich U24-5; U81-13; U88-5
Fettplaque U24-5
Fettpolster **U24**-5; U56-4; U79-11
Fettresorption U46-13; U88-8
Fettsäure U24-5
–, essentielle **U79**-12
–, freie U81-19
–, mehrfach ungesättigte U79-11; U81-24
Fettsäureabbau U78-10
Fettsäureester U82-14
Fettsäuresynthese U78-4
Fettschicht U24-5
–, subkutane U87-8
fettspaltend U78-10
Fettspeicherzellen U24-5
Fettstoffwechsel U24-5

Fettstuhl U46-19; U79-11
Fettsucht **U24**-9; **U56**-5; U89-2
–, konstitutionelle U25-3
–, universelle U56-5
fettsüchtig **U79**-11
–, krankhaft U25-6
Fettvakuole U83-11
Fettverdauung U24-5; U46-11; U109-1
Fettverteilung U24-5
Fettzelle U24-5; U56-5; U86-2
Fettzylinder U112-14
Fetus **U70**-4; **U85**-1
feucht **U105**-13; U139-18
feuchte Kammer U140-5
Feuchtigkeit U56-12; **U105**-13
Feuchtigkeitscreme **U105**-13; U9-8
Feuchtigkeitsgehalt U105-13
feuchtkalt U105-10
feuchtwarme Packung U140-24
Feuchtwarze U50-1
Feuer **U6**-10
Feueralarm U6-10; U123-4
Feuerameise U91-16
Feuerball U6-10
Feuerbestattung U12-16
feuergefährlich **U6**-10
Feuerlöscher U6-10
Feuermal U25-19; U98-15; U114-3
Feuermelder U6-10
Feuern **U42**-6
Feuersbrunst **U6**-10
Feuerwehr U6-10
Feuerwehrmann **U6**-10
Feuerzeug **U10**-18
F-Faktor U69-2; U84-8
F-I **U37**-12
Fiber(endo)skop U128-2; U118-11
Fiberbronchoskopie U118-11
fibrillierend **U110**-7
Fibrin **U37**-12
Fibringerinnsel U37-12; U38-12
Fibrinkleber **U137**-14,11; U127-10
Fibrin-Monomere U37-12
Fibrinnetz U37-12
Fibrinogen **U37**-12
Fibrinogenaufnahmetest U37-12
Fibrinogen-Kryopräzipitat **U37**-12
Fibrinogenmangel U37-12
Fibrinogenspaltprodukte U37-12
Fibrinolyse **U37**-15,12; **U38**-14
fibrinolysehemmend **U38**-14
Fibrinolysehemmstoff U37-12
Fibrinolyseinhibitor U37-12
Fibrinolysin **U37**-15; **U38**-14
Fibrinolytikum **U38**-14; **U92**-16
Fibrinschaum U37-12; U137-14
Fibrinspaltprodukt U81-8
Fibroadenom U98-4
Fibrom(a) **U98**-8
fibromartig **U98**-8
fibromatös **U98**-8
Fibromatose/-sis **U98**-8
Fibromyalgie U98-8

Fibromyom **U98**-8
fibrös **U86**-5
Fibrose, zystische U86-17
Fibrositissyndrom U98-8
Fibula **U28**-24; U23-10
Fibularislähmung U30-17
Fieber **U105**-3
– unbekannter Ursache/Genese **U105**-16,3; U94-19
–, intermittierendes U119-11
–, remittierendes U119-17
–, rheumatisches U105-3
–, wolhynisches U105-3
Fieberabfall **U105**-18
Fieberanstieg, treppenförmiger U94-19
Fieberattacke U103-4
Fieberblase U96-10; U105-3
Fieberdelir U7-16; U105-3
fiebererzeugend **U105**-4
fieberfrei **U105**-3; U108-5
fieberhaft **U105**-3
Fieberkrämpfe U105-3; U113-5
Fieberkurve U20-5; U105-1
Fiebermesser **U105**-6
fiebernd **U105**-3
Fieberschübe U103-4; U105-3
fiebersenkend **U105**-4,18; U92-11
Fieberspitze U105-1
Fiebertherapie **U105**-5
Fieberwahn U105-3
Fieberzacke U105-1,3
fiebrig **U105**-3
Figur (Körper) **U25**-1; U1-15
–, mollige U25-6
–, schlaksige U25-5
–, schlanke U24-6
filamentär **U83**-5
Filmhalter U64-9
Filmoxygenator U125-11
Filmtablette U9-7
Filmverband U140-17
Filter **U49**-1; **U83**-22; **U10**-17
filtern **U49**-1; **U83**-22
Filterpapier(streifen) U83-22
Filtrat **U49**-1; **U83**-22
Filtration **U49**-1
Filtrationsdruck U49-1
Filtrationsfraktion U49-1
Filtrations-Leukapherese U136-15
Filtrationsrate U49-1
–, glomeruläre **U49**-2
Filtratrückresorption U49-1
filtrieren **U49**-1; **U83**-22
Filzläuse U22-8; U90-15
Fimbrien U50-4
finden (richtiges Tempo) U65-6
Finger **U23**-7; U28-18
–, schlanke U25-5
Fingerabdruck U23-7
Fingeramputation U142-6
Fingerballen U87-17
Fingerbeere U23-7; U136-2
Fingerbeuger U31-2
Fingerbreite **U23**-7

Fingerdissektion U87-5
Fingerendphalangen, trommelschlägel-
   förmige U56-16
Finger-Finger-Perkussion U107-8
Fingergoniometer U142-9
Fingergrundgelenk U28-17; U142-8
Fingerknöchel **U23**-7; **U28**-18
Fingerknöchelpolster U23-7
Fingerknochen **U28**-18
Fingerkuppe U23-7; U125-9
Fingernagel **U23**-7
Finger-Nase-Versuch U23-7
Finger-Perkussion U107-8
Fingerplastik U129-1
Fingerpräparation U128-14
Fingerprint-Methode U84-11
Fingerspitze **U23**-7
Fingerspitzenpalpation U107-7
finster **U67**-11
First messenger U83-17
Fisch **U3**-2
Fischgeruch U62-3
Fissur **U28**-6; **U87**-26; **U106**-1,11
Fissura longitudinalis cerebri U41-5
– orbitalis U58-1
– sphenopetrosa U60-7
– sterni U28-13
– Sylvii U41-5
Fissurenbildung U114-14
Fistel U34-6; **U89**-25
Fistelbildung **U89**-25
Fistelgang U89-25
Fistelmund/-maul U89-25
Fitness **U1**-9
Fitnessraum U1-9,18
Fitnesstest U1-9
Fitnesstraining U1-9
Fitness-Zentrum **U1**-18
Fixateur externe U141-4
Fixation **U59**-14; **U129**-7; U64-2
– (Fraktur) **U141**-4
Fixationsbewegung U59-14
Fixationsdisparation U59-14
Fixationsgrip (Trokarhülse) U133-6
Fixationsobjekt U59-14
Fixationspunkt U59-14
Fixationsvorrichtung **U133**-9
Fixationswechsel U59-14
Fixationsweste **U125**-24
fixen **U11**-8
Fixer(in) **U11**-8
fixieren **U59**-14; **U141**-15
Fixierschraube U141-4
fixiert (auf) U75-14; U76-15
Fixierung, mechanische U77-26
flach **U87**-2; U58-5; U59-10
flachbrüstig U22-2
Fläche **U87**-4
Flachmeißel U132-11
Flagellaten U90-2
Flagellum **U83**-5
Flamme **U6**-10
Flanke **U22**-6
Flankenschmerz U22-6; U104-10,15

Flankenschnitt U22-6; U126-9
Flaschenetikett U136-4
Flaschenkaries U14-8
Flaschenkind U71-26
Flaschennahrung, zusätzliche U14-8
Flash **U11**-9
Flashback **U11**-9; **U74**-11
Flatterflimmern U110-7
Flattertremor U113-4
Flatterwellen U110-7
flatulent **U46**-15; **U109**-7
Flatulenz **U46**-15; **U109**-7
Flatus **U46**-15,3; **U109**-7
Flechte **U114**-14
Fleck **U25**-18 f; **U114**-9 f; **U116**-4
–, blauer **U5**-13; U89-26
–, blinder **U58**-14; U59-18
–, gelber **U58**-13
–, milchkaffeefarbener U25-18
–, scharlachroter U95-6
Fleckfieber U90-12; U94-19; U114-9
–, epidemisches U90-15
fleckig **U114**-9
Flecktyphus U94-19; U114-9
Fledermaus U94-4; U122-2
Fledermaustollwut U94-12
Fleisch **U3**-1
–, mageres U24-10
Fleischbolus U46-9
Fleischfliege U90-15
Fleischmole U98-15
flektieren **U31**-2
–, dorsal U87-16
flexibel **U31**-17
Flexibilitas cerea U31-17
Flexibilität **U31**-17
Flexio(n) **U31**-2
Flexor **U31**-2
Flexur **U31**-17
Flexura coli dextra U45-15; U47-1
– coli sinistra U35-4; U45-15
– duodenojejunalis U45-10
– hepatica coli U45-15
– lienalis coli U45-15
Fliege **U90**-15
Fliegerkrankheit U6-17
Fliehkraft U83-20
fließend sprechen U66-8
Fließgleichgewicht **U88**-20; U119-15
Flimmerbesatz, Zylinderepithel mit U86-11
Flimmerepithel U50-4; U83-5; U86-7
Flimmerflattern U110-7
Flimmerhärchen **U83**-5
flimmernd **U110**-7
Flimmerskotom U99-17; U113-11
Flimmerzelle U86-18
floaten **U1**-19
flocken **U81**-27
Flockenbildung **U81**-27
flockig **U81**-27
Flockung **U81**-27
Flockungsreaktion U116-2
Flockungstest U81-27

Floh **U90**-15
floppy infant U31-12
florid **U119**-13
florierend **U1**-4
Flotation **U1**-19
fluchen U66-14
flüchtig **U82**-2; U95-3; U105-14
– (Hautläsion) U114-11
Fluchtmechanismus U77-9
Fluchtreaktion U77-9
Flugangst U77-5
Flügelschlagen U113-4
Flugkrankheit U103-11
Flugrettung U8-5
Flugrettungsdienst U8-1
Flugrettungstransport U8-3
Flugzeugabsturz U6-2
Flugzeugpilot(in) U6-17
Fluor **U82**-22; U79-17; U96-8
– vaginalis U50-8; U88-11
Fluoreszeinmarkierung U84-38
Fluoreszenz **U99**-8
Fluoreszenzangiografie U58-14
Fluoreszenzmikroskopie U86-1
Fluorid **U82**-22
Fluoridapplikator U17-13
Fluoridierung U82-22
Fluorometrie U99-8
Fluorose U82-22
Fluorvergiftung U82-22
Fluorwasserstoffsäure U82-9
Flush **U56**-18
Flushsyndrom U98-2
Flussdiagramm U20-5; U100-27
flüssig **U81**-22; **U82**-4
Flüssigkeit **U81**-22; **U82**-4; **U88**-9; U46-8
–, ätzende U91-10
–, blutig tingierte U82-4
–, hochkonzentrierte U82-4
–, interstitielle U86-19
–, trübe U82-4
Flüssigkeitsabgabe U88-16
Flüssigkeitsabsonderung U89-11
Flüssigkeitsansammlung U5-15; U78-20; U88-15
Flüssigkeitsaufnahme **U46**-1; U82-4
Flüssigkeitsausscheidung U88-16
Flüssigkeitsaustritt, massiver U38-6
Flüssigkeitsbelastung U33-10
Flüssigkeitschromatografie U82-4
Flüssigkeitsersatz U78-22; U82-4
Flüssigkeitshaushalt **U78**-22; U48-9
Flüssigkeitssubstitution U78-22
–, extrazelluläre U136-13
Flüssigkeitstherapie U125-2
Flüssigkeitsverlust U6-15; U136-13
Flüssigkeitszufuhr U82-4; **U134**-12
Flussrate, maximale U52-15
Flusssäure U82-9
flüstern **U66**-16
Flüstern, leises U61-5
Flüsterprobe U66-16
Flüsterstimme U66-16

Flutkatastrophe U6-20
Flutwellen U6-20
Foetor ex ore **U109**-2; U46-17
– uraemicus U112-13
fokal **U89**-3
Fokalinfektion U97-10
Fokus **U89**-3; **U97**-10
Folat **U79**-14
Foley-Instrumententasse U125-20
Folge **U101**-27
Folgebewegungen, glatte U58-16
–, kontinuierliche U58-16
Folgeerscheinung(en) U4-16; **U134**-9
Folgen U4-16
folgend U75-10
Folgestrang U84-11
Folliculi lymphatici aggregati **U35**-11
Folliculus lymphaticus U35-1
– ovaricus maturus **U51**-6
Follikel, atretischer U51-6
–, präovulatorischer U51-6
–, (sprung)reifer U51-6
Follikelatresie U51-6
Follikelflüssigkeit U51-6
Follikelphase **U51**-7; U51-6
Follikelpunktion, ultraschallgesteuerte
 transvaginale U69-12
Follikelreifungsphase **U51**-7
Follikelsprung **U51**-9
Follikelverstopfung U56-13
Follikelwachstum U51-6
follikulär **U51**-6
Follitropin **U55**-14
Folsäure **U79**-14
Folsäureantagonist U92-6
Folsäuremangel U78-21
Folsäuresalz **U79**-14
Folsäuresupplementierung U79-14
Folsäuresynthese U78-4
Folsäurezyklus U78-6
Fontanelle **U28**-7
–, große U28-7; U87-16
–, hintere U28-8
–, kleine U28-8
Fonticulus anterior U28-7; U87-16
– mastoideus U28-7; U60-14
– posterior U28-8
– posterolateralis U28-7; U60-14
Foramen **U28**-6
– apicis dentis U28-6
– interventriculare U41-4
– ischiadicum majus U28-6
– magnum U28-6
– mandibulae U28-6
– mentale U21-6; U28-10
– ovale cordis **U32**-11
–, offenes U32-11; U34-14
– stylomastoideum U60-14
– supraorbitale U58-1
– vertebrale U22-12; U28-6
förderlich **U1**-5; **U132**-1
fördern U79-15
– (Entspannung) U1-10
Forelkreuzung U41-14

Form (Fitness) **U1**-9
Formaldehyd U82-12
Formalin U122-7
formalininaktiviert U122-7
Formatio reticularis U83-8
– reticularis, pontine U41-12
Formation, retikuläre U83-8
formbar **U31**-11
Formbarkeit U82-6
Formel, chemische U81-1
formen **U129**-4
Formicatio **U103**-19
Fornix cerebri **U41**-3
– conjunctivae U58-4
– vaginae U50-8
forsch **U65**-13
Forschung **U101**-2
– betreiben U16-5
Forschungslabor U116-1
Forschungsstadium U101-2
Forschungsstipendiat(in) **U15**-7
Forschungsstipendium **U15**-7
Fortbestehen **U119**-11
Fortbewegung **U65**-2; U53-7
–, amöboide U90-4
forte Tablette U9-7
Fortlaufnaht U137-16
Fortleitung U42-3
–, saltatorische U42-3
fortpflanzen, sich **U42**-4; **U69**-1
Fortpflanzung U116-6
–, assistierte **U69**-11,1
Fortpflanzungsorgane **U52**-1
Fortsatz **U28**-5; **U87**-27
–, fingerförmiger U23-7
fortschreiten (Krankheit) **U97**-7; **U119**-12
fortschreitend U4-12; **U97**-7; **U119**-12
Fortschritt **U97**-7; **U119**-12
Fortschritte (Genesung) U134-7
fortsetzend, sich **U87**-12
Fortsetzung **U87**-12
Fossa **U28**-6; **U87**-26
– condylaris U29-6
– cranii U28-7
– cubitalis U23-4; U28-6; U87-18,26
– hypophysialis U87-26
– iliaca U28-6,22; U87-26
– intercondylaris U29-6
– – (femoris) U28-6
– ovalis U32-11
Fötus **U70**-4; **U85**-1
foudroyant **U119**-13
Fovea centralis **U58**-13
Foveation **U58**-13
Fowler-Lagerung **U63**-12
F-Plasmide U84-8
Fractura radii loco classico **U106**-10
Fragestellung, geschickte U102-14
Fragment **U106**-2
Fragmentation **U39**-3; **U106**-2
Fraktile **U100**-11
Fraktion **U81**-4
Fraktionierung **U81**-4
Fraktur **U106**-1; **U5**-20

Fraktur, dislozierte U64-4
–, stabile U31-15; U125-2
Frakturausläufer U106-11
Praktureinrichtung U141-1
Frakturheilung **U106**-15,1
frakturieren **U106**-1; **U5**-20
Frakturlinie U106-7
Frambösie U142-7
frameshift-Mutation U84-21
Frau **U50**-2
Frauenarzt **U15**-16
Free-Base U11-20
frei von U56-10
frei(mütig) **U75**-13
Freien, im U1-10
Freiendprothese U27-7
freigelegt U129-9
freihalten (Atemwege) U8-2
Freiheitsgrade **U100**-16
freilegen U87-5; U126-7 f
Freilegung (Haut) U114-13; U58-6
– (OP) **U126**-7; U128-1
freiliegend U130-6
freimachen (Atemwege) U123-5
–, sich **U107**-4
Freipräparierung **U126**-7,12
freisetzen **U20**-16; **U54**-2; **U88**-11
–, exozytotisch U83-15
Freisetzung **U20**-16; **U88**-11
Freisetzungsfaktor U55-1
Freisetzungsmediator U83-19
Freitod **U12**-8
Freiwasser-Clearance U49-7
freiwillig **U16**-15; **U40**-6; U73-3
freiwillige(r) Helfer(in) **U16**-15
Freiwilliger U101-10
Freizeit U1-10
Freizeitaktivitäten U142-27
Freizeitbeschäftigung U1-10; U64-18
Freizeitdroge U1-9; U10-9; U11-1
Freizeiteinrichtungen U1-10
Freizeitschuhe **U65**-8
Freizeitsport U116-19
Freizeitzentrum U1-17
fremd **U39**-21
Fremdantigen U39-21
fremdeln U77-5; U102-2
Fremdheit, vermeintliche **U74**-18
Fremdkörper **U8**-10; U12-14; U45-12; U64-12; U140-12
–, festsitzender U109-15
–, intraorbitaler U58-1
–, penetrierender U6-7
Fremdkörperaspiration U8-10; U44-3; U111-4; U127-16
Fremdkörperembolus U8-10
Fremdkörperentfernung U8-10
Fremdkörpergefühl U8-10; U57-3; U103-2
Fremdkörpergranulom U8-10
Fremdkörperobstruktion U123-6
Fremdkörperreaktion U8-10
Fremdkörperriesenzellen U8-10
Fremdproteine U39-21; U79-9

Fremdsubstanz(en) **U8**-10; U39-22
Fremitus **U111**-11
–, tastbarer U62-8
Frenulum **U26**-11
– clitoridis U50-12
– labii U21-9
– labiorum majorum U50-14
Frequency-Urgency-Syndrom **U112**-4
Frequenz, hörbare U61-2
Frequenzbereich U61-6
Frequenzschwankungen U61-6
Fresh frozen Plasma **U136**-16
Fresssucht U2-1
Fresszelle **U39**-17
Freudentaumel U76-16
freudlos **U75**-6
freundlich **U75**-5
– gesinnt U1-3
Friedhof **U12**-18,17
friedlich **U76**-19
Friedreich-Ataxie U113-8
frigid **U68**-7
Frigidität **U68**-7
Friktion U68-2; U142-15
Frischblut **U136**-9,14
frischoperiert U126-1
Frischplasma, tiefgefrorenes **U136**-16; U37-3
Frischverletzte(r) U16-14
Frischverletztenambulanz U14-9
Frischverletztenstation U14-7
froh **U75**-6
fröhlich **U75**-6; **U76**-9; **U67**-6
Fröhlichkeit **U76**-9
Frohnatur U75-6
frontal **U87**-20
Frontalebene U87-2,20
Frontallappen U87-23
Frontalzusammenstoß U6-2
Frontzähne **U26**-2
Froschstellung, (in) **U63**-5
Frostbeule **U5**-12
Frösteln **U105**-9
–, starkes U56-14
fröstelnd U64-6; **U105**-7,9
Frostigkeit **U105**-9
frottieren **U62**-11
fruchtbar **U69**-2; **U70**-1
Fruchtbarkeit **U69**-2; **U70**-1
Fruchtbarkeitsrate U69-2
Fruchtbarkeitsziffer U69-2
Fruchtblase, intakte/stehende U71-9
Fruchtblasenpunktion U85-15
Früchte **U3**-7
Fruchtsack **U85**-15
Fruchtschmiere **U71**-19
Fruchttod, intrauteriner U70-4; U85-1; U91-22
Fruchtwasser U71-6,19; U85-15
–, mekoniumhaltiges U71-19
Fruchtwasserembolie U85-15
Fruchtwasserspiegelung U85-15
Frühabort U119-14
Frühaufsteher U65-17

Früherkennung U74-3; U117-4 f;
 U119-14
–, systematische U102-13
Früherwachen, morgendliches U72-7,16
Frühgeburt U70-8; U71-8; U80-4
Frühmobilisation U64-2; U65-1;
 U134-13; U141-5
Frühpension U80-14
frühreif U51-2
Frührente U80-14
Frühschwangerschaft U70-12; U119-14
Frühsommer-Meningoenzephalitis
 U90-15; U94-13
Frühstadium U97-14; U119-14
Frühsymptom U119-4,14; U103-3;
 U108-1
Frühsyphilis U96-3
Frühwochenbett U71-21
Frustrationstoleranz U76-11
frustriert U76-11
FSH U55-14; U51-6
FSH-Mangel U55-14
FSH-RF U55-14
FSH-Sekretion U55-14
FSH-Spiegel, postmenopausale U55-14
FSME U90-15; U94-13
FT-Faser U30-1; U31-5
Fugue, dissoziative U74-20
Fugue-Zustand, psychogener U74-20
fühlbar U62-8 f
fühlen U57-2,5; U76-1
Fühlen U57-5
führen U61-4
– zu U116-18; U117-6; U140-8
Führungsdraht U141-14
Führungshohlsonde U132-8
Führungsnadel U136-6
Führungsschiene U137-5
Führungsstab U133-12
Fulguration U127-14
Füllmaterial (Darm) U79-16
Füllung, diastolische U33-3
–, frühdiastolische U33-9
Füllungsdefekt, strahlendurchlässiger
 U99-11
–, unscharf begrenzter U87-10
Füllungsdruck (Herz) U33-9
–, erhöhter enddiastolischer U33-9
Füllungsgeräusch, mesodiastolisches
 U110-3
Füllungsperiode U33-9
Füllungsphase U33-9
Füllungszystometrie U49-15
fulminant U119-13
Funda U140-20
Fundus (oculi) U58-12,2
– vesicae U48-11
Funduseinstülpung U129-8
Funduskopie U58-12
Funduskopiebefund U58-12
Fundusreflex U113-1
Fünflinge U70-14
Fünftagefieber U105-3
fünfwertig U81-10

fungiform(is) U90-18
Fungizid U91-8; U17-15; U92-26
Fungus U90-18
Fungusball U90-18
Funiculus spermaticus U52-7
– umbilicalis U71-17
Funken U6-9; U127-14
Funkenerosion U27-21
Funkkontakt U8-6
Funknotruf U6-19
Funkrufempfänger U17-17
Funktionalis U50-6
Funktionsdiagnostik U102-11
Funktionserhaltung U126-13
Funktionsfähigkeit U77-1
Funktionsgips U141-7
Funktionsprüfung U102-11; U117-1
Funktionsschiene U19-14
Funktionsstörung U4-4; U142-3
–, sexuelle U68-7
Funktionsszintigrafie U99-17
Funktionstest U116-3
Furche U85-3; U87-26
– (Helix) U84-11
–, nicht sehr tiefe U87-23
furchig U87-26
Furcht U6-21; U77-5
fürchten U6-21
furchterregend U6-21
Furchung(steilung) U85-3; U51-5
Furchungsstadium U85-3
Fürsorge U1-7; U13-6
Fürsorgeberechtigte(r) U77-25
Fürsorgehelfer(in) U16-15
Fürsorger(in) U16-8
Furunkel U114-16; U56-13
Furunkulose U114-16
Fusionssystolen U33-1
Fusobakterium U90-7
Fuß U23-13; U61-4
Fußabdruck U23-13
Fußballen U23-13; U65-16
Fußdeformität U142-7
Fußende (Bett) U19-3
Fußfesseln U19-2
Fußgänger(in) U6-3
Fußknöchel U23-12
Fußmarsch U65-1,14
Fußpflege U15-15
Fußpfleger(in) U15-15; U16-1
Fußpilz(erkrankung) U90-16
Fußsohle U23-13
Fußsohlenreflex U113-1; U17-9;
 U87-17
Fußsohlenwarze U23-13; U114-17
Fußstapfen U65-4
Fußstütze U19-4; U64-17; U131-11
Fußtieflage U131-13
Fußtritt U64-12
Fußwurzel(knochen) U28-25
Fusus neuromuscularis U57-12; U30-2
– neurotendineus U57-12
füttern U2-3; U17-13; U79-1

G

G/P/A/AR-System U70-8
G0-Phase U83-12
G1-Phase U83-12
G2-Phase U83-12
GABA U82-17
GABAerg U42-11
Gabe U121-3,7
–, orale U118-21
gabeln, sich U34-13
Gähnen U44-1; U72-1
Galle U47-11,1; U45-10
–, extravaskuläre U38-6
–, pleiochrome zähflüssige U47-11
Galleerbrechen U47-11
Gallenabfluss U36-6
Gallenblase U47-7; U22-4; U35-11
Gallenblasenentfernung U47-7
–, laparoskopische U128-3
Gallenblasenentleerung U47-7
Gallenblasenentzündung U47-7
–, akute U109-13
Gallenblasengang U47-8
Gallenblasenhals U47-7
Gallenblasenkarzinom U98-2
Gallenfarbstoff U47-11; U56-7
Gallenflüssigkeit U47-11; U55-13
Gallengang U47-9; U90-17
–, interlobulärer U47-3
–, proximaler U87-14
Gallengangadenom U47-9
Gallengänge U47-5
–, extrahepatische U47-6
–, intrahepatische U47-9
Gallenganghypoplasie U47-6
Gallengangstenose U47-8
Gallengangsystem, durchgängiges
 U34-14
Gallengangwucherung U47-9
Gallenkanälchen U47-11
Gallenkapillaren U34-5; U47-11
Gallenkolik U47-9,11; U104-15
Gallenproduktion U47-11; U54-2;
 U88-11
Gallenrückfluss U46-4
Gallensäfte U46-11
Gallensalz U47-11; U82-5
Gallensalzaufnahme U47-11
Gallensalzmangeldiarrhoe/-ö U47-11
Gallensand U47-11
Gallensäure U47-11; U78-16; U81-2,19
–, (de)konjugierte U47-11; U81-9
–, wasserlösliche U78-4
Gallensäurepool U47-11
Gallensekrete U46-11
Gallensekretion U88-11
Gallenstauung U47-10
Gallensteinauflösung U81-22
Gallensteine U47-7,1; U89-21
–, eingeklemmte U109-15
–, stumme U119-6
Gallensteinerkrankung U47-11
Gallensteinileus U109-6

Gallensteinleiden U89-2
Gallensteinzertrümmerung U13-9
Galleproduktion U47-11
gallertartig U58-10
Gallertkern U85-20
Gallestauung U47-7,11
Gallethromben U47-11
Gallezylinder U47-11
gallig **U47**-11
Galopp(rhythmus) **U110**-6
–, präsystolischer U110-6
–, protodiastolischer U33-6
Gamet **U51**-4; **U85**-2
Gametenentwicklung U85-2
Gametentransfer, intratubarer **U69**-18; U50-4; U85-2
Gametenverschmelzung U85-2
Gametogenese U51-4; U85-2
Gametozid U85-2
Gammaaminobuttersäure U82-17
Gammaglobulin U39-5; U78-18
Gammaglobulinfraktion U81-4
Gamma-Hexachlorhexan U81-7
Gammakamera U99-17
Gang **U65**-1f,4
–, antalgischer U65-2
–, ataktischer U65-2; U113-8
–, auffälliger U107-20
–, breitbeiniger U65-2
–, federnder U1-4
–, innenrotierter U23-14
–, kleinschrittiger U65-2
–, schlurfender U65-2
–, schwankender U65-2; U113-8
–, taumelnder U65-2
–, torkelnder U65-2; U77-7
–, trippelnder U65-2
–, unsicherer U31-15; U65-1
–, zerebellarer **U113**-8
Gangart **U65**-2
Gangataxie U65-2; U113-8
Ganglia trunci sympathici U22-8
Ganglienblocker U40-11; U92-7; U93-6
Ganglienleiste U40-11
Ganglienzelle U40-11
Ganglion **U40**-11
– cervicothoracicum U40-11
– Gasseri U40-11
– geniculatum U40-11
– geniculi U40-11
– semilunare U40-11
– spirale cochleae U60-12
– stellatum U40-11
– superius nervi vagi U40-10
– trigeminale U40-11
ganglionär **U40**-11
Ganglioneurom **U98**-13; U40-11
Gangioplegikum U40-11; U92-7
Ganglioside U40-11
Gangrän **U89**-30
–, diabetische U124-7
Gangschulung U142-18
Gangstörung U65-2; U113-8
Gangunsicherheit U113-8

Gänsehaut **U56**-14; **U105**-8
Gantry U99-19
ganz schlucken U9-14
Ganzkörperbestrahlung U99-4
Ganzkörper-Clearance U49-7
Ganz(körper)packung U1-20
Ganzkörperpeeling U1-20
Ganzkörperscanner U99-18
Ganzvirusimpfstoff U122-2,6
Ganzwaschung (im Bett) U142-20
gären **U46**-12
Gartenkräuter U1-19
Gärung **U46**-12
Gärungsprodukt U46-12
Gas, nitroses U82-16
–, schädliches U82-2
–, übelriechendes U82-2
Gasaustausch **U44**-4; U43-1; U82-2
Gasbildung U46-15
Gasbrand U89-30; U90-3
Gaschromatografie U83-22
Gasembolie U124-13
gasförmig **U46**-15; **U82**-2; U105-14
Gasförmigkeit U46-15
Gasgemisch U82-2
Gasinsufflation U128-10
Gasödem U90-3
Gaster **U45**-8
Gastrektomie, totale **U127**-1
Gastrin **U55**-13
– Releasing Peptide U54-9
Gastrinom **U55**-13
Gastritis U45-8
Gastroenteritis **U94**-18
–, infektiöse U94-1,18
Gastrolith U89-21
Gastroskop U17-6
Gastroskopie **U118**-11
gastroskopisch **U118**-11
Gastrula **U85**-5
Gastrulation **U85**-5
Gasverlust (Pneumoperitoneum) U128-9
Gaszustand **U46**-15
Gating-Strom U42-9
Gattung(en) U90-9
Gaumen **U26**-10; U21-8; U87-7
–, weicher U27-16; U45-3; U66-5
Gaumenbein U28-9
Gaumenbogen U35-6; U26-10; U95-13
–, hinterer U45-4
Gaumenmandel U35-6; U45-4
Gaumensegel U26-10
Gaumensegellähmung U64-15
Gaumenspalte U26-10; U87-26
Gaumenwulst U28-10
Gaumenzäpfchen U63-13
Gauß-Verteilung U100-12
Gaze **U140**-18; U17-13; U132-18
Gazekissen U132-18
Gazestreifen U140-18
– (Ohr) U60-1
Gazetampon U140-18
Gazetupfer U140-18

Gebäck **U3**-10
Gebärde **U67**-1
Gebärdensprache U61-11; U67-1
gebären **U71**-2,4,9,8
Gebärende **U71**-9
gebärfähiges Alter U80-1; U92-33
Gebärmutter **U50**-5; U71-1
Gebärmutterentfernung U50-5
Gebärmutterhals **U50**-7
Gebärmutterschleimhaut **U50**-6; U51-7
Gebärstuhl U71-2
Gebäudebrand U6-10
Gebäudeeinsturz U6-5
geben **U23**-6
gebeugt **U63**-2f
Gebiet, zeckenverseuchtes U90-15
Gebiss **U27**-1
–, bleibendes **U27**-6
–, künstliches **U27**-8
gebläht **U109**-8
gebogen **U23**-4; U132-9
geboren **U71**-1
Geborgenheit U8-4
Gebrechen **U4**-7; **U142**-4
gebrechlich **U4**-7; **U25**-8; U18-7
Gebrechlichkeit U25-8; U103-9; U1-11
gebrochen (Knochen) **U106**-1
Geburt **U71**-3f,9; U85-1
–, bei der **U70**-11; U55-23
–, bis zur U69-12
–, nach der U71-20
–, natürliche U71-9
–, sanfte U71-9
–, vor der U71-21
Geburtenanamnese U102-4
Geburtenkontrolle **U69**-5
Geburtenrate U71-2
Geburtenregelung **U69**-5; U71-8
–, natürliche U69-5
Geburtenziffer U71-2
gebürtig U71-1
Geburtsbeginn U71-3
Geburtseinleitung U71-9
Geburtsfehler U142-4
Geburtsgewicht U24-1; U71-8
Geburtshelfer(in) **U15**-16; **U16**-6; U71-8
–, staatl. geprüfte(r) U13-14
–, (nichtärztl.) **U71**-4
Geburtshilfe U15-16; **U16**-6; U18-1
Geburtskanal **U50**-8; **U71**-8
Geburtsklinik U14-1
Geburtslänge U24-2
Geburtsort U71-2
Geburtsphase **U71**-13
Geburtstermin, errechneter U71-4
–, voraussichtlicher **U70**-10; U117-2
Geburtsurkunde U18-10; U71-2
Geburtsvorbereitungskurs U13-12; U70-10; U71-9
Geburtswehen U71-2
Geburtszange U71-9,14; U132-14
Gedächtnis **U74**-1,8,13
–, akustisches U74-8

Gedächtnis, deklaratives U74-8
–, episodisches U74-8
–, explizites U74-8
–, immunologisches U39-15
–, implizites U74-8
–, mittelfristiges U74-8
–, nachlassendes U74-8
–, prozedurales U74-8
Gedächtnisbildung U74-10
Gedächtnisblockade U74-13
Gedächtnisbrücke U74-13
Gedächtnisfähigkeiten U74-8
Gedächtnisfunktion U74-8
Gedächtnishilfen U74-8,13
Gedächtnisleistung U74-8,13
Gedächtnislücke **U74**-17,8
Gedächtnisschwäche U74-13
Gedächtnisspeicherung **U74**-9 f
Gedächtnisspur U74-9,12
–, dauerhafte U74-12
–, langanhaltende U74-12
Gedächtnisstörung U74-8; U77-13
–, funktionell beeinträchtigende U74-17
Gedächtnisstütze **U74**-2,8,13
Gedächtnistraining U74-13
Gedächtnisverlust U74-17,8
–, vorübergehender **U74**-17
Gedächtniszelle U39-15
gedämpft U7-10f; **U61**-5,11; U89-13
– (Stimme) U66-10
Gedämpftheit **U61**-5
Gedanke(n) **U73**-8; U77-5
Gedankengang U73-1,6
Gedankenlesen U61-10; U74-1
gedeckt **U129**-9
gedehnt **U109**-8
gedeihen **U1**-4
Gedeihstörung U15-12
gedemütigt U68-9; U77-12
gedenken **U74**-8
Geduld **U75**-18
Gefahr **U8**-4; **U124**-2; **U134**-5
gefährden **U4**-11; **U8**-4; **U124**-2; **U89**-4
Gefährdung, fetale U124-2
Gefahrenbereich U91-5
Gefahreneindämmung U91-5
Gefahrengrenze U91-5
Gefahrenlinie U91-5
Gefahrenstoffe U91-5; U124-2
Gefahrenzone U8-4
Gefahrenzustand, fetaler U107-11
gefährlich **U8**-4; **U91**-5
Gefahrlosigkeit **U8**-4
Gefälle, osmotisches U49-4; U88-4
gefältelt U52-2
gefaltet **U87**-8
Gefasel U66-1
Gefäß **U34**-1
–, aberrierendes U34-1
–, abführendes U34-1
–, blutendes **U38**-6
–, kreuzendes U87-7
–, neugebildetes U97-15
–, versorgendes U34-1

Gefäß, zuführendes U34-1
Gefäßabschnitt, aneurysmatischer U110-18
Gefäßanlage U34-1
Gefäßaustritt, massiver U38-6
Gefäßbett U34-1
Gefäßbildung U34-1
Gefäßbündel U130-13
Gefäßchirurg(in) U15-14; U126-3
Gefäßclip **U138**-15; U137-13
Gefäßdurchlässigkeit U36-16
Gefäßerweiterung **U36**-11; **U92**-17
Gefäßformationen, neugebildete **U97**-15
Gefäßgeflecht U34-5; U40-12
Gefäßgeräusch U110-4
Gefäßinfiltration U97-12
Gefäßinjektion, episklerale U58-6
Gefäßklemme **U127**-10; U132-13 f
Gefäßklip **U138**-15; U137-13
Gefäßknospe U34-1
Gefäßkrampf U36-11; U110-15
Gefäßkrankheit U118-16
Gefäßläsion U34-1
gefäßlos U86-7
Gefäßlumen **U34**-14; U87-22
Gefäßnadel U132-5
Gefäßnervenbündel **U40**-12
Gefäßnetz U34-5
Gefäßneubildung U34-1
Gefäßpermeabilität **U36**-16
Gefäßpinzette U132-14
Gefäßplastik **U127**-4
Gefäßruptur U5-7; U64-13
Gefäßschädigung U34-1; U59-16
–, postinflammatorische retinale U87-11
Gefäßstiel U34-1; U87-24
Gefäßsystem **U34**-1
Gefäßtonus U31-10
gefäßverengend U36-11; **U92**-17
Gefäßverengung **U36**-11
Gefäßverschluss **U124**-13; U34-1
Gefäßversorgung U34-1
Gefäßwiderstand **U36**-10; U34-1
–, systemischer U36-10
Geflecht **U34**-5; **U40**-12
geflechtartig **U40**-12
Geflechtknochen U28-2
–, verkalkter U31-14
Geflechtschicht U86-5
gefleckt **U114**-9
geflochten **U137**-7
Geflügelpest U94-9
Geflüster **U66**-16
geformt U9-7
gefriergetrocknet U130-9
Gefrierkonservierung **U136**-17
Gefrierpunkt U82-7
Gefrierschnitt U87-5; U126-10
Gefrier-Tau-Zyklus **U69**-14; U136-16
Gefühl **U32**-1; **U57**-3,5; **U76**-1,3; **U77**-2
–, euphorisches U77-18
–, taubes U57-3
–, würgendes U46-4

Gefühle, abgestumpfte U76-1
–, erotische U68-9
–, versteckte U76-1
gefühllos **U32**-2; **U57**-5,8; **U75**-8; **U76**-1,4; **U93**-4
Gefühllosigkeit U57-3; **U135**-3
Gefühlsausbruch U76-1; U102-2
gefühlsbetont U75-16
gefühlskalt **U68**-7
gefühlsmäßig **U76**-1
gefühlvoll **U76**-1; U77-2
gefüllt U53-3
gefurcht **U87**-26
Gegenanzeige U9-17; **U120**-10
Gegenauge U113-11
Gegendrehung U31-7
Gegengewicht **U88**-19
Gegengift U9-15; **U91**-15,2
gegenläufiger Strang U84-11
Gegenleiste U60-2
Gegenmittel **U9**-15; U91-2
Gegenpulsationsvorrichtung U125-8
Gegenquadrant U26-20
Gegensatz **U59**-11
Gegenspieler **U31**-4
Gegensprechanlage **U17**-17
gegensteuern U88-2
Gegenstoß-Fraktur **U106**-9
Gegenstrom **U88**-18
Gegenstromaustauschsystem U49-10
Gegenstromelektrophorese U88-18
Gegenstrommultiplikation U49-10
Gegenstromprinzip U88-18
Gegenstromsystem **U49**-10; U88-18
gegenüberstehen **U21**-2
gegenüberstellen **U59**-11
Gegenzähne U26-1
Gegenzug U141-3
Gehabe, gekünsteltes **U75**-3
Gehalt **U116**-16
Gehbock **U19**-14
Geheimnis U88-11
Geheimratsecken U25-15
gehemmt **U76**-12; U7-1; **U75**-2,17
Gehen **U19**-12; **U142**-13
– ohne Belastung U65-1
–, rasches U1-6,14; U65-1
gehen **U65**-1,5
–, an Krücken U65-1; U142-13
–, am Stock U65-1
–, auf und ab **U65**-6
–, bergauf U65-1
–, hin und her **U65**-6
–, im Ebenen U65-1
–, leicht gebeugt U63-3
–, wackelig (Kleinkind) **U65**-10
gehfähig **U19**-12; **U65**-1; **U142**-13
Gehfähigkeit U19-14
Gehgestell **U19**-14
Gehgips U19-14; U65-1; U141-6
Gehhilfe **U65**-1; U19-11; U142-29
Gehilfe/-in **U142**-29
Gehirn **U41**-1
Gehirnblutung U41-1

Gehirnentzündung U94-13
Gehirnerschütterung U5-14; U41-2; U124-19
Gehirnhautentzündung U94-13
Gehirn-Rückenmark-Flüssigkeit U41-17
Gehirnschlag U124-14; U41-2
Gehirnstoffwechsel U41-1
Gehirnwäsche U41-1
Gehirnwindung U41-5
Gehör U61-2
– finden, kein U61-9
–, absolutes U61-6
–, scharfes U61-8
Gehörgang U21-15; U61-2
–, äußerer U60-3
–, durchgängiger U60-3
–, innerer U60-3
Gehörknöchelchen U60-5; U28-2
Gehörknöchelchendefekt U60-5
Gehörknöchelchenfehlbildung U60-5
Gehörknöchelchenkette U60-5; U61-3
Gehörknöchelchenunterbrechung U60-5
Gehörlose U61-9
Gehörschutzpfropfen U60-1
Gehörstöpsel U60-1
Gehschule U64-18
Gehstock U19-14
Gehstollen U65-1; U141-6
Gehwagen U19-14
geimpft U122-2
Geimpfte(r) U122-2
Geißel U83-5
Geißeltierchen U90-2
Geißelzelle U83-2
Geist U74-1; U75-7; U77-2
–, reger U31-11
–, wacher U1-6; U75-7
geistesabwesend U74-15,1
Geistesgestörte(r) U77-24
Geisteshaltung U75-4
geisteskrank U77-3,13,24; U4-1
Geisteskranke(r) U77-24
Geisteskrankheit U77-15 f; U14-5
Geistesschärfe U59-8
Geisteszustand U77-1; U119-15
geistig U73-1 ff
gekehrt, in sich U75-14
gekocht U3-23
gekrümmt U63-2
gekürzt U22-1
Gel U9-8
–, spermizides U69-5
Gelächter U66-2
geladen, schwach/stark U81-10
gelähmt U31-12; U113-7
gelappt U87-23
gelassen U75-16; U76-19
Gelassenheit U1-16
gelaunt, schlecht U76-2
Gelbfärbung d. Skleren U58-6
Gelbfieber U94-19; U105-3
Gelbkörper U51-8
Gelbkörper-Hormon U55-19

Gelbkörperphase U51-8
Gelbkreuz U82-2
gelblich U37-3
Gelbsehen U59-9; U113-11
Gelbsucht U108-4; U47-1,13; U58-6
–, chronische U89-8
Gelbverfärbung U108-4
Gelenk U29-1
–, echtes U29-3
–, instabiles U31-15
Gelenkbeweglichkeit, eingeschränkte U142-8
Gelenkbewegung U31-18
Gelenkblockierung U128-7
Gelenkchondromatose U98-12
Gelenkdeformierung U142-7
Gelenkempfindung U57-11
Gelenkerguss U29-1,8
–, blutiger U29-3
–, seröser U29-3
Gelenkersatz U29-1; U127-4
Gelenkfläche U29-1; U87-4
Gelenkflüssigkeit U29-8
Gelenkfraktur U106-1
Gelenkhöhle U28-6; U29-1; U87-26
gelenkig U1-13; U31-11
Gelenkinnenhaut U29-3
Gelenkinstabilität U31-15
Gelenkkapsel U29-9,1
–, pathologisch dünne U29-9
Gelenkkapselschrumpfung U29-9
Gelenkknorpel U29-1 f,7
Gelenkknorren U28-4; U29-6
Gelenkkontraktur U29-9
Gelenkkörper, freier U29-3
Gelenkluxation U29-1
Gelenkmaus U29-3
Gelenkpunktion U29-1
Gelenkreiben U106-14
Gelenkreposition U29-1
Gelenkschiene U141-7
Gelenkschmiere U29-8,3
Gelenkschonung U1-10
Gelenksensibilität U57-11
Gelenkspalt U29-1
Gelenksteifigkeit U103-20
Gelenktuberkulose U94-16
Gelenkversteifung U141-13; U29-3
Gelfiltration U83-22
Gelineau-Syndrom U72-18
gelöst U81-25,3
gemäßigt U10-6
Gemeindepfleger U16-7
Gemeindepsychiatrie U77-16
Gemeindeschwester U16-7
Gemeinschaftsaktivitäten U142-27
Gemeinschaftspraxis U14-2; U18-1
Gemeinschaftssinn U77-2
gemischtdispers U81-22
Gemurmel U66-15
Gemüse U3-6
Gemüt, ausgeglichenes U75-15
Gemütsbewegung U76-1
Gemütsleben U77-2

Gemütszustand U76-2
Gen U84-1
–, geschwulsterzeugendes U97-1
–, genabelt, zentral U114-10
Genamplifikation U84-36,1
genau U75-1
Genauigkeit U120-15
Genbank U84-1
Genbestand U84-1
Genbibliothek U84-1
Gen-Cluster U84-2
Gendosis U84-1
Genduplikation U84-1
genealogische Analyse U84-29
genehmigen U101-24
geneigt U131-13
Generalstabsarzt/-ärztin U13-4
Generationskonflikt U80-8
generisch U121-2
genesen U4-16
Genesung U4-16; U14-3; U134-14
Genesungsheim U14-3
Genesungsprozess U142-21
Genesungszeit U120-14; U134-14
Genetik U84-1
Genetiker(in) U84-1
genetischer Stoffwechseldefekt U89-6
Genexpression U83-16; U84-1
Genfamilie U84-1
Gengruppe U84-2
Genickschlag U6-4
Genickstarre U103-20
genießbar U2-5
genießen U62-7
Genioplastik U21-6; U127-4
Genitale U50-1; U69-11
–, äußeres U52-1
– –, weibliches U50-11,1
–, inneres U50-1
–, intersexuelles U50-1
– –, äußeres U53-12
Genitalfalte U50-1
Genitalhöcker U50-1
Genitalien U51; U52-1; U69-1,11
Genitalleiste U50-1; U85-9
Genitalwarzen U96-14
Genitalwulst U85-10
Genkarte, fortlaufende U84-33
Genkartierung U84-34,1
Genklonierung U84-1
Genkopie U84-1,16
Genkopp(e)lung U84-37,1
Genlokus U84-2
Genmanipulation U84-1
Genmutation U84-20
Genom U84-1
Genomhybridisierung, komparative U84-38
Genomkarte U84-1,34
Genort U84-2
Genotyp(us) U84-10,1
Genregion U84-2
Genspleißen U84-1
Gentechnologie/-technik U84-1,17

Genu **U23**-11
- corporis callosi U41-3
- recurvatum **U142**-8
genügen U76-8
genügsam U76-13
Genugtuung, innere U76-1
genuin **U89**-8
Genuss, sinnlicher U57-9
Genussmittelanamnese U102-4
gepflegt **U19**-10; **U25**-4
Geplapper **U66**-17,19
gepolstert **U17**-13; U131-13; U140-19
-, gut **U19**-5
gepresst U9-7
geprüft U102-17
gepuffert **U81**-20
gerade **U31**-3
Geräte **U132**-1
-, orthopädische **U15**-15
Gerätetauchen U6-17
Geräusch **U61**-3; U33-1; U34-3; **U66**-11
-, blasendes **U110**-4
-, diastolisches U33-3
-, leises U61-1
Geräuscherkennung U74-3
geräuschlos **U61**-3
gereizt (Stimmung) U76-7; U89-10
Gereiztheit **U76**-7; **U108**-13
-, prämenstruelle U71-22
Geriater(in) **U15**-17; **U80**-15
Geriatrie **U15**-17; **U80**-15
geriatrisch **U80**-15
Gerichtsmediziner(in) **U12**-21; **U15**-21
gerichtsmedizinisch U77-3
geriffelt (Branchen) U138-14
gerillt **U87**-26
geringfügig U121-14
geringschätzig U67-16
Gerinnbarkeit U38-10
gerinnen **U38**-10,12; **U127**-10
Gerinnsel **U38**-12
Gerinnung **U38**-10
-, disseminierte intravasale U38-10
-, intravasale U124-3
Gerinnungsfaktor **U38**-13,10
Gerinnungsfaktorkonzentrat U136-17
gerinnungsfördernd **U38**-10
gerinnungshemmend **U38**-14
Gerinnungshemmer **U92**-16
Gerinnungsstörung U38-10,13; U89-1
Gerinnungszeit U38-10
Germinalzellaplasie U53-9
Germinalzellen U53-9
germizid **U90**-5
Germizid **U90**-5
Geroderma U80-15
Gerodontologie U80-15
geronnen (Blut) **U38**-12; U136-10
Gerontologie **U80**-15
Gerontopsychiatrie U15-12
Gerontotherapie U80-15
Gerota-Faszie U30-7

gerötet **U56**-18
Gerotherapie U80-15
Geruch **U62**-1,3; U116-15
- erkennen U74-3
- wahrnehmen U62-2
-, angenehmer U75-5
-, durchdringender U62-4
-, moderiger U62-1
-, scharfer U62-4
-, schwacher U62-3
-, übler **U62**-3
-, unangenehmer U62-1
-, widerlicher U62-1
geruchlos **U62**-3; U49-13; U82-11
Geruchsempfindlichkeit U57-8; U62-1
Geruchsempfindung U57-3; U62-1
-, gestörte U62-1
-, veränderte U62-1
Geruchsrezeptor U62-1
Geruchsschwelle U62-3
Geruchssinn **U62**-1; U57-5 f;
Geruchsstörung U62-1
Geruchstäuschung U62-1
Geruchsvermögen U62-1
Geruchswahrnehmung U62-1
geruchundurchlässig U62-3
Gerüsteiweiß U56-6; U79-9
Gerüstsubstanz U86-19
Gesamtbilirubin U47-13
Gesamtblutmenge **U36**-7
Gesamt-Clearance U49-7
Gesamtdosis, kumulative U91-5
Gesamteisenbestand U82-21
Gesamtgröße U25-3
Gesamthämoglobin U116-9
Gesamtinzidenz U100-7
Gesamtkaliumgehalt U82-18
Gesamtkörperfett U24-5
Gesamtkörperwasser U82-4
Gesamtmortalität U12-3
Gesamtrisiko U124-2; U134-5
Gesäß **U22**-13,2; U30-15; U45-17; U70-16
Gesäßbacke **U22**-13
Gesäßfurche U22-13; U25-17; U30-15
Gesäßgegend U22-13
Gesäßmuskel **U30**-15; U22-13
Gesäßmuskelschwund U22-13
Gesäßspalte U22-13; U87-26
gesättigt **U81**-24
geschädigt **U6**-11; U89-4
Geschädigte(r) **U6**-12
geschäftsfähig U20-14; U73-4,2
Geschäftsunfähigkeit U142-4
gescheit **U41**-1; **U75**-7
geschichtet **U87**-8
Geschicklichkeit U74-2
-, feinmotorische U31-20
-, motorische **U31**-19
geschieden U102-9
geschient U31-2
geschlängelt U110-17
Geschlecht **U68**-1; **U84**-30
-, das andere U68-1

Geschlecht, das schöne U25-13
-, gonadales U54-11; U68-1
-, weibliches U50-2
Geschlechtschromatin U84-6
Geschlechtschromosom **U84**-6; U68-1
geschlechtsgebunden **U84**-27,1; U68-1
Geschlechtshormon U55-1
Geschlechtsidentität U68-1,14; U75-2
Geschlechtskrankheit U96-1
Geschlechtsmerkmale U53-12; U68-1
-, sekundäre U55-17; U84-20
Geschlechtsorgane **U50**-1; **U52**-1; U69-1,11
-, äußere U52-1
Geschlechtsperzentile U100-11
geschlechtsreif U68-1
Geschlechtsreife **U80**-7
-, vorzeitige U68-1
Geschlechtstrieb U68-1; U73-11
Geschlechtsumwandlung U53-12
Geschlechtsverkehr **U68**-1,5; U53-2
-, schmerzhafter U68-5
-, ungeschützter U68-5
-, vorehelicher U68-1
Geschlechtszelle **U85**-2
Geschlechtszuordnung U68-1
geschliffen (Fläche) U27-18
geschlossene Reposition U106-3
Geschmack **U62**-6 f
- verleihen **U62**-7
-, metallischer U82-6
-, voller U62-7
geschmacklos **U62**-7
Geschmacksafferenzen U40-4
Geschmacksempfindung U57-2 f; U62-6 f
-, herabgesetzte U62-6
Geschmacksknospe U62-6
geschmackskorrigiert **U62**-7
Geschmacksnervenendigungen U62-6
Geschmacksorgan U21-11
Geschmacksporus U62-6
Geschmacksprüfung U62-6
Geschmacksqualität U62-6
Geschmacksrezeptor U62-6
Geschmackssinn **U62**-6
Geschmacksstoff **U62**-6
Geschmacksunterscheidung U57-2; U62-7
Geschmacksvermögen U62-7
Geschmacksverstärker U62-7
geschmeidig **U31**-11; U24-6; U86-15
geschmeidige Narbe U140-10
Geschmeidigkeit **U31**-11; U56-11
geschützt, patentrechtlich **U121**-2
geschwächt U139-12
Geschwister U72-18; U95-8
-, HLA-identische U39-20
-, vernachlässigtes U77-11
Geschwisterspender U129-15
geschwollen **U56**-19
-, stark U64-2
Geschwulst **U97**-2; **U89**-16
-, gestielte U87-24

Geschwulst, gutartige U97-2
Geschwür U89-17; **U114**-13; **U5**-5
Geschwürabheilung U140-4
gesellig **U75**-14,13
Gesellschaft, medizinische **U13**-13
Gesellschaftstrinker(in) U10-10
Gesetze, physikalische U15-1
gesetzlicher Vertreter U134-3
Gesicht **U21**-2; **U25**-10; **U67**-8
–, ausgemergeltes U25-7
–, faltiges U25-17
–, finsteres **U67**-11
–, gerötetes U25-10; U56-18; U77-7
–, schmales U24-6
–, sorgenvolles U67-11
–, unbewegtes U64-2
–, verdutztes U67-8
–, verhärmtes U25-7; U64-10
–, verzerrtes U67-8
Gesichter schneiden **U67**-8
Gesichtsmuskeln U56-17
Gesichtsapraxie U113-9
Gesichtsausdruck **U67**-8; **U25**-10; U21-2
–, apathischer U25-10
–, stumpfer U76-17
Gesichtserythem U108-7
Gesichtsfalten U25-17; U56-17
Gesichtsfarbe **U25**-11
–, gesunde **U25**-12,11
Gesichtsfeld **U59**-7
–, binokulares U59-7
Gesichtsfeldausfälle **U113**-11; U59-7; U74-18; U142-4
Gesichtsfeldeinengung U59-7
Gesichtsfelduntersuchung U59-7
Gesichtshautstraffung U64-16
Gesichtslage U71-5
Gesichtslähmung U28-9
Gesichtslinie U59-5,7; U87-9
Gesichtsmuskulatur U30-2
Gesichtspunkt U59-1
Gesichtsröte **U108**-8; U51-11
Gesichtsrötung U67-8
Gesichtsschädel **U28**-9
Gesichtsspalte U66-22; U106-11
Gesichtszelt **U125**-12
Gesichtszüge **U25**-10; U21-2
–, grobe U25-10; U103-3
–, männliche U53-1
Gesinnung **U77**-2
Gesinnungswechsel U32-2
gespalten **U81**-8; **U87**-26; U83-14; **U106**-11
gespannt **U31**-10
– (auf) **U76**-5
gespickt **U141**-14
Gespräch, persönliches U102-14
gesprächig **U66**-18,8
gespreizt U131-12
Gestagenpräparat, reines U55-19; U69-7
Gestagentest U55-19
Gestagenvorläufersubstanzen U55-19

Gestank **U62**-1,4
Gestationsalter U70-6
Geste **U67**-1
gesteigert U92-28
gestielt **U87**-24; U114-3
– (Lappen) **U130**-10f
– (Polyp) U127-11
Gestik U67-1
gestikulieren **U67**-1
–, wild U67-1
gestört **U4**-4,11; **U76**-21; **U142**-4; **U89**-2
– (Okklusion) U27-13
–, psychisch U77-13
Gestose U91-22
Gestotter **U66**-20
gestreift U32-6
gestützt (auf) U63-10
gesund **U1**-1 ff; **U2**-13; **U25**-12
– pflegen U16-2
– sein **U1**-3
–, (geistig) **U77**-3
Gesundbeter(in) U15-23; U140-4
gesunde Seite U131-16
Gesundenuntersuchung U18-9
Gesunder U101-10
Gesunderhaltung U126-13
Gesundheit **U1**-1 f,5,7
–, geistige **U77**-3
–, psychische **U77**-1
–, robuste U1-11
–, schwache U25-8; U103-9
gesundheitlich **U1**-5
Gesundheits- u. Krankenpfleger **U16**-4
– – Krankenschwester **U16**-4
– – Sozialministerium (USA) U13-3
Gesundheitsamt U13-2
Gesundheitsapostel **U2**-17
Gesundheitsattest U1-1; U18-10,15
Gesundheitsbehörde **U13**-2
–, regionale U16-7
gesundheitsbewusst U7-1
Gesundheitsbewusstsein **U13**-1
Gesundheitsdienst **U13**-1
–, öffentlicher **U13**-3
–, präventiver U13-1
Gesundheitseinrichtungen U13-2,8; U14-3; U16-1
Gesundheitserziehung U1-1; U142-18
Gesundheitsfürsorge **U13**-1; **U20**-3; U16-1
Gesundheitsgefährdung **U4**-11
Gesundheitsministerium U13-2
Gesundheitsorganisation U13-1
Gesundheitspflege **U1**-5; **U13**-1
Gesundheitspfleger **U16**-4
Gesundheitspolitik U1-1; U13-1
Gesundheitsrisiko U8-4; U91-5,18
gesundheitsschädlich U1-1; U91-1
Gesundheitsschwester **U16**-4
Gesundheitsverhalten U1-1
Gesundheitsverwaltung **U13**-2
Gesundheitswesen U1-1; U13-1; U16-1
–, Mitarbeiter(in) im **U16**-1
Gesundheitszentrum **U1**-18

Gesundheitszeugnis U1-1; U18-10
Gesundheitszustand U1-1; U107-2
gesüßt U79-6
getapet (Gelenk) **U141**-11
getrampelt, zu Boden U65-5
Getränke **U3**-24
–, alkoholfreie U10-2
–, alkoholische **U3**-27; U10-10
–, harte U10-2
–, kohlensäurehaltige U82-10
getränkt U82-5
Getreideflocken **U3**-12
Getreidestaub U91-7
getrennt **U87**-12
getreu **U75**-10
gewalttätig U73-7
Gewebe **U86**-3
–, angrenzendes U87-9; U97-11
–, benachbartes U87-9; U97-11
–, chromaffines U82-25
–, embryonales U85-1
–, erektiles U53-3; U86-3
–, gesundes U1-2
–, interstitielles U86-3
–, kontraktiles U31-1
–, lymphatisches U35-1; U86-3
–, myxomatöses U98-7
–, sensibilisiertes U39-2
–, spongiöses U52-16
–, undifferenziertes U86-3
Gewebeabbau U86-3
Gewebeaktivator U37-15
Gewebeannahme **U129**-20
Gewebeatmung U44-4
Gewebeauflösung U86-3
Gewebebank U14-12
Gewebedehnung **U129**-10
Gewebedosis U99-9
Gewebeeinschmelzung U89-12
Gewebeentnahme **U118**-5
Gewebeexpander U129-10; U136-13
Gewebefaktor **U37**-14
Gewebefasszange U132-13f
Gewebehomogenisator **U133**-17
Gewebehormon U55-1
Gewebehypoxie U111-3; U123-8
Gewebekonservierung U14-12
Gewebekultur U86-3; U116-6
Gewebelehre **U86**-1
Gewebemakrophagen U37-9; U47-4
Gewebemanschette, gesunde U87-10
Gewebeoxygenation U44-6
Gewebeparasit U90-13
Gewebeplasminogenaktivator U88-12
Gewebeprobe **U118**-5,4; U14-11
Gewebeschaden U86-3
gewebeschädigend U91-1
Gewebeschädigung U6-11; U86-3
Gewebescheibe U87-5
Gewebeschnitt U86-1
Gewebeschrumpfung U89-30
Gewebeschwund U89-29
Gewebespannung **U31**-10; U86-3
Gewebethromboplastin **U37**-14

Gewebetransplantat, freies U130-13
Gewebetrümmer U89-30
Gewebeturgor U56-19
Gewebetypisierung U86-3
Gewebeübertragung, freie U130-13; U129-13
Gewebeverhärtung U89-14
Gewebeverteilung U91-17
Gewebeverträglichkeit U129-20; U136-11
Gewebezerkleinerer U128-16; U133-17
Gewebezerkleinerung U128-16
Gewebezüchtung U86-3
Gewebstod U89-30
Gewicht, spezifisches U81-3
Gewichtheben U24-1; U64-16
gewichtiger (als) U117-17
Gewichtskontrolle U24-1
Gewichtsreduktion U1-15
–, bewußte U24-1
Gewichtsschwankungen U24-1
Gewichtstabelle U24-1
Gewichtstraining U142-18
Gewichtsverlagerung U64-4
Gewichtsverlust U108-14; U24-1
–, unbeabsichtigter U40-6
Gewichtszug U141-3
Gewichtszunahme U24-1
Gewinde U133-12
gewinnen U117-3; U69-12
gewissenhaft U75-10,1; U7-1; U104-6
–, sehr U75-11
gewissenlos U75-11
Gewissensbisse U76-13; U77-10
Gewohnheit(en) U10-11; U11-5; U102-9
–, gesundheitsschädigende U91-1
gewohnheitsmäßig U10-11; U11-5; U73-13
Gewohnheitstrinker U10-3
gewöhnt U10-11
Gewöhnung U11-5; U135-5; U73-13
gewunden U41-2; U60-11
Gewürze U3-20
gewürzt U62-7
GFR U49-2
GIA-Stapler U138-17
Gicht U10-10; U49-14; U84-1; U92-28
Gichtknoten U89-16
Gichtnephropathie U49-14
Giemen U44-7,4; U111-8; U103-2
Giemsa-Färbung U96-6; U116-4
gierig essen U2-4
Gießerfieber U82-29
GIFT U69-18; U85-2
Gift U91-2,4; U9-15; U121-12
–, oral aufgenommenes U91-2
–, pflanzliches U91-4
–, tierisches U91-2,4
Giftblase U91-2
Giftdrüse U91-2
Giftefeu U91-2
Giftelimination U91-23,2,17
Giftgas U91-2
giftig U91-2; U122-8
Giftigkeit U91-11; U121-13

Giftinformationszentrale U91-2
Giftmüll U91-5; U124-2
Giftsack U91-2
Giftschlange U91-2
Giftstachel U5-10; U91-2,14,16
Giftstoff U91-4; U9-15
Giftsumach U91-2
Giftzahn U91-16
Gigantismus U24-4
Gigantomastie U24-4
Gingiva U26-12
Gingivaatrophie U89-29
Gingivahyperplasie, fibröse U98-8
Gingivatransplantat, freies U130-10
Gingivostomatitis herpetica U95-7; U109-2
Ginglymus U29-5
GIP U55-13
Gipfel U105-17
Gips U64-14,2
Gipsbinde U141-10
gipsen U141-6
Gipshandschuh U141-6
Gipshülse U141-6
Gipslonguette U141-7
Gipsmieder U141-6
Gipsschale U141-7
Gipsschere U132-4
Gipsschiene U141-7
Gipsstiefel U141-6
Gipstutor U141-6
Gipsverband U64-14; U141-6; U140-20
Gitter (Krankenbett) U131-18
Gitterfaser U86-5
Gitternetz U17-5
Glandula U54-1
– lacrimalis U58-9
– mucosa U86-17
– parathyroidea U54-7
– parotidea U95-4
– pituitaria U54-5
– praeputialis U52-17
– sebacea U56-8
– seminalis U52-9
– sudorifera U56-10; U105-12
– suprarenalis U54-10
– thyroidea U54-6; U55-6
Glandulae bulbourethrales U52-13; U50-10; U53-6
– ceruminosae U60-15
– endocrinae U54-1
– exocrinae U54-1
– intestinales U45-1
– lacrimales U54-1
– – accessoriae U58-9
– mammaria U54-1
– mucosae U44-9; U54-1
– paraurethrales U50-9
– pyloricae U45-8
– salivariae U45-3; U54-1
– sebaceae U54-1
– sudoriferae U54-1; U105-15
– tarsales U56-8
– urethrales U54-1

Glandulae vestibulares majores U50-10; U54-1
Glans (penis) U52-14
– clitoridis U50-12
Glanz U59-11; U82-6
glänzen (Augen) U59-3
glänzend (Oberfläche) U31-10
glanzlos U31-16
Glanzschicht U56-2
Glasfaserendoskop U118-11
Glasfaserinstrument, lichtleitendes U133-2
Glasfaseroptik U133-3
Glasgow-Komaskala U7-14
Glaskörper U58-10; U86-20; U88-9
Glaskörperabhebung U58-10
Glaskörperablösung U58-10
Glaskörperblutung U58-10
Glaskörperentfernung, operative U58-10
Glaskörperflüssigkeit U58-10
Glaskörperraum U58-10
Glaskörperstränge U58-10
Glaskörpertraktion U58-10
Glaskörpertrübung U58-10
Glaspipette U116-12
Glasthermometer U105-6
glatt U17-14; U62-8
glatte Muskulatur U92-19; U93-16
glätten U132-12
Glatzenbildung, männliche U25-16
glatzköpfig U25-16; U21-1
Glatzköpfigkeit U21-16
Glaubersalz U91-24; U82-18
Glaukom, neovaskuläres U97-15
Gleason-Schema U97-14
gleichaltrig U80-1; U100-3
Gleichaltrige U80-8
gleichbleibend U119-12
Gleichgewicht U88-19; U21-15
–, dynamisches U88-20; U57-18
–, osmotisches U88-19
–, seelisches U77-9,16
Gleichgewichtsdialyse U88-19
Gleichgewichtskonzentration U81-23
Gleichgewichtssinn U57-18,5
Gleichgewichtsstörung U57-18; U113-8
gleichgültig U75-8; U76-15
Gleichgültigkeit U76-15; U77-8
Gleichschritt, im U65-4
Gleichstromimpulse U123-12
–, synchrone U110-14
Gleichstrom-Kardioversion U123-12
Gleichung, chemische U81-1
gleichverteilt U100-12
gleichwertig U81-10
gleichzeitig bestehend/auftretend U119-16
Gleitbruch U45-5; U65-8
gleitend U65-8
gleitfähig (machen) U56-9; U17-14,6
Gleitgel U17-14; U56-9
Gleitgelenk U29-7
Gleithernie U45-5; U65-8,12; U89-23

Gleitlochschraube U141-16
Gleitmechanismus U29-7
Gleitmittel **U17**-14; **U56**-9; U68-5; U92-30
– ohne Wirkstoffe U56-9
–, reizarmes U17-14
–, schmerzstillendes U56-9
–, spermizides U17-14
Glied(maße) **U23**-1
Glied, abgetrenntes U23-1
–, männliches **U52**-14; **U53**-1
Glieder, bewegliche U31-11
Gliederfüßer U90-12
Gliederschmerzen **U104**-5
Gliedmaßenabsetzung **U142**-6
Gliedmaßengürtel U23-1
Gliedmaßenskelett U28-1
Glioblastom **U98**-14
Glioblastoma multiforme U98-14
Gliom **U98**-14
–, malignes U98-14
gliomatös **U98**-14
Gliomatose **U98**-14
Gliose **U98**-14
–, lobäre U41-5
Glisson-Schlinge U141-3
Glisson-Dreieck **U47**-5,3
Globinkette, α- U39-6
Globulin **U78**-18
–, antihämophiles U38-13; U39-5; U78-18
–, cortisolbindendes U55-10
–, thyroxinbindendes U54-6; U55-6
Globulinfraktion U78-18
Globus pallidus U41-10
Globusgefühl **U109**-5
Globussyndrom **U109**-5
Glomerulosklerose U48-6
Glomerulus **U48**-6
Glomerulusbasalmembran U48-6; U86-16
Glomerulusfiltrat **U49**-1; U48-6
Glomus aorticum U34-8
– caroticum U34-10; U37-1; U86-20
Glossa **U21**-11
Glossitis U21-11
Glottis **U43**-7
Glucagon **U55**-12
Glucagonom **U55**-12
Glucagontest U55-12
Glukokortikoid U55-10
Glukonat **U79**-7
Glukoneogenese U47-17; U78-14
Glukosamin **U79**-7
Glukose **U78**-13; **U79**-7
Glukose-Alanin-Zyklus U82-10
Glukoseaufnahme, insulinvermittelte U78-5
Glukose-Laktat-Zyklus U78-6; U81-15
Glukoserest U79-5
Glukoseschwelle U49-5; U79-7
Glukosespiegel U79-7
Glukosetoleranztest U116-2; U118-2
Glukosetransporter U78-17; U79-7

glukoseundurchlässig U36-16
Glukosurie U49-5; U79-7
Glukuronsäure U78-11
Glukuronsäureanteil U81-4
Glukuronsäurebestandteil U81-4
Glutamat **U47**-16
Glutamatdecarboxylase U47-16
Glutamatdehydrogenase U47-16
Glutamat-Oxalacetat-Transaminase U47-16
Glutamat-Pyruvat-Transaminase U47-16
Glutamatsäurereste U47-16
Glutamin **U47**-16
Glutaminmangel U47-16
Glutaminsäurerest U81-9
Glutaminsynthetase U47-16
Glutathion U47-16
gluteal **U22**-13
Glycerol **U82**-13
Glyceroltrinitrat U82-13,16
Glykocholat-Atemtest, 14 C- U47-11
Glykogen **U47**-14; **U78**-13; U79-7
Glykogenabbau U47-14; U78-10,13
Glykogenese **U78**-14; U47-14
Glykogenolyse **U78**-14,10,13; U47-14
Glykogenose U47-14; U78-13
Glykogenphosphorylase U47-14; U78-13
Glykogenspeicherkrankheit U47-14; U78-13
Glykogenstoffwechsel U47-14
Glykogensynthese **U78**-14; U47-14
Glykogensynthetase U47-14
Glykol **U47**-17
Glykolyse **U78**-14
Glykosid, zyanogenes U91-9
Glykosurie U49-5
glykosylieren **U78**-7
Glyzeral U82-13
Glyzerin **U82**-13
Glyzerinaldehyd U82-13
GnRH U55-20
GnRH-Sekretion, pulsatile U55-22
Gold **U82**-28
goldener Schuss **U11**-11
Goldfolie U82-28
Goldgussfüllung U82-28
Goldinlay U82-28
Golgi-Apparat **U83**-10
Golgi-Komplex **U83**-10
Golgi-Region U83-10
Golgi-Sehnenorgan **U57**-12
Golgi-Vesikel U83-10
Gomphosis U29-14
gonadal **U50**-3
Gonade(n) **U54**-11; U52-1; U69-1
–, undifferenzierte U85-11
Gonadenanlage, indifferente U54-11
Gonadendifferenzierung U85-11
Gonadendosis U54-11; U99-9
Gonadendysgenesie U54-11
Gonadenschutz U54-11
Gonadoliberin U55-20

Gonadotropin **U54**-11
–, humanes menopausales U69-17
–, hypophysäres U55-20
Gonadotropinanstieg U55-20
Goniometrie **U142**-9
Gonoblennorrhoe/-ö U96-2
Gonokokkämie **U96**-2
Gonokokkeninfektion **U96**-2
Gonokokkensepsis **U96**-2
Gonorrhoe/-ö **U96**-2; U69-6
gonorrhoisch **U96**-2
Gonosom **U84**-6; U68-1
Goormaghtigh-Zellen U48-6
Gower, Hämoglobin U37-6
GPT **U47**-16
Graaf-Follikel **U51**-6; U55-14
Grad **U97**-11,14
Gradient, osmotischer U49-4
Grading **U97**-14
–, korrektes U97-14
Graefe-Zeichen U67-14; U59-2
grämen, sich **U12**-12 f
Gram-Färbung U116-4
Grammmolekül **U81**-3
Grand mal(-Epilepsie) **U124**-9
Granula, gefriergetrocknete U9-9
granulär **U140**-7
Granulat **U9**-9
Granulationsgewebe **U140**-7
Granuloma inguinale **U96**-6; U89-17
– pediculatum U96-6
– pyogenicum U96-6
– teleangiectaticum U96-6
– venereum **U96**-6
granulozytär **U37**-8
Granulozyten, basophile U37-8
–, eosinophile U37-8
–, junge U37-8
–, neutrophile **U39**-18; U37-8
–, polymorphkernige U37-8; U39-17
–, reife U37-8
–, segmentkernige U37-8; U87-6
–, stabkernige U37-8
–, übersegmentierte U37-8
Granulozytenspeicher U37-8
Granulozytentransfusion U37-8
Granulozytenvorläuferzelle U37-8
Granulozytenzellreihe U37-8
Granulozytopenie U38-5
Granulum melanini U56-7
Graph **U100**-27
Graphit U82-32
Gratiolet-Sehstrahlung U58-15
grätschen (Beine) **U63**-5
Grauen **U77**-5
grausam **U32**-2
Grauwert-Sonografie U118-17
gravid **U70**-5
Gravidität **U70**-6
Gravitation U70-7
Grawitz-Tumor **U98**-2
Gray **U99**-10
grazil **U24**-6
graziös U24-6

Gregg-Syndrom U95-3
greifbar **U62**-9
greifen **U64**-9; U23-6
Greifkraft U31-13
Greifreflex U64-9
Greifzirkel **U24**-12; U17-1
Greis U80-2
greisenhaft **U80**-13
Grenzdebilität U77-22
Grenzdifferenz U100-21
Grenzen **U87**-10
–, deutlich erkennbare U87-10
– erkennen, seine U74-4
Grenzfall U102-13; U116-23
Grenzlinie **U87**-10
Grenzschwellenwert U91-18
Grenzstrang U40-9
Grenzstrangganglien U22-8
Grenzwert **U100**-24
Grenzwert-Hypertonie U116-23
grenzwertig **U116**-23
– (Signifikanz) U100-21
Grenzzone, dermoepidermale U56-2 f
Griff **U64**-9; U23-6; U132-2; U133-1
Grifftechniken U142-12
Grimasse **U67**-8
Grimmdarm **U45**-15
Grinsen **U67**-9
Gripgewinde (Trokarhülse) U133-6
Grippe **U94**-9
– , leichte U62-8; U94-9
grippeähnlich **U94**-9
Grippepneumonie U94-9
Grippe(schutz)impfung U94-9; U122-4
Grippevirus U94-9
Grobgriff U64-9
grobknochig U24-8
grobkörnig U89-30
Grobmotorik **U31**-20
Grocott-Färbung U82-28
Groll **U76**-11
groß **U24**-3
großblasig **U114**-12
Großbrand U6-10
Größe **U24**-2 f; **U97**-11; U89-15
Größenideen U77-18
Größenwahn U77-20
Größenwahnsinnige(r) U75-21
Großhirn **U41**-2
Großhirnhälfte **U41**-3
Großhirnhemisphäre **U41**-3
– dominante U41-3
Großhirnlappen U87-23
Großhirnrinde **U41**-6; U86-23
Großhirnsichel U41-2
großlumig U127-18; U132-5; U136-5
großzügig **U75**-16
GRP U54-9
Grube **U28**-6; **U58**-13; **U87**-26
Grübeln **U109**-3; U73-6
–, zwanghaftes U77-19
Grundbetreuung, medizinische U13-1
Grunderkrankung U4-4; U120-9

Grunderkrankung, bösartige U97-5
Grundglied U87-14
Grundimmunisierung U122-3
Grundleiden U4-4; U89-1
gründlich U5-11; U140-11
Grundphalanx U87-14
Grundumsatz **U78**-2,12; U55-6
Grundwasser, kontaminiertes U91-6
Grünholzfraktur **U106**-12
Gruppe **U81**-4 f
–, hydrophile U81-13
–, hydrophobe U81-13
–, polare U81-13
Gruppenaktivitäten U142-27
Gruppenbindung U75-9
Gruppendeterminante U39-7
Gruppendynamik U11-13
Gruppenentladung, phasische U42-6
–, rhythmische U42-6
gruppensequentielles Design U101-13
gruppiert U95-7; U114-9 f
Guajaktest **U118**-6
Guanosinmonophosphat, zyklisches U81-7; U83-17
gucken U59-1 f; **U67**-12
Gültigkeit **U100**-30
Gültigkeitsprüfung **U100**-30
Gumma U96-3
Gummiharze U81-6
Gummiknoten U96-3
Gummimanschette U17-8
Gummistrümpfe U31-16
Gummizelle **U77**-26
Gummy smile U26-12
Gunn-Zeichen U58-5
günstig U91-18
Gurgellösung, salzhaltige U94-10
Gurgelmittel U21-12; U93-4
Gurgeln **U66**-7; U45-4; U46-4,14
Gurt U131-10; **U141**-8,11
Gürtel U140-26
gürtelförmig U93-3
Gürtellinie **U22**-6
Gürtelrose **U95**-7; U96-10
Gurtverband U141-11
Guss **U19**-10; **U64**-14; U142-20
gustatorisch **U62**-6
gut (für Gesundheit) **U1**-5
– belüftet U44-5
– gebaut **U25**-1
gutartig **U97**-5
Gutartigkeit **U97**-5
Gutenachtgeschichte U72-4
Güterwagen U6-3
gutgehend (Praxis) U1-4
gutherzig **U32**-2; U75-5
gutmütig **U75**-1; U76-2
Guttae **U9**-11
gut tun **U1**-3
guttural **U21**-12
Gutturallaute U66-2
GVHR **U130**-20
Gymnastik **U1**-15
Gymnastik machen U1-12

Gynäkologe/-login **U15**-16
Gynäkologie **U15**-16
Gyrus **U41**-5
– frontalis U28-8

H

H1-Antihistaminika U92-22
H1-Rezeptorenblocker U92-22
Haar **U21**-16; **U25**-15
–, krauses U63-6
Haaransatz **U25**-15; **U87**-9; U21-15 f
–, hinterer U87-20
–, niedriger U25-15
Haarbalg **U56**-13
Haarbruch **U106**-11; U25-15
Haare, einwachsende U25-14
–, wenig U56-13
haarfein **U87**-9
Haarfollikel **U56**-13
Haargefäß **U34**-5
haarig **U25**-15; **U56**-13
Haarnävus U25-19; U98-15
Haarpapille **U56**-13
Haarschaft U56-13
Haarschnitt U25-15
Haarteil U25-15
Haarwurzel U56-13
Haarzunge U21-11; U56-13
Habenula U54-13
Habituation **U73**-13
habituell **U10**-11; **U11**-5; **U73**-13
Habitus **U25**-2; **U107**-10; **U73**-13
–, asthenischer U25-2
Haemangioma **U98**-5
Haematemesis U103-12
Haemophilus influenzae B-Meningitis U94-13
– – Typ b U78-17
Haferkleie U2-17
haftbar U20-13
haften U139-19; **U128**-15
Haftlinse **U58**-8
Haftpflichtversicherung U18-15
Haftschalen, harte U58-8
Haftstiel **U85**-17
Haftzecke U90-15
hager **U24**-10
Hahn **U118**-7
Hahnentritt U65-2
Haken **U132**-9
Hakenbein U28-17
Hakendraht U141-14
Hakenfuß U28-27
Hakenwurm U90-16
Halbantigen **U39**-7
Halbblut **U37**-1
Halbdunkel **U59**-11
halbdurchlässig **U36**-16
Halbierung **U51**-5
Halbleiter U82-30
halbliegend U63-10
Halbmond **U56**-15

Halbschlaf **U72**-1
Halbseitenblindheit **U113**-11; U59-17
Halbseitenlage, (in) **U63**-9
Halbseitenunaufmerksamkeit U77-11
Halbwertbreite U92-5
Halbwertszeit **U92**-5; U88-20
–, biologische U83-1; U91-17
–, physikalische U91-17
halbwüchsig **U80**-8
Halitose **U109**-2
Halluzination(en) **U77**-20; **U73**-10
–, akustische U11-21; U60-7
–, hypnagoge U72-18
halluzinatorisch **U77**-20
halluzinieren **U77**-20
Halluzinogen **U11**-21
halluzinogen **U11**-21
Halluzinose **U11**-21
Haloextension U141-9
Halo-Fixateur U141-9
Halogengruppe U82-23
Halogenkohlenwasserstoff U93-12
Halonävus U98-15
Halothan **U93**-12
halothanbedingte Leberschädigung U93-12
Halothanhepatitis U94-15
Hals **U21**-12 f
–, dünner U24-10
–, geröteter U103-5
–, schlanker U25-5
Halsband der Venus U114-4
Halsentzündung **U103**-5
Halskratzen U62-11; U103-5
Halskrause **U141**-9; U8-15; U21-13
Halskrawatte U141-9
Hals-Nasen-Ohren-Heilkunde **U15**-19
Halsrippe **U28**-14; U21-13
Halsschmerzen **U103**-5; U45-4
Halsschwirren U110-3
Halsspülung U21-12
halsstarrig **U75**-19
Halsstellreflex U57-16
Halsvenen, prominente U110-6
Halsvenenkollaps U110-16
Halswickel U45-4
Halswirbel U28-19
Halswirbelsäule U21-13; U142-12
Halswirbelsäulenschleudertrauma **U124**-18
Haltbarkeit U9-19
Halteband **U30**-8
Haltegriff U64-9
Haltemuskel U30-2
halten **U64**-9
Haltenaht U64-16; U137-1; U138-1
Haltereflex **U57**-16
Haltetremor U113-4
Haltevorrichtung **U64**-9; **U133**-1,9
Haltung **U63**-1; **U65**-3; **U75**-3; **U76**-3
– (Körper) U1-15
–, schlechte U5-17
–, aufgeschlossene U75-16
–, aufrechte U63-1

Haltung, dystone U142-17
–, feindselige U75-3; U77-7
–, gebeugte U25-9; U63-3
–, gebückte U63-3
–, krumme **U63**-2
–, schlechte U63-1
–, starre U63-1
–, versöhnliche U77-2
Haltungsfehler U63-1; U142-12
Haltungsgymnastik U1-15; U142-18
Haltungskorrektur U142-1,12
Haltungsreflexe **U57**-16; U42-12; U63-1
Haltungsschaden U142-7
Haltungsschule U63-1
Haltungstherapie U63-1
Haltungsübungen U63-1; U142-17
Häm **U37**-6; U116-9
Hämadsorption U81-12
Hämagglutination **U38**-11; U39-19
Hämagglutinationshemmtest U38-11
Hämagglutinin U39-19
Hämangiom **U98**-5
Hämangioperizytom U98-5
Hämapherese U136-15
Hamart(omat)ose **U98**-6
Hämarthros U29-3
Hamartoblastom **U98**-6
Hamartochondrom U98-6,12
Hamartom **U98**-6
Hamartoma pulmonum U98-6
hamartomartig **U98**-6
hamartomatös **U98**-6
Hämatemesis U37-1; U111-7
Hämatoblast **U38**-3
Hämatochezie U109-11
hämatogene Infektion U136-9
Hämatokrit(wert) (HKT) **U116**-10
Hämatom **U38**-8; **U89**-26; U5-13; U12-15
–, epidurales U38-8
–, organisiertes U38-8
–, pulsierendes U38-8
Hämatombildung U136-7
Hämatopoese **U38**-1
–, konstitutive U38-1
hämatopoetisch **U38**-1
Hämatotympanon **U60**-4
Hämatoxylin-Eosin-Färbung U116-4
Hämaturie **U112**-3
–, schmerzlose U102-2
Hämeisen U82-21
Hämgruppe U81-4
Hammer **U60**-5
Hammerfinger U23-7; U64-15; U142-8
Hammerstiel U60-5
Hammerzehe U23-14
Hämoccult®-Test **U118**-6
Hämodialysator **U125**-21
Hämodialyseshunt U36-14
Hämodilution **U36**-13,4; U81-23
–, isovolumetrische U36-13
Hämodynamik **U36**-4
hämodynamisch **U36**-4; U4-11

Hämofiltration **U125**-21
Hämoglobin **U37**-6; **U116**-9
–, adultes U37-6
–, embryonales U37-6
–, (früh)fetales U37-6
–, glykolisiertes U37-6
– C-Krankheit U116-9
– –, homozygote U84-5
– S-C-Krankheit U37-6
Hämoglobinderivat U116-9
Hämoglobinkonzentration, mittlere korpuskuläre (MCHC) U37-4; U116-10
Hämoglobin-Sättigung U81-24
Hämoglobinurie U37-6
Hämokonzentration **U36**-13
Hämolysat **U136**-12
Hämolyse **U38**-4; **U136**-12; U36-4
hämolysieren **U136**-12
Hämolysin **U38**-4
hämolytisch **U38**-4
Hämoperfusion **U136**-1
– (mit Aktivkohle) U91-25
Hämophile(r) **U38**-6; **U5**-18
Hämophilie U37-1
– B U38-10,13
Hämopoese **U38**-1
Hämoptoe **U103**-17; **U111**-7
Hämoptyse **U103**-17
Hämoptysis **U111**-7
Hämorrhagie **U5**-18; **U38**-8; **U89**-26
hämorrhagisch **U38**-8
Hämorrhoidenzäpfchen U9-12
Hämospermie U53-7
Hämostase **U38**-10; **U127**-10
–, primäre U38-10
Hämostatikum **U127**-10
Hämostyptikum **U127**-10
Hämothorax **U111**-14
Hämotoxin U91-4
Hämoxymetrie **U125**-9
Hämozyt **U37**-4
Hämozytoblast **U38**-3
Hämozytometer **U83**-21
Hämpräkursor U37-6
Hämsynthese U37-6
Hämvorstufe U78-9
Hand **U23**-6
Handbeatmungsbeutel U8-12
Handbewegung **U67**-5; U142-12
Handchirurgie U23-6
Handdynamometer U142-17
Hände ringen U67-4
Händedesinfektion **U139**-6
Händedruck **U64**-9 f; U23-6
–, feuchter U105-12
–, schlaffer U31-12; U65-11
Händeklatschen **U67**-6
Handelsname U121-2
Händereinigung, chirurgische U131-2
Handfesseln U19-2; U23-5
handfest **U62**-9
Handfeuerwaffe **U6**-8
Handfläche **U23**-6; U106-10

handflächenwärts **U87**-17
Handgelenk **U23**-5; U28-16; U31-2
Handgelenksfessel U77-26
Handgelenksgurte U125-24
Handgelenksumfang U25-3
Handgerät U23-6
Handgeschicklichkeit U23-6
Handgriff **U64**-9; U23-6; U28-13; **U141**-2
Handgriffe U8-11
Handicap **U142**-3
Händigkeit **U23**-6
handlich **U23**-6
Handlinie U87-17
Handlungsanweisungen, festgelegte U20-7
Handlungsvollmacht **U20**-14
Handrücken U22-11; U114-5
Handschrift U23-6
Handschuh, OP- U139-15
handschuhförmig U93-3
Handsteuerung U19-4
Handteller U23-6
Handtuch U140-24
–, zusammengerolltes U64-8
Handvoll **U23**-2
Handwölbung U64-9
Handwurzel **U23**-5; **U28**-17
Handwurzelkanal U23-5
Handwurzelknochen **U28**-17; U23-5
Handzerstäuber U92-14
Hanf U11-15
Hang **U75**-4
Hängebauch U22-4; U45-6; U63-13
Hängebrust U56-19; U63-13; U64-15
Hängelage **U63**-13
Hängen **U56**-19
– (Brust) U71-27
– lassen U64-15
hängend U63-13; **U64**-15
Hängeohren U60-1
Hangman-Knoten U138-4
Hansen-Krankheit **U94**-17
haploid **U84**-9
Haploidentität U84-9
Haploidie **U84**-9
Haplotyp U84-4,9
Happen **U27**-12
Hapten **U39**-7
Haptenkonjugat U39-7
Haptenkonjugation U39-7
harmlos **U6**-11; U39-23
Harn **U49**-12
– lassen U49-16,12
–, 24-Stunden- U49-12; U116-15
–, blutig tingierter U49-12
–, trüber U49-12
Harnabflussbehinderung U48-1
Harnabgang, unwillkürlicher U112-15
harnableitend U49-12
Harnableitung U48-1; U49-12
Harnanalyse **U116**-15
Harnausscheidung **U49**-6; U88-16
–, übermäßige **U112**-2

Harnausscheidung, vermehrte U49-6; **U55**-24
–, verminderte **U112**-2
Harnausstrich U116-5
Harnaustritt U38-6; U136-7
Harnblase **U48**-11
Harnblasenmuskulatur **U48**-11
Harndrang U11-2
–, imperativer **U112**-4; U49-16
–, schmerzhafter **U109**-15
Harnfluss **U49**-17
Harngang **U85**-17
Harngewinnung U116-15
Harninkontinenz **U112**-15
Harnkanälchen **U48**-5,7
harnkontinent U112-15
Harnkonzentration U116-15
Harnkonzentrierung U116-15
Harnkultur **U116**-15
Harnleiter **U48**-10
–, embryonaler **U85**-17
Harnleiterfistelung, retroperitoneoskopische perkutane U128-5
Harnleitermündung U48-10; U87-21
Harnleitersteine U48-10
Harnleiterstenose U89-20
Harnmenge U112-5
–, Überwachung der U125-6
Harnorgane **U48**-1
Harnprobe **U116**-15; U49-12
–, zentrifugierte U83-20
Harnretention U112-10; U48-1
Harnröhrenaufdehnung U48-13
Harnröhrenausfluss U48-13
Harnröhrenbougierung U48-13
Harnröhrendauerkatheter U125-20
Harnröhrenentzündung U48-13
Harnröhrenmündung U48-13
Harnröhrenöffnung U48-13
Harnröhrenschließmuskel **U48**-14
–, äußerer U30-9
Harnröhrenspalte, untere U69-1
Harnröhrensphinkter U48-14
Harnröhrenstriktur U48-13; U89-19
Harnröhrenverengung U48-13
Harnsammelbehälter U19-8
Harnsäure **U49**-14; U92-28
Harnsäureausscheidung U49-14
Harnsäurebestimmung U49-14
Harnsäureclearance U49-7
Harnsäurekonzentration U49-14
Harnsäurekristalle U49-14; U82-5
Harnsäurelöslichkeit U49-14
Harnsäureretention U112-10
Harnsäurestein U81-22
Harnsäuresteinbildung U49-14
Harnsediment U48-1; U49-12; U81-27
–, unauffälliges U107-18
Harnspeicherung **U49**-15
Harnsperre, komplette U112-10
Harnstein U48-1; U49-12; U89-21
Harnstoff **U47**-18; **U49**-13,5; U48-8
– & Elektrolyte U116-12
Harnstoffclearance U47-18

Harnstoffspaltung U47-18; U78-14; U81-8
Harnstoffsynthese U49-13; U78-4
Harnstoff-Zyklus U47-18; U49-13; U78-6; U81-15
Harnstottern **U112**-9; U49-17
Harnstrahl **U49**-17; U48-1
–, schwacher U4-7; U112-7
Harnstrahlabweichung U49-17
Harnstreifentest U49-12
Harntrakt **U48**-1
Harnträufeln U49-17,12; **U112**-15
harntreibend **U92**-21
Harnuntersuchung **U116**-15
Harnvergiftung **U112**-13; U37-2
Harnverhalt(ung) **U112**-10; U48-1
Harnverlust (nach Miktion) U112-11
–, unwillkürlicher U112-15
Harnvolumen **U49**-7; U88-16
Harnwege, ableitende U48-1
Harnwegserkrankung U49-12
–, obstruktive U112-12
Harnwegsinfektion U48-1; U52-18; U94-2
–, fieberhafte U105-3
–, rezidivierende U119-18
Harnwegsobstruktion U89-18
Harnzylinder **U112**-14; U49-12; U116-15
Harnzytologie U83-1; U116-15
hart **U75**-11
harter Gaumen U28-10
hartnäckig **U75**-19; **U120**-13; U14-2
Hartnäckigkeit U75-11
Harz U11-15
–, gallensäurebindendes U47-11
Haschisch **U11**-15
– rauchen U11-1
Haschischzigarette **U11**-14
Hasenscharte U21-9
Hashimoto-Thyreoiditis U124-8
Hashitoxikose U91-20
Hasner-Klappe U58-9
hässliche Narbe U140-10
Hasson-Kanüle **U133**-14
– Trokar(hülse) **U133**-14
Hast **U65**-15
hastig **U65**-15
Hatha-Yoga U1-16
Haubenkreuzung U41-14
Hauch **U62**-2
Häufigkeitsverteilung **U100**-12
Häufung U94-8
–, familiäre U89-7; U102-7
Hauptast **U34**-13
Hauptbeschwerden U102-1; U103-1 f
Hauptbronchus U43-9
Hauptgefäß U34-6
Haupthistokompatibilitätskomplex **U39**-20
Hauptindikation U120-10
Hauptmahlzeit U2-7,2
Hauptmetabolit U78-11
Hauptnahrung U2-12

Hauptrisikofaktor **U124**-2
Hauptstromrauch U91-7
Hauptsymptom(e) U102-1; U103-1
Haupttodesursache U12-7
Hauptveranwortung U131-17
Hauptwirt U94-5
Hauptziel **U134**-4
Hausarzt/-ärztin U15-1; U102-7
Hausbesuch **U18**-7,2
Haushaltschemikalien U11-23
Haushaltshilfe U142-29
hausintern **U15**-5
Hauskrankenpflege U18-7
Hauskrankenpfleger(in) U18-7; U19-11; U140-1; U142-29
häusliche (Kranken)pflege U16-2; U120-9
Hausmeister **U16**-14
Hausmittel U9-2
Hauspflegehelfer(in) **U142**-29
Hauspfleger(in) U16-15
Hausstaubmilbe U90-15
Haustiertollwut U94-12
Haustrenanordnung U45-6
Haustrenbildung **U45**-15; U87-6
Haustrenmuster U45-6
Haustrierung **U45**-15
Haustrum **U45**-15
Haut **U56**-1
–, abgeschilferte **U56**-20
–, behaarte U56-13
–, blasse U25-12
–, faltige U25-17; U56-1
–, fettige U56-8
–, feuchtkalte U56-1; U77-5
–, fleckig verfärbte U56-7
–, geschmeidige U31-11; U56-1
–, rissige U56-1; U87-26
–, runz(e)lige U25-17; U56-1,17
–, schuppige U56-1,11
–, seröse **U86**-9
–, unreine U25-18
–, unverletzte U56-1
–, zarte U25-8
Hautablösung, großflächige U56-20
Hautabschilferung U56-20
Hautabschürfung U56-1; U140-13
Hautanhängsel **U114**-17; U56-1
Hautanhangsgebilde U56-1; U98-17
Hautausschlag **U108**-9; **U114**-2; U56-1
–, ekzemartiger U114-1
Hautbank U14-12
Hautbarriere U56-1
Hautbeschaffenheit U107-10
Hautblutung **U89**-27
Häutchen **U56**-16
Hautdeckung **U129**-9
Hautdehnungsstreifen U70-16
Hautdesinfektion **U139**-14
Hautdesinfektionsmittel U17-15; U139-1
Hautdiphtherie U95-9
Hautdurchblutung U16-11; U36-5; U56-1

Hauteinziehung U56-1
Hautentzündung **U114**-1; U56-3
Hautfacharzt **U15**-10
Hautfalten **U56**-17,1; U22-9; U25-17
Hautfaltendicke U24-12; U25-3; U56-17
Hautfaltenmessung U56-17
Hautfarbe, aschfahle U108-5
Hautfettgewebetransplantat U130-6
Hautfetzen U95-6
Hautflora U46-16
Hautgrieß **U114**-6
häutig **U86**-15
Hautikterus U108-4
Hautirritation U104-3
Hautjucken U92-22
Hautkontakt U62-8; U122-5
Hautkrankheit U15-10; U114-1
Hautlappen **U130**-6; U56-1
Hautläsion U5-5; **U89**-17
–, geschwürige U56-20
–, juckende U103-19
–, verkrustete U114-8
Hautleisten **U56**-11,3
Hautleistenmuster U56-11
Hautmanifestationen U15-10; U117-9
Hautmaulwurf U114-2
Hautplastik U56-3
Hautreizung U108-13
Hautrötung **U56**-18,1; **U108**-7; **U114**-2
–, anfallsweise **U56**-18
–, postvakzinale U122-4
Hautschädigung U65-12
Hautschnitt U126-9
Hautschuppen **U114**-7
Hautsegment **U56**-3
Hautsinn U57-3
Hautspaltlinien **U56**-17; U87-9
Hautstruktur U56-1; U107-10
Hauttemperatur U105-1
Hauttest **U118**-2
Hauttestreaktion U118-2
Hauttransplantat **U130**-6f,1,5
–, zweizeitiges **U130**-7
Hautturgor **U56**-19
Hautunreinheit **U25**-18; U76-4
Hautveränderung, präkanzeröse U97-6
Hautverfärbung, bläuliche **U12**-15
Hautverletzung U140-22
Haverhill-Fieber U90-8
Hb **U37**-6
HCG **U55**-20; U98-16
HCG-Bestimmung U55-20
HCG-Betauntereinheit U55-20
HCG-Test U55-20
HCG-Wert, erhöhter U55-20
HCl U81-19; U82-9
HCN U91-9
HDL-Cholesterin U47-12; U78-16
Hebamme **U71**-4,8; U17-12
–, diplomierte **U16**-6
–, staatl.-geprüfte U13-14
Hebammen-Stethoskop U17-2
Hebekran **U19**-13
Hebel U106-4

Heben **U64**-16; **U110**-4
heben **U46**-5; **U64**-16; **U65**-17; **U116**-19; **U129**-11
– (Bein) U65-17
– (Schulterblatt) U64-16
hecheln **U44**-7
Hefe(pilz) **U90**-18
Hefechromosomen, künstl. U84-6
heften **U138**-17; **U141**-15
Heftnaht U137-4
Heftpflaster **U140**-21 f,3; **U141**-11
Heftpflasterverband U140-21
Hegar-Stift U132-17
heikel (Essen) **U62**-8,11; **U2**-1
heilbar **U9**-2
Heilbarkeit U120-2
Heilberufe, nichtärztliche U13-14
heilen **U9**-2; **U120**-2; **U140**-4
heilend **U15**-23
Heiler(in) **U15**-23; **U140**-4
Heilerde U140-4
Heilgymnastik **U142**-18,1,17; U1-15
Heilhilfsberufe U16-1
Heilkraft U15-23
Heilkräuter U9-1
Heilmassage U142-15
Heilmittel **U9**-2; **U120**-2; U66-5
Heilpraktiker(in) U18-1
Heilquelle **U1**-18
heilsam **U1**-2
Heilsarmee U13-12
Heilstätte **U14**-3
Heilung **U15**-23; **U120**-2; **U140**-4
–, gute U1-3
Heilungsabsicht U120-2
Heilungsaussichten U120-2
Heilungsprozess U140-4
Heilungsrate U15-23; U100-8; U120-2
Heimdialyse U125-21
Heimlich-Handgriff **U8**-11
– bei liegenden Patienten U63-8
Heimtrainer U1-12
Heimtraining U142-17
Heinz-(Innen)körper U37-6
heiser **U103**-6; **U111**-11; **U21**-12
– schreien, sich U67-6
Heiserkeit **U103**-6; **U111**-11; U66-23
Heißhungerattacke U2-1
Heißluftdesinfektion U17-15
Heißluftsterilisation U139-2
heiter **U75**-6; U32-2
Heizdecke **U19**-6; U6-14
Heizkissen **U19**-6; U1-13; U140-19
hektisch **U77**-15
helfen **U1**-3; **U8**-1; **U19**-11
– bei U66-7
–, beim Aufsetzen U142-29
Helfer(in) **U8**-1; **U19**-11; **U142**-29; U8-15
–, ehrenamtliche(r) **U16**-15
–, medizinische(r) **U16**-9
Helferzelle **U39**-14
helikal **U84**-11
Helix U60-2
Helixknäuel U84-11

Helix-Loop-Helix-Motiv U84-3
Helixstruktur U84-11
Helix-Turn-Helix-Motiv U84-3
hell **U25**-13; **U59**-11
– (Bewusstsein) **U7**-3
Helladaptation **U59**-10; U88-17
helläugig U59-11
Hell-Dunkel-Unterscheidung U59-10
hellhäutig U25-11
Helligkeit **U59**-11
Helligkeitsregulation U59-11
Helligkeitssteuerung U59-11
hellwach U7-2; U72-6
Helminthen **U90**-16
Helminthiasis U90-16
Hemianopsie **U113**-11; U59-17
Hemicrania ophthalmica U113-16
Hemipelvektomie U142-6
Hemiskrotum **U52**-2
Hemisphärenkonvexität U41-3
hemmen **U42**-13; **U88**-14; U92-6f;
– (Sekretion) **U74**-14
Hemmer **U42**-13; **U88**-14; **U92**-7
Hemmstoff **U92**-7
Hemmung **U88**-14
–, kompetitive U88-14
–, motorische **U42**-13
–, postsynaptische U40-13
–, präsynaptische U42-13
–, reziproke U42-14
–, rückgekoppelte U42-13
hemmungslos U75-21
Henle-Schleife **U48**-8
Hepar **U47**-1
Heparin U136-14
hepatisch **U47**-1
Hepatitis **U94**-15; U47-1
– amoebiana U90-4
–, autoimmune U94-15
– A-Virus U94-1
– B U94-15
– B-Oberflächenantigen U94-15
– B-Virus U122-1
–, chronisch aggressive U94-15
– D-Virus U94-15
Hepatomegalie U47-1
Hepatotoxizität U91-11
Hepatozyt U47-3
herabgesetzt **U116**-20
herabhängen **U56**-19; **U64**-15
Herabhängen **U64**-15
– (Lid) **U113**-17; U58-3
herabsetzen **U88**-14
heranführen **U31**-6
Heranführen, seitliches **U31**-6
Heranreifen **U80**-10
heranwachsen **U80**-3
Heranwachsende(r) **U80**-8
herausdrücken **U54**-2
heraushebeln U106-4
herausspritzen (Blut) **U38**-7
herausstrecken (Zunge) **U67**-17
herauswachsen aus **U80**-3
herbeiführen **U119**-8

Herbizid **U91**-8
Herd **U97**-10; **U89**-3
Herdbefall U97-10
Herdentrieb U73-11
Herdinfektion U89-3; U97-10
Herdläsion U5-5
Herdsymptome U97-10
hereditär **U89**-7
Heredität **U84**-28
Heredoataxie, spinozerebellare U113-8
Herkunft **U84**-29
Hernia abdominalis U87-16
– diaphragmatica U43-12
– epigastrica U22-3
– glutaealis U89-23
– inguinalis U22-9; U52-8
– umbilicalis U22-5; U71-17
– ventralis U87-16
Herniation, zerebrale U124-19
Hernie **U5**-19; **U89**-23; U137-18
–, reponierte U140-26
Hernienstapler U138-16f
Hernioplastik U129-1
–, laparoskopische U128-3
Heroin **U11**-19
heroinabhängig U11-19
Heroinabhängigkeit U11-19
Heroinersatz U11-19
Herpes genitalis **U96**-10; U95-7
– neonatorum U96-10
– simplex **U96**-10; U5-5; U89-17
– zoster **U95**-7; U96-10
Herpes-Enzephalitis U95-7
Herpes-genitalis-Rezidiv U96-10
Herpesläsion U96-10
Herpesparonychie U96-10; U114-16
herpetisch **U95**-7; **U96**-10
herrisch **U75**-17
herstellen, (künstlich) **U54**-2
Hertwig-Magendie-Syndrom U59-15
herumfuchteln **U67**-5
Herumgehen **U65**-1,6
–, nervöses **U65**-6
herumlaufen U65-14
herumtorkeln U65-9
herunterhängen **U56**-19; **U64**-15
hervorheben (auf d. Tabelle) U107-17
hervorrufen U37-7; U92-2
hervortreten U89-23; U140-16
hervortretend **U87**-27
Herz **U32**-1
Herz(beutel)tamponade U32-3,5
Herz(-Kreislauf-)stillstand U32-3
Herz, künstliches U32-1
–, schwaches U103-9
Herzalarm **U123**-4
Herzanfall **U32**-14,1
Herzarbeit U32-3; U33-2
Herzbasis **U32**-4; U87-25
Herzbeutel **U32**-5
Herzbeutelpunktion U118-15
Herzbeuteltamponade **U110**-8; U125-17
Herzblock, totaler U123-2
Herzdämpfung U33-2

Herzdekompression **U125**-17; U6-17
Herzdruckmassage U123-4f; U125-17
Herzenzym U78-8
Herzfehler, angeborener U108-6
Herzfrequenz **U33**-5; U32-1
–, erhöhte **U110**-2
Herzfrequenzschwankungen U33-5
Herzgegend **U22**-3
Herzgeräusch **U110**-3; U32-1; U33-1
–, diastolisches U33-3
–, frühsystolisches U33-8
herzhaft **U32**-2
Herzhypertrophie **U110**-9; U89-15
Herzindex U33-2
Herzinfarkt **U32**-14,1,6 **U124**-11
Herzinfarktrisiko U32-14
Herzinnenhaut **U32**-5
Herzinsuffizienz **U110**-12
–, dekompensierte **U124**-12
Herzjagen **U110**-2
Herzkammer **U32**-8,3
Herzkatheter U127-19
Herzklappe **U32**-10,3; U34-12
Herzklappenerkrankung U32-3
Herzklappenersatz **U32**-5
Herzklappenfehler U118-15
Herzklappeninsuffizienz U32-10
Herzklappenprothese U32-10
Herzklappenrekonstruktion U32-10
Herzklappenstenose U89-20
Herzklappenzipfel **U32**-10
Herzklopfen **U110**-1; U107-7
Herzkontraktion U31-1
Herzkrankheit, koronare (KHK)
U124-11,12; U32-14
Herzkranzfurche U32-7
Herzkranzgefäß U32-14
Herz-Kreislaufinstabilität **U125**-2
Herz-Kreislaufstillstand **U123**-2
Herzleistung U33-2
herzlich **U32**-1f; U75-13
herzlos **U32**-2
Herz-Lungen-Bypass **U125**-11
– – Maschine **U125**-11; U32-1; U44-6;
U123-4
Herzmassage **U123**-5,4
Herzminutenvolumen (HMV) **U33**-7;
U32-3; U36-10; U88-16
Herzmonitor **U125**-6; U134-8
Herzmuskel **U32**-6; U30-2
Herzmuskelgewebe, gefährdetes U32-6
Herzmuskelriss U32-6
Herzmuskelschwäche **U124**-12
Herzohr **U32**-7
Herzpatienten U32-3
Herzperiode **U33**-2
Herzrasen **U110**-2
Herzrhythmus **U33**-6
Herzrhythmusanalyse U110-6
Herzrhythmusanalysestreifen U33-6
Herzrhythmusaufzeichnungen U33-6
Herzrhythmusstörung **U110**-6
Herzrhythmusüberwachung U33-6
Herzruptur U124-15

Herzschlag **U33**-1; U32-1
Herzschlagfolge, verlangsamte **U110**-2
Herzschlagfrequenz **U33**-5
Herzschlauch, primitiver U85-10
Herzschrittmacher **U123**-13; U32-3; U65-6
Herzschuss U6-8
Herzsilhouette U32-3
Herzspitze **U32**-4; U87-25
Herzspitzengeräusch U32-4
Herzspitzenstoß **U33**-4,1; U32-4; U42-5
–, hebender U33-4
Herzstillstand **U33**-3,1 f; **U123**-2,6
–, (künstlich) induzierter U32-3
–, unbemerkter U6-13
Herztätigkeit U32-1; U33-2; U88-14
–, verlangsamte **U110**-2
Herztod, akuter U123-2
Herzton **U33**-1; U61-3
–, gespaltener U33-1
–, IV. (S4) U110-6
Herztöne U17-2; U32-1
–, (kindliche) **U33**-1; U61-3; U70-4; U85-1
–, gedämpfte U33-1
–, schwache U33-1
Herzvergrößerung **U110**-9
Herzversagen **U110**-12; U32-1,3
Herzvorhof **U32**-7
Herzwandaneurysma U124-15
Herzzeitvolumen (HZV) **U33**-7
Herzzyklus **U33**-2
Heterochromatin **U84**-6
Heterodimer **U81**-6
heterodispers U81-22
Heterogenie, nicht-allelische U84-4
Heterophorie **U59**-15
Heterosom **U84**-6
Heterotropie U59-17
Heterovakzine U122-2
heterozygot **U84**-5; U85-2
Heterozygotennachweis U84-5
Heterozygotie **U84**-5; U85-2
hetzen **U65**-15
Heufieber U94-1,9; U105-3
heulen **U66**-2
Heuschnupfen U9-3; U94-1,9; U105-3
Heuschnupfenpatient(in) U4-3; U104-2
Hexenschuss **U104**-16; U28-20; U30-16
Hiatus aorticus U34-8
Hiatushernie U89-23
Hib **U78**-17
Hibernation, artifizielle U105-5
Hidr(o)adenom U98-4
Hidradenitis U56-10; U105-15
Hidroschesis U105-15
Hidrotikum **U105**-15
high **U11**-10
High-Density-Lipoprotein U82-14
High-Gefühl **U11**-10
high-output failure U124-12
hilär **U43**-4; **U87**-25
Hilfe **U8**-1; **U19**-11; **U142**-29
– benötigen U104-2

Hilfe, ärztliche U19-11
–, unsterile **U131**-9
Hilfeleistung, unterlassene **U20**-13,3
Hilferuf **U6**-19
Hilfestellung **U8**-1; **U19**-11
Hilflosigkeit **U142**-29
hilfsbereit **U142**-29
Hilfseinrichtungen U8-5
Hilfsgüter, medizinische U6-20
Hilfskraft, medizinische U16-15,1
Hilfsmittel **U8**-1; **U142**-29; **U120**-3
–, diagnostische U20-8; U117-11
–, orthopädische **U15**-15
Hilfsorganisation U8-2
Hilfspersonal **U16**-15
–, ärztliches **U16**-1; U8-6
Hilfsschwester U16-2
Hilfsteam, katastrophenmedizinisches U13-1
Hilum/-us **U87**-25
– pulmonis **U43**-4
– renale U48-2; U87-25
– renis U87-25
– splenicum U35-4; U43-4; U87-25
Hilusgefäße U43-4
Hiluslymphknoten U43-4
Hilusvergrößerung U43-4
Himbeerzunge U21-11; U95-6
hin u. hergehen U113-2
hinauftitrieren U116-17
hindämmern, vor sich **U72**-1
Hindernis U65-9
hindeuten (auf) U119-3; U109-8; U134-7
hindösen, vor sich **U72**-1
hineinbeißen U27-11
hinken **U65**-11,5; U31-12; U102-1
–, stark U65-11
hinknien U63-4
hinlegen, sich **U72**-3
hinsehen U67-14
hinstarren, vor sich U59-2
hintanhalten U60-15
Hinterbliebene **U12**-6,13
Hinterbliebenenrente U80-14
Hinterdarm U85-21
hintere(r) **U87**-16
hinterhältig **U75**-12,14
Hinterhaupt U28-7
Hinterhauptbein **U28**-8; U87-20
Hinterhauptlage U71-5
Hinterhauptloch, großes U28-6
Hinterkopf U22-11
Hintern **U22**-13
Hinunterschlingen **U2**-4
hinwegraffen U12-18
hinwegsehen U67-15
Hinweise (auf) **U117**-9
– ergeben, keine U107-17
–, subtile U74-2
hinweisen (auf) U54-13; U66-8
Hinweisreize, monokulare (Tiefensehen) U59-16
Hippokampus **U41**-11
Hippokampusformation U41-11

hippokratischer Eid U18-11
Hirci U56-13
Hirn **U41**-1
– und Rückenmarkhäute **U41**-8
Hirnanhangdrüse **U54**-5
Hirnbasis U87-25
Hirnbeteiligung U124-19
Hirnblutung U41-1
Hirndekompression U6-17
Hirndruckmessung, kontinuierliche U125-13
Hirndruckmonitor **U125**-13,25
Hirndrucksteigerung U125-13
Hirndurchblutung U36-5; U41-2
Hirnembolie U124-13
Hirnentwicklung U41-1
Hirngewölbe **U41**-3
Hirnhaut, harte **U41**-8
–, weiche **U41**-8
Hirnhautbeteiligung U94-13
Hirnhautentzündung **U94**-13; U41-8
Hirnhautreizung U41-8; U94-13
Hirninfarkt, ischämischer U124-13
–, vollendeter U124-14
Hirnkammer(n) **U41**-4
–, liquorgefüllte U125-13
Hirnkontusion U124-19
Hirnlappen **U41**-5
Hirnnerv U28-7; U40-1
–, III. U58-16
–, IV. motorischer U58-16
–, VIII. U40-1; U60-9,13
Hirnödem U110-15; U124-19
Hirnprellung U5-13; U41-2; U124-19
Hirnquetschung U124-19
Hirn-Rückenmarkflüssigkeit U105-16
Hirnsand U54-13
Hirnschaden **U124**-19; U41-1; U74-17
–, irreversibler U6-11
Hirnschenkel U41-5
Hirnstamm **U41**-12; U40-3; U98-14
Hirnstammapoplexie U124-14
Hirnstammaudiometrie U125-14
Hirnstammfunktion U41-12
Hirnstamminfarkt U41-12
Hirnstammkontusion U41-12
Hirnstammläsion U41-12
Hirnstammpotentiale, akustisch evozierte U41-12; U42-5; U60-13
Hirnstammreflexe U42-12; U113-12
Hirnstammschädigung U7-17
Hirnstiel U41-2,13; U87-24
Hirnstoffwechselrate U78-2
Hirnstrom-Biofeedback U142-25
Hirnströme U41-1; U118-12
Hirnszintigrafie U41-1
Hirnszintigramm U118-22
Hirntod **U7**-18; U12-7; U41-1; U124-19
Hirntoddiagnose U7-18
hirntot U12-5; U129-17
Hirntrauma U41-1
Hirnventrikel **U41**-4
Hirnverletzung U41-1
Hirnwindung **U41**-5

Hirnzentrum U41-1
Hirsutismus **U53**-12
His-Bündel **U32**-15,7
– – Elektrokardiografie U32-15
– – Rhythmus U33-6
His-Purkinje-System U32-15
Histamin **U78**-24
Histaminantagonist **U92**-22
Histaminkopfschmerz **U113**-16
Histiozyt **U39**-18
Histochemie U81-1
Histokompatibilität U86-1; U136-11
Histokompatibilitätsantigen U39-8,20
Histokompatibilitätstestung U39-20
Histologe/-in **U86**-1
Histologie **U86**-1; **U87**-1
histologisch **U86**-1
Histopathologie U89-1
historisch **U102**-4
Hitzeakklimatisierung U105-11
Hitzebelastung U105-11
hitzebeständig U105-10
hitzeempfindlich U57-8
Hitzeempfindlichkeit U105-11
Hitzeerschöpfung U6-15; U4-6; U103-8; U105-11
Hitzehyperpyrexie **U105**-11
hitzeinaktiviert U122-7
Hitzekollaps U6-5; U110-11; U105-11
Hitzekrämpfe U105-11
Hitzepickel U62-11
Hitzeschockproteine U105-11
Hitzesynkope U105-11
Hitzewallungen **U51**-11; **U108**-8
Hitzschlag **U105**-11,5; U124-14
HIV U96-15
HIV-Demenz U77-23
HIV-Demenzsyndrom U96-15
HIV-Enzephalopathie U77-23; U96-15
HIV-Kachexiesyndrom U96-15
HIV-Träger U94-4
H-Kette **U39**-6
H-Kettengene U39-6
HLA U39-8
HLA-Antigene U39-20
HLA-Genkomplex U39-9,20
HLA-ident (Zwillinge) U130-4
HLA-Labor **U14**-11
HLA-Locus U39-20; U84-2
HLA-Phänotyp U39-20
HLV-Insuffizienz U54-5
HMG U51-2; U55-20
HMV U88-16
HNO **U15**-19; U21-12; U60-1
HNO-(Fach)arzt **U15**-19,8
HNO-(Patienten)stuhl U15-19
hoch (Wert) **U116**-19
hochauflösend **U99**-14
hochdosiert U120-4; U121-7
Hochdruck-Flüssigkeitschromatografie U83-22
Hochdruckkrise **U124**-6; U110-13
Hochdruckpatient(in) **U124**-6

Hochdrucksterilisator U139-3
hochfrequent U46-14
Hochfrequenzbeatmung U123-9
Hochfrequenzstrom U42-9
Hochfrequenz-Therapie **U142**-23
Hochgefühl **U11**-10
hochgelagert (Bein) U125-22
hochgesättigt U81-24
hochheben U46-5; **U64**-16
hochinfektiös U14-10; U94-1
hochkonzentriert U81-23
Hochlagern U19-3; U23-1; U142-21
hochlagern (Bein) **U64**-16; U129-11
Hochlagerung **U116**-19; U21-1; U141-10
hochmaligne U97-5
hochregulieren **U83**-18
Hochregulierung **U83**-18
–, zytokinvermittelte U83-18
Hochstimmung **U77**-18; U93-11
–, in U19-1
hochtailliert U22-6
Hochton-Hörsenke U61-6
Hochvoltstrahlentherapie, externe U99-5
hochwirksam **U121**-9,5
hochziehen (Schulterblatt) U64-16
Hocke **U63**-4
hocken **U63**-4
Höcker **U87**-27; **U28**-4; **U26**-4
Höckerneigung U26-4
Höckerspitze (Zahn) U26-4,23
Höckerwinkel U26-4
höckrig **U26**-4
Hockstellung **U63**-4
Hoden **U52**-3; U54-11
Hodenbiopsie U53-7; U69-13
Hodenentzündung U95-4
Hodenkanälchen **U52**-4
Hodenpol U87-3
Hodensack **U52**-2
Hodentorsion U52-3; U124-1
Hodgkin-Lymphom U98-10
Hof U59-1; U96-4
–, depigmentierter U98-15
–, geröteter U108-7; U114-2
Hoffnungslosigkeit U77-17
höflich **U75**-5
Höhenadaptation U88-17
Höhenakklimatisation U88-17
Höhenangst U77-5
Höhenkrankheit **U6**-17; U103-11
Höhenlage U111-1
Höhenlungenödem U6-17; U111-13
Höhenschielen U59-4
Höhenschwindel U113-6
Höhensonne U19-6
Höhenstand (Geburt) **U71**-13
Höhentraining U1-12
Höhepunkt (Fieber) **U105**-17
– (sexueller) **U68**-6
Höhle **U28**-6
–, seröse U86-9
Höhlengrau, zentrales U41-7

Hohlfaserdialysator U125-21
Hohlhandbildung U64-9
Hohlmeißel **U132**-11
Hohlnadel **U132**-6,5; U136-2
–, großlumige U17-11
Hohlnagel U56-15
Hohlorgan U86-20f; U87-13
Hohlvene **U34**-7
Hohlwarze U50-18
Höllenstein U82-16
holosystolisch U33-3
Holter-Monitor U125-6
Holzbein U23-8
Holzgeist U82-13
Holzkohle U91-9
Holzschuhherz U32-1
Holzschutzmittel U91-8
Holzspatel U17-3
homologe Rekombination U84-17
Homöobox **U84**-34
Homöodomäne **U84**-3
homozygot **U84**-5; U85-2
Hopkinsoptik **U133**-4
Hopsen **U65**-16; U1-13
Hörabfall (Hochtonbereich) U61-6
Hörbahn U60-7
Hörbarkeit **U61**-2
horchen (auf) **U61**-1
Hören **U61**-1f
Hörer(in) **U61**-1
Hörfähigkeit **U61**-2
Hörgerät U8-1; U61-2; U129-18
Hörhilfe U61-2
Hormon **U55**-1,15
–, adrenokortikotropes **U55**-9,4
–, antidiuretisches (ADH) **U55**-24
–, follikelstimulierendes (FSH) **U55**-14; U51-6
–, gastrointestinales U55-1
–, hypophyseotropes U55-1
–, Interstitialzellen-stimulierndes **U55**-15
–, laktogenes **U55**-22
–, lipotropes U55-1
–, luteinisierendes U51-8
–, melanozytenstimulierendes **U55**-26; U56-7
–, somatotropes **U55**-5
–, thyreoideastimulierendes **U55**-6; U54-6
–, thyreotropes U54-6
hormonabhängig U55-1
Hormonantagonist U92-31
Hormonausschüttung U55-1
Hormonbestimmung U55-1
Hormonentzug U55-1
Hormonentzugstherapie U127-13
Hormonersatztherapie U55-1
Hormonpräparat U55-1
Hormonrezeptor U55-1
Hormon-Rezeptor-Komplex **U55**-2
Hormonsekretion U88-11
hormonsensitiv U57-8
Hormonspiegel U55-1

Hormonspirale U55-19; U69-10
Hormonsubstitutionstherapie U55-1
Hormontherapie, postmenopausale U51-3
Hormonüberschuss U55-1
hornartig **U56**-6
Horner-Syndrom U58-16
Hornhaut **U58**-5; U19-10
Hornhautabschabung U5-8
–, operative U58-5
Hornhautabtragung U56-6
Hornhautentzündung U56-6
Hornhauterosion U114-13
Hornhautgeschwür U58-5
Hornhautkrümmung U58-5
Hornhautnarbe U58-5
Hornhauttransplantation U56-6; U58-5
Hornhauttrübung U58-5
Hornissenstich U91-16
Hornschicht **U56**-6,2
Hornsubstanz **U56**-6
Hornzellen U56-6
Hörprüfung U61-2
Hörrinde U41-6; U60-7
Horrortrip U11-10
Hörschärfe U57-5; U59-8; U60-13
Hörschwelle **U61**-7,2; **U88**-7
– bei Knochenleitung U61-7
– – Luftleitung U61-4
Hörstörung **U113**-13; U61-2
Hörsturz U61-2,9; U113-13
Hörverlust **U113**-13; U61-2
–, akuter U61-2
Hörvermögen **U61**-2
–, vermindertes **U61**-8
Hörverständnis U61-1; U73-5
Hörweite **U60**-1
–, in/außer U60-1f
Hosenbund U22-6
Hospital **U14**-1
hospitalisieren **U14**-1
Hospitalisierung **U14**-1; **U19**-15; **U20**-1
Hospitalismus **U14**-1,5
Hospitalkeim U90-5
Hospiz **U14**-4
Hostel U14-1
HPL **U55**-21
HPL-Werte, erhöhte U55-21
Hpoglykämie, artifizielle U78-13
HPV-Infektion, klinisch inapparente U96-13
HPV-Typen, onkogene U96-13
hufeisenförmig U26-9; U37-9; U54-6
Hufeisenniere U48-2
Hüft(gelenk)dysplasie U28-21
Hüft(gelenk)luxation U22-7; U28-21
Hüft(gelenk)schmerz U22-7; U28-21
Hüftbein **U22**-7; **U28**-21,2
Hüfte **U22**-7
–, gebeugte U28-21
–, schnellende U22-7
Hüften, schmale U24-6
Hüftendoprothese U22-7; U28-21
Hüftgelenk **U22**-7; U28-21

Hüftgelenkersatz U22-7; U28-21
Hüftgelenkpfanne U28-21; U29-4
Hüftgelenksexartikulation U29-1
Hüftgelenksubluxation U106-4
Hüftgurt U22-6
Hüftgürtel U22-6
hüfthoch U22-6
Hüftknochen **U22**-7
Hüftschlagader, gemeinsame U34-3
Hügel, oberer (Sehbahn) U58-13
Hühnerauge **U114**-14; U19-10; U23-14
Hühneraugenpflaster U140-19
Hühnerbrust U22-2
Hülle **U86**-8,15; **U40**-14; U58-5; **U129**-9
–, sterbliche **U12**-14
Humangenetik U84-1
Humerus **U28**-15
Humerusköpfchen U28-15
Humerusschaft U28-15
Humerusschaftfraktur U28-15
Humor **U76**-2; **U88**-9
– aquaeus **U58**-11; **U88**-9
– vitreus U58-10
humoral **U88**-9
humorvoll **U75**-7
humpeln **U65**-11,5; U31-12
Hunger **U2**-11
Hungerdystrophie U108-14
Hungerhypoglykämie U78-13
Hungern U12-6; U78-12; U82-16
hungern **U2**-14f
Hungerödem U45-1
Huntington-Chorea U77-23
Hüpfen U1-13
hüpfen **U65**-16
husten **U103**-16
Husten **U103**-16; **U111**-7; **U66**-6,2
–, bellender U111-7
–, kruppartiger U95-10
–, lästiger U95-5
–, produktiver U103-7
–, starker U1-6
Hustenanfall U103-4,16; U104-14
Hustenfraktur U103-16
Hustenkopfschmerz U111-7
Hustenmittel U103-16
Hustenpastille U9-14
Hustenreiz U62-11
Hustensaft U9-11
–, schleimlösender U103-17
Hustenschlag U110-11
Hustenschmerz U103-16
Hustensynkope U110-11; U111-7
HWS-Schiene **U8**-15
– Stützkrawatte **U8**-15; U31-17
Hybrid **U84**-38,30
Hybridisierung mit Fluoreszenzmarkierung, in-situ **U84**-38
Hybridisierungsanalyse U84-37
Hybridisierungssonde U84-38
Hybridprotein U84-38
Hyd(r)arthros U29-3
Hydrant U6-10

Hydrargyrum **U82**-32
Hydrat **U82**-9
hydr(atis)iert **U56**-12
Hydrocortison **U55**-10
hydroelektrisches Vollbad U142-20
Hydrogenase U78-8
Hydrogenium **U82**-9
Hydrogenkarbonat U116-11
Hydrokolloid **U81**-26
Hydrokolloidverband U81-26
Hydrokortison **U78**-16
Hydrolase U78-8
Hydrolyse **U82**-9; U78-4
Hydrolyseprodukt U46-11
hydrolysieren **U46**-11
Hydromassage U142-15
hydrophil **U81**-13
hydrophob **U81**-13; U56-12
Hydrophobie **U94**-12
Hydrops **U108**-10
– connatalis U108-10
Hydrotherapie **U142**-20; U1-19
Hydrothorax U111-15
Hydroureter U48-10
Hydroxyäthylstärke U136-13
Hydroxybenzol **U82**-13
hydroxylieren **U78**-7
Hydroxylierung U78-7; U82-9
Hydroxysäure U82-9
Hydrozephalus occlusus U125-15
Hygiene **U1**-5; **U19**-10
–, übertriebene U19-10
hygienisch **U1**-5
Hymen **U50**-13
– imperforatus U50-13; U89-18
– septus U50-13
–, intakter U50-13
Hymenalatresie U50-13
Hypakusis **U61**-8
Hypästhesie **U135**-4; U57-3
hyperaktiv **U64**-17
Hyperaktivität U76-17; U113-2; **U7**-12
Hyperakusis **U61**-8
Hyperaldosteronismus **U55**-25
Hyperalimentation **U125**-19
–, intravenöse U45-1
Hyperämie **U89**-28
–, konjunktivale U58-4
Hyperästhesie **U135**-4
Hypercholesterinämie U37-2; U47-12
Hypercortisolismus **U55**-10
Hypercortizismus **U55**-10
hyperdens **U99**-11
Hyperdiploidie U84-9
Hyperekplexie U65-16
Hyperemesis gravidarum **U70**-12,7
Hyperextension U31-3; **U142**-8
Hyperextensionsfehlstellung U142-8
Hyperexzitabilität U42-8; U57-1
Hyperfibrinolyse U38-14
Hyperflexion **U142**-8
Hyperglykämie **U78**-13; U37-2
–, manifeste U112-2
Hyperhydratation **U56**-12; U78-22

hyperhydriert **U78**-22
Hyperkaliämie **U82**-18
Hyperkalzurie U112-1
Hyperkapnie **U111**-3; U123-7
Hyperkarbie U116-11
Hyperkeratose U56-7
Hyperkinese **U113**-2
Hyperkyphose **U65**-11
Hypermagnesiämie **U82**-20
Hypermetropie **U59**-17
Hypermobilität (Gelenk) **U142**-8
hypernasal **U66**-22
hypernatriämische Dehydratation U6-15
Hypernephrom U98-2; U112-3
Hyperopie **U59**-17
Hyperperistaltik U46-6
Hyperpigmentierung U56-7
Hyperpituitarismus U54-5
Hyperplasie **U108**-12; **U89**-15
hyperplastisch **U108**-12
Hyperprolaktinämie **U55**-22
Hyperpyrexie **U105**-3
Hyperreflexie **U42**-12
Hypersalivation **U109**-3; U45-3
hypersensibel **U39**-23; **U76**-4
Hypersensibilität **U57**-8
Hypersensitivitätspneumonitis U94-14
Hypersomnie **U72**-17
Hyperspleniesyndrom U103-3
Hypersplenismus U103-3
Hyperstimulation U57-1
–, ovarielle **U69**-17
Hypertension **U36**-8; **U110**-13; **U124**-6
–, portale U36-3,8; U47-5
–, pulmonale U36-2
hypertensiv **U36**-8
Hyperthermie **U105**-5
Hyperthymiker U1-6
Hyperthyreose **U124**-8
–, apathische U77-8
hypertone Dehydratation U6-15
Hypertonie **U36**-8; **U110**-13; **U124**-6
–, essentielle **U36**-8
–, maligne U36-8
–, muskuläre U36-8
–, primäre U36-8
–, pulmonale U36-2
Hypertoniker(in) **U36**-8; **U124**-6
hypertroph(isch) **U108**-12; **U110**-9
hypertrophe Narbe U140-10
Hypertrophie **U89**-15; **U108**-12
hypertrophieren **U108**-12
Hyperventilation **U111**-5; U81-19
Hyperventilationsalkalose U111-5
Hyperventilationssyndrom U111-5
Hyperventilationstetanie U111-5
hyperventilieren **U111**-5; **U125**-10
Hypervigil **U8**-7
Hypervitaminose U79-13
Hyperzytose **U38**-5
Hyphaema U15-18
Hyphe **U90**-18
Hypnotikum U92-23; **U135**-9

hypnotisch U93-14
Hypochonder **U4**-9
hypochondrisch **U4**-9
Hypochondrium U45-6
hypogastrisch **U22**-8
Hypogastrium **U22**-8
Hypogenitalismus U52-1
Hypogeusie U62-6
Hypoglykämie U47-14
–, ausgeprägte U78-13
–, postprandiale U78-13; U124-7
Hypogonadismus **U54**-11
Hypokaliämie U37-2; U92-21
Hypomanie U77-18
hypomorph (Allele) U84-4
hyponasal **U66**-22
Hyponasalität U66-22
Hyponatr(i)ämie U37-2
Hypoparathyreoidismus U54-7
Hypoperfusion **U36**-5
Hypopharynx U45-4
hypophysär U81-8
Hypophyse **U54**-5; U127-5
– gesteuert, durch die U54-3
Hypophysenadenom U98-4
Hypophysenapoplexie U124-14
Hypophysenentzündung U54-5
Hypophysenfunktionsprüfung U118-3
Hypophysenfunktionstests U116-14
Hypophysenhinterlappen U54-5
Hypophysenhormon U36-1
Hypophysenmittellappen U54-5
Hypophysenstiel U41-9; U54-5
Hypophysenstieldurchtrennung U87-5
Hypophysentumor **U55**-22; U54-5
Hypophysenüberfunktion U54-5
Hypophysenvorderlappen U54-5
– Insuffizienz U54-5
Hypophysenzwischenlappen U54-5; U55-26
Hypophysitis U54-5
Hypopituitarismus U54-5
Hyposomnie **U72**-17
Hypospadie U69-1
Hypotension **U36**-8; **U110**-13; **U124**-6
hypothalamisch **U54**-4
Hypothalamus **U41**-9; **U54**-4
Hypothalamushormone U54-4
Hypothalamus-Hypophysen-Nebennierenrinden-Achse U54-4
Hypothalamus-Hypophysensystem U41-9
Hypothermie **U105**-5
Hypothyreose **U55**-6
Hypotonie **U36**-8; **U110**-13; **U124**-6
–, orthostatische U36-8; U63-1
Hypoventilation **U111**-3
Hypovolämie **U6**-15; **U36**-7
hypovolämisch U49-8
Hypoxämie **U111**-3; **U123**-8
hypoxämisch **U123**-8
Hypoxie **U111**-3; **U123**-8
–, fetale U107-11
hypoxisch **U123**-8

Hysterektomie U50-5
–, pelviskopische U128-4
Hysterie **U77**-6
hysterisch **U77**-6; U74-14

I

iatrogen **U89**-9; **U121**-15
ICD-Schrittmacher U123-12
Ich **U77**-2
ichbezogen U75-2
ICSH **U55**-15
ICSI **U69**-15
Icterus prolongatus U108-4
Id **U77**-2
Idealgewicht U24-1
Ideation **U73**-8
Ideen, paranoide U77-18
Ideenflucht U77-18; U73-8
Identifikationsarmband U74-3
identifizieren **U74**-3; **U117**-4
Identität **U75**-2
Identitätsdiffusion U75-2
Identitätskrise U75-2
–, pubertäre U80-8
Identitätsverlust U75-2
idiopathisch **U89**-8
Idiotie **U77**-24,22
Idiotyp(us) **U39**-5; **U84**-1
Ig **U39**-5
IGF-1 U55-5
ikterisch **U108**-4
Ikterus **U108**-4; U89-8; U94-15
–, extrahepatischer U47-6
–, hämolytischer U38-4
–, klinisch manifester U75-13
Iktus **U113**-5
Ileorektostomie U45-12
Ileozäkalklappe U45-12
Ileum **U45**-12
Ileumblase U45-12
Ileum-Conduit U45-12
Ileus **U109**-6; U45-12
Ilium U45-12
illegal **U11**-1
illoyal **U75**-10
Imbezilität U77-22
Imbiss **U2**-10
imitieren U92-27
Immediatgedächtnis U74-1,8
Immediatprothese U142-6
Immersionsobjektiv U86-1
immobil **U64**-2
Immobilisation **U141**-5
Immobilisationsdauer U141-5
Immobilisationskragen **U8**-15
immobilisieren **U64**-2
immun **U39**-1
Immunabwehr U39-2
Immunadhärenz **U39**-19,2
Immunadsorbens U39-1
Immunantwort **U39**-2; U120-11
Immunassay **U116**-3

Immundefekt U39-1; U78-21; U97-18
Immundefektsyndrom, erworbenes **U96**-15
Immundefizienz U39-1; U78-21
Immundefizienzvirus, humanes U96-15
Immundiffusion U88-4
Immune-response-Gene U39-2
Immunfixationselektrophorese U84-35
Immunfluoreszenztest U39-1; U116-3
Immungenetik U84-1
immungeschwächt U4-11; U95-8
Immunglobulin **U39**-5; U78-18
Immunglobulinklasse U39-5
Immunglobulinkonzentration U39-5
Immunglobulinmangel U39-5
Immunhämagglutination **U39**-19
Immunhämolyse U38-4; U136-12
Immunhistochemie **U116**-7; U81-1
immunisieren **U122**-1
Immunisierung U39-1; **U122**-3
Immunität **U122**-3
–, abnehmende U39-4
–, angeborene U39-4
–, antitoxische U91-15; U122-8
–, bleibende U39-4
–, erworbene U39-4
–, humorale **U39**-4; U88-9
–, kollektive U39-4
–, lebenslange U39-4; U122-3
–, natürliche U39-4
–, persistierende U39-4
–, unspezifische U39-4
–, vakzineinduzierte U39-4
–, zelluläre U39-13
–, zellvermittelte **U39**-4,13
immunkompetent U39-1; U55-27
Immunkomplex **U39**-9; U81-14
Immunkomplexbildung U39-9
Immunkomplexglomerulonephritis U39-9
Immunkomplexkrankheit U39-9
Immunmangelkrankheit U39-1
Immunmodulation **U97**-18
Immunmodulator **U92**-34; U83-19
–, unspezifischer U97-18
Immunogen U39-1
Immunozyt U39-1
Immunphänotyp U84-10
Immunreaktion U39-2; U120-11
–, starke U1-11; U39-2
–, überschießende U39-2
–, verzögerte U39-2
–, zelluläre U39-2
Immunschwächesyndrom, erworbenes **U96**-15
Immunsensibilisierung U88-9
Immunserum, polyvalentes U91-15
Immunstatus U39-1
Immunstimulans U39-2
Immunsuppression U39-1 f; U88-14
Immunsuppressiva U39-1; U97-18
immunsupprimiert U139-9
Immunsystem **U39**-1
Immuntherapie **U97**-18

Immuntoleranz **U39**-22,2,21
Immunzelle U39-1
impaktiert **U109**-15; U47-8
– (Weisheitszahn) U26-8
Impaktion U106-6
– (Speisereste) U109-15
Impedanz, akustische U60-13
Impedanzaudiometrie U61-2
impermeabel **U88**-6
Impetiginisation **U114**-15
impetiginös **U114**-15
Impetigo **U114**-15
– bullosa U114-12
–, großblasige U114-12
Impfanamnese U122-3
impfbar **U122**-1
Impfempfehlungen U18-5
impfen **U122**-1
Impffieber U122-2
Impfling **U122**-2
Impfmaterial U122-1
Impfmethode U122-3
Impfnarbe U122-3
Impfpoliomyelitis U95-8
Impfrichtlinien U20-7
Impfschema U122-3
Impfschorf U122-1
Impfschutz U122-6
Impfstelle U122-1
Impfstoff **U122**-2; U39-2
–, inaktivierter **U122**-7
Impfung **U11**-8; U17-10; U120-10
–, parenterale **U122**-4
Impingement **U113**-15
Implantat **U129**-18
–, kontrazeptives U69-5
Implantation **U70**-3; U85-2; **U129**-18
Implantationsort U70-3
implantieren **U70**-3; **U129**-18
Impotenz **U53**-2
–, erektile U4-4; U53-3; U68-7
–, organisch bedingte U86-20
Imprägnation **U70**-2
Impressionsfraktur U17-3; U106-8
Impuls **U73**-12
Impulsechoverfahren U118-17
impulsiv **U75**-18; **U73**-12
Impulsivkauf U75-18
Impulsiv-petit-mal U124-9
Impulsrate U123-13
Impulsstromtherapie **U142**-23
in vitro **U101**-18
– – Fertilisation U69-2
in vivo **U101**-18
inaktiv **U94**-6; **U119**-6; U101-8
–, biologisch U122-7
inaktivieren **U88**-14
Inaktivität **U64**-18; **U94**-6
Inaktivitätsatrophie U89-29
Inanition **U108**-14
inapparent **U94**-6
–, klinisch U119-6
Incentive-Spirometer U118-3
Incisura U28-6

Incisura, clavicularis U28-11
– ischiadica major U28-6
– jugularis (ossis occipitalis) U28-6
– – (sterni) U28-13; U43-13; U110-16
– ligamenti teretis U22-5
– mastoidea U60-14
– supraorbitalis U58-1
– trochlearis (ulnae) U30-8
– tympanica U60-4
Incus **U60**-5
Index **U100**-5
indifferent **U76**-15
Indigestion **U109**-1
Indikation **U120**-10
Indikator **U100**-5; **U120**-10
Individualität **U75**-2
indiziert U120-10
indolent U96-4; U104-6
indolentes Geschwür U104-6
Induktor-Lymphozyt U39-14
Induration **U89**-13
induriert U96-4
Industrieschadstoffe U91-6
induzieren **U119**-8
ineffizient **U101**-26
infantil **U80**-4
Infantilismus **U80**-4
Infarkt **U124**-11
–, vollendeter U124-14
Infarktlokalisation U124-11
Infarzierung **U124**-11
Infektanfälligkeit U119-1
Infektion **U139**-9
–, aerogene U94-7
–, aszendierende U94-2
–, aufsteigende U94-2
–, bakterielle U94-2
–, endogene U88-10
–, erregerassoziierte U90-5
–, inkubierende U94-6
–, latente U94-2,6
–, mikrobielle U90-1
–, nosokomiale U14-1; U94-2
–, opportunistische U96-15
–, rezidivierende U96-10
infektionsanfällig U119-1
Infektionsanfälligkeit U37-5; U39-1
Infektionsausbreitung U94-3
Infektionserreger U92-2; U94-1
Infektionserregerreservoir **U94**-4
Infektionsherd U94-2
Infektionskrankheit **U94**-1
Infektionsquelle U94-2; U131-4
Infektionsrate U13-4
infektiös **U94**-2
Infektiosität **U94**-1
Infektpseudarthrose U106-15
Inferenzstatistik U100-1
infertil **U69**-3
Infertilität **U69**-2; **U70**-1
Infestation **U94**-2
infiltrierend **U97**-12
Infiltrat **U94**-14; **U136**-7; **U89**-13
–, fleckiges U87-23

Infiltration **U97**-12; **U136**-7; **U89**-13
Infiltrationsanästhesie U93-3; U136-7
infiltrieren **U97**-12; **U136**-7
infizieren **U94**-2
infiziert, mit AIDS U94-2
Influenza **U94**-9
Influenzaepidemie U94-9
Influenzavirus U94-9
Information U18-11; **U101**-15
Informationsplakette, medizinische
 U7-2; U16-9; U17-1,16
Informationsspeicherung U74-10
Infraorbitalrand U28-9
Infrarotlicht **U19**-6
Infrarot-Wärmebehandlung U142-22
Infraschall U61-6
Infundibulum U87-24
infundieren **U136**-1
Infusion **U136**-1
–, intravenöse **U136**-2
Infusionsbesteck **U136**-4
Infusionsbeutel **U136**-4
Infusionsdauer **U136**-1
Infusionsflasche **U136**-4,1
Infusionsgeschwindigkeit U136-1
Infusionskanüle **U136**-3; U132-6
Infusionslösung **U136**-1
Infusionspumpe **U135**-16; U136-1
Infusionsschläuche U136-1,4
Infusionsständer U131-18; U136-4
Ingesta **U46**-1
Ingestion **U46**-1; U91-21
Ingestionsallergen U39-23
Inhalat **U44**-2; **U92**-14
Inhalation **U10**-20; **U92**-14
Inhalationsallergen U39-23
Inhalationsanästhetika, (volatile)
 U10-5; U11-23; U93-4,10; U135-11
Inhalationsapparat **U44**-2
Inhalationsmittel **U44**-2; **U92**-14
Inhalationsnarkose **U93**-10; U135-14
Inhalationsnarkotika U11-23; U44-2
Inhalationsschaden U44-2
Inhalationsstoß **U44**-7
Inhalationstherapie U44-2
Inhalator **U44**-2; **U92**-14
inhalieren **U44**-2
inhibieren **U88**-14
Inhibiting-Faktoren U54-4; U55-1
Inhibiting-Hormone U54-4; U55-1
Inhibition **U88**-14
Inhibitor **U42**-13; **U88**-14; **U92**-7
Initialdosis **U135**-19; U121-7
Initialkörperchen U83-8
Initiation **U84**-19
Initiationsort U84-19
Initiator **U84**-21
Initiatorcodon U84-13
Injektion **U122**-4; U18-1; U76-9
–, konjunktivale U58-4
–, subkutane U17-11; U122-4
Injektionsallergen U39-23
Injektionsbesteck U17-11; U122-4
Injektionsflüssigkeit U17-10

Injektionsmittel U17-1
Injektionsnadel **U17**-11; U122-4
Injektionsnarkotika U11-1
injizieren **U122**-4
– (Drogen) **U11**-8
inkarzeriert U89-23
Inkohärenz U77-20
inkompatibel **U136**-11
Inkompatibilität **U136**-11
inkonsequent **U75**-10
inkontinent **U112**-15
Inkontinenz **U112**-15
Inkoordination **U31**-19
Inkubation (Kultur) U94-6
Inkubationsausscheider U94-6
Inkubationszeit **U94**-6
Inkubator **U116**-6
inkubieren **U116**-6
Innenfläche U87-4
Innenknöchel U23-12; U28-24
Innenohr **U60**-1; U21-15
Innenohrentzündung U60-10
Innenohrschwerhörigkeit U57-2,18;
 U60-10,13; U113-13
Innenrotationsgang U65-2
Innenseite U87-4
Innervation **U42**-1; U88-3
–, aberrierende U42-1
–, inhibitorische U42-1
–, motorische U42-1
–, reziproke **U42**-14,1
–, segmentale U42-1
–, sensible U42-1
–, sensorische U42-1
Innervationsdichte U42-1
innervieren **U42**-1
inokulieren **U122**-1
Inokulum **U122**-1
Inokulummenge U122-1
inoperabel **U126**-1
Insekt **U90**-5
–, flügelloses blutsaugendes U90-15
Insektenbekämpfungsmittel **U91**-8
Insektenschutzmittel **U91**-8
Insektenstich **U5**-10; U90-5
Insektenvernichtungsmittel U90-5
Insektizid **U91**-8
Insektizidresistenz U91-8
Insellappen U130-13
Inselladenom **U55**-12; U98-4
Inselzellkarzinom U98-2
Inselzelltumor **U55**-12
Insemination **U53**-6; **U70**-2
–, artifizielle **U69**-12; U53-6; U70-2
–, donogene U70-2
–, heterologe U69-12
insensibel **U76**-4
inserieren **U30**-3
Insertion **U84**-23
Insertionsmutagenese U91-13
Insertionsmutation U84-20,23
Insomnie **U72**-16,12
Inspektion **U107**-6
– (OP) **U126**-11

Inspiration **U44**-3
Inspirationskapazität U44-11
inspizieren **U107**-6
instabil **U31**-15
–, klinisch **U125**-2
instabiler Thorax **U124**-17
Instabilität **U31**-15; **U142**-8; **U141**-4
–, hämodynamische U125-5
–, klinische **U125**-2
Instillation **U136**-1
instillieren **U128**-10; **U136**-1; U9-11;
 U93-5
Instinkt **U73**-11
Institut **U14**-9
institutionalisieren **U14**-5
instruieren **U107**-3
Instrument **U132**-1 f
Instrumentarium **U132**-1
instrumentell **U132**-1
Instrumentenbestand U132-1
Instrumentenhalter **U133**-1
Instrumentenport **U133**-5
Instrumentensatz **U132**-1
Instrumentenschale U17-12; U19-7
Instrumententray U17-12
Instrumentenwagen **U131**-19
Instrumentieren **U132**-1
Instrumentierschwester **U131**-8
Insufficientia cordis **U124**-12
Insuffizienz, respiratorische **U123**-6
–, zerebrovaskuläre U110-10
Insufflationsanästhesie U128-10
Insufflationsdruck U128-10
Insufflationsdruckanzeige U133-15
Insufflationsgas **U128**-10
Insufflationsgerät **U133**-15
Insufflationsnadel **U133**-13
Insufflationsnarkose **U93**-10
Insufflationsschlauch U128-10
Insufflationsventil U128-10
Insufflator **U133**-15
insufflieren **U128**-10
Insulin **U55**-12
Insulinallergie U55-12
Insulinanalogon U55-12
Insulinantikörper U55-12
Insulinase **U55**-12
Insulinmangel U55-12
Insulinmangeldiabetes U55-12
Insulinom **U55**-12
Insulin-Pen U55-12
Insulinpumpe U55-12
Insulinresistenz U55-12
Insulinschock U55-12
Insulinspritze U55-12
Insulinsubstitution U55-12
Insulintoleranztest U55-12
Insulinvorstufe U55-12
Insult, apoplektischer **U124**-14
–, bilateraler U87-16
–, embolischer U38-12
–, hämorrhagischer **U89**-26
intakt **U4**-11
Integument **U56**-1

Intelligenz **U41**-1; U73-5
Intelligenzalter U77-1; U80-1; U73-2
Intelligenzminderung **U77**-22
Intelligenzstörung **U77**-22
Intensitätsdiskriminationsschwelle U61-7
intensiv (Behandlung) **U125**-1; U1-6
Intensivbeobachtungsstation U14-7
intensivieren **U125**-1
Intensivmedizin **U125**-1
Intensivpatient(in) U125-1
Intensivpflege **U125**-1; U20-3
Intensivpflegepersonal U15-2
Intensivstation **U14**-7; **U125**-1
–, kardiologische U14-7; U32-14
Intensivtherapie **U125**-1; U134-8
Intensivtransport, luftgestützter U125-1
Intensivüberwachung **U125**-5,1
Intensivüberwachungseinheit U125-1,5
Intensivüberwachungsgerät **U125**-6
Intentionstremor U113-4; U73-3
Intention-to-treat Analyse **U101**-20
Interaktion, pharmakokinetische U121-11
Inter-Beobachter-Reliabilität U100-30
– – Varianz U100-14
interdental **U87**-14
Interdentalbürstchen U26-22
Interdentalraum U26-22
Interesse, reges U1-6
Interferenzstromtherapie U142-23
Interferon U97-18
interiktale Periode U113-5
Interimsprothese U27-8
Interkarpalgelenke U28-17
interkostal **U28**-14
Interkostalneuralgie U113-14
Interkostalraum U28-14; U32-4
interkurrent (Erkrankung) U101-29
Interleukin-2 U39-16
Interlobärerguss U43-3
intermediär **U81**-18
Intermediärfilament U83-5
Intermediärinsulin U55-12
Intermediärkallus U106-15
Intermediärstoffwechsel U78-1; U81-18
Intermediärwirt U94-5
Intermediat **U81**-18; U78-11
intermenstruell **U51**-2
intermittierend **U119**-11
intern **U15**-5
Interneuron **U40**-1; U42-13
Internist(in) **U15**-9
internistischer Notfall U6-18
Interokklusalabstand **U27**-14
interphalangeal **U28**-18
Interphalangealgelenk, proximales U28-18
Interphase **U83**-12
Interphasekern U83-4,12
Intersexualität **U68**-1; U52-1; U53-12
interstitiell **U86**-19
Interstitium **U86**-19
Intertrigo U105-13

Intervall, anfallsfreies U113-5
–, fieberfreies U105-3
Intervalltraining U1-12
Intervention **U20**-11
Interventionsradiologie U15-13; U20-11
Interventionsstudie U101-1
intervertebral **U22**-12
interzellulär **U86**-19
Interzellularbrücke U86-19
Interzellularraum U86-19
Interzellularsubstanz **U86**-19; U29-2
intestinal **U45**-1,9
Intima U34-2; U87-8
Intimafibrose U34-2
Intimalappen U34-2
Intimaläsion U34-2
Intimaruptur U106-5
Intimaschädigung U34-2
Intimkontakt U96-1
Intoleranz **U75**-16; **U121**-12
Intonation **U66**-11
Intoxikation **U10**-5; **U91**-14
–, urämische U112-13
Intoxikationspsychose U77-15,21
Intoxikationszeichen U121-13
Intra-Beobachter-Varianz U100-14
intrahepatisch **U47**-6
intrakapsulär **U29**-9
intrakorporal **U138**-3
Intrakutannaht U56-16
Intrakutantest U118-2
intraluminal **U34**-14
intranasal verabreicht U93-5
intraoperative Überwachung U125-5
intraoral **U26**-25
Intrauterinpessar **U69**-10
intravasale Hämolyse U136-12
intravenös **U34**-4
intrazellulär **U86**-19
Intron **U84**-14
introvertiert **U75**-14
Introvertiertheit **U75**-13
Intrusion **U74**-11
Intubation, endotracheale **U123**-10
Intubationsnarkose **U93**-13
Intubationsrohr U135-17
Intubator **U123**-10
intubieren U135-17
Intussuszeption U98-1; **U129**-8
Inulin-Clearance U49-7; U88-16
Invagination **U85**-12; U98-1; **U129**-8
invaginiert **U85**-12
Invalide(r) **U4**-8
Invalidenrente U4-8; U80-14; U142-3
Invalidität **U4**-8; **U142**-3; U13-3
Invaliditätsgrad U117-1; U142-3
Invasion **U97**-12
Invasionsneigung U97-12
Invasionstiefe U97-12
invasiv **U97**-12
invasives Verfahren U126-4
Invasivität **U128**-1
Inversion **U31**-8; **U84**-23

Inversionsverstauchung (Knöchel) U31-8
Invertseife U82-14
In-vitro-Fertilisation **U69**-12
In-vitro-Studie U116-2
Involutionshämangiom U98-5
Inzest U37-1; U84-30
Inzidenz **U100**-7; U13-10
inzidieren **U87**-5; **U126**-9 f
Inzisalpunkt U26-3
Inzision **U5**-6; **U126**-9
Inzucht **U84**-30
Iod **U82**-22; U54-6; U79-17
–, proteingebundenes U82-22
iodiert **U82**-22
Iodintoxikation U82-22
Iodismus U82-22
Iodlösung U82-22
Iodmangelstruma U82-5,22
Iodsalbe U9-8
Iodtinktur U9-10; U82-22
Iodvergiftung, chronische U82-22
Iodwasser U82-22
Iodzahl U82-22
Ion **U78**-23; **U81**-11
–, positiv geladenes **U81**-11; U99-20
Ionenaustausch U99-20
Ionenaustauschchromatografie U83-22
Ionenaustauscher(harze) U78-23; U81-11
Ionenbindung U81-11; U99-20
Ionendosis U99-20
Ionendurchlässigkeit U88-6
Ionenfang U81-11
Ionenfluss U78-23; U81-11
Ionengefälle U42-9
Ionengradient U42-9
Ionenkanal U42-9; U81-11
Ionenkonzentration U42-9
Ionenpermeabilität U36-16
Ionenpumpe U42-9; U78-23; U81-11
Ionenstärke U42-9; U78-23; U81-10 f
Ionenstrom U42-9; U81-11
Ionentrapping U78-23
Ionenwanderung U78-23; U81-11
Ionisation **U81**-11; **U99**-20
Ionisationsdichte U99-20
Ionisationskammer U99-20
ionisch **U78**-23; **U81**-11
ionisierbar U78-23
ionisierende Strahlung U99-20
Ionisierung **U81**-11; **U99**-20
Ipecacuanhasirup U9-11
Ir-Gene U39-2
Iridium **U82**-34
Iridodonesis U58-8
Iridoplegie U58-8
Iris **U58**-8
– tremulans U58-8
Irishamartom U98-6
Iriskolobom U58-8
Irisprolaps U58-8
Irisschlottern U58-8
Iriswurzel U58-8

irreduktibel U142-8
irrelevant **U102**-8
irreponibel U142-8
Irresein **U77**-15
irreversible Reaktion U81-15
irreversibler Ausfall U7-18
Irrigation **U127**-17
Irrigator **U127**-17; U139-2
Irritabilität **U89**-10
Irritans **U81**-1; **U89**-10; U92-14
Irritation **U89**-10; **U104**-3
irritieren **U104**-3
Ischämie **U89**-28; **U124**-14; U36-5
-, tourniquetbedingte U8-8
Ischiasnerv U40-1; U63-12; U142-11
Ischiassyndrom **U104**-16
ischiokrurale Muskulatur **U30**-16
Ishihara-Tafeln U17-5
isochor (Pupillen) **U107**-15
Isochromosom U84-7
Isoenzym U78-8
Isolat **U14**-10
isolieren **U14**-10
Isolierstation **U14**-10; U19-1
Isolierung **U14**-10; U122-5
-, protektive U14-10
Isolierzimmer U19-2
Isotop **U82**-1,10
-, knochenaffines U82-1
Isotopennephrogramm U82-1
Isotopenverdünnungsmethode U82-1
Isotransplantat **U130**-4
Isotyp **U39**-5
Isthmus faucium U45-4
IUD **U69**-10
IUP **U69**-10
IUS **U69**-10
IVF **U69**-12,2
IVF mit Embryotransfer U69-16
-, heterologe U69-12
-, homologe U69-12
IVF-Kryozyklus U69-16
IVF-Zyklus U69-12
Ixodida U90-15

J

Jahresrate, 5- U100-8
jähzornig U76-2
Jalousie **U59**-18
Jamais-vu-Erlebnis **U74**-18
Jammer U75-8
jammern **U66**-3
Ja-Nein Quotient U100-35
Jejunaldivertikel U45-11
Jejunalsonde **U125**-18
Jejunitis U45-11
Jejunostomie U45-11
Jejunum **U45**-11
Jejunumsekret U46-10
Jetinjektion, nadellose U122-4
Jochbein U21-7; U28-9
Jochbogen **U28**-9

Jod **U82**-22
-, proteingebundenes U37-3
Joga **U1**-16
Joggen **U65**-14
- an Ort und Stelle U1-14
Jogginganzug U65-14
Joint **U11**-14
Joint-Stummel **U11**-14
Joule **U79**-4
Jubel(stimmung) **U76**-16; **U67**-6
jubelnd **U76**-16
jucken **U62**-11; U5-9; U89-10
Jucken **U103**-19; U114-1
Juckreiz **U103**-19; U5-9; U114-1
-, starker U96-12
Jugend **U80**-2,8
Jugendfürsorge U80-5
Jugendkriminalität U80-8
jugendlich **U80**-2,8
Jugendliche(r) **U80**-2,8
Jugendpsychiatrie U15-12; U77-16; U80-8
Jugendwohlfahrtsbehörde U13-2
Jugulariseröffnung U127-18
Jugularislymphknoten U34-11
Jugularispuls U36-9
Jugularispunktion U110-16; U118-7
Jugularvenendehnung U34-11
Jugularvenendilatation **U110**-16
Jugularvenenerweiterung **U110**-16
Jugularvenenpuls U34-11; U107-13
Jugum sphenoidale U28-8
jung **U80**-2
Junge **U80**-2
-, präpubertärer U53-1
Jungfernhäutchen **U50**-13
Jungfrau **U68**-11; U50-13
Jungfräulichkeit **U68**-11
Junktionsnävus U56-7; U114-3
Junktionszone, dermoepidermale U56-2f; U114-5
juvenil **U80**-8
Juxtaposition U63-1

K

Kabat-Behandlung U57-11
Kachexie **U108**-14
Kadmium **U82**-33
Kadmiumexposition U82-33
kahl **U25**-16
Kahlheit **U25**-16
Kahnbein U28-17,25
Kaiserschnitt U71-3,9; U87-5
Kalendermethode U69-5
Kaliper **U24**-12
Kaliseife U82-14
Kalium **U82**-18; U79-17; U88-4
- chloratum U82-23
Kaliumaluminiumsulfat **U82**-31
Kaliumaufnahme, zelluläre U78-5
Kaliumausscheidung U49-4
Kaliumchlorid U82-23

Kaliumcyanid U91-9
Kaliumerschöpfung U82-18
Kaliumgleichgewicht U82-18
Kaliumhaushalt U82-18
Kaliumkanal U42-7
-, ATP-abhängiger U42-9; U78-15
Kaliummangel U82-18; U88-15
Kaliumpermanganat U82-18
Kaliumsilikat U82-30
Kaliumspeicher U78-20
Kaliumverarmung U82-18
Kaliumverlust U82-18; U108-14
Kaliumzufuhr U82-18
Kalk, gebrannter **U82**-19
-, gelöschter U82-19
Kalkablagerung U31-14; U82-19
Kalkaneus **U28**-27; U23-13
Kalkaneussporn U23-13; U28-27
kalkbildend **U82**-19
Kalkeinlagerung U31-14
Kallus U106-15
Kallusbildung U106-15
Kalomel U82-32
Kalorie **U79**-4
kalorienarm U79-4
Kalorienbedarf U79-4
kalorienbewusst U79-4
Kalorienverbrauch U79-4
Kalorienzufuhr U81-7
-, empfohlene U79-4
-, erhöhte U46-1
kalorischer Wert U79-4
Kalotte U28-7
Kalottenfraktur U106-8
Kälteablation **U127**-13
Kälteagglutinine U37-16; U39-19
Kälteakklimatisation U88-17
Kälteallergie U39-23
Kälteanästhesie U93-3
Kälteanwendung **U142**-21,1
Kältebehandlung U127-8
kälteempfindlich U76-4
Kälteempfindlichkeit U57-8
Kältegefühl **U105**-9
Kälteintoleranz **U105**-10
Kältepräzipitation U81-27
Kälteschaden U105-10
Kältesonde **U127**-8; **U132**-8
Kälteurtikaria U114-11
Kalzifikation U31-14; **U82**-19; **U27**-22
kalzifizieren **U31**-14
Kalzitonin **U55**-8
Kalzium **U82**-19; U79-17
-, oral zugeführtes U82-19
Kalziumantagonist U82-19; U92-7
Kalziumblocker U42-9; U92-7
Kalziumeinstrom U42-6
Kalziumfolinat U82-19
Kalziumhydroxid U82-19
Kalziumkanal **U42**-9
-, spannungsgesteuerter U42-9
Kalziumkanalblocker U82-19
Kalziumkarbonat U82-19
Kalziumoxid **U82**-19

Kalzium-Phosphor-Quotient U82-19
Kalziumsulfat U82-19
Kalziumtrinatriumdiäthylentriamin-
   pentaessigsäure U49-2
Kamera **U133**-3
Kameraabdeckung, sterile U133-3
Kameragehäuse U133-3
Kamm **U28**-5
Kammer **U32**-8
–, feuchte U140-5
Kammeraktion U110-2
Kammerauswurf **U33**-8
Kammerautomatie U110-6
Kammerflattern U110-7
Kammerflimmern U32-8
Kammerfüllung U33-9
Kammerfüllungsdruck **U33**-9
Kammerscheidewand **U32**-9; U86-15
Kammerseptumdefekt U32-8
Kammerstimulation **U123**-13
Kammersystole U32-8; U33-3
Kammertätigkeit U110-2
Kammervergrößerung U110-9
Kammerwasser **U58**-11,5; U88-9
Kammerwasserabfluss U58-11
Kammerwinkel U58-5,8
kämpfen (mit den Tränen) U59-3
Kanälchen **U47**-6
–, gewundene U52-4
Kanalgase U82-2
Kante **U87**-10
Kanüle **U132**-6; U136-2
Kanülenansatz U17-10f
Kanülenspitze U136-3
kanülieren **U136**-3
Kanülierung **U136**-3
Kanzerogen **U91**-13; U98-2
kanzerogen U98-2
kapillär **U34**-5
Kapillarblut U34-5
Kapillardialysator U125-21
Kapillardruck U34-5
Kapillardurchlässigkeit U88-6
Kapillare **U34**-5
Kapillarendothel U86-14
Kapillargefäß **U34**-5
Kapillarität **U34**-5
Kapillarknäuel, glomeruläres U48-6
Kapillarnetz U34-5
Kapillarpermeabilität **U36**-16; U34-5
Kapillarpuls U34-5
Kapillarschlinge U34-5; U48-6
Kapillarwirkung **U34**-5
Kapitalverbrechen U12-11
Kaplan-Meier Diagramm U100-27
Kaposi-Sarkom U98-3
Kapsel **U97**-9; **U9**-7
–, magensaftresistente U122-6
Kapselbakterien U97-9
Kapseldehnung U29-9
Kapselentfernung, operative U29-9
Kapselmuster U142-14
Kapselriss U64-13
Kapsid U90-10

Kapsid-Antigen, virales U90-10
Kapsulektomie **U29**-9
Kapuzenmuskel **U30**-13
Karbolsäure **U82**-13
Karbonat **U82**-10
karbonisieren **U82**-10
Karbunkel **U114**-16
Kardia U32-3; U45-8; U46-10
kardial U32-3
Kardiomegalie **U110**-9
Kardiomyopathie U32-6
–, hypertroph-obstruktive U110-9
–, kongestive/dilatative U110-15;
   U124-12
–, peripartale U71-21
Kardioplegie U32-3; U125-11
kardiopulmonale Reanimation U32-8
Kardiotechniker(in) **U16**-11
Kardiotoxizität, akute U107-13
kardiovaskulärer Notfall U6-18
Kollaps **U6**-5
Kardioversion **U123**-12; U110-9
–, elektrische U6-14
Kardioverter-Defibrillator, implantier-
   barer U123-12
kardiovertieren **U123**-12
Karenzurlaub U71-22
Karies U26-18
kariesanfällig U27-22
kariös (Läsion) U89-3
Karotis **U34**-10
Karotisangiografie U118-16
Karotisdrüse U34-10; U86-20
Karotisgabel U34-10
Karotiskörper U86-20
Karotispuls U33-4; U34-10
Karotisschwirren U110-3
Karotissinus U34-10
Karotissinusdruckmassage U123-5
Karpaltunnel(syndrom) U28-17;
   U113-15
Karpopedalspasmus U23-5; U28-17
Karte, topografische U87-1
Kartei U18-14
Karteikarte **U18**-14; **U20**-5; **U102**-12
kartieren **U84**-34
Karton **U9**-16
Karyoplasma **U83**-4
Karyosom U83-3
Karyotyp **U84**-10
Karzinogen **U91**-13; U98-2
karzinogen U98-2
Karzinogenität **U91**-13
–, diaplazentare U91-13
karzinoid U97-10
Karzinoid **U97**-10; U98-2
Karzinoidsyndrom U97-10; U98-2
Karzinom **U97**-6
–, adenosquamöses U98-2
–, embryonales **U98**-16
–, hypernephroides U98-2; U112-3
–, (früh)invasives U97-12
–, klarzelliges U98-2
–, kleinzelliges U98-2

Karzinom, klinisch nicht signifikantes
   U97-6
–, latentes U97-6
–, lokal begrenztes U97-6
–, lokalisiertes U97-6
–, präinvasives **U97**-10
–, schlecht differenziertes U98-2
–, undifferenziertes U97-8
karzinomartig **U97**-10
karzinomatös **U97**-10
Karzinommetastasen U98-2
Karzinomrezidiv U97-6
Karzinosarkom **U98**-3
Kassiterit U82-29
kastaniengroß U52-10
Kastration U69-3
Kastrationskomplex U77-12
Kasuistik **U102**-13; U20-2,6; U100-2
katabol(isch) **U78**-3
katabolisieren **U78**-3
Katabolismus **U88**-8; U78-10; U81-16
Katalase U81-16
Katalysator **U81**-16; U78-8
Katalyse **U81**-16
katalysieren **U81**-16
Kataplasma **U140**-25
Kataplexie U72-18
Katastrophe **U6**-20; U13-12
–, (kardio)vaskuläre U124-1
Katastrophengebiet U6-20
Katastrophenhilfe U6-20; U8-1 f
Katastrophenhilfsorganisation U13-12
Katastrophenmedizin U6-20
Katastrophenopfer U6-12
Katastrophenübung U6-20
Katecholamin **U78**-24; U82-17
Kater **U10**-9
Katgut **U137**-9,8
Kathartika U92-13
Katheter **U127**-19,18
– legen **U125**-7
–, doppellumiger U87-22
Katheterablation U127-13
Katheterfieber U105-3; U127-19
Katheterharn U116-15
katheterisieren **U125**-7
Katheterisierung **U127**-19
–, zentralvenöse U125-7
Kathetersepsis U124-5; U125-7
Katheterspitze U127-19
Katheterzugang U136-5
Kation **U81**-11; U99-20
Kationenaustausch U78-6
Katzenjammer **U10**-9
Katzenkratzkrankheit U94-1
Katzenschreisyndrom U77-22
Katzenwelsstich U91-16
Kaubelastung U27-15
Kaubewegung U27-15
kaudal **U87**-19
Kaudalanästhesie U28-20; U87-19
kauen **U27**-15
kauern **U63**-4,6
Kaufläche U26-24

Kaugummi, nikotinhaltiger U10-17
Kaukasier(in) U102-9
Kaukraft U26-7; U27-15
Kauleistung U27-15
Kaumuskulatur U30-2
kausal **U119**-2
Kaustikum **U91**-10
kaustisch **U91**-10; U127-9
Kautabak U10-17
Kautablette U9-7
Kautelen, aseptische U131-9; **U139**-1
Kauterisation **U127**-9
Kauvorgang **U27**-15
Kauzyklusdauer U27-15
Kavafilter U34-7
Kavakatheter **U125**-7
Kavasieb U34-7
Kavaverschluss U124-13
Kavernom U98-5
Kavernosografie U52-15
Kavernosometrie U52-15
Kavernosusthrombose U124-13
Kavografie U34-7
Kayser-Fleischer-Ringe U58-5; U77-16
KCN U91-9
Kegel U127-12
kegelförmig U9-12
Kehldeckel **U43**-7
Kehle **U21**-12
Kehlkopf **U43**-7; U21-14; U66-10
Kehlkopfdiphtherie U95-9
Kehlkopfeingang **U43**-7
Kehlkopfmaske U43-5
Kehlkopfpapillom U98-1
Kehlkopfreflex U43-7
Kehlkopfspiegel U17-4; U43-7
Kehllaute U66-2
Keilabsätze U23-13
Keilbein **U28**-8,25
Keilbeinflügel U28-8
Keilbeinhöhle U43-6
Keilbeinkörper U28-8
keilen (Gipsverband) U141-6
Keilexzision U118-5
keilförmig U28-25; U132-11
Keilresektion U126-15
–, thorakoskopische U128-6
Keim **U86**-20; U17-15; U139-8
–, verursachender U90-1
Keimbahn U51-4; U84-17,30
Keimbahnmosaik U51-4
Keimbahnmutation U84-20
Keimbesiedelung U46-16
Keimblase **U85**-5
Keimblatt **U85**-6; U51-4; U87-8
Keimdrüse **U54**-11; U52-1; U69-1
–, weibliche **U50**-3
Keimdrüseninsuffizienz **U54**-11
Keimdrüsenrest, rudimentärer U54-11
keimen U51-4; **U85**-10; **U90**-7
Keimepithel U50-3; U51-1; U85-6; U86-7
Keimfleck U51-4
keimfrei **U139**-2,14

keimfrei machen U1-5
Keimfreiheit **U139**-1 f
Keimling U70-2; **U85**-1
Keimschädigung U51-4
Keimscheibe **U85**-6,1; U70-4
Keimschicht U87-8
keimtötend **U90**-5; **U139**-1,3
Keimträger **U94**-4
Keimverschleppung **U139**-9
Keimzelle **U51**-4; **U85**-2; U53-9; U54-11; U83-2
Keimzellenbildung U85-2
Keimzellschädigung U85-2
Keith-Flack-Knoten **U32**-15
Kelchdivertikel U48-4
Kelchhalsstenose, renale U48-4
Kelchsystem U48-4
Keloid U140-10
Kenngröße **U100**-5
Kenntnis(se) **U74**-4; **U73**-4 f
Kennzeichen **U117**-16; U38-5
–, charakteristische U103-3
Kennzeichnung U13-9
Kennziffer **U100**-5
Kephalometrie U87-19
Keratektomie U56-6
Keratin **U56**-6
Keratinisation **U56**-6
Keratinisierung **U114**-14
Keratinozyten U56-6
Keratitis U56-6
Keratoplastik U56-6; U58-5
Kerbe **U28**-6
Kern, eingedellter U83-4
Kerne, motorische U42-13
–, subkortikale U41-3
kernhaltig **U83**-4; U37-7
Kernig-Zeichen U108-1
Kernkörperchen **U83**-4
Kernladung U99-22
Kernladungszahl U81-2,10
Kernmembran U83-4
Kern-Plasma-Verhältnis U83-4
Kernpolymorphie U83-4
Kernpore U83-4
Kernrest U83-4
Kernspindel U83-5,13
Kernspinresonanztomografie **U118**-24
Kernspintomografie U83-4
Kernspintomogramm U118-24
Kernteilung U83-4
–, indirekte **U83**-13
Kerntemperatur U105-1
Ketoazidose, diabetische U124-7
Ketobuttersäure, β- **U82**-12
Ketogenese U82-12
Ketogruppe U82-12
Ketolyse U78-14; U82-12
Keton **U82**-12
Ketonämie U82-12
Ketonkörper U82-12
Ketonkörperabbau U78-14
Ketonkörperausscheidung U82-12
Ketonkörperbildung U82-12

Ketonkörperspaltung U82-12
Ketonkörperspiegel U82-12
Ketonkörperverwertung U78-14; U82-12
Ketonreagenzstreifen U82-12
Ketonurie U82-12
Ketosäure U82-12
– Derivat, verzweigtkettiges U81-18
Ketose U82-12
Kette **U81**-7
–, leichte/schwere **U39**-6
Kettenabbruch U81-7
Kettenraucher(in) U10-16
Kettenreaktion U81-15
Kettenverlängerung U84-19
Keuchen **U44**-7; **U111**-8
–, krampfartiges U66-3
Keuchhusten **U95**-5; U103-16
keusch **U68**-12
Keuschheit **U68**-12
kichern **U66**-2
Kick U11-8
Kiefer **U21**-5
–, zahnloser U28-10
Kieferbruch U5-20
Kieferbruchschiene U141-7
Kiefergelenk U118-23
Kiefergelenkknacken U21-5
Kiefer(gelenk)luxation U28-10
Kiefer-Gesichtsprothetik U26-26
Kieferhöhle **U43**-6; U28-10
Kieferhöhlenfensterung **U127**-3
Kieferhöhlensonde U132-8
Kieferknochen **U21**-5
Kiefer-Lid-Phänomen U21-5
Kieferrelation U21-5
Kieferwinkel U21-5
Kieferzyste U89-24
Kielbrust U22-2
Kiemengang U87-26
Kiemenspalte U87-26
Kieselgel U82-30
kieselsauer **U82**-30
Kieselsäure **U82**-30
Kiff **U11**-15
Killerzellen **U39**-16; U12-9; U37-10
–, natürliche U39-16
Kinästhesie **U57**-14
kinästhetisch **U57**-14
Kind **U80**-2,5; **U84**-29
– bekommen **U71**-2; U70-5
– erwarten **U70**-5
– gebären U70-5
–, ausgetragenes U70-11
–, empfindsames U76-4
–, extrem schlaffes U31-12
–, großes U70-10
–, kräftiges U1-6
–, sensibles U76-4
–, übertragenes U70-11
–, widerspenstiges U76-14
Kindbett **U71**-21
Kindbettfieber U71-21; U124-5

Kinderarzt/-ärztin **U15**-17; **U80**-6
Kinderbetreuung U80-5
Kinderbett **U19**-3
Kinderchirurg(in) U80-6
Kinderchirurgie U15-17
Kinderdiätassistent(in) U15-17
Kinderdosierung U15-17
Kinderekzem U114-1
Kinderfürsorge U1-7; U16-8
Kinderfürsorger(in) U13-6
Kindergarten **U16**-2; U14-8; U94-7
Kinderheilkunde **U15**-17; **U80**-6
Kinderheim U14-4
Kinderhort U14-8
Kinderintensivstation U15-17
Kinderkrankenhaus U14-1
Kinderkrankenpfleger U15-17
Kinderkrankenschwester U16-5
–, selbständige U15-17
Kinderkrankheit **U95**-1; U4-5; U80-5 f
–, hochinfektiöse U95-1
Kinderkrippe U14-8
Kinderlähmung **U95**-8
kinderlos **U80**-5
Kindermädchen **U16**-2
Kinderonkologie U97-1
Kinderpsychiater(in) U80-6
Kinderpsychiatrie U77-16
Kinderschänder **U68**-16
Kinderschwestern U14-8
kindersicher U9-16
Kindersitz U80-5
Kinderspielzeug U80-8
Kinderstation U15-17; U19-1
Kindersterblichkeit U12-3
Kindertagesstätte U14-8
Kinderurologie U15-17
Kinderzahnarzt U80-6
Kinderzahnheilkunde U15-17
Kinderzimmer **U16**-2
Kindesalter **U80**-4
–, Einnässen im U95-1
Kindesentführung U123-4
Kindesmissbrauch, sexueller **U68**-16
Kindesmisshandlung U80-5
Kindestötung **U80**-4; U12-8
Kindesvernachlässigung U77-11
Kindheit **U80**-5
kindlich **U80**-4 f
Kindsbewegungen **U70**-13,4; U85-1
–, Zählen der U64-12
Kindslage **U71**-5
Kindspech **U71**-19
Kindsteil, vorangehender (VKT) U71-5
Kindstod, plötzlicher U19-3; U80-4
Kinesiologie **U142**-10
Kinesiotherapie U57-14
Kinesthäsie U142-10
Kinetik **U57**-14; **U142**-10
Kinetochor **U84**-7
Kinetose U57-14; U64-1; U103-11
Kinetosom **U83**-6
Kinn **U21**-6; U25-10
Kinnkante U56-19

Kinnkappe U21-6
Kinnkorrektur **U127**-4
Kinnstütze U21-6
Kinnzittern U105-7; U113-4
kippen **U63**-10; **U64**-5
–, nach vorne U63-10
Kipptisch U63-10
Kirschner-Bohrstift U141-14
Kirschnerdraht-Fixation U141-15
Kissen **U17**-13; **U19**-5; **U140**-19
Kittel, weißer **U17**-16
kitz(e)lig **U62**-11; **U64**-11
kitzeln **U62**-11; **U64**-11
Kitzler **U50**-12
klaffend (Gang, Wunde) **U87**-26; U5-3; **U140**-16
Klage U20-13
klagen **U66**-3 f
– über **U103**-2
Klageweiber U67-10
klamm U105-10
Klammer **U138**-17
Klammergröße U138-17
Klammermagazin U138-17
Klammer(naht)gerät **U137**-12; U138-17
klammern **U138**-17; **U137**-4
–, sich **U64**-9
Klammernaht **U137**-12
Klammerreihe U138-17
Klang **U61**-3; **U66**-11
Klangassoziation U74-5
klanglos U103-6
Klappenapparat U32-10
klappenförmig **U34**-12
klappenlos **U34**-12
Klappenschluss U32-10
Klappensegel **U32**-10
Klappenstenose U89-20
Klappentasche U34-12
Klappenton **U110**-5
Klappenventil U133-8
Klapperschlangenbiss U91-2
klar **U117**-9
– (Bewusstsein) **U7**-3
– sehen U59-17
Klarheit **U7**-3; U77-1
klarkommen mit U12-3
klarwerden, sich **U74**-4
klassifiziert **U97**-14
klatschen **U67**-6
Klauenfuß U23-13
Klauenzehe U23-14
Klaustrophobie U77-5
Klavikula **U28**-11
Klavikulaluxation U28-11
Klebeband **U140**-21,3; U141-11
Klebestreifen U141-11
klebrig U71-19
Klebstoff U11-23
Klebstoffschnüffeln U10-20; U44-2; U62-2
Kleeblattschädel U106-10
Kleiderlaus U90-15
Kleidungsstück U77-26

Kleie U79-16
klein(gewachsen) **U24**-3,2
Kleinhirn **U41**-2
Kleinhirnbrückenwinkel U41-2
Kleinhirnhälfte U41-3
Kleinhirnhemisphäre U41-3
Kleinhirninfarkt U124-14
Kleinhirnrinde U41-6
Kleinhirnstiel **U41**-13; U87-24
Kleinhirntonsillen U41-2
Kleinhirnwurm U41-2
Kleinhirnzeichen U41-2
Kleinhirnzelt U41-2
Kleinkind **U65**-10; **U80**-4 f,2; U8-10
kleinlumig (Kanüle) U136-3
Kleinwuchs **U24**-4,2; U54-5
kleinwüchsig **U24**-4,2
Klemme **U137**-13; **U132**-13 f
klemmen **U62**-11
Klemmzange **U132**-13
Klettergerüst U65-18
klettern **U65**-18
Klick U33-1
–, frühsystolischer U110-5
–, systolischer **U110**-5; U33-3
Klient(in) **U20**-2
klimakterisch **U51**-10
Klimakterium **U51**-10
Klimax **U51**-10; U50-14
Klimmzug **U64**-13
Klinge **U132**-2 f
Klingenhalter U132-3
Klinik **U14**-1
–, psychiatrische **U14**-5; U77-1
Klinikapotheke **U9**-5,4; **U15**-21
Klinikdirektor U15-2
Kliniker(in) **U14**-2
Klinikpackung U9-16
Klinikpersonal **U15**-2
Klinikum **U14**-2
klinisch stumm/inapparent U96-9
klinische Studie **U101**-1
Klipapplikator **U138**-16
klippen **U138**-15
Klistier U134-6
Klitoridektomie U50-12
Klitoris **U50**-12
–, erigierte U50-12
Klitorisbändchen U50-12
Klitoriseichel U50-12
Klitorisentfernung U50-12
Klitorishaube U50-12; U68-2
Klitorishypertrophie U50-12
Klitorisschenkel U50-12
Kloake **U85**-21
Kloakenekstrophie U85-21
Kloakenfehlbildung U85-21
Kloakenmembran U85-6,21
Kloakenpersistenz U85-21
Kloakenseptierung U85-21
Klon **U84**-33
klonal **U84**-33
klonen **U84**-33
Klonierungsvektor **U84**-33

klopfen **U64**-11
–, heftig (Herz) **U110**-1
Klopfen, leichtes **U64**-11
Klopfmassage U142-15
Klopfschall U17-9; **U107**-8
–, trommelartiger **U109**-7
Klopfung U142-15
klug **U75**-7; **U117**-18
Klumpen-Stichprobe U100-4
Klumpfuß U23-13
knabbern **U27**-11
Knabe, präadoleszenter U72-14
Knall, lauter U61-5
Knallgas U82-2
Knallquecksilber U82-32
Knalltrauma U6-9; U61-9
Kneifen **U62**-11; **U64**-10; U56-19
Kneifmal U114-3
Kneiftest U64-10
Kneipe **U10**-2
Kneippbewegung **U1**-19
Kneippkur **U1**-19
Knetmassage **U71**-10; U142-15
knicken U129-13
Knick-Senkfuß, kindlicher U31-17
Knie **U23**-11
Kniebeugen **U63**-4,3
Knie-Ellenbogen-Lage U23-11; U63-1,11
Knieendoprothese U23-11
Knieexartikulation U142-6
Kniegelenk U23-11
Kniekehlenvene U23-9
knien **U23**-11; **U63**-4
– über (mit gespreizten Beinen) U63-4
–, auf U63-3
Kniescheibe **U23**-11; **U28**-24
Knieschützer U17-13; U23-11
Kniestrümpfe U23-11
Knirschen U74-15
knirschen (Zähne) **U27**-18
Knistern U61-3; U107-9
–, krepitierendes U44-7
knisternd **U111**-9
Knisterrasseln **U106**-14; **U111**-9
Knoblauch U1-3
Knoblauchgeruch U62-3
Knöchel **U23**-12; **U28**-24
–, verstauchter **U1**-10
Knöchelband, inneres U30-13
Knöchelchen **U28**-2
Knöchelfraktur U23-12
Knöchelödem U23-12; U108-10; U111-2
Knöchelverstauchungen U65-9
Knochen **U28**-2
–, brüchige U25-8; U28-2; U103-9
–, kurzer U28-2
Knochenabbau **U27**-20
Knochenabsprengung U106-5
Knochenalter U28-1
Knochenanbau U141-1
Knochenapposition, höhengleiche U141-1

Knochenaufbau U129-19
Knochenbälkchen U31-14; U65-13
Knochenbank U14-12
Knochenbau **U25**-3
Knochenbildung U31-14
Knochenbildungszelle U31-14
Knochenbruch **U106**-1,5; **U5**-20
Knochenbrüchigkeit U103-9
Knochendichte U28-2; U82-5,8
Knochendichtemessung U118-3
Knochenende **U28**-3
Knochenentmineralisierung U82-5
Knochenextension U28-1
Knochenfeile U132-12
Knochenfissur U25-15; **U106**-1
Knochenfragment **U106**-2
Knochenfraktur **U106**-1; **U5**-20
Knochenfresszelle U31-14
Knochengerüst **U28**-1
Knochengewebe U86-3
Knochenhaft **U29**-14
Knochenhaut **U28**-2
Knochenheilung **U106**-15
Knochenhöcker **U28**-4
Knochenleitung U60-14; U61-4
Knochenmark **U38**-2; U28-2; U86-3
–, krebsbefallenes U97-6
knochenmarkähnlich **U38**-2
Knochenmarkaspiration **U118**-9; U38-2
Knochenmark-Aufreinigungstechnik U118-9
Knochenmarkbiopsie U38-2; U118-9
Knochenmarkdepression U38-2; U88-14
Knochenmarkempfänger U136-9
Knochenmarkfibrose U38-2
Knochenmarkinfiltration U89-13
Knochenmarkkultur U38-2; U118-9
Knochenmarkriesenzellen **U83**-3; U38-2
Knochenmarktransplantat U38-2
Knochenmarktransplantation U118-9; U129-14; U130-2
Knochenmatrix U86-19
Knochenmeißel U132-11
Knochenmetastasen U97-13
Knochenmineralisationsstörung U28-2
Knochennagel U141-15
Knochennaht U29-14; **U141**-12
Knochenplatte **U141**-17; U87-2
Knochenreifung U28-1
Knochenrinde U86-23
Knochenschaft **U28**-3
Knochenschere U132-4
Knochenschraube U141-16
Knochenspan U129-16
Knochenspanplastik **U130**-9
Knochensplitter **U106**-2
Knochensporn U28-2; U87-27
Knochenstopp U142-14
Knochensubstanzverlust U86-23
Knochenszintigrafie U28-2
Knochenszintigramm U28-2; U118-22
Knochentransplantat U130-9

Knochentuberkulose U94-16
Knochenumsatz U78-1
Knochenverbindung, bewegliche U29-1
Knochenvorsprung U87-27
Knochenzange **U132**-11
Knochenzelle U86-2
knöchern **U28**-2
knochig **U25**-7
Knopflochdeformität U106-10; U142-7
Knopfnaht **U137**-15
Knorpel **U29**-2,12; U28-13; U30-6
–, elastischer U86-5
–, kalzifizierter/verkalkter U31-14
Knorpelbildungszelle U86-2
Knorpelfragment U106-2; U128-7
Knorpelgelenk **U29**-12
Knorpelgewebe U29-12; U86-3
Knorpelgrundsubstanz U29-12; U86-3,19
Knorpelhaft U29-1
Knorpelhaut U29-2
knorpelig **U29**-2
Knorpelkappe U29-12
Knorpelmatrix U29-12; U86-19
Knorpelsarkom U98-3
Knorpelspangen (Luftröhre) U43-8
Knorpelzellen U29-2
Knospe **U85**-10
knospen **U85**-10
Knospenbildung U85-10
Knospung **U85**-10; U90-11
Knötchen **U89**-16; **U94**-16
Knoten **U89**-16; **U97**-3
–, chirurgischer U137-6; **U138**-6
–, indolenter U97-3
–, indurierter U89-14; U97-3
–, laparoskopischer **U138**-2
–, mikrochirurgischer **U138**-6
–, schmerzhafter U104-11
–, tastbarer U62-9; U97-3
Knotenbildung **U89**-16; **U97**-3
knotenförmig **U97**-3; U110-17
Knotenschieber **U138**-13
Knotenstruma, hyperthyreote U91-4
Knotentechnik **U137**-6
knotig **U97**-3
Knüpftechnik **U138**-2
knurren **U46**-14; **U66**-5
Koagulabilität U38-10
Koagulans **U38**-10
Koagulation **U38**-10; **U92**-16; **U127**-10
Koagulationskaskade U38-10
Koagulopathie U38-10
Koagulator **U127**-10
koagulieren **U38**-10,12; **U92**-16
Koagulopathie U89-1; U127-10
–, angeborene U84-28
Koagulum U38-10
Koaptation **U137**-5
Kobalt **U82**-25
– Chrom-Legierung U82-25
– Teletherapie U82-25
Kobaltbestrahlung U82-25
kochen **U82**-7

Kochlea U60-11
Kochleaimplantat U60-11
Kochsalz U82-5,18,23
Kochsalzbläschen-Kontrast U99-15
kochsalzimprägniert U140-18
Kochsalzinfusion U136-1
Kochsalzlösung U9-11; U66-7; U136-10
–, gepufferte U82-5
–, isotone U82-5
–, physiologische U82-5; U88-1,5,19
Kodein U11-18
Kodominanz U84-27
Kodon U84-13
Koenen-Tumor U98-8
Koexistenz U119-16
Kofaktor U100-5; U102-8
Koffein U3-26
Kognition U73-4
Kohabitation U68-5
Kohle U82-10
Kohlendioxid U135-14
Kohlendioxidspannung U82-10
Kohlenhydrate U79-5; U46-11; U82-9
–, komplexe U81-14
Kohlenhydratmalabsorption U46-13; U109-10
Kohlenhydratstoffwechsel U55-10; U78-1
Kohlenmonoxidhämoglobin U82-10
Kohlenmonoxidvergiftung U82-10; U91-2,14
Kohlensäure U81-22
Kohlensäureanhydrase U82-10
Kohlenstaub U91-7
Kohlenstoff U82-10
Kohlenstoffverbindung U81-2
Kohlenwasserstoffe U82-9
–, polyzyklische U81-6
–, ungesättigte aliphatische U82-15
–, aromatische U62-3
Kohorte U100-3; U101-11
Kohortensterbetafel U100-26
Kohortenstudie U101-11
Koilonychie U56-15
Koilozytose U96-14
Koitus U68-1,5; U30-6
–, schmerzhafter U68-5,7
Koitusfrequenz U68-5
Koituspositionen U68-5
Kokain U11-20
– schnupfen U62-2
kokainabhängig U11-4
Kokainbase U11-20
Kokainisierung U11-20
Kokain-Lokalanästhesie U11-20
Kokainlösung U11-20
Kokainvergiftung U11-20
Kokken, grampositive U90-8
kokkenähnlich U90-8
Koks U11-20
kokzygeal U28-20
Kolben U17-10; U34-14
Kolik U104-15; U109-14
kolikartig U109-14; U22-9; U104-15,7

Kolitis, kollagene U86-5
–, pseudomembranöse U86-15
kollabieren U6-5; U65-12; U110-12; U111-15
Kollagen U86-4
Kollagenablagerung U86-5
Kollagenase U86-5
Kollagenfaser U86-5
Kollagenfibrille U86-5
Kollagenkrankheit U86-5
Kollagenose U86-5
Kollagensynthese U86-5
Kollaps U6-5; U65-12; U7-4
kollateral U34-6
Kollaterale U34-6
Kollateralgefäße U34-6,1
Kollateralisierung U34-6
Kollateralkreislauf U34-6; U36-1
Kollateralversorgung U34-6
Kollege/-in U15-2
kollern (Darm) U46-14
Kollern (Herzgeräusch) U110-3
kollidieren U6-2
Kollimation U99-6
Kollimator U99-6
Kolliquationsnekrose U82-14
Kollision U6-2
Kolloid U81-26
–, hydrophiles U81-13
kolloid(al) U81-26
Kolloidmilium U114-6
Kolo(no)skopie U45-15
Kolon U45-15
Kolonflexur, linke U35-4; U45-15
–, rechte U45-15; U47-1
Koloninterposition U45-15
Kolonlavage U45-15
–, intraoperative U118-10
Kolonmassage U45-15
Kolonstumpf, distaler U87-14
Kolontransit U45-15; U46-8; U109-6
Kolonzwischenschaltung U45-15
Kolostomie U127-3
Kolostomiebeutel U45-15
Kolostrum U71-24
Kolpokleisis U50-8
Koma U7-14
–, diabetisches U124-7
–, endokrines U124-8
–, hepatisches U47-1
komatös U124-7; U7-14
Komazylinder U124-7
Kombinations-Chemotherapie U97-17
Kombinationsimpfstoff U122-2
Kombinationspräparat U69-7
Kombinationstherapie U120-3
Kombitubus U123-10
Komedo U114-6
Komedokarzinom U114-6
Komedonenquetscher U114-6
komisch U75-7
kommen, zu sich U7-6
Kommissur U41-3
Kommissurenbahnen U41-3

kommunizieren U66-8
Komorbidität U4-4; U89-2; U119-16
Kompakta U28-2; U86-3
Kompartiment, stromales U86-22
Kompartment-Syndrom U30-7
kompatibel U136-11
Kompatibilitätstestung U136-11
kompatible(r) Spender(in) U136-9
Kompensationsmechanismus U88-2
Kompetenz, alltagspraktische U142-27; U73-7
Kompetenzbereich U15-12
Komplementaktivierung U39-10
Komplementaktivierungsweg, alternativer U39-10
–, klassischer U39-10
Komplementaktivität U39-10
Komplementbindungsreaktion U39-10
Komplementdefekt U39-10
Komplementfaktor U39-10
Komplementinaktivierung U122-7
Komplementkomponente, frühe U39-10
–, terminale U39-10
Komplementmangel U39-10
Komplementproteine U39-10
Komplementsystem U39-10
Komplementverbrauch U39-10
Komplex U81-14
Komplexbildner U81-5
Komplexbildung U81-14
Komplikation U134-9
–, akute U4-11
–, hämodynamische U4-11
–, lebensbedrohliche U124-1
komplikationsfrei U107-18
– (Verlauf) U134-7
Komplikationsrate U134-9
Komponente, chemische U81-1
Kompresse U6-6; U17-13; U140-19,25; U142-22
Kompression U6-6,17
–, digitale U125-17
Kompressionsatelektase U111-15
Kompressionsfraktur U6-6; U106-6
Kompressionslähmung U6-6
Kompressionsneuropathie U113-14
Kompressionsosteosynthese U141-17
Kompressionsplatte, dynamische U141-17
Kompressionsstrümpfe U64-10; U141-10
–, elastische U125-22
Kompressionsverband U38-7; U64-10; U125-17; U140-20
komprimieren U6-6; U64-10
kompulsiv U77-19
Kondensat U82-8
Kondensation U82-8
–, enzymatische U82-8
Kondensationsprodukt U82-8
kondensieren U82-8
Kondensmilch U105-14
Kondition (Fitness) U1-9
Konditionstraining U1-9
kondolieren U12-12

Kondom U69-6
kondylär U29-6
Kondylenabflachung U29-6
Kondylenfraktur U28-4
Kondylenschraube U28-4; U141-16
Kondylom U96-1
–, breites U96-14
–, spitzes U96-14; U114-17
Kondylus U28-4; U29-6
Konfabulation U74-18; U77-4
Konfidenzgrenze U100-17
Konfidenzintervall U100-17
Konfidenzniveau U100-17
Konflikt, unbewusster U77-12
Konfliktlösung U77-12
konfluierend U89-27; U114-10
Konformationsdeterminante U39-7
Konfrontationsversuch U59-7
konfrontiert mit U21-2
kongenital U89-6
kongestiv U110-15
Königswasser U82-4
Koniotomie U123-11
Konisation U127-12,5; U50-7
Konjugat U81-9
Konjugation U81-9; U70-1
konjugiert U81-9
Konjunktiva U58-4
Konjunktivalabstrich U58-4
Konjunktivalbiopsie U116-4
konjunktivale Applikation U92-17
Konjunktivitis U58-4
–, chlamydieninduzierte U90-14
Konkavlinse U59-13
Konkremente U89-21; U54-13
Konsanguinität U84-31
konsekutiv (Patientenreihe) U100-3; U101-11
konsensuell (Pupillen) U107-15
konsequent U75-10
Konsequenz U75-10; U120-15
Konservenblut U136-8
konserviert U14-12
Konservierung U126-13
Konservierungsmittel U2-6
–, nitrithaltiges U82-16
Konsiliararzt U102-14
Konsiliardienst U20-4
Konsiliarius U18-13
Konsilium U18-13; U102-14
Konsonant U66-12
konstante Region U84-2
Konstitution U1-8; U25-3; U107-10
konstitutionell U1-8; U25-3
Konstitutionstyp U1-8; U25-3
Konstriktion U6-6; U89-19
konstriktiv U111-17
Konsultation U15-3; U18-13; U102-14
–, fachärztliche U18-13
–, telemedizinische U18-13
konsultieren (Arzt) U15-3; U18-13,1; U102-14
konsumieren U2-2
konsumierend (Erkrankung) U142-4

Kontagion U94-1
Kontagiosität U94-1
Kontakt U122-5
– bleiben, in U62-8
–, zwischenmenschlicher U75-1
Kontaktallergen U39-23
Kontaktdermatitis U62-8; U122-5
Kontaktekzem U114-1
Kontaktgift U91-2
Kontaktisolation U94-3
Kontaktisolierung U94-3
Kontaktlinse U58-8
Kontaktmetastasen U97-13
Kontaktperson U122-5,3
Kontaktübertragung, direkte U94-3
Kontaminant U91-6; U139-9
Kontamination U91-6; U139-9; U131-7
kontaminiert U13-4; U139-2; U140-12
Kontiguität U87-11
kontinent U112-15
Kontinenzinterval U112-16
Kontinenzperiode U112-16
Kontingenztafel U100-27
Kontinuität U87-12; U5-19
–, makroskopische U87-12
kontrahieren U31-1; U71-3
Kontraindikation U9-17; U120-10
kontraktil U31-1
Kontraktilität U31-1
Kontraktion U31-1
–, reflektorische U17-9
kontraktionsfähig U31-1
Kontraktur U31-1; U140-8; U142-1
kontralateral U87-18
Kontrast U59-11
Kontrastauflösung U99-14
Kontrastaufnahme U99-15
Kontrasteinlauf U99-15
Kontrastfärbemittel U99-15
Kontrastmittel U99-15,20; U59-11
–, hochosmolare U49-9
–, iodhaltiges U82-22
Kontrastmittelausscheidung U91-17
Kontrastmittelaustritt U38-6
Kontrastmittelinjektion U122-4
Kontrast-Myelografie U118-7
Kontrastverstärkung U59-11; U99-15
Kontrazeption U69-5,2
kontrazeptiv U69-5
Kontrazeptivum U69-5
–, orales U69-7,5
–, östrogenhaltiges U55-17
Kontrollabstrich U116-5
Kontrolle U18-9,2
– bringen, unter U54-3
–, ambulante U125-5
–, unter endoskopischer U128-2; U133-2
– –, fluoroskopischer U99-8
– –, sonografischer U118-17
Kontrollgerät U125-5
Kontrollgruppe U101-10; U100-22
kontrollieren U18-9; U107-1; U125-5
Kontrollperson U100-2; U101-10; U134-5

Kontrolltermin U18-2
Kontrolluntersuchung U107-1; U18-2; U120-14
Kontrollzystoskopie U118-11
Kontusion U5-13; U6-6
Konusbiopsie U127-12
konvergent U59-13
Konvergenz (Augenachsen) U59-13
Konvergenznystagmus U59-13
konvergierend U59-13
Konversionshysterie U77-6
Konversionsneurose U77-6,21; U73-8
Konversionsstörung U77-16
Konversionssyndrom, klassisches U77-6
Konvexlinse U59-13
Konvolut, proximales U48-5
Konvulsion U103-20; U64-7
Konzentrat U36-13; U81-23; U116-16
Konzentration U81-23; U116-16;
–, osmolale U81-23
–, steady-state U81-23
Konzentrationsfähigkeit U74-16; U81-23
Konzentrationsgefälle U81-23
Konzentrationsgradient U81-23
Konzentrationsschwäche U108-13
Konzentrationsvermögen U81-23
konzentrieren U36-13; U81-23; U116-16
Konzeption U70-2
Konzeptionsverhütung U69-5
Konzeptus U70-2
kooperativ U120-15
Koordination, fehlende U31-19
Koordinationsstörung U31-4,19; U113-8
koordiniert, gut U31-19
Kopf U21-1; U53-7
–, langer (Muskel) U30-11
Kopfbedeckung U21-1
Kopfbein U28-17; U29-1
Kopfbewegungen, ruckartige U67-3
Kopf-Brust-Gipsverband U141-9
Kopfdrehung U64-8
Kopffortsatz U85-20
Kopfhaare U56-13
Kopfhalterung U141-9,3
Kopfhaltung U71-5
–, schräge U63-10
Kopfhaut U25-15; U21-16; U56-1
Kopfhautabschürfungen U25-15
Kopfhaut-EEG U118-12
Kopfhautmassage U142-15
Kopfhautverletzung U5-5
Kopfkissen U19-5
Kopflage U71-5; U87-19
Kopfläuse U90-15; U94-3
Kopfmuskel, vorderer gerader U30-14
Kopfneigung U63-10; U64-5
Kopfschlagader U34-10
Kopfschmerzen U104-4
–, dumpfe U113-16
–, pochende U113-16
Kopfschuppen U114-7; U25-15

Kopfschuss U6-8
Kopfstellreflex U57-16
Kopfstück (Veress-Nadel) U133-13
Kopfstütze U21-1
Kopfteil (Bett) U19-3
Kopftieflage(rung) **U131**-13; U63-1,13
kopfwärts **U87**-19
Kopie (DNA) **U84**-16
kopieren **U84**-16
Koplik-Flecken U95-2; U114-9
Koppelmedium U81-12
koppeln **U81**-12
Kopp(e)lung **U81**-12
–, elektromechanische U42-8; U81-12
–, chemische U81-1
Kopplungsanalyse **U84**-37
Kopplungsgruppe U84-37
Kopplungskartierung U84-34
Kopplungsungleichgewicht U84-37
Kopremesis U46-20
Koprolalie U66-17
Koprostase **U109**-15
Korallenstein U89-21
Kornährenverband U140-20
Kornea **U58**-5
Kornealreflex U58-5; U67-15; U125-25
Körnerzellenschicht U56-2
körnig **U140**-7
koronar **U32**-14
Koronarangiografie U118-16
Koronararterie U34-3
Koronararterienverschluss U32-14
Koronardilatanzien U32-14
koronardilatatorische Wirkung U92-17
Koronardurchblutung U32-14
Koronargefäß U32-14
Koronarinsuffizienz U32-14; U110-10
Koronarkreislauf U32-14; U36-1
Koronarmittel U32-14
Koronarperfusion U32-14
Koronarstenose U32-14
Koronarthrombose U32-14; U124-13
Körper **U77**-2; **U86**-20
–, lebloser **U12**-14,5
–, straffer U75-11
Körperabsonderungen U139-16
Körperarbeit **U1**-18
Körperbau U25-1; **U87**-1; U107-10
–, schmächtiger U24-6
–, zarter U24-6
Körperbauindex **U24**-7
Körperbau(typ) **U1**-8; **U25**-2
–, athletischer U25-2,4
Körperbehaarung U56-13
körperbehindert U142-3
körperbewusst U97-4
körpereigen **U39**-21
Körperfett **U24**-5; U86-20
Körperfettanteil U24-7
Körperfettdepot U78-20
Körperflüssigkeiten **U88**-9; U86-20
körperfremd U39-21
Körperfunktionen U107-1
Körpergeruch U62-3

Körpergewicht **U24**-1
Körpergröße **U24**-2; U100-11
– Gewicht-Verhältnis U108-14
Körperhaltung **U63**-1; **U65**-3; U1-15
–, aufrechte U65-3
–, entspannte U31-1; U76-19
–, lockere U31-1
Körperkerntemperatur U105-1
Körperkontakt U122-5
Körperkreislauf U36-1; U121-10
Körperlänge U24-2
Körperlängsachse U87-3
körperlich **U25**-1; **U86**-20
– gesund U1-2
Körpermaße U24-2
Körpermasse(n)index U25-3
Körpermasse, fettfreie U24-10; U78-2
Körpermasseindex **U24**-7
Körperoberfläche U24-7; U33-7; U86-20; U87-4
Körperpflege U1-5; **U19**-10; U75-1; U102-9; U142-27
Körperpflegeutensilien U19-10
Körperschema U57-2; U86-20; U73-9
Körperschlagader, große **U34**-8
Körperstellung **U63**-1
Körpertemperatur **U105**-1
Körpertraining **U1**-12
Körperverletzung U5-2 f; U6-11; U20-7,13
Körperzellen U39-1; U83-2
korpulent **U24**-8; U67-19; U110-18
Korpuskularstrahl U82-1
Korrektur **U142**-12
–, operative U127-4; **U129**-2
Korrekturosteotomie U129-2; U142-12
Korrektursakkaden U59-14
Korrekturschiene U142-12
Korrelation **U100**-32
korrodieren **U91**-10
Korrosionsbeständigkeit U82-6
Korrosionsfestigkeit U82-6
Korrosionsmittel **U91**-10
korrosiv **U91**-10
Korsakow-Psychose U77-21
– Syndrom U74-17; U77-21
Korsett **U140**-26,20; **U141**-7
Kortex **U86**-23
kortikal U4-6; **U86**-23
Kortikalis U28-2; U86-23
Kortikalistransplantat U130-9
Kortikoide U55-10
Kortikoliberin U55-9
Kortikosteroide **U55**-4,10
Kortikotropin **U55**-9,4; U54-2
Kortison **U55**-10
kosen U62-10
kosmetisch (Prothese) U142-6
– (Ergebnis) U129-3
Kost **U2**-7,12,16
–, ausgewogene U1-3; U88-19
–, ballaststoffreiche U46-18
–, blähende U46-15
kosten **U62**-6
kostitutionelle Symptome U1-8

Kot **U46**-20
kotartig **U46**-20
Koterbrechen U46-20; U103-12
Kotmasse U79-16
Kotstauung **U109**-15,6
Kotyledo U85-14
Kovarianzanalyse U100-28
Koxalgie U22-7; U28-21
Krabbelkind U65-8
krabbeln **U65**-8,18
Krachen **U110**-5
Kraft **U1**-6; U73-11
–, isotonische U142-17
Kräfteverfall U108-14; U119-12
Kraftfahrzeug U6-3
Kraftgriff U64-9
kräftig U1-4,11; **U25**-4; **U31**-13; **U32**-2
kräftigen **U31**-13
– (Muskeln) **U1**-13
Kräftigung **U31**-13
Kräftigungsübung(en) U31-13
–, isometrische U142-17
Kraftlosigkeit **U103**-8 f
Kraftmesser **U142**-16
Krafttraining U1-12
kraftvoll **U1**-6
Kragen **U28**-11
Kragenknopfpanaritium U114-16
Krallenzehe U23-14
Krampf **U103**-20; **U109**-14; **U112**-8; U64-7
Krampfader **U110**-17; U34-4
Krampfaderbruch U110-17
Krampfanfall, (plötzlicher) **U113**-5
–, klonischer U31-10; U72-12
krampfartig **U103**-20; **U112**-8; **U113**-5
Krämpfe, klonische U64-7
krampfen **U103**-20
krampflösend **U92**-19 f; U93-5
kranial **U28**-7; **U87**-19; U131-13
Kraniotomie U28-7
Kranium **U28**-7
krank **U1**-3; **U4**-1,4; **U89**-2
– melden, sich U18-7
–, akut **U107**-11
–, psychisch **U77**-13, U73-2
–, schwer U125-1
Kranke(r) **U20**-2
–, eingebildete(r) **U4**-9
–, psychisch **U77**-24,1
Krankheitseinsicht U73-5
Krankeitserreger **U90**-5
kränkeln **U4**-5,1
Krankenakte **U18**-14; **U20**-5; **U102**-12
Krankenbett, am U117-1
Krankenblatt **U18**-14; **U20**-5; **U102**-12
Krankengeld U4-1
Krankengeschichte **U102**-4 ff
Krankengymnast(in) U16-12; U120-4
Krankengymnastik U14-3; U142-1
Krankenhaus **U4**-7; **U14**-1 f; **U139**-12
–, allgemeines U14-1
Krankenhausaufenthalt **U19**-15; **U20**-1; **U134**-11; U14-1

Krankenhausbelegung U19-15
Krankenhausbett U19-3
Krankenhauseinweisung U14-1
Krankenhausinfektion U13-10; U94-2
Krankenhauspersonal U15-2; U139-11
Krankenkost U2-12
Krankenpflege U14-8; U16-2
Krankenpflegehelfer(in) U16-14 f,4; U8-1
Krankenpflegekraft, leitende U16-2
Krankenpfleger(in) U14-8,1; U16-2,14
Krankenpflegeschule U16-3
Krankenpflegeschüler(in) U15-7
Krankensaal U19-1
Krankenschwester U14-8; U16-2
–, ausgebildete U15-2
–, diplomierte U16-4
Krankenseelsorger(in) U15-20
Krankenstand U4-1; U18-10
Krankenstation U14-2
Krankentrage U8-16
Krankenträger U8-16
Krankenunterlagen U20-5
Krankenurlaub U4-1; U18-10
Krankenversicherung U13-5; U18-15
Krankenwagen U8-5
Krankenwagenfahrer(in) U8-5
Krankenzimmer U14-2; U19-2
krankhaft U15-21; U89-1 f; U116-1
Krankheit U1-1; U4-1,4 f; U103-11
–, ansteckende U94-1
–, endemische U94-8
–, konstitutionelle U1-8; U25-3
–, lysosomale U83-6
–, manisch-depressive U77-17,16,18
–, meldepflichtige U94-1; U20-6
–, quarantänepflichtige U14-10
–, schwere U102-6
–, sexuell übertragbare U96-1; U94-3
–, tödliche U4-1; U12-1
–, übertragbare U94-1
–, vorliegende U102-1
–, zur Invalidität führende U4-4
Krankheitsausbruch U94-6
Krankheitsbeginn U119-5; U94-6
– in der Kindheit U95-1
–, fulminanter U94-7
–, plötzlicher U94-7
Krankheitsbild U108-2; U14-2
Krankheitserreger U119-2; U89-1; U90-1
Krankheitsfall U20-2
Krankheitsgefühl, allgemeines U95-2; U103-7
Krankheitsgewinn U4-9
Krankheitshäufigkeit U89-2
Krankheitsherd U89-3
Krankheitsüberträger U94-4
Krankheitsübertragung U133-16
Krankheitsursache U119-2; U89-8
Krankheitsverlauf U119-9; U18-6; U107-18
Krankheitszeichen, (objektives) U103-1; U108-1

kränklich U4-1,5
Kränklichkeit U1-1; U25-8
Krankschreibung U18-10
Kranzfurche (Herz) U32-7; U87-26
Kranznaht U29-14
Kranzschlagader U34-3
Krätze U96-12; U103-19
Krätzemittel U96-12
kratzen U5-9; U62-11; U103-19; U114-14
Kratzer U62-11
kratzig U62-11
krätzig U96-12
Kratzlinien U87-9
Krätzmilbe U90-15; U96-12
Kratzspuren U5-9
Kratztest U5-9
Kraulen (Schwimmart) U65-8
Krause-Endkolben U57-15
Krause-Kältekörperchen U57-15
kräuseln (Lippen) U63-6
kraus (Haar) U25-15
Kraut U91-8
Kräuter U3-19
Kräuterbad U1-19
Kräuterkunde U1-19
Kräuterwickel U142-22
Kreatin U78-15
Kreatin(phospho)kinase U78-15
Kreatin-Clearance U78-15
Kreatinin U78-15
Kreatinin-Clearance U49-7; U88-16
Kreatinphosphat U78-15
Krebs U97-6
krebserzeugend U98-2
Krebsgen U97-6
Krebsgeschwulst U97-6
Krebsgesellschaft, Amerikanische U13-13
Krebsheiler U15-23
Krebs-Henseleit-Zyklus U47-18; U49-13; U81-15
krebsig U97-10
Krebskachexie U108-14
Krebsregister U13-10; U97-6
Krebsrisiko U124-2
Krebsspezialist(in) U15-8
Krebssterblichkeit U12-3; U97-6
Krebstote U97-6
Krebsvorsorge U6-22
Krebsvorsorgeuntersuchung U97-6
Krebszelle U92-31
Krebs-Zyklus U78-6; U81-15
Kreisbewegung U31-7
kreischen (vor Angst) U66-14
Kreisdiagramm U100-27
Kreisel U142-19
kreisen U31-7
Kreislauf U36-1; U121-10
–, enterohepatischer U36-1
–, extrakorporaler U16-11; U125-11
–, fetaler U85-1
–, großer U36-1
–, kindlicher U85-1

Kreislauf, kleiner U36-2,1; U43-2
–, mütterlicher U55-21
Kreislaufkollaps U110-12; U6-5; U65-12
kreislaufstabil U75-15
Kreislaufstabilität U125-2
Kreislaufstillstand U36-1; U123-6
Kreislaufstörung U36-1
Kreislauf(unter)stützung U125-3
Kreislaufüberbelastung U36-1
Kreislaufversagen U36-1
Kreislaufzusammenbruch U110-12
Kreißsaal U15-17; U71-2 f,9
Kremation U12-16
Krepitation U106-14; U111-9
Kretinismus U95-1
Kreuz U22-11
Kreuz(bein)wirbel U28-19
Kreuzband U23-11
–, vorderes U30-6; U142-10
Kreuzbandruptur U64-13
Kreuzbein U28-20
kreuzen U41-14; U87-7; U58-15; U84-30
Kreuzimmunität U39-4
Kreuzinfektion U139-11; U94-2
Kreuzkorrelation U100-32
Kreuzlappen U130-11
Kreuzprobe U136-10; U14-12
– machen U37-1
Kreuzreaktion U121-11
Kreuzreaktivität U39-2
Kreuzschmerzen U22-7,11; U104-10,16
Kreuztitration U81-23
Kreuztoleranz U11-5; U39-22; U121-12
Kreuzung U87-7
– (Kleinhirnstiele) U41-14
Kreuzzeichen U67-2
Kribbelgefühl U57-3
Kribbeln U103-19,9; U104-17; U135-3 f
kribbelnd U62-11; U103-19
kriechen U65-5
Kriegsverletzte U14-6
Krikothyreotomie U123-11
Krippentod U19-3
Krise U105-18
–, akute klinische U124-1
–, cholinergische U40-8
–, gastrische U105-18
–, hämolytische U38-4; U124-6
–, hypertone U124-6; U36-8
–, hypothyreote U124-7
–, myasthenische U124-1
–, thyreotoxische U124-8; U54-6
Krisenintervention U20-11; U124-1
Kriseninterventionsdienst U13-3
Krisis U105-18
Kristall U82-5
Kristallablagerung U81-26; U82-5
kristallartig U81-26
Kristallbildung U81-26
Kristallgitter U81-26; U82-5
kristallin U81-26
kristallisieren U82-5

kristalloid **U81**-26
Kriterium, diagnostisches U117-16
Krone **U26**-14
Kropf U82-22; U89-16
Krücken **U19**-14; U134-13
–, Gehen an U142-2,13
Krückengang U19-14
Krückenlähmung U19-14
Krummdarm **U45**-12
krümmen U31-3
– (Rücken) U22-11
– (Zehen) U63-6
Krümmung **U31**-17; **U63**-3; U30-8
Krupp **U95**-10
–, echter U86-15; U95-9 f
Kruppanfall U95-10
kruppartig **U95**-10
Kruppbehandlung U95-10
kruppös **U95**-10
Krupp-Syndrom **U95**-10
Kruste **U114**-8
– (Wunde) **U140**-9,6
krustenbildend U114-1,8
Krustenbildung U114-8
krustös U114-1
Kryoablation **U127**-13
Kryochirurgie **U127**-8; **U126**-3
Kryoglobulin U78-18; U136-17
Kryoglobulinämie U136-17
Kryokauter **U127**-8 f
kryokonservieren U69-14
Kryokonservierung **U136**-17
– (Spermatozoen) U69-13
– (Embryonen) **U69**-14
Kryopräzipitat **U136**-17; U81-27
Kryopräzipitatkonserve U136-17
Kryoprotein U136-17
Kryosonde **U132**-8
Kryosperma U53-6; U69-14
Kryo-TESE U69-13
Kryotherapie **U142**-21; **U127**-8
Krypte, tonsilläre U95-13
Kryptorchismus U52-3
kubital **U23**-4
Küchenkräuter **U3**-19
Kugel U6-8
Kugelblitz U6-10
Kugelgelenk **U29**-4; U31-7
Kugelventil U133-8
kühl **U76**-15; **U105**-9
Kühldecke U19-6
Kühle **U105**-9
kühlen **U105**-9
Kühlsalbe U9-8
Kuhpocken U95-7
Kuldoskopie U50-15
kultivieren **U116**-6
kultiviert U69-16
Kultur **U116**-6
Kulturergebnisse U116-6
Kulturflasche U116-6
Kulturgefäß U116-6
Kulturmedium U82-4
Kulturschale U81-20; U116-6

Kulturverfahren U116-6
Kummer **U12**-12 f; **U32**-1; **U76**-20 f,1; **U104**-2; **U113**-2
kümmern, sich **U8**-1; **U15**-3; **U18**-4; **U20**-3
Kumulation im Körper **U91**-19
Kunstfehler **U20**-13
–, ärztlicher U18-1
Kunstherz U32-1
Kunststoffschlauch U127-20
Kunsttherapie U16-12
Kupfer **U82**-29; U79-17
–, caeruloplasmingebundenes U82-29
Kupferausscheidung, hepatische U91-19
–, vermehrte U82-29
Kupferspeicherkrankheit U91-20
Kupfersulfat U82-29
Kupffer-Sternzellen **U47**-4; U39-18
– –, phagozytierende U47-4
kuppelförmig U50-13; U114-10
Kuppengriff U64-10
Kur **U119**-9; **U120**-2,1,5; U9-1
Kuranstalt **U1**-18
kurativ U120-2,9
Kürette **U132**-10
Kurhotel U1-18
kurieren U9-2
Kurort **U1**-18 f; U120-2
Kurpfuscher **U15**-23
Kurvenblatt **U102**-12; U105-1
Kurvenschreiber **U100**-27
Kurzatmigkeit **U111**-1; U44-1; U102-2
kurzfristig U30-2; U57-4
Kurzinfusion U136-6
Kurznarkotika U93-4
Kurzschluss **U36**-14
Kurzschlussreaktion U6-21; U77-6
kurzsichtig **U59**-17,6
Kurzsichtigkeit **U59**-17
Kurzwellendiathermie U127-9
Kurzzeitgedächtnis U74-8
kurzzeitig U30-2
Kuscheln U68-2
Kuscheltiere U67-7
Kuss **U67**-7
Kussmaul-Atmung **U124**-7; U111-2
kutan **U56**-1
Kutanimpfung U122-1
Kutikula **U56**-16
Kutis **U56**-1
Küvettenoxymeter U125-9
Kyphose, verstärkte **U65**-11
Kystadenom **U98**-4
–, muzinöses U98-4
K-Zellen **U39**-16; U12-9

L

Labia (majora/minora) **U50**-14
labial **U26**-23; **U21**-9
Labialfläche U26-23
Labiallaut U21-9

Labien U50-14; U68-8
Labiensynechie U50-14
labil **U75**-15; U73-2
Labilität **U75**-15; **U108**-13
–, emotionale U75-15
–, vegetative U75-15
Labium **U21**-9
Labor, bakteriologisches U14-11; U116-1
–, gerichtsmedizinisches U14-11
Laborant(in) U16-1; U116-1
Laborassistent(in) **U16**-10
–, (med. techn.) U14-11
Laborbefruchtung U69-12
Laborbefund U116-2; U14-11; U117-6
Laborbericht U14-11; U20-6; U101-16
Labordaten U116-2
Labordiagnostik U14-11; U116-2
Labores uteri **U71**-3
laborieren (an) **U4**-5
Labormantel U17-16
Labortiere U116-1
Laboruntersuchungen U14-11; U116-1 f
Laborwerte U14-11; U116-2
Labyrinth **U60**-10
–, häutiges U57-18; U60-10; U86-15
–, knöchernes U57-18; U60-10
labyrinthär **U60**-10
Labyrintherschütterung U60-10
Labyrinthitis U60-10
Labyrinth-Kopfstellreflex U57-16
Labyrinthreflex U60-10
–, tonischer U57-16
Labyrinthschwerhörigkeit U60-10,13
Labyrinthschwindel U57-18
Labyrinthstellreflex U57-18
Labyrinthus cochlearis U60-10
– membranaceus U57-18; U60-10
– osseus U57-18; U60-10
– vestibularis U60-10
Lac sulfuris U82-24
Lächeln **U67**-9
–, freundliches U75-5
–, müdes U76-18
lächeln, süffisant **U67**-9
Lachen **U66**-2; **U67**-9
–, dröhnendes U22-4
lächerlich **U66**-2
Lachgas **U93**-11; U82-11,16
Lachlinie U67-9
Lachs-Calcitonin, rekombinantes U55-8
Lack U11-23; U91-2
Lackzunge U21-11; U103-5
Lacus lacrimalis U58-9
laden **U33**-10; **U81**-10
Laderampe (Rettungswagen) U8-5
lädiert **U6**-11
Ladung **U81**-10
–, elektrische U79-17; U81-10
Lage **U63**-1; **U65**-3; **U87**-8; **U131**-11
–, anatomische U87-1
–, klinische U108-2
Lageanomalie U89-2
Lagedrainage U63-1,13; U140-15

Lageempfindung **U57**-11,5; U65-3
Lagenystagmus U113-12
lagern **U63**-1
Lagerung **U9**-19; **U63**-1; **U131**-11,10
–, halbsitzende U8-17
Lagerungsschwindel U113-6
Lageschwindel U63-1; U103-13; U113-6
Lageveränderung U63-1
Lageverhältnis **U87**-1
Lageversteilung U126-14
Lagewechsel U63-1; U64-4
lahm **U65**-11
lahmen **U65**-11
lähmen **U135**-11
Lähmung **U31**-12; **U135**-11
–, schlaffe U103-9; U124-18
–, (un)vollständige **U113**-7
Lähmungsschielen U59-4; U113-7
Laie U13-12
Laienhebamme U16-6
Laienverständnis U6-13
Laktatazidose U1-6; U36-4
Laktateliminierung U88-20
Laktation **U71**-25
Laktationsamenorrhoe/-ö U71-25
Laktationsperiode **U71**-25
Laktazidose U1-6; U36-4
laktifer **U71**-25
Laktose **U79**-8,6
Laktosemangel U79-8
Laktosurie **U79**-8
Lakunen, trophoblastäre U85-14
Lallen U66-17
Lallphase U66-17
Lalophobie U66-17
Lambdanaht U29-14
Lamina **U86**-15; **U87**-8
– basalis U86-15
– basilaris U60-12
– cribrosa U87-2
– orbitalis U86-15
– quadrigemina **U41**-13
– spiralis ossea U60-11
– tecti **U41**-13
laminar **U86**-15
Laminar-Flow-System U139-8
Lamination **U86**-15
Laminektomie U125-15
Laminektomie-Stanze U132-11
Lampenfieber U6-21
Landarzt/-ärztin U18-1
Landkartenzunge U21-11
langbeinig **U23**-8; **U25**-9
langdauernd **U119**-10
Längenalter U24-2
Längenwachstum U80-3
Längenwachstumszone **U28**-3
Langer Streifen (EKG) U33-6
Langerhans-Inseln **U54**-8; U55-12
Langerhans-Zelle U39-11,18
Langer-Linien **U56**-17; **U87**-9
Langeweile U66-4
langfristig U16-12; **U100**-15
langjährig **U119**-10

langkettig **U81**-7
langlebig U39-15
Langlochplatte U141-17
Längsachse U87-3
langsam U36-5
langsam-progredient U95-5
Langschläfer U65-17
Längsschnittstudie U101-1
Längsteilung U126-14
Langstreckenlauf U65-14
Langzeitbehandlung U20-3
Langzeit-EKG-Rekorder U125-6
Langzeitergebnisse U100-20; U117-6
Langzeiternährung, parenterale U125-19
Langzeitexposition U122-5
Langzeitfolgen U134-9
Langzeitgedächtnis U74-8
Langzeitimmobilität U141-5
Langzeitinfusion U136-1
Langzeitinsulin U55-12
Langzeitkontrolle U18-9
Langzeitkrankenhaus U14-1
Langzeitmorbidität U120-12
Langzeitnachbetreuung U120-14
Langzeitüberlebende(r) U12-6
Lanolinum anhydricum U82-9
Lanthaniden U82-6
Lanugo(haare) U71-23
Lanzette U17-1
lanzinierend U104-7
Laparoskop **U128**-3; **U133**-2
Laparoskopeur **U128**-3
Laparoskopie, explorative U128-3
Laparotomie **U128**-13; **U127**-2
–, explorative U97-14
Laparotomiebesteck U128-19
laparotomieren **U128**-13
Läppchen **U87**-23
läppchenförmig **U47**-3
Läppchenprobe **U118**-2
Lappen **U87**-23; U130-6; U137-4
– ohne Gefäßstruktur **U130**-12
–, einseitig bedeckter U130-15
–, freier **U130**-10
–, gestielter **U130**-11; U87-24
–, umhüllender **U130**-17
Lappenatelektase U111-15
Lappenbronchus U43-3
Lappendeckung U129-9; U142-6
Lappenentfernung **U87**-23
Lappenpneumonie U87-23; U94-14
Lappenzunge U87-23
Lapra-Ty-Klip U138-15
Lärm **U61**-3
–, gesundheitsschädigender U91-1
–, ohrenbetäubender U61-9
Lärmbelästigung U91-6
Lärmschwerhörigkeit U61-3,9; U113-13
Laron-Syndrom U24-4
Larva migrans cutanea U114-2
larviert **U117**-13
Laryngoskop U17-4; U43-7

Laryngoskop Spatel U17-3
Laryngospasmus **U111**-10; U43-7; U66-9
Larynx **U43**-7; U21-14
Lasègue Test **U142**-11; U31-3
Lasègue-Zeichen U113-1; U142-11
Laser **U127**-7
Laserablation U127-13
Lasersonde U127-7
Laserstrahl U127-7
Lasertherapie **U142**-24
Laservaporisation U127-7
Läsion **U5**-5; **U89**-3; U140-17
–, granulomatöse venerische U96-6
–, hamartomartige U98-6
–, herdförmige U97-10
–, raumfordernde U124-14
Lassa-Fieber U14-10
lässig **U75**-16
Last **U33**-10
–, schwere U24-8
lästig **U104**-3
lasttragend **U24**-1
latent **U94**-6; **U119**-6
Latenz **U94**-6
Latenzphase **U94**-6; U39-2
Latenzstadium **U94**-6
Latenzzeit U94-6; U119-6
–, synaptische U40-13
lateral **U87**-18
Lateralinfarkt U87-18
Lateralisation **U87**-18
Latex(agglutinations)test U39-19; U116-3
Latissimus **U30**-12
– dorsi-Lappen, (freier) U30-12
Laudanum U11-18
Lauf **U1**-14; **U65**-14
Laufband **U65**-5; **U142**-16
– Ergometrie U65-5; U142-16
Laufbandtraining U142-16
laufen **U1**-14; **U65**-1,14
–, um d. Wette **U65**-15
Läufer(in) **U1**-14
Laufgestell U65-1
Laufstall U65-18
Lauftempo, lockeres U76-19
Lauftraining **U1**-14
Lauge **U81**-19
Laune **U76**-2
–, schlechte **U76**-9
Launenhaftigkeit **U76**-2
launisch **U76**-2
Laus, echte **U90**-15
Läusebefall **U90**-15; U96-12
Läusefleckfieber U90-15
Laut U66-10f
Lautbildung **U29**-1; **U66**-10,13
Laute hervorbringen **U66**-1
lauter **U75**-12
Lautersatz U66-11
Lautheit **U61**-5
lautlos **U61**-3
Lautsprecher **U17**-17

Lautstärke **U61**-5; U60-13
Lautstärkeempfindung U61-5
Lautstärkepegel U61-5
Lautunterscheidung U66-11
Lavage **U116**-5; **U118**-10; **U140**-11
–, bronchoalveoläre U91-26
Lavagematerial **U91**-26; **U118**-10
Lavagezytologie (Blase) U83-1
Laxans **U92**-13; U46-20; U91-24
–, salinisches U81-21
Laxanzienabusus U92-13
Laxativum **U92**-13
Lazarett U14-1
LD **U91**-11
LDL-Apherese U136-15
– Cholesterin U47-12; U78-16
Lead-time Bias U100-18
Leben, rechtschaffenes U75-12
–, sorgloses U75-16
–, zurückgezogenes U75-14
lebend **U12**-5
Lebendgeburt U71-8
lebendig **U1**-6; **U12**-5
Lebendimpfstoff U12-5; U122-2,6
Lebendspender **U129**-17
Lebendvakzine U12-5; U122-2,6
Lebendvirus U90-10
Lebensalter, mittleres **U80**-12
lebensbedrohlich **U123**-1; U134-5,9
Lebensdauer **U80**-1
Lebensende U80-11
lebenserhaltend **U125**-3; **U126**-13
Lebenserwartung **U80**-1; U100-18
lebensfähig U129-17; U130-21
Lebensfähigkeit U69-14
lebensgefährlich **U123**-1; U100-15
Lebensgewohnheiten U73-11
Lebensjahr U80-11
Lebensjahrzehnt **U80**-11
lebenslang **U80**-1
Lebensmitte **U80**-12
Lebensmittel **U2**-6
Lebensmitteltoxikologie U91-3
Lebensmittelvergiftung **U91**-21; U94-18
Lebensqualität U80-1
Lebensqualitätsstudie U100-20
lebensrettend **U123**-1; **U126**-4
Lebensretter(in) **U123**-1
Lebensrettung **U123**-1
Lebensversicherung U13-5; U18-15
Lebensweise, gesunde U1-2
lebenswichtig **U1**-6
Lebenswille U73-11
Lebenszeit **U80**-1
Lebenszeitwahrscheinlichkeit U100-31
Leber **U47**-1
Leberabszess U47-6
Leberbiopsie U47-1
Leberegel U90-17
Leberentzündung **U94**-15; U47-1
Leberfleck **U114**-5; U116-23
Leberfunktionstests **U116**-14; U47-1
Lebergalle U47-11
Lebergallengang **U47**-6

Leberglykogen U47-14; U78-13
Leberhilum U87-25
Leberinsuffizienz U10-12
Leberkoma U47-1; U124-7
Leberläppchen **U47**-3,5
Leberlappen **U47**-2
Leberlappenresektion **U47**-2
Leberparenchym U47-1; U86-22
Leberparenchymzelle U47-1,3
Leberpforte **U47**-5; U87-25
Leberrand U47-1
Leberschaden U47-1
Leberschmerz U47-1
Lebersinusoid **U47**-4
Leberszintigrafie U47-1
Lebertoxizität U121-13
Lebervergrößerung U47-1
Leberversagen U47-1
Leberzellbalken **U47**-4
Leberzelle U47-1
Leberzirrhose U47-1
lebhaft **U1**-6
leblos **U12**-5; **U123**-1
Leck **U112**-15; **U135**-15; **U137**-11
lecken (Lippen) **U67**-17
lecker **U2**-11; U21-8
Lederhaut **U56**-3; **U58**-6
Lederzecken U90-15
leer **U46**-8
Leeraufnahme U99-3,19; U118-18
– (Harntrakt) **U118**-19
– (Schädel) U54-13
Leerdarm **U45**-11
Leermedikament **U101**-8
Legastheniker(in) **U113**-9; U74-5
legasthenisch **U113**-9
Legen (Magensonde) U123-10
legen (OP-Tisch) **U131**-11
legieren **U82**-6
Legierung U82-6,29
Lehm U82-30
Lehmpackung U1-20
lehnen, (sich) **U63**-10; **U64**-5
Lehnstuhl U19-13
Lehrkrankenhaus U14-1
Lehrvisite U20-9
Leibbinde U140-20
Leibstuhl U19-13
Leiche **U12**-14,5
Leichenbeschauer **U12**-21,16
Leichenflecke **U12**-15
Leichengeruch U12-14
Leichenhalle **U12**-16; U14-4
Leichenniere U48-2
Leichenöffnung **U12**-20
Leichenorgan U129-17
Leichenorganspende U129-15
Leichenschau U12-21
Leichenschauhaus **U12**-16; U16-14
Leichenspender(in) **U129**-17; U12-14
Leichentransplantat U12-14; U130-1
Leichenzug U12-17
Leichnam **U12**-14,5
leicht U72-18

Leichtkettenkrankheit U39-6
Leichtsinn **U75**-18
leichtsinnig **U75**-18
Leid(en) **U4**-3 f,10; **U12**-12; **U104**-2
leiden an **U4**-3; **U102**-1
Leiden, organisches U86-20
–, unerträgliches U4-3
leidend **U4**-5
Leidende(r) **U4**-3
Leidensdruck U4-3
leidtragend **U12**-13
Leihmutter(schaft) **U69**-19; U71-2
Leinentuch U8-16
Leinsamenkataplasma U140-25
Leiomyom **U98**-9
–, gestieltes U98-9
leise **U61**-5
– sprechen U66-16
Leishmaniose, kutane U89-17; U114-16
Leiste **U22**-9; **U28**-5
Leistenband U22-9; U30-6; U52-8
Leiste(nbeuge) **U22**-9; U56-12; U107-1
Leistenbruch U22-9; U89-23
Leistenbubo U96-5
Leistengegend **U22**-9; U45-6
–, untere U52-8
Leistenhernie U22-9; U52-8
Leistenhoden U22-9; U52-3
Leistenkanal **U52**-8; U22-9
Leistenring U22-9; U52-8
–, innerer U52-7
Leistenschmerz U109-12
Leistung **U8**-16; U11-24; U73-5
Leistungsalter U80-1
leistungsfähig **U1**-11
Leistungsfähigkeit **U142**-4; **U101**-26
–, geistige U77-1
Leistungssport U1-12
leiten **U42**-2; **U61**-4
leitend **U42**-2; U16-10
Leiter (Institut) **U21**-1
Leiter(in), stellvertretende(r) U15-3
Leitfähigkeit **U42**-2; **U61**-4; U82-6
– für Natrium(ionen) U42-2
Leitgeschwindigkeit U42-2; U61-4
Leitplanke U6-2
Leitstrang U84-11
Leitsymptom U103-1; U108-1
Leitung **U42**-2; **U125**-5
–, aberrierende U42-2
–, retrograde U42-2
–, verborgene U42-2
Leitungsanästhesie **U93**-6; U135-2
Leitungsaphasie U66-9; U113-10
Leitungsbahnen U40-3; U42-2
Leitungsblock U123-2
Leitungsgeschwindigkeit U42-2; U61-4
Leitungsstörungen U42-2
Leitungsverzögerung U42-2
Leitungswasser U5-11; U82-4
–, reines U64-11
Lemniscus medialis U41-14
Lende **U22**-6; U30-15
Lendenmuskel **U30**-15

Lendenschmerz U109-12
Lendenstütze (Autositz) U6-3
Lendenwirbel U28-19; U35-8; U45-10
Lendenwirbelsäule U22-12
Lentigines seniles U25-18
lentiginös **U114**-5
Lentigo **U114**-5
– praemaligna U56-7
– maligna-Melanom U98-15; U114-5
Leopard-Syndrom U114-5
Lepra **U94**-17
lepromatös **U94**-17
Lepromintest U94-17
leprös **U94**-17
Leptomeningen U41-8
leptosom **U25**-2,5
Lernbehinderung U74-7; U142-3
lernen **U74**-7
–, auswendig U32-2
Lernen, räumliches U74-7
–, soziales U74-7
–, verbales U74-7
–, kognitives U73-6
Lernprozess U74-7
Lernschwäche U4-8
Lernschwester **U16**-3
Lernstörung U74-7
lesbisch U68-14
Leserasterverschiebung U84-21
Leseschwäche U61-10
Lesestörung U61-10
Leseunfähigkeit **U113**-9
Leseverständnis U61-10; U73-5
letal **U12**-2
letale Dosis U121-7
letaler Ausgang U100-20
Letalfaktoren U12-2; U84-1
Letalgene U12-2
Letalmutation U12-2
Lethargie U7-12; **U113**-3
Leuchten **U59**-11; U17-4
leuchten (hell) **U59**-3
Leuchtschirm U99-8
Leucinzipper U84-3
leugnen **U102**-10
Leukämie, akute undifferenzierte U38-3
–, myeloische U38-2
Leukapherese **U136**-15; U37-7
Leuko(zyto)penie U37-7; U38-5
Leukoderm **U114**-4
Leukodiapedese U37-7
Leukoproteasen U37-7
Leukotomie **U87**-23
Leukozyten **U37**-7; U92-34
–, phagozytierende U37-7
–, zahlreiche U37-7
Leukozyten(gesamt)zahl **U116**-8; U86-2
Leukozytenabbau U37-7
Leukozytenadhäsionsmangel U37-7
Leukozytenantigen U37-7
–, humanes U39-8
leukozytendepletierte Erythrozyten U136-16

Leukozytendifferentialzählung U37-7; U116-8
Leukozytenmanschette **U136**-16
Leukozytenphosphatase, alkalische U37-7; U47-15
Leukozytenwanderung U37-7
Leukozytenzahl, niedrige U116-20
Leukozytenzählung **U116**-8
Leukozytenzylinder U37-7; U112-14
Leukozytose U37-7
Levatorschlinge U30-12
Leydig-Zwischenzellen U53-9; U55-15
LH **U55**-15; U51-8
LH-Anstieg (Zyklusmitte) U55-14
LH-Freisetzung U55-15
LH-Gipfel U51-1; U55-15
LHRH-Analogon U55-15
LH-Wert U55-15
Liaisondienst U20-4
Liberine U54-4
Libido **U68**-4; U73-11
Libidostörung **U68**-7
Libidoverlust U68-4
Lichen (ruber) **U114**-14
lichenartig U114-14
Lichenifikation **U114**-14
lichenoid **U114**-14
Licht brechen U59-10
–, kobaltblaues U82-25
Lichtblitze U59-10
Lichtbrechung **U59**-12
lichtempfindlich **U103**-15
Lichtempfindlichkeit U57-8
Lichtempfindung U57-10
Lichterythem U108-7
Lichthof U59-1
Lichtquelle, starke U17-4
Lichtreaktion U58-8; U107-15
Lichtreflex U42-12; U107-15
Lichtscheu **U103**-15; U95-3
lichtstarre Pupillen U7-7
Lichtstrahl U59-10
lichtundurchlässig U121-9
Lichtwahrnehmung **U59**-6,10
Lid **U21**-3
Lidflattern U110-7
Lidkrampf U31-5; U103-20
Lidocain **U93**-5
Lidödem U108-10
Lidplatte U87-2
Lidrandentzündung U58-3
Lidränder U58-3
Lidrandreflex U135-20
Lidreflex U67-15
–, akustischer U60-2
Lidschlag U58-3
–, seltener U59-3
lidschlagbedingt U99-13
Lidschlussreflex U58-3; U59-3
Lidschwellung U5-15
Lidspalte U58-3; U59-2
Lidspaltenerweiterung (Blicksenkung) U59-2
Lidverschlusspflaster **U125**-25

Lidwinkel **U58**-3
liebenswürdig **U75**-5
Lieberkühn-Krypten U45-1
Liebesentzug **U77**-11
liebevoll U62-10
liebkosen **U62**-10
Liebkosung U62-10; **U67**-7; U68-2
Lieblingsspeise U2-8
liefern **U36**-6; **U88**-3; **U116**-18
Liegen **U63**-7
–, im U63-10
liegend **U63**-10
Liegeposition **U63**-7
Liegestütze **U64**-12
Lien **U35**-4
– accessorius U35-4
Lift **U64**-16
Lifter **U19**-13
ligamentär **U30**-6
Ligamentum **U30**-6
– arteriosum U32-11
– cardinale uteri U50-5
– carpi transversum U87-17
– cruciatum anterius U30-6; U142-10
– – genus U23-11
– deltoideum/mediale U30-13
– falciforme hepatis U47-2
– iliolumbale U30-15
– – inguinale U22-9; U52-8
– – Pouparti U30-6
– latum U50-5
– metatarsale U28-25
– nuchae U30-13
– palpebrale laterale U58-3
– suspensorium U63-13
– teres hepatis U47-2
– – uteri U50-5
– ulnocarpale U28-16
Ligand **U81**-14; U79-17; U92-4
–, extrazellulärer U86-19
Liganden-Rezeptorenbesetzung U81-14
Ligase **U78**-4
Ligatur **U137**-3
Ligaturendraht U137-3
Ligaturklip **U138**-15; U137-13
Ligaturschere U132-4
Ligaturschlinge U137-3
–, vorgefertigte **U138**-5
ligieren **U137**-3; U5-6; U138-3
Limbus corneae U58-5f
Lindan U81-7
lindern **U4**-13; **U8**-2; **U12**-5; U92-18
lindernd **U92**-30; **U120**-9
Linderung **U4**-13; **U104**-19; **U120**-9
Linea **U87**-9
– alba U87-9
– arcuata ossis ilii U30-15
– axillaris U23-3
– – anterior U87-9,16
– mamillaris U50-18; U87-9
– medioclavicularis U87-9
– trapezoidea U30-13
linear **U87**-9
Lingua **U21**-11

Lingua lobata U87-23
- plicata U25-17; U56-17; U87-26
- scrotalis U56-17; U87-26
- villosa nigra U56-13
lingual **U26**-23
Lingualhöcker U26-23
Lingualkippung U26-23
Lingualnerv U26-23
Linie **U87**-9
-, weiße U87-9
Linienblitz U6-14
linienförmig **U87**-9
Linker **U84**-37
Linksherzbelastung U33-10
Linksherzhypertrophie U89-15; U110-9
Links(herz)insuffizienz U110-12; U124-12
Linksherz-Katheterisierung U125-7
Links-Rechts-Shunt U110-12
Linksschenkelblock U123-2
Linolsäure U79-12
-, konjugierte U81-9
Linse **U58**-8; **U133**-2
Linsenfleck **U114**-5
Linsenkapsel U58-8
Linsenkern U41-10
Linsenluxation U58-8
Linsenplakode U85-23
Linsentrübung U58-8
Lipase U46-11
Lipid **U79**-11
lipidbeladen (Histiozyt) U39-18
Lipidspeicherung U78-20
Lipidstoffwechsel U24-5
Lipom **U98**-11
-, abgekapseltes U98-11
lipomartig **U98**-11
lipomatös **U98**-11
Lipomatose **U98**-11
-, schmerzhafte U56-5
lipophil U81-13
Liposarkom **U98**-11
-, myxoides U98-7
Lippen **U21**-9
-, aufgesprungene U87-26
-, sinnliche U68-9
Lippenbalsam U21-9
Lippenbändchen U21-9
Lippenentzündung U21-9
Lippenfurunkel U114-16
Lippenhalter U21-9
Lippeninkompetenz U21-9
Lippenlesen **U61**-10; U67-17
Lippenprofil U21-9
Lippenrot U87-10; **U21**-9
Lippensaum U21-9
Lippenschluss U21-9
Lippenschlusslinie U21-9
Lippenspalte U87-26; U21-9
Lippenwulst **U21**-9
Liquefaktion **U81**-22
Liquor (cerebrospinalis) **U41**-17,2; U93-9; U97-13
Liquoraustritt U28-6; U41-17

Liquordruck U41-17; U118-7
Liquorpassage U41-17
Liquorproteine U41-17
Liquorresorption U41-17
Liquorrhoe/-ö U15-19; U41-17; U106-8
Liquorsediment U81-27
Liquorshunt U36-14
Liquoruntersuchung U41-17
Liquorwege U40-3
Liquorzirkulation U36-1
Liquorzucker(spiegel) U41-17; U79-7
Liquorzytologie U41-17; U83-1
Lisch-Knötchen U98-6
lispeln **U66**-21
Lissosphinkter U48-14
Lithium U82-18,22
Lithiumaugmentation U91-19
Lithocholsäure U47-12
Lithotripsie U89-21
Littré-Drüsen U54-1
livid **U12**-15; U114-10
Lividität **U12**-15
Livores **U12**-15
L-Kette **U39**-6
LKW-Fahrer(in) **U6**-3
Lob U62-9
lobär **U43**-3; **U47**-2
Lobärpneumonie U43-3; U87-23; U94-14
Lobektomie **U47**-2; **U87**-23; U41-5
Lobotomie U87-23
lobulär **U47**-3; **U87**-23
Lobulus **U87**-23
- hepatis **U47**-3
- pulmonis U43-3; U87-23
Lobus **U87**-23
- caudatus U47-2; U87-19
- cerebri **U41**-5
- frontalis U87-23
- hepatis **U47**-2
- - dexter U47-2
- - sinister U47-2
- medius pulmonis dextri U43-3
- parietalis U28-8; U41-5; U87-23
- pulmonis **U43**-3
- quadratus U47-2
- temporalis U41-5
Loch **U28**-6
Lochia alba U71-23
- rubra U71-23
- serosa U71-23
Lochien **U71**-23
-, fötide U71-23
Locke (Haar) U25-13
locker **U76**-19; U27-12
- (Lauf) U1-14
- (Muskeln) U1-20
lockern, sich U27-5
Lockerung **U76**-19; U142-8; U26-1
Lockerungsübungen **U1**-13
Lockstoffe, chemische U81-1
Locus **U84**-2
- caeruleus/coeruleus U41-10
- Kiesselbachi U110-20

Locus-control Region U84-2
Löffel, scharfer **U132**-10,3
Löffelnadel U138-14
Löffelnagel U56-15
Logen-Syndrom U30-7
Logistikleiter(in) (Rettungsdienst) U16-9
logistische Regressionsanalyse U100-33
Logopäde/-in U16-12; U120-4
Logopädie U61-10; **U66**-9
Logorrhoe/-ö U66-9; U77-18
Logrank-Test U100-34
lokal **U121**-5
Lokalanästhesie **U93**-3
Lokalanästhetikum U15-11; U121-5
lokalisieren **U117**-4
Lokomotion **U65**-2
lokomotorisch **U65**-2
Longitudinalachse U87-3
Longitudinalstudie U101-1
Löschmannschaft U6-10
lose (Zähne) U27-12
lösen **U81**-8
-, sich (Knoten) U138-2
lösend U81-22; **U88**-5
losgelöst **U76**-15; **U77**-8
Losgelöstsein **U76**-15; U7-15
Loslassschmerz **U109**-12; U102-3
löslich (machen) **U88**-5; U35-4
Löslichkeit **U88**-5; **U9**-11
Löslichkeitsprodukt U88-5
loslösen **U81**-8; U73-10
Lost U82-2
Lösung U4-14; **U88**-5; **U9**-11
-, (in) **U81**-25
-, gepufferte U88-5
-, gesättigte U88-5
-, hyperosmolare U49-9
-, kolloidale U81-26
-, kristalloide **U81**-26
-, niedermolekulare U81-25
-, verdünnte U81-23,25
-, wässrige U81-22; U82-4
Lösungsgeschwindigkeit (Arznei) U81-22
Lösungsmittel **U81**-22; **U88**-5; U10 20
-, unpolares U81-13
Lösungsmittelintoxikation U11-23
Lösungsmittelvergiftung U11-23
Lösungstablette U9-7
loswerden (Verkühlung) U64-14
Löten U82-28
Lotion **U9**-10
Löwengesicht U25-10
Low-output-Syndrom U33-7
loyal **U75**-10
LSD **U11**-22
LSD-Abhängigkeit U11-22
LSD-Blotter U11-22
LSD-Pappen U11-22
LSD-Sucht U11-22
Lubrikans **U56**-9; U68-5
-, wasserlösliches U17-14
Lubrikation **U17**-14; U56-9

Lücke, amnestische U74-20
lückig (Gebiss) U27-2
Luer-Zange **U132**-11
Lues (venerea) **U96**-3
Luesserologie U96-3
Luffaschwamm U1-20
Luft ablassen **U44**-5
–, verbrauchte U62-5
Luftbefeuchter **U105**-13; U90-18
luftdicht (Verschluss) U44-12; U121-9; U133-6; U137-11
Lufteinschluss **U111**-6; U43-10; U87-6
Luftembolie U43-10; U44-12; U124-13
lüften **U44**-6
Luftfeuchtigkeit **U105**-13; U110-20
Luftgewehr U6-8
Lufthunger U44-12
Luftkrankheit U103-11
Luftleitung **U61**-4; U60-13
Lufträume U43-10
Luftrettung über See U8-2
Luftröhre **U43**-8
Luftröhrenknorpel U43-8
Luftröhrenschnitt **U123**-11; U43-8
Luftschadstoffe U91-6
Luftschlucken U43-10; U46-2; U109-5
Luftströmung U139-8
Luftverlust (künstliche Beatmung) U43-10
Luftverschmutzung U91-6
Luftwege **U43**-5; U44-12
Lumbago **U104**-16; U28-20; U30-16
Lumbalanästhesie U41-15
Lumbalpunktion **U118**-7; U41-15,17
Lumen **U87**-22
–, falsches U87-22
–, verengtes U34-14
Lumendurchmesser U34-14
Lumeneinengung U87-22
Lumineszenz, kurzlebige **U99**-17
Lumpektomie **U97**-3
Lunarmonat **U70**-9,6
Lunge **U43**-1
–, eiserne U43-1
–, feuchte U43-1
–, gut belüftete U43-1
–, kollabierte U111-15
Lungenabszess **U111**-14; U43-1
Lungenatmung U44-4
Lungenausdehnung **U44**-10
Lungenbarotrauma U6-17
Lungenbezirke, periphere U43-1
Lungenbiopsie, thorakoskopische U125-16; U128-6
Lungenblähung **U111**-16
Lungenbläschen **U43**-10
Lungendurchblutung U36-2; U88-3
Lungenegel U90-17
Lungenembolie **U124**-13; U36-2; U43-2
Lungenemphysem **U111**-16
Lungenentzündung **U94**-14; U43-2
–, interstielle **U94**-14
Lungenfacharzt U15-8
Lungenfell U43-11; U86-21; U87-13

Lungenflügel **U43**-1
Lungenfunktionsprüfung **U118**-3; U43-2; U116-14
Lungengefäßwiderstand U36-10; U43-2
Lungenheilstätte **U14**-3
Lungenhilus **U43**-4
Lungeninfarkt U124-11
Lungeninfiltrat U43-2
Lungeninterstitium U86-19
Lungenkapillaren U34-5
Lungenkarzinom, kleinzelliges U97-10
Lungenkollaps **U111**-15
Lungenkontusion U43-2
Lungenkrebs U98-2
Lungenkreislauf **U36**-2,1; U43-2
Lungenläppchen U43-3; U87-23
Lungenlappen **U43**-3
Lungenmetastasen U97-13
Lungenödem **U111**-13; U43-2; U108-10
–, interstitielles U43-1; U111-13
Lungenperfusion U16-11; U36-2,5
Lungenperfusionsszintigramm **U118**-22; U16-11; U99-18
Lungenpest U43-2; U94-14
Lungenreife U43-1; U71-9
Lungensegment **U43**-3; U87-6
Lungenspitze U87-25
Lungenstauung U36-2,12; U124-12
Lungenszintigrafie U43-1
Lungentransplantat U43-1
Lungentransplantation U43-1
Lungentuberkulose U94-16
Lungenüberblähung **U111**-6
Lungenventilationsszintigramm U118-22
Lungenverdichtung U43-2
Lungenwiderstand U31-16
Lungenwurzel **U43**-4; U87-25
Lunula **U56**-15
Lupenbrille **U127**-6
Lupus erythematodes, systemischer U108-7
Lust (auf Essen) U2-11
lustig **U75**-7
lustlos **U76**-17
Lustlosigkeit **U76**-17; **U113**-3; U72-1
lustvoll **U57**-9
Lutealinsuffizienz U51-8
Lutealphase **U51**-8
–, mittlere U51-8
–, späte U51-8
Lutealphasendefekt U51-8
luteinisierend **U55**-15
Lutropin **U55**-15; U51-8
lutschen **U46**-2; U9-14
Lutschtablette **U9**-14
Luxation **U5**-20; **U106**-4
–, instabile U31-15
Luxationsfraktur U5-20; U106-4
luxieren **U5**-20; **U106**-4
Luys-Körper U41-9
Lyell-Syndrom, staphylogenes U90-8
Lymphabfluss U35-1
Lymphadenektomie U35-3; U126-12

Lymphadenom **U98**-10
Lymphangiografie U35-1
Lymphangiom **U98**-5
lymphatisch **U35**-1
Lymphbahnen U35-1; U40-3
Lymphbildung U35-2
Lymphdrainage U35-1; U140-15
–, manuelle **U142**-15; U1-20
Lymphe **U35**-2
Lymphfluss U35-2
Lymphfollikel U35-1
Lymphgefäße **U35**-1; U34-1; U86-14
–, subkutane U56-3
Lymphkapillaren U34-5; U35-1
– (Dünndarm) **U35**-10
Lymphknötchen U35-1
Lymphknoten **U35**-3
–, axillärer U35-3
–, befallener U4-10; U35-3
–, druckdolenter U35-3
–, regionärer U35-3
Lymphknotenausräumung U87-5
Lymphknotenbefall U35-3; U89-4
–, lokaler U97-11
Lymphknotenbeteiligung U4-10; U35-3
Lymphknotenbiopsie U35-3; U118-4
Lymphknotendissektion U126-12
–, axilläre U87-5
Lymphknotenentzündung, venerische U96-1
Lymphknotenmetastasen U97-13
Lymphknotenpaket U128-17
Lymphknotenschwellung **U98**-10
Lymphknotenstrang U35-1
Lymphknotenvergrößerung U35-3
Lymphkreislauf U35-1
Lympho(zyto)penie U78-21
Lympho(zyto)poese U38-1; U55-27
Lymphoblast **U37**-10
Lymphödem **U111**-13; U35-1
Lymphografie U35-1
Lymphogranuloma inguinale **U96**-7
Lymphogranulomatose U98-10
lymphoid **U35**-1
Lymphokine **U37**-10
Lymphom, immunoblastisches U98-10
–, lymphoblastisches U98-10
–, lymphoplasmozytäres U98-10
–, malignes **U98**-10
lymphomähnlich **U98**-10
lymphomatoid **U98**-10
lymphomatös **U98**-10
Lymphopathia venerea **U96**-7
Lymphosarkom **U98**-10
Lymphozyt **U37**-10
–, kurzlebiger U39-12
–, reifer U37-10
–, sensibilisierter U37-10
–, thymusabhängiger U35-5; U39-13
Lymphozytenpool U78-20
Lymphozytenpopulation U37-10
Lymphozytenrezirkulation U37-10
Lymphozyten-Subpopulationen U37-10

Lymphozytentransformation U37-10
Lymphozytentransformationsfaktor U39-12
Lymphstauung U35-2
Lymphweg U97-11
Lyse **U78**-4
Lysergsäurediäthylamid U11-22
Lysis **U78**-4; **U105**-18
Lysosom **U39**-18; **U83**-6
–, eisenspeicherndes U39-18
–, primäres U83-6
–, sekundäres U83-6
Lysosomenmembran U83-6

M

Macrophagocytus stabilis **U39**-18
– stellatus **U47**-4; U39-18
Macula **U114**-9
– lutea **U58**-13
– sacculi U60-9
– utriculi U60-9
Mädchenname U102-9
Madenwurm U90-16
Magen **U22**-4; **U45**-8
–, aufgeblähter U109-8
–, empfindlicher U103-9
–, leerer U45-8
–, nüchterner U45-8
–, voller U109-8
Magenaushebung **U91**-26; U125-18
Magenauskleidung U45-8
Magenbeschwerden U45-8
Magenblähung U46-10
Magen-Darmmotilität **U46**-6
– Darmschleimhaut **U54**-9
– Darm-Passage **U118**-21,18; U45-1
– – Röntgen U99-3
– – Trakt **U45**-1
– Duodenal-Dünndarm-Passage (MDDP) U118-21
Magendie-Schielstellung U59-15
Mageneingang U32-3; U45-8; U46-10
Magenentfernung **U127**-1
Magenentleerung U91-26
–, verzögerte U46-8
Magenentleerungszeit **U46**-8; U45-8
Magenerosion U114-13
Magengeschwür U45-8; U89-17; U109-1
Magengrube **U45**-8; U22-4
Mageninhalt U45-8; U125-18
–, regurgitierter U46-4
Magenknurren **U46**-14
Magenkrümmung **U45**-8
Magenmund U46-10
Magenpförtner **U45**-8
Magenrand, linker/rechter U45-8
Magenreizung U89-10
Magensack U22-4
Magensaft **U46**-10; U45-8; U109-4
magensaftresistent U9-7
Magensäuregehalt U81-19

Magenschlauch U45-8; **U91**-26,25
–, großlumiger U91-26
Magenschleimhaut U86-17
Magenschleimhautbarriere U36-15
Magenschleimhautentzündung U45-8
Magenschmerzen U104-4
Magensekret U45-8
Magensekretion U45-8; U88-11
Magensonde U45-8
–, perkutane U125-18
Magenspiegelung **U118**-11
Magenspülflüssigkeit U91-26
Magenspülung **U91**-26,4; U118-10
Magentropfen U9-11
Magenverstimmung **U109**-1; U10-9
Magenverweilsonde U95-12
Magenvolvulus U109-6
mager **U24**-10
Magersucht U103-10; U108-14
Magnesia **U82**-20
Magnesiamilch U82-20
Magnesium **U82**-20
Magnesiumammoniumphosphat U82-20
Magnesiummangel U82-20
Magnesiumoxid **U82**-20
Magnesiumsubstitution U82-20
Magnesiumsulfat **U91**-24; U82-20
Magnetfeldtherapie **U142**-24
Magnetresonanzspektrometrie U83-21
Magnetresonanztomografie (MRT) **U118**-24; U83-4
mahlen **U27**-18
Mahlzahn **U26**-7
Mahlzeit **U2**-7
–, kräftige U32-2
Mahnschreiben U74-2
Mahnung **U74**-2
Maissiat-Streifen U30-15
Maisstärke U79-5
Majorhistokompatibilitätskomplex **U39**-20,9
MAK U91-18
makellos **U25**-18
Makrogyrie **U41**-5
Makrohämaturie U31-20; U57-4; U112-3
Makromolekül **U81**-2
Makrophage **U39**-18; U37-9
Makrophagenaktivierungsfaktor U39-18
Makrophagenmigrationshemmtest U39-18
Makrophagenmobilität U39-18
makroskopisch U12-20; U101-17
Makrothrombozyt **U37**-11
makrozytär U86-2
Makula **U114**-9
Makuladegeneration U89-29
Makulaerkrankung U17-5
Makulaloch U58-13
makulopapulös U114-9
makulös **U114**-9
Mal **U25**-19; **U114**-3; **U116**-4

Malabsorption **U46**-13; **U109**-10; U88-8
maladaptiv **U77**-9
maladaptives Coping U77-9
Malaria **U94**-20
– quartana U94-20
– tertiana U94-20
– tropica U94-20
Malariaanfall U94-20
Malariagebiet U94-20
Malariapigment U94-20
Malariaprophylaxe U94-20
Maldescensus testis U52-3
Maldigestion **U109**-10; U46-11
Malecot-Körbchen U133-9
maligne **U97**-5
– Entartung U84-21
–, hochgradig U97-5
Malignität **U97**-5
Malignitätsgrad **U97**-14; U99-23
Malignom **U97**-5
–, inoperables U97-5
Malleolus **U23**-12; **U28**-24
Malleus **U60**-5
Malnutrition U16-13
Malokklusion **U27**-13
Malpighikörperchen **U48**-6
Mamillarkörper U41-9
Mamillarlinie U50-18; U87-9
Mamille **U50**-18
Mamillenerektion U50-18
Mamillenpigmentierung U56-7; U114-3
Mamillensekret U50-18
Mamma **U22**-2; **U50**-17
–, laktierende U71-25
Mammaamputation U50-17
Mammaaufbauplastik U50-17
Mammaaugmentation U50-17
Mammabiopsie U50-17
Mammahypertrophie U24-4
Mammakarzinom **U97**-10
–, lokal begrenztes U97-9
Mammaknoten U50-17
Mammografiebefund U50-17
Mammogramm U50-17
Mammotropin **U55**-22
Managed Care **U13**-8
Management, verwaltungstechn. U13-8
Mandel **U35**-6; U95-13
Mandelentzündung **U95**-13; U35-6
Mandelkern **U41**-11
Mandelkernkomplex U41-11
Mandibula **U28**-10; U21-5
Mandibularbogen U28-10
Mandibularreflex U64-7
mandibulomaxilläre Fixation U141-4
Mandrin **U132**-7; U136-2
–, Kanüle mit U136-3
–, stumpfer U133-14
Mangan **U82**-26; U79-17
Manganblau U82-26
manganhaltig **U82**-26
Manganmangel U82-26

Mangansalz U82-26
Manganstaub U82-26
Manganvergiftung U82-26
Mangel **U78**-21; **U142**-4
Mangeldurchblutung **U36**-5; U124-12
Mangelernährung U2-12; **U79**-3
mangelhaft **U78**-21
Mangelkrankheit U79-13
Mangelzustände U2-6
Manie **U77**-18
Manieriertheit **U75**-3
manifest, klinisch **U103**-3; **U119**-7;
 U77-13,16
Manifestation(en) **U117**-9
–, klinische **U103**-3; **U108**-2; U102-1
Manifestationshäufigkeit U84-22
Manifestationsalter U102-1
Manifestationsfrequenz **U84**-26
Manifestationsstärke, phänotypische
 U84-26
Manifestationswahrscheinlichkeit
 U84-26
manifestieren, sich **U103**-3; **U117**-9;
 U102-1
Manipulation **U141**-2
–, geschlossene U142-12
Manipulationsbehandlung **U142**-12
manipulative Physiotherapie U142-12
manisch **U77**-18
manische Phase U92-23
Mann **U53**-1
Mannesalter **U53**-1
männlich **U53**-1
Männlichkeit **U53**-1
Mann-zu-Frau-Geschlechtsumwand-
 lung U53-12
manövrieren **U8**-11
Manschette **U141**-7 f
Manschettenbreite U17-8
Manschettendruck U17-8
Manteltablette U9-7
Manualtherapie U142-12
Manubrium mallei U60-5
– sterni U28-11,13
manuell **U23**-6
Manus **U23**-6
MAO-Hemmer U42-13; U88-14
Marasmus U82-25
Marcus-Gunn-Syndrom U67-25
marfanoid (Habitus) U25-2
marginal **U87**-10
Margo **U87**-10
– anterior U28-17
– – tibiae U28-5,24
– infraorbitalis U28-9; U58-1
Marihuana **U11**-15
Marihuanagebrauch U11-15
Marihuanazigarette U11-15
Mariske U45-16
Mark **U86**-23
–, verlängertes **U41**-14,1
markant **U87**-27
markartig **U38**-2
Marker, gewebsspezifischer U97-16

–, hochempfindlicher U97-16
–, prognostischer U97-16
–, strahlendichter U97-16
Markerkonzentration U97-16
Markerspiegel U97-16
Marker-X-Syndrom U77-22
Markgewebe U86-3
markhaltig **U40**-14; **U86**-23; U42-3
Markhöhle U28-3; U38-2; U86-23
Markierungssequenz U84-12
Marknagel **U141**-16
Marknagelung U141-4,16
markreich **U40**-14
Mark-Rinden-Grenze U86-23
Markscheide **U40**-14; U42-5; U86-8
Markscheidenzerfall U40-14
Markschwammniere U48-2; U86-23
Marksubstanz (Kleinhirn) U41-7,14
Marsch **U65**-14
Marschfraktur U65-14; **U106**-13
marschieren **U65**-14
Masern **U95**-2; U94-2
masernähnlich **U95**-2
Masernenzephalitis U95-2
Masernepidemie U95-2
Masernexanthem U95-2
Masernimpfstoff U17-1
Masern-Mumps-Röteln-Impfstoff
 U95-2
– – – Lebendvakzine, attenuierte
 U122-6
Masernschutzimpfung U122-3
Masernvirus U35-12; U95-2
Masken-Beatmung U8-12; U43-5;
 U123-9
Maskengesicht U25-10
maskieren U39-7
maskulin **U53**-1
Maskulinisierung **U53**-12
Massage **U142**-15
–, klassische U142-15
–, schwedische U142-15
Massagedusche **U1**-19
Massagetisch U142-15
Maßband U17-1; U24-11
Masse **U79**-16
–, teigige U97-3
Massenanziehung U70-7
Massenblutung U37-1; U38-6,9;
 U124-16
Massengrab U12-18
Massenhysterie U77-6
Massenimmunisierung U122-3
Massenpanik U6-21
Massenunfall U6-1; U8-9; U14-6
Masseterreflex U21-5 f; U64-7; U113-1
Masseur **U142**-15
massieren **U123**-5; **U142**-15
mäßigen **U10**-6
Mäßigkeit **U10**-6
massiv **U82**-6; **U119**-14
Massivblutung U38-9
Massivtransfusion U136-8
maßlos **U10**-6

Maßnahme(n) **U64**-1
– vor Ort **U8**-1
–, hygienische U19-10
–, lebenserhaltende **U125**-3; U20-11
–, medizinische U20-11
–, therapeutische **U120**-5; U20-11
–, unterstützende U19-11; U64-16
–, vorbeugende U6-22; U20-11
–, zusätzliche U20-11
Maßstab **U24**-11; **U100**-6
maßvoll **U10**-6
Mastdarm **U45**-16
Mastdarmspekulum U17-6
Mastektomie U50-17
Mastitis U50-17
–, parenchymatöse U54-1
Mastoid **U60**-14; U28-5; U87-27
Mastoidektomie U60-14
Mastoptose U56-19
Masturbation **U68**-8
Mastzelle U83-2
Material, adsorbierendes U81-12
–, körperfremdes **U8**-10
Materie U82-1
Matratze **U19**-5
Matratzenauflage U19-5
Matratzenbezug U19-5
Matratzennaht **U137**-17
Matrix cartilaginea U29-12; U86-19
– unguis U56-15; U86-19
Matrixprotein, extrazelluläres U86-19
Matrize U84-19
matt **U103**-9
Mattheit **U59**-11
Mattigkeit **U103**-8 f; U7-12
Maturität **U80**-10
Maul (Zange) U132-13
Maulbeerstadium **U85**-4
Maulteile U138-13
Maxilla **U28**-10; U21-5
maxillofazial **U26**-26
Maximalkraft U31-13
Mazeration U114-14
MCHC U37-4
MCV U37-4
Meatus acusticus U21-15
– – externus **U60**-3
– – internus U60-3
– urethrae U48-1
Mechanismus **U88**-2
Mechanorezeptor U57-13
Media U34-2
medial **U87**-18
Median **U100**-10
Medianebene U87-2,18
Mediannekrose U34-2
Medianlinie U87-9
Medianschnitt U87-18; U126-9
Medianus U87-18
mediastinal **U43**-13
Mediastinalabszess U111-14
Mediastinalemphysem **U43**-13;
 U111-16
Mediastinalflattern U43-13

Mediastinalverbreiterung U43-13
Mediastinalverschiebung U43-13
Mediastinalverziehung **U124**-17; U43-13
Mediastinoskopie **U128**-6
Mediastinum **U43**-13
Mediator(substanz) **U83**-19
Mediatorfreisetzung U83-19
Medikament **U9**-1,3; **U15**-1
– der Wahl U72-16; U94-4
–, cholesterinsenkendes U78-16
–, hochwirksames U53-2
–, missbräuchlich verwendetes U11-6
–, suchterzeugendes U11-4
–, teratogenes U91-12
Medikamentenabhängigkeit U11-3
Medikamenteneinnahme U46-1
Medikation **U9**-1
Medioklavikularlinie U33-4; U87-9
Meditation **U1**-16
Medium **U77**-2
Medizin, innere **U15**-9,1
–, manuelle U15-22
–, psychosomatische U77-14
medizinisch **U9**-1
– techn. Assistent(in) **U16**-10
Medizinprodukt, neues U101-2
Medizinstudent(in) **U15**-6
Medulla **U86**-23
– glandulae suprarenalis U54-10
– oblongata **U41**-14
– ossium **U38**-2; U28-2
– renalis U48-2
– spinalis **U41**-15; U28-19
medullär **U41**-14; **U86**-23
Meeresalgen U142-20
Meeresfrüchte **U3**-3
Meersalzpeeling U1-20
Megagyrie **U41**-5
Megakaryozyt **U83**-3; U38-2
Megakaryozytenreifung U83-3
Megakaryozytopoese U83-3
Megakolon, toxisches U91-4
Megalomanie U77-20
Megaureter U48-10
Mehl **U91**-7
Mehltau U90-18
Mehrfachanalyse **U84**-34
Mehrfachapplikator U137-13
Mehrfachentnahmeflasche U9-13
Mehrfachinsufflationsnadel U133-13
Mehrfachklipapplikator U138-16
Mehrfachstapler U138-17
Mehrgebärende **U70**-8; U71-20
Mehrlingsgeburt U71-8
Mehrlingsschwangerschaft U70-6
Mehrlochkollimator U99-6
Mehrphasenpille U9-7
Mehrphasenpräparat U69-7
mehrreihig **U86**-10
Mehrweginstrument U133-1
mehrwurzelig (Zahn) U26-19
Mehrzweckinstrument U133-1
Meibom-Drüsen U56-8

Meinung, fachärztliche U18-12
–, zweite **U18**-12; U102-14
Meinungsänderung U32-2
Meiose/-sis **U83**-14; U85-3
meiotisch **U83**-14
Meissner-Tastkörperchen U57-15; U62-8
Mekonium **U71**-19
–, kittartiges U71-19
Mekoniumabgang U71-19
Mekoniumaspiration U71-19; U111-4
Mekoniumileus U71-19
Mekoniumperitonitis U71-19
Mekoniumpfropfsyndrom U71-19
Melaena **U109**-11
Melancholie **U76**-22; U77-17
melancholisch **U76**-22
Melanin **U56**-7
Melaninablagerung U56-7
melaninhaltig **U56**-7
Melaninkörnchen U56-7
Melaninsynthese U56-7
Melaninvorstufe U56-7
Melanoglossie U21-11
Melanokarzinom **U98**-15
Melanom U56-7
–, akrolentiginöses U98-15; U114-5
–, malignes **U98**-15
–, noduläres U97-3; U98-15
–, superfiziell spreitendes U98-15
melanomatös **U98**-15
Melanose, prämaligne U56-7; U114-5
melanotisch **U56**-7
Melanotropin **U55**-26; U56-7
Melanozyt **U56**-7
melden **U8**-7; **U20**-6; **U94**-1; **U102**-2
meldepflichtig **U18**-10; **U20**-6
Meldung **U8**-7
Melzer-Knoten **U138**-8
Membran **U86**-15
–, alveolokapilläre U34-5
–, deziduale **U85**-13
–, gasdurchlässige U36-16
–, postsynaptische U40-13
Membrana cellularis **U83**-2
– synovialis **U29**-11,3; U86-15
– tectoria U60-12
– tympani **U60**-4; **U21**-15; U86-15
– – secundaria U60-8
Membranen, intraösophageale U109-4
membranös **U86**-15
Membran-Oxygenation, extrakorporale U125-3
Membranoxygenator U44-6; U125-11
Membranpotential U42-5
Membranrezeptor U55-2
Membrantransport U78-17
Membrum virile **U52**-14
Memory cell **U39**-15
MEN U97-4
Menarche **U51**-3
– praecox U51-3; U119-14
Mendelsche Vererbung U84-28
Ménétrier-Syndrom U89-15
Meniere-Krankheit U35-2

meningeal **U41**-8; **U94**-13
Meningen **U41**-8
Meningismus U94-13
Meningitis **U94**-13; U41-8
– carcinomatosa U98-2
– tuberculosa U94-13
–, (a)bakterielle U94-13
–, aseptische U94-13
–, eitrige U94-13
–, otogene U95-12
–, therapieresistente U94-13
meningitisch **U94**-13
Meniscus medialis U29-2; U87-18
– tactus **U57**-15
Meniskusriss U23-11
Meniskusteilresektion, arthroskopische U128-7
Mennige U82-32
Menopause **U51**-3,10
Menopausengonadotropin U51-2
–, humanes U55-20
Menopausensyndrom U51-10
Menorrhoe/-ö U51-2
Menostase U51-2
Menotropin U51-2; U55-20
Mensch, geselliger U75-14
–, introvertierter U75-14
–, labiler U75-15
–, perverser **U68**-15
–, scheuer U75-14
–, umgänglicher U75-14
Menschenfloh U90-15
Menschenverstand, gesunder U57-5
Menses **U51**-2
Menstruation **U51**-2,1,7
Menstruationsbeginn U51-2; U119-5
Menstruationsbeschwerden U51-1
Menstruationszyklus **U51**-1
menstruell **U51**-1
menstruieren **U51**-2
mental **U77**-2; **U73**-1
mentale Funktionen U5-14; **U73**-2
Mentation **U73**-1
Mentum **U21**-6
Merkel-Scheibe **U57**-15
Merkel-Tastkörperchen **U57**-15
Merkel-Zelle U57-15
merken, sich **U74**-10
Merkfähigkeit **U74**-10
merklich **U57**-2
Merkmal **U100**-5
–, charakteristisches **U117**-16; U53-1
–, histologisches U86-1
–, klinisches U117-16
–, phänotypisches U25-10
Merkurialismus **U82**-32
MESA **U69**-13
Mescalin **U11**-22
Mesencephalon U41-1
Mesenterialgefäßverschluss U45-7; U124-13
Mesenterialinfarkt U45-7
Mesenteriolum U45-7,13
Mesenterium **U45**-7

Mesh-Graft U130-6
Meshtransplantat **U130**-8; U137-4
mesial **U26**-21
Mesoappendix U45-7,13
Mesoderm, intermediäres U85-6
–, parietales U85-6
–, viszerales U85-6
Mesonephros **U85**-21
Mesopharynx U45-4
Mesothel(ium) **U86**-14
mesothelial **U86**-14
Mesothelzelle U86-14
messen **U20**-11
– (Fieber) U105-1
Messenger-RNA U84-15
Messer, chirurgisches **U132**-3
Messerspitze U132-3
Messerstecherei **U6**-7
Messgerät U17-8; U24-12
Messinglegierung U82-6
Messreihe, oxymetrische U125-9
Messstreifen U24-11
Messwert **U101**-15; U100-12
metabolisieren **U78**-1; U92-4
Metabolismus **U78**-1; U79-7
Metabolit **U78**-11
–, stabiler U78-11
–, toxischer U78-11
–, wasserlöslicher U78-11
Metacarpus U23-5
Metall **U82**-6
Metalldämpfe U82-3,6
Metalldampffieber U82-6
Metallenzym U82-6
metallisch **U82**-6
Metallklang U82-6
Metallklip U138-15
Metalllegierung **U82**-6
Metallnadel U17-11
Metalloprotease U82-6
Metallplatte U141-17
Metallprotein U82-6
Metallstab U133-12
Metamyelozyten U37-8
Metanephros **U85**-21
Metaphase **U83**-13
Metaphyse **U28**-3
Metastasen, hämatogene **U97**-13,12
–, lymphogene U97-13
–, regionäre U97-13
Metastasenexstirpation **U97**-13
Metastasenherd U89-3
metastasieren **U97**-13
Metastasierung **U97**-13,11; U89-4
–, hämatogene U97-11
–, meningeale U98-2
metastatisch **U97**-13
Metatarsus **U28**-25
Metathalamus **U41**-9
Meteorismus **U109**-7
Methadon **U11**-19
Methadonersatztherapie U11-19
Methadonsubstitutionstherapie U11-19
Methamphetamin U11-17

Methanol **U47**-17; U82-13
Methanolvergiftung U47-17
Methenamin-Silbernitrat-Färbung
  U82-28
Methode der Wahl U34-1; U120-3
–, operative **U126**-4
Methoden, manuelle U8-11
Methylalkohol **U47**-17; U82-13
Methylierungsreaktion U81-15
MHC-Antigene U39-20
Mid-Laser-Therapie U142-24
Mieder **U141**-7
Miene **U25**-10; **U67**-8
–, mit gelassener U67-8
–, schuldbewusste U77-10
–, strenge U25-10; U67-8
–, teilnahmslose U77-8
Migräne **U113**-16
–, belastungsbedingte U64-19
Migräneanfälle U113-16
migräneartig **U113**-16
Migräne-Patient(in) **U113**-16
Mikrobe **U90**-1
mikrobenabtötend U90-1
Mikrobenkultur U90-1
mikrobiell **U90**-1
mikrobizid U90-1
Mikrochirurgie **U127**-5
mikrochirurgisch U127-5
Mikroelement **U79**-17
Mikroembolie U86-1
Mikroembolus U86-1
Mikrofilament **U83**-5
Mikroflora **U90**-1
Mikrogliazelle U39-17
Mikrohämaturie **U112**-3; U86-1
Mikroinjektion (IVF) **U69**-15
Mikrokaryozyten U83-3
Mikromanipulator U127-5
Mikromilieu U90-1
Mikroorganismen **U90**-1; U139-8
–, antibiotikaresistente U90-1
–, krankheitsauslösende U90-1
–, pathogene **U90**-5,1; **U119**-2
–, übertragbare U90-1
–, ubiquitäre U90-1
Mikrophage **U39**-18
Mikrophonpotential U60-11
–, endocochleäres U60-11
Mikropille U69-7
Mikroschere **U132**-4
Mikroskop **U86**-1
Mikroskopie **U86**-1
Mikrosom **U83**-8
Mikrosonde U127-5
Mikrospektrophotometrie **U83**-21
Mikrotiterplatte U116-17
Mikrotrauma U86-1
Mikrotubuliduplett U83-5
Mikrotubulus **U83**-5
Mikrotubulusorganisationszentrum
  U83-5
Mikrovilli **U45**-14
Mikrowellenhyperthermie U105-5

Mikrowellentherapie U142-22
Mikrowellen-Wärmetherapie U142-23
Mikrozirkulation **U36**-1
Miktion **U49**-16; U40-7
–, erschwerte/schmerzhafte **U112**-1
Miktionsbeschwerden, irritative
  U112-1
Miktionsfrequenz U112-5
Miktionsreflex U40-3; U49-16
Miktionsreiz U49-16
Miktionsstörung U4-4
Miktionsverzögerung **U112**-7
Miktionszentrum U40-3
Miktionszystourethrografie U49-16
Miktionszystourethrogramm U112-12
Milbe **U90**-15
Milbenbefall U94-2
Milbengänge U96-12
Milch **U3**-4f
– absondern **U71**-25
– trinken U71-27
Milchbrustgang **U35**-7
Milchejektion U55-23
Milchejektionsreflex **U71**-27
milchführend **U71**-25
Milchgang U50-18; U71-25
Milchgangpapillom **U98**-1
Milchgebiss **U27**-2
milchig **U35**-10
Milchprodukte **U2**-2; **U3**-5
Milchproduktion **U71**-25
Milchpumpe U71-26
Milchsaft **U35**-2
Milchsäure U79-8; U81-19; U82-9
Milchsäuregärung U46-12
Milchunverträglichkeit U75-16
Milchzähne **U27**-2
Milchzucker **U79**-8,6
mild **U62**-7
mildern (Schmerz) **U104**-19; **U12**-5
Miliaria (rubra) U56-11; U62-11;
  U105-11
Miliartuberkulose U94-16
Milie/-ium **U114**-6
Milieu, günstiges U70-4
Militärkrankenhaus U14-1
Militärspital U14-1
Milwaukee-Korsett U141-7
Milz **U35**-4; U37-11; U39-12; U54-8
Milzbrand U90-3
Milzbrandbazillus U90-7
Milzentfernung U35-4
Milzhämatom, subkapsuläres U38-8
Milzhilus U35-4; U43-4; U87-25
Milzinfarkt U35-4; U124-11,14
Milzkapsel U35-4
Milzruptur U5-19; U35-4; U124-16
Milzsinus U35-4
Milzszintigrafie U35-4
Milztransplantation U130-2
Milzvergrößerung U35-4; U108-5,12
Mimik U21-2; U25-10
Mimikry **U117**-13
–, molekulares U117-13

Minderdurchblutung **U36**-5
minderjährig U51-2
Minderjährige(r) **U80**-9; U68-17
Minderjährigkeit **U80**-9
Minderwertigkeitsgefühl U76-13; U77-12
Minderwertigkeitskomplex **U77**-12
Minderwuchs U10-13; U24-2; U55-5
–, hypophysärer U54-5
–, konstitutioneller U1-8; U24-3; U25-3
–, primordialer U24-3
–, psychosozialer U24-4; U77-11
Minderwüchsige(r), hypothyreote(r) U24-4
mindestens haltbar bis U2-2
Mineral **U82**-5
mineralisch **U82**-5
Mineralokortikoid U55-10
Minerva-Gips U141-9
Minilaparotomie **U128**-13; U133-14
minimal invasives Verfahren U128-1
Minimalsehschärfe U59-8
Minipille U69-7
Miniplatte **U141**-17
Minivirus, hüllenloses **U90**-11
Minusstrang U84-11
Minutenvolumen (MV) **U33**-7
Miosis **U59**-10; U58-8
Miotikum **U59**-10
miotisch **U59**-10
Mikroelement **U79**-17
mischen **U81**-2; U9-5; U121-1
mischerbig U85-2
Mischgebiss U27-1
Mischling **U37**-1; **U84**-38,30
Mischplasma U136-13
Mischung, unreine (Drogen) U11-15
Miserere U46-20; U103-12
missachten **U77**-11
Missbildung **U142**-7; **U89**-5,2
–, schwere U31-20
missbilligend **U67**-11
Missbrauch **U11**-3; U93-14
–, sexueller **U68**-16; U13-13
missbrauchen **U11**-3,6; U77-11
Missempfindung, subjektive **U104**-17; **U135**-4
missgestaltet **U142**-7
misshandelt U74-2; U77-11
Misshandlung, körperliche U68-16
missmutig **U67**-11; **U76**-9
Missmutigkeit U75-19
missverstehen (Lesen) **U61**-10
Mitarbeiter(in) U15-2
Mitarbeiterstab U15-2
Mitbeteiligung U41-3
Mitella U23-2; U141-8
miterleben **U6**-13
Mitesser **U114**-6
mitfühlend **U75**-8
Mitgefühl **U32**-1 f; **U75**-8; U12-13
– aussprechen **U12**-12
–, aufrichtiges U75-8,12

mitgenommen **U76**-21
mithören **U61**-1
mitklatschen, im Rhythmus U67-6
Mitleid U32-2; **U75**-8; **U76**-20
mitleiderregend **U76**-20
mitochondrial **U83**-7
mitochondriales Genom U84-1
Mitochondrienmatrix U83-7
Mitochondrienmembran U83-7
Mitochondrienschädigung U83-7
Mitochondrium **U83**-7
Mitogene U39-13
Mitose **U83**-13,12; U85-3
–, atypische U83-13
Mitosefehler U83-13
Mitosehemmstoff U83-13
Mitosehemmung U83-13
Mitoseindex U83-13
Mitoserate U83-13
Mitosespindel U83-5,13
mitotisch **U83**-13
mitotische Rekombination U84-17
Mitralklappe U32-10
Mitral(klappen)insuffizienz U32-12; U110-10; U119-13
Mitralklappenprolaps U32-12; U89-22; U110-5
– Syndrom U31-12
Mitralöffnungston (MÖT) U110-5
Mitschwingen (Arme) U23-2; U64-5
Mittagessen **U2**-2
Mittagsbesprechung U20-10
Mitte **U22**-6
– dreißig U80-11
mitteilen **U20**-6; **U94**-1
mitteilsam **U66**-8,18
Mitteilung **U57**-4
Mittel **U9**-3 f; **U92**-2
– (gegen Erkältung) U9-2
– der Wahl U9-3
–, amöbizides U90-4
–, appetitanregendes U11-17; U57-1
–, auswurfförderndes **U103**-17
–, entspannungsförderndes **U31**-1; U76-19
–, entzündungshemmendes **U92**-11
–, erweichendes **U92**-30
–, fiebersenkendes **U105**-4
–, gefäßerweiterndes **U92**-17; U36-11
–, gefäßverengendes U36-11
–, gerinnungsförderndes **U38**-10
–, gerinnungshemmendes **U38**-14
–, harntreibendes U49-6
–, keim(ab)tötendes **U17**-15; **U90**-5
–, oxidativ wirkendes U81-5
–, pilzabtötendes **U91**-8
–, potenzsteigerndes U68-3
–, prolaktinsenkendes U55-22
–, pupillenverengendes **U59**-10
–, quacksalberisches U15-23
–, schmerzstillendes **U104**-20
–, schweißtreibendes **U56**-10
–, spermienabtötendes **U69**-8; U53-7
–, verdauungsförderndes **U46**-11

Mittel, wassertreibendes **U92**-21
–, wehenhemmendes **U71**-3
Mitteldarm U85-7,21
Mittelfell **U43**-13,11
Mittelfuß **U28**-25
Mittelgesichtsfraktur U28-9
Mittelhand U23-5
Mittelhandknochen **U28**-17; U23-6
Mittelhirn U41-1
mittelkettig U81-7
Mittellappen, (rechter) U43-3; U87-23
Mittelohr **U60**-1; U21-15
Mittelohrdruck U60-6
Mittelohrentzündung **U95**-12; U60-6
–, eitrige U95-12; U140-14
Mittelohrschädigung U60-6
Mittelohrschwerhörigkeit U60-6
Mittelschmerz U51-1
Mittelstrahlharn U49-12,17; U116-15
Mittelwert **U100**-10; U116-16
mittelzyklisch **U51**-1
mittlere(r) **U87**-18
mittzyklisch **U51**-1
Mittzyklusblutung U51-1
Mixoploidie U84-9
Mixtur U9-6
Mizelle **U81**-2,9
MKG-Chirurg U26-26
M-Mode-Echokardiogramm U118-15
MMS U86-14
Mneme **U74**-13
Mnemonik **U74**-13
mnemonisch **U74**-13
Mnemotechnik **U74**-13
mnemotechnisch **U74**-13
mnestisch **U74**-13
mobil **U65**-1
Mobilisation **U19**-12; **U134**-13; **U141**-5
–, passive **U142**-13
Mobilisationstherapie U142-13
mobilisieren **U142**-13
Mobilisierung, kontinuierliche passive U142-14
Mobilität **U64**-2; **U142**-13; **U141**-5
Modiolous U60-11
Modulation **U83**-19
–, präsynaptische U42-4
Modulator **U83**-19; U42-4
modulieren **U42**-4; **U83**-19
Mol **U81**-3
molal **U81**-3
Molalität **U81**-3
molar **U81**-3
Molar **U26**-7 f
Molarität **U81**-3
Molekül **U81**-2
Molekülaggregat U81-2,9
Molekularbiologie U83-1
Molekulargenetik U81-2; U84-1
Molekulargewicht **U81**-3
Molekularmasse U81-2
–, relative **U81**-3
Molekularsonde U84-33
Molekularstruktur U81-2

Molekülsonde U81-2
Molkeeiweiß U79-9
Molkereiprodukte **U3**-5
Möller-Hunter-Glossitis U25-16
mollig **U25**-6; U24-8
Molprozent U81-3
Molybdän **U82**-27
Molybdän-Cofaktor U82-27
Molybdänsäure U82-27
Molybdat **U82**-27
Molzahl U81-3
Monatsbinde U140-19
Monatsblutung **U51**-2,1
-, ausgebliebene U117-4
-, (un)regelmäßige U75-9
Mondbein U28-17; U29-1
Mondgesicht U25-10; U67-8
Mongolenfalte U58-3
Monitor **U125**-5; **U134**-8
Monitorableitungen U125-6
Monoamin(o)oxidase-Hemmer U42-13; U88-14; U92-24
monofil **U137**-7
monofiles Nahtmaterial U138-8
Monokin **U39**-18
Monomer **U81**-6
Mononukleose, infektiöse **U94**-10,1
Mononukleosetest U94-10
Monosomie **U84**-25
monosynaptisch **U40**-13
monovalent U81-10
Monozyt(en) **U37**-9; **U39**-18
Monozytenleukämie U37-9
Monozyten-Makrophagen-System **U35**-12; U37-9; U39-17f
Monozytenvermehrung U37-9
Monozytenzahl U39-18
Monozytenzählung U39-18
Monozytose U37-9
Mons pubis **U50**-16; U52-18
- veneris **U50**-16; U52-18
Moorbad U1-20
Moorbehandlung **U1**-20
Moorerde U1-20
Moorpackung U1-20; U140-24
Moortrinkkur U1-20
moralischer Auftrieb U142-26
morbid **U89**-2
Morbidität **U120**-12; **U89**-2
Morbiditätsrate **U100**-9
Morbilli **U95**-2
morbilliform **U95**-2
Morbus Basedow U124-8
- Biermer U38-4
- haemolyticus neonatorum U37-17
- Hodgkin U98-10
- Ledderhose U98-8
- Wilson U91-19
Morcellator **U128**-16; **U133**-17
Morcellement **U128**-16; **U133**-17
Mord **U12**-10; U74-17
Mordabsichten U12-10
Mörder(in) **U12**-9f
Morgenharn U49-12; U116-15

Morgenharnprobe U49-16
Morgensteifigkeit U31-17
Morgentemperatur U105-1
Moro-Reflex U57-16; U65-16; U67-7
Moro-Umklammerungsreflex U65-16
Morphin **U11**-18
Morphinabhängigkeit **U11**-18
Morphinderivat U11-19
Morphinismus **U11**-18
Morphinist(in) **U11**-18
Morphinvergiftung U11-18
Morphium **U11**-18
Morphiumsüchtige(r) **U11**-18
Mortalität **U12**-3,2
-, altersspezifische U12-3
-, krankheitsspezifische U12-3
-, perinatale U12-3
Mortalitätsquotient U100-9
Mortalitätsrate U12-3; **U100**-9
Mortalitätsstatistik U12-3; U100-1
Morula **U85**-4
morulaähnlich U85-4
Morulabildung **U85**-4
Morulastadium **U85**-4
Mosaik **U84**-22
Moschcowitz-Krankheit U136-15
Moskitoklemme U132-14
Motilität **U53**-10
Motilitätsstörung **U46**-6
Motiv(ation) **U73**-12
Motivkonflikt U77-12
Motoneuron U30-4; U31-20
-, spinales U40-1
Motorik U31-20
motorisch **U64**-1
Motorkortex U31-20
Mouches volantes U58-10; U59-5
M-Phase U83-12
MR-Cholangiografie U118-20
MSH-Aktivität U55-26
MTA **U16**-10
Mucilago U92-30
Mucinosis papulosa U114-10
Mückensehen U58-10; U59-5
Mucoid impaction U86-17
Mucus **U86**-17
müde **U76**-18
Müdigkeit **U76**-18; **U103**-8; U4-4
Müdigkeitssyndrom, chronisches U103-8
Müsli **U3**-12
Mühe **U64**-19
Mühlradgeräusch U110-4
Mukoepidermoidtumor U98-17
Mukoid **U86**-17
Mukolytikum U86-17
Mukoperiostlappen U130-17
mukös **U44**-9; **U86**-17
Mukosa **U44**-9; **U86**-17
Mukoviszidose U86-17; U89-24
Mull U17-13
Mullbinde U140-18
Müllentsorgung U139-4
Müller-Gang U85-21
Müller-Gang-Abkömmlinge U85-11

Mullkompresse U140-18,20
multifil U137-7
multifokal U97-10
Multigravida **U70**-7
Multiinfarkt-Demenz U77-23; U124-14
Multipara **U70**-8
multivariat (Analyse) **U100**-28,5
Mumps **U95**-4
Mumpsorchitis U69-3; U95-4
Mumpsvirus-Lebendvakzine U95-4
Mund **U21**-8
- spitzen U21-6
-, sinnlicher U57-9
Mundatmung U21-8
Mund-Blinddarm-Zeit **U46**-8
Mundboden U45-3
Munddusche U127-17
münden **U87**-7,21
Mundflora U46-16
mundgerecht U27-12
Mundgeruch U62-3
- (haben) U44-1
-, übler **U109**-2; U46-17
Mundhöhle **U45**-2; **U21**-8
Mundhygiene U19-10; U142-27
Mündigkeit **U80**-9
Mund-Kiefer-Gesichtschirurg U26-26; U28-10
Mundmilieu U26-25
Mundpflege U19-10
Mundschleimhaut U45-2
Mundschleimhautentzündung U21-8
Mundschutz **U139**-18; U17-1
Mundspatel **U17**-3
Mundsperrer **U27**-16; **U44**-8
Mundspiegel U17-4
Mundspülbecken **U27**-10
Mundspüllösung, fluoridhaltige U82-22
Mundspülung U19-10; U91-26
Mundtrockenheit U103-14
Mündung **U87**-21
Mundvorhof **U21**-10; U26-23
Mundvorhoftiefe U21-10
mundwärts **U46**-7
Mundwasser U66-7; U109-2
Mundwinkel U21-8
Mund-zu-Mund Beatmung **U123**-9,4; U8-2
munter **U1**-6
murmeln **U66**-15
Murphy-Zeichen U123-6
murren **U67**-19
mürrisch **U67**-19
muschelartig U60-2
Musculi fibulares **U30**-17
- levatores costarum U30-12
- peronaei **U30**-17
Musculus **U30**-2
- adductor magnus U31-6
- biceps brachii **U30**-11
- - femoris U30-11,16
- biventer U30-2
- brachialis U23-2
- ciliaris U58-16

Musculus deltoideus **U30**-13
- detrusor vesicae **U48**-11
- erector **U63**-2
- - spinae U63-2
- glutaeus maximus **U30**-15
- - minimus U30-15
- iliopsoas **U30**-15
- ischiocavernosus **U53**-3
- latissimus dorsi **U30**-12; U129-13
- levator ani U30-12
- - labii superioris U30-12
- - prostatae U30-12
- - scapulae **U30**-12
- obliquus abdominis **U30**-14
- papillaris anterior U32-13
- - posterior U32-13
- pectoralis U22-2
- peronaeus longus U30-17
- pronator (teres) **U31**-9
- psoas **U30**-15
- pubovaginalis U30-12
- quadratus femoris U23-9
- quadriceps femoris **U30**-16
- rectus capitis anterior U30-14
- - femoris U30-16
- semimembranosus U30-16
- semitendinosus U30-16
- sphincter **U30**-9
- - ani internus U30-9
- - Oddii U47-8
- - urethrae **U48**-14
- - vesicae internus U48-14
- stapedius U60-5; U61-7
- tensor tympani U60-7
- transversus perinei profundus U48-15
- trapezius **U30**-13
- triceps brachii **U30**-11
- - surae U30-17
- vastus lateralis U30-16
Musikalität U76-4
Musikantenknochen U28-2
Muskel **U30**-2
-, entspannter U76-19
-, zweibäuchiger U30-2
Muskelaktionspotential U31-13
Muskelaktivität, willkürliche U40-6
Muskelansatz U30-3
Muskelanspannung U109-13
-, isokinetische U142-17
Muskelatrophie U142-4
-, bulbospinale U41-15
Muskelausdauer U31-13
Muskelbauch U22-4; U30-2
Muskeldehnungsreflex U31-3
Muskelendplatte U87-2
Muskelentspannung U31-1; U142-25
Muskelermüdung U30-2; U103-8
Muskelerregbarkeit U82-20
Muskelerschlaffung U31-1
Muskelfaserbündel **U30**-1
Muskelfaser(n) **U30**-1
-, rote U30-1
-, weiße U30-1

Muskelfaser(n), zirkulär angeordnete U30-1
Muskelfaserverletzung U30-1
Muskelfaszie **U30**-7
Muskelfunktionsprüfung U142-12
Muskelhartspann U104-16
Muskelhülle **U30**-7
Muskelkater U30-13; U104-11
Muskelkontraktion U31-1
-, reflektorische U42-12
Muskelkopf **U30**-3
Muskelkraft **U31**-13
-, isotonische U142-17
Muskelkrämpfe U103-20; U109-14
-, anfallsartige U104-14
-, tetanische U94-11
Muskellähmung, aufsteigende U113-7
Muskelmasse U30-2; U79-16
-, fettfreie U24-10
Muskeln, ischiokrurale **U30**-16
Muskelplatte **U85**-22
Muskelpumpe U30-17
Muskelrelaxanzien **U93**-16
-, depolarisierende U31-1; U42-6
Muskelrelaxation U142-25
Muskelriss U106-5
Muskelschicht U87-8
Muskelschmerz(en) U30-13; U104-21
Muskelschwäche **U31**-13; U103-9
Muskelschwund **U108**-14; U142-4
Muskelsensibilität **U57**-14
Muskelspannung U30-2
Muskelspindel **U57**-12; U30-2
Muskelstarre U30-2
Muskelsteifigkeit **U12**-15; U30-2
Muskeltätigkeit U25-4
-, willkürliche U40-6
Muskeltonus **U31**-10; U30-2; U93-16
Muskelverspannung U30-2; U104-16
Muskelzelle, glatte U78-6
Muskelzerrung U5-17; U64-19
Muskelzittern U113-4
Muskelzucken **U31**-5; U104-12
- (beim Einschlafen) **U72**-12
Muskelzuckungen U30-1; U31-1,5; U64-7; U113-5
- haben U67-8
-, ruckartige U113-5
muskulös **U30**-2
Muskulatur **U30**-2
-, glatte U30-2; U86-3; U92-19
-, mimische U30-2; U56-17
-, quergestreifte U52-12; U93-16
-, unwillkürliche U40-6
-, willkürliche U30-2
muskulös U25-4; **U30**-2
Musterfragebogen U118-4
Mutabilität U84-20
mutagen **U91**-13
Mutagenese U91-13
Mutagenität **U91**-13; U84-20
mutant **U84**-20
Mutante **U84**-20
Mutantenphänotyp U84-10

Mutation **U84**-20
- , stille U119-6
mutationsauslösend **U91**-13
Mutationshotspots U84-20
Mutationsrate U84-20
mutiert **U84**-20
mutiertes Gen U84-1
mutig **U75**-18
Mutismus **U61**-11
-, akinetischer **U7**-17; U61-11
mutlos **U76**-20
Mutlosigkeit U76-1; U77-17
Mutter werden **U71**-2
-, besitzergreifende U75-21
-, Rh-negative U37-17
-, stillende U71-2
-, werdende U70-13
Mutterband, breites U50-5
-, rundes U50-5
Mütterberatung U14-2
Mutterinstinkt U71-2; U73-11
Mutter-Kind-Beziehung U80-4
Mutterkorn pilz U90-18
Mutterkuchen **U71**-16; **U85**-14
Muttermal **U25**-19; **U98**-15,5; **U114**-3; U71-2,8
Muttermilch U50-17; U71-2
- schießt ein U71-24
-, nährstoffangereicherte U71-27
Muttermilchikterus U71-27; U108-4
Muttermund **U50**-7
-, äußerer U50-5,7; U87-21
-, innerer U50-7; U87-21
Muttermunderöffnung **U71**-12
Mutterschaft **U71**-2; **U84**-31
Mutterschaftsurlaub U18-10; U71-22
Mutterschoß U71-2
Müttersterblichkeit U12-3
Mutterzelle **U84**-29; U83-2
Muzin **U86**-17
muzinös **U86**-17
Myalgie U23-10; U103-7; U104-21
Myasthenie U103-9
Mycobacterium tuberculosis U90-7; U94-16
Myelencephalon **U41**-14,1
Myelinabbau U40-14
Myelinhülle U40-14
Myelinmantel U40-14
Myelinscheide **U40**-14; U86-8
Myeloblast U38-3; U86-2
myelogen U38-2
Myelografie **U118**-7
myeloid **U38**-2
myeloisch **U38**-2
Myelosarkom U98-3
myelotoxisch U92-32
Mykoplasmen U90-2
Mykoplasmen-Pneumonie U90-18
Mykose U90-18
Myocardium **U32**-6
myoelektrische Prothese U142-6
Myofibrille U30-1
Myofilament U30-1

Myokard **U32**-6
Myokardinfarkt **U124**-11; U32-6
Myokardinsuffizienz **U110**-12; **U124**-12
Myokarditis, diphtherische U95-9
Myokardperfusionsszintigrafie U118-22
Myokardrevaskularisation U32-6
Myokardschädigung U32-6
Myokardszintigrafie U32-6
Myoklonie-Syndrom, nächtliches **U72**-12
Myoklonusepilepsie U72-12
Myom **U98**-9
–, submuköses U98-9
–, subseröses U98-9
Myoma in statu nascendi U98-8
– laevicellulare **U98**-9
– striocellulare **U98**-9
– uteri U98-9
myomatös **U98**-9
Myomatose **U98**-9
Myomektomie U98-9
Myomenukleation U98-9
Myometrium **U50**-6
myop **U59**-17
Myopie, passagere U59-17
–, progressive U59-17
myopisch **U59**-17
Myotom **U85**-22
Myxochondrom **U98**-12,7
Myxödem U5-15
Myxödemkoma U124-7
Myxofibrom U98-7
Myxolipom U98-7
Myxom **U98**-7
myxomähnlich **U98**-7
myxomatös **U98**-7
Myxomyzeten U90-18
Myxosarkom U98-7
Myzel **U90**-18
Myzetom U90-18

N

Nabel **U22**-5; **U71**-17; **U85**-7
Nabelbinde U22-5
Nabelbläschen **U85**-7
Nabelbruch U22-5; U71-17; U89-23
Nabelentzündung U71-17
Nabelfalte U22-5
Nabelgefäße U71-17
Nabelring U22-5
Nabelschnur **U71**-17; U22-5; U85-15
Nabelschnurblut U37-1; U136-10
Nabelschnurbruch U71-17
Nabelschnurgeräusch U110-4
Nabelschnurrest U71-17
Nabelschnurvorfall U71-17
Nabelstrang **U71**-17; U85-15
Nabelvene, obliterierte U47-2
Nabelvenenkatheter U71-17
Nachahmung **U117**-13
Nachahmungsmechanismus U117-13
Nachbarherd U89-3

Nachbarorgan U86-20; U87-11
Nachbarzahn U26-1
Nachbehandlung **U13**-1; **U120**-14
Nachbehandlungsplan U120-14
Nachbelastung **U33**-10
Nachbild **U59**-5; U73-9
–, negatives U59-5
Nachblutung U5-18; U38-8; U124-16
Nachdepolarisation U42-6
nachgeben **U64**-3; **U116**-18; U31-16
Nachgeburt **U71**-16
–, ausgestoßene U71-15
Nachgeburtsblutung U89-26
Nachgeburtsperiode U71-13
Nachgeburtsteile, unvollständige U71-6,8
Nachgeburtswehen **U71**-20,16
Nachgeschmack U62-6
Nachhirn **U41**-14,1
Nachkomme(schaft) **U84**-29; U69-1
nachlassen **U4**-14; U105-18; **U119**-17
– (Libido) U68-4
nachlässig **U20**-13; **U74**-15
Nachlässigkeit **U74**-15; **U77**-11
Nachlast **U33**-10
nachlaufen U65-14
Nachmittagsschläfchen U72-2
Nachniere **U85**-21
Nachpotential U42-5
nachprüfen **U18**-9
Nachreplikationsreparatur U84-16
Nachruf **U12**-17
nachsichtig **U11**-5; **U75**-16
Nachsorge **U13**-1; **U18**-9; **U120**-14; **U134**-15
–, ambulante U14-2, U20-2
Nachsorgeeinbestellung U18-14
Nachsorgegespräch U102-14
Nachsorgetermin U18-2
nachsprechen **U74**-7
Nachtangst **U72**-14; U6-21; U66-14
Nachtblindheit U59-18
Nachtdienst U20-4
nachteilig **U6**-11; U91-1
nachtragend sein **U75**-16; U76-11
Nachträufeln U49-16; U112-7
Nachtröpfeln U112-7,9
–, postmiktionelles U112-11
Nachtschicht U64-4
Nachtschiene U66-5
Nachtschlaf U72-5
Nachtschränkchen **U19**-7
Nachtschweiß U55-17; U72-9; U105-12
Nachtsehen **U59**-9,6
Nachtstuhl **U19**-8
Nachttisch **U19**-7
Nachtwandeln **U72**-15
Nachuntersuchung **U18**-9; **U134**-15
Nachuntersuchungstermin U134-15
Nachuntersuchungszeitraum U18-9; U120-14; U100-10
Nachwehen **U71**-20,3
Nachweis **U101**-17; **U116**-3; **U117**-9
–, mikroskopischer U117-4

Nachweis, myelografischer U118-7
–, serologischer U122-11
nachweisbar **U117**-4; **U79**-17
Nachweismethode U116-3
Nachwirkung U101-26
nachziehen **U64**-13; U65-11
–, ein Bein U64-13
Nacken **U21**-13; U22-11
Nackenband U30-13
Nackenhaaransatz U87-20
Nackenrolle **U64**-8
Nackensteifigkeit **U103**-20,2; U21-13; U31-17; U94-13; U113-7
Nacktheit U68-10
NAD U82-19
Nadel **U141**-15
–, 22er U17-11
–, atraumatische U127-6
–, chirurgische **U132**-5
–, spitze U17-11
–, stumpfe U17-11
Nadelansatz U17-11
Nadelaspiration, ultraschallgesteuerte transvaginale U69-18
Nadelelektrode U118-13
Nadel-Faden-Kombination U132-5
Nadelhalter **U132**-15; **U138**-14; U17-11
Nadelspitze, abgeschrägte U17-11
Nadelstich **U17**-11; **U62**-11; U93-15
Nadelstichverletzung U5-2; U17-11
–, akzidentelle U6-1
Naegele-Regel U70-10
Naevus araneus U25-19; U98-5,15
– coeruleus U25-19; U98-15
– flammeus U25-19; U98-15
– pigmentosus **U98**-15; U25-19
– pilosus U25-19; U56-13; U98-15
– Sutton U98-15
– vasculosus U25-19
–, behaarter U56-13
Nagel **U56**-15; **U141**-15
–, brüchiger U31-16; U56-15
–, eingewachsener U56-15
Nägelbeißen U56-15
Nagelbett **U56**-15; U23-7; U86-19
Nageldystrophie U56-15
Nageleindellung U56-15
Nagelfalz **U56**-15f; U23-7; U25-17
Nagelfalzentzündung U56-15
Nagelgeschwür **U114**-16
Nagel(ober)häutchen **U56**-15f
Nägelkauen U27-11; U56-15
Nagellack U11-23; U56-15
Nagelmatrix U56-15; U86-19
Nagelmykose U56-15
Nagelplatte U56-15; U87-2
Nagelrand U56-15
Nagelung **U141**-15f
Nagelwall U56-15
Nagetiere übertragen, durch U90-10
nahelegen **U18**-5; **U74**-2
Nähen **U137**-1; U31-20; **U132**-5
nähern, sich **U59**-13
Nahfixation U59-14

Nahlappen U130-11
Nähnadel U132-5
Nahpunkt U59-13
Nährboden U116-6
nähren **U2**-3; **U79**-1
nahrhaft **U79**-2,1
Nährlösung U79-2; U116-6
Nährmedium U116-6
Nährstoffanreicherung **U3**-22
Nährstoffaufnahme U79-2; U88-8
Nährstoffe **U79**-2; U37-3; U47-4
Nährstoffmalabsorption U109-10
Nährstoffmangel U78-21
Nährstoffmolekül U81-2
Nährstoffresorption, unzureichende U46-13
Nährstoffzufuhr U134-12
Nahrung **U2**-3,6,12; U78-5; **U79**-1 f
– umstellen, auf feste U71-28
–, aufgenommene **U46**-1
–, feste U46-8
–, flüssige U134-12
–, gesunde U1-1
Nahrungsaufnahme **U46**-1; **U134**-12; **U2**-1,6; U109-1
–, orale U45-2
–, perorale U125-19
Nahrungsbestandteile, unverdaute U46-20
Nahrungseisenzufuhr U82-21
Nahrungsentzug U77-11
Nahrungskarenz U2-15; U10-7; U47-11; U78-12; U126-2
Nahrungskette U91-19
Nahrungsmittel **U2**-6,16
–, unsachgemäß konservierte U91-21
Nahrungsmittelallergie U39-23
Nahrungsmittelersatz **U3**-21
Nahrungsmittelunverträglichkeit U105-10
Nahrungspartikel, ingestierte U46-1
Nahrungsreste U46-20
Nahrungszufuhr **U46**-1
–, empfohlene U2-12; U18-5
Nährwert U2-6; U79-2; U116-16
Naht **U29**-14
– (legen) **U138**-1
–, chirurgische **U137**-1
–, eingewendelte **U137**-16
–, fortlaufende **U137**-16
–, seroseröse U86-6
Nahtabszess U38-12
Nahtende U138-1
Nahtfaden U138-1
Nahtgerät U138-1
Nahtintegrität U138-1
Nahtmaterial **U137**-1,7; U138-1
Nahtmethoden, endoskopische **U138**-1
–, laparoskopische **U138**-1
Nahtschere U132-4
Nahtschlinge U132-9
Nahtspannung U129-5
Nahttechnik, minimal invasive U128-1
Nahtverschluss U128-18

Namensschild **U17**-16
Narbe **U114**-8; **U140**-10
–, bläulich verfärbte U12-15
–, eingedellte U17-3
–, linienförmige U87-9
–, wulstige U87-27
Narbenbildung U56-1; U114-8,13; U134-10; **U140**-10,5,8
Narbenbruch U5-19; U89-23; U126-9
Narbenemphysem U111-16
Narbengewebe U69-13; U86-3
Narbenretraktion **U140**-8
Narbenschrumpfung **U140**-8
narbiges Gesicht U140-10
Na-Reabsorption, aldosteronabhängige U55-25
Nares U21-4; U43-5
Narkoanalgetika U72-18
Narkolepsie **U72**-18,5
Narkoleptikum **U72**-18
narkoleptisch **U72**-18
Narkose **U135**-2,6; **U93**-1
Narkoseapparat **U135**-14
Narkose(fach)arzt **U15**-11; **U131**-6
Narkoseeinleitung **U135**-13
Narkoseführung U135-2
Narkosegas U93-4
Narkosegerät **U135**-14
Narkosekater U135-23
Narkosemaske **U135**-15
Narkosemittel **U11**-16
Narkoseprämedikationsraum **U131**-3
Narkoseprotokoll **U135**-22
Narkoseraum **U131**-3
Narkoserisiko **U135**-12,2; U124-2
Narkoseschwester U16-5; U131-6
Narkosesystem **U135**-14; U93-10
Narkosetiefe **U135**-20,2,13; **U131**-6
Narkosevorbereitung, medikamentöse U11-1
Narkosezeichen U135-11
Narkotikum **U72**-18; **U93**-4,1; **U135**-5,1 f; U9-3; U11-1
narkotisch **U11**-1; **U72**-18
narkotisieren **U135**-1
nasal **U43**-6
Nase **U21**-4
– putzen, sich die **U103**-16; U66-6
–, verstopfte U43-6; U110-15
näseln (Sprache) U43-6; U66-17,22
Nasenabstrich U17-13
Nasenausfluss U17-6
Nasenbluten **U38**-6; **U110**-20
Nasenbohren U110-20
Nasendiphtherie U95-9
Naseneingang U21-10
Nasenflügelatmen **U111**-1
Nasenfurunkel U114-16
Nasenhöhle U21-4
Nasenklemme U8-12
Nasenlöcher U43-5; U135-1
Nasen-Magen-Sonde **U125**-18
Nasenmuschel U28-9
Nasennebenhöhlen U43-6; U28-6

Nasennebenhöhlentumoren U43-6
Nasenplastik U15-19, U17-6
Nasen-Rachenpolypen **U35**-6
Nasenrachenraum U45-2
Nasenraspel U132-12
Nasenrücken U59-13
Nasenscheidewand U86-15; U110-20
Nasenschleimhaut U43-6; U86-8
Nasenschleimhautentzündung U15-19
Nasensekret U66-6
Nasenseptum U110-20
Nasenseptumdeviation U43-6
Nasenspekulum **U17**-6
Nasenspiegelung **U17**-6
Nasenspüllösung, salzhaltige U82-5
Nasentamponade U110-20; U140-24
–, hintere U43-6
Nasentropfen U64-15
Nasenverstopfung U124-12
Nasopharyngealtubus U123-10
Nasopharynx U45-2
nässen (Wunde) **U67**-10; **U140**-13
nässend **U67**-10; U114-8
Nasspräparat **U83**-20
Natis **U22**-13
NATO-Lagerung **U8**-17
Natrium **U82**-18; U79-17
Natriumausscheidung U54-3; U82-18
Natriumbelastung, filtrierte U49-1
Natriumbikarbonat U82-18
Natriumchlorid U82-5,18,23
Natriumcyanid U91-9
Natriumfluorid U82-22
natriumhaltig U9-1
Natriumhydrogenkarbonat U82-18
Natriumhydroxid U91-10
Natriumkanal U82-18
Natriumkonzentration U88-2
Natriummangel U49-8
Natriumnitrit U82-16
Natriumpumpe U82-18
Natriumreabsorption, renale U49-4; U88-8
Natriumretention U49-4; U82-18; U112-10
Natriumrückresorption U82-18
Natriumsulfat U91-24; U82-18
Natriumtransport U78-17
Natriumüberbelastung U33-10
Natriumverlust U49-8; U82-18
Natriumzufuhr U125-21
Natriuretikum U82-18
natriuretisch U82-18
Natron, doppeltkohlensaures U82-18
Natur(ell) **U75**-1
Naturarzt/-ärztin U18-1
Naturell **U75**-4; **U76**-2
–, fröhliches U67-6
Naturkatastrophe **U6**-20; U100-19
Nausea **U103**-11
Nävus **U25**-19; **U114**-3; U71-8
–, blauer U98-15
–, epidermaler U56-2

Nävuszellnävus U98-15
-, dysplastischer U98-15
Nebelsehen U59-5
Nebelzelt **U95**-10
Nebenast **U34**-13; U36-3
Nebenhoden **U52**-5
Nebenhodenentzündung **U52**-5
Nebenhodengang U52-5
Nebenhöhlen (Nase) U21-4
Nebenhöhlendurchleuchtung U99-16
Nebenmetabolit U78-11
Nebenmilz U35-4
Nebenniere **U54**-10
Nebennierenadenom, aldosteronpro-
   duzierendes U55-25
Nebennierenhyperplasie U54-10
Nebennierenmsuffizienz U124-6
Nebennierenmark U54-10
Nebennierenrinde U54-10; U86-23
Nebennierenrindeninsuffizienz
   U124-12
-, akute U54-10
Nebenprodukt, degradatives U78-10
-, katabole U78-10
Nebenschilddrüse **U54**-7
Nebenschilddrüsenadenom U54-7
Nebenschilddrüsenhyperplasie U54-7
Nebenschilddrüsenunterfunktion U54-7
Nebenwirkung(en) **U121**-14,11,13;
   U9-3,17 ; U92-24
- , toxische U91-4
Nebulisator U92-14
Necking **U68**-2
negativ **U116**-22
Neglect U19-10
- (-Syndrom) U77-11
-, sensorischer U77-11
neigen U31-2; **U64**-5
- (Kopf) U63-3
- zu (Erkrankung) U89-27; U104-13
-, (sich) **U63**-10; **U64**-5
Neigung **U64**-5; **U75**-4; U77-7
Nekropsie **U12**-20
Nekrose **U89**-30
-, käsige U94-16
nekrotisch U89-30; U140-12
NEL-Wert **U91**-18
Nematoden U90-16; U92-25
nennen, beim Namen **U74**-3
nennenswert **U117**-5
neoadjuvant **U120**-8
Neocortex **U41**-6
Neodym-YAG-Laser U127-7
Neonatologe/-login **U15**-16
Neoplasie **U97**-4
Neoplasma **U97**-4
neoplastisch **U97**-4
Neovaskularisation **U97**-15
-, retinale U97-15
Nephritis, lipomatöse U98-11
Nephrogramm U48-2
Nephron **U48**-5
Nephroptose U113-17
Nephrotom **U85**-22

nephrotoxisch U92-32
Nerv, sensibler U57-7
-, motorischer U40-1
-, sensorischer U40-1; U57-7
-, vasokonstriktorischer U36-11
-, vasomotorischer U34-1
Nervenadaptation **U137**-5
Nervenanspannung U40-1; U113-2
Nervenast U40-1
Nervenbahnen **U40**-3,1
-, motorische U31-20
Nervenbündel U130-13
Nervenendigung(en) U30-4; U40-1
-, freie U57-13
-, postganglionäre U40-11
-, sympathische U40-9; U75-8
-, vagale U40-10
Nervenfasern, adrenerge **U40**-8
-, afferente **U40**-4
-, efferente **U40**-4
-, markhaltige U41-7
-, marklose U41-7
-, motorische **U40**-4
-, parasympathische **U40**-9
-, sekretorische **U40**-7
-, sensible **U40**-4
-, sensorische **U40**-4
-, somatische **U40**-7
-, sympathische **U40**-9
Nervengeflecht, vegetatives U40-6
Nervengewebe U40-1; U86-3
Nervengift U91-2,4
Nervenheilanstalt **U14**-5; U77-3,24;
   U73-2
Nervenimpuls **U42**-5
Nervenkompressionssyndrom U113-15
Nervenlähmung U40-1
Nervenleiden **U113**-14
Nervennaht U137-2
Nervenschädigung U124-14
Nervenscheide U40-1
Nervenschmerz **U113**-14
Nervenstamm U22-1; U40-1
Nervenstimulation, transkutane elektri-
   sche (TENS) U142-23
Nervenstimulator, transkutaner
   U142-23
Nervensystem, animales U40-7
-, autonomes **U40**-6
-, peripheres **U40**-5
-, vegetatives **U40**-6
Nervenversorgung U40-1
Nervenwurzel U28-19; U40-1
-, eingeklemmte U113-15
Nervenwurzelreizung U89-10
Nervenwurzelschädigung U6-11
Nervenzelle **U40**-1
Nervenzusammenbruch U6-5; U76-6
Nervi cavernosi penis U52-15
- craniales U28-7
- olfactorii U62-1
- spinales U22-12; U41-15
nervös U31-10; **U40**-1; **U76**-5 ff;
   U108-13

Nervosität **U76**-6; **U108**-13
nervschonend (Eingriff) U8-18;
   U126-13
Nervtransposition U129-13
Nervus acusticus U40-1
- cranialis U40-1
- ischiadicus U40-1; U113-1
- - Dehnungszeichen U142-11
- lingualis U26-23
- medianus U87-18
- motorius U40-1
- oculomotorius **U58**-16
- olfactorius U40-1
- opticus **U58**-15
- phrenicus U40-1
- spinalis U40-1
- statoacusticus **U60**-13
- supraorbitalis U58-1
- trochlearis U58-16
- ulnaris U28-16
- vagus **U40**-10
- vestibulocochlearis **U60**-13,9,11
Nesselausschlag U108-9
Nesselsucht **U114**-11; U124-3
nett **U75**-5,8
Netz **U45**-7; U56-5
-, großes U45-7
-, kleines U45-7
-, neuronales U40-1
-, soziales U13-6; U16-8
netzartig **U35**-12
Netzbeutel U29-10; U45-7
Netzbruch U45-7
netzförmig **U83**-8
Netzhaut **U58**-13
Netzhautablösung U58-13; U124-1
Netzhautadaptation U59-10
Netzhautbild U58-13; U59-5
Netzhautflecken U58-13
Netzhautperipherie U58-13
Netzhautriss U58-13; U59-5; U107-1
Netzmittel U81-2
Netztransplantat **U130**-8
Netzwerk U56-5
-, retikuläres U83-8
Neuankömmling **U71**-1
Neubeurteilung U117-8
Neubildung **U1**-10; **U97**-4
- (Glukose) U47-17
Neueinpflanzung (Ureter) U48-10
Neuerkrankungsrate **U100**-7
neugeboren **U71**-1
Neugeborenenasphyxie U44-8; U123-7
Neugeborenenerythroblastose U37-17
Neugeborenenikterus U108-4
-, physiologischer U88-1
Neugeborenenintensivstation U14-7;
   U125-1
Neugeborenenkrämpfe U113-5
Neugeborenenstation **U14**-8
Neugeborenentetanus U94-11
Neugeborenes **U71**-1; **U80**-4
-, dystrophes U70-10
-, unreifes U80-10

Neugedächtnis U74-1,8
neugierig blickend U67-8
Neumutation U84-27
Neuorientierung **U107**-12
neural **U40**-1
Neuralfalten U85-18
Neuralgie **U113**-14
neuralgisch **U113**-14
Neuralleiste U40-1,11; U85-18
Neuralplatte **U85**-18
Neuralrinne U85-12,18
Neuralrohr **U85**-18,8
Neuralrohrdefekt U40-1; U85-18
Neuralrohrverschluss U85-18
Neurasthenie U40-1
Neuraxon **U40**-2
Neurilemmom **U98**-13
Neurinom **U98**-13
Neurit **U40**-2
Neuritis nervi optici U58-15
Neuroblastom **U98**-13
Neurochirurg(in) **U15**-14
Neuro-Effektor-Synapse **U30**-4
Neurofibrille U40-1
Neurofibrom **U98**-13,8
–, plexiformes U98-13
Neurofibromatose/-sis **U98**-13
Neurografie U74-12
Neurohormon **U55**-1
Neurohypophyse U54-5
Neurolemm U98-13
Neuroleptikum U74-11; U92-2,23; U135-10
Neurologe/-login **U15**-14
neurologisch **U15**-14
neurologische Ausfälle **U113**-7
Neurolues **U96**-3; U40-5
Neuron(en) **U40**-1
–, adrenerge U40-1
–, cholinerge U40-8
–, präganglionäre U40-1
–, untere motorische U40-1
neuronal **U40**-1
Neuronenkreis U40-1
Neuronenschaltung U40-1
Neuropathie **U113**-14
neurophysiologisch U88-1
Neuropsychologe/-in U15-14
Neuropsychologie U77-21
Neurose **U77**-21
–, depressive U77-17
Neurostatus **U77**-1; U117-1
Neurosyphilis **U96**-3
Neurotiker(in) **U77**-21
neurotisch **U77**-21
Neurotoxin U91-2,4
Neurotoxizität U91-11
Neurotransmitter **U42**-10
Neurotransmitterbahn U42-10
Neutralfette U24-5; U81-20
Neutralisation **U81**-20
Neutralisationswärme U81-20
neutralisieren **U81**-20; U91-15
Neutralsalz U82-5

Nezthautdegeneration U58-13
NF-1/2 U98-13
Nichtansprechbarkeit U5-14
Nichtmetall **U82**-6
nichtmetallisch **U82**-6
Nichtraucher(in) **U10**-16
Nichtselbst **U39**-21
Nichtsinnmutation U84-21
nichtssagend U67-4
Nichttrennung **U84**-24
Nichttrinker(in) **U10**-10
Nickel **U82**-27
Nickelallergie U82-27
Nickelschmelztiegel U82-27
Nickeltetracarbonyl U82-27
nicken **U67**-3; **U72**-2
Nickerchen **U72**-2
– machen **U67**-3
Nicoladoni-Operation U129-13
Nicotin(säure)amid U82-17
Nidation **U70**-3; U85-2
Nidationshemmer U69-7
Nidationsstörung, plazentare U70-3
niederfrequent **U61**-6; U32-13
Niederfrequenztherapie U142-23
niedergeschlagen **U71**-22; **U76**-20,22,2
Niedergeschlagenheit **U77**-17; U76-1
niederknien U63-4
niederkommen **U71**-4
Niederkunft **U71**-4
niederosmolar U81-21
Niederschlag **U81**-27
niederschlagen, sich **U82**-8
niederschreiben **U18**-14; **U102**-12
Niederspannungsverletzung U6-14
niederstoßen **U6**-2
niedertreten **U65**-5
Niednagel U56-15
niedrig **U116**-20
Niere **U48**-2
–, kontralaterale U87-18
–, künstliche **U125**-21
–, gesunde U48-2
–, überzählige U48-2
Nierenbecken **U48**-3; U28-21
–, erweitertes U48-3
Nierenbeckenkelchsystem **U48**-9
–, stark dilatiertes U48-9
Nierenbeteiligung U89-4
Nierendurchblutung U16-11; U36-1
Nierenfunktionsprüfung U116-14
Nierengefäß U34-1
Nierenhilus U48-2; U87-25
Niereninsuffizienz U18-5
–, terminale U119-15
Nierenkanälchen **U48**-5,7
–, gerade U48-2
Nierenkapsel U29-9; U48-2
Nierenkelch **U48**-4
Nierenkelchdivertikel U48-4
Nierenkolik U104-15
Nierenkörperchen **U48**-6
Nierenkreislauf U36-1
Nierenlagerschmerzen U28-14; U109-12

Nierenmark U48-2
Nierenpapillen U48-3
Nierenparenchym U86-22
Nierenpol, oberer U87-3
Nierenpyramiden U48-2
Nierenrinde U48-2
nierenschädigend U92-32
Nierenschale **U17**-12
Nierenschwelle **U49**-5; U88-7
Nierenstein U48-2; U89-21
Nierenstiel U35-9; U48-2; U87-24
Nierenszintigramm U82-1
Nierenverdopplung U48-2
Nierenversagen U48-2; U88-15
–, akutes U119-10
Nierenzellkarzinom U98-2; U112-3
Niesanfall U66-6; U103-16
niesen **U66**-6,2; **U103**-16; U131-4
Niesreflex U66-6
Niesreiz U66-6
Nikotin **U10**-17
Nikotinabhängigkeit U10-17
Nikotinabusus U10-17
Nikotinamidadenindinukleotid U82-19
Nikotinentwöhnung U10-17
Nikotinersatztherapie U10-17
nikotingelb **U10**-17
nikotinhaltig **U10**-17
Nikotinpflaster U10-17
Nikotinsäure U10-17
Nikotinsäureamidadenindinukleotid U47-17
Nikotinsucht U11-2
Nisse U90-15
Nitrat **U82**-16
Nitril **U91**-9
Nitrit **U82**-16
Nitrit-Teststreifen U82-16
Nitrobenzol U82-16
Nitrogenium **U82**-16
Nitroglyzerin U82-13,16
Nitroprussid U91-9
Nitroprussidnatrium U82-18
nitros **U82**-16
Nitrosamin U82-16
Nitrozellulose U82-16
N-Lost U82-16
NNM U54-10
NNR U54-10; U86-23
Nodi lymphatici axillares U35-3
– – cubitales U23-4
– – inguinales U35-1
– – – profundi U35-3
Nodositas **U97**-3; **U89**-16
nodulär **U97**-3
Nodulus **U89**-16
Nodus atrioventricularis U32-15
– lymphaticus **U35**-3
Non-A-Non-B-Non-C Hepatitis U94-15
Nondisjunction **U84**-24
Non-Hodgkin-Lymphom U98-10
Nonnengeräusch U110-3
Nonnensausen U110-3
Non-REM-Schlaf **U72**-11

Non-REM-Schlafphase U72-11
Nonsense-Codon U84-13
Nonsense-Mutation U84-21
Noradrenalin **U42**-11; **U55**-11; U40-8
Norepinephrin **U42**-11; **U55**-11
Norm(wert) **U116**-21
normal **U116**-21
–, (geistig) **U77**-3
Normalbereich **U116**-21
–, im **U107**-19
normalisieren, sich U4-14; **U116**-21
Normalsichtigkeit U59-6,17
Normalverteilung U100-12
Normalwert **U116**-21
Normbereich **U116**-21
–, im **U107**-19
Normoblast(en) U37-5
  U38-3
Normophorie **U59**-15
normoton **U110**-13; U116-21
Normotoniker(in) **U110**-13; U100-22
Normovolämie **U36**-7; U116-21
nosokomial **U139**-12; **U89**-6; **U121**-15
Nosokomialinfektion U13-10; U14-1
Not U107-11
Not(fall)behandlung U6-18; U14-6
Not(fall)dienst U6-18; U13-3; U16-1,9
Not(fall)operation U124-1
Not(lage) **U104**-2; **U113**-2; U75-8
Notamputation U126-5
Notarzt/-ärztin U14-6; U15-1; U126-5
Notarzthubschrauber **U8**-5
Notarztteam U14-6
Notarztwagen U8-5
Notaufnahme **U14**-6; U6-18; U15-15
–, allgemeine U14-6
–, psychiatrische U77-16
Notdienst, ärztlicher U13-3
Note, persönliche U62-8
Noteingriff U6-18
Notfall **U6**-18; **U14**-6; U126-5
–, gynäkologischer U15-16
–, internistischer **U124**-1
–, toxikologischer U91-3
Notfallausrüstung U123-1
Notfallbronchoskopie U118-11; U124-1
Notfallchemo(therapie) U97-17
Notfalldialyse U125-21
Notfallendoskopie U6-18
Notfalllaparoskopie U128-3
Notfalllaparotomie U128-19
notfallmäßig **U6**-18
Notfallmedizin U6-18; U124-1
Notfallverhütung U69-5
Notfallversorgung U120-1
Notfallwagen U131-19
notieren **U20**-6
Nötigung, sexuelle **U68**-17,10
Notiz **U57**-4
Notizblock U17-13
Notlage **U6**-18
notleidend U6-4; **U104**-2
Notmaßnahme U6-18; **U20**-8,11
Notoperation U6-18; U20-8; U126-3

Notruf U6-18f; U14-6; U18-7
Nottracheotomie U123-11
Notzucht **U68**-17
notzüchtigen **U68**-17
novo, de **U119**-5
Noxe U91-1
Nozi(re)zeptor **U57**-13
Nozizeption **U57**-13
nozizeptiv **U57**-13
Nozizeptorenschmerz U57-13
NSA U92-11
N-Terminus U84-3
nüchtern **U46**-8; **U2**-15; U134-6
– (Alkohol) **U10**-4
Nüchternblutprobe U118-4
Nüchternblutzucker U79-6f;
  U116-12,19
–, erhöht U78-13
Nüchternheit **U10**-4
Nüchternschmerz U2-11; U104-7
Nüchternserumgastrinspiegel U55-13
Nüchternzustand U119-15
nuckeln **U46**-2
Nucleus caudatus U41-10; U87-19
– lentiformis U41-10
– nervi hypoglossi U41-14
– pulposus U85-20
– subthalamicus U41-9
nuklear **U83**-4
Nuklearmedizin U83-4; U99-22
Nukleinsäurestoffwechsel U78-1
Nukleokapsid U84-12
Nukleolus **U83**-4
Nukleoplasma **U83**-4
Nukleoprotein U83-4
Nukleosid U84-12
Nukleosom U83-4
Nukleotid **U84**-12
–, zyklisches U83-17
Nukleotidanalogon U84-12
Nukleotidase **U84**-12
Nukleotidsequenz U84-12
Nukleotidstoffwechsel U84-12
Nukleotidtriplett **U84**-13
Nukleus **U83**-4
Nullallel U84-4
Nullhypothese **U101**-19
nullipar **U70**-8
Nulllinie U125-6
Nulllinien-EEG U7-18; U118-12
nullwertig U81-10
Nullzeitpunkt U100-26
Nullzelladenome U39-16
Nullzelle **U39**-16
Nullzelllinie U39-16
nuscheln **U66**-15
Nüsse **U3**-14
Nutzen **U1**-5
nützen **U1**-5
Nyktalopie U59-18
Nykturie **U112**-6,5
Nymphomanie U68-4
Nystagmografie **U113**-12
Nystagmus **U113**-12; U58-2

Nystagmus, latenter U59-15
–, vestibulärer U60-9
Nystagmusintensität U113-12
nystagtisch **U113**-12

O

o.B. (ohne Befund) **U107**-18,20
Obdach **U142**-28
Obduktion **U12**-19f; **U87**-5; **U126**-12
Obduktionsbefund U12-20
Obduktionsgenehmigung U12-20
Obduzent(in) **U12**-20
obduzieren **U12**-20
O-Beine **U23**-8
O-beinig **U23**-8; U25-9
Oberarmknochen **U28**-15
Oberarmköpfchen U28-15
Oberarzt U15-4; U80-13
–, leitender U20-9
Oberbauch(gegend) **U22**-3; U45-8
Oberbauch, Druckgefühl im U109-12
Oberfläche **U87**-4
Oberflächenanästhesie U93-3
Oberflächendosis U99-9
Oberflächenelektromyografie U118-13
Oberflächenepithel U86-7
Oberflächenerwärmung U19-6
Oberflächenimmunglobulin U39-12
Oberflächenkarzinom **U97**-10
Oberflächenrezeptor U55-2
Oberflächensensibilität U57-3
Oberflächenspannung U44-9; U87-4
oberflächlich **U87**-4
Oberhaut **U56**-2
Oberkiefer(knochen) **U28**-10; U21-5
Oberkieferhöhle U28-10
Oberkörper freimachen U22-6
–, mit nacktem U22-2
Oberkörperhochlagerung mit angezogenen Beinen **U63**-11
Oberlappensegment U43-3
Oberlippengrübchen U21-9
Oberschenkel **U23**-9; U22-2; U30-15
Oberschenkelamputation U142-6
Oberschenkelarterie, tiefe U34-3
Oberschenkelbeuger **U30**-16
–, steife U31-17
–, unbewegliche U31-17
–, verkürzte U30-16
Oberschenkelfaszie U30-7
Oberschenkelfraktur U28-23
Oberschenkelgurt U131-13
Oberschenkelhämatom U38-8
Oberschenkelknochen **U28**-23; U23-9
Oberschenkelkopf U21-1
Oberschenkelstrecker **U30**-16
Oberschwester **U16**-2
Oberweite **U22**-2
Obesitas **U24**-9
Obhut **U77**-25
Objekte, unbewegte U59-14
Objektiv U133-4

Objektträger **U17**-13; U86-1; U116-5
Obliteration **U89**-18
obliteriert, (nicht) U85-17
Obsession **U77**-19
obsessiv **U77**-19
Obst **U3**-7
Obstipation **U109**-6; U94-19
obstipiert **U109**-6; U2-1
Obstruktion **U89**-18; **U109**-6
–, subvesikale U112-12
Obstruktionsatelektase U111-15
Obstruktionspneumonie U111-16
obstruktiv **U111**-16; **U112**-12
Obturator **U133**-6
Obturatorspitze U133-6
Obturator-Tubus U123-10
Oddi-Sphinkter U30-9; U47-8
Odds Ratio U100-8
Ödem **U108**-10; **U5**-15
–, eindrückbares U108-10
–, interstitielles U86-19
–, periorbitales U58-1
ödematös **U108**-10; **U109**-9; **U111**-13
Ödipus-Komplex U77-12
Odontoblasten U26-16
Odynophagie U103-6; U109-5
offen **U34**-14; **U75**-12 f
– (Drain) U140-15
–, ganz U32-2
offen-chirurgisch **U128**-3; U126-1
offene Luxation U106-3
– Wunde U106-3
offenhalten U127-20
Offenheit U75-13
Offenherzigkeit **U32**-2
Offenlegung U18-11
offensichtlich **U107**-10; **U117**-9
offiziell **U18**-1
öffnen **U87**-21
Öffnung **U87**-21
–, durchgängige U87-21
–, künstliche U58-2
–, operativ angelegte **U127**-3
Öffnungston U32-4; U33-1
Ohnmacht **U7**-4 f; **U110**-11; U72-7
ohnmächtig werden **U7**-4,6; **U110**-11; U123-3
Ohnmachtsanfall U103-4; U110-11
–, hysterischer U77-6
Ohr **U21**-15
–, äußeres U60-1
Öhr (Nadel) U132-5
Ohr(en)spiegelung **U17**-7
Ohr(muschel)knorpel U29-2
Ohranhänge U60-2
Ohren, abstehende U60-1; U87-27
–, druckschmerzempfindliche U60-1
–, fehlgebildete U63-3
–, tiefsitzende U25-10; U60-1
ohrenbetäubend U60-1
Ohrenfluss U20-16; U60-1,3
Ohrenklingen **U113**-13
Ohrensausen **U113**-13
Ohrenschmalz **U60**-1,15

Ohrenschmalzdrüsen U60-15
Ohrenschmerzen U60-1
Ohrenschützer U60-1
Ohrenspekulum **U17**-7,6
Ohrenspiegel U15-19; U60-1
Ohrfluss U21-15
Ohrgeräusch **U113**-13
–, pulssynchrones U36-9; U113-13
Ohrgrübchen U85-23
Ohrknorpel U60-2
Ohrläppchen **U60**-2; U87-23
–, gedehntes U60-2
Ohrleiste U60-2
Ohrmuschel **U32**-7; **U60**-2; U17-7; U56-4
Ohrmuscheldefekt, angeborener U60-2
Ohrmuscheldeformität U60-2
Ohrmuschelhöcker U60-2
Ohrmuschelknorpel U60-2
Ohroliven U17-2
Ohroxymeter U125-9
Ohrpinzette U132-14
Ohrplakode U85-23
Ohrplastik U129-3
Ohrspeicheldrüse U45-3; U95-4
Ohrthermometer U105-6
Ohrtrompete **U60**-7; U45-4
–, klaffende U60-7
okkludieren **U27**-13
okklusal **U26**-24
Okklusion **U17**-3; U89-18
–, dynamische U29-7
Okklusionsbefund U27-12
Okklusionsbewegung U29-7
Okklusionsdiagnostik U27-12
Okklusionsebene U27-13
Okklusionsstörung **U27**-13
Okklusionsverband U140-5,17
Okklusivpessar **U69**-9
okkult **U119**-6
Okular U21-3; U58-8; **U133**-4
okulär **U58**-2
Okulomotoriuslähmung U58-16
okzipital **U87**-20
Öl **U3**-15
–, ätherisches U82-2
Olecranon **U28**-16
ölen **U17**-14
olfaktorisch **U62**-1
Olfaktus **U62**-1
ölig **U56**-8
Oligodendrogliom U98-14
Oligomer **U81**-6
Oligonukleotid, allelspezifisches U84-4
Oligonukleotidhybridisierung, allelspezifische U84-38
Oligosialie U109-3
Oligospermie U53-7
Oligurie **U112**-2
Oliver-Cardarelli-Zeichen U64-13
Ollier-Erkrankung **U98**-12
Ombudsmann (Gesundheitswesen) U13-1
Omega-3-Fettsäure U79-12

Omentum **U45**-7
Omphalitis **U71**-17
Omphalos **U22**-5; **U85**-7
Omphalozele **U71**-17
onc-Gen U84-1
Onkogen U84-1; U97-1,6
Onkogenexpression U83-16
Onkogenität **U91**-13
Onkogenitätsstudie U91-13
Onkologe/-in **U97**-1
Onkologie **U97**-1
onkologisch **U97**-1
onkostatisch U97-1
Onlay-Plastik U130-9
on-off-Effekt U121-8
Onychodystrophie U56-15
Onychomykose U56-15
Onychophagie U56-15
Oogenese **U51**-5
Oogonien U51-5
Oolemma U51-5
Oozyt U86-2
OP-Anzug **U139**-15
Opazität U99-11
OP-Bedarf U131-9
OP-Einrichtung U131-1
Operateur **U131**-5; **U126**-3
Operation **U126**-2 f,1
Operationsangst U134-4
Operationsassistent(in) U16-10; U131-4
–, techische(r) U16-10
Operationseinwilligung U126-2; **U134**-3
Operationsergebnis U101-27; U126-3
Operationsfeld U8-1; U126-2
Operationshandschuhe **U139**-17
Operationskleidung **U139**-6
Operationsliste U20-6
Operationsmikroskop **U127**-6; U86-1
Operationsnarbe U126-2
Operationspräparat U118-4
Operationsrisiko **U134**-5
Operationssaal **U131**-1; U126-2
Operationssitus U126-2
Operationsteam **U131**-4
Operationstechnik **U126**-4
Operationstisch **U131**-10
Operationstrakt 14-9; **U131**-2
Operationsvorbereitung U126-2
Operationsweg **U126**-6
operativ **U126**-2; U41-5
operieren **U126**-1
Opfer **U6**-12; **U14**-6; U64-6
Opferzahl U6-20
OP-Gehilfe **U131**-9
OP-Handschuhe U17-1; U139-15
OP-Haube U139-18
ophthalmisch **U15**-18
Ophthalmodynamometrie U15-18
Ophthalmologe/-in U58-2
Ophthalmologie **U15**-18
Ophthalmoplegie U15-18
Ophthalmoskop U17-6; U118-11
Ophthalmoskopie **U58**-12,8; U15-18
Opiat **U11**-18

Opiatantagonisten U11-18
Opioide U11-1; U135-5
Opioidererhaltungstherapie U11-18
Opioidrezeptoren U11-18
Opiumalkaloid U11-18
Opiumtinktur, benzoesäurehaltige U9-10
OP-Kleidung **U139**-15; U131-1 f
OP-Mantel **U139**-15
opportunistischer Erreger U139-9
OP-Saal **U131**-2
OP-Schleuse U131-2
OP-Schürze U139-15
OP-Schutzkittel **U17**-16
OP-Schwester **U131**-8; U16-2
Optik **U133**-2 f
–, prograde U133-2
Optiker(in) **U58**-14
Optiktrokar U133-3,5
Optikusatrophie U58-15; U89-29
Optikusgliom U98-14
Optikusschädigung U58-15
optimistisch **U75**-6
optisch **U58**-14
OP-Tisch U126-2
optische Geräte U132-1
– Täuschung U73-10
optisches System **U133**-2 f
OP-Vorbereitungsraum U19-2
oral **U21**-8
Oraltemperatur U45-2; U105-1
Orbita **U58**-1; U21-3; **U28**-8; U29-4
Orbitaboden U28-9; U58-1
Orbitadach U58-1
Orbitadermoid U98-17
Orbitaeingang U58-1
orbital **U58**-1
Orbital U81-2
Orbitarand U58-1
Orchitis U95-4
Orchoepididymitis U52-5
Ordensschwester **U16**-2
Ordination **U18**-1; **U126**-3
Ordinationszeit U18-1; U102-14
Ordnung U90-9
Ordnungszahl U81-2,10
Organabstoßung U86-20
Organanamnese, systematische **U102**-11
organbegrenzt **U97**-9
Organbergung **U128**-17
Organbergungssack **U133**-16
Organbeutel U128-16
Organdosis U99-9
Organe **U86**-20
–, innere U15-9; U86-20; U108-12
–, lebenswichtige U86-20
–, parenchymatöse U86-21 f
Organelle U86-19
organerhaltend **U126**-13
Organerhaltung U86-20
Organersatztherapie U123-9
Organisation, gemeinnützige U13-12
organisch **U86**-20; **U137**-10
Organismus U86-20

Organismus, kultivierter U90-1
–, pathogener **U90**-5
–, ruhender U90-1
Organkonservierung U86-20
Organomegalie U86-20
Organon **U86**-20
Organrejektion U130-21
organrettender Eingriff U126-4
Organsack **U133**-16; U128-17
Organschaden U86-20
Organschädigung U86-20
Organspende U86-20
Organspenderausweis U129-15
Organtoleranzdosis U121-12
Organtoxizität U91-11
Organum **U86**-20
– spirale **U60**-12
Organvergrößerung U129-19
Organversagen U86-20
–, multiples U125-1
Orgasmus **U68**-6; U11-9; U50-14
Orgasmusphase U68-6
Orgasmusstörung **U68**-7,6; U50-2
orgastisch **U68**-6
Orientbeule U89-17; U114-16
orientiert zu Zeit, Raum, Person U7-8
Orientierung **U7**-8; **U107**-12
–, räumliche U41-3
–, sexuelle **U68**-14
Orientierungspunkt **U126**-8
–, anatomischer U87-1
Orientierungsreaktion U107-12
Orientierungssinn U57-5
Orientierungsstörung U77-4; U107-12
Ornithin-Zyklus U49-13; U78-6; U81-15
Oropharyngealtubus U43-5
Orotrachealtubus U45-2
Orthetiker **U141**-9
Orthopäde/-in **U15**-15
Orthopädiemechaniker(in) **U15**-15; **U142**-6
Orthopädietechnik **U15**-15
orthopädisch (Schuhe) **U15**-15; U142-12
Orthophorie **U59**-15
Orthopnoe **U111**-2
orthopnoisch **U111**-2
Orthostase U65-3
Os **U28**-2
– breve U28-2
– capitatum U28-17; U29-1
– coccygis **U28**-20
– compactum U28-2
– coxae **U22**-7; **U28**-21,2
– cuboideum U28-25,27
– ethmoidale **U28**-8
– frontale **U28**-8; U87-20
– hamatum U28-17
– hyoideum U28-2,9
– ilium **U28**-22
– ischii **U28**-22
– lunatum U28-17; U29-1
– naviculare U28-25

Os occipitale **U28**-8; U87-20
– palatinum U28-9
– parietale **U28**-8; U87-13
– pisiforme U28-17
– pubis **U28**-22; U52-18
– sacrum **U28**-20
– scaphoideum U28-17
– sesamoideum U28-2
– sphenoidale **U28**-8
– spongiosum U28-2
– tarsi **U28**-25
– temporale **U28**-8
– triquetrum U28-17
– zygomaticum U21-7; U28-9
Osmolalität **U49**-9; **U81**-21
Osmometrie U49-9
Osmoregulation U49-9; U54-3; U88-2
Osmorezeptor U49-9; U81-21
Osmose **U49**-9; **U81**-21; **88**-4
osmotisch **U49**-9; **U81**-21; **U88**-4
ösophageal **U45**-5
Ösophagitis, erosive U114-13
Ösophagospasmus U109-4
Ösophagotrachealfistel U89-25
Ösophagus **U45**-5
Ösophagusachalasie U109-4
Ösophagus-Breischluck U46-2
Ösophagusersatzsprache U45-5
Ösophagusfremdkörper U109-4
Ösophagusmanometrie U118-3
Ösophagusmotilität U46-6; U109-4
Ösophagusperistaltik U45-5
Ösophagusruptur U45-5
Ösophagussphinkter, unterer U45-5
Ösophagusstimme U45-5; U66-8
Ösophagusvarizen U45-5; U109-4
Ösophagusverätzung U91-10
Ossa carpi **U28**-17; U23-5
– cuneiformia U28-25
– metacarpalia **U28**-17
ossär **U28**-2
Osseointegration U31-14
Ossicula auditus U21-15
Ossiculum **U28**-2
Ossifikation **U31**-14
–, enchondrale U29-2; U31-14
Ossifikationskern U31-14
ossifiziert **U31**-14
ossikulär **U60**-5
Osteoblast U31-14
Osteochondrome **U98**-12
–, multiple U28-2
Osteodensiometrie U118-3
Osteogenese U31-14
Osteogenesis imperfecta U28-2
Osteoid U86-19
Osteoklast U31-14
Osteomalazie **U95**-11; U28-2
Osteopath(in) **U15**-22
Osteopathie **U15**-22
osteopathische Behandlung U142-12
Osteosarkom U98-3
Osteosynthese **U141**-4,12
Osteotom U132-11

Osteozyt U86-2
Ostia U48-12
Ostium U87-21
– atrioventriculare dextrum U87-21
– – sinistrum U87-21
– cardiacum U87-21
– ileocaecale U45-12
– pyloricum U87-21
– ureteris U48-10; U87-21
– urethrae U48-1,13
– uteri U50-5,7; U87-21
– vaginae U50-8; U87-21
Ostium-primum-Defekt U87-21
– secundum-Defekt U87-21
Östradiol U55-18,14
Östradiolbenzoat U55-18
Östradiolvalerat U55-18
Östriol U55-18
östrogenartig U55-17
Östrogenbehandlung U120-5
Östrogene U55-17
–, konjugierte U55-17
–, nichtsteroidale U55-17
–, synthetische U55-17
Östrogenersatztherapie U55-17
Östrogenkur U120-5
Östrogen-Priming U55-17
Östrogenreifung U55-17
Östrogenrezeptormodulator, selektiver U83-19
Östrogensekretion U55-17
Östrogensubstitutionstherapie U55-17
Östron U55-18
Östronsulfat U82-24
Otalgie U60-1
Otitis media U95-12; U15-19; U60-6
– – , seröse U86-9
Otolithenapparat U60-9
Otolithenorgan U60-9
Otoplastik U129-1
Otorhinolaryngologie U15-19
Otorrhoe/-ö U21-15; U60-1,3
Otoskop U17-7,6; U15-19; U60-1
Otoskopie U17-7
Otoskopiebefund U17 7
Otostroboskop U17-7
ototoxisch U17-7
Output U88-16
Ovar U50-3; U54-11
–, polyzystisches U50-3
Ovarektomie U50-3
Ovarialbiopsie U50-3
Ovarialfibrom U98-8
Ovarialhormon U50-3
Ovarialinsuffizienz U50-3; U55-15
Ovarialstroma U86-22
Ovarialtumor U50-3
Ovarialzyklus U50-3
Ovarialzyste U50-3; U98-17
Ovariopexie U50-3
Ovarium U50-3
Overgrowth, bakterielles U46-16; U90-6
Overheadextension U141-14

Ovogenese U51-5
Ovozyt(e) U51-5; U86-2
Ovulation U51-9
–, parazyklische U51-9
Ovulationsblutung U51-2
Ovulationshemmung U51-9
Ovulationsinduktion U51-9
Ovulationsmethode U51-9; U69-5
ovulatorisch U51-9
ovulieren U51-9
Ovum U50-3; U51-5
Oxidans U81-5; U82-11
Oxidanzienbelastung U81-5
Oxidation U81-17; U82-11
–, aerobe U81-17
oxidationsbeständig U82-25
Oxidationsmittel U82-11
Oxidations-Reduktions-Reaktion U81-17
Oxidationsstufe U81-17
Oxidationszahl U81-17
oxidativ U81-17
oxidieren U81-17; U82-11
Oxidoreduktase U81-17; U82-11
Oxygenation U125-11
–, hyperbare U44-6; U125-12
oxygenieren U44-6; U82-11; U125-11
Oxygenium U82-11
Oxyhämoglobin U37-6; U116-9
Oxytocin U55-23
Oxytocinbelastungstest U55-23
Oxytocininfusion U55-23
Oxytozin U55-23
Oxyuris vermicularis U90-16

P

Paar U81-12
paaren, sich U83-14; U8-430
paarig angelegt U86-20
Paarung U84-30
–, meiotische U83-14
Pachygyrie U41-5
Pachymeninx U41-8
Pacini-Körperchen U57-15
packen U64-9
Packung U9-16; U140-24
– (Kompresse) U142-22
–, heiße U1-20
Packungsbeilage U9-17
Pädiater(in) U15-17; U80-6
Pädiatrie U15-17; U80-6
pädiatrisch U80-6
pädophil U80-6
Pädophilie U68-15; U80-6
paffen U44-7
palatal U26-23,10
Palatoschisis U87-26
Palatum U26-10
– durum U28-10; U26-10
– fissum U87-26
Pallästhesie U57-17

Pallästhesiometrie U57-17
palliativ U120-9
Palliativoperation U120-9
Palliativtherapie U104-19
Palliativum U104-19
Pallidum U41-10
Pallor U108-5
palmar U23-6; U87-17
Palmaraponeurose U23-6; U87-2
Palmarerythem U87-17
Palmarflexion U31-2; U87-17
palpabel U62-9; U107-7
Palpation U62-9; U107-7; U110-1
Palpationsbefund U107-7
palpatorisch U62-9; U107-7
Palpebra U58-3
palpieren U62-9; U107-7
Palpitatio cordis U110-1
Palpitation U110-1; U107-7
p-Aminobenzolsulfonsäure U82-4
Panaritium U114-16; U24-5
Pandemie U94-8,7
pandemisch U94-8
Panik U6-21; U77-6
Panikattacke U6-21; U77-6; U103-4
Panikreaktion U77-6
Pankreas U54-8
– anulare U54-8
–, endokrines U54-8
Pankreasenzyme U54-8
Pankreasgang U54-8
Pankreasinselzelltumoren U54-8
Pankreaskopf U54-8
Pankreaskörper U54-8
Pankreaspseudozyste U54-8
Pankreassaft U46-10; U54-8; U55-13
Pankreasschwanz U54-8
Pankreassekret U54-8
Pankreasstein U54-8
Pankreastransplantation U54-8
Pankreatitis U54-8
Pankreolith U54-8
Pankreozymin U55-13
Panniculus adiposus U56-5
Panoramaaufnahme U87-4
Panotitis U95-12
Panthenol U82-13
Panzytopenie U38-5
Pap-Abstrich U17-14
Papageienkrankheit U90-14; U96-9
Papanicolaou-Abstrich U116-5
Papaverin U11-18
Papel U114-10; U95-7
–, erythematöse U108-7
Papelbildung U114-10
Papierchromatografie U83-22
Papilla duodeni major U45-10
– mammae U50-18
– nervi optici U58-14
– pili U56-13
– Vateri U45-10
Papillae linguales U21-11
– renales U48-3
Papillarleisten U56-11,3

Papillarmuskel **U32**-13
Papillendrusen U58-14
Papillenödem U58-14
Papillom **U98**-1
-, blumenkohlartiges U98-1
-, invertiertes U98-1
papillomatös **U98**-1
Papillomatose/-sis **U98**-1
Papillomavirus U114-17
Papillomavirusinfektion, humane **U96**-13
Papovaviridae U96-14
Pappkarton **U9**-16
Pap-Test U17-14
Papula **U114**-10
para laufen **U136**-7
Paraaminohippursäure-Clearance U49-7
Parafango **U1**-20
Paraffin(um) **U82**-15
-, flüssiges U82-15
Paraffinbad U82-15
paraffingetränkte Gaze U140-18
Paraffinpackung **U1**-20
Paraganglien U34-10; U37-1
-, chromaffine U82-25
-, sympathische U82-25
Parainfluenza **U94**-9
Parainfluenzavirus U95-10
Paralyse **U31**-12; **U113**-7; **U135**-11
-, progressive U113-7
paralysiert **U31**-12
Paralysis agitans U64-6
paralytisch **U113**-7
paramedizinisch **U8**-6
paramedizinisches Personal **U16**-1
Parameter **U100**-5,19
Parameterübersicht **U20**-5
Paramnesie **U74**-18
Parapertussis **U95**-5
Paraphasie **U113**-10
paraphasisch U66-9
Paraphile(r) **U68**-15
Paraphilie **U68**-15
Paraplegie **U142**-5; U103-20
Paraplegiker(in) **U142**-5
Parapsychologie U77-2
Parasit **U90**-13; **U94**-5
-, fakultativer U90-13
-, intrazellulärer U90-12
-, obligater U90-13
parasitär **U90**-13
Parasitenbefall **U90**-13; **U94**-2
- (Wimpern) U58-3
Parasitenbelastung U90-13
Parasitenei U90-13
Parasitenreservoir U94-4
parasitieren **U90**-13
Parasitismus U90-13
Parasitose U90-13
Parasomnie **U72**-14
Parästhesie **U104**-17; **U135**-4
Parasympathikotonus U40-9
Parasympathikuslähmung U40-9

Parasympatholytikum **U40**-8,10
parasympatholytisch **U92**-8
Paratendineum U29-11
Parathormon **U54**-7; **U55**-7
-, immunreaktives U55-7
Parathormonrezeptor U55-7
Parathormonspiegel U55-7
Parathormonüberschuss U55-7
Parathyrin **U55**-7
Paratonie U103-20
Paratop **U39**-7
Paratyphus **U94**-19
Paravasat **U136**-7
Paravasation **U136**-7
Parazentese **U118**-8
Parazervikalblockade U93-6
Parenchym **U86**-22
parenchymatös **U86**-22
Parenchymbeteiligung U86-22
Parenchymnekrose U86-22
Parenchymschädigung U86-22
parentales Gen U84-29
parenteral U79-1,3; U121-3
Parese **U113**-7; **U135**-11
Parfüm **U62**-3
parfümiert **U62**-3
Paries mastoideus U60-14
parietal **U28**-8; **U87**-13
Parietallappen U41-5; U87-13,23
Parietalzelle U28-8; U54-9
Parität **U70**-8
- feststellen U70-8
Parkinson-Krankheit U64-6; U105-7
Parkplatz U6-3
Paronychie U56-15
Parosmie U62-1
Parotis U45-3; U95-4
Parotitis acuta U95-4
- epidemica **U95**-4
-, eitrige U95-4
Paroxysmus **U72**-18; **U104**-14
Pars abdominalis U48-10
- - aortae U34-8
- ascendens U48-8
- - aortae U34-8
- cardiaca ventriculi U32-3
- cervicalis U45-5
- convoluta (distaler Tubulus) U48-5
- descendens U45-10; U48-8
- - aortae U34-8
- fetalis U71-16; U85-16
- laryngea U45-4
- materna U71-16
- membranacea (urethrae masculinae) U32-9; U48-13; U86-15
- muscularis U32-9
- nasalis U45-4
- oralis U45-4
- pelvina U48-10
- petrosa ossis temporalis U60-3
- prostatica (urethrae masculinae) U48-13; U52-10
- spongiosa (urethrae masculinae) U48-13; U52-13

Pars superior U45-10
- thoracica U45-5
- - aortae U34-8
- uterina U71-16
Partialdruck, arterieller CO_2 U116-11
Partialthromboplastinzeit U37-14; U116-13
Partikel **U82**-1
-, subvirale **U90**-11
Partnerwechsel, häufiger **U68**-12
Partus siccus U71-3
Parulis **U114**-16
Passage **U86**-13
passive Mobilisation **U142**-13
Paste **U9**-8
Pastille **U9**-14
Pätau-Syndrom U84-25
Patch-Plastik U129-19
Patella **U23**-11; **U28**-24
-, tanzende U65-12
Patellahochstand U28-24
Patellaluxation U28-24
patellar **U28**-24
Patellarsehne U28-24
Patellarsehnenreflex U23-11; U28-24; U30-16; U113-1
pathogen U89-1
Pathogenese U119-2
Pathogenität **U90**-5
Pathologe/-in **U15**-21; **U116**-1
Pathologie **U15**-21; **U116**-1; **U89**-1
Pathologielabor **U14**-11; **U116**-1
pathologisch **U15**-21; **U89**-1f; **U116**-1
Pathophysiologie **U88**-1; U15-21
Patient(in) **U20**-2; **U104**-2
-, ambulante(r) **U20**-2
-, bettlägrige(r) U19-3
-, dehydrierte(r) U56-12
-, depressive(r) U72-17
-, gehfähige(r) U14-2
-, immungeschwächte(r) U20-2
-, obduzierte(r) U12-20
-, stationäre(r) U19-2; U20-1f
-, wache(r) U72-6
Patientenaufklärung U142-18
Patientenbogen **U20**-5
Patienten-Compliance **U120**-15
Patientendaten **U102**-9
Patientendokumentation **U102**-13; U20-5
Patientenerhebungsbogen **U101**-16
Patienten-Fragebogen **U102**-15
patientengesteuerte Analgesie U135-7
Patientengut U18-1
Patientenidentifikation U74-3
Patienten-Identifikationsarmband U19-2
Patientenrekrutierung **U101**-4
Patientenselektion **U134**-2
Patientenserie **U101**-11; U100-3
Patiententestament **U20**-14; U13-5
Patientenüberstellung U64-4
Patientenüberwachung U125-5
Patientenverfügung **U20**-14; U16-1

Patientenverlegung U64-4
Patientenzahl U20-2
Patientenzimmer **U19**-2
Patientenzufriedenheit U20-2
paucibakteriell **U90**-7
Paukenhöhle **U60**-6,14
Paukenhöhlenerguss U60-6
Pausbacken U25-6,10
pausbäckig U21-7
Pause **U64**-17
Pavlik-Bandage U141-8
Pavor diurnus U72-14
– nocturnus **U72**-14; U66-14
PDGF U55-5
Pectoralislappen, gestielter U30-10
Pectus carinatum U22-2
– excavatum U22-2; U28-13
Pediculus **U90**-15
Pedikulose **U90**-15; U96-12
Pediküre **U15**-15
Pedunculus cerebellaris U41-13
– – caudalis U41-13; U87-24
– – inferior U41-13; U87-24
– – medialis U87-24
– – medius U41-13
– – rostralis U41-13; U87-24
– – superior U41-13; U87-24
– cerebri U41-2,13; U87-24
Peeling **U1**-20
PEEP-Beatmung U125-10
Pegel **U116**-16
Pein **U77**-5
peinlich U72-6
Peitschenschlagverletzung **U124**-18
Peitschenwurm U90-16
Pellet **U9**-9; U83-20
pelvin **U22**-7; **U28**-21
Pelvis **U22**-7; **U28**-21
Pelviskop **U128**-4
Pelviskopie **U128**-4,3
Pelvitrainer **U128**-8
Pendel **U63**-13
Pendelhoden U52-3
Pendelnystagmus U113-12
Pendelrhythmus U63-13
Penetranz **U84**-26,22
Penetration **U6**-7
Penetrationstest U53-7
penetrierend **U6**-7
penibel **U75**-11
Penicillamin **U92**-10
Penicillin **U92**-10
Penicillinderivat U81-18; U92-10
Penicillin-Lösung, wässrige U82-4
Penis **U52**-14; **U53**-1
Penisdeviation U52-14
Penisfraktur U52-14
Peniskrümmung U52-14
Penislänge U53-4
Penisneid U52-14
Penisprothese U52-14
Penisschaft U52-14
Penisverdopplung **U52**-14
Peniswurzel U52-14

Penizillinase **U92**-10
penizillinresistent U92-10
Penrose-Drain U140-15
Pension **U80**-14
pensionieren **U80**-14
Pensionierung **U80**-14
Pensionist(in) **U80**-14
Pensionsalter U80-14
pensionsberechtigt U80-14
Pentachlorphenol U82-13
pentavalent U81-10
Pepsinproduktion U40-8
Peptidbindung, schwache U81-8
Peptide, gastrinsezernierende U54-9
–, parathormonähnliche U55-7
–, gastrointestinale U54-9
Peptidhormon U55-1
perfundieren **U16**-11; **U36**-5; **U88**-3; **U136**-1
Perfusion **U16**-11; **U36**-5; **U88**-3; **U136**-1
Perfusionschemotherapie U136-1
Perfusionsflüssigkeit **U36**-5; **U136**-1
Perfusionshyperthermie U136-1
Perfusionsstörung U36-5
Perfusionsszintigrafie **U118**-22
Perfusionsszintigramm U118-22
Perfusor U16-11; U136-1
periampullär **U47**-10
Periarthropathia humeroscapularis U23-3
Periarthrosis humeroscapularis U23-3
Pericarditis constrictiva U110-5
Perichondrium **U29**-2
Periduralanästhesie **U93**-8; U41-8
Periduralraum U41-8
Perikard **U32**-5
Perikardblatt, parietales U87-13
Perikarddekompression **U125**-17
Perikardektomie U32-5
Perikarderguss U32-5; U110-8; U118-15
Perikardfenster U32-5
Perikardiozentese **U125**-17
Perikarditis, konstriktive U110-5
Perikardpunktion **U125**-17; U32-5; U110-8; U118-15
Perikardpunktionsbesteck U125-17
Perikardreiben **U110**-8
Perikardtamponade **U110**-8; U32-3,5; U125-17
Perikardton U110-5
Perilymphe U57-18; U60-8
Perimetrie U59-7
Perimetrium **U50**-6
perineal **U22**-10
Perineoplastik U52-20
Perineum **U22**-10; **U52**-20; U50-1
Periode **U51**-2
Periodenprävalenz U100-7
Periodik, zirkadiane U72-8
periodisch auftretend **U119**-11
perioral (Blässe) U108-5
Periost **U28**-2
peripher **U87**-15

Peripherie **U87**-15
Periportalfeld **U47**-5,3
Peristaltik **U46**-6; U79-16
– , propulsive U46-6 f
peristaltisch **U46**-6
Peritonealdialyse U45-7
–, kontinuierliche ambulante U125-21
Peritonealduplikatur U45-7; U86-9
Peritoneallavage U45-7; U118-10
Peritonealspülung U45-7; U91-26
Peritoneum **U45**-7; U140-14
– parietale U45-7
– viscerale U45-7; U86-9; U87-13
Peritonitis U45-7
peritonsillär **U35**-6
Peritonsillarabszess **U95**-13
Perkussion **U107**-8
–, indirekte/mittelbare U17-9
–, kräftige U17-9
–, leise U17-9
Perkussionsempfindlichkeit U17-9; U107-8
Perkussionshammer **U17**-9
Perkussionsschall U17-9; **U107**-8
perkutan U121-3
– (Spickung) U141-14
– (Stent) U127-20
perkutieren **U107**-8; **U127**-16
permeabel **U88**-6
Permeabilität **U88**-6
–, selektive U36-16
Pernio **U5**-12
perniziös **U6**-11
Peronäuslähmung U30-17
peroral U121-3
perorale Arzneiform U9-6
perplex U7-8
Persistenz **U119**-11
persistieren **U119**-11; U104-6
Person, empfängliche U94-8
–, gepflegte U75-1
–, medial veranlagte **U77**-2
Personal, ärztliches **U15**-2
–, steriles U139-6
Personalausweis U18-14; U74-3
Personalien **U102**-9
Personengedächtnis U74-8
Personenwaage **U24**-11; U19-9
Persönlichkeit, abhängige U75-1
–, anankastische U75-1; U77-19
–, asoziale U75-1
–, histrionische U75-1; U77-6
–, hyperthyme **U1**-6
–, multiple U75-1
–, schizoide U75-1
–, schizotypische U75-1
–, stabile U75-1
–, starke U75-1
–, zwanghafte U75-1; U77-19
–, zyklothyme U76-3
Persönlichkeitsentwicklung U75-1
Persönlichkeitsmerkmal **U75**-1
Persönlichkeitsprofil U102-9

Persönlichkeitsstörung **U77**-24,13; U75-1
-, dissoziale U4-4
Persönlichkeitszerfall U73-5
Persönlichkeitszüge **U75**-1
-, anankastische U77-19
Perspiratio insensibilis U57-8
- sensibilis **U105**-12
Pertechnetat, 99 mTc- U82-34
Pertussis **U95**-5
Pertussisimpfstoff U95-5
Pertussisschutzimpfung U95-5
Pertussistoxin U95-5
Perücke U21-16
Perversion **U68**-15
pervertieren **U68**-15
Perzentile **U100**-11
Perzentilenrang U100-11
Perzeption **U57**-2; **U73**-1
Pes adductus **U23**-14
- calcaneus U28-27
- equinus U23-13
PESA U69-13
Pessar **U69**-9
Pessarbehandlung U69-9
Pessarunterstützung U69-9
Pestizid **U81**-1; **U91**-8
-, chloriertes U91-8
Pestizidrückstand U91-8
Pestpneumonie U94-14
Pestsepsis /-septikämie U124-5
PET U99-19
Petechie **U89**-27; U38-8
Petit mal(-Epilepsie) U124-9
Petri-Schale U17-12
Pétrissage **U71**-10
Petroläther U11-23
Petting U62-10; U68-2
Peyer-Plaques **U35**-11
Pfählungsverletzung U5-2
Pfeife **U10**-19; **U67**-18
pfeifen **U67**-18
pfeifend atmen **U44**-7
Pfeiffer-Drüsenfieber **U94**-10,1; **U54**-1
Pfeifgeräusch U67-18
Pfeiler **U65**-13
pfeilförmig U129-4
Pfeilgift U93-17
Pfeilnaht U28-8; U29-14
Pferdeantitoxin U122-8
Pferdeenzephalitis U94-13
Pferdeschweif **U41**-15
Pferdeserum U91-15; U122-2
Pfiff **U67**-18
Pflanzenschutzmittel **U81**-1
Pflaster **U140**-21 f,3; U121-3; U141-11
Pflasterbinde, elastische **U141**-11
Pflasterverband **U141**-11
Pflege **U16**-2; **U71**-26
-, häusliche U18-7; U20-3; U120-1
-, individuelle U14-7
-, psychiatrische U77-16
-, stationäre U14-5; U15-4
Pflegeanamnese U16-2
Pflegeanweisungen U20-7

Pflegedienst U13-3; U14-3
Pflegedienstleiter(in) U16-2
Pflegeevaluation U16-2; U20-12
Pflegeforschung **U16**-2
Pflegeheim **U14**-3 f,8; U1-10; U16-2
Pflegeheimbewohner(in) U14-4
Pflegehelfer **U16**-14
Pflegeintervention U20-11
Pflegekind **U14**-8
Pflegekostenrückerstattung U14-3
Pflegemutter U16-2
pflegen (Patient) **U14**-8; **U16**-2; **U20**-3
-, sich **U19**-10
Pflegepersonal U15-2; U16-2
Pflegeplan U13-1
Pfleger **U16**-14
Pflegesatz U14-3
Pflegestation U19-1
Pflegevisite U20-9
Pflegeziel U16-2
Pflegschaft **U77**-25
Pflicht **U20**-4
Pflichtverletzung U20-4
Pflichtversäumnis U77-11
Pflugscharbein U28-9
Pfortader U34-4
Pfortaderdruck U36-3; U47-5
Pfortaderentzündung U36-3; U110-17
Pfortaderhochdruck U36-3,8; U47-5
-, intrahepatischer U47-6
Pfortaderkreislauf **U36**-3; U47-5; U82-17
Pfortaderstauung U110-13
Pfortadersystem **U36**-3
Pfortaderthrombose U36-3; U47-5
Pfortaderverschluss U36-3; U124-13
Pförtner **U45**-8
Phagolysosom U39-17; U83-6
Phagosom **U83**-11; U39-17
Phagozyt **U39**-17
Phagozytenaggregation U39-17
phagozytieren **U78**-19; U39-17; U83-11
Phagozytose **U39**-17; **U83**-15
Phagozytoseaktivität U39-17
Phagozytosedefekt U39-17
Phagozytosevakuole U39-17; U83-11
phalangeal **U28**-18
Phalanx **U28**-18
- proximalis U87-14
Phallus **U52**-14
Phänomen **U100**-5
Phänotyp(us) **U1**-8; **U84**-10
phänotypisch **U84**-10
Phantasie **U73**-9
Phantasien, erotische U68-9
Phantomglied U23-1
Phantomschmerz U142-6; U104-10
Pharmakodynamik U92-1
pharmakodynamisches Wirkprofil U121-8
Pharmakogenetik U84-1; U92-1
Pharmakognosie U92-1
Pharmakokinetik U92-1
pharmakokinetische Interaktion U121-11

Pharmakologe/-in **U15**-20
Pharmakologie **U92**-1
Pharmakopoe U15-20; **U92**-1
Pharmakotherapie U15-20
Pharmazeutik **U9**-4; **U92**-1
pharmazeutisch **U15**-20
Pharmazie **U9**-4; **U15**-20; **U92**-1
pharyngeal **U45**-4
Pharynx **U21**-12; **U45**-4
Phase, depressive U77-17
-, disperse U81-22
-, feste U82-6
-, genitale U50-1
-, iktale U74-8
-, phallische U52-14
-, prämitotische U83-12
-, präovulatorische U51-7
-, trockene U10-4
Phasenkontrastmikroskopie U86-1
Phencyclidin U11-15
Phenobarbital U11-16
Phenol(um) **U82**-13
Phenolgruppe U81-5
phenolisiert **U82**-13
Phenollösung, wässrige U82-13
Phenoloxidase U82-13
Phenolphthalein U82-13
Phenolvergiftung U82-13
Pheromone U81-1
Philtrum U21-9
Phimose, erworbene U52-17
Phlebitis **U110**-17
Phlebografie U110-17
Phlebothrombose **U124**-13; U34-4
Phlebotomie **U127**-18; U34-4
Phobie **U77**-5,21
-, soziale U77-5
Phonasthenie U66-10
Phonem U66-12
Phoniatrie U66-10
phonieren **U66**-13
phonisch **U66**-10
Phorbolester U82-14
Phosphatase U82-19
-, alkalische (AP) **U47**-15; U116-14
-, saure **U47**-15
Phosphatclearance U82-19
Phosphatpuffer U81-20
Phosphatstein U82-19
Phosphofruktokinase U82-19
Phospholipid **U47**-12
Phosphor **U82**-19
Phosphoreszenz **U99**-8
Phosphorsäure U82-19
Phosphorverbindung U82-19
Phosphorvergiftung U82-19
phosphorylieren **U78**-7
Phosphorylierung U82-19
-, oxidative U81-12,17; U83-7
Photoallergie U76-4
Photophobie **U103**-15
Photosensibilität U57-8
Phrenikus U40-1
Phrenikusstimulation U42-8

Phthirus pubis U90-15
pH-Wert **U81**-20
Physik **U15**-1
physikalisch **U25**-1
physikalische Medizin U142-1
– Therapie U120-4; **U142**-1
Physiker(in) U15-1
Physiognomie **U25**-10
physiognomisch **U25**-10
Physiologe/-in **U88**-1
Physiologie **U88**-1
physiologisch **U88**-1
Physiotherapeut(in) **U142**-1; U16-12
Physiotherapie **U142**-1; U120-4
–, manipulative U142-12
Physiotherapiebecken U142-1
physisch **U25**-1; **U77**-2; **U86**-20
Phytotoxin **U91**-4
Pia mater **U41**-8
Pick-Atrophie U77-23
Pickel **U25**-18; **U114**-9
Pickelgesicht U25-18
pickelig **U25**-18
Pick-Krankheit U77-23
Piebaldismus **U114**-4
Piepser **U17**-17
Piepssignal **U17**-17
Piepston **U17**-17; U61-3
Pigment **U114**-3
Pigmentepithel (Retina) U86-7
Pigmentfleck **U114**-3
pigmentieren **U114**-3
Pigmentierung, graubraune U56-3
Pigmentmal **U98**-15; **U114**-3
Pigmentmangel U114-3
Pigmentnävus **U114**-3; U25-19
Pigmentzelle **U56**-7
PIH U55-22
pikant **U62**-7
Pille **U69**-7; **U9**-7
– danach U69-7
–, große **U46**-9
–, hochdosierte U69-7
–, östrogenhaltige U69-7
Pillendrehertremor U113-4
Piloarrektion **U56**-14
Piloerektion **U56**-14; **U105**-8
Pilomotorenreaktion **U105**-8
Pilotstudie U101-1
Pilz **U90**-18
pilzabtötend U90-18
Pilzball U90-18
Pilze, essbare U2-1
–, halluzinogene U11-21
Pilzerkrankung U90-18; U92-26
Pilzfaden **U90**-18
pilzförmig U90-18
Pilzgeflecht **U90**-18
Pilzinfektion U90-18; U94-2
Pilzkultur U116-6
Pilzmeningitis U94-13
Pilzpneumonie U94-14
Pilzvergiftung U45-3; U91-2
pineal **U54**-13

Pinealom U54-13
Pinealozytom U54-13
Pinealzellen U54-13
Pink-puffer U111-3
Pinna **U60**-2
Pinozytose **U83**-15
pinseln U139-5
Pinzette **U132**-14,13
Pinzettengriff U64-9
PIP-Gelenk U28-18
Pityriasis U114-7
Pivotshift Test U29-4
Placebogruppe U100-3
Placeboresponder U101-8
plagen **U4**-5
Plakode **U85**-23
–, ektodermale U85-23
plantar **U23**-13; **U87**-17
Plantaraponeurose U23-13; U30-5,7
Plantarfibromatose U98-8
Plantarflexion U31-2; U87-17
Plantarreflex **U113**-1; U87-17
Planum **U87**-2
plappern **U66**-17,19
Plaque **U114**-10
– muqueuses U96-3
–, atheromatöse U78-16
–, lipidhaltige U24-5; U78-6
Plaquefissur U124-15
Plaqueruptur U124-15
Plaques, senile U80-13
Plasma seminis U53-6
–, frisch eingefrorenes U83-20
–, gepooltes U136-13
–, thrombozytenreiches U136-13
Plasmaalbumin U37-3; U78-18
Plasmaaustausch U37-3
Plasmaaustauschtherapie U136-13
Plasmabestandteile U136-13
Plasmacortisol U55-10
Plasmaderivat U37-3; U136-13
Plasmaersatz U37-3
Plasmaersatzstoff **U136**-13; U37-3
Plasmaexpander **U136**-13; U37-3
Plasmafluss, renaler **U49**-2; U36-5
Plasmafraktion U37-3; U136-13
–, kryopräzipitatarme U136-17
Plasmakonserve U14-12
Plasmalemm **U83**-2; U86-15
Plasmaosmolarität U49-9
Plasmapherese **U136**-15; U37-3
Plasmaproteine U37-3
–, phospholipidbindende U47-12
Plasmareninaktivität U88-14
Plasmareninkonzentration U49-11
Plasmathrombinzeit (PTZ) U116-13
Plasmaverdünnung U136-13
Plasmaviskosität **U36**-12
Plasmavolumen U36-7; U37-2 f
Plasmazelldyskrasie U37-10; U39-12
Plasmazellen **U37**-10, **U39**-12; U83-2
–, antikörperbildende U39-12
–, vereinzelte U37-10
Plasmazellenleukämie U39-12

Plasmid **U84**-8
plasmidvermittelt U84-8
Plasmin **U37**-15; **U38**-14
Plasmininhibitor U37-15
Plasminogen **U37**-15
Plasminogenaktivatorinhibitor U37-15
Plasminogen-Streptokinase-Aktivator-
komplex U81-14
Plasmozyt U83-2
Plastik **U127**-4; **U129**-1
Plastikklip U138-15
Plateauphase U42-7; U68-6
Plathelminth U90-16
Platin **U82**-28
Platinverbindung U82-28
Plättchenaggregationstest U38-11
Plättchenantikörper U37-11
Plättchenfaktoren U37-11
Plättchenthrombus U37-11
Plättchenwachstumsfaktor U37-11; U55-5
Platte **U86**-15; **U87**-2,8
– (Osteosynthese) **U141**-17
Plattenepithel **U86**-12; U98-2; U114-7
–, mehrschichtiges U56-2; U86-10,12
Plattenepithelbildung U140-6
Plattenepithelkarzinom **U98**-2,17; U86-12
Plattenepithelzelle U56-20
Plattenepithel-Zylinderepithel-Grenze U86-11
plattenförmig **U87**-2
Plattenosteosynthese **U141**-17
plattfüßig U23-13
Plattwurm U90-16
Platzangst U77-5
platzen **U5**-19; **U6**-9; **U89**-23
– (Follikel) U51-6
platzieren **U63**-1
Platzierung (Trokare) U133-5
Platzwunde **U5**-7
Plazebo **U101**-8
Plazeboresponder U120-11
Plazenta **U71**-16; **U85**-14
– adhaerens U71-16
– mit randständiger Insertion U71-16
–, anhaftende U71-16
Plazenta-AP U47-15
Plazentabarriere U36-15
Plazentabildung **U71**-16
Plazentadurchblutung U71-16
Plazentahormon U55-1
Plazentalaktogen **U55**-21
Plazentalösung, manuelle U71-16
plazentar **U71**-16
Plazentareste U70-2
Plazentaretention U71-16
Plazentaschranke U70-4; U71-16
Plazentation **U71**-16
Plegie **U135**-11
pleiotrop **U84**-22
Pleiotropie **U84**-22
pleomorph **U84**-22
Pleomorphismus **U84**-22

Pleozytose U38-5
Plessimeter **U17**-9; U107-8
Pleura **U43**-11
- costalis U28-14; U43-11
- mediastinalis U43-11
- parietalis U43-11
- pulmonalis U43-11; U87-13
- visceralis U43-11; U86-21
Pleurablatt U28-8; U43-11
Pleuraempyem **U111**-14,12
Pleuraerguss **U111**-12; U89-13
-, seröser U86-21
Pleurahöhle U43-11
Pleurakuppel U43-11
Pleuramesotheliom U86-14
Pleurapunktion U111-12
-, thorakoskopische U128-6
Pleuraraum U125-16
Pleurareiben **U111**-12; U43-11
Pleuraschwarte U43-11; U111-12
Pleuraschwiele U111-12
Pleuraspalt U43-11
Pleuraspülung U91-26
Pleuraverwachsung U29-12
Pleuritis **U94**-14; U111-12
pleuritisch **U43**-11
Pleurodese U128-6
plexiform **U40**-12
Plexus **U34**-5; **U40**-12
- choroidei U40-12; U41-17
- coeliacus U34-5; U40-12
- hypogastricus U22-8
- - inferior U40-12
- myentericus U40-12
- pelvinus U40-12
- solaris U34-5; U40-12
- vasculosus U34-5; U40-12
Plexusanästhesie U40-12
plexusartig **U40**-12
Plexuslähmung U40-12
Plica **U25**-17; **U87**-8; **U129**-8
- axillaris U23-3
- duodenalis superior U45-10
- duodenojejunalis U30-6
- epigastrica U22-3
- glossoepiglottica U45-4
- lacrimalis U58-9
- rectouterina U28-20
- synovialis U29-11; U87-8
- umbilicalis U22-5
- - lateralis U22-3
- - medialis U85-17
Plikation **U129**-8
Plumbum **U82**-32
Plummer-Vinson-Syndrom U109-5
pluriglandulär **U54**-1
Plurigravida **U70**-7
Pluripara **U70**-8
PMS U51-1
Pneumarthrografie U118-23
Pneumokokken-Pneumonie U94-14
Pneumomediastinum **U43**-13
Pneumonie **U94**-14; U43-2
-, interstitielle U86-19

Pneumonie, nosokomiale U94-14
-, persistierende U4-15
Pneumonitis **U94**-14; U43-2
Pneumoperitoneum **U128**-9; U45-7
Pneumoretroperitoneum **U128**-9
Pneumothorax, offener **U124**-17; U46-2
PNS **U40**-5
pochen (Herz) **U33**-1; **U110**-1
pochend U87-20
Pocken **U95**-7
pockenähnlich **U95**-7
Pockenschutzimpfung U122-3
Pockenvirus U90-10
Podologe/-login **U15**-15
Poikilozytose U38-5
Pol **U81**-13; **U87**-3
polar **U81**-13
Polarisationsmikroskopie U86-1
Poleinstellung **U71**-5
Polierpaste U27-19
Poliklinik **U14**-2; U20-2
Polioformolimpfstoff U122-2
Poliomyelitis **U95**-8
-, paralytische U135-11
Polioschluckimpfung U95-8; U122-2
Poliovakzine, inaktivierte U95-8
Politur U91-2
Pollakisurie **U112**-5,1; U70-9
Pollution U53-6,11
Polster **U17**-13; **U19**-5
polstern **U17**-13; **U19**-5; **U140**-19
Polsterschiene U19-5
Polstersessel U19-5
Polsterung **U140**-19; U141-9
Polsterwatte U29-10; **U140**-19
Polus occipitalis U87-3
- posterior U58-13
Polyarthritis, juvenile chronische U95-1
Polydipsie U112-2
Polyesternaht U137-10
Polyglykolsäure U81-6
polyklonal U84-33
Polymer **U81**-6; **U84**-36
-, stark verzweigtes U81-6
Polymerase-Kettenreaktion (PCR)
   U84-36
Polymerdiät U81-6
Polymerisation **U84**-36
Polymerisationstemperatur U82-7
polymerisieren U81-6
Polymerkette U81-6
Polymorphismus **U84**-22
Polyp **U98**-1
-, benigner U97-5
-, gestielter U89-22; U98-1
-, juveniler U98-1
-, neoplastischer U97-4
polyp(en)ähnlich **U98**-1
Polypektomie **U98**-1
-, endoskopische U98-1; U128-2
Polypenabtragung **U98**-1
Polypenschlinge U127-11
Polypeptid, gastrisches inhibitorisches
   U55-13

Polypeptid, vasoaktives intestinales
   U55-13
Polyphänie **U84**-22
polypös **U98**-1
Polypose **U98**-1
-, familiäre adenomatöse U98-1,4
Polyposis **U98**-1
Poly(ribo)som **U83**-9
Polysomnogramm **U72**-16
Polysomnografie U72-12
Polytrauma U5-4
Polyurethanverband U81-6
Polyurie **U112**-2
Pons cerebri **U41**-12
pontin **U41**-12
Pool(ing) **U78**-20
poolen **U78**-20
Poolplasma U136-13
Population **U100**-3
Populationsgenetik U84-1
Pore, erweiterte U56-11
Porenschluss U56-11
Porphyrinring U81-7
Port **U133**-5
Port(katheter)-System **U136**-5
Porta hepatis **U47**-5
portal **U47**-5
Portalkreislauf **U36**-3
Portioerosion U50-7; U114-13
Portiokappe **U69**-9
Portion **U2**-9; **U23**-2
Portografie U36-3; U47-5
Porus gustatorius U62-6
- sudoriferus U56-11
Positio (Foetus) **U71**-5
Position **U131**-11
-, anatomische U87-1
positionieren (Scheidendiaphragma)
   U69-9
Positionsklonierung U84-33
Positionswechsel U131-11
positiv **U116**-22
Positron **U81**-11
Positronenemissionscomputertomo-
   grafie U99-19
post mortem **U12**-19
post(h)um **U12**-19
posterior **U87**-16
postexpositionell **U122**-5
postexpositionelle Prophylaxe U120-6
postinfarziell **U124**-11
postkoital U50-7
Postkoitalpille **U69**-7
postkommotionelles Syndrom U5-14
Postmenopause U51-3
postmortal **U12**-19
postpartal **U71**-21
Postpartalperiode **U71**-21
Postpartum-Thyreoiditis U71-21
Postreplikationsreparatur U84-16
postsynaptisch **U40**-13
Postsynthesephase U83-12
posttransfusionell **U136**-8
Posttransfusionshepatitis U136-8

Posttranslationsmodifikation U84-19
Postulat **U101**-19
Potential, exzitatorisches U42-8
–, postsynaptisches U40-13; U42-8
–, teratogenes U91-12
Potentialdifferenz U42-5
Potentiale, akustisch evozierte (AEP) U61-2; U125-14
–, sensorisch evozierte U40-7
–, somatosensibel evozierte U40-7; U42-5
Potenz (Pharmakon) **U53**-2
–, sexuelle **U121**-9
potenzerhaltend **U53**-2
potenzieren U92-24
Potenzierung **U91**-19
Potomanie U77-18
Pott-Fraktur U106-10
Poupart-Band U22-9; U52-8
Power (Statistik) U100-1
Power-Lasertherapie U142-24
Prä-AIDS U96-15
Präalbumin U78-18
Prächordalplatte U85-20
Prädiktion **U100**-29
prädiktiver Parameter **U100**-29
prädisponiert **U119**-1
Prädisposition **U119**-1; U89-7
–, genetische U84-1
Prädispositionsfaktor U100-5
Präeklampsie U91-22
prägen **U74**-9
Prägung, genomische U84-1
prahlerisch U75-6
Präinfarkt-Angina U124-11
präkanzerös **U97**-5 f
Präkanzerose U5-5; U97-6
präkarzinomatös **U97**-5 f
präklinisch **U14**-1
präkordial **U22**-3
Präkordialgegend **U32**-1
Präkordialregion U22-3
Präkordialschmerz U22-3
Praktiker(in) **U18**-1
Praktikum U15-5
praktisch **U23**-6
praktizieren, als Arzt **U15**-8; **U18**-1; **U74**-6
prall gefüllt U58-14
prallen (auf) **U6**-2
Präludium **U68**-2
Prälungenödem U111-13
prämaligne U98-4
Prämaxilla **U28**-10
Prämedikation U9-1; U134-4; U93-2
prämenopausal U51-10
prämenstruell **U51**-1
Prämenstruum U51-8
Prämolar **U26**-6
prämorbid U75-1
präoperativ U134-6
Präparat **U118**-4; U9-1; U99-13
–, eingebettetes U82-15
–, formalinfixiertes U118-4

Präparation **U126**-12; U93-1
–, exakte U87-5
–, stumpfe U87-5; U128-14
–, weite U87-5
Präparierbesteck U132-1
präparieren **U87**-5; **U126**-12
Präpariermikroskop U86-1; U87-5
Präparierschere U132-4
Präproprotein **U78**-9
Präputium **U52**-17
präsentieren (Symptome) **U102**-1
Präservativ **U69**-6
Präsomitenembryo U85-1,19
prätransfusionelle Untersuchung U136-8
Prävalenz U13-10; **U100**-7
Prävalenzrate U100-7
Prävalenzstudie U101-1
Präventionsprogramm U6-22
präventiv **U120**-6
Präventivmaßnahmen U6-22; U20-11
Präventivmedizin U6-22; U120-6
Praxis **U15**-8,1; **U18**-1; **U126**-3
–, gutgehende U1-4
Praxisablauf U18-1
Praxisalltag **U18**-1
Präzipitat **U81**-27
Präzipitation **U81**-27
präzipitieren **U81**-27
Precursor **U78**-9
Precursorzelle U78-9
Prellung **U5**-13; **U6**-6
Preload **U33**-10
Presbyakusis **U61**-8
Presbyopie U59-12,17
Pressen **U64**-10,12,16; **U71**-11; U49-16
Pressorezeptor U57-10
Presswehen U71-3,11,15
prickeln **U62**-11; U104-17
Prick-Test **U118**-2,7; U5-10
Primar **U15**-3
Primäraffekt, syphilitischer U96-4
Primärantwort U39-2
Primararzt **U15**-3
Primärbehandlung U120-1
primäre Wundheilung U140-5
primärer Wundverschluss U140-3
Primärfollikel U51-6
Primärharn U49-12
Primärheilung U140-4; U141-1
Primärmedaillon U114-10; U119-3
Primärnaht U137-1; U140-3
Primärplaque U114-10
Primärpunktion **U128**-12
Primärreaktion U39-2
Primärtrokar **U133**-5
Primärtumor U97-2
Primärzotten U85-24
Primerverlängerung U84-34
Primigravida **U70**-7
Priming (Dialysator) U125-21
Primitivdarm **U85**-21,8
Primitivgrube **U85**-8
Primitivknoten **U85**-8

Primitivstreifen **U85**-8
primordial **U85**-9
Primordialfollikel U51-6; U85-9
Prinzmetal-Angina U124-11
Prion **U90**-11
Prionenkrankheit U90-11
Prionenprotein U90-11
Prise (Schnupftabak) U10-19
Pritschenwagen U6-3
Privatklinik U14-8; U16-2
Privatleben U102-9
Privatpraxis U18-11
Privatsphäre **U18**-11
Privatversicherung U18-11
Proakzelerin U37-14
Proband **U100**-2
Probe **U74**-6; **U118**-4
Probeexzision U107-6; U118-5; U126-9
Probeinzision U118-5
Probelaparotomie U126-11; U128-19
Probematerial U118-5
proben **U74**-6
Probenentnahme **U118**-4; U117-3
Probenglas **U17**-12
Probenkennzeichnung U118-4
Probepunktion U118-7; U126-11
Probethorakotomie U125-16
probieren **U62**-6
Probleme, psychische U77-1
problemlos U4-16
Problemstoffe U124-2
Processus **U28**-5; **U87**-27
– caudatus (hepatis) U87-19
– condylaris mandibulae U29-6
– coracoideus U30-11
– coronoideus mandibulae U28-10
– – ulnae U28-16
– mastoideus **U60**-14; U28-5
– spinosus U28-5,19
– styloideus U28-16
– xiphoideus U28-13; U30-14
Prodrom **U119**-4
prodromal **U119**-4
Prodromalstadium U119-4
Prodromalsymptom U103-1
produzieren **U54**-2
Proenzym **U78**-8
Proerythrozyt **U35**-12; U119-4
profitieren (von) **U1**-5; U4-4
Progenitorzellen, hämatopoetische U38-1
Progestagen **U55**-19
Progesteron **U55**-19
Progesterontest U55-19
Progesteronzäpfchen U55-19
Progestogen **U55**-19
Prognose **U119**-19
Prognoseindex U119-19
prognostisch **U119**-19
prognostizieren **U119**-19; U125-4
progredient **U4**-12; **U97**-7; **U119**-12
Progredienz **U119**-12
Progression **U119**-12
–, ständige U97-7

progressiv U97-7
Prohormon U55-1; U78-9
Proinsulin U55-12
Prokaryo(n)t U83-3
prokaryont(isch) U83-3
Prokaryontenribosomen U84-15
Prokaryontentyp U83-3
Prokonvertin U37-14
Proktoskopie U45-16
Prolabium U21-9
Prolaktin U55-22,15
Prolaktinbestimmung U55-22
Prolaktinfreisetzung U55-22
Prolaktinhemmer U55-22
Prolaktinkonzentration, erhöhte U55-22
Prolaktinom U55-22
Prolaktoliberin U55-22
Prolaktostatin U55-22
Prolaps U89-22; U113-17
Prolapsus uteri U50-5
Proliferation U92-9
Proliferationsphase U51-7
proliferieren U97-7
Prometaphase U83-13
Prominentia U87-27
- laryngea U21-14; U43-7
Promiskuität U68-12
promiskuös U68-12
Promonozyt U37-9
Promontorium U28-4
Promotionsfeier U17-16
Promotor U84-21
Promotorregion U84-2,21
Pronation U31-9
Pronator U31-9
Pronephros U85-21,9
pronieren U31-9
proniert U31-9
Pronukleusstadium U69-12
Propanon U82-1
Prophase U83-13
prophylaktisch U120-6
Prophylaxe U6-22; U120-6
-, postexpositionelle U122-5
Propriorezeptor U57-11
Propriozeption U57-11,14; U142-19
propriozeptiv U57-11
Proprotein U78-9
Prosektor U126-12
Prosencephalon U41-1
prospektiv U101-6
Prostaglandin U78-24
Prostaglandin(bio)synthese U78-24
Prostaglandinantagonist U78-24
Prostaglandinfreisetzung U78-24
Prostaglandinsynthetase-Hemmer U78-24
Prostansäure U78-24; U82-10
Prostata U52-10
Prostatabeschwerden, chronische U52-10; U112-6
Prostataexprimat U52-10
Prostatagewebe U52-10

Prostatahyperplasie U52-10
-, benigne U89-15; U108-12
Prostatakapsel U29-9; U52-10
Prostatakarzinom U97-10
Prostataleiden, chronisches U52-10
Prostatamassage U52-10
Prostataphosphatase, saure U47-15
Prostatastein U52-10
Prostatavergrößerung U52-10
Prostatektomie U112-12; U22-10
Prostatismus U52-10; U112-6
Prostration U4-6; U103-8; U104-5
Protease U79-9
Protein U79-9
-, mikrotubulusassoziiertes U83-5
-, ribosomales U83-9
Proteinelektrophorese U84-35
Protein-Energie-Mangelsyndrom U79-3; U82-25
Proteinkinase, cAMP-abhängige U83-17
proteinkodierende Region U84-2
Proteinurie U78-18; U79-9
Proteinvorstufe U78-9
Proteoglykan U79-9
Proteohormon U55-1
Proteolyse U78-14,4,10; U81-8
proteolytisch U79-9
Prothese U142-6; U129-2
Prothesenanpassung U142-6
Prothesenbasis U27-8
Prothesenbauer(in) U142-6
Protheseneinbau U129-2
Prothesenrand U26-23
Prothesenreiniger U27-8
prothesentragend U27-8
Prothetik U82-31
Prothrombin U37-13
Prothrombinaktivator U37-13
Prothrombinkomplex U81-14
Prothrombinkomplexkonzentrat U37-13; U136-17
Prothrombinverbrauchstest U37-13
Prothrombinzeit U37-13; U116-13
Protium U82-9
Protokoll U101-7
protokollieren U20-5; U102-12
- (Befund) U117-6
Proton U81-11
Protonenpumpenhemmer U81-11
Protoplasma U83-2
Protoplasmaausstülpung U90-4
Protozoeninfektion U90-2
Protozoon U90-2
Protozoonose U90-2
protrahiert U119-10
Protraktion U141-3
Protrusio bulbi U113-17
Protuberantia mentalis U21-6
- occipitalis interna U87-27
Protuberanz U87-27
Provirus U90-10
Provitamin U78-9; U79-13
- A U78-9

Provokationstest U117-12; U118-2
proximal U26-22; U87-14
Prozentsatz U100-8
Prozess, energieverbrauchender U78-12
prüde U68-10
prüfen U107-1; U116-2
Prüfung U20-12
Prüfvariable U101-10
Pruritus U103-19; U92-22
- ani U45-17; U103-19
- vulvae U50-11
prusten U66-5
PSA U52-10; U97-9
Pseudarthrose U29-1; U106-15
Pseudoaszites U109-9
Pseudobulbärparalyse U113-7
Pseudodemenz U77-23
Pseudohämaturie U112-3
Pseudohermaphroditismus U53-12
Pseudokrupp U95-10
Pseudoleukoderm U114-4
Pseudologia phantastica U74-18
Pseudomembran U86-15; U95-9
Pseudomilium colloidale U114-6
Pseudopodium U90-4
Pseudorubella U95-3
pseudostratifiziert U86-10
Pseudozylinder U112-14
Pseudozyste U89-24
Psittakose U90-14; U96-9
Psoasabszess U30-15
Psoaszeichen U30-15; U113-1
Psoriasis U89-2; U114-7
- guttata, akute exanthematische U114-2
- pustulosa U114-12
Psyche U77-2
Psychedelikum U15-12
Psychiater(in) U15-12,8; U77-16
Psychiatrie U15-12; U77-16
-, dynamische U77-16
-, forensische U15-12
-, kommunale U77-16
-, psychoanalytische U77-16
psychiatrisch U15-12
psychiatrischer Betreuer U16-8
psychisch U15-12
- Kranke(r) U77-13; U73-2
Psychoanalytiker(in) U15-12; U77-21
Psychodelikum U11-21
psychodelisch U11-21; U77-2
Psychodynamik U77-16
Psychodysleptikum U11-21
psychogen U77-2
Psychohygiene U1-5; U77-1
Psychologe/-in U15-12
psychomotorisch U40-4
Psychopath(in) U77-24
Psychopathie U77-24
Psychopharmakologie U77-21
Psychopharmakon U92-23; U9-3
Psychose U77-21
-, affektive U76-2; U77-13

Psychose, bipolare U77-16
-, hypothyroide U77-15
-, organische U77-1,21
Psychosomatik U77-14
psychosoziale Betreuung **U77**-25
Psychostimulans U15-12; U57-1
Psychotherapeut(in) U15-12
Psychotherapie U15-12
Psychotiker(in) **U77**-21
psychotisch **U77**-21
Psychotomimetikum **U11**-21; U15-12
Psychotonikum U15-12
PTB-Unterschenkelschaft U142-6
PTH **U54**-7
Ptose **U113**-17; **U89**-22
Ptosis **U64**-15; U56-19; U58-3
– congenita U113-17
PTT U37-14
Ptyalismus U45-3
Pubarche **U80**-7
puberal **U80**-7
Pubertas praecox U68-1; U80-7
– tarda U80-7
Pubertät **U80**-7
Pubertätsbeginn **U80**-7
Pubertätsgynäkomastie U80-7
pubertierend **U80**-7; U50-17
Pubes **U52**-19; U56-13
Pubis **U28**-22
Pudendum femininum **U50**-11; **U52**-20
Pudendusanästhesie U22-10; U52-20
Pudendusblock U50-11; U52-20; U93-6
Puder **U9**-9,8; **U91**-7
Puerpera **U71**-21
Puerperalfieber U71-21; U124-5
Puerperalsepsis U124-5
Puerperium **U71**-21; U15-16
Puffer **U81**-20
Pufferbase U81-20
Pufferkapazität U81-20
Pufferlösung U81-20
puffern **U81**-20
Puffersystem U81-20
Pulex irritans U90-15
Pulley, A2- U130-8
Pulmo **U43**-1
pulmonal **U43**-2
Pulmonalarterienkatheter **U125**-7
Pulmonaliskatheterisierung U125-7
Pulmonalklappe U32-10; U43-2
Pulmonal(klappen)insuffizienz U43-2; U110-10
Pulmones **U43**-1
Pulpa (dentis) **U26**-18
– (Milz) U35-4
Pulpafreilegung U26-18
Pulpakavum U26-18
Pulpaüberkappung U26-18
Puls(schlag) **U107**-13
Puls, flacher U36-9
–, paradoxer U36-9; U110-8
–, schnellender U33-8; U64-7
–, schwacher U4-7; U7-4; U103-9
–, unregelmäßiger U64-7

Pulsader **U34**-3
Pulsamplitude U107-13
Pulsation(en) **U107**-13
–, epigastrische U36-9
Pulsdefizit U36-9; U107-13
Pulsdruck **U36**-9; U107-13
Pulse, periphere U87-14f
Pulsfeldelektrophorese U84-35
Pulsfrequenz **U107**-13; U33-5; U36-9
pulsierend **U36**-9; **U107**-13
pulslos **U36**-9
Pulsoxymetrie **U125**-9; U36-9 ; U118-3
Pulsqualität U107-13
Pulsschreiber U17-8
pulssynchron **U36**-9; U89-26
Pulsus **U107**-13
– celer U33-8
– – et altus U110-12
– dicrotus U107-13
– paradoxus U107-13; U110-8
Pulswelle **U36**-9; **U107**-13
Pulswellenanstieg U36-9
Pulswellengeschwindigkeit U36-9
Pulswellenlaufzeit U36-9
Pulver **U9**-9; **U91**-7
pulverisiert **U9**-9
pummelig **U25**-6
Pumpversagen **U110**-14
–, therapierefraktäres linksventrikuläres U125-8
Punctum lacrimale U58-9
– maximum **U33**-4
– –, großflächiges U33-4
– proximum U59-13
Punkteschema U100-6
Punktezahl U100-6
Punktion **U6**-7; **U17**-11; **U64**-11; **U118**-7; **U136**-2
–, subdurale U41-8
Punktionsflüssigkeit **U127**-16
Punktionskanüle U136-3,6
Punktionsnarbe U17-11; U114-3
Punktionsschale U118-7
Punktionsstelle U6-7; U132-5; U136-2
Punktionszytologie U83-1; U118-9
Punktmutation U84-20
Punktprävalenz U100-7
Punktschmerz U104-11
Punktschmerz(haftigkeit) U109-12
Pupillarreflex U107-15
Pupille **U58**-8; U21-3; U7-7,14
Pupillen prompt/seitengleich **U107**-15
–, erweiterte U58-8
–, lichtstarre U58-8
–, ungleiche U58-8
–, weite U58-8
Pupillenerweiterung U107-15
Pupillengleichheit U58-8; U107-15
Pupillenöffnung U107-15
Pupillenprüfung U58-8
Pupillenreaktion U58-8; U107-15
Pupillenreflexe U58-8
Pupillenträgheit U58-8
pupillenverengend **U59**-10

Pupillenverengung **U59**-10; U107-15
Purganzien U91-24; U92-13
Purging U38-2
Purinantagonist U78-11
Purinantimetabolit U78-11
Purinbasen U84-12
Purkinje-Fasern **U32**-15
Purpura Schoenlein-Henoch U124-3
–, thrombotisch-thrombozytopenische U136-15
purpuraartig U89-27
purulent **U89**-12; U114-16; **U140**-14
Pus **U89**-12
Pustel **U114**-12; U95-7; U140-9
Pustula **U114**-12
Putamen U41-10
Putreszenz **U46**-17
p-Wert U100-21
Pyelografie, intravenöse **U118**-19
Pyelogramm U48-3
Pyelon **U48**-3; U28-21
Pyelonephritis U48-3
Pyeloplastik U48-3
pyknisch (Körperbau) **U25**-2,6
Pylephlebitis U36-3; U110-17
Pylorus **U45**-8
Pylorusdrüsen U45-8
Pylorusobstruktion U45-8; U109-6
Pylorusstenose U89-20
Pyothorax U111-14
Pyramidenbahn **U41**-16,6; U86-23
Pyramidenbahnläsion U41-16
Pyramidenbahnzeichen U41-16
Pyramidenfasern U41-14
Pyramidenkreuzung **U41**-14
Pyramidenseitenstrangbahn U41-16
Pyramidenzellen U41-16
Pyramides renales U48-2
Pyretikum **U105**-4
Pyrexie **U105**-3
Pyridoxalphosphat U82-19
Pyrimidinbasen U84-12
Pyrogen **U105**-4
–, endogenes U88-10
Pyrolyse U78-10
Pyromane/-in **U6**-10
Pyrosis **U109**-4
Pyruvatdehydrogenase-Komplex U81-14
Pyurie, sterile U112-1

Q

Quacksalber **U15**-23
Quacksalberei **U15**-23
Quaddel **U114**-11; U56-1
Quadrant **U26**-20
Quadratsummen U100-34
Quadriplegie U113-7
Quadrizepssehnenreflex U30-16
Qual **U77**-5; U107-11
Qualitätsbeurteilung **U20**-12
Quallenvergiftung U91-20

Qualm **U6**-10
qualvoll (Schmerzen) U104-9
Quantensprung U65-16
Quantifizierung U83-21
Quarantäne **U14**-10
Quarantänemaßnahmen U14-10
quarantänepflichtig **U14**-10
Quarantänestation **U14**-10
Quarantänezeit U14-10
Quartile **U100**-11
Quarz **U82**-30
Quarzstaub U82-30
Quarzstaublunge **U82**-30
Quecksilber **U82**-32; U105-6
–, flüssiges U82-4
Quecksilberamidchlorid U82-32
Quecksilberdampf U82-3,32
Quecksilberfulminat U82-32
quecksilberhaltig **U82**-32
Quecksilberintoxikation **U82**-32
Quecksilberpräparat **U82**-32
Quecksilbertoxizität U91-11
Quecksilberverbindung **U82**-32
Quecksilbervergiftung **U82**-32
Quecksilberzittern U82-32
Quelle U1-18
–, exogene U88-10
quellen (Naht) U137-7; U138-7
Quellstoffe U79-16
Quellungsreaktion U81-15
quengelig **U64**-17
Querbrücke U78-10
queren **U87**-7
Querfraktur U106-1
quergestreift (Muskel) U48-15; U93-16
Querinzision U126-9
Querlage U71-5
Querschnitt **U87**-5; **U126**-10,14
Querschnittgelähmte(r) **U142**-5
Querschnittsfläche U87-5; U126-10
Querschnittslähmung **U142**-5
Querschnittstudie U87-5; U101-1
Quetelet-Index **U24**-7
quetschen **U64**-10
Quetschung **U5**-13,2; **U6**-6; U64-10
Quetschwunde U5-13; U6-6
Quick-Wert U116-13
Quotient **U100**-8

R

Rabenschnabelfortsatz U30-11
Rabies **U94**-12
Rachen **U21**-12; **U45**-4; U95-6
Rachenabstrich U103-5; U116-5
Rachendiphtherie U95-9
Rachenmandel U21-12; U35-6
Rachenring, lymphatischer U35-5
Rachenspülproben U91-26
Rachitis **U95**-11; **U31**-14; U82-5
Rad (Strahlungsdosis) **U99**-10
Radgelenk **U29**-4
Radialispuls U28-16; U107-13

Radiatio optica U58-15
Radikal **U81**-5
–, freies U78-19; U81-5
Radikalfänger **U78**-19; U39-17
Radikalgruppe **U81**-5
radioaktiv **U99**-21
– markiert U99-1 f
radioaktives Implantat U132-7; U99-21
Radioaktivität **U99**-21
Radioiod U82-22,34
Radioiodaufnahme U55-3
Radioiodtest U99-21
Radioiodtherapie U82-22
Radioisotop **U82**-1,34; U99-22
Radioisotopennephrogramm U82-1
Radioisotopennephrografie **U99**-22
Radiokobalt U82-25
Radiokohlenstoff U82-10
radiolog.-techn. Assistent(in) U16-10
Radiologe/-login **U15**-13; **U99**-1
Radiologie **U15**-13; **U99**-1
radioluzent **U99**-11
Radiomimetikum U99-2
Radionuklid **U82**-1,34; **U99**-22,17
Radionuklidangiografie U118-16
Radioonkologie U97-1
radiopak **U99**-11
Radiopharmakon U99-2,21
Radiosensitizer U99-23
Radium **U82**-34
Radiumtherapie U82-34
Radius **U28**-16
Radiusfraktur **U106**-10
Radiusköpfchenepiphyse U28-3
Radiusköpfchensubluxation U23-4
Radiusperiostreflex U31-9
Radix **U87**-25
– dentis **U26**-19; U87-25
– linguae U21-11; U87-25
– penis U52-14
– pili U56-13
– pulmonis **U43**-4; U87-25
Radon **U82**-34
Radonseed U82-34
Radontochternuklide U82-34
Raffnaht **U137**-18
Ramus **U28**-5; **U34**-13
– ascendens U34-13
– descendens U28-5
– inferior ossis pubis U52-18
– ossis pubis U28-5
– pubicus U22-8
– superior ossis pubis U52-18
Rand(zone) **U87**-10,15; U30-12
Rand, deutlich erkennbarer U87-10
Ränder, erhabene U64-16; U65-17; U96-4
–, schlecht abgrenzbare U97-3
randomisiert U101-12
Randomisierung **U101**-5
Randschärfe U99-14
randständig **U87**-10
Randulkus U89-17
Ranvier-Schnürring **U40**-15; U42-3
Raphe scroti U52-2

Rapport **U102**-16
Raptus U77-7
rasch U59-10
Raschelgeräusch U61-3
rasen **U65**-15
rasend **U77**-15
– (Schmerzen) U104-9
Raserei U94-12
rasieren **U25**-16
Rasierzeug U25-16
Raspatorium **U132**-12
Raspel **U132**-12
Rasse **U84**-30
Rasselgeräusch(e) **U111**-8 f; U44-7
–, pfeifende(s) U67-18
–, feuchte(s) U105-13
Rasseln U107-9
Rastermutation U84-20
Rasterverschiebung U84-21
rastlos **U64**-17; **U76**-8
Rastlosigkeit **U76**-8
Rasur **U25**-16
–, präoperative U139-14
Rat, ärztlicher **U18**-4
–, kompetenter U18-4
Rate **U100**-8
raten **U18**-4 f
Rate-response-Schrittmacher U123-13
Ratgeber, praktischer U18-1
rational **U73**-7
ratsam **U18**-4
Rattenbissfieber U90-8 f
Rattenfloh U90-15
Rattengift U91-2
rau **U103**-6; U62-8
– (Stimme) U21-12
Raubwanze U90-5
Rauch **U6**-10; **U10**-16; **U82**-3; **U91**-7
–, kalter U62-4
Rauchen **U10**-16; U44-7
Raucher(in) **U10**-16
Raucherentwöhnung U10-16 f
Raucherentwöhnungsberatung U16-12; U18-4
Raucherentwöhnungsseminar U14-2
Raucherfinger U10-19
Raucherherz U10-16
Raucherhusten U10-16
rauchfrei **U10**-16
Rauchgas **U82**-3
Rauchgewohnheiten U10-11
rauchig **U44**-1
Rauchmelder U6-10; U91-7
Rauchopiate U11-18
Rauchwolke U6-10
Raum, intervillöser U45-14
–, schalldichter U60-13; U61-3
Raumforderung U89-3; U97-3
–, intrakranielle U125-13
raumfüllend **U79**-16
Raumluft U19-2
Räumung **U8**-3
Rausch, im **U10**-5
Rauschdroge **U9**-3

Rauschgift **U11**-1; **U135**-5
Rauschgiftsüchtige(r) U11-1
Rauschmittel **U10**-5; **U135**-5f; U9-3
Rauschmittelintoxikation U10-5
Rauschzustand **U10**-5; **U91**-14; U11-23
räuspern, sich **U103**-17,5; **U66**-6
Rautenhirn U41-1
Raynaud-Krankheit U110-19
– Phänomen **U110**-19
– Syndrom **U110**-19
reabsorbieren **U49**-4
Reabsorption **U49**-4; **U88**-8
Reagens **U81**-15
Reagenz **U81**-15
Reagenzglas U101-18
Reagenzglasbefruchtung U69-12
Reagenzstreifen U81-15
Reagibilität **U39**-2; **U7**-7
reagieren **U39**-2; **U7**-7
– (auf Therapie) **U120**-11
Reaktion **U120**-11; U57-1
– (chemische/physikalische) **U116**-2
– vom Soforttyp, IgE-vermittelte U39-23
– – Spättyp, zellvermittelte U39-23
–, affektive U113-3
–, alkalische U81-15
–, allergische U39-23
–, anaphylaktische **U124**-3
–, basische U81-15
–, chemische **U81**-15
–, depressive U76-22
–, deziduale U85-13
–, exergone U81-15
–, humorale U88-9
–, hysterische **U77**-6
–, lytische U81-22
–, neurohumorale U88-9
–, reversible U81-15
Reaktionsaudiometrie, elektrische U61-2
Reaktionsfähigkeit **U39**-2; **U7**-7
Reaktionsgleichung, chemische U81-1
Reaktionspartner **U81**-15
Reaktionsunfähigkeit **U7**-11; U135-6
Reaktivität **U81**-15
Realangst **U77**-5
realisieren **U74**-4
Reanastomosierung U69-4
Reanimation **U123**-4; U126-1
–, kardiopulmonale U42-6; U110-9
Reanimationsausrüstung U14-7; U123-4
Reanimationsbescheinigung U18-10
Reanimationsgeräte U14-7
Reanimationsmaßnahmen U8-11
–, erweiterte **U125**-3; U123-4
–, primäre **U123**-4
Reanimationsteam U125-3
Reanimationstechniken U13-12
Reanimationsversuche U123-4
Reanimationsverzicht U117-18
Reanimationszimmer U19-2
Reanimator **U123**-4
reanimieren **U123**-3

Rearrangement **U84**-24
Rebound-Phänomen U124-7
Receiver-Operating-Characteristic Kurve U100-34
Recessus U50-15
– cochlearis U60-11
– pinealis U54-13
Rechnungslegung **U18**-15
rechteckig U130-14
rechthaberisch **U75**-17
Rechtschreibübungen U74-6
Rechts(herz)insuffizienz U124-12
–, dekompensierte U110-12
Rechtsherzbelastung U5-17
Rechtsherzvergrößerung U110-9
Rechts-Links-Shunt U36-14
Rechts-Links-Störung U77-4
Rechtsverschiebung U64-4
Recklinghausen-Krankheit U98-13
Recoveryposition U8-17
Rectus abdominis **U30**-14
Rede U66-8
Rededrang U66-9
Redefluss, ungehemmter U77-18
Redeflussstörung U66-16
Redegewandtheit **U66**-18
redlich **U75**-12
Redoxpaar U81-12,17
Redoxpotential U81-17
Redoxreaktion **U81**-17,15
Redoxsystem U81-17
Redoxzahl U81-17
Redressionsgips U141-6
redselig **U66**-18; U75-5
Reduktion **U81**-17; **U129**-19
Reduktionskost U2-12
Reduktionsteilung **U83**-14; U85-3
Reduplikation **U84**-16
Reduviidae U90-5
reduzieren **U116**-20
–, allmählich U121-6
Reduzierhülse **U133**-11
Reduzierplättchen **U133**-11
Reduzierstück **U133**-11
Reepithelisation U86-7
reepithelisieren **U86**-7
Reexpansionsödem U111-13
Referenzbereich U100-15; U116-9
Referenzwert U116-16
Refertilisierung **U69**-4
reflektorisch **U42**-12; **U113**-1
Reflex **U42**-12; **U64**-7; U102-3
–, bedingter U42-12
–, konditionierter U42-12
–, nozizeptiver U57-13
–, okulokardialer U58-2
–, propriozeptiver U57-11
–, übersteigerter U112-8
–, vasomotorischer U36-11
–, vestibulookulärer U60-9
–, viszeraler U86-21
Reflexabschwächung U42-12
Reflexantwort U42-12; U113-1
Reflexantwort, gesteigerte U112-8

Reflexbahnen U40-3
Reflexbewegung U42-12
Reflexblase U48-11; U112-8; U113-1
Reflexbogen **U42**-12; U17-9
Reflexe auslösen U42-12
–, abgeschwächte U17-3; U42-12
–, erloschene U42-12
–, frühkindliche U80-4
–, gesteigerte U12-12
–, koordinierte U31-19
–, lebhafte U42-12
–, nicht auslösbare U42-12
–, verminderte U116-20
Reflexhammer **U17**-9; U42-12
Reflexhandlung U42-12
Reflexhemmung **U42**-13; U17-9
Reflexinkontinenz U112-15
Reflexion **U73**-6
Reflexionsspektrophotometrie U83-21
Reflexkrampf U42-12
Reflexlatenz U42-12
Reflexprüfung U17-9
Reflexzeit U42-12
Reflexzentrum U42-12
Reflexzonenmassage U142-15
Reflux **U103**-12; **U112**-12; U116-15
–, gastroösophagealer **U109**-4
–, hepatojugulärer U47-1
–, postprandialer U46-4
–, pyelorenaler U112-12
–, vesikoureteraler U48-12; U112-12
Refluxgeräusch U110-10
–, kardiales U110-3
refluxiv **U112**-12
Refluxkrankheit U109-3
Refluxnephropathie U112-12
Refluxösophagitis U109-4
Refluxtest, hepatojugulärer U22-4
Reformkost U1-1; U2-6
refraktär **U120**-13
Refraktärphase **U42**-7
Refraktärverhalten **U42**-7
Refraktärzeit U120-13
Refraktion **U59**-12
Refraktionsamblyopie U59-12
Refraktionsanomalien U59-12
Refraktionsbestimmung U59-12
Refraktur **U106**-1
refundiert U18-15
rege **U7**-2
Regel **U20**-7
Regelblutung **U51**-2f,10
–, ausgebliebene U70-6
–, erste **U51**-3
–, letzte **U51**-3,10
–, starke U51-2
regelmäßig **U33**-6
Regelung **U20**-7; **U88**-2
regen, (sich) **U64**-3
Regenbogenhaut **U58**-8
Regendusche U1-19
Regeneration **U1**-10
regenerieren (sich) **U1**-10
Regio epigastrica U45-8

Regio glutaea U22-13
- hypochondriaca sinistra U22-4
- inguinalis **U22**-9
- scapularis U28-12
Region, genreiche **U84**-2
-, konstante U39-3
-, variable U39-3
Regionalanästhesie **U93**-2
Register (Organtransplantation) U13-10
registrieren **U20**-5; **U74**-9; **U102**-12
Registriergerät U20-5
Regler **U54**-3
Regression **U100**-33; **U119**-17
Regressionsgerade U100-33
Regressionskoeffizient U100-33
Regressionsmodell, lineares U100-35
Regulation **U88**-2
-, enzymatische U54-3
-, humorale U88-9
Regulationsstörung U88-2
Regulatorgen U54-3
Regulatorprotein U88-2
regulieren **U54**-3; **U65**-6; **U88**-2
- (nach oben/unten) **U83**-18
Regurgitation **U46**-4; **U103**-12
Regurgitationsgeräusch U110-10
Regurgitationsvolumen U110-10
Regurgitationswelle U110-10
Regurgitieren **U46**-4; U110-10
-, saures U46-4
regurgitierend **U110**-10
Rehabilitation **U142**-2
-, orale U129-2
Rehabilitationseinrichtung **U11**-13; U142-2,28
Rehabilitationshilfen U142-2
Rehabilitationsmaßnahmen U142-2
Rehabilitationstherapie U142-1 f
Rehabilitationszentrum U142-2
Rehabilitationsziele U142-2
Rehydratation, i.v. U136-5
Rehydratationslösung U78-22
Rehydratationstherapie, orale U78-22
Reibegeräusch **U106**-14; U33-1; U43-4
-, hochfrequentes U111-12
-, hörbares U110-8
-, perikardiales U17-2; U32-5
reiben **U62**-11; **U64**-11
Reiben **U62**-11; U33-1
-, perikardiales U110-8
Reibmassage U142-15
Reibung U17-14; U29-10; U68-2
reich an U2-13; U137-14
reichen **U23**-6
reichlich vorhanden U79-17
reif U85-2
Reife **U80**-10
Reifebestimmung (Neugeborene) U80-4
reifen **U80**-10
Reifenbahre **U19**-4
Reifeprozess **U80**-10
Reifeteilung **U83**-14
-, erste U83-14; U85-3

Reifgeborenes U70-11; U80-4
Reifung U55-14; U69-17; U73-5
Reihe (Patienten) **U100**-3
Reihenuntersuchungen U1-1
reinerbig U85-2
Reinfarkt U124-11
Reinfektion, exogene U88-10
reinfundieren **U136**-1
Reinheit U13-9; U116-3
reinigen U49-7; **U139**-5; U140-1
Reinigung, gründliche U15-13
-, mukoziliäre **U44**-9
Reinigungslotion U9-10
Reinigungsmechanismus U44-9
Reinigungsmittel **U139**-5
Reinkultur U84-30; U116-6
reinnervieren **U42**-1
reinrassig U84-30
Reisediarrhoe/-ö U109-10
Reisefähigkeit U1-9
Reiseimpfung U122-3
Reisekrankheit U6-17; U103-11
Reiserücktrittsversicherung U13-5
reißen **U64**-13; U69-6; **U89**-23
Reithosenfettsucht U24-9
Reitunfall U6-1
Reiz **U42**-5,8; **U57**-1; **U88**-12
-, afferenter U40-4
-, akustischer U42-5; U57-1
-, bedingter U57-1; U88-12
-, konditionierter U57-1; U88-12
-, optischer U57-1
-, propriozeptiver U42-2
-, schädlicher U57-1; U88-12
Reizantwort U57-1
reizbar **U76**-7
-, leicht **U62**-8; **U108**-13
Reizbarkeit **U76**-7; **U108**-13
Reizblase **U112**-4; U48-11
Reizdarm U45-9
Reizdarmsyndrom U103-20
reizen **U42**-8
reizend **U81**-1
Reizgas U81-1; U82-2
Reizgifte U91-2
Reizkolon U45-9,15; U109-6
Reizleitung U42-5
-, verzögerte U42-2
reizlos **U62**-7
Reizmagen U108-13
Reizmittel **U81**-1; U92-14
Reizschwelle U123-13
-, sensorische U57-7
Reizschwellenbestimmung U123-13
Reizstärke U57-1
Reizstoff **U81**-1
Reizstrom **U142**-23
Reizübertragung U42-2
Reizung **U89**-10; **U104**-3
-, galvanische U42-8
Rejektion **U39**-22
Rejektionstherapie U39-22
Rekanalisation U52-6

Rekanalisation (Samenleiter) **U69**-4
rekapitulieren U74-7
Rekombinante **U84**-17
Rekombinanten-DNA-Technik U84-17
Rekombination, genetische **U84**-17
Rekompression **U6**-17
Rekonstruktion **U129**-1
Rekonvaleszent(in) **U4**-16
Rekonvaleszentenserum U4-16
Rekonvaleszenz **U4**-16; **U134**-14,7
Rekrutierungschance U101-5
rektal **U45**-16
Rektalabstrich U45-16
Rektal-Hohlsonde U132-8
Rektaltemperatur U45-16
Rektalzäpfchen U45-16; U103-11
Rektozelen U51-10
Rektum **U45**-16
Rektumbiopsie U45-16
Rektumprolaps U45-16; U89-22
Rektusdiastase U30-14
Rektusscheide U30-14
rekurrent **U119**-18
Relais **U42**-4
Relaiskern U42-4
Relaxans **U31**-1; **U76**-19; U93-16
Relaxation U1-10; **U31**-1
Releasing-Faktor U54-4
Releasing-Hormon U54-4
relevant **U102**-8
Reliabilität **U100**-30,23
REM **U99**-10
REM-Entzug U72-10
Remission **U4**-14; **U119**-17; U104-8
remittierend **U119**-17
REM-Rebound U72-10
- Schlaf **U72**-10,9
- Schlafmuster U72-10
- Schlafphase U72-10
- Zunahme, plötzliche U72-10
Ren **U48**-2
- arcuatus U48-2
- duplex U48-2
- lobatus U87-23
- mobilis U48-2; U64-2
Renin **U55**-25
Reninaktivität U49-11
Renin-Angiotensin-Aldosteron-System **U49**-11; U55-25
Reninausschüttung U49-11
Reninfreisetzung U49-11; U55-25
Renshaw-Hemmung U42-13
Renshaw-Zelle **U42**-13
Rente **U80**-14
Rentenalter U80-14
Rentner(in) **U80**-14
Reoperation U126-1; U134-10
Repellent **U91**-8
repetitiv **U74**-7
Replikation **U84**-16
replikationsfähig U84-16
Replikationsfehler U84-16
Replikationszyklus U84-16
replikativ **U84**-16

Replikator **U84**-16
Replikon **U84**-16
replizieren **U84**-16,8
Repolarisation **U42**-7
Repolarisationsphase U42-7
reponierbar U142-8
reponieren U28-1; **U140**-2,26
Reportage **U8**-7
Reposition U31-3
– (Fraktur) **U141**-2; U106-1; **U140**-2
–, manuelle U142-12
Reproduktion, assistierte U69-1
– –, medizinische **U69**-11
Reproduktionsgedächtnis U74-1
Reproduktionsmedizin U69-11
Reproduktionstoxikologie U69-1
Reproduktionsverfahren, assistierte medizinische **U69**-11
Reproduzierbarkeit **U100**-30
RES **U35**-12; U86-14
RESA U69-13
Resektion **U126**-15; **U127**-13
Resektionsgrenzen U97-11
Resektionsränder U97-11
–, tumorfreie U86-1; U87-10
Resektionsschlinge U138-5
Resektoskop U126-15
Reserve U39-16; U69-14
Reservevolumen U44-12
–, exspiratorisches U44-12
–, inspiratorisches U44-3,12
reserviert **U75**-14,17
Reservoir **U78**-20; **U94**-4
Reservoirwirt U94-4
resezieren **U126**-15
Residentflora U15-4; U90-1
Residualeffekt, Insektizid mit U91-8
Residualharn **U112**-11
Residualkapazität, funktionelle U44-11
Residualvolumen **U44**-12,3
Residuen, neurologische U113-7
Resine U78-23; U81-11
Resistance U43-5; U123-10
resistent **U39**-22; **U120**-13
Resistenz **U120**-13
–, angeborene U39-22
–, erhöhte U39-22
–, erworbene U39-22
–, immunologische **U39**-22
–, plasmiddeterminierte/-vermittelte U84-8
Resistenzbestimmung U57-8
Resistenzfaktoren U84-8
resolut **U75**-11
Resonanzkörper U66-11
resorbierbar **U137**-8
resorbieren **U46**-13; **U78**-5; **U88**-8
Resorption **U27**-20; **U78**-5; **U88**-8
–, enterale U88-8
Resorptionsatelektase U111-15
Resorptionsgeschwindigkeit U46-13; U88-8; **U121**-10
Resorptionsstörung **U46**-13
Resorptionstest U88-8

Resorptionsverzögerung U46-13
Resorptionszeit U137-8
Respiration **U44**-4
Respirationstrakt U43-5; **U44**-4
Respirator **U44**-4f; **U123**-9; **U125**-10
respiratorisch **U44**-4
Respiratorschläuche U125-10
Rest (Säure, etc.) **U81**-4; U85-13,20
Restaffinität U81-12
Restbeschwerden U4-14; U104-1
Restdefizite U113-7
Restharn **U112**-11; U49-12,16
Restitutio ad integrum U4-16
Restless legs-Syndrom U76-8
Rest-N U82-16
Restriktion U100-16
Restriktionsanalyse U84-32
Restriktionsendonuklease **U84**-32; U78-8
Restriktionsfragment-Längen-Analyse U84-32
Restriktionsfragment-Längen-Polymorphismus U84-13,22
Restriktionskarte U84-32
Restriktionskartierung U84-32,34
Restriktionsort U84-32
Restriktionsschnittstelle U84-32
Reststickstoff U82-16
Resttumor U97-2; U132-7
Restwirkungen U135-23
Resublimation **U82**-8
Resultat **U101**-27
resultieren **U116**-18
retardiert, geistig **U77**-22
Retardierung, mentale/geistige **U77**-22
–, psychomotorische U77-22
Retardpräparat U9-3,6f; U121-4
Retentio testis abdominalis U52-3
– – inguinalis U52-3
Retention **U49**-4; **U74**-10; U64-2
– (Speisereste) U109-15
Retest-Stabilität U100-30
Reticulum endoplasmicum **U83**-8
– trabeculare U58-11
retikulär **U35**-12; **U83**-8
Retikularkörperchen U83-8
Retikulin **U83**-8
Retikulinfaser **U86**-5; U83-8
Retikuloendotheliose U35-12
Retikulozyt **U35**-12; U37-5; U83-8
Retikulozytenzahl U35-12
Retikulozytenzählung U116-8
Retikulum, endoplasmatisches **U83**-8
–, sarkoplasmatisches U83-8
Retikulumzelle U83-8
Retina **U58**-13
Retinaculum **U30**-8
– extensorum U30-8
– flexorum (manus) U87-17
– musculorum peronaeorum inferius U30-8
– patellae mediale U30-8
Retinafalte U58-13
retinieren U26-1

Retinolester U82-14
Retinopathia pigmentosa U58-13; U114-3
Retinoskopie U58-13
Retortenbaby U69-12
Retraktion **U64**-13; **U141**-3
Retransplantation **U129**-14
retrobulbär U87-16
retrokaval **U34**-7
Retroperitoneoskopie **U128**-5
retropubisch U87-16
retrospektiv **U101**-6
Retroversio uteri U31-8
Retrovirus U90-10
–, AIDS-assoziiertes U96-15
retten **U8**-2,18
Retter(in) **U8**-2; U63-9
Rettung **U8**-2,18
Rettungsaktion U8-2
Rettungsarbeiter(in) U16-1
Rettungsassistent(in) **U8**-6; **U16**-9
Rettungsboje U8-4
Rettungsbrett U8-16
Rettungsdienst U8-5; U13-3
Rettungshelfer(in) **U8**-6; U13-1; U16-1
Rettungshubschrauber **U8**-5
Rettungskragen U8-15
Rettungsleitstelle **U8**-9
Rettungsmannschaft U8-2
Rettungsmaßnahmen U8-2
Rettungsring U123-1
Rettungssanitäter(in) **U8**-6,5; U16-10
–, ausgebildete(r) U18-10
–, geprüfte(r) U18-10
Rettungsschwimmen **U123**-1
Rettungsschwimmer(in) **U123**-1
Rettungstrage **U8**-16,2; U22-12
Rettungsversuch U8-2
Rettungswagen **U8**-5
Reue **U76**-13; **U77**-10
Revakzination **U122**-3
Revers U18-4
reverse Genetik **U84**-1
– Transkription U84-18
Rezept **U20**-7
– ausstellen U121-1
Rezeptblock U17-1
rezeptfrei U9-2; **U121**-1
rezeptiv **U57**-10
Rezeptor(en) **U57**-5,10; **U81**-14
–, adrenerge U55-11
–, intrazelluläre U55-2
–, membranständige U55-2
Rezeptoraffinität U55-2
Rezeptorbesetzung U55-2
Rezeptorblocker U55-2
Rezeptordichte U55-2
rezeptorgesteuert U55-2
Rezeptorpotential U55-2
Rezeptorprotein U55-2
Rezeptorstellen **U55**-2; U57-10
Rezeptorsuperfamilie U55-2
Rezeptorszintigrafie U55-2

rezeptorvermittelt U55-2; U57-10
rezeptpflichtig U9-3; U121-1
rezessiv **U84**-27
Rezessivität **U84**-27
Rezidiv **U94**-7; **U119**-18,3; U9-1
rezidivfrei **U4**-4
rezidivieren **U119**-18; **U94**-7; U44-9
Rezidivrate U100-8; U119-18
Rezidivrisiko U124-2
R-Faktoren U84-8
Rh **U37**-17
Rhabdomyom **U98**-9
Rhabdomyosarkom U98-3
Rhabdosphinkter **U30**-9; **U48**-14
Rhesusantikörpertiter U37-17
Rhesus-Faktor **U37**-17
Rhesussensibilisierung U37-17
Rheumafaktor U89-16
Rheumaknoten U89-16
Rheumatoidarthritis, juvenile U95-1
Rhinitis U15-19
– acuta **U94**-9
–, allergische U39-23; U94-9
–, saisonale allergische U80-12
–, vasomotorische U94-9
Rh-Inkompatibilität U136-11
Rhinolalie U43-6; U66-17,22
Rhinophonie U66-17
Rhinoplastik U15-19; U17-6
Rhinorrhoe/-ö U17-6
Rhinoskop **U17**-6
Rhinoskopie **U17**-6
Rhodopsin U58-13; U59-5
Rhombencephalon U41-1
Rhonchus **U111**-8
rhythmisch **U33**-6
Rhythmus, atrioventrikulärer U33-6
–, idioventrikulärer U33-6; U110-6
–, zirkadianer **U72**-8
Rhythmusstörung **U33**-6; **U110**-6
–, zirkadiane U72-8
Ribonuklease U83-9; U84-15
Ribonukleinsäure **U84**-15
Ribonukleosidreste U84-15
Ribonukleotid **U84**-15,12
Ribose **U83**-9
Ribosom **U83**-9; **U84**-15
ribosomal **U84**-15
Ribosomenuntereinheit U83-9; U84-15
Ribosyl **U83**-9
Ribotypisierung U84-15
richtig negativ U100-22
Richtlinie **U20**-7
Richtungsventil U135-14
Rickettsia **U90**-12
Rickettsia rickettsii U90-12
Rickettsie **U90**-12
Rickettsienantigen U90-12
Rickettsieninfektion **U90**-12
Rickettsienpocken U90-12
Rickettsiose **U90**-12
Riechbahnen U62-1
Riechen **U62**-1; U57-6
riechen nach **U62**-4,1

Riechepithel U62-1
Riechhärchen U62-1
Riechkolben U62-1
Riechnerv(en) U40-1; U62-1
Riechplakode U85-23
Riechsalz U62-1; U123-3
Riechstörung U62-1
Riedel-Struma U124-8
Riemen U140-26; **U141**-11
Riese **U24**-4
riesenhaft **U24**-4
Riesenhämangiom U98-5
Riesenwuchs **U24**-4
Riesenzelle U24-4
Riesenzellhepatitis U94-15
Riesenzellsarkom U98-3
riesig **U24**-4
rigid **U12**-15; **U31**-17; **U103**-20; **U109**-14
Rigidität **U12**-15; **U53**-4; **U103**-20
–, anhaltende U53-4
Rigiditätsmessung U53-4
Rigor **U12**-15; **U103**-20; **U105**-9
– mortis **U12**-15
Rima ani U87-26
– palpebrarum U58-3
– pudendi U50-14
Rinde **U86**-23; U41-6
–, agranuläre U41-6
–, motorische U31-20
Rindenblindheit U41-6; U59-18
Rindenfeld U41-6
–, akustisches U60-7
–, motorisches U31-20; U40-4
–, sensibles U41-6
–, sensorisches U41-6
Rinden-Mark-Grenze U41-7
Rindenzentrum U41-6
Rinderalbumin U78-18
Rinderwahnsinn U77-15
Ring, aromatischer U81-7
Ringband **U30**-8
–, A2- U30-8
Ringchromosom U84-6
ringen, nach Atem U44-7
Ringerlaktatinjektion U122-4
Ringer-Laktat-Lösung U8-13; U81-25
ringförmig U108-9
Ringknorpel U21-14; U29-2
Ringpankreas U54-8
Ringpessar U69-9
Ringsideroblast U86-2
Ringskotom U113-11
Rinne **U85**-12; **U87**-26
– Stimmgabelversuch U118-2
Rippen **U28**-14
–, echte U28-13
–, falsche U28-14
–, fliegende U28-14
Rippenbogen U28-14; U87-9
Rippenbogenrand U87-10
Rippenbuckel U28-14
Rippenfell U28-14; U43-11
Rippenknorpel U29-2
Rippenrand U28-14

Rippenraspatorium U132-12
Rippenspreizer U28-14
Rippfellentzündung U111-12
Risiko **U8**-4; **U124**-2; **U134**-5
– behaftet, mit einem U64-16
Risikoeinschätzung U8-4; U117-1
Risikogeburt U80-6
Risikokind U80-4; U124-2
Risiko-Nutzen-Abwägung U117-2
– – Verhältnis U124-2; **U134**-5
Risikopatient U134-5
Risikopersonen U100-2
Risikopopulation U122-1
risikoreich **U8**-4; **U91**-5
Risikoschwangerschaft U70-6; U124-2
riskant **U8**-4; **U124**-2
Riss **U5**-19,7; U58-6; **U106**-1,5,11
–, mikroskopisch kleiner U86-1
rissig **U87**-26; U56-18
Risswunde **U5**-7; U107-6
Rist **U23**-13; U28-25
rittlings **U63**-5
Ritual **U73**-13
ritzen (Haut) **U132**-5
Rizinusöl U82-13; U92-13
RNA, ribosomale U83-9
RNA-Bindemotiv U84-3
RNA-Matrize U84-15
RNA-Polymerase **U84**-18,15
RNA-Spleißen U84-15
RNS-Bindemotiv U84-3
Robertson-Translokation U84-23
Roboterarm **U133**-1
robotergestützte Chirurgie U133-1
robust (Konstitution) **U1**-11,8; **U25**-4
Robustheit **U1**-11
Rockbund U22-6
Roeder-Knoten **U138**-7
Roger-Reflex U45-5
rohe Rate U100-8
Röhre, Eustachische **U60**-7
Röhreninstabilität U99-13
Rohwert **U100**-6
Rollbett **U19**-3
Rollbinde U140-20
Rolle **U30**-8
rollen **U64**-8
– (Augen) U58-2
rollenförmig **U28**-15; **U30**-8
Rollhügel **U28**-4
Rolllappen **U130**-15
Rollstuhl **U19**-13; U4-8
Rollstuhl-Rampe U19-13
Rollwagen **U142**-19; U17-12
röntgen **U99**-3
Röntgen(untersuchung) **U118**-18
Röntgenanlage U99-3; U118-18
Röntgenassistent(in) **U15**-13; **U99**-3,1
–, diensthabende(r) U20-4
Röntgenaufnahme **U99**-3; U18-14
Röntgenbefund U99-1; U117-6
–, positiver U116-22
Röntgenbereich U99-1
Röntgenbild **U99**-3; U118-18

Röntgenbildbetrachter U118-18
Röntgendarstellung U99-12
Röntgendiagnostik U99-1
Röntgendurchleuchtung U99-8
Röntgendurchleuchtungskontrolle, unter U15-13
Röntgeneinrichtungen U14-3
Röntgenfluoreszenz U99-8
Röntgenfluoroskopie U118-18
Röntgenröhre U5-20; U118-18
Röntgenstrahler U118-18
Röntgentherapie U118-18
Rooming-in **U19**-2
Rosenthal-Faktor U37-14
Roseola U114-9
– infantum **U95**-2 f; U114-2
rostfreier Stahl U137-12
rot **U25**-12
Rotameter U135-14
Rotation **U31**-7,18
– (VKT) **U71**-14
Rotationsfehlstellung U31-7
Rotationsinstabilität U31-7
Rotationsknoten **U138**-10
Rotationslappen **U130**-19; U29-5
Rotationsstellung U141-1
Rotatorenmanschettenruptur U113-15
rotbackig U25-12
rotblond **U25**-13
Röte **U25**-12
Röteln **U95**-3
–, postnatale U95-3
rötelnähnlich **U95**-3
Rötelnantikörpertiter U95-3
Rötelnarthritis U95-3
Rötelnembryopathie U95-3
Rötelnimmunität U95-3
Roter Hund U56-11; U105-11
Rotes Kreuz, Blutspendedienst U13-12
– –, Internationales Komitee **U13**-12
rotgesichtig U25-12
Rotgrünblindheit U59-18
rotieren **U31**-7
Rot-Kreuz-Gesellschaft U13-12
Rötung U56-18; **U108**-7
Route **U97**-11
Routinetätigkeiten, ärztliche U18-1
Routineuntersuchung U18-9
–, klinische U107-2
Roux-Y Operation U129-6
RPF **U49**-2
R-Plasmide U84-8
RR-Messung **U17**-8
rRNA U84-15
RT-PCR U84-36
Rubella **U95**-3
– Syndrom, kongenitales U95-3
Rubeola **U95**-3
Rubidium U82-18
Ruck **U64**-7; **U65**-9
ruckartig **U64**-7; **U72**-12; **U113**-1
Rückatmungsbeutel U8-12
Rückbildung **U4**-15; **U119**-17; U5-11
–, menopausale U51-10

Rückblende **U74**-11
Rückdiffusion U88-4
Rücken **U22**-11; U87-16
– (liegend), auf dem **U63**-8,10
–, krummer **U63**-3
–, verspannter U22-11; U31-10
Rückenlage **U131**-11 ff,16; U8-17
–, in **U31**-9; **U63**-8
Rückenmark **U41**-15; U28-19; U40-5
Rückenmarkbeteiligung U124-18
Rückenmarkdurchtrennung U124-18
Rückenmarkerschütterung U5-14
Rückenmarkkompression U41-15; U125-17; U142-5
Rückenmarknerv U40-1
Rückenmarkreflexe U41-15
Rückenmarkschädigung U41-15; U124-18
Rückenmarksegment U41-15; U87-6
Rückenmarkshaut, harte **U41**-8
–, weiche **U41**-8
Rückenmarksnerven U22-12
Rückenmarksubstanz, graue U41-7
Rückenmarktumor, intramedullärer U41-14
Rückenmarkverletzung **U124**-18; U5-2; U41-15
Rückenmarkwurzel U41-15
Rückenmassage U62-11
Rückenmuskel, breiter **U30**-12
Rückenmuskulatur U22-11
Rückensaite **U85**-20
Rückenschmerzen **U22**-11
Rückenschule **U142**-18
Rückenstrecker U63-2
Rückentraining **U142**-18
Rückentrainingsprogramm U142-18
Rückfall **U94**-7; **U119**-18,3; U9-1
Rückfallfieber U94-19; U105-3
Rückfallrate U119-18
rückfließend **U110**-10
Rückfluss **U36**-5; **U46**-4; **U112**-12; U110-10
–, maulvoller **U109**-3
–, venöser **U36**-6
Rückgang **U4**-14; U105-18; **U116**-20
–, kontinuierlicher U88-20
Rückgrat U22-12
Rückholfäden U69-10
Rückholversicherung U13-5
Rückkopplungsmechanismus U88-2
Rucknystagmus U113-12
rückresorbieren **U49**-4
Rückresorption **U49**-4; **U88**-8
Rückseite **U22**-11
rückseitig **U87**-16
rücksichtslos **U75**-18
Rücksichtslosigkeit **U75**-18
Rückstau **U49**-4
Rückstreuung U99-6
Rückstrom U110-10
–, venöser **U36**-6; U34-4
–, zentralvenöser U36-6
Rückströmen **U46**-4

Rückströmen, (passives) **U103**-12
Rückversicherung **U13**-5
Rückwärtsinsuffizienz U110-12
Rückzug **U76**-15; U77-8
–, autistischer U77-8
–, sozialer **U77**-8; U76-8,15; U113-3
Ruderergometer U142-16
rudimentär **U85**-9
Ruf U66-1
rufen U18-7; **U66**-14
Ruffini-Körperchen U57-15
Ruhe **U1**-10,16; **U64**-17; **U72**-5; **U76**-19; **U119**-6
–, ewige **U12**-7
Ruhedyspnoe U111-1
Ruhe-EKG U118-14
Ruhe(herz)frequenz U33-5
Ruhekern U83-12
Ruhelage U1-10; U64-17
– (Kiefer) U27-14
Ruhelosigkeit **U64**-17; **U72**-5; **U113**-2
ruhen **U1**-10; **U64**-17; **U72**-5
ruhend (Krankheit) **U94**-6; **U119**-6
Ruhephase U83-12; U119-6
Ruheposition U63-1
Ruhepotential U42-5,8
Ruhepuls U107-13
Ruheschmerz U4-13; U64-17; U104-7
Ruheschwebe(lage) U27-14
Ruhestand **U80**-14
Ruhestellung U64-17
Ruhetonus U1-13; U31-10
Ruhetremor U64-17; U113-4
Ruhezustand **U94**-6; U119-6
ruhig **U61**-11; **U64**-17; **U76**-19
–, äußerlich U76-19
ruhigstellen **U64**-2
Ruhigstellung **U141**-5
Ruhr, bakterielle U90-7
rühren, (sich) **U64**-3
Ruktus **U46**-3
rülpsen **U46**-3; U109-4
Rülpser **U46**-3
Rumination **U109**-3
Rumpel-Leede-Stauversuch U8-8; U17-8
Rumpf **U22**-1; U6-8
Rumpfataxie U22-1; U113-8
rümpfen **U56**-17
–, Nase U25-17
Rumpfmuskulatur U22-1
Rumpforthese U141-7
Rumpftrikotschlauch U141-10
Rumpfverkürzung U24-3
rumpfwärts **U87**-14
rundlich **U25**-6; U24-8
Rundlichkeit **U25**-6
Rundlochplatte U141-17
Rundstiellappen **U130**-15 f
Rund-um-die-Uhr-Betreuung U125-1
Rundwürmer U90-16; U92-25
runzeln **U25**-17; **U56**-17
– (Stirn) **U67**-11; U59-2
runzlig **U25**-17,7; **U56**-17; U24-10

Ruptur **U5**-19,7; U58-6; **U89**-23
-, drohende U124-15
Rutschbrett U142-19
rutschen **U65**-8,12

S

sabbern **U45**-3; **U27**-9,4
Säbelscheidentibia U28-24
Sabin-Schluckvakzine U122-2
SA-Block U32-15; U123-2
Saccharide **U79**-6
Saccharin **U79**-6
Saccharose **U3**-16
Sacculus alveolaris U44-12
Saccus conjunctivae U58-4
– lacrimalis U58-9
– vitellinus **U85**-7
Sachschaden U6-1
Sachverständige(r), medizinischer U6-13
Sack U52-2
Sado-Maso Fesselspiele U68-9
SAEKG U118-14
Saft **U3**-25
Sagittalebene U87-2
Sakkade **U59**-14; U58-16; U113-12
Sakkulus **U60**-9
SA-Knoten **U32**-15
Sakralanästhesie U28-20; U87-19
Sakrum **U28**-20
Salbe **U9**-8; U96-10
-, beruhigende U62-7
-, borsäurehaltige U82-31
-, schwefelhaltige U82-24
-, pflegende U56-9
Salbenkanüle U132-6
Salicylat U78-7
salinisch **U82**-5
Salivation **U27**-9; **U45**-3
Salk-Vakzine U122-2
Salmiak U82-23
Salmiakgeist U47-17
Salmonelleninfektion **U94**-19
Salmonellose **U94**-19
Salpeterpapier U82-16
Salpetersäure U82-4,16
salpetrig **U82**-16
Salpingektomie U69-3
Saluretika U92-21
Salve U42-4
Salz **U82**-5; **U3**-18
– (Harnsäure) **U49**-14
-, basisches U82-5
-, iodiertes U82-5,22
Salzersatz, kaliumhaltiger U82-18
salzhaltig **U82**-5
Salzlösung U128-11
-, isotone U88-5
-, kristalloide U81-26
-, physiologische U88-19
Salzmangel U82-5
Salzsäure U46-10; U81-19

Salzverlust U78-21; U88-15,17
Salzverlustsyndrom, renales U82-5
Samen **U53**-6
Samenbank **U69**-14; U14-12
Samenbläschen **U52**-9
Samenbruch U53-8
Samenerguss, nächtlicher U53-6,11; U72-9,12
-, vorzeitiger U53-11
Samenfaden, reifer **U53**-7
Samenflüssigkeit **U53**-6
Samengänge U52-9
Samenhügel **U52**-12,9
Samenleiter **U52**-6,3
Samenplasma U53-6
Samenstrang **U52**-7; U53-7
Samenstrangtorsion U52-7; U124-1
Samenstrangtumoren U52-7
Samenwege, ableitende U52-9
Sammellinse U59-13
Sammelrohr **U48**-9,5
Sammelsystem (Niere) **U48**-9
Sammelwirt U94-5
Sammlung **U117**-3
Sanatorium **U14**-3
Sandsack U6-4
sanft **U62**-10
sanftmütig U76-2
Sanguis **U37**-1
sanitär **U1**-5
Sanitäter **U16**-14; U8-1
Sanitäterteam U14-7
Sanitätsdienst U8-6
Sanitätssoldat(in) **U16**-9
Sapo kalinus U82-14
– medicatus U82-14
Saponifikation **U82**-14
Saponin U82-14
Saprophyt **U90**-13
Sarcoma botryoides U98-3
Sarcophaga U90-15
Sarcoptes scabiei U90-15
Sarg **U12**-18
Sarggeburt U71-9
Sarkom **U97**-6; **U98**-3
sarkomatös **U97**-6; **U98**-3
Sarkomatose **U98**-3
Sarkoplasma U30-1
Sarkozele U97-6
Satellit **U84**-7
Satelliten-DNA U84-7
Sattelblock U29-6; U93-6
Sattelgelenk **U29**-6
Sattelnase U29-6
sättigen **U81**-24
Sättigung, prozentmäßige U81-24
Sättigungseffekt U11-18
sättigungsfähig **U81**-24
Sättigungsgefühl, vorzeitiges U109-1
Sättigungsgrad U81-24
saturiert **U81**-24
Satyriasis U68-4
Satz **U65**-16; **U81**-27
Satzmelodie **U66**-11

sauber **U1**-5
– abgewischt U139-17
Sauberkeitserziehung U64-18
sauer **U62**-5; **U76**-9f; **U81**-19
Sauerstoff **U82**-11
Sauerstoffaffinität U81-12
sauerstoffarm **U44**-6
Sauerstoffaufnahme U82-11; U125-12
Sauerstoffbindungskapazität U44-11
Sauerstoffdissoziationskurve U81-22; U82-11; U116-9
Sauerstoffgefälle U82-11
Sauerstoffgradient U82-11
Sauerstoff-Lachgas-Gemisch U93-11
Sauerstoffmangel U111-3; **U123**-8
Sauerstoffnot **U111**-3
Sauerstoffpartialdruck U116-11
Sauerstoffradikal U81-5; U82-11
sauerstoffreiches Blut U37-1
Sauerstoffsättigung U34-8; U116-9; U125-9,12
Sauerstoffschuld U82-11; U88-20
Sauerstoffspannung U125-12
Sauerstofftransportkapazität U82-11
Sauerstoff-Überdrucktherapie U82-11; U125-12
Sauerstoffverbrauch U82-11; U125-12
Sauerstoffversorgung U88-3; U125-12
Sauerstoffzelt **U125**-12; U82-11
Sauerstoffzufuhr U88-3; U125-12
saufen **U10**-2
Säufer(in) **U10**-1f
Saufgelage U10-1
Saugakt U46-2
Saugbiopsie U118-5
Saugdrainage U127-16; U140-15
-, geschlossene U125-16
saugen **U46**-2; **U118**-9; U71-27
säugen **U46**-2
Sauger **U46**-2; **U118**-9
Säugetier U90-15
Säugetiermilch U79-8
saugfähig **U88**-8
Saugflasche U2-3
Saugkanüle U132-6
Saugkürettage U70-9; U127-16
Säugling **U46**-2; **U71**-26; **U80**-4f
-, zyanotischer U70-5
Säuglingsbotulismus U91-21
Säuglingsekzem U95-1
Säuglingsernährung U79-3
Säuglingsnahrung U2-6; U70-5
Säuglingspflege **U16**-6
Säuglingsschwester U16-6
Säuglingsstation U14-8
Säuglingssterblichkeit U12-3; U80-4
Säuglingssterblichkeitsrate U100-9
Säuglingszimmer **U14**-8; **U16**-2
Saugreflex U46-2; U113-1
Saug-Spül-Drain U125-16
– Spülvorrichtung, integrierte U128-11
Saugvorrichtung **U127**-16; U140-15
Saugwurm **U90**-17
Säulenchromatografie U83-22

Säulendiagramm U100-27
Saum **U87**-10
Sauna(bad) **U1**-17
Säure **U81**-19
–, selenige U82-21
–, titrierbare U116-17
– Basen-Gleichgewicht U78-22
– – Haushalt U81-19; U88-19
– – Status U119-15
– – Stoffwechsel U78-1
säurebeständig U81-19
säurebildend **U81**-19
säurebindend **U92**-29; U121-2
Säureblocker U46-10
säurefest U81-19
säurefeste Färbung U116-4
Säuregrad U81-19; U92-29
säurehaltig **U81**-19
Säurereflux U109-4
Säurerest U81-19
Säureverätzung U91-10
Scabies **U96**-12
– crustosa U114-8
– scabiei U96-12
Scala vestibuli U60-9
Scan **U99**-18
Scanbreite U99-18
Scanner **U99**-18
Scapula **U28**-12; U23-3
– alata U28-12
Scapus pili U56-13
Scarlatina **U95**-6
Scarlatinella **U95**-6
Scavenger **U78**-19
Scavenger-Zelle U78-19
Schabeisen **U132**-12
schaben **U5**-9
Schädel **U28**-7; U21-1
Schädelbasis U28-7; U87-25
Schädelbasisbruch U124-19; U106-1,8
Schädel-Becken-Missverhältnis U87-19
Schädelbruch **U106**-8
Schädeldach U28-7
Schädeldachfraktur U106-8
Schädeldekompression U125-17
Schädeleröffnung U28-7
Schädelfraktur **U106**-8; **U124**-19
Schädelgrube U28-7
Schädel-Hirn-Trauma **U124**-19; U41-1
Schädelimpressionsfraktur U106-3; U124-19
Schädelindex U87-19
Schädelknochen U28-2
Schädellage U71-5; U87-19
Schädelmessung U87-19
Schädelnaht U28-7; U29-14
Schädelröntgen U21-1; U28-7; U99-3
Schädeltrauma, stumpfes U124-18
Schädelverletzung, gedeckte U124-19
–, offene U28-7
schaden **U6**-11; **U5**-3; **U89**-11
Schaden **U6**-11; **U142**-4
–, bleibender U6-11

Schadenersatz (Kunstfehler) **U6**-11; U18-1
Schadenersatzansprüche U6-11
Schadenersatzprozess U20-13
schädigen **U4**-10; **U91**-1; U36-15
Schädigung **U4**-11; **U5**-5; **U6**-11; **U142**-3; **U89**-3 f
–, neurologische U15-14
schädlich **U4**-1; **U6**-11; **U91**-1,18; U1-5; U121-11 f
schädliche Substanz U92-12
Schädling **U91**-8
Schädlingsbekämpfung U91-8
Schädlingsbekämpfungsmittel **U81**-1; **U91**-8; **U92**-26
Schadstoff **U91**-5 f,1; U6-11; **U139**-9
Schadstoff-Alarmstufe U91-6
Schadstoffbelastung U91-5
Schadstoffkonzentration, höchstzulässige U91-5
Schadstoffpartikel U91-1
Schadstoffprobe U118-4
Schadstoffschutzmaßnahmen U6-22; U91-5
Schadstoffwert U91-6
Schafblattern **U95**-7; U114-12
Schaffellauflagen U19-5
Schafhaut **U85**-15
Schaftfraktur U106-7
Schale **U2**-8; **U17**-12; **U86**-8
Schalenpessar U69-9
Schall **U66**-11
– leiten U42-2
–, dumpfer U61-3
schallarm U118-15
schalldicht U118-15
Schalldruckpegel U61-3
schalldurchlässig U118-15
Schallempfindungsschwerhörigkeit U57-2; U60-13; U61-3,9
Schallenergie U61-3
Schallfeld U61-3
Schallfrequenz **U61**-6
Schallintensität **U61**-5; U60-13
Schallintensitätsschwelle U61-7
Schallleitungsschwerhörigkeit U42-2; U61-3 f; U113-13
Schallmuster U118-15
Schallquelle U61-3
Schallsonde U132-8
Schallstärke U60-13
Schalltrauma U5-4
Schalltrichter U17-2
Schallübertragung **U61**-4
Schallverstärkung U61-3
Schallwechsel U107-8; U109-9
Schallwelle **U61**-3
Scham **U76**-12 f; U77-10
Schambehaarung **U52**-19; U50-2
Schambein **U28**-22; U52-18
Schambeinast U22-8; U28-5
Schambeinfuge **U52**-18; U28-22; U29-12
Schambeingegend U52-20

Schambeinhöcker U28-22
Schambereich/-gegend **U52**-20; **U22**-10
Schamberg U52-18
Schamfuge **U52**-18
Schamhaare U50-16; U52-19
schamhaft U80-8
Schamhügel **U50**-16
Schamläuse U22-8; U90-15
Schamlippen **U50**-14; U68-8
Schamspalte U50-14
Schande **U76**-12; U77-10
schändlich **U76**-12; U77-19; U73-11
Schanker **U96**-4; U89-17
–, harter **U96**-3,1
–, weicher **U96**-4
schankerartig **U96**-4
schankrös **U96**-4
Schanz-Krawatte **U141**-9
scharf **U62**-5,7; **U68**-3
– machen **U68**-3
scharfe Kürette U132-2
scharfes Präparieren U132-2
scharfkantig U132-2
Scharfsichtigkeit **U59**-8
Scharlach **U95**-6
scharlachähnlich **U95**-6
Scharlachexanthem U95-6
Scharlachfriesel U95-6
Scharlachtoxin U95-6
Scharnier U130-19
Scharnierachse U29-5
Scharniergelenk **U29**-5; U23-4
Scharnierprothese U29-5
schätzen **U57**-2
Schätzfunktion U100-18
Schatzki-Ring U109-5
Schätzung **U117**-2
Schätzwert **U100**-29
Schauder **U64**-6; **U105**-7
schaudern **U64**-6; **U105**-7
schauen **U59**-1; **U67**-14
–, in die Ferne U59-2
Schauer **U105**-7
Schaufelbahre **U8**-16
schaufelförmig U28-20
Schaufeltrage **U8**-16
Schaufensterkrankheit **U110**-19
Schaukelbrett **U142**-19
schaukeln **U64**-5
Schaumbad U1-17; U142-20
schaumig U96-8; U103-16
Schaumpolster U140-19
Schaumstoff-Halskrawatte U141-9
Schaumstoffkissen U19-5
Schaumstoffmatratze U19-5
Schaumstoffpolster U141-10
Schaumzelle U39-18
Scheibe **U5**-6
Scheide **U50**-8; **U86**-8
Scheidenabstrich U116-5
Scheidenausfluss U71-7; U88-11
–, blutiger U37-1
Scheidendammschnitt **U71**-18

Scheidendiaphragma **U69**-9
Scheideneingang U50-8; U71-15
Scheidenflora U46-16; U50-8
Scheidengewölbe U50-8
Scheidenjucken U103-19
Scheidenkrampf U50-8
Scheidenlubrikation U17-14
Scheidenpessar **U69**-9; U43-12
Scheidenplastik U50-8
Scheidensekret U88-11
Scheidenspekulum U17-6; U50-8
Scheidenspülung U19-10; U50-8
Scheidenverschluss, operativer U50-8
Scheidenvorhof U50-11
Scheidewand **U86**-15
Scheidewasser U82-4
Scheinapherese U136-15
scheinbar gesund U1-2
scheinen **U59**-3
Scheinfüßchen U90-4
Scheinfütterung U101-8
scheingeschichtet **U86**-10
Scheinmedikament **U101**-8
Scheinschwangerschaft **U70**-6
Scheintod U7-15
Scheitelbein **U28**-8; U87-13
Scheitel-Fersen-Länge **U71**-15
Scheitellappen U28-8; U41-5; U87-13,23
Scheitel-Steiß-Länge U24-2; U71-15
scheitern **U123**-6
Schema **U100**-6
Schenkel **U23**-1,9
–, absteigender U48-8
–, aufsteigender U48-8
Schenkelblock U40-12
Schenkelhals U28-23
Schere **U132**-4
Scherengang U65-2
Scherkräfte U36-12
scheu **U75**-17
Scheuklappen **U59**-3
Schicht **U86**-15; **U87**-8; U99-19
–, auskleidende U86-8
–, dünne U24-10
Schichtaufnahme **U99**-19
schichten **U86**-10; **U87**-8
Schichten, in **U87**-8
Schichtenbildung **U86**-10
Schichtnaht U137-1
Schichtung **U86**-10,15
schichtweiser (Wund)verschluss U128-18; U140-3
Schicksal **U12**-2
Schicksalsschlag **U6**-4
Schiebeknoten **U138**-9; **U137**-6
schieben **U64**-12; **U65**-8
Schieber **U19**-8
Schiefe **U100**-13
Schiefhals U103-20
Schielamblyopie U59-4
Schielen **U59**-4; **U58**-2
–, latentes U59-15
–, manifestes U59-17

schielen U67-14; **U21**-3; **U59**-4
–, auf, verstohlen U65-8
–, (nach innen) **U59**-4
Schielwinkel U59-4
Schienbein **U28**-24; **U23**-10; U106-1
Schienbein(bereich) **U23**-10
Schienbeinkante U28-5
Schienbeinschützer U23-10
Schiene **U141**-7; U106-3; **U140**-26; U142-13
–, gepolsterte U140-19
schienen **U127**-20; U8-4; U18-13
Schienung **U141**-7
schießen **U6**-8; **U11**-8
Schifferknoten U137-6; U138-6
Schilddrüse **U54**-6; **U55**-6
–, vergrößerte U54-6
Schilddrüsendiagnostik U102-9
Schilddrüsenentzündung **U124**-8; U54-6
Schilddrüsenfunktionsprüfung U102-9; U118-3
Schilddrüsenhormon **U55**-6
Schilddrüsenhormonpräparat U55-6
Schilddrüsenhormonresistenz U55-6
Schilddrüsenhormonsubstitution U55-6
Schilddrüsenkarzinom, calcitoninproduzierendes medulläres U55-8
Schilddrüsenlappen U87-23
Schilddrüsenperoxidase U55-6
Schilddrüsenszintigrafie U54-6; U55-3
Schilddrüsenüberfunktion **U124**-8
Schilddrüsenunterfunktion **U55**-6
Schilddrüsenvergrößerung U54-6
Schildknorpel U29-2; **U54**-6
Schildrüsenknoten U54-6
Schildzecke U90-15
Schimmel(pilz) **U90**-18
Schimmelbildung U90-18
schimmeln **U90**-18
Schimmelpilz U92-9
Schimmelpilzspore U90-3
schimpfen **U67**-19
Schinadel U138-14
Schistosoma **U90**-17
Schistosomiasis **U90**-17
Schizont **U90**-4
Schlaf **U72**-5
–, desynchronisierter **U72**-10,9
–, hypnotischer U7-15
–, orthodoxer **U72**-11
–, paradoxer **U72**-10
–, synchronisierter **U72**-11
–, tiefer U1-3; U72-5
–, unruhiger U76-8; U113-2
schlafähnlich **U72**-5
Schlafanfälle U72-18,5
Schlafapnoe **U72**-13; U111-5
Schlafapnoesyndrom **U72**-13
Schlafaufzeichnungen U20-5
Schläfchen **U72**-2
Schlafdauer U72-5
Schläfe U21-2

schlafen **U72**-5 f
– legen (Kind) U72-3
–, fest U72-6
–, lange U72-5
–, tief U72-6
Schläfenbein **U28**-8
Schläfenbeinfraktur U106-8
schlafend **U72**-6
Schlafengehen, beim **U72**-4
–, vor dem U19-3; U72-3 f
Schläfenlappen U41-5
Schlafenszeit(en) **U72**-4; **U19**-3
–, regelmäßige U72-4; U75-10
Schlafentzug U72-5; U77-11
schlaff **U31**-12; **U53**-4; **U64**-15; **U65**-11
Schlaffheit **U31**-12; U142-8
Schlaffheitsgrad U142-14
schlaffördernd U93-14
Schlafforschungslabor U14-11
Schlafkontinuität U72-10
Schlafkrankheit U72-5
Schlaflähmung U72-18; U113-7
Schlaflatenz U72-5,10
schlaflos **U72**-7
Schlaflosigkeit **U72**-16,12; U120-13
–, psychogene U77-14
Schlafmangel U72-5
Schlafmittel **U11**-16; **U93**-14; U72-5; U92-23; **U135**-9
Schlafmütze U72-1
Schlafprofil U102-12
schläfrig **U72**-1 f
Schläfrigkeit **U72**-1; **U7**-5; U77-4
Schlafsedierung U135-8
Schlafspindeln U72-5
Schlafstadien U72-5,10
Schlafstörung **U72**-16,5
Schlafsucht **U72**-17
Schlaftiefe U72-10
Schlaftrunkenheit U72-5
Schlaf-Wach-Gewohnheiten U72-8
– – Rhythmus **U72**-8; U7-16
– – 24-stündiger U72-8
Schlafwandeln **U72**-15; U65-1
Schlafwandler(in) **U72**-15
schlafwandlerisch **U72**-15
Schlag **U6**-4; **U33**-1; U5-13
–, elektrischer **U6**-14
Schlagader **U34**-3
Schlaganfall **U124**-14; U104-2
Schlaganfallpatient(in) U142-26
Schlaganfallrisiko U124-14
schlagen **U6**-4; **U33**-1; U64-11
Schlagvolumen **U33**-7; U36-7
schlaksig **U25**-5
Schlammpackung **U1**-20; U140-24
Schlangenbiss **U91**-16
Schlangengift U91-2
Schlangengift-Antiserum **U91**-15
Schlangengift-Antivenin **U91**-15
Schlangenserum U91-15
schlank **U24**-6; **U25**-5
Schlankheit **U24**-6; **U25**-5
Schlankheitsdiät U2-12

Schlankheitskur U25-5
schlapp **U31**-12
– fühlen, sich U65-11
schlau **U59**-11
Schlauchstethoskop U17-2
Schlauchverband U141-10
Schlaufe **U138**-4
schlechter werden **U4**-12
– Gesundheitszustand U4-1
schleichen **U65**-8
schleichend **U119**-7; U89-18
Schleier U59-7
Schleiersehen U59-5
schleifen **U27**-18; **U64**-13
Schleifendiuretika U48-8; U92-21
schleifenförmig U129-4
Schleifmittel **U5**-8
Schleifpapier U27-19
Schleim **U44**-9; **U86**-17; **U103**-18,12; U92-15,30
–, hochvisköser U36-12
–, zäher U44-8 f
Schleimbeutel **U29**-10,3; U23-11
Schleimbeutelentzündung **U29**-10
schleimbildend **U98**-7
Schleimdrüsen U44-9; U52-13
Schleimhaut **U44**-9; **U86**-17
–, blasse U86-17
–, mastikatorische U27-15
–, rissige U86-17
Schleimhautabstoßung U56-20
Schleimhautauskleidung U86-8,17
Schleimhautbarriere U86-17
Schleimhauteffloreszenzen U96-3
Schleimhautentzündung U86-17
Schleimhauterosion U56-20; U114-13
Schleimhautfetzen U86-17
Schleimhautimmunität U39-4
schleimhautprotektiv U92-29
Schleimhautreizung U104-3
Schleimhauttransplantat U130-1,10
Schleimhautveränderung U86-17
Schleimhautverdickung U86-17
schleimig **U44**-9; **U86**-17; **U98**-7
schleimig-eitrig U44-9
schleimlösend **U92**-15,2
Schleimlöser U86-17
Schleimpfropf U44-9; U71-7; U111-7
Schleimpilze U90-18
Schleimproduktion, übermäßige U44-9
Schleimschicht U44-9
Schleimsekretion, übermäßige U44-9
Schleimstoff **U86**-17
Schleimstraße (Nasenrachenraum) U43-6; U103-16
Schleimverlegung (Bronchien) U86-17
Schlemm-Kanal **U58**-11
schlendern, gemächlich **U65**-7
schleudern **U64**-14; **U65**-12
Schleudertrauma **U124**-18; U5-2; U113-13
Schleuderverband U140-20
Schließmuskel **U30**-9
Schlinge **U64**-14; **U138**-4

Schlinge (Knoten) U137-6,17
– (Verband) **U141**-8; U140-20
–, elektrische **U127**-11; **U132**-9
Schlingenelektrode U127-9; U138-5
schlingenförmig U129-4
Schlingern **U65**-9
schlittern **U65**-8
Schluchzen **U67**-10; **U66**-3; U113-2
Schluck **U46**-2; **U21**-8
Schluckakt **U46**-2; U40-10; U43-7
Schluckangst U77-5
Schluckauf **U46**-3
Schluckbeschwerden U104-6; U109-5
Schlucken **U46**-2; U60-7; U73-13
–, schmerzhaftes U103-6; U109-5
schlucken **U109**-5; U27-15
–, unzerkaut U46-2
Schluckimpfung U45-2; U122-3
Schluckreflex U46-2; U57-10; U113-1
Schluckstörung **U109**-5; U46-2; U113-10
Schluckzentrum U46-2
Schlund(enge) **U21**-12; **U45**-4; U17-3
Schlunddarm U85-21
schlüpfen **U65**-12
Schlüpfhilfe U69-11
schlüpfrig U17-14
Schlupfwarze U50-18
schlurfen **U65**-11
Schlussdesinfektion U139-5
Schlüsselbein **U28**-11; U21-12
Schlüsselbeinbruch U28-11
Schlüsselbeingelenk, äußeres U28-11 f
Schlüsselenzym U78-8
Schlüsselgriff U62-11; U64-10
Schlüssellochchirurgie **U128**-1
Schlüsselrolle U39-20
Schlüsselwert U101-16
Schlusston U33-1
schmächtig **U24**-6; **U25**-8
schmackhaft **U62**-6 f; **U2**-5
Schmackhaftigkeit U62-1
schmal **U24**-6; **U25**-5
schmalbrüstig U25-9
schmalhüftig **U22**-7; **U25**-9
schmalschultrig U25-9
schmarotzen **U90**-13
Schmarotzertum U90-13
schmatzen U67-17
schmecken **U62**-6
Schmeckzellen U62-6
Schmelz **U26**-15
Schmelzauflösung U81-22
Schmelzbildung U26-15
Schmelz-Dentin-Grenze U26-16
Schmelze **U82**-7
schmelzen **U82**-7; U9-12
Schmelzgut U82-7
Schmelzmasse **U82**-7
Schmelzoberhäutchen U26-15; U27-9
Schmelzofen U82-7
Schmelzpulver U26-15
Schmelzpunkt **U82**-7
Schmelztemperatur **U82**-7

Schmelz-Zement-Grenze U26-17
Schmerz **U104**-4 ff; **U104**-21; **U113**-2
–, klopfender U26-1
–, krampfartiger U109-14
–, nozizeptiver U57-13
–, seelischer U77-2
–, stechender **U104**-13; U6-7
–, übertragener U52-3
–, viszeraler U86-21
Schmerzattacke U103-4; U104-14
Schmerzbahnen U40-3; U104-20
Schmerzdauer **U104**-8
schmerzempfindlich U89-14
Schmerzempfindung **U57**-13,2; **U135**-7; **U104**-20
Schmerzen (Oberbauch) **U109**-12
– verursachen U104-18
–, akute **U107**-11
–, heftige U125-1
–, kolikartige U47-8
–, pektanginöse U124-11
schmerzerfüllt **U104**-6
schmerzfrei U104-20
schmerzhaft **U104**-11,4,6; U62-8
Schmerzintensität **U104**-9
Schmerzklinik U14-2
schmerzlindernd **U135**-7
Schmerzlinderung **U104**-19; U4-13
Schmerzlokalisation **U104**-10
schmerzlos U96-4; **U104**-6
Schmerzmittel U7-10; **U135**-7
Schmerzmodulation U42-4
Schmerzqualität **U104**-7
Schmerzrezeptor **U57**-13
Schmerzschwelle U104-18; U61-7
schmerzstillend **U104**-20; U135-7
Schmerzsyndrom, myofasziales U77-14
Schmerztherapie U142-18
Schmerztoleranzgrenze **U104**-18
Schmerzunempfindlichkeit **U15**-11; **U135**-2; U104-6
schmerzverzerrt U104-6,12
Schmerzzustände, neurogene U113-14
schmetterlingsförmiger Ausschlag U108-9
Schmierblutung, postkoitale U68-5
schmieren **U17**-14; **U56**-9
schmierig **U56**-8; U9-8
Schmiermittel U29-8
Schmierseife U82-14
schmollen **U67**-16; **U76**-9
Schmollmund U67-16
Schmuckprothese U142-6
Schmuggler(in) **U11**-7
Schmugglerring U11-7
schmusen **U62**-10; **U67**-7; **U68**-2
schmutzig **U68**-10
Schnabelbecken U22-7
Schnabeltasse U2-3
Schnappatmung **U44**-7; U111-2
schnappen **U64**-9
–, nach Luft U44-7
Schnapphüfte U22-7
Schnaps U10-2

Schnarchen **U44**-1; **U66**-5; **U72**-13
-, habituelles U44-1
-, starkes U72-13
Schnarcher(in) **U72**-13
Schnarchgeräusche U72-13
schnauben U103-16; **U66**-5
schnaufen **U44**-7
schnäuzen U103-16
Schnecke **U60**-11
Schneckenachse U60-11
Schneckenfenster **U60**-8
Schneckengang U60-11
-, häutiger U60-11
Schneckenlabyrinth U60-10
Schneckenspindel U60-11
Schneckenspitze U60-11
Schneeblindheit U59-18
Schneidblätter U132-4
Schneide U87-10; U132-3
Schneidekante U26-3
schneiden **U5**-6; **U6**-7
Schneidezahn U26-3
-, linker mittlerer U87-15
Schnellabstrich U116-5
Schnellinfusion U135-19; U136-1
Schnellinjektion, i. v. U122-4; U136-5
schniefen **U10**-20; **U44**-2; **U62**-2; **U67**-10
Schnitt **U6**-7; **U87**-5; **U126**-10,9; **U127**-2; **U5**-6
Schnitt machen **U87**-5
-, histologischer U86-1
Schnittentbindung U71-3,9; U87-5
Schnittfläche U126-10; U6-7; U87-4
Schnittkonisation U127-12
Schnittrand U5-6; U137-12
-, chirurgischer U126-3; U138-1
Schnittverletzung U5-9
Schnittwunde **U5**-6
Schnüffeln **U10**-20; U11-8; U67-3
- (Lösungsmittel) **U11**-23
schnüffeln **U44**-2; **U62**-2
Schnüffelstellung **U8**-17
Schnüffelsucht **U62**-2
Schnüffler(in) **U10**-20; **U62**-2
schnupfen U103-16
Schnupfen **U10**-20; **U94**-9; U95-3
-, leichter **U62**-2
-, nervöser U94-9
-, starker U94-9
Schnupftabak **U10**-20
Schnupftabakdose U10-20
schnuppern **U44**-2; **U62**-2
Schnurrbart **U25**-14; U21-16
Schock(zustand) **U64**-7; **U124**-4
Schock, anaphylaktischer U124-3
-, elektrischer **U6**-14
-, hämorrhagischer U38-8
-, hyperdynamischer septischer U88-16
-, hypoglykämischer U124-7
-, hypovolämischer **U6**-15
-, kardiogener U110-14
-, septischer **U124**-5; U139-1

Schock, bakterieller U124-5
-, spinaler U124-18
-, toxischer **U91**-22
Schockbehandlung U110-14; U124-4
schockieren U110-14; **U124**-4
Schocklunge U124-4
Schockraum U14-9; U123-4
Schocksyndrom, toxisches U91-4,22
Schockzustand U110-14
schön **U25**-13
schonen **U8**-18; **U126**-13; U28-17
-, sich **U1**-10; U76-19
Schönheitsfehler **U25**-18
Schonkost **U2**-12
Schonung **U8**-18
Schorf **U56**-20; **U114**-8; **U140**-9,6
Schorfbildung U21-9
Schoß **U22**-10; U80-5
schräg U17-4
- stellen **U63**-10
Schrägaufnahme U87-4
Schrägfraktur U106-1
Schräglage U71-5
Schramme **U5**-8 f
Schranke **U81**-20
schrauben U133-10
Schraubenbolzen **U141**-16
Schraubenkopf U21-1
Schreck **U65**-16
Schrecken **U6**-21
schrecken **U124**-4
schreckhaft U65-16
schrecklich **U6**-21; U12-2
Schreckreaktion U65-16; U67-7
Schrei U66-1
Schreibarbeit U15-6
Schreibkraft, medizinische **U102**-17
Schreibkrampf U103-20
Schreibunfähigkeit U113-9
schreien **U66**-14
schreiten **U65**-4
Schreitreflex U65-4
schrill U113-5
Schritt **U22**-10; **U64**-1; **U65**-4 ff
- halten (mit) U65-6
-, langer **U65**-4
-, mutiger U75-18
Schritte, erste U65-4
-, zaghafte U65-4
-, zögernde U65-4
Schrittmacher **U65**-6; **U123**-13
schrittmacherbedingt U99-13
Schrittmachercode U123-13
Schrittmacherelektrode U123-13
Schrittmacherpotential U42-5
Schrittmachersyndrom U123-13
Schrittmachertherapie **U65**-6; **U123**-13
Schrittmacherunterstützung U129-18
schrittweise **U65**-4; U129-4
- Mobilisation U142-13
Schrotflinte U6-8
Schrumpfblase U31-1; U48-11
schrumpfen U140-8; U130-1
Schrumpfgallenblase U47-7

Schrumpfleber U47-1
Schrumpfniere U48-2
Schrumpfung U31-1
Schub **U103**-4
Schüben, in U119-11
schüchtern **U75**-17
Schüchternheit U77-12
-, lähmende U75-17
Schuhe, orthopädische U142-12
Schuheinlage U64-16
Schuhwerk U23-13
Schulangst U77-5
Schuld **U77**-10; U76-1
schuldbeladen U77-10
Schuldbewusstsein, mangelndes U75-21
Schuldgefühle **U76**-13; **U77**-10
- verdrängen U74-14
schuldig **U77**-10; U71-26
Schuldkomplex U77-10
schuldlos **U77**-10
Schuldwahn U77-20
Schulter **U23**-3
-, instabile U23-3
Schulter(gelenk)luxation U23-3
Schulter-Arm-Gipsverband U23-3
Schulterblatt **U28**-12; U23-3
-, flügelförmig abstehendes U28-12
Schulterblatthochstand U28-12
Schulterbreite U23-3
Schultereckgelenk U28-11
Schultergelenkpfanne U28-12; U87-26
Schultergurt U23-3
Schultergürtel **U22**-2; U23-3; U28-11 f
Schulter-Hand-Syndrom U23-3
Schulterheben U67-4
Schulterhöhe U28-12
Schulterkreisen U23-3
Schulterlage U71-5
schultern **U23**-3
Schultern, breite U25-6
-, schmale U23-3; U24-6
Schulterpolster U23-3
Schulterriemen U23-3
Schultersteife, schmerzhafte U23-3
Schulterstütze U131-13
Schulterzucken U67-3
Schuppe(n) **U86**-12; **U114**-7; U56-2,20
schuppenartig U86-12
Schuppenbildung U60-1
Schuppenflechte U89-2; **U114**-7
schuppenförmig **U114**-7
Schuppenshampoo U114-7
Schuppung U60-1; U95-6; U114-1
schuppig **U114**-7; U56-8
Schürfwunde **U5**-6
schürzen (Lippen) U63-6
Schuss **U6**-8
- setzen **U11**-8
-, (i. v.) **U11**-8
-, goldener U122-4
Schussapparat U118-5
Schüssel **U2**-8

Schussverletzung **U6**-8
Schusswaffen **U6**-8
Schusswunde **U6**-8; U86-1
Schüttelfrost **U12**-15; **U105**-9; U94-9
Schüttellähmung U64-6; U105-7
Schüttelmixtur U9-10; U64-6
schütteln **U64**-6; **U105**-7
– (Kopf) **U67**-3
Schütteln, kräftiges U64-6
Schütteltrauma U105-7
schütter (Haarwuchs) **U25**-16
Schutz **U8**-2,4; **U77**-25; U132-2
Schutzbrille U8-4
Schütze **U6**-8
schützen **U8**-2; **U109**-13
Schutzhandschuhe U139-17
Schutzimpfung **U122**-3,1
Schutzmechanismus U88-2
Schutzpolster U17-13
Schutzvorrichtung U6-22; U139-15
schwabblig **U64**-5
schwach **U4**-7; **U7**-4; **U31**-13
– fühlen, sich U103-9
Schwäche **U4**-7
–, körperliche **U103**-9; **U142**-4
Schwächegefühl **U103**-9,13; **U7**-4
schwächen **U31**-13; **U103**-9
Schwachsichtigkeit U59-17
schwachsinnig **U4**-7
Schwachsinnige(r) **U77**-24
Schwächung **U89**-4
Schwammbiopsie U118-5
Schwammgold U82-28
Schwammniere U48-2; U86-23
Schwanenhalsdeformität U142-8
schwanger **U70**-5
– werden U51-9; U69-2,14; U70-2,5
–, im 8. Monat U70-5
Schwangerengymnastik U70-10
schwängern **U69**-2
Schwangerschaft **U70**-6; U73-3
Schwangerschaften, Anzahl der bisherigen **U70**-7
Schwangerschafts- u. Geburtenanamnese **U70**-7
Schwangerschaftsabbruch U70-9
Schwangerschaftsabschnitt, letzter U55-21
Schwangerschaftsdauer U70-2,6
–, errechnete U70-10
Schwangerschaftsdermatose **U70**-15
Schwangerschaftserbrechen U70-7
–, unstillbares **U70**-12
Schwangerschaftshypertonie U110-13
Schwangerschaftsikterus U108-4
Schwangerschaftsstreifen **U70**-16,7
Schwangerschaftstest U70-6
Schwangerschaftstoxikose U91-22
Schwangerschaftsvorsorgeuntersuchung U18-2
Schwangerschaftswoche U85-1
schwanken **U64**-5; **U100**-15
Schwanken U103-13; U110-11
Schwankungen, hormonelle U71-22

Schwannom **U98**-13
Schwann-Scheide U98-13
Schwann-Zelle **U40**-14
Schwanz U52-5; U53-7
schwanzförmig **U41**-15; **U87**-19
Schwanzlarve U90-17
Schwartz-Bartter-Syndrom U55-24; U81-23
Schwärzepilze U90-18
schwatzen **U66**-19
schweben, im Wasser **U1**-19
schwebend U58-11
Schwebetank U1-19
Schwefel **U82**-24
Schwefelatom U81-2
Schwefeldioxid(dämpfe) U82-3,11,24
Schwefelmilch U82-24
schwefeln **U82**-24
Schwefelquelle U82-24
Schwefelsäure U82-24
Schwefelwasserstoff U82-9,24
Schweifkern U41-10; U87-19
Schweigen **U61**-11
– bringen, zum **U61**-11
Schweigepflicht **U18**-11
schweigsam **U61**-11; **U66**-18
Schweineinsulin U55-12
Schweiß **U105**-12,15
Schweißabsonderung **U105**-15
Schweißausbruch U51-11; U105-12
schweißbedeckt **U105**-12
schweißbildend **U105**-15
Schweißdrüse **U56**-10; U105-12,15
–, apokrine U56-10
–, merokrine U42-11; U56-10
Schweißdrüsenadenom U98-4
Schweißdrüsenausführungsgang U56-11
Schweißdrüsenentzündung U56-10; U105-15
Schweißfriesel U62-11
Schweißfüße U105-12
schweißgebadet U56-10; U105-12
Schweißperlen U105-12
Schweißpore **U56**-11
Schweißsekretion U105-12,15
Schweißtest U56-10; U105-12
schweißtreibend U56-10; **U105**-15
Schweißverdunstung U105-14
Schweißverlust U56-10
Schweißzentrum U56-10
schwelgen, in Erinnerungen **U74**-2
Schwelle **U88**-7
–, osmotische U81-21
Schwellenaudiometrie U61-2,7
Schwellendosis U88-7; U99-9
Schwellenpotential U42-5; U88-7
Schwellenreiz U88-7
Schwellenschwundtest U61-3
Schwellensubstanz U88-7
Schwellentraining, anaerobes U1-15
Schwellenwert **U88**-7; **U100**-24; U61-7
Schwellenwertperkussion U107-8
Schwellkörper **U52**-15 f; U53-7

Schwellkörperinsuffizienz U52-15
Schwellung **U5**-15; **U97**-2; **U108**-10
– (Uterus) U71-27
schwenken U9-9
schwer **U24**-8
Schweregrad U92-20; U117-1
– (Verletzung) U8-9
– (Erkrankung) U125-4
schwerelos **U24**-1
schwerfällig **U76**-17
Schwerfälligkeit **U76**-17
Schwergewicht U24-8
schwerhörig **U61**-9,2
Schwerhörigkeit **U113**-13; U61-2
–, psychogene U61-9
Schwerhörigkeitsgrad U113-13
Schwerkettenkrankheit U39-6
Schwerkraft U70-7
Schwermetall U82-6
Schwermetallvergiftung U82-33; U91-2
Schwermut **U76**-22; **U77**-17
–, lähmende U71-22
schwermütig **U76**-22; **U77**-17
Schwermütigkeit **U76**-22
Schwerspat-Staublunge U82-29
schwerstbehindert U66-18
Schwertfortsatz U28-13; U43-13
Schwertfortsatzspitze U22-5
schwerverdaulich U2-7
schwerwiegend **U117**-17; U121-14
Schwesterchromatiden U84-7
Schwesternhelfer(in) U16-2 f,15
Schwesternschüler(in) **U16**-3; U15-7
Schwesternzimmer U16-2
Schwiele U23-6; **U106**-15
schwimmen, obenauf **U81**-27
Schwimmhosennävus U98-15; U114-3
Schwimmweste U6-19; U123-1
Schwindel **U103**-13; **U113**-6; U1-12
–, lagebedingter U63-1
Schwindelanfall **U113**-6; U103-4,13
Schwindelgefühl **U103**-13; **U113**-6,4
schwindeln U75-12
schwindlig **U103**-13; **U113**-6; **U7**-5
Schwindung U31-1
schwingen **U64** 5
Schwingung, niederfrequente U57-17
Schwirren **U110**-3
– (Schilddrüse) U54-6
–, systolisches U33-3
Schwitzen U51-11
schwitzen **U105**-12
–, starkes U119-11
schwul U68-14; U80-8
Schwund **U108**-14; U142-8
– (Zahnfleisch) U26-12
Schwung **U64**-5
schwungvoll **U1**-6; **U76**-17
Score **U100**-6,16
Screening-Test U118-2
Scrotum bipartitum U52-2
Sebolith U56-8
Seborrhoe/-ö U56-8; U114-7
seborrhoisch **U56**-8

Sebum **U56**-8; U98-17
Sechsjahrmolaren U26-7
Sechzigjährige(r) **U80**-16
Seckel-Syndrom U24-4
Second Messenger **U83**-17
Second-look-Operation U126-1
Secretin U55-13
Secretin-Pankreozymin-Test U55-13
Sectio (caesarea) U71-3,9; U87-5
Sedativum **U77**-17; **U135**-9 f; U92-23
sedieren **U135**-10,8
sedierend U11-16; U92-22; U93-14
Sedierung **U135**-8 ff
Sediment **U81**-27
Sedimentbildung **U81**-27
sedimentieren U116-12
seekrank **U103**-11
Seele **U77**-2
Seelenleben U77-2
seelisch **U77**-2; **U73**-1; U15-12
Segel U32-9
–, septales U32-9
Segment **U87**-6
–, übermäßig bewegliches U43-3
segmentär **U87**-6
Segmentatelektase U111-15
Segmentation **U43**-3; **U87**-6
Segmentbildung **U43**-3; **U87**-6
Segmentbronchus U43-9; U87-6
segmentieren **U87**-6
segmentiertes Genom U84-1
Segmentreflex U87-6
Segmentresektion **U87**-6
Segregationsanalyse **U84**-37
Sehachse U59-5,7,15; U87-3,9
Sehbahnen U40-3; U58-14
sehbehindert U59-5; U142-3
sehen **U59**-1; **U67**-14; **U87**-4
Sehen **U59**-6,18; U58-2
–, binokulares **U59**-16
–, peripheres U59-6; U87-15
–, photopisches U59-9
–, räumliches U59-6
–, skotopisches U59-6,9
–, stereoskopisches U59-6
–, trichromatisches U59-9
–, verschwommenes **U103**-14; U59-6; U113-6,11
Sehfeld **U59**-7
Sehhilfe U19-11; U59-5
Sehhügel **U41**-9
Sehinseln U59-7
Sehkraft **U59**-6; U21-3; U58-2
Sehleistung U59-6
Sehne **U30**-5; U5-16; U31-1
sehnen, sich **U11**-2
Sehnenansatz U30-3
Sehnenfäden U30-5; U32-12
Sehnenfädenabriss U32-12
Sehnenfädenverwachsung U32-12
Sehnengleitgewebe U29-11
Sehnenhaut **U30**-5
Sehnenknötchen U30-5
Sehnennaht U30-5; **U137**-2

Sehnenplastik U30-5
Sehnenreflexe U17-9; U31-12; U113-1
Sehnenriss U5-7,19; U64-13
Sehnenruptur U5-7; U64-13
Sehnenscheide U29-3,11; U30-5; U86-6,8
Sehnenscheidenentzündung U30-5
Sehnenschmerz U104-21
Sehnenspindel U57-12
Sehnentransplantation U30-5
Sehnerv **U58**-15
Sehnervenatrophie U58-15; U89-29
Sehnervenentzündung U58-15
Sehnervenkopf U58-15
Sehnervenkreuzung **U58**-15; U41-14
Sehnervenpapille **U58**-14
Sehnervenschädigung U58-15
sehnig **U30**-5
Sehprobentafel(n) **U17**-5; U18-14; U58-2; U59-8; U102-12
Sehpurpur U58-13; U59-5
Sehrinde U86-23
–, (primäre) U41-6
Sehschärfe **U59**-8; U17-5
– in die Ferne U87-11
–, binokulare **U59**-8
–, herabgesetzte U59-8
–, korrigierte U59-8
–, zentrale U59-8
Sehschärfenbestimmung U59-8
Sehschärfenprüfung U59-8
Sehschwäche U59-8,11
Sehstörungen U103-14
Sehtafel U21-3; U102-12
Sehvermögen **U59**-6; U89-4
Sehwinkel U59-5
Sehzentrum, primäres U41-6
Seide U137-10
Seife, antiseptische U82-14
–, medizinische U82-14
seifenartig U82-14
Seifenersatz U82-14
seifig U82-14
Seilbahn U6-3
Seilspringen **U65**-16; U1-13
Seite **U22**-6; **U87**-4
Seitenansicht U87-4,18
Seitenaufnahme U87-4,18
Seitenbandzerrung U5-16
Seitenblickoptik U133-2
Seitenfontanelle U28-7; U60-14
seitengleich (Pupillen) **U107**-15
Seitenkette U81-7
Seitenlage **U131**-16,11; U63-7
–, stabile **U8**-17
Seitenlagerung U8-17
Seitenstechen U104-13
Seitenventrikel U41-4; U87-18
seitlich **U87**-13,18
seitwärts **U87**-18
Seitwärtsbeweglichkeit U142-8
Seit-zu-Seit-Anastomose U129-6
Sekret **U20**-16; **U54**-2; **U88**-11
–, eitriges U58-9; U88-11

Sekret, schleimiges U44-9
–, seröses U86-9
–, übelriechendes U96-6
–, wässriges U82-4; U88-11
–, zähes U88-11
–, zähflüssiges U36-12
Sekretin **U54**-9; **U55**-13
Sekretininfusionstest U55-13
Sekretion **U49**-4; **U54**-2; **U88**-11
–, parakrine U54-2
–, pulsierende U54-2
–, tubuläre U49-4
sekretionsanregend U42-8
sekretionsfördernd U42-8
sekretionshemmend U40-7
Sekretionsphase **U51**-8
– (Menstruationszyklus) U55-19
Sekretionsvakuole U83-11
Sekretolytikum **U92**-15; U86-17
sekretorisch **U54**-2; **U88**-11
Sekretprotein U83-10
Sekretverflüssigung U81-22
Sektion **U12**-20; **U87**-5; **U100**-2; **U126**-12
–, gerichtliche U15-21; U12-20
sekundäre Wundheilung U140-5
sekundärer Bote, G-Protein-gekoppelter U83-17
sekundäres Hauttransplantat **U130**-7
Sekundärkallus U106-15
Sekundärzotten U85-24
Sekundenkapazität U44-12
Selbst **U39**-21
Selbstachtung U76-13; U77-17
Selbstannahme U75-2
Selbstanzeige U20-6
Selbstbefriedigung, sexuelle **U68**-8
Selbstbehalt U18-15
Selbstbehandlung U20-3
selbstbewusst U75-2; U76-12
–, übertrieben U75-17
Selbstbewusstsein U14-5; U75-2
Selbstbewusstseinstraining U75-20
Selbstbild U75-2
Selbstentgiftung U91-23
Selbsterhaltungstrieb U73-11
Selbsterkenntnis U1-16
Selbsterniedrigung U75-2
Selbsthilfe **U8**-1; **U19**-11; **U142**-29
Selbsthilfegruppe U11-13; U142-29
Selbsthilfegruppe für Trauernde U12-13
Selbsthilfevorrichtung U19-11
Selbstinfektion U39-21
Selbstkontrolle U125-5
Selbstkonzept **U75**-2
Selbstkritik U76-13
Selbstlaut U66-12
selbstlimitierend **U119**-12
Selbstmord begehen U12-4,8
Selbstmorddrohung U12-8
Selbstmordgedanken U12-8
Selbst-Nicht-Selbst-Erkennung U39-21
Selbstreduplikation U84-16
Selbstregulation U88-2
selbstsicher **U75**-17,19

selbstständig U76-13
Selbstständigkeit **U142**-28
selbstsüchtig **U75**-2,21
Selbsttötung **U12**-8
Selbsttötungsabsicht U12-8; U73-3
Selbstuntersuchung **U107**-2
– (Brust) U50-17
Selbstvergiftung **U91**-14
Selbstverlegung **U102**-10; U75-21
Selbstvernachlässigung U77-11
Selbstversorgung, Fähigkeit zur U142-28
Selbstverständnis U75-2
Selbstverstümmelung U5-2; U75-2
Selbstverteidigung U12-10
Selbstvertrauen **U75**-17,2; U14-5
–, mangelndes U18-11
selbstverursacht U119-8
Selbstvorwürfe **U76**-13; U75-2; U77-10
Selbstwertgefühl U75-2; U142-28
Selektionskriterien U134-2
Selen **U82**-21; U79-17; U81-5
Selenmangel U78-21; U82-21
Selenocystein U82-21
Selensulfid U82-21
Selenvergiftung U82-21
Sella turcica U54-5
Sellink-Passage U118-18
Semen **U53**-6
Semicanalis tubae auditivae U60-7
Semilunarklappe U32-10
semipermeabel U36-16; **U88**-6
senden **U8**-9
Seneszenz **U80**-13
Senfgas U82-2
Senfpackung U140-25
Sengstaken-Blakemore-Sonde U125-18
senil **U80**-13
Senior **U80**-13
Seniorenheim U14-4; U80-2
Seniorenrunden U80-15
senken **U31**-2; **U116**-20
– (Augenlider) U58-3
– (Kopf) U63-3
–, (sich) **U64**-15
Senkniere U113-17
Senkung **U56**-19; **U64**-15; **U113**-17
Senkwehen U71-3
sensationell **U65**-16
sensibel **U57**-8; **U76**-4; U56-1
sensibilisieren **U39**-23; **U122**-5
Sensibilisierung **U122**-5
Sensibilität **U57**-8; **U76**-4; U135-4
–, epikritische U57-8
–, herabgesetzte U57-3
Sensibilitätsprüfung U26-18
– (mit neurolog. Nadel) U62-11
Sensibilitätsstörung U5-12; U40-4
Sensibilitätsverlust U57-3
sensitiv **U57**-8
Sensitivität **U57**-8; **U100**-23
sensomotorisch U57-7
Sensor **U57**-5
sensorisch **U57**-7,10; U76-4

Sensorium **U57**-7
Sensus **U57**-6
SEP U40-7
Sepsis **U124**-5; **U139**-1
– acutissima U119-13
–, perakut verlaufende U119-13
sepsisbedingt U120-12
Sepsisherd U124-5
septiert **U32**-9; **U86**-15
Septikämie **U124**-5
Septum **U86**-15
– interatriale **U32**-9
– interventriculare **U32**-9; U86-15
– nasi U86-15
– rectovaginale U45-16
– vesicovaginale U86-15
Septumdeviation U86-15
Septumhypertrophie U32-9
–, asymmetrische U110-9
Sequenz **U84**-12
–, codierende U84-13
Sequenzanalyse/-ierung **U84**-12,34
sequenzieren **U84**-2
Sequenztherapie U120-5
Sequenzwiederholung U84-12
Sequesterzyste U89-24
sequestriert U91-17
Serienmörder(in) U12-9
Serienschnitt U87-5; U126-10
Serienszintigramme U99-17
Serientitration U116-17
Serodiagnostik U122-11
Serokonversion **U122**-11; U37-3
Serokonversionskrankheit U122-11
serokonvertieren **U122**-11
Serologie **U122**-11
serologisch **U122**-11
Serom **U86**-9
seropositiv U116-22; U122-11
–, Chlamydien- U90-14
Seropositivität U122-11
Seroreaktion **U122**-11
serös **U86**-9
Serosa **U86**-9
Serosa(ein)riss U86-9
Serosazyste U86-9
seröse Mittelohrentzündung, U86-9
Serositis **U86**-9
Serotonin **U42**-11
Serotoninaktivität U92-3
Serotoninantagonist U42-11
serotoninerg U42-11
Serotoninspiegel U42-11
Serotoninwiederaufnahme-Hemmer, selektiver U42-11
Serotyp **U122**-11
Serovakzination U37-3
Serovar **U122**-11
Sertoli (Stütz)zellen **U53**-9; U52-4
Sertoli-cell-only-Syndrom U53-9
Sertoli-Leydig-Zelltumor U53-9
Sertoli-Zelltumor U53-9
Serum **U37**-3
Serumalbumin U78-18

serumartig **U86**-9
Serumcholesterinspiegel U47-12; U37-2
Serumeisen U37-3
Serumelektrolyte **U116**-7
Serumgastrinspiegel U55-13
Serum-Glutamat-Oxalacetat-Transaminase (SGOT) U116-14
Serum-Glutamat-Pyruvat-Transaminase (SGPT) **U47**-16; U116-14
serumhaltig **U86**-9
Serumhepatitis U94-15
Serumhöchstwert U116-16
Serumikterus U129-16
Serumkrankheit U37-3; U39-9
Serumkupfer U82-29
Serumtherapie U97-18; U122-11
Sesambein U28-2
Seuchenbekämpfung U101-25
seufzen **U44**-1; **U66**-4
Seufzer **U44**-1; **U66**-4
–, müder U76-18
Seufzeratmung U44-4; U111-2
Sexchromatin U84-6
Sexist(in) **U68**-1
sexistisch **U68**-1
Sexologie **U68**-1
Sexualanamnese U68-1; U102-4
Sexualdifferenzierung U85-11
Sexualerziehung U68-1; U142-18
Sexualhormon, weibliches U55-1
Sexualität **U68**-1
Sexualkontakt U62-8
Sexualreife U80-10
Sexualtrieb **U68**-1,4; U11-2
Sexualverhalten U68-1; U75-3
–, abweichendes U68-15
–, promiskuöses U68-12
–, unbeherrschtes U75-18
Sexualwissenschaft **U68**-1
sexuell **U15**-10; **U73**-12
sexuelle Spannkraft U1-6
sexy **U68**-3,9
sezernieren **U49**-4; **U54**-2,8; **U88**-11
sezieren **U87**-5; **U126**-12
Sezieren (Leiche) U12-14
Seziermesser U132-3
SGPT **U47**-16
Shaken-Baby-Syndrom U105-7
Shampoo, medizinisches U9-1
Shigellose **U94**-18; U90-7
Shunt **U36**-14; U129-6
–, arteriovenöser U34-6; U36-14
–, jejunoilealer U45-11
–, portokavaler U36-3; U47-4
–, portosystemischer U36-14; U47-4
–, ventrikuloatrialer U125-15
–, ventrikuloperitonealer U36-14
shunten **U36**-14
Shuntinfektion U36-14
Shuntumkehr U36-14
SIADH U55-24
Sialinsäurerest U81-4
Sialolith U89-21

Sialorrhoe/-ö **U109**-3; U45-3
Siamesische Zwillinge U70-14
sichelförmig U107-1
Sichelfuß(haltung) **U23**-14
Sichelzellen U37-5
Sichelzellen-Hämoglobin U116-9
Sichelzellgen U84-1
sicher U8-2,4; **U75**-17
Sicherheit **U8**-4
Sicherheitsalarm U8-4
Sicherheitsbestimmungen U6-22
Sicherheitseinführschutz **U133**-7
Sicherheitsgurt U6-3; U8-2; U77-26
Sicherheitskontrolle U8-4
Sicherheitsmechanismus **U133**-7
Sicherheitsnadel U8-4; U141-15
Sicherheitsrisiko U8-4
Sicherheitsschild **U133**-7
Sicherheitsventil U8-4
Sicherheitsvorkehrungen **U6**-22;
 U9-18; U132-5; U139-1
sichern U8-2; **U137**-4
sicherstellen U8-2; U44-6; U101-24
Sicherung **U8**-4; U132-2
Sicht **U59**-7; **U87**-4
–, persönliche U75-1
–, schlechte U59-7
–, unter U128-2; U133-2; U135-17
sichtbar **U57**-4; **U59**-6; **U102**-2
– machen **U59**-7; **U99**-12
– werden U87-4
Sichtbarkeit **U59**-7
Sichtkontrolle U132-8
Sichtschutz (Anästhesiebereich) **U131**-7
Sichtung **U8**-19
Sichtweite **U59**-7
Sickerblutung **U38**-7; U5-18; U89-26
sickern **U38**-7
sickernd U67-10
Sick-Sinus-Syndrom U33-5
Sideromakrophage U39-18
Siderophilin **U37**-6
Siderophore U78-19
Siebbein **U28**-8
Siebbeinhöhle U28-6
Siebbeinplatte U87-2
Siebbestrahlung U99-4
Siebzigjährige(r) **U80**-16
sieden U82-7
siedend (heiß) **U5**-11
Siedepunkt **U82**-7
Siegeszeichen U67-2
Sigmatismus **U66**-21
Sigmavolvulus U109-6
Sigmoidvolvulus U109-6
Signal **U67**-2; **U74**-2
–, akustisches U61-2
–, extrazelluläres U83-16
–, hormonales U83-16
signalisieren **U67**-2
Signalmittelungs-EKG U118-14
Signalpeptid U83-16
Signaltransduktion **U83**-16
Signalübertragung(sweg) U83-16

signifikant, statistisch **U100**-21
Signifikanzniveau U100-21
Signifikanztest U100-34
Silbe **U66**-12
Silbenstolpern **U66**-12,20
Silber **U82**-28
Silberblick **U67**-14
Silberfärbung U82-28
Silberglanz U82-28
Silberimprägnation U116-4
Silberimprägnationstechnik U82-28
Silberkolloid U82-28
Silbernitrat U82-16,28
Silber-Palladium-Legierung U82-28
Silicagel U82-30
Silikat **U82**-30
Silikofluorid U82-30
Silikon **U82**-30
Silikongummi U82-30
Silikonimplantat U82-30
Silikonpolymer U81-6
Silikose **U82**-30
Silikotuberkulose U82-30
Silizium **U82**-30; U79-17
Siliziumdioxid **U82**-30
Simonart-Bänder U85-15
Sims-Lage **U131**-15; U87-18
Sims-Position U8-17; U63-12
Simulant(in) **U4**-9
simulieren **U4**-9; U69-18
Singultus **U46**-3
sinken **U4**-14; **U64**-15; **U116**-20
Sinn **U57**-5 f
– für **U74**-4
Sinnenfreude U57-9
Sinnesänderung U74-1
Sinneseindruck **U57**-5
Sinnesempfindung **U57**-5
Sinneslust **U68**-4
Sinnesorgan **U57**-10
Sinnesreiz U57-7; U88-12
Sinnesschärfe U40-4; U57-7
Sinnestäuschung **U73**-10; **U77**-20
Sinneswahrnehmung **U57**-3,2; **U73**-10;
 U40-4
sinnlich **U57**-9; **U68**-9; U76-4
Sinnlichkeit **U57**-9
sinnlos U57-5; U76-8
Sinoatrialknoten U32-15
Sinus **U28**-6
– aortae U32-10
– caroticus U34-10
– ethmoidalis U28-6
– frontalis U28-6,8; U43-6; U87-20
– maxillaris **U43**-6; U28-10
– paranasales **U43**-6; U21-4; U28-6
– sphenoidalis U43-6
– splenici U35-4
– urogenitalis U85-21
– Valsalvae U32-10
– venosus sclerae **U58**-11
Sinusarrhythmie U32-15; U110-6
Sinusboden-Augmentation U129-19
Sinusbradykardie U33-5; U110-2

Sinusknoten **U32**-15
Sinusknotenerholungszeit U32-15
Sinuslift-Operation U129-19
Sinusoidauskleidung U47-4
Sinusoidendothel U86-14
Sinusoid-Erweiterung U47-4
Sinusrhythmus **U33**-6
Sinustachykardie U110-2
Sirup **U9**-11
Sirupus ipecacuanhae **U91**-25
Situation, klinische U108-2
Situationsangst U77-5
Situationsnaht U137-1
Sitzbad U1-17; U22-7; U142-20
Sitzbein **U28**-22
Sitzbeinhöcker U28-22
sitzen, auf d. Unterschenkeln U63-6
–, gerade U63-2
–, rittlings **U63**-5
Sitzfläche U19-13
Sitzhöhe U24-2
Sitzkissen U19-5
Sitzsack **U142**-19
Skabies **U96**-12; **U103**-19
skabiös U96-12
Skala **U24**-11; **U100**-6
Skalpell **U132**-3
Skalpellklinge U17-3
skalpieren **U25**-15
Skapula **U28**-12
Skarifikationstest **U118**-2; U5-9
Skelett **U28**-1
Skelettalter U28-1
skelettartig **U28**-1
Skelettentwicklung U28-1
Skeletthand U28-1
skelettieren **U28**-1
Skelettmuskel U28-1
Skelettmuskelfaser U30-1
Skelettmuskulatur U30-2
Skelettszintigramm U118-22
Skelettverformung U142-7
Skene-Drüsen **U50**-9
Skene-Gänge U50-9
Skiaskopie U58-13
Sklera **U58**-6
Sklerarand U58-6
Skleraruptur U58-6
Sklerektomie U58-6
Sklerenikterus U58-6; U108-4
Sklerodermie U56-3
Skleromyxödem U114-10
Skleroprotein U56-6
Sklerose, multiple U40-15
Sklerosierung U110-17
–, endoskopische U128-2
Sklerotherapie U110-17
–, endoskopische U128-2
Sklerotom **U85**-22
Skoliose U87-18
Skotom **U113**-11; U59-7
Skrotalhämatom U52-2
Skrotalhernie U52-2

Skrotalödem U52-2
Skrotalreflex U52-2
Skrotalwulst U85-10; U52-2
Skrotum **U52**-2
skrupellos **U75**-11
Smegma U52-17
Smith-Fraktur U106-10
Smog **U91**-7
Smog-Alarmstufe U91-6
Snellen-Sehprobentafel **U17**-5
Sodawasser U82-4
Sodbrennen **U32**-1; **U109**-4; U10-9
Sodoku U90-9
Sodomie U68-15
Sofortgedächtnis U74-1,8
Sofortmaßnahmen, lebensrettende **U123**-4; U125-3
Soforttypreaktion U39-23
Soft-Lasertherapie, medizinische U142-24
Sohlenbogen U87-17
Sohlenplatte U65-1
sohlenwärts **U87**-17
Solenopsis saevissima U91-16
solitär **U89**-3
Solitärknoten U89-16; U97-3
Solitärläsion U5-5
Sollgewicht U24-1
Solubilisation **U88**-5
Soma **U77**-2
somatisch **U77**-2
Somatisierung **U40**-7
Somatoliberin U55-5
Somatomedin C U55-5
Somatopleura U85-6
Somatostatin U55-5
Somatotropin **U55**-5
Somazelle U83-2
Somit **U85**-19
Somitenwand U85-19
Sommerdiarrhoe/-ö U95-1
Sommersprossen **U25**-18,13; **U114**-5
somnambul **U72**-15
Somnambulismus **U72**-15
Somniloquie U72-15
somnolent **U72**-1
Somnolenz **U7**-13; **U72**-1
Sonde **U132**-8
–, chirurgische U17-11
–, dreilumige U125-18
Sondenernährung **U125**-19; U2-3
Sonderschule U142-18
sondieren **U132**-8,3
Sonnenbrand U108-7
Sonnengeflecht U34-5; U40-12
Sonnenlicht meiden U103-15
Sonnenschutz U25-11
Sonnenstich **U105**-11
Sonografie **U118**-17
sonografisch **U118**-17
Sonogramm **U118**-17
Sopor **U7**-13
Sorge **U76**-5; U6-21; **U77**-5
–, übertriebene U1-1
Sorgeberechtigte(r) **U20**-3; **U77**-25

Sorgen U104-2 f
sorgen für **U88**-3
Sorgerecht, elterliches U77-25
sorgfältig **U20**-3; U104-6
Sorgfaltspflicht, Verletzung der **U20**-13
SOS-Signal **U6**-19
Sotos-Syndrom U24-4
Southern-Blot Methode **U84**-35
– Hybridisierung U84-35
Sozialanamnese U102-4
Sozialarbeit **U16**-8
Sozialarbeiter(in) **U16**-8,1; U1-7
Sozialbeiträge U13-6
Sozialbetreuer(in) U16-8
soziale Kompetenz U73-4
soziales Netz U16-8
Sozialhilfe **U1**-7; **U13**-6; **U16**-8
Sozialleistungen U13-6
Sozialmedizin U16-8; U13-6
Sozialversicherung U13-5 f; U16-8
SP **U47**-15
spähen **U59**-2
Spalt(e) **U85**-3; **U87**-26; **U106**-11
Spalt, intervillöser U45-14
Spaltbildung (Iris) U58-8
Spalte U45-2; U100-27
spalten **U78**-10; **U81**-8; **U126**-14,9
Spalthauttransplantat U126-14; U130-6
Spaltlampe U58-11
Spaltprodukt U46-11; U78-10; U81-8
Spaltung **U78**-10,7; U39-10
–, enzymatische U78-8
Spaltvakzine U90-11
Spaltzunge U21-11; U126-14
Span (Knochen) U130-9
Spannkraft **U31**-16
–, sexuelle U1-6
Spannung **U31**-10; **U76**-5; U108-13
Spannungsgefühl U57-3
Spannungskopfschmerz U113-16
Spannungspneumothorax U124-17
Spannungszustand **U1**-13; **U31**-10
– (Haut) **U56**-19
Spannweite **U100**-15
Spargel U68-3
Spasmolytikum **U92**-19
Spasmus **U103**-20; **U112**-8
– masticatorius **U94**-11
Spastik **U103**-20; **U112**-8
–, progrediente U103-9
spastisch **U103**-20; **U112**-8
Spastizität **U103**-20; **U112**-8
Spätblutung U38-6; U124-16
Spatel **U17**-3
Spatium episclerale U58-6
– intervaginale U58-6
– subarachnoideum U41-8
Spätkomplikation U134-9
Spätmorbidität U120-12
Spätreaktion U39-23
Spätrezidiv U119-18
Spätschmerz U104-8
Spätschock U110-14
Spätsyphilis U96-3

spatulieren **U17**-3
spazieren gehen **U65**-1; U23-2
Spaziergang **U65**-1,7
Spazierstock U19-14
Spearman'scher Rangkorrelationskoeffizient U100-32
Speedballs **U11**-20
Speibecken **U27**-10
Speiche **U28**-16
Speichel **U45**-3; **U67**-7; **U82**-8
–, zähflüssiger U45-3; U109-3
Speichelbildung **U27**-9
Speicheldrüse **U45**-3; **U54**-1
Speicheldrüsentumor U45-3
Speichelfluss **U27**-9; **U45**-3
Speichelgang U45-3
Speichelsekretion, gesteigerte **U109**-3
–, pathologisch gesteigerte U45-3
–, reflektorische U113-1
Speichelstein U89-21
Speichelsubstitution U45-3; U109-3
Speicher **U74**-10; **U78**-20
Speichereisen U78-20
Speicherfunktion U78-20
Speicherkapazität U49-15; U74-10
Speicherkrankheit U78-20
–, lysosomale U39-18; U83-6
speichern **U49**-15; **U74**-10; **U78**-20
Speischale U17-12
Speise **U2**-8
Speisebrei **U46**-9,7; U55-13
speisen **U2**-4,2
Speisereste U2-6
Speiseröhre **U45**-5
Speiseröhreninhalt **U109**-3
Speisesalz U82-5
Spektrometrie **U83**-21
Spektrophotometrie, hochauflösende U83-21
Spekulumspitze U17-6
spenden **U69**-16
– (Blut) U14-12
Spender (Organ) **U129**-15,17
Spenderareal U129-12
Spenderauswahl U129-15
Spenderblut(gruppe) U136-9
Spendereizelle **U69**-16
Spender-Empfänger-Auswahl U134-2
Spendererythrozyten U136-9
Spenderherz U32-1
Spenderniere U48-2
Spenderorgan U86-20
Spendersamen U53-6
Spenderstelle U129-15
Sperma **U53**-6 f
Spermatide **U53**-8
Spermatogenese **U53**-8
Spermatogonien **U53**-8
Spermatozele U53-8
Spermatozoenaspiration U69-13
Spermatozoenextraktion, testikuläre **U69**-13
Spermatozoengewinnung U69-13
Spermatozoon **U53**-7

Spermatozystitis U52-9
Spermatozyt U53-8
Spermauntersuchung U53-6
Spermide **U53**-8
spermienabtötend **U69**-8
Spermienanzahl U53-7
Spermienaspiration, mikrochirurg. epididymale (MESA) **U69**-13
Spermienbeweglichkeit **U53**-10
Spermiendichte U53-7
Spermienextraktion, testikuläre **U69**-13
Spermiengewinnung U69-13
Spermieninjektion, intrazytoplasmatische **U69**-15
–, subzonale U69-15
Spermienmotilität **U53**-10,7
Spermienzählung U53-7
Spermiogenese **U53**-8
Spermiogramm U53-6
Spermium **U53**-7
Spermizid **U69**-8; U53-7
Sperrgebiet U91-5
Sperrungszustand, katatoner U77-8
Spezialbett U19-3
Spezialbettpfanne für Frakturierte U19-8
Spezialgebiet **U15**-8
spezialisieren, sich **U15**-8
Spezialist(in) **U15**-8
Spezifität **U100**-23
S-Phase U83-12
Sphinkter **U30**-9
Sphinkterhypertonie U30-9
Sphinkterinsuffizienz U30-9
Sphinkterplastik U30-9; U48-14
Sphinktertonus U30-9; U48-14
Sphygmograph U17-8
Sphygmomanometer **U17**-8; U107-14
Spica U140-20
– humeri U23-3; U141-6
Spickdraht **U141**-15
Spickung **U141**-14f,4
Spiegel **U116**-16
Spiegelbild U59-5; U73-9
Spielplatz U1-10
Spieltherapie U16-12
Spina **U22**-12; **U28**-5
– iliaca U28-5
– – anterior U28-22
– ischiadica U71-13
spinal **U28**-19
Spinalanästhesie **U93**-7; U41-15
Spinalganglion U40-11; U87-16,25
Spinalnerv U40-1; U41-15
Spindelfaser **U83**-5; U84-7
Spindelgeräusch U110-3
Spindelpol U83-25
Spine-Board **U8**-16
Spinne U91-2
Spinnennävus U98-5; U114-3
Spinnenstich U91-16
Spinnwebenhaut **U41**-8
Spiralbruch U106-1
Spirale **U69**-10,2

Spirillen-Rattenbissfieber U90-9
Spirillum **U90**-9
spirituell **U77**-2
Spirituosen **U3**-28; **U10**-2; U47-17
Spiritus **U10**-2;U82-13
Spirochaeta muris U90-9
Spirochäte **U90**-9
spirochätenabtötend U90-9
Spirochätose U90-9
Spirogramm **U118**-3
Spirometer **U118**-3
Spirometrie **U118**-3; U44-3
Spirometriebefund U118-3
Spital **U14**-1
Spitze **U87**-25
spitzen (Lippen) U67-17
Spitzfuß U23-13
–, neurologisch bedingter U113-7
Spitzfußprophylaxe, Stiefel zur **U125**-23
Spitzfußstellung U19-4
– (Peronäuslähmung) U64-15
Spitzgaumen U26-10
Spitzgriff U64-10
Splanchnikusanästhesie U93-3
Splanchnomegalie U86-21
Splen **U35**-4
Splenektomie U35-4
Splenium corporis callosi U41-3
Splenomegalie U35-4; U110-9
Splenoportografie U35-4
Splint **U127**-20
Splitter **U106**-7
Splitterfraktur **U106**-7
Splitterpinzette U132-14
Splitterzange U132-14
Spondylodese **U141**-13; U41-15
spongiös U30-3
Spongiosa U28-2; U86-3
Spongiosaplastik **U130**-9
Spongiosaspäne U106-2
Spongiosatransplantat **U130**-9
spontan **U75**-18; U73-12
– abklingend **U119**-12
Spontananfälle U113-5
Spontanatmung U123-9
Spontanfraktur U106-1
Spontangeburt U71-11
Spontanhandlung U73-12
Spontanheilung U4-16; U134-14
Spontanluxation U106-4
Spontanmutation U84-20
Spontanremission U4-15; U119-17
Spontanruptur U5-19
Sporangium U90-3
Spore **U90**-3; U139-2
Sporenbehälter U90-3
Sporenbildner U90-3
Sporenbildung **U90**-3
Sporenfärbung U90-3
Sporentierchen **U90**-2
Sporn U30-3
Sporogenese U90-3
Sporogonie U90-3
Sporozoit **U90**-2

Sporozoon **U90**-2
Sporozyste **U90**-2
Sport **U1**-12
Sportgymnastik, rhythmische U1-15
Sporthalle **U1**-15,18
Sportherz U25-4
Sportler **U1**-12
sportlich **U1**-12; **U25**-4
Sportlichkeit U25-4
Sportmassage U142-15
Sportmedizin U1-12; U142-23
Sportplatz U1-10
Sportverletzung U25-4
Sporulation **U90**-3
Sprachaudiometrie U61-2,10
Sprachäußerungen U66-17
Sprachdiskrimination U61-10
Sprache **U21**-11; **U66**-8
–, verwaschene U61-11; U113-10
Sprachentwicklung U66-8
Spracherkennungsschwelle **U61**-7
Sprachhörschwelle U88-7
Sprachmelodie **U66**-11
Sprachproduktion U66-9; U88-16
Sprachstörung U66-8,9
Sprachverständlichkeit U61-1
Sprachverständnis U66-8
Sprachwahrnehmungsschwelle U61-7
Spraydose **U91**-7
Sprechangst U66-17
sprechen **U66**-8,1
– (im Schlaf) U72-15
Sprechen, lautes U61-5
–, stockendes U76-14
Sprechhilfen U66-8
Sprechlautbildung **U66**-1
Sprechstimme U66-10
Sprechstörung U66-8; U67-17
Sprechstunde U18-13; U102-14
Sprechstundenhilfe **U18**-3
Sprechweise **U66**-1,8
Sprechzimmer U18-13; U102-14
spreizen **U31**-6
–, Beine U23-8
Spreizer **U17**-6
sprengen **U6**-9
Sprengkörper U6-9
springen **U65**-16
–, ins Wasser U1-17
sprinten **U65**-15
Spritze **U17**-10; **U122**-4; U9-11
– (Injektion) **U11**-8; U93-9
spritzen **U38**-7; **U122**-4
–, i. v. **U11**-8
Spritzennadel U17-11
Spritzenpumpe **U135**-16; U136-1
Spritzlacke U11-23
Spritzpistole U6-8
spröde **U31**-16; U82-25
Sprödigkeit **U31**-16
sprossen **U51**-4; **U90**-5
Sprössling **U84**-29
Sprosspilz **U90**-18
Sprossung U90-11,18

Sprühstöße U62-2
Sprühverband U140-17
Sprung U65-16; **U106**-1
Sprungbein **U28**-26; U23-12
Sprungbeinhals U28-26
Sprungbeinkörper U28-26
Sprunggelenk **U23**-12; **U28**-26; **U29**-1
Sprungseil U65-16
Spucke **U103**-17
spucken **U27**-10; **U103**-17
spülen **U19**-10; **U91**-26; **U118**-10; **U128**-11
Spülflüssigkeit U127-17; U140-11
Spülkanal U136-5
Spülkanüle U132-6
Spüllösung **U125**-21
Spülmittel U91-10
Spül-Saug-Drainage U140-15
Spül-Saugvorrichtung **U128**-11
Spülspritze U17-10
Spülung **U19**-10; **U116**-5; **U118**-10; **U127**-17; **U140**-11,1
– (mit Kochsalzlösung) U91-26
–, arthroskopische U128-7
spürbar **U57**-2; **U62**-9
spüren **U74**-4; **U76**-1; **U102**-2
Spurenelement **U79**-17; U82-1
–, metallisches U82-6,33
–, mineralisches U82-5
spurten U65-15
Sputum **U103**-17 f
–, maulvolles eitriges U111-17
Sputumabstrich U103-18
Sputumprobe U103-18
Sputumuntersuchung U103-18
Sputumzytologie U103-18
Squama **U86**-12
squamös **U114**-7
SRH U55-5
SSM U98-15
SST U55-5
Stab U141-16
Stäbchen U58-13; U59-10
–, säurefestes U90-7
Stäbchenbakterium U90-7
stabil **U31**-15; **U75**-15; **U119**-12; **U141**-4
–, klinisch **U125**-2
stabile Seitenlage **U8**-17
stabilisieren **U31**-15
–, klinisch **U125**-2
stabilisiert **U119**-12
Stabilisierung **U31**-15
– (Fraktur) **U141**-4
–, hämodynamische U125-2
–, operative U31-15
Stabilisierungstab U141-4
Stabilität **U31**-15; U9-19
Stablinsenoptik U133-4
Stabsarzt **U16**-9
Stachel **U5**-10; **U91**-16,2
–, steckengebliebener U91-16
stachelförmig **U28**-19
stachelig **U62**-11

Stachelzellenschicht U56-2
Stadieneinteilung **U97**-14
Stadium **U97**-14; **U119**-15
– decrementi U105-18
–, akutes U119-10
–, i. fortgeschrittenen U97-14; U119-15
–, lakunäres U85-4
Staging **U97**-14
– Laparotomie U97-14
– Operation U97-14; U126-4
Stahleinlage U140-26
Stakkatohusten U103-16
Stamm **U22**-1; U87-14; U90-2,7
–, attenuierter U122-6
–, pandemischer U94-8
–, virulenter U90-10
Stammbaum **U84**-29
Stammbaumanalyse U84-29
Stammbronchus U43-9
Stammeln U66-20
stammen **U81**-18; **U85**-11
stammen (von) **U38**-3
Stammfettsucht U22-1; U24-9; U56-5
stämmig **U25**-6; U24-3
Stämmigkeit **U25**-6
Stammskelett U28-1; U87-3
Stammvater **U84**-29
Stammzelle(n) **U38**-3; U85-24
–, pluripotente U38-3
–, aneuploide U84-9
–, embryonale U85-1
–, hämatopoetische U38-1
Stammzellenentnahme U38-3
Stammzellenklon U84-33
Stammzellenleukämie U38-3
Stammzellfaktor U38-3
Stammzotten **U85**-24
stampfen U65-5
Stand **U65**-3
Standardabweichung U100-13
Standard-Echokardiografie U118-15
Standard-EEG U118-12
Standardfehler (Mittelwert) U100-10,18
Standarduntersuchung, biochemische U81-1
Standardwert **U100**-6
Stataxie U113-8
standhalten U128-18
ständig **U75**-10
Standphase (beim Gehen) U65-3
Standpunkt **U65**-3; **U87**-4; U59-1
Standrad U1-12
Stangen U8-16
Stangerbad U142-20,23
Stanniol U82-29
Stannum **U82**-29
Stanzbiopsie U118-4 f
stanzen U132-5
Stapedektomie U60-5
Stapediusreflex U60-11,13; U113-1
Stapelwirt U94-5
Stapes **U60**-5
Stapesfixation U60-5
Stapesfußplatte U60-5

Stapesplastik U60-5
Staphylococcus **U90**-8
– aureus U90-8
Staphylokokken-Clumping-Test U90-8
Staphylokokkeninfektion U90-8
Staphylokokkenpneumonie U90-8
Staphylokokkose U90-8
Staphylokokkus **U90**-8
Stapler U138-17
stark **U24**-8; **U31**-13; **U119**-14
– ausgeprägt U103-7
– gewunden U52-5
– gewürzt **U62**-7
– juckend U70-15
–, überwältigend **U119**-13
Stärke (Harnstrahl) U49-17
Stärkeabbau U84-46
Stärkegelelektrophorese U84-35
stärkehaltig **U79**-5
stärken (Muskeln) **U1**-13; **U31**-13
Stärkezucker U79-5
Starkstromverletzung U6-14
Stärkung **U31**-13
Stärkungsmittel **U31**-10
Staroperation, ambulante U20-2
starr **U12**-15; **U31**-17; **U103**-20; **U109**-14
– (Optik) U133-4
Starre **U12**-15
starren **U59**-2; **U67**-13 f
Starrheit **U31**-17
Startcodon U84-13
Starterlösung U88-5
Startstelle U84-19
Startverzögerung **U112**-7
Staseflecken U56-7
Statine U54-4
Station **U19**-1; U15-6; U20-1,9
–, chirurgische U126-3; U131-17
–, geschlossene U19-1
–, onkologische U97-1
–, psychiatrische U14-5
stationär **U20**-2; **U65**-3
– aufnehmen, zur Beobachtung U125-5
– Behandlung U134-11; U139-12
Stationsgehilfe U15-6
Stationshelferin U15-6
Stationsschwester U16-2; U19-1
–, ausgebildete U15-2
Stationsvisite **U20**-9
Statistik **U100**-1
statokinetischer Reflex U57-16
Statur **U24**-2; **U25**-1
Status **U119**-15
– anginosus U124-11
– asthmaticus **U124**-10
– epilepticus **U124**-9
–, klinischer U108-2
– komplex-partieller U124-9
–, mentaler **U77**-1
–, neurologischer **U77**-1; U119-15
Statuserhebung U107-2; U117-1
stattlich (Statur) U24-2
Staub **U91**-7

Staub, anorganischer U91-7
−, kieselsäurehaltiger U91-7
−, organischer U91-7
−, sporenhaltiger U91-7
Staubbekämpfung U91-7
staubdicht U91-7
Stäube, inerte U82-29
Staubexposition U122-5
Staubfilter U91-7
Staubinde **U8**-8; **U140**-20
Staubpartikel U91-6f
Stauchungsbruch **U106**-6; **U6**-6
Staumanschette **U17**-8; **U135**-18
Stauschlauch **U8**-8; **U17**-8; **U136**-2
Stauung **U124**-12
−, vaskuläre U34-1
−, venöse **U110**-15; U34-4
Stauungshyperämie U89-27
Stauungsinsuffizienz **U124**-12; U110-12
Stauungsleber U47-1; U110-15
Stauungslunge U110-15; U124-12
Stauungsödem U89-19
Stauungspapille U58-14
Stauungszirrhose U110-15
Steady state **U88**-20
− Konzentration U88-20
− Plasmaspiegel U88-20
Steatorrhoe/-ö **U109**-10; U46-19
Stechampulle **U9**-13
Stechapparat U91-16
−, steckengebliebener U91-16
stechen U6-7; **U62**-11; **U104**-13; **U118**-7; **U122**-4
stechend (Schmerz) U113-14
Stechmücke U91-8
Stechwerkzeuge U91-16
Stecknadel **U141**-15
stecknadelkopfgroß U114-10
− (Pupillen) U7-14
stehen **U65**-3
− (über), breitbeinig **U63**-5
steif **U12**-15; **U31**-17; **U53**-4; **U103**-20; **U109**-14
Steifheit **U12**-15; **U31**-17
−, anhaltende U53-4
Steifigkeit **U31**-17; **U105**-9
Steifigkeitsgefühl U31-17
Steigbügel **U60**-5
Steigbügelentfernung U60-5
Steigbügelfußplatte U60-5
Steigbügelmuskel U60-5
steigen **U65**-4,17f
steigern **U88**-12
Steigerung **U88**-12
Steigung **U100**-33
Steilgaumen U26-10
Stein **U89**-21
steinbedingt U89-21
Steinbildner U89-21
steinfrei **U89**-21
Steinimpaktion U89-21
Steinkohleteer U82-10,13
Steinkörbchen U128-17
Steinleiden U104-15

Steinmann-Nagel U141-15
Steinschnittlage **U63**-12; **U131**-14
Steiß(bein)wirbel U28-19
Steißbein **U28**-20
Steißgeburt U71-9
Steißlage U71-5
Steißteratom U98-16
Stelle, narbige U52-19
Stellenbesetzung **U15**-2
Stellreflex **U57**-16
Stellung **U63**-1; **U65**-3; **U131**-11
−, anatomische U87-1
−, korrekte U141-1
−, soziale U75-15
Stenokardie **U124**-11
Stenose **U89**-20,19; **U140**-10
Stent **U127**-20
Stentverlegung U127-20
Stepper U142-16
Steppergang **U65**-4,2
Sterbebegleitung U14-4; U125-1
Sterbebetreuung U14-4
Sterbebett **U12**-7
Sterbehilfe **U12**-9
Sterbeklinik **U14**-4
sterben **U12**-4
Sterben, im **U12**-1
Sterbende **U12**-4
Sterbetafel U100-26
Sterbetafelmethode U100-29
Sterbeziffer U12-2
sterblich **U12**-3
Sterbliche **U12**-3
Sterblichkeit **U12**-3; **U100**-9
Sterblichkeitsziffer **U12**-3,2
Stereotypie U103-19
Stereozilien U60-12
steril **U69**-3; **U139**-1f,7
Sterilbereich **U131**-7
Sterilisation **U69**-3; **U139**-2
Sterilisator **U139**-2
Sterilisierbehälter U139-2
sterilisieren **U1**-5
Sterilisiertrommel U139-2
Sterilität **U69**-2f; **U139**-2
Sterilitätsoperation U69-3
Sterilzone U139-8
Sternalpunktion U28-13
Sternalrand U28-13
Sternfraktur U106-8
Sternnävus U98-5,15; U114-3
Sternotomie, mediane U87-18
Sternum **U22**-2; **U28**-13
Sternumspalte U28-13
Steroid(e) **U55**-4
−, anabole U55-4
−, hochwirksame U55-4
Steroid(bio)synthese **U55**-4
Steroidakne U55-4
Steroidapplikation U55-4
Steroiddiabetes U55-4
steroidinduziert U55-4
Steroidrosacea U55-4
Steroidsalbe U55-4

Steroidzufuhr, exogene U88-10
Stertor U111-2
Stethoskop U17-2
Stethoskopmembran U17-2
Steuerfunktion U54-3
Steuerhormone U54-3
steuern **U54**-3; **U88**-2
Steuerung **U54**-3; **U88**-2
− (Zellzyklus) U83-12
Steuerungshormone U54-3
Steuerungsmechanismus U88-2
ST-Faser U30-1
STH **U55**-5
Stich **U5**-10; **U6**-7; **U62**-11; **U104**-13; U91-11
stichfester Behälter U136-2
Stichinzision **U128**-12; U126-9
Stichprobe **U100**-4
Stichprobenerhebung **U118**-4; **U100**-4
Stichprobenumfang U100-4
Stichprobenverfahren U100-4
Stichwort **U74**-2
Stichwunde U5-3,7; U6-7; U136-2
Stickoxid U82-11,16; U123-8
Stickoxidradikal U81-5
Stickstoff **U82**-16
−, flüssiger U82-4,16; U127-8
Stickstoffausscheidung U49-8
Stickstoffbilanz **U82**-16
−, ausgeglichene U88-19
Stickstoffgleichgewicht **U82**-16; U88-19
stickstoffhaltig **U82**-16; U79-10
Stickstoff-Lost U82-16
Stickstoffmonoxid U81-17; U82-11,16
Stickstoffstoffwechsel U47-18; U82-16
Stickstoffverbindung U81-2; U82-16
Stickstoffverlust im Harn U49-8
Stiegengeländer U65-18
Stiegensteigen U65-18
Stiel **U65**-13; **U87**-24; U130-10f
stielförmig **U87**-24; U41-13
Stieltupfer **U17**-13
Stifneck® U8-15
Stift **U141**-15f,14
Stiftfixation **U141**-15f,4
Stiftimplantation U129-18
Stiftzahn U29-4
Stigma **U108**-1
still **U61**-11; **U76**-19
Still-BH U14-8
Stille **U61**-11; **U76**-19
−, beklemmende U76-11
stillen **U16**-2,6; **U46**-2
− (Kind) **U50**-17; **U71**-25f,20; U69-5
− (Blutung) **U123**-2; U89-26
− nach Bedarf U71-26
−, voll U75-10
stillend **U14**-8; **U71**-25f
stillende Mutter U16-2
Stillkind U71-26; U80-4
Stillschwierigkeiten U71-26
Stillstand **U65**-3; U123-6
stillstehend **U65**-3

Stimmapparat **U43**-7
Stimmbänder U31-6; U66-10
Stimmbandlähmung U113-7; U135-11
Stimmbildung **U66**-10,13
Stimme **U66**-10f,23
–, belegte U44-1
–, gedämpfte U61-5
–, heisere U103-6
–, leise U61-5
–, weinerliche U67-10
–, zaghafte U76-14
–, zitternde U64-5f; U77-5
Stimmengewirr U66-17
Stimmfremitus U111-11
Stimmgabel **U17**-7; U61-1,4
–, schwingende U57-17
Stimmgabelprüfung U17-7
stimmhaft **U66**-10
Stimmklang U66-8
Stimmlippen U66-10
Stimmlippenknötchen U66-14
Stimmlippenlähmung U31-12
Stimmlosigkeit **U66**-23; **U103**-6; **U111**-11
Stimmritzenkrampf U43-7; U66-10
Stimmschwäche U66-10
Stimmstörung **U103**-6; U113-10
Stimmung **U76**-2; U74-1
–, ausgeglichene U75-15
–, ausgelassene U1-6
–, eigenartige U76-2
–, euphorische U76-16
–, gedrückte U17-3
–, gereizte U76-6f
Stimmungsaufhellung U75-5
Stimmungslabilität U75-15; U108-13
Stimmungslage U76-2; U119-15
Stimmungsschwankung(en) U64-4; U76-2; U77-1
Stimulans **U11**-17; **U57**-1; **U88**-12; U92-23
–, rezeptfreies U11-17
Stimulation, kontrollierte ovarielle U69-17
–, QRS-inhibierte U123-13
–, sexuelle **U68**-8
–, transkranielle U142-23
Stimulationstest U55-9
Stimulationszyklus U69-17
stimulierend **U42**-8; **U57**-1; **U88**-12
stimuliert U33-1
Stimulus **U42**-8; **U57**-1; **U88**-12
stinken **U62**-1,4
Stippchengallenblase U47-7
Stirn U21-2; U25-10; U87-20
Stirnbein **U28**-8; U87-20
Stirnglatze U25-15; U87-20
Stirnhöhle U28-6,8; U43-6
Stirnlage U71-5
Stirnlappen U87-23
Stirnlocke U114-4
Stirnreflektor **U17**-4
Stirnrunzeln **U67**-11; U56-17
Stirnspiegel **U17**-4; U21-1
Stirnwindung U28-8

Stöckelschuhe U65-10
stocken (beim Sprechen) U66-12,20
Stockmädchen U19-1
Stockstützen **U19**-14
stocktaub U61-9
Stockzahn **U26**-6
Stoff (Droge) **U11**-1
–, fester **U82**-6
–, gefährlicher U91-5
–, gelöster U49-7
–, knitterfreier U17-16
Stoffauflage U140-25
Stoffkumulation im Körper **U91**-19
Stofftransport **U78**-17
Stoffwechsel **U78**-1; U79-7
–, mitochondrialer U83-7
Stoffwechselabfallprodukte U37-3
Stoffwechselanomalie U107-20
Stoffwechseldefekt, genetischer U84-1
Stoffwechselendprodukte U49-1; U78-1
Stoffwechselenergie U78-12
Stoffwechselkrise U124-1
Stoffwechselnebenprodukt U78-1
Stoffwechselprodukt **U78**-11; U37-1
Stoffwechselprozesse U92-5,11
–, aufbauende **U78**-3
Stoffwechselrate, erhöhte U78-2
Stoffwechselreaktion U78-1
Stoffwechselregulation U78-1; U88-2
Stoffwechselschlacken U37-3
Stoffwechselsteuerung U78-1
Stoffwechselstörung **U88**-19; U78-1
Stoffwechselweg U78-1; U83-16
–, anabol(isch)er **U78**-3
–, anaerober U83-16
–, katabol(isch)er **U78**-3
Stoffwechselwirkung U91-20
Stoffwechselzwischenprodukt **U78**-11,1; U81-18
stöhnen **U66**-4
stolpern **U65**-9
Stolperstein U65-9
Stolz U75-20
Stoma **U127**-3; U87-21
Stomatitis U21-8
– aphthosa U95-7; U109-2
Stomatodynia U109-2
stoned **U11**-10
stopfendes Mittel **U92**-13
Stopfgold U82-28
Stoppcodon U81-7; U84-13
Storchenbiss U114-10
stören **U104**-3
störend U76-21
Störgröße **U100**-18
stornieren **U18**-2
Störung **U4**-4,11; **U77**-13; **U89**-4
–, affektive U76-2f
–, autistische U77-16
–, bipolare affektive U77-18
–, dissoziative U74-20; U77-6
–, hämodynamische U36-4
–, konstitutionelle U25-3

Störung, phobische **U77**-5
–, psychiatrische U14-5; U77-13
–, psychische U14-5; U77-16
–, psychosomatische U40-7; U77-21
–, psychotische U77-21
–, saisonale affektive U77-16; U113-3
–, somatische U77-2
–, visuospatiale U59-6
–, wahnhafte U77-20
Störungen, neurologische U56-14
–, vegetative U40-6
Stoß **U6**-4; **U64**-12; U5-13f
– (mit Knie) U64-12
Stoß-auf-Stoß-Naht U137-5
stoßen **U6**-4; **U8**-11; **U64**-12,14
– auf **U117**-5
Stoßherd U106-9
stoßweise **U64**-7; U48-10
Stoßwelle U6-4
Stottern U113-10
stottern **U66**-20,12
Strabismus **U59**-4,15
– concomitans U59-4
– convergens U59-4,13
– divergens U59-4
– paralyticus U59-4; U113-7
– verticalis U59-4
–, akkommodativer U59-4,12
Strabismusoperation U59-4
strafbar **U12**-11
straff **U31**-10; U60-4
– (Bauch) U1-11
straffällig U80-8
straffen **U76**-5; U30-14; U64-13
straffes Gelenk U29-1
Straffung **U64**-16
Straftat U77-10
Strahl(enbündel) **U99**-5,2
Strahl richten auf U99-5
–, dünner U49-17
–, schwacher U49-17
Strahldusche U1-19
strahlen **U67**-9; **U59**-3
–, vor Freude U67-9
Strahlen, konvergierende U59-13
Strahlenbelastung **U99**-7; U91-5
Strahlenbiologie U83-1
Strahlenchemie U81-1
strahlend U59-11
strahlendicht **U99**-11; U82-33
Strahlendosis **U99**-9
strahlendurchlässig **U99**-11
strahlenempfindlich **U99**-23
Strahlenenteritis U94-18
Strahlenexposition **U99**-7; U91-5
Strahlenfokussierung **U99**-6
strahlengeschädigt U6-11
Strahlenhärtung U99-5
Strahlenhygiene U99-7
Strahlenkater U99-2; U103-11
Strahlennekrose U89-30
Strahlenpneumonie U94-14
Strahlenpneumonitis U94-14
strahlenresistent **U99**-23

Strahlenrisiko U91-5
Strahlenschaden U6-11
Strahlenschädigung **U99**-7
Strahlenschutz U99-2
Strahlenschutzkleidung U99-1
Strahlensensibilität U99-23
Strahlensensitizer U99-23
Strahlensicherheit U8-4
Strahlentherapeut(in) U15-13
Strahlentherapie, interstitielle U86-19
Strahlentrennraster **U99**-5
Strahlenüberdosis **U99**-7
strahlenundurchlässig **U99**-11; U15-13
Strahlung U15-13; **U99**-2
Strahlungsdetektor U99-7
Strahlungsenergie U78-12; U99-4
Strahlungsschwächung U99-3
stramm **U1**-4
strampeln **U64**-12
Strampeln U72-13
Strang **U84**-11
-, fibröser U51-4
Strangbruch U84-11
Strangulationsileus U109-6
Stratum basale U56-2; U87-8
- corneum **U56**-6,2
- functionale U50-6
- germinativum U87-8
- granulosum U56-2
- lucidum U56-2
- papillare U56-3
- reticulare U56-3; U86-5
- spinosum U56-2
- spongiosum endometrii U85-13
strauchen **U65**-12
Streak-Ovar U54-11
Strebe **U65**-13
strecken **U31**-3
-, sich **U63**-6
Strecker **U31**-3
Streckung U31-3; **U141**-3
Streckverband U141-3
Streich U67-13
streicheln **U62**-10; **U64**-11
Streicheln U68-2,8
- (Geschlechtsteile) U62-10
Streichen U142-15
streichen **U62**-10; **U64**-11
Streichholz U10-18
Streichmassage **U71**-10; U142-15
Streifenkörper **U41**-10
Streifenwagen U6-3
Streitbarkeit, ungezügelte U77-7
streitsüchtig **U77**-7
Streptobacillus U90-7
Streptobazillen-Rattenbissfieber U90-8
Streptococcus **U90**-8
- pyogenes U90-8
- viridans U90-8
Streptokokkenangina **U95**-13; U90-8
Streptokokken-Scharlach U95-6
Streptokokkensepsis U90-8
Streptokokkus **U90**-8
Stress, oxidativer U81-5; U82-11

Stress-Echokardiografie U118-15
Stressfaktoren U105-7
Stressinkontinenz U112-15
Stressprotein U105-11
Stressulkusprophylaxe U120-6
Streudiagramm U100-27
Streupuder U9-9
Streustrahlenraster U99-5
Streustrahlung U99-2
Streuung, hämatogene U94-16
Striae cutis atrophicae U70-16
- - distensae U70-16
- gravidarum **U70**-16
-, rötlich-bläuliche U70-16
Striatum **U41**-10
Stridor **U111**-10; U66-23
-, charakteristischer U95-5
-, exspiratorischer U44-3
-, inspiratorischer **U95**-5,10
stridorös **U111**-10
stridulös **U111**-10
Striktur **U89**-19
Strom, elektrischer U127-9
Stroma **U86**-22
Stromaendometriose U86-22
Stromainfiltration U86-22
stromal **U86**-22
Stromatose U86-22
Stromkabel U6-14
Stromstoß **U6**-14
Stromunfall **U6**-14
Strömungsgeräusch **U110**-4; U107-9
-, diastolisches U110-3
Strömungswiderstand U36-10
strotzen, vor Gesundheit U1-4
Struktur **U87**-1; U25-11
Strukturen U84-1
-, virales U90-11
Strukturprotein U79-9
Struma U82-22; U89-16
- lymphomatosa U124-8
-, blande U91-4
-, die Trachea einengende U44-8
-, endemische U94-8
-, hyperthyreote U124-8
strumpfförmig U93-3
Struvit U82-20
ST-Streckenhebung U116-19
Stuart-Prower-Faktor U37-14
Stubenfliege U90-15
Studie, klinische **U101**-1 f; U14-2
-, epidemiologische U13-11
Studienabbruch **U101**-29
Studienabbruchbedingung **U101**-30
Studienabbruchbestimmung **U101**-30
Studienanleitung **U101**-7
Studienbegleitkommission **U101**-25
Studiendesign U101-7
Studienprotokoll U101-7
Studienteilnehmer **U101**-4
Stufe **U65**-4
stufenweise **U65**-4
Stuhl **U46**-19 f; U19-13; U88-11
-, acholischer U46-19; U108-4 f

Stuhl, blutiger U46-19
-, breiiger U109-10
-, dünnflüssiger U46-19
-, geformter U46-19
-, heller U46-19
-, kalkfarbener U46-19
-, lehmfarbener U46-19
-, voluminöser U46-19
-, wässriger U109-10
Stuhlabstrich U109-11
Stuhlbeschaffenheit U109-11; U118-6
Stuhldrang U6-18; U46-18; U72-5
-, imperativer U112-4
-, schmerzhafter **U109**-15
Stuhlentleerung U46-20; U92-13
Stuhlentleerungsprobleme U46-18
Stuhlfarbe U109-11
Stuhlfettausscheidung U88-11
Stuhlflora U46-16
Stuhlgang **U46**-18 f,14; **U64**-1; **U109**-10
-, normaler U46-18
-, regelmäßiger U46-19
-, schmerzhafter U46-18
Stuhlgeruch, intensiver U62-5
Stuhlgewohnheiten U45-9; U46-14
stuhlinkontinent U46-19
Stuhlinkontinenz U46-19 f; U112-15
Stuhlkonsistenz U118-6
Stuhlkultur U109-11; U116-6; U118-6
Stuhlprobe U109-11; U118-6
Stuhlteststäbchen U17-1
Stuhluntersuchung U109-11; U118-6
Stuhlverhaltung U46-19
Stuhlverstopfung **U109**-6
Stuhlzäpfchen U9-12
stumm **U61**-11; U7-11
-, klinisch U87-20; U119-6
Stumme **U61**-11
Stummheit **U61**-11
stumpf U47-1
- (Spitze) U133-6; U132-4
- (Trauma) U16-9; U106-3
Stumpf U137-5; U129-5
- (Amputation) **U142**-6
- (Fraktur) U140-2
Stumpfdeckung U142-6
Stumpfschmerz U142-6
Stumpfstrumpf U142-6
Stupor **U7**-11; U135-6
stuporös **U7**-11
Stupsnase U25-10
stur **U75**-19
Sturz **U6**-5; **U65**-12
stürzen **U6**-5; **U65**-12
Sturzhelm U6-2
Stützapparat **U141**-9
Stütze U19-11,14; **U64**-16
-, seelische U76-1
stützen **U19**-11; **U64**-16; U131-10
- auf, sich **U64**-17
stützend **U125**-3
Stützgewebe U64-16; U86-4
Stützklebeband U140-21
Stützkorsett U28-11; **U140**-26; **U141**-7

Stützstrümpfe, elastische U125-22; U65-17; U141-10
subakut U119-10
Subarachnoidalblutung U41-8
–, aneurysmabedingte U124-15
Subarachnoidalraum U41-8; U93-7
Subarachnoidalschraube U125-13
Subduralerguss U41-8
subfebril U105-3
Subfertilität U69-2; U70-1
Subklaviakatheter U136-5
Subklaviapunktion U127-18
subkutan U56-3f
Subkutannadel U17-11
Subkutis U56-4
Sublimat U82-2
Sublimation U82-8
Sublingualtemperatur U45-2; U105-1
Subluxation U106-4
Subluxationstest U29-4
Submukosa U86-17
Subokzipitalpunktion U41-17
Subserosa U86-9
Substantia alba U41-7
– compacta U28-2; U86-3
– corticalis U28-2
– grisea U41-7
– intermedia centralis U41-7
– nigra U41-10
– spongiosa U28-2; U86-3
Substanz mit hoher Nierenschwelle U49-5
–, adsorbierende U81-12
–, alkylierende U82-15; U78-7
–, antineoplastische U92-31
–, ätzende U91-10
–, chemische U81-1
–, eisenbindende U78-19
–, gametozytenschädigende U85-2
–, gelöste U81-25,23; U116-17
–, graue U41-7,3
–, grenzflächenaktive U81-16
–, halluzinogene U15-12
–, hydrophile U81-13
–, körperfremde U39-22
–, niedermolekulare U81-3
–, oberflächenaktive U81-16
– P U42-10
–, psychotrope U92-23; U77-21
–, spermienabtötende U69-8
–, suchterzeugende U11-4
–, weiße U41-7
–, zellschädigende U39-16
–, zellzyklusspezifische U83-12
–, ZNS-stimulierende U11-17
–, zytotoxische U39-16
Substituent U81-5
substituieren U136-13
Substitution U84-23
Substitutionstherapie U136-13
Substitutionstransfusion U136-8
Substrat U81-16; U92-32
Substratoxidation U81-17
Substratsättigung U81-16

Substratspezifizität U81-16
Substratverbrauch U81-16
Subthalamus U41-9
Subtraktionsangiografie, digitale U118-16
suchen U59-1
Sucht U11-3,5
suchtbildend U11-5
Suchtentwöhnungsbehandlung U11-6
suchterzeugend U11-4f; U10-11
Suchtgefahr U11-3
suchtgefährdet U11-3
Suchtgift U9-3
süchtig U11-4,6; U9-3
Süchtige(r) U11-6
süchtigmachend U11-4
Suchtkrankheit U11-4
Suchtmittel U11-4
suchtmittelabhängig U80-8
Suchtmittelabstinenz U11-12
Suchtmittelprophylaxe U11-6
Suchtneigung U11-3
Suchtpotential U11-3,5
Suchtverhalten U11-4
Sudor U105-15
Sudoriferum U56-10; U105-15
Suizid U12-8
Suizidabsicht U12-8
Suiziddrohung U12-8
Suizidgedanken U12-8 U77-6,17
suizidgefährdet U80-8
Suizidgefährdete(r) U12-8
Suizidphantasien U12-8
Suizidprävention U12-8
Suizidprophylaxe U6-22; U12-8
Suizidrate U12-8
Suizidversuche U12-8
Sukzessivkontrast U59-11
Sulcus U87-26
– calcarinus U41-5
– centralis U41-5; U87-26
– cerebri U41-5
– chiasmatis U41-5
– coronarius U32-7; U87-26
– gingivalis U87-26
– hippocampi U41-11
– intertubercularis U30-11f; U87-26
– lateralis U41-5; U87-26
– nervi ulnaris U87-26
– parieto-occipitalis U87-13
– praecentralis U41-5
– Rolandi U41-5; U87-26
Sulfanilsäure U82-4
Sulfat U82-24
Sulfid U82-24
Sulfon U82-24
Sulfonamid U82-24
Sulfur U82-24
Summationsgalopp U110-6
summen U67-18
Summen U110-3
Sumpffieber U94-20
Superovulation U69-17

Supination U31-9
supiniert U31-9
Suppositorium U9-12; U92-12
Suppression U88-14
Suppressorzellen U37-10; U39-13
supprimieren U88-14
Suppuration U140-14
suprakondylär U28-4
Supravitalfarbstoff U116-4
Surfactant U44-9; U81-16
Surfactantmangel U44-9
Surfactantsubstitutionstherapie U44-9
Surrogatmutter U69-18
Surveillance U120-7; U125-5; U100-3
suspekt U117-8
suspendieren U63-13; U81-25
Suspension U63-13; U81-25; U141-3
Suspensionsdraht U141-3; U129-7
Suspensionsschlinge U129-7
süßen U3-16
Süßigkeiten U3-17
Süßstoff U79-6
Sustenaculum tali U30-8
Sutura U29-14; U137-1
– coronalis U29-14
– cranii U28-7; U29-14
– lambdoidea U29-14
– sagittalis U28-8; U29-14
– serrata U29-14
Swan-Ganz-Katheter U125-7
Sylvius-Furche U41-5; U87-26
Sympathikusausschaltung U40-9
Sympathikusblockade U40-9; U93-6
Sympathikusirritation U40-9
sympathisch U75-8
Sympath(ik)olytikum U40-8f; U92-27
Sympath(ik)omimetikum U92-27; U40-8f
sympatholytisch U40-8
Symphyse U29-12
Symphysis pubis U52-18; U29-12
Symport U49-3
Symptom U103-1ff; U108-1; U117-9
–, klinisches U14-2
Symptomatik, fulminante U119-13
–, schleichende U119-7
symptomatisch (für) U103-1
Symptomatologie U103-1
Symptome haben/zeigen U102-1
–, grippeähnliche U94-9
–, kostitutionelle U1-8
Symptomenkomplex U103-1
symptomlos U103-1; U119-6; U96-9
Synalgie U104-10
Synapse U40-13
–, axosomatische U40-2
–, erregende U40-13; U57-1
–, exzitatorische U40-13; U57-1
–, myoneurale U30-4
–, neuromuskuläre U42-11; U93-17
Synapsenspalt U40-13
Synapsenverbindung U40-13
Synapsis nonvesicularis U40-13
Synarthrose U29-13

Synchondrose U29-12
Synchondrosis sternocostalis U29-12
Syndaktylie, kutane U23-7,14
Syndesmophyt U29-13
Syndesmose/-sis U29-13,1
Syndesmosensprengung U29-13
Syndesmosis tibiofibularis U29-13
Syndrom U103-1
– der unruhigen Beine U76-8
–, adrenogenitales U54-10
–, amnestisches U74-17
–, apallisches U119-15
–, depressives U77-17
–, dienzephales U41-12
–, extrapyramidales U41-16
–, fragiles X- U77-22
–, hämolytisch-urämisches U38-4
–, hyperkinetisches U74-16
–, meningeales U41-8
–, okulopupilläres U58-16
–, prämenstruelles U51-1; U76-5
–, psychovegetatives U40-1; U76-6
Synergie U31-4
Synergismus U31-4; U92-6
Synergist U31-4; U92-6
synergistisch U31-4
syngenes Transplantat U130-1
Synkinese, mandibulopalpebrale U58-5; U67-15
Synkope U110-11; U7-4; U124-2
–, vasovagale U40-10
Synostose U29-14
Synotransplantat U130-4
Synovi(al)tis U29-11
Synovia U29-8,3
Synovialabstrich U29-8
Synovialanalyse U29-8
Synovialfalte U29-11
Synovialflüssigkeit U29-8
Synovialhaut U29-11,3; U86-8
Synovialhernie U29-11
Synovialis U29-11,3; U86-8
Synovialsarkom U98-3
Synovialzotten U29-8
Synthese U78-4
Synthesehemmer U78-4
Synthesephase U83-12
Synthetase U78-4
synthetisch U137-10
synthetisieren U54-2; U78-4
Synzytiotrophoblast U85-14
Syphilis U96-3
– cerebri U40-5
– latens U119-6
syphilitisch U96-3
System, aufsteigendes retikuläres (aktivierendes) U42-4
–, endolymphatisches U35-2
–, extrapyramidales U41-16
–, intrauterines U69-10
–, limbisches U41-11
–, lymphatisches U35-1
System, phagozytäres U39-17

–, retikuloendotheliales U35-12
systemisch U121-5
Systole U33-3; U31-1
–, ausgefallene U33-1
systolisch U33-3
Szintigrafie U99-18,22; U118-22
Szintigramm U99-17
Szintillation U99-17
Szintillationsdetektor U99-17
Szintiscanner U99-18

T

T3-Aufnahme U55-3
Tabak U10-17
Tabakbeutelnaht U137-18
Tabakpflanze U10-17
Tabakrauch U10-17; U91-7
Tabakwaren U10-17
Tabakwarenhändler U10-17
Tabanus U90-15
tabellarisch U100-27
Tabelle U100-27; U102-12
Tablett U19-7
Tablette U19-7
Tachyarrhythmie U110-2
Tachykardie U33-5; U110-2; U32-3
–, supraventrikuläre U33-5
–, ventrikuläre U32-8
Tachypnoe U111-5
Tadel U77-10
tadelnswert U77-10
Tafel U100-27
Tafelmethode U100-29
Tafeln, pseudoisochromatische U17-5
Tafelsalz U82-5
Tagangst U72-14
Tagesbericht U20-6
Tagesheim U14-3
Tagesklinik U14-1,3; U126-3
Tagesmüdigkeit mit Einschlafneigung U72-17
Tagesrhythmus U72-8
Tagessehen U59-9
Tagesstättenbetreuer(in) U16-14
Tagtraum U72-9
tagträumen U72-9; U7-15
Taille U22-6; U131-16
–, schlanke U24-6
Taillenumfang U22-6
tailliert U22-6
Takt, im U65-4
taktil U62-8
Taktilität U57-3
taktlos U75-5
taktvoll U75-5
Talg U56-8; U98-17; U114-6
Talgadenom U56-8
Talgdrüse U56-8; U54-1; U98-17
Talgdrüsenadenom U56-8
Talgdrüsenhyperplasie U56-8
Talgdrüsenstein U56-8
Talgdrüsentumoren U56-8

Talgproduktion U56-8
Talgzyste U56-8; U89-24
Talkum U91-7
Talus U28-26; U23-12
Taluskippung U28-26
Talusrolle U30-8
Tampon U140-24
tamponieren U110-8; U140-24
Tandem-Gang U65-1
Tankrespirator U123-9
tanzende Patella U28-24
Tapen U64-11; U140-21
– (mit Nachbarfinger) U142-13
Tape-Verband U141-11; U140-21
tapsen U65-10
tarsal U28-25
Tarsaltunnelsyndrom U28-25
Tarsus U28-25; U87-2
Tasche U137-16
Taschenklappe (Herz) U32-10
Taschenlampe U17-4; U107-1
Taschentuch U105-12
tastbar U62-8 f; U107-7; U89-3
Tastbefund 107-7
Tastempfindung U62-8
tasten U107-7
Tastfinger 107-7
Tastgefühl U62-8
Tasthaare U62-8
Tastkontrolle, unter U123-10
Tastpapille U56-13
Tastsinn U62-8
Tastzirkel U24-12; U17-1
TATA-Sequenz/-Box U84-12
Tätigkeit U88-14
–, anstrengende U64-19
–, berufliche U142-26,3
–, körperliche U64-18
–, sitzende U142-26
tatkräftig U76-17
tätlich werden U68-17
Tätlichkeit U77-7
tätscheln U62-10; U64-11
taub U61-9; U135-3
– geboren U71-1
– machen U61-9
– stellen, sich U61-9
– werden U61-9
Taube U61-9
taubes Gefühl U104-17
Taubheit U113-13; U72-7
–, angeborene U61-9
–, psychogene U61-9
Taubheitsgefühl U57-3; U103-2
taubstumm U61-9
Taubstumme U61-9
Taubstummheit U61-9
Taucher U6-17
Tauchtiefe U6-16
Tauchunfall U6-1
taumeln U65-9 f
täuschend U75-12
Täuschung U73-10
–, optische U73-10; U58-14

Tauzeit U136-16
TB **U94**-16
TBG U54-6; U55-6
Team **U19**-1
–, notärztliches U14-7
Technetium U82-34
technisch durchführbar U126-4
Teenager **U80**-8
Teenageralter **U80**-8
Teerdämpfe U82-3
Teerheroin, schwarzes U11-19
Teerstuhl **U109**-11
teflonbeschichtet U137-10
TEFNA U69-13
Tegmen tympani U60-4
Tegmentum pontis U41-12
Tegument U84-18
Teigwaren **U3**-11
Teil **U87**-4,6
–, weiter peripher gelegener U87-6
Teilbad U19-9; U142-20
Teilbereich U15-9
Teilchen **U82**-1
– , (el.) geladenes U81-10; U82-1
Teilchenbeschleuniger U82-1
Teilchenfluss, konvektiver **U49**-3
Teilchenstrahlung U82-1; U99-10
Teildosen U121-7
teilen, (sich) **U85**-3
teilinvalid U142-3
teilnahmslos **U7**-10; **U76**-15,17
Teilnahmslosigkeit **U7**-13,12; **U76**-15,17; **U77**-8; **U113**-3
–, schläfrige U72-1
Teilreaktion U120-11
Teilremission U119-17
teilstationäre Behandlung U120-14
Teilung U85-10
–, äquale U85-3
Teilungskerbe U9-7
Teilverrenkung **U106**-4
Teilzeitarbeit U142-28
Teilzeitkrankenschwester U16-2
Teint **U25**-11
Telefonberatung U142-29
Telefonvermittlung U16-15
Telekanthus U58-3
Telenzephalon U41-2
Telogenhaare U56-13
Telomer **U84**-7
Telomerase **U84**-7
Telomerverkürzung U84-7
Telophase **U83**-13
Temperament **U75**-4; **U76**-2
Temperamentsausbruch U76-7
temperamentvoll **U75**-4
Temperatur **U105**-1
–, erhöhte **U105**-1
–, kritische U82-7
Temperaturabfall U105-1
Temperaturablesung U105-1
Temperaturanstieg U116-19
Temperaturanzeige U105-1
Temperaturausgleich U105-1

Temperaturempfindung U57-3,13; U105-1
Temperaturmethode U69-5
Temperaturregulation U105-2
Temperaturrezeptor **U57**-13
Temperatursinn U57-5,13; U105-1,5
Temperaturskala U24-11
Temperatursturz U105-1
Tempo **U65**-6; U1-13
–, lockeres U75-16; U76-19
Temporallappen U41-5
Temporallappenepilepsie U124-9
Tenalgie U104-21
Tendenzen, selbstbestrafende U76-13
Tendo **U30**-5
Tendodynie U104-21
Tendovaginitis U30-5
Tenesmus **U109**-15
Tennisellbogen U23-4
Tennisschuhe **U65**-8
Tenon-Raum U58-6
Tenosynovitis U30-5
TENS-Behandlung U142-23
Tensid U81-2
Tentorium cerebelli U41-2
TEQ U91-4
Teratoblastom U98-16
teratogen **U91**-12; **U92**-33
Teratogen U91-12
Teratogenese **U92**-33
Teratogenität **U91**-12; U98-16
Teratoid U98-16
Teratokarzinom **U98**-16
Teratologie **U98**-16
Teratom(a) **U98**-16
–, embryonales U98-16
–, (un)reifes U97-16; U98-16
–, zystisches U98-16
– adultum U97-16; U98-16
teratomatös **U98**-16
Termin **U18**-2
–, zum errechneten (Geburt) **U70**-11
Terminabsage **U18**-2
terminal **U12**-2
Terminalkranke U14-4
Termination **U84**-19
Terminationscodon U81-7; U84-13
termingerecht **U70**-11
Terminkalender U18-2
Terminvereinbarung U18-2
Tertiärfollikel U51-6
Tertiärzotten U85-24
TESE **U69**-13
Test **U116**-3
–, parameterfreier U100-34
–, toxikologischer U91-3
–, verteilungsunabhängiger U100-12
–, Wilcoxon U100-34
–, zuverlässiger U75-9
Testament U73-3
testen **U107**-1; **U116**-2 f
Testergebnis U117-6
Testgruppe **U101**-10
Testis **U52**-3; U54-11

Testmedikament **U101**-23,2; U9-3
Testnadeln, neurologische U17-1
Testosteron **U55**-16
Testosteroncreme U55-16
Testosteronderivat U55-16
Testosteronpflaster U55-16
Testosteronpräparat U55-16
Testosteronpropionat U55-16
Testperson **U100**-2
Testpflaster U118-2
Testschälchen **U17**-12
Teststamm U122-1
Teststärke, statistische U100-1
Teststreifen (Harnuntersuchung) U116-15
Tetanie U94-11; U95-11; U103-20
–, latente U94-6
tetaniform **U94**-11
tetanisch **U94**-11
tetanoid **U94**-11
Tetanus **U94**-11
Tetanusadsorbatimpfstoff U94-11
tetanusähnlich **U94**-11
Tetanusantitoxin U91-17; U94-11
Tetanusauffrischung(simpfung) U94-11
Tetanusimmunglobulin U39-5; U94-11
Tetanusimpfung U122-4
Tetanusprophylaxe U94-11
Tetanustoxoid U122-8
Tetrachlorkohlenstoff U82-23
Tetrachlormethan U82-23
Tetrahydrocannabinol U11-22
Tetraiodthyronin U54-6
Tetraparese **U94**-11
Tetraplegie **U142**-5; U113-7
Tetraplegiker(in) **U142**-5
Textilpflaster U140-21
Textus nervosus U40-1
T-Gedächtniszelle U39-15
TH1-Zelle U39-14
Thalamus **U41**-9
Thalassotherapiezentrum U1-18
Thallium **U82**-33
Thalliumaufnahme U82-33
Thalliumchlorid U82-33
Thalliumsulfat U82-33
Thalliumszintigrafie U82-33
Thebesius-Klappe U32-10
T-Helfer-Lymphozyt **U39**-14
T-Helferzelle U37-10
–, aktivierte U39-14
T-Helferzellenfunktion U39-14
T-Helfer-Zellzahl U39-14
Theomanie U77-15
Therapeut(in) **U16**-12; **U120**-4
therapeutisch **U16**-12
therapeutische Breite **U121**-13
therapeutische Fenster U120-4
Therapie **U120**-1,4
–, antiskabiöse U96-12
–, experimentelle U118-1
–, lebenserhaltende U123-1
–, manuelle **U142**-12
–, medikamentöse U15-20
–, mobilisierende U64-3

Therapie, physikalische **U142**-1; U25-1
-, unterstützende U125-3
Therapieabbrecher U100-4; U101-14
Therapiearm **U101**-12
Therapiebeginn U14-5
Therapieblock **U101**-11
Therapieeinleitung U14-5
Therapieergebnis **U101**-27
Therapiekontrolle U101-7
Therapiekreisel **U142**-19
therapierefraktär U104-9
Therapiereserve U120-4
therapieresistent **U120**-13; U14-2
Therapieschema U121-1
Therapie-Sitz(sack) **U142**-19
Therapiesitzung U142-18
Therapietreue U101-20; U120-15
Therapieversagen U120-1; U121-11
Therapieversager U101-21
Therapiewechsel **U101**-14
Therapiezugang, erweiterter **U101**-22
Thermalbad U1-18; U82-23
Thermalwasser U105-5
thermisch **U105**-5
Thermodilution U36-13
Thermogenese **U105**-2
Thermografie U105-2
Thermokaustik U105-2
Thermokoagulation U105-2
Thermolyse **U105**-2
Thermometer **U105**-6
Thermophor U136-4
Thermorezeptor **U57**-13; U105-1,2
thermostabil U105-2,10
Thermotherapie **U142**-22; U105-2
Thiaziddiuretika U92-21
Thoracic Outlet-Syndrom U125-17
thorakal **U22**-2
Thorakalatmung U44-4
Thorakoskop **U128**-6
Thorakoskopie **U128**-6
-, videogestützte U125-16
Thorakotomie **U123**-11; **U125**-16
Thorakozentese **U118**-8; U128-6
Thorax **U22**-2
Thoraxapertur, obere U87-21
Thoraxatmung U44-4
Thoraxausdehnung U44-10
Thoraxbeweglichkeit U44-11
Thoraxchirurgie, videogestützte U128-2
Thorax-Compliance U44-10
Thoraxdrain **U125**-16
Thoraxdrainage U125-16
Thoraxexkursion, Behinderung der U44-10
Thoraxexpansion **U107**-16
Thoraxhälfte U43-12
Thoraxinstabilität **U124**-17; U31-15
Thoraxkompression U6-6
Thorax-Kontrollröntgen U118-18
Thorax-Nativaufnahme U118-18
Thoraxperkussion U107-8
Thoraxröntgen **U118**-18; U99-3
- im Stehen U124-16

Thoraxsegment, instabiles U124-17; U125-2
Thoraxwand, instabile U124-17
Thoraxwandexpansion **U107**-16
Thrombapherese U136-15
Thrombenbildung U38-12
Thrombin **U37**-13
Thrombinbildung U37-13
Thrombinzeit U37-13; U116-13
Thromboembolie U124-13
Thrombokinase **U37**-14,13
Thrombolyse U38-4,14; U124-13
Thrombolytikum **U38**-14; **U92**-16
thrombolytisch U38-14
Thrombophlebitis **U136**-7
Thromboplastin U37-14,13
Thromboplastinzeit (TPZ) U37-13; U116-13
-, partielle U37-14
Thrombopoese U37-11
Thromboxan U78-24
Thrombozyt(en) **U37**-11; U38-2
-, histokompatible(r) U37-11
-, zirkulierende(r) U36-1
Thrombozytenabbau U116-13
Thrombozytenadhäsion U116-13
Thrombozytenagglutination **U38**-11; U39-19
Thrombozytenaggregation **U38**-11; **U116**-13; U37-11
Thrombozytenaggregationshemmer U38-11; U116-13
Thrombozytenaggregationstest U38-11
Thrombozytenantigen U39-8
Thrombozytenfaktoren U37-11
Thrombozytenfunktionsprüfung U118-3
Thrombozytenhemmstoff U88-14
Thrombozytenkonzentrat U36-13; U136-17
Thrombozytenlebenszeit U37-11
Thrombozytentransfusion U136-8
Thrombozytenzählung U116-8,13
Thrombozythämie U37-11
Thrombozytopathie U116-13
Thrombozytopoese U37-11
Thrombozytose U38-5
Thrombus **U38**-12; U37-1
-, frei flottierender U38-12
-, wandständiger U38-12
-, weißer U37-11
Thymoleptika U35-5
Thymom U35-5; U54-12
Thymopo(i)etin **U55**-27
Thymosin **U55**-27
Thymozyt U35-5
Thymus **U35**-5; **U54**-12
thymusabhängig **U54**-12
Thymusagenesie U54-12
Thymusanlage, fehlende U54-12
Thymusdrüse **U54**-12
Thymusfaktor, endokriner U54-12
Thymushyperplasie U54-12
Thymusinvolution U35-5; U54-12

Thymusrückbildung U35-5; U54-12
Thymustransplantat U54-12
Thymustumor U35-5; U54-12
Thymusvergrößerung U35-5; U54-12
Thyr(e)otropin **U55**-6
Thyreocalcitonin **U55**-8
Thyreoglobulin U54-6; U78-18
Thyreoiditis **U124**-8; U54-6
Thyreotoxikose **U124**-8
thyreotoxisch U91-4
Thyr(e)otropin **U55**-6; U54-6
- Releasing-Hormon U55-6
- Rezeptor-Antikörper U55-6
- Spiegel U81-8
- Synthese U54-2
Thyroidea **U54**-6
Thyroliberin U55-6
Thyroxin U54-6; U55-6
TIA U41-12; U103-4
Tibia **U28**-24; U23-10
Tibiakopf U106-1
tibial **U28**-24
Tibiofibulargelenk U28-24
Tic(k) **U31**-5; U104-12; U73-13
Tic convulsif U31-5
tief **U61**-6
Tiefenmuskelentspannung **U1**-16
Tiefenperkussion U17-9
Tiefenschmerz U104-10
Tiefensehen U59-6,16
Tiefensensibilität **U57**-11,14; U57-3,8
Tiefenwahrnehmung U59-16
Tiefenwirkung U142-22
Tiefertreten **U71**-14,3
- (VKT) U71-14
-, verzögertes U71-14
Tiefgefrieren (Embryonen) **U69**-14
Tiefschlaf U72-5
-, künstlicher U7-14
Tier, tollwütiges U94-12
Tierfellnävus U25-19
Tierhaare U91-7
Tierkohle U91-25
Tierphobie U77-5
Tierstudie U116-2
Tiertransplantat **U130**-5
Timbre U66-8
Tinctura Opii U11-18
Tinea U90-16
Tinktur **U9**-10
Tinnitus aurium **U113**-13
Tinnitus-Masker U113-13
Tirade **U66**-19
TISS-Bewertungssystem **U125**-4
Tissue engineering U86-3
Titan(ium) **U82**-31
Titanimplantat U82-31
Titanklip U138-15
Titanoxid U82-31
titansauer **U82**-31
Titanschraube U141-16
Titer **U81**-23; **U116**-17
-, erhöhter U81-23
Titeranstieg U81-23; U116-17

Titration **U81**-23; **U116**-17
Titrationsanalyse U116-17
Titrationskurve U81-23; U116-17
titrieren **U81**-23; **U116**-17; U93-10
Titubation **U113**-4
T-Lymphozyt **U39**-13; U35-5; U37-10
T-Lymphozyteaktivierung U39-13
T-Lymphozytenklone U39-13
T-Lymphozytenmangel U39-13
Tm U49-3
TNM-Klassifikation U97-14
tobend U77-26
Tochtergeschwulst **U97**-13
Tochterzelle U83-2
Tod **U12**-7; U101-27
– (elektrischer Strom) **U6**-14
– durch Ersticken U44-8
– – Ertrinken U6-16
– führen, zum U65-15
–, gewaltsamer U12-4
–, vorzeitiger U12-7
Todesanzeige U12-7
Todesfall **U12**-2,7
Todesfolge, Unfall mit U12-10
Todesopfer **U12**-2
–, Zahl der U12-7
Todesröcheln U12-7
Todesstrafe **U12**-11,7
Todestrakt (Gefängnis) U12-11
Todesurteil U12-11
Todfeind U12-3
todkrank **U12**-1
tödlich U12-2 f,5,9; U130-20
Toilette **U19**-9
Toilettenbecken U17-12; U19-9
Toilettenbenutzung **U19**-9
Toilettensitz U19-9
Tokolytikum U71-3
tolerant **U11**-5; **U75**-16
Toleranz **U11**-5; **U75**-16; U10-11
Toleranzentwicklung U11-5; U121-12
Toleranzstadium U135-20
Toleranztest U121-12
tolerieren **U11**-5
tollpatschig U72-15
Tollwut **U94**-12
Tollwut-Antiserum U37-3; U122-2
tollwütig **U94**-12
Tollwutprophylaxe U94-12
Tollwutvirus U94-12
Tomografie **U99**-19
Ton **U61**-3; **U66**-11; U82-30
–, gedämpfter U61-3
–, hoher U61-3
–, klingender U61-3
–, niederfrequenter U61-3
Tonaudiometrie U61-2
Tonerde **U82**-31
Tonfall **U66**-11,13
Tonhöhe **U61**-6; **U66**-11; U107-8
Tonhöhen unterscheiden U61-9
Tonikum **U31**-10
tonisch **U31**-10
tonischer Halsreflex U57-16

tonisierend **U31**-10
Tonizität **U31**-10
tonlos U103-6
Tonometer **U31**-10
Tonschwellenaudiometrie U61-2
Tonsilla adenoidea U35-6
– lingualis U21-11; U35-6; U95-13
– palatina U35-6; U45-4; U95-13
– pharyngealis U21-12; U35-6
– tubaria U35-6; U60-7
Tonsillae cerebelli U41-2
Tonsillarkrypten U35-6
Tonsille **U35**-6; U95-13
–, vergrößerte U95-13
Tonsillektomie U95-13
Tonsillitis **U95**-13; U35-6
Tonsilloadenoidektomie U35-6
Tonus U1-13
–, arteriolärer **U36**-10
Tonuserhöhung U31-10; U112-8
Tonusverlust U31-10
–, affektiver U72-18
Tonusverminderung **U36**-8
Töpfchen U19-13
Tophus arthriticus U89-16
topisch **U121**-5
Topografie **U87**-1
TORCH-Komplex **U96**-11
torkeln **U64**-5,7; **U65**-9
–, hin und her U65-9
Torkildson-Drainage U125-15
torquieren **U31**-7
Torsion **U31**-7; **U5**-16
Torsionsfraktur U106-1
Torsionskräfte U31-7
Torsionsverletzung U31-7
Tor-Strom U42-9
Tortendiagramm U100-27
Torticollis U103-20
Torus palatinus U28-10
tot **U12**-5
– umfallen U64-15
Totalkapazität U111-6
Totalprolaps U89-22
Tote(r) **U6**-12; **U12**-5
töten **U12** 9
Totenbett **U12**-7
Totenflecke **U12**-15
Totengräber U12-18
Totenkälte U12-15
Totenkleid U12-16
Totenschau U12-21
Totenschein U18-10
Totenstarre **U12**-15,14
totgeboren **U71**-1
Totgeburt **U71**-2; U70-8; U80-4
– im 2. Trimenon U70-9
Totimpfstoff **U122**-7
Totraum U12-5
–, physiologischer U88-1
Totschlag **U12**-10; U74-17
Tötung **U12**-10
–, fahrlässige U12-10
Totvakzine **U122**-7

Tourniquet **U8**-8; **U17**-8; U135-18
Tourniquetsyndrom U17-8
Tox(ik)ämie **U91**-22
–, fulminante U91-22
–, massive U91-22
toxigen **U91**-4
Toxikokinetik U91-3
Toxikologe/-in **U91**-3
Toxikologie **U91**-3
toxikologischer Test U121-13
Toxikose **U91**-20
–, exogene U91-20
Toxikum **U91**-4
Toxin **U91**-4; **U122**-8
Toxinämie **U91**-22
toxinbildend **U91**-4
toxisch **U91**-2; **U122**-8
toxische Wirkung **U121**-13
Toxizität **U91**-11; **U121**-13
Toxoid **U122**-8
Toxoidimpfstoff **U122**-8
t-PA U37-15
Trab **U65**-14
–, gemächlicher U65-14
Trabecula U31-14
Trabeculae carneae **U32**-13
Trabekeln **U32**-13
Traben U1-13
traben **U65**-14
Tracer U99-1,21 f
–, radioaktiver U82-34
Tracersubstanz, radioaktive U82-34
Trachea **U43**-8
Trachealkanüle U123-11; U125-16
Trachealrasseln U43-8
Trachearückwand, membranöse U86-15
Tracheobronchialbaum U43-8
Tracheobronchialsekret U43-8
Tracheomalazie U98-12
Tracheostoma **U123**-11,10; **U127**-3
– Anlage, perkutane U123-11
Tracheostomapflege U123-11
Tracheotom **U123**-11
Tracheotomie **U123**-11; U43-8
Trachom **U90**-14
Tractus cerebellovestibularis U41-16
– corticonuclearis U86-23
– corticospinalis **U41**-16,6; U86-23
– iliopubicus U28-22
– iliotibialis U30-15
– opticus U58-15
– spinobulbaris U41-16
– spinothalamicus U41-15
– – lateralis U41-9
– – ventralis U41-9
Trage **U8**-16
träge **U76**-17; U77-8
Tragemutter U69-19
tragen **U64**-16
Träger U23-3; U49-3; U78-17
– (Erbgut) U84-11
–, asymptomatischer U103-1

Träger, heterozygoter U84-5
–, klinisch inapparenter U94-4
–, latenter U94-4
Trägermolekül U81-2
Trägerprotein U78-17
Trägersubstanzen U49-3; U78-17
trägervermittelt U78-17; U83-19
Trägheit U76-17; U7-12
–, geistige U76-17
Tragus U60-2
trainieren U64-18
Training U1-12; U64-18
–, autogenes U1-12; U142-18
–, intensives U64-18
–, isometrisches U142-17
–, isotonisches U142-17
Trainingseinheit U1-12; U142-18
Trainingsplan U1-12
Trainingszustand U5-17
TRAK U55-6
Trakt U14-9
Traktion (Fraktur) U141-3
trampeln, zu Tode U65-5
Trance U7-15
Tränen U58-9; U66-3
Tränenabfluss U58-9
Tränendrüse U58-9; U54-1
Tränenflüssigkeit U58-9
–, künstliche U58-9
Tränengang U58-9
Tränengas U82-2
Tränen-Nasen-Gang U58-9
Tränenpunkt U58-9
Tränensäcke U21-3; U58-9
Tränensackentzündung U58-9
Tränensee U58-9
Tränensekretion U58-9; U45-3
Tränenträufeln U58-9; U5-19
Tränenwärzchen U58-9
Tränenwege U58-9
tränken U19-10
Tranquilizer U92-23; U135-10
transaminieren U82-17
Transaminierung U47-16
Transcortin U55-10
Transfektion U84-39
Transfektionskit U84-39
Transfektionsreagenz U84-39
Transfer (Embryonen) U69-16
Transferrin U37-6
Transfer-RNA U84-15
transfixieren U141-4
transfizieren U84-39
Transformation U84-21
–, maligne U97-5
transformieren U78-6
transfundieren (Blut) U136-8; U37-1
Transfusion, autologe U136-8
transfusionsbedingt U136-8
Transfusionshepatitis U94-15
Transfusionsreaktion, hämolytische U136-12
Transfusionsverweigerung U136-8
Transfusionszwischenfall U136-8

Transfusionszwischenfall, hämolytischer U136-12
Transillumination U99-16
Transitionalzellkarzinom U86-13; U98-2
transitorisch U86-13
transkribieren U84-18
Transkriptase U84-18
Transkriptase-Hemmer U84-18
Transkriptelongation U84-18
Transkription U84-18
Transkriptionsfaktor U84-18
Transkriptionspromotor U84-21
Transkriptionsregulation U84-18
transkutan U121-3
translatieren U84-19
Translation U84-19
Translokation U84-23
Translokationsträger U84-23; U94-4
translozieren U84-23
Transmembrandomäne U84-3
Transmission U94-3
Transmissionsoxymetrie U125-9
Transmitter U42-10
Transmitteragonist U42-10
Transmitterantagonist U42-10
Transmitterfreisetzung U42-10
Transmitterwirkung U42-10
Transpiration U105-12; U51-11
transpirieren U105-12
Transplantat U129-14; U130-1
–, allogenes U130-3
–, autologes U130-2
–, syngenes U130-4
–, xenogenes U130-5
Transplantatabstoßung U39-22; U130-21
Transplantatannahme U130-1,21
Transplantatbett U130-1
Transplantatempfänger U100-24; U129-14; U130-3
Transplantatentnahme U129-12
Transplantat-gegen-Wirt Reaktion U130-20
Transplantationsantigene U39-20
Transplantatlebensdauer U100-25
Transplantatversagen U129-14
Transplantatzerstörung U130-1
transplantieren U129-14; U130-1
transponieren U129-11
Transport U8-3; U20-15; U49-3
–, aktiver U49-3; U78-17
–, ATP-abhängiger U78-15
–, bidirektionaler U49-3
–, carriervermittelter U88-3 f
–, gekoppelter U49-3
–, passiver U78-17; U88-3
–, trägervermittelter U49-3
–, tubulärer U49-3; U78-17
transportieren U8-3; U20-15; U88-3
Transportkapazität U49-3
Transportleistung, maximale tubuläre U49-3
Transportleiter U8-3

Transportmaximum U49-3; U78-17
Transportmedium U78-17
Transportproteine U49-3; U78-17
Transportsystem U78-17
–, mukoziliäres U44-9
Transportwirt U94-4,5
Transpositionslappen U129-13; U130-14
trans-Region U83-10
Transsexualität U68-1
Transsudat U140-13
Transuran U82-1
Transversalebene U87-2
transzendentale Meditation U1-16
Transzytose U83-15
trapezförmig U30-13
Trapezlappen U130-17
Traubenzucker U79-7
Trauer U12-12 f; U76-20,1
Trauerarbeit U18-4; U20-3
Trauerbegleiter(in) U16-1,12
Trauerfall U12-13
Trauerfamilie U12-13
Trauerkleidung U12-12
trauern (um) U12-12; U67-10
Trauernde(r) U12-12
Trauerprozess U12-12
Trauertherapeut(in) U12-12; U16-12
Trauerzeit U12-12 f
Traum U72-9
Trauma U5-2,4; U6-22
–, stumpfes U16-9; U58-1
Traumapatient(in) U5-4; U6-12
traumatisiert U130-7
Traumbilder U72-9
träumen U72-9
Traumerinnerung U72-9; U74-1
träumerisch U72-9
traurig U12-13; U76-9,20
Traurigkeit U12-13
Tray U17-12; U132-1
treffen U6-4
Treibhausgase U82-2
Treitz-Band U30-6
Trematoda U90-17
Trematodenei U90-17
Trematodeninfektion U90-17
Tremor U113-4
– mercurialis U82-32
–, feinschlägiger U31-20
Trendelenburg-Zeichen U30-15
Trendelenburglage(rung) U131-13; U63-1
trennen (chir.) U126-14
Trennungsangst U76-5; U77-5
Trennwand U86-15; U19-1
Trepanation U28-7
Treppengeländer U65-18
Treppensteigen U65-18
treten U64-12; U65-4 f
–, zur Seite U65-3
Treten U72-13
treu U75-10
Treue U75-10

Triage U8-19
Triage-Anhängekarte U8-19
Triageleiter(in) U8-19
Trichlormethan U82-23
Trichomonade U96-8
Trichomonadenurethritis U96-8
Trichomonosis (genitalis) U96-8
Trichophytie U90-16
Trichromat U59-9
–, normaler U59-9
Trichterbrust U22-2; U28-13
trichterförmig U46-9; U48-3
Trichuris trichiura U90-16
Trieb U73-11
Trigeminusneuralgie U104-21; U113-14
Trigger U88-13
Triggerfaktor U88-13
Trigger-Finger U23-7
Triggermechanismus U88-13
triggern U88-13
Triggerpunkt U88-13; U93-5
Triggerreiz U88-13
Triggerzone U88-13
Triglyzeride U35-7; U78-18; U82-13
Trigonum urogenitale U52-1
– vesicae U48-12
Trijodthyronin U55-6
Trijodthyronin-Aufnahme U55-3
Trikarbonsäure-Zyklus U81-15
Trikotschlauch U141-10; U140-17
Trikuspidalklappe U32-10
Trikuspidal(klappen)insuffizienz U110-10
Trikuspidalöffnungston U110-5
Trimenon U70-9
Trimer U81-6
trimmen U24-6
–, sich U25-4
Trimmübungen U1-15
Trinitrotoluol U6-9
trinken U10-1; U46-2
–, in Maßen U10-6
Trinker(in) U10-10
–, starke(r) U24-8
–, notorische(r) U10-3
Trinkgewohnheiten U10-1
Trinkwasser U82-4
Trinukleotidrepeat U84-14
Trip U11-10
Tripelhelix U84-11
Trippelgang U65-11; U113-8
trippelnd U65-11
Tripper U96-2; U69-6
Trismus U94-11
Trisomie U84-25
Tritium U82-9
Tritt U6-4; U64-12; U65-5
Trizeps (brachii) U30-11
Trizepshautfaltenmessung U30-11
Trizepssehnenreflex U23-4; U30-11
trizyklisch U81-7
Trochanter U28-4
– major/minor U28-4
Trochlea U28-15; U30-8
– humeri U30-8

Trochlea tali U30-8
trochlear(is) U30-8
Trochlearislähmung U30-8
trocken U10-4
Trockeneis U142-21
Trockengeburt U71-3
trockentupfen U64-11; U105-13
Trokar U132-7; U133-5
Trokaranordnung U133-5
Trokardorn U133-6; U132-7
Trokarhülse U133-6; U132-7
Trokarventil(mechanismus) U133-8
Trommelbauch U109-7; U45-6
Trommelfell U60-4; U86-15
Trommelfellbeweglichkeit U60-4
Trommelfellcompliance U60-4
Trommelfelleinziehung U60-4; U64-13
Trommelfellperforation U60-4
Trommelfellretraktion U60-4
Trommelfellruptur U60-4; U5-19
Trommelfellspanner U60-7
Trommelschlägelfinger U108-11
trommelschlägelförmig U108-11,6
Trompetenventil U133-8
Tropenkrankheit U94-1
Tröpfcheninfektion U94-3,7
tröpfeln U136-3
Tropfen U9-11; U64-15
–, dicker U94-20
Tropfenzähler U64-15
Tropfer U136-3
Tropfflasche U9-5; U136-4
Tropfinfusion, i.v. U136-3
Tropfkammer U136-3
Trophoblast U85-14,5
Trophoblasttumor U85-14; U97-4
Trophozoit U90-4
Trophozoitenstadium U90-4
Trost U18-6; U104-1
trösten U18-6
Trott, gemächlicher U65-14
trotten U65-14
trotzig U75-18
trüb U58-5; U103-16; U111-14
– (Sekret) U5-3
trüben U59-11
Trübheit U59-11
trübsinnig U75-6,14; U76-9
Trübsinnigkeit U75-17
Trübung U116-15
Trugwahrnehmung U73-10
Trümmer U8-7
Trümmerfraktur U106-7,3; U23-11
Truncation U84-21
Truncus U22-1
– arteriosus U22-1
– – persistens U32-11
– brachiocephalicus U34-9
– bronchomediastinalis U35-9,7
– cerebri U41-12
– coeliacus U34-9,14
– corporis callosi U41-3
– intestinalis U35-9
– lumbalis U35-9

– lumbosacralis U28-20
Truncus pulmonalis U22-1; U34-9; U36-2
– subclavius U35-9
– sympathicus U40-9
– vagalis U40-10
Trunkenheit U10-1
– am Steuer U10-1
trunkieren U22-1; U84-21
Trunksucht U10-1; U77-18
Tschandu U11-18
Tsetsefliege U90-15
TSH U55-6; U54-6
TSH-Anstieg U55-6
TSS U91-4,22
t-Test U100-34
Tuba auditiva U60-7; U45-4
– Eustachii U60-7
– uterina (Fallopii) U50-4; U70-1
Tubarabort U50-4
Tubargravidität U50-4; U70-6
Tube U50-4
Tubendurchgängigkeit U50-4
Tubenende, fimbrienbesetztes U50-4
Tubenkoagulation U69-3
Tubenligatur U69-3; U50-4
Tubenlumen U87-22
Tubenmandel U35-6; U60-7
Tubenplastik U69-4,3; U50-4
–, pelviskopische U128-4
Tubensterilisation U50-4
– rückgängig machen U69-3
Tubenunterbindung U69-3
Tubenverklebungen U128-15
Tubenvernarbung, chlamydienbedingte U90-14
Tuber calcanei U28-27
– ischiadicum U28-22
Tuberculosis cutis U94-16
Tuberculum U28-4
– genitale U50-1
– mentale U21-6
– pubicum U28-4,22; U52-18
Tuberkel U94-16
Tuberkelbakterium U94-16
Tuberkelbazillus U90-7; U94-16
Tuberkulintest U94-16; U118-2
tuberkulös U94-16
Tuberkulose U94-16
Tuberositas U28-4
– deltoidea (humeri) U30-13
– tibiae U28-4
Tubocurare U93-17
Tuboovarialabszess U50-3
Tubuli recti U48-7
– seminiferi U52-4
Tubulus contortus distalis U48-5; U87-14
– – proximalis U48-5
– renalis U48-5
– – colligens U48-9
– – contortus U48-7
–, proximaler U48-5
Tubulusnekrose U48-7
Tubus U123-10; U135-17

Tubusmanschette U17-8
Tuchklemme U132-13; U137-13
tüchtig **U75**-7
Tumeszenz **U53**-5; **U5**-15
Tumor **U5**-5; **U97**-2; **U89**-3,16
-, ACTH-produzierender U55-9
-, benigner U97-5
-, bösartiger **U97**-5; U13-10
-, embryonaler U85-1
-, feminisierender U50-2
-, gastrinproduzierender **U55**-13
-, großer U97-2
-, gutartiger U97-5
-, HCG-produzierender U55-20
-, inaktiver U119-6
-, indurierter U97-3
-, infiltrierender U97-12
-, maligner **U97**-6
-, platinsensitiver U82-28
-, raumfordernder U97-3
-, voluminöser U97-2
Tumorangiogenese **U97**-15
Tumorangiogenesefaktor U97-15
Tumoranteil U87-6
tumorartig **U97**-2
Tumorausbreitung **U97**-11,2
Tumorausdehnung U97-11
Tumorbefall U97-2
tumorbefallen U4-10
Tumorbett U97-2
Tumordissemination U128-17
Tumorembolus U124-13
Tumorerkrankung, klonale U84-33
Tumorgewebeprobe U117-3
Tumorgröße U97-2,11
Tumorinvolution U97-7
Tumorläsion U97-3 f
Tumorlast U97-2,14
Tumorlatenz U94-6
Tumorleiden U97-4
Tumormarker **U97**-16
Tumormasse **U97**-3
-, abgrenzbare U97-3
-, tastbare U97-3
-, verschiebliche U97-3
Tumornekrosefaktor U97-2
tumorös **U97**-2
Tumorpatient(in) U97-1
Tumorploidie U84-9
Tumorprogression **U97**-7
Tumorproliferation **U97**-7
Tumorremission U97-7
Tumorrest U97-2
Tumorrezidiv U97-2; U119-18
Tumorrückbildung U97-7
Tumorrückgang U97-2
Tumorschrumpfung U97-2
Tumorsitz U97-2
Tumorstaging U97-1
-, thorakoskopisches U128-6
Tumorvakzine U97-18
Tumorverkleinerung U97-2
Tumorverschleppung U128-17
Tumorvirus U97-1

Tumorwachstum **U97**-7
Tumorzellaussaat U56-20
Tumorzell-Purging U38-2; U118-9
Tumorzerfall U105-18
tumorzerstörend U97-2
Tunica adventitia **U34**-2
- conjunctiva bulbi U58-2
- - palpebrarum U58-4
- externa **U34**-2
- interna U34-2; U87-8
- intima U34-2; U87-8
- media U34-2
- mucosa U50-6; **U86**-17
- muscularis U50-6
- serosa U50-6; **U86**-9
- submucosa U86-17
- vasculosa bulbi **U58**-7
Tunnel, innerer U60-12
Tüpfelung (Zahnfleisch) U26-12
-, basophile (Erythrozyten) U37-8
Tupfer U17-13,1; **U116**-5; **U132**-18; **U140**-23,11
-, chirurgischer U131-8,19
Tupferträger U132-18
Tupferzange U132-14,18
Tupfpräparat U132-18
Turgor **U31**-10; U86-3
Türkensattel U54-5
Turnhalle **U1**-15
Turnübungen **U1**-12
Turnus **U15**-5
Turnusarzt U15-1,3; U16-9
Tylektomie **U97**-3
Tympanie **U109**-7
Tympanometrie U60-4; U61-7
Tympanon **U60**-6
Tympanoplastik U60-4
Tympanosklerose U60-4
Tympanum **U60**-6
Typ **U75**-1
-, extrovertierter U75-13
Typ I-Faser U30-1
Typ II-Faser U30-1
Typ IV-Immunantwort U39-23
Typhus abdominalis **U94**-19; U90-7
Typhusbakterien U94-19
Typhusimpfstoff U94-19
Typhusträger U94-19
Typhusvakzine U94-19
Typisierung, serologische U122-11
T-Zelle(n) **U39**-13; U37-10
-, antigenreaktive U39-11
-, zytotoxische U37-10; U39-16
T-Zellen-Antikörper U39-13
T-Zell-Lymphom U39-13
T-Zell-Rezeptor U39-13
T-Zell-Subpopulation U39-13
T-Zellzahl U39-13

U

übel **U4**-1
Übelkeit **U103**-11; U46-5; U70-9
-, morgendliche U103-11
übelnehmen U76-11
übelriechend U62-1,3; **U109**-2
üben U18-1; **U64**-18; **U74**-6
überaltert U35-4
überängstlich **U6**-21; **U75**-11; **U77**-6
Überanstrengung U64-19; U24-9
- (Augen) U58-2; U113-16
-, körperliche U76-18
überarbeiten **U74**-7
Überbeanspruchung U113-15
Überbelastung **U5**-17; **U33**-10
Überblähung **U44**-5
überbrücken **U63**-5
überdauern **U12**-6
überdeckt U77-12
überdehnen U5-16 f
Überdehnung **U44**-10; U31-3
überdenken U126-2; U73-6
überdosieren **U11**-11; **U91**-11
Überdosierung **U11**-11; **U91**-11
-, suizidale U91-11
Überdosis **U11**-11; **U91**-11; **U121**-7
-, akzidentelle U11-11
Überdruckbeatmung U44-5
-, intermittierende U123-9
-, kontinuierliche U125-10
Überdruckkammer U64-4
übereinanderschlagen (Beine) U23-8
überempfindlich **U39**-23; **U76**-4
Überempfindlichkeit **U39**-23; **U57**-8; U75-17
- (Haut) U56-1
Überempfindlichkeitsreaktion U122-3
- (Soforttyp) **U124**-3
überengagiert U75-6
Überernährung **U79**-1
übererregbar **U42**-8
Übererregbarkeit **U57**-1
-, neuromuskuläre U94-11; U108-13
überessen, sich **U2**-1
überfahren **U6**-2; U65-14
Übergang **U86**-13
Übergangsepithel **U86**-13,7; U49-12
Übergangsgebiss U27-1
Übergangsstadium U86-13
Übergangszellkarzinom U86-13; U97-9; U98-2
Übergangszone U86-13
-, anorektale U45-17
-, rektosigmoidale U45-16
übergeben, sich **U46**-4 f; **U103**-12
Übergewicht **U24**-8,1
übergewichtig **U24**-8
Überhang **U100**-8
Überheblichkeit **U75**-20
Überich **U77**-2
Überkompensation U77-12
Überkopfwurf U64-14
überkreuzen (Beine) U23-8

überlagern U117-13; U124-19
Überlagerung, psychogene U77-2
überlappende Gene U84-1
überlasten U64-19
Überlastung U33-10
Überlaufinkontinenz U112-15
überleben U12-6; U80-1,16
Überlebende(r) U12-6
Überlebenskurve U12-6
Überlebensrate U12-6; U100-25
–, progressionsfreie U97-7
Überlebensstatistik U100-1
Überlebensvorteil U12-6; U100-25
Überlebenswahrscheinlichkeit U12-6
–, kumulative U100-31
Überlebenszeit U12-6; U100-25
– (Transplantat) U130-21
–, rezidivfreie U12-6; U119-18
Überlebenszeitanalyse U100-26,25; U101-28
Überlegenheitskomplex U77-12
Überleitung, atrioventrikuläre U42-2
übermangansaures Kalium U82-18
übermitteln U42-4
überprüfen U18-9; U107-1
Überprüfung U18-9; U20-12
überreagieren U108-13
Überredungsversuch U75-19
überreizt U76-8
Überreizung U89-10
Überreste U85-13
Übersättigung U81-24
überschießendes Granulationsgewebe U140-7
Überschreitung (Geburtstermin) U70-6
Überschüsse U13-6
überschwänglich U76-16; U75-6
überschwellig U88-7
Überschwemmungen U6-20
übersehen U67-14; U117-4
Übersetzung U84-19
Übersichtsliste (Gesundheitsprobleme) U20-6
übersinnlich U77-2
überspannt U76-6
überspringen U65-16
übersprudelnd U1-6
Überstand U81-27,4
überstehen (Krankheit) U4-16
übersteigen U116-16
Übersteigerung der Hörschärfe U61-8
überstellen U20-15; U64-4
Überstellung U20-15; U64-4
Überstimulation, ovarielle U69-17
Überstimulationssyndrom U69-17
Überstreckbarkeit U142-8
überstrecken (Kopf) U8-17
Überstreckung U31-3; U142-8
–, kompensatorische U142-8
Überstreckungsverletzung U31-3
überstürzt U75-18
übertragbar U94-3
Übertragbarkeit U94-1f

übertragen (Krankheit) U42-2,4; U64-4; U94-2; U129-13
–, durch die Luft U44-12
–, sexuell U96-1
Überträger U94-4
–, mechanischer U94-4
Überträgersubstanz U42-10
Übertragung U94-3; U71-4; U129-13
–, aerogene U94-3
–, diaplazentare U94-3
–, fäkal-orale U94-3
–, germinative U94-3
–, horizontale U94-3
–, iatrogene U94-3
–, neuromuskuläre U42-2
–, sexuelle U15-10; U94-3
–, vertikale U94-3
Übertragungsinfektion U139-9
Übertragungsweg U94-3; U119-2
Übertransfusion U136-8
übertreffen U1-18
Überventilation U111-5
überwachen U125-5; U131-6
Überwachung U54-3; U125-5; U134-8; U142-29; U120-7,14
– (ZVD) U125-6
–, ambulante U65-1
–, anästhesiologische U135-2
–, hämodynamische U36-4
–, immunologische U39-2
–, intraoperative U126-2
–, stationäre U125-5
Überwachungsgerät U125-5; U134-8
Überwanderungselektrophorese U88-18
Überwärmung U105-5
überwässert U78-22
Überwässerung U56-12; U78-22
überweisen U18-12
Überweisung U18-12; U102-14; U13-7; U126-5
–, erwünschte U18-12
Überweisungsklinik U18-12
Überweisungspraxis U18-12
Überweisungsschein U18-12
überwiegen U117-17
überwiesen U102-14
überwinden U4-16
Überwucherung, bakterielle U46-16; U90-6
Überzeugung, feste U75-11
überziehen U86-8; U129-9
Überzug U86-8; U9-6
Ubichinon U81-5
Übung(en) U1-12; U64-18; U74-6
–, anstrengende U76-18
–, isometrische U1-15; U142-17
–, isotonische U142-17
–, therapeutische U14-3
Übungstherapie U16-12
Uhrzeigersinn, Drehung im U31-7
Ulcus U89-17
– corneae U58-5
– duodeni U45-10

Ulcus durum U96-1,3
– molle U96-4
– pepticum U82-27; U92-29
– varicosum/cruris U110-17
– ventriculi U45-8; U109-1
Ulkus U114-13
–, granulierendes U140-7
–, peptisches U82-27
Ulkusabheilung U140-4
Ulkuskrater U89-17
Ulna U28-16
Ulnardeviation U28-16; U106-10
Ultrafiltrat U49-1
– Hämodialysegerät U125-21
Ultrahochfrequenz U61-6
ultrakurze ionisierende Strahlung U99-20
Ultraschall U61-3
– Kardiografie (UKG) U118-15
Ultraschall(diagnostik) U118-17
ultraschallgezielt U118-17
Ultraschallraum U14-9
Ultraschalltherapie U142-23
Ultraschallvernebler U118-17
Ultraschallwellen U118-17
Ultraviolettmikroskop U86-1
Ultrazentrifugation U83-20
ulzerierend U89-17
umarmen U67-7; U68-2
Umarmung U67-7
Umbilicus U22-5; U71-17; U85-7
umbilikal U22-5
umdrehen U64-8
umfallen, tot U12-5
umfassen U67-7
Umfeld, keimfreies U90-5
umformen U78-6; U129-4
Umgang (mit Kranken) U19-7; U75-3
umgänglich U75-14
Umgangsformen U75-3
Umgebung, geschützte U11-13
–, ruhige U76-19
Umgebungstemperatur U82-7; U105-1
umgehen U36-14; U125-11
Umgehung U36-14
umgewandelt U37-12
Umhergehen U19-12; U65-1; U134-13; U142-13; U73-8
umhüllt U86-8
Umhüllung U86-8
Umklammerung U67-7
Umklammerungsreflex U67-7
Umklappeffekt U99-13
umknicken U5-16
umlagern U8-14; U20-15
Umlagern (Patient) U63-8
–, häufiges U63-1; U64-8
Umlagerung U20-15; U63-1; U64-4; U131-11
umleiten U36-14; U53-5
ummantelt U86-8
Ummantelung U86-8
umreißen U87-9
Umriss U99-12

umrühren U9-9
Umsatz (Stoffwechsel) **U78**-1
Umsatzrate U78-1
Umschaltstellen (Geschmacksreize) U42-4
Umschlag **U6**-6; **U140**-25,20,13
-, feuchtwarmer U92-30
Umschlagfalte (Konjunktiva) U58-4
- (Schleimhaut) U21-10
-, peritoneale U45-7
umschneiden **U126**-9
umschrieben (Läsion) U89-3
Umschulung **U142**-18,26
umsetzen, in d. Praxis U74-6
Umsichschlagen U72-13
umsichtig **U75**-7; **U117**-18
umspritzen (Nerv) U93-6
Umstandskleider U71-22
umstechen **U137**-3
Umstechungsligatur U126-14; U137-3
umwandeln **U78**-1,6; **U2**-6; **U55**-10
Umwandlung **U78**-6
-, enzymatische U78-6
Umwelt, rauchfreie U91-7
Umweltbelastung U91-5
Umweltgefahr **U91**-5
Umweltkatastrophe U6-20
Umweltmedizin U91-5
Umweltreize U57-1; U74-11
Umweltschadstoff **U91**-5 f
Unabhängigkeit **U142**-28
Unachtsamkeit U74-16
unangenehm **U75**-5; **U104**-3,1
unangepasst **U76**-21
unansehnlich U5-11
unanständig **U68**-10
unattraktiv U25-5
unauffällig **U76**-19; **U107**-18 f,2
- (Befund) **U134**-9; U99-3
unaufmerksam U74-16
Unaufmerksamkeit **U74**-16
Unausgeglichenheit **U75**-15
unbeabsichtigt U122-1
unbeaufsichtigt U131-18
unbedeutend **U20**-13
unbefugt **U20**-7
unbehaglich U77-5
unbeirrbar U74-1
unbekannt **U74**-3
unbekümmert **U75**-18; **U32**-2
unbemerkt **U57**-4; **U102**-2
unbeobachtet **U6**-13
unbequem U104-1
unberechenbar **U75**-9
Unberührtheit **U68**-12
unbeschwert **U75**-6,16
unbesonnen **U75**-18
unbeständig **U75**-9 f
unbestimmt **U117**-2
unbeteiligt **U76**-15
unbeweglich **U12**-15; **U53**-10; **U64**-1 f; **U103**-20
Unbeweglichkeit **U64**-2
unbewusst U7-1

unblutig **U37**-1
Uncoating U90-10
undeutlich (Sprache) U66-15
undicht sein **U112**-15
undichte Stelle **U137**-11; U135-15
undifferenziert **U97**-8
undissoziiert U81-22
undurchlässig **U88**-6
Undurchlässigkeit (Strahlen) U99-11
uneben U65-9
unehelich U70-6
unehrlich **U75**-12
unelastisch **U116**-18
unempfindlich **U57**-8; **U76**-4; **U93**-4; **U135**-3
Unempfindlichkeit U57-3
unentschlossen **U75**-11; **U76**-14
Unentschlossenheit **U75**-11; U76-13
unergiebig **U116**-18
unerkannt **U117**-10,4
unersättlich U68-4
unerträglich U5-2; U104-2,9
unerwünscht U91-1; U121-14
Unfähigkeit **U20**-14; U142-3
Unfall **U6**-1
Unfallambulanz U6-1
-, allgemeine U14-6
Unfallchirurg(in) U15-15
unfallgefährdet **U6**-1; U119-1
Unfallopfer **U6**-12; **U14**-6
Unfallort U6-1
Unfallstation **U14**-6; U6-12; U19-1
Unfalltod U5-4; U6-1; U12-7
Unfallverhütung **U6**-22,1
Unfallverhütungsprogramm U8-4
unfruchtbar **U69**-3; **U139**-2
Unfruchtbarkeit **U69**-2 f; **U70**-1
-, therapieresistente U69-11
ungeboren **U71**-1
Ungeduld U67-15; U71-22
ungeduldig **U75**-18
ungehalten **U75**-18; U76-10
ungenießbar **U2**-5
ungepflegt U107-10
ungepuffert **U81**-20
ungesättigt **U81**-24
Ungeschicklichkeit U113-9
ungesellig **U75**-14
ungestört **U4**-11
ungestüm **U77**-7; U140-16
ungesund **U1**-5,1 f; **U4**-1
ungetrübt U7-1
Ungewissheit **U8**-4
ungezahnt U132-4
ungezogen U75-3
ungiftig **U121**-13
ungläubig U67-3
Ungleichgewicht **U57**-18
-, osmotisches U88-19
Ungleichheit U88-19
Unglück **U6**-1; **U6**-4; U77-5
unglücklich **U76**-20
Unglücksort U8-4
Unguentum **U9**-8

Unguis **U56**-15
- incarnatus U56-15
ungünstig **U91**-1
unheilbar **U120**-2
unhygienisch **U1**-5
univariat **U100**-5; U100-33
Universalspender(in) U129-15; U136-9
Universalspenderblut U136-14
Unkenntlichkeit U74-3
unklar **U116**-23; **U117**-4
unkonzentriert **U74**-16; U76-15
unkoordiniert **U113**-8
unkorreliert **U100**-32
Unkrautbekämpfungsmittel **U91**-8
Unkrautvertilgungsmittel **U91**-8
unkritisch **U117**-15
unlöslich **U88**-5; U79-11
Unmäßigkeit **U10**-6
unmündig **U80**-9
unpässlich **U1**-3; **U75**-4
Unpässlichkeit **U4**-5; **U103**-7; **U104**-1; U95-2
unphysiologisch **U88**-1
unpolar **U81**-13
unreif **U80**-10,2
Unrichtigkeit **U75**-12
Unruhe **U64**-17; **U72**-5; **U76**-8; U134-4
-, innere U71-22; U77-2
-, motorische U31-20; U64-17
-, psychomotorische **U7**-12; **U76**-8; **U113**-2; U77-16
unruhig **U64**-17; **U76**-6,8; **U113**-2
unschädlich **U6**-11; U39-23
unschöne Narbe U140-10
Unschuld **U68**-11
-, kindliche U80-5
unsicher **U8**-4; **U76**-12; **U91**-5; **U117**-8
Unsicherheit **U8**-4; **U64**-6
- (beim Gehen) U65-2; U113-8
Unsicherheitsgefühl U103-13
unsichtbar U59-6
unsterblich **U12**-3
untadelig **U77**-10
untätig **U76**-17
Untätigkeit **U64**-18
unter direkter Kontrolle U69-13
- Drogen **U7**-9
Unterarm **U23**-2; **U28**-16; **U139**-6
Unterarmbeuger U31-2
Unterarmkrücken U19-14
Unterarmsupination U31-9
Unterbauch(gegend) **U22**-8
unterbesetzt **U15**-2
Unterbewusstsein **U7**-1
unterbinden **U137**-3; U69-4; U138-3
- (Samenleiter) U52-6
Unterbrechung **U119**-11
- (Blutzufuhr) U36-5
unterbrochen **U87**-12
unterdrücken **U74**-14; **U88**-14
Unterdrückung **U88**-14
Untereinheit **U81**-4
-, katalytische U81-16
unterentwickelt **U24**-4

Unterentwicklung (Geschlechtsorgane) U52-1
Unterernährung **U2**-3; U24-1; **U79**-1
Unterfütterungslappen **U130**-18
untergeordnet **U34**-13
Untergewicht **U24**-10
untergewichtig **U24**-10
Unterhaltung **U1**-10
Unterhautbindegewebe U56-4; U86-4
Unterhautfettgewebe **U56**-5,4; U24-5
Unterkiefer(knochen) **U28**-10; U21-5 f
Unterkieferasymmetrie U5-16
Unterkieferkörper U28-10
Unterkieferrand U21-5
Unterkieferverrenkung U28-10
Unterkieferzahnreihe U28-10
unterkühlt U105-9
Unterkühlung **U105**-5
Unterkunft U80-3
Unterlagen **U101**-15
unterlassen **U77**-11
Unterlassung **U77**-11
Unterleib **U45**-6
Unterleibstyphus **U94**-19
untermauern **U117**-12
unterminiert U96-4
unterordnen, sich U77-7
Unterreich U90-2
Unterricht, klinischer **U14**-2
unterscheiden **U117**-15; U62-8
Unterscheidung **U87**-12; **U117**-15
Unterscheidungsmerkmale U103-3
Unterscheidungsparameter U100-5
Unterschenkel **U23**-10,8
Unterschenkelamputierte U142-6
Unterschenkelgeschwür U89-17
Unterschenkelgips U141-6
Unterschied **U87**-12
unterschiedlich U100-14
untersetzt **U24**-8; **U25**-6; U110-18
unterstützen **U8**-1; **U19**-11; **U64**-16; **U120**-8,14
Unterstützung **U117**-12; **U142**-29
–, maschinelle U125-3
–, seelische U19-11
untersuchen **U107**-1; **U116**-2; **U118**-1
–, lichtmikroskopisch U86-1
Untersucher(in) **U107**-1; **U101**-2
Untersuchung **U107**-6; **U118**-1; **U77**-1
–, ambulante U20-2
–, ärztliche **U18**-9
–, bimanuelle U107-7
–, biochemische U81-1
–, diagnostische **U20**-8; **U126**-11
–, digitale rektale U45-16
–, funktionsdiagnostische U102-11
–, gynäkologische U15-16
–, karyometrische U83-3
–, klinische **U101**-1; **U107**-2
–, körperliche U18-9; **U107**-2
–, labordiagnostische **U116**-2; U20-8
–, medizinische U81-8
–, mikroskopische **U86**-1
–, neurologische U15-14

Untersuchung, psychiatrische U77-16
–, serologische U37-3
–, sportmedizinische U1-12
–, wissenschaftliche **U101**-2; U100-16
–, zytologische U83-1
Untersuchungsergebnis U117-6
Untersuchungsformular U116-2
Untersuchungskabine **U19**-1; **U107**-5
Untersuchungsmaterial **U118**-4; U91-3
Untersuchungsobjekt **U100**-2
Untersuchungsraum U19-2; U107-1
Untersuchungstisch **U107**-1
Untersuchungsverfahren U20-8
Untersuchungszimmer U19-2; U107-1
Untertauchen **U6**-16
Untertemperatur U105-1
Unterton **U66**-11; U67-19
unterversichert U13-5
Unterwäsche U107-4
Unterwasser-Druckstrahlmassage U142-15
Unterwassergymnastik U142-17,20
Untreue U12-12
untröstlich **U32**-2; **U76**-20
untypisch U75-1
unverändert **U65**-3
unverdaulich **U46**-11; **U109**-1
unvergesslich **U74**-8
unverhohlen **U75**-13
unverkennbar **U87**-12
unversehrt **U5**-3
unverständlich U66-17
unverträglich **U136**-11
Unverträglichkeit **U136**-11; **U121**-12
unverzerrt **U100**-18
unvollständig (Verbrennung) U81-17
unvorsichtig U65-5
Unwahrheit **U75**-12
unwahrscheinlich **U100**-31
unwesentlich **U20**-13
unwiderstehlich U72-16; U73-11
unwillig **U76**-14
unwirksam **U101**-26,8
unwissentlich U96-9
unwohl **U1**-3; **U4**-1; **U75**-4
– fühlen, sich **U103**-7; U104-1
Unwohlsein **U103**-7
unzerkaut schlucken U9-7; U121-3
Unzucht **U68**-13
unzüchtig **U68**-10
unzugänglich **U128**-1; **U126**-6
Unzulänglichkeit U75-14; U77-10
–, eigene U102-9
unzurechnungsfähig **U18**-10; **U77**-3,13,15; U20-14
Unzurechnungsfähigkeit **U77**-15
unzusammenhängend **U87**-12
– (Sprache) U66-1,17
unzuverlässig **U100**-30
upper-limb-tension-Test **U142**-11
Urachus **U85**-17
Urachusdivertikel U85-17
Urachusfistel U85-17
Urachuspersistenz U85-17

Urachusrest U85-17
Urachussinus U85-17
Urachuszyste U85-17
Urämie **U112**-13; U37-2
Urämiegifte U112-13
urämisch U37-2; **U112**-13
Uran 238 U82-34
Urat **U49**-14
Uratablagerung U49-14
Uratkristalle U49-14; U82-5
Uratnephropathie U49-14
Uratstein U49-14; U81-22
Urdarm **U85**-21,8; U45-9
Urea **U47**-18; **U49**-13,5; U48-8
Ureier U51-5
Ureolyse U78-14
Ureter **U48**-10
Ureterabgang U48-10
Ureterabgangsenge/-stenose U112-12
Ureteranlage U85-10
Ureterknospe U48-10; U85-10
Ureterneozystostomie U48-10
Ureterostomie, retroperitoneoskopische perkutane U128-5
Ureterperistaltik U48-10
Uretersteine U48-10
Ureterstenose U48-10
Urethra **U48**-13
Urethraabstrich U48-13
Urethralklappen U48-13
Urethritis U48-13
–, gonorrhoische U96-2
Urethrorrhoe/-ö U48-13
Urge **U112**-4
– Inkontinenz U112-4,15; U119-2
Urharnsack **U85**-17
Urikosurika **U92**-28; U49-14
Urin **U49**-12
Urinal **U19**-8; **U49**-12
Urinbeutel **U125**-23
Urinbeutelfixierung U125-23
Urinextravasation U136-7
Urinflasche **U19**-8; **U49**-12
urinieren **U49**-16,12; U65-17
Urinkultur **U116**-15
Urinmenge U48-1
Urinprobe **U116**-15
Urinproduktion U48-1
Urinschiffchen U19-8
Urkeimzelle U51-4; U85-9
Urlaubsvertreter(in) **U15**-6
Urniere **U85**-21
Urnierengang U85-21
Urobilinogen **U47**-13
Uroflowmetrie U49-12
urogenital **U48**-1
Urogenitalschistosomiasis U112-3
Urogenitaltrakt U52-1
Urografie, intravenöse **U118**-19
Urokinase **U37**-15
Urokinase-Plasminogen-Aktivator, einkettiger U37-15
Urothel U48-11; U49-12; U86-7
Ursache (Krankheit) U89-8

Ursache, organische U86-20
ursächlich **U119**-2
Ursegment **U85**-19
Ursprung **U30**-3; **U81**-18; **U85**-11
–, embryologischer U85-1
Urteil, ärztliches **U117**-18
urteilen **U117**-18
Urteilsfähigkeit U77-23; U73-5
Urteilsvermögen **U73**-6; U7-12; U77-3
–, beeinträchtigtes U117-18
–, schlechtes U74-16
Urtica **U114**-11
Urtierchen **U90**-2
Urtikaria **U114**-11; U124-3
usuriert U27-21
Uterinageräusch U110-4
Uterus **U50**-5; U71-1
– myomatosus U98-9
– septus U50-5; U86-15
Uterusentfernung, pelviskopische U128-4
Uterushalteapparat U63-13
Uteruskontraktionen U55-23
Uteruskörper U50-5
Uterusmyom U98-9
Uterusruptur U50-5
Uterussonde U132-8
Uterusvorfall U50-5
U-Test (Mann-Whitney) U100-34
Utriculus prostaticus U52-10
Utrikulus **U60**-9
Utrikulusrezeptor U57-18
Uvea **U58**-7
Uveaentzündung **U58**-7
Uveitis **U58**-7
UV-Lampe U19-6
Uvula U26-10; U63-13

V

Vacutainer-Kanüle **U17**-10
Vagina **U50**-8
– carotica U34-10
– duplex U50-8
– synovialis tendinis U29-3
– tendinis U30-5; U86-6
–, blind endigende U50-8
Vaginalabstrich U50-8
Vaginalflora U50-8
Vaginalschaum U69-8
Vaginalschwamm **U69**-9; U50-8
Vaginalsuppositorium **U69**-8
Vaginalverkehr U50-8; U68-5
Vaginalzäpfchen **U69**-8; U9-12; U50-8
Vaginaverdopplung U50-8
Vaginismus U50-8; U68-7
Vaginose, bakterielle U90-6
Vagolytikum U40-10
Vagus **U40**-10
Vagusganglion, oberes U40-10
Vaguspuls U40-10
Vagusreflex U40-10
Vagusreiz U42-5

Vagusstamm U40-10
Vagusstimulation U40-10; U88-12
Vagustonus U40-10
vakuolär **U83**-11
Vakuolen **U83**-11
–, zahlreiche intrazelluläre U39-18
vakuolenartig **U83**-11
Vakuolenbildung **U83**-11
Vakuolen-Protonenpumpe U83-11
Vakuolisierung **U83**-11
Vakuummatratze **U8**-15
Vakuumpumpe U53-5
Vakuum-Schiene U8-15
Vakzination **U122**-3
– parenterale **U122**-4
Vakzine **U122**-2; U39-2
–, inaktivierte zelluläre U122-7
Vakzinetherapie U122-2
vakzinieren **U122**-1
Valenz **U81**-10
Valenzelektron U81-10,11
Valenzwechsel U81-10
Validität **U100**-30
Valsalva-Manöver U40-10; U142-11
Valsalva-Versuch U44-2
Valva atrioventricularis dextra U32-10
– – sinistra U32-10
– semilunaris U32-10
– trunci pulmonalis U32-10; U43-2
Valvula Eustachii U34-12
– sinus coronarii U32-10
– venae cavae inferioris U34-12
– venosa **U34**-12
Valvuloplastik U32-10
Vanadin **U82**-26
Vanadinsäure U82-26
Vanadismus U82-26
Vanadium **U82**-26
Vanadiumvergiftung U82-26
vaporisieren **U82**-3; **U127**-15,5
Variabilität **U100**-14
Variable **U100**-5
variable Region U84-2
Variante **U100**-14
Varianz **U100**-14
Varianzanalyse U100-14
Variation **U100**-14
Variationskoeffizient U100-14
Varicellae adultorum U95-7
Varicella-Zoster-Virus U95-7
varikös **U110**-17
Varikosität **U110**-17
Varikozele U110-17
Variola **U95**-7
Variolavirus U95-7
Varix **U110**-17
Varize **U110**-17; U34-4
Varizellen **U95**-7; U114-12
Varizellen-Pneumonie U95-7
Varizenblutung U38-6; U124-16
Varizenstripping U110-17
Vas capillare **U34**-5
– deferens U52-6,3

Vasa afferentia U34-1
– efferentia U34-1
– lymphatica **U35**-1
– vasorum U34-1
Vasektomie **U52**-6; **U69**-3
–, prophylaktische U69-3
vasektomieren **U69**-3
Vaselin U92-30
vaskulär **U34**-1
Vaskularisation U34-1
Vasodilatanzien **U92**-17; U36-11
Vasodilatation **U36**-11; **U92**-17
Vasokongestion **U110**-15
Vasokonstriktion **U36**-11; **U92**-17
Vasokonstriktor U36-11; U82-17
Vasokonstringenzien U36-11; **U92**-17
Vasoligatur U52-6
Vasomotor U34-1
Vasomotorenkollaps U110-11
Vasomotorentonus U110-15
Vasopressin **U55**-24; U92-21
Vasopressintest U55-24
Vasopressor U82-17
Vasoresektion **U52**-6; **U69**-3
Vasospasmus U36-11; U110-15
Vasostomie **U69**-4
Vasotocin U55-24
Vasovasostomie **U69**-4; U52-6
Vasovesikulografie U52-6
Vater-Ampulle **U47**-10
Vater-Pacini-(Tast-/Lamellen)-körperchen U57-15
Vaterschaft **U84**-31
Vaterschaftsbestimmung U84-31
VDRL-Test U96-1
vegetarisch **U2**-16
Vektor **U94**-4
Vektorübertragung U94-3,4
velopharyngealer Abschluss U66-22
Velum palatinum U26-10
Vena **U34**-4
– azygos U36-3
– cava **U34**-7
– – Ligatur U137-3
– cephalica U87-19
– hemiazygos U36-3
– hypogastrica U22-8
– iliaca interna U22-8
– interlobularis hepatis U47-3
– jugularis U110-16
– – externa **U34**-11
– poplitea U23-9
– portae U34-4
Vena-cava-superior-Syndrom U34-7
Venae brachiocephalicae U34-9
– communicantes U34-6
– fibulares U117-4
– sectio **U5**-6; U34-4; U110-17
Vene **U34**-4
–, oberflächliche U34-4
Venendruck U34-4
–, zentraler U36-8; U107-14
Venenentzündung, oberflächliche **U110**-17; **U136**-7

Venenkatheter **U136**-3,6
–, zentraler **U125**-7; U127-19; U136-5
Venenklappe **U34**-12; U32-10
–, insuffiziente U34-12
Venenklappeninsuffizienz U34-12
Venenpuls U34-4
Venenpunktion **U118**-7; **U136**-2
Venenschnitt **U127**-18; **U5**-6; U34-4
Venenstau(ung) **U110**-15
Venenstripping U34-4
Venenthrombose, tiefe **U124**-13; U34-4
Venenverschluss U34-4
Venenverweilkanüle **U136**-6
Venenverweilkatheter U136-5
–, zentraler U125-7
venerisch **U15**-10; **U96**-1
Venerologie **U96**-1
Venografie U110-17
Venole **U34**-4
Venostase **U110**-15; U34-4
Venter **U22**-4
– musculi U22-4; U30-2
ventilartig U44-3
Ventilation **U44**-5; **U125**-10
Ventilations-Perfusions-Verhältnis U111-3; U123-9
ventilieren **U44**-5; **U123**-9
Ventilpneumothorax U124-17; U123-1
ventral **U87**-16
Ventriculus cerebri **U41**-4
– lateralis U41-4; U87-18
Ventrikel **U32**-8
–, dritter U41-4
–, vierter U41-4
Ventrikelauswurf **U33**-8
Ventrikelblutung U41-4
Ventrikeldrain **U125**-15
Ventrikeldrainage **U125**-15; U41-4
Ventrikelejektionsfraktion U32-8
Ventrikelfüllung U33-9
Ventrikelpunktion U41-4; U125-15
Ventrikelseptumdefekt U32-8
Ventrikelstimulation **U123**-13
Ventrikelsystole U33-3
Ventrikelvolumen U32-8
ventrikulär **U32**-8; **U41**-4
Ventrikulozisternostomie U125-15
Venula U34-4
Venusberg **U50**-16; U52-18
verabreichen **U91**-11; **U121**-3
– (Medikament) U16-7
Verabreichung **U121**-3,1; U21-8
– (Testmedikament) **U101**-23
–, i.v. U136-5
–, subkutane U17-11; U56-4
verächtlich U67-16
veränderlich **U100**-5
Veränderungen **U83**-19
–, tumorähnliche U97-3
–, anatomische U87-1
–, physiologische U88-1
–, postmortale U12-19
verankert U28-25
Veranlagung **U75**-4; **U76**-2; **U119**-1

verantwortlich **U75**-9; U16-10
verantwortungsbewusst **U75**-9
verantwortungslos **U75**-9
Verarbeitung, elaborierte U74-9
verärgert **U76**-9 f,7
verästelt **U34**-13
Verästelung **U34**-13
Verätzung U5-11; U81-1,19; U91-10
Verband **U140**-17,3,20; **U5**-1
–, elastischer U31-16
Verbandmaterial U17-1
Verbandmull **U140**-18,23; U9-8
Verbandraum U140-17
Verbandskasten U8-1
verbessert U69-14
verbeugen, sich **U31**-2; **U63**-3
Verbeugung **U31**-2; **U63**-3
verbinden **U74**-5; **U81**-2,12
– (Wunde) **U140**-17,1,20; U129-5
verbindend **U81**-8
Verbindung **U41**-3; **U74**-5; U47-16; U85-17; **U100**-32; U129-6
– stehen, in U60-14
–, arsenhaltige **U82**-33
–, arteriovenöse U34-6
–, chemische **U81**-2,1; **U84**-37
–, energiereiche U78-12
–, hitzebeständige U81-2
–, künstliche U127-3
–, radioaktiv markierte U81-2
–, synaptische U40-13
–, thermostabile U81-2
–, unlösliche U88-5
–, wasserlösliche U81-2
–, zyklische **U81**-7
Verbindungsäste U34-6
Verbindungsstelle **U41**-3
Verbissenheit U75-11
verbittert **U76**-11
verblassen U74-10; U114-5
verblenden **U87**-4
verblinden U101-9
verblüffen **U59**-3; U7-8
Verblüffung **U77**-4
verbluten **U38**-9
Verblutung **U38** 9; U37-1
Verblutungsrisiko, hohes U38-9
verborgen U119-6
Verbot **U10**-8
verboten U11-24
Verbrauchskoagulopathie U38-10
Verbreitung (Keime) **U94**-3; U139-8
verbrennen (Kalorien) U24-5; U79-4
Verbrennung (Unfall) **U5**-11; **U6**-10
– (Kalorien) **U81**-17; U105-5
–, vollständige U81-17
Verbrennungsmotor U81-17
Verbrennungsopfer U6-12
Verbrennungspatient(in) U6-12
Verbrennungsschock U124-4
Verbrennungsschorf U114-8; **U140**-9
Verbrennungswärme U81-17
Verbrühung **U5**-11; U6-5
verbunden mit **U81**-14; **U87**-12,8

Verdacht (auf) **U116**-23; **U117**-8
– erregen U72-7; U74-2
verdächtig **U116**-23; **U117**-8
Verdächtige(r) **U116**-23; **U117**-8
Verdachtsdiagnose U116-23; U117-8,11
verdampfen **U82**-2 f; **U105**-14
– (Gewebe) **U127**-15,5
Verdampfer **U82**-3
Verdampfung **U105**-14
Verdampfungsgerät **U82**-3
verdauen **U45**-8; **U46**-11
verdaulich **U46**-11; **U109**-1
Verdauung **U46**-11; U2-1
Verdauungsenzym U46-11; U78-8
Verdauungskanal **U45**-1; U46-11
Verdauungssäfte U45-1
Verdauungsstörung **U109**-1,10; U46-11
–, leichte U4-5
Verdauungstrakt **U45**-1; U46-11
Verdauungsvorgang U45-1
verdecken **U117**-13; U58-5
verderben (Magen) U45-8; U109-1
verdichten **U82**-8
Verdichtung **U89**-13
Verdichtungsareale U89-13
Verdickung **U85**-10
– (Basalmembran) U86-16
verdoppeln, sich U84-8
Verdoppelung, identische **U84**-16
– (Niere) U48-9
verdrahten **U141**-14
verdrängen (Erinnerungen) **U74**-14
Verdrängung, unbewusste U74-14; U77-17
verdrehen **U31**-7; U5-16
– (Augen) U58-2
Verdrehung **U31**-7
verdrießlich **U76**-9
verdünnen **U36**-13; **U81**-23
verdünnt **U36**-13; **U81**-23; U82-5
Verdünnung **U81**-23; **U116**-17
Verdünnungsazidose U81-23
Verdünnungshyponatriämie U81-23
Verdünnungsmittel **U81**-23; U91-25
Verdünnungsreihe U81-23
verdunsten **U82**-2 f; **U105**-14; U56-12
Verdunstung **U105**-14; **U127**-15
Vereinbarung, nur nach U18-2
vereinen, sich U58-14
Vereinigung U34-11
vereinzelt U57-15
vereisen U93-3
verengen **U6**-6; **U36**-11; U132-17
Verengung **U89**-19 f
vererben **U20**-14
Vererbung **U84**-28; **U89**-7
–, autosomale U84-6
Vererbungslehre, Mendelsche U84-1
Vererbungsmuster U84-28
Veress-Nadel **U133**-13
verestern **U78**-7; **U82**-14
Veresterung **U78**-7; **U82**-14
Verfahren **U126**-4; U101-1
–, bildgebende U20-8; U118-24

Verfahren, diagnostische **U20**-8; U117-6
–, experimentelle U20-8
Verfahrensanweisungen, festgelegte U20-7
Verfall, geistiger **U4**-12; U77-16,22 f
Verfalldatum U9-19
verfälschende Faktoren U101-9
verfärben **U116**-4; U114-9
Verfärbung (Zähne) U26-12
–, dunkle **U25**-12
–, livide U114-1
Verfassung U74-1
–, geistige U119-15; U73-2
–, körperliche **U1**-8 f; U107-2
verfaulen **U46**-17
Verfestigung **U89**-13
verflacht U76-3
verflüchtigen, sich **U82**-2 f; **U105**-14
verflüssigen, (sich) **U82**-4,8
Verflüssigung **U81**-22; **U82**-4
Verflüssigungsnekrose U82-14
Verfolgungswahn U7-16; U77-12,20
verformbar U141-14
Verformbarkeit U82-6
Verfügbarkeit, biologische **U121**-10
verfügen **U20**-14
verführen **U68**-9
vergären **U46**-12
Vergehen U77-10; U73-3
vergehen, sich an jem. **U68**-17
vergesellschaftet (mit) U119-16
Vergessen **U74**-14 f,1
Vergessenheit **U74**-15
vergesslich **U74**-15
Vergesslichkeit **U74**-15
–, benigne U74-15
vergewaltigen **U68**-17
Vergewaltiger **U68**-17
Vergewaltigung **U68**-17; U12-10
– in der Ehe U68-16
Vergewaltigungsopfer U6-12
vergießen (Tränen) **U64**-15; U67-10
vergiften U91-2,14
Vergiftung **U91**-2,14; U2-1
–, akzidentelle U91-2,22
–, schwere U10-5; U91-14
–, systemische **U91**-20
Vergiftungserscheinung U91-21
Vergiftungsnotfall U9-15
Vergleich anstellen **U59**-11
Vergnügen U66-2
vergnügt **U76**-9; **U67**-6
vergoldet U82-28; U141-14
vergrößern **U136**-13
–, sich **U108**-12
vergrößert **U110**-9
Vergrößerung **U88**-12; **U89**-15; **U129**-19,2; **U127**-2
–, myomatöse U98-9
Verhalt **U49**-4
verhalten, sich **U75**-3
– (Stuhl) U46-19
Verhalten **U75**-3; U20-13; U73-13
–, abweichendes U75-3

Verhalten, aggressives U77-7
–, altersgemäßes U75-3
–, aufmerksamkeitsheischendes U74-16
–, biologisches U83-1
–, eigensinniges U75-19
–, erlerntes U74-7
–, extrovertiertes U75-13
–, gestörtes U76-21
–, gesundheitsgefährdendes U75-3
–, motorisches U31-20; U40-4
–, selbstzerstörerisches U75-2
–, unsittliches **U68**-10
–, verschlossenes U77-8
Verhaltensaktivierung U72-7
Verhaltensänderung U75-3
verhaltensauffällig U76-21
Verhaltensmuster U75-3
Verhaltensnormen U75-3
Verhaltensstörung U75-3,21; U77-13,16
Verhaltenstherapeut U16-12; U120-4
Verhaltenstherapie U75-3
–, kognitive U75-3; U73-4
Verhältnis **U74**-5; **U100**-8
–, molares U81-3
Verhältnisse, geordnete U75-15
–, topografische U87-1
verhärmt **U25**-7
Verhärtung **U89**-14
verhätscheln U80-5
verheerend **U6**-20; U76-12
verheilen **U140**-4; **U120**-2
verhindern **U6**-22; U70-3
verhornt **U56**-6
Verhornung U56-6; **U114**-14
verhungern **U2**-14; U12-4
Verhütung (Giftunfälle) U80-5
Verhütungsmethode U69-5
Verhütungsmittel **U69**-5
Verifizierung **U101**-17
verkalken **U31**-14
Verkalkung U31-14; **U82**-19; **U27**-22
–, stippchenartige U98-12
verkapselt **U97**-9
Verkapselung **U97**-9
Verkäsung U89-29 f
verkatert **U10**-9
Verkehr U68-1; U69-8
Verkehrstote U12-2
Verkehrsunfall U6-1
verkleben **U39**-19
Verklebung **U128**-15; **U134**-10
Verkleinerung **U129**-19
verklumpen **U38**-11; **U39**-19
Verklumpung (Blut) **U38**-11
verknöchert **U31**-14
Verknöcherung **U31**-14
verknorpelt **U29**-2
verknoten U137-6,4,16; **U138**-2
verknüpfen **U137**-6
Verknüpfung **U74**-5
verkohlt U62-4
verkrampfen, (sich) **U103**-20; U31-10
verkrampft **U31**-10

Verkrampfung **U103**-20
verkrusten **U114**-8
verkümmern **U89**-29
Verkürzung **U24**-3; **U64**-13
verlagern **U64**-4; U131-13
Verlagerung **U84**-23; U33-4
Verlangen **U68**-4; **U73**-12
– (Nahrung) U2-11
– (Zigarette) U10-17
–, sexuelles **U68**-4; **U73**-12
–, sinnliches U57-9
–, unbezwingbares **U11**-2
Verlängerung **U141**-3
verlangsamen **U77**-22; U73-2,6
Verlangsamung, gedankliche U77-1
verlassen **U20**-16
–, sich **U75**-9
verlässlich **U75**-9
Verlauf **U87**-7; U89-5; **U134**-7
–, fulminanter U94-14; U119-13
–, gesamter U87-7
–, gutartiger U97-5
–, klinischer U14-2
–, natürlicher **U119**-9
–, postoperativer **U134**-7; U126-2
–, schubweiser U119-18
–, ungünstiger U119-12
verlaufen **U87**-7
Verlaufsbeobachtung U125-5
Verlaufsbericht **U20**-6; U119-12
Verlaufskontrolle **U134**-15; **U120**-14
Verlaufsuntersuchung U101-1
verlegen (Benehmen) U75-14; **U76**-12
– (Patient) **U20**-15; **U64**-4; U19-1
Verlegenheit **U76**-12
verlegt (Kanüle) U136-6
Verlegung **U20**-15; **U64**-4; **U89**-18; **U109**-6; U43-9
verlegungsfähig (Patient) U20-15
verletzen **U5**-1,3; **U6**-11
Verletzte(r) **U6**-12; **U14**-6
Verletzung **U5**-1 ff; **U89**-3; U104-1
–, innere U15-9
–, oberflächliche U87-4
–, penetrierende U6-7
–, selbstzugefügte U6-11
–, stumpfe U8-16
–, tödliche U12-2
Verleugnung **U102**-10; U12-7; U77-9
verlieren **U12**-13; **U49**-8; **U78**-21; **U88**-15; **U142**-4
– (Sehkraft) U59-6
–, persönlicher U102-9
–, schmerzlicher **U12**-13
vermachen (Erbe) **U20**-14
vermännlichen **U53**-1
vermehren, sich U39-15; U90-11
Vermehrung U116-6
vermeiden (Blickkontakt) U59-2
vermiform **U90**-16
vermindern **U4**-13; **U83**-18; U92-18
vermindert **U116**-20; U37-2
Verminderung **U78**-21; U31-1; U54-3

Verminderung (Sehkraft) U59-7
Vermis U41-2
vermischen U121-1
vermitteln U42-4; U54-3; U83-19
Vermittler U83-19
vermuten U116-23; U117-8
vernachlässigen U20-13; U77-11
Vernachlässigung U77-11
–, emotionale U77-11
–, halbseitige U19-10; U113-9
vernähen U132-5; U130-15
vernarben U140-10
Vernarbung U133-13
vernebeln U82-3; U91-7; U135-1
Vernebler U135-14
Vernehmbarkeit U61-2
verneigen, sich U31-2; U63-3
verneinen U102-10
Verner-Morrison-Syndrom U94-21
vernichten U6-20; U12-9
Vernichtungsängste U77-6
Vernichtungsstrahlung U99-2
Vernix caseosa U71-19
vernünftig U72-4; U76-4; U73-1,6
verödet, nicht U85-17
Verödung U89-18; U110-17
Veröffentlichung, postume U12-19
verordnen U20-7; U107-3; U121-1
– (Bettruhe) U4-6
Verordnung U68-10
–, ärztliche U20-7
verpacken U9-16
Verpackung U13-9; U9-16,13
verpflanzen U129-13; U130-1
verpflichtet U20-4
Verrenkung U5-20; U106-4
Verriegelungsnagel U141-16
verringern U116-20
verrotten U46-17
Verruca U114-17
– plantaris U23-13; U87-17
– senilis U80-13
verrückt U77-3,15; U4-1
–, total U77-15
Verrückte(r) U77-15,18,24
Verrücktheit U77-15
verrukös U114-17
versagen U123-6
Versagerquote U69-6
verschalten U42-4
Verschaltung U42-4
verschämt U75-14
Verschattung, diffuse U111-13
–, radiologische U89-13; U99-11
Verschiebelappen U130-14; U65-8
verschieben, (sich) U64-4; U77-26
Verschiebung U64-4; U5-20; U100-13; U106-4
verschlafen U72-2,5
verschlechtern, sich U4-12; U5-17
Verschlechterung U4-12; U89-2; U100-26
–, zunehmende U119-12
Verschleiß U64-13; U5-19

Verschleppung U124-13
verschließen U137-11; U9-13
–, sich U75-14
verschlimmern, (sich) U4-12; U77-14,21
Verschlimmerung U4-12; U119-17
–, akute U119-10
verschlingen U2-4; U46-2
verschlossen U75-14; U76-15; U11-6; U77-16
Verschlucken U46-2
verschlucken (Fremdkörper) U2-1
Verschluss U137-11; U89-18
–, luftdichter U17-6
–, operativer U128-18
Verschlussdruck, pulmokapillärer U36-2
verschlüsseln U74-9
Verschlusshydrozephalus U125-15
Verschlussikterus U108-4
Verschlusskrankheit, arterielle U124-13
Verschmelzung U28-20; U70-1
verschmolzen (Zahn) U26-8
verschmutzen U91-6
Verschmutzung U91-6; U139-9
verschnaufen U44-1
Verschnaufpause U44-1
verschnupft U62-2
verschorfen U140-9; U127-9
verschrauben U141-16
verschreiben (Arznei) U121-1
Verschreibung U20-7
Verschuppung U60-1
verschwinden (Symptome) U4-15
verschwitzt U105-12
verschwollen U108-10; U5-15
verschwommen U58-7
Versehen U6-1
versehentlich U6-1; U5-6; U133-7
Verseifung U82-14
Verseifungszahl U82-14
versetzen (Stoß) U8-11
verseucht U4-2
Verseuchung, radioaktive U139-9
Verseuchungsgefahr U91-5
Versicherer U13-5
versichern U13-5; U18-15,6
Versicherte(r) U13-5; U18-15
Versicherung U13-5; U5-1
–, leistungsbezogene U18-15
–, privatwirtschaftliche U18-15
Versicherungsanstalt U18-15
Versicherungsbeitrag U13-5; U18-15
Versicherungsgeber U13-5; U18-15
Versicherungsgesellschaft U13-5
Versicherungskarte U18-14
Versicherungsnehmer(in) U13-5; U18-15
Versicherungspolice U13-5; U18-15
Versicherungsprämie U13-5; U18-15
Versicherungsschein U13-5; U18-15
Versicherungsschutz U13-5
Versicherungssumme U18-15
Versicherungsträger U13-5; U18-15

Versicherungsvertrag U13-5
Versiegelung U137-11; U82-30
Versiegler U137-11
versinken U64-15
Version U59-16
versöhnlich U75-16
versorgen U15-3; U20-3; U36-6; U42-1; U88-3
versorgend U34-13
Versorgung U8-1; U88-3; U120-1; U129-2
–, arterielle U34-3
–, medizinische U1-1; U20-3; U13-8
–, nervale U42-1; U88-3
–, notdürftige U20-3
–, präklinische U14-1
Versorgungsgebiet U113-14
verspannt U21-13; U30-16
verspüren U102-2
Verstand U74-1; U75-7; U41-1; U73-1
–, bei klarem U77-3; U7-3
verständigen, sich U66-8
verständlich U66-1; U73-5
Verständnis U74-4; U73-5
verständnisvoll U74-4; U75-8,16
verstärken U88-12; U92-24
verstärkt U77-14; U137-15
Verstärkungsnaht U129-8
verstauchen (Knöchel) U1-10; U23-12
Verstauchung U5-16; U142-24
verstehen U74-4; U73-5
versteifen U31-17; U103-20
Versteifung U103-20
–, op. (Wirbelsäulensegmente) U41-15
verstimmt U76-16
Verstimmung U76-9; U89-2
–, depressive U76-22; U77-17
–, postpartale U71-22
verstohlen blicken U67-12
verstopfen U44-8; U89-18
verstopft U56-6; U66-6
–, vollkommen U109-6
Verstopfung U109-6; U92-13
verstorben U12-5,7
Verstorbene(r) U12-5,7
verstört U77-15
verstoßen gegen U68-10
verstreut U114-5
verstümmelt U12-15
Verstümmelung U84-21; U6-8
Versuch U100-16
Versuchsserie U101-6
Versuchsteilnehmer U101-4
Versündigungswahn U77-20
Vertebra U28-19; U141-13
Vertebrae cervicales U28-19
– coccygeae U28-19
– lumbales U28-19
– sacrales U28-19
– thoracicae U28-19; U87-16
Vertebralisangiografie U118-16
verteilen (Salbe) U9-8
–, fein U81-22
Verteilersystem U8-9

Verteilung **U81**-22; U92-1; U100-13
-, kolloidale U81-22
Verteilungschromatografie U83-22
Verteilungsgleichgewicht **U88**-4
Verteilungskoeffizient U100-12
Verteilungsmuster U91-17
Verteilungsvolumen **U91**-17
vertiginös **U113**-6
Vertigo **U113**-6
Vertikalachse U87-3
vertragen **U11**-5; **U45**-8; **U75**-16; **U121**-12
- (Magen) **U109**-1
verträglich **U136**-11
-, gut (Medikament) U1-3
Verträglichkeit U14-11; **U121**-12
Vertragsarzt U15-1
Vertrauen **U18**-11,8; U102-16
-, kindliches U80-5
Vertrauensbasis U18-8; U102-16
Vertrauensbereich **U100**-17
Vertrauensverhältnis **U18**-8; **U102**-16
vertrauenswürdig **U75**-9
vertraulich **U18**-11
Vertraulichkeit **U18**-11
verträumt **U72**-9
Vertrautheit, vermeintliche **U74**-18
Vertretung U15-6
Vertretungsstelle U15-6
verunglücken **U6**-2,1
verunreinigen **U91**-6
verunreinigt U13-4; **U139**-1 f; U140-12
- (Drogen) U11-1
Verunreinigung **U91**-6; **U139**-9; U79-17
Verunsicherung **U8**-4
verunstaltet U6-11
Verunstaltung **U142**-7
verursachen **U68**-2; **U119**-2,8; U1-12
verursacht, durch den Arzt **U89**-9
Verursachung (Krankheit) **U119**-2
Verwachsung **U128**-15; **U134**-10
-, häutige (Finger) U23-7
Verwachsungsstränge U128-15
verwahrlost U77-11
verwandt **U18**-8; **U74**-5; **U84**-31
Verwandte **U18**-8
- 1. Grades U102-7
-, nächste U102-6
Verwandtentransplantat U130-3
Verwandtschaft **U74**-5; **U84**-31
verwegen **U75**-18
verwehren (Zutritt) U102-10
verweigern **U102**-10
Verweigerung U77-9
Verweilkanüle U136-2
Verweilkatheter **U125**-20; U136-3
verweisen **U18**-12
verwesen **U46**-17
verwirklichen **U74**-4
verwirrt **U77**-4
-, geistig U77-13
Verwirrtheit **U74**-16,15; **U7**-8
-, geistige **U77**-4; U14-5; **U73**-2
-, nächtliche U72-12; U77-4
Verwirrtheit, postiktale U77-4

Verwirrtheitszustand U77-4; U119-15
Verwirrung **U77**-4
verwitwet U102-9
verwöhnen (Kind) U80-5
verwunden **U5**-1,3
verwundet, tödlich U12-2 f
Verwundung **U5**-3
verwüsten **U6**-20
Verwüstung **U6**-20
verzahnt U56-3
Verzahnung U17-3
Verzehr **U2**-2
verzerrt (Bild) U74-10; U103-14
- (Gesicht) U5-16
Verzerrung **U100**-18; **U5**-16
-, visuelle U113-11
verzichten **U10**-7
Verzichterklärung **U134**-3
verziehen **U25**-17
- (Lippen) U63-6
verzögern **U77**-22; U9-6; U92-7
- (Heilung) **U119**-18
Verzögerung U101-21
Verzögerungsinsulin U55-12
verzweifelt **U76**-21; **U107**-11
Verzweiflung **U76**-21; U77-17
verzweigen, sich **U34**-13; U40-2
verzweigt, stark U47-14
verzweigtkettig (Aminosäure) U79-10; U81-7
Verzweigung **U34**-13
Vesica biliaris **U47**-7
- fellea **U47**-7
- urinaria **U48**-11
Vesicula **U114**-12
- seminalis **U52**-9
- umbilicalis **U85**-7
Vesikanzien **U136**-7
Vesikel, synaptische U40-13
vesikulär **U114**-12
Vesikulitis U52-9
vestibulär **U21**-10
Vestibularapparat U57-18; U60-9
Vestibularisausfall U60-9
Vestibularisschwindel U57-18; U60-9 f; U113-6
Vestibulum **U60**-9
- labyrinthi **U60**-9
- oris **U21**-10
- vaginae U50-11
Vestibulumplastik U21-10
VH-Region U39-3
Vial **U9**-13
Vibrationsempfindung **U57**-17
Vibrationsempfindungsschwelle U57-17
Vibrationsmassage U142-15,23
Vibratorstimulation U68-8
vibrieren **U57**-17
Vibrioinfektion **U94**-21
Videoendoskopie **U128**-2
Videolaparoskop U133-2
Videoport U133-3,5
Vielgebärende U70-8

Vieraugengespräch U20-10
Vierfuß-Gehhilfe U19-11
Vierhügelplatte **U41**-13
Vierkrallen-Fasspinzette U132-14
Vierlinge **U70**-14
Vierstufen-Triage U8-19
vierwertig **U82**-10
Vigilanz **U7**-2,1; **U73**-1
Vigilanzsteigerung U77-5
Villi intestinales **U45**-14,1; U35-10
- synoviales U29-8
villös **U45**-14
VIP U55-13
Vipernserum, polyvalentes U91-15
viril **U53**-1
virilisieren **U53**-1
Virilisierung **U53**-12
Virion **U90**-11
Virionen-Ausscheidung U90-11
Virionen-Clearance U90-11
Viroid **U90**-10
Virostatikum U90-10; **U92**-9
virulent (Bakterienstamm) U139-11
Virulenz **U90**-10
Virulenzabschwächung **U122**-6
Virulenzfaktor U90-10
Virus **U90**-10
-, attenuiertes lebendes **U122**-6
-, kruppassoziiertes U95-10
-, onkogenes U90-10; U97-1
-, virulenzgeschwächtes U90-10
Virusanheftung U81-12
Virusausbreitung U64-15
Virusausscheidung U96-10
Viruserkrankung U4-1
Virusfreisetzung U90-10
Virusgenom U90-10
Virushülle U84-18; U90-10f
Viruslast U90-10
Virusmeningitis U94-13
Viruspartikel **U90**-11
Virusreplikation U84-16; U90-10
Virusreservoir U90-10
Virusschnupfen **U94**-9
Virusvermehrung U90-10
viruzid U90-10
Viscera **U86**-21
Viscerocranium **U28**-9
Visceropleura U85-6
Visier **U139**-18
Visite **U20**-9; U19-1
-, präop. anästhesiologische U102-14
viskös **U36**-12; U86-17; U93-5
Viskosität U36-12
Visualisierung **U73**-9
Visus **U59**-6
Visusverlust U15-18; U59-6
Visusverschlechterung U40-1
Viszera **U87**-13
viszeral **U86**-21; **U87**-13
Viszeralschmerz U86-21; U87-13
Viszeromegalie **U108**-12; U86-20f
vital **U1**-6
Vitalfärbung U116-4

Vitalfunktionen **U108**-3; U134-8
-, stabile U119-12; U125-2
Vitalindikation U120-10
Vitalität **U1**-6
Vitalitätsprüfung U26-18
Vitalkapazität **U44**-11; U1-6; U118-3
Vitalzeichen **U108**-3; U1-6
Vitamin **U79**-13
- B12-Mangelanämie U38-4
- C **U79**-15; U81-19
- D-Mangel Rachitis U95-11
Vitaminanreicherung U79-13
Vitaminmangel U79-13; U92-25
vitiliginös **U114**-4
Vitiligo **U114**-4
Vitiligoflecken U114-4
Vitrektomie U58-10
VKT auf Interspinallinie U71-13
VLDL-Triglyzeride U82-13
VL-Region U39-3
Vogelgesicht U21-2; U25-10
Vogelgrippe U94-9
Vokal **U66**-10,12
Vokalisation **U66**-8
volar **U23**-6
Volarflexion U31-2; U87-17
volatil **U82**-2; U93-4; U105-14
Völkermord U12-8
Volkmann-Sprunggelenkdeformität U106-10
Vollbad U142-20
Vollbild, klinisches **U119**-14; U94-18
Vollblut **U136**-14,8; U37-1
-, heparinisiertes U136-14
Vollblutgerinnungszeit U136-14
Vollbluthämatokrit U116-10
Vollbluttransfusion U136-14
Völlegefühl **U109**-8,1
-, postprandiales U109-8
Vollhautlappen U130-6
vollinvalide U4-8
Vollinvalidität U142-3
volljährig **U80**-9
Volljährigkeit **U80**-9 f
Vollkornbrot **U2**-13; U3-9
Vollmacht **U20**-14
Vollnarkose **U93**-1
Vollprothese U26-9
Vollremission U4-15; U119-17
vollschlank **U24**-8
Vollspektrum-Licht U59-10
vollstrecken **U12**-11
Vollstreckung **U12**-11
Vollwertprodukte **U2**-13
Volumen U46-19
-, enddiastolisches U33-7
volumendepletiert U49-8
Volumenersatz U123-4; U136-13
Volumenersatztherapie U125-2 f
Volumenmangelschock **U6**-15
Volumensubstitution U36-7; U88-15
Volumenüberlastung **U136**-8,13; U36-7
Volumenverlust U36-7; U136-13
volumetrisch **U36**-7

voluminös **U79**-16
Volvulus U45-9
- intestini **U109**-6
- ventriculi U109-6
Vomer U28-9
Vomitus **U103**-12
- biliosus U47-11
- matutinus **U70**-12
vor(wärts)neigen U31-2
vorausgehend **U119**-4; U71-7
Vorbehandlung U120-5
Vorbereitungsraum **U131**-3
vorbeugen U44-3
-, sich U63-3
vorbeugend **U6**-22; **U120**-6; U9-18
Vorbeugung **U6**-22
Vorbote **U119**-3 f
Vorderdarm U85-8,21
vordere(r) **U87**-16
Vorderhauptlage U71-5
Vorderhirn U41-1
Vorderhorn **U41**-15; U95-8
Vorderhornzellen **U42**-14; U30-4
Vorderhornzellerkrankung U42-14
Vorderwandinfarkt U124-11
Vorderzähne **U26**-2
voreilig **U65**-15; **U75**-18
voreingenommen U100-18
vorenthalten **U77**-11
Vorerkrankung U4-1
Vorerkrankungen, Anamnese der **U102**-6
Vorfahr(e) **U84**-29
Vorfall **U6**-1; **U89**-22; **U113**-17; U100-19
Vorfuß U23-13
vorgefertigt (Knoten) U138-2
vorgeformt **U129**-4
Vorgeschichte U102-6
vorgesetzt **U80**-13
Vorgesetzte(r) U68-16
Vorhang U19-1; U107-5
Vorhaut **U52**-17
Vorhautverengung, erworbene U52-17
vorherrschend U76-2
Vorhersage **U100**-29; **U119**-19
vorhersagen **U119**-19; U125-4
Vorhersagewert U100-29; U119-19
vorhersehen U100-29
Vorhof **U32**-7
- (Mund) **U21**-10
Vorhofextrasystolen U32-7; U110-6
Vorhoffenster **U60**-8
Vorhofflattern **U110**-7; U32-7
Vorhofflimmern **U110**-7; U32-7; U123-12
Vorhofkontraktion U32-7
Vorhoflabyrinth U60-10
Vorhofsäckchen **U60**-9
Vorhofscheidewand **U32**-9
Vorhofseptum **U32**-9
Vorhofseptumdefekt U32-7
Vorhofsystole U33-3
Vorhoftachykardie U33-5; U110-2

Vorhofton U110-6
Vorhoftreppe U60-9
Vorkehrungen U132-5
Vorkernstadium U69-12
Vorlage U140-19
Vorlast **U33**-10
Vorläufer U39-12; **U78**-9; **U119**-4
Vorläufermolekül U78-9
Vorläuferstadium U119-4
Vorläuferzelle **U84**-29; U86-2
Vormilch **U71**-24
Vormund, gesetzlicher **U77**-25; U134-3
Vormundschaft **U77**-25
vorneigen, sich **U63**-3
Vorniere **U85**-21,9
voroperiert (Abdomen) U126-1; U133-13
vorragen **U87**-27
Vorrat **U74**-10
Vorrichtung U132-1; U133-1
vorschieben (Trokar) U133-10
- (Unterkiefer) U8-11
vorschlagen **U18**-5; U66-8
Vorschrift **U20**-7
vorschriftsmäßig U121-1
Vorschub U99-19
Vorschulalter U80-5
Vorsicht **U6**-22; **U9**-18
vorsichtig **U20**-3
Vorsichtsmaßnahme **U6**-22; **U9**-18
Vorsorgemedizin U6-22
Vorsorgeuntersuchung **U18**-9,2; **U107**-1; U13-7
Vorsorgevollmacht **U20**-14; U16-1
Vorspiel **U68**-2
vorspringend **U87**-27; U21-6
Vorsprung **U87**-27
vorstehend **U87**-27
Vorsteherdrüse **U52**-10
vorstellen, sich etwas **U59**-6 f,1
Vorstellung **U59**-6; **U73**-8
Vorstufe **U78**-9; **U119**-4
- (Häm) U37-6
vorstülpen (Lippen) U21-6
vortäuschen **U117**-13
Vortcil **U1**-5
vorteilhaft U1-5
vorübergehend (Besserung) U4-14
Voruntersuchung U118-1
vorverdauen U46-11
vorwarnen **U8**-7
Vorwärtsbewegung U46-7
Vorwärtsinsuffizienz U110-12
Vorwärtsvolumen U33-7
Vorwasser **U71**-6
Vorwölbung **U85**-10; **U87**-27; U22-3
- (Stirn) U87-20
Vorwölbungen (Sklera) U58-6
Vorwurf, bitterer U76-11
vorwurfsvoll **U76**-13
Vorzeichen **U119**-3 f
V-Region U84-2
Vulva **U22**-10; **U50**-11,1
Vulvakarzinom U50-11
Vulvaring U71-15

Vulvektomie U50-11
Vulvitis U50-11
V-Y Plastik U126-4

W

Waage **U24**-11
wabb(e)lig **U31**-12; **U64**-5
Wabenkissen U19-5
Wabenmatratze U19-5
wach **U7**-2; **U72**-6
– und ansprechbar U72-6
–, geistig U77-1
Wache U8-4
wachhalten U72-6
Wachheit **U7**-2,1; **U72**-1; U73-2
Wachheitsgrad U7-2
Wachkoma **U7**-17
Wachperioden, nächtliche U72-7
Wachphasen U72-7
wachsam **U59**-1; **U72**-7; **U117**-7
Wachsamkeit **U117**-7
wachsartig **U60**-15
wachsend, infiltrativ **U97**-12
wächsern **U60**-15; U135-3
Wachstation U125-1
Wachstum **U80**-3; U92-9
–, infiltrierendes U97-12
–, übermäßiges U97-2
Wachstumsakzeleration U80-3
Wachstumsbeschleunigung U80-3
Wachstumsfaktor, epidermaler U56-2
–, insulinähnlicher U55-5,12
wachstumsfördernd **U55**-5
Wachstumsfuge U28-3
Wachstumsgeschwindigkeit U24-2
Wachstumshormon **U55**-5; U83-16
–, hypophysäres U55-5
Wachstumskurve U18-14
Wachstumsschmerzen U80-3; U104-5
Wachstumsschub U80-3
–, pubertärer U24-2; U80-7 f
Wachstumstabelle U17-5; U102-12
Wachstumsverzögerung U1-8; U77-22
Wachstumszone, knorpelige U29-12
Wachszylinder U112-14
Wachtraum **U72**-9
Wachträumen U7-15
Wachzustand U72-6 f; U73-1
–, ruhiger U76-19; U119-15
wackeln **U64**-5 f
– (Zehen) U65-10
Wackeltremor **U113**-4
wacklig **U105**-7
Wade **U23**-10; **U30**-17
Waden(bein)muskeln **U30**-17
Wadenbein **U28**-24; U23-10
Wadenkrampf U30-17; U103-20
Wadenmuskelpumpe U30-17
Wadenmuskelzerrung U30-17
Wadenmuskulatur U23-10
Wadenschmerz U23-10
Waffe **U6**-8

Waffenbesitz U6-8
Waffengesetze U6-8
Wahleingriff U126-3,5
wahllos **U117**-15
Wahn(idee) **U77**-20
Wahn, depressiver U77-20
–, hypochondrischer U4-9; U77-20
–, religiöser U77-15
–, systematisierter U77-20
Wahnerinnerung **U74**-18
wahnhaft **U77**-20; U73-6
Wahnidee **U77**-20
Wahnsinn **U77**-15,24
wahnsinnig **U77**-15,18,24
Wahnsinnige(r) **U77**-18
Wahnstimmung U77-20
Wahnvorstellung **U77**-20; U73-9 f
–, massive U77-18
wahrnehmbar, kaum U57-2
Wahrnehmbarkeitsschwelle U61-7
wahrnehmen **U57**-2,4 f; **U74**-4,15; **U117**-5
–, bewusst U93-4; U131-3
Wahrnehmung **U57**-2 f,10; **U73**-1; U7-1
–, außersinnliche U57-2
–, optische U59-5
–, visuelle U59-5
Wahrnehmungsschwelle U117-5
Wahrnehmungsstörung U57-2; U77-20
Wahrnehmungsverarbeitung U57-2
Wahrnehmungsvermögen **U57**-2,7; U135-3
–, vermindertes U10-14
Wahrscheinlichkeit **U100**-31,1
Wahrscheinlichkeitsverteilung U100-12,31
Waldeyer-Rachenring U35-5
Walken U1-14; U65-1
Wallungen U65-15
Wanderhoden U52-3
Wanderkur U1-18
Wanderlappen **U130**-16
wandern **U65**-1; U85-8
Wanderniere U48-2; U64-2
Wanderschuhe U65-1
Wanderung U65-1
Wandkarte U17-5
wandständig **U28**-8; **U87**-10,13
Wange **U21**-7
Wangenabhalter U132-16
Wangenbein U28-9
Wangenbeißen U21-7
Wangenröte **U108**-8; U56-18
Wangenschleimhaut U21-7; U86-17
wanken **U65**-9; **U105**-7
Wannenbad U19-9; U142-20
Wanze **U90**-5
Wanzenbiss U90-5
Warenzeichen U121-2
Wärme, feuchte U142-22
Wärmeabgabe **U105**-2,14; **U88**-19
Wärmeakklimatisation U88-17
Wärmebehandlung **U142**-22
Wärmebelastung U105-11

wärmebeständig U105-2
Wärmebett U19-3
wärmebildend **U105**-2
Wärmebildung **U105**-2,10
wärmeempfindlich U57-8
Wärmeempfindlichkeit U105-11
Wärmeempfindung U57-3
Wärmeenergie U78-12
wärmeerzeugend **U79**-4
Wärm(e)flasche U19-6; U136-4
Wärmegefühl U57-3
Wärmehaushalt U105-10
Wärmeintoleranz **U105**-10
Wärmelampe **U19**-6; U142-22
Wärmeleitfähigkeit U105-5
Wärmematratze U19-5
Wärmeregulation U105-2
Wärmestrahlung U105-5
Wärmetherapie U105-2
Wärmeunverträglichkeit **U105**-10
Wärmeurtikaria U105-10
warnen **U6**-22; **U7**-2; **U8**-7; **U117**-7
Warnsignal U8-4; U108-1
Warnung **U6**-22; **U8**-7
Warnzeichen U108-1
Wartebereich U18-3
– (OP-Schleuse) U14-7; U131-2
Warteliste U18-3
Warteraum **U18**-3
Wartezeit U18-3
Wartezimmer **U18**-3
Warze **U114**-17
–, anogenitale U96-14
warzenartig **U114**-17
warzenförmig **U60**-14
Warzenfortsatz **U60**-14; U28-5
Warzenfortsatzzellen U60-14
Warzenhof U50-18
Warzenvirus U114-17
warzig **U96**-14
Waschbrettbauch U1-11
Wäsche **U19**-10
waschen U1-17; **U19**-9; **U91**-26; U142-20
Waschlappen **U19**-10
Waschung **U116**-5; U19-9; U142-20
Wasser lassen **U49**-16
– treten U65-5
–, destilliertes U82-4
–, kohlensäurehaltiges U82-4
–, schweres U82-4
–, verseuchtes U91-6
Wasserabgabe, unmerkliche U57-8
wasserabstoßend **U81**-13; U56-12
wasserabweisend (Pflaster) U140-21
Wasser-Aerobic U1-15
wasseranziehend **U81**-13
Wasserbehandlung **U142**-20
Wasserbett U19-3
Wasserdampf **U82**-3
wasserdicht U137-11; U128-18
Wasserdurchlässigkeit U88-6
Wasserentzug **U78**-22
Wassergymnastik U1-15; U142-20

wasserhaltig **U82**-4,9
Wasserhammerpuls U110-12
Wasserhaushalt U55-25
Wasserinjektion U118-7
Wasser-in-Öl-Emulsion U81-25
Wasserintoxikation U10-5
Wasserlassen, häufiges U70-9
–, nächtliches **U112**-6,5
wasserlöslich **U82**-4; U92-10
Wasserlöslichkeit U88-5
wasserscheu U56-12
Wasserstoff **U82**-9; U56-12
Wasserstoffbindung U82-9
Wasserstoffbrückenbindung U82-17
Wasserstoffion U78-23; U81-11
Wasserstoffionenkonzentration U81-23
Wasserstoff(su)peroxid U82-9; U118-6
Wasserstrahldusche U19-10
Wasserstrahlmassage U142-15
Wassersucht **U108**-10
wässrig **U82**-4
wässrige Absonderung U140-13
waten U65-5
Watschelgang U64-5; U65-2,10
watscheln **U65**-10
Wattebausch **U140**-23; U60-1
Wattepfropf U21-15
Wattestäbchen U17-13
Watteträger **U17**-13; U132-14
–, steriler U116-5
wattieren **U17**-13
WC-Muschel U19-9
wearing-off-Effekt U121-8
Wechsel **U64**-4
Wechselbad U19-9
Wechselfieber **U94**-20
Wechseljahre **U51**-10
Wechselklinge U132-3
Wechselschnitt U126-9
Wechselwirkung **U121**-11; U101-21
–, hydrophobe U81-13
Wechselzahl U78-1
Weckamin **U11**-17
weckbar, durch Zuruf U72-1
wecken **U68**-2; **U72**-7; **U74**-2; **U7**-2
 (Erinnerungen) U74-8
Weckreaktion U72-7
Weckschwelle U72-7
Weckzeiten U72-8
Weddelitstein U89-21
Wedge-Druck U36-2
Weg **U83**-16; **U97**-11
wegführen, seitwärts **U31**-6
wegreiben U64-11
wegschneiden **U5**-6
wegtragen U12-18
wegwerfen U64-14; U139-4
wegwischen U9-10
weh **U104**-4
Wehen **U71**-3,2; **U104**-6
– liegen, in den U71-3
–, vorzeitige U70-11; U71-3
Wehenakme U71-15
Wehenanomalien U71-3

Wehenaufzeichnung U71-3
Wehenbeginn U119-5
–, vorzeitiger U96-9
Wehendystokie U71-3
Wehenindukion U71-9
Wehenschreiber U71-3
Wehwehchen **U104**-5,4
Weiberknoten U137-6
weiblich **U50**-2
weich **U31**-12; **U61**-5; U53-4
– anfühlen, sich U62-8
Weichteilauflösung U99-14
Weichteile U86-3; U118-24
Weichteilsarkom U98-3
Weichteilschwellung U108-10
Weichteilstopp U142-14
Weichteilverletzung U5-2
Weichteilzerreißung U106-5
Weigerung, hartnäckige U75-19
Weinen **U67**-10
weinen **U67**-10; **U66**-3
–, sich in den Schlaf U67-10; U72-5
weinerlich **U67**-10; U76-15
Weinfleck U25-19; U114-3
Weingeist **U10**-2; U82-13
Weinkrämpfe U103-4
Weise **U75**-3
weise **U75**-7
Weisheitszahn **U26**-8
Weißarsenik U82-33
Weißfleckenkrankheit U114-4
Weitblick U20-7; U77-10
Weite, lichte **U34**-14; **U87**-22
weiterentwickeln, sich U97-7
weiterleben **U12**-6
weiterleiten **U42**-2,4; U8-9
Weiterleitung U42-3
weitmaschig U140-18
weitsichtig **U59**-17
Weitsichtigkeit **U59**-17
Weitsprung U65-16
Wellen, peristaltische U46-6
Wellenlänge **U61**-3
Wellness **U1**-7
Weltgesundheitsorganisation **U13**-11
Wenckebach-Block U123-2
Wendelappen **U130**-19
wenden **U64**-8
werfen **U64**-14
–, sich zu Boden U64-14
Werfer(in) U64-14
Werkstätte, geschützte **U11**-13; **U142**-28
Werkzeug U132-1
Wernicke-Aphasie U57-10; U113-10
Wert **U101**-15; **U116**-16; **U100**-6,16
–, höchster zulässiger U91-18
Wertepaar U100-32
Wertigkeit **U81**-10
Wertlosigkeit U77-17
wertschätzen **U74**-4
Wertschätzung **U57**-2
Wesen **U75**-1,4; **U76**-2; **U77**-2
–, ausgeglichenes U76-2
–, eigenbrötlerisches U75-1

Wesen, introvertiertes U75-14
–, liebenswürdiges U75-4
–, verschlossenes U75-14
Wesensart **U75**-1,3,6
Wesenszug **U75**-1,4
Wespenstich U6-7; U91-16
Wespentaille U22-6
Westergren (BSG-Bestimmung) U116-12
Western-Blot-Methode U116-3
Wettkampf U1-12
WHO-Empfehlungen U13-11
WHO-Forschungsgruppe U13-11
WHO-Richtlinien U13-11
Wickel U1-20
–, feuchter **U140**-24,20
widerlich U109-2
widerspenstig **U77**-7
Widerstand, kapillärer U36-19
–, peripherer **U36**-10; U87-15
–, venöser U36-10
widerstandsfähig **U1**-11; **U11**-5; **U39**-22
Widerstandsfähigkeit **U1**-11
Widerstandsübungen U142-17
Widerstreben **U75**-11
Widerwillen **U75**-11
widerwillig **U75**-11; **U76**-14
wiederaufbereiten **U78**-6
wiederaufflammend **U94**-7
Wiederauffüllung U49-8
Wiederaufnahme (Klinik) **U20**-1
– (Aktivitäten) **U134**-14
Wiederauftreten **U119**-18; U95-7
wiederbeleben **U123**-3 f
Wiederbelebung **U123**-4; U16-10
Wiederbelebungsmaßnahmen U20-11
wiedereingliedern **U142**-2
wiedererkennen **U74**-3; **U117**-4; **U73**-4
wiedererlangen (Sehkraft) U59-7
– (Unabhängigkeit) U142-28
Wiedererleben, belastendes **U74**-11
wiederhergestellt (Gesundheit) U4-16; U31 13
Wiederherstellung **U129**-1 f; **U142**-2
– (Achsenausrichtung) **U141**-2
Wiederherstellungschirurgie **U129**-3
wiederholen (Lernstoff) **U74**-7
wiederholen, sich **U74**-7
Wiederholung **U74**-6
Wiederholungsimpfung **U122**-3
Wiederholungszwang U77-19
Wiederkäuen **U109**-3
wiederkehrende Blasenentzündungen U18-5
wiederkehrendes Ereignis U100-19
wiedervereinigen **U140**-2
Wiedervereinigung **U129**-5
wiederverwenden U17-11; U139-4
wiederverwerten **U78**-6
wiegen **U24**-1; **U64**-5
Wilcoxon (Rangsummen)test U100-34
wild **U77**-15

wildes Fleisch U140-7
Wildtypallel U84-4
Wille(nskraft) U73-3; U74-19
willensstark U75-19; U73-3
willentlich U40-6; U73-3
Willkürbewegung U64-1; U73-3
willkürlich U16-15; U40-6; U117-15
Wilson-Krankheit U91-19
wimmern U66-3
Wimpern U58-3; U21-3; U25-14
Wimpernfollikel U56-13
Wimper(n)tierchen U90-2
Wind U46-15; U109-7; U46-3
Windabgang U46-15
Windei U51-5
Windelausschlag U108-9
winden, sich U65-10
Windpocken U95-7; U94-1
Wink U67-5
Winkelbeschleunigung U60-9
Winkelblockglaukom, akutes U59-11
Winkelmesser U142-9
Winken U67-5
Winterschlaf U105-5
winzig U127-5
Wippe U142-19
Wirbel U22-12; U28-19; U141-13
–, benachbarter U28-19
Wirbelbogen U28-19
Wirbelbogenresektion U125-15
Wirbelkanal U41-15
Wirbelkörper U22-12; U28-19
Wirbelloch U22-12; U28-6
Wirbelsäule U22-12; U28-19,5
Wirbelsäulenkrümmung U22-12
Wirbelsäulenmobilisation U142-13
Wirbelsäulenverletzung U124-18
Wirbelsäulenversteifung, operative U141-13
wirken U55-2
Wirkort U121-4; U92-3
Wirksamkeit U53-2; U101-26; U121-9,8
wirksam U55-25
Wirkstoff U92-2; U9-3; U91-24
Wirkstofffreisetzung U121-4
Wirkung U53-2; U88-14; U121-8; U122-7
–, antibakterielle U88-14
–, antiemetische U46-6
–, antioxidative U81-5
–, berauschende U10-5
–, biologische U92-3
–, gegensinnige U31-4
–, gerinnungshemmende U38-14
–, hemmende U42-13
–, hustenreizstillende U82-3
–, katalytische U81-16
–, keimtötende U17-15
–, Na-retinierende U55-25
–, reizlindernde U82-3
–, schädliche U6-11
Wirkungsbereich, toxischer U121-13
Wirkungseintritt U121-8; U135-2

Wirkungsfluktuation U121-8
Wirkungsmaximum U121-7
Wirkungsmechanismus U121-8
Wirkungsspektrum U121-8
Wirkungsstärke U121-9,4
Wirkungsverlängerung U92-3
Wirkungsverzögerung U101-21
Wirkungsweise U9-17
wirr U77-4
Wirt U90-13; U94-5
–, abwehrgeschwächter U94-5
–, empfänglicher U94-5
–, gesunder U94-5
–, paratenischer U94-5
Wirtsorganismus U94-5
Wirtsspektrum U94-5
wirtsspezifisch U88-17; U94-5
Wirtswechsel U94-5
Wirtszelle U83-2
Wismut U82-27
Wismutsaum U82-27
Wismutstomatitis U82-27
Wismutverbindung, kolloidale U81-26
Wismutvergiftung, (chronische) U82-27
Wissenschafter U101-2
wissenschaftliche Arbeit U101-3
Wittmaack-Ekbom-Syndrom U23-8
Witz U75-7
witzig U75-7,5
Wochenbett U71-21; U15-16
Wochenbettdepression U71-22; U76-22
Wochenbettfieber U124-5
Wochenbettpsychose U71-21
Wochenfluss U71-23
Wöchnerin U71-21
Wöchnerinnenstation U19-1; U71-22
wohl fühlen, sich (nicht) U1-3; U76-19
wohlauf sein U1-3
Wohlbefinden U1-7; U57-5
Wohlergehen U1-7; U16-8
wohlerzogen U75-15
Wohlfahrt U1-7; U13-6
Wohlfahrtsstaat U1-7
Wohlgeruch U62-3
Wohlgeschmack U62-1
Wohlgestimmtheit, oberflächliche U76-16; U77-18
wohlmeinend U73-3; U75-15
wohlschmeckend U2-5
wohlwollend U75-15
Wohnen, betreutes U11-13
Wohngemeinschaft, betreute U142-28
wohnhaft U15-4
Wohnheim U11-13
Wohnort U15-4
Wölbung U30-8
Wolf U105-13
Wolff-Gang U85-21
Wolfram U82-31
Wolframat U82-31
Wolframkarbid U82-31
Wolfshunger U2-11
Wollen U73-3

Wollwachs U82-9
Wort U66-9
Wortamnesie U113-10
Wortfindung U74-6
Wortfindungsstörung U113-10
wortgewandt U66-18
wortkarg U66-12,18
Worttaubheit U61-9; U113-13
Wrack, nervliches U76-6
Wrackteile U8-7
wuchern U97-7
Wucherung(en) U97-2; U92-31
–, polypöse U98-1
–, warzenartige U97-2; U114-17
–, adenoide U35-6
Wuchs U24-2
Wulst U85-10
Wulstnarbe U140-10
wund U104-11
Wundabdeckung U129-9
Wundanfrischung U140-12
Wundauflage U140-17,3; U5-3
Wundbehandlung U140-1; U20-3
Wundbenzin U10-2
Wundbett U140-11; U130-8
Wundbotulismus U91-21
Wunddehiszenz U140-16; U106-5
Wunddiphtherie U95-9
Wunde U5-3f
–, infizierte U94-2
–, leicht blutende U38-7
–, nässende U38-7; U67-10
–, tiefe U140-1
wunde Stelle U89-17
Wundexzision U140-12
Wundhaken U132-16
Wundheilung U140-5
Wundhöhle U140-3
Wundinfektion U94-2
Wundklammern U138-17
Wundkontrolle U120-7
Wundliegen U63-7; U4-6; U19-3
Wundnaht U140-3
Wundrand U87-10; U140-2,17
Wundrandausschneidung U140-12
Wundrandexzision U140-12
wundreiben U5-8
Wundschorf U114-8
Wundsein U105-13
Wundsekret U5-3; U140-11,23
Wundspreizer U17-6; U132-16
Wundspülung U140-11
Wundstarrkrampf U94-11
Wundtoilette U140-12
Wundverband, antiseptischer U139-1
Wundverschluss U140-3; U137-1,4
Wundversorgung U140-1,5; U5-3
Wunschdenken U73-6
Wurf U64-14
Würfelbein U28-25,27
Würg(e)reflex U27-16; U44-8; U45-4
Würgen U44-8; U123-7; U40-10
würgen U27-16; U44-8; U46-5
Wurm, geschlechtsreifer U90-16

Wurm, unreifer U90-16
wurmabtötend **U90**-16
wurmähnlich **U90**-16
Wurmbefall, geringer U90-16
Wurmeier U118-6
Wurmerkrankung U90-16
Wurmfortsatz **U45**-13
Wurmmittel **U90**-16; **U92**-25
Wurzel **U87**-25
–, motorische U87-25
–, vordere U87-25
Wurzeldekompression U125-17
Wurzeldentin U26-16
Wurzelfüllung U26-19
Wurzelglätten U132-10
Wurzelhaut U26-13
Wurzelkanaleingang U87-21
Wurzelkanalöffnung U28-6
Wurzelkompression U6-6; U87-25
Wurzelresorption U27-20
Wurzelscheide U56-13
Wurzelspitze U26-19; U87-25
Wurzelstift U141-15
Wurzelzement **U26**-17
würzen **U3**-18; **U62**-7
Wut **U76**-10; **U77**-15
–, rasende U94-12
–, stille U94-12
Wutanfall U64-12; U76-2; U103-4
wütend **U76**-10; **U77**-15

X

x^2 Test **U100**-34
Xanthomzelle U39-18
Xanthopsie U59-9; U113-11
X-Beine **U23**-11
X-Chromatin U84-6
X-chromosomaler Erbgang U89-7
Xenobiotika U78-1
Xenotransplantat **U130**-5
X-gekoppelter Phänotyp U84-10
X-gekoppeltes Gen U84-27
Xylen U81-5

Y

Yaws U142-7
Yoga **U1**-16
Y-Stück, Infusionsset mit U136-4

Z

Zackennaht U29-14
zaghaft U32-2
zähflüssig **U36**-12; **U86**-17
zählen, laut U61-5
Zahlengedächtnis U74-8,10
zahlreich U30-9; U83-7
Zahn **U26**-1
–, impaktierter U109-15

Zahn, luxierter U106-5
Zahnarzt U15-8
Zahnarztassistent(in) U16-10
Zahnarzttermin U18-2
Zahnausfall U56-20
Zahnbein **U26**-16
Zahnbeweglichkeit U26-1
Zahnbogen **U26**-9
Zahnbogenbreite U26-9; U27-3
Zahndurchbruch **U27**-1,3 f
Zähne (Wundhaken) U132-16
–, bleibende **U27**-6
–, kariöse U46-17
Zähneklappern U56-14
Zähneknirschen **U27**-18; U74-15
–, habituelles U77-14
Zahnen **U27**-4
Zahnentfernung U27-7
Zähnepressen U21-5
Zahnfach **U26**-13; U29-4
Zahnfehlstellung U26-1
Zahnfleisch **U26**-12; U45-2
Zahnfleischabszess, submuköser U114-16
Zahnfleischbluten U124-16
Zahnfleischfurche U87-26
Zahnfleischmesser U132-3
Zahnfleischrand U26-12
Zahnfraktur U106-1
Zahnhals U26-19
Zahnhöcker **U26**-4
Zahnhöhle U26-18
Zahnkrone **U26**-14
zahnlos **U27**-7; U21-5
Zahnlosigkeit (Zahnentfernung) **U27**-7
Zahnpaste, fluorhaltige U82-22
Zahnpressen **U27**-17
Zahnprothese **U27**-8; U129-18
Zahnpulpa **U26**-18
Zahnradphänomen U103-20
Zahnreihe **U26**-9
Zahnreihen schließen **U27**-13
Zahnschmelz **U26**-15; U132-11
Zahnschmerzen **U104**-4
Zahnschutz U21-8
Zahnspiegel U17-4
Zahnstein U89-21
Zahntechniker(in) U16-10
Zahnverlust U27-7
Zahnwechsel **U27**-5
Zahnwurzel **U26**-19; U87-25
Zäkum **U45**-12
Zäkumhochstand U45-12
Zange U132-14
Zangenextraktion U71-9
Zangengeburt, hohe U71-9
Zäpfchen **U9**-12; U26-10; U92-12
Zapfen U58-13; U59-9
Zapfenzahn U26-1
Zapfhahn **U118**-7
zappelig U64-17; **U76**-6
zappeln **U64**-17; **U65**-10
zart(gliedrig) **U24**-6; **U25**-8
zartbesaitet U56-1

Zartheit **U25**-8,5
zärtlich **U62**-10
Zecke **U90**-15; U14-2
–, infizierte U94-2
Zeckenbiss U5-10; U90-15
Zeckenbissfieber U90-12
Zeckenenzephalitis U90-15; U94-13
Zeckenfleckfieber, amerikanisches U94-19
Zeckenlähmung U113-7
Zeckenrückfallfieber U90-15
Zeckenschutzimpfung U122-1
Zeckenschutzmittel U90-15; U91-8
Zehe **U23**-14; U28-18
–, kleine U28-18
Zehenamputation U142-6
Zehengrundgelenk U28-25
Zehenknochen **U28**-18
Zehennagel **U23**-14
Zehenspitze **U23**-14
Zehenspitzen, auf **U65**-8
Zehenspreizung U23-14
Zehenstrahl U142-6
Zeichen **U67**-2; **U74**-2,9; **U103**-1; **U120**-10
– erkennen U74-2
– geben **U67**-5
–, (klinisches) **U108**-1
–, meningeales U113-1
–, pathognomonisches U108-1
–, ungünstiges prognostisches U108-1
–, unmissverständliches U67-2
–, vereinbartes U67-2
–, verräterisches U67-2
Zeichensprache U66-8; U67-2
Zeichnen (Blutung) **U71**-7
zeichnet, es U71-7
Zeigefinger U23-7; U29-6
zeigen **U102**-3; **U107**-17
–, sich klinisch **U103**-3
zeitaufwändig U136-10
Zeitpunkt der Wahl **U126**-5
Zellabstrich **U116**-5
Zellaggregat U81-9
Zellapherese U136-15
Zellatmung **U44**-4
–, anaerobe U1-15
Zellauflösung U83-1
Zellbank U83-2
Zellbestandteil U83-2
Zellbiologie **U83**-1
Zelldifferenzierung U85-11; U97-8
Zelle(n) **U83**-2
–, ACTH-produzierende U55-9
–, antigenpräsentierende **U39**-11,8,21
–, dendritische **U39**-11
–, eukaryont(isch)e U83-3
–, folliküläre dendritische U39-11
–, hemizygote **U84**-5
–, immunkompetente U39-1
–, inaktive U119-6
–, juxtaglomeruläre U48-6
–, parafollikuläre U55-8

Zelle(n), parasitenbefallene U90-13
-, prolaktinproduzierende U55-22
-, spindelförmige U83-5
-, verhornte U56-2
-, zilienbesetzte U83-5
-, zytotoxische U39-16
Zellenlehre U83-1
Zellfragmente U35-3
Zellgerüst U86-19
Zellgift U92-32
Zellkern U83-4
Zellkonservierung U14-12
Zellkörper U83-2
Zellkultur U83-2; U116-6
Zellkunde U83-1
Zellleib U83-1
Zelllinie U83-2; U84-30
Zellmembran U83-2; U86-15
Zelloberflächenladung U81-10
Zellorganelle U86-20; U83-4
Zellpackungsvolumen U116-10
Zellpol U81-13
zellschädigend U91-4; U92-32
Zellstoffwechsel U83-2
Zellteilung U85-3,10; U83-2; U84-6
-, indirekte U83-13
-, mitotische U85-3
Zelltod U89-30; U83-2
Zelltoxizität U92-32
Zelltrümmer U89-12; U114-8
zellulär U83-2
Zellularpathologie U15-21; U116-1
Zellulosenitrat U82-16
zellvermittelt U78-17; U83-19
Zellwachstum U54-3; U83-2
-, ungehemmtes U97-7
Zellzahl, erhöhte U38-5
Zellzyklus U83-12
Zellzyklusphase, erste/initiale U83-12
Zellzykluszeit U83-12
Zement (der) U26-17
zentral U87-15
Zentralfurche U87-26
Zentralkörperchen U83-6; U84-7
Zentralnervensystem U40-5; U41-17
Zentralwert U100-10
Zentren, vegetative U40-6
Zentrifugalkraft U83-20
Zentrifuge U83-20
zentrifugieren U83-20
Zentrifugierung U83-20
Zentriol U83-6; U84-7
zentrisch (Okklusion) U27-13
Zentromer U84-7
Zentromerprotein U84-7
Zentroplasma U83-6
Zentrosom U83-6; U84-7
Zentrum für selbstbestimmtes Leben Behinderter U142-28
-, motorisches U40-4
zerbersten U6-9
zerbrechlich U25-8; U31-16
Zerbrechlichkeit U25-8; U103-9
zerdrücken U64-10

zerebellar U41-2
zerebral U41-2
Zerebralparese U41-2
Zerebrospinalflüssigkeit U118-7; U1-4; U22-12; U97-13
Zerfall U46-17; U78-10; U81-22; U9-6; U82-1,34
-, radioaktiver U99-22
zerfallen U81-22; U74-10
-, in Bruchstücke U39-3
Zerfallsreaktion U81-22
zerfetzt U5-7
zerfressen U91-10; U114-13
zergehen lassen U9-7
Zerkarie U90-17
zerkauen U27-15
zerkleinern U128-16
Zerlegung der Quadratsummen U100-34
zermahlen U27-18
zerquetschen U64-10
zerreißen U64-13; U5-19; U106-5
Zerreißung U5-7,19; U106-3
zerren U64-13
- (Muskel) U5-17; U64-13
Zerrissenheit U80-8
Zerrung U5-16f; U5-19; U142-24
zerschlagen U6-2
zerschmetternd U6-6; U64-10
Zersetzung U46-17; U78-10; U47-11
-, bakterielle U46-12,17
-, thermische U46-17; U78-10
zersplittern U106-2,7
zerstören U5-19
-, elektrochirurgisch U127-14
Zerstörung (Marksubstanz) U40-14
zerstoßen U64-10
- (Tabletten) U6-6
zerstreut U74-16,1
Zerstreutheit U74-16
Zerstreuung U1-10; U74-16
Zerstreuungslinse U59-13
zerstückeln U128-16
Zerstückelung U128-16; U133-17
zertrampeln U65-5
Zertrümmerung U106-7
Zerumen U60-1,15
-, impaktiertes U60-15
Zeruminalpfropf U9-2; U60-15
zervikal U50-7; U21-13
Zervikobrachialsyndrom U23-3
Zervix U21-13; U137-18
- ist aufgebraucht U71-7
Zervixabstrich U17-13; U50-7
Zervixdilatation U71-12
Zervixhöhlenkarzinom U50-7
Zervixinsuffizienz U50-7
Zervixkonisation U50-7; U127-12
Zervixpolyp U98-1
Zervixschleim, visköser U36-12
Zervixschleimmethode U50-7; U69-5
Zervixverkürzung U71-12
Zeuge/-in U6-13
zeugen U69-1

Zeugenaussage U6-13
Zeugengeld U6-13
Zeugenstand U6-13
Zeugnis U6-13
Zeugungsunfähigkeit U53-1
Ziegenmeckern U111-11
Ziegenpeter U95-4
ziehen U64-13; U87-7
Ziehl-Neelsen-Färbung U116-4
Ziel U55-2; U73-8; U101-3
Ziel(setzung) U135-3
zielführend, nicht U41-17; U73-8
Zielgewebe U55-2; U99-4; U121-4
Zielgröße U100-20
Zielorgan U55-2; U86-20
zielstrebig U74-1; U75-19
Zielzelle U55-2
zierlich U24-6; U25-8
Zierlichkeit U24-6
Ziffer U100-6
Zigarette U10-19
-, brennende U10-18
Zigarettenanzünder U10-18
Zigarettenasche U10-19
Zigarettenspitze U10-19
Zigarettenstummel U10-19
Zigarre U10-19
Ziliarfalten U58-7
Ziliarfortsätze U58-7
Ziliarkörper U58-7
Ziliarkörperentzündung U58-7
Ziliaten U90-2
Zilie U83-5
Zilienbewegung U44-9; U64-1
Zimmer, geschlossenes U19-2
Zink U82-29; U79-17
Zinken U17-7; U61-4; U132-16
Zinkfieber U82-29
Zinkfinger U82-29
Zink-Finger-Motiv U84-3
Zinkmangel U82-29
Zinkoxiddämpfe U82-29
Zinkpaste U9-8; U82-29
Zinksalbe U82-29
Zinksalz U82-29
Zinkvergiftung U91-20
Zinn U82-29
Zinnfolie U82-29
Zinnoxid U82-29
Zinnstein U82-29
Zirbeldrüse U54-13
Zirkadian-Syndrom U101-21
Zirkeltraining U1-14
Zirkulation, extrakorporale U125-11
zirkulierend U36-1
Zirkumduktion U31-7
Zirkumzision U52-17
Zirrhose, biliäre U47-11; U108-11
zischen U66-21
Zischlaute U66-21
Zisterne U83-8
Zisternenpunktion U41-17
Zitratblut U37-1; U136-14
Zitrat-Zyklus U81-15

Zitronensäure U81-19
- Zyklus U78-6; U81-15; U83-7
Zittern **U64**-6; **U108**-13; **U113**-4 f,2
zittern **U57**-17; **U64**-6; **U105**-7
- (Stimme) U66-10
-, am ganzen Körper U67-3
zitternd **U64**-5 f; **U105**-7
Zittrigkeit **U113**-4
Zivilbevölkerung U6-9
ZNS-Infektion U40-5
ZNS-Metastasen U40-5
zögern **U75**-11; **U76**-14
Zökum U45-12
Zölom U85-9
Zona pellucida U51-5
- Dissektion, partielle U69-15
Zone, erogene U68-9
-, sterile U139-8
Zonulae occludentes U53-9
Zootoxin **U91**-2,4
Zorn **U76**-10
-, unterdrückter U74-14
zornig **U76**-10
Zosterneuralgie U95-7; U113-14
Zotten, frühe U85-24
-, verkürzte U45-14
Zottenadenom U45-14
Zottenatrophie U45-14
Zottenbüschel U85-14
Zottenhaut **U85**-16
Zottenpolyp U45-14
zottenreich **U45**-14
zottig U86-15
Z-Plastik U129-3; U130-14
zubeißen **U27**-11
zubereiten (Arznei) **U9**-5
- (Speise) U2-1
Zubereitung U121-1
Zubereitungsform **U9**-6
zublinzeln **U67**-15
Zucht **U84**-30
züchten **U84**-30
Züchtung **U116**-6
zucken **U31**-5; **U64**-6 f; **U72**-12
Zucken **U104**-12; U21-3
- (Achseln) **U67**-4
-, (nervöses) **U31**-5
-, leichtes U31-20
zuckend, schnell **U31**-5
Zucker **U3**-16; **U79**-6
Zuckeralkohol U82-13
Zuckergärung U46-12
Zuckerverbindung U79-5
Zuckung(en) **U31**-5; **U64**-7; **U72**-12
-, faszikuläre **U31**-5; U30-1
Zuckungsfaser, schnelle U30-1
Zufall U100-1
zufällig **U101**-5
zufallsabhängig U100-19
Zufallsbefund U117-6
Zufallsbiopsie U118-5
Zufallsgenerator **U101**-5
Zufallsprinzip U101-12
Zufallsstichprobe U100-4

Zufallszahl U101-5
Zufallszuteilung **U101**-5
Zufluchtsstätten U11-13
Zufluss **U36**-5
Zufuhr **U88**-3; U78-5
- (Nahrungsmittel) U2-1
zuführen **U36**-6; U79-15; **U121**-4
Zufüttern U14-8
Zug **U64**-13
- (Fraktur) **U141**-3
- (trinken) U2-4
-, geschickter U75-7
Zugang **U136**-5; **U126**-6; U127-18
-, direkter U128-1
-, genormter seitlicher U133-8
-, implantierbarer **U136**-5
-, operativer **U126**-6,2
-, retropubischer U52-18
-, vaskulärer U34-1
-, venöser **U136**-5; U14-6; U34-4
-, zentralvenöser U136-5
Zugang(sweg), operativer **U128**-1,6
zugänglich **U128**-1
Zugangsart **U126**-6
Zugangsweg **U126**-6; U136-5
zugeben **U102**-10
Zugehörigkeitsgefühl U57-5
Zügel **U141**-8
zugelassen U13-9; U92-2
zügellos U75-21
Zügellosigkeit **U10**-6
zugeschrieben U39-13
zugeteilt U101-5
Zugfestigkeit U31-10; U137-7
Zuggurtung U141-14
Zugkraft **U64**-13
zuhalten (Mund) U67-6
zuheilen **U140**-4
zuhören U61-1
Zuhörer(in) **U61**-1
Zunahme **U65**-17
zunehmen (Gewicht) U24-1
Zuneigung **U76**-3; U12-19; U67-7
Zunge **U21**-11
-, belegte **U103**-5
Zungenbändchen U26-11
Zungenbein U28-2,9
Zungenbiss U113-5
Zungenbrennen U26-1
Zungenentzündung U21-11
Zungengrund U21-11; **U87**-25
Zungenhalter U21-11
Zungenmandel U21-11; U35-6
Zungenpapille U21-11
Zungenpressen U64-12
Zungenrücken U22-11
zungenseitig **U21**-11
Zungenspatel **U17**-3; U21-11
Zungenverwachsung U21-11
Zungenwurzel U87-25
zunicken U67-3
zuordnen (örtl./zeitl.) **U74**-3
zupacken **U64**-9
zurechnungsfähig **U77**-3,13; U73-7

zurechnungsfähig, geistig voll U12-9
Zurechnungsfähigkeit **U77**-3
zurechtkommen **U77**-9
zurechtschneiden **U129**-4
zurückbilden, sich **U4**-15; U54-12
zurückbleiben U80-8
zurückführen auf U5-7; U79-17
zurückgebildet **U85**-9
zurückgeblieben (Entwicklung) U80-5
-, geistig **U77**-22; U76-21
zurückgelehnt **U63**-10
zurückhalten **U49**-4
zurückhaltend **U75**-11,17,21; **U76**-15,13
Zurückhaltung **U10**-6
Zurücklegen (Stichprobenerhebung) U100-4
zurücklehnend, (sich) **U63**-10
zurückrufen, ins Gedächtnis **U74**-1
zurückschneiden **U137**-13
zurückströmen **U46**-4; **U103**-12
zurückwandeln **U78**-6
zurückwerfen **U119**-18
zurückziehen (Haut) **U64**-13
-, sich **U72**-3; **U77**-8; U7-12; U76-7
Zusammenarbeit U18-8
zusammenballen **U38**-11; **U39**-19
zusammenbeißen **U27**-17; U64-9
zusammenbrechen **U6**-5; **U65**-12; **U110**-12
-, vor Erschöpfung U65-12
Zusammenbruch **U6**-5; U65-12
zusammendrücken **U6**-6; **U64**-10
Zusammendrücken U56-19
zusammenfalten **U25**-17
zusammenfassen, (kurz) **U74**-7
Zusammenfassung, tägliche **U20**-6
zusammenfließend (Hautläsion) U114-10
zusammengerollt **U63**-6; **U64**-8
zusammengesunken **U63**-2
Zusammenhang **U74**-5; **U87**-12; **U100**-32; **U101**-2
- stehen, in U74-5
-, enger U74-5
zusammenhängend **U18**-8; **U74**-5
- reden U66-8
zusammenkauern **U63**-6
zusammenkleben **U38**-11
zusammenkneifen (Augen) **U67**-14
zusammenkuscheln **U67**-7
zusammenlagern **U81**-9; **U37**-5
zusammenlaufend **U59**-13
zusammenpressen (Zähne) **U27**-17; U64-9
zusammenrollen, (sich) **U63**-6
zusammensacken **U63**-2
Zusammensetzung U9-17; U90-11
Zusammenspiel U42-14
Zusammenstoß **U6**-2
zusammenstoßen **U6**-2
Zusammenwirken **U31**-4; **U37**-14
zusammenziehen **U6**-6; **U31**-1; **U36**-11
zusammenziehend U82-28

zusammenzucken (Schmerz) **U104**-12
Zusatzinfusion **U136**-4
Zusatzleitung U136-4
Zusatzmaßnahmen U16-15
Zusatztherapie **U120**-8,4
Zuschauer(in) **U6**-13; **U67**-14
zuschreiben U92-20
Zu-Schwung-Gang (Krücken) U64-5
zusehen **U59**-1
Zuspruch, (ärztlicher) **U18**-6
–, beruhigender U76-19
Zustand **U4**-4; **U119**-15
– nach (Z. n.) U119-19
–, deliranter U10-14
–, erbärmlicher U76-20
–, in schlechtem U27-1
–, konditioneller U1-9
–, kritischer U125-1
–, lebensbedrohlicher **U124**-1
–, psychischer **U77**-1; U73-2
–, schlafähnlicher **U7**-13
–, stabiler U119-12; U125-2
–, tranceähnlicher U7-15
zuständig (für) **U42**-1
zustopfen U140-24
– (Ohren) U60-1
zuteilen **U87**-6; U8-19
Zuteilung **U101**-4
–, blockweise **U101**-11
zuträglich **U1**-5
zuverlässig **U75**-9,15
Zuverlässigkeit **U100**-30,23
zuversichtlich **U75**-6,17
Zuwendung, mangelnde affektive **U77**-11
zuwerfen **U64**-14
zuwinken **U67**-5
zuziehen (Fachkollegen) **U18**-13
–, sich (Erkrankung) **U4**-2
zuzwinkern **U59**-3; **U67**-15
ZVD U87-15
Zwang **U77**-19; U73-11
–, (innerer) **U11**-2; **U77**-19
zwanghaft **U11**-2; **U77**-19
Zwangseinweisung U14-5; U20-1
Zwangsernährung U2-3; U79-3
Zwangsgedanken U77-19
Zwangsidee U77-19; U73-8
Zwangsjacke **U77**-26; U125-24
Zwangslachen U113-3
Zwangsmaßnahme **U77**-26
Zwangsneurose U11-2; U77-19,21
Zwangsstörung U77-19
Zwangsweinen U77-19; U113-3
Zweck **U101**-3; **U73**-8
zweieiig U85-2
Zwei-Etagen-Verletzung U124-18
Zweifel **U117**-8
– zerstreuen U117-7

zweifelhaft **U117**-8; U1-5
zweifellos **U116**-23
Zweig **U28**-5
Zwei-Helfer-Reanimationsmethode U8-2
Zweikammerschrittmacher U123-13
Zweikanal-Goniometrie U142-9
zweiköpfig **U30**-11
zweiteilen **U126**-14
Zweiteingriff U126-1
Zweiterkrankung U100-9
Zweitgutachten **U18**-12; U102-14
Zweiwegventil U133-8
zweiwertig **U81**-10,5; **U82**-19
zweizeitig (OP) U126-4; **U130**-7
Zweizellstadium U85-4
Zwerchfell **U43**-12
Zwerchfellatmung U43-12; U44-4; U45-6
Zwerchfellbewegung U43-12; U44-10
Zwerchfellexkursion U44-3,10; U107-16
Zwerchfellhälfte **U43**-12
Zwerchfellhernie U43-12
Zwerchfellhochstand U43-12; U44-11
Zwerchfellkuppel **U43**-12
Zwerchfelllähmung **U31**-12
Zwerchfellruptur U43-12
Zwerchfellstand U116-16
Zwerchfellwölbung U43-12
Zwerg **U24**-4
zwergenhaft **U24**-4
Zwergwuchs **U24**-4
Z-Wert **U100**-6
zwicken U62-11; **U64**-10
Zwilling(e) **U70**-14
Zwillingsbildung **U70**-14
Zwillingsschwangerschaft U70-14
Zwillingsschwester U70-14
Zwillingstransfusionssyndrom U70-14
zwingen **U11**-2
Zwinkern **U59**-3; **U67**-15; **U72**-2
–, unwillkürliches U59-3
Zwischenblutung U38-8; U51-2
Zwischenergebnis U117-6
Zwischenfall **U6**-1; U11-7
Zwischengewebe U86-3
Zwischenhirn **U41**-12
Zwischenkieferknochen **U28**-10
Zwischenmahlzeit **U2**-10; U79-2
Zwischenneuron **U40**-1; U42-13
Zwischenprodukt **U81**-18
–, reaktionsfähiges U81-15
Zwischenraum **U86**-19; U87-11
Zwischenrippenraum U32-4; U33-4
Zwischenstoffwechsel U78-1; U81-18
Zwischenwirbelscheibe U22-12; U29-2
Zwischenwirt U94-5
Zwölffingerdarm **U45**-10

Zwölffingerdarmgeschwür U45-10
Zwölffingerdarmzotten U45-10
Zyanid **U91**-9
Zyanidverbindung U81-2
Zyanose **U108**-6
–, periphere U87-15
zyanotisch **U108**-6
Zygoma **U28**-9
Zygotän **U85**-2
Zygote **U85**-2; U69-12; U70-1
Zygotentransfer, intratubarer U69-18
zyklisch **U78**-6
Zyklitis U58-7
Zyklus **U51**-1; **U78**-6; **U81**-15; U9-1
Zyklusanamnese U51-1
Zyklusmitte U55-14
Zyklusstörungen U51-1
Zylinder U17-10; U49-12
Zylinderepithel **U86**-11; U50-6
–, hohes zilienbesetztes U43-8
–, mehrreihiges U86-10
Zylinderepithelzellen U86-11
Zymogen **U78**-8
Zystadenom **U98**-4
Zyste **U89**-24
Zystenniere U48-2
Zystikusverschluss U47-8
Zystometrie U49-15
Zystoskop U118-11
Zystoskopie U118-11
Zystotomie **U127**-2
Zystozele U89-23
Zytapherese U136-15
Zytochemie **U81**-7
Zytodiagnostik U83-1
Zytokin **U39**-13; U35-12; U97-18
Zytologe/-in U83-1
Zytologie **U83**-1; **U86**-1
zytologisch **U83**-1
Zytolyse U39-10; U83-1; U105-18
Zytomegalie **U96**-11
Zytomegalievirusimmunglobuline U96-11
–, hochkonzentrierte U39-5
Zytometrie U86-2
Zytopathologie U89-1
Zytopenie **U38**-5
Zytophotometrie **U83**-21
Zytoplasma U83-1
zytoplasmatisch U86-2
Zytoplasmavakuole U83-11
Zytoskelett **U83**-5,1
Zytostatika **U92**-31 f
Zytotoxin **U92**-32
zytotoxisch **U91**-4; **U92**-32
Zytotoxizität **U39**-16; U83-1; U91-11
Zytotrophoblast **U85**-14
Zytotrophoblasthülle U85-14
Zytotrophoblastzelle U85-14

Quellenverzeichnis der Abbildungen

Abb. S. 34: aus Ziegenfuß, T.: Checkliste Notfallmedizin, 2. Aufl. Thieme, Stuttgart, S. 62

Abb. S. 72: aus Faller, A., Schünke, M.: Der Körper des Menschen, 13. Aufl. Thieme, Stuttgart, S. 220

Abb. S. 83: aus Hüter-Becker, A., Schewe, H., Heipertz, W.: Physiotherapie. Band 9 Traumatologie, Querschnittlähmung. Thieme, Stuttgart, S. 50–53

Abb. S. 95: aus Möller, T. B., E. Reif: Taschenatlas der Röntgenanatomie, 2. Aufl. Thieme, Stuttgart, S. 98 u. 99

Abb. S. 115: aus Platzer, W.: Taschenatlas der Anatomie. Band 1 Bewegungsapparat, 7. Aufl. Thieme, Stuttgart, S. 125

Abb. S. 118: aus Platzer, W.: Taschenatlas der Anatomie. Band 1 Bewegungsapparat, 7. Aufl. Thieme, Stuttgart, S. 27

Abb. S. 124: aus Platzer, W.: Taschenatlas der Anatomie. Band 1 Bewegungsapparat, 7. Aufl. Thieme, Stuttgart, S. 251

Abb. S. 130: Kahle, W., Leonhardt, H., Platzer, W.: Taschenatlas der Anatomie. Band 2 Innere Organe, 6. Aufl. Thieme, Stuttgart, S. 9

Abb. S. 138: aus Möller, T.B., E. Reif: Taschenatlas der Röntgenanatomie, 2. Aufl. Thieme, Stuttgart, S. 300

Abb. S. 159: aus Riede, U.-N.: Taschenatlas der allgemeinen Pathologie. Thieme Stuttgart, S. 27

Abb. S. 165: aus Kahle, W.: Taschenatlas der Anatomie. Band 3 Nervensystem und Sinnesorgane, 7. Aufl. Thieme, Stuttgart, S. 31

Abb. S. 166: aus Kahle, W.: Taschenatlas der Anatomie. Band 3 Nervensystem und Sinnesorgane, 7. Aufl. Thieme Stuttgart, S. 11

Abb. S. 175: aus Möller, T. B., E. Reif: Taschenatlas der Röntgenanatomie, 2. Aufl. Thieme, Stuttgart, S. 340

Abb. S. 185: aus Riede, U.-N., Schaefer, H:-E.: Allgemeine und spezielle Pathologie, 4. Aufl. (limitierte Sonderausgabe) Thieme, Stuttgart, S. 712

Abb. S. 196: aus Schwegler, J. S.: Der Mensch: Anatomie und Physiologie, 3. Aufl. Thieme, Stuttgart, S. 318

Abb. S. 202: aus Kahle, W., Leonhardt, H., Platzer, W.: Taschenatlas der Anatomie. Band 2 Innere Organe, 6. Aufl. Thieme, Stuttgart, S. 305

Abb. S. 208: aus Drews, U.: Taschenatlas der Embryologie. Thieme, Stuttgart, S. 29

Abb. S. 209: aus Kahle, W., Leonhardt, H., Platzer, W.: Taschenatlas der Anatomie. Band 2 Innere Organe, 6. Aufl. Thieme, Stuttgart, S. 287

Abb. S. 216: aus Schwegler, J. S.: Der Mensch: Anatomie und Physiologie, 3. Aufl. Thieme, Stuttgart, S. 384

Abb. S. 225: aus Schwegler, J. S.: Der Mensch: Anatomie und Physiologie, 3. Aufl. Thieme, Stuttgart, S. 466

Abb. S. 229: aus Schwegler, J. S.: Der Mensch: Anatomie und Physiologie, 3. Aufl. Thieme, Stuttgart, S. 478

Abb. S. 235: aus Kahle, W.: Taschenatlas der Anatomie. Band 3 Nervensystem und Sinnesorgane, 7. Aufl. Thieme, Stuttgart, S. 339

Abb. S. 246: aus Kahle, W.: Taschenatlas der Anatomie. Band 3 Nervensystem und Sinnesorgane, 7. Aufl. Thieme, Stuttgart, S. 369

Abb. S. 254: aus Ziegenfuß, T.: Checkliste Notfallmedizin, 2. Aufl. Thieme, Stuttgart

Abb. S. 277: © Alexander Alge, Frauenklinik, Medizinische Universität, Innsbruck

Abb. S. 280: © Alexander Alge, Frauenklinik, Medizinische Universität, Innsbruck

Abb. S. 285: aus Kahle, W.: Taschenatlas der Anatomie. Band 2 Innere Organe, 6. Aufl. Thieme, Stuttgart, Abb. S. 327

Abb. S. 287: © Alexander Alge, Frauenklinik, Medizinische Universität, Innsbruck

Abb. S. 353: aus Hirsch-Kauffmann, M., Schweiger, M.: Biologie für Mediziner und Naturwissenschaftler, 4. Aufl. Thieme, Stuttgart, Abb. S. 1

Abb. S. 358: aus Riede, U.-N.: Taschenatlas der allgemeinen Pathologie. Thieme, Stuttgart, Abb. S. 7

Abb. S. 370: aus Drews, U.: Taschenatlas der Embryologie. Thieme, Stuttgart, Abb. S. 104

Abb. S. 374: aus Platzer, W.: Taschenatlas der Anatomie. Band 1 Bewegungsapperat, 7. Aufl. Thieme, Stuttgart, Abb. S. 9

Abb. S. 400: aus Hirsch-Kauffmann, M., Schweiger, M.: Biologie für Mediziner und Naturwissenschaftler, 4. Aufl. Thieme, Stuttgart

Abb. S. 422: aus Hirsch-Kaufmann, M., Schweiger, M.: Biologie für Mediziner und Naturwissenschaftler, 4. Aufl. Thieme, Stuttgart, Abb. S. 357

Abb. S. 437: aus Riede, U.-N.: Taschenatlas der allgemeinen Pathologie. Thieme, Stuttgart, Abb. S. 383

Abb. S. 546: aus Ziegenfuß, T.: Checkliste Notfallmedizin, 2. Aufl. Thieme, Stuttgart, Abb. S. 89 u. 92

Abb. S. 527: aus Möller, T. B., E. Reif: Taschenatlals der Röntgenanatomie, 2. Aufl. Thieme, Stuttgart, Abb. S. 242 u. 248

Abb. S. 554: aus Riede, U.-N., Schaefer, H.-E.: Allgemeine und spezielle Pathologie, 4. Aufl. (limitierte Sonderausgabe) Thieme, Stuttgart, Abb. S. 448

Abb. S. 560: aus Largiadèr, F., H.-D. Saeger: Checkliste Chirurgie, 8. Auflage, Thieme, Stuttgart

Abb. S. 569: aus Janetschek, G., Rassweiler, J., Griffith, D. O.: Laparoscopic Surgery in Urology, Thieme, Stuttgart, Abb. S. 45

Abb. S. 586: aus Janetschek, G., Rassweiler, J., Griffith, D. P.: Laparoscopic Surgery in Urology, Thieme, Stuttgart, Abb. S. 16 u. 20

Abb. S. 604: aus Janetschek, G., Rassweiler, J., Griffith, D. P.: Laparoscopic Surgery in Urology, Thieme, Stuttgart, Abb. S. 71

Abb. S. 620: aus Kisner, C., Colby, L. A.: Vom Griff zur Behandlung, 2. Aufl. Thieme, Stuttgart, Abb. S. 48

Grundsätzliches zur Aussprache

Da in der medizinischen Fachsprache eine Vielzahl von Fachtermini aus dem Lateinischen oder Griechischen hergeleitet sind, ist deren richtige Aussprache selbst für englischsprachige Ärzte immer wieder eine Quelle der Unsicherheit. Dies gilt umso mehr für den deutschsprachigen Arzt, denn viele Fachwörter sind zwar vom Schriftbild her vertraute Internationalismen, deren Aussprache im Englischen deckt sich aber nur selten mit jener im Deutschen. Dadurch wird die Aussprache zu einem wichtigen Faktor für die richtige Verständigung.

Der Benutzer findet die Aussprachehinweise in der weithin bekannten internationalen Lautschrift der International Phonetic Association (IPA). Die verwendeten Symbole, die auf der neuesten IPA-Version beruhen, sind auf der Innenseite der Umschlagklappe übersichtlich mit Beispielwörtern dargestellt. Grundsätzlich wird immer die Aussprache im *Standard American English (AE)* angegeben und durch Hinweise auf Varianten im *British English (BE)* überall dort ergänzt, wo Besonderheiten vorliegen. Als Grundlage für die Aussprache im AE diente vor allem das *Medical Audio Dictionary* (Merriam-Webster, 1997), ergänzt durch Recherchen unserer Mitarbeiter in den USA.

Hinweise zur Aussprache medizinischer Fachwörter		
-itis	[aɪtɪs]	gingivitis, pulpitis, gastritis, meningitis, sinusitis, arthritis, periodontitis
h(a)ema-	[hiːmə]	hematoma, hematemesis, hematocrit, hematuria
hemi-	[hemɪ]	hemifacial, hemiplegia, hemiblock, hemisphere, hemianopsia, hemizygous
syn-, sym-	[sɪn], [sɪm]	syndrome, syndesmosis, synchronous, synthetic, symptom, symphysis, sympathetic
dys-	[dɪs]	dysfunction, dysplasia, dystrophic, dysphagia, dyscrasia, dysostosis
pn-, ps-, pt-	silent [p]	pneumonia, pneumatic, psychologic, psoas, ptosis, ptyalin
ch	[k]	ache, trachea, tachycardia, splanchnic, technique, mechanism, parenchyma
sch	[sk]	ischial, ischemia, schedule, eschar, scheme, school
-myo-	[maɪoʊ]	myocardial, myometrium, myoneural, myotomy, electromyography, fibromyoma
-cyto-	[saɪtoʊ]	cytologic, cytometry, cytoplasm, cytotoxic, cytokine, leukocytosis, thrombocytopenia
pyo-	[paɪoʊ]	pyogenic, pyoderma, pyothorax, pyocyst, pyorrhea
micro-	[maɪkroʊ]	microscope, microsurgery, microbial, microorganism, microflora
bio-	[baɪoʊ]	biologic, biopsy, biochemical, bioavailability, bioassay, biomaterials, biocompatible
eu-	[ju]	euphoria, euthyroid, euthanasia, eugenic
-i *(lat. pl)*	[aɪ]	alveoli, villi, bronchi, stimuli, calculi, emboli, nuclei, rami
-ae *(lat. pl)*	[ɪ]	sequelae, vertebrae [iː‖eɪ], papillae, fistulae, trabeculae, fasciae, conjunctivae
-(s)tomy -graphy -scopy*	main stress on vowel before the suffix!	anatomy, laparotomy; ileostomy; radiography, arthrography, sonography; endoscopy, bronchoscopy, colonoscopy

* Neben diesen hier aufgezählten Nachsilben gibt es noch eine Liste von weniger geläufigen, die durchwegs mit dem gleichen Betonungsmuster verbunden sind: **-lysis** (analysis, dialysis, hemolysis), **-metry/-ter** (cephalometry, thermometer), **-logy/-logist** (radiology/-gist), **-pathy** (neuropathy), **-schisis** (cheiloschisis), **-rrhaphy** (herniorrhaphy).

Unterschiede zwischen AE und BE in der Schreibweise

Standard American English				British English (RP)
fetus, diarrhea, edema, maneuver, esophagus, estrogen	e		oe	*foetus, diarrhoea, oedema, manoeuvre, oesophagus, oestrogen,
pediatric, anemia, hemorrhage, etiology, cecum, feces, anesthesia	e		ae	paediatric, anaemia, haemorrhage, aetiology caecum, faeces, anaesthesia
liter, titer, center, fiber, maneuver, caliber, goiter	-er		-re	litre, titre, centre, fibre, manoeuvre, calibre, goitre
catheterize, paralyze, cauterize, analyze	-ize		-ise	*catheterise, paralyse, *cauterise, *analyse
hospitalization, mobilization, localization	-zation		-sation	*hospitalisation, *mobilisation, *localisation
color, labor, behavior, tumor, favorite, flavor, humor	-or		-our	colour, labour, behaviour, tumour, favourite, flavour, humour
homolog, catalog, dialog, analog	-og		-ogue	homologue, catalogue, dialogue*, analogue
diagram, radiogram, cystogram, milligram, sonogram, cardiogram	-am		-amme	diagramme, radiogramme, cystogramme, milligramme, sonogramme, cardiogramme
leukoplakia, leukopenia, leukocyte	leuko-		leuco-	leucoplakia, leucopenia, leucocyte
*imbed, inquiry, inclose	in-/im-		en-/em-	embed, *enquiry, enclose
offense, license, defense	-se		-ce	offence, licence, defence
counselor, *instal, tranquilizer	-l		-ll	counsellor, install, tranquilliser

* Neben dieser Schreibweise existiert auch die *AE* bzw. *BE* Variante.